o the House of the God of Jacob and He will teach us
n shall go forth the Law and the word of the Lord from
lem

ENCYCLOPAEDIA
JUDAICA

VOLUME 11

LEK-MIL

ENCYCLOPAEDIA JUDAICA

ENCYCLOPAEDIA JUDAICA JERUSALEM

Library of Congress Catalog Card Number: 72-90254

First printing 1972
Second printing 1973
Third printing 1974
Fourth printing 1978

Computerized typesetting, printing and binding by
Keterpress Enterprises, Jerusalem

Printed in Israel

A Clal Project

GLOSSARY

Asterisked terms have separate entries in the Encyclopaedia.

Actions Committee, early name of the Zionist General Council, the supreme institution of the World Zionist Organization in the interim between Congresses. The Zionist Executive's name was then the "Small Actions Committee."

***Adar,** twelfth month of the Jewish religious year, sixth of the civil, approximating to February-March.

***Aggadah,** name given to those sections of Talmud and Midrash containing homiletic expositions of the Bible, stories, legends, folklore, anecdotes, or maxims. In contradistinction to **halakhah*.

***Agunah,** woman unable to remarry according to Jewish law, because of desertion by her husband or inability to accept presumption of death.

***Aḥaronim,** later rabbinic authorities. In contradistinction to **rishonim* ("early ones").

Ahavah, liturgical poem inserted in the second benediction of the morning prayer *(*Ahavah Rabbah)* of the festivals and/or special Sabbaths.

Aktion (Ger.), operation involving the mass assembly, deportation, and murder of Jews by the Nazis during the *Holocaust.

***Aliyah,** (1) being called to Reading of the Law in synagogue; (2) immigration to Ereẓ Israel; (3) one of the waves of immigration to Ereẓ Israel from the early 1880s.

***Amidah,** main prayer recited at all services; also known as *Shemoneh Esreh* and *Tefillah.*

***Amora** (pl. **amoraim**), title given to the Jewish scholars in Ereẓ Israel and Babylonia in the third to sixth centuries who were responsible for the **Gemara.*

Aravah, the *willow; one of the *Four Species used on *Sukkot ("festival of Tabernacles") together with the **etrog, hadas,* and **lulav*.

***Arvit,** evening prayer.

Asarah be-Tevet, fast on the 10th of Tevet commemorating the commencement of the siege of Jerusalem by Nebuchadnezzar.

Asefat ha-Nivḥarim, representative assembly elected by Jews in Palestine during the period of the British Mandate (1920–48).

***Ashkenaz,** name applied generally in medieval rabbinical literature to Germany.

***Ashkenazi** (pl. **Ashkenazim**), German or West-, Central-, or East-European Jew(s), as contrasted with *Sephardi(m).

***Av,** fifth month of the Jewish religious year, eleventh of the civil, approximating to July-August.

***Av bet din,** vice-president of the supreme court *(bet din ha-gadol)* in Jerusalem during the Second Temple period; later, title given to communal rabbis as heads of the religious courts (see **bet din*).

***Badḥan,** jester, particularly at traditional Jewish weddings in Eastern Europe.

***Bakkashah** (Heb. "supplication"), type of petitionary prayer, mainly recited in the Sephardi rite on Rosh Ha-Shanah and the Day of Atonement.

Bar, "son of . . ."; frequently appearing in personal names.

***Baraita** (pl. **beraitot**), statement of **tanna* not found in *Mishnah.

***Bar mitzvah,** ceremony marking the initiation of a boy at the age of 13 into the Jewish religious community.

Ben, "son of . . ."; frequently appearing in personal names.

Berakhah (pl. **berakhot**), *benediction, blessing; formula of praise and thanksgiving.

***Bet din** (pl. **battei din**), rabbinic court of law.

***Bet ha-midrash,** school for higher rabbinic learning; often attached to or serving as a synagogue.

***Bilu,** first modern movement for pioneering and agricultural settlement in Ereẓ Israel, founded in 1882 at Kharkov, Russia.

***Bund,** Jewish socialist party founded in Vilna in 1897, supporting Jewish national rights; Yiddishist, and anti-Zionist.

Cohen (pl. **Cohanim**), see Kohen.

***Conservative Judaism,** trend in Judaism developed in the United States in the 20th century which, while opposing extreme changes in traditional observances, permits certain modifications of *halakhah* in response to the changing needs of the Jewish people.

***Consistory** (Fr. *consistoire*), governing body of a Jewish communal district in France and certain other countries.

***Converso(s),** term applied in Spain and Portugal to converted Jew(s), and sometimes more loosely to their descendants.

***Crypto-Jew,** term applied to a person who although observing outwardly Christianity (or some other religion) was at heart a Jew and maintained Jewish observances as far as possible (see Converso; Marrano; Neofiti; New Christian; Jadīd al-Islām).

***Dayyan,** member of rabbinic court.

Decisor, equivalent to the Hebrew *posek* (pl. **posekim*), the rabbi who gives the decision (*halakhah*) in Jewish law or practice.

***Devekut,** "devotion"; attachment or adhesion to God; communion with God.

***Diaspora,** Jews living in the "dispersion" outside Ereẓ Israel; area of Jewish settlement outside Ereẓ Israel.

Din, a law (both secular and religious), legal decision, or lawsuit.

Divan, diwan, collection of poems, especially in Hebrew, Arabic, or Persian.

Dunam, unit of land area (1,000 sq. m., c. 1/4 acre), used in Israel.

Einsatzgruppen, mobile units of Nazi S.S. and S.D.; in U.S.S.R. and Serbia, mobile killing units.

***Ein-Sof,** "without end"; "the infinite"; hidden, impersonal aspect of God; also used as a Divine Name.

***Elul,** sixth month of the Jewish religious calendar, 12th of the civil, precedes the High Holiday season in the fall.

Endloesung, see *Final Solution.

***Ereẓ Israel,** Land of Israel; Palestine.

***Eruv,** technical term for rabbinical provision permitting the alleviation of certain restrictions.

***Etrog,** citron; one of the *Four Species used on *Sukkot together with the **lulav, hadas,* and *aravah.*

Even ha-Ezer, see Shulḥan Arukh.

***Exilarch,** lay head of Jewish community in Babylonia (see also *resh galuta*), and elsewhere.

***Final Solution** (Ger. *Endloesung*), in Nazi terminology, the Nazi-planned mass murder and total annihilation of the Jews.

***Gabbai,** official of a Jewish congregation; originally a charity collector.

***Galut,** "exile"; the condition of the Jewish people in dispersion.

***Gaon** (pl. **geonim**), head of academy in post-talmudic period, especially in Babylonia.

Gaonate, office of *gaon.

***Gemara,** traditions, discussions, and rulings of the **amoraim*, commenting on and supplementing the *Mishnah, and forming part of the Babylonian and Palestinian Talmuds (see Talmud).

***Gematria,** interpretation of Hebrew word according to the numerical value of its letters.

General Government, territory in Poland administered by a German civilian governor–general with headquarters in Cracow after the German occupation in World War II.

***Genizah,** depository for sacred books. The best known was discovered in the synagogue of Fostat (old Cairo).

Get, bill of *divorce.

***Ge'ullah,** hymn inserted after the **Shema* into the benediction of the morning prayer of the festivals and special Sabbaths.

***Gilgul,** metempsychosis; transmigration of souls.

***Golem,** automaton, especially in human form, created by magical means and endowed with life.

***Ḥabad,** initials of *ḥokhmah, binah, da'at*: "wisdom, understanding, knowledge"; ḥasidic movement founded in Belorussia by *Shneur Zalman of Lyady.

Hadas, *myrtle; one of the *Four Species used on Sukkot together with the **etrog*, **lulav*, and *aravah*.

***Haftarah** (pl. **haftarot**), designation of the portion from the prophetical books of the Bible recited after the synagogue reading from the Pentateuch on Sabbaths and holidays.

***Haganah,** clandestine Jewish organization for armed self-defense in Ereẓ Israel under the British Mandate, which eventually evolved into a people's militia and became the basis for the Israel army.

***Haggadah,** ritual recited in the home on *Passover eve at *seder* table.

Haham, title of chief rabbi of the Spanish and Portuguese congregations in London, England.

***Ḥakham,** title of rabbi of *Sephardi congregation.

***Ḥakham bashi,** title in the 15th century and modern times of the chief rabbi in the Ottoman Empire, residing in Constantinople (Istanbul), also applied to principal rabbis in provincial towns.

Hakhsharah ("preparation"), organized training in the Diaspora of pioneers for agricultural settlement in Ereẓ Israel.

***Halakhah** (pl. **halakhot**), an accepted decision in rabbinic law. Also refers to those parts of the *Talmud concerned with legal matters. In contradistinction to **aggadah*.

Ḥaliẓah, biblically prescribed ceremony (Deut. 25:9–10) performed when a man refuses to marry his brother's childless widow, enabling her to remarry.

***Hallel,** term referring to Psalms 113–18 in liturgical use.

***Ḥalukkah,** system of financing the maintenance of Jewish communities in the holy cities of Ereẓ Israel by collections made abroad, mainly in the pre-Zionist era (see *kolel*).

Ḥalutz (pl. **ḥalutzim**), pioneer, especially in agriculture, in Ereẓ Israel.

Ḥalutziyyut, pioneering.

***Ḥanukkah,** eight-day celebration commemorating the victory of *Judah Maccabee over the Syrian king *Antiochus Epiphanes and the subsequent rededication of the Temple.

Ḥasid, adherent of *Ḥasidism.

***Ḥasidei Ashkenaz,** medieval pietist movement among the Jews of Germany.

***Ḥasidism,** (1) religious revivalist movement of popular mysticism among Jews of Germany in the Middle Ages; (2) religious movement founded by *Israel ben Eliezer Ba'al Shem Tov in the first half of the 18th century.

***Haskalah,** "Enlightenment"; movement for spreading modern European culture among Jews c. 1750–1880. See *maskil*.

***Havdalah,** ceremony marking the end of Sabbath or festival.

***Ḥazzan,** precentor who intones the liturgy and leads the prayers in synagogue; in earlier times a synagogue official.

***Ḥeder** (lit. "room"), school for teaching children Jewish religious observance.

Heikhalot, "palaces"; tradition in Jewish mysticism centering on mystical journeys through the heavenly spheres and palaces to the Divine Chariot (see Merkabah).

***Ḥerem,** excommunication, imposed by rabbinical authorities for purposes of religious and/or communal discipline; originally, in biblical times, that which is separated from common use either because it was an abomination or because it was consecrated to God.

Ḥeshvan, see Marḥeshvan.

***Ḥevra kaddisha,** title applied to charitable confraternity (**ḥevrah*), now generally limited to associations for burial of the dead.

***Ḥibbat Zion,** see Ḥovevei Zion.

***Histadrut** (abbr. for Heb. **Ha-Histadrut ha-Kelalit shel ha-Ovedim ha-Ivriyyim be-Ereẓ Israel).** Ereẓ Israel Jewish Labor Federation, founded in 1920; subsequently renamed Histadrut ha-Ovedim be-Ereẓ Israel.

***Holocaust,** the organized mass persecution and annihilation of European Jewry by the Nazis (1933–1945).

***Hoshana Rabba,** the seventh day of *Sukkot on which special observances are held.

Ḥoshen Mishpat, see Shulḥan Arukh.

Ḥovevei Zion, federation of *Ḥibbat Zion, early (pre-*Herzl) Zionist movement in Russia.

Illui, outstanding scholar or genius, especially a young prodigy in talmudic learning.

***Iyyar,** second month of the Jewish religious year, eighth of the civil, approximating to April-May.

I.Ẓ.L. (initials of Heb. ***Irgun Ẓeva'i Le'ummi;** "National Military Organization"), underground Jewish organization in Ereẓ Israel founded in 1931, which engaged from 1937 in retaliatory acts against Arab attacks and later against the British mandatory authorities.

***Jadīd al-Islām** (Ar.).a person practicing the Jewish religion in secret although outwardly observing Islam.

***Jewish Legion,** Jewish units in British army during World War I.

***Jihād** (Ar.), in Muslim religious law, holy war waged against infidels.

***Judenrat** (Ger. "Jewish council"), council set up in Jewish communities and ghettos under the Nazis to execute their instructions.

***Judenrein** (Ger. "clean of Jews"), in Nazi terminology the condition of a locality from which all Jews had been eliminated.

***Kabbalah,** the Jewish mystical tradition:
- **Kabbalah iyyunit,** speculative Kabbalah;
- **Kabbalah ma'asit,** practical Kabbalah;
- **Kabbalah nevu'it,** prophetic Kabbalah.

Kabbalist, student of Kabbalah.

***Kaddish,** liturgical doxology.

Kahal, Jewish congregation; among Ashkenazim, *kehillah*.

***Kalām** (Ar.), science of Muslim theology; adherents of the Kalām are called *mutakallimūn*.

***Karaite,** member of a Jewish sect originating in the eighth century which rejected rabbinic (*Rabbanite) Judaism and claimed to accept only Scripture as authoritative.

***Kasher,** ritually permissible food.

Kashrut, Jewish *dietary laws.

***Kavvanah,** "intention"; term denoting the spiritual concentration accompanying prayer and the performance of ritual or of a commandment.

***Kedushah,** main addition to the third blessing in the reader's repetition of the *Amidah* in which the public responds to the precentor's introduction.

Kefar, village; first part of name of many settlements in Israel.

Kehillah, congregation; see *kahal*.

Kelippah (pl. **kelippot**), "husk(s)"; mystical term denoting force(s) of evil.

***Keneset Yisrael,** comprehensive communal organization of the Jews in Palestine during the British Mandate.

Keri, variants in the masoretic (*masorah) text of the Bible between the spelling (*ketiv*) and its pronunciation (*keri*).

***Kerovah** (collective plural (corrupted) from **kerovez**), poem(s) incorporated into the **Amidah*.

Ketiv, see *keri*.

***Ketubbah,** marriage contract, stipulating husband's obligations to wife.

Kevuẓah, small commune of pioneers constituting an agricultural settlement in Ereẓ Israel (evolved later into *kibbutz).

***Kibbutz** (pl. **kibbutzim**), larger-size commune constituting a settlement in Ereẓ Israel based mainly on agriculture but engaging also in industry.

***Kiddush,** prayer of sanctification, recited over wine or bread on eve of Sabbaths and festivals.

***Kiddush ha-Shem,** term connoting martyrdom or act of strict integrity in support of Judaic principles.

***Kinah** (pl. **kinot**), lamentation dirge(s) for the Ninth of Av and other fast days.

***Kislev,** ninth month of the Jewish religious year, third of the civil, approximating to November-December.

Klaus, name given in Central and Eastern Europe to an institution, usually with synagogue attached, where *Talmud was studied perpetually by adults; applied by Ḥasidim to their synagogue (*"kloyz"*).

***Knesset,** parliament of the State of Israel.

K(c)ohen (pl. **K(c)ohanim**), Jew(s) of priestly (Aaronide) descent.

***Kolel,** (1) community in Ereẓ Israel of persons from a particular country or locality, often supported by their fellow countrymen in the Diaspora; (2) institution for higher Torah study.

Kosher, see *kasher*.

***Kristallnacht** (Ger. "crystal night," meaning "night of broken glass"), organized destruction of synagogues, Jewish houses, and shops, accompanied by mass arrests of Jews, which took place in Germany and Austria under the Nazis on the night of Nov. 9–10, 1938.

***Lag ba-Omer,** 33rd (Heb. **lag**) day of the **Omer* period falling on the 18th of *Iyyar; a semi-holiday.

Leḥi (abbr. for Heb. ***Loḥamei Ḥerut Israel,** "Fighters for the Freedom of Israel"), radically anti-British armed underground organization in Palestine, founded in 1940 by dissidents from *I.Ẓ.L.

Levir, husband's brother.

***Levirate marriage** (Heb. *yibbum*), marriage of childless widow *(yevamah)* by brother *(yavam)* of the deceased husband (in accordance with Deut. 25:5); release from such an obligation is effected through *ḥaliẓah*.

LḤY, see Leḥi.

***Lulav,** palm branch; one of the *Four Species used on *Sukkot together with the **etrog, hadas,* and *aravah*.

***Ma'aravot,** hymns inserted into the evening prayer of the three festivals, Passover, Shavuot, and Sukkot.

Ma'ariv, evening prayer; also called **arvit*.

***Ma'barah,** transition camp; temporary settlement for newcomers in Israel during the period of mass immigration following 1948.

***Maftir,** reader of the concluding portion of the Pentateuchal section on Sabbaths and holidays in synagogue; reader of the portion of the prophetical books of the Bible (**haftarah*).

***Maggid,** popular preacher.

***Maḥzor** (pl. **maḥzorim**), festival prayer book.

***Mamzer,** bastard; according to Jewish law, the offspring of an incestuous relationship.

***Mandate, Palestine,** responsibility for the administration of Palestine conferred on Britain by the League of Nations in 1922; mandatory government: the British administration of Palestine.

***Maqāma** (Ar., pl. **maqamāt**), poetic form (rhymed prose) which, in its classical arrangement, has rigid rules of form and content.

***Marḥeshvan,** popularly called Ḥeshvan; eighth month of the Jewish religious year, second of the civil, approximating to October-November.

***Marrano(s),** descendant(s) of Jew(s) in Spain and Portugal whose ancestors had been converted to Christianity under pressure but who secretly observed Jewish rituals.

Maskil (pl. **maskilim**), adherent of *Haskalah ("Enlightenment") movement.

***Masorah,** body of traditions regarding the correct spelling, writing, and reading of the Hebrew Bible.

Masorete, scholar of the masoretic tradition.

Masoretic, in accordance with the masorah.

Meliẓah, in Middle Ages, elegant style; modern usage, florid style using biblical or talmudic phraseology.

Mellah, *Jewish quarter in North African towns.

***Menorah,** candelabrum; seven-branched oil lamp used in the Tabernacle and Temple; also eight-branched candelabrum used on *Ḥanukkah.

Me'orah, hymn inserted into the first benediction of the morning prayer (*Yoẓer ha-Me'orot*).

***Merkabah,** *merkavah,* "chariot"; mystical discipline associated with Ezekiel's vision of the Divine Throne-Chariot (Ezek. 1).

Meshullaḥ, emissary sent to conduct propaganda or raise funds for rabbinical academies or charitable institutions.

***Mezuzah** (pl. **mezuzot**), parchment scroll with selected Torah verses placed in container and affixed to gates and doorposts of houses occupied by Jews.

***Midrash,** method of interpreting Scripture to elucidate legal points (*Midrash Halakhah*) or to bring out lessons by stories or homiletics (*Midrash Aggadah*). Also the name for a collection of such rabbinic interpretations.

***Mikveh,** ritual bath.

***Minhag** (pl. **minhagim**), ritual custom(s); synagogal rite(s); especially of a specific sector of Jewry.

***Minḥah,** afternoon prayer; originally meal offering in Temple.

***Minyan,** group of ten male adult Jews, the minimum required for communal prayer.

***Mishnah,** earliest codification of Jewish Oral Law.

Mishnah (pl. mishnayot), subdivision of tractates of the Mishnah.

Mitnagged (pl. ***Mitnaggedim**), originally, opponents of *Ḥasidism in Eastern Europe.

***Mitzvah,** biblical or rabbinic injunction; applied also to good or charitable deeds.

Mohel, official performing circumcisions.

***Moshav,** smallholders' cooperative agricultural settlement in Israel, see moshav ovedim.

Moshavah, earliest type of Jewish village in modern Ereẓ Israel in which farming is conducted on individual farms mostly on privately owned land.

Moshav ovedim ("workers' moshav"), agricultural village in Israel whose inhabitants possess individual homes and holdings but cooperate in the purchase of equipment, sale of produce, mutual aid, etc.

***Moshav shittufi** ("collective moshav"), agricultural village in Israel whose members possess individual homesteads but where the agriculture and economy are conducted as a collective unit.

Mostegab (Ar.), poem with biblical verse at beginning of each stanza.

***Muqaddam** (Ar., pl. **muqaddamūn**), "leader," "head of the community."

***Musaf,** additional service on Sabbath and festivals; originally the additional sacrifice offered in the Temple.

Musar, traditional ethical literature.

***Musar movement,** ethical movement developing in the latter part of the 19th century among Orthodox Jewish groups in Lithuania; founded by R. Israel *Lipkin (Salanter).

***Nagid** (pl. **negidim**), title applied in Muslim (and some Christian) countries in the Middle Ages to a leader recognized by the state as head of the Jewish community.

Nakdan (pl. **nakdanim**), "punctuator"; scholar of the 9th to 14th centuries who provided biblical manuscripts with masoretic apparatus, vowels, and accents.

***Nasi** (pl. **nesi'im**), talmudic term for president of the Sanhedrin, who was also the spiritual head and, later, political representative of the Jewish people; from second century a descendant of Hillel recognized by the Roman authorities as patriarch of the Jews. Now applied to the president of the State of Israel.

***Negev,** the southern, mostly arid, area of Israel.

***Ne'ilah,** concluding service on the *Day of Atonement.

Neofiti, term applied in southern Italy to converts to Christianity from Judaism and their descendants who were suspected of maintaining secret allegiance to Judaism.

***Neology; Neolog; Neologism,** trend of *Reform Judaism in Hungary forming separate congregations after 1868.

***Nevelah** (lit. "carcass"), meat forbidden by the *dietary laws on account of the absence of, or defect in, the act of **sheḥitah* (ritual slaughter).

***New Christians,** term applied especially in Spain and Portugal to converts from Judaism (and from Islam) and their descendants; "Half New Christian" designated a person one of whose parents was of full Jewish blood.

***Niddah** ("menstruous woman"), woman during the period of menstruation.

***Nisan,** first month of the Jewish religious year, seventh of the civil, approximating to March-April.

Niẓoẓot, "sparks"; mystical term for sparks of the holy light imprisoned in all matter.

Nosaḥ (nusaḥ), "version"; (1) textual variant; (2) term applied to distinguish the various prayer rites, e.g., *nosaḥ Ashkenaz;* (3) the accepted tradition of synagogue melody.

***Notarikon,** method of abbreviating Hebrew words or phrases by acronym.

Novella(e) (Heb. **ḥiddush(im)*), commentary on talmudic and later rabbinic subjects that derives new facts or principles from the implications of the text.

***Nuremberg Laws,** Nazi laws excluding Jews from German citizenship, and imposing other restrictions.

Ofan, hymns inserted into a passage of the morning prayer.

***Omer,** first sheaf cut during the barley harvest, offered in the Temple on the second day of Passover.

Omer, Counting of (Heb. *Sefirat ha-Omer*), 49 days counted from the day on which the *omer* was first offered in the Temple (according to the rabbis the 16th of Nisan, i.e., the second day of Passover) until the festival of Shavuot; now a period of semi-mourning.

Oraḥ Ḥayyim, see Shulḥan Arukh.

***Orthodoxy** (Orthodox Judaism), modern term for the strictly traditional sector of Jewry.

***Pale of Settlement,** 25 provinces of czarist Russia where Jews were permitted permanent residence.

***Palmaḥ** (abbr. for Heb. *peluggot maḥaẓ;* "shock companies"), striking arm of the *Haganah.

***Pardes,** medieval biblical exegesis giving the literal, allegorical, homiletical, and esoteric interpretations.

***Parnas,** chief synagogue functionary, originally vested with both religious and administrative functions; subsequently an elected lay leader.

Partition plan(s), proposals for dividing Ereẓ Israel into autonomous areas.

Paytan, composer of **piyyut* (liturgical poetry).

***Peel Commission,** British Royal Commission appointed by the British government in 1936 to inquire into the Palestine problem and make recommendations for its solution.

Pesaḥ, *Passover.

***Pilpul,** in talmudic and rabbinic literature, a sharp dialectic used particularly by talmudists in Poland from the 16th century.

***Pinkas,** community register or minute-book.

***Piyyut** (pl. **piyyutim**), Hebrew liturgical poetry.

***Pizmon,** poem with refrain.

Posek (pl. ***posekim**), decisor; codifier or rabbinic scholar who pronounces decisions in disputes and on questions of Jewish law.

***Prosbul,** legal method of overcoming the cancelation of debts with the advent of the *sabbatical year.

***Purim,** festival held on Adar 14 or 15 in commemoration of the delivery of the Jews of Persia in the time of *Esther.

Rabban, honorific title higher than that of rabbi, applied to heads of the *Sanhedrin in mishnaic times.

***Rabbanite,** adherent of rabbinic Judaism. In contradistinction to *Karaite.

Reb, rebbe, Yiddish form for rabbi, applied generally to a teacher or ḥasidic rabbi.

***Reconstructionism,** trend in Jewish thought originating in the United States.

***Reform Judaism,** trend in Judaism advocating modification of *Orthodoxy in conformity with the exigencies of contemporary life and thought.

Resh galuta, lay head of Babylonian Jewry (see exilarch).

Responsum (pl. ***responsa**), written opinion (*teshuvah*) given to question (*she'elah*) on aspects of Jewish law by qualified authorities; pl. collection of such queries and opinions in book form *(she'elot u-teshuvot)*.

***Rishonim,** older rabbinical authorities. Distinguished from later authorities (**aḥaronim*).

***Rishon le-Zion,** title given to Sephardi chief rabbi of Ereẓ Israel.

***Rosh Ha-Shanah,** two-day holiday (one day in biblical and early mishnaic times) at the beginning of the month of *Tishri (September-October), traditionally the New Year.

Rosh Ḥodesh, *New Moon, marking the beginning of the Hebrew month.

Rosh Yeshivah, see *Yeshivah.

***R.S.H.A.** (initials of Ger. *Reichssicherheitshauptamt*: "Reich Security Main Office"), the central security department of the German Reich, formed in 1939, and combining the security police (Gestapo and Kripo) and the S.D.

***Sanhedrin,** the assembly of ordained scholars which functioned both as a supreme court and as a legislature before 70 C.E. In modern times the name was given to the body of representative Jews convoked by Napoleon in 1807.

***Savora** (pl. **savoraim**), name given to the Babylonian scholars of the period between the **amoraim* and the **geonim*, approximately 500–700 C.E.

S.D. (initials of Ger. *Sicherheitsdienst*: "security service"), security service of the *S.S. formed in 1932 as the sole intelligence organization of the Nazi party.

Seder, ceremony observed in the Jewish home on the first night of Passover (outside Ereẓ Israel first two nights), when the **Haggadah* is recited.

***Sefer Torah,** manuscript scroll of the Pentateuch for public reading in synagogue.

***Sefirot, the ten,** the ten "Numbers"; mystical term denoting the ten spheres or emanations through which the Divine manifests itself; elements of the world; dimensions, primordial numbers.

Selektion (Ger.), (1) in ghettos and other Jewish settlements, the drawing up by Nazis of lists of deportees; (2) separation of incoming victims to concentration camps into two categories—those destined for immediate killing and those to be sent for forced labor.

Seliḥah (pl. ***seliḥot**), penitential prayer.

***Semikhah,** ordination conferring the title "rabbi" and permission to give decisions in matters of ritual and law.

Sephardi (pl. ***Sephardim**), Jew(s) of Spain and Portugal and their descendants, wherever resident, as contrasted with *Ashkenazi(m).

Shabbatean, adherent of the pseudo-messiah *Shabbetai Ẓevi (17th century).

Shaddai, name of God found frequently in the Bible and commonly translated "Almighty."

***Shaharit,** morning service.

Shali'aḥ (pl. **sheliḥim**), in Jewish law, messenger, agent; in modern times, an emissary from Ereẓ Israel to Jewish communities or organizations abroad for the purpose of fund-raising, organizing pioneer immigrants, education, etc.

Shalmonit, poetic meter introduced by the liturgical poet *Solomon ha-Bavli.

***Shammash,** synagogue beadle.

***Shavuot,** Pentecost; Festival of Weeks; second of the three annual pilgrim festivals, commemorating the receiving of the Torah at Mt. Sinai.

***Sheḥitah,** ritual slaughtering of animals.

***Shekhinah,** Divine Presence.

Shelishit, poem with three-line stanzas.

***Sheluḥei Erez Israel** (or **shadarim**), emissaries from Ereẓ Israel.

***Shema** ([Yisrael]; "hear . . . [O Israel]," Deut. 6:4), Judaism's confession of faith, proclaiming the absolute unity of God.

Shemini Aẓeret, final festal day (in the Diaspora, final two days) at the conclusion of *Sukkot.

Shemittah, *Sabbatical year.

Sheniyyah, poem with two-line stanzas.

***Shephelah,** southern part of the coastal plain of Ereẓ Israel.

***Shevat,** eleventh month of the Jewish religious year, fifth of the civil, approximating to January-February.

***Shi'ur Komah,** Hebrew mystical work (c. eighth century) containing a physical description of God's dimensions; term denoting enormous spacial measurement used in speculations concerning the body of the **Shekhinah*.

Shivah, the "seven days" of *mourning following burial of a relative.

***Shofar,** horn of the ram (or any other ritually clean animal excepting the cow) sounded for the memorial blowing on *Rosh Ha-Shanah, and other occasions.

Shoḥet, person qualified to perform **sheḥitah*.

Shomer, *Ha-Shomer, organization of Jewish workers in Ereẓ Israel founded in 1909 to defend Jewish settlements.

***Shtadlan,** Jewish representative or negotiator with access to dignitaries of state, active at royal courts, etc.

***Shtetl,** Jewish small-town community in Eastern Europe.

***Shulḥan Arukh,** Joseph *Caro's code of Jewish law in four parts:
Oraḥ Ḥayyim, laws relating to prayers, Sabbath, festivals, and fasts;
Yoreh De'ah, dietary laws, etc;
Even ha-Ezer, laws dealing with women, marriage, etc;
Ḥoshen Mishpat, civil, criminal law, court procedure, etc.

Siddur, among Ashkenazim, the volume containing the daily prayers (in distinction to the **maḥzor* containing those for the festivals).

***Simḥat Torah,** holiday marking the completion in the synagogue of the annual cycle of reading the Pentateuch; in Ereẓ Israel observed on Shemini Aẓeret (outside Ereẓ Israel on the following day).

***Sinai Campaign,** brief campaign in October-November 1956 when Israel army reacted to Egyptian terrorist attacks and blockade by occupying the Sinai peninsula.

Sitra aḥra, "the other side" (of God); left side; the demoniac and satanic powers.

***Sivan,** third month of the Jewish religious year, ninth of the civil, approximating to May-June.

***Six-Day War,** rapid war in June 1967 when Israel reacted to Arab threats and blockade by defeating the Egyptian, Jordanian, and Syrian armies.

***S.S.** (initials of Ger. *Schutzstaffel*: "protection detachment"), Nazi formation established in 1925 which later became the "elite" organization of the Nazi Party and carried out central tasks in the "Final Solution."

***Status quo ante** community, community in Hungary retaining the status it had held before the convention of the General Jewish Congress there in 1868 and the resultant split in Hungarian Jewry.

***Sukkah,** booth or tabernacle erected for *Sukkot when, for seven days, religious Jews "dwell" or at least eat in the *sukkah* (Lev. 23:42).

***Sukkot,** festival of Tabernacles; last of the three pilgrim festivals, beginning on the 15th of Tishri.

Sūra (Ar.), chapter of the Koran.

Ta'anit Esther (Fast of *Esther), fast on the 13th of Adar, the day preceding Purim.

Takkanah (pl. ***takkanot**), regulation supplementing the law of the Torah; regulations governing the internal life of communities and congregations.

***Tallit (gadol),** four-cornered prayer shawl with fringes *(ẓiẓit)* at each corner.

***Tallit katan,** garment with fringes *(ẓiẓit)* appended, worn by observant male Jews under their outer garments.

***Talmud,** "teaching"; compendium of discussions on the Mishnah by generations of scholars and jurists in many academies over a period of several centuries. The Jerusalem (or Palestinian) Talmud mainly contains the discussions of the Palestinian sages. The Babylonian Talmud incorporates the parallel discussion in the Babylonian academies.

Talmud torah, term generally applied to Jewish religious (and ultimately to talmudic) study; also to traditional Jewish religious public schools.

***Tammuz,** fourth month of the Jewish religious year, tenth of the civil, approximating to June-July.

Tanna (pl. ***tannaim**), rabbinic teacher of mishnaic period.

***Targum,** Aramaic translation of the Bible.

***Tefillin,** phylacteries, small leather cases containing passages from Scripture and affixed on the forehead and arm by male Jews during the recital of morning prayers.

Tell (Ar. "mound," "hillock"), ancient mound in the Middle East composed of remains of successive settlements.

***Terefah,** food that is not **kasher*, owing to a defect in the animal.

***Territorialism,** 20th century movement supporting the creation of an autonomous territory for Jewish mass-settlement outside Ereẓ Israel.

***Tevet,** tenth month of the Jewish religious year, fourth of the civil, approximating to December-January.

Tikkun ("restitution," "reintegration"), (1) order of service for certain occasions, mostly recited at night; (2) mystical term denoting restoration of the right order and true unity after the spiritual "catastrophe" which occurred in the cosmos.

Tishah be-Av, Ninth of *Av, fast day commemorating the destruction of the First and Second Temples.

***Tishri,** seventh month of the Jewish religious year, first of the civil, approximating to September-October.

Tokheḥah, reproof sections of the Pentateuch (Lev. 26 and Deut. 28); poem of reproof.

***Torah,** Pentateuch or the Pentateuchal scroll for reading in synagogue; entire body of traditional Jewish teaching and literature.

Tosafist, talmudic glossator, mainly French (12th–14th centuries), bringing additions to the commentary by *Rashi.

***Tosafot,** glosses supplied by tosafist.

***Tosefta,** a collection of teachings and traditions of the *tannaim*, closely related to the Mishnah.

Tradent, person who hands down a talmudic statement in the name of his teacher or other earlier authority.

***Tu bi-Shevat,** the 15th day of Shevat, the New Year for Trees; date marking a dividing line for fruit tithing; in modern Israel celebrated as arbor day.

***Uganda Scheme,** plan suggested by the British government in 1903 to establish an autonomous Jewish settlement area in East Africa.

***Va'ad Le'ummi,** national council of the Jewish community in Ereẓ Israel during the period of the British *Mandate.

***Wannsee Conference,** Nazi conference held on Jan. 20, 1942, at which the planned annihilation of European Jewry was endorsed.

Waqf (Ar.), (1) a Muslim charitable pious foundation; (2) state lands and other property passed to the Muslim community for public welfare.

***War of Independence,** war of 1947–49 when the Jews of Israel fought off Arab invading armies and ensured the establishment of the new State.

***White Paper(s),** report(s) issued by British government, frequently statements of policy, as issued in connection with Palestine during the *Mandate period.

***Wissenschaft des Judentums** (Ger. "Science of Judaism"), movement in Europe beginning in the 19th century for scientific study of Jewish history, religion, and literature.

***Yad Vashem,** Israel official authority for commemorating the *Holocaust in the Nazi era and Jewish resistance and heroism at that time.

Yeshivah (pl. ***yeshivot**), Jewish traditional academy devoted primarily to study of rabbinic literature; *rosh yeshivah*, head of the yeshivah.

YHWH, the letters of the holy name of God, the Tetragrammaton.

Yibbum, see levirate marriage.

Yiḥud, "union"; mystical term for intention which causes the union of God with the **Shekhinah*.

Yishuv, settlement; more specifically, the Jewish community of Ereẓ Israel in the pre-State period. The pre-Zionist community is generally designated the "old yishuv" and the community evolving from 1880, the "new yishuv."

Yom Kippur, Yom ha-Kippurim, *Day of Atonement, solemn fast day observed on the 10th of Tishri.

Yoreh De'ah, see Shulḥan Arukh.

Yoẓer, hymns inserted in the first benediction *(Yoẓer Or)* of the morning **Shema*.

***Ẓaddik,** person outstanding for his faith and piety; especially a ḥasidic rabbi or leader.

Ẓimẓum, "contraction"; mystical term denoting the process whereby God withdraws or contracts within Himself so leaving a primordial vacuum in which creation can take place; primordial exile or self-limitation of God.

***Zionist Commission (1918),** commission appointed in 1918 by the British government to advise the British military authorities in Palestine on the implementation of the *Balfour Declaration.

Ẓiyyonei Zion, the organized opposition to Herzl in connection with the *Uganda Scheme.

***Ẓiẓit,** fringes attached to the **tallit* and **tallit katan*.

***Zohar,** mystical commentary on the Pentateuch; main textbook of *Kabbalah.

Zulat, hymn inserted after the **Shema* in the morning service.

Initial letter "L" for *Laudate,* the first word of Psalm 135 (Vulgate 134), from the illuminated Latin *St. Albans Psalter* (p. 346), England, early 12th century. The figures illustrate the verse "Who smote the first-born of Egypt, both man and beast" (Ps. 135:8). Hildesheim, Germany, St. Godehard's Cathedral.

LEKERT, HIRSCH (1880–1902), bootmaker, native of a small Jewish town in Lithuania. Lekert was active from his youth in workers' groups and in the *Bund in Dvinsk,

Hirsch Lekert, Lithuanian Jew who attempted to assassinate the governor of Vilna. Courtesy Bund Archives, Jewish Labor Movement, New York.

Kovno, Yekaterinoslav, and Vilna. He became famous for his attempt on the life of the governor of Vilna, wounding him, because the latter had ordered the flogging of 26 demonstrators (among them 20 Jews) on May 1, 1902. After the flogging, the central committee of the Bund published a manifesto calling for revenge; Lekert carried out his attack with the help of a group of workers which organized itself independently, since the Vilna committee of the Bund, headed by M. *Gurevich, refused to support the deed officially—they were opposed in principle to political terror. The flogging gave rise to dejection and confusion among the Jews; the shooting by a simple bootmaker at the anti-Semitic governor was regarded by the Jewish population in general as an act in defense of Jewish honor. Lekert served as an example for P. *Dashewski, especially after the Kishinev pogrom. The Bund, together with Polish and Lithuanian Social Democrats, published a statement on the affair which had international reverberations. In the Russian *Iskra,* V. Zasulich and J. *Martov praised Lekert's reaction, while Lenin dissociated himself from it. In the Bund itself terrorist tendencies were aroused for a time. Its fifth conference in Berdichev in August 1902 adopted a resolution for a policy of "organized revenge" that was encouraged by S. *Gozhanski and A. *Braun. The resolution was rescinded under the influence of the "committee abroad" of the Bund.

Lekert was sentenced to death by a military court and hanged on June 10, 1902. The anniversary of Lekert's death was marked for many years in the Jewish workers' movement. The deed was commemorated in popular songs and in special literary works (H. *Leivick, A. *Kushnirov). On the 20th anniversary of Lekert's death a memorial, which no longer exists, was erected in a square in Minsk.

Bibliography: J. S. Hertz, *Hirsh Lekert* (Yid., 1952), bibliography compiled by E. Jeshurin: 118–35; N. Sirkin, in: *Kunteres*, 6, no. 117 (1922/23), 10–12; A. S. Stein, *Ḥaver Artur* (1953), index; Index to *Mi-Bifnim* (1970), 293. [M.M.]

LEKET, SHIKHḤAH, AND PE'AH (Heb. לֶקֶט, שִׁכְחָה וּפֵאָה; "gleanings, forgotten produce, and the corners of the field"), talmudic designation of three portions of the harvest which the farmer was enjoined to leave for the benefit of the poor and the stranger. *Pe'ah* ("corners") and *leket* ("gleanings") are enjoined in Leviticus 19:9–10, while *shikhḥah* ("forgotten produce") and *leket,* in Deuteronomy 24:19–21 (see also *Poor, Provision for). *Leket* refers to the ears of corn which fall to the ground during the reaping. It was usual for the reaper to grasp the ears of corn with one hand and to cut them with the other. If during the reaping one or two stalks fell to the ground because the reaper was not holding them, he was not to gather them but leave them for the poor (Lev. 19:9–10). Corresponding to *leket* in grain is *peret* in the vineyard. Thus if during the vintage one or two grapes fell to the ground, they constituted *peret* for the poor (Pe'ah 6:5). The *olelot* ("small clusters with few grapes") in the vineyard also belonged to the poor (*ibid.,* 7:4), in accordance with the verse, "Thou shalt not glean thy vineyard, neither shalt thou gather the fallen fruit of thy vineyard; thou shalt leave them for the poor and for the stranger."

Shikhḥah applies to one or two sheaves forgotten in the field by the harvester. The owner may not take them, but "it shall be for the stranger, for the fatherless, and for the widow" (Deut. 24:19). The biblical precept of *shikhḥah* refers to cut sheaves, but the sages extended it to apply also to the standing corn which is forgotten in the reaping (Sif. Deut. 283; Pe'ah 6:7). *Shikhḥah* also applies to trees so that if the harvesting of one or two trees was overlooked, they are *shikhḥah* (Pe'ah 7:1). The Bible (Deut. 24:20) specifies only olive trees: "when thou beatest thine olive trees thou shalt not go over the boughs again, it shall be for the stranger, for the fatherless, and for the widow." The word *aharekha* ("to go over again") was taken to refer to *shikhḥah,* but it was made to apply to all trees (Ḥul. 131a). *Pe'ah,* according to the Bible, applies only to the corner of the field left by the reaper, but it was extended by the rabbis to include the fruit of the trees (Sifra, Kedoshim, 1:7; Maim. Yad, Mattenot Aniyyim 1:2). According to biblical law the command to give the gifts to the poor applies only in Ereẓ Israel, since the Bible says, "And when ye reap the harvest of your land" (Leviticus 19:9); the rabbis, however, applied it to outside Ereẓ Israel as well (Ḥul. 137b), and according to Maimonides (*ibid.,* 1:14) the same ruling applies to the other gifts to the poor. The Bible lays down no minimum quantity for *pe'ah,* and therefore according to the letter of the law, even if one ear of corn has been left, the precept has been fulfilled; the rabbis, however, established a minimum of one sixtieth of the harvest (Pe'ah 1:1–2; Ḥul. 137b). They forbade the farmer to hire gentile workers for the harvest lest, being unaware of the law, they prevent the poor from gathering *leket* and *pe'ah.* Nevertheless, if he does hire them and they reap the whole field, he must give *pe'ah* from the harvest (Tosef. Pe'ah 3:1; BK 94a). R. Simeon, who always "expounded the reasons for the precepts of the Torah," gives four reasons why the Torah enjoined that *pe'ah* be left at the edge of the field: to prevent the poor from being deprived of their rights—that the

farmer should not wait until his field is practically cleared and say to his poor relative, "this is *pe'ah*—hasten and take before others come" (if it is left at the edge of the field, however, the poor see it and come); not to waste the time of the poor—that the poor should not have to wait and watch where the farmer would leave his *pe'ah;* to prevent suspicion—that passersby should not say, "let that farmer who has not left *pe'ah* be cursed" (when they see him reaping the whole field and do not know that he has already given it); and because of swindlers (who will not leave *pe'ah* and say they have already given it; Tosef. Pe'ah 1:6; Shab 23a).

Pe'ah was left standing, and the poor plucked it. They were not permitted to cut it with a scythe nor uproot it with a spade so as to prevent them from assaulting one another (Pe'ah 4:4). The poor were permitted to pick *pe'ah* thrice daily: in the morning, at midday, and in the afternoon. If a poor man came at some other time he was forbidden to pick, in order that all the poor assemble at a prescribed time. These times were chosen because some of the poor were nursing mothers who must eat at the beginning of the day, and some were minors who do not wake up early and cannot reach the field until midday, and some were aged who cannot reach the field until the afternoon (Pe'ah 4:5; Maim. *ibid.* 2:17). The poor thus obtain four gifts from a vineyard—*peret, olelot, pe'ah,* and *shikhḥah;* three from grain—*leket, shikhḥah,* and *pe'ah;* and two from trees—*shikhḥah* and *pe'ah.* Basing themselves on the fact that the Bible does not state "Thou shalt give," but "thou shalt leave," the rabbis held that the farmer was forbidden to select the poor to whom these gifts would be given, any poor person being free to take them (Ḥul. 131a). Although the injunction applies specifically to the Jewish poor, in the interests of peace, it was extended to the gentile poor (Git. 5:8).

See also *Poverty.

Bibliography: D. Hoffmann, *Das Buch Leviticus,* 2 (1906), 36–38, 240f.; S. Lieberman, *Tosefta ki-Feshutah, Zera'im* (1955); Maim, Yad, *Mattenot Aniyyim;* J. Feliks, *Ha-Ḥakla'ut be-Ereẓ-Yisrael bi-Tekufat ha-Mishnah ve-ha-Talmud* (1963), index; E. E. Urbach, in: *Zion,* 16 (1951), 1–27; I. F. Baer, *ibid.,* 27 (1962), 141–55; I. Heinemann, *Ta'amei ha-Mitzvot be-Sifrut Yisrael,* 1 (1954³), 2 (1956). [A.Ar.]

LEKHAH DODI (Heb. לְכָה דוֹדִי; "Come, my friend"), the opening words and name of a hymn with which the Sabbath is welcomed. It consists of nine stanzas; the initial letters of the first eight stanzas acrostically form the name of the author Solomon ha-Levi (*Alkabeẓ), a Safed kabbalist of the early 16th century. The opening line and refrain is: "Come, my friend, to meet the bride; let us welcome the presence of the Sabbath." Inspired by talmudic accounts (Shab. 119a) which describe how the scholars used to honor and welcome the Sabbath (likened to a princess or bride), the Safed kabbalists used to go on Friday afternoons into the fields to meet the "Queen Sabbath" in meditation and song. The hymn *"Lekhah Dodi"* reflects this practice as well as the kabbalistic identification of the Sabbath with the *Shekhinah,* the mystical archetype of Israel. Hence also the messianic motives in the hymn, echoing talmudic concepts associating redemption with the observance of the Sabbath (*ibid.,* 118b).

"Lekhah Dodi" is sung immediately after the recital of Psalms 95–99 and 29, with which the Sabbath eve service starts in Ashkenazi synagogues; the *ḥazzan* stands on the *bimah* ("high platform") and not at his regular place to indicate that this part of the service is not in the original order of prayers. It is customary to turn around at the recital of the last stanza (*"Bo'i ve-shalom"*) to face the

לאחר כך יעמדו כל העדה הקדושה לכבוד סבת מלכתא · לעורר
הפיוט נחה ושובח אשר חברו וסדרו הרב הכולל הצדקי מהר'ר שלמה
הלוי זל חלמקן ושמו חתום בראשי חרוזות שהי כזק לבת ארן גבי תזב ·

רי לקראת כלה פני שבת נקבלה ·
    לבה דודי לקראת כלה פני שבת נקבלה ·
ש מור וזכור בדבור אחד · ה
ה השמיענו אל המיוחד · יי אחד
    ושמו אחד · לשם ולתפאר ולתהלה ·
    לבה דודי לקראת כלה פני שבת נקבלה ·
ל קראת שבת לכו ונלכה · כי היא
    מקור הברכה · מראש מקדם נסוכה ·

Opening of the *"Lekhah Dodi"* hymn from the manuscript *Seder Tikkunei Shabbat,* Vienna, 1715. Cecil Roth Collection. Photo David Harris, Jerusalem.

entrance of the synagogue and bow. The "Sabbath bride" is thus symbolically welcomed. *"Lekhah Dodi,"* among the latest *piyyutim* to be incorporated into the prayer book, is one of the favorite hymns in the Ashkenazi as well as in the Sephardi ritual. In the extant texts, there are only slight variations, although one version has five additional stanzas also attributed to Alkabeẓ. In many rituals, *"Bo'i kallah Shabbat malketa'* ("Come our bride, queen Sabbath"; Shab. 119a) is added at the end of *"Lekhah Dodi."*

The Reform ritual has retained only an abridged version of the hymn consisting of the first, third, fourth, and the last stanzas (*Union Prayer Book,* 1 (1926), 27). *"Lekhah Dodi"* has been rendered into most European languages; among the well-known translations are those of the German poets J. G. Herder and H. *Heine. In his poem *"Prinzessin Sabbat,"* Heine erroneously ascribed its authorship to Judah Halevi. Another version of *"Lekhah Dodi"* was composed by a contemporary of Alkabeẓ, R. Moses ibn Machir, head of the yeshivah in Ein Zeitun near Safed (printed in *Seder ha-Yom* (Venice, 1599), 43).

[M.Y.]

Musical Rendition. The poem was written to be sung, but none of the contemporary sources offers any information about its original melody. In the first printed version of the text, in a Sephardi prayer book, Venice 1583/4, it is headed "To the tune of *Shuvi Nafshi li-Menuḥaikhi* (by Judah Halevi; Davidson Oẓar 3665). This heading was taken over by two much later Sephardi prayer books, Amsterdam 1660/1 and Constantinople 1734/5, but apparently nowhere else. No conclusions can be drawn from it about the melody adopted or created in Safed, or about the ancestry of any one of the melodies presently used. Most of the existing melodies—A. Z. Idelsohn estimated their number at over 2,000—show no distribution over a larger area and are either demonstrably late or the obvious products of musical styles that could not have been available or acceptable at Safed. Of the remainder there emerge three distinct melodies, one of which may well represent the original setting. Type-melody *a* (see mus. ex. 1) is found in Ereẓ Israel, southern Syria, Turkey, and the Balkans and has also been notated from North African informants. It belongs to the *Maqam Nawa,* which dominates the melodic character of the Sabbath eve and morning services in the Eastern Mediterranean communities, and Idelsohn proposed it as the original setting of *"Lekhah Dodi."* Type-melody *b* (see mus. ex. 2) is found in the Sephardi communities of Amsterdam, London, Hamburg, and Leghorn. It is more complex than type *a* and has a definitely oriental flavor. Type-melody *c* (see mus. ex. 3) is found in the Sephardi communities of Bayonne and Bordeaux, in the Comtat Venaissin (i.e., Provence, a non-Sephardi community), and has also been notated from informants from Sarajevo (Yugoslavia) and Meknès (Morocco); its variants are extremely divergent, but all of them contain the elements of a Turkish military march. All these communities also have some strictly local melodies for *"Lekhah Dodi"* and the non-Sephardi Eastern communities have only local and regional melodies. The single example published from Yemen is sung to the general Yemenite pattern of psalm recitation (Idelsohn, *Melodien,* 1 (1914), nos. 20–21). In the Western Ashkenazi area, a certain stabilization was attempted by the melodic linking of *"Lekhah Dodi"* to the particular character of the respective Sabbath, week, or season. There were special melodies for *Shabbat Shuvah* and *Shabbat Sefirah,* and the melody used on the eve of *Shabbat Ḥazon* and during the three weeks between Tammuz 17 and Av 9 was based on *Eli Ẓiyyon.* Many of the ostensibly free compositions also begin with a "seasonal reminiscence," such as the *Ma'oz Ẓur* motive for the Sabbath of the Ḥanukkah week. The completely free compositions are in the majority, and the surviving cantorial

EXAMPLE 1

EXAMPLE 1. Three versions of the *"Lekhah Dodi"* melody common in the Near East. The omission sign in each line represents three repetitions, with slight variations, of the first two bars. I. Notated by J. Parisot in Damascus, 1901. After J. Parisot, *Journal of the American Oriental Society,* 24, 1903. II. Common Jerusalem Sephardi version. Free notation by B. Bayer. III. Rumanian Sephardi version. After Idelsohn, *Melodien* 4, 1922, no. 4.

EXAMPLE 2

EXAMPLE 2. Beginning of the European Sephardi type-melody. From Hamburg (?). After A. Baer, *Ba'al Tefillah*, 1883³, no. 329.

EXAMPLE 3

EXAMPLE 3. Beginning of the Mediterranean and Balkan Sephardi type-melody. From Sarajevo. After Levy, *Antologia* I, 1965, no. 25.

manuals of the 18th century already contain hundreds of melodies which for the most part reflect the style of the gentile environments ("Menuetto," "Polonaise," etc.). They also show the interesting custom of setting each stanza to a different melody, or at least distinguishing *"Hitoreri"* ("Wake Up!") by an energetic melody and *"Bo'i ve-Shalom"* ("Come in Peace, O Sabbath Queen") by a lyrical one. Since the "reception of the Sabbath" in the synagogue precedes the "entrance of the Sabbath" itself, it was possible to accompany the ceremony, and especially the singing of *"Lekhah Dodi,"* with musical instruments. There are references to this practice in several communities, notably Prague, in the 17th and 18th centuries. In Eastern Europe no trace of standardized renditions can be discerned. This complete freedom may account fo Hebrew-Yiddish *"Lekhah Dodi"* "play songs" and parodies. [B.B.]

Bibliography: Elbogen, Gottesdienst, 108, 388, 530; Davidson, Oẓar, 3 (1930), no. 928; Abrahams, Companion, CXXIV–CXXVII. Y. Y. Cohen, *Seder kabbalat Shabbat u-fizmon lekhah dodi* (1969). MUSICAL RENDITION, SEPHARDI TYPE-MELODIES. TYPE *a*: Idelsohn, Melodien, 4 (1923), nos. 3–7; J. Parisot, in: JAOS, 24 no. 2 (1903), 244; A. Baer, *Ba'al Tefillah* (1883³), no. 937; Levy, Antología, 1 (1965), nos. 14, 20, 23; 3 (1968), no. 327. TYPE *b*: A. Baer, *Ba'al Tefillah* (1883³), no. 329; E. Aguilar and D. A. De Sola, *Ancient Melodies of the Spanish and Portuguese Jews' Congregation, London* (1857, 1931), no. 7 (also in: Idelsohn, Melodien, 4 (1923), 110); F. Consolo, *Libro dei Canti d'Israele* (1892), no. 5 (also in Idelsohn, loc. cit.); Levy, Antologia, 1 (1965), no. 18. TYPE *c*: J. S. and M. Crémieu, *Chants Hébraïques suivant le rite . . . de l'ancien Comtat Venaissin* (1887), no. 1; M. J. Benharoche-Baralia, *Chants Hébraïques traditionnels en usage dans la communauté sephardie de Bayonne* (1961), no. 13; S. Foy, *Recueil des Chants . . . en usage dans la Communauté de Bordeaux* (1928); Levy, Antología, 1 (1965), no. 25: 3 (1968), no. 78. OLDER WEST ASHKENAZIC FREE AND SEASONAL MELODIES: A. Nadel, in: EJ, s.v. *Lecha Dodi*: Idelsohn, Melodien, 4 (1923), 217, 219–20, 222, 229; A. Baer, *Ba'al Tefillah* (1883³), nos. 325–7. LITERATURE: Idelsohn, Melodien, 4 (1923), 109–10; Idelsohn, Music, 116, 362, 509 note 54; A. Friedmann, *Der Synagogale Gesang* (1904), 70–71; Adler, Prat Mus, 24, 28–30, 127. "PLAY SONGS" AND PARODIES: S. Lehman, in: *Arkhiv far Yidisher Shprakh-Visenshaft, Literaturforshung un Etnologie*, 1 (1926–33), 430.

LEKHNO, DAVID (d. 1735), scholar living in the Crimean community of *Karasubazar (Belogorsk). His family name indicates his Polish origin. A leader of the Karasubazar community, Lekhno was also respected by the Karaites of Crimea. His extant works include an introduction to *Maḥzor Minhag Kafa*, which contains information on the way of life of Crimean Jewry; *Mishkan David*, on Hebrew grammar; and *Devar Sefatayim*, a history of the kingdoms of the Tatar khans in Crimea (the first chapters were published by Y. D. Markon in *Devir*, 2 (1924, 243–7).

Bibliography: A.A. Harkavy, *Altjuedische Denkmaeler in der Krim* (1876), 230–2. [Y.S.]

°**LELEWEL, JOACHIM (Ignacy;** 1786–1861), historian and Polish freedom fighter. The Polish historian and statesman *Czacki, his teacher at the University of Vilna, entrusted him with the proofreading of his research work on Jews and *Karaites *(Rozprawa o żydach i Karaitach)* in 1807. In 1830, at the time of the Polish uprising, he was appointed vice-minister of education and religions in the provisional national government. After the suppression of the revolt, he emigrated to Paris and settled in Brussels in 1833, and after 1848 he abandoned political activity. He published a comprehensive work on the history of Poland (20 vols., 1823–64). In his important work *Géographie du moyen âge* (5 vols. with atlas, 1849–57), Lelewel deals among other things (vol. 4) with the travels of R. *Benjamin of Tudela. Lelewel also published an article in Eliakim *Carmoly's *Notice historique sur Benjamin de Tudèle* (1852²).

His attitude toward the Jews, which was at first negative, changed from 1832. At the end of that year, Lelewel issued his appeal *Au peuple d'Israël!* (the full text of it was published in Leon Hollaenderski's *Les Israélites de Pologne* (1846), 117–31), which was later translated into Yiddish by Ludwig Joshua Lubliner. Lelewel calls upon the Jews to support the revolt of the Polish nation which will break out in the future. He says that "the Jews will obtain their rights, and if they insist upon returning to Palestine the Poles will assist them in the realization of this aspiration." On Nov. 16, 1859, the Polish periodical *Przegląd rzeczy polskich*, which appeared in Paris, published a "letter from J. Lelewel to Mr. H. Merzbach," in which the author expressed his vigorous opposition to the anti-Semitic campaign, accused the Russian government of having fomented hatred between Poles and Jews, and hoped that an improvement in the condition of the population would result in healing the breach between them. At his funeral in Paris, Lelewel was eulogized by Rabbi Elie-Aristide *Astruc. Jewish students in Warsaw held a memorial service for Lelewel in a synagogue on June 1, 1861.

Bibliography: M. Muenz, *Lelewel, Kaempfer fuer Recht und Wahrheit und die Judenfeinde* (1860); M. Balaban, in: *Miesięcznik Żydowski*, 1 no. 1 (1933), 289–331; J. Shatzky, *Geshikhte fun Yidn in Varshe*, 2 (1951), 164–7, 203, 218; S. Lastik, *Z dziejów oświecenia żydowskiego* (1961), index; A. Eisenbach (ed.) *Żydzi a powstanie styczniowe, materiały i dokumenty* (1963), index; H. Merzbach, *Joachim Lelewel w Brukseli* (1889). [A. CY.]

LELOV (Lelow), ḥasidic dynasty in Poland and Ereẓ Israel. Its founder, DAVID BEN SOLOMON OF LELOV (1746–1813), studied Lurianic Kabbalah in his youth and behaved in the manner of the "great Ḥasidim." He became attracted to Ḥasidism as a result of his contact with *Elimelech of Lyzhansk, and studied under several ḥasidic rabbis, including *Moses Leib of Sasov, becoming the outstanding disciple of *Jacob Isaac Horowitz, ha-Ḥozeh ("The Seer") of Lublin. He earned his living as a grocer. David's teachings stressed love of the Jewish people *(ahavat Yisrael)* and of man in general; he said: "I am not worthy as yet to be called a *zaddik* since I still feel more love for my own children than for other people." He was much appreciated by the prominent ḥasidic leaders of his day. David was both a friend and a relative of Jacob Isaac of *Przysucha, the "Holy Jew." When a controversy broke out between the latter and Jacob Isaac of Lublin, David attempted to reconcile the two sides. The physician, Bernard of Piotrkow, the famous penitent *(ba'al teshuvah),* was his outstanding disciple. David's son, Moses (1778–1850), became the son-in-law of Jacob Isaac of Przysucha, and served as rabbi in several communities. Toward the end of his life he settled in Ereẓ Israel. Since then part of the Lelow dynasty has been connected with Ereẓ Israel, although they did not formally serve as *admorim.* Moses' grandson, David Joseph of Lelov (1827–1907), was a disciple of Menahem Mendel of *Warka (Worki). From 1877 he led a ḥasidic community. The dynasty is still continued through its branch in Ereẓ Israel.

Bibliography: M. Brakman, *Migdal David,* (1930); L. Grossmann, *Shem u-She'erit* (1943), 56; M. Buber, *Tales of the Hasidim: Later Masters* (1961), 185–8; M. Y. Weinstock, *Peri Kodesh Hillulim* (1961). [A.St.]

LELOW (Pol. **Lelów**), village (formerly a town) in Kielce province, S. E. central Poland. Several dozen Jewish families were living in Lelow in 1547, but in 1564 only six families remained; each paid the king one red guilder residence tax and a certain quantity of spices for the right to slaughter cattle. During the 16th and 17th centuries Jews played an important part in the Lelow fairs. In the first part of the 18th century they had grown to a considerable community, paying 741 zlotys poll tax in 1718 and an annual average of 1,050 zlotys in 1733–37. In the district, which included the communities of Lelow, Naklo, Janow, Pilico, Szczekocin, and Zarki, there were 3,415 Jews in 1765, when 335 Jewish poll tax payers were recorded in Lelow and 18 villages were under the community's jurisdiction. By an agreement with the townsmen, in 1778, the Jews were released from the payment of municipal taxes, as well as from the duty of billeting the troops. Between 1823 and 1862 Jewish residence was restricted to a specific quarter. The community numbered 269 (29% of the total population) in 1808, 339 (39%) in 1827, 480 (53%) in 1857, 720 (60%) in 1897, and 638 (52%) in 1921. Before the outbreak of World War II there were about 700 Jews in Lelow. The Jewish community was liquidated in September 1942, when all the Jews were deported to *Treblinka death camp. After the war the Jewish community of Lelow was not reconstituted.

Bibliography: Halpern, Pinkas, index; J. Kleczyński, *Spis ludności dyecezyi krakowskiej 1787* (1894); Warsaw, Archiwum Skarbowe, *Tax Register of 1553, 12:46;* I. Schiper, *Dzieje handlu Żydowskiego na ziemiach polskich* (1937), index; B. Wasiutyński, *Ludność Żydowska w Polsce w. wiekach XIX i XX* (1930), 56; R. Mahler, *Yidn in Amolikn Poyln in Likht fun Tsifern* (1958), index. [EJ/Ed.]

LELYVELD, ARTHUR JOSEPH (1913–), U.S. Reform rabbi and community leader. Lelyveld was born in New York and was ordained at Hebrew Union College in 1939. Rabbi Lelyveld served as national director of the B'nai B'rith Hillel Foundations (1947–56), and from 1958 was rabbi of Fairmount (formerly Euclid Avenue) Temple in Cleveland. He was president of the American Jewish Congress from 1966; a leader of the National Association for the Advancement of Colored People; and served as general chairman of the Jewish Welfare Fund campaign of Cleveland. He wrote *Atheism is Dead* (1968), a response to contemporary radical theology. In 1964 Rabbi Lelyveld went to Mississippi as part of a team of clergy counseling civil rights workers and was severely beaten by racists. For this mission he won the Distinguished Service Award of the NAACP. [J.Ri.]

LEMANS, MOSES (1785–1832), Hebraist and mathematician. Born in Naarden, Netherlands, Lemans was one of the leaders of the Haskalah movement in Holland. He was one of the founders in 1808 of the "Chanogh lanangar ngal pie darkoo" society the aim of which was a reform in Jewish education. He published a pamphlet in which he praised the Sephardi pronunciation of Hebrew, preferring it to the Ashkenazi one. For the society he published Hebrew textbooks, as well as a translation of the Bible into Dutch. He was one of the founders of the Jewish Mathematicians' Association, "Mathesis artium genetrix." In 1818 he was appointed head of the first school for needy Jews in Amsterdam, and in 1828 teacher of mathematics in the Amsterdam gymnasium (secondary school). Lemans published a number of works on Hebrew grammar and mathematics. With S. I. *Mulder, he compiled a Hebrew-Dutch dictionary. Of his Hebrew poems, the most important is an epic on the revolt of the Belgians against the Netherlands (in Ms.). For his activities on behalf of the Jews he was awarded a medal by the Netherlands' government. His works include: *Levensbeschrijving . . . Moses Majemonides* (Amsterdam, 1815); *Rudimenta of gronden der hebreeuwsche taal* (1820); *Gebeden der Nederlandsche Israëliten* (1822), *Hebreeuwsch-Nederduitsch handwoordenboek* (1831); and *Allereerste gronden der Hebreeuwsche taal* (1876).

Moses Lemans, Dutch Hebraist and mathematician. Courtesy Amsterdam University Library.

Bibliography: Ulman, in: *Jaarboeken voor de Israëliten in Nederland,* 2 (1836), 297–312; A. Dellavilla, *Allon Muẓẓav* (1852); Michman-Melkman, in: *Leshonenu la-Am,* 18 (1967), 76–90, 120–35. [J.M.]

LEMBERGER, MOSES BEN AARON (1706–1757), rabbi. At the age of eight Moses left his home in Lvov to be brought up by his grandfather in *Mikulov (Nikolsburg). In 1724 he was appointed rabbi of *Lipnik (Leipnik, Moravia) and in 1729 was appointed to succeed Jehiel Michael Ḥasid as *av bet din* of Berlin. He stayed there for one year, accepting a call in 1730 to the position of *av bet din* of Frankfort on the Oder, a position he held for about 14 years. He returned to Lipnik as *av bet din* in 1745. In 1755 on the death of his uncle Issachar Berush *Eskeles, Moses was elected *Landesrabbiner* of Moravia. Moses' novellae on the tractate *Rosh Ha-Shanah* were published in Frankfort on the Oder in 1731.

Bibliography: S. Buber, *Anshei Shem* (1895), 166, no. 422; W. Mueller, *Urkundliche Beitraege zur Geschichte der maehrischen Judenschaft* (1903), 157–9; H. Gold (ed.), *Juden und Judengemeinden Maehrens . . .* (1929), index s.v. *Lwów, Moses b. Aaron.* [Ed.]

LEMKIN, RAPHAEL (1901–1959), international lawyer who initiated the use of the term "genocide." Educated in Poland, Germany, and France, he became secretary of the Court of Appeal, Warsaw, in 1927. Early in his career he tried to mobilize support for the international penalization of genocide, despite his view that crimes committed by acts of sovereign states are not subject to international jurisdiction. Returning to Warsaw in 1933, after the Madrid Conference for the unification of penal law, he was compelled to give up his official position. He suffered under Colonel Beck's pro-German anti-Semitic government. In the early part of World War II most of his family were murdered in Warsaw by the Germans. Lemkin fought in the Polish underground, eventually escaping and finally reaching the United States in 1941. There he taught at Duke and Yale universities and served on the Board of Economic Warfare, under Henry Wallace. In 1944 he published his *Axis Rule in Occupied Europe: Laws of Occupation, Analysis of Government Proposals for Redress,* in which he first systematized the material under the term *genocide. In 1946, Lemkin succeeded in mobilizing sufficient support to have genocide put on the agenda of the U.N. General Assembly. The Economic and Social Council invited him to present a draft convention. Assisted by Herbert V. Evatt, the Australian president of the General Assembly, he was able to get that body to pass a resolution in December 1948 on the adoption of the Convention for the Prevention and Punishment of Genocide. Although he was not an official of an international organization, Lemkin nevertheless played an important role through his forceful personal insistence.

Bibliography: H. Maza, *Neuf meneurs internationaux* (1965), 341–57; E. Aroneanu, *Le Crime contre l'Humanité* (1961). [J.J.L.]

LEMLEIN (Lammlin), ASHER (16th century), false messiah active in 1500–02. Apparently of Ashkenazi origin, Lemlein began his activities in northeast Italy, later extending them to Germany. According to his statements the redemption was approaching because the Messiah had already come—namely Lemlein himself. His disciples, who circulated this rumor, stimulated a movement of asceticism and repentance hitherto unknown in these areas. Long afterward this year was recalled as the "year of the repentance," even in Christian polemics against the Jews. There is no information on the events of Lemlein's life and his personality, except that he engaged in Kabbalah. The evolution of his movement is also not known. Apparently it ceased to exist with his death. The statements of Gedaliah b. Joseph *ibn Yaḥya in *Shalshelet ha-Kabbalah* (Venice, 1586), on a wave of apostasies from Judaism as a result of the crisis of the Lemlein movement, are not to be accepted, for even his chief enemies among his contemporaries, Abraham *Farissol and *Joseph ha-Kohen, do not mention this fact.

Bibliography: A. Z. Aescoly, *Ha-Tenu'ot ha-Meshihiyyot be-Yisrael* (1956), 249–50, 307–12; A. Marx, in REJ, 61 (1911), 135–8; S. Loewinger, *ibid.*, 105 (1940), 32ff. [Ed.]

°**L'EMPEREUR (Van Oppyck), CONSTANTIN** (1591–1648), Christian Hebraist and theologian of Harderwijk (central Netherlands). Upon the establishment of a special chair for polemics against Judaism at the University of Leiden, L'Empereur became professor of Hebrew language and literature, with the title *controversarium Judaicorum professor.* In addition, he was appointed professor of theology in 1648. He edited the Mishnah tractates *Middot* (1630) and *Bava Kamma* (1637) with Latin translations, the commentaries to Isaiah by Isaac *Abrabanel and by Moses *Alshekh (1631 and 1665), Moses *Kimḥi's *Introductio ad scientam* (1631), Joseph *ibn Yaḥya's paraphrase to Daniel (1633), and the diaries of the traveler *Benjamin of Tudela (1633). His own writings are: *De linguae hebraicae dignitate et utilitate* (1627) on Hebrew language and grammar; *Clavis Talmudica, complectens formulas, loca dialectica et rhetorica priscorum Judaeorum* (1634–1714^{2}), a compendium on talmudic literature; *De legibus Ebraeorum forensibus* (1637), on the Jewish penal code; *Disputationes theologicae Hardevicenae sive systema theologica* (1648); *Commentationes ad Bertramus de republica Ebraeorum* (1651).

Bibliography: Steinschneider, Cat Bod, 971, no. 5032; idem, Handbuch (1937^{2}), 45, no. 561; idem, in: ZHB, 2 (1897), 149, no. 174. [Ed.]

LEMUEL (Heb. לְמוּאֵל, לְמוֹאֵל ; "belonging to God"), apparently a foreign king to whom the instruction in Proverbs 31:2–9 is addressed by his mother. Proverbs 31:1, in which Lemuel is mentioned, should be divided not after *melekh* but after *massa,* thus identifying the man as: "Lemuel, king of Massa," Massa being the North Arabian tribe, known from Genesis 25:14, one of the Kedemite peoples whose wisdom the Israelites held in high esteem (see *Agur son of Jakeh). The Septuagint did not recognize either *lemu/o/el* or *massa* as proper nouns, and some moderns follow it, obtaining with the help of some emendations the sense (in Scott's rendering): (1) Words [of advice] to a king acting foolishly. A solemn injunction which his mother lays on him: . . . (4) It is not fitting for a king to play the fool, etc. But the interpretation of the Septuagint, Torczyner (Tur-Sinai), and Scott all involve dubious readings and/or Hebrew grammar.

Bibliography: See commentaries on Proverbs; N. H. Torczyner (Tur-Sinai), *Mishlei Shelomo* (1947), 3–5; N. H. Tur-Sinai, *Ha-Lashon ve-ha-Sefer,* 3 (1955), 383; W. F. Albright, in: *Studi . . . Giorgio Levi Della Vida,* 1 (1956), 1–14; R. B. Y. Scott, *Proverbs and Ecclesiastes* (1965), 183–4. [M.Fo./H.L.G.]

LENGYEL, JÓZSEF (1896–), Hungarian author and poet, born in Marcali. Lengyel's poetic talents were first discovered in the modernist periodical, *A Tett* ("The Deed"). In 1918 he was one of the founders of the Hungarian Communist Party, and was arrested by the revolutionary authorities of the Károlyi regime before the Bolshevik revolution led by Bela *Kun. After its failure, he fled to Vienna, and thence to Berlin, finally settling in Moscow, where he worked in the circle of Hungarian emigré writers. There he was arrested in 1938 and sent to a Soviet concentration camp. After World War II, Lengyel was exiled to Siberia, but was released and rehabilitated in 1955, when he returned to Hungary. His literary work after his imprisonment describes with profound psychological analysis the horrifying world of those condemned to slow death. His works include *Visegrádi utca* ("Visegrádi Street," 1930^{1}, 1957^{2}), *Prenn Ferenc hányatott élete . . .* ("The Life and Wanderings of Franz Prenn," 1958), and *Elévült tartozás* ("Debt Overdue," 1964).

Bibliography: Magyar Irodalmi Lexikon, 2 (1965), s.v. [B.Y.]

LENGYEL, MENYHÉRT (Melchior; 1880–), Hungarian playwright. Born in Balmazújváros, Lengyel started his career as a journalist but soon began writing for the theater. His most-successful plays included *Próféta* ("The Prophet," 1911), *A cárnö* ("The Czarina," 1913), *Róza néni* ("Aunt Rose," 1913), and *Antónia* (1925). In 1929 Lengyel was appointed director of a Budapest avant-garde theater. He wrote the libretto of the ballet *Csodálatos mandarin* ("The Miraculous Mandarin") for the composer, Béla Bartók. In 1931 he moved to London and then in 1937, to the United States. Lengyel's best-known play, which had a worldwide success, was *Tajfun* ("Typhoon," 1909), in which he dealt with a contemporary political problem—the whirlwind progress of the Japanese and the resulting danger to the world. In a dramatization of *Cervantes' classic, *Don Quixote, Sancho Panza királysága* ("The Reign of Sancho Panza," 1919), Lengyel expressed his own views on the just society. He also wrote the scripts for several famous films, including *Catherine the Great* (1934, starring Elisabeth Bergner); an adaptation of his own *Czarina; The Blue Angel* (1932, with Marlene Dietrich); and *Ninotchka* (1940, with Greta Garbo). Years later, Lengyel published *Das stille Haus* (1957). In his later years he lived in Rome.

Bibliography: *Magyar Irodalmi Lexikon*, 2 (1965), 34–35. [B.Y.]

°**LENIN (Ulyanov), VLADIMIR ILYICH** (1870–1924), Russian revolutionary, leader of the Communist movement, and founder of the Soviet state. At all stages of his career, Lenin had to cope with the Jewish question from ideological, organizational, and political points of view. At the outset of Lenin's activities, the Jewish *Bund, whose representatives took part in Russian Social Democratic congresses, was a factor to be dealt with in his tactics as head of the Bolshevik faction, as the Bund increasingly threw its weight to the Mensheviks and sometimes swung the balance against Lenin. Like every Russian revolutionary in his time, Lenin attacked, possibly with more sincerity and vigor than others, the anti-Jewish policy of the Czarist regime. He never displayed any inclination to exploit the deep-seated hatred of Jews in the Russian masses as "fuel" to advance the revolution, and in both his personal and political behavior. Lenin never differentiated between people—friends and enemies alike—on the basis of their national or ethnic origins. On the other hand, he viewed the assimilation of the Jews and their complete disappearance into the surrounding culture and society as an inevitable and even desirable result of human advancement. He believed that Jewish separateness, even in the modern and secularist image of the Bund and Socialist Zionism, was a remnant of the precapitalist era and had begun to disappear quickly in Western capitalist countries such as Germany, France, and England. He viewed the separate cultural and social existence of the Jews of Russia as a corollary of the anti-Jewish discrimination and persecution and as a symptom of the backwardness of Russia, in which medieval divisions had not yet crumbled. He therefore denounced not only all manifestations of anti-Semitism, but also all forms of Jewish nationalism and separatism as "reactionary" phenomena that deflect the Jewish workers away from revolutionary solidarity with their non-Jewish comrades and from the struggle for the future revolution to overthrow all class barriers and finally solve the Jewish problem. Lenin expounded his views on the Jewish question and on the national question in general in many articles, e.g. "The Position of the Bund in the Party" (1903: *Collected Works*, (1961[4]), 92–103), "Theses on the National Question" (1913; *ibid.*, 19 (1963[4]), 243–51), "Cultural-National Autonomy" (1913; *ibid.*, 503–7), "Critical Remarks on the National Question" (1913; *ibid.*, 20 (1964[4]), 17–51).

After the Revolution, when Lenin took power in Russia (end of 1917), he endorsed the establishment of special departments for Jewish affairs in both the ruling Communist Party (the *Yevsektsiya) and in the relevant ministry (the Commissariat of Nationalities, headed by Joseph *Stalin). Neither did he object to the recognition of Yiddish as the national language of the Jews, since the masses of Jews—especially in the former *Pale of Settlement—were a large ethnic bloc, with its own culture and language, that should be addressed through means—especially linguistic—understood by it. Together with his acquiescence in the de facto recognition of a Jewish "nationality" in Soviet Russia, Lenin campaigned vigorously, both orally and in writing, against anti-Semitism and incitement to pogroms by the anti-Soviet right-wing forces (the White Army, the Ukrainian nationalists, peasant anarchists, etc.) and initiated, soon after the Revolution, the decree outlawing pogroms and their instigators (July 1918). Thus not only did Lenin abide by one of his ideological principles, he also faced and courageously fought the most demagogic challenge of the counterrevolutionary forces that rose against his regime (see *Anti-Semitism, Anti-Semitism in the Soviet Bloc). Despite this position, however, Lenin did not oppose the cruel persecution of Zionists and suppression of the Hebrew language and the Jewish religion by the Soviet authorities, although in his time many arrested Zionists and rabbis were eventually allowed to leave Russia and go to Palestine. The assassination attempt on behalf of the Social Revolutionaries (1918), carried out against him by a Jewish woman, Fanya Kaplan, did not change his approach to the Jews at all.

At the end of his life, during his illness, Lenin attempted to oppose the Russian "great power chauvinism" of the young Soviet regime, which intervened, behind his back, with excessive cruelty in the lives of other nationalities in the country (such as the Georgians) and thus violated his principles on the national question. The Jewish aspect, however, did not play any part in this last struggle, since the anti-Semitism of the Soviet regime appeared undisguised only years after his death. This development is symbolized by the fact that among the eight speeches that Lenin recorded in 1919, seven were rerecorded in the Soviet Union on a long-playing record and marketed in 1961, during the Khrushchev era, but one speech was not rerecorded—his speech against anti-Semitism.

See also *Communism, *Russia, *Martov, *Stalin, *Trotsky.

Bibliography: S. Schwarz, *Jews in the Soviet Union*, (1961), index; Y. Ma'or, *She'elat ha-Yehudim ba-Tenu'ah ha-Liberalit ve-ha-Mahpekhanit be-Rusyah (1890–1914)* (1964), index; A. B. Ulam, *Lenin and the Bolsheviks* (c. 1966). [B.E.]

LENINGRAD (**St. Petersburg** until 1914, **Petrograd** until 1924), capital of Russia until 1918; industrial city and major port on the Baltic Sea. Some apostates or Marranos appeared in St. Petersburg soon after its foundation in 1703. Anton Divier, who was of Portuguese Jewish origin, was appointed the first police minister of the new capital in 1718. "The Portuguese Jew," Jan Dacosta, was one of the jesters at the royal court during the first half of the 18th century. Jewish physicians and financiers held various positions in the city during the 18th century: Lippmann was financial agent of the court during the 1720s. In 1738 the proselyte officer Alexander *Voznitsyn and Baruch Leibov of Dubrovna, who had introduced him to Judaism, were burnt at the stake in St. Petersburg. Because of the intolerant attitude of Czarina Elizabeth (1741–62) the few Jews who lived in St. Petersburg left. *Catherine II, on the other hand, was interested in attracting Jewish contractors, industrialists, and physicians to the city, and issued instructions to the authorities to overlook the presence of those "useful" Jews who lived there with their families and clerks and had the protection of court officials. Toward the end of Catherine's reign, there was a large community in the town; most prominent was the contractor Abraham *Peretz, whose household included Mendel of Satanov and J. L. *Nevakhovich. The latter published the first work of Russian Jewish literature, *Vopl dshcheri iudeyskoy*, in St. Petersburg in 1803.

From the end of the 18th century, when St. Petersburg had become the government center for millions of Jews who

Figure 1. The Leningrad synagogue, completed in 1893. Courtesy C.A.H.J.P., Jerusalem.

were incorporated into the Russian Empire after the partition of Poland, communal workers and *shtadlanim* streamed into the city. Many others arrived as a result of their business activities or in search of a livelihood in the prosperous city. During the years 1798 and 1800–01, *Shneur Zalman of Lyady, the leader of the Ḥabad Ḥasidim, was imprisoned in St. Petersburg. In 1802 a group of Jews leased a plot of land in the Lutheran cemetery, thus laying the foundations of a permanent community in the city. The situation of the Jews worsened with the accession of Czar *Nicholas I. He ordered that all Jews living in the city "without doing anything" be expelled. According to the official estimate, there were 370 Jews living in the city at that time. These included craftsmen, merchants, and various *shtadlanim;* most of them were ordered to leave. Regulations were issued authorizing Jews to stay in St. Petersburg on business for a maximum period of six weeks; by a special permit from the local authorities this could be extended to between six and ten months. Right of residence was granted to a number of physicians (including the czar's dentist and the midwife of the royal court). After 1827 many *Cantonists went to St. Petersburg and some of them brought their families to the city. They maintained a prayer house and those Jews who had to come to St. Petersburg on business found refuge in their homes. The prohibition on Jewish residence was stringently applied; anyone found living in the city without a permit was liable to be pressed into the army. From time to time the police hunted down Jews living in the city illegally. There was a large and increasing number of apostates, most of whom changed their names and disappeared among the general population.

The situation changed once more with the beginning of the reign of *Alexander II, especially after the publication of the laws granting right of residence outside the *Pale of Settlement to merchants of the first guild, intellectuals, and craftsmen. Wealthy Jewish merchants and financiers (the families *Guenzburg, *Polyakov, A. *Varshavski, Friedland, L. *Rosenthal, and others), physicians, advocates, and scientists soon settled in the city. Many Jewish students registered at the university and the other higher schools of the city (326 in 1886 and 848 in 1911). The influence of the wealthy and the *maskilim* was decisive within the community. Jews and apostates played an important role in the life of the city as journalists, publishers, advocates, scientists, artists, and physicians. In 1881 there were 17,253 Jews (c. 2% of the total population) in St. Petersburg. Ten years later, after a period of strict supervision of residence rights under Police Minister Greser, there were 15,331 Jews (1.6%). According to the 1897 census there were 17,254 (including 310 Karaites), forming 1.4% of the population. In fact, the number of Jews in the city was greater at all periods, because many, whose right to reside there was dubious, evaded the census officers.

Despite its small numbers, the St. Petersburg community played an important role in Russian Jewish life, thanks to the riches of individual members and their proximity to and influence at the court. The barons of the Guenzburg family, as well as other rich Jews, were considered as the spokesmen of the whole of Russian Jewry before the central government. From time to time gatherings of rabbis and community representatives were called to St. Petersburg for official and semiofficial meetings, at which vital problems were discussed. From the 1860s an organized community existed in the city. The right of a communal vote depended on payment of 25 rubles tax, thus assuring that the wealthy had control of the community. Several leading personalities held the position of **kazyonny ravvin* ("government appointed rabbi") in St. Petersburg, including A. Neumann, A. *Drabkin, and M. *Eisenstadt. Among the traditional rabbis was Isaac *Blaser, who held office from 1864 to 1878; the last rabbi of the community was David Tevel *Katzenellenbogen (1907–30). The poet J. L. *Gordon was the community secretary from 1872 to 1879. After many endeavors and numerous refusals, a magnificent central synagogue, containing 1,200 seats and built in the Moorish style, was completed in 1893. In spite of prohibitions and unremitting police persecutions, the community continued to grow, numbering 35,000 (1.8% of the population) in 1914. Severe *censorship regulations caused the Jewish press (Hebrew, Russian, and Yiddish) to be centered in St. Petersburg from the 1870s until the 1905 revolution. The newspapers *Ha-Meliẓ* (1871–73 and 1878–1904), *Ha-Yom* (1886–88), *Dos Yudishes Folksblat* (1881–90), and the first Russian daily newspaper in Yiddish, *Der Fraynd* (1903–08), were all published there. Above all, the city was the center of Russian-Jewish journalism and literature. The periodicals *Yevreyskaya Biblioteka* (1871–80), *Razsvet* (1879–83), and *Voskhod* (1881–1906), the Zionist organ *Razsvet* (1907–18), and many other newspapers, were also published in St. Petersburg. One of the outstanding publications was the Russian-Jewish encyclopedia, *Yevreyskaya Entsiklopediya.*

In addition to local cultural and charitable institutions (such as the Society for the Support of Poor Jews, which was established in 1907 to coordinate the activities of the various charitable societies and was recognized as a legal institution under whose aegis their work could be carried out), many nationwide Jewish organizations had their headquarters in St. Petersburg. Oldest of these organizations was the *Society for the Promotion of Culture among the Jews of Russia (founded in 1863). Others included

Figure 2. Prayers in the Leningrad synagogue, 1950s. Courtesy C.A.H.J.P., Jerusalem.

*ORT; the *Jewish Colonization Association (I.C.A.); the Ḥovevei Sefat Ever (called *Tarbut after the 1917 Revolution); the Historical-Ethnographic Society, which published the historical quarterly *Yevreyskaya Starina;* and the Society for Jewish Folk Music. The city's Asian museum housed a valuable Hebrew department, based on the library of the wealthy M. Friedland. The Imperial Public Library (now the State M.E. Saltykov-Shchedrin Public Library) contains one of the world's oldest and most important collections of Hebrew manuscripts. Under the initiative of Baron D. *Guenzburg, courses in oriental studies were opened in St. Petersburg in 1907. It was intended to develop these into a higher institute of Jewish studies. The concentration of public and cultural institutions in the town attracted Jewish authors and intellectuals (these included A. A. *Harkavy, J. L. *Katzenelson, S. *Dubnow, and M. *Kulisher).

With the outbreak of World War I, *YEKOPO ("Jewish Committee for the Relief of War Victims") was established to concentrate all the relief activities on behalf of hundreds of thousands of Jews who were refugees from the battle regions. After the February Revolution in 1917, all residence restrictions affecting the Jews of Petrograd were abolished and the city became a center of the organizational activities of all the parties and factions of Russian Jewry. In June 1917, the seventh conference of the Zionist Organization of Russia was held in the town. Large numbers attended, demonstrating the strength of the movement and the loyalty of Russian Jews to the Zionist ideal even after they had been granted full civic emancipation. Preparations were also made to convene a general Jewish assembly in Petrograd. During the troubled days in the latter part of 1917 a Jewish battalion under the command of J. *Trumpeldor was formed, made up of Jewish soldiers of the local garrison. Around this battalion a self-defense unit was organized, which protected Jewish lives and property during the revolution of October 1917. The transfer of the seat of government from Petrograd to Moscow (1918) and the shortages and famine reigning in the city during the Russian civil war severely affected the Jewish community. Many Jews returned to their families in provincial towns. In 1920 there were 25,453 Jews (3.5% of the total population) in Petrograd. With the consolidation of the Soviet regime, the number of Jews rapidly increased, to 52,373 (4.9%) in 1923 and 84,505 (5.2%) in 1926. The 1926 census listed their occupations as: clerks (40.2%), craftsmen (14%), laborers (13.5%), government and municipal employees (10.2%), and liberal professions (2.5%); the remainder were unemployed. Organized Jewish life was liquidated in Leningrad as in all places throughout the Soviet Union. A small group of Russian-Jewish intellectuals attempted to continue its literary-scientific work under the new regime. They maintained their former cultural societies and continued to publish scientific and literary periodicals in Russian. By the end of the 1920s, these projects were also liquidated by the Soviet regime. Some intellectuals then left Russia (including S. Dubnow and S. *Ginzburg) and others were integrated in Soviet life (I. *Zinberg, Yu. *Hessen). In his poem the Hebrew poet H. *Lenski described the atmosphere of the city during the Soviet period. On the eve of the Nazi invasion, the number of Jews in Leningrad was estimated at about 200,000 persons. During World War II the Jews shared the general suffering and hunger during the German siege. [Y.S.]

The Contemporary Period. In the census of 1959, 162,344 Jews were registered in Leningrad but the real number was probably closer to 200,000; 13,728 of them declared Yiddish as their mother tongue. The city has one large, imposing synagogue, from the prerevolutionary period, a wedding room, a poultry slaughterhouse, and a *mazzah* bakery. Thousands of Jews congregate in the synagogue and its vicinity on the High Holidays. The congregation published a Jewish calendar on the eve of Rosh Ha-Shanah in the 1950s and 1960s. In the 1950s the city's synagogue board had a dynamic chairman, Gedaliah Pecherski, who was not only devoted to the religious needs of his congregation, but also initiated petitions to the Soviet government and the municipal authorities asking to be allowed to organize courses in such subjects as Hebrew and Jewish history. One petition was also signed by scholars, among them the non-Jewish authority on ancient and medieval Hebrew literature, K. B. Starkova. The petitions were rejected out of hand and Pecherski was arrested in 1961 and sentenced to seven years' imprisonment, ostensibly for having "maintained contact with a foreign [Israel] embassy." The rabbi of the synagogue, Rabbi Lubanov, who had been imprisoned in a forced labor camp in the Stalin era, returned to office and was venerated by the congregation as a scholar and spiritual leader.

The department of oriental and Hebrew studies at Leningrad University has been run mostly by scholars, Jewish and non-Jewish, who studied there before the Revolution and who try to continue the tradition of independent research and scholarly publication in the field of Jewish history, archaeology, etc. Joseph Davidovich Amusin published a book on the Dead Sea Scrolls which became popular with the Soviet public at large. The Saltykov-Shchedrin Library contains a rich section of Hebrew and Yiddish books (about 40,000 volumes) and also displays a number of Hebrew and Yiddish periodicals from abroad, including Israel. Jews and non-Jews frequent this section, though it is generally assumed that "excessive interest" in Hebrew language and literature is viewed with suspicion by the security officials. In 1962 a Jewish drama circle was established, but it soon stopped functioning because of lack of funds.

In 1962–64, as in other parts of the U.S.S.R., the baking of *mazzah* in the Leningrad synagogue was discontinued by the authorities. In 1962, with the intensification of the anti-religious drive, directed mainly against Judaism, several Jews were arrested, some of them charged with "illegally" baking *mazzah.* In the same year, on the eve of Simḥat Torah, 25 Jewish youths were arrested while dancing in the street near the synagogue. The local newspaper, *Vecherniy Leningrad,* carried an article (Oct. 27, 1962) condemning the synagogue's activity. In 1963 flour for *mazzah* baking was confiscated in private Jewish homes.

Figure 3. Concert in the Petrograd city hall, September 1917. Among the artists was Chaliapin, who sang *"Ha-Tikvah"* in Hebrew. Jerusalem, J.N.U.L. Photo Collection.

Figure 4. Dedication page of a Pentateuch in the Leningrad public library, written by Isaac the Pious in Ereẓ Israel or Egypt, 1088 C.E. Leningrad, Saltykov-Shchedrin Library. Heb. B. 111 fol. iv.

From 1963 the authorities prohibited the use of the Jewish cemetery, which was finally closed down in 1969. Jews bury their dead in a section allotted to them in the general cemetery. In 1964, when thousands of Jewish youths danced and sang near the synagogue on Simḥat Torah eve, several of them were arrested. Later the militia put up barriers in the street opposite the synagogue to prevent Jewish youth from congregating and dancing on Simḥat Torah.

After the Six-Day War (1967), Jewish youth displayed more openly its identification with Israel in spite of the official anti-Israel campaign. Many started to study Hebrew in private groups; others protested publicly against the refusal to grant them exit permits for Israel and their protests were published abroad. In June 1970 some of them were arrested in their homes and places of work and their trial has not yet taken place (January 1971). Another group of young Jews, mostly from Riga, together with two non-Jews, were tried in Leningrad in December 1970 for allegedly planning to hijack a Soviet plane in order to land abroad and ultimately to reach Israel. Two were sentenced to death and the others to prison terms of 4–15 years. A worldwide storm of protests, including Communist parties and newspapers in the West, preceded the appeal of the condemned in the Supreme Court of the Russian Republic in Moscow 1971; the death sentences were commuted to 15 years' hard labor and some of the other sentences were reduced.

[ED.]

Bibliography: S. Ginzburg, *Amolike Peterburg* (1944); idem, *Meshumodim in Tsarishn Rusland* (1946), 11–53, 194–206, 279–308; Feinberg, in: *Heawar,* 4 (1956), 21–36; B. Dinur, *Bi-Ymei Milḥamah u-Mahpekhah* (1960), 44–304; L. Gordon, in: *Voskhod,* nos. 1–2 (1881); O. S. Grusenberg, *ibid.,* no. 1 (1891); H. A. Soloveychik, *ibid.,* no. 5 (1892); S. Dneproveki (Dubnow), in: *Nedelnaya Khronika Voskhoda,* nos. 35–36 (1893); L. Klyachko, in: *Yevreyskaya Letopis,* 2 (1923), 114–22.

LENSKI, ḤAYYIM (1905–1942), Hebrew poet. Born in the town of Slonim, district of Grodno, Russia, Lenski spent his childhood and early youth in his grandfather's home in the townlet of Derechin. Late in 1921 he left to study at the Hebrew Teachers' Seminary in Vilna, where he published his first poems in a students' magazine. After two years in Vilna, he joined his father in Baku at the end of 1924, following an adventurous journey. In 1925, however, he left his family and went to Moscow and Leningrad, where he settled down as a worker in the Amal factory founded by *He-Ḥalutz. In Moscow he continued to write poetry, which he sent to literary periodicals in Ereẓ Israel. *Bialik warmly encouraged his writing. Lenski was arrested at the end of 1934 for writing in Hebrew, and, after being detained in Leningrad for a few months, he was sentenced to five years' imprisonment with hard labor in Siberia. His poems, however, continued to reach Ereẓ Israel. While in the labor camp near Mrinsk, he appealed to the Russian writer Maxim Gorki to intercede for him ("I am a poet and my only crime is that my poems were written in Hebrew"), but it is doubtful whether the plea ever reached Gorki. In 1937 Lenski was transferred to the forced labor camp of Gornaya Shoriya, near the Soviet-Mongolian border; from that time on, his poems ceased to reach Ereẓ Israel. In 1939 or 1940, having served his term, he returned to Leningrad. Soon afterward he was again arrested and sent to the prison camp of Malaya Vyshera, near Leningrad. From there he was probably sent back to Siberia, where he died.

Lenski proudly declared in his poem *Leshon Kedumim* ("Ancient Tongue") that he launched the armies of the Queen (i.e., of the Hebrew language) across the rivers Don, Neva, and Neman. At the end of 1958, a number of manuscripts reached Israel which contained a nearly complete collection of his lyrical poems, copied out in the poet's fine handwriting and ready for publication. His poems were subsequently published in Israel under the title of *Me-Ever Nehar ha-Lethe* ("Beyond the River Lethe," 1960).

Lenski's poetry comprises mainly short lyrical poems, sonnets, and ballads that are marked by a perspicuity of language, a concreteness of imagery, and sonorous and vibrant music. Influenced by both Pushkin and Yesenin, with a dash of Heine's bitterness, Lenski's poetry reflects the reality he knew at first hand: the landscape of townlets, forests, and rivers of his Lithuanian homeland, scenes from the Leningrad factory, and Siberia's boundless spaces. All this is transmuted into an imagistic idiom, vivid and often boldly modernistic, as when he indulges in playful onomatopoeic effects. Close to folk and popular lore, his writing is tinged with sober humor which,

Ḥayyim Lenski, Soviet Hebrew poet. Jerusalem, J.N.U.L., Schwadron Collection.

in his longer poems, is transfigured into mordant and rebellious satire. In these longer poems, his most important, the fundamentally nonpolitical poet attacks the "world of tomorrow" promised by Communist utopians and demagogues. Two of these, "The Delator" and "Barbers' Gate" (the latter a poem playing on the imagery of Pushkin's "Bronze Horseman"), attest to the remarkable courage of a poet who, himself subjected to "the dungeons of ancient servitude" openly predicts his captors' "imminent downfall."

The "I" in Lenski's poetry is that of the romantic, bohemian poet, proud of his mission but perfectly willing to mock both himself and his trade. He is the uprooted wayfarer, the unhappy lover, and tramp who admits to being "enthralled by the wormwood" thus sharing with many another poet "the fascination of what's difficult."

In Siberia Lenski also translated into Hebrew an adaptation of a Vogul epic, "The Tundra Book," which appeared in the poet's first collection, *Shirei Ḥayyim Lenski* (1939). Here too, his mastery of a rich, concrete, and colorful language is amply manifested in the short and flowing verses modeled on Longfellow's *The Song of Hiawatha.* Lenski also tried his hand at drama and prose, but these were never published. Biographical data on Lenski and critical evaluations of his work by A. Kariv and others appear in the editions of his work already mentioned (*Shirei Ḥayyim Lenski* and *Me-Ever Nehar ha-Lethe*) and in *He-Anaf ha-Gadu'a* (1945).

Bibliography: Holtz, in: *Judaism,* 14 (1965), 491–6; Goell, Bibliography, 33, no. 1005–14; Kressel, Leksikon, 2 (1967), 292–3. [N.Z.]

LENTIL (Heb. עֲדָשָׁה, *adashah,* pl. עֲדָשִׁים *adashim*), the legume *Lens esculenta,* one of the earliest of the flora of Israel. Remains dating to over 3000 years ago have been discovered in excavations and in Egyptian tombs of the 12th dynasty as food for the dead. In the Bible they are mentioned as the red "pottage of lentils" for which Esau sold his birthright to Jacob (Gen. 25:29–34). They were supplied by Barzillai the Gileadite to David's forces (II Sam. 17:28), and were included in the bread mixture that the prophet Ezekiel was commanded to eat for 390 days (Ezek. 4:9–10). In mishnaic and talmudic times, lentils were the most important of the legumes and many details about them occur in this literature. They lie on the surface of the ground, hence the expression "as lowly as the lentil" (TJ, Sanh. 2:5, 20b). The seed is like a discus—"round like a sphere" and has no protuberance—"the lentil has no mouth." The custom therefore obtained of providing mourners with lentils to eat, to symbolize that "the mourner has no mouth," i.e., is obliged to be silent, and that mourning is "a wheel that revolves throughout the world," all men being mortal (BB 16b; Gen. R. 63:14).

Flowering stalk, pod, and seed of the lentil *(Lens esculenta).* Courtesy J. Feliks, Jerusalem.

In addition to the species with a reddish seed there was a dark brown species (TJ, Shab. 7:6–end, 10d). Lentils were essentially the food of the common people; fastidious people who abstained from eating them suffered harm when obliged to do so (Ket. 67b). On the other hand it is mentioned that lentils were served at the table of Rabban *Simeon b. Gamaliel (Beẓah 14b). Like other legumes they leave a bad smell in the mouth but they are noted as a remedy for diphtheria (Ber. 40a). A delicacy called *ashishim* was sometimes prepared from them. It consisted of "ground roast lentils kneaded in honey and fried" (TJ, Ned. 6:15, 40a). This is apparently the scriptural *ashishah* ("sweet cake"; I Chron. 16:3), regarded as a cure for lovesickness (Song 2:5).

Bibliography: Loew, Flora, 2 (1924), 442–52; H. N. and A. L. Moldenke, *Plants of the Bible* (1952), index; J. Feliks, *Olam ha-Ẓome'aḥ ha-Mikra'i* (1968²), 159–61. [J.F.]

°**LEO,** name of 13 popes.

Leo VII (936–39), the only pope who openly advocated forcible measures for the conversion of the Jews. He advised Frederick, archbishop of Mainz from 937 and the pope's vicar in all the regions of Germany, to deliver to the Jews sermons on the Incarnation and the Trinity. If they refused to adopt the Christian faith, the pope authorized the bishop to banish them, "to avoid all contact with the enemies of God." It is true that Leo did not regard expulsion as a forcible measure, for he ended his letter by saying that, at all events, the Jews must not be compelled to accept baptism. It is also true that the initiative once more lay with the archbishop, and perhaps served as one of the weapons in his battle with the emperor Otto the Great, who had never denied his partiality for the Jews.

Leo X (Giovanni de' Medici; 1475–1521), pope, 1513–21, one of the most tolerant of popes, whose reign was a happy one for the Jews. Intervening in the *Reuchlin-*Pfefferkorn controversy, he ensured an outcome of the dispute favorable for the Jews. His personal physician, Jacob b. Emanuel (Bonet *Lattes), was so well regarded that Reuchlin approached him for a recommendation to the pope. In 1514 Leo reconfirmed the privileges of the Jews in *Comtat Venaissin in opposition to the new measures which the bishop of *Carpentras wished to impose. He authorized the establishment of a Hebrew press in Rome and approved the printing of the Talmud. It is also true that the establishment of a chair of Hebrew in the University of Rome (1514) was aimed at promoting conversion, and Leo also granted considerable advantages to converts. [B.Bl.]

Leo XIII (Vincenzo Gioacchino Pecci: 1810–1903), pope, 1878–1903. Archbishop of Perugia from 1846 to 1878, he fought against the anticlerical laws passed in Italy after 1860. While he declared the Church receptive to cultural progress, he considered liberalism its archenemy and Judaism, which he saw as alienated from its own traditions, its driving force. As pope, his attitude toward Jews remained the same and during his pontificate the publication of a series of anti-Semitic articles in the Italian Jesuit organ, *La *Civiltà Cattolica,* did not meet with any papal interference. The *Dreyfus case found his sympathies on the side of the anti-Dreyfusards, who included the French Catholics, though in principle he wanted to see justice rendered to Dreyfus. The anti-Semitic policy of *La *Croix,* a French Catholic daily, did not apparently contradict the pope's own attitude. In 1892 Leo XIII admitted that there was a Jewish problem, but he saw it mainly as economic. Herzl tried to establish contact with Leo XIII but failed. On the other hand, the report that the pope had issued a protest against Zionism (also quoted in Herzl's *Diaries*) was officially denied. [W.P.E.]

Bibliography: Leo VII: P. Browe, *Judenmission im Mittelalter* (1942), 243; B, Blumenkranz, *Auteurs chrétiens latins...* (1963), 219f. Leo X: Vogelstein-Rieger, 2 (1895), 32ff.; Milano, Italia, 238f.; P. Browe, op. cit., 155, 215. Leo XIII: P. Sorlin, *La Croix et les Juifs, 1880–1899* (1967), index; T. Herzl, *Complete Diaries* (1960), index.

°**LEO III** (called **"the Isaurian"**=Syrian; c. 680–741), Byzantine emperor from 717 to 741. Leo emerged a strong ruler after compelling the caliph Suleiman to give up the siege of Constantinople early in his reign. In 721–22 he issued a decree ordering the baptism of the Jews, but, according to a Byzantine source, those that submitted "quickly washed off the baptism." No Jewish source mentions the decree. In 730 Leo forbade the worship of icons, allegedly because of his "saracen mindedness," or, alternatively, persuaded by a Jewish sorcerer. Yet Leo had earlier defended their use to the Caliph Omar II, while direct Jewish influence was, obviously, quite unlikely. However, the fact that Leo's best soldiers came from Phrygia, the home of iconoclasm, partly engendered there by a constant Judeo-Christian syncretism, and his own origins in a monotheistic cultural milieu, might have produced a distaste for images in worship. In this sense there could be a Jewish element in Leo's final choice of iconoclasm rather than another issue for his real purpose—the reassertion of imperial authority over the Church.

Bibliography: J. Starr, *Jews in the Byzantine Empire* (1939), 90–93; G. Ostrogorsky, *History of the Byzantine State* (1956), 142–5; Sharf, in: *Byzantinische Zeitschrift* (1966), 37–46; Baron, Social², 3 (1957), 175–8; A. A. Vasiliev, *History of the Byzantine Empire*, 1 (1965), 255–6. [An.Sh.]

°**LEO VI** (called **"The Wise"**), Byzantine emperor from 886 to 912. His law code, the *Basilica*, contains no innovations concerning the Jews. Leo appears favorably in Jewish sources. A tenth-century Hebrew apocalyptic text, the *Vision of* **Daniel*, refers to him as granting "freedom and relief to the holy people," and the 11th-century chronicle, *Megillat Aḥima'aẓ* written by *Ahimaaz b. Paltiel, states that Leo annulled the decree of forced baptism issued by his father, *Basil I. However, Leo's 55th *novella*, or imperial rescript, declares that "in order to complete my father's work all Jews, baptized or not, must live according to the ceremonies and customs of Christianity"—thus even abrogating the fundamentals of Byzantine Jewish legislation. The probable explanation of this contradiction is that Leo continued Basil's attempt but quickly abandoned it when he saw its ineffectiveness—and it was this which was remembered.

Bibliography: J. Starr, *Jews in the Byzantine Empire* (1939), 6–7, 134, 140–1; B Klar (ed.), *Megillat Aḥima'aẓ* (1946), 23–24; M. Salzmann (tr.), *Chronicle of Aḥimaaz* (1924), 74; Sharf, in: *Bar-Ilan, Sefer ha-Shanah...*, 4–5 (1967), 201–3. [An.Sh.]

LEO BAECK INSTITUTE, organization founded by the Council of Jews from Germany in 1955 in Jerusalem, for the purpose of collecting material and sponsoring research on the history of the Jewish community in Germany and other German-speaking countries. The Institute is primarily concerned with the period from the emancipation to the destruction and dispersion of the Jewish community of Central Europe. It is named for Leo *Baeck.

There are branches of the Leo Baeck Institute in Jerusalem, London, and New York. The New York branch houses a library of about 40,000 books and has extensive

Lobby of the Leo Baeck Institute in New York, with a bust of Leo Baeck by Erna Weill.

archives, which include memoirs, manuscripts, and art work representative of the history of Central European Jewry since the Emancipation. The work of the three branches is coordinated through an international advisory body. The Institute publishes a yearbook (YLBI; 1956 to date). A quarterly in German, *Bulletin des Leo Baeck Instituts* (BLBI), is published in Tel Aviv. The Institute has published about 40 monographs in English, Hebrew, and German. Among the twenty major publications of the series *Schriftenreihe wissenschaftlicher Abhandlungen des Leo Baeck Instituts* are the *History of Prussian Jewry* by Selma Stern-Taeubler, the *Zunz Letters* by Nahum N. Glatzer, and the *Anthology of the Science of Judaism* by Kurt Wilhelm. The Leo Baeck Institute has continued work on *Germania Judaica* started in 1917, a monumental history of all Jewish places of settlement in Central Europe from its earliest days to the 14th century (2 vols. in 3, 1963–68). The 83rd volume of *Monatsschrift fuer die Geschichte und Wissenschaft des Judentums* (1939), of which only one complete copy had been salvaged, was reprinted by the Institute (1963). A series of important memoirs was published in cooperation with the Deutsche Verlags-Anstalt, Stuttgart. [M.Kr.]

LEON, capital of the ancient kingdom of Leon, Spain. The Jewish quarter apparently remained in the same location in the Santa Anna quarter from the beginnings of Jewish settlement. The 14th-century synagogue was situated in the Cal de Moros, now Calle de Misericordia. The *Prado de los Judíos* ("Meadow of the Jews") is on the site of the medieval cemetery. Various sources mention Jews in Leon who became converted to Christianity in the tenth century. One of the apostates, Habaz (or Navaz), bestowed all his property on the local monastery. From the 11th century information becomes more plentiful. A number of Jews resided in the citadel, and owned real estate, fields, gardens, and vineyards in the vicinity. Some engaged in moneylending and commerce. The status of the Jews was regularized by a *fuero* ("charter") granted in 1020. In the 11th century (1091) the Jews of Leon enjoyed special privileges as they were under royal jurisdiction. One concession was the right to have lawsuits with Christians heard by the king or one of the court clergy. When the issue was to be decided by duel, the Jew was entitled to appoint a champion. The charter was subsequently used as a model for the legislation applying to other communities in the kingdom of Leon. The cemetery of Puente Castro near Leon contains tombstones dating from the 11th century, including those of Jews from Leon.

From the 13th century the rights of the Jewish community in Leon were progressively curtailed by a series of royal decrees. In 1260 Alfonso X fixed the rate of interest on loans. Sancho IV included Leon in a royal decree issued to *Palencia in 1286, providing that lawsuits between Jews were to be tried by Jewish judges and lawsuits between Christians by Christian judges so as to prevent the trial of mixed lawsuits by Jewish judges. In 1293 King Sancho acceded to a request by the Cortes in Valladolid that excluded Jews from taxfarming in Leon, and confirmed an order issued by Alfonso X prohibiting the Jews in Leon from acquiring real estate, etc.. Ferdinand IV forbade the Jews in Leon to appear at his court. However, he permitted them to choose a judge for settling their disputes, a privilege for which they paid 400 maravedis to the municipality. In 1305 they concluded an agreement with the municipality that if the royal judges were not local residents, the Jews would be entitled to make recourse to a judge of their own choice. In 1313 the Infante Don Juan, in the name of Alfonso XI, confirmed that the regulations issued by the Cortes of Palencia also applied to Leon. The Jews throughout the kingdom of Leon were now compelled to wear the yellow *badge on their garments; no Jew could be released from paying taxes; and the evidence of a Jew could not be used against Christians. In 1332 Alfonso XI granted the inhabitants of Leon a general moratorium on Jewish loans and in 1365 Pedro ordered both Jews and Moors to pay the *alcabalá* (indirect taxes) like the other residents in Leon.

The troubles experienced by Spanish Jewry in the 15th century also affected the Jews in Leon. The low tax paid by the community in 1439 shows that it had become impoverished: instead of 6,400 maravedis in old coin, they paid only 2,700 maravedis in silver. On May 25, 1449, riots broke out and most of the Jewish quarter was pillaged. However, in this case the crown took action against the aggressors and ordered that they should be arrested and tried, and their property confiscated. In 1481 the Jews in Leon were ordered to leave the Jewish quarter, but in 1488 the crown agreed to allow them to enlarge it. The names of several Jewish taxfarmers from Leon are known from the second half of the 15th century. The Jews in Leon in this period, besides engaging in crafts, commerce, and agriculture, also sold goods in the mountain villages. Some of these merchants complained to the king that their clients had refused to pay for the goods. After the decree of expulsion of 1492, the governor of Leon, John of Portugal, undertook to protect the Jews there in return for a payment of 3,000 maravedis but failed to honor the agreement and seized their property. Jewish property was also looted after the exiles had left, but some was restored to Jews who returned to Leon in 1493 and accepted baptism.

Bibliography: Baer, Spain, index; Baer, Urkunden, index; F. Castro and F. de Onís, *Fueros Leoneses* (1916); C. Sánchez Albornoz, *Estampas de la vida en Leon hace mil años* (1934); F. Cantera, *Sinagogas Españolas* (1955), 237; idem, in: *Sefarad*, 3 (1943), 329–58; Cantera-Millás, Inscripciones (1956), 5–25; Cantera-Burgos, in: *Sefarad*, 24 (1964), 3–11; Gonzales, in: *Hispania*, 3 (1943), 195ff.; J. Rodríguez Fernández, *De Historia Leonesa* (1961); idem, in: *Archivos Leoneses*, 2 (1947), 33–72; 2 (1948), 15–27, 29ff.; 4 (1950), 11–53; González Gallego, *ibid.*, 21 (1967), 375–408; Suárez Fernández, Documentos, index.

[H.B.]

LEON, family name of European and U.S. notables whose progenitors fled the Iberian Peninsula during the Inquisition. The name derives from the kingdom of Leon, Spain. Early in the 1500s, the Marrano PEDRO DE LEON tried to escape the Spanish inquisitors by moving with his family to the West Indian island of Hispaniola. However, he was apprehended and in 1515 brought back to Seville for trial. Others were more fortunate and the name Leon appears in the records of Ancona, Jerusalem, Hamburg, Salonika, London, Venice, Jamaica, Surinam, Amsterdam, and the United States. ISAAC BEN ELIEZER DE LEON of Spain, who is best known for his *Megillat Esther* (Venice, 1592), a commentary to Maimonides' *Sefer ha-Mitzvot*, spent most of his life in Ancona, Italy. He is also the author of a responsum dated 1545 that appeared in Rome. In Greece, the liturgical poet ABRAHAM DE LEON composed *"El Ram al Kol Tehillah,"* a dirge on the capture of Rhodes by the Turks in 1522, which was included in the *Bakkashot* published about 1545 at Constantinople. (The poem is numbered 4042 in Davidson, *Oẓar*, vol. 1, 1924.) JOSEPH DE LEON served as rabbi in Jerusalem c. 1588. At Hamburg, the *ḥakham* of the Portuguese congregation from 1615 to 1656 was JUDAH ḤAYYIM LEON. About 1632, in Salonika, then under Turkish dominion, the *rosh yeshivah* was ISAAC DE LEON.

At London's Spanish-Portuguese synagogue, the assistant to the haham from 1685 to 1707 was ABRAHAM JUDAH LEON. The rabbi of Venice in about 1695 was JOSEPH DE LEON. JACOB DE LEON and JACOB RODRIGUEZ DE LEON resided in Jamaica in 1698. Among the leaders of Surinam's Portuguese Jewish community during the 1780s was MOSES P. DE LEON, coauthor of a history of his community, *Essai historique sur la colonie de Surinam avec l'histoire de la Nation Juive Portugaise et Allemande y établie* (1788), subsequently published also in Dutch (Amsterdam, 1791).

A number of men bearing the name Leon appeared in Amsterdam. In the mid-1600s MEIR DE LEON translated Solomon ibn Verga's *Shevet Yehudah* into Spanish (*La Vara de Judá*, Amsterdam, 1640). The leading figure of Amsterdam's Keter Torah yeshivah was SAMUEL DE LEON. Requests for decisions on matters of Jewish law addressed to the yeshivah were generally referred to him; his responsa were published at Hamburg in 1679. Fleeing from the Inquisition in 1685, the Marrano MANUEL DE LEON, who was born in Leiria, Portugal, arrived in Amsterdam, where he remained until his death in 1712. He produced Spanish and Portuguese verse, published in Brussels (1688), in The Hague (1691), and in Amsterdam (1712). The *ḥakham* of Amsterdam's Gemilut Ḥasadim fund was ELIJAH DE LEON, who was also coeditor of the Bible printed in 1661 by Joseph *Athias.

There were numerous Leons in colonial America. Joseph Rosenbloom's *A Biographical Dictionary of Early American Jews, Colonial Times through 1800* (1960) lists 38, many of them descendants of Abraham de Leon (b. 1702), who settled in Savannah, Georgia, in 1733. The name was prominent in New York City during the 1850s. MOSES LEON was among the leaders of New York's Hebrew Benevolent Society and MORRIS J. LEON was active in the Young Men's Benevolent and Fuel Association; the *ḥazzan* of the Bnai Israel synagogue in 1854 was JOSHUA DE LEON.

Bibliography: Roth, Marranos, 274, 294; H. B. Grinstein, *Rise of the Jewish Community of New York 1654–1860* (1945), 552–4. [ED.]

LEON, HARRY JOSHUA (1896–1967), U.S. classics scholar and historian, Leon, born in Worcester, Massachusetts, taught classical languages at the University of Texas from 1923, was a research professor at the American Academy of Rome 1950–51, and was an active member of many learned societies. Apart from his work on *Tacitus* (1960^2) and translations of classical literature, Leon published a *History of the Jews of Ancient Rome* (1960) which was largely based on a careful analysis of inscriptions in the Jewish *catacombs in Rome.

[ED.]

LEON, ISAAC DE (d. 1486 or 1490), Spanish rabbi and kabbalist. Isaac was born in Leon in the second decade of the 15th century. He was a pupil of Isaac *Canpanton and was friendly with Isaac *Aboab. Abraham b. Samuel *Zacuto in the *Sefer Yuḥasin* (ed. by H. Filipowski (1857), 226) states that Isaac was "experienced in miracles." He was rabbi of Ocaña. Among Isaac's many pupils were Samuel ibn *Sid, who summarized in his *Kelalei Shemu'el* many of the traditions and methods of learning in Spain received from his master; Isaac Giacon, the teacher of the well known kabbalist *Abraham b. Eliezer ha-Levi; Abraham b. Bolat; and Abraham b. Hassan of Salonika. Isaac de Leon became embroiled with Don Abraham *Senior and scornfully termed him *sone or* ("hater of the light") because of heresies which he found in him even before his apostasy. In 1482 De Leon visited Saragossa and became friendly with the Jewish royal courtier, Alfonso de la Caballeria. There he became involved in a violent controversy with the local rabbi Isaac Ziyyat, with reference to the permissibility of certain animal fat, which caused a storm among the Jews of Aragon. A ruling by De Leon on the laws of adjoining owners is extant (in *Sheva Einayim*, ed. by J. London, Leghorn, 1745), with which Isaac Ziyyat disagreed. Some of his rulings are mentioned by Joseph *Caro in his *Beit Yosef*. He wrote a supercommentary to Rashi's Pentateuch commentary. Toward the end of his life he moved to Toledo, where he died.

Bibliography: A. Marx, *Studies in Jewish History and Booklore* (1944), 90–92, 432; G. Scholem, in: KS, 2 (1925/26), 270; I. Ta-Shema, in: KS, 45 (1969/70), 124–5; Baer, Spain, index s.v. *Isaac de Leon.*

[A.D.]

LEÓN, LUIS DE (1528–1591), Spanish poet, humanist, and Augustinian friar. Born in Belmonte, New Castile, he spent most of his life in Salamanca where, as a professor, he dominated the university until some intolerant rivals discovered his *New Christian origin. The fact that his great-grandmother had been burnt at the stake as a relapsed Jewess led to his imprisonment for five years at Valladolid from 1572 at the hands of the Inquisition. Luis de León was accused of Judaizing and of doubting the authority of the Vulgate, the literal accuracy of which he had called into question. His Spanish translation of the Song of Songs reinforced these charges. After his eventual acquittal, Luis de León returned in triumph to Salamanca. These experiences are scarcely reflected in his poetry, which is a model of equilibrium. Apart from original verse and translations from the Bible and from classical and Italian literature, he wrote a number of theological and exegetic works, in which he invoked the support of the Christian Kabbalah. Luis de León's work unites the medieval Christian, biblical Hebrew, and classical traditions in the harmony of the Spanish Renaissance.

Bibliography: A. F. G. Bell, *Luis de León: A Study of the Spanish Renaissance* (1925); J. M. Cohen, *History of Western Literature* (1956), 137f.

[K.R.S.]

LEON, MESSER DAVID BEN JUDAH (1470/72?–1526?), rabbi and religious philosopher. Born in Mantua, Italy, Leon studied in his father's yeshivah in Naples, where he was ordained at the age of 18 by French and German rabbis. He then went to the yeshivah of Judah Minz in Padua. In 1494 he was living in Florence, about 1505 moved to Salonika, and about 1512 was appointed rabbi of Valona, Albania. In this town there were many disputes between the various communities because of the desire of the exiles from Spain and Portugal to impose their customs on the existing communities. He became involved in these disputes, and in one of them excommunicated his opponent, Meir ibn Verga. On the night of the Day of Atonement, during a fierce quarrel between the various communities, he was insulted and banned two scholars among the heads of the community who opposed him. His ruling, which attempted to justify his action and prove that the ban was legally in force, was published under the title *Kevod Ḥakhamim* (ed. by S. Bernfeld, 1899). There is, however, a conjecture that a great part of this work was taken from the responsa of Joseph *Colon (Venice, 1519 ed. no. 170). As a result of these disputes he returned to Salonika where he died.

Leon combined vast erudition in Jewish subjects with a comprehensive knowledge of general culture, particularly in philosophy. In the study of Torah he preferred the method of the rabbis of Germany and France to the methods of the rabbis of Spain. An admirer of Maimonides, Leon, in those of his works that have remained unpublished, *Magen David* (dealing with the problem of the nature of the *Sefirot* and compiled apparently before 1506) and *Ein ha-Kore* (a commentary on the *Guide of the Perplexed*), defended Maimonides' philosophical method and attempted to answer the complaints of his critics. He was opposed to Levi b. Gershom and Isaac Abrabanel, mainly because their views differed from those of Maimonides. His combination of general culture with values originating from Jewish religion and culture is reflected in his query to Jacob b. David *Provençal "on the view of the sages of the Talmud in the study of the natural sciences, logic, philosophy and medicine." The reply (published in the collection *Divrei Ḥakhamim* (1849), 63–74 of Eliezer Ashkenazi), that "each one of the seven sciences is praiseworthy and valued in the eyes of our sages," addressed him as one who would produce "fruit from the tree, but not forsake the root in order to take hold of the husk." Apparently Leon also engaged in Kabbalah. He stated that although his father refused to allow him to engage in it "because of his tender age," he studied Kabbalah in secret. Among his other works worthy of mention are *Tehillah le-David* (Constantinople, 1577), on religious philosophy, published by his grandson Aaron Leon; *Sod ha-Gemul;* and his rulings and responsa, and letters and poems (some also in Latin)—most of which are still in manuscript.

Bibliography: L. Zunz, *Kerem Ḥemed*, 5 (1841), 139; Michael, Or, no. 727; J. Schechter, in: REJ, 24 (1892), 118–38; M. Steinschneider, in: MGWJ, 42 (1898), 263; idem, in: *Festschrift . . . A. Berliner* (1903), 353; idem, *Gesammelte Schriften*, 1 (1925), 219f.; Rosanes, Togarmah, 1 (1930^2), 79, 85–88, 110–3; Assaf, Mekorot, 2 (1931), 99–101; G. Scholem, in: KS, 9 (1932–33), 258; D. Tamar, *ibid.*, 26 (1949/50), 96–100.

[Y.Ho.]

LÉON, XAVIER (1868–1935), French philosopher. Léon founded the important philosophical journal, *Revue de Métaphysique et de Morale*, which he edited from its beginning in 1893 until his death. The journal was not only against positivist trends, but also in favor of speculative philosophy. Léon also founded the *Société française de philosophie* (1901). In both of these ventures he had the collaboration of Élie *Halévy. Léon organized several international congresses of philosophy. He wrote on the German philosopher, Fichte, publishing *La Philosophie de Fichte* (1902) and *Fichte et son temps*, 2 vols. (1922–27).

Bibliography: E. Halévy et al., *Xavier Léon 1868–1935* (Fr., 1937); *Enciclopedia Filosofica*, 2 (It., 1957), 1876f.

[R.H.P.]

LEONARD, BENNY (1896–1947), U.S. boxing champion, considered the greatest lightweight in the history of the sport. Born Benjamin Leiner on New York's Lower East Side, Leonard entered the prize ring in 1911, and won his first important fight in 1915. Two years later he won the world lightweight championship and in 1925 retired from boxing as the undefeated lightweight champion. Hard-pressed financially however, Leonard returned to the ring as welterweight in 1931, but retired permanently in 1932. A master boxer with a powerful punch, Leonard took part in many memorable boxing matches.

Benny Leonard, world lightweight boxing champion, 1917–24. From M. U. Schappes, *The Jews in the United States,* New York, 1958.

Leonard worked for numerous Jewish causes and in 1935 was chairman of the Maccabi National Sports Board which selected the American team for the World Maccabiah Games in Palestine. He served as a lieutenant commander in the United States Maritime Service in World War II and was a boxing referee from 1943 to 1947, when he collapsed and died in the ring. In 1955 his name was included in the Boxing Hall of Fame, and in 1969 *The Ring* magazine named him the outstanding lightweight of all time.

Bibliography: N. Fleischer, *Leonard the Magnificent* (1947); B. Postal et al., *Encyclopaedia of Jews in Sports* (1965), 162–4. [J.H.S.]

LEONE, LEON (Judah) DI (d. 1830), rabbi in Italy. Leone went to Europe from Ereẓ Israel as an emissary of the Hebron community and in 1795 was elected rabbi of Rome. In 1796 he joined other rabbis in Italy in writing a protest against statements current in France and Germany that radical religious reforms were being introduced in the Italian Jewish communities. When the community in Rome was reorganized on the French pattern in 1811, Leone became chairman of the consistory.

Bibliography: Milano, *Ghetto di Roma* (1964), 313, 394; Vogelstein-Rieger, 2 (1896), 400–1. [U.C./Ed.]

LEONHARD, RUDOLF (1889–1953), German essayist and poet. Leonhard, who was born in Lissa, studied law at Goettingen. He subsequently worked as a free-lance writer in Berlin, but in 1927 moved to Paris. Leonhard was a radical pacifist, but, nevertheless, fought in the French underground during the Nazi occupation of France. He returned to East Berlin after World War II. His works include: essays on literary and political topics, some of them in French; two volumes of collected poems entitled *Polnische Gedichte* (1918) and *Katilinarische Pilgerschaft* (1919); a book of aphorisms, *Alles und Nichts* (1920); and a tragedy, *Geiseln* (1946). Leonhard, an accomplished critic, also translated the works of Anatole France.

Bibliography: M. Scheer (ed.), *Rudolf Leonhard erzaehlt* (1955). [R.K.]

LEONI, MYER (d. 1796), English cantor. Born Meir ben Judah Loeb, probably in Poland, he was first known in England as an opera singer named "Meir Leoni." In 1767 he was engaged as cantor at the Great Synagogue, London, on condition that he would conduct himself henceforth as an observant Jew. His tune for the **Yigdal,* known as the "Leoni Yigdal," was heard at the synagogue in 1770 by the Methodist minister Thomas Olivers and adapted for the

Engraving showing Myer Leoni as Don Carlos, with Mrs. Mattocks as Louisa, in the comic opera, *The Duenna,* by Richard Brinsley Sheridan and Thomas Linley.

Christian hymn, "The God of Abraham Praise." Leoni later returned to the stage, stipulating that he should not appear on Friday nights, when he officiated in the synagogue. His relations with his congregation became difficult, however, and when he sang in a performance of Handel's *Messiah* he had to resign. In 1787 he went to Jamaica as reader to the Ashkenazi synagogue in Kingston, where he remained until his death. Some of the synagogal music composed by Leoni and his colleague, Abraham of Prossnitz (d. 1779), the father of John *Braham, figured in the collection of cantorial music made by Aaron Beer of Berlin, while specimens adapted for harpsichord and other instruments were published in London in 1780.

Bibliography: C. Roth, *Great Synagogue, London 1690–1940* (1950), 143–45; Grove, Dict; Idelsohn, Music, 218–26; idem, in: *Hebrew Union College Jubilee Volume* (1925), 415–6; J. Picciotto, *Sketches of Anglo-Jewish History* (1956), 139–49; Sendrey, Music, no. 6216. [C.R.]

LEONTE (Judah) BEN MOSES (12th century), liturgical poet. Leonte, who lived in Rome, is most probably identical with the scholar Judah b. Moses who, in the name of the Roman community, addressed an inquiry to *Judah b. Kalonymus and "the sages of Mainz" (Zedekiah Anav, *Shibbolei ha-Leket,* ed. S. Buber (1886), introd. 11 n. 87). A Leon of Rome in 1210 is mentioned in A. *Zacuto's *Yuḥasin* (ed. by H. Filipowski (1857), 221); Joseph ibn *Ẓaddik (Neubauer, Chronicles, I (1887), 94) mentions a Leon of Rome in the year 1216. Leonte is named as the author of about ten *seliḥot*, which, though formerly common in the Roman ritual, remained nevertheless in manuscript. In the acrostic he signs his name in the Hebrew form, Judah, or in the Romanic form, Leonte, occasionally adding עני or ענו ; he presumably belonged to the Roman-Jewish family *Anav.

Bibliography: Davidson, Oẓar, 4 (1933), 431 s.v. *Lionti b. Moshe;* Landshuth, Ammudei, 157f.; Vogelstein-Rieger, 1 (1896), 227, 372f.; Zunz, Lit Poesie, 314f.; Schirmann, Italiah, 80–81. [ED.]

LEONTOPOLIS, locality in the district of Heliopolis in Egypt, N.E. of *Memphis, 6 mi. (10 km.) N. of Cairo. A settlement of Jewish soldiers was established in Leontopolis under the leadership of the former high priest, *Onias IV, sometime after the outbreak of the Maccabean revolt, in the middle of the second century B.C.E. with the approval of Ptolemy Philometer and his wife Cleopatra (Jos., Ant., 13:62ff.). Its nucleus was made up of emigrants from Judea. The Jewish soldiers of the region subsequently played a role in the political life of Egypt and the area was also called "the land of Onias." Onias erected here a temple to the God of Israel by restoring a ruined Egyptian temple which stood on the site. This temple served the Jewish inhabitants of the region for more than 200 years until it was closed down by the Romans in 73 C.E. (Wars, 7:433–646). The present name of the locality, Tell al-Yahūdiyya, is a survival from this ancient Jewish settlement. In archaeological excavations, Jewish inscriptions were found there. Some wish to associate "Camp of the Jews" mentioned by Josephus (Ant. 14:133), and also the Castra Judaeorum mentioned in the Byzantine era with this region.

Bibliography: Tcherikover, Corpus, 1 (1957), 44–46; idem, *Hellenistic Civilization and the Jews* (1959), 278–9; Delcor, in: RB, 75 (1968), 188–205; Rapaport, in: *Revue de Philologie*, 43 (1969), 80–81. [U.R.]

°**LEONTOVICH, FEDOR** (1833–1911), historian of Russian and Slavic law. Leontovich held the position of professor of the history of law at the universities of Odessa and Warsaw. He was the first to deal with the history of the Russian legislation concerning the Jews, when he published "An Historical Survey of the Regulations concerning the Jews in Russia" in the Russian-Jewish periodical *Sion*. His "The Rights of the Russian-Lithuanian Jews" (Kiev, 1863) was based on original documents and elucidated the outlines of the legal and social situation of the Jews in the grand duchy of Lithuania. I. G. *Orshanski and S. A. *Bershadski were influenced by these works. In 1882 he published an article in the monthly *Nablyudatel* entitled "What We Must Do with the Jewish Problem," where he argued that the Jews could only be granted equality of rights after they had abandoned their "specific nationalist culture"; as this was a process which could continue through several generations, there was no room for emancipation of the Jews at the time. [Y.S.]

LEOPARD (Heb. נָמֵר, *namer*), the strongest carnivorous animal in the Middle East. The leopard has a spotted coat, this being the meaning of its Hebrew name (Jer. 13:23). It is not to be confused with the tiger which, besides being striped, did not inhabit Ereẓ Israel (it is mentioned in Ḥul. 59b). Belonging to the feline family, the leopard, *Felis pardus tullianus* (= *Panthera pardus*), has a body which, excluding the tail, is 120–150 cm. (c. 4–5 ft.) long and a yellowish-fawn coat with black spots. Its bodily structure, with its short forelegs and extremely powerful hindlegs, is especially suited to lying in wait, this habit being referred to in the Bible (Hos. 13:7; cf. Jer. 5:6). In Isaiah's vision of the messianic age, in which he depicts the amity that will exist between the carnivorous animals and their prey, he declares that "the leopard shall lie down with the kid," the latter being the usual prey of the leopard, as the lamb is of the wolf and the calf of the young lion (Isa. 11:6). The leopard's speed and agility are stressed in the Bible (Hab. 1:8), while its strength is referred to in the Mishnah (Avot 5:20): "Be strong as a leopard, swift as an eagle, fleet as a gazelle, and brave as a lion to do the will of your Father in heaven" an aphorism that was illustrated in paintings and engravings in synagogues. In recent years leopards, like other wild animals, have decreased in the Middle East. Occasionally individual or pairs of leopards come down from the Lebanese mountains to Upper Galilee (cf. Song 4:8). In the neighborhood of En-Gedi a family of leopards was killed in the 1960s, and in the Arabah some members of the leopard family were hunted. The cheetah (*Acinonyx jubatus*), which is called *bardelas* in the Mishnah, is enumerated alongside the leopard among the carnivorous animals (BK 1:4). It is apparently included in the Bible under the term *namer* on account of its spotted coat, although in fact its bodily structure differs from that of the leopard, the cheetah having a small head and long legs which enable it to pursue its prey.

Bibliography: Lewysohn, Zool, 71f., no. 116; F. S. Bodenheimer, *Animal and Man in Bible Lands* (1960), 20–22, 26, 43; J. Feliks, *The Animal World of the Bible* (1962), 33. [J.F.]

°**LEOPOLD I** (1640–1705), Holy Roman Emperor (1658–1705), king of Bohemia (1656–1705), and king of Hungary (1655–1705). His treatment of the Jews was determined by his ultra-Catholic attitudes, which led to their expulsion from Vienna in 1670. On his election as Holy Roman Emperor in 1658 he confirmed all charters which had been granted in Austria and in the Holy Roman Empire by his father *Ferdinand III and ordered that Jewish life and property be protected (1660, 1665, 1669). However, his anti-Jewish attitude was intensified by his marriage in 1666 to the Catholic-educated Margaret Theresa, daughter of Philip IV of Spain, who saw in the tolerance of the Jews the reason for the death of her firstborn (1668). In 1670 he responded to the city's request that the Jews be expelled from Vienna, in spite of papal intervention, and swore never to admit them again. He took into account the Hungarian Protestants' claim that they were worse off than the Jews, and he was influenced by Cardinal *Kollonich. When readmitting *Court Jews such as Samuel *Oppenheimer in 1676 and Samson *Wertheimer in 1684, he had the problem of his oath solved by theologians. In 1695 he permitted the printing of the Talmud in Germany. At Oppenheimer's request, he prohibited (1700) the circulation of Johann Andreas *Eisenmenger's *Entdecktes Judenthum*.

Bibliography: D. Kaufmann, *Die letzte Vertreibung der Juden aus Wien* (1889), 65–166; H. Tietze, *Die Juden Wiens* (1935), index; Pillich, in: J. Fraenkel (ed.), *The Jews of Austria* (1967), 5–9; W. Mueller, *Urkundliche Beitraege zur Geschichte der maehrischen Judenschaft* (1903), 25–31; A. F. Pribram, *Urkunden und Akten zur Geschichte der Juden in Wien*, 1–2 (1918), index; M. Grunwald, *Vienna* (1936), index; MHJ, 2 (1937), index. [M.LA.]

LEOVO (Rum. **Leova**), town in S. W. Moldavian S.S.R., in the region of Bessarabia. There were 25 Jewish families living in Leovo in 1817. The community grew as a result of the large Jewish immigration into Bessarabia in the 19th century and numbered 2,773 persons (57% of the total population) in 1897. The Jews there were subject to the legislation restricting Jewish residence in the border zone. The *ẓaddik* Dov Baer, the son of Israel (Friedmann) of *Ruzhyn, whose defection from Ḥasidism to the *maskilim* caused a furor, lived in Leovo in the 1860s. The writers

Judah *Steinberg and Jacob *Fichmann taught there. Among the 434 members registered in the Jewish loan fund in 1925, there were 84 farmers, 102 craftsmen, and 163 businessmen. There were 2,326 Jews living in Leovo (35% of the total population) in 1930. The community then maintained a kindergarten and a school, both belonging to the *Tarbut network. [EL.F.]

Holocaust Period. During the Rumanian evacuation of Leovo in June 1940, the Jewish population, numbering some 600 families, was unharmed. In July 1940, a month after the annexation of Bessarabia by the Soviet Union, all Zionist leaders and wealthy Jews were exiled to Siberia and their property was confiscated. When war broke out between Germany and the Soviet Union in June 1941, Leovo was in the battle zone. Most of the population tried to escape with the help of the Russians, but the majority of the Jews who managed to leave the town were murdered by Rumanian soldiers and gendarmes in the neighboring villages and towns. A few who succeeded in reaching Odessa and the Caucasian Mountains were murdered by the Germans when they reached these areas. Those Jews who stayed in Leovo were all murdered by Rumanian troops. Some of the Jews who were caught on the roads were exiled to *Transnistria, from which only a few returned. Only 30 Jews returned to Leovo after the war.

Bibliography: BJCE. [J.AN.]

LEPEL, city in Vitebsk oblast, Belorussian S.S.R.; before the 1917 Revolution it served as a district town in the province of Vitebsk, Russia. In 1802 the Jewish population of Lepel and district totaled 368. Their number increased to 1,509 in 1847 and 3,379 (53.7% of the total population) in 1897. During World War I the city was on the Russo-German front, and it also suffered greatly in the war between Russia and Poland (1919–20). There were 1,932 Jews (28.9%) in the town in 1926. The Germans occupied the city at the beginning of July 1941 and later established a ghetto there. In February 1942 about 1,000 Jews from Lepel ghetto were shot. There is no information on Jewish life in Lepel after World War II. [Y.S.]

LEPROSY. The Hebrew biblical term for leprosy, *ẓaraʿat*, like its Greek equivalent λέπρα (LXX and New Testament), is not limited to true leprosy, i.e., Hansen's disease. It is a generic name, embracing a variety of skin ailments, including many noncontagious types. Thus, the leprosy of Miriam was transient (Num. 12:10–15) and that of Naaman did not prevent him from mixing freely in society (II Kings 5). Probably only those actually banished from their fellowmen were true lepers, e.g., the four lepers forced to live outside Samaria (II Kings 7:3–10) and King Uzziah, who was permanently quarantined in separate quarters (II Chron. 26:19–21).

"The medical principles of the early Hebrews, as enshrined in the Pentateuch, represent a notable advance upon contemporary theories of disease in that they repudiated magic completely, and sought to consider disease either from an empirical standpoint or else in terms of the personal spiritual relationship existing between the sufferer and his God. The principle of personal and social hygiene contained in the medical sections of Leviticus are unique in antiquity as rational assessments of pathology" (R. K. Harrison, in bibl.). Medical texts of the Ancient Near East attribute disease either to evil magic or the sufferer's sin (R. C. Thompson, *Assyrian Medical Texts* (1923); A. L. Oppenheim, *Ancient Mesopotamia* (1964), 291). In both cases, rituals are prescribed which bear a striking resemblance to those in the Bible (see below), with one critical difference. The pagan employs rituals as

Naaman, commander of the Aramean army, bathing in the Jordan to cure himself of leprosy (II Kings 5:14). From a 12th-century enamel plaque. London, British Museum.

therapy, believing them to be the counter-magic needed to exorcise the disease. The Bible, on the contrary, denies the therapeutic value of rituals, prescribing them only after healing has taken place (Kaufmann). The diagnosis and treatment of leprosy is the paradigm for this Israelite innovation.

The Laws of Leviticus 13–14. Leviticus 13–14 is composed of the following sections: the diagnosis of the afflictions of the skin (13:2–28, 38–39, summarized below), of the hair (13:29–37), and of the scalp (13:40–44); the ostracism of the incurable (13:45–46; cf. Lam. 4:15); the diagnosis of the deterioration of garments, due probably to mildew or fungus (13:47–59); the ritual for the rehabilitation of the healed leper (14:1–32); the diagnosis of the "leprosy" of houses, probably due to the spread of dry rot, mineral precipitates, or the growth of lichens and fungi (14:33–53); and the summary (14:54–57). The structure is logical, with houses, a post-conquest reality, being put at the end (cf. 14:34). Though not all the technical terms are understood (see the commentaries), the symptoms given are capable of precise medical definition. The affliction can occur spontaneously (13:2–17), follow a furuncle (13:18–23) or a burn on the skin (13:24–28), or develop on the head or beard (13:29–45). The first symptoms are those of a swelling (*se'et;* LXX οὐλή), or subcutaneous nodule, a cuticular crust (*sappaḥat,* LXX σημασία), and whitish-red spot (*baheret;* LXX τηλαύγημα). "The crux of the matter lay in the degree of cutaneous penetration which the disease had achieved. If it affected the epidermis or outermost layer of skin and did not produce pathological changes in the hairs, the affliction was not regarded as especially serious. As such it might consist of eczema, leukoderma, psoriasis, or some allied cutaneous disease. But if the affliction had infiltrated the dermis (corium) and had caused hairs to split or break off and lose their color, then leprosy was to be suspected" (R. K. Harrison). This diagnostic principle also applied to disease affecting the scalp (13:29–37) where the affliction was spoken of as *netek (neteq)* (LXX θραῦσμα; JPS "scall").

The Role of the Priest. In contrast to his pagan counterpart, the Israelite priest is not involved in every epidemic (except in emergencies where he intercedes through sacrifices, Num. 17:11ff.; II Sam. 24:25—David officiating as priest) but only in the contagious skin diseases enumerated here (see Deut. 24:8–9, and contrast the laws pertaining to gonorrhea, Lev. 15). Moreover, he is not a healer but a sort of quarantine officer, an ecclesiastical public health official.

The priest was called in to inspect the affliction. If leprosy was only suspected but not certain, the priest imposed a seven-day quarantine. At the end of this period the afflicted was examined again, and if no further degeneration was apparent he was isolated for another week, after which he could be pronounced healed. The priest, however, did nothing to promote the cure. His rituals were performed only after the disease had passed. It was the responsibility of the afflicted himself to pray (I Kings 8:37–38; II Kings 20:2–3) and fast (II Sam. 12:16) in order to win God's healing. Deuteronomy 24:8–9 charges the priests with the diagnosis and containment of leprosy (but no other disease), citing the case of Miriam (see Num. 12:11–16), apparently to prove that this affliction is caused by rebellion against God (so for Uzziah; see below). It is noteworthy that in Miriam's case healing came from God, and not through any priestly intervention, but through Moses' prayer. Thus Israel's priest is a far cry from the pagan physician or magician. Healing comes from God alone, either directly (Ex. 15:26) or through His surrogate, the prophet (e.g., Moses, Ex. 15:25; Elisha, II Kings 2:21; Isaiah, II Kings 20:7–8).

The Ritual. The prescribed ritual for the healed leper illustrates how the Bible eliminated the suzerainty of magic from its world. Three separate ceremonies are required: for the first day (Lev. 14:2–8; also invoked for houses, 14:48–53), the seventh (14:9), and the eighth (14:10–32). The first-day ritual is performed by the priest outside the camp or city from which the leper has been banished. Cedar wood, crimson cloth, and a live bird are dipped into an earthen vessel containing a mixture of fresh water and the blood of a second bird. The leper (or leprous house) is sprinkled with this mixture seven times, after which the live bird is set free. The leper is admitted into the camp or city after he washes his clothes, shaves all his hair, and bathes, but he is not allowed to enter his residence. That is permitted him on the seventh day after shaving, laundering, and bathing again. On the eighth day he brings to the sanctuary oil and sheep for various offerings—whole, meal, purification, and reparation. The whole and purification animals may be commuted to birds if the leper is poor. However, the reparation lamb and *log* of oil may not be changed, as the blood of the lamb and the oil are needed to daub the leper's right ear lobe, right thumb, and right big toe.

This complex ceremonial is elucidated by comparison with similar prescriptions in the ancient world. There is much evidence of the banishment of evil by carriers (J. Frazer, *The Golden Bough*, 6 (1935), 249ff.), especially animals (e.g., Hittite: F. Sommer and H. Ehelolf, *Das hethitische Ritual des Papanikri von Komana* (1924), III 45, Rev. iv, 5ff.; Mesopotamia and Israel: see *Azazel). Aspersions of materials such as cedar, scarlet wool, and hyssop are also known (e.g., J. Laesse, *Studies in the Assyrian Ritual*... (1955); R. C. Thompson, *The Devils and Evil Spirits of Babylon*, vol. 2, 1904). Moreover, a letter of Nergal-sharrani to Esarhaddon cites an apotropaic letter and a ritual for *kamunu* lichen which appeared in the inner court of the temple of Nabû and for the *kattanu* lichen on the walls of storehouses (R. F. Harper, *Assyrian and Babylonian Letters*, 4 (1896), no. 367). Clearly, then, the original purpose of the leper's ritual of the first day was to exorcise the demonic disease and banish it to a place of no return, e.g., the desert (see *Azazel) or the open country in the case of the leper (*ha-sadeh;* Lev. 14:7, 53). However, the Bible has completely severed this rite from its pagan ideological moorings. The ritual is prescribed only after "the priest sees that the leper is healed" (14:3). It is as though exorcism and monotheism were incompatible. The disease is not a demonic entity independent of God, nor is the ritual an intrinsically effective agency of healing. Both disease and healing stem from the one God: the ritual, bereft of its intrinsic power, is transformed into a symbolic purification; it becomes a religious, and not a therapeutic, act. If ritual purification is the purpose of the ritual of the first day, why its week-long extension? Here, in keeping with the priestly system of scaled impurities, a severe defilement endures for eight days after healing and calls for a three-stage purification which reduces and finally eliminates this vestigial impurity (see *Purity and Impurity, Ritual). The rite of the first day enables the leper to mingle with, but not touch, his fellowmen, nor can he enter a confined space lest he defile what it holds (see 14:8b; rabbinic מאהיל, cf. Kelim 1:4; Neg. 13:3, 7, 8, 11; Jos., Ant., 3:261ff.; Jos., Apion 1:279ff.; cf. Num. 19:14). These restrictions are removed only at the end of the seventh day, after he has again shaved, laundered, and bathed.

Having been restored to his community and household, he is still impure vis-à-vis the realm of the sacred: he has to be rehabilitated in the eyes of his God (ten times the text insists that the ritual is "before the Lord," Lev. 14:11–31). In the eighth-day ritual—the third and final stage—he therefore brings to the sanctuary a complex of sacrifices. The purification offering purges the sacred area of the defilement brought on by his leprosy (see *Atonement); the whole and meal offerings expiate the sin that might have caused his affliction (e.g., Miriam, see above); the reparation offering is his expiation in case he has trespassed on sancta (*maʿal*, a sin punishable by leprosy, e.g., Uzziah, II Chron. 26:16–21; cf. Lev. 5:14–19; and see *Sacrifices). The blood of the animal of reparation and the oil are successively daubed on the extremities of his body so that he may have access to the sanctuary and its sancta (as far as allowed to a layman). That sanctification is the purpose of this ritual is demonstrated by the consecration service of the priest (Ex. 29; Lev. 8), where the daubing of the same parts of the body is prescribed and where a mixture of oil and sacrificial blood is used (in sprinkling, not in daubing: note verb *qadesh* "sanctify." Ex. 29:21; Lev. 8:30). Israel's sanctification motif is brought into even sharper relief when compared with similarly structured rituals in the Ancient Near East. There is abundant attestation of daubing (see *Anointing) but its purpose is different. The incantations recited during the ritual smearing of persons, the statues of gods, and buildings testify that its object is purificatory and apotropaic: to wipe off and ward off the incursions of menacing demonic forces. Hence it is always the vulnerable parts of bodies (extremities) and of structures (corners, entrances) that are smeared with magical substances (e.g., Pritchard, Texts, 338). The Bible, however, having eliminated the demonic as a power apart from God has no further need of apotropaic rites or exorcisms. As a result, purificatory and apotropaic rituals have been reinterpreted as steps in the healed leper's rehabilitation which enabled him to return to his community and qualified him to have access to the Sanctuary and God. Ezekiel's ritual of consecration for the altar is strikingly analogous: blood is to be daubed on its horns and the corners of its two gutters, located at its middle and bottom (Ezek. 43:20). These points correspond to a man's ear lobe, thumb, and big toe. There can be no question that the purpose of this altar ritual (as in the consecration of the priests) is sanctificatory; the same must be said of the eighth-day ritual for the leper.

[J.M.]

In the Second Temple and Talmud. The laws of leprosy are given in great detail in the Talmud, and a whole tractate of the Mishnah and Tosefta, **Nega'im,* consisting of 14 chapters in the former and 9 in the latter, is devoted to them. There is no *Gemara* to the tractate. Leprosy was a scourge during the period of the Second Temple. In the courtyard of the Temple itself, on the northwest, there was the Chamber of the Lepers where the lepers remained after they had been cured, and where they bathed on the eighth day of their purification, awaiting their admittance for the anointing of their toes (Neg. 14:8; Mid. 2:5). In the New Testament there are numerous references to lepers. In the two instances in which Jesus is said to have cured lepers (one an individual—Luke 5:12–14; cf. Matt. 8:3; and the other a group of ten—Luke 17:12), he told them, "Go show yourself to the priest," after their cure, and one passage (Luke 5:14) adds, "and make an offering for thy cleansing, as Moses commanded..." This is evidence that the biblical laws were in operation, both as regards the functions of the priest and the obligatory offering. The Apostles are told in general to cleanse the lepers (Matt. 10:8, Luke 7:22).

It is therefore curious that there are hardly any references in the tannaitic period to actual cases of leprosy (see below). The last Mishnah of *Nega'im* reports a question addressed to *Joshua b. Hananiah (in whose early days the Temple still stood, and who officiated in it as a levite) as to the procedure to be adopted when the offerings of two lepers had been mixed up and one of them died before his sacrifice had been offered. An anonymous Tosefta (6:1) actually includes the "house affected by leprosy" (Lev. 14:34–53) among those laws which "never were and never will be," their purpose being merely "to expound and receive reward therefore" (cf. *Rebellious Son). Eleazar b. Simeon, however, adds that there was a site in the vicinity of Gaza which used to be called "the enclosed ruin" (which was presumably a house affected by leprosy which had been destroyed in accordance with the law (Lev. 14:45)), and Simeon b. Judah of Kefar Akko (according to the amendment of Elijah Gaon of Vilna) said that there was a site in Galilee which used to be pointed out as having within its bounds leprous stones. In addition to this, it is definitely stated that according to the *halakhah,* the law of quarantine for lepers fell into abeyance when the Jubilee year (see *Sabbatical year and Jubilee) was not in operation (cf. Tosef., Ber, 5b top), i.e., during the Second Temple period.

Nevertheless Josephus, who was both a priest and lived during the time of the Temple, in his description of the Mosaic laws, states that it was forbidden to the leper to "come into the city at all [or] to live with any others, as if they were in effect dead persons." He makes a sharp contrast between this law and the fact that "there are lepers in many nations who are yet in honor, and not only free from reproach and avoidance, but who have been great captains of armies, and been entrusted with high office in the commonwealth and have had the privilege of entering into holy places and temples" (Ant., 3:261–9). It is possible, however, that this passage is merely a reference to Naaman, the commander of the army of Syria (II Kings 5, especially vs. 5 and 18).

This lack of reference to actual cases is probably connected with the question of the nature of leprosy during the period of the Second Temple. Two scholars who have dealt with the subject at length both refer to the undoubted fact that whereas biblical leprosy was definitely contagious, that of the Mishnah was not. I. M. Rabbinowicz adduces the evidence, among other things, that if a bridegroom detected symptoms of leprosy on his skin he was permitted to postpone his examination until after the seven days of the nuptials, as was a person who observed them on a festival, until after the festival (Neg. 3:2). I. Katzenelson agrees with this, but he adds the interesting point that not all the various types of leprosy mentioned in the Bible are dealt with in the Mishnah. Leviticus 13:2 refers to the *se'et* ("arising"), the *sappaḥat* ("scab"), and the *baheret* ("bright spot"). Yet, apart from a bare mention of the *se'et* in the first Mishnah, its laws are not dealt with at all, while the *sappaḥat* is not even mentioned, and the whole tractate deals only with the *baheret.* Nor is there any mention of the "appearance of the plague which is deeper than the skin" (13:3). Although Rabbinowicz ascribes this difference to the fact that the leprosy of the Talmud was elephantiasis, which is not contagious, I. Katzenelson is of the opinion that the word refers to a group of skin diseases, those called in the Bible "clean *nega'im,*" which were noninfectious and to be distinguished from "unclean *nega'im,*" which were infectious. He maintains, moreover, that in an attempt to minimize the dislocation and inconvenience caused by the strict application of the biblical laws, which at that time were no longer necessary because of the better conditions which prevailed, the rabbis limited the laws of leprosy to one disease, *vitiligo* or *leuce,* which was of rare occurrence, and in addition they superseded the priests as the determiners of the incidence of the disease.

It would seem, however, that by the time of the compilation of the Mishnah and Tosefta, at the beginning of the third century, all practical laws about the disease had been forgotten, and the classification and identification of the disease by the rabbis were dependent not upon medical facts but upon an academic interpretation of the biblical law. In fact, the laws of leprosy were regarded as the most abstruse and complicated of laws. Eleazar b. Simeon on one occasion said to R. Akiva, "What have you to do with *aggadah?* Turn to the subject of leprosy" (Ḥag. 14a). Although, according to the Talmud, leprosy did not exist in Babylon "because they eat turnips and drink beer and bathe in the Euphrates" (Ket. 77b), it certainly existed in Ereẓ Israel in mishnaic and amoraic times. R. Johanan and Resh Lakish stated that it is forbidden to walk four cubits, or 100 cubits (dependent upon whether there was a wind blowing at the time) to the east of a leper; R. Meir refrained from eating eggs which came from a district where lepers lived; R. Ammi and R. Assi never entered such a district; when Resh Lakish saw one he would cast stones at them, exclaiming, "get back to your location and do not contaminate other people"; and R. Eleazar b. Simeon would hide from them (Lev. R. 16:3). As Katzenelson points out, since the segregation enjoined in the Bible no longer applied in talmudic times, this segregation and its consequences were the result of popular feeling, and not a legal requirement. There is a geonic responsum which states explicitly, "among the people of the east, that is, in Babylonia, at the present time, if, God forbid, a scholar should be affected by leprosy, he is not excluded from the synagogue or the schools, since today the injunction, 'thy camp shall be holy' (Deut. 23:15; i.e., the laws of ritual cleanness) no longer applies" (*Sha'arei Teshuvah,* no. 176).

Reference should be made to the allegation first mentioned by the Egyptian historian *Manetho, and repeated by *Chaereman, *Lysimachus, and other Egyptian writers hostile to the Jews, and quoted by *Apion, to the effect that not only was Moses a leper, but the children of Israel were expelled from Egypt because they suffered from leprosy. Indeed, according to Lysimachus the seventh day was called *Sabbaton* because of the leprous disease of the groin which they suffered which is called *Sabbo* in Egyptian (Jos., Apion, 1:227ff., 2:20–21).

In the Aggadah. With the destruction of the Temple and the consequent abolition of sacrifices and the obsolescence of the regulations of ritual cleanness, the laws of leprosy fell into desuetude. The rabbis, however, derived from leprosy a moral lesson. Homiletically interpreting the word *meẓora* as connected with *moẓi shem ra,* "the person guilty of slander or libel," they regarded leprosy primarily as a divine punishment for this evil, an interpretation which receives historical support by the punishment of Miriam for her slander of Moses (Num. 12:1–15), and the rabbis add that Aaron suffered the same punishment for the same reason (Shab. 97a). Among other sins which bring leprosy as retribution are "the shedding of blood, taking oaths in vain, incest, arrogance, robbery, and envy" (Ar. 16a), as well as benefiting from sacred objects (Lev. R. 17:3). From the combination of the cedar, which represents haughtiness, and the hyssop, the symbol of lowliness, in the purification rites for the leper (Lev. 14:4) the rabbis derived the lesson that man should ever humble himself (see Rashi to Lev. 14:4). The leper was one of the four unfortunates considered to suffer a living death (Ned. 64b; Sanh. 47a; cf. Num. 12:12). That leprosy resulted from a lack of hygiene is indicated not only by the reason given for its absence in Babylon, but from such statements as that it comes from flies (Ḥag. 14a) and that the children born from intercourse with a menstruant woman will be afflicted by it (Lev. R. 15:5). The *aggadah* makes a considerable addition to the number of characters mentioned in the Bible as having been struck with leprosy. They include Cain (Gen. R. 22:12), the daughter of Pharaoh (Ex. R. 1:23), Aaron (see above), Doeg (Sanh. 106b), David (Sanh. 107a), Goliath (Lev. R. 17:3), and Vashti (Meg. 12b). According to the Midrash, the reference to the pharaoh who died (Ex. 2:23) actually refers to the fact that he was afflicted with leprosy. His advisers told him that the only cure was to bathe morning and evening in the blood of 150 Hebrew children, but the decree was averted by God, who in his compassion cured Pharaoh (Ex.R. 1:34). [L.I.R.]

Bibliography: Kaufmann, Y., Toledot, 1 (1937), 539–58; Kaufmann Y., Religion, 103–10; R. K. Harrison, in: IDB, 3 (1962), 111–3, 331–4. In The Second Temple and Talmud: I. M. Rabbinowicz, *La Médicine du Talmud* (1880), 107ff.; G. N. Minkh, *Prokaza i pes* (1890); J. Preuss, *Biblisch-talmudische Medizin* (1923[3]), 369–90; J. L. Katzenelson, *Ha-Talmud ve-Ḥokhmat ha-Refu'ah* (1928), 304–53; H. L. Strack and P. Billerbeck, *Kommentar zum Neuen Testament aus Talmud und Midrash*, 14 (1928), 745–63; Ginzberg, Legends, index; A. R. Short, *The Bible and Modern Medicine* (1953), 74–83.

LERER, YEHIEL (1910–1943), Yiddish poet. He was introduced to Yiddish literature by his townsman and mentor, the novelist, I. M. *Weissenberg, with whose literary circle in Warsaw he is generally associated. When, at the age of 18, he composed his first poems, entitled *Tehillim* ("Psalms"), Weissenberg hailed him as the Yiddish Tagore. These poems were later included in the volume *Shtilkeyt un Shturm* ("Silence and Storm," 1932), a volume characterized by religious piety and lyric solemnity. Unsuccessful in various callings, Lerer suffered from privation throughout his short life. His poem *Mayn Heym* ("My Home," 1937), about a family in a small Jewish town, stressed the transformation of its traditional religious and social character under the impact of new forces. Sholem Asch called this poem a "gift of God's grace, one of the most beautiful Jewish books." Lerer was a romantic epigone during the dominance of expressionistic tendencies in Yiddish poetry. After the Nazi occupation of Warsaw, he participated in the ghetto's literary activities under various assumed names, until, in 1943, he was transported to *Treblinka, where he was killed.

Bibliography: LNYL, 5 (1963), 370–2; M. Ravitch, *Mayn Leksikon* (1945), 119–21; M. Grossman, *Heymishe Geshtaltn* (1953), 158–64; *Yizkor-Bukh fun der Zhelekhover Yidisher Kehile* (1954), 181–94; D. Sadan, *Avnei Miftan* (1962), 237–48. [M.Rav.]

LÉRIDA (Leyda, Ilerda), city in Spain on the border between Catalonia and Aragon. In the Muslim period, the Jews of Lérida maintained close contact with those in nearby Barcelona. Their major occupation was tanning, as attested by various documents, but there were several wealthy merchants and a few farmers. The Jewish quarter, dating from the 11th century, was located to the west of the city in a place called Cuiraça. A street still called Judería, located above the quarter, attests to its subsequent expansion.

The Order of Knights Templar had many interests in Lérida and its vicinity, and Jews were connected with its activities. In 1168, the bailiff of Lérida, a Jew named Jafia, was granted several properties in the city. In 1172 his son David was given a workshop and a house near the king's palace in the city. In 1175 Jafia mortgaged a wine cellar he owned in the Jewish quarter and a vineyard to the Templars of Gardeny near Lérida. In 1173 one of the synagogues was converted into a church. Profet Benvenist, the king's *alfaquim*, also owned property in Lérida, including a house in the Muslim quarter (1189). Deeds of sale of houses, gardens, and vineyards owned by Jews, dating from the beginning of the 13th century, have been preserved. One of them mentions a Jew named Abraym Cavalaria of Lérida but it is not known whether he was related to the well-known *Cavaleria family. In addition to his other offices, Benveniste de Porta was bailiff of Lérida. In the controversy over *Maimonides' writings, the Lérida community joined in the ban imposed on *Solomon of Montpellier and his followers in 1232 by the communities of Aragon. Some Jews from Lérida settled in Valencia after the capture of the city in 1238. In 1271 James I appointed a certain Nasi Ḥasdai as rabbi and *dayyan* of the Lérida community. He was authorized to adjudicate all disputes between Jews according to Jewish law in consultation with two of the elders who were bound to accept the rabbi's summons to sit in court. The appointment was unique in Catalonia, similar instances being found only in Castile. The taxes levied upon the community of Lérida amounted to about 5,000 sólidos in 1271, and 3,000 sólidos in 1274. The community was headed by **muqaddimūm* or *adelantados*, a council, and magistrates *(borerim)*. The *muqaddimūm* appointed their own successors in office.

At the beginning of the 14th century several *Conversos returned to Judaism in Lérida, among them a convert from Belmont near Toulouse who was apprehended in 1317 and tried by the Inquisition in Toulouse. Jews from Lérida were among those who went to bury the victims of the *Pastoureaux massacres in *Montclus in 1320, and were accused of demolishing a bridge and cutting down trees there, but were pardoned the same year on payment of a large sum to the crown. During the massacres accompanying the *Black Death in 1348, the community found refuge in the citadel. In 1350 they had to pay 350 Barcelona sólidos to the official appointed for their protection. An agreement between the community and the municipal authorities concerning the import of wine was ratified by Pedro IV in 1353; the document, in which the community undertook not to bring imported wine into the city, contains a long list of the communal leaders. Two Jews from Lérida were accused in 1383 of desecrating the *Host, and the count of Urgel was ordered by the king to investigate the charges.

During the persecutions of 1391 a number of Jews took refuge in the citadel and 78 were massacred. The Jewish quarter was destroyed. The king ordered that measures should be taken to punish the rioters and protect the Jews. In 1400 King Martin gave permission to the survivors to take steps to rehabilitate the community. Newcomers were granted a reduction of taxes and released from their debts, and Jews from other communities were permitted to settle in the city after they had settled their taxes. If their former communities refused to allow them to settle there, the municipal authorities of Lérida would guarantee the payment of their liabilities through mortgages and assist in moving the newcomers. In addition, an electoral procedure was established in which the rights of the newcomers were safeguarded. Stringent measures were passed against *informers. The community was allowed to impose indirect taxes, and its members were permitted to live in other parts of the city until the Cuiraça district had been reconstructed.In 1408 King Martin ordered that the synagogue, which had been converted into a church, should be restored and also provided for the election of two *muqaddimūm* and nine councillors and regulated their authority. An agreement was concluded in 1410 between the city authorities and the community concerning the latter's status and activities. In 1421 Queen Maria wrote to the municipal authorities concerning the establishment of a new community in Lérida. John II granted the community a number of patents of protection and alleviated certain of the restrictions imposed before 1459 on some occupations. In 1490 a district tribunal of the Inquisition was established in Lérida which included Huesca and Urgel within its jurisdiction. An unsuccessful attempt was made to murder the inquisitor in 1514.

Bibliography: J. Pleyan de Porta, *Apuntes de Historia de Lérida* (1873), 135ff., 172, 400; H. C. Lea, *History of the Spanish Inquisition*, 1 (1907), 549; Baer, Urkunden, index; F. Mateu y Llopis, in: *Hispania*, 2 (1942), 407–37; J. Llandoza, *La "Cuiraça" y* *la judería leridana* (1951), 110ff.; Simón de Gilleuma, in: *Sefarad*, 18 (1958), 83–97; A. López de Meneses, *ibid.*, 19 (1959), 101; D. Romano, *ibid.*, 20 (1960), 50–65; Baer, Spain, index; Ashtor, Korot, 2 (1966), 174–6. [H.B.]

LERMA, JUDAH BEN SAMUEL (middle of the 16th century), scholar of Spanish origin living in Italy. The year of Lerma's birth and death are unknown, and all the information on him relates to the years 1553–56. The place and scope of his activity are also not clear, but apparently he never held an official rabbinical post. He states that he attempted to amass wealth but lost all that he possessed. He also complains, as do other contemporary scholars in Italy, that the attitude of the public to him was not as it should be toward a scholar. He is frequently confused with Judah Lerma of Belgrade, author of the *Peletat Bat Yehudah*, but it is doubtful if there was even a family relationship between them. Some think he was the son of Samuel Lerma, the copyist in 1536 of the manuscript glosses on the Mishnah. He wrote *Leḥem Yehudah*, a commentary to *Avot*. The first edition was published in Venice in 1553, but was consigned to the flames in the same year, with the burning of the Talmud (see Burning of *Talmud). A second edition was published in the following year in Sabbioneta, but there are conspicuous differences between the two editions, especially in the first half. He also wrote a commentary on the Book of Job which is frequently quoted in both editions of the *Leḥem Yehudah*, and there are also fragments of *aggadah* with a commentary extant in manuscript. His commentary to *Avot* is quoted in the various 16th-century anthologies of commentaries to *Avot*.

Lerma was a philosopher who followed the Spanish Jewish philosophers, from whom he derived his theories and views. His approach is on the whole moderate and conservative. His main sources, besides the talmudic and midrashic literature and Maimonides, are Joseph Albo, Isaac Abrabanel, and in particular Isaac Arama. Lerma had no direct knowledge of the writings of non-Jewish thinkers and was also most sparing in the use of other Jewish speculative and literary works. His method of writing is nearer in style and form to talmudic than to the philosophical literature (particularly in the second edition). He is more interested in using his sources as the basis of his own views than in explaining the literal meaning of the tractate. Although original neither in his ideas nor in his manner of expressing them, Lerma's views about the influence of the stars upon the world and man, and about predestination in its relation to man's religious autonomy and the Commandments are interesting and unique in content, form, and scope (in both editions). These views met with the opposition of his contemporaries despite their moderate approach. There is a note of arrogance in his work. He frequently disputes the views of earlier authorities and even expressed himself to the effect that the person studying his work "would have no need of any other commentator."

Bibliography: Steinschneider, Cat Bod, 1337, no. 5737; E. Carmoly, *Divrei ha-Yamim li-Venei Yaḥya* (1850), 35, n.109; Epstein, Mishnah, 1286–87. [Jos.H.]

LERNER, ABBA PETACHJA (1903–), U.S. economist. Born in Russia and educated at the London School of Economics, Lerner began to teach there in 1935. In 1942 he went to the United States and soon established himself as an eminent teacher in economics. He taught at the New School for Social Research, New York, Michigan State University, Roosevelt University, and the University of California. During 1953–56 he served as an economic adviser to the government of Israel. Beside his professional interests, which include international trade, welfare economics, labor and employment, price formation, and the gold standard, Lerner is concerned with problems of social reform and foreign policy. His major publications include *The Economics of Control* (1944), *The Economics of Employment* (1951), *Essays in Economic Analysis* (1953), and *Everybody's Business* (1961). [J.O.R.]

LERNER, ALAN JAY (1918–), U.S. lyric writer and librettist who collaborated in several successful musicals. Lerner was born in New York and wrote for advertising agencies and radio before teaming up with the composer, Frederick Loewe. Their first hit was the musical *Brigadoon* (1947) which was followed by *Paint Your Wagon* in 1951. Lerner also worked independently and won an Oscar in 1951 with his screenplay for *An American in Paris*. His greatest success came in 1956 when, with Loewe, he created *My Fair Lady* (based on Shaw's *Pygmalion*). The Lerner and Loewe film musical *Gigi* (1958) won Oscars, and in 1960 their *Camelot* had a two-year run on Broadway.

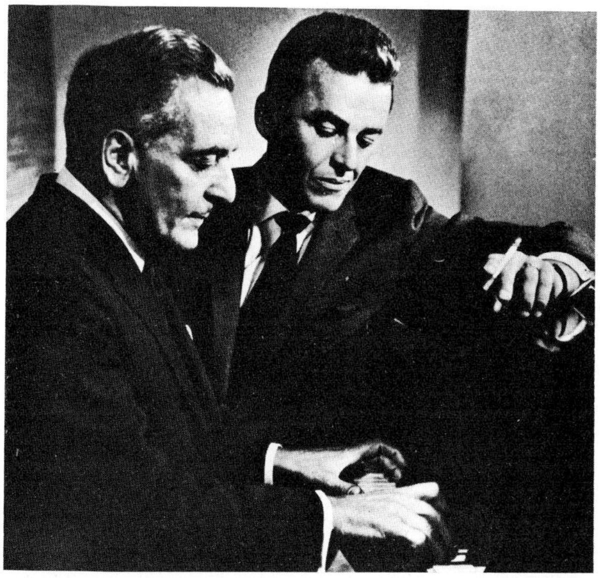

Alan Jay Lerner, U.S. lyric writer and librettist (right), with the composer, Frederick Loewe. From S. Green, *The World of Musical Comedy*, New York, 1968. Photo Karsh.

With the composer Burton Lane, Lerner wrote *On a Clear Day You Can See Forever* (1965) and with André Previn, *Coco* (1969), the story of the "queen" of Paris fashions, Coco Chanel.

Bibliography: D. Even, *Complete Book of the American Musical Theater* (1958), 194–200; I. Martin, *Pete Martin Calls On . . .* (1962), 449–59; *Current Biography Yearbook* (1958), 241–4. [G.E.H.]

LERNER, ḤAYYIM ẒEVI BEN TODROS (1815–1889), Hebrew grammarian and pedagogue. Born in Dubno (Volhynia), he was the pupil of the noted scholar Ze'ev Wolf Adelsohn, under whose influence he studied both Hebrew and secular subjects. He worked as a private Hebrew tutor and became a teacher at the Jewish government school in Berdichev, in 1849, and in 1851, a teacher of Hebrew language and grammar at the government rabbinical seminary in Zhitomir. He was very successful in the latter and held the post until the closing of the institute by governmental decree in 1873.

Lerner's most important work is his Hebrew grammar, *Moreh ha-Lashon* ("Teacher of the Language," 1859) which is based on the principles laid down by his teacher, S. *Pinsker. In Lerner's lifetime, the book appeared in seven editions; these he annotated and supplemented from the fourth edition onward (1879), notably with a supplement of practical exercises. After his death, the book was also printed with the supplement *Yalkut Ḥazal* (1893^{8}), which includes explanations to difficult Bible passages and their commentaries. *Moreh ha-Lashon,* published in 13 editions (1909[13]), was the first of its kind that laid down rules for teaching children the essentials of Hebrew grammar. Lerner also wrote: *Dikduk Leshon Aramit* (1875), and *Toledot ha-Dikduk* (1876), a short history of Hebrew grammar and grammarians up to the 19th century. He also translated into Hebrew S. D. Luzzatto's Italian work on the Aramaic in the Babylonian Talmud, under the title *Dikduk Leshon Talmud Bavli* (1880). The last years of his life Lerner spent in poverty in Zhitomir, supported by his former pupils. He left in manuscript a research work on talmudic texts, *Arba Middot,* and a rich collection of his correspondence with leading Jewish scholars of his time.

Bibliography: N. Sokolow (ed.), *Sefer Zikkaron le-Soferei Yisrael*... (1889), 65–66; *Ha-Meliẓ,* 29 (1889), nos. 76, 79; Skomorovsky, in: H. Lerner, *Moreh ha-Lashon* (1898[10]), iii–v (introd.); *Kol Kitvei A. U. Kovner* (1947), 23–30; A. J. Paperna, *Kol ha-Ketavim* (1952), 197–204. [Y.S./Ed.]

LERNER, JOSEPH JUDAH (1849–1907), writer, dramatist, and scholar. Born in Berdichev, he contributed from an early age to the Hebrew, Russian, and Yiddish press. During the Russo-Turkish war he published *Zapiski Grazhdanina,* a Russian paper in Bucharest, emphasizing the Jewish contribution to that war. There he met Goldfaden's Yiddish theatrical troupe, and on his return to Odessa started a company of his own, intending to raise standards in both the language and content of Jewish plays. Earning his living as an unqualified lawyer, he often came into contact with the world of crime and, at times, became involved in precarious transactions to the extent that in 1873 he was temporarily compelled to seek asylum in Vienna. Among the plays he translated and adapted were *Uriel Acosta* (1885) by Gutzkow, and *The Jewess* (1889) by Scribe. With the ban on the Jewish theater in 1883, Lerner returned to his journalistic and literary career, and contributed to the major Russian newspapers. He became a convert to Christianity in the 1890s. His works include a novel about Jewish life in Russia, *Yamim mi-Kedem* (1868); a Jewish history in Yiddish, *Di Yidishe Geshikhte;* and a study in Russian of the Jews in New Russia, *Yevrei v Novorossiskom *Kraie,* which was based on the archives of the former governor-general of New Russia.

Bibliography: E. R. Malachi, *Massot u-Reshimot* (1937), 71–75; Borovoy, in: *Filologishe Shriftn,* 3 (1929), 472–84; B. Gorin, *Geshikhte fun Yidishn Teater,* 1 (1929), 227–36; Z. Zylbercweig, *Leksikon fun Yidishn Teater,* 2 (1934), 1162–68. [Y.S.]

LERNER, MAX (1902–), U.S. author and journalist. Lerner, who was born in Minsk, Russia, was taken to the

Max Lerner, U.S. author and journalist. Courtesy *New York Post.* Photo Philippe Halsman.

United States at the age of five. He taught at Sarah Lawrence College, Harvard University, Williams College, and, from 1949, at Brandeis University. A liberal social commentator, Lerner became known for his scholarly works on American society and the science of government. Lerner was managing editor of the *Encyclopaedia of Social Sciences* (1927–1933). He also edited the periodical *The Nation* (1936–38). He was a columnist for the newspaper *P.M.* (1945–48), for the *New York Star* (1948–49), and, from 1949, was syndicated by the *New York Post.* His principal works include: *It is Later than You Think* (1938); *Ideas are Weapons* (1939); *Ideas for the Ice Age* (1941); *America as a Civilization* (1957); and *The Age of Overkill* (1962). Lerner's work contains elements of his journalistic style together with more sober academic attempts to analyze American life in his day. [L.H.F.]

LERNER, MAYER BEN MORDECAI OF ALTONA (1857–1930), rabbi. Lerner was born in Czestochowa (Poland). He studied first in Cracow but completed his

Mayer Lerner, rabbi of Altona and Schleswig-Holstein. Courtesy M. Lerner, London.

studies in the Rabbiner-Seminar in Berlin. While still a student at the seminary he wrote his important work *Anlage und Quellen des Bereschit Rabba* (1882). He was appointed rabbi of Wintzenheim, Alsace, in 1884 and remained there until 1890, when he became rabbi of the Federation of Synagogues in London, which then consisted of 23 synagogues. In 1894 he was appointed rabbi of Altona and of Schleswig-Holstein. Lerner vigorously opposed the historical approach of *Graetz and the Reform movement in Germany.

Lerner's main talmudic works are his *Hadar ha-Karmel* (1891), responsa, including some talmudic novellae; and *Ḥayyei Olam* (1905) on the prohibition of cremation. His research works, in addition to the above-mentioned *Quellen* include *"Die aeltesten Mischna—Kompositionen"* (MWJ, 13 (1886), 1–20) and his magnum opus, *Torat ha-Mishnah,* dealing with the origin of the oral tradition, of which, however, only the first part appeared (1915). He also showed an active interest in the Jewish settlement of Palestine and in 1905 founded the association Moriah whose aims were "to restore the ancient ruins, and the national and religious culture of the Jews." The association was opposed both to the Mizrachi and the Zionist movements, and in 1930 merged with the Agudat Israel movement.

Bibliography: E. Duckesz, *Ivvah le-Moshav* (1903), 136–9; Weingarten, in: J. L. Fishman (ed.), *Sefer ha-Mizrachi* (1946), 103–10; Bath-Yehudah, in: AZD, 3 (1965), 266–70. [Y.Al.]

LE ROITH, HAROLD HIRSCH (1905–), South African architect. Born in Grahamstown, he became disciple of the modern school of architects, such as Le Corbusier, Gropius, and Frank Lloyd Wright. Le Roith translated the concepts of functionalism into much of his work in Johannesburg and other South African cities. His specialized area lay in the planning of business and industrial complexes, extensive flat units, and modern-type houses. In these fields his designs attracted international recognition in the professional literature. He practiced in Johannesburg where he served as honorary architect to the United Progressive (Reform) Jewish Congregation and of other Reform communities on the Witwatersrand. He was on the executive committee of the Johannesburg Progressive congregation and was president for several years. [L.Ho.]

LESHNEV (Pol. **Leszniów**), town near Brody, Lvov oblast, Ukrainian S.S.R. Jews first settled there in the early 17th century, and the Jewish cemetery dates from that era. The synagogue, built in the second half of the 17th century, had an Attic roof and pseudo-Tuscan columns. Under the influence of the *ḥerem* proclaimed against the Ḥasidim in Brody, in 1772 an assembly of "select members of the community," including the local rabbi, Menahem Mendel b. Jacob, and R. Akiva of Vladimir-Volynski, passed a decree against the Ḥasidim, which was signed by all the participants. The Leshnev community numbered 696 (32% of the total population) in 1880; 513 (26%) in 1900; and only 179 (about 10%) in 1921. [EJ/Ed.]

The 17th-century synagogue of Leshnev, Ukraine. Courtesy Yad Vashem Archives, Jerusalem.

Holocaust Period. With the German conquest of the town at the beginning of July 1941 attacks against Jewish life and property began. Many fell at the hands of the Ukrainian population. Jewish youth were taken to labor camps in the surrounding area, and many met their deaths there. In 1942 the Jews were concentrated in a special quarter, and in November 1942 a closed ghetto was established. Later some of the Jews were transferred to the Brody ghetto and were sent from there to extermination camps. On April 17, 1943, the remnants of the Leshnev community were liquidated. A few managed to escape from the ghetto and found shelter in the surrounding forests. After the war, Jewish life was not reconstituted in the town. [Ar.W.]

Bibliography: M. Bałaban, *Zabytki historyczne Żydów w Polsce* (1929), index; Dubnow, Ḥasidut, 1 (1960²), index; *Sprawozdania Komisji dla badania historyi sztuki w Polsce*, vol. 5; B. Wasiutyński, *Ludność żydowska w Polsce w wiekach XIX i XX* (1930), 139.

LESKO (Ger. **Lisko;** Heb. and Yid. **Lisk**), town in Rzeszow province, S.E. Poland. Jews lived in Lesko from the town's foundation in the middle of the 16th century. In 1704 the town was burnt down by the Swedish army. In a plague which broke out afterward, 303 Jews perished. In 1718 the community paid 3,400 zlotys poll tax. In the 18th century the community's rabbi was Samuel Shmelke b. Mordecai, who approved the book, *Berit Shalom*, by Phinehas of *Wlodawa. The *Councils of the Lands intervened in a dispute that lasted from 1705 to 1724 between the community of Lesko and the neighboring one of *Sanok. Because of the serious economic plight of the Jewish population, the Polish *Sejm in 1768 declared a moratorium on its debts to the government. The Jewish community numbered 1,976 in 1880 and 2,400 in 1921 (c. 63% of the total population). In the folklore of Galician Jews, Lesko Jews were considered as "wise fools" like those of *Chelm in Congress Poland. In June 1941 the German army entered the town. On Aug. 14, 1941, the entire Jewish population was deported to Zaslaw and was exterminated together with Zaslaw Jews. [Sh.L.K.]

°**LESKOV, NIKOLAY SEMYONOVICH** (1831–1895), Russian author. One of the most controversial and misunderstood writers in Russian literature, he wrote some passages critical of Jews but more frequently criticized his fellow-Russians, often contrasting them unfavorably with the Jews, the Ukrainians, the English, the Americans, the Poles, and the Germans. Leskov's interest in the Jews can be traced throughout his literary career. Jewish themes were especially important in his literary and journalistic writing during the years 1880–87, when he published more than 30 works on the subject, including over 20 newspaper articles explaining Jewish religious beliefs and customs to non-Jewish readers. His fictional works on Jewish themes include *Skazaniye o Fyodore-khristianine i o druge yego Abramezhidovine* ("The Tale of Theodore the Christian and his friend Abram the Jew," 1887), a simple parable on tolerance and brotherhood, which was reprinted by the Petrograd Soviet shortly after the October 1917 Revolution; *Obman* ("Deception," 1883), in which Leskov cleverly attacked anti-Semitism by exposing his fellow-Russians to ridicule; and *Ukha bez ryby* ("Fish Soup without Fish," 1887), an entertaining story in which a learned provincial rabbi achieves poetic as well as economic justice at the expense of the town's leading Russian Orthodox citizens. Two other stories, *Rakushanskiy melamed* ("The Hebrew Teacher from Galicia," 1878), and *Zhidovskaya kuvyrkollegiya* ("Somersaulting Yids," 1882), caused him to be accused of anti-Semitism by readers who failed to realize that Jews had no more claim to protection from Leskov's humorous satire than Orthodox archbishops, czarist bureaucrats, self-centered intellectuals, or despotic revolutionaries. Leskov also wrote anonymously what was possibly the most powerful defense of equal rights for Jews published in 19th-century Russia. *Yevrei v Rossii* ("The Jews in Russia," 1884), a report intended for government circulation only, caused much excitement in Jewish circles in St. Petersburg. When a copy was lent to A. E. Landau, editor of the leading Russian-language Jewish journal *Voskhod,* he immediately devoted a long series of enthusiastic editorials to it and, with unconscious irony, regretted that the author of such a well-written document was not a professional writer. *Yevrei v Rossii* was republished in Petrograd (1919) and in New York (1969), but it does not appear in the 11-volume Soviet edition of Leskov's works published in 1956–58.

Bibliography: A. L. Volynski (pseud.), *N. S. Leskov* (Rus., 1923); L. Grossman, *N. S. Leskov* (Rus., 1945); B. M. Drugov, *N. S. Leskov: ocherk tvorchestva* (1957); W. B. Edgerton (ed. and tr.), *Satirical Stories of Nikolai Leskov* (1963), incl. bibl. [W.B.E.]

LESLAU, WOLF (1906–), U.S. Semitics scholar and philologist. Leslau was born in Krzepice, Poland. He taught at the Ecole des Hautes Etudes in Paris and the Ecole des Langues Orientales. In 1942 he emigrated to the U.S. He taught at several institutions before joining the faculty of the University of California in Los Angeles in 1955, where he continued teaching Hebrew and Semitic languages.

Leslau was a fellow of the American Academy of Arts and Sciences, American Academy of Jewish Research, and other scholarly societies. Leslau undertook eight trips to Ethiopia to do fieldwork on the various Semitic languages of Ethiopia and on the culture and folklore of the country, giving special attention to the *Falashas. His published works deal with descriptive and comparative problems of Ethiopic as well as Semitic linguistics, and include *Falasha Anthology* (1951), which he translated and edited; *Lexique Soqotri* (1938); *Etude descriptive et comparative du Gafat* (1956); *Ethiopic Documents: Gurage* (1950); *An Amharic Conversation Book* (1965); *Amharic Textbook* (1968); *Ethiopic and South Arabic Contribution to the Hebrew Lexicon* (1958); *Etymological Dictionary of Harari* (1963); and *Hebrew Cognates in Amharic* (1969). [W.J.F.]

LESLIE, ROBERT L. (1886–), U.S. typographic expert. Leslie and Sol M. Cantor (1892–1965) formed a typesetting firm, The Composing Room, Inc., in New York specializing in books for publishers throughout the U.S. Leslie introduced novel promotion techniques to further the graphic arts, bringing graphic artists together to form typographic design clinics. The Composing Room provided a wide variety of typefaces. Thousands of separate fonts were available for hand, machine, and photo composition. Among the typographic experts was Ismar *David, designer of the Hebrew type face "David." [I. So.]

LESMIAN (Lesman), BOLESŁAW (1878–1937), Polish poet. Born in Warsaw, Leśmian was raised in Kiev and trained as a lawyer. A master of Polish verse, he was one of the leading representatives of the group of symbolist poets known as Young Poland, in whose organ *Chimera* his earliest works appeared (1901–07). In turn satirical and pathetic, he produced verse full of symbolic description and metaphysical reflection, mingling realistic, fanciful, and grotesque effects. Above all, Leśmian stressed the tragic fate of mankind—a prey to sickness and misery. During his lifetime he published three verse collections: *Sąd rozstajny* ("The Widespread Orchard," 1912); *Łąka* ("The Meadow," 1920); and *Napój cienisty* ("Shady Liquor," 1936). A fourth volume, *Dzieje leśna* ("The Wood Fable"), appeared posthumously in 1938. Leśmian also translated poems by Edgar Allan Poe and published two prose works, *Klechdy sezamowe* ("The Sesame Narrative," 1913), fairy tales; and *Przygody Sindbada żeglarza* ("The Adventures of Sindbad the Sailor," 1915), a popular children's book. Leśmian, whose works often recall those of *Kafka, was a forerunner of the Polish surrealists and his poetry enjoyed a new lease of life in the 1960s, inspiring literary symposia and research. His *Szkice literackie i eseje* ("Literary Sketches and Essays") were published in 1959. [S.W.]

LESS, EMIL (1855–1935), German meteorologist. Born in Koenigsberg (Kaliningrad), Less was director of the Berlin weather bureau (1884–1923) and in 1897 was appointed to the Landwirtschaftliche Hochschule of Berlin. He was also associate professor at the Kaiser Frederick William University of Berlin. Less was among the founders of the Deutsche Meteorologische Gesellschaft. During the years he directed the Berlin weather bureau, he published the annual and general reports on the climatic elements of Germany. In 1914 he was enlisted as an officer in the army, providing meteorological guidance and weather information for the pilots of the Air Force.

Bibliography: J. C. Poggendorff, *Biographisch-literarisches Handwoerterbuch*, 4 (1904); 5 (1926); 6 (1938), s.v., includes bibliography; *Kuerschners Deutscher Gelehrten-Kalender*, 3 (1929); 4 (1931), s.v., incl. bibl. [D.Ash.]

LESSER POLAND (Pol. **Małopolska**), historical region in S.W. Poland. In the structure of Jewish *autonomy and in historical geography, Lesser Poland embraced the provinces (*województwa*) of Krakow and Sandomierz alone; after the first partition of Poland (1772) it passed to Austria and was essentially Western Galicia. According to the 1764 census the Jews in Lesser Poland numbered 18,670 in Krakow province and 42,972 in Sandomierz, around 10.5% of the total Jewish population of Poland. More Jews were actually living there at the time, but since the census was related to a poll tax, the Jews concealed their exact number. About 60% of them lived in the towns and the rest in the countryside. The largest communities in the region had several thousand members; in most of the villages there were only a few Jewish families. Between 1511–14 King Sigismund I appointed Jewish *seniores* as heads of the region and collectors of taxes from the Jews. At the same time he appointed Joseph *Polak as chief rabbi of Lesser Poland. Since the system was unsuccessful the king abandoned it and handed over tax collecting to the Jews in the various regions of the country between 1518–22. Lesser Poland thus became one of the basic units of Jewish autonomy in Poland. However, the king retained the right to nominate the chief rabbis and in Lesser Poland he appointed Moses Fishel. The king's retention of control was resisted by the communities and in 1551 King Sigismund II Augustus allowed them to elect their own rabbis.

The principal communities of Lesser Poland in the *Councils of the Lands were Opatow (Apta), Ḥenchin (Checiny), Sandomierz (Ẓuzmir), Pinczow (Pintshev), and Lhidlov (*Staszow), all in the province of Sandomierz, and Wodzislaw (Voidislav), *Olkusz (Elikush), and Cracow (Kraka), in the province of Krakow. According to the 1717 assessment, Lesser Poland had to pay the Council of Four Lands a share of 27,075 zlotys in the total payment of 226,109 zlotys due from all the Jews in Poland. When the council was dissolved, the committee appointed by the royal treasury to carry out the liquidation drew up a list of debts: a total of 2,314,350 zlotys for the entire Jewish population. Of this the provinces of Krakow and Sandomierz owed 338,089 zlotys on account of loans received for poll tax. Four of the representatives at the Council of Four Lands came from Lesser Poland. The provincial council of Lesser Poland convened every year to determine the apportionment of taxes among the various communities. Other problems of Jewish life were also discussed at these meetings. The provincial council employed a rabbi, who was presiding judge of the provincial court, as well as several clerks, among them a *shammash* who represented the larger communities at the *Breslau fairs. In 1738 the authorities decreed that the numbers of these *shammashim* in Poland should be reduced and the communities of Lesser Poland were allowed to appoint one representative only. The council of Lesser Poland was heavily in debt to rich Jews. When the Council of Four Lands discussed the matter in 1762–63, it resolved to press the provincial council to pay its debts.

Thanks to the standing of the yeshivot of Cracow and its great rabbis, as well as the centrality of the region in the origins and development of the Polish state and culture, the Jewry and leadership of Lesser Poland enjoyed an influence disproportionate to their numbers. Under Austrian rule, Western Galicia developed its own kind of Jewish culture and society.

See also *Great Poland; Moses *Isserles; *Galicia; *Poland, Modern Era; and Osias *Thon. [SH.L.K.]

°**LESSING, GOTTHOLD EPHRAIM** (1729–1781), German dramatist, philosopher, and critic. One of the outstanding representatives of the Enlightenment in Germany, Lessing was devoted to the principle of toleration.

Engraving of Gotthold E. Lessing, German Enlightenment figure, by W. Aarland. New York, Leo Baeck Institute.

One of Lessing's earliest literary ventures was *Die Juden* (1749), a one-act comedy in which for the first time a Jew was presented on the German stage in a reasonably objective manner. Lessing later upheld the play's defense of toleration against the criticism of J. D. *Michaelis. Through a physician, Aaron Solomon Gumpertz, he became a friend and admirer of Moses *Mendelssohn, whom he encouraged to publish his first philosophical work. The outcome of their common interest in aesthetics was *Pope ein Metaphysiker* (1755) and a critical journal, *Briefe, die neueste Literatur betreffend* (1759–60). Their correspondence, mainly on philosophical themes, continued until Lessing's death.

Mendelssohn was the inspiration for Lessing's *Nathan der Weise* (1779), his last play, and once more a plea for toleration. Based on the parable of the three rings, adapted from *Boccaccio's *Decameron,* the play presents Judaism, Christianity, and Islam as three sons of a benevolent father who has given each an identical ring, although each one claims that his ring alone is authentic. Nathan is made the spokesman for the aspirations of the Enlightenment: tolerance, brotherhood, and love of humanity. Lessing's vision of Jewish-Christian amity was ridiculed by Julius von Voss in *Der travestierte Nathan der Weise* (1804), and attacked by the anti-Semites Wilhelm *Marr, Karl Eugen *Duehring, Sebastian *Brunner, and Adolf Bartels. On the other hand Lessing's personal example and ideals were vigorously upheld and emphasized by German Jews such as Gabriel *Riesser, I. H. *Ritter, Berthold *Auerbach, Emil *Lehmann, and Johann *Jacoby. *Nathan der Weise* was translated into Hebrew, notably by Simon *Bacher and D. B. *Gottlober and many of Lessing's other plays were also translated. His ideological and stylistic influence on the *Haskalah was as decisive as that of Friedrich *Schiller.

However, Lessing's attitude toward Judaism was ambivalent. While never forsaking the principle of tolerance, he came to depreciate Judaism in relation to Christianity with his publication of *Fragmente eines Ungenannten* (1774–78), the posthumous writings of the ultra-rationalist theologian H. M. Reimarus. He reached a further stage in his epoch-making *Erziehung des Menschengeschlechts* ("Education of Humanity"), which was published anonymously. In it the Old Testament is described as morally and aesthetically inferior to the New Testament, which itself is on the verge of being superseded by rational enlightenment. The monotheistic and universalistic mission of Judaism as the forerunner of Christianity had been completed. This attitude also appeared in *Nathan der Weise,* in which the brother representing Christianity accuses the Jewish religion of having given birth to intolerance through the concept of a chosen people.

Bibliography: ADB, 19 (1884), 756–802; L. Zscharnack, *Lessing und Semmler* (1905); L. Geiger, *Die deutsche Literatur und die Juden* (1910), 54–58; P. Hazard, *European Thought in the Eighteenth Century from Montesquieu to Lessing* (1954); Ettinger, in: *Zion,* 29 (1954), 182–207; H. E. Allison, *Lessing and the Enlightenment* (1966); P. Demetz (ed.), *G. E. Lessing: Nathan der Weise* (1966); H. M. Z. Meyer, *Moses Mendelssohn Bibliographie* (1965), index, s.v. *Lessing;* EJ, bibliography; see also the exchange of letters between Lessing and Mendelssohn in Moses Mendelssohn's *Gesammelte Schriften* (1932), vol. 11. [M.GRA.]

LESSING, THEODOR (1872–1933), German philosopher. Born in Hanover, he was the son of a prosperous physician and took up history, philosophy, and medicine at Bonn and Munich. He converted to Lutheranism when a student at Freiburg. In 1908 he was appointed instructor at the Technische Hochschule in Hanover but soon became absorbed in the history of ideas. In the years that followed he produced such studies as *Schopenhauer, Wagner, Nietzsche* (1906), *Philosophie als Tat* (1914), *Untergang der Erde am Geist* (1915), and *Geschichte als Sinngebung des Sinnlosen* (1919). With the rise of Zionism, Lessing returned to Judaism and underwent a complete change of outlook. He expressed his views in *Der juedische Selbsthass* (1930), a clinical study of Jewish intellectuals who had succumbed to self-hatred, a malady which he had himself experienced. Lessing saw in the Jews an Asiatic people forced upon the European scene, and made to occupy a position between the cultures of two continents. He discovered the strength of the Jews in their closeness to nature and life's elemental roots: it was their tragedy that against their earthbound instincts history had cut them off from the soil, eventually causing a people of peasants to become over-spiritualized and decadent. In the minority that had begun to trickle back to the eroded soil of Palestine, he saw the eventual recovery of both land and people. In 1925 Lessing expressed opposition to Hindenburg's election as president of the Weimar Republic, was subjected to anti-Semitic attacks, and forced to suspend his lectures. He was living in Marienbad in 1933, and was assassinated by Nazis dispatched there for that purpose. His memoirs, *Einmal und nie wieder,* were published in 1935 and republished in 1970.

Theodor Lessing, German philosopher. Jerusalem, J.N.U.L., Schwadron Collection.

Bibliography: S. Liptzin, *Germany's Stepchildren* (1944), 152–69; E. Hieronimus, *Theodor Lessing, Otto Meyerhof, Leonard Nelson, bedeutende Juden in Niedersachsen* (1964), 9–57. [S.L.]

LESTSCHINSKY, JACOB (1876–1966), Russian-born pioneer in sociology, economics, and demography of Jewish life. Lestschinsky, who was born in Horodicz in the Ukraine, was deeply affected by *Aḥad Ha-Am and became a member of the *Benei Moshe League when he was 17. He and his brother Joseph established a modern Hebrew school in Horodicz which became famous for its tutelage. He studied at Berne and Zurich universities, pamphleteered

Jacob Lestschinsky, demographer of Jewish life. From A. Manor, *Ya'akov Lestschinsky*, Jerusalem, 1961.

for Zionist Socialism, principally in Warsaw, and served as a Zionist delegate at the Sixth Zionist Congress in Basle, where he supported the territorialists. He helped found the Zionist-Socialist (S.S.) Party, writing for it and for other journals on economics under the name Aḥad ha-Kanna'im. "Statistics of a Small Town" (1903) was his first study in the field he was to concentrate on, and was followed by two applications of Marxist methods, *Der Yidisher Arbeter in London* (1906) and *Der Yidisher Arbeter in Rusland* (1906). After 1906 he was not active in party politics, although he remained a Zionist activist. At this period he published two series of studies on conversions in different countries (1911) and on German Jewry (1912). Before 1914 he operated an ORT employment agency for Jewish refugees in Warsaw. During the February Revolution in Russia he helped found the United Jewish Socialist Party and served on the editorial board of *Naye Tsayt*, its official journal.

In 1921 Lestschinsky left Russia and established himself in Berlin, where he was the *Forward* correspondent, a connection he maintained virtually until his death. His *Yidishe Folk in Tsifern* (1922) viewed Jewish demography in worldwide perspective. Early in the 1920s he helped establish the Institute for Research into Contemporary Jewry and Judaism. He served as editor of an important journal, *Bleter far Yidishe Demografie un Statistik*, from 1923 to 1925. His *Probleme der Bevoelkerungs-Bewegung bei den Juden* (1926) has been called "one of the most brilliant investigations of problems of Jewish demography ever published." His study *Die Umsiedlung und Umschichtung des juedischen Volkes im Laufe des letzten Jahrhunderts* (1929–30) was of fundamental importance. In the 1920s he directed *YIVO's economics and statistics section, and his work appeared in YIVO publications. Less than two months after Hitler came to power in Germany, Lestschinsky sent a dispatch to *Forward* which was published in the *New York Times* on March 26, 1933; in it he said: "The Hitler regime flames up with anger because it has been compelled through fear of public foreign opinion to forego a mass slaughter of Jews. It threatens, however, to execute pogroms if Jews in other countries make too much fuss about the pogroms it has hitherto indulged in." Arrested by the Nazis upon publication of the dispatch, he was expelled from Germany. In 1934 he went to Warsaw, but was expelled from there in 1937 for publishing material on the plight of the Jews in Poland. In 1938 he went to the United States. During the war he lived in New York, and worked with the Institute of Jewish Affairs of the World Jewish Congress. One of the earliest students of the Holocaust, he wrote two basic studies in this field, *Di Yidishe Katastrofe* (1944) and *Crisis, Catastrophe, and Survival: A Jewish Balance Sheet, 1914–1948* (1948). In 1959 he moved to Tel Aviv, and in 1964 to Jerusalem, where he remained until he died. His collection of books and papers, which he somehow maintained throughout his wanderings, are at the Institute of Contemporary Jewry of the Hebrew University.

Bibliography: P. Glikson, in: JJSO, 9 (1967), 48–57, incl. bibl.; J. Anilowicz, in: YIVO-Bleter, 10 (1936), 327–39, a bibl.; A. Manor, *Ya'akov Lestschinsky* (Heb. 1961); idem, in: JJSO, 4 (1962), 101–6.

[EH]

LESTSCHINSKY, JOSEPH (**"Chmurner"**; 1884–1935), Jewish socialist leader in Russia and Poland. Both Joseph, who was born in the Ukraine, and his brother, Jacob *Lestschinsky, joined a circle of Zionist youth in Warsaw which acquired in 1903 a socialist character. In 1905 Lestschinsky helped to found the *Zionist Socialist Workers Party and was a member of its central committee. He was a theoretician of *territorialism in the party, edited its publications, and published his articles in them. One of the leaders of the left wing of the *United Jewish Socialist Workers' Party in the Ukraine in 1917, he was its representative on the Central Council of the Ukraine (Rada) and on the Jewish National Council. In 1921 he went to Poland, where he joined the *Bund and became the chief ideologist and publicist of its leftist faction.

Bibliography: *Chmurner-Bukh* (Yid., 1958); LNYL, 5 (1963), 376–80; B. Johnpoll, *The Politics of Futility* (1968), index.

[M.M.]

LESZNO (Ger. **Lissa**), town in W. Poland. Jews settled in Leszno on the foundation of the town in 1534. In 1580 they received their first charter. The community had jurisdiction over the northwestern part of the town, where they lived. The Leszno community had to flee temporarily in 1659 during the second Swedish war. The earliest tombstone preserved in the cemetery dates from 1667. As early as 1650 the Jews of Leszno had close business connections with those of Breslau and from 1688 they attended the Leipzig fairs. A synagogue was established in 1685. In 1740 Jewish merchants exceeded those of the non-Jews. By 1793, 40 of the 53 merchants were Jews, as were 200 of the 201 brokers. In 1800, 32 of the 51 tailors were Jews and 250 Jewish women were lace-workers. There was also a considerable number of smelters, tanners, furriers, and embroiderers.

During the Northern War (1706–07) Leszno Jews suffered from the exactions of both sides. Russian soldiers committed plunder and rape, and the entire Jewish quarter was burned. In the plague of 1709 the Jews were accused of infecting the town with plague by bringing the corpse of a Jew to be buried in the town cemetery. As a result of this libel, the Jews were expelled from the city, but when the plague subsided they returned. In 1767 a fire destroyed the whole Jewish quarter and 20 Jews were killed. After this the Jews were freed from taxes for six years. A new *bet midrash* was built and a library purchased; later a large synagogue

The synagogue of Leszno, Poland, 1939. Courtesy Yad Vashem, Jerusalem.

was built, with the help of other communities. In the summer of 1790 a fire swept through the Jewish quarter once more; 196 of 481 Jewish houses were destroyed, as well as the new synagogue and the *bet midrash*. Another synagogue was completed in 1799. In the second half of the 18th century Leszno became central in Jewish life in *Great Poland following the decline of *Poznan after 1736. The "sages of Leszno" were renowned throughout Europe. At the end of the 18th century students came to Leszno yeshivah from Germany as well as from central and southeastern Poland. Rabbis who served the town included Mordecai b. Ẓevi Hirsch (1721?–53), who was requested to be the main arbitrator in the dispute between Jacob *Emden and Jonathan *Eybeschuetz. After his death his brother and successor, *Abraham Abusch Lissa (1753–59), continued the attempt at arbitration. David Tevele, rabbi from 1774 to 1792, gave strong and eloquent expression to the Orthodox opposition to Haskalah trends of assimilation. In a trenchant sermon he castigated the subservience of N. H. *Wessely to an alien culture, drawing attention to the human and humanistic values inherent in the traditional Jewish culture and way of life. From 1809 to 1821 Jacob *Lorbeerbaum was rabbi, and from 1864 to 1912 Samuel Baeck, father of Leo *Baeck. Akiva *Eger studied in Leszno from 1780 to 1790. Raphael Kosch, a native of Leszno, was first vice-president of the National Council in Berlin in 1848 and headed the procedural committee of the Prussian parliament. Ludwig Kalisch (1814–1882), the humorist who participated in the revolution of 1848 and later moved to Paris, was also a native of the city. The Jewish population in Leszno rose from 400 families in 1656 to 4,989 persons in 1765. However, after the partition of Poland and the Prussian annexation of the town in 1793, the community began to decline. Deprived of their commercial markets in the Polish interior and in Russia, many Leszno Jews moved to central Germany. The numbers fell from 3,960 in 1833 to 2,578 in 1858, 1,206 in 1895, 804 in 1913, and 322 in 1921. [Y.Ro.]

Holocaust Period. Under Nazi occupation, Leszno came under the Regierungsbezirk Posen (Wartheland). No ghetto was created in the town, but a *Judenrat existed. The Jews were obliged to appear daily before the German authorities for hard labor. Jews were driven out of their houses and the synagogue was transformed into a storehouse. In December 1940, 300 Jews were deported to *Grodzisk Mazowiecki in the General Government and in February 1941 were taken together with the Jews of that town to the Warsaw ghetto. In Leszno itself or the vicinity a Jewish labor camp functioned from April 1941 until August 1943, with about 250 inmates. [De.D.]

Bibliography: L. Lewin, *Geschichte der Juden in Lissa* (1904); idem, in: MGWJ, 73 (1929), 179; Jacobson, *ibid.*, 64 (1920), 282; 65 (1921), 45, 47, 158, 162, 235; I. Trunk, in: *Bleter far Geshikhte*, 2 no. 1–4 (1949), 64–75, passim; D. Dabrowska, in: BZIH, 13–14 (1955), 122–84, passim.

LETICHEV, town in Khmelnitsky oblast, Ukrainian S.S.R.; under czarist rule a district town in the province of Podolia. Jews are first mentioned there in a document of 1581. The community was destroyed during the *Chmielnicki massacres (1648). More than a century later (1765) 652 Jews paid the poll tax in Letichev and the vicinity. The community grew, numbering 1,852 in 1847 and 4,108 (56.6% of the total population) in 1897. During the civil war (1919–20) the town and surrounding countryside suffered severely at the hands of rebellious Ukrainian bands. In 1926 there were 2,434 Jews (34%) in the town. After the German occupation in the summer of 1941, those Jews who did not manage to escape were slaughtered. No information is available on Jewish life in Letichev after World War II. [Y.S.]

LETTERIS, MEIR (Max; 1800?–1871), Hebrew poet, writer, and editor. Born in Zolkiew (now Zholkva), Letteris, as a child, was introduced to Nachman *Krochmal whom he henceforth considered his mentor. In spite of

Meir Letteris, Hebrew writer. Jerusalem, J.N.U.L., Schwadron Collection.

fame, professional recognition, public honors, and numerous editions of several of his works, he struggled financially all his life, holding jobs as copyreader in different printing houses (but especially in that of Anton von *Schmid), and lecturing, publishing periodicals, selling subscriptions, writing occasional poems, and, for some time, even receiving charity. In the course of his work as a copyreader in Vienna, Pressburg, and Prague, he edited important reprints and first editions, to which he added notes, explanations, and biographies. The latter, along with his autobiography, letter collections, and the contributions of his contemporaries to his various publications, convey a vivid picture of the Galician-Austrian Haskalah and all its leading personalities.

His works include the following: (1) Books of Hebrew poetry: *Divrei Shir* (1822), original poems as well as translations of Schiller, among others; *Ayyelet ha-Shaḥar* (1824), original poetry and translations of Schiller, Byron ("Hebrew Melodies"), and others; *Afrot Zahav* (1852), original and translated poetry; *Tofes Kinnor ve-Ugav* (1860), his first two volumes of poetry together with other previously published and new poems. (2) Translations: Two of Racine's plays, which are in fact free adaptations in Hebrew: *Athalie* (*Geza Yishai*, 1835) and *Esther* (*Shelom Ester*, 1843); several works by L. A. *Frankl, as well as Goethe's *Faust*, part 1 (*Ben Avuyah*, 1865), probably Letteris' most important work in this field of endeavor: he adapted and hebraized the play (the setting and characters are Jewish), and deleted all christological references. (3) Hebrew literary collections: *Ha-Ẓefirah* (1824)—intended as the first number of a periodical—opening with "*Yonah Homiyyah*," which became the best known of Letteris' poems, set to music and sung for generations; collections of letters including *Mikhtavim* (1827), *Mikhtevei Ivrit* (1847), and *Mikhtevei Benei Kedem* (1866). Further Hebrew collections appeared as supplements to some of his German periodicals. (4) German publications: *Sagen aus dem Orient* (1847), poetic renditions of biblical, midrashic, and talmudic themes, for which he was awarded a gold medal by Emperor Franz Joseph; *Wiener Blaetter*, with the Hebrew supplement *Ẓefirat Tiferet* (1851–52), *Wiener Vierteljahrs-Schrift*, with *Avnei Neẓer* (1853), and *Wiener Mitteilungen* (1854–70). He republished both his Hebrew and German writings, including: *Oestliche Rosen* (1852), *Beitraege zur Literatur- und Kulturgeschichte* (1859), and *Ein Blatt Geschichte* (1869). His German translation of the *maḥzor* (with a Hebrew commentary, 1845–49) and the *Andachtsbuch fuer israelitische Frauenzimmer* (1845) saw numerous editions. He also wrote a *Hebraeische Sprachlehre* (1853). (5) Editions from manuscripts; M. Ḥ. *Luzzatto's *Migdal Oz* (1838) with a Latin introduction by Franz *Delitzsch and notes by S. D. *Luzzatto; Abraham *ibn Ezra's *Sefat Yeter* (1838), and R. Joseph ha-Kohen's *Emek ha-Bakha* (1852), with notes by S. D. Luzzatto. Among his new editions (always with notes, biographies, or text additions) are *Ben-Ze'ev's *Oẓar ha-Shorashim* (1839–44), the works of Isaac *Erter, *Ha-Ẓofeh le-Veit Yisrael* (1858), volume one of *Ha-Me'assef* (1862), and Krochmal's *Moreh Nevukhei ha-Zeman* (1863). (6) Other works: *Ḥikrei Lev* (1837), a treatise on Bible study; contributions to the periodicals *Bikkurei ha-Ittim, Kerem Ḥemed,* and *Bikkurei ha-Ittim ha-Ḥadashim.* In the latter, Letteris published a Spinoza biography (1845, 27b–31b) which aroused controversy because of his plea for the rehabilitation of Spinoza among Jews. Another undertaking, the editing of the Hebrew text of the Old Testament for the British and Foreign Bible Society of London (1852), damaged his reputation among Jews. It was perhaps his most lasting achievement, however, as it resulted in innumerable editions of the "Letteris Bible." Of his autobiography, *Zikkaron ba-Sefer* (1869), only the first part appeared, leading up to 1831, and containing a description of Nachman Krochmal's circle in Zolkiew.

Letteris was a true exponent of the Haskalah, a mediator between Jewish and Western cultures. His free Hebrew renditions of European literary works are probably his greatest contribution to modern Hebrew poetry.

Bibliography: Waxman, Literature, index; Klausner, Sifrut, 2 (1952[2]), 360–400; Lachower, Sifrut, 2 (1953[12]), 7–11; Zinberg, Sifrut, 6 (1960), 83–88; Kressel, Leksikon, 2 (1967), 247–9. [W.W.]

LETTERS AND LETTER WRITERS. The letter holds an honored place in Jewish history and literature and includes diplomatic correspondence, state papers, and letters as vehicles of religious or secular literature and as a means of polemics in communal and spiritual matters, business or private family letters, and so on. In Jewish law and ritual the authoritative opinion in answer to an inquiry has given rise to an entire literature of its own (see *Responsa).

The language of Jewish letters was above all Hebrew, and even after Jews adopted the languages of their homes in the Diaspora, it gained in importance as Jewry's *lingua franca,* apart from remaining the vehicle of all learned communication. At a later stage Yiddish occupied a similar position for European Jews. In style the language often became formalized and adopted the literary conventions of the dominant culture. Letters constitute a valuable source for Jewish history.

Biblical Period. From the very beginning of Israel's history is the famous collection of diplomatic correspondence, the *Tell el-Amarna letters with their first oblique references to the incursion into Canaan by the "Ḥabiru." To approximately the same period also belong letters written on clay tablets found at *Ta'anach. The first biblical letter is the one that sent Uriah to his death (II Sam. 11:14-15), and to the same category belongs the one written by Jezebel arranging the judicial murder of Naboth (I Kings 21:8–11). In both cases the Hebrew word *sefer* ("book") is used for letter; in Ezra (1:1) and II Chronicles (21:12; 36:22) it is *mikhtav* ("letter"); and in Esther (9:26, 29) as well as in II Chronicles (30:1, 6) and Nehemiah (2:7–9; 6:5, 17, 19), *iggeret* ("epistle"). Nehemiah 6:5 speaks of an "open letter" sent by Sanballat to Nehemiah. As the use of *sefer* shows, the dividing line between "book" and "letter" is vague (cf. Isa. 29:11–12, "a sealed letter"; Ezra 2:9–10, "a scroll-letter"; and Zech. 5:1ff.).

Jeremiah wrote or dictated his famous letter to the exiles in Babylonia (29:1ff.), which produced an angry reaction by letter from Shemaiah the Nehelamite (*ibid.,* 24ff.). Among the discoveries in the Dead Sea caves (Wadi Murabba'at) was a papyrus palimpsest on which was probably an eighth-century letter, of which only the greeting formula is still recognizable. From Jeremiah's time are the Lachish Letters, *ostraca referring to Nebuchadnezzar's second campaign against Judah (589). These are the oldest original Jewish letters in existence. II Chronicles 21:12ff. records a letter of Elijah to Joram of Judah, and 30:1ff., proclamations by letter from Hezekiah. The Persian period in Jewish history begins with one by Cyrus to the Jews in Babylonia (*ibid.,* 36:22–23), and the Book of Ezra (ch. 4ff.; cf. Neh. 2:7–9) contains correspondence and state papers in Aramaic concerning the rights of the returnees from Babylon. The first *she'elah u-teshuvah* (inquiry and responsum concerning ritual) is found in Zechariah in 7:1ff., though it is not certain whether even the inquiry was in writing. Mordecai and Esther sent a proclamation by letter concerning the Purim festival to all Persian Jews (Esther 9:20ff.). Letter writing in biblical times required professional writers (I Chron. 2:55) and was no doubt the main occupation of the royal officer called the *sofer* ("scribe"; II Sam. 8:17). The many *seals found in archaeological excavations were used for signing letters, documents, and state papers (I Kings 21:8; cf. Gen. 38:18, 25) and also to close them (Job 41:7).

Persian and Greek Periods. Still close to biblical times are the *Elephantine (Yeb) letters, Aramaic papyri shedding light on the life of the military settlement of Jews on the Upper Nile from the sixth to the fourth centuries B.C.E. The Letter of *Aristeas, written in Greek in the third or second century, describes the origins of the Jewish community of Alexandria and of the Septuagint Bible translation; it includes an exchange of letters between Ptolemy Philadelphus II and Eleazar the high priest. The work, a propaganda tract for Jews and Judaism, is an early Jewish example of the Greek genre of epistolary literature. Other Jewish letters in this period are those found in the first and second book of Maccabees. In the first (12:5ff.), the Hasmonean Jonathan sent a diplomatic message to Sparta; the second (1:1–9 and 1:10–2:18) contains messages sent by the Jews of Jerusalem to those of Egypt in connection with the Hasmonean victories and the institution of the Ḥanukkah festival. *Philo in his "Delegation to Gaius" (Caligula) recorded the moving and historically important letters, which he may have drafted himself, of Agrippa I to the emperor, imploring him to desist from his plan to have his statue erected in the Temple of Jerusalem (ed. E. M. Smallwood, (1961), 122–36). *Josephus included in his works many letters, real or fictitious, among them the charter given to the Jews by Antiochus III in 198 B.C.E. (Ant. 12, 3, 138–44). In his *Life* (364–67) he reports that Agrippa II sent him 62 letters, complimenting him on the accuracy of his histories; two of these letters he quotes verbatim.

New Testament; Bar Kokhba Letters. Of the 21 Epistles in the *New Testament, those of Paul occupy a prominent place. Only 10 out of the 13 ascribed to him are generally recognized as really his; the others were written by other founder-members of the new religion. The most "Jewish" among them is the Epistle of James, which may have been based on some pre-Christian apocryphon. The discovery in 1952 in Wadi Murabba'at and Naḥal Ḥever in 1960/61 of Hebrew letters written during the Bar Kokhba revolt, some signed by Bar Kokhba, have added further specimens of actual letters written in antiquity.

Talmudic Literature. In talmudic literature the earliest letter is the one sent by Simeon b. Shetaḥ (first century

B.C.E.) appealing to his colleague Judah b. Tabbai to return from his self-imposed exile: "From me, Holy Jerusalem (Jerusalem, the Great) to thee, my sister Alexandria (Alexandria, the Small): how long doth my betrothed dwell with you, and I dwell desolate on account of him" (Sota 47a; Sanh. 107b; TJ, Ḥag. 2, 277d; Sanh. 6, 7, 23c). Letters conveying decisions in calendar and other ritual matters were sent to Jewish communities inside and outside Palestine on behalf of the Sanhedrin by Gamaliel I (before 50 C.E.; Sanh. 11b and parallels) and a generation later by his son Simeon and Johanan b. Zakkai (Mid. Tan. to Deut. 26:13). Letters like this are rare in Talmud and Midrash, where the preference was for oral transmission as against written communications. Messages like the one sent by the Jerusalem authorities to *Judah b. Bathyra at Nisibis (Pes. 3b) or to Theodoros (Thodos) of Rome (*ibid.* 53a) may or may not have been in writing, but the constant exchange of information and views between Palestinian and Babylonian scholars in the talmudic era is likely to have been partly in writing. For political reasons some of these messages had to be sent in code (Sanh. 12a). In this period, too, the writing of letters, particularly official ones, was entrusted to special secretaries (*sofer* or *libellarius*).

Belonging to the same period, but from non-talmudic sources, is the letter by *Julian the Apostate (in 363 C.E.) promising to restore Jerusalem and the Temple. Similarly, the brief episode of Empress Eudocia's kindness to the Jews 60 years later led to a flicker of messianic hope, which expressed itself in a letter by the Jewish notables to the Jews of the Diaspora (438; see Nau, in REJ 83, (1927), 196–7). Also in the fourth century the patriarch Gamaliel b. Hillel maintained correspondence with the Syrian Hellenist Libanius, but only Libanius' letters have been preserved.

[ED.]

Medieval Hebrew Literature. Throughout the Middle Ages letters served as a major literary form in all countries in which Jews lived and wrote. Neither the form of the letter nor the fact that it was addressed to a specific person implied that the contents of the letter were private, for letter writing was one of the more usual means of publishing one's views and bringing them to the attention of as wide a public as possible. Letters were delivered by hand, and in many Jewish communities en route it was common practice to stop the messengers in order publicly to read the letters they were carrying. Frequently, it was requested that the messenger allow a local scribe to copy the letter, which would be read by the rabbis and kept in the files of the community. This practice explains why many hundreds of letters found in the Cairo **Genizah* were not addressed to the Egyptian Jewish community, but rather to various communities in North Africa and Europe. It was also common for a man to write several copies of his letter and send them to different places for publication. At the end of their letters, some writers requested the reader to pass the letter on or make additional copies of it. Letters containing messages of importance to the whole community were read aloud in the synagogue; others of more limited interest were read by the *bet din* or the community council.

Treating letters as a means of publishing one's views gave rise to certain literary forms frequently utilized in epistolary literature. For instance, the published letter was an opportunity for the writer to demonstrate his erudition and his mastery of Hebrew language and style, which explains why many letters written in the Middle Ages contain numerous biblical and talmudic phrases and references. The introduction of the letter was often written in rhymed prose, and many letters were composed entirely in this style. The opening phrases of a letter were usually a series of formula descriptions of the addressee's wisdom, generosity, and greatness. These phrases were often employed interchangeably from one letter to another. Therefore, very little individual style is to be found in medieval letters, even those written by the most prominent Jewish thinkers, who developed a personal style in their other writings.

The character of epistolary literature made the distinction between a book and a letter very unclear. The usual word for book, *sefer,* was frequently used to denote a letter, and the word for letter, *iggeret,* was used as the title of many books. Some of the more important books in the Middle Ages were originally written as letters, the most celebrated example being Maimonides' *Guide of the Perplexed.*

Large collections of letters exist in the fields of *halakhah,* polemics, and ethics.

HALAKHIC RESPONSA. From the gaonic period, Jews all over the world addressed halakhic questions to the supreme halakhic authorities of the time. The various *geonim* in Babylonia, Maimonides in Egypt, the tosafists and the Rashi school in Germany, Naḥmanides and Solomon ben Abraham Adret in Spain, Caro in Safed—all received hundreds of halakhic questions which they usually answered in great detail. Occasionally these responsa grew into whole treatises, later published as books (the first being Rav Amram Gaon's answer to a question on the laws concerning prayers, which became the first prayer book or *siddur*). Similar questions were also addressed to many less eminent rabbis, some of whom collected their answers and published them in book form. These responsa presented *halakhah* in a most concrete, everyday way. When writing halakhic exegesis or specialized treatises, the author may be preoccupied with fundamental, theoretical questions, but when writing responsa he is required to solve a specific problem. Accordingly, halakhic responsa are regarded as one of the most important sources of medieval Jewish history (see also *Responsa).

POLEMICAL LETTERS. By nature, *polemical literature is addressed to a specific person with whom the author is in conflict, yet the author wishes his views to be known as widely as possible. Therefore, most medieval Jewish polemical material is found in epistolary literature. Some major conflicts in Jewish life and thought are found solely in collections of polemical letters. In Spain, Italy, and Provence during the 13th and 14th centuries, the great controversies raging over Maimonides and his views, and over the study of philosophy in general, were carried on in hundreds of letters, many of which are extant. Letters written in Hebrew and Arabic were the vehicle for the controversy between the Karaites and Rabbinic Judaism. The controversy about the renewal of *semikhah* (ordination of rabbis) in Safed, Jerusalem, and Egypt was conducted through letters, which have been collected and serve as a primary historical source. Similarly, in the 17th century, the Shabbatean controversy, and the Eybeschuetz-Emden controversy which followed in its wake, was sustained by letters, many of which were later edited and published. Authors sometimes changed the wording of their original letters to suit changed circumstances, a tactic known to have been executed in many other controversies.

Many of these letters are written, partially or wholly, in rhymed prose and include other literary forms developed for argumentation. *Milḥamot Adonai* by Solomon b. Jeroḥam, which was the Karaite's answer to Saadiah Gaon, is among the earliest polemical letters and includes one of the most perfect examples of the use of irony in medieval Hebrew literature. A whole vocabulary of sarcastic phrases and abusive references was developed in this literature. Very frequently the discussion of theological differences gave way to personal abuse.

ETHICAL LETTERS. One of the literary forms which was developed in the Middle Ages within the framework of *ethical literature was the short ethical epistle. This literary form is very close in character to another sort of short ethical treatise—the ethical *will. In medieval times many ordinary as well as eminent Jews wrote letters—usually to their sons, but sometimes to other relatives or to communities—describing the ethical way of behavior, and imploring the readers to follow this path. These writers clearly intended that their letters be published, and that the letters were addressed to specific people is no more than a literary device. Because the letters were usually short, they therefore contained a complete ethical system in a nutshell, revealing what the age thought the most important areas in which behavior had to be corrected. Like other letters, ethical letters also frequently employed rhymed prose.

AGRONIM. One of the major sources for the study of the development of the Hebrew letter in medieval and early modern times is the literature of the *agronim*. An *agron* is a collection of form letters, compiled or written by a scholar for the use of the general public. Included in the collection are form letters of praise, reference, appointments, business requests for charity, for money to marry one's daughters, for money to ransom the release of Jewish prisoners, and for almost every other conceivable occasion in which a Jew may be in need of a special letter. All the user did was to fill in the name(s) and other necessary details and a well-written letter, which would evoke respect from the reader, was ready for sending. The first collection of stereotyped Hebrew letters, *Iggerot Shelomim*, was printed anonymously in Augsburg in 1534. This example was soon followed by others: *Megillat Sefer* or *Mikhtavim* (also anonymous, Venice, 1545–48?), and Samuel Archevolti's *Ma'yan Gannim* (Venice, 1553, Cremona, 1566).

The *agronim*, of which dozens were printed, became a very popular literary form, especially since the 18th century. There are, in manuscript, *agronim* from Spain dating as far back as the 15th century. Many *agronim* also include other literary works, like short poems of praise or riddles, which might be useful to the reader. *Agronim* are of great historical value inasmuch as they reveal the literary and social conventions of a given time and place; for example, the differences between a form of an application for the rabbinate in a small town and a big city are very instructive. Until recently this field had been neglected by scholars and especially historians; therefore, no definitive history of the development of the Hebrew epistle, from a literary and historical point of view, is to be found.

The epistolary form was used in other literary fields. The earliest extant medieval historiographical work, *Iggeret Rav Sherira Gaon* (in: Ḥ. J. D. Azulai, *Shem ha-Gedolim* (1967), 26–59) was probably written by Hai Gaon as an answer to a letter inquiring about the transmission of the *halakhah* from age to age. Letters regarding scientific and philosophical questions are also found in medieval Hebrew literature.

[Y.D.]

SPAIN. In Spain, where letter writing developed into a specific genre, Moses ibn Ezra took pride in the leading position occupied by his countrymen in this art (*Shirat Yisrael*, ed. by B. Z. Halper, 62 (1924; repr. 1967), Halper, 62). An early example is the correspondence of *Ḥisdai ibn Shaprut with the king of the *Khazars. His own letters were drafted by his secretary, the poet and grammarian *Menahem b. Saruk, who inserted an acrostic of his own name in addition to Ḥisdai's in an introductory poem. In contrast to his polished and allusive style, the letter of a Khazar Jew to Ḥisdai, found in the *genizah*, is written in a clear and simple Hebrew. Maimonides made the most intensive use of correspondence, and his influence was largely due to the extensive correspondence he carried on with all parts of the Jewish world. Following his father's example in his "Letter of Consolation," Maimonides exercised his spiritual leadership over the Diaspora by means of pastoral letters, such as the "Letter to Yemen" on true and false messianism. He also was in correspondence with groups of, or individual, scholars, with friends and pupils, apart from the great number of responsa he wrote in answer to inquiries from all over. His style is clear and terse and has a beauty of its own, and found late imitators in Isaac *Abrabanel, Joseph Solomon *Delmedigo and *Manasseh Ben Israel. At the turn of the 14th century Profiat *Duran wrote his anti-Christian epistle *Al-Tehi ka-Avotekha*, typical of the polemic produced by more or less forced baptisms and the emergence of the Marranos.

Modern Period. The expulsion of Jews from Spain in 1492 produced letters from the exiles reporting their experiences in their new homes, particularly in Palestine. There had been antecedents for this, e.g., *Judah Halevi, Maimonides, Naḥmanides, Obadiah of *Bertinoro, and Elijah of Ferrara; but from the 16th century onward a growing volume of such letter reports from Palestine reached a news-hungry Diaspora. Among the most prominent correspondents were Solomon *Molcho in the 16th century, Isaiah *Horowitz in the 17th and some ḥasidic leaders in the 18th (see A. Yaari, *Iggerot Ereẓ Yisrael*, 1943). Interesting, too, is a letter by *Elijah ben Solomon Zalman, the Gaon of Vilna, written before he set out for Palestine.

ITALY. The true heir to Spain in Hebrew epistolary art was Italy, where the spirit of the Renaissance found able and congenial adepts among Hebrew letter writers. Nearly 100 letters by the banker-scholar Solomon da Poggibonzi (ed. by S. Simonsohn in *Koveẓ al Yad*, 6 (1966), 379–417), reveal an accomplished practician of the art. The most prolific of them all was Leone *Modena, who carefully kept copies of his letters, *Leo Modenas Briefe* . . . (ed. by L. Blau (1907)), which reveal his mind and life. Italy remained the home of letter writing, as shown by Modena's younger contemporary *Mahalalel Hallelyah of Ancona, who, like M. Ḥ. *Luzzatto a century later, can be regarded as one of the precursors of the Hebrew revival. In the 19th century J. S. *Reggio and S. D. *Luzzatto in their correspondence with other Jewish scholars made an important contribution to the new Wissenschaft des Judentums. Much of the argument in the battles around Reform and Haskalah at the end of the 18th and beginning of the 19th century took the form of letters (cf. the collections of letters by N. H. Wessely, *Nogah ha-Ẓedek* (1818); *Elleh Divrei ha-Berit* (1819); *Teshuvot be-Anshei Aven* (1845).

GERMANY. S. R. *Hirsch gave his book, which laid the foundations of modern Orthodoxy, the fictional form of 19 letters (*Iggerot Ẓafon; The Nineteen Letters of Ben Uziel* (1899, 1969²)). Moses Hess's *Rom und Jerusalem* (1862) is a call in letter form for a Jewish national renaissance, and Joseph Perl also used "letters" for his anti-ḥasidic satires *Megalleh Temirim* (1919) and *Boḥen Ẓaddik* (1838). The emergence of the Wissenschaft des Judentums produced Hebrew periodicals such as *Kerem Ḥemed* and *Oẓar Neḥmad*, which published scholarly contributions in letter form.

Enlightenment and Wissenschaft des Judentums. In the Enlightenment period the letters written by Moses *Mendelssohn (*Jubilaeumsausgabe*, 11 (1932); 16 (1929)), L. *Zunz (*L. and A. Zunz—an account in letters*, ed. by N. Glatzer, 1958), *I. S. Reggio (*Iggerot YaSHaR*, 1834–36); S. D. *Luzzatto (*Iggerot ShaDaL*, 1882–94, repr. 1967); S. J. *Rapoport (*Iggerot SHIR*, 1845), and others are important sources for the history of that crucial period in Jewish history. Not one of the least achievements of modern Jewish scholarship was the publication of letters of prominent and even ordinary people of the past, such as those of Leone Modena (see above); correspondence between Jews of Prague and Vienna from the time of the Thirty Years' War *Juedische Privatbriefe* ... ed. by A. Landau and B. Wachstein (1911); letters of Ḥ. J. D. *Azulai in *Ha-Ẓofeh le-Ḥokhmat Yisrael* (11, 1927); M. Ḥ. Luzzatto (S. Ginzburg, *RaMaHaL u-Venei Doro* (1937); and some of those written by Akiva *Eger, Moses *Sofer, and members of their families (*Iggerot Soferim*, ed. by S. Schreiber, 1929).

Jewish-Christian Correspondence. A special place in the history of Jewish letter writing is held by Jewish-Christian correspondence. In the 13th century Solomon *Cohen exchanged letters on philosophical themes with his imperial patron Frederick II and the latter's court philosopher Theodorus. In the 16th century Lazarus de *Viterbo corresponded in Latin with Cardinal Sirleto on the Bible, as did Leone Modena with Italian, French, and English scholars. Johannes *Buxtorf (the Younger) maintained a lively correspondence in Hebrew with Jewish scholars, and J. C. *Wagenseil entered into a polemic with R. Enoch ha-Levi. Manasseh Ben Israel wrote hundreds of letters in Latin, Spanish, and English as well as in Hebrew to the leading Christian scholars and theologians of his time. The 49 letters of *Spinoza still extant were all addressed to non-Jews. Nevertheless, they betray, more than any other of his writings, the Jewish roots of a man who had become totally estranged from his people. Anna Maria Schurmann was not the first, but certainly the most able and prolific, Christian women writing letters in Hebrew.

Women Letter Writers. The *genizah* yielded some Hebrew letters written by women. In Yiddish, women's letters stand out for their direct and homely style, such as in the letter of Rachel Ashkenazi, Eliezer Susman Ashkenazi's widow, to her son from Jerusalem in 1567 and that of Sarel Gutmann, the wife of Loeb Gutmann of Prague, writing to her husband in Vienna in 1619. When Esperanza Malchi, chamberwoman to the sultana in Constantinople at the end of the 16th century, wrote on behalf of her mistress to Elizabeth I of England, she wrote in Italian, as did Sara Coppio Sullam in her letters to a fellow poet.

Sullam's platonic love letters have been lost, but one by Salamone Candia written in Judeo-Italian to his bride about 1590 has been preserved. So has one by Shabbetai Ẓevi to his wife-to-be. In the first half of the 18th century Catherine Villareal and Jacob Mendes da Costa exchanged love letters in English, but with few Jewish elements in them.

Collections of Letters. In more recent times the Ḥibbat Zion and Zionist movements have produced much letter writing among their leading figures. For the former A. Druyanow edited a collection of letters, *Ketavim le-Toledot Ḥibbat Ẓiyyon* ... (3 vols., 1919–29). Theodor Herzl's letters of 1895–97 have been published in Hebrew as *Iggerot* (1961, vol. 9 of his collected writings) and those of Chaim Weizmann are being published (first volume *Kitvei* ... series 1: *Iggerot*, 2 vols. (1969–70)). Collections of letters by the great modern Hebrew writers have also been published: J. L. Gordon (2 vols., 1894–5); Aḥad Ha-Am (6 vols., 1923–25); and Ḥ. N. Bialik (5 vols., 1937–39). Of particular importance for modern intellectual and spiritual history are the letters of Chief Rabbi A. I. *Kook, *Iggerot ha-Re'ayah* (3 vols., 1943; 1962–65[2]) and those of Franz *Rosenzweig, *Briefe* (1935). Interesting selections of letters by the philosopher Hermann Cohen and the painter Max Liebermann were issued in the *Schocken Buecherei* (1937, 1939). The experiences of World War I are reflected in *Kriegsbriefe deutscher Juden* (1935, repr. 1961) and in E. Tannenbaum's *Kriegsbriefe deutscher und oesterreichischer Juden* (1915). Letters by Israel soldiers in the Six-Day War of 1967 were collected in *Be-Darkam; Ḥavrei ha-Iḥud she-Nafelu* ... (1968).

The first modern anthology of Jewish or Hebrew letters is S. J. Fuenn's *Soferei Yisrael* (1871), a collection of 55 letters. A pioneer in this field was Franz Kobler (1882–1965), who published *Juden und Judentum in deutschen Briefen* . . . (1935), *Juedische Geschichte in Briefen* . . . (1938), and *Letters of Jews Through the Ages* (2 vols., 1952, with bibliography). A. Yaari's *Iggerot Ereẓ Yisrael* appeared in 1943 and Cecil Roth edited *Anglo-Jewish Letters* (1938). Many Jewish letters are incorporated in such general works as H. Adler's *Miscellany of Hebrew Literature* (2 vols., 1873), J. Winter and A. Wuensche, *Juedische Litteratur* (2 vols., 1894–97), and B. Halper's *Post-Biblical Hebrew Literature* (2 vols., 1921). J. R. Marcus' *American Jewry—Documents—18th century* (1959) contains letters that are preserved in the American Jewish Archives at the Hebrew Union College, Cincinnati, which has specialized in letter collections. The British Museum possesses a great collection of Emmanuel Mendes da Costa's correspondence.

Formulas and Style. Hebrew and other Jewish letters are characterized by certain epistolary conventions, in which *abbreviations occupy a prominent position. The opening formula was ב״ה or בע״ה (בְּעֶזְרַת ה׳ = "with the help of God") or (שיל״ת) (שִׁוִּיתִי ה׳ לְנֶגְדִּי תָמִיד—Ps. 16:8 = "I have set the Lord always before me"). This was followed by the Jewish date, either day, month, and year or the day of the week and the coming weekly Sidra. The latter was often hinted at by a characteristic verse, and the year, by a similar *gematria*. In the period between Passover and Shavuot, the respective day in the Omer counting took the place of the date as would any particular day in the calendar, such as the New Moon and fast days. However, the date was often added at the end. This is followed by an exordium in which the addressee is apostrophized according to his station and worth, usually in flowery and exaggerated terms. The most common greeting, used in the beginning or at the end, was *shalom* ("peace"), or *berakhah* ("blessing"), which is found even in the Lachish ostraca letters.

The epistolary style from the Middle Ages onward became increasingly flowery and allusive (*meliẓah*), and was overloaded with biblical and talmudic quotations, which produced a strong reaction in modern times. Among the enactments of Rabbenu Gershom b. Judah (11th century) was one protecting the secrecy of letters, threatening the unauthorized opener with excommunication. This used to be alluded to in the letters by adding the abbreviation בחדר״ג = (בחרם דרבנו גרשום). [Ed.]

Bibliography: F. Kobler, *Letters of Jews Through the Ages*, 2 vols. (1952); W. Zeitlin, in: ZHB, 22 (1919), 32ff.; J. Buxtorf, *Institutio Epistolaris Hebraica* (Basel, 1629); H. Beinart, in: *Sefunot*, 5 (1961), 73–135; J. Katz, in: *Sefer Zikkaron le-Vinyamin de Vries* (1968), 281ff.

LETTUCE (Heb. חֲזֶרֶת, *ḥazeret* or חַסָּה, *ḥassah*), vegetable. Lettuce is not mentioned in the Bible. According to rabbinic tradition, however, it is included in the term *merorim* ("bitter herbs," Ex. 12:8) which are commanded to be eaten on the night of the Passover *seder* (see *Maror). According to the Mishnah (Pes. 2:6) this obligation can be discharged with five species of vegetable, the first of which is חֲזֶרֶת, which the *Gemara* explains to be *ḥassah* (Pes. 39a). Lettuce when young has soft leaves and a sweet taste, but if left in the field until it begins to flower its leaves harden and become bitter. For this reason the rabbis stated that it is ideal as *maror:* "just as lettuce is first sweet and then bitter, so was the behavior of the Egyptians to our ancestors" (TJ, Pes. 2:5, 29c), or "because the lettuce is first soft and finally hard" (Pes. 39a).

Lettuce was a popular vegetable. It is a winter crop which does not usually grow in summer, but people of wealth endeavored to obtain it out of season too. Thus it is related of *Antoninus and R. Judah ha-Nasi that their tables "did not lack lettuce even in summer" (Ber. 57b). Some think that the lettuce referred to is the wild variety *Lactuca scariola* out of which the cultivated "sweet" lettuce developed. Against this it should be noted that the growing of the cultivated variety is very ancient, it being depicted already in ancient Egyptian paintings, from which it seems that they grew the long leaved lettuce, *Lactuca sativa,* var. *longifolia,* and apparently this variety was also grown in Israel in ancient times. The aforementioned wild variety, which is called the "compass lettuce" because its leaves point north and south, is found in all districts of Israel, particularly near refuse. The Mishnah (Kil. 1:2) calls it *ḥazeret gallim,* i.e., lettuce of the rubbish heaps, and decided that it is of the same species as the cultivated lettuce. The Samaritans have the custom of eating this wild lettuce with their Passover sacrifice. Among Jews of European origin the common custom is to eat as *maror* on the night of the *seder* horseradish, *Armocaria rusticana,* which they identify with the *ḥazeret* or *tamkha* mentioned as a bitter herb (Pes. 2:6), but this vegetable is sharp and not "bitter," nor was it grown in Ereẓ Israel in ancient times.

Bibliography: Loew, Flora, 1 (1928), 424–39; H. N. and A.L. Moldenke, *Plants of the Bible* (1952), 6, 34, 74f., 140; J. Feliks, *Kilei Zera'im ve-Harkavah* (1967), 56–58; idem, *Olam ha-Ẓome'aḥ ha-Mikra'i* (1968²), 194–6. [J.F.]

°**LEUSDEN, JOHANN** (1624–1699), Calvinist theologian and Hebraist. Having numbered Jews among his teachers, in 1650 he became a professor of Hebrew language at the University of Utrecht. In collaboration with the Amsterdam publisher Joseph *Athias, he published the first Hebrew Bible in which the verses are numbered (*Biblia Hebraica,* 1661, 1667²). The edition became well known for its exactness and beautiful print, and served as a model for almost all publications of the Bible up to the 19th century. Leusden was one of the foremost Bible scholars of his time and wrote several treatises on Bible research and Hebrew philology. He also translated (Utrecht, 1656) the catalog of 613 commandments that heads Maimonides' halakhic code.

Frontispiece of the second edition of Johann Leusden's *Philologus Hebraeo-Mixtus,* showing the destruction of the Temple, with Israel represented as a queen being carried off into captivity. Utrecht, 1682. Jerusalem, J.N.U.L.

Bibliography: *New Schaff-Herzog Encyclopedia of Religious Knowledge,* 6 (1910), 466; B. Glasius, *Godgeleerd Nederland,* 2 (1851–56), 365–7; *Nieuw Nederlandsch Biografisch Woordenboek,* 9 (1933), 601–2 (incl. bibl.). [Jo.H./Ed.]

LEV, ABRAHAM (1910–1970), Yiddish poet. He was born in Piaski near Volkovysk, Belorussia and settled with his family in Vilna in 1922. In 1932 he emigrated to Ereẓ Israel and joined kibbutz Givat ha-Sheloshah. His first poem was published by Melech *Ravitch in a Warsaw journal, when he was 16. Thereafter his lyrics appeared in Yiddish periodicals in Poland, France, the U.S., and Israel. Many of his poems were translated into Hebrew and were included in school texts and anthologies. His mature lyrics appeared in the volumes *Heym un Feld* ("Home and Field," 1953) and *Beymer in Vint* ("Trees in the Wind," 1960). Lev is a poet of the kibbutz landscape, who refers to himself as a farmer-poet dreaming his visions in the shade of the trees which he himself planted.

Bibliography: LNYL, 5 (1963), 242–4; M. Ravitch, *Mayn Leksikon* (1958), 233–5. [I.H.B.]

LEV (Lab; Leb), JOSEPH BEN DAVID IBN (also known as the **MaHaRIVaL,** for **Morenu Ha-Rav Yosef ibn Lev;** 1505–1580), Turkish rabbi and *posek.* Lev was born in Monastir (now Bitolj, Yugoslavia). Nothing is known of his early life, but he was appointed *dayyan* in his native town while still quite young. Because of a quarrel with a colleague on the *bet din* he moved to Salonika in 1534, where he became embroiled with Solomon ibn Hasson. Lev fought vigorously against the powerful and wealthy who oppressed the common people. Following his dispute with the Jewish tyrant Baruch of Salonika, his son David was murdered by hired assassins in 1545. His second son Moses drowned. These events and the hostile attitude of his opponents caused him to move in 1550 to Constantinople, where he remained until his death. There he was appointed teacher in the yeshivah founded by Doña Gracia (Mendes) *Nasi. In 1556 he was taken ill and from 1561 was unable to continue regular teaching in the yeshivah. At the instigation of Gracia and Joseph Nasi, in retaliation for the adverse stand of Pope *Paul IV against the Marranos of Ancona, Lev compiled a responsum in which he supported the banning of trade with Ancona and the taking of reprisals against the papal kingdom, in contrast to Joshua Soncino, one of the opponents of the ban.

Lev at first planned the compilation of a work in the manner of the *Beit Yosef* of Joseph *Caro. When in 1551 the *Beit Yosef* was published he forbade its use out of fear that it would lead to a decrease in the study of the Talmud. However, when on one occasion he could not remember one of the sources of the *Arba'ah Turim* and found it in the *Beit Yosef,* he changed his attitude and realized the value of the work. His responsa, in four parts, were first published separately but then together in Amsterdam in 1726. A new edition of the responsa in two volumes appeared in Jerusalem in 1959/60. Lev attributes many glosses to his son David out of a desire to perpetuate his memory, but it is probable that he himself was the author of most of them. He was highly thought of by contemporary scholars.

Bibliography: S. M. Chones, *Toledot ha-Posekim* (1929), 560; C. Tchernowitz, *Toledot ha-Posekim,* 2 (1947), 220; 3 (1948), 35; I. S. Emmanuel, *Histoire des Israélites de Salonique* (1936), 151–64, 219; Rosanes, Togarmah, 2 (1938), 77–78, 80, 82, 89–91; M. S. Goodblatt, *Jewish Life in Turkey in the 16th Century* (1952), 18, 92–93; I. Sonne, *Mi-Paulus ha-Revi'i ad Pius ha-Ḥamishi* (1954), 146, 148, 155, 158; M. Molcho, *Salonika, Ir va-Em be-Yisrael* (1967), 13; idem, in: *Sinai,* 48 (1961), 290–8; S. Assaf, *ibid.,* 1 (1937), 7; A. Danon, in: REJ, 41 (1900), 102–3. [Y.Ho.]

LEVAILLANT, ISAÏE (1845–1911), French civil servant and publicist, born in Hegenheim, Alsace. After the Franco-Prussian war of 1870–71, Levaillant founded a Republican newspaper in Nevers and filled various administrative posts under Gambetta. In 1885 he was appointed head of the Sureté Générale at the Ministry of the Interior. He was dismissed for his pro-*Dreyfus sympathies and subsequently wrote his own defense, *Ma Justification* (1895). After this, he devoted himself to combating anti-Semitism, chiefly through his editorials in *L'Univers Israélite,* which he edited until 1905. When the separation of Church and State in France (1906) made it necessary to revise the organizational structure of French Jewry, Levaillant drew up the new statute. His writings include *La genèse de l'antisémitisme sous la Troisième République* (1907).

Bibliography: *L'Univers Israélite,* 67 (1911/12), 229–39; AI, 72 (1911), 340f., 348. [Ed.]

LEVANDA, LEV OSIPOVICH (1835–1888), Russian author and publicist. Born of a very poor family in Minsk, Levanda studied in a *ḥeder,* a modernized Jewish school, a government school for Jewish children, and finally at the rabbinical school in Vilna (1850–54), from which he graduated as a teacher. From 1854 to 1860 he taught at a government Jewish school in Minsk, and in 1860 he became the Jewish expert *(uchony yevrey)* to the governor-general of Vilna, remaining in this office for the rest of his life. Altogether he spent 32 years in Vilna, a period that he resented as a frustration of his aspirations. He wanted to go to St. Petersburg to study at the university, and to advance in his intellectual life and literary activity. However, he made no resolute move in this direction, and remained a provincial correspondent of publications issued in the capital, and his activities were of local scope. Yet his literary work made him a leading figure in the circles of the Russian-Jewish intelligentsia.

Levanda had a wide acquaintance with Russian and Western literature. He made several trips abroad, and knew Western conditions, including Jewish life in the West from personal observation. Levanda was a sensitive, perspicacious observer, reserved in his contacts with people. His struggles and sufferings, his strong reactions to various aspects of Jewish life, and his passionate idealism brought about a growing nervous tension which made an invalid out of him in the last two years of his life; he died in a mental sanatorium in St. Petersburg.

Lev Osipovich Levanda, Russian author. Jerusalem, J.N.U.L.

Levanda lived during three periods of Russian Jewish history. He grew up under the extreme autocracy and military bureaucracy of *Nicholas I (1825–55), which is reflected in his reminiscences of the "schoolophobia" campaign against modern schools, and was one of the young hotheads of *maskil* progressivism. During the early years of *Alexander II's reign (1855–65)—"years of great reforms" and initial liberalization—feelings of great expectations of general betterment and, in particular, of rapid improvement in the position of Russian Jewry and of their ultimate integration into Russian society with civic equality were common. During this period Levanda became a government official. He was also a sometime editor of *Vilenskiy Vestnik* and a contributor to *Razsvet* (1860–61), the first Russian Jewish journal, presenting in articles and in fiction the critique of inner aspects of Jewish life: poverty, parasitism, the role of women storekeepers with the resulting neglect of children, excessive pursuit of talmudic studies, negative role of rich and retrograde communal leaders, marriages imposed by parents, and other problems. He assisted in unraveling an incipient *blood libel at *Siauliai in 1886. He developed a concept of the Jews in northwest Russia (Lithuania-Belorussia) as prospective carriers of Russian culture and citizenship as against Polish aspirations in the region; the Jews were to become Russians except for their religion *(sliyaniye).* The issue was particularly acute during the Polish insurrection of 1863. Later, he expressed this mood in a novel *Goryacheye Vremya* (1875), in which young Westernized Jews were urged by the hero, Sarin, to abandon Polish orientation (after 500 years of unhappy experience with the Poles) and become Russians.

Levanda unhappily had to witness the growing reaction in Russia and the rise of modern anti-Semitism in the West and its adoption in Russia. He worried about the concentration of Jews in middleman occupations and professions; he urged economic productivization and diversification, and less ostentatiousness on the part of the wealthy. He deplored the fact that Jews had all the obligations, but almost none of the rights, of Russians, and, indeed, suffered from specific restrictions. The Jews wanted a fatherland, and Russia might stand to gain by becoming one (*Voskhod,* February, 1881).

In this period he was primarily a writer of fiction, bitterly denouncing the nouveaux riches (bankers, industrialists, speculators) and the new diploma-intelligentsia crowd with its careerism and greed; he berated the alienation and aloofness of these groups from Jewish interests.

The final stage in the development of his views took place during the wave of pogroms in the early 1880s. Deeply disturbed, he attacked the rich Jews, feeling that the events were really directed against them and that their turn might yet come. He was opposed to the anti-migration stand of the upper class and considered emigration a normal and sound response. He also called for *self-defense. Moving toward agreement with Leon *Pinsker's auto-emancipation, he then joined the ranks of *Ḥovevei Zion as one of their leading figures in literature, propaganda, and organization. Representing Jewish nationalism in an age of national revival and politics, he saw no contradiction between Jewish nationalism and the ideal of a monolithic humanity.

In private correspondence he pointed out that despite his apparent transition from cosmopolitan assimilation to nationalism he had been basically a devoted Jewish patriot who never conceived the dissolution of Jewish group existence or of cultural extinction (Russification being far from assimilation), and to whom the needs of the Jewish masses were always the point of departure. When the pro-Russian hero of his novel is asked, "And what if the Russians do not respond to your aspirations?" he answers, "Then we shall have to reconsider." Levanda wrote later that he clearly remembered that while writing this he had the first glimpse of modern Jewish nationalism.

In the Ḥibbat Zion movement, he considered the awakening of the Jewish masses in Russia, land acquisition in Ereẓ Israel, and entrenchment of Jews on the soil as main tasks. He was against overestimating the value and the claims of the youth movement (e.g., *Bilu), and while opposed to the philanthropic trend, he expected more from middle-class efforts. He sought to counteract Pinsker's tendency to become discouraged, and, unlike Pinsker, did not expect Western Jewry to take a leading role in the movement. He felt that the position of the Jew was dangerously deteriorating. In the past, the Jew had been confronted with an unfavorable law, but now the elemental lawlessness of a violent mob threatened the very life and safety of the Jew. The hope to reeducate these forces was illusory; the safe thing was to avoid the onslaught. Jews must get soil under their feet. Their national culture too would have a normal development once this soil was secured.

Thus Levanda stands out as a reflector and guide of the Haskalah, assimilationism, and nationalism—three stages in the development of the social-political ideology of the intelligentsia, as it abandons traditional messianism and searches for a fatherland to which its energies could be harnessed. As a creative writer, he was gifted and witty in feuilletons, sketches, and in drawing the ethnographic canvas, but he lacked the mastery of characterization and could not develop into a substantial, original artist. In his final years he turned to historical fiction, novels based on the pre-modern history of East European Jewry. [M.PE.]

His brother VITALI OSIPOVICH LEVANDA (b. 1840), a Russian lawyer, was born in Minsk, Belorussia. His study on the question of Jewish agriculture in Russia (in *Yevreyskaya Biblioteka,* vol. 2, 1872) was well received. On the recommendation of Baron H. *Guenzburg, he compiled and published in 1874 his *Polny khronologicheskiy sbornik zakonov...* ("Complete Chronological Collection of Laws and Regulations Concerning Jews from the Time of Czar Alexei Mikhailovich to the Present, 1649–1873"), a valuable guide to the legislation affecting Jews in Russia. He also wrote articles in the periodical *Russkiy Yevrey* on the development of agriculture among the Jews in Russia; he opposed immigration to Ereẓ Israel (in *Razsvet,* no. 40, 1881). [ED.]

Bibliography: WORKS: L. O. Levanda's works are listed in *Sistematicheskiy ukazatel literatury o yevreyakh* (1893). Most appeared in *Razsvet* (1860, 1879–81), *Yevreyskaya Biblioteka, Voskhod* (monthly and weekly), *Russkiy Yevrey,* and *Palestina.* Many were reprinted and translated into Hebrew and Yiddish. GENERAL: S. L. Ẓitron, *Anashim ve-Soferim* (1921), 69–92; idem, in: *Leksikon Ẓiyyoni* (1924), 297–312; S. M. Ginzburg, in: *Minuvsheye* (1923). MEMOIRS: L. Kantor, in: *Ha-Shilo'aḥ,* 1 (1896/97), 255–62; Mordekhai ben Hillel Ha-Kohen, *Olami,* 1–2 (1927); S. M. Ginzburg, in: E. H. Jeshurin (ed.), *Vilne* (1935), 466–71; J. L. Appel, *Betokh Reshit ha-Teḥiyyah* (1936). CORRESPONDENCE, DOCUMENTS: S. M. Ginzburg, in: *Perezhitoye,* 1 (1908), 36–7; A. Druyanov, in: *Yevreyskaya Starina,* 5 (1913), 279–281; idem, in: *Ketavim le-Toledot Ḥibbat Ẓiyyon* (1919–32); N. A. Buchbinder, *Literaturnye Etyudi* (1927), 5–49; M. Perlmann, in: PAAJR, 35 (1967). IDEOLOGY: B. A. Goldberg, *Lev Levanda kak publitsist* (1900); A. Idelson, in: *Razsvet,* 12 (1913); S. Breiman, in: *Shivat Ẓiyyon,* 2–3 (1951–52), 177–205; I. Klausner, *Be-Hitorer Am* (1962); idem, *Mi-Kattowitz ad Basel* (1965). THE WRITER: P. Lazarev, in: *Voskhod* (1885); A. Volynski, in: *Voskhod* (1888–89).

LEVANON, MORDECAI (1901–1968), Israel painter. He was born in Transylvania and in 1921 went to Palestine where he worked for a year as an agricultural laborer. From 1922 he studied painting in Jerusalem and Tel Aviv. He

Self-portrait of Mordecai Levanon, 1942–43, oil on canvas, 38×27 in. (96×68 cm.). Jerusalem, Israel Museum.

moved to Jerusalem in 1939 but from 1963 worked also in his Safed studio.

Levanon, primarily a landscapist, remained faithful to the expressionist concept so widespread in Palestinian art. He brought to this his own individual vision and his work reveals his European background. In his paintings of Jerusalem, Lake Kinneret, and Safed there is an intermingling of mystery and grandeur. [Y.FI.]

LEVEEN, JACOB (1891–), librarian and author. Born in Jerusalem, Leveen studied in England and worked for many years in the Department of Oriental Books and Manuscripts of the British Museum, from 1953–56 as keeper. He was responsible for part 4 of the *Catalogue of Hebrew and Samaritan Manuscripts in the British Museum* (1935). His *Hebrew Bible in Art* (1944, the British Academy's Schweich lectures, 1939) was a pioneer study in this field. Leveen also published a facsimile edition of a unique British Museum manuscript of Zechariah b. Judah Aghmati's digest of commentaries on the three Bava tractates of the Babylonian Talmud (1961). He prepared the second part of a catalog of Hebrew manuscripts in the Cambridge University Library (unpublished). [ED.]

LEVEN, NARCISSE (1833–1915), French philanthropist and public figure. Leven was born in Germany, and his family settled in Paris during his childhood. In 1855 he graduated from the Sorbonne in law. A staunch republican,

Leven acted as secretary to Adolphe *Crémieux, minister of justice during the Franco-Prussian War (1870/71). After the war he practiced law, and in 1879 was elected member of the Paris municipal council, and was its vice-president in 1882. However, he was defeated in the elections in 1887, as a result of an anti-Semitic campaign directed personally against him. Leven had been deeply stirred as a child by the *Damascus affair (1840) and later by the *Mortara case (1858). This influenced him to found the *Alliance Israélite Universelle, together with Charles *Netter, Jules *Carvallo, and others. He was successively secretary, vice-president, and, from 1898 until his death, president of the Alliance central committee. Together with Zadoc *Kahn, Leven also assisted Baron de *Hirsch in formulating his colonization plans, and was the first to preside over the council of the *Jewish Colonization Association (ICA). Leven was a member of the Central Consistory of French Jews for over 50 years. He wrote *Cinquante ans d'histoire: l'Alliance Israelite Universelle, 1860–1910* (vol. 1, 1911; vol. 2, 1920, posthumous).

Bibliography: J. P. Coulon, *Narcisse Leven* (Fr., 1920); A. Chouraqui, *L'Alliance Israélite Universelle* (1965), index. [E.B.]

LEVENE, PHOEBUS AARON THEODOR (1869–1940), U.S. biochemist. Born in Sagor, Russia, as Fishel Aaronovich Levin, he emigrated to New York in 1892, and practised medicine there till 1896. At the same time he studied chemistry at Columbia University and carried out research in the department of physiology. He worked at the Pathological Institute of the New York State Hospitals (1902–05). He joined the newly formed Rockefeller Institute for Medical Research, where he worked for the rest of his life, from 1907 in charge of the Chemistry Division.

His main contribution was in the structural chemistry of nucleic acids, and the isolation of the two sugars (then unknown) which characterize them—D-ribose and its 2-deoxy derivative. His work embraced all classes of tissue constituents, especially proteins and sugar phosphates; in the latter connection he did a great deal of work on fundamental carbohydrate chemistry. He was a pioneer in numerous aspects of biochemistry.

Bibliography: D. D. Van Slyke and W. A. Jacobs, in: National Academy of Sciences of the U.S.A. *Biographical Memoirs*, 23 (1944), 75–126; Tipson, in: *Advances in Carbohydrate Chemistry*, 12 (1957), 1–12; E. Farber (ed.), *Great Chemists* (1961), 1313–24. [S.A.M.]

LEVER, NORMAN HAROLD (1914–), British politician and financial expert. Born in Manchester, Lever practiced as a barrister for several years before entering the House of Commons as a Labor member in 1950. He sponsored the Defamation Act of 1952 as a private member's bill and acquired a considerable reputation as an authority on financial matters. In 1967 he was appointed parliamentary under-secretary for economic affairs, later in the same year was promoted to the post of financial secretary to the Treasury, and finally paymaster general, with a seat in the Cabinet, as second minister in charge of the Ministry of Technology (until the Labor Party went out of office in 1970). Lever represented the United Kingdom at the International Monetary Fund and European "Group of Ten" financial conferences which considered the world currency crises of 1968. Though not prominent in any specific communal institution, he worked unofficially for many Jewish and Zionist causes.

His brother, LESLIE LEVER (1905–), sat in the House of Commons from 1950 and was lord mayor of Manchester in 1957–58. He was active in Jewish affairs as president of the Manchester and Salford Jewish Council and vice-president of the Board of Guardians. [V.D.L.]

LEVERSON, ADA (1865–1936), English novelist. A member of the *Beddington family, Ada Leverson was of Marrano descent. At nineteen she married Ernest Leverson, the son of a diamond merchant; their unsuccessful marriage ended in separation. In addition to novels she wrote many occasional pieces for periodicals, including the humorous weekly, *Punch*. Her salon was frequented by the leaders of the "nineties" movement, such as Aubrey Beardsley, Oscar Wilde, and Walter Sickert, and she contributed stories to *The Yellow Book*. She remained a loyal friend to Oscar Wilde, and took him into her home between his trials. Ada Leverson's six novels, beginning with *The Twelfth Hour*, were published between 1907 and 1916. Typical of the Edwardian era, they were well received, though largely as the work of a gifted dilettante. The diverting conversation of Ada Leverson's characters, often uninterrupted by description, owes much to her love of the theater. Always urbane and gently ironic about the relations between husband and wife, she held strong moral views about loyalty in marriage. Her forte was high comedy and she was a penetrating satirist of the manners of her time. In her later years, she was a close friend of the Sitwells.

Bibliography: A. Leverson, *Little Ottleys* (1962), foreword by C. McInnes; O. Sitwell, *Noble Essences* (1950), 127–62; V. Wyndham, *Sphinx and her Circle* (1962). [RE.W.]

LEVERTIN, OSCAR IVAR (1862–1906), Swedish poet and literary critic, the first Jew to gain eminence in Swedish literature. Levertin, the son of a Stockholm antiquarian, was born in Gryt, near Norrköping. In his student days at the University of Uppsala (where he was a pupil of Johan Henrik *Schück), he joined the literary circle of "Young Sweden." In 1899 he became professor of literature at the Academy (now the University) of Stockholm. As a poet, Levertin was distinguished by his aestheticism and his sophisticated preoccupation with aims and moods. Emotionally drawn to romanticism, he was intellectually a determinist, and the personal struggle engendered by this conflict became the *leitmotiv* of his poetry. He was thus closer to the English Pre-Raphaelites and the French symbolists than to writers of the contemporary Swedish school. His most characteristic verse appears in *Legender och visor* ("Legends and Songs," 1891), which contains a number of poems on Jewish themes. Two other collections were *Nya dikter* ("New Poems," 1894) and *Dikter* ("Poems," 1901). As a critic, Levertin displayed sensitivity, learning, and cultural awareness. In 1897 he joined the reorganized *Svenska Dagbladet*, gaining new fame as the newspaper's principal literary critic. Together with Carl Gustav Verner von Heidenstam, a leader of the Swedish anti-naturalist movement, he formulated a literary program to which he adhered in his own writing.

Levertin's many prose works include novels, novellas, and essays. *Rococo-noveller* ("Rococo Stories," 1899), a collection of pastiches, recreated the courtly 18th-century world of King Gustav III. One of the most beautiful of these tales, *Kalonymos*, describes a Passover celebration in Stockholm, the central character expressing something of the writer's own skeptical humanism. As a young man in 1880, Levertin had published a poem denouncing anti-Semitism. Though thoroughly Swedish in his tastes and sympathies—his family settled in the country in the late 18th century—he remained a conscious Jew, emotionally and historically bound to his people and never quite at home in his Scandinavian environment. For many years he suffered from a lung disease, and he became increasingly obsessed with death and religious problems. His last major work was the verse cycle *Kung Salomo och Morolf* ("King Solomon and Morolf," 1905), whose themes derived from

Jewish, oriental, and medieval sources. His other publications include the novella *Konflikter* (1885), *Diktare och drömmare* (1898), *Teater och drama under Gustav III* (1889), and *Svenska gestalter* (1903). His collected works appeared in 24 volumes (1907–11).

Bibliography: W. Söderhjelm, *Oskar Levertin*, 2 vols. (Swedish, 1914–17); O. Mendelsohn, *Jödiske innslag i Oskar Levertins diktning* (1938); C. Fehrman, *Levertins lyrik* (1945); *Svenskt litteraturlexikon* (1964), s.v.; A. Levertin (ed.), *Den unge Levertin* (1947); B. Julin, *Hjärtats landsflykt* (1962). [H.V.]

LEVERTOFF, PAUL PHILIP (1878–1954), apostate and theologian. Levertoff, who was born in Orsha, Belorussia, into a ḥasidic family, was converted to Christianity in 1895. After studying theology in Russian and German universities, traveling in Europe, Palestine, and Asia Minor, and working for a time in Warsaw and as professor of Old Testament and rabbinics at the Institutum Delitzschianum in Leipzig (1912–18), he was appointed librarian and sub-warden of St. Deiniols Library, Hawarden (Wales; 1919–22). From 1922 until his death, he was director of the London Diocesan Council for work among the Jews (formerly The East London Fund for the Jews), and edited its quarterly journal *The Church and the Jews*. He also took a leading part in the Hebrew Christian movement, translated considerable parts of the Anglican liturgy into Hebrew, and conducted Christian services partly in Hebrew at the North West London church where he was minister. Levertoff was a prolific writer on liturgical and theological subjects in Hebrew, German, and English. He contributed to periodicals and encyclopedias, translated the Midrash Sifre on Numbers (1926), and cooperated with H. Sperling in the translation of the Zohar into English (1933). [R.P.L.]

LEVI (Heb. לֵוִי), third son of Jacob and Leah, born in Paddan-Aram (Gen. 29:34); father of the tribe named after him. The name Levi is explained in the Pentateuch by Leah's words at his birth: "Now this time my husband will become attached to me (Heb. *yillaweh*)."

The Man. In the affair of *Dinah (Gen. 34), Levi and Simeon took the chief part in the slaying of the men of Shechem and the plunder of their city, an act that aroused Jacob's anger against them (Gen. 34, cf. 49:5–7).

The sons of Levi were Gershon, Kohath, and Merari (Ex. 6:16), from whom stemmed the families of the tribe of Levi. Nothing further is recorded of Levi the man.

The Tribe. According to the censuses of the Levites in the wilderness which covered—exceptionally—"all the males from the age of one month up," Levi was the smallest tribe, comprising 22,000 or 23,000 males (Num. 3:39; 26:62). The tribe was singled out during the wanderings in the wilderness for the service of the tabernacle, carrying the Ark and attending to the duties of the sanctuary. Supervising them were descendants of their tribe, the *Aaronides (Num. 1:48–53; 3:5–40). The census of the Levites was conducted separately from the general census of the Israelites in the wilderness (Num. 1:47–49), and it is stated that they were chosen for their service "in place of all the firstborn among the Israelite people" (see *Firstborn), the number of the firstborn being practically identical with that of the Levites (3:40–43).

The story of the *golden calf emphasizes the loyalty of the tribe to Moses. In this affair, too, as in that of Dinah, the Levites stand out as men of zeal who do not spare brother, friend, or kin (Ex. 32:25–30). On the other hand, note should be taken of the rebellion of *Korah and his company, who were Levites, against Moses (Num. 16; the non-Levites in this pericope are followers of *Dathan and Abiram). A reflection of Levi's closeness to the tribe of Judah is to be found in the juxtaposition of the two in the Blessing of Moses (Deut. 33:7–9) as well as in the genealogy of the Levite youth from a Judahite family in Beth-Lehem (Judg. 17:7), and in the story of the Levite from the other end of the hill country of Mt. Ephraim who took a concubine from Beth-Lehem of Judah (19:1). These reports testify to this connection with Judah, as well as to the Levite's lack of a fixed territory, as stated in the Pentateuch (Num. 18:23b). The Levite youth from Beth-Lehem became a priest in the House of Micah on Mt. Ephraim, and Levite priests also served in Dan in the era of the Judges (Judg. 17:10–11; 18:19–30).

THE SERVICE. According to Numbers, the Levites were in attendance upon the priests in the service of the Tent of Meeting, carrying it and its appurtenances. This service was divided between the three families of the tribe—Gershon, Kohath, and Merari (Num. 3–4). The Levites were also entrusted with the task of serving the priests, performing duties for them and for "the whole community before the Tent of Meeting" (3:7). This apparently consisted of guarding the Tent and its furnishings against the laity. It was also their duty to provide a barrier between the tabernacle and the people (1:50–54; 18:22–3). In the course of their work, the Levites were subject to the priests appointed over them and they were not permitted to witness the dismantling of the sanctuary (4:20). The superiority of the Aaronide priests of the tribe of Levi to the Levites is expressly stressed in Exodus, Leviticus, and Numbers, and the division of functions between them is clearly defined (see *Priests and Levites). The Levites were also assigned instructional responsibilities, and it was they who bore the Ark of the Covenant (Deut. 10:8; 31:9), but these functions were primarily intended for the priests, the most select of the Levites (Mal. 2:4–8; 3:3). According to the view of Deuteronomy, all the Levites are fit to serve in the sanctuary, even such as do not have permanent duties in the sanctuary (Deut. 18:6–9). In return for their service they are entitled to receive *tithes (Num. 18:21).

This appointment of the Levites as ministers of God resulted in their becoming wanderers during the period of the Judges, without any permanent possession in the country. They are reckoned in the Bible among those needing support, such as the stranger, the orphan, and the widow. It seems that even at the time of the monarchy the Levites at the gates of the cities still did not possess their own territory but this is explained as a sign of a superior status: "the Lord is their portion" (10:9; 18:2).

MONARCHICAL PERIOD. Possibly, the Levites became state

Levites bearing the Ark of the Covenant across the Jordan, from a 12th-century Greek manuscript, *Kosmas Indicopleustes*, Sinai Peninsula, St. Catherine's Monastery, Ms. 1186, fol. 89r.

officials in the time of David and Solomon when the cult itself was transformed into an instrument for state influence. Chronicles relates a great deal about the high status of the Levites in the time of David, even in the administration of government (I Chron. 23–27). According to Chronicles, Levites were among those who came to transfer the monarchy to David at Hebron (I Chron. 12:27), and their loyalty to the kings of the dynasty of David continued until the destruction of the Temple (II Chron. 23:2–9, 18–19; 24:5–15, et al.). The story of the migration of the Levites from Israel to Judah after the division of the kingdom may reflect a real historical situation that is alluded to in Kings (I Kings 12:31; 13:33; cf. II Chron. 11:13–17; 13:9–12). According to I Chronicles, the Levites took a leading part as overseers in the work of the House of the Lord (23:4), as choristers, musicians, gatekeepers, and guardians of the threshold (9:14–33). Among the choristers mentioned are Heman, Asaph, and Jeduthun, who are also referred to in Psalms. The sons of Korah are also connected with psalmody (cf. Ps. 42:1; 44:1; et al.) and are so mentioned incidentally in II Chronicles 20:19, though they are mostly reckoned in this source among the gatekeepers. The Levites also functioned as officials, judges, craftsmen for the Temple service, supervisors of the chambers and the courts, overseers of the Temple treasuries, and officers in charge of the royal service (I Chron. 9:22, 26–27; 23:4, 28; et al.). The special status of the Levites in the time of Jehoshaphat as disseminators of the Torah and as judges in the towns of Judah and in Jerusalem is understandable in the light of the above (II Chron. 19:8, 11). It would also seem possible from many passages that the Levites mainly ministered alongside the priests, and that the priests were appointed over them (I Chron. 6:31ff.; 23:27–32; et al.). Hence, it seems that in the time of the First Temple the demarcation between Levites and priests was not clearly preserved, and that even among the Levites themselves there existed a certain grading.

The incorporation of the Levites into the monarchical system of Israel found its expression in the setting aside of special towns from the territories of the tribes as levitical towns of residence. According to Numbers (35:1–8), the Israelites were commanded, while still in the plains of Moab, to set aside 48 towns from their territory for the Levites (see *Levitical Cities). In Joshua 21, lists are cited which apparently originated in the same tradition, and current research inclines to regard them as a reflection of a real situation that existed at the time of the First Temple. There is no contradiction between the principle of no territory and the allocation of towns of residence, since these were merely towns and fields for the raising of cattle without agricultural settlement. The houses in the levitical towns were regarded as a substitute for territory, and the laws of the *Jubilee applied to them as to land, in contrast to dwellings in walled cities. Their adaptation to a monarchical regime brought about the fact that the priests did not forbid themselves the ownership of agricultural land too (I Kings 2:26; Jer. 32:7–16; et al.). However, the principle remained in force for many generations, so that even Ezekiel, who says that in the time to come the Levites will no longer be scattered throughout the country but gathered into Jerusalem, outlines for them an area beside the Temple (Ezek. 45:4–5; 48:11–15).

From the time of the return to Zion the boundaries between priests and Levites were firmly established. The Levites acquired an honored status, and even their small number in comparison with that of priests (Ezra 2:40–42) added to their importance in the eyes of the people. In the time of Ezra and Nehemiah it was necessary to bring Levites to Jerusalem from the exile and from the rural towns. From this time on the division between priests and Levites remained permanent.

Concerning the special status of the Levites as well as their functions, see also *Priests and Priesthood. [SH.AB.]

In the Aggadah. Rabbinical *aggadah* greatly expanded the biblical material, sometimes to Levi's detriment, but more frequently it reversed the picture. At the births of Simeon and Levi, Leah prophesied that Simeon would produce an enemy of God (Zimri), but from Levi would come Phinehas and heal the wound inflicted through Zimri (Gen. R. 71:4). The proposal to kill Joseph (Gen. 37:20) came from Simeon and Levi and it was they who sold him. When the brothers came to Egypt, Joseph separated them by imprisoning Simeon (Gen. 42:24), for together they would have destroyed Egypt; the separation caused Levi's strength to ebb away (Gen. R. 97, ed. by Theodor-Albeck, p. 1216).

To Levi's credit is the story of the *Shekhinah* ("Divine Presence"), which originally dwelt in the lowest sphere, but seven wicked persons or generations drove it ever further away to the highest (seventh) heaven. Seven righteous men brought it progressively back to earth, from the highest sphere to the next; one of these was Levi (Gen. R. 19:7; PdRK 2).

The name Levi was prophetic: his tribe would lead (*laveh;* "to escort," "accompany") the Israelites to their Father in Heaven (Gen. R. 71:4). When Phinehas argued before the Almighty that the sin of Zimri did not warrant the condign punishment of the whole nation (Num. 25:9), the angels sought to repell him, but God said to them, "Let him be: he is a zealot and the descendant of a zealot [Levi, who was zealous to defend his sister's honor, Gen. 34:25f.], a wrath-appeaser and a descendant of a wrath-appeaser" (Sanh. 82b; Lev. R. 33:4). The tribe of Levi was the only one that practiced circumcision in Egypt and did not lapse into idolatry (Sif. Num. 67; Ex. R. 15:1; 19:5). On the other hand, it was the only tribe not enslaved and put to degrading work (Ex. R. 5:16). Whereas the Israelites in general were liberated from Egypt for their prospective (but not present) merit in making the tabernacle, the tribe of Levi was liberated for its own immediate merit (Num. R. 3:6), for the whole tribe was righteous in Egypt (*ibid.* 15:12). Scripture gives the genealogy of Reuben, Simeon, and Levi only in Exodus 6:14ff. for three reasons: Because they meekly accepted their father Jacob's rebuke; to lead up to Moses and Aaron; they were the only ones who preserved their family trees in Egypt and did not worship idols (this is one of the few places where this is said of Reuben and Simeon too). These three exercised authority (as individuals) over all the Israelites in Egypt consecutively, but at Levi's death the authority did not pass to Judah (Song. R. 4:7 no. 1). The children of the other tribal ancestors did not uniformly produce righteous descendants, but the descendants of Levi's three sons, Gershon, Kohath, and Merari, were all righteous (Num. R. 3:7). This tribe did not participate in the sin of the golden calf, and taught the Israelites to serve only the one God in Ereẓ Israel *(ibid.)*.

Several reasons are given why Levi was not numbered together with the other tribes: one is because they were not doomed to die in the wilderness, but entered the Promised Land (Num. R. 1:11 and 12). As against this it is pointed out that the tribe of Levi was considerably smaller than the other tribes, because its numbers were depleted through their being grazed by fire when they carried the Ark (Num. R. 5:1; 6:8; see also Yal. on Isa. 428). For this reason God associated His name with Kohath to save them from being entirely consumed (Num. R. 6:8). Jacob predicted of Simeon and Levi, "I will divide them in Jacob, scatter them in Israel" (Gen. 49:7); this was fulfilled by their becoming teachers in the schoolhouses everywhere (Gen. R. 97, ed. by Theodor-Albeck, p. 1207). The tribe of Levi would teach sinners that sacrifice without true repentance does not constitute atonement (Lev. R. 9:5). Originally *shoterim* (officials of the *bet din*) were appointed only from the tribe of Levi (Yev. 86b). When the Almighty purifies the tribes, He will purify the tribe of Levi first (Kid. 71a). Greece (one of the powers that traditionally enslaved Israel) would fall through the Hasmoneans, members of the tribe of Levi (Gen. R. 99, ed. by Theodor-Albeck, p. 1274). Every tribe described as "Mine" will exist for ever and to all eternity—and of the Levites it is said, "the Levites shall be Mine" (Num. 3:12; Yal. I Sam. 124). [H.FR.]

Bibliography: IN THE BIBLE: See *Priests and Priesthood. IN THE AGGADAH: Ginzberg. Legends, 2 (1946[6]), 194–8, 5 (1947[6]), 380.

LEVI (fl. third quarter of the third century), Palestinian *amora*. Generally Levi is mentioned without his patronymic but he may be identical with Levi b. Laḥma (Ḥama) mentioned in the Babylonian Talmud (RH 29b). (However, as the name Levi b. Laḥma never appears in Palestinian sources, he may have gone to Babylon.) He was a contemporary of R. Ze'ira I, R. Abba b. Kahana, and R. Ḥama b. Ukba (Ukva). Levi was primarily an aggadist; his frequent quotations from Ḥama b. Ḥanina suggest that he was his pupil. He and R. Judah b. Naḥman gave popular lectures on alternate Sabbaths in Johanan's academy, for which each was paid two *selas*. On one occasion his lecture, in which he reconciled two opposing opinions, so pleased R. Johanan that he appointed him to a regular lectureship, a post which he held for 22 years. In those days non-ordained scholars apparently lectured standing, while ordained scholars lectured sitting, and R. Johanan expressed the hope that one day he would be privileged to deliver his lectures sitting (Gen. R. 98:11; cf. TJ, Hor. 3:9, 48c; Eccles. R. 6:2). It seems from this that he was not then an ordained teacher.

There are no *halakhot* in his name, but he does sometimes explain *halakhah* (e.g., on Ber. 60b; RH 22a, 29b), though even then his teachings have an aggadic flavor. His lectures were so highly esteemed that R. Ze'ira, who generally did not have a high opinion of *aggadah*, nevertheless advised scholars (*ḥavrayya*, colleagues) to attend his lectures, as they were always instructive (TJ, RH 4:1, 59b). Levi sometimes lectured on the same text for quite a long time and could easily switch from one interpretation to the opposite (TJ, Sanh. 10:2, 28b). He claimed the ability to link together texts from the different sections of the Bible and penetrate to their inner meaning—an ability which he did not concede to most preachers (Song R. 1:10). Frequently he explained different words in biblical texts by reference to Arabic words (Gen. R. 87:1; Ex. R. 42:4; Song R. 4:1) and he may have lived in Arabia for a while. He also composed elaborate parables to elucidate texts, and was regarded as a master of interpretation (Gen. R. 62:5). Among his numerous sayings are: "The punishment for [false] measures is more severe than for incest" (BB 88b); "Living without a wife is not living" (Gen. R. 17); "However much a man does for his soul, he does not fully discharge his obligations, . . . because it comes from on high" (Lev. R. 4:2); "To rob a human is worse than robbing the Almighty" (BB 88b). His yearning for the messianic period is reflected in a number of his statements, such as: "If Israel would keep but one Sabbath properly, the son of David would immediately come" (TJ, Ta'an. 1:1, 64a; see also Song R. 3:1).

Bibliography: Frankel, Mavo, 111; A. Bruell, *Fremdsprachliche Redensarten* (1869), 41–46, 50; Bacher, Pal Amor; Hyman, Toledot, 8, 51, 57; Ḥ. Albeck, *Mavo la-Talmudim* (1969), 256f.

[H.FR.]

LEVI (Bet ha-Levi), prominent, wealthy, and ramified Sephardi family of scholars and rabbis, many of whom served as congregation leaders during the 15th–17th centuries. The family originated from Évora in Portugal, but all that is known of its previous history is the statement of *Solomon II: ". . . my grandfather the expert physician, pious and understanding, Maestro Solomon I, the son of the noble prince Don Joseph, son of the expert physician Maestro Moses, son of the exalted Don Solomon, son of the holy [martyred?] Don Isaac, son of the distinguished physician Maestro Joseph of the House of ha-Levi" (*Bet ha-Levi*, in manuscript). SOLOMON I arrived in Salonika after the expulsion of the Jews from Portugal in 1497 and founded the family which was outstanding in Salonika during the period that followed. The Ha-Levis were one of the richest families of Salonika and continued to be so until 1620. A patriarchal family, its members were proud of their lineage and of their scholarly attainments and position. Several reached outstanding positions of influence and status in the Jewish community of Salonika. They were devoted to study and possessed extensive libraries. The members of the family exhibited variegated talents, excelling as rabbis of communities, as *posekim* and as scholars, as outstanding preachers and poets. Some possessed a thorough knowledge of philosophy, and there were even kabbalists among them.

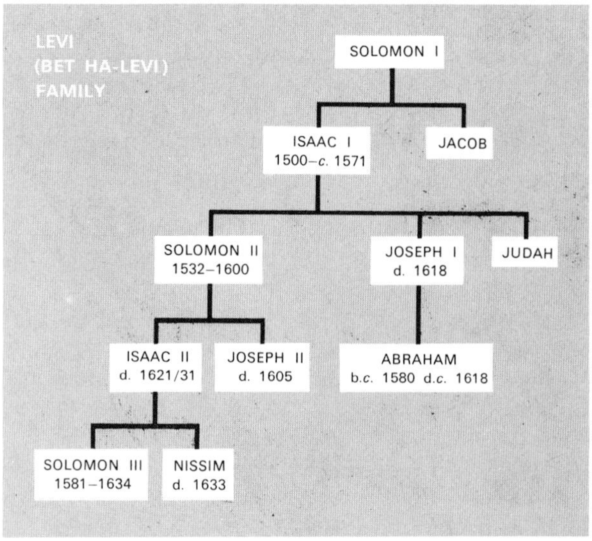

Two of the sons of Solomon I, ISAAC I (1500–1570/71), who was born in Salonika, and JACOB (and perhaps a third son, Joseph) were among the outstanding personalities of the Salonikan Jewish community in the mid-16th century. They were in contact with Joseph Caro after he moved to Safed. Isaac is eulogized in Saadiah Longo's *Seder Zemannim* (Salonika, 1594, 36ff.). He had two sons *Solomon II (1532–1600) and JOSEPH I (d. 1618), who were eminent scholars, and a third son, JUDAH, who died in his youth. Solomon II had two sons, *Isaac II (d. c. 1621/31) and JOSEPH II (d. 1605), who married the daughter of Joseph I, as well as three daughters, one of whom married R. Aaron *Sasson. Isaac II had two sons, *Solomon III (1581–1634), an outstanding scholar, and NISSIM (d. 1633), a *paytan*. Solomon had a son JACOB. Abraham *Levi was the son of Joseph I.

Bibliography: Solomon le-Bet ha-Levi, *Ḥeshek Shelomo* (Salonika, 1600), introductions; Conforte, Kore, index; Ch. Hirschensohn, in: *Hamisderonah*, 2 (1888), 161, 190–2, 219–23, 340–3; D. Pipano, introduction to *Ein Mishpat* of R. Abraham le-Bet ha-Levi (1897); A. Danon, in: *Yerushalayim*, ed. by A. M. Luncz, 7 (1906–07), 351–4; I. S. Emmanuel, *Maẓẓevot Saloniki*, 2 vols. (1963–68), index.

[JOS.H.]

LEVI (Bet ha-Levi), ABRAHAM BEN JOSEPH (after 1580–shortly after 1618), a rabbi in Salonika of the *Levi (Bet ha-Levi) family. At an early age he showed outstanding intellectual abilities and was ordained rabbi at a very young age. Questions were addressed to him from far and wide and his endorsement was requested to the responsa of prominent rabbis older than himself. He studied under R. David ibn Naḥmias, and was a colleague of R. Shabbetai Jonah. He was a member of the *bet din* of Abraham Ḥazzan, together with whom he often gave his approbation to the responsa of R. Joshua Handali. Abraham's colleague with whom he studied was R. Shabbetai Jonah. In addition to his published responsa (the bulk written between 1608–18), other responsa and approbations appear in the works of several of his contemporaries in Salonika and elsewhere. (His novellae, on several talmudic tractates and on the *Arba'ah Turim*, have apparently been lost.)

Bibliography: Abraham le-Bet ha-Levi, *Ein Mishpat* (Salonika, 1897), introduction by editor D. Pipano; Rosanes, Togarmah, 3 (1938), 181–2. [Jos.H.]

LEVI, BEHREND (b. c. 1600), army purveyor during the Thirty Years' War (1618–48) and financial adviser and diplomatic agent to the elector of Brandenburg. In 1650 Frederick William, the great elector, appointed Behrend Levi as overlord of all the Jews in the principalities of Brandenburg west of the River Elbe. This gave him authority to admit Jews, to fix their places of residence and tax rates, and to grant personal and business licenses. He collected the taxes of Halberstadt, Minden, Ravensburg, and Cleves Jewry, and rendered judgments in local disputes. An annual income accompanied the patent, which was renewed regularly. The Jews of Cleves and his rivals, such as the *Gomperz family, protested against his harsh methods and his authority was rescinded in 1652. A year earlier his brother, SALOMON LEVI, had procured for Behrend similar powers over Paderborn Jewry, but he was accused of embezzlement and once more of harsh rule and his authority terminated in 1654. However, the great elector repeatedly supported his favorite and renewed his patent in 1657.

Bibliography: H. Schnee, *Die Hoffinanz und der moderne Staat*, 1 (1953), 97–101; S. Stern, *The Court Jew* (1950), index, s.v. *Levi, Bernd.* [ED.]

LEVI, BENEDETTO (Baruch Isaac; 1846–80), Italian rabbi and scholar. He was born in Ferrara and graduated from the rabbinical seminary in Padua in 1872. From 1872 to 1875 he was in Nizza Monferrato and from 1875 in Ferrara. He wrote: *Cenni bibliografici sulla Bibbia Luzzatto* (1876); *Ḥikkur Din* (1877), on the death penalty in talmudic law; *Il sommo sacerdozio appresso gli antichi ebrei* (1880); *Taḥanunei Benei Yisrael*, 12 penitential prayers (in *Kobez al Jad*, 4, 1888). Among his essays are biographies on Jacob Daniel *Olmo (in *Ha-Maggid*, 16, 1872); Phinehas Ḥai *Anav (*ibid.*, 17, 1873); Azariah de' *Rossi (in Italian, 1869); Isaac *Lampronti (in Italian and in Hebrew, 1871); and on the Jewish poets of Ferrara (in *Kevod ha-Levanon* vols. 10, 11). Together with S. Z. H. *Halberstamm he edited *Takkanot Ḥakhamim* (in *Ivri Anokhi*, 15, 1879), on the regulations adopted at the conference of Jewish delegates held at Ferrara in 1554.

Bibliography: Kressel, Leksikon, 2 (1965) 182. [U.C./ED.]

LEVI, CARLO (1902–), Italian author and artist. Born in Turin, where he studied medicine, Levi became interested in art, literature, and politics. After Mussolini came to power he joined the anti-Fascist underground and was one of the founders of the radical movement Giustizia e Libertà. He was arrested in 1934 and in the following year was exiled to Lucania in southern Italy for a year. In 1939 he fled to France. He returned to Italy in 1942 to join the Resistance and was again arrested. After World War II, he settled in Rome, where he was active in journalism and politics. He was elected a senator in 1963 on the Communist ticket, but retained an independent outlook.

Levi's experiences as a political exile inspired his masterpiece, *Cristo si è fermato a Eboli* (1945; *Christ Stopped at Eboli*, 1947), the first major Italian literary work of the postwar era, which was translated into many languages. In it he describes the society of Lucania, its customs, addiction to magic, and pre-Christian traditions. Accepting their unending miseries and without hope of a

"Three Calabrian Laborers," oil painting by Carlo Levi. From *Von Atelier zu Atelier*, vol. 6, nos. 7 and 8, Dusseldorf, 1958.

better future, the peasants nevertheless show themselves to be lovers of justice, good neighbors, and loyal friends. Levi reveals all the poetry of this primitive world.

Using the documentary techniques of journalism or of a travel diary, Levi wrote about the cultural climate and problems of many countries: Sicily, in *Le parole sono pietre* (1955; *Words are Stones*, 1958); the Soviet Union, in *Il futuro ha un cuore antico* (1956); Germany, in *La doppia notte dei tigli* (1959; *Linden Trees*, 1962); and Sardinia, in *Tutto il miele è finito* (1964). His other works include the essay *Paura della libertà* (1946; *Fear and Freedom*, 1950) and the novel, *L'Orologio* (1950; *The Watch*, 1951). As a painter, Levi exhibited in one-man and collective shows, achieving particular success in the United States.

Bibliography: P. Pancrazi, *Scrittori d'oggi*, 4 (1946), 282–9; C. L. Ragghianti, *Carlo Levi* (It., 1948); L. Russo, *I narratori 1850–1950* (1951²), 335–9; G. Pullini, *Il romanzo italiano del dopoguerra 1940–1960* (1961), 224–7, 263–6. [G.R.]

LEVI, DAVID (1742–1801), English Hebraist and polemicist. Born in London and intended by his parents to be a rabbi, Levi instead was apprenticed to a cobbler, and later worked as a hatter. However, he continued to pursue Jewish studies and interests. He published new translations of the Pentateuch for synagogal use (1787), of the Sephardi liturgy (6 vols., 1789–93) and the Ashkenazi (1794–96); and

David Levi, 18th-century English Hebraist and polemicist. Engraving by Bromley after a painting by Drummond. Cecil Roth Collection. Photo David Harris, Jerusalem.

Lingua Sacra (1785–87), a Hebrew grammar and dictionary. He also wrote *Rites and Ceremonies of the Jews* (1783). Levi was the first Jew to write, in English, polemics in defense of Jews and Judaism. In his *Letters to Dr. Priestley* (1787) he rejected the attempts of the noted scholar Joseph Priestley to convert Jews to Christianity. In the same vein, he answered Thomas Paine's attacks on the Bible and the authenticity of prophecy (*Letters to Thomas Paine in*

Answer to his "Age of Reason," 1797). He also opposed millennarian theories in *Letters to Nathaniel Brassey Halhed in Answer to His Testimony of the Authenticity of the Prophecies of Richard Brothers and His Pretended Mission to Recall the Jews* (1795). Levi's whole life was a struggle to devote himself to scholarship in spite of poverty, and he was ultimately given a small pension by a group of supporters headed by the *Goldsmids.

Bibliography: S. Singer, in: JHSET, 3 (1896), 55–71; J. Picciotto, *Sketches of Anglo-Jewish History* (1956²), 219–20, 243, 270; C. Roth, *Great Synagogue* (1950), 148–9; Roth, Mag Bibl, index; DNB, s.v.; S. Daiches, in: JHSEM, 4 (1942), 28–32. [Y.Ro.]

LEVI, DORO (1898–), Italian archaeologist. Levi, born in Trieste, had a distinguished career as organizer of archaeological expeditions, curator, and administrator. He was a lecturer at Florence University, and in 1935 went to Sardinia to become professor at the Cagliari University and the island's director of art and antiquities. From 1939 to 1945 Levi was in the United States as a guest lecturer at Princeton and Harvard, but returned to Italy in 1945 to become adviser on cultural relations to the Ministry of Education. In 1947 he was appointed director of the Italian School of Archaeology in Athens and led archaeological expeditions in the Levant. He organized excavations at Caesarea in Israel in the late 1950s, and continued the Italian excavations on the Aegean islands, including Crete, Gortyna, Phaistos, and Arkades-Aphrati. His excavations at Iasos, a town in Caria on the Anatolian coast (1960–61), threw light on the origins of the early Cycladic and early Minoan civilizations. He summarized the activities of the Italian school in Athens in: *The Italian Excavations in Crete and the Earliest European Civilization* (1963) and *The Recent Excavations at Phaistos* (= *Studies in Mediterranean Archaeology*, vol. 11, 1964).

Levi's scientific interests embraced the whole of the ancient world from prehistory to late antiquity, with a strong leaning toward mythology and the history of religion. These interests came to fruition in his study, "The Allegories of the Months in Classical Art" in *Art Bulletin* (23 (1941), 251–91), and in his monumental work *Antioch Mosaic Pavements* (2 vols., 1947). [P.P.K.]

LEVI, EDWARD H. (1911–), U.S. educator, legal scholar, and university administrator. Levi, who was born in Chicago, was a descendant of the rabbinical families of *Einhorn and *Hirsch and a son of Rabbi Gerson B. Levi. He received his law degree at the University of Chicago in 1935. Awarded the Sterling Fellowship at Yale Law School, he earned his degree of doctor of jurisprudence in 1938. Levi was appointed professor of law at the University of Chicago and also held several administrative positions. In 1967 he was appointed president of the university. An outstanding administrator, Levi also distinguished himself as a legal expert. In the 1940s he served under Thurman Arnold, head of the U.S. Justice Department's antitrust division. He was active in atomic energy legislation; his work provided the basis for the establishment of the Atomic Energy Commission. Levi's *An Introduction to Legal Reasoning* (1949) is considered a classic work. He coauthored (with Roscoe Steffen) *Elements of the Law* (1950) and wrote *Four Talks on Legal Education* (1951).

Bibliography: *University of Chicago Magazine* (Nov. 1967). [S.Z.L.]

LEVI, EUGENIO (1876–1966), Italian literary critic and essayist. Born in Milan, Levi taught languages and literature for many years in state schools. When he was forced to leave them as a result of Mussolini's anti-Semitic laws, he moved to the Milan Jewish high school, where he exerted a strong influence on his pupils. Until 1938 he taught Arabic at various colleges, including the Philological Institute and the Colonial High School. After World War II he also taught at the Sally Mayer College of Semitic Studies (1951–60), and was from 1960 honorary dean of Milan's Jewish schools.

His vast cultural curiosity and breadth of knowledge led Levi to the writing of essays—a literary genre in which he excelled. Some of his best studies of the theater and of Italian literature were published in the review *Il Convegno* (1919–1938), which he edited and through which he introduced Italian readers to great contemporary writers of Europe and the United States, such as Joyce, Kafka, Hemingway, and Lorca. He did a great deal of research on the theater, some of which resulted in the prizewinning study *Il Comico di Carattere da Teofrasto a Pirandello* (1959). Other notable works include translations into Italian of Molière's *Tartuffe* (1949), and the *History of World Literature* by Gustav *Karpeles (1906); and the study, *Il lettore inquieto* (1964). Levi dealt with Jewish themes in two essays originally published in the *Rassegna Mensile d'Israel:* "Zangwill e l'Ebraismo" (1955), and "Ricordo di Sabatino Lopez" (1968), and in "Italo Svevo e l'anima ebraica" (*Scritti . . . Sally Mayer*, 1956).

Bibliography: *L'Espresso* (April 12, 1959), 31; *Nuovo corriere della sera* (April 3, 1959); RMI, 32 (1966), 427. [G.R.]

LEVI, GIORGIO RENATO (1895–1965), Italian physical chemist. Born in Ferrara, Levi during World War I worked at a dynamite factory and remained in industry until 1921. He was appointed assistant professor at the Polytechnic Institute of Milan, and founded a team doing X-ray diffraction. In 1927 he became professor of general chemistry at the University of Milan. Later he was professor at the University of Pavia, but lost his chair when Mussolini applied the Nuremberg Laws to Italian universities. He went to São Paulo, Brazil, where he worked in a commercial research laboratory and was professor of physical and analytical chemistry at the university. His scientific research was on the structure of inorganic crystals, and the preparation and study of hitherto unknown inorganic compounds, some of industrial significance. A street in São Paulo is named after him. [S.A.M.]

LEVI, GIULIO AUGUSTO (1879–), Italian literary critic. Levi, who was born in Turin, was for some time a secondary-school teacher, but later became professor of Italian literature at the University of Florence. In 1926 he was baptized and became a Roman Catholic. Levi was rescued by private individuals and Christian institutions during the anti-Jewish persecution of the Fascist regime and escaped deportation during World War II. As a critic, he mainly devoted himself to an analysis of Leopardi's works and, with his own method of study, deliberately moved away from both positivism and the idealism of Croce. He wrote for several newspapers and journals and his publications appeared throughout the first half of the 20th century. Levi's critical works include *Studi estetici* (1907); *Storia del pensiero di Giacomo Leopardi* (1911); *Il Comico* (1913); *Breve storia dell'estetica e del gusto* (1924); *Giacomo Leopardi* (1931), his best-known study of the poet; *Da Dante al Machiavelli* (1935); and *Vittorio Alfieri* (1950). [L.C.]

LEVI, GIUSEPPE (1872–1965), Italian neuroanatomist and histologist. A member of a well-known family of Trieste bankers, Levi in 1910 was appointed professor of human anatomy at Sassari, Sardinia. In 1915 he moved to Palermo, and four years later was made director of the Institute of Human Anatomy of the University of Turin.

Levi's long and brilliant research career centered on microscopic anatomy, particularly of the nerve cell. He laid the foundations of much of our knowledge of the factors that determine the size of sensory and motor neurons. He was one of the pioneers of the technique of tissue culture.

Levi was an outspoken anti-Fascist, and in 1933 was imprisoned for several weeks. In 1938, under Mussolini's racial law, he was removed from his post. He took refuge in Belgium, where he set up a laboratory, but his work was cut short by the German invasion and he returned to Turin. There, although in his seventies, he managed to continue his research and writing clandestinely. At the end of the war he was restored to the directorship of the Institute of Human Anatomy. [M.L.G.]

LEVI, GRAZIADIO DAVID (1816–1898), Italian patriot and poet. Born at Chieri in northern Italy into a wealthy family, Levi studied at the universities of Parma and Pisa and joined *Giovane Italia*, the secret nationalist movement of Giuseppe Mazzini. He worked as a journalist in Switzerland and later in Paris where he associated with Italian patriots and came into contact with Hungarian and Polish nationalists. Levi returned to Italy to take part in the revolution of 1848. He supported the Sardinian king against the Austrians, contrary to Mazzini's republican policy of opposition to all monarchies. In 1860 following the unification of Italy he was elected to the Italian assembly as a liberal representative. He fought for equal rights and religious freedom until his defeat in 1879. Levi wrote many poems and war songs including a satire on Pope Pius IX and war songs for Garibaldi's brigades. His romantic dramas include *Il Profeta* (2 parts, 1866–84), an allegorical work based on the story of Jeremiah. All his works were imbued with the spirit of 19th-century European liberalism with which he equated the ethical values of Judaism.

Bibliography: S. H. Margulies, *Dichter und Patriot* (1896) [J.B.S.]

LEVI, HERMANN (1839–1900), German conductor. Born at Giessen, the grandson of a rabbi who had been a representative in Napoleon's Sanhedrin. Levi studied music at Leipzig and Paris. From 1872 to 1896 he was court conductor at Munich. Having at first been close to Brahms, Levi gradually drew nearer to *Wagner's circle, and owing to his position as conductor of the Royal Munich Opera Orchestra, he conducted the premiere of *Parsifal* at Bayreuth in 1882. His relationship with Wagner was marred by the latter's anti-Semitism, and by constant suggestions that Levi submit to baptism because of the Christian implications of *Parsifal*. A composer as well as a conductor, Levi

Portrait of Hermann Levi, 19th-century conductor, by F. Lenbach. Jerusalem, J.N.U.L., Schwadron Collection.

wrote songs and a piano concerto. He revised and edited Lorenzo *Da Ponte's librettos to Mozart's operas, thus contributing to a Mozart renaissance in the late 19th century. His interpretations of the works of Mozart, Brahms, Bruckner, and Wagner distinguished Levi as one of the greatest conductors of his time. In Munich, he acted as unofficial musical adviser to the city's synagogue; he composed a work for the inauguration of the Mannheim synagogue and a *Ve-shamru* for the cantor of Giessen.

Bibliography: E. von Possart, *Erinnerungen an Hermann Levi* (1901); J. Stern, in: *Zeitschrift fuer die Geschichte der Juden*, 7 (1970), 17–25, incl. bibl.; MGG, incl. bibl.; Grove, Dict, incl. bibl.; Riemann-Einstein; Riemann-Gurlitt, incl. bibl.; Baker, Biog Dict, incl. bibl.; Sendrey, Music, nos. 5313–15, 3096. [J.Co.]

LEVI (Bet ha-Levi), ISAAC (II) BEN SOLOMON (II; d.c. 1621/31), halakhist, preacher, kabbalist, and leader of the Jewish community in Salonika from 1610 to 1620. From 1573 to 1600 he studied in the yeshivah of the Évora congregation of Salonika. When his father died he was forced out of the yeshivah, and he was even denied access to his father's works. He moved to the Provencal congregation of the city in 1601, where he established a yeshivah which he headed. Greatly influenced by his father, he was profoundly affected by his death as well as those of other members of his family (1600–05). According to David Conforte (Kore, 44a), Isaac was head of the yeshivah Eẓ Ḥayyim. In 1620–21 his family home was burned and many of his books and manuscripts were destroyed (though some have been preserved). Nothing is known of him afterward. His signature appears on the *haskamot* ("resolutions") of the rabbis and leaders of Salonika from 1614–18. His responsa, which contain some novellae, are preserved in manuscript. Some were published in the works of his contemporaries and relatives (R. Ḥayyim Shabbetai; Jacob, Abraham, and Solomon Bet ha-*Levi). All of them praise his extensive knowledge. From his responsa it is evident that he studied Kabbalah and his contemporaries attest his piety and emphasize his talents as a preacher. He wrote introductions, provided indices, and added poems to the *Ḥeshek Shelomo*, his father's commentary to the Book of Isaiah.

Bibliography: Solomon le-Bet ha-Levi, *Ḥeshek Shelomo* (Salonika, 1600); Ch. Hirschensohn, in: *Hamisderonah*, 2 (1888), 219–23, 340–3; A. Danon, in: *Yerushalayim*, ed. by A. M. Luncz, 7 (1906–07), 351–4; A. Z. Schwarz, *Die hebraeischen Handschriften in Oesterreich* (1931), 71–74, no. 96; I. R. Molho and A. Amarijlio, in: *Sefunot*, 2 (1958), 45–51; I. S. Emmanuel, *Maẓẓevot Saloniki*, 1 (1963), 232–3, no. 527. [Jos.H.]

LÉVI, ISRAEL (1856–1939), chief rabbi of France, scholar, and writer. Lévi graduated from the Ecole Rabbinique in his native Paris. He was appointed assistant rabbi in Paris in 1882, and began teaching Jewish history at the Ecole Rabbinique in 1892 and Talmud and rabbinic literature at the Ecole Pratique des Hautes Etudes in 1896. When the Société des Etudes Juives was founded in 1880, Lévi became its secretary. In 1886 he was appointed editor of the **Revue des Etudes Juives*. He participated in the publication of the French Bible translation, the so-called "Bible du Rabbinat" (2 vols., 1899–1906), which was edited by his father-in-law Zadoc *Kahn and Julien Weill (1906). From 1919 to 1938 Lévi served as chief rabbi of the French central Consistoire.

Lévi's contributions to modern Jewish scholarship covered a wide range, from Bible, Apocrypha, Talmud, and Midrash to liturgy and history—that of the Jews of France in particular. He was a regular contributor to learned periodicals, especially the *Revue des Etudes Juives*, where he also proved himself an expert and painstaking reviewer of almost every publication in the field of Jewish and Hebrew scholarship. Lévi's approach to biblical and talmudic research was without dogmatic prejudice, but he shied away from the radicalism of the higher and lower Bible criticism (cf. his study on the Nash papyrus, in REJ, 46 (1903),

212–7). His main published works include: *Le Roman d'Alexandre* (1887); *L'Ecclesiastique* ... (1898–1901; *The Hebrew Text of the Book of Ecclesiasticus*, 1904); *Le Péché originel dans les anciennes sources juives* (1907); and *Histoire des Juifs de France* (1903). On the occasion of his 70th birthday, Lévi was honored by the publication of "Mélanges offerts à Israël Lévi" (in REJ, 86 (1926), 9–29, incl. bibl.).

Israel Lévi, chief rabbi of France. Jerusalem, J.N.U.L., Schwadron Collection.

Bibliography: J. Miklishanski, in: S. Federbusch (ed.), *Ḥokhmat Yisrael be-Ma'arav Eiropah*, 1 (1958), 297–309. [J.K.M.]

LEVI (Bet ha-Levi), JACOB BEN ISRAEL (second half of 16th century–1636), halakhist and scholar. A member of the famous Bet ha-*Levi family, Jacob grew up in Salonika, where he studied in the local yeshivot. He studied *halakhah* with R. Aaron ibn Ḥasson and philosophy with R. David ibn Shushan (see his approbation (*haskamah*) to the *Sefer Illem* of 1629). He moved from Salonika to Xanthe, where he served as rabbi of the town and its environs, and then went to Venice. Jacob became famous for his responsa (1612; complete edition, Venice, 1632–34), and his sermons and translation of the Koran are extant in manuscript. He translated the Koran from Arabic "to a Christian language [Latin?] and from the latter into the holy tongue." In Italy he was apparently an affluent businessman who established close contact with the authorities, apparently as a result of his intellectual attainments. The great rabbis of Salonika, Greece, and Italy of the early 17th century gave their endorsements to his responsa, and answered the halakhic queries which he addressed to them. Some of his responsa appear in the works of these rabbis, and similarly, his approbations to several books printed in Italy and elsewhere have been published.

Bibliography: Solomon (II) le-Bet ha-Levi, Responsa (Salonika, 1652), OḤ, no. 8; A. Figo, *Binah la-Ittim* (Venice, 1648), 191–3; *Literaturblatt des Orients*, 2 (1841), 606–7; Steinschneider, Cat Bod, 1221, no. 5550. [Jos.H.]

LEVI, JOSHUA JOSEPH BEN DAVID (c. 1700), Venetian Hebrew poet. His elegies on the death of various contemporaries are all distinguished by their excellent style. Among those lamented are: Moses *Zacuto, Abraham Ẓemaḥ (a lamentation for both in 24 octaves, 1692?), Samuel *Aboab (1694?) and Mose Merari. Joshua Joseph's best-known piece is *Kos Tanḥumim* (Venice, 1707), being an elegy on Mose Levi Muggia, part of which was republished by J. Schirmann in his anthology (1934). A prose introduction and a sonnet by Levi are printed in Samson *Morpurgo's *Eẓ ha-Da'at* (Venice, 1704, p.37a–b).

Bibliography: A. Coen, *Saggio di Eloquenza Ebrea*, 1 (1827), 41–3; Ghirondi-Neppi, 171–3, no. 72; Steinschneider, Cat Bod, 1555; Schirmann, Italyah, 342–6; Davidson, Oẓar, 4 (1933), 392. [J.H.Sch.]

LEVI, MARIO GIACOMO (1878–1955), Italian chemist. Born in Padua, Levi worked there until 1906, when he moved to the University of Pisa. In 1909 he became professor of technological chemistry at the University of Palermo, Sicily, and in 1919 was appointed the first director of the Higher Institute for Commercial and Colonial Studies. In 1927 Levi went to Milan as professor of industrial chemistry at the Polytechnic. When Mussolini introduced legislation against Jews in the professions in 1938, he went to live in Lausanne, Switzerland. An Italian patriot, Levi played an important role in the development of his country's chemical industry. His contributions to technical and scientific journals included papers on the Deacon chlorine process, hyposulfites, fuels, the noble gases, radioactivity, electrochemistry, nonaqueous solvents, and catalysis.

Bibliography: J. C. Poggendorff, *Biographisch-literarisches Handwoerterbuch*, 5 (1926), s.v.; 6 (1938), s.v.; *Chimica e Industria* (then *Notiziario Chimico-industriale*), 2 (1927), 4–5. [S.A.M.]

LEVI, PAOLO (1919–), Italian playwright. Born in Genoa, Levi began his career as a dramatic critic, contributing to various Italian and foreign reviews. After spending tne years 1944–46 in Brazil, he returned to Rome where he wrote plays for radio and television and a number of dramas, beginning with *Anna e il telefono* (1951). Levi made his name both in Italy and overseas with *Legittima difesa* (1952; publ. in *Teatro-Scenario*, no. 3, 1952). His later successes included *Scaccomatto* (1953; publ. in *Teatro-Scenario*, no. 11, 1953), *La Fiera* (1956; publ. in *Ridotto*, Feb. 1958), *Il gioco è fatto* (1957), and *Lastrico d'inferno* (1959). Levi's favorite theme—the problems besetting the individual—also dominates *Come per scherzo* (1955), *I Nemici* (1955), and *Il Caso Pinedus* (1954; publ. in *Teatro-Scenario*, no. 2, 1955). *Gli dei di pietra* was staged in Dortmund, Germany, as *Die steinernen Goetter* (1958). Levi won an award for his radio plays in 1952 and codirected several Italian motion pictures during the 1950s.

Bibliography: S. d'Amica, *Palcoscenici del dopoguerra*, 2 (1953), 293–5. [Ed.]

LEVI, PAUL (1883–1930), German socialist politician. A lawyer by profession Levi gained renown by his defense of striking workers (1912) and of Rosa *Luxemburg (1914), who became his mentor and colleague. Levi was one of the founders and leaders of the "Spartacus League," the nucleus of the emerging Communist Party (1919) of which he became the leader, inheriting Luxemburg's mantle. He succeeded in outmaneuvering anti-parliamentary and insurrectionary elements, consolidating the party and substantially increasing its membership. His own position was undermined by his opposition to the interference of the Comintern in German affairs and he resigned from the central committee in February 1921. In March, the party, on Moscow's orders fomented an armed uprising in Saxony which was quelled with much bloodshed. Paul Levi publicly denounced the tactics and methods of the leadership and was expelled from the party. He thereupon formed, with his

Paul Levi, German socialist politician. Jerusalem, J.N.U.L., Schwadron Collection.

adherents, an independent Communist fraction in the Reichstag (parliament) but eventually returned to the fold of the Social Democratic Party where he was leader of its left wing. A collection of Levi's speeches, letters, and essays was edited by C. Beradt and appeared in 1969, *Zwischen Spartakus und Sozialdemokratie.*

Bibliography: W. T. Angress, *Stillborn Revolution* (1963), index.
[Ed.]

LEVI, PRIMO (1919–), Italian author. Levi, who trained as a chemist, was born in Turin. His first book, *Se questo è un uomo?* (1947; *If This is a Man,* 1959), described the Auschwitz extermination camp to which he had been deported by the Nazis in 1944. In 1961 it reappeared under the title *Survival in Auschwitz: the Nazi Assault on Humanity.* In *La Tregua* (1963; *The Truce,* 1965; U.S. ed., *The Reawakening,* 1965), he told of his wanderings and adventures on the return journey to Italy at the end of World War II, when he also traveled through Soviet Russia. Levi broadened his scope in *Storie naturali* (1966), moralistic and fantastic tales published under the pseudonym of Damianos Malabaila.

Bibliography: *Dizionario enciclopedico della letteratura italiana,* 3 (1967), 383; I. Calvino, in: *L'Unità* (May 6, 1948); A. Cajumi, in: *La Stampa* (Nov. 26, 1957).
[Ed.]

LEVI, SAID BEN SHALOM (d. 1917), educator and writer; known as **"Ḥakham Said."** One of the first Yemenite immigrants to Ereẓ Israel, Levi settled in Jaffa in 1888, where he became a teacher in the *talmud torah* Torah Or. From the diary of his school, which is extant, one learns of the modern educational methods which he attempted to adopt. In 1889 he left for Algiers as the emissary of the Sephardim. He was also the secretary of the Yemenite workers' union *Pe'ullat Sakhir,* whose objective was to employ Jewish rather than Arab labor in the settlements. He was a gifted writer and he had an exceptionally fine Hebrew style. His diary of World War I, which relates the sufferings of the *yishuv* during the war, is also extant.

Bibliography: Y. Ratzaby, in: *Shivat Ẓiyyon,* 2–3 (1953), 404–25.
[Y.R.]

LEVI, SHABBETAI (1876–1956), mayor of Haifa. Born in Constantinople, he settled in Ereẓ Israel in 1894. There he first taught at Petaḥ Tikvah and later became one of the Baron de *Rothschild's officials in *PICA. He assisted land reclamation projects throughout the country, including Transjordan, and attempted to establish good relations between the Jewish colonies and neighboring Arab villages. Levi represented the *yishuv* and the inhabitants of Haifa in dealings with the authorities during World War I. A founder of the first Hebrew school in Haifa and of the city's Reali school and *Technion, he was also instrumental in the development of Mount Carmel and the suburbs in Haifa Bay. From 1919 he was a councillor on the mixed Arab-Jewish Haifa Municipality; in 1934 he became deputy mayor of Haifa and in 1940 became the first Jewish mayor of the city, a post he held until 1951.

Bibliography: Tidhar, 2 (1947), 901–2.
[A.A.]

LEVI (Bet ha-Levi), SOLOMON (II) BEN ISAAC (1532–1600), rabbi, commentator, author, and community leader. Solomon was a member of the Bet ha-*Levi family which originated from Portugal. He was born in Salonika. His life and activity can be divided into two main periods. During the first period, until approximately 1568, supported by his wealthy father, he was able to devote himself to study and to writing. He studied Talmud and codes in the yeshivah of Joseph ibn *Lev in Salonica, and secular studies and philosophy from private teachers. He gained a proficiency in various languages, and when only 13 years of age, composed a dialogue in Spanish. He seems also to have had a knowledge of Latin. At about the age of 30 he began to study Kabbalah. He married in 1553; two of his sons, Isaac (II) b. Solomon *Levi (Bet ha-Levi) and Joseph, and a daughter, who married Aaron *Sasson, are known. He wrote commentaries to various books of the Bible (including *Ḥeshek Shelomo,* on Isaiah, Salonika, 1600), on *Avot* (*Lev Avot,* Salonika 1565), and on the *aggadot* of the Talmud (*Leḥem Shelomo,* Venice, 1597). The draft of a work on geography, and one dealing with the genealogy and position of the levites, talmudic novellae, and many of his poems, are still extant in manuscript. He wrote more than 20 works and commentaries on many aspects of Jewish studies.

During the second period, from 1568, he was appointed rabbi of Üsküb (Skoplje), Yugoslavia, and devoted himself assiduously to community affairs there. In c. 1571, after his father's death, he returned to Salonika where he was appointed rabbi to the Provençal congregation. Two years later his rabbinate was extended to include that of the Évora congregation, one of the most prestigious in Salonika. He served as rabbi of both these congregations as well as head of the Évora congregation's yeshivah until his death. He delivered sermons (some of which were published in *Divrei Shelomo,* Venice, 1596) which attracted a large attendance, including the notable members of the congregations, and his name appears as a signatory on the *haskamot* ("resolutions") signed by the religious leaders of the community. He also wrote responsa to communities in Greece and throughout the Balkans (some of which are still preserved in manuscript). He wrote up talmudic novellae on topics which had evolved from the studies in the yeshivah and wrote marginal notes on such works as the *Arba'ah Turim,* the *Midrash Rabbah,* etc. Toward the end of his life, at his sons' urging, he began to collect and edit his writings, but died before he could finish.

Solomon was an unusual person who was imbued with a sense of mission. He possessed comprehensive knowledge, a fine style, and rhetorical ability, and was a dynamic personality. A man of considerable wealth, he consciously regarded himself as a communal leader, but on more than one occasion went out of his way to defend the community against wealthy members and various leaders who attempted, in his opinion, to exploit their positions in their own interests. He had a large library both of printed works and manuscripts, some on parchment (many of which have been preserved). His ramified, scholarly, and honored family basked in the light of his patriarchal figure. His influence in Salonika was inestimable, and his contemporaries referred to him with veneration. They accorded him the title of "the great rabbi," "the chief rabbi." Solomon regarded communal leadership as the duty of scholars, and his writings reveal that he was alive to the local and contemporary conditions. One can detect in his writings the changes and development which took place in his personality, especially in his subsequent editing and amendments of his earlier works. His great vitality and his multifaceted personality reveal an encyclopedist, the product of a superb education. These qualities made possible and brought about his great influence on his surroundings from his youth. Combined with his independent means they made it possible for him to become one of the outstanding leaders of Salonika Jewry in the 16th century.

Bibliography: A. Geiger (ed.), *Melo Ḥofnayim* (1840), 22 (Heb. part); J. Reifmann, in: *Ha-Maggid,* 3 (1859), 151; E. Carmoly, in: *Ben Chananja,* 5 (1862), 67; Steinschneider, Cat Bod, 2363, no. 6944; idem, Uebersetzungen, 88, 110–1, 228; D. Pipano, in: Abraham le-Bet ha-Levi, *Ein Mishpat* (1897), introd.; Rosanes, Togarmah, 2 (1937–8), 108–10; I. S. Emmanuel, *Histoire des Israélites de Salonique* (1936), 188–91; idem, *Maẓẓevot Saloniki,* 1

(1963), 178–9, no. 407; J. Hacker, in: *Zion*, 34 (1969), 43–89; idem, in: *Tarbiz*, 39 (1970), 195–213. [Jos.H.]

LEVI (Bet ha-Levi), SOLOMON (III) BEN ISAAC (II) (1581–1634), rabbi of Salonika and one of the greatest halakhists and writers of responsa of his time. The grandson of Solomon (II) b. Isaac, Solomon engaged in teaching and writing from his youth. He served as head of the *bet din* of the Évora congregation in Salonika in 1631 and was head of the yeshivah of the congregation Eẓ Ḥayyim. A man of many talents, he was well known as a preacher and a poet, and he also wrote talmudic novellae. Of his works there have survived his responsa (published posthumously by his widow; Salonika, 1652), some correspondence, poems, and *haskamot*. Solomon studied at the home of his grandfather and his father as well as under Ḥayyim Shabbetai, whom he revered (he was a member of his *bet din*). He maintained close connections with his relatives of the Aaron *Sasson family, even after they moved to Constantinople. Part of his correspondence with Sasson has been published by Hirschensohn (see bibl.) and that with his father-in-law Tam ibn Yaḥya is still in manuscript. From his youth, Solomon was active in the scholarly life in Salonika, and had many disciples. His responsa and approbations appear in the responsa collections of his contemporaries. His works received the approbations of the great rabbis of Salonika and the surrounding communities, while others addressed their halakhic queries to him. He was deeply involved in the charitable needs both of Salonika Jewry and of institutions in Ereẓ Israel, and elsewhere, and several of the appeals addressed to him are still extant.

Bibliography: Conforte, Kore, 46b; E. Carmoly, *Divrei ha-Yamim li-Venei Yaḥyah* (1850), 40–41; Ch. Hirschensohn, in: *Hamisderonah*, 2 (1888), 161, 190–2, 219–23; A. Danon, in: *Yerushalayim*, ed. by A. M. Luncz (1906–07), 351–4; idem, in: REJ, 41 (1900), 104–5; 257–8, 260–1; M. Wallenstein, in: *Melilah*, 1 (1944), 55, 2 (1946), 138–40; M. Molho, in: *Sinai*, 28 (1950–51), 312–4; I. S. Emmanuel, *Maẓẓevot Saloniki*, 1 (1963), 262–3, no. 599. [Jos.H.]

LÉVI, SYLVAIN (1863–1935), French orientalist, born in Paris. Lévi, known for his *Etude critique sur le théatre indien* (1890), became professor of Sanskrit at the College of France (1894), and later director of the Institute of Indian

Sylvain Lévi, French orientalist. Jerusalem, J.N.U.L., Schwadron Collection.

Studies at the Sorbonne (1904). He published *Le Népal, étude historique d'un royaume hindou* (3 vols., 1905–08); *L'Inde et le monde* (1926); and a study on the Jews in South India (in REJ, 89 (1930), 26–32). Lévi founded the French School of the Far East in Hanoi, and later directed the French-Japanese Institute in Tokyo (1926-28). After his return to France he was elected mayor of Andilly, near Paris. He also joined the Zionist Commission headed by Chaim *Weizmann, and set up discussions with the Allied delegations at the Versailles Peace Conference (1919). He left the commission, however, contending that the Zionist program for Palestine opposed French interests in the Middle East. From 1920 until his death Lévi served as president of the Central Committee of the *Alliance Israélite Universelle and of the Société d'Etudes Juives.

Bibliography: *Hommage à Sylvain Lévi* . . . (1964); C. Weizmann, *Trial and Error* (1949), 267, 304–6. [L.L.]

LEVI, TESTAMENT OF, an ancient Jewish pseudepigraphical work written in Aramaic, probably before 100 the Twelve *Patriarchs, the work referred to in the C.E. A source of the Testament of Levi is the Testaments of Damascus Document of the Dead Sea sect (4:15). Prior to the discovery of the Dead Sea Scrolls, large fragments of a medieval manuscript, containing the Aramaic original, were found in the Cairo *Genizah* and published. New Aramaic fragments, not all of which have been published, were found among the Dead Sea Scrolls. In a Greek tenth-century manuscript of the Testament of the Patriarchs from Mt. Athos, two larger interpolations in the Testament of Levi can be identified as parts of a Greek translation of the present work; a small Syriac fragment also exists. The Aramaic Testament of Levi is put in the mouth of Levi, the son of Jacob, and represents probably his last speech to his descendants. In the extant fragments, Levi talks about his previous life, and about his function as high priest at Beth-El when he was consecrated by angels. The work contains prescriptions about offerings. These moral and ritual prescriptions are explained to Levi by Isaac his grandfather. Levi's prayer is an important document for the history of Jewish prayers.

This work, abbreviated and rewritten, formed a central source of the Greek Testament of Levi. It is ultimately related to Jubilees chapters 20–22. The Aramaic Testament of Levi contained ideas similar to the Book of Jubilees, the Testaments of the Patriarchs, and the Dead Sea sect. Common to all is the idea, expressed in one fragment of the present work from Qumran, that "priesthood is greater than kingdom," i.e., that Levi is superior to Judah. The Aramaic Testament of Levi was produced within a broader movement in ancient Judaism, from which the Dead Sea sect arose.

Bibliography: H. L. Pass and J. Arendzen, in: JQR, 12 (1900), 651–61; R. H. Charles and A. Cowley, *ibid.*, 19 (1907), 566–83; R. H. Charles, *Greek Versions of the Testaments of the Twelve Patriarchs* (1908); P. Grelot, in: REJ, 114 (1955), 91–99; D. Barthélemy and J. T. Milik, *Discoveries in the Judaean Desert*, 1 (1955), 87–91; J. T. Milik, *Ten Years of Discovery in the Wilderness of Judaea* (1959), 34; idem, in: RB, 62 (1955), 398–406; D. Flusser, in: IEJ, 16 (1966), 194–205. [D.Fl.]

LEVIAS, CASPAR (1860–1934), U.S. orientalist and lexicographer. Born in Zagare, Lithuania, Levias studied and was a fellow in the department of oriental languages of Columbia University (1893–94) and in the department of semitic languages of Johns Hopkins University (1894–95). From 1895 to 1905 he was an instructor of Semitic languages at Hebrew Union College, and from 1910 to 1920 he served as principal of the Plaut Memorial Hebrew Free School in Newark, New Jersey. An ardent Zionist, he devoted much time to the propagation of modern Hebrew literature, and together with R. *Brainin and I. *Schapiro he edited and published the literary journal *Ha-Deror*. His main interest, however, was Semitic philology and grammar, about which he contributed numerous articles to scholarly journals. His chief works were the pioneer study *A Grammar of the Aramaic Idiom Contained in the Babylonian*

Talmud (1900), and a Hebrew book on the same subject, *Dikduk Aramit Bavlit* (1930). Only two parts of his *Oẓar Ḥokhmat ha-Lashon*, a study of Hebrew philology, were ever published (1914–15), and a lexicon compiled by him of medical terms in Hebrew literature never appeared at all.

Bibliography: Kressel, Leksikon, 2 (1967), 191. [Ed.]

LEVIATHAN (Heb. לִוְיָתָן, *livyatan*, Ugaritic *ltn*, presumably pronounced *lōtan*). In the Bible and talmudic literature the leviathan denotes various marine animals, some real, others legendary, and others again both real and legendary. The word leviathan seems to derive from the root *lwy*, "to coil," which is further confirmation of its serpentine form. In the Bible it is used interchangeably with several other sea monsters—*tannin* ("dragon"), *rahav*, and *yam* ("sea"; of which the last-named alternates with *neharim* ("flood") in Hab. 3:8)—all of whom are represented as supernatural enemies of God. This hostility directly reflects a myth widely known in pre-biblical sources of a primordial combat between the creator deity and the forces of the sea, personifying chaos, which the former must overcome to create and control the universe (see *Creation). The Hittites knew it as the struggle between the dragon Illuyankas and the mortal Hupasiyas (Pritchard, Texts, 125–6). In Mesopotamia it appears in several forms, of which the most famous is the battle of Marduk and Tiamat in the creation epic (*ibid.*). More relevant is a cylinder seal from Tell Asmar of the 24th century B.C.E., which pictures two men fighting a seven-headed serpent. And recently, the leviathan itself may have been found in a Mesopotamian incantation designed "to revive a serpent" (see van Dijk in bibliography). The closest Near Eastern parallel to the biblical materials, however, and probably their actual source, is the Ugaritic myth(s) of Baal and Anat pitted against various sea monsters, one of which is named Lotan (Pritchard, op. cit.). Not only is this merely another form of the name leviathan, but the same epithets used of leviathan are here prefigured of Lotan, e.g., *btn brḥ* and *btn ʿqltn* as compared with *naḥash bariah* and *naḥash ʿaqallaton* of Isaiah 27:1. [P.Ma.]

In Bible and Talmud. In the Bible Leviathan is a multi-headed (Ps. 74:14) sea serpent, appearing in Isaiah 27:1; Psalms 74:14; 104:26; Job 3:8, and 41:1ff. The detailed description in Job (40:25–32) applies to the *crocodile, although a rabbi, maintaining that the reference is to the leviathan—the legendary animal prepared for the righteous in the hereafter—concludes that "the leviathan is a permitted fish," and regards its *maginnim* (Job 41:7)

Figure 1. The leviathan depicted with the *shor ha-bar* in a folk-art picture from Poland, 19th century. R. Lilientalowa, *Śweita Zydowskie w Przesziośei I Terazniejszosci*, Cracow, 1908.

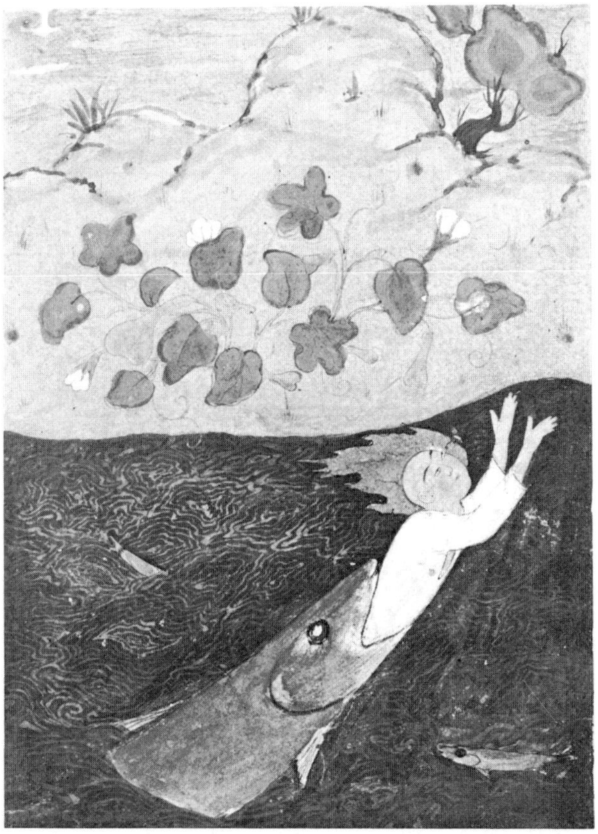

Figure 2. The great fish of the Jonah saga, one of the sea monsters traditionally associated with the leviathan. Turkish miniature from *Qisas al-Anbiya* by Ishaq al-Nashapuri, c. 1560. Dublin, Chester Beatty Library, Ms. 231, fol. 156.

as scales, one of the characteristics of a permitted fish (Tosef., Ḥul. 3:27). On the other hand, *tannin*, which generally denotes the crocodile, sometimes applies to the whale, as would appear from Genesis 1:21. The verse: "Even the *tannin* [*keri: tannim*] draw out the breast, they give suck to their young ones" (Lam. 4:3) may refer to the whale, the female of which suckles its young (according to another view, the reference is to the *jackal). The whale is intended in the literal meaning of the verse describing the great sea: "There go the ships; there is leviathan, whom Thou hast formed to sport therein" (Ps. 104:26). At times the long-headed whale (*Physeter catodon*), which is as much as 20 meters (about 65 ft.) long and feeds on large fish and even sharks, reaches the shores of Israel. This may be the basis of the biblical story about "a great fish" that swallowed Jonah (2:1). On rare occasions the largest of the whales, *Sibbaldus* (*Balaenoptera*) *musculus*, appears off the Israel coast after entering the Mediterranean through the Straits of Gibraltar.

By *tannin* and leviathan the Bible also intends animals which "in days of old" are said to have rebelled against the Creator, Who thereupon destroyed them (Ps. 74:13–14; cf. Isa. 51:10; Job 3:8; 7:12)—similar to the Ugaritic legends mentioned above. Relics of the bones or footprints of prehistoric reptiles may have been found by the ancients (such footprints have been discovered at Bet Zayit in the vicinity of Jerusalem) and these may have served as grounds for the legend of the destruction of these gigantic creatures. Some of these verses were used as a basis for the well-known *aggadah* about the leviathan and the *shor ha-bar* ("the wild ox") intended for the righteous in the hereafter. The passage: "There is leviathan, whom Thou hast formed to sport with" has been homiletically interpreted to mean that God sports with the leviathan (Av. Zar. 3b), while the descriptions of the *behemoth and the leviathan in Job (40:15–41:26) have been construed as referring to the fight between these animals, after which the Almighty will prepare from them a feast for the righteous (BB, 74b–75a; Lev. R. 13:3; 22:10). This struggle is picturesquely depicted in the **Akdamut*, the Aramaic *piyyut* which is said on Pentecost and which describes the great reward in store for the righteous. In later popular works the words leviathan and *shor ha-bar* became synonyms for the reward of the righteous in the world to come. [J.F.]

Bibliography: I. Broydé and K. Kohler, in: JE, 8 (1904), 37–39; H. Wallace, in: BA, 11 (1948), 61–68; T. H. Gaster, in: IDB, 1 (1962), 708; 3 (1962), 116; M. D. Cassuto, in: EM, 4 (1962), 485–6; C. H. Gordon, in: A. Altmann (ed.), *Biblical Motifs* (1966), 1–9; J. van Dijk, in: *Orientalia*, 38 (1969), 541; Lewysohn, Zool, 155–8 (nos. 178–80), 355 (no. 505); H. L. Ginsberg, *Kitvei Ugarit* (1936); M. D. Cassuto, *Ha-Elah Anat* (1953²); J. Feliks, *Animal World of the Bible* (1962), 51, 94, 108; Gutman, in: HUCA, 39 (1968), 219–30.

LEVI BEN ABRAHAM BEN ḤAYYIM (c. 1245–c. 1315), French philosopher, whose teachings were the focus of the anti-philosophical controversy which raged among Jews in Provence and Catalonia between 1303 and 1305. Levi b. Abraham was born at Villefranche-de-Conflent. Persecuted by the opponents of philosophy, Levi was forced to wander from place to place, and was poverty-stricken throughout his life. In 1276 he lived in Montpellier, in 1295, in Arles, and in 1303, in Perpignan, in the home of Samuel of Escalita. The latter, influenced by the reproaches directed against philosophy by Solomon b. Abraham *Adret during this period, and seeing a divine punishment in the death of his daughter, drove Levi out of his house. Levi then sought refuge at the home of his relative Samuel b. Reuben of Beziers, where he remained for a time. In 1314 he was in Arles, where he apparently died soon after.

Levi is the author of two works: (1) *Battei ha-Nefesh ve-ha-Leḥashim* (a title derived from Isa. 3:20), an encyclopedia of medieval science and philosophy, in rhymed prose, written in Montpellier in 1276 (Paris, Ms. héb. no. 978). It is composed of ten chapters of varying length, dealing with ethics, logic, *ma'aseh bereshit* (see *Kabbalah), the soul, prophecy, *ma'aseh merkavah* (the "divine throne-chariot," see *Merkabah Mysticism), mathematics, astronomy, astrology, physics, metaphysics. I. Davidson published the first section of this work together with an anonymous commentary in *Yedi'ot ha-Makhon le-Ḥeker ha-Shirah ha-Ivrit* (vol. 5 (1939), 2–42), and the seventh section in *Scripta Mathematica* (vol. 4 (1936), 57–65). (2) *Livyat Ḥen*, another encyclopedic work composed of diverse scientific treatises. Divided into six parts, the work seems to have been extant in a long and short version. Fragments of the first five parts of both the long and short versions have been preserved, and so have more lengthy fragments of the sixth section, entitled "Boaz." Of the short version the following sections have been preserved: a section on astronomy consisting of 49 chapters (Paris, Ms. héb. no. 1047, fols. 174v–220v), a section on the purpose of metaphysics (Oxford, Ms. Mich. no. 519, fols. 1–17), and fragments of the sixth section, "Boaz" (*ibid.*, fols. 1–127v). Of the long version a section on astrology has been preserved, corresponding to chapter 40 of the short version on astronomy (Paris, Ms. héb. no. 1066, fols. 1–106v), a section on metaphysics (*ibid.*, no. 1050, fols. 60–65), as well as fragments of the sixth section (de' Rossi, Ms. no. 1346, fols. 1–194; Vatican, Ms. héb. 192, fols. 1–147; no. 298, fols. 27–37v).

The fragments of the sixth section, which are lengthier than those of the rest of the work, provide a fairly detailed picture of Levi's views. This section deals with the Bible, the mysteries of faith, *ma'aseh bereshit*, *ma'aseh merkavah*, and *aggadah*. Adopting the methodology of *Maimonides, Levi uses allegorical exegesis extensively in his attempt to reconcile various biblical and talmudic passages with philosophical doctrines. For example, he interpreted the figures of Abraham and Sarah as representatives of form and matter, and the flood as a psychological upheaval that takes place in the soul of man. It was mainly for his allegorical exposition that Levi was criticized. His contemporaries claimed that in interpreting the Bible allegorically he was negating the literal meaning of the Torah. Levi himself protested that he was not negating the literal meaning but finding additional levels of meaning in the text. In the *Livyat Ḥen* one finds many of the allegorical interpretations that Abba Mari *Astruc attacked in his *Minḥat Kena'ot* (1838), but actually Levi's interpretations are no more extreme than those found in the *Guide of the Perplexed* by Maimonides, *Ma'amar Yikkavu ha-Mayim* by Samuel ibn *Tibbon, or *Malmad ha-Talmidim* by Jacob b. Abba Mari *Anatoli.

Like most of the medieval philosophers after Maimonides, Levi agrees with *Averroes on many points, going so far as to accept even his belief in the eternity of the world. Like Maimonides, Levi maintains that the role of the revealed law is to help men acquire moral virtues and to ensure social harmony. He also believes that man's happiness is dependent on the level of his intellectual development, as is the degree of divine *providence accorded him. Levi bases his theory of prophecy on that of Maimonides, but follows Abraham *ibn Ezra in his interpretation of miracles. Like Ibn Ezra, he believes in astrology, although he does not utilize it as much in the long version as in the short version of the work.

While Levi was not an original thinker, his writings are particularly representative of the philosophy of his time. Examination of his philosophical doctrines gives no clue as to why he was the object of such violent opposition. Perhaps it was the encyclopedic nature of his work that seemed so particularly dangerous. It also appears that in his oral instruction Levi was less careful than other philosophers.

Bibliography: Guttmann, Philosophies, 212, 222; Halkin, in: PAAJR, 34 (1966), 65–76; Renan, Rabbins, 628–74; I. Davidson, in: REJ, 105 (1940), 80–94; C. Sirat, *ibid.*, 122 (1963), 167–77; Baeck, in: MGWJ, 44 (1900), 24–41, 59–71, 156–67, 337–44, 417–23.

[C.S.]

LEVI BEN GERSHOM (1288–1344; acronym: **RaLBaG**; also called **Maestre Leo de Bagnols; Magister Leo Hebraeus; Gersonides**), mathematician, astronomer, philosopher, and biblical commentator, born probably at Bagnols-sur-Cèze (Languedoc—now département du Gard, France). He lived primarily in Orange and briefly at Avignon. Little is known about his life beyond the fact that he maintained relations with important Christian persons. Levi had very broad intellectual interests and contributed to many areas of human learning.

Scientific Work. The scientific works of Levi deal with arithmetic, geometry, trigonometry, and astronomy.

His first work, written in 1321, the *Sefer Ma'aseh Ḥoshev* or *Sefer ha-Mispar* ("The Book of the Number"; published with a translation in German by G. Lange, 1909) is divided into two parts: principles and applications. The work deals with addition, subtraction, multiplication, series, permutation, combination, division, extraction of roots, and proportion. In 1343, Levi composed a second book on arithmetic for Philip of Vitry, bishop of Meaux. Only the Latin translation of the book has been preserved, under the title *De numeris harmonicis* (published by J. Carlebach, *Lewi ben Gerson als Mathematiker* (1910), 129–44).

In his commentary on Books 1–5 of Euclid, which resembles his commentaries on *Averroes, Levi attempts to construct a geometry without axioms, but, in place of Euclid's axioms, he unwittingly introduces other axioms of his own.

In his important treatise on trigonometry (translated into Latin in 1342 under the title *De sinibus, chordis et arcibus* and dedicated to Pope Clement VI), Levi rediscovered

Title page of "The Book of the Wars of the Lord," the chief work of Levi b. Gershom, Riva di Trento, Italy, 1560. Jerusalem, J.N.U.L.

independently the sine theorem in the case of plane triangles (proportionality of sines to opposite sides); his sine tables are correct to the fifth decimal.

Talmudic and Liturgical Works. A commentary on the 13 hermeneutical rules of R. *Ishmael (printed in Jacob Faitusi, *Sefer Berit Ya'akov*, 1800) has been attributed to Levi as well as a commentary on the *aggadot* of *Bava Batra*, entitled *Meḥokek Ẓafun*. This attribution is probably erroneous. In his commentary on the Pentateuch, Levi reports that he wrote a commentary on the talmudic treatise *Berakhot*, but this commentary is lost. An eminent talmudist, Levi was consulted on questions of *halakhah* (see REJ, 44 (1902), 82–86). A responsum of his can be found in the *She'elot u-Teshuvot* of Isaac de Lattes (1860). Three poems *(pizmonim)* for the holiday of Shavuot and a *viddui* (confession of sins) composed by Levi were published and translated into French by C. Touati (REJ, 117 (1958), 97–105). Levi is also the author of a parody written for the festival of Purim, entitled *Megillat Setarim* ("Scroll of Mysteries").

Commentaries on Aristotle and Averroes. In one of his first philosophical works, *Sefer ha-Hekkesh ha-Yashar* (1319), translated into Latin under the title *Liber syllogismi recti*, Levi corrects certain inaccurate arguments of *Aristotle in his *Posterior Analytics*. Levi became acquainted with Aristotle's views by reading the paraphrases and commentaries of Averroes, and he himself wrote supercommentaries on a number of them: on the paraphrase of the *Physics* (1321), on the middle commentary of the *Physics* (1321), on the paraphrase of the *De generatione et corruptione* (1321), on the paraphrase of the *De caelo* (1321), on the paraphrase of the *Meterologica* (1321), on the middle commentary of the *Organon* (1323), on the paraphrase of the *De animalibus* (1323), on the paraphrase of the *De anima* (1323), on the paraphrase of the *Parva naturalia* (1324), on two questions of Averroes concerning Aristotelian logic, and on the letters concerning the union of the separate intellect with man. The supercommentaries on the middle commentary of the *Metaphysics* and the *De plantibus* have been lost. The supercommentaries of Levi on Averroes exist only in manuscript. The Latin translation by Jacob *Mantino of one section of the supercommentary on the *Organon* was published in volume one of the Venice edition of the works of Aristotle (1550–52).

In his commentaries on Averroes, which are important for understanding his philosophy, Levi paraphrases the text but frequently inserts notes of varying lengths, preceded by the words: *amar Levi* ("Levi says"). In these notes he develops, criticizes, or corrects aspects of the ideas of Aristotle or Averroes. He manifests an independent spirit in relation to the two philosophers. Several passages from commentaries on Averroes appear in H. A. Wolfson, *Crescas' Critique of Aristotle* (1929).

Biblical Commentaries. Levi wrote commentaries on Job (1325), Song of Songs (1325 or 1326), Ecclesiastes (1328), Ruth (1329), Esther (1329), the Pentateuch (1329–38), the Former Prophets (1338), Proverbs, Daniel, Nehemiah, and Chronicles (1338). All of these were published, some in several editions. The commentary on Job is one of the first books to be printed in Hebrew (Ferrara, 1477).

The biblical commentaries of Levi are the work of an exegete and a philosopher. Certain of his literal explanations are still of interest today. Diverse questions of a philosophical or theological nature are discussed by him, such as the problem of providence, miracles, and the Messiah. From each book of the Bible, Levi extracts the ethical, philosophical, and religious teachings that may be gleaned from the text and calls them *to'alot* or *to'aliyyot*. A collection of these *to'aliyyot* was printed separately (Riva di Trento, 1570). In his voluminous commentary on the Pentateuch, Levi attempts to reconstitute the *halakhah* rationally, basing himself on nine logical principles which he substitutes for the traditional 13 *hermeneutical rules, and condemning allegorical interpretations. In the 15th century in Italy, *Judah Messer Leon wanted to prohibit the study of Gersonides' commentary on the Pentateuch, using the pretext that the latter wished to fabricate a new Talmud.

Sefer Milḥamot Adonai. Levi's major work, to which he constantly refers in his commentaries on Averroes and the Bible, is the *Sefer Milḥamot Adonai* ("The Book of the Wars of the Lord"), begun in about 1317 and completed in 1329. In this work, he treats problems which, in his opinion, have not received a satisfactory solution by preceding philosophers, including *Maimonides. Divided into six parts, the work deals with: the immortality of the soul (first book), dream, divination, and prophecy (second book), divine knowledge (third book), providence (fourth book), celestial spheres, separate intellects and their relationship with God (fifth book), the creation of the world, miracles, and the criteria by which one recognizes the true prophet (sixth book). Numerous manuscripts of the *Milḥamot* are extant, but the book was printed only twice, and then imperfectly (Riva di Trento, 1560 and Leipzig, 1863). The first four books of the *Milḥamot* were translated into German with notes by B. Kellerman (*Die Kaempfe Gottes*, 2 vols., 1914–16), but this translation is unreliable. A French translation of books three and four, based on a critical edition together with an introduction and notes, was made by C. Touati (1968).

The *Milḥamot* is written in a precise and technical Hebrew but, like Levi's other works, it is characterized by repetitiveness. In almost all the questions analyzed, Levi quotes the opinions of his predecessors—Aristotle, *Alexander of Aphrodisias, *Themistius, Al-*Farābī, *Avicenna—with whom he became acquainted largely by reading Averroes, as well as the opinions of Averroes himself and of Maimonides. He enumerates the arguments that, respectively, support and disprove their theses and, finally, he expounds his own theory. Though lacking a systematic structure, the *Milḥamot* contains an almost complete system of philosophy and theology. However, this work cannot be understood unless one is familiar with Levi's commentaries on Averroes and the Bible, which explain and complement the *Milḥamot* on many points. In order to understand the ideas of Levi, one should have recourse to all his philosophical and exegetic works.

His Philosophy. GOD. Demonstrating the existence of God, Levi rejects the proof, favored by many of his Aristotelian predecessors, according to which the existence of God, as prime mover, can be derived from the various motions existing in the world. In its place he presents a proof based on the orderly processes existing in the world, that is, an argument from design. According to this proof, the observed regularity of processes of generation within the sublunar world leads to the conclusion that these processes are produced by an intelligence. This intelligence is the so-called agent intellect (see *Intellect) which governs the sublunar world. This intelligence endows matter with its various forms and is aware of the order it produces. The activities of the agent intellect are mediated by the natural heat which is found in the seeds and sperms of plants and animals and this natural heat in turn is produced by the motions of the various celestial spheres. Since these motions contribute to the perfection of the terrestrial world, they must also be produced by intelligences which know them, that is, they are produced by the intelligences of the celestial spheres. From what has been said, it can be seen that the celestial and terrestrial worlds form an ordered, unitary whole and this requires that there exists a supreme being which produces and knows this order. This being is God.

Unlike Maimonides, Levi maintains that it is possible to ascribe positive attributes to God without reducing or changing His absolute unity and simplicity. Admitting that real multiplicity exists only in beings composed of form and matter, he argues that all the predicates of a proposition dealing with a non-material entity are derived analytically from the subject. According to Levi these predicates are simply an explanation of the subject and introduce no plurality whatever. Opposing Maimonides' doctrine of negative attributes, Levi teaches that man may have a certain positive knowledge of God, based on the observation of His actions. The essential action of God is thinking, and, consequently, the effusion of all forms. All the attributes that man recognizes in his own form are just so many attributes of God. Since the attributes common to both man and God have the relation of cause and effect, it is impossible to consider them absolute homonyms, that is, terms which have nothing in common except their names.

By means of a knowledge that is neither temporal nor changing, God eternally perceives the general law of the universe, that is, those laws governing the movements of the heavenly bodies and, through them, the sublunar beings. God is aware of the fate that awaits all individuals, inasmuch as they are distributed in groups subject to the same celestial determinism which, in principle, governs all the conditions of man. However, this determinism, essentially beneficial, may occasionally cause misfortune. God has therefore accorded man freedom which allows him to liberate himself from the shackles of determinism. An individual who makes use of his freedom is no longer subject to the universal law known by God; he has accomplished an act which is absolutely undetermined and which remains totally unknown to God. God's knowledge, however, does not undergo any modification; it always remains true, since the author of the free act is no longer included in the necessary and universal proposition thought by God. For Levi, God's knowledge embraces all the events of this world, with the exception of free acts that cannot be predicted by any type of knowledge. Levi is convinced that he has finally succeeded in reconciling two contradictory fundamental principles of the Bible: divine omniscience and the freedom of man's will.

The providence of God extends a means of protection that increases in proportion to man's moral and intellectual perfection. Through the determined activities of the stars, God assures a maximum of good to men in general and spares them a maximum of ills. Premonitions, dreams, prophecies and the exercise of free choice save certain individuals from harmful effects of determinism. However, the existence of evil cannot be denied since, at times, the righteous do suffer. But Levi upholds the belief that the true good which is specifically human is the immortality of the soul, and it is this immortality, rigorously proportioned according to one's moral rectitude and intellectual perfection, that constitutes the actual recompense of God.

CREATION OF THE WORLD. In opposition to Maimonides who held that the creation of the world can not be demonstrated philosophically, Levi offers philosophic arguments designed to show that the world came into being. One such is that everything produced by a final cause, ordained to a certain end, and serving as a substratum for accidents, cannot exist eternally. Since the world fulfills all these conditions it follows that it cannot be eternal, that is, that it has a beginning in time. He derives the same conclusion from the state of the sciences. Were the world eternal, he argues, the sciences would be more advanced than they are. He holds further that a large number of Aristotle's arguments designed to prove the eternity of the world beg the question. They are based on the assumption that the physical laws discovered within the world are also applicable to its beginning. However, this assumption is fallacious. For while it is true that there are some similarities between processes within the world and creation (Levi here is more moderate than Maimonides who holds a similar view), creation is also unique. Whereas motions in the world take place in time, creation occurred in an instant. However, since nothing can be created out of nothing, the world has a substratum, an eternal body which is nonetheless a relative non-being, in the sense that it possesses no form whatever. This substratum has no "existence" in the proper sense of the word, since all existence derives from form. Thus the theological difficulty that might give rise to the possibility of more than one eternal being is avoided.

MAN. God has arranged the universe so that man, the most perfect being of the sublunar world, is accorded the greatest good and is spared the greatest amount of ills possible, as we have already seen. Revelations of different types protect him (premonitions, dreams, etc.). His imagination, under the action of one or several celestial bodies, envisions the menace that certain stellar configurations may place upon him. God has equally furnished man with a practical intellect, from which he learns the indispensable arts of self-preservation, and a speculative intellect which permits him to perceive truth and to achieve immortality. The material or potential intellect is not a substance but rather a simple disposition, whose substratum is the imagination. Building on the sensations, the human intellect abstracts concepts; but sensation is only an incidental agent in the production of knowledge, for knowledge in its true sense is the comprehension of intelligibles as they exist in the agent intellect. The human intellect, having understood the intelligible, which is eternal, becomes itself immortal. Differing from Averroes, who maintained that, at this state, the human intellect loses its individuality, Levi held that immortality is individual.

ISRAEL. Providence extends particularly to the children of Israel, chosen by God through His covenant with the Patriarchs. Prophecy is a kind of revelation that is superior to all other types of revelation, and differs from them not in degree but in nature. The prophet must necessarily be a preeminent philosopher who grasps the general laws governing changes in the sublunar world as they exist in the agent intellect. By means of his imagination, he applies this knowledge to given individual or communal situations, announcing the good or evil events that may befall a person, a group, or an entire people, as a result of the operation of the laws of nature. He is also capable of predicting a miracle, which is a violation of nature, not, as Maimonides thought, an event included in the laws of nature at the time of the creation of the world. Levi maintains that a miracle is produced at a particular time and place, and that it occurs when the agent intellect suspends normal, natural law, since it no longer applies to certain circumstances. Though miracles are not part of the laws of nature, or subject to them, they have their own laws. However, since a miracle is produced by the agent intellect, which can only act upon the sublunar world, no miracles can occur in the translunar world. Thus, for example, the sun did not really stand at the order of Joshua; the victory at Gibeon was attained during the short lapse of time when the sun seemingly stood at its zenith.

Through the intermediacy of Moses, the greatest of all prophets, God gave Israel the Torah, which, through its *mitzvot* and speculative truths, aims to help the children of Israel attain the moral and intellectual perfection which makes immortality possible for them. The commandments have various purposes, which Levi expounds in detail, but the purpose of most of them is to remove materialistic tendencies and teach the existence of forms. Finally, the Torah has revealed certain metaphysical truths that the philosophers have never been able to deduce, namely, the creation of the world and the immortality of the soul.

ESCHATOLOGY. Levi's eschatology is based on a tradition that there are two Messiahs. After the Messiah son of Joseph dies, having been assassinated, the Messiah son of David will appear. He will be greater than Moses, not because he will promulgate a new Torah, but because he will accomplish a miracle greater than those of Moses: the resurrection of the dead, an event which will convert all peoples of the earth to the true religion. He predicts the coming of the Messiah for the year 1358. During messianic times, the world will follow its usual pattern, men will die as before, but the earth will be filled with knowledge of God and human liberty will be utilized for good ends.

Views on Levi ben Gershom. On account of his boldness and of the suspicion of heresy fastened to him, Levi was subject to virulent attacks. Certain of his doctrines became the object of harsh criticism on the part of Ḥasdai *Crescas. Abraham *Shalom, while defending him against Crescas, censured him for other reasons. Shem Tov *ibn Shem Tov labeled Levi's major work the "Wars against the Lord." *Isaac b. Sheshet Perfet, though recognizing Levi as a great talmudist, maintains that it is prohibited to accept certain of his theories. Isaac *Abrabanel, in several of his works, also criticizes him. However, even the most vehement critics of Levi, who very often did not understand his real thought, did not hesitate to borrow some of his ideas. His influence continued to exert itself even as late as the 19th century, when he is mentioned in *Malbim's commentary on Job.

[CH.T.]

As Astronomer. *Milḥamot Adonai* contains an astronomical treatise of 136 chapters. This astronomical section (Book V, Part 1) is not included in the manuscripts or printed versions of the rest of the work, but it was translated in its entirety into Latin. There also exists a second Latin version of the first few chapters dedicated to Pope Clement VI. The text covers most of the topics of medieval astronomy: trigonometry (the construction of the sine table and the solution of triangles); the construction and use of various astronomical instruments; an analysis of several schemes for arranging celestial motions; a discussion of solar, lunar, and planetary motions including tables to aid in their computation; and a discussion of the order of the planets and their distances from the earth.

The astronomical treatise was not meant to be an elementary text for students, but presupposes some familiarity with medieval astronomical literature. Although the work is clearly in the Ptolemaic tradition, Levi deals quite critically with his sources and often rejects earlier views in favor of his own. His most important innovation in terms of technical astronomy was his new geometrical model to account for lunar motion, which he describes in chapter 71. He argues that his new model corrects a glaring fault of Ptolemy's lunar model, which brought the moon so close to the earth at quadrature that it appeared twice as large as its observed size. Levi considered agreement with his own observations to be the principal criterion in choosing between alternative models for the motions of the celestial bodies; in this he departed from the widespread medieval dependence on the observations recorded in Ptolemy's *Almagest*. In addition to Ptolemy, Levi relied on al-Battānī, the famous ninth-century Arab astronomer, and to a lesser extent on Abraham *ibn Ezra and *Abraham bar Ḥiyya. Levi carefully described his observations of four solar and six lunar eclipses, as well as observations of the moon and of the planets under different conditions. Such extensive recording of observations were quite rare among medieval astronomers.

Levi's best-known contribution to astronomy is his invention of the Jacob Staff, which was widely used to measure the angular separation between two celestial bodies. This instrument became an important navigational tool and was especially popular in the 16th century among European sailors.

Most medieval scholars accepted the order of the planets presented by Ptolemy in *The Planetary Hypotheses:* Moon, Mercury, Venus, Sun, Mars, Jupiter, Saturn, and the fixed stars. There was, however, some dispute concerning the place of the sun in relation to Mercury and Venus. Levi considered several possibilities in detail, but seems to have preferred the theory that the sun lies below both planets. In another departure from Ptolemy, who set the distance to the fixed stars at 20,000 earth radii, Levi argued that those stars are more than 159×10^{12} earth radii away, a truly astounding distance in terms of medieval science. [B.R.G.]

Bibliography: Renan, Ecrivains, 240–98; Steinschneider, Uebersetzungen, 1060, s.v. *Levi b. Gerson;* idem, *Gesammelte Schriften*, 1 (1925), 233–70; G. Sarton, *Introduction to the History of Science*, 3 pt. 1 (1947), 594–607; M. Joel, *Lewi ben Gerson als Religionsphilosoph* (1862); I. Weil, *Philosophie religieuse de Lévi-ben-Gerson* (1868); Husik, Philosophy, 329–61; Guttmann, Philosophies, 208–24; idem, *Dat u-Madda* (1956), 136–48; G. Vadja, *Introduction à la pensée juive du moyen âge* (1947), 159–69; C. Touati, *Levi ben Gershom, Les Guerres du Seigneur, Livres III et IV* (1968); idem, in: *Revue des sciences religieuses*, 28 (1954), 335–67; Wolfson, in: *M. M. Kaplan, Jubilee Volume* (1953), 515–30 (Eng. sect.); B. R. Goldstein, in: Israel Academy of Sciences and Humanities, *Proceedings*, vol. 3, no. 9 (1969), 239–54.

LEVI BEN ḤABIB (**Ralbaḥ**; c. 1483–1545), rabbi in Jerusalem and principal opponent of the restoration of the **semikhah*. Levi b. Ḥabib was born in Zamora, Spain, and in 1492 was taken to Portugal by his father, R. Jacob *ibn Ḥabib. There he was forcibly baptized. Both he and his father escaped to Salonika where Levi received his education. He succeeded his father, teaching at the congregation of Spanish exiles, called *Gerush Sefarad*, in Salonika. Levi became famous as a talmudist, showing a preference for the use of literal meaning *(peshat)* as opposed to casuistry *(pilpul)*. He never presented his own views

שאלות ותשובות

Title page of *She'elot u-Teshuvot*, a book of responsa by Levi b. Ḥabib (Ralbaḥ), Venice, 1565. Jerusalem, J.N.U.L.

unless they had been given by previous scholars. Levi admitted that he was not well versed in Kabbalah, but he was proud of his knowledge of astronomy. In order to atone for his baptism as a youth, he went to Ereẓ Israel, traveling via Asia Minor, Aleppo, and Damascus. He first settled in Safed and later moved to Jerusalem. For 15 years he officiated there, instituting as rabbi various new regulations for the community. At that time, there was no "ordained" (Heb., *samukh*) *bet din*, like the ancient Sanhedrin, i.e., one which was authorized to sentence to punishment by lashes (*malkot*), prescribe fines, and determine the intercalation of months. Therefore the rabbis of Safed decided to restore the ancient *semikhah* and chose R. Jacob *Berab to ordain rabbis and act as a judge. This act was of great significance, as the ordination was to be reestablished only in messianic times, and it also marked the supremacy of the Safed rabbis. Levi b. Ḥabib refused to accept the authority of Berab and accused the latter of disgracing the honor of Jerusalem. A violent controversy ensued whose details are recalled in an appendix entitled *Semikhat Zekenim o Kunteres ha-Semikhah* ("Ordination of the Elders or Pamphlet Concerning Ordination") printed at the end of Levi's responsa (Venice, 1565). The volume also contains Levi's commentary on Maimonides' *Hilkhot Kiddush ha-Ḥodesh*. In addition to responsa, he completed and published the second part of his father's *Ein Ya'akov*.

See also Jacob *Berab (I).

Bibliography: Frumkin-Rivlin, index; Rosanes, Togarmah, 2 (1938), 156–8; Y. R. Molḥo, in: *Ḥemdat Yisrael... H. H. Medini* (1946), 33–42; Y. Katz, in: *Zion*, 16 (1950/51), 28–45; M. Benayahu, in: *Sefer Yovel... Y. Baer* (1960), 248–69. [S.Mar.]

LEVI BEN JAPHETH (Abū Saʿīd; 10th–11th century), Karaite scholar, son of *Japheth b. Ali. Levi b. Japheth lived in Jerusalem and wrote, in Arabic, a "Book of Precepts," a work which was used by almost all the later Karaite writers. Only fragments of the Arabic original are preserved. Manuscripts of the Hebrew translation, *Sefer ha-Mitzvot*, are extant in Oxford, Leningrad, and Leiden. In his interpretation of the law, Levi distinguished between the views of the early and later *Rabbanites, numbering *Saadiah Gaon among the latter and frequently censuring him severely. He also wrote a short commentary on the Bible (only fragments of this, too, remain), and is said to have compiled an abridged version of David b. Abraham *Alfasi's dictionary, *Agron*.

Bibliography: S. Poznański, *Karaite Literary Opponents of Saadiah Gaon* (1908), 42–46; Z. Ankori, *Karaites in Byzantium* (1959), index, s.v. *Levi b. Yefeth*. [Ed.]

LEVI BEN SISI (end of second and beginning of third century, C.E.), Palestinian and Babylonian *amora*. He is mentioned in the Babylonian Talmud without a patronymic, but with his father's name in the Jerusalem Talmud. He was a colleague-disciple of *Judah ha-Nasi (Ber. 49a; Shab. 107b; Zev. 30b; Men. 80b, et al.), whom he called *Rabbenu ha-Kadosh* ("Our Holy Master," Shab. 156a). Although Judah sometimes scolded him (Yev. 9a), he held his scholarship in high regard (Zev. 30b). So authentic were the traditions handed down by him that the words *lemedin li-fenei ha-ḥakhamim* ("It was taught before the sages") are said to refer to Levi's transmission of the teachings of Judah ha-Nasi (Sanh. 17b). The Talmud gives various details of his intimate position in Judah's household: he was the merrymaker on festive occasions and entertained those present with acrobatic performances. Once he tried to imitate the manner in which the priests used to prostrate themselves in the Temple, but dislocated his hip which resulted in a permanent limp (Suk. 53a). Levi taught that at prayer a person must stand with his feet straight like the angels (TJ, Ber. 1:1, 2c). He used to write down in a notebook the discussions with his teacher (Shab. 156a). Out of those notes came a collection of *beraitot* which is mentioned several times in the Talmud (Yoma 24a; Yev. 10a, Ket. 53b; et al.). Levi was held to possess special power for successful intercession on such occasions as drought (Ta'an. 25a) or danger from bandits (TJ, Ta'an. 3:8, 66d).

Levi seems to have traveled often between Ereẓ Israel and Babylonia and was well acquainted with the cultural conditions of the peoples of Babylonia. After his return from one of these journeys Judah ha-Nasi asked him about their particular characteristics (Kid. 72a). When the citizens of Simonia sought a judge and spiritual leader, Judah ha-Nasi recommended Levi, who, despite his initially disappointing performance, was appointed on the strength of the recommendation (TJ, Yev. 12:7, 13a). After the death of Judah ha-Nasi, when Afess was appointed in his place, Levi discontinued his studies at his master's academy but studied with R. *Ḥanina b. Ḥama outside the walls of the yeshivah. For this behavior he was criticized by many of his contemporaries, and according to legend he was punished for this by exclusion from the "academy in heaven" until Samuel interceded on his behalf and he was admitted (Ber. 18b). After the appointment of Ḥanina b. Ḥama as head of the academy, Levi migrated to Babylonia where he joined the school of *Rav (Beẓah 24b; Ket. 52a) and other former disciples of Judah ha-Nasi (Shab. 59; Ket. 103b).

Levi settled finally in Nehardea where he became a close friend of *Abba b. Abba, the father of *Samuel (Ber. 30a; BB 42b). Both studied in the old synagogue of the town called Shaf ve-Yativ, according to legend built of stones brought from Jerusalem by Jehoiachin, and witnessed there the appearance of heavenly messengers (Meg. 29a). Levi also lectured at the academy there (Song. R. 4:8) and was associate judge at the court of the *exilarch Mar *Ukba (Ukva; Pes. 76b; BB 54a) who held his erudition in very high esteem (Shab. 108b; MK 26b). Levi instructed his friend's son, later the famous Babylonian *amora* Samuel, who transmitted many of his master's teachings (Shab. 108b; Er. 10a, et al.). Among Levi's prominent pupils were *Mattnah (MK 26b) and a number of *amoraim* who later migrated to Ereẓ Israel, including *Assi (Av. Zar. 38b), *Ḥiyya b. Abba (Eccl. R. 1:4), and *Ze'ira (Shab. 108b). After Levi's death Abba b. Abba eulogized him as a scholar whose worth was equal to that of the rest of mankind (TJ, Ber. 2:85a).

Bibliography: Hyman, Toledot, 859–62; Ḥ. Albeck, *Mavo la-Talmudim* (1969), 153–5. [Ed.]

LEVI-BIANCHINI, ANGELO (1887–1920), Italian naval officer and member of the *Zionist Commission. Born in Venice, Levi-Bianchini completed his studies in the naval academy at Leghorn and joined the Italian navy, becoming

Angelo Levi-Bianchini, Italian naval officer and member of the Zionist Commission set up in Palestine in 1918. Jerusalem, J.N.U.L., Schwadron Collection.

a naval officer (a rare occupation among Italian Jews). Afterward he became a lecturer at the naval academy and at the military school in Turin. In 1917 he was appointed to the Navy ministry, on behalf of which he fulfilled several missions. With the establishment of the Zionist Commission, Levi-Bianchini, together with G. Artom, joined as a representative of the Italian Jewish community, in close liaison with the Italian Foreign Office. He arrived in Palestine in the summer of 1918 and immediately strengthened his ties with Chaim *Weizmann, members of the Zionist Commission, and the various circles of the *yishuv*. In addition, Levi-Bianchini won the confidence of many in the British military government and Arab leaders. He also contributed directly and indirectly to the organization of self-defense in the *yishuv* and represented the interests of the *yishuv* and the Zionist Movement before *Allenby and the British military government. In April 1919 he prevented the outbreak of disturbances following the Arab holiday and traditional parade from al-Nabi Mūsā. In May of the same year he left Palestine. He continued his service for the Italian government, participating in the Versailles Conference in 1919 and the San Remo Conference in Italy in 1920, at which he worked to procure the Italian Foreign Office's approval of the British Mandate on Palestine and the *Balfour Declaration in general. In 1920 Levi-Bianchini was sent by the Italian foreign minister, Sforza, to examine the situation in Palestine and Egypt, especially the role of the Zionist Movement in the new political developments in the Middle East. He was killed near Khirbet el Gazale in a bedouin attack on a train making its way from Damascus to Haifa. His body was eventually found near the scene of the attack and was buried in Turin about a year after his death.

Bibliography: S. Minerbi, *A. Levi-Bianchini e la sua opera nel Levante 1918–1920* (1967); idem, in: D. Carpi (ed.), *Ha-Ẓiyyonut*, 1 (1970), 296–356; C. Weizmann, *Trial and Error* (1949), 212. [G.K.]

LEVI-CIVITA, TULLIO (1873–1942), Italian mathematician. Levi-Civita, who was born in Padua, was appointed to the chair of mechanics at the university there at the age of 25. In 1918 he left Padua to become professor of mechanics at the University of Rome. He opposed the rise of fascism in Italy. He was dismissed from his position after the implementation of the anti-Jewish laws of 1938. After this, his health deteriorated rapidly and he was unable to accept any of the offers of asylum which he received from several countries. Levi-Civita was an excellent teacher and his many scientific papers and books are distinguished by their lucidity. He developed, after an initial collaboration with Curbasto Gregorio Ricci, the absolute differential calculus, which was the essential mathematical tool required by Einstein for his development (in 1916) of the general theory of relativity. Levi-Civita's most important contribution in this field was the theory of "parallel displacement." He also produced significant papers on relativity, analytical dynamics, hydrodynamics, and systems of partial differential equations. Levi-Civita was a member of many Italian and foreign mathematical societies. In 1922 he was awarded the Sylvester Medal of the Royal Society.

Bibliography: Hodge, in: Royal Society of London, *Obituary Notices of Fellows*, 4 (1942–44), 151. [B.S.]

LEVI DELLA VIDA, GIORGIO (1886–1967), Italian Arabist and Semitist. Born in Piedmont, della Vida completed his university studies in Rome. In 1914 he began to lecture at the university of Naples, went on to Turin, and in 1920 was appointed professor at Rome University. He taught Biblical Hebrew, Arabic, Syriac, Phoenician and neo-Punic inscriptions, and the histories of the Semitic peoples and their literatures. In all these fields, he published many articles. A number of them, principally in the field of Judaism and Islam, were gathered into the collection *Storia e religione dell'oriente semitico* (1924). He also edited a series of Arabic and Syriac texts with his translations. His catalog of the Vatican Arab-Muslim manuscripts (vol. 1, 1935; vol. 2, 1965), his collection of documents dealing with the relations between the Church of Rome and the oriental churches during the reign of Pope Gregory XIII (1948), as well as a series of detailed articles on the manuscripts of the Vatican collection were the fruits of the years he worked in the Vatican Library. His later works included: *Aneddoti e svaghi arabi e non arabi* (1959), and a book of memoirs *Fantasmi ritrovati* (1966). He was one of the twelve lecturers (out of a total of 1,225 university teachers), who refused, at the end of 1931, to take the oath of allegiance to the Fascist regime and he was therefore dismissed from his position. From 1939–48, he was professor at the University of Pennsylvania, but in 1948 was reinstated in his position in Rome.

Bibliography: G. Strachan, *Giorgio Levi della Vida* (Eng., 1956); *Studi orientalistici in onore di Giorgio Levi della Vida* (1956). [H.Z.H.]

LEVI ISAAC BEN MEIR OF BERDICHEV (c. 1740–1810), ḥasidic *ẓaddik* and rabbi; one of the most famous personalities in the third generation of the ḥasidic movement. Levi Isaac was born into a distinguished rabbinic family and his father was rabbi in Hoshakov (Galicia). After marrying the daughter of a rich contractor he moved to his father-in-law's home in *Lubartow (Poland), where he studied with Joseph *Teomim. At that time he met Samuel Shmelke *Horowitz of Nikolsburg, then rabbi in Richwal (Ryczwol), who acquainted him with the Ḥasidism of *Israel b. Eliezer Ba'al Shem Tov. In 1766 Levi Isaac went to study under *Dov Baer the Maggid of Mezhirech, becoming one of the intimate circle of his pupils. When Shmelke left Richwal Levi Isaac replaced him, though only

Gravestone of the Polish ḥasidic rabbi Levi Isaac ben Meir of Berdichev.

for a short period. He next served as rabbi in Żelechów, where he first emerged as a ḥasidic *ẓaddik;* to his contemporaries he became known as the "rabbi in Żelechów." A testimony dating from 1774 reports that he took a strong and even aggressive stand against the local *mitnaggedim,* but the latter finally triumphed and Levi Isaac had to leave Żelechów. An account of this controversy appears in the *Iggeret ha-Kodesh* by Eliezer the son of *Elimelech of Lyzhansk, published at the end of the latter's *No'am Elimelekh,* 1788. In 1775 he was elected rabbi of Pinsk but there, too, he was dismissed through pressure from the *mitnaggedim* and with the concurrence of *Elijah b. Solomon Zalman of Vilna. Moving to Berdichev in 1785, he served as rabbi there until his death. In Berdichev Levi Isaac won great renown as rabbi, ḥasidic leader, and scholar; even the *mitnaggedim* admitted that he was a noted Torah scholar (*Zemir Ariẓim* (Warsaw, 1798), 3) but complained of his lack of knowledge of the Kabbalah. He made many amendments in communal *takkanot* and took part in public affairs. In 1801(?) he convened a meeting of leaders (in which the *ẓaddik* Baruch b. Jehiel of Medzibezh and the *maskil* writer Menahem Mendel Levin participated) to discuss the government's prohibition on Jewish settlement in the villages and other oppressive measures; in 1807 Levi Isaac's name headed a list of Jewish contributors to the Russian war effort against the anticipated French invasion. During a serious illness in 1793, "he was grieved and his spiritual forces declined" (*Oẓar ha-Ḥayyim ve-Heikhal ha-Berakhah,* introduction to the Book of Numbers). In this crisis he was helped by Israel b. Shabbetai the Maggid of *Kozienice.

The founder of Ḥasidism in central Poland, Levi Isaac consolidated the movement in Lithuania and furthered it in the Ukraine. When he was still in Poland (Żelechów) the *mitnagged* writer, *David of Makow, described him as "rabbi of all that sect" (see M. L. Wilensky, in: PAAJR, 25 (1956), 151), an indication of his widespread popularity. While he was rabbi in Pinsk he engaged in a debate with the fanatic *mitnagged* Abraham *Katzenellenbogen, a rabbi of Brest-Litovsk. At Praga near Warsaw before the month of Elul 1781, they discussed basic precepts of Ḥasidism, both parties later claiming victory. On the fifth of Tammuz 1784, Abraham Katzenellenbogen circulated an epistle summarizing his arguments against Ḥasidism, but Levi Isaac's reply is not extant.

In his teachings Levi Isaac stressed the element of joy in Ḥasidism, the principle of *devekut* ("adhesion") to God, and the necessity for fervent prayer to the point of *hitpashetut ha-gashmiyyut* ("abstraction from corporeality"). When a man prays fervently "with all his heart and his soul then his spirit delights because it is elevated from the material world and only the spirit remains" (*Kedushat Levi,* Va-Yeẓe). It is necessary that "every Jew should worship the Creator with devotion and fervor" (*Kedushat Levi,* Va-Yera). One of the best loved of *ẓaddikim,* Levi Isaac occasionally traveled with great acclaim throughout the land. Accompanied by his *minyan,* he introduced the people to the joy of fulfilling the commandments, winning them over to Ḥasidism. Before the Holocaust, visitors to the *bet midrash* in the "Iron Gate" in Warsaw were shown a column in front of which Levi Isaac used to pray when he visited the city. The *mitnagged* Israel *Loebl also reports on his visits to Warsaw and his fervent prayers: "And here I will tell you the story of R. Levi the rabbi of Berdichev, when he was in Łazienki, the king's pleasure gardens. He boasted that he had never prayed a *Minḥah* like the one he uttered there" (*Sefer ha-Vikku'aḥ* (Warsaw, 1798), 19).

Levi Isaac shared the distress of his people and worked to improve their living conditions. In singing his prayers he addressed the Creator in Yiddish; popular tradition has preserved some of these ("The *Kaddish* of R. Levi Isaac" etc.; see **Kaddish*). He stressed the good that is in man and always pleaded the cause of Jews: "No one has a right to say anything evil about the Jewish people, but only to intercede for them" (*Kedushat Levi,* Ḥukkat). He distinguished between two types of preacher: he who admonishes "with good words," who shows man "his merit and the source of his soul," bringing out his superior qualities and indicating opportunies for him to rise; and he who admonishes "with severe words," awes and subdues. Only he who "admonishes Jewish people gently, elevates their souls and always extols their righteousness is worthy of being their leader" (*ibid.*). Levi Isaac's book of sermons, *Kedushat Levi,* was published during his lifetime (Slavuta, 1798; Zolkiew, 1806) and was supplemented by his sons from manuscripts (Berdichev, 1811).

Although he did not found a dynasty, Levi Isaac had many pupils and left an indelible mark on Ḥasidism. He was a popular hero in Jewish poetry and fiction both in Hebrew and in Yiddish; the following plays are especially noteworthy: Ya'akov Cohen's *Ha-Ẓe'akah ha-Shelishit* (his complete works, vol. 4, 1945); the first play in *Sheloshah Ketarim* by Zevi Cahn (1954); Y. Sela, *Ha-Sanegor ha-Gadol* (1958). Important poems are Z. Shneur's *Din Torah Ḥadash le-Rabbi Levi Yiẓḥak mi-Berdichev* (*Shirim* (1960), 111–4), Uri Zvi *Greenberg's *Be-Keẓ ha-Derakhim Omed Rabbi Levi Yiẓḥak mi-Berdichev ve-Doresh Teshuvat Ram* (in: *Reḥovot ha-Nahar,* 1951), and S. *Meltzer's ballad *Din Torah* (in: *Or Zaru'a,* 1959). He was also depicted in Joseph *Opatoshu's well-known story, *In Poylishe Velder* (1921).

Bibliography: Dubnow, Ḥasidut, 151–7, 193–201, 479–81; idem, *Chassidiana* (Heb.)—supplement to *He-Avar,* 2 (1918); Horodezky, Ḥasidut, 2 (1951³), 71–96; S. Gutmann, *Tiferet Beit Levi* (1909); A. Z. Aescoly, *Introduction à l'étude des hérésies religieuses parmi les juifs. La Kabbale. Le Hassidisme* (1928); C. Lieberman, in: *Sefer ha-Yovel . . . Alexander Marx* (1943), 15–17; M. Buber, *Tales of the Hasidim—the Early Masters* (1947), 203–34; M. E. Gutman, *Mi-Gedolei ha-Ḥasidut* (1953²); I. Halpern, in: *Tarbiz,* 28 (1959), 90–98 (*Yehudim ve-Yahadut be-Mizraḥ Eiropah* (1969), 340–7); J. Twersky, *Ḥayyei R. Levi Yiẓḥak mi-Berdichev* (1960); L. Jung (ed.), *Men of the Spirit* (1964), 403–13.

[A.Ru.]

LEVIN, ALTER ISAAC (pseudonym: **Asaf ha-Levi, Ish Yerushalayim;** 1883–1933), Hebrew writer. Born in Russia, he emigrated to Palestine in 1891, and studied at religious schools in Jerusalem. He worked as an insurance broker, but subsequently became enmeshed in financial difficulties and committed suicide. He was also an art collector. Encouraged by Israel Dov *Frumkin, Levin wrote poems and articles for **Ḥavazzelet* and other newspapers in Palestine. He published a collection of poems, *Megillat Kedem le-Asaf ha-Levi Ish Yerushalayim* (1920), and a booklet of folk songs, *Shirei Am* (1920).

Bibliography: D. Kimḥi, *Massot Ketannot* (1938), 80–86; Y. R. Feldmann (Rabbi Binyamin), *Mishpeḥot Soferim* (1960), 169–72; *Haaretz* (Sept. 28, 1934). [G.K.]

LEVIN, EMANUEL (Menahem Mendel; 1820–1913), author and communal worker, early pioneer of *Haskalah in Russia. A teacher of Russian and German in new schools in Vilna and his native Minsk, Levin wrote *Dikduk Leshon Rusyah* ("Grammar of the Russian Language") in 1846 and published a Russian translation of *Pirkei Avot* with notes in 1868. He founded a school for girls in Minsk, and in 1852 he was appointed as a teacher in the government rabbinical seminary in *Zhitomir. In 1857 he entered the service of the barons Y. and H. *Guenzburg, becoming their confidant and secretary for Jewish affairs. Under their instructions he drafted memoranda and appeals to the authorities, including a memorandum on the pogroms of 1881–82 to the Pahlen Commission, the government committee which discussed the Jewish question (see *Russia). Levin published several collections of the special laws concerning the Jews in Russia (*Sbornik ogranichitelnykh zakonov . . . o yevreyakh*, 1902). He also drafted the constitution of the *Society for the Promotion of Culture among the Jews of Russia and served as its first secretary (1863–72). From 1895 Levin was a member of the historical committee of the society and one of the collaborators in the publication of the collection *Regesty i Nadpisi*. Levin was also the secretary of several conventions of the leaders of Russian Jewry, including the meetings of the communal delegates during the years of the pogroms of 1881–82. He died in St. Petersburg.

Bibliography: Goldstein, in: *Yevreyskaya Starina*, 9 (1916), 253–75. [Y.S.]

LEVIN, JUDAH LEIB (known by the acronym **Yehalel** = *YeH*udah *L*eib *L*evin; 1844–1925), Hebrew socialist poet and writer and one of the first members of Ḥovevei Zion. He received an Orthodox education at home but studied secular subjects and became completely estranged from his former environment. In 1870 he was employed as tutor and secretary by the *Brodskis, the Jewish sugar magnates of Kiev, and worked for them until the Soviet regime closed the enterprise in 1918. In 1871 he published his first collection of poetry, *Siftei Renanot* (Zhitomir, 1871), which was well received by the Hebrew reading public. His socialist views stemmed from reading Russian radical and socialist literature and observing the relations between his employers, the Brodskis, and their employees. He joined the circle of A. S. *Liebermann and helped him publish his newspaper, *Ha-Emet*. Most of his poems which appeared from 1874 to 1880 in *Ha-Shaḥar* dealt with social problems and sharply criticized the existing order and the regime. His poems, actually essays in rhyme, were minor and innovative only in that they were the first to introduce socialist themes into Hebrew literature and poetry. Levin's interest in problems of Jewish life increased when Russian nationalism and anti-Semitism grew stronger. The pogroms in 1881 brought a decisive change in Levin's ideas; he drew even further from the socialist circles and devoted himself to the problems of Jewish life. He joined Ḥovevei Zion, was one of the founders of this pre-Zionist movement in Kiev, and through letters and articles propagandized for the settle-

Judah Leib Levin, Hebrew socialist poet. Courtesy Genazim, Tel Aviv.

ment of Ereẓ Israel. He translated Disraeli's *Tancred* (*Or la-Goyim*, Warsaw, 1884), which visualizes the return of the Jews to their land. Because of this activity he had to leave Kiev and settle in the small town of Tomashpol where he worked for Brodski and continued with his literary work. Living in remote Tomashpol had an adverse effect on Levin. Out of touch with his contemporaries, he did not progress with the mainstream of Hebrew poetry and literature. In 1910, the jubilee of his literary work, he published his memoirs, *Zikkaron ba-Sefer*, including a chronological list of his writings. With the onset of the Russian Revolution Levin returned to Kiev, where he spent his last years in poverty and loneliness. A selection of his memoirs, articles, and poems was published in 1968 as *Zikhronot ve-Hegyonot*.

Bibliography: J. L. Levin, *Zikhronot ve-Hegyonot* (1968), 7–28 (introd. by Y. Slutsky); J. L. Levin, *Ketavim Nivḥarim* (1911), 1–9 (introd. by M. M. Feitelson); S. Breiman, in: *Shivat Ẓiyyon*, 3/4 (1953), 164–77; Klausner, Sifrut, 6 (1958), 118–87 (incl. bibl.); LNYL, 4 (1961), 244f. (incl. bibl.); Waxman, Literature, 3 (1960²), 258–60. [Y.S.]

LEVIN, LEWIS CHARLES (1808–1860), U.S. lawyer, editor, and congressman. Levin, who was born in Charleston, South Carolina, attended South Carolina College (now the University of South Carolina). After studying law, he settled in Philadelphia in 1838 where he was admitted to the bar. There, he achieved prominence as a temperance speaker and editor of the *Temperance Advocate*. He was a founder of the Native American (later "Know-Nothing") Party in 1843 and edited and published its official organ, the *Daily Sun*, in Philadelphia. Elected as a candidate of the Native American Party to the 29th, 30th, and 31st Congresses (March 4, 1845–March 3, 1851), Levin championed a high tariff, expansionism, public works, including a dry dock at Philadelphia, and "Know-Nothing" legislation. After being defeated for reelection in 1850, he resumed his law practice.

Bibliography: J. A. Forman, in: AJA, 12 (1960), 150–94. [P.M.G.]

LEVIN, MAKSIM GRIGORYEVICH (1904–), Soviet Russian ethnologist and physical anthropologist. Levin did extensive field work in Siberia and wrote on the ethnology of Asiatic Russia and Siberia. The expert knowledge accumulated in these expeditions is reflected in his *Narody Sibiri* ("Peoples of Siberia," 1956), which he edited with L. P. Potapov and to which he was himself an important contributor; and in *Istoriko-geograficheskiy atlas Sibiri* ("A Historico-Geographical Atlas of Siberia," 1961), which he again edited with L. P. Potapov. He also wrote *Ocherki po istorii antropologii v Rossii* (1960), a history of the development of anthropology. One of his works, *Etnicheskaya antropolgiya i problemy etnogeneza narodov Dal nego Vostoka* (1958), became available in English translation in 1963 as *Ethnic Origins of the Peoples of Northeastern Asia.* Levin became deputy director of the Institute of Ethnography of the Academy of Sciences of the USSR and head of its physical anthropology section, and edited many of the institute's publications. [E.Fi.]

LEVIN (Lefin), MENAHEM MENDEL (1749–1826), early Haskalah author, translator, and educator. Born in Satanov, Podolia, he had a traditional Jewish education but also studied sciences, mathematics, and medieval philosophy in his youth. From 1780 to 1783/84 Levin lived in Berlin, where he met Moses *Mendelssohn, through whom he established contact with the leaders of the Haskalah. His first popular literary success was a Hebrew translation of Tissot's *Manual of Popular Medicine and Hygiene*, undertaken with Mendelssohn's encouragement. Through a chance encounter, he made the acquaintance of one of Poland's leading statesmen, Prince Adam *Czartoryski, who ultimately became his patron, helping him to publish his work and allotting him a stipend. Levin taught mathematics and philosophy to Czartoryski's children, which was rare at that time, and dedicated his unpublished philosophical treatise, "*Aus dem Nachlass eines Sonderlings zu Abdera,*" to Czartoryski's wife. When the great Sejm met in Warsaw (1788–92), Levin participated in discussions on contemporary problems. Toward the end of the 18th century, he resided in Ustye and in St. Petersburg in the home of the wealthy philanthropist J. *Zeitlin, serving as tutor to his grandson. After 1808 he lived in Brody and Tarnopol, where his influence on the *maskilim* in Galicia, notably N. *Krochmal and J. *Perl, was so considerable that he is regarded as the father of the Galician Haskalah.

Believing that the achievement of the objectives of the Haskalah depended, in large measure, upon making books readily available to the public, he dedicated himself to the publication of both secular and religious works. Like other *maskilim*, Levin derived his views on Judaism primarily from Maimonides, and he prepared a new version of the *Guide of the Perplexed* (Zolkiew, 1829), which he wrote in mishnaic Hebrew, hoping thereby to make the work more accessible to the modern reader. Levin's main contributions to Jewish literature were his use of mishnaic Hebrew, whose style he described as "light and pure," rather than the biblical rhetoric employed by almost all of his literary contemporaries, and his willingness to write works in Yiddish—the anathema of the Haskalah. Thus he directed a number of Haskalah writers toward a more popular Hebrew style and many of his usages and neologisms have entered modern Hebrew. To render certain books of the Bible more easily comprehensible to the East European Yiddish speaker, he produced an idiomatic Yiddish translation of the ethical and poetic books of the Hagiographa: Psalms, Proverbs, Job, Lamentations, and Ecclesiastes. However, the appearance of his translation of Proverbs (Tarnopol, 1813) was bitterly criticized by *maskilim*, especially Tobias *Feder, who objected to the use of Yiddish, denouncing it as a betrayal of Haskalah ideals and a reversion to parochialism. Levin's other Yiddish works either remained in manuscript or were published after his death.

Levin was more of a popularizer than an original writer. Most of his works were translations, popularizations, or proposals designed to improve the condition of the Jews through the use of Enlightenment ideas, i.e., the application of reason to the social, economic, and moral problems of the community. For example, believing that poverty among the Jews stemmed from their involvement in petty commerce, he suggested that the situation could be improved only by Jewish participation in basic industry, the skilled trades, and farming. In spite of his strong opposition to Ḥasidism, he did not hesitate to request help from the leaders of the ḥasidic community in order to achieve communal reforms. Levin's approach to social and cultural problems was particularly influenced by the Edict of Tolerance (1781) of *Joseph II of Austria, and by N. H. *Wessely's *Divrei Shalom ve-Emet* (1782). Advocating the reform of Jewish education, Levin, like Wessely, urged that secular studies, especially the sciences, be added to Torah learning. The language of instruction, he believed, should be Polish, and that the Bible should be taught with the aid of a Polish translation. Although opposing fanaticism, Levin nevertheless held that religion was the driving force in the history of the Jewish people. He, therefore, vehemently opposed those *maskilim* who deviated from traditional observance. Unlike Mendelssohn, he wanted to preserve the wide internal autonomy of the *kehillah* and the jurisdiction of the Jewish rabbinical courts, but recommended the reorganization of the rabbinate so that it include district rabbis who possessed secular as well as talmudic knowledge.

Levin opposed Kabbalah, and Ḥasidism which he claimed to be responsible for lowering morality among the Jews. The first writer to see Ḥasidism as the most powerful opponent of the Haskalah, Levin urged rabbis to attack Ḥasidism and to censor its books as well as kabbalistic works. In his unpublished *Maḥkimat Peti* and *Der Ershter Ḥasid* Levin satirized the "nonsense" in ḥasidic writings, social mores, and theoretical principles. In his opinion the authorities were interested in bringing Enlightenment to the Jews and he suggested the enactment of legislation for this purpose. The best way of combating Ḥasidism was by undertaking educational work among the Jews. Levin died in Tarnopol.

Among his other writings are: *Moda la-Binah*, containing essays on science and excerpts from *Refu'ot ha-Am* and *Iggerot Ḥokhmah* (Berlin, 1789); *Ḥeshbon ha-Nefesh* (Lemberg, 1812), ethical essays patterned on Benjamin *Franklin's *Poor Richard's Almanac; Masot ha-Yam* (Zolkiew, 1818; Lemberg, 1859), a translation of Campe's travel book; *Elon Moreh*, an introduction to the *Guide of the Perplexed* (Odessa, 1867); *Sefer Kohelet* (Odessa, 1873; Vilna, 1930), a Yiddish translation of Ecclesiastes; and *Essai d'un plan de réforme ayant pour objet d'eclairer la nation juive en Pologne et de redresser par là ses moeurs* (1791–92).

Bibliography: Klausner, Sifrut, 1 (1952²), 224–53, includes bibliography; Zeitlin, Bibliotheca, 202–4; J. S. Raisin, *Haskalah Movement in Russia* (1913), 99–101; N. M. Gelber, in: *Abraham Weiss Jubilee Volume* (1964), 271–305, Hebrew part; idem, in: *Aus Zwei Jahrhunderten* (1924), 39–57; J. Weinloes, in: *Ha-Olam*, 13 (1925), iss. 39–42; idem, in: *YIVO Bleter*, 3 (1931), 334–57; J. L. Landau, *Short Lectures on Modern Hebrew Literature* (1938²), 187–92; M. Wiener, *Tsu der Geshikhte fun der Yidisher Literatur in 19ten Yorhundert* (1945), 38–44; S. Katz, in: KS, 16 (1939–40), 114–33; M. Erik (Merkin), *Etudn tsu der Geshikhte fun der Haskale* (1934), 135–51; Ch. Shmeruk, in: *Yidishe Shprakh*, 24 (1964), 33–52; Waxman, Literature, index, s.v. *Leffin*. [A. Ru.]

LEVIN, MEYER (1905–), U.S. novelist. Born and raised in the Chicago slums, Levin became a reporter for the Chicago *Daily News* and in 1925 was sent to cover the opening of the Hebrew University of Jerusalem, and returned to Palestine in 1928 to spend a year on a kibbutz. He had already written short stories of Jewish life, some of which appeared in the *Menorah Journal*, but his *Yehudah* (1931) was one of the first novels about kibbutz life. In *The*

Golden Mountain (1932), reissued in 1966 as *Classic Hassidic Tales*, he retold stories of the Ḥasidim, and in *The Old Bunch* (1937) portrayed his own generation of Chicago Jews. Levin was a correspondent in Spain during the Civil War (1936–39) and later reported the Palestine disorders for the Jewish Telegraphic Agency (1945–46). In 1946 he made the first feature film of the *yishuv*, *My Father's House*, and a documentary, *The Illegals*, in 1947. His autobiography, *In Search*, appeared in 1950.

Meyer Levin, U.S. novelist. Photo Eric Schwab.

Levin's writings covered a wide field—from Jewish mysticism to the modern American scene, which he depicted with realism and vitality. His novels include *Reporter* (1929), *Frankie and Johnny* (1930, reedited as *The Young Lovers*, 1952), *The Fanatic* (1964), and *Stronghold* (1965). Levin was the first writer to dramatize *The Diary of Anne Frank* (1952). His bestseller, *Compulsion* (1956), a study of the *Loeb-Leopold murder case of the 1920s, was dramatized by the author himself (1959) and filmed. *Eva* (1959) told the story of a Jewish girl's escape from Nazi-occupied Poland to Palestine. Levin also published a Passover *Haggadah*, various histories of Israel for juveniles, and books on the synagogue and the Jewish way of life. In 1958 he settled in Israel, which was the setting for his erotic extravaganza, *Gore and Igor* (1968).

Bibliography: S. Liptzin, *The Jew in American Literature* (1966) 218–22. [S.L.]

LEVIN, NATHANIEL WILLIAM (1819–1903), pioneer New Zealand communal leader. Born in London, he arrived at Port Nicholson (Wellington) in 1841, opened a store, and prospered, although the store was destroyed by an earthquake in 1848. He became a dynamic force in local commercial and maritime enterprises, establishing interests in the whaling trade and exporting wool. He built his own wharf and owned a fleet of sailing ships. A justice of the peace and foundation member of many public institutions, he was appointed to the Legislative Council in 1869, but retired to London in 1871. Earlier he took part in the affairs of the embryo Wellington Jewish community, his name appearing as a trustee to the Crown grant of the Jewish cemetery land. He was the father of William Hort Levin M.P. The town of Levin was named after the family.

Bibliography: *Journal and Proceedings of the Australian Jewish Historical Society*, 3 (1949–53), 305a.; L. M. Goldman, *History of the Jews in New Zealand* (1958), index. [M.S.P.]

LEVIN, SHMARYA (Shemaryahu; 1867–1935), Zionist leader, Hebrew and Yiddish author. Born in Svisloch, Belorussia, Levin joined Ḥibbat Zion in his youth, was one of *Aḥad Ha-Am's adherents, becoming a member of the *Benei Moshe society. Levin studied at Berlin University and at the Hochschule fuer die Wissenschaft des Judentums in the same city, joining the Russian-Jewish Scientific Society, which proliferated the idea of Jewish nationalism among Russian-Jewish students in Germany. He served as **Kazyonny ravvin* in Grodno (1896–97) and Yekatrinoslav (1898–1904) and preached in Vilna (1904–06). Throughout his career he worked toward spreading Zionist ideas both orally and in the Hebrew press (*Ha-Shilo'aḥ, Ha-Zeman, Ha-Ẓofeh*) and the Yiddish press (*Der Yud, Der Fraynd*). At the Sixth Zionist Congress (1903), Levin was among the leaders of the opposition to the *Uganda Scheme. He was also among the founders of the League for the Attainment of Equal Rights for the Jewish People in Russia (established in 1905) and a member of its central board. In 1906 Levin was chosen to the first Russian Duma as delegate of the Jewish National List in Vilna (with the support of the Lithuanians). He participated in deliberations in the Duma and delivered two speeches on the pogrom in Bialystok. After the first Duma was disbanded, Levin was among the signators of the Vyborg Declaration, which called for civil disobedience.

Afterward, Levin left Russia and settled in Berlin, from where he traveled to the United States on a number of lecture tours. At the Tenth Zionist Congress (1911), he was elected a member of the Zionist Executive. He took part in the work of the *Hilfsverein der deutschen Juden in Germany and was among the initiators of the establishment of the technical school in Haifa (the *Technion); he also influenced American Jews to contribute to this cause. Levin resigned from the board of governors of the Technion together with Aḥad Ha-Am and J. *Tschlenow after their suggestion to use Hebrew as the language of instruction was rejected. During World War I he lived in the U.S. and directed propaganda work on Zionism and Hebrew culture orally and in writing. Together with Y. D. *Berkowitz he edited the weekly *Ha-Toren* and regularly wrote its editorials. Levin was outstanding as a sharp-witted publicist, and he became particularly famous as a speaker and conversationalist. His speeches were a blend of Jewish heritage and European culture, spiced with Jewish folk wit. He frequently contributed to the Zionist press in all its languages, and some of his articles were collected in *Bi-Ymei ha-Ma'avar* ("In the Days of Transition," 1949).

In 1920 Levin participated in the postwar Zionist Conference in London and was entrusted with the propaganda for *Keren Hayesod. He was among the founders and directors of the Devir publishing house. In 1924 he

Portrait of Shemaryahu Levin by Joseph Oppenheimer, 1931. Oil on canvas, 72.5×96 cm. ($28\frac{1}{2}\times38$ in.). Jerusalem, Israel Museum. Photo David Harris, Jerusalem.

settled in Palestine, traveling from time to time in various countries on missions for the Zionist Movement and its funds. He developed ties of friendship with Sir Arthur *Wauchope, the high commissioner for Palestine. Levin's first book was entitled *Asarah Shirim* ("Ten Poems," original works and translations, 1899). In his last years he began to publish his memoirs in the *Jewish Daily Forward* (New York). A selection of his letters was published in 1966 entitled: *Iggerot Shemaryahu Levin*. A small selection of his articles appeared in English entitled *Out of Bondage* (1919). Levin's autobiography and memoirs appeard in English in three volumes entitled *Childhood in Exile* (1929), *Youth in Revolt* (1930), and *The Arena* (1932). In 1967 it appeared in one volume (abridged by Maurice Samuel) entitled *Forward from Exile* (1967).

Bibliography: L. Lipsky, *A Gallery of Zionist Profiles* (1956), 78–85; Z. Woyslawsky, *Yeḥidim bi-Reshut ha-Rabbim* (1943), 62–75; B. Katznelson, *Be-Ḥavlei Adam* (1964²), 83–88; J. Fichmann, *Be-Terem Aviv* (1959), 310–23; Ch. Weizmann, *Trial and Error* (1949), index. [Y.S.]

LEVIN, THEODORE (1897–1971), U.S. federal district court judge. Born in Chicago, Levin was appointed by President Truman in 1946 to the federal district court in Michigan. From 1959 to 1967 he was chief judge of the eastern district federal court of Michigan, remaining on the court until his death. Levin gave important aid to immigrants. He led the legal fight against an alien registration act which, in 1931, mainly thanks to his efforts, was declared unconstitutional by the U.S. circuit court of appeals, and cooperated actively with local and national agencies aiding immigrants. He started a sentencing counseling system in federal courts. A lifelong Zionist, Levin, who was deeply involved in Jewish organizational work, held numerous national and local offices. At one time, he was president of the Detroit Jewish Welfare Federation, United Jewish Charities, and the Council of Social Agencies. He was a board member of many organizations, among them the Joint Distribution Committee and the National Refugee Service. [F.R.L.]

LEVIN, YIZḤAK MEIR (1894–1971), leader of the *Agudat Israel movement. Born in Gora, Poland, Levin came from a ḥasidic family: his maternal grandfather was the Gerer Rabbi, R. Judah Aryeh Leib Alter *(Sefat Emet)*, and his father-in-law was the Gerer Rabbi, R. Abraham Mordecai Alter. He was active in Agudat Israel when it was formed in Poland after World War I. Agudat Israel in Poland was dominated by the Gerer Ḥasidim, and Levin quickly rose to its leadership. In 1924 he represented his movement on the Warsaw Community Council, and at the Second Great Assembly of Agudat Israel (Vienna, 1929) he was elected to the World Presidium. In 1935 he visited Palestine at the head of a delegation of the Agudat Israel Center in Poland and reorganized the executive there. At the Third Great Assembly (Marienbad, 1937), he was chosen as one of the two deputy presidents of the World Actions Committee.

Levin managed to escape from Poland at the beginning of World War II and in 1940 reached Palestine, where he was active in rescue operations from Nazi-dominated Europe. When the Central Committee of Agudat Israel met in Marienbad (1947), he was put in charge of the Ereẓ Israel branch of the movement. Levin was elected to the First *Knesset and was minister of social welfare in the first Israel government. He served in this capacity until 1952, when he resigned during the controversy over some form of national service for women. At the Fourth Great Assembly (Jerusalem, 1954), he was elected president of the World Actions Committee and chairman of the World Executive of Agudat Israel.

Bibliography: Tidhar, 4 (1950), 1804–05. [M.Fr.]

LEVIN, ẒEVI HIRSCH(-EL) BEN ARYEH LOEB (Hirsch Loebel; Hart Lyon; 1721–1800), rabbi; born in Rzeszow, Galicia. In addition to talmudic scholarship he had a knowledge of Hebrew grammar, Jewish history, philosophy, physics, and geometry. While still young, he took part in the *Emden-Eybeschuetz controversy, siding with Jacob Emden, his maternal uncle. In 1758 he was appointed rabbi of the Great and Hambro synagogues, London (where he was known as Hart Lyon), holding the post for seven years. When in 1764 the leaders of the London community prevented him from publishing a defense of the *sheḥitah* in London in reply to the attack of Jacob Kimḥi, and because of dissatisfaction with the state of talmudic studies, he relinquished his position and went to Halberstadt (Germany), where he was appointed rabbi and *rosh yeshivah*. In 1770 he was appointed rabbi of Mannheim and in 1773 became rabbi of Berlin. Levin was a friend of Moses *Mendelssohn, even writing an approbation for his German translation of the Bible. When the Prussian government requested Levin to write in German an account of Jewish commercial and matrimonial law, Levin asked Mendelssohn to compose it under his supervision. It was published in Berlin (1778) and entitled *Ritualgesetze der Juden*. His friendship with Mendelssohn was impaired when Levin attempted to prevent N. H. *Wessely from publishing his *Divrei Shalom ve-Emet* (Berlin, 1782) and even endeavored to have him expelled from Berlin. When Mendelssohn defended Wessely, Levin sent in his resignation; however, he did not act on it and remained in Berlin until his death. Levin supported and defended his son, Saul *Berlin, in the disputes in which he was involved, especially

Ẓevi Hirsch Levin, 18th-century rabbi in England and Germany. Cecil Roth Collection. Photo David Harris, Jerusalem.

with regard to the forged responsa *Besamim Rosh* (Berlin, 1793).

Levin's commentary on *Avot* was published together with that of Jacob Emden (Berlin, 1834). He also wrote occasional poems, entitled "*Naḥalat Ẓevi*" which were published in *Ha-Maggid* (no. 14, 1870). One of his poems appears at the beginning of his brother Saul's *Binyan Ari'el* (Amsterdam, 1778). He was father of Solomon *Hirschel, subsequently chief rabbi in London.

Bibliography: Adler, in: *Papers Read at the Anglo-Jewish Historical Exhibition* (1888), 280–4; B. H. Auerbach, *Geschichte der israelitischen Gemeinde Halberstadt* (1866), 86–96; C. Duschinsky, *The Rabbinate of the Great Synagogue, London* (1921), 2–73, 274–95; L. Landshut, *Toledot Anshei ha-Shem* (1884), 69–115; Schischa, in: *Ha-Darom*, 12 (1960), 58–67; Samet, in: KS, 13 (1967/68), 430–1; C. Roth, *History of the Great Synagogue, London* (1950), 108–23; idem, *Essays and Portraits in Anglo-Jewish History* (1962), 252–3; M. S. Samet, in: *Meḥkarim be-Toledot Am Yisrael ve-Ereẓ Yisrael le-Zekher Ẓevi Avneri* (1970), 249–53. [SH.T.]

LEVINAS, EMMANUEL (1905–), French philosopher. Born in Lithuania, Levinas went to the University of Strasbourg in 1923. In 1928–29 he studied at Freiburg. During these years he became familiar with the thought of Edmund *Husserl, serving his apprenticeship in phenomenology with Jean Hering. Levinas completed a doctoral dissertation on Husserl's theory of intuition, and was one of the first to introduce the work of Martin Heidegger in France. A practicing Jew, Levinas subsequently headed the Ecole Normale Orientale of the Alliance Israélite Universelle in Paris and taught at the University of Paris at Nanterre.

Levinas' philosophical work is concerned with the significance of the other person for metaphysical inquiry. Rejecting Heidegger's view that man must recover the meaning of being which has been obscured in the history of thought, Levinas maintains that man must transcend ontology through a unique relation with other persons. According to Levinas, traditional metaphysics sustains a distinction between the one and the other but this distinction is incorporated within a single point of view. The radical exteriority that characterizes genuine otherness is lost and the other is merely included within a totality. True otherness can only be experienced in a relation with a being beyond the totality. The subjectivity of the other person is always beyond totality and opens a dimension which can never be incorporated within thought. The being beyond totality which is reflected within it as its eschatological dimension is the infinite. Aspiration directed toward the infinite is metaphysics. Moral experience is the mode in which eschatology, through the experience of the human other, breaks into the totality. Levinas' major works include *De l'existence à l'existant* (1947); *En découvrant l'existence avec Husserl et Heidegger* (1949, 1967[2]); *Totalité et infini* (1961); *Difficile Liberté* (1963); and *Quatres lectures talmudiques* (1968).

Bibliography: J. Martin, in: *Revue Diocésaine de Tournai*, 19 (1964), 226–41; J. Derrida, in: *Revue de Métaphysique et de Morale*, 69 (1964), 322–54, 425–73. [E.W.]

LEVINÉ, EUGENE (**Nissen Berg**; 1883–1919), revolutionary, socialist politician and journalist. Born in St. Petersburg into a wealthy family, Leviné joined the Social Revolutionary Party on the outbreak of the 1905 revolution and was imprisoned by the czarist authorities. He was released in 1908 and allowed to go to Germany for medical treatment. He remained there and joined the Social Democratic Party. Leviné became a German citizen, joined the army on the outbreak of World War I, and was discharged in 1916 for reasons of health. Subsequently, he became a member of the Independent Social Democratic Party and then of the Communist Party, editing the party newspaper, *Rote Fahne*. Following the Bavarian uprising of November 1918, Leviné became chairman of the Council of People's Commissars in the Bavarian Soviet Republic of 1919. Two weeks later, when the republic was overthrown, Leviné was tried for treason and executed.

Bibliography: O. M. Graf, *Prisoners All* (1928); G. Schmolze, in: *Emuna* (1969), 329–36. [ED.]

LEVINE, JACK (1915–), U.S. painter; born in Boston. In 1936 his "Feast of Pure Reason" was included in the Museum of Modern Art exhibition—New Horizons in American Art. It caused a stir because Levine portrayed the millionaire John Pierpont Morgan within an unpleasant underworld setting. "String Quartette" (1934–37) was widely reproduced and reached a vast public. Levine served in the U.S. army during World War II, and then resumed his career in New York. He continued to work in a style that has been called "social realism." Unconcerned with abstract art, Levine continued to paint the uglier aspects of American society. Not all of his works, however, were marked by social indignation. "The Tombstone Cutter" (1947) represents the weariness of all working men. Levine's love extends to the working animals, e.g., in "The White Horse," 1946 and to familiar places as in "Apteka," the neighborhood around the Polish drugstore (1947). He also painted a series of small paintings dealing with the heroes of the Old Testament. In 1958 the New York Graphic Society issued six of them in an album, with a preface by Harvard professor Paul J. Sachs. Levine is a first-rate draftsman and has an unerring color sense. His paintings are characterized by vigorous reds, oranges, and blues, applied in heavy impasto, yet carefully maneuvered, well planned, and controlled so as to glow like stained glass. Levine's wife, the painter RUTH GIKOW (1914–), was born in Russia and

"Hillel" by Jack Levine. The rabbi is depicted as a scribe, with his writing desk in the form of a tower. Oil on panel, 8×10 in. (20×25 cm.). New York, Mr. and Mrs. Nate Spingold Collection. Photo Geoffrey Clements.

raised in the U.S. She studied at Cooper Union art school under Raphael Soyer. During the Depression she achieved eminence as a mural painter and graphic artist on Federal Art Projects. Her swift brush stroke and fresh sparkling color conveyed her warm personal impressions of urban life. Her work attracted wide attention and was acquired by leading U.S. museums.

Bibliography: F. Getlein, *Jack Levine* (1966), includes plates.

[A.W.]

LEVINE, PHILIP (1900–), U.S. immunohematologist. Born in Russia, Levine was taken to the United States when he was eight years old. From 1925 to 1932 he worked at the Rockefeller Institute and in 1935 was appointed bacteriologist and serologist to Newark's Beth Israel Hospital. From 1944 to 1965 he was director of immunohematology at the Ortho Research Foundation in Raritan, New Jersey. Levine did extensive work on human blood groups and blood transfusion. He discovered and codiscovered many blood group factors including the Rh, Hr (c), Cellano (k), M, N, P, Guth (s), Mia (Miltenberger), and the Tj^a factors. He described the specificity of the hemolysin in paroxysmal cold hemoglobinuria (Tj^a), elucidated the Rh null factor with suppressor genes preventing formation of Rh antigens, and characterized hemolytic disease of the newborn (erythroblastosis fetalis) and the phenomenon of isoimmunization through pregnancy. Levine was the author of New Jersey and Wisconsin state laws on blood tests in paternity disputes.

Bibliography: S. R. Kagan, *Jewish Medicine* (1952), 270–1. [F.R.]

LEVINGER, LEE JOSEPH (1890–), U.S. Reform rabbi. Born in Burke, Idaho, Levinger was ordained at Hebrew Union College in 1914. He held several pulpits and was a chaplain with the American Expeditionary Force in France in 1918–19. In 1929 he was national chaplain of the American Legion. Levinger became director of the Hillel Foundation at Ohio State University in 1925 and when in 1935 the National Hillel Commission set up a bureau of research to study the economic and occupational adjustment of Jewish students, it appointed him director. From 1942 to 1947 he was a field worker for the National Jewish Welfare Board and in 1948 he became chaplain of the Veterans Administration Hospital in Palo Alto, California. Levinger wrote a number of books. His *History of the Jews in the United States* which appeared in 1931 was one of the first works of its kind and went through several editions. He also wrote *A Jewish Chaplain in France* (1921); *Anti-Semitism Yesterday and Tomorrow* (1936); and *Folk and Faith* (1942).

In 1916 he married ELMA EHRLICH, author of several books and plays for Jewish children. [S.D.T.]

LEVIN-SHATZKES, YIZHAK (1892–1963), social leader. Born in Dvinsk (Daugavpils), Levin-Shatzkes joined the (illegal) Dvinsk branch of the *Bund in 1912. After Latvia became an independent state, he was elected a member of the Bund central committee, served on the Dvinsk city council (1922–34), and was secretary of the Jewish community council and chairman of the professional societies in Latgale province. By 1913 he had begun contributing articles to Russian-language periodicals appearing in Dvinsk; in 1921 he turned to Yiddish and became a contributor to Riga Yiddish dailies *Dos Folk* and *Frimorgen* and to periodicals published by the Bund. He was also the editor of *Latgalskaya Mysl*, a Russian-language weekly appearing in Dvinsk. After the May 1934 coup in Latvia, he was arrested, but was soon released. He settled in New York in 1936 and two years later became secretary of the *Jewish Socialist Farband of America and editor of *Der Veker*, the Farband organ. He contributed to various Yiddish periodicals published in New York and was active in a number of Jewish organizations and institutions.

Bibliography: *Yahadut Latvia* (1953), index; LNYL, 5 (1963), 281–2. [Jo.Ga.]

LEVINSOHN, ISAAC BAER (1788–1860), Hebrew author, one of the founders of the *Haskalah in Russia. He also was known as Ribal (initials of Rabbi Isaac Baer Levinsohn). Levinsohn was born in Kremenets, Volhynia, Russia, into a wealthy family. Later he moved to Radzivilov, on the border of Austrian Galicia. He taught himself European languages, and served as translator for the Russian forces in the time of the French invasion (1812). From 1813 to 1820 Levinsohn lived in the Eastern Galician towns of Brody, Tarnopol, and Zolkiew where he was befriended by such leaders of the Haskalah as Naḥman *Krochmal, Isaac *Erter, Joseph *Perl, and S. J. *Rapoport, and taught in the modern schools established in Tarnopol and Brody. From 1820–23 he spread the ideas of the Haskalah as a private tutor in wealthy homes in Berdichev and other towns. For reasons of health, Levinsohn returned to Kremenets in 1823. Levinsohn's connections with the Russian government gave him authority in Haskalah circles and protected him against the fury of his fanatical opponents. In his memoranda he tried to persuade the Russian authorities to mitigate the persecution of the Jews (his memorandum against the kidnapping of children for military service) and to introduce reforms in the spirit of the Haskalah. He supported a plan for agricultural settlement of Jews, especially those who had lost their livelihood owing to expulsion from the countryside and border areas. On his advice, the Russian authorities limited the number of Hebrew printing presses to three: Warsaw and Vilna in 1836, and Zhitomir in 1846 and imposed censorship on imported Hebrew books. In 1856, the Russian government decided to support him by buying 2,000 copies of his book *Beit Yehudah* and distributing them to synagogues and Jewish schools.

Levinsohn's literary work was mainly polemical and propagandistic. It dealt with the social, internal, and external position of the Jews in Eastern Europe. He started his public advocacy of the Haskalah by writing satires, mainly imitations of those by Perl and Erter. *Divrei Zaddikim* ("Words of the Righteous," 1830) written in the style of Perl's *Megalleh Temirin*, was published anonymously. In *Emek Refa'im* ("Valley of Ghosts"), *Peloni Almoni ha-Kozevi* ("So-and-So the Liar"), and his Yiddish play *Di Hefker Velt* ("The World of Chaos"), he satirizes not only the Ḥasidim and their *zaddikim*, but also the tyrannical

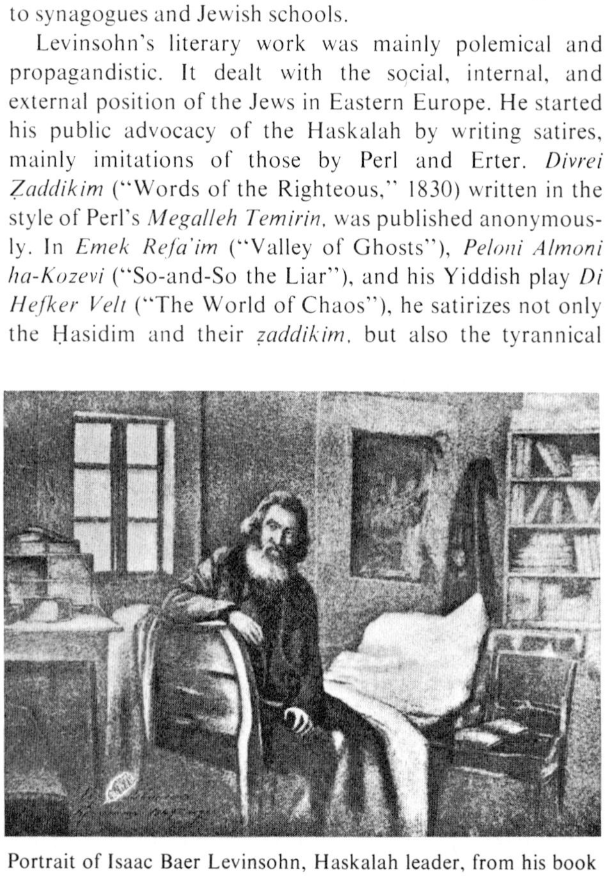

Portrait of Isaac Baer Levinsohn, Haskalah leader, from his book *Te'udah be-Yisrael*, Warsaw, 1901.

leaders of the community, the tax farmers, and the "kidnappers." These works circulated in manuscript among the Jews in Volhynia and Galicia and were only published posthumously, the first in Odessa in 1867; the second in 1880; and the third, *Yalkut Ribal*, in 1878.

In 1823, Levinsohn completed his most influential work *Te'udah be-Yisrael* ("Testimony in Israel") which, because of Orthodox opposition, did not appear until 1828 (Vilna). Levinsohn listed five questions which he intended to discuss: (a) Was it essential to study Hebrew grammatically? (b) Was it permitted to study foreign languages? (c) Was it permitted to study secular subjects? (d) Was there any advantage in the study of sciences and languages? (e) Did the advantage of such studies outweigh the disadvantages? Levinsohn appealed to the authority of talmudic and medieval sources, and to national sentiments. He characterized the Hebrew language as "the bond of religion and national survival," uniting all the dispersions of Israel into one people. He severely criticized the traditional *ḥadarim* ("Hebrew schools") which he dubbed "*ḥadrei mavet*" ("rooms of death"). He denounced their talmudic-centered curriculum, their unsystematic method of instruction, and their employment of corporal punishment. He objected to the use of Yiddish and demanded its replacement by "pure" German or Russian. He demonstrated that great Jews of the past knew foreign languages and studied the sciences, and explained the advantages of such studies, both in business and in relations with the authorities. He devoted considerable space to the advocacy of manual labor, especially farming, and criticized Jewish fondness for petty trading. The book had a great impact on Russian Jewish life. Groups formed in many towns which undertook to carry out Levinsohn's proposals. Even a part of Orthodox Jewry received the book sympathetically; only the Ḥasidim regarded it as a dangerous work. They banned the book and labeled an adherent of the Haskalah with the pejorative epithet *te'udke*. The Russian government awarded him a prize of 1,000 rubles for *Te'udah be-Yisrael*.

Levinsohn's second major book, *Beit Yehudah* ("House of Judah"), was published in Vilna in 1838 after considerable argument with the printers who refused to print it because of rabbinical opposition. The book purports to be a reply to 35 questions asked by "the great Christian nobleman Emanuel Lipen" (the name is a scramble of the Hebrew letters *Peloni Almoni* "So-and-So"). The questions deal with the nature of the Commandments, the Talmud, the Karaites, the Pharisees, the Zohar, Shabbateanism, Ḥasidism, and poses the question: "Is there still hope to reform the House of Israel and how?" In his basic assumptions Levinsohn follows Moses *Mendelssohn's *Jerusalem*. Judaism is a law; it should not be limited to "divine law," rather it should include "civic law," involving the practices of society and the sciences required for its maintenance and development. "Civic law" may be reformed and altered, with the consent of the people, in accordance with the spirit of the times and national needs. "The Jew is free to accept the legends of the Talmud or to reject them." Modern Christians should not be regarded as idolaters because they obey the seven *Noachide commandments and worship God. They are equal to Jews in respect to all the precepts involving the relations between men. The second half of the book is devoted to a historical survey of the teachings of the Jewish sages in all periods, including *Elijah of Vilna and Moses Mendelssohn. His historical survey follows traditional lines and contains numerous errors, demonstrating the backward state of Jewish knowledge at the time. Toward the end of the book, Levinsohn presents a five-point program for the reform of Jewish life in Russia: (a) The establishment of elementary schools for boys and girls of the lower classes. At the same time, boys and girls should learn a trade or a craft. For gifted pupils only, central colleges should be established in Warsaw, Vilna, Odessa, and Berdichev to teach Talmud and Codes, as well as "science, and various languages." (b) The appointment of a *rav kelali* ("chief rabbi"), assisted by a supreme religious court, who would appoint rabbis and preachers in all the towns of Russia, under his supervision. A committee of *parnasim kolelim* ("communal leaders") should also be appointed mainly to defend the poor and the ordinary people "against their leaders and the rich men who suck their marrow and drink their blood." (c) Preachers and orators should be appointed to arouse the people to good behavior, encourage them to take up trades and handicrafts, and explain to them their duties "to the Lord, to themselves, to their fellows, to the State, and to every man." (d) Representations should be made to the government to transfer one-third of the Jews of Russia to agriculture. (e) Luxuries should be forbidden, especially expensive feminine jewelry. These reforms should be carried out without asking for the people's consent.

Efes Damim (1837; "No Blood"), written to refute *blood libel, was published in Vilna in 1837 in the form of a debate between a Jewish rabbi and the Greek patriarch in Jerusalem, supplemented by statements of popes and kings protesting the blood libel. It was translated into English on the occasion of the Damascus blood libel in 1840, and into German and Russian. Another pamphlet called *Shorshei ha-Levanon* (or *Beit ha-Oẓar*, Vilna, 1841), containing minor studies, was published during the author's lifetime. He bequeathed his numerous unpublished works to his nephew Jacob Israel Levinsohn who asked David Bernhard *Nathanson to edit and publish them.

The most important of these posthumous works was *Zerubbavel*, which appeared in an incomplete form in Odessa in 1863, and later in several complete editions. It was written as a reply to *Netivot Olam* (1838–39), Stanislav *Hoga's Hebrew translation of *Old Paths*, a critique of Judaism published by the British missionary, McCaul. Levinsohn demonstrates McCaul's ignorance and the unfairness of his attacks on Judaism. He explains the evolution of the Oral Law from the Written Law, pointing out that in the course of this development reforms have been introduced in accordance with the changing needs of the times. Levinsohn insisted that only the halakhic ("legal") and not the aggadic ("legendary") elements of the tradition are binding for the observant Jew. Unlike Christianity, which is restricted to the spheres of faith and ethics, Judaism encompasses all spheres of individual and public life, and its aim is the strengthening of Jewish society: "The survival of the nation is the greatest of all the commandments." The book served to modify the hostile views about the Talmud and rabbinical literature which were often held by the followers of the Haskalah. Since *Zerubbavel* was intended for publication, Levinsohn phrased his remarks cautiously, so that the book could pass the censor. At the same time he wrote another work containing the rest of his arguments against Christianity. This manuscript was published after his death under the title of *Aḥiyyah ha-Shiloni ha-Ḥozeh* ("Ahijah the Shilonite, the Prophet," 1863). Here Levinsohn condemns the Christians for their persecution of the Jews, and their intolerance toward members of other faiths and various Christian sects, despite the Christian doctrine of forgiveness. As Christians did not carry out the Christian precepts of love, how can they demand that the Jews become Christians? He compares the sobriety and normal family life prevailing among the Jews, with the higher rate of alcoholism among non-Jews. "All these virtues have come to us from the Talmud." He uses the arguments of *Maimonides and others to show that whatever is positive in the New Testament is of rabbinic origin. Jesus himself, he argues, was an observant Jew who fulfilled all the commandments and believed that the Jews are the "chosen people."

Most of Levinsohn's other works were included in the collections *Bikkurei Ribal* (1888), *Yalkut Ribal* (1878), and *Eshkol ha-Sofer* (1891). Levinsohn's work was derivative. His views were drawn mainly from Mendelssohn, and his practical proposals followed those of the earlier Haskalah. The Hebrew readers of his day who belonged to the generation of transition from Orthodoxy to Haskalah enjoyed his defense of Judaism and his easy style, studded with biblical and rabbinic quotations. His books appeared in numerous editions, and Nathanson's biography of Levinsohn, *Sefer ha-Zikhronot* ("Book of Remembrances"), went through nine editions between 1876 and 1900. His contemporaries called him "The Russian Mendelssohn." For the modern reader, only his first book, *Te'udah be-Yisrael,* is of some historical value. By his personality and literary activity, Levinsohn undoubtedly did much to strengthen the moderate Haskalah. Certain ideas formulated in *Te'udah be-Yisrael,* such as educational reform and the transition to a life of labor and agriculture, later became a part of the programs of *Ḥibbat Zion, *Zionism, and other organizations and movements which preached "the productivization" of the Jewish masses and their adaptation to life in the modern world.

Bibliography: L. S. Greenberg, *A Critical Investigation of the Works of Rabbi Isaac Baer Levinsohn* (1930), includes bibliography; J. S. Raisin, *The Haskalah Movement in Russia* (1913), 204–13; S. Spiegel, *Hebrew Reborn* (1930), 167–72; Waxman, Literature, 3 (1960[2]), 202–12; Klausner, Sifrut, 3 (1952[2]), 33–115; S. Halkin, *Modern Hebrew Literature* (1950), 67. [Y.S.]

LEVINSON, ABRAHAM (1888–1955), U.S. pediatrician. Levinson, who studied with Béla *Schick and Heinrich *Finkelstein, was professor of pediatrics at Northwestern University Medical School. He founded the Levinson Research Foundation for research in pediatric neuropsychiatry. Levinson earned an excellent reputation as clinician, teacher, and historian. He pursued fundamental research in pediatric neurology and was a pioneer in the study of cerebrospinal fluid. He also did research on diphtheria, influenza, and tuberculosis. His most significant contribution was a test for diagnosing tuberculous meningitis and his study on the pathological changes in the brain following streptomycin treatment of that disease. Levinson's books include: *Cerebrospinal Fluid in Health and in Disease* (1919), the first book on the subject to appear in English; *Pediatric Nursing* (1925); *Pioneers of Pediatrics* (1936); and a biography of *Tobias Cohn* (1923). Levinson and Isaac Abt co-edited the *Pediatric Year Book* (1916–20).

Bibliography: *Abraham Levinson Anniversary Volume* (1949); *American Medical Association Journal...*, 159 (1955), 1139; S. R. Kagan, *Jewish Medicine* (1952), 369. [S.M.]

LEVINSON, ANDRE (1887–1933), dance critic and foremost writer on ballet in his time. Levinson was a professor of French literature in St. Petersburg, where he was born, and helped to edit a periodical on the imperial theaters. He became known as a brilliant critic of dance and a champion of the classical tradition. Leaving Russia after the 1917 Revolution, he settled in Paris in 1921 where he lectured on Russian literature and contributed to various journals. He was probably the first critic in France to approach ballet purely from the point of view of dance. He opposed the innovations of Fokine and Diaghilev, whom he regarded as having subordinated dancing to music and scenic elements. His biographies of dancers and people connected with the ballet included studies of the designer, Leon *Bakst (1923), the dancers and choreographers Noverre (1935), Marie Taglioni (1929) and Serge Lifar (1934). Among his books were *La danse au théâtre* (1924) and *La danse d'aujourd'hui* (1929). Levinson also wrote studies on the poets Théophile Gautier (1921) and Paul Valéry (1927). [M.B.S.]

LEVINSON, SALMON OLIVER (1865–1941), U.S. lawyer and world peace advocate. Levinson, who was born in Noblesville, Indiana, was admitted to the Illinois bar in 1891, and began to practice law in Chicago. Although subsequently recognized as the successful corporation lawyer who reorganized both the personal affairs and the companies of industrial tycoon George Westinghouse, Levinson became particularly prominent in 1915 for his "outlawry of war" idea and his attempt to start an international peace movement during World War I. He opposed the terms of the Versailles Treaty, which he considered unduly harsh and not conducive to world peace. In 1920 Levinson backed Warren G. Harding, who had espoused Levinson's idea of outlawing war, for the presidency. Although Levinson at first advocated and then opposed U.S. entry into the League of Nations, he did not work with the U.S. delegation to the Disarmament Conference (1921) and later urged U.S. entry into the World Court (1925). In 1927 he presented the Levinson Plan which called for the readjusting of German reparations and allied and interallied debts, and world peace. Levinson sponsored and helped draft the Kellogg-Briand peace pact, later ratified by 15 countries (1928). He donated two large collections of documents to the University of Chicago (1937, 1938) concerning his national and international activities and descriptions of his meetings. [Ed.]

LEVINTHAL, U.S. family, descended from an old rabbinical family. Bernard Louis Levinthal (1865–1952), who was born in Lithuania, went to the United States in 1891 after having studied at the yeshivot of Kovno, Vilna, and Bialystok. Settling in Philadelphia, he succeeded his father-in-law, Eleazar Kleinberg, as rabbi of Congrégation B'nai Abraham, where he served until his death, and as head of the United Orthodox Hebrew Congregations of Philadelphia. Levinthal was an able organizer and was responsible for the establishment of a number of institutions tending to the religious and social needs of the immigrant Jewish community, such as the Central Talmud Torah, out of which later grew the Yeshivah Mishkan

Portrait of Bernard Louis Levinthal by Robert Suzanne. Courtesy Abraham Levinthal from *American Jewish Historical Quarterly*, Vol. 54, New York, 1964.

Israel, and a municipal *va'ad ha-kashruth* to supervise ritual slaughtering. One of the founders of the *Union of Orthodox Rabbis of the United States and Canada in 1902, of which he was the first president, his energy and wide range of interests enabled him to represent the Orthodox point of view in the greater Jewish community. He was a founder of the American Jewish Committee and a member of the delegation sent by the American Jewish Congress to the Paris Peace Conference in 1919. An active Zionist as well, he helped to establish the Mizrachi Organization of America and was an honorary vice-president of the Federation of American Zionists.

His son ISRAEL HERBERT LEVINTHAL (1888–) was ordained by the Jewish Theological Seminary in 1910. He served at Congregations B'nai Shalom and Petach Tikvah in Brooklyn from 1910 to 1915 and from 1915 to 1919 respectively, and after 1919 at the Brooklyn Jewish Center. In addition, he was active in the Zionist movement and served as president of the Rabbinical Association of America. An exceptionally gifted preacher, he was adept at traditionally expounding biblical and rabbinical texts in the English language and several volumes of his sermons have been published. He taught homiletics at the Jewish Theological Seminary. His books include: *Judaism, An Analysis and An Interpretation* (1935); *Point of View: An Analysis of American Judaism* (1958); and *Judaism Speaks to the Modern World* (1963). LOUIS EDWARD LEVINTHAL (1892–), Israel's brother, practiced law in Philadelphia until 1937, when he was appointed judge on the Philadelphia Court of Common Pleas, a position he held until his retirement in 1959. Besides writing a number of legal works, he devoted himself to numerous charitable and civic organizations and to the Zionist Organization of America, of which he was elected president in 1941. He was particularly active in the Jewish Publication Society of America, serving as chairman of its publications committee from 1939 to 1949 and again from 1954 to 1962, and as its president from 1949 to 1954. He was chairman of the Board of Governors of the Hebrew University (1962–66). [S.D.T.]

LEVI-PEROTTI, GIUSTINA, the supposed 14th-century author of two Petrarchan sonnets. In one, the author expresses her longing for the poetic world and her wish to gain experience in writing poetry, instead of engaging in weaving and sewing, tasks normally assigned to women. The sonnets were published in the 16th century and were attributed to Giustina in a collection of the poems of Petrarch (1304–74) assembled by G. F. Tomasini (*Petrarcha redivivus*, Padua, 1635). Tomasini claimed that the sonnet described was directed to Petrarch and that the latter replied with one of his most famous works, *La gola, e'l sonno e l'otiose piume*, encouraging the poet to persevere in a task "undertaken by only a few." On the basis of the obviously Jewish name Giustina Levi (Giusta or Giustina were names common among Italian Jewesses, especially during the Middle Ages), it was assumed that Petrarch had some connection with a Jewish poet of his time. However, only a few Petrarch scholars ever accepted this assumption, which was finally rejected by modern Italian literary critics. The notion of a Jewish poetess exchanging sonnets with Petrarch is in the romantic vogue of *petrarchismo*, which flourished in the 16th century and was based on imitations of Petrarch's verse. It is thus very probable that the poems attributed to Giustina Levi-Perotti were actually written in the 16th century and that she never in fact existed.

Bibliography: Morici, in: *Rassegna Nazionale* (1899), 662–95.

[J.B.S.]

LÉVI-PROVENÇAL, EVARISTE (1894–1956), French orientalist; original name, **Mabkhūsh.** Born in Algiers, where he also studied, Lévi-Provençal became professor (1922) and director (1929) of the Institut des Hautes Etudes Morocaines in Rabat, professor (1928) at the University of Algiers, professor (1945) at the Sorbonne, and director of the Institut des Etudes Islamiques and of the Centre d'Etudes de l'Orient of the University of Paris. He distinguished himself mainly in two fields: in the publication of Arabic texts and as a historian of Muslim Spain. In the libraries of North Africa and Spain he discovered various manuscripts of old texts which shed new light on the history of the Almohads and the Muslim rule in Spain, among them works such as the memoirs of Baydhag, a companion of Ibn Tūmart, and those of Abdallah, the last Zirid king of Granada. He also published other texts, such as old *ḥisba* books, dealing with markets, letters of the Almohad rulers, and writings of the Magreb and Spanish Arabic historians and geographers. His major achievement, however, was his *Histoire de l'Espagne musulmane* (vol. 1, 1944; vols. 1–3, 1950–53²), whose first two volumes give a very clear outline of the political history of Muslim Spain until the downfall of the Umayyad caliphate of Cordoba, whereas the third volume contains a detailed analysis of its social and cultural life. The whole work should have comprised six volumes, but when the author died, he had only collected his materials for the last three volumes. Lévi-Provencal also published Arabic inscriptions from North Africa and Spain (*Inscriptions arabes d'Espagne*, 1931) and many essays on the history and the civilization of the Muslims in Spain. Additionally, he was the founder of the review *Arabica* (Paris, 1953–) and one of the first editors of the second edition of the *Encyclopaedia of Islam*.

For a list of his writings see J. and D. Sourdel, in: *Arabica*, 3 (1956), 136–46. [E.A.]

LEVIRATE MARRIAGE AND ḤALIẒAH.

Definition. Levirate marriage (Heb. יִבּוּם; *yibbum*) is the marriage between a widow whose husband died without offspring (the *yevamah*) and the brother of the deceased (the *yavam* or levir), as prescribed in Deuteronomy 25:5–6:

> If brethren dwell together, and one of them die, and have no child, the wife of the dead shall not marry without unto a stranger [the last words according to AV translation, which is correct]; her husband's brother shall go in unto her, and take her to him to wife, and perform the duty of a husband's brother unto her. And it shall be, that the firstborn that she beareth shall succeed in the name of his brother that is dead, that his name be not blotted out of Israel.

When the levir does not marry the *yevamah*, the ceremony of *ḥaliẓah* (Heb. חֲלִיצָה) takes place, whereby the woman becomes released from the levirate tie (*zikkat ha-yibbum*) and free to marry someone else:

> If the man like not to take his brother's wife, then his brother's wife shall go up to the gate unto the elders, and say: 'My husband's brother refuseth to raise up unto his brother a name in Israel; he will not perform the duty of a husband's brother unto me.' Then the elders of his city shall call him, and speak unto him; and if he stand, and say: 'I like not to take her'; then shall his brother's wife draw nigh unto him in the presence of the elders, and loose his shoe from off his foot, and spit in his face; and she shall answer and say: 'So shall it be done unto the man that doth not build up his brother's house.' And his name shall be called in Israel 'The house of him that had his shoe loosed'" (Deut. 25:7–10).

In the Bible. The events concerning Judah and Tamar (Gen. 38) indicate that the practice of levirate marriage preceded the Mosaic law (cf. Gen. R. 85:5). However, it appears that levirate marriage then differed from that of Mosaic law in that the obligation also appears to have been laid on the father of the deceased husband (Gen. 38:26) and no mention is made of a release by way of *ḥaliẓah*. Some scholars expressed the opinion, following the view of Josephus (Ant. 5:332–5) and several Karaite authorities (*Gan Eden*, Nashim, 13, 30; *Adderet Eliyahu*, Nashim 5), that the events concerning Ruth and Boaz (Ruth 4) also

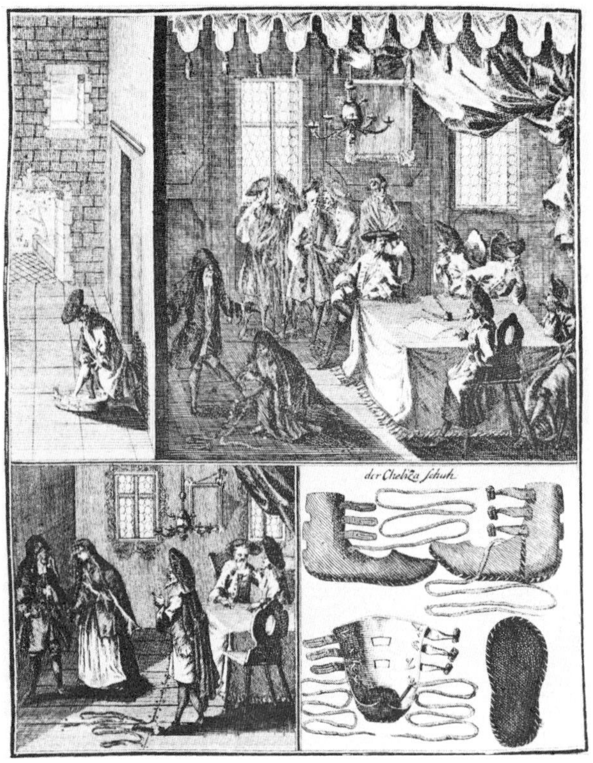

Figure 1. Page showing the *ḥaliẓah* ceremony from *Kirchliche Verfassung*, a book on Jewish rituals by the German Protestant theologian, Johann Bodenschatz, Erlang, 1748. Above left, the brother washes his feet in preparation for the ceremony; above right, the *yevamah* removes her brother-in-law's shoe; lower left, she spits in his face; lower right, the *ḥaliẓah* shoe. Cecil Roth Collection.

indicate a levirate marriage, but it appears that in this case the duty of the *go'el* to marry Ruth was incidental to the laws concerning the redemption of property of the deceased; hence the variation in a number of details from the prescribed levirate marriage laws (Ibn Ezra, Deut. 25:5; Naḥmanides, Gen. 38:8).

In the Talmud. NEED FOR LEVIRATE MARRIAGE AND ḤALIẒAH. The word *ben* ("son") in Deuteronomy 25:5 is interpreted in the Talmud, in the Septuagint, and by Josephus (Ant. 4:254) to mean "offspring" and not only a male child (cf. Gen. 3:16), so that a levirate marriage is only obligatory when the deceased husband leaves no offspring whatever, whether from the *yevamah* or another wife, including a child conceived during his lifetime but not born until after his death, even if that child subsequently died (Yev. 2:5, 22B; Nid. 5:3; and codes). The words, "if brothers dwell together" (Deut. 25:5) have been interpreted by the scholars as confining the application of levirate marriage to the brothers of the deceased who were born prior to his death (Yev. 2:1, 2). Thus if the birth of the levir precedes his brother's death by as little as one day and there are no other brothers, the *yevamah* must wait until he reaches the age of 13 years and a day, when he becomes legally fit either to marry her or grant her *ḥaliẓah* (Nid. 5:3; Yev. 105b; see *Legal Capacity). The law of *yibbum* applies only to paternal not maternal brothers (Yev. 17b). If the deceased is survived by several brothers, the obligation of *yibbum* or *ḥaliẓah* devolves on the eldest but is nevertheless valid if performed by another brother (Yev. 24a; 39a). If the deceased brother had several wives, fulfillment of the obligation in respect of one wife suffices and exempts the other wives (Yev. 4:11, 44a; and codes).

The tie (*zikkah*) between the *yevamah* and the *yevam* arises immediately upon the husband's death. From this stage, until she undergoes levirate marriage or *ḥaliẓah*, the *yevamah* is known as a *shomeret yavam* ("awaiting the levir") and relations between the levir and her kin are prohibited (as incestuous), as if he were married to her. Only a putative marriage can be contracted between a *shomeret yavam* and an "outsider," who is obliged to divorce her, although their offspring are not considered *mamzerim (Yev. 13b; al. Yad, Ishut, 4:14).

The *shomeret yavam* may not undergo levirate marriage or *ḥaliẓah* until three months after the date of her husband's death (Yev. 4:10 and codes) as with any other widow, who must await this period before remarrying. She is therefore entitled to *maintenance from her husband's estate during this period, but not thereafter, according to the *halakhah* of the talmudic period—neither from her husband's estate nor from the levir. However, if the levir evaded her after she had sued him in court either to marry her or grant her *ḥaliẓah* the rabbis fined him to pay her maintenance (Yev. 41b; Rashi, and Tosafot thereto), and this was also the law if he became ill or went abroad (TJ, Ket. 5:4, 29d; Yad, Ishut, 18:16).

In biblical law the levir does not require a formal marriage *(kiddushin)* to the *yevamah* since the personal status tie, the *zikkah* between them, arises automatically upon the death of the husband of the *yevamah*. However, the scholars prescribed that the *yevamah* should be married like all women, in this case by *kiddushei kesef* or *shetar*, these *kiddushin* called "*ma'amar*" (lit. "declaration"): "first he addresses to her a *ma'amar* and then they cohabit" (lit. "he takes her into his home"; Tosef. Yev. 7:2; Yev. 52a). The scholars ruled that the levir who marries the *yevamah* succeeds to the estate of his deceased brother (Yev. 4:7), interpreting the passage "*ve-hayah ha-bekhor asher teled*" (Deut. 25:6) as referring to the firstborn of the brothers on whom the duty of levirate marriage devolved and hence that the continuation of this passage, i.e., "shall succeed in the name of his brother" (meaning "shall succeed to the inheritance") refers to the levir undergoing levirate marriage. This argument was described as "having entirely deprived the text of its ordinary meaning through a *gezerah shavah*" (see *Hermeneutics; Yev. 24a). According to R. Judah (Yev. 4:7), "where there is a father, he inherits the son's property," otherwise the brothers succeed to the estate (Tosef. Yev. 63) and the levir marrying the *yevamah* inherits only a brother's proportional share. He interprets the above passage literally, as referring to the firstborn of the union between the levir and the *yevamah*, who succeeds to the estate of the deceased brother (interpreted similarly by Tar. Yer., Ibn Ezra, and Rashbam, Deut. 25:6, Rashi, Gen. 38:8—from whom Ramban Gen. *ibid.* differs). The *amoraim* commented, however, that R. Judah did not differ from the scholars but merely excepted the case of the deceased who is survived by his father, for the levir is compared to the *firstborn ("ve-hayah ha-bekhor asher teled")*, who does not inherit in his father's lifetime (Yev. 40a). Even according to the scholars whose opinion was accepted, the levir does not succeed to a contingent inheritance *(ra'ui)*, i.e., to property due to come to the deceased brother (such as the proportional share of his father's estate which the deceased, but for his death, would have inherited), but only to property already owned by the brother at the time of his death, as in the case of the firstborn (Bek. 8:9; see *Succession). The *ketubbah*, i.e., the widow's jointure, is a charge on the property which the levir inherits from the deceased and he is prohibited from alienating the latter by way of sale or gift—any such attempted alienation being void (Ket. 82a). In a case where the levir inherits no property from his brother, the scholars determined that the widow must receive her *ketubbah* from the levir's property "so that he shall not consider it easy to divorce her" (Yev. 39a). A levir who chooses to perform *ḥaliẓah* receives no more than a brother's share of the deceased's estate (Yev. 4:7) and upon *ḥaliẓah* the widow becomes entitled to receive her *ketubbah* from her deceased husband's estate (Yev. 85a; Sh. Ar., EH 165:4).

The Duty of Ḥaliẓah. According to the Torah, the duty of *ḥaliẓah* is imposed only when the levir willfully refuses to marry the *yevamah*, and not when he is unable to or prohibited from marrying her, for "whoever is subject [lit. "goes up"] to levirate marriage is subject to *ḥaliẓah*, and whoever is not subject to levirate marriage is not subject to *ḥaliẓah*" (Yev. 3a). Thus, for example, where a levirate marriage is precluded because the relationship would be incestuous, the widow (supposing she is the levir's daughter or his wife's sister) is also exempted from *ḥaliẓah*. According to Bet Hillel, if one of the deceased's several wives is prohibited from marrying the levir she also exempts her co-wives (*ẓarah*, "rival") and the "rivals of her rivals" (if the rival has married another man) from levirate marriage and *ḥaliẓah*, but Bet Shammai's opinion was that the rival is not thus exempted (Yev. 1:1; 1:4; cf. Yev. 16a and TJ, Yev. 1:6, 3a). On the other hand, it was determined that at times the duty of *ḥaliẓah* exists even where levirate marriage is forbidden—as between a priest and divorcee—by a "prohibition of holiness" (*issur kedushah*); in such a case *ḥaliẓah* is still required for, as in all cases of negative precepts, the marriage, even if prohibited, is nevertheless valid once it has taken place (Yev. 2:3 and Rashi ad loc., TJ, Yev. 1:1, 2c; see Prohibited *Marriage). This rule also applies when doubt exists as to whether levirate marriage is incumbent on the widow, in which case *ḥaliẓah* is required (Git. 7:3, et al.). In cases where the levir is seriously ill or there is a big difference in their ages, or the levir is "not suitable" (*eino hagun*) for the widow, etc., efforts were made to arrange for *ḥaliẓah* rather than marriage.

Priority between Levirate Marriage and Ḥaliẓah. In the course of time some scholars accepted the view that the duty of the *ḥaliẓah* always took priority over that of levirate marriage, a view stemming from the attempt to reconcile the prohibition on a man marrying his brother's wife (Lev. 18:16) with the command of levirate marriage. These biblical commandments induced the Samaritans to confine the application of levirate marriage to a woman who had undergone *kiddushin* but not *nissu'in* (see *Marriage)—in which case she would not be considered a relative with whom marriage was prohibited (Kid. 75b–76a; TJ, Yev. 1:6)—while some Karaite scholars were led to interpret the word "brothers" as relatives and not literally (*Gan Eden* Nashim, 13; *Adderet Eliyahu*, Nashim, 5). The two biblical provisions do not conflict, however, for the prohibition in Leviticus 18:16 applies only where the deceased brother is survived by descendants, whereas the *mitzvah* of levirate marriage applies only when the deceased brother dies without issue, in order that the levir shall "succeed in the name of his brother." The *mitzvah* of levirate marriage and the prohibition of marrying a brother's wife "were said as one" (Mekh. Ba-Ḥodesh; Sif. Deut., 233; TJ, Ned. 3:2, 37d). Hence in the beginning, when the parties carried out the precept for the sake of fulfilling a commandment, levirate marriage took priority over *ḥaliẓah*; but when the precept was carried out for other reasons, the scholars said that *ḥaliẓah* took priority over levirate marriage, and "a levir who marries the *yevamah* other than for the sake of fulfilling a commandment commits incest" (Bek. 1:7 and Rashi ad loc.); and ". . . I am inclined to think that the child of such a union is a *mamzer*" (Abba Saul, Tosef. Yev. 6:9; Yev. 39b). The question of priority was much disputed by the scholars. In the third generation of *tannaim*, levirate marriage was customarily upheld (Yev. 8:4), while the Babylonian *amoraim* left the choice between marriage and *ḥaliẓah* to the levir, although some "reenacted the priority of levirate marriage over *ḥaliẓah*" (Yev. 39a–b). The Palestinian *amoraim* apparently held that *ḥaliẓah* took priority (Bar Kappara in TJ, Yev. 109a, makes no mention of the above "reenactment" of levirate marriage priority).

The Order of Ḥaliẓah. *Ḥaliẓah* which releases the widow from the obligation of levirate marriage enables her to marry freely, except that the scholars prohibited a priest from marrying her (Yev. 24a). The *ḥaliẓah* ceremony is designed to shame the levir for not "building up his brother's house" (Deut. 25:9). It has been seen as an act of *kinyan* (*acquisition), whereby the widow buys from the levir the inheritance of his deceased brother (Rashbam *ibid.*; cf. Ruth 4:7–8), or as a form of mourning for the levir's brother "for he shall be forgotten now that no offspring shall be raised in his name" (Jehiel of Paris cited in *Seder Ḥaliẓah* to Sh. Ar., EH 169:57, no. 82; Responsum of Isaac Caro at the end of Responsa *Beit Yosef*). Although the formalities of *ḥaliẓah* are performed by the *yevamah*, the levir is called the *ḥoleẓ*, i.e., "loosener" (Yev. 4:1, 5–8; 5:6; et al.), for the levir "participates in *ḥaliẓah* in that his intention to loosen is required," hence a deaf-mute levir who lacks such intention is called the *neḥlaẓ* and not the *ḥoleẓ* (Yev. 12:4; *Nimmukei Yosef* 104b, and Maim. commentary ad loc.).

Many details are stipulated for the order of the *ḥaliẓah* ceremony (Yev. 12:6; Yad, Yibbum 4:1–23; Sh. Ar., EH 169); essentially they are as follows: The levir and the *yevamah* appear before the *bet din*, the levir wearing on his right foot a special shoe, the "*ḥaliẓah* shoe"; the *yevamah* recites a passage indicating the levir's refusal to perform his duty to marry her; the levir responds by affirming his refusal—all this in Hebrew in the words prescribed in the Bible (Deut. 25:7, 9); the *yevamah* then removes the shoe from the levir's foot, throws it to the ground, spits on the ground before the levir, and utters the final prescribed passage (Deut. 25:9); finally, those present repeat the words "*ḥaluẓ ha-na'al*" three times. The Boethusians held that the *yevamah* is required actually to spit in the levir's face and this is also stated in two manuscripts of the Septuagint, in Josephus' *Antiquities*, and in some of the apocryphal books, but the talmudic scholars held it to be sufficient if the elders see her spitting (Sif., Deut. 291). At the completion of the ceremony, the *dayyanim* express the wish "that the daughters of Israel shall have no need to resort to either *ḥaliẓah* or levirate marriage" (Sh. Ar., EH, 169, "abridged order of *ḥaliẓah*," 56). At first it was

Figure 2. Leather *ḥaliẓah* shoe, Germany, 19th century. Jerusalem, Israel Museum, Feuchtwanger Collection. Photo David Harris, Jerusalem.

customary to issue a deed of *ḥaliẓah* as proof that the ceremony had taken place (Yev. 39b—as distinguished from a deed of divorce where the delivery of the deed constitutes the act of divorce), but in the course of time this practice was abandoned since "the ceremony was performed in public, before ten people, and she does not require documentary proof" (Sh. Ar., EH 169, "abridged order of *ḥaliẓah*," 13; and end of commentary *Seder Ḥaliẓah*, no. 82).

In the Post-Talmudic Period. PRIORITY. In the post-talmudic period, the dispute over the question of priority was continued. In the opinion of the Sura *geonim*, levirate marriage took priority, while those of Pumbedita thought otherwise, as did some of the Sura scholars (R. Hillai and R. Natronai). In the rabbinic period the Spanish scholars—particularly Alfasi (to Yev. 39b), Maimonides (Yad, Yibbum 1:2), and Joseph Caro (Sh. Ar., EH, 165:1)—gave priority to levirate marriage, contending that otherwise there is no reason to shame and to submit the levir to the prescribed indignities and that the kabbalistic scholars said that "levirate marriage is very beneficial for the soul of the dead," and that Abba Saul who held that *ḥaliẓah* took priority, "did not know this kabbalistic mystery," otherwise he would not have come to the conclusion he reached (Isaac Caro, quoted in Resp. *Beit Yosef*, loc. cit.). Such has actually been the custom, until the present day, of the Jews of Spain and of the oriental communities in North Africa from Morocco to Egypt—in Yemen, Babylonia, and Persia. This was also the case in Ereẓ Israel (even at the end of the 1940s; see *Mishpetei Uziel*, EH no. 119) until the matter was settled by a *takkanah* of the chief rabbinate of Israel (in 5710–1949/50, see below). The scholars of northern France and Germany—particularly Rashi, Rabbenu Tam, Asher b. Jehiel (Tur. EH 165), and Moses Isserles (*Rema* EH, 165:1)—held that *ḥaliẓah* takes priority though they did not all assign the same measure of priority to it. The acceptance of Rabbenu Gershom's decree (prohibiting polygamy) among Ashkenazi Jews (see *Bigamy) apparently contributed greatly toward the entrenchment of the rule that *ḥaliẓah* takes priority—in order not to distinguish between a married and an unmarried levir—and Ashkenazi communities gradually came to adopt the practice of *ḥaliẓah* to the exclusion of levirate marriage.

Problems of Levirate Marriage—The Apostate Levir. The scholars devote a great deal of discussion to the solution of problems centering around the laws of levirate marriage and *ḥaliẓah*, arising both from objective factors and from the levir's conduct. The Mishnah (Git. 7:3) relates the case of a childless husband who fell ill and wrote his wife a "conditional" bill of divorce, effected upon his death, so that on his death the divorce would take effect retroactively to the date of delivery of the bill, with the intention of absolving her from the obligations of a *yevamah*. In the case of an "unsuitable" levir, or one suffering from a serious illness, or whose age differed greatly from that of the widow, it was sought to influence the levir in various ways to forego marriage in favor of *ḥaliẓah*. From the geonic period, mention is made (first in the *Halakhot Gedolot*, end of Hilkh. Yevamot) of the problem of the *yevamah* and the *apostate levir "in the land of the Berbers, among gentiles" or "who cannot be reached in a far land," which placed the *yevamah* in the position of an **agunah*. Some of the *geonim* decided that she retained this status until released by the apostate levir, but others ruled that she was exempted from *ḥaliẓah* if at the time of her marriage to the deceased his brother was already an apostate. It seems that the Babylonian academies were also divided on this question, Sura taking a lenient view and Pumbedita a strict one (L. Ginzberg, *Ginzei Schechter*, 2 (1929), 167f.). In later times the view that *ḥaliẓah* was obligatory for the widow in every case became increasingly stronger and a solution for the problem was sought by the imposition—at the time of the *kiddushin* ceremony—of a condition specifying that the wife "shall be considered as not having been married if it shall be her lot to require levirate marriage at the hands of an apostate" (*Rema*, EH 157:4).

Problems of Ḥaliẓah. In an effort to overcome the problem that arose when a levir refused to undergo *ḥaliẓah*, many French and German communities enacted *takkanot* awarding the levir a substantial share of the deceased brother's estate—financed partly at the widow's expense—although according to law the levir was entitled only to a brother's share upon *ḥaliẓah*. The varying terms of these *takkanot* gave rise to frequent disputes, so that in practice the courts sought to compromise between the parties (Sh. Ar., EH 163:2, 165:4). As this, in turn, frequently caused the widow to be left at the levir's mercy, it became increasingly customary for the husband's brothers to write—at the time of the marriage—a "deed of undertaking to grant *ḥaliẓah*" committing themselves to release the widow, whenever the need might arise, in a valid *ḥaliẓah* ceremony, without delay or demand for consideration; this undertaking was enforced by way of a biblical *oath and a severe penalty or *ban. Where the levir was a minor at the time of his brother's marriage and his undertaking consequently unenforceable, his father would write a deed guaranteeing that his minor son would, upon reaching maturity, provide the required undertaking to his sister-in-law. The father backed his guarantee—which was itself lacking in authority (see **Asmakhta*)—by a monetary pledge to his daughter-in-law, which would be canceled on the production of the required undertaking (Gulak, Oẓar, 90–97). Many of the **aḥaronim* decided in favor of obliging the levir to maintain the widow to whom he refused to grant *ḥaliẓah*, despite the lack of unanimity among the *rishonim* on the circumstances and terms on which maintenance should be awarded, as otherwise "she may be kept an *agunah* forever" (*Arukh ha-Shulḥan*, EH 160:8).

In recent years the problem of *ḥaliẓah* arising from the levir being absent abroad has become more acute, particularly in the case of countries in the Soviet bloc. Several halakhic authorities, led by Shalom Mordecai ha-Kohen *Schwadron, head of the Brezen *bet din*, have sought to avoid the widow's need to travel to the *levir* by permitting her to be represented at the *ḥaliẓah* ceremony by an agent (Resp. Maharsham, pt. 1, nos. 14, 135), a view based on confining the prohibition on *agency in *ḥaliẓah* to the levir only (Ket. 74a); however, most of his contemporaries dissented from this. It has also been rejected by modern Ereẓ Israel scholars (e.g., *Mishpetei Uziel* 2 (1938), EH 88; *Kunteres Sheliḥut ba-Ḥaliẓah*) and this problem—like that which arises when the *levir* is a minor, placing the widow in a position of an *agunah* until he reaches the age of 13 years and a day—urgently awaits a solution, possibly along the lines already indicated.

Takkanah of the Chief Rabbinate of Ereẓ Israel. In 1944 the chief rabbinate of Ereẓ Israel enacted a *takkanah* obliging the levir to maintain the levirate widow until he released her by *ḥaliẓah*, according to "law and precept," if a rabbinical court had certified that he refused to comply with its decision ordering him to grant her *ḥaliẓah*. This *takkanah*, which gives expression to the view of those halakhic scholars who would oblige the recalcitrant levir to maintain the widow, has made this obligation part of the law of maintenance, rather than its being a fine for noncompliance. It was prompted by the fact of "much difficulty and suffering arising from the regrettable preva-

Figure 3. Marriage certificate for the levirate marriage of a *yevamah*. Venice, 1735. Cecil Roth Collection.

lence of cases of Jewish women who are in need of levirate marriage and are placed in the position of *agunot* because *ḥaliẓah* has been withheld from them." A further *takkanah* of the chief rabbinate of the State of Israel (1950) completely prohibited the practice of levirate marriage in Israel while making *ḥaliẓah* obligatory. This *takkanah*, extending also to the Sephardi and oriental Jewish communities in Israel, was expressly justified on the grounds that "most levirs do not undergo levirate marriage for the sake of fulfilling a *mitzvah*, and also to preserve peace and harmony in the State of Israel by keeping the law of the Torah uniform for all."

In the State of Israel. The Rabbinical Courts Jurisdiction (Marriage and Divorce) Law, 5713–1953 of the State of Israel confers on the rabbinical court exclusive jurisdiction in a case where a woman sues her deceased husband's brother for *ḥaliẓah*, and also with regard to maintenance for the woman until the day on which *ḥaliẓah* is granted (sec. 5). Section 7 of the same law further provides that "Where a rabbinical court, by final judgment [i.e., when it can no longer be appealed against; sec. 8] has ordered that a man be compelled to give his brother's widow *ḥaliẓah*, a district court may, upon expiration of three months from the day of making the order, on application of the attorney general, compel compliance with the order by imprisonment." A judgment compelling a levir to grant *ḥaliẓah* will be given by the rabbinical court in similar circumstances to those in which it customarily sees fit to compel the grant of a divorce, and in certain additional cases, e.g., where the levir is already married (Tur and Sh. Ar., EH 165), but at all times only where compulsion is supported by halakhic authority so as not to bring about a prohibited "forced *ḥaliẓah*" (Yev. 106a; Yad, Yibbum 4:25–26; Sh. Ar., EH 169:13). This procedure, so far as halakhically permitted, offers an effective means of dealing with a recalcitrant levir. [M.E.]

The Ceremony of Ḥaliẓah. The ceremony of *ḥaliẓah* is invested with a special solemnity. The normal *bet din*, consisting of three ordained rabbis, is augmented for the occasion by two additional members (who can be laymen), "in order to give publicity to the matter" (Yev. 101a–b). The five members of the *bet din* meet at the place where the ceremony is to take place on the previous day, in order to "establish the locum" (Yev. 101b). The ceremony takes place the following morning, and the *yevamah* (more correctly *yavmah*) is enjoined to fast until the ceremony. She and the levir are also instructed, if necessary, to repeat the respective declarations which they have to make, according to Deuteronomy 25:7–10, in the original Hebrew. Questions are put to ascertain that there are no circumstances which might invalidate the ceremony, e.g., to ascertain that both are majors, in full possession of their normal mental faculties, that 91 days have passed since the death of her husband. Although *yibbum*, levirate marriage, is forbidden at the present time, the presiding rabbi nevertheless formally asks the levir which he prefers, to marry his sister-in-law or release her through *ḥaliẓah*, to which he replies confirming the latter alternative. The ceremony proper then commences, the essence of which is that the *yevamah*, in accordance with Deuteronomy 25:9, has to draw a shoe off the foot of her brother-in-law. The *ḥaliẓah* shoe must conform rigidly to the halakhic regulations laid down for it. It is made of leather including the sewing, the loops, and the straps, no metal whatsoever being permitted. It resembles a moccasin, and is fastened primarily with three loops. Long straps are attached to the top of the uppers. Since the shoe must be the property of the levir, it is given to him as an unconditional gift. He tries it on his right foot and is asked to walk in it, to see that it fits, even when it is unlaced; he repeats the procedure after it is tied in the prescribed manner, first by fastening the loops and then winding the straps around it. The laces are then undone.

Until recent times, in Eastern Europe the morbid custom obtained for the levir to lean against an upturned board used for the ritual washing of a corpse in order to emphasize that his status and rights as a levir derived from the death of his brother. This custom has been (largely) abandoned. The levir nowadays leans against a beam or a wall and presses his foot hard on the ground. The *yevamah* then makes the following declaration, in Hebrew: "My husband's brother refuses to raise up unto his brother a name in Israel; he will not perform the duty of a husband's brother unto me" (Deut. 25:7), to which he answers, also in Hebrew, and in one breath, the three words meaning "I like not to take her" (Deut. 25:8). The *yevamah* then bends down, places her left hand on the calf of her brother-in-law and with the right hand undoes the laces and the loops. She then raises his leg, slips off the shoe, and casts it away. She then collects some ordure in her mouth and spits on the floor in front of him (not "in his face"; see Deut. 25:9) and declares, again in Hebrew: "So shall it be done unto the man that doth not build up his brother's house; and his name shall be called in Israel *beit ḥaluẓ ha-na'al* ("the house of him that had his shoe loosened"; Deut. 25:9–10). All those present thrice repeat the last three words. The members of the *bet din* then recite the formula "may it be the divine will that the daughters of Israel shall be liable neither to *yibbum* nor *ḥaliẓah*." [L.I.R.]

Bibliography: A. Geiger, in: *He-Ḥalutz*, 6 (1861), 26–28; I. I. Mattuck, in: *Studies . . . Kohler* (1913), 210–22; I. S. Zuri, *Mishpat ha-Talmud*, 2 (1921), 113–23; Gulak, Yesodei, 3 (1922), 30–33; idem, Oẓar, 90–97; Finkelstein, Middle Ages, 229f., 245–7, 253–6; M. Price, in: *Oriental Studies . . . Haupt* (1926), 268–71; A. A. Judelowitz, *Av be-Ḥokhmah* (1927); Z. Karl, in: *Ha-Mishpat*, 1 (1927), 266–79; L. Ginzberg, in: *Ginzei Schechter*, 2 (1929), 166–81,

270f.; Ḥ. Albeck, in: *Berichte der Hochschule fuer die Wissenschaft des Judentums*, 49 (1932), 66–72; idem (ed.), *Mishnah, Nashim*, 7–10; B.M. Lewin (ed.), *Oẓar ha-Ge'onim, Yevamot* (1936), 34–37, 67–80; H. Tchernowitz, *Toledot ha-Halakhah*, 3 (1943), 186–203; A. H. Freimann, in: *Sinai*, 14 (1943/44), 258–60; idem, *Seder Kiddushin ve-Nissu'in Aḥarei Ḥatimat ha-Talmud* (1945), 385–97; S. Assaf, *Tekufat ha-Ge'onim ve-Sifrutah* (1955), 275–7; M. Elon, in: *Sefer Yovel le-Pinḥas Rozen* (1962), 187f.; idem, Mafte'aḥ, 89–91; idem, *Ḥakikah Datit*... (1968), 31, 162, 172f.; M. Silberg, *Ha-Ma'amad ha-Ishi be-Yisrael* (1965^{4}), 381–6, 391; B. Schereschewsky, *Dinei Mishpaḥah* (1967^{2}), 226–36.

LEVISON, WILHELM (1876–1947), medievalist. Born in Duesseldorf, Germany, Levison taught at Bonn University from 1903, becoming professor in 1912. He specialized in the early Merovingian and Carolingian periods, being the first scholar to treat Rhenish history as an integral part of German and European history (cf. the chapter he contributed to the *Geschichte des Rheinlandes* (vol. 1 (1922), 45–168). He took part, first as assistant and later as coeditor, in editing volumes 3–5 of the *Monumenta Germaniae Historica, Scriptores rerum Merovingicarum*, 5–7 (1910–20); Levison also completely revised and reedited the first part of W. Wattenbach's classic, *Deutschlands Geschichtsquellen im Mittelalter*... (3 vols, 1952–57). Many of his articles were published in his *Aus rheinischer und fraenkischer Fruehzeit* (1948). The rise of Hitler drove Levison from Germany and he accepted a fellowship at the University of Durham, England. In 1943, he delivered the Ford lectures at Oxford, which form part of his best-known book, *England and the Continent in the Eighth Century* (1946). [H.Wi.]

LEVI-STRAUSS, CLAUDE (1898–), French anthropologist. Born in Brussels, Belgium, and educated at the Sorbonne, he was chosen as a member of the French University mission to Brazil in 1934 where he became professor of sociology at the University of São Paulo from 1935 to 1939. During this period he conducted ethnographic field work among the tribes of the Mato Grosso area of central Brazil. On the outbreak of World War II Levi-Strauss served with the French Army from 1939 to 1940 and after the fall of Paris went to New York as visiting professor at the New School of Social Research from 1941 to 1945. He returned to France as professor of primitive religion at the Ecole Pratique des Hautes Etudes at the Sorbonne and in 1959 he was appointed professor of social anthropology at the College de France.

Levi-Strauss' works began appearing in 1948 with the publication of "La Vie Familiale et sociale des Indiens Nambikwara" (*Journal de la Société des Americanistes*, 37 (1948), 1–130). *Tristes Tropiques* (1955, 1968^{2}; *A World on the Wane*, 1961) was a distinguished literary work

Claude Levi-Strauss, French anthropologist. Courtesy Magnim Photo, New York. Photo Henri Cartier-Bresson.

containing elements of autobiography, ethnography, and social anthropology based on his experience in Brazil. His most significant theoretical work *Les Structures Elémentaires de la Parenté* (1949, 1967^{2}; *Elementary Structures of Kinship*, 1969) was a treatise on structural anthropology of the 20th century. His *Anthropologie Structurale* (1958; *Structural Anthropology*, 1963, 1968^{3}) is a collection of essays on language, kinship, and social organization which elucidates his theory of structural anthropology. His later works were *La Pensée Sauvage* (1962, 1964^{2}; *The Savage Mind*, 1966) and *Le Cru et le Cuit* (1964) which dealt with the nature of primitive thought and native mythology. His *Totémisme* (1962, 1965^{2}; Eng. tr. 1963, paperback 1969) is a critical survey of the literature on totemism and advances new interpretations.

Levi-Strauss' most original and significant contribution is his theory of structural anthropology. Taking linguistics as his model of a social science, he conceives of social anthropology as a general science concerned with relations involving logical structure of social phenomena. Ultimately, he maintains, all social phenomena are symbolic expressions of the human mind and it is the function of the social anthropologist to make explicit the implicit, unconscious structural relations inherent in different systems of symbolic forms. All social phenomena are regarded as systems of communication manifested especially in the forms of kinship, economics, and language.

Levi-Strauss also attempted to establish a new science of myth. He maintained it was the function of the structural analysis of myth to make conscious and explicit the logical structure which underlies the concrete images and plots of a given series of myths. Myths, like science, are motivated by an intellectual impulse, a problem to be solved, and differ from science, not in their logic, but only in the kind of objects to which this logic is applied. Myth reveals not the unconscious instinctual nature of man as Freud maintained but rather man's unconscious, rational thought in his attempt to resolve the logical problems which confront him. Myth is really man's first attempt to construct a philosophy and science of nature and culture; it is the wisdom of savages and of the folk expressed in a mode of sensible images.

In agreement with E. B. Tylor, Levi-Strauss is prepared to maintain that if law is anywhere, it is everywhere. The science of social anthropology is based on the assumption that the human spirit is subject to rational law and that freedom of creativity is an illusion. Levi-Strauss' theory of a structural science of social anthropology is highly controversial, but it is also one of the most thought-provoking and influential theories of modern times.

Bibliography: *Current Anthropology*, 7 (1966), 110–11, bibliography of his writings; R. L. Zimmerman, in: *Commentary*, 45 (May 1968), 54–61; C. Levi-Strauss, *Totemism* (1969), introd. by R. C. Poole; E. Leach, *Claude Levi-Strauss* (1971). [E.F./D.B.]

LEVITA, ELIJAH (Baḥur; ben Asher ha-Levi Ashkenazi; 1468 or 1469–1549), Hebrew philologist, grammarian, and lexicographer. Born in Neustadt, near Nuremberg, Germany, he spent most of his life in Italy (Padua, Venice, and Rome) where he taught Hebrew language and grammar. His pupils included Christian humanists, from whom he learned Greek and Latin. Some of the leading Christian Hebraists with whom Levita maintained contact at various times were: Paulus *Fagius, Johannes de Kampen (Campensis), Andreas *Maes, Guillaume *Postel, and Johann Albrecht *Widmanstetter (Widmanstadius). Postel in his *Linguarum duodecim characteribus differentium alphabetum* (Paris, 1538, fol. 3) wrote that he became a close friend of Levita in Venice — *"Elias Germanus, quo usus sum Venetiis."* Among his pupils he counted Sebastian *Muenster, who translated Elijah's works into Latin, and Cardinal *Egidius da Viterbo in whose home in Rome Elijah stayed for 13 years

(1514–27). Before entering the house of Egidius da Viterbo, Elijah also wrote secular literary works in Yiddish. To this period belongs *Bovo d'Antona* (unicum: Isny, 1541, but believed to have first been published in 1507) which became known as the **Bove-Bukh* in later editions. It is an adaptation in verse of one of the Italian versions of an Anglo-French romance, *Sir Bevis of Hampton*. His *Paris un Viene* (apparently written in 1508/09; the unicum with the beginning missing preserved at Trinity College, Cambridge, was printed at Verona in 1594) is evidently based on a medieval Provençal romance. Elijah also adapted two love epics from Italian sources; the first is based on a courtly love legend, and the second is an abridged and free adaptation of an Italian-Provencal literary work, written in *ottava rima* (a stanza of eight iambic lines containing three rhymes) which Elijah introduced into Yiddish literature. Elijah instructed da Viterbo principally in the Kabbalah and translated some manuscripts for him (e.g., the commentary of R. Eliezer of Worms on *Sefer Yeẓirah*). Georges de Selve, another of his pupils, who later became the French ambassador to Venice invited him, in the name of King Francis I, to lecture in Hebrew at the Collège royal in Paris. He declined the offer for two reasons: he neither wanted to be the only Jew allowed to live in France, nor did he feel that under such conditions he could observe the religious precepts.

In 1527, when Rome was sacked by the armies of Charles V, Elijah lost all his property (including some manuscripts). He returned to Venice, where he earned his livelihood as a proofreader in the publishing house of Daniel *Bomberg (1529 to the late 1530s), and remained here, except for an absence of four years (1539/40–44). During that period, he supervised Fagius's press at Isny (in Wuerttemberg), and later accompanied him to Constance (1542–43). At Isny, Levita printed some of his most important works. The rabbis looked with disfavor on Elijah's teaching gentiles the Torah. Elijah rejoined with the claim that earlier Christian Hebraists had upheld Christian and Jewish Hebrew scholarship resulting in a tendency, on their part, to defend Jews and the Jewish community also from physical violence. Two of Elijah's grandchildren, however, converted to Christianity and helped those who calumniated the Talmud. One of them, baptized as Vittorio Eliano, became an ecclesiastical censor of Hebrew books and had some part in the *Cremona (Christian) edition of the Zohar (1558–59). Elijah, despite false allegations brought against him to the contrary, remained an observant Jew.

Elijah wrote many Hebrew grammar works, Hebrew and Aramaic dictionaries, and did masoretic research. In Hebrew grammar, he followed the line of thought of the *Kimḥis: he published Moses Kimḥi's *Mahalakh*, with his own commentary (Pesaro, 1508; in this edition the name of the author is mistakenly given as Benjamin of Rome); and wrote notes and critiques, "*Nimmukim*" (unpublished), on David Kimḥi's *Mikhlol* and on his *Sefer ha-Shorashim*. His own works, written and published in Rome between 1518–19, and translated into Latin by Sebastian Muenster, are: *Sefer ha-Harkavah* (1518); *Ha-Baḥur* (1518; the title is after his own name "R. Elijah Baḥur"); and *Lu'aḥ be-Dikduk ha-Pe'alim ve-ha-Binyanim* (unpublished). *Ha-Harkavah* deals with "the grammar of every foreign and compound word" in the Bible, listed in alphabetical order, and the grammar of the noun and the verb. In *Ha-Baḥur*, which in a later edition became known as *Dikduk Eliyyah ha-Levi* (Isny, 1542), there is an allusion to the name of the author: "Since for every young man it [the book] is good and 'chosen.' And I, my name is Baḥur [= "chosen"], therefore *Baḥur* have I called it." In Rome in 1520, he published *Pirkei Eliyahu*, a work, written partly in verse, on the grammar of the Hebrew letters and vowels; it is a follow-up of *Ha-Baḥur* and completes the study in the latter. In its second edition (Venice, 1546), he added some chapters on the pattern of the nouns and the formative letters. Elijah did not introduce many innovations in his grammatical system; its easy and clear presentation, however, was instrumental in spreading the knowledge of the Hebrew language and grammar among Jews and Christian humanists. His grammatical rule on the five classes of *sheva-na* is still accepted today. His *Masoret ha-Masoret* (Venice, 1538), in which he explains the technical terms and the signs of the masorah, is an important contribution to masoretic study. The preface, written in prose (which follows the foreword in verse and the rhymed introduction), is an historical and original research in Hebrew vocalization and accentuation, and in the masorah. Elijah was the first to point out that the vowels and accents did not originate in the Sinai period (as had been assumed until then, and was still accepted by Moses *Mendelssohn in his *Or li-Netivah* several centuries later), but in post-talmudic times. Elijah's grammatical assertions influenced S. D. *Luzzatto in his *Vikku'aḥ Al Ḥokhmat ha-Kabbalah* (1852). *Masoret ha-Masoret* was last published together with notes and an English translation by Christian David *Ginsburg (1867; repr. 1968). In his work *Tuv Ta'am* (Venice, 1538), Elijah attempted to explain the rules on the accents in the Bible: their grammatical value and their relationship to each other. His dictionary, compiled from the Aramaic translations of the Bible, *Meturgeman* ("The Interpreter," with a Latin foreword by Paulus Fagius), and his lexicon of the Hebrew words in the Talmud and the Hebrew of the Middle Ages *Tishbi*, with a Latin translation by Fagius (Isny, 1541), are of major importance in the research of Hebrew grammar. *Tishbi* is a source on the pronunciation and the vocalization of Hebrew by the German and Italian Jewish communities. Levita's *Meturgeman* and *Tishbi* were extensively used by Christian Hebraists such as Guy *Le Fèvre de la Boderie, a pupil of Postel, who makes glowing reference to Levita in the preface to his *Dictionarium Syro-Chaldaicum* (in the Antwerp Polyglot Bible, 1572). Elijah also composed a concordance to the Bible, *Sefer ha-Zikhronot* (the complete work was never published; see Frensdorff, in MGWJ, 12 (1863), 96–108).

His research into the Hebrew language laid the foundations for the lexicography and etymology of Yiddish. Elijah refers to Yiddish as the "language of Ashkenaz" (Germany) or "Deutsch"; his reference in fact is only to the German dialect used by Jews. *Shemot Devarim* (Isny, 1542) is the first known Yiddish-Hebrew dictionary. It lists 985 words with their Hebrew translation, as well as Latin and German by Paulus Fagius. In *Tishbi*, where Elijah concludes each entry with the translation of the Hebrew radicals into German (he also does this to a certain extent in the *Meturgeman*), there are etymological explanations of several Yiddish words (such as *katavos, meykn, shekhtn*); two (*mashkeyt, sargenes*) are even included in the 712 entries of the dictionary. His Yiddish translation of Psalms (Venice, 1545), the first to be published, is based on earlier translations which closely followed the Hebrew text; it became a popular work, went through several editions, and served as a model to other translators. Extracts from two of his pamphlets, "*Ha-Mavdil*" and "*Oyf di Sreyfe fun Venedig*," written by Elijah against his personal Venetian adversaries, were published in *Tsaytshrift*, 1 (Minsk, 1926), 141–58; these, however, lack any literary value.

See also: *Yiddish Literature.

Bibliography: W. Bacher, *Die hebraeische Sprachwissenschaft* *vom 10. bis zum 16. Jahrhundert* (1892), 104ff.; idem, in: ZDMG, 43 (1889), 206–72; idem, in: MGWJ, 37 (1893), 398–404; S. Buber, *Leben und Schriften des Elias Bachur, genannt Levita* (1856); Kahana, in: *Ha-Shahar*, 12 (1883/84), 498–505, 539–48; J. Levy, *Elia Levita und seine Leistungen als Grammatiker* (1888); J. Shatzky, *Elia Bakhur* (Yid., 1949), includes bibliography; M. A. Szulwas, *Ḥayyei ha-Yehudim be-Italyah bi-Tekufat ha-Renaissance* (1955), 353 index, s.v. *Eliyah Baḥur;* Vogelstein-Rieger, 2 (1895), 86–92; M. Weinreich, *Shtaplen far Etuden tsu der Yidisher Shprakhvisenshaft un Literaturgeshikhte* (1923), 72–86; idem, *Bilder fun der Yidisher Literaturgeshikhte* (1928), 124, 142, 149–91; I. Zinberg, *Toledot Sifrut Yisrael*, 2 (1956), 255–62; 4 (1958), 38–51; Shunami, Bibl, nos. 3452–53b; Waxman, Literature, s.v. *Elijah Bahur;* N. Snaith, *Prolegomenon to "Jacob ben Chajim ben Isaac ibn Adonijah's Introduction to the Rabbinic Bible" and "The Massoreth ha-Massoreth of Elias Levita"* (1968); G. E. Weil, *Elie Levita humaniste et massorète 1469–1549* (1963); J. Perles, *Beitraege zur Geschichte der hebraeischen und aramaeischen Studien* (1884), 32ff.

[M.ME.]

LEVITAN, ISAAC ILITCH (1861–1900), Russian painter, who has been called the father of Russian landscape painting. Levitan, who was born in Wirballen (Virbalis), Lithuania, studied at the Moscow Art School and in 1889 visited Paris. He was one of the first Russian artists to understand the achievement of the Barbizon painters and

"Russian Village" by Isaac Ilitch Levitan. Oil on canvas, 18×30 in. (45.5×76 cm.). Jerusalem, Israel Museum.

the impressionists, and was thus equipped to become the major interpreter of the Russian landscape, with its vastness and its brooding melancholy. Continually seeking to improve his art, Levitan repainted the same subjects many times and altered his techniques. In his later paintings, executed with a thick, soft brush stroke, he succeeded in his aim of combining freedom of expression with solidity of structure. In 1896, Levitan was appointed professor of landscape painting at the Moscow Art Academy, where he taught until his death. His work had a deep influence on Russian painters and won the passionate admiration of his friend Anton Chekhov the dramatist. Examples are "Spring," "After the Rain," "Evening," and "The Hay Harvest."

Bibliography: S. A. Prorokova, *Levitan* (Rus., 1960); V. A. Prytkov, *Levitan* (Rus., 1960); Roth, Art, 630–2; A. N. Benua, *The Russian School of Painting* (1916), 160–3.

[ED.]

LEVITAN, SOLOMON (1862–1940), U.S. merchant, banker, and politician. Levitan, who was born in Taurrogen near Tilsit, East Prussia, immigrated to the United States in 1880. He settled in New Glarus, Wisconsin, a year later and went into business as a pack peddler and horse-and-wagon dealer. Levitan opened his first store in New Glarus in 1887 and subsequently became justice of the peace there. After moving to Madison in 1905, Levitan became a dry-goods merchant, bank officer (1909–40), and investment executive. An active campaigner for Robert M. La Follette, Sr., Republican nominee for governor, Levitan was a La Follette delegate in several Republican state conventions, a Republican presidential elector in 1912, and a delegate to the Republican national conventions of 1920 and 1924. He left the organization with La Follette when the latter formed the Progressive Party. After two unsuccessful attempts, he was elected state treasurer in 1922. Reelected several times, he served six terms (1922–32, 1936–38).

[L.J.SW.]

LEVITICAL CITIES. The ecclesiastical tribe of Levi neither fought in the wars of the conquest of Canaan nor received an allocation of continuous territory as did all the other tribes (see *Priests and Levites). Its economic base was to be the sacred offerings of the Israelites—figuratively speaking, "YHWH was its portion and share among the Israelites" (Num. 18:20, 24; Deut. 18:1–2). Yet since the clergy was not a monastic order but a tribe consisting of families, the Levites required real estate on which to build their houses and land on which to graze their beasts. That need was met by the levitical cities prescribed in Numbers 35:1–8: the Israelites were to assign out of their tribal portions 48 towns with strips of open land outside them to Levites, distributed among the tribal territories in proportion to their varying sizes. The six cities of refuge are included among the 48. The open land is in the form of a square, each of whose sides is at a distance of 1,000 cubits from the town wall at its farthest extension toward each of the four cardinal points of the compass (on this meaning of verses 4–5 see M. Greenberg in bibl.). The legal status of this property differed from that of ordinary property: to prevent the dispossession of the Levites it was ordained that they might at any time redeem houses in their towns that they had been forced by need to sell; moreover, such a house, if not redeemed, reverted to its original Levite owner at the Jubilee (ordinarily, a town house that was not redeemed within a year of its sale became irreversibly transferred to its buyer). No plots of their open land could be sold at all (Lev. 25:29–34).

From Joshua 21:11–12 it emerges that the assignment of a town to Levites did not include either its unwalled suburbs or its fields (beyond the levitical open land); these remained tribal property. How the assignment was done is described in Joshua 21, where the list of towns is also given. The Levites received by lot four towns in the portions of each of the 12 tribes, excepting Judah and Simeon which together supplied nine, and Naphtali which supplied only three. The priests were concentrated in 13 southern towns in the portions of Judah, Simeon, and Benjamin; all the rest of the Levites were assigned towns of the other tribes to the north. A variant of the list in Joshua appears in I Chronicles 6:39–66; W. F. Albright's close study has led him to conclude that both derive from a single original.

Two features of the plan of Joshua 21 indicate its artificiality: its schematic nature—the number and distribution of the towns and the clean separation of priests from Levites (in the spirit of the priestly stratum of the Pentateuch); and obliviousness of the real impulse behind the Levites' scattering through the land of Israel—the necessity of finding employment at local sanctuaries. Not only does the list omit many early sanctuary towns (e.g., Beth-El, Nob, Jerusalem, Beer-Sheba) while mentioning towns in which the presence of Israelites, let alone a sanctuary, is dubious (e.g., Gibbethon, Eltekeh), but the whole scheme to which the list belongs aims at solving the problem of settling the Levites without reference to their sacred vocation. Had the scheme envisioned them serving at sanctuaries, it could never have been content with only four

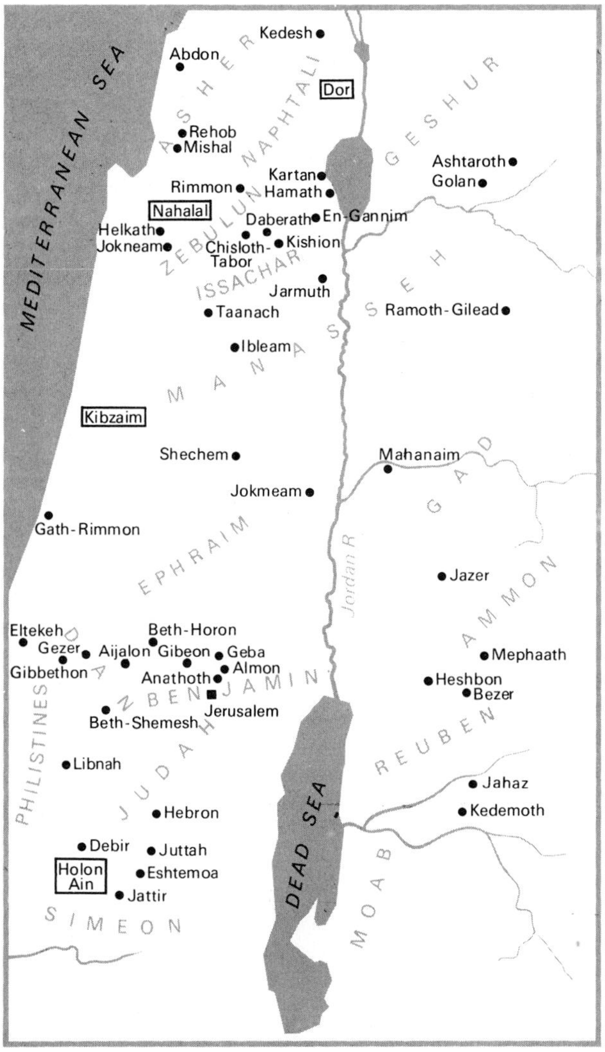

Sites of the levitical cities. Names within frames are of places as yet unidentified, though their general location is known from the sources. Based on Y. Aharoni in *Carta Atlas of the Bible*, Jerusalem, 1964.

towns per tribe. (The real situation of Levites—namely, dispersal throughout the countryside—is rather reflected in Deuteronomy's allusion to them "in any of the settlements throughout all Israel"; 18:6; cf. 16:11, 14.) The visionary arrangement of Ezekiel 45:1–5; 48:8–14 gives more consideration to the reality of levitical needs in that it settles the priests and Levites in a sacred "oblation" adjacent to the future temple in which they are to serve (on the analogy of their position around the desert tabernacle in the Pentateuch). Granting the unreal character of the scheme of Joshua 21, one may still ask whether any historical situation underlies the town list. J. Wellhausen regarded it as a post-Exilic "echo of the general recollection that there were once in Israel many holy places and residences of priesthoods," the influence of Jerusalem being reflected in the concentration of priests in Judah and Benjamin—this in accord with his view of the lateness of the entire priestly stratum of the Pentateuch. On the other hand, Y. Kaufmann regarded the list as a very early solution to the problem of the future of the Levites after the break up of the unified camp of Joshua's time; he dates it to a time before sanctuaries had been established throughout the country, and characterizes it as wholly utopian and never put into practice. Other scholars sought to interpret the list in the light of the fact that the United Monarchy (under David and Solomon) was the sole period in which all the towns were in Israel's possession. The list was taken as a reflex of the royal regulation of the settlement of Levites throughout the newly extended kingdom (S. Klein, W. F. Albright). B. Mazar considered the Levites an arm of the civil service of the United Monarchy (suggested by I Chron. 26:30–32), settled in strategic locations and provincial capitals around the country to manage royal estates, collect taxes, and strengthen borderlands with prevailingly non-Israelite populations. Even this interpretation, however, cannot mitigate the theoretical and unreal character of the scheme of Joshua 21, although its representation of the dispersal of the Levites throughout the land of Israel is in principle historically true (cf. M. Haran).

Bibliography: J. Wellhausen, Proleg, 159–64; D. Hoffmann, *Die wichtigsten Instanzen gegen die Graf-Wellhausensche Hypothese*, I (1903), 148ff.; S. Klein, in: *Kovez ha-Ḥevrah ha-Ivrit le-Ḥakirat Erez-Yisrael ve-Attikoteha* (1935), 81–107; W. F. Albright, in: *L. Ginzberg Jubilee Volume* (1946), 49ff. (Eng. sect.); Y. Kaufmann, *Sefer Yehoshu'a* (1959), 270–82; B. Mazar, in: VT Supplement, 7 (1960), 210ff.; M. Haran, in: JBL, 80 (1961), 45ff., 156ff.; M. Greenberg, in: JAOS, 88 (1968), 59ff.

[Mo.G.]

LEVITICUS, BOOK OF (Heb. וַיִּקְרָא; LXX *Λευιτικόν*), more aptly described by its tannaitic name, *Torat Kohanim*, "the Priests' Manual," the third book of the Pentateuch. Leviticus is thematically an independent entity. *Exodus contains the story of the construction of the cultic implements—the Tabernacle and the priestly vestments—whereas Leviticus converts this static picture into scenes from the living cult. *Numbers, on the other hand, is set chronologically during the wanderings of Israel in the wilderness and therefore concentrates upon the cultic laws of the camp in motion, e.g., the military arrangement and census of the tribes, the transport of the sancta, and their protection against encroachment. Since the latter is the main function of the Levites, it is striking that all the laws pertaining to the Levites are in Numbers and none is in Leviticus.

The "Priests' Manual" of Leviticus indeed focuses on the priests. Few laws, however, apply only to the priests (these are Lev. 8–10; 16:1–28; 21:1–22:16). The role of the priest is defined in pedagogic terms: to teach the distinctions "between the holy and profane between the pure and impure" (10:10; cf. 14:57; 15:31; Ezek. 22:26; 44:23). This they must do lest Israel's defilement, brought about by its moral sins and physical impurities, defile the sanctuary and cause its abandonment by God. The underlying postulate is that God will not reside in a defiled sanctuary (see *Day of Atonement). The priests are thus charged with a double task: to instruct Israel not to cause defilement and to purge the sanctuary whenever its defilement occurs. However, Leviticus is not just ritual laws. On the contrary, the ethical fuses with and even informs the ritual so that there is justification to seek a moral basis behind each ritual act.

From the point of view of literary criticism, Leviticus is relatively uncomplicated: it is a single source. Even if another stratum is recognized (see below, Holiness Source), it has been thoroughly assimilated by P (see *Pentateuch). The text has been excellently preserved; the few divergences in the versions are nearly all secondary in relation to the Masoretic Text. The difficulty lies in only one area: the terminology, which deals with the cult, an ancient institution with its peculiar, conservative vocabulary whose meaning was sometimes lost upon the age of the Second Temple, not to speak of subsequent generations.

The impact of Leviticus upon Judaism can be comprehended by realizing that nearly half (247) of the 613 commandments (Gen. R. 3:5) and about the same proportion of the material of the Talmud are based upon

BOOK OF LEVITICUS – CONTENTS

1:1–7:38	**The sacrificial system.**
1:1–2	General introduction.
1:3–17	The whole offering *(ʿolah).*
2:1–16	The tribute (cereal) offering *(minḥah).*
3:1–17	The well-being offering *(shelamim).*
4:1–35	The purification offering *(ḥaṭṭaʾt).*
5:1–13	Borderline cases requiring the purification offering.
5:14–26	The reparation offering *(ʾasham).*
6:1–7:38	Supplementary instructions on sacrifices.
8:1–10:20	**The inaugural service at the sanctuary.**
8:1–36	The installation of the priests.
9:1–24	The priests assume office.
10:1–11	The sin of Nadab and Abihu.
10:12–20	The consumption of the initiatory offerings.
11:1–16:34	**The laws of impurities.**
11:1–47	Animal impurities.
12:1–8	The impurity of childbirth.
13:1–14:57	The impurity of skin diseases (leprosy).
15:1–33	The impurity of genital discharges.
16:1–34	The impurities of the sanctuary and the nation.
17:1–26:46	**The holiness source.**
17:1–16	Killing for food.
18:1–20:27	On being holy.
21:1–22:33	The disqualifications of priests and sacrifices.
23:1–44	The festivals.
24:1–23	Miscellanea.
25:1–26:46	The Sabbatical and Jubilee Years.
27:1–34	**Commutation of gifts to the sanctuary.**

Leviticus. Furthermore, Leviticus was traditionally the first book taught to school children (Lev. R. 7:3), stemming probably from the historical fact that the priestly school preceded the lay school in origin. The priority of Leviticus in the life of rabbinic Judaism is also attested by the title of its tannaitic commentary: *Sifra,* "The Book," as against *Sifrei* (on Numbers and Deuteronomy), i.e., "Other Books."

CONTENTS

Chapters 1–7. The Sacrificial System. In chapters 1–5, the sacrifices are listed from the point of the donor: chapters 1–3, the spontaneously motivated sacrifices: *ʿolah, minḥah, shelamim;* chapters 4–5, the sacrifices required for expiation: *ḥaṭṭaʾt* and *ʾasham.* Chapters 6–7 regroup these sacrifices in order of their sancity and priority in the daily ritual, i.e., most sacred: *ʿolah, minḥah, ḥaṭṭaʾt, ʾasham;* sacred: *shelamim.* The common denominator of the sacrifices discussed in these chapters is that they arise in answer to an unpredictable religious or emotional need, and are thereby set off from the calendrically fixed sacrifices of the public feasts and fasts (Lev. 9, 16, 23; cf. Num. 28–29). Many prophets sharply criticized the sacrificial system when it failed to lead to a more ethical life, but their lonely isolation in this respect and the positive evidence of the folk literature make it amply clear that the people themselves were convinced that it met their spiritual needs. Chapters 1–7 will be summarized in terms of their literary structure and main ideas (see *Sacrifice, for details).

1:1–2: General Introduction. The Hebrew particles for introducing general and particular statements in legal formulation indicate that chapters 1 and 3 were originally a single unit which was later split by the insertion of chapter 2. The conditional construction of 1:2a underscores the voluntary basis of the sacrifices.

1:3–17: The Whole Offering (ʿolah). This is the only sacrifice which is entirely consumed on the altar (favoring the translation "whole," cf. Deut. 33:10; I Sam. 7:9; Ps. 55:21). Verses 1:3–4 encapsulate the major concepts of the sacrificial system: laying on of hands, acceptance, expiation, slaughter, blood manipulation, and entrance to the Tent of Meeting (see Sacrifice). The donor is an active participant in the ritual; he is responsible for the presentation, hand-laying, slaughter, skinning, quartering, and washing of the animal. The priest executes the blood rite and the burning of the animal, i.e., everything which relates to the altar. The whole offering must be chosen from male, unblemished, and eligible species of the herd, flock, and birds. The *ʿolah* is probably the oldest and most popular sacrifice (Tosef., Zev. 13:1). Its function here is expiatory (1:4; cf. 9:7; 14:20; I Sam. 13:12; Job 1:5, 42:8; C. H. Gordon, *Ugaritic Textbook* (1965), text 9, line 7) but in P, whenever it is offered by an individual, the motivation is joyful (e.g., Lev. 22:17ff.; Num. 15:1–11).

Chapter 2: The Tribute (Cereal) Offering (minḥah). In the nonpriestly texts, it connotes both "a present made to secure or retain goodwill" (S. R. Driver; e.g., Gen. 32:20) and a tribute brought by subjects to their overlords, both human (Judg. 3:15–18) and divine and could be either animal or vegetable (Gen. 4:3–4; I Sam. 2:17). In P, however, it is exclusively cereal, either choice flour (Lev. 2:1–3), cakes of choice flour (2:4–10), or wasted grain (2:14–16). Because leaven and honey (fruit syrup) ferment, whereas salt preserves, they were respectively proscribed and prescribed on the altar (2:11–13). The former, however, were permitted as a first fruit offering to the priest (23:17; II Chron. 31:5). The restriction to cereal emphasizes that man's tribute to God should be from the fruit of his labors on the soil. In daily life, however, the aspect of "appeasement" may also have been present (I Sam. 26:19; "A Dialogue about Human Misery," Pritchard, Texts, 439, line 51). Because cereal was abundant and cheap, it became the poor man's *ʿolah* (Philo, Spec. 1:271; Lev. R. 8:4) and probably replaced it in popularity and function.

Chapter 3: The Well-being Offering (shelamim). This offering never serves as expiation. Its basic function is simply to permit the consumption of flesh. It was usually prompted by a joyous occasion, specified in 7:11ff. as: spontaneous (always in a happy context, e.g., Num. 15:3; Deut. 16:10–11), votive, and thanksgiving (motivated by elation, e.g., Ps. 116:17–19). The rules are similar to those of the whole offering, except that the victims may be female but not birds. Also, being of lesser sanctity, they were not slaughtered at the altar, and portions were assigned to the priests and the donor as well as to God. The choicest internal fats (suet) were turned to smoke.

Chapter 4: The Purification Offering (ḥaṭṭaʾt). Its purpose is to remove the impurity inflicted upon the sanctuary by the inadvertent violation of prohibitive laws (but not laws against man, i.e., ethical violations). The deliberate violation of these laws is punishable by *karet* (Num. 15:27–31), death through divine agency. The loci of *karet*—all in P—specify the nature of the violations: holidays (e.g., Passover, Day of Atonement), contamination of sancta (e.g., Lev. 7:20–21), prohibited cultic acts (e.g., 17:4, 9), and illicit sex (18:29). The last mentioned is also a ritual sin: it leads to the pollution of the land (18:27–28). The procedure for the purification offering falls into two categories: 4:3–21 where the blood is brought into the sanctuary by the high priest, but the flesh of the victim is burned outside the camp, and 4:22–35, sins requiring cheaper animals, scaled to the social and financial status of the offender, where the blood is not brought into the sanctuary, and the flesh is not burned but must be eaten by the officiating priest (6:19; 10:17). Verses 4:3–21 comprise two cases that are really one. The first instance (4:3–12) presumes that the high priest's inadvertent error has caused harm to his people (e.g., through his negligence, Num. 18:4b–5) or has caused them to expropriate sancta (e.g., Lev. 5:14–16; 22:14–16). In the second instance (4:13–21), the community as a whole has erred—probably by blindly following the high priest's instruction—and must bring its own purification offering when the error is discovered (4:14). The individuals liable to the purification offering are the tribal chieftain (4:22–26) and the commoner (4:27–35). Whereas the ruler brings a he-goat, the commoner offers a she-goat or a she-lamb.

5:1–13: BORDERLINE CASES REQUIRING THE PURIFICATION OFFERING. Rabbinic tradition distinguishes between the purification offering of chapter 4 and 5:1–13, calling the latter *ʿoleh we-yored,* "the scaled offering," geared to the means of the offender (not his status, as in chapter 4). This *ḥaṭṭa'ṭ* probably arises from the failure or inability to cleanse impurity immediately upon its incurrence. "The sin of which he is guilty" (5:6, 10, 13), in distinction to chapter 4, is not the contraction of impurity but its prolongation. In three out of the four given cases (5:2, 3, 4,), the offender has knowingly contracted impurity or uttered an oath—acts in themselves guiltless—but due to a lapse of memory has unknowingly contaminated sancta or violated his oath. The case of 5:1, where the offender withheld testimony, may be explained by assuming either that he never entered into oath but only heard its public proclamation, thereby putting him out of the jurisdiction of the court (but not of God for having defied the imprecation) or that his reluctance to be an "informer" is considered to be inadvertent, precisely like the amnesia cases which follow (for details see *Sacrifice).

5:14–26: THE REPARATION OFFERING (*'ASHAM*). It is enjoined for trespassing *(maʿal)* upon the property of God or man, the latter through the use of a false oath. The sin is *desecration *(ḥillul)*: the sancta or the name of God have become desanctified (as opposed to the purification offering, chapter 4, where the sin is the contamination of sancta). Three cases are given: 1) 5:14–16: For inadvertent trespass of sancta, the offender pays the sanctuary an amount equal to the value of the desecrated sanctum plus a 20% fine and brings a ram, commutable into currency, for his expiation. 2) 5:17–19: This case complements the preceding. Both deal with unintentional poaching upon sancta; the first real, the other suspected (so R. Akiva in Ker. 5:2). The general wording of Leviticus 5:17 makes it clear that every suspected violation is liable to the *'asham.* 3) 5:20–26: The reparation offering, which in 5:15–19 was imposed for inflicting real or suspected damage to sacred property, is now transferred to the human sphere where the Lord, through an oath, has been made a party to the defrauding of man. Fraud, being a deliberate sin, would ordinarily be unexpiable by sacrifice. However, the offender has voluntarily confessed his wrong and relinquished his illicit gain. The usual penalties (e.g., Ex. 21:37; 22:6) are mitigated. He is treated as an inadvertent offender: full restitution plus 20% for the material loss and a reparation offering to the Lord for desecrating His name in a lying oath are required of him.

CHAPTERS 6–7: SUPPLEMENTARY INSTRUCTIONS ON SACRIFICES. Since the well-being offering is chiefly consumed by the donor, the rules pertain mainly to him (7:11–34; esp. 7:23, 29). Otherwise they are the concerns of the officiating priest. The subjects are: the altar fire (6:1–6); the manner and place for eating the tribute offering (6:7–11); the daily tribute offering of the high priest and the voluntary one of the ordinary priest (6:12–16); safeguards in sacrificing the purification offering (6:17–23); the ritual for the reparation offering (7:1–7, missing in chapter 5); the priestly share in the whole and tribute offerings (7:8–10); the types of well-being offering (see chapter 3, above) and their taboos (7:11–21); the prohibition against consuming suet and blood (7:22–27); the priestly share of the well-being offering, set aside by the donor (7:28–36); the summation (7:36–38). The inclusion of the consecration offering before the well-being offering suggests that a section based on Exodus 29 originally preceded 7:11.

Chapters 8–10: The Inaugural Service at the Sanctuary. This section follows logically and chronologically upon Exodus 35–40: the priests are inducted into service after the priestly vestments and the Tabernacle are completed. Not Aaron, however, but Moses dominates the scene. It is he who conducts the inaugural service, consecrates the priests, and apportions all tasks. Aaron is clearly answerable to him, as seen from their confrontation in Leviticus 10:16–20. Strikingly, the superiority of prophet over priest is insisted upon by the priestly document.

CHAPTER 8: THE INSTALLATION OF THE PRIESTS. "To ordain you" (8:33) is literally "to fill your hands." In Scripture, this phrase is used exclusively for the ordination of priests (Ex. 32:29; Judg. 17:5, 12; I Kings 13:33), but in the archives of Mari dating from the time of Hammurapi it refers to the distribution of booty. Thus, the Hebrew idiom indicates that installation rites officially entitle the priests to their share of the revenues and sacrifices brought to the sanctuary. "As the Lord commanded Moses" concludes each phase of the ordination ceremony, a reminder that this chapter is a repetition of the instruction in Exodus 29.

CHAPTER 9: THE PRIESTS ASSUME OFFICE. On the eighth day following the week of consecration, the priests begin their official duties. They offer up special sacrifices for the people, "that the presence of the Lord may appear" (9:6; also verses 4, 23). Indeed, the whole purpose of the sacrificial system is revelation, the assurance that God is with His people. God's presence was never assumed to be a coefficient of the cult, as did the pagans; it was always an act of His grace.

10:1–11: THE SIN OF *NADAB AND ABIHU. That the fire was "alien" could be debited either to the offering or the offerer. Most likely, the fire was taken from elsewhere than the altar (16:12; Num.17:11).

10:12–20: THE CONSUMPTION OF THE INITIATORY OFFERINGS. This is the continuation of chapter 9. The tribute- and well-being offerings are eaten by the priests in accordance with 6:9 and 7:28–34. But the procedure for the purification offering is switched from the individual to the communal form: the disposal of blood (9:9, 15; 10:18) has been executed according to 4:30 but not the disposal of flesh which follows 4:12, rather than 6:19, and despite 6:23. The death of Nadab and Abihu has intervened. Aaron follows the more stringent procedure of destroying, rather than eating, the sacrificial meat because it has been doubly contaminated by the death and by the sin of his sons; its consumption will not be "acceptable in the sight of the Lord" and must be burned outside.

Chapters 11–16: The Laws of Impurities. An empiric knowledge of contagion must be credited to biblical man, as demonstrated in the example of washing: 1) Lustration is limited to impurities arising from animal cadavers and certain human skin diseases and fluxes, all prime sources of putrefaction and infection. 2) One who contracts the impurity from a human washes himself at once (antisepsis through washing is effective only the first few hours) even though his ritual impurity lasts till nightfall; the one who is afflicted is removed from camp (Num. 5:2–5) and washes only after he is healed. (Lustration serves no medical purpose once infection sets in.) 3) In regard to animals, the living never transfer impurity (not so the swine in Egypt, Herodotus, 2:47). The carcass, however, must be disposed of; hence its handling is never prohibited, but one contaminated thereby must purify himself with water. For details see *Purifications.

CHAPTER 11: ANIMAL IMPURITIES. The food prohibitions are certainly older than the rationale given them. Regardless of their origin—as yet undetermined—the fact remains that no punishment befalls anyone who violates them. The demoniac has been banished. The laws themselves offer but one reason: holiness (Lev. 11:44–47; 20:22–26; cf. Ex. 22:30; Deut. 14:21), a word which bears the dual connotation of "sanctification" (by emulating God's nature, Lev. 11:44a) and "separation" (from the impurities of the pagans, 20:23–26). The food prohibitions taken together with the blood prohibition form a united dietary code whereby man may indulge his lust for meat and not be brutalized in the process. Chapter 11 is but the culmination of the system. It begins at Creation where man was meant to be a vegetarian (Gen. 1:28–30). The sons of Noah are permitted meat on the condition that they do not eat the blood (Gen. 9:3–4). The sons of Jacob, however, are directed to a higher rung in the level of holiness (Ex. 19:6a) by further narrowing their diet to a few living creatures, those of the tame, herbivorous species. Knowing that the taking of animal life is a divine concession, and the spilling of its lifeblood a divine prohibition, biblical man is thus disciplined to revere all of life.

11:1–8: Land Animals. Compare Leviticus 11:3–4 with Deuteronomy 14:4–7, where the permitted quadrupeds are named and classified.

11:9–12: Fish. That neither the prohibited nor permitted fish are enumerated (nor in Deut. 14:9–10) may be explained by the little contact Israel had with the sea. Fish—alone among the creatures—were not named by Adam (Gen. 2:19–20).

11:13–23: Birds and Winged Insects. No classification is given for birds because none was probably known. A number of identifications are conjectural.

11:24–40: Impurity by Contact with Carcasses. This section could be an insertion from another source as it interrupts the fourfold classification (11:46) of creatures that may not be eaten. Nonporous articles are defiled by cadavers of the eight species listed in verses 29–30 and must be washed, but contaminated earthenware (porous and absorbent, 6:21) may never be refused. Food and seed grain are immune to impurity except when moist, since water is an impurity carrier.

11:41–47: Swarming Things and Summation. Continues 11:23.

CHAPTER 12: THE IMPURITY OF CHILDBIRTH. Parturition marks the onset of impurity: seven days following the birth of a male and 14 days for a female during which no conjugal relations are allowed. For an additional period of 33 and 66 days, respectively, contact with sancta is proscribed. That the sacrifices are brought after the defilement has passed is clear proof that their purpose is not apotropaic. The puerperal period is not feared as being governed by the demoniac (comment on chapter 4). Only ritual impurity adheres which time alone removes and whose removal is certified by rite. The latter is scaled to economic circumstances (cf. 5:7–13; 14:21–32).

CHAPTERS 13–14: THE IMPURITY OF SKIN DISEASES (LEPROSY). The word translated as "leprosy" actually refers to a variety of skin diseases. The noncontagious kind, described as an outbreak of dull white spots, is probably vitiligo or, less likely, psoriasis. This, rather than true leprosy—Hansen's disease—is what afflicted Naaman (II Kings 5) for he mingled freely in society. Verses 13:1–44 diagnose the various symptoms of the affliction and 13:45–46 require the incurable to put on the habiliment of a mourner and demands his removal outside the city (cf. Num. 5:2–5). Verses 13:47–59 describe the deterioration of garments due probably to mildew or fungus and 14:33–53 describe the infection of houses due to the spread of saltpeter or moss, in which quarantine procedures are also enforced. Unusual considerations for property are reflected in 14:36: the priest clears the house prior to his inspection lest the house be condemned with its contents. The ritual is described in verses 14:1–32. Three separate ceremonies are prescribed: the first day (14:2–8), the seventh (14:9) and the eighth (14:10–32). The ritual of the first day is also applied to "leprosy" of houses (14:48–53). Details are given in *Leprosy.

CHAPTER 15: THE IMPURITY OF GENITAL DISCHARGES. This chapter is divided logically into two sections: natural discharge of men and women (15:16–18, 19–24, respectively) whose impurity is simply removed by bathing, and pathological discharges (15:2–15, 25–30, respectively) which require sacrificial expiation.

CHAPTER 16: THE IMPURITIES OF THE SANCTUARY AND THE NATION. According to 16:1, chapter 16 follows upon chapter 10. Thus chapters 11–15 are an insert listing the specific impurities that will contaminate the sanctuary (15:31) for which the purification ritual of chapter 16 is mandated. Verses 16:1–28 represent a fusion of two rites: the first to purge the sanctuary according to procedures administrated in 4:3–21, and the second to expiate the people for the defilement they have caused the sanctuary through the confession and transference of their sins onto a live purification offering, a goat banished to *Azazel. The sins expiated by this ritual are exclusively within the religious sphere, i.e., between man and God (comment on chapter 4). Ethical violations require prior rectification with the one who was wronged, before God's forgiveness may be sought (comment on 5:20–26). For the ritual, see *Day of Atonement; for the process see *Atonement.

Chapters 17–26. The Holiness Source. The remainder of the Book of Leviticus, it is averred, consists largely of an independent code in which moral and ritual laws alternate and whose motivation is holiness (e.g., 19:2; 20:7–8, 26; 21:8, 23; 22:16, 32; 23:3, 4, 7, 21, 24, 35, 37; 25:10, 12). This, however, is to be doubted. The alleged beginning of the code, chapter 17, is connected thematically and verbally with preceding chapters. The alleged conclusion, chapters 25 and 26, forms an independent scroll, to judge by its unique vocabulary (e.g., 25:18, 19; 26:5), theme (25:8–13; 26:34–35, 43), and redaction (25:1; 26:46); it was probably affixed in its present position at a later stage. Nonetheless, much of the language and some of the ideas in chapters 17–26 differ from the first part of Leviticus. Most likely, P incorporated into these chapters an earlier document which might be called the Holiness source. (For the prevailing view and a summary of the contents of these chapters, whose main themes follow in brief outline, see *Holiness Code.)

CHAPTER 17. KILLING FOR FOOD. The entire chapter (except the last two verses) is of one piece. It declares that, whosoever kills a domestic animal outside the sanctuary is guilty of murder (17:3–4). Two ends are thus achieved: sacrifice to "satyrs" is abolished (17:5–9), and expiation is assured through a ritual by which the lifeblood of animals may be returned to its creator either upon the altar (17:10–12), in the case of sacrificial animals, or by being drained and covered by earth, in the case of animals that are hunted (17:13–14; cf. Deut. 12:16). The inescapable conclusion to be drawn from the context of the blood prohibition is that 17:11 has nothing to do with the expiation of general sin. The only time one runs the risk of eating blood is while consuming the *shelamim* (see above on ch. 3). That is why the blood prohibition occurs solely in *shelamim* passages (3:17; 7:26–27). However, it is the only sacrifice which plays no expiatory role (see *Atonement). The only "sin" (the word does not even occur here) is the charge of murder (17:4) levied against him who kills for food outside the Sanctuary, i.e., without properly restricting the lifeblood to God: "and I have assigned it [the *shelamim* blood] to you upon the altar to expiate [i.e. ransom] for your lives" when you take the animal's life for its flesh (see *Blood).

CHAPTERS 18–20. ON BEING HOLY. Though these three chapters were originally independent scrolls they are thematically united: chapter 20 prescribes the penalties for the illicit relations and homicidal cult practices of chapter 18 (see 20:1–5) and the practice of magic prohibited in 19:31 (see 20:6). Moreover, this unit is framed by the identical reasoning: separation from the Canaanites, whose idolatrous and immoral practices contaminate the divinely-chosen land (18:3, 24–30; 20:22–24). The arraignment of Ezekiel 22 contains a mixture of ethical and ritual sins based solely on these chapters, and shows that their written formulation is pre-Exilic. The concept of negative holiness—separation from heathens—figures in these chapters. The key word in this section is *kadosh* (*qadosh*, "holy"). In Semitic polytheism, holy means "that which is unapproachable except through divinely imposed restrictions" or "that which is withdrawn from common use." Material objects, such as specific trees, rivers, stones, and the like, are believed to be invested with natural, independent holiness. But for Israel, holiness stems solely from God. If certain things are holy—such as lands (Canaan), persons (priests), places (Sanctuary), or time (festivals)—they are so by divine dispensation. Moreover, only in the Bible is holiness enjoined upon a whole people: Israel is commanded to separate itself from all defiling contact with man (i.e., idolatrous worship, 20:6–7; cf. Deut. 7:4–6; 14:1–2) and beast (so the dietary laws, Lev. 11:44–45; 20:25–26).

A *qadosh*-cluster is found in but one other context—the rules concerning the priesthood, 21:6–8. This fact is significant. The priesthood, Israel, and man, respectively, form three concentric rings of decreasing holiness about the center, God. The term "holy" is never used with man nor statically applied to Israel. The biblical ideal is that all Israel shall be "a kingdom of priests and a holy *[qadosh]* nation" (Ex. 19:6). If Israel is to move up to a higher sphere of holiness, it is enjoined to observe a more rigid code of behavior than that practiced by the nations, just as the priest lives by more stringent standards than his fellow Israelites. Holiness, then, implies separation and is so defined in Leviticus 20:26. The positive aspect of holiness is discussed in chapter 19.

Chapter 18. Illicit Sexual Relations. This chapter is encased by an introduced and peroration (18:1–5, 24–30) which castigate the Egyptians and the Canaanites for the depravity of their sexual mores. The pagan world worshiped and deified sex. It reserved the term "holy ones" for its cult prostitutes. No wonder Israel is charged with an exacting code of family purity whose violation means death (cf. 20:11–16). Furthermore, H (the Holiness Code) is the only source which proclaims the sanctity of the land of Canaan, a doctrine which explains the equal responsibility of both resident Israelites and strangers to maintain its sanctity (18:27; 20:2; and comment on 24:15–22) as well as the moral justification for its conquest (18:27–28; 20:22–23). But Israel's ideological sword is two-edged: if guilty of the same infractions, it, too, will be "vomited out."

Another presupposition of the chapter—one shared by the entire Torah literature—is that all peoples are held accountable for gross immorality (Gen. 6:11; 9:5–6; 15:16; 18:1–19:38, etc.). Moreover, though idolatry is allowed them (e.g., Deut. 4:19), Moloch worship is emphatically proscribed (Lev. 18:21; 20:1–5). It is the only idolatrous practice explicitly listed. Presumably, all other practices cannot be charged against the Canaanites as justification for their expulsion (18:27–29). Indeed, in view of Genesis 9:6, this is what we would expect: Moloch worship, requiring child sacrifice, is murder, punishable solely with death. Leviticus 18:6–18 is concerned with incest. In the cases cited, affinity has the same force as consanguinity. In marriage, each partner transfers his set of incest taboos to the other. Verses 19–23 enumerate sexual aberrations; they transmit "impurity" to the offender and to the land (18:24–30), and must be excised.

Chapter 19. Imitatio Dei—Positive Holiness. In the Bible there is no animism. Holiness is not innate; it is the extension of God's will. Thus, for Israel, holy means more than that which is "unapproachable" and "withdrawn." It becomes a positive concept, an inspiration and a goal associated with God's nature and his desire for man: "You shall be holy, for I . . . am holy" (19:2). That which man is not, nor can ever fully be, that which he is commanded to emulate and approximate is what the Bible calls *qadosh.* Holiness means *imitatio dei*—the life of godliness.

How can men imitate Him? The answer of Leviticus 19 is given in a series of ethical and ritual commands; no distinction is made between them. Similarly, in the entire Ancient Near East, morality is inseparable from religion (for Egypt, Pritchard, Texts, 34–35; for Babylonia, *Šurpu,* 2). Indeed, precisely within a ritual context, biblical ethics rise to their summit. Not only is the decalogue encompassed (1–5 in 19:3–8; 6–10 in 19:9–22; cf. Lev. R. 24:5) but soaring above it is the commandment to love man—all men, citizens (19:18) and aliens (19:34) alike. This leveling of society stems partly from the sanctity which, for P, God's land imposes upon all its inhabitants (comment, above, on ch. 18). But, there is more. The law of love is no verbal ideal. It must be expressed in deeds; equality in justice, civil (20:12; 24:16, 22; Num. 35:15) and religious (Lev. 16:29; 17:15; Ex. 12:19; 49; Num. 9:14—all P); and equality in mercy, e.g., free loans (Lev. 25:35–58; cf. Deut. 10:18) and free gleanings (Lev. 19:9–10; cf. Deut. 24:19–22). Moreover, that the law of love may be implemented, the vitiating components in the nature of man, callousness (Lev. 19:14, 33) and hatred (19:16–18), are also proscribed.

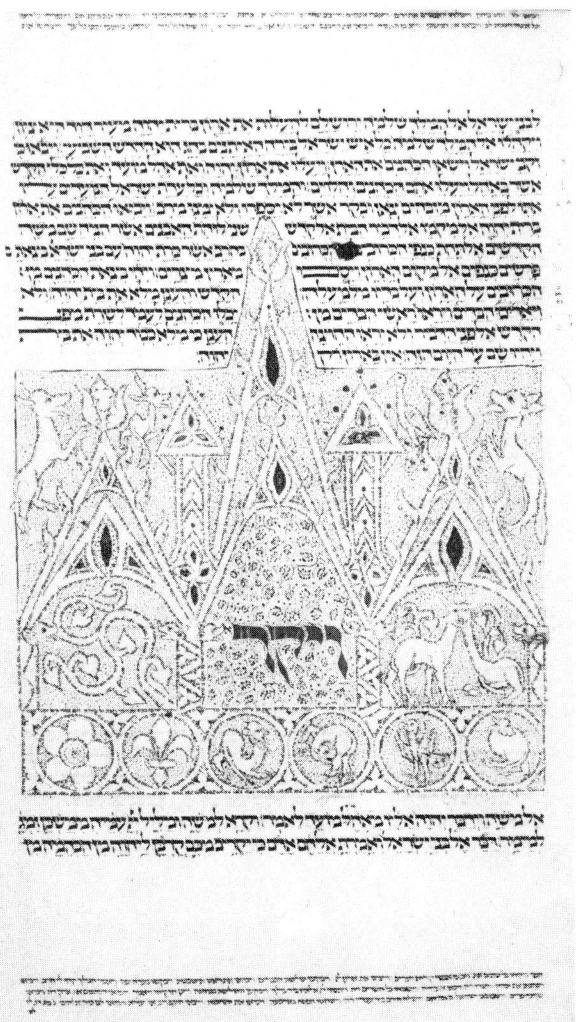

First page of Leviticus with micrographic masorah, written by the Bavarian scribe Moses of Ebermannstadt, 1290. From a manuscript containing the Pentateuch and the Five Scrolls, 15½×11½ in. (39.5×29.5 cm.). Copenhagen, Det Kongelige Bibliotek, Cod. Heb. XI, fol. 104v.

Chapter 20. Penalties for Certain Infractions in Chapters 18–19. Illicit sex relations are graded according to the severity of the punishment: verses 9–16 death by man, verses 17–19 death by God *(karet),* verses 20–21 childlessness. Missing are marriages with a stepsister, grandchildren, and two sisters (18:9, 10, 18), but these are marginal cases. Interestingly, the offenses of 20:17–21, which do not call for the death penalty, were practiced in early Israel. With such notable precedents as Abraham and Ammon (20:17), Milcah and Amram (20:19), and Onan (20:21), the offender could be reprimanded but not punished by man. God alone would settle with him. Of the idolatrous varieties, only Moloch worship and oracles through mediums are singled out, the former because of its monstrousness (see *Moloch) and the latter because of its prevalence (Deut. 18:9–12; I Sam. 28:9; Isa. 8:19). That the lofty pronouncements of chapter 19 are not in this list is mute evidence that ethics are really unenforceable.

CHAPTERS 21–22. THE DISQUALIFICATIONS OF PRIESTS AND SACRIFICES. The priest, ranking highest in human holiness, could enter the sanctuary to handle its objects and eat of its gifts. These privileges had commensurate restrictions, especially for the high priest. They were intended as safeguards against moral and ritual defilement which might inflict dire consequences on him and his people (22:9, 15–16; cf. 4:3; 15:31). These restrictions pertain to death and marriage (21:1–15), to physical blemishes of officiants and sacrifices (21:16–24; 22:17–33), and to the eating of the sacred food (22:1–9, 10–16).

CHAPTER 23. THE FESTIVALS. P's listing of the festivals is distinguished from that of JE (Ex. 23:14–17; 34:21–23) and D (Deut. 16) in its emphasis on natural and agricultural data: the Feast of Unleavened Bread starts and the Feast of Weeks closes the grain harvest, and the Feast of Booths follows the "ingathering" and is celebrated by the use of branches.

CHAPTER 24. MISCELLANEA. 24:1–4. THE LAMP OIL. A repetition of Exodus 27:20–21 except that the latter command is set in the future. Since the lampstand stood inside the Sanctuary building, its greater sanctity required pure oil and that it be lighted by the high priest (Ex. 30:7–8; Num 8:1–4; "sons" in Ex. 27:21 is a probable error). The lampstand is described in Exodus 25:31–40 and Numbers 8:1–4.

24:5–9. The Shewbread. Twelve wheat loaves, symbols of God's covenant with the twelve tribes, were set in two rows of six on the table which stood before the Holy of Holies. Being of the inner sancta, like the lampstand above, it was tended only by the high priest. Each Sabbath he renewed the loaves and offered up the incense placed at their side (24:7) together with the daily incense (Ex. 30:7–8) upon the golden *altar. Both incense offerings, like the oil above, called for pure *frankincense (Lev. 24:7; Ex. 30:34), again for the same reason (Lev. 2:2, 15). The shewbread is called a fire offering (24:9) because originally, as Ancient Near Eastern parallels indicate, it was entirely consumed by fire.

24:10–14, 23. The Law of Blasphemy. The law is introduced by a case. Blasphemy means more than speaking contemptuously of God, for which there is no stated penalty (Ex. 22:27). It must involve the additional offense of uttering the Tetragrammaton (because of the derogatory context it is called "the Name," cf. II Sam. 12:14; Job 2:9 for other euphemisms), and it is the combination of the two (24:15–16) that warrants the death penalty. The Tetragrammaton's power affects not only the speaker but his hearers; their contamination is literally transferred back to the blasphemer by the ritual of the laying on of hands.

24:15–22. An Appendage of Civil Damage Laws. It begins with the law of blasphemy and culminates in the equalization of the resident alien and citizen before the law—an unmistakable hallmark of P (Ex. 12:49; Num. 15:15–16, 29). In this pericope, the inclusion of the stranger is even more significant: his equality applies to civil as well as religious law (see comment on chapter 18 for P's motivation). That lex talionis (Ex. 21:23–25; Deut. 19:21) was extended to the stranger is one of the great moral achievements of P's legislation. Not only is every distinction eradicated between the powerful and the helpless but even between the Israelite and the non-Israelite. The interpolation of these civil statutes with their emphasis upon the resident alien is due to the legal status of the half-Israelite offender.

CHAPTER 25. THE SABBATICAL AND JUBILEE YEARS.

25:1–7. The Sabbatical Year. Each seventh year is a Sabbath of liberating rest for Israelite slaves (Ex. 21:2–6; Deut. 15:12–18), debtors (Deut. 15:1–11), and the land (Ex. 23:10–11). In P, this "full" Sabbatical is reserved for the Jubilee, whereas the seventh year Sabbatical applies only to the land. For details consult *Sabbatical Year.

25:8–34. The Jubilee Year. At the sound of the *shofar*—Jubilee means (horn of a) ram (25:10; Josh. 6:4)—a year of emancipation is proclaimed. Land must lie fallow, landed property (except for town houses) is restored to its original owner, and all Israelite slaves are set free. The basis for the Jubilee is clearly stated: Israel and the land belong solely to God (comment on ch. 18); neither can be owned in perpetuity. Thus, absolute ownership of natural property is abolished: man and land may be leased, not sold—a sublime safeguard against the pauperization of society.

25:35–55. Indebtedness and the Jubilee. A defaulting Israelite debtor distrained by an Israelite creditor (perhaps with his family, 25:41, 54) is neither charged interest for his room and board, verses 35–38; nor treated as a slave if forced to enslave himself (until the Jubilee), verses 39–46; and should be redeemed if enslaved to an alien creditor, verses 47–55. The language and terminology of this pericope are paralleled in Old and Middle Babylonian laws (18th–17th century Alalakh and 15th–14th century Nuzi, respectively), which permeated the milieu of the Patriarchs; however, they were no longer understood in post-Exilic times.

Chapter 26. The Concluding Exhortation. The threat of total destruction and exile appears in three other books of the Bible: Deuteronomy, Jeremiah (only while a deuteronomic evangelist), and Ezekiel (whose eschatology is largely based on Lev. 26). These also share with chapter 26 the preprophetic view that cultic sins alone determine the nation's collapse. (Idolatry verse 1, and the neglect of the sabbatical system, verses 2, 34–35, are specified here. Chs. 18, 20 are gross sexual violations, but these, too, are ritual impurities.)

Chapter 27. Commutation of Gifts to the Sanctuary. The following gifts are discussed: persons (27:1–8), animals (27:9–13), houses (27:14–15), land (27:16–25), firstlings (27:26–27), "devoted" things (27:28–29), and tithes (27:30–33). The commutability of sacred gifts is an ancient practice (comment on the *ʾasham*, 5:15) underscored throughout this chapter by technical language no longer understood in post-Exilic times (e.g., 27:2, 3, 12). The commutation of vows of persons is taken for granted as an established practice in II Kings 12:5. Certainly, the **ḥerem*, in its meaning of death to persons (Lev. 27:29), bespeaks an early provenance.

Bibliography: COMMENTARIES: S. R. Driver (Eng., 1898); D. Hoffmann (Ger., 1905–06, Heb., 1953); M. Noth (Eng., 1965); K. Elliger (Ger., 1966); N. Snaith (Eng., 1967). DATE: Y. Kaufmann, in: ZAW, 48 (1930), 23–43; 51(1933), 35–47; idem, in: VT, 4 (1954), 307–13; H. L. Ginsberg, in: *Commentary*, 10 (1950), 282ff.; M. Greenberg, in: JAOS, 70 (1950), 41–47; E. A. Speiser, in: *Y. Kaufmann Jubilee Volume* (1960), 29–45 (Eng. sect.); D. Lieber, in: *Jewish Education*, 34 (1963), 254–61; J. G. Vink, *The Date of the Priestly Code in the Old Testament* (1969), includes comprehensive bibliography. [J.MI.]

LEVITICUS RABBAH, one of the oldest Midrashim extant, probably composed in the fifth century in Palestine. Like other ancient Midrashim it has many passages in Palestinian Aramaic and contains a considerable number of Greek and Latin words. Many of the stories and folktales interwoven in its homilies reflect a Palestinian locale, especially that of the Sea of Galilee and its surroundings, and conditions in Palestine in the first four centuries C.E.; often the *halakhah* and customs referred to are specifically Palestinian. Much of the aggadic material presented is quoted in the names of Palestinian *amoraim* or of *tannaim*. The Midrash knows and quotes the Mishnah, Tosefta, and other tannaitic material. The editor either made use of the Palestinian Talmud (Albeck) or had access to similar (oral) traditions as were embodied in it, though differing from it in style and details (Margulies).

Leviticus Rabbah is a homiletical Midrash; it is composed of separate homilies, 37 in number, each of them based on the beginning of one of the *sedarim* ("orders") i.e., the weekly pericopes according to the so-called triennial cycle (though in a good many cases the division in *Leviticus Rabbah* differs from the lectionary as known from other sources). Hence *Leviticus Rabbah* does not provide a running commentary on the entire book of Leviticus but limits itself to developing one theme (or, sometimes, several themes) related to the beginning of the *seder*. However, the subject of the homily is by no means always identical with the main content of the pericope itself; thus, while the first *seder* of Leviticus deals mainly with the burnt-offering, the Midrash devotes its entire first homily to the first verse and, accordingly, deals with Moses' outstanding qualities as a man and a prophet. Hence the author retained, to a large extent, freedom in choosing and arranging his material. He avoided, on the whole, matters of ritual, to which most of Leviticus is devoted, e.g., details of different categories of sacrifices, and developed instead homilies on subjects such as God's preference for the poor, their offerings and their prayers (ch. 3, relating to 2:1), the dangers of drunkenness (ch. 12, on 10:8–9), the praise of peace (part of ch. 9, on 7:11; the rest of the homily is devoted to "peace-offerings"), etc. Though the editor is not in fact the author of the aggadic material, which came to him through tradition, he nevertheless attempts, usually successfully, to present homilies which are homogeneous thematically; moreover he strives to attain in the composition of each homily full integration and a balance between its component parts. If in chapter 3 he quotes a series of tales which express the contempt felt by the aristocracy and especially by the priests for the meager sacrifices offered by the poor ("What is there in this to eat? What is there in this to offer up"? 9), he counterbalances them by concluding with a hymn of praise for the ideal priests, who are without a share in the land and take their portion from the hand of God Himself, and who are thus themselves the poorest of the poor and yet are devoted wholeheartedly to the service of God. Or, if in the beginning of chapter 9 (3) the story is told of R. Yannai who had invited a man to his house believing him to be a scholar and then insulted him when he discovered him to be an ignoramus, it has its counterpart at the end of the chapter (9) in the tale of R. Meir who allowed himself to be insulted in order "to make peace between a man and his wife." Most of the homilies thus testify to the skill of the editor and to his art, which express themselves in the degree of unity which he achieves even though using heterogeneous material. Often the various elements of the homily, as well as different homilies dealing with similar themes, are linked together dialectically, expressing different, even contrasting aspects of one and the same subject. Thus the picture drawn in chapter 3 of the ideal priest is again qualified in chapter 5 (relating to Lev. 4:13), where the merits of the common people and their true leaders—the sages—are extolled (7–8) in contrast to the shortcomings of the priests, who frequently failed in their high office and, at times, even led the people astray (5–6). It is not to them that the people must look for atonement, but, instead, they can rely on their own good deeds (especially their generosity in providing funds for scholars (4)) and their prayers; for "Israel knows how to placate its Creator" (9).

Each homily in *Leviticus Rabbah* is constructed according to a definite pattern; it opens with a number of proems, then follows the "body of the sermon" (which does not possess any standard form), and, lastly, a peroration, devoted mostly to the messianic hope. These homilies, though their material was drawn mainly from sermons as preached in the synagogue, are by no means identical with the latter; thus, e.g., it stands to reason that a preacher used no more than one proem in each sermon (see also: *Preaching). This new structure found in *Leviticus Rabbah*—which is a composite of materials drawn from a number of sermons and welded together into a new artistic unit, the "literary homily"—may well be the creation of the author of this Midrash, which appears to be the oldest of the homiletical Midrashim in which it occurs. It may have been this new form which enabled the author to shape his Midrash as he did, to arrange the traditional material freely to suit his own purposes, to deal with subjects suitable for a wider circle of readers, and to enrich his work by the inclusion of numerous folktales and parables.

Leviticus Rabbah is similar in character to *Pesikta de-Rav Kahana*, which was composed at about the same time (and possibly by the same author (Margulies)); though others believe it to be somewhat later (Albeck). The structure of the homily is identical in both; but the plan of construction of the two Midrashim as a whole is completely different: while *Leviticus Rabbah* deals with all *sedarim* of one book of the Pentateuch consecutively, *Pesikta de-Rav Kahana* presents homilies for all the special days in the calendar, festivals and special Sabbaths, relating to their respective lections, taken from different books of the Pentateuch or the Prophets. A curious feature is the appearance of no less than five identical homilies in both these Midrashim; in *Leviticus Rabbah* as sermons on pericopes of Leviticus, in *Pesikta de-Rav Kahana* as sermons for festivals on which those same sections were read. It can hardly be maintained that the author of either Midrash simply transferred whole chapters from the other; rather is it due to copyists, who were tempted by the identical structure of homilies in both works to augment the one by drawing upon the other. Chapter 28 may be considered as an authentic part of *Leviticus Rabbah*, because it appears to be superfluous in *Pesikta de-Rav Kahana*; on the other hand, chapters 20, 29, and 30 and, perhaps, 27 would seem to have originated in the latter. Another query arises regarding the three cases, where *Leviticus Rabbah* has two separate chapters relating to one and the same *seder*, viz. chapters 1 and 2 (on Lev. 1: 1ff.); chapters 4 and 5 (relating, seemingly, to 4:2); and chapters 20 and 21 (on 16: 1–2). However, chapter 20 originally belonged to *Pesikta de-Rav Kahana* (see above), whereas chapter 4 was mistakenly ascribed to 4:1–2 and belongs in reality to a *seder*—otherwise unknown—beginning at 4:13. Hence the one remaining case of two homilies on the same pericope appears suspect, too; presumably chapter 2 is not authentic either in *Leviticus Rabbah*. Moreover, even after these "deductions" of 4 or 5 chapters from the total of 37, the number still appears too large, considering that Leviticus is divided traditionally into only 20 to 25 pericopes. It appears likely that the division of pericopes underlying the composition of *Leviticus Rabbah* differed considerably from the one accepted eventually as the custom of most congregations; hence the need was felt to supplement the Midrash by supplying the "missing" ones. This would also explain why quite often the beginnings of pericopes indicated in the Midrash as it stands are distant from one another by as few as five, eight or nine verses only. However, if some of the homilies of *Leviticus Rabbah* are not original, they must have been added at a very early stage, for they are common to all manuscripts, including the ones from the Cairo *Genizah*. A critical edition of *Leviticus Rabbah* by M. Margulies has been published (Jerusalem, 1953–60); an English translation by J. Israelstam and J. Slotki appeared as part of the Soncino edition of *Midrash Rabbah* (1939).

Bibliography: D. Kuenstlinger, *Die Petichot des Midrasch rabba zu Leviticus* (1913); H. L. Strack, *Introduction to the Talmud and Midrash* (1931), 211f.; Albeck, in: *Louis Ginzberg Jubilee Volume* (1946), 25–43 (Hebrew section); Zunz-Albeck, Derashot, index; M. Margulies, *Midrash Va-Yikra Rabbah*, 5 (1960), introduction; Heinemann, in: *Tarbiz*, 37 (1968), 339–54; Goldberg, *ibid.*, 38 (1969), 184–5.

[J.HEI.]

LEVITSKY, JACOB (1904–1956), mathematician. Born in Ukraine, Levitsky was taken to Palestine as a child. He studied mathematics at Goettingen and Yale, and began to lecture at the Hebrew University in 1931. Under the influence of Emmy Noether he engaged in abstract algebra,

Jacob Levitsky, Israel mathematician. Courtesy Hebrew University, Jerusalem. Photo Frence Grubner, Jerusalem.

notably in the theory of noncommutative rings. His work on the laws of rings with the minimum condition is regarded as a classic. In 1953 he and a pupil were awarded the first Israel Prize for exact sciences for their research on the law of identities of rings. The radical in associative rings—known as the Levitsky Radical—is named after him.

[SH.AM.]

LEVITSKY, LOUIS MOSES (1897–), U.S. Conservative rabbi. Levitsky was born in Kremenchug, Russia, and was taken to Montreal as a child, then emigrated to the United States in 1916. He was ordained at the Jewish Theological Seminary (1923), then led a congregation in Wilkes Barre, Pennsylvania (1922–40). Since 1940 he led Oheb Shalom Congregation in South Orange, N.J. Levitsky also served as director of the Seminary School of Jewish Studies (1940–65). He taught Jewish history and theology at Rutgers and other colleges. A leader in Conservative Judaism and in civic life, Levitsky was president of the Rabbinical Assembly (1942–44) and chairman of its Ethics Committee, and also served as a member of the National War Labor Board Panel of Mediators and the New Jersey Labor Mediation Board. He wrote *A Jew Looks at America* (1939). He was especially concerned with adult Jewish education.

[J.R.]

LEVITT, U.S. family of builders and philanthropists. ABRAHAM LEVITT (1880–1962), born in Brooklyn, New York, the son of Polish immigrants, was a real-estate lawyer for 27 years. In 1929 he founded the building firm, Levitt and Sons, Inc., which pioneered in community planning, assembly-line techniques, and mass production. In the late 1940s the firm built three whole communities, all called Levittown, in Long Island, New Jersey, and Pennsylvania. The family established the Levitt Foundation, Inc., to provide scholarships and donate funds to medical and welfare funds in 1949. Levitt was president of the Founders Society of the Albert Einstein Medical College at Yeshiva University and chairman of several fund drives for the UJA. His son WILLIAM JAIRD LEVITT (1907–), born in Brooklyn, was president of the family firm; shortly after its merger with International Telephone and Telegraph Corporation he became chairman of the board of Levitt and Sons, Inc., and also of Levittown. During his presidency the firm began building houses in Europe. Levitt engaged in extensive civic and charitable activities. A younger son of Abraham Levitt was Alfred S. Levitt (1912–1966). He was associated with his father as vice-president of Levitt and Sons, until 1954, when he organized his own firm, Levitt House Inc., based in Queens, New York. His sons John and Andrew took it over in 1959. [Ed.]

LEVNER, ISRAEL BENJAMIN (1862–1916), Hebrew writer. Born in Trudolyubovka, a Jewish colony in the Russian province of Yekaterinoslav, Levner taught in various parts of Russia. In the early 1880s he published his first articles, in **Ha-Meliẓ*, which dealt with educational subjects and descriptions of Jewish life in the communities he had visited. His stories, first published in 1895, attracted wide attention. *Ben-Avigdor invited him to join the Tushiyyah publishing house, where he edited a series of storybooks for children (especially *Bibliotekah li-Yla-*

Masthead of the children's Hebrew weekly *Ha-Peraḥim*, edited and published by Israel Levner. Courtesy Uriel Ofek, Herzliyyah.

dim—the first proper readers for Hebrew-reading children). His major work, *Kol Aggadot Yisrael*, which has retained its popularity to the present day, contains the legends of the Talmud, written in biblical style and arranged in chronological order. First published in 1895, the book has had a great many editions in Ereẓ Israel and abroad, and has been translated into various languages. Levner continued writing children's literature, especially for *Ha-Peraḥim*, a weekly which came into existence in 1908 and continued publication until the eve of World War I (he was also its editor and publisher); these works have earned an important place in Hebrew literature for children (see *Children's Literature). Together with Judah Steinberg—one of the major contributors to *Ha-Peraḥim*—he published the first of two volumes of *Kereistomatyah* ("Chrestomathy," 1908[3]). Among other works by Levner are a version of the Shulḥan Arukh (1906) and an edition of *Ein Ya'akov* (1909), both for youth.

Bibliography: Ofek, in: *Moznayim*, 16 (1963), 137–8; Kressel, Leksikon, 2 (1967), 170–1. [G.K.]

LEVONTIN, JEHIEL JOSEPH (1861–1936), Hebrew writer. Born in Orsha, Belorussia, he graduated from the University of Moscow as an engineer, and worked on railroad construction in Persia and Russia. He was among the early Ḥovevei Zion and a founder of the Benei Zion association in Moscow (1884). His letters about the life of Jews in Persia appeared in *Ha-Meliẓ* (1891) signed Ḥushai ha-Arki, which became his permanent pen name. He contributed stories about Jewish life outside the Russian Pale of Settlement, such as "*Ha-Kabbelan*" and "*Ha-Anus*," to *Ha-Meliẓ* and other literary publications, and wrote a novelette about the early days of Ḥibbat Zion in St. Petersburg, "*Yemei ha-Ma'aseh*" (*Ha-Shilo'aḥ*, vols. 2, 3). His other novels, *Shimon Eẓyoni* (1899), *Mi-Bein ha-Arafel* (1914), and *Ha-Shevu'ah* (1931), are concerned with the dispute between assimilationists and Zionists in prerevolutionary Russia. He published one of the earliest modern Hebrew books about agriculture (*Ha-Ikkarut*, 1915). During World War I, he lived in Moscow and served on the executive of the Russian Zionist movement. He was arrested together with the other participants in the illegal Zionist convention which took place in Moscow in 1920. In 1922 he migrated to Palestine. Two volumes of his stories and articles were published posthumously: *Min ha-Meẓar* (1938) and *Bein Tikvah ve-Ye'ush* (1938).

Bibliography: Lachower, Sifrut, 3 pt. 2 (1963), 37f.; J. L. G. Kahanovitz, *Me-Homel ad Tel Aviv* (1952), 66–68. [Y.S.]

LEVONTIN, ZALMAN DAVID (1856–1940), a pioneer of Jewish settlement and banking in Ereẓ Israel. Born in Orsha, Belorussia, the son of a Ḥabad ḥasidic family, Levontin received a religious education and was tutored privately in languages and secular studies, after which he worked as a clerk in a commercial bank in Kremenchug. He was one of the first members of *Ḥovevei Zion and established a settlers' association in his town and in Kharkov. The two associations sent him to Ereẓ Israel to purchase lands, and after a short tour of the country Levontin convened a meeting of the representatives of the settlers' associations from Russia and Rumania, as well as local public leaders. This conference established the Va'ad Ḥalutzei Yesud ha-Ma'alah, which decided to found a settlement by the name of *Rishon le-Zion. In 1882 Levontin, with the assistance of his wealthy uncle, Ẓevi Levontin, purchased 3,340 dunams (835 acres) and founded Rishon le-Zion there; he later served as head of the settlement's first committee.

In 1883, lack of funds forced Levontin to sell his land to Baron Edmond de *Rothschild and return to his family in Russia, where he served as branch bank manager in various towns in the *Pale of Settlement. Levontin joined the Zionist Movement upon its establishment and, in 1901, was

Zalman David Levontin, pioneer of Jewish settlement and banking in Ereẓ Israel. Jerusalem, J.N.U.L., Schwadron Collection.

summoned by *Herzl to become one of the directors of the *Jewish Colonial Trust in London. In 1903 he went to Ereẓ Israel to establish a bank under British auspices, to be known as the Anglo-Palestine Company (see Bank Leumi le-Israel in *Israel, Banking and Commerce). Under his directorship this bank became the central financial and credit institution in the new *yishuv* and engaged in banking activities with the Turkish authorities and the Arabs. When World War I broke out, Levontin went to London and Paris to mobilize funds in order to overcome the economic crisis that had beset the *yishuv*. When he was about to return, Turkey joined the war against Britain and France, and Levontin remained in Alexandria, where he opened a temporary branch of the Anglo-Palestine Company which extended aid to refugees and exiles from Palestine. He participated in the negotiations with the British authorities leading to the establishment of the *Zion Mule Corps, commanded by Joseph *Trumpeldor. In the spring of 1918, Levontin returned to Palestine and continued his banking work; six years later he retired from the bank's board of directors. He published his memoirs, *Le-Ereẓ Avoteinu* (vol. 1, 1884, revised edition, 1963; vol. 2, 1925; vol. 3, 1928), in which he advocated the employment of capitalist methods of agricultural settlement and criticized the settlement methods of the Zionist Organization, particularly those of the labor movement. Jehiel *Levontin was his brother.

Bibliography: Y. Ya'ari Poleskin, *Z. D. Levontin* (Heb., 1932); D. Idelovitz, *Sefer Rishon le-Ẓiyyon* (1941), index; *Terumah la-Kohen ... (Z. D. Levontin)* (1926); Y. Ḥurgin, *Z. D. Levontin* (Heb., 1943); Tidhar, 2 (1947), 813–5; Kressel, Leksikon, 2 (1967), 159–60.

[Y.S.]

LEVY, wealthy family of Portuguese refugees in Morocco. MEYER (d. 1520) established an important spinning mill in Safi; the carpets woven there were famous. In about 1510 the king of Portugal appointed Meyer "royal treasurer." In 1520 the sharif of the Saʿadi dynasty accused him of espionage and had him put to death. His brother ISAAC (d. after 1555), who was the "confidential Jew" of the sharifs of the Saʿadi dynasty, played an active role in their foreign policy. Meyer's son JOSEPH (d. after 1560) entered the service of the Portuguese and was their official interpreter from 1535. A talented negotiator, he received a pension from the king of Portugal. His grandson JUDAH (d. c. 1635) was entrusted with important functions during the reign of Aḥmed al-Manṣur (1578–1603) and became one of the favorites of the ruler's successors, during whose reigns he was responsible for "marine and commercial affairs" and was appointed *rentero* of the port of Safi, then the most important one in the kingdom. He was a merchant and was as well known in London and Amsterdam as in Morocco. Toward the end of his life the sultan entrusted him with the administration of the funds of the royal treasury. He died in Safi. His brother MOSES (d. after 1620) was an important financier. In about 1600 the title of *nagid* was bestowed upon him and for a time he presided over the activities of Moroccan Jewry. In 1603 he signed the *takkanot* of Fez. In 1617 the sultan sent him on an economic mission to the Netherlands with credentials addressed to the Estates-General and Maurice of Nassau. His family played an important role in the international commerce of Morocco and the leadership of the Jewish communities until about 1720. The family's descendants were known from their *ketubbot* in Safi, Mogador, and Gibraltar until the 19th century.

Bibliography: D. Cazès, *Notes bibliographiques* ... (1893), 44–50, 237–9; J. M. Toledano, *Ner ha-Ma'arav* (1911), 193; J. Abensur, *Mishpat u-Ẓedakah be-Ya'akov*, 1 (1894), no. 92; 2 (1894), nos. 123–4; SIHM, index.

[D.Co.]

LÉVY, family of French publishers. MICHEL (1821–1875) was born in Phalsbourg, Lorraine. He studied at the Paris music conservatory, but, finding that he lacked talent, abandoned his studies and became a secondhand bookseller. Lévy first sold books in the street and then on a stall. In 1842 he and his brothers ALEXANDRE NATHAN LÉVY and CALMANN LÉVY (1819–1891) founded the Lévy publishing firm. Their first success was a new edition of Goethe's *Faust* and, within a short time, Michel Lévy Frères became established as one of the largest publishing houses in France. They issued the works of great French authors such as Balzac, Lamartine, Anatole France, and Ernest Feydeau. When Feydeau included an anti-Semitic reference in his novel *La Comtesse de Chalis* (1867), the Lévy brothers refused to allow their name to appear as publishers. They also published books on biblical subjects and comparative religion. For a long period they issued the famous *Revue de Paris*. On the death of Michel Lévy in 1875, Calmann Lévy assumed control of the firm, which was renamed Calmann-Lévy. In 1878 he published Ernest David's French translation of George *Eliot's *Daniel Deronda*. After the death of Calmann Lévy, his three sons, PAUL, GEORGES, and GASTON took over the management of the firm. [J.M.S.]

LEVY, AARON (1742–1815), U.S. merchant and land speculator. Levy was born in Amsterdam. He went to Pennsylvania about 1760, where he established himself as an Indian trader and merchant. His major interest was in land speculation; he was one of the most active speculators in the colonies. He had large holdings in Northumberland and Centre counties and owned land in every other county of Pennsylvania. During the Revolution Levy made loans to the Continental Congress which, according to Robert Morris, superintendent of finance from 1781 to 1784, were never fully repaid. In addition, Levy helped to supply the colony's regular troops. After the war, in 1786, Levy announced plans for Aaronsburg, a town to be built in Penn Valley, Centre County. This was the first community in the United States founded by and named after a Jew. Although Levy actively promoted Aaronsburg, it was not a success. The failure left Levy land-poor, and to obtain cash he became an agent for other speculators. In 1796 he settled in Philadelphia, where he lived until his death.

Bibliography: S. M. Fish, *Aaron Levy* (1951); Rosenbloom, Biogr Dict. [N.O.]

LEVY, AARON (1771–1852), U.S. army officer and land speculator. Levy, the son of Hayman *Levy, was born in New York City. He was commissioned a paymaster of infantry in 1800 and served as a captain of artillery in 1812. He was appointed a lieutenant colonel of artillery in 1816 and resigned from the army in 1819. Levy, after having been licensed as an auctioneer in 1807, went into partnership with his father-in-law Isaac Moses. Levy was active in real estate transactions in the Lake George area of New York State. He served as president of Congregation Shearith Israel, New York, in 1803 and 1804.

Bibliography: Rosenbloom, Biogr Dict; AJHSP, 27 (1920), 335–44.

[L.HE.]

LEVY, SIR ALBERT (1864–1937), English philanthropist. After a successful business career as founder, chairman, and managing director of the Ardath Tobacco Co., he retired in 1931 to devote himself to philanthropy. He was knighted in 1929. His special interest was hospitals. He donated £10,000 for hospitals to mark King George V's coronation in 1911, and in 1928, £100,000 to the Royal Free Hospital, London, of which he was treasurer from 1927 to 1937. The Albert Levy Benevolent Fund, which he founded, donated £400,000 to about 125 institutions. Among many offices he held were president and treasurer of the Eastman Dental Clinic. [J.M.S.]

LÉVY, ALFRED (1840–1919), chief rabbi of France, scholar, and author. Lévy, who was born in Lunéville,

France, graduated from the Paris Ecole Rabbinique in 1866 and subsequently served as rabbi at Dijon (1867–69), Lunéville (1869–80), and Lyons (1880–1905). In 1905 he succeeded Zadoc Kahn as chief rabbi of the Consistoire Central de France, in which capacity he presided over the reorganization of French Jewry following the separation of State and Church in 1905. In 1932 a street in his native Lunéville was named after him. Lévy, whose main scholarly interest was in French-Jewish history, wrote: *Les Juifs de la Comté au xive siécle* (in: *Archives Israélites*, 30 (1869), 182ff., 214ff., 245ff.); *Les Juifs du duché de Bourgogne au moyen-âge* (*ibid.*, 1869); and *Notice sur les Israélites de Lyon* (1894). Levy also wrote on Al-Ḥarizi's *Taḥkemoni* (in: REJ, 59 (1910), *Actes et Conférences*, VII–XXV); *Le deuil et les cérémonies funéraires chez les Israélites* (1874); and published a volume of sermons *Les doctrines d'Israël* (1896).

Alfred Lévy, chief rabbi of France. Jerusalem, J.N.U.L., Schwadron Collection.

Bibliography: *L'Univers Israélite* (June 22, 1914; July 25, 1919; Aug. 1, Aug. 8, 1919); *Archives Israélites* (June 21, 1917; July 31, 1919).

[G.WE.]

LEVY, AMY (1861–1889), English poet and novelist. Amy Levy published her first book in 1881, while still an undergraduate at Cambridge. This was *Xantippe and Other Verse*, the title poem being a defense of the wife of Socrates. A Londoner by birth and upbringing, she is remembered chiefly for *A London Plane Tree* (1889). Throughout her life, Amy Levy suffered from melancholy, and her second volume, *A Minor Poet and Other Verses* (1884), conveys her despair. As a novelist, she wrote the experimental *The Romance of a Shop* (1888) and, in the same year, the more competent *Reuben Sachs*, which was criticized for its unsympathetic portrayal of the wealthier Jewish classes. More genial, but slight, was her *Miss Meredith* (1889), the story of a governess. *Cohen of Trinity*, published in *The Gentleman's Magazine* (1889), a story arresting in its psychological delineation, was written a few months before she committed suicide.

Amy Levy, English poet and novelist. From *Transactions of the Jewish Historical Society of England*, Vol. II, 1924–27, London. Jerusalem, J.N.U.L.

Bibliography: M. F. Modder, *Jew in the Literature of England* (1939), 261, 317–8, 323–4, 380.

[ED.]

LEVY, ASSER (d. 1681), New York merchant and landowner. Levy was a member of the first group of Jews to arrive in New Amsterdam, in September 1654. In the following years he successfully contested a tax assessed against Jews who were refused the right to serve in the militia and he also achieved for his coreligionists the right to carry on trade in the community. Levy was made a freeman in 1657, and became the most prominent of 17th-century New York Jews. He purchased land in various sections of New York and developed an extensive trade, principally in the city and in the Hudson River Valley, dealing in all types of merchandise. He opened a butcher and tanning shop in New York City in 1678.

Bibliography: J. R. Rosenbloom, Biogr Dict, 88; J. R. Marcus, *Early American Jewry*, 1 (1951), 30–31; Huehner, in: Karp, ed., *Jewish Experience in America*, 1 (1969), 51–65.

[L.HE.]

LEVY, BENJAMIN (c. 1650–1704), founder of the London Ashkenazi community, son of Loebel or Levy Moses of Hamburg. He arrived in London in about 1670, made a fortune, and in 1697 became one of the 12 original Jewish brokers in London. He is said to have been instrumental in procuring the charter for the reorganized East India Company and was a "proprietor" (i.e., member of the board) of the company in charge of New Jersey. Though attached to the Sephardi congregation, he purchased the original cemetery for the Ashkenazi community in 1696. On his death, leadership of this community was assumed by his kinsman Moses *Hart (1675–1756). The latter's daughter JUDITH (1707–1803) married Benjamin's son ELIAS (d. 1750). In 1790 Judith Levy defrayed a large part of the cost of reconstructing the Great Synagogue which her father had rebuilt in 1722.

Another BENJAMIN LEVY (d. 1693), born in Cracow, lived in Recife (Brazil), before becoming *ḥazzan* and *shoḥet* of the London Sephardi community from about 1664. He was the recipient in London of enthusiastic communications regarding *Shabbetai Zevi.

Bibliography: C. Roth, *History of the Great Synagogue* (1950), passim; A. M. Hyamson, *Sephardim of England* (1951), 41–44, and passim; L. D. Barnett, *Libro de los Acuerdos* (1931), passim; J. Sasportas, *Ẓiẓat Novel Ẓevi*, ed. by Y. Tishbi (1954), 71 (44b).

[C.R.]

LEVY, CHAPMAN (1787–1850), U.S. lawyer. Levy, who was born in Camden, South Carolina, was admitted to the South Carolina bar in 1806. He served in the War of 1812, and reached the rank of colonel. Levy was in the state legislature from 1829 to 1833. He was elected to the state convention which passed the nullification of the federal tariffs of 1828 and 1832, despite Levy's negative vote. He again served in the legislature from 1836 to 1838. Levy then moved to Mississippi where he operated a plantation at Camden until his death. [N.O.]

LEVY, CLIFTON HARBY (1867–1962), U.S. Reform rabbi. Born in New Orleans, his family had settled in the American colonies in 1740. Levy was ordained at Hebrew Union College, was rabbi of Congregation Gates of Hope, New York City (1890–91), and superintendent of classes for immigrant children established by the Baron de Hirsch Fund. He later served congregations in Lancaster, Pa. (1892–94) and Baltimore, Md. (1894–96). He founded Tremont Temple, Bronx, N.Y., and was its rabbi from 1906 to 1921. In 1924 he organized the Center of Jewish Science, New York City, which sought to counter the influence of Christian Science among middle-class Jews. While still a student, Levy published a five-act Purim play, *Haman and Mordecai* (1886). During his stay in Baltimore he edited *Jewish Comment*. He edited *The Bible in Art* (1936), and *The*

Bible in Pictures (1942), and served as art editor of the *Universal Jewish Encyclopedia.* [ED.]

LEVY, FELIX ALEXANDER (1884–1963), U.S. Reform rabbi and scholar. Levy was born in New York, son of parents of Alsatian origin. He was ordained at Hebrew Union College (1907). From 1908 until his retirement in 1955, Rabbi Levy served Emmanuel Congregation, Chicago. He influenced his colleagues in modifying the attitude of Reform Judaism to *halakhah* and the nature of Jewish identity. These changes were embodied, inter alia, in the 1937 Columbus Platform adopted by the Central Conference of American Rabbis under Levy's leadership as president (1935–37). After his retirement, Rabbi Levy served as editor of *Judaism* and as dean of the Academy for Higher Jewish Learning in New York. A selection of his papers and sermons appeared in *His Own Torah* (ed. S. D. Temkin, 1969).

Bibliography: S. D. Temkin (ed.), *His Own Torah* (1969), 3–43. [W.KE.]

LEVY, HAYMAN (1721–1789), New York merchant and landowner. Levy was born in Hanover, Germany, and went to New York shortly before 1748. He was naturalized and made a freeman of New York in 1750. During the Seven Years' War he had a considerable Indian trade and he owned trade ships engaged in privateering. Early in the Revolutionary War Levy left the British-occupied city for Philadelphia, where he served in the militia. After the war he returned to New York and opened a commission store. Very much involved in Jewish affairs, Levy served as president of Congregation Shearith Israel six times. He had 11 children who became important members of the New York community.

Bibliography: J. R. Rosenbloom, *Biographical Dictionary of Early American Jews* (1960), s.v. *Levy* and *Sloe Myers;* L. Hershkowitz (ed.), *Wills of Early New York Jews* (1967), 165–85. [L.HE.]

LEVY, HYMAN (1889–), British mathematician. Levy was born in Edinburgh and was professor of mathematics at the Imperial College of Science, London, from 1923 to 1955, and was dean of the Royal College of Science (1948–54). During World War I he worked on aerodynamics at the National Physical Laboratory. Always deeply interested in social affairs, Levy was a pioneer in explaining and interpreting the social impact of science. He was chairman of the Labor Party's science advisory committee from 1924 to 1930. He became a leading member of the British Communist Party, particularly active among scientists. After a visit to the Soviet Union in 1957 he published a pamphlet "Jews and the National Question" (1958), which criticized the Soviet attitude to the Jews and Jewish culture in the U.S.S.R., whereupon he was expelled from the Communist Party. [M.GOL.]

LÉVY, ISAAC (1835–1912), French rabbi, born in Marmoutier, Alsace. Lévy was rabbi of Verdun in 1858, of Lunéville in 1865, and of Colmar in Upper Alsace in 1869. After the annexation of Alsace by Germany following the Franco-Prussian war of 1870–71, Lévy chose to remain French, and the French government created a new chief rabbinate for him at Vesoul. In 1887 he became chief rabbi of Bordeaux. Lévy wrote *Récits bibliques* (1864), *Défense du Judaïsme* (1867), and *Histoire sainte à l'usage de la jeunesse Israélite,* the standard biblical history for Jewish children in France (1869; 16th ed. 1931). [ED.]

LÉVY, ISIDORE (1870–1954), historian of religion. Born in Rixheim, Alsace, Lévy taught at the Ecole des Hautes Etudes (1905–28) in the departments of religion and historical and philological sciences, as well as at Lille (1919–23), the Sorbonne (1923–27), the Université Libre in Brussels (1929), and the Collège de France (1932–40; 1944–45). His studies are devoted to the ancient history of religion, extending from Asia Minor to Egypt and particularly the western Semites. Lévy's books include *Recherches sur les sources de la Légende de Pythagore* (1926), *La Légende de Pythagore de Grèce en Palestine* (1927), and *Recherches esséniennes et pythagoriciennes* (1965).

Bibliography: Brussels, Université Libre, Institut de Philologie et Histoire Orientales et Slaves, *Annuaire,* 13 (1953), v–xix, incl. list of his works. [V.A.M.]

LEVY, JACOB (1819–1892), rabbi and lexicographer. Born near Poznan, Poland, he studied under his father, Rabbi Isaac Levy, and under Rabbi Akiva *Eger by whom he was ordained. He also studied philology and Middle Eastern languages at Breslau and Halle universities. For several years he served as rabbi of Rosenberg, Upper Silesia, but resigned from this post in 1850, in order to devote himself exclusively to scientific work. He settled in Breslau where he became assistant rabbi (*dayyan*) in 1857; in 1864 he was appointed to the Breslau court to administer the *oath *more judaico* ("Jewish Oath"). From 1878 to his death, he also served as lecturer at the Mora-Salomon Leipziger Foundation.

Levy's first major work was the *Chaldaeisches Woerterbuch ueber die Targumim und einen grossen Teil des rabbinischen Schrifttums,* 2 vols. (1867–68, 1881[3]). For this work the Prussian government awarded him the title of "professor." A second monumental work, *Neuhebraeisches und chaldaeisches Woerterbuch ueber die Talmudim und Midraschim* (4 vols., 1876–89), is of particular importance because of the comparative study of its quotations: various versions from different manuscripts are given, explained, and translated. Both dictionaries were annotated by the Leipzig Arabist H. L. Fleischer. In 1924 the second of the two works was republished by L. *Goldschmidt in a revised and enlarged version. Levy was the outstanding scholar of his time in the field of talmudic and rabbinical lexicography, and his successors, including Alexander *Kohut, the author of *Arukh ha-Shalem,* based their scholarship on his work.

Bibliography: Schwab, Repertoire, 281 (bibliography of articles); Zeitlin, Bibliotheca, 207–8; W. Bacher, in: ZDMG, 47 (1893), 495ff.; A. Kohut, *ibid.,* 723; A. Heppner and J. Herzberg, *Aus Vergangenheit und Gegenwart der Juden . . . in den Posener Landen* (1909), 315, 373. [B.SU./ED.]

LEVY, JEFFERSON MONROE (1852–1924), U.S. congressman and lawyer. Levy, who was born in New York City, served three terms in the U.S. House of Representatives (1899–1901, and 1911–1915). He was a leader of the "Gold Democrats" during his first term, and sponsored the Reserve Bank Bill during his second and third terms. Levy advocated the maintenance of a large navy, led the fight that resulted in higher wages for the nation's postal clerks, was instrumental in codifying New York State's election laws and reforming the surrogate courts, and exposed instances of waste and extravagance in Mayor John Purroy Mitchel's generally reformist and efficient administration (1913–17) in New York City. He was the nephew of Uriah P. *Levy, from whom he inherited Monticello, Thomas Jefferson's home. [ED.]

LEVY, JONAS PHILLIPS (1807–1883), U.S. naval officer and communal leader. Levy, the brother of Uriah Phillips *Levy and the father of Jefferson Monroe *Levy, was born in Philadelphia. He took up a career in the U.S. navy, reaching the rank of commander. Unlike his brother Uriah, he seems to have adapted well to naval life and encountered no recorded anti-Semitism. In 1847 he was commander of the steamer America, ferrying troops to and participating in the naval battle for Veracruz during the Mexican War. He was appointed captain of the captured city. Levy was active in Jewish life. His greatest contribution to progress in equal rights for Jews was in his work to rectify the disabilities imposed on Jews in Switzerland. When news of the U.S.-Swiss treaty drawn up in 1850 reached American Jews, Levy led the struggle to alter the treaty, writing letters and working with his friend, Senator Lewis Cass, to delete the provision disallowing equal rights of travel and settlement to Jewish nationals and non-nationals in Switzerland. When Levy moved to Washington, D.C., in 1852, there were about 25 Jewish men in the city, meeting haphazardly for services. Levy supported the movement for a permanent synagogue. Discovering that the local laws were ambiguous on the rights of Jews so to organize, Levy called on his political friends, and in 1855 an act of Congress gave full rights to the Washington Hebrew Congregation and other congregations to organize.

Bibliography: H. K. Meier, *United States and Switzerland in the Nineteenth Century* (1963), 33–38, 58–66; C. Adler, *Jews in the Diplomatic Correspondence of the United States* (1906); C. Adler and A. M. Margalith, *With Firmness in the Right: American Diplomatic Action Affecting Jews, 1840–1945* (1946); S. Stroock, in: AJHSP, 11 (1903), 7–11. [AB.K.]

LEVY, JOSEPH LEONARD (1865–1917), U.S. Reform rabbi. Levy was born in London. He graduated from the University of London in 1884 and was trained for the Orthodox ministry at Jews College, London. From 1885 to 1889 he served the Bristol Hebrew Congregation. In 1889 he went to the United States as rabbi to a congregation in Sacramento, California, and from 1893 to 1901 he was assistant rabbi at Congregation Keneseth Israel, Philadelphia. From 1901 to 1917 he was rabbi of Congregation Rodef Shalom, Pittsburgh. During the Spanish-American War he was an army chaplain for a short period. Levy was famous in his day as a preacher; about 16 volumes of his sermons were published. He was active in local and international peace associations and in health, housing, and other welfare organizations in Pittsburgh. [S.D.T.]

LEVY, JUDAH (Mercado) BEN MENAHEM (c. 1790–c. 1875), rabbi in Ereẓ Israel. Levy was born in Sarajevo from where he moved to Ragusa, immigrating to Jerusalem in his youth. He was appointed rabbi of Jaffa in 1825 by the Jerusalem rabbinate and may be regarded as the real founder of the Jewish community in Jaffa. Later the Turkish government recognized him and conferred on him the title *ḥakham bashi.* He was responsible for the consecration of the first Jewish cemetery in Jaffa (previously its Jews had been buried in Jerusalem). Levy assisted Charles *Netter in founding the *Mikveh Israel agricultural school.

Bibliography: Brill, in: *Ha-Levanon*, 2 (1865), 56; M. D. Gaon, *Yehudei ha-Mizraḥ be-Ereẓ Yisrael*, 2 (1938), 320f.; Frumkin-Rivlin, 3 (1929), 309 no. 13. [SH.A.H./ED.]

LEVY, LEONARD WILLIAMS (1923–), U.S. historian. Born in Toronto, Canada, he taught at Brandeis University, serving as dean of the Graduate School of Arts and Sciences (1958–63) and dean of the Faculty of Arts and Sciences (1963–66). From 1958 he held the chair in American constitutional history. Levy contributed to the history of American constitutional law and to the early history of American law, with emphasis on the background of the Bill of Rights. His main works are: *The Law of the Commonwealth and Chief Justice Shaw* (1957); *Legacy of Suppression: Freedom of Speech and Press in Early American History* (1960); *Jefferson and Civil Liberties . . .* (1963). His *Origins of the Fifth Amendment . . .* (1968) was awarded a Pulitzer Prize. Levy was also editor of several historical series. He was a member of both the American Jewish Committee and the American Jewish Congress, serving on the latter's Commission on Law and Social Action. [R.B.M.]

LEVY, LOUIS EDWARD (1846–1919), U.S. chemist, inventor, communal leader, and newspaper editor. Levy, who was born in Pilsen, Bohemia, was brought to the U.S. at the age of eight. In 1875 he invented the photochemical engraving process known as "Levytype," permitting newspapers to print halftone pictures from the stereotype plate, and founded the Levytype Company in Baltimore. The company moved to Philadelphia in 1877. Levy, the first U.S. citizen to receive a patent in this field, also invented the Levy acid blast, an etch-powdering machine, and the Levy line screen. He published and edited the Philadelphia *Evening Herald*, an independent Democratic daily (1887–1890), the *Mercury*, a Sunday paper (1887–1891), and *The Jewish Year* (1895). Levy was a leader of the Philadelphia Jewish community and, reflecting his deep interest in the problems of Jewish immigration to the U.S., was a founder (1884) and president of the Association for Relief and Protection of Jewish Immigrants. He wrote: *The Russian Jewish Refugees in America* (1895), a pamphlet; *Business, Money and Credit* (1896); and (with Hugo Bilgram) *The Cause of Business Depressions as Disclosed by an Analysis of the Basic Principles of Economics* (1914). [ED.]

Louis Edward Levy, Philadelphia inventor, newspaper editor, and communal leader. Jerusalem, J.N.U.L., Schwadron Collection.

LEVY, LUCIEN (1853–1912), French mathematician. He was born in Paris, taught mathematics at the Lycée Louis le Grand. He wrote many articles and contributed to the French edition of the Mathematical Encyclopedia; he published textbooks and two works on applied mathematics. From 1910 to 1911 he was president of the Mathematical Society of France. His son PAUL LEVY (1886–) became a high official in the administration of mines (1925). In 1941 after the occupation of France by the Nazis, he was exempted from the anti-Jewish statutes because of his distinguished work and permitted to teach both at the Ecole Polytechnique and at the Ecole Supérieure de Mines. He published several textbooks. In 1964 he became president of the Mathematical Society of France. [ED.]

LEVY, MARION JOSEPH, JR. (1918–), U.S. sociologist. Born in Galveston, Texas, Levy was professor of sociology at Princeton University from 1947. His scholarly work was devoted to the study of the family and to the investigation of social and cultural change in the Far East, both within the framework of system analysis. He further formulated the concepts, propositions, and methodological premises of the structural-functional approach to social phenomena in his major work, *Structure of Society* (1952). His other works are *Family Revolution in Modern China* (1949); *Rise of the Modern Chinese Business Class* (1949); *Aspects of the Analysis of Family Structure* (1965); and *Modernization and the Structure of Societies*, 2 vols. (1966). [W.J.C.]

LEVY, MOSES (c. 1665–1728), New York merchant and landowner. Levy arrived from England sometime before 1695. In that year he was made a freeman of the city, enabling him to embark on a noteworthy mercantile career and became probably the most prominent and wealthiest New York Jew of the early 18th century. He was elected constable in 1719, but paid a fine rather than serve.

Moses Levy, colonial American merchant and landowner. Portrait by an unknown artist, oil on canvas, 45×36 in. (114×91 cm.). Waltham, Mass., American Jewish Historical Society. Gift of N. Taylor Phillips.

President of the Jewish congregation of New York shortly before his death, Levy contributed to the building of Shearith Israel on Mill Street, but did not live to see its completion.

Bibliography: J. R. Rosenbloom, *Biographical Dictionary of Early American Jews* (1960), 94. [L.He.]

LEVY, MOSES (1757–1826), U.S. judge. Born in Philadelphia, Levy was the son of Samuel Levy, a Philadelphia merchant. In 1778 he was admitted to the Philadelphia bar, the first Jew to qualify as a lawyer in the United States. Levy became one of the outstanding lawyers of Philadelphia and was one of the defense counsel in the trial of Bache, editor of the anti-federalist *Aurora* for "libeling the President and the Executive Government in a manner tending to excite sedition and opposition to the laws." From 1802 to 1806 he was a member of the Pennsylvania legislature and subsequently was a judge of the district court of Philadelphia. Levy acquired a considerable reputation in the legal profession and at one time was considered for the post of attorney general of the United States. When he died the members of the Philadelphia bar wore a black armband for 30 days.

Bibliography: H. S. Morais, *Jews of Philadelphia* (1894), index. [J.J.M.]

LEVY, MOSES ELIAS (c. 1782–1854), pioneer Jewish settler in Florida, visionary exponent of Jewish colonization and educational schemes, and father of the first congressman and senator of Jewish birth, David L. *Yulee. Levy led a life which was fascinating in its variety. Born in Mogador, Morocco, and brought up in Gibraltar, Levy settled in St. Thomas, Virgin Islands, about 1800, achieving some success in business. He left St. Thomas and moved to Havana, Cuba, where he established himself as a government contractor and invested heavily in real estate which was located in Florida (then still under Spanish rule). After the cession of Florida to the United States in 1821, Levy took up residence in the new American territory and registered for American citizenship. Levy developed a number of plantations in Florida but never succeeded in attracting the settlers, including Jews, he had envisaged. In 1821 he also undertook a campaign for the establishment of a Jewish boarding school, which, however, aroused little interest. It is ironic that this champion of Jewish education so alienated his two sons that the one, David, eagerly adopted Christianity, not merely for convenience prior to his marriage as some have thought, and the other, Elias, was at one time a missionary minister of the Swedenborgian sect. Levy spent a number of years in London during the late 1820s and engaged in public debate over Jewish theological questions; several pamphlets on various themes of Jewish interest were published in his name at this time. Hard luck pursued Levy's agricultural and mercantile ventures; fire, war, and litigation devoured his assets. The wealth that Florida had seemed to promise always eluded him. Levy had close contacts with a number of important Jewish merchants and communal leaders of his day, including Moses Myers of Norfolk and Mordecai M. Noah and the Rev. M. L. M. Peixotto of New York City.

Bibliography: L. Huhner, in: *Florida Historical Quarterly*, 19 (1941), 319–45; B. W. Korn, *Eventful Years and Experiences* (1954), 152–3, 199–200; S. Proctor, in: *Proceedings of the Conference on the Writing of Regional History in the South* (1956), 81–115. [B.W.K.]

LEVY, NATHAN (1704–1753), colonial American merchant. Levy, who was born in New York City, moved to Philadelphia in 1738 where he established a business with his brother Isaac. Primarily distributors of dry goods, hardware, and general goods, the brothers also placed indentured servants with employers, and, to a limited extent, traded slaves. He and his brothers are the first known practicing Jews to settle in Philadelphia. In 1741 Nathan and Isaac Levy formed a partnership with David and Moses Franks, which entered the shipping business. As a founder of Philadephia's Jewish community, he obtained land for its first Jewish cemetery in 1740. [N.O.]

LÉVY, PAUL (1887–1962), French linguist and historian. Lévy, who was born in Alsace, became a specialist on the linguistic history of Alsace and Lorraine and taught at the Lycée Kléber in Strasbourg. From 1933 he taught at the Lycée Rollin (later Jacques Ducour) in Paris. During the German occupation of France in World War II he refused an offer of exceptional reinstatement in his post. After the war, Lévy directed the investigation of the secret archives of the Third Reich. Among his major works were: *Histoire linguistique d'Alsace et de Lorraine* (1929), *La Langue allemande en France* (1950–52), and *Les Noms des Israélites en France* (1960). [Ir.M.]

LÉVY, RAPHAËL (c. 1612–1670), victim of a *blood libel in France. Born in Chelaincourt, near Metz, Lévy was a livestock merchant in the village of Boulay, though the anonymous Christian account of his trial describes him as "filling the office of rabbi" there. He was accused of having abducted a Christian child in the village of Glatigny, on the eve of Rosh Ha-Shanah 1669, when he was on his way to Metz to buy a *shofar*. Giving himself up voluntarily ("to save the house of Israel"), he was condemned to death by the *parlement* of Metz after a scandalous trial, even though the remains of the child, devoured by wolves, had in the meantime been found. On Jan. 17, 1670, he was burned at the stake in Metz. The tribunal also demanded the permanent expulsion of the Jews from Metz. The latter belatedly laid the affair before the royal council which, on the basis of an address by Richard *Simon, concluded that there had been a judicial error.

Bibliography: J. Reinach, *Raphaël Lévy, une erreur judiciaire sous Louis XIV* (1898); R. Clément, *Condition des juifs de Metz* (1903), 52–66.
[G.C.]

LEVY, REUBEN (1891–1966), British orientalist. Born in Manchester, Levy became lecturer in Persian language and literature at Oxford University (1920–23). From 1923 to 1926 he taught biblical literature at the Jewish Institute of Religion, New York. On his return to England he taught Persian at Cambridge University, and was appointed professor in 1950. During both world wars Levy served in British Intelligence. From 1918 to 1920 he was in the Iraq political service.

Apart from editing and translating a number of classical Persian and Arabic texts, Levy wrote two textbooks: *The Persian Language* (1951) and *Persian Literature* (1923, repr. 1955); a two-volume work *Introduction to the Sociology of Islam* (1931–33; second edition, *The Social Structure of Islam*, 1957); and a commentary with introduction on *Deutero-Isaiah* (1925). [Ed.]

LEVY, RUDOLF (1875–1944), German painter. Levy, who was born into an Orthodox Jewish family in Stettin (Pomerania), studied cabinetmaking in Berlin and Karlsruhe, and painting in Munich. In 1903 he went to Paris, where he was strongly influenced by Matisse, with whom he

Rudolf Levy, self-portrait. Photo Lee Brian, Palm Beach, Fla.

worked. During World War I, Levy served in the German army and received the Iron Cross. After the war he settled in Berlin but in 1933 left Germany, going first to Paris and then to Italy, where he settled in Florence. Though forewarned by the German consul and by the Italian police, Levy remained in his atelier and in December 1943 was arrested by the Gestapo, sent to a concentration camp, and killed either in Auschwitz or Dachau. Levy was one of the few German painters of his generation who did not join the expressionist movement, but remained under the influence of Matisse and Cézanne. His work, lyrical in nature, was molded by the Mediterranean atmosphere which inspired some of his finest oils.

Bibliography: W. Haftmann, *Painting in the Twentieth Century*, 1 (1965^2), 79–80, 401–2; 2 (1965^2), 295.
[A.W.]

LEVY, SAM SAADI (1870–1959), journalist. Levy was born in Salonika, but at an early age he went to live in Paris, returning in 1898 to Salonika, where he collaborated in the periodicals *La Epoca* (Judeo-Spanish), founded in 1875, and *Journal de Salonique* (French), founded in 1895. He also wrote and edited the most brilliant part of the satirical *El Kirbatch* ("The Riding Whip"), which was very popular with the public. In 1905, wishing to escape all censorship, he settled in Zemlin (Austria) where he founded two periodicals, *Le Rayon* (French) and *El Luzero* (Judeo-Spanish), both intended to be circulated in Turkey. With the Young Turk revolution of 1908, he returned to Salonika, again taking up the editorship of *La Epoca* and *Journal de Salonique*. In 1912, with the Hellenization of northern Greece, he sold his newspapers. He then settled first in Lausanne, and later on in Paris, where he set up the *Guide Sam*, a publication which for years constituted the directory of all industrial and commercial enterprises in the Near East. In Paris, he also founded the *Cahiers Sefardis*, in which many historical, social, and economic studies on the Jewish communities of the Near East were published. [J.N.]

LÉVY, SAMUEL (b. 1678), rabbi and financier. After studying in Metz and in Poland, in 1702 Lévy was appointed rabbi of Upper Alsace (later the Haut-Rhin department) by Louis XIV and served there until 1709. Subsequently he engaged in financial transactions, purchasing abroad corn and specie on behalf of Duke Leopold of Lorraine. In 1715 Lévy was appointed tax-collector for Lorraine, where he effected cuts in public expenditure and introduced new taxes which antagonized the nobility. In 1716 he was removed from office at the instigation of his opponents and faced total bankruptcy. His creditors, whose claims amounted to three million livres, had him arrested, together with his wife. He was in prison for several years; following his release in 1722, he was expelled from Lorraine and moved to Paris, where he died in complete poverty.

Bibliography: H. Baumont, *Etudes sur le règne de Léopold* (1894), 400f.; 493–4; M. Aron, in: REJ, 34 (1897), 107–16; M. Ginsburger, *ibid.*, 65 (1913), 274–300; 66 (1913), 263–84; 67 (1914), 82–117; 262–87; 68 (1915), 84–109; C. Pfister, *Histoire de Nancy*, 3 (1909), 316–7.
[EJ]

LEVY, URIAH PHILLIPS (1792–1862), U.S. naval officer. Levy was born in Philadelphia, into a distinguished family of U.S. patriots. Running away to sea at ten, he became a sailing master in the United States navy at 20 and a midshipman four years later. Commissioned as lieutenant in 1816 and captain in 1844, he saw little active duty in the years 1827–57 because of disciplinary problems. In 1857 he was reinstated by a naval Court of Inquiry and ordered to the Mediterranean, where in 1859 he served for six months as commodore of the U.S. fleet. Most of what is known about Levy is from the record of six court-martials and the proceedings of his fight against an order in 1855 dropping him from the navy lists, together with 200 fellow officers. He was certainly an excellent sailor, a good disciplinarian, a progressive officer, and a brave patriot. He was also extremely sensitive about his Jewishness, exhibited some peculiar mannerisms, and was extremely pugnacious. The proceedings established beyond a doubt that his career had suffered because of anti-Semitism. On the other hand, any officer with his record of six court-martials and his unorthodox methods of maintaining discipline might have

Captain Uriah Phillips Levy exhibiting the cat-o-nine-tails to Washington statesmen during his successful campaign for the abolition of flogging in the U.S. navy. Courtesy Mariners' Museum, Newport News, Virginia.

had the same difficulties. Moreover, he had begun his career as a sailing master, unlike the "gentlemen" who received their commission as midshipmen directly. In spite of these handicaps and an array of petty accusations against him, an imposing list of high naval officers testified to his honorable character and his professional ability. Levy's greatest liability, so far as popularity with his fellow officers went, but his greatest claim to lasting fame as well, was his active espousal of a law to prohibit corporal punishment in the navy. Senator John Parker Hale sponsored such a bill (1850), and Levy was one of a small group of naval officers who supported him. Indeed, Levy had long previously advocated such a change, not only in numerous writings, but as captain of the S.S. *Vandalia,* the first ship to sail with discipline maintained without recourse to the lash. Levy wrote extensively on the problems of naval discipline. He also published *A Manual of Informal Rules and Regulations for Men-of-War* and several navigation charts. While on active duty, he found time to explore the Rio Grande from Veracruz as far up as Matamores. During his years of inactive service Levy acquired, and at great expense refurbished, Thomas Jefferson's estate at Monticello, which eventually became the summer home of his nephew, J. M. *Levy, until purchased by a public organization and made into a historic monument. His mother is buried along the walk approaching the main house. During the 1855 proceedings, Levy testified that his "parents were Israelites and I was nurtured in the faith of my ancestors." He was a member of Congregation Shearith Israel in New York and a charter member of Washington Hebrew Congregation. He sponsored (1854) the new Seminary of the Bnai Jeshurun Educational Institute in New York. Levy received a traditional Jewish funeral and is buried in the Cypress Hill Cemetery of Congregation Shearith Israel in Brooklyn, New York.

Bibliography: A. Kanof, in: AJHSP, 39 (1949/50), 1–66. [AB.K.]

LEVY-BACRAT, ABRAHAM BEN SOLOMON (late 15th–16th century), poet of Spanish origin. Bacrat took refuge in North Africa in 1492. In his native town of Malaga he had been a disciple of Judah Gabbai, to whom he dedicated several poems. At first he settled in Tlemcen, together with Abraham *Benzamero, Abraham *Gavison, and Moses *Alashkar. He wrote an elegy on the Spanish Expulsion. His major work, a supercommentary on Rashi, is called *Sefer ha-Zikkaron* ("Book of the Memory") and was completed in 1507 in Tunis, where he became a close friend of Abraham *Zacuto. This work was known from its copies but it remained in manuscript until its publication in Leghorn in 1845. The author's introduction contains an instructive autobiography which contains information on Bacrat's tribulations after the Spanish Expulsion.

Bibliography: D. Cazès, *Notes bibliographiques sur la littérature juive-tunisienne* (1893), 234–6; H. H. Ben-Sasson, in: *Tarbiz,* 31 (1962), 59–71; Hirschberg, Afrikah, 1 (1965), 300, 325. [D.Co.]

LÉVY-BRUHL, LUCIEN (1857–1939), French anthropologist, philosopher, and psychologist. Born and educated in Paris, Lévy-Bruhl taught philosophy at the Lycée Louis-le-Grand (1885–95), and later at the Sorbonne where he was appointed to the chair of history of modern philosophy. Here he was a colleague of Emile *Durkheim, and wrote a series of anthropological works on various aspects of preliterate culture to demonstrate the nature of primitive mentality. Lévy-Bruhl endeavored to show that the primitives' thought was indifferent to the laws of logic and was essentially mystical. Later in his notebooks published posthumously he retracted this idea and stated that prelogical and preliterate societies would employ logical thought to meet the practical demands of natural environment. Lévy-Bruhl's works on this subject evoked criticism from Durkheim in *Les formes élémentaires de la vie religieuse* (1912; *The Elementary Forms of the Religious Life,* 1947) and from Franz *Boas. Lévy-Bruhl revised this idea in later books but further developed the idea of a "special sense" or mysticism. Although his views on primitive mentality are not accepted, Lévy-Bruhl's theories have had diverse influence on some Jungian psychologists in their interpretations of the relation of archetypes of the unconscious to primitive mentality, and of the phenomenon of "participation." [E.F.]

Lucien Lévy-Bruhl, French anthropologist. Jerusalem, J.N.U.L., Schwadron Collection.

His son HENRI (1884–), born in Paris, taught law successively at Grenoble, Lille, and Paris until he was deposed during the German occupation of France in World War II. After 1945, he founded with G. Gurvitch and G. LeBres the Centre d'Etudes Sociologiques, recreated the *Année Sociologique,* and became one of the directors of the Division of Social Sciences at the Ecole Pratique des Hautes Etudes. Henri Lévy-Bruhl belonged to the Durkheimian School in French sociology; he specialized in the sociology of law, particularly Roman law and the ethnology of law, and he also worked in the field of criminology. Among his major works are: *Le témoignage instrumentaire en droit romain* (1910), *Histoire de la lettre de change en France* (1933), *Quelques problèmes du très ancien droit romain* (1934), *Initiation aux recherches de sociologie juridique* (1947), and *Aspects sociologiques du droit* (1955). [W.J.C.]

Bibliography: *Les carnets de Lucien Lévy-Bruhl* (1949), preface; J. Cazeneuve, *Lucien Lévy-Bruhl, sa vie, son oeuvre, avec un exposé de sa philosophie* (1963), incl. bibl.; idem, in: IESS, 9 (1968), 263–6; *Mélanges Henri Lévy-Bruhl* (1959), incl. bibl.

LEWALD, FANNY (1811–1889), German novelist and champion of women's rights. The eldest daughter of a Koenigsberg businessman who had all his children baptized, Fanny Lewald spent most of her life in Berlin, where her cousin, August Lewald, editor of the periodical *Europa*, encouraged her first literary efforts. In 1842, she published her first novel, *Clementine*. Its success prompted others, including *Jenny* (1843), *Eine Lebensfrage* (1845), and *Prinz Louis Ferdinand* (1849).

During a trip to Italy in 1845, she met the classical philologist Adolf Stahr, whom she married ten years later.

Fanny Lewald, German novelist. Jerusalem, J.N.U.L., Schwadron Collection.

She then established a salon in Berlin, where her circle included such prominent literary figures as Karl Gutzkow, Varnhagen von Ense, Henriette *Herz, Berthold *Auerbach, and Bettina von Arnim.

Fanny Lewald's work was greatly influenced by the French novelist George Sand, but it also shows the impact of Goethe and of the "Young Germany" school. Her novels, which enjoyed enormous popularity, dealt with contemporary issues, advocating anti-romanticism, political liberalism, feminism, religious toleration, social reform, and anti-militarism. Her most important novel was *Von Geschlecht zu Geschlecht* (8 vols., 1864–66), and she also published an autobiography, *Meine Lebensgeschichte* (3 vols., 1861–63).

Bibliography: M. Steinhauer, *Fanny Lewald, die deutsche George Sand* (1937). [S.L.]

LEWANDOWSKI, LOUIS (1821–1894), choral director and composer. Born in Wreschen, near Posen, Lewandowski became a singer at the age of 12 with *ḥazzan* Ascher Lion's choir in Berlin. Later he studied with Adolph Bernhard *Marx at Berlin University and with Rungenhagen and Grell at the Academy of Fine Arts. After 1840 he served as conductor of the choir at the Old Synagogue in the Heidereutergasse, and after 1866 at the New Synagogue. Lewandowski, the most significant composer of synagogue music after Solomon *Sulzer, reproduced the traditional melodies in a more classical form and treated the organ accompaniment with greater freedom than did his predecessor. His style, which was more harmonic than contrapuntal, was calculated to appeal to a wide public, and together with the soulful quality of his melodic idiom, gained great popularity for his compositions. The traditional foundations of his work were, on the one hand, the liturgy of the Old Synagogue established by the *ḥazzanim* Lichtenstein and Rosenfeld, and, on the other hand, the East European *nusaḥ* which Lewandowski received from immigrant *ḥazzanim* and singers. Outstanding examples of these

Louis Lewandowski, composer of synagogue music. Courtesy Department of Musicology, J.N.U.L., Jerusalem.

influences are his choral work *Ki ke-Shimcho;* and his chief works *Kol Rinah U'T'fillah* (for one and two voices, 1871); *Todah W'simrah* (for four voices and soli, optional organ accompaniment, 2 vols., 1876–82); and *18 Liturgische Psalmen* (for solo, choir, and organ; n.d.) Lewandowski also served as singing teacher at the Jewish Free School and the Jewish Teachers Seminary in Berlin. He rose slowly to a prominence which made him, in the last 20 years of his life, the greatest influence on Western Ashkenazi synagogal music for almost 50 years after his death. Although his recitatives were based mostly on tradition, the choral parts followed the style of Mendelssohn's oratorios and choruses, both in melodic idiom and harmonic structure. The adaptable musical and instrumental settings of his works allow them to be utilized by small ensembles and even by communities without an organ, yet at the same time suiting the large and prosperous centers which had spacious "temples" and professional synagogue choirs, grand organs, and musically trained *ḥazzanim*. Lewandowski's style was early transferred to the Conservative and moderate Reform congregations in the great urban communities of the United States.

Bibliography: Sendrey, Music, indices; Idelsohn, Music, 269–84; M. Davidsohn, in: *Proceedings of the Fifth Annual Conference-Convention of the Cantors Assembly* (1952), 30–34. [B.B.]

LEWI, MAURICE J. (1857–1957), U.S. physician and educator. Lewi held several positions in his native Albany as physician and educator, including that of professor of medical jurisprudence at the Albany Law School, before becoming secretary of the New York State Board of Medical Examiners in 1892, a position he held until 1913. In that same year, he became first president of the First Institute of Podiatry in New York City. The institute became the Long Island University College of Podiatry in 1948 and the New York College of Podiatry in 1955. Lewi edited: *Text Book of Chiropody* (1914); *Surgery, With Special Reference to Podiatry* (1917); *Practical Podiatry* (1918); and *Foot Orthopaedics* (1927). [Ed.]

LEWIN, AARON BEN NATHAN OF RZESZOW (1879–1941), rabbi, author, and communal worker. When he was 15 years old, his talmudic novellae were published and when he was 19, his sermons, in *Davar be-Itto* (1899). At the age of 24, he was elected rabbi of Sambor. He subsequently refused invitations from several other communities. Accorded the title of *Kaiserlicher Rat* (crown councillor), he was able to render many services to the refugees of World War I who streamed into Vienna. In 1922 he was elected to the Polish Sejm as representative of the "Jewish bloc" and was a member of its cultural commission. An outstanding speaker, he captivated his audience with his brilliant style. He was one of the leaders of *Agudat Israel, and delivered the opening addresses at its conventions in 1929 and 1937. In 1926 he was elected rabbi of Rzeszow, succeeding his father. In 1931 he was again elected to the Polish Sejm, but in 1935, because of government pressure, he failed to obtain reelection. Lewin participated in every sphere of communal activity in Poland. When the Germans invaded Poland in World War II he fled to Lemberg and then to Radzyn. He returned to Lemberg, where he was arrested by the Nazis and murdered. As well as his numerous communal activities, he was a prolific writer. In addition to *Davar be-Itto*, he published *Birkat Aharon*, on tractate *Berakhot* (1903); *Ha-Derash ve-ha-Iyyun* on Genesis (1927); on Exodus (1931), on Leviticus (1937); on Numbers (1939); responsa *Avnei Ḥefeẓ* (1934); and "Speeches in the Sejm" in Polish (1926). The second volume of *Avnei Ḥefeẓ* as well as *Ha-Derash ve-ha-Iyyun* on the end of Numbers and on Deuteronomy were lost in the Holocaust.

Bibliography: I. Lewin, in: *Elleh Ezkerah*, 1 (1956), 40–63; idem, in: L. Jung, *Guardians of Our Heritage* (1958), 583–601; *Kehillat Reisha* (1967), 86.

[Y.AL.]

LEWIN, ADOLF (1843–1910), German rabbi and historian. Lewin, who was born in Pinne, Prussian Posen, studied in Breslau at the Jewish theological seminary and at the university there, obtaining his doctorate for the thesis *Die Makkabaeische Erhebung* (1870). He served as rabbi at Koschmin (from 1872), Coblenz (1878), and Freiburg im Breisgau (from 1885). Among Lewin's works are a prize-winning essay, "*Die Religionsdisputation R. Jechiel von Paris ...*" (in MGWJ, 18, 1869); *Juden in Freiburg im Breisgau* (1890); and *Geschichte der badischen Juden* (1909). He contributed the section on the historical, geographical, and travel literature of the Jews in the rabbinic period to Jakob Winter and August Wuensche's well-known handbook *Die juedische Literatur seit Abschluss des Kanons* (in: 3, 1896, 287–473). In his many articles and book reviews for Jewish papers and periodicals, Lewin dealt with Jewish-Christian relations and anti-Semitism as well as with miscellaneous historical subjects.

Bibliography: M. Brann, *Geschichte des Juedisch-Theologischen Seminars* (1905), 179–80; G. Kisch (ed.), *Breslau Seminary* (1963), 425, incl. bibl.; Koebner, in: *Ost und West*, 10 (1910), 335–7; L. Jung (ed.), *Guardians of Our Heritage* (1958), 581–601.

[S.NE.]

LEWIN, BENJAMIN MANASSEH (1879–1944), rabbinic scholar, educator, and authority on geonic literature. Born in Gorodets, Russia, into a wealthy ḥasidic family and orphaned at an early age, Lewin studied at various yeshivot and for a time served in the Russian army. He came under the influence of A. I. *Kook, who was then rabbi at Bausk, Latvia, and served as a tutor in his house. When Kook left to become rabbi in Jaffa (1905), Lewin continued his studies at the Berlin Rabbinical Seminary and Berne University. In Berne he edited the journal for Jewish studies and Jewish religious thought *Taḥkemoni* (1910–11). In 1912 he went to Ereẓ Israel, where he served as a teacher and later as head of the religious schools network Neẓaḥ Yisra'el. He edited volumes 9–14 of Z. *Jawitz's *Toledot Yisrael* (1932–40) and the sixth volume (biblical period) of I. Halevy's *Dorot ha-Rishonim* (1939). He also founded the short-lived Alummah Society for Jewish Studies, for which he edited the publication *Alummah* (1936). Lewin's major and pioneering work was in the field of geonic studies, in particular his *Oẓar ha-Ge'onim* (13 vols., 1928–62), an arrangement—with notes, references, and indexes—of geonic responsa and commentaries in the order of the Talmud tractates (to *Bava Meẓia*). The material for this monumental work was scattered over many works and responsa collections, some retrieved from the Cairo *Genizah treasures. Lewin also published a critical edition of Sherira Gaon's famous "Epistle on the origins of rabbinic tradition" (1921), and of the early *Ḥillufei Minhagim ...* ("Differences of Custom Between Palestinian and Babylonian Jewries," 1937). He also reconstructed from Genizah material and early rabbinic literature parts of the lost *Sefer Metivot* (1934). Lewin contributed many articles on the geonic period in learned periodicals, and edited the five volumes of *Ginzei Kedem* (1922–34), devoted to geonic studies, the major part of the contributions being his own.

Bibliography: Y. Werfel, in: *Sefer ha-Yovel* (1939), 17–32, includes bibliography; Y. Raphael (Werfel), in: *Sinai*, 35 (1955), 66–73.

[ED.]

LEWIN, GERSHON (1868–1939), physician and publicist in Yiddish and Hebrew. Son of a Lublin *ḥazzan*, Lewin graduated from the faculty of medicine of Warsaw University. In 1891 he joined the group around the writer I. L. *Peretz and, encouraged by the latter, was active in propagating popular Jewish culture among the assimilationists. He contributed to the newspaper *Haynt*, and published articles in *Ha-Ẓefirah* and *Ha-Ẓofeh*. Settling in Warsaw in 1895, he participated in Jewish public life and was a member of the executive committees of Ha-Zamir, the Yidishe Kultur-Gezelshaft, and the Jewish health organization *TOZ (Towarzystwo Ochrony Zdrowia). His published works include recollections of I. L. Peretz (1919); *In Velt Krig* (1923), his memoirs as a medical officer in World War I; *In di Alte Gute Tsaytn* (1925), memories of his youth; his reminiscences of Shalom Aleichem (1926); *Iberlebenishn, Epizodn un Ayndrukn fun Rusish-Yapanishn Krig* (1931), memoirs of a physician; and *Dos Bukh fun Mayn Lebn* (1937).

Bibliography: J. Glatstein, *In Tokh Genumen*, 1 (1947), 213–23; J. Shatzky, *Geshikhte fun Yidn in Varshe*, 3 (1953), 275; LNYL, 5 (1963), 267–8.

[A.CY.]

LEWIN, JOSHUA HESHEL BEN ELIJAH ZE'EV HA-LEVI (1818–1883), Lithuanian talmudist and author. Lewin was born in Vilna and studied under Elijah *Ragoler. In his youth he was friendly with Mordecai Aaron Gunzberg, Samuel Joseph *Fuenn, and Julian Klaczko. In addition to his extensive talmudic learning, he acquired a knowledge of secular subjects. He married a granddaughter of Isaac b. Ḥayyim of Volozhin, in which town he took up residence. His opposition to the teaching methods at the yeshivah of Volozhin brought him into conflict with its heads, Eliezer Isaac and Eliezer's brother-in-law, Naphtali Ẓevi Judah *Berlin. Lewin had hoped to become head of the yeshivah and to make fundamental changes in its curriculum and direction. When his differences with Berlin were brought before the trustees of the yeshivah, however, they decided against Lewin, who thereupon felt compelled to leave Volozhin. Subsequently he lived an unsettled life. For a year he acted as rabbi of Praga (a suburb of Warsaw). After lecturing in various provincial towns on his new approach to the functions of the rabbi, he went to St. Petersburg and called a rabbinical conference where, with the participation of the *Society for the Promotion of Culture Among the Jews, the founding of Jewish elementary schools was discussed. From 1875 to 1876 he was the preacher at a synagogue in Minsk. Lewin was a supporter of the *Ḥovevei Zion movement, favored the establishment of an Orthodox rabbinical seminary, and initiated with the encouragement and participation of some of the most eminent rabbis of his day the publication of a rabbinic journal, *Peletat Soferim*, of which, however, only one number appeared (1863). Articles not published in other pamphlets were published by Y. Raphael (see bibliography). In 1882 he succeeded Israel *Lipkin of Salant as rabbi of the Russian community in Paris, but died in the following year.

Lewin was the author of: (1) glosses to the *Midrash Rabbah*, published with the commentary of Ze'ev Wolf Einhorn to *Genesis Rabbah* (1835); (2) *Mevasseret Ẓiyyon* (1866), prospectus to his book *Ẓiyyon Yehoshu'a;* (3) *Aliyyat Eliyahu* (1856), a biography of *Elijah b. Solomon, the *gaon* of Vilna; (4) *Ẓiyyun Yehoshu'a* (1869), parallel passages in the Jerusalem Talmud which shed light on the Babylonian; (5) *Mareh Yehoshu'a* (1869), glosses to the Jerusalem Talmud: (6) *Tosefot Sheni le Ẓiyyon* (1886), passages from the Babylonian Talmud paralleling and clarifying passages in the Jerusalem Talmud; (7) *Davar be-Itto* (1878), a rabbinical anthology; (8) *Mizpeh Yehoshu'a*, an extract from his commentary on *Avot*, entitled *Ma'yenei Yehoshu'a* was printed in the *Ru'aḥ Ḥayyim* (1859) of *Ḥayyim b. Isaac of Volozhin. His other works remain unpublished. Lewin also published the prayer book *Derekh ha-Ḥayyim* (1845) of Jacob *Lorbeerbaum of Lissa. His planned new edition of the Jerusalem Talmud to include the commentary of Moses b. Simeon *Margolioth *(Penei Moshe)* and his own *Mareh Yehoshu'a* was not realized (see **Ha-Maggid*, 3 (1859) no. 18).

Bibliography: Ḥ. N. Maggid-Steinschneider, *Ir Vilna* (1900), 277–81; Citron, in: *Reshumot*, 1 (1925), 123–35; Y. Raphael, *Rishonim va-Aḥaronim* (1957), 342–6; idem, in: *Aresheth*, 1 (1958), 327–95, *Yahadut Lita*, 1 (1959), 211f.; 3 (1967), 60.

[SH.A.H./ED.]

LEWIN, JUDAH LEIB (1894–1971), Russian rabbi. Born in Yekaterinoslav, where his father, Eliezer Shemuel, was rabbi, Lewin studied at the Slobodka yeshivah. During World War I he became rabbi of the Ukrainian town Grishino (now Krasnoarmeisk, Ukraine), and later, for a short period, rabbi of his native Yekaterinoslav. Because of the high taxes imposed on religious clergy and conflicts with the leaders of the congregation he gave up the rabbinate and, returning to Krasnoarmeisk, engaged in the work of a religious scribe for various Jewish communities, particularly in Georgia. In 1957, when Rabbi Solomon *Schliefer inaugurated the yeshivah in the Moscow Great Synagogue, Lewin was appointed principal. The head of the yeshivah was, according to official regulations, Rabbi Schliefer himself. Several months after Schliefer's death Lewin was appointed his successor, both as rabbi of the Great Synagogue and as head of the yeshivah. He did his best to fulfill his difficult task—to serve as semiofficial spokesman and apologist for the Soviet policy in matters of Judaism and at the same time to be a genuine spiritual leader to his

Judah Leib Lewin, rabbi of Moscow. Courtesy Israel Sun, Tel Aviv.

congregation and refrain from acts and statements blatantly contradicting Jewish interests and the real sentiments of Soviet Jewry (as, e.g., condemning Israel's "aggression against the Arabs"). In spite of his age and poor health, he undertook a journey to the U.S. in 1968 at the invitation of the *American Council for Judaism. In February 1969 the Committee of the Great Synagogue in Moscow invited rabbis from Israel and Western countries to attend the celebration of Lewin's 75th birthday. [M.CH.]

LEWIN, KURT ZADEK (1890–1947), psychologist and author. Lewin, who was born in Mogilno, Germany, was professor of psychology at the University of Berlin until 1932 when he foresaw the rise of the Nazi regime and went

Kurt Lewin, psychologist. Courtesy Simon Herman, Jerusalem.

to the United States. He taught at Stanford, Cornell, and Iowa universities (1935–45) and organized and directed the research center for group dynamics at the Massachusetts Institute of Technology (1945–47). Lewin was considered one of the most original psychologists of his generation. He was a pioneer in group dynamics; he introduced field theory, and his writings on the nature of causation all were innovations. From his earlier collaboration with the Gestalt school he moved to problems affecting group life. In his books *Principles of Topological Psychology* (1936), *The Conceptional Representation and Measurement of Psychological Forces* (1938), he tried to develop a systematic theory of psychology by a mathematical description of behavior in a "life space," using vectors, geometry, and topology to interpret psychological situations. Lewin applied his dynamic theories to Jewish psychosocial needs. Zionism was to him a sociological necessity. He contended that in order to belong, develop normally, and have contact with nature, the Jews must have their own country. He visited Palestine several times. He accepted a chair at the Hebrew University, to organize its department of psychology but the plan did not materialize because of lack of laboratory funds. He then devoted himself to research on the problems of Jewish maladjustment and self-acceptance as a member of a minority group. In 1945 he established the Commission on Community Interrelations of the American Jewish Congress, a research action program to combat anti-Semitism. He also planned to organize an international Jewish institute of action-research. He outlined plans for a United Nations' international organization of group dynamics. Lewin was associated with Jewish educational work all his life. His philosophy was that "an early buildup of a clear and positive feeling of belongingness to the Jewish group is one of the few effective things that Jewish parents can do for the later happiness of their children. In this way parents can minimize the ambiguity and the tension inherent in the situation of the Jewish minority group, and thus counteract various forms of maladjustment resulting therefrom." In addition to his numerous papers and 70 experimental studies published with his students, Lewin's principal works include: *A Dynamic Theory of Personality* (1935); *Field*

Theory in Social Science (1951); and "Bringing up the Jewish Child," in *The Menorah Journal*, 28 (1940), 29–45.

Bibliography: Tolman, in: *Psychological Review*, 55 (1948), 1–4; R. Segalman, *A Test of the Lewinian Hypothesis on Self-Hatred Among the Jews* (1967—thesis, N.Y. University); J. Rothman, *Minority Group Identification and Intergroup Relations: an Examination of Kurt Lewin's Theory of Jewish Group Identity* (1967); Alfred J. Marrow, *The Practical Theorist: The Life and Work of Kurt Lewin* (1969).

[M.M.Br.]

LEWIN, LOUIS (1868–1941), German rabbi and historian. Lewin, who was born in Znin (province of Posen (Poznan), Poland), graduated from the Berlin Rabbinical Seminary. He served as rabbi in several communities of his native province and neighboring Silesia such as Inowroclaw (Hohensalza), Pinne, Kempen, and Kattowitz (1905–25), and as head of a boarding school in Breslau (1925–37). In 1937 he settled in Palestine. Lewin made important contributions to the history of the Jews in Germany and Poland. He published: *Aus der Vergangenheit der juedischen Gemeinde Pinne* (1903); *Geschichte der Juden in Lissa* (1904); and *Die Landessynode der grosspolnischen Judenschaft* (1926). Lewin's numerous studies on local history appeared in learned and regional periodicals. He also contributed articles to the history of Jewish physicians *"Juedische Aerzte in Grosspolen"* (in JJLG, 9, 1911, 367–420). His valuable library, including many manuscripts, passed to Yeshiva University, New York.

Bibliography: J. Heilperin, in: KS, 19 (1943), 114–6, a list of his works; A. Heppner and I. Herzberg, . . . *Juden . . . in den Posener Landen* (1909–29), 478, 520, 687, 1032; G. Kisch, in: HJ, 4 (1942), 177–8; 5 (1943), 85.

[I.Ha.]

LEWIN-EPSTEIN, ELIAHU ZE'EV (1863–1932), Ereẓ Israel leader. Born in Vilkaviskis (Russian Lithuania), the son of a prosperous bookseller, Lewin-Epstein joined Ḥovevei Ẓion after the 1881 Warsaw pogrom and was one of the founders of the Warsaw *Benei Moshe. Together with Z. *Gluskin, he established the Menuḥah ve-Naḥalah society whose aim was to establish an agricultural settlement in Ereẓ Israel financed by the settlers themselves that would serve as a model in its efficiency and leadership. He was sent by the society to deal with the purchase of land and the establishment of the settlement, called *Reḥovot (1890), and during its early years he was its spritual leader and head of the settlement committee. One of the founders of the Carmel Society for the marketing of the wine produced in the Ereẓ Israel settlements he visited the U.S. on its behalf and there served as a director of the *United Hias Service and treasurer of both the Federation of American Zionists and the Provisional Zionist Committee which organized the relief work for the *yishuv* in Palestine in World War I. Lewin-Epstein then settled permanently in Palestine, where he served as a member of the Zionist Commission in 1919. He frequently traveled to the U.S., England and Germany to promote Palestine Jewish interests. His memoirs, *Zikhronotai*, appeared in 1932.

Bibliography: D. Idelovitch (ed.), *Rishon le-Ẓiyyon* (Heb., 1941), 304–8; M. Smilansky, *Reḥovot* (Heb., 1950); Tidhar, 1 (1947), 78; S. S. Wise, *Challenging Years* (1949), index.

[Y.S.]

LEWINSKY, ELHANAN LEIB (1857–1910), Hebrew writer and Zionist leader. Born in Podberezye, Russia, Lewinsky, like many others of his generation, was swept up by the Haskalah movement in his youth and turned to secular studies, including Russian. Roaming from town to town in the Russian Pale, he supported himself by giving private lessons. In 1880 he registered at the University of Kharkov, but after the pogroms of 1881 he traveled to Palestine and came back an ardent Zionist. He became an active propagandist and organizer of Ḥovevei Zion groups, settled in Odessa, and befriended its circle of Hebrew

Elhanan Leib Lewinsky, Hebrew writer and Russian Zionist leader. Courtesy Genazim, Tel Aviv.

writers. In 1889 he joined the *Benei Moshe society founded by *Aḥad Ha-Am. He wrote the Zionist utopia *"Massa le-Ereẓ Yisrael bi-Shenat Tat la-Elef ha-Ḥamishi"* in: *"Pardes"* 1 (1892), 128–72. In 1896 he became representative of the Palestinian "Carmel" wine company in Russia, and on his travels through various Russian communities, he combined Zionist propaganda with his occupation as distributor of wines from Palestine. He was the moving spirit behind much of the Jewish community work in Odessa. He was one of the founders of the Moriah publishing house, served as treasurer and preacher in the Zionist synagogue, Yavneh, and supported various literary enterprises. He was one of the founders of Ivriyyah, a movement for the revival of the Hebrew language, and also published the first Yiddish daily paper in Odessa, *Gut Morgen* (1910). He gained his place in Hebrew literature through his popular feuilletons. His first articles in this style were published in *Ha-Meliẓ* in 1891–92. Subsequently, they appeared in *Ha-Ẓofeh*, *Ha-Ẓefirah* in Hebrew, and in *Gut Morgen* under the pseudonym Darshan Zaken ("Old Preacher") in Yiddish. His most important feuilletons appear in *Ha-Shilo'aḥ*, 1–23 (1897–1910) under the title *Maḥashavot u-Ma'asim* ("Thoughts and Actions") and under the pseudonym Rabbi Karov. The high standard of the journal impelled Lewinsky to improve and polish his feuilletons so that although they deal with passing affairs of his day, they have retained their literary value. They are marked by good-natured humor, perceptive response to current events, and extensive use of material drawn from the Midrash and from Jewish folklore. His works were published posthumously in three volumes (1911–13), edited by Ḥ. N. Bialik, J. Klausner, and J. Ḥ. Rawnitzky. The Lewinsky Teachers Seminary in Tel Aviv (originally situated in Jaffa) is named after him.

Bibliography: J. Klausner, in: *Kitvei E.L.L.*, 1 (1911), V-XXIV; J. Klausner, et al., in: *Ha-Shilo'aḥ*, 23 (1910), 481–589; Lachower, Sifrut, 3 (1932), 39–40, 215; Kressel, Leksikon, 2 (1967), 214–5.

[Y.S.]

LEWINSKY, YOM-TOV (1899–), Hebrew writer. Born in Zambrow, Poland, Lewinsky settled in Ereẓ Israel in 1935, where he taught for ten years, and then joined the Devir publishing house. A founder of Yeda Am (1942), the folklore society, he remained one of its leaders, and, from 1948, editor of its publication, *Yeda Am*. In the 1920s Lewinsky began writing, in Yiddish and Hebrew, on current as well as historical subjects. In Ereẓ Israel he engaged primarily in the study of Jewish folklore over the ages and published articles on this subject in most of the newspapers and periodicals. His books are: *Keiẓad Ḥikku et Haman bi-Tefuẓot Yisrael?* (1947); a memorial book for the communities of *Lomza (1952) and *Zambrow (1963); *Sefer ha-Mo'adim* (1956 and after, completion of vol. 2 and editing of vols. 3–8; a series of books on the Jewish festivals containing a wealth of material from various sources); *Haggadah shel Pesaḥ* (1960, versions of the **Haggadah* from different Jewish communities, with explanations and commentary); and an encyclopedia of Jewish tradition, customs, and folklore (2 vols., 1970).

Bibliography: Kressel, Leksikon, 2 (1967), 215–6; LYNL, 5 (1963), 318–9. [G.K.]

LEWINSTEIN, JOSEPH BEN ABRAHAM ABUSH (b. 1840), Polish rabbi. Born in Lublin, Lewinstein was rabbi in Chorzele from 1860 to 1868, in Zaklikow from 1868 to 1878, and from 1878 in Serock. He engaged in genealogical and biographical studies and published many articles in this field in *Ha-Ẓefirah, Ha-Goren, Ha-Eshkol,* etc., as well as supplements to the works of other authors (Buber's *Anshei Shem;* Feinstein's *Ir Tehillah;* Riedenstein's *Ir Gibborim;* and Nissenbaum's *Le-Korot ha-Yehudim be-Lublin*). He also corresponded with numerous Jewish scholars in Eastern and Western Europe. He was the author of *Dor Dor ve-Doreshav* (Warsaw, 1900), on the anniversaries of the deaths of outstanding Jewish personalities from ancient times to his own. In addition he published two works by his ancestor Abraham Abush b. Ẓevi of Lissa, both of which he entitled *Birkat Avraham* (Warsaw, 1881 and 1884 respectively). The first consists of novellae to *Eruvin, Pesaḥim, Beẓah, Ḥagigah,* and *Mo'ed Katan* and has an appendix by Lewinstein himself; the second is a commentary on Genesis and on *Avot.*

Bibliography: L. Owtschynski, *Naḥalat Avot,* 1 (1894), letter Yud, no. 52; B.-Z. Eisenstadt, *Dor, Rabbanav ve-Soferav,* 1 (1895), 36; L. Lewin, *Geschichte der Juden in Lissa* (1904), 188; S. N. Gottlieb, *Oholei Shem* (1912), 365. [Sh.A.H./Ed.]

LEWIS, SIR AUBREY JULIAN (1900–), psychiatrist. Born in Adelaide, Australia, he first became a physician and then a psychiatrist. He studied in the United States under Adolf *Meyer. He continued his studies in Germany and obtained a research grant at Maudsley psychiatric hospital in London, where he was appointed clinical director in 1936. During World War II, Lewis worked with military patients and served on service psychiatry committees. He was a member of the Medical Research Council's brain injuries committee and prepared a report for the council on neurosis in wartime. In 1943 he was appointed civilian consultant to the Royal Air Force. In 1946 Maudsley hospital was designated a university teaching center and Lewis was appointed professor. He wrote extensively on diverse topics. His contributions on depression and obsessional states were widely recognized. He also wrote on postcontusional states of the brain "Discussion on Differential Diagnosis and Treatment of Post Contusional States" (1942), and on effort syndrome and postoperative conditions. Lewis maintained that psychiatry should be an integral part of medicine, and stressed the potential contribution of the social scientist to psychiatry. He explored many socio-medical and social-psychiatric problems such as aging, occupational adjustment, and public attitudes to mental illness. He contributed to the literature of psychiatric genetics and the history of psychiatry. An example of the latter is "Letter from Britain" (1953). He was knighted in 1959. Among his books were *Inquiries in Psychiatry* (1967), and a collection of essays and lectures *The State of Psychiatry* (1967).

Bibliography: M. Shepherd, in: P. H. Hoch and J. Zubin (eds.), *Comparative Epidemiology of the Mental Disorders* (1961), ix–xiv; A. Grinstein, *Index of Psychoanalytic Writings,* 3 (1958), 1228; 7 (1964), 3637. [Lo.M.]

LEWIS, BERNARD (1916–), British orientalist, and historian of the Islamic Near East. Born in London, he was appointed assistant lecturer at the University of London in 1938. During World War II he served in the army and then was seconded to the foreign office. In 1949 he was promoted to professor of Near and Middle East history in London University's School of Oriental and African Studies. His scholarly work dealt primarily with Arab and Turkish history, but he also translated Hebrew prose and poetry. Among his books are: *The Origins of Ismailism* (1940); *The Arabs in History* (1950); *The Emergence of Modern Turkey* (1961); *Istanbul and the Civilization of the Ottoman Empire* (1963); *The Middle East and the West* (1964); and *The Assassins* (1967). Works edited, compiled or translated by him include: *Handbook of Diplomatic and Political Arabic* (1947); *Land of Enchanters* (1948); *The Kingly Crown* (1947); and *Historians of the Middle East* (with P. M. Holt, 1962). He also served as an editor of *The New Encyclopedia of Islam* and the *Cambridge History of Islam.* [N.I.]

LEWIS, DAVID (1909–), Canadian lawyer and socialist politician. Born in Svisloch, Belorussia, where his father was a member of the *Bund, Lewis was taken to Montreal at the age of 12. He won a Rhodes scholarship to Oxford and became president of the Oxford Union. On his return to Canada, he was one of the founders of the Cooperative Commonwealth Federation (CCF), serving as national secretary. Later he became successively vice-chairman, chairman, and president of the CCF Party and represented its successor, the New Democratic Party (NDP), in Parliament from 1962 to 1963 and from 1965 onward. In 1971 he was elected leader of the NDP. He also achieved prominence as a lawyer and was made a queen's counsel in 1963. Lewis was active in Jewish affairs and was vice-president of the Jewish Labor Committee of Canada. [B.G.K.]

LEWIS, OSCAR (1914–1970), U.S. anthropologist. Born in New York City, Lewis was a research associate at Yale (1942–43), a propaganda analyst for the U.S. Department of Justice (1943), and a social scientist in the Department of Agriculture (1944–45). He also taught at various institutions, and, from 1948, at the University of Illinois. Lewis' chief interests were in the fields of cultural change and applied anthropology. His particular contribution was the application of the anthropological method to the study of the urban family unit, especially among poverty-stricken Mexicans and Puerto Ricans. In this connection he originated the idea of the "culture of poverty," a concept which achieved wide currency in the 1960s, a decade of profound social and racial turmoil when the problem of the urban poor became a primary governmental concern. In his research, Lewis made wide use of tape recordings to take down the case histories and reactions of his subjects. His study of a poor family in Mexico City, published as *The Children of Sanchez* (1961), achieved wide popularity both among sociologists and the general reading public. His other books include: *Five Families: Mexican Case Studies in the Culture of Poverty* (1959); *Pedro Martinez: a Mexican Peasant and his Family* (1964); and *La Vida: a Puerto-Rican Family in the Culture of Poverty, San Juan and New York* (1966). [E.Fi.]

LEWIS, TED (formerly **Gershon Mendeloff;** also known as **Kid Lewis;** 1893–1970), British boxer and world welterweight champion. Born in London's East End, Lewis was 15 when he began to box professionally. In 1913 he won the British featherweight title, the youngest boxer ever to win a British championship. In 1914 he gained the European title. In 1915, by now a welterweight, he won the world open championship in a 12-round fight in Boston, Massachusetts, with Jack Britton. Lewis held the title until 1919, when Britton knocked him out in the ninth round in Canton, Ohio. In all, the pair met 20 times between 1915 and 1921, Lewis winning three fights, losing four, and drawing two. They had 11 no-decision contests.

Between 1920 and 1924 Lewis was at various periods the welterweight and middleweight champion of Britain, the British Empire, and Europe. He retired from the ring in 1929 with a record of 155 victories (65 by knockouts), six draws, 24 defeats, and 65 no decisions. He was voted into the U.S. Boxing Hall of Fame in 1964.

Bibliography: H. Carpenter, *Masters of Boxing* (1964), 163–78; *Encyclopedia of Jews in Sports* (1965), 166–7. [J.H.S.]

LEWISOHN, U.S. family of industrialists and philanthropists. LEONARD LEWISOHN (1847–1902) was born in Hamburg, Germany, the son of Samuel Lewisohn, a prominent merchant. After arriving in New York City in 1865, he and his brothers JULIUS and ADOLPH (1849–1938), who came from Hamburg to New York City in 1867, founded Lewisohn Brothers. Originally active in the ostrich feather and allied import-export activities, the firm soon pioneered in the development of copper mines in the United States and moved into worldwide sales of copper and lead. Leonard's philanthropies included the Hebrew Sheltering Guardian Society and the Jewish Theological Seminary, as well as general leadership in New York Jewish community affairs.

In 1898, Adolph and Leonard, with Henry H. Rogers and William Rockefeller, formed the United Metals Selling Company. Among the other firms with which Adolph was associated were the General Development Co., the American Smelting and Refining Co., Tennessee Copper and Chemical Co., and Adolph Lewisohn and Sons. Adolph rapidly accumulated a fortune in these enterprises and became prominent in civic, communal, and cultural affairs. He was especially interested in child care, crime prevention, and prison reform and served as president of the National Committee on Prisons and Prison Labor. Adolph Lewisohn was also president of the Hebrew Sheltering Guardian Society for over 30 years, was one of the founders of the American ORT in 1924, and made generous contributions to Columbia University, the Federation for the Support of Jewish Philanthropic Societies in New York, Mount Sinai Hospital, and Brooklyn Museum. He was also a noted art and rare book collector. Adolph's best-known gift was the 6,000-seat athletic stadium he gave to City College of New York in 1915. He stipulated in his will that the college allow it to be used for concerts in the summer, and for almost 50 years (to 1966) it was the setting for inexpensive musical events. Leonard's son FREDERICK (1882–1959) entered the family business in 1898 and participated in the formation of American Smelting and Refining Company and Anaconda Copper Company. His interests also included gold and platinum mines in Colombia and the Lewisohn Copper Corporation of Arizona. Lewisohn was a member of the New York Stock Exchange and a director of the New York Central Railroad.

Adolph's son SAM ADOLPH (1884–1951) was born in New York City. After working briefly as a lawyer, he decided in 1910 to devote himself to his family's mining and financial

Adolph Lewisohn, industrialist and philanthropist, with granddaughters. Courtesy Joan L. Simon.

enterprises. He continued his father's interests in child welfare and prison reform and made distinguished contributions in industrial relations; he was a founder and the first president (1923–26) of the American Management Association and worked with the American Association for Labor Legislation, the U.S. Employment Service, and the New York City Industrial Relations Board. He was actively associated with the municipal reform movement and served as an officer of Citizen's Union of New York for many years. His cultural interests were expressed in art collecting and contributions to the Metropolitan Museum and the Museum of Modern Art. He was prominent in Jewish communal affairs, including the Hebrew Sheltering Guardian Society, Jewish Child Care Association, Federation for the Support of Jewish Philanthropic Societies of New York, and the United Jewish Appeal. Lewisohn was the author of *New Leadership in Industry* (1926), *Painters and Personality* (1937), and *Human Leadership in Industry* (1945). Sam Adolph married MARGARET SELIGMAN (1895–1954), the daughter of Isaac Newton *Seligman. Her principal activities were with the Public Education Association of New York, which she led for over 30 years. She was one of the founders of Bennington College in 1932 and also served as a trustee of Vassar College.

Bibliography: JE (on Leonard); DAB, 22 (1958), 383–4 (on Adolph); S. Birmingham, *Our Crowd* (1967); B. E. Supple, in: *Business History Review*, 31 (1957), 143–78; *National Cyclopedia of American Biography*, vol. 11, 263–4 (on Sam Adolph); *National Cyclopedia of American Biography*, vol. 44, 148 (on Margaret Seligman). [Mo.Ro.]

LEWISOHN, LUDWIG (1882–1955), U.S. novelist and essayist. Born into a middle class Berlin family, Lewisohn was taken to Charleston, South Carolina, in 1890. In his autobiography, *Up Stream* (1922), he wrote of his student years at Columbia University, where he had specialized in English literature with a view to taking up college teaching, but was shocked to find anti-Jewish prejudice barring his way. He was professor of German at Ohio State University

(1911–19) and won recognition as a literary scholar with his translation of Hauptmann, Rilke, and Sudermann and critical works such as *The Modern Drama* (1915) and *The Spirit of Modern German Literature* (1916). During World War I Lewisohn's pacifism and pro-German sympathies ended his academic career, which was only resumed 30 years later with his appointment as professor of comparative literature at Brandeis University in 1948. From 1919 to 1926 he was an associate editor of *The Nation*.

Between 1924 and 1940 Lewisohn lived mostly in Paris, where the singer and poet Thelma Spear (1903–1968) kept house for him and maintained a literary salon. Meanwhile, he had become deeply interested in Zionism. He visited Palestine in 1925 and recorded his impressions of its transformation by Jewish colonists in *Israel* (1925). In another volume of autobiography, *Mid-Channel* (1929), and in *The Answer: the Jew and the World* (1939), he told of his discovery of his Jewish heritage and its effect on his outlook. Lewisohn negated the common American assumption that, for Jews, the United States was a home and not merely another exile, insisting that it could never fully replace Zion. The country's non-Jewish majority determined what was American or un-American, and had the power to impose its will and thinking on the Jewish minority. He therefore called upon American Jews to repudiate assimilation and find their way back to their own sources in the land of Israel, where Jews first underwent the group experience which stamped them eternally as a people.

Lewisohn wrote several novels most of which dealt either with marital problems or with Jewish themes. Among the latter are *The Island Within* (1928, 1968[2]), *The Last Days of Shylock* (1931), *Trumpet of Jubilee* (1937), and *In a Summer Season* (1955). His other works include *Don Juan* (1923), *Stephen Escott* (1930), *The Case of Mr. Crump* (1931), *This People* (1933), *Breathe Upon These* (1944), *Among the Nations* (1948), and *Goethe* (1949). He edited *Creative America* (1933), *Rebirth; A Book of Modern Jewish Thought* (1935), *Jewish Short Stories* (1945), and *Theodore Herzl: a Portrait for This Age* (1955). Between 1943 and 1948, Lewisohn was editor of *The New Palestine*, and from 1947, of the *American Zionist Review*. His last works include *The American Jew: Character and Destiny* (1950) and *What is the Jewish Heritage?* (1954). His son JAMES LEWISOHN (1929–) was poet in residence at the University of Maine.

Ludwig Lewisohn, U.S. writer. Courtesy S. Liptzin, Jerusalem.

Bibliography: F. A. Levy, in: JBA, 14 (1956/57), 46–55; S. Liptzin, *Generation of Decision* (1958), 224–33; Chyet, in: AJA, 11 (1959), 125–47; idem, in: AJHSQ, 54 (1964–65), 296–322. [S.L.]

LEWITE, LEON (1878–1944), Polish Zionist. Born in Warsaw, Lewite joined the Zionist Movement as a youth. After the revolution of the Young Turks (1908), Lewite made it possible, through a donation of a considerable sum (5,000 rubles), to establish a Zionist political and information center in Constantinople with the participation of Victor *Jacobson, Vladimir *Jabotinsky, and Richard *Lichtheim. With the outbreak of World War I (1914), he moved to Moscow, where he joined the leadership of the Zionist Movement and of the Jewish community. After the establishment of independent Poland (1918), Lewite returned to Warsaw and served in the front line of Jewish and Zionist affairs. He was a representative of Polish Jewry on the Comité des Délégations Juives which represented Jewish interests at the Paris Peace Conference, and took part in the first Zionist conference held after the war in London (1920). Lewite concerned himself basically with practical affairs, especially with the organization of *aliyah* from Poland to Palestine. In 1925 he established a Polish-Palestinian chamber of commerce and remained its president until 1939. His outlook—encouragement of private middle-class initiative and lack of sympathy for the collective and cooperative labor economy in Palestine—placed him among the right-wing *General Zionists. He steered the policy of the Zionist movement in Poland in this direction for many years until the "radical" faction, under the leadership of Yiẓḥak *Gruenbaum, prevailed and caused him to resign from the presidency of the organization. The General Zionists in Poland then split, in effect, into two factions: one termed itself Et Livnot ("This is the Time to Build") and remained under the direction of Lewite; the other, Al ha-Mishmar, was led by Gruenbaum. Lewite did not devote much attention to Jewish policy on the Polish scene; he devoted himself mainly to encouraging *aliyah* to Palestine, especially during the years of the middle-class Fourth Aliyah in the 1920s. With the outbreak of World War II (1939) Lewite succeeded in reaching Palestine, where he was completely restricted from public activity by a severe illness.

Bibliography: I. Gruenbaum, *Penei ha-Dor*, 1 (1957), 193–9.
[A.TAR.]

LEWKO (or **Lewek**), **JORDANIS** (d. 1395), the wealthiest Jew of Cracow (and Poland) in his time; he acted as court banker of the kings of Poland. The son of a wealthy merchant and owner of real estate who lived in Cracow from about 1324, Lewko is mentioned in documents of the early 1360s as the owner of houses and building plots in the city. He apparently amassed great wealth in dealing with these properties and began to lend money to the townsmen and the feudal lords (among others to the princes of Masovia).

King Casimir III the Great, who put much confidence in him, entrusted him with the administration of the royal salt mines of Bochnia and Wieliczka and the mint of Cracow in 1368. In appreciation of his services, the king presented him with two houses in the Jewish quarter of Cracow. Lewko, who also acted as tax collector for Archbishop Bodzanta, who was in charge of the royal estate in Cracow, aroused the anger of the townsmen (1369), but their complaints were rejected by the king. From 1374 Lewko was assisted in the administration of his local affairs by the Jewish agent Gosma. At the same time he entered into partnership with Jewish bankers and merchants in Cracow in order to carry out large loans and commercial dealings. During the early 1380s he opened commercial relations with the Jewish banker of Breslau, David Falken, and his son Israel (or Azriel). The greatest sums of money which Lewko lent were his loans to King Louis I of Hungary and Poland (Louis of Anjou). His financial power and influence at court led the nobleman Clemens of Kuzow to address a complaint against him to Pope Boniface IX (1392). Lewko's heirs were his widow Swenka, his sons Abraham, Canaan, Jordan, and

Israel, and his daughter Golda. For about 15 years the heirs worked together in order to collect the debts owed. After that, each managed his business affairs independently. Of Lewko's grandsons Jordan ranked among the leaders of the community of Cracow in 1465.

Bibliography: I. Schiper, *Studya nad stosunkami gospodarczymi Żydów w Posce podczas średniowiecza* (1911), 115–26; M. Bałaban, *Historja, Żydow w Krakowie i na Kazimierzu*, 1 (1931), 17–23; S. Kutrzeba, in: *Przewodnik naukowo-literacki* (1901), 1155. [A.Cy.]

LEWKOWITZ, ALBERT (1883–1954), philosophical and pedagogical writer and scholar. Lewkowitz, who was born in Georgenberg (Miasteczko), Silesia, studied at Breslau University and Jewish Theological Seminary, becoming lecturer at the latter in the philosophy of religion and pedagogics in 1914. During World War I, he served as a chaplain in the German army. Taking refuge in Holland from Nazi Germany, he lectured from 1939 at the Ashkenazi Rabbinical Seminary in Amsterdam, but was interned in 1943 at the *Westerbork concentration camp and from there was transferred to *Bergen-Belsen. Surviving the ordeal, he settled in Haifa, where he served as rabbi to the Aḥavat Zion congregation (he was an adherent of moderate Reform), as lecturer at the Even Pinnah Teachers' Seminary, and taught at the Reali school.

Lewkowitz' scholarly activities date from the publication (1910) of his thesis dealing with *Hegels Aesthetik im Verhaeltniss zu Schiller*. This was followed by studies on neo-Kantianism (in *Zeitschrift fuer Philosophie und philosophische Kritik*, vol. 144, no 1, 1911) and on the classical theory of law and state (*Die klassische Rechts- und Staatsphilosophie*, 1914), and other works. He soon turned to the study of the philosophy of religion and of Judaism in particular, devoting special studies to the relationship to Judaism of such philosophers as *Spinoza, *Mendelssohn, and *Kant. Lewkowitz' major work was *Das Judentum und die geistigen Stroemungen des 19. Jahrhunderts* (1935), which was preceded by two similarly titled articles which appeared in the 1928 *Jahresbericht* ("Annual Report") of the Breslau seminary and in the seminary's 75th anniversary volume (1929). In this work, Lewkowitz compares Jewish and general philosophies and points out their similarities and divergencies. He also wrote *Hauptrichtungen der Paedagogik* (1933).

Bibliography: G. Kisch (ed.), *Breslau Seminary* (1963), 130, 281, 398f. (bibliography). [Ed.]

LEWY, ISRAEL (1841–1917), rabbi and scholar. Born in Inowroclaw (Hohensalza), Poland, Lewy studied at the Breslau Jewish Theological Seminary. At the opening of the

Israel Lewy, talmudic scholar. Jerusalem, J.N.U.L., Schwadron Collection.

*Hochschule fuer die Wissenschaft des Judentums in Berlin in 1872, he became its lecturer in Talmud. In 1883 he returned to the Breslau Seminary in the same capacity and as *Seminarrabbiner*. Apart from his erudition in all branches of Jewish and general scholarship, Lewy brought a keen analytical sense and conjectural brilliance to the field of talmudical studies. He combined this freedom of enquiry with deep piety and strict observance. Lewy's scholarly output is relatively small in quantity, but terse in style and free of polemics. It mainly appeared in the annual reports of the Hochschule and the Breslau seminary. His important works include: *Ueber einige Fragmente aus der Mischna des Abba Saul* (1876), a study in the sources of the Mishnah which has been called a classic example of modern talmudic research; *Mechilta des R. Simon* (1889), a study preparing the way for D.*Hoffmann and J. N. *Epstein in this field; and the first six chapters of *Bava Kamma* in the Jerusalem Talmud, with commentary and introduction (1895–1914). A *Festschrift* in Lewy's honor was published in 1911 (ed. by M. Brann and I. Elbogen).

Bibliography: M. Brann, *Geschichte des juedisch-theologischen Seminars* (1904), 110, 131 (bibliography); *Jahresbericht des ... Seminars Breslau* (1917), 1ff.; I. Elbogen, in: AZDJ, 8 (1917), 460ff. (bibliography); E. E. Urbach, in: G. Kisch (ed.), *Das Breslauer Seminar* (1963), 177–82 (Heb.). [Y.Ro.]

LEWY, JULIUS (1895–1963), philologist and Assyriologist. Born in Berlin, he taught at the University of Giessen from 1922 (professor, 1930). From 1929 to 1936, he was curator of the Hilprecht collection of cuneiform tablets at

Julius Lewy, philologist and Assyriologist. Courtesy American Jewish Archives, Cincinnati, Ohio. Photo Jack Warner Studio, Cincinnati.

the University of Jena. Dismissed from his post by the Nazis, he left Germany in 1933 and in 1934 settled in the United States, where he was professor at Hebrew Union College, Cincinnati, from 1936.

His principal works are: *Untersuchungen zur akkadischen Grammatik* (1921); *Studien zu den alt-assyrischen Texten aus Kappadokien* (1922); *Die Kültepetexte aus der Sammlung Frida Hahn* (1930); and in collaboration with G. Eissler, *Altassyrische Rechtsurkunden von Kültepe* (2 vols., 1930–35). Lewy also published many articles dealing with philological questions, Akkadian grammar, the study of Assyrian-Babylonian religion, and problems concerning the study of Assyrian documents of Cappadocia which were discovered in Kültepe (the ancient Kanish). Lewy's works are of special importance for the study of old Assyrian texts. In this branch of Assyriology, Lewy was one of the most important modern researchers. In several of his works, he discusses problems arising out of the study of the ancient history of the Jewish people and biblical questions; for example *Chronologie der Koenige von Israel und Juda* (1927) and the problems of the Habiru and the Hebrews, on which he wrote in the periodical *Hebrew Union College Annual* (1939, 1940, and 1957). [H.Ta.]

LEWY, YOḤANAN (Hans; 1904–1945), classical scholar. Lewy studied at the university of his native Berlin. After doing research in Russia, Armenia, and Palestine, he settled in Palestine in 1933, becoming lecturer in classical languages at the Hebrew University. He made his chief scholarly contribution in the field of Jewish Hellenism (e.g., his articles in *Encyclopaedia Judaica* and *Eshkol Enziklopedyah Yisre'elit*), with particular emphasis on Philonic studies (*Neue Philontexte in der Ueberarbeitung des Ambrosius* (1932); *Von den Machterweisen Gottes* (1935); *The Pseudo-Philonic De Jona* (vol. 1 only, 1936); *Philosophical writings; Philo, Selections* (1946), repr. in *Three Jewish Philosophers* (1960). He edited volume 6 of I. Heinemann-M. Adler's *Die Werke Philos von Alexandria* (1938). A collection of his articles on Judaism in the Greco-Roman world appeared in 1960 under the title of *Olamot Nifgashim* ("Worlds Meet"). His untimely death cut short a brilliant scholastic career (see collected eulogies published by the Hebrew University in 1946 with a partial bibliography). A memorial volume, *Sefer Yoḥanan Lewy. Meḥkarim be-Helenismus Yehudi*, edited by M. Schwabe and J. Gutman, appeared in 1949 (with bibliography by M. M. Plessner).

Yoḥanan Lewy, classical scholar. Courtesy Hebrew University, Jerusalem.

Bibliography: Kressel, Leksikon, 2 (1967), 183, incl. bibl. [ED.]

LEWYSOHN, ABRAHAM (1805–1860), Polish rabbi and scholar. Lewysohn, a native of Schwerzenz (Swarzec), Poznania, served as rabbi in Peiskretscham (Pyskowice), Silesia. He belonged to the pioneering generation of modern Jewish scholars, and his *Mekorei Minhagim* (1846), a study of the origin of religious customs in rabbinic literature, was a considerable contribution to scholarship. A shortened version with the same title was plagiarized by J. Finkelstein in 1874. He wrote numerous biographies of *tannaim* and *amoraim*, in both Hebrew and German, and also talmudic novellae, grammatical studies, poetry, and Hebrew and German sermons. [ED.]

LEWYSOHN, YEHUDI LEIB LOUIS (1819–1901), rabbi and scholar. Lewysohn, who was born in Schwerzenz, (Swarzec), Poznania, taught at Frankfort on the Oder (1848–51) and served as rabbi and preacher in Worms (1851–59) and rabbi in Stockholm (1859–83). He was a regular contributor to the Hebrew press, particularly *Ha-Maggid*, and also wrote on Jewish subjects in German, English, French, and Swedish. Lewysohn's most important book, *Zoologie des Talmuds* (1858), was the first scientific attempt by a Jewish scholar to collate all talmudic and midrashic references to animal life. He published many addenda to this work, some in Hebrew periodicals and anthologies including: *Gan Peraḥim*, 3 (1891); *Ner ha-Ma'aravi*, 1 pts. 1 and 3 (1895); *Kadimah*, 1 (1899); *Oẓar ha-Ḥokhmah ve-ha-Madda*, 2 (1854); *Ha-Mizpeh; Oẓar ha-Sifrut* (1887–1902), and G. A. Kohut (ed.), *Semitic Studies in Memory of Rev. Dr. Alexander Kohut* (1897). Lewysohn also published a book of epitaphs from the Jewish cemetery of Worms, *Nafshot Ẓaddikim* (Ger., 1855); sermon collections in German and Swedish; and textbooks.

Bibliography: M. Reines, *Dor va-Ḥakhamav* (1890), 123–32; K. Wilhelm, in: HJ, 15 (1953), 49–58. [G.K.]

LEZAJSK (Pol. **Leżajsk;** Yid. **Lyzhansk**), town in Rzeszow province, S. E. Poland. The Jews of Lezajsk are first mentioned in 1538. In the middle of the 17th century the community possessed a wooden synagogue and a cemetery. During the 17th and 18th centuries the Jews of Lezajsk engaged in the grain trade, the weaving of woolen cloth, and the brewing of beer, and were contractors of estates and inns. According to the census of 1765, 909 Jewish poll tax payers lived in Lezajsk and its environs. When the *zaddik* R. *Elimelech settled in Lezajsk in 1775, it became an important center of *Ḥasidism in Poland and Galicia. Each year (until the Holocaust) on the anniversary of his death (21st of Adar), thousands of Jews used to journey to pray at his grave in Lezajsk. Fires in 1834 and again in 1873 severely affected the economic situation of the community, but toward the end of the century conditions began to improve. The Jewish population fluctuated between 1,868 (38% of the total) in 1880, 1,494 (28%) in 1900, 1,705 (32%) in 1910, and 1,575 (31%) in 1921. In the interwar years Zionist parties and youth movements were active in the town. There were Tarbut, Yavneh, and Beth Jacob schools in the town. [A.CY.]

Holocaust Period. The number of Jews in Lezajsk in 1939 rose to more than 3,000. With the outbreak of the war in September, the Poles began to loot stores and attack the Jews. Jewish self-defense was organized. The Germans entered Lezajsk on the eve of Rosh Ha-Shanah (September 1939), set synagogues afire, and burned sacred books in the town square. On the eve of Sukkot the Jews were deported by the Germans to the area under Soviet control on the other side of the San River. Part of the community went into hiding and was later allowed to remain in the city. They were concentrated in the ghetto, and in 1942 many of them were transported to work or death camps. Those who were deported to the Soviet zone lived there in very difficult economic conditions. In the summer of 1940 many of them were deported to the Soviet interior. A few hundred Jews, mostly from those who were in the U.S.S.R., survived. The old Jewish cemetery was destroyed by the Nazis and in its place a park was later made. Only the grave of the *zaddik* Elimelech remained. The main synagogue housed the town museum. [AR.W.]

Bibliography: D. Rabin (ed.), *Lizhansk, Sefer Zikkaron;* Halpern, Pinkas, index; M. Schorr, *Żydzi w przemyślu do końca XVIII wieku* (1903), index; B. Wasiutyński, *Ludność żydowska w Polsce* . . . (1930), 116.

LIABILITY (Torts). Every person of full mental capacity, male or female (BK 15a) when causing injury to another person, is liable to the injured party for any damage which his negligent conduct causes the latter to suffer (see *Torts), even a husband to his wife (BK 32a). A person who lacks mental capacity—such as a deaf-mute, idiot, or minor—is exempt from liability for damage caused by the act of his person because he is incapable of foreseeing damage, whereas the injured party is required to take care, for most people know that one must be on guard against a person lacking in understanding as he tends to cause damage. For this reason too the latter's guardian or parents are not liable on his behalf (BK 87a).

A principal who commissions an agent to commit a tort is exempt from liability, but the agent is liable, for the latter, having discretion, should foresee resulting damage, whereas the principal cannot be required to know that the agent will carry out his evil mandate (Tos. to BK 56a; 79a). Where, however, the agent cannot foresee that the damage will result from the carrying out of his mandate—as in the case of an agent lacking mental capacity, or an animal incited by the principal, or in a case where the agent could not have known that he was doing wrong because, for example, the principal told him to fetch a chattel for him telling him that it was his—the agent is no more than a tool in the principal's hand, and the latter is liable for the damage caused by the agent (loc. cit.; BK 9b). Where the principal himself could not have foreseen that the agent would cause injury in carrying out the mandate, he too is exempt from liability, as in the case where he puts a glowing coal in the hands of a minor, who burns another's article (BK 59b).

If a slave, having full mental capacity, causes injury, the sages exempt his owner from liability—although he knows that slaves are in the habit of causing injury yet retains him despite the fact that he is unable to guard the slave—on the ground that no person can afford payment of such heavy damages as the slave is likely to cause (BK 4a). On the other hand the tortfeasant slave is personally liable, for—having understanding—he is liable for his negligence. As long as he is a slave and has no independent means he is treated in the same way as a poor man who does not have the wherewithal to pay for damage he has caused; but once he is manumitted and acquires his own means, he is obliged to pay for the damage. Such, too, is the law in the case of a married woman, who generally does not have the means to pay for damage she has caused, but is obliged to pay for the damage when she is able to do so, as for instance after being divorced (BK 87a).

His own negligence notwithstanding, the injuring party is exempt from liability for damage resulting from conduct which is licensed, whether consented to and authorized by the injured party or by the court. The injuring party is also exempt from liability if the damage caused is not of a physical nature, such as economic damage.

The law of the State of Israel (Civil Wrongs Ordinance, 1947) renders a person over the age of 12 years liable in tort. The law imposes vicarious liability on a person for the acts of his servants and for acts done by others authorized by him. [SH.A.]

LIACHO, LÁZARO (1898–), Argentine poet and essayist. Born in Buenos Aires, Liacho was the son of JACOBO SIMON LIACHOVITZKY (1874–1937), a noted Yiddish journalist, who emigrated from Lithuania to Argentina in 1894, founded the first Argentine Yiddish daily, *Der Tog*, and the weekly *Der Tsionist*, and in 1904 helped to establish the Argentine Zionist Federation. Liachovitzky wrote a successful play, *Judíos en la Patagonia*, and short stories. Lázaro Liacho was associated with the periodicals *Mundo Israelita* and *Judaica*, but won recognition mainly as poet. His *Bocado de pan* (1931), *Pan de Buenos Aires* (1940), and *El hombre y sus moradas* (1961), reflect his outlook both as a Jew and as an interpreter of Latin American culture. In his later poems, notably *Entre Dios y Satán* (1966), a collection of 101 sonnets, Liacho turned to biblical, religious, and metaphysical themes. His other works include *Palabra del hombre* (1934) and *Dinámica porteña* (1936). He edited *Anecdotario judío* (1939). [P.LI.]

LIBEDINSKI, YURI NIKOLAYEVICH (1898–1959), Soviet Russian novelist. Libedinski was born in Odessa, but his father's medical practice took him to a factory in the Urals, and most of Libedinski's works are set in the distant provinces. *Nedelya* (1923; *A Week*, 1923) firmly established Libedinski as one of the founders of Soviet proletarian prose, and he has enjoyed wide popularity ever since. Though somewhat marred by inept imitation of the literary mannerisms of the Symbolists, this short novel is still considered one of the most effective and honest descriptions of the early days of the Soviet regime, under which Libedinski served as a Bolshevik political commissar. While the author's unconditional support of the Communist cause is emphatically stated, he does concede the fact that most of the population, and particularly the peasantry, was implacably hostile to Soviet rule. *A Week* ends with a description of an uprising in which most of the communists are killed. Suspicion with regard to the allegiance of Russia's peasantry was a basic tenet of Trotskyism, and Libedinski's next novel *Zavtra* ("Tomorrow," 1924), showed even closer ties to the teachings of *Trotsky: the disillusionment within the ranks of the Communist Party was curable only if a revolution were to take place in Germany. *Komissary* ("The Commissars," 1925, 1935[14]) is of interest as a social document; it gives an insider's view of the milieu of communist functionaries. The hero, Mindlov, is a Jew and a former Menshevik. *Rozhdeniye geroya* ("The Birth of a Hero," 1930) attempts to tackle an ambitious theme: the dehumanization of human relationships under the impact of demands made by a society which puts a premium on industrial and bureaucratic efficiency and on political orthodoxy. Though not very successful, the novel was one of the few works of Soviet prose that tried to probe some of the basic dilemmas of the human condition. Of Libedinski's later works—other than some effective wartime reporting — the most noteworthy is a trilogy set in the Caucasus immediately before and during the Revolution: *Gory i lyudi* ("Mountains and People," 1947); *Zarevo* ("Dawn," 1952); and *Utro Sovetov* ("The Morning of Soviet Power," 1957). It is commonly agreed that Libedinski narrowly escaped imprisonment or death on at least two occasions: first, as a Trotskyite in 1938, when he was actually expelled from the Party, though reinstated shortly afterward; and again in the late 1940s, as a "Jewish cosmopolitan." Little information about either period can be found in his book of reminiscences entitled *Sovremenniki* ("Contemporaries," 1958). *Ob uvazhenii k literature* ("On Respect for Literature," 1965) includes further reminiscences and articles by him. [M.F.]

LIBER, MARC (pseudonym of **Michael Goldman;** 1880–1937), leader of the *Bund, born in Vilna. Liber's father, Isaac, a Hebrew poet and a Ḥovev Zion, did not provide his children with a Jewish education. All became active in the revolutionary movement. The eldest son, Boris (Gorev), was active in the Russian Social Democratic Labor Party, and Leon (Akim) was a founder of the Bund and later one of its opponents and an active Menshevik; of the sisters, Olga joined the Social Democrats and Julia became a Bundist. At secondary school Liber made contact with Lithuanian Social Democratic circles and became friendly with Feliks Dzerzhinski, the future head of the "Cheka." From 1900 he was active in the Bund, appearing as an extremist representative of its national wing in the fourth congress of the Bund (1901), and its chief spokesman at the second congress of the Russian Social Democratic Labor Party (1903). He was later attacked by Lenin. An excellent speaker, Liber became one of the most popular leaders of the Bund. He was among the less doctrinaire members of the Bund who supported its return to the Social Democratic Labor Party (1906), and was elected to its central committee. In the revolution of 1905 he represented the Bund in the Workers' Soviet in St. Petersburg. In 1906 he went on behalf of the Bund to the United States.

Belonging to the wing of the party which regarded legal activities within the framework of the law as its most important task during the period of reaction in Russia, he took part in legal and open activities in Vilna. In 1910 he was imprisoned for political activities and escaped abroad, returning in 1914 to St. Petersburg. He was among those in favor of defending Russia during the war ("Oborontsy"). In 1915 he was again arrested and not freed until after the February Revolution of 1917. During the period of the Kerensky government Liber became prominent as leader of the rightist Mensheviks and the Bund, which he represented at the executive of the Petrograd Soviet. Even after the October 1917 Revolution he actively opposed the Bolsheviks. He was imprisoned in 1923 and spent the rest of his life in exile. Seriously ill and crippled, he was executed during the purges of November 1937.

Bibliography: J. S. Hertz (ed.), *Doyres Bundistn,* 1 (1956), 196–225; idem et al. (eds.), *Geshikhte fun Bund,* 3 (1966), index; I. Getzler, *Martov; a Political Biography of a Russian Social Democrat* (1967), index. [M.M.]

LIBER, MAURICE (1884–1956), chief rabbi of France and scholar. Born in Warsaw, Liber went to Paris with his parents at the age of four. He graduated from the Ecole Rabbinique de Paris in 1907 and began lecturing on Jewish history there. In 1911 he was appointed assistant to the chief rabbi of Paris, serving as an army chaplain and receiving the Croix de Guerre during World War I. In 1920 Liber became rabbi at the Rue de la Victoire synagogue, in 1921 lecturer in the history of rabbinic Judaism at the Ecole Pratique des Hautes Etudes, and in 1927 succeeded his teacher Israël Lévi as professor. He was appointed director of religious education by the Paris Consistoire in 1930 and, two years later, head of the Ecole Rabbinique. In 1934 Liber was appointed chief rabbi of France *par interim,* to assist the aging Israël Lévi in his task. Under the German occupation of France during World War II, he strove hard to safeguard the Ecole Rabbinique—which had been evacuated to unoccupied southern France—and the religious character of the Consistoire. He also strove to maintain some sort of Jewish education, both legal and underground.

Liber's chief field of research was French-Jewish history. He is best known by his biography of Rashi (1905; Eng. tr. 1906). He wrote a series of articles, based on archival sources, under the title "Les Juifs et la convocation des Etats Généraux" (in REJ, vols. 63–66, 1912–13), and another series, "Napoléon et les Juifs" (*ibid.,* vols. 71–72, 1920–21). On liturgy he wrote, among other works, *La Récitation du Schema . . .* (1909); "La Formation de la liturgie Synagogale" (in *Annuaire de l'Ecole des Hautes Etudes,* 1933/34); and "Structure and History of the Tefilah" (in JQR, 40 (1949/50), 331–57). Liber also wrote an extensive introduction to the reprint of M. Schwab's French translation of the Palestinian Talmud (1932).

Absorbed into the French cultural climate, Liber opposed Zionism, calling it a national theory unacceptable to those who believe that emancipation resolved the national question for the Jews. Though deeply religious, he felt compelled to compromise with the facts of French synagogue life, such as the use of an organ.

Bibliography: R. Sommer, in: REJ, 118 (1959/60), 95–119; 125 (1966), 9–20; Z. Szajkowski, *Analytical Franco-Jewish Gazetteer, 1939–1945* (1966), 44, 55, 57; G. Vajda, in: *Annuaire de l'Ecole Pratique des Hautes Etudes, Section des Sciences Religieuses* (1957/58), 26; REJ, 15 (1956), 5–7. [G.We./Ed.]

LIBEREC (Ger. **Reichenberg**), city in N. Bohemia, Czechoslovakia. There were 60 Jews in Liberec in 1582. There was no community in the city during the 18th and first half of the 19th centuries. Although there were 57 Jews in Liberec in 1811, no community was permitted and their residence there was illegal (see *Familiants Law). The Jewish wool dealers, among them Simon von *Laemel, were among the developers of the textile industry. The Jews were permitted to remain in the town only during the week—the church authorities published an ordinance on the subject in 1776. In 1799 and 1810 the Jews were officially evicted from private houses and were allotted special inns, but after 1848 Jews settled in the town. Later, a congregation was founded (1863), a synagogue was dedicated (1889), and an Orthodox prayer room, Achdus Yissroel, was established. In 1912 there were 1,240 Jews in the town (3.4% of the total population) and in 1930 there were 1,392 (3.6%). At the time of the Sudeten crisis (1938) the Jews left Liberec; some 30 remained behind and were arrested. The synagogue was demolished on Nov. 10, 1938. A community was refounded in 1945, with most of the members coming from *Subcarpathian Ruthenia. By 1948 it numbered 1,105, and in 1954 a memorial tablet for Holocaust victims was erected.

Bibliography: Hofmann, in: H. Gold (ed.), *Die Juden und Judengemeinden Boehmens in Vergangenheit und Gegenwart* (1934), 529–69; Klein, *ibid.,* 7; Lamed, in: BLBI, 8 (1965), 302–14; R. Iltis, *Die aussaeen unter Traenen . . .* (1959), 36–39. [J.Her.]

LIBERMAN, YEVSEY GRIGORYEVICH (1897–), Soviet economist. Liberman studied at the Kharkov Engineering Economics Institute and began his teaching and research career in 1933. From 1947 to 1963 he held the chair of economics and organization of machine-building industry at the Institute. In 1963 he was appointed professor of statistics and accounting at Kharkov University. Liberman received worldwide notice for his pronouncements in a debate which started in 1962 on the need for economic reforms in the U.S.S.R.

Liberman's ideas represented a school of thought among Soviet economists who demanded more rationality in the planning process, new criteria of success, and more freedom of decision-making or autonomy for management. Thus, Liberman represented a reaction against the overcentralization of economic administration in the U.S.S.R., against the insufficiency of material incentives for management and workers, and against many arbitrary criteria of success of individual enterprises. According to Liberman the old system inflicted heavy costs upon the state by obstructing useful innovations and insufficiently stimulating progress, and upon the welfare of the workers and consumers. Liberman assumed that administrative reforms would introduce greater flexibility in the system, and self-interest on the part of management and workers would improve both the quantity and quality of production. Liberman argued that the reforms would not limit the basic political decisions but rather improve the efficiency of the basic economic plans. The goal of every enterprise and the criteria of its success should be the maximization of profits from which the incentive payments for workers and management should be drawn. Thus profits would become, under the Soviet conditions, primarily an index which measures the efficiency of the performance of the enterprise, reflecting the increase of the quantity and quality of production, the growth of labor productivity and utilization of resources, and simultaneously a measure of the reward of society for successful performance.

Encouraged by the promises of liberalization in economic administration made by Kosygin but also frustrated that most of his proposals were not introduced in practice, Liberman continued to advocate direct links between the industrial enterprises and the trade organizations, so as to make the industrial production more responsive to the needs and wishes of the consumers. He continued to demand a decrease of centralization by suggesting the reduction of the number of products centrally planned and spoke up against imposing an a priori wage fund upon the enterprises.

Yevsey Grigoryevich Liberman, Soviet economist, depicted on a cover of *Time* Magazine. Courtesy Time Inc., 1965.

Bibliography: M. Dobb, *Soviet Economic Development Since 1917* (1966[6]), 379–81; *Prominent Personalities in the U.S.S.R.* (1968), s.v. [Ar.K.]

LIBIN, Z. (pseudonym of **Israel Zalman Hurwitz;** 1872–1955), Yiddish novelist. Libin emigrated from Russia to London in 1891, and soon after to New York, where he spent three years working in sweatshops. He was a pioneer of Yiddish literature in the U.S. In over half a century of creative work, he wrote and published hundreds of realistic, compassionate stories and sketches about early immigrant life, and about the struggles and the sufferings of sweatshop workers.

His first story was published in 1892; afterward he contributed to newspapers, periodicals and, above all, to the Yiddish *Jewish Daily Forward*, writing stories and light articles about daily events. Libin also wrote about 50 plays, which were produced in the U.S. and Europe. His most famous play, *Di Gebrokhene Hertser* ("Broken Hearts"), was produced in 1903 with Jacob and Sarah *Adler in the main parts, and was later played by various companies throughout the Jewish world. It was filmed in 1926 by Maurice *Schwartz, who inaugurated his Yiddish Art Theater in 1918 with Libin's play *Der Man un Zayn Shotn* ("The Man and His Shadow"). Many of Libin's stories and plays remained uncollected. Among his published books are: *Geklibene Skitsn* (1902); *Geklibene Shriftn* (2 vols., 1910); and *Gezamelte Werk* (4 vols., 1915–16). His tragicomedy *Kolegn* was translated into English (*Colleagues*, 1915).

Drawing of Zalman Libin, Yiddish novelist, by Bernard Gussow, 1901. From M. U. Schappes, *The Jews in the United States*, New York, 1958.

Bibliography: Rejzen, Leksikon, 2 (1927), 113–6; LNYL, 5 (1963), 44–49; Z. Zylbercweig, *Leksikon fun Yidishn Teater*, 2 (1934), 1026–38; S. Niger, *Dertseylers un Romanistn* (1946), 204–16; B. Bialostotzky, in: JBA, 11 (1952/53), 169–71. [E.Sch.]

LIBNAH (Heb. לִבְנָה). (1) Station of the Israelites on the route of the Exodus, between Rimmon-Perez and Rissah (Num. 33:20–21). It is perhaps identical with Laban (Deut. 1:1). (2) Canaanite city-state in the Shephelah which Joshua conquered and destroyed after Makkedah and before Lachish (Josh. 10:29ff.; 12:15). It was allotted to the levites (Josh. 21:13; I Chron. 6:42) and was included in the fourth district of Judah which extended over the eastern Shephelah (Josh. 15:42). The city revolted against Joram, king of Judah, at the same time as Edom, but was subdued (II Kings 8:22; II Chron. 21:10). Hamutal, the mother of kings Jehoahaz and Zedekiah, was a native of Libnah (II Kings 23:31; 24:18; Jer. 52:1). It was attacked by Sennacherib after the fall of Lachish (II Kings 19:8; Isa. 37:8). Eusebius identifies it with Lobana, a village of Eleutheropolis (Onom. 120:23ff.). The identification of the ancient city with Tell al-Ṣāfī, the crusader *Blanche-Garde* ("the white tower"; cf. Heb. *lavan*, "white"; see *Gath, now identified with this site), has been superseded in scholarly opinion by that with Tell Birnāt, 2 mi. (3.2 km.) northwest of Bet Guvrin or with nearby Tell-al-Judayda.

Bibliography: Albright, in: BASOR, 15 (1924), 9; Elliger, in: PJB, 30 (1934), 58ff.; Z. Kallai, *Naḥalot Shivtei Yisrael* (1967), 319–20; Abel, Geog, 2 (1938), 369–70; EM, 4 (1962), 421–3. [M.A.-Y.]

LIBOWITZ, SAMUEL NEHEMIAH (1862–1939), writer on Jewish subjects. Born in Kolno, Poland, he emigrated to America in 1881. He traded in precious stones and was so successful that he could afford to print over twenty books in limited editions. He corresponded with eminent Jewish scholars including Israel *Davidson, to whom he wrote 107 letters, which he later published himself in 1933. His works include: *Peni'el* (1914), a collection from Jewish literature on the subject of death; *Ha-Mavet be-Fanim Soḥakot* (1917); *Sefer Sha'ashu'im* (1927); and *Ha-Shome'a Yiẓḥak* (1907), sharp-witted jokes and original interpretations of the rabbis and from the Middle Ages; *Judah Aryeh Modena bi-Demuto ve-Ẓivyono* (1896); *Kitvei ha-Rav Yehudah Aryeh mi-Modena* (1936); and *Doresh Reshumot ha-Aggadah* (1893, 1920[2], 1929[3]), explanations of several *aggadot* of the Talmud. He also edited and published *Oẓar ha-Ḥokhmah ve-ha-Madda* (1897), in collaboration with Jacob Reifmann, Moses Reicherson, Solomon Rabin, and others. In several of his works he violently polemized against such scholars as R. Isaac Hirsch Weiss, Ze'ev Schorr, Radkinson, Saul Tchernichowsky, and Joseph Klausner. He emigrated to Palestine in 1927, but his longing for his children took him back to America.

Bibliography: S. Bernstein, *N. S. Libowitz* (Heb., 1931); D. Persky, in: *Hadoar*, 21 (1940/41), 656–8; Kressel, Leksikon, 2 (1967), 251–2. [H.R.R.]

LIBRARIES. In antiquity, whatever books there were were kept in public *archives, attached to temples or royal palaces. II Maccabees 2:13–14 speaks of a "treasury" of books established by Nehemiah (in the Temple?) which contained "books about the kings and prophets, the books of David (Psalms) and royal letters about sacred gifts." The community living at *Qumran shortly before and after the beginning of the present era had a library (see *Dead Sea Scrolls). The Cairo **Genizah* has revealed the existence of both public and private libraries of the geonic period (for private libraries and book collectors see *Bibliophiles).

Communal Libraries. Communities and their synagogues and *battei midrash* were anxious to build up libraries. In Italian communities almost every *talmud torah* possessed a library. The rules of the Verona *talmud torah* of 1650

Figure 1. Library of the American Jewish Historical Society, Waltham, Mass. Courtesy Harrison and Abramowitz, New York. Photo Alexandre Georges, Pomona, N.Y.

require a special room to be set aside for the library. The present library of the *Rome community, which has a fine collection of manuscripts and early printed books, is the direct successor of a medieval *talmud torah* library. The same is true for a number of other communities such as Ferrara, Reggio Emilia, Pisa, and Leghorn. These libraries were often enriched by the acquisition of private collections. The library of the Talmud Torah School of the Sephardi congregation of *Amsterdam is mentioned by the bibliographer Shabbetai *Bass in his *Siftei Yeshenim* (1680).

Public Libraries. The 19th century saw the development of public libraries. These took on various forms: (1) communal libraries; (2) voluntary libraries; (3) libraries attached to rabbinical seminaries; (4) departments of Hebraica and Judaica in national, university, and municipal libraries.

COMMUNAL LIBRARIES. The first of the modern Jewish communal libraries was established at Mantua at the end of the 18th century, and was followed by others. In Germany many communities established their own libraries, intended mainly for the use of teachers and young people. Berlin, Frankfort, Hamburg (reestablished after World War II), Munich, and Breslau possessed numerous libraries, as did the communities of Vienna, Prague, Warsaw, Vilna, and Zurich. The library at Zurich is still in existence. Synagogue libraries in the United States developed differently from those of European Jewish communities. Most U.S. synagogue and temple libraries are school libraries, designed to work closely with the synagogue religious schools. There are three large congregational libraries which serve the needs of the entire congregation and, by extension, the entire community: the Temple Library in Cleveland, Ohio; the Wilshire Boulevard Temple Library in Los Angeles, California; and the Temple Emanu-El Library in New York City, New York.

ORGANIZATIONAL LIBRARIES. A number of Jewish organizations have developed substantial libraries. Their holdings vary considerably according to the requirements of the particular organization. They include the American Jewish Archives in Cincinnati, Ohio; the American Jewish Committee Blaustein Library in New York City; the American Jewish Historical Society Library in Waltham, Massachusetts; the Biblioteka Żydowskiego Instytutu Historycznego in Warsaw; the Bibliothèque Centrale Juive in Geneva; the Bibliothèque de l'Alliance Israélite Universelle in Paris; the Centre de Documentation Juive Contemporaine in Paris; the Jewish Education Committee in New York City; the Jewish Public Library in Montreal; the Leo Baeck Institute Library in New York City; the Mosaiska Forsamlingens Bibliotek in Stockholm; the Mount Scopus War Memorial College Library in Melbourne (destroyed by fire in 1970); the Wiener Library in London; the YIVO Institute for Jewish Research Library with branches in Buenos Aires and New York; and the Zionist Archives and Library in New York City. Other voluntary bodies interested in cultural work established popular reading and lending libraries, such as Jewish trade unions, Zionist and Socialist societies, women's organizations, and youth movements, etc. Originating with the Haskalah movement, these were frequent in Eastern Europe whence they spread to wherever Jews emigrated in Europe and the Americas. The persecution of Jewish religion and culture as well as of Zionism in Soviet Russia led to the closure of most of these libraries, though some Yiddish ones continued to operate—at least until 1948.

RABBINICAL SEMINARIES. In Italy, too, the first rabbinical seminary library was established, at the Collegio Rabbinico Italiano which was located first in Padua, and moved from there to Rome, Florence, and again back to Rome. The Breslau Jewish Theological Seminary followed: its library attained considerable importance, incorporating among others the Saraval collection. The Berlin Rabbinical Seminary too had a fine library, and so had the Hochschule (Lehranstalt) fuer die Wissenschaft des Judentums, which received A. Geiger's collection. Then followed Jews' College, London, owning the Montefiore, Green, Loewy, Zunz, and Buechler collections; the Ecole Rabbinique de France in Paris; the Sephardi, Ashkenazi, and Eẓ Ḥayyim seminaries in Amsterdam; the Israelitisch-Theologische Lehranstalt in Vienna, and the Budapest rabbinical seminary. The Mocatta Library in London is housed at University College, London, and administered by the college in association with the Jewish Historical Society of England. It was destroyed in a German air raid in 1940, but was reconstructed on a modest scale. In the U.S. the library of the Jewish Theological Seminary has the most important collection of Hebraica and Judaica of both manuscripts and printed books outside Ereẓ Israel. In 1966 a disastrous fire—and the water used to put it out—destroyed a large section of it, which as far as possible was reconstituted. Among the collections it received were those of Sulzberger, Steinschneider, Halberstamm, and E. N. Adler. Other important libraries are attached to Hebrew Union College-Jewish Institute of Religion, Cincinnati and New York (Klau Library and E. Hirsch—G. Levi Library), Dropsie College, Philadelphia, and others. Jewish teachers' seminaries too, particularly in the United States, have developed their own libraries.

Nazi Persecution. The persecution of European Jewry by Nazi Germany (1933–45) brought with it the wholesale confiscation of both public and private libraries. Some of the books were moved to the Institut zur Erforschung der Judenfrage in Frankfort on the Main. Toward the end of World War II, the looted books were brought by the Nazis to central stores in southern Germany and western Czechoslovakia. When recovered after the war, mainly by a body called "Jewish Cultural Reconstruction," they were returned wherever possible to the heirs of their owners; the over 1,000,000 volumes that remained were distributed to Jewish libraries and cultural or educational organizations in Israel, America, and other parts of the Diaspora. However, the incunabula and manuscripts that belonged to these Jewish libraries were not recovered after World War II. It is assumed that these materials were hidden by the Nazis in unused mines. Non-Jewish circles organized the Germanica Judaica library in Cologne in 1958.

JEWISH SECTIONS IN GENERAL LIBRARIES. The importance of the Hebraica and Judaica collections in the great national libraries for the preservation of Jewish literary and scholarly treasures can hardly be exaggerated. In antiquity the famous library of Alexandria contained the Septuagint and other Judeo-Hellenistic works. Medieval monastery libraries frequently contained Hebrew, particularly Bible, codices; records of persecutions, expulsions, book burnings and confiscations filled their shelves, as well as those of episcopal and princely palaces and of medieval universities. The interest in Hebrew studies produced by the age of Reformation and Humanism led many Christian scholars such as Johann *Reuchlin and J. A. Widmanstad (1506–1557) to collect Hebrew manuscripts and books. Here again priority belongs to Italy, where until the 19th century the most important collections were to be found in Rome, in the Vatican Library, the Biblioteca Casanatense, Biblioteca Angelica, Biblioteca della Pia Casa dei Neofiti, Biblioteca Vittorio Emanuele (originally in the Collegio Romano), and the Biblioteca Nazionale (some very valuable Mss.). The Biblioteca Palatina in Parma incorporates the famous Rossi and also the Foa collections. Mention should also be made of the Biblioteca Mediceo-Laurentiana at Florence, the University Library of Bologna, the Royal Library at Modena, the Biblioteca Marciana at Venice, and the Ambrosiana at Milan. The valuable manuscript collection at Turin was destroyed by fire in 1904.

Italy lost its primacy in this field to England when the Bodleian Library acquired the great collections of D. *Oppenheim and H. *Michael and the British Museum, the Almanzi Collection of Hebrew manuscripts. These two libraries have since been systematically completed and expanded. The Cambridge University Library is famous for its Cairo *Genizah* treasures, the largest such collection in the world. Also at Cambridge is the W. H. Low Library of Hebraica in Trinity College. In France the Bibliothèque Nationale in Paris and the Strasbourg University Library have important Hebraica and Judaica collections. In Germany the state libraries in Berlin, Munich, and Hamburg, and the municipal libraries of Frankfort and Leipzig have Hebrew collections, as has the Academy Library of Leyden (rich in Karaitica) and the Amsterdam University Library which includes the Rosenthaliana; the Royal Library in Copenhagen with the Bibliotheca Judaica Simonseniana; the Austrian National Library at Vienna (before 1918 the Kaiserliche und Koenigliche Hofbibliothek); the Hungarian National Library at Budapest (with the Kaufmann Collection); the Asiatic Museum (containing the Friedland and Chwolson collections, by Firkovich and Antonin) and the Saltykov-Shchedrin Library at Leningrad; the Lenin Library, and the Oriental Institute of the Academy of Sciences Library, both at Moscow.

In the U.S., the New York Public Library and the Boston Public Library possess particularly important Jewish departments, as does the Library of Congress in Washington, D.C. U.S. university libraries that have substantial Jewish collections include the following: Brandeis University, Brown University, Columbia University, Cornell University, Harvard University, Indiana University, New York University, Ohio State University, Princeton University, Rutgers University at New Brunswick, University of California at Berkeley, University of California at Los Angeles, University of Chicago, University of Michigan, University of Southern California, University of Texas, University of Wisconsin at Madison, Wayne State University at Detroit, and Yale University.

From 1968 an Association of Jewish Libraries was active in the U.S.—a merger of the Jewish Librarians Association and the Jewish Library Association consisting of two divisions: a synagogue, school, and center library division, and a research and special library division. It issues the *AJL Bulletin* as well as an annual volume of *Proceedings*.

See also *Books; *Bibliophiles; Mattityahu *Strashun.

[Is.So./M.A.S./Ed.]

In Israel. In 1867, Albert Cohen, the representative in Palestine of Baron Rothschild, established a small library in Jerusalem, which was administered by Dr. London, physician in the Rothschild Hospital. Before the end of the century two more libraries were founded: the Abrabanel Library in 1884 (see J. *Chasanowich) which developed into the Jewish National and University *Library; and the Sapir Public Library in Petaḥ Tikvah. Up to the establishment of the State of Israel development was slow, being left to the private initiative of individuals or such bodies as the Histadrut, which in the 1920s had a central library with tens of thousands of volumes, serving labor settlements. After the establishment of the State of Israel great advances were made. The expansion of the school network, of local government, the research needs of scientific institutions, the expansion of agriculture and industry, all these made necessary the establishment (or development) of public or special scientific libraries as well as university and school libraries.

University Libraries. The Jewish National and University Library fulfills a double function: to collect all books, periodicals, etc. which bear on Jewish subjects and serve the general reading public; and to provide staff and students of the university with the required literature and textbooks. The Technion in Haifa, the universities of Tel Aviv, Ramat Gan (i.e., Bar Ilan), Haifa, Beersheba, and the Weizmann Institute in Reḥovot operate their own libraries. In most university libraries individual departments have built up their own specialized collections. The total number of books in all these institutions in 1970 was estimated at seven million. University libraries maintain contact with and assist and advise each other as well as other libraries and serve a circle of readers far beyond their own staff and students.

Public (Municipal) Libraries. In 1968, 733 Jewish locations in Israel were served by 441 public libraries with 611 service points, covering 97% of a population exceeding 2,300,000. Library service was available in 209 urban centers and 400 village settlements, the mobile libraries of WIZO serving both types at the same time. Kibbutzim have also built up libraries. Kibbutz *Kefar Giladi (population c. 700) had a library with 35,000 volumes. There were seven district libraries, each with responsibility for no less than ten settlements. The number of volumes in these public libraries (1968) was 4,328,700, of which 42% was fiction, 41.3% nonfiction, and 16.7% children's books. Of all these 84.6% were in Hebrew, 6.5% in English, and 8.9% in other languages. The number of registered readers was 227,300, 42.7% of whom were under 13.

The public libraries department of the Ministry of Education and Culture supports the setting up of public libraries, in particular in development areas and settlements established since 1948. In conjunction with the Israel Library Association and the Graduate Library School of the Hebrew University, the Ministry has formed a Guidance Center for Public Libraries, which assists with basic

Figure 2. Senior Library at Mount Scopus War Memorial College, Melbourne, Australia. Photo Allen Studios, Collingwood.

and current catalogs, publishing *Yad la-Koré*, a quarterly for librarianship and bibliography, arranging training, refresher courses and seminars for librarians, centralized book buying, etc.

The U.S. Information Centers and those set up in Jerusalem, Tel Aviv, and Haifa by the British Council, the (Italian) Dante Alighieri Society, and the Centres de Civilisation Française also serve the purpose of public libraries.

SPECIALIZED LIBRARIES. In 1970 280 specialized libraries with 2,700,000 volumes operated in Israel, among them the Knesset Library, those of various ministries, public corporations, museum libraries (the Bezalel Library of the Israel Museum holds 30,000 volumes), hospital libraries for the use of doctors and nurses; trade associations, factories, and economic concerns too have their own specialized libraries. All these were organized by the Israel Society of Special Libraries and Information Centers of 1966. Of particular importance in this connection are libraries devoted to Judaic and rabbinic studies such as (1) the Jewish Theological Seminary-Schocken Library (55,000 volumes, 200 manuscripts, 20,000 photostats); (2) the Central Rabbinical Library, attached to Hechal Shelomo, which received important collections saved from the Holocaust as well as from other sources (50,000 volumes and many valuable manuscripts); the libraries of (3) the Mosad ha-Rav Kook (60,000 volumes and many manuscripts) and of (4) Yad ha-Rav Herzog (40,000 volumes; 10,000 microfilm copies of Talmud texts and commentaries, also from the *Genizah*); (5) the Yeshurun Synagogue Library, all of these in Jerusalem; and (6) the Rambam Library in Tel Aviv, and others. In Jerusalem, too, are several valuable libraries of the various oriental research institutes: (1) the William Foxwell Albright School of Oriental Research (45,000 volumes); (2) the Ecole Biblique et Archéologique Française (Dominicans, 40,000 volumes); (3) the Monastery of the Holy Savior (Franciscans; 30,000 volumes, 150 manuscripts); (4) the Studium Biblicum Franciscanum (10,000 volumes); (5) the Gulbenkian Armenian Library (50,000 volumes, 3,700 manuscripts); (6) the library of the Department of Antiquities in the Rockefeller Museum (30,000 volumes); (7) the library of the Greek-Catholic Seminary of St. Ann (16,000 volumes, 125 manuscripts); (8) the library of the Institut Biblique Pontifical (11,000 volumes); (9) the library of Ratisbonne Monastery (8,000 volumes); (10) the Al-Aksa Mosque Library (10,000 volumes, 1,000 manuscripts); and (11) the Khalidiya (Moslem) Library (5,000 volumes, 5,000 manuscripts). Mention too should be made of: (1) the library of the Central Zionist Archives (54,000 volumes and 165,000 smaller items); (2) the Yad Vashem (Holocaust) Library (40,000 volumes; periodicals); and (3) the B'nai B'rith and (4) Y.M.C.A. libraries (two) in Jerusalem, with 25,000 volumes each.

LIBRARIANS. In 1970 there were over 1,500 librarians in the country, of whom nearly 80% were organized in the Israel Library Association, founded in 1952 and associated with the International Federation of Library Associations (IFLA). The Association is not only concerned with the material conditions of library staff but also with the level of their professional training, holding courses and arranging examinations for a librarian's diploma. [M.Z.B./M.A.S.]

Catalog. Catalogs in the modern sense were first published in the 17th century, but book lists are much older (see *Books, *Book Trade). Some belonging to the 12th century were found in the Cairo *Genizah*. *Immanuel of Rome (13th century) mentions a catalog arranged according to subject matter. The first to introduce a systematic division according to subjects was *Manasseh Ben Israel. From the end of the 17th century sale catalogs began to be printed, such as those of S. Abbas and Solomon *Proops, both of Amsterdam, or later the famous collection of David Oppenheimer. In modern times M. *Steinschneider did pioneering work in this field. The first scientific listing was his catalog of the Hebrew books of the Bodleian Library (1852–60). J. *Zedner followed with his catalog of the Jewish books in the British Museum (1867).

Figure 4. Library at the Mosad ha-Rav Kook in Jerusalem. Photo K. Weiss, Jerusalem.

Figure 3. Traveling library of the Ḥabad movement. From *Challenge*, London, 1970.

The most popular method of dividing Jewish catalogs is in two sections: (1) Hebraica, including books written in Hebrew or any other Jewish language; (2) Judaica, including books on Jewish topics in any language. The catalogs of large collections (both private and public), especially of non-Jewish collections, contain a section, not always separate, of Orientalia, together with the Jewish works.

Lately some major libraries have issued photoreproductions of their card catalogs, e.g., New York Public Library, Hebrew Union College (Cincinnati), and Harvard University. For a list of catalogs see Shunami, Bibl. nos. 86–208, 209–481 (public collections); 4485–92 (private collections), 4493–99 and 4503–06 (booksellers' and publishers' catalogs).

See also *Archives. [B.Y.]

Bibliography: GENERAL: JBA (1942–); A. Marx, in: *Studies in Jewish History and Booklore* (1944), 198–237; S. Abramson, in: KS, 26 (1949/50), 72–92; J. Fraenkel (ed.), *Guide to the Jewish Libraries of the World* (1959); D. Z. Baneth, in: *Tarbiz*, 30 (1960/61), 171–85; S. Shunami, *Al Sifriyyot ve-Safranut* (1969). ISRAEL: Israel Center of Scientific and Technological Information, *Directory of Special Libraries in Israel* (1964²); Center for Public Libraries in Israel, *Aims and Activities* (1967); Golan, in: *Yad la-Koré*, 10 (1969); Irgun Safranei Israel, *Du'aḥ Pe'ullot ha-Irgun* (1969). OUTSIDE ISRAEL: H. M. Rabinowicz, *Jewish Literary Treasures of England and America* (1962).

LIBRARY, JEWISH NATIONAL AND UNIVERSITY, the national library of Israel and the Jewish people, also serving as the library of the *Hebrew University in Jerusalem. The library dates from 1892, when *B'nai B'rith founded a public library in Jerusalem to which in 1895 a Bialystok physician, Joseph *Chasanowich (Chazanowicz), presented his collection of 8,800 books, mostly in Hebrew. Other gifts followed and by 1920, when the library was taken over by the Zionist organization, the number of volumes had reached about 30,000. Under the direction of the philosopher Samuel Hugo *Bergman, who was librarian from 1920 till 1935, the number of volumes increased to 300,000. Between 1936 and 1946, under Gotthold *Weil, about 150,000 books were added. When the Hebrew University was opened on Mount Scopus in 1925, the library was transferred to it, and in 1930 it was installed in the Wolffsohn building.

In 1948, when communication with Mount Scopus was broken off as a result of the War of Independence, the library contained nearly half a million books. Curt *Wormann, who had been appointed librarian only a few months earlier, had to build it up anew in western Jerusalem, where it was housed in the Terra Sancta building. With the help of friends and supporters in Israel and abroad, it acquired tens of thousands of books and was brought back into working condition. In the years following World War II, the university (later joined by the Ministry of Religious Affairs) salvaged hundreds of thousands of books in Europe, as well as hundreds of manuscripts (chiefly Hebraica and Judaica), the remnants of Jewish public and private libraries looted by the Nazis. Many of these were incorporated into the National Library; the rest were distributed among university, public, synagogue, and yeshivah libraries throughout the country.

Following an agreement with the Jordanian government in 1958 (through the mediation of the secretary-general of the UN, Dag Hammarskjöld), about 350,000 books from Mount Scopus were gradually transferred to the Israel-held sector of Jerusalem. In 1960 a library building was opened on the new campus at Givat Ram. At the beginning of 1968, the library possessed about 1,500,000 volumes, over a quarter of them Hebraica and Judaica, together with 6,100 Hebrew and 800 other manuscripts. In 1962, the Institute of Microfilms of Hebrew Manuscripts was transferred to the library from the Ministry of Education and Culture. From then until 1971 it had acquired 25,000 photocopies of Hebrew manuscripts from 18 countries, together with thousands of photographs of **genizah* fragments. From 1924 the library published a bibliographical quarterly, **Kirjath Sepher,* listing all current publications in Palestine and Israel and all Judaic publications appearing elsewhere. An Institute of Hebrew Bibliography in the library records all books published in Hebrew characters. Since 1956, a graduate library school has been functioning at the library.

Main reading room of the Jewish National and University Library (J.N.U.L.) at the Hebrew University of Jerusalem. Photo David Rubinger, Jerusalem.

The library possesses a number of special collections: the Zalman Schocken collection of Hebrew incunabula; the Ignaz Goldziher collection of Orientalia (especially of Islamica and Arabica); the Harry Friedenwald collection on Jews in medicine; the Abraham Schwadron (Sharon) collection of Jewish autographs and portraits; the Immanuel Loew collection of Judaica and Hebraica (including his personal archives); and the A. S. Yahuda collection of Orientalia, Hebraica, and Judaica. The library also has the personal archives of Aḥad Ha-Am, Martin Buber, Joseph Klausner, Stefan Zweig, and S. J. Agnon.

Bibliography: A. Ya'ari, *Beit ha-Sefarim ha-Le'ummi ve-ha-Universita'i bi-Yrushalayim* (1942); *The Hebrew University of Jerusalem* (1966), 234–50; Y. Haezrahi, *Beit ha-Sefarim ha-Le'ummi ve-ha-Universita'i* (1967).

[SHL.SH.]

LIBSCHITZ, BARUCH MORDECAI BEN JACOB (1810–1885), Polish rabbi and author. Libschitz occupied successively rabbinical positions at Siemiatycze, Volkovysk, and Novogrudok, before he was appointed rabbi of Siedlce in 1876. He was acknowledged as a leading halakhic authority and many turned to him with their halakhic questions. Although Siedlce was a ḥasidic community, as a Lithuanian Libschitz was opposed to Ḥasidism and often came into conflict with the members of his community who were used to ḥasidic rabbis. He was one of the first to support the Ḥovevei Zion movement and in his letters to Joseph Friedland, the first propagandist of the Zionist movement, he gave him much encouragement. He was also one of the main supporters of the establishment of the Eẓ Ḥayyim yeshivah in Jerusalem. He published *Berit Ya'akov,* responsa on the Shulḥan Arukh (pt. 1 ḤM; pt. 2 EH, 1876–77); and *Beit Mordekhai,* sermons and memorial addresses (1881). His *Minḥat Bikkurim,* talmudic novellae, has remained in manuscript. He had two sons, MEIR EZEKIEL, who settled in Jerusalem and died there in 1909, and JACOB ZALMAN (d. 1915); their talmudic novellae appear in the works of R. Elijah *Klatzkin, the rabbi of Lublin who had settled in Jerusalem.

Bibliography: Ḥ. N. Maggid-Steinschneider, *Ir Vilna* (1900), 164; Frankel, in: *Yizkor li- Kehillat Siedlce* (1956), 296f.

[Y.AL.]

LIBYA, country in N. Africa, consisting of the regions of Tripolitania, Cyrenaica (see *Cyrene), and Fezzan. Isolated finds of Jewish origin from pre-Exilic Ereẓ Israel were discovered both in Cyrenaica and Tripolitania, but there is no reliable evidence of Jewish presence in those countries before the time of Ptolemy Lagos (ruled Egypt 323–282 B.C.E.); he is reported to have settled Jews in the Cyrenean Pentapolis to strengthen his regime there, probably in 312 B.C.E. The phrases used consistently in the sources point to their distribution around Cyrene presumably as military settlers on royal land. The temporary extension of Ptolemaic control into Tripolitania in the early third century B.C.E. may have occasioned similar Jewish settlement in that area; there are Jewish finds from this date at Busetta and Zliten.

Early History. After the Maccabean breakthrough to Jaffa commerce between Ereẓ Israel and Cyrene appears to have been strengthened (147–43 B.C.E.). II Maccabees is an abbreviation of a work by Jason of Cyrene. With the political reunion of Egypt and Cyrene under Ptolemy Euergetes II in 145 B.C.E., a fresh wave of Jewish immigration reached the latter country; the Jewish community of Teucheira, evidenced by their epitaphs, and composed probably of military settlers linked with Egypt, must have originated late in the century. In 88 B.C.E., after Cyrene had been freed from Ptolemaic control, the Jews of the country were involved in an undefined civil conflict perhaps to be connected with contemporary manifestations

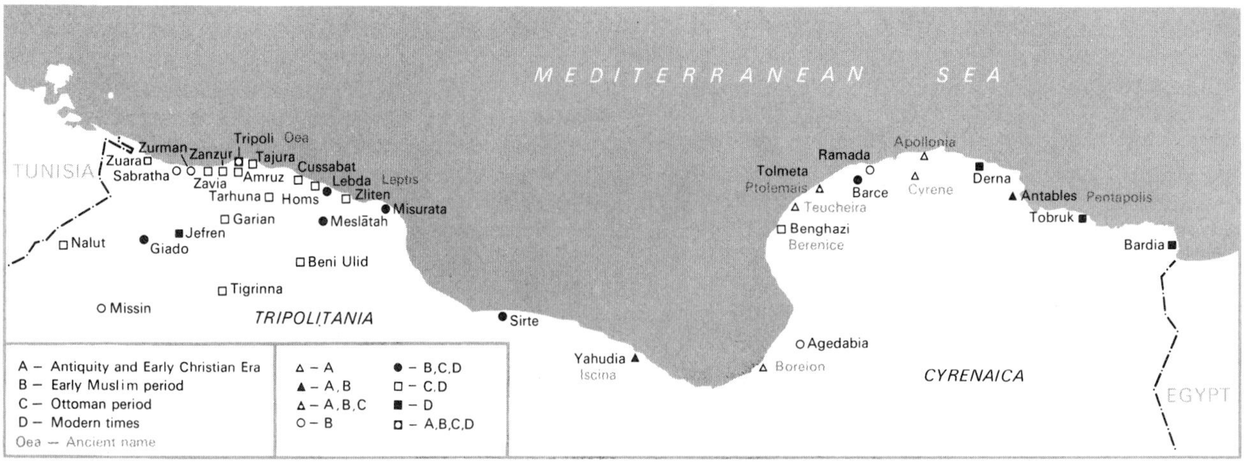

Jewish settlements in Libya, from antiquity to modern times.

of Greek anti-Jewishness in Alexandria and Antioch. The Roman exploitation of the royal domains at the expense of their cultivators would have involved numerous Jews, ultimately expropriated, perhaps one of the social bases of the risings of 73 and 115 C.E.

Cyrene became a Roman province in 74 B.C.E.; inscriptions of the reigns of Augustus, Tiberius, and Nero at Berenice (Benghazi) indicate a wealthy, well-organized community with an executive board and its own amphitheater for assembly, as well as a synagogue. Jewish urban communities prior to 115 C.E. are further evidenced at Apollonia and Ptolemais. Cyrenean Jewry under Augustus was compelled to defend its right—attacked by Greek cities—to send the half-shekel to Jerusalem, but its privileges were confirmed by the Roman power. A section of the Cyrenean community at this point seems to have obtained improved civic status, and Jewish names appear among graduates of city gymnasia both at Cyrene and Ptolemais, but it is clear that the bulk of the community was considered intermediate between alien residents and citizens. Cyrenean Jewry was nevertheless preponderantly rural; sites of Jewish rural settlement are known at Gasr Tarhuna, Al-Bagga, in the Martuba area, at Boreion (Bu-Grada) in the south (the site of an alleged "temple"), and at an unlocated place called Kaparodis. The Teucheira group was largely agricultural and a Jewish rural population probably existed around Benghazi. The occupations of Cyrenean Jewry included, besides agriculture, those of potter, sailor, stonemason, bronze-worker, and possibly weaver. Commercial elements are likely to have existed at the ports of Benghazi, Apollonia, and Ptolemais. The Jewish aristocracies of Benghazi, Ptolemais, and Cyrene were highly hellenized (cf. a Jew, Eleazar son of Jason, who held municipal office at Cyrene under Nero); though Jewish graduates of gymnasia appear at Teucheira, most of the Jews there were relatively uncultured, and suffered a high rate of child mortality. Cyrenean Jews maintained a synagogue in Jerusalem in the first century C.E.

In 73 C.E. Jonathan the Weaver, a "desert prophet" of the Qumran type and a Zealot refugee from Ereẓ Israel, incited the poorer element of the Jews of Cyrene to revolt, leading them to the desert with promises of miraculous deliverance. Jonathan was apprehended and his followers were massacred; the Roman governor L. Valerius Catullus also took the opportunity to execute some 3,000 wealthy Jews and to confiscate their property. The Zealot movement was not confined to the city of Cyrene, and the removal of the hellenized Jewish aristocracy led to the radicalization of the rest of the community. Under Vespasian (69–79 C.E.) the recovery and redistribution of the extensive Cyrenean state lands began, resulting in increased friction with the seminomadic transhumant Libyan elements. To the same period belongs the Jewish settlement of Iscina (Scina) Locus Augusti Iudaeorum (Medinat al-Sultan) on the shore of eastern Tripolitania, an imperial foundation which may plausibly be held to reflect a forcible removal of disaffected Jewish elements from Cyrene to the desert borders—a view which finds support in Jewish historical tradition. A Jewish-Libyan rapprochement on the desert borders may well have taken place prior to the rising of 115.

In 115—during Trajan's Second Parthian campaign—the Jewish revolt broke out in Cyrene, Egypt, and Cyprus. The very heavy gentile casualties in Cyrene and the scope of the destruction wrought by the Jews at Cyrene, probably at Apollonia, Balagrae (Zwiat Beda), Teucheira, and in the eastern areas, suggest that the rebels, under their leader *Lucuas (or Andreas), who was called by the gentile historians "King of the Jews," intended to quit the country for good. The wholesale destruction of the Roman temples testifies to the Zealot content of the rising. At the end of 116 the Jews broke into Egypt, but cut off from Alexandria were defeated by Marcius Turbo; Lucuas is thought to have been killed in Judea.

Jews may have already been again living in Ptolemais in the third century, and, in the later part of the fourth century, Jewish ships were reaching Cyrene from Egypt. There is much evidence for the existence of a Jewish population in the country on the eve of the Muslim conquest (642), and presumably the numerous Jewish traditions attached to ancient sites throughout the country relate to the Byzantine period. In Tripolitania, except for the appearance of Iscina, the Jewish record is blank until the fourth century. In Africa Vetus (Tunisia) Jewish settlement cannot be proven before the early second century C.E., and the Talmud (Men. 110a) seems to imply a gap in Jewish settlement east of Carthage; Jerome nevertheless believed that in the late fourth century Jewish settlement was continuous from Morocco to Egypt, and numerous place-names on the Tripolitanian coast suggest a very ancient Jewish tradition. A Christian cemetery of the fourth century at Sirte contained chiefly Jewish names, perhaps of people connected with imperial domains of the area. A Jewish community at Oea (now *Tripoli), which possessed competent scholars, is attested by Augustine (fifth century). The Boreion community indicates longstanding settlement; its "temple" was converted into a church, and its Jews were forced to accept Christianity by Justinian (527–65). Ibn Khaldūn (14th century) thought the Berbers on Mount Nefusa were Judaized, and derived from the Barce area (Cyrene)—like the Jarawa of the Algerian Aurès—but his statement is tentative and the traditions of Judaizing Berber tribes, despite the extensive modern literature concerning them, have been shown not to be pre- or early Islamic. [SH.AP.]

Arab Period. According to late Arabic sources, the Jews were dispersed among the Berbers who lived around Mount Nefusa before the Arab conquest, but in Jewish sources the Jews of this district are only mentioned from the tenth century onward. The Jews also believed that the Jewish population of the entire region originated there. From the frequent repetitions of the surname al-Lebdi in 11th- and 12th-century sources, it can be concluded that there was also an important Jewish population in Lebda, near the harbor town of Homs, and also in the oasis of G(h)adames. There was also a Jewish population in Barce and in other localities. Between 1159 and 1160 the Jewish population suffered as a result of the victory of the Almohads but the rulers did not take any lives or force conversion.

There is no extant information on Libyan Jewry during the next 400 years. According to a later source, 800 Jewish families fled from Tripoli to Tajura—situated to the east of the latter—and to Jebel Gharyān (Garian)—in the interior of the country—as a result of the Spanish invasion of 1510. After the Turkish conquest the Jews prospered again. At that time, R. Simeon *Labi, a Spanish refugee, settled in Tripoli and strengthened the position of Judaism and introduced Jewish learning. According to a manuscript which belonged to M. Gaster (now BM. Or. 12368), "A sad and bitter event happened to the people of the Mahgreb," i.e., the Jews of Libya were in great distress during the years 1588–89 as a result of the revolt against the Turks which was fomented by the mahdi Yaḥyā b. Yaḥyā. Many of them were forcibly converted to Islam, but with the suppression of the revolt, they returned to Judaism. There is, however, no mention or allusion in Jewish sources to this period of persecution.

The community of Tripoli gained in strength with the arrival of Jews from *Leghorn. In 1663 the Shabbatean Abraham Miguel *Cardozo arrived there and conducted his Shabbatean campaign. From the second half of the 17th century until the Italian conquest (1911) the Jews of Libya were led by *qā'ids* ("leaders"). During the famine and plague of 1784–85, there was much suffering among the Jews and they were threatened with grave danger when Ali Gurzi, known as "Burgul," was appointed pasha of Libya. After a year and a half he was banished from the town, and in commemoration of their deliverance the Jews of Tripoli celebrate "Purim of Burgul" every 29th of Tevet. The Jews of Libya lived in special quarters (*ḥāra*) in the various towns. In the two villages of Jebel Gharyān and Tigrinna, they lived in below-ground-level caves until their emigration to Israel in 1950–51. The *Ḥārat al-Yahūd* ("Jewish quarter") in Tigrinna contained about 300 Jews. They earned their living as goldsmiths, blacksmiths, and peddlers among the Bedouin in the area.

The traveler Benjamin the Second found about 1,000 Jewish families (about a third of the population) in Tripoli. There were four competent *dayyanim* and eight synagogues. In 1906 N. *Slouschz visited Libya and his descriptions have become a historical source of information. Most of the information in his books about the 18th and 19th centuries stems from his guide Mordecai Hacohen, whose history based on earlier sources is still in manuscript. At the end of Ottoman rule there were no important incidents in the history of Libyan Jewry, apart from the fact that in 1909 they, like all citizens of the Ottoman Empire, were subject to the compulsory military service law. Jews—of an Orthodox religious background—feared the law because they were forced to desecrate the Sabbath in the course of military service. However, the law was only in force for a short time, since Libya shortly thereafter fell to the Italians. [H.Z.H.]

Italian Rule. On Oct. 11, 1911, Tripoli fell to the Italians, and two months later the rest of Libya. The first 25 years of Italian rule passed peacefully for the Jews. They retained equal rights, and the number of those in government employment grew, as did the numbers of those who became prosperous and attended school. During this period Zionist activity went unhindered. The Jewish population of Libya in 1931 was 21,000 (4% of the total population). They were dispersed in 15 localities, with about 15,000 of them in Tripoli. In 1936 the Italians began to enforce fascist anti-Jewish legislation, and started to hinder the freedom of the Jews. Jews were removed from municipal councils, some were sent away from government schools, and their papers were stamped with the words "Jewish race." They were forced to open their shops on the Sabbath, and those who refused to do so were punished. When the Benghazi area fell to the British in February 1941, the Jews were overjoyed. [H.J.C.]

Holocaust Period. In March 1941 the Italian governor of Tripoli took discriminatory measures against all Jews and ordered Jewish organizations to cease activities. On April 3, 1941, young Arabs ran wild and assaulted the Jews of Benghazi. The British reoccupied Benghazi briefly at the end of 1941. In February 1942, the reoccupation of *Benghazi by Axis forces was followed by the systematic plunder of all Jewish shops and the promulgation of a deportation order: 2,600 persons were deported into the desert to Giado, 149 mi. (240 km.) south of Tripoli, where they were forced to do hard labor in road construction while living under extremely bad conditions. During their 14-month exile 562 people died of starvation or typhus. In April 1942 the Jews of Tripoli were compelled to declare all their property, and those between 18 and 45 years of age were sent on forced labor: some 1,400 persons to Homs, and 350 to lay the railway line linking Libya and Egypt. They were subject to severe bombing by the Royal Air Force. [R.AT.]

During this period, Zionist activity was paralyzed. In general the relations with the Muslim population did not worsen, and village Muslims sometimes gave sanctuary and shelter during the three years to Jews who fled to them, although in the towns fascist propaganda reached and influenced the young Muslims. During World War II the men of the Jewish Brigade conducted various political and cultural activities among the Jewish population.

The British Occupation. The Jews were able to reopen their schools, although in this period they suffered from persecution by Muslims which was unparalleled in the past. On July 4, 1945, there were Muslim riots against the Jews of Tripoli and other towns. In Tripoli the masses ran wild, killing and wounding many Jews, looting their property, and setting fire to five synagogues. On January 6 troublemakers from Tripoli arrived in Zanzur (c. 30 mi. (48 km.) from Tripoli) and incited the Muslim population against the 150 local Jews, of whom half were murdered. Jews were also killed at Meslātah, Zaniah, Tajura (10 mi. (16 km.) from Tripoli), and at Amruz ($2\frac{1}{2}$ mi. (4 km.) from Tripoli). According to various estimates, from 121 to 187 Jews were killed and many were wounded during these incidents. Nine synagogues were burned down and damage to property was half a million pounds sterling, a very large sum for a poor community. The British authorities did not succeed in immediately stopping the excesses because they had Arab soldiers and policemen in their service who gen-

Jews of Tripoli offering thanks in public prayer, following the entry of the British Eighth Army in 1943. Courtesy Joint Distribution Committee, New York.

erally joined in the riots with the masses when sent to protect Jews; only when forces came from outside, especially Sudanese soldiers, were the rioters dispersed. After the riots about 300 rioters were brought to trial, of whom two were sentenced to death. The leniency of the sentences and the incitement by the Arab countries, regarding Palestine, encouraged the Libyan Muslims again to persecute the Jews in June 1948 in Benghazi and Tripoli. However, this time some of the Jews were ready to defend themselves, since after the 1945 attacks a Jewish defense organization was set up by emissaries from Palestine (1946). Tripoli Jews used hand grenades and repelled marauders trying to enter the Jewish quarter; before the rioters could be stopped the police arrived, but 14 Jews had already been killed. Most of the persecutors were Tunisian volunteers on the way to the Palestinian front.

Contemporary Period. After the first pogroms, Jews began leaving Libya, most of them emigrating to Palestine. Between 1919 and 1948 about 450 Jews emigrated to Palestine from Libya, most of them during the years 1946 and 1947 when about 150 emigrated there. When the State of Israel was established, Jewish flight from Libya increased; they left by way of Tripoli and Tunisia; between May 1948 and January 1949 about 2,500 left the country. Only in 1949 did the British permit legal emigration to Israel, and many immediately registered to emigrate. Until the end of 1951, 30,000 Jews emigrated, only about 8,000 Jews remaining in Libya. Most of them lived in Tripoli and about 400 in Benghazi, while the townlets and villages were almost entirely emptied of Jews. Under the independent Libyan regime (from January 1952) Jews did not suffer from persecution and equal rights were guaranteed them under the Libyan constitution. Nevertheless, Libyan citizens were forbidden to return home if they visited Israel (June 1952), and in 1953 the authorities closed the Maccabi club. In June 1967 after the Six-Day War there were anti-Jewish riots and the Jews locked themselves inside their houses for fear of attack; 17 Jews were murdered and many were arrested. After a time, most of the remainder left, some of whom emigrated to Israel. With the outbreak of the coup by Col. Qaddafi on Sept. 1, 1969, the 400–500 Jews remaining in Libya were concentrated in a camp in Tripoli. These included Libyan citizens, bearers of foreign citizenship (British, French, Italian), and those bearing no citizenship. The government claimed that this step was taken to defend the Jews against incursions on their property. After the coup Jews were not allowed to leave Libya, although all of them were released and some of them succeeded in leaving Libya. On July 21, 1970, the revolutionary regime announced the nationalization of Italian and Jewish property, mostly of Jews who had left Libya indefinitely.

Demographically, it should be noted that Libyan Jews, of whom there were about 20,000 in 1911, were mainly concentrated in the town of Tripoli (c. 12,000), but many of them were scattered in towns, townlets, and villages all over the country. According to the 1931 census there were 24,534 Jews, and in 1948 about 38,000 Jews in Libya, of whom about 20,000 were in Tripoli. This shows that there was no mass emigration before 1948, nor was there considerable migration within the country. At the end of 1970 only some 90 Jews remained in Libya.

Social, Economic, and Religious-Cultural Conditions. The wide dispersal of Libyan Jewry into dozens of communities, many comprising only a few families, sometimes affected their economic and educational circumstances. The Alliance Israélite Universelle opened a school only in Tripoli, although hundreds more Jews preferred to send their children to Italian schools in Tripoli and Benghazi; in small towns they made do with study at a *ḥeder*. For this reason a large proportion of Jewish children outside the main towns received no modern education, and sometimes no education whatsoever. However, in comparison to the beginning of the century, the younger generation contained far fewer illiterates. The Jews also opened a private high school in Tripoli in 1936, when they were expelled from Italian high schools; they were forced to close it in 1939. In 1947 a Hebrew teachers' seminary was opened in Tripoli, but it was closed after the large-scale emigration.

Libya's most prominent rabbis included: R. Masʿud Hai *Rakaḥ, author of the work *Ma'aseh Roke'aḥ* on Maimonides; R. Abraham Ḥayyim Adadi, author of *Va-Yikra Avraham;* and R. Isaac Hai Bukhbaza (d. 1930).

Apart from the Tripoli community which contained a number of important merchants and officials, most Libyan Jews were occupied as artisans; a few were peddlers and farmers and thus worked hard for their living. The statements of 6,080 breadwinners who emigrated to Israel from Libya between 1948 and 1951 show that 15.4% were merchants, 7.5% were clerks and administrators, 3.0% were members of the liberal professions (including teachers and rabbis), 6.1% were farmers, 47% were artisans, and 7.1% were construction and transport workers. The remainder (13.9%) worked in personal services or were unskilled laborers.

As a result of their poverty, disease was widespread among Libyan Jewry; they suffered mainly from trachoma, tuberculosis, and eczema, so much so that children in school had to be classified according to illness. O.S.E. began work in Tripoli to care for schoolchildren and convalescents were sent to a *talmud torah* in the town, where healthy children were kept. However, in April 1950 only 30% of the 2,000 Jewish schoolchildren were healthy; thus, the Israel immigration authorities had to screen potential immigrants for illness and provide them with medical care before permitting them to immigrate.

Zionist Activity. A short time after Libya was conquered by Italy, contact was made between Libyan Jewry and the Italian Zionist Organization, mainly due to the newspapers that reached Tripoli and Libya. In 1913 some of the readers of these newspapers, led by Elijah Neḥaisi, tried to found a Zionist organization. At first only an evening *talmud torah* was founded (1914) in order to spread the Hebrew language, and then the Zion Society was established (May 1916), and the committee of this Zionist association succeeded in entering the Tripoli community committee, gaining 11 of the 31 places as members of their association (June 1916). The Zion Society published the first Zionist newspaper in Libya, *Degel Ẓiyyon* (1920–24). In 1923 the association changed its name to the Tripolitanian Zionist Federation. The Ben Yehuda Association, established in 1931, was very active in spreading the Hebrew language. In 1933 it published a weekly entitled *Limdu Ivrit!* ("Learn Hebrew!"). The association also opened a Hebrew school in Tripoli in 1931, which was attended by 512 pupils (1933); their numbers rose to 1,200 in 1938/39. In 1939 the school was closed and the association disbanded on government orders.

When Libya was conquered by the British (1943) and Jewish Palestinian soldiers came to the country, Zionist work was able to continue. A number of Zionist youth organizations were established and several Hebrew newspapers were published (*Ḥayyeinu,* a Hebrew monthly, 1944; *Niẓzanim,* Hebrew monthly, 1945–48; *Ḥayyeinu,* Hebrew, Italian, and Arabic weekly, 1949–50). In 1943 the He-Ḥalutz organization was set up, and an agricultural training farm was established; it was abandoned in November 1945 when the pogroms against the Jews broke out; the ten trainees emigrated to Israel (1946). Subsequently, agricultural training was renewed, until the 23 trainees were forced to abandon the farm during the June 1948 pogroms.

In May 1946 an emissary from Ereẓ Israel founded a defense organization, which was trained in the use of weapons and manufactured homemade "bombs"; it defended the Jewish quarter in Tripoli during the June 1948 pogroms. In 1946 illegal emigration to Ereẓ Israel also began, achieved by illegally crossing the frontier into Tunisia, and from there to Marseilles. In 1948 illegal immigration to Ereẓ Israel was organized through Italy. Hundreds emigrated in this way, until legal immigration became possible (1949).

Since Libyan Jews were observant, most of the Zionist organizations were religious, including the youth groups founded after 1943. These were affiliated to Ha-Poel ha-Mizraḥi. [H.J.C.]

Attitude Toward Israel. When the UN General Assembly resolved (Nov. 21, 1949) that Libya become independent before Jan. 1, 1952, Israel, itself a newcomer to the UN, cast its vote for the resolution. This gesture of goodwill received no reciprocation, and Israel did not repeat it in the case of any other Arab state. Anti-Jewish outbursts accompanied the announcement about the impending independence, and Israel took all precautions to enable Libya's Jews who wanted to settle in Israel to reach their destination before the critical date. Close to 90% of Libyan Jewry settled in Israel up to the end of 1951. Independent Libya joined the Arab League in 1952 and adopted a hostile attitude toward Israel, though it was mainly declaratory. Libya took part in Arab summit conferences, joined the Arab boycott, conducted anti-Israel propaganda, and attacked Israel at the UN. The situation became more critical during the Six-Day War (1967), when widespread strikes of Libyan oil workers, as an expression of Arab solidarity, brought the flow of oil to a temporary stop, hitting the U.S. and Western Europe, which allegedly aided Israel, and shaking the conservative rule of King Idris.

After the war, Libya allowed Palestinians to live and work inside its territory, but only in limited numbers. It permitted collections for the terrorist organizations, founded a school for al-Fatḥ orphans, and played host to several delegations from these organizations. Libya, like the other two Arab oil states (Saudi Arabia and Kuwait), contributed an annual share ($8,000,000) to Egypt and Jordan, according to the resolution of the 1967 Arab summit conference in Khartoum.

A drastic change occurred in Libya's attitude toward Israel after the overthrow of the monarchy on Sept. 1, 1969, and the rise of a revolutionary regime. Libya now adopted the militant line of the extreme Arab states in regard to Israel, as well as against the West in general. Muammar al-Qaddafi, chairman of the Revolutionary Council, announced from the start that the new regime opposed political solutions to the Israel-Arab conflict and did not believe in the possibility of a successful peaceful settlement. He promised to mobilize all Libya's rich resources in order to assist the armed confrontation with Israel. At the Arab summit conference in Rabat (Dec. 21–23, 1969), he also promised to extend a considerable part of Libya's oil revenues (which amount to $1,000,000,000 annually) to reinforce the Arab front. Libya set up a "holy war fund" out of state grants, special taxes, and individual donations.

The following meeting in Tripoli (Dec. 25–27, 1969) of the presidents of Egypt, Sudan, and Libya, who agreed to establish an alignment of the three countries, proved even more forcefully the new regime's desire to integrate into the Arab struggle against Israel. Libya drifted more and more into the sphere of influence of *Nasser, who exploited the situation to deepen the Egyptian military and economic penetration into Libya, a step which became possible after the liquidation of the American and British military bases there and expulsion of foreigners. The regime acquired considerable quantities of arms which may serve the Arab cause at the front. On Nov. 8, 1970, the presidents of Libya, Egypt, and Sudan decided to establish a "union," or federation, of their countries in order to bring about closer military, economic, and political links; Syria later joined this bloc. Libya assisted the Palestine terrorist organizations financially and politically. [R.Co.]

Bibliography: Early Period: P. Monceaux, in: REJ, 44 (1902), 1ff.; N. Slouschz, *Travels in North Africa* (1927); S. A. Applebaum, *Yehudim vi-Yvanim be-Kirene ha-Kedumah* (1969); Hirschberg, in: *Journal of African History,* 4 (1963), 313ff.; *Zion,* 19 (1954), 52–56 (a bibl.). Modern Period: F. Suarez et al. (eds.), *Yahadut Luv* (1960); I. M. Toledano, *Ner ha-Ma'arav* (1921), 88; I. S. Bernstein, in: *Sinai,* 19–20 (1946–47); G. Scholem, *Iggeret Avraham Mikha'el Cardozo le-Dayyanei Izmir* (1954); Hirschberg, Afrikah, 1 (1965), 5–17, 11, 173–206; idem, in *Bar-Ilan,* 4–5 (1967), 415–79; R. Attal, in: *Sefunot,* 9 (1965), a bibl.; I. J. Benjamin, *Acht Jahre in Asien und Afrika* (1858[2]), 230–7; M. Cohen, *Gli ebrei in Libia, usi e costumi* (1928); M. Eisenbeth, *Les Juifs de l'Afrique du Nord* (1936); G. V. Raccah, in: *Israel,* 23 (Florence, 1938); S. Groussard, *Pogrom* (1948). Holocaust Period: Rabinowitz, in: *Menorah Journal,* 23 (1945), 115–26; E. Kolb, *Bergen-Belsen* (Ger., 1962), 64; P. Juarez et al. (eds.), *Yahadut Luv* (1960), 197–201.

LICHINE (Lichtenstein), DAVID (1910–1972), Russian-born dancer and choreographer who carried on the ballet tradition of Diaghilev and Massine. He studied ballet with Lubov Egorova in Paris after emigrating from Russia and he first won attention when engaged by Bronislava Nijinska in 1928 to appear with Ida *Rubinstein's company. He later danced with Pavlova. From 1932 to 1940 he was a leading dancer and choreographer with Colonel de Basil's Ballets Russes de Monte Carlo. World War II brought Lichine and his wife, the ballerina Tatiana Riabouchinska, to the United States. In 1952 they settled in Los Angeles, where they established their own school and company. Lichine was at various times guest choreographer for American Ballet Theater, the Royal Danish Ballet, the Festival Ballet of London, and other companies. His ballets include *Protée* (1938), *The Prodigal Son* (1939), *Graduation Ball* (1940), and *Helen of Troy* (1942).

Bibliography: F. Gadan-Pamard and R. Maillard (eds.), *Dictionary of Modern Ballet* (1959). [M.B.S.]

LICHT, ALEXANDER (1884–1948), Zionist leader in Yugoslavia. Licht was born in the Croatian village Sokolovac. Except for one year of study in Vienna, he was educated in Zagreb, where he also graduated as a lawyer. He was the founder and spiritual leader of the "Zagreb school" in Yugoslav Zionism, which consisted mainly of young people and intellectuals and transformed the Zagreb community from a center of assimilationism into a dynamic focal point of Zionism. As a young man he was elected chairman of the Jewish youth circle Literarni Sastanci, which soon became a Zionist society. In Vienna he was the chairman of Bar Giora, a Zionist group of students from the areas which became Yugoslavia. He also organized in 1906 the second conference of Jewish academic youth in Osijek and wrote articles on Zionism in the Croatian press that won the sympathy of the gentile intelligentsia. He translated the "Ghetto songs" of Morris Rosenfeld into Croatian and edited the Zionist monthly *Židovska Smotra* ("Jewish Review"). In 1909 he was elected secretary of the Zionist Organization for the southern Slavic countries (Dalmatia, Bosnia, Croatia, and Slavonia). He served on the front during World War I, and after returning in 1918 he addressed a memorandum to the Yugoslav National Committee expounding the Zionist attitude to the problems arising from the disintegration of the Hapsburg Empire. In 1919 he was instrumental in preventing dangerous frictions between Sephardi and Ashkenazi Jews and the expulsion of Jews from Bosnia and Vojvodina. Between the world wars, Licht served as chairman of the Zionist Executive and later of the Zionist Organization of Yugoslavia. In 1929 he became a member of the Zionist General Council. In 1941 he was arrested and, after spending several months in prison in Graz, Austria, he wandered from one refugee camp to another in Slovenia, Italy, and Switzerland, where he finally managed to settle with his family. He died in Geneva and in 1955 his remains were transferred to Jerusalem. [Y.Ev.]

LICHT, FRANK (1916–), U.S. jurist and governor. Licht, who was born in Providence, R.I., the son of Russian immigrants, was active in Jewish youth organizations in

David Lichine, dancer and choreographer. From M. Seymour, *Seymour on Ballet*, New York, 1947.

Providence. At Brown University he was founder of the Menorah Society. In 1948 Licht was elected to the Rhode Island senate, serving until 1956, when he was appointed associate judge of the Rhode Island superior court. He resigned from the bench in 1968 to accept the Democratic nomination for governor, scoring an upset victory against a popular Republican incumbent to become governor in 1969. At the time of his election he was president of the General Jewish Committee of Rhode Island (the Jewish federation) and active in other Jewish affairs. [B.P.]

LICHT, MICHAEL (1893–1953), Yiddish poet and essayist. Born and raised in a Ukrainian village, he emigrated to the United States in 1913. At first he wrote English poems, but in 1916 he began to publish Yiddish lyrics. Soon afterward he joined the Inzikhist group (see *In-Zikh) and, together with the Inzikhist poets Jacob *Glatstein and N. B. *Minkoff, edited avant-garde journals in 1925 and 1926. He continued to write during 20 years of illness, but he published only three small volumes of poems during his lifetime. His collected poems and essays, as well as his translations of modern American poetry, appeared posthumously in *Gezamlte Verk* (1953). Licht is a poet of the American metropolis, with original insights and satiric undertones.

Bibliography: LNYL, 5 (1963), 138–40; Minkoff, in: M. Licht, *Gezamlte Lider* (1957), 9–14, introduction; S. Bickel, *Shrayber fun Mayn Dor* (1958), 63–68. [Sh.B.]

LICHTENBAUM, JOSEPH (1895–1968), Hebrew writer. Born in Warsaw, Lichtenbaum moved to Moscow, where he was one of the co-founders of *Habimah in 1918. In 1920 he immigrated to Ereẓ Israel. He published poems and essays on writers and books of both Hebrew and general literature, and also translated a great deal of poetry and prose from world literature. Among his works are: *Sefer ha-Shirim* (1944); *Sha'ul Tchernichowsky* (1946, 1953); *Sofereinu* (1949); *Soferei Yisrael* (1959 and after); *Bi-Netivei Sifrut* (1962), essays and reflections; *Sifrutenu ha-Ḥadashah* (1963), the development of poetry and prose in Hebrew literature; *Meshorerim Olamiyyim* (1966); and *Yosef Ḥayyim Brenner* (1967). He also published anthologies, including: *Ha-Sippur ha-Ivri* ("The Hebrew Story," vol. 1 (1955), from Mapu to Shneur; vol. 2 (1960), from Burla to the present) with an introduction in each volume discussing the development of the Hebrew story; *Tekumah* (1958), Israel poetry and prose, including bibliographical notes; and *Shiratenu* (2 vols. (1962), from M. Ḥ. Luzzatto to Bialik, and from Bialik to the present) including an introduction on the development of modern Hebrew poetry.

Bibliography: Kressel, Leksikon, 2 (1967), 264–6. [G.K.]

°**LICHTENBERG, BERNHARD** (1875–1943), German Catholic priest and anti-Nazi. He served as military chaplain during World War I and was a member of the Berlin municipal council. As early as 1935 he protested against the cruelties in the concentration camps. In 1938 he became provost of St. Hedwig's Cathedral in Berlin. Following the burning of the synagogues in 1938 (see **Kristallnacht*), Lichtenberg used to close his evening services with a prayer for the persecuted Jews. He also protested against the "euthanasia" program. Arrested on Oct. 23, 1941, he insisted on joining the Jews "in the East" to pray for them. In 1942 he was sentenced to two years' imprisonment, and after serving his time, was moved to *Dachau concentration camp, but died on the way (Nov. 5, 1943).

Bibliography: A. Leber, *Conscience in Revolt* (1957), 198–202; G. Lewy, *Catholic Church and Nazi Germany* (1964), index; A. Erb, *Bernhard Lichtenberg, Dompropst von St. Hedwig zu Berlin* (1949).
[Y.Re.]

LICHTENFELD, GABRIEL JUDAH (1811–1887), Hebrew author and mathematician. Born in Lublin, he lived most of his life in Opatow, Poland. Having taught himself sciences and European languages, he wrote for *Ha-Shaḥar, Ha-Ẓefirah, Izraelita,* and Polish newspapers, mostly on mathematical topics. In 1865 he published *Yedi'ot ha-Shi'urim* ("Science of Measurement"), by which a reader might "learn the elements of surveying, without the aid of a teacher." In 1874–75 he published polemic tracts against Ḥ. S. *Slonimski, questioning the latter's competence in scientific matters. With I. L. *Peretz, whose first wife was Lichtenfeld's daughter, he co-edited *Sippurim be-Shir ve-Shirim Shonim me'et Shenei Ba'alei Asufot* ("Stories in Verse and Sundry Poems From Two Anthologists," Warsaw, 1877), incorporating a long original poem by the editors called *Ḥayyei Meshorer Ivri* ("Life of a Hebrew Poet"). Lichtenfeld's book on mathematics, *Bo'u Ḥeshbon,* was published posthumously (1895). Some of the terminology which he coined has been generally accepted.

Bibliography: Rejzen, Leksikon, 2 (1927), 980; Kressel, Leksikon, 2 (1967), 266–7.
[Y.S.]

LICHTENSTADT, ABRAHAM AARON (d. 1702), *Court Jew and *primator* ("leader") of the Bohemian *Landesjudenschaft. Lichtenstadt has been identified with Aaron Schlackenwerth (d. 1694) and also with Abraham Aaron of Frankfort, but Tobias *Jakobovits established that he was the son of the physician Naphtali Hirz Oettingen of Przemysl (Poland). He took his family name from his place of residence, Hroznetin (Lichtenstadt). First mentioned as agent of the court of Saxony, he became the *shtadlan* of Bohemian Jewry in 1673. In 1680 he persuaded *Leopold I to cancel the order expelling the Jews from the Planá community (see *Chodová Planá), and later secured for the Jews the right to attend the Leipzig fairs. He was instrumental in having Abraham *Broda appointed as chief rabbi *(Landesrabbiner)* of Bohemian Jewry in 1689. As a result of internal strife in the Jewish community, he was denounced for abusing his position when determining the allotment of taxes. Legal proceedings were opened in 1692, and although a case could not be established against him, Leopold I removed him from his post and had him, his son Solomon, and the secretary *(Landschreiber)* of the Landesjudenschaft imprisoned. The complicated trial which followed was one of the most prominent of its kind at the time. In 1693 he was released from prison and restored to office in 1701; those who had denounced him were imprisoned.

Bibliography: T. Jakubovits, in: MGWJ, 74 (1930), 35–41; 76 (1932), 511–2; idem, in: JGGJČ, 5 (1933), 79–136, passim.
[M.La.]

LICHTENSTADT, BENJAMIN WOLF BEN JUDAH (c. 1755–1827), Moravian rabbi. Lichtenstadt, a student of R. Joseph Liberles and of R. Ezekiel *Landau of Prague, became the teacher of R. Baruch Jeiteles. He served as rabbi of *Myslice (1787–92) and Neuraussnitz (1792–96) in Moravia, preferring a small-town position in order to have more time for study. Thereafter, he transferred to Hungary, serving as rabbi in Trenčín from 1797 until his death. His *Kedushat Yisrael* (Brno, 1788) is a halakhic work, the first part of which deals with several tractates of the order of *Nashim* and comments on some rabbinic authorities *(posekim)*; the second part (1829) is on the tractate *Gittin.*

Bibliography: J. J. Greenwald, *Ha-Yehudim be-Ungarya* (1912), 49 no. 31; P. Z. Schwartz, *Shem ha-Gedolim me-Ereẓ Hagar,* 1 (1913), 28a no. 7; M. Stein, *Even ha-Me'ir* (1909), 38a no. 192.
[J.H.]

LICHTENSTEIN, HILLEL BEN BARUCH (1815–1891), Hungarian rabbi. Lichtenstein was one of the outstanding pupils of Moses *Sofer. He first served as rabbi of Margarethen and in 1854 was elected rabbi of Kolozsvar, the capital of Transylvania. After 18 months he was compelled to leave the locality without officially assuming office, owing to his opposition to Abraham Friedman, rabbi of Transylvania, and because of the internal frictions in the community which were aggravated as a result. His refusal to go to Gyulafehérvár (*Alba-Julia), where the district rabbi had his seat, to receive his sanction to take up his post, as was then the custom, served as the formal reason for his departure. Between 1865 and 1867 he was rabbi of Szikszó, also in Hungary. He then moved to Galicia and became rabbi of Kolomyya (Kolomea). Lichtenstein was one of the dominant figures of the Orthodox community in their struggle with the reformers both before and after the great schism of 1869. He fought against any suspicion of reform in the life of the Jews, and sharply criticized those Orthodox Jews, including rabbis, who inclined to any kind of innovation in religious practices. He especially attacked those who attempted to preach in German, and even censured Azriel *Hildesheimer on this account. Lichtenstein's pupils also served as uncompromising fighters against religious reforms. At rabbinical conventions in Hungary, called on his initiative, the main principles of extremist Orthodoxy for Hungarian Jewry were laid down. The first convention of this kind assembled in Sátoraljaújhely in 1864 but the main one took place in 1866 in Nagymihály (Michalovce) where resolutions were adopted excommunicating Reform Judaism and any rabbi preaching in German or any other European language. Ten *takkanot* were also enacted, which to this day serve as the basis of the separation between Orthodox Jews and reformers in Hungary. Lichtenstein wrote many books, including *Maskil el Dal,* 4 parts, sermons (1860–69); *Shirei Maskil,* on ethics (1877); *Avkat Rokhel,* responsa, 2 parts (1883–85); and *Et La'asot,* in Yiddish, on ethics, 2 parts (1878).

Bibliography: Aaron of Nadvornaya, *Zekher Ẓaddik* (1891); Z. H. Heller, *Beit Hillel* (1893); Rejzen, Leksikon, 2 (1927), 147–50; N. M. Gelber, in: *Pinkas Kolomey* (1957), 41–48.
[Y.Mar.]

LICHTENSTEIN, WALTER (1880–1964), U.S. educator, economist, and public official. Lichtenstein, who was born in Brunswick, Germany, was taken to the U.S. at the age of two. He served as editor of the *New International Encyclopaedia* (1902–03) and curator of Harvard University's Hohenzollern Collection (1905–06). From 1908 to 1919 he was again curator of the collection and also held the positions of associate professor (1908–11) and professor of history (1911–18) at Northwestern University, Evanston, Illinois. Although Lichtenstein, in the course of his career, was consultant to several large U.S. companies and a longtime officer of the First National Bank of Chicago, he also had an extensive public service career. His positions included: secretary to the Federal Advisory Council of the Federal Reserve System (1926–48); member of the U.S. Monetary Plan Commission (1936–54); and economic adviser to the American Military Government for Germany (1945–47). Lichtenstein edited a number of historical works, including *Ulrich Zwingli, Latin and German Works* (1912). [Ed.]

LICHTHEIM, RICHARD (1885–1963), Zionist leader in Germany. Lichtheim was born in Berlin of an assimilated family and completed his studies in economics in Freiburg, where he also joined the Zionist movement. At first he aided the Zionist Organization's Palestine department, which was established in Berlin after the Fifth Zionist Congress (1907). He eventually became one of the outstanding ideologists and publicists in the Zionist movement, and his work *Das Program des Zionismus* (1911, 1913²) made a lasting impression. After D. *Wolffsohn's resignation (1911) and the transfer of the Zionist center to Berlin, Lichtheim became the editor of the central Zionist organ, *Die* **Welt*, and remained in this post until 1913. In that year he went to Constantinople as a representative of the Zionist Executive. At first he worked together with Victor *Jacobson, and when the latter had to leave Constantinople at the outbreak of World War I, Lichtheim, who was a German citizen, remained (until 1917). During that period he did much to curb the physical persecution of the Jews in Ereẓ Israel through the influence of the German and American representatives in the Ottoman capital.

At the end of the war, Lichtheim returned to Germany, and his memoranda on the methods of upbuilding Ereẓ Israel under the British Mandate aroused Chaim *Weizmann's interest. From 1921 to 1923 he was a member of the Zionist Executive and head of its Organization Department. Afterward he left the Executive in opposition to Weizmann's policy, and in 1925 he joined the *Revisionist movement, which he left in 1933 joining for a while the *Jewish State Party which seceded from it. Lichtheim worked in an insurance company in Germany and continued in this field after settling in Palestine in 1934 by establishing the Migdal Insurance Company together with G. *Halpern. He was in Geneva throughout World War II and set up a network of contacts with occupied European countries for the Zionist Organization. At the end of the war, Lichtheim returned to Jerusalem and during his last years wrote his memoirs, *She'ar Yashuv* ("A Remnant Shall Return," 1953), and *Toledot ha-Ẓiyyonut be-Germanyah* ("A History of Zionism in Germany," Heb., 1951, Ger., 1954), and an autobiographical volume *Rueckkehr* (1970), on his activities in Zionist diplomacy before World War I. [G.K.]

Richard Lichtheim, German Zionist leader. Photo David Harris, Jerusalem.

His son, GEORGE LICHTHEIM (1912–), historian and political scientist, was born in Berlin and in 1933 went to Jerusalem, where he spent most of the Hitler years as foreign editor of the *Jerusalem Post* and as a translator. From 1946 he lived in London, except for two periods spent in the U.S. as associate editor of *Commentary* (1957–58) and as visiting lecturer and research associate at Columbia and Stanford universities (1964–66). Besides serving as London editor of *Commentary* from 1960 and as a correspondent for the *Jerusalem Post*, he was a leading scholar in the fields of socialism and political science, and has contributed to a number of leading scholarly and intellectual publications. His works include: *Marxism, an Historical and Critical Study* (1964²), *Europe and America* (1963), *The New Europe* (1963), *Marxism and Modern France* (1966), and *The Concept of Ideology and Other Essays* (1967). [I.R.]

Bibliography: A. Ruppin, *Pirkei Ḥayyai* (1969), passim; G. Herlitz, in: *Ha-Olam*, (Feb. 15, 1945); P. Rosen, in: *Ha-Boker* (June 7, 1963); Tidhar, 11 (1961), 3786–87.

LICHTSTEIN, ABRAHAM BEN ELIEZER LIPMAN (18th–19th century), Polish rabbi. He functioned as rabbi in Wolkowysk, Lida, and Przasnysz, and as *dayyan* and preacher of the small town of Lask where he went to have more leisure to devote himself to his scholarly endeavors. Lichtstein is the author of the following works: *Kanfei Nesharim* (1881), a commentary on the Pentateuch containing explanations and homilies, some of them inspired by Naḥmanides, Gersonides, and Isaac Arama; *Ammudei Shamayim* (Warsaw, 1803), a commentary on Maimonides' formulation of the 13 articles of faith; *Ge'ullat Olam* (Grodno, 1822) on the *Haggadah; Iggeret ha-Ẓofeh* (Bialystok, 1806), a commentary on the *Halakhot* of Isaac Alfasi, explaining the latter's methodology; *Or ha-Even* (Sklow, 1822) on religious ethics and morals; and a commentary on the pseudo-Aristotelian *Sefer ha-Tappu'aḥ*. A commentary of his on Alfasi is still in manuscript.

Bibliography: Steinschneider, Uebersetzungen, 1 (1893), 268; P. Z. Glicksman, *Ir Lask va-Ḥakhameha* (1926), 66–68. [J.H.]

LICHTSTEIN, ABRAHAM JEKUTHIEL ZALMAN BEN MOSES JOSEPH (second half of 18th century), Polish rabbi. Lichtstein served as *av bet din* of Plonsk (Warsaw district). He was the author of *Zera Avraham*, an extensive commentary to the *Sifrei* (pt. 1 to Numbers, Dyhrenfurth, 1811; pt. 2 to Deuteronomy, Radzivil, 1820). It gives the source references to biblical verses in the text under the title *Mikra Meforash*, and to talmudic parallels, under the title *Mevo ha-Talmud*. The work was completed in 1788, but was published posthumously by his son Moses, who also added the glosses of a Jerusalem manuscript by a Sephardi scholar as well as his own additions. Lichtstein's introduction to the *Divrei Kohelet* (Nowy Dwor, 1785) of his son Solomon, who died in his youth, was also published by Moses. It contains expositions of Maimonides' *Mishneh Torah*, novellae on the laws of **terefah* and the Talmud, a eulogy of his son called *Emek ha-Bakha*, and novellae by Moses called *Darash Moshe*.

Bibliography: A. Walden, *Shem ha-Gedolim he-Ḥadash*, 1 (1864), 2b no. 47; 2 (1864), 14b no. 29; S. Wiener, *Kohelet Moshe* (1918), 272 no. 2237; S. Hazan, *Ha-Ma'alot li-Shelomo* (1899), 29a; *Sifri . . . im Be'ur . . . Emek ha-Neẓiv me'et . . . N. Z. J. Berlin*, 1 (1959), 325n. [Y.Ho.]

LIDA, town in Grodno oblast, Belorussian S.S.R. According to a decision of the Lithuanian council (see *Councils of the Lands) of 1623, the Jewish community of Lida was subordinated to the Grodno *kahal*. The files of the Lithuanian financial commission contain records of the quarrels between the Lida *kahal* and the Jews of the neighboring villages. In 1766 there were 1,167 Jewish poll-tax payers in Lida and the vicinity. The community numbered 567 (73.6% of the total population) in 1817; 1,980 in 1847; 5,166 (68%) in 1897, when there were 24,813 Jews (12%) in the whole district; and 5,419 (40.4%) in the town, with 16,551 (8.5%) in the district in 1921. In the 1880s the 13 prayerhouses in the town were grouped in one large square; they were all damaged in a fire. Until World War II the butchers' synagogue contained an Ark with undamaged ancient doors. In 1921, there were 302 Jewish workshops in Lida, over half of them family enterprises. There were 37 Jewish farms in 1927. Between the two world wars the community maintained a secular elementary school and a children's home, both affiliated to the Central Yiddish School Organization. There was also a *Tarbut school.

Among rabbis of Lida were R. *David b. Aryeh Leib of Lida (later in Amsterdam), his son Pethahiah, and his grandson, the *zaddik* David Benjamin. R. Elijah Schick (Elinke Lider) officiated in the 19th century, and I. J. *Reines, the Mizrachi leader, at the beginning of the 20th century. The latter founded a modern yeshivah in Lida which functioned until World War I. [EJ]

Holocaust Period. In 1940 the number of Jews in Lida had risen to 15,000. During the period of Soviet rule (1939–41), Jewish community institutions were closed, the activities of Jewish parties was forbidden, and the basis of the Jewish economy from the prewar period was demolished. A large part of the Jewish refugees from western Poland who found shelter in Lida were deported to the Soviet interior in the summer of 1940. Groups of deportees were brought to Soviet camps in the Rybinsk area. With the outbreak of the war between Germany and the U.S.S.R. (June 22, 1941), the Germans bombed Lida; the center of the town, which was inhabited principally by Jews, was burned, and there were hundreds of Jewish casualties. On July 5, 1941, the Germans collected the Jews of the city in the main square and took away all the rabbis, *shohatim*, doctors, and teachers—the leadership of the community—to near the village of Stoniewicze where they were murdered; 200 men fell at that time. In the autumn of 1941 the Jews were concentrated in a special quarter and were joined by the Jews from Lipniszki, Juraciszki, Traby, and Duoly. On May 8, 1942, an *Aktion* was carried out. Only 1,250 people were left; all the rest were killed near the village of Stoniewicze. About 200 people succeeded in escaping the scene of the slaughter, returned to the ghetto, and told of the Germans' horrifying acts. A group of youths succeeded in leaving the city on May 21, 1942 and entered the forests of Naliboki. The youth in the ghetto also organized and armed themselves with weapons. At the end of 1942 contact was established with the partisans in the *Novogrudok area. The Jewish partisans from Lida fought with the unit of an experienced Jewish fighter, Tuvia Bielski, and another unit called "Iskra." The ghetto was destroyed on Sept. 17–19, 1943. The city was liberated on July 5, 1944, and about 300 Jews were rescued. Most of those who had been with the partisans were mobilized into the Soviet army and continued to fight in Germany until the end of the war.

In the mid-1950s the Jewish cemetery was confiscated and converted into a building site. The Jewish population of the town in 1970 was estimated at a few families. [AR.W.]

Bibliography: S. Dubnow (ed.), *Pinkas ha-Medinah* (1925), index; Vilenskaya Kommissiya dlya razbora drevnikh aktov, *Akty*, 29 (1902), nos. 183, 206; *Słownik geograficzny Królestwa Polskigo*, s.v.; B. Wasiutyński, *Ludność żydowska w Polsce*... (1930), 80, 84, 87; Jewish Colonization Association, *Rapport pour l'année 1928;* Yad Vashem Archives.

LIDIN (Gomberg), VLADIMIR GERMANOVICH (1894–), Soviet Russian novelist. Born and educated in Moscow, Lidin began his literary career in 1915. His first collection of short stories, published on the eve of the Revolution, described the Russian intelligentsia and was markedly influenced by Chekhov, Bunin, and Maupassant. *Idut korabli* ("The Ships are Sailing," 1926) is of interest primarily as a document of life in the new Russia's demimonde and is reminiscent of L. L. Leonov's *Vor* ("The Thief," 1927). Varied backgrounds continued to attract Lidin in later years. *Mogila neizvestnogo soldata* ("The Tomb of the Unknown Soldier," 1932) is set in Paris in the 1920s, while *Velikii ili Tikhii* ("The Great or the Silent," i.e., the Pacific, 1933) describes the fishermen and reindeer breeders of the Soviet Far East. During World War II Lidin was a war correspondent. Lidin's two postwar novels, *Izgnaniye* ("Exile," 1947) and *Dve zhizni* ("Two Lives," 1950), are undistinguished, and his memoirs, *Lyudi i vstrechi* ("People I Have Met," 1962) are very circumspect and far less revealing than those of some of his contemporaries, such as Ilya *Ehrenburg and Samuel *Marshak.

Bibliography: *Russkiye Sovetskiye Pisateli Prozaiki*, 2 (1964), index. [M.F.]

LIDZBARSKI, MARK (Abraham Mordecai; 1868–1928), Semitist. Lidzbarski was born in Plock, Russian Poland, and received a strict Orthodox education. At 14 he ran away from home and went to Posen, Prussian Poland, where he studied at the gymnasium. He continued his studies at the University of Berlin, living in difficult conditions. As a student he converted to Protestantism. In 1896 he began lecturing in oriental languages at the University of Kiel; in 1907, at the University of Greifswald, and in 1917, at the University of Goettingen. He was a corresponding member of the Goettingen Gesellschaft der Wissenschaften from 1912 to 1918, when he became an ordinary member.

Lidzbarski was a scholar of high repute in several branches of Semitic studies. He may be considered the founder of Semitic epigraphy; several of his articles and books are still standard works in this field, including *Die neuaramaeischen Handschriften der Koeniglichen Bibliothek zu Berlin* (2 vols., in 3, 1896), *Handbuch der nordsemitischen Epigraphik* 2 vols., 1898, repr. 1962), *Ephemeris fuer semitische Epigraphik* (3 vols., 1900–15), and *Kanaanaeische Inschriften* (1907) in the series *Altsemitische Texte.* His contribution to the 29th edition of Gesenius' *Hebraeische Grammatik* is of major importance. Lidzbarski also contributed much to Mandean studies. His theory that the gnostic Mandeans originated in Palestine in pre-Christian times was in vogue among scholars for a time but is no longer accepted. However, his editions of the Mandean texts *Das Johannesbuch der Mandaeer* (2 vols., 1905–15, repr. 1966), *Mandaeische Liturgien:* in the series *Abhandlungen der Koeniglichen Gesellschaft der Wissenschaften zu Goettingen* (1920, repr. 1962), and *Altaramaeische Urkunden aus Assur:* in the series *Wissenschaftliche Veroeffentlichungen der Deutschen Orient-Gesellschaft* (1921) have made these accessible to scholars. Lidzbarski's autobiography, *Auf rauhem Wege* (1927), was published anonymously.

Bibliography: W. Baumgartner, in: *Neue Zuercher Zeitung* (July 14, 1968), 51. [D.D.]

LIEBEN, ADOLPH (1836–1914), Austrian organic chemist. Born in Vienna, he went to work with C. A. Wurtz in Paris, and then became professor of chemistry successively

Detail from a bust of Adolph Lieben, Austrian chemist. Courtesy Photo Archive of the Austrian National Library, Vienna.

in Palermo (1864), Turin (1867), the German University of Prague (1871), and finally Vienna (1875). He discovered the iodoform test for alcohol and ketones, did pioneering work on aliphatic alcohols, on the aldol reaction and other condensation reactions of aldehydes, and on chelidonic acid. He was made a member of the Austrian upper chamber, and was vice-president of the German Chemical Society. When he retired, a *Festschrift* was published in his honor.

Bibliography: *Festschrift Adolf Lieben zur Feier des siebzigsten Geburstages*... (1906); M. Kohn, in: *Journal of Chemical Education*, 20 (1943), 471–3; 22 (1945), 562–4; *Oesterreichische Chemiker-Zeitung*, 59 (1958), 262; 60 (1959), 220. [S.A.M.]

LIEBEN, KOPPELMANN (1811–1892), Prague scholar and bibliophile. Lieben, who was on the board of the Jewish community and a member of the assembly of notables convened in 1850 by the governor of Bohemia, earned his living as registrar of the community and actuary of the *ḥevra kaddisha*. With Simon *Hock he published in 1856 a collection of tombstone inscriptions from the old Prague cemetery Gal-Ed, and 100 biographies of outstanding personalities buried in Volšany (Wolschan) cemetery in Prague. This collection, *Die Eroeffnung des zweiten Israelitischen Wolschaner Friedhofes* (ed. D. Lieben, 1890), is a valuable source for the history of Prague in the first half of the 19th century. Lieben willed his valuable library to the community. Because of his strict adherence to German, Lieben was attacked by the Czech-speaking Jews.

See *Čechů-Židů, Svaz. [Ed.]

LIEBEN, ROBERT VON (1878–1913), scientist and inventor. He was born in Vienna, where his father, vice-governor of the Austro-Hungarian state bank, was ennobled. Lieben went to work at the Institute for Physical Chemistry in Goettingen, Germany, where he studied under Walter Nernst, a founder of modern physical chemistry. Later he worked in his own laboratory, where he built a private telephone system. In 1906 he invented the amplifying valve and in 1910 the grid tube (with Eugen Resz and Siegmund Strauss as co-inventors). This led directly to modern radio and later developments in electronics such as sound tracks for films and television. In 1936 the Austrian Government issued a stamp commemorating his contribution to research in the field of sound. Lieben had little contact with the Jewish community and referred to himself as an atheist.

Robert von Lieben's invention of the amplifying valve, commemorated by the Austrian postal service, 1936. Jerusalem, B. M. Ansbacher Collection.

Bibliography: H. von Hoffmannsthal, *Die prosaischen Schriften gesammelt*, 3 (1917), 48–53; W. Nerst, in: *Telefunken Zeitung*, 6 (1923); S. Kaznelson, *Juden im Deutschen Kulturbereich* (1959), 412–31. [Ed.]

LIEBEN, SALOMON (1884–1942), Prague physician and communal functionary. A member of *Agudat Israel, Lieben represented Orthodox Jews on the board of the Prague community. With the establishment of Czechoslovakia in 1918, he cooperated with the Zionists and joined the Jewish National Council. He was one of the moving spirits behind the foundation of the Židovská ústředna pro sociální péči (Central Jewish Welfare Board) in 1932. As a military physician in Galicia during World War I, he organized Jewish welfare activities there, and then in Prague for refugees from Eastern Europe. He founded a Jewish outpatients clinic and a soup kitchen, and was among the administrators of several charitable institutions. Lieben conducted scientific research in defense of *sheḥitah against the numerous "humanitarian" attacks on it throughout Europe, publishing several papers in veterinary and medical periodicals claiming that *sheḥitah* is the least cruel method of slaughtering animals. When the Nazis entered Prague in 1939 and ordered the immediate expulsion of Jewish patients from the general hospitals, Lieben organized a hospital in the Jewish orphanage. He also saw to the religious needs of Prague Jews, organizing, for example, the illegal distribution of unleavened bread. In 1942 he was deported with his family to a concentration camp, where he died.

Bibliography: *Dos Yidishe Vort*, 16 no. 139 (1970), 27–29. [M.La.]

LIEBEN, SALOMON HUGO (1881–1942), historian of Bohemian Jewry, cousin of Salomon *Lieben. Lieben received his general and Jewish education in his native Prague and taught religion in Prague German-language secondary schools. In 1906 he founded and directed the Prague Jewish museum in the *ohel tohorah* ("the purification hall") of the old cemetery, around which the Nazis later ordered the organization of the Central Jewish Museum (now the Prague State Jewish Museum; see *Museums, Jewish); Lieben was among its scientific workers. He published research papers on Bohemian Jewish history in many Jewish scientific publications, concentrating on its outstanding personalities and events, such as David *Oppenheim, Ezekiel b. Judah *Landau, Eleazar *Fleckeles, Jewish printing in Prague, and the expulsion by *Maria Theresa (1745). He exposed the Ramshak chronicle, allegedly from the *Hussite period, as a falsification by Marcus Fischer (see Moses *Fischer). On the board of the Society for the History of the Jews in Czechoslovakia and coeditor of its yearbooks (JGGJČ) and of *Die Juden in Prag* (1927), he edited *Die juedischen Denkmaeler in der Tschechoslowakei* (1933) and collaborated with Hugo *Gold in editing his books on the communities of Bohemia and Moravia. Lieben died in Prague.

Bibliography: O. Muneles, *Bibliographical Survey of Jewish Prague* (1958), contains list of his publications; H. Volavková, *Story of the Jewish Museum in Prague* (1968), passim. [M.La.]

LIEBERMAN, CHAIM (Herman; 1890–1963), Yiddish essayist and literary critic. Born in Kolki (Volhynia) he emigrated to the U.S. in 1905. His first articles, on education, appeared in the New York Yiddish daily *Tageblatt*. On the eve of World War I, he helped to found the Farband's Yiddish secular schools and the Jewish Teachers' Seminary affiliated with the Farband. He taught Yiddish and Yiddish literature and espoused Labor Zionism. Lieberman's critical articles on Jewish and non-Jewish writers, combining vast knowledge and enthusiastic, positive appraisals, were collected in three volumes (1923, 1924, 1930). In the 1930s Lieberman underwent a spiritual crisis, became extremely pious, and joined the religious Zionists. His former fervent championship of writers he liked gave way to sharp and cutting polemics against writers he disliked. He began with attacks on Jewish pro-communists, proceeded to assail Chaim *Zhitlowsky and S. *Niger, and reached a climax of vituperation in his articles and books against Sholem *Asch's christological novels, which were translated into English as *The Christianity of Sholem Asch* (1953). There followed attacks upon Satmar Ḥasidim because of their anti-Israel approach, *Der Rebe un der Sotn* ("Rabbi and Satan," 1959); against the American Council of Judaism, published in English as *Strangers to Glory* (1955); and, finally, ten articles against Ben *Hecht, published in English translation in book form (*The Man and his "Perfidy,"* 1964).

Bibliography: LNYL, 5 (1963), 66–71; J. Glatstein, *In Tokh Genumen* (1947), 428–34; A. B. Shurin, *Keshet Gibborim* (1964), 147–52. [SH.B.]

LIEBERMAN, ELIAS (1883–1969), U.S. educator and poet. Lieberman, who was born in St. Petersburg, Russia, went with his family to the United States at the age of seven. He began teaching in the New York public school system in 1903. Lieberman served as principal of Thomas Jefferson High School in Brooklyn from 1924 to 1940, and then as associate superintendent of schools. He published four volumes of poetry and was a contributor to various periodicals. His patriotic poem "I am an American," which first appeared in 1916, has been reprinted in numerous anthologies and school books. Among the literary magazines that he at one time helped edit were *Puck, Current Literature*, and *The American Hebrew*. [H.H.]

LIEBERMAN, HERMAN (1870–1941), Polish lawyer and Socialist politician. Born in Drogobycz, Galicia, into an assimilated family, Lieberman joined the Polish Socialist Party of Galicia and Silesia and became one of its leaders. In 1907 he entered the Austrian parliament, where he was considered one of its most gifted speakers. During World War I he fought in the Polish Legion on the Russian front. When Poland regained her independence at the end of the war, he became a member of its parliament (1919–30), and was one of the authors of the democratic constitution of 1921. He was a member of the Central Council of the Polish Socialist Party from 1920 to 1929. He was a noted advocate, and distinguished himself as defense counsel in the famous case of Polish legionnaires in Mármaras-sziget (Sighet) in 1918. After the Pilsudski coup d'état in 1926, Lieberman led the opposition to the regime in parliament. In 1930 he was sentenced to three years' imprisonment, but escaped to Czechoslovakia and later went to France. He was the spokesman for the radical wing of the Polish Socialist Party in exile and cooperated with the Communists in organizing help for the Republicans during the Spanish Civil War. In 1940 he moved to London and a year later was appointed minister of justice in the Polish government-in-exile, thus becoming the first Jew in a Polish cabinet. [A.WE.]

Sketch of Herman Lieberman, Polish lawyer and Socialist politician. Jerusalem, J.N.U.L., Schwadron Collection.

LIEBERMAN, MYRON (1919–), U.S. educator. Lieberman was instrumental in raising and protecting the status of the teacher. Born in St. Paul, Minnesota, he taught at the universities of Illinois and Oklahoma, and was appointed chairman of the department of education at Yeshiva University. In 1963 he became chairman of the professional studies division, Rhode Island College, and from 1965 directed its educational research and development. He was author and coauthor of a number of books, monographs, and articles, including (jointly with M. Moskow) *Collective Negotiations for Teachers...* (1966), *Education as a Profession* (1956), and *The Future of Public Education* (1960). He contended that national professional groups should replace local school boards as arbitrators of educational problems. [R.E.O.]

LIEBERMAN, SAUL (1898–), talmudic scholar. Born in Motol, near Pinsk, Belorussia, he studied at the yeshivot of Malch and Slobodka. In the 1920s he attended the University of Kiev, and, following a short stay in Palestine, continued his studies in France. In 1928 he settled in Jerusalem. He studied talmudic philology and Greek language and literature at the Hebrew University, where he was appointed lecturer in Talmud in 1931. He also taught at the Mizrachi Teachers Seminary and from 1935 was dean of the Harry Fischel Institute for Talmudic Research in Jerusalem. In 1940 he was invited by the Jewish Theological Seminary of America to serve as professor of Palestinian literature and institutions. Nine years later he was appointed dean, and in 1958 rector, of the Seminary's rabbinical school.

Combining vast erudition in all fields of talmudic and rabbinic literature with a penetrating knowledge of the classical world, Lieberman opened new pathways to the understanding of the life, institutions, beliefs, and literary products of Jewish Palestine in the talmudic period.

He made his debut in scholarly literature in 1929 with the publication of *Al ha-Yerushalmi*, in which he suggested ways of emending corruptions in the text of the Jerusalem (Palestinian) Talmud and offered variant readings to the text of the tractate of *Sotah*. This was followed by: a series of text studies of the Jerusalem Talmud, which appeared in *Tarbiz*; by *Talmudah shel Keisaryah* (1931), in which he expressed the view that the first three tractates of the order *Nezikin* in the Jerusalem Talmud had been compiled in Caesarea about the middle of the fourth century C.E.; and by *Ha-Yerushalmi ki-Feshuto* (1934), a commentary on the treatises *Shabbat, Eruvin*, and *Pesaḥim* of the Jerusalem Talmud.

His preoccupation with the Jerusalem Talmud impressed him with the necessity of clarifying the text of the tannaitic sources, especially that of the Tosefta, on which no commentaries had been composed by the earlier authorities and to whose elucidation only few scholars had devoted themselves in later generations.

In the comparatively short period of three years (1937–39) he published the four-volume *Tosefet Rishonim*, a commentary on the entire Tosefta with textual corrections based on manuscripts, early printings, and quotations found in early authorities. During that period he also published *Tashlum Tosefta*, an introductory chapter to the second edition of M. S. *Zuckermandel's Tosefta edition (1937), dealing with quotations from the Tosefta by early authorities that are not found in the text.

Years later, Lieberman returned to the systematic elucidation of the Tosefta. He undertook the publication of

Saul Lieberman, talmudic scholar. Courtesy Jewish Theological Seminary, New York.

the Tosefta text, based on manuscripts and accompanied by brief explanatory notes, and of an extensive commentary called *Tosefta ki-Feshutah*. The latter combined philological research and historical observations with a discussion of the entire talmudic and rabbinic literature in which the relevant Tosefta text is either commented upon or quoted. Between 1955 and 1967 ten volumes of the new edition appeared, representing the text and the commentaries on the orders of *Zera'im* and *Mo'ed* and on part of the order of *Nashim*.

In *Sifrei Zuta* (1968), Lieberman advanced the view that this halakhic Midrash was in all likelihood finally edited by Bar Kappara in Lydda.

His two English volumes, which also appeared in a Hebrew translation, *Greek in Jewish Palestine* (1942) and *Hellenism in Jewish Palestine* (1950), illustrate the influence of Hellenistic culture on Jewish Palestine in the first centuries C.E.

Other books of his were *Sheki'in* (1939), on Jewish legends, customs, and literary sources found in Karaite and Christian polemical writings, and *Midreshei Teiman* (1940), wherein he showed that the Yemenite Midrashim had preserved exegetical material which had been deliberately omitted by the rabbis. He edited a variant version of the *Midrash Rabbah* on Deuteronomy (1940, 1965²). In his view that version had been current among Sephardi Jewry, while the standard text had been that of Ashkenazi Jewry. In 1947 he published *Hilkhot ha-Yerushalmi* which he identified as a fragment of a work by Maimonides on the Jerusalem Talmud. Lieberman also edited the hitherto unpublished Tosefta commentary *Ḥasdei David* by David *Pardo on the order *Tohorot*. The first part of this work appeared in 1970.

A number of his works have appeared in new and revised editions. Lieberman served as editor in chief of a new critical edition of Maimonides' *Mishneh Torah* (vol. 1, 1964), and as an editor of the Judaica series of Yale University. He also edited several scholarly miscellanies.

He contributed numerous studies to scholarly publications as well as notes to books of fellow scholars. In these he dwelt on various aspects of the world of ideas of the rabbis, shed light on events in the talmudic period, and elucidated scores of obscure words and expressions of talmudic and midrashic literature.

He was for many years president of the American Academy for Jewish Research. He was an honorary member of the Academy for the Hebrew Language, a fellow of the American Academy of Arts and Sciences, and a fellow of the Israel Academy of Sciences and Humanities. In 1971 he was awarded the Israel Prize for Jewish Studies.

His wife, JUDITH LIEBERMAN (1904–), was a daughter of Rabbi Meir Berlin (*Bar-Ilan), leader of the Mizrachi. She served from 1941 first as Hebrew principal and then as dean of Hebrew studies of Shulamith School for Girls in New York, the first Jewish day school for girls in North America. Among her publications were *Robert Browning and Hebraism* (1934), and an autobiographical chapter which was included in *Thirteen Americans, Their Spiritual Autobiographies* (1953), edited by L. Finkelstein.

Bibliography: E. S. Rosenthal, in: PAAJR, 31 (1963), 1–71 (Heb.); idem, in: *Hadoar*, 43 no. 23 (1963); T. Preschel, *Dr. Sha'ul Lieberman*... (Heb., 1963); A. Marx, in: *Proceedings of the Rabbinical Assembly of America*, 12 (1949).

[T.P.]

LIEBERMANN, AARON SAMUEL (known as **Bar Derora, Daniel Ish Ḥamudot, Arthur Freeman**; 1845–1880), pioneer of Jewish Socialism and Hebrew writer. He was born in Lunna, Lithuania, the son of Eliezer Dov Liebermann, scholar, *maskil*, and Hebrew author. His family moved to Bialystok and from there to Suwalki. He obtained his teacher's diploma at Vilna (1867), and returned to Suwalki, where he was appointed secretary of the community and teacher. In 1870 he enrolled as an occasional student at the Technological Institute of St. Petersburg. While there he wrote a geography of Ereẓ Israel, but the manuscript was destroyed. In his distress he returned to Vilna, where he worked with an insurance company and in draftsmanship, while continuing to show talent in graphics and drawing. From 1872 he was one of the most active leaders of the local revolutionary group, whose ranks included the future noted members of the Narodnaya Volya, A. *Zundelewicz and V. *Jochelson, and the future Hebrew authors L. Davidowicz and J. E. Triwosch. In this circle Liebermann already evinced enthusiastic attachment to the Hebrew language, and it was there that his idea of initiating special Socialist activities among the Jews was born. When the group was discovered by the authorities in 1875, Liebermann escaped abroad. He joined Socialist circles in Berlin and then moved to London, where he worked as a typesetter for the Socialist periodical *Vpered*, its editors P. Lavrov and V. Smirnov supporting his projects both in theory and in practice. In the articles which Liebermann published in *Vpered* on Vilna and Bialystok (1875–76), he also described the life of Jewish workers in the region. He pointed out progressive social elements in ancient Jewish culture, and in his propaganda sought to employ messianic themes. In January 1876 he

Aaron Samuel Liebermann, pioneer of Jewish Socialism. Jerusalem, J.N.U.L., Schwadron Collection.

drew up regulations for the establishment of a Socialist-revolutionary organization among the Jews of Russia, and in May of that year he founded the *Aguddat ha-Soẓyalistim ha-Ivrim in London. In a Hebrew manifesto addressed to the *shelomei emunei Yisrael* ("wholesome and faithful Jews"; summer 1876), which was also translated and published in *Vpered*. Liebermann dissociated himself from the assimilationist Socialist intelligentsia who were out of touch with the people. He regarded the supporters of Socialism among the working classes or the *maskilim*, who were close to the people, as the potential principal activists of the movement and in this respect placed much hope in students of the yeshivot. Liebermann also contributed to the German-language Socialist press. At the beginning of 1877 he settled in Vienna, and that summer published three issues of his monthly **Ha-Emet*, writing most of the articles himself. Their publication aroused considerable interest in the Hebrew press. He formed and led a group of authors who shared his views, such as J. L. *Levin (Yehalal), M. Kamyonski, I. *Kaminer, Ẓevi ha-Kohen Scherschewski, and M. Adelman-Meyuḥas. He established contact with supporters in southern Russia and succeeded in moderating the extremist anti-Jewish outlook prevailing among Ukrainian Socialists in Vienna. When *Ha-Emet* ceased to appear, Liebermann contributed to the newspapers published by P. *Smolenskin, *Ha-Mabbit* and *Ha-Shaḥar*, in which he published as early as 1874 a story, *Ḥazut ha-Kol*, criticizing organized Jewish life, the exploitation of the poor by rich Jews, and the *maskilim* who derided Jewish tradition. After being imprisoned and tried in Austria for revolutionary activities (February 1878–January 1879) he was expelled to Germany. There he was immediately arrested, and at the end of the year was expelled and reached London. His endeavors to participate in the activities of the Narodnaya Volya were unsuccessful. In the summer of 1880 he established, in conjunction with *Vinchevsky, the short-lived Jewish Workingmen's Benefit and Educational Society. In 1880 Liebermann followed the woman he loved to the United States, but she refused to leave her husband. In New York he was associated with the Agudat Shoḥarei Sefat Ever. Subsequently he committed suicide. In 1934 his remains were buried next to those of Vinchevsky in the cemetery of the Arbeter Ring (Workmen's Circle) in New York.

Liebermann was influenced by cosmopolitan ideas. He was nevertheless imbued with Jewish consciousness and a sense of responsibility toward the fate of the Jewish masses. He interpreted the Narodniks' principle of "going to the people" as going out to the Jewish people. He was depressed when his projects for Jewish Socialist activity clashed with the prejudices against Jewish "parasitism" and "exploitation" he encountered within the Russian revolutionary movement, while on the other hand his activity found little response among the Jewish public. It was not until several decades after his death that the personality of Liebermann was fully appreciated. His memory was particularly revived with the establishment of the labor movement in Ereẓ Israel.

Bibliography: D. Weinryb, *Be-Reshit ha-Soẓyalizm ha-Yehudi* (with Eng. summary, 1940); Ẓ. Kroll, *Ha-Rishon* (1945); K. Marmor (ed.), *Aron Libermans Briv* (1951); Klausner, Sifrut, 5 (1949), index; 6 (1958²), 220–74; LNYL, 5 (1963), 61–65; Leksikon, 2 (1967), 254–8; B. Sapir, in: *International Review of Social History*, 10 no. 3 (1965), 1–20; A. Patkin, *The Origins of the Russian Jewish Labour Movement* (1945), index.

[M.M.]

LIEBERMANN, CARL THEODOR (1842–1914), German organic chemist. He did research in his native Berlin with Adolf von Baeyer, and in 1873 succeeded him as professor at the Gewerbeinstitut, which grew into the Berlin Technische Hochschule. Liebermann's main field was dyestuffs, and he worked out the synthesis of alizarin, an industry which came to be worth hundreds of millions of marks to Germany. He worked on azo dyes, naphthalene, naphthoquinone, anthracene, chrysene, and the constitution of natural dyestuffs. He also worked on alkaloids. A list of his numerous publications was collected in the *Festschrift* produced in honor of his 70th birthday. Liebermann was president of the German Chemical Society.

Carl Theodor Liebermann, German organic chemist. Jerusalem, J.N.U.L., Schwadron Collection.

Bibliography: *Berichte der deutschen chemischen Gesellschaft*, 48 (1915), 4f.; Wallach, *ibid.*, 51 (1918), 1135–60; Bistrzycki, in: *Chemiker Zeitung*, 39 (1915), 165–7.

[S.A.M.]

LIEBERMANN, FELIX (1851–1925), medievalist, brother of Max *Liebermann, the artist. Born in Berlin, he was on the editorial staff of the *Monumenta Germaniae Historica* (1877–85) and worked on the edition of English historical sources for vols. 11 and 27 of its *Scriptores* series. He edited volume 28, which contains excerpts from English sources relating to 13th-century German history. Liebermann also published *Ungedruckte anglo-normannische Geschichtsquellen* (1879) and a number of articles on related subjects. His numerous studies on early English law published from 1893 through 1902 culminated in his most important work, *Die Gesetze der Angelsachsen* (3 vols., 1898). Another study was *The National Assembly in the Anglo-Saxon Period* (1913).

Bibliography: H. D. Hazeltine, *Felix Liebermann 1851–1925* (1939); Davis, in: *English Historical Review*, 41 (1926), 91–97; *Festgabe fuer F. Liebermann . . .* (1921).

[H.Wi.]

Portrait of Felix Liebermann by Jan Pieter Veth, 1905. Jerusalem, J.N.U.L., Schwadron Collection.

LIEBERMANN, MAX (1847–1935), German painter. Liebermann, the son of a Berlin industrialist, studied at the Weimar Academy. He was only 23 when his picture of *The Boy Jesus in Dispute with the Rabbis* was attacked by critics, some of whom appear to have been motivated by anti-Semitism. Two years later his *Women Plucking Geese* received high praise when it was exhibited in Hamburg and Berlin.

Liebermann was a very Nordic painter. Photographic naturalism was as abhorrent to him as expressionism, and although he has often been called an impressionist he never regarded himself as one. He spent much of his life in Holland and was heavily influenced by its gray skies. He used cool, austere colors to paint the bleak, flat Netherlands landscapes in which he discovered the excitement of changing atmosphere, sunlight intermingling with mist,

Self-portrait by the German painter, Max Liebermann, 1920. Oil on canvas, 30×20 in. (75×50 cm.). Jerusalem, Israel Museum. Photo David Harris, Jerusalem.

blue hazes, and empty spaces. While his early work tended to be static, he gradually loosened up as regards form and color, reversing the traditional pattern by growing freer and more spontaneous as he became older. In his fifties he began painting athletes in action, rearing horses, and the colorful vegetable markets of the Amsterdam Jewish quarter.

In 1898 Liebermann became a member of the Berlin Academy and helped to found Sezession, an association of progressive artists. In 1920 he became president of the Berlin Academy of Art. His *Gesammelte Schriften* ("Collected Writings") appeared in 1922. By this time he was too frail for his regular trips to Holland and did much of his painting at his summer home in Wannsee, outside Berlin. He became a celebrated and expensive portraitist, painting his sitters with a broad virtuosity, but not often probing deeply into their personality. Among them were Hermann *Cohen, Georg *Brandes, and Walter *Rathenau. He also did thousands of rapid sketches in pen, pencil, crayon, and chalk.

Liebermann considered himself first and foremost a German and had little interest in Jewish affairs, although he described himself as being "very much aware of belonging to the Jewish people" and as watching the goals of Zionism with "the greatest interest." Apart from his paintings and drawings of the Amsterdam ghetto, virtually his only work on Jewish subjects was a series of lithographs for an edition of Heinrich *Heine's *Rabbi of Bacharach* and two oils on the Samson and Delilah theme. When the Nazis came to power in 1933 he was ousted from presidency of the Academy and his paintings were removed from all German museums. His death two years later was completely ignored by the German press. In 1943 his widow was told that she was to be deported by the Gestapo, and she committed suicide. The Liebermann house in Pariser Platz was looted and its valuable collection of paintings stolen and scattered.

Bibliography: M. J. Friedlaender, *Max Liebermanns graphische Kunst* (1922[2]); K. Scheffler, *Max Liebermann* (Ger., 1953); F. Stuttmann, *Max Liebermann* (Ger., 1961), includes plates; E. Hancke, *Max Liebermann, sein Leben und seine Werke* (1923), includes plates.

[A.W.]

LIEBERT (Levy), ARTHUR (1878–1946), German philosopher. Born in Berlin, he was coeditor of *Kant-Studien*, the publication of the Kant Society. From 1925 to 1933 he was professor of philosophy at the High School for Commercial Sciences, Berlin. When the Nazis came to power, he moved to Belgrade. There he founded and edited *Philosophia*, which appeared from 1936 to 1938. Its purpose was to unite around him the anti-Nazi philosophers. During World War II Liebert lived in England; shortly after the end of the war, he returned to Berlin where he died in 1946. Liebert's philosophy developed from that of the neo-Kantian Marburg school, led by Hermann *Cohen. Liebert's own contribution was that he attached great importance to the concept of "value." Philosophers should be concerned with the "evaluation" of being, and not only its existence. Reality not only exists, but "value" is found in it: it symbolizes something, and its own purpose is concealed in it. Liebert regarded metaphysics as necessary for investigating the totality of being. Through reason's dialectical activity, a metaphysical system is built up, but it can never achieve perfection. In this process, spirit and reason are the basic foundation of life itself. Liebert's major works include: *Das Problem der Geltung* (1914); *Der Geltungswert der Metaphysik* (1915); *Vom Geist der Revolutionen* (1919); *Die geistige Krisis der Gegenwart* (1923); *Die Krise des Idealismus* (1936); *Der universale Humanismus* (1946); *Von der Pflicht der Philosophie in unserer Zeit* (1938). [A.Gr.]

Arthur Liebert, German philosopher. Jerusalem, J.N.U.L., Schwadron Collection.

LIEBMAN, JOSHUA LOTH (1907–1948), U.S. Reform rabbi. Liebman, who was born in Hamilton, Ohio, was ordained by Hebrew Union College in 1930. In 1931,

Liebman took up his first position as rabbi in Lafayette, Indiana. At approximately the same time, he was appointed an instructor at Hebrew Union College. In 1934 he was appointed to Kehilath Anshe Maarab Temple, Chicago,

Bookplate of Joshua Loth Liebman, U.S. Reform rabbi. Courtesy Hebrew Union College, Cincinnati, Ohio.

and in 1939 to Temple Israel in Boston. During his ministry in Boston, Liebman became widely known as a radio preacher. He also taught at Boston University and Andover-Newton Theological Seminary. For the last two years of his life, Liebman was a nationally famous figure through the phenomenal success of his book *Peace of Mind* (1946). This had an instant appeal to a generation which had been harassed by the experience of Word War II. Its popularity helped to encourage a closer working relationship between psychology and religion. [S.D.T.]

LIEBMANN, JOST (**Judah Berlin;** c. 1640–1702), *Court Jew. His first wife, Malka, was the niece of *Glueckel von Hameln. Together with Ḥayyim Hameln, Glueckel's husband, Liebmann originally traded in precious stones and metals. His second wife, Esther Schulhoff, whom he married in 1677, was the widow of Israel Aron, the Brandenburg court supplier and founder of the Berlin Jewish community. Since Esther held a letter of protection which was still valid after her second marriage, Liebmann was able to settle in Berlin. In 1678 he began supplying gems to Frederick William, the elector of Brandenburg, and from then on was court jeweler in Berlin. Being more circumspect than his predecessors, he occupied himself solely with the sale of jewels and precious metals. Toward the end of the century he was considered one of the richest Jews in Prussia. In 1690 Glueckel von Hameln estimated his fortune at 100,000 thalers. The luxury-loving King Frederick I owed large sums of money to Liebmann, who assisted him in acquiring a sizable collection of precious stones, a safe investment in difficult times. In 1684 Liebmann was released from payment of the body tax *(Leibzoll)* and in 1694 his books were recognized as legal evidence in court.

Liebmann was also influential in the Jewish community and secured positions as rabbis in various communities in Prussia for his sons and other members of his family. As he was the owner of the only synagogue in Berlin, he was able to exert pressure on his opponents within the community, led by Moses Benjamin Wulff.

After Liebmann's death, his wife successfully carried on his business and supplied ever-increasing amounts of jewelry to the court. Part of her payment was a license to mint and issue large amounts of coinage. In 1713, with the accession of the frugal soldier-king, Frederick William I, she was put under house arrest and released only after she had paid the king large sums. Her sons, Isaac Liebmann and Liebmann Jost, were also court purveyors of jewels, but they did not attain the wealth and position of their parents.

Bibliography: S. Stern, *The Court Jew* (1950), 49–55; idem, *Der preussische Staat und die Juden* (1962), index; H. Schnee, *Die Hoffinanz und der moderne Staat*, 1 (1953), 47ff.; H. Rachel and P. Wallich, *Berliner Grosskaufleute und Kapitalisten*, 2 (1937), index. [R.M.]

LIEBMANN, OTTO (1840–1912), German philosopher. Liebmann, who was born in Loewenberg, Silesia, was appointed lecturer at Tuebingen in 1865, in 1872 professor at Strasbourg, and in 1882 professor at Jena. In 1870–71 he was in the Prussian army at the siege of Paris, and published a patriotic memoir, *Monate vor Paris* (1871). Liebmann was one of the founders of neo-Kantianism. His *Kant und die Epigonen* (1865) attacked post-Kantian metaphysical theories and advocated a return to Kant's philosophy. For Liebmann, Kant's transcendental idealism, the recognition of the intimate and necessary correlation of the subjective and objective, of empirical reality and transcendental ideality, sufficed to explain the world. He opposed metaphysical theories about the "thing-in-itself" as well as empirical, positivistic, and materialistic views. In his later works, he tried to develop his neo-Kantianism with regard to metaphysics, experience, science, psychology, and ethics and aesthetics. His chief works were *Ueber den individuellen Beweis fuer die Freiheit des Willens* (1866); *Ueber den objektiven Anblick* (1869); *Zur Analysis der Wirklichkeit* (1876); *Die Klimax der Theorien* (1884); *Gedanken und Tatsachen* (2 vols.; 1882–1904) and *Immanuel Kant* (Ger., 1904). He also wrote poetry, collected in *Weltwanderung* (1889).

Bibliography: *Kantstudien*, 15 (1910), 1–151, contains a festschrift in Liebmann's honor; Campo, in: *Encyclopedia of Philosophy*, 4 (1967), 466–7; Rossi, in: *Enciclopedia Filosofica*, 3 (It., 1957), 50. [R.H.P.]

LIÉGE (Flemish **Luik,** Ger. **Luettich**), capital of Liége province, E. Belgium. There is no evidence that a Jewish community existed in Liége in the Middle Ages. During the 11th century Bishop Wazon, the overlord of the city, had a religious disputation with a Jewish physician at the court of Emperor Conrad II. In 1138 a Jewish physician, Moses, cured a cleric Rodolphe de Saint Trond in Liége, but there is nothing to attest to his residence there. In 1573 a Jew in Liége became converted to Christianity, and in 1722 a German rabbi and his family were baptized. The first real evidence of the existence of a Jewish community in Liége postdates the French occupation at the end of the 18th century. There were 24 Jews living in the city in 1811, and 20–30 Jewish families in the second half of the 19th century. The oldest tombstone in the Jewish cemetery, with a Hebrew inscription, dates from 1842. The community in Liége had a synagogue and established communal institutions. On May 11, 1940, during the Nazi occupation, the Jewish population numbered 2,000 (according to the Gestapo report, it numbered 3,000 in 1939). An order issued by the Germans on Oct. 29, 1941, designated Liége as one of the four cities from which Jewish residence in Belgium was not excluded, along with Brussels, Antwerp, and Charleroi. On the liberation of Liége by the United States army on Sept. 8, 1944, there were 1,200 Jews in the city.

In 1959 the population numbered 594. There was then a *ḥazzan*-minister in Liége, but no rabbi, and no local source of *kasher* meat. The synagogue was reform in tendency. About 25% had intermarried; Jewish religious observance was weak and tendencies to assimilate strong. However, Israel and Zionism, as a means of expressing Jewish identity, played a large role in community life. Liége had four Zionist societies and other fund-raising organizations on behalf of Israel. In 1968 its Jewish population was 1,500.

Bibliography: E. Ouverleaux, *Notes et documents sur les juifs de Belgique* . . . (1885); E. Ginsburger, *Les Juifs de Belgique au XVIII*[e] *siècle* (1932), 1, 97; J. Stengers, *Les juifs dans les Pays-Bas au Moyen Age* (1950), index; W. Bok, *Aspects de la Communauté Juive de Liège* (1959).

[Ed.]

LIEN (Heb. שִׁעְבּוּד נְכָסִים, *Shi'bud Nekhasim*). **The Concept.** Jewish law enables the creditor to exercise a lien over all the debtor's property, in addition to his remedies against the debtor personally. This lien automatically comes into existence on the creation of the obligation and is called *aharayut* or *shi'bud nekhasim* (i.e., "property bearing responsibility" or the "encumbrance of property"). Sometimes the parties may limit the application of the lien to a specified part of the debtor's property, in which event it may operate either in addition to the general charge on the debtor's property or so as to release the remaining property from any such encumbrance. A limitation of the lien to a specified asset may be effected in two ways: firstly, by the asset remaining in the debtor's possession, in which event the lien is called *apoteke* (see below); secondly, by the debtor surrendering possession of the asset to the creditor, this being called *mashkon*, i.e., pledge. The law relating to the latter is dealt with fully under *pledge.

Import of the Term Aḥarayut Nekhasim. Originally, the general lien applied only to the real estate (*karka*, "land") of the debtor because land could not be carried away or spoiled and was therefore deemed "property bearing responsibility" (Kid. 1:5). Chattels were regarded as incapable of being preserved and were therefore deemed property "not bearing responsibility" *(ibid.)*. The special reasons for the availability in Jewish law of the automatic lien in respect of all obligations will be dealt with below and in the article on *Obligation.

The concept of a charge on assets is already mentioned in a *takkanah* from the time of Simeon b. Sheṭaḥ, concerning a husband's written undertaking to his wife that all his property shall be charged in her favor to secure the repayment of her **ketubbah* (Ket. 82b); it may be assumed that a charge of this nature was known at that time in respect of other obligations as well. In the third century the *amoraim* Ulla and Rabbah disputed the question whether a charge of this nature originated from Pentateuchal law *(shi'buda de-oraita)* or from rabbinical enactment *(de-rabbanan)*. According to some of the *rishonim*, this dispute related only to the question of seizing assets which had been alienated by the debtor to a third party, and that as long as the assets remained with the debtor all agreed that they were subject to the Pentateuchal lien (Tos. to BB 175b and *Bet ha-Beḥirah* thereto). Other *rishonim* were of the opinion that the dispute was one of principle, whether or not the encumbered assets had been alienated, namely: whether the right of recovery of the debt in this way flowed from the personal aspect of the obligation, as was the case when the creditor recovered payment out of the chattels of the debtor, or whether in relation to land the creditor acquired a lien also in the nature of a rent right, in addition to the personal obligation (Rashbam, Tos. to BB 175b; Nov. Rashba, *ibid.*; Nov. Ritba Kid. 13b; see also Elon, Ḥerut ha-Perat ... 21). The *halakhah* was decided in accordance with the view of *shi'buda de-oraita* (Yad, Malveh, 11:4; Sh. Ar., ḤM 111; Sma *ibid.*, n. 1).

Substance of the Creditor's Right in the Debtor's Property. The creditor's general lien over the debtor's property does not allow him a full proprietary right *(zekhut kinyanit)*. This finds expression mainly in two respects. Firstly, the right of lien does not preclude the debtor from validly transferring ownership of his property to another, albeit subject to the the fact that the creditor, when seeking to recover payment, is entitled to seize the property from the party who acquired it (this right of seizure is known as *terifah*, from the *nekhasim meshu'badim*, i.e., the "encumbered and alienated property"). As will be seen below, special rules were laid down governing the right of seizure from any such transferee. Secondly, the lien is subordinate to and dependent on the debtor's own ownership in the property, and hence the latter, in certain circumstances, is able to oust or extinguish the creditor's lien over his property.

Recovery of the Debt out of Encumbered Assets. It is a substantive principle that a debt may not be satisfied out of the *nekhasim meshu'badim* (see above) as long as the debtor is possessed of other assets, i.e., *nekhasim benei ḥorin* ("free property"), even if the remaining assets are inferior to those to which the creditor is entitled (e.g., the free assets are *beinonit* or average, whereas the obligation is tortious and must therefore be satisfied from the *iddit*, or best). If the debtor has sold the encumbered property to several purchasers, the creditor must first recover from the last purchaser since the anterior one may plead: "I have left you room to recover from him." Similarly, the purchaser retains the right to pay in cash rather than surrender the encumbered property. Where there are several creditors, a preferential right of lien over the debtor's property will be enjoyed by the creditor to whom the debtor first became indebted (Git. 48b; BK 8a; Sh. Ar., ḤM 104; see also *Execution (Civil)).

Creation of the Debt. As long as the debtor's property remained in his possession there would be no need to limit the creditor's lien therein, as mentioned above. However, there was good reason for limiting the right of seizure from the transferee of the encumbered assets only to cases where the debt was originally evidenced in writing (i.e., *milveh bi-shetar*, "loan by deed") and not orally *(milveh be-al peh)*. The *amoraim* disputed the legal justification of this limitation (BB 175b). In the opinion of Ulla, the law entitled the creditor to seize encumbered land from the purchaser even for an orally established debt, except that the scholars had regulated against it in order not to cause loss to the purchaser of such land, since an "oral" debt had no *kol* ("publicity," lit. "voice") and the purchaser would therefore have no notice of the land's encumbrance in favor of the creditor. On the other hand, Rabbah was of the opinion that the law did not recognize the institution of *aḥarayut nekhasim* at all and the creditor's right to recover from the debtor's property, including land, derived from a personal liability only, which could not be enforced except against the debtor's free property (see above). However, the scholars enacted that, in the case of a debt evidenced in writing and constituting notice, the creditor could seize the debtor's property from the purchaser, for otherwise the creditor would have no security for the repayment of the debt and thus no borrower would ever be able to obtain a loan. The need to secure repayment of the debt in such a firm manner so as to forestall any reluctance to grant a loan most probably stemmed from the fact that in Jewish law the prohibition against interest precluded the earning of any profit from the actual loan, and accordingly the principal at least had to be adequately secured. From its application to a liability originating from loan, this rule was also extended to other obligations (L. Auerbach, *Das juedische Obligationenrecht*, 1 (1870), 172). Since the reason for precluding seizure from the purchaser in the case of an oral debt was to avoid loss because he had no notice of the debt's existence, R. Pappa decided that the creditor could seize the land of the debtor if the third party into whose hands it had passed was the heir of the debtor (BB 176a; but cf. the opinion of Rav, TJ, BK 10:1, 7b and BM 1:6, 8a; BB 175a and the opinion of Samuel there); the *halakhah* was decided accordingly in the codes (Yad, Malveh 11:4, Sh. Ar., ḤM 107:1).

In post-talmudic times various *takkanot* were enacted laying down that a debt was not to be considered a written one unless the deed was written and signed by a scribe and witnesses specially appointed for the purpose (see Sh. Ar., ḤM 61:1), whereby the maximum notice and warning were thus afforded to potential purchasers—in much the same way as mortgages are registered in land registry offices at the present time.

A debt established by deed provided the right of exacting payment out of encumbered property, even if not so expressly stipulated—the omission being attributed to "an error of the scribe" (BM 14a; 15b). With regard to an obligation stemming from the *ketubbah*, this rule was specifically endorsed in a special enactment (Ket. 4:7). An exception to the rule distinguishing between oral obligation and one by deed was recognized in the case of land sold with a guarantee (i.e., in respect of claims by third parties against the land) in the presence of witnesses, even without a deed. In this event the purchaser could exact the purchase price from the encumbered property, it being considered that a sale of land before witnesses would become known even in the absence of a written instrument (BB 41b and codes). Similarly, and for the same reason, the creditor could exact payment from the debtor's encumbered property if there was an obligation established by way of a *kinyan* before witnesses (see *Acquisition; BB, 40a; Sh. Ar., ḤM 39:1).

Seizure for a Debt of Fixed Amount Only. The scholars regulated "for the sake of good order" *(mi-penei tikkun olam)* that recovery could be made out of encumbered assets only for a debt of a fixed amount and not otherwise, e.g., in respect of maintenance for a wife and daughters (Git. 5:3, 50b and codes).

Debts Stemming from Tort. According to tannaitic law, an injured party could recover all the various measures of compensation from *nekhasim meshu'badim* (even though not stipulated in the deed; Tosef., Ket. 2:2). However, the *amoraim* disputed the question of whether an obligation imposed by law was subject to the same rules as one agreed upon in a deed (Bek. 49b et al.). In the light of the rule that a debt for an unspecified amount was not recoverable from encumbered assets, it would seem that there was room for extending the limitation also to a debt stemming from tort, for precisely the same reasons. The matter remained a disputed one, however, even in the codes (see e.g., Tos. to BK 8a s.v. כול ; *Beit Yosef* ḤM 119 n. 4).

Any obligation not recoverable out of *nekhasim meshu'badim* becomes recoverable in this way in consequence of a judgment of the court on a claim submitted (BB 175b; BK 104b–105a).

Encumbrance of Assets. Originally, the law was that a lien extended only to assets in the possession of the debtor at the time the debt was created (cf. the ancient wording: "all the property that I have," Ket. 4:7; Tosef., Ket. 4:7; Tosef., Ket. 12:1), and property later acquired could not be seized by the creditor once it had been transferred to a third party (Yad, Malveh 18:1; Sh. Ar., ḤM 112:1). In order to increase the creditor's security, however, the scholars prescribed that if, at the time the debt was created, the debtor agreed that property he might acquire in the future would also be subjected to the lien, this would also form part of his encumbered assets, i.e., from the time it came into his possession (TJ, Ket. 4:8, 29a; BB 44b). This rule was discussed in the light of the principle that a person could not transfer ownership of something not in his possession (*reshut;* see *Contract), but the distinction was made that one could nevertheless encumber property in this manner (BB 157 a/b; Yad, Malveh 18:1; Sh. Ar., ḤM 112:1). The opinion is expressed in the codes that, in view of the rule of "the scribe's error" (see above), the lien also extended to assets acquired by the debtor after the creation of the debt, even if not expressly agreed to by him when the obligation came into being (Rema, ḤM 112:1).

Chattels as Nekhasim Meshu'badim. In the amoraic period the rule that a lien extended only to the debtor's land underwent a variation: it was laid down that if, at the time of creation of the debt and as security for it, the debtor expressly charged the chattels incidental to his land (*agav karka;* see *Acquisition), the lien would also extend to such chattels, whether they were in his possession or acquired thereafter (BB 44b; Yad, Malveh 18:2; Sh. Ar., ḤM 113:1–2). The extension of the lien in this manner was due to the fact that the number of landowners had diminished and the lien, if limited to land alone, would have failed to provide adequate security for the repayment of a debt. With the intensification of this economic trend in geonic times, the practice was accepted of *kinyan* ("acquisition") incidental to land—even if the debtor owned none at all—involving the doctrine of the "four cubits *[arba ammot]* in Ereẓ Israel" said to be possessed by every Jew. For the same reason a special *takkanah* was enacted in the geonic period, making it possible—contrary to talmudic law (see Ket. 92a)—for the creditor also to exact payment out of the debtor's chattels acquired by his heirs (*Ḥemdah Genuzah* no. 65; cf. justification of the rule on similar grounds, Rashbam BB 174a; see also Yad, Malveh 11:11; Sh. Ar., ḤM 107:1).

This *takkanah* concerning the seizure of the debtor's chattels after they passed into the hands of his heirs was unlikely to create difficulty, since it was only proper that the heirs should fulfill the obligations of the deceased. However, so far as purchasers were concerned, the growing practice whereby even one's chattels were charged on the creation of an obligation, caused the creditor's consequent right of seizure to be a serious obstacle to business transactions. Accordingly, the earlier practice was reverted to and it became accepted that the creditor would not recover from chattels sold to a third party, even though the debtor had expressly agreed in the deed to charge such of his chattels as were incidental to land—this being justified by the *takkanat ha-shuk* ("market overt")—for otherwise no person would be able to buy any chattel from his neighbor for fear that a lien existed in favor of his creditors (Resp. Rosh 79:5; also 4 and 6; Tur, and Sh. Ar., ḤM 60:1; but cf. also *Siftei Kohen* ḤM 60, n. 4, where the custom is contested).

To counter the fear of prospective purchasers that property acquired from a seller was subject to being seized by the latter's creditors, the practice was adopted—in terms of a *takkanah* enacted in the Middle Ages and observed in many communities—whereby at the time of the sale of land any person claiming a right or lien over the property in question was publicly called upon to come forward within a period of 15 days (Resp. Rashba, vol. 6, nos. 6–7) or 30 days (idem, vol. 2, no. 95) and establish his claim, failing which he would lose his right and thenceforth be precluded from raising any objection to the sale and from making any claim by way of lien or otherwise over the property (see also Resp. Rosh no. 18:16; Tur, ḤM 104:3; Resp. Ritba, no. 156).

Cancellation and Extinction of Lien. The creditor's lien over the debtor's property is extinguished by the cancellation of the underlying obligation—i.e., by the repayment of the debt or the debtor's release from it—and hence "a deed which has been borrowed on and repaid cannot be borrowed on again, since release has already been granted from its lien" (Ket. 85a). The creditor may, however, relinquish his lien in favor of one purchaser while retaining it in respect of other purchasers (Ket. 95a and codes), and he may also release part of the encumbered assets from the operation of the lien, while retaining it in respect of other parts (Tur and Sh. Ar., ḤM 111:12). In both cases the release has no validity unless formally effected by way of *kinyan (ibid.;* also 118:1).

As mentioned above, the creditors' lien does not amount to an independent proprietary right, but is subject to the debtor's own ownership of the encumbered property. Hence, the termination of the latter's ownership of the property may, in certain circumstances, automatically extinguish the creditor's lien therein. The Talmud mentions three cases in which the creditor's lien is extinguished as a result of the debtor's loss of ownership of the encumbered property: when the proprietor has made an irredeemable consecration (*kedushat ha-guf;* see **Hekdesh*) of the property, in which event it is thereafter and for all time placed beyond the ownership of the common man (*hedyot;* Git. 40b; Tur and Sh. Ar., ḤM 117:7)—according to Maimonides a redeemable consecration (*kedushat dammim*) also extinguishes the lien, save that the creditor may seize the property if and when it is redeemed (Yad, Malveh 18:6–7; Arakhin 7:14–16); when there is a prohibition against deriving benefit from the property, e.g., *ḥameẓ* ("leaven") during Passover, which has the effect of nullifying ownership of the property; and when the property in question is a slave manumitted by his owner, since thereupon the right of ownership is totally extinguished (Git., Yad; Sh. Ar., *ibid.;* and see below).

A person who causes a lien over his property to be extinguished is nevertheless liable to the creditor for any loss resulting to the latter (see also **Gerama;* *Tort).

Apoteke (אַפּוֹתֵיקִי). *Apoteke* is distinguished from the implied general lien by the fact that it is limited to a specific part of the property of the debtor, in whose possession it remains. The term is of Greek origin and in several tannaitic sources is rendered as "הִיפּוֹתֵיקִי"(*hippoteke;* Tosef., Shev. 8:6; Tosef., 11:8; Tosef., BM 1:8). Despite this Greek origin, however, in its substance and legal rules *apoteke* is in Jewish law similar to the general lien, and in fact it differs from the Greek hypothec (ὑποθήκη) in essential principles (see below). In effect, *apoteke* does not create a new charge on the property in question since all the debtor's property is included in the implied, comprehensive charge that comes into existence upon creation of the obligation, but merely serves to restrict an already existing charge to particular assets. For this reason, Jewish law sources make no specific mention of the term *shi'bud apoteke,* but speak of "defining" or "setting aside" a field (Git. 37a; Ket. 54b, 55a, 81b; BB 50a; TJ, Shev. 10:1, 39b), i.e., singling out of a particular asset from the generally charged property. The *rishonim* interpreted the term *apoteke* as a *notarikon (from אפה תהא קאי , i.e., "on this it shall stand": *Arukh ha-Shalem,* s.v. אפתק; Rashi BK 11b; Rashbam BB 44b; or from פה תַּקָּנָה —Maim., Comm. to Git. 4:4). The rule is that the creditor may only exact payment from the hypothecated property in respect of such obligations as would serve to create in his favor a general lien over the debtor's property, i.e., a debt by deed and not an oral one, etc. (*Beit Yosef,* ḤM 117, n. 3). Talmudic sources indicate that the *apoteke* itself had to be created by deed (Tosef., Shev. 8:6); but it was later laid down in the codes that an *apoteke* could be created before witnesses without deed, although the underlying obligation itself had to be under deed (*Beit Yosef,* loc. cit.).

The hypothecated property generally consisted of land, but instances are also mentioned where the *apoteke* attached (*inter alia*) to slaves (Git. 4:4) and to a bond of indebtedness, e.g., the *ketubbah* (Tosef., Ket. 11:1; Rashi's interpretation, in commenting on Ket. 54a, that the *apoteke* is effected specifically in relation to the land of the wife included in the *ketubbah* does not accord with the plain meaning of the Tosefta statement, but shows the influence of Rava's ruling; see below); and to chattels collectively (to a *ḥavilah*, "bundle"; Tosef., Ket. 11:8). In the fourth century it was laid down by Rava in Babylonia that a hypothecated slave who had been sold could be seized by a creditor in recovery of his debt, since the sale of a slave carried a "voice" and purchasers would have warning, whereas the sale of a hypothecated ox or ass carried no "voice" and therefore these were not recoverable from a purchaser in settlement of the vendor's debt. Even then, however, a hypothecated slave afforded only limited security for the creditor, since already in the Mishnah it was prescribed that a slave manumitted by his owner, i.e., the debtor, could not be seized in recovery of the latter's debt (Git. 4:4) because his manumission extinguished the charge (TJ, Yev. 7:1, 8a and see above). This was in accordance with the fundamental doctrine of human liberty that "a slave, once liberated, does not return to servitude" (TJ, Pes. 2:29a). Hence it was not common to execute *apoteke*, not even in respect of slaves, and *apoteke* came to be equaled with the general lien, attaching to land only and not to chattels. Later this was enshrined in the codes in absolute manner, to the effect that no (alienated) hypothecated chattels of any kind were recoverable in payment of a debt since they carried no "voice," even if the *apoteke* was executed by deed and the purchaser had notice of it (Tur and Sh. Ar., ḤM 117:3; see also Sma, ḤM 117, n. 13).

Simple and Express Apoteke (apoteke setam and apoteke meforash). Jewish law recognizes hypothecation of a specific asset in two different ways, each having its own rules concerning the creditor's right of recovery from such an asset. In the first case, referred to in the codes as *apoteke setam* (Tur, ḤM 117:1), the debtor gives a written undertaking to his creditor that if he should fail to repay the debt, "you may recover from this asset." As long as the debtor fails to repay the debt in cash and the asset remains in his possession, the creditor is entitled to exact payment out of such an asset and the debtor is not entitled to offer substitute assets. If the hypothecated asset should not suffice to repay the debt, or becomes spoiled, or ceases to exist, the creditor may recover payment out of the debtor's other assets (Git. 41a; Yad, Malveh 18:3; Sh. Ar., ḤM 117:1). Just as the general lien does not preclude the debtor from selling his assets, so he is also free to sell assets subject to a simple hypothecation. As long as he retains any free property, the creditor may not recover his debt out of such hypothecated assets alienated by the debtor (TJ, Yev. 7:1, 8a; Git. 41a). If the debtor has no free property, the creditor may recover from the hypothecated property in a purchaser's hands, even if other encumbered assets were alienated by the debtor after his alienation of the hypothecated property; in this respect *apoteke* gives the creditor a right that ranks in preference to that available to the creditor under the general lien (see above). However, the purchaser of hypothecated property—like the debtor himself—retains the right to repay the debt in cash (Yad, Malveh 18:4, 8, and *Maggid Mishneh*, ad. loc. Sma, ḤM 117 n. 8).

Simeon b. Gamaliel expressed the opinion that alienation was forbidden of assets hypothecated in favor of a woman's *ketubbah*, since "a woman is not in the habit of having recourse to the courts," and that she could recover her *ketubbah* from the hypothecated property only, and not from the remaining property in her husband's possession (Git. 41a). Apparently, however, he too was of the opinion that if the hypothecated property did not equal the value of the *ketubbah* or if it depreciated, the wife could recover from the remaining property of her husband (cf. Ket. 4:7; Tosef., Ket. 11:8; see Gulak, *Ha-Ḥiyyuv ve-Shi'budav*, 55). The *halakhah* was decided in accordance with the opposing view of the scholars, so that no difference is recognized between the *ketubbah* obligation and any other obligation (Yad and Sh. Ar., loc. cit.).

Express *apoteke* (termed *apoteke meforash* in the codes) is constituted when the debtor makes a written declaration to the creditor that "you shall not recover payment except out of this [asset]" (*lo yehe lekha pera'on ella mi-zo*, Git. 41a; BM 66b; TJ, Ket. 10:6, 34a). In this event no charge attaches to the debtor's remaining property and hence if the hypothecated property should be spoiled the creditor may not recover payment out of the debtor's free property nor out of other property alienated by him to a third party (Git. 41a). Expressly hypothecated property also does not provide the creditor with an absolute proprietary right therein. Thus, if its value exceeds the amount of the debt, the creditor must return the balance to the debtor. Furthermore, while the *amoraim* of Ereẓ Israel disputed the question of whether the debtor could alienate expressly hypothecated property (TJ, Shev. 10:1, 39b), it appears from the Babylonian Talmud that he may do so, except that the creditor can exact payment out of the hypothecated assets in the purchaser's possession even if the debtor has any free property, and except further that the purchaser is not entitled to pay in cash in lieu of the hypothecated property, as he may do in the case of simple hypothecation (BK 96a; the debtor himself retains the right to pay in cash in both cases). The *halakhah* was decided in the codes in accordance with the latter view (Tur and Sh. Ar., ḤM 117:1; Sma ḤM 117, n. 5 and 6). Basically, therefore, express hypothecation afforded the creditor no greater rights than did simple hypothecation, whereas it did serve to deprive him of the general lien over all the other property of the debtor, and Gulak (*Ha-Ḥiyyuv* . . . p. 59f.) correctly surmises that its main purpose was to promote the free transaction of land sales by freeing all but a distinct part of the debtor's property from the creditor's lien.

In the State of Israel. The law in Israel recognizes no implied general lien of the kind known in Jewish law, but allows for the bonding of a specified asset in the creditor's favor by way of pledge or mortgage. A real estate mortgage is registered in the Land Registry Office, whereupon the mortgagor may not transfer ownership of the property without the consent of the mortgagee.

For further particulars see *Pledge.

Bibliography: I. S. Zuri, *Mishpat ha-Talmud*, 4 (1921), 61–67; Gulak, Yesodei, 1 (1922), 141f., 149–65; 2 (1922), 8–10; idem, in: *Madda'ei ha-Yahadut*, 1 (1925/26), 46–48; idem, Oẓar, 235–8; idem, *Das Urkundenwesen im Talmud* . . . (1935), 114–25; idem, *Toledot ha-Mishpat be-Yisrael bi-Tekufat ha-Talmud*, 1 (*Ha-Ḥiyyuv ve-Shi'budav*, 1939), 31–61; Herzog, Instit, 1 (1936), 339–63; ET, 1 (1951³), 216–20; 2 (1949), 130–4; 5 (1953), 121–32; M. Elon, *Ḥerut ha-Perat be-Darkhei Geviyyat Ḥov* (1964), 1–23; idem, Mafte'aḥ, 391–6.

[M.E.]

LIEPAJA (Ger. **Libau**; Rus. **Libava**), city in Latvian S.S.R.; one of the oldest Baltic ports. Jews were not permitted there up to the 18th century, and in 1797 there were only 19 Jewish inhabitants. Under czarist rule Liepaja was excluded from the *Pale of Settlement, and only merchants of the first guild, artisans, and Jews who had lived in *Courland before 1881 were permitted to reside there. The Jewish population numbered 1,348 in 1835 and 1,218 in 1850. In 1840, 13 families (78 persons) left to join the agricultural settlements in *Kherson province. By 1881 it had increased to 6,651 following the completion of the Libava-Romny railroad, linking Liepaja with the leading industrial and commercial centers of the Ukraine. By 1897 the community had risen to 9,454 (c. 14% of the total population), consisting of the old-established residents of Courland among whom German cultural influences predominated, and Jews who had moved to Liepaja from various parts of Russia. Jews were prominent in the export trade in grain and lumber. They also owned about one-quarter of the industrial enterprises in the city, and about the same proportion of factory workers were Jews. When Latvia became independent after World War I, Liepaja lost its Russian hinterland, which was a severe setback for the development of the city. The Jewish population declined, from 9,758 (19%) in 1920, to 7,908 (13.81%) in 1930, and 7,379 (12.92%) in 1935. It nevertheless remained the third-largest Jewish community in the country, after Riga and Daugavpils (Dvinsk). Before World War I and under democratic government in Latvia (1918–34) a number of social and political groups, prominent rabbis, and communal leaders (including N. *Katzenelson) were active in the community. The Hebrew writer J. L. *Kantor was **kazyonny ravvin* from 1890 to 1904. He was succeeded in 1907 by Aaron Nurock, who later served as community rabbi until 1937. He was also a member of the Latvian parliament for one term. Yiddish and Hebrew schools, charitable institutions, and other communal organizations existed in Liepaja.

Holocaust Period. After the outbreak of the Soviet-German war, Liepaja was occupied by the Germans on June 29, 1941. This was followed at once by anti-Jewish excesses and mass arrests. On July 24, 1941, 3,000 Jews from Liepaja, mostly men, were taken to the lighthouse at Schkeden and put to death. Jews from the surrounding towns and villages were concentrated in Liepaja, and on Dec. 15 and 16, 1941, another 3,500 were murdered. Four hundred Jews lost their lives in February 1942. In June of that year, a ghetto was set up, where 816 Jews were confined; it was liquidated on October 8, 1943 (the eve of the Day of Atonement), and the remaining Jews were deported to concentration camps.

Only a few dozen Liepaja Jews survived the war. The city was liberated by the Red Army on May 9, 1945, but most of the Jewish survivors did not return, preferring to stay in Displaced Persons' camps, from where they eventually left for Israel and other countries overseas.

Bibliography: M. Schatz-Anin, *Di Yidn in Letland* (1924), 19–24; L. Ovchinski, *Di Geshikhte fun di Yidn in Letland* (1928), 123–32; *Le-Korot ha-Yehudim be-Kurland,* (1908); *Yahadut Latvia* (1953), 241–3; 359–61; M. Kaufmann, *Die Vernichtung der Juden Lettlands* (1947), 299–304.
[Jo.Ga.]

LIES, MAN OF (Heb. אִישׁ הַכָּזָב, *Ish ha-Kazav*), a person mentioned in some of the Qumran texts because of his opposition to the *Teacher of Righteousness. In the Damascus Document the figure of approximately 40 years marks the interval "from the day that the Unique Teacher was gathered in until the consuming of all the men of war who returned with the Man of Lies" (6QD 20.14ff.). In view of the fact that the members of the Qumran community called themselves "the poor," it may be that they derived the term "Man of Lies" from Proverbs 19:22, "A poor man is better than *ish kazav*." The reference to the consuming of all the men of war is probably based on Deuteronomy 2:14–16, where all the "men of war" who came out of Egypt perished within 38 years. The identification of the scriptures underlying the Zadokite author's language, however, does not help much to identify the persons he has in mind. The Man of Lies may have been the leader of a rival sect; sometimes the bitterest expressions of hostility and charges of apostasy are made between groups which an outsider could hardly distinguish one from another. One possibility that has been aired is that the Man of Lies is the Pharisaic leader *Simeon b. Shetaḥ, who returned from exile to enjoy a position of influence in Judea when Alexander *Yannai died in 76 B.C.E.; the "men of war" might then be his fellow exiles who came back with him.

The Habakkuk Commentary from Qumran Cave I has two references to the Man of Lies: one in which the words of Habbakkuk 1:5 ("a work . . . which ye will not believe if be told you") are interpreted as "the traitors (apostates) with the Man of Lies, because they did not [listen to the words] of the Teacher of Righteousness from the mouth of God" (1QpHab. 2:1–3); the other in which the words of Habakkuk 1:13 ("wherefore lookest Thou, when they deal treacherously, and holdest Thy peace when the wicked swalloweth up the man that is more righteous than he?") are said to concern "the house of Absalom and the men of their counsel, who were struck dumb when the Teacher of Righteousness was chastised, and did not aid him against the Man of Lies, who rejected the Law in the midst of all their congregation" (1QpHab. 5:9–12). Some help might be expected from the mention of the "house of Absalom," but in every generation from the Hasmonean revolt to the war of 66 C.E. an Absalom can be produced—from an envoy sent by Judah Maccabee to Lysias in 164 B.C.E. (II Macc. 11: 17) to a lieutenant of *Menahem in 66 C.E. (Jos., Wars 2:448). If the Man of Lies could be confidently identified with the Prophet of *Lies, then it might be possible to think of a rival religious teacher to the Teacher of Righteousness, whose rejection of the latter's interpretation of scripture would be tantamount in the eyes of the community to rejection of the Law itself. Otherwise he could be any enemy of the Teacher and the community, and thus identified according to the period in which the Teacher is dated; thus H. H. Rowley thinks of Antiochus IV, W. H. Brownlee of John Hyrcanus, A. Dupont-Sommer of Hyrcanus II (identical with the *Wicked Priest), C. Roth of Simeon Bar Giora, G. R. Driver of several possibilities, including Agrippa II and John of Giscala.

Bibliography: H. H. Rowley, *Zadokite Fragments and the Dead Sea Scrolls* (1952), 33, 40, 43, 60, 70; G. R. Driver, *Judaean Scrolls* (1965), 152ff., 271ff.
[F.F.B.]

LIES, PROPHET OF (Heb. מַטִּיף הַכָּזָב, *Mattif ha-Kazav*, "spouter of falsehood"), a person mentioned in some of the Qumran texts, whose identity with the *Man of Lies cannot be assumed as certain in the present state of knowledge of the *Dead Sea Scrolls. The designation given to him is derived from Micah 2:11, "If a man walking in wind and falsehood do lie, 'I will preach *(attif)* unto thee of wine and of strong drink'; he shall even be the preacher *(mattif)* of this people!" (quoted 6QD 8:13). He is also called the "man of scoffing" near the beginning of the Zadokite Admonition: about the same time as the rise of the *Teacher of Righteousness, it is said, "there arose the man of scoffing, who preached [*hittif,* "spouted"] to Israel water of falsehood and led them astray in a trackless wilderness" (6QD 1:14f.). The reference is probably to a rival religious leader, probably to a leader of the Pharisees, for the Prophet of Lies and his associates "interpreted with smooth things" (1:18)—adopted a less exacting *halakhah* than did the followers of the Teacher of Righteousness—and other passages which mention the *Seekers after Smooth Things indicate that this is a description of the Pharisees. Later in the same document these people are called "the builders of the wall" who "walked after *ẓav*" (a reference to Hos. 5: 11). The enigmatic *ẓav* is explained in terms of a "preacher" *(mattif)*, in whom a variant and inferior reading of Micah 2:6 (*hattef yattifun,* as against the masoretic text, *al tattifu yattifun*) is seen as fulfilled: he leads his followers astray by his interpretations of the marriage law and the law of purity (see Book of Covenant of *Damascus).

In the Qumran commentary on Micah the denunciation of Samaria in Micah 1: 5–7 is interpreted of "the Prophet of Lies who [leads astray] the simple." In the commentary on Habakkuk, the denunciation of "him that buildeth a town with blood" (Hab. 2:12) is interpreted of "the Prophet of Lies *(mattif ha-kazav)* who has led many astray, to build a worthless town with blood and to raise up a congregation with falsehood for the sake of its glory"; but he and his followers "will come to fiery judgments for having reviled and defamed God's elect ones" (1QpHab. 10:9–13). This language is akin to the condemnation in the Zadokite Admonition of those who, at the instance of the Prophet of Lies, "built the wall and daubed it with plaster" (6QD 8:12; cf. Ezek. 13:10ff.).

Although it is fairly certain that this Prophet of Lies is a

Pharisaic teacher, his identity remains in doubt. Simeon b. Shetaḥ is one possibility, but since the Prophet appears to have been contemporary with the Teacher of Righteousness, the identity of the former must depend on the date assigned to the latter.

Bibliography: G. R. Driver, *Judaean Scrolls* (1965), 307–10; Roth, in: JSS, 4 (1959), 339ff. [F.F.B.]

LIESSIN, ABRAHAM (pseudonym of **Abraham Walt;** 1872–1938), Yiddish poet and editor. He was born in Minsk, Russia, and studied at yeshivot where he showed an interest in philosophical problems and in the Haskalah literature. He agitated for a Jewish Socialism and contributed to the emergence of the Jewish Labor *Bund in 1897. That year Liessin arrived in the United States and immediately became an active Socialist. He participated in the newly founded Yiddish daily *Forward* writing editorials as well as feature articles. Although not a Zionist, Liessin demanded of the Jewish Labor Bund a more positive approach to Jewish nationalism and Jewish values and culture, and later fought against its neutrality toward Jewish nationalism. From 1913 until his death Liessin edited the *Zukunft,* making it the leading Yiddish literary and cultural monthly, and publishing the works of the most important Yiddish writers in the United States and Europe. He contributed a signed editorial to each issue. Liessin is known primarily as a poet. His verses are intense, melodious and linguistically pure. Throughout his career he wrote a great deal of narrative lyric poetry which he regularly published in his journal. Steeped in Jewish history and tradition, and imbued with a spirit of revolt against social injustice, he wrote about the heroes and martyrs of the past as well as the heroes of his own time. He glorified *Judah Maccabee, *Bar Kokhba, Solomon *Molcho, Rabbi *Meir of Rothenburg, and Hirsch *Lekert. Liessin translated Russian and German poets, as well as Bialik and Walt Whitman, who influenced his own ballads and lyrics. His memoirs *Zikhroynes un Bilder* (1954) are of great literary value. The first collection of Liessin's poems *Moderne Lider,* in a hectographed edition, appeared illegally in Minsk in 1897. *Lider un Poemen,* his complete poetry, was published in three volumes in New York in 1938.

Bibliography: Rejzen, Leksikon, 2 (1927), 259–66; LNYL, 5 (1963), 179–91; B. Bialostotsky, *Lider un Eseyen* (1932), 79–130; E. Schulman: *Geshikhte fun der Yidisher Literatur in Amerike* (1943), 200–6; Z. Shazar, *Or Ishim* (1955), 195–207; H. Leivick, *Eseyen un Redes* (1963), 167–74; B. Rivkin, *Yidishe Dikhter in Amerike* (1959), 72–79; S. Bickel, *Shrayber fun Mayn Dor* (1965), 210–4; Waxman, Literature, 4 (1960²), 1023–28; I. Ch. Biletzky, *Essays on Yiddish Poetry and Prose Writers* (1969), 15–22. [E.Sch.]

LIFE AND DEATH. In Jewish thought both life and death are part of the divine plan for the world.

Life. The opening chapter of Genesis states that all things are created by God. They are, therefore, all purposeful. They all have some value, as is clearly implicit in God's judgment on the created order: "God saw everything He had made, and behold, it was very good" (Gen. 1:31). But it is man who is at the apex of creation and the highest level in the order of value. All other things were created for his sake and constitute the theater of his operation and creative ingenuity.

Since life is the highest good, man is obliged to cherish it and preserve it. Every person is under mandate to marry and procreate in order to share in perpetuating the human species (Yev. 63b). He must preserve himself in a state of health. The Talmud includes many rules of hygiene and cautions against making one's home in a community where there is no competent physician (Sanh. 17b). Maimonides included a chapter on rules of health in his code *Mishneh Torah,* since "the preservation of the health of the body is one of the godly ways" (Yad 4). The rabbis ruled that the preservation of life supersedes the fulfillment of all commandments, except the prohibitions against murder, unchastity, and idolatry (Yoma 82a). One should be concerned as much with the preservation of others' lives as with one's own life. Rabbi Akiva regarded the commandment to love one's neighbor as oneself the most fundamental precept of the Torah (Sifra 19:18). Whoever sustains a single person, taught the rabbis, is as one who sustains the whole world, and whoever destroys a single person is as one who destroys the whole world; for every person bears the divine image, and every person was created unique and irreplaceable. Each one, therefore, has a right to say: "For my sake was the world created" (Sanh. 4:5). Indeed, man's obligations are not limited to his fellowmen. They extend to all existence. He must not wantonly and unnecessarily destroy any object in the world nor inflict pain on any living creature. In this spirit the 18th-century rabbi Ezekiel Judah *Landau forbade hunting (S. Wind, *Rav Yeḥezekel Landau* (1961), 54).

In stressing the sanctity of human life, the rabbis often went beyond biblical precedent. For example, the Bible calls for *capital punishment for a wide variety of crimes, but the rabbis limited such punishment to conditions which in effect made the law inoperative. The Mishnah brands a court that imposes a sentence of capital punishment once in seven years, or according to another tradition, once in 70 years, a murderous court (Mak. 1:10).

Death. In view of the high value attached to man, death, which puts an end to man and his achievements, is the most baffling phenomenon. The account of Adam's sin (Gen. 2) is the biblical attempt to deal with the problem. Rabbinic literature contains a variety of views on the subject. Some rabbis regarded death as a punishment meted out to Adam and his descendants because of his sin in the Garden of Eden (Gen. R. 16:6), but others held that death was an appropriate termination for a finite creature and that it had been preordained at the time of creation (Gen. R. 30:8; Ex. R. 2:4). Death is the price paid for new birth, for the continued emergence of a new generation. Death must be deemed a good, noted Maimonides, since it is the means of "perpetuating existence and the continuity of individual beings through the emergence of one after the withdrawal of the other" (*Guide* 3:10).

Death was also robbed of its terror by the belief that after death individuals survive as incorporeal spirits (Ket. 103a; Ber. 18b). Related to this was the belief in retributive judgment. The righteous would be rewarded with eternal bliss in paradise and the wicked, punished in hell (see *Garden of Eden, *Gehinnom, and *Beatitude).

The final mitigation of the terror of death in rabbinic literature was the belief in the *resurrection of the dead and the world to come. At the end of the historical process God will create the dead anew reuniting body and soul, and then the resurrected dead will enjoy the bliss of the "world to come." The literalness of the belief in the resurrection appears to have been questioned by some rabbis. Thus, one view expressed in the Talmud states that in the world to come "there is no eating or drinking, no begetting children, no commerce, envy, hatred, or competition, but only this: that the righteous sit with crowns on their heads and delight in the splendor of God's presence" (Ber. 17a). The technical term for resurrection is *teḥiyyat ha-metim,* literally, "the revival of the dead." But there were Jewish philosophers, beginning with Philo, who interpreted this figuratively as referring to the immortality of the soul. Maimonides, especially, inveighed against the notion of a physical restoration as man's final state, and insisted that ultimate happiness consists of the incorporeal existence of men's intellect, attained by pursuing a life of virtue and wisdom.

To accentuate the rejection of a belief in physical resurrection, the Reform liturgy drops the praise of God as the *meḥayyeh ha-metim* ("He who revives the dead") from the *Amidah* and substitutes *note'a be-tokhenu ḥayyei olam* (". . . who has implanted within us eternal life"). The Reconstructionist prayer book substitutes for *meḥayyeh ha-metim, zokher yeẓirav le-ḥayyim be-raḥamim* (". . . who in love rememberest Thy creatures to life"). But many Jewish modernists use the traditional text, interpreting it, no doubt, as an allusion to the soul's *immortality.

Bibliography: E. Fackenheim, in: *Commentary*, 39 (1965), 49–55.
[B.Z.Bo.]

LIFSHITS, SHIYE-MORDKHE (1829–1878), pioneering Yiddish lexicographer, author, and a theoretician of the Yiddishist movement in the 19th century. With a solid intellectual background (a student of mathematics, physics, chemistry, languages) Lifshits propounded the idea of a secular Jewish culture on the basis of Yiddish. As a close friend of *Mendele Mokher Seforim, it is thought that Lifshits was instrumental in convincing the "Grandfather of modern Hebrew and Yiddish literature" to switch from Hebrew to Yiddish as a means of literary expression. A pioneer of the idea of Yiddish press, it is also assumed by some that under Lifshits' influence A. *Zederbaum began to publish the epoch-making Yiddish periodical *Kol Mevasser*, where Lifshits became a literary contributor on various topics.

Lifshits' lexicographic achievements are to a large extent unsurpassed in their quality and reliability, especially in depicting the South-Eastern (Volhynian) Yiddish dialect. The manuscript of one of his dictionaries (Yiddish-German, German-Yiddish) unfortunately was lost. His excellent *Rusish-yidisher verter-bikh* went through four editions (1869–86). The Yiddish-Russian dictionary, *Yidish-rusisher verter-bikh*, was published in 1876.

A man of progressive ideas, Lifshits opened a tailor shop in the 1870s in Berdichev (where he died and was probably born) and shared the profits with the girls who worked there. He was deeply respected as a man of high ethical standards and admired even by his opponents. Although paralyzed in his later years, he continued his creative work to the very end.

Bibliography: N. Shtif, in: *Di Yidishe Shprakh* (July–Oct., 1928); Rejzen, Leksikon, 2 (1930), 180–9; LNYL, 5 (1963), 210–5.
[Mor.Sch.]

LIFSHITZ, DAVID (1907–), U.S. *rosh yeshivah* and rabbinical leader. Lifshitz was born in Minsk and studied under Simeon *Shkop in the Grodno yeshivah and at the Mir yeshivah. In 1935 he succeeded his father-in-law, Joseph Joselowitz, as rabbi of Suwalki where he soon established a yeshivah. Lifshitz became active in all communal affairs and assisted Ḥayyim Ozer *Grodzinski of Vilna in safeguarding the interests of Orthodoxy. After the deportation of the Jews of his community by the Nazis, Lifshitz succeeded in emigrating to the United States, where in 1942 he became a *rosh yeshivah* at Chicago's *Hebrew Theological College. In 1945 he was appointed to a similar position at *Yeshiva University. Lifshitz was active in guiding Orthodox Jewry in its relationship to the State of Israel and urged the religious parties to form a united religious front. He was a member of the presidium of the *Union of Orthodox Rabbis, the rabbinical advisory board to *Torah u-Masorah, and a director of Ezrat Torah, which aided rabbis and scholars throughout the world.

Bibliography: O. Rand, *Toledot Anshei Shem* (1950), 76f.
[Ed.]

LIFSHITZ, NEHAMAH (1927–), folk singer of Yiddish and Hebrew songs. Born in Kaunas (Kovno), Lithuania, where she started her schooling at the Hebrew high school, Nehamah Lifshitz was evacuated with her parents during

Photo portrait of Nehamah Lifshitz by A. Agor, Tel Aviv. Courtesy Giora Godik, Tel Aviv.

World War II to Uzbekistan. After returning in 1946 to Soviet Lithuania, she studied at the Vilna conservatoire and in 1951 she gave her first concert. At an all-Soviet competition in 1958 she received the title of laureate of *estrada* (folk) artists. She traveled throughout the U.S.S.R., giving concerts of Yiddish (and some Hebrew) songs, drawing large crowds, including many young Jews. In 1959 and 1960 she visited France, Belgium, and Austria. In 1969 she was allowed by the Soviet authorities to immigrate to Israel where she was enthusiastically received as "the voice of the Jews of silence." [B.E.]

°**LIGHTFOOT, JOHN** (1602–1675), English Hebraist and Bible scholar. Lightfoot, a Puritan, was master of Catherine Hall, Cambridge, from 1650 and three years later he became vice-chancellor of Cambridge University. He began studying Hebrew after his ordination, but at first gave his attention to Bible research on scientific lines, publishing works such as *Harmonia, Chronica et Ordo Veteris Testamenti* (1647). However, he soon turned to rabbinical literature, a field in which he became the outstanding Christian authority of his time, showing a remarkable expertise in talmudic and midrashic scholarship. He published a *Descriptio Templi Hierosolymitani* (1650), on the Temple of Herod, and *Horae Hebraicae et Talmudicae* (1658–74), a study of the rabbinic sources of and background to the New Testament gospels. His first venture in Hebraica, published at the outset of his career, had been *Erubhin; or Miscellanies, Christian and Judaical, and others . . .* (London, 1629), and as a result of his unusual and objective investigation of rabbinic literature Lightfoot was accused of "rabbinism." He contributed to Bryan *Walton's *Biblia Sacra Polyglotta* (London Polyglot Bible; 1654–57), revising the Samaritan Pentateuch and specially preparing a geography of Palestine for the work. A Latin edition of his complete writings was later issued by his contemporary, Johann *Leusden, professor of Hebrew at Utrecht.

Bibliography: D. M. Welter, *J. Lightfoot, the English Hebraist* (1878); DNB, 33 (1893), 229ff.
[G.E.S.]

LIKKUT AẒAMOT (לִקּוּט עֲצָמוֹת, lit., "gathering of the bones"). In ancient Ereẓ Israel, the interment of the corpse did not take place immediately after death. First the body was left in the sepulchral chamber for some time until it was reduced to a mere skeleton, and afterward the bones were gathered together and then solemnly interred in the final resting place (TJ, MK 1:5; 80c–d; Sem. 12). This duty was generally performed one year after death by the children of the deceased and the laws of mourning were practiced on the day of the final interment (MK 8a; Sem. 12). Mourning was not continued the next day even if the gathering of the remains was only then completed. It was forbidden to deliver mournful eulogies on this occasion, and public condolences were not extended. However, the departed was praised and private condolences were conveyed (MK 8a; Sem. 12-13). The remains had to be reverently handled, and they could not, for example, be transported to their final resting place in a saddle bag (Ber. 18a). It was not considered respectful for the son to touch the remains of his parents directly with his bare hands (Sem. 12). Those engaged in the meritorious deed of *likkut aẓamot* were exempt from reading the **Shema*, and from all other positive commandments (Sem. 13). The gathering of the bones could not take place during the intermediate festival days since such an event would infringe upon the joy of the festival (MK 1:5). The laws pertaining to *likkut aẓamot* are also applicable in instances when *disinterment is permissible. However, when the coffin is still intact and is not opened during the disinterment procedure, the laws of mourning do not apply (TJ, Sanh. 6:11, 23d).

See also *Burial.

Bibliography: S. Krauss, in: REJ, 97 (1934), 1–34; J. M. Tukacinsky, *Gesher ha-Ḥayyim*, 1 (1960²), 276–82; 2 (1960²), 183–91; J. J. (L.) Greenwald, *Kol Bo al Avelut*, 1 (1947), 223–49; 2 (1951), 75–94. [Ed.]

LILIEN, EPHRAIM MOSES (1874–1925), Austrian illustrator and printmaker. Lilien was born in Drohobycz, Galicia. He studied art in Cracow for a short time, but lack of funds forced him to return home. He eventually earned enough as a sign painter to go to the Academy of Fine Arts in Vienna. In 1895 he worked in Munich as a cartoonist; three years later he moved to Berlin, where he soon became known as a book illustrator. Lilien was the first artist to become involved in the Zionist movement. He took an active part in three consecutive Zionist Congresses and was a member of the *Democratic Fraction, which stressed the need to foster Jewish culture. He was one of the founders of the Berlin publishing house, *Juedischer Verlag*, which he served not only as an illustrator but also as editor, manager, and publicity agent. In 1902 the firm published *Juda*, a volume of ballads on Old Testament themes by a pro-Zionist German poet, Boerries Freiherr von Muenchhausen, illustrated by Lilien. He collaborated closely with Theodor *Herzl; Lilien's photograph of the Zionist leader on the Rhine bridge, his Herzl portraits, and his decorations for the Golden Book of the Jewish National Fund became familiar to Zionists all over the world. In 1905 Lilien, along with Boris *Schatz and others, was a member of the committee formed to establish the *Bezalel School of Art in Jerusalem. He taught there for some months in the following year and revisited Palestine three times, on the last occasion as a lieutenant in the Austro-Hungarian army during World War I. In 1908 Lilien turned from book illustration to etching. Many of his etchings are views of Austria and Hungary, while others record his impressions of Palestine, Damascus, and Beirut. His drawings, executed mainly in india ink, show a crisp, elegant line and a strong contrast between black and white areas.

Ephraim Moses Lilien, Austrian illustrator and printmaker. Courtesy Central Zionist Archives, Jerusalem.

Bibliography: M. S. Levussove, *The New Art of an Ancient People: The Work of Ephraim Mose Lilien* (1906), includes plates; L. Brieger, *E. M. Lilien* (1922), includes bibliography. [A.W.]

LILIENBLUM, MOSES LEIB (1843–1910), Hebrew writer, critic, and political journalist. Born in Kedainiai, near Kovno, Lilienblum was one of the leaders of the Haskalah in its last period and a leader of Ḥibbat Zion.

His Life and Public Activity. His first teachers were his father, R. Ẓevi, a poor cooper, and his maternal grandfather, who was a teacher. Steeped in Talmud, Lilienblum established two yeshivot at the age of 22. At the same time, he began studying the Haskalah literature, secular subjects, and Russian and disseminated his views in public. In 1866 fanatic religious elements in Wilkomir, where he was then living, began to persecute him for his beliefs. Lilienblum retaliated in articles and an exchange of letters published in *Ha-Karmel* and **Ha-Meliẓ*. In 1868 he published his articles *"Orḥot ha-Talmud"* and *"Nosafot le-Orḥot ha-Talmud"* in *Ha-Meliẓ*, advocating reforms in religion and in society. Lilienblum stated that the Talmud contains progressive ideas modified to suit time and place, while the Shulḥan Arukh is rigid in tone and out of touch with life. He criticized the outstanding rabbis of his time through the pages of *Ha-Levanon* and *Kevod ha-Levanon*. In 1869 Lilienblum moved to Odessa, where he published his political satire, *Kehal Refa'im* (1870), in which he attacked many of his contemporaries, rabbis, writers, and editors, and called for the normalization of Jewish life through agricultural labor and the rational organization of work in industry, crafts, and commerce.

In 1871 Lilienblum began to edit the Yiddish journal, *Kol Mevasser*. In a series of articles he drew a grim picture of Jewish education in the *ḥeder* and in the yeshivot of the time. In articles written in 1871–73 he raised the problems of the emancipation of women, the mismanagement of Jewish community life, and religious and individual freedom. In his article *"Olam ha-Tohu"* (1873), a critique of Abraham *Mapu's book *Ayit Ẓavu'a*, he wrote of the need to reflect life as it really is, without romanticism, superstition, mysteries, or imagination, "a material view of life." In

1873–76 Lilienblum wrote his masterful autobiography *Ḥatte'ot Ne'urim*, in which he described his struggles and suffering and the development of his beliefs. In 1874–81 Socialism became the main subject of his writing. He

Moses Leib Lilienblum, Hebrew writer, critic, and political journalist. Jerusalem, J.N.U.L., Schwadron Collection.

published his article *"Mishnat Elisha ben Avuyah"* in Liebermann's *Ha-Emet*, urging the importance of labor in the life of the individual and the nation. He deliberately dated the article "The Day of Atonement, 1877." The year of the pogroms (1881) marks a radical shift in Lilienblum's career. He became a nationalist and a leader of the Ḥibbat Zion movement in Russia. He was one of the founders of the Odessa committee in 1883, and two years later was appointed its secretary and secretary of the Odessa *ḥevra kaddisha* ("burial society").

Lilienblum the Publicist. Lilienblum's career as a journalist had three stages: (a) 1866–70, the period of his struggle for religious reform. Lilienblum believed that the Jewish religion was stagnating and hindering the development of the nation. During this period Lilienblum advocated the introduction of the evolutionary principle into the field of religious practice. His main desire was to create close cooperation between Jews and their non-Jewish neighbors to be expressed in moderate reform of the more rigid religious precepts. (b) 1870–81, abandonment of the principle of religious evolution and the adoption of the demand for equal rights to be granted by the state as a prerequisite for the renaissance of Judaism in the spirit of the Haskalah. The Haskalah and progress are not a guarantee against anti-Semitism, and civil equality cannot be created only as a result of internal reforms in Judaism. (c) From 1881 until his death, the belief that the roots of anti-Semitism lie in the Aryan society's instinctive enmity toward the Semitic Jews. Legal equality is no guarantee of social equality. The aim of nationalist movements is either total assimilation of the Jews or their expulsion from their countries of residence. The source of the trials of the Jewish people lies in their constituting a nation within a nation. There is no basis for the hope that progress will bring about the end of anti-Semitism. The process of assimilation will not be implemented because of the firm stand of the Jewish people against the forces of disintegration, nor does it provide a solution to the problems of the Jewish people. Lilienblum concluded that it was necessary to concentrate the nation as one group in its own territory, and regarded Palestine as the suitable location, since there the nation would not constitute a foreign body; he opposed the creation of a Jewish haven in the U.S. His proposal was that land be purchased from the Turks and a quasi-governmental entity be established. It was not sufficient merely to establish settlements. In his view, the solution to the Jewish problem lay in the elimination of the Diaspora, and in the attainment of the status of an independent nation. The return to Zion could be implemented if the nation willed it. Lilienblum placed great hopes in the masses and in a certain stratum of the Jewish intelligentsia, whose task would be to arouse the desire for national independence. From 1889 onward he conducted a debate in the pages of *Ha-Meliẓ* and *Ha-Shaḥar*, with *Aḥad Ha-Am, *Ben-Avigdor, Zalman *Epstein, S. I. *Hurwitz, and *Dubnow, developing the ideology of the Ḥibbat Zion movement and practical Zionism. He grasped the dynamic and aggressive character of anti-Semitism, as did *Smolenskin, and foresaw the threat of total physical destruction of the Jewish people. Lilienblum rejected as artificial the autonomist approach, advocated by Dubnow, for the solution of the Jewish problem and regarded the theories of Aḥad Ha-Am and his disciples as making the existence of the Jewish people dependent on metaphysical speculations. He stressed that the Jewish people wanted to live for the sake of living and not for any purpose beyond life.

Lilienblum, the Critic and Writer. In his literary criticism Lilienblum adopted the concepts of critical realism, bordering on nihilism, as advocated by Pisarev, Dobrolyubov, and Chernyshevski, even after having abandoned their political and social ideology. His literary and lyrical talent was small. *Kehal Refa'im*, his satirical work, is, in its way, an imitation of *Erter's satires, and the motifs are common ones in Haskalah literature. His only real contribution to literature is *Ḥatte'ot Ne'urim* (Vienna, 1876), his autobiography. Despite the sparsity of plastic description, the work is distinguished by its pathos and its insight into the inner emotional and moral conflict of the protagonist who struggles with social mores and the Jewish tradition.

Lilienblum wrote his literary criticism from the pragmatic viewpoint with the aim of educating the Jewish people to a true material view of life and freeing them from the useless life of the imagination. He admired only "real things." This anti-aesthetic pragmatic approach runs throughout his work and his critical articles. All art must be examined in the light of its usefulness to society. Lilienblum attached no importance to style and language as an integral part of artistic expression. He was contemptuous of imagination. He dismissed most love poetry as lacking innovation, and regarded any deviation from rational logic to mysticism, such as the Kabbalah and Ḥasidism, as constituting a dangerous deviation from reality. He therefore rejected the Nietzschean revolt as expressed by Berdyczewski, his *Ha-Kera'im she-ba-Lev*, and the worship of hidden impulses. Lilienblum's philosophy is that "there is no aim in life except life itself."

His Books. Lilienblum prepared his own works for publication and they were published posthumously by J. Klausner in four volumes, *Kol Kitvei Lilienblum* (1910–13). *Derekh Teshuvah* (1899) and *Derekh La'avor Golim* (1899) were not included in this collection. Some of Lilienblum's letters were printed in *Hed ha-Zeman*, in *Ha-Olam*, in *Reshumot*, and in *Ketavim le-Toledot Ḥibbat Ẓiyyon*, edited by A. A. Druyanow in *Beḥinot* and in *Perakim*. His letters to J. L. Gordon were published in 1968, edited by S. Breiman, who also edited his autobiographical writings (3 vols., 1970). Lilienblum wrote a play in Yiddish entitled *Zerubbavel* (1887); he also edited the fifth volume of *Lu'aḥ Aḥi'asaf* (1897).

Bibliography: J. S. Raisin, *The Haskalah Movement in Russia* (1913), index; Klausner, Sifrut, 4 (1953), 190–300; Breiman, in: *Shivat Ẓiyyon*, 1 (1950), 138–68; 2–3 (1953), 83–113; idem, introd. to *Ketavim Autobiografiyyim*, 1 (1970), 7–74 (incl. bibl.); A. Shaanan, *Ha-Sifrut ha-Ivrit ha-Ḥadashah li-Zerameha*, 2 (1962), 19–34; S. Streit, *Penei ha-Sifrut*, 1 (1938), 155–72; D. Ben-Nahum, *Be-Ma'aleh Dorot* (1962), 277–90; P. Lipovetzky (Ben Amram), *Ra'yon ha-Avodah ba-Sifrut ha-Ivrit* (1930), 54–68; S. Zemaḥ, *Eruvin* (1964), 37–50; Waxman, Literature, index; Spiegel, *Hebrew Reborn* (1962), 199–205. [S.O.]

LILIENTHAL, DAVID ELI (1899–), U.S. attorney, public official, and specialist in the development of natural resources. Lilienthal, who was born in Morton, Illinois, was admitted to the Illinois bar in 1923. He practiced law in

David Eli Lilienthal, U.S. public figure. Photo Ulli Steltzer.

Chicago and was special counsel to that city in litigation concerning telephone rates until 1931. From 1926 to 1931, when he was appointed to the Wisconsin Public Service Commission, he also edited the journal *Public Utilities and Carriers Service*. In 1933 he was chosen by President Roosevelt to be director of the Tennessee Valley Authority. He held this post until 1941 when he was promoted to TVA chairman. In these capacities he defended TVA against attacks by Wendall L. Willkie and the power companies, resisted attempts to undermine the nonpolitical nature of appointments to the agency, and strove for decentralization of administration, voluntary cooperation of local communities, and planning in response to their needs. In 1946 he left the TVA to assume the chairmanship of the U.S. Atomic Energy Commission. His "Lilienthal Plan" called for an end to the nuclear arms race through international control of all atomic energy. He also publicly questioned the wisdom of America's decision to produce the hydrogen bomb. In the wake of controversy created by these views, Lilienthal returned to private life in 1950. In 1955 he formed the Development and Resources Corporation, a private venture in the designing and execution of development plans for backward countries. He served as a consultant on the utilization of human and natural resources to the governments of Colombia, Italy, and Iran for various periods after 1955. His books include: *TVA: Democracy on the March* (1944); *Big Business: A New Era* (1953); and the four-volume *Journals of David E. Lilienthal* (1964–1969).

Bibliography: J. Daniels, *Southerner Discovers the South* (1938), 46–97; Brooks, in: *New Yorker* (April 29, 1961), 45–90; P. Selznick, *TVA and the Grass Roots* (1949), which presents conclusions different from Lilienthal's own.

[B.St.]

LILIENTHAL, MAX (Menahem; 1815–1882), educator, author, and rabbi. Born in Munich, Bavaria, Lilienthal completed his studies at the university of his native town, and in 1839, on the recommendation of Ludwig Philippson, was appointed director of the Jewish school of Riga. He succeeded in this position, and also became known for the sermons which he delivered in German at the Riga synagogue (published as *Predigten in der Synagoge zu Riga*, 1841). He formed a friendship with the Russian minister of education S. S. *Uvarov, to whom he dedicated the above work.

In 1841, on the recommendation of Uvarov, the czarist government invited Lilienthal to draw up a project for the establishment of state schools for Jews providing a European-type education. Lilienthal set out upon his task by attempting to persuade the community leaders in the *Pale of Settlement to accept the project. His mission encountered opposition and mistrust among Jews there. Orthodox circles, and particularly the Ḥasidim, considered the project an attempt by the government to destroy traditional Jewish education, and possibly even to convert the Jews, while the *maskilim* also expressed misgivings. Lilienthal's meetings with the representatives of the Jews of Vilna, one of the main centers of Russian Jewry, ended in failure. His attempts to issue threats in the name of the government (it is not clear whether he was authorized to do so) aroused revulsion, while his strategy of contacting the representatives of the Orthodox and Ḥasidim and ignoring the *maskilim* alienated the latter from him. The publication of his proposals to invite teachers from Germany for the projected schools was a cause of further mistrust. In *Minsk Lilienthal found open hostility accompanied by personal abuse. His reaction, in 1842, was an appeal to Uvarov to enforce "educational reform" on the Jews through a series of laws. The minister of education refused to do so, but by means of a decree (June 22, 1842) he hinted to the Jews that the czar himself was in favor of the reform.

In order to sever the connection between the projected "reforms" and the personality of Lilienthal, Uvarov appointed a commission composed of Jewish personalities to study the proposals. Lilienthal was called upon to undertake an extensive journey through the Jewish centers to assess public opinion and guide it in the desired direction. Having learned from his previous experiences, Lilienthal on this occasion did not repeat his former suggestions, such as the employment of teachers from abroad and the imposition of a tax on the *melammedim* (*ḥeder* teachers), and succeeded in winning sympathy. However, his tactics in seeking an alliance with the Orthodox against the *maskilim* once more led to his failure. Lilienthal's appeal in *Maggid Yeshu'ah* (Vilna, 1842) brought a sharp retort from Mordecai Aaron *Guenzburg in the pamphlet *Maggid Emet* (Leipzig, 1843). The Commission for the Education of the Jews completed its task in 1843, and in 1844 a law for the establishment of state schools for the Jews was issued. In 1844, however, at the height of his success, Lilienthal had to leave Russia secretly. It appears that he had become convinced that intentions of the czarist government were insincere and that it was scheming to exploit the network of schools as an instrument for eventual conversion to Christianity. The government's demand to exclude the study of Talmud from the curriculum marked the turning point in his outlook.

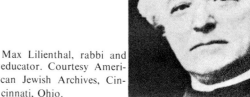

Max Lilienthal, rabbi and educator. Courtesy American Jewish Archives, Cincinnati, Ohio.

Additionally, the law for the establishment of the schools was accompanied by other anti-Jewish laws in various spheres.

In 1845 Lilienthal emigrated to the United States, settling

in New York City where he conducted a private boarding school for a few years. In 1849 he became rabbi of a short-lived union of the city's German congregations and directed their day schools. From 1855 until his death Lilienthal was rabbi of the important Bene Israel congregation of Cincinnati, which he led in the direction of moderate Reform. As a civic leader in his city on friendly terms with its Christian clergy, he was a member of its board of education (1860–69) and a trustee of the University of Cincinnati from 1872 until his death. He was perhaps the leading Jewish exponent in his day of the rigorous exclusion of all religious teaching from the public schools. Lilienthal actively cooperated with his fellow townsman Isaac Mayer *Wise in promoting Reform Judaism throughout the West, and was the publisher of *The Sabbath Visitor* from 1874, founder of the scholarly Rabbinical Literary Association, and taught at *Hebrew Union College from its opening in 1875. In 1857 he published *Freiheit, Fruehling und Liebe*, a collection of poems.

Bibliography: D. Philipson, *Max Lilienthal, his Life and Writings* (1915); idem, *The Reform Movement in Judaism* (1931²), index; D. Kahana, in: *Ha-Shilo'aḥ*, 27 (1913), 314–22, 446–57, 546–56; J. S. Raisin, *The Haskalah Movement in Russia* (1915); P. Wengeroff, *Memoiren einer Grossmutter*, 1 (1908), 123–43; J. Shatzky, *Yidishe Bildungs-Politik in Poyln fun 1806 biz 1866* (1943), 71–80; H. B. Grinstein, in: HUCA, 18 (1943/44), 321–52; *The Sabbath Visitor* (April 14, 1882); *Der deutsche Pionier*, 14 (1882), 162–70, 211–6.

[EH/ED.]

LILIENTHAL, OTTO (1848–1896), German inventor and aeronaut. Born in Anklam, Pomerania, Lilienthal and his brother, Gustav, studied the flight of birds and while still at school succeeded in constructing a glider. During the next few years the brothers built many gliders and executed a large number of flights. Lilienthal demonstrated the superiority of arched wings over flat-surfaced types, and brought gliding flight into a regular practice. He made over 2,000 flights, but finally while in flight his machine was upset by a sudden gust of wind, and he was killed near Rhinow. He wrote *Der Vogelflug als Grundlage der Fliegekunst* (1939³), and *Die Flugapparate* (1894). Lilienthal also made technical improvements in steam boilers, and designed children's building blocks. The Lilienthal brothers' Jewish origin has been disputed.

Otto Lilienthal, 19th-century German aeronaut and inventor. Jerusalem, J.N.U.L., Schwadron Collection.

Bibliography: G. Halle, *Otto Lilienthal* (1936), incl. bibl., 186–90; A. and G. Lilienthal, *Die Lilienthals* (1930); S. Kaznelson, *Juden im deutschen Kulturbereich* (1962³), 1053.

[EH]

LILITH, a female demon assigned a central position in Jewish *demonology. The figure may be traced to Babylonian (possibly even Sumerian) demonology, which identifies similar male and female spirits—Lilu and Lilitu respectively—which are etymologically unrelated to the Hebrew word *laylah* ("night"). These *mazikim* ("harmful spirits") have various roles: one of them—the Ardat-Lilith—preys on males, while others imperil women in childbirth and their children. An example of the latter kind is Lamashtu, against whom incantation formulas have been preserved in Assyrian. Winged female demons who strangle children are known from a Hebrew or Canaanite inscription found at Arslan-Tash in northern Syria and dating from about the seventh or eighth century B.C.E. Whether or not Lilith is mentioned in this incantation, which adjures the stranglers not to enter the house, is a moot point, depending on the addition of a missing letter: "To her that flies in rooms of darkness—pass quickly, quickly, Lil[ith]." In Scripture there is only one reference to Lilith (Isa. 34:14), among the beasts of prey and the spirits that will lay waste the land on the day of vengeance. In sources dating from earlier centuries, traditions concerning the female demon who endangers women in childbirth and who assumes many guises and names are distinct from the explicit tradition on Lilith recorded in the Talmud. Whereas the Babylonian Lilu is mentioned as some kind of male demon with no defined function, Lilith appears as a female demon with a woman's face, long hair, and wings (Er. 100b; Nid. 24b). A man sleeping in a house alone may be seized by Lilith (Shab. 151b); while the demon Hormiz, or Ormuzd, is mentioned as one of her sons (BB 73b). There is no foundation to the later commentaries that identify Lilith with the demon Agrath, daughter of Mahalath, who goes abroad at night with 180,000 pernicious *angels (Pes. 112b). Nevertheless, a female demon who is known by tens of thousands of names and moves about the world at night, visiting women in childbirth and endeavoring to strangle their newborn babes, is mentioned in the *Testament of *Solomon*, a Greek work of about the third century. Although preserved in a Christian version, this work is certainly based on Judeo-Hellenistic *magic. Here the female demon is called Obizoth, and it is related that one of the mystical names of the angel *Raphael inscribed on an *amulet prevents her from inflicting injury.

Midrashic literature expands the legend that *Adam, having parted from his wife after it had been ordained that they should die, begat demons from spirits that had attached themselves to him. It is said that "he was encountered by a Lilith named Piznai who, taken by his beauty, lay with him and bore male and female demons." The firstborn son of this demonic union was Agrimas (see the Midrash published in *Ha-Goren*, 9 (1914), 66–68; *Dvir*, 1 (1923), 138; and L. Ginzberg, *Legends of the Jews*, 5 (1925), 166. The offspring of this Lilith fill the world. A transmuted version of this legend appears in the *Alphabet of *Ben Sira*, a Midrash of the geonic period, which sets out to explain the already widespread custom of writing amulets against Lilith. Here she is identified with the "first Eve," who was created from the earth at the same time as Adam, and who, unwilling to forgo her equality, disputed with him the manner of their intercourse. Pronouncing the Ineffable Name, she flew off into the air. On Adam's request, the Almighty sent after her the three angels Snwy, Snsnwy, and Smnglf; finding her in the Red Sea, the angels threatened that if she did not return, 100 of her sons would die every day. She refused, claiming that she was expressly created to harm newborn infants. However, she had to swear that whenever she saw the image of those angels in an amulet, she would lose her power over the infant. Here the legend concerning the wife of Adam who preceded the creation of Eve (Gen. 2) merges with the earlier legend of Lilith as a demon who kills infants and endangers women in childbirth. This later version of the myth has many parallels in Christian literature from Byzantine (which probably preceded it) and later periods. The female demon is known by different names, many of which reappear in the same or in slightly altered forms in the literature of practical *Kabba-

Amulet for the protection of a newborn child against Lilith, Persia, 18th century. Lilith is represented with arms outstretched and bound in fetters. On her body is written, "Protect this newborn child from all harm." On either side of her are the names of Adam and Eve and the patriarchs and matriarchs, while above are the initial letters of a passage from Numbers 6:22–27, and below from Psalms 121. $3\frac{1}{2}\times2\frac{1}{2}$ in. (9.1×6.7 cm.). Jerusalem, Israel Museum, Feuchtwanger Collection, donated by Baruch and Ruth Rappaport.

lah (as, for example, the name Obizoth from the *Testament of Solomon*), and the place of the angels is taken by three saints—Sines, Sisinnios, and Synodoros. The legend also found its way into Arabic demonology, where Lilith is known as Karīna, Tabi'a, or "the mother of the infants." The personification of Lilith as a strangler of babies is already clear in Jewish incantations, written in Babylonian Aramaic, which predate the *Alphabet of Ben Sira*. A late Midrash (*Ba-Midbar Rabbah*, end of ch. 16) also mentions her in this respect: "When Lilith finds no children born, she turns on her own"—a motif which relates her to the Babylonian Lamashtu.

From these ancient traditions, the image of Lilith was fixed in kabbalistic demonology. Here, too, she has two primary roles: the strangler of children (sometimes replaced in the Zohar by Naamah), and the seducer of men, from whose nocturnal emissions she bears an infinite number of demonic sons. In this latter role she appears at the head of a vast host, who share in her activities. In the *Zohar, as in other sources, she is known by such appelations as Lilith, the harlot, the wicked, the false, or the black. (The above-mentioned combination of motifs appears in the Zohar I, 14b, 54b; II, 96a, 111a; III, 19a, 76b.) She is generally numbered among the four mothers of the demons, the others being Agrat, Mahalath, and Naamah. Wholly new in the kabbalistic concept of Lilith is her appearance as the permanent partner of Samael, queen of the realm of the forces of evil (the *sitra aḥra*). In that world (the world of the *kelippot*) she fulfills a function parallel to that of the **Shekhinah* ("Divine Presence") in the world of sanctity: just as the *Shekhinah* is the mother of the House of Israel, so Lilith is the mother of the unholy folk who constituted the "mixed multitude" (the *erev-rav*) and ruled over all that is impure. This conception is first found in the sources used by *Isaac b. Jacob ha-Kohen, and later in *Ammud ha-Semali* by his disciple, *Moses b. Solomon b. Simeon of Burgos. Both here, and later in the *Tikkunei Zohar*, there crystallizes the conception of various degrees of Lilith, internal and external. Likewise we find Lilith the older, the wife of Samael, and Lilith the younger, the wife of *Asmodeus (see Tarbiz, 4 (1932/33), 72) in the writings of Isaac ha-Kohen and thereafter in the writings of most kabbalists. Some of these identify the two harlots who appeared in judgment before Solomon with Lilith and Naamah or Lilith and Agrat, an idea which is already hinted at in the Zohar and in contemporary writings (see Tarbiz, 19 (1947/48), 172–5).

Widespread, too, is the identification of Lilith with the *Queen of Sheba—a notion with many ramifications in Jewish folklore. It originates in the Targum to Job 1:15 based on a Jewish and Arab myth that the Queen of Sheba was actually a jinn, half human and half demon. This view was known to *Moses b. Shem Tov de Leon and is also mentioned in the Zohar. In *Livnat ha-Sappir* Joseph Angelino maintains that the riddles which the Queen of Sheba posed to Solomon are a repetition of the words of seduction which the first Lilith spoke to Adam. In Ashkenazi folklore, this figure coalesced with the popular image of Helen of Troy or the Frau Venus of German mythology. Until recent generations the Queen of Sheba was popularly pictured as a snatcher of children and a demonic witch. It is probable that there is a residue of the image of Lilith as *Satan's partner in popular late medieval European notions of Satan's concubine, or wife in English folklore—"the Devil's Dame"—and of Satan's grandmother in German folklore. In the German drama on the female pope Jutta (Johanna), which was printed in 1565 though according to its publisher it was written in 1480, the grandmother's name is Lilith. Here she is depicted as a seductive dancer, a motif commonly found in Ashkenazi Jewish incantations involving the Queen of Sheba. In the writings of Ḥayyim *Vital (*Sefer ha-Likkutim* (1913), 6b), Lilith sometimes appears to people in the form of a cat, goose, or other creature, and she holds sway not for eight days alone in the case of a male infant and 20 for a female (as recorded in the *Alfabet de-Ven Sira*), but for 40 and 60 days respectively. In the Kabbalah, influenced by astrology, Lilith is related to the planet Saturn, and all those of a melancholy disposition—of a "black humor"—are her sons (Zohar, *Ra'aya Meheimna* III, 227b). From the 16th century it was commonly believed that if an infant laughed in his sleep it was an indication that Lilith was playing with him, and it was therefore advisable to tap him on the nose to avert the danger (Ḥ. Vital, *Sefer ha-Likkutim* (1913), 78c; *Emek ha-Melekh*, 130b).

It was very common to protect women who were giving *birth from the power of Lilith by affixing amulets over the bed or on all four walls of the room. The earliest forms of these, in Aramaic, are included in Montgomery's collection (see bibl.). The first Hebrew version appears in the *Alphabet of Ben Sira*, which states that the amulet should contain not only the names of the three angels who prevail over Lilith, but also "their form, wings, hands, and legs." This version gained wide acceptance, and amulets of this type were even printed by the 18th century. According to *Shimmush Tehillim*, a book dating from the geonic period, amulets written for women who used to lose their children customarily included Psalm 126 (later replaced by Ps. 121) and the names of these three angels. In the Orient, also amulets representing Lilith herself "bound in chains" were current. Many amulets include the story of the prophet *Elijah meeting Lilith on her way to the house of a woman in childbirth "to give her the sleep of death, to take her son and drink his blood, to suck the marrow of his bones and to eat his flesh" (in other versions: "to leave his flesh"). Elijah excommunicated her, whereupon she undertook not to harm women in childbirth whenever she saw or heard her names. This version is doubtless taken from a Christian Byzantine formula against the female demon Gyllo, who was exorcised by the three saints mentioned above. The transfer from the Greek to the Hebrew version is clearly seen in the formula of the 15th-century Hebrew incantation from Candia (see *Crete), which was published by Cassuto

(RSO, 15 (1935), 260), in which it is not Elijah but the archangel Michael who, coming from Sinai, encounters Lilith. Though the Greek names were progressively corrupted as time elapsed, by the 14th century new Greek names for "Lilith's entourage" appear in a manuscript of practical Kabbalah which includes material from a much earlier date (British Museum Add. Ms. 15299, fol. 84b). The story of Elijah and Lilith included in the second edition of David Lida's *Sod ha-Shem* (Berlin, 1710, p. 20a) is found in the majority of the later amulets against Lilith, one of her names being Striga—an enchantress, either woman or demon—or Astriga. In one of its mutations this name appears as the angel Astaribo, whom Elijah also encountered; in many incantations he takes the place of Lilith, a substitution found in a Yiddish version of the story dating from 1695. Also extant are versions of the incantation in which Lilith is replaced by the *Evil Eye, the star Margalya, or the demon familiar in Jewish and Arab literature, Maimon the Black. In European belles lettres, the Lilith story in various versions has been a fruitful narrative theme.

Bibliography: G. Scholem, in: KS, 10 (1934/35), 68–73; idem, in: *Tarbiz*, 19 (1947/48), 165–75; R. Margalioth, *Malakhei Elyon* (1945), 235–41; Y. Schachar, *Osef Feuchtwanger—Masoret-ve-Ommanut Yehudit* (1971); H. Von der Hardt, *Aenigmata Judaeorum religiosissima* (Helmstedt, 1705), 7–21; J. A. Eisenmenger, *Entdecktes Judentum*, 2 (1700), 413–21; J. Montgomery, *Aramaic Incantation Texts From Nippur* (1913); R. Dow and A. Freidus, in: *Bulletin of the Brooklyn Entomological Society*, 12 (1917), 1–12, (bibl. on Sammael and Lilith); I. Lévi, in: REJ, 67 (1914), 15–21; D. Myhrmann, *Die Labartu-Texte* (1902); Ch. McCown, *The Testament of Solomon* (1922); M. Gaster, *Studies and Texts*, 2 (1925–28), 1005–38, 1252–65; F. Perles, in: *Orientalistische Literaturzeitung*, 18 (1925), 179–80; I. Zoller, *Rivista di Antropologia*, 27 (1926); Ginzberg, Legends, 5 (1955), 87f.; H. Winkler, *Salomo und die Karīna* (1931); J. Trachtenberg, *Jewish Magic and Superstition* (1939), 36f., 277f.; Th. Gaster, in: *Orientalia*, 12 (1942), 41–79; H. Torczyner (Tur-Sinai), in: *Journal of Near Eastern Studies*, 6 (1947), 18–29; M. Rudwin, *The Devil in Legend and Literature* (1931), 94–107; T. Schrire, *Hebrew Amulets* (1966); E. Yamaūchi, *Mandaic Incantation Texts* (1967); A. Chastel, in: RHR, 119–20 (1939), 160–74; A. M. Killen, *Revue de littérature comparée*, 12 (1932), 277–311. [G.Sch.]

LILLE, city in Nord department, N. France. The Jewish community of Lille was formed in the 19th century. From 1872 Lille was the seat of a chief rabbinate; the first incumbent was Benjamin Lippmann, formerly chief rabbi at Colmar, who had refused to remain in Alsace after it was annexed by Germany. According to the census of the Jewish population in occupied France carried out at the beginning of 1942, there were 1,259 Jews then living in Lille, only 247 of whom were born there. The sinister Commissariat Générale aux Questions Juives (CGQJ) had an office there. The Germans executed five Jews in Lille in March–April, 1942, in a reprisal for an underground raid. Of the 461 Jews (French and foreign) deported from the whole of the Nord department, 336 disappeared. Leon Berman (1892–1943), son of a ḥasidic rabbi (Reb Ḥayyim), was rabbi of Lille from 1936 to 1939. In 1937 he published his *Histoire des Juifs de France*. He was arrested along with his wife and son in October 1943, interned at the camp of Drancy, then deported to a death camp. In 1969 there were 2,800 Jews in Lille, which was the seat of the Association cultuelle israélite and the rabbinate for the Nord department; R. Jacques Ouaknine was then the incumbent. The Lille community possessed a synagogue, erected in 1874, and a community center, and published a bulletin.

Bibliography: Z. Szajkowski, *Analytical Franco-Jewish Gazetteer 1939–1945* (1966), index; R. Berg, *Guide juif de France* (1968), index. [Ed.]

LIMA, ancient capital of the Peruvian viceroyalty and capital of *Peru, population over 1,700,000 (1961). Ninety-eight per cent of Peru's Jewish population of about 6,000 lives in the city. Lima was one of the most important centers of *Crypto-Jews during the Colonial period. Following the establishment of the Inquisition in Lima (1570), Crypto-Jews, the majority of whom were Portuguese, were condemned to death (in 1581, 1605, 1625, and 1639). Of the 63 Jews brought to trial in 1639, 12 were put to death. The remaining families became assimilated with the local population and scarcely a trace of them exists. Street names still surviving today suggest the presence of Jews in the city during the days of the viceroyalty. A handful of Jews from Alsace settled in Lima around 1870, and they established a benevolent society (Sociedad de 1870). The descendants of these immigrants assimilated completely, but the Sociedad was continued by other German-speaking immigrants. Its cemetery still serves the community. Individual Jews, most of whom were on government commission as engineers, scientists, etc., also arrived during the 19th century. Jews from Turkey, North Africa, and Syria settled in Lima about the time of World War I; afterward a much larger wave of immigrants arrived from the disintegrating Turkish Empire and the small Rumanian border town of Novoselitsa. The next mass influx occurred during World War II, Peru's relatively stringent immigration laws notwithstanding.

NOSOTROS

PUBLICACION QUINCENAL, DEDICADA PREFERENTEMENTE A CUESTIONES JUDIAS DEL PERU Y EL EXTRANJERO

Año XXXII — Lima, Abril 30 de 1963 — Nº 405

Fallecimiento del Presidente Ben Zwí, en vísperas del XV Aniversario de Israel, enluta a nuestra comunidad

Excmo. Señor Don IZJAK BEN ZWI.

PREMIER DE ISRAEL

Sr. DAVID BEN GURION

EN SU GIRA POR PAISES DE AMERICA ESTA POR LLEGAR A LIMA EL REPRESENTANTE DEL CONGRESO JUDIO MUNDIAL, SR. MARK TURKOW.

Nos informan que el 10 de mayo próximo llegará a Lima el representante del Congreso Judio Mundial, Sr. Mark Turkow, quien se halla actualmente en gira por varios paises del continente.

Fue suscrito Tratado de Mútua Ayuda Técnica entre el Perú é Israel

Salió para Israel el segundo grupo de becados peruanos

Front page of a 1963 issue of *Nosotros*, the Lima Jewish community's monthly publication. Jerusalem, J.N.U.L.

The three sectors of the Jewish community—the Ashkenazi, the "1870," and the Sephardi, are united under a roof organization, the Asociación de Sociedades Israelitas, and each maintains its own synagogue and communal institutions. Lima's Jewish school, León Pinelo, named after the 17th-century Peruvian lawyer, scholar, and writer, was established in 1946. In 1966 it had an enrollment of 800, which is 80% of all school-age children within the Jewish community. The community publishes a monthly, *Nosotros*

(1931). In addition, *The Jewish Telegraphic Agency Bulletin*, which appears daily, supplies world Jewish news.

See also *Peru.

Bibliography: *Comunidades Judías de Latinoamérica* (1968), 109–12, passim; EJC. [Ed.]

LIMA, MOSES BEN ISAAC JUDAH (?1605–1658), Lithuanian rabbi and halakhist. Lima studied at the yeshivah of Joshua *Falk in Cracow, where he became friendly with many who later were leaders of the generation. In 1637 he served as rabbi of Slonim and in 1650 was *av bet din* of Vilna, his colleagues being *Ephraim b. Jacob ha-Kohen and *Shabbetai Kohen, author of the *Siftei Kohen*. In 1655 he was appointed rabbi where he served until his death. One of his three sons, Raphael, published his father's work *Ḥelkat Meḥokek* (Cracow, 1670), a commentary on the Shulḥan Arukh, *Even ha-Ezer*, outstanding for its critical perceptiveness and profundity and acknowledged as one of the best halakhic works of the later generations. It was accepted as an authorative work in its field, despite its difficult style, which at times makes a super-commentary necessary. The *Beit Shemuel* of *Samuel b. Uri Shraga Phoebus is devoted largely to a discussion of Lima's book. For the benefit of rabbis and *posekim* Lima and Samuel compiled *Kunteres ha-Agunot*, appended to chapter 17 of *Even ha-Ezer*, containing the essence of hundreds of books and responsa concerning the permission of *agunot* to remarry. Some later authorities expressed reservations as to whether it was permissible to base oneself on the work for practical decisions without reference to the sources. Of Lima's other works, there remain only a number of responsa in various collections.

Bibliography: H. N. Maggid-Steinschneider, *Ir Vilna* (1900), 4f.; S. J. Fuenn, *Kiryah Ne'emanah* (1915²), 76–78; H. Tchernowitz, *Toledot ha-Posekim*, 3 (1948), 158–63; Szulwas, in: I. Halpern (ed.), *Beit Yisrael be-Polin*, 2 (1954), 21; Wilenski, in: *Sefunot*, 3–4 (1959–60), 541f.; Eidelberg, in: *Sinai*, 60 (1967/68), 188; Kahana, in: *Sinai*, 34 (1954), 311–24. [I.T.-S.]

LIMERICK, seaport in southwestern Ireland. Jews began to settle there after the beginning of the Russian persecutions at the close of the 19th century. The attitude of the townspeople was hostile, and attacks on the Jews occurred in 1884. Nevertheless, immigration continued and a synagogue was established in 1889. The majority of the newcomers engaged in the drapery business; others in grocery and furnishing, trading partly on the "hire-purchase" system. In 1904, owing to the preaching of Father Creagh of the Redemptorist Order, an anti-Jewish riot broke out, followed by a boycott, and many Jews left. The community is now extinct.

Bibliography: B. Shillman, *Short History of the Jews in Ireland* (1945), 136f.; C. H. L. Emanuel, *Century and a Half of Jewish History* (1910), 119, 160, 164; JC (Jan. 15, 1904). [C.R.]

LIMITATION OF ACTIONS. The Concept and its Substance. In the talmudic period, Jewish law generally did not recognize the principle that the right to bring an action could be affected by the passage of time (i.e., extinctive prescription); in the post-talmudic period, it came to be recognized as a principle that there was a limit to the claimant's right of instituting action on account of the passing of time, without extinction of the underlying right itself. In Jewish law, the principle of limitation of actions is grounded on the reasoning that delay in instituting action serves to cast doubt on the reliability of the claimant's evidence. Consequently, prescription serves to deprive the plaintiff of a remedial action only if the defendant denies the existence of the right forming the subject matter of the action, but not if he admits its existence.

In the Talmudic Period. In the Talmud, the principle of limitation of actions—apart from two exceptional cases—was wholly unrecognized: "a creditor may recover his debt at any time, even if it has not been mentioned" (Tosef., Ket. 12:3; cf. the version in TJ, Ket. 12:4, 35b and TB, Ket. 104a).

The Widow's Claim for her Ketubbah. One exception to the general rule is the claim of a widow for her *ketubbah*, which becomes prescribed under certain circumstances. In a dispute with R. Meir, the scholars held that "a widow, as long as she lives in her husband's house, may recover her *ketubbah* at any time; when, however, she lives in her father's house [and not with the heirs, and is therefore not inhibited from claiming her *ketubbah* from them], she may recover her *ketubbah* within 25 years only" (from the date of her husband's death; Ket. 12:4). Thereafter, her right to recover the *ketubbah* is extinguished, on the assumption that she has waived it, taking into account the great delay in instituting action and the fact that the *ketubbah* "is not like a loan and therefore she has not suffered any loss" (Ket. 104a and Rashi ad loc.). R. Meir expressed the contrary opinion that as long as she lives in her father's house she may recover her *ketubbah* at any time, but as long as she lives in her husband's house, she may only recover her *ketubbah* within 25 years, for "25 years suffices for her to extend favors in exhaustion of her *ketubbah*" (as it may be assumed that during this period she made use of the assets of the estate to render favors (gifts) to her neighbors in an amount corresponding to the value of her *ketubbah*: Ket. 12:4 and Rashi ad loc.). In the opinion of R. Ishmael, the period is three years only (Tosef., Ket. 12:3). The *halakhah* was determined according to the first view (Yad, Ishut, 16:21–24; Sh. Ar., EH 101:1–4). In talmudic times, this limitation of action in the case of a widow seeking to recover her *ketubbah* after the lapse of 25 years from the date of her husband's death already applied only where she was not in possession of the *ketubbah* deed; there was no limitation of action if she was in possession of such a deed at the time her claim was brought. Similarly, her right of action for recovery of the *ketubbah* remained intact even though she lived in her parents' home after her husband's death, provided that the attitude of the heirs toward her was particularly favorable ("delivering her maintenance to her on their shoulders"), on the presumption that the nature of this relationship had served to inhibit her from demanding her *ketubbah* from them (Ket. 12:4; 104b). On the widow's death her heirs too could recover her *ketubbah* only within 25 years (Ket. 12:4), commencing, according to some of the *posekim*, from the date of their succeeding to her right, i.e., on her death (Tur and Sh. Ar., EH 101:1), and according to others, from the date that the cause of action arose, i.e., on the death of the husband (Rashi and Hananel, Shevu. 48a; *Beit ha-Beḥirah*, Ket. 104b).

The Widow's Claim for Maintenance. Another exception to the general rule is to be found in a halakhic ruling from amoraic times stating that a delay of two years on the part of a poor widow—or three years on the part of a rich one—in claiming *maintenance from the estate of the deceased husband, barred her from recovering maintenance for the period which had elapsed (Ket. 96a; TJ, Ket. 11:2, 34b has two or three months respectively). The reasoning behind this quasi-limitation of action is likewise based on the assumption that the widow, by virtue of her delay, has waived her claim for maintenance (Rashi Ket. 96a; *Beit ha-Beḥirah ibid.*; Yad, Ishut, 18:26; Tur and Sh. Ar., EH 93:14). If, during the aforesaid period, the widow has borrowed for her maintenance or if she has been in possession of a *pledge, she cannot be presumed to have waived her claim for maintenance and it does not become prescribed (TJ, loc. cit.).

Roman Law. Roman law of that period also did not recognize the principle of limitation of actions, although there were the *actiones temporales*, which had to be brought within a fixed period, mostly within one year (the *annus utilis*). However, the reason for the limitation of those actions lay in the fact that they were founded on a right "granted" by the praetor who limited in advance the period within which an action could be brought for enforcement. Consequently, once this period had elapsed, the remedial action as well as the underlying right itself became extinguished. In contradistinction to this, actions based on civil law (*actiones civiles*), as well as those praetorian rights in respect of which the praetor had not determined any fixed period for instituting action, were numbered among the *actiones perpetuae*, which could be brought at any time (save for a number of exceptions). It was only in 424 C.E., in a law of Honorius and Theodosius, that the principle of prescription was recognized in respect of all actions. The general period of prescription was fixed at 30 years and, in certain exceptional cases, at 40 years (R. Sohm, Institutionen (1949[7]), 709–15).

In the Post-Talmudic Period. From the begining of the 13th century, Jewish law began to give limited recognition to the principle of limitation of actions. While the principle was preserved that limitation of the right of action could not extinguish the underlying right itself, the doctrine evolved that delay in bringing an action served to cast doubt on the credibility of the evidence adduced in proof of the claim.

EFFECT OF DELAY ON CREDIBILITY OF CLAIMANT'S EVIDENCE. Thus at the end of the 13th century Asher b. Jehiel, dealing with a claim based on old deeds, expressed the fear that an unduly long silence might serve as a subterfuge to enable deceit to go unnoticed or to be forgotten; he accordingly demanded that a suit of this nature be thoroughly investigated if the defendant should plead that he paid the debt or deny its very existence and, "if I assess as a strong probability *(umdenah de-mukhah)* that the suit is a fraudulent one and unfounded, I say that no *dayyan* in Israel should grant relief in this suit, and this I write and sign for delivery into the hands of the defendant" (Resp. Rosh, 68:20; 85:10). However, this view was not generally accepted at once and in the 14th century *Isaac b. Sheshet of Spain and North Africa gave his opinion that a plea by a defendant based on the plaintiff's long delay in bringing his action was "an idle plea, lacking in substance, and served neither to prove nor disprove the existence of the debt" (Resp. Ribash no. 404). In time, however, Asher b. Jehiel's view on the effect of delay in bringing an action came to be generally accepted, and even supplemented by various further details. In the 15th century, Joseph *Colon (of northern Italy) decided that overlong delay carried with it a suspicion of fraud, which obliged a careful investigation of the matter, even if it was written (in the deed) that the defendant would "raise no plea against the deed and took this upon himself on ban and oath" (Resp. Maharik no. 190; *Darkhei Moshe* ḤM 61, n. 5: *Rema* ḤM 61:9). The *halakhah* was decided accordingly by Joseph *Caro and Moses *Isserles (Sh. Ar., ḤM 98:1–2). In the 16th century Samuel di *Medina (of the Balkan countries and Turkey) decided that where no reasonable justification could be found to account for the delay, the court should endeavor to effect a compromise between the parties (Resp. Maharashdam, ḤM 367), while Isaac *Adarbi, Medina's contemporary and compatriot, charged the court with compelling the parties to a compromise in a suit based on a long-delayed claim (*Divrei Rivot* no. 109). Until this time, i.e., the beginning of the 17th century, no fixed period of prescription had been determined and the court would investigate and determine each case on its merits.

FIXED PERIODS FOR LIMITATION OF ACTIONS. From the beginning of the 17th century, the need became increasingly felt for precise legal directions concerning the period within which a defendant could expect a particular action to be brought against him. Jewish law accordingly came to recognize the principle—by way of *takkanah* and custom (see **minhag*)—that the mere lapse of time sufficed to impugn the credibility of the evidence in support of the claim, without the need for any particular investigation by the court. Consequently, if the defendant denied the existence of the debt, he was absolved from liability when he delivered an oath as to the truth of his plea. At the same time the substantive principle, basic to prescription in Jewish law, that the lapse of time did not operate to extinguish the underlying right itself, was preserved, so that a debtor who did not deny the existence of the debt—and certainly one who admitted it—was obliged to make repayment notwithstanding prescription of the right of action. The period of prescription was determined in advance—generally three years and in certain cases six (*Pinkas ha-Medinah, Lita*, ed. by S. Dubnow (1925), *Takkanah* 205 of 1628; Benjamin Ze'ev Wolf, *Misgeret ha-Shulḥan*, 61, n. 16; Ẓevi Hirsch b. Azriel, *Ateret Ẓevi*, to Sh. Ar., *ibid.*; Jacob Lorbeerbaum, *Netivot ha-Mishpat, Mishpat ha-Kohanim*, n. 18). Once more, this new development with regard to the law of prescription was not immediately accepted by all the halakhic scholars. Thus Abraham *Ankawa (19th century, Morocco), in commenting on this development in Polish and Lithuanian Jewish centers, remarked that it was "a great innovation, and presumably a *takkanah* they enacted for themselves, although contrary to the law, for whatever reason they had at the time" (*Kerem Ḥamar* ḤM no. 33). So too, at the beginning of the 18th century, Jacob Reicher (Galicia) had decided in accordance with the principles laid down in the Shulḥan Arukh, in a matter concerning an old deed (*Shevut Ya'akov*, vol. 3, no. 182). His younger contemporary, Jonathan *Eybeschuetz expressed the opinion that "at this time much scrutiny is required, to keep the court from giving effect [in the case of an old deed] to a fraudulent suit" (*Urim* ḤM 61, n. 18). In the course of time, however, this development came to be accepted as part of the law of prescription, and was even refined and supplemented by certain additional rules, namely: if the debt cannot be recovered from the debtor on account of his impoverishment, prescription is interrupted for the period of his impoverishment; prescription does not apply during the period in which either the plaintiff or defendant is a minor; prescription does not bar the institution of an action if the debtor has waived such a plea in writing, in clear and unequivocal terms, even after completion of the period of prescription (*Kesef ha-Kedoshim* 61:9).

In the State of Israel. A substantial number of the various provisions of the Prescription Law, 5718/1958, accord with the principles of prescription in Jewish law, including the principle that "prescription shall not per se void the right itself" (sec. 2). On the other hand, this law includes the provision that an admission by the defendant of the plaintiff's right shall only have the effect of nullifying the period of prescription already accrued if the admission is not "accompanied by a plea of prescription" (sec. 9). This provision is at variance with the Jewish law principle that the defendant—if he has admitted the existence of the plaintiff's right—is not entitled to void the claim by pleading that the period within which the action may be instituted has lapsed.

For prescription with regard to immovable property, see **Ḥazakah*.

Bibliography: I. S. Zuri, *Mishpat ha-Talmud*, 7 (1921), 15f.; M. Elon, in: *Ha-Peraklit*, 14 (1957/58), 179–89, 243–79; idem, in: ILR, 4 (1969), 108–11; Z. Warhaftig, *Ha-Ḥazakah ba-Mishpat ha-Ivri* (1964), 263–85.

[M.E.]

LIMOGES, capital of the Haute-Vienne department, central France. A Jewish source, *Sefer Yeshu'at Elohim* (in A. M. Habermann, *Gezerot Ashkenaz ve-Ẓarefat* (1945), 11–15) contains an account of a semilegendary anti-Jewish persecution in Limoges in 992 resulting from the activities of an apostate from Blois. The Christian writer Adhémar of Chabannes relates that in 1010 Bishop Alduin of Limoges gave the Jewish community the choice of expulsion or conversion. It is possible that both sources refer to the local manifestation of the general anti-Jewish persecutions which occurred around 1009 and which were followed by baptisms and expulsions. At any rate, whether or not the Jews were expelled from Limoges, the expulsion order was no longer in force from the middle of the 11th century; a certain Petrus Judaeus is mentioned in a local document between 1152 and 1173 and Gentianus Judaeus in 1081. Around the middle of the 11th century R. Joseph b. Samuel *Bonfils (Tov Elem) headed the Jewish community of Limoges and Anjou. The beginnings of the modern Jewish community in Limoges date from 1775. During World War II, Limoges became the largest center of refuge for Alsatian Jews; about 1,500 families and many institutions were transferred to the town. The present community, which was formed in 1949, numbered over 650 in 1970 and possessed a synagogue and community center.

Bibliography: Gross, Gal Jud (1897), 308–9; J. de Font-Reaulx (ed.), *Cartulaire du Chapître de St.-Etienne de Limoges* (1919), passim; *La Vie Juive*, no. 51 (1959), 15; B. Blumenkranz, *Juifs et Chrétiens* . . . (1960), index; Z. Szajkowski, *Analytical Franco-Jewish Gazetteer* (1966), 286; Roth, Dark Ages, index. [B.BL.]

LIMOUX, town in the department of Aude, *Languedoc, southern France. The existence of a Jewish community there is confirmed toward the end of the 13th century. Its privileges were withdrawn in 1292, as were also those of a number of other Jewish communities in Languedoc, but were restored in 1299. In 1302, the Jews of Limoux, again together with those of other localities in Languedoc, were freed by *Philip IV (the Fair), from liability to prosecution by inquisitors. At the beginning of the 14th century, some Jews from Limoux were living in Narbonne. A new community may have been constituted after 1315; this would be the one referred to in the *Shevet Yehudah* (ed. by A. Shochet, p. 149) under the name לשמאדש as having been massacred by the *Pastoureaux in 1320.

Bibliography: G. Saige, *Les Juifs du Languedoc* (1881), 29, 33, 286; Gross, Gal Jud, 313–4; REJ, 2 (1881), 31; *ibid.*, 38 (1899), 106.

[B.Bl.]

LIMPIEZA DE SANGRE (Sp.; "purity of blood"), an obsessive concern in Spain and Portugal from the 15th century, based on the mythical goal of a society in which all but the most humble functions would be exercised by "pure-blooded" Christians. In varying degrees this obsession afflicted Spain until well into the 19th century; blood purity was still a requirement for admission to the military academy until 1860, when it was legally abolished. In Portugal all legal distinctions between Old and *New Christians were officially removed in 1773. *Limpieza de sangre* continues to be a matter of concern on the island of Majorca, where Christians of Jewish ancestry are disdainfully referred to as **chuetas* and frequently suffer discrimination because of their "impure blood."

Although the pure-blood statutes established by the various communities of Spain in the 16th century adopted a routine formula directed against all Christians descended from Moors and heretics as well as Jews, the problem, both in its historical origins and in its later consequences, mainly concerned those of Jewish ancestry. The first such measure of which details are known, the so-called *Sentencia-Estatuto* adopted in Toledo in 1449 in the course of a popular uprising under the leadership of Pedro *Sarmiento against royal authority, was directed solely against the Toledan *Conversos. It prohibited them from testifying in legal proceedings and excluded them from all public office, especially notaryships which were most frequently in their hands, "under penalty of death and confiscation of all their goods."

This extraordinary measure against the Conversos or New Christians was a direct consequence of a series of anti-Jewish riots which swept through Spain in 1391. Protests against and denunciations of the *Sentencia-Estatuto* arose both among the affected converts as well as distinguished ecclesiastics of non-Jewish origin, including Pope Nicholas V. Nevertheless, the pure-blood statutes spread to such an extent that by 1500 most Spanish organizations, secular or religious, insisted on "blood purity" as a qualification for membership. The controversy concerning the legality and propriety of the *limpieza de sangre* discriminations continued until well into the 17th century, and Conversos were excluded from an increasing number of guilds, religious confraternities, most colleges, religious and military orders, and residence in certain towns. Churches and cathedrals reserved even their most humble benefices for Christians "without the stain of Jewish blood," leading one polemicist to observe that Jesus himself would have failed to qualify as a porter in Toledo Cathedral.

Spain's obsession with blood purity in the 16th and 17th centuries led to considerable social turmoil. As generations passed and the memory of the Jewish ancestry of Converso Spaniards faded, efforts were redoubled to unearth the traces of their long-forgotten "impure" forefathers. Communities vied with one another in the severity of their pure-blood statutes. The Old College of Saint Bartholomew of Salamanca, the source of Spain's most important leaders, took pride in refusing admittance to anyone even rumored to be of Jewish descent. Hearsay testimony and words spoken in anger to the effect that someone was a Jew, or a descendant of Jews, sufficed to disqualify a man, a kind of "civil death" understandably feared by Spaniards. As investigations into ancestries ranged even farther into the distant past, until "time immemorial" as some put it, even families considered Old Christian lived in constant fear lest some remote, forgotten "stain" be brought to light or a hostile rumormonger destroy their reputation.

Since no one could be absolutely certain of his blood purity "since time immemorial," *limpieza de sangre* ultimately became a qualification negotiated through bribed witnesses, shuffled genealogies, and falsified documents.

See also *Inquisition; *Marranos.

Bibliography: J. Caro Baroja, *Los judíos en la España moderna y contemporánea*, 1 (1961), ch. 6; 2 pt. 4 (1961), chs. 2–7; A. Domínguez-Ortiz, *La clase social de los conversos en Castilla en la Edad Moderna* (1955); H. C. Lea, *A History of the Inquisition of Spain*, 1 (1906), ch. 3; A. A. Sicroff, *Les controverses des statuts de "pureté de sang" en Espagne* (1960).

[Al.A.S.]

LINCOLN, town in eastern England. The medieval Jewish community (first mentioned in 1159) was probably the second in importance in England after London. During the crusader riots which swept the country in March 1190, the Jews were attacked and took refuge under the protection of the sheriff. The citizens were subsequently fined for their unruly conduct. St. Hugh, the great bishop of Lincoln, protected the Jews, who later joined their fellow townsmen in mourning his death in 1200. The most prominent Anglo-Jewish financier of the time was *Aaron of Lincoln (c. 1123–86), whose operations extended over every part of the country but were especially important in Lincolnshire. R. Joseph of Lincoln is mentioned as a scholar (c. 1125–36). In the second half of the 13th century, the outstanding Lincoln Jews were *Hagin (Ḥayyim), son of R. *Moses b. Yom Tov of London, who was *archpresbyter of English Jewry (1258–80), and his brother *Benedict of Lincoln (d. 1276?), identical with the tosafist R. Berachiah of Nicole, who has left some significant literary remains. The latter was absolved at the time of the ritual murder accusation in 1255 associated with the name of "Little" St. *Hugh of Lincoln when 91 Lincoln Jews were sent to London for trial and 18 executed. Notwithstanding this, the community continued to be important. In 1266, during the Barons' Wars, the "Disinherited Knights" attacked the Lincoln Jewry, sacked the synagogue, and burned the records registering debts. On the expulsion of Jews from

A medieval building in Lincoln known as Jews' Court which was probably a synagogue. Photo Leslie H. Hare, Lincoln.

England in 1290, assets were registered of 66 householders (not all still alive), and the property which fell into the king's hands exceeded £2,500, in addition to 30 houses. Specimens of medieval Jewish architecture, including a building which was probably the synagogue, may still be seen in the former Jewry (now Steep Hill). A small Jewish community existed again in Lincoln at the beginning of the 19th century. There was a small community of evacuees during World War II.

Bibliography: J. W. F. Hill, *Medieval Lincoln* (1948), 217–38; Davis, in: *Archeological Journal*, 38 (1880), 178ff.; C. Roth, in: JHSET, 9 (1918–20), 28; idem, in: JJS, 1 (1948), 67–81; idem, *Medieval Lincoln Jewry and its Synagogue* (1934); Rosenau, in: *Archeological Journal*, 94 (1937), 51–56; JHSET, 1 (1893–94), 89–135; 3 (1896–98), 157–86; C. W. Foster (ed.), *Registrum Antiquissimum of the Cathedral Church of Lincoln*, especially vol. 7 (1931).

[C.R.]

°**LINCOLN, ABRAHAM** (1809–1865), 16th president of the United States; first president to become officially involved in national questions of Jewish equality and anti-Jewish discrimination. Lincoln participated in two matters of Jewish historic significance. The first related to the appointment of Jewish chaplains for the army and for

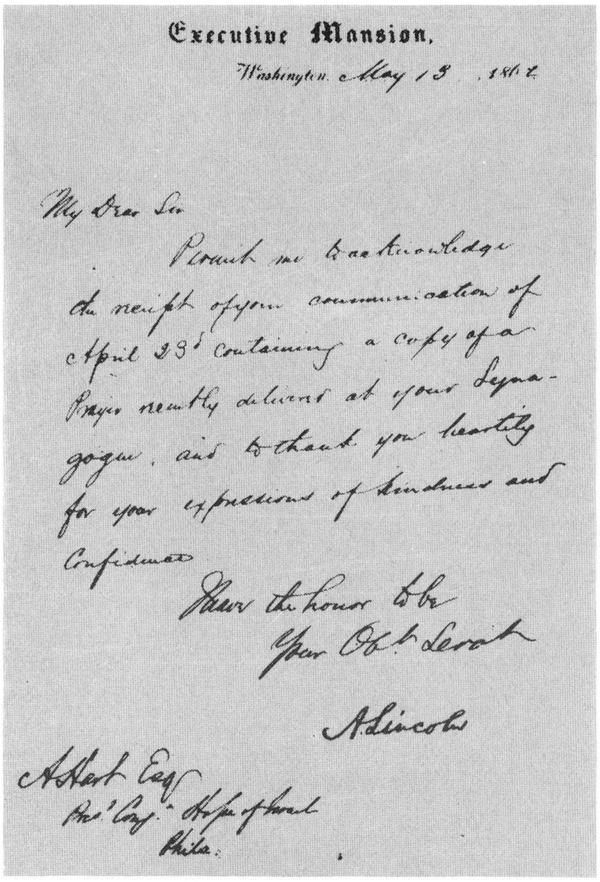
Executive Mansion,
Washington, May 13, 1862.
My Dear Sir
Permit me to acknowledge the receipt of your communication of April 23d containing a copy of a Prayer recently delivered at your Synagogue, and to thank you heartily for your expressions of kindness and Confidence.
I have the honor to be
Your Obt. Servant
A. Lincoln
A. Hart Esq
Prest. Congn. Hope of Israel
Phila.

Letter from Abraham Lincoln to Congregation Mikveh Israel in Philadelphia, thanking them for their prayers for the Union cause, 1862. Courtesy American Jewish Archives, Cincinnati, Ohio.

military hospitals. Legislation passed by the House of Representatives in July 1861 required that a chaplain be a "regularly ordained minister of some Christian denomination." Although a Jewish layman, Michael Allen, did serve as chaplain, he resigned his commission after being accused of serving illegally. A campaign of public pressure was undertaken to change the law, and in December 1861 the Rev. Arnold Fishel of New York went to Washington, under the aegis of the Board of Delegates of American Israelites, to act as lobbyist and civilian chaplain. He secured an appointment with Lincoln who wrote him promising to use his best efforts "to have a new law broad enough to cover what is desired by you in behalf of the Israelites." New legislation was introduced in both the House and the Senate. By July 1862, a new law made it possible for rabbis to serve as military chaplains alongside Protestant ministers and Catholic priests, for the first time in history—a major step in the Americanization of the Jewish religion. Had Lincoln ignored Fishel's representations, or actively opposed them, it is unlikely that either house of Congress would have passed the legislation.

In December 1862, General Ulysses S. *Grant issued an order expelling all Jews from the area of his command, on the alleged grounds that Jews were engaging in illegal trade. This was brought to Lincoln's attention by a Jew from Paducah, Kentucky, Cesar Kaskel, in January 1863, and Lincoln, recognizing the injustice of the order, issued instructions for its immediate cancellation. General-in-Chief H. W. Halleck, in the second of a series of telegrams, explained to Grant that "as it in terms proscribed an entire religious class, some of whom are fighting in our ranks, the President deemed it necessary to revoke it." Lincoln, consenting to see another Jewish delegation after he saw Kaskel, assured the group, which included Rabbis Isaac M. *Wise and Max *Lilienthal, that "to condemn a class is, to say the least, to wrong the good with the bad. I do not like to hear a class or nationality condemned on account of a few sinners."

Lincoln was a close friend and political associate of Abraham *Jonas, a Jew from Quincy, Illinois, and their correspondence reveals a warm mutual appreciation and common political loyalties.

American Jews have felt especially attracted to Lincoln as the emancipator of the Negro slave, as a victim of violence, as a dreamer of peace, and as the spokesman of a way of life "with malice towards none, with charity for all," which matches the idealism of the prophets.

Bibliography: B. W. Korn, *American Jewry and the Civil War* (1951); I. Markens, in: AJHSP, 17 (1909), 109–65; E. Hertz (ed.), *Abraham Lincoln, the Tribute of the Synagogue* (1927). [B.W.K.]

LINDAU, town in Bavaria, W. Germany. Jews are first mentioned in tax lists of 1242. The 13th-century town charter allowed Jews to trade in pledges on loans and the local Jewish *oath was short and humane. In 1344 the Jews offered to make loans at very advantageous terms ($43\frac{1}{3}\%$ interest instead of the $216\frac{2}{3}\%$ demanded by Christians) if they were offered civic rights. Individual Jews were granted special civic status in 1385 and 1409. In 1348 *Charles IV granted the town the local Jewish tax; in that same year the community was destroyed during the *Black Death persecutions. However, they were again in residence by 1358. In 1430, 15 Jews, accused of the murder of a boy, were burned and the rest were expelled. In 1547 the city was granted the right to exclude the Jews, a privilege reaffirmed in 1559. Even during the 18th and early 19th centuries Jews were only allowed to stay for short periods on special permits. The group of Jews who settled in Lindau, seven in 1810, never numbered more than 30 and had fallen to only four in 1939. In 1967 two elderly Jews were still living in Lindau.

Bibliography: Schweizer-Weitersheim, in: *Der Israelit* (Nov. 18, 1909), 2–5; Germ Jud, 1 (1963), 505; 2 (1968), 488–90; PK Bavaria.

[Ed.]

LINDHEIM, IRMA LEVY (1886–), U.S. Zionist leader. She was born in New York City to a wealthy, assimilated family. She was educated in social work at Columbia University. During World War I she served as an ambulance driver, and in 1919 became president of the

Seventh District of the Zionist Organization. She entered the Jewish Institute of Religion in 1922 and was accepted as a candidate for a rabbinical degree, while continuing her studies at Columbia under John Dewey. Irma Lindheim first visited Palestine in 1925 and incorporated her experiences into her book *Immortal Adventure* (1928). On her return to the U.S. she devoted herself to work with the Jewish National Fund. She became president of Hadassah (1926–28), and simultaneously was national vice-president of the Z.O.A. Attracted by the *ḥalutz* philosophy, Irma Lindheim joined the Labor Zionist group in 1930 and helped organize the League for Labor Palestine in 1932. In 1933 she decided to settle in Israel, and moved to kibbutz Mishmar ha-Emek. She wrote many articles, and her autobiography, *Parallel Quest*, was published in 1962.

[Gl.R.]

LINDO, English family descended from Isaac (Lorenço Rodrigues) Lindo (1638–1712), who was born in Badajoz. After being penanced in 1656 as a Judaizer by the Inquisition in the *Canary Islands, he settled about 1670 in London, where he became an elder of the synagogue and was a signatory of the **Ascamot* of 1694. He was one of the earliest "Jew Brokers" of the city (1697). His descendants continued in that capacity until the 19th century and the entire series of their brokers' medals is preserved. Other members of the family included: Moses (1712–1774) who emigrated in 1756 to South Carolina and became inspector general and surveyor of indigo, drugs, and dyes. He experimented scientifically with dyes and was responsible for some ambitious projects. Abraham Alexander, formerly of Jamaica, wrote pamphlets on the affairs of the island, and, in England, against the Reform movement. He delivered an address in the Sephardi Synagogue on the death of William IV in 1837. David Abarbanel (1772–1852), an active English communal worker, was at one time president of the elders of the Sephardi community. He was connected by marriage to the Disraeli family, and was the *mohel* of Benjamin *Disraeli. His daughter Abigail (1803–1848) wrote *Hebrew and English and English and Hebrew Vocabulary, also Hebrew and English Dialogues* (1837; other eds. 1842, 1846) which displayed considerable learning as well as awareness of the potentialities of Hebrew as a spoken language. Elias Ḥayyim (1783–1865) settled in London after a mercantile career in St. Thomas (West Indies) where he was president of the Jewish community. He published an English translation of *Manasseh Ben Israel's *Conciliador* (1842), *A History of the Jews of Spain and Portugal* (1848), and a *Jewish Calendar for Sixty-four Years* (1838) containing much historical information. Some of his unpublished translations of Jewish classics are in the library of Jews' College, London.

Bibliography: Roth, Mag Bibl, index; A. M. Hyamson, *Sephardim of England* (1951), index; B. A. Elzas, *Jews of South Carolina* (1903), 47–67; L. Wolf, *Jews in the Canary Islands* (1926), index; Abrahams, in: JHSEM, 3 (1937), 80–94; J. A. P. M. Andrade, *Record of the Jews in Jamaica* (1941), passim; C. Reznikoff and U. Z. Engelman, *Jews of Charleston* (1950), 23–34; C. Rabin, in *Leshonenu la-Am*, no. 137 (1963).

[C.R.]

LINETZKY, ISAAC JOEL (1839–1915), Yiddish writer. He was born into a ḥasidic family in Podolia, Ukraine, but in his youth rebelled against this milieu and became a spokesman of the radical wing of the Haskalah. Linetzky published his first Hebrew article in *Ha-Meliẓ* in 1865 and his first Yiddish article in *Kol Mevasser* in 1867. In the same

The brokers' medals of the Lindo family, bearing the royal and City of London coats of arms. London, Guildhall Museum.

weekly he published his novel *Dos Poylishe Yingl* ("The Polish Boy," 1869), criticizing Jewish life and satirizing Ḥasidim. His language was coarse, colorful, and grotesque. The novel appeared in 30 editions—the last in Kiev in 1939. A sequel appeared in 1888 in Shalom Aleichem's almanac, *Di Yidishe Folksbibliotek*, under the title *Der Vorem in Khreyn* ("The Worm in the Horseradish") and in book form as *Nit Toyt, nit Lebedik, oder Dem Poylishen Yingl's a Zuhn* ("Neither Dead nor Alive, or the Polish Boy's Son," 1898). Linetzky also published various collections under the title *Linetzkys Ksovim* (1876), as well as pamphlets and brochures. Among these are *Der Beyzer Marshelik*, satirical poems (1879); *Amerika tsi Erets Yisroel, and Di Kurtse Geografie fun Palestine* (both 1888). In the collections *Linetzkys Ksovim* he formulated his positive approach to Yiddish, regarding the language not only as a vehicle for enlightenment, but as a medium of literary expression. Linetzky translated into Yiddish part of Graetz's history of the Jews (1883–89); Lessing's *Nathan der Weise* (1884), and from the Hebrew *Kozo shel Yod* by Gordon. Though Linetzky's vogue faded with the rapid development of Yiddish literature and the emergence of great writers of the classical period, his major novel, *Das Poylishe Yingl*, retains an enduring place in Yiddish literature.

Bibliography: Rejzen, Leksikon, 2 (1927), 165–74; LNYL, 5 (1963), 163–8; S. Niger, *Dertseylers un Romanistn* (1946), 77ff.; R. Granovsky, *Linetzky un Zayn Dor* (1941); S. Liptzin, *Flowering of Yiddish Literature* (1963), 77–78.

[E.SCH.]

LINOWITZ, SOL MYRON (1913–), U.S. ambassador, lawyer, and business executive. Linowitz, who was born in Trenton, New Jersey, practiced law privately, in New York and served as assistant general counsel to the Office of Price Administration (1942). From 1944 to 1946 he served in the U.S. Navy. After the war, Linowitz resumed his legal practice and began an association with Xerox Corporation. Linowitz eventually was appointed board chairman and head of Xerox International, Inc. Throughout his association with Xerox, Linowitz consistently tried to establish the image of the company as one dedicated to public service as well as profits. He served as chairman of the State Department's Advisory Committee on International Organizations, a member of the Business Advisory Committee to the federal poverty program, and co-founded (with David Rockefeller) the International Executive Service Corps formed to assist business administration in underdeveloped countries. Linowitz helped to establish Rochester's antipoverty agency after the 1964 Negro riots there. President Johnson appointed Linowitz the U.S. representative to the Organization of American States (OAS) and the Inter-American Committee of the Alliance for Progress in 1966. Linowitz also served as a trustee of the American Jewish Committee.

Bibliography: *Current Biography Yearbook 1967* (1968). [J.O.R.]

LINZ, capital of Upper Austria. Jewish moneylenders are recorded in Linz in 1304; a Jewish settlement in the growing market town is probably a century older. In 1335 a synagogue is mentioned; two Jews were baptized a year earlier. Jews were accused of desecrating the *Host in 1338. Although the community was not harmed during the *Black Death persecutions of 1348, a local persecution occurred in 1371. In 1396 Duke Albert IV permitted Jews to conduct only fiscal transactions with the burghers; the decree was renewed in 1412. The Jews were expelled from Linz in 1421, and in 1426 the synagogue was turned into a church. Jews were permitted to attend the biannual markets in the town in 1494, and Jewish horse dealers and feather and wool merchants, mainly from Moravia, continued to trade at the fairs until their entry was forbidden at the end of the 17th century. Only in 1783 were the markets officially declared open and in 1824 the Jews opened their own prayer room. A cemetery was consecrated in 1863, when the modern community was established. In 1869 there were 391 Jews (1.3% of the total population) and 533 in 1880. A new synagogue was opened in 1877 by Rabbi Adolf *Kurrein (1876–82), publicist and author. His son, Rabbi Viktor Kurrein (1923–38), wrote the history of the community.

In 1923 there were 1,238 Jews in Linz, 671 in 1934 (0.6%), and in 1938, before the *Anschluss*, 650. On Nov. 10, 1938, the synagogue was burned down by the S.S.; the 65 remaining Jews were arrested and ordered to leave within three days for Vienna. The Nazis claimed that the Jews must leave the town because it was the capital of the province of Hitler's birth. Jewish shops were not looted because they had already been "Aryanized." Shortly after the end of the war, 2,400 Jewish refugees were housed in the nearby Bindermichen camp. A new community was reorganized, which numbered 238 in 1949 and 145 in 1961. In October 1957, an anti-Semitic demonstration was sparked off by a performance of "The Diary of Anne Frank." Protests against a ban on *sheḥitah* were lodged in 1958. A new synagogue was consecrated in 1968.

Bibliography: *Festschrift anlaesslich der Einweihung des neu erbauten Bethauses in Linz* (1968); V. Kurrein, *Die Juden in Linz* (1927); idem, in: *Menorah* (1927), 309–44; idem, in: JGGJČ, 2 (1930), 497–500; 4 (1932), 481–4; idem, in: *Juedisches Archiv*, 1 no. 5–6 (1928), 3–7; Germ Jud, 2 (1968), 490–1; L. Moses, *Die Juden in Niederoesterreich* (1935), 185–6, no. 274, 279; H. H. Rosenkranz, *Reichskristallnacht—9 November 1938 in Oesterreich* (1968), 51; PK Germanyah.

[H.W.]

LION. Called in the Talmud "the king of the beasts" (Ḥag. 13b), the lion has many Hebrew names: אַרְיֵה *(aryeh)* or אֲרִי *(ari)*, and לָבִיא *(lavi)* fem. לְבִיאָה *(levi'ah)*, both of which are used for the lion in general, כְּפִיר *(kefir)*, usually a young lion, לַיִשׁ *(layish)*, mostly poetical, and according to some, "an old lion"; שַׁחַל *(shaḥal)*, general name for the lion in poetry, though like שַׁחַץ *(shaḥaẓ)* perhaps the intention is any fierce animal; and גּוּר *(gur)* almost always meaning "a lion's whelp." The first five are all mentioned together by Eliphaz the Temanite (Job 4:10–11), on which Rashi comments that *ari* is the large lion, *shaḥal* the medium-sized one, and *kefir* the small lion, while the first six are cited in Sanhedrin 95a. In the Bible the lion has more than 150 references, many of them descriptive, metaphoric, and allegorical. To the lion were compared the tribes of Judah (Gen. 49:9) and Dan (Deut. 33:22); Balaam said of the Israelites: "Behold a people that riseth up as a lioness *(lavi)*, and as a lion *(ari)* doth he lift himself up" (Num. 23:24); the mother of the kings of Judah was compared to a lioness and her sons to young lions (Ezek. 19:2–9). David, of whom it was said that his "heart is as the heart of a lion" (II Sam. 17:10), declared in his lament over Saul and Jonathan that "they were swifter than eagles, they were stronger than lions" (*ibid.* 1:23). This combination of the lion, the king of the beasts, and the *eagle, the king of the birds (the biblical reference is to the *vulture), is very common in later Jewish art, particularly on the Holy Ark, and occurs in Ezekiel's vision of the lion, the ox, the eagle, and the cherub (Ezek. 1:10; 10:14). In Solomon's Temple there were carvings of "lions, oxen, and cherubim" (I Kings 7:29), while a lion with eagle's wings symbolized in the Book of Daniel (7:4) the kingdom of Babylonia. The lion is mentioned several

Figure 1. Pair of marble lions, partly restored, from the synagogue of Sardis, Turkey. Carved in the fifth century B.C.E., they are believed to have been taken from a shrine of the goddess Cybele to stand guard on either side of the *bimah* of the synagogue. Courtesy Sardis Expedition.

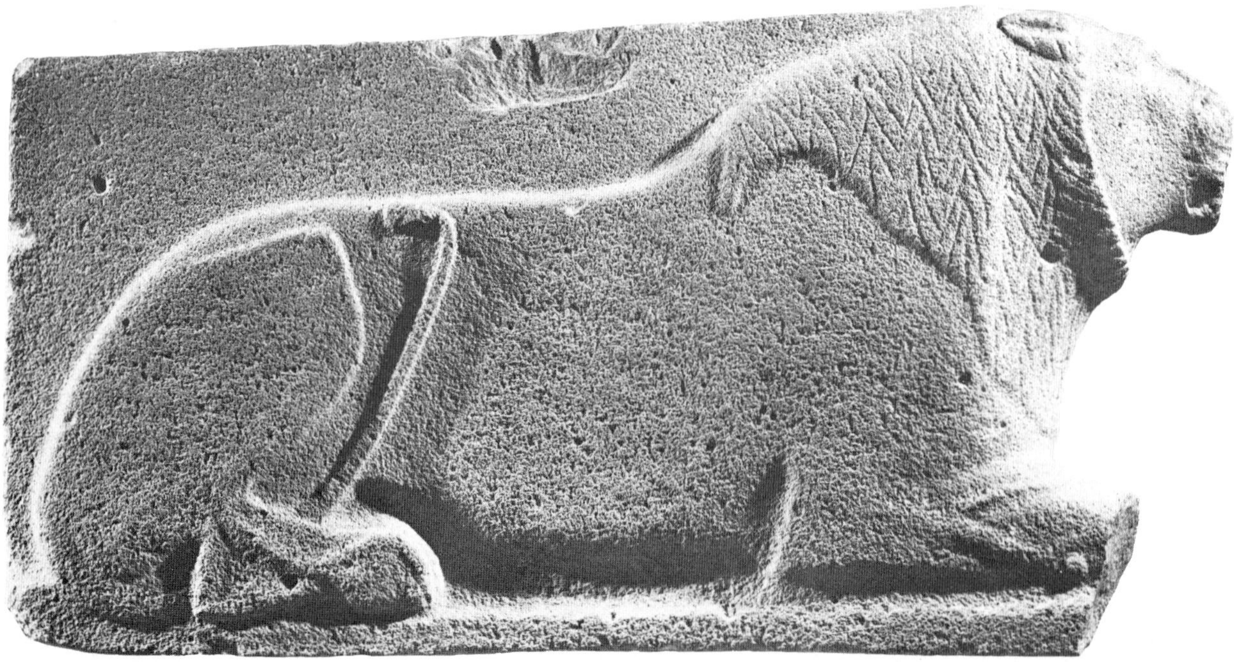

Figure 2. Canaanite orthostat lion found in a temple at Hazor, Upper Galilee, 14th–13th century B.C.E. Jerusalem, Israel Museum, Israel Department of Antiquities.

Figure 3. Lions used as decoration on an amulet depicting the sacrifice of Isaac. Italy, 17th century. Formerly New York, M. Zagayski Collection.

Figure 4. Ritual laver in the form of a lion, Augsburg, Germany, 17th century. Courtesy Sotheby and Co., London.

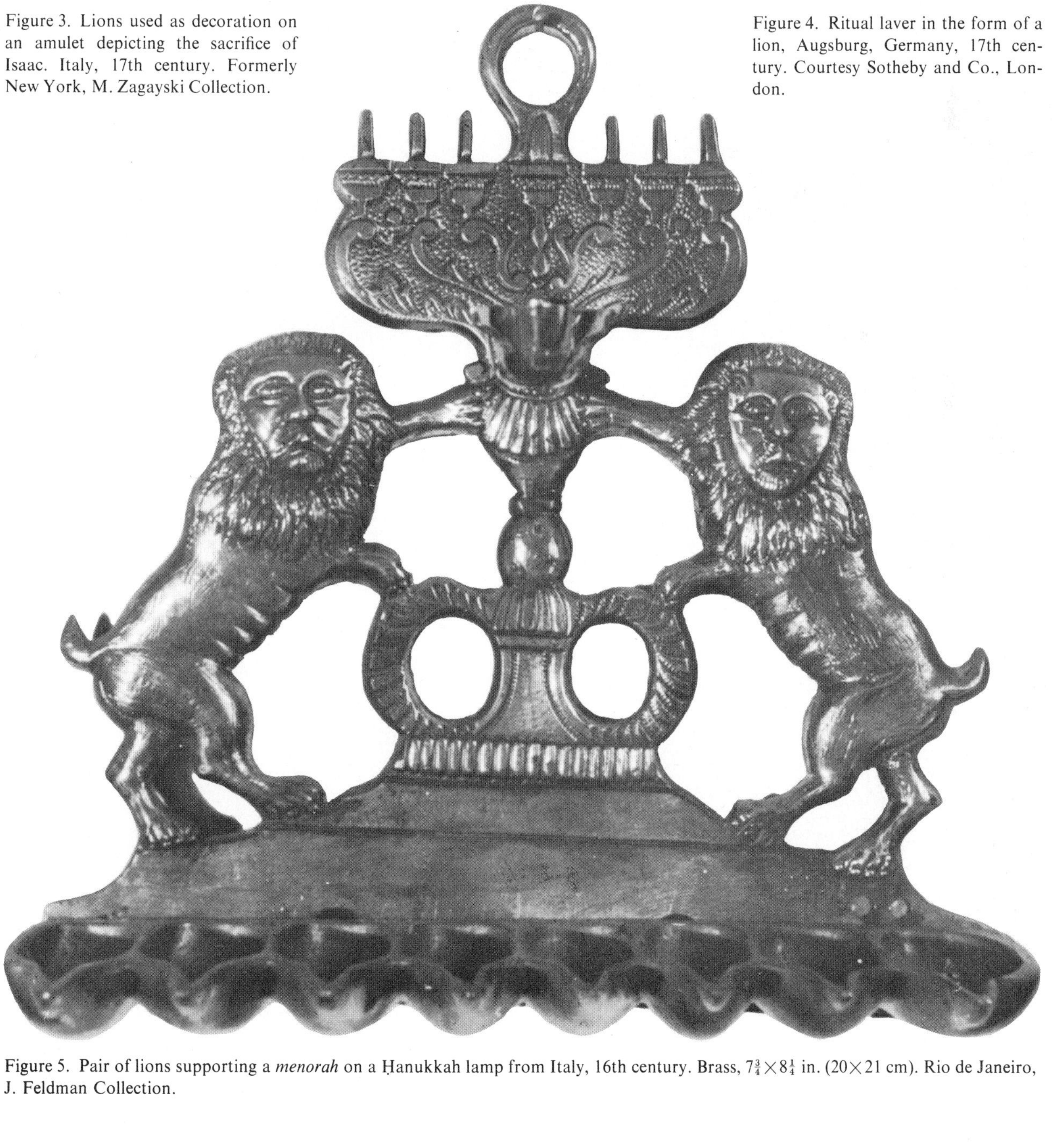

Figure 5. Pair of lions supporting a *menorah* on a Ḥanukkah lamp from Italy, 16th century. Brass, $7\frac{3}{4}\times8\frac{1}{4}$ in. (20×21 cm). Rio de Janeiro, J. Feldman Collection.

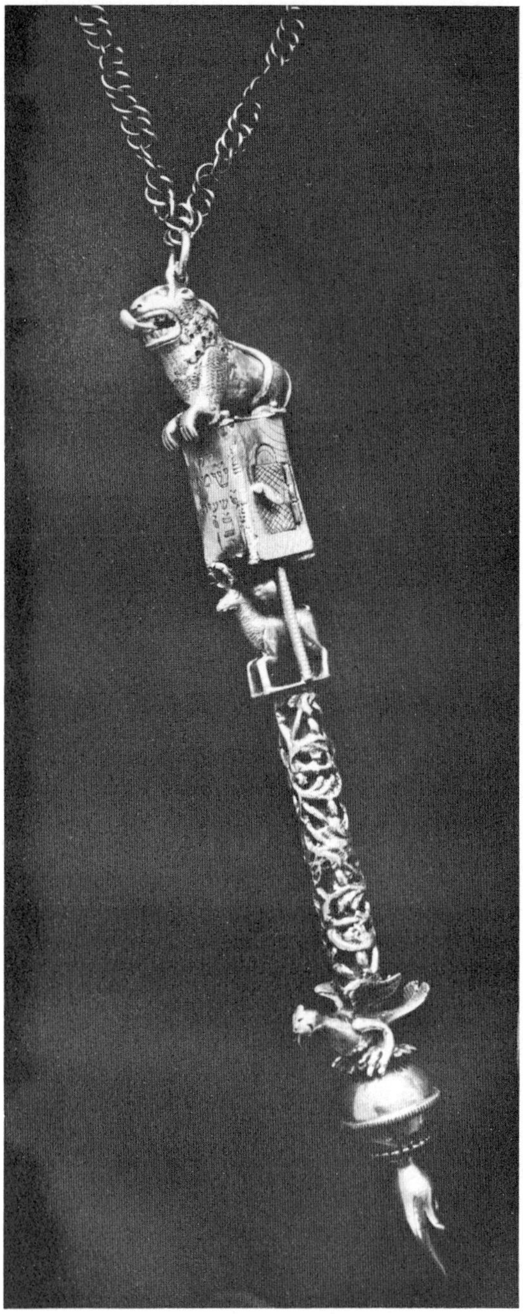

Figure 6. Lion as base of a silver Torah pointer, 16th century. Prague, State Jewish Museum.

Figure 7. Lion carved in high relief on ivory box from Megiddo, Israel, 12th century B.C.E. Jerusalem, Rockefeller Museum, Israel Department of Antiquities.

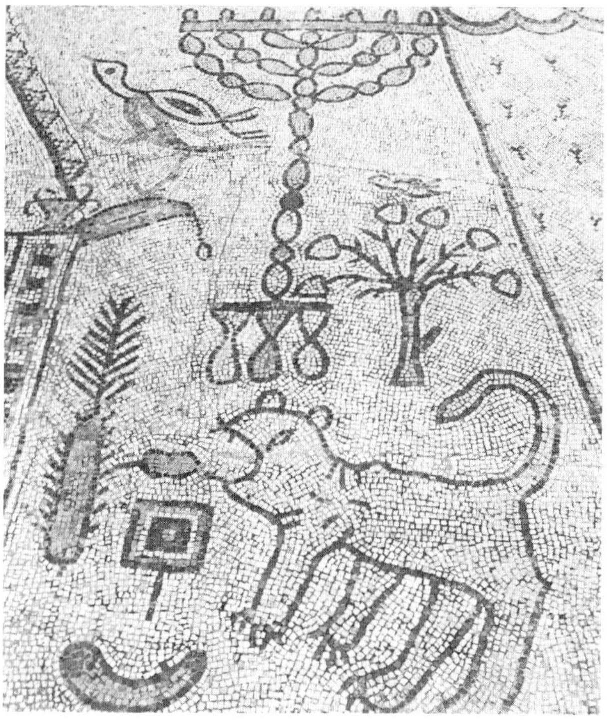

Figure 8. Detail showing lion from the mosaic floor of the Bet Alfa synagogue, sixth century C.E. Courtesy Government Press Office, Tel Aviv.

Figure 9. Pair of lions painted on a tombstone in Volovets, Ukraine, 1789. After H. Guttmann, *Hebraica, documents d'art Juif*, Paris, 1932.

Figure 10. Lion from the mosaic floor of the synagogue of Hammam-Lif, Tunisia, second half of fifth century C.E. New York, Brooklyn Museum.

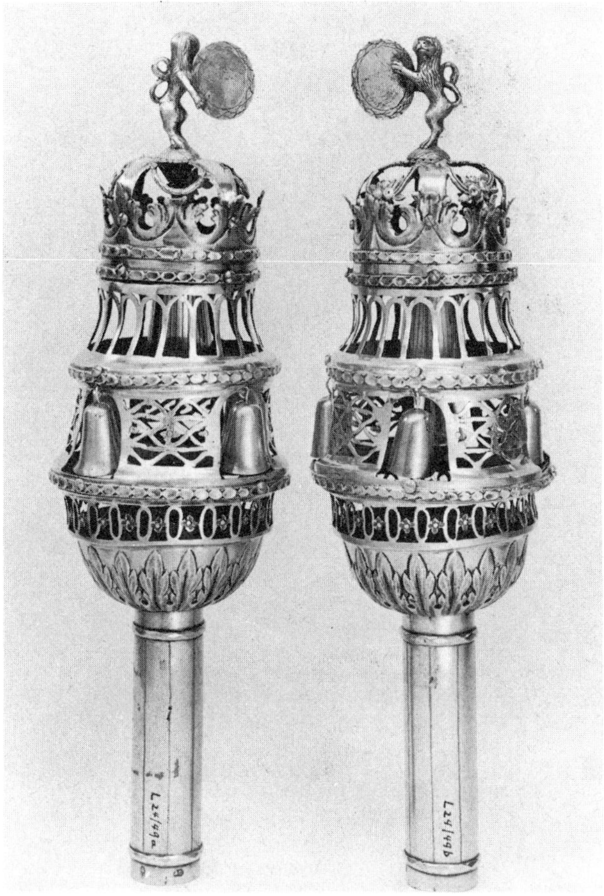

Figure 11. Lions topping a pair of Torah finials, silver, parcel gilded, Augsburg, Germany, 1803. New York, Jewish Museum.

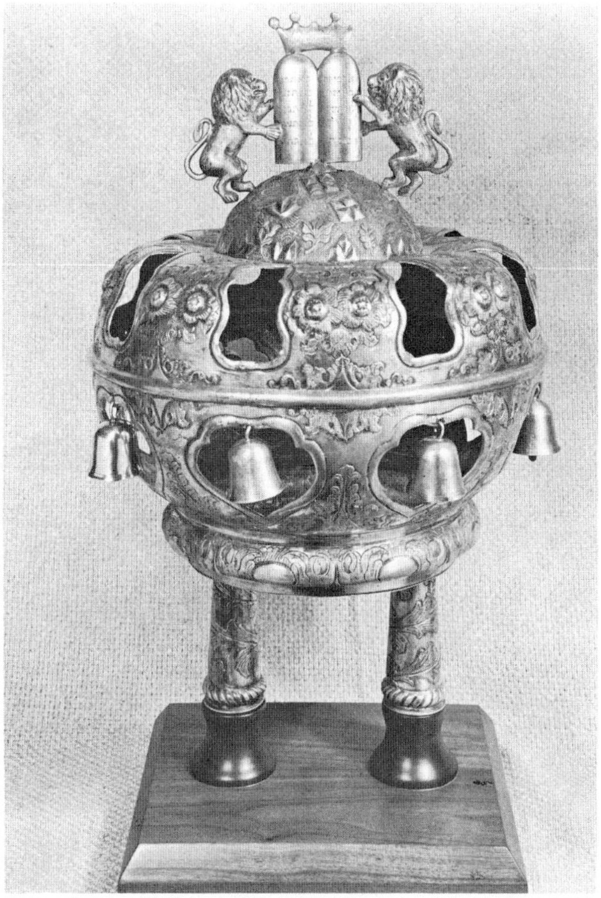

Figure 12. Torah crown with lions, Russia, 1869. Formerly Feinberg Collection, Detroit. Photo Manning Bros.

Figure 13. Rampant lions bearing the candleholders on a pair of Sabbath candlesticks, Germany, 19th century. Wrought and repoussé silver, height 5½ in. (14 cm.). Formerly Feinberg Collection, Detroit. Photo Manning Bros.

Figure 14. Lions supporting a *menorah* in a paper-cut *mizraḥ* from the Ukraine, 19th/20th century. $17\frac{1}{4}\times15$ in. (44×38 cm.). Jerusalem, Israel Museum, Photo David Harris, Jerusalem.

Figure 15. Rococo Torah breastplate with pair of lions supporting the crown. Germany, 19th century, wrought gilded silver, height $13\frac{1}{2}$ in. (34 cm.). Formerly Feinberg Collection, Detroit. Photo Manning Bros.

Figure 16. Lion in micrographic writing, at the beginning of the masorah to the Book of Ezekiel, Germany, 13th century. Vienna, National Library, Cod. heb. 16, fol. 226.

Figure 17. Lions embroidered on the *parokhet* covering the Ark of the Law, from the synagogue of Bamberg, Germany, 1809. Jerusalem, Israel Museum Photo Archives.

times together with the bear as the most powerful beasts of prey (Lam. 3:10; Prov. 28:15; I Sam. 17:34; et al.). When a lion attacks its prey there is no escape from it, being mentioned in many parables, as when Amos (3:12) declares that a shepherd can rescue out of its jaws no more than "two legs, or a piece of an ear." Nor is a lion in the least frightened even when shepherds gather to chase it away (Isa. 31:4). An encounter between a man and a lion is usually fatal to the former (I Kings 13:24; 20:36), lions having killed new settlers in the cities of Samaria (II Kings 17:25), and having claimed victims, according to Jeremiah (5:6), in the land of Judah. Only in exceptional instances was a lion slain in such a clash, as when encountering a man of great personal courage such as Samson (Judg. 14:6), David (I Sam. 17:34), and Benaiah the son of Jehoiada (II Sam. 23:20).

From the Bible it is clear that lions did not permanently inhabit populated areas, their haunts having been the mountains of Lebanon (Song 4:8), Bashan (Deut. 33:22), the thickets of the Jordan (Jer. 49:19), and the desert regions of the Negev (Isa. 30:6). From there they invaded populated areas, penetrating deeply and regularly, in particular at times of drought when wild animals, their usual prey, had decreased in number. Lions also multiplied when the country lay destroyed and derelict. In the neighborhood of Ereẓ Israel long- and short-maned lions were to be found. There are evidences that there were lions in the country in mishnaic and talmudic and even in crusader times (in the Negev). The last lions in the Middle East were destroyed in the 19th century. [J.F.]

In Folklore and Art. The lion figures prominently in folklore as a result of two main references to it in the Bible: the appellation of Judah as "a lion's whelp" (Gen. 49:9; Dan is also so called in Deut. 33:22, but the lion is always associated with Judah) and as one of the figures in the divine chariot of Ezekiel (Ezek. 1:10). A secondary motif is connected with the statement of Judah b. Tema (Avot 5:20) "Be as strong as a leopard, light as an eagle, fleet as a hart and brave as a lion to perform the will of thy Father who is in heaven."

Based on the image of the Lion of Judah in Genesis, the name Aryeh ("lion") became a common Jewish personal name mostly in all combinations with Judah and with Leib (Loeb), its German or Yiddish translation, thus giving the composite names Judah Aryeh, Judah Leib, and Aryeh Leib. The Judah mentioned in the verse, however, is associated not only with the son of Jacob of that name, but with the tribe, and particularly with the House of David (cf. Rashi ad loc.), and as a result the Lion of Judah became one of the most common of Jewish symbols. It is also one of the appellatives of the king of Ethiopia, who according to Ethiopian tradition is descended from Solomon and the Queen of Sheba. The rampant Lion of Judah is a favorite embellishment of the synagogue ark, the mantle covering the scroll of the Torah, etc. The Lion of the Divine Chariot is one of the four figures of Ezekiel's *merkavah* (divine chariot) which consisted of a human being, a lion, an ox, and an eagle. Different opinions are expressed in the Talmud as to the permissibility of reproducing these figures, but the general consensus is that the only reproductions wholly forbidden are either the four together or the complete human form (see *Art). On the other hand, almost complete freedom was accorded in the reproduction of the lion, possibly both because of its national association as described above and because of the figures of lions upon the laver in Solomon's Temple (I Kings 7:29) and especially in the steps leading to his throne and on its sides (*ibid.* 10:20).

*Jacob b. Asher opens his *Tur Oraḥ Ḥayyim* with the above-quoted passage of Judah b. Tema, and the four animals mentioned in it have often been made the subject of paintings. The word lion is often employed figuratively in a laudatory sense, mostly referring to an outstanding scholar. Thus Joshua b. Hananiah refused to controvert the ruling of Eliezer b. Hyrcanus after the latter's death because "one does not answer a lion after its death" (Git. 83a). Ḥiyya is called "the lion of the brotherhood" (Shab. 111a); a scholar, the son of a scholar, is called "a lion, son of a lion," while one of no such distinguished parentage is called "the lion the son of a jackal" (BM 84b), and Simeon b. Lakish expressed his admiration for the learning of Kahana, who had come to Ereẓ Israel from Babylon, in the words "a lion has come up from Babylon" (BK 117a). In one instance, however, it is used in a pejorative sense. Proselytes to Judaism who convert for selfish personal motives are called, in contradistinction to *gerei ẓedek*, righteous proselytes, "the converts of lions" (e.g., Kid. 75b), the allusion being to the Samaritans who adopted Judaism only because of their fear of lions (II Kings 17:25–28). [L.I.R.]

Bibliography: Lewysohn, Zool, 68–70, no. 114; Y. Aharoni, *Zikhronot Zo'olog Ivri*, 2 (1946), 222; F. S. Bodenheimer, *Animal and Man in Bible Lands* (1960), passim.

LION OF WRATH (Heb. כְּפִיר הֶחָרוֹן, *kefir he-ḥaron*), character mentioned in the Nahum and Hosea commentaries from Qumran Cave 4 (4QpNahum). In the comment on Nahum 2:12ff., where Nineveh is described as "the den of the lions . . . the feeding-place of the young lions *(kefirim)*," to which the lion brought home his prey—"he filled his caves with prey and his dens with torn flesh." These last words, says the Qumran commentator, refer to "the lion *(kefir)* of wrath, who smote with his mighty ones and the men of his counsel" and "took vengeance on the *Seekers after Smooth Things, in that he proceeded to hang them up alive [which was never done] in Israel before, for concerning one hung up alive on wood the Scripture says . . ." What the Scripture says is that he is an "affront to God" (Deut. 21:23). But the Scripture envisages the hanging of the body of an executed criminal on a tree until sunset; the commentator on Nahum has in mind something much more atrocious—hanging men up alive, or crucifying them. That such a thing "was never done in Israel before" implies that the perpetrator was an Israelite—not that he was a gentile ruler mistreating Israelites thus, like Nebuchadnezzar (Lam. 5:12) or Antiochus IV (Jos., Ant. 12:256). If he was an Israelite, the first Israelite ruler recorded to have crucified his enemies is Alexander Yannai, who in 88 B.C.E., having defeated his rebellious subjects who enlisted the aid of Demetrius III (Eukairos) against him, made an example of 800 of their leaders by crucifying them in Jerusalem (Jos., Wars 1:97; Ant. 13:380). This identification is supported by the commentator's reference in the same context to "[Deme-]trius, king of Javan, who sought to enter Jerusalem by the counsel of the Seekers after Smooth Things"—especially if the latter group should be identified with the Pharisees, whose sufferings at the hands of Yannai were long remembered in rabbinical tradition. Other identifications, however, have been suggested for the Lion of Wrath, ranging from Antiochus IV (preferred by H. H. Rowley) to John of Gischala (so C. Roth) and Simeon Bar Giora (so G. R. Driver).

Bibliography: Allegro, in: JBL, 75 (1965), 89ff. (containing the editio princeps of 4QpNahum); Rowley, in: PEFQS, 88 (1956), 107ff.; C. Roth, *Historical Background of the Dead Sea Scrolls* (1958), 40ff., 84; G. R. Driver, *Judaean Scrolls* (1965), 288ff.

[F.F.B.]

LIOZNO (Pol. **Lozniany**), town in Vitebsk oblast, Belorussian S.S.R.; under czarist rule it was included in the province of Mogilev. Jewish settlement in Liozno dates from the 18th century. The founder of Ḥabad Ḥasidism, R. *Shneur Zalman of Lyady, was born there in 1745. There were 82 Jewish poll-tax payers in the town in 1766. The community increased in the 19th century; in 1847 the Jewish population of the town and vicinity totaled 2,137, and in 1897 the community of Liozno numbered 1,665 (67.3% of the total population); by 1926 it had fallen to 1,204 (46.3%). After the German occupation (1941) those Jews who did not escape were murdered. No information is available on Jewish life in Liozno after World War II. [Y.S.]

LIPCHITZ, JACQUES (**Chaim Jacob**; 1891–), U.S. sculptor. He was born in Druskieniki, Lithuania. He attended school in Bialystok and in 1909 went to Paris, where he adopted the name Jacques. There he studied and became a French citizen in 1925. In 1930 he had a large retrospective exhibition which gave him his international reputation. In 1940 the German advance compelled him to leave Paris and seek refuge in unoccupied France. In 1941 he went to the United States, and settled in Hastings-on-Hudson, New York.

Lipchitz was one of the foremost cubist sculptors—his first pure cubist sculpture is dated 1913. He was influenced by the painters Picasso and Braque, and by the visionary El Greco. He developed an interest in African wood carvings which he collected. During this early period, Lipchitz frequently worked in stone. These pieces, with their sharp edges, flat planes, and solid mass came very close to pure abstraction.

In the 1930s, Lipchitz abandoned cubism for a markedly baroque manner of expression. At the same time, he became interested in social and philosophical themes, as distinguished from the harlequins and dancers, bathers, and musicians he had fashioned in his youth. One of the most celebrated baroque pieces is based on the Prometheus myth. His first sketches, made about 1933, show Prometheus a triumphant figure, the guardian of the flame. The second Prometheus, slightly different in feeling, shows a warrior, still in the thick of battle and unsure of triumph. This was destroyed. Lipchitz recreated it in 1943–44 for the Brazilian government, to decorate the facade of a government building in Rio de Janeiro. The final version, made for the Philadelphia Museum of Art—the superman's battle with the vulture—was Lipchitz's own rendering of the myth, since no such battle is described in ancient literature.

Lipchitz often derived inspiration from his Jewish background. Beginning in the 1930s, he frequently turned to biblical episodes or themes taken from Jewish life and

Jacques Lipchitz during his visit to the Youth Wing of the Israel Museum, Jerusalem, 1971. Photo Emka, Jerusalem.

history to interpret tragic or joyous events. "Man is wrestling with the Angel," he said about his "Jacob Wrestling with the Angel": "It is a tremendous struggle, but he wins and is blessed." Similar sentiments are expressed in "David and Goliath," made under the impact of the Nazi destruction. "The Prayer" (an old man swinging a rooster in the *kapparot* ritual) is a grim reminder of the slaughter of Jews in Europe. "The Miracle" is inspired by the happy news of the creation of the Jewish state—an exultant figure with raised arms faces the Tablets of the Law, out of which grows the seven-branched candelabrum, the finials of which might be tiny flames, or young leaf buds of a tree.

Lipchitz's work is represented in important museums, particularly in the United States and Israel. He left all his casts to the Israel Museum, Jerusalem.

Bibliography: A. M. Hammacher, *Jacques Lipchitz, his Sculpture* (1961); I. Patai, *Encounters: the Life of Jacques Lipchitz* (1961); H. H. Aranson (ed.), *Jacques Lipchitz* (1970). [A.W.]

LIPINER, SIEGFRIED (1856–1911), Austrian poet and playwright. Born in Jaroslaw, Galicia, and raised in Tarnow, he moved to Vienna in 1871, devoting himself to literature and philosophy. Lipiner's first epic poem *Der entfesselte Prometheus* (1876) aroused much favorable comment. It was followed by the epic *Renatus* (1878), by a volume of lyrics entitled *Buch der Freude* (1880), and by a libretto, *Merlin* (1886), for which Karl *Goldmark wrote the music. The last work was staged by the Viennese Royal Opera in 1886. From 1881 until his death, Lipiner was librarian and archivist of the Austrian *Reichsrat*. Although he converted to Christianity in 1891 and avoided all reference to his Jewish descent, Lipiner was described by his admirer, Nietzsche, as a Polish Jew capable of imitating the various forms of European lyric fastidiously and "almost genuinely." His original poetry was much influenced by Schopenhauer, Wagner, and Nietzsche. He also published a German translation of Adam *Mickiewicz's *Pan Tadeusz*. Three of his plays were *Der neue Don Juan* (1880), *Adam* (1911), and *Hippolytos* (1911). Lipiner's fame reached its peak while he was in his early twenties, but his verse later lost its popularity, though it often received mention in literary histories. He was a close friend of the composer Gustav *Mahler.

Bibliography: H. von Hartungen, *Der Dichter Siegfried Lipiner* (Dissert., Munich, 1935). [S.L.]

LIPKANY (Rum. **Lipcani**), small town in N. Moldavian S.S.R., in the region of Bessarabia. There were 82 Jewish families in Lipkany (out of a total of 203) in 1817, 4,410 persons (63% of the total population) in 1897, and 4,693 in 1930 (79.8% of the total). During the first half of the 19th century the *ẓaddik* Meir of Peremyshlyany lived in the town for several years. The writers Judah *Steinberg and Eliezer *Steinbarg were born in Lipkany. [El.F.]

Holocaust Period. When the town was taken on July 8, 1941, by German-Rumanian forces, they carried out a pogrom the same day in which many Jews were killed (no figures are available on the number). The soldiers went from house to house, robbing and murdering the inhabitants. The survivors (about 4,000) were taken to a forest near Vertyuzhany and from there were sent on a death march which took them to *Sekiryany, *Yedintsy, and *Khotin, and back to Yedintsy; the old, the sick, and the children, who were unable to withstand the pace, were shot on the journey. From Yedintsy, the survivors were deported to *Transnistria, where most of them died. Only a few dozen Jewish families from Lipkany were saved by the arrival of the Soviet army. Almost all the young Jews from the town who joined the Soviet army at the beginning of the war were either killed or returned as invalids. One Jew from Lipkany, Abram Schneider, was decorated as a "Hero of the Soviet Union." [J.AN.]

Bibliography: M. Carp, *Cartea Neagră*, 3 (1947), index; BJCE; Herz-Kahn, in: *Eynikeyt* (Oct. 2, 1945).

LIPKIN (Salanter), ISRAEL BEN ZE'EV WOLF (1810–1883), founder and spiritual father of the *Musar movement. His father, author of the glosses *Ben Aryeh* on the Talmud and *rishonim*, served as rabbi in Goldingen, Latvia and Telz, Lithuania, and he was later appointed rabbi of Zhagare, where Israel was born. At the age of 12, Israel went to the yeshivah of Ẓevi Hirsch Broida in Salant, and his reputation there was such that his teacher referred to him as "the little *Alfasi"; other great contemporary scholars applied similar laudatory appellations to him. His chance meeting with R. Zundel of Salant, who though a great scholar was an unusually humble and modest man, had a decisive influence on him. Powerfully impressed by Zundel's personality, Israel attached himself to him, regarding him from then on as his principal teacher, and conducting himself according to Zundel's ethical principles. He refused to accept rabbinical office, even that of Brest-Litovsk—the major community in Lithuania.

During his whole life, Israel Lipkin sought the best way in which to influence the community. Deciding to become a preacher or a *mashgi'aḥ* ("spiritual mentor") in a yeshivah, he accepted the position of head of a yeshivah in Vilna, where he was quickly renowned for his profound acumen. He soon resigned this post, however, and established his own yeshivah in Vilna. When his fame spread he began to preach sermons giving expression to the doctrine of *musar*, a moral movement based on the study of traditional ethical literature. These sermons attracted huge audiences. He proceeded to found groups for the study of *musar* on the lines of various ethical works. With the consolidation of these groups he established a special institution called a Bet Musar, in which he delivered his *musar* discourses and these became the pattern for similar discourses delivered in all the yeshivot of the Salanter school. These discourses were never recorded apart from several individual ones published by his pupil Shneur Zalman Hirschovitz in *Even Yisrael* (1883).

During the cholera epidemic which swept Vilna in 1848, Lipkin was in the forefront of all the most dangerous relief activities. He gave instructions that every kind of work was to be done on the Sabbath by Jews and was not to be relegated to non-Jews. On the Day of Atonement during the epidemic he ordered the congregation to partake of food, and set a personal example by mounting the pulpit and publicly eating. This dramatic action made a powerful impression both in contemporary and in later literature. His name was put forward to head the rabbinical seminary of Vilna, founded in 1848, but he refused to accept despite the attractive terms offered and the government pressure that was brought to bear upon him. As a result of this pressure he left Vilna and went to Kovno, where he founded a Musar yeshivah, which expanded greatly, attaining a roll of 150 students, many of whom were to become outstanding Lithuanian rabbis. His most important activity during this period was the improvement of the living conditions of the yeshivah students. He abolished the custom of the students being given daily hospitality in private homes, arranged suitable accommodation for them, and insisted that they be properly and neatly dressed. He also taught deportment and aesthetics. The period of study in his yeshivah was highly valued by the students, who saw themselves under "a new heaven and a new earth and an individual superior to all" (*Tenu'at ha-Musar*, p. 175). Salanter obtained his livelihood from communal posts in Kovno. Opposition to his methods began during the period of his yeshivah in Kovno, and among his opponents were Joshua Hoeschel of Janow, Abraham Samuel of Rossiyeny, Mordecai Eliasberg of Bauska, and Isaiah of Salant.

In 1857, to the surprise of many, Lipkin moved to Germany—first to Halberstadt for medical attention and later to Koenigsberg, where he lectured to university students on Judaism. In 1860 he went to Memel near the German-Lithuanian border. There he published his periodical *Tevunah*, for the dissemination of Torah and *musar*, to which all the outstanding scholars of Lithuania and Galicia contributed; 12 numbers were published. In Memel he acquired German citizenship, adopted German dress, and even preached in German. He also mastered various secular subjects. He visited several German cities, including Tilsit, Berlin, Frankfort, and Halberstadt. During this period he maintained contact with his pupils in Lithuania by correspondence. These letters constitute the main source for his system of *musar*. In 1877 he founded a **kolel* for young married students in Kovno; similar institutions were also set up in various towns. Salanter's pupils began to establish large yeshivot in Volozhin, Kelme, Telz, and Slobodka, in which *musar* teaching was predominant. In 1880 he went to France in order to disseminate Judaism. Although he suffered greatly there because of his straitened circumstances, he did not cease his activity. He stayed in Paris two years and succeeded in strengthening its Jewish institutions. From Paris he returned to Koenigsberg where he died.

In general Lipkin was revolutionary in his ideas. He proposed the compilation of an Aramaic-Hebrew dictionary for the better understanding of the Talmud, the translation of the Talmud into Hebrew, its printing in one volume, its translation into European languages, its teaching in universities, and the provision of religious books in Russian. Lipkin was also active in the communal and political spheres. He left no large works. He published an article in the *Ez Peri* (1881) and a number of articles from *Tevunah*, were later collected in a special work called *Imrei Binah* (1878). His well-known *Iggeret ha-Musar* ("ethical letter") was first published in Koenigsberg in 1858 and repeatedly republished. Twenty-two letters were collected by Isaac *Blaser, who published them under the title *Or Yisrael* (1900). A collection of his discourses recorded by pupils was published under the title *Even Yisrael* (1883); letters and collections appeared in various organs such as *Beit Yisrael*, *Ḥut ha-Meshullash*, etc. All these deal with his system of *musar* which spread throughout Lithuania and was adopted by all the yeshivot.

Among Lipkin's sons were YOM TOV LIPMAN *LIPKIN, a scientist with an international reputation; ARYEH LEIB HOROWITZ, author of the *Ḥayyei Aryeh* (1907) and rabbi of Choroszcz, Janow, and Brezhin; and ISAAC LIPKIN, rabbi of Janow, Korets, and Prosnitsa.

Bibliography: S. Rosenfeld, *R. Yisrael Salanter* (Heb., 1911); L. Ginzberg, *Students Scholars and Saints* (1928), 145–94; K. Rosen, *Rabbi Israel Salanter and the Musar Movement* (1945); M. G. Glenn, *Israel Salanter* (1953); D. Katz, *Tenu'at ha-Musar*, 1 (1958[3]), 137–38b; L. Jung (ed.), *Jewish Leaders*, 1 (1953), 197–211.
[Y.AL.]

LIPKIN, YOM TOV LIPMAN (1845–1875), Russian mathematician, son of Israel Salanter (see Israel *Lipkin). In his early youth Lipkin demonstrated great interest and promise in the exact sciences, studying higher mathematics on his own. Leaving his family for Koenigsberg, he was admitted to the university there. After finishing at the Berlin Gewerbe-Akademie, he was accepted at the University in Jena, where he presented his dissertation, *"Ueber die*

Raeumlichen Strophoiden," in 1870. Moving to St. Petersburg, he demonstrated his mechanical device for changing linear motion into circular motion, which he had previously written about in *Mélanges mathématiques de l'Academie Impériale à St. Petersbourg* (1870). His kinematic system

Yom Tov Lipman Lipkin, Russian mathematician. Jerusalem, J.N.U.L., Schwadron Collection.

was included in many Russian and foreign textbooks.

Bibliography: Slonimski, in: *Vestnik russkikh yevreyev*, nos. 17, 19 (1871); *Ha-Ẓefirah*, 22 (1874); nos. 22, 24 (1875). [Ed.]

LIPMAN, EUGENE JAY (1919–), U.S. Reform rabbi. Lipman was born in Pittsburgh, Pennsylvania. He was ordained at Hebrew Union College in 1943 and served for a year at Temple Beth-El in Fort Worth, Texas. As a chaplain in the U.S. army (1944–46, 1950–51) and as liaison officer for the U.S. army and the Jewish Agency for Palestine (1947–48), he was instrumental in aiding the flight of Jews from Eastern Europe through Czechoslovakia. From 1951 to 1961 he was director of the Commission on Social Action and the Commission on Synagogue Activities of the Union of American Hebrew Congregations, and from 1961 he was rabbi of Temple Sinai, Washington, D.C. Lipman was active in a number of causes concerned with civil rights; with A. Vorspan, he wrote *Justice and Judaism* (1956) and coedited *A Tale of Ten Cities* (1962). [Ed.]

LIPMAN, JACOB GOODALE (1874–1939), U.S. soil chemist and bacteriologist. Lipman was born in Friedrichstadt, Latvia. His parents were expelled from Moscow in 1888, and went to the U.S. In 1898 he joined the New Jersey State Agricultural Experimental Station, and was its director from 1911. In 1910 he became professor of soil fertility and bacteriology at Rutgers and from 1913 to 1939 was professor of agriculture. Among the books he wrote were *Bacteria in Relation to Country Life* (1908), and *A Laboratory Guide of Soil Bacteriology* (1911, with P. E. Brown). He edited several journals including *Soil Science* which he founded in 1916.

Jacob Goodale Lipman, U.S. soil chemist. Jerusalem, J.N.U.L. Schwadron Collection.

Lipman was director of the *Jewish Agricultural Society. In 1927 he was on the commission of experts surveying Palestine, and in 1929 he became a member of the Jewish Agency for Palestine.

Bibliography: *Industrial and Engineering Chemistry*, 27 (1935), 103; *Soil Science*, 40 (1935); S.A. Waksman, *Jacob G. Lipman* (1966). [S.A.M.]

LIPMAN, LEVI (**Isaac Libman;** first half of 18th century), merchant of Courland and financial agent for the imperial Russian court. Lipman's name is found in documents from the reigns of Peter II (1727–30) and Anna (1730–40), occasionally with the addition of the titles *Ober-Hof-Kommissar* and *Kammeragent*, as a purveyor of various goods and precious stones to the imperial court. His name is sometimes mentioned as a *shtadlan* active on behalf of the Jews. He was a favorite of Prince Dmitri Golitsyn and later of Count Biron, the "strong man" at Czarina Anna's court. When Biron was appointed duke of Courland in 1737, he entrusted Lipman with all the financial affairs of the duchy. He pursued his commerce in St. Petersburg and maintained his relations with the imperial court even after the fall of Biron. As he was the sole Jewish figure at the court of St. Petersburg, his contemporaries exaggerated the extent of his influence. (One ambassador wrote of him: "Lipman is the actual ruler of Russia".) In fact, Lipman was merely one of the *Court Jews who were characteristic of that period in Europe.

Bibliography: R. J. Wynderbar, *Geschichte der Juden in den Provinzen Liv- und Kurland* (1853), 23; Yu. Hessen, in: YE, 10, 224–5. [Y.S.]

LIPMANN, FRITZ ALBERT (1899–), U.S. biochemist and Nobel Prize winner. Lipmann was born in Koenigsberg, Germany. From 1927 to 1931 he pursued research at

Fritz Albert Lipmann, biochemist and Nobel Prize winner. Courtesy Israel Medical Association, Jerusalem.

the Kaiser Wilhelm Institute in Berlin and at Heidelberg. With the rise of the Nazi regime he left Germany and went to Denmark, working at the Biological Institute of the Carlsberg Foundation in Copenhagen from 1932 to 1939. He then emigrated to the United States and worked at Cornell University from 1939 to 1941, at the Massachussetts General Hospital from 1941 to 1947 and at the Harvard University Medical School, where he was professor of biological chemistry from 1949 to 1957. In 1957 he was appointed professor at the Rockefeller Institute for Medical Research in New York.

In 1953 Lipmann was awarded the Nobel Prize for Medicine and Physiology, which he shared with Hans *Krebs, for his discovery of coenzyme A and its importance for intermediary metabolism. This substance plays an important role in the "Krebs cycle" through which food is converted into carbon dioxide, water, and energy. Lipmann found that coenzyme A contains pantothenic acid, one of the vitamin B group. His hundreds of contributions to scientific journals include papers on metabolism, vitamin function, and cell structure.

Bibliography: T. N. Levitan, *Laureates: Jewish Winners of the Nobel Prize* (1960), 173–5; *Chemical and Engineering News*, 26 (March 1948), 860. [S.A.M.]

LIPMANN, OTTO (1880–1933), German psychologist and expert in vocational guidance. Lipmann was one of the pioneers in Germany of psychological counseling for the selection of a profession. According to Lipmann, effective counseling came from a knowledge of the individual's

Otto Lipmann, German psychologist. Jerusalem, J.N.U.L., Schwadron Collection.

characteristics and this determined the profession suitable for him. Lipmann suggested a method of examining the individual by means of tests and questionnaires, followed by an analysis of professions. Lipmann was the first psychologist to employ statistics in his work. He prepared several "psychograms" of professions such as telegraphist, typesetter, businessman, metal worker, academic worker, etc. Lipmann was the founder of the Institute for Applied Psychology in Berlin and editor (together with William Stern) of the *Zeitschrift fuer angewandte Psychologie*. His works include: *Psychische Geschlechtsunterschiede* (2 vols., 1917, 1924[2]); *Wirschaftspsychologie und psychologische Berufsberatung* (1918, 1921[2]); *Die psychologische Analyse der hoeheren Berufe* (1920); *Grundriss der Arbeitswissenschaft und Ergebnisse der arbeitswissenschaftlichen Statistik* (1926).

Bibliography: *American Journal of Psychology*, 46 (1934), 152–4. [H.O.]

LIPNIK NAD BECVOU (Czech. **Lipník nad Bečvou;** Ger. **Leipnik**), town in N.E. Moravia, Czechoslovakia. A synagogue is first mentioned there in 1540, though a Jewish settlement existed at least a century before. Most of Lipnik's Jews were engaged in textile production and in the import of livestock from Poland. In 1570 an economically injurious obligation to lend horses to the local gentry was

The former Jewish quarter of Lipnik, Moravia. Courtesy Czechoslovak State Archives, Prague.

abolished and the Jews' right of residence in perpetuity acknowledged in return for a payment. The community grew to 40 households in 1665. The rabbinate was founded in the late 16th century. Renowned rabbis included Moses Samson *Bacharach (1632–44), who composed a *seliḥah* on the sack of the town by Swedish troops in 1643, Isaac *Eulenburg (1652–57), and Isaiah b. Shabbetai Sheftel *Horowitz (1658–73). Under the rabbinates of Baruch *Fraenkel-Teomim (1802–28), Solomon *Quetsch (1832–54), and Moses *Bloch (1856–77), the yeshivah attracted pupils from all Europe. Rabbi F. Hillel (1892–1928) wrote the history of the community. In 1567 a third cemetery was opened (a fourth in 1883). The community was constituted as one of the political communities (see **Politische Gemeinde*) in 1850, where 485 Jews and 453 gentiles lived in 1880, and 294 Jews and 711 gentiles in 1900. Outside it, lived 288 Jews in 1880 and 240 in 1900. The number of families permitted to live in Lipnik by the *Familiants Laws was 255 in 1788. The community grew from 975 in 1794 to 1,259 in 1830, and 1,687 in 1857, but declined to 212 in 1921. In 1930 the community numbered 154 (2% of the total population). The community came to an end when its members were deported to the Nazi extermination camps in 1942. The synagogue equipment was sent to the Central Jewish Museum in Prague. Community life was not renewed after World War II. Lipnik was the birthplace of the industrialists David and Wilhelm *Gutmann, who established an institution for the poor in their mother's house in 1903.

Bibliography: A. Springer, *Juedische Kulturbilder* (1904), 34–56; F. Hillel, *Die Rabbiner und die verdienstvollen Familien der Leipniker Gemeinde* (1928); idem, in: H. Gold (ed.), *Die Juden und Judengemeinden Maehrens* (1929), 301–6; A. Kohut, in: AZDJ, 78 (1914), 499–501. [Ed.]

LIPNO, town in Bydgoszcz province, central Poland. Jews are first mentioned in Lipno in 1677. In 1736 the community paid a poll tax of 150 zlotys. In 1808 there were 777 Jews (85% of the total population) in the town. Between 1824 and 1864 the authorities compelled the Jews to reside in a separate quarter. The Jewish population numbered 892 in 1827, increasing to 1,558 (40%) in 1857, and 2,079 (36%) in 1897. At that time more than 50% of the town's commerce was in Jewish hands. In 1921 there were 2,443 Jews (29%) in the town itself and 4,795 (5.2%) in the district. There were 102 Jewish industrial enterprises. [EJ/Ed.]

Holocaust Period. During World War II, Lipno belonged to Reichsgau Danzig-Westpreussen, included in the Reich by Hitler's decree of Oct. 26, 1939. Before the war, Lipno had about 1,300 Jews. When the war broke out many Jews fled to the east, mainly to the western towns of the General Government. The Warsaw ghetto in August 1940 had about 300 Jewish refugees from Lipno. By the end of December 1939, the town was declared **Judenrein*.

Bibliography: Warsaw, Archiwum Akt Dawnych, *Akty Komisji rządowej do spraw wewnętrznych*, no. 107; E. Heller, *Żydowskie przedsiębiorstwa przemysłowe w Polsce* . . ., 1 (1922); B. Wasiutyński, *Ludność żydowska w Polsce* . . . (1930), 23; I. Schiper, *Dzieje handlu żydowskiego na ziemiach polskich* (1937), index. [De.D.]

LIPOVETS, town in E. Vinnitsa oblast, Ukrainian S.S.R. An early Jewish community was completely destroyed during the *Chmielnicki massacres (1648–49). Reestablished, it increased from 1,802 in 1847 to 4,135 (47.6% of the total population) in 1897, but fell to 3,605 (41.7%) in 1926. After the German occupation in the summer of 1941, all the Jews remaining in the town were slaughtered. [Y.S.]

LIPPE (Lippe-Detmold), former state in N.W. Germany. Jews are first mentioned in 1345 when they were ordered by Bernard V to bring their cases before his ducal court and not the *Feme* or private courts, an order which promised them greater security. The capital Detmold became the leading community after Jews were permitted to settle there in 1500. In 1583, 12 Lippe families moved to Altona. During the late 17th and 18th centuries, *Court Jews, who generally controlled the tobacco monopoly, exercised broad executive power over the Jews of Lippe, filled the office of rabbi, and were court financiers as well. Though no dynasty of Court Jews established itself, Joseph Isaac was the most prominent and powerful. In 1732 complaints were lodged against the growing number of Jews. Family *names were imposed on the 175 Jewish families in the county (27 in Detmold) in 1810. Civil rights were granted in 1858 and 1879. Twelve communities were included in the regional union of communities. The number of Jews in Lippe declined from 1,024 in 1885 to 900 in 1904, 780 in 1913, and 607 (0.32% of the total population) in 1928. Until 1742 services were held in a rented prayer room; after that a barn was converted into a synagogue, and a new building was not erected until 1904. Lippe had no rabbi after 1879. After the Nazi rise to power (1933), the Jewish population came to an end through emigration, persecution, and deportation. The tiny neighboring principality of Schaumburg-Lippe was notable for its dynasty of Court Jews founded by Isaak Heine, who received a letter of protection in 1682. In 1705/06 he and his cousin, *Behrends Leffmann, successfully averted an expulsion order. His family continued to serve the rulers of the principality for three generations; most distinguished of his descendants were the financier Salomon *Heine and the poet Heinrich *Heine.

Bibliography: A. Feilchenfeld, in: MGWJ, 43 (1899), 273f.; FJW, 419–21; AVJW (May 28, 1965), 3; Germ Jud, 2 (1968), 492; H. Schnee, *Die Hoffinanz und der moderne Staat*, 3 (1955), 93–124; H.-H. Hasselmeier, *Die Stellung der Juden in Schaumburg-Lippe von 1648 bis zur Emanzipation* (1967).

[ED.]

LIPPE, KARPEL (1830–1915), early member of Ḥovevei Zion and the Zionist movement. Born in Stanislav, Galicia, Lippe became a physician in Jassy, Rumania. From 1865 he published many articles as well as pamphlets and books on science, defense of the rights of Rumanian Jews, apologetics on Judaism, the Jewish religion and its attitude toward Christianity, etc. He also composed poetry, which he would sometimes read at gatherings instead of delivering a speech. When a society to settle in Ereẓ Israel was established in Rumania, Lippe became its chairman

Karpel Lippe, physician and early Zionist. Jerusalem, J.N.U.L., Schwadron Collection.

(1880). From that time he was active in the *Ḥibbat Zion movement, especially on behalf of the settlements of *Zikhron Ya'akov and *Rosh Pinnah, which were established by Rumanian Jews. He was a participant at the conference of Ḥovevei Zion in Kattowitz (1884). When Theodor *Herzl's *Judenstaat* appeared, Lippe wrote an article in the Berlin monthly *Zion* (1896) in which he rejected the idea of a Jewish state. Instead, he counseled the Jews to settle in Ereẓ Israel as Turkish citizens and strive for autonomy similar to that of the Austrian Empire in Galicia. Lippe nonetheless joined the new Zionist movement, was elected to the First Zionist Congress in Basle, and, being its senior delegate, delivered the opening speech. He considered himself one of the three initiators of the Zionist idea, together with Leon *Pinsker and Isaac *Ruelf, and as such he published the book *Meine 25-jaehrige Zionistische Agitation* (1902). He was elected chairman of the Jassy Conference of Rumanian Zionists (1903). In 1911, Lippe returned to Galicia and settled in Przemysl, but with the outbreak of World War I he fled to Vienna, where he died. Among his works are *Symptome der antisemitischen Geisteskrankheit* (1887) and *Zwei Vortraege ueber Unsterblichkeit und Spiritismus* (1907).

Bibliography: I. Klausner, *Ḥibbat Ẓiyyon be-Rumanyah* (1958), index.

[I.K.]

LIPPMANN, EDMUND OSKAR VON (1857–1940), German industrial chemist. He was born in Vienna and was director of sugar refineries in Duisburg (1881–86) and Halle (1890–1926). In 1926–32 he was honorary professor of chemical history in Halle. He wrote the standard books of his period on sugar, *Chemie der Zuckerarten* (1900[3]), *Geschichte des Zuckers* (1890, 1900, 1929), and *Entwickelungen der deutschen Zuckerindustrie von 1850–1900* (1900). He was a leading historian of chemistry, writing *Entstehung und Ausbreitung der Alchemie* (1919, 1931), *Geschichte der Ruebe als Kulturpflanze* (1925), *Geschichte der Naturwissenschaften* (two volumes, 1923), *Geschichte des Wismuts zwischen 1400 und 1800* (1930), and others.

Bibliography: J. C. Poggendorff, *Biographisch-literarisches Handwoerterbuch der exakten Naturwissenschaften*, 7a (1959), 111.

[S.A.M.]

LIPPMANN, EDUARD (1842–1919), Austrian organic chemist. Born in Prague, Lippman worked for a time with the French chemist, Charles Wurtz in Paris, and in 1868 became an instructor at the University of Vienna. In 1873 he went to teach at the Technische Hochschule at Brno, Moravia, but returned to Vienna in 1875 to become professor of chemistry at the university. In 1877 he was appointed professor of analytical chemistry at the Handelsakademie and from 1881 held the same position at the Technische Hochschule. Lippmann developed in 1886 what became the standard technique for determining carbon and hydrogen in organic compounds. Among the subjects dealt with in his numerous publications were benzyl alcohol, diethyltoluene, azobenzenes, anthracene, and alkaloids.

Bibliography: J. C. Poggendorff, *Biographisch-literarisches Handwoerterbuch* ..., 4 (1904), s.v.; 5 (1926), s.v.

[S.A.M.]

LIPPMANN, GABRIEL (1845–1921), French physicist and Nobel Prize winner. Though born in Luxembourg, Lippmann spent most of his life in Paris. His association with the *Annales de chimie et de physique*, for which he prepared summaries of the articles written in German, enabled him to keep abreast of innovations in electricity. After working in Heidelberg and under the brilliant H. L. F. von Helmholtz in Berlin, Lippmann was appointed professor of probability and mathematical physics at the Sorbonne (1883–86). From 1886 he was professor of experimental science and director of the Sorbonne's research laboratories, a position which he held until his death. Lippmann was responsible for much basic work in classical physics. His early research at Heidelberg was concerned with the effects of electrical charges on surface tension leading to the development of the "capillary-electrometer." In 1879 he presented before the Académie des Sciences, to which he was elected 7 years later, his work dealing with the effective mass of a charged body, in which he

Gabriel Lippmann, French physicist and Nobel Prize winner. Jerusalem, J.N.U.L., Schwadron Collection.

claimed that the moment of inertia in a charged body was higher than that of an uncharged body. This conclusion is of fundamental importance in the study of the electron. He also devised various scientific instruments: in astronomy his outstanding contribution was the development of the coelostat, an instrument for obtaining a stationary image of the sky, and the uranograph, an instrument for obtaining a map of the sky with lines of longitude at equal time-intervals. He achieved fame in 1891 through his production of color photographs based on the phenomenon of interference, although the three-color system proposed by J.C. Maxwell was preferred. Lippmann was nevertheless awarded the Nobel Prize for Physics for the results of this research. His most important works were his *Cours de thermodynamique* (1886), and *Cours d'acoustique et d'optique* (1888). Lippmann was elected president of the Académie des Sciences in 1912.

Bibliography: E. Lebon, *Savants du jour: Gabriel Lippmann* (1911), incl. bibl.; T. Levitan, *Laureates: Jewish Winners of the Nobel Prize* (1960), 56–58; N. H. de V. Heathcote, *Nobel Prize Winners in Physics, 1901–50* (1953), 65–69. [A.Co.]

LIPPMANN, WALTER (1889–), U.S. journalist, whose writing exerted influence on public policy. Born in New York, Lippman was for several years an assistant to the philosopher George Santayana. In 1914 he began his journalistic career as founder and associate editor of *New Republic*, a journal of liberal opinion. He left at the

Walter Lippmann, U.S. journalist and author. Jerusalem, J.N.U.L., Schwadron Collection.

outbreak of World War I to serve as an assistant to Newton D. Baker, secretary of war in the Wilson administration, and later helped to prepare data for the Peace Conference at Versailles. Lippmann in 1921 joined the staff of the *New York World*, a crusading newspaper noted for its attacks on corruption, poverty, and injustice. He served as editor from 1929 until the paper ceased publication two years later. He then wrote a column on public affairs for the *New York Herald-Tribune*, which was syndicated to more than 250 papers in 25 countries and made him widely known and respected. He was awarded two Pulitzer prizes, in 1958 and 1962. His political philosophy, as expressed in his newspaper writing and nearly thirty books, showed a gradual modification from socialism to liberalism to independent conservatism. His volumes include *Preface to Politics* (1913), *Public Opinion* (1922), *The Phantom Public* (1925), *Preface to Morals* (1929), *Good Society* (1937), *Cold War* (1947), *Essays in the Public Philosophy* (1955), and *Drift and Mastery* (1961).

Bibliography: C. Rossiter and J. Lare (eds.), *Essential Lippmann* (1963); M. Childs and J. Reston (eds.), *Walter Lippmann and his Times* (1959); D. E. Weingast, *Walter Lippman* (Eng., 1949). [I.R.]

LIPPOLD (d. 1573), *Court Jew to Joachim II (1535–71), elector of Brandenburg. When in 1556 he was appointed "supervisor" of *Brandenburg Jewry and collector of all monies paid by it to the court for ten years, the elector called him "our beloved, faithful Lippold." Nine years later he was elevated to the position of mintmaster, a post which involved clipping, devaluating, and reminting coins to the benefit of the elector. Lippold exploited Joachim's insatiable passion for women, alchemy, and money to attain a position of confidence and power. Ruthless and rapacious toward Jews and Christians alike, as private moneylender he charged an exorbitant interest rate (54%), borrowed large amounts with no intention of repaying them, and practiced embezzlement and extortion at will. Immediately after Joachim's death (Jan. 2, 1571) disorders broke out in *Berlin and Lippold was arrested. At his trial his crimes, real and alleged, were revealed; he was also accused of sorcery and of poisoning the elector. On Jan. 28, 1573, he was executed and quartered, after refusing baptism and withdrawing his confession. The Jews were expelled from Brandenburg soon after.

Bibliography: H. Schnee, *Die Hoffinanz und der moderne Staat*, 1 (1953), 38–47; A. Ackermann, *Muenzmeister Lippold . . .* (1910); G. A. Kohut, *Court Jew Lippold . . .* (1893); H. Rachel, *Berliner Wirtschaftsleben im Zeitalter des Fruehkapitalismus . . .* (1931). [ED.]

LIPSCHITZ, JACOB HA-LEVI (1838–1921), Hebrew writer and opponent of the Haskalah. Born in Vilkomir (Ukmerge), Lithuania, Lipschitz was the secretary, assistant, and representative on public affairs for R. Isaac Elhanan *Spektor from 1870 to 1896. He was one of the organizers of the fact-finding mission on the 1881–82 pogroms and persecutions of Russian Jewry which sent reports to the Jewish centers of Western Europe. He wrote sharply-worded articles (usually anonymous) against the Haskalah and its leaders, gradually becoming the leading Orthodox journalist and Orthodoxy's spokesman in its polemics against the religious reforms proposed by the Hebrew writers M. L. *Lilienblum and J. L. *Gordon. He encouraged the publications of the religious press (e.g., *Ha-Levanon, Ha-Kerem, Ha-Peles, Ha-Modi'a*), to which he contributed regularly. He issued manifestos and lampoons against the Zionist movement from his office in Kovno ("the Black Office" to his opponents). His books include: *Divrei Shalom ve-Emet* (1884), against the proposal to establish a rabbinical seminary in Russia; and a biography of Spektor (*Toledot Yiẓḥak*, 1897; also in Yid. as *Ge'on Yiẓḥak*, 1899). His Orthodox ideology is presented in *Sefer Maḥazikei ha-Dat* (1903). His *Zikhron Ya'akov* (3 pts., 1924–30), which he wrote during his World War I exile in the Ukraine, contains historical notes and personal memories. It was published after his death by his son Nathan Nata Lipschitz and is an important source for the history of the Jews in Russia during the 19th century.

Bibliography: B. Dinur, *Be-Olam she-Shaka* (1958), 86–92; Kressel, Leksikon, 2 (1967), 282–3; Rejzen, Leksikon, 2 (1927), 178–9. [Y.S.]

LIPSCHITZ, RUDOLF OTTO SIGISMUND (1832–1903), German mathematician. Born in Koenigsberg, he later taught in the secondary schools of Koenigsberg and Elbing. In 1857 he was appointed a lecturer at the University of Bonn and later became rector. Lipschitz's work was greatly influenced by his teachers Peter Dirichlet (1805–1859), and G. F. B. Riemann. His contributions to mathematics and physical mathematics were mostly in the theory of numbers, the computation of variations, progressive series, and the theory of potential and analytic mechanics. With the French mathematician Augustin Louis Cauchy (1789–1857), he proved the theorem of prime importance in differential calculus and equations concerning the existing solutions to the equation $dy/dx = f(x,y)$. [A.Co.]

LIPSCHITZ, SOLOMON ZALMAN (1765–1839), Polish rabbi, first chief rabbi of Warsaw, known as "Ḥemdat Shelomo" after his works of that name. Lipschitz, who was of a wealthy family whose members included the kabbalist Solomon Zalman Auerbach (17th century), was born in Poznan. Until he was 40 years old he lived and studied there, and therefore was also known as Solomon Zalman Posner. In 1804, after he had lost his fortune and his father-in-law was unable to continue to support him, he became rabbi of Nasielsk, where he also founded an important yeshivah. Lipschitz was unable to bear the atmosphere of Nasielsk, which was becoming increasingly ḥasidic. In 1806 he received a call to be rabbi of his home town, but he refused in order to protect his children from the influence of the Haskalah, which had spread from Germany. In 1819, he was elected rabbi of Praga (a suburb of Warsaw) where there was a large Jewish population. With the development of the Warsaw *kehillah*, he was appointed rabbi of the community (1821). There, too, he founded an important yeshivah. Among its students were many who later became Polish rabbis. As chief rabbi of Warsaw, he led the opposition to the Haskalah movement, the assimilationists, and the rabbinical seminary established there, which became a stronghold of assimilation under the direction of Anton *Eisenbaum. During the Polish insurrection against the czarist regime in 1831, Lipschitz opposed Jews joining the city guard as they would have been obliged to shave off their beards. He was in halakhic correspondence with many contemporary rabbis, including R. Akiva Eger, Moses Lorbeerbaum, R. Jacob of Lissa (Leszno), R. Meir Weyl of Berlin, R. Abraham Tiktin, and R. Aryeh Leib Zinz, and many rabbis turned to him with their halakhic problems. His responsa and decisions are cited in the halakhic works of many Polish rabbis. When he died, a month of mourning was proclaimed. A special announcement issued by the community forbade women to wear jewelry during that month. Lipschitz is the author of three works, all entitled *Ḥemdat Shelomo:* responsa (Warsaw, 1836); novellae on various tractates of the Talmud (3 pts., 1851–92), and sermons (1890). Some of his original letters were saved from the Holocaust but have not been published.

Bibliography: A. I. Bromberg, *Rishonei ha-Rabbanim be-Varsha* (1949), 9–79; J. Shatzky, *Geshikhte fun Yidn in Varshe*, 2 vols. (1947–48), index; D. Flinker, in: *Arim ve-Immahot be-Yisrael*, 3 (1948), 105–6; H. Seidman, in: *Velt Federatsie fun Poylishe Yidn. Amerikaner Ekzekutive Yorbukh*, 1 (1964), 242–7; Dubnow, Ḥasidut, 461f. [Ed.]

LIPSCHUETZ (Lipschutz, Lifschitz, Lifshyts, Lipszyc, Liebschuetz), widely dispersed Jewish family, which provided a large number of rabbis and scholars. The name is probably an indication of their origin and points to either Loebschuetz (Lubczyce; now Glubczyce) in Silesia, Liebschuetz in Thuringia, or to Liebeschitz in Bohemia. The derivation from the feminine name Liebscha is not acceptable. According to M. *Brann (see bibl.), the first well-known bearers of this name were the 16th-century R. Moses ben Isaac Lipschuetz of Brzesc-Kujawski and Gdansk (Danzig), and Isaac Lipschuetz of Poznan. In the first half of the 17th century members of this family included: R. Benjamin Benush, rabbi in Brest-Litovsk, son-in-law of R. Saul *Wahl and perhaps the son of the aforementioned R. Moses; R. Israel Mordecai ben Elijah, who was one of those who approved in 1609 the Prague edition of R. Eliezer b. Nathan's *Even ha-Ezer* (1610); R. Ḥayyim ben Isaac, *ḥazzan* in Poznan, who published additions to a commentary on the *kinot* by the *ḥazzan* Asher b. Joseph (Lublin, 1617); R. Moses ben Noah Isaac in Poznan and R. Gedaliah b. Solomon *Lipschuetz from Lublin. In the second half of the 17th century R. Elijah lived in Brest-Litovsk, R. Moses ben Enoch in Burgpreppach. From Gedaliah Lipschuetz (see Israel b. Eliezer *Lipschuetz and his son Gedaliah), who lived in Ostrava at the beginning of the 17th century, descended an unbroken line of learned rabbis right to modern times. Among the last members of this learned family were the Mishnah commentator R. Israel b. Gedaliah *Lipschuetz and his son R. Baruch Isaac *Lipschuetz.

Bibliography: Ẓ. H. Edelmann, *Gedullat Sha'ul* (1854), 24a; I. T. Eisenstadt and S. Wiener, *Da'at Kedoshim* (1897–98), 57, 83; D. Kaufmann, *Die letzte Vertreibung der Juden aus Wien...* (1889), 203; H. N. Maggid-Steinschneider, *Ir Vilna* (1900), 38–40; J. L. Feinstein, *Ir Tehillah* (1886), 23f., 154f., 202; S. Z. Kahana, *Anaf Eẓ Avot* (1903), 23; M. M. Biber, *Mazkeret li-Gedolei Ostraha* (1907), 62; I. de Terni, *Sefer ha-Makhri'a* (1897), introd.; A. J. L. Lipschuetz, *Avot Atarah le-Vanim* (1927), 46, 144; E. Kohan, *Kinat Soferim* (1892), 92a; J. Perles, *Geschichte der Juden in Posen* (1865), 49; A. Berliner, in: MGWJ, 50 (1906), 215–7; M. Brann, *ibid.*, 218f.; L. Lewin, in: JJLG, 5 (1907), 101ff. [Sh.A.H./Ed.]

LIPSCHUETZ, BARUCH ISAAC BEN ISRAEL (1812–1877), rabbi and author. The son of Israel b. Gedaliah *Lipschuetz, Lipschuetz was born in Wronki where his father was rabbi. In 1833 he was appointed to succeed his

Baruch Isaac b. Israel Lipschuetz, rabbi and author. Jerusalem, J.N.U.L., Schwadron Collection.

father there, but had to relinquish the appointment because of Akiva *Eger's resolute opposition to a young unmarried man of 21 functioning as religious leader of a community. He subsequently became rabbi of Landsberg, where he served until 1853, when he was invited to Mecklenburg-Schwerin to succeed David *Einhorn, the reform rabbi, because the central government wished to strengthen the Orthodox section of the community. In 1858 he was compelled to resign because of his firmness in religious matters. Henceforth he accepted no other communal appointment, and lived first in Hamburg and then in Berlin, where he died. He was the author of: *Ḥosen Shemu'el* (n.d., n.p.) an abstract of the Shulḥan Arukh *Even ha-Ezer* (incomplete), and *Torat Shemu'el* (1867), a devotional work. His *Beit Shemu'el* and *Shemesh u-Magen* remain in manuscript. He edited and republished his father's famous commentary on the Mishnah, *Tiferet Yisrael*, to which he made many editions. Some of his sermons are published in Ettlinger-Enoch's *Shomer Ẓiyyon ha-Ne'eman*.

Bibliography: A. Walden, *Shem ha-Gedolim he-Ḥadash*, 1 (1864), 40b, no. 319; H. N. Maggid-Steinschneider, *Ir Vilna* (1900), 39; E. Duckesz, *Chachme AHW* (1908), 126 (Heb. section); Berliner, in: MGWJ, 50 (1906), 217. [SH.A.H./ED.]

LIPSCHUETZ, ELIEZER MEIR (1879–1946), Hebraist, religious educator, and historical writer in Ereẓ Israel. Lipschuetz was born in Skole (Galicia). He was a businessman in Lemberg, but influenced by S. *Buber, he began studying medieval Jewish history and literature. Lipschuetz had early devoted himself to the revival of Hebrew, not only as a literary medium, but also and above all as a spoken language (in the Sephardi pronunciation). He attracted a circle of like-minded friends, such as Joseph *Babad, A. *Barash, Ḥ. *Yalon, Mordecai Ben-Ezekiel, and, especially, S. Y. *Agnon. His wife, too, spoke Hebrew and his child was the first in Lvov to grow up with Hebrew as his mother tongue. In 1910 Lipschuetz began teaching Hebrew and Jewish history at the *Ezra teacher's seminary in Jerusalem. As the result of the Hebrew versus German conflict, he left to take up a post with the Hebrew Teachers Seminary. In 1917 he was expelled from Palestine by the Turks and found refuge in Berlin, where he continued studying and writing to Jewish scholars. In 1920 he returned to Palestine and the following year founded the Mizrachi Teachers' Seminary, which he headed until his death. Lipschuetz worked actively in the religious education department of the Zionist Organization and was one of the

Eliezer Meir Lipschuetz, religious educator in Ereẓ Israel. Jerusalem, J.N.U.L., Schwadron Collection.

architects of the Mizrachi school network. He was also an active member of the Va'ad ha-Lashon, now the Academy of the Hebrew Language. In addition to Lipschuetz' *Raschi* (1912), a classic biography, he wrote a great number of essays on scholarly educational, literary, and linguistic subjects. Among these is one on S. Y. Agnon (1926), whose importance he was one of the first to recognize. A large part of his work was reissued in his collected writings, *Ketavim* (3 vols., 1947–57) but much remains in manuscript, including a voluminous correspondence.

Bibliography: A. B. Posner, *E. M. Lipschuetz* (Heb., 1941); O. Wolfsberg (Aviad), *Deyokena'ot* (1962), 152–4; A. J. Brawer, *Zikhronot* (1966), 214–5; 441–6; Kressel, Leksikon, 2 (1967), s.v. [ED.]

LIPSCHUETZ, GEDALIAH BEN SOLOMON ZALMAN (16th–17th century), Polish scholar, author, and Jerusalem emissary. Lipschuetz was a pupil of *Meir b. Gedaliah (the Maharam) of Lublin. In 1618 he immigrated from Poland to Ereẓ Israel. On the way he stayed in Prague where he obtained from the local scholars, Solomon Luntschitz and Isaiah ha-Levi *Horowitz (the Shelah), commendations for his work *Eẓ Shatul*, a commentary on the *Ikkarim* of Joseph *Albo. That same year he proceeded to Venice, where he published that work, and where he also proofread the collection of responsa of his teacher Meir, which were published that year, with the title *Manhir Eynei Ḥakhamim*. From there he continued to Ereẓ Israel and settled in Jerusalem. He was there in 1626 during the oppression of the Jews of Jerusalem at the hands of the tyrannical governor Muhammad ibn Farukh. When Farukh was dismissed the following year, and the heads of the Jerusalem community sent emissaries to the Diaspora to solicit aid in reconstructing the community, Lipschuetz was sent to the Balkans. At the beginning of the summer of 1629 he was in Belgrade, where he endorsed a halakhic responsum of Judah Lerma (see the latter's responsa *Peletat bat Yehudah*; no. 27, end).

Bibliography: Frumkin-Rivlin, 2 (1928), 45f.; Ya'ari, Sheluḥei, 268. [A.Y.]

LIPSCHUETZ, HILLEL ARYEH LEIB BEN ZE'EV DOV (1844–1907), Lithuanian rabbi and author. Lipschuetz studied under his father, who was rabbi of Srednik. In 1868 he became rabbi of Popelnya, then of Plunge, and later of the important town of Suvalki from 1880 to 1893, when he was elected rabbi of Lublin. He had a sound knowledge of many languages and an extensive general education. He is the author of *Beit Hillel*, novellae on the Shulḥan Arukh, *Ḥoshen Mishpat* (1890). A gifted writer, he contributed essays to the periodical *Ha-Levanon*, using the pseudonym Ha-Le'eh (from his initials), and translated into Hebrew the historical novel *Suess Oppenheimer* by Markus Lehmann (1873). His sons, Ezekiel, Eliezer, and Jacob also held rabbinical positions, Ezekiel being rabbi of Kalisz.

Bibliography: S. B. Nissenbaum, *Le-Korot ha-Yehudim be-Lublin* (1900²), 128; B. Eisenstadt, *Dor, Rabbanav ve-Soferav*, 4 (1902), 21. [Y.AL.]

LIPSCHUETZ, ISRAEL BEN ELIEZER (d. 1782), German rabbi, studied under Ezekiel *Katzenellenbogen. In the responsa of his father entitled *Heshiv R. Eliezer* (Nevewirth, 1649), there are included several items by the son, Israel, who is mentioned as being the rabbi of "Diez, Hadamar, and the environs." Later he served as rabbi in Cleves. In 1766–67 he came into prominence with regard to the cause célèbre known as the *Cleves *get*. Lipschuetz himself in 1770 published a collection of responsa supporting his standpoint under the title *Or Yisrael* (Cleves, 1770) in answer to the *Or ha-Yashar* published by *Aaron Simeon of Copenhagen in Amsterdam a year previously in support of the opposing side.

His son GEDALIAH (d. 1826) eked out a meager living serving as rabbi to various smaller Jewish communities in East Prussia, among them Obrzycko and Chodziez (now in Poland). In 1809 he came into conflict with the local authorities when he opposed an edict forbidding the settlement of conflicts by recourse to Jewish courts. Gedaliah was the author of *Ḥumrei Matnita* (Berlin, 1784) in six parts: comments on the Talmud and its main commentaries with special attention given to the tractates *Nazir* and *Nedarim*; an explanation of unusual words in the Talmud; novellae on *Asher b. Jehiel entitled *Ateret Rosh*; notes on Isaac *Alfasi entitled *Ma'aseh Ilpas*; *Minei Targimon*, comments on *Targum Onkelos* and Rashi's

Pentateuch commentary; *Mirkevet ha-Mishnah*, comments on difficult passages in the Mishnah. In his approbation of this work the father mentions 17 works of his son as existing in manuscript form. Gedaliah also wrote *Regel Yesharah* (Dyhernfurth, 1777), containing a list of unusual words left unexplained by Rashi in his commentary on the Talmud, referring to other passages where an explanation is found; comments on the order *Nezikin* and the minor tractates of the Talmud; an excursus on talmudic weights and measures; and an elucidation of the geometrical matter in chapters three and five of the tractate *Kilayim*. The allegedly presumptuous tone of this work, combined with the conceit and contentious disposition of its author, led to its disparagement among the *maskilim* who coined the saying, "the author of the *Regel Yesharah* ("Straight Foot") is a twisted blockhead."

Bibliography: Berliner, in: MGWJ, 50 (1906), 215–8; S. B. Freehof, *Responsa Literature* (1955), 158ff.; D. Kaufmann and M. Freudenthal, *Familie Gomperz* (1907), 74; Tal, in: *Sinai*, 24 (1948–49), 152–67. [J.H.]

LIPSCHUTZ, ARYEH LEIB (d. c. 1849), talmudist and ḥasidic rabbi. He was born in Jaroslaw and was the pupil of Aryeh Leib b. Joseph ha-Kohen *Heller, author of *Keẓot ha-Ḥoshen* and of Jacob Isaac *Horowitz of Lublin. Aryeh was the son-in-law of Moses *Teitelbaum, rabbi of Ujhely, and himself served as rabbi in several Galician communities. His last post was at Brigal, where he died. He is the author of two books of novellae, *Ari she-ba-Ḥavurah* (1852), on *Ketubbot* and *Ḥiddushei Aryeh de-Vei-Ilai* (1880), on *Kiddushin*, *Yoma*, *Menaḥot*, *Kinnim*, and *Niddah*. In addition he published a book of responsa *Aryeh de-Vei-Ilai*, (1874) on the four parts of the Shulḥan Arukh.

Bibliography: A. Walden, *Shem ha-Gedolim he-Ḥadash*, 1 (1965), 82. [Ed.]

LIPSCHUTZ, ELIEZER BEN SOLOMON (d. 1750), rabbi and talmudist. When he was over the age of 30 he became the rabbi of *Ostrowiecz (Poland). There he had many pupils, but he left for Germany where he wandered from post to post because of differences with his communities. Through the influence of his wife's uncle, Simeon Jolles, the leader of the community, he obtained a position in Cracow. There also he made enemies and after Jolles' death he left Cracow. Finally he secured a position at Neuwied where he remained until his death. He published *Heshiv R. Eliezer ve-Si'aḥ la-Sadeh* (Neuwied, 1749) in two volumes: (1) responsa with notes by his son Israel; and (2) (subtitled *Dammesek Eliezer*), novellae on *Yoreh De'ah* and *Ḥoshen Mishpat*. He carried on correspondence with noted authorities of the time. Another member of his family was R. Israel b. Gedaliah *Lipschutz, the author of *Tiferet Yisrael*.

Bibliography: S. Chones, *Toledot ha-Posekim* (1910), 602; H. N. Dembitzer, *Kelilat Yofi*, 2 (1893), 133b. [Ed.]

LIPSCHUTZ, ISRAEL BEN GEDALIAH (1782–1860), German rabbinic scholar. Lipschutz served as rabbi in the towns of Wronki (1821), Dessau and Colmar (1826–37), and Danzig (1837–60). His fame rests upon his commentary to the Mishnah, entitled *Tiferet Yisrael*, one of the finest of its class. In this work, he explains the words of the Mishnah briefly, offers new interpretations to difficult passages, particularly in the orders of *Zera'im*, *Kodashim*, and *Tohorot*, and adds everywhere the halakhic ruling as decided on in the Shulḥan Arukh and its commentaries. To each of the orders of *Mo'ed*, *Kodashim*, and *Tohorot*, he prefaces general introductions comprising a methodic summation of all the principles of the order, after the manner of *Maimonides in his introduction to his commentary on the Mishnah. A considerable portion of the commentary is taken from that of his son, Baruch Isaac *Lipschutz as well as from Akiva *Eger, *Elijah b. Solomon (the Gaon of Vilna), and others. *Tiferet Yisrael* became the most widespread Mishnah commentary, and is regarded as an invaluable adjunct to that of Obadiah *Bertinoro. Lipschutz's commentary to *Zera'im*, *Zera Emunah*, and to *Tohorot*, *Ta'am ve-Da'at*, with a general preface entitled "*Yevakkesh Da'at*," was published in Hanover (1830). His commentary to *Nashim*, *Ḥosen Rav*, was published later (Danzig, 1843). Appended to it was *Avi Ezer*, a work by Lipschutz's father on the Shulḥan Arukh, *Even ha-Ezer*. The commentary to *Mo'ed*, *Davar be-Itto* (*ibid.*, 1844), included an introduction dealing with topics relevant to the Sabbath and intercalations. *Nezikin* was published in Danzig in 1845, along with a treatise on immortality and the resurrection. *Kodashim*, under the title *Ḥokhmat Elohim* (Koenigsberg, 1850), includes laws of the order entitled *Ḥomer ba-Kodesh* at the beginning and diagrams of the Temple and altar at the end. The commentary was republished in its entirety (Berlin, 1862) with additions by Lipschutz's son Baruch Isaac. Lipschutz also composed an extensive commentary to the order *Tohorot*, *Ateret Tiferet* (Vilna, 1887–95), in which he separated the plain interpretation from the *pilpul*, calling the former "*Yakhin*" and the latter "*Bo'az*," and added a section giving the halakhic rulings, "*Hilkheta Gevirta*," at the end of each chapter. In later editions of the Mishnah *Tiferet Yisrael* was similarly divided. He also published a brief commentary to the Mishnah called *Zera Yisrael* (Vilna, 1852), and his ethical will was published in Koenigsberg in 1861. His son mentions that Lipschutz left in manuscript sermons, notes on the Talmud, on Maimonides and on the Shulḥan Arukh, and many responsa. He apparently also compiled *Rashei Avot*, a commentary on *Avot*, and *Megillat Setarim*.

Bibliography: B. I. Lipschuetz, in: *Ha-Maggid*, 4 (1860), 170–1; H. N. Maggid-Steinschneider, *Ir Vilna*, 1 (1900), 38–39; Brann, in: MGWJ, 50 (1906), 375; Ḥ. Albeck, *Mavo la-Mishnah* (1959), 253; Posner, in: *Shanah be-Shanah*, 4 (1963), 395–401. [A.D.]

LIPSCHUTZ, SHABBETAI BEN JACOB ISAAC (1845–1929), rabbi, kabbalist, and author. Lipschutz was born in Rohatyn, Galicia, and from 1907 served as a rabbi in Bereg-Ilosva (now Irshava, Sub-Carpathian Ruthenia, U.S.S.R.). He wrote *Berit Avot* (also entitled *Sharvit ha-Zahav he-Ḥadash*), on the laws of circumcision (1898; with supplement, 1912); *Pidyon Nefesh* (also entitled *Sha'arei Pedut*), on the redemption of the firstborn (1899); *Segullot Yisrael* (also entitled *Sefer ha-Ḥayyim*) on healing by sympathetic treatment (1905); a second edition together with Sussman Sofer's *Even Segullah* (1908); notes on the *Shemirat ha-Nefesh* (1872) of Israel Mattathias Auerbach (1901); *Kol Todah*, a commentary on the Book of Esther (1884 and 1888); *Tiferet Ya'akov*, homilies on the Pentateuch (1912); *Sha'arei Raḥamim*, a commentary on Ephraim Zalman Margaliot's *Sha'arei Efrayim* (1932); and *Likkutei Shoshannim* (also entitled *Sefer ha-Eshel*), on various halakhic matters (1949). A number of his works have remained unpublished.

Bibliography: S. N. Gottlieb, *Oholei Shem* (1912), 212; A. Stern, *Meliẓei Esh*, 3 (1962[2]), chapter *Adar*, 57b, no. 263. [Sh. A.H./Ed.]

LIPSCHUTZ, SOLOMON BEN MORDECAI (d. 1736), Dutch rabbi. Born and educated in Lisse, Lipschutz was appointed rabbi of the Ashkenazi community in The Hague during the incumbency of David Nunes (c. 1700) as rabbi of the Sephardi community. About 1710 he was appointed rabbi of Rotterdam, remaining there until his death. His query in connection with the *eruv* of Rotterdam, based on the fact that the river could be regarded as its boundary, is published in Jacob *Poppers' responsa *Shav Ya'akov* (1702, pt. 1, no. 17). Having received conflicting rules from Ezekiel Katzenellenbogen and Jacob *Reischer, to whom he had first turned, he addressed himself to Jacob Poppers for a decision, and he appears to have written a book for which he obtained Poppers' approbation. The large Boompjes synagogue in Rotterdam was built while he was rabbi. After his death Solomon was succeeded as rabbi of Rotterdam by his son JUDAH (d. 1754) whom Jonathan Eybeschuetz called "a righteous and upright man who increased peace in the world and was pleasing to his brethren." Judah's son ABRAHAM (d. 1780) was also appointed a rabbi of Rotterdam, but his appointment stirred up a great controversy because two of the lay leaders were his relatives. The leaders of the community turned to Jonathan Eybeschuetz and David Berlin for a decision, and they decided in Abraham's favor.

Bibliography: Z. H. Horowitz, *Kitvei ha-Ge'onim* (1928), 21–25.

[Y.AT.]

LIPSET, SEYMOUR MARTIN (1922–), U.S. sociologist. Born in New York City, Lipset taught at Columbia University, the University of Toronto, Canada, and at Berkeley, California, before becoming professor in the department of social relations at Harvard University. Lipset is one of the foremost representatives of political sociology in the United States; he combines a "middle range" theoretical orientation with verification in research. In his major work, *Union Democracy* (with M. A. Trow and J. S. Coleman, 1956), he provides a negative proof for Roberto Michels' contention that large-scale organizational structures make bureaucratic procedures inevitable: this rule does not apply to the American Typographical Union, which Lipset investigated, because of its relatively small size and the high educational standards of its members. Other important publications of Lipset, apart from numerous scholarly papers, are *Agrarian Socialism* (1950, 1968²), an analysis of Canadian socialist movement; *Class, Status and Power* (edited with R. Bendix, 1953, 1966²); *Social Mobility in Industrial Society* (with R. Bendix, 1959); *Social Mobility and Occupation Career Patterns* (with R. Bendix, 1952); *Political Man* (1960); *Berkeley Student Revolt* (1965); *The First New Nation* (1967), and *Revolution and Counterrevolution* (1968). He edited *Sociology and History: Methods* (with R. Hofstadter, 1968). Lipset was a leading member of American Professors for Peace in the Middle East and author of *The Left, the Jews and Israel* (1969). [W.J.C.]

LIPSHITZ, ISRAEL LIPPY (1903–), South African sculptor. Born in Lithuania, Lipshitz was taken to South Africa in 1908, and, apart from a period of study in Paris, spent most of his life in Cape Town. He was regarded as a leader of the modern school in sculpture and, from 1950 to 1968, was associate professor at the Cape Town University's School of Fine Art. Lipshitz worked in a variety of media, e.g., marble, bronze, stone, and wood. He drew many of his subjects from nature and from the Bible including Lot's wife, Jacob wrestling with the angel, and a massive head of Moses, carved out of a fossilized tree trunk, acquired by the National Art Gallery in Salisbury, Rhodesia. [L.S./L.H.]

LIPSKI, ABRAHAM (1911–), Polish engineer and inventor. Born in Lodz to a Zionist family, Abraham Lipski settled in Belgium. A highly successful construction engineer, he specialized in techniques of "presolicitations"—a modern method in construction. In 1951 he won international renown with his invention of the "preflex" construction beam. In 1958 at the Brussels World Fair he acted as assistant general commissioner for the Israel pavilion. Among a vast variety of public and private constructions he erected are the Transport Pavilion at the 1958 Brussels Exhibition; wharf constructions at Ostend and Ghent; the Midi Tower in Brussels; the funicular railway in Haifa, the Carmelit; and the Shalom-Meyer Tower in Tel Aviv. He participated in the construction of the Lydda International Airport and the Tel Aviv bus station. Lipski devoted a great deal of time to Jewish affairs. [RO.B.]

LIPSKY, LOUIS (1876–1963), U.S. Zionist leader, journalist, and author. Lipsky, who was born in Rochester, New York, and edited a weekly periodical *Shofar* there, was an active Zionist even before the opening of the First Zionist Congress (1897). In 1901 Lipsky founded *The Maccabean* (later *The New Palestine*) magazine in New York, the first English-language Zionist periodical in the U.S. Under Lipsky's editorship, the magazine often exercised a powerful influence on Zionist actions in the U.S. Lipsky also edited *The American Hebrew* (1900–14). Lipsky served first as secretary, then chairman of the executive committee of the Federation of American Zionists, which was replaced by the Zionist Organization of America (ZOA) in 1917. In the ensuing Brandeis-Weizmann rift over the financial support and control of Jewish Palestine, Lipsky backed Weizmann. Lipsky was ZOA president from 1922 to 1930, and then became president of the Eastern Life Insurance Company (1930–59).

Louis Lipsky at the U.S. National Conference of the World Jewish Congress, 1941. Courtesy Zionist Archives, New York.

Lipsky was a founder of the Keren Hayesod, the Jewish Agency, and the American and World Jewish congresses. In 1915 he had advocated the establishment of an American Jewish Congress, directly elected by American Jews which would support the concept of a Jewish national home. In 1918 the first American Jewish Congress was elected. Lipsky subsequently served as its vice-president and chairman of its governing council, and from 1934 to 1945 was deeply involved in the organization's attempts to call attention to the plight of European Jewry and to organize their rescue. A prolific author, Lipsky's three-volume *Selected Works* consisting of *Thirty Years of American Zionism*, *Stories of Jewish life*, and *Shields of Honor*, a selection of his plays and short stories, was published in 1927. He also wrote *A Gallery of Zionist Profiles* (1956).

His son ELEAZAR LIPSKY (1912–) was for many years head of the Jewish Telegraphic Agency in New York City. A second son, JOEL CARMICHAEL (1915–), wrote widely on subjects concerning Jewish history, the Middle East, and Russia. Among his books are *The Shaping of the Arabs* (1967), *A Short History of the Russian Revolution* (1964), and *Death of Jesus* (1962).

Bibliography: M. W. Weisgal, *Louis Lipsky* (Eng. 1964); S. S. Wise, *Challenging Years* (1949), passim; A. Friesel, *Ha-Tenu'ah ha-Ẓiyyonit be-Arẓot ha-Berit ba-Shanim 1897–1914* (1970), index; S. Halperin, *The Political World of American Zionism* (1960), index. [M.G.]

LIPSON, EPHRAIM (1888–1960), English economic historian. Born in Sheffield, and educated at Cambridge, Lipson was a reader in economic history at Oxford from 1921 to 1931. He was instrumental in founding the Economic History Society, and the *Economic History Review*, serving as editor until his resignation in 1934. His major works, some of which went through numerous editions, were: *Economic History of England* (3 vols., 1915–31; 1959[12]); *Europe in the Nineteenth Century* (1916, rev. ed. 1962); *The History of the Woollen and Worsted Industries* (1921); *Europe 1914–1939* (1940[2]); *The Growth of English Society—A Short Economic History* (1949). In *A Planned Economy or Free Enterprise: The Lessons of History* (1944), he pleaded for a policy aiming "to preserve best in our present economic system, the spirit of enterprise, and fuse it with the team spirit, so that self-interest was held in check by the ideal of public service and devotion to the Commonweal." His brother DANIEL LIPSON (1886–) was housemaster of the Jewish House at Cheltenham College, one of England's leading boarding schools. He served as mayor of Cheltenham from 1935 to 1937 and was Independent member of Parliament for Cheltenham from 1937 to 1950. He was an opponent of Zionism and frequently expressed his anti-Zionist views in parliamentary debates. [B.J.K.]

LIPSON, MORDEKHAI (1885–1958), Hebrew writer and folklorist. Born in Bialystok, he was ordained as a rabbi in 1903. After teaching for several years, he immigrated to the United States in 1913. There he wrote for the Hebrew and Yiddish press and edited the Hebrew weekly *Ha-Ivri* (1916–21). He founded and edited the New York Hebrew daily *Hadoar* (1921–23), which was the only modern Hebrew daily to appear in the U.S. When the newspaper was taken over by the Histadrut Ivrit and turned into a weekly, Lipson served for a period as editor. He immigrated to Ereẓ Israel in 1930 and edited the religious daily *Ha-Ẓofeh* from its inception, in 1937, until 1944. For more than a generation he collected Jewish folklore which appeared in *Mi-Dor-Dor* (3 vols., 1928–29), *Anshei Middot* (5 vols., 1927–34), *Midrash Zuta* (1951), and *Emshol Lekha Mashal* (1956). He also translated many books from Hebrew to Yiddish and from Yiddish to Hebrew, including works by I. J. *Singer, I. *Bashevis Singer, and J. *Opatoshu. [G.K.]

LIPTON, MAURICE (1916–), Canadian air commodore and chief of operations of the Royal Canadian Air Force (RCAF). Lipton was born in Sydney Harbour, Nova Scotia. He joined the permanent air force in 1938 and was on active duty during the whole of World War II. Lipton served as commanding officer of a night fighter squadron in Britain (1941–42), commanding officer of the Central Flying School (1943), and director of Air Force Training (1944–45). He was awarded the Air Force Cross for distinguished service in 1944. After the war he returned to Canada and held several positions at the RCAF Staff College. In 1957 he became director of strategic planning, and in 1959 was appointed chief of operations of the air force. [ED.]

LIPTON, SEYMOUR (1903–), U.S. sculptor and educator. Lipton was a practicing dentist in New York City for many years. From the mid-1950s he devoted himself

"Archangel" by Seymour Lipton. Metal sculpture, in the east foyer of Philharmonic Hall in Lincoln Center, New York. Height 9 ft. (274 cm.). Courtesy Lincoln Center for the Performing Arts. Photo Bob Serating.

fully to sculpture. Following the dominant art trends, he used socialist-realist themes in his carvings in the 1930s and welded abstract forms together in the 1940s. The decorative, but strangely menacing, spiked bronze totems he evolved won him an award at the São Paulo Biennial in 1957. His sculptures decorate several important industrial buildings in the U.S. as well as the Philharmonic Hall, Lincoln Center, New York, the Dulles International Airport, Washington, D.C., Temple Israel, Tulsa, Oklahoma, and Temple Beth-El, Gary, Indiana. Lipton has taught sculpture at the Cooper Union, New York, Newark State Teachers College, New Jersey, Yale University, Connecticut, and the New School for Social Research, New York.

Bibliography: Elsen, in: *Art Journal*, 24 (1964), 113–8. [R.BRO.]

LIPTOVSKY MIKULAS (Slovak **Liptovsky Mikuláš;** Hung. **Liptószentmiklós**), town in N. Slovakia. A Jewish settlement in Liptovsky was founded by peddlers and merchants from Holesov, who were avoiding the 1726 *Familiants Laws. The first synagogue was built in 1731 and enlarged in 1770. The office of rabbi was first held by a layman merchant, who established the *talmud torah*, followed by R. Loeb Kunitz, who founded a yeshivah in 1776 (in existence till 1862). From 1821 to 1830 Eleazar *Loew was rabbi of the community. In 1845 the community established a German-language Jewish elementary school where Simon *Bacher taught. A private Jewish secondary school was founded in 1860. Although it existed for only 15 years it had a number of outstanding students, including the scholars E. *Baneth and W. *Bacher, the publisher Samuel *Fischer, the journalist Albert Sturm, and Simon Goldstein, the first Jewish lawyer in Hungary. The community numbered approximately 300 families in 1840. It was the first Slovakian community in which a dispute arose over Reform, especially in 1843 when the controversy centered around the location of the *bimah* in the new synagogue. Liptovsky Mikulas was known for its good relations between Christians and Jews, which found expression in the fact that the local nobility sent their children to the Jewish schools. The first Jewish mayor in Hungary, Isaac Diner, was elected in Liptovsky Mikulas; thereafter the office was held by Jews on several occasions. Banks and factories in the town were owned by Jews. The community totaled about 1,200 persons in 1933 and 957 in 1941, most of whom perished during the Holocaust. A community was reestablished after the war.

Bibliography: E. Herzog, *A zsidók története Liptó-szt.-Miklóson* (1894); M. Lányi and H. Propperné Békefi, *Szlovenszkói zsidó hitközségek története* (1933), 179–224; Y. L. Bato, in: *Das neue Israel*, 21 (1968), 471–5; *Israelitische Annalen*, 3 (1841), 19–20; 181, 231–2; *Jews of Czechoslovakia*, 1 (1968), 72, 74, 77, 91; A. Schnitzer, *Juedische Kulturbilder* (1904); *Magyar Zsidó Lexikon* (1929), 536, s.v. *Liptószentmiklós;* MHJ, 7 (1963), s.v. *Liptószentmiklós.*

[ED.]

LIPTZIN, SOL (1901–), literary scholar and educator. Leaving his native Satanov, Russia, as a boy, Liptzin was raised in the U.S. He taught at City College, New York, where he became professor of German in 1948 and served as chairman of the department of Germanic and Slavonic languages (1943–58). His interest in the mutual interaction of 19th-century German and English literature finds reflection in works such as *Shelley in Germany* (1924), and *The English Legend of Heinrich Heine* (1954). He also wrote *Lyric Pioneers of Modern Germany* (1928), *Arthur Schnitzler* (1932), and *Richard Beer-Hofmann* (1936). Liptzin turned his attention to Yiddish literature in *Peretz* (1946), *Eliakum Zunser* (1950), *The Flowering of Yiddish Literature* (1963), and *The Maturing of Yiddish Literature* (1970). Active in Jewish affairs, he was honorary president of the Jewish Book Council of America (1953–) and editor of the *Jewish Book Annual* (1953–56). Liptzin was a visiting professor at Yeshiva University (1929–40), and, after settling in Israel in 1962, at Tel Aviv University (1962–63), Haifa Technion (1962–66), and The American College in Jerusalem. His other works include *Germany's Stepchildren* (1945), on German-Jewish writers, and *The Jew in American Literature* (1966). [ED.]

LISBON, capital of *Portugal.

The Middle Ages. Jews were apparently settled in Lisbon in the 12th century, at the time of the conquest of the territory from the Moors and the establishment of the kingdom of Portugal by Affonso I (1139–85). For a period of two centuries they appear to have lived in tranquility, sharing the lot of their coreligionists in the rest of the country. Many Jews were prominent in court circles as tax farmers, physicians, or astronomers; the *almoxarife* Dom Joseph ibn Yaḥya, descendant of a family founded by a Jew who accompanied the first king on his conquest of the country, constructed a magnificent synagogue at his own expense in 1260. When the religious and political organization of the communities of Portugal was revised by Affonso III (1248–79), Lisbon became the official seat of the **arraby mór*, or chief rabbi. The most important incumbent of this office was Dom Moses Navarro, physician to Pedro I (1357–67), who, with his wife, acquired a large landed property near Lisbon.

This initial period of prosperity came to an end in the reign of Ferdinand I (1367–83). When Lisbon was captured by 1373, the Jewish quarter was sacked and many Jews killed. After the king's death, the Jews were considered by the populace to be at the root of the rapacious policies of the queen dowager Leonora—notwithstanding the fact that she had deposed the Jewish collector of taxes at Lisbon, as well as Dom Judah, the former royal treasurer. A popular revolt led to the accession to the throne of the master of Aviz, the first of a new dynasty. The feeling in Lisbon against the Jews became extreme, and the people wished to take violent steps to discover the treasures left by the late instrument of royal greed. An anti-Jewish reaction followed in the political sphere. Nevertheless, the new king (known as John I) did his best to protect the Jews against actual violence, though they were henceforth excluded from the positions of trust they had formerly occupied and were forced to make disproportionate contributions to the gift exacted by the city for presentation to the new king. Toward the close of his life, the latter became a little more tolerant. There was a reaction, however, under his son, Duarte (1433–38), who attempted to enforce the complete separation of Jews and Christians. This led to a protest by the community of Lisbon, and as a consequence the severity of the recent decree was mitigated (1436).

Persecution and Expulsion. Popular feeling, nevertheless, continued antagonistic. In 1455, the Côrtes of Lisbon demanded restrictions against the Jews. The Portuguese sovereigns had not permitted the wave of rioting which swept through the Iberian Peninsula in 1391 to penetrate into their dominions. Nevertheless, as a result of some disorder in the fish market, there was a serious anti-Jewish outbreak in Lisbon toward the close of 1449 which led to many deaths, and another (in the course of which Isaac *Abrabanel's library was destroyed) in 1482. Owing to the tolerant if grasping policy of John II, a number of the exiles from Spain were allowed to enter Lisbon after the expulsion of 1492. Their crowded living conditions led to an outbreak of plague and the city council had them driven beyond the walls. Royal influence, however, secured the exemption from this decree of Samuel Nayas, the procurator of the Castilian Jews, and Samuel Judah, a prominent physician.

When in 1496/97 the Jews were to be expelled from Portugal, Lisbon alone was assigned to them as a port of embarkation. Assembling there from every part of the country, they were herded in turn into a palace known as Os Estãos, generally used for the reception of foreign ambassadors; here the atrocities of forced conversion were perpetrated. Simon Maimi, the last *arraby mór*, was one of the few who was able to hold out to the end. Thus, the community of Lisbon, with all the others of Portugal, was driven to embrace a titular Christianity. In the period immediately before and after the general expulsion, however, some individuals managed to escape. They probably contributed a majority of the members to the "Portuguese" synagogues in various places in the Turkish Empire, such as Smyrna (*Izmir), while at *Salonika and elsewhere they established separate congregations which long remained known by the name of "the *kahal* of Lisbon."

Lisbon was the seat of the most tragic events in *Conversos history during the course of the subsequent period. On Whitsunday, 1503, a quarrel in the Rua Nova (the former Jewish quarter) between some *New Christians and a riotous band of youths led to a popular uprising, which was suppressed only with difficulty. In 1506, on the night of April 7, a number of New Christians were surprised celebrating the Passover together. They were arrested, but released after only two days' imprisonment. On April 19 trouble began again, owing to the conduct of a Converso who scoffed at a miracle which was reported to have taken place in the Church of Santo Domingo. He was dragged out of the church and butchered, and a terrible massacre began—subsequently known as *A Matança dos Christãos Novos* ("The slaying of the New Christians"). The number of victims was reckoned at between two and four thousand, one of the most illustrious being João Rodriguez Mascarenhas, a wealthy tax farmer and reputedly the most hated

A carpet page from the *Lisbon Bible*. The larger framing text and the micrography form the final part of an allegorical poem on the battle between the Bible and the Talmud. The three-volume manuscript was written by Samuel bar Ibn Musa at Lisbon in 1483. London, British Museum, Or. ms. 2628 (and 2626–7) fol. 185 (12 × 9½ ins / 30.5 × 24 cm.).

עזר אלהי קדם שוכן
מעונה : אחל לפרש
תפלות כל השנה ::

First page of *Perush ha-Berakhot ve-ha-Tefillot* by David b. Joseph b. David Abudarham, printed in Lisbon by Eliezer Toledano in 1489. The book, written in 1370, is a commentary on the complete synagogue liturgy. *Incunabula list, no. 107.

man in Lisbon. Sailors from the Dutch, French, and German ships lying in the harbor landed to assist in the bloody work. The king, Manoel, sharply punished this outbreak, temporarily depriving Lisbon of its erstwhile title "Noble and Always Loyal," fining the town heavily, and executing a number of the ringleaders.

The Inquisition. The visit of David *Reuveni (c. 1525), and the open conversion to Judaism of Diogo Pires (subsequently known as Solomon *Molcho), created a great stir amongst the Lisbon Conversos. They were foremost in attempting to combat the introduction of the Inquisition into Portugal, but their efforts were in vain. Lisbon itself became the seat of a tribunal of the Holy Office and on Sept. 20, 1540, the initial Portuguese auto-da-fé took place in the capital—the first of a long series which continued over more than two centuries. Throughout this period, the Lisbon tribunal was the most active in the whole country. Inquisitional martyrs who perished there included Luis *Dias, "the Messiah of Setúbal" together with his adherents, the pseudo-prophet Master Gabriel, and the mystical poet Gonçalo Eannes Bandarra, an "Old Christian" (1542 etc.); Frei Diogo da Assumpção (Aug. 3, 1603); António *Homem, the *"Praeceptor Infelix"* and others of his circle (May 5, 1624); Manuel Fernandes *Villareal, the statesman and poet (Dec. 1, 1652); Isaac de *Castro Tartas, with other Conversos captured in Brazil (Dec. 15, 1647); António Cabicho, with his clerk Manoel de Sandoval (Dec. 26, 1684); Miguel (Isaac) Henriques da Fonseca, with António de Aguiar (alias Aaron Cohen Faya), and Gaspar (Abraham) Lopez Pereira, all of whom were mourned by Amsterdam poets and preachers as martyrs (May 10, 1681).

At times during the Inquisition period, the New Christians as such suffered. Thus, for example, when in 1630 a theft occurred at the Church of Santa Engrácia at Lisbon, suspicion automatically fell on the New Christians. A youth named Simão Pires Solis was cruelly put to death; the streets of the capital were placarded with inflammatory notices; the preachers inveighed from the pulpits against the "Jews"; and 2,000 persons are said to have fled from Lisbon alone. Similarly, in 1671, when a common thief stole a consecrated pyx from the Church of Orivellas at Lisbon, suspicion again fell on the Conversos and an edict was actually issued banishing them from the country (but not put into effect). From the accession of the House of Bragança in 1640 the power of the Portuguese Inquisition had been restrained in some measure, and its suspension by Pope Clement X in 1674 gave the New Christians some respite, but it proved little less terrible than before on its resumption in 1681. After the outbreak of the War of the Spanish Succession (1701–14), there seems to have been a recrudescence of inquisitional power, and, in the subsequent period, it became customary to send to Lisbon for punishment all those persons found guilty by the other tribunals of the realm. An auto-da-fé held at Lisbon in 1705 was the occasion of the famous and savage sermon of the archbishop of Cranganur, which in turn provoked David *Nieto's scathing rejoinder. At the Lisbon auto-da-fé of Sept. 24, 1752, 30 men and 27 women were summoned—all but 12 for Judaizing. In addition to these, three persons were burned in effigy.

The Lisbon earthquake of 1755 allowed many Conversos, together with those incarcerated in the dungeons of the Inquisition to escape, and prompted others to make their way to open communities overseas. After this, no further Judaizers suffered in the capital; the last victim of the Lisbon tribunal was Father Gabriel Malagrida—a Jesuit. The reforms of the Marquês de Pombal put an end to all juridical differences between Old Christians and New (1773), and the Conversos of Lisbon disappeared as a separate class, although there were many families who continued to preserve distinct traces of their Jewish origin.

The Renewed Community. The close association of Portugal with England, and the position of Lisbon as an intermediate port between Gibraltar and England, made it inevitable that a Jewish settlement would be established in the city as soon as Jews could land with safety. By the middle of the 18th century, some individuals had found their way there and began to practice Jewish rites privately, under the security of British protection. Most of them originated from Gibraltar, though there were some from North Africa and one or two families direct from England. In 1801, a small piece of ground was leased for use as a cemetery. The services rendered to the city by certain Jewish firms at the time of the famine of 1810 improved their status, and in 1813, under the auspices of a certain R. Abraham Dabella, a congregation was formally founded. The condition of the Jews in Lisbon at this period is unsympathetically portrayed by George Borrow, in his classical *The Bible in Spain* (1843); while Israel Solomon, an early inhabitant, gives an intimate glimpse in his memoirs (F.I. Schechter in AJHSP, 25 (1917), 72–73). A little later in the century, two other synagogues (one of which is still in existence) were founded. In 1868, the community received official recognition for the first time. It was, however, recognized as a Jewish "colony," not "community," and the new synagogue (Shaare Tikvah) constructed in 1902 was not allowed to bear any external signs of being a place of worship. Complete equality was attained only with the revolution of 1910. Until the outbreak of World War I, the vast majority of the community were Sephardim, mostly from Gibraltar and North Africa, and many of them still retained their British citizenship. Subsequently, however, there was a very large Ashkenzi influx from Eastern

Europe. During World War II, about 45,000 refugees from Nazi persecution arrived in Portugal, and passed mainly through Lisbon, on their way to the free world. In Lisbon they were assisted by a relief committee headed by M. Bensabat *Amzalak and A. D. Esagny. The Jews of Lisbon numbered 400 in 1947, and 2,000 in 1970. In addition to the two synagogues, there was a school and a hospital, as well as charitable and educational institutions.

Scholars. In the Middle Ages, Lisbon did not play a very important part in Jewish scholarship. The most illustrious scholars associated with it are the *Ibn Yaḥya family. It was also the birthplace of Isaac Abrabanel, who did much of his literary work there, while Joseph *Vecinho, Abraham *Zacuto, and other notable scholars are associated with the city in the period after the expulsion from Spain. *Levi b. Ḥabib also passed his early years in Lisbon. Many of the most illustrious Conversos who attained distinction in the communities of Amsterdam or elsewhere were also natives of Lisbon—men like Moses Gideon *Abudiente, *Zacutus Lusitanus (Abraham Zacuto), Paul de Pina (Reuel *Jesurun), Abraham Farrar, Duarte Nunes da Costa, Duarte da Silva, and perhaps *Manasseh Ben Israel. The outstanding figure in the modern community of Lisbon was Moses Bensabat Amzalak, who was important in public, economic, and intellectual life, as well as being a prolific writer on Jewish subjects.

Hebrew Printing. A Hebrew printing press was active in Lisbon from 1489 to at least 1492 (see *Incunabula) and was closely connected with that of *Híjar, Spain, from which it took over the excellent type, decorated borders, and initials. After 1491 a new type was used. The founder of the Lisbon press was the learned and wealthy Eliezer b. Jacob Toledano (in whose house it operated), assisted by his son Zacheo, Judah Leon Gedaliah, Joseph Khalfon, and Meir and David ibn *Yaḥya. Their first production was Naḥmanides' Pentateuch commentary (1489); in the same year Eleazar Altansi brought out David Abudraham's prayer book. Other works printed in Lisbon are Joshua b. Joseph of Tlemcen's *Halikhot Olam* (1490); the Pentateuch with Onkelos and Rashi in 1491 (text with the vowel and cantillation signs); Isaiah and Jeremiah with David Kimḥi's commentary (1492); Proverbs with David ibn Yaḥya's commentary *Kav ve-Naki* (1492); *Tur Oraḥ Ḥayyim* (also 1492?) and Maimonides' *Hilkhot Sheḥitah.* No other productions have been preserved apart from a fragment from a Day of Atonement *maḥzor,* which may have come from this press. On the expulsion from Portugal in 1497, the printers—taking their type, tools, and expertise with them—found refuge in *Constantinople, *Salonika, and *Fez where they continued to produce beautiful books.

Bibliography: Roth, Marranos, index; J. Mendes dos Remédios, *Os judeus em Portugal,* 2 vols. (1895–1928), index; S. Schwarz, *Inscripções hebraicas em Portugal* (1923); M. B. Amzalak, *Tipographia hebráica em Portugal no século XV* (1922); M. Kayserling, *Geschichte der Juden in Portugal* (1867); J. L. d'Azevedo, *História dos Christãos Novos Portuguêses* (1921), index; King Manuel (of Portugal), *Early Portuguese Books: 1489–1600* (1929), 1, 23–43; J. Bloch, *Early Printing in Spain and Portugal* (1938), 32–35; B. Friedberg, *Toledot ha-Defus ha-Ivri be-Italyah* (1956^2), 102–4.

[C.R.]

LISHANSKY, YOSEF (1890–1917), member of the clandestine intelligence organization *Nili in Ereẓ Israel. Lishansky was born in the district of Kiev, Ukraine. He was orphaned, taken to Ereẓ Israel at the age of six, and raised by relatives living in Metullah. He joined the *Po'alei Zion Party, and for three years he worked as a watchman for *Ha-Shomer in Galilee, but was not accepted as a member of the organization. At the end of 1915 he joined Nili. In January, 1917 he and Avshalom *Feinberg tried, on behalf of Nili, to cross the Sinai Desert to reach the British lines in Egypt. Feinberg was killed en route by Bedouins, but Lishansky, though wounded, reached Egypt. Upon his return to Ereẓ Israel, he joined Sarah *Aaronsohn in organizing the group's espionage work. When Nili was uncovered by the Turks, Lishansky sought refuge with former comrades in Ha-Shomer, who, however, decided

Yosef Lishansky, member of the Nili spy group. Courtesy Haganah Archives, Tel Aviv.

that the safety and security of the Jewish population necessitated his death. Emissaries of Ha-Shomer set out to assassinate Lishansky, but succeeded only in wounding him, and he managed to escape. He tried to reach Egypt but was caught on the way and sentenced to death by the Turkish authorities in Damascus. He was hanged on Dec. 16, 1917, together with his Nili comrade Na'aman *Belkind, and was buried beside him at Rishon le-Zion.

Bibliography: A. Engle, *Nili Spies* (1959), index; Dinur, Haganah, 1 (1954–56), 358–78, 409–11, 733–78; E. Livneh (ed.), *Nili, Toledoteha shel He'azah Medinit* (1961), index.

[Y.S.]

LISITZKY, EPHRAIM E. (1885–1962), U.S. Hebrew poet and educator. Born in Minsk, he emigrated to the United States at the age of 15. In 1918, after peregrinations which took him to Boston, New York, Central Canada, Buffalo, and Milwaukee, he finally settled in New Orleans, where he spent the rest of his life. He became principal of the city's Hebrew School, one of the best in the United States.

Lisitzky was a prolific Hebrew poet. Though not marked by originality, he made lasting contributions to the thematic wealth of Hebrew literature. *Medurot Do'akhot* ("Dying Campfires," 1937), a story of two Indian tribes, is based on Indian legends and contains fine descriptions of the American landscape. It is written in the unrhymed trochaic tetrameter of *Hiawatha* and *Kalevala.* Out of Negro folktales and folk songs, sermons and spirituals, habits and customs, he composed *Be-Oholei Kush* ("In the Tents of Cush," 1953). In his narrative poem *Ki-Teko'a Shofar* (1922) he contrasts the spiritual aridity of the small town American Jew with the deep religiosity of Eastern European Jewry (*Shirim* (1928), 241–80). His dramatic poem *Naftulei Elohim* (1934), despite some happy phrases, must be

Ephraim Lisitzky, U.S. Hebrew poet. Courtesy Genazim, Tel Aviv.

considered a failure, overburdened with the poet's mythological inventions and with Jewish, Christian, Islamic, and Buddhist doctrine. Similarly unsuccessful is *Bi-Ymei Sho'ah u-Mesho'ah* (1960), which deals with the European Holocaust. Lisitzky's occasional articles on literature and educational matters in the Hebrew press were collected in his book, *Bi-Shevilei Ḥayyim ve-Sifrut* (1961). Lisitzky's reputation will ultimately rest on his moving autobiography *Elleh Toledot Adam* (1949; *In the Grip of Cross-Currents*, 1959), his book of Negro poems, and his Indian epic.

Bibliography: A. Epstein, *Soferim Ivrim ba-Amerikah*, 1 (1952), 39–65; Waxman, Literature, 4 (1960²), 1063–65; Silberschlag, in: JBA, 21 (1963/64), 66–71. [El.S.]

LISMANN, HERMANN (1878–1943), German painter. Born in Munich, he studied in his native town and in Lausanne, and later went to Rome and to Paris (1904). Here he belonged to the group of artists that met regularly at the Café du Dôme. After serving in the German army in World War I he settled in Frankfort, where many of his works were acquired by the local museum, and where for several years he taught aesthetics at the university. After the rise of Hitler he emigrated to France, residing in Tours. He was interned by the French at the outbreak of World War II as an enemy alien, but managed to escape to Montauban near Toulouse, in the unoccupied zone. However, in 1943 he was deported to his death in the extermination camp of Maidanek. His post-impressionist works, in the Staedelsches Museum at Frankfort and in the museum of Wuppertal, were confiscated by the Nazis and disappeared. Nevertheless, a memorial exhibition held by the Frankfort Kunstverein in 1959 was able to assemble 132 of his works. [A.W.]

LISSAUER, ERNST (1882–1937), German poet and playwright. Born in Berlin, his earliest publications were two volumes of verse: *Der Acker* (1907), and *Der Strom*

Ernst Lissauer, German poet. Jerusalem, J.N.U.L., Schwadron Collection.

(1912). Lissauer is, however, remembered as the composer of the "Hymn of Hate" (*Hassgesang gegen England*, 1915), which German troops sang at the front during World War I. From 1924 he lived in Vienna and supported the German nationalsts. He insisted that the Jews were not one people and that he, as a German Jew, had nothing in common with the Jews of Eastern Europe. Lissauer opposed Zionism and advocated complete assimilation. He wrote a number of plays including *Yorck* (1921), *Das Weib des Jephta* (1928), and *Luther und Thomas Muenzer* (1929).

Bibliography: A. Schwadron, in: *Der Jude*, 1 (1916–17), 490–2; G. K. Brand, *Ernst Lissauer* (1923); D. Sadan, *Ha-Namer vi-Ydido ha-Menamnem* (1951), 124–5, 129–32, 188–91. [S.L.]

LISSER, JOSHUA FALK (d. 1807), rabbi and talmudist. Joshua studied under Moses Zerah *Eidlitz of Prague. As *dayyan* at Lissa he was involved in the decision to condemn and burn Naphtali Herz *Wessely's *Divrei Shalom ve-Emet*, which called on Jews to emancipate themselves. Lisser published *Binyan Yehoshu'ah* (Dyhernfurth, 1788), commentaries, including textual emendations, on the minor tractates *Avot de-Rabbi Nathan*, *Semaḥot*, *Derekh Ereẓ Zuta*. The commentary on *Avot de-Rabbi Nathan* was reprinted in 1858–64 in Zhitomir and in Romm's Vilna editions of the Talmud. Bearing in mind the spirit of opposition to critical scholarship at the time, Lisser apologized in the preface of his commentary for his suggested textual emendations. In defense of his work he pointed to the precedents of Solomon *Luria and Samuel *Edels, who had also suggested variant readings in their commentaries.

Bibliography: L. Lewin, *Geschichte der Juden in Lissa* (1904), 271f. [Ed.]

LISSITZKY, EL (Lazar; 1890–1941), Russian painter. Born in Smolensk province, where his parents were hatters, he earned his living by giving drawing lessons. He was unable to enter the Academy of Art in St. Petersburg because the Jewish quota was filled. Instead he left for Germany, to study in Darmstadt. At the outbreak of World War I he returned to Russia. It was only after the 1917 Revolution that he could develop his original and versatile talent. When *Chagall was appointed director of the school of art at Vitebsk, Lissitzky joined him there as professor of architecture and graphic arts. In common with Chagall, he was deeply interested in Jewish folklore. Examples of this interest were his watercolor illustrations to the *Legend of Prague* by M. Broderzon, and his color lithograph illustrations to the **Ḥad Gadya*. These were distinguished by the bright, childlike colors of folk art. He also collaborated in the production of Jewish children's books, developing new ideas for typography and layout. Strongly influenced by Casimir Malevich, leader of the Russian cubists, Lissitzky was a major force in a related movement, constructivism. In this movement, which believed that the purpose of art was not necessarily to beautify, he tried to integrate his aesthetic concepts into the Marxist theory. In 1919 he painted his first "prouns," a generic term he was to apply to his mature work which is based on stereometric elements, fusing aspects of painting with architecture. In 1921 he was appointed professor at the Moscow Academy. However, angered by the government's hostility to the new trends, he joined the artists who left Russia for countries more receptive to radical aesthetic ideas. He lived and worked in Germany, France, Holland, and Switzerland, and at one time collaborated with Ilya Ehrenburg in the publication of a constructivist magazine. In 1925 the progressive museum director, Alexander Dorner, commis-

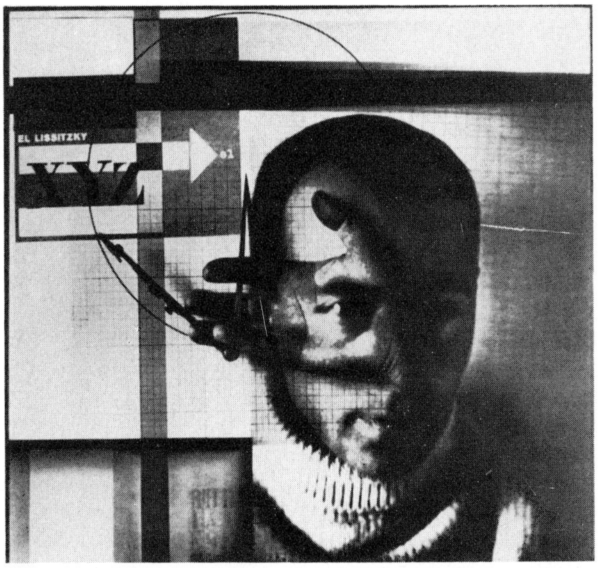

Self-portrait, "The Constructor," by El Lissitzky, 1924. From S. Lissitzky-Kueppers, *El Lissitsky, Life and Letters*, London, 1968.

sioned Lissitzy to install a special gallery for the showing of abstract art in the Landesmuseum at Hanover. The room was later destroyed by the Nazis. Lissitzky maintained his links with the Soviet regime, and in 1928 returned to Russia. The government however, employed him only to design pavilions at a number of international exhibitions abroad, and also the restaurant at the Soviet section of the 1939 New World's Fair. He died of tuberculosis.

Bibliography: S. Lissitzki-Kueppers, *El Lissitzky* (1968); Roth, Art, 800f.

[A.W.]

LIT, U.S. family, prominent in Philadelphia, Pennsylvania, in the 19th–20th centuries. The Philadelphia department store operation known as Lit Brothers was first established in 1891 as a dress and millinery shop by RACHEL P. LIT (1858–1919; later Wedell, still later Arnold), who was soon thereafter joined by her brothers Colonel SAMUEL D. LIT (1859–1929) and JACOB D. LIT (1872–1950). Samuel's only experience had been as an apprentice plumber and book salesman. However, he and Jacob brought tremendous energy and ambition to their task. The store expanded yearly, and by 1906 covered the entire city square on Market Street from Seventh to Eighth, where a new building was erected in 1907. Samuel served as a member of the Delaware River Bridge Commission and of the Board of City Trusts; he was also a member of the boards of Mikveh Israel Congregation and of the Jewish Hospital. Jacob was active in the leadership of the YMHA and was founder-president of the downtown Mt. Sinai Hospital (1900). In 1928 Lit's was purchased by City Stores, in which Albert M. *Greenfield was the controlling figure. After World War II, the business expanded into suburban areas of Pennsylvania and New Jersey, and in 1962 absorbed the four branches of Snellenburg's, thus becoming the largest department store chain in the Delaware Valley area. Rachel's daughter ETTA (d. 1953) was the wife of JULES E. MASTBAUM (1872–1926), motion picture exhibitor and executive who gave his magnificent collection of Rodin sculptures, drawings, and letters to the city, together with $1,000,000 for the erection of a museum to contain them, opened to the public as a landmark on the Benjamin Franklin Parkway in 1929. Another brother, JONKER LIT (1853–1919), had a daughter Juliet, who married J. DAVID STERN (1886–) the publisher of *Philadelphia Record* (1928–47), *Camden Courier-Post* (1919–47), and *The New York Post* (1933–39).

[B.W.K.]

LITERATURE, JEWISH. Literature on Jewish themes and in languages regarded as Jewish has been written continuously for the past 3,000 years. What the term Jewish literature encompasses however demands definition since Jews have lived in so many countries and have written in so many different languages and on such diverse themes. In this article it will be understood to include the following categories: (1) works written by Jews on Jewish themes in any language; (2) works of a literary character written by Jews in Hebrew or Yiddish or other recognized languages, whatever the theme; (3) literary works written by writers who were essentially Jewish writers, whatever the theme and whatever the language. This entry covers the subject up to the threshold of the modern period. The continuation will be found in other entries including *Hebrew Literature; *Yiddish Literature; *Ladino Literature.

This article is arranged according to the following outline:

EARLY BEGINNINGS TO THE MEDIEVAL PERIOD

BIBLICAL LITERATURE

The earliest, greatest, and most enduring Jewish literary works are the books of the Bible, known collectively in Hebrew as *Tanakh,* made up of the initial letters of *Torah* ("Pentateuch"), *Nevi'im* ("Prophets"), and *Ketuvim* ("Hagiographa"). The Bible consists of either 25 or 39 books, depending on whether the 12 prophets are counted as one or 12 books and whether Samuel, Kings, and Chronicles are counted as one or two books, respectively.

The Pentateuch comprises five volumes and offers an account of the creation of the world, the early history of mankind, the life and experience of the forefathers of the Jewish people, the experiences of Israel in Egypt, the Exodus, and their wanderings in the desert for 40 years under the leadership of Moses. Extended sections are devoted to laws governing individual and social behavior, to ethical principles, to theological statements, and to details of ritual for priest and layman. The underlying theme is that God has entered into a covenant with the patriarchs and subsequently, in a revelation at Mount Sinai, with the Jewish people as a whole. The covenant demands that the people of Israel worship God exclusively and abide by the law as set forth in the Torah; God, in turn, undertakes to make them "His own peculiar treasure" among the nations and to give them the Land of Canaan. The Jews thus became a choosing and a chosen people.

The *Nevi'im* are subdivided into two sections: Early Prophets and Later Prophets. The Early Prophets are historical works, portraying: the experiences of Israel when entering Canaan (Book of Joshua), a period of turmoil and settlement (Judges), a period of consolidation under the kings (Samuel and Kings), and the period of division of the land into two kingdoms down to the destruction of the Northern Kingdom by the Assyrians and the Southern Kingdom by the Babylonians (Kings). These books are selective history and reflect a point of view and philosophy of history which seems to be that of the prophets. The Latter Prophets include the three large books of the major prophets: Isaiah, Jeremiah, and Ezekiel, and the 12 books of the minor prophets (so named because of the brevity of the books). The themes which unite the books are: that the prophets present revelations from God whose substance is that Israel has strayed from true worship, has departed from proper ethical behavior, both individually and socially, and that it is called upon to repent its ways. The penalty for obduracy will be the destruction of the polity. The hope is, however, offered that "a saved remnant" of righteous people will have the opportunity to renew and continue the covenant with God. This prophetic preachment seems to have been a continuous element in Jewish life from the time of Moses (13th century B.C.E.) to the time of Malachi (450 B.C.E.) and seems to have been the concern and responsibility of "schools of prophets" or of a prophetic party.

The *Ketuvim* comprise works as diverse as the lyrics of the Psalms, the searching dramatic exploration of suffering of the Book of Job, the skepticism of Ecclesiastes, the love poetry of the Song of Songs, the laments attributed to Jeremiah, and such historical works or semi-historical works as the Chronicles, Ezra, Nehemiah, Esther, Ruth, and the foreshadowing of an apocalyptic literature in the Book of Daniel.

The books of the Bible were written over a period extending from the 11th century B.C.E. (upon the basis of traditions perhaps several centuries older) to the third century B.C.E. Although the canon was substantially closed by 250 B.C.E., an argument as to the propriety of including the Song of Songs and Ecclesiastes in the Bible was apparently not settled until about the year 90 C.E. The authorship of the various books of the Bible is rarely clear. The talmudic assumption is that all the books were written under the influence of "the holy spirit" which means that they are attributed to figures who were the recipients of divine revelation. Thus where no author is indicated, as in the Book of Judges, the Talmud ascribes it to the prophetic figure Samuel, more or less a contemporary, and in the case of the Book of Kings makes the assumption that it was the work of Jeremiah. The major books of the Bible, in terms of their significance for Jewish life, are the Five Books of Moses. The traditional view, which is used as an underlying assumption by the Talmud, and subsequently by Jewish law, is that they were a direct revelation from God to Moses and that every word, therefore, has chosen and special meaning. Biblical critical scholarship of the 19th and 20th centuries has assumed that the Pentateuch is the work of man and has proposed that its five books are an amalgam of several distinct and ancient versions which no longer exist and which are denominated as the J, E, and P documents. Presumably they were put together in one document by a redactor or a body of editors known as R sometime between the end of the seventh century B.C.E. and the middle of the fifth century B.C.E.

While the Bible is the only extant literature of the early centuries of Jewish existence, the Bible itself indicates that there were other works such as the "*Book of the Wars of the Lord" (Num. 21:14) and the "*Books of the Chronicles of the Kings of Judah and Israel" (II Chron. 25:26; 28:26; 32:32). It is also probable that there were works of "true prophets," writings of "false prophets," and a great many lyrical poems, like the Book of Psalms and the Song of Songs, which have not survived (see *Bible; *Pentateuch; the individual books of the Bible; *Allegory; *Poetry, Biblical; *Fable; *Parable).

APOCRYPHAL WORKS

From the third century B.C.E. the literary creativity manifested in the Bible continued undiminished in works called *Apocrypha (*Sefarim Ḥizonim*, meaning "excluded" or "hidden" works). These writings, usually of unknown authorship, included fictional and moralistic works (*Tobit); didactic books (*Ben Sira or Ecclesiasticus); disguised historical allegories (the Book of *Judith); historical works (the Books of the *Maccabees); and apologetic works (IV Maccabees). Some of them, such as the Addition to Esther, were designed as supplements to the Bible to fill in apparent lacunae in that text. Some were imitations of biblical patterns, or conceived as continuations of biblical traditions, like Ben Sira which is in the vein of the books of Proverbs and Ecclesiastes, and the recently discovered Dead Sea *Thanksgiving Psalms Scroll which is in the tradition of the biblical psalter. Some were already early Midrashim, homiletic and moral extensions of biblical material, like the *Dead Sea Scrolls: the Genesis Apocryphon and the *Pesher Habakkuk which applies the prophetic statement of an earlier age to the Jewish-Roman confrontation of the first century B.C.E. and the first century C.E.

The extent of this literature is not known. The discovery of the Dead Sea Scrolls has made it clear that there were many works, perhaps sectarian books, which were not preserved as part of the literary and religious mainstream. Moreover, even the previously known works of the Apocrypha were excluded and hidden from Jewish literature, apparently in an attempt to prevent competition with the canon and to suppress dissident sectarian points of view. Consequently, most of them did not survive in their original language, whether Hebrew or Aramaic, but were preserved in Greek versions by Christians who invested them with semisanctity.

More striking than the literary quality of the works is the appearance of certain themes. The arguments about religious practices and philosophies and the emergence of new doctrines, such as immortality, resurrection, and Messianism are present in the Apocrypha. The confrontations of Jews with the Hellenistic world and the need to authenticate the Jewish tradition is reflected both in historical works and in apologetic books, like IV Maccabees and the Letter of *Aristeas. A nationalistic, revolutionary literature appears in the Dead Sea Scrolls, such as the War of the Children of Light against the Children of Darkness, and from the same source there are new indications of the stresses and strains within the Jewish community. It is a literature of dignity and beauty whose merit does not depend upon anything but its intrinsic quality (see *Apocrypha and Pseudepigrapha; *Dead Sea Scrolls; *Dead Sea Sect; *Hebrew Language of the Dead Sea Scrolls).

APOCALYPTIC LITERATURE

During the period of the Apocrypha (c. 200 B.C.E. to about the end of the first century C.E.) another body of literature, apocalyptic works, also developed. Like the Apocrypha, they were set aside by later Jewish authorities and were preserved in the Christian tradition surviving either in Greek or Ethiopic revisions. Features common to these works were: a claim to be revealed books and to reveal the future, and their pseudepigraphy, purporting to be the writings of ancient heroic or saintly figures. Clearly reactions to political events of the time as well as to theological problems, their essential themes were eschatological—the question of evil and of suffering, the vision of the Messiah, Messianic times, the Day of Judgment, and the vision of a new world. IV *Esdras, a national Job, was probably written right after the destruction of the Temple. The author's solution to the tragedy of the Jewish people is to assert that while God's will is inscrutable, His love for Israel is abiding. After evil has run its course, there will be a 400-year Messianic period to be followed by the Day of Judgment, the resurrection and the creation of a new world. Similarly, the Testament of the Twelve Patriarchs hesitates between a Messiah out of the tribe of Levi and one from the tribe of Judah and presumably represents a reaction, first positive then negative, to the rule of John *Hyrcanus, the Hasmonean ruler.

Another characteristic of the apocalyptic books is their tendency to employ elaborate allegories and embellish the biblical stories with much legendary material designed to fill the lacunae in the biblical text. Mainly Pharisaic (although the Book of *Jubilees differs in places, particularly in calendar dating, from authoritative doctrine), these works often depict the Messiah as a supernatural being and much is made of angels. The Book of *Enoch, in particular, with its view of the Messiah as "the son of man," its portrayal of fallen angels, and its vision of final judgment foreshadowed much of Christian thinking.

Ten books are regarded as apocalyptic works, to which must be added some of the Dead Sea Scrolls, particularly The War of the Children of Light against the Children of Darkness, and the so-called *Zadokite fragments. It is probable that there were others as well and that they, and perhaps some of the known works, were of a sectarian character. The rabbinic attitude of the times led to their disappearance in their original language of Hebrew and Aramaic. Some polemical works, however, such as the *Sibylline Oracles and the Assumption of *Moses were written in Greek in Alexandria, but have come down with many Christian interpolations. Thus the style of the apocalyptic books cannot really be gauged, but the sweep of imagination and the structure of several of them is of a very high order (see *Apocalypse; *Apocrypha and Pseudepigrapha; *Dead Sea Scrolls).

HELLENISTIC LITERATURE

While some books, written originally in Greek and probably the works of the Alexandrian community, have already been referred to as apocryphal or apocalyptic literature, a large body of writings was the product of the several million Jews who between the third century B.C.E. and the first century C.E. took up their residence outside Ereẓ Israel in lands dominated by Hellenistic culture. They produced a considerable and distinctive body of literature, much of which has been lost. The Bible was translated into Greek and upon these translations were written exegeses and interpretations, all of them designed to meet the needs of Jews in Hellenistic lands and to offer apologetics for the Jewish religion which was under assault from within and from without. As an extension of these needs, Jewish philosophy developed with the aim of harmonizing Jewish and Hellenistic thoughts. At the same time, historical and belletristic works were composed both for the benefit of the Jewish population and for apologetic purposes. Thus a body of writings developed which were to be a prototype for an elaborate literature to be produced whenever Judaism, in later centuries, came into contact with other dynamic civilizations. Simultaneously, in Palestine, a literature designed essentially for Jews free from the problems of acculturation and assimilation was being developed in Hebrew and Aramaic. Its objective was the explication of Judaism in religious, legal, and homiletic terms; it was also a prototype for the expansive Jewish literature of the ages (see *Hellenistic Jewish Literature, *Apologetics).

BIBLE TRANSLATIONS

Greek. Literary undertakings of Hellenistic Jewry started in the third century B.C.E. with the translation of the Bible into Greek (*Septuagint). According to the Letter of Aristeas, which purports to be the account of the emissary of the king of Ptolemy, Philadelphus (285–246 B.C.E.), to Eliezer, the high priest, Ptolemy II commanded that 70 translators be engaged to render the Bible into Greek. The facts seem to be that the Bible translation was undertaken by savants of Egyptian Jewry to meet the needs of the Jewish population. The Septuagint, as the first translation of the Bible, had a significant effect and was employed as a pattern for subsequent translations. The Greek style is not distinguished since it relied heavily on Hebrew constructions. It was not a literal translation, however, since it incorporated commentary in the text, consciously attempted to harmonize biblical and Greek thoughts and to include halakhic and aggadic ideas which were current in Palestinian commentary. Some interesting features of the text are its deletion of all anthropomorphic expressions and the provision of many readings of the text which are different from the standard masoretic version. Whether this was because the translators worked with different texts is not clear, but the variants have provided fruitful interpretations of difficult biblical passages and material for speculation on how the biblical text developed.

Two other translations into Greek were undertaken in subsequent centuries because Palestinian rabbis deemed the Septuagint not to be altogether authentic and because it had become subject to interpolations and manipulations by Christians. At the behest of R. Eliezer b. Hyrcanus and R. Akiva, *Aquila, a Greek-speaking native of Pontus and a proselyte, undertook a new translation at the beginning of the second century C.E. The result was a literal translation, incorporating many of the rabbinic interpretations. It was widely used and approved, but has disappeared and only fragments are retained in the writings of *Origen (185–254 C.E.), one of the Church Fathers. The translation of Theodotion (about 200 C.E.), another proselyte, has also been lost, except for his version of the Book of Daniel. It was however integrated by the Church into a revised version of the Septuagint (see *Bible, Translations).

Aramaic. The translations of the Bible into Greek, undertaken in Alexandria, was paralleled in Palestine by translations (Targums) into Aramaic. Presumably, the same need for understanding the Hebrew text motivated the Aramaic translations and in consequence, particularly in Babylonia, it became customary to read the Targum together with the original text. The standard Aramaic translation of the Pentateuch is Targum Onkelos which is printed in almost every edition of the Hebrew Bible. The

Talmud ascribes it to a proselyte named Onkelos who worked under the direction of Joshua b. Hananiah and Eliezer b. Hyrcanus at Jabneh in the first third of the second century C.E. More probably, however, it was a standardization of translations which had continued for decades or even centuries. Like the Aquila translation, it gives a literal rendition of the text but adds halakhic interpretations and aggadic embellishments wherever they are deemed necessary so as to present the Bible in the best possible light. Anthropomorphisms are thus avoided and the biblical figure Rachel "takes" the teraphim rather than "steals" them (Gen. 31:19); the phrase "visiting the iniquity of the fathers upon the children" (Ex. 34:7) is rendered with the addition "when the children follow the sinful ways of their fathers." Another translation called the Targum Yerushalmi (the Palestinian Targum), known also as Pseudo-Jonathan (probably due to an early printer's error), is essentially a compilation of freely rendered passages of the Pentateuch rather than a translation. It bears the homilist stamp and is replete with midrashic, aggadic, and halakhic statements. From internal evidence it appears that it must have been finally redacted in the seventh century in Palestine, but that it contains layers of interpretations from centuries past.

The standard Aramaic translation of the Prophets though ascribed, by the Talmud, to *Jonathan b. Uzziel, a pupil of Hillel, was probably an ordering of earlier material rather than the work of one man. It resembles the Onkelos in phrasing but makes more frequent use of aggadic material. It is particularly important for exegesis because it deviates frequently from the masoretic text and agrees with the Septuagint and with other sources which are unknown.

The translations of the third section of the Bible, the Hagiographa, are of uncertain origin and authorship and are incomplete. Except for the translation of Proverbs, which is quite literal, they make extensive use of the *aggadah*. The books of Daniel, Ezra, and Nehemiah, which were partly written in Aramaic, were not translated (see *Bible, Translations).

EXEGESIS

The great exegete of Hellenistic Jewry, *Philo of Alexandria (c. 30 B.C.E.–42 C.E.), sought to provide an interpretation of the Bible which would be acceptable in terms of Hellenistic thought. He wrote or began a commentary on the entire Pentateuch, but only parts of the commentary on Genesis and Exodus have survived (in an Armenian translation and a Latin translation). He also undertook an outline of Mosaic legislation which was supplemented by treatises on politics, on teaching virtue, and on the creation. A commentary on Genesis, his major exegetical work, consists of essays on various subjects such as the immutability of God and the value of sobriety. Philo's approach to the Bible was allegorical. Thus he interprets "Adam, where are thou?" as Adam being the symbol of wicked man who hides from the voice of Reason. *Ḥameẓ* is a symbol of passion and *maẓẓah* of purity of soul. Despite his allegorical view, he insisted that the laws be obeyed literally and his interpretations show an awareness of the halakhic and aggadic interpretations which were current in Palestine (see *Bible, Exegesis).

PHILOSOPHY

Formal Jewish philosophy begins in the Hellenistic world as a result of the confrontation with another culture. Among the first philosophers is *Aristobulus (c. 150 B.C.E.) who sought to demonstrate the dependence of peripatetic philosophy upon Mosaic law. Philo, the major philosophic figure, exerted little direct influence upon Judaism, but much upon the history of philosophy and upon Christian thought. Concerned with the problem of the relation of a perfect God to an imperfect world, Philo proposed a series of intermediate causes of which the main one is the Logos, described variously as the word of God, the supreme manifestation of divine activity, and as moral law. It is the chief medium through which God created the world. In Philo's philosophy there is in man, as in the universe, a dualism between the soul and the body, the spiritual which is good and the material which is evil. The greatest good for man is contemplation, but the basis of practical ethics is duty, induced by education and habit (see Jewish *Philosophy).

HISTORY

Between 200 B.C.E. and 100 C.E. a considerable body of Jewish historical works were written, but after this 300-year period Jewish historiography lapsed for almost two millennia, not to be taken up again until the 19th century. There are records and fragments of the work of *Demetrius, an Alexandrian (early third century B.C.E.), on the kings of Judah, and of *Eupolemus (middle of the second century B.C.E.), a Palestinian, on the same subject. The Letter of Aristeas is the source of the familiar story about the Septuagint, although it was probably written between 200–100 B.C.E. Philo also wrote history, describing contemporary events, and several poets apparently took events in Jewish history as themes, the most notable being *Ezekiel whose drama *Exagoge* ("The Exodus") appeared about 250 B.C.E.

The most notable historian of the period was *Josephus whose major works *The Wars of the Jews* (seven vols.), the *Antiquities of the Jews* (20 vols.), *The Life*, and *Against Apion* were widely read and quoted throughout the ages. The books were at once a defense of the conduct of Josephus in the war against Rome (66–70 C.E.), a generally affirmative presentation of Judaism to the pagan world, and a defense of the doctrines of Judaism. One of the few Jewish sources for the post-biblical period, Josephus' works incorporate a great deal of aggadic material, but fail to give a sufficient view of the spiritual life of Jewry at the time. Essentially a political history, the material on the Great *Synagogue, the *soferim*, a group of scribes, and the nonpolitical talmudic sages is quite meager. His contemporary, *Justus of Tiberias, who wrote on the same themes, may have offered a different account, but his works were lost. The historical works of the period generally attempted to evolve a philosophy of Jewish history and through their apologetics show Judaism to be historically more significant and of a truer religious perception than the paganism which dominated the ancient world (see *Historiography).

HALAKHAH AND AGGADAH

The Bible, as the fundamental document of Judaism, became, in the course of time, the base of an inverted pyramid out of which a vast and varied literature developed that included law, theology, ethics, philosophy, poetry, and grammar. The most significant body of literature, extending over a period of 1,000 years (500 B.C.E.–500 C.E.), was a corpus of writing called **halakhah* and **aggadah*. Based on the Pentateuch, it was rooted in the tradition (set forth in the Mishnah, Avot 1:1) that Moses received not only a Written Law at Sinai but also an Oral Law which was transmitted to leading figures, including the prophets, of successive generations.

Save for stray references, there is no knowledge of the Oral Law during the First Temple period. Talmudic traditions, however, ascribe the beginning of great expansion in the Oral Law to Ezra (c. 450 B.C.E.), the *soferim*, and to the Great Synagogue. Employing the method of Midrash (from the root *darash*, to search out), they established the process of extending and detailing the law and set the pattern of finding biblical support for new practices and for some which had already become normative. Among their enactments were the public reading of the Torah with accompanying interpretation, the organization of the daily worship pattern, and the building of "fences" (cautionary rules and legislation) around the Torah.

A supreme court, the *Sanhedrin, headed by **zugot*, pairs of scholars, continued the work of the *soferim* from about 200 B.C.E. The last pair, *Hillel and *Shammai (fl. 20 B.C.E.–20 C.E.) were two of the greatest figures in the development of the law. During this 200-year period religio-political parties developed in Palestine whose differences were partially based on the interpretation and application of Jewish law. The major parties, the *Pharisees and the *Sadducees, alternated in ascendancy, but dominance in the religious legal field ultimately fell to the Pharisees, while the Sadducees became the major force in civil affairs. When the Jews lost their independence, the sphere of the Pharisees ultimately became primary and the talmudic record of the period reflects their dominance. Nonetheless, there were different strands of thought within the Pharisaic movement and the leading figures, Hillel and Shammai, represent different emphases which were perpetuated by their disciples. On the whole, the school of Hillel tended to be broader and more lenient in its interpretation of the law than the school of Shammai which was more literal in the application of biblical texts. The convention of the Talmud ultimately became that the ruling of the school of Hillel (presumably the majority) was accepted as law.

Hillel formalized the development of the *Oral Law by establishing seven rules of interpretation of the Torah which he and others employed as a measuring rod for the *halakhot* or laws which were being developed. The effect of the method and the authority of figures like Hillel became evident with the acceptance of the Hillelite ruling of prosbul which, in response to the economic needs of the time, enabled debtors and creditors to circumvent the explicit biblical law of the sabbatical year limitation on debts. His great disciple, *Johanan b. Zakkai, in the last decade of his life when the Temple was destroyed, initiated one of the great revolutions in Jewish history by transferring the seat of Jewish authority to Jabneh. He established there a Sanhedrin, which functioned like a senate, for Jews both inside and outside of Palestine. The need to define Jewish patterns anew led to a marked expansion of the Oral Law, which was accomplished by five generations of *tannaim*. Leading figures were: Eliezer b. Hyrcanus and Joshua b. Hananiah in the first generation; their disciples Akiva and Ishmael; R. Akiva's disciples Meir, Judah, Simeon, and Yose b. Halafta. The major personality of the fifth generation was Judah ha-Nasi (135–219).

Simultaneously with the growth of the *halakhah*, another oral tradition, that of *aggadah* (from *hagged*, to impart instruction) was developed. A vast body of literature, it may be grouped under two major headings: legendary-historical material and ethicoreligious literature.

The legendary-historical material has ancient origins and comprises stories and chronicles in which the lives of biblical figures and biblical episodes are elaborated and accounts of national and personal trials, crises, and salvations are given. It often suggests a kernel of historical fact. Much of this material made its way into the Apocrypha and into the Targums. But, there were, in addition, special collections of the early talmudic period: the **Megillat Ta'anit*, organized around special days celebrated as minor feast days and special fast days; **Seder Olam* ("The Order of the World"), a chronicle of events in Jewish history from creation to the time of Alexander, which both records and interprets events and is ascribed to Yose b. Ḥalafta (middle of the second century).

The ethicoreligious *aggadah* concentrates on a philosophy of life and faith, with practical and metaphysical implications. Often cast in a semi-poetic form or in an aphoristic style, it includes fables and parables. Though some has been lost, much *aggadah* has been preserved in the Talmud and in the collections of Midrashim. Two of its finest works are *Pirkei *Avot* ("The Sayings of the Fathers"), a work of the Mishnah, and the **Avot de-Rabbi Natan* ("The Teachings of the Fathers According to the Collection of Rabbi Nathan"). Written in an aphoristic style, the works include much of the ethics and some of the theology of the talmudic sages. The *aggadah* generally employs the Bible as its frame of reference and represents the homiletic interpretations of preachers in the synagogue on Sabbath afternoons. They also resorted to **gematria* (using the numerical value of the letters for interpretation) and other devices. Since they were the works of preachers, they responded to events of the time, to the mood of people, and to the need to communicate faith and values. Stories, parables, and epigrams are therefore characteristic forms employed in the literature.

The oral tradition in *halakhah* and in *aggadah* became too complex as the decades went by and the difficult circumstances in Palestine with periodic revolutions and the disruption of academies finally made it imperative that the material be reduced to writing. This process essentially, though not entirely, concentrated on the halakhic material which represents the actual laws by which life was governed.

Halakhah. The compilation of the oral *halakhah* resulted in three bodies of works: "motivated *halakhot*," the Mishnah, and the Tosefta.

"MOTIVATED HALAKHOT." In "motivated *halakhot*" a rule of law was set forth together with the appropriate biblical verses and their interpretations. They include the **Mekhilta*, organized around the Book of Exodus and attributed to R. *Ishmael b. Elisha of the third generation of *tannaim;* the **Sifra*, a collection based on Leviticus attributed to R. Judah of the fourth generation; and the **Sifrei* material on the Books of Numbers and Deuteronomy, collected by R. Simeon of the same generation. In all probability these men were the original compilers and redactors, while the finished products were the work of later hands (see **Halakhah*).

MISHNAH. The greatest body of law, the Mishnah, is a compilation of "unmotivated *halakhot*," that is, material not related to a text. The work was begun in various academies, notably those of Akiva of the third generation, and of his disciple, Meir, in the second century C.E. Meir apparently developed a very complete work. The final redaction of the Mishnah however was by Judah ha-Nasi who was head of the court, the academy, and the Jewish civil government. He was a man of wide culture and organizing talent and while he based himself on the compilation of Meir, he studied in various academies and assembled different collections of *mishnayot* before he began his own work. In the Mishnah he redacted, which was the product of a collegium, the Oral Law was organized into six major orders *(sedarim):* (1) *Zera'im* ("seeds"), detailing agricultural laws and precepts connected with agriculture (e.g., *berakhot*, prayers, and blessings); (2) *Mo'ed* ("festival"), on the laws of holidays and the Sabbath; (3) *Nashim* ("women"), involving family law; (4) *Nezikin* ("damages"), including civil and criminal law, courts, and legal procedure; (5) *Kodashim* ("holy things"), dealing with sacrifices, the Temple service, and dietary laws; (6) *Tohorot* ("purifications"), on ritual purity and impurity. The *sedarim* were divided into tractates *(massekhtot)* of related materials; a total of 66 tractates were compiled. These were subdivided into chapters *(perakim)* which were divided into sections *(mishnayot)*.

The Mishnah was designed to organize a body of scattered material, to set forth a code for practice and for judgment, and to provide a code for study. It was intended to be all-inclusive in the sense that it dealt even with matters which were no longer observed, such as the laws of sacrifice. Simultaneously, however, it was exclusive in that it set an order of importance and left out thousands of *halakhot*. It was decisive in that it made rulings on matters which had been in dispute. But it was designed to promote development, as well, and therefore included minority opinions, and cited their proponents. While the Mishnah was essentially a legal document, it devoted a tractate *(Pirkei Avot)* to ethical statements and emphasized, in various tractates, certain dogmas, such as the unity of God, providence, reward and punishment in this world and the hereafter, freedom of will, the doctrine of the Messiah, and resurrection. Fundamental to its thinking was the notion that the Torah was revealed and every word of it was subject to interpretation; that the Oral Law was equally revealed and had been transmitted; that the Mishnah, which embodied it, therefore enjoyed authority; and that the sages had a right to interpret the law. The entire work, written in a direct and lucid Hebrew, was completed about 200 C.E. The Mishnah with later elaborations, the *Gemara*, represents hundreds of years of lawmaking and is the decisive corpus of writings in Jewish life for almost two millennia (see *Mishnah).

THE TOSEFTA ("ADDITIONS"). This body of literature includes many of the *halakhot* omitted from the Mishnah, as well as elucidations of mishnaic statements and some *aggadah*. The work was begun by *Ḥiyya b. Abba and Oshaiah (Hoshaya) Rabbah, disciples of Judah ha-Nasi, but the final redaction probably took place about 500 C.E. (see *Tosefta).

TALMUD. The Mishnah had scarcely been completed when the process of expanding the Oral Law began. This activity resulted in a vast body of literature known as the *Gemara* (from the Aramaic *gamar*, to learn). The impetus came from the fact that the Mishnah was concise and, therefore, needed explanation; that there were thousands of *halakhot*, known as *beraitot (baraita)*, which had not been included in either the Mishnah or the Tosefta and had to be reconciled with the Mishnah; and that new problems arose in daily living which demanded new solutions. These elements were particularly evident in Babylonia where the problem of maintaining Jewish law in the midst of a society governed by other laws was immediate. The classic formulation of R. *Samuel (Mar; 180–254), *dina de-malkhuta dina* ("the law of the land is law") so far as nonreligious matters are concerned, is an attempt at dealing with the question. There were, however, many other problems and the need to deal with them, as well as the conviction that the Jew's highest purpose was to study God's law, produced an extensive body of debates, decisions, obiter dicta, and historical material.

Two *Gemarot* were formulated: a shorter work developed in Palestine and known as the Jerusalem Talmud; a longer body of writing, the product of the Babylonian community where perhaps a million Jews lived and which was studied throughout the ages. These *Gemarot* together with the Mishnah are collectively known as the Talmud.

There are *Gemarot* for 39 mishnaic tractates in the Jerusalem Talmud and for 37 tractates in the Babylonian Talmud. Presumably, there must have been *Gemarot* for all of the 66 tractates of the Mishnah but some of them may have been lost and others, such as the tractates dealing with *tohorot* (laws of purity and impurity) and *zera'im* (agricultural laws, tithes and sabbatical year), may have been discarded as no longer pertinent to post-Temple days. The missing *Gemarot* are not necessarily the same in the two Talmuds. Thus the Babylonian Talmud has *Gemarot* for the order of *Kodashim* (dealing with the Temple cult), while those of the Jerusalem Talmud, mentioned by early authorities, were lost. The Jerusalem Talmud has *Gemarot* to the 10 tractates of the order of *Zera'im*, whose laws were observed in Palestine in post-Temple days, and there is only one such *Gemara (Berakhot)* in the Babylonian Talmud.

The pattern of the text in both Talmuds is to record a Mishnah and to follow it with the *Gemara* discussion and debate. While the Mishnah bases itself upon the Bible, the *Gemara* bases itself upon the Mishnah as its authority, although in certain matters requiring clarification or in developing new *halakhot* it refers back to the Bible. The usual order of the text is to analyze the Mishnah and to broaden the debate by citing a *baraita* (an external *halakhah* not recorded in the Mishnah) which may then also be subject to analysis and to opposing statements. Connections are often loose because the oral tradition relied heavily upon memory. In consequence, while a series of unrelated statements of one man may be cited in full, probably only one of them is connected with the matter under discussion. This may expand into an explanation of the meaning of the other statements and their application which may prompt aggadic interpolations for several lines or pages. Then the halakhic theme is picked up once again, and usually, but not always, a halakhic decision is rendered. Both Talmuds contain much of *aggadah:* stories, philosophizing, proverbs, ethical maxims, historical information, medical and scientific observations, and practical advice for daily living. There is a certain amount of humor, considerable wit, and some sharp satirical comments. Approximately one third of the Babylonian Talmud and one sixth of the PalestinianTalmud are comprised of *aggadah*. The style of both Talmuds tends to be terse.

Jerusalem Talmud. The Jerusalem Talmud is the product of five generations of *amoraim* who conducted their studies at various academies. The major centers at first were Sepphoris, Galilee, the seat of the patriarchate, Judea, and later Tiberias whither the patriarchate was transferred. Leading figures of the first generation were Ḥanina b. Ḥama, Yannai, Bar Kappara, Oshaiah Rabbah, and *Joshua b. Levi. *Johanan Nappaḥa and *Simeon b. Lakish were second generation notables in whose lifetime the academy at Tiberias became the major center, attracting students from Babylonia as well as from all over Palestine. This period represents the peak of creativity for the Jerusalem Talmud. The succeeding generations also produced men of note, among them Ammi, Assi, *Eleazar b. Pedat, Zeira, and *Abbahu (of Caesarea) who was the acknowledged leader of Palestinian Jewry. He was a diplomat and a formidable controversialist in polemics with Christians.

By the beginning of the fourth century, the condition of Jews in Palestine had begun to deteriorate due to heavy taxes, a worsening of the economic situation, more frequent persecutions, and the hegemony of Christianity which had now been established by a decree of Constantine. The situation was not propitious to learning or to the maintenance of the academies and many scholars emigrated to Babylonia. The decision was therefore made to reduce to writing the oral debates and decisions of the past five generations. The redaction seems to have been undertaken by Yose b. Bun and to have been completed about 365 C.E.

The Jerusalem Talmud is only about one eighth the size

of the Babylonian Talmud and its intellectual, dialectical, and logical quality is inferior. Its explanations of the Mishnah tend to be direct and terse but at times seem cryptic. This was partly because subjects which called for debate in Babylonia were self-evident in Palestine where the terrain and the conditions were better known, and partly because of indifferent editing. Subjects are often juxtaposed without any connection between them; *halakhot* are neither introduced nor elaborated, and only parts of quotations are given. Clearly, the redaction was undertaken by a community under stress which was losing its grasp and authority to the extent that it abandoned the fixing of the calendar by witnesses and resorted to mathematical calculation.

Babylonian Talmud. The Babylonian Talmud was composed under more felicitous conditions. The community enjoyed size and stability, academies like Nehardea and Sura, later Pumbedita and Maḥoza, and an autonomous government under the leadership of the exilarch. The foundations of the Babylonian Talmud were laid by *Rav who had studied with Judah ha-Nasi, and by Samuel (Mar). Rav was a specialist in religious law, an aggadist, and a liturgist of note, while Samuel, the major authority in civil law at the time, was also famed as an astronomer and physician. Their disciples included Rav *Huna and Rav *Judah b. Ezekiel, who founded the academy at Pumbedita and developed the dialectical method which won for the sages of Pumbedita the reputation that they could cause "an elephant to go through the eye of a needle." Huna expanded the academy at Sura so that it had 800 students. Their successors, *Rabbah Nahamani and *Joseph b. Ḥiyya, developed their methods. Rabbah evolved the dialectical approach to a point where the subject matter of the Talmud increased to such an extent that in part it became independent of the Mishnah. Joseph excelled in accumulated knowledge, basing his teachings upon tradition, thus providing a rein to the exuberance of Rabbah. The fourth generation of scholars, in the first part of the 4th century, *Abbaye and *Rava, also expanded the subject matter and dialectical acuteness of talmudic study. The succeeding generations produced such notable figures as *Papa (b. Naḥman) and *Naḥman b. Isaac. It came to be clear, however, that the mass of material was too great for oral transmission and that systemization was needed. The redaction was undertaken by *Ashi (335–427), who became president of the academy of Sura at the age of 23, but a large group of scholars who met twice a year in Adar and in Elul, known as the *kallah* months, also engaged in the work which lasted 30 years. At this time full academic sessions were held for the dispersed students who were often business and professional men and who otherwise pursued their studies at home. A tractate was edited at each session. After the edition was completed, all the tractates were revised, a process which apparently lasted another 30 years. Further editing and supplementation of the basic material was under the leadership of *Mar Bar Rav Ashi,*Meremar, and particularly *Ravina b. Huna who died in 499. In the following year (500) *Yose, his successor, declared the Talmud officially closed.

The Babylonian Talmud is much better edited than the Jerusalem Talmud. It was redacted over a period of 100 years, so that there was ample time for editing and revision. Logical connections are sought, quotations are complete, editorial explanations abound, and decisions on law are given. While the style is often verbose, the approach is subtle ahd highly dialectical. Material is analyzed minutely, hypotheses are offered and tested, and discussions are carried through. As in the Jerusalem Talmud, the language is Aramaic, but while the Palestinians employed the Western Aramaic dialect the Babylonians used Eastern Aramaic. In both there is an admixture of Hebrew, but the Babylonian text has a great deal more. The completed Talmud is more than a legal work; it reflects the Jewish view of God, man, and society; of theology and ethics; of Jewish values and of the way they were exemplified in daily life. While it is the work of many generations, it represents only the elite fraction of the population both in ability and in considerateness for the people. The Talmud in its time elevated religious scholarship to the highest calling in Jewish life, and the long-term effects of this view have been evident ever since. For 15 centuries the Talmud has been the major concern of Jewish studies and the major guide to Jewish life. Judaism is far less the child of the Bible than that of the Talmud. If the the Bible is the base of the Jewish structure, the Talmud is the house within which the Jews have dwelt (see *Talmud).

Aggadah. MIDRASHIM. The same concern for preservation which led to the compilation of the Oral Law caused the *aggadah* to be organized and committed to writing. While much of it was contained in the Talmud, it was widely scattered and not suitably arranged for reference. Both the scholar and the ordinary Jew had a need for works in which the interpretations of the Bible would be arranged according to books, chapters, and verses. The scholars required it to facilitate finding and comparing interpretations; the laymen needed it because the aggadic statements were major formulations of Jewish ethics, theology, and values, but at the same time were light reading and provided assurances and comfort in the dark hours which Jews, particularly those in Palestine, were experiencing.

The midrashic literature was compiled in places as diverse as Palestine, Babylonia, and Italy, approximately between the sixth and twelfth centuries, although much of the material is of an earlier date. Written largely in Aramaic, though some of the compilations have a considerable admixture of Hebrew, it consists largely of homilies preached by rabbis in synagogues on Sabbaths and festivals and at study classes. Unlike modern preachments, they involved not only the Pentateuch and the books of the Prophets, but the Hagiographa which was read in the synagogue on Saturday afternoons, the time when sermons were given. The Midrash does not contain complete sermons, but rather the core of ideas, insights, illustrations, and special interpretations upon which the sermon was based. The sermonic technique was to take a point of interest to the listener and to cast new light upon it or to relate it to other matters. The universal subjects of discourse were the Bible or Jewish observance and law. The sermon usually began by pointing out contradictions or similarities in widely scattered parts of the Bible or by raising a question of law, resolving it, and then proceeding to consider moral and religious aspects of the matter. Stories, poetic statements, parables, and epigrams were employed by gifted preachers (see *Aggadah, *Midrash).

Midrash Rabbah. The first major compilation was the **Midrash Rabbah* ("The Large Midrash"), so designated because of its length. It consists of Midrashim to each of the books of the Torah and to each of the five *megillot.* Internal evidence indicates that the earliest Midrash, **Genesis Rabbah,* dates from the sixth century and the latest, **Numbers Rabbah* from the 12th. Most of them were composed in Palestine, although several seem to have been subjected to Babylonian re-editing. In many of the *Rabbah* Midrashim the homiletic commentary technique is used whereby a series of comments refer to a specific verse. **Leviticus Rabbah, Numbers Rabbah,* and **Deuteronomy Rabbah,* however, use the sermon method. They select a verse or two from the Torah reading of the Sabbath, adduce various comments, skip the rest of the verses, and proceed to verses derived from the next Sabbath reading. The triennial cycle, customary in Palestine, is the Torah order followed.

Tanḥuma-Yelammedenu. Another major midrashic compilation is the **Tanḥuma-Yelammedenu* cycle on the Pentateuch of which three versions are extant, either in part or whole. The original version was probably compiled in Palestine in the sixth century; the other two also seem to be products of Palestine but are probably late ninth century. It is possible, however, that they may be from Babylonia and southern Italy. The *Tanḥuma* title is derived from Tanḥuma b. Abba, a noted Palestinian aggadist of the fourth century who is frequently quoted. The title *Yelammedenu* ("let our master teach us") refers to a formula frequently employed in the book which involved the raising and answering of a halakhic question after which the discussion branched off into *aggadah* and commentary.

Pesikta. The midrashic cycle *Pesikta* (*paska*, "to divide") has two versions: the **Pesikta de-Rav Kahana*, probably compiled in Palestine before the end of the seventh century, and the **Pesikta Rabbati*, which records the year 845 as the date of composition and in its use of Hebrew and of snatches of rhymed poetry gives evidence of having been influenced by the Palestinian Hebrew poetry school which began to flourish in the seventh century. The material consists of homilies on the Torah and prophetic readings for festivals and for special Sabbaths.

Other Homiletic Midrashim. In addition to these general compilations, there seem to have been in earlier times Midrashim on all the prophetic and hagiographic books, most of which have been lost. Extant are: **Midrash Tehillim*, consisting of homilies; **Midrash Proverbs* which is more in the nature of an aggadic commentary and is replete with parables, apothegms, and short homiletic interpretations; **Midrash Samuel*, a Midrash on Samuel I and II, a collection of sermons involving references to one or two verses. All three works are of 10th- or 11th-century origin and were probably compiled in southern Italy.

The characteristic patterns of all the midrashic cycles is their focus, either by way of commentary or sermon, on biblical verses and their reflection of the thinking and experiences of many generations. They are interrelated in a peculiar sense; they plagiarized from one another, sometimes even to the extent of bodily lifting passages. The *Tanḥuma* borrows from the *Pesikta de-Rav Kahana* and the *Pesikta Rabbati* from the *Tanḥuma;* the later books of the *Midrash Rabbah*, on Exodus, Numbers, and Deuteronomy, borrow heavily from the *Tanḥuma*. All of them derive a great deal of material from the scattered references in the Talmud (see *Homiletic Literature; *Preaching).

Non-Homiletic Midrashim. In addition to the homiletic Midrashim, there are midrashic works of another kind, e.g., the eighth-century Hebrew work **Pirkei de-Rabbi Eliezer*, in which biblical narratives serve to teach ethical and religious lessons on such themes as the Sabbath, reward and punishment, paradise and hell, and Messianic doctrine. It also discusses cosmogony, astronomy, and the calendar; abounds in legends and stories, many of them ancient and similar to stories in the Apocrypha; and is written in a poetic style. The resort to numbers as a form of organization is an interesting device and the use of numerical groups, especially of seven and ten, is common. It was probably written in Palestine. A book of a similar stamp, *Seder Eliyahu*, by Abba Elijah, a tenth-century Palestinian, is divided into two parts (*Rabbah*, large and *Zuta*, small) and includes a moral discourse on Torah, the love of Israel and of mankind, and the love of God. Written in Hebrew in a poetic style, it makes great use of stories and parables. Other midrashic compilations of the eighth, ninth, and tenth centuries, of undetermined authorship and provenance, are about Moses, Solomon, the Messiah, and paradise and hell. Later midrashic works rearranged traditional material and supplemented it. Such works were composed by *Moses ha-Darshan of Narbonne and Rabbi Tobiah of Germany, both of the 11th century. A more significant work, **Yalkut Shimoni*, by Simeon Karo (13th century), drew heavily on the Talmud and on many midrashic compilations. Karo organized a compendium of aggadic statements and commentaries on all the 25 books of the Bible.

In a sense midrashic literature has never ended since homily, commentary, and elaboration on biblical themes continue to be creative activities. Jewish and Christian traditions have drawn heavily on the midrashic literature whose roots are in deep antiquity. The Midrash lent color and variety to Jewish tradition; concentrated on ethical and theological problems; recorded and interpreted difficult episodes of Jewish history; and enriched Jewish culture. It was particularly sustaining to the average Jew, man and woman alike, who was not at home in halakhic literature. He drew his philosophy and his sense of worth and purpose from the stories, parables, proverbs, and intuitive insights in which midrashic literature abounded.

MEDIEVAL PERIOD (500–1750)

A characteristic feature of Jewish history is that while Jews lacked stability and experienced declining fortunes in one land, they prospered or were tolerated in another. In consequence, there was always one major center, and usually two or three, where Jewish literary creativity continued unabated. In the 1200-year period which constitutes the Jewish Middle Ages, Babylonia, North Africa, Spain and Provence, the Franco-German area, and Italy were the major centers. There were intermittent periods of significant literary activity in Palestine and, after the expulsion of the Jews from Spain, in the Eastern Levant, including Palestine, Turkey, and Egypt, which became centers for a century or two. From the 16th century onward Germany declined for about two centuries while the Slavic countries rose to a prominence both in literary productivity and in Jewish population which they retained until the 20th century.

On the whole, Jewish productivity was greatest and most varied in lands which were part of the mainstream of history and declined as it began to bypass those countries. The most notable examples are Babylonia and Spain at the height of Arab culture and the most marked exceptions are Slavic countries where the general cultural level was low, but where Jewish literary productivity, concentrating almost exclusively on rabbinics, was high. One important factor which should be noted is that contact between Jewish communities was considerable and that what was produced in one land had an effect upon Jewish literature in other countries. There seems, in the earlier period, to have been two particular streams of influence—one flowing from Palestine into Italy and then into the Franco-German area and the other, stemming from Babylon, flowing through North Africa into Spain.

In the Middle Ages, as in antiquity, Jewish literature constituted several layers. As the Bible was the basis for the Mishnah and the Mishnah for the *Gemara*, the total tradition was the basis for the literary labors of the Middle Ages, much of which concentrated on the explication of the Bible and the Oral Law through grammar, exegesis, commentary, philosophy, mysticism, and liturgical and didactic poetry. Secular poetry, prose, and science were ornaments of the religious tradition which by the Middle Ages had become complex and stratified. Fundamental to the literature was a belief in the revealed Torah, God's providence, the chosenness of Israel, the coming of the Messiah, and the restoration to the Land of Israel. These ideas were examined, but never seriously disputed until the modern era. They reflected a national characteristic, manifested both in law and literature, which called for life to be lived and coped with, no matter what the circumstances, and which assumed that the details of living, according to the Torah, could be spelled out. In the same spirit, the many *kinot* ("lamentations") written during the Middle Ages were rarely overwhelmingly pessimistic and despairing.

The literature will be organized here into categories of writing. Obviously, there were interrelationships and effects which, however, cannot be noted; only highlights can be mentioned. Thus grammatical writing influenced Bible exegesis and poetry; rabbinics influenced Bible exegesis; and the impact frequently was all the greater because many of the writers were versatile, writing in many fields. Thousands of works have been lost and thousands more cannot be mentioned. The literary productivity of a small group, highly literate and dedicated to study, was phenomenal.

The question of language also deserves attention. Jews wrote in many languages, but mostly in Hebrew, Aramaic, and toward the end of the period in Yiddish and Ladino. Much, however, was written in Arabic and some in other languages. This multiplicity of languages points to another feature of Jewish literary activity which cannot be dealt with here. Since Jews were dispersed through many countries, were multilingual, and moved from land to land, they performed a major function as cultural intermediaries, translating from one language to another and making the riches of one culture available to the other. A third linguistic feature of significance is that the Hebrew language after the talmudic era, when it lapsed as a literary language, suddenly came to life in the early Middle Ages, notably in Palestine and Spain. Most of the great works during the entire 1200-year period were written in Hebrew.

GRAMMAR AND LEXICOGRAPHY

The formulation of rules of grammar prompted by a need to study and understand the Bible was basic to the revival of Hebrew as a literary language. The renewed interest in Bible study due to a controversy with the Karaites, who rejected the Oral Law and insisted that the Bible alone was authoritative, was sparked by the realization that the rabbinic position had to be defended. Such an examination inevitably led to the formulation of rules of language. It was further motivated by the fact that the correct reading of the Bible, in its vowels, accents, and *keri* (the way a word was read), as against *ketiv* (the way a word was written), was an oral tradition and needed to be set down since Jews were dispersed in many lands. Finally, Arabic culture which stressed poetry, and consequently grammar, had a major impact in those centers of Jewish life—Babylon, Palestine, and Spain—which came under Arab rule.

The first philological effort was the *masorah, a collective work of many generations. While its origins date back to Ezra, significant masoretic activity began in the sixth century, continuing to the tenth, and was concentrated in Palestine and Babylonia. The work resulted in a definition of vowels, accents, *ketiv*, and *keri*. It noted all exceptions in spelling and peculiarities of words and orthography. Through the use of accents, correct relationship of words and thought were achieved and the chant for biblical reading was fixed. In effect, the relating of words was itself a form of biblical commentary. Ultimately, all the masoretic works were compiled by Jacob b. Ḥayyim, an Italian scholar, and printed in the *Bomberg edition of the Bible (1525). The notes which were designed to clarify the text and to prevent further errors were of three kinds: the masorah *parva* ("small"), printed in the outer margin; the masorah *magna* ("large"), printed in the inner margin, or above, or below the text; and the masorah *finalis* at the end of the text, which also included an alphabetical list of word peculiarities. Since the masorah is a collective undertaking, few of the scholars who worked on it are known. However, the Tiberian school, where the major work was done, recorded the names of Pinḥas (eighth century) and Asher the elder (eighth century), the first of a family who for six generations labored on the masorah. Aaron *Ben-Asher (beginning of the tenth century) substantially brought the masoretic work to a close. Literary work on the masorah is found in Europe as late as the 12th century and still later Elijah *Levita (1468–1549) published the *Masoret ha-Masoret* in which he explained how to read and use the masoretic material.

The formal foundations of grammar and lexicography were laid in Babylon by *Saadiah b. Joseph Gaon (tenth century) in *Agron*, a dictionary, and in *Sefer ha-Lashon* ("Book of the Language"), a work on grammar. His most notable successors were *Menahem b. Jacob ibn Saruq of Spain whose Hebrew work *Maḥberet* ("Joined Words") is a dictionary of biblical language and a grammar. Judah *Ḥayyuj (end of the tenth century), writing in Arabic, established the principle of the bilateral Hebrew root and Jonah *ibn Janaḥ almost completed the structure of Hebrew grammar in *Book of Critique* (in Arabic) in which he laid the groundwork of Hebrew syntax. A century later David *Kimḥi of Provence rearranged and expanded Ibn Janaḥ's study in his *Mikhlol* ("Compendium"), a grammar and dictionary of roots. In the 14th century Joseph ibn *Kaspi of Provence attempted a logical structuring of words and grammar, a venture which was repeated more elaborately by Isaac Profiat *Duran (15th century) who in *Ma'aseh Efod* ("The Work of the Ephod") combined logical structure with an elaborate philosophy of language. The last major grammatical authority of the Middle Ages was Elijah Levita whose *Meturgeman* ("The Interpreter") is the first dictionary of the Targum (see *Hebrew Language, in the Supplementary Entries).

BIBLE EXEGESIS

Simultaneously with literary creativity in grammar there was a development of biblical exegesis. The same scholars were often active in both fields. Four major methods of commentary were developed: *peshat* ("plain sense"), *derash* ("aggadic interpretation"), *remez* ("allegory and philosophy"), and *sod* ("mystical interpretation"). Here, too, the versatile Saadiah b. Joseph Gaon laid the foundations with his translation of the Bible and his commentaries in Arabic in a work most of which has been lost. The greatest figure of the era, *Rashi, wrote a phrase-by-phrase commentary on almost the entire Bible which was a harmonious blend of *peshat* and *derash*. His commentary was popular for many generations so that *Ḥummash* (Pentateuch) and Rashi became almost synonymous. His major rival, Abraham *ibn Ezra (12th century) of Spain, a poet, grammarian, and scientist, who was a master of grammar and Hebrew, chose the path of *peshat*. His commentary is lucid although occasionally he permitted himself veiled allusions to doubts he entertained about the text. He commented on the entire Bible but only the works on the Pentateuch, Isaiah, and some of the Hagiographa have survived. Preeminently an intellectual's commentator, Ibn Ezra was the subject of supercommentaries.

Another major commentator who is usually associated with the above-mentioned scholars is David Kimḥi who emphasized *peshat,* but also resorted to aggadic and philosophic interpretations in his commentaries on the prophets, Psalms, Genesis, and the Books of Chronicles.

While the above are the best exponents of the *peshat* and *derash* methods, they based themselves on precursors. There were also contemporaries who pursued the same paths, and successors who adopted their methods. Thus, Rashi's grandson, R. *Samuel b. Meir, wrote extensive commentaries on the Bible in the *peshat* method. As mystical and philosophic tendencies were manifesting themselves in the Jewish world, the other two approaches (*sod* and *remez*) also began to be employed. *Sod* owed much to the rise of *Kabbalah, of which the *Zohar (itself a sort of commentary on the Torah) was the outstanding work of the period. Meanwhile the approach and spirit of *Maimonides' *Guide of the Perplexed* which centered about the philosophic exposition of many biblical passages, gave impetus to *remez.* The major commentary in the mystical spirit was the work of *Naḥmanides (13th century), a major figure of Spanish Jewry. His commentary on the Pentateuch reflects the belief that the Torah is capable of yielding many meanings to the initiated and he therefore offers multiple interpretations in the spirit of *halakhah, peshat,* and mysticism. His mysticism is, however, limited since he believed that mystic teachings in their full strength should be confined to an elect and that the masses should be taught a Judaism based upon faith, piety, and reason. His younger contemporary, *Baḥya b. Asher, took the mystical approach further in his commentaries, and *Jacob b. Asher, the noted codifier, utilized the techniques of *gematria* (devising meanings from the numerical value of the words) and *notarikon* (employing initial or final letters of words to discern hidden meanings).

The outstanding exponent of the philosophic school was *Levi b. Gershom of Provence. Commenting on all the Bible, except the Latter Prophets, he attempted to find speculative truths in it, to ascertain the principles of ethics, and to supply reasoned interpretations of biblical precepts. His commentary enjoyed a high repute among Jewish intellectuals. To a lesser degree, the commentaries of Joseph b. Abba Mari Kaspi employed the same approach and enjoyed a similar reputation.

The last great commentator of the period was the statesman and financier, Don Isaac *Abrabanel of Spain. At home in both Christian and Jewish exegesis and in general literature, he brought all of these into play in his commentaries, which covered the entire Bible. In his approach he first posed a series of questions arising out of the text and then proceeded to resolve them through the use of philosophy, theology, history, and modified mysticism. Apart from his singular method, he is noted for devoting considerable attention to the problems of political philosophy and historical chronology (see *Bible, Exegesis).

POETRY

The Arabic influence and the renaissance of the Hebrew language also led to a remarkable flourishing of Hebrew poetry in the Middle Ages. An equally important factor was the structuring of the prayer book and the liturgy (at that time still fluid) which occurred during these centuries, when thousands of poems which became part of the liturgy were being composed. In this field there was continuity rather than innovation, since the composition of liturgy had persisted throughout the talmudic period. However, the writing of secular poetry: love songs, wine songs, didactic poetry, epigrams, and the like represented a new development whose immediate origins may be traced to Arabic influence and whose remote roots may be found in the poetry of the Bible.

The characteristic forms of medieval Hebrew poetry are partly influenced by the Bible, but more by Arabic literature and, at the end of the period in Italy, by European forms like the sonnet and the tercet. Biblical poetry, based on parallelism, had occasionally used both the alphabetical form and rhyme. Medieval Hebrew poetry, while using some parallelism, employed the alphabetical form (forward or backward), the acrostic, rhyme, and meter as its characteristic elements. Rhyme, both in poetry and prose, was relatively easy due to the Hebrew suffixes; thus variant and more complicated forms developed. Palestinian and West European poetry tended to use the simple rhyme, while Babylonian and notably the Spanish poetry used the two- and three-syllable rhyme. Masters of the language, they prided themselves on the ability to use the same word, with different meanings, for rhyming. Meter, introduced by *Dunash b. Labrat (tenth century) and current mainly in Spain, was essentially spondaic and iambic, but was employed in complicated forms so that 19 (or according to some 52) different meters developed. Trick poetry was also composed, often of surprisingly high quality, such as the *"Elef Alfin"* of Abraham *Bedersi in which each word of a 1,000-word poem begins with the letter *alef.*

The major types in medieval Hebrew poetry, secular verse and *piyyut,* ranging from doggerel to moving lyrics and to long, beautiful philosophical poems, were frequently composed by the same poets. The combination, however, was largely confined to Spain, Provence, and Italy. The Palestinian and Franco-German poets were essentially *paytanim* and their poetry was generally inferior in quality to that of their Iberian coreligionists. Both secular and religious poetry drew extensively on the same sources and employed biblical and aggadic phrases allusively in order to display technical mastery.

The liturgical poems composed in Palestine in the seventh and eighth centuries mark the beginnings of medieval Hebrew poetry. Some were anonymous, like "All the World Shall Come to Serve Thee" of the Day of Atonement service, but most of them can be attributed to three poets, *Yose b. Yose, *Yannai, and Eleazar *Kallir (ha-Kallir). Their compositions are standard prayers in the High Holy Days *maḥzor* and in the festival services. Yose is the author of the *Avodah* (a Temple service poem) recited on the Day of Atonement and Kallir wrote the *Geshem* ("rain") prayer recited on Sukkot. The influence of Palestine was felt most notably in Italy (and from that country in the Franco-German area) which always maintained close ties with the Palestinian developments and learning. In both areas there were families of *paytanim* who continued to compose *piyyutim, seliḥot* ("penitential verse"), and *kinot* in successive generations. Notable among them was the *Kalonymus family whose founder, *Meshullam, composed works in Italy and whose descendants moved to Germany at the end of the tenth century. In Germany Meshullam (c. 976), his son Kalonymus (c. 1000), the author of *U-Netanneh Tokef,* a prayer in the High Holy Days *maḥzor,* the latter's son, *Moses (c. 1020), and grandsons Kalonymus and Jekuthiel (c. 1050), were prolific in their writing of *piyyutim.* Other prominent poets in France and Germany were *Gershom b. Judah and *Ephraim of Bonn, the author of the *Hymn of Unity.* In later periods these countries produced hundreds of *paytanim.* Virtually every scholar tried his hand at this form of writing, including Solomon *Luria, Samuel *Edels, and Yom Tov Lipmann *Heller.

Spanish, Provençal, and later Italian poetry can claim many distinguished poets who wrote both religious and secular poems. They were men of varied accomplishments, very much at home in all the intellectual and social worlds of their time. The first major Hebrew poet of Spain, *Samuel ha-Nagid (11th century), vizier of Granada, a military commander and a talmudist, wrote extensively but his works have only recently become fully known. They include sacred poetry, reflections on war, love poems, wine songs, elegies, and three volumes on imitations of the books of Psalms, Proverbs, and Ecclesiastes. His younger contemporary, Solomon ibn *Gabirol, who died at an early age, is one of the outstanding figures of Hebrew poetry. Dextrous in the use of language and a master of every form of rhyme and meter, Gabirol wrote on all themes. His few surviving secular poems on nature, love, wine, and death are gems of their kind. His poetic genius found, however, full expression in his religious poetry and in several long philosophical poems of which *Keter Malkhut* ("The Royal Crown") is his most consummate work. The poem masterfully integrates the poet's great philosophical and scientific knowledge to create a lofty ode to God.

Moses *ibn Ezra covered the gamut of secular and religious poetry. Author of more than 6,000 verses, he wrote about "wine and the delights of men," "the world and its vicissitudes," and "poems in praise of the creator." Many of his verses are reminiscent of Omar Khayyam, although Ibn Ezra's range, his delicacy of fancy, and use of imagery exceed the poetic quality of the Persian poet. His masterpiece, *Tarshish*, composed of 1210 verses, shows a great variety in language and themes. His religious poems are at once philosophical and deeply moving.

The peak of Spanish poetry is found in the harmonious verse of *Judah Halevi. Rejoicing in life, love, and friends and passionate in his quest of God, Halevi wrote of God and man with equal felicity. Love of Zion, expressed in several poems whose theme is "I am a harp for thy [Zion] songs," also characterizes the work of Halevi. These poems, as well as his religious verse, have been incorporated into the liturgy.

Another great Spanish poet, Abraham ibn Ezra, wrote on a wide variety of subjects. His secular poetry while embracing conventional themes displayed a mastery of style, form, and language, and a great capacity for wit and satire turned as frequently against himself as against others. His religious poetry however is deeply fervent and moving, ranging from the lyrical to the philosophical. A restless traveler whose journeys took him to Babylonia and Persia, Ibn Ezra also roamed through the realms of the imagination. "The Letter of Hai ben Meliẓ" is an allegory in rhymed prose of a journey through three worlds.

The last major poet of Spain, Judah b. Solomon *al-Ḥarizi, the author of *Taḥkemoni* ("Book of Wisdom"), wrote in *maqāma* form (rhymed prose) frequently interspersed with verse. The poems embraced devotional and love poetry, satire and narrative; some were riddles, others proverbs. The *Taḥkemoni*, consisting of 50 chapters, each devoted to a different subject and treated in a variety of forms, displays remarkable linguistic skill, manipulation of biblical phrases to serve unusual ends, wit, and great literary variety.

While poetry continued to be written in Spain for another two centuries, the golden age had passed. The poets of southern Spain, like Meshullam *da Piera, engaged largely in polemical verse as part of the *Maimonidean controversy; others, like Abraham b. Samuel *ibn Ḥasdai and Shem Tov b. Joseph *Falaquera, wrote didactic poetry. In northern Spain, Solomon *da Piera (14th century) made his mark primarily as a religious poet, although he composed secular poetry as well. Solomon *Bonafed (15th century) wrote secular poetry. In one of his poems lamenting the decline of poetry, he incidentally left a record of Hebrew literature of the 14th and 15th centuries. Provence medieval Jewish literature was distinguished by the Bedersis: Abraham (13th century) and Jedaiah (14th century), his son.

The major center of Jewish poetry from the 13th century onward was Italy where *Immanuel of Rome wrote his *Maḥbarot*, following Al-Ḥarizi in the use of the *maqāma* form. Buoyant, gay, and sorrowing by turns, employing varied meters and diverse forms (including the sonnet), the *Maḥbarot* touches on widely different subjects and satirizes and parodies other poets. Two unusual features are that his love songs are highly erotic, and that the last of the 28 chapters is an imitation of Dante's *Divine Comedy*. Immanuel of Rome had no immediate successors of distinction; Moses *Rieti (15th century) however modeled his *Heikhal* on Immanuel's imitation of Dante. After a period of decline, Italian poetry revived with Leone *Modena (mid-17th century) and notably with the brothers, Jacob and Emmanuel *Frances (17th century). While Jacob wrote excellent caustic polemic poetry directed against the Shabbatean movement, his brother composed religious and secular verse in various styles, including a substantial number of epigrams. With Moses *Zacuto (17th century) Italian medieval poetry came to an end. Although he introduced poetic drama into Hebrew literature, Zacuto was a poet rather than a dramatist: *Yesod Olam* ("Foundations of the World") and *Tofteh Arukh* ("Hell Prepared"), his two dramas, resemble the medieval miracle play in form and development of plot.

A brief period in the composition of poetry in Palestine developed under the influence of the kabbalists. Israel *Najara wrote a substantial body of religious poetry. Employing Turkish, Arabic, Greek, and Italian forms and meters, Najara's themes were on God, Israel, and the redemption. Many of his works are essentially love poems to God and a considerable number were incorporated in the liturgy including the Sabbath table hymn, *Yah Ribbon* (see *Poetry, Medieval; *Prayer).

RABBINIC LITERATURE (500–1250)

The most voluminous body of writings in the medieval period was the legal rabbinic literature consisting of commentaries, codes, and responsa. The number of writers probably runs into the thousands. Beginning with the *geonim* in Babylonia, the activity extended into every country, embracing the Slavic states, which became the major centers toward the end of the period. Due to its scope and quantity, this literature will be divided into two chronological sections: 600–1250 and 1250–1750.

Commentary. The first activity took place in Babylonia where in the ninth century the *gaon* *Ẓemaḥ composed an *arukh* ("A Prepared System") which was both a dictionary and a commentary on talmudic phrases and selected passages. Not long thereafter, Saadiah wrote brief commentaries (in Arabic), which have been lost, on several tractates. *Hai Gaon in his commentaries on large parts of the Talmud (not all are extant) explicated words and phrases and paraphrased passages in the Talmud. This pattern became the model for the commentaries of the North African and Spanish schools which were in close contact with Babylonia.

In Babylonia, the talmudic tradition was kept alive in the very institutions where it had been nurtured and the need for commentary, therefore, was not great. However, in the newly developing centers, commentary was essential. Abraham *ibn Daud associates the beginning of talmudic learning and academies outside Babylonia with four rabbis who set out from southern Italy, were captured, and ultimately dispersed to Cordova, Kairouan, and Alexandria. According to another tradition, at the end of the eighth or ninth century the Kalonymus family migrated to Mainz, in Germany, where an academy was founded. Whatever the case, by the tenth century talmudic learning was established in all these places.

From Babylonia, commentary activity passed first to Kairouan where R. *Hananel b. Ḥushi'el (11th century), employing the method of Hai, commented on several *sedarim* of the Talmud. He was however more elaborate in his paraphrase, often compared the discussion on the same subject in the two Talmuds, and gave a *pesak* ("decision") at the end of each discussion. His contemporary, *Nissim b. Jacob, pursued the same method in elucidating the Babylonian Talmud, but made more extensive comparisons with the Palestinian Talmud and tannaitic Midrashim. Other distinguished 11th-century figures were Spanish Jewish scholars. Isaac b. Jacob *Alfasi, the most eminent among them, had emigrated to Spain from Fez in 1088. His great work, *Halakhot,* a compendium of the Talmud, is a combination of code and commentary; it became a basic text for talmudic studies and was the subject of numerous supercommentaries. His immediate disciple, Joseph ha-Levi *ibn Migash, also employed the method of paraphrase in his commentaries on many tractates.

A new method was introduced by *Maimonides of whose commentaries on three talmudic *sedarim* only fragments have survived, but whose commentary (in Arabic) on the Mishnah is complete. Maimonides applied logic and systematization to the Mishnah, analyzing the principles of Oral Law, classifying the *halakhot,* offering logical sequence for the order of the Mishnah, and providing a historical survey. He was concerned with aiding the ordinary student and in consequence was at pains to indicate the law in each case and to incorporate the relevant material from the *Gemara.*

In the Franco-German region, commentary was developing along different lines. At the academy of Mainz, headed by *Gershom b. Judah, hundreds of students engaged in the study of the Talmud. They took notes *(kunteresim)* on the lectures delivered and the Commentary of Rabbi Gershom is in fact a collection of several generations of such *kunteresim* based on the teachings of R. Gershom b. Judah or his disciples. The academy developed the Franco-German system of running commentary on words and phrases, a method for the training of scholars, in contrast to the Spanish method which sought general principles under which particulars were organized and were designed as a resource for students who only learned periodically. The most notable representative of the Franco-German method is Rashi whose commentary on almost all tractates appears side by side with the text in every major edition of the Talmud. It reflects his capacity for lucidity, brevity, penetration to the heart of a matter, and is a notable example of pedagogy. Several commentators, members of Rashi's family, followed his method and rounded out his work. Among them were *Judah b. Nathan and Samuel b. Meir. Talmudic commentary in the Franco-German region however took a different turn in the commentaries known as the **tosafot* ("additions"). The tosafist undertook to restore the *Gemara* method: he raised questions about the text and resolved them, following the order of the *Gemara* page by page. The *tosafot,* a product of several generations, appear side by side with the text in all the standard editions. The major scholars who initiated the method and are quoted frequently were *Meir b. Samuel of Ramerupt and his three sons Samuel, *Isaac, and particularly Jacob (Rabbenu *Tam). The next generation produced the great luminary *Isaac b. Samuel of Dampierre who is quoted almost as frequently as Jacob b. Meir. Under the leadership of figures like *Samson b. Abraham of Sens, *Moses b. Jacob of Coucy, and *Meir b. Baruch of Rothenburg, tosafist activity flourished until the beginning of the 14th century.

Simultaneously with Franco-German scholarship there was considerable talmudic activity in Italy where *Nathan b. Jehiel of Rome (11th century) wrote the *Arukh,* a dictionary-encyclopedia of the Talmud which is the basis for all modern talmudic lexicography. Nathan explicated words and passages, quoted and cited authorities and comments which would otherwise have been lost, and in his explications and elucidations used comparative philology. Contemporaries and successors have imitated him and the tosafist school. A major figure of the next generation was *Isaiah b. Mali di Trani, the author of *Tosafot Rid.* In Provence, situated midway between the Spanish and Franco-German centers, academies also flourished and the methods of both northern and southern schools were employed. Zerahiah b. Isaac *Gerondi ha-Levi (12th century) in *Sefer ha-Ma'or* composed an analytical commentary on Alfasi which combined critical evaluations of earlier and contemporary commentaries with additions to Alfasi. *Abraham b. David of Posquières (12th century), the leader of the anti-Maimonides school, commented on several tractates of the Talmud and on the *Sifra,* and wrote a severe criticism on Maimonides' code.

Codes. The need for codes arose out of the demands of life: the Jewish community was dispersed and thus lacked readily available authority; the law had also become increasingly complex and required codification. The first responsa were written in Babylonia and were often intended for far-flung Diaspora communities. *She'iltot* by R. *Aḥa (Aḥai) *gaon* of Shabḥa (eighth century) deals with the *mitzvot* as they are arranged in the Pentateuch and organizes the relevant talmudic material under those headings. It is assumed that the work, consisting of 171 discourses, originally dealt with the entire 613 commandments. Rabbi Aḥa initiated the method of codification in which decisions and sources are given. Another method is that of *Yehudai Gaon, head of the academy of Sura (757–761) in whose **Halakhot Pesukot* ("Halakhic Decisions") only decisions are handed down. The third major codification, the **Halakhot Gedolot* ("Large *Halakhot*"), ascribed by some to Simeon Kayyara (eighth century), piled and organized under one heading the scattered material in the Talmud on a given *mitzvah.* The order of the talmudic tractates is followed, except for the laws relevant to the Temple which are omitted, with the author modeling himself on the *She'iltot* and quoting extensively from the Talmud. During the following century, *Amram b. Sheshna Gaon, adopting the method of Yehudai Gaon, wrote his *Seder* ("Ordering"), a code on the prayer book. Starting with general principles, Amram deduced subsidiary laws, which he subsequently divided into classes. Hai Gaon, the last *gaon* of Pumbedita, wrote a series of codes on civil law.

The great codes, however, were the products of other lands. Isaac b. Jacob Alfasi's *Halakhot,* partly commentary but mainly code, is an abridgment and paraphrase of the Talmud section by section which adheres to the main line of discussion of the Mishnah and comes to a conclusion about the law. Alfasi thus provides a basis for decisions, but fails, as the Talmud does, to achieve an orderly systematic discussion of all aspects of a subject. Such a systematization is the work of Maimonides in his *Mishneh Torah* ("The Second Law"). The code brings the entire body of Jewish law into an orderly and systematic arrangement, including laws which were omitted by Alfasi and his predecessors. It sets forth divergent opinions, decides between them, and renders clear decisions. Maimonides' work encompasses the Talmud, the *geonim,* and the works of other scholars. He bases himself upon the 613 precepts, but organizes them according to his own system: God and man, the life of the individual, laws relating to the Land of Israel, and laws relating to society. While the work was widely accepted and remains one of the monuments of Jewish literature, it also evoked opposition from those who feared it would supplant the study of the Talmud. It has one grave drawback, however, in that it fails to indicate the sources for the rulings and it was this deficiency, plus the fact that new problems constantly arose, which led to the development of other codes (see *Maimonidean Controversy).

The Franco-German school followed different criteria and did not attempt to formulate an overall code of the scope and system of that of Maimonides, but many less comprehensive codes were written. *Isaac b. Abba Mari of Marseilles (12th century) in *Ittur Soferim* ("The Crowning of Scholars"), a code on civil law, on marriage and divorce, and on dietary laws, adopts the source method, including under each subject treated the relevant talmudic, geonic, and Alfasi discussions. *Ha-Terumah* ("The Heave-Offering") by *Baruch b. Isaac of Worms, dealing with dietary, Sabbath, and marriage laws, uses the code method; the work presents a selection of the best scholarship of his generation. More decisive was the **Maḥzor Vitry* of Simḥah of Vitry. Organized around the liturgy and the religious cycle, it cites prayers and laws and is a major work in the history of liturgy, as well as a significant source for geonic and midrashic texts which have otherwise disappeared.

An effort on a broader scale was made by *Eliezer b. Samuel of Metz in *Sefer Yere'im* where he attempted a complete code; he organized the material along the lines of Maimonides but cited sources verbatim. A code distinctively Franco-German in tone is that of *Eleazar b. Judah of Worms, *Roke'aḥ* ("A Compound of Spices"), which deals with the entire body of religious laws. The work, a pure code, without quoting sources, is at the same time a compendium of customs and practices which reflect the daily life of the period. Its pervading spirit, neither intellectual nor purely legal, is one of deep medieval piety which mirrors the effect of the Kabbalah in daily life (see *Codification of Law).

Responsa. Huge and varied, responsa literature is usually precisely what the name implies, responses to legal questions which were asked by individuals and communities. It is rarely an organized or systematic body of scholarship. Many responsa were written but many were undoubtedly lost and others have never been printed. Only a small amount of this vast body of writings is extant. The importance of the responsa is not only legal, but historical. They constitute source material for virtually every phase of Jewish life, since the responsa often involved comments upon community conditions.

The gaonate in Babylonia, the recognized authority for world Jewry for several centuries, produced a vast body of responsa of which only a few hundreds have survived. On the whole they are very brief and direct. Many of them standardized synagogue practices and worship throughout the Jewish world. The famous responsum of Amram Gaon to a Spanish community was of this order. Other major writers of responsa were *Sherira Gaon and Hai Gaon. In North Africa, Alfasi left a considerable collection of responsa in Arabic as did his Spanish student, Joseph ibn Migash, and Maimonides who wrote in Arabic as well as in Hebrew. *Mikhtav li-Yhudei Teiman* ("Letter to the Jews of Yemen") is a famous example of Maimonides' responsa. In France, Rabbi *Gershom b. Judah and Rashi wrote numerous responsa, which, however, were not collected, but are referred to and quoted by others, as are the responsa of Kalonymus and Meshullam. By the 12th century, responsa had become lengthy essays written in Hebrew and incorporating an analysis of relevant material. They also began to be preserved by the author himself. There are collections of Jacob b. Meir Tam and of Solomon b. Abraham *Adret (13th century) of Spain who wrote approximately 7,000 responsa. Meir of Rothenburg (13th century) of Germany, Jacob b. Moses *Moellin (14th–15th century), and Israel *Isserlein (beginning of 15th century) of Vienna also wrote extensively. Moellin insisted that responsa, as case law, were more important than the codes. In the 14th and 15th centuries Joseph *Colon, the great writer of responsa of Italy, *Isaac b. Sheshet, and his younger contemporary Simeon b. Ẓemaḥ *Duran of North Africa, greatly enriched responsa literature (see *Responsa).

RABBINIC LITERATURE (1250–1750)

The second half of the Jewish Middle Ages was marked by a heightening of persecution, an increased physical, social, and intellectual isolation of the Jews in most countries, and a consequent turning inward to peculiarly Jewish studies. It was characterized, too, by the rise to eminence of new Jewish centers, most notably those in Eastern Europe and the Turkish Empire, embracing Palestine. The production of rabbinic literature was vast, numbering thousands of works. Only a few of the major efforts can be considered here and they will be discussed chronologically rather than by countries. This approach may be adopted the more readily since by the end of the 15th century Spanish Jewry had disappeared or been dispersed and German Jewry had declined in creativity.

Commentary. The significant commentators of the 13th century were Spanish Jews. Naḥmanides, a pupil of *Jonah b. Abraham Gerondi, adopted the French method and wrote extensive *novellae on three major orders of the Talmud, providing decisions, as well as raising and resolving difficulties found in the Talmud. His disciple Solomon b. Abraham Adret wrote novellae to 16 tractates of the same three major orders of the Talmud but was more analytical than his master and more given to straight commentary. He selects passages from virtually every page of the Talmud for his novellae. At the beginning of the 14th century *Asher b. Jehiel was the most eminent commentator. Originally from Germany, he became rabbi of Toledo in 1304 and enjoyed a reputation which brought students to his academy from all over Europe. Unconcerned with the sciences, opposed to philosophy, he concentrated his attention on the Talmud. His greatest achievement was a code, but he also wrote *tosafot* (glosses and remarks), which are characterized by simplicity and logic, to 17 tractates and commentaries to several tractates of the Talmud and to several orders of the Mishnah. Other scholars of the period were Meir b. Todros ha-Levi *Abulafia of Toledo whose *Yad Ramah* followed the old Spanish method of summary and comment, and Menahem b. Solomon *Meiri don Vidal of Provence who wrote commentaries on all the tractates of the Talmud. Lucid and systematic in style, he adopted the approach of Maimonides. He introduced each section—whether tractate, chapter, or Mishnah—with a statement of its themes and while his discussion centers around the Mishnah, he also gives the gist of the *Gemara* and the decision.

In the 14th century, Rabbi *Yom Tov b. Abraham Ishbili, a disciple of Solomon b. Abraham Adret, continued the novellae method, writing on the three major orders of the Talmud. His contemporary, *Nissim b. Reuben Gerondi, a major force in Spanish Jewry, not only wrote novellae on the same orders but composed one of the two major commentaries on Alfasi. His student Joseph *Ḥabiba completed the work on Alfasi and concentrated particularly on the classification of decisions, a practice which made him a favorite of later codifiers.

During the 15th century, a period of turmoil, significant scholarship declined but was again prominent in new centers in the 16th century. Obadiah of *Bertinoro, who had moved from Italy to Jerusalem, wrote his major exposition on the Mishnah, which is the standard commentary included in all editions. It discusses every order and does not only explain the words, but explicates entire passages, illuminating them with the discussions of the *Gemara.* Another commentator of the East, Bezalel *Ashkenazi of Egypt, in *Shitah Mekubbeẓet* excerpted and arranged the interpretations of a large number of commentators on difficult passages of the Talmud. He employed *tosafot,* Arabic commentaries, and commentators who were not well known and whose work would otherwise have been lost.

The 16th century also saw the rise of Poland as a major center of Jewish learning. The migration of German scholars to Poland initiated a period of activity which continued until the tragic end of Polish Jewry in the 20th century. In 1507 Jacob b. Joseph *Pollak, the most eminent of these scholars, headed the academy at Cracow where he continued his work for three decades. He developed the method of *ḥilluk* in the study of Talmud, i.e., division and analysis. It consisted of taking an apparently unified talmudic subject, dissecting it into its component parts, drawing shades of distinction and building up a new subject out of the newly defined parts. Pollak, however, left no books. His younger contemporary, Solomon b. Jehiel *Luria, the first important talmudic commentator of Poland, wrote *Yam shel Shelomo* which is essentially a code and partly a commentary, on seven tractates of the Talmud, presented in a plain, non-pilpulistic style. A second work, *Ḥokhmat Shelomo,* consists of glosses and comments on the entire Talmud, on Rashi, and on *tosafot.* The great merit of the work is in its corrections of the texts and it is considered so significant that the relevant comments are incorporated at the back of each talmudic tractate. The novellae of Meir b. Gedaliah *Lublin and Samuel Eliezer *Edels, two important scholars of the next generation, were essentially comments on Rashi and *tosafot* rather than on the *Gemara.* Those of Edels, more deeply penetrating, applied the tosafist method of posing challenges to the text in order to arrive at a new and more cogent answer.

Leading lights of the 17th century were Yom Tov Lipmann *Heller and Meir b. Jacob ha-Kohen *Schiff. Heller, in response to the need of Mishnah study groups which had become common and to what he felt were inadequacies in previous commentaries, composed a major commentary on the Mishnah, entitled *Tosafot Yom Tov* ("The Glosses of Yom Tov"). Basing himself upon Obadiah of Bertinoro's commentary, he expanded the material and introduced philosophic and ethical views. Schiff wrote extensive and very terse novellae on the entire Talmud with the intention of setting forth plain meaning, but only the comments on ten of the tractates remain, the others having been destroyed in a fire in 1711.

Penei Yehoshu'a, an 18th-century collection of novellae to most of the Talmud by Jacob Joshua *Falk is distinguished by keen analysis and brilliance. The work has remained an accepted reference book to students of the Talmud. Ezekiel b. Judah *Landau (18th century), whose major reputation is that of a writer of responsa, and who was considered the leading rabbinic authority of his time, also wrote a highly pilpulistic collection of novellae, *Ẓelaḥ* (in Hebrew the initials of "Monument to a Living Soul").

Codes. Works of codification exceeded books of commentary during this period. The code of Maimonides, since it lacked sources and was a specifically Sephardi work, did not end the process of code making. Codes continued to be written among Franco-German and Spanish Jews, and, at the end of the period, among Jews in Poland. The form followed the pattern of the previous era: a compendium, a digest of the talmudic discussion, arrangement according to the precepts of the Torah, arrangements according to the order in the Pentateuch, and compilation of groups of kindred laws. In the Franco-German region the first great code of the period was *Sefer Mitzvot Gadol* ("The Large Book of Precepts," also called *Semag*), by *Moses b. Jacob of Coucy (13th century). Basing himself on the 613 precepts, which he divided into affirmative and negative precepts, Moses distinguishes six categories of laws and in giving both the law and the sources, relies not only on the Talmud, but on later authorities as well. He does not limit himself to legal matters only, but discusses beliefs and ethics and cites Jewish philosophers. The Hebrew style is clear and excellent, and is similar to that of Maimonides. The *Semag* was inevitably followed by the *Semak* (*Sefer Mitzvot Katan,* "The Small Book of Precepts") by *Isaac b. Joseph of Corbeil (late 13th century). The book, designed for the scholarly layman rather than the scholar, classifies Jewish law into seven categories, but is much more sparing in the citation of sources than the *Semag.* Two other distinguished codes of the 13th century were *Or Zaru'a,* by Isaac b. Moses of Vienna, and *Mordekhai,* by *Mordecai b. Hillel ha-Kohen of Nuremberg. *Or Zaru'a,* a compendium rather than a code, cites sources copiously. It is intended for scholars, and is particularly useful because of its extensive resort to post-talmudic sources and decisions. *Mordekhai* is badly arranged and seems to be a source book for a code rather than the finished product. It comprehends, however, a great mass of material and cites many responsa on the subjects it treats. Both works were employed extensively by later codifiers as sources.

The 13th-century Italian school is represented by the *Shibbolei ha-Leket* of Zedekiah b. Abraham *Anav in which the author limits himself to the rituals and festivals. Employing the code method, he also presents a selection of material from other codes and responsa, including the opinions of Italian scholars. A digest of it, entitled *Tanya,* designed for popular use, was prepared by Jehiel b. Jekuthiel *Anav.

The great codes of the period were composed by Spanish Jews. They tend to be more systematic, less rigorous in decision, and less guided by custom than the Franco-German works. Among the 13th-century codes were some small works by Naḥmanides and the *Torat ha-Bayit* ("Household Laws"), by Solomon b. Abraham Adret, devoted to laws of the Jewish home. Adret, applying the same method, commented and interpreted extensively. He also wrote a résumé which appears in the margin of the book. Particularly noteworthy is the pedagogical work, *Sefer *ha-Ḥinnukh* ("Book of Education") attributed to Aaron ha-Levi of Barcelona which arranges the *mitzvot* according to the weekly portions of the Torah, discusses their origin, their ethical meaning, and their application. He does not quote sources, but indicates where they may be found. The book, written in excellent Hebrew, was and continues to be popular. The first major 13th-century code, *Piskei ha-Rosh,* the compendium of Asher b. Jehiel, a German-trained scholar who emigrated to Spain, bears the imprint of both the German and the Spanish schools. Its great value is that while it follows the Alfasi method of paraphrasing the Talmud section by section, it goes far beyond that. Alfasi relies on the Talmud, the *geonim,* and himself. Asher b. Jehiel brings to bear all the weight of preceding codes, commentaries, and responsa, with particular emphasis on the discussions of the Franco-German schools. Enjoying great authority the decisions of the work are quoted in later codes and were used as a basis in *Sefer ha-Turim* (Tur) written by Jacob, Asher b. Jehiel's son. *Sefer ha-Turim* takes the rulings of Asher b. Jehiel as a basis for an entire code of Jewish law, excluding those which ceased to operate with the destruction of the Temple. The title refers to the four rows *(turim)* on the breastplate of the high priest. Jacob b. Asher consequently divided his code into four sections: (1) *Tur Oraḥ Ḥayyim* on daily religious conduct, the Sabbath, and the festivals; (2) *Tur Yoreh De'ah* on prohibited and permitted things, e.g., dietary laws, laws of purity, etc.; (3) *Tur Even ha-Ezer* on the laws of family relations; (4) *Tur Ḥoshen Mishpat* on civil law. The code provides decisions without sources and includes Franco-German and Spanish views. Clear in content, style, decision, and authority, it was accepted as the authoritative code for a large segment of Jewry for several centuries. The attempt by *Jeroham b. Meshullam of Provence, a pupil of Asher b. Jehiel, to codify *Piskei ha-Rosh* resulted in a pure code on all of Jewish law, except civil law, which is entitled *Toledot Adam ve-Ḥavvah.* The work was well regarded, but did not win general acceptance.

The work which finally became the decisive code of Jewry was that of Joseph b. Ephraim *Caro who was born in Spain, moved to Bulgaria, and ultimately to Safed. His great work, *Beit Yosef,* which Caro conceived of as a commentary to *Sefer ha-Turim,* was designed to include other opinions and to expand the source references in *Sefer ha-Turim.* It emerged, however, as an independent work which utilized the fourfold form of organization of *Sefer ha-Turim,* traced the development of laws, cited various opinions and the reasons for them, and finally concluded with Caro's decision. As a preparatory manual of study for the work, Caro composed the *Shulḥan Arukh which is arranged in the same way, but generally gives only one opinion and one decision and limits each paragraph to a specific point of law, a pattern which facilitates study and decision. In formulating decisions, Caro was guided by three earlier codes: Alfasi, Maimonides, and Asher b. Jehiel. His approach was to rely on any two opinions against the third. The code, essentially Sephardi in outlook, became the definitive code of Jewry and has remained so to the present day.

As it was written the Shulḥan Arukh was not acceptable to Franco-German and Polish (Ashkenazi) Jewry. Solomon Luria protested against it and a way of meeting this protest was devised by Moses b. Israel *Isserles. Apart from other works, Isserles undertook an addition to the Shulḥan Arukh, *Mappat ha-Shulḥan,* in which he set forth the Ashkenazi view and, in case of controversy, rendered decision according to that outlook. In addition, he noted customs prevalent among Ashkenazi Jewry, raising many of them to the status of law. On the whole, he was more rigorous than Caro. But there are many instances where he is more lenient, notably in the case of *hefsed merubbeh,* instances involving a considerable loss. It was the Caro-Isserles Shulḥan Arukh which became the universal code.

While it was still struggling for universal acceptance, other codes were being formulated. The most important was *Levush* by Mordecai b. Abraham *Jaffe of Prague and Poland. He set out to create a code, midway between *Beit Yosef,* which he deemed too lengthy, and the Shulḥan Arukh, which he thought too brief. His method was to state a decision and to give the history of the law. His decisions frequently differed from those of Caro and Isserles. For a time, it appeared that this work might supplant the Shulḥan Arukh but in the end the Shulḥan Arukh prevailed both because of the errors in *Levush* and the power of the combined authority of Caro and Isserles.

Although a definitive code had finally been produced, it proved, like all the others, to be imperfect both in itself and because new situations continued to arise for decision and codification. The result was that an entire field of commentaries on the various codes arose of which 186 commentaries on the Maimonidean code alone have survived, and there were doubtless many more. The first important commentary on the Maimonidean code, that of Shem Tov b. Abraham *ibn Gaon (14th century) of Spain, entitled *Migdal Oz,* sought to classify Maimonides' way of reasoning in the code. Don *Vidal Yom Tov of Tolosa, Spain, defended the Maimonidean system in his *Maggid Mishneh* as did Caro in his *Kesef Mishneh. Sefer ha-Turim* was equally the subject of commentaries, the best known (apart from *Beit Yosef*) being *Darkhei Moshe* ("The Ways of Moses") by Isserles, which was essentially a polemic against Caro and was the foundation of his later glosses to the Shulḥan Arukh. The best commentaries on *Sefer ha-Turim* were those of Jacob Joshua Falk and *Bayit Ḥadash* by Joel *Sirkes. Falk added explanations, decisions, and sources to *Sefer ha-Turim,* while Sirkes sought to reestablish it as the decisive code in place of the Shulḥan Arukh.

The Shulḥan Arukh was also the subject of numerous commentaries which finally set the seal of authority upon it. David b. Samuel ha-Levi in *Turei Zahav* (abbr. as *TaZ* and meaning "Golden Rows") defended the rulings of the Shulḥan Arukh, quoted contrary opinions, and arrived at final decisions. *Siftei Kohen* (abbr. as *ShaKh* and meaning "The Lips of the Priest") was similarly motivated; it explained the sources of the code and attempted to harmonize the difference between Caro and Isserles. Characterized by intellectual brilliance and logical acumen, both works became the standard commentaries on the Shulḥan Arukh (see *Codification of Law).

Responsa. In the third major category of rabbinic literature of the period, responsa, there was remarkable productivity; the number of collections runs into several thousands, and thousands of others are still in manuscript. They were composed because life outstripped the codes and new problems arose which were either not properly dealt with in the codes or not included in them. Since the early Middle Ages every major rabbinic figure answered questions and the responsa, essentially essays in law, were either collected by himself or by others. These served as supplements to the codes and as bases for later codes.

Medieval responsa should be divided into two time periods: the 13th century to the end of the 15th, during which the rabbis responded to conditions in the Franco-German region and in Spain, and the 16th century through the 18th when Jewish life was centered in the East, in Germany, and in Poland. Responsa reflect Jewish life of the times and thus differ greatly in content. The responsa from Spain and the East where Jewish life was in greater contact with the surrounding world and enjoyed a larger measure of autonomy testify to greater judicial authority, more severe punishments, better communal organization, and more cases dealing with moral behavior than other parts of the Jewish Diaspora. Spanish responsa also discussed questions of philosophy and theology, whereas the German-Polish questions centered mostly around law. The greater seclusion in Germany and Poland and the greater persecution are reflected in the frequent cases dealing with taxes, special levies, religious questions, cases of women whose husbands had disappeared *(agunot)* and the like (see *Responsa).

Responsa (1250–1500). The most important collections of Spanish responsa are those of Solomon b. Abraham

Adret and Asher b. Jehiel. Adret's extant responsa number 3,000 of a possible original 7,000. Almost one-half of them deal with civil law and commercial affairs and thus reveal much about Jewish life in Spain. They reflect strong community organization, the power of leaders to fix prices, regulate promissory notes, and establish and prohibit study patterns. Philosophic and theological questions comprise another large section, including discussions on the relation between *mitzvot* and intention *(kavannah)*. A third group deals with religious and family problems. Asher's 1,500 responsa are concerned essentially with *halakhah*. They indicate that Jews had and exercised the power of capital punishment and that the community had great power to regulate economic, spiritual, and moral life. Two other collections of the period, those of Isaac b. Sheshet Perfet (14th century), a Spaniard who ultimately became rabbi of Algiers, and his successor Simeon b. Ẓemaḥ Duran, a mathematician and grammarian, reflect, apart from other matters, the turbulence of life in Spain at the end of the 14th century and the complicated problem of the Marranos. Duran also responded to many questions on mathematics and grammar.

The number of surviving collections of responsa from Germany (13th to 15th centuries) is not extensive but those that are extant are illuminating. Meir of Rothenburg wrote several thousand responsa on questions of lending with interest to gentiles, the duties and salaries of teachers, the import and export business. Jacob Moellin left some 200 responsa on civil law and family life and Jacob b. Judah *Weil, his disciple, deals extensively with community affairs. The responsa of Israel b. Pethahiah *Isserlein and Israel b. Ḥayyim *Bruna mirror the rigorous piety of medieval Germany, indicating the importance that customs assumed and their endorsement by the writers of responsa. During the same period Joseph Colon was writing responsa which reflect contemporaneous life in Italy. Among other things they point to the low scholarly level of the rabbinate in Italy, to the state of the medical profession among Jews, and to the fact that some physicians formed partnerships. The responsa of Judah b. Eliezer ha-Levi *Minz and Meir b. Isaac *Katzenellenbogen (16th century) broaden the picture of Italian Jewish life, indicating that the moral tone was rather lax in the upper stratum. The general tenor of the Italian responsa reflects, in contrast to Germany, a spirit of liberalism and a readiness to deal with problems arising out of the confrontation of Jews with the life of the general society.

Responsa (1500–1750). With the expulsion from Spain a large part of Spanish Jewry migrated to the East where an indigenous Jewish community had continued to exist. As a result intellectual activity greatly increased. Even before the exile, R. Elijah b. Abraham *Mizraḥi, a native of Constantinople and the chief rabbi of Turkey, had won a reputation as a major figure both in Jewish and secular learning. His responsa, reflecting Jewish life in Turkey, testify to the great autonomy enjoyed by the community. The rabbi was the recognized intermediary between the government and the community and the assessor of taxes for the Jews. Soon afterward *David b. Solomon ibn Abi Zimra, a native of Spain who had served as chief rabbi of Cairo for 40 years, became the leading Jewish authority in the East. His 3,000 responsa (of which 1,300 have been preserved) present a picture of life in Eastern lands. They indicate that polygamy was practiced, that the Jewish laws of emancipation regarding slaves were still in force, and that relations with Karaites were closer than they had been in earlier centuries, but had deteriorated since the time of Maimonides. Theological questions point to varied beliefs about dogma. Other important collections of the 15th and 16th centuries are those of Moses b. Isaac *Alashkar of Cairo, Jacob *Berab, *Levi b. Ḥabib, and Moses b. Joseph *Trani. The responsa of Trani have some particularly interesting comments about the role of Jews in the export trade and about a boycott organized by Turkish Jewish traders, at the instigation of Dona Gracia *Nasi, against the papal port of Ancona, Italy, as a reprisal against the pope for the burning at the stake of Marranos there (see *Responsa).

Methodology. A fourth area of rabbnic study, methodology, namely the rules of talmudic logic, the terms employed, and how decisions are made, which had scarcely been touched during the early Middle Ages, developed considerably in the 18th century. *Samson b. Isaac of Chinon (France) and *Jeshua b. Joseph ha-Levi of North Africa had dealt with the subject in the 14th and 15th centuries, respectively. The first major work on methodology however was *Yad Malakhi*, by *Malachi b. Jacob ha-Kohen (middle of the 18th century), which discusses 667 talmudic rules and terms, arranged in alphabetical order. Some sections are extended essays, such as the essay on the authenticity of halakhic statements which were transmitted by disciples in the name of their teachers. Another part of the book discusses the methods of the great codifiers. Isaac *Lampronti of Italy, in *Paḥad Yiẓḥak*, the second major work of the period, has arranged all the subjects and terms treated in talmudic and rabbinic literature in alphabetical order. Included are also talmudic sources and the views of codifiers and writers of responsa.

PHILOSOPHY AND THEOLOGY

Jewish philosophy in the Middle Ages while quantitatively less than exegetical, halakhic, and poetic writings was nonetheless substantial and of high quality. As in the Hellenistic period, medieval Jewish philosophy was born out of a confrontation with other cultures. By the eighth century, Aristotle and Plato had been translated into Arabic and Islam tried to reconcile religion and reason through the philosophy of *Kalam* (meaning "word"). Judaism was also experiencing internal problems: the Karaites rejected the Talmud and *Ḥiwi al-Balkhi (late ninth century) represented a school of thought which violently attacked the Bible. Jewish philosophy, primarily theological, sought to defend Jewish religion against philosophic attack, and to found the principles of belief on a speculative basis. Scholarly writings thus were directed toward metaphysics and related fields and to a philosophical interpretation of the Bible. These literary activities were undergirded by writings and translations in logic, psychology, and the sciences. Jews also made a significant contribution in these disciplines and other spheres as cultural intermediaries between the Islamic and Christian worlds.

The earliest Jewish medieval philosophers (9th to 11th centuries) wrote in Arabic. David ibn Marwān *al-Mukammis of Babylon in *Book of Twenty Tractates* advances proofs for the existence of God; Isaac b. Solomon *Israeli of Kairouan, in *Book of the Elements*, sought to defend the doctrine of creation against the theory of the eternity of matter. *Emunot ve-De'ot* ("Doctrines and Beliefs"), by Saadiah Gaon, attempts to prove the compatibility of revelation, Torah, and reason. Saadiah posited ten basic principles, founding them on a theory of knowledge through which he established the existence and nature of God, the need for revelation, and the reasons for revealed doctrines and *mitzvot*. In his ethics he advocated the middle road between the contending forces in human nature. With regard to the Jewish people, he asserted that it was a people only by reason of the Torah. After Saadiah, Spain became the center of Jewish philosophy where the first philosopher of note was the brilliant young poet Solomon ibn Gabirol whose major philosophic work *Mekor Ḥayyim* (originally Arabic, Latin *Fons Vitae*, 1150) had until the 19th century been ascribed to an Arab named "Avicebron." The book deviates from traditional medieval Jewish philosophy, being closer in tone to neoplatonism. It is a religious philosophic work concerned with personal salvation and with man's purpose and its thesis is that the human soul, which has been united with matter, seeks to return to its source through reason and contemplation. In this connection it discusses God, a theory of emanations, the world (composed of matter and form), and creation. *Mekor Ḥayyim*, which had a considerable effect in Christian circles, was rather less accepted among Jews, although Ibn Gabirol's thinking, often unattributed, was incorporated into Jewish mystical thought. About the same time, *Baḥya b. Joseph ibn Paquda, in *Ḥovot ha-Levavot* ("The Duties of the Heart"), primarily ethical in content, and in *Torat ha-Nefesh* ("The Doctrine of the Soul"), a philosophic work, advanced the theory of design as a proof of God's existence. He proposed the doctrine of negative attributes of God and developed a theory of emanations.

The first philosophic book in Hebrew is *Abraham b. Ḥiyya's *Hegyon ha-Nefesh ha-Aẓuvah* ("Meditation of the Sad Soul") where he sets forth the theory that the world was first created in potentiality and then actualized by the word. The microcosm doctrine was propounded by *Joseph b. Ẓaddik (in his *Olam Katan*—"the Microcosm"): man is a microcosm and can know the world by knowing himself. With Judah Halevi the emphasis in Jewish philosophy shifted. His *Kuzari* is a philosophy of Judaism which seeks to prove that the truths of revealed religion are superior to those of reason and that God is best understood through Jewish history. It is also a philosophy of history whose theme is that Israel is the heart of the nations, endowed with a prophetic capacity, and that the Torah is the expression of the Will of God. Within the framework of Jewish and human endeavors, he assigns a central role to the Land of Israel. Literarily, the *Sefer ha-Kuzari* is distinctive in Jewish philosophy since it is composed as a dialogue and is founded on a historical event (the conversion of the Khazars to Judaism). Abraham ibn Ezra, however, reverting to the more conventional approach, proposes that God's Will flashing through the upper, middle, and lower worlds is the staying power for everything and that spirituality is resident in everything in the universe. Abraham ibn Daud (12th century) of Toledo also discusses familiar themes along Aristotelian lines, but pays great attention to the problem of free will and providence. Asserting that God knows man's options but not his choice, Ibn Daud discusses providence and suggests that there are gradations in providence which depend upon how earnestly a man strives for the knowledge of God.

The master work of Jewish philosophy, a synthesis of the Jewish philosophic process, is Moses Maimonides' *Guide of the Perplexed* which was written in Arabic in 1190. Studied by Christians and Moslems, it had a deep effect on scholastic literature apart from its influence on all of Jewish thought. Maimonides, indicating that he is writing for those who know philosophy but are perplexed about contradictions between philosophy and religion, touches upon specific problems and often takes the biblical verse and expressions as his framework. Discussing anthropomorphism, he deals with proofs for the existence of God and with His attributes which, he asserts, can only be understood negatively. He rejects the doctrine of the eternity of matter as unproved and propounds the concept of *creatio ex nihilo*, in accordance with the Torah which he holds to be immutable. He contends that the Torah is designed to guide the body, the body politic, and the soul and to help a man endowed with sufficient contemplative capacity to achieve union with the active intellect in the universe and thus gain immortality. Other major themes in *Guide of the Perplexed* are Divine providence, which is presented as graduated according to man's capacity; evil, which is largely the work of man; and ethics, to which the Torah directs man.

The Maimonidean synthesis was almost immediately challenged in commentaries and in different systems as Jewish philosophy expanded its scope and embarked upon new ventures. Two main factors contributed to this development: (a) The major Arabic works in philosophy, translations and commentaries of the Greek philosophers, and original works of the Arabic philosophers, were translated into Hebrew along with the works of the Jewish philosophers. Thus *Plato, *Aristotle, Al-*Farabi, *Avicenna, Al-*Ghazali, and *Averroes became available to Hebrew readers in Christian Spain and Provence who did not know Arabic. Among the distinguished translators were Judah ibn *Tibbon (12th century), his son Samuel, and his son Moses. Other translators were Jacob b. Abba Mari *Anatoli (13th century), Jacob b. Machir Tibbon (13th century), and Kalonymus b. Kalonymus (14th century), all of Provence. In the same period the task of translating Latin philosophic works into Hebrew was also undertaken (see *Translators and Translations). (b) A Hebrew philosophic terminology was created. The way was now open to Jews, whose major literary language was Hebrew and whose audience read Hebrew, to engage in philosophic writing.

Once the basic philosophic language was developed and works were translated into Hebrew, several new spheres were open to Jewish philosophy, one of which was commentary. Some scholars wrote commentaries on Arabic and Greek philosophers, among them: Levi b. Gershom (14th century), on Averroes; *Moses b. Joshua of Narbonne on Averroes and Al-Ghazali, and Joseph *ibn Shem Tov and *Judah b. Jehiel Messer Leon on Aristotle. *Guide of the Perplexed* frequently served as the basis for commentaries which were often original works. The earliest commentary, *Moreh ha-Moreh* ("The Guide of the Guide"), by Shem Tov Falaquera compiles extensive excerpts from Arabic and Jewish philosophers on subjects treated by Maimonides. *Maskiyyot Kesef* by Joseph *Kaspi represents the highly rationalistic Provençal school which set philosophic principles above tradition. Kaspi denies that *creatio ex nihilo* is a Jewish dogma and interprets the creation story, not literally, but in philosophic terms. Other commentaries, which are essentially explanatory and are usually printed with the text of *Guide of the Perplexed*, were those of Profiat Duran and Asher (Bonan) b. Abraham *Crescas.

Another field developed from the 13th century onward but treated only cursorily in the past is psychology. Averroes' restatement of Aristotle reflects the basic problem of psychology. For Averroes, the active intellect is not an integral part of the soul, but an immaterial substance, derived from the universal intellect, which unites with the soul during a man's life and returns to its source at death, without retaining any individuality. Thus the religious beliefs in personal immortality and reward and punishment came under attack. *Hillel b. Samuel of Verona, Italy, discusses these problems and related points in *Tagmulei ha-Nefesh* ("The Rewards of the Soul"). He attempts to establish that the intellect is not only part of the soul, but is the actual form of the soul which directs all its forces. It is at once eternal and yet retains its individuality so that it is subject to reward and punishment which he conceives as elevation to a higher level of contemplation or awareness of degradation. In proving and pursuing his contentions, Hillel necessarily deals with the question of free will and

God's foreknowledge which he resolves by asserting that necessity and possibility are inherent in the very nature of man and that God conceives every human action as a possibility. Approaching the same question from another point of view, Shem Tov Falaquera composed his *Sefer ha-Nefesh* ("The Book of the Soul") in the spirit that "knowledge of the soul leads to knowledge of God." Like Hillel, he concludes that the soul is immortal and individual and ultimately unites with the universal intellect. Through these works psychology became part of Jewish philosophic speculation and it has been reflected in the mainstream of Jewish philosophy since the 13th century.

The first major philosophic figure after Maimonides was Levi b. Gershom, also a translator and Bible commentator, whose main work, *Milḥamot Adonai* ("The Battles of the Lord"), like Maimonides' is Aristotelian in outlook, but differs from his in that it gives precedence to philosophic conclusions over biblical teachings. He substitutes for *creatio ex nihilo* the notion that the world, created in time and by the will of God, was shaped out of chaos or formless matter. He further asserts that positive attributes apply both to God and to man, though in different degree. Levi b. Gershom deals with a wide variety of problems, including psychology and the immortality of the soul, freedom of will, divine providence, and cosmology. In general he follows the Aristotelian view of the world and the soul, as modified by Arabic philosophers and by neoplatonists. He affirms the immortality of the individual soul in terms of his system in which the sum total of a man's thoughts of God and the order of the universe constitute the immortal soul whose reward, after death, consists not of new knowledge but of greater clarity about knowledge acquired during life. Providence, he contends, equally depends upon man's attainment and consists not in miracles but in prior awareness of potential difficulties. Man has individual freedom because God knows and predetermines the general order of events and of possibilities, but not which of the possibilities available to a man will be realized in a single life.

Aristotelianism runs its course with Levi b. Gershom; his major successor, Ḥasdai *Crescas of Barcelona, a man of highly critical and innovative faculties, no longer blindly accepts either "the philosopher" or Maimonides but criticizes them both. His major work, *Or Adonai* ("Light of the Lord," completed 1410, published in Ferrara, 1555), designed as a section of a two-part work embracing both *halakhah* and philosophy, is essentially a work on dogmatics in which, after extended philosophic analysis, Crescas sets forth dogmas of the Jewish faith that differ, both in detail and in emphasis, from many of those of Maimonides. He is motivated partly by his emphasis on emotion and action in religion, rather than speculation, and partly by a desire to dispute certain Christian teachings. Attacking Maimonides' proof of the existence of God, which is based upon Aristotelian doctrine that there cannot be infinite space or infinite causes, Crescas offers a novel proof, that there is a being, God, who is the necessary cause of all existence. The existence of God is one of the basic roots that Crescas posits. In his theory of attributes, he asserts that the attributes of God are essential, positive, and infinite in number and extent. God is goodness and he speaks of God's infinite happiness in His infinite love for His creatures. Crescas applies critical analysis and originality to the themes of free will, reward and punishment and immortality, and providence, all of which he affirms. His views were challenged by the talmudist and writer of responsa Simeon b. Ẓemaḥ Duran of Algeria whose *Magen Avot* ("The Shield of the Fathers") defends the Maimonidean viewpoint. Essentially concerned with dogmatics, Duran uses the Mishnah Sanhedrin 10:1 "All Israelites have a share in the world to come . . ." to classify Maimonides' 13 principles under three major headings: the existence of God, the divine origin of the Torah, and reward and punishment. His philosophic statement is basically a synthesis of Maimonides and Levi b. Gershom, though he is more conservative than either in asserting that Divine providence extends to all men regardless of intellectual capacity.

A contemporary of Duran, Joseph *Albo of Spain, evolved a philosophic system which borrowed largely from Maimonides and Crescas, but added new ideas to the field of dogmatics. Albo reacting to the strong pressure of Christianity upon the Jewish population, sought to standardize the principles of Jewish religion, and to demonstrate that philosophy and religion go hand in hand. In *Ikkarim* ("Principles") he employs the same threefold classification of Jewish dogmas as Duran but takes the classification further. He defines God, revelation, and reward and punishment as universal characteristics of divine religion and distinguishes between a conventional religion rising out of social life and a divine religion which is revealed. He asserts that these three principles must be accepted on faith if necessary, although they can be buttressed by reason. What distinguishes an individual religion, however, is a series of secondary dogmas which must be justified by reason. Besides these, a Jew must accept another six doctrines which though obligatory are not principles: *creatio ex nihilo*, the *sui generis* nature of the prophecy of Moses, the immutability of the Torah, the capability of even one precept to perfect the human soul, resurrection, and the coming of the Messiah. The entire work is written in a lucid and popular style, and became a favorite Jewish work.

The last of the Spanish philosophers, Don Isaac Abrabanel, wrote a considerable number of philosophic works on specific topics. Widely read in Jewish, Arabic, and Christian philosophy, Abrabanel draws on his extensive and versatile knowledge to explicate and give a full view of the philosophical problems which he discusses. Following his exegetical method, Abrabanel in his philosophic works also poses a series of objections to a theory and then proceeds to answer them one by one. While he tends toward Maimonides' philosophic view, he is even more traditional in his concept of Providence, rejecting the idea that Providence depends on the intelligence of man. He also repudiates the rational theories of prophecy and miracles, regarding prophecy as a direct influence from God, not dependent on intellectual excellence. *Dialoghi di Amore* (1535), a philosophical work by his son, Judah *Abrabanel, which is written in Italian and in dialogue form, alludes profusely to classical mythology. Renaissance in tone, its theme is outside the conventional stream of Jewish philosophy and centers mainly around the concept of love of God and how it affects the soul and the concept of the beautiful. Love is the principle which permeates and unites the universe, extending from God through all creation and back to Him. The influence of the treatise was greater in general thought than in Jewish life since it discusses only few distinctly Jewish themes.

The severe criticism of the rationalistic tendency in the development of philosophy throughout the 13th, 14th, and 15th centuries elicited defenses by scholars who also partly shared the view that rationalism had gone too far. They attempted to indicate that philosophy and religion were separate domains and to assert that while philosophic truths were worthy of study and were proper guides, the Torah pointed to still higher truths and ways of life. The notable proponents of this view were the 15th-century

Spanish thinkers Abraham *Bibago b. Shem Tov and Joseph ibn Shem Tov. The latter cautioned, however, that the basic principles of religion must agree with logical truth. In the interpretation of the Torah he distinguished between law, which he accepted, and opinion, which need not necessarily be accepted.

The last major philosophic figure of the Jewish Middle Ages was Baruch *Spinoza. Though the *Ethics* belong to the sphere of general rather than Jewish philosophy, it was clearly influenced by Jewish thought, most notably by Crescas, from whom he borrowed much. Spinoza's pantheistic view, however, at odds with the Jewish philosophic approach took him in different philosophic directions. Nevertheless *Tractatus-Theologicus-Politicus* is a distinctly Jewish work which examines the Old Testament critically and, in effect, initiates modern biblical criticism. Spinoza discusses exhaustively the election of Israel, prophecy, miracles, the dogmas of faith, the constitution of the Hebrew state, and the authority of the state in religious matters. His purpose was to defend freedom of thought against religious authority, thus establishing a distinction between religion and philosophic speculation. He contends that prophecy is characterized by imagination and not by speculation, and proceeds to work out the dogmas of universal religion which very much resembles those of Crescas. Having distinguished between religion and philosophy, Spinoza proceeds to a discussion of the state which he conceives as founded upon a social contract that protects the right of every man to freedom of thought. Since Spinoza is clearly fighting with the Jewish authorities and attempting to show that they are misrepresenting Judaism, the book is partly a polemic. A fundamental point developed in the work is that the scriptural laws were given for the Jewish body politic and lost their cogency, as did of course rabbinic law, after the destruction of the state. Even for the Jews only the moral laws remain binding. In this approach Spinoza foreshadows Reform Judaism (see *Philosophy).

ETHICS

The distinction between philosophy and ethics in the Jewish Middle Ages was not very clear, since both fields centered around religious premises and Torah and the application of these to life. Accordingly, most of the philosophic works also discussed ethics or at least, were ethical in their implications. Nonetheless, there was a considerable corpus of writings whose purpose was distinctly ethical. Most of them are essentially pietistic or, like the *aggadah*, infused with the moral implications of biblical verses. Some of them, however, primarily works from Spain and Provence, presented formal ethical systems. Solomon ibn Gabirol's *Tikkun Middot ha-Nefesh* ("Improvement of the Moral Qualities"), written in Arabic, was the first noteworthy effort in this field. Predicated on psychological and physiological bases rather than religious premises, Gabirol's thesis conceives the soul as consisting of two parts: the higher, which strives for union with God, and the lower, the seat of the moral qualities of daily life. He proposed to teach the art of training and cultivating the soul. *Ḥovot ha-Levavot*, by Baḥya ibn Paquda, a more important and accepted work, has as its central thesis man's gratitude and relationship to God which the author posits as the yardstick of moral behavior. After establishing a metaphysical foundation for his analysis in the first portal (section), Baḥya devotes nine portals to such virtues as sympathy, action for its own sake, meekness, and the harmonization of reason and passion. Altogether different in tone is **Sefer Ḥasidim* ("The Book of the Pious"), a 12th-century Franco-German work attributed to *Judah b. Samuel he-Ḥasid of Regensburg (c. 1200). Comprised of manuals on ethics and piety, it contains detailed instructions for daily living in the spirit of talmudic and aggadic literature. Its subjects range from worship to marital life, to treatment of servants, to table manners and is abundantly illustrated with stories. Though marked by strong superstition, the work is imbued with a spirit of piety and ethical sensitivity. It enjoyed great popularity in its time and for many generations. An equally popular, though distinctly formal work, was the *Shemoneh Perakim* ("Eight Chapters") of Maimonides which constituted the introduction to his commentary on *Pirkei Avot*. Writing as though he were "a doctor of the soul," Maimonides suggests that there are good dispositions and bad ones, that man is a free agent and a *tabula rasa*, and that he can be educated to the good. He proposes "the middle way" as the norm of conduct.

By the 13th century, ethical literature began to proliferate, although formal, analytical systems were on the decline. Among the important books of the century were *Sha'arei Teshuvah* ("The Gates of Repentance") by *Jonah b. Abraham Gerondi and *Kad ha-Kemaḥ* by Baḥya b. Asher. Gerondi discusses the ways that arouse a man to repentance, the nature of repentance and forgiveness, and the obligatory precepts incumbent upon a Jew. He is particularly forceful in his demand for the observance of community enactments which, he says, are designed to strengthen the Jewish community and religion and thus to sanctify the name of God. Baḥya, like Jonah, writing from a religious point of view, arranges his subject matter alphabetically and discusses a wide variety of themes. Among his observations is the view that Jews are dispersed so that they may fulfill the mission of living like a model nation and spreading the knowledge of the One God and His Providence. Once the mission is fulfilled redemption will come.

**Sefer ha-Yashar*, an anonymous ethical work which was mistakenly attributed to Jacob b. Meir Tam and to *Zerahiah ha-Yevani, is of the 14th century. The author saw the people of his time as being so engrossed in the pursuit of riches and pleasure that they needed to be redirected to the love of God and right conduct. Making an appeal both to reason and piety, he emphasizes, in the manner of Baḥya, the awe of God, the wonder of the world, and the need to imitate God and thus fulfill the purpose of creation and of perfecting man. Less theoretical, and more given to the practical exposition of behavior, are: the 14th-century work, *Menorat ha-Ma'or* ("Candelabrum of Light") by Israel b. Joseph *al-Nakawa of Spain, which concentrates on the meaning and application of specific *mitzvot* like loving-kindness and the Sabbath, and the anonymous 15th-century treatise, *Orḥat Ẓaddikim* ("The Way of the Righteous"), stemming from Germany, which examines the art of training the soul to seek the good.

The major work of the period, also called *Menorat ha-Ma'or*, by Isaac *Aboab of Toledo, enjoyed great popularity. In contrast to contemporary trends, Aboab stressed the importance of the *aggadah* whose teachings were concerned with the education of the soul. The author, as stated in his preface, wrote the book with the explicit purpose of giving instruction to all in practical ethics. He bases his work on three principles set forth in Psalm 34:15 "Depart from evil, and do good; seek peace and pursue it," which he divides into seven categories characterized as the seven *nerot* (lamps) that make up the "candelabrum of light." Avoiding evil involves neither desiring nor speaking evil; doing good demands the observance of the *mitzvot*, the study of the Torah, and repentance; pursuing peace calls for love and meekness. Fusing philosophic speculation and mysticism, the book is an exposition of the meaning and application of these seven qualities. The text is richly interwoven with allegories and parables drawn from the *aggadah* which serve as illustrations to the author's instruction. A spate of other books appeared in subsequent centuries. Among them, *Reshit Ḥokhmah* ("The Beginning of Wisdom") of Elijah b. Moses de *Vidas, written in a mystical spirit, and the many commentaries on *Pirkei Avot* which elaborated the ethical approach to life. Notable among the latter, in addition to the commentaries of Rashi, Maimonides, and Bertinoro, were those of Simeon Duran, Joseph b. Ḥayyim *Jabez and Judah b. Samuel *Lerma.

A novel note in ethical works, heralding a new era, appeared about 1705 with *Kav ha-Yashar* ("The Measure of Righteousness") by Ẓevi Hirsch *Koidonover. Neither well ordered nor particularly distinguished, the work is important because it reflects the vigorous and mystical spirit of Polish Jewry, and was written both in Hebrew and in Yiddish (see *Ethical Literature).

ETHICAL WILLS

A body of literature which had a great vogue during the entire Jewish Middle Ages, but most notably from the 11th century onward is the corpus of documents known as "ethical wills." This literature had its precursors in the Bible, the Apocrypha, and the Talmud, but it became common only in the Middle Ages. Ethical wills were written in the form of the communication of a father's experience, insights, and mandates to his son and vary in length, some of them being as large as a small book. These works are important testimonies to the thinking and values of eminent men and reflect the life of different periods and places. One of the earliest extant wills, that of *Eliezer b. Isaac of Worms (11th century), examines the attitude of man to his fellowmen, the fulfilling of *mitzvot*, the rules of hygiene, and the religious tone of life. Judah ibn Tibbon (12th century) in his "testament" urges the study of Torah and science, gives moral and scientific advice to his son, a physician, in the practice of medicine, and offers guidance on how to treat one's wife, children, and books. Writing from Palestine to his oldest son, Naḥman, Naḥmanides advises him on the practice of ethical virtues, especially emphasizing humility so that "every man should seem in thine eyes as one greater than thyself" in some respect. He enjoins his younger son, Solomon, who held a position in the king's court, not to be ensnared by glamour, but to cling to Jewish practice and study and to purity of conduct.

The testament of Asher b. Jehiel addressed to his children is a long work divided into 155 sections and written in an epigrammatic style, stressing honesty and humility, and the giving of charity. His two sons *Judah and *Jacob b. Asher also left testaments. Judah's will, divided into three parts, relates episodes of his life, urges his son to study, enjoins the virtues of truthfulness and humility, and discusses financial matters. In the third section he outlines a scheme for distribution of charity, which constitutes valuable historical data; reckons his salary for 23 years as rabbi of Toledo and directs that as a return his library be dedicated to the use of students. He also incorporates a family agreement to observe the practice of tithe and charity. Suffused with profound piety, the testament of Jacob b. Asher urges love of God to the point of being ready to undergo martyrdom, enjoins against consulting fortune-tellers, and advocates the diligent study of Talmud and the avoidance of casuistry. *Sefer ha-Musar* ("The Book of Morality"), by Joseph Kaspi, a short systematic work on proper behavior written in the form of a will, attempts to enjoin a combination of belief, piety, and ethical behavior based on rational principles. Kaspi discusses the fundamental principles of Judaism which every Jew must apprehend by means of proof and logical reasoning. He, therefore, sets a curriculum of study including Bible, Talmud, mathematics, ethics, law, physics, and logic, culminating with the study of philosophy and theology from the age of 20 on. The work concludes with a defense of the study of philosophy.

The testaments of the 14th and subsequent centuries were written by laymen rather than scholars. Thus *Eliezer b. Samuel ha-Levi (14th century) of Mainz urges his children to live in large Jewish communities so that their offspring may receive a proper Jewish education, warns against card playing and dances, and enjoins the giving of charity and the conduct of household affairs in an orderly manner. Another layman, Solomon Isaac of Provence, is much concerned with study and advises his son always to have a volume of Talmud open so that he might be moved to study.

After the 16th century, testaments are clearly influenced by kabbalistic thought. The most important wills written during the following centuries are by Abraham, Jacob, and Sheftel Horowitz, in the 17th century, and Moses Ḥasid, Alexander Sueskind, Joel b. Abraham Shemariah of Vilna, *Israel b. Eliezer the Ba'al Shem Tov, and *Elijah b. Solomon Zalman, the Gaon of Vilna, in the 18th century. Ethical will literature did not end with the 18th century, but continued to be written down to our own day and to be circulated within families (see Ethical *Wills).

PHILOSOPHIC EXEGESIS

The extensive literature which attempted to harmonize philosophy and religion led to interpretations of the Bible that were extreme, to allegorical explanations, and to commentaries which were basically homiletic. While the approaches of Levi b. Gershom and Isaac Abrabanel were systematic, the works of other scholars were either loosely organized or concentrated on limited themes. The 13th-century work, *Yikkavu ha-Mayim*, by Samuel ibn Tibbon of Provence, is a major example of this type of literature. Starting with the question of creation and committed to proving the truth of the Bible, Ibn Tibbon, with much ingenious philosophic explanation and a moderate use of allegory, discusses angels, Divine providence, and creation. Provence produced a school which interpreted the Bible allegorically, but unfortunately the works have been lost. There is however some knowledge of their exegetical explanation: Abraham and Sarah represent form and matter while Isaac and Rebekah stand for the active and passive intellect. The most important work in philosophic exegesis, *Akedat Yiẓḥak* by Isaac b. Moses *Arama (15th century) of Spain, is a compilation of the author's sermons and philosophic discourses. Arama's avowed purpose is not only to explain words, a method which characterized most commentaries, but to elicit the full philosophic teachings of the Bible. In this, he claims to follow the approach of Christian preachers. Through his method, resembling that of Isaac Abrabanel—to pose a series of questions and to answer them—he discusses the soul, the symbolic meaning of paradise and the four rivers (Gen. 2:8–15), justice in the state, the Sabbath, and family life. The stories of the Bible are interpreted allegorically and the author refers extensively to Jewish literature and to general works on ethics, science, and politics to elucidate his arguments. *Akedat Yiẓḥak* was widely influential and served as a source for generations of preachers (see *Bible, Exegesis).

MYSTICAL LITERATURE

Throughout the Middle Ages, particularly the later medieval period, rationalist philosophy was supplemented by a great body of mystical literature. Its origins, found in the Apocrypha, the Talmud, and the *aggadah* center around the theophany *(Ma'aseh Merkavah)* in the first chapter of Ezekiel (see *Merkabah Mysticism). Initially regarded as secret doctrine, it was transmitted orally from one generation of initiates to the next. The first mystical books, pseudepigraphically assigned to early *tannaim*, such as R. Ishmael and R. Akiva, appear in the middle of the geonic period: *Alef-Bet de-Rabbi Akiva*, the *Heikhalot* texts, the *Ma'aseh Bereshit* literature and the Book of Enoch. The first systematic mystical work, *Sefer *Yeẓirah*, was written in Hebrew by an unknown author (probably in Palestine between the second and sixth centuries). The great development of mystical literature began in the 13th century in the south of France and the north of Spain. By then the influence of mystical doctrines known as *Kabbalah ("tradition") had become apparent in exegesis and philosophic literature. One of the most influential personalities in its formative period was *Isaac the Blind (12th–13th century), the son of Abraham b. David of Posquières. There are, however, indications of direct influences from both Babylonia and Palestine especially on the circles of *Ḥasidei Ashkenaz. The kabbalistic works of Eleazar b. Judah of Worms express the group's teachings in this sphere. They are also reflected in *Sefer Ḥasidim*.

Pre-Zohar and Zohar Literature. The literature of the "speculative Kabbalah" *(Kabbalah iyyunit)*, which arose in Spain and Provence is distinguished by originality of thought, aggadic style, and frequent pseudepigraphic ascriptions of the writings. In the nature of Midrashim, these works are written either in Hebrew or Aramaic or a combination of the two. The oldest kabbalistic text, the obscure *Sefer ha-*Bahir*, is attributed to a second-century *tanna*, but was probably edited in Provence in the 12th century. Other influential 12th-century works were the treatise *Massekhet Aẓilut* and the works of *Azriel of Gerona. Significant in the 13th century were the **Ma'arekhet ha-Elohut* and the central figure of ecstatic kabbalism Abraham b. Samuel *Abulafia, whose main works were written at the same time as the *Zohar.

The latter, the most distinguished work of speculative, indeed theosophic, Kabbalah, the *Zohar* is written in Aramaic and attributed to Simeon b. Yoḥai of the second century; it is now taken to have been written by the Spanish kabbalist *Moses de Leon (13th century). During the succeeding two centuries the Zohar gave rise to an extensive mystical literature including the works of Menahem b. Benjamin *Recanati of Italy, Moses b. Isaac *Botarel, Shem Tov b. Joseph *ibn Shem Tov, and Judah b. Jacob *Ḥayyat of Spain.

The next great flowering in kabbalistic speculation centered around Safed in the 16th century, and especially Moses b. Jacob *Cordovero, Isaac *Luria, and Ḥayyim b. Joseph *Vital. Luria's original and far-reaching conceptions, as presented by his disciples, reshaped kabbalistic thought and dominated it in subsequent centuries. Through Luria's essentially messianic doctrine, kabbalistic ideas acquired mass popularity.

The numerous kabbalistic works of the next two centuries, largely commentaries and compilations, though reflecting classical kabbalistic thinking and the Lurianic school, were original in thought. The most notable writers were Joseph Solomon *Delmedigo and Isaiah b. Abraham ha-Levi *Horowitz. The major work of the period, Isaiah Horowitz' *Shenei Luḥot ha-Berit*, a combination of code and kabbalistic commentary on the Pentateuch, profoundly influenced religious life in Eastern Europe and introduced practices and prayers whose sole source and authority was the Kabbalah. Later kabbalistic writing is reflected in the *Pitḥei Ḥokhmah* of Moses Ḥayyim *Luzzatto and especially in the practices and writings of *Ḥasidism. (For a full description see *Kabbalah. See also *Anthropomorphism, *Allegory, *Emanation, *Eschatology, *Immortality of the Soul, **Shekhinah*.)

PROSE LITERATURE

History. The dispersion of the Jews, a scarcity of reliable documents, and the fact that medieval scholars did not have a historical sense made the writing of Jewish history and geography difficult. The works of the period are often inaccurate and frequently credulous in their reliability on sources. Together with responsa, however, they provide sources for modern Jewish historical studies. Among the historical works of the early Middle Ages was the anonymous *Seder Olam Zuta*, a history of the Babylonian exilarchs from Zerubbabel down to the eighth century which emphasizes the Davidic line but ignores the most glorious exilarch of the seventh century, *Bustanai b. Ḥaninai. **Josippon* (tenth century), a widely read anonymous work, is a summary of Jewish history starting with Adam down to the destruction of the Temple. Relying primarily on Josephus, it also drew on non-Jewish sources and on Jewish legends. More factual contemporary accounts, emphasizing the history of the gaonate and the spiritual life of Babylonian Jewry, were provided by Saadiah Gaon (10th century) and his contemporary *Nathan b. Isaac ha-Kohen who depict Babylonian life. An apparently authentic account of Jewry in southern Italy was provided by the family chronicle *Aḥima'aẓ* (1054; *Ahimaaz b. Paltiel) which testifies to the judicial autonomy enjoyed by Italian Jews and to the close relationship existing between southern Italy and Palestine over the centuries. The chronicles of Jews in France and Germany centering around the Crusades afford authentic and moving accounts of Jewish life in those areas; they include the works of Solomon b. Simeon and *Eliezer b. Nathan, both of Mainz (about 1140), and that of Ephraim of Bonn (after 1196). Abraham ibn Daud's *Sefer ha-Kabbalah* ("Book of Tradition"), a work of broader scope, includes a history of the political parties in the second commonwealth, the talmudic tradition, the geonic period, and Jewish intellectual life in Spain. Ibn Daud based himself on known sources and sources unknown today with the avowed intent of showing the superiority of the *Rabbanites over the *Karaites.

The historical works of the later Middle Ages are both far more numerous and more detailed than those of the earlier period. They also attempted to place Jewish history in the context of general history and were superior in orderly arrangement and, sometimes, in critical treatment of the material. They too, however, mixed fact and fancy and were parochial or tendentious in their themes and outlook. The works of the period included a considerable number of chronicles of communities, families, or specific events. Much of the writing, centering about the lives of Jewish heroes or about persecutions, was not history for its own sake, but served as a background to halakhic or aggadic works designed to show the continuity of Jewish tradition or to provide a history of scholarship. Social and economic histories were noticeably lacking. Among the chronicles of tradition were those of Menahem b. Solomon *Meiri of Provence (1287), whose work takes the history of Jewish tradition up to his own time and is a source of information on scholarship in Provence and in the Franco-German area. A century later Isaac de Lattes of Provence wrote *Sha'arei Ẓiyyon* which takes Menahem Meiri's work as a source. The work of Joseph b. Ẓaddik on the Spanish Jewish community provides full data about Spanish scholars up to 1487. *Abraham b. Solomon of Torrutiel in his *Book of Tradition* (1510) not only deals with scholarly accomplishment from the 12th century onward, but also describes the period of the expulsion from Spain. His eyewitness account of the expulsion is especially valuable as is his invective against the upper classes of Spanish Jewry and his accounts of the events after his exile. *Divrei Yosef* (1673), by Joseph b. Isaac *Sambari of Egypt, discusses the Jews of the East. Emphasizing the history and life of Egyptian Jewry, the author also lists scholars in other Eastern cities and persecutions in the area. The book contains a wealth of data, including legends, not found in other sources.

Another type of historical literature dealt with the frequent persecutions of the period. Two major works were *Shevet Yehudah*, by Solomon *ibn Verga, written on the basis of the notes of his relative Judah, supplemented by the notes of his son Joseph; and *Emek ha-Bakha*, by *Joseph ha-Kohen (16th century) of Italy. While Ibn Verga's account of the persecutions is unsystematic and inaccurate, his eyewitness account of the Spanish expulsion, particularly the events following it, is both detailed and moving. He is particularly informative on the religious debates which took place in Spain in connection with which he relates the story of the three rings which Lessing also was to employ in his drama, *Nathan der Weise*. The material in *Emek ha-Bakha* is much better arranged and goes up to 1575; it is particularly informative about contemporary Italian Jewish life. The book is also noteworthy because of its account of Joseph *Nasi and his attempt to rebuild Tiberias.

The major histories of tradition during the period, written in the vein of Ibn Daud, are combinations of chronologies and biographies which gained importance because they threw light on creative activities in different countries at successively later periods. The first such history, *Sefer Yuḥasin* (1505), by Abraham b. Samuel *Zacuto, begins with the men of the Great Synagogue and takes history down to the author's own time. The work contains frequent and detailed citations and such interesting additional material as the diary of *Isaac b. Samuel of Acre about the authenticity of the Zohar. To place his writing in perspective, Zacuto devotes the last of his five sections to universal history. *Shalshelet ha-Kabbalah*, by Gedaliah b. David ibn Yaḥya (16th century) of Italy and Turkey, is an encyclopedic mélange of the history of Jewish tradition. It is a series of essays on aspects of Jewish history and on subjects ranging from embryology to the history of persecution. Confusing fact and fancy, the work was nonetheless popular because it marshaled a host of legends about major Jewish historical personalities and because of its eclectic character which afforded room for many historical oddities. *Ẓemaḥ David*, by David b. Solomon *Gans (16th century), on the other hand, is dry, factual, and well organized. Discussing both historical events and figures, he is particularly informative about Polish and German Jewish history and provides chronological tables and citations of sources which are still of value today. An equally systematic approach characterized David *Conforte's *Kore ha-Dorot* (17th century), which is a history of Jewish scholars and scholarship from the period of the Talmud to the author's own day and is especially informative about the tosafists and Eastern scholarship of the 16th and 17th centuries. Its value as a reference source was enhanced by the fact that the author made considerable use of responsa. The primary value of *Seder ha-Dorot* by Jehiel Heilprin (17th–18th century) is also as a technical reference source, particularly in the field of bibliography. The work is also exceptionally detailed in its treatment of talmudic figures. Thus in his discussion on Judah b. Ilai, he lists almost 3,000 statements attributed to him. As in other books of the period, a critical approach to history is lacking and thus while Heilprin adds to a knowledge of Jewish tradition, particularly in rabbinics, he mixes fact and legend uncritically in the biographies which are the warp and woof of the work.

Other noteworthy works dealing with literary history and bibliography of the period were those of Joseph Solomon *Delmedigo (17th century), Shabbetai b. Joseph *Bass (17th and 18th centuries), and Ḥayyim Joseph David *Azulai (18th century). In a letter in rhymed prose, *Iggeret Aḥuz*, Delmedigo reviewed medieval Jewish literary history, except for rabbinics. He discusses every field of literature and its principal figures. His style is epigrammatic and often mordantly witty, and he characterizes many of the personalities and books with a single phrase. Bass and Azulai did notable work in *bibliography; while Bass listed over 2,400 works in his *Siftei Yeshenim*, Azulai recorded 3,000 short biographies and bibliographical items. Almost all the historical works discussed above were also based on non-Jewish sources in an attempt to place Jewish history in historical perspective; they lacked, however, critical insight. The scholar who best combined general knowledge, a critical approach, and a historical sense with intensive Jewish knowledge was Azariah dei *Rossi (16th century) of Italy. In *Me'or Einayim* he used the short essay form to analyze critically some aspects of Jewish history, literature, and institutions. Dealing with the chronology of the Second Temple period, he disputes both the Talmud and his predecessors and arrives at a new chronology. In his analysis of the *aggadah* he questions the method of the rabbis in arriving at religious and ethical truths. Discussing science in the Talmud, he indicates errors in view and knowledge and lays down the principle that rabbinic authority applies only to the areas of law and tradition. It is the first work of critical history and initially engendered much controversy because it was considered radical in its views.

During the 16th century Jewish scholars were beginning to turn their attention also to general history, with illuminating side references to Jewish history. Thus while *Seder Eliyahu Zuta* (1523), by Elijah *Capsali, of Crete, is essentially a work on the history of the Ottoman Empire, the author provides valuable data about the history of the Jews of Spain, Turkey, and Rhodes. Similarly, the history of the kings of France and the Ottoman Turks by Joseph ha-Kohen (16th century) contains much Jewish material, including an account of David Reuveni and Solomon Molcho (see *Historiography).

Geography and Travel. Current events, history, and legend fused in the literature of geography and travel of the 1,000-year period. A book which fired the Jewish imagination is the record of *Eldad ha-Dani who appeared in Kairouan in 890 with detailed accounts of independent Jewish kingdoms in East Africa, Arabia, Khazaria, and Persia, which he described as the *Ten Lost Tribes. Mingling fact and legend he buttressed Jewish hopes and ego for many centuries. Equally bolstering was the correspondence between Ḥisdai ibn Shaprut (tenth century), a leader of Spanish Jewry, and *Joseph, king of the *Khazars, about the conversion of the latter's ancestor to Judaism. The king's answer, with a document from the Cairo *Genizah*, provide a fascinating picture of a bypath of Jewish history and Jewish proselytizing efforts.

The great Jewish travel book of the Middle Ages is *Benjamin of Tudela's account of his travels, depicting life in Southern Europe and in the East (1159–73.) An eyewitness account of the life in many lands, which the author supplemented with data on Slavic lands, Persia, and India, he portrays a vital Jewish life in many communities and a record of such oddities of history as the black Jews of Malabar and the false messiah, David Alroy. The accounts of Benjamin's near contemporary *Pethahiah of Regensburg which record his travels in Slavic lands, Babylon, and Palestine between the years 1175 to 1185 are less detailed and more credulous. He confirms Benjamin's observations, adds data, and notes the presence of a great number of Karaites in Crimea.

From the 13th century onward there is a considerable body of literature devoted to trips to Palestine and to a description of communities visited en route. While many are merely descriptions of religious sites and legends centering about holy people and places, others contain illuminating bits of information. Thus *Elleh ha-Massa'ot* by Jacob of Paris records the anomaly that he was sent to Palestine to raise money for a yeshivah in Paris. Meanwhile, he gives an account of Jewish life in Damascus and Baghdad. *Estori ha-Parḥi of Provence (14th century) has extensive topographical material on Palestine and his contemporary, Isaac Ḥilo, provides an illuminating picture of Jewish life in Palestine. He notes that there are many scholars from France and Germany among the Jews of Haifa, that the Jews of Acre are quite rich, and that the Jews of Jaffa possess a fine library.

The varied character of Jewish life and the relatively rapid changes in it are mirrored in 15th- and 16th-century Jewish travel chronicles. Meshullam b. Menahem, an Italian, visiting Egypt in the 1480s reports that the Cairo community has 850 Jewish families, several hundred Karaites, and 50 Samaritans, but he deprecates their way of life. Obadiah of Bertinoro, the commentator on the Mishnah, writing in the same decade, gives a detailed and affirmative description of these communities and also mentions that 50 former Marrano families settled in Cairo. On the other hand while he is negative about the Jews of Sicily whom he describes as artisans, workers in the fields, and morally lax, he indicates that they are a tightly organized Jewish community enjoying great autonomy. Of Jerusalem, he reports that there are but 70 families, all of them poor and ignorant, which is a completely different account from that of Ḥilo of 150 years earlier. Later works include *Gelilot Ereẓ Yisrael* (1624), by Gershon b. Eliezer of Prague, a book replete with bizarre legends and wonder stories; several books by the Karaite *Samuel b. David (1642) of the Crimea who gives a glowing account of Karaite life in the East; Benjamin Yerushalmi (1786), and the itinerary of Simḥah b. Joseph of Poland who reports that the Constantinople Jewish community would annually charter a boat for pilgrimage to Palestine for the High Holy Days. The most fascinating travel book of all is that of David Reuveni (16th century) who appeared in Italy in 1523 claiming to be the brother of King Joseph, ruler of a small Jewish kingdom in the Arabian desert, and sent to negotiate with the pope about waging war against the Muslims. Describing his travels to Alexandria and thence to Italy, much of the book is devoted to his reception by Jews and gentiles in Europe, to his extended negotiations with the pope and the king of Portugal, and to his contacts with the Marranos in Portugal. Reuveni made a considerable impression upon Jews and gentiles, but he was ultimately arrested by the authorities and the book ends in *medias res* (see *Travelers and Explorers).

Biographies and Autobiographies. Reuveni's work could also be classified in the memoir genre which began to appear in the 17th century. An early example of this kind, *Shivḥei ha-Ari,* composed by one of Luria's followers Solomon Shlumil of Dreznitz, is partly biographical, but primarily an account of the wonders performed by Isaac Luria. *Sefer Ḥezyonot,* by Luria's disciple, Ḥayyim Vital, is a similar mixture and centers about Vital himself, with some references to Luria.

There were, however, two autobiographies of distinction, one by Leone *Modena (16th–17th century) and the other by *Glueckel of Hameln (17th–18th century). Modena, who claimed 26 occupations, provides a fascinating account of his life, and, incidentally of contemporary Italian Jewry. Writing in Hebrew he indicates that he was instructed in Latin, in music, and in dancing. He wrote on many themes, served as rabbi, gambled unsuccessfully, engaged in polemics and, in general, fitted the picture of a Renaissance man. Glueckel's memoir is notable on several scores. It is one of the few works by a woman, was written in Yiddish, and presents a lively picture of the life of a well-to-do Jewish woman of the time and the community in which she lived. She tells of her childhood, the few years she studied in *ḥeder,* her marriage, her widowhood, the education of her children, business practices, study patterns, and religious observance among Jews. She avows a philosophy of faith in God's Providence, displays a rich knowledge of Judaism garnered from reading and listening, and sets the study of Torah as primary. She relates that she sent her children to yeshivot and then gave them in marriage. Her book is a rich portrayal of contemporary German-Jewish life and values (see *Biographies and Autobiographies).

Fiction. As the field of Jewish literature broadened it came to comprehend belletristic prose which included tales, fables, and didactic works in which the ethical content is combined with satire, humor, proverbs, and apothegms for the sake of entertainment and aesthetic pleasure. While much of it was based on Arabic models, since the basic tales and proverbs tend to be universal on which national or cultural forms were superimposed, there were also Jewish models taken from the Bible, the Apocrypha, and the *aggadah.* The bulk of these works, until the middle of the 14th century, were written in Spain and thereafter in Provence and Italy.

TALES. The earliest book of fables, *Sefer ha-Ma'asiyyot,* by *Nissim b. Jacob b. Nissim ibn Shahin of Kairouan, written in Arabic, was based largely on aggadic legends. The most notable early work, however, was the Hebrew book, *Sefer Sha'ashu'im,* by the physician, Joseph *ibn Zabara (12th century). A mélange of folktales, epigrams, and short passages of philosophy and science, the story centers around Zabara's encounter with a stranger who proves to be a devil. In their travels, they debate with one another, tell stories, and compete with one another in the telling of proverbs and epigrams. Characterized by wit, humor, and satire the style resembles that of the **maqāma;* it is, however, not poetic in form.

Another major work, *Ben ha-Melekh ve-ha-Nazir,* by Abraham b. Samuel ha-Levi *ibn Ḥasdai, is a Hebrew adaptation of an Arabic version (which has been lost), of an Indian tale based on the life of Buddha, whose theme is the vanity of the world and the value of the ascetic life. The Indian tale had already been adapted in many European languages. Ibn Ḥasdai's treatment of the material is original and many of the parables and the content of the last 11 chapters, which reflects the moral and psychological teachings of 12th-century philosophy, appear in no other version. Written in rhymed prose, interspersed with poetry, abundantly ornamented by proverbs and poetry, the book is the story of a prince who through the instruction of a hermit is converted to an ascetic life.

Meshal ha-Kadmoni (1281), by Isaac ibn *Sahula, is another important work of the period. Based on aggadic stories but also including original tales, it is written in rhymed prose and embellished with puns and parodies based on biblical and aggadic expressions. The author indicates that his motive was to show Arabic-reading Jews that the Hebrew language was an equally suitable vehicle for entertainment. About the same time *Berechiah b. Natronai ha-Nakdan published his *Mishlei Shu'alim* ("Fox Fables"). Animal stories of this type were a familiar genre in medieval literature and much resemble Aesop's fables. The distinctive Hebraic character of Berechiah's version derives from the play of language. The animals converse in biblical Hebrew, interspersed with talmudic quotations, and readily resort to biblical puns and to parodies upon Jewish characters. A similar book which, however, was a direct translation from the Arabic was the *Iggeret Ba'alei Ḥayyim*, by Kalonymus b. Kalonymus (see *Fiction; *Animal Tales; *Exemplum; *Exempla of the Rabbis; *Hagiography).

Satire and Humor. The major medieval work of satire and humor, Al-Ḥarizi's *Taḥkemoni*, was the precursor of a considerable body of literature of lesser worth, one of which is *Sone Nashim* ("Hater of Women," 1298) by Judah ibn Shabbetai of Spain. Its obvious theme is elaborated with parodies on the Bible, on the liturgy, and on the marriage contract. A rejoinder, much inferior in quality, was written almost a century later by Jedaiah b. Abraham Bedersi (ha-Penini) under the title of *Ohev Nashim* ("Lover of Women").

The parodying of familiar literary forms, notably the Bible and the Talmud, centered about Purim which was an occasion for merrymaking and wine drinking. Of the large volume of literature written in this vein, the most representative are: *Massekhet Purim* by the 14th-century *Kalonymus b. Kalonymus which parodies the talmudic style, and the rather more witty *Megillat Setarim*, by Levi b. Gershom, which celebrates wine and merrymaking. Similar works were composed in subsequent centuries, most of them centering about Purim, but a few parodying the Passover *Haggadah*. Kalonymus b. Kalonymus was also the author of the satirical and didactic work *Even Boḥan* in which he portrays the Jews of Provence and characterizes their formal religiosity as devoid of spirit. He attacks the doctors and holds the upper classes up for ridicule. Other parts of the book, however, are dedicated to the theme of the vanity of the world and are in the form of fine parables (see *Parody, Hebrew).

Didactic Literature. *Mivḥar ha-Peninim*, a book of proverbs culled from Arabic literature and intended to provide ethical instruction, attributed to Ibn Gabirol, is the precursor of a large body of ethical works, most of which were didactic, and of works in which ethical systems were formulated. What distinguished didactic from ethical works was essentially a form and a style which were light and popular rather than formal since the intention of the author was to provide entertainment as well as instruction to his audience. *Milḥemet ha-Ḥokhmah ve-ha-Osher*, by Judah ibn Shabbetai, claims that both wisdom and wealth must be pursued. Its form is that of a dialogue between contending parties before a court and its style involves the use of puns and parody. *Ha-Mevakkesh* (1264), by Shem Tov b. Joseph ibn Falaquera, is a more serious work in which the author discusses various professions and crafts, reviews philosophy, ethical theory, and poetry and concludes with a discussion on religion, science, and philosophy. The book, he asserts, is designed to instruct people in proper conduct and is written in dialogue form with the morals being brought home in short poems and proverbs. The conclusion is that a true understanding of religion depends upon a knowledge of science and philosophy.

Beḥinat Olam, written in the earlier part of the 14th century by Jedaiah Bedersi (ha-Penini) is altogether more solemn and is written in a poetic prose. Its themes are the pursuit of immortality and the cultivation of the soul toward that pursuit. Happiness, he asserts, resides in the observance of the Torah and in following the path of moderation in daily life.

POLEMICAL AND APOLOGETIC LITERATURE

From the 12th century onward, as a result of the confrontation of Judaism with Islam and Christianity, the literature of polemics and apologetics developed. Although having its roots in biblical and Hellenistic sources, this literature reached its zenith in the Middle Ages primarily in response to Christian attempts to proselytize Jews by force or persuasion, and to involve them in theological debates. The problem of confrontation was considerably less severe in Muslim countries where the central issues were usually biblical exegesis and articles of faith with which almost all medieval philosophers and theologians dealt, either in their major works or in separate treatises. In addition, within Judaism itself there was a tradition of polemical literature: between the Rabbanites and the Karaites, between philosophers and their critics, and between kabbalists and their opponents. Polemical efforts are, however, found as early as the ninth century in parts of David ibn Marwān *al-Mukammis' larger works in which he attacks both Christianity and Islam. He scores the former for undermining pure monotheism and the latter on the grounds that the style of the Koran does not prove divine origin. In the tenth century Saadiah Gaon took much the same line, questioning the validity of Christian and Muslim exegesis of the Bible and asserting the immutability of the Torah. Expressing his criticisms of the other faiths in the form of a debate with Christians and Muslims, Judah Halevi, in his *Sefer ha-Kuzari* (12th century), extensively elaborates the points of his Jewish polemical predecessors in accusing Christianity and Islam of retaining many elements of pagan idolatry. Maimonides, in his letter to the Jews of Yemen, defends Judaism and denies that there are biblical references presaging Muhammad.

The first polemical work as such, however, is *Sefer ha-Berit* by the 12th-century writer, Joseph *Kimḥi of Provence. Written in the form of a dialogue, the author presents a debate between a Jew and a Christian on such issues as the interpretations of biblical passages, original sin, the role of Jesus, and the traditional charges Christians had leveled against Jews, i.e., deicide and usury. Kimḥi's arguments were the same as those which had been commonly adduced by Jews, namely, that the doctrine of original sin contradicts the biblical view, that the Jews did not kill Jesus, and that Christian biblical exegesis is mistaken. In addition, Kimḥi asserts that the Jews had an elevated moral sense and a decent communal life.

The talmudic debate held in 1240 before the king in Paris is recorded in *Vikku'aḥ* by one of the disputants, Rabbi *Jehiel b. Joseph of Paris. The rabbi defends the Talmud against the charge that it contains anti-Christian statements by claiming that the passages in question refer to an earlier Jesus and not the Jesus of the New Testament. Jehiel further contends that irrational statements in the Talmud and Midrash belong to the *aggadah*, which need not be accepted. *Kol Nidrei* and the laws relating to gentiles are also explained.

Another important disputation records Naḥmanides' debate with Pablo *Christiani at Barcelona in 1263. The polemic deals primarily with such questions as to whether the Messiah has come, whether the Messiah is divine or human, and whether Judaism is a just and true religion. Naḥmanides, referring to the familiar biblical passages, asserts that "the suffering servant" implies the Jewish people; he attacks the doctrine of original sin and, in terms similar to those of Jehiel, describes the non-halakhic nature of the *aggadah*.

In the 14th century the increase of forced conversions and attacks on Judaism by apostates caused Solomon b. Abraham Adret to write a dialogue denouncing the dogmas of Islam and denying the divine origin of the Koran, while defending Jews from the charge of having eliminated references to Muhammad from the Bible. Vis-à-vis a Christian antagonist, Solomon repudiates the allegorical interpretations of the Bible, defends the immutability of the Torah, and explains certain talmudic passages.

More significant are Isaac Profiat Duran's two polemical works, the ironic letter *Al Tehi ka-Avotekha* ("Be not Like your Fathers"), and the lengthy *Kelimmat ha-Goyim* ("The Shame of the Gentiles"). The first is addressed to a Jew who, like Duran himself, was forcibly converted in 1391, and who reneged on an agreement with Duran to flee Spain and to abandon Christianity. Heavily satirical, the letter urges the friend not to be like his fathers who believed in the pure unity of God, but to accept the notion of corporal embodiment. In the same ironic manner of apparent advocacy, Duran attacks many Christian doctrines. He continues his criticism in a more detailed and systematic way in his second work where literary and historical methods rather than irony are employed to establish his views. Ḥasdai Crescas composed a no less powerful polemic, *Bittul Ikkarei ha-Noẓerim* ("Refutation of the Dogmas of Christianity"), which elicited Christian replies.

A major polemical work which evoked considerable controversy and many Christian retorts is the comprehensive *Sefer ha-Niẓẓaḥon* by Yom Tov Lippman *Muelhausen (15th century) of Prague. The book is both an attack on Christianity and a defense of Judaism and its dogmas. Lippman sharply refutes Christian interpretations of the Bible and the doctrines derived from them, and incidently provides many exegetical insights. His statement of Jewish dogmas is couched in philosophical terms. A contemporaneous work by Simeon b. Zemaḥ Duran, *Keshet u-Magen*, attacks both Islam and Christianity. In his criticism of Christianity, he makes the significant point that Paul's abrogation of the law was not intended for Jews, but only for gentiles in order to attract them to the new faith.

The debates of the 15th and the 16th centuries are more notable for their polemic nature than for any new insights. Thus contentiousness marked the debate, held at the invitation of the pope, at Tortosa, Spain, in which an apostate Jew argued with Joseph Albo, whose views are summarized in his *Ikkarim*, and with Don Vidal Benveniste, who headed a delegation of the leading Jewish scholars of Spain. Don Isaac Abrabanel dealt at length with Christian doctrines. In the latter part of the 16th century, Joseph *Nasi, Duke of Naxos, and his brother, David, who was the business agent of a cardinal of Crete, and Abraham ibn Migash, the physician of Sultan Suleiman, all wrote polemics against Christianity.

The 17th century saw the renewal of accusations against Jews by apostates and of proselytizing by Catholics and Protestants. These activities were condemned by Zalman Ẓevi Oppenhausen of Germany, Jacob of Venice, and Leone Modena. Public disputations were still being held as, for example, in Ferrara in 1617, which was recorded by an anonymous Jewish scholar in his book about the immutability of the Torah; and later in the century, Isaac Lupis participated in a debate in Marseilles. By the end of the century, however, the number of polemics against Christianity began to decrease. The only such production of note in the 18th century was Moses *Mendelssohn's famous letter to Johann Casper Lavater (see *Apologetics; *Polemical Literature; *Disputations; *Apostasy).

YIDDISH LITERATURE

The late Middle Ages witnessed the development of a new literary language—a mixture of German and Hebrew and other languages ultimately known as Yiddish. In the course of time, Yiddish not only became the lingua franca of North European Jewry, but also the language in which a great and creative literature, which mirrored the folk spirit, was written. Apparently emerging some time in the 13th century, literary Yiddish was at first the medium of a secular literature which brought German popular romances, songs, and entertainment forms to the Jewish community. Subsequently acquiring Jewish character and themes, *Yiddish literature was initially designed for women and less educated men whose Hebrew was poor. Nevertheless, the language became a medium for everyone and, in consequence, not only was a religious and pietistic literature produced but, in the modern era, a major secular literature as well. Since Yiddish has always been written in Hebrew characters, its connection with the Hebrew language was maintained, and as the pronunciation of words taken from German became modified, the original connection with German became more remote.

The first Yiddish work extant dates from the late 15th century, but it is probable that works were composed as early as the 14th century. The dominant facts about early Yiddish literature are that it was written principally for women, frequently under their direct patronage, usually by men of inferior literary ability. Accordingly, Yiddish works centered on subjects which were amusing or instructive to women. Most of the material was translated from Hebrew or the European languages, and was modified to suit the taste of the feminine audience. Yiddish writing, therefore, usually took the form of tales or romances, and in the religious field of translations of the Bible, the prayer book, petitional prayers (**teḥinnot*), Apocryphal books, and ethical and moralistic literature (e.g., Baḥya ibn Paquda's *Ḥovot ha-Levavot*). Legal and philosophical literature was not translated. Special books emphasizing women's religious duties and status were written or compiled.

Often changed to fit the feminine temperament, Yiddish translations of the *teḥinnot*, for example, emphasize God as a loving father rather than as a stern judge; the merit of the matriarchs rather than that of the patriarchs; and define rewards in terms of pious and virtuous children. The tone of the writing is romantic and sentimental, its style verbose and popular, and, in general, represents a folk literature which mirrored daily life in the home and the ghetto. It is significant to note that the authors of works of this kind included a considerable number of women, a phenomenon very rare in Hebrew writing.

The earliest extant writing in Yiddish consists of glosses on biblical writing, which included both translations and aggadic commentaries. From the beginning of the 14th century, there exists a separate Yiddish glossary to most of the Bible. Yiddish literary activity expanded to the translation of the Bible and to the compilation of lexicons. An early 15th-century anonymous Yiddish translation of Psalms and Proverbs exist. The first printed Yiddish translation of the Pentateuch and *haftarot* (1544) was by a convert to Christianity, Michael Adam. In the same year another convert, Paulus Aemilius, published another translation. In 1560 Judah Leib *Bresch appended an abbreviated version of the Rashi commentary to the Adam translation. Thereafter several editions of the *Teutsch-Khumesh* appeared in which aggadic and interpretive embellishments were mixed with the text. The first edition was prepared by *Isaac b. Samson ha-Kohen of Prague in 1608, followed by other versions which appeared in the 17th and 18th centuries.

These efforts merely foreshadowed a richer and more creative biblical literature in Yiddish. Its avowed purpose was to provide both entertainment and traditional Jewish spiritual enrichment for women and for men who could not read Hebrew and to wean them away from reading German romances and card playing. The point is continually made that while scholars and intellectuals may despise works in the vernacular, such works are a labor of piety.

Three types of biblical works were produced with the above aims in mind. The first, Yiddish translations of biblical books other than the Pentateuch, included a translation of Psalms, attributed to Elijah Baḥur *Levita (1545); of Proverbs by Mordecai Teplitz (1582); and of Isaiah, together with an abridged version of David Kimḥi's commentary (1586). The second type was a rhymed Yiddish translation of biblical books in eight-line strophes which could be read or sung. Judges was so rendered in 1564; Moses Stendal translated Psalms in this vein in 1586; and some years later, both Daniel and Kings were also published in this form. In 1644 a biblical anthology, *Mizmor le-Todah* by David b. Menahem ha-Koḥen, appeared.

The third type of work, which complemented the second, involved a rewording of the biblical stories into rhymes and epic poems with the inclusion of much aggadic material. The most notable example, the **Shemuel Bukh*, which appeared as early as 1544, but may be 100 years older, is an epic poem about David based on the Book of Samuel and on aggadic material. Written in eight-line strophes, and accompanied by a special melody for singing, the poem was widely copied. Among its imitators are Jacob Siegel's *Book of Kings* (1543) and *Kehillat Jacob* (1692) by Jacob b. Isaac ha-Levi of Roethelsec, comprising the Pentateuch, Joshua, and Judges.

The most notable and influential Yiddish paraphrase of the Bible, the **Ẓe'enah u-Re'enah* became a major source of Jewish knowledge for women. Composed at the end of the 16th century by Jacob b. Isaac *Ashkenazi of Janov, it was a skillful interweaving of Pentateuch translation, *aggadah*, Midrash, exegesis, and mysticism. Furthermore, desiring to emphasize moral instruction, the author organized his material to that end. Ashkenazi complemented this work with *Ha-Maggid*, a similar interpretation of the rest of the Bible.

Ultimately, the enterprise was rounded out by a literal (*peshat*) Yiddish translation of the entire Bible. Two versions, that of Jekuthiel b. Isaac Blitz and a superior effort by Josef Witzenhausen, appeared almost simultaneously about 1676. While translation of works into Yiddish enriched the language, this process was reinforced by works in lexicography. The first such work, *Mirkevet ha-Mishneh* or *Sefer shel Rabbi Anshel*, a combination of biblical concordance and dictionary, appeared in 1534 and was widely used for generations. Eight years later, *Shemot Devarim*, by Elijah Baḥur Levita, a four-column arrangement of Yiddish (in Hebrew characters), Latin, Hebrew, and Yiddish in German script, was issued. Other similar works are the *Be'er Moshe* by Moses Serles (1604), an interlinear Yiddish translation of the Bible, and the *Safah Berurah* ("Clear Language") by Nathan Hannover, a four-language dictionary, which includes Italian as well as Hebrew, Yiddish, and Latin.

Another major activity of early Yiddish was the translation of the prayer book. The earliest such work, which includes a complete translation of the High Holiday *maḥzor*, dates from the 15th century. However, the first complete translation of the prayer book, which was produced by Joseph Yakir, appeared in 1544. The numerous subsequent translations elaborated and expanded the contents, the most complete being Jehiel M. *Epstein's *Derekh Yesharah* (1697) which contained a digest of all the laws and customs pertaining to the liturgy and the synagogue. At the same time other groups of prayers and the *Haggadah* were translated into Yiddish and published in various collections. One of the most remarkable features of these endeavors was that several translations were undertaken by women. The name of Elis, daughter of Mordecai of Slutzk (second half of 17th century), appears in this connection.

The composition of Yiddish *teḥinnot* for every phase of life offered writers greater freedom of expression. Couched in personal and intimate language, these prayers reflect both piety and the heartfelt sentiments of Jewish women. While the first collections were composed by men, including those of Abraham Apotekev in 1590 and *Aaron b. Samuel somewhat later, subsequent efforts were largely those of women. The most famous authoress, Sarah, daughter of Mordecai, wrote prolifically under the name Sarah bat Tovim.

To accompany the *teḥinnot*, many manuals for women on religious life and conduct were written. The first such manual, *Mitzvot ha-Nashim* or *Frauen Buchlein* ("The Laws of Women"; Venice, 1552), was written in rhyme and enjoyed great popularity. In the 18th century its popularity was matched by Simon Frankfurter's *Sefer ha-Ḥayyim* ("The Book of Life"), which appeared in 1703.

Ethical and Musar Literature. The extensive ethical literature in Yiddish developed a style distinct from its Hebrew prototypes, even when it was only a translation from the latter. Directed principally, although not entirely, toward women, this literature was written in a popular vein, rich in stories, parables, and legends. Catering to the needs of the common folk, it reflects the life, spirit, and physical conditions of the ghetto and is, therefore, a significant historical source. *Sefer Middot* ("The Book of Good Qualities"), the first such book, is an adaptation of the anonymous German moralistic work in Hebrew, *Orḥot Ẓaddikim* ("The Ways of the Righteous," 1542). The book was dedicated to a woman, Murda of Ginzburg, who is described as a doctor of medicine. In 1546 the first of several Yiddish translations of *Jonah b. Abraham Gerondi's *Sefer ha-Yirah* was published. The composition of original works soon followed—the earliest being *Der Brant Spiegel* (1602) by Moses Ḥanoch of Prague in which the author, purporting to hold a mirror to the life about him, prescribes good behavior in practical terms, e.g., how to train children, how to treat servants. *Lev Tov* (1620) by *Isaac b. Eliakim of Posen, which discusses Jewish law and manners, was also widely read.

Women made their debut as writers of ethical literature in Yiddish with the publication of Rebekah Tiktiner's *Meineket Rivkah* (1609), a compilation of statements gathered from aggadic and *musar* literature. A century later Elhanan Hendel Kirchan in his *Simḥat ha-Nefesh* ("The Joy of the Soul") discusses manners and etiquette in the context of German Jewish life and emphasized the joys of living. To promote the joy he spoke of, the author included poems and folk songs for all occasions accompanied by their musical notation.

The numerous smaller ethical works of the period were complemented by aphoristic books on ethical themes. One of the more memorable works of this genre is Seligman Ulma's *Der Zuchts Spiegel* (1610), which is a collection of culled proverbs and *bon mots* from Jewish literature.

Romances. Secular works in Yiddish, following hard upon religious works in that language, began to appear in the 15th century. The first secular works to appear were Yiddish translations or recastings of romances from other literatures. Based on the oral renditions by Jewish equivalents of the German *spielman*, whose material was often sung to melodies which became standardized, these romances circulated in manuscript and ultimately appeared in print. The most popular romances were *Dietrich von Bern*, *Herzog Ernst*, and the *Hildesbrandslied*, all of which recount much the same theme—the adventures of a valiant knight who overcomes obstacles, and ultimately gains the lady of his choice. The *Arthurian legends, too, circulated widely in manuscript in the early 15th century. In the 16th century, new romances achieved wide popularity, two of which, rendered into Yiddish from the Italian by Elijah Levita, were the *Bove Bukh* (written in eight-line rhymed strophes) and *Paris un Viene*. The title of the first work became the synonym for any fantastic tale and left its mark as a Yiddish expression, "the *Bobe-Mayse*." While both works were typical romances of the period, Levita invested his characters with Jewish attitudes and behavior. These romances were followed, in turn, by Yiddish translations of many other popular European romances and stories, including Boccaccio's *Decameron*.

Concurrently, original romances on similar themes from ancient or medieval legends were being written in profusion. One of the most important, *Ma'aseh Beri'ah ve-Zimrah*, is the story of the daughter of a high priest who is a counsellor to a Jewish king and a pope. Anachronistic though it is, the novel gained wide popularity after it was printed in 1597. Other well-known collections of tales and short stories include Yuspa Shammash's *Ma'aseh Nissim* (1670), based on legends that arose around the city of Worms, its distinguished Jewish figures, and the anonymous *Ma'aseh Bukh* (see *Ma'aseh Book). The latter, an earlier work edited about 1580, included 257 tales taken from the Talmud, the Midrash, and more contemporary folktale sources.

Drama. Plays based upon biblical themes and written in the manner of medieval miracle plays also began to be produced in Yiddish. The first, "The Sacrifice of Isaac," appeared in the 15th century. Somewhat later, another genre of dramatic presentation in Yiddish, the **Purim-shpil*, using satire and burlesque, drew upon the Bible for its themes. *Purim-shpils* were usually written in poetic form and were presented publicly to enthusiastic audiences. Plays on contemporary themes, staged toward the end of the 18th century, appear to have been less successful.

Original Yiddish poetry—humorous and satiric songs, historical and ethical verse, love poems and festival songs—began to be written in great abundance. Many of these poems were composed by anonymous "fools" (jesters) who recited or sang humorous and satirical compositions. Few collections of this material have survived, but specimens appear in anthologies such as that of Isaac Wallich, which appeared in 1681.

Prose and Poetry. Yiddish didactic poets whose compositions survive include Isaac of Vilna, and Shlome Singer of Prague (17th century), who composed both words and melodies. These poems, produced in great numbers, are not of high quality and their authors are often unknown. However, a true expression of folk literature, these poems, jingles, and songs long enjoyed popularity. As in other branches of Yiddish literature, women, e.g., Rebekah Tiktiner, Roesil Fishel (16th century), Toybi Pan (c. 1700), and Hannah Katz also wrote in this genre.

Prose literature also began to appear in Yiddish in these fruitful centuries. Many works were translated from Hebrew, like *Sefer ha-Ma'asim* (1625) by Ḥayyim b. Nathan, which contained translations of nine of the apocryphal books. Other translations include such popular historical works as *Josippon* (1546), *Shevet Yehudah* (1591), and *Ẓemaḥ David* (1695). The travel books of Benjamin of Tudela and Pethahiah of Regensburg were also early translated into Yiddish. Original Yiddish prose comprises historical works such as *She'erit Yisrael* ("The Remnant of Israel"), which consists of excerpts from Jewish and non-Jewish history, 70 C.E. to 1740. Other works based on history are the memoirs of Glueckel of Hameln and Yom Tov Lippman Heller, and the *Lider* or poems commemorating events in more contemporary Jewish history such as *Megillat Vinẓ* (see *Fettmilch). Inevitably, textbooks on arithmetic, geography, hygiene, practical medicine, etc., also began to appear in Yiddish (see *Yiddish Literature).

[ME.WA./M.WAX]

LADINO LITERATURE

The beginning of Ladino literature may be traced to the 13th century with the translation of the Bible into Ladino. These translations, however, were in Latin script and it is only after the expulsion of the Jews from Spain that Ladino translations of the Bible were written in Hebrew script and the language acquired a distinctly Jewish character (see *Bible, Translations, Ladino). Another major literary activity in religious Ladino literature was the translation of exegetical and ethical works, moral handbooks, and prayer books. A number of original works were also produced such as *Almosnino's popular *Il Regimiento de la Vida* (Salonika, 1564), an ethical treatise which included a long dissertation on dreams. Most of Almosnino's works, however, were in Hebrew, although his compilation of data on Constantinople in Ladino, which Jacob *Cansino of Oran later published in Spanish under the title *Extremos y Grandezas de Constantinopla*, is a major work in Spanish Jewish literature and a significant historical source.

By the end of the 17th century poetry, mystical writings, biblical exegesis, history, and ethics were written in Ladino. **Me-Am Lo'ez*, the monumental ethical-religious work of Ladino literature, is an elaborate encyclopedic commentary on the entire Bible which in 1730 was initiated by Jacob *Culi who wrote the commentary on Genesis and a portion of Exodus. It is assumed that the subsequent commentaries are in part based on his manuscripts. The work, written in a popular style, was intended to make the Bible and Jewish learning readily understandable to the layman who no longer was able to use the Hebrew texts. Among original works of religious poetry in Ladino are *Proverbios morales* by Shem Tov (*Santob) de Carrion (14th century) and the *Poema de Yosef*, probably composed at the beginning of the 15th century, which is an adaptation of the story of Joseph and his brethren from the Midrash and *Sefer ha-Yashar*. The poem's strophic and metric form, influenced by the Hebrew *piyyut*, is also reminiscent of the *cuaderna via* literary structure which was developing at the time. Written also in Spanish in Arabic characters, the poem became an integral part of Spanish literature. The popular Ladino poem on the same subject, *Coplas de Yosef ha-Zaddik*, by Abraham de Toledo (1732), is known in two distinct versions: one written in Constantinople (1732) and the other in Belgrade (1861) which is based on the lost Salonika version (1755). The poem, consisting of 400 quatrains, was also sung on Purim. The *copla* genre which flourished in Ladino in the 19th century was mainly the poetic expression of minor works written for Purim (*Coplas de Purim*).

A distinctly secular mode of expression in Ladino literature is the *romancero* which formed part of the oral tradition of Jews in Spain. The Ladino *romancero* is largely a continuation and an adaptation of the Spanish *romancero* of the Middle Ages and the Renaissance. The original *romancero*, a traditional Spanish ballad widely popular in the 14th and 15th centuries, was often sung. There are also many original romances and songs in Ladino or later composition. The different types of *romanceros* found in

Spanish literature (historical, tragic, humorous, amorous, satirical) were also found in Ladino to which have been added three specifically Jewish types: wedding songs, religious hymns, and laments.

Other secular literature in Ladino are adaptations and translations of plays and novels, mainly from French literature. This led to the writing of original plays and novels, most of which, however, are of an inferior quality. There is a rich Ladino folk literature but most of it has neither been collected nor studied.

See also *Ladino Literature; *Judeo-Arabic Literature. For modern literature see Modern *Hebrew Literature, Hebrew Literary *Criticism, *Drama, *Prosody; *Yiddish Literature. [Ed.]

Bibliography: Waxman, Literature: see bibliographies at end of each volume; Winter and Wuensche, *Die juedische Literatur* (1906); see also bibliographies for each relevant entry in the encyclopaedia.

LITHUANIA (Lithuanian **Lietuva;** Pol. **Litwa;** Rus. **Litva;** Heb. **Lita** ליטא or ליטה; Yid. **Lite** ליטע), southernmost of Baltic states of N.E. Europe; from 1940 Lithuanian S.S.R. (for early period, see *Poland-Lithuania). With the partition of Poland at the close of the 18th century the territories of Lithuania passed to Russia. Subsequently, for over 120 years, Lithuania ceased to exist as a political or administrative unit. It was divided up into six or seven provinces in which the history of the Jews was similar to that of the Jews throughout *Russia. Lithuanian Jewry nevertheless retained its specific character, and its influence on Russian Jewry—and on world Jewry in general—extended beyond the boundaries of historic Lithuania. Lithuanian Jewry was particularly oppressed during World War I. The attitude of the Russian military authorities toward the Jews was one of suspicion and hostility; rumors were spread that they were traitors, and the army therefore perpetrated pogroms against them. In the spring of 1915 expulsions of Jews from the provinces of *Suwalki, Kovno (*Kaunas), *Courland, and *Grodno began. During the fall of the same year, northern and western Lithuania were occupied by the German army. The population suffered from lack of food and unemployment. Limited aid arrived from the Jews of Germany and the United States and a ramified Jewish assistance organization was set up. A network of Hebrew and Yiddish schools, including secondary schools, was established. After the end of World War I, a considerable number of refugees returned to their former places of residence. Lithuanian Jewry was henceforward divided among three states: independent Lithuania, Belorussian S.S.R. (see *Belorussia), and Poland.

Character and Influence on the Diaspora. The notion of "Lithuanian" ("*Litvak*" in Yiddish) to be found in speech, folklore, and Jewish literature in all its languages applies to the Jewish community which developed within the boundaries of historic Lithuania, the region which formed part of the greater Polish kingdom during the 16th to 18th centuries. From the close of the 18th century until World War I this area came under the rule of czarist Russia and included the provinces of Kovno, *Vilna, Grodno, and northern Suwalki, which were essentially of Lithuanian-Polish character, and of *Vitebsk, *Minsk, and *Mogilev, which were Belorussian-Russian in character. A distinction is sometimes made between Lithuanian Jews in a restricted sense (from the provinces of Vilna, Kovno, and the northern parts of the provinces of Suwalki and Grodno) and the Belorussian Jews ("province of Russia"). At the close of 19th century, about 1,500,000 Jews lived in this region; they constituted more than one-eighth of the total population. The Jews were mainly concentrated in the towns and villages, where in the main they were in the majority. There were over 300 communities in Lithuania with over 1,000 persons, including 12 large communities each numbering over 20,000 persons: Vilna, Minsk, *Bialystok, Vitebsk, Dvinsk (*Daugavpils), *Brest-Litovsk, Kovno, Grodno, Mogilev, *Pinsk, *Bobruisk, and *Gomel; but even the smaller settlements with only some dozens of Jewish families had a vibrant and full Jewish life.

Both economic and historical factors were responsible for the unique character of Lithuanian Jewry. Lithuania was a poor country, and the mass of its inhabitants, consisting of Lithuanian and Belorussian peasants, formed a low social stratum whose national culture was undeveloped. The Jews who had contacts with them as contractors, merchants, shopkeepers, innkeepers, craftsmen, etc. regarded themselves as their superior in every respect. Lithuanian Jewry was relatively less affected by the *Chmielnicki massacres that devastated the Jews of Ukraine in 1648–49, and those perpetrated by the *Haidamacks during the 18th century. Even when the wave of pogroms swept Russia during the last decades of czarist rule, there were only isolated manifestations of anti-Jewish violence in Lithuania (Gomel, Bialystok). These circumstances gave the Lithuanian Jews a feeling of stability and security, as a result of which they developed no desire to adopt the language and culture of the surrounding peoples.

The Jews of Lithuania maintained their own way of life. They spoke a special dialect of Yiddish—Lithuanian Yiddish—which differed from the Yiddish spoken in Poland and Volhynia mainly in the pronunciation of the vowels (and in certain districts in the pronunciation of the שׁ (*shin*) as שׂ (*sin*) or ס (*samekh*). The world outlook and way of life of Lithuanian Jewry were based on the Written Law and the Oral Law. The Shulḥan Arukh and its commentaries guided them in their everyday life. Torah learning flourished among wide circles, and love of Torah and esteem for its study was widespread among the masses of Jews. The Jews who lived in the region bordering Lithuania, the "Poles" in the west and the "Volhynians" in the south, associated specific characteristics with the Lithuanian Jews: a certain emotional dryness, the superiority of the intellect over emotion, mental alertness, sharp-wittedness, and pungency. Their piety was also questioned (hence the popular derogatory appellation for the Lithuanian Jews, "*tseylem-kop*"). It was also a feature of Lithuanian Jewry that *Ḥasidism did not strike roots in northern Lithuania, while in the provinces of Belorussia it assumed a different nature and content—the Ḥabad trend—from the original Ḥasidism of Ukraine and Poland (see below). Lithuanian Jews were considered the "prototype" of the **Mitnaggedim*.

Spiritual Trends and Leaders. Until the 16th century the Jews of Lithuania were on the outer fringe of European Jewry. During the 16th and 17th centuries, they were influenced by Polish Jewry, and adopted its organizational methods (Lithuanian Council; see *Councils of the Lands), its educational system, and its mode of learning. The first prominent rabbis who were called upon to officiate in the large Lithuanian communities, such as Mordecai b. Abraham *Jaffe, author of the *Levushim*, and Joel *Sirkes, author of *Bayit Ḥadash* (the "Baḥ"), came from outside Lithuania. Solomon b. Jehiel *Luria (the Maharshal), who was of Lithuanian origin and promoted Torah learning there for a number of years, acquired most of his education and was mainly active beyond the borders of that country. It was only during the 17th century that leading Torah scholars emerged from the yeshivot of Lithuania. Among them were the commentators on the Shulḥan Arukh, *Shabbetai b. Meir ha-Kohen (the Shakh), and Moses b. Naphtali Hirsch *Rivkes, author of *Be'er ha-Golah*.

Map showing Jewish communities in Independent Lithuania and in the Vilna region ceded to Lithuania in October 1939.

List of alternative names for places shown on map.

Lithuanian Name	Russian Name	Yiddish Name
Alytus	Olita	Alite
Anyksciai	Onikshty	Aniksht
Balberiskis	Balkerishki	Balbirishok
Birzai	Birzhi	Birzh
Butrimonicai	Butyrmantsy	Butrimants
Darbenai	Dorbyany	Dorbian
Dusetoi	Dusjaty	Dusyat
Gargzdai	Gorzhdy	
Jonava	Janovo	Yanove
Joniskis	Yanishki	Yanishok
Jurbarkas	Jurburg	
Kaisiadorys	Koisedary	Kashedar
Kalvarija	Kalvariya	
Kaunas	Kovno	
Kedainiai	Keidany	Keidan
Kelme	Kelmy	Kelm
Klaipeda	Memel	
Krakiai	Kruki	Krok
Krakinava	Krakinovo	
Kretinga	Kretinga	Kretingen
Kudaros-Naumiestis	Vladislavov	
Kudirkos-Naumiestis	Novoe Mesto	Nayshtat
Kupiskis	Kupishki	Kupishok
Kursenai	Kurshany	Kurshan
Kybartai	Kibarty	Kibart
Lazdijai	Lozdzee	Lazdey
Linkuve	Linkovo	
Luoke	Lavkov	Luykeve
Maletai	Maljaty	Malat
Marijampole	Mariampol	
Mazeikiai	Mazheiki	Mazheik
Merkine	Meretsch	
Nemaksciai	Nemokshty	Nemoksht
Obeliai	Abeli	Abel
Pandelis	Ponedeli	Ponedel
Panevezys	Ponevezh	
Pasvalys	Posvol	
Pilviskiai	Pilvishki	Pilvishok

Lithuanian Name	Russian Name	Yiddish Name
Plunge	Plungyany	Plungyan
Prienai	Preny	Pren
Radviliskis	Radzivilishki	
Raguva	Rogov	Rogove
Raseiniai	Rossieny	Rasseyn
Rietavas	Retovo	Riteve
Rokiskis	Rakishki	Rakishok
Sakiai	Shaki	
Salakas	Soloki	Salok
Salantai	Salanty	Salant
Seda	Syady	Syad
Seduva	Shadov	Shadove
Seirijai	Seree	Serey
Siauliai	Shavli	Shavl
Silale	Shileli	Shilel
Simnas	Simno	
Sirvintos	Shervinty	Shirvint
Skaudvile	Skadvile	Shkudvil
Skuodas	Shkudy	Shkud
Sveksna	Shvekshni	
Taurage	Taurogen	Tavrig
Telsiai	Telschi	Telz
Trakai	Troki	
Ukmerge	Vilkomir	
Utena	Utsjany	Utyan
Uzpaliai	Uschpol	
Varniai	Vorni	Vorne
Veisijai	Veisee	
Vieksniai	Wekschni	Vekshne
Vilkaviskis	Vilkovishki	Vilkovishk
Vilkija	Vilki	
Virbalis	Verzhbolov	Virbaln
Zagare	Zhagory	Zhager
Zarasai	Novo Aleksandrovsk	Ezherene
Zasliai	Shosli	Zasle
Ziezmariai	Zhizhmory	Zezmer
Zydikiai	Zhidiki	Zidik

1

2

Figure 1. Purim party at the kindergarten in Kedainiai.

Figure 2. A corner of the cemetery of Gruzdžiai, Siauliai District.

Figure 3. *Bimah* in the Jurbarkas wooden synagogue.

Figure 4. The synagogue of the small Karaite community of Panevėžys.

Figure 5. Wooden synagogue in Jurbarkas, built 1790, destroyed by the Nazis, September 1941.

3

4

5

Figure 6. Training as *ḥalutzim* for Ereẓ Israel in Utena. The entire Jewish population of this town was murdered by the Nazis in August 1941.

However, the personality which symbolized the supremacy of Torah learning within Lithuanian Jewry and determined its character for several generations was that of the Gaon of Vilna, *Elijah b. Solomon Zalman, who lived during the second half of the 18th century. He established his own method of study. Its main features were abstention from casuistic methods, close examination of the talmudic text and accuracy in its interpretation, a comprehensive knowledge of all the sources, and the study of grammar and the sciences which were essential for profound understanding of the teachings of the Torah.

R. Elijah appeared on the Lithuanian scene when winds of change were beginning to blow across that country. In the south, Ḥasidism blazed a trail, and the disciples of *Dov Baer the Maggid of Mezhirech arrived in *Shklov, Vitebsk, Vilna, and other communities, winning over a large following. From the West came the ideas of the *Haskalah; these at first were moderate in character and sought to adapt themselves to the old school (like the scholars of Shklov, R. Baruch b. Jacob *Schick, or Phinehas Elijah *Hurwitz, author of *Sefer ha-Berit*), but their revolutionary nature was rapidly revealed. R. Elijah's circle of disciples consolidated against these new forces; they regarded Torah study as a guarantee for the continued existence of the nation in its traditional form and converted religious learning into a popular movement, in which the great central yeshivot played a leading role. The first of these was the yeshivah established by Ḥayyim *Volozhiner in 1803 in the townlet of Volozhin. In its wake, both large and small yeshivot were founded in many towns and villages, as well as *kolelim* and *kibbuẓim* ("groups") for young men and *perushim* ("abstinents"), whose students prepared themselves for the rabbinate through self-instruction (the *kibbuẓ* of Eisiskes (Eishishok), near Vilna, was well known). During the 19th century, large yeshivot were established in *Mir, Telz (*Telsiai), *Slobodka (near Kovno), and other townlets. The personality of *Israel Meir ha-Kohen (the Ḥafeẓ Ḥayyim) left its imprint on his yeshivah in the little town of Radun, where Torah learning was combined with the study of *musar* (ethical literature). An attempt to adapt these studies to the spirit of the modern era was made by Isaac Jacob *Reines, a founder of the *Mizrachi organization, who in 1904 established a yeshivah in *Lida where secular studies were taught and modern Hebrew literature was studied.

During the middle of the 19th century, the *Musar movement emerged from within the ranks of Orthodox Jewry. Initiated by R. Israel (Salanter) *Lipkin, it endeavored to strengthen traditional Judaism against the dangers of the modern era by fostering the study of ethics. The "Musarniks" established several yeshivot (Keneset Yisrael in Slobodka; the yeshivah of *Novogrudok where an extremist, fanatical, and ascetic wing of the movement emerged). Their attempt to introduce this trend into other yeshivot gave rise to sharp polemics from their opponents, who feared that the study of *musar* would result in a neglect of Torah study.

The yeshivot of Lithuania attracted young men throughout Russia. They trained rabbis and religious communal workers for Jewish communities all over the world. Many who later abandoned traditional Judaism, including Ḥ. N. *Bialik and M. J. *Berdyczewski, were also educated in them. Over the last century, the rabbis of Lithuania became known throughout the Jewish world. They included Isaac Elhanan *Spektor of Kovno, Joseph Baer *Soloveichik of Brest, *Meir Simḥah ha-Kohen and Joseph *Rozin of Dvinsk, Ḥayyim Ozer *Grodzinski of Vilna, Jeruham Judah Leib *Perelmann ("Ha-Gadol mi-Minsk"), Isser Zalman *Meltzer of Slutsk, Abraham Isaiah *Karelitz (the Ḥazon Ish), and many others.

Ḥasidism did not spread through Lithuania to the same extent as in the other parts of Eastern Europe. Only one branch, Ḥabad Ḥasidism, struck roots in Belorussia. The descendants and disciples of its leader, *Shneur Zalman of Lyady, scattered in many towns and townlets and formed an energetic organization of Ḥasidism whose influence spread beyond the borders of Lithuania. Their headquarters were in the townlet of *Lubavich. This trend in Ḥasidism was of a scholarly, philosophical nature. It considered Torah study to be one of the fundamentals of

Ḥasidism, to be combined with the study of ethical and ḥasidic works. At the close of the 19th century, the Ḥabad movement established its own network of yeshivot (*Tomekhei Temimim*). A more popular branch of Ḥasidism which developed in the region situated between Lithuania and Volhynia was centered around the *ẓaddikim* of the *Karlin-*Stolin dynasty.

An important cultural factor in Lithuania from the close of the 18th century was the Hebrew press. The first printing presses were founded in Shklov (1783) and Grodno (1788). During the 19th century Vilna became one of the world's leading centers for the printing of Hebrew books (of the *Romm family and other presses). It was here that the famous Vilna Talmud was printed, as well as a multitude of religious and ethical works, and Haskalah and popular literature in Hebrew and Yiddish.

Although Lithuania played an important role in the preservation of traditional Judaism, it also contributed largely to the movements which shook the Jewish world in recent generations and brought many changes in it. These were Haskalah, the Zionist movement, and the Jewish Socialist movement.

Haskalah. From neighboring Prussia Haskalah penetrated Lithuania, first to the small border towns and the cities of Vilna and Minsk, and from there to other localities. In Lithuania Haskalah assumed a particular character. The manifestations of national disavowal and *assimilation to other cultures which left their imprint on Haskalah in Western Europe, as well as in Poland and southern Russia, were absent in Lithuania. Circles of *maskilim* who adhered to their people and its language were formed. A Hebrew literature which spread Haskalah and its ideas developed. This literature was not confined to Jewish studies (Wissenschaft) but encompassed every aspect of life. Its exponents were poets such as Abraham Dov (Adam ha-Kohen) *Lebensohn, and J. L. *Gordon, novelists such as Abraham *Mapu and Perez *Smolenskin, publicists and critics such as A. U. *Kovner, A. J. *Paperna, M. L. *Lilienblum, and J. M. *Pines, scholars in Jewish studies (Joshua *Steinberg, E. *Zweifel), authors of popular works on general history and geography (M. A. *Guenzburg; K. *Schulman), and natural sciences (H. S. *Slonimski, Ẓevi *Rabinowitz, and S. J. Abramowicz, known as *Mendele Mokher Seforim). The *maskilim* assisted the Russian government in its efforts to spread Russian culture among the Jews and cooperated with it in the establishment of a network of Jewish state schools, at the center of which stood the government rabbinical seminary of Vilna. They laid the foundations of both the Russian-Jewish literature (L. *Levanda) and modern Yiddish literature (I. M. *Dick, *Shomer (N. M. Shaikevich), J. *Dineson, and Mendele Mokher Seforim). They also paved the way for the *Ḥibbat Zion and Zionism on the hand and the Jewish Socialist movement on the other.

Ḥibbat Zion and Zionism. Lithuania was a fertile ground for the development of Ḥibbat Zion and Zionism. The Jews of Lithuania had been attached to Ereẓ Israel by powerful ties since the immigration there of the Ḥasidim and the disciples of the Gaon of Vilna from the end of the 18th century. Natives of Lithuania such as D. *Gordon, in the periodical *Ha-Maggid*, P. Smolenskin, in *Ha-Shaḥar*, J. M. Pines, and E. *Ben-Yehuda had already discussed Jewish nationalism and settlement in Ereẓ Israel in the 1870s. With the inception of Ḥibbat Zion, the movement spread to many towns and townlets, one of its centers being Bialystok, the residence of Samuel *Mohilever, one of the leaders of the movement. Natives of Lithuania were among the most prominent propagators of the Ḥibbat Zion ideology throughout Russia and beyond (S. P. *Rabinowicz, Hermann *Schapira, etc.). In 1902 the second convention of Russian Zionists was held in Minsk. This was the only Zionist convention to be held openly and attended by the public in the czarist period. From 1905 to 1912 the center of Russian Zionism was Vilna. The Zionists headed the movement for the revival of the Hebrew language and the establishment of modern Hebrew schools (*ḥeder metukkan*, "reformed *ḥeder*"). The first Diaspora institution for the training of Hebrew teachers was opened in 1908 in Grodno ("the Grodno courses"). The development of Hebrew literature in Lithuania and the activities of Hebrew authors

Figure 7. Market day in Pilviskiai, in the Vilkaviskis district.

and poets such as Z. *Shneour, Yaakov *Cahan, and I. D. *Berkowitz were closely connected with Zionism.

Jewish Socialist Movement. Lithuania was the cradle of the Jewish Socialist movement. It was characteristic that the Jews of Lithuania found it necessary to publish a Socialist literature, at first in Hebrew (A. S. *Liebermann and his colleagues) and later in Yiddish. The background to this was the existence of the many thousands of poor and oppressed Jewish workers and craftsmen who did not know Russian or Polish; the *maskilim* and Socialists were therefore compelled to address them in their own language. From the close of the 19th century, there rapidly developed an ideology in which revolutionary Socialism was allied to fragmentary and propitiatory nationalist formulae which in practice called for the fostering of a secular literature in Yiddish (Yiddishism) and Jewish cultural autonomy, centered on a secular community organization and Jewish schools giving instruction in the language of the masses (Ch. *Zhitlowsky). In order to mobilize the Jewish workers for revolutionary activities the *Bund was organized. The Bund rapidly extended its activities into Poland and Ukraine but its influence was essentially felt in Lithuania. Its emissaries gained adherents among the poverty-stricken Jews of the towns and townlets, and created a sense of self-confidence in the Jewish apprentices and workers and mobilized them into the service of the revolution. The Bund played a major role in the destruction of traditional Judaism and in opposition to Hebrew culture and Zionism.

The influence of Lithuanian Jewry on Russian and world Jewry gained in impetus from the middle of the 19th century. The Lithuanian yeshivot attracted students from every part of Russia, as well as from abroad. Religious and secular books from Vilna were sold throughout the Disapora. Rabbis of Lithuanian origin served many of the world's communities and Lithuanian *melammedim* (teachers of elementary religious studies) were recognized as capable teachers in Poland and southern Russia.

One of the causes of the spread of Lithuanian influence was the dire poverty in the country, which led to a constant stream of emigration toward southern Russia and Poland and later to the countries of Western Europe and America. Wherever the Lithuanian Jews arrived, they brought with them their spiritual heritage and learning and thus contributed toward strengthening traditional Judaism and the forging of closer links among the Jewish people and its culture. They were also prominent among the Jewish populations of St. Petersburg and Moscow. Large numbers settled in Warsaw and Lodz. They streamed to America and formed a special concentration in South Africa. They also made an extensive contribution to the modern development of Ereẓ Israel.

Lithuanian Jewry was severely affected by World War I and the revolutions and border changes which ensued, bringing dissolution and economic and spiritual chaos. When the Jews were expelled from Kovno province, many communal leaders and activists there left for the interior of Russia, where they continued their activities. Once the regimes and their borders had consolidated, Lithuanian Jewry found itself divided among states: independent Lithuania, Belorussian S.S.R., and Poland.

In Belorussian S.S.R. There were some 400,000 Jews living in Belorussian S.S.R. between the two world wars. The authorities adopted a policy of systematic repression of traditional Judaism, the Hebrew language and culture, and the Zionist movement, assisted in this by the *Yevsektsiya. During the 1920s, the elements remaining faithful to Judaism still carried on a difficult struggle and maintained clandestine yeshivot and *ḥadarim*, Zionist youth movements

Figure 8. Carved wood Ark of the Law in the 16th-century synagogue in Vezaitiai, Utena district.

Figure 9. Jewish soldiers as *seder* guests of a Utena family.

Figure 10. The shoemakers' synagogue, in the northern Lithuanian town of Biržai.

and *Heḥalutz organizations. The Jewish Communists endeavored to provide a substitute for Jewish culture. In Belorussia there even existed a trend among the Yevsektsiya which attempted to consolidate the national position of the Jews in this region by promoting Yiddish schools, Jewish publishing houses and newspapers, and the establishment of a higher institute for Jewish studies in Minsk which engaged in research on the history of the Jews in Lithuania, their dialect, and their popular culture. These experiments flickered out and were liquidated during the 1930s because the authorities did not support them and the Jewish masses were indifferent to them.

In Poland. After World War I the majority of the former Lithuanian Jews came within the boundaries of newly independent *Poland on the border strip extending from the north of Vilna to the Polesye marshes. They continued to develop independent cultural activities in every sphere. Yeshivot flourished in this region (among them, the great yeshivah of Mir with its hundreds of students, and those of Radun, *Slonim, *Lomza, *Kletsk, etc.). Hebrew schools, including secondary schools and excellent training colleges for teachers, founded by the *Tarbut organization were concentrated there. The network of Yiddish schools of the Central Yiddish School Organization (CYSHO) was also developed in this area, and in 1925 the Institute for Jewish Research (Yiddisher Visenshaftlicher Institut, *YIVO) was founded in Vilna. It became a world center for research into the Yiddish language and the history of the Jews and their culture in Eastern Europe. The Vilna theatrical company (*Di Vilner Trupe*) was established and a Yiddish press and literature flourished (the *Yung Vilner* group of poets included Chaim *Grade and A. *Suzkever). The Zionist and pioneer youth movements expanded in this region. When both independent and Polish Lithuania were annexed by Russia in 1939–40, the Jewish institutions were rapidly liquidated. The German invasion of June 1941 brought the physical annihilation of Lithuanian Jewry. [Y.S.]

In Independent Lithuania. About a year before the end of World War I, on Sept. 18–23, 1917, precisely two years after the capture of Vilna by the Germans, the Lithuanians were given permission by the German occupation force to hold a congress in Vilna to consider the future political fate of Lithuania. The congress put forward the demand for an independent Lithuanian state within its ethnographic boundaries with Vilna as the capital. The Vilna congress

Figure 11. The old *bet ha-midrash* in Žydikiai.

Figure 12. Main street of Alytus, a town with one of the oldest Jewish communities in Lithuania. The community was wiped out by the Nazis in 1941.

also elected a national council, Lietuvos Taryba, which on Feb. 16, 1918, proclaimed Lithuania an independent state. The Germans maintained their occupation of Lithuania until the end of 1918.

Population. According to the census held on Sept. 17, 1923, the Jewish population numbered 153,743 (7.5% of the total), and was the largest national minority. They formed just under one-third of the total population of the larger towns, 28.7% of the small-town population, and only 0.5% of the village inhabitants. In the following five towns the census showed the Jewish population to be:

Table 1.

	Jewish population	% total population
Kaunas (Kovno)	25,044	27.1%
Panevezys (Ponevezh)	6,845	35.6%
Siauliai (Shavli)	5,338	24.9%
Ukmerge (Vilkomir)	3,885	37.5%
Vilkaviskis (Volkovyshki)	3,206	44.1%

In *Memel (Klaipeda), which with its district belonged to Lithuania from 1923 to 1939 as an autonomous region, there were 2,470 Jews in 1929. Their number in the Memel region rose as a result of migration from other parts of Lithuania. At the beginning of 1939, shortly before the seizure of Memel by Germany, the territory had about 9,000 Jewish inhabitants. Statistics of 1937 show 157,527 Jews (75,538 males, 81,989 females; or 98% of the total) as having declared their nationality as Jewish, an indicator of the strength of Jewish consciousness among the Jews of Lithuania and the slight influence of assimilation.

Jews mainly spoke Yiddish among themselves, but a number of the professional intelligentsia used Russian. Although in time practically all Jews were able to speak Lithuanian, this did not become their regular spoken language.

Economic Position. The agrarian reforms which the Lithuanian constituent assembly adopted in 1922 also affected the few Jewish owners of farms of over 80 hectares in extent. The Lithuanian government, however, did little to satisfy the claims of Jews who had any rights to the ownership of land. The agrarian reforms only partly satisfied the land hunger of the poor peasants, and in addition to emigration abroad there was also a considerable migration from the rural districts to the towns. This general process of urbanization came into conflict with the long-established economy of the Jewish inhabitants of the town and *shtetl*. In this growing economic competition, the administration of the young Lithuanian republic actively took the part of the Lithuanians. To develop agrarian economy, the government assisted in the formation of cooperatives, which accumulated control of the entire export trade, including

Figure 13. Staff and pupils of the *Tiferet Baḥurim* school in Kaisiadorys. Trakai district, southeastern Lithuania.

the trade in agricultural products. Thus many Jews were deprived of their livelihood.

In 1923 there were 25,132 Jews engaged in trade and credit banking, 18,107 in industry and crafts, 4,996 in agriculture, 4,180 in the liberal professions, and 2,348 in transport. Jewish commerce was largely concentrated in small trade, while industry and crafts were mainly carried on in small factories or workshops.

During the early years of Lithuanian national independence the Jews had a predominant part in the export-import trade. However, shortly before World War II Jewish participation in the export trade amounted to only 20%, and in the import trade to 40%. In 1923 there were nearly 14,000 Jewish shops and 2,160 non-Jewish shops; in 1936 the respective numbers were approximately 12,000 and 10,200. The majority of Jewish shops were small-scale establishments. Jewish traders were unable to compete with the Lithuanian cooperatives, which enjoyed great privileges especially in respect of taxation. They increased rapidly and, between 1919 and 1925, the number of such competitive enterprises ranged against Jewish trade doubled in number.

About one-third of the Jews earned their livelihood in crafts. There were Jews also in the professions, but their numbers continually decreased, and their places were taken by Lithuanians. At the beginning of 1931 there were 88 Jewish cooperative people's banks having more than 20,000 members and functioning in conjunction with an association of Jewish people's banks. The Jewish people's banks owned a portion of the working capital of the central bank for the support of Jewish cooperatives.

Emigration. Both open and unofficial measures aiming at ousting Jews from their economic positions led many Jews to emigrate. Between 1928 and 1939, 13,898 Jews emigrated from Lithuania, of whom 4,860 (35%) went to South Africa; 3,541 (25.5%) to Palestine; 2,548 (18.3%) to Latin America; 1,499 (10.8%) to the United States; 648 (4.6%) to Canada; and 602 (5.8%) elsewhere. It is estimated that between 1923 and 1927 at least 6,000 to 7,000 Jews emigrated from Lithuania, and between 1919 and 1941, 9,241 Lithuanian Jews emigrated to Palestine (3.07% of all those who settled there in that period).

Jewish Autonomy. In the early period of the republic, Lithuanian policy was concerned that Jewish influence in Lithuania and abroad, especially in the United States, should be exercised for the benefit of their country. In the first Lithuanian cabinet formed in Vilna, there were three Jews, J. Wygodsky (minister for Jewish affairs), Shimshon Rosenbaum (deputy foreign minister), and N. Rachmilewitz (deputy minister of commerce). At the end of 1918 the Germans evacuated Lithuania, and in January it was occupied by the Bolsheviks. The Lithuanian government then moved from Vilna to Kaunas (Kovno). Wygodsky remained in Vilna, which in 1920 was captured by the Poles under General L. Zeligowski, and the city and district of Vilna became a part of Poland. The other two members of the cabinet accompanied the government to Kaunas, and in 1919 Wygodsky was replaced as minister of Jewish affairs by the Kaunas communal leader and Zionist Max Soloveichik (*Solieli).

On Aug. 5, 1919, the Lithuanian delegation to the Peace Conference at *Versailles sent to the *Comité des Délégations Juives in Paris a letter in which the Lithuanian government guaranteed to the Jews of Lithuania the "right of national-cultural autonomy." This official declaration made possible the rise and development in Lithuania of institutions of Jewish national autonomy. As a result there arose a widespread system of legally recognized *communities *(kehillot)*. On Jan. 5, 1920, the first communal conference was held in Kaunas with the participation of 141 delegates. A Jewish National Council was appointed and given the task, in conjuction with the Ministry of Jewish Affairs, of administering the Jewish autonomous institutions. Shimshon Rosenbaum was elected head of the Jewish National Council. The minister for Jewish affairs received directives from the National Council and was responsible to it. The National Council conducted widely ramified activity in all areas of Jewish life. During the early years of its existence it was much occupied with assistance to the Jewish war refugees who had returned from Russia, and also with helping immigrants. It obtained financial means from the *American Jewish Joint Distribution Committee and other Jewish aid organizations.

A statute concerning the communities was promulgated in March 1920 and recognized the community *(kehillah)* as a regular, obligatory, public, authorized institution, competent to impose taxes and issue regulations in order to meet the budgets for religious affairs, charity, social aid, educational institutions, and the like. The community was also responsible for the registration of Jewish births. The community administration, the community council, was elected on democratic principles. Every citizen whose documents showed him to be a Jew was automatically a member of the community. Only by conversion to another religion or on proof that his document was invalid, could anyone cease to be a member of the *kehillah*. The second communal congress, which opened in Kaunas on Feb. 14, 1922, was attended by 130 delegates representing all the Jewish communities in the towns and small towns in Lithuania. One of the focal problems of the congress was the question of the Jewish educational system, especially in respect of the school curriculum and the right of the pupils' parents to determine the ideological spirit of the school.

On the admission of Lithuania into the League of Nations, the Lithuanian government, in May 1922, signed a declaration that Lithuania would fulfill all obligations regarding her national minorities as formulated in the agreement concerning *minority rights in the newly established states. On Aug. 1, 1922, the Lithuanian Constituent Assembly accepted the constitution which assured national rights to the larger national minorities in the country. The years 1919 to 1922 were the golden age of Jewish national autonomy in Lithuania, when the political and citizenship rights of the Jews were recognized and confirmed. The end of 1922 and the start of 1923 saw the beginning of the erosion of Jewish autonomy. The reactionary clerical groups then standing at the helm of state launched a campaign, at first covertly and later openly, against Jewish autonomy and Jewish interests in general. There were many reasons for this new course taken by the Lithuanians in respect of their Jewish fellow citizens. Once the Lithuanian republic had found its feet, the Lithuanians no longer felt that they needed the help of Jews either at home or abroad. When the Constituent Assembly, in dealing with the draft constitution, removed the clauses relating to ministries for the affairs of the national minorities and the right of the minorities to use their mother tongue for public matters, the minister for Jewish affairs, M. Soloveichik, resigned from the cabinet. His portfolio was then held for a short time by Julius (Judah) *Brutzkus.

On Nov. 20, 1923, the Jewish National Assembly opened in Kaunas, consisting of delegates elected by the Jewish population by democratic proportional voting. The composition of the newly elected National Council was: General Zionists 11; *Mizrachi 10; *Ẓe'irei Zion (Hitaḥadut) 6; Zionist-Socialist 5; Craftsmen 4; *Po'alei Zion Left 2; *Folkspartei 2. The *Agudat Israel groups in general boycotted the elections. In dealing with the national budget for the year 1924, the Lithuanian parliament struck out the provisions for the Ministry of Jewish Affairs. In protest, Rosenbaum resigned from his portfolio in February 1924. The new cabinet, formed in April 1924, included no minister for Jewish affairs. The National Council continued in

Figure 14. The Kaunas (Kovno) Maccabi soccer team.

Figure 15. A Jewish porter in Jurbarkas.

Figure 16. A Jonava Jew.

Figure 17. Jewish fire brigade in the town of Plunge.

existence for a short time but when it met for a special session on Sept. 17, 1924, it was dispersed by the police, and subsequently ceased to exist. The democratically organized *kehillot* were also later dissolved. The government passed a new law for the *kehillot*, depriving them of their Jewish-national content. The Jews then boycotted the elections to these *kehillot* and they were not constituted. Later, as a result of the efforts of the Jewish parliamentary faction, two bodies were formed with limited functions: Ezra (for social aid) and Adass Yisroel (for religious needs). All that remained as remnants of autonomy were the Jewish people's banks and the Hebrew-Yiddish school system.

EDUCATION. The educational system set up in independent Lithuania was one of the most important achievements of the Jewish national autonomy. Teachers in the Jewish elementary schools who had teaching certificates approved by the ministry of education received their salaries from state funds in common with non-Jewish teachers in the general state schools. The running expenses of the schools were met by city government institutions. The three school systems comprised *Tarbut which was Zionist-orientated; "Yiddishist" schools for the Socialist trend; and Yavneh, the religious traditional schools. The language of instruction was Hebrew in the Tarbut schools, Yiddish in the Yiddishist schools, and Hebrew, and to some extent also Yiddish in the Yavneh schools. Each school system was supported by its own political-ideological groups. The Tarbut schools were in the front rank of Jewish schools in Lithuania. Because of the large number of its Hebrew schools of all grades, Lithuania acquired its reputation among Jews as the "second Ereẓ Israel." There were 46 Tarbut elementary schools in 1922, 72 in 1924, and 84 in 1932. The Agudat Israel and Mizrachi groups confined their interest to the Yavneh schools. There were also *ḥadarim*, *talmud torah* institutions, and *yeshivot. Apart from the celebrated yeshivot in Slobodka and in Telz there were large yeshivot also in *Panevezys (Ponovezh), *Kelme (Kelmy), and other communities. The Culture League (Kultur-Lige), founded in 1919, also had its schools, where at first the moderate Yiddishist elements were represented but later the Communists set the tone. These schools ignored Hebrew and introduced the phonetic spelling of Yiddish. The Culture League was closed down by the government in 1924, and some of its institutions (elementary schools, evening schools, and libraries) were abolished. Those that survived had no formal central management. However, an illegal organization of Yiddishist schools was maintained in Kaunas. In 1926 the Folkspartei created a Jewish educational association, and some of the Yiddishist schools were under its supervision.

The number of Hebrew and Yiddish elementary schools in Lithuania reached 108 in 1936, having 13,607 pupils and 329 teachers. There were in addition Hebrew and Yiddish kindergartens. In the school year 1935/36, there were 60 secondary schools, of which 28 were state schools and 32 private. Among the latter there were 14 Jewish secondary schools. Jewish pupils in the Jewish and non-Jewish secondary schools amounted to 18.9% of the total school attendance. There were also Hebrew and Yiddish pre-secondary schools which provided the first four grades of the secondary school course. The Jewish secondary and pre-secondary schools had to be largely maintained by the parents; the Ministry of Education reduced its subsidy to the Jewish educational institutions year by year. The medium of instruction in the Hebrew secondary schools was Hebrew in all eight grades. There were two secondary schools giving instruction in Yiddish, the *Vilkomir (Ukmerge) Reali school, and the Kaunas Commercial School.

Kaunas University in 1922 had a student body of 1,168, including "free auditors" or occasional students, among them 368 Jews (31.5%). In 1935 the student body (including occasionals) numbered 3,334, among them 591 Jews (16.4%). A *numerus clausus was unofficially introduced in the medical faculty in the course of time, and in 1936 not a single Jewish medical student gained admittance. Because of the difficulties facing Jews trying to qualify in law, and the deterioration of prospects in the liberal professions generally, the proportion of Jewish students in the other faculties also fell sharply. Among the 411 professors, lecturers, and other members of the teaching staff of Kaunas University, there were no more than six Jews. The chair of Semitic studies was held by Ḥayyim Nachman *Shapira.

POLITICAL POSITION. During the democratic period of the independent Lithuanian republic (1919–26) there were four parliamentary elections. The constituent assembly (May 1920–November 1922) included six Jewish deputies, S. Rosenbaum, M. Soloveichik (both Zionists), N. Rachmilewitz, Rabbi A. Poppel (Aḥdut, i.e., *Agudat-Israel), and N. *Friedman and E. Finkelstein (both advocates and non-party democrats). N. Friedman was succeeded on his death by S. Landau. There was Jewish representation in parliamentary committees, and in the praesidium, and the Jews played their part in drawing up the basic citizenship laws of the young Lithuanian state. Their main task, however, was to safeguard the interests of the Jewish natonal minority. The Jewish parliamentary faction maintained close contact with the Jewish National Council.

On the basis of the election results for the first parliament (which sat from November 1922 to March 1923) the Jews were entitled to six seats, but because of a deliberately false interpretation of the election law, only three Jewish seats were recognized. The same happened with the Polish representation. The Jewish and Polish deputies, together with the other opposition members, thereupon expressed "no confidence" in the newly established government. The first parliament was accordingly dissolved. In the elections for the second parliament (which sat from May 1923 to May 1926), the Jews and other national minorities formed a nationalities bloc, and seven Jewish deputies were elected: M. Wolf, J. *Robinson, S. Rosenbaum, all Zionists; I. Brudny (Ẓe'irei-Zion, World Union) L. Garfunkel (Ẓe'irei-Zion, Hitaḥadut); E. Finkelstein (Folkspartei) and Rabbi Joseph *Kahaneman. For various reasons there were subsequent changes in the Jewish representation. The last democratically elected parliament lasted in all just over half a year, and the coup d'état of Dec. 17, 1926 put an end to democracy in Lithuania. Power then fell into the hands of the extremist nationalists (*Tautininkai*) who introduced an authoritarian regime. The parliament was dissolved in April 1927, and a temporary constitution was promulgated in May 1928, abolishing the most important democratic principles of the previous constitution.

The social and economic contrasts existing between the Lithuanians and Jews influenced their relationship and aggravated anti-Semitism. Economic anti-Semitism found its most conspicuous expression in the organization of Lithuanian traders and workers known as the Verslininkai ("skilled workers"). The organization was formed in 1930 and its slogan was "Lithuania for Lithuanians." Its attitude toward the Jews became increasingly aggressive, and although there were no pogroms in Lithuania as in Poland and Rumania, anti-Semitic demonstrations occurred from time to time. The Jewish press played a great part in the struggle of the Jewish population for national political rights. Lithuanian Jewry, though small in number, published a number of newspapers and periodicals which

Figure 18. A wedding group in the little town of Alsediai, in the Telšiai district.

Figure 19. Ḥasidic synagogue in Kaunas (Kovno).

Figure 20. A Jewish blacksmith.

Figure 21. Punting timber on the Neman river near Jonava.

helped to form Jewish public opinion both at home and abroad.

Soviet Rule in Lithuania, 1940–41. The U.S.S.R.-German Pact of Aug. 23, 1939, brought Soviet dominance to the Baltic area. On Oct. 10, 1939, the U.S.S.R. and Lithuania concluded an agreement in Moscow for "the transfer of Vilna and the Vilna province to the Lithuanian Republic and mutual assistance between the Soviet Union and Lithuania," which came into effect on the following day. With the incorporation of Vilna, the Jewish community of Lithuania grew by about 100,000. Previously the 160,000 Lithuanian Jews constituted 7% of the population, but with the annexed portions they totaled over a quarter of a million, about 10% of the total population of the enlarged country. The number of Jewish refugees from Poland grew considerably (to 14,000–15,000) in the following months. About 10,000 stayed in Vilna and the rest in Kovno (Kaunas) and other places. About 5,000 refugees managed to emigrate from Lithuania. The Lithuanian Jews made every effort to assist refugees. On June 15, 1940, Soviet troops crossed the Lithuanian border and a "people's government" was established on June 17, which included two Jews, L. Kogan, minister of health, and H. Alperovitch, minister of commerce. On July 14, "elections" to the People's Sejm ("parliament") took place. Five Jews were among the deputies elected. On August 3 the Supreme Soviet acceded to the Sejm's "request" to become the 16th Soviet Republic. Shortly afterward, the provisional Lithuanian government was replaced by a soviet of people's commissars. All industrial and commercial enterprises, private capital, and larger dwelling houses were nationalized, and a new agrarian reform carried out. All social groups and organizations, general as well as Jewish, had to cease their activities, with the exception of those belonging to the Communists (who had been illegal until the Russian invasion), and the press (again excepting the Communist newspapers) was closed down. A wave of arrests swept over the country. At the same time a considerable number of Soviet officials entered Lithuania. Many of the former owners of the nationalized houses, firms, and factories were forced to settle in the provinces. The effect of the introduction of Soviet rule upon the Jewish population was particularly strong. The new Communist regime was in urgent need of experience and abilities possessed by the Jewish intelligentsia, so that Jews were given prominent positions in the economic, legal, and administrative apparatus. At the same time, although nationalization of all important branches of the economy applied equally to all citizens, irrespective of their ethnic origin, large segments of the Jewish population were affected with special harshness. A total of 986 industrial enterprises were nationalized, of which about 560 (57%) belonged to Jews; of 1,593 commercial firms nationalized, no less than 1,320 (83%) were owned by Jews. Jews were also strongly hit by the nationalization of houses and bank accounts.

The phase before the German attack on Lithuania was marked by deportations to Siberia. In the spring of 1941 the Soviet security services compiled lists of "counter-revolutionary elements" and submitted secret reports on those listed, which also included Jews in the following categories: leaders and journalists of various Zionist political groups; leaders of the Bund and Bundist journalists; leaders of Jewish military and "fascist" formations—e.g., of the Jewish veterans of Lithuania's war of independence, of the Jewish war veterans, of *Betar, the *Revisionists, and their affiliated bodies.

In mid-June 1941, one week before the German-Soviet war, many people, including Jews, were hastily deported as politically unreliable to Siberia and other parts of Soviet Asia. They were interned in forced labor camps and set to work in coal mines, wood cutting, and other heavy labor. Some of those deported were tried for "crimes" committed prior to the Soviet occupation. Although large numbers of Jews were also among the deportees, Lithuanian anti-Semites alleged that the deportations were the result of Jewish revenge on the local non-Jewish majority, carried out by "Jewish" security officers in charge of the deportations.

German Occupation, 1941–44. The entire country was occupied by the Germans within one week, so that only a handful of Jews managed to escape into the Soviet interior. Lithuania, called Generalbezirk Litauen, was included in the administrative province of the Reichs Kommissariat Ostland which also included the other Baltic republics, Estonia, Latvia, and also Belorussia. Hinrich Lohse was appointed Reich Commissar of Ostland, with headquarters in Riga. The Generalbezirk consisted of three districts: the Šiauliai (Shavli) district, the Kaunas (Kovno) district, and the Vilna district. Adrian von Renteln, the commissioner general for Lithuania, had his seat in Kaunas (called Kauen by the Nazis). The Germans also established a local administration, composed of pro-Hitler elements. Lithuanian "councillors general" (a sort of minister) were appointed, headed by Petras Kubiliūnas, a former general in the Lithuanian army.

On Aug. 13, 1941, Lohse issued secret "provisional regulations" to the general commissioners of Ostland specifying how to deal with Jews pending the application of the "final solution" of the "Jewish question" in Ostland. These orders applied to all the Jews in Ostland—former citizens of Germany, Czechoslovakia, Poland, the Baltic states, and other parts of the Soviet Union. There were special instructions for the treatment of foreign Jews and persons of mixed parentage. The commissioners general were required to register all the Jews under their regional jurisdiction and to issue compulsory orders to them to wear two yellow badges (one on the chest and one on the back). Jews were prohibited from moving from their house or place of residence without permission from the district or city commisioner; using the sidewalks; using public transportation; residing in spas; visiting parks and playgrounds, theaters, cinemas, libraries, museums, or schools; owning cars or radios. Ritual slaughter was also prohibited. Jewish doctors were permitted to treat only Jewish patients; pharmacies owned by Jews were turned over to Aryan pharmacists; Jews were not permitted to function as veterinarians, lawyers, notaries, bank officials, or commercial agents, nor could they deal in real estate or freight forwarding. All Jewish property was confiscated. Persons holding Jewish property had to report to the German administration which dealt with its confiscation. Only the bare necessities of furniture, clothing, and linen were left in Jewish possession, and an allowance of no more than 20 pfennig (about $0.05) per day per person was permitted to the Jews. Finally, the regulations provided for the concentration of the Jews in ghettos, where food and other necessities were supplied to them only insofar as no shortage resulted for supplying the general population. Inside the ghettos, the Jews were permitted "autonomy" in their affairs, subject to the supervision of the regional commissioner, and had their own *Ordnungsdienst* ("police force"). The ghettos were sealed off from the outside world and put under the guard of auxiliary police recruited from among the local population. Able-bodied Jews were put on forced labor, inside or outside the ghetto. Private persons or enterprises utilizing Jews in forced labor paid the regional commissioner directly. The commissars general were authorized to issue orders based on these regulations.

EINSATZGRUPPEN. The *Einsatzgruppen* (Action Units)

Figure 22. The *shammash* of a *bet midrash*.
Figures 1–22 are from the Y. D. Kamson Collection, Yad Vashem Archives, Jerusalem, photographed or collected in 1937–38.

played a major role in the destruction of the Jews in the occupied eastern territories, including Lithuania. *Einsatzgruppe A* was attached to the Northern German army and operated in the Baltic states and Leningrad area. Details of the murder of the Jews in Lithuania are contained in some of the 195 *Einsatzgruppen* reports regularly submitted to the *R.S.H.A. (Reichssicherheitshauptamt) in Berlin from the end of June 1941 to April 24, 1942. The following is an extract of these reports:

> . . . a detachment of *Einsatzkommando* 3, assisted by a Lithuanian *Kommando*, has carried out actions in the following towns: Raseiniai, Rokiskis, Zarasai, Birzai, and Prienai. These executions bring the total number to date of persons liquidated by *Einsatzkommando* 3 (with the assistance of Lithuanian partisans), to 46,692 . . . (Report No. 88, Sept. 19, 1941).

Important data on the extermination of Lithuanian Jewry is contained in a report by *SS-Brigadefuehrer* Stahlecker, commander of *Einsatzgruppe A*. The report, covering the activities of his group on the northern Russian Front and in the occupied Baltic states, dates from the beginning of the war against Russia until Oct. 15, 1941. On June 23, 1941, *Einsatzgruppe A* joined the German forces on the northern Russian front. By June 25 Stahlecker, with a detachment of the *Einsatzgruppe*, reached Kovno, which was taken by the Germans the previous day. The following is an extract from his report:

> . . . In the very first hours after the entry of German troops, local anti-Semitic forces were organized, despite the considerable difficulties involved, to carry out pogroms against the Jews. The security police received appropriate orders and were in fact prepared to solve the Jewish problem by all available means and with utmost severity. It seemed desirable, however, that at least in the beginning, the extraordinarily harsh means [to be employed] should not be recognized for what they were, for that would have caused concern even in German circles. On the surface the impression had to be created that it was the local population which had initiated the anti-Jewish measures as a spontaneous reaction to their oppression by the Jews for many years and to the Communist terror to which they had been exposed in the recent past.
>
> . . . Partisan groups formed in Lithuania and established immediate contact with the German troops taking over the city. Unreliable elements among the partisans were weeded out, and an auxiliary unit of 300 men was formed under the command of Klimaitis, a Lithuanian journalist. As the pacification program progressed, this partisan group extended its activities from Kovno to other parts of Lithuania. The group very meticulously fulfilled its tasks, especially in the preparation and carrying out of large-scale liquidations.
>
> . . . As the Baltic population had suffered from the Jews and the Communists during the Bolshevik occupation, it was to be expected that they would take their own measures against those of their [Jewish and Communist] enemies remaining in their midst. It was the task of the German security police to ensure the speedy completion of this goal. Furthermore, evidence had to be created in order to prove, at a later stage, that it was the local population which had squared their own accounts with the Jews and the Communists. The orders given by the German sources had to be concealed . . .
>
> In Lithuania the initiative was taken by the Lithuanian partisans. On the night of June 25–26, the partisans in Kovno, under the command of Klimaitis, staged a pogrom in which 1,500 Jews were killed. Several synagogues were burned down or otherwise destroyed and a Jewish neighborhood of 60 houses went up in flames. The next night, an additional 2,300 Jews were rendered harmless in the same manner. Kovno has served as a model for similar actions in other parts of Lithuania.
>
> . . . Pogroms, however, could not provide a complete solution to the Jewish problem in Ostland. Large-scale executions have therefore been carried out all over the country, in which the local auxiliary police was also used; they cooperated without a hitch . . .
>
> . . . Simultaneously with the executions ghettos had to be established. There were 30,000 Jews in Kovno. After the first pogroms and killings, a Jewish committee was formed, mainly to organize the transfer to the ghetto . . . In the establishment of the ghettos the security police were in charge of police matters, while the newly established ghetto administration [the Judenrat] was responsible for the provision of forced labor, food supplies, etc.

Appendix No. 8 of Stahlecker's report is contained in Table 2, giving the number killed by *Einsatzgruppe A* in Lithuania (up to the end of October 1941).

Table 2.

Place	Jews	Communists	Total
Kaunas (Kovno) (and vicinity)	31,914	80	31,994
Siauliai (and vicinity)	41,382	763	42,145
Vilna (and vicinity)	7,015	17	7,032
Grand total	80,311	860	81,171

A map drawn up by *Einsatzgruppe A* to show the number of Jews killed in the Baltic states up to the end of December 1941, indicates that 136,421 Jews were murdered by that date in Lithuania (excluding Vilna), with 16,000 Jews remaining in the Kovno ghetto and 4,500 in the Šiauliai ghetto. A comparison of these figures with the Stahlecker report reveals that in this area alone, 56,110 Jews were killed in the last two months of 1941.

Destruction of Jewish Communities in the Provinces. Most of the Jewish communities in the provinces were totally destroyed in the period from August to September 1941. Many communities were wiped out by sudden attack, not a single person surviving to tell the story of their martyrdom. The sparse material available conspicuously points to the active participation of Lithuanians from all walks of life, side by side with the Germans in the slaughter. Most of the Lithuanians who took part in the murder of Jews fled to Germany in the summer of 1944, when the Soviet army liberated Lithuania. After the war they were classified as Displaced Persons and were aided as Nazi victims.

At the first conference of liberated Lithuanian Jews in Germany, held in Munich in April 1947, a resolution was adopted on the "Guilt of the Lithuanian People in the Extermination of Lithuanian Jewry."

HELP FROM NON-JEWS. There were among the Lithuanians a few individuals who in the face of the Nazis extended a helping hand to the Jews, despite the mortal danger to which they thus exposed themselves. In Kovno, those who helped the Jews included E. Kutorgienė, P. Mažylis, the writer Sofija Čiurlionienė, the priest Paukštys, the nun Ona Brokaitytė, and the opera singer Kipras Petrauskas. In Vilna, Ona Simaitė was of the greatest help, while in Siauliai the daughter of the lawyer Venclauskas, the poet Jankus, the priest Lapis, and former mayor Saneckis were among those who distinguished themselves in aiding the Jews.

War Crimes Trials. On Dec. 20, 1944, the Soviet press published the "Declaration of the Special Government Commission Charged with the Inquiry into Crimes Committed by the German-Fascist Aggressors in the Lithuanian Soviet Socialist Republic." This lengthy document also includes a report on the mass murders committed at Ponary, near Vilna, and at the Ninth Fort near Kovno. In its final chapter the declaration lists a substantial number of Nazi war criminals responsible for the murders carried out in Lithuania during the German occupation. The list includes Von Renteln, commissioner general for Lithuania; Wysocki, chief of police in Lithuania; Fuchs, chief of the security police and the SD; Ditfurt, commandant of Vilna; Weiss, chief of the Vilna prisons; Kramer, city commissioner for Kovno; Lentzen, Kovno regional commissioner; Gewecke, Šiauliai regional commissioner; Buenger, Gestapo chief in Kovno; Goecke, commandant of the Kovno concentration camp (formed of remnants of the ghetto; in the fall of 1943 the Kovno ghetto was turned into a concentration camp). Lithuanians who collaborated with the occupying power are not listed at all.

In addition to the major Nazi war criminals who were tried by the International Military Tribunal in Nuremberg and the *Einsatzgruppen* commanders tried by the U.S. Military Court at Nuremberg (case no. 9), a number of Nazi criminals who had had a hand in the destruction of Lithuanian Jewry were tried by the U.S. Military Courts at Dachau and elsewhere. After the war, some trials also took place in Soviet Lithuania. On the whole, however, only a small number of the criminals were brought to account, as most of them succeeded in evading trial. Notable among the trials was the trial at Ulm, Germany (April 28–September 1958) against a group of *Einsatzgruppen* who in 1941 murdered 5,500 Jews in various places near the German border. The accused were sentenced to various terms of imprisonment.

Liberation. Lithuania was liberated by the Soviet army in the summer of 1944 (Vilna on July 13, Šiauliai on July 27, Kovno on August 1). The Jewish survivors consisted of several hundred Jewish partisan fighters, and a few families and children who had been hidden by gentiles. Jewish refugees who at the beginning of the war escaped to Soviet Asia also began to make their way back.

At the beginning of 1945, when Soviet troops liberated the Stutthof concentration camp, several hundred Jewish women from Lithuania were listed among the survivors, and when Dachau was liberated by the Americans, some Lithuanian Jewish men were found alive there. Both the women and the men had been deported from Lithuania in the summer of 1944, 80 of whom found their death in German concentration camps.

Some of the survivors returned to Lithuania, but the majority stayed in the *Displaced Persons (DP) camps established after the war in Germany, Austria, and Italy. Later, they were joined by other Lithuanian Jews who had escaped from Soviet Lithuania via the Jewish underground escape route (see *Beriḥah*). When the DP camps were dissolved, the Lithuanian Jews settled in Israel, the United States, and other countries overseas together with other Jewish DPs.

After the War. The 1959 Soviet census report indicated the Jewish population of Lithuania at 24,672 (11,478 men and 13,194 women), constituting less than 1% of the total population (2,880,000). Of these, 16,354 Jews lived in Vilna, 4,792 in Kovno, and the rest in other urban areas. At the time the census was taken, 17,025 declared Yiddish as their native tongue (the highest percentage in all the areas where the census was taken), 6,912 Russian, 640 Lithuanian, and 95 specified other languages. In the academic year 1960/61 there were 413 Jewish students at institutions of higher learning (1.67% of the total Jewish population of Lithuania). Lithuania was one of the centers from which pressure came to establish a revival of Jewish cultural life after the war. The Soviet authorities eventually agreed to establish an amateur Yiddish theater group there.

For details on Jewish life in the modern period see *Vilna, *Kaunas. [JO.GA.]

Bibliography: *Yahadut Lita*, 3 vols. (1959–71); J. Shatzky, *Kultur Geshikhte fun der Haskole in Lite* (1950); W. Z. Rabinowitsch, *Lithuanian Hasidism* (1970); D. Katz, *Tenu'at ha-Musar*, 5 vols. (1958–63[3]); S. K. Mirsky (ed.), *Mosedot Torah be-Eiropah be-Vinyanam u-ve-Ḥurbanam* (1956), 1–354; M. A. Szulwas, in: I. Halpern (ed.), *Beit Yisrael be-Polin*, 1 (1954), 13–35; A. Kariv, *Lita Mekhorati...* (1960), 7–16. INDEPENDENT LITHUANIA: *Lite*, 1 (1951), index; 2 (1965), index; J. Gar, in: *Algemeyne Entsiklopedye: Yidn*, 6 (1964), 330–41, 402; Kaunas, Centralinis Statistīkos Biuras, *Lietuvos Gyventojai* (1923); *Der Idisher Natsional Rat in Lite: Barikht vegn Zayn Tetikayt* (1922); *Barikht fun der Idisher Seym-Fraktsie fun Tsveytn Litivishn Seym 1923–26* (1926); *Farband fun di Idishe Folks-Baynk in Lite* (1929); *Di Idishe Handverker in Lite in Tsifern* (1936); B. Kagan, in: Z. Scharfstein (ed.), *Ha-Ḥinnukh ve-ha-Tarbut ha-Ivrit be-Eiropah bein Shetei Milḥamot ha-Olam* (1957); EJ, 10 (1934), 1022–290. HOLOCAUST: IMT, *Trial of Major War Criminals*, 23 (1949), index; R. Hilberg, *Destruction of the European Jews* (1961), index; G. Reitlinger, *Final Solution* (1968), index; A. Dallin, *German Rule in Russia 1941–1945* (1957), 182–8; Embassy of the U.S.S.R., Washington, *Information Bulletin* (Feb. 1945); Werner, in: *The American Scholar*, 27 (1957/58), 169–78; N. Grinblat (Goren), in: *Tav Shin He* (1946), 557–79; E. Oshri, *She'elot u-Teshuvot mi-Ma'amakim* (1959), 221–300; idem, *Khurbn Lite* (1951); *Lite*, 1 (1951), vols. 1645–1840; M. Segalson et al. (comps.), *Vernichtung der Juden in Litauen: Tatsachen aus den Jahren 1941–1945* (1959); *Anlageschrift* of the Ulm Trial (1958); *Sudebny protsess po delu o zlodeyaniyakh nemetskofashistskikh zakhvatchikov na territorii Latviyskoy, Litvoskoy i Estanskoy S.S.R.* (1946); J. Gar, in: *Algemeine Entsiklopedie: Yidn*, 6 (1964), 341–74, 402–3; idem, *Azoy is es geshen in Lite* (1965); M. Joffe (ed.), *Hitlerine okupacija Lietuvoye* (1961); S. Binkiene (ed.), *Ir be ginklo kariai* (1967); A. Z. Bar-On and D. Lewin, *Toledoteha shel Maḥteret* (1962).

LITIN, town in Podolia, Ukrainian S.S.R., N.W. of Vinnitsa. In 1578 the king of Poland, Stephen Bathory, permitted the owner of the estate of Litin to establish a town on his land and to hold two annual fairs which "all the citizens of the land, Christians, Jews, and merchants from foreign countries," would be permitted to attend. In 1616 there were 88 houses in the town; 12 belonged to Jews. In 1765 there were 481 Jews; in 1847, 1,804, and in 1897, 3,874 (41% of the total population). In May 1919 a Ukrainian gang conducted pogroms in Litin and 180 Jews were killed and Jewish property looted. In 1926, 2,487 Jews lived in the town (30% of the total). With the Nazi occupation (July 1941) the Jews of Litin were gathered in the ghetto in the district capital of Vinnitsa and killed, together with the other residents of the ghetto (Sept. 22, 1941).

Bibliography: Ẓe'irei Ẓion. Rusyah, *Naftulei Dor*, 2 (1955), 142. [Y.S.]

LITOMERICE (Czech. **Litoměřice;** Ger. **Leitmeritz**), town in N. Bohemia, Czechoslovakia. Jews are mentioned in the town's founding charter (1057) as salt merchants, thus making Litomerice the first town in Bohemia, after Prague, in which Jews are mentioned. There was a Jewish quarter in 1411. In 1514 the city council protected its "poor Jewish artisans" against financial demands of outside lords, and in 1529 the Bohemian royal authorities demanded that the town mayor provide proper protection for the Jews. Ferdinand I canceled a permit allowing free trade of wine in 1540, and in the following year, after a massacre, the Jews were expelled. The town was granted the privilege *de non tolerandis Judaeis* in 1546; the synagogue was turned into a hospital (a Hebrew inscription on the building was preserved). In 1584 Jews were permitted to attend fairs. Six Jewish families settled in Litomerice in 1851. In 1863 there were 100 Jews. The community was constituted in 1875 and a synagogue was dedicated in 1883. There were 616 Jews in 1921. Between the two world wars there was a training center for settlement in Ereẓ Israel at the Litomerice agricultural school. The Zionist politician Emil *Margulies lived in the town. In 1930 the community numbered 425 (2.3% of the total population), of whom 143 declared their nationality as Jewish. At the time of the Sudeten crisis (1938) nearly all of the community left the town, the few men who remained being deported to concentration camps.

A Jewish community also existed in LOVOSICE (Lobositz) on the opposite bank of the Elbe. According to tradition the community was founded by the Jews who had been expelled from Litomerice in 1541. The first documentary evidence on the community is from 1704. There were 17 Jewish houses there in the 18th century. The *Hoenigsberg family lived in the town for some time. Lovosice Jews developed the business of shipping products to Germany on the Elbe, dealing in the production of chocolate. There were 201 persons in the community in 1930. At the time of the Sudeten crisis nearly all the community left the town. The few remaining males were sent to concentration camps.

Bibliography: H. Ankert, in: H. Gold (ed.), *Die Juden und Judengemeinden Boehmens in Vergangenheit und Gegenwart* (1934), 363–9; Germ Jud, 1 (1963), 157; 2 (1968), 478. [J.HER./M.LA.]

LITTAUER, LUCIUS NATHAN (1859–1944), U.S. industrialist, congressman, and philanthropist. Littauer was born in Gloversville, New York, the son of an immigrant from Breslau, Prussia. Upon his graduation from Harvard College in 1878 Littauer entered his father's glove factory. He assumed directorship of the company in 1883, and under him it became the largest manufacturing enterprise of its kind in the country. An entrepreneur, he founded and participated in many other business enterprises, including public utilities, banking, textiles, and transportation.

Littauer became active in Republican politics and served in the U.S. House of Representatives from 1896 to 1907, representing predominantly non-Jewish upstate constituencies. An intimate friend and close political adviser of President Theodore Roosevelt, he was a leading member of the important House Appropriations Committee. From 1912 to 1914 he served as a member of the Board of Regents of the University of the City of New York. During the remainder of his life, Littauer devoted himself to the management of his widespread business interests, and, above all, to an increasing range of philanthropic activities. His initial gift in 1894 for the Nathan Littauer Hospital in Gloversville was followed by many substantial contributions for the building and support of numerous institutions in the area, including the Jewish Community Center. A statue of him was erected in Gloversville in 1929.

His donations helped social welfare, health, recreation, education, and the financial support of needy students aspiring to higher education. He contributed extensively to medical care and research, aiding medical schools and hospitals in New York City, Albany, Paris, and Breslau, where he endowed the Nathan Littauer Stiftung at its Jewish Hospital. At the New York University College of Medicine he endowed a professorship of psychiatry; he also gave a building to the National Hospital for Speech Disorders. In 1937 he made a large gift to the New School of Social Research, New York, for the support of its newly established University in Exile, where many distinguished refugee Jewish intellectuals and scholars found a haven to continue their teaching and research. An abiding interest in public affairs motivated his largest single gift: the erection and endowment at Harvard of the Littauer Center of Public Administration, and the establishment of the Graduate School of Public Administration. The Lucius N. Littauer Foundation, established in 1929, gives grants to a wide variety of causes, including the advancement of Jewish studies and Jewish learning.

Throughout his life, Littauer remained a faithful Jew in the Reform tradition. While in Congress, he advocated legislation to liberalize the immigration laws in order to help the victims of religious persecution in Eastern Europe. He firmly believed in the role of Jewish culture in U.S. intellectual life and supported the **Menorah Journal* and the Menorah movement. In 1925 Littauer endowed the Nathan Littauer professorship of Hebrew literature and philosophy at Harvard—the first of its kind in the U.S.—later augmented by other gifts to Harvard for publications, fellowships, and the acquisition of collections of rare Hebraica and Judaica. He contributed to the Central Conference of American Rabbis for scholarly studies. In 1938 he founded the Institute of Social and Religious Studies at the Jewish Theological Seminary of America. At New York University he initiated the endowment of a chair in Jewish and Hebrew studies. Littauer received a variety of awards and honors for his philanthropic and public activities.

Bibliography: L. Littauer, *Louise Littauer, Her Book*, ed. by L. N. Littauer (1924); *The Letters of Theodore Roosevelt*, ed. by E. E. Morison, 2 (1951), 967; 7 (1954), 502; L. Einstein, *Roosevelt—His Mind in Action* (1930); J. A. Blanchard (ed.), *The H Book of Harvard Athletics...* (1923). [H.STA.]

LITURGY.

IN THE BIBLE AND THE SECOND TEMPLE PERIOD

The beginnings of Jewish liturgy are obscure. The prayers found occasionally in the Bible are spontaneous reactions to personal events or experiences, e.g., the short prayers of Moses (Num. 12:13), Jethro (Ex. 18:10), and Hannah (I Sam. 1:11), and the extended prayer of Solomon at the inauguration of the Temple (I Kings 8:15ff., 23ff.). The only formal prayers are the confessions to be recited when bringing the first fruits (*Viddui Bikkurim*) and the tithe (*Viddui Ma'aser;* Deut. 26:5–15), and that of the high priest which had no prescribed formula (Lev. 16:21). Pious individuals seem to have prayed thrice daily (Dan. 6:11; cf. also Ps. 55:18), and some of the psalms may have served as

Figure 1. Title page of *Maḥzor Romania*, prayers according to the rite followed by the Jews of the Byzantine Empire. Venice, 1586. Cecil Roth Collection.

texts for the levitical service twice a day in the First and Second Temples (I Chron. 23:30). There is no evidence, however, of communal prayer in the Temple. There was only a short liturgy for the priests on duty which comprised a benediction, the recitation of the **Shema* and the *Decalogue, three additional benedictions and the *priestly blessing (Tam. 5:1). The laymen present for the sacrifices participated in the ritual by prostrating themselves (Tam. 7:3; cf. Ber. 11b) and at appropriate pauses, probably chanting such responses as "O give thanks unto the Lord, for He is good" (Ps. 136:1). This ceremony might have been one of the sources out of which the liturgy later developed.

The rise of the synagogue, the frequent fasts prescribed in times of drought for which a special liturgy was fixed in the Mishnah (Ta'an. 2:1–5; see *Fasting), and the *ma'amadot* institution (Ta'an. 2:7; 4:1–4) contributed to the development of liturgy. The *ma'amad* consisted of representatives of the people, part of whom were present at the sacrifices and the rest assembled at home, both conducting prayers four times a day—**Shaḥarit*, **Musaf*, **Minḥah* and *Ne'ilat She'arim* (see **Ne'ilah*, **Mishmarot*, and **Ma'amadot*). The hours later fixed for the *Shaḥarit*, *Minḥah* and **Arvit* prayers were in accordance with the times (of prayer of the members of the *ma'amadot* and thus) of the sacrifices as well as in accordance with the practices of pious individuals who fixed their prayer schedule according to the position of the sun (TJ, Ber. 4:1, 7b; Ber. 26b).

TALMUDIC PERIOD

During the tannaitic period there already existed a somewhat fixed order for prayers, which is found in the Mishnah and the Tosefta and whose composition is attributed to the men of the Great *Synagogue (Ber. 33a). Recorded is the original prayer formula: i.e., *berakhah* ("the benediction") with its wording *Barukh Attah Adonai* ("Blessed are Thou, O Lord") which serves both for prayers of adoration and of petition; the obligation derived from the Pentateuch, to recite the *Shema* twice daily (the recitation was by heart; Ta'an. 4:3) with its benedictions (three in the morning and four in the evening); and the daily **Amidah*, known as *Tefillah*, comprising 18 benedictions (Ber. 4:3) and recited twice daily.

The *Amidah* was most probably composed and edited over a long period; its first three and last three benedictions seem to be the most ancient. On the Sabbath and holidays, the 12 middle benedictions were replaced by the blessing sanctifying the particular occasion ("Sanctity of the Day"; RH 4:5). On Rosh Ha-Shanah only nine benedictions in the *Amidah* were recited because of the numerous additions to the liturgy on that day (i.e., **malkhuyyot*, **zikhronot*, and **shofarot*). The *Amidah* was originally designed for public worship (L. Ginzberg (Ginzburg), *Perushim ve-Ḥiddushim ba-Yerushalmi*, 3 (1941), 237), and the congregation simply answered "Amen" to the reader's recitation. Later, however, it was adapted for individual prayer, and one tannaitic opinion already regarded the practice as obligatory (Ber. 4:3). The *Shaḥarit* (morning) and *Minḥah* (afternoon) *Amidot* were correlated to the sacrifices; the *Arvit* (evening) *Amidah*, however, lacked such correlation and it was therefore at first considered (at least theoretically) not to be obligatory. Ultimately, it became a formal part of the daily liturgy (Ber. 27b). On days when an additional sacrifice *(Musaf)* was prescribed, an *Amidah* was added. Originally it consisted of the same text, but gradually it was elaborated upon with a special section dealing with the restitution of sacrifices and the pilgrimages to Jerusalem.

After reciting the obligatory service, private prayers including personal requests (known as *devarim;* Tos. to Ber. 3:10, also called *teḥinnah* or *taḥanunim*), could be offered. The *teḥinnot* of a number of *tannaim* and *amoraim* are preserved in the Talmud (Ber. 16b–17a). Later, certain psalms (6 and 25) were also used as *teḥinnot*. There is no evidence, however, that psalms were frequently used in the ancient liturgy. The early sources only mention the **Hallel* psalms (RH 4:7) and the *Hallel ha-Gadol* in connection with special feasts (Ta'an. 3:9).

The public reading of portions from the Torah and Prophets was already considered an old institution in mishnaic times. Some texts for these readings (Meg. 3:4ff.) and the number of persons called to the reading (4:1–2) were fixed. The public reading of the Aramaic translation (Targum) of the Torah was likewise a permanent practice in the tannaitic and amoraic periods, and it was still considered obligatory by R. *Amram (Gaon) b. Sheshna (ninth century). The old tradition which ascribes the Sabbath morning reading to Moses (TJ, Meg 4:1, 75a) and the Sabbath *Minḥah*, the Monday and the Thursday reading to Ezra (*ibid.*, BK 82a) is indicative of the great antiquity of the institution of Torah reading.

During the amoraic period little change seems to have taken place in the liturgy. There may have been slight differences between the Palestinian and Babylonian rites in that the latter stressed the superiority of public worship and community prayer (Ber. 6a). All that is known from the sources about these periods concerns the structure and form of the liturgy, while almost nothing is recorded about the texts. Texts which do occasionally occur in the Talmud are the **Havdalah* prayer recited between the Sabbath and a festival following it (Ber. 33b), the seven marriage benedictions (Ket. 7b–8a), the blessing of the new moon (Sanh. 42a), and *Raḥem*, a special prayer for the Ninth of *Av (TJ, Ta'an. 2:2, 65c). These prayers, all essentially *piyyutim*, did not yet have a fixed formula at that time and variant readings of the same prayer were common. Ultimately, one of these readings received general acceptance, sometimes through a combination of two or more formulas, in accordance with the well-known practice of R. *Papa (Sot. 40a., Ber. 11b (cf. Dik. Sof., ad loc.), 59b, Meg. 21b). *Massekhet Soferim* (geonic period) also contains only a few prayer texts.

As early as the tannaitic period the service was elaborated with *piyyutim;* whole prayers were rendered poetically and existing ones were supplemented with piyyutic insertions. Consequently, the exact demarcation line between "ordinary prayer" and *piyyut* is blurred, and many of what are considered ordinary prayers are actually piyyutic in form. The *piyyut* flourished mainly in Palestine; Babylonia was less productive and even resisted its adoption.

GEONIC PERIOD

By early geonic times, two different rites had already developed: the Palestinian and the Babylonian. The old Palestinian rite, which flourished until the 12th century C.E. at least, became known in modern times only after the discovery of the Cairo *Genizah. While there are considerable differences between the Palestinian usage and the other known rites, the discovered texts do not always show whether they were destined for private or public prayer.

The Palestinian texts were mainly published by the following scholars: S. Schechter, in: JQR, 10 (1898), 654–9; I. Lévi, in: REJ, 53 (1907), 231–41; I. Elbogen, *Studien zur Geschichte des juedischen Gottesdienstes* (1907), 1–48; idem, in: JQR, 18 (1906), 587–99; 19 (1907), 229–49; 704–20; idem, in: MGWJ, 55 (1911), 426–46, 586–99; J. Mann, in: HUCA, II (1925), 269–338; S. Assaf, in: *Sefer Dinaburg* (1949), 116–31; A. Scheiber, in: *Ignaz Goldziher Memorial Volume*, 1 (1948), Heb. pt. 27–40; N. Wieder, in: JJS, 4 (1953), 30–37, 65–73. Palestinian liturgical poetry in the *Yedi'ot* of Ha-Makhon le-Ḥeker ha-Shirah ha-Ivrit. Poems of *Yannai were published by M. *Zulay (1938). The Israel Academy of Sciences has been concerned with the registering and publishing of the *Genizah* material under the direction of E. *Fleischer.

Among the characteristics peculiar to the Palestinian rite are: the triennial cycle of the Torah reading; the ending *Ẓur Yisrael ve-Go'alo* for the **ge'ullah* benediction after the *Shema* (morning and evening); *illu finu* (with the benediction *El ha-Hoda'ot*) or *Yehallelukha* (with the benediction *Mehullal ba-Tushbaḥot*) or both, after the **Pesukei de-Zimra;* different texts for several benedictions including the **Birkat ha-Torah;* a totally different recension of the 18 (not 19) benedictions of the *Amidah* in which the (otherwise also known) benedictions *Elohei David u-voneh Yerushalayim, she-Otekha be-yirah na'avod, ha-tov lekha lehodot, oseh ha-shalom* occur; a special benediction before the *Shema, Asher kiddeshanu be-mitzevotav ve-ẓivvanu al mitzvat keri'at Shema* and the addition of *Ya'aleh ve-Yavo* to the *Musaf Amidah.*

The old Babylonian rite is mainly known from geonic treatises; the oldest, the *Seder R. Amram* (ninth century), comprises the text of the prayers together with respective halakhic prescriptions (ed. by N. N. Coronel, 1865; A. L. Frumkin, 1912; D. Hedegard, 1951, pt. I only). The only earlier source is the responsum of *Natronai b. Hilai concerning the 100 benedictions (L. Ginzberg, *Geonica*, 2 (1909), 114ff.). Unfortunately the extant text of the *Seder R. Amram* is in a badly altered form due to the arbitrary modifications of its many copyists (Ginzberg, *ibid.*, 1 (1909), 124, Elbogen, Gottesdienst, 359). The morning service comprises, as do all later compilations, the following well-known compositions: *birkot ha-shaḥar* (*morning benedictions), *Pesukei de-Zimra* with two benedictions, *Shema* with the three benedictions, the *Amidah, taḥanunim,* the Torah reading for certain days, and the **Kedushah de-Sidra.* The other prayers are also arranged according to current usage.

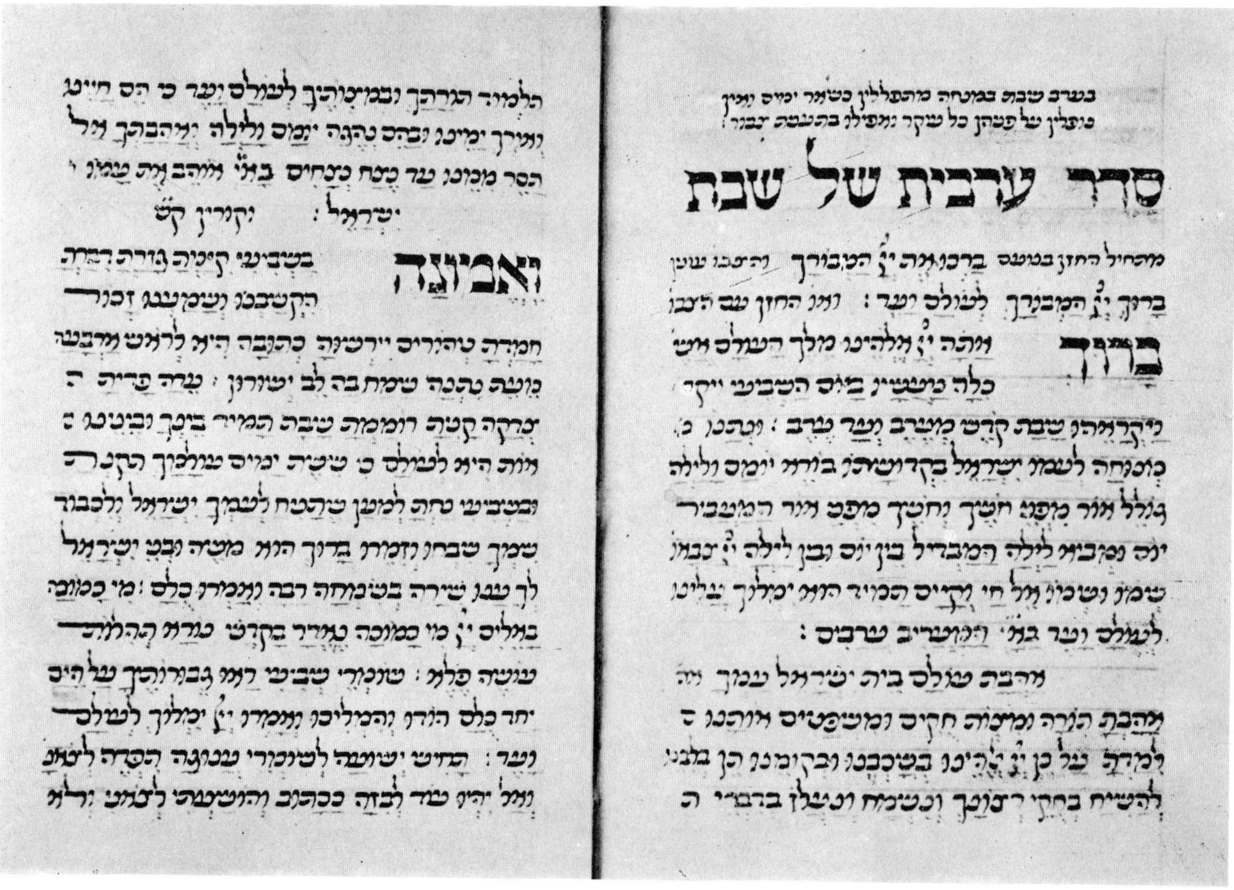

Figure 2. Opening of Sabbath evening service from a manuscript copy of prayers according to the Roman rite, used primarily by the Jews of the Italian peninsula. Italy, 15th century. Cecil Roth Collection.

Figure 3. Page from a *maḥzor* according to the Ashkenazi rite. Weckelsdorf, 1680. Jerusalem, J.N.U.L.

The *seder* was followed (a century later) by the *siddur* of *Saadiah (Gaon) b. Joseph with prescriptions in Arabic (ed. by I. Davidson, S. Assaf, and B. I. Joel (1941)) which, despite some influences of Palestinian usage, is a good example of geonic prayer books; and later still by *Siddur Rashi* (without texts of prayers; ed. S. Buber and J. Freimann (1910–11); **Maḥzor Vitry* (11th century, interpolated with insertions from 13th and 14th centuries, ed. by S. Hurwitz (1923[2])); and Maimonides' *Seder Tefillot* (part of *Mishneh Torah;* see Goldschmidt, in: YMHSI, 7 (1958), 183–213). A *siddur* of Solomon b. Nathan of Sijilmassa (North Africa, 12th century), also containing instructions in Arabic, is still in manuscript (Neubauer, Catalogue of Hebrew Manuscripts in the Bodleian Library, cat. no. 896–9).

With the exception of the **Avodah* of the *Day of Atonement, **azharot,* and **hoshanot,* the Babylonian rite adopted very little Hebrew poetry. In later times, however, when Babylonian communities were established in Palestine and Egypt, *piyyutim* were also introduced in those circles (see M. Zulay, *Zur Liturgie der babylonischen Juden* (1933), passim).

LITURGICAL RITES

From these two ancient usages—the Palestinian and the Babylonian—all the various rites of Jewish liturgy developed. According to some scholars their differences are mainly in the *piyyutim* adopted by the various communities, and they therefore tend to divide the rites into two groups: the Palestinian (comprising Italy, the Balkans, and the French-German countries) and the Babylonian (comprising the Spanish and Yemenite rites). This division may be justified from the historical point of view since the Jews of the first group, originating from the Byzantine Empire, accepted the Palestinian *piyyut* and retained some of the original wording of regular prayers; the Jews of the second group did not accept the Palestinian *piyyut* and were later influenced by the liturgical poetry of the great Spanish poets. The division is, however, not justified from a textual point of view insofar as the statutory prayers are concerned. The wording and order of prayers in all known rites follow the *Seder R. Amram,* i.e., the usage of the two great Babylonian academies, Sura and Pumbedita, and, indirectly, the Babylonian Talmud. In contradistinction, the influence of the old Palestinian rite is hardly noticeable. Obviously, the rites themselves influenced each other, so that not a single rite remained in its original form.

At the same time it would also be incorrect to state that the various rites differ only in the *piyyutim* that they adopted. Distinctions in the regular prayers of the rites were introduced, such as variant readings in the text, which occurred even after the invention of printing; the deletion or inclusion of certain passages; and differences in the order of the prayers in the ritual. All communities tended to shorten or omit entire *piyyutim,* or to combine various liturgical poems, even those of different authors. In some rites the opposition of the halakhic authorities caused the abolition of certain types of *piyyutim.*

PALESTINIAN GROUP

Romanian (Romaniot) Rite. The first ancient rite in the so-called "Palestinian" group is the Romanian (Greek) rite followed by the Jewish communities of the Byzantine Empire. In use in Greece and in European Turkey, at least until the end of the 16th century, and perhaps even later, it was superseded by the Sephardi rite. Four editions of *Maḥzor Romania* appeared in the 16th century, and many more of smaller prayer books *(siddurim)* of the rite. Distinctive features of the rite are: *Hodu* before *Barukh she-Amar;* in the **Kaddish,* the addition *Ve-Yaẓmaḥ purkaneh vi-karev Meshiḥeh u-farek ameh be-raḥmateh;* several elaborations of the weekday *Amidah; Le-Dor va-Dor* for the third benediction of the *Amidah* (instead of *Attah Kadosh*); the short *Emet ve-Yaẓẓiv* on the Sabbath; *Keter* for the *Kedushah* in *Musaf. Maḥzor Romania* contains a large collection of *piyyutim* for *Shaḥarit (*petiḥah, *reshut, *Kaddish, *Barekhu, *yoẓer, ofan, zulat, mi-khamokha); Ma'arivim* for every festival (including the Day of Atonement); **kerovot* for fast days, Purim, the Day of Atonement, Rosh Ha-Shanah (in Mss. also for the other holidays and Ḥanukkah); and a large collection of **seliḥot* and **kinot.* Differences in the manuscripts and the printed editions show that the rite was edited in its final form at a comparatively late date.

(For a description of this rite see: Zunz, Ritus, 79ff., and D. Goldschmidt, in: *Sefunot,* 8 (1964), 205–36.)

The ritual of the Jews of Corfu (their *maḥzor* was never printed) is almost identical with the Romaniot rite. The rite of the Jews of Kaffa (Feodosiya) and Karasubazar (Belogorsk) in the Crimea has, despite many elaborations of the texts, all the distinctions of the *Maḥzor Romania.* While their *siddur* was printed twice (last edition Kala, 1735), their *maḥzor* was never printed. I. Markon (in: *Festschrift . . . A. Harkavy* (1908), 449–69), lists 315 *piyyutim* from their *maḥzor.*

Roman Rite. The Roman (Italian) rite, also called *Minhag ha-Lo'azim,* is in use in Rome, in the interior of Italy, in a few communities in Salonika and Constantinople, and also in the Italian synagogue in Jerusalem. Peculiar to this rite are: *Le'eila Le'eila* in the usual *Kaddish; Keter* in all *Kedushot;* different wording to the *Amidah;* different *taḥanunim* (*ve-Hu Raḥum* is missing); a special piyyutic version of the *Arvit* for Friday evening *(Asher Killah Ma'asav)* and its *Amidah (U-me-Ahavatkha); kerovot* for the Day of Atonement and all the fast days, but not for Rosh Ha-Shanah and other festivals. A number of *piyyutim* had already been removed from the *maḥzor* before the invention of printing.

The first edition of this rite was that of Soncino, printed at Casal Maggiore, 1485/86. An introduction to this *maḥzor* was published by S. D. Luzzatto (1856) entitled *Mavo le-Maḥzor Benei Roma* (new edition, with supplement by D. Goldshmidt and a bibliography of the printed *maḥzor* and *siddur* by J. J. Cohen, Tel Aviv, 1966).

Northern France and Ashkenazi Rites. The Northern French and Ashkenazi rites may be considered as one unit. They are known to have been followed as early as the tenth century at least. The rite of Northern France was never printed because it ceased to exist with the persecutions during the 13th and 14th centuries. It differs from the Ashkenazi rite only in certain additional *piyyutim:* a *kerovah* for the second day of Rosh Ha-Shanah, and some *ma'arivim* (two treatises of the 13th century, *Sefer ha-Maḥkim* and *Siddur Troyes,* record these peculiarities). Until the 1290 expulsion, English Jews also followed the ritual of Northern France. A complete *siddur* with a few *piyyutim* is contained in *Eẓ Ḥayyim* (printed in the edition of I. *Brodie, 1 (1962), 63–138), by R. Jacob Ḥazzan of London. Part of this rite remained in use in three communities in Piedmont (Northern Italy): Asti, Fossano, Moncalvo (אפ"ם) until modern times. These communities had accepted the Ashkenazi rite upon their establishment in Italy, but on the High Holy Days continued to recite the *piyyutim* of the French *maḥzor* from handwritten copies. The community of Asti continued to hold High Holiday services in accordance with its ritual until about 1965.

The *maḥzor* of these communities (known as APM: אפ"ם) is described by D. Goldschmidt, in: KS, 30 (1954–55), p. 118–36, 264–78; and a list of the *piyyutim* is given by I. Markon, in: *Jewish Studies ... G. A. Kohut* (1935), Heb. pt., 89–101. The *Avodah* of the French *maḥzor ... ke-Fi Minhag Italiani,* 2 (1856), 212ff., and additional *piyyutim* were published by A. Rau, in: *Festschrift *Freimann* (1937), Heb. pt. 128–48, and S. *Bernstein, in: *Tarbiz,* 10 (1939), 13–25. The whole material of High Holidays *piyyutim* of the French *maḥzor* found in manuscript is by now included in the *Maḥzor la-Yamim ha-Nora'im,* ed. D. Goldschmidt, Jerusalem, 1970.

The Ashkenazi rite, originally used by the German or German-speaking Jews, was the most widely followed and its *siddur* and *maḥzor* have been printed since the 16th century. Only fragments of the Palestinian texts (e.g., *Ẓur Yisrael* or the short *Emet ve-Yaẓẓiv* in connection with *piyyutim*) have been retained. The *maḥzor* contains *yoẓerot* for the special *Sabbaths and all festivals; *kerovot* for the Four Parashiyyot, *Shabbat ha-Gadol,* all the festivals, Purim (in some communities also for Ḥanukkah), and the Ninth of Av; and a large collection of *seliḥot* and *kinot.* Most of the *piyyutim* are by Palestinian or German authors. The rite is now followed in Germany (from the Elbe River westward), Switzerland, Holland, Belgium, northern France, and in a number of communities of Northern Italy.

During the Middle Ages, the Eastern European communities that followed the rite separated from the rest. This branch comprised the eastern part of Germany, Poland, Lithuania, Bohemia, Moravia, Hungary, and the rest of Austria, all of Russia, Rumania, and the rest of the Balkan countries, and later included also the Ashkenazi Jewish communities of Denmark, England, America, and Palestine. Differences between the two branches—the Western, called *Minhag Rainus* ("Rhine usage") in the Middle Ages; and the Eastern, called *Minhag Oystraikh* or *Minhag Peihem* ("Austrian or Bohemian usage"), today generally known as *Minhag Polin*—are hardly noticeable in the regular prayers; the main variances are in some special *piyyutim.* Different editions of *Minhag Ashkenaz* (Western) and *Minhag Polin* (Eastern) were published from the 16th century onward. The *seliḥot* point to local differences. Thirteen different rites have been printed (see the *Seder ha-Seliḥot* edition of D. Goldschmidt (1965), introd. 7).

Until the 18th century this rite was generally followed by all Ashkenazi Jews, but since the rise of Ḥasidism, the rite of Isaac Luria *(Nosaḥ ha-Ari)* was accepted in ḥasidic communities. Though retaining some of the Ashkenazi usage (e.g., the *taḥanunim,* the *Kedushah* for the *Shaḥarit* of Sabbath, Grace after Meals), *Nosaḥ ha-Ari* generally resembles the Sephardi rite (see below) and is therefore popularly called *Nosaḥ Sefarad.* The *piyyutim* used by the ḥasidic communities are, however, according to the Ashkenazi (Polish) rite. Through the negligence of printers, the texts of this rite were badly emended. The special editions for the *Ḥabad Ḥasidim (after the revision of R. *Shneur Zalman of Lyady) are explicity marked *Nosaḥ ha-Ari.*

BABYLONIAN GROUP

The so-called "Babylonian" group is mainly represented by the Sephardi (Spanish) rite. Originally dominant in the Iberian Peninsula, after the Jewish expulsion it spread to North Africa, Italy, Holland, some communities in Germany (e.g., Altona, Vienna), England, the Balkans, and countries in the Near East, including Palestine. Later it reached North and South America and superseded the local rites of such communities as Greece and Turkey (*Maḥzor Romania,* see above), Persia, Aleppo, and Crimea. In the 16th century it was redacted and altered according to the *"Kavvanot ha-Ari."*

Sephardi (Spanish) Rite. The Sephardi rite differs from the Ashkenazi by putting *Hodu* before *Barukh she-Amar,* inserting *Ve-Yaẓmaḥ Purkaneh* in the *Kaddish;* introducing the *Kedushah* with *Nakdishakh* and *Keter*; different versions of the ninth benediction of the *Amidah* for summer and winter; minor differences in the general wording of the *Amidah;* and the formula *Le-Moshe Ẓivvita* (instead of *Tikkanta*) for the Sabbath *Musaf.* The Sephardi (Castilian) rite has only a few *piyyutim* since most of them had been deleted by the time of David *Abudarham (see his commentary to the *piyyutim, Tashlum Abudarham,* ed. by L. Prins (1900)). Even in the Day of Atonement *Amidot* there are only one or two *piyyutim* for the introduction of the *Kedushah,* and the *seliḥot* come after the *Amidah.*

North African Rites. Both the rich literary output of the Sephardi poets and the characteristic form of the *Sephardi Maḥzor* were preserved by the communities of North Africa where the expelled Jews settled. The *maḥzorim* of Tunis, Algiers, and Oran-Tlemcen are very similar, containing *yoẓerot* and *kerovot* for Rosh Ha-Shanah, and the Day of Atonement, fast days, the Four Parashiyyot, and also *tal* (*dew), and *geshem* (*rain), prayers. The printed *maḥzor* for Constantine (1872) does not contain the larger collection of poetry contained in the manuscript which S. Bernstein discovered (see *Aresheth,* 1 (1959), 9–43). The community of Tripoli (its *maḥzor* was already printed in 1711 in Venice entitled *Siftei Renanot*) has an entirely different Day of Atonement liturgy in which the repetition of each *Amidah* contains a different *ma'amad* (it also occurs in a printed book which Davidson entitled *Maḥzor Bilti Noda* ("Unknown *Maḥzor*"; see below)) written by Isaac b. Judah *ibn Ghayyat. The *maḥzor* of Tripoli also has many *seliḥot.*

Catalonia and Aragon Rites. The *maḥzorim* of the rites of Catalonia and Aragon (identical with the Castilian rite in daily prayers) were printed several times (first editions: Catalonia (Salonika, 1627), Aragon (Salonika, 1629)) for the Catalonian and Aragon Jews who settled in Salonika after the expulsion. The two *maḥzorim* are similar but differ from the rites of North Africa in *piyyut* (see Zunz,

Ritus, 41ff., and a detailed description of these *maḥzorim* in *Sefunot,* 11).

Provençal Rite. The Provençal rite (southern France) is nearly identical with the Sephardi rite and was followed by the communities of Avignon, Carpentras, L'Isle sur la Sorgue, and Cavaillon until the 19th century. The text shows some additions due to the influence of the rite of northern France, e.g., the three *Kedushot* begin with *Nekaddesh, Na'ariẓakh, Keter;* in all the *Amidot, Shalom Rav* is used instead of *Sim Shalom.* The *maḥzor* of Avignon was printed in Amsterdam (4 vols., 1765ff.; a detailed description of it was given by Zunz, in: *Allgemeine Zeitung des Judentums,* II (1838)–IV (1840)). The *maḥzor* of Carpentras, which abbreviated almost all the *piyyutim,* was printed in Amsterdam (1739–62, 4 vols.). The *maḥzorim* of L'Isle and Cavaillon, preserved only in manuscript, contain numerous *piyyutim* for festivals and Sabbaths, but only *kerovot* for the fast days, Rosh Ha-Shanah, the Day of Atonement, and the prayers of dew and rain. These *kerovot* were recited after the *Amidah* in accordance with the practice of the North African communities. A *siddur* with selected *piyyutim* for these communities was edited by M. Milhaud (*Rituel des Prières en Hébreu à l'Usage des Israélites de l'Ancien Comtat.* 2 vols., 1855).

Yemenite Rite. *Minhag Teiman,* the rite of the Jews of Yemen who emigrated from southern Arabia, exists today only in Israel. It follows the *Seder Tefillah* of Maimonides which is based on the *siddur* of Saadiah Gaon, but shows the influence of Sephardi elements (see L. Goldschmidt, in: YMHS 7 (1958), 188). A small number of *piyyutim* such as *Avodah, hoshanot,* and *seliḥot* are taken from the Sephardi prayer book. The Yemenite liturgy was first printed in Jerusalem (2 vols., 1894) entitled **תכלאל** from which a handwritten (mimeographed) edition elaborated with many *piyyutim* was edited by J. S. Hobareh (**תכלאל קדמונים**(1964)).

Persecutions and migrations of Jews from country to country resulted in the disappearance of a number of rites, such as the old Palestinian, Romanian, Persian, and French rites. Besides the rites used by the few Italian and Yemenite communities, the Ashkenazi and Sephardi rites are the two most widely followed today. The need for a uniform rite—already foreseen by S. D. Luzzatto (*Mavo le-Maḥzor Benei Roma,* end) and Zunz (Ritus, 178)—has been discussed in the last few years. Particularly in Israel, the need for a unified prayer book in the schools and army is felt, but until now no satisfying results have been achieved.

OTHER RITES

There are a number of rites which are difficult to categorize. Among them are the liturgy of the Persian Jews (preserved only in manuscripts and insufficiently described by E. Adler, JQR, 10 (1898), 601–25); the rite of the Jews of Aleppo (*Maḥzor Aram-Zova;* printed Venice, 1523–27) whose High Holy Days prayers, very similar to those of the Persian prayer book, were also influenced by the Romanian and Roman rites; the liturgy of the so-called *Maḥzor Bilti Noda* ("Unknown *Maḥzor*") described by Bernstein (JJB, 3 (1942), 32–42), a *maḥzor* for the Day of Atonement which, like the Tripoli *maḥzor,* contains the *piyyutim* of Ibn Ghayyat, but consists of an entirely different rite in the regular prayers. According to Sonne (*ibid.,* 84–89), it was printed as a supplement to the *Ḥizzunim* of the Jews of Sicily (Constantinople, 1585), which is the only work to provide information about the rite of this community after it settled in Salonika. It contains *piyyutim,* most of which are not included in other rites for many of the different Sabbaths and festivals, except for the Day of Atonement. They are listed by Davidson, in *Livre d'Hommage . . . S. Poznański* (1927) Heb., pt. 59–77 (see also *Sefunot* 11). [D.G.]

Figure 4. Page of the service for Simḥat Torah according to the Cochin rite, S. India. From a manuscript on rice paper, 17th/18th century. Cecil Roth Collection.

REFORM

Dissatisfaction began to be felt with the traditional liturgy and the need to make it more relevant to the new conditions obtained after the Emancipation, especially in Western Europe, from the beginning of the 19th century. As a result there was a proliferation of new liturgies, based on the old, but, as the Reformers saw it, having now a more refined, spiritual, and intellectual approach. The early Reformers were unduly influenced by the *Zeitgeist;* they were eager to model Jewish prayer on the patterns of Protestant worship and keen to make the Jewish service "respectable" to the gentile neighbors. They had, however, real difficulties with some of the forms that had been handed down from the past and, since they disagreed with the Orthodox view which regarded the liturgy as sacrosanct, they were moved to introduce changes so that, as some of them were fond of saying, man might not speak lies to his Maker.

The Reformers felt the need to make the service more intelligible to the average worshiper. Less Hebrew was used; some of the traditional prayers were translated; and new prayers in the vernacular, as well as in Hebrew, were introduced. The services were shortened by omitting some of the lengthier prayers, *piyyutim,* and study portions.

Other changes were governed by Western standards of decorum and by aesthetic considerations. For instance, the Torah, the prophetic readings, and some of the prayers were declaimed rather than chanted as in the traditional mode. New melodies, influenced by the musical tradition of the West, were introduced to the accompaniment of organ and choir. A determined effort was made to rid the service of such anachronisms as the *Yekum Purkan* prayer in Aramaic in which God is entreated to bless the exilarch and scholars of Babylon. Aramaic was generally abandoned in favor of Hebrew and this included in many congregations the famous Aramaic *Kaddish* prayer. Typical of 19th-century fastidiousness is the omission from the prayer service (even in communities which retained the account of the compounding of the incense; Singer, Prayer Book, 219–20), of the discussion found in the traditional liturgy, whether urine can be used in the mixture. The *priestly blessing was generally omitted partly because it was held that the priesthood was an anachronism and partly because of the superstitions surrounding it (i.e., that anyone who gazes at the hands of the priests will become blind). On the other hand it became not at all unusual for the rabbi to adopt the priestly role by blessing the congregation with uplifted hand at the end of the service, an obvious imitation of church worship.

שַׁחֲרִית לְיוֹם שִׂמְחַת תּוֹרָה   רי״ח

כָּבוֹד יַנְחִילוּ וְכוֹנֵן כִּסְאוֹ וִירוֹמֵם מֶמְשַׁלְתּוֹ אֱלֹהִים
חַיִּים וּמֶלֶךְ עוֹלָם יָשִׂים יָם וְקֶדֶם מִשְׁלוֹחַ יָדוֹ וְצָפוֹן וְיָמִין
מִשְׁמְעָתוֹ ׀ וְאַחֲרִיתוֹ יֵיטַב בְּאוֹרֶךְ יָמִים בְּעֹשֶׁר נְכָסִים
וְכָבוֹד ׀ יָרוּם הוֹדוֹ וְיִשָּׂא וְגָבַהּ עַד מְאֹד ׀ יַגְדִּיל
כִּסְאוֹ אֱלֹהִים חַיִּים וּמֶלֶךְ עוֹלָם ׀ וְיֹאמְרוּ בְּכָל מָחוֹז
וּפֶלֶךְ יְחִי אֲדוֹנֵנוּ הָאַפִּיוֹר פָּאפָּא פְּלוֹ לְעוֹלָם ׀ חֲלוֹ נָא
פְּנֵי אֵל וִיחָנֶּהוּ ׀ יָאֵר פָּנָיו אֵלָיו וְיִשְׁמְרֵהוּ ׀ הַמָּקוֹם
בְּרַחֲמָיו ׀ שָׁלוֹם יַעֲשֶׂה לּוֹ מְרוֹמָיו ׀ וְיִשְׁמְרֵהוּ וִיחַיֵּיהוּ ׀
וּמִנַּפֶּשׁ אוֹיְבָיו יִצְּרֵהוּ ׀ וְיַאֲרִיךְ יָמָיו וּשְׁנָיו ׀ דִּבְרֵי שָׁלוֹם
וֶאֱמֶת מְהֵרָה תִּשָּׁמַעְנָה אָזְנָיו ׀ וְיִשְׁלַח בְּרָכָה בְּכָל מַעֲשֵׂה
יָדָיו ׀ וְיַצְלִיחֵהוּ בְּכָל דְּרָכָיו וּמַעֲבָדָיו ׀ וְיַטֶּה לִבּוֹ
לְעוֹזְרֵנוּ ׀ לְרַחֵם עַל פְּלַטָרְנוּ ׀ וּלְהָתֵנוּ מְהֵרָה
כַּעֲבוֹדָתֵנוּ ׀ בְּכָל אֲשֶׁר יִפְנֶה יַשְׂכִּיל וְדָבָר כְּעִתּוֹ ׀ גַּם
אוֹיְבָיו יַשְׁלִים אִתּוֹ ׀ וְהָיְתָה מְנוּחָתוֹ כָּבוֹד דָּשֵׁן וְשָׁמֵן ׀
וְכֵן יְהִי רָצוֹן וְנֹאמַר אָמֵן :

מִי שֶׁבֵּרַךְ אַבְרָהָם יִצְחָק וְיַעֲקֹב דָּוִד וּשְׁלֹמֹה
וּנְבִיאֵי יִשְׂרָאֵל וְכָל חֲסִידֵי עוֹלָם ׀ הוּא
יָבָרֵךְ וִירוֹמֵם וְיִשָּׂא מַעְלָה מַעְלָה הָאָדוֹן הָאַפִּיוֹר
פָּאפָּא פְּלוֹ וְכָל הָאֲדוֹנִים הַסְּגָנִים לְעוֹלָם ׀ הַמָּקוֹם
בְּרַחֲמָיו שָׁלוֹם יַעֲשֶׂה לָהֶם מִמְּרוֹמָיו ׀ וְיִשְׁמְרֵם וִיחַיֵּם
וִישִׁיעֵם וּמִנֶּפֶשׁ אוֹיְבֵיהֶם יְפָדֵם וְיִצְּרֵם ׀ וְיַאֲרִיךְ יְמֵיהֶם
וּשְׁנוֹתֵיהֶם ׀ וְיִשְׁלַח בְּרָכָה בְּכָל מַעֲשֵׂה יְדֵיהֶם ׀ דִּבְרֵי
שָׁלוֹם וֶאֱמֶת תִּשָּׁמַעְנָה אָזְנֵיהֶם ׀ וְיַצְלִיחֵם בְּכָל דַּרְכֵיהֶם ׀
יַטֶּה לִבָּם לְעוֹזְרֵנוּ ׀ לְרַחֵם עַל פְּלַטָרְנוּ ׀ וּלְהָתֵנוּ
                              נה ב ב ‟ מחזה

שַׁחֲרִית לְיוֹם שִׂמְחַת תּוֹרָה

וָאֶהְיֶה : וְעוֹד כְּתִיב פִּצְחוּ רַנְּנוּ יַחְדָּו חָרְבוֹת יְרוּשָׁלַיִם
כִּי נִחַם יְיָ עַמּוֹ גָּאַל יְרוּשָׁלָיִם : וְעוֹד כְּתִיב חָשַׂף יְיָ אֶת
זְרוֹעַ קָדְשׁוֹ לְעֵינֵי כָּל הַגּוֹיִם וְרָאוּ כָּל אַפְסֵי אֶרֶץ אֵת
יְשׁוּעַת אֱלֹהֵינוּ :

פִּזְמוֹן לַמְצַלְאִין לַאֲדוֹנֵנוּ הַפְּפִיוֹר יִרְאֶה

לְנוּ חָרְדוּ רֵעֵינִי

יִקְרְאוּן מֵי בְרָכוֹת תְּהִלּוֹת הֲגִיוֹנֵנוּ וְעַל גּוֹיִם וּמַמְלָכוֹת
נְשַׁחֵר פְּנֵי קוֹנֵנוּ ׀ וּלְמַעַן הַבְּרָכוֹת ׀ נַמְלִיךְ מִמְּעוֹנֵנוּ ׀
וְנָבִיא שִׁירוֹת עֲרוּכוֹת ׀ לְבָרֵךְ אֶת אֲדוֹנֵנוּ :

מְצַלְאִין אֲנַחְנָא וּתְבָעִין רַחֲמֵי מִן קֳדָם אֱלָהּ שְׁמַיָּא
מָרֵי דְרַחֲמֵי לְחַיֵּי אַב הֲמוֹן אֲדוֹנֵנוּ הָאַפִּיוֹר
פָּאפָּא פְּלוֹ אֲנַחְנָא בְּנֵי גָלוּתָא עַבְדוֹהִי לְמֶלֶךְ שְׁמַיָּא
דִּי קְשׁוֹט מַעֲבָדוֹהִי ׀ אָתוֹהִי כַּמָּה רַבְרְבִין וְכַמָּה
תַּקִּיפִין תִּמְהוֹהִי :

כִּכְתוּב יְיָ יְיָ אֵל רַחוּם וְחַנּוּן אֶרֶךְ אַפַּיִם וְרַב חֶסֶד
וֶאֱמֶת נוֹצֵר חֶסֶד לָאֲלָפִים נוֹשֵׂא עָוֹן וָפֶשַׁע
וְחַטָּאָה וְנַקֵּה :

הַנּוֹתֵן לַמְּלָכִים תְּשׁוּעָה ׀ הַפּוֹצֶה אֶת דָּוִד עַבְדּוֹ
מֵחֶרֶב רָעָה ׀ הַנּוֹתֵן רוֹזְנִים לָרוּם וְכוֹכְבֵי
מֶמְשַׁלְתּוֹ יַנְהוּ ׀ וְאֶת מְלָכִים לַכִּסֵּא וְיוֹשִׁיבֵם לָנֶצַח וַיִּגְבָּהוּ
הוּא כְרַחֲמָיו יַגְבִּיהַּ וִירוֹמֵם וְיִשָּׂא מַעְלָה מַעְלָה אֲדוֹנֵנוּ
הָאַפִּיוֹר פָּאפָּא פְּלוֹ הוּא יִשְׁלַח מַלְאָכוֹ אִתּוֹ וּמִכָּל פֶּגַע
רַע יִשְׁמְרֵהוּ ׀ מֹשֶׁה וְרַב יְגַטְּלֵהוּ וְנִשָּׂאֵהוּ ׀ וְכִסֵּא
כָבוֹד

Figure 5. Pages from the Simḥat Torah prayers of the Carpentras *maḥzor,* with a prayer for the health of the Pope. Amsterdam, 1739. Cecil Roth Collection.

There were moral objections to the few vestiges found in the traditional liturgy for the downfall of enemies (e.g., the *Av ha-Raḥamim* prayer, Singer, 206). Many communities also omitted the *Kol Nidrei* declaration on the eve of the Day of Atonement on the grounds that it lent credence to the accusation that the Jew's word was not his bond and that the recitation of a bare juridical formula was historically and religiously an inappropriate beginning for the most solemn day in the Jewish calendar. Instead, *"O Tag des Herrn!"* an anthem by Leopold Stein, one of the early Reformers, was substituted, or its haunting melody was set to the words of a psalm. The early morning benediction in which a man thanks God for not having made him a woman was omitted. The word *nokhri* ("stranger," "pagan") was substituted for *goi* ("gentile") in a similar benediction: "who hath not made me a *goi.*" The statement that the "uncircumcised" do not rest on the Sabbath in the Sabbath morning prayer was changed so as to read the "wicked" do not rest.

Many changes were introduced on theological grounds. The most far-reaching one, which especially aroused the ire of the Orthodox, was the deleting of all references to the return to Zion. The Reformers believed that these references frustrated the universalistic aspect of Judaism and that the dispersion of the Jews was neither "exile" nor punishment for Israel's sins. Since the emphasis was placed on the messianic age rather than on a personal messiah, the necessary changes were introduced, e.g., instead of "He bringeth a Redeemer," "He bringeth redemption." Prayers for the peace of Israel were extended to embrace all mankind. Superstitious references were excised: e.g., the prayer for the sick in which the name of the sick person is changed so as to avert the evil decree; references to angels and demons. A theological question which greatly bothered not only the Reformers but some of the Conservatives and Orthodox as well, was whether a modern Jew could sincerely pray for the restoration of the ancient sacrificial cult. The tendency was either to omit references to it entirely or to change the wording so as to commemorate it historically rather than as a hope for the future (e.g., "and there our fathers offered . . ."). Most of these changes are still to be found in the Reform liturgy and some of them in the Conservative and Orthodox liturgies. A marked tendency is, however, to be observed in a wish to restore the prayers for the rebuilding of Zion.

See also: *Prayer Books; *Piyyut; *Prayer; *Amidah; *Benedictions; *Reform Judaism.   [L.J.]

Bibliography: Zunz, Ritus, passim; Elbogen, Gottesdienst, passim; Idelsohn, Liturgy, passim; J. Heinemann, *Ha-Tefillah bi-Tekufat ha-Tanna'im ve-ha-Amora'im* (1962²), passim; J. J. Petuchowski, *Prayerbook Reform in Europe* (1968).

LITVAKOV, MOSHE (1875–1938?), Yiddish writer and editor, and communist leader. Litvakov was born in Cherkassy, Ukraine. At the age of 17 he abandoned talmudic studies for secular learning, attending the Sorbonne in Paris from 1902 to 1905. At first he drifted from *Aḥad Ha-Am Zionism to Socialist Zionism and wrote in Russian, Hebrew, and Yiddish on social and literary problems. After the revolution of 1905 he was a member of the central committee of the territorialist Socialist-Zionist (S.S.) Party (see *Socialist Zionism), and edited its various periodicals in Vilna. Litvakov also published the pamphlet *Der Zionismus un di Ugande Frage* (Yid., 1905).

After 1917 he contributed to the Yiddish journals in Kiev. In 1919 he joined the Communist Party, and in 1921 he assumed a leading role in Moscow's *Yevsektsiya. From 1924 he edited *Emes*, the principal Yiddish organ of the Communist Party. In its columns he demanded the uprooting of Jewish religious observances and Jewish national aspirations. Litvakov attempted to place Yiddish literature at the service of the regime. Nevertheless, in his critical articles and as professor of Yiddish literature and Jewish history in the Jewish section of the Moscow Pedagogical Institute, he was often unable to avoid touching on the Jewish past. His *In Umruh*, a collection of essays (vol. 1, 1918; vol. 2, 1926), dwelt on the cultural tradition which Jewish proletarian writers in the Soviet Union inherited from prerevolutionary writers, such as M. *Rosenfeld, A. *Reisen, *Shalom Aleichem, and I. L. *Peretz, insisting on the hegemony of the new Soviet Yiddish literature. Litvakov also published a booklet on the Yiddish Chamber Theater in Moscow (Yid., 1924). With *Esther (Frumkin) he edited a Yiddish edition of Lenin's selected writings in eight volumes. In the ideological polemics between Yiddish writers he was attacked for his essays which allegedly contained fragmentary remnants of Jewish separatism and chauvinism. Outmaneuvering efforts to purge him through self-accusations in 1931–32, he continued editing *Emes* until the major purges of 1937, when he was arrested as an enemy of the people, perishing in prison.

Bibliography: Rejzen, Leksikon, 2 (1927), 35–41; LNYL, 5 (1963), 90–94; Z. Schneour, *Bialik u-Venei Doro* (1958), 340–8; S. Bickel, *Shrayber fun mayn Dor*, 1 (1958), 287–304.

[S.L.]

LITVIN, A. (pseudonym of **Shmuel Hurwitz**; 1862–1943), Yiddish journalist and folklorist. Born in Minsk, he was self-educated. Believing in "redemption through physical labor," he tried to earn a living as street paver, carpenter, and typesetter, meanwhile contributing articles on miscellaneous subjects to Russian, Hebrew, and Yiddish periodicals. In 1901 he emigrated to the U.S., where he worked in a shoe factory and wrote for Yiddish journals. During the 1905 Revolution, he returned to Russia, edited the Vilna monthly *Lebn un Visenshaft* (1909–12), and published studies on *Shomer (1910) and on I. M. *Dick (1911). Returning to New York in 1914, he wrote for radical and Labor Zionist organs as well as for the Yiddish dailies, the *Jewish Daily Forward* and the *Jewish Morning Journal*. During travels through the Polish, Lithuanian, and Galician Jewish communities (1905–14) he had accumulated vast material on Yiddish folklore and on strange folk characters and half-forgotten villages, part of which he utilized in his main work *Yidishe Neshomes* (6 vols., 1916–17), a panorama of exotic, picturesque Jewish life in preceding generations. Selections from these volumes were translated into Hebrew by A. *Kariv and published in 1943. The greater part of Litvin's collection of Yiddish folk songs, folktales, and folk humor was deposited in the archives of the *YIVO, Institute for Jewish Research in New York, and forms a rich treasure for scholarly research.

Bibliography: Rejzen, Leksikon, 2 (1927), 142–6; LNYL, 5 (1963), 94–97; B. I. Bialostotsky, *In Kholem un Vor* (1956), 409–16; Kressel, Leksikon, 2 (1967), 263.

[S.L.]

LITVINOFF, EMANUEL (1915–), English poet. A Londoner by birth and upbringing, Litvinoff served in the army during World War II. Apart from his journalism (as editor of the periodical *Jews in Eastern Europe*), Litvinoff wrote poems, some of which were collected in two volumes, *The Untried Soldier* (1942) and *A Crown for Cain* (1948), and a novel, *The Lost Europeans* (1959). His work was largely concerned with the problems of the Diaspora Jew, mostly because he was influenced by the vigorous Jewish culture of London's East End and the anti-Semitism of the British Fascists in the thirties, and was deeply affected by the Holocaust and its aftermath. Litvinoff's most significant poem is, perhaps, "To T. S. Eliot," a protest against Eliot's occasionally sneering attitude toward Jews and a passionate self-identification of himself with the dead of Treblinka. In *The Lost Europeans*, Litvinoff describes the experience of a Jew in postwar Berlin, and in his second novel, *The Man Next Door* (1968), the workings of an anti-Semite's mind. His brother, BARNET (1917–), journalist and Zionist worker, wrote a biography of David Ben-Gurion, *Ben Gurion of Israel* (1954); *Road to Jerusalem* (1965), on the development of the Zionist movement; and *A Peculiar People* (1969), about contemporary Jewish communities.

[J.S.]

LITVINOV, MAXIM MAXIMOVICH (**Wallach, Meir Moiseevitch**; 1867–1951), Russian revolutionary and Soviet diplomat. Born in Bialystok, Litvinov joined the illegal Social-Democratic Party in 1899 and was arrested and exiled. In 1902 he escaped to Switzerland and in 1903, after having joined the Bolshevik faction, he returned clandestinely to Russia and took part in the 1905 Revolution. He collaborated with Maxim Gorki on the newspaper *Novaya Zhizn* ("The New Life"). After the failure of the revolution he fled from Russia and lived in France and England. While in England he became closely associated with *Lenin and was instrumental in various underground operations of the Bolsheviks, including the smuggling of arms to the Caucasus. In London Litvinov married Ivy Low, niece of the English historian Sir Sidney *Low. Following the October Revolution in 1917 Litvinov was made Soviet diplomatic agent to Britain, but he was detained by the British government and exchanged for Bruce Lockhart, the British diplomatic agent in Soviet Russia. In 1921 he became deputy commissar for foreign affairs under Chicherin and from then until 1939 he was at the center of Soviet diplomacy, particularly with the West. In 1919 he negotiated the first peace treaty of Soviet Russia (with Estonia), took part in the international conference in Genoa in 1922, which resulted in the Rapallo Treaty with Germany and headed the Soviet delegation to the subsequent conference at the Hague and the disarmament conference in Geneva (1927). In 1930 Litvinov became commissar for foreign affairs and in 1933, at Franklin D. *Roosevelt's invitation,

Maxim Litvinov, Russian revolutionary and Soviet diplomat. Photo Lotte Jacobi, Hillsboro, New Hampshire.

he personally conducted the negotiations for the establishment of American-Soviet diplomatic relations. In the period of Moscow's anti-Nazi policy (1934–39), Litvinov became the chief Soviet spokesman at the League of

Nations where he demanded the establishment of a collective security system. However, in May 1939, when *Stalin decided to reverse his policy and to effect a rapprochement with Hitler at the expense of the West, Litvinov, being a Jew and known as a protagonist of a pro-Western orientation, was replaced by Stalin's closest collaborator, V. M. Molotov; in February 1941 he was even dropped from the party's central committee. Following the German invasion of the Soviet Union, in June 1941, Litvinov was appointed Soviet ambassador to the United States, where he remained until 1943. He was reappointed assistant commissar for foreign affairs for a short period in 1946, but retired soon afterwards. His publications include *The Bolshevik Revolution, its Rise and Meaning* (1918) and *Against Aggression, Speeches by Maxim Litvinov* (1939). Litvinov was never self-conscious about being a Jew. He became a lonely, forgotten figure in the last years of his life when Stalin's anti-Semitic campaign was in full swing.

Bibliography: A. U. Pope, *Maxim Litvinoff* (Eng., 1943); G. A. Craig and F. Gilbert (eds.), *Diplomats 1919–1939* (1953), 344–77; D. G. Bishop, *Roosevelt-Litvinov Agreements: the American View* (1965); B. D. Wolfe, *Strange Communists I Have Known* (1965), 207–22; G. F. Kennan, *Russia and the West* (1960), index.

[B.E.]

LITVINOVSKY, PINḤAS (1894–), Israel painter. He was born in Novo-Georgiyevsk, Ukraine. In 1912 he was persuaded by Boris *Schatz, who was visiting with a Bezalel exhibition, to go to Ereẓ Israel. He began to study at the Bezalel School of Art in Jerusalem, but was disappointed and returned to Russia to study at the St. Petersburg Academy. In 1919 he returned to Jerusalem. He participated in the first group exhibitions of Palestinian artists in Jerusalem from 1923 and in Tel Aviv from 1926. A sure draftsman, he makes brilliant use of color and form, often juggling several styles to recreate a traditional Jewish theme. Though he is best known for his portraits, his group pictures, such as "The Market Place" (in the Tel Aviv Museum), show traces of cubism in the almost plastic quality of the figures. [Y.Fi.]

"A Rabbi," oil painting by Pinḥas Litvinovsky.

LITWAK, A. (pseudonym of **Ḥayyim Yankel Helfand;** 1874–1932), popular publicist and propagandist of the *Bund. Born in Lithuania, he studied in yeshivot there. In 1894 he joined Social Democratic circles in Vilna, taking a leading part in the "Jargon Committees" for publishing and circulating popular educational and informational literature in Yiddish. Exiled to Siberia for revolutionary activities, on his return in 1904 he became active in the Bund in Vilna and Warsaw, and from 1910 a member of its central committee. A prolific and sharp-edged writer and lively speaker, Litwak was warmly attached to Jewish folk culture and way of life, and became known as the *"talmid ḥakham* of the Bund." He was a leader of the "hard" group in the Bund which stood out for preserving its independence from the Russian Social Democratic Party in 1906, and later criticized the doctrine of national neutralism put forward by Vladimir *Medem. For two years Litwak stayed in Vienna, and in 1915 went to the United States. Returning to revolutionary Russia in July 1917 he became a leader of the anti-Bolshevist faction in the Bund, and after its split, a leader of the "Social Democratic" Bund. After trying to settle down in Poland, where he moved in 1921, he proceeded to the United States (1926). There he was active in the *Jewish Socialist *Farband,* edited its organ *Veker,* and promoted secular education in Yiddish. He met with difficulties in his attempts to associate himself with the American Jewish Labor Movement.

Bibliography: LNYL, 5 (1963), 83–90; B. Johnpoll, *The Politics of Futility* (1968), 134–5.

[M.M.]

LIUZZI, GUIDO (1866–1942), Italian soldier. Born in Reggio Emilia, Liuzzi was commissioned in a Bersaglieri regiment in 1885. He lectured at the Military Geographical Institute from 1905 to 1907 and commanded a battalion in the Turkish War of 1911–12. On Italy's entry into World War I he was appointed chief of staff of an army corps in the Italian Fourth Army. He commanded the Vallarsa sector of the Italian front from July 1917 to February 1918. Subsequently Liuzzi was made head of the Army Service Corps and after World War I became director of the military academy which trained officers for the general staff. Under his direction the academy became one of the leading army schools of Europe. In 1928 Liuzzi was promoted lieutenant general and given command of the crack Udine army corps. He retired in 1932. His son, GIORGIO LIUZZI (1896–), also followed a military career. He fought in World War I but was dismissed by Mussolini in 1939. Reinstated in 1944, he was chief of staff of the Italian army 1956–58. [Mo.K.]

LIVERIGHT, HORACE BRISBIN (1886–1933), U.S. publisher and theatrical producer. Liveright was born in Osceola Mills, Pennsylvania. He worked briefly in Philadelphia in a broker's office and as a margin clerk, and then turned to selling bonds, which he did with great flair. In 1911 he established a paper-manufacturing company, and in 1917 he joined Charles Boni to form the publishing house Boni & Liveright. They published the Modern Library, which reproduced classics and near-classics, from 1918 to 1925, when it was sold to Bennet *Cerf, their editor. The Boni & Liveright list also included such political radicals as Max Eastman, Michael Gold, and John Reed. When Boni left the firm after a few years, Liveright added many U.S. authors to the list, including such luminaries of American letters as Theodore Dreiser, Sherwood Anderson, Ernest Hemingway, William Faulkner, Hart Crane, Eugene O'Neil, E. E. Cummings, Ezra Pound, T. S. Eliot (Boni & Liveright first published *The Waste Land* in 1922), Lewis Mumford, and Conrad Aiken, as well as famous European writers. Liveright sold these distinguished authors' works with flamboyant publicity and for about ten years the publishing company was a stupendous success. A leading opponent of pornography laws, he successfully set out to defeat a "clean books" bill before the New York State legislature which would have prohibited many publications (1924). As a theatrical producer and president of Stonelea Players, Liveright produced *Hamlet in Modern Clothes* (1925); a dramatization (1926) of Dreiser's *An American Tragedy* which was a big success; and *Dracula* (1927), among other plays. After the successful bustle of the '20s, Liveright, who was maneuvered out of the publishing firm in 1930, spent his last three years in penury and isolation. Noel Coward's *The Scoundrel,* turned into a movie by Ben Hecht and Charles MacArthur in 1935, was partly based on Liveright's life and character.

Bibliography: W. Gilmer, *Horace Liveright, Publisher of the Twenties* (1970); W. D. Frank, *Time Exposures* (1926), 111–7. [ED.]

LIVERPOOL, seaport in N.W. England. It seems probable that Jews settled there before 1750, since in 1752 there was a "Synagogue Court" off Stanley Street and a Jewish place of worship, as the 1753 *Liverpool Memorandum Book* confirms. The site of this early synagogue and a picture of its facade have also been discovered in a map of Liverpool dated 1765. John Wesley refers to the excellent relations which the local Jews enjoyed with their Christian neighbors (*Journal,* entry of April 14, 1755). About 20 Jews are listed in the Liverpool Directory for 1790, some of whom bear names that inspired the unsubstantiated theory that the original community was Sephardi. They were mostly peddlers and traders catering to the seafaring population and included Benjamin Goetz (or Yates), a seal-engraver described as the "Jews' High Priest" (*ḥazzan?*).

The "Old" Hebrew Congregation was organized, or reorganized, at Turton Court in 1780. Its first cemetery was acquired nine years later and its Yiddish regulations drawn up in 1799. The first synagogue, built on a site in Seel Street donated by the Liverpool Corporation, was consecrated in 1808. The congregation's present handsome building on Princes Road was constructed in 1874. In the early 19th century the congregation's preacher was Tobias *Goodman, whose sermons are thought to have been the first delivered in English at a synagogue in the British Isles. Internal conflicts led to a secession in 1838, and to the subsequent establishment of a rival congregation at Hope Place. By about 1860, Liverpool's Jewish community, then numbering around 3,000, was second in size to London's. Toward the end of the 19th century, Russian and Polish refugees reached Liverpool on their way to America; a number remained to modify the character of Liverpool Jewry. A Levantine Sephardi community also existed between 1892 and 1914, and a small Liberal synagogue was established in 1928. A Liverpool and District Rabbinate was set up in 1904, its first two incumbents being Samuel Jacob *Rabinowitz, an early Zionist leader, and Isser Yehudah *Unterman, later chief rabbi of Israel. Other communal institutions include a pioneer Jewish welfare board (founded 1875), a philanthropic society (1811), a yeshivah (1915), and Hebrew-endowed schools (1840). During the first quarter of the 20th century British Jewry's first Hebrew day school flourished in Liverpool under the direction of Jacob Samuel *Fox. In 1971 there were in Liverpool nine congregations serving an estimated Jewish population of 7,500 (1% of the total). Some 700 Jewish children received their education at the King David schools.

Charles Mozley became the city's first Jewish mayor in 1863, and there have since been four Jewish lord mayors.

Synagogue of the "Old" Hebrew Congregation of Liverpool, consecrated in 1874. Photo Stewart Bale, Liverpool.

Important civic and other dignities have been filled by the *Benas and *Cohen families and by Lord *Cohen of Birkenhead. Isaiah *Raffalovich and Izak *Goller were other prominent figures in recent communal history. The monthly *Liverpool Jewish Gazette* (1947–) mirrors the local scene, while the Zionist Central Council (1898) and the Merseyside Jewish Representative Council (1944) coordinate the community's activities.

Bibliography: Roth, Mag Bibl, index; Lehman, Nova Bibl, index; L. Wolf, *History and Genealogy of the Jewish Families of Yates and Samuel of Liverpool* (1901); P. Ettinger, *"Hope Place" in Liverpool Jewry* (1930); C. Roth, *Rise of Provincial Jewry* (1950), 82; B. B. Benas, in: JHSET, 17 (1953), 23–37; Goodman, in: *In the Dispersion,* nos. 5–6 (1966), 52–67; G. E. Silverman, in: *Niv ha-Midrashiyyah* (Spring 1970), 74–81, English section. [ED.]

LIVESTOCK, TRADE IN. The laws of ritual slaughter (**sheḥitah*) made it necessary for Jews to buy cattle for their own consumption. In Muslim countries the gentile population bought meat from Jewish butchers. In Christian countries many charters granted to the Jews contained articles regulating the slaughter of livestock by Jews as well as the right to sell meat to non-Jews. This was necessary because the surplus, ritually unclean, parts of animals had to be sold to the Christian populace, to the great resentment of the guild of Christian butchers. Churchmen also were indignant that Jews sold to Christians meat that they considered unfit to eat according to the law. Protests by butchers against the irregular sale of meat by Jews were common occurrences in most medieval cities, often resulting in limitations in Jewish trade which had been beneficial both to Jews and to most Christians. Trade in livestock became much more intensive following the expulsions of the 15th and 16th centuries, which had resulted in a considerable section of Central European Jewry adopting a rural mode of life. Henceforth their main occupations were as *peddlers, traders, brokers in agricultural products, and livestock traders. Many villages were composed largely of traders in cattle, goats, and horses. For example, in Eichstetten, Baden, four-fifths of the 68 Jewish families were livestock traders in the 19th century. In *Poland-Lithuania Jews traded in cattle on a larger scale. Herds of cattle, often numbering thousands of heads, were driven for sale to the west. In the *Arenda system the Jewish lessee would obtain both ritually clean and unclean animals. The problems arising from the maintenance and sale of the latter are dealt with in much of the halakhic literature of the 17th and 18th centuries.

Jewish participation in the livestock trade was a mainstay of the activity of military *contractors. Supplies from

Poland-Lithuania helped boost this trade among German and Austrian Jews. Herds of draft oxen, cattle for meat, and horses for the cavalry were supplied by Samuel *Oppenheimer and Samson *Wertheimer of Vienna and many other *court Jews. In Poland the *Nachmanovich family specialized in supplying large quantities of horses to the armies. The thousands of beasts necessary were amassed through a system of contractors and subcontractors, reaching down to the petty rural livestock trader. Isaac, son of Daniel *Itzig, became bankrupt in 1795 when he did not receive payment from *Cerfberr for delivering 8,835 out of 10,000 horses contracted for. The livestock trade was a predominantly Jewish occupation in Bohemia-Moravia, Hungary, and Eastern Europe. The familiar presence of the Jewish livestock trader made him a common figure in local folksong; a Westphalian example goes:

> Jew Itzig bought a cow
> and a calf as well;
> Itzig Jew didn't notice,
> the calf was *mo'beres.*

The use of a Hebrew word (*mo'beres-me'ubberet,* "pregnant") is typical, for the professional livestock traders' language in most of Europe was full of Hebrew and Yiddish expressions. The vocabulary of non-Jewish livestock traders in Holland after World War II consisted of about 90% corrupted Hebrew and Yiddish words. Jewish horse traders developed a secret trade dialect which non-Jewish horse traders first tried to understand and then eventually adopted for their own mercantile purposes.

Cattle was not only bought and sold but was also raised for meat and dairy products by Jews living in villages. The problem of the *firstborn animal was solved in *Hesse and neighboring regions in a unique manner: ritually pure calves and kids were sent to graze in the *Frankfort on the Main cemetery and on their eventual death, of old age, were buried wrapped in a white sheet. These animals were butchered by Vincent *Fettmilch's mob and saved during the 1711 fire. This custom, mentioned by Ludwig *Boerne, was also followed in various communities in Eastern Europe.

In Switzerland, from which the Jews had been expelled in the 15th and 16th centuries and finally in 1622, Jewish livestock traders were nevertheless present throughout the country. Pacific Switzerland attracted the Jewish horse traders supplying the armies of neighboring states. The various cantons were forced to accept and encourage their presence, or to suffer stagnation in the livestock trade. Attempts were made to differentiate between the needed livestock buyers and unwanted traders and peddlers. The few Jewish communities that existed in Switzerland in the 18th and early 19th centuries subsisted primarily from livestock trading. In Endingen, of 144 heads of families, 48 were engaged in livestock trading and 5 were butchers. In relatively isolated Endigen and Lengnau a special horse-traders' language persisted into the 20th century without passing through a process of de-Hebraization and Germanization.

When in 1689 the *Nuremberg council wanted to prohibit all trade between Jews and Christians, the Christian butchers protested and the council was forced to make an exception for the livestock trade. As against 1,590 transactions in cattle conducted by Jews between 1784 and 1800 in Winterborn (in the *Palatinate), only 82 were conducted by Christians. This predominance in rural markets had its anti-Jewish ramifications. Jewish livestock traders were frequently accused of trickery, primarily of *usury and exploitation, for the animals were generally bought and sold on credit. Accusations against Jewish livestock traders were particularly common in Alsace-Lorraine, Bavaria, Hesse, and Eastern Europe. Through channeling the resentment of the farmers in backward rural Hesse against Jewish livestock traders, Otto Boeckel was elected to the Reichstag. This type of anti-Semitic agitation was later adopted by the Nazis, particularly by the party's agricultural experts. Immediately after the Nazi seizure of power concerted steps were taken to break the Jews' dominant position in livestock markets, both on the local, regional, and national levels. Traditional markets were boycotted and special *judenfreie* ones were established, where farmers were urged to bring their livestock. Eventually, heavy pressure, both public and legal, had to be exerted in order to induce the farmers to sever their ties with Jewish traders. The campaign was intensified in the middle and late 1930s. On Jan. 26, 1937, only pure-blooded Germans were permitted to deal in livestock, and on Nov. 12, 1938, after the **Kristallnacht,* Jews were totally forbidden to attend markets and fairs.

Goats and cattle were raised on a small scale by many Jewish households; in the **shtetl* the owner of a few cows or goats supplied kosher milk and dairy products. Tales of such men were common in folklore and literature, the most famous being Tevyeh the milkman by *Shalom Aleichem.

See also *Agriculture; *United States; *Meat.

Bibliography: A. Kapp, *Die Dorfjuden in der Nordpfalz* (1968), 257ff.; U. Jeggle, *Judendoerfer in Wuerttemberg* (1969), index, s.v. *Viehhandel;* J. Picard, *The Marked One* (1956); F. Guggenheim-Grunberg, in: *The Field of Yiddish,* 1 (1954), 48–62; P. J. Diamant, in: *Zeitschrift fuer die Geschichte der Juden,* 1 (1964), 79–83; M. Shaḥaf, in: *Yeda Am,* 2 (1954), 42–46; B. Brilling, *ibid.,* 3 (1955), 15ff.; H. Bloom, *The Economic Activity of the Jews of Amsterdam* (1935), index, s.v. *Livestock;* H. Genschel, *Die Verdraengung der Juden aus der Wirtschaft im dritten Reich* (1966), index, s.v. *Viehhandel;* B. Rosenthal, in: MGWJ, 79 (1935), 443–50; M. Grunwald, *Samuel Oppenheimer und sein Kreis* (1913); Z. Szajikowski, *Franco-Judaica* (1962), index s.v. *Horses, Cattle;* L. Davidsohn, *Beitraege . . . Berliner Juden . . .* (1920), 52–56; G. L. Weisel, *Aus dem Neumarker Landestor* (1926), 105f; O. Donath, *Boehmische Dorfjuden* (1926); A. Weldler-Steinberg, *Geschichte der Juden in der Schweiz* (1966); A. Hertzberg, *The French Enlightenment and the Jews* (1968), index, s.v. *Horses, Cattle, Alsace;* S. Ettinger, in: *Zion,* 21 (1956), 107–42; H. H. Ben-Sasson, *ibid.,* 183–206.

[H.W.]

LIZARD (Heb. לְטָאָה), reptile included among the eight creeping things that are prohibited as food and whose dead body defiles anything with which it comes into contact (Lev. 11:30–39). Talmudic literature states that its tail moves convulsively when cut off (Oho. 1:6), that in intense heat it remains immovable, stirring only when water is poured over it (Pes. 88b). Both features are characteristic of various species of lizard, but the reference is apparently mainly to those belonging to the family Lacertidae, of which four genera (that include ten species) are to be found in Israel. Of the *Lacerta,* the most common are the brown lizard (*Lacerta laevis*) and the great green lizard (*Lacerta viridis*) which is the largest and most beautiful of this family, is commonly found in the mountainous regions, and feeds on insects. The dab lizard, which belongs to another family, is apparently to be identified with the צָב (*ẓav*), likewise included among the unclean creeping things see *Tortoise).

Bibliography: Lewysohn, Zool, 221f., no. 272; J. Feliks, *The Animal World of the Bible* (1962), 96; M. Dor, *Leksikon Zo'ologi* (1965), 177f.

[J.F.]

LJUBLJANA (Ger. **Laibach**), capital of Slovenia, Yugoslavia; until 1918 in Krain, Austria. Individual Jews are mentioned in Ljubljana during the 12th century, and the repair of a synagogue is attested in 1217. A "Jewish Road" and a "Jewish Street" are remains of the former Jewish quarter. The Jews of Ljubljana were merchants, money-lenders, and artisans, and were allowed to own real estate. During the Middle Ages they were from time to time accused of child murder, well poisoning, etc. They were not expelled together with the rest of the Jews from Carinthia and Styria in 1496; in 1513, however, Emperor Maximilian gave in to the burghers' claims and forbade the Jews to engage in commerce, and in 1515 expelled them from Ljubljana. Under Leopold II in 1672 the whole of Krain was forbidden to Jews. Later Joseph II allowed them to visit the fairs.

During the Napoleonic Kingdom of Illyria, Abraham Heimann from Bavaria settled in Ljubljana with two relatives under protection of the French governor and opened an official money changer's office. When Ljubljana reverted to Austria in 1814, the emperor confirmed Heimann's right of residence, but he had to fight with the municipal authorities until the 1848 Revolution. After the *emancipation in 1867 Jews again settled in Ljubljana, and by 1910 there were 116 of them, but without an organized community. They were attached to the community of Graz in Austria until 1918, and after Slovenia became a part of the new Yugoslav kingdom, they were attached to the Zagreb community. The Ljubljana community, founded after World War II, had 84 members in 1969.

Bibliography: L. Šik, in: *Židov* (April 29, 1919); I. Vrhovec, in: *Jevrejski Glas* (May 20, 1938). [Ed.]

LLERENA, city in W. Spain, near the Andalusian border. Jews lived in Llerena throughout the 13th–15th centuries, up to the expulsion in 1492. In 1474 the annual tax paid by the community amounted to 3,500 maravedis. It increased to 35,820 maravedis in 1491, probably because Jews recently expelled from Andalusia had settled in the city. A Jew of Llerena, Gabriel-Israel, served as interpreter to Ferdinand and Isabella during the war with Granada, and won the king's esteem. There were also Conversos living in Llerena. Toward the end of the 16th century a permanent tribunal of the Inquisition was established there which became one of the most active in Spain. David *Reuveni was imprisoned in the inquisitional dungeons in Llerena from 1532, and from 1631 onward a large group of fugitives from Badajoz was tried by the Llerena tribunal with tragic results. As late as 1652 six fugitive judaizers were burned in effigy, at an auto-da-fé in Llerena, together with the bones of a woman who had died in prison.

Bibliography: Baer, Spain, 317; Baer, Urkunden, 2 (1936), 233, 349, 398; H.C. Lea, *History of the Inquisition in Spain*, 1 (1906), 549–50; Suárez Fernández, Documentos, 36, 68, 81, 256, 257.

[H.B.]

°**LLOYD GEORGE, DAVID (Earl Lloyd-George;** 1863–1945), British prime minister (1916–1922) under whose government the *Balfour Declaration was approved. Lloyd George first came into contact with the Zionist movement in 1903, when the firm of solicitors for whom he worked prepared, at the request of Leopold *Greenberg, a draft connected with the *Uganda Scheme. After Britain's declaration of war on Turkey in November 1914, he told Herbert *Samuel that he "was very keen to see a Jewish State established in Palestine," so that when he first met Chaim *Weizmann in December 1914, he was already in a receptive mood toward Zionism. Lloyd George, the Welshman, was drawn toward Zionism both by his religious upbringing ("I was taught far more about the history of the Jews than about the history of my own people," he wrote) and by his belief that "it is the small nations that have been chosen for great things."

Although sentiment played no small part in Lloyd George's approach, on strictly rational grounds he was determined to make Palestine British, at a time when the Zionists regarded British administration of the country as vital to their aims. Before Sir Mark *Sykes left for Egypt in April 1917 to become *Allenby's political adviser, Lloyd George impressed upon him three main points: (1) Palestine was to be under British rule; (2) no pledges should be given to the Arabs concerning Palestine; (3) nothing should be done to prejudice the Zionist aspirations with regard to Palestine. In the cabinet, Lloyd George enthusiastically supported the pro-Zionist Balfour Declaration, viewing it as a step toward the possible establishment of a Jewish state. A few days before the issue of the declaration, he told Weizmann: "I know that with the issue of this Declaration I shall please one group [i.e., the Zionists] and displease another [i.e., the assimilationists]. I have decided to please your group because you stand for a great idea." He also brought about ratification of the Balfour Declaration at the *San Remo Conference and its inclusion in the *Mandate for Palestine.

David Lloyd George, speaking at a Zionist Federation dinner in London, 1931. Courtesy Topical Press Agency, London.

Lloyd George appointed Herbert Samuel as the first high commissioner for Palestine and fought vehemently against the Passfield White Paper of 1930 (see *White Papers). In his testimony before the Royal Commission for Palestine in 1937 he said: ". . . it was contemplated [in 1917] that when the time arrived for according representative institutions for Palestine, if the Jews had meanwhile responded to the opportunity afforded them and had become a definite majority of the inhabitants, then Palestine would thus become a Jewish commonwealth." He told the Royal Commission that halting Jewish immigration to Palestine would be "a fraud." He took the same firm stand against the anti-Zionist White Paper of 1939. An entire chapter on Palestine is included in his *Memoirs of the Peace Conference* (2 (1939), 721–74).

Bibliography: L. Stein, *The Balfour Declaration* (1961), index; C. Weizmann, *Trial and Error* (1949), index; F. Owen, *Tempestuous Journey* (1954), index; R. Lloyd George, *Lloyd George* (1960), index; C. Sykes, *Crossroads to Israel* (1965), index. [D.Ef.]

LOAN (Heb. הַלְוָאָה, *halva'ah*), a transaction in which a thing, usually money, is given by one person, called the *malveh* ("lender"), to another, called the *loveh* ("borrower"), for the latter's use and enjoyment, and in order that such thing or its equivalent be returned by the borrower at some later date. In halakhic literature the term *halva'ah* is often used to describe an obligation or debt (*ḥov*) in general—i.e., not necessarily one originating from a transaction of loan—and many of the *halakhot* applying to debt in the wide sense of this term apply to loan, and vice versa (see Gulak, Yesodei, 2 (1922), 5f.; see also *Obligation, Law of). In this article loan is treated in the restricted sense of the term defined above

Oral Loan (milveh be-al peh) and Loan in Writing (milveh bi-shetar). A loan established orally is distinguished from one established in writing in two main respects: (1) in the former case the borrower's plea that he has repaid the loan is believed, whereas in the latter case such a plea by the borrower is not believed when the bond of indebtedness is in the lender's possession; (2) in the case of a loan in writing, the creditor has the right to levy on the debtor's *nekhasim meshu'badim* ("alienated and encumbered" assets, see *Lien; Obligation, Law of), a right not available to him in the case of an oral loan. The term *milveh be-al peh* is apparently a post-talmudic creation, although the distinction between the two forms of loan was recognized as early as tannaitic times (Gulak, loc. cit.; Herzog, Instit, 1 (1936), 352).

Mitzvah of Lending. The precept of lending to the poor of Israel is based on Exodus 22:24: "If thou lend money to any of my people that is poor by thee" (see Mekh., Mishpatim, s. 19), and is included in the enumeration of the *mitzvot* (*Sefer ha-Mitzvot,* Asayin no. 197; *Semag,* Asayin no. 93; *Sefer ha-Ḥinnukh* no. 66). Some scholars derived this precept from other biblical passages (*She'iltot* no. 114; *Semak* no. 248). The lender, if he apprehends that he may not be repaid, may make his loan conditional on the receipt of a *pledge from the borrower (Tos. to BM 82b; *Ahavat Ḥesed,* 1:13). The merit of fulfilling this precept was lavishly extolled by the scholars—even beyond the act of *charity (Shab. 63a). The duty was held to cover also a loan to a rich man in his hour of need (Sh. Ar., ḤM 97:1, *Sma* thereto, n. 1), but some scholars restricted its application to the case of a poor man only (*Even ha-Ezer,* Malveh ve-Loveh 1:1). In certain circumstances a person is prohibited from lending money to another. This is so if there are no witnesses to a loan (BM 75b), lest the borrower is tempted to deny his indebtedness or the lender to forget that he gave the loan; it nevertheless became customary for a loan, even an oral one, to be given in the absence of witnesses, and the *aḥaronim* sought to explain the custom and reconcile it with the talmudic *halakhah* (*Pilpula Ḥarifta* to BM 75b; Resp. *Ben Yehudah,* 1:153). Similarly prohibited is a loan given to a poor man for the repayment of another debt, since—but for such loan—the creditor might come to his relief on account of his poverty (Tos. to Ḥag. 5a).

Nature of the Repayment Obligation. The nature of the borrower's obligation to repay the loan was a matter of dispute among the *amoraim.* R. Papa took the view that the duty of repayment was no more than a *mitzvah*—just as it was a *mitzvah* for the lender to give a loan—whereas R. Huna b. Joshua held that repayment was a legal duty (Ket. 86a; BB 174a; Nov. Ritba, Kid. 13b; Resp. Mabit, vol. 1, no. 51; *Semag,* Asayin 93). It seems that alongside the legal duty, R. Huna recognized also the existence of a religious duty to repay the debt (Resp. Ribash 484; M. Elon (see bibl.), 20f. and n. 44, 45; for an opinion that the duty was a *mitzvah* only, see Nov. Ramban BB 173b). Some scholars held this *mitzvah* to be of Pentateuchal origin (Ritba, loc. cit.; Mabit, loc. cit., *Resp. Pitḥei Teshuvah,* ḤM 97, n. 4), while others interpreted R. Papa's statement as relating only to oral loan (Rashbam BB 174a). A borrower who fails to repay the loan is described as *rasha* ("wicked"; Ps. 37:21; *Semag,* Asayin no. 93; see also *Contract; Obligation, Law of).

Halva'ah and She'elah. *She'elah* (loan for use and return) relates to "utensils" *(kelim),* and *halva'ah* (loan for consumption) to money or "produce" *(perot).* Utensils are things which are not counted by weight and measure, nor exchangeable one for the other; things which are counted and exchanged in this way are "produce" (Gulak, Yesodei, vol. 1, p. 95; vol. 2, pp. 20, 171). The *sho'el* (borrower for use and return) must return the subject matter of the loan in specie, whereas the *loveh* need not do so. Unless otherwise stipulated, a loan is for consumption and the borrower will only be liable for payment of the equivalent in produce or other property (see also *Shomerim).

Establishment of Loan. A loan transaction is concluded upon handing over of the money (or "produce") to the borrower. In post-talmudic times the opinion was advanced that a contract of loan might be established upon performance of a formal *kinyan* alone (see *Acquisition), without handing over of the money, and that thereupon the borrower would become obliged to repay the money (Tur, ḤM 39:19 and *Beit Yosef* ad loc.); however, this opinion was not accepted by scholars (*Beit Yosef* loc. cit.; ḤM 89:17). Once the money of the loan has been given to the borrower, the lender will no longer have any right to retract and demand its return, even if it is still intact in specie (*Baḥ,* ḤM 39:19; *Siftei Kohen,* ḤM 39, n. 49). Where the lender has undertaken to give a loan and the borrower has already written a deed on the former's instruction, some scholars hold that as long as the money has not yet passed to the borrower the lender remains free to retract from the loan (Resp. Rashba, vol. 1, no. 1054; Sh. Ar., ḤM 39:17), while others preclude him from so doing (*Sefer ha-Terumot* 48:1; *Maggid Mishneh,* Malveh, 23:5). In the case of an oral loan, the lender may withdraw at any time before handing over of the money (*Netivot ha-Mishpat,* Mishpat ha-Urim, 39, n. 17).

Repayment Date. When Specified. If a specified date was stipulated between the parties, the lender may not reclaim the loan prior to that date (Mak. 3b; Yad, Malveh, 13:5). Some scholars maintain that the lender—even in circumstances where he has reason to fear the borrower's imminent departure abroad, or is aware that the latter may be squandering his assets and therefore unable to repay the debt on due date—is not entitled to anticipate the day of repayment (*Teshuvat ha-Ge'onim* no. 45; *Sefer ha-Terumot* 16:3; Tur, ḤM 73); other scholars invest the court with discretion in the matter and the power to order distraint of the property in the borrower's possession (Resp. Rif. no. 113; Resp. Rashba, vol. 1, no. 1111). It was held that the court might do this only if the borrower is squandering his assets, otherwise—even though his financial position may be steadily deteriorating for other reasons—the court will not have the power to intervene prior to the due date of repayment (*Yam shel Shelomo* BK 1:20; *Siftei Kohen* ḤM 73, no. 34, see also below; *Execution (Civil)).

When Unspecified. A loan for an unspecified period is given for 30 days (Yad, Malveh 13:5), and may not be reclaimed within this period. If it is customary in a locality to retain a loan of unspecified duration for a longer or a shorter period, that custom is followed (Sh. Ar., ḤM 73:1, *Sma* and *Siftei Kohen* ad loc.). Some scholars expressed the opinion that in this matter even the gentile custom is followed (*Sma,* loc. cit.)—but others disputed this (*Siftei Kohen,* loc. cit., n. 1 and 39).

Further Differences. (1) In the case of a loan for a specified period, the borrower's plea that he has made repayment within the term of the loan is not believed, since "a person is not likely to make payment before due date" (BB 5a), whereas in the case of a loan for an unspecified period the borrower's plea that he has paid within the 30 days as required is believed (Tos. to BB 5a). This distinction has been justified by the scholars on many grounds. Some hold that in the case of a specified repayment date, the borrower, for no particular reason, knows that he will have no money available until the due date, but not so in the case of an unspecified repayment date (Resp. Rosh, 76:3); others hold that when no date is specified, the borrower will feel ashamed if he should have money before the end of the 30 days and fail to make repayment—hence it is presumed that he will repay the loan, even within the said period, if he has the money (*Shitah Mekubbezet,* BB 5a); yet another view is that in the case of an unspecified repayment date, the borrower is liable for repayment of the loan before expiry of the 30 days—save that he cannot be obliged by the court to make payment before then—hence he is likely to repay earlier if he has the money (*Devar Avraham,* vol. 1, no. 32). A minority opinion holds that in the case of a loan for an unspecified period the borrower is not likely to anticipate payment, and his plea to this effect is not to be believed (Nov. Ramban BB 40a). (2) Apparently even those who adhere to the opinion that the property of a borrower—even when it is being squandered by him—cannot be distrained until due date of payment of the loan agree with all other scholars that as regards a loan for an unspecified period, the court may distrain the property in the debtor's possession even before expiry of the 30 days (*Keneset ha-Gedolah,* ḤM 73; *Beit Yosef* 20b).

Anticipation of Payment by the Borrower. Since determination of the repayment date is for the borrower's benefit (Ran to Ket. 81a, s.v. *vegarsinan*), it is permissible for him to repay the loan before the due date, regardless of the lender's wishes (Ran, loc. cit.). He may not, however, anticipate payment without the lender's consent when there is a substantial apprehension of an imminent and official change in currency values (*Sefer ha-Terumot* 30:2; see also below).

Acceptance of Payment. Payment made to the lender against the latter's will is a valid payment; if the latter refuses to accept the money and the borrower throws it to him, he will be discharged (*Sefer ha-Terumot* 50:1; Tos. to Git. 75a). However, when the lender is prepared to accept payment, the borrower must make the payment into his hands and may not throw it to him (Git. 78b; Yad, Malveh 16:1). Payment to the lender's wife is held by some scholars to discharge the borrower, provided that she is accustomed to transacting her husband's business (see *Husband and Wife; Resp. Maharam of Rothenburg, ed. Prague, no. 225; *Rema,* ḤM 120:2), but other scholars dispute that this is a valid discharge (*Yam shel Shelomoh* BK 9:39).

Place of Payment. The lender may claim repayment at any place, even in the wilderness (BK 118a; Sh. Ar., ḤM 74:1). Upon due date the borrower may oblige the lender to accept payment at any settled place (*yishuv*), even if this is not the place where the loan was transacted nor the place of residence of the lender or borrower (*Sefer ha-Terumot,* 30:1; Sh. Ar., loc. cit.). If the loan was transacted in the wilderness, the borrower may oblige the lender to accept payment there (*Rema* ḤM 74:1).

Method and Means of Payment. A debt not yet due may be repaid little by little (BM 77b; *Mordekhai* BM no. 352; *Ittur,* vol. 1, pt. 2, s.v. *iska*); according to some scholars payment in this manner, although initially forbidden, is valid in retrospect (*Bedek ha-Bayit* ḤM 74; *Siftei Kohen* ḤM 74, n. 17). After due date the lender may, in the opinion of all scholars, refuse to accept payment in the said manner (*Mordekhai,* loc. cit.). The borrower must repay in money, and, if he has none, in land. The lender may refuse to accept the land and offer to wait until the borrower has money—even if this is after the due date (Resp. Rosh, 80:9; Sh. Ar., ḤM 74:6, 101:4). If the borrower has no money, the lender may not instruct him to sell his assets in order to receive money for them, but must either take the assets as payment or wait until the borrower has money (Tos. to BK 9a). If payment in money entails a loss for the borrower, he may repay the loan in land (Tos. Ket. 92a and Ran ad loc.). If the borrower has money, land, and chattels, and wishes to pay in money, while the lender asks for land or chattels, some scholars hold the law to favor the lender and others the borrower (*Sefer ha-Terumot* 4:2; see also *Execution Civil)).

Fluctuation in Currency Values. In case of official withdrawal and replacement of the existing currency, the position is as follows: If the new currency is of the same kind, the borrower pays in the currency in circulation at the time of payment (BK 97). If, however, the withdrawn currency is circulating in another country on the same terms as it formerly did in the country of its withdrawal, the lender—if he has the means of reaching such a country and there is no particular difficulty in transferring the old currency—will be obliged to accept the withdrawn currency in payment (BK 97; Sh. Ar., ḤM 74:7). If as a result of a change in the value of the currency there is a reduction in the price index of the commodities ("produce"), the borrower pays in accordance with the new currency value and deducts for himself the excess (BK 97b, 98a); if the reduction in prices result from factors unconnected with a currency revaluation, the borrower pays in the stipulated currency, without any deduction (Sh. Ar., YD 165). The view that the rules stated with reference to a currency revaluation must also be extended, by analogy, to the case of a currency devaluation (*Aferet Zahar* no. 165) was accepted as *halakhah* (*Piskei ha-Rosh,* BK 9:12; *Ḥikrei Lev,* Mahadura Bafra, ḤM 9) in preference to a contrary opinion (*Piskei ha-Rosh,* loc. cit.; Resp. Rashba, vol. 3, no. 34).

In many Jewish communities **takkanot* were enacted which were aimed at reaching a compromise in disputes between parties relating to the manner of debt-payment in case of a change in currency values, and a decisive majority of the *posekim* inclined toward adjudging and compromising between the parties in terms of these *takkanot* (see Kahana, bibl.; **Takkanot ha-Kahal*).

Plea of Repayment (*Parati;* "I have repaid"). An oral loan is repayable without witnesses; a loan in writing, before witnesses. In a claim for repayment of an oral loan, the borrower's plea that he has already made repayment is believed (Sh. Ar., ḤM 70:1); such a plea is regarded as a general denial of the claim, and—on taking a solemn *oath (*shevu'at hesset*)—the borrower is exempted (Sh. Ar., ḤM 70:1). Where there is a bond of indebtedness, the borrower's plea that he has made repayment is not believed, and the lender—on swearing an oath that he has not been repaid—proceeds to recover the debt (*ibid.*). (As regards the borrower's plea of payment prior to the due date, see above.) As a means of protecting the lender against such a possible plea of repayment, it became customary to stipulate, at the time of the loan, that credence be given to the lender upon his denial of a repayment plea by the borrower—such stipulation availing to dismiss the latter plea (Sh. Ar., ḤM 71:1). For the similar protection of the lender, the practice was adopted of stipulating at the time of the loan that it be repayable only before witnesses—the borrower's plea of repayment being thus deprived of credibility unless attested by witnesses (*ibid.,* 70:3). In the latter case it still remained possible for the borrower to plead that he had repaid the debt before witnesses A and B, who had since gone abroad, and—upon making a solemn oath—become exempted; to forestall this possibility the practice was adopted of stipulating, "You shall not repay me except before witnesses so and so, or before the court"—thus precluding the borrower from pleading that he made repayment before some other witnesses (*ibid.,* 70:4).

Multiple Loans. If a lender has given the same borrower two separate loans and the latter seeks to repay on account of one of them, the lender may appropriate the payment toward whichever loan he pleases without any right on the borrower's part to protest or maintain that he intended otherwise (Tur., ḤM 83:2 and *Beit Yosef* ad loc.; *Sefer ha-Terumot* 20:2). This rule only applies when both loans have already fallen due for payment (*Sefer ha-Terumot*, loc. cit.); if one loan has fallen due but not the other, the payment is deemed to have been made on account of the former (Resp. Radbaz, 1252 (181)); if neither has fallen due, the law is apparently the same as for two loans already due (Radbaz, loc. cit.; *Keẓot ha-Ḥoshen* 83, n. 1).

Conversion into Loan of Other Contractual Obligation. At times the practice was adopted, for various reasons, of converting an obligation originating from a transaction other than loan into an obligation of loan. This practice is referred to as *zekifat ḥov be-milveh* and was adopted—for instance in the case of a purchaser indebted to the seller for the purchase price—because of the restricted number of pleas possible against a claim for a loan-debt as compared to a claim for a debt originating from the sale of goods (BM 77b; ḤM 190:10). *Zekifat ḥov* takes place in one of the following ways: (1) by the writing of a special bond of indebtedness for an already existing debt; (2) by the stipulation of a date for the repayment of an existing debt; and (3) by the gradual accumulation of a debt, for instance by purchase on credit from a shop. In this way the original obligation is largely—or even entirely—extinguished and converted into a new obligation. From the time of such *zekifah* the debt is an obligation of loan only, the new obligation retaining none of the legal characteristics of the old (Gulak, Yesodei, vol. 2, pp. 116–8).

Minor as Party to a Loan. By pentateuchal law, a minor has no legal capacity to lend. As long as the subject matter of such a loan is still intact (in specie), it must be returned by the borrower; hence in case of loss resulting from **ones* (force majeure) the borrower is exempt from liability as the property is deemed to be in its owner's possession for purposes of loss arising from *ones*. The rabbis enacted that a loan given by a minor should be valid, the borrower being liable also for loss resulting from *ones* (Gulak, Yesodei, vol. 1, p. 40). A minor who has borrowed is exempt from returning the loan, even after reaching his majority. According to some scholars, a minor who has borrowed for his own maintenance can be recovered from even during his minority (Gulak, loc. cit.; see also *Legal Capacity).

Measures to Prevent "Bolting the Door" to Borrowers. Hillel the Elder instituted a *Prosbul designed to overcome reluctance to lend to a borrower at the approach of the *shemittah* (sabbatical) year (Shev. 10:3; Rashi Git. 37a; see also **Takkanot*). Although according to pentateuchal law the need for *derishah* and *ḥakirah* (examination of witnesses) extends also to civil law (*dinei mamonot*) matters, the scholars enacted for the obviation of this procedure in the latter cases, so as not to bolt the door before borrowers (Sanh. 3a; see also *Practice and Procedure; *Witness). Despite an opinion upholding the need, by the pentateuchal law, for three expert judges in matters of *hoda'ot* ("acknowledgements") and loans, the scholars enacted for the competence of a court of three laymen, lest the door be bolted before borrowers for fear that no expert judges be found to enforce the law (*ibid.*; see also **Bet Din*). The scholars enacted that in certain circumstances the judges, if they erred, were not to be exempted from liability, in order not to discourage people from lending to others (*ibid.*). According to pentateuchal law, the creditor recovers the debt out of the *zibburit* ("worst land") of the debtor, but the scholars enacted that he might do so from the *beinonit* ("medium land"), for the reason mentioned above (Git. 50a; see also *Execution (Civil)). According to those who held that the doctrine of *shi'bud nekhasim* was non-pentateuchal, the scholars enacted for a lender on a bond to recover from the debtor's *nekhasim meshu'badim* ("encumbered and alienated property"; see *Lien; BB 175b).

Bibliography: Gulak, Yesodei, 1 (1922), 145f.; 2 (1922), 33–35, 42f., 83–88, 105–9, 113–8, 170–2; 3 (1922), 102–6; 4 (1922), 85–90; idem, Oẓar, 205f., 208; J. Rappaport, in: *Zeitschrift fuer vergleichende Rechtswissenschaft*, 47 (1932/33), 256–378; Herzog, Instit, 1 (1936), 121–4, 219f., 359f.; 2 (1939), 57f., 186f., 215f.; J. S. Kahana, in: *Sinai*, 25 (1949), 129–48; ET, 1 (1951[3]), 263–6; 4 (1952), 110–4; 5 (1953), 92–132; 9 (1959), 215–40; M. Silberg, *Kakh Darko shel Talmud* (1961), 71–75; M. Elon, *Ḥerut ha-Perat* . . . (1964); idem, Mafte'aḥ, 48–57.

[SH.SH.]

LOANZ, ELIJAH BEN MOSES (1564–1636), one of the outstanding kabbalists of Germany in the late 16th and early 17th centuries. Born in Frankfort on the Main, he was a grandson of *Joseph Joselmann b. Gershom of Rosheim. His teachers included Akiva Frankfurter, Jacob Guenzberg of Friedberg, *Judah Loew b. Bezalel of Prague, and *Menahem Mendel b. Isaac of Cracow. Serving as rabbi in *Fulda, *Hanau, *Friedberg, and *Worms successively, he was also *rosh yeshivah*, preacher, and *ḥazzan* in Worms for a time. Because he was well known as a writer of kabbalistic amulets and incantations, early in his career he acquired the cognomen Elijah Ba'al Shem. Only one of his books, *Rinnat Dodim*, a kabbalistic commentary on the Song of Songs, was printed during his lifetime (Basle, 1600). Other published works include *Mikhlol Yofi*, a commentary on Ecclesiastes (Amsterdam, 1695). He was the author of occasional liturgical poetry and his secular poem, *Vikku'aḥ Yayin im ha-Mayim*, was translated into German. Among his works still in manuscript (Oxford Bodleian Library) are an incomplete commentary on Midrash *Genesis Rabbah; Ma'gelei Ẓedek*, a supercommentary on *Baḥya b. Asher's commentary on the Pentateuch; *Adderet Eliyahu*, a commentary on the Zohar; *Ẓafenat Pa'ne'aḥ* on *Tikkunei Zohar;* and a commentary on Baḥya ibn Pakuda's *Ḥovot ha-Levavot*. Some of his kabbalistic amulets and formulae are included in the collections *Toledot Adam* (Zolkiew, 1720) and *Mifalot Elohim* (*ibid.*, 1727). Loanz also prepared for press a number of halakhic works, notably *Darkhei Moshe* by Moses Isserles. He exchanged learned correspondence with the Christian Hebraist, Johannes *Buxtorf.

Bibliography: M. Mannheimer, *Die Juden in Worms* (1842), 61; Landshuth, Ammudei, 16–17; L. Lewysohn, *Nafshot Ẓaddikim; Sechzig Epitaphien* . . . (1855), 59; I. Tishby, in: *Sefer Asaf* (1953), 515–28; Neubauer, Cat. 1829–32; D. Kaufmann, *R. Jair Chajjim Bacharach* (1894), 33–34; A. Epstein, *Mishpaḥat Luria* (1901), 47ff.

[TH.F.]

LOBATO (Cohen Lobato), Marrano family prominent in Amsterdam, Hamburg, and London. Of especial importance were the following: ABRAHAM COHEN LOBATO, Portuguese Marrano born in Lisbon where he was known as Diego Gomez Lobato. In 1599, when his kinsman, Paul de Pina (alias Reuel *Jesurun) set out for Rome with the intention of becoming a monk, Lobato wrote to Elijah *Montalto at Leghorn, who dissuaded him from his plan. Lobato subsequently went with De Pina to Brazil. On their return to Europe, they both settled as professing Jews in Amsterdam. Abraham Cohen Lobato is not to be confused with another person of the same name (perhaps his grandson) who died in Hamburg in 1665. The name Rehuel (Reuel) remained common among his descendants. REHUEL COHEN LOBATO, probably his son, and father of Isaac Cohen, was cotranslator, with Moses *Belmonte, of *Avot*, published in Spanish in Amsterdam (1644). ISAAC COHEN LOBATO filled the role of "Mount Zion" in the original presentation of Reuel Jesurun's "Dialogue of the Seven Mountains" in 1624, and was one of the founders of the society Sha'arei Ẓedek in Amsterdam in 1678. REHUEL

Lobato (1797–1866), a Dutch mathematician, was author of scientific and statistical works.

Bibliography: Roth, Marranos, index; M. Kayserling, *Sephardim an der unteren Elbe* (1859), 176; Kayserling, Bibl, 27, 64, 89; M. Grunwald, *Portugiesengraeber auf deutscher Erde* (1902), 115; M. De Barrios, *Casa de Jacob* (1685), 18, 24; H. Brugmans and A. Frank, *Geschiedenis der Joden in Nederland,* 1 (1940), 220, 264, 267. [C.R.]

LOCKER, BERL (1887–1972), Labor Zionist leader. Locker was born in Kriwiec, Galicia, and from 1902 he began to contribute to the Lemberg Labor Zionist newspaper, *Der Yidisher Arbeiter,* of which he later became editor. He organized the *Po'alei Zion party in the Austrian Empire before World War I. During the war Locker spent some time in the United States and from 1916 ran the world office of Po'alei Zion at The Hague. At the world conference of Po'alei Zion in Vienna (1920) he supported the split which brought about the separation of the pro-Communist wing and headed the World Union of Po'alei Zion ("right wing"). He was a member of the Zionist and Jewish Agency Executives in London from 1931 to 1936, when he settled in Palestine. Locker was a member of the *Histadrut Executive from 1936 to 1938, and from 1938 headed the political bureau of the Jewish Agency in London during the period of the struggle against the policy embodied in the White Paper of 1939 and for Jewish statehood. He tried to effect a rapprochement with the British government, particularly after the Labor Party took office in 1945.

Berl Locker, Labor Zionist leader. Courtesy Jewish Agency Photo Service, Jerusalem.

From the establishment of the State of Israel (1948) until 1956, Locker served as chairman of the Jewish Agency Executive in Jerusalem. He was a member of the Third Knesset on the *Mapai list. Locker wrote many articles and pamphlets in Yiddish, German, Hebrew, and English. For the most part, he devoted himself to Zionist propaganda in England, and during the *yishuv's* struggle in Palestine he published the pamphlet, *A Stiff-Necked People—Palestine in Jewish History* (1946; the American edition is called *Covenant Everlasting,* 1947). A Hebrew translation and selections of his articles were published in *Be-Ḥevlei Kiyyum u-Tekumah* (1963). Among the various newspapers and publications of the Labor Zionists, he edited a selection of Ber *Borochov's work in Yiddish (1928). He also wrote *Mi-Kitov ad Yerushalayim* (1970).

Bibliography: N. M. Gelber, *Toledot ha-Tenu'ah ha-Ẓiyyonit be-Galiẓyah* (1958), 771-3; Tidhar, 11 (1961), 3779. [Ed.]

LOCKER, MALKE (1887–), Yiddish poet and essayist. Born in Eastern Galicia, she learned German, Polish, and Ukrainian as well as Hebrew and Yiddish in her youth. She married the Labor Zionist leader Berl *Locker. Her predilection for romantic and symbolist poets found expression in her Yiddish biography *Rimbaud* (1950; translated into French, 1965), and in her book of Yiddish essays on German, English, and French romantic writers, *Romantiker* (1958; Fr. *Les Romantiques,* 1964). She also wrote Yiddish lyric poetry, beginning with *Velt un Mentsh* (1931) and *Du* (1932), and culminating in *Yerushalayim* (1967). The poems of her volume *Di Velt is on a Hiter* (1947) were translated into Hebrew by Avigdor *Hameiri.

Bibliography: LNYL, 4 (1961), 463; M. Ravitch, *Mayn Leksikon,* 3 (1958), 219f.; Vigée, in: M. Locker, *Les Romantiques* (1964), 7–14 (introd.). [S.L.]

LOCKSPEISER, SIR BEN (1891–), British scientist and industrial expert. Born in London of Hungarian immigrant parents, Lockspeiser was engaged in aeronautical research at the Royal Aircraft Establishment in Farnborough from 1920 to 1937 when he became head of the government air defense department. During World War II he was in charge of research at the Air Ministry and the Ministry of Aircraft Production and later became director general there. From 1946 to 1949 he was chief scientist in the Ministry of Supply. He was secretary to the Department of Scientific and Industrial Research (1949–56) and a member of the international council of scientists set up by *Einstein and Bertrand Russell to prevent nuclear destruction. He was also president of the Council of the European Organization for Nuclear Research (1955–57), an organization for the development of atomic energy for peaceful purposes. In 1956 he became adviser to the Ministry of Development in Israel and as U.N. representative served as chairman of the Israel Technological Advisory Board. Lockspeiser was knighted in 1946. [S.A.M.]

His brother Edward Lockspeiser (1905–), conductor and musicologist, was born in London. In 1934 he founded the Toynbee Hall Orchestra. He served as music critic to the *"Yorkshire Post"* and *"Musical America,"* and in 1942 became Overseas Information and Research Assistant to the Music Department of the B.B.C. His writings include *Debussy, His Life and Mind,* 2 vols. (1962–65) and studies of Berlioz (1939) and Bizet (1951). [Ed.]

LOCUST (Heb. אַרְבֶּה, *arbeh*), one of the four insects which, having "jointed legs above their feet, wherewith to leap upon the earth," are permitted as food (Lev. 11:21–22). The locust was one of the ten plagues of Egypt (Ex. 10:4–19). The reference is to the Sudanese locust, *Schistocerca gregaria,* a pest that reached Ereẓ Israel in large numbers every few years causing havoc to agriculture. The Bible and talmudic literature describe the plague of locusts as one of the worst visitations to come upon the country. Its gravity and extent varied from time to time, one of the severest plagues having taken place in the days of the prophet Joel who devoted most of his prophecy to it. His precise descriptions of the locusts' development, sweep, and damage were confirmed in the extremely serious plague of

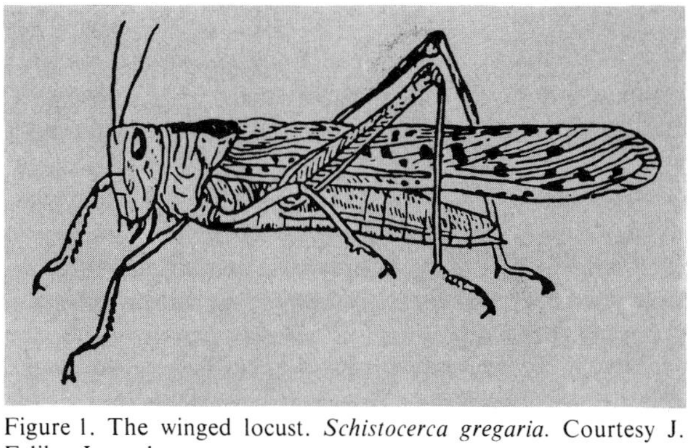

Figure 1. The winged locust. *Schistocerca gregaria.* Courtesy J. Feliks, Jerusalem.

locusts that visited Ereẓ Israel in 1915 when the crops were entirely destroyed in most parts of the country.

During the plague the locust undergoes various metamorphoses from the larva to the fully-grown, the stages of its development being given in Joel (2:25) in the expressions אַרְבֶּה *(arbeh)*, יֶלֶק *(yelek)*, חָסִיל *(ḥasil)*, and גָּזָם *(gazam)*, the last of these being the fully grown male or female. After being fertilized, the female lays a cluster of eggs in a hole which it makes in the ground. From the eggs, dark wingless larvae, the size of tiny ants, are hatched, these being the *yelek*, a word apparently connected with לָקַק, "to lap," "lick up." Eating the tender vegetation of the field, the *yelek* grows rapidly, and since (as with all insects) its epidermis does not become bigger, it sheds it at various stages of its growth, during which it changes the color of its skin. The next stage, during which its skin is pink, is the *ḥasil*, which word, from the root חסל, refers to its total destruction of the vegetation of the field, for at this stage it consumes enormous quantities; hence *ḥasil* is used as a synonym for *arbeh*. Thus in Solomon's prayer at the dedication of the Temple he declared that during a plague of *arbeh ḥasil* people would come there to pray for its riddance (I Kings 8:37; cf. Ps. 78:46). It now casts its skin twice, grows short wings, and becomes the *gazam*. At this juncture, when no more vegetation is left in the field, it "cuts off" (this being the meaning of גָּזָם) and chews the bark of trees with its powerful jaws; as Joel (1:7) says: "he hath made it (the fig-tree) clean bare . . . the branches thereof are made white"; and Amos (4:9): it devours "your gardens and your vineyards and your fig-trees and your olive-trees." Finally, after casting a further epidermis, it becomes the fully grown, long-winged *arbeh*, the yellow-colored female which is fit to lay its eggs. This cycle of the locust's development extends from spring until June when the swarms of locusts return to their place of origin or are blown by the wind to the Mediterranean or Dead Sea (Joel 2:20).

Joel refers to the locust as "the northern one," which is seemingly strange since it comes from the south. But in contemporary times (especially in 1915) it was found that swarms of locusts reach Jerusalem from the north. The means of fighting an invading swarm of locusts were very limited. While attempts were made to drive them away by making a noise (Job 39:20), reliance was chiefly placed on the mercy of the Lord by praying and proclaiming a fast and a solemn assembly (Joel 2:15). In talmudic literature, locusts are included among the disasters for which the alarm of the ram's horn *(shofar)* was sounded and a public fast held (Ta'an. 3:5). A plague of locusts brought famine in its wake, sometimes even in the following years by reason of the damage done to fruit trees. Having no other source of food, the people collected the locusts, dried and preserved them as food. The Mishnah cites divergent views on whether the blessing "by whose word all things exist" is to be said when eating locusts (in the Mishnah גּוֹבַאי *(govai)*, in the Bible גּוֹבָי *(govai)*; Nah. 3:17), one view being that since it "is in the nature of a curse, no blessing is said over it" (Ber. 6:3). In ancient times however they were regarded as a frugal meal and especially associated with *asceticism, as when John the Baptist ate only "locusts and wild honey" (Matt. 3:4; Mark 1:6). Some Yemenite Jews still eat fried locusts. In recent years swarms of locusts have at times visited countries neighboring on Israel, frequently originating in Africa and the Arabian peninsula, but modern methods have succeeded in destroying them in time by spraying from the air or by poison on the ground.

Figure 2. Detail from an illumination in the *Golden Haggadah*, Spain, 14th century, showing Moses and Aaron watching the locust plague in Egypt. London, British Museum. Add. Ms. 27210, fol. 13r.

Bibliography: Lewysohn, Zool, 285ff., 370; Whiting, in: *National Geographic Magazine*, 28 (1915), 511–50; F. S. Bodenheimer, *Studien zur Epidemologie, Oekologie und Physiologie der afrikanischen Wanderheuschrecke* (1930).

[J.F.]

LO-DEBAR (Heb. לְדְבִר ,לוֹ דְבָר ,לֹא דְבָר), city on the border of Gad in the northern part of Gilead (Josh. 13:26; Lidbir). Mephibosheth son of Jonathan lived there when Saul's family fled to Gilead after the disastrous battle at Mt. Gilboa (II Sam. 9:4ff.). Lo-Debar apparently fell into the hands of the Arameans during their wars with Israel and was recovered by Jeroboam (cf. Amos 6:13 where the name is translated as "a thing of nought"). The ancient name may be preserved in Umm al-Dabr in the eastern Jordan Valley 10 mi. (16 km.) south of the Sea of Galilee.

Bibliography: Abel, Geog, 2 (1938), 304, 370; M. Noth, in: PJB, 37 (1941), 87; Press, Ereẓ, 3 (1956²), 517; EM, 4 (1962), 409–10.

[M.A.-Y.]

LODEVE, town in the department of Hérault, S. France. In 1092, Bernard III, bishop of Lodève, renewed the ancient canonical prohibition on mixed marriages. The Jewish community of Lodève, which a medieval document describes as having been flourishing and with many scholars (although no works from them have been preserved), appears to have dwindled away from the end of the 13th century; Jews originally from Lodève are subsequently found in Montpellier and later in Perpignan. During the 18th century, Jews from Avignon traded in Lodève. In June 1941, about 100 Jews were living there, according to the census of Jews carried out at that time. There is a Rue des Juifs in Lodève, and in the vicinity a grotto known as Pons des Jésiaous ("Well of the Jews").

Bibliography: Gross, Gal Jud, 273ff.; REJ, 14 (1887), 73; 22 (1891), 265; 43 (1901), 295; G. Paris, *Histoire de Lodève* (1851), passim; Z. Szajkowski, *Analytical Franco-Jewish Gazetteer 1939–1945* (1966), 200.

[B.Bl.]

LODI, town in N. Italy, in the former duchy of Milan. Jewish moneylenders were possibly invited to Lodi in about 1420. In 1541 the Jews of Lodi and of other cities of the duchy obtained the protection of Pope *Paul III against the anti-Jewish preachings of the friars. Copies of the Talmud were burnt by order of the Inquisition in Lodi in 1559, and in 1597 other works were destroyed. The Jews were expelled from the duchy in 1597, only two families remaining in Lodi for a time to settle outstanding financial details.

Bibliography: Roth, Italy, index; Milano, Italy, index; Milano, Bibliotheca, index; Pavoncello, in: REJ, 119 (1961), 131–42; Joseph ben Joshua ha-Kohen, *Emek ha-Bakha* (1945[2]), passim; Dimitrowski, in: *Zion*, 20 (1955), 179–81; idem, in: *Talpioth*, 6 (1955), 708–22; Cremascoli, in: *Israel* (Jan. 24, Feb. 14, March 21, 1957).

[Ed.]

°**LODS, ADOLPHE** (1867–1948), French Protestant Bible scholar and historian. Lods was born in Courbevoie, near Paris. After lecturing on Hebrew at the Faculté Théologique of Paris, in 1906 he began teaching Hebrew language and literature at the Sorbonne. He was elected to the Academie des Inscriptions in 1935. Lods published a study of Proverbs, *L'Ecclésiaste et la philosophie grecque* (1890); an edition of the book of Enoch from Greek fragments with variants from the Ethiopian text, translation, and notes, *Le livre d'Hénoch* (1892); and his major study, *La croyance à la vie future et le culte des morts dans l'antiquité Israelite* (2 vols., 1906). After the publication of *Jean Astruc et la critique biblique au 18ième siecle* (1924), Lods concentrated on more general studies, including *Israël, des origines au 8ième siecle* (1930; English trans. *Israel from the Beginning to the Middle of the Eighth Century* by S. H. Hooke, 1932) and its continuation *Des Prophètes a Jésus* (1935; English trans. of the first part, by S. H. Hooke, *Prophets and the Rise of Judaism*, 1937); *La religion d'Israël* (1939; Spanish trans. by A. Spivak, 1940); and *Histoire de la littérature hébraïque et juive* (to 135 C.E.; 1950).

Bibliography: Bayet, in: *Comptes Rendus de l'Académie des Inscriptions et Belles Lettres* (1957), 315–27; H. F. Hahn, *The Old Testament in Modern Research* (1956), 166–9.

[Ed.]

LODZ (Pol. **Łódź**), city in central Poland, center of the textile industry. In 1793 there were 11 Jews in Lodz; by 1809 (when the city was under Prussian rule) the number had risen to 98. A community was organized at that time and a wooden synagogue erected which was renovated in subsequent years. After 1820 (under Russian rule) Lodz became an important industrial center and consequently the Jewish population increased rapidly, until the community became the second largest in independent Poland.

Year	General Population	Jewish Population	% Jews
1820	767	259	33.8
1823	799	288	36.0
1856	24,655	2,886	11.7
1897	310,302	98,676	31.8
1910	409,405	166,628	40.7
1921	452,623	156,155	34.5
1931	604,470	202,497	33.5

Wishing to develop the textile industry in Lodz, the Russian government invited German weavers to settle on very favorable terms. To avert the possibility of Jewish competition, the Germans insisted that the same limitations on Jewish settlement as applied in *Zgierz should prevail in Lodz. According to these restrictions, Jews were not allowed to settle and acquire real property, nor were they allowed to sell liquor; only those who had previously kept inns were allowed to continue to do so without a special permit. However, the Jews were largely successful in preventing the Zgierz limitations being applied. When the local authorities planned the town, they set aside the two streets near the market, Walburska and Nadrzeczna, for the Jews. In 1825 they declared that as from July 1, 1827, Jews would be permitted to acquire building sites, to build, and to live on the southern side of the Podrzeczna and Walburska streets and the market only. The only Jews allowed to settle outside this quarter were those who established factories employing Jewish workers, wholesale merchants, members of the liberal professions who built houses, and two families who each possessed 20,000 zlotys. All Jews granted exceptional residence rights had to know Polish, French, or German, and their children over the age of seven had to attend general schools along with non-Jewish children. They were also forbidden to wear the traditional Jewish dress. For a time the authorities continued to harass even those Jews who fulfilled all these conditions. Anxious to eliminate competition from the growing number of Jewish weavers, the German textile workers pressed for the expulsion of the Jews. From 1832 Samuel Ezekiel Salzmann led the battle to extend the rights of Jewish settlement. As the number of Jews continued to grow he built many houses to alleviate the overcrowding and rising rents in the Jewish quarter.

In 1848 the czar abolished the limitations on Jewish settlement in Polish cities. By decrees of 1861 and 1862 the concept of a specific Jewish quarter in Lodz was finally abolished. Jews settled throughout the city, although many of them continued to be concentrated in the former Jewish quarter, the "Altstadt." A synagogue was erected on Wilki Street, outside the old quarter. Large numbers of Jewish craftsmen, peddlers, and factory workers were concentrated in the suburb of Balut (Baluty). This settlement began early in the 19th century, when Balut was still a separate village and Isaac Blauwatt and Isaac Birnzweig leased lands from its owner to sublet to Jews. Although no industrial enterprises were established in Balut itself, many Jewish weavers who worked for the large enterprises on a contractual basis lived there. Until 1916 Balut was officially a village outside the Lodz municipality, and hygienic conditions were consequently poor. Conditions remained the same when it was incorporated into the municipality. With rising unemployment and worsening conditions for handloom weavers, life in Balut steadily deteriorated in the interwar period.

Throughout the 19th century and up to 1939 Jews were active in much of the trade in Lodz, especially in supplying raw materials for the textile industry. Wholesale and retail traders, agents, and brokers formed over one third of the Jewish earners in Lodz. In the 20th century Jews entered industry on a considerable scale; by 1914, 175 factories (33.3% of the total) were owned by Jews; 150 of these were textile mills. Jews also owned 18,954 small workshops (27.7%); 18,476 of them textile enterprises. Of the 27,385 Jewish workers (32.9% of the labor force), 26,845 were employed in textile industries. Thus the majority of Jewish enterprise and workers was employed in the small workshops of the Jewish textile industry. Jewish mills produced mainly cotton although there were some woolen and linen mills. The most prominent industrialists were Poznański, Hayyim Jacob Wiślicki, Asher Cohen (Oskar Kohn), the brothers Ettingon, Jacob Kastenberg, and Tuvia Bialer.

Lodz was badly destroyed during World War I when the German residents collaborated with the German invaders. With the break-up of czarist Russia and the creation of independent Poland, the large Russian market was lost and consequently new markets were needed. The Polish government did not grant Jewish industry financial aid for reconstruction. In the early 1920s the anti-Jewish fiscal policies of Polish Finance Minister W. Grabski further hindered the recovery of Jewish industry. Those firms which managed to recover were again hit by the world crisis of

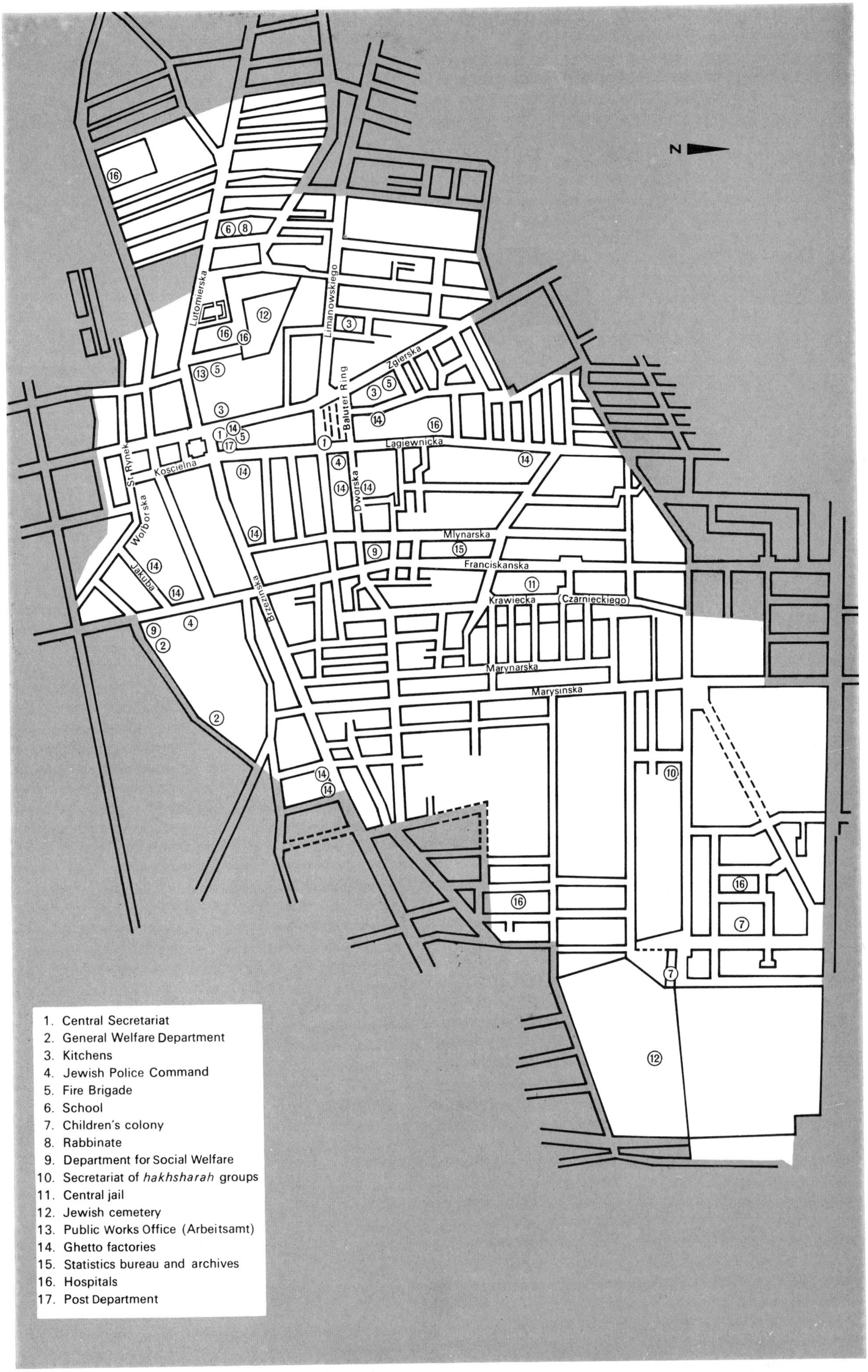
N
Lutomierska
Limanowskiego
Baluter Ring
Zgierska
Lagiewnicka
St. Rynek
Koscielna
Wolborska
Jakuba
Dworska
Brzezinska
Mlynarska
Franciskanska
Krawiecka
(Czarnieckiego)
Marynarska
Marysinska
1. Central Secretariat
2. General Welfare Department
3. Kitchens
4. Jewish Police Command
5. Fire Brigade
6. School
7. Children's colony
8. Rabbinate
9. Department for Social Welfare
10. Secretariat of *hakhsharah* groups
11. Central jail
12. Jewish cemetery
13. Public Works Office (Arbeitsamt)
14. Ghetto factories
15. Statistics bureau and archives
16. Hospitals
17. Post Department

Plan of the Lodz ghetto, 1940–44. From J. I. Trunk, *Lodzher Geto,* 1962.

Figure 1. Italianate synagogue built in Lodz in 1888 and destroyed during World War II. Courtesy YIVO, New York.

1929. During the 1930s, anti-Jewish economic policies were intensified throughout Poland. Jewish workers were squeezed out of industry, even the enterprises owned by Jews. Every growth in the scale of a plant or increasing mechanization meant that Jewish workers were likely to lose their jobs, both because Polish workers were opposed to their employment and because anti-Jewish government policy encouraged this opposition. Between the wars, ready-made tailoring in Lodz was almost entirely in Jewish hands. Jews were also engaged in building and related trades such as paving, making steps, and carpentry, working on a contractual basis. Polish anti-Jewish policy attempted to replace Jewish weavers by Polish craftsmen. In 1910 the First Union of Jewish Craftsmen was organized, also including large-scale Jewish industrialists, on the initiative of the Jewish Bank for Mutual Assistance. In 1912 it was renamed the Union of Industrialists. Craftsmen and middle-range industrialists joined its ranks. After World War I a union of craftsmen and industrialists was organized as was a union of Jewish merchants in 1925. Small tradesmen and retailers had their own unions. In 1926 a union of both Jewish and non-Jewish traders and retailers was formed; however, the non-Jews soon left it. The Jews formed their unions in collaboration with *Ort. The *Bund, the *Po'alei Zion, and the Polish Socialist Party (the *P.P.S.) competed in organizing trade unions among the Jewish laborers in Lodz. In 1901, at a funeral of one of its members, the Bund held a demonstration in which 2,000 persons participated. During the revolution of 1905, the Bund was very active in Lodz. At the end of 1903, a Jewish section of the P.P.S. was organized in the city on the initiative of the famous Polish leader Józef *Pilsudski. Jewish craftsmen in Lodz, as elsewhere in Poland, were faced in 1927 with a law which demanded examinations for craftsmen and a diploma awarded by a union of artisans.

Social Life and Culture. The official enactments against and intrusions into Jewish communal institutions from the 1820s (see *Russia, *Poland, *Community, **Kazyonny ravvin*) had little effect in Lodz. The community maintained its *autonomy in difficult circumstances. With the official recognition of Jewish communal autonomy in independent Poland the first democratic elections for the community council of Lodz were held in 1924; seven of the members were Ḥasidim of *Aleksandrow, six Zionists and *Mizrachi, three Bund, 11 *Agudat Israel, one *Po'alei Agudat Israel, two representing the craftsmen, two left Po'alei Zion, one *Folkspartei, and one each from two Communist lists. The first chairman was the Zionist Dr. Uri Rosenblatt. In 1931 the authorities dissolved the community council and announced new elections. The results were: one Po'alei Agudat Israel, four Zionists, 12 Agudat Israel, two Ḥasidim of Aleksandrow, one Folkspartei, one representing the small tradesmen, and one each of the four leftist lists. Leib Minzberg of Agudat Israel was elected chairman, a position he occupied until the Holocaust. The community maintained a kosher slaughterhouse, a **mikveh*, and a **talmud torah* for the poor, and collaborated with *T.O.Z. and other charitable organizations. The most prominent was Gemilut Ḥasadim (Pol. Dobroczynność), founded in 1899 by Jewish philanthropists such as Israel Poznański as a roof organization for many charitable societies. Rabbis of Lodz included Mendel Wolf ha-Kohen Jerozolimski (1825–32) and Ezekiel Nomberg (1832–56), a *Kotsk Ḥasid who was opposed by many in the community. (His great-grandson was the Yiddish writer Hirsch David *Nomberg.) With the growth of Jewish Lodz, the rabbinical seat gained in importance. After a heated election campaign, Moses Lipshitz, also a Kotsk Ḥasid, was chosen in 1857. He was followed by the famous Lithuanian rabbi, Elijah Ḥayyim *Meisel (1873–1912), who enhanced the stature of the office by becoming the recognized leader of the Jews of Lodz. His successor was Eliezer Leib Treistman, a Gur Ḥasid, and former rabbi of Radom. After Treistman's death in 1920, because of disagreement between the parties, no other community rabbi was elected. Last of the Reform synagogue preachers and rabbis was Markus (Mordecai) *Braude, the founder of the Hebrew schools network (see below).

*B'nai B'rith established a lodge in Lodz in 1926 which supported the Ort vocational school, the orphanage, and various cultural institutions. A *bikkur ḥolim* organization was founded in 1881; in 1908 it was incorporated into the Dobroczynność. Between the two world wars, the convalescent home for sufferers from pulmonary diseases was particularly well known. There was also a *Linat ha-Ẓedek* society which visited Jewish patients in Lodz hospitals. In the course of time its activities were extended; between the two world wars it established a hospital for children and a *Linat ha-Ẓedek* pharmacy which was subsidized by the municipality of Lodz and the Jewish community. The synagogues organized societies for the relief of the sick and other charitable organizations, such as the Malbish Arumim which provided clothing for poor children. It subsequently undertook a variety of services: legal aid, the organization of cooperatives, and medical assistance. In the interwar period, there were soup kitchens for the needy which also distributed free meals to school children.

Jewish education in Lodz shared in the development and crises of the traditional Orthodox Jewish education system in modern times (and see **Ḥeder*, *Yeshivah). There were many yeshivot; some, e.g., Beth Israel of the Aleksandrow Ḥasidim and the Lithuanian-style Torat Ḥesed, were

Figure 2. Lodz Jews with a German soldier, 1915.

Figure 3. Stamp issued in the Lodz ghetto at the beginning of World War II, depicting the *Judenaeltester,* Chaim Mordecai Rumkowsky. Jerusalem, B. M. Ansbacher Collection.

influential. The *talmud torah* founded by R. Elijah Ḥayyim Meisel in 1873 provided education for children of elementary school age. Some subjects were taught in Polish and some in Hebrew. A diversified network of educational institutions, from kindergarten to secondary school, existed in Lodz. A "reformed" *ḥeder* (known as the Jaroczyński School after the philanthropist of this name) was founded in 1890 and included secular subjects in its curriculum. The first Jewish gymnasium in Russia was established in Lodz by Markus (Mordecai) Braude in 1912. In accordance with the requirements of Russian law, it was named after a private person, Dr. D. B. Rabinovich. In it too some subjects were taught in Polish and some in Hebrew. Another secondary school was headed by Itzhak *Katzenelson, the noted Hebrew poet who perished in the Holocaust. In 1918 the first Yiddish school was established, named after B. Borochov. The Jaroczyński *talmud torah* was converted into a vocational school in 1921 and in 1927 it became a secondary vocational school for the study of mechanics, electricity, and weaving. A *Beth Jacob school for girls was founded in 1924.

Although Lodz was not a leading Jewish cultural center, there was considerable creativity in the city. The Hebrew authors and poets, Itzhak Katzenelson, David *Frischman, and Jacob *Cohen lived and worked in Lodz, as did the scholars J. N. *Simchoni, Philip *Friedman, Aryeh *Tartakower, and Ḥayyim Isaac *Bunin. Yiddish authors and poets included Isaiah Uger, the editor of the newspaper *Lodzher Togblat,* J. I. *Trunk, H. L. *Fuks, and Ḥayyim Krol. Most famous of the many Jewish musicians were Chemjo *Vinaver, the conductor, and the composer I. Goldstein. Jewish drama companies were formed at the close of the 19th century, and from among these emerged the theater known as the "Great Theater," where the famous Yiddish actors, Julius Adler and Zaslavski, appeared. There were also well-known satirical theaters, directed by the Yiddish poet Moshe *Broderzon and actor Shimon *Dzigan.

Many Zionist societies were organized in Lodz soon after the First Zionist Congress of 1897, such as the Ohel Ya'akov, Ateret Zion, and Tikvat Zion, structured around synagogues. During World War I, Agudat Israel, whose main supporters were the Ḥasidim of Gur, engaged in numerous activities. The Zionist organizations were active in the propagation of the Hebrew language and Hebrew culture, initiated and organized by the historian J. N. Simchoni. The Hebrew cultural activities operated within the framework of the literary-musical society, Ha-Zamir, founded in 1899. It maintained a choir, a dramatic circle, and a library, and in 1915 formed a philharmonic orchestra. The D. B. Borochov Library was established by Po'alei Zion in 1914 and the Bund established the Grosser Library, named after the Bundist leader by the same name. Jewish newspapers included the Zionist *Lodzher Togblat* (1908), *Lodzher Morgnblat* (1912), *Lodzher Folksblat* (1915), *Nayer Folksblat* (1923), and other periodicals in Yiddish and Hebrew.

Until the Nazis began to disseminate anti-Semitic propaganda among the German minority in Lodz (from the mid-1930s) the anti-Semitic movement in the city followed the customary Polish pattern (see *Endecja, *Rozwój); from April 1933 there were many cases of murderous attacks on Jews. In May 1934 and in September 1935 Jews were wounded or killed in organized attacks. The anti-Semitic parties gained an overwhelming majority in the municipal elections of 1934 after conducting an election campaign on the platform of purging the town of Jews. Their rule was shortlived, for in the elections of 1936 the Polish and Jewish Socialist parties won a majority. Under different pretexts controllers and officials were introduced by the Polish authorities into the factories of Cohen, Ettingon, Poznański, and others. Rich Jews were arrested in 1938 and imprisoned in the camp of *Bereza-Kartuska. Guards were placed outside Jewish shops in order to prevent non-Jewish customers from entering them. In vain, the town's Socialist administration tried to prevent the growth of anti-Semitism and the accompanying agitation.

[SH.L.K.]

Holocaust Period. At the outbreak of World War II, Lodz had 233,000 Jews, about one third of the city's population. As soon as the war broke out many Jewish inhabitants, including the social and cultural elite, the youth, and wealthier circles, left Lodz out of fear of persecution. Their exodus continued up to May 1940. They sought refuge in Warsaw and other towns in the General Government (see *Poland, Holocaust) and many escaped to the territories occupied by the U.S.S.R. The German army entered Lodz on Sept. 8, 1939. In October–November 1939 Lodz was annexed to the Reich as part of Warthegau (Wartheland), and given a German name, Litzmannstadt. The Jewish community council, now understaffed, reinstated its activities a few days after the capitulation (Sept. 12, 1939). The council mainly extended assistance, as it did formerly, to the ever-increasing number of impoverished Jews, to refugees from the vicinity, to the sick, and to victims of Nazi terror. In October 1939 the Germans disbanded the council and appointed its former vice-chairman, Chaim Mordecai *Rumkowsky as *Judenaeltester.* He formed an advisory but short-lived body, "Beirat," of 31 Jewish personalities. On Nov. 11, 1939, the Nazis deported the Beirat members to the nearby Radogoszcz camp (Radegast). After some time another purely formal body was set up, completely subordinate to *Gestapo orders and to the *Judenaeltester.* The brutal liquidation of the first Beirat was an indication of further acts of terror to come that November, when the Nazis burned down the great synagogue and publicly hanged two Poles and a Jew.

In December 1939 the Germans evicted many Jews living along the central streets of the town to settle *Volksdeutsche* in their place. On December 12–14 the authorities deported a few thousand Lodz Jews to the General Government, after which a mass "spontaneous" exodus of Jews occurred as a result of the fear of deportation. In January 1940 the Jews were segregated into the Old City and Bałuty quarter, the area of the future ghetto, officially founded by a police order on Feb. 8, 1940. The ghetto (less than 2 sq. mi.; 4 sq.

km.) generally lacked sewage disposal and its houses were fit for demolishing. To speed up confinement of the Jews into the ghetto, the Nazis organized a pogrom on March 1, 1940, known as "bloody Thursday," during which many Jews were murdered. Thousands of Jews were then driven into the ghetto without being permitted to take their property with them. On April 30, 1940, the ghetto was closed off. Its small area contained the 164,000 Jews still living in Lodz, for between Sept. 1, 1939, and May 1, 1940, 70,000 Jews had left the city. The ghetto was separated from the rest of the city by barbed wire, wooden fences, and a chain of "Schupo" (Schutzpolizei) outposts. The Jewish administrative body and the German ghetto council (Ghettoverwaltung) headed by Hans Biebow communicated with each other at the so-called Bałuty market, where some German and the central Jewish offices were located. The ghetto was crossed by two thoroughfares which did not, however, belong to the ghetto area. These streets divided the ghetto into three parts connected to one another by several gates (for traffic) and three bridges (for pedestrians). The isolation of the ghetto was strengthened by the fact that it was deliberately surrounded by a German population according to the "Germanization policy."

Up to October 1940 the local German authorities counted on the deportation of the ghetto inmates to "reserves" in the Lublin District or to Madagascar (see *Madagascar Plan). But German plans changed and the Lodz ghetto remained. The ghetto inhabitants were subjected to starvation, alleviated in part by the smuggling of foodstuffs (1940–41), but smuggling activities were vigorously combatted by the ghetto branch office of the German Kriminalpolizei. The little food supplied by the authorities was rationed out on even lower standards than those applied in Nazi prisons. Apart from this a large quantity of the foodstuffs arrived in spoiled condition. In 1940 the majority of the ghetto population was left with no means of subsistence. Hunger demonstrations and riots resulted in the early fall. The economic situation of the inmates improved a little after some time, when a ghetto factory network was organized to produce goods, mainly for the Wehrmacht. In August 1942 there were 91 factories with 77,982 employees. Many of the workers earned too little to be able to buy even the inadequate food rations allotted to them, and working conditions were unbearable. Apart from starvation and exhaustion, the population underwent roundups for the forced labor camp at Warthegau. In 1940–44 the Germans sent 15,000 Jews from the ghetto to labor camps, but only very few ever returned, and they arrived back in a state of exhaustion. The branch office of the ghetto Kriminalpolizei carried out extensive robbery of the remaining Jewish possessions. It terrorized the ghetto inmates with house searches, requisition, and torture to uncover any hidden property. The extremely crowded living quarters, combined with bad hygienic conditions, starvation and overwork, caused epidemics of dysentery, typhus, and typhoid fever, but mortality was due mostly to tuberculosis, the death rate for which was 26 times higher than it had been among Lodz Jews in 1936. The overall average death rate per month reached 7.23 per 1,000, whereas in 1938 it had been 0.91 per 1,000, i.e., the rate increased eightfold since prewar time.

In these appalling conditions, Rumkowski tried to organize the life of the Jewish community. He created a wide-spread network of Jewish self-administration, which included departments that provided for the needs of the population as far as possible (the former Jewish social institutions having been liquidated by the Nazis), and other departments that fulfilled German orders, some sections performing both tasks. From 1940 to September 1942, the health department of the ghetto ran five to seven hospitals, five pharmacies, and several special infirmaries. The education department ran 45 primary religious and secular schools, two high schools, and one vocational school. The food supply department organized public kitchens in factories, offices, and schools. Apart from the general food control system (ration cards), an additional ration system

Figure 4. Child workers in a carpet-weaving factory in the Lodz ghetto, from a diary-album for the period July 1941–July 1942 compiled by Yehoshua Klugman, founder and director of the factory, which employed some 3,000 people. Jerusalem, Yad Vashem Archives.

was introduced for various categories of people (for those engaged in hard labor, excrement carriers, police and firemen, physicians, pharmacists, persons in leading positions, the sick, and confined women). The department for social welfare handed out regular small pittances for the unemployed and for those with meager income. There were two old age homes, a home for invalids, and a home for the chronically ill; however, conditions in these homes were extremely bad and the death rate very high. An orphanage and a children's camp were organized for 1,500 children as well as a morning camp for the summer period.

The agricultural department alloted small garden plots to the population. The factories, called Arbeitsressorte, exploited Jewish labor, but on the other hand gave the employees certain wages and additional food rations. The statistics department gathered—for the needs of the ghetto and the Germans—data on all branches of life in the ghetto. The archives department collected valuable documents and kept daily chronicles of ghetto life. (The majority of these documents found their way to the *Jewish Historical Institute in Warsaw.) The rabbinate oversaw the semi-legal religious life of the ghetto up to September 1942. On the other hand a department known as the Arbeitsamt (Arbeitseinsatz) supplied the Germans with Jewish manpower for the forced labor camps, and a special "purchasing department" bought Jewish property at the lowest prices and handed it over to the Ghettoverwaltung. These sales enabled the Jewish authorities to obtain the means for the purchase of foodstuffs for the ghetto (the Germans supplied food only in exchange for real goods, i.e., Jewish labor or Jewish property), and therefore the Jews found such sales were preferable to the outright requisitions made by the Kriminalpolizei. The Jewish police (Ordnungsdienst) administered order in the ghetto, but also took part in deportations and roundups of Jews for forced labor camps. A special police group (Sonderabteilung) under the orders of the Kriminalpolizei confiscated Jewish property. Its commander, David Gertler, and later M. Kligier, took orders from the Gestapo. A court and prison functioned. The latter was the collection point for those sent on forced labor or to extermination camps. Persons who returned from labor camps or who were held by the Gestapo were kept in the ghetto prison.

Several political and social groups (e.g., some Zionist organizations, WIZO, Bund, the communist "Trade Union Left," the organization of ex-combatants and invalids) held secret meetings, taught and provided self-education, organized demonstrations against the *Judenaeltester* Rumkowsky (1940) and strikes in factories, engaged in production sabotage, and listened in to the radio. Certain parties (Bund, Po'alei Zion), with Rumkowsky's approval, ran their own "kitchens" (1940–41) where they fed their members and held cultural gatherings. During the mass deportations these organizations engaged in saving their active members. The He-Ḥalutz ("pioneer") youth groups, in the spring of 1940, organized a *hakhsharah* (Zionist pioneer training program) on the outskirts of the ghetto (Marysin). The *hakhsharah* served different organizations and had 1,040 members, including non-Zionists such as members of the Bund and Agudah. Apart from farm work, the youth held cultural activities and provided self-education. In September 1940 several Zionist groups formed the Ḥazit Dor Benei Midbar, which continued its activities in the ghetto even after the liquidation of the *hakhsharah* in mid-1941.

The German authorities gave orders which imposed the sequence of events to come in Lodz Ghetto. They allowed a period of relative autonomy (May 1940–September 1942) but ended it with a wave of mass deportations to the extermination camp at *Chelmno on the Ner. During January–April 1942 the Germans deported over 44,000 Jews. In May 1942, 11,000 Jews originally from Prague, Vienna, Luxembourg, and various cities from the "Old Reich" were rounded up and deported for extermination. These Jews (20,000), mostly elderly and sick, had been taken in the fall of 1941 to Lodz Ghetto, where they lingered on in terrible conditions, were crowded into unheated, mass quarters, and endured more severe hunger than the local population. By 1942, 5,000 among them died of typhus and starvation. After their deportation, the notorious *"Gehsperre" Aktion* was carried out to exterminate 16,000 Lodz Jews, including children up to ten years old, persons above 60, and the sick and emaciated. With this mass murder action, the population decreased from 162,681 in January 1942 to 89,446 on October 1, 1942, i.e., by nearly half. This decrease was in fact greater because 15,500 refugees from the liquidated provisional ghettos had been brought to Lodz Ghetto in spring/summer 1942.

After the mass liquidation campaign the Germans transformed the ghetto de facto into a labor camp. There followed the reduction and liquidation of the Jewish administrative bodies which had served the needs of the population, e.g., health, food supply, welfare, education and records departments, and the rabbinate. The orphanages, old-age homes, the majority of the hospitals, schools, and children's homes no longer existed. The number of factories increased to 119 (August 1943) and employed 90% of the population. Children from the age of eight worked in these factories. The Germans held control over all internal matters in the ghetto, such as food supply (additional rations), and they limited Rumkowsky's power to allow Kligier, chief of the Sonderabteilung, and Jakubowicz, chief of the Arbeitsressorte (factories), more sway.

Under these conditions the ghetto lingered on until its

Figure 5. Jewelry made in the Lodz ghetto. The articles in the top row depict ghetto structures. Courtesy S. Adler-Rudel, Jerusalem.

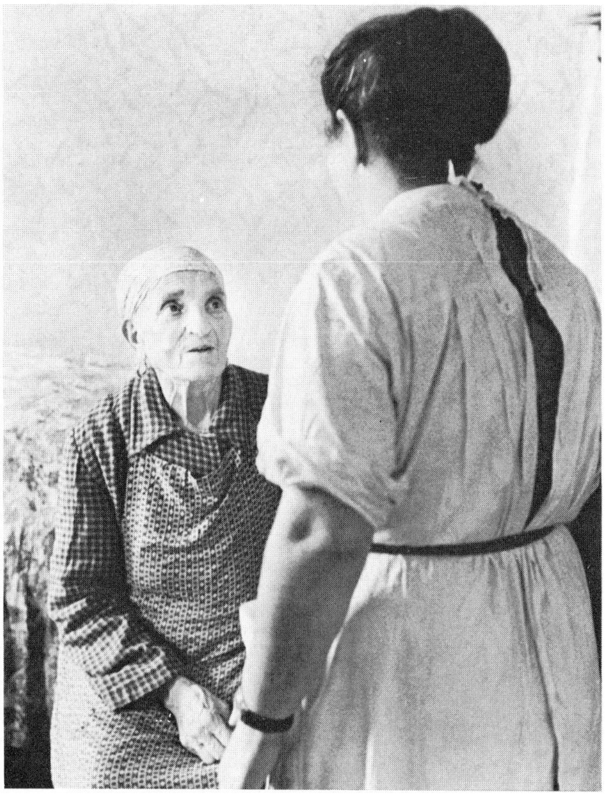

Figure 6. Resident of an old-age home in Lodz, 1960. Courtesy Joint Distribution Committee, New York.

final liquidation in June–August 1944. By Sept. 1, 1944, the whole population, 76,701 (June 1, 1944 registration), was deported to *Auschwitz. By January 1945, only an Aufraeumungskommando (800 Jews) remained in the ghetto joined by some Jews who were hiding in the area of the former ghetto. They were liberated when the Soviet army arrived on Jan. 19, 1945. [De.D]

Contemporary Period. When the Soviet army entered Lodz only 870 Jewish survivors were left in the city. Nevertheless, within the next two years Lodz became the largest reconstructed Jewish community in Poland. Over 50,000 Jews settled there by the end of 1946, of whom the overwhelming majority had survived the Holocaust period in the Soviet Union. A number of Jewish institutions began to function, including the Central Jewish Historical Commission, a Jewish theater, editorial staffs of a number of Jewish (Yiddish, Hebrew, and Polish-language) papers. Zionist organizations conducted intensive activity, with the support of the majority of Jews. A number of "kibbutzim" (homes for Jewish youth who prepared themselves for *aliyah*) were established. All these activities were stopped in 1950, when the Sovietization of Poland was completed. Over a half of the city's Jewish population left Poland during 1946–50. After the second wave of *aliyah* to Israel during 1956–57, only a few thousand Jews remained. A club of the government-sponsored Jewish Cultural Society and a Jewish public school continued to function until 1968–69, when almost all remaining Jews left Poland. [S.Kr.]

Bibliography: A. Z. Aescoly, *Kehillat Lodzh: Toledot Ir va-Em be-Yisrael* (1948); A. Alpern, *Żydzi w Łodzi: początki gminy żydowskiej, 1780–1822* (1928); idem, in: *"Haynt" Yubiley-Bukh* (1928), 106ff.; idem, in: *Rocznik Łódzki*, 1 (1928); F. (P.) Friedman, *ibid.*, 2 (1930), 319–65; idem, *Dzieje Żydów w Łodzi od początków osadnictwa Żydów do r. 1863* (1935), incl. bibl.; B. Weinryb, in: *YIVO Ekonomishe Shriftn*, 2 (1932), 34–55; idem, *Neueste Wirtschaftsgeschichte der Juden in Russland und Polen*, 1 (1938); A. W. Yasny, *Geshikhte fun der Yidisher Arbeter-Bavegung in Lodzh* (1937); M. Zer-Kavod, in: *Sinai*, 28 (1950/51), 241–78; A. Tenenbaum-Arazi, *Lodzh un Ire Yidn* (1956). Holocaust Period: A. W. Yasny, *Geshikhte fun Yidn in Lodzh in di Yorn fun der Daytsher Yidn-Oyszrotung*, 2 vols. (1960–66); *Lodzher Yizker-Bukh* (1943); J. I. Trunk, *Lodzher Geto* (1962); Y. L. Gersht, *Min ha-Meẓar: Zikhronot ... be-Getto Lodzh ...* (1949); S. Zelver-Urbach, *Mi-Ba'ad le-Ḥalon Beiti: Zikhronot mi-Getto Lodzh* (1964); D. Dąbrowska (ed.), *Kronika getta Łodzkiego ...*, 2 vols. (1965–66); *The Last Journey of the Jews of Lodz* (photo album, 1967).

LOEB, ISIDORE (1839–1892), French rabbi and scholar. Loeb, who was the son of a rabbi in Soultzmatt, Alsace, studied at the Ecole Rabbinique of Metz (which was later transferred to Paris). After tutoring in Bayonne and Paris, he became rabbi at Saint-Etienne (1865). In 1869 Loeb was appointed secretary of the *Alliance Israélite Universelle in Paris, a post he held until his death. As a result of his initiative, the Alliance increased its network of schools in Mediterranean countries and the Balkans and intervened in international conferences on behalf of oppressed Jewish minorities (cf. his *La situation des Israélites en Turquie, en Serbie et en Roumanie* (1877), and *Les Juifs de Russie* (1891)). The Alliance bulletins became, under his editorship, a main source of information to all those who were engaged in the fight for Jewish emancipation. Loeb founded and developed the library of the Alliance. From 1878 he taught Jewish history at the École Rabbinique. Loeb's scholarly work covered biblical and talmudic literature, medieval historiography, and the history of the Jews in France and Spain. His articles appeared in various journals including the short-lived *Revue Israélite*, which he edited from 1870 to 1872. He was also publication manager of the *Revue des Études Juives*, to which he contributed some 50 articles, and wrote for the *Grande Encyclopédie* (articles on Judaism from A to C). He prepared a French edition of the *maḥzor* (1869), and wrote mathematical works including *Tables du Calendrier* (1886). He also wrote *La Littérature des Pauvres dans la Bible* (REJ, 20 (1890); 21 (1890); 23 (1891); 24 (1892), which also appeared separately in 1892), Loeb contended that certain biblical books contain several passages (on whose dating scholars disagree), expressing the idealization of poverty and suffering. This Renan-inspired view has been discussed. A collection of his sermons was published in 1865.

Bibliography: REJ, 24 (1892), 1–4; Z. Kahn, *ibid.* 161–83; J. Levi, *ibid.*, 184–224; M. Liber, *ibid.*, 105 (1940), 16–22; A. Neubauer, in: JQR, 5 (1892/93), 1–4. [G.We.]

Isidore Loeb, French rabbi and scholar. Jerusalem, J.N.U.L., Schwadron Collection.

LOEB, JACQUES (1859–1924), U.S. physiological chemist. Born near Strasbourg, Alsace, into a family of Portuguese and Italian origin, Loeb studied medicine. He emigrated to the U.S. and became professor of physiology at the University of California (1902–10), and then head of the division of general physiology at the Rockefeller Institute for Medical Research in New York (1910–24). He founded and edited the *Journal of General Physiology* from 1918. A brilliant experimentalist, he was a pioneer in explaining vital processes on a basis of physical chemistry. Some of his special fields of work were the physiology of the

Jacques Loeb, U.S. physiological chemist. Jerusalem, J.N.U.L., Schwadron Collection.

brain, tropism, antagonistic salt action, the duration of life, and colloidal behavior. He wrote *The Organism as a Whole* (1916), *Regeneration from a Physico-chemical Viewpoint* (1924), and *Proteins and the Theory of Colloidal Behaviour* (1924²).

Bibliography: Osterhout, in: *Journal of General Physiology*, 8 (1925–28), ix–lix; Armstrong, in: *Journal of General Physiology*, 8 (1928), 653–70; Kobelt, in: *Journal of General Physiology*, 8 (1928), lxiii–xcii, bibl. [S.A.M.]

LOEB, JAMES (1867–1933), U.S. banker, philanthropist, and translator. Loeb, who was born in New York, joined his father's well-known banking firm of Kuhn, Loeb & Co. in 1888. He left the firm in 1901 and in 1912 established his residence in Murnau, Germany. The institutions which Loeb founded and endowed include: the Institute of Musical Art in New York, later a part of the Juilliard Musical Foundation; the Deutsche Forschungsamstalt fuer Psychiatrie in Munich, for research into the various causes of mental disorders; and the famed Loeb Classical Library (1912), consisting of classic Greek and Latin works in the original, faced by English translations. Among the works which Loeb translated into English were: Maurice Croiset's *Aristophanes et les partis a Athènes;* Phillippe Ernest Legrand's *Daos;* and Auguste Couat's study of Alexandrian poetry. He was also a competent cellist.

Bibliography: *Festschrift fuer James Loeb . . .* (1930). [Ed.]

LOEB, LEO (1869–1959), pathologist and pioneer in cancer research. Loeb, who was born in Mayen, Germany, emigrated to the United States in 1900 and held a variety of academic and research posts until 1910, when he settled in St. Louis, Missouri. From 1915 to 1937 he was professor of pathology at St. Louis' Washington University. Loeb made significant contributions to cancer research. In a series of experiments on rats and mice, he and his co-workers found that the growth energy of cancer cells may be experimentally decreased and increased. They also showed that hormones may induce cancer in a mouse's mammary gland, vagina, and cervix. They studied growth and retardation factors influencing the thyroid gland. Loeb's papers included studies of blood coagulation and thrombosis, pathology of the circulatory organs, kidneys and stomach, experimental cell fibrin tissue, old age, and the analysis of cell death. Leo Loeb was the brother of the physiologist and biologist Jacques *Loeb.

Bibliography: S. R. Kagan, *Jewish Medicine* (1952), 229f. [S.M.]

LOEB, MORRIS (1863–1912), U.S. physical chemist and philanthropist; brother of James *Loeb. Loeb was born in Cincinnati, Ohio. In 1891 he became professor of chemistry at New York University, and was also attached to Clark University. In 1910 he resigned his chair to devote himself to research and his public activities. His main fields of research were on osmotic pressure, electrolysis, and the molecular weight of iodine. He was chairman of the New York section of the American Chemical Society and president of the Chemists' Club of New York City. His public and philanthropic work was carried out against the background of the intensive immigration of Jews into the United States at the time. He was director of the Jewish Agricultural and Industrial Aid Society and he created a Jewish Agricultural Experimental Station in New Jersey. He was president of the Hebrew Technical Institute, trustee of the Jewish Theological Seminary of America, and founder of the American Jewish Committee and of the Educational Alliance.

Bibliography: T. W. Richards (ed.), *The Scientific Work of Morris Loeb* (1913); *Morris Loeb Memorial Volume* (1913); L. H. Baekeland, in: *Industrial and Engineering Chemistry*, 4 (1912), 784–5; C. L. Sulzberger, in: AJHSP, 22 (1914), 225–7. [S.A.M.]

LOEBEL, ISRAEL (late 18th century), preacher and *dayyan*, opponent of Ḥasidism. He was probably born in Slutsk, or at least lived there in his childhood, was preacher in Mogilev, and in 1787 was appointed permanent preacher and *dayyan* in Novogrudok. While he was still in Mogilev, his opposition to the Ḥasidim grew as a result of his brother's joining their ranks. When *Elijah b. Solomon, the Vilna Gaon, issued a proclamation against the Ḥasidim in 1797, Loebel obtained from R. Saadiah, an emissary and disciple of the Gaon, a letter of recommendation authorizing him to preach against the sect wherever possible, and approval for the publication of his books. He was likewise granted the approval of the **parnasim* of the Slutsk community, and at the gathering of the leaders of the Lithuanian communities at Zelva he was evidently authorized to travel throughout Poland and beyond, in order to disseminate anti-ḥasidic propaganda. His two booklets against Ḥasidism, *Sefer Vikku'aḥ* and *Kivrot ha-Ta'avah*, were printed in Warsaw in 1798; the latter is no longer extant. In his preachings in the communities of east Galicia, Loebel conducted anti-ḥasidic propaganda. According to his own testimony, Loebel was granted an audience with Emperor Francis II at Vienna in early 1799, as a result of which public meetings of Ḥasidim were prohibited in all the provinces of Poland which had then come under Austrian rule. There is, however, no historical evidence for this.

Sefer Vikku'aḥ describes a disputation between a Ḥasid and a *Mitnagged.* The author compared the Ḥasidim with heretical sects that had arisen within Judaism throughout its history. He denied the ḥasidic principle that considers prayer more important than Torah study and the ḥasidic emphasis on joy as a basic element in prayer; and objected to such ḥasidic customs as the acceptance of the Sephardi prayer rite and not observing the fixed times of prayer. He likewise attacked the ḥasidic leaders, claiming that they were ignoramuses whose every command was obeyed, who exploited the masses and enjoyed a rich life at their expense, and who deluded them with the belief that the *ẓaddik* atoned for their sins. *Sefer Vikku'aḥ* and its author became the target of attacks by the Ḥasidim, who prepared to reply with a pamphlet entitled *Mul Maggid Peti* ("Against the Foolish Preacher"), though it is not clear if this was in fact printed. They bought up practically the whole edition of *Sefer Vikku'aḥ* and tried to destroy it "by tearing up the book and trampling on it as on mud in the streets." In the

1820s the Hebrew writer Joseph *Perl made an unsuccessful attempt to reprint the book.

Loebel also wrote a booklet in German, *Glaubwuerdige Nachricht von einer neuen und zahlreichen Sekte unter den Juden, die sich Chassidim nennt* . . . (Frankfort on the Oder, 1799). Though the original is not extant, it has been preserved in a reprint in the journal *Sulamith*, 2 (Dessau, 1807), 308–33. His homiletic works are: *Ozer Yisrael* (Shklov, 1786), printed anonymously; *Takkanat ha-Mo'adim* (before 1787); *Iggera de-Hespeda* (possibly unpublished; the last two works are not extant); *Middot Ḥasidut;* and *Ta'avat Ẓaddikim* (both Warsaw, 1798); the latter, which is ambiguous in the original, includes a chapter against Ḥasidism. His *Even Boḥan* (Frankfort on the Oder, 1799) is a polemic against the *maskilim*.

Bibliography: M. Wilensky, *Ḥasidim u-Mitnaggedim* (1970); Dubnow, Ḥasidut, 278–86 and index; G. Scholem, in: *Zion*, 20 (1955), 153–62; I. Bacon, *ibid.*, 32 (1967), 116–22; H. Liberman, in: KS, 26 (1950), 106, 216; M. Mahler, *Ha-Ḥasidut ve-ha-Haskalah* (1961), index. [E.Z.]

LOEBL, EUGEN (1907–), Czechoslovak economist and politician. Loebl was born in Holič, Slovakia, into a wealthy Jewish family. In 1934 he became a member of the Communist Party. In March 1939, when the Germans invaded Czechoslovakia, Loebl fled to England, where he served as economic consultant to Jan Masaryk, the foreign minister of the Czechoslovak government-in-exile. After World War II, he became a departmental head in the Ministry of Foreign Trade and a leading member of the Communist Party's economic council. In 1947 he headed the Czechoslovak mission to Moscow which negotiated the first postwar political and economic agreement with the U.S.S.R. and in the following year, after the Communist seizure of power, became first deputy in the ministry of foreign trade. Loebl supported Czechoslovakia's acceptance of the American Marshall Aid Plan and also initiated the Czechoslovak-Israel transfer agreement. In November 1949 Loebl was arrested and put on trial together with Rudolf *Slansky. Under duress he confessed his guilt and in 1952 he was sentenced to life imprisonment. In 1963 he was rehabilitated and appointed director of the state bank in Bratislava. From 1965 onward, he campaigned for the implementation of economic reforms and the democratization of the Czechoslovak Communist regime. Following the Soviet invasion of Czechoslovakia in 1968, Loebl emigrated to the United States where he worked as an economist. His writings include *Geistige Arbeit—die wahre Quelle des Reichtums* (1966), *Hinter den Kulissen des Slansky Prozesses* (1968), an account of the Slansky trial, and *Stalinism in Prague* (1969). [E. Ku.]

LOEB-LEOPOLD CASE, U.S. murder case in 1924 which involved one of the most sensational crimes of the century. Richard Loeb (1905–1936), 18, a graduate of the University of Michigan and Nathan Freudenthal Leopold (1904–1971), 19, a graduate of the University of Chicago, the well-educated scions of wealthy Chicago Jewish families, attempted, as they said at their trial, to perpetrate the perfect crime, when they kidnapped and killed a 14-year-old neighbor, Bobby Franks. After a thorough investigation and a highly publicized trial, in which the famous attorney Clarence Darrow represented the young men, they were sentenced to life imprisonment plus 99 years, the court recommending that they never be released. In jail the young men developed a correspondence school in which many subjects were taught to the inmates of 19 penitentiaries. In 1936 Loeb was murdered by an inmate. Leopold worked ceaselessly at his prison activities. Possessing a remarkably high I.Q., he was a participant in the famous wartime malaria experiments and mastered 27 languages. His book, *Life Plus 99 Years* (1958), tells the story of his imprisonment. For a period of years there were unsuccessful efforts to release him. In 1957 Attorney Elmer Gertz took over the case and the parole board finally paroled Leopold in 1958 to Puerto Rico, where he worked at the Castaner General Hospital. Leopold earned a master's degree, taught at the University of Puerto Rico, and published a book on birds. The case was described by Meyer *Levin's novel *Compulsion* (1956; which Leopold characterized as unwarranted invasion of his privacy).

Bibliography: M. McKernan, *Crime and Trial of Leopold and Loeb* (1925); C. S. Darrow, *Plea . . . in Defence of Richard Loeb and Nathan Leopold* (1924). [El.G.]

LOEW, ELEAZAR (1758–1837), rabbi in Poland and Hungary. Loew was born in Wodzislav (Poland) and when only 17 years of age was appointed *dayyan* in his native city. At the age of 20 he was appointed rabbi of Pilica (Poland) and in 1800, on the recommendation of Mordecai *Banet, became rabbi of *Trest (Triesch). Subsequently he held positions as district rabbi of *Pilsen (1812–15), *rosh yeshivah* of Trest (1815–20), rabbi of Liptovsky Mikuláš, Slovakia (1821–30) and finally, from 1830 until his death rabbi of Santo (Abaujszanto), Hungary. Loew played a vigorous part in the fight against religious reform, and was an active opponent of Aaron *Chorin. Loew is best known mainly for his many scholarly works in all areas of *halakhah*, which are written with a rational approach, avoiding casuistry, and for his critical commentaries to early works.

Eleazar Loew, rabbinical authority in Poland and Hungary. Courtesy M. Lamed, Ne'ot Mordekhai.

Among his halakhic works are *Shemen Roke'aḥ*, 3 volumes of responsa (1788–1902), and under the same title novellae to the tractates *Berakhot, Pesaḥim, Beẓah* (Prague, 1812); *Torat Ḥesed*, on talmudic methodology (Vienna, 1800); *Sha'arei Ḥokhmah*, on various halakhic topics (Prague, 1807); *Zer Zahav*, annotations to *Hai Gaon's *Ha-Mikkaḥ ve-ha-Mimkar* (Vienna, 1800); *Sha'arei De'ah*, on the Shulḥan Arukh, *Yoreh De'ah*, pts. 1 and 2 (1821–28); and *Zikhron Aharon*, on *ḥazakah* ("legal presumption"; 1834). His homiletic works include *Sama de-Ḥayyei* (Warsaw, 1796), *Yavin Shemu'ah* (Prague 1814), and *Minḥat Erev* (1911).

Bibliography: Michael, Or, no. 484; L. Muenz, *Rabbi Eleasar, genannt Schemen Rokeach* (1895); A. Schnitzer, *Juedische Kulturbilder* (1904), 45f.; J. J. Greenwald, *Ha-Yehudim be-Ungarya* (1913), 45; I. Muenz, *Stammtafel des Rabbi Eleasar, genannt Schemen Rokeach* (1926); H. Gold (ed.), *Die Juden und Judengemeinden Maehrens in Vergangenheit und Gegenwart* (1929), 542f.; A. Klein, in: *Nachlath Z'vi*, 7 (1937), 139–47; M. M. Glueck (ed.), Eleazar Loew, *Zikhron Elazar* (1937), introd. 7–18; W. G. Plaut, *The Rise of Reform Judaism* (1963), 35f. [EH]

LOEW, IMMANUEL (1854–1944), Hungarian rabbi and scholar. Loew was the son of Leopold *Loew whom he succeeded in 1878 as rabbi of Szeged, Hungary, and whose collected works he published (5 vols., 1889–1900). He studied at the Hochschule fuer die Wissenschaft des Judentums in Berlin and at the Leipzig university. The new synagogue in Szeged, one of the most beautiful in the world,

Immanuel Loew, Hungarian rabbi and scholar. Jerusalem, J.N.U.L., Schwadron Collection.

was built in 1903 according to Loew's plans (the architect was L. Baumhorn) and its stained-glass windows were made according to his designs. During the "white terror" and counterrevolution in Hungary (1920–21), Loew was imprisoned for 13 months on the allegation that he had made statements against Admiral Horthy. During his imprisonment he worked on his four-volume work, *Die Flora der Juden* (1924–34). From 1927 he represented the Neolog (non-Orthodox) communities in the upper chamber of the Hungarian parliament and also was a member of the Jewish Agency for Palestine. Soon after his 90th birthday, the Germans occupied Hungary and Loew was first sent to a brick factory in the local ghetto and then put on a deportation train. In Budapest, however, he was freed by Zionist workers. He died that year in Budapest.

Like his father, Loew was a great preacher in the Hungarian language, and several hundred of his sermons were published in four volumes between 1900 and 1939. On the occasion of his congregation's centenary he published (with Z. Kulinyi) the congregation's history (1885) and that of its *ḥevra kaddisha* (with S. Klein, 1887). In 1883 he published a prayer book (in Hungarian) for women, and rendered the Song of Songs and some psalms into the same language.

Loew's fame as a scholar rests above all on his pioneering work in the field of talmudic and rabbinic lexicography and in the study of *realia* (artifacts, such as a coin from talmudic times). He contributed to W. Gesenius' famous Bible dictionary (10th ed., 1886; 11th ed., 1890), and to K. Brockelmann's *Lexicon syriacum* (1895). Loew made critical annotations to S. Krauss's *Griechische und lateinische Lehnwoerter im Talmud, Midrash und Targum* (1899), and to the same author's supplement volume to Kohut's *Arukh ha-Shalem* (1937) and to his *Talmudische Archaeologie* (1910–12) which was dedicated to Loew and thus saved the author many etymological errors. There are also notes of his in J. Theodor-Ḥ. Albeck's edition of *Genesis Rabbah*, 3 pt. 2 (1965), 127–48ff. He also wrote on Jewish folklore. The special direction of Loew's scholarly interest in *realia* is already evident in his doctorate thesis *Aramaeische Pflanzennamen* (1879), and in his *Meleagros aus Gadara und die Flora Aramaea* (1883). Half a century later this line of research found its triumphant achievement in *Die Flora der Juden* (4 vols., 1924–34). Loew systematically uncovered the basis of flora terminology in the Hebrew and Aramaic of different periods and mastered the latest descriptive and terminological methods prevailing in this field of science. He familiarized himself with the literary sources for flora and made meticulous use of manuscript material. He clarified etymologies with the help of Semitic languages, especially Syriac. The result is a flood of light shed on biblical, talmudical, and rabbinical botanical terms; not only the past flora but also that of present-day Israel is brought to life. It was only natural that Loew should proceed to the realm of fauna and of minerals, and in both these fields he published a number of studies in various periodicals and other learned publications. The manuscript of a *Mineralien der Juden*, ready for publication, became a victim of the tragic events of 1944. Loew's other literary remains in these fields passed partly to the National and University Library of Jerusalem and partly to the **Landesrabbinerschule*, Budapest. His essays on fauna and minerals were reissued in 1969 (*Fauna und Mineralien der Juden*) together with an introduction by Alexander Scheiber.

Bibliography: E. Frenkel, in: *Festschrift I. Loew* (1934), 236–55 (a bibl.); idem, in: A. Scheiber (ed.), *Semitic Studies in Memory of I. Loew* (1947), 6–11 (bibl.); A. Scheiber, *ibid.*, 1–6 (Hung.), 357 (bibl.).

[AL.SCH./M.Z.KA.]

LOEW, LEOPOLD (**Lipót**; 1811–1875), Hungarian rabbi and scholar, the first Reform rabbi in Hungary. Loew, who was born in Czernahora, Moravia, was a descendant of *Judah Loew b. Bezalel. In his childhood Loew showed talent in music; he studied in Moravian yeshivot, translated Schiller into Hebrew, and also acquired a knowledge of Italian, French, Latin, and Greek. He was ordained as a rabbi by Solomon Judah *Rapoport, Aaron *Chorin, and Low *Schwab, later marrying Schwab's daughter. In 1840 Loew was elected rabbi of Nagykanizsa.

In 1844 he began to deliver his sermons in Hungarian. A strong advocate of Hungarian Jewish emancipation, he argued that the liberation of the Jews should not be made dependent upon abandonment or reform of their religion; in this he opposed the views of the great Hungarian liberator, Louis Kossuth. In 1846 Loew began serving as rabbi of Papa, where he was severely attacked by the Orthodox, who disapproved of his having studied at the Protestant High School and even produced false witnesses that Loew was not ritually observant. During the Hungarian revolution of 1848–49 he served as a chaplain in the army of the Hungarian revolutionaries, spurring them on with inflammatory speeches. Because of his patriotic stand he was arrested in 1849 and served three months in jail.

From 1850 until his death Loew served as the rabbi of Szeged. Loew was in favor of Reform but insisted that reforms be instituted within the framework of the rabbinic tradition. His viewpoint made it possible for him to participate in the *rabbinical conferences in Breslau in 1845 and Leipzig in 1870. He also wrote a biography of Aaron Chorin, who had approached the cause of Reform in the same spirit. Though he did not participate in the Hungarian

Leopold Loew, the first Hungarian Reform rabbi. Jerusalem, J.N.U.L., Schwadron Collection.

Jewish congress of 1868, which had been called to draw up the constitution of Hungarian Jewry and at which Hungarian Jewry was divided into two camps—Reform and Orthodox—he expressed his views on the issues in his *Die*

Juedischen Wirren in Ungarn (1868). The medieval form of the Jewish oath was abolished in Hungary on the basis of a lecture he delivered at the Hungarian Academy of Sciences, *A zsidó eskü* (1868). He was first to suggest a Hungarian translation of the Bible for Jews, and published the Book of Joel in the translation of I. Bleuer (in *Magyar Zsinagoga*, 1, 1847). Loew served as the editor of the periodical *Ben-Chananja* from 1858 to 1867. He was the first to deal with the history of Hungarian Jewry; among his works are "*Schicksale und Bestrebungen der Juden in Ungarn*" and "*Kalender und Jahrbuch fuer Israeliten*" both in *Jahrbuch des deutschen Elementes in Ungarn* (1846/7) and *Zur neueren Geschichte der Juden in Ungarn* (1874). He contributed such pioneering works in the study of Jewish antiquities and folklore as *Ha-Mafte'aḥ* (1855), *Beitraege zur juedischen Alterthumskunde*, 1: *Graphische Requisiten und Erzeugnisse bei den Juden* (2 vols., 1870–71), and *Lebensalter in der juedischen Literatur* (1875). His collected writings were edited by his son and successor, Immanuel *Loew, under the title *Gesammelte Schriften* (5 vols. 1889–1900).

Bibliography: A. Hochmuth, *Leopold Loew als Theologe, Historiker und Publizist* (1871); W. N. Loew, *Leopold Loew: A Biography with a Translation of the ... Tributes Paid to His Memory* ... (1912); I. Loew and Zs. Kulinyi, *A szegedi zsidók* (1885), 172–240; I. Loew, *Gesammelte Schriften*, 5 (1900), 3–19 (bibl.); W. Bacher, in: *Magyar Izrael*, 4 (1911), 90–97; L. Venetianer, in: *Zsidó Plutarchos*, 1 (n.d.), 5–26.

[Al.Sch.]

LOEW, MORITZ (1841–1900), German astronomer. Born in Mako, Hungary, Loew joined the University Observatory at Leipzig. He was appointed head of the department in the Prussian Geodetic Institute of Berlin, and later professor. He wrote on the elements of planets and comets; studies on the theory of the transit instrument in the first vertical; and on astronomical-geodetical determinations of geographic positions. [A.Be.]

LOEW-BEER, family of textile manufacturers in *Brno (Bruenn), Czechoslovakia. Three cousins, who originated from *Boskovice, began their career in the *textile industry as wool buyers for the Brno textile factories. In the 1840s various members of the family opened independent spinning-mills. One firm, founded by Aaron and Jacob (d. 1866) in 1853, employed 1,200 workers. Another firm was set up by Moses and later directed by Max Loew-Beer (1829–1887), who also established sugar refineries. The firm founded by Samuel (d. 1884) was later directed by Ignaz Loew-Beer. Other members of the family founded textile firms at the end of the 19th century. The whole family was active in Jewish and public life. A soup kitchen founded by Jonas Loew-Beer for World War I refugees was taken over by the community in 1924. The various firms remained in existence until the German occupation in 1939.

Bibliography: H. Heller, *Maehrens Maenner der Gegenwart*, 4 (1890), 102–3; *Jews of Czechoslovakia*, 1 (1968), 413. [M.La.]

LOEWE, FRITZ PHILIPP (1895–), meteorologist. Loewe, who was born in Berlin, went in 1923 to work in the Light, Climate, and Radiation Observatory at Davos, Switzerland, with Carl Dorno. The following year he worked at the Oceanography Institute in Berlin. From 1925 to 1929 he was a member of the party of scientists at Tempelhof Airport investigating problems of meteorological flight research and carried out hundreds of experimental flights to heights of 20,000 ft. In 1929 Loewe was a member of the preparatory expedition of Alfred Wegener to Greenland and was one of the first researchers to measure the thickness of the ice by means of artificial seismic waves caused by explosions in the ice. From 1930 to 1932 he was a member of the temporary directorate of the expedition wintering in Eismitte in the center of Greenland on the 2–3 km.-thick ice cap which was thought up to that time to be the coldest spot on earth. Loewe's legs suffered severely from frostbite there. However, he recuperated and returned to the meteorological office at Tempelhof, until 1933. With the rise to power of the Nazis, he was dismissed from his position and went to England. From 1934 to 1936 he was a research member of the Robert Scott Institute for Polar Research at Cambridge. In 1937 Loewe went to Australia, and was lecturer in meteorology at the University of Melbourne until the early 1960s. From 1948 on he participated in several expeditions to Antarctica and in 1962 and 1964 he took part in new expeditions to Greenland. [D.Ash.]

LOEWE, HEINRICH (Eliakim; 1867–1950), one of the first Zionists in Germany, scholar in Jewish folklore, and librarian. Born in Wanzleben, Germany, into an assimilated family, Loewe was raised without a Jewish education

Heinrich Loewe, early German Zionist and authority on Jewish folklore. Courtesy Central Zionist Archives, Jerusalem.

and at the age of 13 began to study in a Protestant high school in Magdeburg. Afterward he studied at Berlin University and at the Hochschule fuer die Wissenschaft des Judentums in Berlin. Together with Shmarya *Levin, Yosef *Lurie, Naḥman *Syrkin, and Leo *Motzkin he established the Zionist group known as the Russian Jewish Scientific Society and was the only one among this group who was born in Germany. In 1892 Loewe founded Jung Israel, the first Zionist group in Germany. He was also among the founders of the Vereinigung Juedischer Studierender, which gave rise in 1914 to the *Kartell Juedischer Verbindungen, the roof organization for Zionist students in Germany. Loewe edited the *Juedische Volkszeitung* in Berlin from 1893 to 1894 and, from 1895 to 1896, the monthly *Zion*.

In 1895 Loewe visited Ereẓ Israel for the first time and became known to *Herzl even before the publication of *Der Judenstaat*. Two years later he returned to Ereẓ Israel with the intention of settling there, but he returned to Europe in August 1897 as a delegate from Ereẓ Israel to the First Zionist Congress. After the Congress he remained in Germany and established the Zionist Federation there. From 1899 Loewe worked as a librarian in the University of Berlin. He quickly rose in professional status until he was appointed professor in 1915. From 1902 to 1908 he was the first editor of **Juedische Rundschau*, the central organ of the German Zionists. In 1905 he gave impetus to Joseph *Chasanowich's idea to establish a Jewish national library in Jerusalem by writing a memo to the Seventh Zionist Congress. His proposal was accepted unanimously.

Throughout his career he worked for the library and was the moving spirit of the Verein der Freunde der Jerusalem-Bibliothek.

In 1933 Loewe settled in Palestine and assumed the post of librarian of the municipal library Sha'ar Zion in Tel Aviv. In 1948 he prepared a collection of his writings on Zionism formerly published in part under the pseudonym Heinrich Sachse as *Antisemitismus und Zionismus* (1894) and *Zionistenkongress und Zionismus eine Gefahr?* (1897). He frequently published works in the field of Jewish folklore such as *Die Sprachen der Juden* (1911), *Die Juden in der katholischen Legende* (1912), *Schelme und Narren mit juedischen Kappen* (1920), and *Reste vom alten juedischen Volkshumor* (1922).

Bibliography: J. L. Weinberg, *Aus der Fruehzeit des Zionismus: Heinrich Loewe* (1946). [Y.Ro.]

LOEWE, HERBERT MARTIN JAMES (1882–1940), English orientalist. Loewe was born in London, the grandson of Louis *Loewe. After completing his studies at Cambridge, he lived for a time as teacher in the Middle East and then held academic appointments in England. After his return from military service in India (1917–1919), he became lecturer in rabbinic Hebrew at Oxford, and in 1931 he taught rabbinics at Cambridge and was lecturer in Hebrew at the University of London. For a generation, he was regarded in English academic circles as the representative of Jewish scholarship, in the same way as Israel *Abrahams had been regarded before him. His home in the two university cities was a focus of Jewish life. Within the Jewish community he represented informed and tolerant Orthodoxy, moving freely in liberal (Reform) Jewish circles and collaborating closely with C. G. Montefiore, the founder of Liberal Judaism in England. His works include: *A Catalogue of the Aldis Wright MSS. in Trinity College, Cambridge* (1926), *"Render unto Caesar"* (1940), *Mediaeval Hebrew Minstrelsy* (1926), *Some Mediaeval Hebrew Poesy* (1927; on the **Zemirot*) and a volume of annotations to Abrahams' and Stokes' *Starrs and Jewish Charters in the British Museum*, 2 vols. (1930–32). He collaborated with C. G. Montefiore in *A Rabbinic Anthology* (1938, 1968^2), a widely used source book.

Herbert Loewe's elder son Raphael James Loewe (b. 1919), after fighting in World War II and being awarded the Military Cross, pursued interests similar to his father's and taught in Leeds and Cambridge before becoming lecturer in Hebrew at University College, London. He wrote widely on Jewish subjects, in particular on the English Christian Hebraists of the Middle Ages.

Bibliography: *The Times* (London, Oct. 12, 1940), 6; JC (Oct. 18, 1940), 5. [C.R.]

LOEWE, JOEL (Bril; 1762–1802), Hebrew writer, grammarian, and biblical exegete in the Moses *Mendelssohn circle in Berlin. Born in Berlin, Loewe studied under Isaac *Satanow and soon joined Mendelssohn's enlightenment movement. Together with Aharon *Wolfsohn, he edited **Ha-Me'assef* (1784–97), and was a frequent contributor to it. He signed his Hebrew works בריל״ (Ben R. Yehudah Leib Loewe). Mendelssohn helped him obtain a position as tutor in David *Friedlaender's household. In 1791, he was appointed principal of the Wilhelms-Schule in Breslau, serving in this capacity until his death.

Loewe's major contribution is his introduction and commentary to Mendelssohn's German translation of Psalms (1785–88), which includes a study on the structure and style of Hebrew poetry and on the history of ancient Jewish music. He wrote *Ammudei Lashon*, an attempt at a scientific grammar of biblical Hebrew of which only the first part was published (Berlin, 1794). He took an active part in Mendelssohn's Bible translation project, writing, in addition to his work on Psalms, commentaries to Ecclesiastes, Jonah, and with Wolfsohn, the Song of Songs. Loewe was the first Haskalah writer to publish original epigrams in the style of the Book of Proverbs, and was the first to translate the Passover *Haggadah* to German.

Bibliography: P. Sandler, *Ha-Be'ur la-Torah shel Moshe Mendelssohn ve-Si'ato, Hithavvuto ve-Hashpa'ato* (1940), index; Fuenn, Keneset, 433f.; Lachower, Sifrut, 1 (1963^{12}), 79f., 146; Zeitlin, Bibliotheca, 215; Waxman, Literature, 3 (1960^2), 127. [Ed.]

LOEWE, LOUIS (Ha-Levi, Eliezer; 1809–1888), orientalist. Loewe was born in Zuelz, Germany, and studied at the yeshivot of Lissa and Pressburg; later he specialized in oriental languages at the universities of Vienna and Berlin.

Louis Loewe, British orientalist and educationist. Jerusalem, J.N.U.L., Schwadron Collection.

In 1833 he moved to London. At the suggestion of the scholarly Duke of Sussex (son of King George III) and of several leading French and English orientalists, Loewe decided in 1837 to undertake an expedition to Egypt, in preparation for which he had mastered Egyptology and the Nubian and Ethiopic languages. On this journey he deciphered various inscriptions on the banks of the Nile, at Thebes, Alexandria, Cairo, and elsewhere.

From Egypt he proceeded to Palestine, but had the misfortune to arrive there during the revolt of the Druze; when he was in Safed they robbed him and destroyed 13 of his notebooks, already prepared for publication. He stayed in Shechem for a short time, studying Samaritan customs and literature. In Damascus he acquired a valuable collection of rare ancient coins. In Constantinople he studied the customs of the Karaite community and acquired many rare books and manuscripts of this sect. His impressions of his visit to Palestine were published in a series of letters in the German-Jewish weekly *Allgemeine Zeitung des Judenthums* for the year 1839 (in an abridged Hebrew translation by M. A. Guenzburg in his *Devir*, vol. 1, 1844).

From 1839, he accompanied Montefiore on all his journeys as his interpreter and secretary in oriental languages, including Hebrew, and was Montefiore's devoted assistant in all his public activities. At the time of the Damascus Affair (1840) he accompanied Montefiore, Adolphe Crémieux, and Salomon Munk who went to Egypt and Turkey in an effort to intervene on behalf of the Jews. His command of Arabic enabled him to suggest a change in the wording of Muhammad Ali's firman, which resulted in the substitution of the term "honorable acquittal" for "pardon" (with its implication of guilt). Loewe accompanied Montefiore on visits to Russia in 1846 and 1872 and also on five trips to Palestine.

On his return to London in 1839 the Duke of Sussex offered him the post of director of the oriental section of his extensive library, a position which he held for about 15 years. From 1856 to 1858 he was principal of *Jews' College in London. At Brighton in 1861 he established a school for Jewish boys, many of whom came from abroad. From 1869 to 1888 he was principal of Ohel Moshe vi-Yhudit, a theological seminary founded in 1869 by Moses Montefiore at Ramsgate. Loewe edited the *Diaries of Sir Moses and Lady Montefiore* (2 vols., 1890). His other works include *The Origin of the Egyptian Language* (1837); an English translation of and lengthy introduction to *Efes Damim* by I. B. Levinsohn (*No Blood*, 1841); an English translation of *Ha-Kuzari ha-Sheni o Matteh Dan* by David Nieto (1842); and *A Dictionary of the Circassian Language* (1854).

Bibliography: J. H. Loewe, *A Descriptive Catalogue of a Portion of the Library of the Late Dr. Louis Loew* (1895), introduction; J. Kurrein, in: JJGL, 27 (1926), 148–61; I. Trywaks and E. Steinmann, *Sefer Me'ah Shanah* (1938), 97–121; A. Yaari, *Iggerot Erez Yisrael* (1943), 379–408; *Enziklopedyah shel ha-Ziyyonut ha-Datit*, 3 (1965), 95–98. [G.El.]

LOEWE, LUDWIG (1839–1886) and **ISIDOR** (1848–1910), German industrialists. They were born in Heiligenstadt, Thuringia, sons of an indigent teacher. Ludwig Loewe became a wealthy machinery merchant in Berlin. In 1860 he was elected to the City Council, in 1876 to the Prussian Landtag, and in 1878 to the Reichstag as a Social Democrat, opposing Bismarck. In 1870 Ludwig visited the United States and studied American business and production methods. By introducing these into his sewing machine factory he set a pattern which led to a vast improvement in German industrial techniques. In 1872 he began to manufacture rifles for the German army and later exported them on a large scale.

Isidor Loewe joined his brother's firm in 1875, and became its director in 1878. After Ludwig's death he effected a merger with the Mauser factory in order to fulfill orders for over a million rifles for Prussia and Turkey. In 1892 the anti-Semite Hermann *Ahlwardt wrote several scurrilous pamphlets on "Jew rifles," accusing Loewe of being a traitor to Germany by using such poor materials that the rifles were a greater hazard to the user than to his enemy. Ahlwardt was charged with libel and sentenced to a term of imprisonment. Further mergers resulted in 1896 in the formation of the Deutsche Waffen- und Muntionsfabrik A.G., with the largest rifle factory in the world. In 1892, together with an American company, Isidor Loewe established a firm which built electric streetcars for German and Belgian cities. He also made automobiles and began to manufacture aircraft.

Bibliography: K. Zielinziger, *Juden in der deutschen Wirtschaft* (1930); F. Wegeleben, *Die Rationalisierung im deutschen Werkzeugmaschinenbau* (1924). [S.A.M.]

LOEWENSON, JEAN (Hans; Lavi, Yoḥanan; 1898–1966), Israel author and journalist. Born in Toruń, Poland, Loewenson was taken to Switzerland in 1907. After working as a newspaper correspondent in Paris and Geneva, he settled in Jerusalem in 1934. From 1936 he was correspondent for Havas, and then for Agence France-Presse until 1949. Later he worked for the French publications department of the Jewish Agency. Loewenson's literary quality shows best in his translations from German into French. His knowledge of Hebrew and of Jewish philosophy enabled him to produce outstanding versions of works by Martin *Buber and Gershom *Scholem. Loewenson's original poetical and philosophical prose works include *Variations sur le destin* (1944), *Femmes en Israël* (1950), *Virtualités* (1961), and *Pièces pour une armature* (1966).

Bibliography: Gottgetreu, in: *Mitteilungsblatt* (Feb. 11, 1966); Catane, in: *Israelitisches Wochenblatt fuer die Schweiz* (April 1, 1966); idem, *Gazette de Lausanne* (April 5–6, 1966). [M.C.]

LOEWENSTAMM, 18th-century family of Dutch rabbis. ARYEH LOEB BEN SAUL LOEWENSTAMM (1690–1755) was born in Cracow, where his father SAUL had been rabbi; in 1707 Saul was appointed Ashkenazi rabbi of Amsterdam in succession to Moses Judah b. Kalonymus Kohen (known as Leib Ḥarif), but he died in Glogau on the way to take up his position. That same year Aryeh Loeb married Miriam, the oldest daughter of Ẓevi Hirsch Ashkenazi (the Ḥakham Ẓevi), then rabbi of Altona, Hamburg, and Wandsbeck. He accompanied his father-in-law to Amsterdam but later went to Poland, where he was appointed rabbi of Dukla and subsequently of Tarnopol (1720). This appointment was obtained by the intervention of the government, influenced by Loewenstamm's relatives, to have the incumbent deposed so that he could be appointed. As a result his appointment was not received favorably by the community, and he himself was deposed shortly after. He served as rabbi of Rzeszow (1724–28) and then of Glogau (1734–39), where he was involved in the dispute with regard to Moses Ḥayyim *Luzzatto, against whom he issued a ban in 1735, at the request of the rabbis of Venice. In 1740 he was appointed rabbi of Amsterdam, where he remained for the rest of his life.

Loewenstamm left no works. Some of his responsa, novellae, and notes, however, are to be found in the responsa of his father-in-law (no.76); in Mordecai of Dusseldorf's *Ma'amar Mordekhai* (Bruenn, 1790; nos. 62, 63); in David Meldola's *Divrei David* (Amsterdam, 1753; nos. 10, 53, 81); and in his son Saul's *Binyan Ari'el* (see below). In 1711 he published, together with Shemariah b. Jacob of Grodno, a second edition of the responsa of Moses Isserles, to which he added a *kunteres aḥaron*. He is also mentioned in the *takkanot* and minutes of the *Council of Four Lands. He took an active part in the Emden-Eybeschuetz controversy. Naturally siding with his brother-in-law Jacob *Emden (the son of Ashkenazi), he was unsparing in his language against Eybeschuetz (see J. Emden, *Sefat Emet* (1876), 16).

Loewenstamm had two sons: one, known as Hirschel b. Aryeh Loeb *Levin, was rabbi of Berlin. The other, SAUL (1717–1790), born in Rzeszow, succeeded his father as rabbi of Amsterdam, having previously served as rabbi of Lakacz, Hungary, and Dubno, Lithuania. In Amsterdam he devoted himself to the yeshivah established by his father. Ḥ. J. D. Azulai, who met him in Amsterdam, refers to him in glowing terms. In 1754 he participated in the session of the Council of Four Lands in Jaroslaw. Saul Loewenstamm's most famous work is his *Binyan Ari'el* (Amsterdam, 1778), which is divided into three parts: on the Pentateuch, on the Five Scrolls, and comments on various talmudic passages. His glosses to tractate *Niddah* were published in the Amsterdam edition of the Talmud (1765). Saul was succeeded as rabbi of Amsterdam by his son JACOB MOSES (1747–1815), previously rabbi in Filehne (Poznania) and Cleves. When the "progressive" congregation Adat Yeshurun appointed as their rabbi Aaron Moses Isaac Graanboom, a proselyte whose father was also a proselyte, Loewenstamm debarred him from the rabbinate because of his association with Reform tendencies. Jacob's son, JEHIEL ARYEH LOEB (d. 1807) was appointed rabbi of Leeuwarden, and died in his father's lifetime.

Bibliography: Michael, Or, no 535; A. L. Landshuth, *Toledot Anshei ha-Shem u-Fe'ulatam be-Adat Berlin* (1884), 72–75, 111, 118f.; Ḥ. N. Dembitzer, *Kelilat Yofi*, 1 (1888), 128a–136b; 2 (1893), 83a–b; S. Buber, *Anshei Shem* (1895), 37–40, 234; I. T. Eisenstadt and S. Wiener, *Da'at Kedoshim* (1897–98), 105f., 113, 121f.; J. Emden, *Megillat Sefer*, ed. by D. Kahana (1897), 65–69, 154; P. Pesis, *Ir Dubna ve-Rabbaneha* (1902), 22f.; H.Z. Margoles, *Dubna Rabbati* (1910), 14f.; J. Maarsen, in: HḤY, 6 (1922), 15–19, 134–58; Z. Horowitz, *Kitvei ha-Ge'onim* (1928), 74–81, 115, 136;

idem *Le-Korot ha-Kehillot be-Polanyah* (1969), 138, 181–96; Halpern, Pinkas, index, s.v. *Aryeh Loeb b. Sha'ul;* idem, *Yehudim ve-Yahadut be-Mizraḥ Eiropah* (1969), 396f.; EG, (1955), 31–34; *Rzeszów Jews Memorial Book* (1967), 43ff. [L.I.R.]

LOEWENSTEIN, BERNHARD (1821–1889), rabbi, preacher, and pioneer of the Reform movement. Born in Mezhirech, western Poland, he was active in spreading *Haskalah and the ideas of the Reform movement. On the recommendation of Ludwig *Philippson, in 1845 he was appointed preacher and headmaster of a school in Liptó-Szent-Miklós, Hungary. In 1857 he became rabbi of the community of Bucovice in Moravia. His most important congregational work was done in Lemberg, where in 1862 he was officially elected rabbi and preacher of the community, and also served as teacher of religion at the high school and registrar of the community. His sermons attracted a large congregation, occasionally including even non-Jews. Loewenstein was involved in the opening of a new type of **talmud torah*, called Ohel Moshe, where Jewish and secular studies were taught. This was closed, however, after two years because of the opposition of the Orthodox. He was also active in the *Shomer Israel society which sought to disseminate culture among the mass of Jews in order to bring them closer to the culture of their surroundings. In addition to sermons, he published a collection of poems entitled *Juedische Klaenge* (Bruenn, 1862), translated into Hebrew by Judah Rohatiner. His son, Nathan *Loewenstein, was an assimilationist leader in Galicia.

Bibliography: N. Samuely, *Rabbiner und Prediger Bernhard Loewenstein* (1889); Z. Karl, in: EG, 4 (1956), 439–40; J. Tenenbaum, *Galitsye Mayn Alte Heym* (1952), index. [M.LAN.]

LOEWENSTEIN, KARL (1891–), U.S. political scientist, Loewenstein practiced law in his native Munich and lectured at the university there from 1931 to 1933. He emigrated to the United States in 1934 and two years later became professor of jurisprudence and political science at Amherst College and in 1961 emeritus professor. In 1956 he was appointed professor of law at the University of Munich. During and after World War II, he served first as special assistant to the attorney general (1942–44) and then as legal adviser to the U.S. Military Government in Germany (1945–50). Lowenstein wrote extensively, in three languages, in the fields of public law and comparative government on European and American political systems. His earliest work, *Volk und Parlament nach der Staatsauffassung der franzoesischen Nationalversammlung von 1789* (1922) remains a standard work in the subject. His major work deals with U.S. constitutional law and practice, *Verfassungsrecht und Verfassungspraxis der Vereinigten Staaten* (1959). He also wrote a political science textbook *Political Power and the Governmental Process* (1957), *Hitler's Germany* (1939), *Brazil under Vargas* (1942), *Die Monarchie im modernen Staat* (1952), and many others, as well as numerous articles, some of which are collected in his book *Beitraege zur Staatsoziologie* (1961). [E.E.G.]

LOEWENSTEIN, LEOPOLD (1843–1924), German rabbi and historian. Loewenstein, who was born in Gailingen, south Baden, studied at the University of Wuerzburg and with Ezriel *Hildesheimer in Eisenstadt. He served as district rabbi in Gailingen (1872–87) and then in Baden (1887–1924). He made important contributions to the study of German-Jewish history in his *Geschichte der Juden am Bodensee* (1879), *Geschichte der Juden in der Kurpfalz* (1895), *Geschichte der Juden von der babylonischen Gefangenschaft bis zur Gegenwart* (1904), *Familie Aboab* (1905), and *Zur Geschichte der Juden in Fuerth* (3 vols., 1909–13; repr. 1967), among other works. From 1899 to 1904 he edited the *Blaetter fuer juedische Geschichte und Literatur*, a monthly supplement to the Orthodox Jewish newspaper published in Mainz, *Der Israelit*.

Bibliography: ZHB, 22 (1919), 71–76, bibl., Wininger, Biog. [M.A.M.]

LOEWENSTEIN (Von Opoka), NATHAN (1859–1929), lawyer and political leader, born in Bucovice, Moravia. Loewenstein was the son of the preacher of Lemberg, Bernard *Loewenstein. He became leader of the assimilationists of Galicia, and editor of the Polish nationalist-oriented weekly *Ojczyzna.* Between 1881 and 1886 he was a member of the community council, the municipality of Lemberg, and the Galician Sejm (parliament). From 1907 he was a deputy to the Austrian parliament as a member of the "Polish club." In 1906 he conducted an inquiry into the living conditions of the Jews of Galicia which served as the basis for his speech in the Galician Sejm (1907) on the gravity of the economic situation. During the parliamentary elections of 1911 there were bloody clashes in *Drogobych (Drohobycz) between his supporters and Zionist opponents over the question of his candidacy; the army intervened, and a number of Jews were killed. Loewenstein withdrew his candidacy, but after a few months he ran again and was reelected, retaining his seat until World War I. With the creation of independent Poland, he was automatically given a seat in the Polish Sejm, as deputy of the region where elections could not be held since there was a military and political struggle between the Poles and Ukrainians over the control of eastern Galicia. In the first Sejm he was prominent for his conservative approach as a landowner and an assimilationist, ignoring the Jewish deputies' campaign on behalf of the needy Jewish population. Having lost public support, he retired from political life after the elections of 1922. Loewenstein gained note at the *Steiger trial (1924–25) for his brilliant speeches in defense of the accused and his resolute struggle against the authorities, who introduced false evidence into their indictment. Loewenstein wrote a book on the Steiger affair, *O sprawe Steigera*, which was published in 1926.

Bibliography: *Almanach Żydowski* (1937). [M.LAN.]

LOEWENSTEIN, RUDOLPH MAURICE (1898–), psychoanalyst and psychoanalytic theoretician. Loewenstein, who was born in Lodz, Poland, worked in Berlin from 1923 to 1925 and in Paris from 1925 until the outbreak of World War II, when he served with distinction in the French army. He settled in the United States in 1943. Together with Heinz *Hartmann and Ernst *Kris, Loewenstein staked out important aspects of psychoanalytic theory as propounded by *Freud, and developed them further, particularly in the field of ego psychology. In 1951 Loewenstein published, in French and English, *Christians and Jews: a Psychoanalytic Study*. In this he traced the historical and cultural roots of anti-Semitism. He viewed Christians and Jews as a mutually interdependent pair, and suggested that the impossibly difficult ethic of the Christian religion may make the use of the Jew as a scapegoat a necessity for the Christian. Loewenstein collaborated with Princess Marie Bonaparte in translating some of Freud's works into French, and edited a series of psychoanalytic essays, *Drives, Affects and Behavior*, published in the princess's honor in 1953. He was an early coeditor of the anual *Psychoanalytic Study of the Child*, and served as president of both the New York Psychoanalytic Society and the American Psychoanalytic Association.

Bibliography: A. Grinstein, *Index of Psychoanalytic Writings* 3 (1958), s.v. [R.Mo.]

LOEWENSTEIN-STRASHUNSKY, JOEL DAVID (1816–1850), *ḥazzan.* Born in Lemberg, he was the son of the *ḥazzan* of Vilna, Ẓevi Hirsch Loewenstein. At an early age, he became known for his fine voice and his mastery of the violin. After the death of his father in 1830, the 15-year-old lad succeeded him as *ḥazzan* and became known as "Der Vilner Balabesl" (the Little Householder of Vilna). After 1839 he began studying with the composer Moniuszko. In 1842, Loewenstein was invited to Warsaw where he gave recitals accompanied by a chorus and orchestra, which deeply impressed his audience comprised of the town's aristocratic and wealthy classes. The passage from the narrow ghetto world to a cosmopolitan atmosphere produced a mental shock on Loewenstein. Legend attributes it to a tragic infatuation with a Polish woman singer. He went into "voluntary exile" and for several years wandered through the communities of Central Europe, appearing in synagogues only on rare occasions. His life became the subject of legends and literary works including Mark Orenstein's *Der Vilner Balabesl* (Yid., 1908), and J. J. Wohl's *La-Menaẓẓe'aḥ bi-Neginot* (in *Aḥi'asaf,* 7 (1899), 177–97). Several of his prayer melodies have been preserved; *Ve-Havi'enu le-Shalom,* for example, was published by A. Nadel in *Ost und West* (5 (1905), 103–6).

Bibliography: Sendrey, Music, 3533, 5678–84; Idelsohn, Music, 299–302; Ḥ. N. Steinschneider, in: *Talpiyyot* (1895), pt. 12, 8–13; E. B., in: *Ost und West,* 5 (1905), 102–8; Y. Appel, *Be-Tokh Reshit ha-Teḥiyyah* (1936), 565–77; M. S. Geshuri, in: *Ba-Mishor,* 1 (1940). [EH]

LOEWENTHAL, EDUARD (1836–1917), German political theorist. Born in Ernsbach, Prussia, Loewenthal advocated a new religion based on scientific truth and rejecting metaphysical concepts. He expounded his ideas in *System und Geschichte des Naturalismus* (1861, 97⁶; *System and History of Nature,* 1882) which achieved considerable popularity. He founded the "Cogitant" religious society to propagate his views in 1865 and in 1869 formed the European Union, a Pan-European society dedicated to the abolition of war. Following the outbreak of the Franco-Prussian war in 1870, Loewenthal was forced to leave Prussia but he returned in the following year to reorganize the European Union with a program of a world court and the compulsory arbitration of disputes. In 1874 he was forced to leave Prussia for a second time but continued to preach his pacifist philosophy abroad. He was nominated for the Nobel peace prize toward the end of his life but, to his chagrin, was not given the award.

Bibliography: E. Loewenthal, *Mein Lebenswerk ...* (1910); Wininger, Biog, 4 (1925) s.v., includes bibliography; EJ, s.v., includes bibliography. [Ed.]

LOEWI, OTTO (1873–1961), biochemist and Nobel Prize winner. Loewi, who was born in Frankfort, studied at Strasbourg and later worked in the Pharmacological Institute at Marburg and then in Vienna. From 1909 to 1938 he was professor of pharmacology at the University of Graz, Austria. In 1902 he showed that the nitrogen requirements of mammals could be supplied solely by the amino acids obtained from protein hydrolysis without direct supply of proteins. He studied the stimulation and retardation of the frequency and strength of the heartbeats of frogs when the nerve trunk was electrically stimulated, and showed that the effects were related to the release of various chemicals, particularly acetylcholine. A test for pancreatic insufficiency is known as Loewi's test. He was awarded the Nobel Prize in Physiology and Medicine in 1936 (jointly with Sir Henry Dale), "for discoveries relating to chemical transmission of nerve impulses." After the Germans took over Austria in 1938, he was imprisoned for two months and deprived of all his possessions before being allowed to leave. During 1939–40 Loewi worked at Oxford. In 1940 he went to the U.S. where he was appointed professor of pharmacology at the College of Medicine of New York University.

Otto Loewi, biochemist and Nobel Prize winner. Photo Reportagebild, Stockholm.

Bibliography: *British Journal of Pharmacological Therapy,* 18 (1962); C. Singer and E. A. Underwood, *A Short History of Medicine* (1962), 262; I. Asimov, *Biographical Encyclopedia of Science and Technology* (1964), 461; C. Brooks and P. Cranefield (eds.), *The Historical Development of Physiological Thought* (1959), 170–5. [S.A.M.]

LOEWINGER, DAVID SAMUEL (1904–), Hungarian biblical and talmudic scholar and bibliographer. Loewinger was born in Debrecen, Hungary. While still a student he published with D. *Friedmann the *Alphabet of Ben Sira* (1926) from a manuscript and *Darkhei ha-Nikkud ve-ha-Neginot* (1929, 1969²), ascribed to Moses ha-Nakdan. He also contributed the commentary on Habbakuk to A. Kahana's edition of the Bible (1930). From 1931 he lectured at the Budapest rabbinical seminary on Bible and Talmud and became its director in 1942. After World War II he was responsible for the reconstruction of the seminary and the resumption of its scholarly activities. In the prewar years Loewinger was one of the editors of *Ha-Soker* (1933–40) and **Magyar Zsidó Szemle* and also edited a number of jubilee volumes, e.g., on S. *Hevesi (*Emlékkönyv,* Hg. and Heb., 1934), E. Mahler (*Dissertationes in honorem Dr. E. Mahler,* 1937), M. Guttmann (*Jewish Studies in Memory of M. Guttmann,* 1946), and I. Goldziher (*I. Goldziher Memorial Volume* 1, 1948). In *Germánia prófétája* ("The Prophet of Germany," 1947) Loewinger attempted to trace Germany's Nazi anti-Semitic ideology to F. Nietzsche. With A. *Scheiber he published *Ginzei Kaufmann* (*Genizah Publications in Memory of D. Kaufmann,* 1949).

After emigrating to Israel in 1950, Loewinger became the scientific secretary and then director of the Institute of Microfilms of Hebrew Manuscripts at the National and University Library in Jerusalem. He was also associated with various projects relating to the Bible text. He specialized in the problems of Bible manuscripts, particularly of the famous Bible codex *Keter Aram Ẓova* ("Aleppo Codex"; in *Textus,* 1 (1960), 59–111). With others he prepared several manuscript catalogs, which were published by the Institute, including the catalog of the

Hebrew manuscripts in the Vatican library (list of photocopies in the Institute, part 3: *Hebrew Manuscripts in the Vatican*, Jerusalem, 1968, Heb.). With B. D. Weinryb he published *Catalogue of the Hebrew Manuscripts in the Library of the Juedisch-Theologisches Seminar in Breslau* (1965). [B.Y.]

LOEWINSON-LESSING, FRANZ YULYEVICH (1861–1939), Russian geologist, pioneer of magmatic petrology. Loewinson-Lessing occupied the chair of geology, petrology, and mineralogy first at the University of Dorpat (now Tartu), Estonia, and from 1902 until his retirement in 1930, at the Polytechnic Institute of St. Petersburg (Leningrad). In 1925 he was elected a member of the Soviet Academy of Sciences, where he was appointed director of the newly established Petrographical Institute. As early as 1897, in a paper presented to the international geological congress held in St. Petersburg, Loewinson-Lessing introduced a chemical classification of igneous rocks. This was followed by shorter papers on petrochemistry, in which he discussed the role of assimilation in the origin of magmatic rocks and applied the "phase rule" of physical chemistry to substantiate his synthetic-liquational theory of differentiation. In his later years he also dealt with the physical properties of rocks and the tectonic movements of igneous masses. The two books on petrography which he published in 1923, *Uspekhi petrografii v Rossii* ("Advances in Petrography in Russia"), and *Voedeniye v geologiyu* ("Introduction to Geology"), became standard textbooks in the U.S.S.R.

Bibliography: P. I. Lebedev, *Akademik P. Yu. Loewinson-Lessing kak teoretik petrografii* (1947); A. A. Zvorykin (ed.), *Biograficheskiy slovar deyateley yestestvoznaniya i tekhniki*, 1 (1958), 502–3.
[L.Pi.]

LOEWISOHN, SOLOMON (1789–1821), Hebrew writer. Born in Mor, Hungary, he received a Jewish education but at the same time studied secular subjects in a Capuchin monastery. With the aid of his relative Solomon Rosenthal, a wealthy scholar, he studied in Prague at a yeshivah and at the university. In 1811 and 1812 he published two grammatical studies which were collected and annotated by A. B. Lebensohn and J. Behak under the title *Meḥkerei Lashon* (1849). He wrote his first important poem, an elegy on the death of his friend Baruch *Jeiteles, in 1814.

In Prague Loewisohn eked out a meager living by giving private lessons. But the five years, between 1815 and 1820, were the most productive and the most "affluent" years of his life. He became proofreader and counselor of Anton von *Schmid. After 1820, he became mentally ill. Insanity led to his untimely death. He published his chief work in 1816; *Meliẓat Yeshurun*, the first aesthetic interpretation of the Bible in the Hebrew language. It discusses in detail various poetic devices including allegory, irony, metaphor, and hyperbole. The work is prefaced by a remarkable hymn to beauty and poetry. Loewisohn allotted 27 pages of his book to an analysis of the Song of Songs which he regarded as a love song of King Solomon. Loewisohn also used non-biblical passages to illustrate figures of speech. In the chapter on apostrophe he quoted from the second part of *King Henry IV* (Act 3, Scene 1)—the first translation of Shakespeare into Hebrew. In 1819 he published *Meḥkerei Areẓ*, the first Hebrew geographical handbook for the biblical period. It utilized Josephus, Eusebius, Pliny, and Strabo. Translated into German two years after its publication, the book served as a handbook for generations of readers, developed a geographical terminology, and pioneered the way for utilization of rabbinic sources.

Loewisohn had also a keen interest in Jewish liturgy. He annotated and translated the *kinot* and also annotated the *Shir ha-Yiḥud* ("Hymn of Unity") and wrote a preface on the value of prayer for the *siddur* of Judah Leib *Ben-Zeeb (1816). Loewisohn also wrote in German and published several articles in the periodical *Sulamith*, and a history of the Jews, *Vorlesungen ueber die neuere Geschichte der Juden* (1820) which was praised by *Graetz.

Bibliography: S. Klein, *Toledot Ḥakirat Ereẓ Yisrael ba-Sifrut ha-Ivrit ve-ha-Kelalit* (1937), 74–80; J. Fichmann, *Anshei-Besorah* (1938), 50–56; Ḥ. N. Schapira, *Toledot ha-Sifrut ha-Ivrit ha-Ḥadashah* (1939), 454–78; Schwartz, in: *Moznayim* (1963), 373–83; J. L. Landau, *Short Lectures on Hebrew Literature* (1938), index; Waxman, Literature, 3 (1960), 147–53.
[El.S.]

LOEWITH, KARL (1897–), German philosopher of Jewish origin. His teachers were E. *Husserl, M. *Geiger and M. Heidegger in philosophy, and H. Spemann in biology. From 1928 he was privatdocent at Marburg University; from 1934 to 1936 a Rockefeller fellow at Rome; then professor at Sendai, Japan; from 1941 at the Hartford Theological Seminary; from 1949 at the New School for Social Research, New York; from 1952 at Heidelberg, Germany. Loewith's philosophy has its main non-contemporary sources in Hegel and in the development of thought after Hegel, which was one of the main subjects of his studies. His thinking shows the influence of Nietzsche and of Heidegger, whose existentialist-historicist ontology was later heavily criticized by Loewith. He tries to move back from modern thought with its anthropocentricism—through its Christian (biblical-Augustinian) origins—toward a predominantly Aristotelian horizon of thought: the horizon of a pure theory being knowledge for knowledge's sake—theory of nature (including human nature) and of the "cosmos" in its eternal being and becoming. Thus searching for the lost way of a really cosmological—and in Kantian language, "dogmatical"—philosophy, Loewith confronts the Greek *logos* of the cosmos with modern thinking in two papers presented in 1960 and 1964 to the Heidelberg Academy; and he further elaborates this search in his book on metaphysics from Descartes to Nietzsche, the last chapter of which deals with Spinoza's "Deus sive natura." Loewith's books include: *Das Individuum in der Rolle des Mitmenschen* (1928); *Kierkegaard und Nietzsche* (1936); *Nietzsches Philosophie der ewigen Wiederkehr des Gleichen* (1935); *Jacob Burckhardt* (1956); *Von Hegel zu Nietzsche* (1941; *From Hegel to Nietzsche*, 1964); *Meaning in History* (1949), later published in German as *Weltgeschichte und Heilsgeschehen* (1953); *Heidegger, Denker in duerftiger Zeit* (1953); *Wissen, Glaube und Skepsis* (1956); *Gesammelte Abhandlungen zur Kritik der geschichtlichen Existenz* (1960); *Vortraege und Abhandlungen zur Kritik der christlichen Ueberlieferung* (1966); *Nature, History and Existentialism* (1966), a collection of Loewith's essays; *Gott, Mensch und Welt in der Metaphysik von Descartes bis zu Nietzsche* (1967); *"Philosophie der Vernunft und Religion der Offenbarung in H. Cohens Religionsphilosophie"* (*Sitzungsberichte der Heidelberger Akademie der Wissenschaften*, 1968).

Bibliography: *Natur und Geschichte: Karl Loewith zum 70 Geburtstag* (1967).
[O.I.S.]

LOEWY, EMANUEL (1857–1938), Austrian classical archaeologist. Loewy was born in Vienna and then traveled extensively in Greece and Asia Minor. In 1882 he took part in the excavations of a Lycian burial site, the "Heroon" of Gjölbaşi-Trysa, in which important Greek reliefs were found from the late fifth century B.C.E. In 1887 he began his academic career as lecturer in Vienna, becoming a professor in Rome in 1889. He returned to Vienna after World War I and was professor for classical archaeology. His early writings on the history of ancient Greek artists were influenced by the philology-oriented Seminary in Vienna.

His later activity was influenced by contemporary art historiographers of the "Vienna School" such as F. Wickhoff and A. Riegl: in the place of the philologico-antiquarian interpretation of ancient works of art, came the form and style analysis, together with a reevalution of pre- and post-classical style periods. Loewy contributed essentially to the comprehension of the then underestimated archaic art of Greece with his *Naturwiedergabe* and *Typenwanderung*. Loewy considered the archaic style not as a preliminary to the classical period, but as an artistic creation, complete in itself. Apart from numerous scholarly works, Loewy reached a wide general public with his popular scientific works *Die Griechische Plastik* (2 vols., 1911, 1924^4) and *Polygnot, ein Buch von griechischer Malerei* (2 vols., 1929). His works include: *Inschriften griechischer Bildhauer* (1885); *Naturwiedergabe in der aelteren griechischen Kunst* (1900; Eng., 1907); *Typenwanderung* (Yearbook of the Austrian Archeological Institute, 12 (1909); 14 (1911); *Neuattische Kunst* (1922). [P.P.K.]

LOEWY, ISAAC (1793–1847), industrialist; founder of the town of Ujpest. Born in Nagy-Surány (now Surány), Hungary, Loewy studied at the yeshivah of Pressburg. He also learned his father's trade, that of tanner, and with his brothers Joachim and Bernát took over the family business in 1823. When in the early 1830s he tried to establish his workshop in Pest, the town council and guilds refused to admit him. At about that time some uncultivated lands to the north of the town were being parceled out for sale by the proprietor, Count István Károlyi; Loewy, his family, and his workmen settled on them. The terms of the sale stipulated that there would be no religious discrimination in the new settlement and that the traditional craft guilds would not be established there. By 1834 Loewy's new factory had started production, and the first residential building was erected in 1835. Several wealthy Jews of Pest followed Loewy, building rows of houses on the new settlement. In 1839 and 1840 a synagogue and school were built. In 1840 the settlement was officially declared a borough, with the name Ujpest ("New Pest"). This was mainly due to the efforts of Loewy, who was elected the first

Isaac Loewy, Hungarian industrialist and founder of Ujpest. From *Beth-El, Ehrentempel Verdienter Ungarischer Israeliten*, Pest, 1867.

president of the town council of the new town. He also suggested the development of a port on the Danube at Ujpest. After his death a street in Ujpest was named after him.

Bibliography: I. Reich, in: *Beth-El; Ehrentempel verdienter ungarischer Israeliten*, 1 (1868), 8–20; E. Ballagi, in: *Egyenlöség*, 41 (Dec. 16, 1922), 14; Gy. Ugró, *Ujpest* (1932), 19–21. [J.Z.]

LOEWY, JACOB EZEKIEL BEN JOSEPH (1814–1864), rabbi and author. Born in Hotzenplotz, Moravia, Loewy went at the age of nine to study with Baruch Te'omim Fraenkel in Leipnik. After Fraenkel's death in 1827, he studied at various yeshivot including those of Benjamin Wolf in Tepelstein and Jacob Meshullam *Ornstein in Lemberg, he spent one year in Berlin where his studies included secular learning. After his marriage he engaged in business, studying in his spare time. In 1846 he was appointed rabbi of Wadowice, his seat being in Oswiecim (Auschwitz). In 1854 he accepted the position of rabbi in Beuthen where he died. Among his works are *Tisporet Lulyanit* (1839) attacking the *Ma'amar ha-Tiglaḥat* (1835) of Isaac Samuel *Reggio who had permitted the cutting of the beard during the intermediate days of a festival; and *Bikkoret ha-Talmud* ("*Kritisch-talmudisches Lexicon*," vol. 1, Vienna, 1863). The latter purports to be a critical encyclopedia on the Oral Law and tradition, alphabetically arranged. The volume covers articles under the letter *alef*. In conformity with his conservative approach, Loewy attempted in his work to harmonize scientific criticism with tradition. In the article on marriage (pp. 155–65) he strongly attacks the extreme reform views of *Holdheim in his *Ma'amar ha-Ishut* and their qualified approval by Reggio. His halakhic work, *Shorshei Halakhah*, remains in manuscript. He also published a series of studies in *Ha-Maggid*, *Ha-Meliẓ*, and other periodicals.

Bibliography: Fuenn, Keneset, 552. [Ed.]

LOEWY, MAURICE (1833–1907), astronomer. Loewy was born in Pressburg (Bratislava), where he trained in the local observatory. In 1861 Loewy was appointed assistant

Maurice Loewy, astronomer. Jerusalem, J.N.U.L., Schwadron Collection.

astronomer of the Paris observatory and astronomer in 1864. After the death of Amédée E. B. Mouchez in 1892, he was put in charge of the great international enterprise of the photographic "Carte du Ciel," and later became director of the observatory. He devised several new observational methods. His particular interest was the moon, and together with his collaborator, P. H. Puiseux, he produced a large photographic atlas, which has remained a masterpiece. He was a pioneer in astronomical photography, and the inventor of the "elbow" telescope. He received many honors including the Gold Medal of the Royal Astronomical Society in London.

Bibliography: Royal Astronomical Society, *Monthly Notices*, 68 (1907–08), 249–52; (1942), 166–7, incl. list of major works. [A.Be.]

LOGGEM, MANUEL VAN (1916–), Dutch author and critic. A psychotherapist, Van Loggem taught drama in Brussels, but is mainly known as the author of numerous dramas and television plays in which the characters are drawn with great psychological skill. His outstanding plays include the prizewinning *De Chinese fluitspeler* ("The Chinese Flutist," 1947) and *Jeugdproces* ("Youth Trial," 1965), which was translated into many languages. His plays for television include *Een zon op Hiroshima* ("A Sun over Hiroshima," 1962). Van Loggem also wrote novels and short stories, some of them on Jewish themes. Van Loggem's novel *Mozes* (1960^2; shortened version, 1968) describes the genesis of the Jewish people. His short story "*Deze plek komt me bekend voor*" from the collection *Het tijdperk der zerken* ("The Age of Memorials," 1968) introduces the figure of the *Wandering Jew after the Israel capture of the Western Wall in Jerusalem in June 1967. His theoretical and critical prose includes *Oorsprong en noodzaak* ("Origin and Necessity," 1951), and *Inleiding tot het toneel* ("Introduction to the Theater," 1953[2]).

[G.A.-T.]

LOGIC (Heb. חָכְמַת הַדִּבּוּר or מְלֶאכֶת הַהִגָּיוֹן), the study of the principles governing correct reasoning and demonstration. The term logic, according to Maimonides, is used in three senses: to refer to the rational faculty, the intelligible in the mind, and the verbal expression of this mental content. In its second sense, logic is also called inner speech, and in its third, outer speech. Since logic is concerned with verbal formulation as well as mental content, grammar often forms a part of logical writings. Shem Tov ibn *Falaquera, for example, prefaces his *Reshit Ḥokhmah* with an account of the origin of language, its nature, and its parts. As Maimonides had done in the introduction to the *Guide of the Perplexed,* Falaquera classifies terms into distinct terms, synonyms, and homonyms, a classification which was very important in the medieval philosophic exegesis of the Bible.

The two mental acts which are basic to logic are conception and judgment. The former is involved in the apprehension of the essence of things, the latter, in deciding whether propositions are true or false.

Maimonides does not consider logic a part of philosophy proper as the Stoics did, but follows the Peripatetics in viewing it as the instrument and auxiliary of all the other sciences.

Although some of the methods of biblical exegesis and legal interpretation *(middot)* employed by the rabbis of the talmudic period rest upon the rules of logic (see *Hermeneutics), it is doubtful that the rabbis had a formal knowledge of the subject. However, beginning with Saadiah, who refers to Aristotle's categories, proving that they are not applicable to God (*Emunot ve-De'ot,* 2:8), Jewish thinkers have been acquainted with the *Organon*—the title traditionally given to the body of Aristotle's logical treatises which formed the basis of logic—as propounded by the logicians of Islam. During the Islamic period, few works on logic were written by Jews. While Isaac *Israeli and Joseph ibn *Ẓaddik appear to have written works on logic, the first extant work on logic written by a Jew is Maimonides' *Maqāla fī-Ṣināʿat al-Manṭiq* (ed. by M. Turker (1961); Arabic text in Hebrew characters published by I. Efros in PAAJR, 34 (1966), 9–42 (Hebrew section); translated by the same into English under the title *Maimonides' Treatise on Logic* in: PAAJR, 8 (1937/38), 34–65). It was only when the setting of Jewish philosophy shifted to Christian countries and Arabic ceased to be the language of the Jews that logical works were translated into Hebrew and a greater number of Hebrew works on logic were written by Jews.

In the *Maqāla fī-Ṣināʿat al-Manṭiq* Maimonides offers concise exposition of the 175 most important logical, physical, metaphysical, and ethical terms used in the discussion of logical theory. The popularity of this treatise is attested by the fact that it was translated into Hebrew three times, under the title *Millot ha-Higgayon* or *Shemot ha-Higgayon:* once in a florid style by *Ahitub, a physician in Palermo in the 13th century; again, by Joseph ben Joshua ibn Vivas (of Lorca) in the 14th century; and by Moses b. Samuel ibn *Tibbon (all three translations appear in: PAAJR, 8 (1937/38), 23–129). This last translation was by far the most popular and has gone through many editions. Maimonides' work served not only as a handbook of logic, but, until comparatively recent times, also as an introduction to general philosophy. Of the commentaries written on it, those of Mordecai b. Eliezer *Comtino and Moses *Mendelssohn may be singled out.

While there is little information on the logical authorities used by the Jews up until the middle of the 12th century, it is known that by this time al-Fārābī was the acknowledged authority on logic. Maimonides, in a famous letter to Samuel ibn Tibbon, the Hebrew translator of his *Guide,* advises him to study logic only from the works of al-Fārābī, and, as M. Tucker has shown, Maimonides in his *Maqāla fī-Ṣināʿat al-Manṭiq* relied heavily on four works by al-Fārābī. During the first half of the 13th century, *Averroes too came to be regarded as an authority on logic, soon superseding al-Fārābī. Thus, Judah ben Samuel ibn *Abbas, in his *Ya'ir Nativ,* suggested that in order to learn the principles of logic, a student should read the works of al-Fārābī or Averroes.

While it appears that there were no translations into Hebrew of any of the books comprising the *Organon,* all the commentaries of al-Fārābī and Averroes were translated and annotated. Jacob b. Machir translated Averroes' *Epitome* of the Organon, and Jacob *Anatoli, Averroes' middle commentaries, which he completed in 1232. *Kalonymus b. Kalonymus and Moses b. Samuel ibn Tibbon were among some of the others who undertook to translate the logical writings of al-Fārābī and Averroes. Anatoli's translation of the middle commentaries was utilized by Joseph *Kaspi in his compendium of logic, entitled *Ẓeror ha-Kesef.*

The Jews were also familiar with the logical writings of Avicenna. Their knowledge of Avicenna's writings did not come from translations of Avicennian works, but rather through the logical portions of al-*Ghazālī's "Intentions of the Philosophers" *(Maqāṣid al-Falāsifa).* In addition to the Islamic tradition, a work by a Christian scholar, Peter of Spain's *Summulae Logicales,* was also popular, as the four or five Hebrew translations or extracts of it, which are still extant, testify.

These translations are of great importance because in many instances the original Arabic texts of the commentaries are no longer extant. Moreover, many of these texts were translated from the Hebrew into Latin by Jews who served as the intermediaries between the logicians of Islam and the scholastics. *Levi b. Gershom wrote supercommentaries on the middle commentaries and epitomes of Averroes, as well as an independent work on logic entitled *Ha-Hekkesh ha-Yashar* ("The Correct Syllogism"), which drew upon itself the attention of gentile scholars and was translated into Latin under the title *Liber Syllogismi Recti.* In the 15th century, *Judah b. Jehiel Messer Leon wrote a supercommentary on Averroes' middle commentaries which shows the influence of the scholastic Walter Burleigh.

Bibliography: L. Jacobs, *Studies in Talmudic Logic and Methodology* (1961), 3–50; A. Hyman, in: *Actes du quatrième congrès international de philosophie médiévale* (1969), 99–110; I. Husik, *Judah Messer Leon's Commentary on the "Vetus Logica"* (1906); Steinschneider, Uebersetzungen, 43–168; Waxman, Literature, 1 (1960[2]), 319–20, 2 (1960[2]), 213.

[J.H.]

LOGOS, a Greek word meaning "speech," "organization," "rational order," "rational relationship," or "rational expression," common in Greek philosophical writings. As the word of God in all its manifestations, it appears in Jewish and Christian theological texts in Greek from the Hellenistic period. *Aristobulus of Paneas, Wisdom of *Solomon, and *Philo are the Jewish sources, and the Gospel of John, the earliest representative of the Christian ones. The later history of the term belongs to Christian theology, where, following John, logos is the Son, or the preexistent Messiah. Logos as an independent entity appeared in Jewish literature suddenly in the writings of Philo. Because of the connection between Philo's use of the term and the Johannine innovation, according to which logos is an intermediary between God and the world, scholars sought parallels elsewhere in Jewish writings, both for the word of God as a distinct concept and for its appearance as a divine intermediary. The *memra* ("word") of the Lord, one of the terms used to paraphrase the name of the Lord in the Targums, has been mistakenly viewed as such a parallel.

Greek Philosophy. Among early Greek philosophers Heraclitus (fifth century B.C.E.) considered logos as (1) the order in the universe, (2) the organizing force that originates and maintains that order, and (3) human apprehension and reasoned expression of it. All these things for him are one and the same, and are, it seems, to be identified with heat. Plato used the term primarily for logical discussion. However, in *Epinomis* (986c4), a dialogue probably not written by Plato himself, logos is identified with the intelligence that governs and imposes rational structure in the world; in the Sixth Letter (323d2f.), whose authenticity is also disputed, the son of the true god is identified as "the divine governor and origin of all things present and future," which may point to some notion of the logos as an intermediary between true reality and the world in Greek sources. In Stoic thought logos again has the threefold role of (1) being responsible for fashioning things, (2) accounting for the disposition of things (and so for the rational faculty in man), and (3) expressing reality in language.

Bible. The Word of God *(devar Adonai)* appears in the Bible as divine teaching, i.e., the medium of revelation and guidance (Gen. 15:1; I Sam. 3:21; Isa. 55:10–11; Ezek. and Zech. passim), the instrument of creation (Ps. 33:6; Gen. 1, though the technical term is not used), and the instrument that controls nature (Ps. 107:20; 147:18). This usage parallels in some ways the threefold, normative Greek philosophical identification of logos, except that the biblical emphasis is on moral, instead of natural, philosophy. The Word of the Lord is identified directly with Torah in Psalms 119 *(passim)*, and the attributes of the Word or Torah (Ps. 89; 119) are ascribed to Wisdom in the first nine chapters of Proverbs. Indeed, Torah and Wisdom are identified in the apocryphal books Ben Sira (24:1–21, 22ff.) and Wisdom of Solomon (6:18ff.) in all the same aspects.

Jewish Hellenistic Literature. Aristobulus (fl. 160 B.C.E.) speaks of the voice of the Lord as the natural law, according to which the universe functions (Eusebius, *Praeparatio Evangelica,* 13:12). Thus, a rapprochement of the Jewish and Greek notions has occurred. In *Wisdom of Solomon* (7:17–21) also, Wisdom teaches natural philosophy to man. In the same work logos personifies divine Mercy (Wisdom 16:12), and slays the first-born of Egypt. In the *Haggadah* of Passover the Messenger (sometimes identified with logos by modern scholars), who was excluded from any role in the Exodus, may, if that passage is early and if it is a polemic against Wisdom of Solomon, point to an early popular hypostatization of logos; but the bulk of the evidence is opposed to such an early personification. The author of Wisdom of Solomon seems to distinguish between *sophia* ("wisdom") and logos, as two aspects of God's word, the former being human thoughts and actions in consonance with reality, and the latter, God's speech seen as a messenger, or angel. In addition, the former teaches natural philosophy, not logos.

Philo. Logos is central to Philo's thought. It is the chief power of God; it unites His strength and His goodness, and hence it is the rational term which connects opposites, another meaning of the Greek word. In this function, logos brings God to man and man to God. It is the representative of the Governor to His subjects; and its position is intermediate between created things and the uncreated (Her. 205). Logos is a copy (Gr. *eikon*) of God (I Spec. 81, etc.) through which the world was made (*ibid.*, III L.A. 96, etc.), and human intelligence is a copy of it (Her. 230, Fug. 68, Op. 69). Philo applies the term logos, or the holy logos, to Scripture itself, i.e., the Law (IV *Quaestiones et Solutiones in Genesin,* 140; I Som. 229). It is not a person, according to Philo, nor is it an intermediary between God and man, although it is identified with the biblical angel of the Lord (Mig. 174, etc.). Rather, it is sometimes the same as wisdom (I L.A. 65, etc.), because it is the most inclusive expression of the thoughts and ideas of God, which in turn are identified with the Law, or the Torah, with the pattern of all creation, and with the law that directs and maintains all things. Philo's identification of logos with Wisdom and Torah parallels the identification of Torah and Wisdom and the Word of God in rabbinic literature, and conforms to the roles assigned to each in Scripture and rabbinic sources.

Gospel of John. The prologue to the Gospel of John follows biblical and apocryphal sources in portraying the preexistent logos dwelling on earth; but the presentation of logos as an independent agent, and furthermore, as the preexistent messiah is a radical innovation. Apparently, Philo did not think of either notion (I Som. 228f. is not evidence that such a belief existed earlier). Rabbinic and Christian Gnostic speculations, all of later date than John, do, however, understand logos as a second god. Some accounts of *Gnosticism, whose doctrine implies a logos-hypostasis, would even date gnostic sources before John. Among the rabbis a belief in a "second God," or divine intermediary, is represented in the heretical views of *Elisha b. Avuyah (cf. also *Metatron). His views seem related to speculations about Creation, in which the voice, or Word, of the Lord on the waters (Ps. 29:3 and Gen. 1) and at the revelation on Sinai (Ex. 20) are hypostatized. All this, however, is later than the use of the Greek word "logos" in Philo and in the fourth Gospel.

The *memra* of the Targums, whether it is used in an attempt to express the otherness of God, to avoid anthropomorphisms, or for some other reason, was not thought of as an intermediary between man and God, was certainly not personified in rabbinic thought, and was not identified with Torah regularly. In later rabbinic writing *ha-dibbur* ("the speech") is used to refer to God, but that phenomenon seems unrelated to the Jewish-Hellenistic logos.

Bibliography: W. Kelber, *Die Logoslehre von Heraklit bis Origenes* (1958); H. Strack and P. Billerbeck, *Kommentar zum Neuen Testament aus Talmud und Midrasch,* 2 (1924), 353–5; H. Leisegang, in: Pauly-Wissowa, 25 (1926), 1047–81; H. A. Wolfson, *Philo,* 1 (Eng., 1947), 200–82.

[D.E.G.]

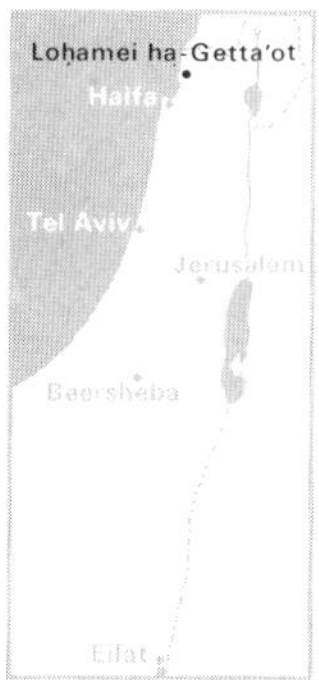

LOḤAMEI HA-GETTA'OT (Heb. לוֹחֲמֵי הַגֶּטָאוֹת; "The Ghetto Fighters"), kibbutz in the northern Coastal Plain of Israel, 3 mi. (5 km.) N. of Acre, affiliated with Ha-Kibbutz ha-Me'uḥad. Loḥamei ha-Getta'ot was founded in 1949 as one of the first villages to be erected in the framework of the comprehensive settlement scheme for Acre Plain and Western Galilee, by a group from Poland composed of survivors of the resistance against the Nazis in Polish and Lithuanian ghettoes, among them Yizḥak (Antek) *Cukierman and Ziviah *Lubetkin. The kibbutz is located near an aqueduct built by Aḥmad Pasha al-Jazzār at the end of the 18th century to lead the *Kabri spring waters to Acre. Farming at Loḥamei ha-Getta'ot is highly intensive and fully irrigated. The kibbutz runs a factory producing condensers

Holocaust Museum at kibbutz Loḥamei Ha-Getta'ot, seen through an arch of the nearby aqueduct. Courtesy Government Press Office, Tel Aviv.

and other electronic equipment. The Ghetto Fighters' House in memory of Yitzḥak *Katznelson, the Holocaust Museum, and an educational center named after Janusz *Korczak are located in Loḥamei ha-Getta'ot. The kibbutz also publishes a research bulletin, *Yedi'ot* (1951–60). At the end of 1969 the population of Loḥamei ha-Getta'ot numbered 341. [E.O.]

LOḤAMEI ḤERUT ISRAEL (Leḥi, or "Stern Group"), armed underground organization in Palestine founded by Avraham *Stern. In June 1940, after the *Irgun Ẓeva'i Le'ummi (IẒL) decided on a truce of underground armed activities during World War II, the Stern group broke away from IẒL. At first it called itself Irgun Ẓeva'i Le'ummi be-Israel and declared a continuation of war against the British, opposed the voluntary enlistment of Jews into the British army, and even attempted to contact representatives of the Axis. This attitude gained it the reputation of a "fifth column" in official circles, and the British Palestine police and secret service were mobilized against it. During January and February 1942 the clashes between members of the Stern group and the British military and civil authorities reached their peak, and the British forces reacted by arresting and killing leading Stern group members. On Feb. 12, 1942, Avraham Stern himself was caught in his hiding-place and was killed on the spot by British police officers. Considerably weakened, the group was on the verge of complete disintegration when some of its detainees managed to escape from prison and regrouped their forces. They then gave themselves the new name of Loḥamei Ḥerut Israel. In early 1944 Leḥi resumed its operations under a triumvirate leadership (Yiẓḥak Shamir, Nathan *Yellin-Mor, and Israel Eldad-Scheib), continuing them with short interruptions until the end of the Mandate in 1948. Members of the group were ordered to be continually armed. Those who were caught admitted in court to being its members, refused to recognize the court's authority, and made political statements. In November 1944 two Leḥi members, Eliahu Ḥakim and Eliahu Bet-Ẓuri assassinated Lord Moyne, British minister of state for the Middle East, in Cairo. They were caught, tried, and hanged in Cairo in March 1945. In July 1945 Leḥi and IẒL agreed to cooperate

THE GRESHAM Life Assurance Society Ltd. COMPETITIVE TERMS FOR ENDOWMENT ASSURANCE PLANS

LATE Edition

JERUSALEM TUESDAY, APRIL 22, 1947

THE PALESTINE POST

PRICE: 15 MILS VOL. XXII. No. 6387

WE ARRANGE SHIPPING SPACE FOR YOU FROM AND TO ALL PARTS AND PORTS OF THE WORLD. ATID NAVIGATION Co. Ltd. HAIFA – JAFFA – TEL AVIV – JERUSALEM

Column One By David Courtney

INDIA is a test case in the fundamental issues of democracy. In its way, it is the greatest experiment in Sovereign rehabilitation ever undertaken. The signs at the moment are not propitious and it looks as if Congress and the Moslem League will be as far apart as ever when, some 14 months from now Britain hands over. The news is still of high feeling, which any day may erupt again into murder and arson: It is the tragedy of this apparently sophisticated age that the road to national rebirth should so often be beset by murder, arson and repression. There have been 60 arrests in Bombay and the prisons of the country must be pretty full; but that is not the end of the protest. Prison room for a good many more will be needed before the year is out. Reports from Bombay, New Delhi and Calcutta make it pretty obvious that the occasion of imminent independence has roused not hopes and pride alone but also the ambitions and cupidity of what can only be described as reactionary and anachronistic element in both the Hindu and Moslem sections of the population. To many of these men the great experiment is seen as a great personal opportunity and their working upon a people illiterate and hungry has been a main cause of the unrest.

IN greater or lesser degree, much the same can be said of other countries aspiring to the sovereign rights of an independent people. As a result, the main issue and the fundamental purity of just causes become obscured; and in their obscurity are weakened against the challenge of imperialism. This is seen very near at hand and can be said of more than half the new states of the Middle East; for these states have some times been built, not upon the historic and spontaneous urge of common people, but on the deals of ambitious men, with ambitious concessioners: the sovereignty of one state after the other in this part of the world is the sovereignty of oil and pipeline.

In India, the problem is complicated beyond anything known among the recent and other nascent autonomies. Since the irrevocable decision of the British Government to resign its power in India in June 1948, the communal rift between the opposing sections of India's vast population, seems rather to have widened than to have narrowed. The official hope that the prospect of early British withdrawal would have brought Congress and the Muslim League nearer to a working agreement, has not been ful-

CONDEMNED MEN COMMIT SUICIDE
BARAZANI AND FEINSTEIN BLOW SELVES UP ON EVE OF HANGING

Moshe Barazani and Meir Feinstein committed suicide at the Jerusalem Central Prison last night while preparations were being made to carry out their death sentences.

They apparently obtained a small quantity of high explosives which they placed against their chests and detonated at 11.40 p.m. by some means not yet known. There were two simultaneous explosions which killed them instantly, but caused slight damage to the cell in which they were both kept, but not to the rest of the building. An inquiry is being held.

An official statement announced that the two men were due to be executed today (April 22).

The Prison Chaplain, Rabbi Jacob Goldman, had been summoned to the prison at 9.15 last night, and curfew was enforced at 10 o'clock.

The two men's sentences were confirmed by the G.O.C. last Thursday.

Barazani and Feinstein had earlier in the day been visited by their parents who persuaded them to petition the High Commissioner to commute their sentences. They agreed to sign appeals.

Last Minute Plea

An appeal had been sent to His Excellency by Prof. Chaim Weizmann. A last-minute plea was also made by the Chief Rabbi, Dr. I. H. Herzog, who telephoned to the A.D.C. to the High Commissioner last night and asked him to convey to His Excellency his urgent appeal for reprieves.

Meir Feinstein, whose family claimed that he was under 18, but whose age was stated to be at least 21 by R.A.M.C. specialists, was sentenced by the Jerusalem Military Court on April 3 for taking part in the blowing up of the Jerusalem Railway Station last October. Barzani, who was 21, was sentenced to death by the same court on March 17 after a 90-minute trial for carrying a hand grenade in Jerusalem a week before.

Feinstein, whose left arm was amputated above the elbow after he had been found badly hurt following the attack on the station sat through an eight-day trial reading books and papers. Daniel Azulai was sentenced to death with him, but this sentence was commuted to life imprisonment last Thursday. Bouton and Horowitz, tried at the same time, were acquitted of all charges.

Stern Gang Member

Barazani, who declared in court that he was a member of the Stern Gang, was arrested near the Middle East H.Q. of the Royal Army Pay Corps (the Syrian Orphanage). The Military Prosecutor said that the Military Commander of the Hippo Area, Brig. E.F. Davies, passed the spot frequently on his way to and from the area. Sentence was passed 16 minutes before the ending of Martial Law.

OFFICIAL COMMUNIQUE No. 116

In view of statements in the Press that the right of appeal from the judgment of a Military Court has been taken away by recent legislation, it appears desirable to point out that this right has not existed since 1937 when Military Courts were first established. The amendments made to the relevant Regulation in 1945 and last week do not do more than expand the provisions of Regulation 30 so as to secure that the original intention is fully covered.

MILITARY CARS ATTACKED

Hurled by the blast of hand-grenades in Nebi Samuel Road in Jerusalem yesterday morning, this jeep smashed into the metal shutters of a greengrocer's stall in the market. (Mendelsohn Photo)

Palestine Post Staff

Mines, grenades and automatic weapons were used in three attacks on military vehicles yesterday. Three soldiers and a civilian were injured.

Tel Aviv was cordoned off early in the evening, and the feeling was general that a curfew was imminent. None had been declared by midnight, however.

Rocked by two hand-grenades suddenly thrown at them in Nebi Samuel Road, Jerusalem, in the morning, two jeeps, each manned by two soldiers, continued to roll for a few yards until automatic fire was directed against them. With his wind-screen shattered by bullets, the driver of the first jeep lost control and the vehicle careered off the road, jumped the pavement and smashed into the closed metal shutters of a greengrocer's stall in the Bokharan Market.

and from the ropes, and tracked to Aliyah Street, where the trail was lost."

There were no casualties when a land-mine exploded under a military vehicle on the Ramleh-Aqir road about two miles from Ramleh at 7 o'clock yesterday morning. The truck was slightly damaged. Another mine harmlessly exploded three hours later on the same road.

About 30 minutes later, the last vehicle of a military convoy travelling toward Haifa was blown up by a road-mine north of Hadera. The driver of the truck, which was completely burnt out, escaped with slight injuries. Two men are reported to have been detained following the incident.

Checking identity cards in Petah Tikva shortly before midnight on Sunday, a police patrol opened fire on a 15-cwt. pick-up which failed to

Refugees Strike CYPRUS FAST CONTINUES

By SHABE GLUEBENLIAN, Palestine Post Correspondent

NICOSIA, Monday. — Officials at the Caraolos Camp this evening confirmed that the hunger strike, which is still continuing after more than 72 hours, is being observed by all the refugees, with the exception of the latest batch who arrived here from the Theodor Herzl.

Asked whether "all the immigrants" included the children also, the authorities stated that they did not know.

The body of Moshe Lehrer, the refugee who was shot on Friday, was buried this afternoon at the Margo cemetery, Rabbi Hellpern conducting the service. It was officially announced that 75 of the Caraolos Camp detainees were allowed to attend the funeral.

Reports from the camps indicate that the "Children's Village" at Xylotymbou Camp has not joined the hunger strike, although the children in Caraolos Camp are reported to be observing it. At the same time, as the military are not being allowed into the camps, the food situation among the children at Xylotymbou is stated to be acute, and welfare workers are desperately trying to cope with the situation. Nursing mothers were previously supplied with milk from the children's rations, but these are now exhausted and several cases have been reported of mothers' milk drying up.

No Hospital Cases

Many of the refugees in the camps fainted in the summer heat today, but none has asked to be transferred to hospital.

The extreme reticence on the part of the authorities here was today deplored in the Cyprus, English-language, daily newspaper. Commenting on the fact that journalists were being refused permission to visit the camps, the paper added:

"The authorities apparently consider that they can dispose of the matter with a few sparsely-worded communiques."

An appeal was addressed to the fasting detainees by the Vaad Leumi Executive last night urging them to end their hunger strike.

"The entire Yishuv is with you in your struggle and your hope," the message ran. "It regards you as its sons. The closed gates will yet open."

It was reported in Jerusalem yesterday afternoon that the Chief Rabbi, Dr. I. H. Herzog, had cabled the refugees in the Cyprus camps, requesting them to end their hunger strike.

Higher Pay for U.S.

BIG FOUR MAKE NO PROGRESS
Both Normal, Secret Sessions Fruitless

By SYLVAIN MANGEOT, Reuters Diplomatic Correspondent

MOSCOW, Monday. — The Foreign Ministers, during a two hour meeting this morning failed to make any headway on action to be taken on the report of the special four power Financial Commission which they appointed last December in New York, to investigate the financial position and prospects of the Trieste Free Territory.

Since the Commission submitted its report on February 27, three new documents have been added for consideration.

They recommend that: the commission's report be sent to the Security Council for action and early consideration by the Governor of Free Trieste; that the attention of the U.N. be drawn to the possibility of foreign exchange deficit in the free territory during the period between July and September this year, (estimated at around 5,000,000 dollars); that the Foreign Ministers recommend that the U.N. provide assistance up to this sum, if a request for external assistance is received from Trieste.

M. Molotov resisted all these proposals, which were supported by Britain, and it was finally resolved that the disagreed points in the Commission's report, together with the Italian and Yugoslav comments and the British proposals, be referred to the Deputies for consideration.

Yugoslavia has no Food

Mr. Bevin said earlier that the Soviet delegate to the Commission had reported that a substantial part of Trieste's food requirements could be met from Yugoslavia against purchases of industrial products from Trieste. Yugoslavia herself, he said, had to seek aid from UNRRA, the U.S. and Britain. There was no doubt that Yugoslavia was no longer in a position to guarantee food deliveries, and Mr. Bevin declared that the Foreign Ministers must not gamble on feeding Trieste, whose integrity and independence were assured by the Security Council. Both the Italians and Yugoslavs recognized the possibility of a need for outside assistance during the early months, he added.

This afternoon the Ministers unexpectedly went into closed session after a 100-minute discussion of points of the Austrian treaty.

The closed session broke up at nine o'clock tonight with no announcement on any possible progress made.

The Ministers will meet again at 11 o'clock tomorrow morning, in a normal open session. The deputies will also meet in the morning to consider the report of the Trieste Commission which was handed to them by the Ministers today.

AUSTRIAN DEPUTIES MAKE PROGRESS

MOSCOW, Monday (Reuter). — The Big Four Deputies for Austria made considerable progress today, reaching agreement on several important questions, among them the withdrawal of Allied troops from Austria.

Clause 36 (Restitutions to be made by Austria) and part of Clause 45 (Austrian Property on U.N. Territory) were also satisfactorily settled.

Regarding the latter item, "Allied and associated powers declare their intention to return Austrian property, legal rights and interests in the shape in which they at the present time exist in their territories," it is laid down. In cases where such property rights or interests had been liquidated, disposed of or realized in other ways, the income accrued from their liquidation is to be returned to Austria.

FIRST FIGURES ON GERMAN ELECTIONS

BADEN BADEN, Monday. — The first unofficial figures on the allocation of seats in the newly elected "Landtag" in the British zone of Germany put the Christian Democrats in the Rhine-Westphalia district ahead of both the Socialists and Communists with 91 seats to their respective 64 and 23 seats.

In Lower Saxony, the Socialists are ahead with 66 seats with the Christian Democrats a late second, with only 31. The Communists there ran last, after both the small Moderate and Liberal parties, and won only 8 seats.

In Schleswig-Holstein, too, the Socialists are ahead, with 44 seats, exactly double the number won by the Christian Democrats.

These figures put the Socialists ahead in the over-all picture with 174 seats to 144 for the Christian Democrats and 31 for the Communists.

(See more on Page 4)

New Danish King Proclaimed

COPENHAGEN, Monday (Reuter). — Denmark's new King, Frederick IX, was proclaimed by the Prime Minister at four o'clock this afternoon from the balcony of Chris-

Call to Youth PRINCESS BROADCASTS

CAPETOWN, Monday (Reuter). — Princess Elizabeth, broadcasting to the Empire tonight on the occasion of her 21st birthday, urged all young men and women of her own age not to be daunted by the anxieties and hardships the war has left behind.

The Princess, who with her father, mother and sister has just completed a 10,000-mile tour of South Africa, hinted that she may make more journeys to other parts of the Empire. "There are homes ready to welcome us in every continent of the earth," she said. "Before I am much older, I hope I shall come to know many of them."

To the young men and women of her own age she said: "Now that we are reaching manhood and womanhood, it is surely a great joy for us to think we shall be able to take some of the burdens off the shoulders of our elders, who have worked and suffered to protect our childhood.

"We know that we cheerfully undertook hardships during the war to pay for the high honour of standing alone seven years ago in the defence of the world's liberty," the Princess declared. "Let us now say with Rupert Brooke:

Now God be Thanked who has Matched
Us with this Hour.

"I declare before you that my whole life shall be dedicated to you and to the service of our great Imperial Family, to which we all belong, but I shall not have the strength to carry out this resolution alone, unless you work in it with me, as I now invite you to do," she concluded. "I know your support will unfailingly be given. God help me to make good my vow."

Merlin Sought in Paris For Whitehall Bomb

By GEORGE LICHTHEIM, Palestine Post Correspondent

LONDON, Monday. — The responsibility for last week's abortive bomb attempt in Dover House has now been fixed by the authorities on one Samuel Merlin, described as an emissary of the I.Z.L. political branch abroad.

The "Daily Herald," which today gives prominence to this story, also reports that Merlin "has vanished from the Hotel Lutetia, his Paris headquarters." Merlin is also known as a member of the "Bergson Group" of New York.

This is only one of a number of circumstantial reports surrounding the Colonial Office bomb affair, which during the past week have pointed to Pa-

Issue of *The Palestine Post* of April 22, 1947, reporting the suicide of Moshe Barazani, a member of Loḥamei Ḥerut Israel, and Meir Feinstein, a member of Irgun Ẓeva'i Leumi. Jerusalem, J.N.U.L.

in their struggle against the British, and in November 1945 Leḥi joined the Haganah and IẒL in the Hebrew Resistance Movement (Heb. Tenu'at ha-Meri ha-Ivri), which existed for nine months. During and after this period, Leḥi carried out sabotage operations and armed attacks on military objectives and government installations (army camps, airfields, police stations, railway trains), while also attacking individual members of the British police and army and organizing expropriations to secure funds. Its clandestine radio station waged a continual propaganda campaign, and posters and declarations were distributed.

In April 1947 Leḥi began sabotage operations outside Palestine, mailing bombs to British statesmen. The Mandatory authorities reacted by making administrative arrests of anyone suspected of belonging to or helping Leḥi and by passing severe sentences on those caught in operations or even merely carrying arms. On March 17, 1947, Moshe Barazani was sentenced to death for having a hand grenade in his possession. Together with Meir Feinstein, a member of IẒL, Barazani blew himself up in the Jerusalem prison before the sentence could be carried out. The history of Leḥi was marked by frequent prison breaks and escapes from arrest in Palestine (Mazraʿa, Latrun, Jerusalem, Acre, Athlit) and from the countries of forced exile (Eritrea, Sudan, and Kenya). After the United Nations resolution on the partition of Palestine in November 1947, Leḥi participated in attacks on Arab regular and irregular forces, including the attack on the village of Deir Yāsīn near Jerusalem, which they captured together with IẒL (April 9, 1948).

On May 29, 1948, two weeks after the establishment of the State of Israel, members of Leḥi joined the Israel army. In Jerusalem, however, they continued to fight separately for a time. After the assassination of the U.N. mediator, Count Folke *Bernadotte, in Jerusalem on Sept. 17, 1948, an act which a group of Leḥi members were suspected of perpetrating, the Israel authorities enforced the final disbanding of Leḥi in Jerusalem. After its leading members were arrested and investigated for a short period, Leḥi ceased to exist. Its leaders took part in the elections to the First Knesset as the Fighters' List and Nathan Yellin-Mor was elected as representative. Memorial meetings in the memory of Avraham Stern are held annually by an association of Leḥi members.

Bibliography: *Loḥamei Ḥerut Yisrael*, 2 vols. (1959); J. Banai (Mazal), *Ḥayyalim Almonim* (1958); G. Cohen, *Sippurah shel Loḥemet* (1962); I. Scheib (Eldad), *Ma'aser Rishon* (1950); D. Niv, *Ma'arkhot ha-Irgun ha-Ẓeva'i ha-Le'ummi*, 3 (1967); Y. Bauer, *Diplomacy and Resistance* (1970). [D.N.]

°**LOISY, ALFRED FIRMIN** (1857–1940), French biblical commentator and theologian. Born in Ambrières (Haute-Marne), Loisy was ordained as a Catholic priest in 1879. He studied at the Institut Catholique de Paris, where he later lectured in Hebrew and exegesis. He was dismissed in 1893 on the order of the pope for the publication of his article "La Question biblique et l'inspiration des Ecritures," which took a view opposed to the traditional teaching of the Church. His special approach to biblical research and interpretation aroused the suspicion of the Catholic Church authorities, who also condemned his essay *La religion d'Israël* (1900; *The Religion of Israel*, 1910). In 1902 he published *L'Evangile et l'Eglise* (1902; *The Gospel and the Church*, 1903) which, though intended as a Catholic answer to the work of Adolph von Harnack, was unacceptable to the Church. The work was favorably received throughout Europe, but was placed on the Church Index of forbidden books. From 1901 onward he taught the history of the Christian religion at the Ecole des Hautes Etudes Pratiques. Loisy's polemics with the Church attracted considerable attention in Europe, especially after he was excommunicated in 1908. From 1909 to 1932 he was professor of Church history at the Collège de France.

Loisy is considered the leading exponent of biblical "modernism" and of the critical approach in the study of the New Testament and the problems of the Christian faith. He denied the supernatural inspiration of the Bible and based his research on a critical study of the sources and philological analysis. After World War I he became active in a new field of religious meditation, which paved the way for a progressive and humanistic sociology of religion. The majority of his works were banned by the papal orders of 1932 and 1938. Loisy founded and directed the bimonthly *Revue de l'enseignement biblique* until 1894, and from 1896 to 1922 edited the *Revue d'histoire et de littérature religieuse*. The most important of his works are: *Histoire du Canon de l'Ancien Testament* (1890); *Les Evangiles synoptiques* (2 vols., 1907–08); *Les origines du Nouveau Testament* (1936; *The Origins of the New Testament*, 1950); and *Les mystères païens et le mystère chrétien* (1919, 1930²).

Bibliography: M. Lepin, *Les Théories de M. Loisy: Exposé et Critique* (1909); N. Y. Lagrange, *A. Loisy et le Modernisme* (1932); Petre, in: *The Hilbert Journal*, 39 (1940), 5–14; F. Heiber, *Der Vater des Katholischen Modernismus: A. Loisy* (1947); A. Moutin, *La question biblique au XIX siècle* (1902); A. Détrez, *L'Abbé Loisy* . . . (1909), includes bibliography. [Z.B.]

LOMBARDY, region of N. *Italy; the political and physical borders, in which *Mantua also would be included, have not always coincided. References to Jews in Lombardy (*Milan) date to the fourth century; subsequently there is only slight evidence down to the very end of the 12th century, when Jews are found engaged in moneylending. In 1225 the Jews were expelled from *Pavia and *Cremona; in 1278 they began to be harassed by the conversionist sermons of the *Dominicans. Before the end of the 13th century, Jews of German origin arrived in Lombardy and engaged in moneylending, mainly settling in Cremona as the Jews were expelled from Milan in 1320. In the 14th century and during the first decades of the 15th, small communities were constituted in *Pavia, *Vicenza, and *Como. In general, however, the Jewish population in the region remained small. Although Jews were accorded favorable treatment by the Visconti and Sforza dukes of Milan, the populace in general remained hostile.

The Cremona community remained important in the 16th century; its talmudic academy and printing establishment were famous. Further groups of Jews were by now settled in *Alessandria and *Lodi. In 1452, Pope Nicholas V authorized Duke Francesco Sforza to maintain their existing privileges on condition that the restrictive ecclesiastical regulations were strictly enforced. However, the Jews were compelled to maintain loan banks in every town in Lombardy, even where they incurred losses, and to pay the government an exceptionally heavy annual tax. Even after the duchy of Milan passed under Spanish rule in 1535, the Jews there continued to have their residential permit renewed about every ten years, although they were not permitted to reside permanently in Milan itself. In 1565, Philip II of Spain decided to expel the Jews from the duchy. After lengthy negotiations in Madrid, permission was given for them to remain until 1597, when the 900 Jewish residents had to leave. Two families were allowed to remain in each of the three towns of Cremona, Lodi, and Alessandria. In the course of time, the Jews disappeared from the first two, but in Alessandria the Jewish population had increased to 230 by 1684. After Lombardy passed to Austria in 1713 a few Jews again settled in the region. Their number increased after 1800, and reached 500 by the middle of the 19th century, mainly concentrated in Milan.

After the incorporation of Lombardy in the Kingdom of Italy in 1859–61, and the commercial and industrial transformation of the region which followed, there was a considerable increase in the Jewish population. Former members of now disintegrating small Italian communities, as well as industrialists from Germany and Austria, settled in Lombardy. In the middle of the present century, there was Jewish immigration from Germany and after 1947 from Libya, Egypt, and Iraq. The Jewish population numbered 3,500 in 1901 (almost all living in Milan), and 11,000 in 1938. Reduced during the Holocaust, it numbered 8,500 in 1966.

Bibliography: Roth, Italy, index; Milano, Italia, index, s.v. *Lombardia;* Milano, Bibliotheca, index; Rota, in: *Bollettino della società parese di storia patria,* 4 (1906), 349–82; Levi Minzi, in: *Israel* (Feb. 11, 1932); Scharf, in: RMI, 2 (1926/27), 33–49.

[A.Mil.]

LOMBROSO, CESARE (1835–1909), Italian physician and criminologist. Born in Verona, Lombroso took degrees in medicine and surgery. While at the University of Vienna he studied psychology and psychiatry, as well as the anatomy and physiology of the brain. For 30 years he advocated his revolutionary theories of criminology. During his four years of army service he made systematic measurements of physical differences among soldiers from various regions of Italy, and of differences between well-disciplined and aggressive or criminal soldiers. He concluded that certain innate physical characteristics are connected with social behavior. His conception of the "born criminal" resulted from his observations, physical measurement, and comparisons of mentally ill and sane people, and of criminals and law-abiding citizens. All men, including the "born criminal," are born with certain faculties, both mental and physical, which decisively influence their behavior. Lombroso published his theory, asserting that the "true criminal" was atavistic, in his controversial *L'Uomo delinquente* ("The Criminal Man," 1876). The first edition of *L'Uomo delinquente* comprised 252 pages, the fifth 1,203 pages in three volumes. It was in 1876 that Lombroso became professor of legal medicine and public hygiene at Turin University, which appointed him professor of psychiatry in 1896, and ten years later created a chair in criminal anthropology for him.

Cesare Lombroso, Italian physician and criminologist. From G. Simson, *Fuenf Kaempfer fuer Gerechtigkeit,* Munich, 1951.

While Lombroso gradually came to admit the existence of acquired criminogenic factors, pathological or environmental, he continued to claim that the true criminal was a subspecies of man of an atavistic origin. In his later period he gave more attention to environmental factors as causes of crime, and developed an inclusive typology of the various forms of crime which recognized that a great deal of criminality is not organic or endogenous but a product of diverse exogenous and environmental factors. In the field of penology Lombroso supported such reformist ideas as the compensation of the victims of crime from the prison work of the malefactor. Despite his views on inherited delinquency he was against capital punishment, favoring the rehabilitation of the criminal by a "symbiosis" with his society, whereby the latter would make constructive use of the evildoer and his work potential.

Although the idea of the "born criminal" is no longer accepted, Lombroso remains an important figure in the history of the behavioral sciences. Scholars honor him as a pioneer, and even his critics credit him with shifting the emphasis in criminology from the crime itself to the criminal and his origins.

A friend of Max *Nordau he had an interest in Zionism and espoused this doctrine in 1900. In 1894, he published a monograph on anti-Semitism in which he analyzed the manifestations of atavism in anti-Semites and their folly.

Lombroso published a considerable number of books and articles of which only a few have been translated. His only important book translated into English is *Crime, Its Causes and Conditions* (1911).

Bibliography: H. Mannheim, in: *Sociological Review,* 28 (1936), 31–49; Wolfgang, in H. Mannheim (ed.), *Pioneers in Criminology* (1960), 168–227; Vervaeck, in: *Archives de l'anthropologie criminelle,* 25 (1910), 561–83.

[Z.H./E.F.]

LOMZA (Pol. **Łomża;** Rus. **Lomzha;** Yid. **Lomzhe**), town in N. E. Poland. In 1556 the Jews were compelled to leave after the privilege *de non tolerandis Judaeis* was granted to the town, giving it the right to exclude Jews. They did not return there until after the Congress of Vienna (1815). Once their presence was authorized, the number of Jews increased, to 737 in 1826, 2,574 in 1852, 9,244 (54.8% of the total population) in 1897, and 11,088 in 1915 (including 1,500 refugees from the surrounding towns). The numbers later declined to 9,131 (70.8%) in 1929, and 8,912 (56.7%) in 1931. During the 19th century they were integrated in the life of the country and took an active part in the Polish uprising of 1863. They played a major role in the economic life of Lomza, owned factories, and were the leading wholesalers in the grain and timber trade. Between the two world wars, Jews played an important part in the municipal administration. In the municipal elections of 1919, and again in 1926, they won half the seats. After this, however, as a result of the Polish policy of restricting Jewish influence in the town, the number of seats allocated to the Jews was limited. In 1921 there were 498 Jewish workshops in Lomza, 295 of them with salaried employees. During this period the Jews engaged in various crafts, but they were ousted from these by the anti-Semitic measures introduced by the Polish government. As a result of the economic crisis and the anti-Jewish *boycott imposed by the anti-Semitic trade unions and parties, the Jews were greatly impoverished, and many left Lomza. The community administration, which maintained social and educational institutions, was unstable after World War I. Following the elections to the community administration in 1939, interparty dissensions brought its activities to a complete standstill, and the government subsequently appointed an official commissioner to take charge of its affairs.

Educational institutions, such as the *talmudei torah* and the *ḥadarim,* had already been established in Lomza during the 19th century. Under independent Poland, pressure was exerted on the Jews to send their children to the Polish government schools. A Jewish-Polish secondary school had already been established in 1916. The Great Yeshivah,

Mastheads of the Jewish papers published in Lomza. From *Sefer Zikkaron li-Kehillat Lomza,* Tel Aviv, 1952.

founded in 1883 by R. Eliezer Szuliawicz, was transferred to Ereẓ Israel (Petaḥ Tikvah) in 1926, where it became known as Yeshivat Lomza. Jewish parties active in Lomza included *Agudat Israel, the *Bund, and the Zionist organizations. These published regular and occasional periodicals, including the *Lomzher Shtime, Lomzher Veker,* and *Lomzher Lebn* in Yiddish and others in Polish. The Great Bet Ha-Midrash was erected during the early 1840s and the Great Synagogue in 1880. The last rabbis of Lomza were Aaron Bakst and Moses Shatzkes. [SH.L.K.]

Holocaust Period. On the outbreak of World War II there were about 11,000 Jews in Lomza. In September 1939 the Red Army entered the city. With the outbreak of the German-Soviet war, the Germans occupied the town on June 24, 1941, and established the ghetto on Aug. 12, 1941. On September 17 a large-scale *Aktion* took place and 3,000 Jews were killed. On Nov. 2, 1942, the deportations to *Zambrow camp began, and between Jan. 14 and Jan. 18, 1943 the inmates of Zambrow camp were deported to *Auschwitz. Thousands of Jews were brought out of the city and killed in the woods of Galczyn near Lomza. After the war, the Jewish community of Lomza was not reconstituted. Organizations of former residents of Lomza are active in Israel, France, Australia, and the United States. [ED.]

Bibliography: *Sefer Zikkaron le-Kehillat Lomza* (1952).

LONDON, capital of *England and seat of what has always been the largest Jewish community in the country.

Medieval Period. There is no reliable evidence for the presence of Jews in London until after the close of the Saxon period. After the Norman Conquest of 1066, a few Jews, attracted by the economic opportunities that now offered themselves, came over from the adjacent areas of the continent (in the first instance presumably from the duchy of *Normandy, including *Rouen) and established themselves in London. The earliest recorded mention of the London community dates from the reign of William Rufus (1087–1100), who appears to have favored the Jews to some extent. In his reign, a religious *disputation took place at Westminster between the abbot and a Jew from Mainz who did business with the abbey. A Jewish quarter *(vicus Judaeorum)* is first mentioned in the *Terrier* of St. Paul's (c. 1128). In 1130 the Jews of London were accused of killing a sick man—possibly some sort of *blood libel—and were forced to pay the then enormous fine of £2,000. Intellectual life in the period was sufficiently flourishing to attract a visit from Abraham *ibn Ezra, who wrote his *Iggeret ha-Shabbat* and his *Yesod Mora* in London in 1158. Until 1177 the relative importance of the community was so great that its cemetery served the whole of Anglo-Jewry.

During the reign of Henry II (1154–1189), the community flourished and was augmented by fresh arrivals from abroad. The anti-Jewish riots which broke out at the coronation of Richard I (Sept. 3, 1189) began at Westminster and soon spread to London, where the Jewish quarter was set afire and 30 persons died—including the tosafist R. *Jacob of Orleans. The community soon recovered, however, and in 1194 contributed approximately one quarter to the levy raised by the Jews of the country toward the king's ransom. The reorganization which was then undertaken by the Ordinance of the Jewry confirmed London as the administrative center for the communities of the country. The first *archpresbyter of the Jews of England under the new system was Jacob of London. Anti-Jewish feeling again manifested itself in London during the reign of John (1199–1216) who rebuked the mayor on that account. The baronial opposition, both in his reign and in that of his son Henry III (1216–72), considered the Jews, not without justification, to be royal financial instruments and maltreat-

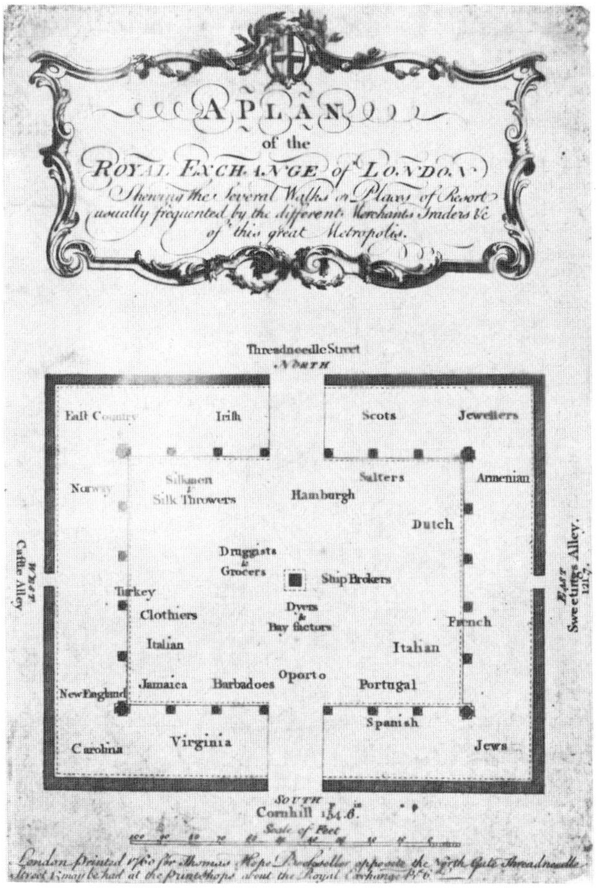

Figure 1. Plan of London's Royal Exchange in 1760, showing the places occupied by various categories of merchants and traders. The Jews are in the southeast corner of the building.

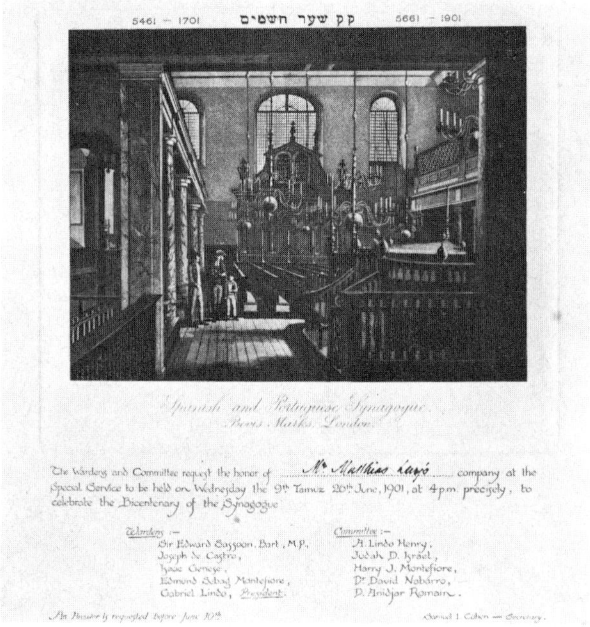

Figure 2. Invitation to the bicentenary service of the Spanish and Portuguese Synagogue in Bevis Marks, 1901, incorporating an aquatint of the synagogue executed in 1817. Cecil Roth Collection.

ed them accordingly. There was a baronial attack on London Jewry in 1215.

During the period of maladministration under Henry III, the Jews of London, with those of the rest of the country, were oppressed and mulcted of enormous sums. The climax came in 1244 when it was alleged that some gashes found on the body of a dead child constituted Hebrew characters and the Jews were accused of ritual murder. This resulted in a savage punitive levy on the Jews of the realm to the amount of 60,000 marks. On the outbreak of the Barons' War (1263–65), they suffered greatly at the hands of the insurgents under Simon de Montfort. During Easter week 1263, as the result of a trivial dispute between a Jew and a citizen concerning interest on a debt, the Jewry was sacked and several of its inhabitants killed. Later, on hearing a report that the Jews had manufactured Greek fire for the royal troops, Simon de Montfort returned to London and put the Jewry systematically to the sword. In 1266, another attack was made by the so-called "disinherited knights" on the remnants of the community, who sought refuge in the Tower of London.

The Jews of London profited from the period of pacification which followed the war. Edward I's *Statutum de Judaismo* of 1275, however, which prohibited Jewish moneylending, inevitably drove some into dishonest ways of making a living. In 1278 a number of London Jews were included in the 680 from all over the country who were imprisoned in the Tower of London on the charge of clipping the coinage. Nearly 300 are said to have been hanged (though this figure has been doubted). In the meantime, theological odium against the London Jews had been increasing. In 1232 Henry III confiscated their principal synagogue on the pretext that the chanting could be heard in a neighboring church. In the same year he founded the London *Domus Conversorum to encourage conversions. A further ritual murder accusation was followed by a civic order restricting the Jews henceforth to houses in the Jewry (1281). In 1283 the bishop of London ordered all the synagogues in his diocese to be closed, only one being subsequently reopened. Finally, in 1290, the Jews were expelled from England and the London community ceased to exist.

The number of Jews in London in the Middle Ages probably did not exceed 500, though contemporary Jewish writers speak of 2,000 households. The original Jewish quarter, which contained a number of strong stone houses, was situated in and near what is still known as the Old Jewry. In the 12th century, the Jews began to give up their houses here and to move a little distance westward, where the Church of St. Laurence Jewry commemorates their residence. The cemetery was in what is now known as Jewin Street and the surrounding area. Prominent medieval London scholars included Joseph b. Jacob, known as "Rubi Gotsce" (fl. 1130–1160), the host of Abraham ibn Ezra and the outstanding English Jew of his day, *Jacob b. Judah, of London (late 13th century), author of *Ez Ḥayyim*, R. Moses of London (d. 1268), grammarian and halakhist, and his son the illustrious *Elijah Menahem of London (d. 1284), who also enjoyed considerable repute as a physician.

Middle Period. The Domus Conversorum, established by Henry III in 1232, housed nearly 100 converts at the period of the expulsion, and never remained entirely empty in subsequent years. There was a constant, though slender, stream to London of poor foreign Jews who qualified for emoluments by the formal adoption of Christianity. In addition, a few isolated Jews visited London without being baptized: for example, the physicians Elias b. Sabbetai (Sabot) of Bologna, who came in 1410 with ten followers to attend Henry IV, and Master Samson de Mirabeau who attended the wife of Richard Whittington, mayor of London, in 1409. After the expulsions from Spain and Portugal, a few Marrano refugees settled in London. At the close of the reign of Henry VIII, the crypto-Jewish community comprised some 37 householders, and religious services were held in the house of one Alves Lopes to whom newly arrived fugitives would come for assistance and advice. In 1542, the group was disturbed in consequence of disclosures made during proceedings against Marrano fugitives on the continent. It was largely dispersed as a result of the Catholic reaction in the reign of Mary. Under Elizabeth, however, it attained again significant proportions. One of its leading members was Roderigo *Lopez, the queen's physician. When an envoy of Alvaro Mendes (Solomon *Abenaes), duke of Mytilene, was in London on an official mission in 1592, services were held at his house. Toward the end of the century, the importance of the secret community diminished, and in 1609 the Portuguese merchants living in London, who were suspected of Judaizing, were again expelled.

Figure 3. Silver salver presented to the lord mayor by the elders of the Spanish and Portuguese Synagogue, 1702. London, Jewish Museum. Photo Warburg Institute.

Figure 4. Tombstone in London's first Ashkenazi cemetery, recording the burial of the early leaders of the community, headed by Benjamin Levy, who purchased the ground in 1696.

Resettlement Period. Nevertheless, when in 1632 the Marrano community of Rouen was temporarily broken up, some fugitives, the most important being Antonio Fernandez *Carvajal, found a home in London. Other Marrano settlers went directly from Spain and Portugal. Thus, when *Manasseh Ben Israel went to England in 1655, there was already established a secret community numbering several families. Though the Whitehall Conference convened by Oliver *Cromwell in December 1655 proved abortive, they were emboldened to begin organizing their religious life on a more formal basis. A petition was presented to Cromwell asking for protection (March 1656). A house was rented and adapted for use as a synagogue in the following December. A few months later, a piece of ground was acquired for use as a cemetery. After Cromwell's death various attempts were made to procure the suppression of the community. Charles II, however, intervened in its favor, and it henceforth enjoyed de facto recognition. The original synagogue, in Creechurch Lane, was enlarged and remodeled in 1674, and in 1701 a new place of worship in Bevis Marks—still one of the architectural monuments of the city—was erected.

As its spiritual leaders, the newly established community appointed a succession of foreign scholars. They were: Jacob *Sasportas (1664–65), who fled because of the great plague of London, in which several members of his flock perished, Joshua da *Silva (1670–79), Jacob *Abendana (1681–85), Solomon *Aylion (1689–1701), and David *Nieto (1701–28). The congregation was continually reinforced by fresh Marrano refugees from Spain and Portugal. After the accession of William of Orange (1689), there was a considerable influx of Spanish and Portuguese Jews from Holland. The majority of the communal magnates at this time were brokers, importers, and wholesale merchants, with a sprinkling of physicians. In the course of the reorganization of the Royal Exchange in 1697, it was arranged to admit 12 Jews—the so-called "Jew brokers" who remained a feature of the City of London until the beginning of the 19th century. In order to secure the favor of the lord mayor, a purse containing 50 guineas was presented to him each year on a valuable piece of plate by the elders of the congregation.

Meanwhile, the original Sephardi settlers had been followed by Ashkenazim who arrived for the most part via Amsterdam or Hamburg. They organized their own congregation around 1690, and in 1696 a burial ground for their use was purchased by the wealthy Benjamin *Levy. The first rabbi of the congregation, Judah Loeb b. Ephraim Anschel ha-Kohen, subsequently of Rotterdam, left as a result of internal dissensions. His place was taken, first by R. Aaron b. Moses the Scribe, of Dublin, and then by R. Uri Phoebus b. Naphtali Hirsch, known as Aaron *Hart. The latter's brother, Moses Hart, was the maecenas of the community. In 1722 he reconstructed the synagogue in Duke's Place. Further enlargement and reconstruction took place in 1766 and in 1790. In 1706 a secession had taken place in the Ashkenazi community, headed by Mordecai b. Moses of Hamburg, called Marcus Moses (a son-in-law of Glueckel von Hameln). This led to the organization of a rival body, which constructed its own synagogue (known as the Hambro' Synagogue) in 1726. The historic synagogal organization of the metropolis was completed in 1761, when another rival body, still called the New Synagogue, came into existence.

The primacy of the parent body (by now known as the Great Synagogue) was, however, generally recognized—not only by the other Ashkenazi communities in London, but also by those which had by now sprung up elsewhere in the country. R. Aaron Hart was followed in the rabbinate by R. Hirschell *Levin, known in England as Hart Lyon (1758–64), R. David Tevele *Schiff (1765–91), R. Moses Myers (who also officiated at the New Synagogue (1792–1802), and R. Solomon *Hirschell, son of Hart Lyon (1802–42), who was the first formally recognized chief rabbi of the Ashkenazi communities of the whole of England. The Ashkenazim were by now the most numerous and influential element in the London Jewish population. The lower classes, however, mainly peddlers and dealers in old clothes, who were mostly recently arrived immigrants, were not greatly esteemed. P. Colquhoun, in his *Treatise on the Police of the Metropolis* (1800), asserted that they were responsible for a disproportionate amount of petty crime.

The 19th century was a period of expansion and reorganization. The first synagogue outside the City (later the Western Synagogue) had been organized in Westminster around 1761. The Borough Synagogue, on the south side of the river, owed its origin to a *minyan* begun about the middle of the 18th century. The board for *sheḥitah*, in which Sephardim and Ashkenazim cooperated, was organized through the advocacy of Baron Lyon de Symons in 1792–1804.

As early as 1760, the Sephardi community admitted representatives of the Ashkenazim to their committee of *deputados*, which was appointed from time to time to represent the community vis-à-vis the government. This ultimately developed into the *Board of Deputies of British Jews, on which, until 1838, only the London communities were represented. The old *talmud torah* of the Ashkenazi community, established in 1732 and placed on a broader basis in 1788, was reorganized in 1817 as the Jews' Free School, originally intended to meet the menace presented

Figure 5. Monmouth Street, a hub of London's old clothes trade in the 19th century, as depicted by the caricaturist George Cruikshank. Cecil Roth Collection. Photo David Harris, Jerusalem.

Figure 6. Cooking class at the Jews' Free School, 1902. Founded in 1817, the school served the East End community until World War II. Courtesy J.F.S., London.

Figure 7. Interior of the Great Synagogue, Duke's Place. Drawn and engraved by Pugin and Rowlandson; aquatint by Sutherland, 1809. Cecil Roth Collection.

ספר
לחם עוני
פי׳ על הגדה של פסח
כתר ענ״א עניותא אזלא עני המהפך
בתרא תפוכי מסרתא פשט
את ידו יד כהה לדקדק עם חס״רין
דקדוקי עניות אעיל ד״ך ואפיק
ש״ח אסמולהכי יאה עניותא
לחם עוני
בשמו ובמעשיו
ובמקומו
מלתא דאתיא מק״ל וחו״מר קל שבקלי׳
זנב לשועלים האיש הלוה גברא
הוא דלא חזי חלא ריחיה וטעמיה זגין וחרצן:
הצעיר רפאל חסאן
ואת עמ״לנו אלו הכנים כל אחד ואחד
לפי מנהגו ספרדים ואשכנזים
סים לפי מהללו ילד״קו ויהללו כל זרע
ישראל:

ברשות אנשי המעמד
בבית ובדפוס
אלכסנדר בר יהודה ליב זצ״ל
בלונדן
בשנת [illegible] לבנ״י ביום ההוא לפ״ק

Figure 8. Title page of *Leḥem Oni,* a commentary on the *Haggadah* by Raphael Hassan, printed by Alexander Alexander, pioneer of the London Hebrew press, 1784. Jerusalem, J.N.U.L.

Figure 9. Memorial in Willesden Jewish Cemetery, London, to British Commonwealth servicemen who died in the two World Wars. Photo M. Ninio, Jerusalem.

by the schools which were now being set up for Jewish children by Christian conversionists; this developed in due course into one of the largest schools in Europe. The struggle for Jewish *emancipation in England centered in London. In 1831 Jews were admitted to the freedom of the city, and hence to the privilege of carrying on retail trade, from which they had hitherto been barred. In 1835, David *Salomons was elected a sheriff of the city, the first Jew to attain that distinction. In 1847 he was the first Jewish alderman, and in 1855 the first Jewish lord mayor of London. From 1830 the City of London had shown sympathy with Parliamentary emancipation of the Jews, and its persistence in electing Baron Lionel de *Rothschild, notwithstanding the fact that he could not take his seat because of the form of the statutory oath, was in a large measure responsible for the admission of the Jews to Parliament in 1858.

The growing Anglicization of London Jewry hastened the reorganization of the community. A Reform congregation was established, nearer the fashionable centers of population in 1840. To meet this challenge, both the Sephardi and the Ashkenazi congregations established branch synagogues in the West End. Nathan Marcus *Adler, appointed in 1844, initiated a new period in the history of the Chief Rabbinate. Under his auspices, a modern theological seminary, *Jews' College, was founded in 1855, and a model charitable organization, the Board of Guardians for the Relief of the Jewish Poor, was established in 1859. In 1870 a union of the principal Ashkenazi congregations of the metropolis was formed under the title, the "*United Synagogue." Newer congregations in other parts of the metropolis later attached themselves to this organization, which is now perhaps the largest and the best organized of its kind in the world.

With the mass emigration from Russia which started after 1881, there was a great influx especially to London, and the population rose in the course of the next quarter of a century from some 47,000 to approximately 150,000, of whom about 100,000 lived in the East End. Thus, alongside the more or less "native" community, a new, essentially foreign, community grew up. A majority of the newcomers was absorbed by the tailoring, shoemaking, and cabinet-making industries. Fresh charities were created to meet their requirements. A Yiddish press and an active trade union movement came into being. Numerous minor synagogues, with their related institutions, were created. In 1887 Sir Samuel Montagu (later Lord Swaythling) created the Federation of Synagogues to coordinate their religious activities. The strike of 10,000 Jewish tailors in London in 1889, lasting for six weeks, attracted great attention and ended the period of the unmitigated exploitation of the Jewish immigrants. The Royal Commission on Alien Immigration, as well as the various inquiries into slum life, dealt to a large extent with the conditions of the new Jewish life which had sprung up in the East End of London, and was arousing some antagonisms. The Aliens Act of 1905 stemmed the tide of immigration, though it continued in modified form until the outbreak of World War I in 1914. The Jew of the East End, as he became more well-to-do, tended to move away to the newer suburbs, particularly in the northeast (Stamford Hill) and northwest (Golders Green), where important congregations sprang up. The progress of the Reform movement, indeed, was comparatively slow, though the radical Liberal Jewish Synagogue, which grew out of the Jewish Religious Union (1902), was established in 1910.

The period between the two wars witnessed a considerable economic and geographical expansion of London Jewry, as it attained a greater degree of well-being, extended

Figure 10. Science class at the J.F.S. comprehensive school, 1963. This successor to the Jews' Free School was opened in Camden Town, London, in 1961. Courtesy J.F.S., London.

its interests and hastened the movement from the traditional center of the East End into the northern suburbs. At the same time, there was some degree of organizational consolidation. The United Synagogue, in particular, extended its activities. A communal center for the major London Jewish institutions and a Jewish museum were established at Woburn House in the Bloomsbury area. The beginning of the persecutions in Germany in 1933 brought about a considerable influx of refugees who did a good deal to stimulate certain aspects of London Jewish life and to consolidate the organization of the extreme Orthodox wing.

Anti-Semitic movements were active during the 1930s, notably Sir Oswald Mosley's British Union of Fascists. The "Blackshirt" march through London's East End in October 1936 provoked massive disorders which led to the Public Order Act banning the political use of uniforms. The Mosleyites' march left a deep impression on the consciousness of London Jewry. [C.R.]

Contemporary Period. ECOLOGY. Between the two world wars, London Jewry experienced its first substantial population shift from the East End, a trend heightened during World War II, when, due to long periods of enemy bombing and extensive damage to the inner districts of London, Jews (together with the rest of the population) moved in large numbers to less vulnerable areas further from the center. With a rise in the standard of living in Britain, considerable urban renewal and suburban development took place.

During the 1950s and 1960s, Jews, who by this time had generally risen rapidly on the socioeconomic scale, settled in ever-increasing numbers in suburban areas, particularly in the north and northwest of London. It has been estimated that the East End, which at the beginning of the 20th century contained about 125,000 Jews and in 1929 still had some 85,000 Jews, was left with no more than 30,000 Jews within a few years after World War II. The northwest London area alone was said to have contained some 85,000 Jews by 1950. The vast majority of Jews always lived to the north of the Thames, and by the end of the 1960s they were spread along and below a suburban arc stretching from Wembley, Harrow, Stanmore, and Edgware in the west through Finchley and Palmers Green in the north to Ilford in the east. Below this arc were heavy concentrations of Jews in what may be termed "gilded ghettos," such as Golders Green, or semi-decaying "zones of transition," such as Stamford Hill, where newer non-Jewish immigrants settled in the 1960s in increasing numbers. The total Jewish population of Greater London in 1970 was estimated at 280,000.

The pattern of settlement and the movement of London Jewry were of particular importance for their effect on Jewish identification. Evidence suggests that throughout the 20th century, the directions of the major shifts were strongly influenced by developments in transport facilities vis-à-vis the place of work, that is the industrial and commercial areas in the city. The fanning out of the transport system and the improvement in highways, however, made incursions into the traditional pattern of settlement symbolized by the Jewish district. Whereas some of the new suburbs were still thickly inhabited by Jews—Edgware with 10,000 Jews representing 40% of the local population was a case in point—in 1970 there were larger numbers of Jews living in a more scattered fashion away from Jewish districts and throughout the Home Counties in and around Greater London. Not only was the lack of proximity to Jewish centers and the negative effects of living in predominantly non-Jewish areas bound to affect the identification of such Jews, but the problem also arose of how to cater to this more fluid and spread-out Jewish population from the organizational point of view.

ORGANIZATIONS. Most observers of Anglo-Jewish life highlighted the fact that the community was over-organized, a situation that led to duplication, inefficiency, and waste. The organizational aspect of communal life came to the fore even more starkly in the case of London Jewry, first because it contained the headquarters of many organizations catering to Anglo-Jewry as a whole (e.g., Board of Deputies of British Jews, Anglo-Jewish Association, Association of Jewish Ex-Service Men, National Union of Hebrew Teachers, Jewish Initiation Society, Central British Fund for Jewish Relief, and so on), and secondly because the problems of organizational efficiency were greater in a large community, particularly one which had become more scattered. The latter point may best be illustrated by the fields of religious and educational organization. The closing of some synagogues in the older areas of London in the late 1960s, such as the branches of the United Synagogue in Dalston and Bayswater, was more than compensated by the construction of new synagogues in the many areas where Jews settled in the postwar period and more recent years. A proliferation of synagogues was further brought about by the fact that all the main synagogal bodies representing the various streams had their own building programs. Thus, most of the 200 synagogues in London belonged to the five major synagogal organizations. A somewhat similar situation obtained for day schools, which were in the hands of the London Board of Jewish Religious Education, the Zionist Federation, the Jewish Secondary Schools Movement, Yesodei Hatorah Schools, and the Lubavitch Foundation, plus a number of independent schools.

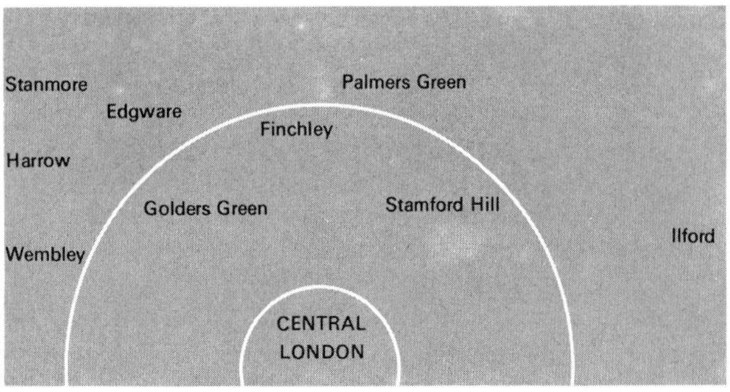

Map of London showing shift of Jewish population according to establishment of Hebrew congregations.

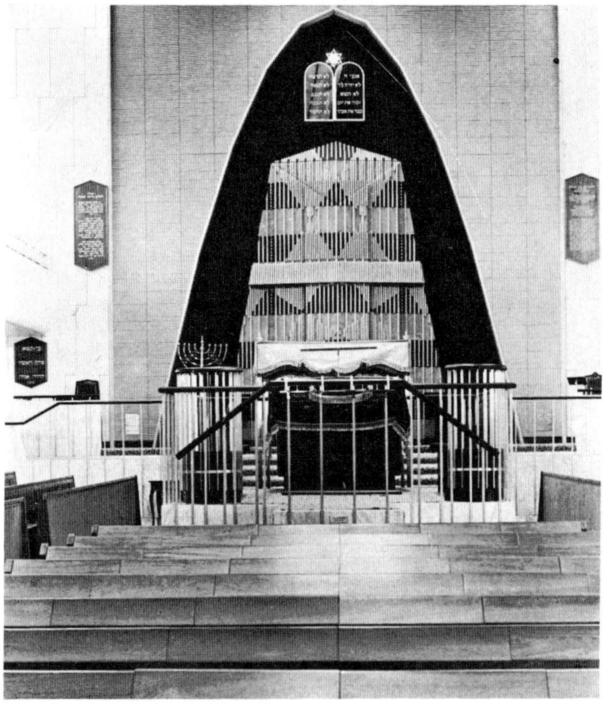

Figure 11. Ark of the Law in the new St. John's Wood Synagogue, built in the late 1950s. Photo M. Ninio, Jerusalem.

By contrast, there was greater efficiency and centralization in London in the sphere of welfare work. The London Jewish Welfare Board, which operated 19 homes for the aged and a host of other services for the needy, was the largest Jewish welfare institution in the country. London also had numerous societies concerned with the amelioration of physical and mental handicaps, e.g., the Jewish Blind Society, the Jewish Deaf Association, schools for the mentally retarded and handicapped children, and Jewish hospitals. The various charitable institutions, friendly societies, and professional associations added further to the well-being of London Jews. The younger generation of the community was well provided for by the large number of youth clubs and societies, including some famous ones such as the Jewish Lads' Brigade (founded in 1895), the Brady Club (1896), and the Bernhard Baron Settlement (1914). The renewal and improvement of premises in the form of Jewish youth centers, however, progressed slowly. The large number of Jewish students in London, for instance, were provided by B'nai B'rith with a new and much enlarged Hillel House only in 1970. Finally, London Jewry had a whole array of Zionist organizations and a large number of bodies supporting Israel institutions (in 1970 there were 65 such organizations in London, most with branches in provincial communities).

CULTURE AND RELIGIOUS LIFE. The leading part played by London Jewry in English Jewish life was particularly apparent in the cultural sphere. The largest number of publications on Jewish themes— newspapers, magazines, journals, or books—emanated from London, which also had ten libraries and museums with Jewish collections open to the public. The permanent residence of the chief rabbi engaged by the United Synagogue, the largest synagogal body in the country with a membership of 40,000 and 80 synagogues, further added to London's leading position. These factors generally had the effect of centralizing the administration of communal affairs. Thus, the Chief Rabbinate and its *bet din* tended to administer the religious life of large sections of provincial Jewry through other *battei din* and rabbis. The two leading bodies dealing with religious education, the London Board of Jewish Education and the Central Council for Jewish Religious Education dealing with the provinces, both operated from London. The pattern was similar in the political and philanthropic spheres. However, after World War II, and particularly in the 1960s, there was a growing trend toward decentralization. For example, the second largest synagogal body, the Federation of Synagogues, with 17,000 members in some 50 branches, as well as the smaller religious groups, i.e., the Union of Orthodox Hebrew Congregations, the Reform and Liberal movements, and the Sephardim, set up independent *battei din*. Growing decentralization was also manifest in other fields, including Jewish education, despite efforts, mainly from the center, to maintain some overall organizational unity in the Jewish community of Britain.

London's position appeared even less formidable when a number of other important facts were taken into account. Although strict Orthodoxy made important strides there, particularly through the growing strength of the ḥasidic groups in the Stamford Hill area, the largest and most successful yeshivah was in the small provincial community of Gateshead in the northeast corner of England. As for Jewish day schools, Manchester undoubtedly took the leading position. However, when London Jewry was set in the proper perspective in relation to the rest of Britain's Jewish community, it became clear that it was a very strong force not only in that community but in world Jewry.

[E.Kr.]

Hebrew Printing. Some Hebrew printing on wood blocks appeared in works printed in London from 1524, when a few isolated words and phrases figured in R. *Wakefield's *Oratio de utilitate . . . trium linguarum*. Movable Hebrew type was apparently first used in 1563 in W. Musculus' *Common Places of Christian Religion*, and consecutive Hebrew printing (a 14-line "sonnet") appeared in 1588 in a single-sheet broadside of poems in various languages by Theodore Beza celebrating the defeat of the Spanish Armada. In the 17th century a few books mainly or partly in Hebrew were published by Christian Hebraists, such as a Hebrew text of Psalms (1643), a vocalized text of *Avot* (1651), and Bryan *Walton's Polyglot Bible (1653–57). Communal controversies in the early 18th century produced the first Hebrew publications printed for (though not by) Jews, particularly the dispute that raged around haham David *Nieto's disputed Orthodoxy (1705) and a dispute concerning a divorce two years later (Aaron Hart's crudely produced *Urim ve-Tummim*, 1707). In 1714–15, some works by Moses Hagiz and Joseph *Ergas aimed against the Shabbateans appeared in London, presumably because of the unfavorable atmosphere in Amsterdam; and in the same year Nieto's classical *Matteh Dan* was brought out by Thomas Ilive's printing house in three editions—in Spanish alone, Spanish and Hebrew, and Hebrew alone. Thereafter there was a long hiatus in London Hebrew printing, though Ephraim *Luzzatto's poems *Elleh Benei ha-Ne'urim* appeared there in 1766 with a reprint in 1768. In 1770, printing by and for Jews at last began, possibly in consequence of the removal of some trade restriction. A consortium of Jewish printers from Amsterdam (who, however, failed after a few years) set up a printing house which produced ambitious editions of the Jewish liturgy (3 vols., 1770; other eds., 1771, 1785) and many other works. Simultaneously, A. *Alexander began his printing activity which was continued by his son Levi (mainly liturgical works) well into the 19th century. Other printers, Jewish and non-Jewish, appeared in the following years. In 1820 J. Wertheimer set up his Hebrew press, which was active for over a century, subsequently under the name of Williams, Lea, and Company. With the increase in the London Jewish population, especially after the immigration from Eastern Europe from the 1880s onward, Jewish printers and printing in London proliferated, though learned works were mainly produced at the presses of the universities of Oxford and Cambridge. [C.R.]

Bibliography: Roth, Mag Bibl, index; idem, England, index; Lehmann, Nova Bibl, index; E. N. Adler, *[History of the Jews in] London* (1930); M. Gaster, *History of the Ancient Synagogue . . . Bevis Marks* (1901); C. Roth, *Federation of Synagogues* (1947); idem, *Great Synagogue, London, 1690–1940* (1950); A. B. Levy, *East End Story* (1951); A. M. Hyamson, *Sephardim of England* (1951); idem, *London Board for Shechita, 1804–1954* (1954); V. D. Lipman, *Social History of the Jews in England* (1954); idem, *Century of Social Service* (1959); idem, in: JHSET, 21 (1968), 78–103; idem, (ed.): *Three Centuries of Anglo-Jewish History* (1961); A. Barnett, *Western Synagogue through Two Centuries* (1961); idem, in: JHSET, 20 (1964), 1–50; S. Stein, *ibid.*, 63–82; A. Rubens, in: J. M. Shaftesley (ed.), *Remember the Days* (1966), 181–205; A. Ziderman, in: JJSO, 8 (1966), 240–64; E. Krausz, *ibid.*, 10 (1968), 83–100; 11 (1969), 75–95, 151–63; R. Apple, *Hampstead Synagogue* (1967); A. S. Diamond, in: JHSET, 21 (1968), 39–63; C. Bermant, *Troubled Eden* (1969); J. Gould and S. Esh (eds.), *Jewish Life in Modern Britain* (1964); C. Duschinsky, *Rabbinate of the Great Synagogue, London, from 1756–1842* (1921, 1971[2]).

LONDON, city in S.W. Ontario, Canada, with a Jewish community numbering 1,500 in 1969 and constituting approximately 0.83% of the total population. In 1871, 35 Jews were listed as living in London. One early settler from Poland, Isaac Hellmuth, converted to Christianity and became the first Anglican bishop of Huron. By 1899 there were 144 Jews. In 1886 a cemetery plot was acquired and a *minyan* established and in 1899 a synagogue structure built. Reflecting various schisms this congregation was known by various names, until it settled on "B'nai Israel." A more lasting split occurred in 1906 which was not repaired for 60 years. As a result, two synagogues existed, both Orthodox (later both Conservative) and each with its own *talmud torah*. The second synagogue was named "B'nai Moses Ben Judah," after its founder Moses Leff. From 1926 to 1966 Rabbi David Kirshenbaum, who was also an author, served as rabbi of that congregation.

Another new element in the community were the anti-czarist radicals. Despite their radical ideology and nonreligious outlook, they were community minded and contributed to overseas fund raising, the formation of a free loan agency and other projects, and participated actively in Jewish (especially Yiddish) cultural life. London had a Zionist group as far back as 1900 and has been closely linked with the Zionist movement. In 1966 the two synagogues were reunited under the name of Or Shalom. An Orthodox congregation, Beth Tefila, was established in that year. Dr. Isidore Goldstick (1890–1961), who taught high school in London for more than 40 years, was the community historian. The London Jewish Community Council unites all segments of the community.

Bibliography: Canadian Jewish Congress, *The Jewish Community of London, Ontario* (1959). [B.G.K.]

LONDON, ARTUR (1915–), Czechoslovak statesman and Communist leader. He was born in Ostrava. In 1937 he went to Spain and joined the Communists within the International Brigade fighting in the Spanish Civil War. After the defeat of the Republican cause, London lived in France. Following the fall of France in 1940, he was arrested by the Nazis and deported to Buchenwald. London returned to France in 1945 where he represented the Czechoslovak information board. He was a prominent figure in the Czech Communist Party and following the Communist coup d'état of 1948 he was recalled to Prague to become a member of the central committee of the Communist Party. In the same year he became deputy minister of foreign affairs and as director of the ministry was responsible for the appointment of the diplomatic service. In 1951 London was arrested and charged with being a Zionist and a Trotskyite. He was one of the accused at the *Slansky Trial and in 1952 was sentenced to life imprisonment. He was released in 1955, however, and was later rehabilitated, becoming a member of the editorial staff of the monthly *Mezinárodní Politika*. In 1963 he left Czechoslovakia to join his family in France and in 1969 published his book *L'Aveu–Dans l'engrenage du procès de Prague* (Ed. Gallimard), an account of the Slansky Trial, which was made into a film in 1970.

Bibliography: P. Meyer et al., *Jews in the Soviet Satellites* (1953), index; *Procès des Dirigeants du Centre de Conspiration contre l'État dirigé par Rudolf Slansky* (1953), 200–20; E. Loebl, *Sentenced and Tried* (1969), 143–50; S. Orenstein, *Lefi Pekuddah mi-Moskvah* (1969), 165–74. [E.Ku.]

LONDON, FRITZ (1900–1954), German theoretical physicist. London was born in Breslau, and was at the University of Berlin till driven out by the Nazis. In 1927, together with Walter Heitler of Zurich, he wrote a basic paper for physicists and chemists, on the homopolar chemical bond, interpreting valency in terms of electronic spin. This was followed by studies of activation energy, the tetravalency of carbon, and van der Waals forces. From 1933 to 1936 he worked in a laboratory in Oxford mainly on superconductivity at temperatures near absolute zero, and from then until 1939 he was director of research at the College de France in Paris. From 1939 he was professor at Duke University (Durham, North Carolina), first of theoretical chemistry, and finally of physical chemistry.

Bibliography: *New York Times* (March 31, 1954), 27; *Nature*, 174 (July 10, 1954), 63. [S.A.M.]

LONDON, JACOB BEN MOSES JUDAH (first half of 18th century), rabbi and scholar. Born in Wesel, Germany, Jacob was taken to London as a child, when his father was appointed cantor there. There are those, however, who maintain he was born in London. When his father died, Jacob settled in Frankfort, where he attended the yeshivah of Samuel Schotten. After the fire in the Frankfort Jewish quarter in 1711, London moved to Leszno, Poland, where he became cantor and director of the Jewish school. For several years he lived in Prague, holding the post of inspector of the Talmud Torah schools, but he returned to Leszno in 1728. For the next six years he was engaged in writing an allegorical work, *Hista'arut Melekh ha-Negev im Melekh ha-Ẓafon* (Amsterdam, 1737), describing the struggle between the evil and the good inclination. He later traveled to Italy, where he published *Meginnei Shelomo* (Venice, 1741) by *Joshua Heschel b. Joseph of Cracow and *Shivah Einayim* (Leghorn, 1745), which consisted of halakhic writings by *Naḥmanides, Isaac *Alfasi, Isaac *Aboab, *Judah de Leon, Isaac *ibn Ghayyat, and Abraham Bulat. While on a journey to Piedmont, London was suspected of espionage on account of the Hebrew manuscripts that he had in his possession. In his introduction to *Meginnei Shelomo*, London mentions that he wrote a halakhic work entitled *Pegi'at Ya'akov*, which is no longer extant. He also wrote *Eẓ Ḥayyim*, a two-part work on moral precepts that was never published.

Bibliography: Steinschneider, Cat Bod, 1230; Ghirondi-Neppi, 124; Landshuth, Ammudei, 108; Fuenn, Keneset, 553; Zunz, Lit Poesie, 450; Carmoly, in: *Revue Orientale*, 2 (1842), 334; L. Lewin, *Geschichte der Juden in Lissa* (1904), 289ff. [Sh.A.H./Ed.]

LONDON, MEYER (1871–1926), U.S. lawyer and Socialist leader. London was born in Gora Kalvaria, Poland, and followed his father to New York City in 1891. He was immediately drawn into radical politics, in large measure because of his father's involvement with anarchist and Socialist groups. Initially an adherent of the Socialist Labor Party, he joined the opposition to its leader, Daniel *De Leon, in 1897, and ultimately became a member of the Socialist Party of America.

London had a significant influence on the needle trades unions of New York City in their formative period prior to World War I. Admitted to the bar in 1898, he served as legal counsel for a multitude of unions and union members.

Meyer London, U.S. lawyer and Socialist. From M. U. Schappes, *A Pictorial History of the Jews in the United States*, New York, 1958.

London was intensely pragmatic in labor matters, and despite his Socialist ideology, he helped to formulate the Protocol of 1910, which attempted to establish collective bargaining and arbitration in the women's cloak trade. London resisted the argument of some Socialists that such agreements substituted mutuality of interest for class struggle. He favored unemployment insurance, the abolition of child labor, and other social-reform legislation designed to improve the conditions of life and labor for the worker.

In 1914, after repeated attempts at elective office, London won election to the House of Representatives as a Socialist from a largely immigrant Jewish district on the Lower East Side in New York City; he was reelected in 1916 and 1920. Although he was a moderate Socialist, he endured the full brunt of bitter anti-Socialist attacks.

As a congressman he was active and argued strongly for reform. He voted against restrictive immigration and the Fordney tariff and actively supported nationalization of the coal industry. One bill of his became law: an act protecting the employees of bankrupt firms.

Although he strongly opposed American entrance into World War I and fought efforts to curb the civil liberties of opponents of the war, London refused to resist all wartime activities without qualification. This position alienated him from many of his friends and associates in American radicalism. He also had little sympathy for Zionism, believing that the emancipation of the Jew had to be accomplished not through nationalism but by uplifting the working class. London died as the result of a car accident.

Bibliography: H. Rogoff, *East Side Epic: Life and Work of Meyer London* (1930); A. Gorenstein, in: AJHSP, 50 (1961), 202–38; M. Epstein, *Profiles of Eleven* (1965), index. [I.Y.]

LONDON, SOLOMON ZALMAN BEN MOSES RAPHAEL (1661–1748), author, translator, and bookseller. London was born in Nowogrudok (Lithuania). Between 1709 and 1735 he published and sold books in Amsterdam, London, and Frankfort on the Main. He is best known for *Kohelet Shelomo* (1722), a devotional handbook which included occasional and domestic prayers and benedictions together with ritual laws and instructions both in Hebrew and Yiddish. It became popular in Western Europe and was reprinted many times, including later editions in which the Yiddish was replaced by German (cf. the Ger. ed. of 1919(?) and that by A. Sulzbach, 1908). *Kohelet Shelomo* also contains a Passover *Haggadah* with Leone de Modena's commentary *Ẓeli Esh*. This *Haggadah* also appeared separately (1733) and was reprinted several times. *Ḥinnukh Katan*, a small Hebrew-Yiddish vocabulary, was added to some of the editions.

London's *Zokher ha-Berit* (1714), which followed the same lines, detailed the ceremonies and laws of circumcision and redemption of the firstborn, with Yiddish translation. He also published a *siddur*, according to the German-Polish rite, under the title *Tikkun Shelomo* (1712, 1733[2], often reprinted), with Yiddish text added; it included the *Tikkunei Shabbat* of Isaac Luria. London prepared a number of ethical and halakhic compendia by various authors, providing a Yiddish translation. These included such works as *Orḥot Ẓaddikim* (author unknown, 1735); Jonah Gerondi's (13th century) *Iggeret ha-Teshuvah* (1742); and Isaac b. Eliezer's (15th century) *Sefer ha-Gan* (1747). [Ed.]

LONG BEACH, U.S. city in California, south of Los Angeles along the Pacific Coast. An estimated Jewish population of 15,000 persons resides in the Long Beach area (out of a total population of 400,000), which includes the neighboring communities of Rossmore, Los Alamitos, and Lakewood. The origins of the Jewish community go back to the first Jewish resident in 1898. Samuel Heller visited the city, liked its potentialities, and stayed to engage in real estate development. When the city introduced a municipal produce market in 1913, a number of Jewish produce men moved to Long Beach to operate stalls. By 1915 the population included 25 Jewish families. The first permanent Jewish organization was established after World War I with the chartering of B'nai B'rith Lodge 870 with 33 members. In 1922 the Community Building Association was established. It was dissolved in 1923 and reconstituted as a Reform congregation, Temple Israel, with Julius Liebert as its first full-time rabbi. In 1924 Temple Sinai (Conservative) was established with Lazar Friedland as its rabbi. Rabbis of Temple Israel included Harvey Franklin (1930), Elliot Grafman (1938), Walli Kaelter (1955). Temple Sinai had Jacob Friedman (1929), Shalom Ravetch (1935), and Sidney Guthman (1959). Jewish Welfare Fund campaigns began in 1929. In 1945 a Jewish Federation was established. A Jewish community center was organized in 1948. Its present center building was dedicated in 1960. In 1952, with 6,300 Jews in the rapidly growing city, a second Conservative congregation was formed with Maurice Schwartz as rabbi, followed in 1962 by Rabbi Joseph Miller. The Jewish community is a residential community of higher than average economic status. In 1962, 82% owned their own homes with an average income of $8,500, higher than in neighboring Los Angeles. Approximately 25% of the men were professionals, 18% were proprietors, 14% managers, and 25% were in clerical or sales work. There were few skilled or unskilled workers.

Bibliography: S. A. Hartman, *A History of the Long Beach Jewish Community* (1957); F. Massarik, *A Study of the Jewish Population of Long Beach, Lakewood and Los Alamitos* (1962). [M.V.]

LONGO, SAADIAH (first half of 16th century), poet. Born in Turkey, Saadiah lived in Salonika, where he was a member of the Ḥakhmei ha-Shir ("scholars of poetry"), a group of poets supported by Gedaliah ibn Yaḥya, a wealthy Salonikan. In addition to his *Shivrei Luḥot* (Salonika, 1594), consisting of poems of elegy and lament, he composed poems of friendship and jest in the spirit of his age. He also wrote poems of "beliefs," a type of poem which commences in a serious vein and then goes on to deal with the self-evident; they are banal and lack originality. Poems of this kind were composed in a spirit of rivalry by the poets of the group, who disagreed on the method of composition and the use of poetic conventions. The poets sharply criticized each other's work, and their criticism sometimes degenerated into personal attack. Longo's disputant in these poems was Jacob Tarfon, a local contemporary.

Bibliography: H. Brody, in: *Minḥah le-David* (1935), 205–20; A. M. Habermann, *Toledot ha-Piyyut ve-ha-Shirah* (1970), 232–4; EJ, s.v. [A.M.H.]

LONS-LE-SAUNIER, capital of the department of Jura, in *Franche-Comté, E. France. A *vicus Judeorum* ("Jewish quarter") is mentioned in Lons in 1220; the establishment of the community therefore preceded this date. The Rue des Juifs (later the Rue de la Comédie and Rue de la Balerne) is mentioned down to the 14th century. The Jews of Lons owned a cemetery, but there is no record of a synagogue. During the 14th century, Jews from Lons are found in numerous other localities of Franche-Comté. During World War II, a large number of Jews from Alsace and Lorraine who took refuge in Lons established a community numbering approximately 1,300 members. Lons also became the seat of a regional rabbinate. There was no organized community in Lons by the 1960s.

Bibliography: B. Prost and S. Bougenot, *Cartulaire de Hugues de Chalon . . .* (1904), 496; L. Gauthier in: *Mémoires de la société d'émulation du Jura*, 3 (1914) passim; J. Brelot and G. Duhem, *Histoire de Lons-le-Saunier* (1957), 74; Z. Szajkowski, *Analytical Franco-Jewish Gazetteer* (1966), 208–9. [B.Bl.]

LONZANO, ABRAHAM BEN RAPHAEL DE (late 17th–early 18th century), kabbalist, and Hebrew grammarian. It seems that he was a descendant of the renowned kabbalist Menahem de *Lonzano. Abraham became well known through his *Kinyan Avraham* (Zolkiew, 1723) on Hebrew grammar, from which it appears that he came from Zakinthos (Zante), one of the Greek isles. Following the attacks of the local inhabitants against the Jews, many troubles befell him and he began to wander from country to country. He studied at the yeshivah Eẓ Ḥayyim in Amsterdam. At a later date, he appears to have been in Prague where he was persecuted by the scholars of the yeshivah because he criticized them sharply for studying Torah without a knowledge of the Hebrew language. He wrote a declaration against Neḥemiah Ḥiyya *Ḥayon in Genoa in 1715 (published in *Sefunot;* see bibliography). He was in Lemberg in about 1723. In one of his poems, which appeared in his book, he angrily attacked those who regard themselves as poets without having any knowledge of even the form and arrangement of a poem. He also wrote *Ḥamishah Kinyanim* (unpublished), a commentary to the *Sefer Yeẓirah*. He subsequently converted to Christianity in the Prussian town of Idstein and adopted the name Wilhelm Heinrich Neumann.

Bibliography: Steinschneider, Handbuch, 85 no. 1201; J. F. A. de le Roi, *Die evangelische Christenheit und die Juden*, 1 (1884), 393; M. Friedman, in: *Sefunot*, 10 (1966), 602–6; Frumkin-Rivlin, 2 (1928), 156–7. [A.D.]

LONZANO, MENAHEM BEN JUDAH DE (1550–before 1624), linguist, poet, and kabbalist. Little is known about his life, but it is assumed that he was born in Constantinople. At the age of 25 he emigrated to Jerusalem and later moved to Safed. Forty years later, he went to Turkey and to Italy, and in 1618 he returned to Jerusalem.

Lonzano was best known for *Shetei Yadot* (Venice, 1618), which is divided into two sections (*Yad Ani* and *Yad ha-Melekh*). The first contains his original writings and the second the midrashic literature which he intended to edit. Each section is called *yad* ("hand") and has five *eẓba'ot* ("fingers"). *Yad Ani* includes the following: (1)*Or Torah* (also separately, Amsterdam, 1659), notes on the masorah ("text") of the Torah according to the weekly portions, comparing the printed Venice editions with important manuscripts which he knew. Because his work relates only to the Torah, it became second in importance to *Minḥat Shai*, by his contemporary Solomon *Norzi, which treats the entire Scripture. Despite this fact Lonzano's work was reprinted in many editions with additions and interpretations. (2) *Ma'arikh* (also separately, Leipzig, 1853), additions to the talmudic dictionary *He-Arukh* by *Nathan b. Jehiel of Rome. The work is based on his knowledge of Greek and Arabic and other languages (Turkish and Persian) used by his Jewish contemporaries. (3) *Avodat ha-Mikdash* (also separately, Constantinople, 1572), prayers for the order of worship in the Temple, with additions according to "the wisdom of the Zohar." (4) *Derekh Ḥayyim* (also separately, Constantinople, 1573), moralistic poetry. (5) *Tovah Tokhaḥat*, a long moralistic poem. From *Yad ha-Melekh*, he only managed to publish the first section, *Aggedata de-Bereshit*, which was reprinted many times. He intended to conclude the publication of *Midrash Agur*, which had begun to appear in Safed in 1587, and also planned to publish other important Midrashim according to manuscripts which he himself discovered, but this material has been lost.

Lonzano's other works treat Lurianic Kabbalah and aroused bitter opposition: (1) *Omer Man*, a commentary on the *Idra Zuta* and the *Sifra de-Ẓeni'uta* (Vilna, 1883); (2) *Imrei Emet*, a critique of Luria's interpretation of *Sifra de-Ẓeni'uta* and repudiations of Ḥayyim *Vital. According to Lonzano, Luria wrote his commentary before he received divine inspiration and "if he could, he would have changed or hidden this work" (Ms. British Museum 9167). Other works planned by Lonzano were hidden and only parts of them were preserved in manuscripts or published posthumously. They include: (1) a commentary on the Zohar (fragment, in manuscript); (2) comments on *Tikkunei Zohar* (Ms.); (3) *Haggahot le-Zohar Ḥadash* (Venice, 1643); (4) *Haggahot le-Talmud Yerushalmi* (Warsaw, 1737); (5) *Adi Zahav*, annotations on the book *Ha-Levushim* by Mordecai Jaffe; (6) comments on the prayer book (lost). Lonzano's originality caused him to suffer from the attacks of his opponents. In this matter his dispute with Gedaliah *Cordovero is of interest, but its background is still not clear. He was a thorough scholar. In search of manuscripts he made several trips abroad where he met with many scholars. As a poet, Lonzano was involved in a quarrel with Israel *Najara whom he criticized because of his use of erotic language and words such as "adulterers say to one another" (*Shetei Yadot*, 142) to describe the relationship between Israel and God.

Bibliography: Frumkin-Rivlin, 1 (1928), 134–45; Davidson, Oẓar, index; G. Scholem, *Kitvei Yad be-Kabbalah* (1930), 115–6, 152, 156; M. Kasher, *Sarei ha-Elef* (1959), 16, 18; A. Yaari, *Ha-Defus ha-Ivri be-Kushta* (1967), 116; Rosanes, Togarmah, 2 (1938), 182–6; M. Wander, *Derekh ha-Ḥayyim* (1931), 1–29, introduction; I. Sonne, in: *Kovez al Yad*, 5 (1950), 197–204; S. H. Kook, *Iyyunim u-Meḥkarim*, 1 (1959), 241–5; R. Elitzur, in: KS, 42 (1967), 511.

[D.S.Loe.]

LOOKSTEIN, JOSEPH HYMAN (1902–), U.S. rabbi and educator. Lookstein, who was born in Russia, was taken to the U.S. as a child. He became assistant rabbi of Congregation Kehilath Jeshurun in 1923 and rabbi in 1936. Lookstein was ordained at the Rabbi Isaac Elchanan Theological Seminary (1926). In 1929 he helped found the Hebrew Teachers Training School for girls and was its principal for ten years. He founded the Ramaz School in 1936 and was its principal for over 30 years. In 1958 Lookstein became acting president of Israel's Bar-Ilan University and also served as chancellor. Lookstein, who taught at Yeshiva University from 1931, was professor of sociology, homiletics, and practical rabbinics at that institution. He was chairman of the Jewish Welfare Board's Chaplaincy Commission (1954–57), president of both the Rabbinical Council of America (1941–43) and the New

Joseph Lookstein, U.S. rabbi and educator. Photo Fabian Bachrach, New York.

York Board of Rabbis, and was deeply involved in the Mizrachi movement. His philosophy of the integration of Judaism with the best of Western culture is expressed in the schools that he founded and in his articles and books, among which are *Judaism in Theory and Practice* (1931), *Sources of Courage* (1943), and *Faith and Destiny of Man* (1967).

[L.Be.]

LOPES, English family whose assimilated descendants attained distinction in English life. Manasseh Lopes (early 18th century), a prominent broker, made a fortune by speculation on false reports of Queen Anne's death. Manasseh Masseh (Massey) Lopes (1755–1831) was born in Jamaica. He converted to Christianity with his father, the West Indian merchant Mordecai Rodrigues Lopes in 1802, became a member of parliament, and was created a baronet in 1805. He was heavily fined and imprisoned in 1819 for corruption in a parliamentary election but was nevertheless later returned for Westbury. He resigned in 1829 in favor of Sir Robert Peel. Subsequently, he was recorder of Westbury. Sir Ralph Lopes (formerly Raphael Ralph Franco; 1788–1854), a descendant on the male side of the Leghorn *Franco family, succeeded his uncle, Manasseh Masseh Lopes, in the baronetcy. Sir Lopes Massey Lopes (1818–1908), eldest son of Ralph Lopes, was a civil lord of the Admiralty from 1874 to 1880. Sir Henry Charles Lopes (Baron Ludlow; 1828–1899), third son of Ralph Lopes, was a lord justice of the Court of Appeal 1885–1897. The head of the family held the title of Baron Roborough from 1938.

Bibliography: DNB, s.v.; J. Picciotto, *Sketches of Anglo-Jewish History* (1950[3]), 55, 209, 296–8, 407; A. M. Hyamson, *Sephardim of England* (1951), 201–4.

[C.R.]

LOPEZ, AARON (1731–1782), American merchant-shipper. Born in Portugal, Lopez went in 1752 to Newport, Rhode Island, where, renouncing his Marrano past, he remarried his wife Abigail in a Jewish ceremony, underwent circumcision, and in time became a leader of the Yeshuat Israel Congregation. Lopez' ties to the well-established *Gomez and Rivera families and the British America's economic boom during the French and Indian War assured him the credit he needed to expand his business beyond Rhode Island. Jacob Rodriguez *Rivera, whose daughter Sarah he married in 1763 after Abigail's death, often acted as his partner. Though a specialist in the whale oil and spermaceti candle industries, Lopez' business included: livestock, groceries, lumber, rum, ships, and clothing. He was also among the few American Jews active in the slave trade. The credit he secured during the 1760s and 1770s from his English suppliers enabled Lopez to build an extensive transatlantic mercantile empire. Lopez had trading connections with the Caribbean, Western Europe, and West Africa and on the eve of the American Revolution, was Newport's leading merchant and her

Detail from a painting of Aaron Lopez, Newport, Rhode Island merchant. From *American Jewish Historical Society Quarterly*, Vol. 27, New York, 1920.

largest taxpayer. Lopez supported the rebel cause and withdrew from British-threatened Newport to Leicester in central Massachusetts. This diminished his business and he did not survive to recoup his losses. The Newporters, to whose prosperity he had contributed so signally before the Revolution, mourned him, wrote Stiles, with a "demonstration of universal sorrow."

Bibliography: Bigelow, in: *New England Quarterly*, 4 (1931), 757–76; *Commerce of Rhode Island*, 2 vols. (1914–15); M. Gutstein, *Aaron Lopez and Judah Touro* (1939); J. Marcus, *Colonial American Jews*, 3 vols. (1970); S. F. Chyet, *Lopez of Newport* (1970). [S.F.C.]

LOPEZ, ROBERT SABATINO (1910–), U.S. medieval historian, son of Sabatino *Lopez. Born in Genoa, Italy, Lopez began his teaching career at the teachers' colleges of Cagliari, Pavia, and Genoa, and at the University of Genoa. As the Fascist regime in Italy became more oppressive Lopez migrated to the U.S. in 1939 and continued his studies. He was appointed professor at Yale university in 1955 and chairman of Medieval Studies (1963). Lopez was a prolific author and is particularly well known for several highly significant books and articles on various aspects of the economic history of the Middle Ages. Among his books are: *Studi sull'economia genovese nel medioevo* (1936); *Storia delle colonie genovesi* (1938); *Medieval Trade in the Mediterranean World* (with I.W. Raymond, 1955); *Il ritorno all'oro nell'Occidente duecentesco* (1955); *La prima crisi della banca di Genova* (1956). He served on various Jewish committees concerned with Zionism and Israel. [H.L.A.]

LOPEZ, RODERIGO (1525–1594), Portuguese Marrano physician. After graduating at Salamanca, he settled in London early in the reign of Queen Elizabeth. He became a

Elizabethan etching showing Roderigo Lopez plotting to poison the queen.

member of the College of Physicians and was the first house physician at St. Bartholomew's Hospital. Subsequently, he was appointed physician to the earl of Leicester and in 1586 to Queen Elizabeth. He was connected by marriage with Alvaro Mendes (Solomon *Abenaes), duke of Mytilene, the adviser of the Turkish sultan. Lopez worked closely with the earl of Essex, the Queen's favorite, and participated in an intrigue to secure English intervention on behalf of Dom *Antonio, pretender to the throne of Portugal. Later, he broke with Dom Antonio and began to work for an understanding with Spain. The Spanish court secretly negotiated with him and offered a heavy bribe if he would murder the pretender. Early in 1594 he was arrested and accused of plotting to poison Elizabeth, was found guilty, and executed at Tyburn (June 7, 1594). There is little doubt that he was innocent, though his aims and methods were not above suspicion. The case attracted much attention, and it is generally believed that Lopez was the prototype of Shylock in *Shakespeare's *Merchant of Venice*.

Bibliography: G. Harvey, *Lopez the Jew* (1920); Roth, England [3], 140ff.; Hume, in: JHSET, 6 (1908–10), 32–55; Wolf, *ibid.*, 11 (1924–27), 1–34; Gwyer, *ibid.*, 16 (1945–51), 163–84; Kohler, in: AJHSP, 17 (1909), 9–25; DNB, s.v. [C.R.]

LOPEZ, SABATINO (1867–1951), Italian playwright, critic and novelist. Born in Leghorn, Lopez spent some years as a teacher before devoting himself to the theater and dramatic criticism. A playwright of Italy's realistic school, he wrote about 70 plays, including such successful comedies

Sabatino Lopez, Italian author. Courtesy Guido Lopez, Milan. Photo Ghitta Carrell, Milan.

as: *La buona figliola* (1909), *La nostra pelle* (1912), *Il brutto e le belle* (pub. 1913), *Parodi & C.* (1925), and *La Signora Rosa* (1928). Faithful to Italian theatrical tradition, Lopez was essentially an actor's writer, and his plays are full of scintillating dialogue. In the earlier ones, where the emphasis is on drama, he relied on French realistic fiction and Italian *verismo;* his mature works incline to satire and ironic, though superficial, criticism of late 19th-century bourgeois morals, the irony and comedy skillfully balanced by humane sentimentality. Lopez also wrote some plays in collaboration with other writers, a book of memoirs, *S'io rinascessi* (1950), and stories of stage life, *Le Loro Maestà* (1920). Between 1911 and 1919 he directed the Italian writers' guild. Lopez took an active part in Jewish communal life and was for many years the chairman of the Zionist Organization in Milan. The historian Robert Sabatino *Lopez was his son. Another son was GUIDO LOPEZ (1924–), journalist and author. He was editor of the literary section of the weekly *Epoca* (1953–) and wrote the novels *Il Campo* (1948) and *La prova del nove* (1952) and a popular guidebook to Milan, *Milano in mano* (1965).

Bibliography: L. Tonelli, *Sabatino Lopez* (It., 1920); S. D'Amico, *Il teatro italiano* . . . (1932), 184–7; B. Curato, *Sessant'anni di teatro in Italia* (1947), 156–61; I. Sanesi, *La Commedia*, 2 (1944), passim; G. Pullini, *Teatro italiano fra due secoli* (1958), passim;

Ghilardi, in: *Il Dramma* (1967), nos. 371–2; Levi, in: RMI, 34 (1968), 131–7; *Enciclopedia dello spettacolo*, 6 (1959), s.v. [G.R.]

LOPEZ ROSA, Marrano family, members of which suffered at the hands of the Inquisition; possibly to be identified with the family of the same name who had a printing establishment in Lisbon in the middle of the 17th century. The following are noteworthy: MOSES (DUARTE) LOPEZ ROSA (second half of 17th century), a native of Beja, Portugal, Marrano physician and poet. In maturity he emigrated, first to Rome and then to Amsterdam, where he openly embraced Judaism. He became "arbiter" of the Academia de los Floridos, founded by the Baron de *Belmonte in 1685. A facile poet, he composed complimentary verses in honor of the English and Portuguese sovereigns and other prominent personalities. He is not to be confused with another DUARTE LOPEZ ROSA of Beja, likewise a physician, reconciled by the Inquisition in 1723. SIMON LOPEZ ROSA (alias Abraham Farrar, "the elder," first half of 17th century), a Marrano physician, was an early warden of the Beth Jacob community in Amsterdam. In common with some of his contemporaries, he was critical of the authority of the rabbis; and it was in consequence of a dispute in the congregation, occasioned by an episode in which he figured, that the Beth Israel synagogue was established. Appeal was made to R. Joel *Sirkes of Brest-Litovsk, who recommended that he should be excommunicated; a similar case, in which his cousin Dr. David Farrar was implicated, led to an appeal to the rabbinate of Salonika and to Leone *Modena in Venice. Lopez Rosa was among the Marranos judaizing in Amsterdam who were denounced to the Lisbon Inquisition in 1617.

Bibliography: M. Kayserling, *Geschichte der Juden in Portugal* (1867), 319; Kayserling, Bibl, 44, 95; idem, in: REJ, 44 (1901), 275f.; M.B. Amzalak, *Abraham Pharar: notícia biobibliográfica* (1927); C. Roth, *Life of Menasseh Ben Israel* (1933), ch. 7; idem, in: HUCA, 18 (1943/44), 221–4; Brugmans-Frank, 1 (1940), 678.
[C.R.]

LOPIAN, ELIJAH (1876–1970), rabbi, educator, and exponent of *musar*. Born near Grajewo, Poland, Lopian studied at Lomza and at Kelme, where he came under the influence of Simḥah Zissel *Broida. Broida's doctrine of *musar*, which emphasized the need for constant soul-searching and moral scrutiny, left a deep impression on Lopian. In Kelme he founded a yeshivah which he headed until he received an invitation in 1926 to teach at the Etz Chaim Yeshivah in London. He served there both as *mashgi'aḥ* (moral tutor) and, for a short time, as principal, until his retirement in 1950. During his years in England, he was instrumental in training many English rabbis. Lopian emigrated to Israel at the age of 74, but even then spent the

Elijah Lopian, rabbi and educator. Courtesy B. D. Klien, London-Jerusalem.

last 20 years of his life as *mashgi'aḥ* of the Keneset Ḥizkiyyahu Yeshivah at Kefar Ḥasidim. Although he never published any works, Lopian was renowned both as an orator of considerable power, and the greatest exponent of the old *musar* school. Of his nine sons three were heads of yeshivot: ḤAYYIM SHEMU'EL LOPIAN (1909–) at Sunderland, author of *Ravḥa de-Shemateta;* LEIB LOPIAN (1910–) at Gateshead; ELIEZER LOPIAN (1911–) at Torat Emet Yeshivah, London; as were two of his sons-in-law: Leib Gurwicz (1906–) at Gateshead, and Kalman Pinski at the Kamenitz yeshivah in Jerusalem. [A.U.]

LORBEERBAUM, JACOB BEN JACOB MOSES OF LISSA (c. 1760–1832), Polish rabbi and halakhist. His father, the rabbi of Zborow, died before Lorbeerbaum was born and his relative, Joseph *Te'omim, brought him up. After his marriage he settled in Stanislav and engaged in business, but devoted most of his time to study. He frequently attended the lectures of Meshullam *Igra. When after a few years his business failed, he accepted the rabbinate of Monasterzyska where he founded a yeshivah. He was later appointed rabbi of Kalisz where he wrote most of his books and with exceptional humility published anonymously his work on parts of Shulḥan Arukh, *Yoreh De'ah: Ḥavvat Da'at*, a name by which he himself became known in scholarly circles when his authorship came to light. This work was accepted in the rabbinic world as a compendium of practical *halakhah*, and won him the reputation of an outstanding *posek*. In 1809 he was invited to become rabbi of Lissa, long a center of Torah in Poland. Lorbeerbaum enlarged the yeshivah, to which hundreds of students streamed, among them many who later became great scholars and pioneers of the Ḥibbat Zion movement such as Elijah *Gutmacher, Ẓevi Hirsch *Kalischer, and Shraga Feivel *Danziger. Many of Jacob's contemporaries turned to him with their problems. During his time the war between the reformers and the rabbis flared up, and Lorbeerbaum, together with Akiva *Eger and Moses *Sofer, unleashed a vehement attack against the *maskilim* and the reformers. In Lissa, however, as in other towns of Great Poland that came under Prussian rule after the partition of Poland, the influence of the Berlin reformers grew continually stronger. The schism between Lorbeerbaum and a large section of the community eventually became so great that in 1822 he decided to leave Lissa and return to Kalisz. There he devoted his time to study, rejecting all offers of rabbinic posts from large and ancient communities such as Lublin. In 1830 he quarreled with a powerful member of the community who denounced him to the government, compelling him to leave Kalisz. On the way to Budapest, where he had been invited to become *av bet din*, he passed through the regional town of Stryj and was persuaded to remain there.

The following of his works have been published: *Ḥavvat Da'at* (Lemberg, 1799); *Ma'aseh Nissim* (Zolkiew, 1801), on the Passover *Haggadah; Mekor Ḥayyim* (*ibid.*, 1807), novellae and expositions of the laws of Passover in the Shulḥan Arukh together with the glosses of *David b. Samuel ha-Levi and Abraham Abele *Gumbiner on the *Oraḥ Ḥayyim* and novellae to tractate *Keritot; Netivot ha-Mishpat* (*ibid.*, 1809–16), on *Ḥoshen Mishpat; Torat Gittin* (Frankfort on the Oder, 1813), the laws of divorce and novellae on tractate *Gittin; Beit Ya'akov* (Hrubieszow, 1823), expositions on *Even ha-Ezer; Kehillat Ya'akov* (1831), on *Even ha-Ezer* and some sections of *Oraḥ Ḥayyim; Derekh ha-Ḥayyim*, an anthology of liturgical laws for the whole year, first published with the prayer book (1828) and then separately (1860 or 1870); *Naḥalat Ya'akov* (1849), expositions of the Pentateuch; *Emet le-Ya'akov* (1865), expositions of talmudic *aggadot; Imrei Yosher*, commentaries on the five *megillot*, each published at a different place and time; his ethical will (1875) and *Millei de-Aggadeta* (1904), sermons and responsa.

Bibliography: Z.Y. Michelsohn, *Toledot Ya'akov* (1913); L. Lewin, *Geschichte der Juden in Lissa* (1904), 168f., 204–22; Landau, in: HHY, 6 (1922), 310–2; Fuenn, Keneset, 554f.;

H. Tchernowitz, *Toledot ha-Posekim,* 3 (1947), 252–8; A. I. Bromberg, *Mi-Gedolei ha-Torah ve-ha-Ḥasidut,* 12 (1957); I. Lewin, in: *Sefer ha-Yovel . . . A. Jung* (1962), 167–85 (Heb. part). [E.K.]

LORGE, IRVING (1905–1961), U.S. educator. Born in New York, Lorge joined the Institute of Educational Research, Teachers College, Columbia University, as a research assistant in 1927, working closely with Professor Edward L. Thorndike. In 1946 he became professor of education and executive officer of the Institute of Psychological Research. Lorge pioneered in research in mental measurement and the capacity for human learning. His major work was on the nature of giftedness, the formulation of indexes of readability and of word frequency, the assessment of intellectual functioning of elderly adults, and the measurement of intelligence in young children. Some of the leading American psychologists and educators of the mid-twentieth century received their research training under him. During World War II, Lorge was special consultant to the secretary of war, the chief of the Corps of Engineers, and the Army Specialized Training Division. From 1944 to 1948 he was expert consultant to the adjutant general's office. His research for the armed forces brought radical changes in the service methods of teaching illiterates. Lorge's many publications include *The Lorge-Thorndike Intelligence Tests* (1954); *A Semantic Count of English Words* (1938); and in collaboration with J. Tuckman, *Retirement and the Industrial Worker: Prospect and Reality* (1953). [A.J.T.]

LORIA, ACHILLE (1857–1943), Italian economist. Loria, a native of Mantua, was a professor at the universities of Siena, Padua and Turin. He considered man's relationship to the amount of available free land to be a vital factor in the history of mankind, holding that the relative scarcity of free land condemned men to subjugation and exploitation by land owners. His deterministic economic theory of history reflects the influence of many 19th-century schools of thought, including those of Karl *Marx and Herbert Spencer. He seems also to have been influenced by the Irish land-reform debate.

Loria's voluminous writings include *Analisi della proprietà capitalista* (1889), *Verso la giustizia sociale* (1914–20), and *Ricordi di uno studente settuagenario* (1927). He was regarded by his contemporaries as one of the foremost scholars of his time, and his appointment to the Italian Senate in 1919 was only one of the many honors conferred on him. His stress on the importance of free land in the history of the United States had considerable influence on such economic interpreters of U.S. history as Charles Beard and Frederic Jackson Turner.

Bibliography: L. Einaudi, in: *La Riforma Sociale,* 43 (1932), list of his works; idem, in: *Economic Journal,* 56 (1946), 147–50.

[J.O.R.]

LORJE, CHAIM (1821–1878), founder of the first society for the settlement of Ereẓ Israel (Kolonisations-Verein fuer Palaestina). Born in Frankfort on the Oder, Lorje was an educator there and headed a children's boarding school. In 1864 he moved to Berlin where he lived until his death. He considered himself a descendant of the Safed kabbalist Isaac *Luria; he had a tendency toward mysticism throughout his life and this was probably the source of his initiative to establish the first society for the agricultural settlement of Ereẓ Israel in Frankfort on the Oder (1860). Opposition from the old *yishuv* immediately arose against the scheme for they feared that Lorje's society would divert part of the *ḥalukkah* funds from abroad. On the other hand, the early harbingers of the Zionist idea, namely Z. *Kalischer, Y. *Alkalai, M. *Hess, David *Gordon, and others, joined Lorje. The society also published Kalischer's programmatic book *Derishat Ẓiyyon* (1862). At the close of the book is an appendix by Lorje on the society and its rules.

The center of the society was then moved to Berlin. At first it was successful and collected substantial funds;

Chaim Lorje, a founder of the first society for settlement in Ereẓ Israel. Jerusalem, J.N.U.L., Schwadron Collection.

however, Lorje's egocentrism and aggressive tone toward his adversaries brought about the gradual weakening of the society until it ceased to exist in 1864. When other societies were established afterward, Lorje's group was honored as the direct and indirect inspiration for these societies and the Ḥibbat Zion movement in the West.

Bibliography: Kressel, in: *Zion,* 7 (1942), 197–205. [G.K.]

LORKI (i.e., of Lorca), **JOSHUA** (d.c. 1419), physician and writer who converted to Christianity and became an implacable enemy of Judaism. His father was Joseph Abenvives (or Ibn Vives) of Lorca, near Murcia in Spain. In his youth Lorki apparently studied in Alcañiz under Solomon ha-Levi (*Pablo de Santa María), and was greatly influenced by his teacher's conversion. Deeply impressed by the letter sent by Pablo to R. Joseph *Orabuena concerning the fulfillment of the messianic prophecies through Jesus, Lorki wrote to Pablo disclosing his own doubts in the Jewish faith and analyzing the causes of Pablo's conversion. Lorki nevertheless remained in the fold of Judaism until 1412, when he became converted under the influence of the Dominican preacher Vicente *Ferrer. On baptism, Lorki assumed the name Hieronymus de Sancta Fide (or Gerónimo de Santa Fé). Immediately after his conversion, Lorki conceived the idea of convening a disputation with the leading Jews of Alcañiz. He submitted his proposal to the antipope *Benedict XIII, whose personal physician he became. Benedict recommended that the disputation should be held at *Tortosa, and that the foremost Jews of Aragon should take part in it. During the disputation Lorki treated his former coreligionists with contempt and threatened them with punishment by the Inquisition. The Jews referred to him as "*Megaddef*" ("The Blasphemer"), a combination of the initials of Maestre Gerónimo de [Santa] Fé. After the disputation, Lorki traveled widely, trying everywhere to win Jews to Christianity.

Probably when still a Jew, Lorki wrote a book in Arabic on plants and herbs and their therapeutic qualities at the request of Don Benveniste de la *Cavallería. It was translated into Hebrew by Don Vidal Joseph, son of Benveniste (*Gerem ha-Ma'alot,* Vienna Ms. 154). After his conversion, Lorki wrote two polemics against Judaism: *Contra perfidiam Judaeorum,* in which he cites aggadic passages allegedly attesting to the coming of Jesus, and *De Judaeis erroribus ex Talmuth* (Augsburg, ca. 1468; Zurich, 1552; later Hamburg, n.d.; both in *Bibliotheca Maxima Veterum Patrum,* vol. 3, Frankfort, 1602), under the name *Hebraeomastix.*

One of Lorki's sons, Pedro de Santa Fé, was a favorite of Queen María, the wife of Alfonso V of *Aragon. Another descendant, Francisco de Santa Fé, filled various important public offices. At the end of 1485 Francisco was accused of being implicated in the murder of Pedro de *Arbues, the inquisitor of Saragossa, and arrested. He committed suicide in the prison of the Inquisition. His body was burned and its ashes thrown into the Ebro River.

Bibliography: Baer, Spain, index s.v. *Joshua Halorki;* Baer, Urkunden, 1 (1929), 809ff., 833ff.; L. Landau, *Das Apologetische Schreiben des Josua Lorki* (1906); A. Lukyn Williams, *Adversus Judaeos* (1935), 235ff.; A. Pacios López, *La Disputa de Tortosa*, 2 vols. (1957), index; J. Amador de los Ríos, *Historia Social... España y Portugal* (1960), 836ff.

[H.B.]

LORM, HIERONYMUS (pseudonym of **Heinrich Landesmann;** 1821–1902), Austrian poet and novelist. The son of a prosperous Moravian merchant, Lorm was born in Nikolsburg and raised in Vienna. He studied music until he lost his hearing at the age of 15. Shortly afterward his sight began to fail and he eventually became totally blind. Throughout the 1840s, Lorm wrote liberal lyrics and articles, using various pseudonyms in order to avoid political persecution. Moving first to Leipzig and then to Berlin, he became the literary correspondent of the influential periodical *Die Grenzboten*, but returned to Vienna in 1848. Here he befriended the young composer Anton *Rubinstein and the novelist Berthold *Auerbach. Auerbach, who married Hieronymus' sister, inspired the character of the young Jewish intellectual in *Gabriel Solmar*, Lorm's most popular novel, which originally appeared in 1855 as *Ein Zoegling des Jahres 1848. Gabriel Solmar* tells of a Jew's disillusionment with the panacea of general emancipation and of his return to his own people though not to religious Orthodoxy. It also deals with the political intrigues of the revolutionary period. Other novels of Jewish interest are *Am Kamin* (2 vols., 1857), *Todte Schuld* (1878), *Der Ehrliche Name* (1880), and *Ausserhalb der Gesellschaft* (1881). Since Lorm could communicate only by a touch system, he gradually reconciled himself to a life devoted solely to literary pursuits. He wrote several volumes of short stories, and some touching poems deeply influenced by Nicolaus Lenau's *Weltschmerz*. His last volume of poems, *Nachsommer*, appeared in 1896 and was filled with pessimism. The publication of his *Philosophisch-kritische Streifzuege* (1873) gained him an honorary doctorate from the University of Leipzig. From 1873 to 1892 Lorm lived in Dresden, where he worked as a journalist and published a dozen novels, the best known of which was *Die schoene Wienerin* (1886). He moved to Bruenn in 1892 and from then until his death devoted himself to philosophical writing, including his main work in this field, *Der grundlose Optimismus* (1894).

Hieronymus Lorm, Austrian poet and novelist. Jerusalem, J.N.U.L., Schwadron Collection.

Bibliography: K. Kreisler, *Hieronymus Lorms Schicksal und Werk* (1922); J. Straub, *Hieronymus Lorm* (Ger., 1960). [S.L.]

LORRAINE (Heb. לוֹתִיר), region in E. France, formerly Lotharingia. Although the region of Mainz-Speyer did not form part of Lotharingia, the Hebrew sources use *"Gedolei Lotar"* to denote not only *Gershom b. Judah, who was born either in Metz or Mainz, but also apparently his disciples in these two towns and the tosafists of Speyer as well as those of Metz, Toul, and Verdun. The Jews are only mentioned in the duchy proper from the time of Simon II (1176–1205), who is said to have expelled them. There is evidence for the presence of the Jews in *Trier from as early as the fourth century and in *Metz, *Toul, and Verdun in the Carolingian period. At the beginning of the 13th century, a group of Jews was driven out of Saint-Dié on the pretext that one of them had practiced sorcery. In 1286 Duke Ferri III (1251–1304) permitted a number of them to live in Lorraine (in exchange for a quitrent of pepper) and to acquire a cemetery in Laxon, near Nancy, to serve the whole of the duchy. In charters granted to towns in the duchy (e.g. Neufchâteau, Sierck) he stipulated the right to admit Jews. In *Sarreguemines, Duke Raoul took three Jews under his protection in 1336, and acquired some land from another in Laneuve-ville-devant-Nancy, while many Jews who had been expelled from France settled in neighboring Barrois.

From that date the Jews seem to have disappeared from the duchy, probably as a result of the *Black Death, but Lorraine appears to have admitted some of the refugees from France at the end of the 14th century (according to Joseph ha-Kohen, *Emek ha-Bakha*, ed. Vienna (1852), 74). In about 1455 Duke John II (1453–70) sold to many Jewish families the right to reside in the market towns of *Nancy, Neufchâteau, Pont-à-Mousson, *Lunéville, Rosières-aux-Salines, and Sarreguemines. Duke René II (1473–1508), however, confiscated their belongings and expelled these families in 1477 as a way of "giving thanks to God" for his victory over Charles the Bold in the same year. In theory this expulsion decree remained in force until the 18th century, but from as early as the 16th century the duke, his officers, and his vassals turned a blind eye to the arrival of a few isolated individuals, as well as attracting the financier Maggino Gabrieli to Nancy in 1597 and authorizing a large group to reside in Saint-Hippolyte, on the Alsatian slope of the Vosges. Jews are also mentioned in various villages, especially of German-speaking northern Lorraine: first in Vaudrevange, Sierck, *Morhange, Vaudoncourt, and Faulquemont in about 1600; then in *Boulay, Dieuze, Frauenberg, Sarreguemines, and Puttelange under French rule (1633–97); and finally during the reign of Leopold I (1658–1705), to whom the territory was restored by the Treaty of Ryswick in 1697.

As he was in debt to the Jewish bankers of Metz, Leopold even authorized some of them, including Samuel *Lévy and Moses Alcan, to settle in Nancy, entrusting the former with the administration of his finances (1715). After Lévy's downfall Leopold turned against the Jews: his decree of August 1720 subjected the movements of foreign Jews to strict control and that of April 1721 expelled all those who had arrived in the duchy after 1680. A list of the 74 families authorized to remain was published. They were spread out in small groups (with the exception of 19 families in Boulay) in 24 localities, mostly in German-speaking Lorraine. All formed a single community with one officer, Moses Alcan of Nancy, and a central synagogue in Boulay. In 1733 their number was increased to 180 families and the officers, then three in number, were charged with raising an annual tax of 100,000 livres. The Jews of Lorraine were authorized to appoint a rabbi by Stanislaus I, duke of

Lorraine and Bar (1736–66), but it was not until 1785 and 1788 that those of Lunéville and Nancy were able to open synagogues and cemeteries. Stanislaus interpreted liberally the restricted number of 180 families. A decree of 1753 shows that Jews had then settled in 28 new localities, including Lunéville, Etain, and Bar; those exceeding the official quota were granted special authorizations or, after the reunion of the territory with France (1766), were naturalized. In 1789 there were about 500 Jewish families in Lorraine, 90 of them in Nancy, where bankers, army purveyors, and merchants were able to develop the cloth trade and to establish industries; one member of the Cerfberr family even acquired the seigniory of Tomblaine. During the preparation of the Estates-General (1788–89) most of the memoranda of complaints *("cahiers de doléances")* from *Alsace and Lorraine were bitterly anti-Jewish. From many villages of Lorraine came such suggestions as that the Jews should be forced to engage in manual labor, that usury should be forbidden, and even that the Jews should be totally expelled from France.

In 1789 *Berr Isaac Berr led a delegation of the Jews of Lorraine, Metz, and Alsace at the National Assembly and published two pamphlets calling for the emancipation of the Jews. After the dissolution of the single community of the Jews of Lorraine (1790) and the constitution of independent communities in Lunéville, Sarreguemines, Lixheim, etc., the two *consistories of Metz and Nancy, with 6,500 and 4,200 Jews respectively, included most of the Jews of Lorraine (1808). The number of rabbis increased and synagogues were also established in *Phalsbourg, Sarreguemines, Verdun, Epinal, and Toul. After 1871 many Jewish refugees from Alsace and Moselle settled in that part of Lorraine which remained French after the Franco-German War. The department of Vosges, which by then had 2,500 Jews, was incorporated in a new consistory formed in *Vesoul (subsequently transferred to Besançon). In the remainder of French Lorraine, the number of Jews rose to between 7,000 and 8,000 in 1900, 4,000 of whom lived in Nancy. In the part of Moselle annexed by Germany after 1871 there were 7,015 Jews in 1900 (in comparison with 8,571 in 1870). The Jews who remained in this department left many of the villages for Metz or the newly industrialized regions, where they were joined by immigrants from the rest of Germany and Eastern Europe. After Alsace-Lorraine had been ceded to France by the Treaty of Versailles (1919) more immigrants came to the region. The Jewish population of Lorraine was greatly reduced by assimilation and the massive deportations of World War II, especially in the south, although it was slightly augmented by the arrival of some 200 families from North Africa after 1962. In 1970 rabbinates were to be found in Metz, Nancy, and Sarreguemines only: other communities numbering more than 100 persons were in Thionville, Lunéville, Forbach, Epinal, Sarrebourg, and Saint-Avold.

See also *Alsace, *France.

Bibliography: Germ Jud, 1 (1937), 160ff.; Gross, Gal Jud, 293–305; C. Pfister, *History of Nancy*, 1 (1902), 678–81; 3 (1908), 311–38; L. Vanson, in: *Revue juive de Lorraine*, 10 (1934); 11 (1935), passim; A. Hertzberg, *French Enlightenment and the Jews* (1968); Z. Szajkowski, *Economic Status of the Jews in Alsace, Metz and Lorraine* (1954); B. Blumenkranz, in: *Annales de l'Est* (1967), 199–215.

[G.C.]

LOS ANGELES, city in S. California with approximately 4,000,000 inhabitants occupying 455 square miles of territory; the third most populous city in the U.S. and the largest city in area in the world. Los Angeles is the home of 510,000 (1967) Jews, second only to New York City.

Beginnings. The origins of the city go back to the early

Figure 1. The plot bought for the first Jewish cemetery in Los Angeles, 1855. From M. Vorspan and L.P. Gartner, *The History of the Jews of Los Angeles*, San Marino, Calif., 1970.

Spanish colonization of California. Los Angeles was formally dedicated as a pueblo on Sept. 4, 1781, with 44 inhabitants. The town grew slowly to 1,100 inhabitants by 1840. A year later the first party of pioneers traveled overland to Los Angeles from the Middle West. With them was Jacob Frankfort, the first Jewish resident of Los Angeles. The accession of California to the U.S. in 1850 as an aftermath of the Mexican War and the discovery of gold brought a surge of Jews from Western Europe and the Eastern U.S. to seek a quick fortune. The majority did not engage in gold mining but opened stores in the small towns and mining camps of northern California. The prosperity filtered down to the rancho country of southern California and to the small town of Los Angeles which was its marketing and commercial center. A Los Angeles census of 1850 revealed a total of 1,610 inhabitants of which eight are recognizably Jewish: Morris Michaels, aged 19, Portland, Oregon; Abraham Jacobi, 25, Poland; Morris L. Goodman, 24, Germany; Philip Sichel, 28, Germany; Augustine Wasserman, 24, Germany; Felix Bachman, 28, Germany; Joseph Plumer, 24, Germany; and Jacob Frankfort, 40, Germany; all were unmarried and merchants, except for Frankfort who was a tailor. The Jewish population, in the wake of economic expansion, increased rapidly. Jews came from San Francisco and the East and directly from Germany and promptly set up businesses, or, procuring carts and wagons, began to trade with the prosperous Spanish rancheros. Jewish services probably began on the High Holidays in 1851 and were more formally established with the arrival of Joseph Newmark (1799–1881) in 1854. Rabbinically trained and traditionally oriented, he was the patriarch of the Jewish community until his death. Services were held in various rented and borrowed places until the first synagogue was built in 1873 at 273 N. Fort Street (now Broadway).

The first visit of the artist S. N. Carvalho, in 1854, directly stimulated the founding of the Hebrew Benevolent Society of Los Angeles. Carvalho influenced his host, Samuel Labatt, to establish a philanthropic society and a Jewish cemetery. Thirty charter members elected S. K. Labatt as president; Charles Schachno, vice-president; Jacob Elias, secretary and treasurer; and S. Lazard and H. Goldberg, trustees. This was the first social welfare organization in Los Angeles. A year later the society procured land from the City Council in Chavez Ravine for the Jewish cemetery which served until 1900. In addition to furthering their economic interests and "the holy cause of benevolence," the Jewish merchants during these early years were also active in such civic affairs as the

Figure 2. B'nai B'rith Congregation on S. Broadway, the first synagogue built in Los Angeles, 1873. From *History of the Jews of Los Angeles.*

founding of the Masonic order, the first Library Association, the Odd Fellows order, the German Turnverein, and as elected members of the City Council and County Board of Supervisors. Jews participated freely in every facet of social and economic as well as communal life. From 1850 until 1880 one or two Jews continuously served as elected officials. In 1873 they took the initiative in organizing the first Chamber of Commerce. Jewish business, concentrating on wholesale and retail merchandising, was among the largest in town. In 1865 I. W. Hellman (1843–1920) ventured into the banking business to become ultimately the leading banker in Los Angeles and among the dominant financial powers in the state. By the 1890s I. W. Hellman and Henry Huntington became the two financial giants of southern California. In 1861 Beth El, a congregation of Polish Jews, was formed. It soon was replaced by the German Congregation B'nai B'rith, which invited the Orthodox Rabbi A. W. Edelman (1832–1907), a Hebrew school teacher in San Francisco, to become its first rabbi. Congregation B'nai B'rith's first officers were Joseph Newmark, president; Wolf Kalisher, vice-president; M. Behrend, secretary; and Elias Levinthal, Isadore Cohen, and Louis Levy, trustees. It functioned as a traditional congregation until the middle 1880s, when it began moving to an unequivocal Reform position. Ephraim Schreiber of Denver became the rabbi from 1884 to 1889; Abraham Blum, 1889–95; M. G. Solomon, 1895; and Sigmund Hecht, 1900–19. The position of the Jewish community in Los Angeles was expressed by an editorial in the local *Daily News* in 1873, which summed up the prevailing attitude toward the Jewish population: "We commend them for their commercial integrity and their studied isolation from prevalent vices of gambling and inebriation. We commend them for their general business and personal probity . . . they are among our best citizens and the city suffers nothing in their hands . . ." The population of Los Angeles rose sharply during the 1880s with the arrival of the transcontinental railroad service and following a concerted program of promotion by the Chamber of Commerce. The population, only 11,000 in 1880, multiplied five fold in a few years during a land boom of vast proportions. With the arrival of large numbers of Middle Westerners the easygoing, socially integrated society began to change. Jewish social life became more ingrown. Jews established separate social outlets including a Young Men's Hebrew Association for the young and the Concordia Club for the card-playing parents. Jews lost their places in the Blue Book, the local social register, which in 1890 listed 44 Jews, 22 in 1921, and in recent years, no discernible Jews.

Population Growth and Communal Development. At the beginning of the 20th century large numbers of Eastern European Jews began to migrate to Los Angeles to begin in their turn the ascent to prestige, status, and security. Their movement to Los Angeles was aided by the Industrial Removal Office in New York, which sent them as part of a grand dispersal design. Approximately 2,000 Jews went to Los Angeles through this source of assistance, and subsequently brought their families. In 1900 the Los Angeles population was 102,000 and the Jews numbered 2,500. Twenty years later the Jews constituted 40,000 out of 576,000, and by 1930 the Jews numbered 70,000 out of 1,200,000. The rapid increase of population created for the first time recognizably Jewish neighborhoods. By 1920 the three major areas of Jewish concentration were: Temple Street, Boyle Heights, and the Central Avenue district. The early Jewish community organizations, Congregation B'nai B'rith, B'nai B'rith Lodge No. 224, which had been established in 1874, the Ladies Hebrew Benevolent Society established in 1870, and the Hebrew Benevolent Society were by this time insufficient to meet the needs of a new era. The high percentage of Jews coming West for their health made the establishment of medical institutions the first order of communal business. In 1902 the private home of Kaspare Cohn was donated to become the Kaspare Cohn Hospital. A few years later, the hospital was forced to move outside the city when the treatment of tuberculosis, its main business, was declared illegal within the city limits. In 1911 the Jewish Consumptive Relief Association was established and began to build a sanitarium at Duarte for consumptives who came to seek relief. For the elderly people the Hebrew Sheltering Home was established, to become the Jewish Home for the Aged. In 1910 B'nai B'rith was the moving force for the establishment of the Hebrew Orphans Home, whose name ultimately became Vista Del Mar. In 1912 the Federation of Jewish Charities was established to unite all fund raising for Jewish institutions. The Kaspare Cohn Hospital gradually transformed itself into a general hospital. It gradually altered its character as a charity hospital and began to charge patients. In 1926 it moved to its present facilities on Fountain Street near Vermont Avenue, and was renamed the Cedars of Lebanon Hospital. The first meeting of the Federation of Jewish Charities was held in 1912 with

Figure 3. The Wilshire Boulevard Temple, formerly Congregation B'nai B'rith. From *History of the Jews of Los Angeles.*

Ben R. Meyer, the son-in-law of Kaspare Cohn, as president, and included Dr. David W. Edelman, son of Rabbi Edelman and the president of the Reform congregation; Louis M. Cole, son-in-law of I. W. Hellman; M. N. Newmark and Isaac Norton, members of pioneer families; and S. G. Marshutz of B'nai B'rith, the founder of the Orphans Home. They typified the local Jewish leadership, to whom philanthropy was central in Jewish community life. The first decade of the 20th century was marked by a transition from charity aid to social welfare. During World War I overseas needs began to assume a large role in the philanthropy of the Jewish community. In 1934 the United Jewish Community was organized alongside the United Jewish Welfare Fund and the United Community Committee which was established to fight anti-Semitism. The new leaders were mostly lawyers and not men of inherited wealth. Men like Lester W. Roth, Harry A. Holzer, Benjamin J. Scheinman, and Mendel B. Silberberg succeeded the Newmarks and the Hellmans. In 1937 the United Jewish Community was incorporated as the Los Angeles Jewish Community Council, with the United Jewish Welfare Fund as its fund-raising arm. The United Community Council became the Community Relations Committee of the Jewish Community Council. The Federation of Jewish Philanthropies continued as a separate entity until 1959, when a merger was effected between the Jewish Community Council with its pro-Israel interest and overseas concerns, and its orientation toward Jewish education, and the Federation of Jewish Welfare organizations typifying the earlier Jewish community, with its primary concern for local philanthropies. A few years later the Cedars of Lebanon Hospital and Sinai Hospital, which was established during the 1920s by the Eastern European community, also merged.

Religious Developments. In the early 1900s Congregation B'nai B'rith, which had served the entire community since 1861, was joined by the first Orthodox congregation, Beth Israel or the "Olive Street Schul." In 1906 Congregation Sinai, the first Conservative congregation, was organized, and built its first edifice three years later. Isadore Meyers was rabbi and his successors included Rudolph Farber, David Liknaitz, Moses Rosenthal, and others. The congregation grew and moved in 1930 to an imposing edifice at 4th and New Hampshire streets. Two rabbis and two congregations towered over the religious life in Los Angeles Jewry until World War II. Wilshire Temple was founded in 1860. It was classical Reform, with a magnificent structure on Wilshire Boulevard representing the affluence of its membership, including many of the movie colony. It was the "established" congregation of the Jewish community. Hushed worship, the garments of the minister, the mixed choir, the centrality of the sermon, and the absence of bar mitzvah, all marked the Reform temple. Its rabbi was Edgar F. Magnin (1890–). Under his influence membership rose from 300 to 2,000, to become reputedly the largest congregation in the United States. In 1930 Dr. Jacob Kohn (1881–) arrived at Congregation Sinai. He became renowned for his liberal forthrightness, philosophical depth, and Jewish scholarship. At the end of World War II 150,000 Jews lived in Greater Los Angeles, an increase of 20,000 since the war began. The major growth of the Jewish population in Los Angeles began after 1945 when thousands of war veterans and others moved West with their families. The city's population multiplied and the Jewish community grew apace. By 1948 the Jewish population was a quarter of a million, representing an increase of 2,000 people a month as Jews moved West in one of the great migrations in Jewish history. The Middle West was the major area of origin; perhaps 38% of the Jewry in Los

Figure 4. Abraham W. Edelman (with beard), the first rabbi of Los Angeles, photographed with his family, 1886. From *History of the Jews of Los Angeles.*

Angeles in 1951 were from the Chicago area. In 1951 it was estimated that 330,000 Jews lived in Los Angeles. Dozens of suburban communities founded during this period were swiftly absorbed in the spreading Los Angeles metropolis. By 1965 the Jewish population of Los Angeles had reached half a million and the community had become one of the largest centers of Jewish population. The vast increase in Jewish population resulted in a proliferation of congregations, synagogues, and religious functionaries. The national movement of the religious denominations "discovered" Los Angeles as the United Synagogue established its Pacific Southwest Region, the Union of American Hebrew Congregations established its Southern Pacific Region, and rabbis by the dozen wended their way West. By 1968 there were 150 congregations and even more rabbis in Los Angeles. The largest congregations were Wilshire Temple, Temple Israel of Hollywood, Temple Emanuel, Temple Beth Hillel, and Temple Isaiah (Reform); Temple Beth Am, Valley Jewish Community Center, Sinai Temple, Hollywood Temple Beth El, and Temple Beth Sholom (Conservative); and Beth Jacob and Beth Tfillah (Orthodox). All three branches of Judaism established schools of higher Jewish learning after 1945. The Jewish Theological Seminary established the University of Judaism, which in turn developed a Hebrew Teachers' College, a School of the Fine Arts, the Graduate School, and an extensive program of adult Jewish studies. Hebrew Union College similarly developed a branch in Los Angeles with a rabbinical preparatory school, cantors' training school, and a Sunday school teachers program. Yeshiva University established a branch specializing in teacher training and adult education. All three institutions had extensive programs of public education and public lectures and exercised a maturing effect on the growing Los Angeles Jewish community. Brandeis Camp Institute, near the city, with a college camp, children's camp, and weekend cultural retreats exerted a cultural influence on the Jewish community; other summer camps were educational influences for children. The Bureau of Jewish Education did much to raise the level of teaching and encouraged and subsidized Hebrew secondary schools. By 1968 the Los Angeles Hebrew High School, the largest, had more than 500 students. The community centers were organized under the Jewish Centers Association, founded in 1943. By 1968 there were the following neighborhood centers: The Olympic Jewish Center and the Valley Cities Jewish Center, the Los Feliz Jewish Center and the Bay Cities Jewish Center, the West Valley Jewish Center and the North Valley Jewish Center, all under professional direction. The directors of the Jewish Centers Association since the Second World War were Meyer E. Fichman, Bertram

H. Gold, and Charles Mesnick. Los Angeles has been the capital of the movie industry. The development of films moved from New York to Los Angeles beginning in 1912. Film distributors or exhibitors like Marcus Loew, Adolph Zukor, William Fox, Carl Laemmle, Lewis Selznick, Samuel Goldfish (later Goldwyn), and Louis B. Mayer, many of whom had started in the clothing business, came to the suburb of Hollywood to make films. By 1925 the Hollywood movie colony was famous throughout the world. The advent of talking pictures was sparked by the Warner Brothers, Albert, Jack, Sam, and Harry, who produced *The Jazz Singer*, a film about a Jewish cantor. This ushered in a new era in the movies. In 1930 three of the eight major production companies were partly owned by Jews, and 53 of 85 production executives were Jewish. When television production established itself in Hollywood from 1950, Jews were again a considerable proportion of the writers and producers in the industry. The biggest Jewish business in town, however, was not entertainment but construction and financing. Many Jews were involved in one or another aspect of real estate, financing, and other elements of the building trade. They built some of the large suburban areas and tract cities such as Lakewood, La Mirada, Panorama City, and Santa Susanna. Jews, too, were strongly represented in the research, electronic, aircraft, and educational institutions which dotted southern California. The University of California at Los Angeles, for instance, which reputedly had only one Jewish professor in the 1930s, had over 400 Jewish scholars on its faculty 30 years later. As elsewhere, Jews founded thriving practices in medicine, law, and accounting, and were heavily concentrated in furniture, food, sportswear, and retail merchandising. By 1968 Jewish mobility had brought an end to the formerly Jewish Boyle Heights, Adams Street, Temple Street, Wilshire District, and other areas of Jewish concentration. Jews settled in the western and newer sections of sprawling Los Angeles—Westwood, Santa Monica, Beverly Hills. In the San Fernando Valley 100,000 Jews resided in communities from North Hollywood westward to the city limits. Other Jewish communities had been established in the San Gabriel Valley, while thousands moved to Orange County.

Bibliography: M. Vorspan and L. P. Gartner, *History of the Jews of Los Angeles* (1970); H. Newmark, *Sixty Years in Southern California* (1930[3]); M. R. Newmark, in: *Historical Society of Southern California Quarterly*, 24 (1942), 77–97; 25 (1943), 5–65; 38 (1956), 167–84; S. Reichler, in: J. Meltz (ed.), *Mount Sinai Year Book* (1946); I. Soref, in: *Reconstructionist*, 18 (1952/53), 8–12; A. Laurie, *Social Adjustments of German Jewish Refugees in Los Angeles* (Thesis, University of Southern California, 1953); F. Massarik, *Report on the Jewish Population of Los Angeles* (1953); D. Bin Nun, *Religious and Other Cultural Factors Affecting the Assimilation of Jews in Los Angeles* (Thesis, University of Southern California, 1954); R. Glantz, *Jews of California from the Discovery of Gold until 1880* (1960); E. Lipman and A. Vorspan, *Tale of Ten Cities* (1962); J. Turner, in: AJHSP, 54 (1964/65), 123–64; N. B. Stern, *California Jewish History; a Descriptive Bibliography* (1967). [M.V.]

Figure 5. Mass rally at the Hollywood Bowl in Los Angeles at the end of the Six-Day War, June 11, 1967. From *History of the Jews of Los Angeles*.

LOSICE (Pol. **Łosice;** Rus. **Lositsy**), town in Lublin province, E. Poland. Jews probably settled in Losice at the end of the 17th century. At the beginning of the 18th century the townsmen complained to the king about competition from Jewish craftsmen. A synagogue was erected in the 18th century against an annual payment of 200 zlotys. In 1765 there were 389 Jewish poll tax payers in Losice and the vicinity. The community numbered 654 (42% of the total population) in 1827 and 917 (54%) in 1857. From then on their numbers increased considerably due to the horse markets in the town in which large numbers of Jewish dealers took part. The Jewish population numbered 2,396 (71%) in 1897 and 2,708 (70%) in 1921. Before the outbreak of World War II there were about 2,900 Jews in Losice. The community was liquidated on Aug. 22, 1942, when the Jews were deported to *Treblinka camp.

Bibliography: Halpern, Pinkas, index; B. Wasiutyński, *Ludność żydowska w Polsce w wiekach XIX i XX* (1930), 34; ICA, *Rapport pour l'année 1925;* M. Baliński and T. Lipiński, *Staro żytna Polska* (1845), IIIa; Yad Vashem Archives. [EJ]

LOSTICE (Czech **Loštice;** Ger. **Loschitz**), village in N.W. central Moravia, Czechoslovakia. The first documentary mention of a Jew in Lostice is from 1571. A large number of Lostice Jews attended the Leipzig fairs in the 18th century. In 1798 the number of heads of families allotted to Lostice was 71 (see *Familiants Laws). There were 22 Jewish houses in the village in 1834. Their numbers declined sharply after emancipation allowed the Jews freedom of movement; from 483 Jews in 1848, they had fallen to 284 in 1869, and 115 in 1900. In 1928 most of the Jewish quarter was destroyed by fire. The community numbered 55 in 1930 (20% of the total population). By 1938 only six families remained; all were deported during the Holocaust and only one survived. The synagogue was destroyed on Nov. 11, 1938. The appointment of Abraham *Neuda as rabbi of Lostice in 1831, against the wishes of the Chief Rabbi Nehemiah *Trebitsch, created a conflict which spread throughout Moravia.

Bibliography: Gold-Wachstein, in: H. Gold (ed.), *Die Juden und Judengemeinden Maehrens in Vergangenheit und Gegenwart* (1929), 318–20. [M.La.]

LOST PROPERTY (Heb. *avedah u-meẓi'ah;* lit. "lost and found").

The Basis of the Law. Lost property, called *avedah*, is property which has passed out of its owner's possession and whose whereabouts are unknown to him. Both criteria must exist together for the property to be designated as an *avedah* (Rashi and Tos. to BM 30b, and see 31a). The Pentateuch enjoins that an *avedah* be returned to its rightful owner (Deut. 22:1–4). When the owner has clearly despaired of finding an *avedah* and of having it restored to his possession (see **Ye'ush*) his ownership in it ceases, and the finder is not obliged to return it but may retain it for himself (BM 21b). Even in the absence of the owner's *ye'ush*, the same consequence follows if there is no possibility of the *avedah* being restored to him (Tos. to BM 22b; Ran, Nov. Ḥul. 38b). The laws of *avedah u-meẓi'ah* comprise two categories: (1) laws forming part of property law, namely the determination of what constitutes an *avedah* and the point at which ownership thereof ceases so as to enable the property to be acquired by the finder *(zekhiyyah);* and (2) laws circumscribing the *mitzvah* of restoring the lost property, i.e., laws not appertaining to property law, since the finder who fails to return an *avedah* and who leaves it where it was found, transgresses the law but is not obliged to compensate the owner. However, the finder who takes an *avedah* and appropriates it for himself is considered a thief (BM 26b).

Avedah with Retention of Ownership. In accordance with the above definition, it may be noted that, for instance, an animal grazing on public land without the knowledge of the owner and where it is not kept from getting lost is considered an *avedah,* although not if it is grazing on a path when he is aware of its presence there (Ravad, in: Asheri BM 2:26). Similarly, a garment lying in a public thoroughfare is an *avedah,* but not one lying behind a fence (BM 31a). Nor would a vessel that is covered, even though found in a refuse heap, be deemed an *avedah* (BM 25b).

Restoration. The fact that an article has been lost does not in itself involve loss of ownership. Accordingly, a person who comes across property that appears to be lost is duty bound to take it into his custody and care until it can be restored to its owner. In certain circumstances, however, the finder is exempt from this duty. Thus a kohen is prohibited from entering a cemetery and therefore cannot be responsible for an *avedah* which he has seen there (BM 32a). Similarly a person is also exempt if he would not normally take the object, even if it were his own, such as an elderly person for whom such an action would be considered undignified (BM 30a). Furthermore, the finder of property which is of negligible value (i.e., less than a prutah; BM 27a), or a finder who would be involved in expense in restoring the property to its rightful owner (BM 30b), are also exempt. All other finders of lost property, however, must take charge thereof and seek out the owner, to whom it must be returned. Some scholars are of the opinion that the finder's degree of responsibility for an *avedah*—as long as it is in his care—must be the same as that of an unpaid bailee, while others equate the standard of care required to that of a paid bailee (BM 29a; see *Bailment). In the case of an animal, if the expense of its upkeep should prove to be too high to make its return to the owner worthwhile, the finder may sell the animal after a certain period, but has to account for the proceeds to the owner (BM 28b). Inanimate property may not be used by the finder except to prevent its deterioration (BM 29b).

When the owner's identity is unknown to the finder, he must bring the *avedah* to the notice of the public, i.e., by announcing it. If the claimant owner offers notable identification marks *(simanim),* the property is returned to him, but if he is suspected of being an impostor he must also produce evidence of his ownership (BM 28b). Before the destruction of the Temple, the announcement was made from a stone platform in Jerusalem, during the three festivals when the people were gathered there. In later times the announcement was made in the synagogues and it was also enacted that, in places where the secular authorities expropriated all lost property, it would suffice if a finder made the matter known to his neighbors and acquaintances only (BM 28b). If no claimant responds to the announcement, the finder must retain the *avedah,* in trust for the owner, indefinitely (Sh. Ar., ḤM 267:15).

The *mitzvah* to restore lost articles to their owners is not limited to physical objects that are found, but it is extended to include the wider concept of preventing loss to one's fellow. Thus, if a man sees water flooding a neighbor's field and he is able to stop it he has a duty to do so; or if he sees an animal destroying a vineyard he has a duty to drive it away (BM 31a). Furthermore, this wider concept even extends to the person of an individual so that if anyone finds that another has lost his way, it is a *mitzvah* to set him right or to guide him as may be necessary (BK 81b).

Related to the *mitzvah* of returning an *avedah* is that of "loading and unloading" *(perikah u-te'inah),* which also involves saving one's neighbor from suffering losses. A person is required to come to the aid of a neighbor in the unloading and reloading of a heavily laden beast of burden (Ex. 23:5; Deut. 22:4; BM 32a–33a). In view of their common halakhic source, the laws of loading and unloading and of returning lost property are similar and interrelated (see Ḥ. Albeck, *Hashlamot* to *Mishnah,* BM 2:10).

Avedah with Loss of Ownership. When the owner despairs of having lost property restored to him, his ownership thereof ceases (see **Ye'ush*) and title to the property vests in the finder. *Ye'ush* may be inferred from speech or conduct, or may be assumed from the circumstances in which the lost property is found. For instance, an *avedah* which has no identification marks, or which is found in a public thoroughfare, or which appears to have been lost a long time before—factors which make it impossible for the property to be returned—are instances in which *ye'ush* would be inferred. Often it is doubtful whether under certain circumstances the owner is presumed to have despaired, and the sages disagree as to whether the finder has to restore the lost property or acquires ownership in it; e.g., where the lost property has identification marks but they are liable to be erased by being trodden upon, or when the property has marks which were not made intentionally, or whether the place in which the property was found can be an identification mark (BM 23a).

A second category of lost property which becomes ownerless and may therefore be appropriated by the finder, is that of *avedah mi-da'at* ("intentional loss"), i.e., when it appears from the circumstances that the property has been intentionally abandoned or thrown away by its owner and that he no longer desires it, e.g., scattered fruit on a threshing floor, figs which have dropped from a tree alongside a road, open jars of wine or oil left in a public place (BM 21a, , 23b). Finally, lost property which can no longer be restored to its owner ceases to be owned by him and belongs to the finder, even if in the absence of the owner's *ye'ush.* Thus an *avedah* carried away by the river is lost to the owner and "to the whole world," even if the owner is unaware of his loss and even if he does not despair (Tos. to BM 22b). Some scholars nevertheless establish the owner's *ye'ush* in these circumstances, on which ground they justify the above rules (TJ, BM 2:1; 8b; Maim. Yad, Gezelah va-Avedah, 11:10). Similarly, geese and fowl which escaped from their owner and can no longer be restored to him belong to the finder (Ran on Rif Ḥul. ch. *Shillu'aḥ ha-Ken,* introd.).

In talmudic times it was already customary, as a matter of equitable law, to return certain classes of lost property, even if ownership thereof had already ceased, as in the case of an *avedah* dropped in a public thoroughfare (BM 24b). In post-talmudic times the communities of Europe adopted the practice of returning property carried away by a flood or similarly "lost to the world," either in terms of rabbinical enactments *(*takkanot)* or in accordance with the principle of **dina de-malkhuta dina* (Mordecai, BM no. 257; Rema, ḤM 259:7; see also **Shomerim*).

The laws of the State of Israel require all lost property to be handed over to the police, but the finder may claim it for himself if after a certain period the owner is not found.

Bibliography: T. Lampronti, *Paḥad Yiẓḥak,* s.v. *Avedah;* Gulak, Yesodei, 1 (1922), 137ff.; 2 (1922), 190 n. 3; 3 (1922), 34, 40, 67f.; Herzog, Instit, 1 (1936), 299–317; ET, 1 (1951[3]), 11–15; 11 (1965), 53–100; H. E. Baker, *Legal System of Israel* (1968), 132–4. [Sh.A.]

LOT (Heb. לוֹט), son of Haran, grandson of Terah, and nephew of *Abraham (Gen. 11:27). Upon Haran's death in Ur, Terah took Lot with him when, with Abraham and Sarah, he left the city for the land of Canaan. After Terah's death in Haran (11:32), Abraham accepted Lot into the fold of his family in accordance with his patriarchal responsibility to the son of his deceased brother (12:4). Lot accompanied Abraham in his journeys from Haran to Canaan, from Canaan to Egypt, and from Egypt back to Canaan (12:5; 13:1). Abraham and Lot then passed through the Negev into the Benjamite hill country seeking pasture for their livestock which had multiplied in Egypt (12:16; 13:2). A personal quarrel then broke out between their respective shepherds, for "the land would not support them staying together" (13:6). In order to avoid strife, particularly between "kinsmen," Abraham suggested to Lot that they part company. He gave his nephew first choice of the land, whereupon Lot chose the fertile Jordan plain, and settled near Sodom (13:8–12). The biblical narrative tacitly contrasts Abraham's benevolence with Lot's self-interest, and points out that Lot chose to reside with the people of Sodom who "were very wicked sinners against the Lord" (13:13). Abraham continued to show concern for Lot even after their separation. When Lot and his property were captured by *Chedorlaomer and his allies, Abraham pursued them, rescued Lot, and brought him back safely to Sodom (14:1–16).

Lot's separation from Abraham depicted in a Byzantine mosaic, late fourth century. Lot is shown going to his right, Abraham to his left. Rome, S. Maria Maggiore. Photo Alinari, Florence.

Parallels have been pointed out between Noah's position in the *Flood story and that of Lot in Sodom's destruction (19:1–29). In both cases, God's natural, destructive forces act against man because of his wickedness, and both narratives emphasize God's choice in saving the one worthy person of that generation. Lot's righteousness is not mentioned but his hospitality forms a clear contrast to the perversions and wickedness of the people of Sodom (19:2–10). Lot carried his hospitality so far in protecting his visitors, that when the Sodomites demanded to "become intimate" with them he offered his virgin daughters in their place (19:8). Lot is rescued from Sodom for the sake of Abraham (19:29), but his personal merit is implied in the contrast with his sons-in-law who frivolously disbelieved in the destruction of Sodom (19:14), and with his wife who, disobeying orders, looked back, only to become a pillar of salt (19:17, 26).

After the destruction of Sodom and Gomorrah, Lot, who had found protection in Zoar, took to the hills and lived in a cave with his two daughters (19:23, 30). Here, the girls, believing all other males to have become extinct, got their father drunk and without his knowledge committed incest with him (19:31–35). As a result, Lot's older daughter became the mother of *Moab and his younger daughter the mother of *Ben-Ammi (19:36–38). The name "sons of Lot" (Deut. 2:9, 19; Ps. 83:9) in biblical reference to Moab and Ammon is probably based on this etiological story.

The narrative of Lot and his daughters may be an indication of retributive punishment of Lot for offering his daughters to the Sodomites in place of his visitors. Just as he had allowed the claims of courtesy to transcend morality, so his daughters permitted their concern for the propagation of the species to outweigh moral considerations.

The present form of the Lot narrative leaves an unmistakable impression of Israelite ascendancy over Ammon and Moab: Haran, Lot's father and the grandfather of Ammon and Moab, was the youngest of Terah's sons, while Abraham was the oldest; Lot was continually in need of Abraham's protection and help; the incestuous union between Lot and his daughters disgraces their offspring, the Ammonites and Moabites.

The Dead Sea Scroll's Genesis Apocryphon (20–21), written in Aramaic, embroiders the scriptural narrative. According to this source, Lot not only accompanied Abraham to Egypt but also functioned there as spokesman to Pharaoh's agent. He acquired great possessions, obtained a wife, and built himself a house in Sodom.

In the Aggadah: The rabbis often represent Lot in an unfavorable light although in some sources he is praised for his virtues, the word *ẓaddik* of Genesis 18:23 being applied to him. When, however, he separated himself from Abraham, he at the same time separated himself from God (Gen. R. 41:5–7). He chose to settle in Sodom because of his lustful desires (*ibid.*). There he became a usurer (51:6). He was appointed head of the local tribunal (50:3), according to some, because he was the worst of all the five judges there (Tanḥ. B; Va-Yera 21). Although Lot owed his deliverance from Sodom to Abraham's intercession (Mid. Hag. to Gen. 13:11), it was also his reward for not having betrayed Abraham in Egypt when he said that Sarah was his sister (Gen. R. 51:6). A greater reward, however, is that the Messiah will be descended from him through Ruth the Moabite and Naamah the Ammonite (see Gen. R. 51:8 and Naz. 23b–24a). Lot had learned the virtue of hospitality from Abraham and invited the angels to his home although in Sodom this was punishable by death (PdRE 25). As a reward for this act, Israel was forbidden to wage war against his descendants (Yalkut 2 (1877), 782 on Is. 15). The whole night Lot pleaded in favor of Sodom (Lev. R. 23:9). Only the two unmarried daughters of Lot followed him when he left the city (Gen. R. 51:9). Lot is condemned for the negligence which caused him to sleep with his two daughters (Gen. 19:30–38). Although he was not aware of what he was doing he allowed himself to become intoxicated again after he had found out what had happened to him with his elder daughter. However, his daughters' intention was honorable (Hor. 10b). [Ed.]

Islam. Lūṭ (Lot) accompanied Abraham when he left Aram-Naharaim (Sura 29:25), but Muhammad has set aside an important place for him in his prophecies because he regards him to have been, like himself, a prophet sent to rebuke the wicked (22:43; 26:160; 37:133). The name of Sodom, however, is not mentioned in the Koran. It appears that the positive description of Lot in the Koran was influenced by Christian literature, because in the Jewish Midrashim there is no such appreciation. Muhammad's attitude toward the wife of Lot is negative (66:11). The later descriptions found in the works of Ṭabarī, Thaʿlabī, and al-Kisāʾī show an extensive familiarity with the events of Lot's life. They particularly deal at length with the description of the wickedness of Lot's wife, who reported the good deeds of her husband to the men of Sodom. The influence of the Jewish Midrash (Gen. R. 51:5) is obvious. Islamic legend, however, also influenced subsequent Jewish *aggadot*.

For Lot in the arts see *Sodom and Gomorrah. [H.Z.H.]

Bibliography: J. Skinner, *Genesis* (ICC, 1912), 251–67, 306–14; S. E. Loewenstamm, in: EM, 4 (1962), 447–9; N. Sarna, *Understanding Genesis* (1967), index; S. R. Driver, *The Book of Genesis* (1911), 151–5, 197–205; G. von Rad, *Das erste Buch Mose* (1952), 142–6, 184–92. In the Aggadah: Ginzberg, Legends, index. In Islam: Tabarī, *Ta'rīkh*, 1 (1357, A. H.), 205–16; Thaʿlabī, *Qiṣaṣ* (1356 A.H.), 86–90; Kisāʾī, *Qiṣaṣ* (1356, A.H.), 148–9; M. Gruenbaum, *Neue Beitraege zur semitischen Sagenkunde* (1893), 193ff.; H. Speyer, *Die biblischen Erzaehlungen im Qoran* (1931, repr. 1961), 157–8; J. W. Hirschberg, *Juedische und christliche Lehren im vor- und fruehislamischen Arabien* (1939), 58, 122–4; Kuenstlinger, in: *Rocznik Orientalistyczny*, 9 (1930), 281–95 (Ger.); Heller, in: *Shorter Encyclopedia of Islam* (1953), s.v.

LOTAN, GIORA (**Georg Lubinski,** 1902–), Israel social welfare expert. Born in Berlin, Lotan practiced as a lawyer. From 1933 to 1938 he headed the division of vocational training for youth and adults in the Organization of German Jewry, wrote many articles on social welfare in Germany and was coeditor of a journal on social welfare. Immigrating to Ereẓ Israel in 1938, he succeeded Henrietta *Szold as director of the social welfare department of the *Va'ad Le'ummi. During World War II Lotan established and directed the Committee for the Welfare of the Families of Jewish Soldiers and carried out a similar assignment during the War of Independence. In 1948 he was a member of the Government of Israel Social Insurance planning committee. He was the first director general of the National Insurance Institute (1954–69). From 1959 to 1961 he also served as the director general of the Ministry of Social Welfare and later, director general of the Ministry of Labor. Lotan wrote many articles and published a study of social insurance in Israel (*National Insurance in Israel*, 1969). [J.N.]

LOTHAR, ERNST (pseudonym of **Ernst Lothar Mueller;** 1890–), Austrian novelist, author, and stage director. Lothar was born in Bruenn and after studying law entered the Austrian civil service and became state attorney and counsellor at the Ministry of Trade. After World War I Lothar was the theater critic of the Viennese *Neue Freie Presse* and in 1935 he succeeded Max Reinhardt as director of Vienna's "Theater in der Josefstadt." He also staged a number of plays at the Salzburg festivals.

Although he converted to Catholicism and was at pains to sever all connections with Judaism and the Jewish community, Lothar was forced in 1938 to resign his post and leave Austria. He eventually emigrated to the U.S. and became professor of comparative literature at Colorado College. In 1945 he returned to Vienna as theater and music officer in the U.S. army of occupation. He later again became a stage director in Vienna. Lothar was a prolific and versatile writer. His works include the novels *Der Feldherr* (1918), *Der Hellseher* (1929; *The Clairvoyant*, 1931), and a trilogy entitled *Macht ueber alle Menschen* (1921–25). His most famous work in this genre, *Der Engel mit der Posaune* (1946, and frequently republished), was first published in English as *The Angel with the Trumpet* (1944); it deals with the problem of the Jewish wife in several generations of a non-Jewish family. *Unter einer anderen Sonne* (1961; first published in English as *Beneath Another Sun*, 1943) was an American best seller. Lothar's autobiography, *Das Wunder des Ueberlebens* (1960), deals largely with his years in exile.

Bibliography: J. W. Nagl and J. Zeidler, *Deutsch-Oesterreichische Literaturgeschichte*, 4 (1937), 1377. [S.L.S.]

LOTHAR, RUDOLF (pseudonym of **Rudolf Spitzer;** 1865–c. 1936), Austrian playwright and journalist. Lothar, a native of Budapest, became a contributor to the Viennese *Neue Freie Presse*. He wrote many dramas and comedies, some in verse. Erotic in content, they reveal clever psychological insight. The most popular were *Koenig Harlekin* (1900), *Casanovas Sohn* (1920), and *Der Werwolf* (1921). Lothar also wrote operas and the libretto for D'Albert's *Tiefland* (1904). His historical study, *Das Wiener Burgtheater*, was expanded in several editions from 1899 to 1934. His essays on the drama, which include *Henrik Ibsen* (1902), and *Das deutsche Drama der Gegenwart* (1905), maintain the view that drama is applied psychology. Lothar's interest in recording techniques inspired *Die Sprechmaschine* (1924) and his work as editor of the *Jahrbuch fuer Phonotechnik und Phonokunst* (1925). A travel book, *Zwischen drei Welten* (1926), includes an account of his trip to Palestine and a study of Jewish culture.

Bibliography: J. W. Nagl and J. Zeidler, *Deutsch-Oesterreichische Literaturgeschichte*, 4 (1937), 1448. [S.L.S.]

LOTS. Biblical Data. The Bible records the practice of casting lots as a means of arriving at decisions on a variety of problems. These may be grouped into two main categories: (a) the selection of one or more members from a group; (b) the division of goods among members of a group. To the first category belong: the election of a king (I Sam. 10:20, 21); the election of cult functionaries (I Chron. 24–26); the selection of the "scapegoat" for the atonement ritual (Lev. 16:8–10); the selection of residents for Jerusalem (Neh. 11:1); the allocation of responsibility for supplying the wood for the altar (Neh. 10:35); the identification of a party guilty of some sacrilege (Josh. 7:10–26; I Sam. 14:41ff.; cf. Jonah 1:7); the assignment of a tribe as the first wave of troops in a military campaign (Judg. 20:18; cf. 20:9); the selection of a date for some future action (Esth. 3:7; 9:24; note the use of Akk. *pūru*, "lot" glossed by Heb. *goral*, "lot," and the survival of the former in the name of the festival Purim).

The second category involves the distribution of goods, usually booty (Isa. 17:14; Nah. 3:10; Ps. 22:19) or conquered territory. The latter instance accounts for most biblical references to the casting of lots. The division of one's land and its reapportionment to others by lot is cited as a divine punishment in Isaiah 34:17, Joel 4:3, and Obadiah 11. The apportionment of Canaanite territory by lot among the Israelites is related in Numbers 26:52–56; 33:54; 34:13; 36:2, and Joshua 14–19; 21:4–12 (the apportionment of levitical cities, cf. I Chron. 6:39ff.). Distribution of land by the casting of lots is paralleled in both ancient Mesopotamian legal documents and the customs of Palestinian Arabs. Although the Bible provides few details concerning the procedure adopted in the casting of lots, evidence can be supplied from several outside sources (see below; in Talmud and Midrash). It would seem that various objects might serve as lots, the most common ones being of wood and stone (cf. the element *GIŠ* "wood") in the Sumerian *GIŠ.ŠUB.BA* ("lot") and the determinative NA^4 ("stone") describing a lot). A die said to have been cast by the Assyrian official Jaḫali in 833 B.C.E. in the ceremonial selection of the annual eponym is in the form of an inscribed terra-cotta cube.

The technique of casting lots involved throwing lots to the ground and interpreting the results on the basis of a prearranged understanding. The element of "throwing" is also evident in the above-mentioned Sumerian term *GIŠ.ŠUB.BA*, "wood which is cast." So, too, the verbs regularly employed with "lot" in both Akkadian and Hebrew denote "to throw, cast down." In the *Iliad* (3:314ff.) there is preserved a rather detailed description of the procedure: the lots are placed in a helmet and shaken to the ground, the shaker averting his eyes by looking backward. The determination in such cases was based on whose lot fell to the ground first (cf., e.g., Josh. 21:10), each lot having been previously marked to identify its owner (cf. the inscribed names on the lot of the Assyrian eponym and the inscribed shards at Masada). This method is most appropriate in contests, and might be applied to any problem where a choice between participating parties or defined options was involved. In more complex cases, such as the division of land, the area is measured off and the options for partition decided upon (cf., e.g., Josh. 18:4–6), it being understood that specific parcels of land correspond to the lots thrown. It is in this way that words denoting "lot" come to denote that which is decided by the casting of a lot, e.g., a parcel of land, an assigned function, or, more generally, one's destiny.

The biblical notion that the divine will is reflected in the fall of the lots is most clearly expressed in Proverbs 16:33: "The lot is cast from (one's) bosom, but all of its decisions (derive) from the Lord." Divine guidance is also implied by the fact that the lots were cast "before the Lord" (Josh. 18:6; 19:51). Further, the sacral usage of the *Urim and Thummim would also seem to stress the role of lots as a divine means of communication (cf., e.g., I Sam. 14:41, 42). So, too, in Isaiah 34:17 it is the Deity who actually casts the lot determining the inherited portion. The same concept, identically expressed, is attested at Qumran (see the restoration of 1QS 4:26 in J. Licht's *Megillat ha-Serakhim* (1965), 105). In sharp contrast to this notion is the ancient Mesopotamian idea that the gods, as well as men, are subject to the fall of the lots. [Mu.L.]

In the Second Temple Period. The lot was extensively used during the Second Temple period, and particularly in the Temple itself in order to determine the allocation of duties among the priests. No biblical sanction, however, seems to have been sought for this practice, and, as the following passage shows, it was an arrangement of expediency arrived at through experience. "Originally whoever wished to clear the ashes from the altar did so. If they were many they used to run up the ramp and he that came first within four cubits secured the privilege . . . It once happened that both reached the decisive point simultaneously; and one of them pushed the other, and he fell and broke his leg. When the *bet din* saw that danger was involved they ordained that (the privilege of) clearing the altar should be done only by casting lots" (Yoma 2:1–2). The Mishnah goes on to detail the other three lots which were cast for the Temple service. The first covered 13 tasks connected with the sacrifice, from the actual slaughter of the animal to the bringing of the wine oblation, the second for offering the incense, and the third the carrying of the members of the sacrificial animal from the ramp to the altar (*ibid.*, 3–4). The order to cast the lots was given by the overseer (*ibid.*, 4; Tam. 1:2). The Talmud discusses whether or not the priests wore their sacred garments while casting the lots (Yoma 24b). According to the Tosefta (Ta'an. 2:1) the extension of the priestly watches (see **Mishmarot* and *Ma'amadot*) from the four which returned to Zion (Neh. 9:5; 11:10) to the 24 in the Second Temple was also decided by lot.

Whereas there is nothing in the Bible regarding the manner in which the lots were cast (see above) the Talmud gives details. The urn (Heb. *kalpei;* Gr. κάλπη) in which the lots were placed for choosing the scapegoat was originally of boxwood *(eshkero'a)*, but Ben Gamala made one of gold (Yoma 3:9). The urn was shaken and the two lots were taken, one in each hand. If the one bearing the inscription "For the Lord" came up in the right hand, it was regarded as a good omen (4:1). The lot could be made of any material, e.g., olive wood, walnut wood, or boxwood (Yoma 37a). According to the Jerusalem Talmud (Yoma 4:1, 41b), they were made of black and white pebbles. The above, however, refers to the biblically ordained throwing of lots for the scapegoat. For other lotteries it would appear that pieces of paper, or shards, such as those found at Masada (see below), were used. They are referred to as *pitka'ot* (Gr. πιττάκιον).

Josephus gives a number of historical incidents in which choice was made by lot. According to his own, suspect, account, he saved himself from death at Jotapata by arranging that the last ten leaders of the besieged city, of whom he was one, should cast lots, the second one to draw the lot putting to death the previous one, and so on, the last one left having to immolate himself. When he was left with the last other survivor, he persuaded him to abandon the plan (Wars 3:387–91). A similar system was employed for the suicide of the last ten defenders of Masada. Ten were chosen by lot to be the executioners of the defenders, and then the ten drew lots among themselves to determine who should slay the remaining nine, the last then committing suicide (*ibid.*, 7:396ff.). A series of ostraca bearing the names of men found at Masada have been connected by Yadin with this episode. Josephus also states that the Zealots, during the last days of the Temple, in order to mock at the aristocratic families from whom the high priest was usually selected, elected *Phinehas b. Samuel by lot (*ibid.*, 4:155).

The *aggadah* extends the use of the lot to many instances of biblical history. The fact that although Eldad and Medad were "of them that were recorded" but they remained in the camp (Num. 11:26) is explained by stating that Moses chose the 70 elders mentioned in the context by placing 72 slips in an urn; on 70 of them the word "elder" was written, while two were blank, and six were selected from each tribe (Sanh. 17a). A similar lot was drawn to select the 22,000 firstborn *(ibid.)*. The Midrash also adds that Jacob's sons drew lots to decide who was to bring the bloodstained coat of Joseph to Jacob (Gen. R. 84:8). Details are given of the manner in which the territory of Israel was divided among the tribes (BB 122a), and that brothers can divide by lot an estate bequeathed to them is laid down as the law (BB 106b).

Post-Talmudic Times. According to Jewish thought a decision arrived at by lot is not regarded as the result of blind choice. Only once is an objection taken to deciding matters by lot and, peculiarly enough, it has been included in the Shulḥan Arukh. The tosafists apparently had a reading to the *Sifrei Deuteronomy* 18:13: "From what do we learn that it is forbidden to enquire by casting lots? Since the Bible says Thou shalt be wholehearted with the Lord thy God" (see Tos. Shab. 156a). The statement does not occur in the present editions of the *Sifrei*, which give an entirely different deduction from this verse (in Pes. 113b the doctrine that "one should not enquire of the Chaldeans" is deduced from this verse, a reading which is

One of the eleven ostraca found at Masada, thought to be the lots used to select the men to kill their comrades in the doomed fortress in 73 C.E., as described by Josephus (*Wars*, 7:395f.). This ostracon is inscribed *Ben Ya'ir*, possibly Eleazar ben Jair, commander of the Zealot garrison. Courtesy Yigael Yadin, Jerusalem.

supported by the context in which it occurs). Either the *tosafot* had a different reading, or, as appears probable, the deduction is based upon I Samuel 14:41, where the word *tammim* ("wholehearted" in Deut. 18:13) is taken to mean "lots" (see 14:42). Whatever the case may be, this statement has been incorporated in the Shulḥan Arukh (YD 179:1) in the laws against witchcraft. It is, however, an isolated statement; a tolerant and even positive view has been taken throughout the ages with regard to lotteries (but see *Gambling). A possible reflection of this is seen in the fact that although games of chance and gambling are not permitted in the State of Israel, the National Lottery is sponsored by the government and the proceeds of the weekly Mifal ha-Payis (payis is the talmudic word for lottery) are designated for hospitals and schools. [L.I.R.]

Bibliography: S. Bergheim, in: PEFQS (1894), 194; A. Bea, in: *Biblica*, 21 (1940), 198–9; A. L. Oppenheim (ed.), *The Assyrian Dictionary*, 7 (1960), 198–202, s.v. *isqu;* idem, *Ancient Mesopotamia* (1964), 99–100; Y. Yadin, *Masada* (1966), 201.

°**LOUIS,** name of 18 kings of France. Of particular importance in Jewish history are: LOUIS I (the *Pious; 778–840), king of Aquitaine (from the age of three), emperor of the West from 814. Of the Carolingian emperors, Louis was the best disposed toward the Jews. He retained several Jewish merchants at his court in the capacity of "merchants of the palace" who enjoyed extremely favorable privileges, part of which were no doubt also valid for all the Jews in the empire. These privileges guaranteed to their holders and their households (including near relatives, slaves, and servants) the widest liberty of movement, the right to acquire and sell property, and exemption from a variety of tolls and imposts affecting persons and goods in transit. Missionary activities by Christians among pagan slaves owned by these Jewish merchants were prohibited. They were authorized to employ Christians on condition that they were freed from work on Sundays and Christian holidays. Their real property and movable goods were safeguarded. In the judicial sphere, the holders of these privileges were exempted from "question" (torture) and trial by ordeal and could take the oath according to Jewish custom. These privileges later became the model for several privileges granted by local lords (such as Bishop *Rudiger to the Jews of Speyer) or by German emperors (*Henry IV to the Jews of Worms). However, the most serious consequences for the future legal status of the Jews, especially those of France and Germany, were contained in the provisions in Louis' privileges, which placed the Jews under the immediate jurisdiction of the emperor. These enabled him to benefit from the fines and indemnities imposed on persons who injured or killed one of these merchants, who were in the service of the palace or the imperial chamber and had been taken under the emperor's protection (*Mainbour*). Some scholars have concluded that this was the origin of the principle of "imperial servitude" of the Jews, the **servi camerae regis*.

That the greater part of the provisions in these privileges benefited not only the "merchants of the palace" but the whole of the Jewish population is evident from the efforts of *Agobard, bishop of Lyons, to have them repealed when the Jews of Lyons and other towns of his diocese took advantage of them. Louis had moreover appointed an imperial official, the *Magister Judaeorum*, who was responsible for the protection of the Jews. Toward 826–8 this position was held by a certain Evrard. Even before attacking the privileges held by the Jews, Agobard had already, in about 820, clashed with Louis over the Jews, when the bishop had attempted to baptize Jewish children in Lyons, Chalon, Mâcon, and Vienne. At the time, Louis accorded the Jews his full protection. His goodwill toward the Jews was not even weakened when his own deacon, *Bodo, fled to Muslim Spain and embraced Judaism. Texts erroneously attributed to Louis, in particular the "forged capitularies," include enactments less favorable to the Jews, as well as the formula for an oath to be taken in a humiliating manner; these are forgeries belonging to a later period.

Louis VI, king of France from 1108 to 1137. During his reign jurisdiction over the Jews (and their revenues) gradually passed from royal control to the hands of the Church. The Abbey of Saint-Denis, in 1112, obtained from the king judicial control over the Jews in the town. In 1119 Louis ceded half his income from the Jews of *Tours to the Abbey of Saint-Martin there; and in 1122 he granted five houses belonging to Jews to Abbot Suger of Saint-Denis.

LOUIS VII (called the Young), king of France from 1137 to 1180. In 1144, Louis banished from the kingdom those Jews who had been converted to Christianity and had later returned to Judaism. In 1146, Louis authorized the Jews to return to Sens, from where they had been expelled. During the preparations for the Second Crusade, of which he became one of the principal leaders, Peter the Venerable of Cluny wrote to Louis, advising him to confiscate the possessions of the Jews; however, Louis followed the more tolerant counsel of Bernard of Clairvaux, who suggested that only the interest on the debts that Crusaders owed to Jewish moneylenders should be canceled.

LOUIS VIII, king of France from 1223 to 1226. On Nov. 8, 1223, Louis published an edict on the Jews, which had strong fiscal motives. Even though only a number of barons signed this decree, it was declared to be equally binding upon those who had not. The edict, the first attempt by the monarchy to affirm its legislative power over all the baronies of the kingdom, ordained the suppression of all interest due on debts toward the Jews, and the repayment of these debts within three years, on the condition that they were registered. Nonregistered debts as well as those which had been pending for more than five years were to be considered as canceled. The king evidently received a quota of the debts collected in this way, which explains why the fiscal income from the Jews increased to a total of 8,682 livres in 1226. The seal which had served to authenticate debts toward the Jews was abolished. Furthermore, Jews were no longer allowed to move from one seigniory to another. This edict had extremely serious consequences for the future legal position of the Jews.

LOUIS IX, king of France from 1226 to 1270. In his attitude toward the Jews, Louis differed from his predecessors and successors solely in that he placed the interests of the Church before his personal concerns and those of the kingdom in general. This was especially evident in the material assistance he granted to converts: expenses on their behalf often exceeded the income derived from the Jews of France. On other occasions, when this income could not be used for this purpose because the king considered that it was defiled by the sin of usury, he tried to restore the money to the victims of usury or their heirs.

In all other respects Louis' attitude toward the Jews was characterized by implacable enmity, which endured throughout his long reign. As early as 1230, he issued the famous Ordinance of Melun which forbade the Jews to engage in any moneylending activities; at the same time, it was stipulated that no one was allowed to detain a Jew who was the property of another lord. However, Louis was compelled to bow to the economic pressures that rendered dependence on Jewish credit indispensable. In 1234 he seized one-third of the debts owed to the Jews and decreed that in the future they would be permitted to take pledges only in the presence of trustworthy witnesses. There is reason to believe that Louis took no measures to protect Jews persecuted by would-be crusaders in 1236 in several provinces (Anjou, Poitou, Mançois, Touraine, Berry). When in 1239 Pope Gregory IX requested the kings of France and Portugal to order the seizure of Jewish books for examination, Louis was the promptest and most zealous to comply; 24 cartloads of Jewish books were burned in 1242. The resolute and clear-sighted defense conducted by *Jehiel b. Joseph of Paris at the famous Paris *disputation in 1240 was to no avail, for the judgment was virtually predetermined. However, the king's outburst, reported by his biographer Jean de Joinville, that rather than discuss questions of faith with a Jew a layman should plunge his sword into him, was probably caused by his anger at the courageous arguments advanced by R. Jehiel (who was compelled to flee). When *Innocent IV, moved by the protests of the Jews that they could not teach the Bible without the Talmud, ordered it to be examined again, Odo (Eudes) of Chateaurous, chancellor of the University of Paris, opposed the pope and the condemnation stood. In December 1254 Louis threatened with expulsion any Jew who kept copies of the Talmud or other banned books; at the same time he forbade them to engage in any kind of moneylending and ordered them to earn a livelihood in manual toil or any other lawful trade. When he decreed in 1257 or 1258 that the profits of usury should be restored to its victims, the commissioners who carried out the task were authorized to sell the real properties of the Jews to raise the required sums of money. In 1268 Louis called for the arrest of all the Jews and the confiscation of their property in preparation for their eventual expulsion; however, this extreme measure remained in abeyance. A year later, under the influence of the apostate Pablo Christiani, the king ordered the Jews to wear a distinctive *badge and instructed his officers to assist the apostate in compelling Jews to listen to missionary sermons.

It is noteworthy that no Jewish historian mentions Louis on any occasion. Joseph ha-Kohen briefly describes his expulsion project of 1254 but without mentioning the king's name. A contemporary Christian author, Matthew of Paris, makes the most succinct comment on Louis' attitude to the Jews: "See how the king of France hates you and persecutes you."

LOUIS X (called Le Hutin: "The Quarreler"), king of France from 1314 to 1316. Soon after his accession, Louis paved the way for the return of the Jews expelled from the kingdom of France in 1306. On April 1, 1315, he suspended the collection of the debts owed to them which were still outstanding from the time of the expulsion. An ordinance was issued on May 17, 1315, regulating the jurisdiction of the Jews in the eventuality of their return to France, which he authorized on July 28, 1315. It permitted them to resettle in the localities where they had lived previously; ordered that their synagogues, cemeteries, and books, with the exception of the Talmud, should be restored to them; and prohibited them from moneylending against interest, allowing them only to take pledges. However, they were permitted to trade freely. The ordinance concluded with the king's guarantee to take the Jews under "his special protection and administration." In fact, in authorizing the return of the Jews, Louis was principally motivated by monetary interests. The duration of this right of residence was set for 12 years, with the possibility of prolongation and one year's notice of revocation. However, a new expulsion order was isssued less than seven years later (1322) by Charles IV while the delay of one year's notice to enable the Jews to dispose of their possessions was not observed.

LOUIS XI, ruler of Dauphiné from 1440 (as Louis II), and king of France from 1461 to 1483. As dauphin, Louis tried to keep the Jews in his province and even to attract newcomers, offering them in 1449 advantageous privileges if they would settle in Crémieu. On several occasions he defended the Jews against the nobility of Dauphiné, confirming their privileges, and even granting them new ones in 1451, 1453, and 1455. However, after his accession to the throne of France, he imposed a heavy fine of 1,500 gold crowns on them in 1463, because "they had spoken ill of the king during his absence." Nevertheless, he reconfirmed the privileges of the Jews of Dauphiné in 1476, that is, 80 years after they had been banished from the kingdom.

LOUIS XII, king of France from 1498 to 1515. Louis ordered the final expulsion of the Jews from *Provence in 1501. In order to compensate for the loss to his revenues caused by the departure of the Jews from Provence, Louis introduced a tax in 1512 on the remaining Jews there, who had accepted baptism. Known as the "tax of the neophytes," it amounted to a total of 6,000 livres. Down to the 18th century, a number of noble Provençal families were held in discredit because they were reputedly descended from these "neophytes."

LOUIS XIII, king of France from 1610 to 1643 with his mother Marie de Medici as regent until he was declared of age in 1614. On April 23, 1615, Louis signed letters patent renewing the expulsion order "against not only Jews but also those who profess and practice Judaism." This order appears to have been directed especially against Marranos and possibly also against those Jews who had come to Paris with Concini (Maréchal d'Ancre), the young king's minister, and his wife, Leonora Galigai. The letters patent were recorded by the *parlement*, but as far as it is known they were not put into effect in any way. However, after the assassination of Concini at Louis' command, in 1617, Leonora Galigai was tried for sorcery and the charge of practicing Judaism was also brought against her. During Louis' reign, the Jews of *Comtat Venaissin could bring action against defendants living in the kingdom of France and even win their cases. When Louis visited Metz in 1632, he granted the Jews letters patent which declared their presence in the town a necessity. [B.Bl.]

Louis XVI, king of France from 1774 to 1792. Among Louis' ministers were Turgot, Choiseul, and *Malesherbes, who were favorably inclined toward the Jews. On his order a census was taken of the Jews of *Alsace in 1784; letters patent concerning them were issued during the same year. Their delegate, Herz *Cerfberr, was received at Louis' court, although he had no official status, and notice was taken of his representations. The first important step toward improvement of the status of the Jews was the abolition of the body tax in 1784. Other projects to alleviate their situation were under study when the Revolution broke out. [R.N.-B.]

Bibliography: Louis the Pious: G. Kisch, *Forschungen zur Recht- und Sozialgeschichte der Juden in Deutschland waehrend des Mittelalters* (1955), 47–55; Baron, Social², 4 (1957), 48–49; B. Blumenkranz, *Juifs et Chrétiens dans le monde Occidental* (1960), index s.v. *Louis le Pieux*. Louis VI: A. Luchaire, *Louis VI* (1890), 146; Suger, *Vie de Louis VI*, ed. by H. Waquet (1929), 265. Louis VII: H. Gross, in: REJ, 4–5 (1882), 171; W. Williams, *Saint Bernard of Clairvaux* (1935¹, 1953²), 267; Fr. Olivier-Martin, *Histoire du droit français* (1951), 119; R. Anchel, *Les Juifs de France* (1946), 100–2. Louis VIII: C. Petit-Dutaillis, *Etude sur Louis VIII* (1894), 414ff.; G. I. Langmuir, in: *Traditio*, 16 (1960), 215–21. Louis IX: L. Berman, *Histoire des Juifs de France* (1937), 95–105; Gross, Gal Jud, 503–5; Baron, Social², 10 (1965), 58ff.; S. Grayzel, *The Church and the Jews . . .* (1966²), index. Louis X: *Ordonnances des Roys de France*, 1 (1723), 554, 571f., 595ff. Louis XI: E. Pilot de Thorey, *Catalogue des actes du Dauphin Louis II*, 1 (1889), 261, 334, 392, 395, 452; 2 (1889), 237, 411. Louis XII: L. Brunschvicg in: REJ, 33 (1896), 91; E. Camau, *La Provence à Travers les siècles*, 4 (1930), 348, 350; R. Anchel, op. cit., 136–8. Louis XIII: REJ, 12 (1886), 101 n. 4; R. Clément, *La condition des Juifs de Metz sous l'ancien régime* (1903), 33; R. Anchel, *Les Juifs de France* (1946), 128, 135, 147. Louis XVI: A. Hertzberg, *French Enlightenment and the Jews* (1968), index; R. Anchel, op. cit., index.

LOUISIANA, south-central U.S. state at the mouth of the Mississippi River. In 1969 its population was estimated at 3,800,000, including about 15,700 Jews. The largest Jewish communities are *New Orleans (10,000), Shreveport (2,000), and Baton Rouge, the state capital (1,400); there are also organized communities in Alexandria, Bogalusa, Lafayette, Lake Charles, Monroe, Morgan City, Natchitoches, New Iberia, and Opelousas. Jewish welfare federations function in New Orleans (1913), Alexandria (1938), Monroe (1938), and Shreveport (1941). There are approximately 20 congregations in the state; about 25 rabbis serve these congregations and the Hillel Foundation at Tulane University in New Orleans.

Early New Orleans. It has generally been assumed that the Louisiana Black Code, promulgated in Paris in 1724 and excluding settlement by Jews and the practice of any religion other than Catholicism in the French colony of Louisiana, compelled a few Jews to live underground and discouraged the immigration of other Jews to the area. However, no documents attest the actual presence of Jews in the colony until 1757–58. By January 1759, there were already said to be six Jews in New Orleans. One of these

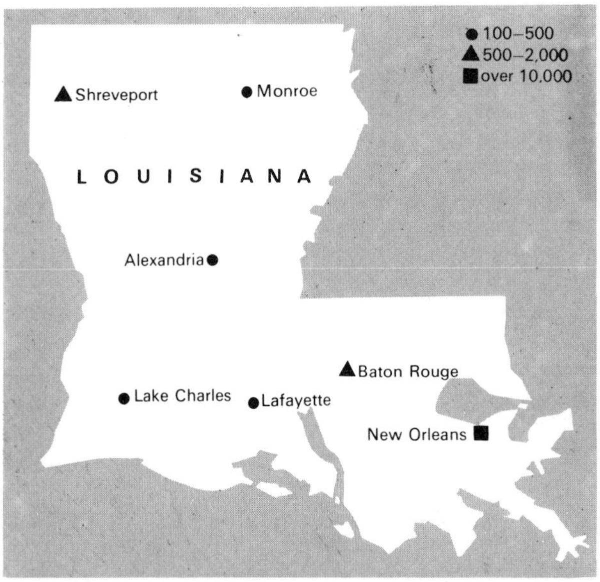

Total Jewish population of Louisiana 15,630
% of Jews in general population of Louisiana 0.42
% of Louisiana Jews in Jewish population of U.S.A. 0.27

Jewish communities in Louisiana. Population figures for 1968.

was Isaac Rodriguez Monsanto, a Dutch-born merchant who had taken his brothers and sisters to Curaçao before moving his headquarters to New Orleans. Between 1757 and 1769 Monsanto conducted successful business operations with settlers and merchants throughout Louisiana, the Illinois country, Atlantic and Caribbean ports, and Europe. Probably the first Jew to set foot in almost every settled village or trading and/or military post in the Louisiana area was Isaac Monsanto or one of his entourage—his brothers Manuel, Jacob, and Benjamin, his partners Manuel de Britto and Mets, and Isaac Henriques Fastio, another associate. In 1769, when Monsanto and his family and associates were expelled from New Orleans under the rigorous Spanish rule of Governor Alejandro O'Reilly, the Monsantos took refuge in British West Florida, but all gradually filtered back into Spanish Louisiana. They were known to be Jews but participated in the rituals of the Catholic Church without baptism.

Judah *Touro arrived in New Orleans in late 1801 or early 1802 and became, through diligence and his simple manner of living, a wealthy man. He was indifferent to Judaism until late in life, when he was persuaded by Gershom Kursheedt to build a synagogue for the second New Orleans congregation, Nefutzoth Yehudah, organized in 1845. Other early settlers were equally unconcerned about the preservation of Jewish identity.

Of the approximately 15 Jews who were in New Orleans in January 1815, when the famous battle for the city between General Andrew Jackson and the British took place, at least ten and possibly 11 had some part in the action, Touro suffering a near-fatal wound. Of these 15, seven remained bachelors, seven intermarried, and one, Manis Jacobs, married a Christian woman after his first (Jewish) wife died. It was Manis Jacobs who became the first president of Shaarei Chassed (1827), the first congregation in Louisiana and indeed anywhere on the Gulf Coast or in the Mississippi Valley south of Cincinnati. This congregation, Sephardi at the outset, later became Ashkenazi as increasing numbers of Jews arrived in the town from the German-speaking lands. But Jewish life did not prosper in New Orleans. The wealthiest men did not support any of the three congregations in existence by 1850. (Gates of

Prayer Congregation was established in the Lafayette suburb of New Orleans in January of that year.) Touro's building of a synagogue did not inspire others to do likewise. Intermarriage continued apace in New Orleans, perhaps more than in any major city in the United States.

German Jews at the port of New Orleans fanned out from that city into more rural areas and became peddlers and artisans. Significant numbers of Jews were country merchants and traders in small Louisiana towns before the Civil War. They established benevolent societies, cemeteries, or congregations in Alexandria (1854), Donaldsonville (1856), Baton Rouge (1858), and Monroe (1861). But the most significant Jewish institution in Louisiana was the Association for the Relief of Jewish Widows and Orphans of New Orleans (1854), the earliest agency of its kind in the United States. Made necessary by the frequent deaths from yellow fever in the New Orleans area, this association was supported from its inception by assimilated Jews who demonstrated no other concern with their Jewish identity. The free-wheeling atmosphere of the state, dominated by New Orleans, encouraged the full participation and integration of Jews; there was then little anti-Jewish prejudice, which seems to have gained momentum only in the late 19th century. Among Louisiana's notable assimilationist Jews were U.S. Senator Judah P. *Benjamin (1853–61); Henry M. Hyams, Benjamin's cousin, lieutenant governor of Louisiana in 1859; and Dr. Edwin Warren Moise, speaker of the Louisiana legislature at the same time and later state attorney general. It was apparently no accident that each of these men intermarried. To those who are aware of the sharp social distinctions obtaining in New Orleans during the 20th century, it seems difficult to believe that the first rex of Mardi Gras, in 1872, was Louis J. Salomon, a great-grandson of Haym *Salomon, the well-known Revolutionary War patriot.

The Civil War and After. More than 200 Louisiana Jews are known by name to have served in the Confederate forces, but the true number is probably three times that large. Three of these men, S. M. Hymans, Edwin I. Kursheedt, and Leon R. Marks, achieved the rank of colonel. Benjamin Franklin Jones, the son of one of Lincoln's closest friends, served as a private; he became the second Louisiana Jew to serve in the U.S. Senate (1879–85). Joseph Bensadon, who was the first medical director of Touro Infirmary (1854), was a surgeon in the Confederate army from 1862 to 1865.

The distinctive leader of the Jews of New Orleans after the Civil War was Rabbi James K. *Gutheim. However, he was apparently so troubled by the dismal future of New Orleans Jewry after the Civil War that he consented to go to New York City in 1868. He returned to New Orleans four years later in response to the creation of a new, Reform congregation by his friends. At the same time the Reform movement was attempting to stem the tides of intermarriage and conversion in other communities, and most of the congregations in Louisiana had become Reform by 1885.

Rabbi Isaac Leucht of the Shaarei Chassed congregation assisted in relief work during the yellow fever epidemic of 1866, as well as in civic work; he became president of the Red Cross Society and a member of the State Board of Education.

In 1882 the Hebrew Foreign Mission Society of New Orleans, in conjunction with the Hebrew Emigrant Aid Society, sponsored an agricultural colony of Russian Jews at Sicily Island in Catahoula Parish. But the project failed when the Mississippi River overflowed and flooded the entire area that year.

Jewish Life in the 19th and 20th Centuries. Beginning in the mid-19th century, Jewish merchants and traders organized communities throughout the state. The largest, except for New Orleans, was Shreveport, where a synagogue, Har El, was founded in 1859 and an Orthodox congregation was organized in 1892. One of the marks of the development of intolerance was a local ordinance (1873) prohibiting Jews from opening their stores on Sunday. Zionist, B'nai B'rith, and other communal organizations were formed, and in 1914 the Reform temple was dedicated. A Shreveport attorney, Sidney Herold, in 1915 successfully persuaded the State Court of Appeals to prohibit the reading of the Bible in public schools.

Baton Rouge, the state capital, was settled by Jews in the early 19th century, but not until 1868 was their number sufficient to form the small congregation which became B'nai Israel in 1879. In Alexandria a Young Men's Hebrew Association was organized in 1882, and the city has Reform and Orthodox synagogues. Jewish communities appeared in Morgan City in 1875, in Opelousas in 1877, and in Lake Charles in 1895. In Bogalusa, an Orthodox congregation was organized in 1925. Communities also functioned in Plaquemine (1856–1932), St. Francisville (1877–1905), and Bastrop (1877–1923). Bastrop and other small communities are served by the United Jewish Charities of Northeast Louisiana, organized in 1938 in Monroe. From 1915 to 1933 Mendel Silber of New Orleans ministered to congregations in New Iberia, Morgan City, and Plaquemine.

In the 20th century movement from smaller to larger communities occurred among Louisiana Jews. Moreover, the total population of Louisiana Jewry declined somewhat after 1940, when there were about 16,000 Jews in the state. But despite the continuing small proportion of Jews in the state population, many Louisiana Jews have attained statewide or national prominence, including the 19th-century philanthropist Isidore *Newman; Isaac Delgado, a charter member of the Louisiana Sugar Exchange who contributed to the art museum and Charity Hospital memorial building; the actress Adah Isaacs *Menken; U.S. congressman Adolph Meier (1891–1908); and state legislators George Joel Ginsberg (1928–32), who sought the impeachment of Governor Huey P. Long before the State Senate in 1929, and Norman Bauer, speaker of the House of Representatives in 1942. Henry A. Lazarus was a member of the state Supreme Court (1880) and Emile Godchaux (1909–18), Max Dinkelspiel (1919–24), and I. D. Moor served on the state Court of Appeals. New Orleans, Alexandria, Monroe, Crowley, Donaldsonville, and Morgan City have elected Jewish mayors, and many Jews have served as school board members and presidents.

Jews have prospered financially in Louisiana, and the Jewish professional and managerial classes have grown significantly since 1940.

Bibliography: L. Shpall, *Jews in Louisiana* (1936); B. Kaplan, *Eternal Stranger* (1957), 39–43; B. Lemann, *Lemann Family of Louisiana* (1965); B. Korn, *Early Jews of New Orleans* (1969); Louisiana Historical Records Survey, *Inventory of Jewish Congregations and Organizations* (1941); A. P. Nasatir and L. Shpall, in: AJHSQ, 53, no. 1 (1963), 3–43.

[B.W.K./E.GR.]

LOUISVILLE, the largest city in Kentucky. The estimated Jewish population of Louisville is 8,500. Louisville was among the first inland communities to contribute to indigenous American Jewish life. It has one of the oldest B'nai B'rith lodges (1852) and Y.M.H.A.-J.C.C.'s (1862); it also has a representative and comprehensive Conference of Jewish Organizations (1934), which now sponsors a Jewish vocational service and a bureau of Jewish education, and supports a community Hebrew school, day school, social service agency, home for the aged (Four Courts), a Jewish children's home, a Jewish hospital, and other local and national agencies. The city has two Orthodox, one Conservative and two Reform congregations, each operating a Sunday school. Practically every national Jewish organization is represented in the city. Four years before its foundation Joseph Simon of Lancaster, Pennsylvania, and his partners John Connolly and John Campbell laid claim to much of what is now Louisville. George Rogers Clark, whose expedition was partially financed by Barnard and Michael *Gratz, occupied the area in 1778 and Clark's men named the settlement Louisville. The owners appealed against the Clark "usurpation" to the Virginia Assembly (at the time exercising jurisdiction over Kentucky), which on Oct. 20, 1783, ruled that nothing shall "affect or prejudice the title of said John Campbell and Joseph Simon to the land aforesaid." Evidence abounds of Jewish fur traders, explorers, and peddlers in the area even before the founding of the city (see *Kentucky for Daniel Boone and his Jewish contacts). In the Arthur Lee Campbell manuscript collection at the Louisville Filson Club there is an 1830 reference to an "Israelite cemetery" in the city. As early as June 4, 1828, a Manis Jacobs of New Orleans wrote to a Jacob A. Solis "to find donors near Louisville" for a synagogue in the Louisiana city. In 1832 the Louisville Directory contained a score or more Jewish names. The *Journals of the House of Representatives* (Kentucky) record on Feb. 12, 1834, that Mr. (Abraham) *Jonas presented a "petition of sundry citizens of Louisville . . . praying an act of incorporation of an Israelitish Congregation there." The first formal and sustained synagogue in the city was organized in 1836. It later became known as Adath Israel. The late 1840s and the 1850s brought small waves of German Jews to the city. The 1880s and the succeeding years attracted mostly East European groups. Many Jews caught in the Gold Rush of the mid-19th century stopped in Louisville on their way to California. Some chose to remain in the city. Among the outstanding Jewish personalities in Louisville were Louis D. *Brandeis, who is interred on the campus of the University of Louisville; Lewis N. *Dembitz; I. W. Bernheim, a philanthropist who enriched the cultural life of the city by an art collection in the public library, the Thomas Jefferson statue by Moses *Ezekiel in front of the Old Court House, and other gifts; Rabbi Emil G. *Hirsch; Rabbi Hyman G. *Enelow; Rabbi B. H. Gotthelf, the second Jewish chaplain in the Union army, 1862; Rabbi Adolph Moses; Rabbi Ignatius Mueller; Rabbi S. J. Scheinfeld; Rabbi A. L. Zarchi; Rabbi Joseph Rauch, for whom a planetarium on the campus of the University of Louisville is named; and Charles W. Morris, founder of the Louisville Conference of Jewish Organizations and a national vice-president of the American Jewish Committee and of the Jewish Welfare Board. Louisville, the metropolis of a border state during the Civil War, has maintained the moderate political tradition of a border city. In its Jewish life, too, the community has no excessive wealth, nor dire poverty, no ultra-Orthodoxy, nor extreme Reform. The main congregations are: Adath Israel (Reform, founded 1836); Brith Sholom (Reform, 1881); Adath Jeshurun (Conservative, 1884); Anshei Sfard (Orthodox, 1893); Keneseth Israel (Orthodox, 1926). Being among the first cities in the South to integrate its schools and public institutions, Louisville rarely exhibited virulent anti-Semitism. Even the vestiges of some early socioeconomic discrimination are apparently dissipating. Jews who in the younger days of the city tended to become artisans and small shopkeepers now take part in every economic, social, political, literary, artistic, and scientific activity, including the tobacco, liquor, and horse racing industries. Several Louisville Jews hold high offices in national organizations and in eminent academic bodies.

Statue of Thomas Jefferson by Moses Ezekiel, in front of the old courthouse of Louisville, Kentucky. Courtesy *Louisville Courier-Journal.*

Bibliography: L. N. Dembitz, in: AJHSP, 1 (1892), 99–101; J. R. Marcus (ed.), *Memoirs of American Jews*, index; I. T. Naamani, in: *Jewish Frontier*, 22, no. 4 (1955), 8–13; AJHS (1914), index; *A History of the Jews of Louisville* (n.d.), publ. by AJHS.

[I.T.N.]

LOUNY (Ger. **Laun**), town in N.W. Bohemia, Czechoslovakia. Jews are first mentioned in Louny in 1254—one year after it received its freedom as a town—as living on a Jewish street and having a synagogue and a cemetery. The city records for 1380–92 contained a special section for Jewish lawsuits. In 1505 there were 12 Jewish houses. A Jew, accused in 1541 of having acquired a monstrance, was burned and the community was expelled from the town. From 1655 only one Jewish family was protected by the town, but in 1680 a cemetery was established. At the end of the 18th century there were 43 "bad Jews" in Louny, i.e., Jews who did not have permission under the *Familiants Law to live there, and the first Jew to settle there in 1849 was forcibly returned to his former town by the crowd. Thereafter, Jews came to Louny, a synagogue was built, and in 1874 a German-language Jewish school was founded (given up in 1897); a new cemetery was built in 1875 (which still existed in 1970). In 1893 the community adopted Czech as the official language. In 1876 there were 44 taxpayers; in 1902 there were 666 Jews in Louny and the 18 surrounding villages; and in 1930 there were 205 (1.8% of the total population). The community was deported to the Nazi death camps in 1942 and the synagogue's equipment was sent to the Central Jewish Museum, Prague. The community was not reestablished after World War II.

Bibliography: K. Linhart, in: H. Gold (ed.), *Die Juden und Judengemeinden Boehmens in Vergangenheit und Gegenwart* (1934), 348–61; F. Štědry, *Dějiny města Loun* (1930); Abeles, in: *Juedisches Centralblatt*, 3 (1884), 115–6.

[J.HER.]

LOURIE, ARTHUR (1903–), Israel diplomat. Born in Johannesburg, South Africa, Lourie practiced as a barrister-at-law and lectured in Roman-Dutch law at Witwatersrand University. He served as political secretary of the Jewish Agency in London from 1933 until 1948, working under Nahum *Sokolow and Chaim *Weizmann. He spent most of World War II in the United States, engaged in Zionist political work. In 1945 he was a member of the Jewish Agency delegation at the San Francisco U.N. Conference and, from 1946 to 1948, was director of the Jewish Agency U.N. Affairs Office in New York. From 1948 Lourie was a member of the Israel foreign service: from 1948 to 1953 he was Israel consul general in New York, from 1957 to 1959 he was ambassador to Canada, from 1960 to 1965 ambassador to the United Kingdom, and deputy director-general, Israel foreign ministry, 1965–72. A member of several Israel delegations to the U.N. General Assembly, he was head of the delegation in 1959. [B.J.]

LOURIE, NORMAN VICTOR (1912–), U.S. social worker and government official. Born in New York, from 1937 to 1939 Lourie was a research associate with the Russell Sage Foundation and from 1939 to 1943, an assistant director of the Bronx House and Madison House settlements in Manhattan. After serving in World War II as director of the social work section of the U.S. Army School for Military Neuropsychiatry, he became the director of the Hawthorne Cedar Knoll School for the correction of juvenile delinquents (1946–51). In 1951 he moved to Philadelphia to direct the work of the Association for Jewish Children and from 1955 onward was executive secretary of Pennsylvania's Department of Public Welfare. He took part in the White House Conferences on Children and Youth in 1950 and 1960 and was a member of the advisory council of the President's Committee on Juvenile Delinquency. He was president both of the National Association of Social Workers and the Academy of Certified Social Workers during 1961 to 1963 as well as of the American Orthopsychiatric Association, 1967. Lourie was chairman of the editorial board of the *Journal of Jewish Communal Service* (1952–58) and *Child Welfare* (1962–64). [Ed.]

LOUSE (Heb. כִּנָּם, כִּנִּים in plural. Talmud כִּנָּה, singular), insect; one of the ten plagues with which Egypt was smitten (Ex. 8:13–14; Ps. 105:31) was the plague of lice. The כֵּן in Isaiah (51.6): "They that dwell therein shall die *kemo-khen*" may refer to the louse; i.e., "like a louse." The louse caused much suffering to people of all classes in former times. A distinction was made between the dark-colored head louse and the light-colored clothes louse (Pes. 112b), two strains of the *Pediculus hominis,* against which people sought to protect themselves by constantly changing and washing their clothes—although they were also compelled to search their garments to kill the lice (Tosef., Shab. 16:21, where the louse is called *ma'akholet,* i.e., the eater). Lice nits were regarded as the smallest of creatures, and hence the statement that "the Holy One blessed be He feeds the whole world, from the horned buffalo to the lice nits" (Av. Zar. 3b). Some maintained that "the louse does not multiply and increase" (Shab. 107b) but generates spontaneously.

Bibliography: Lewysohn, Zool, 324–6; J. Feliks, *The Animal World of the Bible* (1962), 131. [J.F.]

LOVE.

In the Bible. In the Bible, "love" has, like the word "love" in most languages, many and various shades of meaning.

Hebrew Words for "Love." It is represented by Hebrew words which range from sensuous, and often evil, desire or passionate love between man and woman (II Sam. 13:4; Jer. 2:33), through family affection, up to theological conceptions of God's love for Israel, and of Israel's love for God. In most of the passages, "to accept, adopt, or recognize," could profitably be substituted for "to love," and "to reject, disown," or "repudiate," for "to hate." The root most commonly used is *ʾahav.* Another verb *riḥam* and the noun *raḥamim* point to the family feeling through their connection with *reḥem,* the mother's womb; they express the *compassion presupposing the suffering, distress, or weakness of the other party. The root *ḥafeẓ* means "wish for" or "delight in," but is also used, with a person as object, in the sense of "feel inclined." A similar meaning is attached to *raẓah,* "to be pleased with," and "accept." The root *ḥashak (ḥashaq)* involves instead the sense of personal attachment. As for the verb *ḥanan* and the noun *ḥen,* both express the idea of concrete favor, rather than warm affection. Finally, the often-used word *ḥesed* means "loyalty," but sometimes designates the "real love" (Gen. 20:13; 47:29; I Sam. 20:8; II Sam. 9:1; Jer. 2:2; Ruth 2:20), which is evinced in acts of devotion and friendship, and is conditioned by the fact that there are two parties connected with each other by ties of family, tribe, nationality, treaty, covenant, etc.

Love as a Spontaneous Relationship. The word "love" is first of all used to denote the father's or mother's love (Gen. 22:2; 25:28; 37:3; 44:20; Prov. 13:24; Ruth 4:15), the love between young people intending to marry (Gen. 29:18, 20; I Sam. 18:20), or between husband and wife (Gen. 24:67; 29:30, 32; Judg. 14:16; 16:15; I Sam. 1:5; Prov. 5:19; Eccles. 9:9; II Chron. 11:21). This use is largely attested in the Song of Songs, whose unique obvious theme is love between man and woman, celebrated in glowing colors and passionate words (e.g., 1:3, 4, 7; 2:5; 3:1, 2, 3, 4; 5:8). "Love" designates also the specifically sexual desire for a woman (II Sam. 13:1, 4, 15). The verb *ʾahev* denoted also affection and esteem. It is used in this sense for David and Jonathan, to express natural friendship (I Sam. 18:1, 3; 20:17; II Sam. 1:26; cf. I Sam. 16:21), for a servant, to denote his attachment to his master's family (Ex. 21:5); and for the people, to signify their enthusiastic sympathy for David (I Sam. 18:16, 22, 28). The participle *ʾohev* means "friend" at least 17 times out of the 62 occurring in the Bible. On the other hand, Isaac, for instance, is said to "love" game as Rebekah knew to prepare it (Gen. 27:4, 9, 14). The verb *ʾahev* seems to express there a preference, as in several other texts (Gen. 25:28; 37:3, 4; Deut. 21:15; I Sam. 1:5).

The rendering of *reʿa* in Leviticus 19:18 ("Love your *reʿa* as yourself"), and similar passages, by "neighbor" is hallowed by tradition; but "fellow citizen" would be more enlightening, since the reference here to one's fellow Israelite is obvious from its identification by parallelism with "kinsmen" *(bene ʿammekha)* in Leviticus 19:18 and the fact that an additional verse, verse 34, was needed in order to include the metic (*ger,* but see Love of Neighbor, below). Common sense tells that the "love" that these verses require the Israelite to extend to his fellow citizen and to the metic residing in Israel is consideration, or, as Jewish tradition realistically defines it, not treating them in a manner in which one would resent being treated (so the interpretation of Pseudo-Jonathan, Lev. 19:18, 34, in accordance with the famous saying attributed in Shab. 31a to Hillel but in Eusebius, *Praeparatio evangelica,* 8:7, 8, to Philo, and also to be found in Arist. 207; Tob. 4:15; Test. Patr., Iss. 5:2; Test. Patr., Dan 5:3).

The Reciprocal Love of God and People. In the Bible, the object of the divine love is generally the people of Israel. The two passages where Jerusalem is presented as the object of God's love (Ps. 78:68; 87:2) are only variants of that fundamental aspect. The relation of God to His people is conceived as a union marked by love on one side and demanding a corresponding love on the other. This reciprocal love of God and the people is expressed in categories of familial or social unity: father-son relationship, marriage analogy, or covenantal love.

The doctrine of God's love for Israel, and the imperative necessity of Israel's love for God are rarely found in the first four books of the Bible, but they constitute the basic principles of the Deuteronomic teaching. The Lord's love for Israel is there viewed as the result of His election, manifested in the covenant and sanctioned by it. This clearly appears in Deuteronomy 7:7–8, where the divine love for Israel is mentioned paralleling the oath sworn by God in the rite of the covenant-making, and is ultimately justified by God's free choice. His free and personal love to Israel is manifested above all in the deliverance from Egypt. This primal love of the Lord for Israel (Deut. 4:37; 7:13; 10:15; 23:6) is the basis for the obligation of Israel's love in return (Deut. 6:5; 7:9; 10:12; 11:1, 13, 22; 13:4; 19:9; 30:6, 16, 20). Love in Deuteronomy is therefore a love that God can command: "You shall love the Lord your God with all your heart, and with all your soul, and with all your might" (Deut. 6:5; cf. 10:12; 11:1; 30:6). It is also a love intimately related to fear and reverence (Deut. 4:10; 5:29; 6:24; 8:6; 10:12; 14:23; 17:19; 31:13). Above all, it is a love which must be expressed in obedience to the requirements of the law. For to love God is to be loyal *(davak)* to Him (Deut. 4:4; 10:20; 11:22; 13:5; 30:20), to walk in His ways (Deut. 10:12; 11:22; 19:9; 30:16), to keep His commandments (Deut. 10:13; 11:1, 22; 19:9), to fulfill them (Deut. 11:22; 19:9), to heed them or His voice (Deut. 11:13; 13:5), and to serve Him (Deut. 6:13; 10:12; 11:13; 13:5). It is, in brief, a love defined by and pledged in the covenant. If the people appear to be unworthy of the divine love because of its ingratitude or infidelity, the love will change into wrath.

W. L. Moran has established the relationship of this Deuteronomic concept of love with the ideology and the terminology of ancient oriental treaties, from the 18th to the 7th centuries B.C.E., in which the term "love" is used to describe the loyalty and friendship joining independent and equal rulers (cf. I Kings 5:15), overlord and vassal, or king and subject. This use of the term "love" is no innovation of the author of Deuteronomy 6:5, which is generally considered the earliest reference to the love of God in Deuteronomy. Since Judges 5:31 belongs most likely to the original Song of Deborah and uses the expression "those who love Him," it is probable that the term "love" goes back to a very early period in the Israelite covenant tradition. The formula "those who love Me" appears also in the passage of Exodus 20:6 and Deuteronomy 5:10, which belongs to the Decalogue. The father-son relationship in Deuteronomy, which reflects the very ancient Israelite concept of Israel as the Lord's son (cf. Deut. 32:6, 10–11, 18–20), is also found in the body of the Book of Deuteronomy (Deut. 1:31; 8:5; 14:1). If there is tenderness in this relationship as seen in Deuteronomy 1:31; 32:10–11; Isaiah 63:16; Jeremiah 3:19; 31:9, and Hosea 11:1, the Lord is in Deuteronomy 8:5 the father who does not spare the rod, but this divine chastening is considered in Proverbs 3:11–12 as a sign of the divine love. Israel appears as a disobedient son also in Isaiah 1:2 and 30:9. He is disloyal even to the point of turning away from the Father to other gods (Deut. 32:18–20), just as a faithless vassal abandons his sovereign for another overlord. God intervenes then as one who is angry with his sons for their disloyalty (Deut. 32:19), and who is, therefore, ready to punish them (Isa. 30:1–5, 8–14). In Deuteronomy 14:1, the relationship between father and son as applied to God and Israel is a motive to obey a particular command. It is thus clearly akin to the covenantal love, which should exist between the suzerain and the vassal, called respectively father and son in the diplomatic terminology of the ancient Near East (cf. E. Lipinski, *Le poème royal du Psaume LXXXIX*, 1–5, 20–38 (1967), 57–66). Malachi 1:6 parallels the son with the servant, and expects reverence from each. Since covenantal love involves reverential fear, there may be here a later offshoot of the same tradition. It may reasonably be inferred, therefore, that the ancient Israelite concept of Israel as God's son is very close to the Deuteronomic conception of covenantal love between God and Israel, though it is also associated with the current imagery of father and son. It can be influenced too by the idea of divine Fatherhood, expressed in personal names of the type *ʾaviyyah* (Abijah), *ʾaviyyahu* (Abijahu), "the Lord is my Father." Occasionally, the affection of God for His people is also depicted as the love of a mother for her child (Isa. 49:15; cf. 66:13; Deut. 32:11).

The husband-wife metaphor of Hosea 2 recurs in the earliest poems of Jeremiah (Jer. 2–3; 31:2–6), who had most likely been influenced in his youth by the Hoseanic tradition. Ezekiel, too, knew the symbolism of the marriage (Ezek. 16; 23), which recurs again in Deutero-Isaiah as a means of describing Israel's restoration after the Exile: Zion was a deserted wife (Isa. 49:14; 54:6; cf. 60:15; 62:4), without children (Isa. 49:20; 51:18; 54:1), and reduced to captivity (Isa. 40:2; 52:2), because she has been repudiated by the Lord (Isa. 50:1); but the Lord had decided to take her back (Isa. 54:5–8). YHWH's wrath required the rejection of the people—the repudiation of the unfaithful wife. This was the historical turning point with which the prophets were confronted. Nevertheless, the people was the Lord's people, the chosen people, the object of God's love. What would become of the election and of the divine plan for Israel if the "repudiation" became definitive? A tension ensued between God's love and God's wrath. Even the end of Judah as an independent state did not mean the complete annihilation of the nation. The reason is that Israel is precious in the Lord's eyes, and is loved by the Lord. In Hosea 14:5 it is expressly said that God of His own free will and love will heal the faithlessness of His people. Ezekiel emphasizes that the Lord will restore Israel, but not because of her fidelity to the covenant (Ezek. 16:60–68); and Deutero-Isaiah (under the influence of Ezekiel, e.g. ch. 36) says that God blots out the transgressions of His people not because of their sacrifices, but "for His own sake," i.e., His sovereign love (Isa. 43:22–44:5).

A few texts affirm that God loves the righteous (Ps. 146:8; Prov. 15:9; cf. 3:12), and some psalmists refer to God's compassion (Ps. 25:6; 40:12; 51:3; 69:17; 119:77) for all His creatures (Ps. 145:9). Such texts are relatively rare: the Lord's love is almost exclusively love for Israel, the elect people. Even the prophets never say that the Lord "loves" other peoples, or that mankind is an object of His love; but God's actions in Israel's history are dictated by His love. The same is true of His punitive educative work as well as of His gracious gifts in the continued course of history. This is the main theme of the biblical theology of love, probably because the divine love is generally conceived as related to the covenant. The use of the word *ḥesed* reveals indeed that this term also belongs to the covenantal terminology.

The love for God is sometimes signified in an indirect way, without mentioning the divine name. Thus when Amos 5:15 exhorts the people to "love the good," he intends the justice demanded by the divine law (cf. Micah 6:8; Ps. 52:5), which is mentioned 11 times in Psalm 119 as object of love (vs. 47, 48, 97, 113, 119, 127, 140, 159, 163, 165, 167). Of course, the author meant by law, the stipulations of the covenant. The love of wisdom (Prov.

8:17, 21; cf. 4:5–6; 7:4; 29:3; Eccles. 4:11–14) is also interpreted as love of the law (Wisd. 6:17–18; cf. 6:12; 7:10), but this theme probably has an Egyptian origin: the personified divine wisdom seems to be an Israelite adaptation of the Old Egyptian Maat, whose love was also highly recommended in texts celebrating this deified idea of truth and justice (cf. Ch. Kayatz, *Studien zu Proverbien 1–9* (1966), 98–102). The biblical passages mentioning the love for the Temple or Jerusalem (Isa. 66:10; Ps. 26:8; 122:9) express instead the desire for the divine familiarity, more vividly felt in the holy places. [E.Li.]

Post-Biblical. The Song of Songs has been called the world's greatest love poetry. In range of imagery, lyric quality, and personal insight, it has taught the true nature of love to much of mankind. While it was admitted to the Bible only after a struggle, and then, apparently, because it was seen as an allegory of the love of God for Israel, the manifest content of the poems could never be denied. Thus an intimate link was established in Jewish literature between human love and the love of God. Jewish mysticism made this a major motif in its esoteric teaching. Rabbinic literature likewise reveals its appreciation of love only tangentially but with the same deep feeling: "A man once said, 'When love was strong, we could have made our bed on a sword-blade; Now that our love has grown weak, a bed of 60 cubits is not large enough for us'" (Sanh. 7a).

It is not the love in itself, or the passion associated with it, or its sexual fulfillment which are valued in these writings, as much as the understanding and the generosity which love creates and sustains. Thus, understanding and generosity become the highest ideals for human relationships. Love between man and woman is almost always connected with marriage, which is either the goal of love or the motive which brings it into being. This ideal of love in marriage which leads to understanding and generosity, though influenced by the various cultural circumstances among which Jews found themselves, remained relatively stable over the centuries. Though the ideal of romantic, courtly love did penetrate the Jewish community in the 11th and 12th centuries, unrequited passion never became a major Jewish concern.

Following the Aristotelian denigration of the senses and passion, the Jewish philosophers, *Maimonides in particular, tended to denigrate sexual love, and to intellectualize the love of God. They viewed the love of God as an essentially cognitive matter. Maimonides explains that "And thou shalt love the Lord thy God with all thy heart" means that "you should make His apprehension the end of all your actions." (*Guide of the Perplexed,* 1:39; see also 3:33; Yad., Teshuvah, 10:3–4, 6). The mystics, though they had a similar anti-corporeal, ascetic strain in their teaching, nevertheless, had a more emotional understanding of love, and, following the Song of Songs, could see in the sexual passion between man and wife the model of the reintegration of the presently fragmented divine unity (Zohar, 1:49b–50a). In modern times, Jewish thinkers have tended to accept the general, gradual reaffirmation of the physical aspects of human existence as essentially healthy. In the 19th and early 20th century, before this change of attitude toward the physical aspects of love, most Jewish discussions of love remained under the influence of German idealistic philosophy. Love was understood and valued primarily as the most embracing principle of ethics. After World War I, Franz *Rosenzweig and Martin *Buber, in creating Jewish existentialism, introduced a new concern for the whole person and placed their major emphasis on man's relationships. For them, love becomes the very ground of one's being, the source of all meaning and the guide to all action.

Love and Fear of God (Heb. אַהֲבַת ה׳; יִרְאַת ה׳). In his morning prayer the Jew asks God to "unify our hearts to love and fear Thy Name." This request indicates the recognition, prevalent in Judaism since a century or two before the destruction of the Second Temple, that the love and fear of God are the major motives for serving Him, and that there is some tension between them.

Both terms are widely used in the Bible, but the concept of fearing God appears much more frequently than that of loving Him. It is not clear, however, exactly what the biblical writers sought to convey about their faith by using a word for it which, when related to normal experience, regularly describes emotions of dread and fright (Josh. 10:2; Jer. 42:16). In many of its uses, the term loses all denotations of fear, and conveys a broad sense of one's religion, one's god, or one's pattern of worship (II Kings 17:28; Isa. 29:13). In some cases the term occurs in conjunction with the love of God, so that the two appear to have a similar content (Deut. 10:12). Some scholars have therefore argued that the terms are identical in meaning, but this interpretation seems unlikely in view of the heavy biblical emphasis on God's punishing sin and His utter transcendence of man. He is never described as simply loving man, though He does love Israel; rather the emphasis is on His mercy and benevolence, that is, though He is the master, He deals kindly. Hence, while the primitive denotations of fear have been sublimated in much biblical usage to a more intimate relationship with God, there is good reason to believe that the fear of God is a primary Hebrew response to God as the transcendent one, but it shades off into the love of God as the benevolent one. In both terms, however, the immediate connotation is action. Neither is used to commend an emotional state, worthy because of the feelings it arouses. Both are used as motivations for doing the will of God. They are means to observance.

By early rabbinic times, the emphasis on love had risen to parity with that on fear. Throughout talmudic times, the emphasis was increasingly placed on love as the most appropriate motive for the service of God. This is in accord with the rabbinic stress on carrying out the commandments for their own sake *(li-shemah).* The implication arises that, in doing them out of fear, it is reward and punishment which move the doer, which, to the rabbis, are extrinsic and inferior motives. They do not insist that doing the commandments for their own sake is the only acceptable way for Judaism, but rather accommodate themselves to human frailty by reasoning that from extrinsic motivation people will come to intrinsic motivation, which indicates their preference. Hence, though a number of rabbinic dicta make a distinction between the two motives, none of them prefers service from fear to service from love. The following are typical: "the reward of the lover is two portions; that of the fearer is one" (SER 28:140–1); "Act out of love, for the Torah makes a distinction between one who acts out of love and one who acts out of fear . . . In the former case his reward is doubled and redoubled" (Sif. Deut. 32).

A major addition to the meanings of loving God is the rabbis' association of martyrdom with the term. Love would naturally seem to imply a willingness to do anything for one's beloved. With R. Akiva as the model, the rabbis saw the will to give one's life for God and His teaching as the highest expression of love for Him (Ber. 61b; Sif. Deut. 32). The rabbis, however, considered martyrdom an end in itself, and placed severe restrictions on the conditions under which one had to give one's life for the love of God. This idea became a major part of the medieval Jew's sense of the right motive from which to serve God.

With the advent of Muslim-Jewish philosophy, with its

rigorous, abstract evaluation of motives, a full-scale preference for the love of God over the fear of God began to pervade Jewish literature. For Maimonides, the rigorous philosophical estimate of all things led to a disparagement of the fear of God as a motive worthy of women and children alone (Maim., Yad, Teshuvah, 10:1). Only the love of God, because it seeks nothing for itself, should be considered the motive which men ought to strive to achieve as the basis for their action. Yet Maimonides' Aristotelianism did not permit him to accept love in all its emotional connotations. What he carried over of love's normal meaning is its singleness of focus and its comprehensive relation to its object. In terms of man's inner state, however, since thinking was for Maimonides the most significant thing one can do, love was completely reinterpreted in terms of reason and cognition (*ibid.*, 10:6). Even where Maimonides used the symbols of the love of God, his meaning always related to an intellectual activity which concentrates utterly on its object and seeks to carry that fixation into every other aspect of existence (*Guide of the Perplexed*, 3:51).

Ḥasdai *Crescas, as part of his general attack on the Maimonidean system, rejected this intellectualization of man's fundamental relationship to God. In great measure this is due to Crescas' insistence that positive attributes may be postulated about God (see *God, Attributes of). Since he then connects will and goodness with God, it is obvious that the appropriate response to such a benevolent God is love (*Or Adonai*, 1:3, 3). This feeling becomes for Crescas the desired basis of man's service to God (*ibid.*, 2:6, 1–2).

In Jewish mysticism, by contrast, though there are continual references to the fear and love of God, no clear-cut emphasis on one or the other becomes dominant in any of the major movements. The Zohar, for example, esteems both very highly. The concept of *devekut* calls on man to intimately associate his being with God and to be linked to Him in every activity of his life. This concept incorporates aspects of the traditional ideas of both the love and fear of God. It carries over the closeness of the former, yet maintains a sense of the distance and greatness of God.

Modern Jewish thinkers have avoided discussing the fear of God, since it seems too closely associated with the image of man as passive and abject. Wishing to ascribe to man an active role in his relationship with God, they have almost universally made the reciprocal love of God and man central to their teaching. Since this idea can easily be extended to the point where the distance between God and man is obliterated, as in various schools of humanism, some thinkers have begun to suggest that a concern for the fear of God is not incompatible with the dignity of man and is required by the transcendence of God.

Love of Neighbor. Leviticus 19:18 commands: "Love your neighbor (*re'akha*) as yourself: I am the Lord." The surrounding verses qualify this commandment. They prohibit unfair dealing and defrauding even of the defenseless, and forbid vengeance and the bearing of a grudge.

It is not clear whether the commandment to love one's neighbor applies to Jews only or to non-Jews as well. There is no substantial data from the Bible concerning the practice of the commandment. From the parallel term in the first part of the verse, *benei ammekha* ("children of your people"), it would seem that *re'akha* ("your neighbor") in the second part of the verse refers to specifically Jewish neighbors (see for example, Maim. Yad, De'ot, 6:3), though the word *re'a* is used elsewhere in the Bible to refer to non-Jewish neighbors as well. The fact that the love of the resident stranger (*ger*) is enjoined in the same chapter in a separate verse (19:33–34) would seem to indicate further that "neighbor" in verse 18 refers specifically to Jews. It is clear that according to the interpretation of the rabbis of the talmudic period the commandment of loving one's neighbor does not refer to idolaters. Idolatry is, of course, the classic wickedness in Jewish eyes. While there is no commandment to hate idolaters, and while there are in rabbinic literature many stories about the positive relations between Jews and idolaters, the law places so many restrictions on association with idolaters and their goods that the commandment of neighborly love cannot easily be said to apply to them.

The rabbis had a clear appreciation of the significance of this commandment. Akiva called it the epitome of the Torah. Ben Azzai, in preferring the verse: "In the day that God created man, in the likeness of God made He him" is not denying Akiva's assertion of the importance of this commandment (Sifra 19:18). If anything, he is seeking a more inclusive verse, for "neighbor" might be understood literally or locally, but "creation in the image of God" excludes no human being. Similarly, both Hillel (Avot 1:12) and R. Meir (*ibid.* 6:1) enjoin that one should love all mankind ("creatures"). Concern for the non-Jew and his welfare is understood to be part of the Jewish goal of promoting peace among men, *mi-penei darkhei shalom* ("in the interest of peace"). From this commitment a whole range of moral responsibilities toward gentiles devolves upon Jews. Maimonides, in a typical ruling from the many in medieval writings, writes: "We bury the dead of heathens, comfort their mourners, and visit their sick, as this is the way of peace" (Yad, Avel, 14:12).

In modern times, when the Jew's neighbor for the first time is truly all humanity, the understanding of neighborly love by Jewish thinkers has been, correspondingly, universalized. Samson Raphael *Hirsch makes the love of all mankind a condition for being a true Israelite, and Hermann *Cohen considers it the necessary and unique concomitant of Jewish *monotheism. Leo *Baeck writes: "In Judaism neighbor is inseparable from man . . . there is no 'man' without 'fellowman,' no faith in God without faith in neighbor . . ." (*Essence of Judaism* (1936), 193). Martin *Buber posits the I-Thou relationship, which entails love of neighbor and sympathy for him, as a cornerstone of his philosophy, and he goes so far as to hold that it is through these interpersonal relationships that God is encountered.

[E.B.B.]

Bibliography: IN THE BIBLE: B. J. Bamberger, in: HUCA, 6 (1929), 39–53; D. W. Thomas, in: ZAW, 57 (1939), 57–64; E. Jacob, *Theology of the Old Testament* (1958), 108–13; W. Eichrodt, *Theology of the Old Testament*, 1 (1961), 250–8; 2 (1967), 290–301; W. L. Moran, in: CBQ, 25 (1963), 77–87; N. H. Snaith, *The Distinctive Ideas of the Old Testament* (1964[3]), 94–142; D. J. McCarthy, in: CBQ, 27 (1965), 144–7. ḤESED: A. R. Johnson, in: *Interpretationes ad Vetus Testamentum pertinentes Sigmundo Mowinckel septuagenario missae* (1955), 100–12; N. Glueck, *Ḥesed in the Bible* (1967). POST-BIBLICAL: N. Glatzer, *Franz Rosenzweig, His Life and Thought* (1961), xxiii–xxv; M. Buber, *Between Man and Man* (1948), 28–30, 51–58; M. Harris, in: JQR, 50 (1959/60), 13–44; idem, in: *Conservative Judaism*, 14 (1959/60), 29–39. LOVE AND FEAR OF GOD: A. Buechler, *Studies in Sin and Atonement in the Rabbinic Literature of the First Century* (1928), 119–75; Scholem, Mysticism, 233–5, and index, s.v. *Love of God;* G. Vajda, *L'Amour de Dieu dans la théologie du moyen âge* (1957); F. Bamberger, in: HUCA, 6 (1929), 39–53. LOVE OF NEIGHBOR: S. R. Hirsch, *Horeb: A Philosophy of Jewish Laws and Observances* (1962), 52–54; H. Cohen, *Religion der Vernunft* (1929[2]), 144ff.; M. Buber, *I and Thou* (1937), passim.

LOVELL, LEOPOLD (Leo) SOLOMON (1905–), South African politician who was the only white man in the first cabinet of independent Swaziland. Born of Russian immigrant parents, he practiced law in Benoni in the Transvaal. During the 1930s he became prominent in the Labor Party, organized resistance to the Gray Shirt (pro-Hitler) movement, and had its gangs expelled from the town. Lovell represented Benoni (S. Transvaal) in the House of Assembly from 1948 until 1957 when the Labor Party ceased to be represented in Parliament, and was an outspoken opponent of the Nationalist Government's apartheid policies. He took up residence in Swaziland in 1961 and was admitted to the bar there. In 1967 he became a member of its Parliament and was appointed minister of finance, commerce, and industry. [L.S.]

LOVESTONE, JAY (Liebstein, Jacov; 1898–), U.S. Communist Party leader; architect of U.S. organized labor's post-World War II anti-Communist foreign policy. Lovestone, who was born in Lithuania, was taken to the

Jay Lovestone, U.S. labor leader. Courtesy A.F. of L.-C.I.O., New York.

United States as a child and grew up on New York's Lower East Side.

Lovestone joined the Socialist Party as a youth and was active in that party's left wing. Lovestone later was a founder of the American Communist Party in response to the Bolshevik Revolution and served as its executive secretary from 1927 to 1929. While American Communism's top bureaucrat, Lovestone outlined the notion of "American Exceptionalism," i.e., that the United States did not fit into the general Communist theory. However, he and his theory were reviled and ostracized after Stalin's Comintern declared a "third period" of capitalist crisis and revolutionary upsurge, which included the United States. Following the Stalinization of American Communism, Lovestone formed an opposition Communist Party (later the Independent Labor League) and during the Depression fought Communists in the auto workers' and ladies garment workers' unions. In 1944 Lovestone was chosen to head the Free Trade Union Committee. Thereafter, Lovestone guided the American Federation of Labor's anti-Communist foreign policy. He constructed a worldwide intelligence network which, throughout the Cold War era, worked closely with the CIA. When the AFL and CIO merged, Lovestone continued his anti-Communist activities within the merged labor movement's Department of International Affairs. During the 1960s he vigorously supported American military intervention in Cuba, the Dominican Republic, and Vietnam, and opposed the concepts and practitioners of neutralism and revolutionary nationalism.

Bibliography: T. Draper, *American Communism and Soviet Russia* (1960); L. Velie, *Labor U.S.A.* (1959); Lens, in: *The Nation* (July 5, 1965). [K.W.]

LOVY, ISRAEL (Lowy; Israel Glogauer; 1773–1832), *ḥazzan* and composer. Born near Danzig, Lovy received his talmudic education in Glogau, where his father officiated as *ḥazzan*. From the age of 13 he acted as assistant *ḥazzan* in various communities of Moravia, Bohemia, Saxony, and Bavaria. In 1799 Lovy was employed in Fuerth, where he continued his education in European music. After temporary employment in Mainz, Strasbourg, and London, he went to Paris in 1818 and in 1822 became the chief *ḥazzan* of the newly founded synagogue in the Rue Notre Dame de Nazareth. There he organized a four-voiced choir, for which he composed his *Chants religieux . . . pour les prières hébraïques* (1862). He had already appeared as a concert singer in Germany, and in Paris was urged to go on the stage, but refused. His tunes were popular among the German cantors, but his priority as a "reformist" passed to Solomon *Sulzer whose innovations had a wider influence. The "Polish airs" notated at the end of his *Chants* (149–57) are the first appearance in print of the "ḥazzanic-klezmeric" (folk) repertoire for weddings and other family rejoicings and an important relic of 18th-century traditions.

Bibliography: E. Manuel, in: *Archives Israelites*, 11 (1850), 298–306, 344–52 (abbreviated version in the preface of Lovy's *Chants . . .*); Idelsohn, Music, 219, 226–9, 287; Sendrey, Music, 5687–88, 6260, 6707. [B.B.]

LOW (Loewe), British family of Hungarian origin which became prominent in journalism and literature.

MAXIMILIAN LOEWE (1830–1900) was born in Hungary and joined the Nationalist party led by Louis Kossuth. After the failure of the 1848 revolution in Hungary, Loewe fled to England where he engaged in business. Within a short time he acquired a considerable fortune as a result of speculation but in 1878 lost it all. Loewe became interested in the Theist movement and helped to establish its church. He was a profound admirer of British culture and imbued his children with a love of English literature.

His son, SIR SIDNEY JAMES MARK LOW (1857–1932), became a lecturer at King's College, London. His bent was for literature but the state of the family finances compelled him to earn his living as a journalist which he successfully combined as literary editor of the *Standard* (1904). He edited, with F. S. Pulling, the *Dictionary of English History* in 1884 and 20 years later published his second and most important work, *The Governance of England* (1904). As a journalist, Low achieved a high reputation for his style and sense of history and was given access to the papers of eminent statesmen such as Lord Milner and Leopold S. *Amery. From 1888 to 1897 he achieved fame as editor of the *St. James Gazette*. During World War I, Low wrote a series of books on the British Empire in which he took a strict imperialist line with high propaganda value. He was knighted in 1918. An ardent patriot and confidant of leading statesmen, he was compelled to resign his official position as editor of the wireless service of the Ministry of Information in order to forestall a House of Commons question on his "Central European origin."

Maximilian's second son, SIR MAURICE LOW (1860–1929), was also a well-known journalist. He emigrated to the U.S. when the family fortunes waned and became Washington correspondent of the *Boston Globe* and subsequently of the London *Daily Chronicle* and *Morning Post*. He was considered one of the best correspondents in the United States and by his writing and lectures did much to arouse American public opinion to an awareness of the German menace and to improve the image of Britain. For these services, he was knighted in 1922. He wrote studies of the United States, of which the best known is *The American People* (2 vols., 1909–11), as well as books concerning World War I and a political novel.

Maximilian Loewe had six sons and five daughters. One daughter, Edith, who was a leader of *WIZO, married Montague David *Eder, psychologist and Zionist leader.

Ivy, a daughter of Sir Sidney Low, married Maxim *Litvinov, the Soviet political leader.

Bibliography: D. Chapman-Huston, *Memoir of Sir Sidney Low* (1936); DNB 1931–40 (1949), s.v. *Low, Sidney; The Times* (June 18, 1929), 18 (obituary of Maurice Low). [Ed.]

LOWE, ADOLPH (1893–), economist. Born in Stuttgart, he was a civil servant in Germany's ministries of labor and economic affairs and in the central statistical office (1919–26). From 1926 to 1931 he was a professor of economics and sociology at the University of Kiel, where he became director of research at the Institute for World Economy. In 1931 he was appointed professor of economics at the University of Frankfort and in 1933 with the advent of the Nazis went to England, where until 1940 he was a lecturer in economics and political science at the University of Manchester. In 1940 he settled in New York City and began teaching at the New School for Social Research. From 1943 to 1951 he directed research at the Institute of World Affairs in New York City. General economic theory, economic development, and business fluctuations were his main professional interests. His major publications include *Economics and Sociology* (1935); *The Price of Liberty* (1937); *The Classical Theory of Economic Growth* (1954); *Structural Analysis of Real Capital Formation* (1955); and *On Economic Knowledge* (1965). [J.O.R.]

LOWENSTEIN, SOLOMON (1877–1942), U.S. social work executive and Reform rabbi. Lowenstein, who was born in Philadelphia, was ordained by Hebrew Union College in 1901. He was successively employed as: superintendent of the United Jewish Charities in Cincinnati (1901–1904); assistant manager of the United Jewish Charities in New York (1904); superintendent of the Hebrew Orphan Asylum (1905–18); deputy commissioner of the American Red Cross in Palestine (1918–19); and director of the Federation of Jewish Philanthropic Societies (1920–35). In 1935 he became the Federation's executive vice-president and held this post until his death. During this period, coinciding with the depression of the 1930s, Jewish philanthropy greatly expanded and shifted and Lowenstein coordinated and systematized its operations. Lowenstein was president of the National Conference of Social Work (1938), and was also a trustee of both the American Jewish Committee and the American Jewish Joint Distribution Committee, and a vice-president of the American Friends of the Hebrew University. [Ed.]

LOWENTHAL, MARVIN (1890–1969), U.S. Zionist writer. Born in Bradford, Pennsylvania, Lowenthal was sent by Louis D. *Brandeis to the West Coast to organize the Zionist movement there (1916–18). From 1924 to 1929 he traveled abroad as European editor of the *Menorah Journal*, and for part of this time also represented the American Jewish Congress. During these years he wrote extensively on literature, politics, and Zionism, evincing affection for the secular elements in Jewish culture. He became widely known in the United States through his essays and lectures, but his most enduring works are his travel and historical books. His craftsmanship and urbanity of style appear at their best in *The Jews of Germany* (1936; includes bibliography of his works). Lowenthal served on the Zionist Advisory Commission (1946–49), and was editor of *The American Zionist* (1952–54). His works include a book on Jews in Europe and North Africa, *A World Passed By* (1933); and he edited *Henrietta Szold: Life and Letters* (1942), and the one-volume precis of the *Diaries of Theodor Herzl* (1956). He translated and edited *Memoirs of Glueckel of Hameln* (1932) and a one-volume abridgment of Montaigne's *Autobiography* (1935).

Bibliography: C. Madison, in: JBL, 28 (1970/71). [L.W.Sch.]

LOWICZ (Pol. **Łowicz**), town in the province of Lodz, central Poland. The Jews began to settle there at the beginning of the 16th century. In 1516 they were expelled by Archbishop Jan Laski and established themselves in the surrounding towns. Until 1797 the presence of Jews in Lowicz was authorized only on market days and during fairs. At the regional church synod held in Lowicz in 1556 it was decided to inflict severe punishment on four Jews of *Sochaczew who had been accused of *Host desecration. At the close of the 16th and during the 17th centuries Jewish merchants played an important role in the Lowicz fairs. From the beginning of the 19th century the Jewish population of the town increased rapidly. The 60 Jews (2.5% of the population) who lived in Lowicz in 1808 earned their livelihood mainly as innkeepers and craftsmen. With the renewal of the Lowicz fairs in 1820 much of the trade in the town was in Jewish hands. In 1827 the Jewish community of Lowicz numbered 405 (11% of the population). In 1829 a wooden synagogue was erected; the local Jewish cemetery was founded in the early 1830s. In 1897 the construction of the Great Synagogue was completed. During the years 1828–62 the Jews were allowed to live only in the Jewish quarter. In the course of time Ḥasidism gained influence in the community. In 1863 some Lowicz Jews contributed funds to the Polish rebels and collaborated with them in smuggling arms.

The Jewish population increased from 1,161 in 1857 (21% of the population) to 3,552 in 1897 (35% of the total). Their principal sources of livelihood were shopkeeping, trade with the neighboring peasants and the soldiers of the local Russian military camp, and crafts. A considerable part of the Jewish poor was employed in the textile, stocking, and food manufacturing industries. Under the influence of the *Bund, Jewish workers and students participated in the revolutionary incidents which took place in Lowicz in 1905. From the beginning of the century Zionist groups were organized. At the end of 1914 there were Jewish victims and severe damage to property as a result of the battles which were fought in the town and its vicinity. In 1917 six Jewish delegates were elected to the municipal council, forming half of its members. In 1921 there were 4,517 Jews (30% of the total population) in Lowicz. In the inter-war period CYSHO (Central Yiddish School Organization) and Beth Jacob schools functioned. From 1935 to 1939 the weekly *Mazovsher Vokhenblat* was published in Lowicz. In 1931, 4,339 Jews (25% of the total population) lived in the town. In 1933 anti-Jewish riots occurred, which were repelled by the Jewish *self-defense. [A.Cy.]

Holocaust Period. On the outbreak of World War II there were about 4,500 Jews in Lowicz. The German army entered the town on Sept. 9, 1939. That day all Jewish males were ordered to assemble in the market place. They were imprisoned in the synagogue and tortured for two days. During 1940 about 3,500 Jews from the towns of Lodz province, which had been incorporated into the Third Reich, were forced to settle in Lowicz. In May 1940 a ghetto was established there. On June 17, 1941, a decree forbidding Jews to live in the town or country of Lowicz was issued. All the Jews were transferred to the *Warsaw ghetto and shared the plight of Warsaw Jewry. No Jewish community has been rebuilt in Lowicz. [S.Kr.]

Bibliography: B. Wasiutyński, *Ludność żydowska w Polsce w wiekach XIX i XX* (1930), 20, 45, 70, 75; W. Tarczyński, *Łowicz, wiadomości historyczne* (1899); I. Schiper, *Dzieje handlu żydowskie-*

go na ziemiach polskich (1937), index; *Lowicz, A shtat in Mazovie* (1966). HOLOCAUST: T. Brustin-Bernstein, in: BŻIH, 1 (1952), 83–125.

LOWIE, ROBERT HARRY (1883–1957), U.S. anthropologist. Born in Vienna, Lowie was taken to the U.S. and educated in New York. He studied anthropology under Franz *Boas, and served two institutions, the American Museum of Natural History (1907–17) and the University of California at Berkeley (1917–50). He did field work among various American Indian tribes, especially the Crows. His early interest in comparative mythology led to his publishing several works, notably *Primitive Society* (1920) and *Primitive Religion* (1924). Lowie's contribution to anthropology was widely recognized and he edited the *American Journal of Anthropology*. During World War II he taught an "area" course on Germany and this experience, combined with ethnographical field trips, led to his publication of *The German People—a Social Portrait to 1914* (1945), and *Towards Understanding Germany* (1954), which assessed the impact of the war on the German personality. Though generally a follower of the Boas school, which insisted on the scientific method, Lowie contended that more importance ought to be allotted to the biological factor in accounting for differences among individuals as well as groups. He also resisted Freudian generalizations, and envisaged the possibility of applying correlation techniques to culture variables. In his ethnographical studies Lowie was concerned to illuminate the interaction between social organization, religion, and folklore. He has been considered by some the precursor of structural anthropology. [E.Fi.]

LOWN, PHILIP W. (1890–), U.S. shoe manufacturer and philanthropist. Lown arrived in New York in 1907, later attending the University of Maine and obtaining a degree in chemical engineering (1918). Lown went into shoe manufacturing, eventually heading Lown Shoes Inc. (from 1933) and Penobscot Shoe Co. Settling in Lewiston, Maine, in 1935, he became active in civic and Jewish communal affairs, especially educational. Lown served as a longtime board member, vice-president, and president of the American Association for Jewish Education from 1950 on, and was one of the leading philanthropists of Jewish education in the United States. He endowed a chair in Jewish philosophy at Brandeis University and founded the Lown School of Near Eastern and Judaic Studies. He was president of the Hebrew Teachers' College of Brookline, Massachusetts (1962–), and vice-president of the American Friends of the Hebrew University. He served as a national cabinet member of the U.J.A. (1950–), and was treasurer of the Combined Jewish Philanthropies of Boston. A jubilee volume edited by Judah Pilch was published in his honor in 1967. [Ed.]

°**LOWTH, ROBERT** (1710–1787), Hebraist. Appointed professor of poetry at Oxford in 1741, Lowth devoted a series of 34 Latin lectures to the literary qualities of biblical poetry. Originally published as *Praelectiones de sacra poesi Hebraeorum* (Oxford, 1753), these were translated into English as *Lectures on the Sacred Poetry of the Hebrews* (London, 1787). Lowth was the first modern scholar to formulate the theory of parallelism as the metrical basis of biblical Hebrew poetry, a discovery in which he had been partially anticipated in the 16th century by Azariah de *Rossi, whom Lowth quoted. Renaissance scholars, relying on classical and contemporary verse forms, had tried unsuccessfully to scan poetic passages in the Bible as though they were classical hexameters, but Lowth showed that Hebrew poetry was fundamentally antiphonal, the latter part of each verse echoing the idea of the first by corroboration or contrast—"The mountains skipped like rams / the hills like children of the flock." His translation of the Book of Isaiah (1778) was also original in biblical translation, distinguishing between the prose and poetry of the original Hebrew. Lowth is notable for having stressed the sublimity of Old Testament literature and the vividness of its imagery in an era of prudery and circumlocution. He was bishop of Oxford 1766–67 and thereafter bishop of London.

Bibliography: S. H. Monk, *The Sublime* (1935); M. Roston, *Prophet and Poet* (1965). [M.Ro.]

LOZINSKI, SAMUEL (1874–1945), Russian historian. Born in Bobruisk, Belorussia, Lozinski specialized in the history of Western Europe, writing studies on the modern history of France, Austria, Holland, and Belgium. He collaborated in editing and translating standard historical works into Russian, including E. Renan's *Histoire du peuple d'Israël* and H. C. Lea's *History of the Inquisition of Spain*. He also did research in Jewish history and edited the sections on Jewish culture in Europe and the history of the Jews in France and England in the Russian-Jewish encyclopedia (*Yevreyskaya Entsiklopediya*). Under the Soviet regime, Lozinski lectured in history at the universities of Leningrad, Minsk, Rostov, and other cities. During the 1920s he belonged to the small circle which was active in Jewish historical research under the conditions of the new regime. He edited a collection of documents, *Kazyonnye yevreyskiye uchilishcha* ("Jewish Governmental Schools," 1920), and co-edited the collections *Yevreyskaya Starina* and *Yevreyskaya Letopis*. He also engaged in research on the history of the Church. His two works *Svyataya Inkvizitsiya* ("The Holy Inquisition," 1927) and *Istoriya Papstva* ("History of the Papacy," 1934) were published by the Academy of Sciences of the U.S.S.R.

Bibliography: S. Lozinski, *Istoriya Papstva* (1961), preface; *Bobruisk* (Heb. and Yid., 1967), 521–2. [Y.S.]

LOZOVSKI (Dridzo), SOLOMON ABRAMOVICH (1878–1952), Soviet statesman and trade union leader. Born into a poor family in Danilovka, Yekaterinoslav province, Lozovski went to work at the age of 11 and completed his studies on his own. He joined the Russian Social-Democratic Party in 1901 and in 1905 attached himself to the Bolshevik wing. Lozovski participated in the Revolution of 1905, and several times was arrested, but escaped. In 1909 he arrived in France where he was active in the socialist movement until 1917. Lozovski returned to Russia following the outbreak of the February Revolution and was immediately elected secretary of the Trade Union Council. His opposition to Lenin's policies during and after the October Revolution led to his expulsion from the party in March 1918 and until December 1919, when he rejoined the Bolsheviks, he was a leader of the Internationalist Social-Democrats. From 1920 on, he was appointed to a series of important posts, serving as head of the Communist Trade Union International (Profintern; 1921–37), director of the state publishing house (1937–39), deputy commissar of foreign affairs (1939–46), and deputy director and later director, of the Soviet Information Bureau. From 1939 to 1949 he was a member of the central committee of the Communist Party.

In his capacity as head of the Soviet Information Bureau, Lozovski was responsible for the work of the Jewish *Anti-Fascist Committee and was concerned with world Jewish affairs. It is believed that in 1944 he supported the plan to set up a Jewish autonomous settlement in the Crimea and that this led to his arrest in 1949, when the authorities began to liquidate Jewish culture in the Soviet Union. Lozovski was tried together with 24 other Jewish writers and intellectuals in July 1952, and was executed with them on August 12, 1952. He was posthumously rehabilitated in 1956.

Bibliography: J. B. Salsberg, in: *Jewish Life* (Feb. 1957); I. Ehrenburg, *Memoirs 1921–1941* (1964), 498; vol. 2, p. 11, 120; H. E. Salisbury, *To Moscow and Beyond* (1960), 72; *Deyateli Sovetskogo Soyuza,* vol. 1, p. 333–7; *Bolshaya Sovetskaya Entsiklopediya,* 51 (1958²), 180; *Sovetskaya Litva* (March 30, 1963); *Sovetskaya Istoricheskaya Entsiklopediya,* 8 (1965), 760–1; *Voprosy istorii KPSS,* 10 no. 7 (1966), 24.

[B.PI.]

LUBACZOW (Pol. **Łubaczów**), town in Rzeszow province, S. E. Poland. Jews are mentioned in Lubaczow as early as 1498. When confirming the municipal rights of the town in 1523, King Sigismund I granted a privilege according to which the Jews were forbidden to trade in the surrounding villages. In 1562 only two Jewish houses were mentioned in Lubaczow; there were three Jewish houses in the first half of the 17th century, but in 1662 there were no Jews at all, probably a result of the Swedish wars and the wars against the Cosssacks (in 1655 the town was burned down by the Cossacks). In 1717 the Jews of Lubaczow paid 560 zlotys poll tax, 425 in 1719, and 500 in 1721; in addition they were to pay the king a yearly "kettle tax" of 1,200 zlotys, and for cattle slaughtering the shoulder blade duty *(łopatkowe)*. In 1765 the community of Lubaczow together with the townlet of Potylicz and surrounding villages numbered 687 poll tax payers. In 1880 the community numbered 1,503 (34% of the total population), 1,911 in 1900, 2,171 in 1910, and 1,715 (32%) in 1921. At that time Lubaczow had 106 Jewish workshops, 33 of which had salaried workers.

Holocaust Period. Before the outbreak of World War II there were about 2,300 Jews in Lubaczow. The majority of them were deported in the autumn of 1942 to *Belzec death camp. The remaining Jews were exterminated on Jan. 6, 1943. After the war, the Jewish community of Lubaczow was not reconstituted.

Bibliography: J. Kleczyński and F. Kluczycki, *Liczba głow żydowskich w Koronie z taryf 1765 r.* (1898); A. Prochaska, *Materyały archiwalne* (1899), no. 217; E. Heller (ed.), *Żydowskie przedsiębiorstwa przemysłowe w Polsce . . .*, 6 (1923); B. Wasiutyński, *Ludność żydowska w Polsce . . .* (1930), 114; Yad Vashem Archives.

[R.MA.]

LUBARSKY, ABRAHAM ELIJAH (1856–1920), early member of *Ḥovevei Zion in Russia. Born in Balta, Ukraine, Lubarsky was engaged in business. From 1893 he was agent for Wissotsky Tea in Odessa and traveled throughout the large communities in Russia, making connections with the prominent figures in Hebrew and Yiddish literature in the late 19th century. He was especially close with *Aḥad Ha-Am, whom he stimulated to write his famous first essay, *Lo Zeh ha-Derekh*. Lubarsky was one of the first members of the secret society *Benei Moshe and influenced K. Z. *Wissotsky to support the Hebrew monthly *Ha-Shilo'aḥ*. He contributed to the Hebrew press throughout this period. In 1903 he emigrated to the United States, where he became the moving spirit of the Hebrew movement. Lubarsky was a founder there of the Histadrut Ivrit and its newspaper, *Ha-Toren*.

Bibliography: P. Friedman, in: *Haaretz* (Oct. 21, 1920); Epstein, *ibid.* (Oct. 9, 1931); *Sefer ha-Congress* (1950²), 374–5. [Y.S.]

LUBARTOW (Pol. **Lubartów;** Rus. **Lyubartov**), town in Lublin province, E. Poland. The poll tax paid by the Jewish community rose from 1,500 zlotys in 1717 to 2,400 zlotys in 1736. In 1765 there were 764 Jewish poll-tax payers. The community also had jurisdiction over 217 Jews in the neighboring villages and 37 Jews in the townlet Kamionka. Among the 218 heads of families were 14 contractors, 20 merchants, 34 tailors, 5 hatters, and 9 carters. The community maintained two synagogues and a *mikveh;* 164 houses were owned by Jews. In 1796 the owner of the town granted the Jews a privilege defining the status of the *kahal* and the Jewish craftsmen's guilds. Among the town's wealthiest Jews were the merchant family *Peretz and the chief contractor, Solomon Kosiowicz. In the first half of the 19th century the Jews were allowed to keep taverns only with the permission of the local overlord. The community numbered 2,074 (58% of the total population) in 1827; 1,820 (56%) in 1857; 2,623 (53%) in 1897; and 3,269 (54%) in 1921. In that year there were 176 Jewish workshops in the town, about half of them employing salaried workers.

Holocaust Period. About 3,500 Jews lived in Lubartow before World War II. In November 1939 over 2,500 Jews were ordered to leave the town and settle in Parczew and Ostrow. Most of them came back within a year. In May 1942 about 1,000 Jews from Slovakia were deported to Lubartow. On Oct. 11, 1942, Jews from Lubartow were deported to the Sobibor and Belzec death camps. Near Lubartow two Jewish-partisan units were active for more than a year, under the command of Samuel Jegier and Mietek Gruber.

Bibliography: Halpern, Pinkas, index; R. Mahler, *Yidn in Amolikn Poyln in Likht fun Tsifern* (1958), index; B. Wasiutyński, *Ludność żydowska w Polsce w Polsce w wiekach XIX i XX* (1930), 34, 62, 72; J. Bartyś, in: *Bleter far Geshikhte,* 8, no. 3–4 (1955), 88–105; *Die juedischen industriellen Unternehmungen in Polen* (1921); *Khurbn Lubartow: A Matseyve . . .* (1947).

[EJ/ED.]

LUBAVICH (Lyubavichi), small town in Smolensk oblast, Russian S.F.S.R.; until 1917 it was in Mogilev province, Belorussia. The Jewish population numbered 1,164 in 1847 and 1,660 (67.3% of the total) in 1897. Lubavich became the center of *Ḥabad Ḥasidism in Lithuania, Belorussia, and the eastern Ukraine after Dov Ber, the son of the founder of the *Ḥabad system, *Shneour Zalman of Lyady, moved from Lyady to Lubavich in 1813. His nephew and son-in-law Menahem Mendel (the *"Ẓemah-Ẓedek"*) extended the influence of the dynasty (see *Schneersohn). The Jews in the town mainly earned their livelihood from the flax trade, and in providing for the many Ḥasidim who visited their "rabbi" there. His grandson Shalom Baer established the yeshivah Tomekhei Temimim in 1897 in Lubavich. He left Lubavich in 1915, but the name of the town remained connected with the Ḥabad movement (the "Lubavich Ḥasidim"). After the 1917 Revolution the town's economy declined and the Jews suffered from persecution by the *Yevsektsiya. In 1926 there were only 967 Jews in Lubavich (50% of the total population). The Germans entered the town in August 1941, and almost immediately established a ghetto. In November 1941, about 700 Jews from Lubavich ghetto were shot.

Bibliography: Z. Har-Shefer, in: *He-Avar,* 2 (1954), 86–93; B. Dinur, *Be-Olam she-Shaka* (1958), 145–55; M. Fainsod, *Smolensk under Soviet Rule* (1958), 441–3.

[Y.S.]

LUBETKIN, ZIVIA (1914–), fighter in the Warsaw ghetto uprising. Born in Beten, near Slonim, Zivia Lubetkin was a member of the Zionist labor youth movement Deror and a representative of *He-Ḥalutz on the National Jewish Council. She married Yiẓḥak *Cukierman. In the summer of 1939, she attended the Zionist Congress in Basle and returned to Warsaw in September. At the time of the Warsaw ghetto uprising (April 1943), she was among the fighters in the central ghetto while her husband was one of the leaders of the revolt. On May 8, 1943, after the main bunker, which housed the command of the Jewish fighters' organization headed by Mordecai *Anilewicz, fell, Zivia Lubetkin escaped from the ghetto with the other surviving

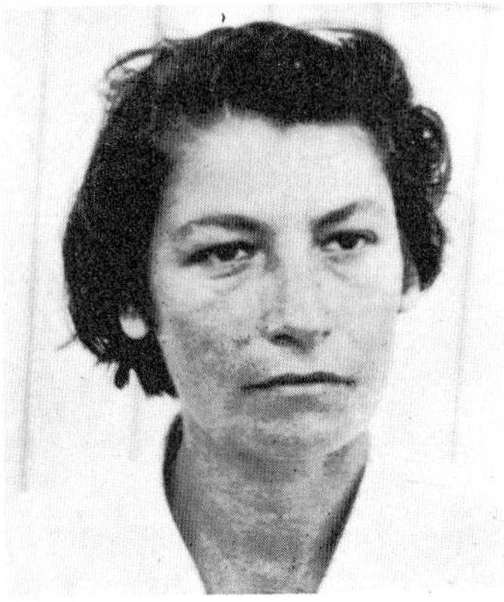

Zivia Lubetkin, Warsaw ghetto fighter. Courtesy kibbutz Loḥamei ha-Getta'ot.

fighters through the sewage system. In August of the same year, she and her husband sent Isaac Schwarzbart, a member of the Polish National Council in London, a telegram that reported the results of the revolt in the ghetto, called for help, and included a warning to the Jews of Western Europe of the fate awaiting them after deportation to Poland. Zivia Lubetkin fought with the partisans and participated in the Polish revolt of October 1943, together with other survivors of the Warsaw uprising. After Poland was liberated from Nazi occupation by the Soviet army in January 1944, Zivia Lubetkin settled in Palestine. She and her husband were among the founders of kibbutz *Loḥamei ha-Getta'ot and were active in the ghetto fighters' organization in Israel. As a member of the executive of *Kibbutz ha-Me'uḥad, she was appointed to the Executive of the *Jewish Agency (1966–68). In her testimony at the *Eichmann trial, she described the uprising in the Warsaw ghetto.

Bibliography: Y. Cukierman and M. Basok (eds.), *Sefer Milḥamot ha-Getta'ot...* (1954), index; *Ha-Yo'eẓ ha-Mishpati la-Memshalah Neged Adolf Eichmann: Eduyyot*, 1 (1963), 242–61; N. Blumenthal and J. Kermisz, *Ha-Meri ve-ha-Mered be-Getto Varshah* (1965). [B.M.A.]

LUBETZKY, JUDAH (1850–1910), French rabbi. Lubetzky was born in Russia. He went to Paris in 1880 and was appointed rabbi of the Eastern European Jews there the following year and a member of the Paris *bet din* in 1904. He published his edition of parts of the *Sefer ha-Hashlamah* of Meshullam b. Moses of Béziers from a manuscript in the Paris library of Baron *Guenzburg, together with his own commentary, entitled *Torat ha-Hashlamah*, and an introduction giving the biography of Meshullam and of other Provençal scholars (3 vols., 1885–1910). In 1896 he published *Bidkei Battim*, comprising: (1) notes and amendments to the *Sefer ha-Hashlamah* on tractates *Berakhot, Ta'anit, Yevamot*, and *Megillah*, with a biographical introduction on some Provençal rabbis; (2) Meshullam's criticism of Maimonides' laws of *Eruvin* and *Shevu'ot*, from a manuscript, with Lubetzky's own notes; (3) a critique of Mordecai Horowitz with regard to the *Cleves *get*.

Lubetzky became famous for the vigorous stand he took against the proposal to introduce a conditional clause into Jewish marriages in France, with the aim of making civil divorce effective in the dissolution of Jewish marriages. The proposal was first made in 1885 and again in 1893. By his articles in the Hebrew periodicals and by enlisting the opposition of the great rabbis of the time he was successful in having it rejected. In 1907 an assembly of French rabbis resolved to adopt the proposal. Lubetzky then collected the opinions of more than 400 eminent scholars and, supported by Baron Rothschild, succeeded in having the resolution rescinded. He prepared all the material relevant to the proposal for publication and sent it to Ḥayyim Ozer *Grodzinski. When the proposal was again raised, Grodzinski gave the material to Aaron D. A. Waronovski, who published it with the title, *Ein Tenai be-Nissu'in* (1930).

Bibliography: Schapira, in: *Ha-Yehudi*, 14 (1910/11), nos. 35–36; *Der Israelit* (Sept. 29, 1910). [S.Z.H.]

LUBIN, ISADOR (1896–), U.S. economist. Born in Worcester, Massachusetts, Lubin taught economics for a year at the University of Missouri (1917–18) and left to serve as statistician for the U.S. Food Administration, from which post he moved to the U.S. War Industries Board as a special expert. He returned to teaching in 1926, at the universities of Michigan and Missouri and Brookings Institute (1922–33). Subsequently, he served many public and semipublic institutions including governmental agencies and the Allied Reparations Commission, the International Labor Organization, and the U.S. Mission to the United Nations. From 1946 to 1951 he was president and board chairman of the research organization Confidential Reports, Inc., and from 1950 chairman of the executive committee of the Franklin Delano Roosevelt Foundation. During 1959–61 he was professor of public affairs at Rutgers University. From the 1960s Lubin was consultant to the United Israel Appeal, Inc. (a U.S. body representing the Jewish Agency for Israel), in which capacity he paid frequent visits to Israel. He was also a member of the boards of the Weizmann Institute in Israel and Brandeis University. His publications include *The British Coal*

Isador Lubin, U.S. economist. Photo Blackstone-Shelburne Inc., New York.

Dilemma (1927), *The British Attack on Unemployment* (with A. C. C. Hill, 1934), and *Our Stake in World Trade* (with F. D. Murden, 1954), all of which reflect his interests in labor economics, economic development, and trade policy. [J.O.R.]

LUBIN, SIMON JULIUS (1876–1936), U.S. economist, business executive, and public servant. Lubin, who was born in Sacramento, California, entered the Sacramento firm of Weinstock, Lubin & Company after his graduation from Harvard in 1903 and rose to become its president. Lubin drafted the California State Immigration and Housing Law and in 1913 Governor Hiram Johnson named him to head the California State Commission of Immigration and Housing. In that position he strove to improve conditions among migrant farm workers. In 1934 Lublin was appointed to a National Labor Board commission to settle agricultural strife in California's Imperial Valley. Lubin also was consultant to the California Emergency Relief Administration; founder (1926) and president of the Sacramento Region Citizens Council; and founder (1931) and president of the Pan-American Institute of Reciprocal Trade. Although a Republican, he vigorously supported much of the New Deal. [ED.]

LUBITSCH, ERNST (1892–1947), film producer and director. Lubitsch was born in Berlin and gained early acting experience in Max *Reinhardt's troupe. From 1913 he played comic parts in the movies, creating the role of "Meyer" or "Moritz" (archetypical Jewish names in Germany), the butt of good-natured low comedy in a series of successful films. Lubitsch progressed from actor to director and from 1914 to 1917 made many slapstick comedies. Having been persuaded to make serious motion pictures, he produced several successful films which brought Pola Negri to the screen. In 1922 he moved to Los Angeles to direct *Rosita* with Mary Pickford. Many other successes followed, but Lubitsch really made his name with the advent of the "talkies," and especially with his film *The Love Parade* (1929), which starred Maurice Chevalier and Jeanette MacDonald. Lubitsch was a master of subtle humor which, when combined with fanciful situations, came to be regarded as the "Lubitsch touch." His pictures had a zany, implausible quality which appealed to millions of film-goers. His later successes included *The Smiling Lieutenant* (1931); *Trouble in Paradise* (1932); *The Merry Widow* (1934); and *Ninotchka* (1939), starring Greta Garbo.

Bibliography: H. G. Weinberg, *The Lubitsch Touch* (1968), incl. bibl.; A. Sarris (ed.), *Interviews with Film Directors* (1967), 281–5; L. Jacobs, *The Rise of the American Film* (1939), index. [S.KA.]

LUBLIN, city in E. Poland, center of the district of the same name. In the 16th and 17th centuries Lublin was famous for its fairs (see *Market Days and Fairs). Annexed by Austria in 1795, it was incorporated in Russian Poland in 1815. From 1918 to 1939 it was in Poland and from 1939 to 1945 under German occupation; after World War II it was again in Poland.

Jews were first mentioned as transients in Lublin in 1316. The city denied Jews the right to settle there on the basis of its privilege *de non tolerandis Judaeis.* In 1336 King Casimir III permitted them to settle on land adjacent to the city, later known as Piaski Żydowskie ("Jewish sands"). Josko (Joseph) Sheinowicz, a rich tax-farmer for southeast Poland, built a house in Lublin in 1500. Later King Sigismund I permitted Jews to found a settlement in the vicinity of the castle, afterward known as Podzamcze. In the second half of the 16th century the community was given land for its institutions and for a cemetery. The Jews were allowed to set up movable stalls for shops but not to erect buildings. In 1602 there were 2,000 Jews in Lublin. The population figures did not change greatly until the second half of the 18th century; in 1787 there were 4,321 Jews in the city. Tension with the citizenry continued, largely centered around the right of the Jews to live within the city walls. Jews settled mainly in houses belonging to clergymen and feudal lords, who were outside the jurisdiction of the city council, paying them substantial sums for the privilege. They were very active at the Lublin fairs, engaged in local trade, and some were tailors, furriers, manufacturers of brushes, brewers, and bakers, despite the bitter opposition of the Christian merchants and artisans. The rivalry between the Christian and Jewish tailors ended in 1805 when a united guild was founded. In 1780 King Stanislaus II (Poniatowski) ordered the expulsion of the Jews from Lublin. As a result of the intervention of Jewish leaders the expulsion did not take place until 1795, when Lublin was annexed by Austria.

Figure 1. Lublin in the 1920s. Courtesy YIVO, New York. Photo R. Vishniak.

Tensions in the 16th to 18th centuries were aggravated whenever the Polish High Court convened in Lublin, especially when trying a *blood libel case. The court hearings were then followed by attacks on the Jews; some were murdered and their property stolen. If the High Court sentenced the accused Jew to death the execution usually took place on a Saturday in front of the Maharshal Shul synagogue, and elders of the *kehillah* and other Jews had to attend. An execution was often followed by an attack on the Jewish quarter. Like the whole of Jewry in Poland-Lithuania, Lublin Jews suffered greatly during the *Chmielnicki uprisings in 1648–49. Another period of hardship followed in the second half of the 18th century with the disintegration of the Polish state.

In spite of hardships, the fairs and yeshivah of Lublin became central in Jewish communal and cultural life in Poland (see *Councils of the Lands). The first known rabbi of Lublin was Jacob b. Joseph *Pollak; *Shalom Shakhna b. Joseph was nominated by the king of Poland in 1541 as rabbi for Lublin and district. Other rabbis were Solomon b. Jehiel *Luria, in office for 15 years; Mordecai b. Abraham *Jaffe; and Meir b. Gedaliah *Lublin, known in halakhic literature as Maharam of Lublin. Lublin communal institutions included a well-organized *ḥevra kaddisha* and a "preacher's house" which provided visiting preachers with food and lodging. The fortified Maharshal Shul, the most famous synagogue in Lublin, was built in 1567. It burned down in the great fire of 1655 but was later rebuilt.

In the 16th century Lublin had several well-known physicians. At the beginning of the century the king of Poland exempted one, Ezekiel, from various taxes in recognition of his services. Another famous physician of that century was Solomon Luria, author of a medical treatise. Physicians in Lublin in the 17th century were Samuel b. Mattathias, Moses Montalto, and Ḥayyim Felix Vitalis, who graduated from Padua in 1658 and served as physician to the Polish king. During the 19th century Lublin became an important commercial center through the exploitation of the economic opportunities created by the vast Russian markets. The Jews expanded their wholesale commerce and their industrial establishments. One of the largest cigarette factories was founded by a Jew in 1860 and employed about 100 workers; 95% of the tanning industry was owned by Jews. The increased number of Jewish workers became an important factor in Jewish social life: workers' unions were established in various trades, and the first groups of the *Bund emerged at this time. In 1806 there were 2,973 Jews in Lublin, increasing to 8,747 (56% of the total population) in 1857. In 1862, just before the annulment of the prohibition on Jewish residence within the city, they numbered 10,413; by 1897 they had increased to 23,586.

*Ḥasidism played a prominent role in Lublin, mainly through the influence of the local *ẓaddikim,* such as *Jacob Isaac ha-Ḥozeh ("the seer") of Lublin, and the Eiger dynasty from the middle of the 19th century. At the same time some of the community rabbis strongly opposed the Ḥasidim, particularly Azriel Horovitz (late 18th century) and Joshua Heshel Ashkenazi who was nominated in 1852. As the latter was rich and economically independent he led the struggle against Ḥasidism without any regard for the opinions of the *kehillah* members. In the 19th century traditional education in the *ḥeder* and yeshivah continued, although Lublin lost its communal and cultural prominence with the abolition of the Councils of the Lands and the predominance of Ḥasidism. From the second half of the 19th century, the first Jewish schools with instruction in Russian or Polish were founded. In 1897 the first Hebrew school was opened.

In independent Poland there were no substantial changes in the occupational structure of the Jewish community but the percentage of Jews in the population decreased. In 1921 there were 37,337 Jews in the city (34.7% of the population as opposed to 50.9% in 1897). The numbers remained steady; 38,937 in 1931 and 37,830 in 1939 (according to the German census). Many Jewish workers were engaged in the *leather industry; in 1939 the biggest leather factory in the city belonged to a Jew and half the employees were Jews. Consequently the trade union of Jewish leather workers had a membership of above 500. In Lublin, as in the whole of Poland, the Jews suffered from the hatred of the Poles and the anti-Jewish policies adopted by independent Poland between the two world wars. In the 1930s attacks on Lublin Jews were led by students of the Lublin Catholic University, whose rector was the author of anti-Semitic pamphlets. Anti-Semitic propaganda was the main topic of the leading Polish newspaper in the city, *Głos Lubelski* ("Voice of Lublin").

In spite of this Lublin Jews led an active social and cultural life between the wars. Trade unions were influenced by the Bund and the Left Po'alei Zion. In the middle-class sector the Orthodox *Agudat Israel and the *Folkspartei—both anti-Zionist—were influential. Branches of all the Zionist parties were active. The focus of local political interest until 1936, except in the Bund, was the community organization. In education the traditional *ḥeder* system was joined by *Beth Jacob schools for girls and by an Orthodox Zionist Yavneh school. The secular Zionist *Tarbut Hebrew school had its first graduates in 1933. Cultural activities included dramatic societies, libraries, orchestras, and a sports organization. A Jewish daily, *Lubliner Togblat*, was published. The most famous yeshivah of that period in Lublin was the Yeshivah Ḥakhmei Lublin, founded by Meir *Shapira, rabbi from 1925 to 1933. After the death of Shapira a court of three *dayyanim* functioned instead of a rabbi. [Sh.L.K.]

Figure 2. The expulsion of Jews from Lublin by the Nazis. Courtesy Yad Vashem Archives, Jerusalem.

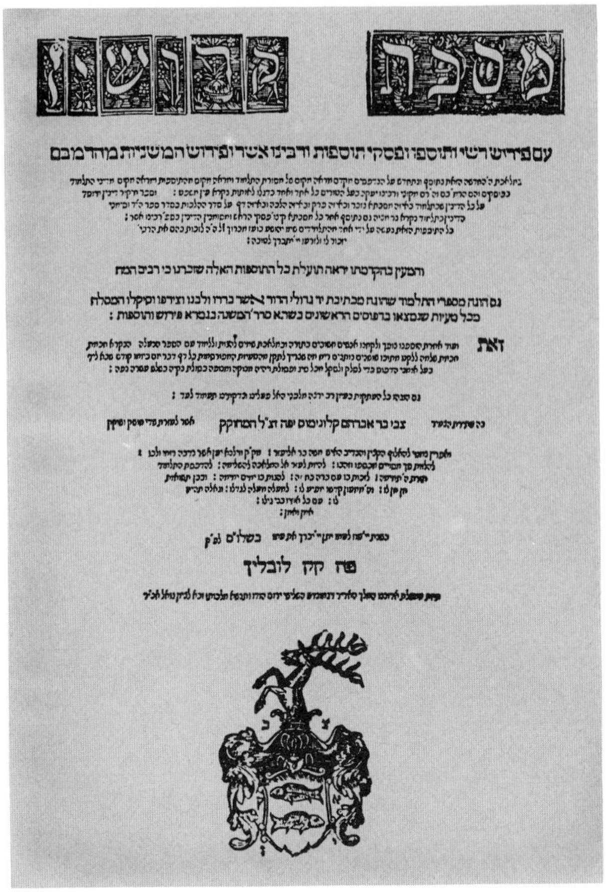

מסכת קדושין

והמעין בהקדמתו יראה תועלת כל התוספות האלה שזכרנו כי רבים המה

צבי בר אברהם קלונימוס יפה זצ"ל המחוקק

פה קק לובליך

Figure 3. Title page of the tractate *Kiddushin*, printed in Lublin in 1618 by Ẓevi b. Abraham Kalonymus Jaffe. From A. M. Habermann, *Title Pages of Hebrew Books*, Safed, 1969.

Hebrew Printing. The wandering printer Ḥayyim Schwarz (Shaḥor), his son, and son-in-law went to Lublin around 1547, where they began printing, with periodically renewed privileges (1550, 1559, 1578). Their first productions were liturgical items, notably the *maḥzor* of 1550. With the help of *Eliezer b. Isaac (Ashkenazi) of Prague they brought out a fine Pentateuch in 1557, and a (complete?) Talmud edition (1559–77), partly printed in nearby Konsha Wolowie when the plague broke out in Lublin in 1559. With a fresh outbreak of the plague in 1592, the printers moved temporarily to Bistrowitz. Kalonymus b. Mordecai *Jaffe, who had married Ḥayyim Schwarz's granddaughter and whose name appears in the Pentateuch mentioned above, took over when Eliezer b. Isaac and his son left for Constantinople around 1573. Kalonymus managed the printing house till his death in about 1603, and it was continued (with interruptions) under his descendants to the end of the century and possibly beyond. A fire destroyed the plant and most of the books in 1647, but printing was resumed soon after. A great variety of works—liturgical, homiletical, and rabbinical—were issued there, among them Mordecai Jaffe's *Levushim* (1591–), a Mishnah (1594–96), the Talmud (1611–39), the first editions of Samuel Edels' *Novellae* (1617), and the Zohar (1623–24). Jacob Hirschenhorn and Moses Schneidermesser opened a Hebrew printing press in 1875 (from 1910 Hirschenhorn and Streisenberg); Feder and Setzer were active from 1894; and M. Schneidermesser in the 1920s. [Ed.]

Holocaust Period. At the beginning of 1941 the Jewish population of Lublin was about 45,000, including some 6,300 refugees. The city was captured by the Germans on Sept. 18, 1939. In the very first days of the occupation, Jews were forcibly evicted from their apartments, physically assaulted, and put on forced labor. Some Jews were taken as hostages, and all the men were ordered to report to Lipowa Square, where they were beaten.

For a while, the Nazis entertained the idea of turning the Lublin district into a Jewish reservation for the concentration of the Jews from the German-occupied parts of Poland

and other areas incorporated into the Reich. At the end of 1939 some 5,000 refugees arrived in Lublin, and another 1,300 came in February 1940 (from Stettin). The group from Stettin did not remain in Lublin. In April 1940 the plan of a Jewish reservation was officially discarded; at a later stage, Lublin became one of the centers for the mass extermination of Jews. For a while, the city was the scene of the activities of Odilo *Globocnik, commander of the police and the S.D. and head of *"Aktion Reinhardt"* (see *Poland, Holocaust Period).

The existing Jewish community council remained in office until Jan. 25, 1940, when the Judenrat was appointed. The composition of the Judenrat did not differ greatly from the former community council; it consisted of 24 members, most of them prewar political figures, and was headed by Henryk Bekker, an engineer. The outstanding leader in the Judenrat however, was its deputy chairman, Mark Alten who later became its chairman, when the Judenrat was reconstituted, on March 31, 1942, and restricted to 12 members. During the first period of its existence, the Judenrat did not confine itself to the execution of Nazi orders (such as the provision of forced labor) but initiated a number of projects designed to alleviate the harsh conditions. Public kitchens were established and provided meals for the local poor and the refugees; the ghetto was divided into a number of units for the purpose of sanitary supervision, each unit run by a doctor and several medical assistants. There were also two hospitals with a total of over 500 beds and a quarantine area in the Maharshal Shul with 300 beds. Hostels were established to house abandoned children, but the Judenrat did not succeed in reestablising the Jewish school system, and the schooling that was available to the children was carried on as a clandestine operation.

In March 1941 the Nazis ordered a partial evacuation of the Jews in preparation for the official establishment of the ghetto. About 10,000 Jews were driven out to villages and towns in the area in the period March 10–April 30, 1941, and at the end of March the ghetto was created, with a population of about 34,000. On April 24, 1941, exit from the ghetto was restricted.

At the beginning of 1942, when the extermination campaign entered its decisive stage, the Jews of Lublin were among its first victims. Their deportation began on March 16, and in its course 30,000 Jews were despatched to the death camp at *Belzec or were murdered on the way. The rate of deportation was fixed at 1,500 per day, and attempts by the Jews to hide were of no avail. The remaining 4,000 Jews were taken to *Majdan Tatarski, where they lived for a few more months under unbearable conditions. On Sept. 2, 1942, 2,000 Jews were murdered, as were another 1,800 at the end of October. Some 200 survivors were sent to the *Majdanek death camp. Some Jews, who were skilled craftsmen, were still employed in Lublin, but in May 1943 the workshops were liquidated and the Jewish workers sent to Majdanek. Another 300 were kept in the Lublin Fortress, where they were employed in a few remaining workshops until July 1944, when they too were put to death a few days before the Nazis evacuated the city.

Figure 4. Drawing of the *bimah* of the Maharshal Shul of Lublin. From M. Balaban, *Die Judenstadt von Lublin*, Berlin, 1919.

Lublin was also the site of a prisoner of war camp for Jews who had served in the Polish army. The first prisoners arrived in February 1940. Those who came from the area of the General Government were set free, but some 3,000, whose homes were in the Soviet-occupied area or in the districts incorporated into the Reich, remained in detention. The Judenrat tried to extend help to the prisoners, and there was also a public committee which provided the inmates with forged documents in order to enable them to leave the camp. When the Germans stepped up the extermination campaign, there were some attempts to escape from the camp, to which the Germans responded by imposing collective punishment upon the prisoners. Nevertheless, there were continued efforts to obtain arms, and some prisoners succeeded in escaping to the nearby forests, where they joined the partisans; some of the escaped prisoners assumed senior command posts in the partisan units. On Nov. 3, 1943, the last group of prisoners was deported to Majdanek. [AR.W.]

Contemporary Period. On July 24, 1944 the Red Army liberated Lublin. The next day Polish regular army and guerilla units entered the city. A few thousand Jewish soldiers served in those units, and among the guerillas was a Jewish partisan company under Captain Jechiel Grynszpan. Until the liberation of Warsaw in January 1945, Lublin served as the temporary Polish capital. During that time some Jewish cultural and social institutions were established there, among others the Central Committee of Polish Jews. Several thousand Jews, most of whom survived the holocaust in the Soviet Union, settled in Lublin, but the majority of them left during the years 1946–50 due to the anti-Semitic attitude of a great part of the Polish population. A club of the Jewish Cultural Society was still functioning in the city until 1968, when all remaining Lublin Jews left Poland. [S.KR.]

Bibliography: S. B. Nissenbaum, *Le-Korot ha-Yehudim be-Lublin* (1900); M. Balaban, *Di Yidn-Shtot Lublin* (1947); N. Shemen, *Lublin, Shtot fun Torah, Rabones un Khasides* (1951); S. Wojciechowski, in: *Bleter far Geshikhte*, 7 pt. 1 (1952), 124–7; B. Mandelsberg-Schildkraut, *Meḥkarim be-Toledot Yehudei Lublin* (1965); Friedberg, in: *Yerushalayim*, ed. by J. Kreppel, 1 no. 3 (1900), 95–104. HEBREW PRINTING: Ḥ. D. Friedberg, *Le-Toledot ha-Defus ha-Ivri be-Lublin* (1900); idem, *Toledot ha-Defus ha-Ivri be-Polanyah* (1950[2]); idem, in: *Ha-Ẓofeh*, 10 (1926), 282–5; Steinschneider-Cassel, *Juedische Typographie* (1938), 36ff. HOLOCAUST PERIOD: N. Blumental, *Te'udot mi-Getto Lublin* (1967), Eng. summary; EG, 5 (1957), Lublin volume; *Dos Bukh fun Lublin* (1952), memorial book.

LUBLIN, MEIR BEN GEDALIAH (Maharam of Lublin; 1558–1616), Polish talmudist and halakhic authority. His acronym, **MaHaRaM**, stands for Moreinu **Ha-Rav Meir**,

"Our teacher the Rabbi Meir." Meir was apparently born in Lublin. His principal teacher was his father-in-law, Isaac b. David ha-Kohen Shapiro, head of the yeshivah and *dayyan* of Cracow. Meir's eminence in learning was such

Meir b. Gedaliah of Lublin, known as "Maharam," Polish talmudist and halakhic authority. From J. Elias (ed.), *The Jewish Face*, New York, 1947.

that he became the head of the yeshivah at Lublin (1582–87) at the age of 24, and before he was 30, he was appointed *dayyan* and head of the yeshivah at Cracow (1587–95). He was rabbi in Lemberg from about 1595 until 1613, when he was appointed rabbi as well as head of the yeshivah at Lublin, where he died. Meir of Lublin was one of the greatest teachers of his generation. Wherever he settled, he established a yeshivah to which numerous pupils flocked from all parts of Poland and beyond. From all over Europe rabbis turned to him with halakhic questions, problems of communal concern, or for advice. He encouraged them by stressing his readiness "to reply to anyone putting a problem to me, for in this I find pleasure" (Responsa No. 18).

In the introduction to his responsa, his son Gedaliah states that Meir wrote seven works, which he enumerates (see below). Only two, however, have been published. *Me'ir Einei Ḥakhamim* ("Illuminating the Eyes of the Wise") was published by his son Gedaliah (Venice, 1619). Regarded as a most important talmudic work and often republished, it was later printed in all editions of the Talmud. It is a commentary on most of the tractates of the Talmud and mainly centers around the statements of Rashi and the tosafists. In it Meir displays profound acumen, and although he treats the remarks of the tosafists with every respect as embodying the truth and not to be controverted, he was nevertheless sometimes critical of them and emended various passages which he maintained had been wrongly inserted by copyists. His commentary, unlike the lengthy lectures he gave to his pupils, is distinguished by its brevity.

The other published work, *Manhir Einei Ḥakhamim* ("Enlightening the Eyes of the Wise"; *ibid.*, 1618), containing 140 responsa, throws light on the religious, economic, and political life of the Jews of Poland and of other countries (cf. Responsa 13, 15, 40, 56, 81, 86, 118, 128, 137, et al.). These responsa reflect his method, temperament, and qualities. Although he was influenced in his halakhic decisions by French, German, and Polish scholars, he displayed independence and was critical of his predecessors. Despite the importance of the Shulḥan Arukh as a supreme halakhic authority, Meir refrained from "building the basis of any ruling upon the implications of its words, since they were not derived from a single source, but were . . . compiled from unconnected collections of sayings" (Responsa No. 11). On several questions, particularly in cases involving loss of money or livelihood, he adopted a lenient view (*ibid.* 50), and he showed concern for the status of women (*ibid.* 81) and for protecting the rights of widows and orphans (*ibid.* 109). Insistent that his decisions be accepted, he more than once declared that his opinion was "the clear truth" (*ibid.* 92, 111, et al.).

Although Meir, like his contemporaries, was given to casuistry in his responsa, a thread of clear thought and logic runs through all his statements. His responsa are one of the earliest sources for knowledge of the *Council of the Lands (*ibid.* 40, 125) to which he ascribed great importance and in whose meetings he participated on several occasions (*ibid.* 84, 88). Meir had hundreds of pupils, the most distinguished of them being Isaiah *Horowitz and *Joshua Heschel of Cracow. The five unpublished works mentioned in Gedaliah's introduction are: *Ma'or ha-Gadol*, a commentary on the *Arba'ah Turim* of Jacob b. Asher; *Ma'or ha-Katan*, a commentary on *Sha'arei Dura*; *Ner Mitzvah*, on the *Sefer Mitzvot Gadol* (Semag) of Moses of Coucy; *Torah Or*—a commentary on the Pentateuch; and *Or Shivat ha-Yamim*.

Bibliography: S. Buber, *Anshei Shem* (1895) 132f.; J. Loewenstein, in: *Ha-Goren*, 1 (1898), 39–54; S. A. Horodezky, *ibid.*, 55–61; idem, *Le-Korot ha-Rabbanut* (1911), 175–82; idem, *Shelosh Me'ot Shanah Shel Yahadut Polin* (1946), 68–72; S. B. Nissenbaum, *Le-Korot ha-Yehudim be-Lublin* (1900), 31f.; Halpern, Pinkas, index; Z. Karl, in: *Arim ve-Immahot be-Yisrael*, 1 (1946), 312f.; C. Tchernowitz, *Toledot ha-Posekim*, 3 (1947), 120f.; I. Rivkind, in: *A. Marx Jubilee Volume* (1950), 427f.; N. Shemen, *Lublin* (Yid., 1951), 365 ff.; I. Rosenthal, in: *Sinai*, 31 (1952), 311–38; B. Z. Katz, *Rabbanut, Ḥasidut, Haskalah*, 1 (1956), 65–69; Zinberg, Sifrut, 3 (1958), 190f.; J. Meisl, *Geschichte der Juden in Polen und Russland*, 1 (1921), 312f.; Waxman, Literature, 2 (1933), 117f., 187. [S.E.]

LUBLINSKI, SAMUEL (1868–1910), German playwright, literary historian, and philosopher of religion. Born in Johannisburg, East Prussia, Lublinski began work as an apprentice bookseller in Italy. He then started to write for various German journals and eventually devoted himself entirely to literature. His work took him to Berlin, Dresden, and finally to Weimar. Lublinski was at first influenced by Ibsen and the dominant naturalistic movement but he soon veered to the neoclassical theories and techniques of Paul Ernst. His plays on historical and mythological themes include *Der Imperator* (1901), *Hannibal* (1902), *Elisabeth und Essex* (1903), *Peter von Russland* (1906), and *Kaiser und Kanzler* (1910). He was best known, however, for his critical insight into literary trends and for his work as a philosopher of religion. Lublinski's views on naturalism and impressionism and his sociological approach to the study of literature appear clearly in *Literatur und Gesellschaft im neunzehnten Jahrhundert* (4 vols., 1899–1900), *Die Bilanz der Moderne* (1904), and *Der Ausgang der Moderne* (1909). His Jewish loyalties are evident in the essay, *Juedische Charaktere bei Grillparzer, Hebbel, und Otto Ludwig* (1899), and in two somewhat unscientific religious works, *Die Entstehung des Judentums* (1902) and *Der urchristliche Erdkreis und sein Mythos* (2 vols., 1910). Lublinski was one of the earliest Zionists in Berlin.

Bibliography: T. Lessing, *Philosophie als Tat* (1914), 343–52; A. Soergel, *Dichtung und Dichter der Zeit*, 2 (1925), 140–3. [S.L.]

LUBNY, city in Poltava oblast, Ukrainian S.S.R. Jews settled in Lubny at the end of the 18th century. From 361 in 1847, their numbers increased to 3,006 (30% of the total population) in 1897, and 5,341 (25%) in 1926. After the German occupation in World War II those Jews who did not manage to escape were murdered. The Jewish population numbered about 600 (2%) in 1959 and was estimated at about 250 in 1970. Although there was no organized Jewish religious life, once a year the Jews assembled at the mass grave of the Holocaust martyrs. [Y.S.]

LUBOSHITZKI, AARON (1874–1942), Hebrew writer, poet, and educator. Born in Poland, he became a member of the Hebrew literary circle in Warsaw at the turn of the century. He served as headmaster of a Hebrew school and established Aviv, an educational publishing house. Later, he taught in Smolensk, Russia, again in Warsaw (where in 1922 he set up the Barkai publishing house), and then in Brest-Litovsk, Volkovysk, and Lodz. After Lodz fell to the Germans during World War II, he was sent to the Warsaw Ghetto, and was active in clandestine cultural activities until his death at the hands of the Nazis.

Luboshitzki began his literary career at the age of 15, and published articles and poems in most of the Hebrew journals of the time. His first volume of poetry *Pizei No'ar* was published in 1894. Among his other works are *Pirkei Shirah* (originals and translations, 1897), *Yosele ha-Matmid* (1899), a story in verse, and *Viddui* (1899), poems with national themes. He wrote many children's poems, some of which were very popular, stories and plays for children and adults, and he translated poetry. His textbooks in Jewish history were widely used in Hebrew schools in Poland and elsewhere.

Bibliography: Ofek, in: *Moznayim*, 17 (1963), 61–63; Kressel, Leksikon, 2 (1967), 174–5. [G.K.]

LUBRANIEC (Rus. **Lyubranets;** Yid. **Lubrentsk**), small town in Bydgoszcz province, central Poland. The Jewish community was founded in the first half of the 17th century. Jewish merchants of Lubraniec had commercial ties with Danzig and Leipzig. The Brest overlord granted Lubraniec Jews a privilege in 1780, permitting them to engage in commerce and crafts. The Jewish population numbered 241 in 1765. The stone synagogue was considered one of the oldest buildings in the town. The Jewish community numbered 475 (47% of the total population) in 1808; 1,148 (60%) in 1827; 987 (58%) in 1857; 816 (39%) in 1897; and 834 (38%) in 1921. Between the two world wars the town contained a children's home of the Central Yiddish School Organization (CYSHO; see *Education). Before the outbreak of World War II there were about 880 Jews in Lubraniec. The Jewish community was liquidated in the spring of 1942, when the Jews were deported to *Chelmno death camp.

Bibliography: M. Freudenthal, *Die juedischen Besucher der Leipziger Messen in den Jahren 1675–1699* (1902), index; B. Wasiutyński, *Ludność żydowska w Polsce w XIX i XX wiekach* (1930), 22; I. Schiper, *Dzieje handlu żydowskiego na ziemiach polskich* (1937), index. [EJ/Ed.]

LUCCA, city in N. Italy. It was probably in the ninth century that the *Kalonymus family settled in Lucca and founded a talmudic academy there. About the year 1000 members of the family moved to Mainz, thereby establishing talmudic studies in the Rhineland. In 1145 Abraham *ibn Ezra wrote some of his works in Lucca. When *Benjamin of Tudela visited the city about 20 years later, he found some 40 Jewish families. Around 1431–32 Angelo di Gaio (= Mordecai b. Isaac) of Forlì opened a loanbank at Lucca; later the poet David b. Joab of Tivoli settled there. When the opinion of Savonarola was asked, he stated that while Jews should not be invited in order to lend at interest it was no sin if they did so once they came. As a result of the anti-Jewish preaching of *Bernardino da Feltre a **Monte di Pietà* was founded in 1489 and the Jewish bankers were fined heavily. Since they did not pay, they were expelled. Around the middle of the 16th century a few Jews returned but after 1572 they were not allowed to stay for more than 15 days at a time. This restriction was set aside in individual cases from 1738. Since then, however, no more than a handful of Jews have lived in Lucca.

Bibliography: Roth, Italy, index; Milano, Italia, index; Milano, Bibliotheca, s.v.; U. Cassuto, *Ebrei a Firenze nell' età del Rinascimento* (1918), index s.v. *David di Dattilo da Tivoli*, and *Lucca;* Roth, Dark Ages, index. [A.Mil.]

LUCENA, town in Andalusia, in S. Spain, S. of Córdoba; important Jewish community in the 11th century. During the period of Muslim rule Lucena was famous as "the entirely Jewish city," and a tradition states that it was founded by Jews. Several prominent families, including that of the historian Abraham *ibn Daud, claimed that their settlement in Lucena dated from the time of Nebuchadnezzar. Isaac *Abrabanel linked the derivation of the name of the town with the biblical town of Luz. Until the 12th century Lucena was a cultural center of Andalusian Jewry. In 853 Natronai Gaon wrote "that Alisana (Arabic for Lucena) was a Jewish place with no gentiles at all." In another responsum the *gaon* asked, "Is there a gentile who prohibits your activities? Why do you not establish an **eruv ḥazerot*?" (*Teshuvot Ge'onei Mizraḥ u-Ma'arav* (1888), para. 26). The 12th-century Arab geographer Idrīsī also commented on the Jewish character of Lucena and stated that while Muslims lived outside the city walls, Jews generally lived in the fortified part within the walls. Menahem b. Aaron ibn Zerah reports the same information at the end of the 14th century (*Ẓeidah la-Derekh* (Ferrara, 1554), 150). The Jews earned their living from olive groves, vineyards, agriculture, commerce, and crafts. Lucena was distinguished by its scholars. In the mid-ninth century *Amram Gaon sent his prayer book in response to a question by a scholar of Lucena. His contemporary Eleazar b. Samuel Ḥurga of Lucena received the titles *alluf (demin Ispania)* and *rosh kallah*, and became famous in the Babylonian academies (see A. Harkavy, *Teshuvot ha-Ge'onim*, Berlin, 1887, para. 386, p. 201, pp. 376–7). In the 11th century Isaac b. Judah *ibn Ghayyat taught in the yeshivah of Lucena. He was succeeded by Isaac *Alfasi who was followed by Joseph *ibn Migash. In 1066 the widow of *Joseph b. Samuel ha-Nagid and her son Azariah were among the refugees who came to Lucena in the wake of the anti-Jewish outburst in Granada (Abraham ibn Daud, *Sefer ha-Qabbalah—The Book of Tradition*, ed. G. Cohen (1967), 77). The last king of the Zirid dynasty, Abdallah, reported an uprising of the Jews of Lucena during his reign—at the time of the expedition against the Almoravides (c. 1090). At the turn of the century a contemporary of Ibn Migash, the *Almoravide ruler, Yusuf ibn Tāshfīn (1061–1106), demanded that the Jews convert to Islam. But the community was saved in exchange for a heavy bribe. The grammarian Jonah ibn Janāḥ and the poets Moses and Abraham *ibn Ezra, *Judah Halevi, and Joseph *ibn Sahl were active in Lucena at some time during their lives. The 11th-century Hebrew poet Abu-ar-Rabia b. Baruch, known throughout Andalusia, lived in Lucena. In 1146 during the Almohad wars, the Jews were persecuted and many were forced to convert to Islam. The community was not able to recover. Lucena was conquered by Castile in 1240. The fate of its Jewish community during the riots of 1391 resembles that of the other Andalusian communities.

Bibliography: M. Maimonides, *Iggeret Teiman*, ed. by A. S. Halkin (1952), xxix, 100f.; Neuman, Spain, index; Ibn Daud, Tradition, index; Baer, Spain, index; Ashtor, Korot, 1 (1966^2), 202f.; 2 (1966), 88–91; H. Schirmann, in: *Sefer Assaf* (1953), 496–514; E. Lévi-Provençal, in: *Al-Andalus*, 4 (1936), 113–6 (Fr.);

Cantera Burgos, in: *Sefarad*, 13 (1953), 112–4; 19 (1959), 137–47; Cantera-Millás, Inscripciones, 168–70; Torres-Balbas, in: *Al-Andalus*, 19 (1954), 190. [H.B.]

LUCENEC (Slovak **Lučenec**; Hung. **Losonc**), town in S. Slovakia, Czechoslovakia. The first Jews in the town settled in the suburb of Tugar—under the jurisdiction of the Szillassy family—in 1808, and at first the Lucenec community was known by the name of the suburb. From the beginning of Jewish settlement there were serious internal conflicts over the allocation of the taxes due to the chief constable. The latter reprimanded the Jews, ordering them to live in peace or he would put the community under Christian jurisdiction. The Jewish community suffered greatly when the Russians occupied the town in 1848. From 1851 Lucenec Jewry had all communal institutions, and in 1862 a synagogue was built. Following a controversy resulting from the delivery of the dedication sermon in Hungarian, a separate Orthodox community was founded in 1868 (officially recognized by the Czechoslovakian authorities in 1920). A school was established in 1878 and a new synagogue was built in 1925. There were 2,278 Jews in the town in 1930 and about 2,200 (c. 15% of the total population) in 1938 when the town came under Hungarian rule and the anti-Jewish laws were applied. Men up to the age of 45 were taken to labor camps and later many Jews were deported to Nazi death camps.

Bibliography: *Magyar Zsidó Lexikon* (1929), s.v. *Losonc;* M. Lányi and H. Propperné Békefi, *A szlovenszkói zsidó hitközségek története* (1933), 229–34. [M.La.]

LUCERNE (Ger. **Luzern**), city in the canton of the same name, central Switzerland. Jews were first mentioned in Lucerne in 1252, when the terms of their protection were defined. During the 14th century, a fine was prescribed for anyone perpetrating a blood libel against the Jews without previously notifying the council. A regulation of 1310 deals with the sale of meat from animals slaughtered by Jews. The Jews, who were authorized to possess real estate, were principally engaged in moneylending. During the massacres following the *Black Death (1348–49) the community came to an end; the town was compelled to indemnify the duke of Austria for the losses he had thus incurred. In 1381, there were once more Jews living in Lucerne. A few Jewish physicians practiced there during the 15th and 16th centuries. In the mid-17th century, Jewish livestock merchants again appeared at the local markets. After the

The synagogue of Lucerne. Photo E. Lande, Lucerne.

proclamation of the Helvetic Republic (1798), some Jews, mainly from Alsace, settled in Lucerne, though not without arousing a certain degree of opposition. The local community was founded in 1867, but never developed to any considerable extent. There was a yeshivah in the canton for some years.

Bibliography: Schweizerischer Israelitischer Gemeindebund, *Festschrift zum 50-jaehrigen Bestehen* (1954); A. Weldler-Steinberg, *Geschichte der Juden in der Schweiz* (1966); Germ Jud, 2 (1968), index s.v. *Luzern.* [S.Sch.]

LUCKMAN, SIDNEY (1916–), U.S. football player and member of both the College and Professional Football Halls of Fame. Born in Brooklyn, N.Y., Luckman became a professional with the Chicago Bears of the National Football League in 1939. A single-wing halfback, Luckman became football's first great T-formation quarterback. The T became football's basic formation, and the T quarterback the game's dominant figure, after Luckman and the Bears won the 1940 championship game.

Sidney Luckman, U.S. football player. From B. Postal et al. (eds.), *Encyclopedia of Jews in Sports*, New York, 1965.

With Luckman guiding the Bears they were division leaders again in 1941–43, and league champion in 1941 and 1943. The league honored him as its most valuable player in 1943.

During World War II, Luckman continued to play quarterback for the Bears while serving as an ensign in the U.S. Merchant Marine. Luckman retired as a player after the 1950 season. In 1965 he helped the U.S. Committee Sports for Israel raise money to send a U.S. team to the World Maccabiah Games in Israel.

Bibliography: B. Postal, et al. (eds.), *Encyclopaedia of Jews in Sports* (1965), 267–9; H. V. Ribalow, *The Jew in American Sports* (1949), 199–221. [J.H.S.]

LUCUAS (early second century C.E.), Jewish "king" and leader of the Jewish rising in Cyrene (115–117 C.E.). The sources are divided as to the name of the Jewish leader; whereas Eusebius (Historia Eclesiastica 4:2) refers to the Jewish king Lucuas, Dio Cassius (68:32) calls him Andreas. It has been suggested, therefore, that the "king" had a double name: Λουκούας ὁ καὶ Ἀνδρέας. Mention of a Jewish "king" perhaps signifies the Messianic overtones of the Jewish revolt in Egypt and Cyrene. One of the "Acts of the Alexandrine Martyrs" describes a dispute between a Greek and Jewish embassy before the Roman emperor Hadrian, and from its contents it is apparent that the subject under debate is connected with the Jewish revolt in Alexandria. A certain king of the stage and mime is mentioned as being brought forth by the Alexandrians to be mocked by the Roman prefect. Tcherikover, in analyzing the papyrus, points out that although it is possible that the "king" described is Lucuas, "he certainly would have been a prisoner in the hands of the Romans, and not of the Alexandrians" as is implied in the text. Furthermore, it is difficult to ascertain why Hadrian should be angry with the Alexandrians, if the object of their mockery was "the Jewish king" responsible for the uprising.

Bibliography: Schuerer, Hist, 291f.; Tcherikover, Corpus, 1 (1957), 86, 89, 90 n. 83; 2 (1960), 87–99. [I.G.]

LUDO, ISAC IACOVITZ (1894–), Rumanian author, journalist, and translator. Ludo began his literary career in his native Jassy, but soon moved to Bucharest, where he contributed to the Jewish review *Lumea evree* and to leading Rumanian periodicals. When the Jewish daily *Mântuirea* was founded in Bucharest in 1919, Ludo joined the staff and became one of its chief contributors. He also directed the Zionist daily *Şitri* and the periodical *Palestina ilustrată*, later editing the Jewish weekly *Adam*. A prominent figure in Rumanian Jewish life, Ludo played a leading part in the fight against anti-Semitism, and in all his writings bitterly attacked both Jewish assimilationists and opponents of the Jews. He spent the two years before World War II in France.

Most of Ludo's works are concerned with Jewish problems. *Doi mari poeţi—Heinrich Heine ş A. C. Cuza* ("Two Great Poets—Heinrich Heine and A.C.Cuza," 1934), first published in *Adam*, mordantly satirizes the Rumanian anti-Semitic leader Cuza, who fancied himself as a poet and claimed that the Jews were incapable of artistic creativity. In *Jurul unei obsesii* ("Around an Obsession," 1936), a lengthy analysis of Cuza's and the Nazis' anti-Jewish claims, he dealt incidentally with the scurrilous portrayal of Rumanian Jews in Ionel Teodoreanu's popular novel *La Medeleni* (1926). Ludo also wrote several more books against the Nazis and Fascists, such as *Hitler salvează echilibrul istoric* ("Hitler Preserves the Balance of History"), *Nae Ionescu apără pe Ebrei impotriva jidanilor* ("Ionescu Defends the Hebrews against the Jews"), and *Dela Rasputin la Hitler* ("From Rasputin to Hitler"). After World War II, he continued to write polemical works against the pre-Communist regime, the old political parties, and the defunct Rumanian dynasty. He also published Rumanian translations of Jewish classics, such as *An-Ski's *Dybbuk* (1927), *Zangwill's *King of the Schnorrers* (1934), and many short stories by *Shalom Aleichem.

Bibliography: G. Călinescu, *Istoria Literaturii Romîne . . .* (1941), 712. [A.FE.]

LUDOMIR, MAID OF (1805–1892), popular name of a ḥasidic "woman-*zaddik*." Her real name was Hannah Rachel, the only child of Monesh Werbermacher of Ludomir in the Ukraine. She prayed with ecstatic emotion, and studied Midrash, *aggadah*, and *musar*. During a serious illness she experienced a vision in which she received "a new and sublime soul." Subsequently she began to observe the religious duties of males, donning *tallit* and *tefillin* when she prayed. She also recited *Kaddish* for her deceased father. A synagogue was built with an adjoining apartment for her. At the **Se'udah Shelishit* repast on the Sabbath, the door to her room was opened and she delivered an erudite discourse to her Ḥasidim. Although she was betrothed at an early age, the betrothal was later annulled. Prominent *zaddikim* attempted to persuade her to marry, and at the age of 40 she wed a scholar whom the *zaddik* of *Chernobyl highly recommended. Her popularity waned after her marriage, and she later emigrated to Ereẓ Israel, where she continued her mystical studies and engaged in rituals designed to hasten the appearance of the Messiah. Y. Twersky's novel *"Ha-Betulah mi-Ludomir* (1949) is based on her.

Bibliography: Horodezky, Ḥasidut, 69–71; Rabinowicz, *World of Hasidism* (1970), 205–7. [ED.]

LUDVIPOL, ABRAHAM (1865–1921), Hebrew journalist. Born in Novograd-Volynsk, he was active in the *Ḥibbat Zion movement in Odessa. In 1890 he sailed for Ereẓ Israel but was not permitted to land. After a sojourn in Alexandria he went to Paris, where he studied and began his career as a journalist, writing in Hebrew for *Ha-Meliẓ*, as well as in French and Yiddish for other papers. His reputation as a leading Hebrew journalist grew during the Dreyfus affair. When the daily **Ha-Ẓofeh* was founded in 1903 he was invited to take up the post of editor. In 1907 he settled in Ereẓ Israel to establish a Hebrew daily of Ḥovevei Zion, but the project fell through. He was active in public affairs in Tel Aviv, and when the daily **Haaretz* appeared at the end of World War I, he became a member of its editorial staff.

Bibliography: J. Fichmann, *Be-Terem Aviv* (1959), 219–22; E. E. Friedman, *Sefer ha-Zikhronot* (1926), 283–8; Waxman, Literature, 4 (1960[2]), 443; Kressel, Leksikon, 2 (1967), 177–8. [G.K.]

LUDWIG (Cohn), EMIL (1881–1948), German biographer and author. The son of Hermann *Cohn, a famous ophthalmologist, Ludwig was born in Breslau. After 1907 he spent most of his life in Switzerland. He began his literary career as a playwright and novelist, but became internationally popular through his colorful biographies, which were translated into many languages. His vast output included *Goethe* (3 vols., 1920), *Napoleon* (1925), *Bismarck*,

Emil Ludwig, German biographer, Jerusalem, J.N.U.L., Schwadron Collection.

and *Wilhelm II* (1926), *Lincoln*, and *Michelangelo* (1930), *Hindenburg* (1935), *Cleopatra* (1937), *Roosevelt* (1938), *Simon Bolivar* (1939), and *Stalin* (1945). He also wrote shorter essays on Rembrandt, Beethoven, and Balzac, and character studies of three eminent German Jews, Sigmund *Freud, Ferdinand *Lassalle, and Walther *Rathenau. Like Lytton Strachey in England and André Maurois in France, Ludwig regarded a biography as a work of art. He did not pretend to compete with the scholars on whose research he based his presentation of historical figures and his personal views often cast doubt on the objective truth of his writing. Nevertheless, he always showed keen insight into the personalities of his subjects and into the historical and social conditions in which they lived, and his work was distinguished by a dynamic literary style. Among Ludwig's other books were one on Jesus, *Der Menschensohn* (1928), *Drei Diktatoren* (1939), and a study of the abdication of King Edward VIII (1939). He also wrote some geographical books, including *Der Nil* (1935, "The Nile," 1936), and *Am Mittelmeer* (1923, *On Mediterranean Shores*, 1929). Ludwig was baptized in 1902, but 20 years later, after the assassination of Walter Rathenau, he publicly renounced Christianity.

Bibliography: N. Hansen, *Der Fall Emil Ludwig* (1930). [S.L.]

LUDWIG, REUBEN (1895–1926), Yiddish poet. Born in the Ukraine, Ludwig emigrated to New York at the age of 15. Suffering from tuberculosis he moved in his twenties to the drier areas of New Mexico, Arizona, California, and Colorado, meanwhile making a meteoric appearance among the *In-Zikh group of Yiddish poets. Ludwig's poems emphasize the imminence of death, expressing sadness and hopelessness while longing for joy and glorious adventure. His *Gezamelte Lider* ("Collected Poems," 1927) include songs of the Rockies and of the American Southwest, then still undiscovered by Yiddish poets. He sympathized with exotic characters, and wrote of various minorities including Indians, Mexicans, Chinese, and Negroes.

Bibliography: Rejzen, Leksikon, 2 (1927), 90ff.; LNYL, 5 (1963), 6ff. [S.L.]

LUDZA (Rus. **Lyutsin**), town in E. Latvian S.S.R., in Vitebsk province within czarist Russia. Jews were living in Ludza as early as the end of the 18th century, and in 1802 there were 582 Jews in the town and district. The Jewish population numbered 2,299 in 1847; 2,803 (54% of the total) in 1897; 2,050 (40.6%) in 1920, 1,634 (30.4%) in 1930; and 1,518 (27.4%) in 1935. The community suffered greatly during and after World War I. The Jewish population also decreased because many Jews there moved to Riga, the capital of Latvia, and other larger population centers, or emigrated. Most of the Jews in Ludza were occupied as shopkeepers or artisans.

Ludza was famous for its rabbis and scholars. The best known were those of the Ẓioni family, and later the Don Yaḥya family, related by marriage. David Ẓioni officiated as rabbi from 1806 to 1808; he was succeeded by his son Naphtali (1808–56), who was followed by Aaron Zelig (1856–76), author of the responsa *Ẓioni* (1875). A prominent member of the Ẓioni family was Itzele Lutẓiner, author of *Olat Yiẓḥak* (1–2, 1885–97), who served as rabbi in *Rezekne. Eliezer b. Shabbetai Don Yaḥya, author of responsa on the Shulḥan Arukh, *Even Shetiyyah* (1893), was a disciple and son-in-law of Aaron Zelig Ẓioni and his successor in the rabbinate of Ludza (1870–1926). Eliezer's son, Ben Zion, was the son-in-law of Isaac Ẓioni, and for 26 years officiated as rabbi in Vilaci; after the death of his father he succeeded him in the rabbinate in Ludza (1926–41). Ben Zion, who perished in the Holocaust, was the author of halakhic books and historical articles. Because of the high standard of Jewish learning the community was known as the "Jerusalem of Latvia."

Holocaust Period. During World War II most of the Jews of Ludza were murdered by the Germans shortly after the occupation of the town in the summer of 1941. The remaining Jews, numbering approximately 300, were interned in the synagogue, which served as the ghetto. Later they were taken to Dvinsk (*Daugavpils) ghetto. Jews lived there after World War II but there was no synagogue in 1970.

Bibliography: *Yahadut Latvia* (1953), 286–300; M. Kaufmann, *Die Vernichtung der Juden Lettlands* (1947), 286–94. [Ed.]

LUEBECK, Baltic port in W. Germany. An imperial city and capital of the Hanseatic League, Luebeck did not permit Jews to reside within its gates, although in the 17th century Jewish peddlers were common and their presence highly resented. In 1680 the city, in need of competent money changers, permitted two **Schutzjuden* to live there; in 1701 their number was restricted to one. Jewish peddlers, dealers in old clothes and secondhand goods, settled in the nearby village of Moisling, and in 1697 received permission to establish a recognized Jewish community. The attempts of the Luebeck authorities to restrict their activities met with little success. From 12 families in 1709 the settlement in Moisling had grown to 70 by the end of the century. In 1724 a rabbi was engaged and a cemetery opened; the community was under the jurisdiction of the *Altona rabbinate. Although Moisling was annexed to Luebeck in 1806 the commercial and civil restrictions were not abolished until 1810, by the French occupation forces. A synagogue was dedicated in Luebeck itself in 1812. The downfall of Napoleon and the retreat of the French army threatened the Jews' newly acquired rights. C. A. *Buchholz, a Luebeck lawyer, attempted to defend them at the Congress of Vienna (1815) but in vain. After a protracted legal battle, in 1824 they were forced to leave the city proper, returning to Moisling, where they built a new synagogue (1827) and opened a school (1837). Emancipation granted during the 1848 Revolution gave the Jews the right to settle in Luebeck, where a synagogue was opened in 1850; a new one was consecrated in 1880. The last five rabbis who served in Luebeck and Moisling were: Ephraim Fischel Joel (1825–51), his son-in-law Alexander Adler (1850–69), his son-in-law Solomon Carlebach (1870–1919), who wrote a history of the Jewish community, succeeded by his son Joseph *Carlebach (1920–22), and David A. Winter (1922–38). The Jewish population in the city rose from 522 in 1857 to 700 in 1913, but after the advent of the Nazis, declined to 250 in 1937. The last 85 Jews were deported to Riga in 1941–42. After the war a new community was established, which numbered 250 in 1948; by 1952 only 30 remained.

Bibliography: S. Carlebach, *Geschichte der Juden in Luebeck und Moisling* (1899); E. Baasch, in: *Vierteljahresschrift fuer Sozial und Wirtschaftsgeschichte*, 6 (1922), 370–98; S. Goldmann, in: *Zeitschrift fuer die Geschichte der Juden*, 6 (1969), 159–64; D. A. Winter, *Geschichte der juedischen Gemeinde in Moisling Luebeck* (1968); A. Winter, in: *Jahrbuch fuer die juedischen Gemeinden Schleswig-Holsteins und die Hansestaedte*, 4 (1932/33), 23–31; 6 (1934/35), 41–43; 7 (1935/36), 51–57; 8 (1936/37), 59–89; 9 (1937/38), 59–89; *Jeschurun*, 11 (1865), 267–76, 307–13; 12 (1866), 11–18, 123–33.

[Y.Ro.]

°**LUEGER, KARL** (1844–1910), leader of the anti-Semitic *Christian Social Party in Austria. Born in Vienna into a lower middle-class family, he qualified as a lawyer. He began his political career with the left wing of the Progressive Party and was elected as their candidate to the city council in 1875. There he associated with Jewish members, among them Ignaz Mandl, a Jewish lawyer who remained his friend and political adviser even after Lueger had ousted him from the Democrats in 1889. In 1884 he sponsored the Democrats' electoral demand for "equality of all faiths." Elected to the parliament in 1885, he cooperated with the political anti-Semite Georg von *Schoenerer but denied being himself an anti-Semite. A year later he berated the Liberal majority in the city council for refusing to deliver a congratulatory address to Adolf *Fischhof on the occasion of his 70th birthday. In spite of this, Lueger made a violently anti-Semitic speech in 1887 in support of Schoenerer's bill against Jewish immigration from Russia and Rumania. After allying himself with Karl von *Vogelsang, in 1893 he united the different Christian factions into the Christian Social Party, which he led until his death. Lueger was extremely popular with the lower middle classes, largely because of his folksy and vulgar speeches uniting popular economic and religious anti-Semitic prejudices. He succeeded in forging a party which channeled social discontent, depicting capitalism and Marxism alike as products of the Jewish mind and fusing these new themes with the centuries-old hatred of the Jews stemming from Church doctrine. In 1897 *Francis Joseph I confirmed Lueger as mayor of Vienna after he had refused to do so on three previous occasions. In this office, which he held until his death, he effected many social reforms. His administration pursued discriminatory practices against Jews, mainly through not employing them in the city services and limiting their numbers in high school and the university. Nevertheless he was in the habit of doing petty favors for poor Jews, even appearing in a synagogue wearing the mayoral chain. In his administration he employed, besides Mandl (who was baptized at the age of 72), the partly Jewish vice-mayor Julius Porzer and the renegade Max Anton Loew. He accepted invitations to Jewish homes and is reported to have said: *"Wer ein Jude ist, bestimme ich"* ("It is up to me to decide who is a Jew").

Lueger's anti-Semitism was opportunistic rather than racist, but he had a profound influence on the young Adolf Hitler in his formative years, and established on a firm footing the Viennese anti-Semitic tradition.

Bibliography: P. G. J. Pulzer, *The Rise of Political Antisemitism in Germany and Austria* (1964), index; D. van Arkel, *Antisemitism in Austria* (1966), 67–80 and passim; O. Karbach, in: *Zeitschrift fuer die Geschichte der Juden*, no. 1 (1964), 1–8; no. 2–3 (1964), 103–16; no. 4 (1964), 169–78—all passim; J. S. Bloch, *My Reminiscences* (1923), 227–58 and passim; J. Fraenkel (ed.), *The Jews of Austria* (1967), index; A. Fuchs, *Geistige Stroemungen in Oesterreich 1867–1918* (1949), index; W. A. Jenks, *Vienna and the Young Hitler* (1960), index; F. Heer, *Der Glaube des Adolf Hitler* (1968), index; idem, *Gottes erste Liebe* (1967), index; S. Mayer, *Wiener Juden* (1917), index; K. Skalnik, *Karl Lueger* (Ger., 1954); T. Heuss, in: ESS, 9 (1954[2]), 629–30; H. Halborn, *A History of Modern Germany 1840–1945* (1969), 714. [ED.]

LUENEBURG, city in W. Germany. The mention of a *Judenstrasse* in 1288 indicates that Jews were living there earlier. They maintained a synagogue and *mikveh* in the 14th century. The Jews dealt in moneylending and were under the protection of the dukes of Lueneburg. In 1350, during the *Black Death, the Jews were massacred, only a few managing to escape despite the feeble attempt of the duke to protect them. The houses of the Jews were subsequently sold by the duke to the very burghers who had participated in the massacre. By the late 14th century, Jews were again living in Lueneburg. Community life was repeatedly interrupted by expulsions in the 16th century (1510, 1553, and 1591). Jacob, son of Leffmann Behrends the Hanover *Court Jew, was allowed to settle there in 1680; a number of **Schutzjuden* were subsequently permitted to reside there. The Jewish population increased slowly from 27 in 1811 to 145 in 1910. Between 1927 and 1930 the large synagogue, consecrated in 1894, was repeatedly desecrated and bombed by local anti-Semites and Nazis. By Oct. 1, 1936, only 36 Jews remained and on Oct. 30, 1938, final services were conducted in the synagogue which was then closed down. During World War II, 11 Jews were deported and lost their lives.

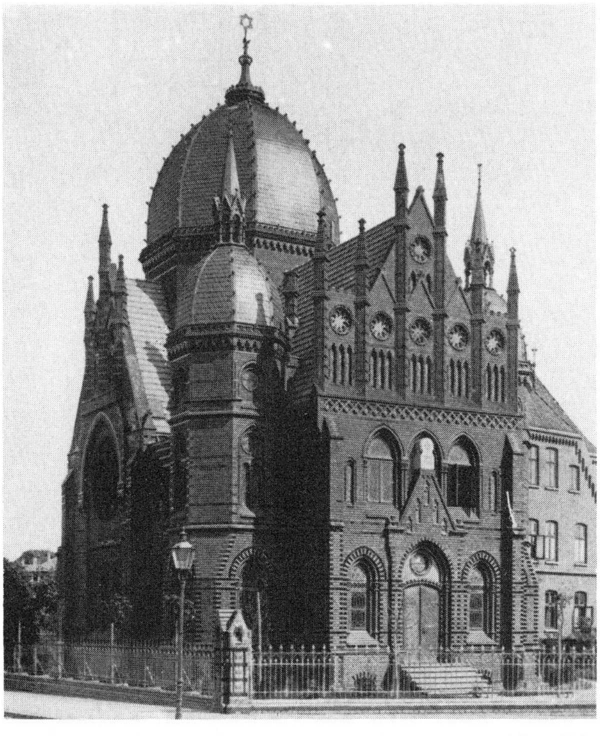

The Lueneburg synagogue, consecrated in 1894, closed in 1938, and later demolished. Courtesy Lueneburg Municipality. Photo Makovec, Lueneburg.

Bibliography: Germ Jud, 2 (1968), 498–501. [ED.]

LUGANSK (1935–58, **Voroshilovgrad**), city in the Lugansk oblast, Ukrainian S.S.R. Before the Revolution of 1917 it was a district town of the administrative province of Yekaterinoslav. The town was founded at the end of the 18th century and in 1897 there were 1,505 Jews (7.5% of the population) living there. From 1908 to 1916 the position of **kazyonny ravvin* ("government-appointed rabbi") of Lugansk was held by the Hebrew writer J. B. Lerner. There he published two newspapers for Jewish children, one in Hebrew *(Peraḥim)* and another in Russian. In 1926 there were 7,132 Jews (c. 10%) in Lugansk. The city was occupied by the Germans in June 1942. During the eight months of the occupation, those Jews who had not succeeded in leaving the city were murdered. There were 5,500 Jews (2.5%) in the city in 1959. [Y.S.]

LUGO, small town in N. central Italy. The first record of a Jewish settlement in Lugo is a tombstone inscription of 1285. The rule of the House of Este (1437–1598) and the famous fairs of Lugo made the community prosperous. After Lugo came under direct papal rule in 1598, conditions deteriorated. A decree of 1639 concentrated the Jews of the former duchy of *Ferrara in three ghettos, one of which was at Lugo; 600 Jews, some from neighboring towns, were confined there. In 1703 this number had been reduced to 54 families, among whom the *Finzi, the *Senigallia, and the Del *Vecchio were prominent. The Del Vecchio and later the *Fano families produced several eminent rabbis, more than would be expected from so small a community, though by 1797 it had grown to 648 members. In 1796 the French authorities granted emancipation to the Jews, but during the reaction following the temporary withdrawal of the French troops the ghetto was plundered three times. When papal rule was restored in 1814, the old interdictions again came into force and became even harsher under Pope *Leo XII, with the result that several families left Lugo. In 1853 there were no more than 400 Jews there. Later they followed the drift to the larger cities. Twenty-six Jews were murdered there during the Holocaust period. In April 1945 the town was liberated by the Jewish Brigade. In 1969 there was only one Jewish family in Lugo.

Bibliography: Milano, Bibliotheca, index; Roth, Italy, index; Servi, in: *Corriere Israelitico*, 6 (1867/68), 335–6; Volli, in: RMI, 23 (1957), 65–76; Sierra, *ibid.*, 24 (1958), 451–9. [A.MIL.]

LUGOJ (Hung. **Lugos**), city in W. Rumania, until 1918 in Hungary. Jews settled in Lugoj and its surroundings at the beginning of the 18th century. An organized community was founded between 1780 and 1790, and a *ḥevra kaddisha* in 1790. Jews played an important role in the development of the extensive textile industry and the processing of natural silk there. The Jewish population numbered 550 in 1851, 1,303 in 1891, 1,878 in 1910, 1,774 in 1924 (8.9% of the total population), and 1,418 in 1930 (6% of the total). During World War I, 173 members of the community served in the Hungarian army. Simon *Hevesi was the local rabbi between 1897 and 1905. With non-Jewish intellectuals, he organized popular educational institutions, the first of their kind in southern Hungary. An elementary school, founded in 1833, functioned until 1944. A large synagogue was erected in 1842. There were also some smaller synagogues. After the split within Hungarian Jewry in 1868 (see *Hungary), the community defined itself as neologist (see *Neology). A charitable organization of Jewish women functioned from 1875 and a *talmud torah* from 1903. Zionist organizations were active in Lugoj, and from 1934 the Zionists were the dominant element in the community leadership. Between 1941 and 1942, the period of the Rumanian Fascist regime, some of the Jewish men were conscripted for forced labor. The Jewish population numbered 1,043 in 1942. After World War II the Jewish population increased, as Jewish refugees from the surrounding districts and northern Bukovina settled there (1,620 in 1947). The number of Jews declined from the 1950s through emigration to Israel, and 220 Jews lived there in 1971.

Bibliography: *Magyar Zsidó Lexikon* (1929), 546; O. Kálmán, in: *Magyar Zsidó Szemle*, 51 (1934), 79–106; PK Romanyah, 1 (1969), 316–8; T. Schwager, in: *Revista Cultului Mozaic*, no. 243 (Dec. 15, 1970). [Y.M.]

LUIDOR, JOSEPH (d. 1921), Hebrew writer. Born in Galicia, Luidor settled in Ereẓ Israel as a youth, working as an agricultural laborer in various places, including Reḥovot and Ein-Ḥai (Kefar Malal). He was especially close to J. Ḥ. *Brenner, and, along with Brenner, was murdered by Arabs in 1921 in Jaffa. His body was never found. Luidor's stories, published in *Ha-Ẓefirah, Ha-Shilo'aḥ, Ha-Toren,* and *Ha-Po'el ha-Ẓa'ir,* were among the first writings to deal with the workers of the Second *Aliyah. He also wrote literary reviews. No collection of his works has yet been published, and some of his longer stories were lost.

Bibliography: Y. Yaari-Poleskin, *Ḥolemim ve-Loḥamim* (1946), 473ff. [G.K.]

LUKA (Ger. **Luck**), small town in W. Bohemia, Czechoslovakia. According to tradition, Jews from Bavaria founded the town in the 11th century, and they are mentioned in local records for 1198. Luka Jews had to supply a chalice for King *Premysl Ottakar II (1253–78) when he visited the pope. A Jewish "place of worship" is mentioned in 1432. During the Thirty Years' War (1618–48) the community was almost decimated by the plague. Luka Jews, like those of Hroznetin (Lichtenstadt), did business in nearby *Carlsbad. The synagogue and community records were destroyed in a fire in 1842. In 1850, 1,150 Jews lived in Luka (80% of the total population). In the 19th century Feibel (Phillipp) Kohn was mayor of Luka for 28 years. Both an Orthodox rabbi and a Reform preacher served in the town. Even before the 1848 Revolution allowed them freedom of movement, Jews had begun to leave Luka; there were 446 in 1869, but by 1930 there was no *minyan*. On Nov. 10, 1938, the synagogue was burned down. Gravestones in the Jewish cemetery were sold by the Nazis to a stonemason.

Bibliography: F. Ullmann, in: *Zeitschrift fuer die Geschichte der Juden*, 3 (1966), 117–23; H. Gold, *Die Juden und Judengemeinden Boehmens* (1934), 388–90. [ED.]

LUKÁCS, GEORG (**György**; 1885–1971), Hungarian philosopher, literary critic, and Socialist. Born in Budapest into a family of bankers, Lukács first attracted public attention through his collection of essays on art and philosophy entitled: *Die Seele und die Formen* (1911) and he founded a new theater in Budapest for the production of modern plays. He left Judaism at this period. During World War I, Lukács championed the cause of the proletariat and joined the Communist Party in 1918. When the Communist regime of Bela *Kun came to power in 1919 Lukács was made commissar for education. In this post he established a national council for culture to impose communist ideas on Hungarian literature and culture. After the collapse of the Kun regime Lukács fled to Vienna where he wrote *Geschichte und Klassenbewusstsein* (1923; *History and Class Consciousness*, 1971), a controversial volume of essays reinterpreting cultural values from a Marxist viewpoint which criticized Communism as it had developed in Russia. His biography, *Lenin* (1924), restored him to favor as an orthodox Marxist. In 1933, when Hitler came to power in Germany, Lukács fled to Russia where he edited several Communist journals including *Internationale Literatur* and the Hungarian literary journal *Uj Hang* ("New Voice").

Lukács returned to Hungary after World War II and was elected a member of Parliament. He was made president of the Academy of Sciences and professor of aesthetics and

Georg Lukács, Hungarian Marxist writer. Courtesy Soziologische Texte, Neuwied.

cultural philosophy at the University of Budapest. His unorthodox views led to frequent clashes with the Hungarian Communist Party and after the abortive rising in 1956, he was forced to hide in the Yugoslav embassy. He was restored to favor in the following year and was the recipient of many tributes and honors on his 80th birthday in 1965.

A prolific writer, Lukács was well known for his Marxist interpretations of literature. He was much influenced, however, by the humanitarian concept of Socialism as preached by the Jewish Socialist, Moses *Hess. His writings, especially his autobiography *Mein Weg zu Marx* (1933), reflected his opposition to the militant revolution of the orthodox Marxists and advocated humanitarian Socialism based on respect for the individual. His study of Hess, *Moses Hess und das Problem der idealistischen Dialektik*, was published in 1926.

Bibliography: H. Althaus, *Georg Lukács* (1962); V. Zitta, *Georg Lukács' Marxism, Alienation, Dialectics, Revolution* (1964); F. Benseler (ed.), *Festschrift zum 80. Geburtstag von Georg Lukács* (1965); G. Lichtheim, *G. Lukács* (1971); G. H. R. Parkinson (ed.), *Georg Lukács: The Man, His Work and His Ideas* (1971). [S.L.]

LUKOW (Pol. **Łuków**; Rus. **Lukov**), town in the province of Lublin, E. Poland. By the 15th century there was considerable Jewish settlement in Lukow with a developed autonomous organization. A responsum (no. 59) of R. Meir b. Gedaliah *Lublin (1558–1616) mentions the synagogue of Lukow, which was destroyed by fire. Joel *Sirkes (the Baḥ) served as rabbi of the community at the end of the

16th or the beginning of the 17th century. At the time of the *Chmielnicki massacres (1648–49) the community suffered heavy material losses and the new synagogue was burned down. In 1659 the Jews of Lukow were granted a royal privilege which confirmed their former rights to live in the town, to acquire land and houses, and to engage in commerce and crafts; they were also authorized to erect a synagogue and maintain a cemetery. In 1727 a poll tax of 120 zlotys was imposed on the community. With the progress of economic activities in the town during the second half of the 18th century the Jewish population considerably increased. In the middle of the 18th century a dispute broke out between the communities of Lukow and Miedzyrzec Podlaski over the question of their authority over the small neighboring communities. According to the census of 1765, there were 543 Jews (137 families) there. During the 1780s the rabbi of the community was Samson Zelig b. Jacob Joseph ha-Levi, the author of *Teshu'ot Ḥen* (Dubno, 1797).

After the Congress of Vienna (1815), Lukow passed to Russia, being in Congress Poland. The Jewish population numbered 2,023 (c. 60% of the total population) in 1827, 2,114 (c. 68%) in 1857, and 4,799 (c. 55%) in 1897. In this period many of the Jews were Ḥasidim and followers of the *ẓaddikim* of Kotsk, Aleksandrow, Radzyn, and Gur. Between 1906 and 1920 the *ẓaddik* Hershele Morgensztern, the great-grandson of R. Menahem Mendel *Kotsk, lived in Lukow. The Jewish population increased to 6,145 (49% of the total) by 1921; there were then 348 Jewish workshops in Lukow. Of the 24 members of the municipal council, ten were Jews (five being delegates of the *Bund). Between the two world wars the Jews of Lukow struggled against anti-Semitism, and an anti-Jewish economic boycott was organized. The last rabbi of the town (from 1937) was Aaron Note Freiberg, who perished with the members of his community in a death camp. [A.Cy.]

Holocaust Period. About 6,000 Jews lived in Lukow at the outbreak of World War II. In May 1942 over 2,000 Jews from Slovakia were deported to the town. In October 1942 they were sent, together with over 2,000 Jews from Lukow, to the *Treblinka death camp and exterminated. At the beginning of December 1942 a closed ghetto for the remaining Jews in Lukow was established. On May 2, 1943, the ghetto was liquidated by extermination of its inmates. [S.Kr.]

Bibliography: Halpern, Pinkas, 17, 27, 109, 151, 480, 481, 511; B. Wasiutyński, *Ludność żydowska w Polsce w wieku xix i xx* (1930), 35; R. Mahler, *Yidn in Amolikn Poyln in Likht fun Tsifern* (1958), index; idem, in: *YIVO Historishe Shriftn,* 2 (1937), 644–5; T. Brustin-Bernstein, in: *Bleter far Geshikhte,* 3, no. 1–2 (1950), 51–78, passim.

LULAV (Heb. לוּלָב ; "a shoot" or "a young branch of a tree"), a term applied in the Mishnah to all trees, e.g., "the *lulavim* of the terebinth, the pistachio, and the thorn" (Shev. 7:5) and to the vine (Or. 1:7). Its use, however, was particularly confined to the *palm branch, one of the components of the *Four Species (*Arba'ah Minim;* cf. Mish., Suk. 3 and 4). Its use in Jewish ritual is on the Feast of *Sukkot. [Ed.]

LUMBROSO, Italian-Tunisian family of scholars, diplomats, leaders, and rabbis of Castilian origin. Jacob and Raphael, sons of Daniel Lumbroso, intervened on behalf of their community in 1686, after a heavy tax had been imposed upon it by the bey. They were the leaders of the *Gornim community (of Leghorn origin) in Tunis.

Isaac ben Jacob (d. 1752) was one of the most brilliant representatives of Tunisian Jewry. He promoted talmudic studies and was largely responsible for the numerous rabbis of eminence who lived in 18th-century Tunis. During his period of office as chief rabbi, the split between the Tuansa (native Tunisian Jews) and Gornim occurred (1710). He attempted to find a compromise solution to the difficulties which arose between the two groups. For a long time he acted as the bey's tax collector; the bey also appointed him *qā'id* (=leader) of the Jews. Wealthy and generous, he gave his financial support to many students. His principal work, entitled *Zera Yiẓḥak* ("Seed of Isaac," 1768), was published in Tunis after his death. It is a voluminous didactic commentary on several parts of the Talmud and also contains funeral eulogies delivered by the author, as well as some scholarly notes on several passages in the Bible. The second part of the book *Benei Joseph* by Joseph *Tanuji, consisting of notes on several tractates of the Talmud and seven responsa by Isaac Lumbroso, which were found by the editor after Lumbroso's *Zera Yiẓḥak* had been printed, is also entitled *Zera Yiẓḥak*. To this day, Isaac is widely renowned among Jews of Tunisian origin as having been a scholar and a mystic.

Isaac Vita (1793–1871), who was born in Tunis, was known especially for his philanthropy. For several decades he was the undisputed leader of the Leghorn Jews in Tunis and president of the "Portuguese" congregation. He was also a *dayyan*.

His son Abram ben Isaac Vita (1813–1887), who was also born in Tunis, was appointed personal physician of the bey and minister of health in the Tunisian government. He established learned societies, and under the patronage of his sovereign he propagated Western culture in Tunisia. He was also a philanthropist. He wrote several authoritative scientific studies in the field of medicine. The king of Italy granted him the title of baron. His brother Giacomo was

Buying *lulavim* in Jerusalem in preparation for Sukkot. Photo Zwy Bassey, Jerusalem.

one of the most prominent merchants of Marseilles, where until 1881 he was the exclusive representative of Tunisia for the whole of France, with the rank of consul general. DAVID (1817–1880), who was born in Tunis, was an important financier and diplomat. He played a prominent role in Tunisian politics. ACHILLE (1858–1914), who was born in Mahdia, was a shipowner in Gabès, where he represented Italy. He was known especially as a poet and author. [D.Co.]

Abram's son, GIACOMO LUMBROSO (1844–1925), was a classical historian and archaeologist. Born in Tunis, he taught at the universities of Palermo, Pisa, and Rome, and was elected to the famous ancient Accademia dei Lincei. A specialist in the hellenistic civilization of Egypt, he was widely recognized as an expert in the ancillary disciplines of papyrology and epigraphy. His major published works were *Recherches sur l'économie politique de l'Egypte sous les Lagides* (1870) and *L'Egitto al tempo dei Greci e dei Romani* (1882, 1895[2]). He also compiled a glossary in ten folio volumes, *Testi e commenti concernenti l'antica Alessandria.* After his death, publication of this work was begun under the auspices of the Italian journal *Aegyptus* (serie scientifica, vol. 4), but only a small part was printed (1934, 1936) before wartime priorities ended the project.

His son was ALBERTO EMMANUELE LUMBROSO (1872–1942), Italian historian, who was born in Turin, and like his father, turned from law to history. He specialized in the Napoleonic period, on which he wrote numerous articles and books. His first major work was a Napoleonic bibliography (1894–96) that was followed by a study of the continental system, *Napoleone I. e l'Inghilterra* (1897) and *Napoleone II* (2 vols., 1902–05). In 1903 he became director of the *Revue Napoléonienne* (published in Paris). In 1904, after the National Library in Turin suffered a disastrous fire, Lumbroso donated his personal library as the core of a new collection. In 1916–18 he was Italian military attaché to Greece. In his *Le origini economiche e diplomatiche della guerra mondiale* (2 vols., 1926–28), he argued that World War I represented a triumph of Anglo-Saxon imperialism. His *Bibliografia ragionata della guerra delle nazioni* was published in 1920. [F.D.G.]

Bibliography: D. Cazès, *Notes bibliographiques*... (1893), index; M. Eisenbeth, in: *Revue Africaine*, 96 (1952), 360–1; J. Ganiage, *ibid.*, 99 (1955), 153–73; Hirschberg, Afrikah, index.

LUMINA, Jewish Social Democratic group in Rumania in the 1890s. Its founders were M. *Wechsler, L. *Gelerter, L. Geller, M. Haimovitz—later well known in the "Arbeter Ring" (*Workmen's Circle) in the United States—and R. Schwartz. Lumina originated in *Jassy in 1893 as an opposition group to the leadership of the Rumanian Social Democratic Party. It rejected the latter's tendency to closer cooperation with the liberal bourgeois party, which was the main factor in anti-Semitism in the country, and also demanded a clear stand on the "Jewish problem." The circle developed into a solely Jewish body which in 1895 emerged as an independent group. It published the periodical *Lumina* (1895–97) in Rumanian and *Veker* ("Awakener") in Yiddish. The society criticized the Social Democratic Party for contenting itself with a demand for general voting rights for all citizens while the Jews were still regarded as "aliens without rights." Lumina considered that one of its functions was to organize the Jewish workers for an independent struggle for political and civic rights, on the assumption that the "liberation of a nation is impossible if it is dormant and frozen." The society, which also had contact with Jewish Social Democrats in Russia, favored the principle of organizing special unions for workers of differing nationalities to function in cooperation. The Jassy group had connections with similar groups in other places in Moldavia (northern Rumania). It sent a memorandum (in German) to the congress of the Socialist International in London in 1896, in which it set out its principles and requested a discussion of the problem of the Jews in Rumania. The memorandum also explained that the Jewish proletariat and bourgeoisie, though in opposition from the class aspect, had a common interest in obtaining civil and political rights. Lumina had reservations on Zionism and religious attitudes, but *Veker* claimed that a man "who is unable to raise himself to love and sacrifice for his own people, can certainly not be such an idealist as to sacrifice himself for strangers."

Bibliography: B. Liber, *A Doctor's Apprenticeship* (1957[2]), index; *Tazkir Aggudat Lumina la-Congress ha-Internazyonal be-London* (Heb. and Ger., 1969); J. Kissman, *Shtudiyes tsu der Geshikhte fun Rumenishe Yidn*... (1944), 63–86 (incl. Eng. summary). [M.M.]

LUNCZ, ABRAHAM MOSES (1854–1918), author, publisher, and editor of geographical works on Ereẓ Israel. Luncz emigrated in 1869 from Kovno, where he was born, to Jerusalem, and was accepted as a pupil in the Eẓ Ḥayyim yeshivah. The director, R. Moses Nehemiah Kahana, was in favor of secular education and the use of Hebrew as a spoken language. Because of this, Luncz was able to continue his secular studies and his reading of Haskalah books. The head of the Jerusalem *maskilim* at that time was Israel Dov *Frumkin; Luncz began to associate with him and took part in the founding of the Maskilim Circle and the Moses Montefiore Library (1873–74). In 1873 he began to write in Frumkin's *Ha-Ḥavaẓẓelet*, and like the latter, he criticized the methods of the **ḥalukkah* and its administrators. However, he did not always oppose the traditional community. When H. *Graetz attacked the Jerusalem community after his visit of 1873, during which he was insulted by religious fanatics, Luncz defended it in 1874 in his *Ivri Anokhi* ("I am a Hebrew"). After having already written several geographical articles, Luncz published in 1876 a guide to Jerusalem, *Netivot Ẓiyyon vi-Yrushalayim* ("Paths of Zion and Jerusalem"), the first work of this kind in Hebrew. From then until his death he worked tirelessly to perfect his geographical knowledge. In his search for

Abraham Moses Luncz, authority on the geography of Palestine, with his daughter Hannah, 1910. Jerusalem Municipality Historical Archives. Photo Ben Dov, Jerusalem.

books he visited the libraries of Christian institutions, a revolutionary step for a Jew in the Jerusalem of those days. In 1877 Luncz's sight began to fail. He went to Vienna and Paris to seek medical help, but it was of no avail; by 1879 he was blind. His misfortune did not deter him from his projects. In Vienna he contacted Perez *Smolenskin, in connection with the publication of his projected yearbook of Ereẓ Israel. The first volume appeared in Hebrew and English in 1882, after a second trip to Vienna, under the title *Jerusalem, Yearbook for the Diffusion of an Accurate Knowledge of Ancient and Modern Palestine.* Only 12 volumes appeared by the time of his death 36 years later. The first volume, of which both the Hebrew and the English part were written mostly by Luncz himself when he still had his sight, is the best. The second volume was printed in 1887 on Luncz's own press in Jerusalem. The articles of the second volume were written by some of the greatest scholars of Palestine and other countries. The material in the Hebrew section dealing with the history of the Jewish settlement is unique. Here again, Luncz was the main contributor. Volumes one and two appeared in Hebrew and English; three and four in Hebrew and German. In 1895 he began to publish the *Lu'aḥ Ereẓ Yisrael,* a literary almanac, which appeared yearly until 1915. Among the books which he published in improved editions with his own notes, the most important are *Kaftor va-Feraḥ* of R. *Estori ha-Parḥi; *Pe'at ha-Shulḥan* of R. *Israel of Shklov; and *Tevu'ot ha-Areẓ* of R. Jehoseph *Schwartz. In the three volumes of *Ha-Me'ammer* he published documentary material on Ereẓ Israel. A courageous experiment for a blind man was his publication of the Jerusalem Talmud according to a manuscript that he found in the Vatican Library. By the time of his death, he had reached the tractate *Shevi'it.* Luncz also wrote *Die juedischen Kolonien Palaestinas* (1902) and edited *Ha-Ikkar* ("The Peasant"), 1894–96. Besides these literary activities, he was an active member of the *Va'ad ha-Lashon ha-Ivrit ("Committee for the Hebrew Language") and in 1902, with two of his friends, he founded the Educational Center for the Blind.

Bibliography: H. Luncz, in: *Yerushalayim,* 13 (1919), 329–50 (incl. list of works); Rivlin and Malachi, in: *Yerushalayim,* ed. by I. Press and E. L. Sukenik (1928), 1–16 (Heb. pt.); Rivlin, in: *Kovez Ma'amarim le-Divrei Yemei ha-Ittonut be-Ereẓ Yisrael,* 2 (1936), 66–81; I. Trywaks and E. Steinman (eds.), *Sefer Me'ah Shanah* (1938), 285–98; Malachi, in: *Talpioth,* 4 (1950), 759–69; idem, in: *Genazim,* 1 (1961), 276–89; BIES, 19 (1955), 1–28; H. Luncz-Bolotin, *Me'ir Netivot Yerushalayim* (1968); Kressel, in: *Netivot Ẓiyyon vi-Yerushalayim* (1970).

[A.J.Br.]

LUNEL, town in Hérault department, S. France, home of a medieval Jewish community renowned for its scholars. According to local tradition the town was founded by inhabitants of Jericho who arrived there after the conquest of their native city. Tourist brochures also claim that this community was outstanding for its medical studies and that its physicians carried out the first surgical operation in Europe. The nearby remains of the synagogue seem to have greater historical validity. The earliest historical evidence on the Jewish community of Lunel is recorded by *Benjamin of Tudela (1159). The community had probably been founded some time before, because by then it numbered at least 300 persons (or perhaps 300 families). Scant information on the Jewish community appears in non-Jewish sources. Toward the close of the 12th century, a Jew of Lunel, David ha-Kohen, son of Solomon, granted a loan to Agnète, wife of Guilhem VIII, lord of Montpellier. On the other hand, in 1293 the lord of Lunel sold part of the incomes from his barony to a Jew of Montpellier named Thauros. The existence of a cemetery is attested in documents dating from the end of the 13th century. On the eve of the expulsion in 1306, six Jews from Lunel were arrested and imprisoned in the Châtelet of Paris. The community must have been reconstituted after the return of the Jews to France in 1315 for, on Aug. 22, 1319, King Philip V the Tall ordered proceedings against the Jews of Lunel who, during Lent, had supposedly insulted the cross. A considerable amount is known about the Jewish scholars of Lunel. Benjamin of Tudela praised them for their erudition, piety, and generosity, not only toward the students who came to study at the yeshivah but also to every Jew in distress. *Meshullam b. Jacob was *rosh yeshivah* and a well-known halakhic authority. Of his five sons, the best known were Jacob, a commentator; *Aaron b. Meshullam of Lunel, impassioned defender of the philosophy of Maimonides; and *Asher b. Meshullam ha-Kohen of Lunel, a mystic and a brilliant talmudist. Meshullam b. Jacob's son-in-law, Moses b. Judah of Béziers, was living in Lunel at the time of Benjamin of Tudela's visit, as was Judah b. Saul ibn *Tibbon, who settled there after persecution forced him to leave Granada. Many scholars, such as Zerahiah b. Isaac ha-Levi *Gerondi and *Abraham b. David of Posquières, stayed in Lunel for varying periods of time. Others more intimately connected with the town included *Abraham b. Nathan ha-Yarḥi (second half of the 12th century); the talmudist *Jonathan b. David ha-Kohen of Lunel; Manoah, commentator on Maimonides' *Mishneh Torah;* and Abba Mari b. Moses, also known as *Astruc of Lunel, a halakhic authority and vigorous opponent of science and philosophy. His main supporters were Isaac b. Avigdor, *Simeon b. Joseph of Lunel, and Meir b. Isaiah; and his staunchest adversary was Solomon b. Isaac of Lunel, referred to as Nasi, who lived in Montpellier. Meshullam b. Machir, also known as Don Bonet Crescas of Lunel (d. 1306), is the last scholar known to have been a native of the town. Throughout the 14th and 15th centuries, however, there were several scholars who bore the name "de Lunel" or "Ha-Yarḥi," especially in Provence. The name was later found among families in Comtat Venaissin and the author Armand *Lunel belonged to one of these.

Bibliography: Gross, Gal Jud, 277–90; T. Millerot, *Histoire de la ville de Lunel* (n. d.), 87, 96f., 113; A. A. Rouet, *Etudes sur l'école juive de Lunel au Moyen Age* (1878); G. Scholem, *Ursprung und Anfaenge der Kabbala* (1962), index.

[B.Bl.]

LUNEL, ARMAND (1892–), French novelist. The descendant of an old Provençal Jewish family, Lunel was born in Aix-en-Provence. After studying law he later taught

Armand Lunel, French novelist. Courtesy Moshe Catane, Jerusalem.

philosophy in Monaco. Writing in his spare time he made his name with his sensitive and imaginative portrayals of Provence and its colorful inhabitants, both Jews and non-Jews. Lunel's major works include *L'Imagerie du Cordier* (1924); *Nicolo-Peccavi, ou l'Affaire Dreyfus à Carpentras* (1926); *Noire et grise* (1930); *Le Balai de sorcière* (1935); *Jérusalem à Carpentras* (1937), a collection of short stories; *La Maison de la femme peinte* (1946); *Les Amandes d'Aix* (1949); and *La Belle à la fontaine* (1959).

Lunel wrote librettos for his childhood friend, the composer Darius *Milhaud, notably the text of *Esther de Carpentras* (1926), on which Milhaud later based his *opéra-bouffe*, *Barba Garibo* (1950), and the oratorio *David* (1954), which was performed for the 3,000th anniversary of Jerusalem. "Esther," inspired by an old Provençal Purim play, evokes the humor and drama of Jewish life in Carpentras during the Middle Ages. Lunel also initiated a series of books on the French provinces, to which he himself contributed *J'ai Vu Vivre La Provence* (1962).

Bibliography: A. Spire, *Quelques Juifs et demi-Juifs* (1928); *Guide Religieux de la France* (1967), 596. [M.C.]

LUNEL, JACOB DE (18th century), Provençal poet. In 1737 he was one of the scholars of Carpentras who approved the publication of the prayers for Rosh ha-Shanah and the Day of Atonement according to the local rite. He revised and enlarged a Purim play by Mardochée Astruc written in Provençal, which he published in 1774 (new edition by E. Sabatier, 1877). Some of his liturgical poems appear in the *Seder ha-Kunteres (Maḥzor Avignon)*. He also composed a Hebrew ode on the occasion of Louis XV's escape from assassination in 1757; this poem was recited with musical accompaniment in the synagogue of Avignon.

Bibliography: Zunz, Gesch, 467; idem, in: AZDJ, 3 (1839), 682 no. 47; Neubauer, Cat, 899 no. 2506; Lipschutz, in: REJ, 84 (1927); Davidson, Oẓar, 4 (1933), 414. [J.H.Sch.]

LUNÉVILLE, town in the Meurthe-et-Moselle department, N.E. France. Several Jews were mentioned in Lunéville in 1470–72, just before the expulsion from the

The synagogue of Lunéville, built in 1785. From E. Kronker (ed.), *Souvenirs Israélites de France*.

duchy of Lorraine. From 1702 Lunéville was the seat of the ducal court of Lorraine; Samuel Lévy took charge of the court's commercial interests in 1705. Two Jewish families were authorized to live in the town by an edict of 1753; there were 16 families residing there when the synagogue was constructed in 1785. A cemetery was not consecrated until 1791. The community numbered 315 persons in 1808 and 400 in 1855; from 1870 it was augmented by a number of manufacturers from Alsace. Among the Hebrew printing presses established in France in the latter part of the 18th century and early in the 19th was one belonging to Abraham Brisach, who produced in Lunéville a *maḥzor* with Judeo-German translation in 1797 and a *Likkutei Ẓevi* in 1798. A hospital, established in 1857, was in use until 1944. Alfred *Lévy, later chief rabbi of France and a native of Lunéville, was rabbi there from 1869 to 1880. During World War I the incumbent minister, S. Weill, and several other Jews were among the civilians slaughtered at Lunéville (1914); 18 other Jews from Lunéville fell in battle in this war and six in World War II. One hundred and thirty-nine Jews (including the patients in the hospital) arrested in Lunéville during the German occupation died in the deportations. In 1969 there were about 200 Jews in Lunéville, half of them from North Africa.

Bibliography: H. Baumont, *Histoire de Lunéville* (1901), 210, 299–301, 559–61; P. Lang, in: *Revue Juive de Lorraine*, 11–14 (1935–38), passim; N. Gruss, in: REJ, 125 (1966), 90. [G.C.]

LUNIETZ (Ilintsky), GEDALIAH BEN ISSAC OF (d. 1785), ḥasidic preacher and *ẓaddik* in Ukraine, son of a *dayyan* in Polonnoye. An ardent preacher who stirred his listeners, Gedaliah was one of the sources of ḥasidic legend. His mentors in Ḥasidism were *Dov Baer the Maggid of Mezhirech and *Jacob Joseph of Polonnoye. Gedaliah was the most outstanding disciple of *Aryeh Leib of Polonnoye. He served as rabbi in *Ostropol, Miropol, and Ilintsy. His *Teshu'ot Ḥen* (Berdichev, 1816) includes sermons, some of them on the importance and holiness of Ereẓ Israel, expressing a profound sense of the bitterness of exile and anticipation of redemption.

Bibliography: L. Grossmann, *Kunteres Shem u-She'erit* (1943), 52. [Ed.]

LUNTS, LEV NATANOVICH (1901–1924), Russian playwright and literary theorist. Lunts was born into a well-educated St. Petersburg family which emigrated to Germany after the 1917 Revolution. He himself, however, remained in Russia for a time, suffered from malnutrition, and died in Hamburg at the age of 23. Lunts was a founder and spokesman of the important young writers' group in Petrograd known as the Serapion Brothers and named after a hero in one of the novels of E.T.A. Hoffmann, the 18th-century German romantic. The group's aims were to free art from political pressures and to win tolerance for artistic dissent. In his articles Lunts argued that Russian literature was unduly tendentious and uniformly realistic, and recommended that it emulate Western models. His play *Vne zakona* ("Outside the Law," 1923) is set in Spain and its central theme is that power corrupts. It was translated into many languages and became part of the repertoire of several Western European theaters. Two of his stories, "*V pustyne*" ("In the Desert," 1922) and "*Rodina*" ("Homeland," 1923), deal with ancient Jewish historical events.

Bibliography: M. Slonim, *Modern Russian Literature* (1953), 294–6; G. Struve, *Soviet Russian Literature—1917–1950* (1951), 46–52, 61, 107. [Y.Ma.]

LURIA (Lourie, Lurje, Loria, Lurja), well-known family traceable to the 14th century. The Luria family spread throughout Germany, Bohemia, Eastern Europe, Italy, and oriental countries. The name perhaps derives from Loria, a small town near *Bassano in the Vicenza region of Italy, but this is by no means certain. All who bear this name did not necessarily belong to one family, and there is certainly no connection between this family and the Luria family (who were levites) to which Isaac *Luria (the Ari) belonged. The main Luria family is descended from *Rashi and legend extends its descent to the *tanna* *Johanan ha-Sandelar. The source of the family history is the genealogical document compiled by Johanan b. Aaron Luria (see later) which *Joseph b. Gershom of Rosheim received from the author and incorporated in his *Sefer ha-Miknah*. Solomon b. Aaron b. Jehiel, Johanan's grandson, sent a copy to his relative, Solomon *Luria (Maharshal), who made an addition to the copy detailing his connection with Jehiel, brother of the author of the document. This copy is important for determining the link between the German and Polish branches. The document passed to Solomon Luria's descendants from generation to generation, each successive member adding his own name. One copy was published, after 300 years, in *Ha-Maggid* (vol. 1 (1857), 178) by Moses Eliezer *Beilinson, himself a member of the Luria family. This copy, which completed the German branch, was published in Solomon Luria's responsa (Fuerth, 1767; Lemberg, 1859).

The founder of the family was SOLOMON SPIRA (a son-in-law of Mattathias Treves; see *Treves family). It is related of his daughter MIRIAM (1350—the second generation) that she taught *halakhah* from behind a curtain in the yeshivah. Nothing is known of Samson of Erfurt (third generation), Jehiel (fourth), and Nethanel (fourth) but their names, but Nethanel's son, AARON LURIA (1450), was known and honored as a rabbinical authority. He was one of the opponents of the convention of rabbis called by Seligman Oppenheim in Bingen in 1456 and his responsum on the subject was printed in the responsa of R. Moses *Mintz (no. 63) along with the views of other opponents. A number of the responsa (16, 19, 23, and 24) of Mintz and Israel *Bruna (nos. 259–61) are addressed to him. JOHANAN (late 15th–early 16th centuries), who compiled the genealogical table, was Aaron's son. He was given the right to establish a yeshivah in *Strasbourg or *Colmar. Losing all his wealth in the Burgundian wars of 1475, he passed the last years of his life in *Worms. He is the author of *Meshivat Nefesh*, a homiletical and kabbalistic commentary on the Pentateuch (Mss. Bodleian, nos. 257–8) with an appendix, *Teshuvat ha-Minim u-She'ar Inyanim*, which is a defense of Judaism against Christian criticism. His didactic ethical poem *Hadrakhah* has been published a number of times. His grandson SOLOMON (d. before 1583) compiled the second version of the Luria family tree for Solomon Luria. His only son, JOSHUA MOSES (d. 1591), who was responsible for the third version, served as rabbi in Worms. He is referred to in the customal of Worms (Mss. Breslau Seminary LXXXVII, 123) and in other works. His son AARON (d. 1613) was a *dayyan* in the *bet din* of Isaiah *Horowitz in Frankfort. After him, unbroken knowledge of the German branch of the family ceases, but the family history does not come to an end then. Joseph of Rosheim was related to the head of the family, Solomon Spira, and his grandson, Elijah b. Moses *Loans (1564–1636), was also the maternal grandson of Johanan Luria.

The name Luria is found in Prague until the end of the 16th century and still later, but the connection between this branch and the German one cannot be established. It is doubtful if the kabbalist Jehiel *Luria of Safed (late 16th–early 17th centuries) belonged to this family. Some identify him with Jehiel Ashkenazi *Luria, author of the *Heikhal ha-Shem* (Venice, 1601). The founder of the Russian-Polish branch was JEHIEL LURIA, brother of Johanan (above). Around 1470 he left Germany and died in Bassat, Lithuania, where he had apparently served as rabbi. His great-grandson was Solomon Luria (the Maharshal). JACOB MOSES BEN ABRAHAM HELIN ASHKENAZI, a grandson of the Maharshal, compiled a commentary, *Yedei Moshe*, on the *Midrash Rabbah* (Frankfort on the Oder, 1705). SOLOMON LURIA (early 17th century), "the physician of Lublin," was a cousin of the Maharshal. Jehiel *Heilprin, author of *Seder ha-Dorot*, was the eighth generation from the Maharshal, and Abraham *Gombiner, author of *Magen Avraham*, the sixth generation. David b. Judah Judel *Luria (Radal) was the tenth generation. His nephew, David b. Jacob Aaron *Luria (1800–73), devoted himself to improving Jewish education in Minsk.

In the 19th century, when the Jews of Russia were compelled to adopt surnames, many chose the name Luria without having any connection with the family. It is unclear what connection, if any, there is between bearers of the name Loria in Italy and the Luria family, and it is possible that the genealogical tree of this branch, transmitted by Z. *Margolioth in his *Ma'alot ha-Yuḥasin* (1900), 61–63, is a 17th-century forgery intended to connect the Italian family with the more renowned one.

Bibliography: A. Epstein, *Mishpaḥat Luria, Shoshelet Yiḥusah*... (1901); JJLG, 5 (1907), 91ff.; A. Lourié, *Die Familie Lourié (Luria)* (1923); J. Cohen-Ẓedek, *Dor Yesharim* (1898).

[Y.Ro.]

LURIA, ALEXANDER ROMANOVICH (1902–), Soviet psychologist. In 1945 Luria was appointed professor in the department of psychology at the Moscow State University, a full member of the Academy of Pedagogical Sciences in 1947, and director of the Laboratory of Experimental Psychology and Restoration of Higher Cortical Functions, U.S.S.R. Academy of Medical Sciences, Moscow. The most frequently translated Soviet psychologist, Luria was familiar to psychologists the world over having acted as the program chairman of the 18th International Congress of Psychology, held in Moscow in 1966. He had wide professional interests which included brain mechanisms of mental operations (neuropsychology), with special reference to disturbances associated with brain lesions, the role of speech in mental development and control of child behavior, and mental retardation. He was a prolific writer and his books include *Sovremennaya psikhologiya v yego osnovnykh napravleniyakh* ("Basic Trends in Modern Psychology," 1928); *Rech i intellekt derevenskogo, gorodskogo i besprizornogo rebyonka* ("Speech and Intellect of Country, City, and Homeless Children," 1930); *The Nature of Human Conflicts*... (1932); *Rech i razvitiye psikhicheskikh protsessov u rebyonka* (with F. Ya. Yudovich, 1956; *Speech and the Development of Mental Processes in the Child*, 1959); *The Mentally Retarded Child* (ed. and coauthor, 1961); *Higher Cortical Functions in Man* (1966); and *The Mind of a Mnemonist* (1968). [J.Bro.]

LURIA, DAVID BEN JACOB AARON (1800–1873), educationalist; a pioneer of Haskalah in Russia. He was born in Minsk into a wealthy family. Influenced by the program of Max *Lilienthal, Luria concentrated on reform of the educational system of the community of Minsk. In 1843 he transferred the *talmud torah* of Minsk to new premises, provided its pupils with clothing, introduced European methods of study and order into the institution, engaged new teachers, and added secular studies and the Russian language to the traditional curriculum. The success of the institution encouraged the establishment in 1845 of a school for the children of "house owners" under the name of "Midrash Ezraḥim" ("School for Citizens") which was attended by about 100 children. At the end of 1846 the Russian authorities, who were about to open a government school for Jews of the town, closed Luria's educational institutions. He continued to spread the ideas of Haskalah in Minsk, and his house was regarded by Orthodox circles as a "meeting place for heretics." He contributed to the periodicals *Ha-Maggid* and *Kokhavim* and published a collection of commentaries to verses of the Bible, and other essays, in the spirit of Haskalah, *Omer ba-Sadeh* (Vilna, 1853).

Bibliography: L. Levanda, in: *Yevreyskaya Biblioteka*, 3 (1873), 365–77; J. L. Levin, *Zikhronot ve-Hegyonot* (1968), 43–46; *Ha-Shaḥar*, 4 (1873), 569. [Y.S.]

LURIA, DAVID BEN JUDAH (1798–1855), Lithuanian rabbi and scholar. Luria was born in Bykhow, Mogilev region. He studied under Saul *Katzenellenbogen in Vilna, but in 1815 returned to his native town, where he remained for the rest of his life and where he founded a yeshivah. A false accusation that grew out of a family quarrel in Bykhow, supported by letters forged in his name attacking the czarist government, led to his imprisonment in the fortress of Schluesselburg, from which he was released when the forgeries came to light (1837/38). Luria was active in communal affairs and together with Isaac *Volozhyner met with Sir Moses *Montefiore when the latter visited Vilna in 1846 to investigate the condition of the Jews in Russia. Luria corresponded with I. B. *Levinsohn, encouraging the translation of his book, *Zerubavel*, as a useful weapon against the calumnious attacks on the Talmud by anti-Semites and the *maskilim*. In one of his responsa to the rabbis of Mantua, he vehemently attacked the reformists for their attempts to delete from the liturgy the prayers for the coming of the Messiah and the future redemption (Responsa, RaDal (1898) 21c–d).

Luria was regarded as one of the Torah leaders of his generation, particularly after the death of his spiritual mentor, *Elijah b. Solomon (Gaon of Vilna). His literary works embrace almost all the books of the Oral Law. They are chiefly textual glosses, notes, source references, and expositions of the sayings of the talmudic scholars, reflecting extraordinary knowledge of Torah together with a feeling for scientific criticism and an understanding of the plain meaning reminiscent of the methods followed by the Gaon of Vilna.

Of his works the following are particularly worthy of note: his commentary to the Mishnah (Vilna, 1886–90); his notes to most of the Talmud, and his glosses to the *Midrash Rabbah*, which were published in the large Vilna (Romm) editions; his commentaries to the *Midrash Samuel Rabbati* (1852); to the *Pesikta Rabbati de Rav Kahana* (1893), to the *Pirkei de-Rabbi Eliezer* (1852) with an extensive and detailed introduction; *Kokhevei-Or* (1877), notes to *Sefer Yuḥasin* and to *Seder ha-Dorot; Kadmut Sefer ha-Zohar* (1856), notes to the Zohar, aimed at proving that its author was indeed Simeon b. Yoḥai; notes to the *She'iltot* of *Aḥai Gaon (1861); *Nefesh David* (appended to the *Yahal Or* (1882) of the Vilna Gaon), expositions of the Zohar and the *Zohar Ḥadash;* a commentary on the Book of Esther (1887); and several responsa (1898). Luria also arranged for the publication of several works of the Vilna Gaon, adding to them his own notes: *To'elet Eliyahu* (1856) on the *aggadot* to *Bava Kamma*, the glosses of the Gaon on the Jerusalem Talmud; order of *Zera'im*, and Luria's own glosses on the order *Mo'ed* (1858). He also wrote notes on *Aliyyot Eliyahu* (1882), Joshua H. *Levin's book on the Gaon.

Bibliography: S. Luria, in: D. Luria, *Kadmut Sefer ha-Zohar* (1887[2]; repr. 1951), 2–16; I. B. Levinsohn, *Be'er Yizḥak* (1899), 163–5; Ḥ. N. Maggid-Steinschneider, *Ir Vilna* (1900), 157–9; S. Ginsburg, *Ketavim Historiyyim* (1944), 28–39. [Y.Ho.]

LURIA, ISAAC BEN SOLOMON (1534–1572), kabbalist, referred to as **Ha-Ari** (האר"י; "the [sacred] lion" from the initials of האלוהי רבי יצחק: *Ha-Elohi Rabbi Yiẓḥak*, "the divine Rabbi"). This cognomen was in use by the end of the 16th century, apparently at first in kabbalistic circles in Italy, but Luria's contemporaries in Safed refer to him as R. Isaac Ashkenazi (הריא"ש), R. Isaac Ashkenazi Luria (הריא"ל), also as De Luria. His father, a member of the Ashkenazi family of Luria from Germany or Poland, emigrated to Jerusalem and apparently there married into the Sephardi Frances family. As he died while Isaac was a child, his widow took the boy to Egypt where he was brought up in the home of her brother Mordecai Frances, a wealthy tax-farmer. Traditions concerning Luria's youth, his stay in Egypt, and his introduction to Kabbalah are shrouded in legend, and the true facts are difficult to distinguish. Contradicting the widely accepted belief that he went to Egypt at the age of seven, is his own testimony recalling a kabbalistic tradition which he learned in Jerusalem from a Polish kabbalist, Kalonymus (see *Sha'ar he-Pesukim*, para. *Be-Ha'alotekha*).

In Egypt, Luria studied under *David b. Solomon ibn Abi Zimra and his successor, Bezalel *Ashkenazi. Luria collaborated with the latter in writing halakhic works such as the *Shitah Mekubbeẓet* on tractate *Zevaḥim*, which according to Ḥayyim Joseph David *Azulai was burned in Izmir in 1735. Their annotations of some of Isaac *Alfasi's works were printed in *Tummat Yesharim* (Venice, 1622). M. Benayahu has conjectured that commentaries on passages in tractate *Ḥullin* and other talmudic tractates, extant in a manuscript written in Egypt not later than 1655 in the academy of a *ḥakham* named Mohariel, derive from notes made by pupils of Luria's yeshivah in Egypt. However, this is doubtful since the manuscript mentions *Sefer Pesakim*, a collection of halakhic decisions by the same author, and there is no evidence to indicate that Luria was the author of such a book, certainly not before he was 20 years old. It is

Ark of the Law in the Ashkenazi synagogue in Safed named after Isaac b. Solomon Luria, Ha-Ari. It is the work of a 19th-century wood carver from Galicia. Courtesy Government Press Office, Tel Aviv.

certain, however, that Luria was familiar with rabbinical literature and was believed to be outstanding in the non-mystical study of the law. As well as religious study, he also engaged in commerce while in Egypt as attested by documents in the Cairo *Genizah. A document relating to his business in pepper dating from 1559 had been published by E. J. Worman (REJ, 57 (1909), 281–2), and a second, relating to grain, by S. Assaf (*Mekorot u-Meḥkarim* (1946), 204). Assaf connects this with Luria's sojourn in Safed, but there is no doubt that it was written in Egypt. The entire document is in Luria's handwriting, the only extant specimen to date. This material supports the evidence of Jedidiah Galante (in Leon Modena's *Sefer Ari Nohem*, ed. by S. Rosenthal; Leipzig, 1840) that, like many of the Safed scholars, Luria conducted business in the town; three days before his death he made up his accounts with his customers. Many of the scholars of Safed similarly engaged in business activities.

While still in Egypt, Luria began his esoteric studies and retired to a life of seclusion on the island Jazīrat al-Rawḍa on the Nile near Cairo. This island was owned by his uncle, who in the meantime had become his father-in-law. It is far from clear whether this retirement, which is reported to have lasted for seven years, took place in his youth at the beginning of the 1550s or when he was older. Legend antedates it considerably. In 1558, Luria endorsed a halakhic decision jointly with Bezalel Ashkenazi and Simeon Castellazzo. In his mystic study, he concentrated on the *Zohar and works of the earlier kabbalists, and of the works of his contemporaries made a particular study of Moses *Cordovero. According to evidence dating from the end of the 16th century, it was during this initial period of kabbalistic study that he wrote his single work, a commentary on the *Sifra di-Ẓeni'uta* ("Book of Concealment"), a short but important section of the Zohar (published in Vital's *Sha'ar Ma'amrei Rashbi*). The book gives no hint of the original kabbalistic system that Luria expounded at the end of his life, and shows some influence of Cordovero. In Egypt he met Samuel ibn Fodeila, a kabbalist, to whom Luria wrote a lengthy letter on kabbalistic topics. Here he refers to his own book and asks him to examine it in his brother's house, evidently in Egypt. Luria may have made a pilgrimage to Meron before going to settle in Safed, since there are references to his presence at the *Lag ba-Omer festival in Meron. In 1569, and perhaps at the beginning of 1570, he settled in Safed with his family and studied Kabbalah with Cordovero for a short time. Some of his glosses on passages of the Zohar were evidently written while Cordovero was still alive and some after his death, since Luria refers to him both as "our teacher whose light may be prolonged" and "my late teacher." On the other hand, he had already begun to impart his original kabbalistic system to a number of disciples in Safed, among them distinguished scholars. After Cordovero's death at the end of 1570, Ḥayyim *Vital drew particularly close to Luria, becoming his principal and most celebrated disciple.

Luria may have gathered around him in Safed an academy whose members engaged in exoteric and esoteric studies. The names of some 30 of his disciples are known. Vital confirms (in the manuscript on practical Kabbalah, holograph in the Musajoff collection, Jerusalem) that a week before his preceptor died they had been studying the tractate *Yevamot*. He also gives some information about Luria's system of study in the non-mystical parts of the law. Luria occasionally delivered homilies in the Ashkenazi synagogue in Safed, but generally refrained from religious teaching in public. On the other hand, he often took long walks with his closest disciples in the neighborhood of Safed pointing out to them the graves of saintly personages not hitherto known, which he discovered through his spiritual intuition and revelations. At this period, he had already become famous as a man who possessed the "holy spirit" or received the "revelations of Elijah." He taught his disciples orally, instructing them both in his original system of theoretical Kabbalah, and also in the way to communion with the souls of the righteous (*ẓaddikim*). This was accomplished by "unification" of the *Sefirot* and exercises in concentration on certain of the divine names and their combinations, and especially by means of *kavvanah*, i.e., mystical reflection or meditations in the act of prayer and the fulfillment of religious precepts. He himself wrote down little of his teaching, apart from an attempt to provide a detailed commentary on the first pages of the Zohar and glosses on isolated passages. These were collected from his autography by Vital and assembled in a special book, of which a number of handwritten copies are extant.

Luria acknowledges his inability to present his teachings in written form since the overflow of his ideas did not lend itself to systematization. Nor did he select the various subjects for study in his doctrine in a logical sequence but at random. He guarded the secret of his system and did not permit its propagation during his lifetime, therefore becoming celebrated at first mainly for his conduct and saintly qualities. Some who applied to study under him were rejected, including Moses *Alshekh. His relations with the scholars of Safed were friendly; a halakhic consultation addressed by him to Joseph *Caro appears in the responsa entitled *Avkat Rokhel* (no. 136). Luria undoubtedly regarded himself as an innovator, preeminent among contemporary kabbalists. Certain allusions made to his disciples suggest that he believed himself to be "the Messiah, the son of Joseph," destined to die in the fulfillment of his mission. The period of his activity in Safed was brief, for he died in an epidemic on July 15, 1572. His grave in Safed was and remains a place of pilgrimage for successive generations.

Both in enthusiastic descriptions by his disciples and their pupils, written in the decade after his death, and in their careful preservation and collection of his teachings and faithful rendering of his personal traits, Luria's striking personality is attested. The relevant details are scattered in the writings of his disciples, particularly those of Vital. Some have been assembled in book form, such as the *Shulḥan Arukh shel R. Yiẓḥak Luria*, compiled from the writings of Jacob Ẓemaḥ and published a number of times (first in Poland, 1660–70), the *Orḥot Ẓaddikim*, on the precepts of Luria from the writings of Vital (vol. 2, Salonika, 1770), and in *Patora de Abba* (Jerusalem, 1905). In addition, a wealth of legend accumulated around his personality, with historical recollection and authentic fact being mingled with visionary pronouncements and anecdotes of other holy men. Such mythical elements already appear in works written 20 years after Luria's death, such as the *Sefer Ḥaredim* of Eliezer *Azikri, *Sefer Reshit Ḥokhmah* by Elijah de *Vidas, and the books of Abraham *Galante. The legend is crystallized in two important documents, whose sequence of publication is a matter of controversy. One is the collection of three letters written in Safed between 1602 and 1609 by Solomon (Shlomel) Dresnitz, an immigrant from Moravia, to his friend in Cracow. The letters were first published in 1629 in *Ta'alumot Ḥokhmah* by Joseph Solomon *Delmedigo, and circulated from the end of the 18th century under the title *Shivḥei ha-Ari* ("The Tributes of Ha-Ari"). The second document, **Toledot ha-Ari* ("Biography of Ha-Ari"), appears in numerous manuscripts from the 17th century; one version is published under the title *Ma'asei Nissim* ("Miracles") although inside it is called *Shivḥei ha-Ari;* it appeared at the beginning of *Sefer ha-Kavannot* (Constantinople, 1720). This version of the legend was generally regarded as the later one, based on the Safed letters. However, M. Benayahu has published a complete edition of this recension (1967) and argued that it served as the basis for the source of Dresnitz' letters. Benayahu considers that the book was compiled between 1590 and 1600 by one of the scholars of Safed, and its various recensions circulated widely in the Orient and Italy. This, the first kabbalistic hagiography, compounds fact and imagination in its biographical account of the life of the saintly man.

There is no doubt that the legend of the Ari was widespread, and circulated earlier than the written sources treating his kabbalistic teaching. These compositions form an extensive literature. Although frequently described by kabbalists as *Kitvei ha-Ari,* "the writings of Luria," they are in fact the works of his disciples and their own disciples, edited and sometimes condensed. While most remained in manuscript, a few were published between 1572 and 1650. Moved by mystical inspiration, Luria expounded his ideas with many variants. His hearers seem to have noted down some of his teachings during his lifetime but mainly transmitted them from memory after his death, frequently superimposing their own interpretation. The conventicle of Luria's disciples included some important kabbalists who rated themselves highly and considered themselves faithful recorders of their master's doctrine. Personal friction and rivalry were not unknown. In the annals of the Kabbalah Ḥayyim Vital has won the laurels as Luria's chief disciple; the works of his associates and rivals have been passed over or erroneously attributed to Vital himself, in which case they acquired the reputation of authoritative sources of Luria's teachings. In fact, a number of variants of these are extant which, in the main, are not interdependent but represent independent traditions recorded by his disciples, including one which must be considered spurious. There are four such principal traditions:

(1) That of Moses *Jonah of Safed, crystallized in *Sefer Kanfei Yonah.* The complete authentic text is extant in numerous manuscripts, particularly in Ms. Sasson 993, copied by the author himself in Constantinople in 1582. A defective edition was compiled by Menahem Azariah *Fano in Mantua (first printed in Korzec, 1786). This is an important source for the study of Lurianic Kabbalah and as yet no satisfactory evaluation of it has been attempted. The author has omitted some of Luria's teachings, such as the doctrine of **ẓimẓum* ("withdrawal"), although, compared with Vital's rendering, his exposition of other teachings of Luria excels in clarity.

(2) That of *Joseph ibn Tabul who, after Luria's death, taught Lurianic Kabbalah to several pupils, among them Samson Bacchi, an Italian kabbalist. Ibn Tabul compiled a systematic exposition of Lurianic Kabbalah divided into *derushim* ("homilies"), with a number of supplements. The homilies are extant in manuscript and for a long time were attributed to Vital under the title *Derush Ḥefẓi-Bah* and were also published in his name (1921, at the beginning of *Simḥat Kohen* by Masʿūd ha-Kohen al-Ḥaddād). This text is most important for the version of the doctrine of *ẓimẓum* that it includes, parts of which were omitted by Vital.

(3) That of Ḥayyim Vital. In contrast to the comparatively limited scope of the preceding disciples, Vital rendered his preceptor's teachings in detail. He augments the words which he specifically quotes as Luria's or propounded according to what he heard, with numerous additions of his own. He also wrote his first versions immediately after Luria's death, although he confirms that certain expositions were only very briefly noted after he had heard them. Luria's teachings, in a book which he calls *Eẓ Ḥayyim* ("The Tree of Life"), were mainly written approximately between 1573 and 1576. However, he sometimes added a different version of the chapters, so that occasionally four variants on the same theme are found. The existence of these differing recensions has introduced considerable confusion into Vital's writings. The original sequence in *Eẓ Ḥayyim* falls into eight parts (called "Gates"): (a) all material in Luria's hand collected by Vital; (b) *Sha'ar ha-Derushim,* a systematic presentation of Luria's theosophical doctrine; (c) *Sha'ar ha-Pesukim,* explanations of biblical passages, arranged in a sequence that follows the Bible; (d) *Sha'ar ha-Gilgulim,* the mystical doctrine of metempsychosis, *gilgul,* and its source; (e) *Sha'ar ha-Kavannot,* on the mystical intentions and meditations required for prayer (*kavvanot ha-tefillah*); (f) *Sha'ar ha-Mitzvot,* the reasons for the religious precepts; (g) the doctrine of amends for sins (*tikkunei avonot*); (h) instructions for mystical "unifications" (*yiḥudim*), which Luria transmitted to each disciple individually. This version of *Eẓ Ḥayyim* remains in manuscript. Using it, Ḥayyim Vital's son Samuel *Vital compiled eight further "gates" in which Luria's own literary heritage is distributed according to its contents. These are: (a) *Sha'ar ha-Hakdamot;* (b) *Sha'ar Ma'amarei Rashbi;* (c) *Sha'ar Ma'amarei Razal;* (d) *Sha'ar ha-Pesukim;* (e) *Sha'ar ha-Mitzvot;* (f) *Sha'ar ha-Kavannot;* (g) *Sha'ar Ru'aḥ ha-Kodesh;* (h) *Sha'ar ha-Gilgulim.* The first edition of this compilation, *Shemonah She'arim,* was published, without the title *Eẓ Ḥayyim,* in the above sequence in Jerusalem (1850–98; new ed. 1960–63). Many kabbalists, in particular among the Sephardim, recognized this version only as authoritative and rejected the rest of Luria's writings including books which were assembled from Vital's own later recensions. Since "the eight gates" remained in the home of Vital and his son and were only rarely copied by others before 1650, kabbalists wishing to study Lurianic Kabbalah used other recensions of Vital's books and eclectic anthologies of Lurianic kabbalism which circulated from 1586. Several of these, which were compiled in Safed itself, are extant (such as Schocken Ms. 97 of 1586 in Jerusalem), in the handwriting of Moses Jonah, and the manuscript of 1588 (Enelow collection 683, in the Jewish Theological Seminary, New York). Copies of Vital's writings that had remained in Jerusalem, where he stayed for several years in the 1590s, were also in circulation from the middle of the 17th century, and various collections have been compiled from them: *Sefer ha-Derushim, Sefer ha-Kavvanot,* and *Sefer ha-Likkutim.* It was not until the end of the 17th century that a comprehensive edition of Vital's writings relating to Luria's Kabbalah was made. This was compiled in Jerusalem by Meir *Poppers of Cracow with a few additions from Luria's other associates. Poppers divided his edition into *Derekh Eẓ Ḥayyim, Peri Eẓ Ḥayyim,* and *Nof Eẓ Ḥayyim,* which in fact includes all the subjects covered in the *Shemonah She'arim.* It was in this recension that Vital's writings became widely disseminated, especially in Europe, and became familiar long before the bulk of them were first published in Korzec in 1784. The printed book thereafter entitled *Eẓ Ḥayyim* is actually the *Derekh Eẓ Ḥayyim* of Popper's recension. A number of books stemming from traditions compiled by Vital have been published in his name, such as *Mevo She'arim,* an introductory section (Korzec, 1784); *Oẓerot Ḥayyim* (*ibid.,* 1783); and *Arba Me'ot Shekel Kesef* (*ibid.,* 1804), part of which is undubitably a forgery.

(4) Superimposed on the tangled web of the three preceding traditions and their mutually interfused forms is a fourth deriving from the works of Israel *Sarug (Saruk), who propagated Lurianic Kabbalah in Italy and several

other European countries after 1590. He is actually the author of *Sefer Limmudei Azilut* ("Doctrines on Emanation"), published in Vital's name (Munkacs, 1897), which contains an entirely different interpretation of the doctrine of *zimzum* and the origin of divine emanation. Since Sarug was the first to spread this teaching in Italy, his version was accepted in wider circles, although there is no doubt that he added original speculations of his own to it. Sarug was not one of Luria's disciples in Safed but based his reconstruction on those works of Luria's principal disciples that reached him. He may have known Luria personally in Egypt, since there are grounds for assuming that he was born there and his signature is appended to a kabbalistic manuscript written in Egypt in 1565 (British Museum, Almanzi 29) for Isaac Sarug (his father?). The innovations in his version in particular made a considerable impression, and for a long time it was the one accepted as authoritative, furnishing the basis for most of the earlier works on Lurianic Kabbalah; for example the *Ta'alumot Ḥokhmah* and *Novellot Ḥokhmah* of Joseph Solomon Delmedigo (Basle, 1629–31), the *Emek ha-Melekh* of Naphtali *Bacharach (Amsterdam, 1648), and *Ma'ayan ha-Ḥokhmah* (*ibid.*, 1652)—which is in fact *Sefer Hatḥalot ha-Ḥokhmah*, a treatise originating in Sarug's circle. Lurianic Kabbalah, therefore, won adherents in the 17th century through the propagation of a version far removed from his original teaching. The inconsistencies in the different versions and the contradictions in Vital's own renderings gave rise to an exegetic literature which flourished particularly among the kabbalists in Italy, North Africa, and Turkey. Throughout these metamorphoses, however, the Lurianic system remained the crucial factor for the development of later Kabbalah. Apart from these variants, there are also a number of treatises and essays extant in manuscript, written by other disciples of Luria, such as Joseph *Arzin, Judah Mish'an, *Gedaliah ha-Levi, and Moses *Najara.

Before Luria's theoretical teachings became known, he won fame as a poet. A number of his liturgical hymns, only a few with mystical content, were published in the collection *Yefeh Nof* (Venice, 1575–80). Best known of his mystical poems are three hymns for Sabbath meals which have been included in most prayer books. Written in the language of the Zohar they describe, in kabbalistic symbolism, the meaning of the Sabbath and the special relationship between man and the world above on this day. Also published in Venice in 1595 were his *Tikkunei Teshuvah*, "penitence rituals" (entitled *Marpe le-Nefesh*), and in 1620 his *Sefer ha-Kavvanot*, an anthology of mystical meditations on prayers and rules for behavior. There is a characteristic contradiction between Luria's theoretical Kabbalah, with its numerous bold innovations in theosophical doctrine and the concept of creation which changed the face of Kabbalah (see **zimzum*; *Kabbalah), and his marked tendency to extreme conservatism when interpreting Jewish ritual customs and folkways. He upheld all the traditional usages, reading a mystical significance into them. He taught that each of the tribes of Israel could be regarded as having its own special entrance to heaven, which had resulted in differences in custom and liturgy, so that no particular usage could be considered superior to others. However, Luria did prefer the Sephardi liturgy, and the mystical meditations on prayer in which he instructed his disciples were based on Sephardi ritual. This was why only the Ashkenazi kabbalists and Ḥasidim accepted the Sephardi liturgy in prayer, as they adopted many of his other observances.

Luria himself attempted to clarify his position in relation to the Kabbalah of Moses Cordovero, and the question has occupied a number of other kabbalists. Answering inquiries on the difference between the two kabbalists, he replied that Cordovero treated of *olam ha-tohu*, "the world of confusion," while his own teaching dealt with *olam ha-tikkun*, "the world of restitution,"—i.e., each was concerned with entirely different planes and states of being in the spiritual realm of emanation, and so Cordovero's province did not impinge on that of Luria. Most kabbalists refrained from attempting to mix or combine the two kabbalistic systems. Vital too, who at first was Cordovero's disciple, wrote that he paved "the plain way *[derekh ha-peshat]* for beginners in his wisdom" while Luria traced the "inner, most important path" (stated in a dream in 1573 recorded in Vital's *Sefer ha-Ḥezyonot*). In reply to Vital's question (according to testimony in *"Sha'ar Ru'aḥ ha-Kodesh"*) as to why he had penetrated more deeply into the mysteries than Cordovero, Luria said that this did not come about through reliance on divine revelation or similar phenomena but because "he took greater pains than the rest of his contemporaries."

The entire structure of Lurianic Kabbalah is permeated with messianic tension. The introduction of the eschatological element into his basic concept of Kabbalah fundamentally changed later thinking. This element is implicit in his doctrine of *Tikkun*, restitution or restoration of the inner and outer cosmos. In no small measure it prepared the ground for the messianic ferment of the Shabbatean movement (see *Shabbetai Ẓevi). The deeds of man are invested with mystical significance, not only because they are linked with the secret workings of creation, but also because they are integrated into a vast cosmological drama which is inacted in order to rectify the original blemish in the world and to restore everything to its proper place. It is not the role of the Messiah to accomplish the *redemption; the task of cosmological restitution is imposed on the entire Jewish people through strict observance of the precepts and prayer. When this spiritual restitution has been effected the Messiah's appearance is inevitable, for it signifies the consummation of the cosmic process. The primary concepts of Lurianic Kabbalah provide an explanation for the existence of evil and impurity in the world and relate at every stage to the Jewish national and messianic mission.

There is no justification for the theory, widely held by modern historians, that the principles Luria introduced are based on the traditions and ethical doctrine of the *Ḥasidei Ashkenaz. Nor should Lurianic Kabbalah be viewed as the epitome of "practical" Kabbalah in contrast to "theoretical," or speculative, Kabbalah. The theoretical and practical aspects are blended in every kabbalistic system, particularly in that practiced by the scholars of Safed. Luria's originality does not lie in his stress on the practical aspects of man's adhesion to his Creator, or on the performance of good deeds, but in his pioneer conception of the theoretical aspect of Kabbalah.

For further details on the teachings of Luria, see *Kabbalah.

Bibliography: Azulai, 1 (1852), s.v. *Yiẓḥak Luria;* D. Kahana (Kogan), *Toledot ha-Mekubbalim ha-Shabbeta'im ve-ha-Ḥasidim*, 1 (1913), 22–42; Kaufmann, in: *Yerushalayim* (A. M. Luncz ed.), 2 (1887), 144–7; S. A. Horodezky, *Torat ha-Kabbalah shel Rabbi Yiẓḥak Ashkenazi ve-Rabbi Ḥayyim Vital* (1947); idem, in: EJ, 10 (1934), 1198–1212; I. Tishby, *Torat ha-Ra ve-ha-Kelippah be-Kabbalat ha-Ari* (1942); Scholem, Mysticism, 244–86, 407–15; Scholem, Shabbetai Ẓevi, 1 (1957), 18–60; idem, *Kitvei Yad ba-Kabbalah* (1930), 103–6, 115–43; idem, in: *Zion*, 5 (1940), 133–60, 214–43; idem, in: KS, 19 (1953/54), 184–99; 26 (1860/61), 185–94; R. Margulies, *ibid.*, 17 (1951/52), 248, 423; M. Benayahu, *Sefer Toledot ha-Ari* (1967); idem, in: *Sefer ha-Yovel le-Ḥanokh Albeck* (1963), 71–80; idem, in: *Aresheth*, 3 (1961), 144–65; idem, in: *Sefunot*, 10 (1966), 213–98; D. Tamar, *Meḥkarim be-Toledot ha-Yehudim* (1969); P. Bloch, *Die Kabbala auf ihrem Hohepunkt und ihre Meister* (1905); S. Schechter, *Studies in Judaism*, 2nd series (1908), 202–306, 317–28; Rosanes, Togarmah, 2 (1938), 198–203.

[G.Sch.]

LURIA, JEHIEL BEN ISRAEL ASHKENAZI (16th–17th century), kabbalist; scholar of Safed and its emissary to Western Europe. It may be assumed that Luria was a relation of Isaac Ashkenazi *Luria (ha-Ari). In 1599 he was in Worms and in 1601 in Venice, apparently on his return journey to Ereẓ Israel. That year he published three works in Venice: *Heikhal ha-Shem* containing early Kabbalah fragments on the ten *Sefirot*, with an appendix of several sayings in the name of Isaac Luria and two *piyyutim* (the *Bar Yoḥai piyyut* and "an elegy on the desolation of the Temple to be said in the early morning vigil"); *Asis Rimmonim*, an abridgment of the *Pardes Rimmonim* of Moses Cordovero; and *Ḥaredim* of Eleazar *Azikri, the first edition from the manuscript. He returned to Ereẓ Israel from this mission and in 1604 was again sent out by the Safed community, on this occasion together with Solomon ibn Ẓur, to the countries of North Africa. Several letters about the mission are extant that were written from Safed to philanthropists in Algeria, and in these the conditions of the Jews of Safed at that time are described. A responsum by Luria on kabbalistic topics is cited by Abraham *Galante (in *Kol Bokhim* on Lam. 1:6).

Bibliography: Yaari, Sheluḥei, 245–6, 248–9; S. Assaf, in: *Koveẓ Al Yad*, 13 (1940), 134–9; E. Loans, *Mikhlol Yofi* (a commentary on Ecclesiastes, 1695), ch. 14; Neubauer, Cat, no. 2578.

[A.YA.]

LURIA, NOAH (Lurye, Noyekh; 1886–1960), Soviet Yiddish writer. Born in Blashne, Belorussia, Luria joined the *Bund in 1905, was imprisoned in 1907–08, and joined the Russian army in 1917 after the February Revolution. From 1918 he was an official of the Yiddish Kultur Lige in Kiev. He began to write in his early 20s, first in Hebrew and later in Yiddish. He wrote widely for children and translated European children's classics into Yiddish. From 1930 Luria mainly wrote realistic tales of Soviet Jewish life. His last Yiddish work to appear in his lifetime was a review in *Heymland* 6 (July–August 1948) and in 1957 a Russian translation of one of his works appeared. He died in Moscow, reportedly leaving behind many unpublished critical studies. Luria's story *"Oys Khaver"* was reprinted in the first issue of *Sovetish Heymland* (January–February 1962).

Bibliography: Ch. Shmeruk et al. (eds.), *Pirsumim Yehudiyyim bi-Verit ha-Mo'aẓot, 1917–1960* (1961); LNYL, 5 (1963), 33–35.

[L.P.]

LURIA, SALVADOR EDWARD (1912–), U.S. biologist and Nobel Prize winner. Born in Turin, Luria studied medicine at the university there working under Giuseppe *Levi, and from 1938 to 1940 did research at the Institute of Radium in Paris. After the fall of France in 1940, Luria emigrated to the U.S., where he taught at Columbia (1940–42), Indiana University (1943–50), and the University of Illinois (1950–59), before becoming a professor of microbiology at the Massachusetts Institute of Technology in 1959. In 1964 he was appointed professor of biology at M.I.T. He was an associate editor of the *Journal of Bacteriology* (1950–55), editor of *Virology* from 1955, and published *General Virology* (1953–67[2]). Luria was one of the pioneers of microbial genetics. In 1943, with Max Delbrueck, he showed that the appearance of bacteriophage-resistant strains of bacteria was the result of spontaneous mutations. The reasoning and design of this classic experiment became a model for subsequent research in viral and bacterial genetics. He dealt with lysogeny (the attachment of viral DNA to the bacterial chromosome), transduction (the transfer of genetic material from one bacterium to another by a virus), and the control of phage properties by the bacterial host. Luria's later experiments, employing novel techniques, extended the principles of genetics to viruses and bacteria and formed an essential part of the foundation of the new science of molecular biology. In 1969 Luria was a corecipient (with Max Delbrueck and Alfred Hershey) of the Nobel Prize for Physiology and Medicine.

Bibliography: *McGraw-Hill Modern Men of Science* (1966), s.v.

[M.L.G.]

LURIA, SOLOMON BEN JEHIEL (?1510–1574), *posek* and talmudic commentator (known as **Rashal** or **Maharshal** = **M**orenu **h**a-**R**av Shelomo Luria). Few biographical details are known of him. He was probably born in Poznan (Poland). His family was related to many of the important families of the time, including *Katzenellenbogen and *Minz of Padua. Luria was orphaned in his youth. He was educated by his maternal grandfather, Isaac Klober, a well-known scholar, and Luria took pride in the fact that he received most of his learning and traditions from him. When 40 years old he was appointed rabbi and *rosh yeshivah* of Ostrog. About 20 years later he moved to Brisk (Brest-Litovsk) where he may also have been rabbi before he went to Ostrog, and then to Lublin where he served as a *rosh yeshivah*, at first in the yeshivah founded by *Shalom Shachna. However, after becoming involved in a quarrel with Israel, the son of Shalom, he left and in 1567—with the permission of the government—founded his own yeshivah where he was able to teach in accordance with his own system. Although Luria raised many pupils who became rabbis in Poland and Lithuania during his own and the following generation, some left his yeshivah and went to

אשרי האיש ירא את יי
במצותיו חפץ מאד
מהר"ר שלמה לוריא זצ"ל בן כבוד
פה בבסיליאה הגדולה והמהוללה:

Title page of *Ammudei Shelomo*, by Solomon b. Jehiel Luria. The book contains expositions of Moses of Coucy's *Sefer Mitzvot Gadol*, together with comments by Luria's pupil, Moses Lunz. Basle, 1600. Jerusalem, J.N.U.L.

R. Israel. Luria felt this desertion deeply and complained about it in harsh words. Among his outstanding pupils were Mordecai *Jaffe and Joshua *Falk.

Luria was unique for his time in the complete independence he showed in halakhic ruling and in the critical method which he employed. It was based on a comparison of all the vast commentative and halakhic material—both that compiled before and during his time—with the talmudic sources, showing remarkable profundity while strictly avoiding the *pilpul* and hairsplitting which then dominated the yeshivot of Poland, particularly that of Shalom Shachna. His criticism also included the quality of the printed text of the Talmud of which the first good and complete editions had been published in the preceding generation. His rulings were accepted by most of his contemporary scholars with whom he was in correspondence and exchanged responsa. However, his extraordinary firmness—as well as his public accusations that many of the rabbis who were stringent in their rulings had their eye on monetary gain and "the benefit it brought them and their scribes" (responsum 21)—roused many opponents against him.

There is no doubt, as he himself states, that the method of *pilpul* was also used in Luria's yeshivah, but he distinguished between the oral teaching in the yeshivah which was designed to sharpen the minds of the pupils and that whose aim was purely to arrive at the truth, as well as between both these methods and the ability to posit the *halakhah*. His independence in his rulings was tempered with a great reverence for the school of Rashi and the tosafists and the early Franco-German authorities generally, and in particular for their traditions and customs, which he always accepted. In addition he relied heavily in *halakhah* on the decisions of Israel *Isserlein, the author of the *Terumat ha-Deshen* (Venice, 1519), even though he does not refrain at times from taking an independent line from him (responsum 39). Luria's works include an exceptionally wide range of literary sources, commentative and halakhic, from the *geonic* period down to his own time, of which he had an extensive collection in his rich library—both of published works and manuscripts. In addition to his glosses and textual emendations of the Talmud, he also wrote on the liturgy, Maimonides' *Mishneh Torah*, the *Turim* (see *Jacob b. Asher), the *Semag* (see *Moses b. Jacob of Coucy), Rashi's biblical commentary, and other works. His interest encompassed many fields, including grammar and Kabbalah, to which he was greatly inclined, although he made very little use of it in his halakhic decisions. To philosophy and its study he was greatly opposed, and hard words on this subject passed between him and Moses *Isserles, his younger relative whom Luria held in high esteem despite the bitter dispute which arose between them toward the end of Isserles' life. Joseph *Caro's commentary to the *Turim*, *Beit Yosef*, was published at that time. Luria, though valuing the work for its own sake, was strongly opposed to the *halakhah* being decided in accordance with it since it was not primarily based upon the tosafists and the Franco-German scholars. Luria seems to ignore the Shulḥan Arukh, although there is no doubt that he knew it.

Only part of Luria's works have been preserved, including: (1) *Yam shel Shelomo* on the Talmud (on *Bava Kamma*; Prague, 1616–18; on *Ḥullin*; Cracow, 1633–35; etc.). It is not certain how comprehensive the original work was, only his comments to a few tractates having been preserved. The book is distinguished for its clarity and for its remarkably detailed, orderly, and erudite presentation of each topic. From it one can clearly follow the manner in which the *halakhah* with which he is dealing developed from the geonic period until his time; (2) *Ḥokhmat Shelomo* (Cracow, 1582 or 1587), glosses on the text of the Talmud together with short comments. This work was published in most editions of the Talmud in a very abridged—and many times corrupt and meaningless—form, after many of his emendations had already been inserted into the actual text of the Talmud; (3) *Ammudei Shelomo* (Basle, 1600), expositions of the *Semag*; (4) *Yeri'ot Shelomo* (Prague, 1609), glosses and expositions of Rashi's Bible commentary and glosses to Elijah *Mizraḥi's supercommentary to it; (5) *Ateret Shelomo* (Basle, 1599/1600), a commentary on the *Sha'arei Dura* (see *Dueren, Isaac Ben Meir); (6) responsa (Lublin, 1574–75). These responsa are exceptionally valuable for the insight they afford into the culture of the Jews of Poland and Lithuania in this period of their efflorescence, and the status and moral standard of the rabbinate of his time. Responsum 29 contains an early historical document on the chronology of the scholars of Germany from the time of *Gershom b. Judah, until the middle of the 14th century. Luria also wrote a commentary to the Grace after Meals (Venice, 1603); to the Sabbath *Zemirot* (Lublin, 1596); expositions of scriptural verses; a critique of Abraham ibn Ezra's Pentateuch commentary; and other works.

Bibliography: Assaf, in: *Sefer ha-Yovel... L. Ginzberg* (1946), 45–63 (Hebrew section); Graetz-Rabbinowitz, 7 (1899), 338–42; S. A. Horodezky, *Kerem Shelomo* (1897); idem, *Le-Korot ha-Rabbanut* (1911), 123–44; S. Hurwitz (ed.), *The Responsa of Solomon Luria* (1938); R. N. Rabinovitz, *Ma'amar al Hadpasat ha-Talmud* (1952²), 62f.; Raphael, in: *Sefer ha-Yovel... S. Federbush* (1961), 316–29; Shulvass, in: I. Halpern (ed.), *Beit Yisrael be-Polin*, 2 (1954), 16; *ibid.*, 239 n. 14; A. Siev, *Ha-Rama* (1957), 49–59; Sonne, in: KS, 8 (1931/32), 128f.; H. Tchernowitz, *Toledot ha-Posekim*, 3 (1947), 74–91. [I.T.-S.]

LURIE, HARRY LAWRENCE (1892–), U.S. social worker. Lurie, who was born in Goldingen, Latvia, was taken to the U.S. in 1898. During 1913–14, Lurie was employed as a staff member by the Federation of Jewish Charities in Buffalo, New York. After service with the Detroit Department of Public Welfare (1915–22), he was subsequently employed as: faculty member at the University of Michigan (1922–24); superintendent of the Chicago Jewish Social Service Bureau (1925–30); lecturer at the University of Chicago (1926–30) and the New York School of Social Work (1931); executive director of the Bureau of Jewish Social Research (1930–35); and executive director of the Council of Jewish Federations and Welfare Funds (1935–57). In the latter capacities, he was a leader in orienting Jewish social work toward the main currents of the American profession. He became editor of the *Encyclopedia of Social Work* in 1962 and wrote *A Heritage Affirmed* (1961), a history of the federation movement in American Jewish philanthropy. [ED.]

LURIE, JOSEPH (1871–1937), Zionist leader and Hebrew educator. Born in Pumpenai, Lithuania, Lurie studied at the University of Berlin, where, together with Leo *Motzkin and Shemaryahu *Levin, he established the first Russian Jewish students' group (1889) and joined the *Benei Moshe association. Lurie was a delegate to the First *Zionist Congress. From 1899 to 1904 he edited the Zionist weekly *Der Yud* ("The Jew"), gathering around him the best of the Yiddish writers. He stressed the importance of the Yiddish language as a national heritage in a series of articles in the St. Petersburg daily *Der Fraynd*, the literary supplement of which he edited until 1906. In that year he was elected to the central committee of the Zionist Organization in Russia and became editor of the Zionist organ *Dos Yidishe Folk* ("The Jewish People") in Vilna. In 1907 he went to Ereẓ Israel, joining the staff of the Herzlia

High School in Tel Aviv. Lurie was a key figure in the language controversy with the *Hilfsverein der deutschen Juden, which tried to introduce German as a language of instruction. During World War I he was banished by the Turkish authorities. From 1919 he headed the education department of the Zionist Organization, later of the Va'ad Le'ummi (National Council of the Jews in Palestine). An advocate of an understanding with the Arab national movement as vitally important to the Zionist movement, he was a member of *Berit Shalom in its early days. His book, *Ereẓ Yisrael* (1914), is a collection of his articles about life in Ereẓ Israel.

Bibliography: D. Kimḥi (ed.), *Nefesh le-Doktor Yosef Lurie* (1938); I. Klausner, *Opoziẓyah le-Herzl* (1960), index; B. Dinur, *Benei Dori* (1965), 156–60; LNYL, 5 (1963), 27–29 (incl. bibl.). [Y.S.]

LURIE, ZVI (1906–1968), *Mapam labor leader in Israel. Born in Lodz, Poland, Lurie went to Palestine in 1925 and worked as an agricultural laborer in *Petaḥ Tikvah. In 1925 he joined the *hakhsharah* group of Ha-Shomer ha-Ẓa'ir at Ein Gannim and settled with them at kibbutz Ein Shemer in 1927. From 1929 to 1931 he was an emissary for Ha-Shomer ha-Ẓa'ir in Poland, and from 1935 to 1937 he

Zvi Lurie, Mapam labor leader in Israel. Courtesy Jewish Agency Photo Service, Jerusalem.

was secretary of the world leadership of Ha-Shomer ha-Ẓa'ir in Warsaw and editor of its weekly. In the following years he was active on all the central bodies of the movement in Palestine. From 1941 to 1948 Lurie served on the Va'ad Le'ummi and on its executive from 1946 to 1948 as director of the Information Department. In 1948 he joined the Provisional Council of the State of Israel and was a signatory of the Declaration of Independence. Lurie was on the *Jewish Agency Executive in New York from 1948 to 1955 and was member of the Executive in Jerusalem and head of the Organization Department from 1956. A collection of his speeches entitled *Mi-Devarav* appeared in 1968.

Bibliography: *Zvi Lurie, le-Zikhro* (1969). [B.J.]

°**LUSCHAN, FELIX VON** (1854–1924), German archaeologist, ethnologist, explorer, and anthropologist. Von Luschan studied at the universities of Vienna and Paris and then joined the Berlin Museum fuer Voelkerkunde, of which he was the director from 1904 until his death. He undertook numerous expeditions to the Balkans, North and South Africa, and New Guinea and Anatolia. In 1881 he began anthropometric work in Lycia in western Asia and for three decades continued to assemble data on the physical evolution of man there. On the basis of his research and studies of the cephalic indices of a large number of Jews, Von Luschan came to the conclusion that the notion of a distinct Jewish race was fallacious. Early in his career he formulated a theory that the Jewish people was racially an amalgam of Semites, Hittites, and Aryan Amorites, a view he later recanted after it was espoused by anti-Semites like Houston *Chamberlain.

Von Luschan energetically combated all forms of racism and in his *Voelker, Rassen, Sprachen* (1922), particularly attacked anti-Semitism. Writing from the anthropological perspective, he rejected the notion of the biological inferiority of any given race and criticized the popular confusion of such distinct, autonomous entities as race, nationality, and culture.

Bibliography: ESS, 9 (1933), 631. [E.Fi.]

LUSTIG, ARNOŠT (1926–), Czech author, whose writings are based largely on his experiences as a youth in 16 Nazi concentration camps. On his return to Prague after World War II, Lustig studied journalism, became editor of several teen-age periodicals, and began to write short stories based on his experience of the death camps. Collections of these stories include *Noc a naděje* (1959; *Night and Hope*, 1962) and *Démanty noci* (1958; *Diamonds of the Night*, 1964). The same theme dominates his novel, *Modlitba pro Kateřinu Horovitzovou* ("A Prayer for Catherine Horowitz," 1964). A number of his stories were made into films, and he also wrote the screenplay for a film about the *Golem. During the brief period of liberalization in Czechoslovakia in 1967–68, Lustig was elected to the Central Committee of the Czechoslovak Writers' Union. After the Soviet invasion in August 1968, he went first to Israel and then to the United States. His works were translated into several languages, including Hebrew.

Bibliography: Iltis, in: *Jewish Quarterly*, 13, no. 2 (Summer 1965). [Av.D.]

°**LUTHER, MARTIN** (1483–1546), German religious reformer. During the first period of his activity (approximately 1513–23), Luther often condemned the persecution of the Jews and recommended a more tolerant policy toward them, based on the spirit of true Christian brotherhood. Commenting on Psalm 22 (around 1519), he roundly condemned the "Passion preachers [who] do nothing else but exaggerate the Jews' misdeeds against Christ and thus embitter the hearts of the faithful against them." Speaking of the controversy between Johann *Reuchlin and Johann *Pfefferkorn, he strongly disapproved of the confiscation of the Talmud and rabbinic literature. Even in later times he referred to Reuchlin as his predecessor and teacher. Although declaring that it was impossible to expect the conversion of the whole Jewish people, he nevertheless nurtured the belief that, after listening to his teachings, many Jews would acknowledge the truth and accept Christianity.

Luther directly considered the Jewish question first in his pamphlet *Dass Jesus Christus ein geborener Jude sei* ("That Christ Was Born A Jew," 1523). Arguing that the Jews, who were from the same stock as the founder of Christianity, had been right in refusing to accept the "papal paganism" presented to them as Christianity, he added, "If I had been a Jew and had seen such fools and blockheads teach the Christian faith, I should rather have turned into a pig than become a Christian." Partly because of his polemics against the use of images in churches, he himself was branded a "half-Jew" *(semi-Judaeus)* by the church authorities. Perhaps encouraged by his conversion of one of the two Jews who had reportedly visited him at the Diet of Worms (1521), Luther had high hopes for the success of his mission among the Jews. Early missionary attempts had failed "not so much [because of] the Jews' obstinacy and wickedness, as rather [through] the absurd and asinine ignorance and the wicked and shameless life of the popes, priests, monks, and scholars." Pending their seeing the light, the Jews should be treated more considerately and given greater opportunities to gain a livelihood.

At first, Luther's disruptive impact on Roman Catholicism (which the Jews equated with the detested kingdom of

*Edom) was welcomed by Jews as a break in the monolithic power of the Church. Others hoped that the turmoil arising in the Christian world through the spread of Lutheranism would lead to toleration of all forms of worship. Moreover they expressed the view that a partial reform of the Church was welcome since it led the Church away from its former evil. There were even some, like Abraham *Farissol, who regarded Luther as a Crypto-Jew, a reformer bent on upholding religious truth and justice, whose anti-idolatrous innovations were directed toward a return to Judaism. Some scholars, particularly of the Sephardi diaspora, such as Joseph ha-Kohen (1496–c. 1575), had strongly pro-Reformation sympathies.

However, although appreciating Luther's apparent kindliness toward them, the Jews resisted his message. Whether through irritation at their refusal to accept his truth or for some other reason, Luther grew increasingly hostile toward the Jews. In 1526 he complained of the Jews' stubbornness in clinging to their traditional interpretation of Scripture. His repeated attacks on usury began to assume an anti-Jewish bias and his successive *Table Talks* of the 1530s contain frequent complaints about "the stiffnecked Jews, ironhearted and stubborn as the devil." The increasing vehemence of his attacks is apparent in his "Letter Against the Sabbatarians," in which he harshly condemns that Protestant sect for adopting Jewish customs. Openly anti-Jewish and couched in Luther's characteristic style of extreme vituperation are two pamphlets written in 1542 and 1543, "On the Jews and Their Lies" and "On the Shem Hamephoras" ("The Ineffable Name"). Repeating the accusations and invective of medieval anti-Jewish polemics and making use of the works of the apostates Antonius *Margaritha and Bernhard Ziegler, he subjects the Jews to a torrent of vile abuse, calling them "venomous and virulent," "thieves and brigands," and "disgusting vermin." Although Luther poured out such violent language on the heads of all his enemies—princes, lawyers, bishops, and especially the pope—in the case of the Jews he also made practical suggestions, ranging from forced labor to outright banishment. As many of the Protestant rulers of the times relied on Luther's political advice, his attitude resulted in the expulsion of the Jews from Saxony in 1543 and the hostile *Judenordnung* of Landgrave Philip of Hesse in the same year. The tenor of his suggestions was equally virulent in his "Admonition against the Jews," a sermon preached in 1546, shortly before his death.

In Germany in particular, Luther's volte-face in his attitude toward the Jews caused bitter disappointment in Jewish circles. After his request to answer Luther's calumnies had been turned down by the authorities of Strasbourg in 1543, *Joseph (Joselman) b. Gershom of Rosheim expressed undisguised hostility to the Reformation, calling Luther "the unclean" (לא טהאר, a word play on his name). Among Reformation thinkers, a certain group (notably the Swiss Heinrich Bullinger and the Nuremberg preacher and Hebraist, Andreas *Osiander) criticized his anti-Jewish stance.

Despite his fight against Judaism, Luther had a deep and abiding love for the Hebrew Bible. Although his Hebrew was weak and his Greek little better, his translation of the Bible into German was one of the most significant in literary history. He accepted the Hebrew language as the only one adequate for the expression of religious truth and sentiment. However, in his translation of and commentaries on the Bible he laid greater stress on intuition and revealed religion than on grammatical or linguistic questions. "I am not a Hebraist with respect to grammar [he said], nor do I wish to be one . . . I rather translate freely . . . . Accurate interpretation is a special gift of God." Although he often used, perhaps unwittingly, the interpretations of Rashi and recognized the importance of Moses and David *Kimḥi, on the whole he rejected rabbinic authorities, feeling that not only *Jerome but also *Nicholas de Lyre (on whom he relied heavily) were misled by them.

Inconsistency and violence characterized Luther's utterances in all fields, but perhaps in none with more disastrous consequences than in his statements on the Jews. Due to his vituperative anti-Jewish polemics, the Lutheran Church, unlike that which owed its foundation to John *Calvin, retained all the superstitious abhorrence of the Jews inherited from the medieval Catholic Church. Indeed Luther's attitude was worse, for he recognized no duty to protect the Jews. Throughout the subsequent centuries Luther's ferocious castigation of the Jews provided fuel for anti-Semites and the vicious force of that legacy was still evident in Nazi propaganda.

Bibliography: H. H. Ben-Sasson, *Reformation in Contemporary Jewish Eyes* (1970); idem, in: HTR, 59 (1966), 385–9; Baron, Social[2], 13 (1969), 216ff.; 421ff.; C. Cohen, in: JSOS, 25 (1963), 195–204; L. I. Newman, *Jewish Influence on Christian Reform Movements* (1925), 617–30; R. Lewin, *Luthers Stellung zu den Juden* (1911); S. Stern, *Josel of Rosheim* (1965), index; Mauser, *Kirche und Synagoge* (1953), 39–51, 88–105.

[Jo.H./B.M.A.]

LUTOMIERSK, a suburb of Lodz, central Poland (formerly a town). Jews first settled in Lutomiersk, which had then an independent municipal status, at the end of the 17th century, and an organized community existed from the 18th century. In 1765, there were 404 Jews living in the town and 41 in eight surrounding villages. Lutomiersk belonged to the Sieradz and Wielun areas, where, according to decisions of the Sejmik (provincial parliament) of 1786, 1787, and 1788, Jews were forbidden to lease inns, taverns, and breweries. At the end of the 18th century four Jews founded a tannery; another Jew, Pinkus Israel, established a cloth factory in 1787, employing 20–30 workers. In 1796 this factory was commissioned by the Prussian government to supply cloth to the army in the province. The wooden synagogue, built in the 18th century by Hillel Benjamin of Lask, burned down during World War I (1915). The Jewish community numbered 657 (53% of the total population) in 1808 and 1,102 (51%) in 1827. Apart from shopkeeping, they were engaged mainly in weaving, tanning, tailoring, and carpentry. In 1857 their number had declined to 999 (46%) because many had moved to Lodz. They numbered 992 (38%) in 1897 and 775 (35%) in 1921. A 1921 report of the *American Jewish Joint Distribution Committee mentioned 58 Jewish enterprises in Lutomiersk, 36 of which employed salaried workers. [EJ]

Holocaust Period. When World War II broke out there were about 2,000 Jews living in Lutomiersk. The anti-Jewish terror began with the arrival of the Germans. Jews were kidnapped in the streets for hard and humiliating labor, their beards were cut off, and their property was requisitioned. Just before the occupation and within its first weeks, nearly 1,300 Jews escaped and by October 1939, only 750 Jews remained in Lutomiersk. In the summer of 1940 an open ghetto was created, but a year later it was closed off and no one could leave without a pass. Groups of Jews were daily led out of the ghetto for hard labor. At the end of 1941, the German authorities established a tailor shop for 20 Jewish tailors, which took many orders and provided the Jews with a small income. Lutomiersk Ghetto was liquidated at the end of July 1942, when the surviving Jews were deported to the death camp in *Chelmno. [De.D.]

Bibliography: Warsaw, Archiwum Główne, Departymenta pogłównego żydowskiego: *Contribution to the Jewish Question*, no.

741; Warsaw, Archiwum Skarbowe, *Memoranda to the Finance Commission*, nos. 36 fol. 227, 38 fol. 103; I. Schiper, *Dzieje handlu żydowskiego na ziemiach polskich* (1937), 321, 324; B. Wasiutyński, *Ludność żydowska w Polsce . . .* (1930), 51; A. Breier, M. Eisler, and M. Grunwald, *Holzsynagogen in Polen* (1934), 28, 30, 35, 36, 39; E. Heller (ed.), *Żydowskie przedsiębiorstwa przmysłowe w Polsce . . .*, 2 (1923); R. Mahler, *Yidn in Amolikn Poyln in Likht fun Tsifern* (1958), index; D. Dabrowska, in: BŻIH, 13–14 (1955), 122–84 passim; Yad Vashem Archives, IM-837, IM-1209/4.

°**LUTOSTANSKI, HIPPOLYTE** (1835–1915), anti-Semitic agitator of Polish origin, born in Lithuania. Lutostanski was originally a Catholic priest but converted to the Greek Orthodox Church after he had been unfrocked on charges of corruption. When Russian society became increasingly anti-Semitic at the end of the 1870s, he wrote several libelous books, including "The Problem of the Use of Christian Blood for Religious Purposes by Jewish Sects" (1876) and "The Talmud and the Jews" (1879). Scholars and public figures such as D. *Chwolson and Z. *Minor revealed his ignorance and distortions of fact. Lutostanski, who knew no Hebrew, drew the material for his books from the Christian anti-Jewish literature of Western Europe, and enjoyed the protection of prominent members of the court. In 1880 he was denounced as an impostor and forger by Alexander *Zederbaum, the editor of *Ha-Meliẓ*. Lutostanski sued Zederbaum but lost the case. From time to time he attempted to extort money from wealthy Jews by promising to put an end to his anti-Jewish activities, but in fact with the support of the authorities, he continued to bring out new editions of his books. These editions included new material mainly calculated to "prove" the responsibility of the Jews in general, and the Zionist Movement and the *Bund in particular, for the rise of the revolutionary movement in Russia.

Bibliography: Z. Minor, *Rabbi Ippolit Litostanski* (Rus., 1879); N. Cohn, *Warrant for Genocide* (1967), 55–57. [Y.S.]

LUTSK (Pol. **Łuck**), city in Volhynia, Ukrainian S.S.R.; until the end of the 18th century in Poland; under Russia until the end of World War I; between the two world wars again in Poland; and in 1939 taken by the U.S.S.R. Nazi Germany occupied Lutsk in 1941, and after World War II it became again part of the Soviet Union. There were Jews in Lutsk in the tenth century, and in the 13th century a community of *Karaites settled there. Both they and the *Rabbanites enjoyed the rights granted to the Jews of Lithuania in general and later of Poland-Lithuania. The importance of Lutsk as a political and economic center grew after the union of Poland and Lithuania in 1569. The Jews benefited by this new situation, some being engaged in large-scale commerce, some leasing the customs revenue, breweries, and potash production plants, while others traded in forest and *agricultural products. Lutsk Jews participated in the fairs of Lithuania and Poland, and established their own craft guilds. In 1576 the city became part of the kingdom of Poland, and in 1580 the king ordered that the municipal taxes collected from the Jews should not exceed their proportionate share in the general population. He also renewed their right to live in Lutsk, and allowed representatives of the Jewish community to attend the meetings of the city council when it debated the levying of the city taxes. During the *Chmielnicki massacres of 1648–49 both Rabbanites and Karaites suffered heavily, but the community was soon reconstructed. By royal order in 1649 and in 1664 the Jews of Lutsk were permitted to trade freely in shoes; it was again established that they should pay no more than a third of the municipal taxes, this being their proportion of the general population. In the 18th century

The synagogue of Lutsk, built in 1626. Jerusalem, J.N.U.L., Schwadron Collection.

Lutsk suffered from the *Haidamack uprising, and from a *blood libel in 1764.

The Lutsk community participated in the regional *(galil)* council of *Volhynia, as well as in the *Councils of the Lands. The city was a center of Torah study and had many yeshivot. Among its famous rabbis in the 17th and at the beginning of the 18th centuries were Moses b. Judah ha-Kohen (formerly of Cracow), Jacob Schor, the son of Ephraim Solomon *Schor, and Joel b. Isaac Halpern, known as the Great Rabbi Joel. Part of the fortress built by Prince Witold was rebuilt as a fortified synagogue, with the permission of King Sigismund III. From the gunmounts on the roof, Jews served as gunners during enemy attacks on the city, while underground tunnels led from the synagogue to other key buildings in the city. This building withstood the fires and enemy attacks of centuries. Under Russian rule during the 19th century the number of Jews in Lutsk was increased when the Jews were expelled from the rural communities following the czar's regulation of 1804. However, they lived under constant threat of expulsion, since Jews were prohibited from settling within 50 versts of the Russian border, and Lutsk was included in this category in 1844.

During World War I the Jews suffered both from the armies and from war devastation, as the city changed hands several times and was occupied by Russian and German troops. Under the rule of *Petlyura in 1918 many Jews were massacred, and when the Polish armies entered Lutsk they looted Jewish houses and organized anti-Jewish riots under the pretext that the Jews had helped their enemies. In the face of these assaults the Jews organized themselves in *self-defense. Between the two world wars the Lutsk community shared in the troubles and struggles of Polish Jewry, facing anti-Semitism and hostile economic and social legislation. For instance "Bata," the shoe factory opened in Lutsk with the assistance of the government, caused many Jewish shoe factories to close down.

The Jewish population grew in the 1920s. According to official figures, 14,800 Jews lived in Lutsk in 1921 (about 70% of the general population) whereas in 1931 they numbered 17,366 (48.5%). In 1937, however, they numbered only 15,880 (36.5%). The Jews took part in the civic life of the city and had their elected representatives in the city council. Between the world wars the Lutsk community led a rich religious and cultural life. Its last rabbi was Zalman *Sorotzkin. It had a hospital as well as several social and medical organizations, some of which were assisted by Lutsk *Landsmanshaften* in the U.S. A printing press attached to a Dominican monastery in Lutsk apparently produced some Hebrew books. Jewish schools were maintained by various organizations, among them the *Tarbut schools run by the Zionist organization and the Beth Jacob girls' school by the Agudat Israel. [SH.L.K.]

Holocaust Period. By 1939 the Jewish population of Lutsk had increased to an estimated 20,000. Under Soviet occupation (1939–41) Jewish public life was repressed, Jewish organizations were disbanded, and private enterprises nationalized. Some Jewish businessmen were ordered to leave the town. In June 1940 the Soviet authorities uncovered the Zionist Gordonia underground and imprisoned its leaders. Many refugees who had fled to Lutsk from Nazi-occupied western Poland were deported to the Soviet interior. When the German-Soviet war broke out on June 22, 1941, many young Jews left together with the retreating Soviet forces. The town fell to the Germans on June 26, and a few days later some 2,000 Jews were murdered. On July 4, 3,000 Jews were put to death in the nearby fortress *(zamek)* of Lubart. A ghetto was established in December 1941 and the Jewish leaders made every effort to alleviate starvation and control epidemics. An orphanage, an old age home, and public kitchens were established in the ghetto, but the degree of suffering was hardly diminished. In the spring of 1942 a group of young Jews attempted to escape from the ghetto to the forests, but most of them were caught and murdered by the Ukrainians. A few, however, managed to join the Soviet partisans and fought the Germans as part of the Kowpak units. One of the refugees of the Lutsk ghetto, Joel Szczerbato, became the commander of the seventh battalion of the partisans. Meanwhile the Germans carried out the large-scale *Aktion* in which the majority of the Lutsk ghetto was murdered (Aug. 19–23, 1942). About 17,000 Jews were led to the Polanka hill on the outskirts of the city and massacred. The remaining 500 Jews, who were employed as artisans in the labor camp, were executed on Dec. 12, 1942. However, the Germans encountered armed opposition on the part of these Jews, who had fortified their building and repeatedly repulsed German attacks. With German reinforcements the labor camp was taken, with some German losses. When the Soviets captured Lutsk on Feb. 2, 1944, only about 150 Jews came out from their hideouts or the nearby forests. No organized Jewish life was renewed in Lutsk. There are Lutsk societies in the United States and in Israel, *Sefer Lutsk* being published in 1961 by the Israel Lutsk society. In the late 1960s there was a Jewish population of about 1,500, but there was no synagogue, the former old synagogue having been converted by the authorities into a movie theater.

Bibliography: *Sefer Lutsk* (Yid. and Heb., 1961). [AR.W.]

LUTZKY, A. (pseudonym of **Aaron Zucker;** 1894–1957), Yiddish poet. Born in a small town near Lutsk, Volhynia, he was privately educated and prepared for a career as a cantor. From the name of his birthplace Abraham *Cahan, editor of the Yiddish daily *Forward,* derived the pseudonym "Lutzky" for the young poet, when in 1918 he engaged him to write a weekly poem for the newspaper. Before arriving in the United States in 1914, Lutzky had visited Warsaw and recited his poems to I. L. *Peretz, who was so delighted with them that he tried to retain him in Warsaw. Life was not easy for the young immigrant who worked as peddler, teacher, and violinist. When he published his first poems in 1917 in the *Tageblatt* and in *The Day* Abraham Cahan recognized his talent and weaned him away from the rival dailies. A few months later, Lutzky was drafted into the U.S. army and fought before Verdun. When he returned from overseas, he astonished his readers with a strange, bizarre style. Special evenings, which increased his popularity, were arranged at which he acted out his new poems. Soon Herz Grossbard, Joseph *Buloff, and other famed actors discovered the dramatic quality of his work and spread his fame throughout the Yiddish world. Four books of lyrics appeared during Lutzky's lifetime, of which the best known was *Bereshis-Inmitn* (1932), in which he philosophized on creation and destruction. A fifth volume, *Fun Aldos Guts* (1958), appeared posthumously and includes a bibliography. Some of Lutzky's lyrics were translated into Hebrew and into English.

The pessimistic poet learned to transmute adversity into gay rhymes and images. His poems are playful parables, often devoid of any moralizing intent. They are theatrical narratives that animate the inanimate world through carefully chosen words and phrases. When Lutzky projected the drama of the waters that flow all over the world, or of pieces of paper that flutter about in the wind, or of beans that discourse before disintegrating in a seething pot, lifeless nature became poetically and dynamically alive.

Bibliography: Rejzen, Leksikon, 2 (1927), 98–100; LNYL, 5 (1963), 20–24; S. Bickel, *Schrayber fun Mayn Dor* (1958), 58–63; B. Rivkin, *Yidishe Dikhter in Amerike* (1959), 172–90; J. Leftwich, *The Golden Peacock* (1961), 300–5. [SH.B.]

LUX, STEFAN (1888–1936), film producer. Born in Vienna, he was twice wounded during World War I as a volunteer in the Austrian army. He worked in his profession in Germany, but emigrated to Prague in 1933 after *Hitler's advent to power. Alarmed by the world's indifference to Nazism's and Fascism's increasing influence, Lux decided to sacrifice his life to alert humanity. On July 3, 1936, he shot himself in the press gallery of the League of Nations Assembly Hall in Geneva, after leaving warning letters to Anthony Eden and other leaders.

Bibliography: A. Hahn, *Vor den Augen der Welt! Warum starb Stefan Lux? Sein Leben—seine Tat—seine Briefe* (1936); Levani, in: *The Jewish Digest,* 12 no. 2 (1966), 16–20. [Y.RE.]

LUXEMBOURG (Luxemburg), grand duchy, formerly a county, bordered by France, Germany, and Belgium. Jews were first noted in the city of Luxembourg, capital of the country, in 1276. In the early 14th century immigrants from the neighboring region of Trier formed several small Jewish settlements. During the *Black Death (1349) many of the Jews were massacred and the remainder expelled from the cities of Luxembourg and Echternach, notwithstanding the protection of Count Charles IV. They must have returned soon after, for in 1367 the existence of a *Porte des Juifs* ("Jews' Gate") is mentioned in the capital. The total expulsion of the Jews was decreed in 1391, but as early as 1405 some few individuals were once more living there. The homes of the Jews were destroyed and their possessions looted following an uprising in 1478. After that only two Jewish families remained, but by 1515 the number of families had grown to 15, residing in Luxembourg, Echternach, and Arlon, which was then still part of the county. The expulsion decreed in 1530 was fully implemented with the exception of some Marranos and a few traders at the fairs. Jews disappeared from Luxembourg until the Napoleonic period, when about 15 families from *Lorraine settled there. In 1808 the number of Jews was 75.

Under Napoleonic legislation they were subject to the Trier consistory until the establishment of Luxembourg's own consistory in 1838. The first synagogue was built in 1823 and the first chief rabbi, Samuel *Hirsch, was appointed in 1843, serving until 1866. There were 87 Jewish families (369 persons) in the city of Luxembourg in 1880 and 63 families in the rest of the duchy. The growth of this population necessitated the construction of a new synagogue in Luxembourg in 1894, and another in Esch-sur-Alzette in 1899. The Jewish population, numbering 1,171 persons in 1927, increased considerably with the arrival of refugees from Germany; in 1935, 3,144 Jews were resident in the duchy. [S.SCH.]

Holocaust Period. At the time of the invasion of Luxembourg on May 10, 1940, over 1,000 of the 4,000 Jews in the grand duchy (among them about 1,000 refugees) managed to flee to France. A new consistory was formed on the initiative of Rabbi Serebrenik, and in August 1940 the Nazis set up a civil administration under *Gauleiter* ("district head") Gustav Simon. After the German annexation, discriminatory racial laws operating throughout the Reich were extended to the grand duchy (Sept. 5, 1940), and 355 commercial enterprises were handed over to "Aryans." On Sept. 13, 1940 the *Gestapo announced that all the Jews would be deported on the following Day of Atonement if the consistory did not succeed in arranging their emigration prior to that date. Due to the consistory's efforts, particularly through a petition sent to *Himmler, this measure was postponed, but emigration remained the sole road to survival. Between Aug. 8, 1940 and May 26, 1941, when Rabbi Serebrenik was forced to leave in peril of his life, 700 Jews possessing more or less authentic visas fled overseas. In another operation, about 1,000 people were secretly evacuated to France in small groups. After these rescue operations the consistory became the Aeltestenrat der Juden and administered the remaining 850 Jews. Of these, 127 emigrated in January 1942 and the rest were deported; only 35 of the latter survived.

Contemporary Period. After World War II approximately 1,500 Jews returned to Luxembourg. Mostly merchants, they succeeded in renewing their business activities and, with financial assistance from the state, devoted themselves to reconstructing their community. The community's institutions were revived and a new synagogue built, the old one having been destroyed in 1943. Instrumental in these achievements was the consistory presided over by Edmond Marx, in cooperation with Rabbi Kratzenstein, who served the community from 1946 to 1948, and Rabbi Lehrmann (1949–1959). In Esch-sur-Alzette a community of 40 families established itself with a new synagogue as its center. Maurice Levy was president of the consistory from 1961 to 1968 and was succeeded by Edmond Israël. From 1959 the chief rabbi was Emmanuel Bulz. In 1970, there were 1,200 Jews in Luxembourg. It was in the city of Luxembourg that the chancellor of the German Federal Republic, Konrad Adenauer, and Israel's foreign minister, Moshe *Sharett, signed on Sept. 10, 1952, the agreement on German reparations to Israel. [E.BU.]

Relations with Israel. Luxembourg's relations with Israel have always been cordial. Luxembourg voted in the UN in Nov. 1947 in favor of the partition of Palestine and has maintained full diplomatic relations with Israel. Israel is represented in Luxembourg by her ambassador in Brussels, while Luxembourg's interests in Israel (as in most other countries) are represented politically by the Dutch embassy and economically by the Belgian embassy. Official visits of the foreign ministers of both countries were exchanged in 1969. Luxembourg, which plays a central role in the European Economic Community, always wholeheartedly supported Israel's application for association with the Common Market. [ED.]

Bibliography: J. Stengers, *Les Juifs dans les Pays-Bas au moyen-âge* (1950); C. Lehrmann, *La communauté juive du Luxembourg dans le passé et dans le présent* (1953); H. Monneray, *La persécution des Juifs en France et dans les autres pays de l'Ouest* (1947), index; *Algemeyne Entsiklopedye*, 7 (1966), 217–20.

LUXEMBURG, ROSA (1871–1919), German economist and revolutionary. Born into a family of merchants in Zamosc, Russian Poland, Rosa Luxemburg joined the Polish revolutionary movement as a schoolgirl in Warsaw. She studied political economy and history at the University of Zurich and worked in the underground Socialist movement of Polish emigrés in Switzerland. In the early 1890s she helped to found the Social Democratic Party of Poland and Lithuania which cooperated for a time with the Marxist Russian Social Democratic movement. Migrating to Germany in 1898, she obtained German citizenship through a formal marriage with a printer. She became active among Polish workers and joined the editorial staff of the Saxony *Arbeiter-Zeitung* and later of the *Leipziger Volkszeitung*, and was a regular contributor to the *Neue Zeit*. Rosa Luxemburg was a leading figure in the revolutionary left wing of the German Socialist movement. She participated in the revolution of 1905–06 in Warsaw, was imprisoned, but escaped and resumed her political activity in Germany, devoting a large part of her attention to the general strike as a revolutionary weapon. She was active in both the Polish and the German Labor movements and was a prominent figure in the Socialist International. She opposed World War I as an imperialist enterprise and spent a long period in prison as a consequence. With Franz Mehring and Karl Liebknecht she founded the "Spartakusbund," a revolutionary organization which at the end of 1918 was transformed into the Communist Party of Germany. She was on friendly terms with Lenin but they disagreed on a number of issues. She was very critical of the Bolshevik reign of terror in the Soviet Union. With Karl Liebknecht she edited the Communist daily *Die Rote Fahne*, and was arrested with him in Berlin on January 15, 1919. While they were being taken to the Moabit prison both were murdered by army officers.

As an economist, Rosa Luxemburg is widely known for her theory of imperialism. She was convinced that in a pure capitalist society the inadequacy of the local market would lead to a search for markets in countries with more primitive methods of production. There would be a struggle for foreign markets, and imperialism would thus become the guiding principle of foreign policy. Although capitalism must

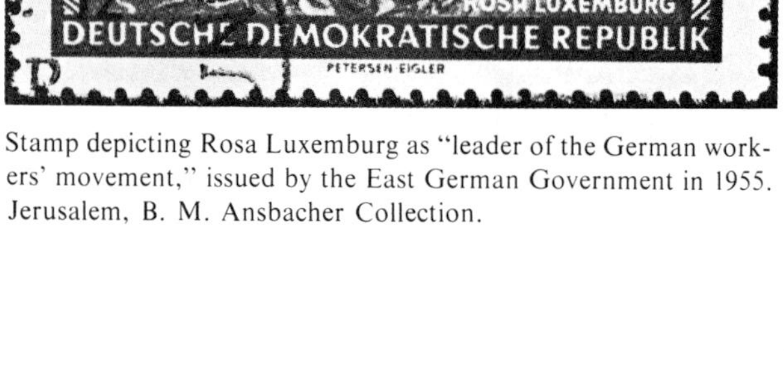

Stamp depicting Rosa Luxemburg as "leader of the German workers' movement," issued by the East German Government in 1955. Jerusalem, B. M. Ansbacher Collection.

automatically disappear with the exhaustion of external non-capitalist markets, it would collapse before reaching this limit, because expanding capitalism would produce profound social conflicts leading to a victorious proletarian revolution. She developed this theory in *Die Akkumulation des Kapitals* (1913). Of great interest are Rosa Luxemburg's views on nationalism. For her, Socialism and national self-determination were conflicting ideas. She opposed Poland's independence; her "fatherland" was the international working class, her aim the Socialist revolution. Jewish in appearance and fond of Yiddish stories, she was indifferent to the frequent anti-Semitic attacks on her. She had no interest in a specifically Jewish labor movement. Rosa Luxemburg's important publications include: *Die industrielle Entwicklung Polens* (her doctoral thesis, 1898), *Sozialreform oder Revolution* (1899), *Massenstreik, Partei und Gewerkschaften* (1906), *Die russische Revolution* (ed. by Paul Levi, 1922), *Briefe aus dem Gefaengnis* (1922[3]), *Briefe an Karl und Luise Kautsky* (1923). Of her *Gesammelte Werke*, three volumes (3, 4, and 6) have appeared.

Bibliography: J. P. Nettl, *Rosa Luxemburg*, 2 vols. (Eng., 1966); P. Froelich, *Rosa Luxemburg* (Eng., 1940). [ED.]

LUZ (Heb. לוז), an old name for *Beth-El, first mentioned in the account of Jacob's dream there (Gen. 28:19). Beth-El is again called Luz in Genesis 35:6; in his blessing of Joseph's sons, Jacob refers to God's appearance at Luz, meaning Beth-El (Gen. 48:3). In the description of the borders of Ephraim, however, the two cities are treated as separate entities (Josh. 16:2); in the parallel account of Joshua 18:13, Luz is mentioned first, then the "side" *(katef)* of Luz, "the same is Beth-El." The man who delivered the city to the Israelites went into the land of the Hittites and built there another Luz (Judg. 1:26). According to later sources, Luz and Beth-El are the same city (Eusebius, Onom. 4:28ff.; 40:20; 120:8ff.; also Madaba Map). Eusebius locates Beth-El 12 mi. (c. 19 km.) north of Jerusalem on the left ("west") side of the road to Neapolis (Onom. 40:20). Some scholars have concluded from the biblical references that Luz remained the name of the city until the time of Jeroboam and that Beth-El was originally the name of the sanctuary to the east of it. A more probable view is that Luz was the ancient name of neighboring *Ai (Heb. *Ha-Ai*, "the ruin"); Beth-El, which was founded in the Middle Bronze Age, doubtless inherited the role and area of the prominent Early Bronze city only about 1 mi. ($1\frac{1}{2}$ km.) distant.

Bibliography: Elliger, in: ZDPV, 53 (1930), 304; W. F. Albright, *The Vocalization of the Egyptian Syllabic Orthography* (1934), 9. [M.A.-Y.]

LUZ (Lozinsky), KADISH (1895–1972), Israel labor leader and third speaker of the *Knesset. Born in Bobruisk, Belorussia, Luz studied economics and social sciences at the University of St. Petersburg, later concentrating on science and agriculture at Odessa and Dorpat, Estonia. He served in the Russian army during World War I and was appointed an officer at the outbreak of the Russian Revolution. Luz was a founder of the organization of Jewish soldiers in Russia and of the Zionist pioneer movement *He-Ḥalutz, both initiated by Joseph *Trumpeldor. In 1920 he settled in Palestine, where he worked on land reclamation at *Kiryat Anavim and *Be'er Toviyyah and on road building in the Jezreel Valley. In 1921 he joined *Deganyah Bet. He was one of the leaders of the *kibbutz movement and the *Histadrut.

From 1951 until 1969 Luz was a Mapai member of the Knesset. He was minister of agriculture in 1955–59 and then became speaker of the Knesset (1959–69). His moderation and impartiality, which made him popular with all parties, helped to maintain the prestige of the office. His published works include *Avnei Derekh* ("Milestones," 1962),

Kadish Luz, speaker of the Israel Knesset, 1959–69.

a book of memoirs *Eḥad mi-Sheneim-Asar* (1970), and numerous articles and booklets on labor problems and the kibbutz movement. [M.L.]

LUZKI (Lucki), ABRAHAM BEN JOSEPH SOLOMON (1792–1855), Karaite scholar and poet in Crimea. He was born in *Lutsk (Luzk) and moved as a child with his father Joseph Solomon b. Moses *Luzki to Yevpatoriya where the latter was *ḥakham*. He was subsequently sent to Constantinople, where he entered the service of a Karaite merchant. Luzki devoted much time to study of the Talmud and rabbinical literature and acquired an extensive knowledge of languages before returning to Yevpatoriya. When in 1827 his father succeeded in obtaining exemption of the Karaites from military service, Luzki composed a poem in honor of Czar Nicholas I. In 1835 he was elected *ḥakham* of Yevpatoriya, but declined the office. The same year he founded a Karaite school there which gained a distinguished reputation under his guidance. His published works include: *Iggeret Zug ve-Nifrad* (Yevpatoriya, 1837), a decision concerning marriage law, mitigating former more severe Karaite rulings; liturgical poems, of which eight are included in the Karaite prayer book (Vienna ed. (1854), 168ff.); *Mishlei Musar*, a translation of fables into Judeo-Tatar (Yevpatoriya, n.d.) and a translation of Joseph *Ha-Efrati's drama, *Melukhat Sha'ul* ("The Reign of Saul") from Hebrew into Turkish. His works in manuscript include *Shoshannim Edut le-Yosef*, a collection of poems, lamentations, sermons, and obituaries, left in the possession of his grandson Samuel Ne'eman in Yevpatoriya.

Bibliography: A. Firkovich, *Avnei Zikkaron* (1872), preface; Fuerst, Karaeertum, 3(1869), 138; Mann, Texts, 2(1935), 472 n.10, 474 n.11, 501. [J.N.S.]

LUZKI (Lutzki, Lucki), JOSEPH SOLOMON BEN MOSES (d. 1844), Karaite scholar, born at Kukizow near Lvov. He later lived at Lutsk, Volhynia, and in 1802 moved to Yevpatoriya in the Crimea where he became *ḥazzan* (=rabbi) of the Karaites. Luzki went with the *ḥakham* Simḥah *Babovich to St. Petersburg where they succeeded in obtaining exemption for the Karaites from compulsory military service, imposed on the Jews in 1827. A detailed account of their journey and activities is given by Luzki in *Iggeret Teshu'at Yisrael* (Yevpatoriya, 1840; with a Tatar translation by the author's brother-in-law, Abraham *Firkovich). A thanksgiving prayer he composed on that occasion was subsequently recited by the Karaites every year on the anniversary. In 1831 Luzki went to Ereẓ Israel.

He later returned to Yevpatoriya and remained there until his death. His works include: *Sefer ha-Ḥinnukh le-Petaḥ Tikvah,* a didactic manual in two parts: (a) *Petaḥ ha-Tevah,* a primer and Hebrew prayers for children with Tatar translation; (b) *Zekher Rav,* by Benjamin *Mussafia, with Lutzki's translation of the Hebrew words into the Tatar language (Constantinople, 1831); and *Tirat Kesef,* a comprehensive supercommentary on the *Sefer ha-Mivḥar* by the Karaite *Aaron b. Joseph (printed with *Sefer ha-Mivḥar,* Yevpatoriya, 1835). Luzki is also the author of a calendar for the years 1859 to 1901 (printed posthumously, probably in Yevpatoriya), and of liturgical poems, prayers, and hymns, some of which were incorporated in the Karaite prayer book.

Bibliography: S. Poznański, *Karaite Literary Opponents of Saadiah Gaon* (1908), 90; Mann, Texts, 2 (1935), s.v. *Jos. Sol. b. Moses Lucki.* [I.M./Ed.]

LUZKI (Lucki), SIMḤAH ISAAC BEN MOSES (d. 1766), Karaite writer and bibliographer. Luzki was born in Lutsk at the close of the 17th century. About 1751 he moved to Chufut-Kale in the Crimea, where he was appointed head of a *bet midrash,* holding that position until his death. Well versed not only in Karaite literature but also in rabbinical literature and Kabbalah, he was a diligent copyist of early Karaite manuscripts, of which there were many in the Karaite community of Chufut-Kale. He also made a valuable contribution to Karaite literature, writing about 20 works on theology, philosophy, *halakhah,* Kabbalah, and a book of precepts. His kabbalistic works include *Livnat ha-Sappir,* on the ten *Sefirot,* and *Sefer ha-Tappu'aḥ,* on creation, which is in the spirit of later Kabbalah. Only two of his works were published: *Or ha-Ḥayyim* (Yevpatoriya, 1847), an extensive commentary on the philosophical work by *Aaron b. Elijah of Nicomedia, *Eẓ Ḥayyim,* and *Oraḥ Ẓaddikim* (Vienna, 1830), an abridged history of the Karaites with a biobibliographical compendium of their works which was published by Mordecai b. Nisan of Kokizow together with his own *Dod Mordekhai.* In this latter work Luzki also gives a list of Karaite scholars which is arranged according to their countries of origin. The bibliography is of special importance, for even though Luzki appears to lack critical instinct and the work contains many errors, it is the first effort in this field. He also wrote *piyyutim,* five of which were included in the Karaite prayer book. His predilection for Kabbalah also found expression in his commentary on the *Eẓ Ḥayyim.* Luzki considered that the Zohar was compiled before the Mishnah, basing his opinion on the rabbinical literature.

Bibliography: Mann, Texts. [S.K.]

LUZ OF THE SPINE, a bone which, according to the rabbis, is to be found at the base of the spine, an addition to the 18 vertebrae. Called the *luz she-ba-shidrah,* it is indestructible and is the source of the future resurrection of the body. R. Joshua b. Hananiah demonstrated it to the Emperor Hadrian, in answer to his questions as to how the resurrection would take place. "They put it in water and it did not dissolve, in fire and it was not consumed, on a mill and it was not ground. They placed it on an anvil and struck it with a hammer. The anvil cracked and the hammer split, but it remained whole" (Eccl. R. 12:5, no. 1; Lev. R. 18:1). It is apparently the statement that the *luz* is an addition to the 18 vertebrae which is the basis of the statement of the Talmud that the **Birkat ha-Minim,* the 19th blessing added to the original 18 of the daily **Amidah,* corresponds to the *luz* of the spine (Ber. 28b). On the other hand, the enumeration of the bones of the body in the Mishnah (Oho. 1:8) lists only the 18 vertebrae and does not mention the *luz.* There is no scientific basis for this legend. It may be connected with the statement that in the second city of *Luz (Judg. 1:26), which was still identified as existing in talmudic times as a place where the **tekhelet,* the blue dye for the ritual fringes (Num. 15:38), was manufactured, "the Angel of Death had no permission to pass through it, and when old men there become tired of life, they go outside the city to die." In Genesis Rabbah 69:8, the reading is, "they are carried out beyond the city walls to die." The belief in the indestructibility of the *luz* was linked with Ps. 34:21, which was translated, "He keeps all his bones; one of them cannot be broken." The Church Fathers Origen and Jerome also regarded it as a pointer to resurrection, and this was accepted by non-Jewish scholars in the Middle Ages, and they spoke of the "Jews' bone" (Judenknoechlein) and identified it with the last vertebra of the spinal column.

Bibliography: Baer, S., Seder, 87n.; Kohut, Arukh, 5 (1926²), 24–25, s.v. *Luz shel Shidrah,* and introd., lxii. [L.I.R.]

LUZZATTI, LUIGI (1841–1927), Italian statesman and economist; the first Jew to become prime minister of Italy. Born in Venice, he graduated in law from the University of Padua. Luzzatti's devotion to economic and social studies arose from his desire to improve the condition

Luigi Luzzati, prime minister of Italy, 1910–11.

of the poor. He began by founding a mutual aid society for the gondoliers of Venice which was opposed by the Austrian police and in 1863 he was expelled from Venice as a revolutionary. He went to Milan where he became professor of economics at the Instituto Tecnico and then professor of constitutional law at the University of Padua (1867). In 1869 Luzzatti became general secretary of the Ministry of Agriculture, Industry, and Commerce. He was elected to Parliament in 1871 and sat continuously for 50 years until 1921 when he was raised to the Senate. He was minister of the treasury on three occasions (1891–92, 1896–98, and 1904–06) and together with Sidney *Sonnino reduced the Italian treasury deficit and secured the conversion of the public debt, thus restoring Italy's finances. In 1909 Luzzatti became minister of agriculture and was prime minister (1910). His ministry introduced numerous reforms aimed at winning popular support, but his right-wing administration was defeated by a combination of Liberals and Socialists the following year. An outstanding orator and expert economist, Luzzatti founded the Banca Popolare in Milan and founded the first cooperative store in Italy. He also negotiated many of Italy's principal commercial treaties. During World War I, Luzzatti established the National Foundation for the sons of peasants fallen in the war and in 1922 presented a plan for international currency stabilization. Though religiously nonobservant, he retained his Jewish sympathies and acted on behalf of oppressed European Jews, intervening through diplomatic channels for the granting of civic rights to the Jews of Rumania. Luzzatti supported Zionist enterprises in Palestine, particularly the agricultural settlements which he much admired. Luzzati's writings were collected under the title *Opere di Luigi Luzzatti* (1924–), including *Grandi Italiani: grandi sacrifizi per la patria* (1924), and *Dio nella libertà: studi sulle relazioni tra lo Stato e la Chiesa* (1926; *God in Freedom* . . ., 1930), a collection of essays on religious liberty.

Bibliography: F. Catalano, *Luigi Luzzatti: la figura e l'opera* (1965); Villari, in: H. Bolitho (ed.), *Twelve Jews* (1934), 123–52; L. Luzzatti, *God in Freedom* (1930), xvii–xxv (biography by D. Askowith).

[G.R.]

LUZZATTO (sometimes **Luzzatti**), Italian family. The name is probably derived from Lausitz (Lat. Lusatia), from where according to tradition the family emigrated into Italy in the mid-15th century, settling in the Venetian territories. One of the seven Venetian synagogues bore the name "Scuola Luzzatto," and many members of the family are buried in the cemetery of the community on the Lido. Others lived in the towns and townships around Venice. The poet and kabbalist Moses Ḥayyim *Luzzatto derived from the Paduan branch of the family. In 1595 the two brothers Abraham and Benedetto Luzzatto, from Venice, settled in *San Daniele del Friuli. From this branch of the family were descended the brothers Ephraim *Luzzatto and Isaac *Luzzatto, both poets. Another descendant, Marco (Mordecai b. Nathan; 1720–1799), was an author and translator. All of his works are in manuscript, and include a Hebrew-Italian dictionary. When the Venetian government introduced its policy of excluding the Jews from the smaller places under its rule in 1777, the San Daniele community became dispersed. The scholarly carpenter Hezekiah Luzzatto settled in Trieste, where his son Samuel David *Luzzatto was born, the first historian of the family. His son Philoxenus (Filosseno; 1829–1854) was an orientalist. He published many works, including studies on *Ḥisdai ibn Shaprut, the Falashas, and Hebrew inscriptions. The most recent member was Federico Luzzatto (1900–1961) who, after a distinguished career in the Italian navy, settled as a farmer in Ereẓ Israel, and did valuable research on Italian Jewish history. Today members of the Luzzatto family, sometimes no longer professing Judaism, are to be found in most important Italian cities and scattered throughout the world.

Bibliography: S. D. Luzzatto, *Autobiografia preceduta da alcune notizie storico-letterarie sulla famiglia Luzzatto* . . . (1882), 7–36; Roth, Italy, index; Milano, Italia, index; Milano, Bibliotheca, index; *Volume . . . Federico Luzzatto* (1962); F. Luzzatto, *Cronache storiche della Università degli ebrei di San Daniele del Friuli* (1964); Zoller, in: REJ, 94 (1933), 50–56; G. Bedarida, *Ebrei d'Italia* (1950), index.

[U.C./Ed.]

LUZZATTO, EPHRAIM (**Angelo**; 1729–1792), Italian Hebrew poet and physician. Born in San Daniele del Friuli, he studied medicine in Padua, and after practicing at various places in Italy, was appointed physician in London's Portuguese community hospital where he worked for nearly 30 years. His loose way of life in England was much criticized. He died in Lausanne returning to Italy.

His collected poems, most of them written in Italy, *Elleh Benei ha-Ne'urim* (1765), were often republished, and influenced the poetry of M. J. *Lebensohn and J. L. *Gordon. They include occasional poems, moralistic poetry, and some erotica. Most important, however, are his love sonnets which have, for the period, a remarkable lyrical quality. These display a variety of moods: indulgent, satirical and passionate. His poems reflect individual experience, and are thus an innovation and a precursor of the Hebrew lyric poetry of the Haskalah.

Bibliography: Klausner, Sifrut, 1 (1952[2]), 295–306; J. Fichmann, in: *Shirei Ephraim Luzzatto* (1942), V–XX (introd.); H. Schirmann, *ibid.*, 2 (1942/43); R. N. Salomon, in: JHSET, 9 (1922), 85–102; C. Roth, in: *Sefer Ḥayyim Schirmann* (1970), 367–70.

[El.K.]

LUZZATTO, GINO (1878–1964), Italian Socialist and economic historian. Born in Padua, Luzzatto graduated in philosophy and law and then lectured in economic history successively at the universities of Bari, Trieste, and Venice. He held a professorship from 1910 to 1953 except for the years 1938–45, when he was suspended because of Italy's anti-Semitic laws. Luzzatto supported the Socialist cause and was an indomitable opponent of Fascism. He was imprisoned by the authorities and on his release joined the underground resistance movement. During the period of anti-Semitic reaction in Italy his works were published under a pseudonym, Giuseppe Padovan, or with his name omitted. From 1946 to 1951 he was councillor and assessor of the municipality of Venice.

Luzzatto was active in Jewish affairs as vice-president of the Venice Jewish community and president of the Italian *ORT. He also wrote several essays on the economic situation of Italian Jewish communities (e.g., *I banchieri ebrei in Urbino nell' età ducale*, 1903[2]), as well as on the economy and the cooperative movement in Israel.

Luzzatto's writings extended over half a century. His main economic works include *Storia del commercio dall' antichità al Rinascimento* (1914); *Storia economica dell' età moderna e contemporanea* (2 vols., 1934, 1948) and *Studi di storia economica veneziana* (1954) and various volumes of *Storia Economica d'Italia* (1949–63).

Bibliography: *Studi in onore di Gino Luzzatto*, 4 vols. (1950); Nuova Rivista Storica, 49 (1965).

[G.R.]

LUZZATTO, ISAAC (1730–1803), Italian poet and physician. Born in San Daniele del Friuli (Italy), Isaac, like his brother Ephraim *Luzzatto, graduated in medicine at Padua (1750). Upon the expulsion of the Jews from San Daniele, as from other rural localities in the Venetian Republic (September 1777), he alone was allowed to remain with his family and practice there. In the summer of 1779, Luzzatto traveled to Vienna and successfully petitioned Maria Theresa to authorize his fellow townsmen to continue living in the rural districts of Austria where they had established themselves. His *Toledot Yiẓḥak*, a collection of poetry, was first published in 1944 by D. J. Eckert and M. Wilensky, with a biography and notes. It includes Hebrew poems, mostly sonnets, on religious and ethical themes, conundrums, and a parody of a mishnaic treatise satirizing the customs of his community (*Mishnayyot San Daniele*, or *Massekhet Derekh Ereẓ*). Luzzatto also translated into Hebrew *La Libertà*, by the Italian poet Metastasio, at the latter's request. Isaac Luzzatto's second wife, Tamar, was a sister of Hezekiah, father of Samuel David *Luzzatto.

Bibliography: F. Luzzatto, *Cronache storiche della Università degli ebrei di San Daniele del Friuli* (1964), index; S. D. Luzzatto, *Autobiografia* . . . (1882), 22, 23.

[Ed.]

LUZZATTO, JACOB BEN ISAAC (16th century), rabbi and author. Luzzatto was born apparently in Safed where he spent his childhood. He later moved to Europe where he lived in Basle and probably also in Posen and Cracow. Luzzatto was the author of *Kaftor va-Feraḥ* or *Yashresh Ya'akov* (Basle, 1581; also called in another version *Kehillat Ya'akov*, Salonika, 1584), an attempt to defend talmudic *aggadot* attacked by the Christian censors as anti-Christian. Luzzatto explained the *aggadot* according to Rashi, the *tosafot*, Solomon b. Abraham Adret, and R. Nissim, citing also parallel readings in the Jerusalem Talmud, Midrashim, and kabbalistic works, giving them allegorical meanings. He was also probably the final corrector, after the censor, of the Basle Talmud (1578–81), since it contains some of his glosses. He edited (including a preface and index) the *Ta'amei ha-Mitzvot* (Basle, 1581) of Menahem Recanati and Solomon Molcho's *Sefer ha-Mefo'ar* (Cracow, 1570). A copy of the latter in Luzzatto's own handwriting is extant (Ms. Oxford, 1660). Luzzatto is identified with the Jacob b. Isaac Luzzat of Posen who corrected the *Toẓe'ot Ḥayyim* (Cracow, n.d.) of Elijah Vidas. He probably died in Ereẓ Israel, though some believe he died in Venice.

Bibliography: S. D. Luzzatto, *Autobiografia*... (1882), 8–10; Brann, in: *Samuel David Luzzatto. Ein Gedenkbuch* (1900), 29, 31–33; Rosanes, Togarma, 3 (1938²), 288; J. Perlis, *Geschichte der Juden in Posen* (1865), 40.

[U.C./ED.]

LUZZATTO, MOSES ḤAYYIM (Heb. acronym **RaMḤaL**; 1707–1746), kabbalist, writer of ethical works, and Hebrew poet; leader of a group of religious thinkers, who were mainly interested in the problems of redemption and messianism and probably tried to use their mystical knowledge to hasten the era of redemption. Luzzatto was born in Padua, Italy, into one of the most important, oldest, and most respectable families in Italian Jewry (see *Luzzatto family). Regarded as a genius from childhood, he knew Bible, Talmud, Midrash, halakhic literature, and classical languages and literature thoroughly. He also had an extensive knowledge of contemporary Italian culture. Luzzatto had a good scientific education, but his chief interest in Western culture was in literature. His main teachers were Isaac *Cantarini, who taught him poetry and secular sciences, and Isaiah Bassan, who taught him mainly Kabbalah and became his friend and protector. Luzzatto's achievements, personality, and great knowledge of mysticism made him a leader of a group of young men in Padua, many of whom came there to study at the city's famous university and thus represented the more open and aware element among young Jews in Italy and in Eastern Europe. The group was formed originally for collective study, but eventually a more active line was adopted.

Probably the most important event in Luzzatto's personal life occurred in 1727. While he was immersed in kabbalistic speculations, he suddenly heard a divine voice, which he believed to be that of a **maggid* (i.e., a divine power inclined to reveal heavenly secrets to human beings). From that moment, the *maggid* spoke to Luzzatto frequently and he noted these revelations, which comprised his kabbalistic writings for a few years. Most of them have not survived; only a few are known and have been published. Luzzatto used the *maggid's* revelations in his teachings to the members of the group around him, which by then had become a secret group dealing in messianic speculations and activity. One of the members of this group, Jekuthiel *Gordon, described in some letters the activities and character of the group. One of these letters fell into the hands of Moses *Ḥagiz, who believed it to be a description of a typical Shabbatean heretical group. Ḥagiz addressed the rabbis of Venice, warning them of the danger he believed this activity signified, and the rabbis turned to Isaiah Bassan, Luzzatto's teacher, who tried to defend his beloved pupil. A vehement controversy followed, in which many of the leading rabbis of Italy took part, and numerous personal attacks were made on Luzzatto. It was believed that only a perfect scholar and kabbalist could receive a revelation from a *maggid*, and many thought that the young, unmarried Luzzatto did not measure up to that standard. According to a later testimony, a search was made at his home, and evidence of dealings in magic were uncovered. After a long struggle, Luzzatto yielded (1730) and agreed to give his kabbalistic writings to Bassan for safekeeping, to refrain from writing the *maggid's* revelations (at least while out of the Holy Land), and not teach Kabbalah.

This compromise did not resolve the conflict. In 1731 Luzzatto married. The continuing controversy in Italy forced him to leave for Amsterdam in 1735. While breaking his journey in Frankfort, he asked for the protection of Jacob ha-Kohen. The latter, instead of helping him, used threats to make Luzzatto sign a statement denouncing the *maggid's* revelations and his kabbalistic teachings as false (the rabbis of Venice had meanwhile announced that these writings should be burned). Luzzatto's writings were handed over to Jacob ha-Kohen, who probably burned some of them and hid the rest. Settling in Amsterdam, where he was left in peace, Luzzatto wrote on many subjects, but he did not openly teach Kabbalah. In 1743 he went to Ereẓ Israel, probably in order to escape from the prohibition on teaching Kabbalah. He lived a short time in Acre, and died there, with his family, in a plague.

Luzzatto's Messianic Doctrine. When Luzzatto formulated his messianic doctrine, the circle around him began actively to seek messianic redemption. The first "code" of the group, which has survived (signed by the members in 1731), includes ten laws, dealing with the methods of study, the relationship between the members and Luzzatto, and a declaration of the group's aim: "That this study [or speculation] will not be regarded as a private *tikkun* of the members nor will it be atonement for personal sins, but its only *kavvanah* will be wholly dedicated to the *tikkun* of the holy *Shekhinah* and all of Israel." Seven members had

ספר
מסילת ישרים
כולל כל ענייני מוסר ויראת ה׳
חברו החכם הנעלה כמוהר״ר
משה חיים לוצאטו
נר״ו:
הובא לבית הדפוס והוגה בעיון נמרץ
על ידי החכם הנעלה כמוהר״ר
יעקב בכ״ר אברהם בשן ז״ל
ומסנהו החכם הנעלה כמוהר״ר דוד בן
החכם השלם הרב הגדול והמובהק כמוהר״ר
רפאל מילדולה נר״ו:
בבית ובדפוס של האלוף כהר״ר נפתלי
הירץ לוי רופא· בן האלוף והקצין פ״ו
כהר״ר אלכסנדר זיסקינר
לוי מעמדין:
בשנת כי עת לחננה כי בא מועד לפ״ק

Title page of the first edition of Moses Ḥayyim Luzzatto's main work on ethics, *Mesillat Yesharim*, Amsterdam, 1740. Cecil Roth Collection. Photo David Harris, Jerusalem.

signed this "code," including Jekuthiel Gordon. Other members joined later, among them Luzzatto's brother and Moses David *Valle, who became one of the group's leaders. He was the writer of the group, author of a voluminous commentary on the Bible, which is extant in a few manuscripts. The members of this group believed that the process of redemption had already begun, and that it was going to reach its culmination in a few years. Their saintly way of life and kabbalistic speculations were intended to facilitate this process. Moreover, they were sure that they, personally, had an important part to play in the process.

The writings of Moses David Valle seem to hint that Valle saw himself as the Messiah, son of David. Jekuthiel assumed the role of Serayah of the tribe of Dan, who was to be the commander of Israel's army in the messianic era. Other messianic roles were distributed among the other members. Luzzatto's own role becomes clear from a unique document preserved in his own handwriting—his commentary on his own *ketubbah*, which he wrote at the time of his marriage. This document proves that Luzzatto understood his marriage to signify a mystical event in the heavenly worlds, the union between Moses and Zipporah (which happened to be the name of his wife), who represent the elements of masculinity and femininity in the divine realm. The earthly marriage ceremony he understood as only a symbol of the redemption of the *Shekhinah* and her union with her divine husband. It is evident, therefore, that Luzzatto saw himself as a reincarnation of Moses, the man who rescued his people from the exile in Egypt and would redeem them from this last *galut* as well.

Luzzatto's opponents understood the messianic nature of his circle, and were afraid of the Shabbatean overtones which such activity might contain. The problem of whether Luzzatto's ideas and activities can be called "Shabbatean" or not is unsolved. Luzzatto himself admitted to being influenced by the writings of *Shabbetai Ẓevi's "prophet," *Nathan of Gaza. However, he maintained that the good element in them should be separated from the heretical context. In some of Luzzatto's kabbalistic ideas, elements of Shabbatean influence can be found, for he maintained that the Messiah must descend to the realm of Satan, the Shabbatean explanation for their Messiah's conversion. However, Luzzatto insisted that this should not involve the Messiah's earthly body; it should be a spiritual experience only, involving no sin. Luzzatto was also moderately inclined toward the Shabbatean idea that a sin might serve a holy purpose, but he always made radical changes in the Shabbatean ideas which avoided their heretical and antinomian nature.

His Kabbalistic Writings. Luzzatto's writings in the field of Kabbalah are divided into two groups: some are general works describing central kabbalistic ideas and emphasizing the importance of Kabbalah for attaining full religious life; the other writings convey his own original kabbalistic concepts. Most of the latter works were written under the influence of the *maggid*.

The outstanding work of the first group is *Kelaḥ* (= 138) *Pitḥei Ḥokhmah*, a systematic theosophical exposition of the Lurianic Kabbalah. Luzzatto's tendency in this work is to minimize the mythological aspects of Isaac *Luria's teachings and to emphasize the theosophical aspects. He developed his own interpretation of the main features of Luria's mythology and interpreted them as symbols, not as actual events. The idea of the *ẓimẓum*, God's withdrawing into Himself prior to the emanation of the divine *Sefirot*, was explained by Luzzatto as an act of divine justice, reflecting God's wish to establish a contact with the created world, whereas originally, in Luria's Kabbalah, this event was a mythological necessity. (Luzzatto's interpretation, by the way, was widely accepted, and even the early Ḥasidim adopted it.) The introduction to this work, also printed separately, *Derekh Eẓ ha-Ḥayyim*, explains the religious merits of kabbalistic study. This small work was widely read and accepted. Another work belonging to the same category is *Ḥoker u-Mekubbal*, designed as a dialogue between a philosopher and a Lurianic kabbalist. In this work, Luzzatto answers, point by point, many criticisms against the Kabbalah which were current among the rationalists in Italy, and tries to prove that only Lurianic Kabbalah can give a satisfactory answer to Judaism's religious problems.

The most important of the writings influenced by the *maggid* was the *Zohar Tinyana*, which was written in Aramaic, the language of the original *Zohar. Most of the work is now lost; parts were printed as *Razin Genizin*, *Megillat Setarim*, and *Tikkunin Ḥadashim* (*Tikkunei Zohar* being one of the later parts of the original Zohar). Although Luzzatto used the Zohar's language and literary form, his main and almost sole idea expressed and studied in these works was the idea of the redemption. Luzzatto employed older kabbalistic ideas about the redemption but gave them a new form and new structure. Detailed study was devoted to the duties of the various messianic figures in the process of the redemption—the Messiah son of Joseph, Messiah son of David, and Moses. Luzzatto studied the function of the various heavenly *Sefirot* in this process, especially the third *Sefirah*, *Binah*, whose revelation and influence on this world would bring about the culmination of the redemption. Recently, a part of Luzzatto's diary describing the first revelations of the *maggid* was discovered, and the theological problems discussed there are the same as those in the other known parts of the *Zohar Tinyana*. Problems of the redemption and the history and adventures of the Messiah's soul are also dealt with in Luzzatto's short treatises, *Addir ba-Marom* and *Ma'amar ha-Ge'ullah*.

Luzzatto's Ethical Works. Long after his death, and after the controversy around him had subsided, Luzzatto became a saint in the eyes of most of Eastern European Jewry. This did not come about because of his kabbalistic writings, but because of his major works on ethics. His chief work in this field, and his best-known book, is *Mesillat Yesharim*, written in Amsterdam (English translation *Mesillat Yesharim: The Path of the Upright* by M. M. Kaplan with Hebrew text and introduction, 1936, 1964[2]), which uses as a framework the famous *baraita* of R. *Phinehas b. Jair (Sot. 9:15). Luzzatto instructs the reader in the path of ascent from the foresaking of sinful ways, through moral behavior, to the peak of prophecy and contact with the divine spirit. The popularity of the book resulted from its systematic exposition of every problem which might prevent the attainment of religious and ethical perfection. The author explains the importance and meaning of every step on the way, describes the means by which it can be made, and warns the reader of the dangers which might obstruct his way. Luzzatto wrote the book in a simple, rabbinic style, using some philosophical terms, but no kabbalistic element is evident, though detailed analysis reveals some underlying kabbalistic assumptions. This work was printed many times, translated into many languages, and alongside *Baḥya ibn Paquda's *Ḥovot ha-Levavot*, became the most influential ethical work in Judaism. In some yeshivot in Eastern Europe where the book was studied, pupils were expected to know it by heart.

In other ethical and theosophical works Luzzatto studied some basic theological questions, using philosophical language, although the underlying kabbalistic approach is apparent. In his *Derekh ha-Shem* and *Da'at Tevunot*,

Luzzatto studied in detail the problems of the aim of creation, original sin, the ways of divine justice, the relationship and mutual dependence between the just and the sinner, the next world and the world of the redemption, etc., alongside discussions of everyday problems of religious and ethical behavior—prayer, the Commandments, the ways to overcome evil desires, etc. All his works in this field were widely read and accepted, and contributed to his metamorphosis to sage and saint, instead of a controversial figure suspected of Shabbateanism.

Poetry and Letters. Luzzatto wrote numerous poetical works. Many of them were lost, and many are still in manuscript. A collection of his poems, published by S. Ginzburg (1945) includes mainly works written in honor or in memory of friends or for weddings. His talent is revealed through his rich and flowing imagery, and his use of the Hebrew language is masterly. These poems were written according to the ancient tradition of Hebrew poetry in Italy, which relied on the traditions of Hebrew poetry in both Muslim Spain and Renaissance Italy. Besides these, Luzzatto's published poems include a few religious pieces, all of which contain kabbalistic and messianic overtones; sometimes he added a mystical commentary to his own religious poems. He also wrote many prayers, and it seems that he wrote 150 religious poems in the form of the Psalms, but this work has not survived.

However, Luzzatto's most famous poetic works are his verse dramas. His first play *Ma'aseh Shimshon* was written before he was 20 years old to exemplify the rhetorical laws he propounded in his *Leshon Limmudim*, a treatise on rhetorics, in which he made use of his knowledge of classical and contemporary Italian literature. It seems that Luzzatto felt close to Samson, his tragic hero, possibly for messianic reasons, and that gave the play some poetic depth. His second and most important play, *Migdal Oz*, was written while he was still in Italy. It was composed in the form of contemporary Italian pastoral drama, but Luzzatto gave the plot such Jewish overtones that some critics think that the play is in fact a kabbalistic allegory. His third and last play *La-Yesharim Tehillah*, written in Amsterdam, is one of Luzzatto's last works. The play is an allegory, which probably gives expression to the feelings of persecution he experienced at the time of controversy around him, and at the same time reflects his belief in the ultimate victory of the just. In *Migdal Oz* and *La-Yesharim Tehillah*, Luzzatto used commonplace love plots to give expression to poetic sentiments far beyond the conventional plots. Luzzatto's plays were accepted and admired by Hebrew writers and intellectuals in Italy and Western Europe, and many were influenced by them. Luzzatto's works, especially *Migdal Oz*, exercised a strong influence on Haskalah literature, especially its poetry and drama. These *maskilim*, who were inimical to the kabbalists, were so impressed by the plays that they forgot Luzzatto's kabbalistic writings and messianic aspirations and adopted him as if he were one of their own.

A vast amount of Luzzatto's personal writings was discovered and printed by S. Ginzburg. This collection includes many of Luzzatto's letters, as well as letters addressed to him or concerning his activities and the controversy around him. The collection includes his personal revealing letters to his teacher and defender, Isaiah Bassan. Among other documents this collection includes the texts of the regulations of Luzzatto's circle, texts of the accusations against him, etc. The details make possible a chronological reconstruction of Luzzatto's bibliography, though many of the works mentioned are unknown today.

Kinat ha-Shem Ẓeva'ot, a polemical work of a personal nature, was written in answer to the accusation that his theology and activities were Shabbatean in nature. A portion of this work was printed in Koenigsberg in 1862. Luzzatto clearly expresses his negative attitude toward Shabbatean heresy and antinomian practices, but he does not deny that there is truth in some Shabbatean kabbalistic ideas. However, he explains that these should be studied with care, to divide "the fruit from the husk."

Luzzatto's place in the history of Hebrew literature was the subject of a long argument, which still persists. Some scholars (e.g. *Lachover), seeing him as the first "modern" Hebrew writer, begin the history of Hebrew modern literature with the study of his dramatic poems. Others maintain that, as modern Hebrew literature was a revolutionary development which rebeled against the religious character of medieval literature, Luzzatto cannot be included among its creators because of his strong ties with such past ideologies as Kabbalah and messianism. Yet others, however, see the development of modern Hebrew literature as an evolutionary process, which never broke completely from traditional ideas and concepts. These regard Luzzatto's works as a compromise between old and new, signifying the start of a new era in Hebrew literature.

It cannot be doubted that Luzzatto's works as a whole are a typical product of 18th-century culture: his Kabbalah was Lurianic Kabbalah, which was the accepted theology of the time; his strongest emotions were aroused by messianic problems, in common with most of the more aware thinkers of his age; and he accepted the conventions of 18th-century Italian literature. However, Luzzatto's work is unique for two reasons. The first is that unlike previous Jewish-Italian thinkers, such as Leone *Modena or Azariah de *Rossi, Luzzatto did not doubt the fundamental Jewish beliefs despite his close connections with Italian secular culture. He could be, at the same time, both a Jewish traditionalist and a writer of dramatic poems in the Italian manner. Secondly, unlike any other writer of the 18th century, Luzzatto, though persecuted when alive, was accepted by the three main 19th-century Jewish movements, which were fighting bitterly among themselves: the Ḥasidim saw him as a saintly kabbalist and used some of his kabbalistic ideas; their opponents, the Mitnaggedim, regarded his ethical works as the clearest pointers toward a Jewish ethical, rabbinic way of life; and the Haskalah writers saw Luzzatto as a progenitor of their own movement, and his works as the beginning of Hebrew aesthetic writing. Every facet of Luzzatto's work, therefore, remained alive and creative in the divided and confused Jewish culture of the 19th century.

Bibliography: A full bibliography of Luzzatto's printed works is to be found in: N. Ben-Menahem, *Kitvei Ramḥal* (1951); S. Ginzburg, *The Life and Works of M. H. Luzzatto* (1931); idem, *R. Moshe Ḥayyim Luzzatto u-Venei Doro* (1937); I. Almanzi, in: *Kerem Ḥemed*, 3 (1838), 112–69; J. Schirmann, *Gilyonot*, 21 (1947), 207–17; F. Lachover, *Al Gevul ha-Yashan ve-he-Ḥadash* (1951), 29–96; I. Tishby, *Netivei Emunah u-Minut* (1964), 169–203; idem, in: KS 45 (1970), 127–254, 300, 628; M. Benayahu, in: *Sefunot*, 5 (1961), 299–336; Waxman, Literature, 3 (1960²), 90–107; Y. David, introd. to Moshe Ḥayyim Luzzatto, *Ma'aseh Shimshon* (1967), incl. bibl.

[Y.D.]

LUZZATTO, SAMUEL DAVID (often referred to by the acronym of **SHaDaL** or **SHeDaL**; 1800–1865), Italian scholar, philosopher, Bible commentator, and translator. His father, Hezekiah, was an artisan at Trieste and a scholarly Jew who could claim descent from a long line of scholars (see *Luzzatto family). He wrote his first Hebrew poem at the age of nine. His mother died when he was 13 and his father's pecuniary status declined seriously making it necessary for the young Luzzatto to assist his father in his work. His own wife died after a long illness, and he eventually married her sister. He survived two of his children—one Philoxenus (or Filosseno), had been a young man of especially great promise. Samuel David's translation of the Ashkenazi prayer book into Italian appeared in 1821/22, and that of the Italian rite in 1829. He established

Lithograph of Samuel David Luzzatto, Italian Judaic scholar. Jerusalem, Israel Museum.

a regular correspondence with the Jewish scholar, Isaac Samuel *Reggio, and through the efforts of the latter, Luzzatto was appointed professor of the newly established rabbinical college of Padua in 1829. There he spent the rest of his life teaching Bible, philology, philosophy, and Jewish history. His versatility and the scope of his learning are best seen in the mass of letters written to all the outstanding Jewish savants of the day—to *Geiger, *Zunz, *Rapoport, *Steinschneider and others. Almost 700 of these letters were published and many run into several pages; some are in themselves dissertations. He wrote a Hebrew commentary on the Pentateuch (5 vols., with Italian translation, 1871–76; new ed. by P. Schlesinger, 1965) and the *Haftarot*, on the Book of Isaiah (together with a translation into Italian, 1845–97; new ed. by P. Schlesinger and completed by A. M. Hovev, 1970), on Jeremiah, Ezekiel, Proverbs, and Job and a long dissertation in Hebrew on Ecclesiastes (1876; repr. 1969). It is in this type of work that his attitude to Judaism is revealed. He was a traditionalist and had a great veneration for Rashi in particular. His antagonism toward Abraham ibn Ezra is asserted boldly in his letters and Bible commentaries. He maintained that his own dislike for Ibn Ezra did not stem so much from the latter's departure from tradition as from his insincerity (see: Letters nos. 83, 242, 272, 275 and 543). Luzzatto had his grievances against Maimonides too, but in the case of the latter his language is more restrained. Luzzatto, as he himself wrote, divided seekers of truth into two groups—those who follow Rashi and Samuel b. Meir and those who are the disciples of Maimonides and Ibn Ezra (Letters nos. 272 and 275). His own commentary on the Pentateuch is not fundamentalist, and whereas he himself did not take the first chapters of Genesis literally, he criticizes those who treat them as an allegory (Letters no. 83). He believed them to be meant as model lessons from which we are to derive moral and ethical values. In his writings, he readily quotes the views of his pupils, mentioning their names when so doing. Although denying the Solomonic authorship of Ecclesiastes he upholds the unity of the Book of Isaiah. He maintained a firm belief in revelation and treated the text of the Torah with sacred regard although he occasionally allowed himself to depart from the traditional phrasing of the words as reflected in the Masorah and the Talmud. A natural corollary of his attitude to the classical authorities is Luzzatto's high regard for the Aramaic translation of Onkelos to which he devoted his *Ohev Ger* (the "Lover of the Proselyte," 1830), an allusion to the conversion of Onkelos to Judaism. He named his son Philoxenus (the Latin equivalent of *Ohev Ger*). He divided the work into two parts. The first demonstrates the method of Onkelos when the latter seems to depart from the literal translation of a text, especially when he wants to avoid anthropomorphisms. The second part of *Ohev Ger* deals with matters of text and is technical.

Luzzatto's philosophy may be compared with that of Judah Halevi. "I esteem Maimonides very greatly" he wrote (Letters no. 83), "but Moses the Lawgiver never dreamed of philosophy and the dreams of Aristotle." He lists his objections to the *Guide* of Maimonides and to some remarks in *Sefer ha-Madda* and to others in Maimonides' commentary on Mishnah *Sanhedrin* (ch. *Ḥelek*) and in the *Shemonah Perakim* (commentary on *Avot*). He was opposed to Maimonides' enumeration and formulation of the 13 principles of faith and his condemnation of those who did not subscribe to these (Letters no. 238). Luzzatto's attitude to Greek philosophy was negative and even hostile. And his negative views on Kabbalah are found in his *Vikku'aḥ al Ḥokhmat ha-Kabbalah* (1852). He blames rationalistic philosophy for having brought about—as a reaction—the flowering of Kabbalah and mysticism. As for the Zohar, he rejected the authorship of Simeon b. Yoḥai as did Jacob *Emden and Leone *Modena before him, and Luzzatto was apparently influenced by the latter's *Ari Nohem* (1840). Luzzatto's religious thinking does not rest at the rejection of "atticism"—Hellenism—as diametrically opposed to Judaism; and of a moral rationalism as represented in the Middle Ages by Maimonides and in modern times by Kant. For him the idolizing of "progress" and the utilitarianism which speaks from the craving for (outer but not inner) emancipation of modern Jewry were the very antithesis of free Jewish thinking and living. He had nothing but contempt for the rotten European civilization. In his theological writings, most of them published lectures such as *Teologia Morale israelitica* (1862; English translation by S. Morais in *Jewish Index*, 1872) and in his *Yesodei ha-Torah* (1880; repr. 1947; English translation by N. H. Rosenbloom *Foundations of the Torah*, 1965) as well as in his letters, he develops his own positive system of Jewish theology and religious philosophy, based on the firm belief in revelation, tradition, and the election of Israel. These he wants to see protected from the prevailing winds of Christian-Protestant criticism and an evolutionary historical relativism. The Torah and the Commandments must not be rationalized and submitted to such relativism, nor can one separate morality from religion. They both flow from the same innate human quality of *ḥemlah* (empathy). The Jewish people is both the carrier and guarantor of this revealed, national religion which embodies its own universalism and humanitarianism. Hebrew language and literature, the main object of Luzzatto's scholarly work, help to foster and deepen Jewish spirit and loyalties. This romantic and nationalistic conception of Judaism embraces a sort of religious Zionism; while rejecting the "false holiness" of the idle *ḥalukkah* Jew. Luzzatto wants the youth of the *yishuv* to return to the soil and the soil of the Holy Land to its former productivity. This conception is apparent in his liturgical researches, in particular by his edition of the *Maḥzor Roma* which he provided with a comprehensive introduction (1856; new edition of the introduction by E. D Goldschmidt, 1966).

Luzzatto also edited the medieval chronicle *Seder Tanna'im ve-Amora'im* (1839); and the prolegomena to an edition of *Joseph ha-Kohen's *Emek ha-Bakha* (1852), ostensibly by M. Letteris, are essentially Luzzatto's work. He also did pioneering work in his editions of Judah Halevi's poetry (*Betulat Bat Yehudah*, 1840; *Diwan Rabbi Judah Halevi* 1, 1864) and his anthology of medieval Hebrew poetry (*Tal Orot*, 1881) and thus contributed greatly to the revival of interest in medieval Hebrew poetry. His own Hebrew poetry had great merit. The same intimate acquaintance with and fine feeling for the Hebrew language, the result of intensive biblical studies, helped Luzzatto with his linguistic and grammatical researches (see *Prolegomeni ad una grammatica ragionata della lingua ebraica* (1836; *Prolegomena to a Grammar of the Hebrew Language*, 1896); *Grammatica della lingua ebraica* (1853–69; Hebrew 1901); *Elementi grammaticali del caldeo biblico . . .* (1865; *Grammar of the Biblical Chaldaic Language . . .*, 1876)). Of bibliographical importance are his *Opere del De Rossi* (1868²) and *Yad Yosef* (1864), a catalog of the Almanzi collection. Luzzatto also published *Avnei Zikkaron*, on the Hebrew tombstone inscriptions of Toledo (1841), being the first to treat epitaphs as an important primary source for Jewish historical research. An autobiography of Luzzatto appeared in 1882 (Hebrew in *Ha-Maggid* 1858–62; German 1882), and memorial volumes in Italian (*Commemorazione . . .*, 1901) and in German (*Luzzatto-Gedenkbuch*, 1900). There are a number of collections of his articles such as *Beit ha-Oẓar* (3 vols., 1847, 1888, 1889) and *Peninei Shadal* (1888); but much of his scholarly work remains scattered over various periodicals, pamphlets, works of other authors, and much has never been published. An edition of all his Hebrew writings was begun in 1913 (*Ketavim Ivriyyim*) but was not completed.

Bibliography: I. Luzzatto, *Catalogo ragionato con riferimenti agli altri suoi scritti e inediti* (1881); S. Baron, in: *Sefer Assaf* (1953), 40–63; N. Rosenbloom, *Luzzatto's Ethico-Psychological Interpretation of Judaism* (1965); S. Werses, in: *Me'assef le-Divrei Bikkoret ve-Hagut*, 5–6 (1965), 703–15; D. Rudavsky, in: *Tradition*, 7 (1965), no. 3, 21–44; *Samuel David Luzzatto 1800–1865. Exhibition on the Occasion of the 100th Anniversary of his Death*, arranged by B. Yaron, Catalog (Heb. and Eng., Jerusalem, 1966); RMI, 32 (1966), no. 9–10 (all articles dedicated to studies of Luzzatto); S. Morais, *Italian Hebrew Literature* (1926), 78–152. [A.T./Ed.]

LUZZATTO, SIMONE BEN ISAAC SIMḤAH (1583–1663), Italian rabbi and author. He was born, probably in Venice, of a well-to-do family of German origin already established in the region for many generations. Luzzatto was ordained in 1606 and served as rabbi in Venice for 57 years. The affluent circumstances of his family made it unnecessary for him to waste his energies in miscellaneous work to supplement his livelihood, as was the case with his contemporary and associate Leone *Modena, after whose death in 1648 he became senior rabbi of the community. Unlike Modena he objected to the presence of gentiles at his sermons in the synagogue, though he had some non-Jewish pupils, including, for a month in 1646, the French mystic Charles de Valliquierville. Shortly after this, he became involved in a drawn-out dispute with the lay leaders of the community over the question of rabbinical ordination, on which he insisted in having a deciding voice. Among his responsa was one (no longer preserved) which permitted travel by gondola in Venice on the Sabbath. His work *Socrate overo dell'humano sapere* dedicated to the Doge (1651), written in dialogue form with Socrates as the principle interlocutor, is an attempt to demonstrate that human reason is impotent unless assisted by revelation. There is nothing specifically Jewish about this work, which shows a considerable degree of competence in philosophy and in the classical literature (though not in Greek), and is a remarkable exemplification of the degree of culture prevailing at this time in the Italian ghettos. His most important publication, however, was his work, *Discorso circa il stato de gl' hebrei et in particolar dimoranti nell'inclita città di Venetia* (1638) in which he put forward reasoned arguments for the toleration of the Jews especially on economic grounds. He argued that they performed functions that could be achieved by no other element, while on the other hand, unlike foreign merchants, they were completely under the control of the government and would not transfer their profits outside the state. This was the first apologetic work of its type and the first in which economic arguments were brought forward systematically in order to advocate the toleration of the Jews. A reply to the work was published by the Christian priest Melchior Palontritti under the title *Breve Risposta a Simone Luzzatto* (1642). A Hebrew translation was published in Jerusalem in 1950; and an English translation was prepared early in the 18th century by the English deist John *Toland (though not published), who used Luzzatto's arguments lavishly in his book of 1714 advocating the naturalization of the Jews. It is now known that the book was written at great speed when a dangerous crisis developed for the Venetian Jews owing to the discovery of large-scale commercial frauds in which some leading families were implicated.

Luzzatto also wrote an Italian treatise in which he vindicated the authority of tradition and of the Oral Law (now lost, but referred to by Samuel Aboab in his responsa, *Devar Shmuel* (1702) n. 152). He is said to have also written *Trattato delle opinioni o dogmi degli ebrei e dei riti loro principali* (Fuerst, Bibliotheca, 284) and, together with Leone de Modena, a work on the Karaites (Wolff, Bibliotheca, vol. 3, 347). He is also reputed to have had considerable competence as a mathematician. Luzzatto's pupil, the apostate Giulio Morosini, reports in his *Via della Fede* several instances of his liberal mind and outspokenness in matters of religion, shown for example when in 1649 he arbitrated in a dispute between two former Marranos about the "seventy weeks" of Daniel. He is also said to have spoken contemptuously of the Kabbalah and to have disbelieved in the preservation of the Lost Ten Tribes. Christian contemporaries, misunderstanding his freedom of spirit, reported that he was prevented by force from embracing Christianity on his deathbed.

Bibliography: S. D. Luzzatto, *Autobiografia . . .* (1882), 12–17, 33–36; Y. F. Baer, *Galut* (1947), 83–92; L. Blau, *Leo Modenas Briefe und Schriftstuecke* (1907), index; S. Luzzatto, *Ma'amar al Yehudei Veneẓyah* (1951), prefaces by Bachi and Szulwas; *In Memoria di A. Sacerdoti* (1936), 99–113; C. Roth, *Venice* (1930), 227–31; F. Secret, *Kabbalistes Chrétiens de la Renaissance* (1964), 328; Szulwas, in: HUCA, 22 (1949), 18–20 (Heb. pt.); Steinschneider, in: MGWJ, 43 (1899), 418f. [C.R.]

LVOV (Pol. **Lwów**; Ger. **Lemberg**), main city of Lvov oblast, Ukrainian S. S. R.

The Early Settlements. It is thought that the first Jews in Lvov arrived from Byzantium and the southeast. After the conquest of the town by Casimir III of Poland (1340), they were joined by Jews from Germany and Bohemia who gave the settlement its Ashkenazi character. At the end of the 14th century, there were two communities in Lvov: the older and larger, the "Holy Congregation Outside of the Walls," founded in 1352; and the second, the "Holy Congregation Within the Walls," situated in the Jews' Street and first mentioned in 1387. Large fires occasionally swept both communities and they were only able to repair their quarters after controversies with the townspeople (this occurred in 1494, 1527, 1571, 1616, etc.). In 1550, 352 Jews lived inside the city walls in 29 houses, while 559 lived in 52 houses outside the town. In the vicinity of this suburban quarter, a *Karaite settlement existed until 1457.

The Jews of Lvov played an important role in trade between the Orient and the West, for which the town was an important transit center. They were equally well represented in the wholesale trade with the interior of the country. They also leased estates, operated brandy distilleries and breweries, acted as customs and tax agents, and loaned money to the nobility and the king. During the second half

Figure 1. Drawing of the Taz Synagogue of Lvov, built in 1582, after the plan of an Italian architect. Donated by Isaac b. Naḥman. From I. Halperin (ed.), *Beit Yisrael be-Polin,* Jerusalem, 1954.

of the 16th century, the commercial agents of Don Joseph *Nasi were active in Lvov. However, the number of Jews who engaged in international trade and in large concerns was very limited and the majority earned their livelihood as shopkeepers, peddlers, and craftsmen. The rights of the Jews of Lvov were based on letters patent granted by the kings of Poland. They were in constant conflict with the townsmen over their rights to trade, especially in the retail branch, and to engage in crafts. Fortunately the royal decrees issued as a result of pressure from the townsmen were rarely absolute and the nobility often succeeded in having them amended. In 1493 King John Albert restricted the Jews to two branches of the wholesale trade: *textiles and *livestock. In 1503 and 1506 King Alexander Jagellon granted the Jews freedom to trade at the markets and fairs as well as the right to benefit from the reductions accorded to other citizens. King Sigismund I restricted Jewish trade (1521), then accorded unlimited trading rights (1527), and finally revoked the permit (in the same year). This uncertain state of affairs continued throughout the whole period. Temporary compromise agreements on the question of trading rights were concluded between the municipality and the Jews in 1581, 1592, and 1602. The renewal of these agreements and the determination of their exact contents were usually accompanied by protests from the townsmen. The Jewish craftsmen were also under constant pressure from Christian artisans.

The Community and its Institutions. The two congregations of Lvov maintained separate synagogues, *mikva'ot,* and charitable institutions. They shared the cemetery (first mentioned in 1411), and the Karaites were also buried there. From 1600 to 1606 there was a violent conflict between the Jews and the Jesuits over the synagogue which had been constructed (in late Gothic style, after the plan of an Italian architect) by the philanthropist Isaac b. Naḥman (founder of the famous *Nachmanovich family) in 1582. The Jesuits claimed that the land on which the synagogue was constructed was their property. The Jews were victorious and the synagogue, which was named the Taz (or "Di Gildene Roiz" after one of the daughters of the Nachmanovich family who died mysteriously), remained standing until the Holocaust. Lvov was the center of "Red Russia" (Galicia, i.e., Western Ukraine) and Podolia-Bratslav region, and its community leaders represented the whole region at the *Councils of the Lands. By the electoral system of the community, a limited number of the wealthy descendants of noble families were assured of long periods in office.

From 1684 to 1772. In the *Chmielnicki massacres of 1648–49 and the successive wars of the second half of the 17th and early 18th century, the Jews of Lvov, especially those who lived outside the town, suffered great losses in life and property. Their houses were at the mercy of the enemy and they were compelled to seek refuge within the town. Generally the Jews played an active part in the defense of the town. During Chmielnicki's siege in 1648 and the Russian siege of 1655, the attackers demanded that the Jews be delivered into their hands. Meeting with the refusal of the townsmen, they settled for a large ransom. During the whole of this period, the townsmen's struggle against the control of trades and crafts by the Jews continued. The latter's efforts to expand their quarter came under special attack. The Jewish quarter consisted of only 49 building lots and the houses built on them were too small to accommodate the established inhabitants and the refugees from many wars. All the efforts of the townsmen to confine the Jews to their quarter and to restrict their trade were in vain, for the nobles usually supported the Jews. At this time the Jews also opened shops in the center of town. During this period, war damages, ransom payments, the costs of court cases, the necessity to rebuild damaged houses, and the decline of Lvov in favor of other commercial centers brought about severe economic crises. In 1727 the community owed the municipality 438,410 zlotys, while in 1765 their debts to the noblemen, the clergy, and the religious orders amounted to 381,999 zlotys, and those to the municipality to 820,409 zlotys. Although direct and indirect communal taxes were raised the community was unable to become solvent. According to the census of 1764/65, 6,142 Jews lived in Lvov—over two-thirds of them outside the town walls—and only 57 of the 3,060 men were self-supporting.

When Shabbateanism began to spread in Russia, David Halevi (d. 1667), *av bet din* of the congregation outside the walls, sent his son and stepson to *Shabbetai Ẓevi; they returned his enthusiastic supporters. After Shabbetai Ẓevi's apostasy, his adherents in Lvov were excommunicated (1722). In 1754 Leib Krisse (Kriss), right-hand man of the pseudo-messiah Jacob *Frank, came to Lvov to propagate the Frankist message. Frank himself arrived in the town in December of 1755, but he was compelled to leave. A disputation with the Frankists was held in 1759. The spokesman for the Jews was R. Ḥayyim Kohen Rapoport, *av bet din* of the town and region.

During the 18th century, the importance of the Lvov community declined and its authority was reduced. The limits of the provincial council's authority were also restricted after the annexation of Podolia to Turkey (1772). In Galicia itself, the expansion of the surrounding communities (Zholkva, Brody) further limited the authority of the Lvov community. At the meeting of the provincial council in 1720, it was declared that "we, the men of the province, have no further portion or inheritance in the holy congregation of Lvov and the rabbi who will be nominated by it." At the meeting of the council in Berezhany in 1740 the rabbinate of the province was divided into two regions and the *av bet din* of Lvov held office in only one of them. Conflicts within the community over the distribution of taxes, the election of rabbis, and other affairs resulted in the intervention of the secular authorities to a greater degree than in the past. Menahem Simḥah Emmanuel de Jonah (d. 1702), a member of a large family of physicians

Figure 2. The Great Synagogue outside the walls of Lvov, following the pogroms of 1918. Courtesy Israel Museum Photo Archives, Jerusalem.

and himself court physician to King John III Sobieski, was highly influential during the second half of the 17th century. He was the "*nesi Ereẓ Israel*" (the chief treasurer of the funds for Ereẓ Israel collected in Poland), a *parnas* of the Councils of the Lands, and the holder of many public offices.

From 1772 to 1914. The Jewish population of Lvov rose from 18,302 in 1800 to 26,694 in 1869, and 57,000 (28% of the total population) in 1910. According to the 1820 census, 55% of the Jews engaged in commerce (the majority as shopkeepers and retail traders) and 24% in crafts. The 745 Jewish craftsmen included 249 tailors, 133 furriers, 51 bakers, and 34 goldsmiths. The Jews of Lvov controlled the wholesale trade between Russia and Vienna. Some were army purveyors, or wholesale dealers in tobacco, cereals, and salt; others owned flour mills; and Jews pioneered industry and banking in the town. Lvov Jewry suffered as a result of the economic crisis in Galicia during the 19th century. After 1772 the townsmen's struggle to restrict Jewish rights of residence and trade were supported by the Austrian authorities. From the beginning of the 19th century only the wealthy and educated merchants who had adopted the German way of life were authorized to live outside the Jewish quarter. In 1848 the Jews were allowed to participate in the elections to the municipal council, but their representation was limited to 15% and later to 20%. In spite of the religious equality granted in the Austrian Empire in 1849, the municipality continued to evict the Jews from the retail trade, and the Christian artisans' guilds struggled against Jewish artisans. The prohibition on acquiring real estate was abolished in 1860, and after the *Sejm of Galicia had revoked all discrimination against Jews the municipality of Lvov was compelled to annul those restrictions opposed to the Austrian constitution of 1867. Intensified anti-Semitic tendencies then prevalent among the Poles and Ukrainians of Lvov and the vicinity were partly caused by the assimilation of the upper strata of the Jews to the ruling German culture.

TRENDS WITHIN THE COMMUNITY. Ḥasidism made headway in Lvov at the end of the 18th century, and although no *ẓaddikim* settled there they occasionally visited the town. In 1792 and in 1798 there were open clashes between Ḥasidim and their opponents. During the 1820s, a ḥasidic *shtibl* was founded and in 1838 there were seven such prayer rooms. As the *Haskalah movement penetrated Lvov, an anonymous *ḥerem* was proclaimed in 1816 against a group of *maskilim* and especially against Solomon Judah *Rapoport, Benjamin Ẓevi Nutkis, and Judah Leib Pastor; it was only as a result of pressure from the authorities that it was rescinded by the *av bet din,* Jacob Meshullam Orenstein. During the 1830s a violent dispute broke out over the question of a change in the traditional Jewish dress. In 1844 a Reform Temple was opened and Abraham Kohen of Hohenems, Austria, was appointed as preacher. He was also made director of the German-Jewish school opened during the same year. The Orthodox were vigorously opposed to him and their opposition gained momentum after the authorities confirmed him as rabbi of the province in 1847. A year later he and his family were poisoned and Orthodox fanatics were accused of having committed the crime.

The assimilationist intelligentsia circles of Lvov identified themselves with German culture, and in 1868 the *Shomer Israel organization was formed, with its ideological organ, *Israelit.* The movement was opposed by the Doresh Shalom society, founded in 1878 and disbanded a short while later, and after it by the *Aguddat Aḥim (1883), which called for assimilation into Polish culture. Its organ was the *Ojczyzna* ("Fatherland"). Toward the end of the century, the move toward Polish assimilation gained in strength and the Jewish representatives from Lvov in the Austrian parliament joined the Polish camp. During the 1870s Orthodox circles organized themselves within the framework of the *Maḥzike Hadas, in which the Ḥasidim were predominant. Lvov was the home of Hertz *Homberg. Within the framework of his educational activities, four schools for boys, three for girls, and a teachers' seminary headed by Aaron Friedenthal were founded there. All were closed down with the liquidation of Homberg's educational network in Galicia in 1806. Jewish children, however, began to attend general schools. Legal restrictions against the attendance of Jews in secondary schools and universities were removed in 1846. There were then many Jews in the liberal professions, including distinguished lawyers and physicians. From the emancipation period, there were numerous cases of apostasy in Lvov. Between 1868 and 1907, 713 Jews abandoned their faith, while 86 Christians were converted to Judaism. In 1874 there were 69 registered *ḥadarim* in the city and the first "reformed *ḥeder*" *(ḥeder metukkan)* in which 381 pupils studied, was founded in 1885. An institute for religious studies opened in 1910.

During the Austrian period the two congregations in Lvov merged into a single community, which from the 1830s was led by moderate assimilationists. These included Immanuel *Blumenfeld, Meir Jerahmeel Mieses, and Emil *Byk. Rabbis who held office in this community were Joseph Saul Nathanson, Ẓevi Hirsch Orenstein, Isaac Aaron Ettinger (see *Ettinger Family), Isaac *Schmelkes, and Aryeh Leib Braude. The preachers at the temple were Dr. S. A. *Schwabacher, Dr. Y. B. Lewinstein, Dr. Ezekiel Caro (who in 1909 was confirmed as rabbi of the community together with R. Isaac Schmelkes), and Dr. S. Gutmann. During the late 19th and early 20th centuries, the power of the assimilationists declined and nationalist-Zionist influence began to be felt. The first Zionist societies, Mikra Kodesh and Zion, were formed in 1883 and 1888. They formed the nucleus of the all-Galician Zionist organization. Periodicals and newpapers were published: *Przyszlość, Wschód, Ha-Karmel, Der Veker,* and *Togblat.* Activists in the Zionist societies included Reuben Birer, Joseph Kobak, David Schreiber, Abraham and Jacob Kokas, and Adolph *Stand. The first moves were made toward a Jewish workers' movement and artisans' unions, while some joined the P.P.S., the Polish workers' movement; the representative of this group was Herman *Diamand.

From 1914 to 1939. With the outbreak of World War I, thousands of refugees arrived in Lvov from the regions bordering on Russia. The entry of the Russian army into the city in August 1914 was accompanied by robbery and looting, the closure of Jewish institutions, and the taking of hostages. With the return of the Austrians in June 1915, Jewish life was resumed, assistance to the refugees was organized, and the public institutions functioned once more. In November 1918, when the Poles and the Ukrainians fought for control of eastern Galicia, pogroms broke out in Lvov; 70 Jews lost their lives and many were wounded. It was then, when the German, Polish, and Ukrainian nationalistic cultures were in conflict, that the inherent risks of assimilation were made manifest to the Jews.

During the period of independent Poland (1918–39), the community of Lvov was the third largest in Poland and one of its most important centers. From 99,595 in 1910 the number of Jews increased to 109,500 (33% of the total population) in 1939. In the struggle between the Poles and the Ukrainians, each side accused the Jews of supporting the other. The rise of anti-Semitism and the severe economic situation were reflected in every sphere of Jewish life. The economic crisis was also illustrated by the reduction in community taxes: from 497,429 zlotys in 1929 to 310,481 zlotys in 1933. During this period, Lvov had three Jewish secondary schools with instruction in Polish; a Hebrew college for advanced studies in Judaism (founded in 1920), first directed by Moses *Schorr; a nationalist-religious school, MaTaT (Mi-Ẓiyyon Teẓe Torah); a vocational school; many *ḥadarim*, and a *talmud torah*. There were many Ashkenazi synagogues and ḥasidic prayer rooms. The newspapers *Chwila* ("The Moment"), *Lemberger Togblat*, and *Opinia* were published. The community was governed by assimilationists in coalition with the Orthodox, while for the greater part of this period the Zionists formed the opposition. In national politics, the Lvov members of the Polish parliament adopted a moderate line. They opposed the minorities bloc and were among the initiators of the *Ugoda (see also O. *Thon and H. *Rosmaryn), the agreement with the Polish government (1925). The Orthodox, especially the Ḥasidim of *Belz, as well as the rich Jews, supported the government majority list. [A.Ru.]

Hebrew Printing. After the first partition of Poland (1772), which brought Galicia under Austro-Hungarian rule, the government forced Jewish printers to transfer their presses from *Zolkiew (Zholkva) to the Galician capital of Lvov in order to facilitate their *censorship. The first to move were W. Letteris and H. D. Madpis, the latter producing Elijah Levita's *Pirkei Eliyahu* in 1783. The house of Madpis brought out a new edition of the Talmud (1859–68) and a seven-volume Shulḥan Arukh with standard commentaries (1858–61), still one of the best editions (a similar one was printed by J. L. *Balaban and his son, who began printing in 1839). In 1785 J. S. Herz set up his press, which produced a good edition of Maimonides' *Mishneh Torah* (1805–11). Madpis' granddaughter, Judith Mann-Rozanes, also moved from Zolkiew, while her son, M. H. Grossmann, continued printing until 1858. About 20 other printers were active in Lvov in the century and a half before the outbreak of World War II, making the city one of the main centers for the production of Hebrew books, not only for Eastern Europe but for the Balkans as well. [Ed.]

Holocaust Period. In September 1939, at the beginning of World War II, Poland was partitioned between Germany and the U.S.S.R., and Lvov became part of Soviet Ukraine. But after the outbreak of the German-Soviet War, the Germans captured the city (July 1941); it then had a Jewish population of about 150,000, including thousands of refugees from the Nazi-occupied western part of Poland. The local Ukrainian population welcomed the German troops, while Stefan Bandera's units joined up with the invading forces and played a major role in stirring up hatred of the Jews and in murdering them. An incited mob attacked the Jews for three days. Thousands of Jews were put in jail, where they were tortured and murdered. During July several hundred Jewish public figures and youth were put to death; over 2,000 Jews were shot in "*Aktion* Petliura" (July 25–27). On July 15, the Jews were ordered to wear the yellow badge, and at the beginning of August a fine of 20,000,000 rubles ($4,000,000) was imposed upon them. Jewish property was confiscated and looted and in August the desecration and destruction of synagogues and Jewish cemetries was carried out.

A Judenrat was appointed by the authorities, headed by Joseph Parnes, who was killed shortly afterward when he refused to supply the Nazis with a quota of men for forced labor. A similar fate was in store for two of his three successors; the last chairman of the Judenrat, Ebersohn, was executed together with the other members of the council in February 1943. Under German supervision, the Judenrat handled taxes, social welfare, and food and housing control. A Jewish police force came into being as a special department of the Judenrat; in the course of time it was manipulated by the Nazis to serve their own aims. On Aug. 1, 1941, Eastern Galicia was incorporated into the General Government, Poland, and all anti-Jewish restrictions that had been in force in western Poland for the past two years were now also applied to the Jews of Lvov (see *Holocaust, General Survey). Labor camps were set up in the city and vicinity, where many Jews were either murdered outright (especially young people) or died as a result of the inhuman conditions prevailing in the camps. In November 1941 the Jews of Lvov were all concentrated in a special quarter of the city and subjected to starvation.

In March 1942 about 15,000 Jews from Lvov were deported to *Belzec extermination camp. The big *Aktion*, however, took place from August 10 to 23, in which 40,000 Jews perished. Following the *Aktion* the S.S.-Gruppenfuehrer Fritz *Katzmann ordered the establishment of a ghetto, completely sealed off and surrounded by a barbed-wire fence. The overcrowding caused a series of epidemics which killed thousands of ghetto inmates. In further *Aktionen* (November 1942 and January 1943), another 15,000 Jews were murdered, some in Belzec and others in the Janowska Road camp. The rest of the ghetto inmates, some 20,000 people, were restricted to a portion of the ghetto designated as the Jewish camp and the Judenrat was liquidated. In the last *Aktion* (June 1943), which resulted in the death of most of the surviving Jews, the Jews offered armed resistance. In places where the Nazis encountered gunfire and hand grenades, they poured gasoline on the Jewish houses and set them in flames. The 7,000 Jews who survived the massacre were dispatched to the Janowska Road camp. Apart from a few Jews in labor camps, Lvov and the environs were made *judenrein*. A few hid in the "Aryan" part of the city.

Figure 3. Farm in the Lvov region, c. 1925. Courtesy Jewish Colonization Association, London.

Nr. 7237 a LWÓW, CZWARTEK, 18. MAJA 1939. ROK XXI

CHWILA

WYDANIE PORANNE

Cena egzemplarza 15 gr.

DZIENNIK DLA SPRAW POLITYCZNYCH, SPOŁECZNYCH I KULTURALNYCH

„BIAŁA KSIĘGA"

Strejk generalny Żydów w Palestynie

W Tel Awiwie strejk potrwa 10 dni!

Figure 4. Masthead and headlines of the Lvov Jewish newspaper, *Chwila* ("The Moment"), May 18, 1939, with news of a Jewish general strike in Palestine protesting the British White Paper. Courtesy Central Zionist Archives, Jerusalem.

JANOWSKA ROAD CAMP. The camp, a place of torture and murder, was set up on Janowska Road in October 1941. One part of the camp contained quarters for the S.S. men and camp police, and a prison barracks (the latter also served as a transit camp for deportees to Belzec extermination camp). The other part contained workshops which in the course of time developed into a special unit, the German Armament Works (DAW; see *S.S., Enterprises in the East). Designed as a forced labor camp for Jews from Lvov and the area, Janowska in fact became an extermination camp. Tens of thousands of Jews from Eastern Galicia were brought there, some of whom were murdered on the spot and others sent on to Belzec. Prisoners were killed in many instances for the "entertainment" of the murderers. Yet in spite of the conditions, the Jews created cultural activities in the camp and prepared for armed resistance. The Germans, under the threat of possible resistance, liquidated the camp in a surprise *Aktion* on Nov. 20, 1943. Only a few individuals escaped. The special conditions prevailing in Lvov—a hostile Ukrainian population, the lack of forests in the area to provide shelter, and the absence of a local partisan movement—precluded the rise of organized Jewish resistance. However, a few sporadic and isolated attempts to resist were made. Some Jews fled to the remote forests, but in most instances the local peasants handed them over to the Nazis. Some instances of resistance have been recorded, e.g., during the liquidation of the ghetto and one in the Janowska road camp. In one instance, a group of camp prisoners charged with the disposal and cremation of corpses attacked and killed several of the German guards. A few dozen prisoners then escaped, but most of them were caught and murdered.

When the Soviet forces entered in July 1944, a Jewish committee was established to help the survivors. Of the 3,400 Jewish survivors who registered with the committee by the end of 1944, only 820 were from Lvov ghetto itself. Most of the survivors settled in Israel, after wandering through Europe, while the rest emigrated to other countries overseas. Some of the ashes of the Lvov martyrs were taken to Israel and interred at the Naḥalat Yiẓḥak cemetery near Tel Aviv.

Contemporary Period. A monument to the memory of Jewish victims of the Nazis, with inscriptions in Hebrew, Yiddish, and Russian, was erected shortly after World War II. In the 1959 census 29,701 Jews were registered in the Lvov oblast, 5,011 of whom declared Yiddish to be their mother tongue. In the city, a center of Ukrainian nationalism, an anti-Jewish atmosphere prevailed in most spheres of life. In 1957 several Jewish students were arrested for "Zionist activities." Organized *maẓẓah* baking was prohibited in 1959, and in the same year pressure was brought to bear on the local *mohalim* to induce them to sign a declaration promising to abandon circumcision. In the Jewish cemetery only a small section was kept intact and used for burials. In 1962 several hundred Jews were arrested for "economic crimes." In that year several articles were published in the local Ukrainian newspaper, *Lvivska Pravda*, demanding the closure of the only remaining synagogue on the pretext that it served as a meeting place for "speculators" and other criminals. It was in fact closed toward the end of that year, and all synagogue officials were arrested and charged with "economic crimes." The community slaughterhouse was handed over to a local municipal organization. In 1965 local Jews addressed a petition to Prime Minister Kosygin asking to be given a place for worship. They were allotted a building site, but the financial burden of erecting a new synagogue was too great. In 1969 the militia broke into private *minyanim* and dispersed them by force. [E.BR.]

Bibliography: J. Caro, *Geschichte der Juden in Lemberg* (1894); S. Buber, *Anshei Shem* (1895, repr. 1968); Dubnow, Hist Russ, index s.v. *Lemberg;* S. An-ski, *Ḥurban ha-Yahadut be-Polin u-Bukovina* (1929), 119–28, 183–203, and passim; *Lwów, Żydowska gmina wyznaniowa* (1928); M. Balaban, *Żydzi lwowscy na przełomie 16 i 17 wieków* (1906); idem, in: *Studja lwowskie* (1932), 41–65; idem, *Geshikhte fun Lemberger Progresivn Templ* (1937); Neiwelt, in: *Pinkes Galitsye 1925–45* (1945), 117–26 and passim; Yaari, in: KS, 17 (1939/40), 95–108; 21 (1945), 299–300; L. Chasanovich (ed.), *Les Pogromes anti-juifs en Pologne et en Galicie* (1919), 47–73; Karl, in: I. L. Fishman (ed.), *Arim ve-Immahot be-Yisrael*, 1 (1946), 290–344 (incl. bibl.); J. Tenenbaum, *Galitsye Mayn Alte Heym* (1952), index; Thon, in: *Pirkei Galiẓyah* (1957), 343–85; N. M. Gelber (ed.), EG, 1 (1956), incl. bibl.; idem, *Toledot ha-Tenu'ah ha-Ẓiyyonit be-Galiẓyah, 1875–1918* (1958), index; Ḥ. N. Dembitzer, *Kelilat Yofi* (1960), 1–156. PRINTING: Bałaban, in: *Soncino-Blaetter*, 3 (1929/30), 17–21; A. Yaari, in: KS, 17 (1939/40), 95ff.; 21 (1945), 299f.; Ḥ. D. Friedberg, in: EG 4 (1956), 539ff. HOLOCAUST: S. Szende, *The Promise Hitler Kept* (1945), 9–179; L. Weliczker-Wells, *Janowska Road* (1963); I. Lewin, *Aliti mi-Spezia* (1947); P. Schneck, in: *Davar* (Nov. 5, 1946); E. Brand, in: *Yedi'ot Yad Vashem*, 25–26 (1961), 17–18; EG, 4 (1956), 539–766; *Eduyyot*, 1 (1963), 195–216; *Forfaits hitlériens: Documents officiels* (1945), 201–32; M. M. Borwicz, *Uniwersytet zbirów* (1946); idem, *Literatura w obozie* (1946); J. Hescheles, *Oczyma dwunastoletniej dziewczyny* (1946); S. Gogołwska, *Szkoła okrucieństwa* (1964).

LVOVICH, DAVID (known as **Davidovich;** 1882–1950), leader of the territorialist-Socialist movement and of *ORT. Born in southern Russia and brought up in an assimilationist environment, Lvovich first became acquainted with Jewish affairs and the Jewish workers' movement when he visited Minsk in 1903 and came into contact with the *Po'alei Zion. After he left Russia he maintained relations with the Ḥerut group founded by N. *Syrkin. In 1905 he visited Ereẓ Israel and on his return he abandoned general Zionism in favor of territorialism. After joining the *Zionist-Socialist Workers' Party (S.S. or Z.S.), he founded the S. S. League abroad and established student groups in Germany. A member of the party's committee in Odessa from late 1905, he was the leader of its *self-defense group during the October pogrom. At the S.S. convention in Leipzig (1906), he represented that trend which connected the future realization of territorialism with the unavoidable turn of the course of Jewish emigration from the towns toward agriculture and concentrated colonization. He later worked for an active policy in the organization and regulation of emigration. As the representative of the S.S. at the conventions of the Jewish Territorialist Organization (see *Territorialism) he was elected to the Angola Committee (Vienna, 1912). In 1907 he was the representative of the S.S. at the Socialist International Congress in Stuttgart. Lvovich tried to promote cooperation between S.S., the *Jewish Socialist Workers' Party ("Sejmists"), and the Po'alei Zion. In 1917 he was elected to the Social-Revolutionary list by Jewish colonists of southern Ukraine as the only delegate of the *United Jewish Socialist Workers' Party at the constituent assembly. Turning his energies to working for ORT in Russia, he traveled abroad (1919) as its emissary, along with L. *Bramson, in order to establish the world ORT league (1921). Becoming a member of its executive council in 1937 he was elected vice-president and in 1946 co-president. He published his memoirs in *Sotsialistisher Teritorializm* (1934), 79–89.

Bibliography: *ORT khronik* (Yid., Oct. 1950); *Akhtsik Yor "ORT"* (1960), 119–41. [M.M.]

LWOFF, ANDRÉ MICHEL (1902–), French biologist and Nobel Prize winner. Born in the Allier department, France, Lwoff became head of the Microbial Physiology Laboratory of the Pasteur Institute in Paris in 1938. Lwoff's

André Lwoff, French biologist and Nobel Prize winner. Courtesy Israel Medical Association, Jerusalem.

earlier work dealt with the morphology and biology of the ciliate protozoa, and particularly the problem of the genetic continuity of cell structures. His later research dealt with the biology of viruses, the genetics of bacteria, and the mechanisms by which viruses are replicated in the course of a viral infection. During World War II he was awarded the Medal of the Resistance for his work in the French underground. After the war Lwoff and his collaborators began a study of lysogeny. Lwoff demonstrated that in this condition the bacterial cell harbors a "prophage" which is harmless to the host cell and is transmitted genetically. It can be induced by external factors, such as ultraviolet light, to become virulent, causing destruction of the host cell and liberation of infectious virus particles. This discovery led to entirely new ideas as to the evolution and biological role of viruses. Lwoff was corecipient of the 1965 Nobel Prize for Medicine and Physiology. Among his books were *Problems of Morphogenesis in Ciliates* (1950); *Biological Order* (1962). He was also editor of *Biochemistry and Physiology of Protozoa* (3 vols., 1951–64). [M.L.G.]

LYADY, small town in Vitebsk oblast, Belorussian S.R.R.; under Polish rule until 1772, when it was incorporated into Russia and was included in the Mogilev province. A Jewish settlement in Lyady is mentioned in documents of 1731. In 1766 there were 207 Jewish poll tax payers. During the 19th century, Lyady became a "Jewish" townlet, the Jews forming the majority of the population. There were 2,137 Jews registered with the community in 1847, and 3,763 (83.9% of the total population) in 1897. Lyady became known as the home of *Shneour Zalman, the founder of the Ḥabad movement, who lived there during the last 12 years of his life, and was referred to as the "Rabbi of Lyady." His son, Dov Baer, also lived there at first. In 1869 the great-grandson of Shneour Zalman, Shneour Ḥayyim Zalman, settled in Lyady. He and his sons maintained a ḥasidic "court" in the town. In 1926 there were 2,020 Jews (56% of the total population). Lyady was the birthplace of Alexander Siskind *Rabinovitz (Azar) and Reuben *Brainin. The community of Lyady was annihilated after the German occupation in 1941.

Bibliography: R. Brainin, *Fun mayn Lebens Bukh* (1946), 31–99; *Regesty i nadpisy*, 2 (1910), 301–02. [Y.S.]

LYAKHOVICHI (Pol. **Łachowicze;** Yid. לעכוויטש), city in Brest-Litovsk oblast, Belorussian S.S.R. Jews were living in Lyakhovichi by the first quarter of the 17th century. According to a decision of the Lithuanian Council of 1623 (see *Councils of the Lands), the community was subordinated to the *kahal* of *Pinsk. During the second half of the 18th century the city's annual fairs were an important meeting place for Jewish merchants. There were 729 Jewish poll tax payers in 1766; in 1847 the community numbered 1,071, increasing to 3,846 (76.6% of the total population) in 1897. The chaos during World War I and the immediate postwar years caused a drop in the Jewish population and in 1921 they numbered only 1,656 (58.7%). [EJ]

Holocaust Period. On the eve of the German occupation (June 24, 1941) the community consisted of 6,000 Jews. On June 28 a number of Jewish community leaders were murdered in the nearby forest, following which a pogrom broke out in which 82 Jews were killed (July 1). In fall 1941 the Jews were ordered to assemble in the market place, where a *Selektion* was made to separate the able-bodied from the "nonproductive." The latter were taken to a trench and murdered; some tried to escape but most of these were shot. The "productive" persons were interned in a ghetto. A group of young persons, led by Zalman Rabinowicz, Josef Peker, and Haim Abramowicz, organized resistance units. In summer 1942, a second *Aktion* was carried out in which 2,500 Jews were murdered. Some attempts at resistance were then made. When an *Aktion* to liquidate the entire ghetto was carried out the Germans met with armed resistance. Some ghetto inmates escaped to the forests and joined the partisans, among them Shmuel Mordkowski, who was an outstanding resistance fighter. Less than ten Jews survived in Lyakhovichi. About 80 Jews from the town who had joined the Soviet army in 1941 also survived. A society of former residents of Lyakhovichi functions in Tel Aviv. [AR.W.]

Bibliography: *Lachowicze, Sefer Zikkaron* (Heb. and Yid., 1949); Halpern, Pinkas, index; S. Dubnow (ed.), *Pinkas ha-Medinah* (1925), index; B. Wasiutyński, *Ludność żydowska w Polsce w wiekach XIX I XX* (1930), 84; I. Schiper (ed.), *Dzieje handlu żydowskiego na ziemiach polskich* (1937), index.

LYCK (Pol. **Elk**), town in Poland; before 1945 in E. Prussia. During the late 17th century Jewish tradesmen visited the market town and subsequently established a community which, in 1713, numbered 29 persons. Its *shoḥet*, Eliezer Lipmann *Silbermann, founded the Hebrew weekly **Ha-Maggid* which was printed in Lyck from 1856 to 1891. The *Mekiẓei Nirdamim Society was also founded by Silbermann and, between 1864 and 1874, 15 of its publications were printed in Lyck. Among them was S. D. *Luzzatto's 1864-edition of *Judah Halevi's *Diwan*, S. *Buber's edition of the *Pesikta de Rav Kahana* (1868), and parts of I. *Lampronti's *Paḥad Yiẓhak* (1864–74). In the second half of the 19th century many Hebrew books were printed in the town and smuggled across the border to Russian Jewry. The community of Lyck increased from 90 persons in 1845 to 250 (3.65% of the total population) in 1880, then declined to 137 in 1933 and 16 in 1939.

Bibliography: Neufeld, in: AUJW (May 7, 1965), 6; PK Germanyah; *Du'aḥ shel Mekiẓei Nirdamim* (1935). [Z.F.]

LYDDA (Heb. לֹד, Lod), town in the coastal plain of Israel, 10 mi. (16 km.) S.E. of Tel Aviv-Jaffa. Lydda first appears in the Canaanite period (1465 B.C.E.) when it is mentioned in Thutmosis III's list of towns in Canaan. According to the Talmud (Meg. 1:3b–4a; TJ, Meg. 1:1), the city was fortified "in the days of Joshua the son of Nun," but according to the Bible, it was built by Shemed, a Benjamite (I Chron. 8:12). It appears with Ono and Hadid in the list of places resettled after the return from the Babylonian Exile (Ezra 2:33; Neh. 7:37), and it occurs with Ono and Ge-Harashim in the list of Benjamite settlements (Neh. 11:35).

In the Hellenistic period the town was outside the boundaries of Judea; it was detached from Samaria and given to Jonathan the Hasmonean by Demetrius II in 145 B.C.E. (I Macc. 11:34; Jos., Ant., 13:127), becoming a toparchy of Judea (Jos., Wars, 3:55). In Maccabean times it was a purely Jewish town; Julius Caesar restored the privileges of the Jews of Lydda (Jos., Ant., 14:208). In the Roman period it was counted as a village, although it was as populous as a city (Jos., Ant., 20:130). In 43 B.C.E. its inhabitants were sold into slavery by Cassius, the governor of Syria (Jos., Ant., 14:275). Quadratus, the Syrian governor in the time of Claudius, executed several Jews there; Cestius Gallus, the Roman proconsul of Syria, burned it on his way to Jerusalem in 66 C.E. It was within the command of John the Essene at the beginning of the First Jewish War (66–70); Vespasian occupied it in 68 C.E.

According to talmudic sources, Lydda was situated on the boundary of the Shephelah and the coastal plain, one day's journey from Jerusalem; other sources call the plain around it the Shephelah of Lydda (Ma'as. Sh. 5:2). The town flourished between the First and Second Jewish Wars. It had a large market; cattle were raised in the area; and textile, dyeing, and pottery industries were established. A Christian community existed there in the time of Peter (Acts 9:32–35). It was the seat of a Sanhedrin; famous talmudic scholars, such as R. Tarfon, R. Eliezer b. Hyrcanus, R. Akiva, Joshua b. Levi, Judah b. Pazi, Eleazar bar Kappara, and Ḥanina bar Ḥama taught there. Among its synagogues was one specially maintained by a community of Tarsians. After the war of Bar-Kokhba (132–135), Jews remained in

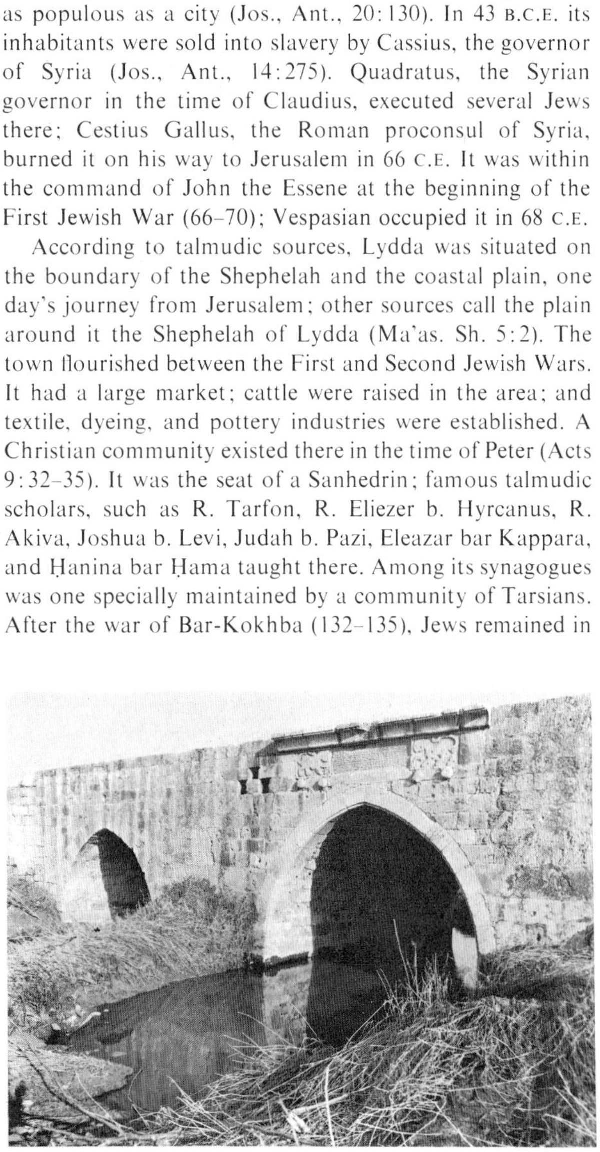

The bridge at Lydda, built in 1278 C.E. by the Mamluk Sultan Baybars. Photo Werner Braun, Jerusalem.

Lydda, though its agricultural hinterland had been destroyed. The patriarch R. Judah I leased estates in its plain.

In 200, the emperor Septimius Severus established a Roman city at Lydda, calling it Colonia Lucia Septimia Severa Diospolis. Its territory consisted of the combined toparchies of Lydda and Thamna. The town remained partly Jewish. It took part in the revolt against the emperor Gallus in 351 and was punished when the revolt failed; according to one Midrash, out of ten measures of poverty in the world, Lydda had nine. The Samaritan element became more powerful in Byzantine times, although the town, part of Palaestina Prima, was predominantly Christian and had a bishop. Justinian built a church there. It was the legendary birthplace of St. George; hence its name Georgiopolis in late Byzantine and crusader sources. It was captured by the Muslim general ʿAmr ibn al-ʿĀṣ in 636 and until the foundation of Ramleh (c. 715) it served as headquarters of the province of Filasṭīn. In 1099 it was occupied by the crusaders and became a *seigneurie* with a vicomte in charge. The crusaders built a Church of St. George there, still partly preserved. In 1170, Benjamin of Tudela found only one Jewish family there. After Saladin's reconquest of the town in 1191, more Jews settled in it. In the 14th century, Estori ha-Parḥi found a Jewish community there. Under the Mamluks Lydda was the seat of an administrative district. The town seems not to have been inhabited by Jews during the early Ottoman period. Ancient remains in modern Lydda include a mound, a Jewish tomb, and a Greco-Samaritan inscription. [M.A.-Y.]

Modern Period. In the 19th century a small Jewish community existed in Lydda, but the 1921 Arab riots compelled the last of its Jewish inhabitants to leave. Further attempts to reestablish the community during the British Mandate failed because of ensuing violence. The town, which numbered only a few hundred families at the beginning of the century, expanded quickly and in 1919 became an important railway junction. In 1944, Lydda numbered about 17,000 Arab inhabitants, one-fifth of them Christians and the rest Muslims.

During Israel's War of Independence, Lydda was occupied by Israel forces in "Operation Dani" on July 10, 1949, and the great majority of its inhabitants abandoned the town. The first Jewish settlers went to Lydda at the end of 1948 when its population numbered 1,200, with 1,050 of them Arabs. In 1949 it received municipal council status. At the end of 1969 its population was 28,000, including 2,900 Muslims and Christian Arabs.

The new parts of Lydda contrast with its ancient nucleus, which has preserved an oriental character and retains its mosques and churches.

The nearby airport, Israel's international airport for passengers and freight, was originally built by the Mandatory government in 1936, with the Israel government greatly expanding its facilities. It serves as the home base for *El Al Israel Airlines. New passenger sections were completed in 1970. Some 115,000 passengers passed through the airport in 1950 and in 1970 the number was over a million. The airport serves the town as an important source of employment, as do the Israel Aircraft Industries. The town's own industrial enterprises include manufacture of paper and cardboard, food preserves, electrical appliances, cigarettes, and oil refining.

Bibliography: Press, Ereẓ, s.v.; EM, 4 (1962), 430–1 (incl. bibl.); S. Abramsky, *Ancient Towns in Israel* (1963); Benvenisti, *Crusaders in the Holy Land*, index. [S.H.]

LYDIA, LYDIANS (Heb. לוּד, לוּדִים, לודיים; Ass. *Luddu*), people who, together with the Phrygians and other Anatolian peoples, infiltrated Anatolia after the decline of

לְכָל לְרֹאשׁ שֶׁבָּחַר בְּאוֹבְרַלְתָּרֹאשׁ בְּבִימוֹרָה בַּתָאֵינָה בְּרֹאשׁ בִּיטְהַ
יֹאוֹתָה דְרוֹשׁ מִפְלֹאוּם לְפָרוּשׁ לַנְשֹׂאָה עַל כָל רֹאשׁ גוּעֵלָה תֵשִׁיתְ
מִיצֹד רֹאשׁ וְהִיא אִתְרִים רֹאשׁ בְּכִסֵּא כָּבוֹד מֵרֹאשׁ

An arcaded initial-word panel from the *Worms Maḥzor*. The illustration and text refer to the Sabbath of the portion of *Shekalim* (Ex. 30:11–16), one of the four special Sabbaths. A man is shown weighing the *shekels* for payment in the Temple. The panel is from the first of two volumes of a lectern festival prayer book, which was written in the Upper Rhine area in 1272 by the scribes Judah of Ernburg, Simḥah, and Shemaiah the Frenchman. For many centuries the two volumes belonged to the Worms community. Jerusalem, Jewish National and University Library, ms. Heb. 4° 781, vol. 1, fol. 39v ($15\frac{3}{8} \times 12\frac{1}{4}$ ins/39×31 cm.).

the *Hittite Empire at the beginning of the 12th century B.C.E., and settled in the vicinity of the Maeander River (modern, Buyuk Menderes) and the western part of the Anatolian heights. After their infiltration, the Lydian tribes assimilated within the local Hittite population and partly took on its language. It is significant to note that one of the kings of the first dynasty is called by the Hittite name Muršiliš (Gr. Myrsilus), a name which was common among the Hittite kings. This dynasty ended with a court uprising, when the head of the royal guard, Gyges, took over the rule. Gyges established the second Lydian dynasty, which ended with the reign of Croesus, when Lydia was conquered by the Persian king Cyrus. During the time of Gyges, relations were established between Lydia and the kingdom of Assyria, because Gyges sought the aid of the latter against the Cimmerians. An important part of this episode has been preserved in the Annals of Ashurbanipal, which records a request for aid by "Guggu king of Luddu (Lydia)" from the Assyrian king (Rassam Cylinder, 2:95). The name of Gyges, in its Hebrew form, *Gog, found its way into Ezekiel (38:2–3). He is referred to here as the head of two Anatolian peoples, Meshech and Tubal. It may thus be concluded that legends about Gyges were popular in both the classical world and the Assyrian empire. Gyges attempted to gain control of central Anatolia and its western coast. The Lydian capital was at this time already in *Sardis. The last Lydian king was Croesus, known throughout the Greek world for his legendary wealth; he was defeated by the Persian army in 547. This brought an end to the Lydian kingdom, which became a province of the Persian empire. The name of the area was preserved as Lydia until a later period, and appears in its biblical Hebrew form, Lud, in talmudic sources as well. The name appears in the Bible together with the names of the Anatolian peoples who were known in the Ancient Near East in the eighth and seventh centuries. In Genesis 10:22, Lud is considered a son of Shem and listed together with Elam, Assyria, etc. This ethnic juxtaposition reflects the geographic relationship of the whole northeastern territory as well as an ethnic unity. The parallel list in I Chronicles 1:17 also includes Meshech, which emphasizes the geographic-ethnic orientation of the list. There is an interesting report in Jeremiah 46:9 which speaks of the army of Pharaoh Neco and which also mentions the Lydians as bowmen serving as auxiliaries of the Egyptian forces. Some scholars regard *Ludim* (Lydians) as a distortion of *Luvim* (Libyans), but it is more reasonable to assume that the verse refers to mercenary forces of Lydians who, like the Greeks, served in the Egyptian army. [AA.KE.]

Jews in Lydia. The beginning of Jewish settlement in Lydia is connected with the establishment of Jewish military settlements by Antiochus III. Josephus relates that during Antiochus' campaign in the East in 209–204 B.C.E. a revolt broke out in Lydia and Phrygia, and Antiochus decided to transfer 2,000 Jewish families from Mesopotamia to the rebellious regions. Each family received a plot of land upon which to build a house and for cultivation. They were to be exempt from taxation for ten years, and during the initial period their needs were to be provided for. They received special authority to live according to the customs of their ancestors. The authenticity of the document quoted by Josephus (Ant., 12:147ff.) is denied by some, but since Jews served as soldiers and dwelt in military settlements as early as in the Persian era, it can be regarded as genuine. These settlements became the nucleus of the Jewish settlement in Asia Minor generally and in Lydia in particular. Lydia remained in the possession of Antiochus until the battle of Magnesia in 190 B.C.E. when it was given by the Romans to Eumenes II king of Pergamum. In 133 B.C.E. Attalus III bequeathed the kingdom to the Romans and an Asian province was created which included Lydia. Information about the Jews of Lydia derives chiefly from the Roman era. Many documents having reference to the Jews of Sardis have been preserved. From a resolution about the Jews by the citizens of Sardis it is clear that the Romans granted the Jews the right to live according to their customs and even to be judged by their own laws. The ancient synagogue of Sardis was discovered and excavated in the 1960s.

The sending of the half shekel to the Temple in Jerusalem was a source of friction between Jews and gentiles, who did not look favorably upon the export of the moneys from their city to a foreign country. The proconsul, Gaius Norbanus Flaccus (in the time of Augustus, 27 B.C.E.–14 C.E.), wrote to the authorities of Sardis ordering them not to prevent the Jews from collecting the moneys and sending them to Jerusalem. There is extant from a still later period, the time of Trajan, an inscription from the city of Thyatira in Lydia (Frey, Corpus, 2 (1952), 16, no. 752). In this inscription the word *Sambatyon* occurs. Some consider it to be a Jewish inscription, while others regard it as being connected with "The God fearing ones" who were not regarded as full Jews. There is already reference to a "God fearing" woman from this city in an earlier period in Acts 16:14. [L.Ro.]

Bibliography: G. Radet, *La Lydie et le Monde Grec*... (1892); A. Goetze, *Kleinasien* (1957²), 206–9; A. Heubeck, *Lydiaka* (1959); G. Neumann, *Untersuchungen zum Weiterleben hethitischen und luwischen Sprachgutes* (1961); R. D. Barnett, in: CAH², vol. 2, ch. 30 (1967). JEWS IN LYDIA: A. Buechler, *Die Tobiaden und die Oniaden* (1899), 144ff.; Schuerer, Gesch, 3 (1909⁴), 12–15, 75; Juster, Juifs, 1 (1914), 190; Pauly-Wissowa, 26 (1927), 2197; Frey, Corpus, 2 (1952), 16–18, nos. 750, 751, 752; Schalit, in: JQR, 50 (1959/60), 289–318; V. Tcherikover, *Hellenistic Civilization and the Jews* (1959), 288.

LYNN, city in N.E. Massachusetts, on the north shore of Massachusetts Bay. The city of Lynn has a population of 90,500; Greater Lynn, which includes the towns of Lynnfield, Swampscott, Nahant, Saugus, and Marblehead, numbers about 153,000, with a Jewish population of 14,000 (estimated, 1969). The first and oldest Jewish organization in Lynn was the Hebrew Benevolent Society (1884), a fraternal organization providing burial grounds and sick benefits for its ten German and Lithuanian member families. By 1900 the Jewish population had grown to about 100 families. The first synagogue was Ahabat Shalom (1901), whose ritual was Orthodox. In 1903 Anshe Sfard synagogue (Orthodox) was established by about 35 Ukrainian families. With the waves of immigration in the 1920s, another Orthodox synagogue, Hevra Thillim, was formed. Greater Lynn Jewry of Reform and Conservative leanings organized Temple Beth El in 1927. From World War II a constant influx of Jewish families from metropolitan Boston augmented the number of Jewish residents of Greater Lynn and led to the formation of Temple Israel of Swampscott (Conservative), Temple Sinai of Marblehead (Conservative), and Temple Emanu-El of Marblehead (Reform). With widened roads, the Jewish communities of Wakefield, Salem, Peabody, and Beverly turned to Greater Lynn for schools and social service. The Jewish Community Federation has endeavored to integrate these communities into a Jewish community of the north shore. The central Jewish institution in Lynn is the Jewish Community Center. Five of the congregations of Greater Lynn have religious schools. There is also a communal Jewish day school, Hillel Academy, in Swampscott, which has an enrollment of 100 ranging from kindergarten to the sixth grade. Philanthropic activities are carried on by the Jewish Community Federation, the Jewish Social Service Agency, and the Jewish Rehabilitation Center, and women's organizations.

Prior to World War II, the Jews of Greater Lynn were well represented in shoe manufacturing and allied industries. There was also a considerable Jewish working class, whose cultural life centered around the Yiddishe Shulle. But in the early 1940s the shoe industry moved north and southwest and Jewish workers retired without being replaced. Jews of Greater Lynn are now in the clothing business, real estate, the leather industry, and chemical manufacturing. Jews are prominent in the practice of law, accountancy, engineering, and, above all, in medicine.

[I.HAR.]

LYON-CAEN, CHARLES LÉON (1843–1935), French jurist. The son of a tailor, Lyon-Caen spent some time on his father's business before studying law. His doctoral thesis, *Partages d'ascendants* (1867), earned him a considerable reputation as a jurist and he became professor of law at the Sorbonne in 1872, a post he held for nearly half a century. Lyon-Caen was an authority on commercial and international law and was the author of important works on both subjects. His *Precis de droit commercial* (2 vols., 1885) and *Traité de droit commercial* (8 vols., 1885), written with Louis Renault, became standard works, while his *Droit international privé maritime* (1883) was one of the first textbooks on maritime law as a separate branch of the law. His other works include: *De la condition légale des sociétes étrangères en France* (1870). Lyon-Caen was elected to the Académie des sciences morales et politiques in 1884 and became its permanent secretary in 1893. He was active in Jewish affairs as president of L'oeuvre des orphelins Israélites and the Comité d'aide aux émigrants juifs.

[S.C.]

LYONS, capital of the Rhône department, E. central France. According to a medieval Jewish legend one of the three boats loaded with Jewish captives taken at the fall of Jerusalem docked at Lyons. Herod Antipas, tetrarch of Galilee, was exiled to the city by Caligula in 39 C.E. Lyons seems to have had a Jewish population in the second century but little more is known until the beginning of the ninth century when there was a large, prosperous, and powerful Jewish community in the city. The Jews owned slaves and also employed a number of Christian laborers in their homes and commercial or agricultural enterprises. The wine they produced was sold to Christians too, who also were customers of the Jewish butchers. The Jews, who were among the purveyors to the imperial palace, received luxurious clothing from the ladies of the court as gifts for their wives. Some Jews were employed in public service, especially as collectors of imposts and taxes. Their religious services also appear to have been attended by Christians, who declared that they preferred the preaching of the Jews to that of the Catholic priests. Such opinions could only have been an extreme irritant to the bishop, *Agobard, who had hoped to find a receptive ear to the Christian message among the Jews. A first attempt—involving the use of a measure of force—around 820 at leading Jewish children to Christianity encountered determined resistance from the parents and the vigorous intervention of the emperor. *Louis the Pious had to intervene on several other occasions against this troublesome bishop, when necessary despatching his special envoys in charge of Jewish affairs, the *missi* or *magister Judaeorum*. *Amulo, Agobard's successor, also attempted to oppose the Jews of Lyons, but without success. In the Middle Ages the Jews lived in the Rue Juiverie at the foot of Fourvière hill. When they were expelled in 1250 they were living in the present Rue Ferrachat. For a century Jews only visited Lyons for short periods, but in the second half of the 14th century there

Ḥanukkah lamp found at Lyons, bronze, 14th century. Paris, Musée de Cluny.

were once more Jewish settlers in the city, contributing toward the municipal taxes, and special officials were appointed with jurisdiction over them. As the city was not part of the Kingdom of France this new community was not affected by the expulsion order of 1394, but they were expelled some years later, probably in1420; most of them moved to neighboring Trévoux. From the 16th century, Jews reappeared in Lyons sporadically as merchants at the fairs and probably also as correctors of Hebrew printing. A group of Jews arrived in Lyons in 1548 (perhaps from Spain and Portugal), but they too were forced to leave. Apparently Joseph *Nasi opened a bank there for some time, but it was closed down by Henri II. A community was gradually formed, consisting of families from Comtat Venaissin, Alsace, and Bordeaux, but mainly from Avignon. In 1775, the community officially requested permission to open a cemetery. At first they purchased space in the vaults of the city hospital. Twenty years later they were able to purchase a cemetery at La Guillotière. Nevertheless, the number of Jews remained insignificant, and they had no synagogue or permanent prayer room.

[B.BL.]

The community was attached to the *Consistory of Marseilles in 1808. With the influx from Alsace and Lorraine the numbers rose to 300 in 1830, and 700 in 1840, the majority living in very modest circumstances and inhabiting two mean quarters in the Rue Lanterne and Rue de la Barre. From 1838 a prosperous industrialist, Samuel Heyman de Ricqulès, was leader of the community; he attempted to endow schools and charitable institutions with the intention of reforming them, but in the face of general hostility he retired after a few years. The number of Jews grew to 1,000 in 1848 and 1,200 in 1854. The community acquired the services of a salaried rabbi in 1850 and in 1857 formed its own consistory, which also included Saint-Étienne (116 Jews), Chalon-sur-Saône (125), Besançon (379), and Montbéliard (202). Among its presidents were Solomon *Reinach and Generals Levy and Worms. Solomon *Munk represented Lyons at the Central Consistory. In 1864 the first synagogue was opened, on the Quai Tilsitt. At the beginning of the 20th century, with the arrival of immigrants from the Mediterranean area, a Sephardi community was formed in the suburb of Saint-Fons. On the eve of World War II Lyons had 500–600 Jewish families. [M.C.]

Holocaust and Postwar Periods. During the war Lyons, in the heart of France, was a "free" city after the Franco-German agreement (June 1940) and became a refuge for Jewish organizations, particularly the offices of the Central Consistory, and for philanthropic and Zionist bodies. Information, official and unofficial, instructions to the Jewish communities in France, protests against anti-Jewish measures, and secret orders of the resistance all emanated from Lyons. A large number of Jewish leaders were arrested there. A center for Jewish studies for refugee intellectuals, to which Léon *Algazi notably contributed, and a reception center for Jewish physicians were set up in the city, on the initiative of *OSE. However, Lyons' most important role in the Occupation was that it provided sanctuary for large numbers of Jews. It was also a large center of the Jewish resistance, which not infrequently operated in total isolation, but sometimes gained the cooperation of Catholic and Protestant bodies, or of the civil and administrative authorities. It was probably in Lyons that Catholic resistance to Nazi persecution was strongest, perhaps as a result of the pastoral letter which Cardinal Gerlier had read on Sept. 6, 1942, in all churches in Lyons and his diocese. The Nazis fought ruthlessly against members of the resistance and Jews. The arrests, torture, and deportations reached a peak in August 1944. Prisoners from the "Jewish quarters" in the Monluc Fort prison were taken to Bron airfield to de-mine the area after the bombardment. After the war their remains, 109 bodies of both sexes, were uncovered.

After the war many Jewish refugees settled permanently in Lyons, but the community, with an estimated 7,000 Jews, was hardly any larger than in 1939. With the city's economic expansion and the influx of immigrants from North Africa, the Jewish population had increased to over 20,000 in 1969. In 1961 one of the first and foremost community centers in France was inaugurated in Lyons. A full-time school was maintained. The various community bodies—consistorial, Sephardi, and Orthodox—worked in close cooperation, and a new synagogue was inaugurated in 1966 in La Duchère, a new quarter of the city. A regional consistory was also founded in 1961. The community institutions included an ORT vocational school. There were several congregations in the vicinity, notably at Villeurbanne, with a Jewish population of 1,800 and a synagogue built in 1965 with the help of Aktion Suehnezeichen ("Repentance Society"), a group of young Germans anxious to expiate Nazi crimes; and at Saint Fons-Vénissieux, with a Jewish population of about 1,200 industrial workers who settled there from North Africa between the world wars. They maintain a synagogue and community center. [G.Le.]

Bibliography: A. Lévy, *Notice sur les Israélites de Lyon* (1894); idem, in: *Univers Israélite*, 48–49 (1892/93–1893/94); T. Reinach, in: REJ, 50 (1905), lxxxi–cxi; S. Reinach, *ibid.*, 51 (1906), 245–50; B. Blumenkranz, *Juifs et Chrétiens dans le monde occidental* (1960), index; A. Coville, *Recherches sur l'histoire de Lyon* (1928), 538ff.; J. Kling, in: *Revue de Psychologie des peuples*, 13 (1958), 199ff.; E. Dreyfus and L. Marx, *Autour des Juifs de Lyon* (1958); F. Delpech, in: *Cahiers d'Histoire* (1959), 51ff.; H. Amoretti, *Lyon . . . 1940–1944* (1964), 142ff.; Z. Szajkowski, *Analytical Franco-Jewish Gazetteer* (1966), 252f.

LYONS, ISRAEL (c. 1700–1770), English Hebraist. Lyons, who was born in Poland, settled in Cambridge (c. 1732), worked as a silversmith, and became an authorized teacher of Hebrew at the university. He contributed Hebrew verses to the volume of elegies (1738) on the funeral of Queen Caroline and published *The Scholar's Instructor, or Hebrew Grammar* (1735; many subsequent editions) and *Observations Relating to Various Parts of Scripture History* (1768). His son ISRAEL LYONS (1739–1775) was an astronomer, botanist, explorer, and mathematician. At the age of 19 he published *A Treatise on Fluxions* (1758), and a *Fasciculus Plantarum circa Cantabrigiam Nascentium* (1763). In 1773 he was appointed principal astronomer to the expedition of Captain Phipps to the North Pole. Lyons appears in a most flattering light in Maria Edgeworth's novel, *Harrington* (1817).

Bibliography: H. P. Stokes, *Studies in Anglo-Jewish History* (1913), 224–6; C. Roth, *Rise of Provincial Jewry* (1950), 42–44; Roth, Mag Bib, index. [C.R.]

LYONS, JACQUES JUDAH (1813–1877), *ḥazzan*, rabbi, and communal leader. Lyons was born in Surinam. He served as a *ḥazzan* of Congregation Neve Shalom in Paramaribo (1833–37). Emigrating to the United States, he served for two years as *ḥazzan* of Congregation Beth Shalom of Richmond, Virginia, and in 1839 began his ministry at the oldest Jewish congregation in the United States, the Spanish-Portuguese congregation Shearith Israel of New York City. Lyons, who was unyielding in his orthodoxy, served as superintendent of the Polonies Talmud Torah School attached to his congregation, as president of Hebra Hased va-Emet, the congregation's benevolent society, and as a director of the Sampson Simson Theological Fund, and was a founder of the Jews' Hospital. Lyons and Abraham *de Sola of Montreal prepared and published *A Jewish Calendar for Fifty Years* (1854), including an essay on the Jewish calendar system and historical data about Jewish communities in the United States, Canada, and the West Indies. From before 1861 to the end of his life, Lyons gathered data and sources on the history of the Jews of the U.S. Although he died before completing the work, this collection was donated to and calendared by the American Jewish Historical Society (see bibl.) and is a most significant source for students of early North American Jewish history.

Portrait of Jacques Judah Lyons, *ḥazzan* and communal leader. Portrait by Jacob H. Lazarus, 1850. From *American Jewish Historical Quarterly*, 1913, Vol. 2, New York.

Lyons is memorialized in the poem "Rosh Ha-Shanah, 5638" by his niece Emma *Lazarus.

Bibliography: AJHSP, 21 (1913), xxiii–xxviii; 27 (1920), 144–9; D. and T. de Sola Pool, *An Old Faith in the New World: Portrait of Shearith Israel, 1654–1954* (1955), 178–82. [I.S.M.]

LYONS, SIR JOSEPH (1848–1917), English caterer and founder of J. Lyons and Company. Lyons was born in London, educated in a Jewish school and started his career as a watercolor painter, exhibiting at the Royal Institute. In 1887 he joined Alfred *Salmon, the brothers Montague, and Isidore *Gluckstein in founding the catering firm of J. Lyons and Company, of which he became the chairman. This concern began by catering at exhibitions, and in 1894 opened the first of many tea shops. It pioneered popular catering and developed into the largest catering establishment in Britain. Sir Joseph Lyons was deputy-lieutenant for the County of London. He was knighted in 1911.

Bibliography: P. H. Emden, *Jews of Britain* (1943), 486–90.

[Ed.]

°**LYSANIAS** (d. c. 36 B.C.E.), son of Ptolemy (son of Mennaeus), king of Chalcis in the region of the Lebanon. On the death of his father (c. 40 B.C.E.), Lysanias inherited the principality of Chalcis and continued to support the Hasmonean prince, Antigonus, in the latter's attempt to oust the house of Herod from Judea. To this end Lysanias induced the Parthian satrap of Syria, Barzapharnes, to restore Antigonus to his throne, offering the Parthian 1,000 talents and 500 women (cf. Jos., Wars, 1:248; according to Jos., Ant., 14:331 the offer was made by Antigonus himself). The ensuing Parthian conquest of Judea (40 B.C.E.) was shortlived, and with the defeat of the Parthians Lysanias lost his kingdom, which was presented by Mark Antony to the Egyptian queen Cleopatra (37–36 B.C.E.). Lysanias was subsequently accused by Cleopatra of supporting the anti-Roman invasion, and was executed by order of Antony.

Bibliography: Schuerer, Gesch, 4 (1911[4]), 75 (index), s.v. [I.G.]

°**LYSIAS** (d. 162 B.C.E.), Syrian general during the Hasmonean War. When in the spring of 165 B.C.E. Antiochus IV went on an expedition to the east he appointed Lysias ruler of the western sector of the Seleucid empire, from the Euphrates to the border of Egypt. Lysias was charged, among other things, with the care of the heir apparent and the crushing of the revolt of Judah Maccabee during the emperor's absence (I Macc. 3:31–37). Lysias accordingly sent an army under *Gorgias against Judah, but the defeat of Gorgias in the battle of Emmaus compelled him to march in person against Judea. According to I Maccabees (though some scholars cast doubt on the veracity of this account) fortune did not favor Lysias, and as a result of his failure the persecutions were abolished and a general amnesty proclaimed by Antiochus IV. On the death of Antiochus shortly afterward, Lysias became regent and de facto ruler of the empire, in the name of Antiochus V who was a minor. Judah's attempt to capture the *Acra compelled Lysias to come again to Judea, this time with a large army, and accompanied by the king. At the battle of Bet Zekharyah (163 B.C.E.) the Syrians gained the upper hand and Lysias besieged Judah and his followers who had fortified themselves within the Temple. He was, however, forced to raise the siege in order to fight against Philip, who had been appointed heir by Antiochus before his death. Lysias, whose influence with the young king was paramount, made peace with Judah and in addition to rescinding the edicts, restored the Temple to the Jews. The evidence in II Maccabees 11 completes the general picture and confirms Lysias' willingness to pacify the Jews not only by military means but also by rescinding the decrees and restoring religious freedom. When Demetrius I was appointed to the Syrian throne, Lysias was put to death.

Bibliography: Schuerer, Hist., 31f., 36–39. [U.R.]

°**LYSIMACHUS OF ALEXANDRIA** (of uncertain date), author of several mythographical works and a book on Egypt. In addition to the scurrilous versions of the Exodus given by *Manetho and *Chaeremon, Josephus adds the account of Lysimachus, who, he says, "surpasses both in the incredibility of his fictions" (Apion, 1:304–20). According to Lysimachus' version, in the reign of Bocchoris (perhaps a corruption of *bekhor*, in allusion to the plague of the first-born during which the Jews left Egypt), king of Egypt, the Jews (see also *Tacitus, *Historiae*, 5:3), afflicted with leprosy and scurvy, took refuge in the temples. A dearth ensued throughout Egypt, and an oracle of Ammon informed the king that the failure of the crops could be averted only by purging the temples of impure persons, driving them out into the wilderness and drowning those afflicted with leprosy. After the lepers had been drowned, the others, numbering 110,600 were exposed in the desert to perish. A certain Moses, however, advised them to proceed until they reached inhabited country, instructing them to show goodwill to no man, to offer not the best but the worst advice, and to overthrow any temples which they found. When they came to the country now called Judea, they built a town called Hierosyla ("town of temple-robbers"). At a later date they altered the name to avoid reproach and called the city Hierosolyma. Josephus attempts to refute the account, not by offering other evidence, but by showing its intrinsic improbability.

Bibliography: A. Gudeman, in: Pauly-Wissowa, 27 (1928), 32–39; Reinach, Textes, 117–20; Schuerer, Gesch, 3 (1909[4]), 535f.

[D.W.]

LYUBESHOV (Pol. **Lubieszów;** Yid. **Libeshey**), ḥasidic dynasty established in Lithuanian Polesie in the early 19th century, originating in Volhynia. Its founder, Shemariah Weingarten (d. 1846), was the son of Abraham Abba-Joseph of Soroca (Soroki) and son-in-law of the celebrated Volhynian *zaddik* David ha-Levi of Stepan. His leadership was acknowledged in Pinsk, *Kobrin, Lyubeshov, Janow, Telekhany, Motol, and Khomsk among other places. Shemariah, who was also a scholar, was given a special right to the rabbinate in Kobrin and the surrounding villages, a unique case in the annals of Ḥasidism in Lithuania. The establishment of the dynasty helped to spread Ḥasidism in this part of Polesie. Shemariah's successor in Lyubeshov was his son Jehiel Michael, and later, his other son Abraham Abba (d. 1861), who served as rabbi of the nearby town of Janow and in Lyubeshov. At that time the influence of the Lyubeshov dynasty, especially in Kobrin, passed to the ḥasidic "court" of Kobrin. After Abraham Abba's death, his son Ḥayyim Isaac served as *zaddik* from 1861 to 1879, and his grandson Jacob Loeb from 1879 to 1922. In 1886 the second son of Ḥayyim Isaac, Abba (d. c. 1924), served as *zaddik* in Janow, which caused a split among the Lyubeshov Ḥasidim. The successor of Jacob Loeb in Lyubeshov was his son Isaac Aaron, who lived in Pinsk and gathered around him the Lyubeshov Ḥasidim. Between the two world wars he visited his Ḥasidim in the U.S. He and his followers perished during the Holocaust.

It was characteristic of Lyubeshov Ḥasidim that their *zaddikim* served as rabbis of towns in Lithuania (Kobrin, Janow, and Lyubeshov). Essentially it was a branch of the Volhynian Ḥasidism. Their *zaddikim* left no written works. An important principle of Lyubeshov Ḥasidim was the holiness of the *zaddik*. They opposed fasting, emphasized the virtue of joy, and had their own melodies. They were concerned with settlement in Ereẓ Israel and during the 19th century set up a Lyubeshov **kolel* there.

Bibliography: W. Z. Rabinowitsch, *Lithuanian Ḥasidism* (1970), index. [W.Z.R.]

LYUBOML (Pol. **Luboml**), city in Volyn oblast, Ukrainian S.S.R. Jews were living in the city in 1516. Under King Sigismund II Augustus in 1557 they obtained a privilege which freed them from any jurisdiction except that of the governor of the province, and guaranteed them the right of appealing to the king. In 1558 the community prohibited the Jews from buying houses and land within the city walls from gentiles, fearing that Jewish homes might be set on fire or the Jews expelled. King Michael Wiśniowiecki confirmed the privileges of Lyuboml Jewry in 1671. The poll tax of 1721 amounted to 833 zlotys, but because of a fire which destroyed much Jewish property in 1729 it was reduced to 544 zlotys; 1,226 poll tax paying Jews then lived in Lyuboml and the settlements under the community's jurisdiction. In 1847, 2,130 Jews lived in the city, and by 1897 there were 3,297 (73% of the total population). In 1921 there were 3,141 Jews (94% of the total population) in the city of Lyuboml and 5,604 (10% of the population) in the surrounding area. The 16th-century synagogue was one of the fortress type which served for defense in the eastern regions of Poland. [EJ]

Holocaust Period. Before the outbreak of World War II there were about 3,500 Jews in Lyuboml. The German army entered the town on Sept. 17, 1939, but, according to the German-Soviet agreement, it withdrew after three days when the Red Army entered the town. The Soviet administration remained there till the outbreak of the German-Soviet war. The Germans occupied the town on June 27, 1941, removed the Jewish population to the fields and nearby villages, and burned part of the town. A series of pogroms took place in Lyuboml in which hundreds of Jews were killed. The remaining Jews were executed on Oct. 1–2, 1942. Altogether, all the 10,000 Jews from Lyuboml and its vicinity were killed in the town and the surrounding woods. After the war, the Jewish community of Lyuboml was not reconstituted. [ED.]

Bibliography: Halpern, Pinkas, index; B. Wasiutyński, *Ludność żydowska w Polsce* . . . (1930), 84; M. Balaban, in: *Yevreyskaya Starina*, 3 (1910), 189; *Yalkut Vohlin*, no. 16–17 (1953), 60–62.

Initial letter for the word *Miserere mei,* "Have mercy upon me," at the beginning of Psalm 51 (Vulgate Ps. 50) from the 12th-century *Psalter of York*. Seen here are David, with Bath-Sheba behind him, being admonished by Nathan. Uriah the Hittite lies dead, stoned by an Ammonite. Copenhagen, Royal Library, Thott, 143, fol. 68r.

MAACAH (Heb. מַעֲכָה), (1) one of David's wives, daughter of Talmai King of Geshur, mother of Absalom (II Sam. 3:3; I Chron. 3:2); (2) one of Rehoboam's wives, daughter of *Absalom or Abisalom son of David, mother of Abijam or Abijah (I Kings 15:2; II Chron. 11:20, 22) and Asa (I Kings 15:11; II Chron. 15:16).

The references to the second Maacah pose certain problems, for a literal reading of all the passages related to her indicates that she is the daughter of Absalom, who, according to II Samuel 14:27, had only one daughter, Tamar. The above references also indicate that Maacah is the mother of Abijah. According to II Chronicles 13:2 (MT), Abijah's mother is Micaiah, daughter of Uriel. Finally the references show Maacah also to be the mother of Asa.

In order to resolve these contradictions, the Masoretic Text of II Chronicles 13:2 must be corrected in accordance with the Septuagint, which reads "Maacah daughter of Uriel." (Everywhere else in the Masoretic Text as well as in the Septuagint Abijah's mother is called Maacah daughter of Absalom.) With this correction the problems are more easily resolved. Maacah is then the granddaughter of Absalom, the daughter of Uriel and Tamar, the mother of Abijah, and the grandmother of Asa. Some of the original confusion results from the fact that the Bible often used the term "children" for "grandchildren" and even descendants who are generations removed (cf. Gen. 31:28; I Kings 15:11, et al.).

W. Rudolph (see bibl.) adopts the view of M. Noth (see bibl.) that II Chronicles 13:2 represents the original text of I Kings 15:2 which is now influenced by I Kings 15:10. Then Abijah would be the son of Rehoboam's wife Micaiah daughter of Uriel, and Asa the son of Abijah's wife Maacah, who would have been the literal daughter of an unknown Absalom, not the granddaughter of David's son Absalom. King Asa deposed Maacah from being queen mother because of an abominable image she had made for Asherah (I Kings 15:13). S. Yeivin maintains that Maacah is Abijah's mother, while Micaiah daughter of Uriel is Asa's mother, and that Asa is Rehoboam's son, and Abijah's half brother.

Bibliography: S. Yeivin, in: BJPES, 10 (1943), 116–9; M. Noth, *Ueberlieferungsgeschichtliche Studien* (1943), 143; W. Rudolph, *Chronikbuecher* (1955), 231–3; EM, 5 (1968), 193–4 (incl. bibl.).

[ED.]

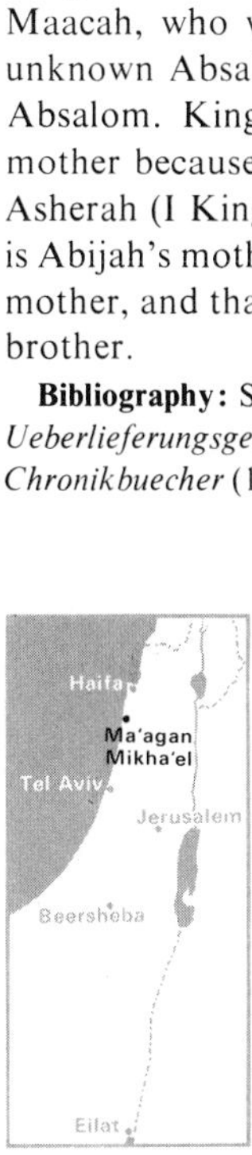

MA'AGAN MIKHA'EL (Heb. מַעֲגַן מִיכָאֵל; "Michael's Anchorage"), kibbutz on the seashore of Israel at the southern end of the Carmel Coast, affiliated with Ha-Kibbutz ha-Me'uḥad. Ma'agan Mikha'el was founded in 1949 by the first group of graduates of the Israel boy scout movement, who were later joined by immigrants from different countries. In 1969 Ma'agan Mikha'el had 665 inhabitants. Its economy is based on fruit plantations, crops, livestock, carp ponds, and an injection molding plant for plastic products.

Fishponds near kibbutz Ma'agan Mikha'el. Photo Werner Braun, Jerusalem.

A nature reserve is located at Ma'agan Mikha'el, at the split mouth of the Tanninim ("crocodiles") River. The reserve, rich in water fowl, comprises the Yonim ("doves") islet in the sea and the former Kabāra swamps which were drained by the *Palestine Jewish Colonization Association (PICA). Prehistoric finds were made in the nearby Kabāra caves. The name of the kibbutz commemorates Mikhael Pollak, a director of PICA. [E.O.]

MA'ALEH AKRABBIM (Heb. מַעֲלֵה עַקְרַבִּים; JPS, "ascent of Akrabbim"; "ascent of the scorpions"), locality mentioned several times in the Bible as being at the southern boundary of the Promised Land. According to Numbers 34:4, the border started "at the end of the Salt [Dead] Sea eastward" and turned south of Ma'aleh Akrabbim, continuing toward the wilderness of Zin"; the account in Joshua 15:3 is similar. The border of the Amorites apparently ran from Ma'aleh Akrabbim, "from Sela, and upward" (Judg. 1:36). Abel identified it with Naqb al-Ṣafī to the west of the Arabah, while Mazar locates it to the east, on the road to Sela. The Akrabattine of I Maccabees 5:3 apparently refers to the district of Acraba to the north of Jerusalem.

Rock formation on the Ma'aleh Akrabbim road in the Negev. Courtesy Government Press Office, Tel Aviv.

Ma'aleh Akrabbim is now the name of a section of a road to Eilat that snakes down into the canyon of Naḥal Ẓin, about 2½ mi. (4 km.) west of the "Small Crater" (Makhtesh ha-Katan). Until the road to Eilat that passes through Ma'aleh ha-Aẓma'ut by Miẓpeh Ramon was built, all traffic to Eilat passed through Ma'aleh Akrabbim. The spot is an excellent lookout point over Naḥal Ẓin and the Arabah.

Bibliography: Abel, Geog, 2 (1938), 46–47; W. J. Phythian-Adams, in: PEFQS, 65 (1933), 143ff.; EM, 5 (1968), 195f.
[M.A.-Y.]

MA'ALEH HA-ḤAMISHAH (Heb. מַעֲלֵה הַחֲמִשָּׁה, "Ascent of the Five"), kibbutz in the Judean Hills, 8 mi. (13 km.) W. of Jerusalem, affiliated to Iḥud ha-Kevuẓot ve-ha-Kibbutzim, founded in 1938 as a *tower and stockade settlement by pioneers of the Gordonia youth movement from Lodz, Poland. In the weeks before setting up their village, the group, then living at nearby Kiryat Anavim, worked in reclaiming the site and planting forests. Arab terrorists killed five members of the group in an ambush. The name of the new kibbutz was chosen to commemorate them. In the Israel *War of Independence (1948), it held out in its advanced position against the Arab Legion, which had taken possession of the nearby "Radar Camp." Until the *Six-Day War, the armistice border passed close by. On the evening of June 5, 1967, Israel forces launched an attack from the kibbutz on the Radar Camp, thereby opening the operations which eventually brought all of Jerusalem and Judea-Samaria under Israel control. The kibbutz economy is based on deciduous fruit orchards and vineyards, dairy cattle and poultry, on a sweets and confectionery factory, a large rest home, and a public swimming pool. Extensive forests have been planted in the vicinity. Its population in 1968 was 290. [E.O.]

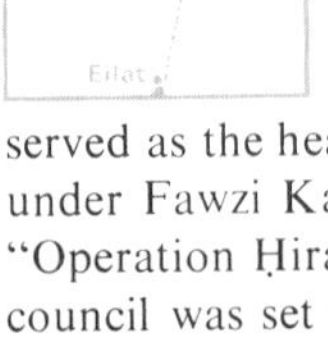

MA'ALOT-TARSHĪḤĀ (Heb. מַעֲלוֹת-תַּרְשִׁיחָה, Arab. ترشيحا; "Heights"), urban community in western Upper Galilee, 12 mi. (20 km.) E. of Nahariyyah, founded in 1957, to replace two *ma'barot* in the vicinity. In 1963 Ma'alot was united with the Arab village Tarshīḥā lying over 1 mile (2 km.) further west. Tarshīḥā was a center of western Galilee, and antiquities found in its vicinity date back to the Roman and Byzantine periods. In the Israel *War of Independence, Tarshīḥā served as the headquarters of the Arab "Liberation Army" under Fawzi Kaukji until it was taken by Israel forces in "Operation Ḥiram" on Oct. 30, 1948. In 1965 a municipal council was set up in Ma'alot-Tarshīḥā. In 1969 the town had 4,750 inhabitants including 3,160 Jews in Ma'alot, the majority of whom originated from North African countries, and 1,590 Arabs at Tarshīḥā, some Muslim and some Christian. Although several industrial enterprises (textile, plastic, food, and building material) existed at Ma'alot in 1969, its economy was not yet firmly established due to the high percentage of welfare cases and the inadequacy of a local labor force. Tarshīḥā's economic situation was far better, as many of its inhabitants were employed as skilled laborers in the Nahariyyah and Haifa areas or maintained lucrative farmsteads. [E.O.]

MA'AMAD or **MAHAMAD,** council of elders in a Sephardi community or congregation in the West after the expulsion from Spain, corresponding to the **kahal* (in the sense of the supreme community council) in the Ashkenazi communities. Schooled by bitter memories of the crisis in Spain on the eve of the expulsion, the policy of the *ma'amad* tended to be conservative and authoritarian in the extreme. One of the characteristic features of *ma'amad* policy was that on completion of its term of office the *ma'amad* itself appointed its successors. A nominee was obliged to accept the assignment. Those who disobeyed the directives of the *ma'amad* were fined heavily, and in some cases were even excommunicated.

Bibliography: Baron, Community, 2 (1942), 52. [N.E.]

MA'ANIT (Heb. מַעֲנִית; "furrow"), kibbutz in central Israel, E. of Pardes Ḥannah, affiliated with Kibbutz Arẓi Ha-Shomer ha-Ẓa'ir. It was founded in 1942 by pioneers from Czechoslovakia. In the Israel *War of Independence (1948), the village, lying close to the Samarian Hills, was exposed to Arab attack. Ma'anit has intensive, irrigated mixed farming, and is a partner in a nearby starch and glucose factory. Ma'anit lies near the site of ancient *Narbata where, in 66 C.E., Jews from Caesarea sought refuge when the war against Rome broke out (Jos., Wars, 2:5, 14). In its initial years, the kibbutz bore the name Narbata. [E.O.]

MA'ARAVOT (Heb. מַעֲרָבוֹת, also *ma'aravim,* sing. מַעֲרָבִית *ma'aravit*), an arrangement of *piyyutim* that embellish the *Ma'ariv (*Arvit)* prayers for festivals and special Sabbaths. The *piyyutim* are topical and conclude with an allusion to all the blessings recited before the **Amidah.* Originally these *piyyutim* were used in place of the regular prayers, but in the course of time the regular prayers were reinstated and the *piyyutim* were offered at the end of each prayer just before its blessing. Except for the lengthy *piyyut* recited before *Mi Khamokha* ("Who is like Thee"), the *piyyutim* are brief. This lengthy *piyyut* is composed in the form of a single or double alphabetical acrostic with the name of the author appearing at the end. Some communities customarily added a *reshut* ("prelude") to the *Ma'ariv.* On the eve of Shavuot, *Tosefet Bikkur* ("Addition of First Fruit") or simply *Bikkur,* a *piyyut* whose subject is the bringing of the first fruits, is recited. The *ma'aravot* are in current usage in most Ashkenazi communities, but there are no *ma'aravot* in the Sephardi rite.

Bibliography: Elbogen, Gottesdienst, 212; Idelsohn, Liturgy, 194, 330f. [A.M.H.]

MA'AREKHET HA-ELOHUT (Heb. מַעֲרֶכֶת הָאֱלֹהוּת; "The Order of God"), an anonymous systematic book of early Kabbalah literature. Moses Cordovero attributed it to Todros *Abulafia while Jacob Reifmann believed the author to be *Baḥya b. Asher. In the first edition, published in Ferrara in 1557, the book is attributed to *Perez the tosafist, but no author is named on the title page of the Mantua edition of 1558. The annotator remarks in his preface that "it is written that the author is the *gaon* Perez the tosafist, but the truth is not known." There is no doubt whatsoever that the book cannot be ascribed to any of these writers. It was written at the end of the 13th or the beginning of the 14th century by a man who associated with the disciples of Solomon b. Abraham *Adret, in whose name and that of the kabbalist R. Isaac (probably Adret's colleague Isaac b. Todros) the author introduces some kabbalistic interpretations. There is reason to believe that he made use of *Keter Shem Tov* by Shem Tov (b. Abraham) ibn Gaon, which was written around that time.

Because of its systematic nature, *Ma'arekhet ha-Elohut* became one of the classical books of Kabbalah. The many commentaries on it, most of which were composed in Italy in the 15th and early 16th centuries, show the great interest it aroused. About ten commentaries were written, two of which were printed: the anonymous commentary which Judah *Ḥayyat called *"Paz"* (*Perush Zulati,* "commentary not by me"), and the commentary written by Judah Ḥayyat at the request of the elders of Mantua. The identity of the first commentator has not been established; recently it has become apparent that he was probably Reuben Ẓarefati, author of *Perush ha-Yeri'ah ha-Gedolah* and *Perush ha-Yeri'ah ha-Ketannah.* According to Judah Ḥayyat, and as indicated by the many extant manuscripts, this commentary circulated widely in Italy during the late 15th century. *"Paz"* was printed in full in Ferrara and in a considerably abridged version in the Mantua edition (1558). The two commentaries are largely independent works and in their thematic discussions they go beyond the framework of a commentary. The systematic analysis of *Ma'arekhet ha-Elohut* by David Neumark (see bibl.) contributes very little to the understanding of the work, and Neumark's belief that it exerted a great influence on the Zohar is chronologically impossible and conceptually incorrect.

In general, the author's main aim was to remove, or at least weaken, the mythical elements which are basic in the Kabbalah and in certain rabbinic sayings. The author's theosophical tendency is not made apparent in the first two chapters, which are essentially theological and do not constitute a consistent theory. The author's purpose in the first chapter is to indicate that true faith is based on the concept of a personal God, the Creator of the world and its supervisor. God acts in the world and He can alter the laws of nature, as proven by the miracles related in the Bible. The second chapter, however, stresses the absolute unity of God, which is based on the denial of any corporeality, plurality, or change within Him. In God there is neither modification of thought nor of action. There is no change in Him and none in His deeds. The changes revealed by worldly events are caused by the actions of man. Man is a vessel which contains God's action, which is simple and undifferentiated but is received differently by different people, each one according to his merit.

The author's theosophical speculations first appear in the third chapter. The Divinity is here defined as the totality of the ten *Sefirot,* which constitute God's direction of the world. This aspect of God alone is expressed in the Bible and Talmud while the Divinity Itself, referred to as *Ein-Sof* ("infinity"), is hinted at only to initiates. *Ein-Sof,* the infinite, the hidden aspect of the Divine, is expressed neither through the order of nature nor in the laws of the Torah. The act of emanation itself, which is the emergence of the *Sefirot* from *Ein-Sof,* does not constitute an innovation or a change in the Divine: it is simply the revelation of what had been hitherto concealed. The author attempts to explain through reasoning and homily that both the legends of the rabbis on the modification in God's thought regarding the ways in which the world should be conducted and the description of the dynamic relations among the diverse *Sefirot* in Kabbalah literature are simply a projection of human experience upon Divinity. Because it is observable in human experience that man decides on the most desirable alternative by a process of choice and deliberation, he therefore ascribes to divine leadership an ideal synthesis of Justice and Mercy, as if it resulted from a similar process. In a similar manner, he expounds the aggadic legend concerning the waning of the moon which the kabbalists related to an act occurring in the world of the *Sefirot;* other legends are also given a kabbalistic interpretation.

The chapter entitled *"Sha'ar ha-Harisah"* (about the nature of sin) is of particular interest. According to this, the sins related in the Bible as committed by individuals or generations are essentially sins of a mystical character. Though the sin was actually committed its essential significance lies in the thought connected with it. In some instances the sin is brought about by an excess of meditation, while in others it results from the sinner's wish to disrupt the pattern of relationship of the *Sefirot.* Most of these themes had already appeared in earlier kabbalistic literature but here they are given a systematic description, and the book is also a systematic summary of most themes treated in early Kabbalah literature.

Bibliography: D. Neumark, *Toledot ha-Filosofyah be-Yisrael,* 1 (1921), 192–206; G. Scholem, in: KS, 21 (1943/44), 284–95; Scholem, Mysticism, index; E. Gottlieb, *Ha-Kabbalah be-Khitvei Rabbenu Baḥya ben Asher* (1970), index; idem, in: *Sefer Zikkaron le-Binyamin De Vries* (1968), 295–304. [E.G.]

MAARIV (Heb. מַעֲרִיב), Hebrew afternoon newspaper published in Tel Aviv. *Maariv* was founded in 1948 by the journalist Ezriel *Carlebach after he and a group of editorial colleagues left the evening paper **Yedi'ot Aḥaronot.* Carlebach was the first to separate entirely the publication of afternoon and morning newspapers (most morning papers having published their own evening papers at one time or another). He created a special style for his paper which was versatile and lively in its news reportage, journalism, and features. *Maariv* achieved the largest circulation of any newspaper in Israel. This success resulted from the paper's coverage of every sphere of life in Israel, its network of correspondents throughout the world, the young generation of newspapermen it trained, and the articles contributed by public figures, literary men, and scientists. The paper appears daily (in fact, in the late morning) composed of 30 to 40 pages and on Fridays of almost 100 pages, which include supplements on literature, culture, entertainment, and sports. After the death of E. Carlebach, A. Dissentchik served as chief editor. In 1970 *Maariv's* average weekday circulation was 160,000 and on Friday 210,000.

מעריב
עתון ערב
המחיר 10 מא"י
העורך: דר. עזריאל קרליבך
יום א' א' אלול, תש"ח א' למדינת ישראל
נציגי רוסיה בארצות המזרח התיכון אוספים חומר נגד ברנדוט ומשקיפיו
מעריב מהיום בהוצאה אחת
מקדונלד אצל רמז
העירקים פתחו באש על משקיפי או"ם
קונסול ארה"ב דן עם עבדאללה על הכרה אמריקנית בעבר הירדן
שליח לברנאדוט בענין הרצח בעזה
שומאן הצליח להרכיב קבינט
הקונסול הבריטי בירושלים מכיר במטבע שלנו
דנים על חלוקת התפקידים בהנהלת הסוכנות
500 עולים
הוראות חדשות לפיקוח על יהלומים
"הבימה" חוזרה
ברנדוט – למצרים
"ההפוגה גוזלת את הנצחון מישראל"
מכריז ציר הקונגרס האמריקני סומרס
טיפוס בבירות
פעולה נגד פריצות בירושלים
זעקה בשכם
משרד למסירה
למכירה
ר' אפרים קורנמהל ז"ל

An early edition of *Maariv,* September 1948. The main headline reads: "Russian representatives in the Middle East gathering material against Bernadotte and his observers."

Bibliography: *Maariv* (Feb. 14, 1958; Feb. 17, 1961; Feb. 16, 1968); G. Kressel, *Toledot ha-Ittonut ha-Ivrit be-Ereẓ Yisrael* (1964), 191–3. [G.K.]

MAARSEN, ISAAC (1893–1943), Dutch rabbi, chief rabbi of The Hague. Maarsen was born in Amsterdam, where he studied at the Amsterdam rabbinical seminary and at the university, graduating in classical philology. He was ordained as rabbi in 1918 and became teacher of Talmud in the high school department of the rabbinical seminary. In 1919 he was appointed a *dayyan* and member of the Amsterdam rabbinate. Five years later he was appointed chief rabbi of The Hague, then the second-largest community in Holland. He excelled chiefly as preacher and lecturer, and in his writings against Reform Judaism. He translated the tractate *Avot* and medieval and modern poetry from Hebrew into Dutch, and engaged in research on the history of the Dutch rabbinate. His reputation rests on his studies in the fields of rabbinical literature, which appeared in various Hebrew periodicals. His main works are: *Tiferet le-Moshe* (1928), notes to Naḥmanides' commentary on the Pentateuch; *Parshandata* (1930–36), a critical edition of Rashi's commentary to the Prophets and Hagiographa, which he did not complete, only three parts appearing, on the Minor Prophets, Isaiah, and Psalms; and *Muḥlefet ha-Shitah* (1940), on the difference between Rashi's comments on the Bible and the same verses when quoted in the Talmud. He met his death in the Holocaust.

Bibliography: *Elleh-Ezkerah,* 1 (1956), 304–8. [B.D.-V.]

MA'ARUFYA (מַעֲרוּפְיָא), medieval Hebrew concept signifying the tie between a Christian client and the Jew who was his permanent supplier, moneylender, or financial administrator. The *din ha-ma'arufya* ("law of *ma'arufya*") was never generally prevalent; where it applied it specified that the relationship between the Jewish merchant and his client was the exclusive prerogative of that Jew alone, which the *community *(kehillah)* protected by means of the **ḥerem* (ban). According to some scholars the term derives from the French while others consider that it comes from Arabic. Some scholars have drawn a distinction between the implications of *ma'arufya* and *ma'arifa,* considering that the first denotes a non-Jewish customer who maintains commercial relations with a certain Jew while the second denotes the exclusive right to trade with him. However, this view is untenable since both forms are used indiscriminately.

Ma'arufya was known in the communities of France and Germany in the tenth century. It is possible that this usage originated in the privileges granted to merchants by the municipal councils or lords of various European towns during the 10th and 11th centuries guaranteeing them trading monopolies. From the responsa of *Gershom b. Judah (Me'or ha-Golah), it appears that the *din ha-ma'arufya* was applied in almost every community. However, 11th-century sources indicate that by then the custom was not accepted everywhere: "there are places where the *ma'arufya* is enforced and there are places where it is not enforced" (Joseph Bonfils (Tuv Elem) in: *Haggahot Maimoniyyot* of Meir ha-Kohen, *Hilkhot Shekhenim*, 6:8). As Jewish business activites were narrowed down to *moneylending in Ashkenazi areas toward the end of the 12th century, *ma'arufya* lost much of its former importance. The *din ha-ma'arufya* is not explicitly recorded in the communities of Spain, although in them too the trend against competition is evident. The essence of *ma'arufya*, and often the term itself, was operative in the communities of Poland-Lithuania and Russia until the modern era. Because of the variety of occupations there, the scope of the concept was applied to give craftsmen and artisans exclusive rights over their customers. The regulations of the crafts' associations included articles intended to assure the established rights of artisans to their clients. If a craftsman had done work for the *ma'arufya* of another craftsman, he was obliged to remit all his profits to him without deducting his own expenses. These rights were bequeathed from father to son, and when there were no heirs the rights were transferred to the dead man's guild.

See also *Arenda, **Ḥazakah*.

Bibliography: I. Levitats, *Jewish Community in Russia* (1943), 235ff.; Sh. Eidelberg, in: HJ, 15 (1953), 59–66; Baron, Social², 4 (1957), 185; Dinur, Golah, 1 pt. 1 (1958²), 382; 2 pt. 2 (1966²), 250ff.; I. Agus, *Urban Civilization in Pre-Crusade Europe*, 2 vols. (1965), index.

[Ed.]

MA'AS (Heb. מַעַשׂ; "Action" or "Deed"), moshav in central Israel, near *Petaḥ Tikvah, affiliated to Tenu'at ha-Moshavim, founded in 1934 in the framework of the Thousand Families Settlement Scheme by veteran agricultural workers. They gradually enlarged their holdings from auxiliary to full-fledged farms while earning their living as hired laborers in the Petaḥ Tikvah citrus groves (therefore calling their village, until the 1950s, Be-Hadragah, "Gradually"). Citrus groves constitute the prominent farm branch in Ma'as. In 1968 its population was 400. [E.O.]

MA'ASEH (Heb. מַעֲשֶׂה), a factual circumstance from which a halakhic rule or principle is derived; as such it constitutes one of the Jewish law sources. A legal principle originating from *ma'aseh* is formally distinguished from those originating from one of the other legal sources of Jewish law—such as Midrash (see *Interpretation), **takkanah*, **minhag*, and **sevara* (see **Mishpat Ivri*)—by the fact that in the latter cases the legal principle appears in selfstanding form, whereas in *Ma'aseh* it is integrated with and bound to a particular set of concrete facts, from which it must be separated and abstracted if it is to be enunciated. As will be seen below, this formal distinction is also of substantive importance. The term *ma'aseh* is customarily used in tannaitic sources (Shab. 24:5; BB 10:8; Eduy. 2:3); in the Babylonian Talmud the equivalent term is *uvda* and in the Jerusalem Talmud sometimes *dilma* (see, e.g., TJ, Ber. 1:1, 2c, Pe'ah 3:9, 17d; et al.).

Substance of Ma'aseh. Ma'aseh constitutes a legal source in two ways: one is represented by the judgment given in a concrete "case" before the court or competent adjudicator (halakhic scholar)—as in other legal systems; the other, by the specific act or conduct of a competent halakhic scholar, not necessarily in his capacity as judge or *posek*. In either case *ma'aseh* serves as a source for the determination of a halakhic principle as regards both civil law *(dinei mamonot)* and ritual law *(dinei issur ve-hetter)*.

Citation of a halakhic principle by way of *ma'aseh* does not in every case warrant the conclusion that such *ma'aseh* is necessarily the source from which the principle was evolved—since the principle may possibly have been in existence before and the halakhic scholar only have applied it in such case. In this event, the *ma'aseh* is not constitutive but only declarative of the existence of the particular halakhic rule (see below). However, *ma'aseh*—even when only declarative—lends the particular halakhic principle a special validity, as *ma'aseh rav* ("an act is weightier," Shab. 21a) or *ma'aseh adif* ("an act is preferred," BB 83a), since a rule tested in the crucible of practical life is regarded by the scholars as having a different force from one for which there is no evidence of its practical application. Hence, once a particular halakhic principle has been followed in practice—even though its application is subject to dispute—it may no longer be varied, since "what has been done is no longer open to discussion" (RH 29b, concerning blowing of the *shofar* on Rosh Ha-Shanah when it falls on a Sabbath).

The particular force of a halakhic principle originating from *ma'aseh* is tied to the substantive principle underlying the entire halakhic system, namely that the Torah was entrusted to the authority *(al da'atan)* of the halakhic scholars (see *Authority, Rabbinical; **Mishpat Ivri*), it being presumed that the judicial decision and conduct in daily life of the competent halakhic scholar are the outcome of his penetration and correct understanding of the *halakhah*. The scholars were fully aware of the power attaching to an act of deciding the law and for this reason exercised great care before doing so (Git. 19a, 37a, and Rashi thereto). In particular, the halakhic scholar is held to reveal, by his conduct, the active image of the *halakhah* and therefore "the service of the Torah is greater than the study of it" (Ber. 7b); one of the ways by virtue of which the Torah is acquired is "attendance on the sages" (Avot 6:6), since practical application of the Torah leads to appreciation of the living and active *halakhah*, its correctness and creative force. For this reason it was required of the halakhic scholars to act with much forethought in their day-to-day conduct of halakhic matters (Tosef., Dem. 5:24 concerning the discussion between R. Gamaliel and R. Akiva); R. Ishmael explained his particularly careful approach toward a certain rule concerning the *Keri'at Shema* in these words: "lest the pupils see and lay down *halakhah* for generations" (Ber. 11a; Tosef., Ber. 1:6).

In Jewish law, *ma'aseh* constitutes a legal source, not because it has the force of binding precedent which (as will be seen below, the Jewish legal system generally does not recognize as a principle), but because the scholars recognized it as a lawmaking source from which to derive halakhic principles becoming part of the general halakhic system. The fact that it remained permissible to dispute a halakhic principle derived from *ma'aseh* did not serve to deprive it of its substantive character as one of the legal sources of Jewish law—just as, for instance, Midrash remained such notwithstanding the fact that different and contradictory halakhic principles were often derived from it by the use of different methods of Bible exegesis.

An Act of Deciding the Law. The laws derived from *ma'aseh* form a very substantial part of the general system of Jewish law—the latter representing, in its nature and path of development, a classic example of a legal system founded on a series of legal acts or "cases," adding up to a comprehensive system of case law (see also *Codification of Law). This character was already stamped on the *halakhah* in the Torah, in which there are many laws enjoined in relation to a particular act or event, as, e.g., in the matter of the blasphemy of the Name (Lev. 24:10–23), the gathering of sticks on the Sabbath (Num. 15:32–36), the law of inheritance concerning the daughters of Zelophehad (Num. 27:1–11), and the law of the second Passover (Num. 9:1–8).

Talmudic sources are replete with *halakhot*, in all fields of the law, quoted in the form of an act of legal decision or in the form of an independent ruling which is, however, either preceded or followed by the facts of the relevant case. The case described does not always form the original source of the halakhic rule, but frequently, and in various ways, it is possible to prove that the rule was actually created as an outcome of the case. Sometimes this fact is expressly stated. Thus, with reference to the law that a bill of divorce must be prepared by the husband for delivery to his wife, the Mishnah states that it suffices if the bill be prepared by the wife provided that the husband procures the signature of witnesses to it since what matters is the signature and not the person by whom the bill is drawn up (Git. 2:5). This principle was learned from a case that occurred in a small village near Jerusalem, a case in which the scholars decided that it was only necessary for a bond of indebtedness to be signed, and not drawn up, by the witnesses (Eduy. 2:3). Similarly, the *amoraim* derived from earlier cases a number of halakhic principles concerning the laws of proselytization (Yev. 46b) and the laws of restoring a loss (*hashavat avedah:* cf. BM 25b with TJ, BM 2:4, 8c—the rule of Abba b. Zavda).

Sometimes derivation of a halakhic principle from the *ma'aseh* is not expressly acknowledged, but from the content it may be deduced that the principle was derived from the adjacent case description. Thus, according to ancient *halakhah,* suretyship for a loan undertaking was valid only if made prior to establishment of the principal debt, i.e., the creditor as it were agreeing to grant the loan on the strength of such suretyship. However, R. Ishmael, in a case that came before him, extended the scope of suretyship by holding it valid in certain circumstances, even if made after grant of the loan, i.e., if the person standing *surety signed after signature by the witnesses of the deed of loan. Ben Nanas differed, maintaining that the suretyship had to precede grant of the loan. The new principle enunciated by R. Ishmael is earlier stated in the Mishnah, in the form of a selfstanding legal rule (BB 10:8; for further examples, see Ned. 8:5; BM 30a).

Conduct of a Halakhic Scholar. Talmudic sources also contain a great number of *halakhot,* in all fields of the law, stated in the form of a description of the conduct of a halakhic scholar and in like manner to the statement of acts of legal decision. Thus in one instance the Mishnah (Shab. 24:5) first quotes several *halakhot* concerning permissible labors on the Sabbath in the form of independent rules: "they may stop up a light-hole or measure a piece of stuff or a *mikveh*"; in continuation, it is stated that in the time of R. Zadok's father and in the time of Abba Saul b. Botnit there occurred a case in which such labors were done on the Sabbath and in conclusion it is stated that from such occurrence the permissibility of these labors on the Sabbath was learned. An analysis of the *halakhot* thus stated offers proof that even when the selfstanding halakhic ruling is stated in the Mishnah before the *ma'aseh,* it does not exclude the possibility that chronologically speaking the *ma'aseh* preceded such a ruling and that the former is the source of the latter—except that the compiler of the Mishnah saw fit to state first the ruling and then the *ma'aseh.* At times disputes concerning a tradition entertained by the halakhic scholars and relating to the conduct of a particular halakhic scholar led in turn to disputing opinions as regards the halakhic principle to be derived from the aforesaid conduct (see, e.g., Suk. 2:7 concerning the dispute between Bet Shammai and Bet Hillel, arising in connection with the *ma'aseh* of R. Johanan b. ha-Ḥorani).

Distinguishing Ma'aseh. Just as a halakhic principle acquires special force and significance from the fact that it has been applied in a practical case, so the latter fact entails the risk of possible error in the manner of deduction of the principle from the practical case. Hence, in deduction of the principle it is required that two important distinctions be made: first, the factual aspect of the case must be precisely distinguished from the legal aspect; secondly—and more difficult—the part that is not material and has no bearing on the halakhic conclusion must be distinguished from the material part which leads to the halakhic conclusion. This distinguishing process is sometimes directed toward a specific purpose, for instance toward restriction of the halakhic principle derived from a case when the need for it arises in a concrete matter for decision. In English law—which has the system of case law—the process of distinguishing is also greatly developed, and here too one of the main functions of the process is to distinguish between the *ratio decidendi* and mere *obiter dictum.* The distinguishing process has been of primary importance to the development of both legal systems.

The phrase commonly employed in the Mishnah for the act of distinguishing is *einah hi ha-middah,* "that is not the inference" (Pes. 1:6–7), and in the Talmud, "This was not stated explicitly but by implication" (BM 36a, et al.; see also BB 130b and Rashbam thereto s.v. *halakhah adifah*), or "Tell me what actually transpired!" (BM 70a, et al.). The process of distinguishing is well illustrated in Bava Meẓia 36a. Rav is quoted as holding that a bailee who entrusted a bailment to another bailee is not liable—i.e., for any more than he would have been liable had he kept the bailment himself—since he entrusted it to a person having understanding *(ben da'at);* however, R. Johanan is recorded as holding the first bailee liable for all damage occasioned to the bailment while it is deposited with the second bailee, since the owner might say to the former that he entrusted the bailment to his personal care and did not wish it entrusted to another (see **Shomerim*). In the continuation of the discussion it is stated, "R. Ḥisda said: this was not stated by Rav explicitly but by implication," i.e., that Rav's rule was deduced by implication from a legal decision he gave in a practical case, but that the rule was deduced in error because no proper distinction had been made. The facts of the case decided by Rav were as follows: Gardeners used to deposit their spades every day, on completion of their work, with an old woman; one day they deposited their spades with one of their members and the latter, wishing to join in some festivity, deposited them with the old woman, from whom they were stolen; when the other gardeners sought compensation from the bailee gardener for the loss of their spades, Rav held the latter exempt from liability. From his decision it had been erroneously concluded that the latter held in favor of exempting a first bailee from liability for damage occasioned to a bailment he had entrusted to a second bailee, for Rav had only exempted the first bailee in that particular case because of the fact that the gardeners had generally been accustomed to deposit their spades with the old woman, and were therefore precluded from saying that they wanted their spades entrusted to the gardener only. Generally, however, if the facts were different, a bailee would be liable if damage resulted to the bailment he entrusted to another, even in Rav's opinion. In this manner the Talmud records how the deduction of an erroneous legal conclusion from a particular case is illuminated by the process of distinguishing.

The Talmud (BB 130b) provides basic guidance on the manner of deriving a legal conclusion from a case without apprehension of error: "The *halakhah* may not be derived either from a theoretical conclusion or from a practical decision (without knowing the facts of the case) unless one has been told that the rule is to be taken as a rule for practical decisions; once a person has asked and been informed that a *halakhah* was to be taken as a guide for practical decisions (and therefore knows the facts), he may continue to give practical decisions accordingly" (see Rashbam, ad loc.). In the 13th century the approach to *ma'aseh* and the distinguishing process was expressed in these terms: "Not in vain were the many practical cases embracing various rules written into the Talmud, not so that the law concerning the relevant matter be applied in accordance with what is stated there, but so that the scholar, by having frequent reference to them, shall acquire the art of weighing his opinion and a sound approach in giving practical decisions" (Resp. Abraham b. Moses b. Maimon no. 97).

In Post-Talmudic Times. *Ma'aseh,* both as an act of legal decision and as conduct of a halakhic scholar, continued to serve as an important legal source in post-talmudic times. The halakhic scholars of this period derived many legal conclusions from practical cases in talmudic literature. Thus Maimonides decided that a person engaged in study of the Torah shall stop studying and recite the *Keri'at Shema* whenever it is the time to do so; however, a person engaged in public matters shall not desist from such activity, even if meanwhile the time for *Keri'at Shema* passes (Yad, Keri'at Shema, 2:5). Maimonides derived this *halakhah* from an account in the Tosefta stating that R. Akiva and R. Eleazar b. Azariah omitted to recite *Keri'at Shema* because they were preoccupied with public matters (Tosef., Ber. 1:4; see comment of Elijah Gaon to Sh. Ar., OḤ 70:4).

In like manner, *ma'asim* of the post-talmudic scholars, in the form of both practical decisions (see below) and conduct, served as a legal source for the deduction of *halakhot* by subsequent scholars. *Ma'asim* of the latter kind are frequently quoted in post-talmudic halakhic literature in the form of testimony by pupils to the conduct of their teachers in different matters of the *halakhah.* Special books of *halakhah* were even compiled in which a considerable part of the material was based on the author's observation of the conduct of his eminent teacher, for he had not only acquired the latter's teachings but also served him in daily life. An example of such a work is the *Sefer Tashbeẓ* of Simeon b. Ẓemah *Duran, a pupil of *Meir b. Baruch of Rothenburg, which deals mainly with the laws in the Shulḥan Arukh's *Oraḥ Ḥayyim* and *Yoreh De'ah,* and to some extent also with matters of family and civil law, largely quoted by the author as the manner in which he had seen his teacher conduct himself (see, e.g., sections 1, 7, 18–23, et al.).

The Responsa Literature. With the development in post-talmudic times of one of the main branches of the literary sources of Jewish law, namely the responsa literature, *ma'aseh* came to fulfill an important role as a lawmaking source. The responsa literature represents the case law of the Jewish legal system. A concrete problem that arose in daily life—whether in matters between individuals or in matters of man's relationship to the Almighty, in matters of civil or ritual law—was brought before the local *dayyan* or halakhic scholar, and they, whenever they experienced any doubt or difficulty in reaching a solution to the problem at hand, turned to the distinguished halakhic scholars of their generation. Certain matters, particularly disputes between the individual and the public or its representative bodies, came directly before the most prominent halakhic scholars. They deliberated all the factual and legal aspects of the case and submitted their findings and conclusion in a written responsum to the questioner. The *she'elah u-teshuvah*—question and response—accordingly represents a classic example of an act of legal decision, and answers to all the requirements set by the talmudic sages for recognition of *ma'aseh* as a legal source, since this procedure is a true application of "having asked and been informed that a *halakhah* is to be taken as a guide for practical decisions..." (above; BB 130b). This character of the responsa literature has served to lend the legal principle emerging from it a particular standing and force exceeding that of a principle derived from the commentaries and novellae and even, in the opinion of the majority of halakhic scholars, exceeding that of a principle derived from the books of *halakhot* and *pesakim* (see *Codification of Law) in cases of inconsistency between the two. Hence, "more is to be learned from the conclusions stated in the responsa than from those stated by the *posekim* [in the codes], since the latter did not write their conclusions in the course of deciding the law in a concrete instance" (Resp. Maharil no. 72). Similarly, "when *halakhah* is laid down in practice there is greater penetration to the heart of the matter than in the course of theoretical study; there is also greater divine guidance *(sayata di-shemaya)* in a practical case... for a conclusion that comes in answer to a practical case is preferable and more directed to the real truth than what is forthcoming from mere theoretical study" (*Meshiv Davar,* pt. 1, no. 24).

Jewish Law and Binding Precedent. Recognition in Jewish law of *ma'aseh* as a legal source from which may be derived the principles that emerge from it is unconnected with the question of whether any conclusion so derived has the force of binding precedent for the purpose of deciding the law in a similar case. In fact, as will be seen below, Jewish law does not recognize the principle of binding precedent.

PRECEDENT IN OTHER LEGAL SYSTEMS. The legal "case" occupies a very modest place in the source hierarchy of the Roman legal system; certainly the latter does not recognize at all the principle of binding precedent. Justinian expressly laid down that judgments be given according to laws and not precedents: *"non exemplis, sed legibus iudicandum est"* (C. 7. 45. 13; see J. Salmond, *Jurisprudence* (1966[12]), 141f.; C.K. Allen, *Law in the Making* (1964[7]), 342f.). Most continental legal systems, following that of Rome, exemplify the codificatory system of law, and in these the decisions of the courts represent no more than material of a theoretical and persuasive nature, without binding force (Salmond, *ibid.*). The position is different in English law: "The importance of judicial precedents has always been a distinguishing characteristic of English law. The great body of the common or unwritten law is almost entirely the product of decided cases, accumulated in an immense series of reports extending backward with scarcely a break to the reign of Edward I at the close of the 13th century... A judicial precedent speaks in England with authority; it is not merely evidence of the law but a source of it" (Salmond, p. 141). As regards the extent to which the courts are bound by precedent, Salmond goes on to say: "It is necessary to point out that the phrase 'the doctrine of precedent' has two meanings. In the first, which may be called the loose meaning, the phrase means merely that precedents are reported, may be cited, and will probably be followed by the courts. This was the doctrine that prevailed in England until the 19th century, and it is still the only sense in which a doctrine of precedent prevails on the continent. In the second, the strict meaning, the phrase means that precedents not only have great authority but must (in certain circumstances) be followed. This was the rule developed during the 19th century and completed in some respects during the 20th" (p. 142). The merits of this development toward the strict meaning of precedent have not remained unquestioned, and in recent times there has been increasing discussion of the correctness and efficacy of this approach (*ibid.*, p. 143 and see note, p. ix, concerning the extra-judicial statement made in the House of Lords in 1966, relaxing the rule of being bound to follow its own previous decisions "when it appears right to do so").

COMPARISON OF PRECEDENT IN ENGLISH AND IN JEWISH LAW. At their respective starting points the two legal systems have much in common in their approach to precedent but they diverge in their manner of development. In both "case" constitutes a source of law; both are, to a large extent, built up around case law, and have developed in consequence of concrete legal decisions in daily life; the basic material at the heart of most Jewish law codifications is likewise the product of legal principles derived from day-to-day legal decisions (see *Codification of Law), and from this point of view the main difference between the two legal systems is that the Jewish law equivalent of the "immense series of reports," namely the responsa literature, dates from the geonic period onward, i.e., from the middle of the eighth century and not, as in England, from the end of the 13th century (see **Mishpat Ivri*). On the other hand, Jewish law has not accepted the doctrine of precedent in the strict meaning of the term—as has English law, commencing from the 19th century—and the power of *ma'aseh* in Jewish law has been confined to that of precedent in the loose meaning of the term, as described by Salmond, "precedents are reported, may be cited, and will probably be followed by the courts." For two reasons, each of which will be dealt with below, Jewish law has been unable to adopt the doctrine of a binding precedent which imposes its inherent halakhic conclusion on the *dayyan* when deciding the matter before him: first, because of this legal system's conception of the substantive nature of a judgment given between the two parties to a suit; secondly, because of the method and approach of Jewish law toward deciding of the *halakhah* in general.

SUBSTANTIVE NATURE OF A JUDGMENT IN JEWISH LAW AND THE PROBLEM OF PRECEDENT. In Jewish law, the finality of a judgment is subject to many reservations, even in relation to the instant parties themselves. According to the original Jewish law, no judgment is absolute and final in the sense of *res judicata* in Roman law, except in so far as it accords with the true objective state of affairs as regards both the facts and the law. Hence, it always remained possible for a judgment given by the court on the available facts to be set aside, and for the matter to be heard afresh when either of the parties was able to produce new evidence. Since this possibility posed a serious obstacle to the due administration of justice and to orderly economic life, which demand an end to litigation, the practice was introduced of having the parties acknowledge—in court and prior to judgment—that they had no further evidence whatever to adduce, thereby annulling in advance the efficacy of any further evidence they might later wish to bring (see Sanh. 31a; Yad, Sanhedrin, 7:6–8; Sh. Ar., ḤM 20). Similarly, the original law held that any judgment which transpires to be wrong in law—i.e., in case of error as regards decided and clear *halakhah*—is inherently invalid, although not so in case of an erroneous exercise of discretion. Here again the way was found to ensure the stability and finality of a judgment (Sanh. 33a; Yad, Sanhedrin 6:1; Sh. Ar., ḤM 25:1–3 and Rema thereto; see also Gulak, Yesodei, 4 (1922), 175–83, 201–3; and see *Practice and Procedure (Civil)).

A judgment in Jewish law accordingly has a dual nature: theoretically it is not final until the truth has been fully explored; in practice reservations were laid down—which would be accepted by the parties and normally would apply automatically—aimed at ensuring an end to litigation between the parties to a dispute and at acceptance of the judgment as decisive and as determining the respective rights of the parties.

The stated theoretical nature of a judgment, which applies even as regards determination of the law for the instant parties themselves, has necessarily entailed the conclusion that a judgment shall not have the force of a binding precedent in relation to a similar problem arising between different parties; hence "if another case comes before him even if it be a like case in all respects—he may deal with it as he sees fit, since the *dayyan* need only act according to what his own eyes see" (Nov. Ran to BB 130b; Nov. Ritba, BB *ibid.*).

METHODS AND APPROACH OF JEWISH LAW CONCERNING DECIDING OF THE HALAKHAH AND THE PROBLEM OF PRECEDENT. The doctrine of binding precedent also conflicts with the very method and approach of Jewish law concerning deciding the *halakhah* (see **Mishpat Ivri;* *Authority, Rabbinical; *Codification of Law). The fact of halakhic difference of opinion, as the latter developed in the course of time, is regarded as a phenomenon that is not only legitimate but also desirable and indicative of the vitality of the *halakhah* and of the possibility of different approaches, based on common general principles, in the search for solutions to new problems that arise. The decisive yardstick in a case of halakhic dispute, is the correctness of each opinion "in accordance only with the Talmud of R. Ashi" (i.e., the Babylonian Talmud: *Piskei ha-Rosh*, Sanh. 4:6) and based "with definite proof on the Talmud, as well as the Jerusalem Talmud and Tosefta, when there is no definite decision in the Talmud" (*Yam shel Shelomo*, introd. to BK). For this reason no codification of Jewish law was accepted which laid before the *dayyan* deciding the law one single, arbitrary, and final opinion on any given matter. For the same reason Jewish law accepted the doctrine of *hilkheta ke-Vatra'ei* ("the law is according to the later scholars"), which was designed to ensure freedom of decision for later scholars—albeit with due reference to and regard for the decisions of earlier scholars. The basic rule applicable is that the judgment of a person who has erred because he was unaware of the decisions of earlier scholars shall be of no force as soon as that person gains such knowledge and realises his error; however, "if he does not find their statements correct and sustains his own view with evidence that is acceptable to his contemporaries—the authority of Jephthah in his generation was as that of Samuel in his, and there is only the judge that 'shall be in those days'—he may contradict their statements, since all matters which are not clarified in the Talmud of R. Ashi and Ravina may be questioned and restated by any person, and even the statements of the *geonim* may be differed from . . . just as the later *amoraim* differed from the earlier ones; on the contrary, we regard the statements of the later scholars to be more authoritative since the latter knew not only the legal thinking of their contemporaries but also that of the earlier scholars, and in deciding between the different views they reached the heart of a matter" (*Piskei ha-Rosh*, loc. cit.).

This conception of a flexible and dynamic legal order naturally left no room for the doctrine that especially a conclusion springing from a practical decision should impose itself on the judicial process. The court which is apprised of a matter has the task of referring to, and taking into proper consideration, all the available relevant laws and certainly the rules emerging from earlier practical decisions, particularly when the halakhic principle emerging from the practical decision has been accepted without exception in a series of legal decisions ("daily practical acts of decision," Ket. 68b; BB 173b; etc.). However, if after such study the judge should, in reasonable manner and in reliance on the halakhic system itself, come to a different legal conclusion from that reached by earlier scholars, he will have not only the right but also the duty to decide as he sees fit; such decision will take precedence over an earlier decision in a like matter, since the judge will also have known the legal thinking of earlier scholars and have decided as he did by going to the root of the matter.

Thus *ma'aseh* constitutes one of the significant lawmaking sources of the Jewish legal system, and every principle emerging from it becomes part of the accumulated body of laws comprising this system, in accordance with which the judge must decide. In standing and validity such principles are like any others deriving from the statements of *posekim* and halakhic scholars, and embraced by the common rule that the judge must consider every law on its substantive merits and decide, in the concrete case before him, according to his own knowledge and understanding deriving from due examination of all the relevant rules of Jewish law.

Bibliography: Epstein, Mishnah, 598–608; J. M. Guttmann, in: *Devir,* 1 (1922/23), 40–44; Ch. Tchernowitz, *Toledot ha-Halakhah,* 1 pt. 1 (1934), 189–96; A. Kaminka, *Meḥkarim ba-Mikra u-va-Talmud...* (1951), 1–41; A. Weiss, *Le-Ḥeker ha-Talmud* (1954), 111–67; Ḥ. Cohn, in: *Mishpat Ve-Khalkalah,* 3 (1956/57), 129–41; Ḥ. Albeck, *Mavo la-Mishnah* (1959), 92f.; E. Ẓ. Melamed, in: *Sinai,* 46 (1959/60), 152–65; B. de Vries, *Toledot ha-Halakhah ha-Talmudit* (1962), 169–78; M. Elon, in: ILR, 2 (1967), 548–50.

[M.E.]

MA'ASEH BOOK (from Heb. מַעֲשֶׂה, "story"; Yid. *Mayse Bukh,* "Book of Stories"). Like many other folk-books the *Ma'aseh Book* is a vast anonymous collection of stories and folktales, jests and merry tales, legends and oral traditions handed down from generation to generation by word of mouth and later recorded in writing in Yiddish. The book contains much of the talmudic *aggadah* and Midrash translated into the vernacular and copied and recopied by various writers who also adapted and Judaized material from other literatures.

The Old-Yiddish *Ma'aseh Book* was first published in Basle in 1602 under the title *Ayn Shoyn Mayse Bukh* by *Jacob b. Abraham of Mezhirech (also known as Jacob Pollak), who is known to have been a compiler of religious textbooks, printer, publisher, and bookseller. The *Ma'aseh Book* with its 254 (the Basle edition with 255) stories was compiled in the latter part of the 16th century, certainly not before 1580, the year when the book *"Kaftor va-Feraḥ"* by the mystic Jacob Luzzatto was published in Basle and from which the author of the *Ma'aseh Book* borrowed several stories to supplement his collection. However, it is clear that much of the narrative lore contained in the book was handed down from generation to generation before this time; extant manuscripts of Yiddish *Mayses* ("stories") bear witness to a lively and continuous productivity in the field of creative narrative traditions.

The *Ma'aseh Book* is part of the folk-literature in Yiddish designed for the use of the ordinary man and woman untutored in the holy language and its literature. Hence, its author uses a simple style and language. The book aims to provide a substitute for the widely circulated popular secular literature of the period, which the compiler of the *Ma'aseh Book,* like many others before him, considered ungodly. His collection, intended to replace this literature and provide a new kind of an *"aggadah* in the vernacular," is permeated with a spirit of piety to strengthen the reader's faith.

The *ma'aseh* corresponds to the Christian *exemplum* and serves to teach conduct and ethical principles, and also to provide entertainment for the masses. As such the *Ma'aseh Book* follows the example of numerous medieval Hebrew

Title page of the Old-Yiddish *Ayn Shoyn Mayse Bukh,* by Jacob b. Abraham of Mezhirech, Basle, 1602. Jerusalem, J.N.U.L.

collections designed to inculcate a moral dictum by way of a narration. It thus had a powerful influence on the didactic literature in Old-Yiddish of the time. The moral of the story was usually appended at the end of the tale and concluded with the hope for an early arrival of the Messiah. But even the pious compiler of the *Ma'aseh Book* could not entirely resist the trend of his time, and had to make some concessions to the popular taste by including various anecdotes, merry tales and fabliaux, often in keeping with the Italian or French *conte* and the German collections, with their licentious, sometimes satirical tone. The author drew profusely on extraneous sources, altering the plot or its characters where possible and adapting the tale to suit the Jewish feeling. In this rich collection oriental themes mingle with Western material, and midrashic stories with legendary lore. Between the first edition of Basle in 1602 and the year 1763, 12 subsequent editions were published. Even in the 19th century several shorter and modernized versions of the *Ma'aseh Book* were published. The popular *Ma'aseh Book* nourished to a great extent the ethical literature in Yiddish and served as a model for similar collections which were later composed and incorporated in the folk-literature.

The *Ma'aseh Book* consists of three parts. The main section is devoted to stories from Talmud and Midrash, drawn from the **Ein Ya'akov.* The second contains a cycle of 27 legends and narrative traditions centered around R. Samuel and his son R. *Judah he-Ḥasid (the "Pious"), the great mystics of medieval Germany, and the authors of the *"Sefer *Ḥasidim."* These stories early entered the oral stream and were later recorded in Hebrew as well as in Yiddish. The third part consists of a variety of narrative material: medieval stories about *Rashi, *Maimonides, and the story of the Jewish pope.

See *Yiddish Literature, *Exemplum.

Bibliography: M. Gaster, *Ma'aseh Book*, 2 vols. (1934); idem, in: *Jewish Studies . . . G. Kohut* (1935), 270ff.; J. Meitlis, *Ma'aseh in the Yiddish Ethical Literature* (1958); idem, *Das Ma'asebuch* (1933), incl. list of editions; Minkoff, in: *The Jewish People, Past and Present*, 3 (1952), 157f.; I. Zinberg, *Geshikhte fun der Literatur bay Yidn*, 6 (1943), 210–26; M. Erik, *Geshikhte fun der Yidisher Literatur* (1928), 353–64. [Y.Y.M.]

MA'ASEROT (Heb. מַעַשְׂרוֹת; "Tithes"), seventh tractate in the order *Zera'im*, in the Mishnah, Tosefta, and Jerusalem Talmud. It is sometimes referred to as *Ma'aser Rishon* ("First Tithe"—*genizah* fragments, Cambridge Ms., Tosefta Ms., and Maimonides' introduction to the Mishnah), but Albeck points out that this is a misnomer influenced by the name of the tractate following it, *Ma'aser Sheni* ("Second Tithe"). *Ma'aserot* deals chiefly with the precepts connected with the separation of the tithes to be given to the levites from the produce of the land (see Num. 18:20–24), and the prohibition against making use of produce before the tithe has been separated.

The selection of lambs for tithe, illustrating the tractate *Ma'aserot*. Title page engraving by Mich. Richey from a Hebrew-Latin edition of the Mishnah, Amsterdam, 1700–1704. Jerusalem, J.N.U.L.

The tractate contains five chapters. Chapter 1 defines the types of produce liable to tithing (1–4), the stage of growth at which they become liable, and when, after harvesting, untithed produce becomes forbidden. Chapter 2 gives circumstances in which casual eating of untithed produce is allowed, i.e., by the laborer. Chapter 3 continues with laws of tithe as they concern the laborer, and deals with the tithing of produce found on the road or in the field and the buildings or localities which render the produce brought there liable to tithe. Chapter 4 deals with the tithing of preserved fruits, liability for tithing arising through the onset of the Sabbath, chance eating from a vat of olives or a winepress, and the eating of insignificant parts of the produce. Chapter 5 deals with the liability for tithing of replanted produce, the selling of produce to those not trusted to tithe, and kinds of vegetables exempt from tithing.

The Tosefta has three chapters, supplementing the Mishnah with numerous accounts and decisions of the *tannaim*. Its editing appears to have been late, since it contains accounts (ch. 3) of Judah and Hillel, the sons of Rabban Gamaliel III. The order of the paragraphs does not correspond to that of the Mishnah, and there is no corresponding Tosefta to *mishnayot* 2:2, 6, 7; 4:4; and 5:6, 7. The Jerusalem Talmud covers about 14 columns of the Krotoszyn edition. It includes an interesting debate regarding the role of *aggadah* between Ze'eira and his colleague, who goes so far as to say that aggadic books are none other than "black magic" and attacks the aggadic method as being illogical (3:9, 51a). The Babylonian Talmud has no *Gemara* to *Ma'aserot*, as it has none on the whole of the order *Zera'im*, except for tractate *Berakhot*. This tractate was translated into English by H. *Danby, *The Mishnah* (1933), 66–73. [D.J.B.]

MA'ASER SHENI (Heb. מַעֲשֵׂר שֵׁנִי; "Second Tithe"), eighth tractate of the order *Zera'im*, dealing with the incidence and disposal of the second tithe (see **Terumot* and **Ma'aserot*). The tractate is based upon those biblical verses (Lev. 27:30–31 and Deut. 14:22–26) which clearly refer to a tithe different from that of the levites (Num. 18:21–24). It deals also with the law as to when the produce may be exchanged for money, when the fifth of the value (Lev. 27:31) must be added to the principal, and how the money may be spent. Since the fruit of trees in their fourth year of planting have the same sanctity as second tithe (Lev. 19:24), such fruit is also included in the discussion, as is declaration of having removed all sanctified products from the house (Deut. 14:28 and 26:13–15), made after the termination of the third and sixth years of the seven-year cycle. The Mishnah consists of five chapters: Chapter 1 deals with the prohibition of business transactions with second-tithe produce or with firstborn cattle, what coins may not be used for exchanging second tithe, and what may be purchased with the money. Chapter 2 discusses the uses of various second tithes, second-tithe money which becomes mixed with ordinary money, and the changing of second-tithe money for other money. Chapter 3 deals with payment made with second tithe, the purchase of other sacred foods with the money, the exchange of second tithe in Jerusalem for produce or money outside it, trees or buildings partly inside and partly outside Jerusalem, the redemption of unclean second tithe, and the neutralization of second tithe. Chapter 4 discusses the rate at which second tithe may be exchanged, the duty of adding a fifth of the value and how this addition may be avoided, changes in the price of the produce, the need to designate second-tithe money, produce eaten against second-tithe money, produce or articles found with markings indicating second tithe, etc. Chapter 5 deals with the marking of a field to indicate that its fruit is **orlah*, the redemption of fruit in the fourth year and the method of assessing its value, the removal of sacred produce in the fourth and seventh years, the declaration then made, and its abolition by John Hyrcanus.

The antiquity of some of the *mishnayot* in *Ma'aser Sheni* has long been a subject for discussion among scholars. Albeck, on the basis of the structure of the Mishnah (cf. Yev. 12:6; Sot. 8; San. 10:4–6), claims that the first part of Mishnah 4:8—about the redeeming of the second tithe—antedates the schools of Shammai and Hillel. Z. Frankel considers Mishnah 5:10–13, about the declaration (*viddui*) of *Ma'aser* in the Temple on the last day of Passover—to be one of the most ancient of *mishnayot*, originating from the period of the *soferim*. Albeck disagrees with Frankel. Although in the fifth chapter the first three *mishnayot* and the fourth belong to two opposing schools, the compiler of the Mishnah does not mention any disagreement. On this basis Albeck maintains that the editor of the Mishnah limited himself to collecting and arranging *mishnayot* without adding his own comment. The Tosefta of *Ma'aser Sheni* consists of five chapters. Its contents do not always correspond to that of the Mishnah, and there are 15 *mishnayot* to which there is no corresponding Tosefta.

Engraving for the tractate *Ma'aser Sheni*, showing pilgrims eating the second tithe in Jerusalem, from a title page of the Hebrew-Latin Mishnah illustrated by Mich. Richey, Amsterdam, 1700–04. Jerusalem, J.N.U.L.

There is no *Gemara* to *Ma'aser Sheni* in the Babylonian Talmud, but in the Jerusalem Talmud it covers no less than 17 columns of the Krotoszyn edition. The Mishnah, Tosefta, and the Jerusalem Talmud contain aggadic sayings which emphasize the supreme importance of tithing. According to Lieberman's reconstruction, Tosefta 5:25 refers to the story about R. Mana who declared a fast because of a drought; he requested a man who had been meticulous in separating tithes to pray and recite the declaration of *ma'aser*, which included the phrase "bless your nation with dew and rain," so that this supplication would be answered by God (S. Lieberman, *Tosefta ki-Feshutah*, 2 (1955), 788f.).

In Mishnah 5:15 it is stated that Johanan the high priest (John Hyrcanus) did away with three ritual acts that had previously been performed in the Temple—the declaration of *ma'aser* and the acts of "awakening" and "knocking." These ritual customs and the reason for their abrogation are explained in Tosefta *Sotah* 13:10–11 (cf. Sot. 48a; TJ, Sot. 9:11; 24a). According to the Tosefta the declaration was abolished in order to prevent people who did not fulfill the *mitzvah* of tithing (or who fulfilled it only with regard to *terumah*) from uttering a lie in the Temple. The Tosefta defines "awakeners" as those who in the Temple used to proclaim the verse: "awake, why sleepest Thou, O Lord?" (Ps. 44:24), a practice known to have taken place in Egyptian temples (Lieberman, see bibl.). The "knockers" were those who struck the calf between its horns. The reason given for the high priest's abolishing the "knockers" was that the animal became unfit for sacrifice after it was stunned and another method was instituted to hold the animal (while it was being slaughtered—TJ, Sot. 9:11, 24a). It is known, however, that this "knocking" was performed as part of idol worship (Lieberman). This tractate was translated into English by H. *Danby, *The Mishnah* (1933), 73–82.

Bibliography: Geiger, Urschrift, 176ff.; Ḥ. Albeck, *Das Buch der Jubilaeen und die Halacha*, in: *Siebenundvierzigster Bericht der Hochschule fuer die Wissenschaft des Judentums in Berlin* (1930), 30–32; idem, *Shishah Sidrei Mishnah, Seder Zera'im* (1958), 243–5; idem, *Mavo la-Mishnah* (1959), 88–91, 266f.; Frankel, Mishnah (1923), 5f.; Halevy, Dorot, 1 pt. 3 (1923), 153; A. Schwartz, *Ha-Tosefta*, 1 (1890), 340ff.; S. Lieberman, *Hellenism in Jewish Palestine* (1950), 139–43. [D.J.B.]

MA'BARAH (Heb. מַעְבָּרָה; plural **ma'barot**), transitional immigrants' camp or quarter in the early 1950s in Israel. At the end of 1949, 100,000 immigrants were living in camps, receiving accommodation, meals and services free, under demoralizing conditions. As the government and the *Jewish National Fund started large-scale development programs, and the newcomers began to earn their keep, the communal dining halls were closed down, and the inmates

A *ma'barah* under construction at Talpiyyot, Jerusalem, in the early 1950s.

enabled to make their own domestic arrangements. Camps which were not suitable for this system were closed down and new ones—*ma'barot*—set up, with a wooden, asbestos, or tin shack, or at least a tent, for each family, wherever there was a demand for labor, near the towns.

Although the *ma'barot* were a great improvement over the early camps, the primitive accommodation gave rise to serious social problems. They were gradually cleared by providing the newcomers with permanent housing and, from 1954, sending immigrants straight from the ship or plane to the villages or towns where they were to settle permanently.

Bibliography: *Israel Government Year Book*, (1958), 356–7; Zionist Organization Executive, *Reports to Zionist Congress*, 24 (1956); 25 (1960).

[M.L.]

MA'BAROT (Heb. מַעְבָּרוֹת; "Fords"), kibbutz in central Israel, near the Alexander River, affiliated with Kibbutz Arẓi ha-Shomer ha-Ẓa'ir. It was founded in 1933, as one of the first villages in the Ḥefer Plain by immigrants from Rumania, Germany, Bulgaria, and Hungary, and later joined by others. In 1969 Ma'barot had 575 inhabitants. Its economy is based on fully irrigated farming and on industrial enterprises—a plant producing electrical clocks and motors; a milk substitute plant for animal feeding; and a pharmaceutics plant.

[E.O.]

°**MACALISTER, ROBERT ALEXANDER STEWART** (1870–1951), Irish archaeologist. From 1899 to 1900 he participated with F. J. Bliss in the excavation of mounds in the Shephelah and in 1902–05 and 1907–09 directed the excavation of Gezer, publishing a three-volume report single-handedly in 1912. In 1925 he directed an excavation on the hill of Ophel in Jerusalem. In his later years, he was professor of Celtic archaeology at Dublin (1909–43). He was one of the pioneers of Palestinian archaeology, being the first to publish his finds in an exact manner and laying the foundations for comparative dating by ceramics and context dating. His works include *The Philistines* (1914) and *A Century of Excavation in Palestine* (1925).

[M.A.-Y.]

°**MACAULAY, THOMAS BABINGTON (Lord Macaulay**; 1800–1859), English historian and politician. A member of a family which had been in the forefront of antislavery agitation, Macaulay was elected to parliament in 1830. His maiden speech in the House of Commons was in support of a bill for the removal of the political disabilities affecting Jews in England. In an article (subsequently translated into several languages) in the *Edinburgh Review* of January 1831, he argued the same cause, supporting it again in the House of Commons in 1833 and 1841. Macaulay argued that, "The points of difference between Christianity and Judaism have very much to do with a man's fitness to be a bishop or a rabbi. But they have no more to do with his fitness to be a magistrate, a legislator, or a minister of finance than with his fitness to be a cobbler." He also urged that it was inconsistent to deny formal political rights to Jews in a society where they had acquired the substance of political power. Rarely had the case for Jewish emancipation been presented with the literary force of Macaulay's essays and speeches; the support of one of England's leading men of letters had a significant effect on public opinion.

Bibliography: T. B. Macaulay, *Essay and Speech on Jewish Disabilities*, ed. by I. Abrahams and S. Levy (1909); Roth, Mag Bibl, 55, 56, 60.

[S.D.T.]

MACCABEANS, ORDER OF ANCIENT, a friendly benefit society in Britain whose members are Zionists. Founded in 1896 by Ephraim Ish-Kishor and registered under the Friendly Societies' Act, the Order of Ancient Maccabeans still exists. Its aims are those of all British friendly societies, namely, to assist members in distress, provide free medical aid, etc. Its special character is laid down in its rules concerning membership: all persons "of the Jewish faith who declare themselves adherents to the Zionist Movement" can become members. From its inception the order was a firm supporter of Zionism, contributed to its various funds, and became a champion of practical Zionist work in Ereẓ Israel. In 1914 a Maccabean Land Company was founded to enable its shareholders to acquire land in Ereẓ Israel. The organization of the order displays masonic features. A grand beacon and high degree council supervise its work; branches are called beacons, of which there are 25 (there once were beacons in Palestine as well); the principal officers are called grand commander, grand treasurer, and grand secretary. Members are called upon to obey the decisions of their order and are forbidden to inform nonmembers of the order's activities.

The revised statutes of the Zionist Organization passed by the Tenth Zionist Congress (1911) permitted the establishment of so-called *Sonderverbaende* (separate unions), in addition to the existing territorial organizations, on the condition that every *Sonderverband* numbered at least 3,000 shekel-buying members and that it professed special views on Zionist work. The Order of Ancient Maccabeans applied for this status, and though its claim was opposed by the English Zionist Federation, the order prevailed. In 1912 the Zionist Executive decided in favor of the order's status as *Sonderverband* on the condition that a Joint Zionist Council be formed, comprising representatives of both the order and the federation. In the 1930s, however, the order lost its special status. Prominent members of the order were Herbert *Bentwich, who served as grand commander; Chaim *Weizmann, who represented the order at Congresses; and Selig *Brodetsky, who served as grand commander.

[I.Ph.]

MACCABEE, the additional name given to Judah, son of Mattathias, military leader of the revolt against Syria in 168 B.C.E. The name Maccabee is also applied loosely to other members of the family, as well as to the Hasmonean dynasty as a whole. For suggestions as to its derivation, see *Judah Maccabee and *Hames. The name is also given in Christian tradition to the seven children martyred by Antiochus Epiphanes when they refused to commit idolatry. Shrines to their memory and that of their mother Salome (in Jewish tradition Hannah) were established in many parts of the Christian world (see *Hannah and her Seven Sons).

[Ed.]

MACCABEES, FIRST BOOK OF (I Maccabees), a historical work extant in Greek, covering the period of 40 years from the accession of Antiochus Epiphanes (175 B.C.E.) to the death of Simeon the Hasmonean (135 B.C.E.). Its name in the Septuagint and in the writings of the Church Fathers (Eusebius and Clement) is Τα Μακκαβαϊκά, i.e., "Maccabean matters" or "the Book of the Maccabees." The original Hebrew name of the book is unknown. According to Origin it was "Sarbeth Sabaniel." Different hypotheses have been suggested to explain these words, which should perhaps read: סֵפֶר בֵּית סַרְבָנֵי אֵל *(Sefer Beit Sarevanei El)*, the words *Sarevanei El* ("who strive for God") being a translation into contemporary (mishnaic)

Hebrew of Jehoiarib, the name of the priestly order (see I Chron. 24:7; Neh. 12:6, 19) to which the Hasmonean family belonged. In support of this conjecture is the fact that in later times, after the glamor of the Hasmonean dynasty had become tarnished, the name Jehoiarib is found translated by the above word in its Aramaic form מסרבי (*mesarevei;* TJ, Ta'an. 4:8, 68d) though it is there used in a pejorative sense as "rebellious," "fractious."

I Maccabees is the main, and at times the only historical source for the period. The book opens with the conquest of Alexander the Great, but immediately after this relates the activities of Antiochus Epiphanes and the Jewish Hellenizers (whom the author calls "the sons of Belial"—the reprobates) and summarily reviews the causes of the Hasmonean rebellion. From this point on it gives a more detailed account of the events of Mattathias' revolt, through the rededication of the Temple, down to the time when John *Hyrcanus, the eldest son of Simon the Hasmonean, was appointed ruler.

The many expressions in the Greek version which occur only in biblical Hebrew (e.g., from the hands of the gentiles: *mi-yad ha-goyim;* and his heart was raised: *va-yarom libbo;* before his face: *al panav;* and the matter found favor in their eyes: *va-yitav ha-davar be-eineihem*) clearly confirm the testimony of the Church Fathers that the original language of the book was Hebrew. The style was biblical Hebrew (including use of the *vav* conversive), and particularly that of the historical books of the Bible. Like Joshua and Judges, it begins with the *vav* conversive, but reflects the style of Ezra and Nehemiah in including historical documents and similar testimony. Like these biblical books, although it is written largely in prose, now and again it includes poetry, such as the Lamentation of Mattathias (2:7–13), prayers (3:18–22; 4:30–33; 7:41–42), and a hymn (14:8–15). Unlike II Maccabees it does not contain explanations of historical or personal psychological motivation, of the sort usually found in the works of the contemporary Greek historians.

The writer achieves a high degree of objectivity. He even refrains from censuring the *Hassideans who opposed the Hasmoneans, though it is clear where his sympathies lie since he regards the Hasmoneans as chosen by Providence "to give deliverance unto Israel" (5:62). The course of events described is not considered as diverging from the natural order, and supernatural intervention is almost entirely absent from the narrative, even though the basic assumption underlying the entire book is that Israel's success is a direct result of their faith and their steadfastness in their loyalty to the Torah and the keeping of the commandments. The author is very circumspect about mentioning God's name. In place of the Tetragrammation or the biblical *Elohim*, he either writes "Heaven" (3:18, 50, 60; 4:10, 40, et al.) or else uses a circumlocution in order to avoid the use of a proper name altogether (e.g., 2:21, 26; 3:22, 53; 4:10, et al.).

The book ranks high as an accurate historical source, and even the numbers it contains are not exaggerated. In spite of scholarly arguments to the contrary, the idiomatic constructions typical of this book incontrovertibly prove it to be the work of a single author. His name is unknown, but he almost certainly was an eyewitness to the events he describes (cf. 6:39). He avoids expressing outright partisanship, but the fact that he wrote at the beginning of John Hyrcanus' rule, when the latter was still a Pharisee, and lauds Mattathias' decision to permit defensive military action on the Sabbath—which was approved by the Pharisaic school (Jos., Ant., 12:276; 14:63; Tosef., Er. 4:6–7)—indicates that he was close to this circle.

The literary sources used by the author include both letters from official archives (such as those from the Seleucid kings and Roman officials to the Hasmoneans), and public documents (such as the people's declaration assigning the high priesthood and the chief executive position to Simeon), as well as other literary sources in Hebrew (among them the various poems). Thus it is that the author employs two different systems of dating: one for external affairs (where he starts the year in the fall, in the month of Tishri), and one for internal events (which he dates according to the calendar starting in the month of Nisan).

The original Hebrew version seems to have disappeared quite early. The Church included I Maccabees in its canon together with the rest of the Septuagint and this was ratified by the Catholic Church Council of Trent. After the Reformation, the Protestants removed it from their Bible and relegated it to the Apocrypha. A Hebrew translation was made in the 11th century (published by D. Chwolson).

Bibliography: Charles, Apocrypha, 1 (1913), 59–124; O. F. Fritzsche, *Libri Apocryphi Veteris Testamenti Graece* (1871); A. Rahlf, *Septuaginta*, 1 (1935); H. B. Swete, *The Old Testament in Greek*, 3 (1894); W. Kappler, *Septuaginta, Vetus Testamentum Graecum*, 9 pt. 1 (1936); A. Geiger, *Urschrift und Uebersetzungen der Bibel* (Breslau, 1857); G. Rawlinson, in: H. Wace (ed.), *Apocrypha*, 2 (1888), 373ff.; B. Niese, *Kritik der beiden Makkabaeerbuecher* (1900); Schuerer, Gesch, 1 (1901[3]), 32–40; H. Ettelson, *The Integrity of I Maccabees* (1925); Y. Baer, in: *Zion*, 33 (1964), 101–24; F. Bickermann, *Der Gott der Makkabaeer* (1937); A. Kahana, *Ha-Sefarim ha-Ḥiẓoniyyim*, 2 (1937), 72–94; J. Heinemann, in: MGWJ, 82 (1938), 145–72; F. M. Abel, *Les Livres des Maccabées* (1949); P. Churgin, *Meḥkarim bi-Tekufat ha-Bayit ha-Sheni* (1949), 190–202; K. D. Schunck, *Die Quellen des I. und II. Makkabaeerbuches* (1954).

[Y.M.G.]

MACCABEES, SECOND BOOK OF (II Maccabees), known in Greek as Τά Μακκαβαϊκά, that is, the narratives about (Judah called) the Maccabee. It was this title which gave the title to the other books of the *Apocrypha bearing the same name. It is an abridgment of a larger work of five books written by a *Jason of Cyrene who is otherwise unknown (see 2:23–28). Traces of the original division may be preserved in the similar conclusions in several chapters (3:40; 7:42; 10:9; 13:26; 15:37–39). Unlike I *Maccabees which was written in Hebrew, the original language of this book was Greek; and unlike the former, which begins with an account of the revolt of Mattathias and tells of the wars of his sons the *Hasmoneans up to the days of John Hyrcanus, this book deals solely with the deeds of *Judah Maccabee, and only until his victory over *Nicanor on 13 Adar II, 164 B.C.E. ("Nicanor Day"). However, the main account is prefaced by a lengthy introduction on the actions of the Hellenizers, Simeon of the priestly division of Minyamin (Bilgah), who wanted to be the *agoranomos* (the market overseer) in Jerusalem, and Jason the brother of the high priest Onias, and Menelaus the brother of Simeon, both of whom wanted to be high priests. Their acts of plunder and bribing the king caused the people to rise against them, but their contacts with kings led to the intervention of the Syrian king Antiochus IV Epiphanes and to the religious persecutions which were in fact the direct cause of the Maccabean revolt.

The events related subsequently are in general similar to those in I Maccabees, although the two books are independent of each other. However, chapters 8–12 present a different order: the death of Antiochus IV (10:1–9) and the arrival of Lysias at Beth-Zur (ch. 11) here precede the purification of the Temple. The epitomizer for some reason or other altered the original order (8:29, 34–36; 10:1–8; 8:30–33; 9:1–29; 10:9; he apparently thought that the

Beginning of II Maccabees, from the *Conradin Bible,* southern Italy, 13th century. Baltimore, Md., Walters Art Gallery. Ms. W. 152, fol. 42v.

letter in 11:22, in which Antiochus IV is regarded as having died, belonged to the same period as the other letters in that chapter which, however, preceded it by a year). If the original order is restored, however, the events accord with those in I Maccabees. In its extant form, II Maccabees begins with an addendum to the main body of the book, consisting of two letters sent at different times from Judea to Alexandria which request that the festival of Ḥanukkah be observed. The first was written, according to its date, in 124 B.C.E. (in the days of John Hyrcanus), while the second, undated one (which has all kinds of aggadic stories and is regarded as largely apocryphal) was written earlier, and is a letter from Judah (Maccabee) to Aristobulus, the tutor of King Ptolemy (Philometor, 180–145 B.C.E.)

The main part of the book commences with 2:19, at a time when Onias (III) was high priest, Seleucus ruled in Asia, and peace and tranquility reigned in Ereẓ Israel; however, the avarice of several high priests led to a complete reversal of the situation. Simeon of the priestly division of Minyamin (see above) informed the king's strategus in Syria and Phoenicia that there were vast treasures in the Temple. The king's mission to take the treasure failed (the envoy Heliodorus saw angels smiting him and fainted), and Jason and Menelaus (see above) then began to compete for the high priesthood. As a result of their rivalry and the base acts accompanying it in Jerusalem and Antioch (where Onias the high priest was killed), the people revolted, and Antiochus instituted religious persecutions against them. At first many suffered martyrdom. Then Judah Maccabee rose in revolt together with his men, defeating first the local governor, then the commanders Nicanor and Gorgias (8:8–29), and in the month of Xanthicus (Adar, March) 164 B.C.E. (11:1–15) triumphed over the commander in chief Lysias near Beth-Zur and purified the Temple (10:1–8). There follows a description of wars with various neighboring countries (8:30–33; 10:15–38; 12:2–9, 17–31), and an account of Antiochus IV's death (ch. 9: described here as a punishment from heaven) and his contrition (the author cites a letter from him to the Jews of Antioch (9:19) and interprets it as addressed to all the Jews). After this comes an account of the wars against Antiochus Eupator (13:1–27), the mission of the priest Alcimus, and Judah's victory over Nicanor (15:36).

In its literary form, as well as in its language, this book is entirely different from I Maccabees. Unlike the latter, which uses simple, matter-of-fact language, II Maccabees is written in the style of Greek historians: in ornate language, rich in idioms and poetic metaphors, and in expressions filled with pathos, drama, and rhetoric, stirring the reader. Also, as was usual with these historians, the book is full of various stories of miraculous events, of the intervention of heavenly creatures, directly (by angels) and indirectly (by signs in heaven and on earth presaging evil).

The purpose of the book is religious propaganda, the basic idea being that the sin of the nation is the cause of the divine punishment ("For it is not a light thing to do wickedly against the laws of God: but the time following shall declare these things"; 4:17). Yet the suffering that comes upon Israel is only to chasten the people (6:12–17), and is itself a sign of the divine providence—to warn them against sin. The aim of the introduction is to show that the sin of the priests lay in serving alien forces. In this book—for the first time—Judaism stands as an antipode to *Hellenism (2:21, 8:1, 14:38), and the Greeks are represented as barbarians, avid for plunder and pillage (4:8, 23, 32, 42; 5:16). In contrast, the strength of the Jews lies in the fulfillment of the practical *mitzvot* (the observance of the Sabbath—6:11; 8:26; 12:38; the precaution against ritual uncleanness—5:27), and outstanding examples of such acts of bravery are given. One is the story of the elderly Eleazar, who steadfastly refused to eat forbidden food despite all the torture inflicted on him; another is of the woman and her seven sons who suffered martyrdom for the sanctification of the Divine Name (6:18ff.; ch. 7—see *Hannah and her Seven Sons). Much emphasis is also laid on the belief in the resurrection of the dead (7:14; 12:43). Although his views are very close to those of the Pharisees, it is impossible to tell whether the author, Jason, was one of them. He was apparently a contemporary of Judah Maccabee, as several incidents sound as if they emanate from an eyewitness.

Bibliography: Charles, Apocrypha, 1 (1913), 125–54; C. L. W. Grimm, *Kurzgefasstes exegetisches Handbuch zu den Apocryphen des Alten Testaments,* 3 (1853); R. Laqueur, *Kritische Untersuchungen zum zweiten Makkabaeerbuch* (1904); idem, in: *Historische Zeitschrift,* 136 (1927), 229–52; W. Kolbe, *Beitraege zur syrischen und juedischen Geschichte* (1946); E. Bickerman, in: Pauly-Wissowa, 14 pt. 1 (1928), 779–97; idem, in: ZNW, 32 (1933), 233ff.; H. Bévenot, *Die beiden Makkabaeerbuecher* (1931); M. Hak, in: *Sinai,* 12 (1943), 92–99. For further bibliography, see *Maccabees, First Book of. [Y.M.G.]

MACCABEES, THIRD BOOK OF (III Maccabees), apocryphal book, included in the *Septuagint, probably dating from the first century B.C.E. It has nothing to do with the Maccabees, but relates a legend to explain why the Jews in Egypt have a Purim-like festival in the summer (the Egyptian date is given). It may have been grouped with the books of the Maccabees, because it, too, relates a persecution of Jews by a Hellenistic king and their miraculous rescue. In it, Ptolemy IV Philopator (221–204 B.C.E.), after his victory over Antiochus III at Rafa, visited neighboring temples. When he insisted upon entering the

Temple of Jerusalem by force, the high priest's prayer brought down upon him the scourge of God. Returning to his capital, he took his anger out on the Alexandrian Jews. He ordered a census of the Jews, which was an infringement of their civil rights, and ordered that they be branded with the emblem of Dionysus. Those resisting initiation to Dionysus' mysteries were to be put to death, and those consenting were to be granted full citizenship. As most Alexandrian Jews remained loyal to their faith, the king ordered all the Jews of the country to be brought to Alexandria and put to death. Clerks attempted to register them but failed for shortage of writing material. Crowds of Jews were then concentrated in a hippodrome where they were to be trampled to death by intoxicated elephants. Their destruction was twice miraculously averted. On the third attempt two angels appeared and struck terror into the king, his army, and the elephants, the beasts turning about and falling upon the soldiers. In the end the king repented and prepared a banquet in honor of the rescued Jews. There are serious objections to the historicity of this story. The king's decree combines an infringement of civil rights that could apply only to Alexandrian Jews, with a census of the Jews of the whole country. Moreover, the only purpose of the census could be to institute a poll tax. However, this would become meaningless if the whole Jewish population were to be put to death; it is probably for this reason that the author had to find a device to stop it. The story of the elephants is told by Josephus (Apion, 2:53–55), but about another Ptolemy. The account of the two angels, as well as that of the king's intrusion into the Temple of Jerusalem, is derived from II Maccabees 3. The theme of the king who is instigated by his counselors to annihilate the Jews is from the Book of Esther. These and other details of the story can be put down as commonplaces of persecution literature. By prefacing his patchwork with a description, albeit irrelevant, of the battle of Rafa, taken from a reliable historian, the author manages to concoct an etiology for a festival, the original meaning of which had been forgotten. The book was written in Greek and its style is characterized by its many rare words and neologisms.

Bibliography: Charles, Apocrypha, 1 (1913), 155–73; M. Hadas, *The Third and Fourth Books of Maccabees* (1953), includes bibliography. For further bibliography see *Maccabees, First Book of.

[Y.AM.]

MACCABEES, FOURTH BOOK OF (IV Maccabees), apocryphal book, included in the Septuagint. It presumably dates from the first century C.E., and is erroneously ascribed by Christian tradition to *Josephus. It does not deal with the warriors of the Maccabean revolt, but with the story of the martyrs of the preceding religious persecution, as related in II Maccabees 6–7. It is of special interest as the only surviving major piece of Greek rhetoric in Jewish literature. IV Maccabees is a philosophical sermon on the theme "pious reason masters passion." This theme, stated at the outset, is frequently repeated in the course of the sermon. After an initial inquiry along the lines of standard Stoic doctrine into the nature of reason and the varieties of passion, the preacher offers historical examples of the ability of reason to control passion. He finally comes to examples provided by the "occasion of this day," the heroic death of the victims of Antiochus' persecution. After a short historical exposition, he describes old Eleazar and the mother (later known as *Hannah) with her seven sons, whom the king tries to force to eat ritually forbidden food. They refuse and each defends his refusal in a fervent speech in the face of cruel torture before being put to death. It seems that the details, as far as they are not drawn from II Maccabees, emanate from the author's own imagination. He spares no pains to excite the emotions of his audience, incorporating detailed descriptions of the torture instruments, delicate analysis of the mother's inner struggle, and great exclamations of admiration for the martyrs. This sermon is one of the outstanding specimens of the "Asianic" school of rhetoric, known for its linguistic excesses, neologisms, redundance of language, and overemphasis.

A most interesting feature is the interweaving of Greek philosophical and Jewish traditional motifs. Not only are moral conflicts and temptations illustrated by biblical stories but in line with the concept that the Torah is the "philosophy" of the Jews, biblical laws are presented as practical means of Stoic self-education and are thus classified according to the different cardinal virtues they help to develop. It passes unnoticed that in the course of this presentation the ideal of the Stoic sage is replaced by that of the God-fearing man, and that heroism is interpreted as the endurance of hardship. The martyr reaps all the glory. He is called an athlete and his ability to endure suffering is the apex of all the moral virtues. The author regards firmness in bearing pain as the victory of reason and as virtually destroying the tyrant's power. The principal religious motivation of the martyr is loyalty to God's law. Eleazar makes no distinction between greater and lesser commandments. Violation of either constitutes contempt for the Lawgiver. The martyrs are certain that God will reward their faithfulness after their death and that He will inflict eternal punishment on the godless king.

The sermon was obviously intended for delivery; otherwise, the mention of its "occasion" would be meaningless. However it may not have been a synagogue sermon, since, in Hellenistic (as in rabbinical) Judaism, such sermons seem always to have been based on a biblical verse. Perhaps it was a Ḥanukkah sermon, but in the absence of any known association of that festival with the martyrs, it may be more correct to think of it as intended for an assembly at their supposed tomb (at Antiochia?) on a traditional commemoration day.

No traces of IV Maccabees have been detected in later Jewish tradition, but Christianity adopted it, together with the "Maccabean Saints" (see *Hannah and her Seven Sons), to whom both the Eastern and the Western Church dedicated a Commemoration Day. Sermons delivered on that day, sometimes referring expressly to IV Maccabees, have been preserved from Gregory of Nazianzus, Augustine, and other Church Fathers. The heroism of the "Maccabees" left its mark on Christian martyr worship, although the Jewish source lacks the special note of longing for torments characteristic of Christian martyrology.

Bibliography: Charles, Apocrypha, 2 (1913), 653–85; M. Hadas, *The Third and Fourth Books of Maccabees* (1953), including detailed bibliography. For further bibliography, see *Maccabees, First Book of.

[Y.AM.]

MACCABIAH, international games, recognized and approved by the International Olympic Committee, held every four years in Israel and open to athletes of the Jewish faith from all countries. The aim of the Maccabiah is to raise the standard of physical culture and sports among Jewish youth and to encourage and foster a sense of belonging to the Jewish people.

The idea of Jewish Olympics was conceived by one of the founders and veteran leaders of the Maccabi movement in Palestine, Joseph Yekutieli, who advocated it with zeal from 1921. After he had succeeded in persuading the mayor of Tel Aviv, Meir *Dizengoff, to build the first sports stadium in the country, he brought his plan before the Maccabi World Congress at Ostrava, Czechoslovakia, in

Figure 1. Calisthenics exhibition by Palestinian participants in the first Maccabiah, Tel Aviv, 1932. Courtesy Keren Hayesod, United Israel Appeal, Jerusalem.

1929 and it was enthusiastically approved. In 1932 the first Maccabiah was held in Tel Aviv, with contingents from 23 countries and 500 athletes.

A great number of the athletes and accompanying personnel remained in Palestine after the Maccabiah and thus the games became not only a tool for stimulating sports but also an important means for promoting Aliyah. The second Maccabiah in 1935 was even more of an "Aliyah Maccabiah," since most of the 1,700 sportsmen from 27 countries, and their escorts, remained in Palestine because of the anti-Semitism which was sweeping Europe following the Nazis' access to power in Germany. The third Maccabiah could not be held until 1950.

In 1953 the fourth Maccabiah was held. The Maccabi World Union congress which followed it adopted a resolution to build a Maccabiah village to house the visiting contingents. Since then the Maccabiah games have been held regularly every four years, the fifth in 1957, the sixth in 1961, the seventh in 1965, and the eighth in 1969, with an ever-increasing participation of athletes from over 30 countries. The main sports embraced by the Maccabiah are track and field events; gymnastics; swimming and water polo; boxing, wrestling, and fencing; tennis and table tennis; soccer, basketball, and volleyball.

The Maccabi World Union Executive, which sponsors and organizes the Maccabiah games, appoints the International Maccabi Games Committee (IMGC). This generally includes the chairmen of the territorial Maccabi organizations. In countries where no organization exists, leading Jewish sportsmen and people connected with athletes are appointed to select and arrange the training of the various teams. Since the third Maccabiah, *Ha-Po'el Israel has taken an active part with its general secretary a member of the IMGC. The *Betar and *Eliẓur sports organizations also participate in the Maccabiah games.

Figure 2. A swimming event at the seventh Maccabiah, 1965. Courtesy Government Press Office, Tel Aviv.

The program for the Maccabiah games includes festive opening and closing ceremonies under the patronage of the president and the prime minister of the State of Israel, with contingents parading under their national flags.

Bibliography: J. Yekutieli, *My Road to the First Maccabiah* (1969); Maccabiah, the 8th, *Maccabiah Omnibus* (1969). [M.Sa.]

MACCABI WORLD UNION. The international Jewish sports organization which bears the name of *Judah Maccabee had its origin in the belief of young Eastern European Jews involved in the growing movement for a national home in Palestine at the end of the 19th century that one essential prerequisite was the improvement of the physique of ghetto youth. To this end, gymnastics clubs were founded in a number of Eastern and Central European countries. They were not immediately called Maccabi. The first club, opened in Constantinople, Turkey, in 1895, was called the Israel Gymnastics Club, while others were named after another hero, Bar Kokhba, or were known by the Hebrew names "Ha-Ko'aḥ" ("strength") or "Ha-Gibbor" ("strong man"). The Bar Kokhba club published a monthly journal *Juedische Turnzeitung* later called *Der Makkabi;* it first appeared in 1900 and promoted athletics and national Jewish education. In 1897 the first of a series of Bulgarian clubs were opened in Plovdiv; a club was organized in Berlin in the following year and in Vienna in 1899. 1901 saw the establishment of a Polish club in Lemberg.

The concept of a nationalist sports movement received impetus in 1898 from a stirring address by the well-known Zionist leader, the physician Max *Nordau, at the second Zionist Congress in Basle, in which he proclaimed:

> . . . gymnastics and physical training are exceedingly important for us Jews, whose greatest defect has been and is a lack of discipline . . . nature has endowed us with the spiritual qualities required for athletic achievements of an extraordinary quality. All we lack is muscle, and that can be developed with the aid of physical exercise . . . The more Jews achieve in the various branches of sport, the greater will be their self-confidence and self-respect.

The truth of Nordau's contention was demonstrated in 1903 at the fourth Zionist Congress in Basle, where a group of 35 outstanding gymnasts from various European clubs staged an impressive display. It was at this Congress that the foundations were laid for the *Juedische Turnerschaft*—the Union of Jewish Gymnastics Clubs—which united all the existing sports clubs, beginning with a membership of some 1,500. It was headed first by Ernst Tuch and later by Theowald Sholom, both of them from Germany. During the first decade of the 20th century the movement spread to more countries on the European continent and to Palestine, where clubs were formed in Jaffa (1906) and Jerusalem (1911). The first real approach to Zionism came in 1912, when at a Maccabi conference in Berlin it was decided to organize group excursions to Palestine (1913 and 1914). By this time there were over 100 affiliated clubs in Europe, with a membership running into several thousands, and the movement had come to be accepted, unofficially, as part of the Young Zionist movement. World War I halted Maccabi activities, but with its close they were renewed everywhere in Europe. As the movement grew, so did the need for firmer integration and in 1921, at a convention in Carlsbad, Czechoslovakia, the World Maccabi Union was formed, and the first Maccabi World Union congress elected Dr. Heinrich Kuhn of Germany as its first president. With ten affiliated countries, the Maccabi World Union started its operations as an organic part of the Zionist movement. By the time of the second Maccabi congress a year later, under the presidency of Heinrich Lellever (1891–1947) of Germany, no less than 22 territorial organizations had affiliated, and the world membership had grown to nearly 100,000.

The first headquarters of the movement were in Vienna, but in 1927 they were moved to Brno, Czechoslovakia, and in 1929 to Berlin, where the movement flourished under the energetic leadership of Dr. Lellever. In 1929 the first international sports meeting was held in Prague; another was held in Antwerp, Belgium, the following year. These were forerunners of the world *Maccabiah games which were to be staged in Palestine from 1932 onward. In 1935 headquarters were transferred from Nazi Germany to London, where Selig *Brodetsky took over the presidency of the World Union, and the second Lord Melchett (*Mond) became honorary world president. In 1939 the world executive was divided into two sections, one operating in Britain and the other, under Lellever, in Palestine. By the time World War II broke out, the world membership was estimated at 200,000 with branches located in most countries of Europe and in Palestine, Turkey, Egypt, China, Australia, South America, and South Africa. It was in 1939 that a nucleus of refugees from Europe established Maccabi in the U.S.

During the war, the activities of the constituent branches of the World Union virtually ceased. Immediately following the war Maccabi leaders in England and Palestine revived the clubs still in existence and helped survivors of the Holocaust to get to Ereẓ Israel. In the countries that now came under Russian control, Jews were forbidden to engage in sports activities as Jews, although a Maccabi group did exist for a short period in the Russian zone of Berlin. In 1946 the first of the annual European Maccabi conferences was held in Basle. The decimation of Jewish communities by the Nazis and the prohibitions of the Iron Curtain countries reduced the number of young recruits to Maccabi in Europe, but new branches were springing up in North and South America, South Africa, and Australia. The birth of the State of Israel gave the movement a new focus and a new impetus, and from 1948 onward all the activities of Maccabi were oriented toward Israel, where the headquarters of the entire movement were established in Tel Aviv. By 1969, 38 countries were affiliated to the World Union, and the membership was estimated to be about 200,000.

A Maccabi world congress is held every three years. The congress elects a president, a chairman, and an executive which consists of representatives from continental and territorial organizations in addition to a number of World Maccabi leaders, who reside in Israel. From 1957 the president was M. W. U. Heth and the chairman Pierre Gildesgame (1903–) who lived in London.

For details on Israel see *Sports.

Bibliography: Maccabi, *Chairman's News Letter; Maccabi Bulletin; Maccabi World Review; Yedi'ot ha-Maccabi ha-Olami;* D. Rimon, *Ḥamishim Shenot ha-Maccabi ba-Olam 1894–1944* (1944).

[M.SA.]

MACCOBY, ḤAYYIM ZUNDEL (1858–1916), Zionist preacher, one of the first members of Ḥovevei Zion (see *Ḥibbat Zion) in England. Born near Kobrin, Poland, Maccoby decided to become a preacher when he discovered his oratorical talents, and he attracted many followers. In 1873 he was accepted as the preacher of Kamenets and from that time on was called "The Maggid from Kamenets." In 1875 he left Kamenets and was a preacher in several places until he became the first regular preacher of the Ḥibbat Zion movement, in 1883. In this office he traversed Russia, Lithuania, and Poland. About 300 societies for the settlement of Ereẓ Israel were founded because of his influence and in spite of the opposition of many rabbis. In 1890 he left Russia for England, where he also attracted large audiences to his sermons and was thus a pioneer of the Ḥibbat Zion movement in the country. Maccoby was one of the strongest opponents of *Herzl for religious reasons. In 1929 a collection of his sermons entitled *Ḥayyim* was published with a detailed biography.

Bibliography: H. R. Rabinowitz, *Deyokena'ot shel Darshanim* (1967), 297–303; EZD, 3 (1965), 501–5; *Ha-Ma'or* (Sept. 1966–Dec. (1967); M. Temkin, in: *Jewish Review* (Feb. 3/Mar. 3, 1971).

[G.K.]

°**McDONALD, JAMES GROVER** (1886–1964), first U.S. ambassador to Israel. McDonald, who was born in Coldwater, Ohio, was assistant professor of history at the University of Indiana, before moving to New York. From 1919 to 1933 McDonald served as chairman of the Foreign Policy Association. During the 1920s he made numerous trips abroad for this organization becoming, in the process, a familiar figure at the League of Nations headquarters in Geneva. McDonald's interest in Zionism was sparked by his experiences as League of Nations high commissioner for refugees from Germany. He held this post from 1933 to 1935 when he resigned and issued a dramatic statement accusing the German government of planning a policy of race extermination and attacking League members for their indifference to the plight of the German refugees. In 1938 he was elected to head the newly created Presidential Advisory Committeee on Political Refugees (PACPR), a quasi-official agency whose main task was to serve as a conduit for funneling the names of prominent refugees to be considered for special visitor's visas to the State Department. In September 1940 McDonald clashed with officials in the State Department who were imposing ever stricter regulations to halt the influx of refugees. When the White House was finally called upon to mediate in the conflict, McDonald asked for and received Eleanor Roosevelt's support. However, despite her intercession, Roosevelt supported the State Department. In May 1943, seemingly affected by the lack of administration support for the refugee cause, McDonald rejected an opportunity to head the U.S. delegation to a refugee conference at Bermuda. During the next two years, he frequently advocated that Palestine be opened to immigration, "limited only by the absorption capacity of the area." In 1945 his efforts were partly rewarded when the Anglo-American Comittee of Inquiry on Palestine, of which he was a member, recommended the admission of 100,000 displaced Jews. President Truman

James G. McDonald (left), the first U.S. ambassador to Israel, presenting his credentials in Tel Aviv, March 29, 1949. Courtesy Government Press Office, Tel Aviv.

appointed McDonald U.S. special representative to Israel in 1948 and ambassador in 1949. McDonald served in this post until his retirement in 1951. He wrote: *My Mission to Israel 1948–1951* (1953). After his retirement, McDonald devoted much time to Zionist-sponsored causes, especially the sale of Israel bonds.

Bibliography: D. S. Wyman, *Paper Walls: America and the Refugee Crisis, 1938–1941* (1968); A. D. Morse, *While Six Million Died* (1968), passim. [H.L.F.]

MACEDONIA, region of southeastern Europe where Alexander the Great was born. As a result of the latter's conquests and subsequent Greek rule in Palestine, the Hebrew term "Javan" as it appears in the Bible was generally translated by the rabbis "Macedonia" (cf. Targum Pseudo-Jonathan to Gen. 10:2; Yoma 10a). Although the origins of a Jewish community in Macedonia are unknown, it is certain that such a colony existed toward the end of the Second Temple period. Philo, in the list of Jewish communities quoted from the correspondence of Agrippa I to Caligula, refers also to the Jews of Macedonia (The Embassy to Gaius, 281). Moreover, the fact that Paul and his followers made a number of journeys to Macedonia, and that their doctrines were readily accepted there, tends to substantiate the existence of a Jewish colony (cf. Acts 16:9; 18:5; 20:1; I Cor. 16:5; II Cor. 1:16; 2:13; 7:5). Josephus, in describing the Jewish community of Alexandria, claims that the Jewish residents there were granted the right to be called "Macedonians" (Wars 2:487–88; Ant. 12:8; Apion 2:35). However, papyrological research has shown that the phrase "Macedonian" eventually lost its original ethnic significance, and is in fact a designation of specific military status.

For later periods see also *Bulgaria; *Byzantine Empire; *Greece; *Yugoslavia.

Bibliography: Schuerer, Gesch, 3 (1909^4), 5; Juster, Juifs, 1 (1914), 187. [I.G.]

MACHADO, family name of Portuguese *Marranos. The best known is perhaps David Mendez Machado (d. 1753), who left his native Lisbon in 1732 after he had aroused the suspicions of the *Inquisition that he practiced Judaism in secret. He arrived in Savannah, Georgia—by way of London—during 1733. Within that year he married Zipphorah Nuñez (c. 1714–1799), daughter of the former Portuguese court physician Samuel *Nuñez; Machado was then appointed *ḥazzan* at New York City's Spanish-Portuguese synagogue, Shearith Israel, serving from 1734 to 1753. His daughter, Rebecca (1746–1831), married Jonas *Phillips (1736–1803), the revolutionary war patriot. Among David Machado's descendants were Uriah Phillips *Levy and Mordecai Manuel *Noah. The record of freemen in New York City for 1739 lists an Aaron Machado, probably the brother of the *ḥazzan*. The Machado family name appears also in the earliest records of the Mexican Inquisition: Antonio Machado and his daughter Isabel were inculpated during the trial of Jorge de Almeida in 1600.

Bibliography: Stern, Americans, index; D. de S. Pool, *Portraits Etched in Stone; Early Jewish Settlers, 1682–1831* (1952); Rosenbloom, Biogr Dict, 105; J. R. Marcus, *Early American Jewry*, 2 (1955), 59, 335. [Ed.]

MACHAERUS, Transjordanian fortress erected by the Hasmonean king Alexander *Yannai in southern Perea, E. of the Jordan and adjacent to the border of Nabatean Arabia (Jos., Wars 1:161; 3:46). The place served as one of the depositories for his treasures (Jos., Ant., 13:417). It was one of the strongest fortresses

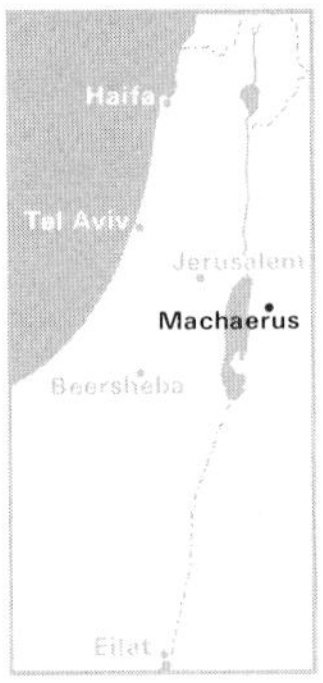

in Judea and served as a base for Alexander and *Aristobulus in their resistance against the Romans. Pliny describes it as the strongest point in Judea after Jerusalem (Plinius, *Historia Naturalis*, 5:16, 72) and Strabo lists the fortress among the Hasmonean strongholds (16:2, 40). Herds, mainly of goats, were raised in the mountains of Machaerus (Tam. 3:8). According to Christian tradition, *John the Baptist was executed there on the orders of *Herod Antipas (Matt. 14:10; Mark 6:14ff.). The place served as one of the stations for signaling the appearance of the new moon and the arrival of holidays (Tosef., RH 2:2). In the Jewish War against the Romans the fortress was taken over by the Zealots (Jos., Wars, 2:485) and remained one of their strongholds even after the fall of Jerusalem (Jos., Wars, 4:555). In 72 C.E. the governor L. Bassus captured it after a short siege (Jos., Wars, 7:164ff.; includes a description of the site). Machaerus is the present-day al-Mukāwir, a ruin 14 mi. (c. 22 km.) southwest of Madaba.

Bibliography: F. M. Abel, *Une Croisière autour de la Mer Morte* (1911), 31ff.; A. Haefeli, *Samaria und Peraea* (1913), 114ff.; Glueck, in: AASOR, 18–19 (1939), 131ff.; Ploeger, in: ZDPV, 71 (1955), 151–5; Baldi, in: LA (1955), 234ff.; Press, Ereẓ, s.v. [M.A.-Y.]

MACHAUT, DENIS DE (late 14th century), Parisian Jew who converted to Christianity. The provost of Paris decreed that his youngest child was to remain under the father's guardianship and receive a Christian upbringing, while the other three children were entrusted to Christian families. De Machaut was to be allowed to visit them but not his wife, who had remained Jewish. After a period of time determined by the provost, the children were to be interrogated on their intention to become Christians or not. A short while later, when Denis de Machaut disappeared, the Jews were accused of having seized him in order to attempt to bring him back to Judaism. Seven of the community's leaders were condemned to be burned at the stake. On April 6, 1394, parliament commuted the sentence to imprisonment until De Machaut was returned. The sentence was accompanied by repeated, severe corporal punishment, and the Paris community was also fined 10,000 livres. It has been claimed that this affair was a decisive factor in the expulsion decree against the Jews or France issued in 1394.

Bibliography: L. Berman, *Histoire des Juifs de France* (1937), 206f.; R. Anchel, *Juifs* (1946), 117–9. [B.Bl.]

MACHIR (Heb. מָכִיר), son of Manasseh and grandson of Joseph. Although Machir appears to have been an only son according to Numbers 26:29–34 (cf. Gen. 50:23), other traditions ascribe more sons to Manasseh (Josh. 17:2), and name Asriel as a brother (I Chron. 7:14). Machir's mother is said to have been an Aramean (*ibid.*). He married *Maacah who bore him Peresh and Sheresh (I Chron. 7:16). He also had a daughter (I Chron. 2:21). He is most frequently described as the father of Gilead (Num. 26:29; Josh. 17:1; I Chron. 2:21; 7:14). Machir is the eponym of one of the most important clans of the tribe of Manasseh, the special status of which is acknowledged in Genesis 50:23. In the Song of Deborah, Machir is mentioned along with Ephraim and Benjamin (Judg. 5:14) while Manasseh is missing, indicating that this powerful tribe is represented by Machir. Further, the Song distinguishes between this tribe and the Gilead who resides in Transjordan and who, along with the tribe of Reuben, did not participate in the war (Judg. 5:15, 17). However, the location of Machir west of the Jordan contradicts other sources which state that the Machirites captured the Gilead and the Bashan in Moses' time before the Israelites crossed the Jordan (Num. 32:39–40; Josh. 17:1). It is reasonable to suppose that at first the entire clan dwelt west of the Jordan. Later, a part of it crossed to the eastern side (cf. Josh. 13:31, "A part of the sons of Machir"). It was subsequent to this settlement that Machir became head of Gilead. According to Numbers 32:39–42, the clan settled in the northern Gilead from the Jabbok to the Yarmuk, while *Jair, son of Manasseh, and Nobah were located even farther north, in the Bashan (cf. Deut. 3:14). In contrast to this, Joshua 13:29–31 and 17:1–2 record that the Machirites settled both in the Gilead and in the Bashan, whereas Jair was situated in the land of Gilead (I Chron. 2:22). These contradictions may be reconciled by assuming that Jair was another branch of the larger clan of Machir or, in the course of time, became affiliated with it. Indeed, in I Chronicles 2:21 Jair is considered Machir's descendant. Further, Maacah's being Machir's wife (I Chron. 7:16) suggests that the Machirites settled north of the Yarmuk bordering the land of Maacah. The reference in I Chronicles 7:14 apparently hints at an ethnic assimilation of the families of Machir with the Aramean population north of the Yarmuk.

Bibliography: A. Bergman, in: JAOS, 54 (1934), 169–77; idem, in: JPOS, 16 (1936), 224–54; J. Liver, in: EM, 4 (1962), 960–1.

[B.O.]

MACHIR BEN JUDAH (first half 11th century), younger brother of *Gershom b. Judah, "the Light of the Exile." Machir was the author of *Alef Bet de-Rabbi Makhir*. This work was in the possession of Rashi and the tosafists, who quote from it (Rashi, Gen. 43:11; Pes. 50a; Er. 22a; Tos. Nid. 7b s.v. *shammuti*, et al.), but it is now lost. It was the first talmudic dictionary to be compiled in Europe, not unlike the *Arukh* of *Nathan b. Jehiel of Rome. Its chief function was to connect words used in the Talmud with Scripture, to explain them, and to translate them into French. In consequence it also engaged in biblical exegesis. All the explanations in Machir's book were, evidently, given anonymously, no authorities being mentioned in it.

Machir had four sons: Nathan, Menahem, Nehemiah, and Yakar. These four collected the rulings, customs, and responsa of the great scholars of their locality. Menahem included all the material in a work which is referred to in the literature of the **rishonim* as *Ma'aseh ha-Makhiri* (Rabban—*Eliezer b. Nathan—Prague, 1610, 84c). Most of the material in his book, since lost, was included in the works of the *De-Vei Rashi* ("school of Rashi") and the whole book may have been used as the foundation for the *Ma'aseh ha-Ge'onim* (Berlin, 1909), certainly in respect of the information it affords about the customs of Speyer, Worms, and Mainz. The majority of the material in the *Ma'aseh ha-Ge'onim* is from these four brothers.

Bibliography: A. Epstein, *Ma'aseh ha-Ge'onim* (1909), x–xiii (introd.).

[I.T-S.]

MACHLUP, FRITZ (1902–), U.S. economist. Born in Wiener Neustadt, Austria, in 1923, Machlup was a partner in a paper manufacturing enterprise. In 1929 he began lecturing at the Volkshochschule in Vienna. In 1933 he emigrated to the U.S. He was a research fellow at the Rockefeller Foundation in New York City, which he left in 1935 to become professor of economics at the University of Buffalo. In 1947 he was appointed professor of political economy at Johns Hopkins and in 1960 became professor of economics and international finance at Princeton University, serving at the same time as director of Princeton's international finance section. During the 1960s one of Machlup's principal interests was the expansion of international liquidity. Among the offices he held in academic organizations were the presidencies of the American Association of University Professors (1962–64); and the American Economic Association (1966). His many publications include *Boersenkredit, Industriekredit und Kapitalbildung* (1931; *The Stock Market, Credit and Capital Formation*, 1940); *Fuehrer durch die Krisenpolitik* (1934), *The Political Economy of Monopoly* (1952), *The Production and Distribution of Knowledge in the United States* (1962), *Essays on Economic Semantics* (1963), and *International Payments, Debts, and Gold* (1964).

[J.O.R.]

MACHPELAH, CAVE OF (Heb. מְעָרַת הַמַּכְפֵּלָה). The word "Machpelah," which in the Bible always appears with a definite article, is variously the name of a cave (Gen. 23:9; 25:9); a field, "the cave which is in the field of Machpelah" (Gen. 49:30); and a place, "the field of Ephron, which was in Machpelah" (Gen. 23:17). The actual meaning of "Machpelah" is understood by all the early translations (Targum, Septuagint, et al.) as well as by the rabbis to mean "double" (from the Hebrew root *k-p-l*) and is interpreted in rabbinical literature as referring either to a double cave or to the "couples" buried in the cave. Machpelah is situated near Mamre, identified with Hebron (Gen. 33:19). The Bible relates that Abraham, wishing to bury Sarah, purchased Machpelah from Ephron the Hittite for 400 silver shekels. Abraham himself, Isaac and Rebekah, Jacob and Leah were all later buried there. Jacob specifically commanded his sons not to bury him in Egypt but to lay him to rest with his fathers in the cave of Machpelah (Gen. 47:28–31; 49:30).

[ED.]

The site of the cave is today identified with Ḥaram el-Khalīl in modern Hebron. Surrounding the area, to a height of 39 ft. (12 m.), is a magnificent wall, distinguished by its hewn stones which are up to 23 ft. (7.5 m.) in length. Because of their style they have been attributed to Herod even though this style of stonecutting existed previously. Josephus, who describes the tombs of the patriarchs as "of really fine marble and exquisite workmanship" (Jos., Wars 4:532), does not, however, mention the surrounding wall. The earliest source on the arrangement of the graves is in the Book of Jubilees (36:21) which states that "Leah is buried to the left of Sarah." According to the Jerusalem Talmud, the graves of the patriarchs are situated in the form

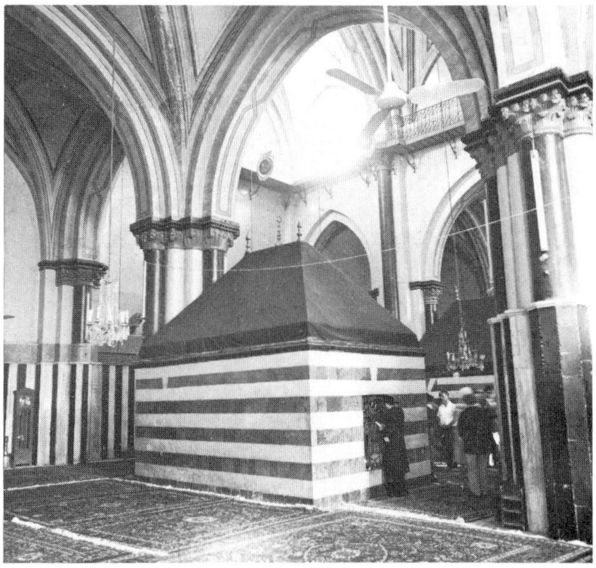

Traditional tomb of Rebekah in the cave of Machpelah at Hebron. Photo Werner Braun, Jerusalem.

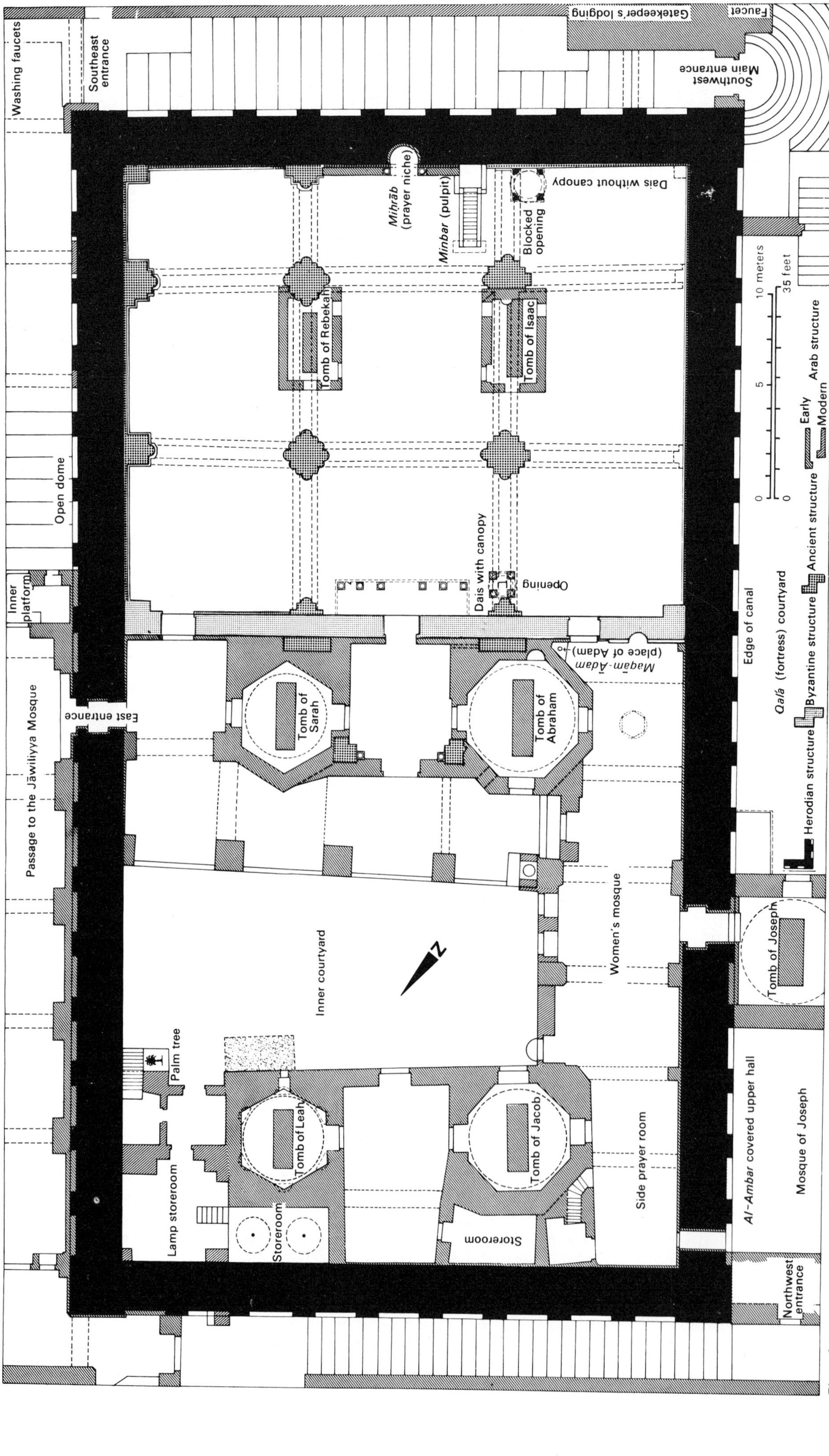

Plan of the mosque above the Cave of Machpelah. After L. H. Vincent *et al.*, *Hebron, Le Haram El-Khalîl, Sépulture des Patriarches*, Paris, 1923.

used for the partaking of a meal; the most prominent reclining at the head, on the middle couch, the second above him and the third below him (TJ, Ta'an. 4:2). The two structures, which today mark the tombs of Abraham and Sarah, are indeed in the center of the compound area. The tombs of Jacob and Leah are at the northwestern end so that when facing the tombs from the southwest—the probable original entrance—the tomb of Leah is in fact to the left of Sarah's. The area inside the compound was evidently originally left roofless. The Byzantines built a church, later converted by the Muslims into a mosque, at the southeastern extremity, which left the two constructions marking Isaac and Rebekah's tombs inside, while those for Abraham and Sarah were outside, at the entrance. In the floor, inside the mosque, are two openings leading to the cave underneath. One of these, at the southeast wall, is covered by stone slabs fixed with iron hooks. The other, at the opposite wall, is open, as a Muslim custom requires the lowering of an oil lamp which is continually lit. The actual form of the cavern is uncertain but from the accounts of travelers it seems safe to conclude that there are at least two caves joined by a passage and possibly a third inner chamber. The entrance to the caves (apart from the two openings) is not known today. Rabbinic sources mention the burial of Adam and Eve in the Machpelah and the alternative biblical name for Hebron, Kiriath-Arba ("the town of the four"), is explained to refer to the four couples buried there. According to Josephus and apocryphal sources, the sons of Jacob were also buried in the Machpelah. A Muslim tradition maintains that Joseph was buried here, his tomb and the Mosque of Joseph being just outside the southwest exit of the compound. This tradition is probably due to a corruption of the Arabic name for Esau, whose head, according to aggadic sources, fell within the cave after he had been killed in a battle for the right of burial in the Machpelah (Sot. 13a; PdRE 39).

During the Byzantine period, the Jews were authorized to pray within the area. The Christians entered through one gate and the Jews through another, offering incense while doing so; when the Arabs conquered the country they handed over the supervision of the cave of Machpelah to the Jews, in recognition of their assistance. During the late 11th century, the official responsible for the area bore the title of "The Servant to the Fathers of the World." The Jews of Hebron were accustomed to pray daily in the cave of Machpelah for the welfare of the head of the Palestinian gaonate. Many Jews sought to be buried in the vicinity of the cave of Machpelah. It was then written of them that "their resting-place was with that of the Fathers of the World." *Benjamin of Tudela, the 12th-century traveler, relates that "many barrels, full of the remains of Jews, were brought there and they are still laid to rest there to this day." The Mamluk sultan Baybars prohibited the Jews and Christians from praying within the area (1267). Jews, however, were permitted to ascend five, later seven, steps on the side of the eastern wall and to insert petitions into a hole opposite the fourth step. This hole pierces the entire thickness of the wall, to a depth of 6 ft. 6 in. (2.25 m.). It is first mentioned in 1521, and it can almost certainly be assumed to have been made at the request of the Jews of Hebron, possibly on payment of a large sum, so that their supplications would fall into the cave situated under the floor of the area. The extremity of the hole is below the blocked opening in the mosque floor and leads to the cave.

Following the Six-Day War of 1967 the Machpelah became a popular center of pilgrimage, and Jews, after a period of 700 years, were once more able to visit the tombs of the patriarchs, and regular services were held there.

[Jo.Br.]

Bibliography: I. S. Horowitz, *Ereẓ Yisrael u-Shekhenoteha* (1923), 248–63; L. H. Vincent, E. J. H. Mackay and F. M. Abel, *Hébron, Le Haram El-Khalîl, Sépulture des patriarches* (1923); Braslavi, in: *Eretz Israel*, 5 (1958), 220–3; idem, in: *Beit Mikra*, 14 (1969), I, 50–56; Luria, *ibid.*, 13 (1968), iii, 10–11; M. Ha-Kohen, *Me'arat ha-Makhpelah ba-Mekorot u-va-Masorot* (1965); O. Avisar (ed.), *Sefer Ḥevron* (1970).

MACHT, DAVID I. (1882–1961), U.S. pharmacologist. Macht, who was born in Moscow, was educated in the U.S. He graduated from Johns Hopkins Medical School where he lectured in pharmacology from 1912 to 1932. From 1933 to 1941 he served as visiting professor of general physiology at Yeshiva College (see *Yeshiva University) and from 1944 onward was consultant and research pharmacologist at Sinai Hospital in Baltimore. Macht published over 900 scientific studies in his field and introduced a number of new methods of treatment of diseases. He discovered the curative qualities of benzyl alcohol as a substitute for cocaine; he found that morphine and codeine have a sedative or depressant effect on the respiratory center as opposed to other narcotic drugs that act as stimulants; he proved that a difference exists in the biological effects produced by Roentgen rays of varying wavelength and introduced a cure for pemphigus by application of "deep" X-rays; he made a special study of the thromboplastic properties of various medical agents, especially of antibiotics. He also did extensive research on the pharmacology of blood and spinal fluid of psychotic patients. An Orthodox Jew, Macht constantly attempted to show the harmonious relationship between religion and science. He studied medical descriptions appearing in the Bible and the Talmud and showed that many of the so-called "miracles" or "medical stupidities" were in reality accurate descriptions of either diseases or their treatments. (Some of these are listed in Friedenwald, *The Jews and Medicine*, 2 (1967[2]), index.)

Bibliography: S. R. Kagan, *Jewish Medicine* (1952), 217–9; *New York Times* (Oct. 16, 1961), 29. [S.M.]

MACHTA, LESTER (1919–), U.S. meteorologist. Born in New York, Machta served in the U.S. Air Force as an instructor in meteorology and lectured in mathematics at the University of Illinois in 1941. He served as research associate at the Massachusetts Institute of Technology until he was appointed head of the special projects branch and director of meteorological research in the U.S. Weather Bureau in Washington in 1948. From 1962 Machta headed the Institute for Atmospheric Sciences and directed the Air Research Laboratories of the Environmental Science Services Administration (E.S.S.A.). [D.Ash.]

MACK, JULIAN WILLIAM (1866–1943), U.S. judge and Zionist leader. Mack, who was born in San Francisco, graduated from Harvard Law School in 1887, studied at the universities of Berlin and Leipzig, entered law practice in Chicago, and served as professor of law at Northwestern University (1895–1902) and the University of Chicago (1902–40). He was elected judge of the circuit court of Cook County, Illinois, in 1903, was judge of the Chicago juvenile court (1904–07), and the U.S. commerce court (1911–13). In 1904 he became president of the National Conference of Social Workers. His interest in the welfare of children was recognized in his appointment as one of the chairmen of the White House conference on children in 1908. Mack was appointed to the U.S. circuit court of appeals in 1913 and presided over hundreds of civil and criminal cases until his retirement in 1941. As a judge in Chicago and subsequently, Mack fought for a progressive approach to the problem of juvenile delinquency. During World War I, he performed ably on several national assignments, including the establishment of standards for reasonable treatment of conscientious objectors. A member of the Harvard University Board of Overseers for 18 years, he was influential in blocking a proposal in 1922 for a *numerus clausus* for Jewish students.

Julian Mack, U.S. judge and Zionist leader. Jerusalem, J.N.U.L., Schwadron Collection.

Mack's interest in Jewish affairs was deep and abiding. In addition to active participation in social work and charitable endeavors, he was among the founders of the American Jewish Committee in 1906 and on its executive committee for 12 years. Influenced by *Brandeis, Mack became an ardent Zionist, served as president of the first American Jewish Congress in 1918, and first chairman of the *Comité des Délégations Juives at the Versailles Peace Conference in 1919. Mack was elected president of the *Zionist Organization of America in 1918, but resigned with Brandeis in a dispute over methods of developing Palestine. He continued his efforts, however, holding high posts in the Palestine Endowment Fund, World Jewish Congress, Jewish Agency for Palestine, United Palestine Appeal, and the Hebrew University. The Israel settlement Ramat ha-Shofet ("Judge's Hill") was so called in his memory. Mack's credo, "We ask no more for the Jew than we do for anyone else," expressed both his sense of justice and loyalty to his people. He wrote *Americanism and Zionism* (1918).

Bibliography: Kallen, in: AJYB, 46 (1944–45), 35–46; *New York Times* (Sept. 6, 1943), 17:1; S.S. Wise, *As I See It* (1944), 178–83.

[Mo.Ro.]

MACNIN (Cohen ben Maknin), Moroccan family of Mogador which at the close of the 18th century was at first appointed "merchants of the sultan." MAC'ŪD MACNIN (d. 1832) was sent to Europe in 1809 by Sultan Mulay Suleiman in order to acquire a large amount of military equipment for the defense of the Moroccan ports. In 1813 he arrived in London as minister plenipotentiary. From 1795 his brother MEIR (d. c. 1830) headed an important firm of Mogador, whose principal agencies were in Marseilles and London. From 1799 the latter agency was directed by his nephew Solomon Sebag, the father of the future Sir Joseph Sebag-Montefiore. From the beginning of his reign Mulay Abd al-Raḥman (1822–59) granted Meir Macnin the exclusive right to export certain products and foodstuffs from Tetuán and Tangier and opened on his behalf the port of Tit to the maritime commerce of cereals. The port of Mazagan was put under his authority. From 1823 the sultan appointed him as his representative and envoy to the Christian courts, with the right of appointing consuls wherever he found the necessity. In 1826 he left on a special mission to London, and in 1828 he was appointed minister plenipotentiary.

Bibliography: Hirschberg, Afrikah, 2 (1965), 369; Miège, Maroc, 2 (1961), 40–41, and passim. [D.Co.]

MÂCON, capital of the department of Saône-et-Loire, E. France. The first *Church council of Mâcon (583) issued a series of decisions concerning the Jews. However, the first specific record of the presence of Jews in Mâcon dates from about 820, when *Agobard, archbishop of Lyons, began missionary activity among Jewish children at Mâcon who were sent to Arles for safety; he also arranged for the delivery of sermons condemning friendly relations between Christians and Jews. From 886 Jews are mentioned as owners of fields, and especially vineyards, on the outskirts of Mâcon and its surroundings, in at least 15 villages and places where they cultivated the land themselves. The Jewish quarter grew up in Bourgneuf. The cemetery was situated not far from Pont Jeu, formerly known as Pont des Juifs. Several medieval Hebrew tombstones have been discovered, some of which are preserved in the Museum of Mâcon. Not far from the site of the cemetery, there was a house commonly known by the name Sabbat, a term sometimes employed in Burgundy for the synagogue. In 1378, the municipality attempted to compulsorily segregate the 18 Jews still living in Mâcon in a separate quarter. They were expelled from the town in 1394. During the 17th and 18th centuries, Jews of Avignon visited Mâcon and its surroundings to trade. At the beginning of World War II, there were about 50 Jewish families living in Mâcon, but they were not organized into a community. The present community, consisting mainly of arrivals from North Africa, numbered 200 in 1969.

Bibliography: Gross, Gal Jud, 339f.; B. Blumenkranz, *Juifs et chrétiens ...* (1960), index s.v. *Mâcon* and *Concile de Mâcon;* idem, in: *Bulletin philologique et historique 1959* (1960), 129–36; G. Jeanton, in: *Annales de l'Académie de Mâcon,* 20 (1917), 381ff.; idem, *Le Vieux Mâcon* (1934), 9ff., 81ff.; Loeb, in: REJ, 5 (1882), 104ff.; Z. Szajkowski, *Analytical Franco-Jewish Gazetteer 1939–1945* (1966), 255.

[B.Bl.]

MADABA, MEDEBA (Heb. מֵידְבָא), Moabite city, situated about 5½ mi. (9 km.) S. of Heshbon in the center of a fertile plain, the biblical Mishor, 2,550 ft. (785 m.) above sea level. The city was captured by the Israelites from the Amorite king Sihon and was allocated to the tribe of Reuben (Num. 21:30; Josh. 13:16). Near Medeba, David defeated the Aramean allies of Ammon (I Chron. 19:7). Israel lost its hold on the city when the monarchy was divided. Omri recaptured it, but the Moabite king Mesha restored it to Moab. In the Hasmonean period, the city fought against Jonathan. It was finally conquered by Hyrcanus I; Hyrcanus II ceded it to the Nabateans. In 106 C.E. it was incorporated into Provincia Arabia. Jews lived there in mishnaic times (Mik. 7:1). It was a flourishing Christian city in Byzantine times, when the town spread around the ancient mound. It had no less than 13 churches, most of which were paved with mosaics. The best known of these is the northern church with a mosaic pavement designed as a map of the Holy Land. Medeba is now a town in Jordan with c. 5,000 inhabitants, mostly Christian.

The Madaba Mosaic Map. In 1884 a mosaic map was discovered during the erection of a new Greek Orthodox church, but only in 1896, when part of it was already ruined, was it brought to the notice of scholars. The map was laid in the transept of a sixth-century church and originally measured 72 ft. (22 m.) × 23 ft. (7 m.). It represented the biblical Holy Land and neighboring regions, from Byblos (Gebal) in the north to No-Ammon (Thebes in Egypt) in the south. The map was oriented toward the east, with the Mediterranean Sea at the bottom. The scale is uneven, largest for the more important areas (central Judea—1:15,000; Jerusalem—1:1,650). In general,

The Madaba map, with Jerusalem in the center and the Jordan River and the Dead Sea above. Sixth century C.E. Photo Sir Herbert Samuel Album, State Archives, Jerusalem.

it follows the *Onomasticon* of Eusebius; it was based on a Roman road map, with the addition of vignettes representing the principal cities. The Greek texts give biblical and contemporary names, sometimes with a historical note or verse from the Septuagint. Important places and tribal areas are marked in red. The extant part of the map covers an area from Neapolis (Nablus) to Egypt. The most valuable section is the detailed plan of Jerusalem, showing two colonnaded streets, the Tower of David, many churches and monasteries, including the Church of the Holy Sepulcher and that on Mount Zion, baths and perhaps even the Western Wall. Most of the other cities indicated on the map are fragmentary. It notes many names in the Negev which are not recorded elsewhere. A few natural features are indicated on the map, as well as ships in the Dead Sea, animals in the deserts, and ferries across the Jordan. In some details, the Madaba map shows clear evidence of the influence of Jewish lore, as in the location of the mountains Ebal and Gerizim near Jericho (although a second Tur Gerizim is placed in its true position near Nablus). The mosaic was restored and recorded in color by a German expedition in 1965–66.

Bibliography: Abel, Geog, 2 (1938), 381–2; Aharoni, Land, index; P. Palmer and H. Guthe, *Die Mosaikkarte von Madeba* (1906); A. Jacoby, *Das geographische Mosaik von Madaba* (1905); O'Callaghan, in: DBI, 5 (1957), s.v.; M. Avi-Yonah, *The Madaba Mosaic Map* (1954); Donner, in: ZDPV, 83 (1967), 1ff.; U. Lux, in: ZDPV, 84 (1968), 106–42.

[M.A.-Y.]

MADAGASCAR, island off Africa. Legends and theories about alleged Jewish descent of and influence on inhabitants of Madagascar are current and widespread, but the resemblance of certain customs is probably a consequence of contact with Islam through trade activities in the late Middle Ages. Various theories and suppositions regarding affinities to the ancient Hebrews were published by a French Lazarist missionary, Joseph Briant, in a booklet entitled *L'hebreu à Madagascar*.

Madagascar never had a sizable Jewish population. A few score of Jewish families settled in Tananarive during the French colonial period, but no community was created.

Relations with Israel. The State of Israel was among the very first (and still few) countries to establish an embassy in the newly proclaimed Malagasy Republic (1960), and, over the years, Presidents Tsiranana and Ben-Zvi exchanged visits and Israel Prime Minister Eshkol and Foreign Minister Golda Meir also visited Madagascar. Israel activities in Madagascar include the construction of the first luxury hotel, and agricultural experts have helped to produce citrus and improve poultry breeding and corn production. In addition, about 200 people from the Malagasy Republic have undergone technical training in Israel. Relations between the two countries were close, although the intimate relationship between France and Madagascar cast a shadow over the picture after the 1967 change in French policy toward the Arab-Israel conflict.

[Z.Lo.]

MADAGASCAR PLAN, proposal for Jewish settlement. Like most of the Nazis' devices for treatment of the Jews, the Madagascar Plan had already been conceived by others. In 1885 Paul de *Lagarde, the well-known German anti-Semitic nationalist, had advocated solving the Jewish question in the East, which he believed had to be colonized by Germany, by deporting the Jews of Poland, Russia, Rumania, and Austria. He preferred the French island colony on the east coast of Africa over Palestine. In 1926 and 1927 Poland and Japan, respectively, investigated Madagascar as a possible solution to the problem of over-population; both dismissed the idea as not feasible. Ten years later, in 1937, a new Polish commission was sent to Madagascar to assess if Jews could be forced to settle there. Leon Alter, the director of *HICEM in Warsaw, and Salmon Dyk, an agricultural engineer from Tel Aviv, took part in the mission. The estimates of the commission's leader, Major M. Lepecki, and those of Alter differed widely, but it was obvious that the available area, with bearable climatic conditions, was very restricted and the danger of endemic tropical diseases was considered extreme. This point was specially stressed by the French governor-general of the island, Marcel Olivier, who wrote and spoke publicly against the proposal. Nevertheless, the idea was taken up by the French foreign minister, Georges Bonnet, who told Joachim *Ribbentrop on Dec. 9, 1938, that in order to relieve France of 10,000 Jewish refugees, it would be necessary to ship them elsewhere. According to Ribbentrop, "They were actually thinking of Madagascar for this."

Even before the November *Kristallnacht,* on March 5, 1938, when the Germans were still considering mass emigration, Adolf *Eichmann was commissioned to assemble material to provide Reinhardt *Heydrich with "a solution of foreign policy as it had been negotiated between Poland and France," i.e., the Madagascar Plan. Thus this project was by no means new when it was again taken up after the fall of France in the summer of 1940. Eichmann prepared a detailed official report on the island and its "colonization" possibilities based on information gathered from the French Colonial Office. An evacuation plan calling for 4,000,000 Jews to be shipped to Madagascar over a period of four years was added. Eichmann also advocated a "police reserve," a sort of giant ghetto *("Gross-Getto").* The plan was to be financed by a special bank managing confiscated Jewish property and by contributions of the rest of world Jewry. The idea was also ventilated by Martin Luther's department of the German Foreign Office.

The plan leaked out and was published in Italy in July. The *American Jewish Committee was alarmed enough to commission Eugene Hevesi to make a special investigation of the conditions prevailing on Madagascar in order to prove that Jews, like other Europeans, could not be settled there. The subsequent report was published in May 1941. At that time the Nazis were already preparing a completely different "*Final Solution." In August 1940, when the Madagascar Plan was officially endorsed, it was probably meant to camouflage the Nazis' true intentions by means of a smoke screen. The 20-page proposal elaborated a detailed plan for which the consent of even the French could not be attained. The operation, whose code word was *"Endloesung,"* was repeatedly discussed. Only when the extermination program was already well in operation and the German ministries had been brought in on the secret of true "Final Solution," at the *Wannsee Conference, was the Madagascar Plan officially shelved (Feb. 10, 1942) and substituted by "evacuation to the East."

Bibliography: G. Reitlinger, *Final Solution* (1968²), 23, 49, 79–82; J. Robinson, *And the Crooked Shall be Made Straight* (1965), index; E. Hevesi, in: *Contemporary Jewish Record,* 4 (1941) 381–94.

[L.Y.]

°**MADISON, JAMES** (1750–1836), fourth president of the United States. The son of a prominent Episcopalian family, Madison graduated from the College of New Jersey in 1771. Because he was then considering a career in the ministry, he spent an additional year studying theology and Hebrew. Throughout his political career, he contended that complete religious liberty was essential for a harmonious society and that religious institutions established by the state engendered "ignorance and corruption." During the Virginia constitutional convention in 1776, he opposed a provision for full religious "toleration," proposing instead that the law declare "the full and free exercise of it [religion] according to the dictates of conscience." In 1784 he successfully led the opposition to a resolution in the Virginia House of Delegates for a tax in "support of the Christian religion, or of some Christian church" and warned that "Instead of holding forth an asylum to the persecuted, it is itself a signal of persecution." As president he vetoed two bills in 1811 which would have granted legal prerogatives to certain churches.

While serving as a congressman from 1780 to 1783, Madison borrowed money from the Jewish broker Haym *Salomon, whom he later referred to gratefully in a letter. Writing to Mordecai M. *Noah in 1818, he expressed delight at the blessings conferred upon Jews by religious liberty in America, while in 1820 he wrote to Jacob De La *Motta that while being little known, "the history of the Jews must be forever interesting." During his presidency he appointed several Jews to government posts, including John *Hays as collector for the Indian Territory in 1814, Mordecai Noah as consul general at Tunis in 1813, and Joel *Hart as consul at Leith, Scotland in 1817.

Bibliography: G. Hunt, *The Life of James Madison* (1902), 8–12, 77–86; S. K. Padover (ed.), *The Complete Madison* (1953), 298–312; Kohler, in: AJHSP, 11 (1903), 60–65.

[E.GR.]

MAḌMŪN BEN JAPHETH BEN BUNDĀR (d. 1151), son of the first *nagid* of the Jews of South Yemen. Maḍmūn continued in his father's position as the "official of the merchants" in Aden, representing the merchants who traded with India, and in this capacity was also the leader of the Jews and the *nagid* of the communities of South Yemen. Dozens of letters have been preserved in the *Genizah* which were written to or by him, as well as court actions connected with his name and poems in his honor. More details are known about him than about any other *nagid* of Yemen from the 11th to the beginning of the 14th centuries. He was in charge of the port of Aden and supervised the customs payments. He formulated the agreements about prices of merchandise and his house served as a post office for the Jewish merchants, as well as a warehouse for merchandise. He owned ships which sailed from Aden to Ceylon. Among his wide-ranging activities, he jointly owned a ship with a vizier in Yemen. In a court action he is named "the confidant of rulers whether on the sea or in the desert," which means that he was held in esteem by the Muslim rulers and drew up agreements with tribal leaders and the leaders of pirates in order to assure free navigation on the sea routes between Egypt and India. In the above-mentioned court action it is stated that he was "appointed on behalf of the *rashei galuyyot* ["exilarchs"] and the *rashei yeshivot* ["academy heads"]." It is not clear whether the reference here is to the exilarch in Babylon or to a person representing the exilarch who lived in Yemen; there is an hypothesis that the reference is to the *bet din* in San'a. *Rashei yeshivot* refers to the Palestinian academy in Egypt.

Maḍmūn maintained close contact with the *gaon* Maẓli'aḥ b. Solomon ha-Kohen, who was active in 1127–39 as head of the Palestinian academy which moved to Egypt as a result of the conquest of Palestine by the Crusaders. Maḍmūn sent the *gaon* questions on *halakhah,* together with expensive gifts which were also given to the scholars of his academy. He ordered that the name of the *gaon* be mentioned in the *reshut* prayer after the name of the exilarch. His attachment to the Palestinian academy aroused the opposition of the supporters of Babylonia. In documents he is called "the *nagid* of God's people, the minister of ministers, head of the communities." The Tunisian merchant Abraham b. Peraḥyah b. Yiju writes of him in his eulogy: "with seven names given by the exilarch," among which are mentioned, *alluf, nagid,* and friend of the academy. When he died, his eldest son, Ḥalfon, who is also called *nagid,* continued in his father's position in economic and public life.

Bibliography: J. Mann, in: HUCA, 3 (1926), 301–3; E. Strauss, in: *Zion,* 4 (1939), 217–31; S. D. Goitein, in: *Sinai,* 33 (1953), 225–37; idem, in: *Sefer ha-Yovel . . . M. M. Kaplan* (1953), 45, 51–53; idem, in: *Tarbiz,* 31 (1962), 357–70; idem, *Bo'i Teiman* (1967), 15–25; idem, in: JQR, NS, 53 (1962), 97; E. Subar, *ibid.*, 49 (1958/59), 301–9. [El.B.]

MADON (Heb. מָדוֹן), Canaanite city in the north of Ereẓ Israel whose king was defeated by Joshua in the battle at the waters of Merom (Josh. 11:1; 12:19). It is usually identified with the tell at Qarn Ḥiṭṭīn (Horns of *Hittin), a peak about 4 mi. (7 km.) west of Tiberias. Remains of walls, including one of cyclopean masonry, and potsherds from the Canaanite and Israelite periods were found on this tell. The identification is based on the similarity between the names Madon and Khirbat Madīn, situated south of Qarn Ḥiṭṭīn, which Arabic tradition connects with Moses' father-in-law Jethro, the priest of Midian, whose grave is venerated nearby. Some scholars, however, question the form of the name Madon, which is the sole basis for the identification. No town with this name is known from any other source; the Septuagint calls it Marron and identifies it with the city Merom near the site of the battle (in LXX: *Hydor Marron,* "waters of Merom"). *Merom is known from various sources as an important city in Upper Galilee and Madon may be a corrupt form of its name.

Bibliography: Abel, Geog, 2 (1938), 372f.; J. Garstang, *Joshua, Judges* (1931), 102, 187ff.; Aharoni, Land, index; idem, *Hitnaḥalut Shivtei Yisrael ba-Galil ha-Elyon* (1957), 91f. [Yo.A.]

MADRAS, city in S. India. Formerly known as Fort St. George, Madras was the first territorial acquisition of the English East India Company in 1639. In the last decades of the 17th century its diamond trade attracted Anglo-Portuguese Jewish merchants, who were allowed by the Company to establish a merchant colony which continued until the end of the 18th century. In the Madras corporation, established in 1688, the "Hebrew merchants" were represented by Jewish aldermen. Among the Jewish merchants prominent in the early days were Bartholomew *Rodrigues, Domingo do Porto, Alvaro da *Fonseca, Jacques *Paiva, Francis *Marques, Isaac do Porto, Joseph d'Almanza, and Isaac Sardo *Abendana. In the 18th century many Ashkenazi Jews from London participated in the profitable trade, including Marcus *Moses and his family, Ephraim Isaac, the *Franks, and later the Portuguese family De *Castro and Salomon *Franco. The Jewish merchants in Madras were integrated into the English society and were on good social terms with several of the governors.

The fluctuating nature of the merchant colony apparently prevented the organization of a Jewish community and the only communal institution seems to have been a cemetery. Some tombstones still remain, but they have been transferred to a new municipal site in Madras called "the People's Park," the entrance of which bears a tablet inscribed in Hebrew *Beit ha-Ḥayyim.* Only 20 Jews were living in Madras in 1968. Unlike those of *Cochin, *Bombay, and *Calcutta, the Jews in Madras did not create any literary works. It was only due to the Christian mission that some Hebrew books were published there in the 19th century. A noteworthy Jewish literary event there was the publication of the *Travels from Jerusalem . . .* of *David d'Beth Hillel in 1832.

Bibliography: Fischel, in: *Journal of the Economic and Social History of the Orient,* 3 (1960), 78–107, 175–95 (incl. bibl.); Roth, Mag Bibl, 106; H. D. Love, *Vestiges of Old Madras,* 4 vols. (1913); A. Yaari, *Ha-Defus ha-Ivri be-Arẓot ha-Mizraḥ,* 2 (1940), 98–99. [W.J.F.]

MADRID (Magerit), capital of Spain. Mentioned as a Moorish stronghold, it was a tiny town in the Middle Ages. A small Jewish community existed there in the 11th century. Most of the Jews there were apparently merchants during the Muslim period. Nearby was located the small town of Alluden, whose name is derived from the Arabic *al-Yahūdiyīn* ("the Jews"). Madrid was captured from the Muslims by Alfonso VI in 1083. [H.Z.H.]

The Community's Status. The community began to flourish during the 13th century, the Jewish quarter being located on the present Calle de la Fé ("Street of the Faith"). The synagogue, which was destroyed during the persecutions of 1391 (see below), was situated next to the Church of San Lorenzo. In 1293 a copy of the resolutions passed by the Cortes in Valladolid was sent to Madrid, in which Sancho IV ratified a series of restrictions concerning the Jews. They were barred from holding official positions, the rate of usury they were permitted to charge was defined, and they were prohibited from acquiring real estate from Christians or from selling them properties already acquired, among other limitations. In 1307, when Ferdinand IV confirmed these prohibitions at the Cortes in Valladolid, a copy of them was passed to Madrid. They were endorsed by Alfonso XI in 1329. A directive from the time of *Asher b. Jehiel (early 14th century) permitting action to be taken against an *informer who had harmed the community is extant (Asher b. Jehiel, Responsa, Constantinople (1517), ch. 17, no. 6).

The Jews of Madrid owned goods and real estate in the town and its environs. In 1385 John I acceded to the request of the Cortes and delivered a copy of its resolutions to Madrid. He then imposed a series of restrictions concerning the relations between Jews and Christians, prohibiting Jews from holding official positions, canceling debts owed them by Christians for 15 months, and abrogating the right to acquire stolen goods, among other regulations.

Persecutions and Expulsion. The persecutions of 1391 were disastrous for the Madrid community. Most of its

Figure 1. Calle de la Fé, "The Street of the Faith," formerly the Jewish street of Madrid. Photo M. Ninio, Jerusalem.

members were massacred, some adopted Christianity, and community life came to an end. The municipal authorities, in a report sent to the Crown, complained of the *pueblo menudo* ("little people") who continued the rioting and pillaging for a whole year. Several of the rioters were arrested and tried, but many escaped justice. Apparently the community was later reestablished, although it was greatly impoverished.

During the early 1460s, *Alfonso de Espina preached in Madrid against the *Conversos. It was there that he turned to *Alfonso de Oropesa, the head of the Order of St. Jerome, to enlist his support in eradicating judaizing tendencies among them. In 1478 the municipal council complained that the Jews and the Moors there were not wearing a distinctive sign (*badge). The Crown answered the complaint on November 12 and ordered that the offenders should be punished in the prescribed manner. On February 2, Ferdinand and Isabella renewed the restriction issued by John II in 1447 which prohibited the Jews of Madrid from trading in foodstuffs and medicaments and from practicing as surgeons.

No details are known as to how the community fared after the decree of expulsion of the Jews from Spain was issued in March 1492. However, on Oct. 7, 1492, Ferdinand and Isabella ordered an investigation into reports of attacks on local Jews by various persons who had promised to assist them in reaching the frontiers in order to go to the kingdoms of Fez and Tlemcen. On Nov. 8, Fernando Nuñez Coronel (Abraham *Senior) and Luis de Alcalá were authorized to collect the debts still owing to Jews.

The Conversos. Several Conversos of Madrid were tried by the Inquisition. They were at first tried in Toledo; however, in 1561 when Madrid became the capital of the kingdom during the reign of Philip II, the supreme tribunal of the kingdom was established there and subsequently numerous *autos-da-fé were held in the city. During the 17th century, many Portuguese Conversos were tried there and one of the large autos-da-fé in this period has been painted by Rizzi de Guevara. During the 1630s, Jacob *Cansino negotiated with the Conde-Duque de Olivares concerning the possible return of the Jews to Madrid, after the example of the Jewish community in Rome. However, the talks had no results because of opposition from the Inquisition. Throughout this period, Madrid was the principal center of the activities of the Portuguese Conversos, several of whom were connected with the court, while others developed diversified business enterprises and maintained relations with the Converso centers outside the Iberian Peninsula.

Figure 2. One of the two synagogues of the Madrid community center, opened in 1968. The center also comprises a kindergarten, school, kosher restaurant, a club, and community offices. Photo M. Ninio, Jerusalem.

The Reestablished Community. Jewish settlement in Madrid was gradually renewed from 1869, with the conferment of the constitution and the arrival of Jews from North Africa, who were joined by Jewish immigrants from Europe. However, it was only during the 1920s that a community was organized. During World War I, Madrid gave asylum to a number of refugees, and Max *Nordau and A. S. *Yahuda, who lectured there in Semitic philology, lived there during this period. Among the first Jews to settle in Madrid was the Bauer family, whose members played an important part in the organization and development of the community. The law of 1924 which granted citizenship to individuals of Spanish descent encouraged the further development of the community, and in the early 1930s there was an addition of refugees from Nazi Germany. During the Spanish Civil War, the community underwent much suffering and most of its members dispersed.

In 1941, the Arias Montano Institute for Jewish Studies was founded and a department of Jewish studies headed by Professor Francisco Cantera-Burgos was organized within the University of Madrid. It was later headed by Professor F. Perez Castro. Madrid also gave asylum to war refugees, who were supported by the *American Jewish Joint Distribution Committee. After the war, the community began reorganization. A synagogue was founded in Calle del Cardinal Cisneros. In 1958, a Jewish center with a synagogue was opened. In 1959, while the representative of the World Sephardi Federation, Yair Behar Passy, was visiting Madrid, an exhibition of Jewish culture in Spain was held at the National Library of Madrid. An Institute for Jewish, Sephardi, and Near Eastern Studies was founded jointly by the Higher Council for Scientific Research and the World Sephardi Federation in 1961. (In 1968 the institute amalgamated with the Arias Montano Institute.) Within the framework of the institute, the first symposium on Spanish Jewry was held in Madrid in 1964. Leaders of the Madrid community in the late 1960s included A. Bauer, H. Cohen, L. Blitz, and M. Mazin (the president of the community). In that year the community numbered over 3,000. It served as a center for Jewish students from abroad coming to study in Madrid. Some Jewish immigrants from North Africa have been integrated within the Madrid community. In 1968 the community inaugurated its new communal center and synagogue. Dr. B. Garzon was appointed first rabbi of the community, which had a recognized school and a Jewish scout movement.

See also *Spain. [H.B.]

Bibliography: Baer, Spain, 2 (1966), index; Baer, Urkunden, 2 (1929), index; Fita, in: *Boletín de la Academia de la Historia, Madrid,* 8 (1885), 439–66; F. Cantera, *Sinagogas españolas* (1955), 241–2; R. T. Davies, *Spain in Decline* (1957), 76–77; AJYB, 63 (1962), 318–22; J. Gomez Iglesias (ed.), *El Fuero de Madrid* (1963); Suárez Fernández, Documentos, index; Ashtor, Korot, 2 (1966), 145; H. Beinart, *Ha-Yishuv ha-Yehudi he-Ḥadash bi-Sefarad* (1969).

°**MAES, ANDREAS** (**Masius;** 1515?–1573), Flemish Hebraist and orientalist. A lawyer and a diplomat, Maes spent much of his life in Italy, where he met Guillaume Postel, under whom he studied Arabic and with whom he thereafter maintained an interesting correspondence. In Venice Maes joined the humanist circle of Daniel Bomberg and was in touch with the pioneer grammarian Elijah Levita. Maes contributed to the Antwerp polyglot Bible (1568–72), in which he published an edition of the Targums and the first printed grammar and lexicon of Syriac. His Hebrew-Greek edition of Joshua, *Josuae imperatoris historia . . .* (Antwerp, 1574), which appeared posthumously,

הַשִּׁירִים אֲשֶׁר לִשְׁלֹמֹה
יִשָּׁקֵנִי מִנְּשִׁיקוֹת פִּיהוּ
כִּי טוֹבִים דֹּדֶיךָ מִיַּיִן
לְרֵיחַ שְׁמָנֶיךָ טוֹבִים
שֶׁמֶן תּוּרַק שְׁמֶךָ עַל כֵּן
עֲלָמוֹת אֲהֵבוּךָ מָשְׁכֵנִי
אַחֲרֶיךָ נָּרוּצָה הֱבִיאַנִי
הַמֶּלֶךְ חֲדָרָיו נָגִילָה וְנ
וְנִשְׂמְחָה בָּךְ נַזְכִּירָה דֹדֶיךָ
מִיַּיִן מֵישָׁרִים אֲהֵבוּךָ
שְׁחוֹרָה אֲנִי וְנָאוָה בְּנוֹת
יְרוּשָׁלַ͏ִם כְּאָהֳלֵי קֵדָר
כִּירִיעוֹת שְׁלֹמֹה אֵל

An initial-word panel for the Song of Songs from the *Tripartite Maḥzor,* depicting King Solomon on his throne. The panel is from the first volume of a three-part *Maḥzor,* written by Ḥayyim the Scribe in South Germany, about 1320. Budapest, Library of the Hungarian Academy of Sciences, Kaufmann Collection, ms. A384, fol. 183 ($12\frac{1}{4} \times 8\frac{1}{2}$ ins/31×21.5 cm.).

aroused controversy because of its independence in regard to the masoretic text. This work lists the rabbinic and kabbalistic manuscripts in Maes' library, which must have been one of the major collections of Judaica in the Renaissance. Maes was apparently a member of the heretical Flemish sect ("The Family of Charity") led by Postel, Arias Montano, and the printer Christophe Plantin. Maes opposed the papal condemnation of the Talmud and the burning of rabbinic books at Rome in 1559.

Bibliography: J. Perles, *Beitraege zur Geschichte der hebraeischen und aramaeischen Studien* (1884), index; M. Lossen (ed), *Briefe von Andreas Masius und seinen Freunden, 1538 bis 1573* (1886); U. Cassuto, *I Manoscritti Palatini Ebraici della Biblioteca Apostolica Vaticana* (1935), 48, 65f.; C. Roth, *The Jews in the Renaissance* (1959), 149; B. Rekers, *Benito Arias Montano* (Dutch, 1961), index; F. Secret, in: *Bibliothèque d'Humanisme et Renaissance*, 23 (1961), 524–40; idem, *Les Kabbalistes Chrétiens de la Renaissance* (1964), 54–56. [G.E.S.]

MAFTIR (Heb. מַפְטִיר; "one who concludes"), name given to the three or more concluding verses of the weekly Sabbath *sidrah* ("Torah portion") as well as to the final verses of the portions read on festivals and public *fast days. The person who is called up to the reading from the Torah of these passages and who then recites the **haftarah* from the Prophets is also called *maftir*.

See also *Torah, Reading of; *Masorah, Masoretic Accents. [Ed.]

MAGDALA, city on the Sea of Galilee, mentioned several times in the New Testament, sometimes with variations on the name, such as Magadan or Dalmanutha (Matt. 15:39; Mark 8:10). It was the hometown of Mary the Magdalene (Matt. 27:56; Mark 15:40). In talmudic sources it appears as Migdal Nunaiya, a center for fishing and the preserving industry (Pes. 46a), four miles (c. 7 km.) from Tiberias. The talmudic identification of the place with Migdal Zobaiya (TJ, Ta'an. 4:8, 69a) has been disputed. R. Isaac and R. Judah were two of the *amoraim* living in Magdala. Resh Lakish sought refuge there against the wrath of the patriarch Judah II. After the destruction of the Temple, the priests of the family of Ezekiel settled there. A local synagogue is mentioned in the *Pesikta de-Rav Kahana* 90c.

On the basis of Josephus' descriptions (see below), talmudic Migdal Nunaiya is generally identified with the city of Taricheae (a name meaning "place where fish were salted"), despite Pliny's erroneous setting of the latter on the southern part of the lake, leading some scholars to look for it at Bet Yeraḥ. Taricheae, one of the centers of the Zealots in Galilee during the Jewish War against Rome, was situated west of Capernaum (Jos., Life, 59, 72). It was walled on the land side and contained a stadium. The city was attacked by the Roman army, which advanced from Sennabris to Tiberias and then to Taricheae, four miles (c. 7 km.) from Tiberias (Jos., Wars, 3:462–505, 532–542). The place fell to the Romans after a strenuous fight on land and sea. However, it continued to exist as a Jewish city. It is identified with present-day Majdal, a ruin on the shores of the Sea of Galilee, north of Tiberias.

Bibliography: Albright, in: AASOR, 2–3 (1922), 29ff.; G. Dalman, *Sacred Sites and Ways* (1934), index; Lickenberger, in: ZDPV, 57 (1934), 281ff. [M.A.-Y.]

MAGDEBURG, city in E. Germany. The Jewish community of Magdeburg is the oldest in East Germany and one of the oldest in Germany as a whole. As early as 965 there were Jews living in the town and they were placed under the jurisdiction of the archbishop by Otto the Great. They traded in the "clothing-court" *(Kleiderhof)*, in the merchants' quarter, and conducted their trade even beyond the Oder River. Their quarter, the *Judendorf*, was situated in the south of the city, in the archbishop's domain. The Jews took part in the funeral procession of Archbishop Walthard von Magdeburg in 1012. The cemetery dates from the 13th century—the oldest gravestone bears the date 1268—later enlarged in 1312 and 1383. In 1213 the soldiers of Otto IV destroyed the *Judendorf*, and four years later the Jews moved to nearby Sudenburg, where numerous other Jews already lived. Demanding jurisdiction over the Jews in 1260 the canons of the cathedral laid claim to the fines they paid in silver, while those paid in gold were to remain the property of the archbishop. Prominent in the city were R. Hezekiah b. Jacob who corresponded with R. *Isaac Or Zaru'a, and R. *Ḥayyim b. Paltiel, rabbi in Magdeburg in 1291, who was in correspondence with R. Meir of Rothenburg. The Jews were persecuted in 1302 and again during the *Black Death disturbances of 1349, despite the attempts of the archbishop and the city authorities to protect them. They were attacked again in 1357 and 1384 when another epidemic broke out. Archbishop Dietrich employed a Jewish court banker between 1361 and 1367. In 1410 Archbishop Guenther issued a letter of protection *(Schutzbrief)* for a period of six years, at a cost to the community of 40 silver marks. During the 15th century the community maintained a flourishing yeshivah. In 1493 the Jews of Magdeburg were expelled; the synagogue was converted into a chapel and the cemetery destroyed.

When the great elector, Frederick William, readmitted Jews to *Prussia (1671), *Schutzjuden* settled once more in Magdeburg. From 1703 they were to be found in Sudenburg, from 1715 in the newer part of town (the *Neustadt*), and from 1729 in the *Altstadt*. A religious school was founded by the modern community in 1834 and a *ḥevra kaddisha* in 1839. Rabbis of the community included Ludwig *Philippson, editor of **Allgemeine Zeitung des Judentums*, Moritz *Guedemann, and Moritz Spanier, both of whom wrote a history of the community. Eduard *Lasker and Otto *Landsberg were repeatedly elected to parliament from Magdeburg. The prosperous community, which included 45 doctors (who founded their own club in 1903), had about 20 social, cultural, and charitable organizations in 1933. The number of Jews increased steadily from 330 in 1817 to 559 in 1840; 1,000 in 1859; 1,815 in 1885; 1,843 in 1910; and around 3,200 in 1928, then dropped to 2,361 (0.6% of the total population) in 1933. The synagogue, built in 1851 and enlarged to seat 900 in 1897, was burned down on Nov. 10, 1938. The men were interned in *Buchenwald. By May 17, 1939, only 679 Jews remained in the town and the majority were transported to concentration camps. On July 1, 1944, there were still 185 Jews living in Magdeburg, mainly partners of mixed marriages, who managed to survive the war. After the war some Jews returned to Magdeburg, and the Jewish population numbered about 100 in 1965.

Bibliography: M. Guedemann, in: MGWJ, 14 (1865), 241–56, 281–96, 321–35, 361–70; M. Spanier, *Geschichte der Juden in Magdeburg* (1928); idem, in: ZGJD, 5 (1892), 273, 392–5; Vogelstein-Rieger, 1 (1895), 315; D. Kaufmann and M. Freudenthal, *Die Familie Gomperz* (1907), 236–42; MGADJ, 1 (1909), 110; 3 (1911/12), 164; S. Neufeld, *Die Juden im Thueringisch-Saechsischen Gebiet* . . ., pt. 2 (1927), 8, 14–16, 168–70; Germ Jud, 1 (1963), 163–70; 2 (1968), 505–10; FJW (1932); PKG; E. Forchheimer, in: *Geschichtsblaetter fuer Stadt und Land Magdeburg*, 46 (1911), 119–78, 328–40; O. Simon, in: *AJR Information*, 15 (Nov. 1960): S. Stern, *Der preussische Staat und die Juden*, 1 (1962), Akten, no. 135–9, 371–410a; 2 (1962), Akten, no. 496–571. [L.Lew./Ed.]

MAGDEBURG LAW, term applied to the constitutional and commercial urban law which developed in *Magdeburg in the Middle Ages and became a pattern for new city constitutions in Central and Eastern Europe. Magdeburg law was adopted by most cities in central, eastern, and northern Germany, Bohemia, and Moravia. Magdeburg, the mother town of the constitutions, possessed a supreme court, to which appeals and queries were addressed, including litigation between Christians and Jews. These cases were treated fairly, without discrimination and with no accompanying degrading oaths. In the 14th century the charters of many towns in Galicia were copies of this law, as were those of Lublin (1317), Sandomierz (1356), Lemberg (Lvov; 1356), Vilna (1387), Brest (1370), and Grodno (1391); in the following century it was extended to several towns in southern Poland, among them Lutsk (1432) and Minsk (1496), and in the 16th century to the towns of Pinsk (1511), Kovel (1518), Tarnopol (1550), Mogilev (1578), Vitebsk (1582), and others. Originally, the privileges enshrined in the law were granted only to German craftsmen and merchants, Jews and all other non-German town dwellers being excluded. However, in the charter granting the law to the city of Lemberg (June 17, 1365), the Jews, Armenians, and other nationals were free to decide whether they wished to avail themselves of it or whether they preferred to abide by their own laws and remain subject to the jurisdiction of their elders, under the chairmanship of the local bailiff. Later the law was granted to all the townspeople, including Jews (as in Kiev and Podolia). One of the paragraphs of the Magdeburg law which was of importance for the Jews provided that no Jew could be forced to stand warranty for objects he had bought or received as a pawn, i.e., to reveal from whom he had bought or received them. The Jews were therefore not responsible for receiving stolen property.

Bibliography: Kisch, Germany, 62–70, index; idem, *Jewry Law in Medieval Germany* (1949), index; I. Bershadski, *Litovskie Yevrei* (1888), 221, 234, 241–3. [Ed.]

MAGEN DAVID (Heb. מָגֵן דָּוִד; "shield of David"), the hexagram or six-pointed star formed by two equilateral triangles which have the same center and are placed in opposite directions.

From as early as the Bronze Age it was used—possibly as an ornament and possibly as a magical sign—in many civilizations and in regions as far apart as Mesopotamia and Britain. Iron Age examples are known from India and from the Iberian peninsula prior to the Roman conquest. Occasionally it appears on Jewish artefacts, such as lamps and seals, but without having any special and recognizable significance. The oldest undisputed example is on a seal from the seventh century B.C.E. found in Sidon and belonging to one Joshua b. Asayahu. In the Second Temple period, the hexagram was often used by Jews and non-Jews alike alongside the pentagram (the five-pointed star), and in the synagogue of Capernaum (second or third century C.E.) it is found side by side with the pentagram and the swastika on a frieze. There is no reason to assume that it was used for any purposes other than decorative. Theories interpreting it as a planetary sign of Saturn and connecting it with the holy stone in the pre-Davidic sanctuary in Jerusalem (Hildegard Lewy, in Archiv Orientální, vol. 18, 1950, 330–65) are purely speculative. Neither in the magical papyri nor in the oldest sources of Jewish *magic does the hexagram appear, but it began to figure as a magical sign from the early Middle Ages. Among Jewish emblems from Hellenistic times (discussed in E. Goodenough, *Jewish Symbols in the Greco-Roman Period*), both hexagram and pentagram are missing.

The ornamental use of the hexagram continued in the Middle Ages, especially in Muslim and Christian countries. The kings of Navarre used it on their seals (10th and 11th centuries) and (like the pentagram) it was frequently employed on notarial signs in Spain, France, Denmark, and Germany, by Christian and Jewish notaries alike. Sometimes drawn with slightly curved lines, it appears in early Byzantine and many medieval European churches, as, for example, on a stone from an early church in Tiberias (preserved in the Municipal Museum) and on the entrance to the Cathedrals of Burgos, Valencia, and Lerida. Examples are also found on objects used in the church, sometimes in a slanted position; as on the marble bishop's throne (c. 1266) in the Cathedral of Anagni. Probably in imitation of church usage—and certainly not as a specifically Jewish symbol—the hexagram is found on some synagogues from the later Middle Ages, for example, in Hamelin (Germany, c. 1280) and Budweis (Bohemia, probably 14th century). In Arab sources the hexagram, along with other geometrical ornaments, was widely used under the designation "seal of Solomon," a term which was also taken over by many Jewish groups. This name connects the hexagram with early Christian, possibly Judeo-Christian magic, such as the Greek magical work *The Testament of Solomon.* It is not clear in which period the hexagram was engraved on the seal or ring of Solomon, mentioned in the Talmud (Git. 68a–b) as a sign of his dominion over the demons, instead of the name of God, which originally appeared. However, this happened in Christian circles where Byzantine amulets of the sixth century already use the "seal of Solomon" as the name of the hexagram. In many medieval Hebrew manuscripts elaborate designs of the hexagram are to be found, without its being given any name. The origin of this use can be clearly traced to Bible manuscripts from Muslim countries (a specimen is shown in Gunzburg and Stassoff, *L'ornement hèbraïque* (1905), pl. 8, 15). From the 13th century onward it is found in Hebrew Bible manuscripts from Germany and Spain. Sometimes parts of the masorah are written in the form of a hexagram; sometimes it is simply used, in a more or less elaborate form, as an ornament. Richly adorned specimens from manuscripts in Oxford and Paris have been reproduced by C. Roth, *Sefarad,* 12, 1952, p. 356, pl. II, and in the catalog of the exhibition "Synagoga," Recklinghausen, 1960, pl. B. 4.

In Arabic magic the "seal of Solomon" was widely used, but at first its use in Jewish circles was restricted to relatively rare cases. Even then, the hexagram and pentagram were easily interchangeable and the name was applied to both figures. As a talisman, it was common in many of the magical versions of the *mezuzah* which were widespread between the tenth and 14th centuries. Frequently, the magical additions to the traditional text of the *mezuzah* contained samples of the hexagram, sometimes as many as 12. In magical Hebrew manuscripts of the later Middle Ages, the hexagram was used for certain amulets, among which one for putting out fires attained great popularity (see Heinrich Loewe, *Juedischer Feuersegen,* 1930).

The notion of a "shield of David" with magical powers was originally unconnected with the sign. It is difficult to say whether the notion arose in Islam, where the Koran sees David as the first to make protective arms, or from inner traditions of Jewish magic. From earlier times there is only one instance connecting the hexagram with the name David on a sixth-century tombstone from Tarento, southern Italy. There seems to have been some special reason for putting the hexagram before the name of the deceased. The oldest text mentioning a shield of David is contained in an explanation of a magical "alphabet of the angel *Metatron" which stems from the geonic period and was current

1

2

3

Figure 1. Hexagram carved on a stone frieze of the synagogue of Capernaum, second–third century C.E. Photo Werner Braun, Jerusalem.

Figure 2. Six-pointed star carved on a marble slab as decoration for the episcopal throne in the Cathedral of Anagni, Italy, 12th/13th century. From E. Hutton, *The Cosmati,* London, 1950.

Figure 3. A six-pointed star (lower right) as one of the patterns on a page of masoretic text in micrographic writing, Germany, 1299. Paris, Bibliothèque Nationale, Heb. 5, fol. 117.

Figure 4. A *magen David* fashioned from Psalm 121 on an amulet for a woman in childbirth, Germany, 18th century. Jerusalem, Israel Museum (Feuchtwanger Collection, donated by Baruch and Ruth Rappaport). Photo R. Milton, Jerusalem.

Figure 5. The *magen David* used as the basic design for a kabbalistic drawing, Italy, 17th century. Vellum, $9\frac{1}{2}\times9\frac{1}{2}$ in. (24×24 cm.). Formerly Feinberg Collection, Detroit. Photo Manning Bros., Highland Park, Mich.

Figure 6. *Magen David* used as a printers' mark on *Seder Tefillot*, the first Hebrew book published in Central Europe, Prague, 1512. From A. Yaari, *Hebrew Printers' Marks from the Beginning of Hebrew Printing to the End of the 19th Century*, Jerusalem, 1943.

Figure 7. *Magen David* on a boundary stone found in Vienna, 1656. Vienna, Staedtisches Museum.

8

9

Figure 8. *Magen David* decorating the exterior of the wooden synagogue of Przedborz, Poland, c. 1760. From M. and K. Piechotka, *Wooden Synagogues,* Warsaw, 1959.

Figure 9. Carved and painted wooden holder in the shape of a *magen David,* possibly used as a receptacle for the *kahal maẓẓah* brought to the synagogue by members of the community before Passover. Alsace, 1770. Strasbourg, Alsace Museum.

Figure 10. *Traustein* (marriage stone) incorporating a *magen David,* from Kochendorf, Germany, 18th/19th century. Courtesy Yad Vashem Archives, Jerusalem.

Figure 11. An "illegal" immigrant to Ereẓ Israel still wearing the Nazis' Jewish badge, 1944. Courtesy J.N.F., Jerusalem. Photo Diner.

Figure 12. Israel flags carried in the Three-Day March, Jerusalem, 1970. Courtesy Government Press Office, Tel Aviv.

11

10

12

among the *Ḥasidei Ashkenaz of the 12th century. But here it was the holy Name of 72 names which was said to have been engraved on this protective shield, together with the name MKBY, which the tradition of the magicians connected with Judah Maccabee. In cognate sources this tradition was much embellished. The name of the angel Taftafiyyah, one of the names of Metatron, was added to the 72 holy names, and indeed an amulet in the form of a hexagram with this one name became one of the most widespread protective charms in many medieval and later manuscripts. (From c. 1500 onward the name *Shaddai* was often substituted for the purely magical one.) This must have provided the transition to the use of the term *"magen David"* for the sign. What caused the substitution of the figure instead of the "great name of 72 names" is not clear, but in the 16th century instructions can still be found stating that the shield of David should not be drawn in simple lines but must be composed of certain holy names and their combinations, after the pattern of those biblical manuscripts where the lines were composed of the text of the masorah. The oldest known witness to the usage of the term is the kabbalistic *Sefer ha-Gevul,* written by a grandson of Naḥmanides in the early 14th century. The hexagram occurs there twice, both times called *"magen David"* and containing the same magical name as in the aforementioned amulet, demonstrating its direct connection with the magical tradition. According to other traditions, mentioned in Isaac Arama's *Akedat Yiẓḥak,* the emblem of David's shield was not the image known by this name today, but Psalm 67 in the shape of the *menorah.* This became a widespread custom and the *"menorah* Psalm" was considered a talisman of great power. A booklet from the 16th century says: "King David used to bear this psalm inscribed, pictured, and engraved on his shield, in the shape of the *menorah,* when he went forth to battle, and he would meditate on its mystery and conquer."

Between 1300 and 1700 the two terms, shield of David and seal of Solomon, are used indiscriminately, predominantly in magical texts, but slowly the former gained ascendancy. It was also used, from 1492, as a printers' sign, especially in books printed in Prague in the first half of the 16th century and in the books printed by the Foa family in Italy and Holland, who incorporated it in their coat of arms. Several Italian Jewish families followed their example between 1660 and 1770. All these usages had as yet no general Jewish connotation. The official use of the shield of David can be traced to Prague, from where it spread in the 17th and 18th century through Moravia and Austria and later to southern Germany and Holland. In 1354, Charles IV granted the Prague community the privilege of bearing its own flag—later called in documents "King David's flag"—on which the hexagram was depicted. It therefore became an official emblem, probably chosen because of its significance as a symbol of the days of old when King David, as it were, wore it on his shield. This explains its wide use in Prague, in synagogues, on the official seal of the community, on printed books, and on other objects. Here it was always called *magen David.* Its use on the tombstone (1613) of David Gans, the astronomer and historian, was still exceptional, obviously in reference to the title of his last work *Magen David.* Except one tombstone in Bordeaux (c. 1726), no other example of its being used on tombstones is known before the end of the 18th century. A curious parallel to the development in Prague is the one case of a representation of the Synagogue as an allegorical figure, holding a flag bearing the *magen David* in a 14th-century Catalan manuscript of the *Breviar d'amor* by Matfre d'Ermengaud (Ms. of Yates Thompson 31 in the British Museum).

The symbol early moved to other communities. Its use in Budweis has been mentioned above, and the Vienna community used it on its seal in 1655. In the following year it is found on a stone marking the boundary between the Jewish and the Christian quarters of Vienna (according to P. Diamant) or between the Jewish quarter and the Carmelite monastery (according to Max Grunwald). Apparently they were both officially recognized symbols. When the Viennese Jews were expelled in 1670 they took the symbol to many of their new habitats, especially in Moravia, but also to the Ashkenazi community of Amsterdam, where it was used from 1671, first on a medallion permitting entrance to the graveyard. Later it became part of the community's seal. Curiously enough, its migration eastward was much slower. It never occurs on official seals, but here and there during the 17th and 18th centuries it appears as an ornament on objects for use in synagogues and on wood carvings over the Torah shrine (first in Volpa, near Grodno, 1643).

The use of the hexagram as an alchemical symbol denoting the harmony between the antagonistic elements of water and fire became current in the later 17th century, but this had no influence in Jewish circles. Many alchemists, too, began calling it the shield of David (traceable since 1724). But another symbolism sprang up in kabbalistic circles, where the "shield of David" became the "shield of the son of David," the Messiah. Whether this usage was current in Orthodox circles too is not certain, though not impossible. The two kabbalists who testify to it, Isaiah the son of Joel Ba'al Shem (Jacob Emden, *Torat ha-Kena'ot,* p. 128) and Abraham Ḥayyim Kohen from Nikolsburg, combine the two interpretations. But there is no doubt that this messianic interpretation of the sign was current among the followers of *Shabbetai Ẓevi. The famous amulets given by Jonathan *Eybeschuetz in Metz and Hamburg, which have no convincing interpretation other than a Shabbatean one, have throughout a shield of David designated as "seal of MBD" (Messiah b. David), "seal of the God of Israel," etc. The shield of David was transformed into a secret symbol of the Shabbatean vision of redemption, although this interpretation remained an esoteric one, not to be published.

The prime motive behind the wide diffusion of the sign in the 19th century was the desire to imitate Christianity. The Jews looked for a striking and simple sign which would "symbolize" Judaism in the same way as the cross symbolizes Christianity. This led to the ascendancy of the *magen David* in official use, on ritual objects and in many other ways. From central and Western Europe it made its way to Eastern Europe and to oriental Jewry. Almost every synagogue bore it; innumerable communities, and private and charitable organizations stamped it on their seals and letterheads. Whereas during the 18th century its use on ritual objects was still very restricted—a good specimen is a plate for *mazzot* (1770), reproduced on the title page of *Monumenta Judaica,* catalog of a Jewish exposition in Cologne, 1963—it now became most popular. By 1799 it had already appeared as a specific Jewish sign in a satirical anti-Semitic engraving (A. Rubens, *Jewish Iconography,* no. 1611); in 1822 it was used on the Rothschild family coat of arms when they were raised to the nobility by the Austrian emperor; and from 1840 Heinrich Heine signed his correspondence from Paris in the *Augsburger Allgemeine Zeitung* with a *magen David* instead of his name, a remarkable indication of his Jewish identification in spite of his conversion. From such general use it was taken over by the Zionist movement. The very first issue of *Die Welt,* Herzl's Zionist journal, bore it as its emblem. The *magen David* became the symbol of new hopes and a new future for the Jewish people, and Franz Rosenzweig also interpreted it in *Der Stern der Erloesung* (1921) as summing up his philosophical ideas about the meaning of Judaism and the relationships between God, men, and the world. When the Nazis used it as a badge of shame which was to accompany millions on their way to death it took on a new dimension of depth, uniting suffering and hope. While the State of Israel, in its search for Jewish authenticity, chose as its emblem the *menorah*, a much older Jewish symbol, the *magen David* was maintained on the national (formerly Zionist) flag, and is widely used in Jewish life.

Bibliography: G. Scholem, in: *The Messianic Idea in Judaism and Other Essays* (1971); J. Leite de Vasconcellos, *Signum Salomonis* (Portuguese, 1918); Mayer, Art, index s.v. *Magen David;* M. Avi-Yonah, in: *Quarterly of the Department of Antiquities in Palestine*, vol. 14, pp. 64–65, pl. 23; P. Diamont, in: *Reshumot*, 5 (1953), 93–103; I. Feivelson, in: *Ha-Levanon, Me'assef Sifruti* (Warsaw, 1912), 53–56; Goodenough, Symbols, 7 (1958), 198–200; J. L. Gordon, *Iggerot J. L. Gordon*, 2 (1894), 36–37; M. Grunwald, in: HJ, 9 (1947), 178–88; J. M. Millás Vallicrosa, in: *Sefarad*, 17 (1957), 375–8; T. Nussenblatt, in: *YIVO-Bleter*, 13 (1938), 460–76, no. 583–4; P. Perdrizet, in: *Revue des Etudes Grecques*, 16 (1903), 42–61; E. Peterson, *Heis Theos* (Goettingen, 1926), 121; J. Reifman, in: *Ha-Shaḥar*, 2 (1872), 435–7; C. Roth, in: *Scritti in Memoria di Leone Carpi* (1967), 165–84; A. Scheiber in: *Israelitisches Wochenblatt fuer die Schweiz*, 66, no. 3 (Jan. 21, 1966), 33–35; B. Vajda, in: *Mitteilungen zur juedischen Volkskunde* (1918), 33–42; Wolf, Bibliotheca, 3 (1727), 997, 1214.

[G.Sch.]

MAGEN DAVID ADOM (Heb. "Red Shield of David"), Israel first-aid society (equivalent of the Red Cross). It was founded in Tel Aviv in 1930 as the medical wing of the *Haganah. In the State of Israel it operates under a law passed by the Knesset on July 12, 1950, and is the sole recognized first-aid organization in the country. It is a nonpolitical, nonprofit, benevolent society, offering free first-aid services to all. The governing bodies are the national conference of 150 delegates; the national council, with 39 members, of whom 13 are appointed by the Israel government; and a national executive of 13 members. Its presidents have been Vera *Weizmann (1954–66) and Eliyahu *Elath (from 1968). In 1968 the Magen David Adom had 63 branches, about 6,000 trained volunteer first-aiders manning its stations, and 230 ambulances in use with a further number in reserve. During the *Six-Day War of June 1967, 180 ambulances were placed at the disposal of the Civil Defense and the Army Medical Corps, while many more, with civilian drivers, operated in battle areas, particularly in and around Jerusalem. The Volunteer Blood Donors' Association, formed in 1935, assures a regular supply of fresh blood for transfusion. Blood banks in Jerusalem, Tel Aviv, Haifa, and Tiberias issue plasma on request to hospitals and Magen David Adom first-aid stations, while the David Marcus Blood Fractionation and Plasma Drying Institute at Jaffa processes blood for longer storage.

In 1948 at the international diplomatic conference which drafted the Geneva Conventions of 1949, Israel requested that the Red Shield of David be recognized as an official emblem, similar to the three others, i.e., the Red Cross, the Red Crescent (for Sunnite Muslims), and the Red Lion and Sun (for Iran). This request was rejected by a one-vote majority. Thus, Magen David Adom is the only national first-aid society which is not a member of the International League of Red Cross Societies (not to be confused with the International Committee of the Red Cross). Israel decided to persist in using its own emblem and made the relevant reservations while ratifying the Geneva Conventions. However, Magen David Adom fulfills all the duties of a national Red Cross Society and cooperates with the International Red Cross in taking care of and providing comforts for prisoners of war, and in the repatriation of wounded prisoners.

The Magen David Adom budget for 1967–68 was IL6,000,000 ($2,000,000), excluding the income in equipment and cash that accrued at the time of the Six-Day War. Of this, IL5,000,000 ($1,667,000) was raised in Israel, partly through the annual lottery authorized by the government. The remaining IL1,000,000 ($333,000) was raised by the Friends of Magen David Adom abroad. Such societies exist in Argentina and other Latin American countries, Australia, Belgium, Canada, France, Great Britain, and the U.S. Donations to Magen David Adom from abroad consist largely of ambulances, medical supplies, and funds for first-aid stations.

Magen David Adom publishes two periodicals: *Be-Sherut ha-Ezraḥ* ("In the Service of the Citizen"; 1957–) for its volunteers, and the *M.D.A. Quarterly* (1961–) for Friends of Magen David Adom abroad. [E.S.]

MAGGID (Heb. מַגִּיד; pl. *maggidim*), literally "one who relates" (cf. II Sam. 15:13). The term, however, has two special connotations in later Hebrew. a) A popular—and often itinerant—preacher, and b) an angel or supermundane spirit which conveys teachings to scholars worthy of such communication in mysterious ways.

The Maggid as Preacher. Itinerant preachers appear in Jewish history long before the emergence of the specific term. Descriptions of the life and social standing of some *tannaim* and *amoraim* depict them as leading the lives of itinerant preachers. During the geonic period, however, there is no record of them and it is not until the 11th century that one finds mention of them. Tales about some of the *Ḥasidei Ashkenaz show them as begging itinerant preachers. The tradition of itinerant *maggid* developed during the late Middle Ages. The 14th-century anonymous author of the *Sefer ha-Kaneh* and *Ha-Peli'ah* sets much of his bitter social and moral criticism in the context of his experiences while wandering and preaching in various communities. In the second half of the 16th century *Ephraim Solomon b. Aaron Luntschitz was a typical, if much respected and influential itinerant *maggid*. He relates that "in my later years, yielding to the importunities of prominent men, I preached in Lublin, especially during the great fairs, where Jewish leaders as well as large masses of the people gathered. There I used to express myself quite freely covering the shortcomings of the rabbis as well as of the laity, undeterred by any consideration or fear. This boldness, naturally enough, created for me numerous enemies who heaped slander upon my name and otherwise persecuted me . . . Of course, I could well have avoided all this wrath and uproar had I been willing to be more restrained in my utterances, or were I more chary of my personal honor. But I had long resolved to put the honor of God above my own" (*Ammudei Shesh* (Prague, 1617), introduction). In this, as in many other passages, Luntschitz shows his strength of character and the troubles that beset a courageous itinerant preacher, attuned to the mood and spiritual needs of his public but fearless in criticizing them. Use of the parable *(mashal)* is already much in evidence in his writings, which also show a conscious effort to stimulate his public and impress them through a show of wit and learning. All these traits were common from the 18th century on when the name *maggid* came into regular use to denote both an itinerant and non-itinerant preacher. There are records of salaried *maggidim* appointed by the community. Some historians have ascribed a considerable part in the social and religious upheavals of the end of the 17th and during the 18th centuries to the influence of

itinerant *maggidim*, who, they consider, functioned as a kind of "non-establishment intelligentsia," having much of the learning and influence of the regular scholars but largely without their connections in the upper strata of Jewish society. They have thus attributed the rise and early success of *Ḥasidism to the influence of such *maggidim*, pointing out that several of the early ḥasidic leaders were called *maggid* or the synonym for *maggid*, *mokhi'aḥ* ("morals preacher"), such as *Dov Baer of Mezhirech or *Jacob Joseph of Polonnoye. Others, however, note that even the most radical of the 18th-century *maggidim*, *Berechiah (Berakh) b. Eliakim Getzel the Younger, considered himself, despite his outspoken social criticism, to be allied by the nature of his office to that of the communal rabbi. They show also that much of the anti-ḥasidic propaganda was conducted by *maggidim*, chief among them being Jacob *Kranz "the Maggid of Dubno," an admiring pupil of *Elijah b. Solomon Zalman, the Gaon of Vilna, who expressly followed the advice of the Gaon on the method of preaching. Kranz, who was celebrated for his parables, exemplifies the type of *maggidim* who were associated with the **Mitnagged* leadership in Lithuanian Jewry. Lithuania and the *Mitnagged* culture remained throughout the 19th and into the 20th centuries the field of activity of the *maggidim*. Sometimes the office of *maggid* was combined with that of *dayyan*, hence the modern titles, mostly in Eastern Europe, of *maggid meisharim u-moreh ẓedek* (the *maggid* of uprightness (cf. Is. 45:19) and teacher of righteousness, the latter being a synonym for a *dayyan*). Sometimes the *maggid* was appointed to a town, with the official title of *maggid de-mata*, in Yiddish *Shtotmagid*. Vilna had a *Shtotmagid*, usually a respected and outstanding scholar, until recent times. Men like Ezekiel b. Isaac ha-Levi *Landau, the *Shtotmagid* of Vilna; the great itinerant *maggid* *Moses Isaac Darshan, the "Kelmer Maggid"; or the *maggid* suspected of Haskalah leanings, Ẓevi Hirsch b. Ze'ev Wolf *Dainow, the "Slutzker Maggid," continued a tradition of preaching expressly intended for the masses, which contained much social criticism but also provided social guidance. Their preaching was also characterized by the mournful sing-song intonation of their delivery (see also *Musar movement). Their direct successors were the "Zionist *maggidim*" like Z. *Maccoby the "Kamenitzer Maggid," and Ẓevi Hirsch *Masliansky. Many of the *meshullaḥim (*Sheluḥei Ereẓ Israel)* for the yeshivot and Ereẓ Israel actually filled the function of *maggidim*. Wherever *Mitnagged* communities were established in other countries, *maggidim* accompanied the immigrants. In modern Ereẓ Israel, Ben Zion Yadler and Benzion *Alfes were in the tradition of the great *maggidim*. A few *maggidim* are still active in the State of Israel and the United States (see also *Darshan; *Preaching).
[H.H.B.-S.]

In Kabbalah. The angel or heavenly force called the *maggid* passes secrets to a kabbalist, when he is asleep or awake, speaks words from his mouth, or dictates to him when he is writing. This revelation is one of the outstanding phenomena in Kabbalah in the 16th to 18th centuries. Throughout the history of Kabbalah, kabbalists relied on heavenly inspirations, the revelations of Elijah, *Metatron, and other angels, or even on heavenly forces such as the Holy Spirit, in addition to questions in dreams and magical means of communication with heavenly forces. An early stage of this phenomenon may be seen in the questioning in dreams practiced before the formation of the Kabbalah, and even regarding the problems of Kabbalah, e.g., by Jacob of Marvège (Provence), author of *She'elot u-Teshuvot min ha-Shamayim* (commentary by R. Margulies, Lvov, 1929). The *maggid* of the 16th to 18th centuries is simply another version of the previous occurrence, though at times the phenomenon seems, in particular cases, to have personal psychological roots.

The image of the *maggid* who reveals heavenly secrets was apparently first crystallized in the circle of Joseph *Taitaẓak, who lived at the time of the Spanish expulsion and whose circle included many of the great kabbalists and preachers of Safed. The revelations of Taitaẓak (or those attributed to him) were written prior to the expulsion and were presented as coming from God Himself. In the Safed literature, the main expositions of the essence of the *maggid* are found in the writings of Moses *Cordovero and Ḥayyim *Vital. In this circle the most outstanding phenomenon was the appearance of the *maggid* of Joseph *Caro. Recording the words of the *maggid*, Caro wrote *Sefer ha-Maggid*, of which only a fragment has survived, called by the printers *Maggid Meisharim*. The major statements of Caro's *maggid* were sermons interpreting the secrets of the Kabbalah and biblical commentary, but many of his pronouncements have a personal and practical meaning. The *maggid* guided Caro in his wanderings in Turkey and directed him to emigrate to Ereẓ Israel. He stimulated Caro to write his halakhic works and to behave morally, promising him achievements in *halakhah* and in his personal life, toward attaining his great dream—martyrdom, like Solomon *Molcho. Caro's *maggid* was the *Shekhinah* ("Divine Presence"), the tenth *Sefirah* in the kabbalistic system, which took on the form of the Mishnah, the Oral Law. To bring about the appearance of the *maggid*, Caro would study *mishnayot*. The *maggid* spoke to him while he was awake, often just as he awoke. Scholars have not reached a conclusion concerning the psychological nature of this revelation, but it is clear that it did not affect the relation of Caro's personality to reality; it was one aspect of his personality which neither contradicted nor harmed the whole.

The Shabbatean movement gave great impetus to appearances of *maggidim* and many revealed secrets to the Shabbateans. The revelations of a *maggid* to Isaac Ẓurgeon, an associate of *Shabbetai Ẓevi in Adrianople in 1668 who confirmed the latter as Messiah and defended his apostasy, have been published (R. Schatz, in: *Sefunot*, 12). There also exists particularly detailed information on the appearance of a *maggid* in the house of study of Abraham *Rovigo, leader of a Shabbatean circle in Modena, Italy, from 1675 to 1691. The first *maggid* to appear in his house of study was that of Baer Perlhefter whose revelation had a great impact on him. Many letters of Meir Rofe who directs his questions to the *maggid*, and their answers, are in existence. The central question discussed in the revelations concerns the reason for Shabbetai Ẓevi's death and a prediction of his return in a year's time. Apparently, a *maggid* was later revealed to Rovigo himself. The most detailed revelations in this house of study have been transmitted by Mordecai Ashkenazi, a pupil of Rovigo's from Zolkiew who was neither a scholar of Torah nor of esoteric matters but who astounded Rovigo with his Shabbatean revelation. Ashkenazi's notebook and other documents relating the revelations of his *maggid* have survived. This *maggid* always revealed himself in a dream; at first only his voice was heard and afterward his form was seen. Scholem has suggested that this was a projection of the image of Rovigo, Ashkenazi's teacher. His revelations include Shabbatean theories, and together with them private advice, mostly on routine matters and on Ashkenazi's education and studies. Apparently they even included criticism of the former *maggid*, that of Baer Perlhefter, based on suspicions of Perlhefter's sins toward the end of his life, whose nature is not clear. Ashkenazi's *maggid*—like Caro's—encouraged his master and teacher to emigrate to Ereẓ Israel and gave him practical advice on ways of realizing this aim, whose background was Shabbatean messianism.

A lengthy and stormy dispute was caused by a *maggid* who revealed himself to Moses Ḥayyim *Luzzatto in Italy in 1727. The *maggid* dictated to Luzzatto, in the language of the Zohar, *Razin Genizin, Tikkunim Ḥadashim*, and other works, which were meant to become a second Zohar (*Zohar Tinyana*). The *maggidim* of Ashkenazi and Caro also spoke the language of the Targum, i.e., Aramaic. The record of the first revelation of Luzzatto's *maggid*, who appeared on Wednesday, Rosh Ḥodesh (the New Moon of) Sivan 1727, still exists. This *maggid* was a voice without an image who spoke to the recipient while he was awake and not in a dream, and alone. This angered Moses *Ḥagiz and others, because they thought that the young Luzzatto was not worthy of such a heavenly revelation and also because they suspected the Shabbatean character of the revelations.

The nature of the phenomenon apparently must be examined in the general context of kabbalistic mysticism, which consistently seeks heavenly confirmation for the secrets revealed to the kabbalist. At different times, various forms were given to these confirmations—some by pseudepigraphy and some by a divine revelation. In general, it appears that there was no fraudulent basis to these revelations, that their source lay in the kabbalist's complete conviction of the hidden heavenly truth in the secrets revealed to him, and that his testimony that he heard them from a divine source is honest. In addition, it seems that the *maggid* is also connected with the parapsychological phenomenon of the materialization of part of the kabbalist's soul which, acquiring an independent form, disassociates itself from the rest of his person and, confronting him objectively as it were, speaks to him. [Y.D.]

Bibliography: Baron, Community, index; I. Bettan, *Studies in Jewish Preaching* (1939), 273–315; B. Z. Dinur, *Be-Mifneh ha-Dorot* (1955), 97–100, 133–6; J. Katz, *Massoret u-Mashber* (1958), index; H. H. Ben-Sasson, *Hagut ve-Hanhagah* (1959), 34–54, 254–6; idem, in: *Zion*, 31 (1966), 68–69, 200–3. In Kabbalah: G. Scholem, *Ḥalomotav shel ha-Shabbetai, R. Mordecai Ashkenazi* (1938); R. J. Z. Werblowsky, in: *Tarbiz*, 27 (1958), 310–21; idem, *Joseph Karo, Lawyer and Mystic* (1962); M. Benayahu, in: *Sefunot*, 5 (1961), 299–336; I. Tishby, *Netivei Emunah u-Minut* (1964), 81–107; G. Scholem, in: *Sefunot*, 11 (1970), 67–112.

MAGGID, DAVID (1862–1942?), scholar and writer. Maggid was born in Vilna; son of Hillel Noah *Maggid-Steinschneider. As secretary to S. J. *Fuenn, he assisted him in writing *Ha-Oẓar* ("The Treasury," 1884–1903) and *Keneset Yisrael* ("Assembly of Israel," 1886–90), a biographical dictionary of Jewish authors and scholars. Later, in St. Petersburg, he taught Jewish religion in government secondary schools. The author of numerous articles on Jewish history and art, he was also a contributor to the *Yevreyskaya Entsiklopediya*. His research encompassed Jewish music of antiquity and the Middle Ages as well as the folklore of the Jews of Crimea. In 1919 he succeeded A. A. *Harkavy as librarian of the Jewish and Oriental department of the National Library of Petrograd. In 1921 he was appointed professor of art history at the Russian Institute in Petrograd and in 1925 became professor of Hebrew at the university. He continued to publish articles and works outside the Soviet Union. Notable are his reminiscences of his father and the first *maskilim* of Vilna, published in *Fun Noenten Ovar* (1937). Other works include *Toledot M. Antokolski* ("The Life of M. Antokolski," 1897), *Rabbi Mordekhai Aharon Guenzburg* (1897), and the completion of his father's work *Toledot Mishpeḥot Guenzburg* ("The History of the Guenzburg Families," 1899).

David Maggid, scholar and writer. Jerusalem, J.N.U.L., Schwadron Collection.

Bibliography: Rejzen, Leksikon, 2 (1927), 356–9; LNYL, 4 (1963), 535–7.
[Y.S.]

MAGGID-STEINSCHNEIDER, HILLEL NOAH (1829–1903), Hebrew scholar and writer. Maggid-Steinschneider, born in Vilna, owed the first part of his name to his grandfather Phinehas, who was *maggid* in Vilna, and the second part to his profession, stonemasonry (*Steinschneider*). He also was a bookdealer. As a stonemason he often composed tombstone inscriptions, which led to an interest in and research about the lives of well-known Vilna families and personalities, particularly those buried in the old and new cemeteries of the town. He published *Ir Vilna* (part 1 only, 1900), a biographical work containing hundreds of biographies of famous Vilna personalities. Maggid also assisted S. J. *Fuenn in collecting material for his history of Vilna Jewry, *Kiryah Ne'emanah* (1860), and also prepared its second edition with numerous additions and a biography of the author (1915). He wrote a history of the *Guenzburg family completed by his son (*Toledot Mishpeḥot Guenzburg*, 1899) and a biography of David Oppenheim (in Y. ben Ḥayyim Mezah (ed.), *Gan Peraḥim*, 1882); with his father-in-law J. Gordon he composed a Thousand Year Calendar, *Lu'aḥ al Elef Shanim* (1854).

Maggid contributed numerous biographical and genealogical articles to Hebrew periodicals, such as *Ha-Shaḥar*, *Ha-Karmel*, and *Ha-Maggid*. He was put in charge of the *Straschun and S. J. Fuenn libraries when they were given to the Vilna community. Maggid's biographical and bibliographical research, much of which remained unpublished, was of importance, though like other works of the transitory period from the old to modern scholarship, his writings lacked organization and literary form.

Bibliography: Kressel, Leksikon, 2 (1967), 314ff.; Rejzen, Leksikon, 2 (1927), 356ff.; H. N. Maggid, *El ha-Kore* (1900), 7–10, introd.; D. Maggid, in: *Fun Noentn Over*, 1 (1937), 3–12; *Budushchnost*, 4 (1903), 248–52.
[Y.S.]

MAGHAR, AL- (Arab. المغار), Druze village in northern Israel, 10 mi. (16 km.) N.W. of Tiberias. One of the major Druze centers, the village in 1969 had 5,750 inhabitants, of whom a minority were Christian and Muslim Arabs. Its economy was based on hill farming and on local workshops. The place is possibly identical with Ma'ariyyah or Me'arot where a priestly family lived in talmudic times (*Baraita of the Twenty-Four Mishmarot*). [E.O.]

MAGHREBI-MA'ARAVI, name of Jewish personalities and congregations originating from North Africa. The Arab geographers designate North Africa and Spain as Maghreb, the West. The name Maghreb-Ma'arav ("West"), Maghrebi-Ma'aravi ("the Westerner"), occurs in geonic literature and later. It continues to be applied to North African congregations and their rites. The Maghrebis speak a different Arabic dialect, which in addition to special rites and patterns of life, distinguishes their tongue from other Eastern Judeo-Arabic dialects and their customs from other congregations.

See also *Musta'rab.

Bibliography: Hirschberg, Afrikah, 1 (1965), 59, 344; idem, in: *Bar Ilan*, 4/5 (1967), 475–79. [H.Z.H.]

MAGIC. Ancient man saw himself surrounded by mysterious and miraculous forces, both benevolent and hostile. He believed that it was possible to exert an influence on many of these forces by means of a suitable action or an appropriate word (i.e., an incantation). In anthropology, the actions taken by ancient man to influence the mysterious forces of the world are known by the general term "magic." All peoples differentiated between mischievous, illegal magic, known as "black magic," and beneficent, legal magic, or "white magic," whose purpose was to afford protection against the harm of evil magic.

In the Bible. In the Bible the most common term for magic is derived from the root *kshp,* which occurs also in Akkadian. In Akkadian this root always indicates black magic, whereas in Hebrew the distinction between black and white magic is not so definite, and only the word *mekhashefah* can be said to refer specifically to black magic. On the other hand, the Hebrew concept does not cover all the Babylonian sorcerer's areas of activity, such as raising the spirits of the dead, which was practiced in ancient Israel by "one who has a ghost *(ʾov)* or a familiar spirit *(yiddeʿoni).*" The blurring of the distinction between black and white magic in the Bible may be due to the Bible's opposition to all kinds of magic and not only to that which is explicitly intended to be injurious.

Another biblical term is *ʾashaf* ("enchanter"). The *ʾashafim* are named in Daniel 2:2 together with *mekhashefim* ("sorcerers"; Heb. אַשָּׁפִים , Dan. 1:20; 2:2; Aram. אַשָּׁף, אָשְׁפַיָּא, אָשְׁפִין, Dan. 2:10, 27; 4:4). The Hebrew and the Aramaic forms are borrowed from the Akkadian *āšipu. Šiptu*-utterers are those who practice white magic, being skilled in counter-magic ceremonies and in adjurations.

The term *ḥover ḥever* ("charmer") occurs in Deuteronomy 18:11 and Psalm 58:6, and *ḥavarim,* "charms," occurs in Isaiah 47:9, 12 together with *keshafim,* "magic." The combination, which gives the impression of being ancient Semitic, occurs also in the Akkadian *Maqlû* text (e.g., tablet 1, lines 4–5). It may be conjectured that the Israelite magic rite resembled that described in the *Maqlû* texts and that the victim of a *ḥover ḥavarim* was no longer in control of his own life but was under the spell of the *mekhashef* ("sorcerer").

The term *laḥash* ("incantation") is connected with the *ḥover ḥavarim* (Jer. 8:17; Ps. 58:6; Eccles. 10:11; Ecclus. 12:13). One who uses incantations is called *nevon laḥash* (Isa. 3:3). The characteristic activity of the Hebrew incantator was charming snakes, an art known also from the Hittites, Babylonians, and Egyptians as the special and exclusive occupation of experts.

The term *havvot (hawwot)* often alludes to an injurious utterance, and in several passages its meaning approximates that of a black magic formula (cf. e.g., Ps. 5:10; 52:4). The meaning of the biblical *hawwot* approximates the Neo-Babylonian expression *amât limuttim* ("an evil utterance") or injurious magic word. The word *hawwot* presumably belongs to an earlier Semitic linguistic stratum and is not borrowed directly from the Akkadian, since it commences with the gutteral *h,* which the Akkadian had lost. This interpretation of *hawwot* helps to explain *howah* in Isaiah 47:11.

In Psalm 31:21 the root *rks* occurs. This verse is explained as alluding to magical plots, and the root *rks* is regarded as analagous to the Akkadian concept *rikistu,* which means plotting for the purposes of magic.

In the Bible the most comprehensive list of various kinds of practitioners of magic occurs in Deuteronomy 18:10–11. Except for the first expression in this list—"one who consigns his son or daughter to the fire"—which does not directly refer to an act of magic (see *Moloch), three types of magicians may be distinguished: a) those whose main function is the prediction of the future by various signs: the soothsayer *(meʿonen),* the augurer *(kosem kesamim; qosem qesamim),* and the diviner (*menaḥesh;* see *Divination): b) those who engage in actual magic: the sorcerer *(mekhashef)* and one who casts spells *(ḥover ḥever);* c) those who engage both in prediction and in actual magic, obtaining their information by raising the spirits of the dead. These listings of magicians occur several times in the Bible with minor differences, parallel terms being sometimes employed (II Kings 21:6 = II Chron. 33:6; Micah 5:11; cf. Jer. 27:9). Magicians are mentioned collectively in the account of the plagues of Egypt (Ex. 7:11), where they are said to have imitated the miracles performed by Moses and Aaron. In Genesis 41:8, 24 the "wise men" *(ḥakhamim)* and "magicians" *(ḥarṭummim)* of Egypt are mentioned as having been summoned to interpret the king's dreams. Although Daniel deals with the interpretation of dreams (Dan. 2:12, 27; 4:4), there is no precise distinction made in the specific functions of the magicians mentioned in the book, probably because these distinctions were not known to the ancient Israelite narrator. Thus reference is made to *Chaldeans alongside a general term such as "wise men": to fortune-tellers and astrologers of the Babylonian type alongside Egyptian magicians and fortune-tellers and *gāzerīn* who are probably also fortune-tellers. Together with these are mentioned indubitable magicians—sorcerers *(mekhashefim)* and enchanters *(ʾashafim).*

The religion of Israel flourished in a cultural milieu permeated with magical concepts, as is reflected in the strong biblical opposition to sorcery. Any belief in the efficacy of magic is seen as contradicting the Israelite belief in the exclusive and supreme rule of the one God Whose will cannot be influenced by any human means. Hence magic as a whole is regarded as an abomination of the non-Israelites (Ex. 22:17; Lev. 20:27). Witchcraft and divination by teraphim are identified with rebellion (I Sam. 15:23). Sorcerers and astrologers are vanity (Isa. 47:8–15; Jer. 10:2–3). Hence the repeated drama in the biblical narratives of the clash between the two outlooks: between Joseph and the magicians of Egypt (Gen. 41); Daniel and the sorcerers at the Babylonian royal court (Dan. 2); and in particular Moses and Aaron and the magicians and sorcerers of Egypt (Ex. 7). This last instance illustrates the difference between apparently identical acts. Whereas the magicians of Egypt employ their secret arts, Moses and Aaron perform miracles at the command of God Who changes the laws of nature in order to bring about the miracle (*ibid.* 7:9–10). The Bible thus accepts *miracles, but not such as are performed with the aid of occult science.

Externally, the Bible derides the non-Israelites, particularly the Babylonians, who rely on magic (e.g., Isa. 43:9). Internally, it strives to eradicate from among the Israelites the tendency to resort to various magical practices. In Deuteronomy 18:9ff. there occurs a detailed statement whose purpose is to prevail on the people to shun an entire series of magical acts. These acts are abhorrent to the Lord, since they are characteristic of the pagan world and brought about the expulsion of the peoples of Canaan from the land. Yet the Deuteronomist is conscious of the needs that induce the Israelites to have recourse to divination. It therefore adds (Deut. 18:15) that the prophet of the Lord will furnish in a legitimate manner the guidance which others seek by augury. Even more basic and profound is Ezekiel's denunciation of the sorceresses and their sympathetic magic practices (Ezek. 13:17–23). The main point of this prophecy is God's declaration that He will save His people from them. Hence for the prophet the harm caused by the sorcerers—which is principally moral—is more dangerous than the sin of sorcery.

While repudiating the power of sorcery, biblical religion at times utilizes means and methods which were borrowed from magical practice, but were subordinated to the new faith and hence not regarded as acts of sorcery. Notable examples are healing with the aid of the *copper serpent (Nehushtan) and the examination of the woman suspected of infidelity (*Adultery; *Ordeal).

The struggle against sorcery was characterized directly by executing judgment against the sorcerer himself and indirectly by taking legal measures against members of the community who resorted to sorcerers. A third way—that of the prophets—was that of rebuke and education. The commandment "You shall not tolerate a sorceress" (Ex. 22:17) is apparently aimed against women who engage specifically in black magic, as the severity of the penalty attests. Its literal meaning refers to capital punishment although some scholars have suggested it is merely a general prohibition. The severity of the law relating to the sorceress is also evidenced by its being juxtaposed to the grave offences of lying with a beast and sacrificing to other gods (Ex. 22:18–19).

The indirect means consists of prohibiting the people from resorting to magic. Accordingly the law forbids not only black magic but every act based on a magical element. This prohibition is stated in Deuteronomy 18:9ff., in Leviticus 19:26: "You shall not practice divination or soothsaying," and in Leviticus 20:6: "And if any person turns to ghosts, and familiar spirits, ... I will set My face against that person ..."

The Mosaic laws did not eradicate sorcery from among the people, as is evident from the reproofs of the prophets. The various magical acts were regarded as tantamount to idolatry and false prophecy (see Isa. 3:2–3; Jer. 27:9; Mal. 3:5, et al.). The alien cults introduced in the reign of certain kings apparently encouraged the sorcerers: Jezebel herself is regarded as a sorceress (II Kings 9:22); of Manasseh it is said that he "practiced soothsaying, and divination, and dealt with those that divined by a ghost or a familiar spirit" (II Kings 21:6; cf. II Chron. 33:6). Josiah eradicated from Judah, along with other manifestations of idolatry, those who divined by a ghost or a familiar spirit (II Chron. 34:3–7). S. Mowinckel has suggested that the "wicked" and "workers of iniquities" who are the subject of numerous psalmists' denunciations are sorcerers. N. M. Nicolsky has also claimed to find in several Psalms (7; 31; 35; 41; 57; 58; 59; 69; 91; 109; 121, et al.) indications of a cultic system against sorcerers.

In the Apocrypha. The apocryphal books do not contain a uniform attitude toward magic. Ben Sira mentions the worry caused to a father by an aging daughter who devoted herself to magic (quoted in the Talmud, Sanh. 100b). The Jewish sibyls denounce the "soothsayers, sorcerers, and conjurers" and "the augurs and ventriloquists" (3:224–26). The Second Maccabees (12:40) tells of the Jewish warriors who kept amulets taken from the idols of Jamnia under their tunics. These amulets "which the Law prohibits to Jews," resulted in the warriors being punished by meeting their death in the battle against Gorgias. The Book of Enoch tells of the fallen angels who instructed the daughters of man in the knowledge of magic formulas and charms (7:1). In the Book of Tobit, the Angel Raphael teaches Tobit's son that the smoke of a burning heart and liver from a certain fish cures a person possessed of a demon and the anointing of the eyes of a blind person with the gall of the same fish restores his eyesight (6:5ff.; 8:2–3; 11:10–11). *Asmodeus, king of the demons, is mentioned in chapter 3 of Tobit. Josephus (Ant. 8:46–49) relates that he was witness to a scene in which a Jew, Eleazar, called up a spirit in the presence of Vespasian, using a ring whose seal contained a miraculous root prescribed by King Solomon. The Jews of Alexandria, who accepted syncretism, took great interest in magic. It was probably among them that the book of magic attributed to Moses, "The Eighth Book of Moses" (or "The Key of Moses") came into being. Another ancient Jewish book of magic is *Sefer Mafte'aḥ Shelomo* (*Book of the Key of Solomon,* facsimile, 1914). *Ḥerev Moshe* (*The Sword of Moses,* ed. M. Gaster, 1896), also an ancient occult Hebrew work, contains many descriptions of magic practices and magic formulas. A large number of jars, dating from the first century C.E., bearing Hebrew and Syrian inscriptions, among them long lists of the names of demons and spirits, were discovered in Babylonia (most of the inscriptions were published in *Aramaic Incantation Texts from Nippur,* J. A. Montgomery, 1913). The introduction of Jewish names of God into magic formulas found on papyri must also have been the work of Jewish magicians. According to Origen (*Contra Celsum,* 4: 520, end) pagan necromancers also used Jewish names of God in their incantations. The Romans, too, were familiar with Jewish names of God used in exorcism. Many Jewish prisoners in Rome, especially women, earned their livelihood by practicing magic (see Juvenal, *Satires,* 6:542–7).

Talmudic Period. The strict prohibition against magic found in the Bible also finds expression in the Talmud, especially the Mishnah, which equates magic with idolatry (Sanh. 7:7). Magic remedies are denounced as being "the customs of the Amorites" (Shab. 6:10). A person who pronounces a magic formula over a wound loses his share of the world to come (Sanh. 10:1). The *tannaim* define the magicians listed in Deuteronomy 18 in greater detail (Sanh. 65a), although at times their interpretations differ from one another. For example *"Ov"* (אב), according to one opinion, is the designation applied to the magician who speaks out of his armpit (Rashi's comment at this point: "The spirit called up by the magician places himself in the magician's armpit and speaks from there"), while according to another opinion, it stands for the magician who poses questions to a skull and relates the answers he receives from it. Similar differences exist in the meaning of other terms, *yidoni, me'onen,* etc. The biblical command to exterminate witches is broadened to apply to male sorcerers as well (Sanh. 67a): "The Torah mentions only witches, because as a rule it is women who practice magic." However, magic was punishable by death only when a magical act was performed *(ibid.)* and not when it consisted of a mere delusion. In order to enable the members of the Jerusalem High Court (Sanhedrin) to determine whether a magician appearing before the court was liable to death punishment or not, they were obliged to study magic (*ibid.* 17a; see also Rashi). One kind of "delusion" which was nevertheless prohibited was the so-called "cucumber lore," demonstrated by R. Eliezer b. Hyrcanus to Rabbi Akiva when they were both in the fields. Eliezer enunciated the magic word, and the whole field was covered with cucumbers; a second magic word collected all the cucumbers into one heap. In reply to the question how could such magic be permitted, the Talmud states that the prohibition did not apply to magic practiced for the sake of study (*ibid.* 68a). The belief in the power of magic, based on the belief in the existence of demons, was shared not only by the common people, but by most scholars as well, except that the latter regarded it as a patrimony of the pagans, and not of the Jews. Of the origin of magic it is said that Abraham communicated the "impure name" (i.e., of the demons) to the sons of his concubine, Keturah, i.e., to the pagans. R. Judah ha-Nasi, the redactor of the Mishnah, held a different opinion: "Only a person who believes in the interpretation of signs, is pursued by magic"; while Ahavah b. Zeira said that "he who is free from superstition attains an eminence in the world to come which is beyond the reach even of the serving angel" (Ned. 32a). On another occasion (Sot. 48a) the Talmud states: "Harlotry and magic have caused the destruction of all": Abba Arikha is quoted as saying: "He who acquires a single item of knowledge from a magician, forfeits his life" (Shab. 75a). Yet in spite of the denunciation of magical practices by the spiritual leaders and the existing religious prohibitions, there was considerable preoccupation with magic in the talmudic period. To some degree, this was the result of the Persian influence upon the Jews. It was primarily women who engaged in black magic (see Avot 2:7; Er. 64b, end). Rabbi Naḥman's daughters, who were given to the practice of magic, were able to stir a pot of boiling water with their bare hands (Git. 45a). The widow Joḥani, a Jerusalem faith healer, was able to delay a birth by magical means (Sot. 22a; see also Rashi). In order to suppress the widespread practice of magic by women, the *tanna* Simeon b. Shetaḥ (first century) is said to have ordered the hanging of 80 witches in a single day (Sanh. 6:6). But there were also occasions when learned and pious men resorted to magic, although they did so for a good purpose. Ḥoni ha-Me'aggel (Ḥoni "the drawer of circles"), a contemporary of Simeon b. Shetaḥ, whose prayer for rain remained unanswered, drew a circle, and entering it, swore that he would not leave the circle until God would have mercy upon His children; and then the rains came. He repeated this practice on frequent occasions and thus earned the epithet of "Ha-Me'-aggel." Such "drawing of circles" was clearly an act which belonged to the world of magic, and Simeon b. Shetaḥ, who sought to stamp out magic among the Jews, told Ḥoni: "If you were not Ḥoni, whom God loves like a son, I would excommunicate you" (Ta'an. 19a). [Ed.]

In Medieval Hebrew Literature. Terminology. The terms "magic" *(kishuf)*, "magician" *(mekhashef)*, and "witch" *(mekhashefah)* are relatively rare in medieval Hebrew literature, especially when compared with the frequency with which magic practices are mentioned. The underlying reason is undoubtedly the explicit biblical prohibition against the practice of magic (repeatedly dwelt upon in medieval Hebrew literature) and the Bible's abhorrence of magicians and soothsayers. There is, therefore, no favorable allusion to magic practices in medieval literature, and they are rarely dealt with in a purely informative manner. Such terms as *kishuf, mekhashef*, and *mekhashefah* were descriptive of the wicked, sinners, and non-Jews. Magic was, however, discussed in medieval Hebrew literature, but surreptitiously, under the guise of different names, such as *segullot* ("remedies" or "charms"), *kame'ot* ("amulets"), *refu'ot* ("cures"), *goralot* ("destinies" or "fortunes"), *simanim* ("signs" or "omens"), and *refafot* ("bodily itches as a portent"). The medieval writer thus was able to circumvent the term "magic" and eschew a direct confrontation with the biblical prohibition. The terms *mekhashef* ("magician") and *mekhashefah* ("witch") in medieval literature designate two very different categories. A *mekhashef* is a person possessed of secret knowledge in magic which he uses for his own profit or to help others. He is considered a professional and is paid for his services. While in medieval Hebrew literature there are few records of a Jew being described as a *mekhashef*, in the early modern period the usage is much more frequent but under the name *Ba'al Shem (i.e., "owner of the Holy Name").

Mekhashef designates a certain psycho-pathological state, often connected with cannibalism. The term alludes to women and men who wander in forests, singly or in groups, or sometimes live in a community and kidnap babies or even grown-ups in order to eat them or suck their blood. While the term *mekhashefah* frequently recurs in medieval Hebrew literature, the actual phenomenon it represents seems to have been rare. In the 12th and 13th centuries in Central Europe these vampires were called *"shtria"* for the female (from the Latin *strix, striga*) and werewolf for the male. Such vampires do not necessarily possess any supernatural powers or secret knowledge. In *Sefer* *Ḥasidim*, a 13th-century ethical work, there is a description of a baby born with teeth and a tail. The rabbi of the community advised that these be cut, so that when he grew up he would not eat people. This seems to testify to a case where a child was considered to have been born a werewolf, and could be cured naturally. No supernatural elements seem to be involved either in the birth of the werewolf or the proposed cure. A community where women ate children is also described in *Sefer Ḥasidim*. When threatened that if they continued their practice their teeth would be ground on the stones of the well, they stopped. The story is told as a clinical fact (which it probably was) and there seems to be neither any supernatural nor religious connotation or implication. On the other hand, in other stories from 13th-century Central Europe such creatures are immortal. They never die naturally but are killed in a prescribed manner. In one case, a witch was offered divine forgiveness if she were to reveal the secret of how she might be killed. Thus the person who committed the sin of cannibalism could religiously be saved. The phenomenon, apparently pathological in nature, was, in some cases, explained supernaturally—as if such cases were already dead, and therefore could not be killed. The *mekhashefah* does not belong to magic in the strict sense but designates a species of abominable creatures who form a category in themselves to which should be added the beliefs associated with them such as the belief in the "mare," a woman who strangles men in their sleep (hence the word "nightmare"). Other unnatural creatures who do not fit into either of the above categories should be classed somewhere between demons and magicians, or demons and witches. The term *mekhashefah* and the literature that evolved around it had relatively little influence on the development of medieval Jewish culture; the term *mekhashef*, however, is much more prominent.

Sources and Dissemination. Literature on magic is universal in its character, its methods, and its structure. Each society, each language, and every period contributed toward magic literature enriching it or modifying it in the light of the particular characteristics of the society, the culture, and the times. The main themes and methods in magic were, however, transmitted from country to country, from language to language throughout the ages without any basic changes being wrought. In the Middle Ages, Jewish magic literature differs very little from the magic literature of other nations. Hebrew works on magic quote extensively from non-Jewish magic literature, citing especially sources that medieval scholarship attributed to ancient Greek authors. The basic terminology and methods found in Hebrew works are similar to those dominant in non-Jewish works. In some Hebrew works a term may be used which was originally Hebrew but is applied in such a way as to show that it was copied from a non-Hebrew work, its

Hebrew origin had apparently been unknown to the Hebrew writer, for example, the term *Elo'i Sabaot* derived from the Hebrew *Elohei Zeva'ot*. Angelology and magic formulas in Hebrew, Greek, and Latin of the Hellenistic period were basic to the development of medieval magic literature. Since this period led to the fusion of Hebrew and non-Hebrew formulas, the process continued throughout the Middle Ages when terms and formulas from Arabic, German, French, Slavic, and other languages were added to medieval Hebrew magic literature. To date there is no serious study on the sources on which medieval Hebrew magic works drew. The various influences have neither been defined nor classified and no clear distinction can therefore be made between the following sources: the Assyrian and Babylonian (which apparently also influenced the Talmud), the Hellenistic (Jewish-Hellenistic and Greek), the ancient Egyptian and their later adaptations during the syncretistic periods of the Roman Empire, the original Arabic and their fusion with the Persian and Indian, and the European which were intermingled with Arabic and other sources. Principally, however, there is as yet no way to distinguish in every case between traditional Hebrew magic, derived from the biblical and talmudic periods, and the magic elements which reached Jewish writers from foreign sources. Until such studies are made, only impressions and generalizations can serve as basis for any assumption as to the nature of medieval Hebrew magic works.

Though there are no detailed studies on hand, there is no doubt that Jewish medieval magic drew on all the abovementioned sources. Some medieval Hebrew works correspond very closely to non-Jewish magic writings. Others, for example a number of 18th-century collections of Hebrew magic formulas, differ little from magic formulas which survived from the geonic period. Collections which originated in North Africa are very similar to works on magic by Jews in Germany. There is thus no essential difference in the basic magic formulas and the attitude toward magic between the various nations, countries, and periods. The same fusion of ancient and medieval sources is to be found in each of these works, all of which contain Arab, European, and authentic Jewish elements.

THE CHARACTER OF HEBREW MAGIC LITERATURE. The character of Hebrew magic literature was influenced not only by the biblical prohibition on witchcraft but by the nature of this literature. Works on magic neither use nor are identified by terms denoting magic, but were written under the guise of concepts which neither reveal their special character nor their contents. There are hundreds of collections on magic, in print and in manuscripts, appearing under such names as *simanim, refafot, refu'ot, goralot,* and *segullot*. These works are usually not devoted only to one branch of magic or popular superstition, but to a variety of practices such as dream interpretation, popular medicine, and amulets.

Many of these works are anonymous; in others the name of the editor or compiler appears in the introduction. (The term "author" is not applicable to such works, which are nothing but collections drawn from various sources.) Rarely is there anything known of them from other sources; most of them were obscure writers who did not engage in scholarly activities. This may be the underlying reason for the low level of the language and literary merit of most of these works. Some of the writings on magic are attributed to ancient sages and scholars; thus, for example, works which are partly devoted to the interpretation of dreams are often ascribed to the biblical figures Daniel or Joseph; works on *goralot* ("destinies" or "fortunes") are attributed to the wise *Ahithophel the Gilonite, etc. Babylonian *geonim* and early scholars, from Saadiah b. Joseph Gaon to Naḥmanides, have had works on magic ascribed to them. Though widely disseminated, works on magic were mostly not written within the framework of medieval and early modern scholarly Hebrew literature. Some of the better known works that discuss magic are: *Nishmat Ḥayyim* by *Manasseh Ben Israel in which the author devotes a long chapter to the description of magical practices; *Derekh ha-Shem* by Moses Ḥayyim *Luzzatto, has a section on magic; the commentaries on the Pentateuch by Naḥmanides; and *Shalshelet ha-Kabbalah,* an important historical work in which the author, Gedaliah b. Joseph *ibn Yaḥya, a Renaissance scholar, also discusses magic.

The literature of the *Ḥasidei Ashkenaz, probably more than any other medieval corpus of Hebrew scholarly writings, is a source on medieval magic (12th and 13 centuries), especially *Sefer Ḥasidim* and the esoteric works of *Judah b. Samuel ha-Ḥasid of Regensburg and of his disciples, of which *Ḥokhmat ha-Nefesh,* a work on psychology by *Eleazar b. Judah of Worms, is a prime example. The concern of the Ashkenazi Ḥasidim with magic practices and phenomena has its roots in some of their theological ideas.

MAGIC AND MEDIEVAL DISCIPLINES. Medieval man, as reflected in the literature on magic, did not clearly differentiate between magic and other branches of knowledge, especially between medicine and magic. Most of the collections dealing mainly with magic do not distinguish between the treatment of an ailment according to the accepted norms of popular medicine, such as the application of heat, herbs, and certain foods, and magic means, calling for the help of angels and demons to heal the patient. This failure of distinction was not only due to the lack of a scientific framework but to the desire to lend authority and legitimacy to magic formulas when combined with medical practice. These works also do not clearly distinguish between astrology and magic. Works on *goralot* ("destinies" or "fortunes") include astrological calculations which portend the fate of a man according to the constellations at his birth, and determine his character traits and religious, economic, and social status. The same works also contain magic instructions on how to use the auguries of the constellations for other purposes and how to change a man's fate through incantations and amulets, etc.

Most of the magic in the extant collections is devoted to *simanim* which derives from the fact that the Talmud, contrary to its injunction against the practice of magic, allows the practice of "signs." This literature describes various events, feelings, or even the itching of various parts of the human body *(refafot),* which are indicative of an oncoming event. Incantations are often chanted and charms used in an attempt either to nullify an ominous portent or to enhance a benign prophecy. To this category also belongs the literature of "dream interpretation" which describes in detail various occurrences within dreams thought to reveal the future to the dreamer. Sometimes advice is tendered in the use of magical means to prevent the bad dreams from being realized.

The *segullah* is basic to all magic formulas and is the main magic means used by the person himself. Knowledge of many charms is the professional distinction of the expert magician. The central element in the *segullah* is a name or a series of names which is considered holy. The common appellation of a magician in Eastern Europe in the 17th and 18th centuries as *Ba'al Shem* or *Ba'al Shem Tov* ("owner of the Holy Name" or "owner of the Holy Good Name") is rooted in this practice. The name used is most frequently that of an angel, or sometimes one of the many names of God.

Sometimes even the name of a demon is resorted to which

would seem to make this form of magic "black magic." The demon invoked in such charms is, however, thought to be a "bad angel" *(malakh ḥabbalah)* who should be addressed when the magician intends to harm someone, kill an enemy, cause damage, find the whereabouts of a thief and make him return his loot, etc. Some of the names in the *segullah* are common biblical or talmudic-midrashic names, mostly polysyllabic so as to awe the hearer and to seem as strange as possible. Many of the names were culled from *heikhalot* and Merkabah writings, the Hebrew mystical literature of the talmudic and geonic period from which the major part of Hebrew medieval angelology is derived; sometimes even from non-Hebrew sources; others were created anagrammatically according to a definite system, either from other known names or from biblical verses.

The name, which is the essence of the *segullah*, is supplemented with various elements which differ from book to book and even from page to page in the same work. The *segullah*, or the petition for magical intercession (of a supernatural power), must be written in a clear form or enunciated clearly and loudly. Sometimes the time at which the deed should occur (a certain hour of the day or night or a certain day of the month) is also given; an astrological element was thus added to the magical charm. Certain substantive elements are also added, such as bits of flesh, bone, or skin from various animals (or even the human body), or certain herbs or plants. In the classic cases of sympathetic magic sometimes the performer of the act of magic, when he directs an incantation against a certain person, draws a pricture of the latter or writes his name, or even molds his likeness in clay. These means were especially resorted to in the case of a thief. The suffering inflicted by sympathetic magic on the thief caused him to reveal the cache of the stolen goods and give them back. Through these means demons could also be compelled to serve man, when an incantation with the name of the culprit proved ineffective.

The *segullah* is used both as a direct magic act to attain a certain aim and as an auxiliary to medical aid, to reveal a man's fate, to appease or prompt the auguries of a "sign," or to interpret a dream. An amulet, for instance, is usually nothing more than a *segullah* written in a certain form, so that a person could carry it with him always. Such a charm is usually protective, invoking the heavenly powers to safeguard the wearer against any harm.

The contents of works on *segullot* are arranged according to their purposes. A title states the function of the charm after which there is a description of the charm including the holy names and the other necessary elements. Another type of *segullot* literature, sometimes called *shimmushim* ("uses"), is arranged according to the holy names indicating the purpose and uses to which each name can be put. Thus, for instance, *Sefer ha-Ḥeshek* lists 70 names of the archangel *Metatron, after each of which the author gives the use that it can be put to and what magical purpose can best be served by using one particular appellation of this angel. The holy divine names, composed either of 42 letters or 72 letters, which are comprised of units of three or six letters, serve many magic purposes; each name can be the means of achieving a specific magic goal. *"Shimmushei Tehillim"* (The Uses of the Psalms"), another body of magic writings, describes the magic power inherent in certain verses and chapters in the Psalms and in some other Scriptures. The Bible was also used for the purpose of "sign" magic, i.e., prophecies. A person practicing this magic would open the Bible, put his finger at random on a certain verse and the content of this verse would reveal the attitude of the Divine Powers to the question or request of the person inquiring.

RELATIONSHIP BETWEEN MYSTIC AND MAGIC LITERATURES. Historical circumstances rather than literary or conceptual affinities have created an impression, especially in modern times, that there is a similarity or even identity between mystic literature and magic in Jewish life and thought. One expression of this view is the term *"kabbalah ma'asit"* ("practical tradition"), which is magic, and *"kabbalah iyyunit"* ("theoretical tradition"), which is mysticism. "Kabbalah" in this context means nothing more than tradition and does not denote any special mystical system. 19th-century scholars of Jewish studies who were fiercely opposed to *Ḥasidism, which is one derivation of the Kabbalah proper (the mystical ideology), saw Ḥasidism and Kabbalah as representing medieval superstition, and did not try to differentiate between mystical thought and magic practice, which to them seemed to derive from the same source. Their ideas were accepted even by some 20th-century scholars. A detailed examination of magic literature clearly shows that most of those who practiced magic, or the authors of works on magic, did not know anything about mysticism in general, or Kabbalah in particular. It is therefore very unlikely that kabbalistic symbolism of the holy *Sefirot*, or the kabbalistic concept of evil would appear in magic charms. When the Zohar became part of the holy literature and widely known, it was used for magic purposes, but no more than the Book of Psalms. The use that both works were put to does not reflect their original content. Many kabbalists, from those in the Gerona circle (13th century) on, did not practice magic at all. The doctrines of medicine and astrology are undoubtedly nearer to that of magic than the doctrines of Jewish mysticism.

Still, there is some connection between the development of magic literature and mystical literature. In talmudic times there undoubtedly existed a unique magic literature to which such works as *Sefer ha-Razim*, published in a scholarly edition (by M. Margalioth, 1966), clearly testify. The book is an example of early Jewish magic which did not have any mystic tendency, and which is influenced mainly by non-Hebrew sources. Aside from this type of works, some elements of magic were included, sometimes prominently, in the writings of the *heikhalot* and the Merkabah. Included are works of a clear magical character, e.g., *Hakkarat Panim ve-Sidrei Sirtutim*, a work on chiromancy. Even major works of this literature, such as *Sefer Heikhalot Rabbati*, include some material concerning prophecies, signs, and even incantations. According to the conceptual view of *heikhalot* and Merkabah literature, when the angels revealed heavenly mysteries (revelations which constitute the body of this literature) to the talmudic sages they also made esoteric magic disclosures in which they described the divine worlds and eschatological secrets. Medieval scholars, the Ḥasidei Ashkenaz, and the kabbalists who resorted to *heikhalot* and Merkabah literature in their esoteric and mystical speculations also accepted the magic tradition that it embraced and sometimes even practiced it. The Ḥasidei Ashkenaz discussed magic in their works at length and also had some magic works attributed to them. The relationship they established between esoteric theology and magic speculation was rooted in a peculiar theological development. The Ashkenazi ḥasidic theology is based on the concept that God, far away from the natural world and the laws that govern it, is revealed, according to these laws, within the world of man in specific, well-defined phenomena which confirm to man His existence. Such phenomena, miraculous in character, including magic, witchcraft, and demonology, defy the laws of nature and reveal the power of the hidden Godhead. The Ḥasidei Ashkenaz consequently tried to collect in their writings as many descriptions of such phenomena as possible which they analyzed and on which they commented in the light of their own esoteric doctrine. The inference, however, cannot be drawn that they dealt in practical magic more or less than other scholars of that period. The implication is merely that they were theologically interested in such matters more than others, and therefore included them in their literature.

The Ḥasidei Ashkenaz thus became famous as scholars possessed of magic knowledge, and many legends revolved around them, such as the story about a competition in magic between *Samuel b. Kalonymus he-Ḥasid, and three non-Jewish magicians; the story about the ability of Eleazar b. Judah of Worms to get very quickly from place to place *(kefiẓat ha-derekh)* by the power of a magical formula; the tale of Judah b. Samuel he-Ḥasid who overpowered an evil magician; and many others. How far the legends woven about scholars were removed from the actual lives of these scholars may be seen by the fact that Abraham *Ibn Ezra, the Spanish Jewish philosopher and commentator, became the hero of many magic stories (probably because of his astrological works).

Magic is relatively little treated in theoretical Kabbalah writings, especially in works which concentrated on matters concerning the structure of the divine worlds, the *Sefirot,* and the developments within the divine realm (themes central to Kabbalistical literature). Supernatural knowledge and powers were, however, attributed to many kabbalists. Even *Isaac the Blind, one of the earliest kabbalists who lived in Provence, was described as having the power to distinguish between a new soul, which appeared for the first time in the world, and an old soul which had been reincarnated. This tradition of magic and supernatural hagiography of prominent kabbalists developed continually up to the times of Isaac *Luria and *Israel Ba'al Shem Tov.

Magic in Kabbalah literature is touched upon in discussion of earthly or demonological matters, but even in this literature it was cautiously treated and circumscribed. Few magic elements are found in the Zohar, and in the writings of other early kabbalists there are even less. Later magic literature and kabbalistic doctrine were also seldom fused. Ḥayyim *Vital describes some magic practices in his autobiographical work *Sefer ha-Ḥezyonot* ("Book of Visions"), which, however, he does not relate to the special kabbalistic doctrine of his teacher, Isaac Luria. In his theological works, magic is a marginal theme. Though he accepted magic, it did not impinge on his innermost spiritual beliefs expressed in the kabbalistic myth which he set down in many books. The same applies to the writings of many other kabbalists.

Some 19th-century scholars described modern Ḥasidism, founded by Israel Ba'al Shem Tov, as a prime example of magic and superstition. While many leaders of the ḥasidic movement believed in magic and practiced it, especially in giving amulets (the Ba'al Shem Tov himself dealt in magic and probably made his living as a popular healer and magician), ḥasidic theoretical literature, the vast homiletic literature which describes its ideology, is devoid of all magic elements. Ḥasidic tales might contain elements of the use of magic or of overcoming magic deeds performed by evil non-Jews, but ḥasidic doctrines eschewed magic elements even more than the kabbalistic literature which the Ḥasidim had inherited and developed. The difference between the "practical tradition" of Ḥasidism, which practiced magic, and the "ideological (theoretical) tradition" of the movement is probably more pronounced in modern Ḥasidism than in any other mystic movement.

Magic in Medieval Jewish Society. Judaism never considered magic either as an ideological or social challenge which had to be dealt with. The belief in the power of magic was apparently universal in Jewish society, both in the East and in the West, from the beginning of the Middle Ages up to early modern times. Opposition to magic was voiced by but a few which, when expressed in writing, formed a minor element within their work. While Maimonides, like some other Jewish philosophers, rejected magic, he was not deeply concerned with it and only devoted a few passages to the problem in *Guide of the Perplexed,* much less, for instance, than to his argument with astrology on which he wrote a special treatise. Among others who repudiated magic were Saadiah Gaon and Hai Gaon; they too, however, did not stress the question in their writings. As a consequence belief in magic hardly ever called forth any defenders in Hebrew literature. In the great 13th-century controversy the rabbis of France in their criticism also denounced Maimonides for his opposition to magic; it was, however, a very minor point. Menahem Ẓiyyoni's short treatise on the defense of magic and the belief in demons, *Ẓefunei Ẓiyyoni* (in Ms.), is written from a kabbalistic point of view as were similar treatises by other kabbalists. Magic, however, never was a major issue in medieval Jewish thought.

The practice of magic (which is quite different from a belief in magic) was also not a major problem in Judaism, though magic as such was condemned outright because of the biblical prohibition and it therefore was practiced under the guise of different names. The practice of "signs," "charms," amulets, astrology, and popular medicine was never a subject of serious scholarly discussion. Halakhic literature tried to delimit the scope of permitted and forbidden magic, but this was always very much a secondary problem. Due to the biblical prohibition on magic the most vulgar and "black" forms of magic did not become common in Judaism and such practices as necromancy were very rare. While some books on magic contain formulas for killing an enemy by magic means, for love potions, etc., there is no evidence that these were practiced. These formulas were probably copied from non-Jewish sources.

As a result magic was not a legitimate and commonly accepted profession in medieval Jewish society and the religious convictions of a man who practiced magic were suspect. Formulas were thus written down since there was no oral transmission within a special class of practitioners of magic. Many Jews, especially in the East, usually consulted non-Jewish magicians rather than Jewish magicians.

The Christian injunctions against magic and witchcraft and the fierce persecutions against those who practiced magic, which started around the end of the 15th century, do not have their parallel in Judaism. There are few examples in Judaism of Jews persecuting Jews because of magic practices. In those rare cases where there is evidence of such persecutions, the accusation served as a camouflage for more fundamental reasons. Thus the accusations of the rabbis of Venice against Moses Ḥayyim Luzzatto for dealing in magic were a guise for their suspicion that he had Shabbatean tendencies. In those Jewish communities where Christian anti-witchcraft persecutions had an influence, such as Italy, the relationship between Jews and non-Jews was closer than elsewhere.

The only social sphere of Jewish life in which magic practice attained legitimacy was in the formulas of the *ḥerem* ("excommunication"). Many *ḥerem* texts have incantations with a clear magic undertone.

In the 17th and 18th centuries in Eastern Europe the position of magicians *("ba'alei Shem")* began to emerge on the Jewish social scene. The *ba'alei Shem* practiced magic and popular medicine, used amulets, drove away demons and prophesied. Due to the power inherent in the names they knew to use, they could discover thieves, retrieve lost articles, purify houses from evil spirits, etc. From the historical point of view, however, these magicians were of special significance in that many of them disseminated Shabbatean ideas throughout Eastern Europe; magicians were also instrumental in the development of the ḥasidic movement

The insignificant purpose to which magic was applied is probably one of the reasons why magic played such a minor role in medieval Jewish literature. There are few records of major significance in which magic featured, such as *Joseph della Reina's attempt to hasten the redemption through magic means. Magic literature centers around such minor matters as toothaches and lost articles, and some attempt at prophecy of private persons' destiny. It thus did not relate to the major historical and ideological problems of medieval Jewish society. The private character of the practice rendered it unimportant in the eyes of both its supporters and opponents so that it never became a major issue of dispute.

The relatively insignificant influence that magic had on medieval Jewish life and thought is in direct contradiction to its role as a cause for anti-Semitism and hatred toward the Jews in the Middle Ages. The belief that every Jew was an evil magician, possessed of supernatural evil powers, was almost universal among Christians in the Middle Ages and early modern times. Jews were believed to be the people of Satan and they thus possessed supernatural secrets. This concept was one of the major sources of persecutions and blood libels throughout that period. Jewish reality in the Middle Ages hardly gave any substance to such accusations or to such an impression of the Jewish people. The basis for it was Christian theology, which described the Jews as deicides, therefore Satanic, and therefore possessors of magic.

See also *Demonology: *Kabbalah: *Sorcery: *Folklore.

[Y.D.]

Bibliography: Bible: H. Zimmern, *Beitraege zur Kenntnis der babylonischen Religion* (1901), 91–95, and passim; A. Erman, *A Handbook of Egyptian Religion* (1907), 148–64; R. C. Thompson, *Semitic Magic* (1908); F. Cumont, *Oriental Religions in Roman Paganism* (1911), 138; J. Pedersen, *Der Eid bei den Semiten* (1914), 1–2; A. Jirku, in: ZAW, 37 (1917–18), 109–25; W. O. Oesterley, *Immortality and the Unseen World* (1921), 125–36; S. Mowinckel, *Psalmenstudien* (1921²); Pedersen, Israel, 1–2 (1926), 430ff.; N. Nicolsky, *Spuren magischer Formeln in den Psalmen* (1927); A. S. Cook, *The Religion of Ancient Palestine in the Light of Archaeology* (1930), 66–86, 200–1, 213; A. Falkenstein, *Die Haupttypen der sumerischen Beschwoerung* (1931); H. Birkeland, *Die Feinde des Individuums in der israelitischen Psalmenliteratur* (1933); G. Meier, *Die assyrische Beschwoerungssammlung maqlu* (1937); A. Guillaume, *Prophecy and Divination* (1938), 26, 34, 233ff., 387–90; idem, in: JRAS, 2 (1942), 111–31; C. H. Gordon, in: AFO, 12 (1937–39), 115–17; Kaufmann Y., Toledot, 1 (1937), passim; S. H. Hook, *The Origins of Early Semitic Ritual* (1938); W. F. Albright, in: BASOR, 76 (1939), 5–11; 150 (1958), 36; Th. H. Gaster, in: *Orientalia*, 11 (1942), 41–79, 186–8; H. Torczyner (Tur-Sinai), in: JNES, 6 (1947), 18–29; H. Tur-Sinai, *Ha-Lashon ve-ha-Sefer*, 1 (1954²), 53–65; M. D. Cassuto, *Ha-Elah Anat* (1950), 66–67, 80; J. Wilson, *The Culture of Ancient Egypt* (1951), 117–8, 142–3; A. Falkenstein and W. von Soden, *Sumerische und akkadische Hymnen und Gebete* (1953), 23–24, 214–7, 295–354; R. Malinowsky, *Magic, Science and Religion* (1954), 17–87; J. Liver, in: *Eretz-Israel*, 3 (1954), 99ff.; E. Reiner, in: JNES, 15 (1956), 129–49; A. Goetze, *Kleinasien* (1957²), 151–61; J. Gray, in: VTS, 5 (1957), 11, 36, 42, 147; Pritchard, Texts, 326–8, 346–58, 383–91; R. O. Gurney, in: *Iraq*, 22 (1960), 221–7; P. Artzi, in: EM, 4 (1962), 348–65. Medieval Hebrew Literature: J. Trachtenberg, *Jewish Magic and Superstition* (1939, incl. bibl.); S. Lieberman, in: *Tarbiz*, 27 (1958), 183–9; Y. Dan, *ibid.*, 32 (1963), 359–69; idem, *Torat ha-Sod shel Ḥasidut Ashkenaz* (1968), 184–202; N. Golb, in: *American Philosophical Society Year Book* (1965); H. J. Zimmels, *Magicians, Theologians and Doctors* (1952).

MAGIDOV, JACOB (1869–1943), Yiddish writer and editor. Born in Odessa, he received both a traditional and a secular education. Emigrating to the United States in 1886, he worked in a shirt factory and studied law at night, passing the bar examination in 1904 and for a time practicing law. Active in the Jewish labor movement from his arrival, he played an important role in 1888 in the founding of the United Hebrew Trades, a central body intent upon organizing Jewish workers into unions. He was also active in the Socialist Labor Party. Magidov began his career as a writer and editor in the Jewish socialist press in 1894. He wrote for *Arbeiter Zeitung* on American politics and became city editor of the *Abend Blatt* at the end of the 1890s. After writing for the *Forward* for a short time he joined the *Jewish Morning Journal* in 1901 and remained associated with it for the rest of his life. His book *Der Shpigl fun der Ist Side* ("The Mirror of the East Side," 1923) contains valuable insights into Jewish personalities of his generation. Magidov was one of the many immigrant intellectuals who felt it their duty to bridge the gap between the Yiddish-speaking masses and their new environment. Especially as the *Jewish Morning Journal* city editor, he served them as an interpreter of events in the new homeland.

Bibliography: LNYL, 5 (1963), 389ff. [H.To.]

MAGINO, MEIR (late 16th century), Venetian inventor. In 1587 Pope Sixtus V invited him to introduce into the Papal States his process of extracting silk thread from the cocoon twice a year. Concerning this new process, Magino published an Italian work entitled *Dialoghi di M. Magino Gabrielli Hebreo venetiano sopra l'utili sue invenzioni circa la seta* (Venice, 1588); this elegantly printed book contains numerous illustrations, among them a portrait of the author, and a Hebrew poem written by him with an Italian translation by S. Tellarino. A second patent secured for Magino the rights to a new process for polishing mirrors and colored cut glass with a special kind of oil. He was also granted the exclusive right to produce special wine bottles, which are still in use in Roman wineshops. One of his children, Gabriel induced Ferdinand I of Tuscany to issue the famous appeal to Jews to come and settle in Leghorn (1593). He was promised the office of consul general of the Jews in Pisa and Leghorn, but the appointment did not materialize.

Bibliography: Roth, *Jews in the Renaissance* (1959), 238f.; A. Milano, *Ghetto di Roma* (1964), 81f. [A.Mil.]

MAGNES, JUDAH LEON (1877–1948), U.S. rabbi and communal leader. He was chancellor and first president of the *Hebrew University of Jerusalem. Magnes was born in San Francisco, California, to parents who emigrated from Poland and Germany in 1863. He attended the Hebrew Union College, where he was ordained as a Reform rabbi in 1900. Magnes spent the years 1900–03 studying in Berlin and Heidelberg. During his years in Germany he traveled widely in Eastern Europe and was profoundly moved by the intensive Jewish life he found. It strengthened his earlier sympathetic feeling toward Zionism and brought him to the commitment to make Zionism and service to his people his mission in life.

On his return from Germany he became rabbi of Temple Israel in Brooklyn (1904–05) and afterward the assistant rabbi of Temple Emanu-El in New York (1906–10). At the same time he served as the secretary of the American Zionist Federation (1905–08) and later became the president of the Kehillah of *New York City from its founding in 1908 until its demise in 1922; he left for Palestine in the same year. Founded to advance and coordinate Jewish life in New York City, the Kehillah dealt vigorously with such internal problems as religious life and Jewish education; in the latter area its Bureau of Jewish Education, directed by Samson *Benderly, pioneered in the centralization and modernization of Jewish education in the U.S. The Kehillah was active and effective in labor arbitration and helped to repress crime in the immigrant Jewish areas in cooperation with the city's police department. It provided a nexus for cooperation between "uptown" and "downtown" Jews and a forum for Jewish public opinion. Magnes was the Kehillah's moving spirit and most competent leader,

Judah L. Magnes, U.S. rabbi and first president of the Hebrew University of Jerusalem.

spokesman, peacemaker, fund raiser, and philosopher, and thus a leading figure in the metropolis. In 1905 he participated in the Zionist Congress at Basle as a member of the U.S. delegation. It was there that he came face to face with the leaders of Russian Jewry and through them he reached a greater understanding of East European Jewry. Back in New York (after his first visit in Palestine) he headed the greatest Jewish demonstration against the Kishinev pogroms and established the Self-Defense Association which collected funds for the purchase of arms to be smuggled to the Jewish *self-defense bodies in Russia. In 1904 he joined Solomon *Schechter's inner circle and moved toward religious traditionalism. In Zionism he became a disciple and follower of *Aḥad Ha-Am, whom Magnes called "The Harmonious Jew." After the Kishinev pogroms he helped Cyrus *Sulzberger and Louis *Marshall in establishing the *American Jewish Committee. In 1908 he married Beatrice Lowenstein, the sister-in-law of Louis Marshall, and this brought him closer to the leading Jewish circles. At the same time he strengthened his ties with the East European Jews.

Magnes' shift toward religious traditionalism brought him to break with Temple Emanu-El. His unfulfilled demands for religious changes led him to resign in 1910. From 1911 to 1912 he was rabbi of B'nai Jeshurun, a leading Conservative congregation, after which he left congregational work altogether to devote himself to Jewish public service. However, Magnes' opposition to U.S. entry into World War I in 1917 out of pacifist convictions, and his activity in the peace movement during the war, undermined his leadership of a Jewish community firmly committed to the war and concerned over possible imputations of disloyalty. His brilliant U.S. Jewish communal career actually ended in 1917. In 1922 Magnes emigrated with his family to Palestine, where he continued his activities in establishing the *Hebrew University of which he was the chancellor (1925–35) and first president (1935–48) until his death. He was active in raising funds for the university, in securing the donation of several personal libraries, and in developing several of its major divisions, especially the Institute for Jewish Studies which was inaugurated in 1924, even before the official opening of the Hebrew University in 1925. The Hebrew University honored him first by publishing *Sefer Magnes* in 1938 and later by naming one of the Chairs of Bible and the press of the University after him, as well as by granting him and Chaim Weizmann the first honorary degrees of the university. With the beginning of World War II, in spite of his pacifistic outlook on life, he called for war against Nazi Germany, serving as chairman of the Supply Board Scientific Advisory Committee of the War. He also helped his life-long friend Henrietta *Szold in her Youth Aliyah work and became the chairman of an Emergency Council of Hadassah in Palestine, as well as the chairman of the Middle East Advisory Council of the *American Joint Distribution Committee which he had helped found in World War I. During World War II he helped Jews who escaped to Turkey from Nazi-occupied countries, became responsible for the direction of relief work amongst the Jews throughout the Orient. Out of his pacifist convictions and the belief that the Jews are not like all nations, he sought an accord with the Palestinian Arabs and entered the political arena with the conviction that Jewish-Arab accord is of the greatest importance not only for the peaceful building of the country but also for the Jewish spirit. He started his political agitation immediately after the 1929 disturbances (see *Israel: Historical Survey 1880–1948), stating, "One of the greatest cultural duties of the Jewish people is the attempt to enter the promised land, not by means of conquest as Joshua, but through peaceful and cultural means, through hard work, sacrifices, love and with a decision not to do anything which cannot be justified before the world conscience" (Opening Speech of the Hebrew University Academic Year 1929/30). Magnes renewed his activities after the riots in 1936 and opposed the Royal Commission's suggestion for the partitioning of Palestine, always believing in the policy of establishing Palestine as a binational state and feeling that it was his personal mission to bring the Arabs and Jews together (see *Berit Shalom; *Palestine Partition and Partition Plans; *Palestine, Inquiry Commissions on). With this belief he carried on his political activities until his death in New York in 1948 while on a visit there. He was later reinterred in Jerusalem. A Judah L. Magnes Memorial Museum was set up in Oakland, California, in 1961. Magnes' writings and speeches were collected in *War-Time Addresses 1917–1921* (1923), *Addresses by the Chancellor of the Hebrew University* (1936), and in *The Perplexity of the Times* (1946).

Bibliography: N. Bentwich, *For Zion's Sake—A Biography of Judah L. Magnes* (1954); A. Goren, *New York Jews and the Quest for Community: The Kehillah Experiment 1908–1922* (1970); S. L. Hattis, *The Bi-National Idea in Palestine During Mandatory Times* (1970), 64–71, 169–72, 258–71 and index; L. Roth, in: *Jewish Education*, 20 (1949); S. H. Bergman, *Faith and Reason* (1961); Z. Szajkowski, in: *Conservative Judaism*, 22 no. 3 (1968); H. Parzen, in: JSOS, 29 (1967), 203–33; 32 (1970), 187–213.

[L.P.G./D.EF.]

MAGNIN, EDGAR FOGEL (1890–), U.S. Reform rabbi and communal leader. Magnin was born in San Francisco of a well-known mercantile family. He was ordained at Hebrew Union College (1914). After a year as rabbi in Stockton, California (1914), Magnin led Congregation B'nai B'rith (from 1929, the Wilshire Boulevard Temple) in Los Angeles, which grew under his leadership to become one of the largest and most influential congregations in the country. Outspoken, colorful, forceful, Rabbi Magnin was for many decades the unofficial voice and representative of the Los Angeles Jewish community in a variety of religious, governmental, social, educational and cultural organizations and institutions. Within the Jewish community he has been a leader in the Los Angeles Jewish Community Council, Cedars-Sinai Hospital, University Religious Conference, Los Angeles Hillel Council, Hebrew Union College-Jewish Institute of Religion, and B'nai B'rith, among many others. Rabbi Magnin was a lecturer in history at the University of Southern California (1934–55) and at the California School of Hebrew Union College. Author of *How to lead a Richer and Fuller Life* (1951), he was columnist for the *Los Angeles Herald Examiner* and the Anglo-Jewish weekly *Heritage*. [M.V.]

MAGNUS, English family. SIR PHILIP MAGNUS (1842–1933) was an educator and politican. Born in London, he was a minister of the West London Synagogue of British Jews (Reform) from 1866 to 1880, and lectured in applied mathematics at University College, London. In 1880 Magnus was appointed organizing secretary and director of the newly established City and Guilds of London Institute. He served on the Royal Commission whose report led to the Technical Education Act of 1884. Magnus was responsible for inclusion of a faculty of engineering at the reconstructed London University in 1889. From 1906 to 1922, he was the university's member of parliament. He was knighted in 1886 and created a baronet in 1917. Magnus played a leading part in Anglo-Jewish affairs, as chairman of the council of the West London Synagogue and as a vice-president of the *Board of Deputies of British Jews and the *Anglo-Jewish Association. He was violently opposed to Zionism and was one of the founders of the anti-Zionist League of British Jews. Sir Philip's wife KATIE MAGNUS (1844–1924) was a writer. She published traditional and historical tales for young readers and her often reprinted *Outlines of Jewish History* (1886) was an especially successful evocation of the past. Her *Jewish Portraits* (1888) included studies of *Judah Halevi, *Heine, and Moses *Mendelssohn. Sir Philip and Lady Magnus' son, LAURIE MAGNUS (1872–1933), began his writing career mainly with studies of English poetry. In 1902 he wrote *Aspects of the Jewish Question*, which revealed him to be an anti-Zionist like his father. Four years later, in *Religio Laici Judaici* ("The Faith of a Jewish Layman"), he again propounded the view that Judaism was a religion and not a nationality. For 14 years, from its inception in 1917 to its suspension, he edited the anti-Zionist *Jewish Guardian*. He was active in Jewish communal life as a warden of the West London Reform Synagogue, a member of the council of Jews' College, London, and president of the Union of Jewish Literary Societies. His most important books were *Dictionary of European Literature* (1926), and *The Jews in the Christian Era and their Contribution to its Civilization* (1929). As Laurie Magnus shortly predeceased his father, the baronetcy devolved directly upon his son SIR PHILIP MONTEFIORE MAGNUS (1906–). He was the author of a number of successful biographies: *Edmund Burke* (1939), *Sir Walter Raleigh* (1952), *Gladstone* (1954), *Kitchener* (1958), and *King Edward VII* (1964). He severed his connections with Judaism, and in 1951 formally added his wife's family name to his own, becoming Sir Philip Magnus-Allcroft.

Bibliography: F. Foden, *Philip Magnus, Victorian Educational Pioneer* (1970). [V.D.L.]

MAGNUS, EDUARD (1799–1872), German painter. Born in Berlin, Magnus studied medicine, philosophy, and architecture and traveled in France, Italy, Spain, and England before turning to painting. His work reflected the evolution of German art in his time. Beginning as a Nazarene (see Philipp *Veit), he developed a romantic neoclassicism influenced by the French painter Ingres, and finally a realistic style. He had a good reputation as a portrait painter. Among his subjects were the singer Jenny Lind, the composer Mendelssohn, the sculptor Thorwaldsen and members of the Prussian royal family. Magnus also left some paintings recording his travels. He was baptized as a child.

Bibliography: Wininger, Biog; M. Bryan, *Bryan's Dictionary of Painters and Engravers* (1904); Roth, Art, 546. [ED.]

MAGNUS, HEINRICH GUSTAV (1802–1870), German chemist and physicist. Magnus, who was born in Berlin into a wealthy family, left Judaism. He began teaching at the University of Berlin in 1831. From 1845 to 1869 he was

Heinrich Gustav Magnus, German chemist and physicist. Jerusalem, J.N.U.L., Schwadron Collection.

professor of physics and technology at Berlin, and in 1861 became rector of the university. His numerous discoveries include the first platinum-ammonia complex, Magnus' green salt ($(Pt(NH_3)_4)PtCl_4$) and the "Magnus Effect." The latter referred originally to projectiles which, subjected to rapid rotation, are turned aside from their original direction by forces which act upon them crosswise. It has important aerodynamic applications.

Bibliography: Huntress, in: *Proceedings of the American Academy of Arts and Science*, 81 (1952), 70f. [S.A.M.]

MAGNUS, MARCUS (also known as **Mordecai ben Manlin Dessau, Raubach,** and **Weisel;** d. 1736), court agent of the Prussian crown prince, later King Frederick William I. In his struggle for power in the *Berlin community, his great rival was Jost *Liebmann and later Liebmann's widow, Esther. In 1709 he became head of the community and in 1720 the spokesman for provincial Jewry before the Prussian authorities. After a protracted quarrel, in which both sides appealed to the king, Magnus persuaded the community to erect one public synagogue instead of the three private ones maintained by Liebmann (1714). In 1722 he was appointed salaried permanent chief elder of the Berlin community, a position he held until his death.

Bibliography: L. Geiger, *Geschichte der Juden in Berlin*, 1 (1871), 19, 21; H. Schnee, *Die Hoffinanz und der moderne Staat...*, 1 (1953), 68, 110–1; L. Stern, *Der preussische Staat und die Juden*, 1 (1962), index; 2 (1962); S. Stern, *The Court Jew* (1950), 181, 185. [M.LA.]

MAGNUS, PAUL WILHELM (1844–1914), German botanist. His father, Meyer Magnus, was a member of the Berlin City Council. Under the influence of the botanist Paul *Ascherson, the young Magnus abandoned the thought of a medical career and turned to the study of botany. After obtaining his degree, Magnus was invited by the Ministry of Agriculture to participate in scientific surveys of the North and Baltic Seas. His studies of specimens brought back from these expeditions led to important contributions on the growth patterns of algae as well as to pioneering investigations of the chytrids, an obscure and still poorly understood group of fungi. Magnus joined the faculty of the University of Berlin in 1875 and was promoted to the rank of *Professor Extraordinarius* in 1880. In 1911 the honorary title of *Geheimer Regierungsrat* was conferred upon him. His most important work was concerned with the systematics and life histories of a number of parasitic fungi.

Paul Wilhelm Magnus, German botanist. Jerusalem, J.N.U.L., Schwadron Collection.

Bibliography: G. Lindav, in: *Berichte der deutschen botanischen Gesellschaft*, 32 (1914), 32–63. [M.L.G.]

MAGNUS, RUDOLPH (1873–1927), German physiologist and pharmacologist. Magnus, who was born in Brunswick, became one of the foremost co-workers of the famous physiologist Sir Charles Sherrington in Oxford. He investigated the mechanisms governing the posture and balance of the body and discovered its center of reflexes in the brainstem up to the midbrain. He became lecturer in pharmacology at Heidelberg until his appointment at Utrecht (1908), where he founded the first pharmacological institute in Holland. Magnus studied the pharmacology and physiology of the intestines, and worked on digitalis. In 1924 he collected the works of his institute in *Koerperhaltung; Koerperstellung, Gleichgewicht und Bewegung bei Saeugern*, with A. de Klein (1930); and *Lane Lectures on Experimental Pharmacology and Medicine* (1930). Other works are *Vom Urtier zum Menschen* (1908) and *Wilhelm Boelsche* (1909).

Bibliography: S. R. Kagan, *Jewish Medicine* (1952), 215–6; I. Fischer, *Biographisches Lexicon*, s.v. [N.Ko.]

MAGYAR ZSIDO SZEMLE ("Hungarian Jewish Review"), Hungarian Jewish monthly journal which was established in 1884 and appeared until 1948 in a total of 65 volumes. During the first decade each volume of *Magyar Zsidó Szemle* contained more than 600 pages, but the number was subsequently reduced; in the period of crisis following the two world wars only individual issues were published annually. The aims of the journal were: to serve as a platform for Hungarian Jewry; to deal in Hungarian with Jewish scholarly subjects; to publish sources of the history of Hungarian Jewry; to discuss problems of religious education; and to review works on Judaica and Jewish history published outside Hungary. The editorial board was headed by professors and directors of the Budapest rabbinical seminary: W. *Bacher (1884–90), L. *Blau (1891–1930), and D. S. *Loewinger (1931–48). The first associate editors did not belong to the seminary (J. Bánóczi, 1884–90; F. Mezey, 1891–95), but the subsequent ones were professors and lecturers at that institute: J.M. *Guttman, H. *Guttman, S. *Hevesi, F. Hevesi, D. Friedmann, J. Hahn, A. *Scheiber, and M. *Weiss.

Attempts were made to transfer some of the many and varied subjects covered by the journal to periodicals devoted to special topics: *Yavneh*, which dealt with problems of religious education (1928–30, vols. 1–3), and *Moriah*, in which sermons were published (1930, vol. 1). Of the appendices to the journal, the most important is the Hebrew supplement *Ha-Ẓofeh me-Ereẓ Hagar* which appeared from 1911 onward. Among its contributors were distinguished Judaic scholars in the world. Until the outbreak of World War I its first four volumes appeared as a supplement to *Magyar Zsidó Szemle*. Subsequently from 1921 to 1930 it was published separately as a quarterly, under the title of *Ha-Ẓofeh le-Ḥokhmat Yisrael*.

During this decade the circle of its scholarly contributors widened still further and the journal became a focal point of scholarship of prime importance in the Jewish world. After *Ha-Ẓofeh* ceased publication, its role was continued by *Ha-Soker*, which appeared between 1933 and 1940 (i–vi) under the editorship of D. S. Loewenger, with J. M. Guttman, F. Hevesi, and D. Friedmann as associate editors. Between the two world wars a change also took place in the contents of *Magyar Zsidó Szemle*, in which there began to appear articles not only in Hungarian but also in other European languages, as well as in Hebrew. The authors of these articles were Hungarian Jewish scholars, as well as Jewish and non-Jewish scholars from Hungary and other countries.

Bibliography: S. Eden, in: S. Federbush (ed.), *Ḥokhmat Yisrael be-Ma'arav Eiropah*, 1 (1958), 554–9; S. Weingarten, *ibid.*, 2 (1963), 380–402. [D.S.Loe.]

MAḤAL, abbreviation of *Mitnaddevei Ḥuẓ la-Areẓ* (Foreign Volunteers), the term used for volunteers from abroad, mainly Jews, who enlisted in the Israel Defense Forces (IDF) and participated in the *War of Independence, 1948/49. In practice the Maḥal section of the IDF Manpower Branch handled volunteers who were citizens or residents of countries outside Eastern and Central Europe. No reliable statistics are available, but it was officially estimated that Maḥal comprised about 5,000 volunteers. Of these, about 1,500 were from U.S.A. and Canada, about 500 from South Africa, and about 1,000 from Great Britain. The small Jewish community of Finland contributed the largest proportion of volunteers, a total of only 30, but 2% of its strength.

The first groups of volunteers were organized after the UN General Assembly recommended the partition of Palestine in November 1947. In some instances, the initiative was spontaneous and local. This was the case in Canada, where two Jewish ex-servicemen issued a call for volunteers for Israel. The same was true in Scandinavia. In South Africa, the movement was organized after the arrival of two representatives of the *Jewish Agency who contacted the South African Jewish servicemen's association. By the beginning of 1948, volunteer organizations were at work in most Jewish communities in the Western world. In many countries the activities were under cover: the official destination of the volunteers was France. A small number of volunteers, mainly with military skills urgently needed by the *Haganah, were smuggled into the country before the State of Israel was proclaimed. The majority of the volunteers were channeled through training camps in France and Italy, organized by the Haganah European Command (with headquarters in Paris) and staffed by instructors from Palestine. Most were World War II veterans, and some had been officers. Transport facilities across the Mediterranean were difficult to arrange.

On arrival, the Maḥal volunteers were absorbed in IDF units according to the need for reinforcements, not fighting in separate formations. They thus fought on all fronts. Their contribution was not in numbers but in quality and experience, most necessary in a new army whose fighting tradition was that of an underground movement. Maḥal's major contribution was to the air force, which was organized, commanded, and to a large degree, staffed by overseas volunteers and by foreign air force veterans on special contract. Maḥal volunteers also played an important part in staffing the army medical corps. Individual volunteers also made important contributions to the engineers' corps, the signal corps, the armored units, and the artillery. Approximately 150 Maḥal volunteers were killed in action, the majority from U.S.A. and Canada. About 300 remained in Israel or returned later to settle there, but the majority went, fought, and returned to their countries of origin. [H.Pu.]

MAHALALEL BEN SHABBETAI HALLELYAH (d. after 1675), rabbi, kabbalist and Hebrew poet. Born at the beginning of the 17th century in Civitanova, Mahalalel suffered many hardships in his youth in Italy as a result of which he seems to have been compelled to wander to various places. Before 1660, he was appointed rabbi of Ancona. He was known primarily for his collection of poems and *piyyutim, Hallelyah,* recited in synagogues on Sabbaths and festivals. This collection also included prayers which were kabbalistic in spirt. Mahalalel and his community were ardent believers in *Shabbetai Ẓevi even after his apostasy in 1666. Two completely different versions of his hymn to Shabbetai Ẓevi and his prophet, *Nathan of Gaza, appear in *Hallelyah,* one version, apparently, composed before and the other after the apostasy. Some of the poems from this collection were published by S. Bernstein (see bibliography). From those of Mahalalel's letters which were also included in this collection and published in part by Bernstein, it seems that he had close ties with the great contemporary scholars in Italy. The following works by him remain in manuscript: *Kodesh Hillulim,* a commentary on the Pentateuch, and *Hallel Gamur.* Sixty-eight halakhic rulings, his responsa, are included in manuscripts (Mantua, Municipal Library, Ms. 88; Ferrara, Talmud Torah, Ms. 20/1).

Bibliography: S. Bernstein, in: *Mizraḥ u-Ma'arav,* 3 (1929), 200–2; idem, in: HUCA, 7 (1930), 497–536; idem: *Mi-Shirei Yisrael be-Italyah* (1939), 66–73, 154–6; M.Wilensky, in: *Sinai,* 25 (1949), 66; G. Scholem, *Shabbetai Ẓevi,* 2 (1957), 404f.; idem, in: *Sefer ha-Yovel Z. Wolfson* (1965), 225–41.
[A.D.]

MAHALLA AL-KUBRA, town of Lower Egypt, halfway between Alexandria and Damietta. There was a flourishing Jewish community in Mahalla al-Kubra under the Fatimids. *Benjamin of Tudela, the 12th-century traveler, relates that he found 500 Jews living there (E. N. Adler (ed.), *Jewish Travellers* (1930), 74). According to a list of contributions to ransom Jewish prisoners, the sum donated by the Mahalla community was the largest of the Delta communities (Mann, Egypt, 2 (1922), 290). Many documents written in Mahalla during the 12th and early 13th centuries have been found in the Cairo *Genizah.* The Jews of Mahalla were engaged in handicrafts and commerce, such as the silk trade. According to a *takkanah,* in 1187 R. Peraḥyah b. Joseph was *dayyan* in Mahalla. *Joseph Sambari, the 17th-century Egyptian chronicler, mentions the *Sefer Torah* in the synagogue of Mahalla, which was read only on the New Moon and on which people took the oath (Neubauer, Chronicles, 1 (1887), 119). According to popular tradition, the tomb of R. Ḥayyim ibn al-Amshatī is situated under the synagogue and pilgrimages (Arabic *ziyāra*) were held there every year on the first day of Iyyar. According to Jacob *Saphir (*Even Sappir,* 1 (1866), 21b), in the middle of the 19th century there were 20 Jewish families in the town. As was the case with other Egyptian Jewish communities, Mahalla's Jewish population increased considerably at the end of the 19th century, and by 1897 there were 200 Jews there. When the Zionist movement spread in the beginning of the 20th century, the Jews of Mahalla established a Zionist association. The Jewish population fell to 91 by 1927, and further declined to ten families by 1937.

Bibliography: J. Blau (ed.), *Teshuvot ha-Rambam,* 1 (1957), 177–8, no. 105; 2 (1960), 624–5 no. 348; Mann, Egypt, index; Worman, in: JQR, 18 (1905/06), 10; Assaf, in: *Sefer Klausner* (1937), 232–4; idem, in: *Tarbiz,* (1937/38), 34; idem, in: *Melilah,* 3–4 (1950), 224–9; Ashtor, in: JJS, 18, pp. 38ff.; Ashtor, Toledot, 1 (1944), 251; Goitein, in: *Tarbiz,* 20 (1948/49), 201–2; 32 (1962/63) 192–4; J. M. Landau, *Ha-Yehudim be-Miẓrayim* (1967), 148–9.
[E.A.]

MAHANAIM (Heb. מַחֲנַיִם), locality east of the Jordan which was named by Jacob before he crossed the Jabbok on his way to *Penuel; according to the etiological version in Genesis 32:3, he named it "God's camp" after he saw the angels of God there. It was on the border between the territories of the half-tribe of Manasseh and of the tribe of Gad (Josh. 13:26, 30); it also appears as a levitical city in Gad (Josh. 21:38; I Chron. 6:65). After the disastrous battle of Mt. Gilboa, Abner son of Ner, captain of Saul's army, took Ish-Bosheth, Saul's son, to Mahanaim and established it as the capital of the dynasty of Saul (II Sam. 2:8); from Mahanaim he started out on his ill-fated expedition to Gibeon and to it he later returned (2:12, 29). It was also chosen by David as his capital during Absalom's rebellion; here he received supplies from Barzillai and other Gileadites (17:24, 27), set out for battle with the rebels, and received the news of Absalom's death. It appears for the last time in the Bible as the capital of Solomon's seventh district with Ahinadab the son of Iddo as its governor (I Kings 4:14). In Shishak's list of conquered towns, it occurs as one of the cities captured during his campaign in the fifth year of Rehoboam. All sources point to its location in the vicinity of the Jabbok in central Gilead, but its exact identification is disputed. The earliest identification of the place with Khirbat al-Makhna 2.5 mi. (4 km.) north of Aijalon, following Estori ha-Parḥi (13th century), has been discarded by modern scholars. Dalman was the first to point to the twin site of Tulūl al-Dhahab on the Jabbok; Glueck, however, would look there for Penuel. Aharoni suggests that the western mound of Tulūl al-Dhahab is Mahanaim and that the eastern mound is Penuel. De Vaux and Noth suggest Tell al- Ḥajaj, uphill and to the south of the Jabbok.

Bibliography: Glueck, in: AASOR, 18/19(1939), 232–5; EM, s.v. (incl. bibl.); Aharoni, Land, index.
[M.A.-Y.]

MAḤANAYIM (Heb. מַחֲנַיִם; "Two Camps," allusion to Gen. 32:3 and other verses, although biblical *Mahanaim was in Transjordan), kibbutz in northern Israel in the Ḥuleh Valley, affiliated with Ha-Kibbutz ha-Me'uḥad. First founded as a moshavah for Orthodox Jews in 1898, but soon abandoned. In 1902, the *Jewish Colonization Association (ICA) settled a small group there whose economy was to be based on tobacco cultivation. The attempt failed, as did another plan to settle Jews from the Caucasus on the site to raise beef cattle. A further attempt was made in 1918, when a laborers' group set out to establish a moshav there. Finally, in 1939, the present kibbutz was established, when the Jewish institutions stepped up settlement on the land as a reply to the British *White Paper (1939). In 1969 Maḥanayim's economy was based on intensive farming. Nearby is the Maḥanayim airfield, servicing the northeastern part of the country. [E.O.]

MAHER SHALAL HASH BAZ (Heb. מַהֵר שָׁלָל חָשׁ בַּז), traditional vocalization of the name which, according to Isaiah 8:3–4, *Isaiah was commanded by the Lord to give to the son who was born to him during the Aramean-

Ephraimite war against Judah (734/3–732 B.C.E.), with the explanation that "before the lad is able to call 'father!' and 'mother!' the wealth of Damascus and the spoils of Samaria shall be carried off before the king of Assyria." Since the four words express twice the idea of speed and booty, it is easy to understand how the name can signify that, but the traditional vocalization leaves the parallelism imperfect; for according to it the words mean literally "Hurry, spoil! Booty has rushed." It therefore seems probable that either the vocalization of the third word is to be corrected to *ḥush,* in which case the name will mean, literally, "Hurry, spoil! Rush, booty!" or the vocalization of the first word is to be corrected to *mihar,* yielding the literal sense, "Spoil has hurried, booty has rushed." Such prophetic namings as portents of the future notoriously not only portend the future but help to bring it about, exactly like other prophetic acts that symbolize what they predict (see *Prophecy). Accordingly, the writing involving the four words in 8:1–2 is also intended at once to portend and to effectuate the early plundering of Damascus and Samaria by the Assyrians; on some problems of detail, see *Isaiah A, Panel 3, Field A. [H.L.G.]

MAHLER, ARTHUR (1871–1916), classical archaeologist and Zionist parliamentarian. Born in Prague, from 1902 Mahler was a professor of classical archaeology at the German University in Prague. He joined the Zionist Movement at the beginning of the 20th century, and in the elections of 1907 he was elected, together with A. Stand and H. *Gabel, to the Austrian parliament on a pro-Zionist ticket. Together they established the Jewish Club headed by B. Straucher, which was the first of its kind in parliamentary history. Because of the Austrian government's intrigues and the influence of Jewish assimilationists, however, the pro-Zionist list lost the 1911 elections. Mahler then left Prague and settled in Vienna. [G.K.]

MAHLER, EDUARD (1857–1945), Hungarian orientalist, mathematician, and astronomer. Mahler was born in Cziffer, Hungary. In 1882 he became assistant to the astronomer Theodor Oppolzer at the Vienna Observatory and, in 1885, assistant at the Institute of Weights and Measures. The same year he published his *Astronomische Untersuchungen ueber die in der Bibel erwaehnte aegyptische Finsterniss* and *Astronomische Untersuchung ueber die in hebraeischen Schriften erwaehnten Finsternisse.* He had already written some important mathematical studies, particularly on the theory of surfaces, but his interest turned more and more to astronomy and chronology of the ancient orient, as is evident in his *Biblische Chronologie und Zeitrechnung der Hebraeer* (1887) and his translation of and commentary on Maimonides, *Kiddush ha-Ḥodesh* (1889). In 1896 Mahler went to Budapest as assistant at the Institute of Trigonometry. Two years later he became assistant keeper in the department of archaeology of the Hungarian National Museum and also began lecturing on oriental history and languages at Budapest University; in 1914 he was appointed professor there. In 1912 he became director of the newly founded Egyptological Institute and, in 1922, director of the Oriental Institute. Mahler explored the date of the Exodus and tried to demonstrate that the biblical data relating the Exodus are accurate in *Der Pharao des Exodus* (1896), and in various articles. He wrote the "Bibel-Babel" controversy, on the *Elephantine documents, and on calendar reform. Further chronological studies culminated in his classic *Handbuch der juedischen Chronologie* (1916, repr. 1967), in which he established the systems of the different Jewish calendars and chronologies in the light of ancient Near Eastern and medieval reckonings. He also provided comparative tables which make possible the conversion of a date in one system to the corresponding date in another system, especially the Christian calendar. Mahler later took up the problem of the Easter date and that of Jesus' death. He was associated with the excavations of an old Roman settlement at Dunapentele, where evidence for the earliest presence of Jews in Hungary was discovered.

Bibliography: *Jubilee Volume . . . E. Mahler* (1937), incl. bibl.
[ED.]

MAHLER, GUSTAV (1860–1911), composer and conductor. Born in Kalischt, Bohemia, Mahler began his career as a conductor of operettas in Bad Hall. He rose through positions in Ljubljana, Olomouc, Kassel, Prague, Leipzig, Budapest, and Hamburg and progressed to become, in 1897, the director of the Vienna Court Opera. (He had to convert to Catholicism to secure this position, and was baptized in the spring of 1897.) His tenure in Vienna brought the opera to a level of artistic achievement previously unknown there. However, he resigned in 1907 because of hostile intrigues. His remaining winters were spent in New York where he conducted the Metropolitan Opera and the New York Philharmonic. He died in Vienna

Gustav Mahler medal by Benno Elkan. Jerusalem, J.N.U.L., Schwadron Collection.

Mahler, although one of the most popular symphonic composers today, was overshadowed as a composer in his lifetime by his successes as a conductor. His attempts to compose opera were abortive despite his genius as opera director. His libretto *Ruebezahl* survives, without music, and unpublished. Though no opera by Mahler exists, his sense of musical drama is evident in his ten symphonies and his "symphony in songs," *Das Lied von der Erde.* Four of the symphonies contain substantial vocal sections; in fact, the Eighth is a gigantic choral work. Mahler did not live to complete his Tenth Symphony; however, Deryck Cooke's "performing version" has been widely accepted as an authentic presentation. Mahler's songs, often written to folk texts, show deep understanding of the voice. Many themes from the songs were reworked in the symphonies. The most important song cycles are *Lieder eines fahrenden Gesellen* (1884) and *Kindertotenlieder* (1900–02).

Bibliography: MGG; Grove, Dict; Riemann-Gurlitt; Baker, Biog Dict; O. Klemperer, *Minor Recollections* (1964), 9–41; A. M. Mahler, *Gustav Mahler, Memories and Letters* (1968); B. Walter, *Gustav Mahler* (1970); D. Mitchell, *Gustav Mahler: The Early Years* (1958); D. Newlin, *Bruckner-Mahler-Schoenberg* (1947, rev. ed. 1971).

[Di.N.]

MAHLER (née **Schoenberger**), **MARGARET** (1897–), child psychiatrist and psychoanalyst. Born in Sopron, Hungary, in the early 1930s she directed in Vienna the first psychoanalytically oriented child guidance clinic. In 1938 she settled in New York and in 1941 was appointed associate in psychiatry at Columbia University College of Physicians and Surgeons. In 1955 she was appointed clinical professor of psychiatry at the Albert Einstein College of Medicine. She was a training analyst at the New York Psychoanalytic Institute and in 1957 became the director of research of Masters Children's Center, where parallel studies of psychotic and normal children and their mothers are conducted. A comprehensive summary of Mahler's work of the 1940s appeared in the *Psychoanalytic Study of the Child,* vols. 3–4, 1948. Two main concepts with her name are: the symbiotic infantile psychosis and the separation-individuation process of normal development during the first three years of life. In her book *On Human Symbiosis,* vol. 1 (1968), Margaret Mahler sees the core of infantile psychosis as "faulty or absent individuation" resulting from a deficiency in the child's intrapsychic utilization of the mothering partner during the symbiotic phase.

Bibliography: A. Grinstein, *Index of Psychoanalytic Writings,* 3 (1958), 1295–97, and 7 (1964), 3687–88. [M.B.Ah.]

MAHLER, RAPHAEL (1899–), historian. Mahler, who was born in Nowy Sącz, eastern Galicia, Poland, studied at the rabbinical seminary and the university of Vienna until 1922. He served as a teacher of general and Jewish history in Jewish secondary schools in Poland. In 1937 he immigrated to the United States and was a teacher in various educational institutions in New York. He was a member from his youth of the left Po'alei Zion party and was connected with *YIVO in its research studies and administration, both in Poland and in the U.S. In 1950 he went to Israel, where he lectured on the history of Israel at Tel Aviv University and in 1961 was appointed professor

Raphael Mahler, historian. Photo Erde, Tel Aviv.

there. He wrote many studies on the history of the Jews in Yiddish, Polish, German, English, and, after going to Israel, chiefly in Hebrew. Among his works are the following: *Di Yidn in Amolikn Poyln* (New York, 1946, in the publication *Di Yidn in Poyln*); *Ha-Kara'im* (1946), on the Karaites; *Yidn in Amolikn Poyln in Likht fun Tsifern* (Warsaw, 1958); *Yehudei Polin bein Shetei ha-Milḥamot* ("Jews in Poland Between the Two World Wars," 1968). Among his articles is *"Torat Borochov ve-Shitato be-Yameinu Anu"* (in: *Ba-Derekh,* 1965). His major work, *Divrei Yemei Yisrael; Dorot Aḥaronim* ("History of the Jewish People in Modern Times"), has been published only in part: first part (on 1789–1815) in 4 vols. (1956–62), and the first volume (1970) of part two (on 1815–48). In his introduction to the work Mahler explains his theory of Jewish history in accordance with historical materialism, his division of Jewish history in the modern period in conformity with social and economic evolution, and the class war and changes of governments during these years. His scientific work is based upon an abundance of sources and a rich bibliography.

Bibliography: Kressel, Leksikon, 2 (1967), 319; LYNL, 5 (1963), 393–7.

[Ed.]

MAHLON AND CHILION (Heb. מַחְלוֹן and כִּלְיוֹן), the two sons of Elimelech and Naomi (Ruth 1:2ff.; 4:9–10). They were Ephrathites of Bethlehem who migrated to Moab, together with their parents, during a drought in the time of the Judges. After their father's death, the two brothers married Moabite women, Chilion marrying Orpah, and Mahlon, *Ruth. Both died childless. Their names ("sickness" and "destruction") have been explained as symbolic of their untimely death.

In the Aggadah. Mahlon and Chilion are identified with Joash and Saraph of I Chronicles 4:22, the different names indicating their characteristics and destiny. Joash was so called because he lost hope (from the root יאש, "to give up hope") of the messianic era; Saraph because he was condemned to be burned (from the root שרף, "to burn"); Mahlon, because he committed acts of profanation (from the root חלל, "to profane"); and Chilion because he was condemned by God to destruction (כלה "to destroy"; BB 91b). They sinned in leaving Ereẓ Israel (BB 91a), and in that they neither proselytized their wives nor ensured that they performed ritual immersion (Ruth R. 2:9). Before they died, they were rendered penniless (Ruth R. 2:10).

Bibliography: Noth, Personennamen, 54, 249; Ginzberg, Legends, 4 (1925), 31; 6 (1925), 189; Y. Ḥasida, *Ishei ha-Tanakh* (1964), 258–9.

[Ed.]

MAH NISHTANNAH (Heb. מַה נִּשְׁתַּנָּה; "What is different?"), first words of the four questions asked at the Passover *seder* service. The questions come at the beginning of the recital of the **Haggadah* and are usually asked by the youngest participant. The first sentence reads: "Why is this night different from all other nights?"

According to the Ashkenazi rite, the questions come in the following order: (1) Why on this night is only *maẓẓah* ("unleavened bread") eaten? (2) Why are bitter herbs consumed? (3) Why are herbs dipped twice (in salt water and in *ḥaroset*) during the *seder* meal? (4) Why do we sit reclined at the *seder* table? The text of the answers "We were slaves unto Pharaoh in Egypt . . . ," follows the set of four questions. The reply is usually made by the father, or the person conducting the *seder*.

The *Mah Nishtannah* dates back to mishnaic times (Pes. 10:4) and originated in contemporaneous dining customs (manners and sequence) at festive meals. The questions were made part of the *seder* celebration as an introduction and reminder to the father to fulfill the biblical injunction: "And thou shalt tell thy son in that day, saying: it is because of that which the Lord did for me when I came forth out of Egypt" (Ex. 13:8; see also Ex. 13:14, 15). The Mishnah enumerates four questions to be asked during the *seder* (Pes. 10:4); the third, "Why do we eat only roasted

דישראל השתא עבדי לשנה
הבאה בני חורין
נשתנה הלילה הזה
מכל הלילות
שבכל הלילות אנו אוכלין
חמץ ומצה הלילה הזה
כלו מצה שבכל הלילות
אנו אוכלין שאר ירקות ה
הלילה הזה מרור שבכל
הלילות אין אנו מטבילין
אפילו פעם אחת הלילה
הזה שתי פעמים שבכל

Beginning of the *Mah Nishtannah* from the *Prague Haggadah*, 1526. From a facsimile edition.

meat [of the paschal sacrifice]?" was omitted after the Destruction of the Temple and the consequent cessation of sacrifices, and for it was substituted another question which is not mentioned in the Mishnah (Why do we recline?). The Sephardi ritual retained the geonic order of the four questions: (1) dipping, (2) unleavened bread, (3) bitter herbs, (4) reclining.

In the geonic literature (and as late as *Rashi and *Maimonides, Yad, *Ḥamez u-Mazzah*, 8:2) the *Mah Nishtannah* was probably recited by the person conducting the *seder* and not asked by the children. Where there is no child present at the *seder* table, the questions should be asked by the housewife, and if only men participate, they must ask each other, even if they are learned scholars (Pes. 116a). The *Mah Nishtannah* questions form part of the *Haggadah* ritual of all trends and segments in Judaism, including the Reform.

Bibliography: E. D. Goldschmidt; *Haggadah shel Pesaḥ* (1960), 10–13; J. Levy, *A Guide to Passover* (1958), 27, 31. [ED.]

MAḤOZA, town on the River Tigris (Ber. 59b), on the bank of the Nahar Malka (Fluvius Regum), one of the canals connecting the Euphrates with the Tigris. Maḥoza was a suburb of Be-Ardashir, situated on the left bank of the Tigris, and of the town of Ctesiphon, situated on its right bank (Er. 57b). Ctesiphon, established by Seleucus Nicator, the founder of the Seleucid dynasty about 300 B.C.E., was destroyed by the Roman commander Avidus Cassius in 165 C.E. On its ruins Ardashir I (226–240 C.E.) erected a new city after his name, the Be-Ardashir mentioned occasionally in the Talmud. Both cities served as the capital. Maḥoza's importance derived also from the fact that it was situated on a central trading route through which caravans passed, as well as considerable merchandise which passed on the rivers. The Jews of Maḥoza took a very active part in the commercial life, both within the town (BB 29b) and beyond it (Git. 6a). The merchants were very successful. They ate well (Shab. 109a), drank much wine (Ta'an. 26a), and were hedonists (RH 17a). Of the women of Maḥoza it is related that they were lazy (Shab. 32b) and wore many ornaments (BK 119a). Among the Jews of Maḥoza were also successful farmers. Some of them possessed fields and orchards, irrigating their fields from the waters of the Tigris (Ber. 59b; Ket. 67a). They reared cattle (Er. 26a; BB 36a, Rashbam ad loc.) and also traded in grain (Git. 73a). A Jewish settlement in Seleucus and Ctesiphon during the first century C.E. is mentioned by Josephus (Ant., 18:310ff.).

Maḥoza is mentioned for the first time as a center of study after the destruction of the academy of *Nehardea in 259 (*Iggeret R. Sherira Gaon*, ed. by B. M. Lewin (1921), 82). Maḥoza attained the height of its fame after the death of *Abbaye in 338 when the academy of Pumbedita together with its scholars moved to Maḥoza, where dwelt Rava who headed the academy for 14 years from 338–352 (*ibid.*, 88f.). During this period Maḥoza had a considerable Jewish population. They constituted the majority of its inhabitants and Abbaye was surprised that there was no **mezuzah* on the city gate (Yoma 11a). It also contained many proselytes (Kid. 73a). Because of Maḥoza's proximity to Be-Ardashir, Rava had close relations with the government (see *Shapur II). When the emperor Julian invaded Babylon in 363, Maḥoza was destroyed. However on his death and the withdrawal of the Romans, it was rebuilt. Maḥoza declined as a Jewish settlement in the second half of the fifth century as a result of the uprising of the Nestorian Christians.

Bibliography: Neubauer, Géogr, 356f.; A. Berliner, in: *Jahres-Bericht des Rabbiner-Seminars zu Berlin* (1882–83), 39–43; J. Obermeyer, *Die Landschaft Babylonien* (1929), 161–78. [M.BE.]

MAH TOVU (Heb. מַה טֹּבוּ; "How goodly"), the opening words of a prayer recited by Ashkenazi Jews upon entering the synagogue. The initial words are a quotation from Numbers 24:5. The remainder of the prayer consists of Psalms 5:8; 26:8; 69:14; and 95:6 (with Ps. 95:6 modified from the plural to the singular form). The Talmud interprets the "tents" and "dwellings" of Numbers 24:5 to refer to synagogues and schools (Sanh. 105b), and the "time of grace" mentioned in Psalms 69:14, to mean the time of public worship (Ber. 8a). At one time, the rabbis apparently intended to include Balaam's blessing of the children of Israel (Num. 22–24) in the recitation of **Shema;* however, they decided that it was too lengthy for the congregation (Ber. 12b).

Sephardi Jews recite Psalms 5:8 on entering the synagogue, and Psalms 5:9 on leaving.

See *Liturgy; **Shaharit*.

Bibliography: Elbogen, Gottesdienst, 87, 526; Idelsohn, Liturgy, 73f.; E. Levy, *Yesodot ha-Tefillah* (1952[2]), 76, 131. [ED.]

MAḤZIKE HADAS (Maḥazikei ha-Dat), organization in Galicia and Bukovina, representing the first attempt of the Orthodox to unite for political action in order to foster its beliefs in the sphere of Jewish social life. The organization was initiated by a meeting of the larger Jewish communities which was convened by *Shomer Israel in Lvov (Lemberg), in 1878, in connection with their opposition to the founding of a rabbinical seminary and to the organizational changes in the communities. The Maḥzike Hadas society was founded primarily to ward off the dangers that lay in such new plans. It was headed by Simon *Sofer (Schreiber) of Cracow (son of the Ḥatam Sofer) and Joshua Rokeaḥ, the rabbi of *Belz. The founding convention took place on March 13, 1879. There the statutes of the new organization were determined and the bi-monthly *Maḥzikei ha-Dat* which appeared in both Hebrew and in Yiddish and which was directed against the publication **Izraelita* was founded. The organization came out with a special list of candidates for the elections of the Austrian parliament of 1879. Of the four candidates it put forward only one, Simon Sofer, was elected. Sofer joined the "Polish club" in opposition to the Jewish assimilationist representatives. In 1882 the organization convened a large conference which was attended by 200 rabbis and 800 representatives of communities. The purpose of the conference was to protect the religious character of the communities from the reform tendencies of the progressives. The conference passed a resolution that only Jews observing the precepts of the Shulḥan Arukh were to be granted full voting rights for communal elections. The death of Simon Schreiber in 1883 temporarily weakened the movement, but in 1908 the rabbi of Belz renewed its vigor by publishing a proclamation *Kol Maḥazikei ha-Dat* which denounced any attempt to introduce a progressive spirit into the communities according to the patterns of Western Europe or, under the influence of Zionism and socialism, to inject into them a secular national content. The rabbi of Belz also denounced the efforts of the Vienna community to set up a central union for Austria. After World War I, when Poland became independent, a section of the Orthodox community, under the influence of the rabbi of Belz, organized an independent political party, calling itself Maḥzike Hadas. The party was founded at a convention which was attended by representatives from 100 communities and which took place in Grodek Jagiellonski (Gorodok), on Dec. 22, 1931. Its influence was chiefly felt throughout Galicia as a rival to *Agudat Israel.

Bibliography: N. M. Gelber (ed.), in: EG, 4 (1953), 310ff.; M. Busak, in: A. Bauminger et al. (eds.), *Sefer Kraka* (1959), 103–7; Z. Fischer-Schein (Zohar), *Be-Sod Yesharim ve-Edah* (1969), 125; I. Schiper (ed.), *Zydzi w Polsce odrodzonej*, 1 (1932), 410; 2 (1933), 258.

[A.RU.]

MAḤZOR (Heb. מַחְזוֹר, *maḥazor;* "cycle"), festival prayer book. The word is similar to the term *Maḥzarta* of the Syrian Church, which means a breviary, and was originally applied to the poetical insertions to be recited in prayers throughout the yearly cycle. In Ashkenazi usage, it came to refer distinctly to the festival prayer book, as distinct from the *siddur* (the daily prayer book). The term is also used by Sephardi Jews.

See *Liturgy; *Prayer Book. [ED.]

Maḥzorim, Illuminated. Illuminated *maḥzorim* flourished in the Ashkenazi world throughout the 13th and 14th centuries, mainly in southwest Germany, in the Rhine valley, making their appearance soon after an authoritative "cycle" of prayers emerged. In the 15th century the fashion moved to northern Italy, where many Ashkenazim had settled, and influenced Italian Jewish illumination. While the Ashkenazi *siddur* contained the daily and personal prayers, both for home and synagogue, the *maḥzor* contains the synagogal communal prayers for the festivals and the seven special Sabbaths of the Jewish year. In the Italian rite, the term *maḥzor* embraced both the daily and festival prayers. Primarily intended for the use of the *ḥazzan*, the German *maḥzorim* are usually large—written in clear, bold letters—and contain a large selection of *piyyutim* ("liturgical poems") for each festival, offering the cantor a variety of choice. A large number of German *maḥzorim* are illuminated with initial-word panels and with illustrations of a ritual and textual nature. These *maḥzorim* were executed over a period of some 100 years, from the mid-13th to the mid-14th century.

The earliest surviving illustrated *maḥzor* manuscript of the 13th century is the two-volume codex of the Michael Collection in the Bodleian Library (Mss. Mich. 617 and Mich. 627), written in 1258 by Judah b. Samuel, called Seltman. Though it is not extensively illustrated it is important, since it proves that illuminated *maḥzorim* existed prior to this date. It was probably illuminated by a gentile, since the first initial-word panel was painted upside down, as though it was a Latin manuscript. However, despite this, the manuscript contains motifs which became traditional in later *maḥzorim* and which could not have been invented by gentiles. The finest examples of *maḥzorim* from the south of Germany are the first volume of the *Worms Maḥzor* of 1272 (see below); the *Laud Maḥzor* of about 1290 (Bodleian Library, Ms. Laud Or. 321); the *Leipzig Maḥzor* of about 1300 (see below); the *Double Maḥzor* in Dresden (Saechsische Landesbibliothek, Ms. A 46a) and Breslau (State and University Library Cod. Or. I. 1); the *Tripartite Maḥzor* of about 1320 (Budapest, Hungarian Academy of Sciences, Ms. A. 384, British Museum, Add. Ms. 22413, and Bodleian Library, Ms. Mich. 619), and the *Darmstadt Maḥzor* of 1340 (Hessische Lands- und Hochschulbibliothek, Cod. Or. 13).

Figure 1. Illustration from a *maḥzor* showing a goat drawing water in a combination of the zodiacal signs of Capricorn and Aquarius, *Worms Maḥzor*, Germany; 1272, fol. 97v. Jerusalem, J.N.U.L.

These *maḥzorim* illustrate both the development of style in southern Germany and the use of a special Jewish *iconography. An example of such development in both style and in motif is found in the distortion of human figures. In all manuscripts before 1300, the use of animal-headed people is consistent; in the *Leipzig Maḥzor*, people have birds' beaks instead of a nose and mouth; but the artists of the later *Tripartite Maḥzor* did not understand the reason for such distortions, and painted all the male figures with ordinary human heads and all the females with animal heads.

Southern German *maḥzorim* have a very wide range of text illustrations. Most of them begin with the prayers for the four special Sabbaths before Passover, continuing with Passover, the Feast of Weeks, the New Year, the Day of Atonement, and the Feast of Tabernacles. Four of the *megillot* ("scrolls") are also usually included in the *maḥzor*—sometimes placed together, at other times appended to the particular celebrations with which they were associated. The Book of Esther was usually written separately on a scroll, to be read at the festival of Purim.

Most German *maḥzorim* have illustrations of the signs of the zodiac for each of the verses of a *piyyut* in the prayer for dew recited on the first day of Passover (*Leipzig Maḥzor*, vol. 1, fol. 133; *Worms Maḥzor*, vol. 1, fol. 95v.; Ms. Mich. fols. 49–51). The signs of the zodiac are depicted in small medallions in the margin. In the *Worms* and the *Tripartite* manuscripts, the labors of the months are depicted in medallions next to the signs of the zodiac. Some specifically Jewish elements have developed in the zodiac illustrations, such as a bucket instead of Aquarius; in some cases a draw well is depicted instead of a mere bucket, and in some *maḥzorim* a kid is shown next to the well to illustrate both Capricorn and Aquarius, which are referred to in one verse of this *piyyut*. In one *maḥzor* (Bodleian Library, Ms. Opp. 161, fol. 84), 11 signs of the zodiac are depicted in one large roundel divided into 12 sections, similar to the arrangements of the signs of the zodiac in floor mosaics of early synagogues (e.g., Bet Alfa). This example may be an indication of a traditional way of depicting the astronomical zodiac *circulus*, which survived into the Middle Ages.

The illustration for the Feast of Weeks traditionally depicts Moses receiving the Tablets of the Law and giving them to the Israelites, who are standing at the foot of Mount Sinai (e.g., *Leipzig Maḥzor,* vol. 1, fol. 130v.; British Museum, Ms. Add. 22413, fol. 3v.; *Worms Maḥzor,* vol. 1, fol. 151). In the *Land Maḥzor* (fol. 127v.) the giving of the Law is combined with an illustration of Moses sprinkling the blood of the Covenant over the Israelites. In the *Leipzig Maḥzor* (vol. 1, fol. 130) the Israelites are standing as though within the mountain, illustrating the Midrash which states that God erected a mountain over the Israelites until they agreed to accept the Torah.

The second volume of an Ashkenazi *maḥzor* normally starts with the prayers for Rosh Ha-Shanah, illustrated by the sacrifice of Isaac, with the ram caught in a thicket by his horns. The sounding of the ram's horn (*shofar*) on New Year's day is a commemoration of God's covenant with Abraham at the time of the sacrifice (e.g., *Leipzig Maḥzor,* vol. 2, fols. 26v., 66; Bodleian Library, Ms. Laud Or. 321, fol. 184, and Ms. Reg. 1, fol. 207v.; *Double Maḥzor,* Breslau, fol. 46v.). In some *maḥzorim,* a horned and claw-footed devil is depicted next to a *shofar* blower, who sometimes supports his right foot on a three-legged stool in order to ward off the earthly influence of evil. This is in accordance with the common superstition that a three-point object keeps evil spirits away (e.g., Budapest, Ms. A. 388, vol. 2, fol. 12v.; Paris, Bibliothèque de l'Alliance Israélite Universelle). Openings of prayers from the Day of Atonement are usually illustrated by initial words and by parts of prayers written within full-page arches resembling doors, an allusion to the Gates of Mercy, now opened to accept the individual prayers of every Jew (e.g., *Leipzig Maḥzor,* vol. 2; Berlin, Preussischer Kulturbesitz, Ms. Or. Fol. 388, fol. 69; *Worms Maḥzor,* vol. 2; *Double Maḥzor,* Breslau, fol. 89).

The prayers for the Feast of Tabernacles are sometimes illustrated by a man holding the fruits of the Holy Land: the *lulav* ("palm branch"), the *etrog* ("citrus fruit"), *hadas* ("myrtle"), and *aravah* ("willow").

Some *maḥzorim* are merely decorated and contain no illustrations at all. An example is the *Nuremberg Maḥzor* of 1331, which for six centuries was owned by the municipality of Nuremberg and is now in the Schocken Library in Jerusalem (Ms. 24100). Its large initial-word panel for the first day of Passover is decorated with foliage scrolls, grotesques, and an architectural top. In the 15th century, the illumination of large-sized *maḥzorim* was no longer fashionable. The smaller-sized illuminated prayer book which became more common continued to be called a *maḥzor.* One such example is the *Maḥzor of Rabbi Friedman of Ruzhin.* This mid-15th century eastern German prayer book was probably intended for use in the synagogue and at home by a wealthy member of the Jewish community. Though the system of illustration remained Ashkenazi, the decoration shows the influence of Italian motifs, evident in the marginal miniatures, initial-word panels, and human busts emerging from flowers. An example of the fusion of the two traditions is the *Schocken Italian Maḥzor* of 1441 (Ms. 13873), which is a large volume, written and decorated in Roman style, of the Roman rite, but with illustrations following the Ashkenazi tradition.

Most of the 15th-century Italian *maḥzorim* are personal rather than synagogal prayer books, stressing the daily prayers, and containing a *Haggadah* which was recited at home. They are therefore small, handy to carry to and from the synagogue, with the prayers arranged for the individual, starting with the daily and Sabbath prayers and the Festival ones. These illuminated small *maḥzorim* were not usually extensively illustrated; besides the decorated openings of prayers, they contained fairly simple marginal pen drawings. Good early examples are those related to famous families of northern and central Italy. Such are *maḥzorim* executed at the order of Daniel b. Samuel ha-Rofe b. Daniel ha-Dayyan, one at Bertinoro in 1390 (Bodleian Library, Ms. Can. Or. 81) and another at Forli in 1393 (British Museum, Add. Ms. 26968). In these works, as in others done for the same patron, the tinted drawings are of Lombard style. A *maḥzor* from Pisa of 1397 ordered by another well-known patron, Jehiel b. Mattathias of the Beit-El family (Sassoon Ms. 1028), is in the same style. Some of the text illustrations in these *maḥzorim* resemble those of the traditional Ashkenazi ones: a horn-blower for the New Year; a *sukkah* for Tabernacles; the balance for Sabbath *Shekalim;* a crescent and star for Sabbath *Ha-Ḥodesh;* and more detailed illustrations for the Passover *Haggadah.*

The same system of illustration was also used by the Ashkenazi scribe and illuminator *Joel b. Simeon. Of the three *maḥzorim* executed in his workshop in the third quarter of the 15th century, the last was probably made for a woman, since it contains several marginal pen drawings of a ritual nature in which a lady called Maraviglia is the main character. Closely related to the Florentine style of Joel b. Simeon are some more elegant *maḥzorim* which have pen and colored decorations on almost every page. Such is the *Rothschild Maḥzor* of 1492 from Florence (Jewish Theological Seminary in New York, Ms. 03225), which was illuminated in three different styles and techniques, with elaborate illuminated opening pages, illustrations to each section, and tinted decorations on each page. Moses receiving the Tablets of the Law illustrating the opening to the mishnaic tractate *Avot* (fol. 139) is an example of the second kind. Other *maḥzorim* with a similar system of illustration are fairly common, though some are richer than others.

The *maḥzor* in the *Rothschild Miscellany,* Ms. 24, Israel Museum, Ms. 180/51, which has sumptuous Ferrarese illuminations from about 1470, consists of textual illustrations for each festival and prayers for special occasions. In fact, it contains a wealth of material illustrating almost every custom of daily life in a rich Jewish Renaissance household. No other manuscript equals the richness and scope of the illumination of this miscellany, though only a portion of its 473 leaves is a *maḥzor.* The *Pesaro Maḥzor* of 1480 (Sassoon Ms. 23), containing almost as many pages as the *Rothschild Miscellany,* consists only of a prayer book of Roman rite. Its borders are very richly decorated by a Ferrarese artist, but there are fewer text illustrations, mostly within a wreath in the lower part of the border.

Two of the outstanding Ashkenazi *Maḥzorim* are described in detail below.

The Leipzig Maḥzor (Leipzig, University Library, Ms. V. 1102) is the most sumptuous of the south German illuminated *maḥzorim* and has the most extensive array of text illustrations. Almost all the special Sabbaths, feasts, and festivals are illustrated. The first volume was written by Menahem, who decorated his name (fols. 113, 137) in the same way as Menahem the scribe who copied the *Birds' Head Haggadah* (see Illuminated *Haggadot*). The second volume was copied by a scribe called Isaac. The two volumes were wrongly bound with additions and corrections in later dates. The

Figure 2. Opening of the prayers for Rosh Ha-Shanah with an initial word panel showing the blowing of the *shofar* and an illustration of a ram caught in a thicket, from Volume II of the *Leipzig Maḥzor,* South Germany, c. 1320. Leipzig University Library, Ms. V. 1102, fol. 26v.

giant manuscript was probably intended initially for a *ḥazzan* of a very rich community on the Upper Rhine. The first volume of the *Leipig Maḥzor* opens with a frontispiece representing Samson rending the lion, possibly an allusion to the phrase "Grow strong like a lion to fulfill the will of your Maker," sometimes referring to the *ḥazzan* (vol. 1, fol. 19). At the end of the short introductory prayers, there is a miniature depicting the *ḥazzan* standing covered with his *tallit* ("prayer shawl") in front of a marble pulpit, on which a large open book rests. This probably represents the first volume of the Leipzig manuscript. The second volume is shown in the hands of a young man wearing a Jewish hat, who is standing behind the *ḥazzan* accompanied by a bearded Jew (vol. 1, fol. 27). A man holding a scale is a common illustration for the Sabbath of *Parashat Shekalim,* referring to the payment of the annual half-shekel for the Temple sacrifices (Ex. 30:11–16).

Most illustrations in the *Leipzig Maḥzor* are common to other south German *maḥzorim,* such as the tall tree from which Haman and his ten sons are hanging (vol. 1. fol. 51v.), illustrating a *piyyut* for Purim; a red heifer illustrates *Parashat Parah* (1, 53v); the sun and moon illustrate *Parashat ha-Ḥodesh* (1, 59); a betrothed couple sitting on a bench illustrates a *piyyut* for the "Great Sabbath" before Passover, alluding to the Torah as the bride of the people of Israel (1, 64). The Egyptians pursuing the Israelites illustrate the Passover Eve prayer (1, 72v.–73), the signs of the zodiac the prayer for dew recited on the first day of Passover (1, 85–87), and Moses receiving the tablets of the Law illustrating Shavuot (1, 130v.). An additional illustration (1, v. 131) depicts the contemporary custom of initiating children into the study of the Torah. The child is brought to his teacher's lap to lick the honey-covered alphabet tablet in order to sweeten his introduction to the study of the Torah, while the other children, in celebration of his initiation, receive eggs and cakes. The first volume ends with the *kinot* ("dirges") for the Ninth of Av, which are hardly ever illustrated. As is common in Ashkenazi *maḥzorim,* the second volume begins with the prayers for Rosh Ha-Shanah, with illustrations of the **akedah* and the ram caught in a thicket. The opening prayers for the Day of Atonement are illustrated with the customary arches resembling doors, alluding to the Gates of Mercy (2, fols. 74v., 85, 164v.), but one of the arches has in the lower margin the additional midrashic illustration of Abraham being saved from the fire of the Chaldeans because of his belief. The feast of Sukkot is illustrated by a man holding the prescribed "four species," and in the lower margin the legendary beasts, the leviathan and behemoth are fighting, an event which is supposed to take place before the end of time. The style of the *Leipzig Maḥzor* is related to south German illumination around 1300. A fascimile of 68 illuminated pages from the *Leipzig Maḥzor,* with an introductory volume, was published in 1964.

The Worms Maḥzor (Jerusalem, Jewish National and University Library, Ms. Heb. 4781/I–II) consists of two unrelated volumes,

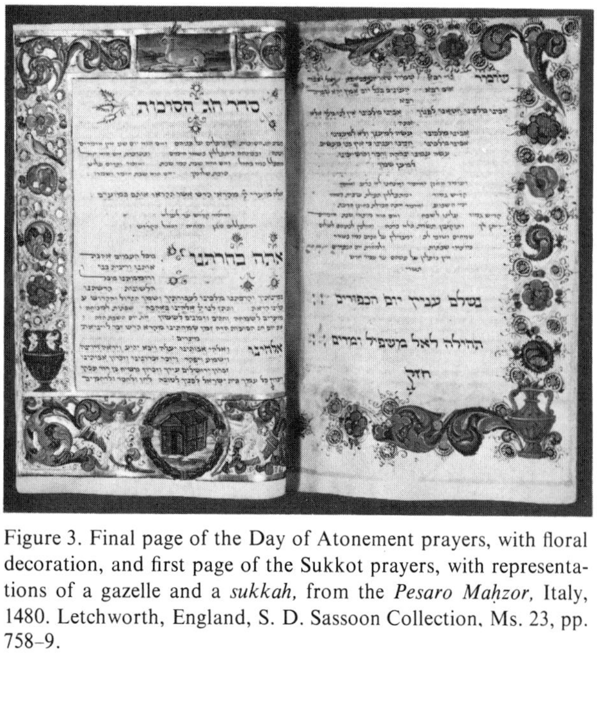

Figure 3. Final page of the Day of Atonement prayers, with floral decoration, and first page of the Sukkot prayers, with representations of a gazelle and a *sukkah,* from the *Pesaro Maḥzor,* Italy, 1480. Letchworth, England, S. D. Sassoon Collection, Ms. 23, pp. 758–9.

which were kept together in the Worms Synagogue from 1578. The fact that the page size, text area, and style of script are different in each volume, and that Ecclesiastes is repeated in both, indicates that they were executed independently. Only the first volume is dated, through a colophon (fol. 34v) stating that it was completed on Jan. 1, 1272, written by Simḥah b. Judah for his uncle R. Baruch b. Isaac. Another entry mentions the scribe, his father Judah of Nuremberg, and Shemaiah the Frenchman, who may have been the artist. Neither volume was intended for the Worms community, since they both contain *piyyutim* and prayers which are not included in the Worms rite while one *piyyut* was common in the rite of Mainz. The first volume of the *Worms Maḥzor* is one of the earliest dated illuminated *maḥzorim* from southern Germany. Associated with the colored initial-word panels are many text illustrations for the special Sabbaths, Passover, and Shavuot. The illustration for *Parashat Shekalim* depicts a man holding a balance, weighing the half-shekels for the payment in the Temple (fol. 39v.) Although the illumination of the *Worms Maḥzor* is somewhat crude, it resembles south German Latin illumination of the second half of the 13th century. Another link with the south German Jewish school of illumination is the style of the animals, birds, and distorted heads of human figures. The second volume contains a very few decorations of a somewhat later south German style.

See also Illuminated Hebrew *Bibles; Hebrew *Illuminated Manuscripts; and *Books (section on Illustration). [B.N.]

Bibliography: M. Steinschneider, *Jewish Literature* (1857, 1965), 165ff.; Idelsohn, Liturgy, xiiif. ILLUMINATED MAḤZORIM: Mayer, Art, 1792 (J. Mueller); 1496 (J. Leveen); 2246 (S. Rothschild); 2846, 2876 (R. Wischnitzer-Bernstein); 857 (E. D. Goldschmidt); 2239, 2240 (E. Roth); 2969 (J. Gutmann); 1222A (B.Narkiss); 2232 (C. Roth); 58 (Z. Ameisenowa); 2933 (B. Ziemlich); 393 (N. Bruell, p. 115–8); 2074 (Recklinghausen); 730 (Frankfort); 523 (Monumenta Judaica); J. Gutmann, in: *Art Journal,* 27 (1967/68), 172; B. Narkiss, in: *Haaretz* (May 15, 1957); idem, *Hebrew Illuminated Manuscripts* (1969), 30–33, 37–39, pls. 26, 27, 33, 34, 35, 44, 49, 52, 53, 56; idem, in: *Papers of the Fourth World Congress of Jewish Studies,* 2 (1968), 129–33; idem, *Hebrew Illuminated Manuscripts from Jerusalem Collections,* The Israel Museum, Exhibition Catalog no. 40 (1967), nos. 5, 10; M. Beit Arié, in: *Leshonenu,* 29 (1965), 27–46, 80–102; Margoliouth, Cat, 2 (1899), 285–8, no. 662; A. Wurfel, *Historische Nachrichten von der Judengemeinde Nuernberg* (Nuremberg, 1755), 97–105; D. S. Sassoon, *Ohel David,* 1 (1932), 289–93; Neubauer, Cat, no. 2373; I. Levi, in: REJ, 89 (1930), 281–92.

MAḤZOR VITRY, halakhic-liturgical composition by *Simḥah b. Samuel of Vitry, a small town in the department of Marne, France. Simḥah was an outstanding pupil, or even a colleague, of Rashi and apparently died during his teacher's lifetime (i.e., before 1105—see Gross, Gallia Judaica, 196). His son Samuel married Rashi's granddaughter and he was the grandfather of the famous tosafist, *Isaac of Dampierre (Urbach, Tosafot, 115). Like his colleague Shemaiah, Rashi's secretary, he occupied himself with the arrangement of his master's halakhic rulings, and later authorities sometimes confused their names. There is however no basis for the assumption of some scholars that there existed two works, one by Shemaiah and one by Simḥah, both entitled *Maḥzor Vitry* (Urbach, *ibid.,* 33). *Maḥzor Vitry* belongs to the group of works from the school of Rashi (e.g., the *Pardes, Sefer ha-Orah, Siddur Rashi*) which are based upon Rashi's rulings and usages, but which are expanded with additions from other authorities, sometimes even discussing and criticising their views, in order to defend those of Rashi. *Maḥzor Vitry* is in the form of a halakhic-liturgical work, the purpose of which was to give the halakhic rulings of the liturgy for the whole circle *(maḥzor)* of the year, weekdays, Sabbaths, and festivals, and connect them with the accepted formula of the prayers. The fact that it also includes laws of Sabbath, **eruv,* marriage, and ritual slaughter makes it wider in scope than the *siddurim* of *Amram and *Saadiah Gaon, which were also sent to various communities at their request. The *Maḥzor Vitry*, referred to by 13th-century authorities, such as the *Sefer Mitzvot Gadol* of *Moses b. Jacob of Coucy (Positive Commandments 27) and the *Or Zaru'a* (part 1, p. 55) of *Isaac b. Moses of Vienna exist in various versions which differ considerably from one another both in scope and arrangement. Apparently it gained instant acceptance and it was enlarged, as was the custom of that time, by successive additions. There does not yet exist a critical edition based on all available manuscripts. The published edition (by S. Hurwitz, 1889, 1923²) is from the London manuscript (Margolioth, Cat, no. 655) containing many additions, some indicated by the letter ת, most of them apparently from Isaac b. Durbal, a contemporary of Jacob Tam, but also including later responsa and extracts from the *Sefer ha-Terumah* of Baruch b. Isaac. It reflects the state of the work in the 13th and 14th centuries. The Oxford manuscript (Bodleian Library, Ms. Opp. 59) omits most of these additions in those fragments preserved in two manuscripts. On the other hand, they contain compilations which have no connection with the *maḥzor*. A more original text occurs in the Reggio manuscript (now in the library of the Jewish Theological Seminary of America) which has as yet not been examined because of its poor state of preservation, and the Parma manuscript (B. Pal. 2574).

Contents and Form. The halakhic portion of the *Maḥzor Vitry* precedes the liturgical formulae, and includes commentaries to the prayers taken from the *aggadah*. The Reggio manuscript includes the following topics: weekday prayers (with their relevant laws), the night prayer, the order of prayers for the Sabbath and its conclusion, the New Moon, the Sanctification of the Moon, Ḥanukkah, Purim, Passover *Haggadah*, and the Aramaic translation of the reading for the 7th day of Passover (Ex. 13:17–15:26) and the laws of Shavuot with a similar Aramaic translation. (Both these Aramaic translations are much enlarged and are to be found in many medieval *maḥzorim*.) There follow *Avot* with a commentary, *Hilkhot Derek Erez*, *Pirkei Ben Azzai*, a commentary on the *Kaddish* and on the Ten Commandments, the order of service for the Ninth of Av, the laws of fasts and mourning, Rosh Ha-Shanah, the Day of Atonement, Sukkot and the *Hoshanot with a commentary, the order of service for Simḥat Torah, the order of service for marriage and circumcision, and the laws of **shehitah* and **terefot*. In the enlarged text in the London manuscript there have been added the laws of *Niddah*, *Ẓizit*, *Tefillin*, *Mezuzah*, *Sefer Torah*, the complete text of tractate *Soferim*, tractate *Kallah* and the laws of divorce, and **ḥaliẓah*. In addition there are many *piyyutim* and *aggadot*. The main sources of *Maḥzor Vitry* are the decisions and customs of Rashi. Simḥah apparently based himself on the *Siddur Rashi* with whose text the *maḥzor* is often identical (see Buber, *Siddur Rashi*, introd. p. 54) but it excludes all the texts of the prayers. In the halakhic portion the sources, in addition to the Talmud, are the geonic literature, especially the **Halakhot Gedolot* and **Halakhot Pesukot*, and the *siddur* of Amram Gaon, which is often quoted verbatim, without giving the source. The talmudic quotations often differ from those in the existing text. *Maḥzor Vitry* is an important source for the historical study of *halakhah* and liturgy, particularly according to the French tradition. The *piyyutim* in the *maḥzor* differ in the various manuscripts, making it difficult to determine which were current during the period when the *Maḥzor Vitry* was composed. The text of these *piyyutim* which were apparently collected at a later period and appended to the London manuscript have been published separately under the title *"Kunteres ha-Piyyutim"* by H. Brody (Berlin, 1894).

Bibliography: S. Hurwitz and A. Berliner, *Mafte'aḥ u-Mavo le-Maḥzor Vitry*, in: S. Hurwitz (ed.), *Maḥzor Vitry le-rabbenu Simḥah*, (1923²); S. Buber (ed.), *Siddur Rashi* (1906), introd. liv-lv; Urbach, Tosafot, 33; Gross, Gal Jud, 196. [D.G.]

MAIER, JOSEPH (1911–), U.S. sociologist. Born in Leipzig, Germany, the son of a rabbi, Maier studied in Germany and in the U.S. In 1947 he was appointed professor of sociology at Rutgers University and became chairman of the department. Among his published works are *On Hegel's Critique of Kant* (1939) and *Sociology* (with J. Rumney, 1953). Maier was a specialist in the sociology of religion and became widely known as the author of a weekly column in the New York German-language Jewish newspaper *Aufbau* dealing with the application of halakhic wisdom to contemporary social problems. [W.J.C.]

MAILER, NORMAN (1923–), U.S. novelist and essayist. Born in New Jersey, Mailer grew up in New York City and attended Harvard College. His two years with the U.S.

Norman Mailer, U.S. writer. Photo Fred McDarrah, New York.

Army in the Pacific theater during World War II provided him with the background for his best-selling novel *The Naked and the Dead* (1948), whose violent dialogue and often lyric prose that evoked the fears and passions of men at war, made him an overnight literary celebrity. *Barbary Shore* (1951) was a semi-surrealistic political novel set in a Brooklyn rooming house, and *The Deer Park* (1955) a novel about Hollywood; in both of these books, which he himself called "existential," he revealed his growing fascination with the individual who intellectually, physically, or morally feels compelled to drive himself to extremes beyond the norms of human conduct in order to experience his own individuality. Mailer's increasing impatience with the novel as a medium for expressing his extraordinarily fertile if undisciplined mind and his ability to yoke together ideas of the most varied political, psychological, and philosophical nature led him in the 1950s to turn more and more to the essay, of which he published several collections: *Advertisements for Myself* (1959), *The Presidential Papers* (1965), and *Cannibals and Christians* (1966). *Why Are We in Vietnam?* (1967) represented an experiment to deal in symbolic fictional terms with a burning political issue of the day. In the same year Mailer wrote *Armies in the Night*, an eyewitness account of an anti-Vietnam demonstration held in front of the Pentagon in Washington whose melange of reportage, social and political speculation, and personal confession, written in a wildly exuberant prose, established his reputation by general critical consensus as the most brilliant virtuoso stylist in the United States. A second documentary, *Miami and The Siege of Chicago* (1968), about the Republican and Democratic nominating conventions of 1968, was again a masterpiece of its kind. *A Fire on the Moon* (1970) was about the implications of the U.S. space program.

Mailer's interest in radical politics took him from Socialism to anarchism to a generalized hostility toward the regimentation and mechanization of modern life that he labeled "radical conservatism." Always partial to publicity, he sought to popularize his ideas by running in the New York mayoralty campaign of 1969.

Bibliography: R. J. Foster, *Norman Mailer* (Univ. of Minn. Pamphlets on American Writers, 1968), incl. bibl.; H. M. Harper, *Desperate Faith* (1967), 96–136, incl. bibl.; J. Flaherty, *Managing Mailer* (1970); H. Breit, *Writer Observed* (1956), 199–201; S. J. Kunitz (ed.), *Twentieth Century Authors,* first suppl. (1955); *New York Times Book Review* (May 5, 1968), 1, 2; Dupee, in: *Commentary,* 29 (1960), 128–32.

[H.H.]

MAIMI, SIMON (d. 1497), chief rabbi *(*arraby moor)* of Portugal. Maimi was martyred when *Manuel I, king of Portugal, tried to force him to accept Christianity, thinking that if the chief rabbi set the example all the Jews could soon be baptized. The attempt to convert Portuguese Jewry occurred during the spring of 1497, following the promulgation of the edict of expulsion on Dec. 4, 1496. Maimi and about eight leading personalities—including his son-in-law, and probably Abraham b. Jacob *Saba, Abraham b. Samuel *Zacuto, and Isaac b. Joseph *Caro were thrown into a dungeon and immured up to their necks. The group refused to yield, and when the wall was torn down a few days later Maimi was dead. His body was stealthily taken by several Marranos who, at the risk of their lives, succeeded in burying him in the Jewish cemetery near Lisbon.

Bibliography: Roth, Marranos, 60; N. Slouschz, *Ha-Anusim be-Portugal* (1932), 9, 63.

[Ed.]

MAIMON (Fishman), ADA (1893–), leader of the women's labor movement in Ereẓ Israel, sister of Judah Leib *Maimon. Born in Marculesti, Bessarabia, she settled in Ereẓ Israel in 1912, and worked on the land and also as a teacher. She represented *Ha-Po'el ha-Ẓa'ir (and later Mapai) in the *Histadrut, the Va'ad Le'ummi, Zionist Congresses, the Zionist General Council, and the First and Second Knesset. She was a founder of *Mo'eẓet ha-Po'alot and its secretary for 12 years, as well as being active on the Executive of World *Wizo and in the struggle for women's rights; the Age of Marriage Law (1950) is known by her name. In 1930 she founded the Ayanot Agricultural School, which she headed for many years. Ada Maimon wrote

Ada Maimon, Israel women's labor leader. Courtesy Government Press Office, Tel Aviv.

Tenu'at ha-Po'alot be-Ereẓ Yisrael (1929), *Ha-Ḥaluẓah be-Ereẓ-Yisrael* (1930), *Ayanot, Mi-Meshek Po'alot le-Veit Sefer Ḥakla'i Tikhon* (1946), and *Ḥamishim Shenot Tenu'at ha-Po'alot, 1904–54* (1955).

Bibliography: Y. Harari, *Ishah va-Em be-Yisrael* (1959), 347–50; M. Braslavsky, *Tenu'at ha-Po'alim ha-Ereẓ-Yisre'elit,* 4 (1963), 367 (index).

[G.K.]

MAIMON (Fishman), JUDAH LEIB (1875–1962), rabbi and leader of religious Zionism. Born in Marculesti, Bessarabia, Maimon studied in Lithuanian yeshivot and, after being ordained, served as a preacher *(maggid meisharim)* in Marculesti and in 1905–13 as rabbi in Ungeni. In 1900 he met Rabbi Isaac Jacob *Reines, founder

Judah Leib Maimon, religious leader in Israel.

of *Mizrachi, and afterward took an active part in the founding conference of Mizrachi, which was held in Vilna, and in its first world conference in Pressburg (Bratislava). Beginning with the Second Zionist Congress, he participated in all the subsequent Congresses and was for many years a member of the Zionist General Council. From 1935 he served as Mizrachi's representative on the Zionist Executive, was vice-chairman of the Executive, and headed the Department for Artisans and Retail Business as well as the Department of Religious Affairs.

Maimon settled in Ereẓ Israel in 1913 and was among the founders of the educational network of Mizrachi there. At the outbreak of World War I he was imprisoned and expelled by the Turkish authorities. He went to the United States, where he was active in the effort to strengthen Mizrachi and published hundreds of articles in the press. He returned on the first ship to reach the shores of Palestine after the war and met Rabbi *Kook, with whom he became very friendly. Together they established the chief rabbinate of Palestine, and Maimon formulated the rabbinate's constitution and organized its founding ceremony. In 1936 he established the Mosad ha-Rav Kook, which published hundreds of books. His private library contained over 40,000 volumes, among them many very rare books, first editions, incunabula, and the only extant copies of many important manuscripts.

Although he maintained his adherence to the organized framework of the *yishuv,* Maimon often expressed his sympathy with the secessionist organizations, Irgun Ẓeva'i Le'ummi (I.Ẓ.L.) and Loḥamei Ḥerut Israel (Leḥi), and gave evidence on behalf of I.Ẓ.L. prisoners. He proclaimed the right of every Jew to bear arms in his own defense and in the defense of Jewish rights in Ereẓ Israel. When the Haganah began actively to suppress I.Ẓ.L. (1944–45), Maimon expressed his opposition to these activities. On "Black Saturday" (June 1946) he was interned as acting chairman of the Jewish Agency Executive. His imprisonment aroused a great furor, since the British had compelled him by force to desecrate the Sabbath, and after great pressure he was released by special order of the high commissioner.

In the first years after the establishment of the State of Israel, Maimon advocated the institution of a Sanhedrin as a supreme religious authority, but this attempt aroused opposition in many religious circles. He was appointed minister of religions and minister in charge of war casualties both in the provisional government and in the first elected one; and was a member of the First Knesset. He later relinquished his political activities and devoted himself entirely to literary work.

Maimon was a prolific author. His first work was *Ha-Noten ba-Yam Derekh* (1903). His second work *Hadar Horati*, a collection of articles on *halakhah*, Maimonides, and *aggadah*, was published ten years later. He also published other articles and biblical investigations. In 1907 he began to publish the talmudic-literary journal, *Ha-Yonah*, which was banned by censorship, however, and its publication discontinued. In 1921 Maimon founded the Mizrachi weekly, *Ha-Tor*, whose publication was continued for 15 years. He later founded and edited the monthly *Sinai*, of which he issued 50 volumes. His major work, *Sarei ha-Me'ah* (6 vols., 1942–47), describes the greatest Jewish scholars of the last century. His other writings include: *Le-Ma'an Ẓiyyon Lo Eḥesheh* (2 vols., 1954–55); *Middei Ḥodesh be-Ḥodsho* (8 vols., 1955–62); *Ḥaggim u-Mo'adim* (1950[3]); *Ha-Ẓiyyonut ha-Datit ve-Hitpatteḥutah* (1937); *Rabbi Moshe ben Maimon* (1959); *Toledot ha-Gra* (1954); and an edition of Judah b. Kalonymus' *Yiḥusei Tanna'im ve-Amora'im* (1942).

Bibliography: G. Bat-Yehudah, *Elleh Toledot Rabbi J. L. Maimon* (1964); EẒD, 3 (1965), 422–94 (incl. comprehensive bibl.).

[Y.Go./Ed.]

MAIMON, SOLOMON (c. 1753–1800), philosopher. Maimon was born in Sukoviboeg, Poland. He was a child prodigy in the study of rabbinical literature. Married at the age of 11 and a father at 14, Maimon supported his family by working as a tutor in neighboring towns. In his spare time he studied Jewish philosophy and Kabbalah; he adopted the name "Maimon" in honor of Maimonides. His attempt to demonstrate that the Kabbalah is based on philosophy caused the Ḥasidim with whom he associated to regard him as a heretic. He turned to the study of secular subjects and left his home and family to study in Berlin. In about 1779 after many hardships he arrived at the gates of Berlin but was refused entry by officials of the Jewish community. After six months as a mendicant he arrived in Posen (Poznan), where he was received and aided by the rabbi, Ẓvi Hirsch b. Abraham. He taught for two years in Posen, but finding the religious atmosphere of the community stifling, he went by carriage to Berlin; this time he was able to enter the city.

In Berlin he became a member of Moses *Mendelssohn's circle but was abandoned by Mendelssohn a few years later because of the dissolute life he led. Forced again to leave Berlin, he moved to Hamburg and then to Amsterdam. In Hamburg he beseeched a Lutheran pastor to convert him to Christianity, but he confessed his disbelief in Christian doctrines. The pastor retorted that Maimon was too much a

Solomon Maimon, 18th-century philosopher. Jerusalem, J.N.U.L., Schwadron Collection.

philosopher to be a Christian. Thereafter, with the help of some benefactors, he was able to study at the gymnasium of Altona for two years. Still poverty-stricken, he moved from Altona to Berlin, then to Breslau, and in 1786 back to Berlin. There he studied Kantian philosophy and under its influence wrote his first work in German; *Versuch ueber die Transzendentalphilosophie* (1790; Heb., 1941), a manuscript of which he sent to Marcus *Herz and Herz sent it to Immanuel *Kant. Kant remarked in a letter to Herz (May 26, 1789) that, even though he had not read the whole book, it was clear to him from a cursory study of it that its value was very great, and that of all Kant's critics nobody understood his philosophy as well as Maimon (E. Cassirer (ed.), *Immanuel Kants Werke*, 9 (1918), 415). Kant's letter determined Maimon's future. He found a publisher for his book and scientific journals accepted his articles for publication. From 1790 to 1795 Maimon was supported by a benefactor, Count Adolf Kalkreuth, at whose residences near Berlin and near Freistadt, Silesia, he lived. When Maimon died, he was buried ouside the Jewish cemetery as a heretic.

Other Works. In 1791 Maimon published a philosophical lexicon, containing a series of essays on the principal points of philosophy (new edition 1970). In 1793 he published his *Streifereien im Gebiete der Philosophie*, followed by three works on the history of philosophy: *Ueber die Progresse der Philosophie* (1793); *Versuch einer neuen Logik* (1794; 1812[2]), in which he attempted to expound a system of logic; and *Die Kategorien des Aristoteles* (1794, 1798[2]). In 1797 his work *Kritische Untersuchungen ueber den menschlichen Geist* was published.

Maimon also wrote the following works in Hebrew, but only the first was published: *Givat ha-Moreh* (1791; ed. by S. H. Bergman and N. Rotenstreich, 1966), a commentary on the first part of Maimonides' *Guide of the Perplexed; Ta'alumot Ḥokhmah*, on mathematical physics; and *Ḥeshek Shelomo*, which was divided into four parts, namely "*Ma'aseh Nissim*," on the 12 sermons of Nissim b. Reuben Gerondi, "*Eved Avraham*," on Ibn Ezra's commentary on the Pentateuch and Psalms, "*Ma'aseh Livnat ha-Sappir*," which are reflections, and "*Ma'aseh Ḥoshev*," on algebra. Maimon's autobiography (*Solomon Maimons Lebengeschichte, von ihm selbst geschrieben*), his only book to win wide acclaim, was published in Berlin in 1793 (Eng. trans. by M. Hadas (1947) and S. H. Bergmann (ed.; 1954); Heb. trans. (1942). It is an important source for the study of Judaism and Ḥasidism in Eastern Europe in that period. The 12th chapter describes Mendelssohn and his thought.

Philosophy. Maimon's achievements as a philosopher were in general, rather than Jewish philosophy. To account for the origin of knowledge and its objectivity, the German philosopher Kant had posited the "thing-in-itself" as something existing outside the mind but unknowable in itself. Maimon's main contribution was to give a new direction to Kant's discussion of it. Maimon agreed with Kant that the cognition process must have a cause and that this cause must also guarantee the objectivity of the knowledge. But he differed from Kant by holding that this cause exists in the mind, not outside it. Invoking Kant's distinction between sensibility and understanding, Maimon affirmed that the concepts of understanding arise from perceptions of sensibility, which he appears to assume are the same for everyone, and which therefore guarantee their objectivity. Maimon maintained further that sensibility is a kind of understanding but more limited and imperfect than understanding itself.

The "thing-in-itself" had another meaning for Maimon, namely, the final goal toward which all cognition tends. Our knowledge is always fragmentary, but as it increases it approaches an ideal knowledge. This may be illustrated by a polygon, which approaches a circle as sides are added, but does not reach it.

Infinite Intellect. While Maimon rejected Kant's extra-mental "thing-in-itself" as the cause of knowledge and the guarantor of its objectivity, he still had to answer

Kant's question of how knowledge is related to a world outside the mind. In his words, "To find a passage from the external world to the mental world is more important than to find a way to East India, no matter what statesmen may say." Maimon bridged this gap by assuming that our sensibility is only an imperfect expression of intellectual reality which underlies the world. Hence the objects of the outside world presented to sensibility are concepts and their relations. But since concepts and their relations must inhere in some intellect, Maimon posits an infinite intellect. Our intellect is derived from this infinite intellect. As finite creatures we can only comprehend a small portion of this rational structure of the world.

The assumption of an infinite intellect permits Maimon to bridge the gap between the intra-mental and extral-mental worlds. But the infinite intellect, in turn, does not receive concepts from objects lying outside of it; rather, it creates objects from within itself. There is no distinction between the form of knowledge and its content. Maimon summarized his position: "We posit ... an infinite intellect ... which creates out of itself all possible kinds of relations of things. Our intellect is the very same intellect, but in a more limited degree."

LAW OF DETERMINABILITY. Maimon had to face the further problem of how to describe the mode of thinking of the infinite intellect, that is, how the concepts cohere to create the structure of the rational world. To answer that question Maimon formulated the "law of determinability" *("Satz der Bestimmbarkeit").* One account of this complex notion was based on Kant's distinction between analytic and synthetic judgments. Analytic judgments, whose form is "A is A," are tautological and they do not produce knowledge; synthetic judgments, whose form is "A is B," produce certain knowledge. Maimon criticizes Kant's notion that synthetic judgments were certain, since in his view subject and predicate in these judgments are foreign to one another. Against Kant's two kinds of judgments, Maimon posited a third which he called the "law of determinability." According to it, there exists a judgment which is both analytic and synthetic. Using the proposition "the color is blue," Maimon states that the subject (the color) can exist without the predicate (blue), and, hence, the relation between subject and predicate is synthetic; on the other hand, the predicate (blue) cannot exist alone but only in connection with the subject and, hence, it is analytic. Maimon had hoped that through this law he could open new possibilities for metaphysics, but he was too careful a philosopher to attempt to build this speculative structure himself.

MAIMON'S SKEPTICISM. Despite the rationalist structure of his idealist philosophy, Maimon exhibited a skeptical streak. While he claimed that the hypothesis of an infinite intellect and the discovery of the law of determinability provide the possibility of viewing the world as a rational structure, he never claimed that one could know with certainty that this rational structure in fact exists in the world. The kind of doubts raised by such skeptical philosophers as David Hume remained. Philosophy can only show that it is possible to construct a rational structure for the world, but it cannot show that this rational structure exists in fact. Hence, one can only philosophize "conditionally."

Maimon's philosophy strongly influenced the philosopher Johann Fichte and, through Fichte, German idealist philosophy. During the 19th century, Maimon was neglected. But, as a result of the efforts of the historian of philosophy J. E. Erdmann (in his *History of Philosophy* (1892[3]), index) interest in Maimon has been revived in the 20th century. In recent years several basic books dealing with his system have appeared. A new photostatic edition of his collected works began to appear in 1965.

Bibliography: N. J. Jacobs, in: KS, 41 (1965/66), 245–62 (bibl. of his writings and writings about him); S. H. Bergman, *The Philosophy of Solomon Maimon* (1967); S. Atlas, in: *Encyclopedia of Philosophy*, 5 (1967), 127–9; idem, *From Critical to Speculative Idealism* (1964); idem, in: HUCA, 21 (1948), 105–52; 23 pt. 1 (1950–51), 517–47; idem, in: *Journal of the History of Ideas*, 13 (1952), 168–87. [SH.H.B.]

MAIMON BEN JOSEPH (d. 1165/1170), Spanish rabbi and *dayyan;* father of *Maimonides. Maimon studied in Lucena under Joseph *ibn Migash, and transmitted his teachings, both oral and in writing, to his son, who utilized them as the basis for his own halakhic works. Maimon was a *dayyan* of Cordoba for many years, until he and his family were compelled to leave, in consequence of the edict of forced conversion issued by the *Almohads after their conquest of the city about 1149. For about ten years he wandered through Spain and probably also Provence. About 1160 he emigrated with his family to Fez, Morocco, where it was easier for forced converts to preserve their Judaism. In Fez he forbade the people to follow the false messiah, Moses Dari, who was popular there at the time. In 1165 he proceded to Ereẓ Israel, where he died, possibly in the following year. According to one tradition his grave is in Tiberias. Some scholars think, however, that he went to Egypt with his son and died there.

Maimon was one of the most outstanding and influential scholars of his generation and the first of his distinguished family of whom a written work is known. His *Iggeret ha-Neḥamah,* written in his second year in Fez (published in the original Arabic by M. Simons, see bibliography; and in a scholarly Hebrew translation by B. Klar, 1945), was designed to comfort and guide the forced converts of Islam in their effort to preserve their Judaism. "We who are in exile can be compared to a man who is drowning. The water has reached our nostrils but we still grasp hold of something ... and as the water threatens to engulf us, behold, a rope consisting of God's precepts and His Torah dangles from heaven to earth. Whoever seizes hold of it still has hope of living ... and surely he who holds on even only with the tips of his fingers has more hope than he who lets go completely."

Maimon's fundamental premise—later adopted by his son Maimonides and accepted as law among Jews in Islamic countries—is that Islam, in that it is free from personification of the Deity, is not to be regarded as idolatry. In keeping with this view, he opposed martyrdom to avoid conversion to Islam. Unlike other scholars, who left the people without hope, Maimon asserts that those who perform the precepts in secret will be rewarded, laying particular stress on the value of reciting the **Amidah* three times daily, even in its abridged form, and even in Arabic. He also places great emphasis upon the importance of belief in the divinity of the mission of Moses, to whose virtues the work is largely devoted, comparing such belief to belief in God Himself. This principle, later embodied by Maimonides in his 13 principles, was designed to nullify belief in the divine mission of Mohammed, for which reason Maimon also stresses that Daniel was the last of the prophets. Maimon's work reflects the spirit of despair that had seized the Jews of the countries during the time of the Almohads, and it fortified his readers that the tyrannical rule would not continue for long, as had been promised by the prophets. Maimon also wrote commentaries to the Talmud, from which his son quotes abundantly; a book on the laws of prayer and the festivals, from which only isolated quotations have been preserved (Simon b. Zemaḥ Duran,

Tashbeẓ, 1, no. 2); responsa, a number of which have been published by A. H. Freimann (see bibl.); a commentary on the Torah; a work on the laws of ritual purity; and, apparently, an exposition of an Arabic astronomical book. With the exception of the responsa, all his works were written in Arabic.

Bibliography: Marmorstein, in: *Sefer ha-Rambam shel ha-Tarbiz* (1935), 182–4 (= *Tarbiz*, 6 (1934/35), 426–8); Freimann, *ibid.*, 164–76 (= *Tarbiz*, 6 (1934/35), 408–20; idem, in: *Alummah*, 1 (1936), 9–13; J. L. Fishman, in: Maimon b. Joseph, *Iggeret ha-Neḥamah*, tr. by B. Klar (1945), introd.; Halkin, in: *Joshua Starr Memorial Volume* (1953), 102–3; Hirschberg, Afrikah, 1 (1965), 100f., 122–4, 263; Simons, in: JQR, 2 (1890), 62–66, 335–69; J. M. Toledano, *Sarid u-Falit*, 1 (1960), 7–8. [I.T.-S.]

MAIMONIDEAN CONTROVERSY, a vast complex of disputed cultural, religious, and social problems, focusing around several central themes. Some of the elements of this controversy considerably antedate *Maimonides (1135–1204); and of the questions brought into sharp relief by his ideas and writings, some have remained topical in many Jewish circles. Vast fields of human experience and thought are encompassed by it: reason and philosophy in their relation to faith and tradition; what components are permitted and what prohibited in the education of a man following the Torah; the proper understanding of *anthropomorphism as expressed in the Bible and Talmud; central theological concepts such as the *resurrection of the body; and the very form of Maimonides' *Mishneh Torah* and its attitude toward talmudic discussion. The question of hierarchical leadership versus intellectual, personal leadership was one of the early causes of this controversy. In the Middle Ages the controversy had three climaxes: around 1180 (in the lifetime of Maimonides); around 1230–32 (involving David *Kimḥi, *Solomon b. Abraham of Montpellier, *Naḥmanides and others, and centering in *Provence); and around 1300–06 (in connection with Abba Mari b. Moses *Astruc, Solomon b. Abraham *Adret, *Asher b. Jehiel, *Jedaiah b. Abraham Bedersi (ha-Penini), and Menahem b. Solomon *Meiri, and centering in Christian Spain and Provence). In between these moments when the conflict flared up anew, tensions and disputes continued. The crisis of Spanish Jewry in the 15th century accentuated the main educational and social themes of the old controversy. In Renaissance Italy and in the diversified and flourishing Jewish center of Poland-Lithuania the old quarrel again became topical, though in a milder form. With the enlightenment (*Haskalah) of the 18th century the "Maimonidean side" of the controversy was given a new, greatly secularized, and radical expression by Moses *Mendelssohn and his followers—an expression that could scarely have been imagined by the former protagonists. In German *neo-Orthodoxy, the "Maimonidean side"—particularly in its striving for a synthesis of Jewish faith and "general culture," as well as in certain of its social tendencies—found a new, conservative expression. In Yemen in the 19th century and well into the 20th, there was a distinct "Maimonidean camp" and a struggle against it (see *Kafaḥ).

The First Clash. Through the charisma of his personality and the trend of his thought and leadership Maimonides himself initiated this. An exile from Muslim Spain, he met in the Near East the hierarchical traditions of the exilarchate and the **geonim*. Maimonides was willing and ready to respect the *exilarch as scion of the royal house of David and as the proper authority, from the halakhic point of view, to appoint and ordain judges.

His mind and heart vehemently opposed the claims of the *geonim*. He criticized sharply the way they:

> fixed for themselves monetary demands from individuals and communities and caused people to think, in utter foolishness, that it is obligatory and proper that they should help sages and scholars and people studying Torah ... all this is wrong. There is not a single word, either in the Torah or in the sayings of the [talmudic] sages, to lend credence to it ... for as we look into the sayings of the talmudic sages, we do not find that they ask people for money, nor did they collect money for the honorable and cherished academies (commentary to Avot 4:5).

This attempt to undermine the economic and social foundations of the leadership of the Babylonian *geonim* went hand in hand with Maimonides' opposition to their program of studies and his contempt for their very office. The *gaon* at Baghdad at this time was *Samuel b. Ali, a strong and authoritarian personality. In an ironic "apology" for Samuel b. Ali's attacks on the *Mishneh Torah*, Maimonides explains to one of his pupils:

> Why, my son, should you take offense that a man whom people accustom from his youth to believe that there is none like him in his generation; when age, high office, aristocratic descent, the lack of people of discernment in this town, and his relationship with individuals, all have combined to produce this execrable consequence that each and every individual hangs expectantly on each word pronounced from the academy in anticipation of an honorific title from there ...—why do you wonder that he has acquired such [evil] traits? How, my son, could you imagine that he should love truth enough to acknowledge his weakness? ... This is a thing that a man like him will never do, as it was not done by better men who preceded him (letter to Joseph b. Judah in: D. H. Baneth (ed.), *Iggerot ha-Rambam* (1946), 54f.).

The gaonate is represented as corrupt, and typical academy study as being of questionable value. Concerning Zechariah, the son-in-law of the *gaon*, Maimonides writes:

> He is a very foolish man. He studies very hard at this talmudic discussion and its commentaries, and thinks that he is the greatest of his generation, having already attained the peak of perfection. My esteemed son knows that my appreciation of the greatest of the sages of Israel is such that I evaluate their worth according to their own criteria. They themselves have defined 'the argumentations *[havayot]* of *Abbaye and *Rava [as] a small matter.' If this is a small matter, why should I pay attention to an old man who is really miserable, an ignoramus in every respect? To my eyes he is like a newborn baby; one has to defend him, according to the measure of his [Zechariah's] foolishness (*ibid.*, 56ff.; the bulk of this passage has been erased in most manuscripts).

This vehement revolt against the authority of the *geonim* came at a time when Samuel b. Ali was attempting to minimize the authority of the exilarch on the grounds that what the people needed then was no more than the leadership of the *geonim* and the guidance of their study in the academy. Small wonder that such a revolt aroused reciprocal anger, coming, as it did, in defense of Maimonides' *Mishneh Torah* which claimed expressly (in the introduction) to supersede the Talmud in popular usage, replacing its deliberations—the very core and substance of the life of academies and *geonim*—by his systematic code. The claim of the intellectual to replace an aristocratic hierarchy seemed to be combined with an attempt to impose Greek systematic modes of codification in place of the traditional many-voiced flow of talmudic discussion. It is hardly suprising that Samuel b. Ali, Zechariah, and *Daniel b. Saadiah ha-Bavli all sought and found halakhic flaws in this code. Some of their arguments have philosophical and theological overtones, but these were to come to the forefront only in the second stage of the controversy. In the main, in this phase, it was Maimonides' creativity which was found provocative, as well as his attitude to Talmud study and to the leadership of established institutions, all of which were being defended against him.

The First Stage in Europe. Maimonides' works reached Europe, chiefly in the southwest—Spain and Provence—entering a cultural and social climate very different from the one in which they had been created in Egypt. His authority in *Mishneh Torah* was impugned halakhically by *Abraham b. David of Posquières and *Moses ha-Kohen, among others. The Christian Reconquest was proceeding apace in the Iberian peninsula. Mystical tendencies and visionary approaches began to find explicit and strong expression in the developing *Kabbalah of Provence and Spain. Jews everywhere were suffering from the impact of the *Crusades, with martyrdom (**Kiddush ha-Shem*) in their wake. Maimonides' grandiose attempt at a synthesis between the Jewish faith and Greek-Arabic Aristotelian philosophy was received with enthusiasm in some circles, mainly of the upper strata of Jewish society, and with horror and dismay in others, imbued with mysticism and dreading the effects of Greek thought on Jewish beliefs. The old and continuously smoldering issue of "Athens versus Jerusalem" conceived in the Talmud as the problem of *ḥokhmah yevanit* (BK 82b–83a; Meg. 9a–b), now burst into flames. Essentially the problem is one of the possible synthesis or the absolute antithesis between monotheistic revealed faith and intellectually formulated philosophy. This problem is interwoven in the great monotheistic religions with the clash between rationalistic religious belief, inclining in the main toward synthesis, and mystic belief, which is largely opposed to it.

The problem was not new in Judaism. In Islamic countries in the tenth century it was in the main decided in favor of rationalism and synthesis. Maimonides was not the only one in the 12th century who expressly sought a synthesis between Greek philosophy and Judaism; a philosophic approach was attempted by Abraham *ibn Daud (see, e.g., his *Sefer ha-Emunah ha-Ramah* (1852), 2, 58), and he was preceded by *Saadiah Gaon and *Samuel b. Hophni who denied the historical veracity of the incident of Samuel and the Witch of Endor.

Yet in that same century changes were taking place. The influence of the Christian environment became more pervasive. Increasingly Christianity was involved in similar problems, as the conflict between Peter *Abelard and *Bernard of Clairvaux clearly shows. Social upheavals in Jewish society during the 12th and 13th centuries added communal tension to the spiritual strife. When Maimonides was still young, most of his work as yet unwritten, *Judah Halevi warned: "Turn aside from mines and pitfalls. Let not Greek wisdom tempt you, for it bears flowers only and no fruit . . . Listen to the confused words of her sages built on the void . . . Why should I search for bypaths, and complicated ones at that, and leave the main road?" (from his poem beginning "*Devarekha be-Mor Over Rekuḥim*").

This opposition hardened and developed with the passage of time. Against it stood the rationalistic attitude of the upper circles. Meir b. Todros ha-Levi *Abulafia, in many respects a sincere admirer of Maimonides, was shocked at the implication that Maimonides did not affirm the resurrection of the body as a halakhic principle. In an angry letter sent to the scholars of *Lunel he not only sought to prove by copious quotations the dogmatic truth of bodily resurrection, but also added passionately that if there is no such resurrection, "to what end did the bodies stand watch for their God, did they go in darkness for the sake of their God? If the bodies are not resurrected, where is their hope and where are they to look for it?" (*Kitāb al-Rasā'il* (1871), 14). Abulafia also attacked Maimonides on other halakhic points. While some of his correspondents agreed with him, others tried to convince him that he had misunderstood the purport of Maimonides' teaching on resurrection, and this latter view was accepted wholeheartedly by the *nasi* Sheshet b. Isaac of Saragossa, who in a very radical sense gave expression to Maimonides' rationalism and philosophic synthesis. Writing about 1200, he attacked sharply and derisively what he regarded as the simplicism and materialism of Abulafia's view (A. Marx, in: JQR 25, (1934/35), 406–28). To speak about bodily resurrection is "to bring down our saintly fathers from the highest level—the status of the angels who enjoy divine glory and live forever—to the status of man, through their returning to the impure body which cannot exist except through food and drink, and must end in dust and worms . . . but the life of wisdom is greater than foolishness, as light is greater than darkness. These notions seem to me like the words of one confused" (*ibid.*, 418). The only correct conception of resurrection, he thought, is the one also accepted by the pagan philosophers. Resurrection means the eternal life of the soul of the sage-philosopher. "If the soul—while still in the body—was yearning for its Creator, subordinating its passion to its reason, [then] when it leaves the body, [it] will attain the highest status, for which it yearned while still in the body; and over it God will emanate of His spirit. This, in the view of the sages, is the resurrection of the dead and the reward of the just at the end of days" (*ibid.*, 421ff.). All pronouncements in the Bible and the Talmud about bodily resurrection are only for the simple men who constitute the majority of mankind and who understand only material rewards, and the same holds true for the Muslim paradise (*ibid.*, 424).

> I ask this fool who maintains that the souls will return to the dead corpses and that they are destined to return to the soil of Israel. Into which body will the soul return? If it is to the body from which it has departed, [then this will] already have returned to its elements thousands of years earlier; [it is now] earth, dust, and worms. Where it has been buried, a house has been built, a vineyard planted, or some other plants have taken root and you cannot find the earth or the dust or the worms into which the body has turned. If, however, this soul is to return to another body, which God will create, then it is another man who will be created in his own time, and has not been dead; how, then can you say that he is being resurrected and that God rewards him, as he has not as yet achieved anything? (*ibid.*, 426).

Sheshet records opposition to the *Mishneh Torah* by reporting the opinion of one of the judges who quarreled with him and refused to judge according to Maimonides: "As he does not adduce proofs from the sayings of the talmudic sages for his decisions, who is going to follow his opinion? It is far better to study Talmud. We will have nothing to do with his books and his writings." In Sheshet's view this opposition stems from the fact that until the *Mishneh Torah* the whole matter of legal decision was so confused that the vast majority of Jews, being ignorant of the Talmud, had to obey their judges, whereas now people had before them a clear and open code and were not dependent on judges alone (*ibid.*, 427).

Despite common admiration for Maimonides and his all-embracing devotion to Torah and the Jewish faith, there was in reality no common language between the two radical positions. Gradually the opponents of Maimonides began to attack his very conception of a synthesis between Greek philosophy and Jewish faith. When David Kimḥi traveled about the communities of Provence to rally the supporters of Maimonides, he was greatly surprised to be answered by the physician and courtier, Judah *ibn Alfakhar, with a bitter attack on Maimonides' very attempt to rationalize and explain away miracles and wondrous tales. Ibn Alfakhar was against half acceptance; logical proofs were

A large decorated initial-word panel from the *Nuremberg Maḥzor* for a *piyyut* of the first day of Passover. From 1499 the manuscript belonged to the Municipality of Nuremberg. In 1951 Salman Schocken obtained it for his library in Jerusalem, where he had already collected four other illuminated leaves from the *Mahzor*. The manuscript was written for R. Joshua bar Isaac in South Germany, in 1331. Jerusalem, Schocken Library, ms. 24 100, fol. 78 ($19\frac{3}{4} \times 14\frac{5}{8}$ ins/50 × 37 cm.).

not so important, "for each true proof needs great checking, since sometimes it may include misleading elements of that false wisdom called sophistry in Greek, and when a proof is joined to this it misleads even sages." Maimonides' "erroneous" intention was to explain matters according to the laws of philosophy and nature "so as to put the Torah and Greek wisdom together, to make out of them one whole. He imagined that the one would live with the other like two loving twin deers. In reality this has resulted in sorrow and dissension, for they cannot live together on the earth and be like two sisters, for the Hebrew women are not like the Egyptian ones. To this our Torah says: 'No, my son is the living one, and yours is the dead' (I Kings 3:22) and her rival angers her. I want peace; if I start to talk to them, they go to war" (letter to Kimḥi, *Iggerot Kena'ot*, in: *Kovez Teshuvot ha-Rambam* (1859), 2a). Thus, through radical rationalistic argumentation, this physician and courtier in Spain rejects the synthesis of the physician and courtier in Egypt and the logical compromise it involves.

The demand for logical consistency was also answered from the Maimonidean camp. Increasingly they inclined toward extreme allegoristic explanations of talmudic and even biblical expressions and tales. Their opponents accused them of even inclining to explain away as no more than symbols certain practical commandments, which need be fulfilled only by simple men, but not by educated people. The rationalists denied this. Social overtones became stronger. The anti-Maimonideans berated their upper-class opponents for their hedonistic, luxurious, and sinful way of life. The Maimonideans countered by accusing their adversaries with anarchy, harshness, ignorance, simplicity of mind, and of being under Christian influence.

The anti-Maimonidean camp turned to the great sages of northern France. Never having been acquainted with Aristotelian philosophy, they never felt the need for synthesis with it; therefore, they unhesitatingly pronounced a *ḥerem* on Maimonides' philosophical works. Some report that they excommunicated even parts of his halakhic code. In Provence and Spain the anti-Maimonidean camp was led by Solomon b. Abraham of Montpellier, *Jonah b. Abraham Gerondi, the poet Meshullam *da Piera, and above all Naḥmanides. The position of Naḥmanides is remarkable for its simultaneous flexibility in expression and rigidity of mental attitude. Seeing that the extreme anti-Maimonidean stance taken by the rabbis of northern France and by Solomon of Montpellier had no chance of finding support among the leading circles of Jewish society in Provence and Spain, he therefore advised the anti-Maimonidean camp to adopt a moderate stand in order to achieve at least what was possible. Writing to the north French rabbis (printed in: MGWJ, 9 (1860), 184–95) he expresses his devotion and admiration, but he humbly submits that they "are nourished in the bosom of [true] faith, planted in the courts of tradition," and therefore had to understand Maimonides in his peculiar cultural and social circumstances. The situation he describes is actually that of Spanish and Provençal Jewish upper society in the early 13th century:

> They have filled their belly with the foolishness of the Greeks ... they ... make fun ... of the trusting souls ... They did not enter profoundly into the ways of our Torah; the ways of alien children suffice for them. But for the words of [Maimonides], but for the fact that they live out of the mouth of his works ... they would have slipped almost entirely.

It is not only a matter of false spiritual pride and alien culture; it is also a case born of social necessity:

> God save and guard us, my teachers, from such a fate. Look about and see: is there a pain like our pain? For the sons have been exiled from their fathers' tables; they have defiled themselves with the food of gentiles and the wine of their feasts. They have mixed with them and become used to their deeds ... courtiers have been permitted to study Greek wisdom, to become acquainted with medicine, to learn mathematics and geometry, other knowledge and tricks, so that they make a living in royal courts and palaces.

This intrinsically hostile description of the life of the upper classes of Jewish society in Provence and Spain is given in order to put Maimonides in the light of a great talmudic sage who—argues Naḥmanides—would certainly and gladly have written and lived as the northern French rabbis did. Alas, it was not granted him: "Did he trouble himself for your sake, you geniuses of the Talmud? He saw himself compelled and constrained to structure a work which would offer refuge from the Greek philosophers . . . Have you ever listened to their words, have you ever been misled by their proofs?" He goes on to explain that extremism would bring about an irreparable split. It is far better to educate gradually this misled society and bring it back to the right way of northern France, by partial prohibitions only. The region most afflicted is Provence; Spain he considers to be in far better order.

Naḥmanides was merely temporizing in his writings to the northern French rabbis. His true temper and the temper of the entire anti-Maimonidean camp is revealed in his commentary on the Torah, which is basically a mystical work against Maimonides and Abraham *ibn Ezra. The very concept of a system of laws of nature ordained by God in His wisdom to be admired by man through his reason, as expressed by Maimonides (see, e.g., *Mishneh Torah, Sefer ha-Madda*), he and his colleagues believe to be sheer heresy. The workings of nature are to be conceived of only and always as "hidden miracles." God performs extraordinary *miracles in order that we should understand the miraculous nature of all existence and life:

> Through the great and famous miracles man recognizes the hidden foundation of the entire Torah. For no man has a share in the Torah of Moses until we believe that all our matters and accidents are miracles, the product neither of nature nor of the way of the world, whether for the multitude or for the individual; but if a man fulfills the commandments his reward will bring him success, if he transgresses them his punishment will strike him—all by divine decree (Comm. to Ex. 13:16).

Though their tactics might thus vary, dogmatics were radical and clearly defined on both sides. *Ḥerem* was hurled against *ḥerem*, as the authority of northern France was met by the authority of local scholars and communal leaders in Provence and Spain. Emissaries of both camps traveled about, rallying their supporters. A profusion of letters and counter-letters, sermons and counter-sermons, commentaries and counter-commentaries poured out. The weapons in the campaign were polemics, original and translations, and the Ibn *Tibbon and *Anatoli families made their name in both. In the work of men like Jonah Gerondi the struggle against Maimonides was merged with a general reforming spirit in morals and community leadership. This battle was ended by a terrible shock when Maimonides' books were burned by the *Dominicans in 1232. Jonah Gerondi relented in his views and many adherents of the anti-Maimonidean camp followed suit.

The controversy returned to the Muslim countries in the East. Maimonides' son, *Abraham b. Moses b. Maimon, was outraged at what had happened in the West. He attacked "many overseas [scholars who are] mistaken. They cling to the literalistic sense of biblical verses, Midrashim, and *aggadot*. This pains our heart; at the sight of this our eyes have darkened, and our fathers are dumbfounded: How could such an impurity, so like the impurity of idol worship, come to be in Israel? They worship idols, deny God's teaching, and worship other gods beside Him." Flinging these accusations against Maimonides' opponents in Europe, Abraham holds that through their exegetical explanations they are guilty of pagan-like anthropomorphism (*Milḥamot ha-Shem*, ed by R. Margalioth (1953), 52). He compares their faith to that of the Christians (*ibid.*, 55). Continuing his father's line of thought, he attacks the European antirationalistic scholars for their exclusive devotion to talmudic studies only, while neglecting the philosophical and philological foundations of the faith (*ibid.*, 49). They are among "those that walk in the darkness of their understanding and in the paucity of their wisdom" (*ibid.*, 50). He expressly prefers Islamic surroundings and influence—conducive to a rationalistic-monotheistic faith—to a Christian environment, which influences men in the direction of antirationalism and anthropomorphism (*ibid.*, 51). Abraham restates the basic rationalistic principle of faith and exegesis:

> Know ye God's people and His heritage, that God differentiated men from animals and beasts through the reason, wisdom, and understanding which He granted them. He also differentiated Israel from the gentiles through the Torah He gave them and the precepts He commanded them. Hence reason preceded Torah, both in creation of the world, and in each and every one living in it. Reason has been given to a man since the six days of creation; Torah was given to man 4,448 years after creation. Should someone say to you, But the sages have explained that the Torah was created two thousand years before the world,' you should reply that this Midrash needs many commentaries to justify it. It is impossible to take it in its simple sense . . . Reason was implanted in each and every one of the seed of Israel before his knowledge of Torah. Know and understand that it is because the child's reason is not yet ripe, that God did not oblige him to fulfill commandments (*ibid.*, 57–58).

While this blast was going forth from the East, extremists from the West caused the desecration of Maimonides' tomb at Tiberias, which shocked not only the Maimonidean camp but also the majority of the anti-Maimonideans. When in the early 1240s the Disputation of Paris and the burning of the Talmud added shock to shock, public quarrels among Jews were set aside for several decades. It remains a much disputed point whether the Dominicans set fire to Maimonides' writings on their own initiative, scenting heresy wherever they could find it, or whether their action resulted from a denunciation by Jews, as contemporary Maimonideans believed. Neither the social nor the cultural motivating forces of the controversy disappeared with the cessation of polemics. The rise of kabbalistic circles and literature (see *Zohar) on the one hand, and the continuing philosophical activity and way of life of the upper and "professional" circles of Jewish society on the other implied a continuation and an intensification of the struggle between rationalists and anti-rationalists.

The Renewed Outbreak. When the controversy flared up again at the end of the 13th and beginning of the 14th century, the immediate catalyst was the extreme allegorical exegesis of certain rationalists. However, it came to encompass the whole range of the content of Jewish education and the question of the possibility or impossibility of synthesis between "Greek wisdom" and the Torah of Moses. Abba Mari Astruc of Lunel turned to Solomon b. Abraham Adret for guidance on these allegorical interpretations, to his mind heretical ones (see the exchange of letters initiated by him in his *Minḥat Kena'ot* (1838); this collection has been altered to a large extent by tendentious editing). After much hesitation, and spurred on by the influence of Asher b. Jehiel, Solomon b. Abraham Adret and the Barcelona community issued a *ḥerem* on July 26, 1305, against "any member of the community who, being under the age of 25 years, shall study the works of the Greeks on natural science or metaphysics, whether in the original language or in translation."

Works by Jewish philosophers were excepted, as was the study of medicine. The ban was intended to prevent young men from being influenced by Greek philosophy to turn away "from the Torah of Israel which is above these sciences. How can any man dare to judge between human wisdom based on analogy, proof, and thought, and the wisdom of God, between whom and us there is no relation nor similarity? Will man, who is embodied in a vessel of clay, judge . . .

God his creator to say, God forbid, what is possible and what he cannot do? Truly this, sometimes leads to utter heresy" (Resp. Rashba pt. 1, no. 415). A ban was also pronounced against all who "say about Abraham and Sarah that in reality they symbolize matter and form; that the 12 tribes of Israel are [an allegory] for the 12 planets . . . [and] that the Urim and Thummim are to be understood as the astrolabe instrument . . . Some of them say that everything in the Torah, from *Bereshit* to the giving of the law, is entirely allegorical" (*ibid.*, no. 416).

The condemnation of extreme allegory did not arouse opposition, but the prohibition on the study of "Greek wisdom" until the age of 25 was sharply opposed on grounds of principle, though to Adret and his group this formula was certainly in many respects a compromise. Among the many communities and individual sages in Provence and Spain who opposed the ban, the great talmudic scholar Menahem b. Solomon Meiri was one of the most eloquent voices. In his counter-*ḥerem* (printed in excerpts in *Jubelschrift . . . L. Zunz* (1884), Heb. pt. 153–72) he reminded Adret of the failure of the early 13th-century attacks against Maimonides. Rejecting insinuations that the study of philosophy causes heresy, he pointed to many talmudic scholars who were students of philosophy. Meiri stressed that sciences such as mathematics were necessary for the understanding of many passages in the Talmud. He regarded the prohibition against certain types of study as self-defeating: "Each individual [nature] will search for what suits him according to his natural inclination." This trait of human intellect and nature, he maintains, will even cause the second generation of the excommunicating community to seek ways out of this prohibition. Meiri was well aware that there was a more radical wing among the rationalists, which he opposed (see his commentary to Psalms, ed. by J. Cohn (1936), e.g., ch. 36, p. 78f., and many passages in his commentary to Proverbs and to Mishnah Avot).

Finally, Jedaiah b. Abraham Bedersi (ha-Penini) wrote Adret a "letter of apology"—actually a sharp attack against the anti-rationalists—basing himself on the spiritual greatness of Provençal Jews and praising rationalism and philosophy. He daringly proclaims:

> My rabbis, please look into the mighty pattern of the benefits of philosophy to all of us, even to those who despise it. For it is extremely well-known that in ancient times anthropomorphism was widespread, one may say almost in the entire Diaspora of Israel . . . but in every generation there arose *geonim* and sages—in Spain, in Babylonia and in the cities of Andalusia—who, thanks to their familiarity with the Arabic language, had the great opportunity to smell the perfume of the sciences, some much, some a little, for they are translated into this language. It is thanks to this that they began to elaborate and clarify many of their opinions on the Torah, above all as to the unity of God and the abolition of anthropomorphism, especially by the philosophical proofs taken from scientific works.

He goes on to list this rationalistic literature, from the days of Saadiah Gaon onward (Resp. Rashba pt. 1., no. 418). This long epistle concludes:

> Relinquish your *ḥerem* for the heart of this people will not turn away from philosophy and its books as long as there is breath in their frame and soul in their bodies, especially as together with it [i.e., with devotion to philosophy], they are true to Torah and commandments. Even if they had heard it from the mouth of Joshua bin Nun they would never have accepted it, for they intend to do battle for the honor of the great teacher [i.e., Maimonides] and his works; and for the holiness of his teaching they will sacrifice fortune, family, and soul as long as there is a breath in their bodies. And thus they will teach and command their children in generations to come *(ibid.)*.

On this sharp though inconclusive note, the great controversy of the early 14th century petered out.

Aftermath of the Controversy. The tension between rationalists and antirationalists never abated throughout the Middle Ages. Among the beleaguered Jews of 15th-century Christian Spain, Maimonidean rationalism was seen by many as the root cause of the misfortunes and the reason for *apostasy. On the other hand a man like Abraham *Bibago, throughout his *Derekh Emunah,* defended rationalism, not only as being justified but as the very essence of Judaism. Proudly calling himself "a pupil of Maimonides," he believed that the Jewish people is the bearer of reason—weak in this world as reason is weak against the unreasonable passions. Generalizing the traditional rationalistic view, he stated:

> The reasonable creature having reason has to study the sciences; and being a believer, he will study Torah and acquire faith and its roots and dogmas. The first study will be a kind of carrier and vessel to bear the second study. In the same way that life is an assumption and carrier by which humanity and speech are carried, so through the form of reason—by whose accomplishment one studies and acquires the sciences—Torah study will be assumed and carried. Thus faith will be complete and without doubt, and the one attitude [faith], will not conflict with the other [philosophy]. Therefore did the sage say, 'Reason and faith are two lights.' To solve all doubts we must explain that 'Greek wisdom' cannot be the above-mentioned wisdom of reason belonging to man insofar as he is a man. Hence it is a human wisdom and not a Greek one. The wisdom called [by talmudic sages] 'Greek wisdom,' must be something peculiar to the Greeks and not to another nation (see above, pt. 2, ch. 3, 46a).

That views like this were acceptable also among 16th-century Ashkenazi Jewry is proved by the fact that the *Sefer ha-Miknah* by *Joseph b. Gershom of Rosheim is in reality a kind of synopsis of Bibago's *Derekh Emunah.* In Renaissance Italy Jehiel b. Samuel of *Pisa wrote a detailed treatise *(Minḥat Kena'ot)* against rationalism, while the life and works of many of his contemporaries and countrymen constituted a clear espousal of it. In Poland-Lithuania in the 16th–17th centuries the tension between Maimonideans and anti-Maimonideans likewise continued, as evidenced, for example, by the dispute between Moses *Isserles and Solomon b. Jehiel *Luria (see Moses Isserles, Resp., nos. 687; and see also his *Torat ha-Olah*).

The problems of the synthesis between Judaism and other cultures, of the proper content of Jewish education, and of the right way to God—through reason or through mystic union—has remained, though formulations and expressions have changed considerably. The old hierarchical basis of Jewish leadership, wholeheartedly hated by Maimonides, has disappeared, but the leadership of the individual scholar, even after Maimonides, retained many hierarchical and sacral elements (see **Semikhah*). The *Mishneh Torah* did not supersede the Talmud, and Maimonides' aristocratic opposition to monetary support for Torah study failed completely. So strong was his personality, however, that most of his opponents made great efforts to say that they opposed not Maimonides himself but some element of his teaching or, better still, some misguided interpretation or citation of his work. The Maimonidean controversy is both very specifically at the heart of Jewish culture and, at the same time, part of a set of problems central to Judaism, Islam, and Christianity alike.

See also *Heresy.

Bibliography: D. J. Silver, *Maimonidean Criticism and the Maimonidean Controversy, 1180–1240* (1965), bibl., 199–210; S. Z. Halberstam, in: *Jeschurun* (Kobak), 8 pt. 1–2 (1871), Heb. pt. 17–56; pt. 3–4 (1895), Heb. pt. 89–100; J. Sarachek, *Faith and Reason: the Conflict over the Rationalism of Maimonides* (1935); H. H. Ben-Sasson, in: *Ha-Ishiyyut ve-Dorah* (1963), 93–106; idem, *Toledot Am Yisrael,* 2 (1969), 155–8, 216–23, 303–6; I. Twersky, *Rabad of Posquières* (1962); idem, in: *Journal of World History,* 11 (1968), 185–207; A. S. Halkin, in: *Perakim,* 1 (1968), 35–55; Baer, Spain, index; Schatzmueller, in: *Zion,* 34 (1969), 126–44; idem, in: *Meḥkarim le-Zekher Ẓevi Avneri* (1970), 129–40; Dinur, Golah.

[H. H. B.-S.]

MAIMONIDES, MOSES (**Moses ben Maimon;** known in rabbinical literature as **"Rambam";** from the acronym **R**abbi **M**oses **B**en **M**aimon; 1135–1204), rabbinic authority, codifier, philosopher, and royal physician.

BIOGRAPHY

The most illustrious figure in Judaism in the post-talmudic era, and one of the greatest of all time, Maimonides was born in Cordoba, Spain, to his father *Maimon, *dayyan* of Cordoba and himself a renowned scholar and pupil of Joseph *ibn Migash. He continues his genealogy, "the son of the learned Joseph, son of Isaac the *dayyan,* son of Joseph the *dayyan,* son of Obadiah the *dayyan,* son of the rabbi Solomon, son of Obadiah" (end of commentary to Mishnah); traditions extend the genealogy to R. Judah ha-Nasi. Posterity even recorded the day and hour and even minute of his birth, "On the eve of Passover (the 14th of Nisan) which was a Sabbath, an hour and a third after midday, in the year 4895 (1135) of the Creation" *(Sefer Yuḥasin)*. Maimonides' grandson David gives the same day and year without the hour (at the beginning of his commentary to tractate *Rosh Ha-Shanah*).

As a result of the fall of Cordoba to the *Almohads in May or June, 1148, when Moses had just reached his 13th birthday, and the consequent religious persecution, Maimon was obliged to leave Cordoba with his family and all trace of them is lost for the next eight or nine years, which they spent wandering from place to place in Spain (and possibly Provence) until in 1160 they settled in Fez. Yet it was during those years of wandering, which Maimonides himself describes as a period "while my mind was troubled, and amid divinely ordained exiles, on journeys by land and tossed on the tempests of the sea" (end of commentary to Mishnah) that he laid the strong foundations of his vast and varied learning and even began his literary work. Not only did he begin the draft of the *Sirāj,* his important commentary on the Mishnah, in 1158, but in that same year, at the request of a friend, he wrote a short treatise on the Jewish calendar *(Ma'amar ha-Ibbur)* and one on logic *(Millot Higgayon)* and had completed writing notes for a commentary on a number of tractates of the Babylonian Talmud, and a work whose aim was to extract the *halakhah* from the Jerusalem Talmud (see below Maimonides as halakhist). According to Muslim authorities the family became formally converted to Islam somewhere in the period between 1150 and 1160. But Saadiah ibn Danan (Z. Edelmann (ed.), *Ḥemdah Genuzah* (1856), 16a) relates that

Figure 1. Traditional portrait of Maimonides from Ugolinus' *Thesaurus Antiquitatum Sacrarum*, Venice, 1744.

the Muslims maintain the same about many Jewish scholars, among them Dunash ibn Tamim, Ḥasdai b. Ḥasdai, and others. In any case in the year 1160 Maimon and his sons, Moses and David, and a daughter, were in Fez. In his old age ʿAbd al-Muʾmin, the Almohad ruler, somewhat changed his attitude to the Jews, becoming more moderate toward those who were living in the central, Moroccan, part of his realm. It was probably on account of this that in 1159 or early in 1160 Maimon deemed it worthwhile to emigrate with his family to Morocco and settle in Fez. Living in Fez at that time was R. Judah ha-Kohen ibn Susan, whose fame for learning and piety had spread to Spain, and Maimonides, then 25, studied under him. Many Jews had outwardly adopted Islam and their consciences were troubling them, and this prompted Maimon to write his *Iggeret ha-Neḥamah* ("Letter of Consolation") assuring them that he who says his prayers even in their shortest form and who does good works remains a Jew (*Ḥemdah Genuzah*, pp. LXXIV–LXXXII). Meantime his son worked at his commentary on the Mishnah and also continued his general studies, particularly medicine; in his medical works he frequently refers to the knowledge and experience he gained among the Muslims in North Africa (see Maimonides as physician). Here also he wrote his *Iggeret ha-Shemad* ("Letter on Forced Conversion") also called *Iggeret Kiddush ha-Shem* ("Letter of the Sanctification of the Divine Name"). These letters of father and son, as well as Maimonides' utterances after leaving Morocco, do not point to outrages and bloody persecutions. Although Maimonides in the opening lines of the *Iggeret ha-Shemad* most strongly deprecates the condemnation of the forced converts by "the self-styled sage who has never experienced what so many Jewish communities experienced in the way of persecution," his conclusion is that a Jew must leave the country where he is forced to transgress the divine law: "He should not remain in the realm of that king; he should sit in his house until he emigrates . . ." And once more, with greater insistence: "He should on no account remain in a place of forced conversion; whoever remains in such a place desecrates the Divine Name and is nearly as bad as a willful sinner; as for those who beguile themselves, saying that they will remain until the Messiah comes to the Maghreb and leads them to Jerusalem, I do not know how he is to cleanse them of the stigma of conversion" (*Iggeret ha-Shemad*, in: Z. Edelmann (ed.), *Ḥemdah Genuzah*, 11b–12a).

Maimon and his sons acted in accordance with this advice, as certainly did many others. Maimonides' departure from the country of the Almohads is commonly assumed to have taken place in 1165; according to Saadiah ibn Danan (*Seder ha-Dorot*, in: *Ḥemdah Genuzah*, 30b.), it was promoted by the martyrdom of Judah ibn Susan, who had been called upon to forsake his religion and had preferred death to apostasy. R. Maimon and his family escaped from Fez, and a month later they landed at Acre. The day of his departure as well as that on which the ship was saved from a tempest were instituted as a family fast enjoined on his descendants, and that of his arrival in Ereẓ Israel as a festival (E. Azikri (Azcari), *Sefer Ḥaredim*; Maim. Comm. to *Rosh Ha-Shanah*, ed. Brill, end).

The family remained in Acre for some five months, striking up an intimate friendship there with the *dayyan* Japheth b. Ali. Together with him they made a tour of the Holy Land, visiting Jerusalem where Maimonides states, "I entered the [site of the] Great and Holy House and prayed there on Thursday the 6th day of Marḥeshvan." Three days later they paid a visit to the Cave of Machpelah in Hebron for the same purpose. Maimonides also appointed both these days as family festivals. The family then left Ereẓ Israel and sailed for Egypt. After a short stay at Alexandria they moved to Cairo and took up residence in Fostat, the Old City of Cairo.

Maimon died at this time either in Ereẓ Israel or in Egypt. It has been suggested that the reason for the choice of Alexandria was the existence at that time "outside the town" of "the academy of Aristotle, the teacher of Alexander" to which "people from the whole world came in order to study the wisdom of Aristotle the philosopher" mentioned by Benjamin of Tudela (ed. by M. N. Adler (1907), 75). It is not certain what prompted the move to Cairo. That Maimonides' influence was decisive in virtually destroying the hitherto dominating influence of the Karaites who were more numerous and wealthy than the Rabbanites in Cairo is beyond doubt (see below) and in the 17th century Jacob Farajī, a *dayyan* in Egypt, states that it was this challenge which impelled Maimonides to move to Cairo (see Azulai, letter M150).

For eight years Maimonides lived a life free from care. Supported by his brother David who dealt in precious stones, he was able to devote himself entirely to preparing his works for publication and to his onerous but honorary work as both religious and lay leader of the community. His *Sirāj*, the commentary to the Mishnah, was completed in 1168. The following year he suffered a crushing blow. His brother David drowned in the Indian Ocean while on a business trip, leaving a wife and two children, and with him were lost not only the family fortune but moneys belonging to others. Maimonides took the blow badly. For a full year he lay almost prostrate, and then he had to seek a means of livelihood. Rejecting the thought of earning a livelihood from Torah (see his commentary on *Avot* 5:4, and especially his letter to Joseph ibn Sham'un in 1191, "It is better for you to earn a drachma as a weaver, or tailor, or carpenter than to be dependent on the license of the exilarch [to accept a paid position as a rabbi]"; F. Kobler (ed.),

Figure 2. Traditional birthplace of Maimonides in the old ghetto of Córdoba. Courtesy H. Schieber, Netanyah.

Letters of Jews Through the Ages, 1 (1952), 207) and he decided to make the medical profession his livelihood.

Fame in his calling did not come to him at once. It was only after 1185 when he was appointed one of the physicians to al-Faḍil, who had been appointed vizier by Saladin and was virtual ruler of Egypt after Saladin's departure from that country in 1174, that his fame began to spread. It gave rise to a legend that Richard the Lionhearted "the King of the Franks in Ascalon" sought his services as his private physician. About 1177 he was recognized as the official head of the Fostat community. Ibn Danan says of him, "Rabbenu Moshe [b. Maimon] became very great in wisdom, learning, and rank." In the so-called *Megillat Zuta* he is called "the light of east and west and unique master and marvel of the generation."

These were the most fruitful and busy years of his life. His first wife had died young and in Egypt he remarried, taking as his wife the sister of Ibn Almali, one of the royal secretaries, who himself married Maimonides' only sister. To them was born their only son Abraham to whose education he lovingly devoted himself, and an added solace was his enthusiastic disciple Joseph ibn Sham'un (not Ibn Aknin, as often stated), whom he loved as a son, and for whom he wrote, and sent chapter by chapter, his *Guide of the Perplexed*. It was during those years, busy as he was with the heavy burden of his practice and occupied with the affairs of the community, writing his extensive correspondence to every part of the Jewish world (apart from the Franco-German area), that he wrote the two monumental works upon which his fame chiefly rests, the *Mishneh Torah* (compiled 1180) and the *Guide* (1190; according to Z. Diesendruck, in: HUCA, 12–13 (1937–38), 461–97, in 1185), as well as his *Iggeret Teiman* and his *Ma'amar Teḥiyyat ha-Metim*.

The following passage in the letter to the translator of the *Guide*, Samuel b. Judah ibn *Tibbon, in which he describes his multifarious cares and duties, with the aim of dissuading Ibn Tibbon from coming to visit him, has often been quoted:

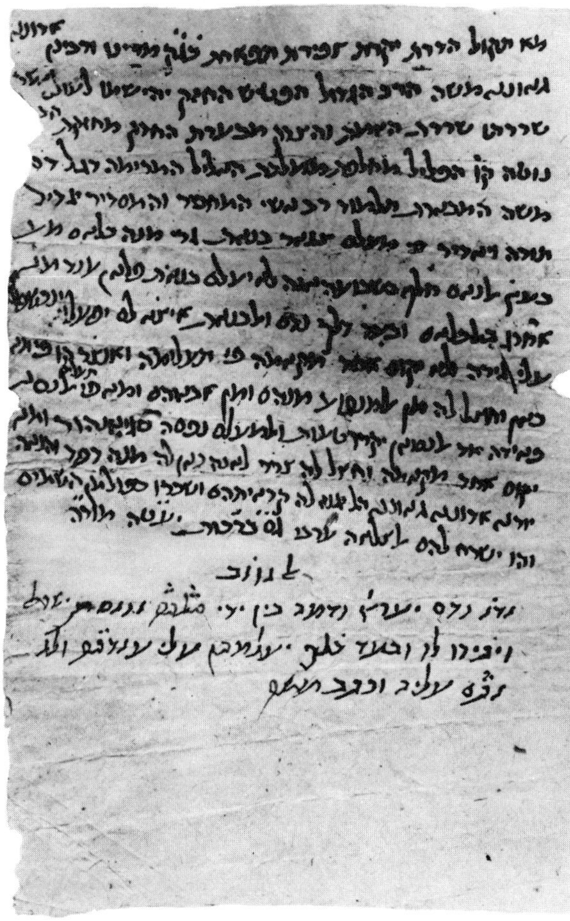

Figure 3. Autograph responsum of Maimonides, written in Hebrew and Arabic in Hebrew characters, found in the Cairo *Genizah*. London, British Museum, Ms. Or. 5519B.

I dwell at Miṣr [Fostat] and the sultan resides at al-Qāhira [Cairo]; these two places are two Sabbath days' journey distant from each other. My duties to the sultan are very heavy. I am obliged to visit him every day, early in the morning; and when he or any of his children, or any of the inmates of his harem, are indisposed, I dare not quit al-Qāhira, but must stay during the greater part of the day in the palace. It also frequently happens that one or two royal officers fall sick, and I must attend to their healing. Hence, as a rule, I repair to al-Qāhira very early in the day, and even if nothing unusual happens, I do not return to Miṣr until the afternoon. Then I am almost dying with hunger . . . I find the antechambers filled with people, both Jews and gentiles, nobles and common people, judges and bailiffs, friends and foes—a mixed multitude who await the time of my return.

I dismount from my animal, wash my hands, go forth to my patients, and entreat them to bear with me while I partake of some slight refreshment, the only meal I take in the twenty-four hours. Then I go forth to attend to my patients, and write prescriptions and directions for their various ailments. Patients go in and out until nightfall, and sometimes even, I solemnly assure you, until two hours or more in the night. I converse with and prescribe for them while lying down from sheer fatigue; and when night falls, I am so exhausted that I can scarcely speak.

In consequence of this, no Israelite can have any private interview with me, except on the Sabbath. On that day the whole congregation, or at least the majority of the members, come to me after the morning service, when I instruct them as to their proceedings during the whole week; we study together a little until noon, when they depart. Some of them return, and read with me after the afternoon service until evening prayers. In this manner I spend that day.

The two major works will be described below, but something must be said of the two letters. The Arab ruler in Yemen, who, unlike the sultans in Egypt who were Sunnites, belonged to the sectarian Shiʿites, instituted a religious persecution, giving the Jews the choice of conversion to Islam or death. Not only did many succumb, but there arose among those Jews a pseudo-Messiah, or a forerunner of the Messiah who, seeing in these events the darkness before the dawn, preached the imminent advent of the Messianic Age. In despair the Jews of Yemen turned to Maimonides, who probably in 1172 answered their request with the *Iggeret Teiman (al-Risāla al-Yamaniyya)*. It was addressed to R. *Jacob b. Nethanel al-Fayyumi, with a request that copies be sent to every community in Yemen. Deliberately couched in simple terms, "that men, women, and children could read it easily," he pointed out that the subtle attack of Christianity and Islam which preached a new revelation was more dangerous than the sword and than the attractions of Hellenism. As for the pseudo-Messiah, he was unbalanced and he was to be rejected. These trials were sent to prove the Jews.

The effect of the letter was tremendous. In gratitude for the message of hope, combined with the fact that Maimonides also used his influence at court to obtain a lessening of the heavy burden of taxation on the Jews of Yemen, the Jews of Yemen introduced into the *Kaddish a prayer for "the life of our teacher Moses b. Maimon" (Letter of Naḥmanides to the rabbis of France, in: *Kitvei Ramban*, ed. by C. B. Chavel (1963), 341).

This remarkable tribute, usually reserved for the exilarch,

has an indirect connection with the third of his public (as distinct from his private) letters, the *Ma'amar Teḥiyyat ha-Metim* ("On Resurrection"; 1191). Maimonides wrote the letter with the greatest reluctance. It was the direct result of his *Mishneh Torah* and constituted his reply to the accusation leveled against him that in this work he denied, or did not mention, the doctrine of personal resurrection which was a fundamental principle of faith among the Jews of his time. An objective study of his work does lend a certain basis to the allegation. It is true, as he indignantly protests, that he included this doctrine as the last of his famous Thirteen Principles of Judaism, but in his *Mishneh Torah* the undoubted emphasis is on the immortality of the soul and not on individual bodily resurrection. That the allegation was not based upon mere malice or envy of his work is sufficiently proved by the fact that anxious queries were addressed to him from the countries in which he was most fervently admired, Yemen and Provence, and Maimonides answered them. Abraham b. David of Posquières wrote: "The words of this man seem to me to be very near to him who says there is no resurrection of the body, but only of the soul. By my life, this is not the view of the sages" (Comm. to Yad, Teshuvah 8:2). Some Jews from Yemen however, unsatisfied, wrote to *Samuel b. Ali the powerful and learned *gaon* in Baghdad who sent a reply, which although couched in terms of respect to Maimonides, vigorously denounced his views. It would appear that the vehemence of this reply was connected with Samuel's desire to assert his authority as *gaon* over Egypt, which he thought was being usurped by Maimonides. On the other hand, Maimonides held the exilarch Samuel (of Josiah b. Zakkai's line), the successor of the exilarch Daniel b. Ḥisdai, in higher esteem than the *gaon* Samuel b. Ali. Thus the relations between Maimonides and the *gaon* remained strained, although there was never open hostility. Joseph ibn Sham'un, in Baghdad, who had also queried Maimonides' views on resurrection, sent a copy of Samuel's reply to Maimonides and with great reluctance Maimonides felt himself compelled to write his *Ma'amar Teḥiyyat ha-Metim* in which he asserted and confirmed his belief in the doctrine.

Maimonides was active as head of the community. He took vigorous steps to deal with the Karaites, and as a result brought about the supremacy of the Rabbanites in Cairo. On the one hand he emphatically maintained that they were to be regarded as Jews, with all the attendant privileges. They might be visited, their dead buried, and their children circumcised, their wine permitted; they were however not to be included in a religious quorum (Resp. ed. Blau, 449). Only when they flouted rabbinic Judaism was a barrier to be maintained. One was particularly to avoid visiting them on their festivals which did not coincide with the dates fixed by the rabbinic calendar. One of the inroads which they had caused in orthodox observance was with regard to ritual immersion for the **niddah*. Their view that an ordinary bath was sufficient had been widely adopted among the Rabbanites. Maimonides succeeded in restoring rabbinic practice in this matter, but generally his policy toward the Karaites was more lenient in his later years, and was continued by his son Abraham. (For an exhaustive treatment of this subject see C. Tchernowitz, *Toledot ha-Posekim* (1946), 197–208.)

Figure 4. Traditional likenesses of Maimonides used as stamp designs. Right, issue by the Israel Post Office to mark the International Congress of the History of Science, 1953. Left, issue by the Spanish Post Office, 1967. Jerusalem, B. M. Ansbacher Collection.

Maimonides made various changes in liturgical custom, the most radical of which was the abolition of the repetition of the **Amidah* in the interests of decorum. With the completion of the *Guide* Maimonides' literary work, apart from his extensive correspondence, came to an end. In failing health he nevertheless continued his work as head of the Jewish community and as court physician. (It is doubtful whether he actually held the appointment of *nagid* as is usually stated; see M. D. Rabinowitz, Introduction to *Ma'amar Teḥiyyat ha-Metim* in *Iggerot ha-Rambam*, 220-7.)

It was during this period however that he engaged in his correspondence with the scholars of Provence in general and with Jonathan of Lunel in particular. In some instances the border line between responsum and letter is not clearly defined (e.g., his letter to Obadiah the Proselyte, see below), but, as Kobler comments, the letters of Maimonides mark an epoch in letter writing. He is the first Jewish letter writer whose correspondence has been largely preserved. Vigorous and essentially personal, his letters found their way to the mind and heart of his correspondents, and he varied his style to suit them. But above all they reveal his whole personality, which is different from what might be expected from his *Mishneh Torah* and the *Guide*. The picture of an almost austere and aloof intellectual above human passions and emotions derived from there is completely dispelled.

Maimonides died on December 13, 1204. There were almost universal expressions of grief. Public mourning was ordained in all parts of the Jewish world. In Fostat mourning was ordained for three days and in Jerusalem a public fast and the Scriptural readings instituted concluded with the verse "the glory is departed from Israel, for the Ark of the Lord is taken" (I Sam. 4:22). His remains were taken to Tiberias for burial, and his grave is still an object of pilgrimage.

Influence. The influence of Maimonides on the future development of Judaism is incalculable. No spiritual leader of the Jewish people in the post-talmudic period has exercised such an influence both in his own and subsequent generations. Despite the vehement opposition which greeted his philosophical views the breach was healed (see *Maimonidean Controversy). It is significant that when Solomon *Luria strongly criticised Moses Isserles for his devotion to Greek philosophy, Isserles answered that his sole source was Maimonides' *Guide*, thus giving it the cachet of acceptability (Resp. Isserles 7). It was probably due to his unrivaled eminence as talmudist and codifier that many of his views were finally accepted. They were very radical at the time. To give but one example, the now universally accepted doctrine of the incorporeality of God was by no means accepted as fundamental before him and was probably an advanced view held by a small group of thinkers and philosophers. Even Abraham b. David of Posquières protested the statement of Maimonides that

Figure 5. Opening page of the first book of the *Mishneh Torah, Sefer ha-Madda*. South Germany, 1310. Budapest, Library of the Hungarian Academy of Sciences, Kaufmann Collection, Ms. A 78 I, fol. 8v.

anyone who maintains the corporeality of God is a sectarian: "Why does he call him a sectarian? Many greater and better than he accepted this idea [of the corporeality of God] basing themselves on Scripture" (Yad, Teshuvah 3:7). C. Tchernowitz (*Toledot ha-Posekim*, 1 (1946), 193) goes so far as to maintain that were it not for Maimonides Judaism would have broken up into different sects and beliefs, and that it was his great achievement to unite the various currents, halakhic and philosophic.

Maimonides is regarded as the supreme rationalist, and the title given by Aḥad Ha-Am to his essay on him, *"Shilton ha-Sekhel"* ("The Rule of Reason"; in: *Ha-Shilo'aḥ*, 15 (1905), 291–319) included in his collected works, *Al Parashat Derakhim* (1921), has become almost standard in referring to him, and so long as one confines oneself to his three great works, the commentary on the Mishnah, the *Mishneh Torah*, and the *Guide*, a case can be made out for this view.

In the *Mishneh Torah* Maimonides rigidly confines himself to a codification of Jewish law, refraining almost entirely from allowing his personal views to obtrude. Where he does advance his own view to which he can find no talmudic authority, he is careful, as he explicitly states in a letter to Jonathan of Lunel, to introduce it with the words "it appears to me" (cf. Yad, Sanhedrin 4:11). From his knowledge of medicine he was aware that certain disabilities in animals which in the time of the Talmud were regarded as fatal were susceptible to cure, while some which were not so regarded were in fact fatal, yet he lays it down that the talmudic view must be applied (Sheḥitah 10:12 and 13). Among the few exceptions the most striking is his outburst against belief in witchcraft and enchantment. After faithfully giving in their minutest details the talmudic description of, and laws concerning, these practices, he adds: "All these and similar matters are lies and falsehood ... it is not fitting for Jews, who are intelligent and wise, to be attracted by them or believe that they are effective ... whosoever believes in them, and that they are true, only that the Bible has forbidden them, belongs to the category of fools and ignoramuses and is in the class of immature women and children" (*Avodat Kokhavim* 11:16). In his work on the calendar included in the *Mishneh Torah* (*Hilkhot Kiddush ha-Ḥodesh*) he maintains vigorously that one should have recourse to works written by non-Jewish astronomers (11:1–6). At the end of *Hilkhot Temurah*, he defends the search after reasons for the biblical commandments (4:13).

In the *Guide* he allows himself more freedom, but the main difference between the two works lies in their different purpose and aim. The *Mishneh Torah* was written for the believing Jew untroubled by the apparent contradictions between revealed law and current philosophy, and its aim was to tell him how he should conduct himself in his desire to live according to the law. The *Guide*, as its name conveys, was designed for those whose faith had been weakened by these doctrines and its aim was to tell him why he should adhere to traditional Judaism. This helps to explain the contradictions between the two.

In both works one sees only the unemotional man of intellect. It is in his letters that Maimonides emerges as the warm human being, his heart open to the suffering of his people, and expressing and responding to both affection and hostility. It comes almost as a shock to read in his letter to Japheth b. Ali, when he informs him of the death of his brother David, that he remonstrates with him for not sending a letter of condolence to him on the death of his father which took place 11 years earlier though he had received innumerable such messages from all over the Jewish world, repeating the complaint twice. The letter was

Figure 6. Title page, with list of contents, of the fifth book of the *Mishneh Torah*, Portugal, c. 1472. London, British Museum, Harl. 5698, fol. 252b.

Figure 7. Title page of Maimonides' *Moreh Nevukhim (Guide of the Perplexed)*, Warsaw, 1872. Jerusalem. Courtesy B. M. Ansbacher.

written eight years after his brother's death, yet he writes, "I still mourn, and there is no comfort . . . Whenever I come across his handwriting or one of his books, my heart goes faint within me, and my grief reawakens" and in that letter he continues that he will never forget those days which he passed in Ereẓ Israel with his correspondent (Kobler 192–3). The personal human element is equally to the fore in the above-quoted letter to Samuel ibn Tibbon, while his letter-responsum to Obadiah the Proselyte reveals Maimonides' spirit to the full. It was surely only to his intimate disciple that he could open his heart and declare, "when I see no other way of teaching a well-established truth except by pleasing one intelligent man and displeasing ten thousand fools, I choose to address myself to the one man and take no notice whatsoever of the condemnation of the multitude" (Introduction to the *Guide*). On the other hand Maimonides is almost virulent in his opposition to songs and music: "song and music are all forbidden, even if unaccompanied by words . . . there is no difference between listening to songs, or string music, or melodies without words; everything which conduces to the rejoicing of the soul and emotion is forbidden." It is immaterial whether they are in Arabic or in Hebrew. "A person who listens to foolish songs with musical accompaniment is guilty of three transgressions, listening to folly, listening to song, and listening to instrumental music. If the songs are sung with accompaniment of drinking, there is a fourth transgression, if the singer is a woman there is a fifth." The references in the geonic sources to singing are only to liturgical hymns (Resp. ed. Blau, 224. cf. 269; Guide 3:8; Yad, Ta'anit, 5:14). Despite this last permission he was opposed to the insertion of *piyyutim* in the prayers (180, 207, 254, 260, 261). If the ignorant insist on them and their ways prevail, they should be said before the *Shema*, the beginning of the essential service (207).

No praise can be too high for the outer form of his works, both in language and logical method. The *Mishneh Torah* was the only work which he wrote in Hebrew, and the language is superb, clear, and succinct. He regretted that he did not prepare Hebrew versions of his other works. In answer to Joseph b. Gabir's request written in 1191 that he translate the work into Arabic, not only does he state that it would thereby lose its specific character, but that he would have liked to translate his works written in Arabic into Hebrew (Kobler 199); and when the rabbis of Lunel asked him to translate the *Guide* into Hebrew, he stated that he wished he were young enough to do so (*ibid.*, 216).

The *Mishneh Torah* is a model of logical sequence and studied method, each chapter and each paragraph coming in natural sequence to its preceding one. More impressive is the fact that in his earliest work one can so clearly discern the seeds of the later, so that it can confidently be stated that his whole subsequent system and ideas were already formulated in his mind when he wrote it. The *Shemonah Perakim* which form the introduction to his commentary on *Avot* is almost a draft of the first portion of *Sefer Madda*, the first book of the *Mishneh Torah*. When attacked on his views on resurrection he pointed out that he had included it in the Thirteen Principles which he evolved in his commentary to the tenth chapter of *Sanhedrin*. The radical view found in the very last chapter of the *Mishneh Torah* that the messianic age is nothing more than the attainment of political independence in Israel is stated in detail in that same excursus, and his original view on the possibility of the reestablishment of the Sanhedrin, which he carefully puts forward as his own ("it appears to me") and which he qualifies by the statement "but the matter must be weighed up" (Sanhedrin 4:11), is already expressed in his commentary on the Mishnah (Sanh. 1:1). [L.I.R.]

AS HALAKHIST

Maimonides' halakhic activity began during his youth with his commentary to some tractates of the Talmud (introduction to commentary to the Mishnah). Only fragments on several tractates have survived (see S. Asaf, in: *Sinai*, 6 (1940), 103–32, on *Shabbat*; M. Kamelhar (1956) on *Yoma*): the commentary to *Rosh Ha-Shanah*, published in its entirety (by J. Brill, 1865; Y. A. Kamelhar, 1906), is of doubtful authenticity (see M. J. L. Sachs, *Ḥiddushei ha-RaMBaM la-Talmud* (1963), introd. 13–23). His *Hilkhot ha-Yerushalmi* ("Laws of the Palestinian Talmud"), alluded to in his commentary to the Mishnah (Tamid 5:1), is not extant; the authenticity of the fragments published by Saul Lieberman (1947) has been challenged (Benedikt in: KS, 27 (1950–51), 329–49). It is interesting to note, in view of the fact that his famous code, the *Mishneh Torah*, embraces the whole of

Figure 8. Tomb of Maimonides in Tiberias. Photo Zev Radovan, Jerusalem.

Jewish law, both practical and theoretical, that in both these works he confined himself to the practical *halakhah*, his commentary on the Talmud being confined to the orders **Mo'ed*, **Nashim*, and **Nezikin* and the tractate **Hullin*, which deals with dietary laws.

Commentary to the Mishnah. It is through his commentary to the Mishnah that one can begin to review Maimonides as a halakhist. In his commentary, Maimonides sets out to explain to the general reader the meaning of the Mishnah, without having recourse to the involved and lengthy discussions in the *Gemara*, the language of which was more difficult than the Mishnah itself (*Mishneh Torah*, introd.). Out of the mishnaic and other tannaitic texts and corresponding passages in the *Gemara*, often widely scattered throughout the Talmud, Maimonides evolves the underlying principles of the subjects discussed, which a particular Mishnah, chapter, or entire tractate presupposed. In some cases he interprets the Mishnah differently from the *Gemara* (cf. in Sanh. 1:1). It has been asserted that even during his early work as a commentator, Maimonides was at the same time a codifier, a role which he later successfully developed in the *Sefer ha-Mitzvot* and the *Mishneh Torah* (M. Guttmann, in: J. Guttmann et al. (eds.), *Moses ben Maimon*, 2 (1914), 306–30; idem, in: HUCA, 2 (1925), 229–68). Following his explanatory glosses to the mishnaic passage, Maimonides gave the halakhic decision in each Mishnah based on his reading of the discussion in the *Gemara*.

Of special significance are the lengthy introductions he included in his commentary. The general introduction which heads his commentary to the order of *Zera'im* is in reality an introduction to and history of the Oral Law from Moses until his own days. The introduction to *Avot*, known as the *Shemonah Perakim* ("Eight Chapters") is a philosophical and ethical treatise in which its author harmonized Aristotle's ethics with rabbinical teachings. In the introduction to Mishnah *Sanhedrin* (10:1), which begins with the words "All Israel has a portion in the world to come," Maimonides dealt at length with the fundamental doctrines of Judaism which are formulated in the Thirteen *Articles of Faith. Especially extensive and exhaustive is the introduction to the difficult order *Tohorot*, in which Maimonides systematizes all that had been said in talmudic literature on the subject of ritual purity and impurity. The standard Hebrew translation, the work of a number of hands, is a poor rendering of the Arabic original. A new and more faithful translation was made by Y. Kafaḥ, *Mishnah im Perush ha-Rambam* . . . (1963–68).

The Responsa of Maimonides. The publication of the critical editions of the responsa of Maimonides (ed. by A. Freimann, 1934; J. Blau, 1957–61) affords a better opportunity to appraise his role in the communal life of the Jews of Egypt and neighboring countries. The responsa, which were in the language of the questioner, whether Hebrew or Arabic, number 464; some of them soon found their way into halakhic literature. Although not all responsa bear the date of composition, it has been ascertained that Maimonides' responsa extend from about 1167, a short time after his arrival in Egypt, until a little before his death. The questioners include prominent scholars like R. Anatoli and R. Meshullam, *dayyanim* in Alexandria; *Jonathan ha-Kohen of Lunel; Joseph b. Gabir; Nissim of Damascus; and Samuel b. Ali, *gaon* of Baghdad. From these responsa one learns of the growing tension between the *gaon* of Baghdad and Maimonides in connection with traveling on the high seas on the Sabbath, prohibited by Samuel b. Ali but permitted by Maimonides (ed. Blau, no. 308–9). Some of the responsa to Jonathan of Lunel, who was a disciple of *Abraham b. David of Posquières, are in essence rejoinders to the latter's criticisms, for his questions coincide with the language and style of these criticisms (ed. Freimann, introd. xliv = ed. Blau, 3 (1961), 43).

The bitter experience of his youth failed to nurture in Maimonides rabid anti-Muslim feelings, and he consistently declined to classify Muslims as idolators. Even the ritual practices connected with the Ka'ba stone in Mecca did not in his opinion deny Islam its purely monotheistic nature (ed. Freimann, no. 369 = ed. Blau, no. 448; see S. Baron, in: PAAJR, 6 (1935), 83f.). In reply to an inquiry by Saadiah b. Berakhot about the authenticity of the gnostic work, *Shi'ur Komah*, Maimonides writes: "Heaven forfend that such work originated from the sages; it is undoubtedly the work of one of the Greek preachers . . . and it would be a divine act to suppress this book and to eradicate its subject matter" (ed. Freimann, no. 373 = ed. Blau, no. 117; see Scholem, Mysticism (1946^2), 63ff.). Of special interest is his responsum to Obadiah the Proselyte (ed. Freimann, no. 42 = ed. Blau, no. 293), who inquired if he was permitted to say in the blessings and prayers, "Our God and God of our Fathers," "Thou who has chosen us," "Thou who has worked miracles to our fathers," and similar expressions. Maimonides' responsum, apart from its halakhic merit, is a unique human document displaying grave concern for the feelings of this lonely proselyte who was so unsure of himself. Obadiah was advised that he was to recite all those prayers in the same way as one born a Jew, that he must not consider himself inferior to the rest of the Jews. The major part of this responsum has been translated into English by F. Kobler (see also S. B. Freehof, *Treasury of Responsa* (1962), 28–34). These responsa, although confined to halakhic decisions, nevertheless display Maimonides' views on matters of doctrine and fundamentals of Judaism.

Sefer ha-Mitzvot ("Book of the Commandments"). Maimonides found all previous attempts at enumerating the traditional 613 *commandments unsatisfactory. He therefore composed the *Sefer ha-Mitzvot* in which he gave his own enumeration of the 248 positive and the 365 negative commandments. As an introduction to this work, he laid down 14 principles which guided him in the identification and enumeration of the commandments. He severely criticized the work of his predecessors, such as the enumeration of the **Halakhot Gedolot* and of R. Ḥefeẓ, as well as those *paytanim* like Solomon ibn Gabirol, who composed the *Azharot*, religious hymns based on enumeration of the commandments.

Maimonides' sharp criticism of the *Halakhot Gedolot* evoked a defense of the latter by Naḥmanides, a staunch apologist "for the ancients," who in his *Hassagot* strongly criticized Maimonides, accusing him of inconsistencies. He was also challenged by Daniel ha-Bavli, a disciple of Samuel b. Ali, the anti-Maimonist. His criticisms took the form of questions which he sent to Abraham, the son of Maimonides, who replied to them. The *Sefer ha-Mitzvot*, however, was generally accepted, and a whole body of literature was produced in defense of it, apart from the general works on the 613 commandments according to Maimonides' classification and enumeration (see A. Jellinek, *Kunteres Taryag*, 1878).

The *Sefer ha-Mitzvot*, originally written in Arabic, was translated several times into Hebrew. The version by Abraham ibn Ḥasdai is no longer extant, while the translation by Moses ibn Tibbon, in its critical edition by H. Heller, is accepted as the standard text (1946).

The Mishneh Torah ("Repetition of the Law"). The *Sefer ha-Mitzvot* was not an end in itself but an introduction to the *Mishneh Torah* (Responsa, ed. Freimann, no. 368 = ed. Blau, no. 447), on which Maimonides labored for ten successive years. The purpose of the work is explained by Maimonides:

In our days, many vicissitudes prevail, and all feel the pressure of hard times. The wisest of our wise men has disappeared; the understanding of our prudent men is hidden. Hence, the commentaries of the *geonim* and their compilations of laws and responsa, which they took care to make clear, have in our times become hard to understand, so that only a few individuals fully comprehend them. Needless to add that such is the case in regard to Talmud itself, both Babylonian and Jerusalem, and the *Sifra, Sifrei,* and Tosefta, all of which require, for their comprehension, a broad mind, a wise soul, and considerable study. Then one might learn from them the correct way to determine what is forbidden and permitted, as well as other rules of the Torah. On these grounds, I, Moses the son of Maimon the Sephardi bestirred myself, and relying on the help of God, blessed be He, intently studied all these works, with the view of putting together the results obtained from them ... all in plain language and terse style, so that thus the entire Oral Law might become systematically known to all without citing difficulties and solutions of differences of view ... but consisting of statements, clear and convincing, that have appeared from the time of Moses to the present, so that all rules shall be accessible to young and old ... (introduction to *Mishneh Torah*).

Maimonides then set for himself the task of classifying by subject matter the entire talmudic and post-talmudic halakhic literature in a systematic manner never before attempted in the history of Judaism. The *Mishneh Torah* was divided into 14 books, each representing a distinct category of the Jewish legal system. (In Hebrew 14 is *yad* and hence the alternative name of the work *Yad ha-Ḥazakah*, i.e., "the strong hand.")

Even though the *Guide of the Perplexed* was written after the completion of the *Mishneh Torah*, Maimonides succeeded in incorporating many of its philosophic and scientific aspects into this purely halakhic work. Philosophy and science were handmaidens to theology. Hence Book 1 contains a complete system of metaphysics, Book 3 the astronomical calculations for reckoning the calendar, and Book 14 a discussion of the doctrine of the Messiah and a refutation of Christianity, Islam, and their founders. These digressions, which technically speaking are not halakhic in essence but rather ethical and philosophic, occur frequently in the halakhic writings of Maimonides.

Unlike the commentary to the Mishnah and *Sefer ha-Mitzvot* which were written in Arabic, the *Mishneh Torah* was written in a beautiful and lucid Hebrew, the like of which had not been known in halakhic literature since Judah ha-Nasi composed the Mishnah. The *Mishneh Torah* influenced the language of later codes, including the Shulḥan Arukh (see J. Dienstag, in: *Sinai*, 59 (1966), 54–75).

Opposition to the Code. The entire structure, form, and arrangement of the *Mishneh Torah* was a cultural and historical phenomenon unprecedented in Jewish dogmatic jurisprudence (see *Codification of Law) which both awed and shocked the scholarly world for centuries (see *Maimonidean Controversy). The architectural beauty of its structure, its logical arrangement, and ready-reference nature were the main targets for criticism, for it was feared that students would turn away from the study of the Talmud and commentaries, the source and wellspring of dynamic halakhic creativity. The severest criticism came from Abraham b. David of Posquières, an older contemporary of Maimonides, who probably equaled him in talmudic scholarship. The most serious of his charges was that Maimonides neglected to cite the sources and authorities from which his decisions were derived:

He [Maimonides] intended to improve but did not improve, for he forsook the way of all authors who preceded him. They always adduced proof for their statements, citing the proper authority; this was very useful, for sometimes the judge would be inclined to forbid or permit something and his proof was based on some other authority. Had he known there was a greater authority who interpreted the law differently, he might have retracted ... hence I do not know why I should reverse my tradition or corroborative views because of the compendium of this author. If the one who differs from me is greater than I, fine; and if I am greater than he, why should I annul my opinion ... ? Moreover, there are matters on which the *geonim* disagree and the author has selected the opinion of one.... Why should I rely on his choice.... It can only be one that an overbearing spirit is in him (Abraham b. David's *Hassagot* to introduction of *Mishneh Torah*).

These charges were not motivated by personal animosity, as claimed by some scholars of the Haskalah period, for on many occasions Abraham b. David traces certain sources of laws in the Code or comments upon it. At other times he is overwhelmed by this compendium (see I. Twersky, in: *Sefer ha-Yovel ... Ẓevi Wolfson* (1965), 169–86). Abraham b. David's objections were shared by lesser-known scholars (I. Twersky, in: A. Altmann (ed.), *Biblical and other Studies* (1963), 161–82), who added their own criticism. During the 19th century, opposition to the *Mishneh Torah* was still a subject of controversy between S. D. Luzzatto, N. Krochmal, and others (J. Dienstag, in: Bitzaron, 55 (1967), 34–37).

In a series of letters Maimonides replied to his criticism that his intention in writing the *Mishneh Torah* was not to discourage talmudic studies, including the *halakhot* of Alfasi. On the contrary, he had lectured to his pupils on these subjects (A. Lichtenberg (ed.), *Kovez Teshuvot ha-Rambam* (1859), pt. 1, no. 140 p. 25, b–c). He regretted the omission of his sources and hoped to include them in a supplement (*ibid.*). Maimonides never realized this hope. However, practically every commentary on the *Mishneh Torah* attempted to trace its sources. If his aim in compiling the Code was "so that no other work should be needed for ascertaining any of the laws of Israel," the more than 300 commentaries and novellae which have been written on it—and their number is growing—is an ironic phenomenon that could not have been anticipated by Maimonides. The *Mishneh Torah* did not become the definitive code its venerated creator had hoped. Actually, it surpassed his hopes, for it became the major source of halakhic creativity and talmudic research equaled only by the Talmud itself.

Maimonides the Halakhist in Modern Jewish Scholarship. Finally, it is interesting to note that no other halakhic authority has been the subject of so much modern Jewish scholarship as Maimonides. The tendentious, albeit subtle, anti-halakhic orientation of many of the exponents of the Wissenschaft school and the scholars of the Haskalah (including the leaders of Reform Judaism) has dampened, if not outright discouraged, intensive research in *halakhah* per se. Some of those who did engage in this discipline, such as A. Geiger, N. Bruell, J. H. Schorr, and others, were motivated by their anti-traditional bias and sought to undermine its authority and advance the cause of modernism and reform. The preoccupation of modern Jewish scholarship with Maimonides as halakhist is out of proportion to its interest in rabbinic literature and the stream of systematic studies on the subject has continued unabated. [J.I.D.]

PHILOSOPHY

Maimonides was, by general agreement, the most significant Jewish philosopher of the Middle Ages, and his *Guide of the Perplexed* is the most important philosophic work produced by a Jew. The Arabic original *Dalālat al-Ḥā'irīn* was completed about 1200 and shortly thereafter was twice translated into Hebrew as *Moreh Nevukhim*. The first translation, a literal one, was made by Samuel ibn Tibbon with Maimonides' advice and was completed in 1204. The second, a freer translation, was made by the poet Judah *al-Ḥarizi a little later. In its Hebrew translations the *Guide* determined the course of Jewish philosophy from the early 13th century on, and almost every philosophic work for the remainder of the Middle Ages cited, commented on, or criticized Maimonides' views.

While the *Guide* contained the major statement of Maimonides' position, his philosophic and theological views appeared in a variety of other writings, among which the most important are the three lengthy essays in his commentary to the Mishnah (see above), first book of the *Mishneh Torah, Sefer ha-Madda* which is devoted to God and His attributes, angelic beings, the structure of the universe, prophecy, ethics, repentance, free will and providence, and the afterlife, and the last section of the work, *Mishneh Torah, Hilkhot Melakhim* which includes a discussion on the Messiah and the messianic age.

Influences on Maimonides. In his philosophic views Maimonides was an Aristotelian (see *Aristotle), and it was he who put medieval Jewish philosophy on a firm Aristotelian basis. But in line with contemporary Aristotelianism his political philosophy was Platonic. In his works he quotes his authorities sparingly (see "*Shemonah Perakim,*" introduction, end), but in a letter to his translator Samuel ibn Tibbon (A. Marx, in: JQR, 25 (1934–35), 374–81) he indicated his philosophic preferences explicitly. In this letter he advises Ibn Tibbon to study the works of Aristotle with the help of the Hellenistic commentators *Alexander of Aphrodisias and *Themistius and of Maimonides' contemporary *Averroes. It appears, however, that Averroes' commentaries reached Maimonides too late to have any influence on his *Guide.* He recommends highly the works of the Muslim al-*Fārābī, particularly those on logic, and he speaks of the writings of the Muslim *Avempace (Ibn Bāja) with approval. The works of *Avicenna (Ibn Sīnā) in Maimonides' view are also worthy of study, but they are inferior to those of al-Fārābī. Of Jewish philosophers he mentions only Isaac *Israeli, of whose views he disapproves, and Joseph ibn *Ẓaddik, whom he praises for his learning, though he states that he knew only the man, not his work. He also mentions some other philosophers of whose views he disapproves. Al-Fārābī, Avempace, and Averroes interpreted Aristotle rationalistically, and it appears that Maimonides preferred their interpretations to the more theologically oriented one of Avicenna, though he relied on Avicenna for some of his views.

(For a full discussion of sources, see S. Pines, *Guide of the Perplexed* (1963), translator's introduction lvii–cxxxiv.)

Maimonides considered himself in the tradition of the Aristotelians, adapting and developing their teachings in accord with his own views; but he differed from them in the works he produced. While the Muslims had composed commentaries on Aristotle's works, summaries of his views, and independent philosophic treatises, Maimonides produced no purely philosophic work of his own, the early *Treatise on Logic* excepted. He held that the extant philosophic literature was adequate for all needs (Guide 2, introd., proposition 25, and ch. 2), and he devoted himself to specific issues, particularly those bearing on the interrelation of philosophy and religion.

Distinction between Intellectual Elite and Masses. Fundamental to Maimonides approach is a division of mankind into two groups: an intellectual elite, who, using reason, can understand by means of demonstrative arguments, and the masses (including those scholars who study only religious law), who, using imagination, understand by means of persuasive arguments. In the light of this distinction Maimonides' works may be divided into two kinds: *Guide of the Perplexed,* addressed primarily to an intellectual elite, and his other writings, addressed to the masses.

This distinction had one further consequence for Maimonides. Maimonides identified *ma'aseh bereshit* (the account of the creation) and *ma'aseh merkavah* (the account of the divine chariot of Ezekiel) with physics and metaphysics respectively. According to the Mishnah, however (Ḥag. 2:1) one may not teach the former to two persons, nor the latter even to one, unless he is wise and able to understand by himself. Maimonides codifies this as *halakhah* (Yad, Yesodei ha-Torah, 2:12; 4:10–13) and in his commentary to the Mishnah gives as the reason for the prohibition the current philosophical opinion that the teaching of abstract matters to someone who cannot grasp them may lead to unbelief.

This prohibition against the public teaching of *ma'aseh merkavah* and *ma'aseh bereshit* posed a problem. How could he write the *Guide,* a book devoted to these esoteric topics, when putting something in writing is equivalent to teaching it in public? Maimonides solved this problem by making use of certain literary devices. First, Maimonides addressed the book to his disciple, Joseph ben Judah ibn Sham'un, who after studying with him left for Baghdad. Hence, the *Guide* in its formal aspect is a personal communication to one student. Moreover Maimonides, in a dedicatory letter at the beginning of the *Guide,* relates Joseph's intellectual history, showing that he had acquired some philosophic wisdom and that he was able to reason for himself. Hence, Joseph had fulfilled the conditions necessary for studying the esoteric disciplines.

But Maimonides was well aware that persons other than Joseph would read his work. Hence, he had to make use of other devices. Invoking modes of esoteric writing also current among Islamic philosophers, Maimonides wrote his work in an enigmatic style. Discussing the same topic in different passages, he would make contradictory statements about it. He describes this method in the introduction to the *Guide,* where he speaks of seven types of contradictions which appear in literary works, stating explicitly that he will make use of two of them. It is left to the perceptive reader to discover Maimonides' true views on a given issue.

The enigmatic nature of the *Guide* imposed great difficulties on medieval and modern commentators, and two schools of interpretation arose. Some, while aware of Maimonides' method, consider him a philosopher who attempted to harmonize the teachings of religion with those of philosophy. Others, however, considered Maimonides a philosopher, whose views were in agreement with those of the rationalistic Aristotelians, and who expressed religious opinions largely as a concession to the understanding of the masses. For example, Maimonides, according to the first interpretation, believed that the world was created, while according to the second, his true view was that the world is eternal.

With all these distinctions in mind one may proceed to an exposition of Maimonides' philosophy based largely on the *Guide.*

Purpose of the Guide. Maimonides wrote his work for someone who was firm in his religious beliefs and practices, but, having studied philosophy, was perplexed by the literal meaning of biblical anthropomorphic and anthropopathic terms. To this person Maimonides showed that these difficult terms have a spiritual meaning besides their literal one, and that it is the spiritual meaning that applies to God. Maimonides also undertook in the *Guide* the explanation of obscure biblical parables. Thus, the *Guide* is devoted to the philosophic interpretation of Scripture, or, to use Maimonides' terms, to the "science of the Law in its true sense" or to the "secrets of the Law" (Guide, introd.).

God. Maimonides' first philosophical topic is God. In line with his exegetical program he begins by explaining troublesome biblical terms, devoting the major portion of the first 49 chapters of the first part of the *Guide* to this task. Representative of his exegesis are his comments on the term "image of God" (*ẓelem Elohim*), found in the opening section of Genesis. Some have argued, Maimonides states, that since man was created in the image of God, it follows that God, like man, must have a body. He answers the objection by showing that the term *ẓelem* refers always to a spiritual quality, an essence. Hence, the "image of God" in man is man's essence, that is his reason but not physical likeness (Guide 1:1).

Divine Attributes. Maimonides then takes up the question of God's attributes (Guide 1:50–60). The Bible describes God by many attributes, but it also states that God is one. If He is one in the sense of being simple, how can a multiplicity of attributes be ascribed to Him? Medieval philosophers held that attributes applied to substances are of two kinds: essential and accidental. Essential attributes are those that are closely connected with the essence, such as existence or life; accidental attributes are those that are independent of the essence and that may be changed without affecting the essence, such as anger or mercifulness. Medieval logicians generally agreed that accidental attributes introduce a multiplicity into that which they describe, while they disagreed concerning essential attributes. Some held that essential attributes are implicitly contained in the essence and, hence, do not introduce multiplicity; others held that they provide new information and, hence, produce multiplicity. Avicenna was an exponent of the latter view, holding that essential attributes, particularly existence, are superadded to the essence. Maimonides accepted Avicenna's position on this point. Maimonides came to the conclusion that accidental attributes applied to God must be interpreted as attributes of action, that is, if it is said that God is merciful, it means that God acts mercifully; and essential attributes must be interpreted as negations, that is, if God is said to be existing, it means that he is not nonexistent.

(See also *God, Attributes of).

Existence, Unity, and Incorporeality of God. Prior to Maimonides, Islamic and Jewish *Kalām philosophers had offered arguments for the existence, unity, and incorporeality of God and for the creation of the world. Maimonides summarized the teachings of the Kalām philosophers in order to refute them (Guide 1:71–76). In the case of the existence, unity, and incorporeality of God, Maimonides held that these are legitimate philosophic issues, but that the Kalām philosophers, relying on categories of the imagination rather than reason, had not solved them correctly. In the case of creation he held that to demonstrate the creation or eternity of the world lies outside the competence of the human mind.

Maimonides prefaces his own proofs for the existence, unity, and incorporeality of God with 25 metaphysical and physical propositions, which he considers to have been demonstrated in the philosophic literature of his days. To these he adds a 26th proposition, namely, that the world is eternal. However, it appears that this proposition does not reflect Maimonides' own belief concerning the origin of the world (see below), but serves, rather, a methodological function. It can be seen readily, Maimonides implies, that if it is assumed that the world is eternal, the existence of God can still be demonstrated (Guide 2, introd.).

Existence. To demonstrate the existence of God, Maimonides makes use of four proofs current in his day: from motion, from the composition of elements (also a kind of argument from motion), from necessity and contingency, and from potentiality and actuality (causality). The common structure of all of them is that they begin with some observed characteristic of the world, invoke the principle that an infinite regress is impossible, and conclude that a first principle must exist. For example, Maimonides begins his first proof, that from motion, by noting that in the sublunar world things constantly move and change. These sublunar motions, in turn, are caused by celestial motions which come to an end with the motion of the uppermost celestial sphere. The motion of that sphere is caused by a mover that is not moved by another mover. This mover, called the Prime Mover, is the last member in the chain of causes producing motion. Maimonides uses the following example as an illustration. Suppose a draft of air comes through a hole, and a stick is used to push a stone in the hole to close it. Now the stone is pushed into the hole by the stick, the stick is moved by the hand, and the hand is moved by the sinews, muscles, etc., of the human body. But one must also consider the draft of air, which was the reason for the motion of the stone in the first place. The motion of the air is caused by the motion of the lowest celestial sphere, and the motion of that sphere, by the successive motions of other spheres. The chain of things moved and moving comes to an end with the last of the celestial spheres. This sphere is set in motion by a principle which, while it produces motion, is itself not moved. This is the Prime Mover, which for Maimonides is identical with God.

Maimonides then turned to the nature of the Prime Mover. Four possibilities exist: Either the Prime Mover exists apart from the sphere, and then either corporeally or incorporeally; or it exists within the sphere, and then either as distributed throughout it or as indivisible. It can be shown that the Prime Mover does not exist within the sphere, which rules out the last two possibilities, nor apart from it as a body, which rules out the third. Hence, it exists apart from the sphere and must be incorporeal. Maimonides shows, further, that there cannot be two incorporeal movers. Thus, it has been established that the Prime Mover exists, is incorporeal, and is one.

Maimonides' proof from necessity and contingency rests on the observation that things in the world are contingent, and that they are ultimately produced by a being that is necessary through itself. This proof was first formulated by Avicenna and was rejected by Averroes (Guide 2:1; for a more popular discussion of Maimonides' conception of God, and his attributes, see Yad, Yesodei ha-Torah, 1–2).

Creation. Maimonides next turned to the incorporeal intelligences, which he identified with the angels to the celestial spheres (Guide 2:2–12), and then to creation (Guide 2:13–26). On the last subject he begins by enumerating three theories of the origin of the world: that of the Torah, that the world was created by God out of nothing; that of Plato and others, according to which God created the world out of preexistent matter; and that of Aristotle, according to which the world is eternal. A major portion of the discussion is devoted to showing that Aristotle's and his followers' proofs of the eternity of the world are not really proofs. From an analysis of Aristotelian texts Maimonides attempted to show that Aristotle himself did not consider his arguments as conclusive demonstrations but only as showing that eternity is more plausible than creation. Maimonides' own position is that one can offer plausible arguments for the creation of the world as well as for its eternity. From this it follows that a conclusive demonstration of the creation or the eternity of the world lies beyond human reason; the human mind can only offer likely arguments for either alternative. However, an examination of these arguments reveals that those for creation are more likely than those for eternity, and on this basis Maimonides accepts the doctrine of creation *ex nihilo* as his own. An additional reason is that Scripture also teaches creation. Maimonides' intellectual daring is apparent in his statement (ch. 25) that had the eternity of the world been demonstrated philosophically, he would not have hesitated to interpret the Bible accordingly, just as he did not hesitate to interpret anthropomorphic terms in the Bible allegorically. He also states that the principle of creation is the most important one after that of God's unity, since it explains the possibility of miracles and similar occurrences. It should be noted, however, that some interpreters understand Maimonides' esoteric teaching as propounding the eternity of the world.

If the world was created, will it come to an end at some future time? He answers in the negative and adds that the future indestructibility of the world is also taught in the Bible (Guide 2:27–29). Maimonides concludes this phase of the discussion with an explanation of the creation chapters at the beginning of Genesis and a discussion of the Sabbath, which in part is also a reminder of the creation.

Prophecy. In the introduction to the *Guide* Maimonides incidentally discussed the nature of the prophetic experience, likening it to intellectual illumination. In the present section (Guide 2:32–48) he is interested in the psychology of prophecy and its political function. He begins by listing three possible theories of how prophecy is acquired: that of the unsophisticated believer, who holds that God arbitrarily selects someone for prophecy; that of the philosophers, according to which prophecy occurs when man's natural faculties, particularly his intellect, reach a high level of development; and that of Scripture, which specifies the same development of natural faculties but adds dependence on God, Who can prevent someone from prophesying, if He so desires. According to this last view, God's role in prophecy is negative, rather than positive.

Maimonides defined prophecy as an emanation from God, which, through the intermediacy of the Active Intellect, flows first upon man's intellectual faculty and then upon his imagination. While a well-developed imagination is of little significance for the illuminative experience of the prophet, it is central to his political function. In line with the views of the Islamic Aristotelians, particularly al-Fārābī, Maimonides conceives of the prophet as a statesman who brings law to his people and admonishes them to observe it. This conception of the prophet-statesman is based on Plato's notion, found in the *Republic*, of the philosopher-king who establishes and administers the ideal state. For Maimonides the primary function of prophets other than Moses is to admonish people to adhere to the Law of Moses; this requires that the prophets use the kind of imaginative language and parables that appeal to the imagination of the masses. Maimonides characterizes three personality types: philosopher, who uses only his intellect, the ordinary statesman, who uses only his imagination, and the prophet, who uses both.

Though he discusses the phenomenon of prophecy extensively, Maimonides mentions Moses, the chief of the prophets, only in passing in the *Guide*. However, in his halakhic writings he singles out Moses for special discussion. Moses, he states, differed so much from other prophets that he and they had virtually only the name "prophet" in common. Moses' prophecy is distinguished from that of the other prophets in four ways: other prophets received their prophecy in a dream or vision, Moses received his while awake; other prophets received their prophecy in allegorical form, Moses received his directly; other prophets were filled with fear when they received prophecy, Moses was not; other prophets received prophecy intermittently, Moses received it when he wished (*Hakdamah le-Ferek Ḥelek*, Principle 7; Yad, Yesodei ha-Torah, 7:6; cf. Guide 2:35). Moses also differed from other prophets and legislators in that he conveyed a perfect law, that is, one that addressed itself not only to man's moral perfection but also to his intellectual perfection by requiring the affirmation of certain beliefs.

Nature of Evil. Maimonides begins the third part of the Guide (introd. ch. 1–7) with a philosophic interpretation of the divine chariot (*merkavah*); this exposition brings to a close that part of the *Guide* that deals with speculative matters, that is, physical and metaphysical topics (Guide 3:7–end). Next he turns to practical philosophy, discussing evil and providence first.

Maimonides accepts the neoplatonic doctrine that evil is not an independent principle but rather the privation, or absence, of good. Like the Neoplatonists and other monists he had to accept this position, for to posit an independent principle of evil was to deny the uniqueness and omnipotence of God. There are three kinds of evil: natural evils, such as floods and earthquakes, which man cannot control, social evils, such as wars, and personal evils, the various human vices, both of which man can control. Natural evils are infrequent, and, hence, the majority of evil in the world, which is caused by man, can be remedied by proper training. Maimonides also argues against those who hold that the world is essentially evil, stating that if one looks at the world at large, rather than at one's own pains and misfortunes, one finds that the world as a whole is good, not evil (Guide 3:8–12).

Divine Providence. Maimonides discusses divine omniscience and then turns to the related question of divine providence. He distinguishes between general providence, which refers to general laws regulating nature, and individual providence, which refers to God's providential concern for individual men. He lists four theories of providence that he rejects: the theory of *Epicurus (see *Epicureanism), which states that everything that happens in the world is the result of chance; that of Aristotle (really that of the commentator Alexander of Aphrodisias), which states that there is only general, not individual, providence; that of the Islamic Asharites (see *Kalām), which states that the divine will rules everything—this is equivalent to individual providence extended to include all beings, animate and inanimate; and that of the Muʿtazilites (see *Kalām), which states that there is individual providence extending even to animals but not to inanimate objects. Last, Maimonides discusses the attitude toward providence of the adherents of the Torah. They all accept man's free will and God's justice. To these principles some more recent scholars (Maimonides had in mind the *geonim*, most likely Saadiah) have added the principle of *yissurin shel ahavah* ("afflictions of love"), which explains that God may cause suffering to a righteous person in order to reward him in the hereafter. Maimonides rejected it, however, stating that only an unjust God would act in this manner, and asserted that every pain and affliction is a punishment for a prior sin. Finally, Maimonides gave his own position: there is individual providence, and it is determined by the degree of development of the individual's intellect. The more developed a man's intellect, the more subject he is to divine providence (Guide 3:16–21). Maimonides used this theory of providence in his interpretation of the Book of Job, in which the characters of that book represent the various attitudes toward providence discussed above (Guide 3:22–23).

Nature of Man and Moral Virtue. Maimonides' final

undertaking in the *Guide* is his explanation of the Law of Moses and its precepts. But this account is based on his philosophy of man, which he summarizes only in his *"Shemonah Perakim."* From this summary it is clear that Maimonides' philosophy of man was one current among Muslim Aristotelians. Man is composed of a body and a soul, the soul, particularly the intellect, being the form of the body. The soul, which is unitary, contains five basic faculties: nutritive, sensory, imaginative, appetitive, and rational. Of these faculties, the appetitive and rational are important for the good life and for happiness on earth and in the hereafter. Man attains happiness through the exercise of moral virtues to control his appetites and by developing his intellectual powers. In Maimonides' discussion of morality he follows Aristotle in holding that virtuous action consists of following the mean, but he holds that all should go to the extreme to avoid pride and anger (Yad, Deot, 2:3). While in his halakhic writings Maimonides embraced a morality of the mean, in the *Guide* he advocates a more ascetic life, and he particularly recommends curbing the sexual drive. As in Aristotelian thought, the moral virtues serve only a preliminary function, the final goal being the acquisition of intellectual virtues.

(For another discussion of Maimonides' moral philosophy, see Yad, Deot.)

Law of Moses. In the *Guide* 3:26–49 Maimonides discusses the reasons of the commandments. Maimonides considers a distinction made by Muʿtazilite philosophers, *Saadiah among them. These philosophers had divided divine law into two categories: rational commandments, such as the prohibitions against murder and theft, which the human mind can discover without revelation; and revealed commandments, such as prayer and the observance of holidays, which are neutral from the point of view of reason and can be known only through revelation. Maimonides understands this position as implying that the revelational commandments come from God's will rather than His reason. Against this view, Maimonides argues that all divine commandments are the product of God's wisdom, though he adds that some are easily intelligible *(mishpatim)*, and others intelligible only with difficulty *(ḥukkim)*. However, Maimonides adds that particular commandments have no rational principle behind them and are commandments only because God willed them.

Maimonides postulates two purposes of the Law: the well-being of the soul (intellect) and the well-being of the body, by which he means man's moral well-being. The former is acquired through true beliefs; the latter, through political and personal morality. The beliefs which a man must accept are graded according to his intellectual ability. There are also true beliefs, such as the existence of God, His unity, and His incorporeality, which everyone must accept regardless of intellectual ability; and there are beliefs, such as that God gets angry at those who disobey Him, which have primarily a political function and are considered necessary beliefs. Ordinary men will accept the Law only if they are promised rewards or threatened with punishment, and it is the function of the necessary beliefs to provide such motivation. They are unnecessary for the philosopher, who obeys the Law because it is the right thing to do regardless of consequences.

Although reasons for general moral laws can readily be found, it is more difficult to explain the numerous ritual laws found in the Bible. Maimonides explains many of them as reactions to pagan practices, and he makes use of his extensive familiarity with such books as the *Nabatean Agriculture*, which describe such practices (see *Commandments, Reasons for). Thus, for example, he explains the biblical prohibition against wearing garments made of wool and linen combined as a reaction to a pagan practice requiring priests to wear such garments. Maimonides also considers certain commandments as concessions to historical situations, such as those dealing with sacrifice. Worship without animal sacrifices is preferred, but it would have been unrealistic to require the Israelites leaving Egypt to give up sacrifices altogether. Hence the Bible commanded sacrifices, restricting, however, the times and places for them and permitting only priests to offer them. We should not infer from this, however, that Maimonides believed in a progressive development of Jewish law; in fact, he codifies all of rabbinic law in his *Mishneh Torah*. The *Guide* concludes with a supplementary section on the perfect worship of God and man's perfection.

Eschatology. Eschatology is barely mentioned in the *Guide*, although Maimonides developed it fully in other works. Following traditional Jewish teachings, he deals with the Messiah and messianic times, the resurrection of the dead, and *olam ha-ba* ("the world to come"). He proceeds characteristically by stripping these occurrences of supernatural qualities as much as possible. The Messiah is an earthly king, descended from the house of David. He will bring the Jews back to their country, but his major accomplishment will be to bring peace and tranquility to the world, thereby facilitating full observance of God's commandments. The Messiah will die of old age and be succeeded by his son, the latter, by his son, and so on. No cataclysmic events will take place during messianic times, but the world will continue in its established natural order. Maimonides calculated the year of the coming of the Messiah *("Iggeret Teiman")*, although he generally opposed speculations of this kind (*Hakdamah le-Ferek Ḥelek*, principle 12; Yad, Melakhim, 12:2—uncensored edition).

During messianic times the dead will be resurrected with body and soul reunited though later they will die again. (For his affirmation of this doctrine in reply to criticism that he rejected it, see above.) Undoubtedly, the central notion of Maimonides' eschatology is his account of *olam ha-ba*. In his view the intellect, but not the body, has an afterlife, and in that afterlife the intellect is engaged in the contemplation of God. Generally, he speaks of incorporeal intelligences (plural), implying that immortality is individual, but there are passages which suggest that immortality is collective, that is, in the world to come there exists only one intellect for all mankind (*Hakdamah le-Ferek Ḥelek;* Yad, Teshuvah, 8–10, Guide 1:41; *Treatise on Resurrection*).

Basic Principles of Judaism. Maimonides' intellectualism is reflected in the formulation of 13 principles that in his view every member of the Jewish community is bound to accept (see *Articles of Faith). Did he intend these principles as a means of developing the intellects of the masses, thus enabling them to share in *olam ha-ba*, or as a political expedient, that is, to make the masses aware of intellectual issues so that philosophers can live safely in their midst? Proponents of both views are found among Maimonides' interpreters (see A. Hyman, in: A. Altmann (ed.), *Jewish Medieval and Renaissance Studies* (1967), 119–44).

Influence. Maimonides' *Guide*, as has been noted, profoundly influenced the subsequent course of medieval Jewish philosophy. Among the extensive literature that arose were numerous full and partial commentaries on the *Guide*, most of them still unpublished. However, four of these have been printed and they appear many times with the Hebrew text of the *Guide*. They are those of Profiat *Duran (Efodi), Shem Tov ben Joseph *Ibn Shem Tov, Asher *Crescas, and Isaac *Abrabanel. In addition, the following commentaries have appeared in print: *Moreh ha-Moreh* by Shem Tov ibn *Falaquera, which also contains corrections of Ibn Tibbon's Hebrew translation based on the Arabic original (edited by M. L. Bisseliches, 1837); *Ammudei Kesef* and *Maskiyyot Kesef*, exoteric and esoteric commentaries respectively, by Joseph *Kaspi (edited by J. F. Bach, 1848); and a commentary by Moses *Narboni (all three reprinted in *Sheloshah Kadmonei Mefareshei ha-Moreh*, 1961). Samuel ibn Tibbon composed a philosophic glossary on the *Guide* entitled *Perush me-ha-Millot ha-Zarot asher be-Ma'amarei ha-Rav*, which has also been printed many times. One aspect of the commentary literature is the attempt to reconcile Maimonides' views with the divergent ones of his contemporary Averroes. Of commentaries and notes that have appeared on the *Guide* in more recent times are those of Solomon Maimon's *Givat ha-Moreh* (edited by Samuel Hugo Bergman and N. Rotenstreich, 1966), the notes in S. Munk's French translation of the *Guide*, and the Hebrew commentary in Ibn Shmuel's edition.

In addition to its significance for medieval Jewish philosophy, the *Guide* also had a formative influence on modern Jewish thought. Maimonides provided a first acquaintance with philosophic speculation for a number of philosophers of the Enlightenment period and served as a bridge for the study of more modern philosophy. Moses *Mendelssohn is a case in point. In addition, Maimonides became a symbol for their own philosophic endeavors; he had attempted to introduce the spirit of rationalism into Jewish teachings during medieval times, just as they tried to do in their own time. Among modern thinkers influenced in some way by Maimonides are, in addition to Mendelssohn and Solomon Maimon (c. 1752–1800), Nahman *Krochmal, Samuel David *Luzatto (who opposed Maimonides' rationalism), S. L. *Steinheim, Hermann *Cohen, and *Aḥad Ha-Am.

Maimonides exercised an extensive influence on Christian scholastic thought. Among these scholastics are *Alexander of Hales, *William of Auvergne, *Albertus Magnus, Thomas *Aquinas, Meister *Eckhart, and *Duns Scotus. These scholastics generally quote Maimonides by name, but sometimes they cite his views anonymously. Giles of Rome composed a treatise entitled *Errores philosophorum* about 1270 (edited by J. Koch, with an English translation by J. O. Riedl, 1944), the 12th chapter of which is devoted to a refutation of Maimonides' views. (For Maimonides' influence on scholastic philosophy, see B. Geyer, *Die patristische und scholastische Philosophie* (1928), index; E. Gilson, *History of Christian Philosophy in the Middle Ages* (1955), index; Kaufmann, Schriften, 2 (1910), 152–89; Jacob Guttmann, in: *Moses ben Maimon*, J. Braun et al. (editors), 1 (1908), 135–230; and see also other studies by Jacob Guttman, Issachar Joel, and Isaac Husik.)

In early modern times Maimonides influenced the secular philosophers Baruch *Spinoza (see H. A. Wolfson, *The Philosophy of Spinoza* (1954), index) and Gottfried Wilhelm Leibnitz. [A.Hy.]

AS PHYSICIAN

Maimonides was probably first taught medicine by his father, but, as stated above, during the seven years which his family spent in Fez, Maimonides probably had the opportunity to pursue his medical studies and mingle with well-known physicians. In his "Treatise on Asthma" he describes discussions with the Jewish physician Abu Yūsuf b. Mu'allim and with Muhammad, son of the famous Avenzoar, and others. From his commentary on drugs it may also be concluded that he received his basic medical education in Morocco. He refers to "our physicians in the West" and to Morocco and Spain. Most of the names of drugs are given there not only in Arabic but also in Berber and Spanish. The only authors quoted by name are Spanish-Moroccan physicians (Ibn Juljul, Ibn Wāfid, Ibn Samajūn), who lived one to two centuries before him, and his older contemporary al-Ghāfiqī. Maimonides was certainly very familiar with Arabic translations of the writings of Greek physicians as well as with the writings of the older Arab physicians, for he himself condensed some of them.

That Maimonides was highly regarded as a physician among the Muslims is evident from the statements of the historians Ibn al-Qifṭī (c. 1248) and Ibn Abi Uṣaybiʿa (c. 1270) as well as of the physician ʿAbd-al-Laṭīf of Baghdad, who visited Maimonides when he was in Cairo in 1201. A song of praise which was written by a grateful patient, Saʿīd b. Ṣanāʿ al-Mulk, has been preserved by Ibn Abi Uṣaybiʿa:

Galen's art heals only the body
But Abu-Amran's [Maimonides'] the body and the soul.
His knowledge made him the physician of the century.
He could heal with his wisdom the sickness of ignorance.
If the moon would submit to his art,
He would free her of the spots at the time of full moon,
Would deliver her of her periodic defects,
And at the time of her conjunction save her from waning.
(Translation taken from B. L. Gordon, *Medieval and Renaissance Medicine* (1959), 235.)

Moreover, from certain statements made by Ibn Abi Uṣaybiʿa, it is clear to us that Maimonides also lectured on medicine and taught disciples such as his own son Abraham, as well as Joseph b. Judah ibn Shamʿun, and Rashīd al-Dīn.

Maimonides classified medicine into three divisions: preventive medicine; healing of the sick; and care of the convalescent, including invalids and the aged. His medical teachings, based on the then prevailing humoral pathology as taught by Hippocrates and Galen, are of a strictly rational character. He disapproved strongly of the use of charms, incantations, and amulets in treating the sick, and was outspoken against any blind belief in authority. He encouraged his disciples to observe and reason critically and insisted on experiment and research. In his "Treatise of Asthma" Maimonides stresses that the physician is important not only during sickness but also when the body is healthy. Unlike any other craftsman, the physician must use art, logic, and intuition. Maimonides also added that the physician must be able to take a comprehensive view of the patient and his circumstances in order to make a diagnosis of both his general condition and of diseases of individual organs.

Except for part of his Galen compendium, all of Maimonides' medical writings, most of which were apparently written in Arabic in Cairo during 1190–1204, have been preserved. The majority of these works were translated into Hebrew and Latin and helped to spread his fame in the West.

(1) *Al-Mukhtaṣarāt* is a compendium of the works of Galen for teaching purposes, of which only three, in Arabic, have been preserved.

(2) A commentary by him on the *Aphorisms* of Hippocrates, which had been translated into Arabic by the ninth-century translator Ḥunayn ibn Isḥāq, in general follows Galen's commentary; it has been only partially preserved in two defective Arabic manuscripts.

(3) *Fuṣūl Mūsā* ("The Aphorisms of Moses") is possibly the most famous and most widely quoted of all Maimonides' medical writings. It was translated into Hebrew under the title *Pirkei Moshe*, in the 13th century. In this work Maimonides included a large number of medical aphorisms and sundry information, mostly from Galen's own writings or his commentaries on Hippocrates, but also from Arab authors. On speaking of the relation between the right-hand part of the heart and the lungs

(1:55), Maimonides seems to have touched on the lesser circulation, without, however, venturing further afield. The passages in 1:19 as well as 8:57 and 62 strongly indicate that he was speaking of arterioles connecting the arteries and the veins.

(4) *Sarḥ asmā' al-ʿuqqār* is a commentary on drugs, the manuscript of which was found in Istanbul in 1932. It consists of 56 pages of 17 lines each. In the introduction Maimonides deals with the necessity of identifying drugs by their popular names. He then lists, in alphabetical order, about 350 remedies, mainly derived from plants. The Arabic names are often followed by Greek and Persian terms as well as colloquial Spanish, Moroccan, Egyptian, and Berber names. The so-called "Prayer of a Physician" was not written by Maimonides but was added later.

(5) *Fī al-Bawāsīr* is a work on hemorrhoids and was written for a young aristocrat.

(6) *Fī al-Jimāʿa,* a treatise on sexual intercourse, was written for the sultan Omar son of Nur al-Dīn.

(7) *Maqāla Fī al-Rabw* ("Treatise on Asthma") was written in 1190. Maimonides regards bronchial asthma as largely due to nervousness, and believes that some people thus inclined react strongly to certain irritants. Correct diet and spiritual treatment, he says, have a beneficial effect on the asthmatic.

(8) *Kilāb al-Sumūm wa al-Mutaḥarriz min al-Adwiya al-Qitāla* ("On Poisons and Their Antidotes"), a very famous manuscript, includes a classic description of the various symptoms of poisoning and is of value even today. Maimonides is the first to distinguish between the various types of snake venoms and suggests the establishment of collections of antidotes in state pharmacies. For snakebites he advises cautery, local tourniquets, rest, and general treatment against shock.

(9) *Fī Tadbīr al-Ṣiḥḥa* ("Guide to Good Health"), a treatise on hygiene, is one of the most popular of Maimonides' works. It was written in 1198 for the Egyptian sultan Afḍal Nūr al-Dīn Ali, who suffered from attacks of depression accompanied by physical symptoms. Maimonides teaches that physical convalescence is dependent on psychological well-being and rest. He stresses the necessity of hygienic conditions in the care of the body, physical exercise, and proper breathing, work, family, sexual life, and diet, and suggests that music, poetry, paintings, and walks in pleasant surroundings all have a part to play toward a happy person and the maintenance of good health.

(10) *Maqāla Fī Bayān al-Aʿrāḍ* ("Explanation of Coincidences") was also written for the sultan Afḍal Nūr al-Dīn Ali, who requested an explanation of the causes of his continued depression. It is a short treatise on the subject, in 22 chapters.

In the formation of his opinions on man's spiritual well-being, Maimonides' scientific and psychological experiences are closely interwoven with his religious principles. Physical and biological rules are integrated with moral and ethical principles in his world of values. To integrate oneself consciously into the natural biological laws of the world represented for Maimonides the fulfillment of the idea of walking in the paths of science and wisdom and achieving true knowledge and perfect bliss. [S.M.]

AS ASTRONOMER

Maimonides did not compose a systematic treatise on astronomy, but his competence in the subject is well illustrated by a number of passages in the *Moreh Nevukhim (Guide of the Perplexed)* and by his treatise on the calendar, *The Sanctification of the New Moon* (*Kiddush Rosh Ḥodesh* in *Mishneh Torah*). In the *Guide* there are references to technical aspects of Ptolemaic astronomy, and it is revealed that Maimonides' disciple Joseph ibn Sham'un had studied Ptolemy's *Almagest* under him. Maimonides states that he was acquainted with the son of Jābir ibn Aflaḥ of Seville (d. c. 1150), the author of a well-known astronomical text which takes exception to some Ptolemaic principles. He also refers to a lost work of Ibn Bāja (d. 1139), concerning the principles of astronomy, that he had obviously read with care. According to Maimonides, the physical difficulties of eccentric and epicyclic spheres need not concern the astronomer, whose task is merely to propose a theory in which the motions of the planets and the stars are uniform and circular, and conform to observation. In the *Sanctification,* Maimonides describes the calendric rules that were used in the time of the Sanhedrin, the rules of the fixed calendar that apply to this day, and the astronomical determination of the beginning of the month. The third section again shows Maimonides to be competent in the technical aspects of Ptolemaic astronomy, although he made no original contribution to the subject. In 1194 Maimonides wrote a letter addressed to the rabbis of southern France strongly denouncing *astrology as a pseudoscience opposed to the true science of astronomy, an opinion rarely expressed by Jewish scholars in the Middle Ages. In this letter Maimonides stated that astrology was the first secular subject he studied, and that he had read everything available in Arabic on the discipline. [B.R.G.]

TRANSLATIONS

Among Maimonides' halakhic works, Y. Kafaḥ published a new Hebrew translation of the *Sefer ha-Mitzvot* (1958) from the original Arabic, on which C. B. Chavel based his English version, *The Commandments: Sefer ha-Mitzvoth of Maimonides,* 2 vols. (1967). An English translation of the entire *Mishneh Torah, The Code of Maimonides,* started to appear in 1949 in the Yale Judaica Series, and by 1971, ten volumes had appeared.

The Arabic original of the *Guide* was edited, with a French translation, by S. Munk (*Le guide des égarés,* 3 vols. (1856–66); ed. by I. Joel, based on Munk's text, 1931). Samuel ibn Tibbon's Hebrew translation was first printed in Rome before 1480, and again in Venice, 1551, Sabionetta, 1553, and frequently thereafter. Yehudah Even-Shemuel (Kaufmann) edited part of this text with introductions and a commentary in three volumes (1935–59). The translation of Judah al-Ḥarizi was edited, with notes, by L. Schlossberg in three parts (1851–79; 1912[3]). Both versions were translated into Latin: that of Ibn Tibbon by J. Buxtorf (Basel, 1629) and Al-Ḥarizi's edited by A. Justinianus (Paris, 1520). The *Guide* was translated into English by M. Friedlaender, 3 volumes (1885; 1904[2]; repr. 1956), and by S. Pines (1963), with introductions by L. Strauss, and the translator C. Rabin published an abridged translation with an introduction by J. Guttmann (1952). German translations were undertaken in the 19th century (R. Fuerstenthal, pt. 1, 1839; M. Stern, pt. 2, 1864; S. Scheyer, pt. 3, 1838), all based on the Hebrew version of Ibn Tibbon. There is also a modern Hebrew translation from the Arabic by A. Siman and E. Mani (1957), and versions in Italian, Spanish, and Hungarian.

I. Efros published an English translation of Maimonides' *Treatise on Logic* (in: PAAJR, 8, 1938), together with part of the Arabic original and three Hebrew versions. He also published a revised edition of the full Arabic text (in Hebrew alphabet) based on the edition of M. Tuerker (in: PAAJR, 34 (1966), 155ff.). J. Gorfinkle translated the *Shemonah Perakim* into English under the title *The Eight Chapters of Maimonides on Ethics* (1966). The *Iggeret Teiman* was translated by Boaz Cohen, *Moses Maimonides' Epistle to Yemen* (1952), edited by A. S. Halkin. S. Muntner edited versions of many of Maimonides' medical works: *Perush le-Firkei Abukrat* ("Commentary on the Aphorisms of Hippocrates" (1961), with an Eng. introd. (*Pirkei Moshe bi-Refu'ah* ("Maimonides' Medical Aphorisms" (1959), with Eng. introd.); *Sefer ha-Kazzeret* (1940; *Treatise on Asthma,* 1963); *Sammei ha-Mavet* (1942; *Treatise on Poisons and Their Antidotes,* 1966); and *Hanhagat ha-Beri'ut* ("Guide to Good Health" (1957); *Regimen Sanitasis,* Ger., 1966). Volume I of *The Medical Aphorisms of Moses Maimonides* (ed. F. Rosner and S. Muntner) appeared in 1970. Selected letters of Maimonides are to be found in English translation in F. Kobler (ed.) *Letters of Jews Through the Ages,* 1 (1952), 178–219 (see also introduction, lx–lxi).

[ED.]

Bibliography: GENERAL: D. Yellin and I. Abrahams, *Maimonides* (1903; repr. 1936); J. Guttmann et al. (eds.), *Moses ben Maimon, sein Leben, seine Werke und sein Einfluss,* 2 vols. (1908–14); Graetz-Rabbinowitz, 4 (1916), 326–406, 459 n. 2, and appendix by A. E. Harkavy, 51–59; A. Cohen, *Teachings of Maimonides* (1927; repr. 1968); I. Epstein (ed.), *Moses Maimonides* (1935); B. Dinur, *Rabbenu Moshe ben Maimon* (1935); S. Baron (ed.), *Essays on Maimonides* (1941); A. S. Halkin, in: *Joshua Starr Memorial Volume* (1953), 101–10 (Heb.); M. D. Rabinowitz (ed.), *Iggerot ha-Rambam* (1960), introductions to the three letters; J. L. Maimon, *Rabbi Moshe ben Maimon* (1960); Hirschberg, Afrikah, 1 (1965), index; A. Neubauer, in: JQR, 8 (1896), 541–61. ALLEGED CONVERSION: On the question of his alleged conversion: those who maintain it are A. Geiger (*Nachgelassene Schriften,* 3 (1876), 42), S. Munk (*Notice sur Joseph ben-Iehouda* (1842), and in: AI, 12 (1851),

319ff.), and Graetz. The allegation is examined and opposed by M. Friedlaender (*Guide for the Perplexed* (1904²), xviii), D. S. Margoliouth (JQR, 13 (1901), 539–41), and S. P. Rabbinowitz (Graetz-Rabbinowitz, 4 (1916), 332, 462). See also J. L. Maimon, op. cit., 235–50; D. Corcos, in: *Zion,* 32 (1967), 138–60. As HALAKHIST: I. Epstein (ed.), op. cit., 59–82; I. Herzog, *ibid.*, 137–53; A. Marmorstein, *ibid.*, 157–74; Levey, in: CCARY, 45 (1935), 368–96; C. Tchernowitz, *Toledot ha-Posekim,* 1 (1946), 193–307; J. Levinger, *Darkhei ha-Maḥashavah ha-Hilkhatit shel ha-Rambam* (1965); A. Zuroff, *Responsa of Maimonides* (Diss., Yeshiva University, 1966); M. Havazelet, *Ha-Rambam ve-ha-Ge'onim* (1967); J. T. Dienstag, in: *Talpioth,* 9 (1968); idem, *Ein ha-Mitzvot* (1968). As PHILOSOPHER: Guttmann, Philosophies, 152–82 and index; Husik, Philosophy, 236–311 and index; D. Rosin, *Die Ethik Maimonides* (1876); I. Efros, *Philosophical Terms in the Moreh Nebukim* (1924); L. Roth, *Spinoza, Descartes, and Maimonides* (1929); J. Sarachek, *Faith and Reason: the Conflict over the Rationalism of Maimonides* (1935); F. Bamberger, *Das System des Maimonides* (1935); L. Strauss, *Philosophie und Gesetz* (1935); idem, in: MGWJ, 81 (1937), 93–105; idem, in: Baron (ed.), op. cit., 37–91 (repr. in: L. Strauss, *Persecution and the Art of Writing* (1952), 38–94); idem, in: PAAJR, 22 (1953), 115–30; G. Vajda, *Introduction à la pensee juive du moyen âge* (1947), 129–51; J. Becker, *Mishnato ha-Filosofit shel ha-Rambam* (1956); L. V. Berman, *Ibn Bājjah ve-ha-Rambam: Perek be-Toledot ha-Filosofyah ha-Medinit* (1959); H. A. Wolfson, in: JQR, 1 (1911/12), 297–339; 25 (1934/35), 441–67; 26 (1935/36), 369–77; 32 (1941/42), 345–70; 33 (1942/43), 40–82; idem, in: *Essays... Linda R. Miller* (1938), 201–34; idem, in: PAAJR, 11 (1941), 105–63; idem, in: *Louis Ginzberg Jubilee Volume* (1945), 411–46; idem, in: *Mordecai M. Kaplan Jubilee Volume* (1953), 515–30; Z. Diesendruck, in: *Jewish Studies... Israel Abrahams* (1927), 74–134 (Ger.); idem, in: HUCA, 5 (1928), 415–534 (Ger.); S. Rawidowicz, in: I. Epstein (ed.), *Moses Maimonides* (1935), 177–88; E. Rosenthal, *ibid.*, 191–206; I. Heinemann, in: MGWJ, 79 (1935), 102–48; A. Altmann, *ibid.*, 80 (1936), 305–30; idem, in: BJRL, 35 (1953), 294–315; A. J. Heschel, in: *Sefer ha-Yovel... Levi Ginzberg* (1945), 159–88; A. Hyman, in: *La filosofia della natura nel medioevo* (1966), 209–18; S. Pines, in: *Encyclopedia of Philosophy,* 5 (1967), 129–34; A. J. Reines, *Maimonides and Abrabanel on Prophecy* (1970). As PHYSICIAN: W. M. Feldman, in: I. Epstein (ed.), *Moses Maimonides* (1935), 107–34; F. Rosner, in: *Bulletin of the History of Medicine,* 43 (1969); S. Muntner, in: *Ha-Refu'ah* (1954); idem, in: *Korot,* 3 (1964), 7–8; W. Steinberg and S. Muntner, in: *American Journal of Obstetrics and Gynaecology,* 91 no. 3 (1965); I. Jakobovits, *Jewish Medical Ethics* (1959); F. Rosner and S. Muntner, *The Medical Aphorisms of Maimonides,* 1 (1970). As ASTRONOMER: A. Marx, in: HUCA, R. Lerner and M. Mahdi (eds.), *Medieval Political Philosophy* (1963), 227–36. HIS VIEWS ON MUSIC: H. G. Farmer, *Maimonides on Listening to Music* (1941); E. Werner and I. Sonne, in: HUCA, 16 (1941), 281–3, 313–5; B. Cohen, *Law and Tradition in Judaism* (1959), 167–81.

MAIMUNA, celebration held by all Maghrebi Jews and many Eastern communities at the end of the last day of Passover which according to tradition is the anniversary of the death of *Maimonides' father *Maimon b. Joseph who lived for a time in Fez. In every home, tables are set with foods and drinks having a symbolic significance, varying according to local custom. These include fresh pitchers of sweet milk, garlands of leaves and flowers, branches of fig trees, and ears of wheat. Usually a live fish (a symbol of fertility) is placed on the table, swimming in a bowl. The menu includes lettuce leaves dipped in honey, buttermilk, and pancakes spread with butter and honey. There is a "lucky dip," a bowl of flour in which golden objects are placed. In some places a plate of flour is set on the table with five eggs and five beans and dates set in it. In Oran, vessels of silver and gold are included in the table decoration. On this night people eat only dairy foods and wafers made of fried dough resembling pancakes, known as *muflita.* No meat is to be consumed. The Jews visit each other, taking gifts of food. On the day following the holiday, the actual day of Maimuna, people go out to the fields, cemeteries, or the beaches and organize large social gatherings. In modern Israel Jews of Moroccan extraction celebrate the day after Passover with communal outings and picnics, and a central gathering is held in Jerusalem. The exact meaning of the word Maimuna is unknown. A suggestion that it is connected with the name of Maimun, the king of the jinns, does not seem acceptable.

A group of Moroccan immigrants celebrating the Maimuna in Jerusalem. Courtesy Government Press Office, Tel Aviv.

Bibliography: H. Z. Hirschberg, *Me-Ereẓ Mevo ha-Shemesh* (1957), 77. [R.KA.]

MAINE, northernmost New England state, with a Jewish population of 8,300 out of a total of 1,000,000 in 1969. Nearly half the Jews lived in Portland (3,600), the largest city. Other substantial Jewish communities were in the twin cities of Lewiston-Auburn (1,400) and Bangor (1,300). There were smaller Jewish settlements in Biddeford (375); Waterville (210); Calais (135); Rockland, Bath, Augusta, Rumford Falls, Caribou, and Gardner; in Aroostook County (120) around the U.S. Air Force Base at Presque Isle, and in the resort towns of Old Town, Old Orchard Beach, and Bar Harbor. Of the 16 congregations in the state, four were in Portland, three in Bangor, and two in Lewiston. There were also synagogues in Biddeford, Bath, Auburn, Caribou, Old Orchard, Old Town, and Rockland. There were Jewish community centers and federations in Portland, Lewiston, and Bangor. A Jewish home for the aged was located in Portland, a Jewish high school in Bangor, and a community Hebrew school in Portland. One of the only three community-owned Jewish funeral chapels in the U.S. was in Bangor. B'nai B'rith maintained a Hillel Foundation at the University of Maine, in Orono.

The first known Jewish resident was Susman Abrams, of Hamburg, Germany, who settled at Waldborough during the Revolutionary War. He also lived at Union and Thomaston. There is no evidence that he embraced Christianity but he was married to a Christian. Families with Sephardi Jewish antecedents, such as the Campanals and Decosters, have been prominent Maine folk for two centuries. Joseph Israel, of Portland, lost his life in 1804 in a daring naval exploit against the Tripolitan pirates in Tripoli harbor. Jewish peddlers from Massachusetts trudged through the southern Maine villages in the late 1700s and early 1800s, before Maine was separated from Massachusetts. An 1832 history of Maine makes no mention of Jews among the state's sects but there were enough Jews in Bangor to form Congregation Ahabat Achim in the 1850s, the first in the state. The earliest modern Jewish settler was Haiman Philip Spitz, who had been one of the founders of the Boston Jewish community. Spitz, who went to Bangor in 1848 when it was the center of the state's lumbering

	Total Jewish population of Maine **8,185**
M A I N E Calais • ▲ Bangor Waterville • Augusta • ▲ Lewiston-Auburn Portland ■ Saco • Biddeford	% of Jews in general population of Maine **0.84**
• —100–1,000 ▲ —1,000–2,000 ■ —2,000–4,000	% of Maine Jews in Jewish population of U.S.A. **0.14**

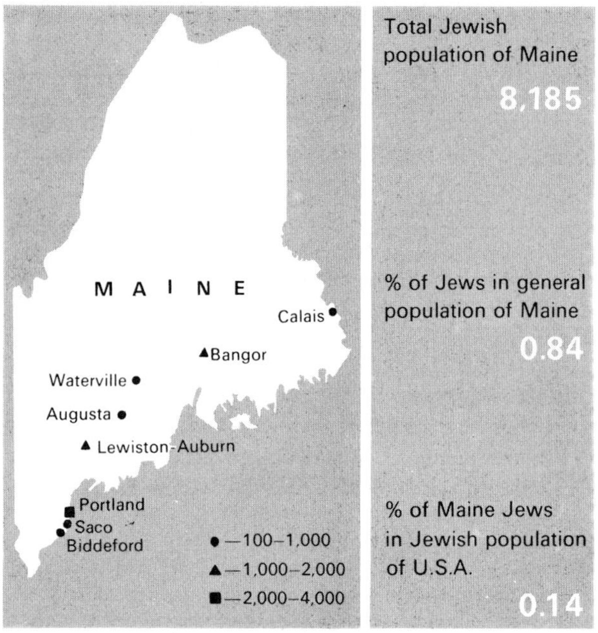

Jewish communities in Maine. Population figures for 1968.

industry, opened a clothing store that catered to the lumber workers. He was followed by five other Jewish families whose living came from clothing and dry goods stores and peddling. Moses Silber was the first president of Ahabat Achim and Spitz was vice-president. The congregation and the community disintegrated when the lumber industry declined during the panic of 1856–57. A Captain A. Goldman, of Bangor, who served with Maine's 17th Regiment during the Civil War, was probably a member of one of the Bangor families.

The bulk of the Maine Jewish community dates from the late 1880s and early 1890s when immigrants from Eastern Europe settled in Portland, the factory towns of Lewiston, Auburn, Bangor, Biddeford, and Watertown, and later spread into the resort and mining areas. By 1884 they were sufficiently numerous for the state legislature to liberalize the Sunday closing laws to permit those who kept their places of business closed on Saturday to engage in their normal occupational pursuits on Sunday. There is no agreement on which synagogue congregation is the oldest in the state. An 1877 census by the Union of American Hebrew Congregations listed a synagogue in Portland. However, the U.S. Census of 1890 reported no synagogue anywhere in Maine. The Portland Hebrew School was founded in 1884 and Congregation Beth Israel in Bangor erected the state's first synagogue in 1890. The Biddeford congregation dates from 1892 and the one in Auburn from 1897. The Isaac L. Rice collection of French literature and music in Bates College, Lewiston, was a gift from the eminent inventor and chess master. In 1969 Louis Bernstein, of Portland, son of one of the 1880 immigrants, was elected president of the board of overseers of Bowdoin College, the state's oldest university. Abraham H. Rudman, of Augusta, was the first Jew named to the Maine Superior Court, in 1934.

Bibliography: B. Postal and L. Koppman, *A Jewish Tourist's Guide to the U.S.* (1954), 207–9; Haiman Philip Spitz, *An Autobiography,* in the files of the American Jewish Archives.

[B.P.]

MAINTENANCE (Heb. מְזוֹנוֹת, *mezonot*), generally speaking, the supply of all the necessaries of the party entitled thereto, i.e., not only food, but also matters such as medical expenses, raiment, lodging, etc. (Sh. Ar., EH 73:7; see *Husband and Wife). When, however, the maintenance

obligation is based on a personal undertaking (see below) and not on the operation of law, it will not cover raiment and perhaps not even medical expenses, unless the contrary is indicated by the terms of the undertaking (Sh. Ar., EH 114:12; *Rema,* ḤM 60:3; *Siftei Kohen* thereto n. 14). The liability of maintenance exists generally by virtue of law, but in the absence of any legal duty it may also be based on a voluntary undertaking (e.g., by the husband toward his wife's daughter by a previous marriage). Even though it is normally for an unfixed amount, such an undertaking will be binding and be governed by the general law of obligations (Sh. Ar., ḤM 60:2, contrary to the opinion of Yad, Meḥirah 11:6; see also *Contract; *Obligation, Law of).

The liability of maintenance by virtue of law is imposed on (1) a husband toward his wife; (2) a father toward his small children; and (3) the heirs of the deceased toward his widow. A divorced wife is not entitled to maintenance from her former husband (Sh. Ar., EH 82:6; see *Divorce), nor, generally speaking, a betrothed woman from the bridegroom (Sh. Ar., EH 55:4 and *Rema* thereto). Only maintenance between husband and wife, as a liability by virtue of law, will be discussed below (see also *Widow; *Parent and Child).

Scope of the Maintenance Obligation. The husband's duty to maintain his wife is one of the duties imposed on him by virtue of his marriage as *obligatio ex lege* (Yad, Ishut 12:2; Sh. Ar., EH 69:2). He has to provide her with at least the minimal needs for her sustenance in accordance with local custom and social standards (Yad, Ishut 12:10; Sh. Ar., EH 70:3). In addition and subject to the aforesaid, the wife's right to maintenance is governed by the rule that she "goes up with him but does not go down with him" (Ket. 61a; Tur, EH 70), i.e., the wife, regardless of the standard of living she enjoyed prior to the marriage, is entitled to a standard of living which matches that of her husband and to be maintained in accordance with his means and social standing. At the same time, she is not obliged to suffer having her standard of living reduced to one below that which she enjoyed prior to her marriage, at any rate not as compared with the standard of living customary in her paternal home with regard to family members backed by means similar to those available to her husband, even if he should choose a lower standard of living than he can afford (Yad, Ishut 12:11; Sh. Ar., EH 70:1, 3 and *Ḥelkat Meḥokek* thereto n. 1). In addition to providing for all the domestic needs of the common household and as part of his duty of maintenance in its wider sense, the husband must give his wife a weekly cash amount for her personal expenses, again in accordance with their standard of living and social custom (Sh. Ar., EH 70:3; *Ḥelkat Meḥokek* thereto n. 7). In return for this obligation, the husband is entitled to his wife's "surplus handiwork," i.e., to her earnings from work done beyond the call of her legal duty toward him (*Ma'aseh Yadeha*). The said obligation being imposed on the husband as part of his duty to maintain his wife, she may, of her own choice, waive her right to the weekly allowance in order to retain for herself such surplus earnings, just as she may waive her maintenance in order to acquire for herself the proceeds of her handiwork (*Ḥelkat Meḥokek* loc. cit.). The unspent balance of the money given the wife for her maintenance belongs to her husband, since he is only required to give her an amount sufficient for her needs (Ket. 65b; Yad, Ishut 12:13; *Pitḥei Teshuvah,* EH 70 n. 1). However, if such balance results from the wife's spending less than she requires for her own needs, it belongs to herself; she need not invest the amount of it and if she should do so, the fruits of such investment would belong to her alone (see *Dowry). Another opinion is that money given by the husband for his wife's maintenance always remains his own, except insofar as she actually expends it on the household or on her own maintenance, and therefore any balance, even if saved, belongs to him (see *Rema,* EH 70:3; *Pithei Teshuvah,* EH 70 n. 1; PDR 2:229 and 289).

The wife's right to be maintained in the manner described above is independent of the fact that she may be able to maintain herself out of her own property and the fact that her husband may be in financial difficulties. She will accordingly not be obliged to sell her property or to use fruits thereof, to which her husband has no right, in order to facilitate his fulfillment of his obligation to maintain her, since he has undertaken the obligation on the marriage and it is also expressed in the *ketubbah* deed in the phrase, "I shall work and support you" (see below, Sh. Ar., loc. cit. *Pithei Teshuvah,* EH 70 n. 2; PDR 1:97, 101f.).

Separated Parties. In general, the husband is only obliged to maintain his wife as long as she lives with him or, at any rate, if he is not responsible for the fact that they are separated (*Rema,* EH 70:12). Hence in the case of separation of the parties, it is necessary to establish which of them has left the common home.

When the Husband Leaves the Home. In principle the wife's right is not affected: "She was given to live and not to suffer pain" (Ket. 61a) and the husband remains responsible for her maintenance (*Mordekhai,* Ket. no. 273). To frustrate her claim, the husband must prove a lawful reason for his absence and refusal to maintain her, e.g., her responsibility for a quarrel justifying his departure (*Rema,* EH 70:12). However, even in circumstances where the husband is responsible for maintaining his wife despite their separation, it will nevertheless be presumed that he has left her with sufficient means to support herself for a reasonable period during his absence and therefore, in general, she will not be awarded maintenance during the first three months following his departure (Ket. 107a; Sh. Ar., EH 70:5). For the wife to succeed in a claim brought within this period, she must prove that her husband has left her without any means at all, or will have to rebut the above assumption in some other manner, e.g., by proving that her husband left the home as a result of a quarrel or with the intention of returning after a short interval but for some reason failed to do so (*Rema,* EH 70:12; *Beit Shemu'el* 70 n. 11; *Hut ha-Meshullash.* 1:6, 4).

The husband is not entitled to demand that his wife should work and support herself out of her earnings during his absence unless she has expressly or by implication consented to do this (Yad, Ishut 12:20; *Maggid Mishneh* thereto; Sh. Ar., EH 70:9; *Helkat Mehokek* 70 n. 33). This is so regardless of whether or not she has been accustomed to working prior to his departure and making over her earnings to her husband, according to law. The court will not of its own initiative investigate the matter of the wife's earnings from her own handiwork, but will take this into account only if it emerges out of the wife's own arguments. However, if after his return the husband can prove that the wife has been working and earning during his absence, he will not be obliged to repay a loan his wife has taken for her maintenance (see below), to the extent that he proves that she was able to support herself from such earnings during his absence. In this event he will similarly be entitled to demand that she refund to him all amounts she has recovered out of his property for the purposes of her maintenance (Yad, Ishut 12:16; Sh. Ar., EH 70:5).

When the wife is entitled to maintenance but her husband leaves her without sufficient means and she does not maintain herself out of her own earnings, she has the right to borrow for her maintenance and to hold her husband liable for the repayment of such a loan (Ket. 107b; Yad, Ishut 12:19; Sh. Ar., EH 70:8). This is not the case if prior to his departure she was supporting herself by her own efforts and remained silent when he publicly disavowed responsibility for debts she might contract, thus seeming to have consented to this (*Rema,* EH 70:12; *Beit Shemu'el* 70 n. 32). The husband's duty to repay such a loan is toward his wife only and he is not directly liable to the creditor. If, however, the wife has no property of her own, or if for any other reason the creditor might have difficulty in recovering from the wife, he may claim repayment of the loan from the husband directly, in terms of the **Shi'buda de-Rabbi Nathan* (permitting the creditor to recover the debt directly from a third party who owes money to the principal debtor if the creditor has no other means of recovering from the latter; (Yad, Ishut 12:19; *Rema,* EH 70:8)).

If the wife has sold some of her own property to support herself, she will be entitled to recover from her husband the equivalent of the amount realized, provided that the facts do not demonstrate any waiver of this right on her part, such as an express declaration to this effect made by her before witnesses at the time of the sale, or if at that time there was a suit for divorce pending between the parties. If proof to this effect is forthcoming, the wife will not be entitled to recover anything from her husband since it is presumed that as long as the marriage tie is in existence, she will not do anything which might bring about its complete severance and will therefore also be prepared to waive her pecuniary rights against her husband (*Rema,* EH 70:8; *Beit Shemu'el* 70 n. 29; PDR 2:289, 291f.). Whenever the wife is not entitled to a refund of the amounts she has expended, during the period of her husband's absence, the earnings from her handiwork will be loans to her (*Rema,* EH 70:8).

Third parties who of their own accord assist the wife in respect of her maintenance are not entitled to be refunded for their expenditure—neither from the wife since she has not borrowed from them, nor from her husband since he has not instructed them to do so—but they are in the position of one who "has put his money on the horns of a deer" (*Rema,* EH 70:8; see also *Unjust Enrichment). If the wife can prove that the assistance was given her in the form of a loan, the question of repayment will be governed by the aforesaid ordinary rules concerning a loan for purposes of the wife's maintenance, even if the assistance was given by her own parents (*Mordekhai,* Ket. no. 273).

When the Wife Leaves the Home. In principle the husband is not obliged to maintain his wife unless she lives with him (see above). Hence the mere fact of her leaving him, or her refusal to return to him after she has left him lawfully, provides the husband with a *prima facie* defense against her claim for maintenance, since by living apart from him she precludes herself from carrying out her marital duties, on due fulfillment of which her right to maintenance is dependent. Therefore, to succeed in a claim for maintenance in these circumstances, the wife must discharge the onus of proving facts justifying her absence from the marital home (*Rema,* EH 70:12; *Beit Shemu'el* 70 n. 34; PDR 6:33, 52f.). These may arise either from the husband's bad conduct toward her—e.g., his reponsibility for a quarrel justifying in law her refusal to continue living with him together in the marital home (*Beit Yosef,* EH 70, end; Sh. Ar., EH 70:12)—or from other circumstances which are independent of the husband's blameworthy conduct toward her, such as his refusal to comply with her justified demand to move to another dwelling or to live away from her husband's relatives who cause her distress (see *Husband and Wife). In general it may be said that any reason sufficient to oblige the husband to grant his wife a divorce will entitle her to claim maintenance from him even though she may have left the home, since the fact that the husband is obliged to grant her a divorce means that he must acquiesce in their living apart; therefore her refusal to live with him entails no breach of her duties toward him. Moreover, by unlawfully withholding a divorce from his wife the husband prevents her from marrying someone else who could maintain her, and there is a rule that a husband who, contrary to law, prevents his wife from marrying another man renders himself liable to maintain her until he grants her a divorce (PDR 1:74, 77–80). If the wife leaves the home on account of a quarrel she has unjustifiably caused, and generally when she has no justifiable reason for living apart from her husband, she will not be entitled to maintenance from him.

For other cases in which the wife forfeits her right to maintenance, see *Husband and Wife (s.v. *moredet*); *Divorce.

Claim for Maintenance Cannot Be Assigned or Set Off. The husband is not entitled to set off against her claim for maintenance any pecuniary claim he may have against his wife, such as one arising from her sale, contrary to law, of her husband's property for purposes of her maintenance during his absence. His duty to maintain his wife means to provide her with the necessities of life with him, i.e., entails responsibility for her daily needs with regard to food, raiment, lodging, etc. This affords the wife a right against which pecuniary debts cannot be set off, since those two differ in their legal nature and her daily needs cannot be satisfied by a reduction of the debt she owes him (PDR 1:333, 338; 2:97, 99). If, however, the wife's claim is based on a right whose legal nature is purely pecuniary, e.g., her claim for repayment of a loan she has taken for her maintenance, there will be no bar to the husband setting off against such claim any other pecuniary claim he may have against her, if, for instance, she is indebted to him for a loan she obtained from him for the purpose of supporting her relatives—he may also set off such pecuniary claim against her claim with regard to payment of her *ketubbah* at the time of their divorce (see PDR 1 loc. cit.). The same reason that entitles the wife to receive actual payment of her maintenance prevents her from assigning this right to others (*Beit Shemu'el* 93 n. 18).

Arrear Maintenance. If the wife, although entitled to maintenance, does not bring an action for it in the court, she will be unable to claim maintenance for any period preceding the date of bringing her suit, since it will be presumed that she preferred to suffer rather than unfold her troubles before the court and her silence will therefore be interpreted as a waiver of her right for such a period (Yad, Ishut 12:22; Sh. Ar., EH 70:11). This presumption may be rebutted by evidence showing that she insisted on her rights, e.g., that she demanded her maintenance from her husband and refrained from instituting action only because of his promise to comply without recourse to the court (*Rema*, EH 80:18; *Beit Shemu'el* 80 n. 27); institution of action has the same effect for any period thereafter even if a considerable amount of time elapses before judgment is given (*Rema* 70:5; *Beit Shemu'el* 70 n. 12; see also *Limitation of Actions).

Nonpayment of Maintenance: Consequences. On the husband's failure to maintain his wife in the manner to which she is entitled, the court—at her instance—will order him to do so, whether he refuses payment although he has the means to meet it or whether he lacks the means because he does not work although he is able to work and earn this amount. In other words, the husband will be ordered to pay maintenance in accordance with his potential working and earning abilities, and not necessarily his actual earnings, for he has undertaken in the *ketubbah* to work and to maintain his wife (*Rema*, EH 70:3; *Ḥelkat Meḥokek* 70 n. 12). If he has sufficient for his own needs only for a single day, he must still share this with his wife since he is liable to maintain her "with himself" (*Rema*, EH 70:3). On the other hand, as he has to maintain her "with him" only, i.e., to no greater extent than he is able in respect of himself, he will be exempt from maintaining her if he cannot afford it because he is in a position of utter poverty and unable to work and earn for reasons beyond his control (*Pitḥei Teshuvah*, EH 70 n. 2; *Perishah*, ḤM 97 n. 41). For the same reason, inability to pay maintenance is excused on grounds of the husband's need to repay regular debts, these taking preference over the former (*ibid.*). If the wife should not wish to content herself with a claim for maintenance, she may possibly be entitled to demand a divorce.

In the State of Israel. Maintenance for the wife is a matter of personal status within the meaning of article 51 of the Palestine Order in Council, 1922, and is therefore governed by Jewish law (sec. 51 thereof) even when claimed in a civil court by virtue of section 4, Rabbinical Courts Jurisdiction (Marriage and Divorce) Law, 5713–1953. So far as a Jewish wife is concerned, the above position was left unchanged by the Family Law Amendment Maintenance Law, 5719–1959, which expressly provides that the question of her maintenance shall be governed solely by Jewish law (sec. 2; see Supr. PD 15 (1961), 1056, 1058). If the husband refuses to comply with a judgment of the court for the payment of maintenance, he may be imprisoned for a period not exceeding 21 days for every unpaid instalment (Executive Law 5727–1967, sec. 70ff.); see also *Imprisonment for Debt.

Bibliography: Gulak, Yesodei, 1 (1922), 37; 2 (1922), 68–70; 3 (1922), 37–39; Gulak, Oẓar, 149–58; ET, 1 (1951^{3}), 324f.; 4 (1952), 80–83, 91f.; 6 (1954), 656; Regional Rabbinical Court, Tel Aviv, Judgment, in: *Ha-Torah ve-ha-Medinah*, 9–10 (1957/59), 185–99; B. Cohen, in: PAAJR, 20 (1951), 135–234; republished in his: *Jewish and Roman Law*, 1 (1966), 179–278; addenda: *ibid.*, 2 (1966), 775–7; B. Schereschewsky, *Dinei Mishpaḥah* (1967^{2}), 117–40; Elon, Mafte'ah, 122f.; idem, *Ḥakikah Datit...* (1968), 44–46, 60–62; H. Baker, *Legal System of Israel* (1968), index.

[B.-Z.SCH.]

MAINZ (**Mayence; Heb.** מגנצא, מגנץ, מענץ), city on the Rhine in W. Germany.

The Medieval Settlements. Mainz is one of the oldest Jewish communities in Germany. It is presumed that Jews came to the city as merchants in the Roman era and may even have founded a settlement there. The date of the first medieval community is uncertain. A church council in Mainz declared in 906 that a man who killed a Jew out of malice must make amends like any other murderer, and presumably there were some Jews in the city at the time. The *Kalonymus family of Lucca is believed to have moved to Mainz in 917 but the date is not completely reliable. Evidence of the existence of a Jewish community is indisputable only from the middle of the tenth century. Archbishop Frederick (937–54) threatened the Jews with forcible conversion or expulsion. They were in fact expelled by Emperor Henry II in 1012 after a priest had converted to Judaism. Soon after, however (according to Jewish sources only a month), they were allowed to return and continued to play a lively part in the trade of the city, which was a commercial center on the Rhine and Main rivers. An organized community was in existence in the late tenth century (when *Gershom b. Judah was teaching in Mainz; his son apostatized in 1012), although land for a cemetery was not acquired until the time of the expulsion (gravestones dating from the 11th–14th centuries, discovered in 1922 in the fortified inner city, came from this cemetery). Many Jews left the city in 1084 after they had been accused of causing a fire in which their quarter was also damaged; settling in *Speyer they founded the community there.

Figure 1. Reconstructed section of the Kalonymus House in Mainz.

At the beginning of the First *Crusade (1096) the Mainz *parnas*, Kalonymus b. Meshullam, obtained an order from Emperor *Henry IV protecting the Jews, but nonetheless, and in spite of an armed and spirited resistance, on May 27 over 1,000 died—some at the hands of the crusaders and many by suicide as an act of **kiddush ha-Shem*. Kalonymus escaped with a group to Ruedesheim, but committed suicide the next morning during an attack led by Count Emicho. The synagogue (first mentioned in 1093) and Jewish quarter were burned down on May 29. Twelfth-century Jews immortalized the Mainz martyrdom as an example of supreme **akedah*. The community slowly recuperated in the following years after Henry IV had permitted those forcibly converted to return to Judaism, decreeing that the Jews were also to enjoy the "king's peace" (*Landfrieden*). During the Second Crusade (1146–47) it suffered several casualties (see also *Bernard of Clairvaux). During the Third Crusade (1189–92) the Jews of Mainz were unharmed because of the resolute protection of Frederick I Barbarossa; large numbers temporarily went into hiding in Munzanberg (near *Friedberg). In 1259 Mainz Jews were ordered to wear the Jewish *badge. In 1281 and 1283 numerous Jews fell victim to the *blood libel; the synagogue was also burnt in these years. As a result of these repeated persecutions some Jews of Mainz, along with those of other German cities, wished, in 1285, to emigrate to Ereẓ Israel under the leadership of *Meir b. Baruch of Rothenburg; others escaped the boundaries of the empire. During the *Black Death (1349) almost the whole community perished; some of them in a battle against the mob, and the majority (6,000 persons) in the flames of their burning synagogue and quarter, set on fire by their own hands in *kiddush ha-Shem*.

In the next decade (following the charter of the German Empire known as the Golden Bull of 1356) Jews again began to settle in Mainz. The community did not attain its former standing, even though a considerable number of Jews settled (in 1385 they presented the council with 3,000 gulden "out of gratitude" for its protection during the anti-Jewish disturbances which had broken out in various places). With the gradual transfer, in the later Middle Ages, of *Judenschutz* ("guardianship over the Jews") to the cities, their financial obligations grew heavier. The Jewry taxes, granted to the city in 1295 and renewed in 1366, became henceforth ever more burdensome. In 1438 Mainz Jews left the city after a dispute with the council (they may in fact have been expelled); synagogue and cemetery were confiscated and the tombstones utilized for building. In 1445 they were readmitted, only to be expelled in 1462; permitted to return in 1473, they were finally forced to leave the city ten years later. The synagogue was converted into a chapel.

The Community in the Middle Ages. Until the second half of the 12th century, the Jews conducted lively mercantile activities and from a very early date attended the *Cologne fairs. Discoveries in the area of the oldest Jewish settlement in Mainz provide evidence of commercial connections with Greece and Italy. From this period onward *moneylending became of increased importance in Mainz, as in all German communities. Records of the 12th, and especially of the 13th century, often reveal that churches and monasteries owed money to Jews. In 1213 Pope *Innocent III released all Christians in the Mainz province who were about to set out on a Crusade from paying interest on debts to Jews. Mainz Jewry also suffered when Emperor *Wenceslaus annulled debts owed to Jews (1390).

Until the Black Death Jews were allowed to possess land in the city and were recognized as owners of houses. Mainz Jews were probably permitted to reside outside the Jewish quarter, for the protective wall, customary in other cities, was missing. A *Judengasse* is mentioned in 1218 and at the end of the century 54 Jewish houses are recorded. The Jewish community was led by a so-called *Judenbischof*, nominated by the archbishop, and by not less than four elders (Vorsteher) who together constituted the Judenrat ("Jews' council") from 1286 until the end of the 14th century. The supreme non-Jewish juridical authority was the archbishop (from 1209). A yeshivah was founded in the tenth century by the Kalonymides, and became central under R. *Gershom b. Judah and his pupils and comtemporaries, Judah ha-Kohen, *Jacob b. Yakar, Isaac ha-Levi, and *Isaac b. Judah. Gershom's **takkanot* ("regulations"), which were applicable to the Rhenish cities, were acknowledged by all the other German communities and even by other European ones, thereby achieving the force of law, a fact which enhanced the reputation of Mainz. The chronicle of *Solomon b. Samson recounting the *kiddush ha-Shem* of 1096 regards Mainz as the main, most ancient, and most famous Jewish community on the Rhine; he praises its learning and pious way of life (see A. M. Habermann (ed.), *Sefer Gezerot Ashkenaz ve-Ẓarefat*).

From the early 12th century on, *Speyer, *Worms, and *Mainz (in Jewish sources named שו"ם (*shum*), an abbreviation made up of the first letter of their names) were recognized as the leading Jewish communities in Germany. Synodal assemblies were held in Mainz (1150, 1223, 1250), in which primarily representatives of the three leading communities took part; their resolutions, the *takkanot Shum*, were acknowledged by the rest of the communities of Germany. The Mainz rabbi, Jacob b. Moses *Moellin (1356–1427; known as Maharil) promulgated *takkanot* (chiefly concerned with ritual matters) aimed at the German and primarily the Rhenish communities. His collection of **minhagim* (compiled by his pupil Zalman of St. Goar), which rely mainly on Mainz traditions, are connected with all German and some non-German communities and were used to a large extent

Figure 2. The main synagogue of Mainz, consecrated in 1912 and burned by the Nazis on *Kristallnacht*, 1938. From *Magenza . . . im 500. Todesjahre des Mainzer Gelehrten Maharil.* Mainz, 1927.

in the Shulḥan Arukh, *Oraḥ Ḥayyim*. Outstanding among the many notable scholars and personalities in medieval Mainz are, in addition to those already mentioned, Nathan b. *Machir b. Judah (c. 1100), *Eliezer b. Nathan (c. 1150), *Meshullam b. Kalonymus (c. 1150), *Judah b. Kalonymus b. Moses (c. 1175), and Baruch b. Samuel (1200).

Resettlement and the Modern Community. In the early modern era only a few Jews lived in Mainz. In 1513 the archbishop designated Weisenau, near Mainz, as the seat of the rabbinate for the diocese of Mainz, presumably because few resided in the city itself. These few were expelled in 1579, but a new community was reconstituted in 1583, reinforced by emigration from *Frankfort (1614), Worms (1615), and *Hanau. A rabbi was subsequently engaged and a synagogue built (1639; see also *Landesjudenschaft*). During the French occupation (1644–48) the Jews suffered and were subsequently subjected to ever-harsher restrictions. The permitted number of Jewish families was limited to 20, and later 10 (1671); they were allowed to inhabit one special street only (ghetto).

Influenced by the *Toleranzpatent* (1784) of *Joseph II, the archbishop-elector improved the legal position of the Jews, and allowed them to open their own schools and attend general ones. After the revolutionary French occupation of Mainz (1792) the *Leibzoll* ("body tax") was abolished and on September 12 the gates of the ghetto were torn down. Until the end of the occupation (1814) the Jews of Mainz were French citizens (they sent delegates to the *Sanhedrin in Paris). The Napoleonic edict of May 17, 1808 remained in force until 1848. After the German war of liberation (1813–15) Mainz passed to *Hesse-Darmstadt. Full civil rights, promised in June 1816, were not granted.

In the mid-19th century, the community split when R. Joseph *Aub introduced ritual reforms in the newly built synagogue (1853). The Orthodox founded the Israelitische Religionsgesellschaft, with its own synagogue, and engaged Marcus *Lehmann as rabbi; he founded a Jewish school (a high school with instruction in foreign languages) in 1859. Until the Prussian law of 1876 regulating secession from religious communities, the Orthodox remained within the community and seceded only later. In modern times, too, a number of scholars originated from Mainz, notably Michael *Creizenach, Isaac *Bernays, Joseph *Derenburg, and Ludwig *Bamberger. Among the former communal institutions were the Israelite Home for the Sick and Disabled, the Jewish Sistership Organization for the Care of Jewish Antiquities, and the *talmud torah*. The Israelitische Religionsgesellschaft possessed a school (eight classes and 68 pupils), a library, and supplied religious instruction to 30 children. The communal budget totaled 220,000 marks in 1931. Twelve communities from the surrounding district were administered by the Mainz rabbinate. In the 19th century the Jewish population of Mainz increased but its percentage of the general population remained steady: 1,620 Jews in 1828 (5.3% of the total population); 2,665 in 1861 (5.8%); 2,998 in 1871 (5.8%). From then on both numbers and ratio declined, to 3,104 (3.7%) in 1900, 2,738 (2.5%) in 1925, and 2,730 (1.8%) in 1933.

Holocaust and Contemporary Periods. On Nov. 9/10, 1938 the main synagogue (including the museum and library) was looted and burned down. The Orthodox and Polish synagogues suffered similar treatment. On May 17, 1939 only 1,452 Jews remained, 70% of whom were 40 years or over. A steady flow of emigrants was partly balanced by an influx of refugees from the countryside. In March and September 1942 the majority of the community was deported to Poland and *Theresienstadt. On Feb. 10, 1943 the final liquidation of the community, which had been moved to the hospital, took place. After the war a new community was organized, which numbered 80 persons in 1948 and 122 in 1970 (with an average age of 53).

Bibliography: Aronius, Regesten; K. A. Schaab, *Diplomatische Geschichte der Juden in Mainz* (1855); M. Wiener, *Regesten* (1862); Germ Jud, 1 (1963), 174–223; 2 (1968), 512–21; Salfeld, Martyrol, index; idem, *Bilder aus der Vergangenheit der juedischen Gemeinde in Mainz* (1903); idem, in: *Festschrift . . . A. Berliner* (1903); idem, in: *Festschrift . . .Hermann Cohen* (1912), 347–76; idem, in: *Festschrift . . . Martin Philippson* (1916), 135–67; E. Carlebach, *Die rechtlichen und sozialen Verhaeltnisse der juedischen Gemeinden Speyer, Worms und Mainz* (1901); L. Rothschild, *Die Judengemeinden zu Mainz, Speyer und Worms von 1349–1438* (1904); Finkelstein, Middle Ages, index, s.v. *Mayence;* S. Levi, *Beitraege zur Geschichte der aeltesten juedischen Grabsteine in Mainz* (1926); idem, in: *Menorah* (Vienna-Frankfort), 5 (1927), 705–16; idem, in: ZGJD, 5 (1934), 187ff.; idem et al. (eds.), *Magenza* (1927); *Mitteilungsblatt des Landesverbandes der israelitischen Religionsgemeinden Hessens,* 5, no. 3 (1930), 9–10; 6, no. 1 (1931), 7; no. 12, 1; 7, no. 1 (1932), 4; J. S. Mencel, *Beitraege zur Geschichte der Juden in Mainz im XV. Jahrhundert* (1933); A. M. Habermann (ed.), *Gezerot Ashkenaz ve-Ẓarefat* (1946); Baron, Social[2], 4 (1957), 65–75; E. L. Rapp, in: *Jahrbuch der Vereinigung "Freunde der Universitaet Mainz"* (1958; 1959; 1962); K. Schilling (ed.), *Monumenta Judaica,* 2 (1963), index; A. M. Klein (ed.), *Tagebuch einer juedischen Gemeinde 1941–43* (1968). [B.D.W.]

MAISEL, ELIJAH ḤAYYIM (1821–1912), Polish talmudist and rabbinic leader. Maisel studied at Volozhin and at the age of 20 was appointed rabbi of Gorodok. After serving for two years he resigned the office, devoting the next ten years to study. After serving as rabbi in a number of small communities he was appointed to the important rabbinate of Lomza, and then in 1874 to the even more important one of Lodz. He was an erudite scholar, with a great understanding of and sympathy for humanity. Though a *Mitnagged,* he was loved by the people of Lodz, most of whom were Ḥasidim. He was a firm and fearless leader, taking an active part in all the community's philanthropic and religious institutions, to assist which he devoted most of his income. When they lacked money he would borrow and himself guarantee the repayment. If the wealthy members of the community refused to meet these debts, he changed his post, making it a condition that the new town paid his charitable debts in his old community. On one occasion the community of Bialystok offered to pay his debts in Lodz. However, not wishing to lose him, the community of Lodz immediately paid the debts. He kept open house and none who came for help was turned away empty-handed. Though lenient to others in personal religious matters, he strove with all his energies to prevent the breakdown of public religious life. He once stood on the Sabbath at the entrance of a Jewish shop until its owner promised to keep it closed in future.

Bibliography: O. Feuchtwanger, *Righteous Lives* (1965), 12–15.
[Mo.Ha.]

MAISELS, ISRAEL AARON (1905–), South African lawyer and communal leader. Born and educated in Johannesburg, Maisels was admitted to the bar in 1930. During World War II he served in the South African Air Force with the rank of major. In 1948 he became king's counsel and was leader of the Johannesburg, as well as the South African, Bar for several years. He was appointed a judge of the High Court of Southern Rhodesia, retiring in 1963, and later acted as a part-time judge of appeal for Botswana, Lesotho, and Swaziland. He served as arbitrator in disputes of public concern. Maisels was at various times president of the South African Jewish Board of Deputies, the South African Zionist Federation, and the United Hebrew Congregation in Johannesburg. [L.Ho.]

MAISELS, MOSES ḤAYYIM (**Misha;** 1901–), Hebrew writer. Born in Warsaw, Maisels, as a member of the staff of the Hebrew papers *Ha-Yom* and *Ha-Ẓefirah* in his native city, contributed numerous articles on contemporary and literary problems. In 1930 he emigrated to the United States where, from 1932, he was a member of the staff of the

Moses Ḥayyim Maisels, Hebrew writer.

Hadoar and, after the death of M. *Ribalow, its editor. In 1959 he emigrated to Israel where he became one of the editors of Mosad Bialik, the scholarly publishing house of the Jewish Agency for Israel. His major work, *Maḥashavah ve-Emet* (1939), is a two-volume essay: the first deals with philosophy in the past and its implications for the present; the second, with Judaism in the context of general philosophy. An abridged edition appeared under the pseudonym of M. Ḥ. Amishai (1961) and an English translation and condensation was published by A. Regelson under the name: *Thought and Truth, a Critique of Philosophy* (1956). Among Maisels' translations are Upton Sinclair's *Oil*—published under the pseudonym of M. Avishai (1929); M. Balaban's Polish studies on the history of the Jews (1930–33), and on the Frankist movement (1934–35); and Louis M. Epstein's *The Jewish Marriage Contract* (1954). Maisels' passion for anonymity led him to publish under numerous pseudonyms.

Bibliography: Kressel, Leksikon, 2 (1967), 343. [El.S.]

MAIUMAS, a popular licentious feast connected with water festivals in various places (13 according to Lev. R. 5:3, et al.); four localities were named after it. (1) Maiumas near Gaza served as the port of that city. It is first mentioned in the Zeno Papyri (259 B.C.E.; Cairo Papyrus 59.006). In the fourth century it became a Christian city called Constantia Neapolis, and was consequently freed from dependence upon the pagan city of Gaza. It is identified with al-Mīnā, $2\frac{1}{2}$ mi. (4 km.) from Gaza, on the Mediterranean coast. A synagogue with a mosaic pavement representing King David as Orpheus and dated to 508/9 C.E. was excavated there in 1967. (2) A Maiumas located on the coast near Ashkelon is mentioned by Antoninus Placentinus. It is perhaps to be identified with Khirbat al-Ashraf at the entrance to the Shikma Valley (Wadi Sikrayr). (3) Khirbat Miyāmās has been identified with al-Shūna, east of Caesarea, where the ruins of a Roman theater are visible. (4) Betomarsea in the vicinity of Charachmoba (al-Karak) is called Maiumas on the Madaba Map and was connected in ancient sources to the Baal-Peor of Numbers 25:3–9.

Bibliography: Strabo, *Geographia,* 16:2, 21; Ptolemaeus, 5:15, 5; Jerome, *Vita Hilarionis,* 3; Eusebius, *Vita Constantini,* 4:38; G. A. Smith, *Historical Geography of the Holy Land* (1896[4]), 190; Avi-Yonah, in: BIES, 30 (1966), 221–3; idem, *Madaba Mosaic Map* (1954), no. 14; A. Ovadyah, *Qadmoniot,* 1 (1968), 124–7, pls. 3–4. [M.A.-Y.]

MAJDAL AL-SHAMS, Druze village in the N. Golan, at the foot of Mt. Hermon. Under Israel military administration after the *Six-Day War (1967), Majdal al-Shams was the largest of all Druze villages in the region. In 1968 it had 3,500 inhabitants whose social and economic services were greatly improved after 1967. Profits from its rich fruit orchards increased and new sources of income were created in tourism, construction of new roads (e.g., the one leading from the village to the top of Mt. Hermon), etc. Majdal al-Shams maintained friendly contact with the Israel administration and close contact with the Druze community in Israel. [ED.]

MAJD AL-KURŪM (Arab. مجد الكروم). Arab village in northern Israel, 10 mi. (16 km.) E. of Acre. In the Israel *War of Independence, the village capitulated to Israel forces (Oct. 30, 1948). In 1969 it had 3,690 inhabitants, most of whom were Sunnite Muslims. The village economy is based on hill farming, with olive groves, deciduous fruit tree orchards, and vegetables and local workshops, stone and marble quarries, and factories particularly for food processing. Its site is assumed to be identical with the talmudic Bet Kerem ("House of Vineyards"), known for its fertile soil and rich water resources (Nid. 2:7; Tosef., Nid. 3:11). [E.O.]

MAJDANEK (Maidanek), concentration and extermination camp on the southeastern outskirts of *Lublin, Poland. Originally set up on July 21, 1941 for prisoners of war, it was soon turned into a camp for Jews and Poles with a maximum capacity for 35,000 inmates. The Germans planned further expansion. The camp commandants were the SS officers Karl Otto Koch, Max Koegel, Hermann Florstedt, Martin Weiss, and Arthur Liebenschel, but in fact final authority rested with Anton Thumann. The first transport, consisting of 5,000 Soviet prisoners of war, arrived in the autumn of 1941. They died of starvation and exposure. All the following transports consisted mainly of Jews, and to a lesser extent, Poles. The first groups of Jews arrived from Slovakia and the Protectorate of Bohemia and Moravia (15,000) and then Poland (36,500). Early in 1943,

Stamp commemorating the Majdanek death camp, issued by the Polish Post Office in 1946. Jerusalem, B. M. Ansbacher Collection.

6,000 Dutch and Greek Jews arrived, followed by 74,800 Polish Jews, mostly from *Warsaw, *Bialystok, and Lublin. Altogether 130,000 Jews were sent to Majdanek in 1942–43, of whom about 60% (women and children, the sick and elderly) were either shot or gassed upon arrival. By November 1943, an additional 37,000 victims had either succumbed to the unbearable living conditions or to sadistic treatment by camp guards. Until the spring of 1942 prisoners were usually shot in a nearby forest, but afterwards two of the camp's four Zyklon B gas chambers were used and the bodies then cremated. Jewish prisoners who were not liquidated were employed in various work projects in the camp or in the Lublin area. In the summer of 1943, 10,000 able-bodied Jews were transferred from Majdanek for work in "Hasag" camp and Auschwitz.

Toward the end of 1943 a strong partisan movement developed in the Lublin district. At the same time, the Jewish prisoners at the death camp of *Sobibór revolted. In retaliation, the Germans carried out a massacre (euphemistically named the "Harvest Festival") of 42,000 Jews, some of whom had been brought from the nearby work camps. This "action" included the machine-gunning of 18,000 Jews in a single day (Nov. 3, 1943) in front of the ditches that the victims were made to dig to serve as their own graves. Following this, only 612 Jews remained in Majdanek, to be exploited in such work as obliterating the traces of the massacre by exhuming and burning the victims, and in sorting the victims' clothing. The number of Jews killed in Majdanek is estimated at 125,000 (of them 100,000 were Polish). When the camp was liberated by the advancing Soviet armies (July 24, 1944), only a few hundred prisoners of various nationalities were still alive. In 1947 the Polish authorities established a museum and research institute at Majdanek.

Bibliography: E. Gryn and Z. Murawska, *Majdanek Concentration Camp* (1966); IMT, *Trial of the Major War Criminals*, 23 (1949), index; A. Werth, *Russia at War 1941–1945* (1964), 889–99, and index; G. Reitlinger, *Final Solution* (1968[2]), index; Z. Lukaszkiewicz, in: *Biuletyn Głównej Komisji Badania Zbrodni Hitlerowskich w Polsce*, 4 (1948), 63–105; T. Berenstein and A. Rutkowski, in: BŻIH, no. 58 (1966), 3–57; *Zeszyty Majdanka*, 3 vols. (1965–69) with Eng. sum. [De.D.]

MAJORCA (Sp. **Mallorca**), largest and most important of the Balearic Isles. It is difficult to determine when Jews first arrived in Majorca, but it may be assumed that the settlement was ancient because of the island's location at the crossroads of the maritime trade routes and its proximity to the coasts of both North Africa and the Iberian Peninsula. The presence of Jews on the nearby island of *Minorca during the fifth century implies their presence on Majorca also, and several lead tablets (attributed to the fourth–fifth centuries) bearing the name of Samuel b. Ḥagi (or Ḥaggai) have recently been found. Practically nothing is known of the history of the island from the sixth to the eighth centuries—and even less of the history of the Jews there during that period. It appears that the Jewish settlement was destroyed when the Byzantine general Belisarius overcame the Vandals and took Majorca (534 C.E.). Similarly, few details are available on the period of the Muslim conquest. When the *Almohads attacked southern Spain (12th century), refugees from Andalusia arrived in Majorca and it may be assumed that there were some Jews among them. The earliest evidence for the presence of Jews on the island during the Muslim period is from 1135, when Ramón Berenguer III, count of Barcelona, took some Jews of Majorca under his protection.

The Beginning of Aragonese Rule. When James I of Aragon conquered *Palma de Mallorca (1229–32), there

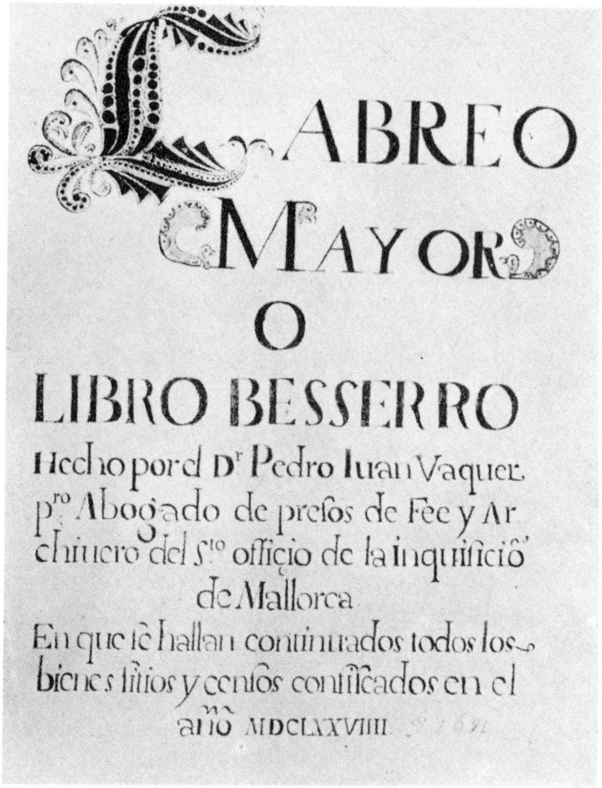

Figure 1. Title page of the first volume of the manuscript account books of the property confiscated by the Inquisition in Majorca from descendants of Jews in 1679 and 1691. From A. L. Isaacs, *Jews of Majorca*, London, 1936.

were several Jews in his retinue and when the distribution of properties took place after the conquest they were among the beneficiaries, notably Samuel *Benveniste, *alfaquim* of Count Nuño Sánchez of Roussillon. Properties were also granted to Jews who settled in other parts of the island: Inca, Petra, and Montiori. In Palma (then named Majorca, like the island itself), a residential area was set aside for the Jewish settlers in the fortress of Almudaina which was later known as "the fortress of the Jews." With the consolidation of Christian rule, Jews arrived from Marseilles and other towns of southern France, from North Africa, and even from Alexandria in Egypt. The king, who controlled settlement on the island, undertook to protect the permanent residential area of the Jews in the same way as other places. The Jews, however, rapidly left the fortress of Almudaina, settling in the vicinity, a move which later led to disputes. Besides the communities mentioned above, there were others in Felanitx, Sineu, Alcudia, Sóller, and Pollensa. James I also gave letters of protection to Jewish settlers from North Africa, among whom was Solomon b. Amar of Sijilmassa (1247).

From the start the Jewish settlers integrated into the economy of the island; they owned Muslim, Turkish, and Tatar slaves, whom they were accustomed to convert to Judaism, although the civil authorities and the church issued a series of decrees designed to prevent this. The Jews of Majorca developed a ramified commercial activity, especially during the second half of the 14th century, when the island reverted to the kingdom of Aragon. They engaged in the international maritime trade and became renowned for their skill in crafts such as gold- and silversmithery and shoemaking. In 1250 James I confirmed the rights of the Jewish settlers, granting them further privileges in conformity with his Jewish policy in the kingdom of Aragon. The problem of interest rates was one of the most severe in the relations between Jews and Christians on the island. Many royal ordinances dealt with the subject: restrictive decrees were issued; rates which had been fixed were cancelled; and occasionally the Jews were obliged to return the interest. In other matters, James I authorized the Jews of Majorca to address their complaints directly to himself and assured them of his protection. In 1254, he assessed their property, along with that of the Jews of Minorca and Ibiza, and constituted them as an independent taxation group. The community of Barcelona nevertheless continued to influence the island communities in their administrative affairs, as well as in all other aspects of communal life. In 1269 the Jews of Palma were granted an important privilege authorizing them to purchase houses, vineyards, and any other property in and around the town and to live in the houses which they had acquired or rented. Toward the close of the 13th century, the Jews in Palma lived in the area between Temple and Calatrava streets and this quarter became the focus of Jewish life in the town until the destruction of the community.

During the early 1270s, James I authorized the Jews to trade on a credit system with the Christians in textiles, cereals, oil, linen, saffron, and other goods. The Jews of Majorca were already fairly prosperous during this period. About 1271 the community of Palma paid an annual tax of 5,000 sólidos. During the same year, together with those communities of Catalonia, *Perpignan, and *Montpellier, it granted the king the sum of 25,000 sólidos toward the expenses of his campaign in Leon. He nevertheless forbade Jews to live side by side with Christians (1273), although he authorized them to purchase new houses. James I also renewed the permit for a separate *sheḥitah* on the island. During this period, the preacher Raimon Lull, who wielded considerable power on Majorca, was active there, conducting religious disputations with the Jews with the aim of bringing them over to Christianity.

From the Time of Alfonso III (1285–95) Until the Rule of Pedro IV (1343). James I divided the kingdom of Aragon in his will, setting up the independent kingdom of Majorca under his second son James II (of Majorca). Reigning from 1276, James II confirmed the privileges which had been granted by his father. In 1285 his nephew Alfonso III seized the island from him, ruling it until 1295. Alfonso confirmed a series of privileges and decrees issued by James I and further exempted the Jews from various taxes. The Jews of Majorca granted the king a special allowance of 10,000 sólidos for his own use, and Alfonso authorized them to appeal to him against legal decisions taken by his officials, provided that the town's interests were not prejudiced by these appeals (1286). During that year, he also borrowed 20,000 sólidos from the trustees of the community. A year later, the Jews of Majorca had to assist the king with a special contribution of 30,000 sólidos. At the same time, Alfonso showed concern for the regular payments of the debts owed to them by Christians, although he occasionally granted to the latter a remission of debts for a given period. Continuing to make yearly demands for support from the Jewish community in addition to the annual tax, in 1290 he imposed a payment of 37,000 sólidos in reparation for the offense of taking excessive interest; he also collected 12,000 sólidos for the right of establishing a "Jewish street," surrounding it with a wall, and installing gates at the points of entry.

James II returned to the island in 1295, reigning there until his death in 1311, when he was followed by his son Sancho I. The situation of the Jews further deteriorated until the island was reconquered by Pedro IV (1343). From the earliest days of the independent kingdom, they were compelled to pay tithes whenever they acquired land and houses from Christians. Anti-Jewish riots broke out in 1305, and in 1309 the first *blood libel occurred on the island when several Jews were accused of the murder of a Christian child. Riots ensued; the king ordered the attackers of the Jews to be punished and the activity of Christians within the Jewish quarter to be restricted. During the same year, similar riots broke out in Inca and many Jews were killed. Nevertheless the island admitted several Jewish settlers who had been expelled from France (1306). Among these was R. Aaron ha-Kohen who studied under R. Shem Tov Falcón in Majorca and later wrote his *Orḥot Ḥayyim* there. The king even sent an emissary to reassure the Jews of their security, and this assurance was reiterated by his son, Sancho I, in 1311. When several Christians from Germany arrived in Majorca in 1314 the community of Palma accepted them as proselytes (even though they had previously been rejected by the communities of *Lérida and *Gerona), thereby arousing considerable ill feeling on the island. Under the influence of Majorca's bishop, Sancho ordered the confiscation of the synagogue of Palma, which was converted into a church, and imposed a heavy fine on the community. A year later he ordered the confiscation of the property of the Jews of Palma, but left them with enough for subsistence. After the fine was paid, Sancho was again willing to take the Jews under his protection. During the same year, a long series of regulations dealing with Jewish matters was issued. The regulations concerned community administration, taxes on foodstuffs and wine, and commerce. It was prohibited to try Jews on their festivals; any Jew who expressed his desire to convert while imprisoned was to be confronted with two other Jews, before whom he had to declare that his conversion was of his own free will; if he reconsidered his decision, he would be authorized to remain a Jew. It was also stated that the Inquisition's investigations against Jews would not take place without the consent of the king; the trustees of the community would be authorized to seize those who disregarded communal regulations and imprison them; a Jew from abroad who came to trade in Majorca would be authorized to carry on to Minorca with his goods

Figure 2. The Calle del Sol, formerly the Jewish street of Majorca. From A. L. Isaacs, *Jews of Majorca,* London, 1936.

without having to pay any additional taxes. A year later, Sancho allowed the Jews of Majorca to import goods and property acquired in Moorish countries even though he was at war with them. He also authorized the erection of a new synagogue to serve as a house of prayer and *bet midrash* but stipulated that it be less splendid then the former building. In 1331 James III, Sancho's nephew, ordered the viceroy on the island to assist the Jews in the erection of the synagogue in spite of the opposition of Pope John XXII.

After the death of Sancho in 1325, the regent Philip, who ruled in the name of James III, confirmed the existing privileges of the Jews on the island and granted them civic rights. Treating them with tolerance, he stopped the legal action against several Jewish merchants accused of smuggling goods to North Africa (after the merchants had promised to pay him a considerable sum) and in 1327 he prohibited the forced conversion of Jews and their pagan slaves. During the reign of James III (1327–43) a poll tax was imposed on the Jews of Majorca. When the Palma community refrained from paying this in 1332, the king imposed a fine on it; after some time, he reduced the fine for several families. In 1337 he granted the trustees of the Majorca community the right to punish those guilty of religious or moral offenses, but they were forbidden to expel them or to administer corporal punishment. In spite of the restriction in the rights of the Jews of Majorca to try cases of criminal law, the *dayyanim* strictly adhered to Jewish law and the customs of Spanish Jewry.

The Organization and Administration of the Majorca Communities. Details of the organization of the Palma community have come down from the close of the 13th century. In 1296 the community was authorized to elect three *muqaddimūn* or trustees; the right of jurisdiction over the Jews was at first in the hands of the communal leaders, who were even authorized to expel any Jew for disreputable conduct. Throughout the period of the independent kingdom, the community was generally headed by six trustees and an executive council of eight "good men," though this council does not seem to have functioned regularly. In 1327, when the regent Philip allowed four of the trustees to dismiss a fifth who had been appointed by Sancho I, he recognized the exclusive right of the Jews of Palma to elect their own officers without any outside intervention, even from the king himself. When Pedro IV conquered Majorca in 1343, he confirmed the existing arrangements. When in 1348 the trustees wished to coopt one of the "small taxpayers" on to the committee distributing charity funds, one of the "large" taxpayers complained to Pedro IV who supported him, declaring that it was preferable that charity be distributed by those who had contributed it. In 1356 Pedro confirmed a communal regulation excluding physicians and brokers from serving as trustees. At that time, the governor of the island appointed a "Council of Thirty" which functioned until 1374, when the king ordered that the former communal leaders were to be responsible for its administration. Members of the council were to be elected by the community itself, and assisted by members appointed on the recommendation of the wealthier taxpayers. Several regulations on the assessment of the communal taxes, which indicate an attempt to create a reasonably objective assessment system, were confirmed by Pedro in 1378. Under the influence of R. Jonah *Desmaestre, Pedro issued in 1383 a series of instructions on the organization of communal life: the right to judge criminal law was restored to the community; the right of individuals to draw up testaments was not to be infringed upon; Jews were not to be compelled to hold disputations with apostates; no Jew of Majorca would be exempted from communal taxes, nor woufd any extraordinary tax be imposed upon him; no Jew might claim office in the community nor would he be exempted from public office if such was imposed upon him. Confirming these regulations John I granted the trustees of Palma the additional right of trying criminal law cases with the assistance of five rabbis, either according to Jewish law or Roman law. The community of Majorca benefited from these regulations until its destruction in 1391. When the Jewish settlement on the island was renewed, it appears that these regulations were again applied until it ceased to exist.

From the Reign of Pedro IV (1343–87) Until the End of the Jewish Settlement. After Pedro IV conquered the Balearic Isles (1343), the situation of the Jews of Majorca improved. The king's retinue included the physician Maestre Eleazar ibn Ardut of Huesca and Ḥasdai Crescas, the grandfather of R. Ḥasdai *Crescas. Immediately after the conquest, Pedro exempted the Jews of Majorca from the taxes imposed upon them by James III and canceled the bonds for the payment of the poll tax. He reconfirmed the privileges which had been granted by James II, Alfonso III, and the regent Philip, and ordered that those Jews who had left the island and newcomers also be given favorable opportunities to settle there. One of the supporters of James III was an alchemist named Menahem who was brought to trial in 1345; later he entered the service of Pedro as alchemist, physician, and astrologer. In 1346, Pedro decreed that a separate quarter be built for the Jews in Inca, in order to prevent both undue familiarity and quarrels between Jews and Christians. However, it appears that this separation did not apply in practice. The island communities suffered extensively at the time of the *Black Death and during the plagues which also broke out in the 1370s and 1380s. Rioting occurred as an aftermath of the plagues, and in 1374 the Christians called for the expulsion of the Jews from the island, but both the king and the infante John endeavored to restore order.

At the end of the 1340s, the Jewish physician and scholar Judah *Mosconi (Leo Grech) left Greece to settle in Majorca. From then until the close of the century, a school of Jewish astronomers and cartographers developed on the island. Among them were Abraham *Cresques (d. 1387), who was made a *magister mapa mundorum et buxolarum*, and his son Judah. Both were also granted by royal decree the privilege of appointing all the ritual slaughterers on the island. In 1359 R. Isaac *Nifoci, an astronomer, was chosen as the companion of the king of Aragon (in 1390 he joined the rabbis of the island). At the end of the 1360s, R. *Isaac b. Sheshet corresponded with R. Solomon Zarfati, the talmudist, who was invited to come to Majorca by Jucef Faquim. R. Vidal Ephraim Gerondi, astrologer to the infante John and Solomon Ẓarfati's rabbinical rival, died a martyr's death in 1391. During the 1380s, R. Jonah Desmaestre did much to strengthen religious observance on the island and acted as *rosh yeshivah* in Palma (Simeon b. Ẓemaḥ *Duran was his son-in-law). Together with R. Ḥasdai Crescas, he undertook the reconstruction of the communities which had been destroyed during the persecutions of 1391. The physician Maestre Aaron Abdal-Ḥagg was also well-known; in spite of the prohibition of 1356, he was appointed as trustee of the community of Palma. In 1381 Pedro IV appointed Solomon b. Abraham Benallell as *mustaçaf* ("town market supervisor") over the Jews of Majorca in appreciation of his services, also leasing him the right to manufacture soap on the island. Granting him a "rabbinical" position in Palma, he authorized him to appoint a ritual slaughterer or to slaughter for the requirements of the community.

During the second half of the 14th century, the island communities developed to the point of gaining the regard of the communities of Aragon, and in 1354 Majorca was invited to send a delegate to the supreme council of the communities of Aragon. In all this period, the Jews of Majorca carried on an intensive local trade and supplied goods from North Africa to the Spanish mainland. Others continued to engage in agriculture and crafts, but small craftsmen and owners of small plots of land were compelled to sell their land in times of difficulty; in an effort to help them Simeon b. Ẓemaḥ Duran (Resp. 1, no. 51) attempted to modify the Jewish *usury laws so that they would be able to take loans. During the 14th century, the Jews of the island still owned slaves and the problems connected with their possession which had arisen during the 13th century persisted. Essentially the prominence of the leading Jewish merchants was based on their maritime trade in the Mediterranean, with Alexandria, Sicily, Sardinia, and other places. It was these merchants who imported grain to the island in times of famine and scarcity, although they were not shipowners; there was even a series of privileges which declared that Christian shipowners must not refuse cargoes loaded on their ships by Jews. Eminent among these merchants was Don Jucef Faquim (Joseph Ḥakim) whose family had arrived on the island in 1332. In 1365 he argued before the king that he should be exempted from taxes because his property consisted of goods scattered over many countries and these possessions were insecure; the king ordered the trustees to appoint two merchants to assess his payments. In 1370 Jucef Faquim supplied grain to the army, which was quartered on Sardinia. When the Jews of Majorca complained to Pedro IV in 1351 about sailors who took some of their number into captivity and removed them elsewhere if they were not redeemed in time, he ordered that the captives be set free against the payment of a ransom of 30 livres of silver. During this period Majorca Jews also engaged in moneylending and frequent governmental measures attempted to reduce the interest rates.

The form of the Jewish *oath in force in Majorca, established by Pedro in 1352, required them to swear on a text containing the Ten Commandments only, without the addition of the reproof sections. In 1359 the king renewed the privilege which stipulated that Majorca Jews could not be tortured without explicit royal approval. In the same year, he authorized the Jews of North Africa to enter and to leave the island, against a payment of one-eighth of the price of goods which they bought or sold on the island. After the inhabitants of the town of Inca had attacked the Jews in 1373, many left the island. After several conversions had taken place, the Jews of Majorca complained to the king, who in 1373 ordered the bishop of Majorca to pay heed to the ancient decree concerning the conversion regulations (see above). In 1376 the Jews of Porreras were set upon by the local population. However, the following year Pedro intervened in favor of the Jews, ordering them to present their claims in person before the mercantile court (*consulado del mar*). During this period the king continued to impose compulsory loans on the Jewish communities (especially in 1380 and 1383).

The 1391 Persecutions. When news of the anti-Jewish riots sweeping Spain in 1391 reached Majorca, the leaders of the Jews appealed to Francisco Sa Garriga, viceroy of John I, to find a way of preventing the outbreak of similar riots on the island. It was decided to cordon off the Jewish quarter and allow no weapons inside. As soon as they heard reports of the riots in Valencia, Jews began to leave the island and those who lived in the villages moved to the towns, into the fortified Jewish quarters. In Palma the riots broke out on July 10; youths bearing crucifixes infiltrated the Jewish quarter. Although the gates were closed the mob broke them down and massacred scores of Jews. The next day the authorities made attempts to mitigate the storm, but on August 2 the riots broke out again. The community of Inca was completely wiped out, as were those of Sóller, Sineu, and Alcudia. Several leaders of the riots were captured, but the mob set them free; villagers traveled to the towns in order to share in the pillage. Many Jews died as martyrs, notably R. Vidal Ephraim Gerondi, and several distinguished personalities accepted baptism; among these were R. Isaac Nifoci, who later atoned for his act by emigrating to Ereẓ Israel, and Judah Cresques, who became a prominent courtier. A list of 111 heads of families who were converted is still extant; they were given the names of their baptismal godfathers (several of the converts were named after the viceroy, Francisco Sa Garriga). In spite of the governor's prohibition on leaving the island, many Jews fled to North Africa, among them Simeon b. Ẓemaḥ Duran, who settled in Algiers and held rabbinical office there. In September the peasants demanded that the surviving Jews be baptized or put to death; in rejecting this demand the authorities explained that Christianity sought to achieve conversion through free will and not by force. However, the peasants renewed their demands a month later and it appears that there were numerous converts at that time.

At the beginning of 1392, the authorities took steps to normalize the situation. The populace was ordered to hand back plundered property; surviving Jews and forced converts were required to provide within ten days a written list of the debts owing to them; the forced converts were called upon to appear before the viceroy and declare whether they desired to continue to live in the Jewish quarter or rent houses to Jews who had been left homeless; and the inhabitants were ordered to return the doors which they had removed from Jewish houses. The bailiff of Palma, one of the leaders of the riot, was executed in January 1392. Fearing that the island's peasants might rebel, the crown granted an amnesty to the rioters and canceled debts to Jews contracted over the previous ten years. Despite the governor's decree forbidding the forced converts to leave the island, many fled to North Africa and returned to Judaism; among them were members of the Najjār family. In January 1393, the governor prohibited further assaults on Jews; anyone molesting them would be hanged if he was of the lower class and flogged if he belonged to the nobility. Nevertheless, a new amnesty was granted to the rioters. As early as 1393, there are instances of the authorities prosecuting forced converts who had returned to Judaism.

In an attempt to reestablish the Jewish communities of the island, in 1394 the authorities invited 150 families from Portugal to settle there, and they arrived in 1395. At the same time the crown granted a writ of protection and exemption from special taxes to all Jews who had fled to North Africa and other places and wished to return to Majorca. However, their resettlement was doomed to failure. In 1413, Vicente *Ferrer visited the island and induced several members of the community to accept baptism. Seeking to undermine the position of the Jews of Majorca, Ferdinand I issued in 1413 a series of restrictions resembling the 1412 decrees of Valladolid with an additional provision prohibiting the emigration of forced converts to North Africa. There was a slight alleviation in the situation during the reign of Alfonso V, who included the Jews of Majorca in his favorable decree of 1419 which ordered that copies of the Talmud be returned to the Jews; that the system of Jewish jurisdiction be set in order; that their synagogue be restored; and that they be exempted from forced attendance at sermons. A *blood libel was perpetrated in Majorca in 1432, and in 1435 the community ceased to exist: 200 persons were converted and the remainder fled to join their coreligionists in North Africa.

The Fate of the Conversos of Majorca. The papal Inquisition was already active in Majorca during the 13th century, but it was only from the beginning of the 15th that its activities really made themselves felt. In 1407 a *Converso who had twice returned to Judaism was condemned to be burnt at the stake, and in 1410 Benedict XIII ordered that measures be taken against the Conversos of Majorca. Antonio Murta, the inquisitor of the Balearic Islands from 1420 to 1436, was responsible for the conversion of many Jews in 1435. The Spanish *Inquisition began to operate in Majorca in 1488. From the start, many Conversos were brought back to the Church. Until the close of the 15th century, 346 trials were held and 257 persons were handed over to the secular arm for the death penalty. During the 16th century, especially after 1520, the tribunal's activities decreased, but they were resumed with renewed ferocity in 1675 and 1677. In 1675, a large group of Conversos from Majorca, referred to by the Inquisition as "Portuguese," was brought to trial. Martyrs included Alonso López; others were sentenced in absentia and burned in effigy. Among those sentenced in 1677 were Pedro Onofri Cortes and Raphael Valis, who were prominent members of the Converso community. The tribunal's activities reached their peak in 1691, when 86 Conversos (including 46 women) were sentenced and another 39 reconciled with the church. From then on its activities appear to have waned. By 1771 the Inquisition had sent a total of 594 Conversos to the stake and reconciled a further 460 with the church. During the 18th century, tribunal officials occasionally arrested Jewish travelers on the Balearic Isles on the suspicion that they were Conversos. In 1718 Jacob Cardozo Nuñez of Bayonne, and Samuel Nahon and his relative Solomon Nahon of Tetuán were arrested. Cardozo was imprisoned until 1721.

Conversos in Majorca were given the name of **chuetas*, a name which persisted into the mid-20th century. They continued to live in separate quarters and all social and public advancement were denied to them. They formed a closed society in which the overwhelming majority secretly observed Jewish rites, for which they were often brought to trial. It was not until the end of the 18th century that the government attempted to alleviate their condition and in 1782 the Conversos were permitted to settle in any part of the town or the island; at the same time it became an offense to molest them by word or deed. After the French conquest of the island, the Inquisition was abolished in 1808 and the Conversos were granted further concessions. However, when Ferdinand IV returned to power (1814) the Inquisition was reintroduced and its final abolition barely improved the lot of the Conversos. In 1856 riots broke out against them once more when several prominent members of the community sought to join the exclusive *Circulo Balear* club. There was a renewed debate on the place of the *chuetas* within the island's society toward the close of the 19th century with the publication of the work of the priest José Tarongi in 1877, condemning their social ostracism and explicitly blaming the clergy for this. Also influential was the work of Vicente Blasco Ibañez, *Los muertos mandan* (1916). Jews began to take an interest in their condition. During the Republican regime in Spain (1931), a work by Garao, *La Fe Triunfante*, was republished. Written a century before it sought to stress the Jewishness of the *chuetas* as grounds for their total rejection. In 1970 there were about 300 members of this community (although some estimates were higher): most were silver- and goldsmiths and a few were small merchants. Some were successful businessmen and a few even left for Spain, where they managed to find a place in Spanish society.

Bibliography: B. Braunstein, *Chuetas of Majorca* (1936); A. L. Isaacs, *Jews of Majorca* (1936), incl. bibl.; Baer, Spain, index; Baer, Urkunden, 1 (1929), index; M. Kayserling, *Juden in Navarra . . .* (1861), 153–89; J. Amador de Los Rios, *Historia política . . . de los Judíos en España . . .*, 3 (1876), 638ff.; J. Rullan, *Historia de Sóller*, 2 vols. (1875–76); H. C. Lea, *A History of the Inquisition of Spain*, 3 vols. (1906), index; F. Fita, in: *Boletín de la Real Academia de la historia*, 36 (1900=*La España hebrea*, 1889–98); J. M. Millás Vallicrosa and J. Busquets Mulets, in: *Sefarad*, 4 (1944), 275–86; A. Pons, *ibid.*, 15 (1955), 69–87; J. M. Millás Vallicrosa, *ibid.*, 18 (1958), 3–9; 21 (1961), 65–66; J. Goñi, *ibid.*, 22 (1962), 105f.; F. L. Lacave, *ibid.*, 23 (1963), 375–6; L. Torres Balbás, *Al Andalus*, 19 (1954), 194; Cantera-Millás, Inscripciones, 319–21, 389–91, 393–4; A. Pons, in: *Hispania*, 78 (1960), 3–54; 79 (1960), 163–266; 80 (1960), 368–540 (incl. bibl.); R. Patai, in: *Midstream*, 8 (1962), 59–68; J. N. Hillgarth and B. Narkis, in: REJ, 120 (1961), 297–320; M. Fortoza, *Els descendents dels jueus conversos de Mallorca* (1966). [H.B.]

MAJORITY RULE, deciding a matter according to the majority opinion. In the field of the *halakhah* this rule is applied in three principal instances: (a) determination of the binding law according to (the view of) the majority of halakhic scholars; (b) adjudication of dispute by the majority decision of the courts' judges; and (c) imposition by majority decision of the community, or its representatives, of a communal enactment (see **Takkanot ha-Kahal*), binding on all members of the community. The basis for the majority rule is to be found in the exegesis of the scriptural phrase, *aḥarei rabbim lehattot* (to "follow a multitude . . ." Ex. 23:2).

In Deciding the Halakhah. In the Talmud the phrase *aḥarei rabbim lehattot* was converted into a decisory canon: "where there is a controversy between an individual and the many, the *halakhah* follows the many" (Ber. 9a). The sages of the Talmud explained the existence of this rule as a practical necessity, for if the Torah had been given in the form of an exhaustive codex, "the world could not have existed" (TJ, Sanh. 4:2, 22a; cf. Mid. Ps. 82:3). The halakhic opinion that has prevailed is that the law is decided in accordance with the view expressed by a majority of the scholars, and this is so even if in a particular matter a heavenly voice (see **Bat-Kol*) should declare that the law is according to the minority opinion (BM 59a).

The individual may continue to express his opinion that the majority has erred, but may not instruct in practice according to the minority opinion; if he actually instructs others to follow the minority opinion, he becomes (when there is a Sanhedrin) a **zaken mamre* (i.e., a "rebellious scholar"; Maim. Yad, Mamrim, 3:5–6). If a majority of scholars should arrive at the same conclusion but each for a different reason, some scholars hold this to be a majority opinion which is binding while other scholars hold the contrary view (*Maggid Mishneh*, Ishut 7:12; Maharik, resp. nos. 41, 52, 94, 102).

Some of the *geonim* and *rishonim* took the view that a minority opinion is to be preferred above a majority opinion of scholars of lesser wisdom. This question first arose in a responsum of Hai Gaon concerning a court decision on the concrete matter in issue, and not as concerns deciding of the *halakhah* in general (*Ge'onim Kadmoniyyim*, resp. no. 144; Ramban nov. Sanh. 23a; *Sefer ha-Ḥinnukh*, no. 67). Some of the scholars opposed this opinion, holding that the law is always as decided by the majority (*Haggahot Asheri*, Av. Zar. 1:3; *Siftei Kohen*, supplementary note to YD 242), while other scholars laid down that whenever the minority opinion is qualitatively superior to the majority opinion, the position is as if opinions are divided equally and either may be followed (Ramban nov. Sanh. 23a; Ritba, RH 14b). In the Shulḥan Arukh, the most authoritative code of Jewish law, determination of the *halakhah* is generally made by application of the majority rule, the author (Joseph Caro) having adopted for himself the principle that the binding *halakhah* was to accord with the opinion held in common by any two of three great halakhists preceding him, namely Alfasi, Maimonides, and Asher b. Jehiel—or with the majority opinion selected on a different basis if a particular matter had not been dealt with by the three above-mentioned scholars. See *Law, Codification of.

Decision by the Court. Within its plain meaning and read within its context, the above-mentioned scriptural passage (Ex. 23:2) has reference to a judgment of the court. The sages of the Talmud derived therefrom an additional interpretation relating to the field of criminal law—in which there is need for a specific majority, i.e., of two at least: "Thou shalt not follow after the many to do evil—I conclude that I must be with them to do well. Then why is it written [To follow] after the many to change judgment? [It means that] thy verdict of condemnation shall not be like thy verdict of acquittal, for thy verdict of acquittal is reached by the decision of a majority of one, but thy verdict of condemnation must be reached by the decision of a majority of two" (Sanh. 1:6 and cf. Mekh., Kaspa 20). Some scholars explain the need for a specific majority in matters of the criminal law on the basis that in matters of the civil law no judgment solely condemns or solely absolves, since any suit involves two litigants and what is to the one's benefit is to the other's detriment; whereas in criminal law matters the judgment is condemnatory, i.e., to the detriment of the accused (Tos. to Sanh. 3b).

A majority is only required in the event that a judicial decision has to be made in a concrete case before the court, whereas in deciding the *halakhah* in the criminal law field—outside the context of instant litigation—a simple majority of one suffices as it does in all other cases (Resp. Radbaz, *Li-Leshonot ha-Rambam*, no. 1690).

The *amoraim* question how a judgment in a civil law matter, arrived at by majority decision, should be worded. It was decided, in accordance with the opinion of R. Eleazar, that the judgment must be written in the name of the court without mention being made of the names of the judges favoring one view or the other (Sanh. 30a; Maim. Yad, Sanh. 22:8); similarly, that a judgment given by a majority decision must be signed also by the judge dissenting therefrom (TJ, Sanh. 3:10; *Avkat Rokhel*, no. 19; Mabit, vol. 2, pt. 1, resp. no. 173; ḤM 19-*Urim*, n. 4). Hai Gaon's opinion (see above) that a preponderance of wisdom should be preferred above numerical majority, also with reference to court decisions, and even that the opinion of one individual may prevail against that of the many, remained generally unaccepted in later generations. Even those who favored wisdom above a numerical majority as the basis for deciding the *halakhah*, agreed that the majority opinion was to be preferred as the basis for a judgment by the court in the concrete matter before it (*Sefer ha-Ḥinnukh*, no. 67; Ramban nov. Sanh. 23a).

Communal Decisions and Enactments. The view that has prevailed in Jewish law is that communal resolutions and enactments are passed by a decision of the majority and bind the minority (see Elon, in bibl., 11 n. 34).

This general view was dissented from by Rabbenu Jacob *Tam, who held that only after an enactment had been passed by the whole community might the majority lay down fines for transgression thereof, and that the minority could not be compelled by the community to comply with a decision of the majority to which it had been opposed (*Mordekhai*, BK 179 and BB 480). The doctrine of *aḥarei rabbim lehattot* has been relied upon by the scholars in support of the right to pass a communal enactment by majority decision (Rosh, resp. no. 6:5).

According to some of the scholars, the ordinances of a guild or an association—as distinguished from communal enactments—must be passed with the consent of all members in order to be binding (Ramban, nov. BB 9a; *Nimmukei Yosef*, BB 9a; *Leḥem Rav*, no. 216).

In the case of a judicial tribunal, it was laid down that a majority decision is not binding unless all the judges have participated in the proceedings and the judgment is that of the majority of the full complement (Sanh. 5:5). Some scholars deduced therefrom that also a communal enactment passed by majority decision is not binding unless the minority has participated in the proceedings (Rashba, vol. 2, resp. no. 104; Maharik, resp. no. 180; Maharit, vol. 1, resp. no. 58). Since this ruling, if followed, might enable the minority to impose its will on the majority by absenting itself from the discussions of the community, it came to be laid down in the course of time that the decision of the majority shall be binding despite the minority's nonparticipation in the discussions leading thereto. The scholars supported the conclusion either on the basis of a presumption that the absentee minority impliedly agrees to accept the decision of the majority which exerts itself to participate (*Mishpat Shalom*, no. 231; *ibid.*, *Kunteres Tikkun Olam*, "vav"), or on the basis that the minority impliedly delegates authority to the majority (*Ḥatam Sofer*, ḤM, resp. no. 116); custom too is relied upon by some scholars in support of the majority rule of those participating in the proceedings in communal legislation (Mabit, vol. 1, resp. no. 264). If the community has delegated authority to its representatives, the latter decide by majority decision, but only if the minority too is present (*Penei Moshe*, vol. 2, resp. no. 110; *Birkei Yosef*, ḤM 13:7).

Bibliography: A. H. Freimann, in: *Yavneh*, 2 (1947/48), 1–6; I. A. Agus, in: *Talpioth*, 5 (1950), 176–95; 6 (1953), 305–20; B. Reicher, in: *Sinai*, 33 (1953), 174–7, 244–6, 383f.; A. I. Zaslanski, *ibid.*, 36 (1954/55), 451–4; I. A. Agus, in: JQR, 45 (1954/55), 120–9; ET, 9 (1959), 241–339; B. Lipkin, in: *Ha-Torah ve-ha-Medinah*, 2 (1960), 41–54; S. Federbusch, in: *Mazkeret... T. H. Herzog* (1962), 575–81; M. Elon, in: *Meḥkarei Mishpat le-Zekher A. Rosenthal* (1964), 1–54; M. P. Golding, in: JSOS, 28 (1966), 67–78; A. J. Blau, in: *Torah she-be-al Peh*, 10 (1968), 128–34. [SH.SH.]

MAKAI (Fischer), EMIL (1870–1901), Hungarian poet and playwright. Born in Mako, Makai was the son of Rabbi Enoch Fischer. In 1884 he entered the Budapest rabbinical seminary, but during his years there he spent much of his time writing. Finally, in 1893, after much heart searching and with the encouragement of the great Jewish poet József *Kiss, he decided to give up his rabbinical studies and devote himself entirely to writing.

Makai began the first, exclusively Jewish phase of his literary career with a collection of lyric verse, *Vallásos énekek* ("Religious Hymns," 1888). This was followed by a biblical drama, *Absalon* (1891), and *Zsidó költők* ("Jewish Poets," 1892), translations from the works of leading Hebrew writers in medieval Spain. These had an epoch-making effect on Hungarian literature, and established Makai's reputation as a poet. In 1893, his paraphrase of the Song of Songs (*Énekek éneke*) was published. Unlike almost all his contemporaries, Makai was an "urban poet," a type virtually unknown in Hungarian literature.

In his second, "worldly" phase of creative writing, Makai wrote primarily about love, notably in the collection *Margit* (1895). His plays include the three-act verse comedy *Tudós professzor Hatvani* ("The Learned Professor Hatvani," 1900), depicting the life of a humorous Faustian character. From 1892 Makai translated more than 100 operettas which, by reason of his masterly metrical technique, established the style of the Hungarian operetta. They included Abraham *Golfaden's *Sulamit* and *Bar Kochba*, the former a major success on the Hungarian stage. A two-volume selection of Makai's writings was published in 1904.

Bibliography: *Magyar Zsidó Lexikon* (1929), s.v.; *Magyar Irodalmi Lexikon*, 2 (1965), 178; F. Ványi (ed.), *Magyar Irodalmi Lexikon* (1926), s.v.; N. Várkonyi, *A modern magyar irodalóm*

1880–1920 (1928), index; K. Sebestyén, *Makai Emil* (Hung., 1923); *Makai Emil munkái* (1904), introd. by G. Molnár; *Révai nagy lexikona*, 13 (1915), s.v.; Mezey, in: IMIT (1912), 158–69.

[P.B./Ed.]

MAKAROV, town in Kiev oblast, Ukrainian S.S.R. Before the Revolution of 1917 it was a small town in the province of Kiev. In 1765, 217 Jews were counted there as paying poll tax. The Jewish community had grown to 848 in 1847. During the 1840s, R. Nahum *Twersky, the grandson of Menahem Nahum the Maggid of *Chernobyl, established his court in Makarov and the town became a center of Ḥasidism. The number of Jews had risen to 3,953 (c. 75% of the total population) in 1897. In July 1919, a band of peasants invaded the town and looted for eight days. When this was followed in September of the same year by a pogrom which claimed over 100 victims, perpetrated by the soldiers of *Denikin's army, the Jewish population left for *Kiev and other towns in the vicinity. Only 152 Jews remained in Makarov in 1923. In 1970 the Jewish population was estimated at about 150 (30 families). The synagogue was unused, having been closed down by the authorities. [Y.S.]

MAKHSHIRIN (Heb. מַכְשִׁירִין), eighth tractate in the order *Tohorot*, in the Mishnah and Tosefta. The word *makhshirin*, the causative *hiphil* form of *kasher* ("to be fit"), means "those things which render fit," but it is here used in a technical sense. In accordance with Leviticus 11:34, 37–8, that food can become liable to ritual impurity only if it has been moistened by water, *makhshirin* is employed to refer to all liquids which have this quality. For the same reason, the tractate is sometimes called *Mashkim* ("Liquids"). It is laid down on the basis of verse 38 that there must be some intention or desire on the part of the owner that the food be so moistened, and the tractate deals primarily with these two points— the liquids which render food liable to ritual impurity and the intention of having the food moistened. Every possible cause of foods becoming moist is detailed— from rain, ordure, damp walls, absorption of water in the food's vicinity, dripping through a leak in the roof, bilge water, steam caused by rain dripping on hot iron, the juice

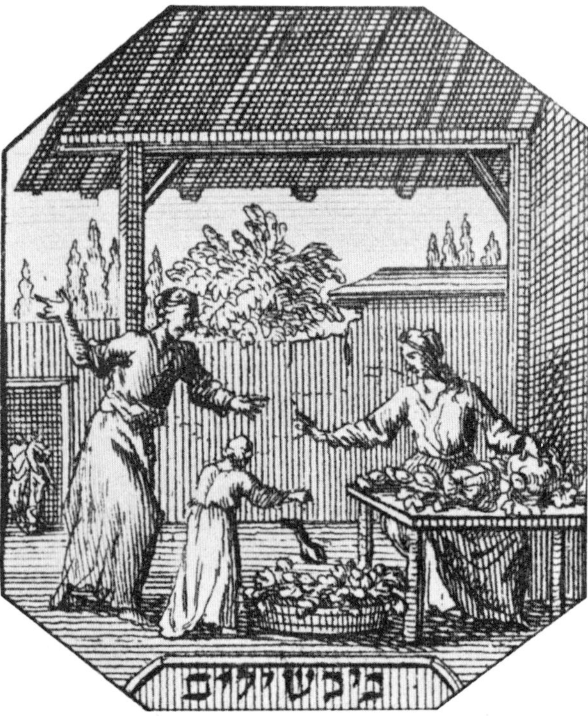

Engraving for the tractate *Makhshirin*, from a title page of the Hebrew-Latin Mishnah, Amsterdam 1700–04. Jerusalem, J.N.U.L.

of grapes, etc. The tractate concludes (6:4–8) with a discussion of liquids other than water which render produce susceptible to impurity. Epstein has pointed to various layers which can be detected in *Makhshirin*. According to him 1:3 belongs to the Mishnah of R. Joshua; 1:4 to that of Akiva; 5:2 and 6:2 to Meir; and 6:3 to Judah b. Ilai, Akiva's disciple. He maintains that Joshua's ascription of Mishnah 6:4 (Ter. 11:2) to "the sages" is evidence that it is an early one. Mishnah 6:8 is interesting in that although *mishnayot* and *beraitot* usually contain only the discussions of colleagues, this Mishnah also gives disciples' questions and Akiva's reply (cf. Epstein, Tanna'im, 88). The standard text of *mishnah* 5:1 deals with a drunken man who pushes someone into the water. S. Lieberman has shown that the text is corrupt. The correct reading should be "if he pushed him in order to injure him" (*leshovero*, לשוברו not *leshokhero*, לשכרו), and is one of several mishnaic references to the prevalent custom of dangerous water sports, of which the rabbis strongly disapproved. In the Tosefta there are some passages of historical interest. One tells of the overruling by the rabbis of Joshua b. Peraḥyah's ruling declaring all Alexandrian wheat (a major source of supply) unclean (3:4) and the alterations made by the farmers of Sepphoris in their methods of harvesting in order to remove the suspicion of defilement from their produce (3:5–6). *Genizah* fragments of the tractate have been found and their alternate readings throw light on several passages (JJLG, 18 (1927), 28ff.).

Bibliography: S. Lieberman, in: *Sinai*, 4 (1939), 57–58; Epstein, Tanna'im, passim; Ḥ. Albeck, *Shishah Sidrei Mishnah*, 6 (1959), 411–3, 512–6. [Ed.]

MAKKEDAH (Heb. מַקֵּדָה), Canaanite city in the Shephelah which marked the farthest limit of the Israelite pursuit of the five kings who united to punish Gibeon but were defeated at Aijalon (Josh. 10). The kings fled to a cave at Makkedah where they were captured and executed by hanging in the Israelite camp. The city was afterward conquered and destroyed and, accordingly, the king of Makkedah is mentioned in the list of defeated Canaanite cities (Josh. 12:16). In the topographical description of Judah, it is located, with Lachish, in the southern Shephelah (Josh. 15:41). Eusebius places the city 8 mi. (c. 13 km.) to the east of Eleutheropolis (Bet Guvrin; Onom. 126:22ff.). The identification of the ancient site is uncertain.

Bibliography: Abel, Geog, 2 (1938), 378; Aharoni, in: *Atlas Yisrael* (1956), Map IX: 4c; J. Garstang, *Joshua-Judges* (1931), 394; Aharoni, Land, index. [M.A.-Y.]

MAKKOT (Heb. מַכּוֹת; "Flagellation"), fifth tractate in the order *Nezikin*, in the Mishnah, Tosefta, and Babylonian and Jerusalem Talmuds. The tractate deals with three separate topics and is a continuation of the preceding tractate *Sanhedrin*, as it also deals with judicial punishments administered by the courts. The first chapter discusses the laws of plotting witnesses (*"zomemim"*; Deut. 19:16–20), the kind of testimony that constitutes such plotting, when such witnesses are punishable by the sentence they intended the court to impose upon the accused, and when their punishment is merely flogging. Chapter 2 contains an exhaustive treatment of circumstances under which the inadvertent murderer is banished to a city of refuge (Num. 35:6f.; Deut. 19:2f.), those liable and those exempt from banishment, the character of the cities of refuge and the protection they afford, and the connection between the death of the high priest and the return of the manslayer to his hometown (Num. 35:25). Chapter 3 gives a list of offenses for which the penalty is flogging; discusses whether flogging is incidental to offenses punishable by death, and

Engraving for the tractate *Makkot,* showing a flogging, from a title page of the Hebrew-Latin Mishnah, Amsterdam, 1700–04. Jerusalem, J.N.U.L.

describes in detail the imposition of the penalty. The tractate ends with an aggadic passage on the value to Israel of the commandments and a summation of the principles which inspire them. An interesting *mishnah* (1:10) deals with capital punishment: "R. Eliezer b. Azariah says: A Sanhedrin that effects a capital punishment once in 70 years is branded a destructive tribunal. R. Tarfon and R. Akiva say: Were we members of the Sanhedrin, no person would ever be put to death. [Thereupon] Rabban Simeon b. Gamaliel remarked: If so, they [these rabbis] would multiply shedders of blood in Israel."

The Tosefta consists of five chapters (ch. 2 is found only in the Erfurt manuscript published by Zuckermandel). Chapter 1 of the Tosefta parallels chapter 1 of the Mishnah; chapter 2, Mishnah 2:1–4; chapter 3, the remainder of chapter 2; while chapters 4 and 5 correspond to chapter 3. De Vries maintains that the Mishnah and Tosefta in this case both derive from an earlier compilation which the Tosefta follows closely, but from which the Mishnah deviated considerably. In his opinion the Mishnah was originally divided into five chapters—as is the Tosefta—and that it was later abridged into three chapters. The Babylonian Talmud has *Gemara* on all three chapters, but the Jerusalem Talmud only on the first two. In addition, the Babylonian Talmud on *Makkot* is much richer in aggadic material. It concludes with the moving story of a group of rabbis who were shocked to see a jackal emerging from the recess of the Holy of Holies. All with the exception of Akiva, burst into tears, while he laughed. He explained his joy with the observation that with this calamity the worst prophecy about the Jews had been fulfilled, and one could now anticipate that the comforting prophecy of Zechariah: "There shall yet old men and old women sit in the broad places of Jerusalem" (Zech. 8:4), would likewise be fulfilled.

Although the printed editions of the Jerusalem Talmud have no *Gemara* to the third chapter, Lieberman has shown that such a *Gemara* existed, but since the topics with which it dealt were discussed in the *Gemara* to Mishnayot in other places, the copyists omitted these duplicated discussions from the third chapter of the tractate. In fact, the early authorities quote passages from the Jerusalem Talmud to *Makkot* which do not occur elsewhere in the existing text. A fragment from the Jerusalem Talmud to chapter 2 of *Makkot* found in the Cairo *Genizah* has been published by S. Wieder. Published translations of the Mishnah include one in Latin, with extracts from the *Gemara,* by J. Coccejus (Amsterdam, 1629), one in German by H. L. Strack (1910), and one in English by Danby (1933). The Babylonian Talmud was also translated into English by H. M. Lazarus in the Soncino edition (1935). Although the imposition of the penalties discussed in *Makkot* was not practiced directly in the Diaspora, yet because of its importance for the theoretical discussion of criminal law it is much discussed and frequently referred to in rabbinic literature.

Bibliography: Ḥ. Albeck, *Shishah Sidrei Mishnah, Seder Nezikin* (1959), 211–8, 461–7; Epstein, Tanna'im, 417; B. De Vries, in: *Tarbiz,* 26 (1956/57), 255–61 (=*Meḥkarim be-Sifrut ha-Talmud* (1968), 102 ff.); S. Klein, in: *Kovez̧ ha-Ḥevrah ha-Ivrit la-Ḥakirat Erez̧ Yisrael ve-Attikoteha,* 3 (1935), 81–107; S. Lieberman, *Hilkhot ha-Yerushalmi le-Rabbenu Moshe b. Maimon* (1947), 67f.; S. Wieder, in: *Tarbiz,* 17 (1947), 129–37. [D.J.B.]

MAKLEFF, family of Erez̧ Israel pioneers. ARYEH LEIB (1876–1929) was born in the Grodno district of Russian Poland and settled in Erez̧ Israel in 1891. At the age of 18 he moved from Jerusalem to Petaḥ Tikvah and worked on his brother's land. Eventually he settled in Moz̧a and put many years of labor into the vineyard planted by his father-in-law Yehiel Chemerinski, one of the founders of the Maḥaneh Yehudah quarter in Jerusalem. As an agricultural expert he was instrumental in choosing the land for Ḥuldah before the Jewish National Fund purchased it. For 25 years his home was the center of the settlement of Moz̧a. During the riots of 1929, the sheikh of the nearby Arab village, Qālūnya, promised him that Moz̧a would not be attacked. Nonetheless, the settlement was stormed by its Arab neighbors, and Makleff was killed along with his wife, BATYAH ḤAYYAH (b. in Jerusalem, 1877); his son, AVRAHAM (b. 1907); and his daughters MINNAH (b. 1905) and RIVKAH (b. 1910).

MORDECHAI (1920–), Aryeh Leib's youngest son, survived the slaughter of his family by taking shelter in a neighbor's home and grew up to become chief of staff of the Israel Defense Forces. Born in Jerusalem, he received a religious education and graduated from the Reali school in Haifa in 1938. He joined the Special Night Squads led by

Mordechai Makleff, Israel chief of staff, 1952–53. Courtesy Government Press Office, Tel Aviv.

Orde Wingate against the Arab terrorists. In 1940 he joined the British army and was sent to officers' school. He saw action in World War II with the *Jewish Brigade in Italy. In 1948 he was the officer of the Haganah unit that captured Haifa and represented the Haganah in its negotiations with the Arabs of the city. He then took part in the battle for Mishmar ha-Yarden and the lightning operation to capture eastern Galilee. He headed the Israel delegation to the armistice talks with Lebanon and Syria. In 1949 Makleff became assistant chief of staff under Yigael *Yadin, and in 1952 he received the appointment of chief of staff, a post which he held for a period of one year. In 1958 he became managing director of the Dead Sea Works, and ten years later was appointed director of the Citrus Marketing Board of Israel. [Ed.]

MAKO (Hung. **Makó**), town in S. Hungary. Jews were first authorized to settle in Mako in 1740. In 1748 they founded a *ḥevra kaddisha* in the town, and the community was probably organized at that time. A Jewish school was also opened. The first synagogue was erected in 1814, and the magnificent great synagogue was built in 1914. After 1868 the community was split into two factions and in 1870 the Orthodox built a synagogue. There were 158 Jews in Mako in 1773, earning their livelihood mainly from trade, especially in onions which grew abundantly in the surroundings. There were also Jewish craftsmen. From 154 in 1824 the Jewish population increased to 1,200 by 1858. The Jews numbered 1,928 in 1918, 2,380 in 1920, and 1,125 in 1941. The first rabbi of the town was Jacob Selig (1773). Others were Solomon *Ullman (1826–1863), who maintained a yeshivah, and Enoch Fischer (1864–1896), the father of the poet Emil *Makai. The last rabbis were the historian A. *Kecskeméti (1898–1944) and M. Vorhand (Orthodox). The renowned journalist and publisher Joseph *Pulitzer was born in this town. After the German invasion (March 19, 1944) the local Jews were deported to *Auschwitz and some to Austria; only 324 of 946 survived. The synagogue was demolished in the late 1960s. In 1970 there were 98 Jews in Mako.

Bibliography: Á. Kecskeméti, *A csanádmegyei zsidók története* (1929); A. Scheiber, in: MHJ, 12 (1969), 5–18. [Al. Sch.]

MAKOW MAZOWIECKI (Pol. **Maków Mazowiecki;** Rus. **Makov**), town in Warszawa province (before 1795 Mazovia province), Poland. An organized Jewish community is traceable to the second half of the 16th century. At the end of the 17th century a Jew, Nachman ben Nathan, was executed as a result of a blood libel. King Augustus III (1733–63) confirmed the rights of the Jewish community. According to the 1765 census, 1,258 poll tax payers, of whom 827 lived in neighboring villages, were under the jurisdiction of the Makow *kahal.* Of the 113 Jewish families (431 persons) living in Makow, 54 owned their houses; 21 families earned their livelihood as craftsmen (tailors, carpenters, tinsmiths). The Jewish population numbered 2,007 (72% of the total population) in 1808; 4,090 (90%) in 1827; 4,100 in 1856; and 4,400 in 1897. Of rabbis in Makow in the 18th century the following are known by name: Moshe ben Gershon, Abraham Abish and David ben Ben Zion Jehezkel (d. 1815), *dayyan* and *maggid,* who was a central figure in the historical controversy between Ḥasidim and *Mitnaggedim.* Of the 19th century rabbis mention should be made of: Arye Leib Zunz, Eliezer Hakohen Lipschutz, and Judah Leib Graubard. Nathan Chilinowicz founded a yeshivah at the end of the 19th century which existed until 1939. [Ed.]

Holocaust Period. At the outbreak of World War II, there were about 3,500 Jews in Makow Mazowiecki. Shortly after the German invasion of Poland, another 500 Jews settled there. At the end of 1940 several hundred young Jewish men were deported to the nearby forced-labor camp in Gasiewo. In September 1941 the ghetto was established. On Nov. 5, 1942, the Germans concentrated Jews still living in the smaller places of Makow county in the ghetto. A few days later (Nov. 14–18, 1942) the first deportation to the *Treblinka death camp took place, and over 500 Makow Jews were exterminated there. On Dec. 8–12, 1942, all the remaining Jews (over 4,000) were deported to Treblinka and exterminated there. No Jewish community was reconstituted in Makow Mazowiecki. [S.Kr.]

Bibliography: R. Mahler, *Yidn in Amolikn Poyln in Likht fun Tsifern* (1958), index; B. Wasiutyński, *Ludnosć Zydowska w Polsce w wiekach XIX i XX* (1930), 18, 25, 48, 70, 75, 78, 184; A. Eisenbach et al. (eds.), *Żydzi a powstanie styczniowe, materiały i dokumenty* (1963), index; *Sefer Zikkaron li-Kehillat Makov Mazovyetsk* (Yid. and Heb., 1969).

MALACH, LEIB (pseudonym of **Leibl Salzman;** 1894–1936), Yiddish author. Born in Zwolen, Poland, he lived in Warsaw from 1907 to 1922 and worked at various trades until his literary talent was discovered by the novelist H. D. *Nomberg. From 1922 until his death in Paris, he lived in a number of countries, his longest stay being in Argentina. He began his literary career with songs and ballads, later turning to prose and drama. His travel sketches were widely read, and his drama *Ibergus* about white slave traffic helped in the struggle against this social evil in Buenos Aires. His novel *Don Domingo's Kraytsveg* ("Don Domingo's Crusade," 1930) is an epic of adventurous and idealistic Jewish life in Latin America.

Bibliography: Rejzen, Leksikon, 2 (1927), 431–4; LNYL, 4 (1965), 4–8; M. Ravitch, *Mayn Leksikon* (1945), 135–7; *L. Malach Bukh* (1949); *Bleter tsum Ondenk fun L. Malach* (1936), includes bibliography. [M.Rav.]

MALACHI, BOOK OF, the last (12th) book of the section of the Bible called *Minor Prophets. It contains "The pronouncement of the word of the Lord to Israel by Malachi" (Mal. 1:1). The Hebrew word מַלְאָכִי *(mal'akhi)* means "My messenger." According to A. von Bulmerincq, the word could be a shortened form of מַלְאָכְיָה (*mal'akhiyyah,* "messenger of the Lord"). However, since this name is not found elsewhere in the Bible, the Septuagint, in which it appears as *mal'akho* ("by the hand of His messenger"), is probably right in not regarding it as a personal name. The Targum follows the masoretic text, but adds a note to the effect that "My messenger" is *Ezra: "by the hand of My messenger whose name is called Ezra the scribe." The same tradition is mentioned and accepted by Jerome. Had Ezra been the author of the book, however, it is unlikely that his authorship would have been thus concealed. In fact, the occurrence of the word in the title is naturally explained as derived from Malachi 3:1: "Behold, I send My messenger" (cf. Mal. 2:7). The book, therefore, must be regarded as anonymous, the title having been added by the compiler who had given similar editorial titles to the anonymous oracles beginning with *Zechariah 9:1 and 12:1. The reason behind the separation of the Book of Malachi from the preceding Book of Zechariah is that the "Malachian" chapters constitute a characteristic unit, different from Deutero- and Trito-Zechariah (Zech. 9–11; 12–14).

The contents of the Book of Malachi fall into six clearly marked sections introduced by a statement of the Lord or of the prophet, which is then challenged by the people or the priests, and defended by the Lord Himself in words of reproach and doom. The Lord's love for Israel, in contrast with His treatment of Edom, is emphasized at the outset (Mal. 1:2–5). The second speech reproaches the priests for their neglect of the sacrificial cult (1:6–2:9): their attitude should express a proper regard for the ritual of the Lord's worship, yet any offering, however imperfect, has been thought good enough for His altar. In this, as no doubt in

A page from the *Laud Maḥzor* for Shavuot (the Feast of Weeks). The giving and receiving of the Tablets of the Law is depicted on top of the arch. Within the arch, Moses sprinkles the blood of the covenant on the Israelites (Ex. 24:8); and below it, the baking of *mazzah* is depicted. South Germany, late 13th century. Oxford, Bodleian Library, ms. Laud Or. 321, fol. 127v ($17\frac{1}{2} \times 12\frac{1}{4}$ ins/44.5 × 31 cm.).

other matters, the priests show themselves unworthy of their forefather Levi, by misleading "the many" into sin with their lax rulings. Let the priests, therefore, take warning, and return to their ancient ideals. This section seems to have been subsequently expanded by the insertion of 1:11–14. The aspect of God as their common father should inspire correct relations between Jew and Jew, and not such conduct as repudiating Jewish wives for the sake of marrying non-Jewish women (2:10–16). In its present form, this speech reproaches the Jews for contracting mixed marriages. The view of Ch. C. Torrey (JBL, 17 (1898), 1–15) and F. F. Hvidberg (*Weeping and Laughter in the Old Testament* (1962)) that a reproach for the adoration of foreign gods is actually meant has little to commend it. A problem, however, arises from the secondary character of 2:11b–13a, or 11–12. Several modern scholars have challenged the genuineness of this passage for literary reasons and consider it a later addition. Without these verses, 2:10–16 contains no reference to mixed marriages, but rather attacks the abuse of divorce by Jews, exhorting them to remain loyal to the wives of their youth (cf. Prov. 5:15–20). If the sacredness and religious value of marriage are implied, the reproach indicates that men were divorcing wives casually and callously.

The prevalence of wrongdoing had provoked skepticism about divine justice. The fourth section asserts against these doubts that the Lord is the God of judgment and will restore the rights of the people; His messenger is already at hand to purge indifferentism from worship and immorality from conduct (Mal. 2:17–3:5). A. von Bulmerincq's assumption that Ezra is the "messenger" of 3:1 is unlikely, because the conception here is rather that of a heavenly being. According to the next section, the people's neglect in paying tithes and other sacred dues has been punished with drought, locusts, and failure of crops; however, the punctilious payment of the withheld tithes will be rewarded with abundance (3:6–12). This fifth section thus enforces the duty of giving tithes. The last section promises the despondent pious Jews vindication for themselves and punishment for the ungodly ones on the Day of Judgment (3:13–21). Religion may seem useless, warns the author, but the Lord remembers His own, and will soon distinguish them openly from the irreligious. The book closes with an appeal to observe the Law that the Lord gave to Moses at Horeb, and with the announcement that the prophet Elijah will come before the threatened judgment (3:22–24). These concluding words are probably an addition, namely a later interpretation of 3:1, saying that the "messenger" is Elijah. However, it shares with the body of the book its deuteronomic orientation: the book evidently regards the entire tribe of Levi as priestly, the closing appeal names Horeb instead of Sinai as the mount of revelation. These facts favor an early rather than a late post-Exilic date. Other features bear this out.

Like Haggai and Zechariah 1–8, the Book of Malachi is an expression of the changed outlook of prophecy in post-Exilic times. The topics noted above clearly relate the book to the post-Exilic period, when the Temple had been rebuilt (1:10; 3:1, 10), the province of Judea was ruled by a representative of the Persian government (1:8), and there had been time enough for the loss of earlier religious enthusiasm. The three main abuses attacked in the text are the degeneracy of the priesthood (1:6–2:9), intermarriage with foreign women (2:11), and the people's remissness in the payment of tithes (3:8). These abuses, especially the second and the third, are mentioned prominently in the Book of Ezra and Nehemiah, and are those which both reformers strenuously set themselves to correct (Ezra 9:2; 10:3, 16–44; Neh. 10:31, 33–40; 13:10–14, 23–29). The independent character of Malachi's attack against divorcing Jewish wives in order to marry foreign women (Mal. 2:10–16) suggests a date of composition prior to that of the work of Ezra (Ezra 9:2; 10:3, 16–44). This earlier date is made still more likely if the reproach against mixed marriages in Malachi 2:11b is a later insertion, one which precisely reflects the preoccupations of the time of Ezra and Nehemiah. The time of Ezra's activity, unfortunately, is uncertain. Following A. van Hoonacker and S. Mowinckel, above all, many scholars have assumed that Ezra did not work under Artaxerxes I (in 458 B.C.E.), but under Artaxerxes II (in 398 B.C.E.; cf. Ezra 7:8). The problems of mixed marriages and unpaid tithes, however, existed also in the time of Nehemiah (Neh. 10:31, 33–40; 13:10–14, 23–29), i.e., between 445 and about 424, the year Artaxerxes I died (cf. Neh. 2:1; 13:6). The insertion of Malachi 2:11b–13a may thus date from that period, and it may reasonably be inferred, therefore, that the original Book of Malachi dates prior to the age of Nehemiah and Ezra. In fact, most modern scholars agree that the prophet prepares the way for the work of those reformers.

There is no evidence of sufficient strength to substantiate a later date. The assumptions of H. Winckler (*Altorientalische Forschungen,* 2 (1898), 531ff.) and O. Holtzmann (ARW, 29 (1931), 1–21), who date the book to the first half of the second century B.C.E., are highly speculative and, at the present state of knowledge, inadmissible. The opinion

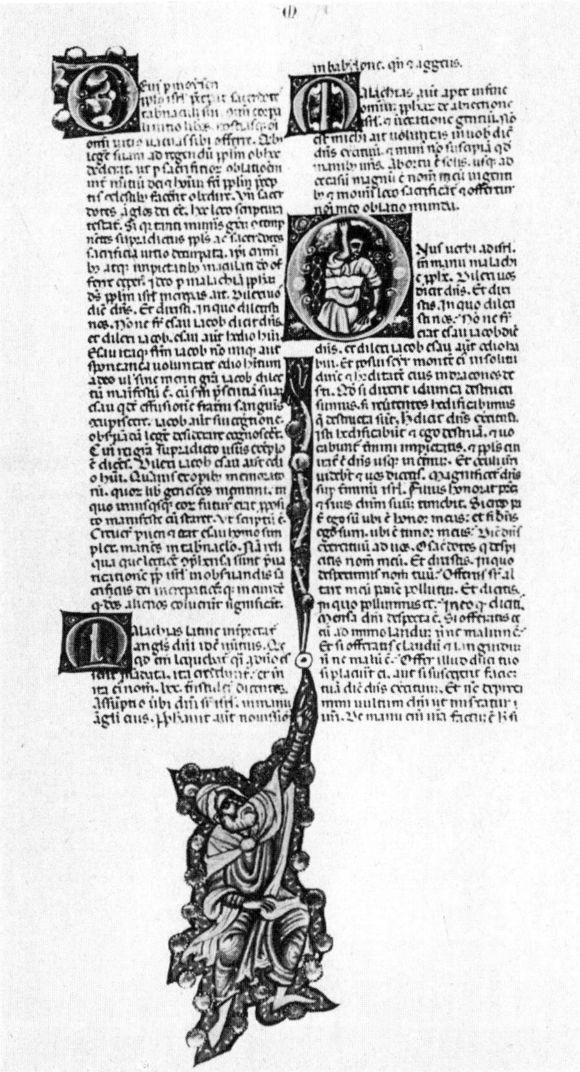

The opening page of the Book of Malachi in the *Conradin Bible,* S. Italy, 13th century. Baltimore, Md., Walters Art Gallery, Ms. W. 152, fol. 28v.

of A. von Bulmerincq, who identifies the "messenger" of Malachi 3:1 as Ezra, becomes still more doubtful if Nehemiah is considered to have preceded Ezra. The period of Nehemiah's absence at the Persian court in approximately 430 B.C.E. (Neh. 13:6) has been proposed as the time of composition by S. R. Driver (*An Introduction to the Literature of the Old Testament* (1897[6]), 357) and A. Gelin (*Introduction à la Bible,* 1 (1957), 572), but an earlier date is the most likely. One of the chief duties of the priest was still the proclamation of the Oral Law (Mal. 2:6–9), and not as yet the solemn reading of the Written Law, as in Nehemiah 8–10. In fact, the prophet seems to be influenced by earlier deuteronomistic theories concerning the priests; on the other hand, it is doubtful whether he knew the Priestly Code regulations on tithes found in Numbers 18:20–32, where the tithe is designated in its entirety for the maintenance of the levites (whereas, according to deuteronomic legislation (Deut. 14:22–29; 26:12–15), the levites only took part of the tithe). It appears that the Priestly Code, in its present form, is not presupposed by the Book of Malachi.

An earlier date for the composition of Malachi is also suggested by the allusion to the destruction of Edom in Malachi 1:3–4. The Arab invasion of this Transjordanian kingdom cannot be dated with precision, but Edom was apparently entirely taken over by Arab tribes toward the end of the sixth century B.C.E. Since the remaining Edomites still expected a restoration of their ruined country (1:4), approximately 500 B.C.E. is a more probable date for the composition of the Book of Malachi than the first half of the fifth century. A. C. Welch even thought that the book dated from the age of the prophet Haggai (520 B.C.E.). The bad harvests and locust plagues alluded to in 3:11 would then reflect the same situation as in Haggai 1:6, 9–11; 2:16–17. However, the existence of the Temple as implied by Malachi indicates a somewhat later date. All things considered, it may reasonably be assumed that the book dates from approximately 500 B.C.E.

The work reflects the various currents of thought and modes of life in the Jerusalem of about 500 B.C.E., affording an interesting and valuable glimpse of the post-Exilic community in the period between the age of Haggai and Zechariah on the one hand, and the time of Nehemiah and Ezra on the other. The situation in Judea was one of depression and discontent. The expectations which earlier prophets had aroused had not been fulfilled. The return from Babylon had brought with it none of the ideal glories promised by Deutero-Isaiah. The completion of the Second Temple (515 B.C.E.) had been followed by disillusionment over the anticipated prosperity announced by Haggai in 520 B.C.E., by consequent indifference to worship, skepticism as to divine justice, and moral laxity. In view of these conditions, the message of Malachi is to reassert the true relation of the people to their God, and to recall the nation to religious and moral earnestness, especially in regard to questions of ritual and marriage. Yet the author is no formalist. Ritual observances are of value in his eyes only as expressions of spiritual service; for example, he supposes that God does not accept offerings presented by disloyal husbands (2:13b–14). Moral and social offenses are fiercely condemned by the prophet (3:5), and from the concept of the brotherhood of all Jews under one Father (2:10), he deduces the duties which they have toward each other, and the wrongfulness of the selfish practice of divorce prevalent in his day (2:14–16).

The Book of Malachi is a significant landmark in the religious history of Israel. Despite its emphasis on the observance of ritual, it shows genuine prophetic spirit. Its denunciation of those who divorced their Jewish wives to marry "the daughter of a strange god" reflects the prophetic ideal of a permanent covenant between God and His people, which has often been represented as a marriage contract. The denunciation also involves a protest against the influences of foreign marriages, the prohibition of which was to be made effective by the reforms of Nehemiah and Ezra. The influence of the closing words of the book (3:22–24) on later messianic expectation is apparent in the Jewish post-biblical literature (Ecclus. 48:10; Suk. 52b; Mid. Ps. to 42:1; Targ., Lam. 4:22; Targ. Yer., Deut. 30:4) and in the New Testament (Matt. 17:3, 4, 10–13; 27:47, 49; Mark 9:4–5, 11–13; 15:35–36; Luke 9:30, 33; John 1:21, 25). [E.Li.]

In the Aggadah. The author of Malachi was considered the last of the prophets, along with Haggai and Zechariah. Upon their death, the spirit of prophecy departed from Israel (Yoma 9b). Malachi was identified with Ezra by R. Joshua b. Korḥa and with Mordecai by R. Naḥman. The sages, however, declared that Malachi was his proper name (Meg. 15a). Targum Jonathan to the words "by Malachi" (1:1) added the gloss "who is known by the name of Ezra the scribe." R. Joshua validated this viewpoint by explaining the references in Malachi to the "daughter of a strange god" (2:11) as identical with the "foreign women" described by Ezra (10:2; Meg. 15a). Malachi was a member of the Great Synagogue, and traditions were later reported in his name (cf. RH 19b).

See also *Minor Prophets. [Ed.]

Bibliography: W. Nowack, *Die kleinen Propheten* (1922[3]); S. R. Driver, *The Minor Prophets: Nahum, Habakkuk, Zephaniah, Haggai, Zechariah, Malachi* (1906); G. L. Robinson, *The Twelve Minor Prophets* (1953); A. Gelin, in: *La Sainte Bible . . . de l'Ecole Biblique de Jérusalem* (1960[3]); W. L. Sperry, in: *The Interpreter's Bible,* 6 (1956); D. R. Jones, *Haggai, Zechariah and Malachi. Introduction and Commentary* (1962); E. G. Kraeling, *Commentary on the Prophets,* 2 (1966). Special Studies: K. Budde, in: ZAW, 26 (1906), 1–18; O. Holtzmann, in: ARW, 29 (1931), 1–21; A. C. Welch, *Post-Exilic Judaism* (1935), 113–25; A. Pautrel, in: DBI suppl., 5 (1957), 739–46; H. J. Boecker, in: ZAW, 78 (1966), 78–80; L. Kruse-Blinkenberg, in: *Studia Theologica,* 20 (1966), 95–119; 21 (1967), 62–82; Kaufmann, Y., Toledot, 4 (1967[5]), 366–77; M. Margalit, in: Kahana (ed.), *Sefer Terei Asar* (1930), 193–212.

MALACHI, ELIEZER RAPHAEL (1895–), U.S. Hebrew scholar and bibliographer. Born in Jerusalem, Malachi emigrated to the United States at the age of 17. A conscientious and diligent scholar, he began his literary career with original and translated stories, but in early life switched to scholarship. Though he wrote profusely, he published only two books of essays: *Massot u-Reshimot* (1937) on contemporary and past writers, and *Ẓilelei ha-Dorot* (1940), on historical occurrences.

His first publication, as a boy of 15, was an essay on Hebrew newspapers, which appeared in Luncz's *Lu'aḥ Ereẓ Yisrael* (1910). His succeeding work embraced Diaspora Hebrew periodicals, the Yiddish press, Hebrew poetry in America, Hebrew literature, historical essays, and individual bibliographies of Hebrew scholars and writers. His bibliographies of scholars include A. M. Luncz, J. N. Simhoni, S. A. Horodetsky, S. Krauss, N. Slouschz, S. Dubnow, A. Elmaleh, J. Schatzky, and S. Tchernowitz, the last of which also appeared separately as *Peri Eẓ Ḥayyim* (1946). His bibliographies of writers include such Haskalah figures as J. L. Gordon and Mendele Mokher Seforim and such late Hebrew writers as Bialik, Tschernichowsky, Shneur, Sokolow, Peretz, H. Zeitlin and Kabak, while his bibliographies of Hebrew writers in America—containing much information in a generally neglected field—include S. B. Maximon, N. Touroff, B. N. Silkiner, Ẓ. Scharfstein, S. Halkin, M. Ribalow, and H. Bavli. The latter was reprinted separately (*Zekher le-Hillel,* 1962). Malachi also published *Iggerot David Frischmann* (1927), a book of David Frischmann's letters, and *Iggerot Soferim* (1932), miscellaneous letters of other writers, with notes and introductions. In addition, he edited a book on the State of Israel and its history, *Yisrael* (1950).

Bibliography: Shunami, Bibl, 925–6. [Ei.S.]

MALACHI BEN JACOB HA-KOHEN (d. 1785–1790), Italian scholar. Little is known of his life. He was the pupil of Abraham Ḥayyim Raphael Rodrigues and of the kabbalist R. Joseph *Ergas, whom he succeeded as rabbi of Leghorn after the latter's death in 1730. He arranged Ergas' work *Divrei Yosef* for publication (Leghorn, 1742). He also drew up an order of service *Shivḥei Todah* ("Praises of Thanksgiving"; Leghorn, 1744), for the 22nd day of Shevat, an annual fast day proclaimed to commemorate the rescue of the Leghorn community from the earthquake of 1742. He lived to an old age, dying in Tripoli, where he had apparently served as an emissary for Ereẓ Israel. Malachi is best known through his work *Yad Malakhi* (*ibid.,* 1767), which deals with the methodology of the Talmud and the codifiers. Part 1 contains principles of the Talmud in alphabetical order; Part 2, principles of the codifiers in chronological order; and Part 3, principles of various laws in alphabetical order. His novellae and responsa are found in the works of contemporary scholars. A manuscript of his responsa, *Teshuvot Yad Malakhi,* was published by E. *Gruenhut in *Ha-Me'assef,* 5 (1900). Malachi was also a liturgical poet. He composed *Sefer Shirei Zimrah,* which includes poems and dirges, part of which was published by S. Bernstein (*Mizraḥ u-Ma'arav,* 3 (1929), 245–61). His poem written on the occasion of the inauguration of the synagogue in Leghorn in 1742 was also published in Piperno's *Kol Ugav* (Leghorn, 1846).

Bibliography: Landshuth, Ammudei, 173–6; S. Bernstein, *Mi-Shirei Yisrael be-Italyah* (1939), 81–86; N. Slouschz, *Massa'i be-Ereẓ Luv* (1937), 246; J. Schirmann, *Mivḥar ha-Shirah ha-Ivrit be-Italyah* (1934), 399–400; A. Toaff and A. Lattes, *Gli Studi ebraici a Livorno* (1909), 25ff. [A.D./Ed.]

MÁLAGA, port in Andalusia, S. Spain. A Phoenician-Punic necropolis has been discovered there. In the Muslim period, the Jewish quarter was located in the eastern part of the city: the cemetery was on the slopes of Gibralfaro. In 863, at the time of the heresy of the bishop of Málaga, Hostegesis, he was alleged to have attached Jews from Málaga to the regional clerical councils as specialists in the principles of Christianity. Málaga served as a refuge for *Samuel ha-Nagid and other Jews who reached there in 1013 after the Berbers captured Córdoba. Solomon ibn *Gabirol was born in Málaga (c. 1021). In the mid-11th century the Jews numbered 200 out of a population of approximately 20,000.

When Málaga was captured by Ferdinand and Isabella in 1487 there were 100 Jewish families living there, and another group of 55 Jews were living in nearby Vélez-Málaga. All these were taken captive. The Jews of the kingdom had to pay 10 million maravedis for their ransom. Abraham *Senior and Meir of Segovia traveled through Andalusia to raise the money, and Solomon *Ibn Verga was also active.

The Catholic Monarchs had already ordered in 1490 that Málaga should be settled by Christians. The Jews and Moors, excepting certain Moors named in the royal edict, were ordered to leave Málaga within 15 days. Sixty-two exiles whose names were stated left Málaga, most of them persons in poor circumstances. Judah b. Jacob *Ḥayyat in his introduction to *Ma'arekhet ha-Elohut* records how on leaving Portugal in 1493 his ship was seized by Basque pirates and brought to Málaga, where local clergy attempted to convert the captives. The community of Málaga was revived in the early 1960s by Jews from North Africa. It has a community center and is affiliated to the organization of Jewish communities in Spain.

Bibliography: Baer, Spain, 2 (1966), index; Baer, Urkunden, 1 (1929), index; Ashtor, Korot, 1 (1960), 29, 63–64; idem, in: *Zion,* 28 (1963), 52–53; J. Millás Vallicrosa, in: *Sefarad,* 1 (1941), 316; A. Garcia y Bellido, *ibid.,* 2 (1942), 25f., 52, 83, 90, 286f.; L. Torres Balba, in: *Al Andalus,* 19 (1954), 197; J. Wiseman, *Roman Spain* (1956), 200; Suárez Fernández, Documentos, index; M. A. Ladero Quesada, in: *Hispania,* 27 (1967), 76–83 (Sp.). [H.B.]

MALAKH, ḤAYYIM BEN SOLOMON (between 1650 and 1660–1716 or 1717), leader of the Shabbatean sect. Malakh was born in Kalish. Nothing is known about his early career, but he became a highly respected rabbinic scholar, kabbalist, and preacher. He was soon attracted by the Shabbatean movement and became closely associated with the Shabbatean prophet Heshel *Ẓoref in Vilna. In 1690 he went to Italy, probably on a mission on behalf of the movement, staying there several months with Abraham *Rovigo and Benjamin *Cohen, the heads of the Italian Shabbateans. They studied the writings of Isaac *Luria and *Nathan of Gaza, and Ḥayyim Malakh received their secret traditions concerning Shabbetai Ẓevi. From 1692 to 1694 he was back in Poland, active as a Shabbatean missionary among rabbinic circles. One of his students (about 1693) was the famous talmudist Mordecai Suskind *Rotenburg, rabbi of Lublin. During this period he attracted the attention of R. Ẓevi *Ashkenazi, the father of Jacob *Emden, who became Malakh's bitter foe. Possibly because of a ban due to his heretic activity or possibly because of his own doubts concerning the Shabbatean theology, he went to Turkey. He stayed for two to three years with Samuel *Primo in Adrianople, becoming his fervent follower and receiving the traditions and secrets of the circle of Shabbetai Ẓevi's personal pupils. He went to Bursa (Turkey) where some outstanding Shabbateans lived, and toward the end of his stay, had a vision which caused him to return to Poland and join with another Shabbatean leader, *Judah he-Ḥasid. He arrived in Zolkiew, late in 1696, and stayed for some time, finding many influential followers. From Zolkiew he sent a letter to his Italian masters informing them that he was leaving their camp since he had found the authentic spring of Shabbatean teaching in Turkey. It is quite possible that he went back to Turkey in 1697 where he seems to have met Abraham *Cardozo in Adrianople. Malakh took Primo's side in the discussions with Cardozo whose speculative dissertations he refused to read. It is not clear whether at this time or later he came into contact with the young leader of the most radical wing of the *Doenmeh sect in Salonika, Baruchiah Russo (Osman Baba), several of whose sayings were quoted by Malakh to one of his pupils (in a Shabbatean notebook, probably written in Damascus, now in Columbia University Library).

After his return he became one of the founders of the new "Association of the Ḥasidim" which advocated an immigration of ascetic scholars to Jerusalem to await the imminent coming of the Messiah. Privately this Messiah was understood to be Shabbetai Ẓevi whose return in 1706, forty years after his apostasy, had been predicted by Malakh. Apparently during these years, Malakh acquired the surname Malakh "the angel." He became generally known by this title from the late 1690s on: whether this was because of his gifts as a preacher or because of his asceticism is unknown. Certainly he was considered the chief kabbalist of the group. In connection with the "ḥasidic" propaganda which attracted many secret Shabbateans in Poland, Germany, and the Hapsburg Empire, he spent some time in Germany and Moravia, where, at the end of 1698, he attended a council of the Shabbatean leaders of the Ḥasidim in Nikolsburg (Mikulov), an eyewitness report of which has survived. He also went to Vienna and announced that he would discuss the Shabbatean belief and teachings with any duly initiated kabbalist. Abraham *Broda, the rabbi of Prague, sent his pupils, Moses Ḥasid and Jonah Landsofer, but the dispute, which lasted two weeks, ended inconclusively. Malakh then went to Ereẓ Israel where, after the sudden death of Judah he-Ḥasid in October 1700, one faction of the Ḥasidim chose him as its leader. What exactly happened in the Shabbatean circle in Jerusalem is unknown or blurred by biased and half-legendary reports. At any rate, internal dissensions between moderate and radical Shabbateans contributed to the break-up of the group, but the precise date of Malakh's expulsion from Ereẓ Israel is unknown. It is probable that he went to Constantinople and again to Salonika, meeting with Baruchiah. Since that meeting Malakh acquired the reputation of being an emissary of the antinomian wing of Shabbateanism. This led to his prolonged persecution by the rabbinical authorities. A circular letter of the Constantinople rabbis, written in 1710, denounced him vehemently. He returned to Poland where he founded the radical sect in Podolia from which the Frankist movement sprang (see Jacob *Frank), but he also served as an emissary for some Ashkenazi groups in Ereẓ Israel. As such he is mentioned in the records of the community of *Tiktin (Tykocin) in 1708. In public he denied any Shabbatean connections, preferring to divulge his doctrine in private. Forced to leave Poland, he wandered through Germany and Holland. In 1715 he was in Amsterdam where a letter from Abraham Broda, then rabbi of Frankfort, urging Malakh's immediate expulsion arrived soon after his departure. He died shortly after his return to Poland in 1716 or 1717. He was generally considered an expert in Kabbalah and a persuasive spokesman for the Shabbatean movement after it was forced to go underground. None of his writings has survived.

Bibliography: J. Emden, *Torat ha-Kena'ot* (1871), 50, 70–71; D. Kahane, *Toledot ha-Mekubbalim, ha-Shabbeta'im ve-ha-Ḥasidim*, 2 (1913), 175–80; C. Bernheimer, in: JQR, 18 (1927/28), 125; G. Scholem, in: *Zion*, 6 (1941), 123–4; 11 (1946), 168–74; idem, in: RHR, 143 (1953), 209–20; M. Benayahu, in: *Sefer Ḥida* (1957), 73–74; idem, in: *Sefunot*, 3–4 (1960), 136–8; idem, in: *Eretz-Israel*, 10 (1971). [G.Sch.]

MALAMUD, BERNARD (1914–), U.S. novelist. Born in New York City, Malamud began to teach in 1939, went west to Oregon State College (an experience used in his third novel, *A New Life*, 1961), and later taught at Harvard. One of the most significant of the younger generation of mid-20th century American writers, Malamud was profoundly influenced by realistic novelists such as Dostoievski. His first novel, *The Natural* (1952), about the rise and fall of a baseball hero, was a brilliant tour de force, displaying a characteristic mixture of realistic detail, vernacular language and free-ranging symbolism and fantasy. Malamud found his true voice, however, with his second novel, *The Assistant* (1957), and a collection of short stories, *The Magic Barrel* (1958). With magnificent virtuosity and integrity, he (like Saul *Bellow) used a dialect of American English mixed with Yiddish, and succeeded in transferring to the American scene the intense moral concern, the comic yet pathetic irony, and the traditional situations of East European Jewish culture. Within the narrower Jewish world, he wrote with special love about the idealistic *shlimmazel*, the obscure and the lonely and the suffering, as in the title story of *Idiots First* (1963); this is also the case with Morris Bober, the grocer protagonist of *The Assistant*. Another recurring theme is the relations between Jews and gentiles: the New York Italian assistant falls in love with Bober's daughter and finally becomes a Jew; stories set in Italy deal with love between Jewish men and gentile women;

Bernard Malamud, U.S. novelist. Courtesy Farrar, Straus and Giroux, New York. Photo Seymor Linden.

and "Angel Levine" and "Black is My Favorite Color" are concerned with Jews and Negroes. Malamud was deeply conscious of the role of the Jew as a symbol of the human tragedy. All his concerns were fused, and grew in scope and significance, in *The Fixer* (1966), which won the National Book Award and the Pulitzer Prize in 1967 and was made into a motion picture. Yakov Bok, a Russian-Jewish handyman falsely accused of ritual murder, is based on Mendel *Beilis, victim of the notorious Kiev Blood Libel of 1913. An obscure little man in flight from his heritage, Bok is thrust into a situation requiring unusual courage. The stages by which he comes to a full understanding of his responsibility, and develops the strength of will to face his ordeal, are powerfully described. Malamud said of this novel: "The drama is as applicable to the American people as it is to the Russian." *Pictures of Fidelman* (1969), subtitled "An Exhibition," uses three previously collected stories, and adds three more, about the picaresque misadventures of an American-Jewish artist in Italy. In Rome, Milan, Florence, and Venice, Arthur Fidelman seeks both "perfection of the life" and "of the work"; in each city, he works at a different art or problem, and lives with a different woman. At the end, "Prometheus Fidelman" has learned his limitations: back in the U.S., "he worked as a craftsman in glass and loved men and women." In "Pictures of the Artist," a "Jewish refugee from Israel" named Susskind is imagined preaching a sort of parody of the Sermon on the Mount.

Bibliography: S. Richman, *Bernard Malamud* (1967), incl. selected bibl. of criticism; Hoyt, in: H.T. Moore (ed.), *Contemporary American Novelists* (1964), 65–79; Solotaroff, in: *Commentary*, 33 (1962), 197–204; R. Alter, *ibid.*, 42 no. 3 (1966), 71–76; L. Trilling, *The Experience of Literature* (1967), 809–11.

[S.J.K.]

MALAYSIA, federation of states in S.E. Asia formerly under British protection. A few Jews settled in Penang, of whom the first was Ezekiel Menassah from Baghdad, in 1895. Although remaining the only Jew in the whole area for nearly 30 years he continued Jewish observances, kept a *kasher* household and welcomed visiting coreligionists. Other Jews arrived there after World War I, mostly poor peddlers. During World War II the community was evacuated to *Singapore, subsequently occupied by the Japanese. Of the Jews who settled in Penang after the war, some 20 families remained by 1963. Only three families lived there in 1969.

Bibliography: I. Cohen, *Journal of a Jewish Traveller* (1925), 207–8. [Ed.]

MALBEN (Heb. initials of מוֹסְדוֹת לְטִפּוּל בְּעוֹלִים נֶחֱשָׁלִים, *Mosedot le-Tippul be-Olim Neḥshalim*—"Institutions for the Care of Handicapped Immigrants"), agency of the *American Jewish Joint Distribution Committee (JDC) for the care of aged, infirm, and handicapped immigrants in Israel. Its funds are derived mainly from the *United Jewish Appeal. The mass immigration after Israel declared its independence included thousands of old people—often the last survivors of families destroyed by the Nazis; victims of tuberculosis acquired in the concentration camps or Middle East ghettos; and others physically or emotionally incapacitated by poverty, wartime suffering, or Nazi persecution. In 1949, Malben was founded by the JDC to relieve the Israel government of the burden of caring for these immigrants. It constructed a network of about a hundred institutions, converting army barracks and whatever buildings were available into old-age homes, hospitals, TB sanitoriums, sheltered workshops, and rehabilitation centers.

Once emergency needs were under control, Malben began to consolidate its programs of direct care, while cooperating with other agencies to create more municipal and regional facilities for the aged and handicapped, and to develop indirect services which would enable elderly people to live on their own as long as possible. These measures include cash relief, constructive loans to help the aged and handicapped to earn a living, employment assistance, home medical care and housekeeping services, and the establishment of "Golden Age" clubs to provide elderly people with facilities for social and community life. Malben also cooperates with the government, the Jewish Agency, and the municipalities in the fields of mental health, chronic illness, and the care of physically and mentally handicapped children and adults among the settled population. Between 1949 and 1968, Malben-JDC helped some 250,000 immigrants—every fifth newcomer and one in ten of the population—at a total cost of $164 million. It maintains a hospital for chronic invalids, 12 old-age homes and villages with 3,000 beds, and extramural services for some 48,000 persons. Some of the homes, hospitals, and other programs initiated by Malben have been handed over to the government and local authorities.

Occupational therapy at the Malben institution at Maḥaneh Israel, 1960. Courtesy Keren Hayesod, United Israel Appeal, Jerusalem.

Bibliography: American Joint Distribution Committee, *Doors to Life* (1968). [M.L.]

MALBIM, MEIR LOEB BEN JEHIEL MICHAEL (1809–1879), rabbi, preacher, and biblical exegete. The name Malbim is an acronym formed from Meir Loeb ben Jehiel Michael. Born in Volochisk (Volhynia), Malbim was a child when his father died. He studied in his native town until the age of 13, with Moses Leib Horowitz, among others. He married at the age of 14, but after a short time divorced his wife. He went to Warsaw, where he became widely known as the "*illui* from Volhynia." From there he went to Leczyca, where he married the daughter of the local

Meir Loeb ben Jehiel Michael Malbim, rabbi and biblical commentator. Jerusalem, J.N.U.L., Schwadron Collection.

rabbi Ḥayyim Auerbach, who maintained him, and he was thus able to devote himself to literary work. In 1834 he traveled to Western Europe to obtain commendations from contemporary rabbis for his *Arẓot ha-Ḥayyim* (1837), visiting, among other places, Pressburg, Amsterdam, and Breslau. In 1839, on the recommendation of Solomon Zalman Tiktin of Breslau, he was appointed rabbi of Wreschen (district of Posen), where he remained for seven years. From there he went to Kempen and was therefore sometimes referred to as "The Kempener." While in Kempen he was invited to the rabbinate of Satoraljaujhely in Hungary but refused the offer. He finally agreed to accept the call of the Bucharest community, and in the summer of 1858 he was officially inducted as chief rabbi of Rumania.

Because of Malbim's uncompromising stand against Reform, disputes broke out between him and the communal leaders of the town, leading to his imprisonment. He was freed only on the intervention of Sir Moses *Montefiore and on condition that he leave Rumania and not return. M. Rosen has published various documents which disclose the false accusations and calumnies Malbim's Jewish-assimilationist enemies wrote against him to the Rumanian government. They accused him of disloyalty and of impeding social assimilation between Jews and non-Jews by insisting on adherence to the dietary laws, and said, "this rabbi by his conduct and prohibitions wishes to impede our progress." As a result of this the prime minister of Rumania issued a proclamation against the "ignorant and insolent" rabbi for his effrontery in "publishing libelous letters against those eating meat from any butcher shop and he has preached against the idea of progress and freedom." In consequence the minister refused to grant rights to the Jews of Bucharest, on the grounds that the rabbi of the community was "the sworn enemy of progress" (from the official newspaper *Monitorul* March 6, 1864). Determined to refute the false accusations made against him, Malbim went to Constantinople to lodge a complaint against the Rumanian government, which was then under Turkish domination. Following the rejection of his appeal and his failure to obtain the help of the Alliance Israélite Universelle (in transmitting a memorandum written in 1864 in Paris in which Malbim, with the help of Adolphe Crémieux, addressed himself to the Rumanian ruler, stressing his patriotism), he was compelled to leave Rumania (1864). During his wanderings in the following years he suffered persecution and calumny. He served as rabbi intermittently in Leczyca, Kherson, and Mogilev and was persecuted by the assimilationists, the *maskilim*, and the Ḥasidim. He was invited to Mainz, and on his way stopped at Koenigsberg, where he remained for about four years. In 1879 he received an invitation from Kremenchug, Poltava oblast, to serve as its rabbi, but died in Kiev on his way there.

Malbim's fame and his immense popularity rest upon his commentary on the Bible, which was widely esteemed. His first commentary published was on the Book of Esther (1845), followed by one on Isaiah (1849). In 1860 his commentary *Ha-Torah ve-ha-Mitzvah* on the Sifra was published in Bucharest. His commentary on the Song of Songs, *Shirei ha-Nefesh*, was published first in Krotoszyn and then in Bucharest in 1860. The remaining commentaries to the books of the Bible were completed and issued during the years 1867–76. Malbim's commentary on the Bible was motivated by his opposition to the Reform movement, which in his view could potentially undermine the very foundation of Judaism. He wished to strengthen the position of Orthodox Judaism in the spheres of exegesis, knowledge of Hebrew, and the exposition of the Bible according to its plain meaning, and thereby counteract and weaken the Reformers in precisely those three spheres, in which they had made appreciable achievements. In his long introduction to the commentary *Ha-Torah ve-ha-Mitzvah* (1860) on the Book of Leviticus and the Sifra, Malbim refers to the Reform Synod at Brunswick in 1844 calling it a gathering of "rabbis and preachers as well as readers who butcher their communities." Because of these Reformers' negative approach Malbim decided that "it was time to act for the Lord, and to fortify the wall around the Law, Written and Oral . . . so that violators could not assail and desecrate it." From that time he began to compose commentaries on the Bible with the aim of proving "that the Oral Law is the law given from heaven, and that all its words are necessary and implicit in the plain meaning of the verse and in the profundity of the language, and that the interpretation is only the plain meaning based upon accurate, linguistic rules."

His commentary to the Bible is based upon three fixed principles: in the text of the Torah and the figurative language of the prophets there are no repetitions of mere synonyms; consequently every word in a sentence is essential to the meaning in accord with the rules of the language despite the fact that they seem to be mere synonymous repetitions. Every statement conveys a sublime thought: all the metaphors are of importance and replete with wisdom for they are the words of the living God (introduction to Isaiah). In Malbim's opinion the sages had "important principles and fixed rules for the grammatical forms and the foundations of the language and of logic," according to which they understood all the words of the revelation transmitted at Sinai. He arranged these rules and principles in a special work, *Ayyelet ha-Shaḥar*, which he prefaced to his commentary on the Sifra. In it he noted 613 paragraphs (248 on linguistic usage and 365 in explanation of the verbs and synonyms) that are the foundations of tradition and the Oral Law. He stresses the superiority of the literal interpretation and complains that the commentators after David Kimḥi—except for Isaac Abrabanel—were exponents of homiletical exegesis "and no one exerted himself to breathe life into the verses by the literal method" (end of his introduction to Joshua). It should be noted that at the end of his commentary to Daniel, Malbim devotes himself to the calculation of the date of the redemption, which was to have been in the period 1913–1928: "We are writing these words in 1868 and according to our calculation the time of the redemption will be removed a further 60 years . . . for the rise of a scion of the house of David, the building of the Temple, and all the promises of the prophets will be fulfilled at the same time, and their luster will shine forth from the year 1913 to the year 1928, when the Temple will already have been established."

The following of his talmudic works are noteworthy: *Arzot ha-Ḥayyim*, contains novellae and expositions on Shulḥan Arukh, *Oraḥ Ḥayyim* (Part 1, on chapters 1–24, 1837; Part 2, on chapters 25–31, 1861), with the novellae of his son-in-law Elijah Joel Heilprin. The work, in three parts, comprises novellae on the responsa of Moses Isserles with source references and a pilpulistic exposition of the Shulḥan Arukh. *Yalkut Shelomo* (1938; 1966^2) was a collection of his novellae on the tractates of the Talmud, published (1966^2) after editing by Solomon Drillich, who also prepared and arranged a new edition of *Ha-Torah ve-ha-Mitzvah*, on the Pentateuch, with the title *Sefer ha-Torah ve-ha-Mitzvah ve-ha-Ḥinnukh*, in three parts (1967). *Alim li-Terufah* (1904) is a small work consisting of an exposition of the fourth chapter of *Hilkhot De'ot* in Maimonides' *Mishneh Torah*. *Arzot ha-Shalom* (1838) contains nine sermons which reveal the profundity of his homiletical ideas. Characteristic of this work is the fact that the sermons are based upon biblical verses only and do not rely upon rabbinic dicta. Each sermon encompasses a specific subject and is preceded by a poetic introduction. This method was regarded by some as an innovation in sermonic literature. His oral sermons were distinguished by verbal precision and strict logic. His *Erez Ḥemdah* (Warsaw 1882) contains sermons on the Pentateuch and expositions of *aggadot*. His works on language, poetry, and logic include: *Ya'ir Or* (1892), on synonymous nouns and verbs, containing 662 synonymous nouns; selections from his commentaries on synonyms are found in the *Likkutei Shoshannim* (1875), and *Ha-Karmel* (1900) arranged by J. Greenbaum; *Yesodei Ḥokhmat ha-Higgayon* (1900), a textbook on logic in 20 chapters comprising a survey on the principles of logic; *Mashal u-Melizah*, first published by Jehiel Brill (1867), a visionary poem on the vice of hypocrisy. His autobiography was published in serial form in *Ha-Levanon* (vol. 2, 1865).

Bibliography: C. H. Brawermann, in: *Keneset Yisrael*, 3 (1888), 207–12; J. Meisl, in: *Jeschurun*, 12 (1925), 112–26; J. Mark, *Gedolim fun unzer Tsayt* (1927), 147–52; idem, *Bi-Meḥizatam shel Gedolei ha-Dor* (1957), 129–33; A. Guenzler, in: *Ozar ha-Ḥayyim*, 6 (1930), 35–37; A. A. Hartstein, *ibid.*, 150f.; H. H. Tscharnotschepki, *ibid.*, 10 (1934), 21–23, 38f.; S. D. Posener, *Eshed ha-Nahar* (1932), 130–42; S. J. Glicksberg, *Ha-Derashah be-Yisrael* (1940), 402–7; E. Herbert, in: *Journal of Jewish Bibliography*, 2 (1940), 112–5; D. Druck, *Di Meforshim fun der Torah*, 3 (1941), 164–80; M. D. Ḥaklai, in: *Talpioth*, 4 (1949/50), 364–70; A. Schischa, *ibid.*, 6 (1953), 498–505; H. R. Rabinowitz, *Deyokna'ot shel Darshanim* (1967), 336–8; M. Rosen, in: *Hagut Ivrit be-Eiropah* (1969), 376–410; J. J. Cohen, in: KS, 44 (1969), 152f.

[Y.Ho.]

MALCA (ben, ibn Malkah), Jewish-Moroccan family name, known from the early 14th century through the kabbalist Nissim ibn Malca, the author of *Zenif Melukhah*. His son was the philosopher, Judah ben Nissim ibn *Malkah. He was strongly influenced by neoplatonic doctrines and wrote several works of which only one has been published *Uns al-Gharīb*. This was completed in 1365 probably in Fez. Lengthy extracts from it were translated into French and published by G. Vajda (see bibl.). For further details see col. 827.

Jacob ben Joseph ben Malca (d. 1771) was a rabbinical authority in Morocco. At first, he was *dayyan* in Fez, together with Judah *Benatar and Jacob *Abensur. Of a quarrelsome disposition, he was often in conflict with his colleagues, who nevertheless respected his profound erudition in the fields of rabbinical law and casuistry. During the famine which struck Fez in 1738 he moved to Tetuán, where he was appointed *av bet din*. He left a large number of decisions on various religious subjects, some of which have been published in the works of various Moroccan authors.

Khalifa ben Malca (d.c. 1750) was a member of a wealthy family of Safi. He studied in Fez with Judah Benatar and Samuel *Sarfaty and later continued his studies in his native town with Joseph Bueno de *Mesquita, where Abraham *ibn Musa and Jacob Abensur were his fellow students. Having lost his fortune, he settled in Agadir, where he represented Moses Guedalla of Amsterdam. He married Deborah, the daughter of the wealthy scholar Isaac *Mendes. In 1728 a plague claimed many vicitims, among them his wife and one of his daughters. In 1737 he lost large sums of money when the community was plundered and its synagogue set on fire. He then traveled to Holland and London. He wrote a commentary on the *siddur* entitled *Kav ve-Naki,* and also wrote commentaries to the Shulḥan Arukh, which he entitled *Rakh va-Tov.* He was particularly remembered for his piety, and both Jews and Muslims regarded him as a saint. Up to the 1960s regular pilgrimages were still made to his tomb in Agadir.

Bibliography: Azulai, 66, 81; I. Bloch, in: REJ, 14 (1887), 114–6; J. M. Toledano, *Ner ha-Ma'arav* (1911), 41, 143–4; J. Ben-Naim, *Malkhei Rabbanan* (1931), 64a, 80a; G. Vajda, *Judah ben Nissim Ibn Malka* (Fr., 1954). [D.Co.]

MALDONADO DE SILVA, FRANCISCO (1592–1639), Marrano martyr in Peru. Son of the physician Diego Nuñez de Silva (d. 1616) who was reconciled by the Inquisition in 1605, Francisco was born in Tucuman (now Argentina) and studied at the University of San Marcos in Lima, Peru. He was reared as a devout Catholic, and educated as a physician. His reading of the anti-Jewish *Scrutinium Scripturarum* by the apostate Pablo de *Santa Maria (Solomon ha-Levi) led him to pose questions to his father on the relative merits of Judaism and Christianity. His father acknowledged that he was still a Jew at heart, and guided his son in studying Judaism. Maldonado was persuaded to become a secret Jew. After his father's death he moved to Chile, where he married and in 1619 was appointed surgeon of the hospital in Santiago. He continued practicing Judaism, but was denounced to the Inquisition in 1627 by his two sisters, whom he had sought to convert. Despite continued efforts by the Inquisition to shake his faith, including 14 attempts by theologians to better him in religious debates, he held fast to Judaism. After each hearing he signed his testimony "Eli Nazareno, unworthy servant of the God of Israel, alias Silva." He circumcised himself with a pocketknife and scissors and resorted to long and agonizing fasts. Though suffering from numerous ailments, he used an improvised rope made from corn husks to lower himself into other cells, where he found some Judaizers whom he fortified in their faith, also converting Catholics to Judaism. Using scraps of paper and a pen made from a chicken bone, he wrote several tracts in support of his beliefs. He was burned at the stake in Lima at the conclusion of the auto-da-fé of 1639. News of his death made a profound impact on writers like Isaac *Cardozo and Daniel Levi (Miguel) de *Barrios, although the latter confuses him with Tomás *Treviño de Sobremonte.

Bibliography: B.Lewin, *Mártires y conquistadores judíos en la América Hispana* (1954), 177–207; idem, *El Santo Oficio en América* (1950), 142–52, 182; Roth, Marranos³, index s.v. *Silva;* H. C. Lea, *Inquisition in the Spanish Dependencies . . . Peru . . .* (1908), index. [M.A.C.]

°**MALESHERBES, CHRÉTIEN GUILLAUME DE LAMOIGNON DE** (1721–1794), liberal French statesman. As minister of the Maison du Roi in 1787, he was responsible with Turgot for the decree granting civic status to "non-Catholics," thus opening the way for effective action by the Jews on their own behalf. Malesherbes' main reason for wanting an improved treatment of the Jews was his belief that it would lead to their conversion; he was opposed to the organized Jewish community, considering it as a state within the state. Jewish individuals were not free to convert, said Malesherbes, because they were so closely tied to the whole community. He therefore proposed that Jews be enabled to use public legal registers for their personal status, thus weakening their ties with Jewry. In spring 1788 Malesherbes set up an informal committee to study the question, coopting as advisers men well-disposed toward the Jews, including Pierre Louis *Roederer. Eight Jewish leaders were summoned to the committee, among them *Cerfberr for Alsace, Berr Isaac *Berr for Lorraine, Abraham *Furtado and D. Gradis for Bordeaux. The purpose of the committee was to conduct a preliminary inquiry on a new system for regulating the condition of French Jewry, and to prepare a memorandum. However, meetings were few and the differences between the two delegations, the "Portuguese" and the "German," were so marked that they could not reach agreement. The "Portuguese" memorandum in answer to Malesherbes' questionnaire on the current state of Judaism was later to influence the one presented by Napoleon's representatives to the *Assembly of Jewish Notables and the French *Sanhedrin. In July 1788 the delegates returned home, without having come to any decision. Malesherbes remained a staunch royalist and was later guillotined.

Bibliography: Szajkowski, in: *Zion,* 18 (1953), 31–79; idem, in: PAAJR, 25 (1956), 119–35; idem, in: JQR, 49 (1958), 63–75; A. Hertzberg, *The French Enlightenment and the Jews* (1968), 323–6; P. Grosclaude, *Malesherbes—témoin et interprète de son temps* (1961), 631–49. [S.Sch./Ed.]

MALIK AL-RAMLĪ (of Ramleh in Ereẓ Israel; mid-ninth century), founder of the sect of Ramlites or Malikites. Like some other sectarians, Malik taught that Shavuot must fall only on a Sunday, that the fat tail of the sheep comes under the heading of forbidden fat, and that marriage to a niece is incestuous. Within a century or so the Ramlites went out of existence, being probably absorbed into the larger sect of *Karaites.

Bibliography: Nemoy, in: HUCA, 7 (1930), 330, 389; idem, *Karaite Anthology* (1952), 53, 335; Mann, Texts, 2 (1935), 6, 11, 65 n. 117; Z. Ankori, *Karaites in Byzantium* (1959), 276n., 371n. [L.N.]

MALINES (Mechelen), camp established by the Nazis in Belgium in October 1941 to concentrate Jews before transporting them to Eastern Europe. The first transport from Mechelen was on Aug. 4, 1942, and arrived in *Auschwitz on August 6. According to a list in the Mechelen archive, between Aug. 4, 1942, and July 1944 there were 26 transports to the east with more than 25,000 Jews. All the inmates of the camp had to wear identification badges. The badges differed for the Jews in the camp. The various known symbols were: *T* = *Transport-Juden* (Jews who would be sent to the east), *Z* = citizens of the Allied countries or neutral countries, *E* = citizens whose identity required further investigation, *G* = *Gefaehrliche Juden* (dangerous Jews to be sent to punishment camps). Members of the Committee for Jewish Defence (CDJ) which was in contact with the Belgian resistance movement, and the Catholic fighters' organization, penetrated into Mechelen a number of times in order to warn the inmates and try to liberate them. The camp was finally liberated by the Allies in September 1944; a few hundred Jews had managed to survive.

See *Belgium, Holocaust.

Bibliography: J. Robinson, *And the Crooked Shall Be Made Straight* (1965); Belgium, Ministère de Justice. Commission des crimes de guerre, *Les Crimes de guerre, commis sous l'occupation de la Belgique 1940–1945. Persécution antisémitique en Belgique* (1947); *Belgium. Nuremberg document UK-76* (undated); *Nuremberg Trials Documents: Case 11, NG5219;* International Tracing Service, Arolsen, Germany, *Vorlaeufiges Verzeichnis der Haftstaetten unter dem Reichsfuehrer-SS 1933–1945* (1969). [B.M.A.]

MALINOVSKI, JOSEPH BEN MORDECAI (Troki; d. after 1624), Polish Karaite scholar. Joseph was the pupil of Isaac b. Abraham *Troki, and completed his *Ḥizzuk Emunah* on Isaac's death (1594). He had extensive knowledge of both Karaite and rabbinic scholarship. Several of his hymns and an outline of ritual customs (*Sefer Minhagim*) were included in the Karaite prayer book. *Manasseh Ben Israel's press printed his prayer *Ha-Elef Lekha* (Amsterdam, 1643). His *Kizzur Inyan Sheḥitah* on the ritual slaughter of animals was printed together with Mordecai b. Nissan's *Dod Mordekhai* (Vienna, 1830). Joseph died in Lutsk.

Bibliography: Mann, Texts, 2 (1935), index. [L.N.]

MALKAH, JUDAH BEN NISSIM IBN (mid-14th century), philosopher, probably living in Morocco. Three of his works written in Judeo-Arabic have been preserved, all unpublished except for one extract (H. Hirschfeld, *An Arabic Chrestomathy in Hebrew Characters* (1892), 19–31); (1) *Uns al-Gharīb* ("Familiarity with the Unfamiliar"), consisting of the author's own views and of a commentary on the *Sefer Yeẓirah,* preceded by a long introduction; (2) a commentary on the *Pirkei de Rabbi Eliezer;* (3) *Tafsīr al-Ṣalawāt,* a commentary on the liturgy (fragment). Besides these, Judah refers to a work which he wrote on astrology, which probably bore the title *Kitāb al-Miftāḥ* ("The Key Book"). Of the first of these works there exists also an anonymous abridgement. The doctrine of Judah b. Nissim rests on two fundamental theses: the unknowability of God and universal astral determinism. From the first there flows an emanation metaphysics having at its apex the prime intellect, to which the functions of the first cause, and consequently those of the God of religion, have been transferred; from the second flows a view of the world according to which even revealed religions are completely determined by astral influences. In the light of this, the superiority of Judaism is that it is best adapted to the demands of astral determination. The only ones who can penetrate this mystery, however, are the philosophers who are adept in the allegorical exegesis of religious texts, whereas the masses are obligated to observe the letter of the law. Judah's philosophy is in many ways similar to the neoplatonic speculations adopted by the Muslim sect of Ismāʿīliyya in constructing their theology, but no precise historical connection can be established between them. His views on astral determinism are not alien to the Jewish thought of the Middle Ages (particularly that of Abraham *ibn Ezra and certain Averroists), but they are brought to conclusions which no one else had perhaps dared to formulate with such boldness. On the other hand, the deductions which Judah drew from the unknowability of God are similar to the Kabbalah. In fact, the author was familiar with the Kabbalah and referred to it; although, besides the *Sefer Yeẓirah,* he cites only the *Bahir* and the *Razi'el,* it has been possible to establish that he availed himself of the kabbalists of *Gerona (*Azriel, Jacob b. Sheshet *Gerondi, and *Naḥmanides), even of the Zohar, and perhaps also of Joseph *ibn Waqar. Nevertheless, he did not consider the teachings of the Kabbalah superior to those of philosophy, but rather identified the Kabbalah with philosophy. More precisely, he regarded the Kabbalah as a particular symbolic expression of God's unknowability and of astral determinism. It appears that Judah had no influence on subsequent Jewish thought; he is rarely mentioned, with the notable exception of Samuel ibn *Motot.

Bibliography: S. Munk, *Les Manuscrits Hébreux de l'Oratoire* (1911), 15–17; Steinschneider, Uebersetzungen, 405–6; J. M. Toledano, *Ner ha-Ma'arav* (1911), 41; G. Sarton, *Introduction to the History of Science,* 3 pt. 2 (1947), 1444; G. Vajda, *Juda ben Nissim Ibn Malka, philosophe juif marocain* (1954); idem, in: *Homenaje a Millás-Vallicrosa,* 2 (1956), 483–500; idem, in: REJ, 15 (1956), 25–71; 16 (1957), 89–92. [G.V.]

MALKHI, EZRA BEN RAPHAEL MORDECAI (d. 1768), Safed talmudist and emissary. Ezra was the son of a well-known physician and scholar in Jerusalem, who had emigrated from Italy. His brother, Moses, became head of the Safed community and he was a brother-in-law of *Hezekiah da Silva and Moses *Ḥagiz. In 1749–50 Ezra went to Turkey and the Balkans as an emissary of Safed. While in Salonika he published his *Malkhi ba-Kodesh* (Salonika, 1749), laws for the night of Passover, and a commentary on the *Haggadah,* together with some halakhic novellae. He appended a note apologizing for the many errors in the work because he could not stay in the town during the printing, but was again in Salonika in 1750 when he had halakhic discussions with Joseph Samuel Modigliano. Owing to the bad economic situation in Safed, Ezra did not return there on the completion of his mission, and was appointed rabbi of Rhodes, where he remained for the rest of his life. In 1752 his signature appears on the *takkanot* of the community. His other books are: *Shemen ha-Ma'or* (Salonika, 1755), on the novellae of *Zerahiah ha-Levi and *Naḥmanides on *Bava Meẓia; Ein Mishpat* (Constantinople, 1770), responsa, many of which were written during his mission, published by his disciple Raphael Jacob de Mayo; and *Einat Mayim* (Salonika, 1811), exposition and novellae on various tractates of the Talmud.

Bibliography: Yaari, Sheluḥei, 438–40, 884. [A.Ya./Ed.]

MALKHI, MOSES (b. Ezra?; mid-18th century), emissary of Safed. Malkhi had the distinction of being the first emissary of Ereẓ Israel to visit the New World. He was in New York in the summer of 1759 for four and a half months, and it is assumed that he remained there at the request of the members of the Sephardi community "Shearith Israel" who had no rabbi, in order to arrange their religious affairs. In the account book of that community it states that they gave the emissary 18 pounds sterling for 18 week's accommodation and for provisions and traveling expenses to Newport, Rhode Island, which was then the wealthiest Jewish community in America. There he met the Christian theologian Ezra *Stiles who was greatly interested in the emissary from Ereẓ Israel. Stiles relates that Malkhi was born and brought up in Safed, and he sent a letter in Latin through him to one of the heads of the Greek Church in Ereẓ Israel requesting exact information on the geography of the country and its inhabitants which he needed for his researches on the *Ten Tribes. This Malkhi must be distinguished from his namesake, Moses (b. Raphael Mordecai *Malkhi). He may have been the son of Ezra *Malkhi.

Bibliography: Yaari, Sheluḥei, 446; D. de Sola Pool, in: *Brandeis Avukah Annual* (1932), 356–7; G. A. Kohut, *Ezra Stiles and the Jews* (1902). [A.Ya.]

MALKHI, MOSES BEN RAPHAEL MORDECAI (d. 1747), head of the Safed community in the first half of the 18th century. Moses was a brother of Ezra *Malkhi. He was head of the Jewish community of Safed for many years, and as such his signature appears first on the letters of appointment of various Safed emissaries. Malkhi was one of the intermediaries between Sheikh Ẓāhir al-Omar and Ḥayyim Abulafia for the renewal of the Jewish community in Tiberias in 1740. He died in Acre and was buried in Kafr-Yasīf. In the letter of the community of Safed reestablishing the Jewish community of Kafr Yasīf written in Elul of that year, the tomb of "the distinguished rabbi Moses Malkhi of blessed memory" and that of Moses Ḥayyim Luzzato, who died that year in the plague in Acre and was buried in Kafr-Yasīf, is listed together with those of *tannaim* and *amoraim*. It may be conjectured that Malkhi also died in that plague during a visit to Acre in connection with the affairs of the Safed community.

Bibliography: Yaari, Sheluḥei, 431, 432, 437, 438, 501, 850.

[A.YA.]

MALKHUYYOT (Heb. מַלְכֻיּוֹת; verses describing God's "sovereignty"), name of the first part of the central section of the **Musaf* prayer for *Rosh Ha-Shanah. It consists of 10 verses, four from the Pentateuch, three from Psalms, and three from the Prophets; all of them proclaim God as King and anticipate the realization of His kingdom on earth. According to the Talmud (RH 32a) the number ten symbolized the ten praises sung by David (Ps. 150), or the Ten Commandments, or the "ten sayings" by which God created the world (cf. Avot 5:1). The *Malkhuyyot* prayer and two similar sections, **Zikhronot* and **Shofarot*, form the *Teki'ata de-Vei Rav*. At the end of each section during the Reader's repetition (and in some rites during the congregation's silent reading), the *shofar* is sounded. The recital of *Malkhuyyot-Zikhronot-Shofarot* verses dates back to mishnaic times (cf. RH 4:5, 6) and was, most probably, part of the prayer service in the Temple. The Talmud, however, does not specify which verses had to be chosen for this purpose (RH 32a–b). The present selection and order of the verses is ascribed to the Babylonian scholar *Rav (175–247 C.E.), as are the introductory and concluding passages.

Bibliography: Elbogen, Gottesdienst, 141–4; Idelsohn, Liturgy, 213–4.

[ED.]

MALKIEL, YAKOV (1914–), U.S. philologist. Born in Kiev, Russia, educated in Berlin, Malkiel emigrated to the United States in 1940. From 1942 he was a faculty member at the University of California (Berkeley) and later professor of linguistics and Romance philology. In 1947 Malkiel was founder and editor in chief of the journal *Romance Philology*. He was president of the Linguistic Society of America in 1965. He was author of numerous articles and monographs dealing with historical linguistics, Hispanic lexicology, and the theory of etymology and lexicography, and he constantly attempted to mediate between general linguistics and Romance philology. Among his works are *Studies in the Reconstruction of Hispano-Latin Word Families* (1954), *Essays on Linguistic Themes* (1968), and the editing of *Directions for Historical Linguistics: A Symposium* (1968), with Winfred P. Lehmann.

[J.C.G.]

MALLER, JULIUS BERNARD (1901–1959), U.S. educator and sociologist. Born in Vobolniki, Lithuania, Maller went to the U.S. in 1921. Having received both a secular and religious higher education, Maller's professional life was divided between teaching posts at Howard University, Washington, D.C. and Yeshiva University (1949–59). He was also active in Jewish organizations. Maller devised (1929) the "Guess Who" technique, a sociometric test for use with children. His personality tests, known as the "Maller Personality Sketches" (1936) and the "Maller Character Sketches" consisted of cards with descriptions of personality or character traits, to be sorted into groups. He demonstrated that intelligence test scores at the fifth grade level were closely related to socioeconomic levels. A close relationship was shown between delinquency, density of population, and economic level. His chapter on personality tests in *Personality and the Behavior Disorders* (1944) was a standard treatment. Later he became a consultant to various government agencies in addition to his interests in Jewish education, his work with Jewish service organizations and his teaching activities. His most important publications were: *Cooperation and competition: an experimental study of motivation* (1929); *Studies in the nature of character:* volume 2; *Studies in service and self-control* (with Hartshorne and May, 1929); and *Testing the Knowledge of Jewish History* (1932). He was also a frequent contributor to Jewish educational periodicals. [M.M.BR.]

MALLOW, plant of the genus *Malva*. Six species are found in Israel, the most common, found in almost every part of the country, being the *Malva nicaensis, Malva silvestris,* and *Malva parviflora*. During the siege of Jerusalem in 1948 the citizens of Jerusalem picked them and prepared from them a variety of dishes. The mallow is popularly known by its Arabic name *khubeiza* which means "small loaf," because its edible seeds are flat and round like the Arab bread *(pittah)*. Job characterizes "the juice of *ḥallamut*" ("mallow") as insipid, so that even in his distress "my soul refuses to touch them; they are as the sickness of my flesh" (Job 6:6). Despite this, the name *ḥallamut* or *ḥelmit* in the Mishnah appears to be connected with *ḥalam* meaning "healthy." It may be, however, the same as *laḥmit*, through transposition of letters, which has the same connotation as its Arabic name "small bread." The Mishnah refers to *ḥelmit* as a vegetable (Kil. 1:8) and the *Arukh* of Nathan b. Jehiel identifies it with *Malva* (mallow). The leaves of some mallows are sensitive to light, and Rashi in his commentary on the vegetable *adani* (Shab. 35b) notes: "It is a vegetable called *malva* whose leaves turn to the sun. In the morning they incline eastward, at midday they are upright, and in the evening they incline westward." The identification of the *ḥallamut* of the Bible with mallow is not certain, and it has been identified with many other plants. The JPS renders *ḥallamut* as "mallow" (AV: "white of egg"), while the AV renders *malu'aḥ* in Job 30:4 as "mallow" (JPS correctly as "saltwort"; see *Orach).

Bibliography: Loew, Flora, 1 (1928), 292–4; N.H.Tur-Sinai, *Sefer Iyyov*, 1 (1941), 85f.; H.N. and A.L. Moldenke, *Plants of the Bible* (1952), 53f.; J. Feliks, *Olam ha-Ẓome'aḥ ha-Mikra'i* (1968²), 188–90.

[J.F.]

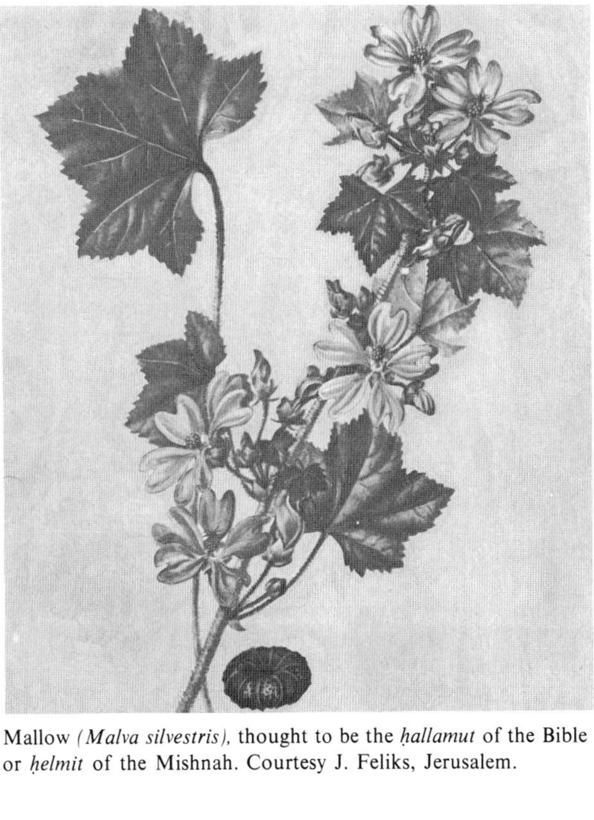

Mallow *(Malva silvestris)*, thought to be the *ḥallamut* of the Bible or *ḥelmit* of the Mishnah. Courtesy J. Feliks, Jerusalem.

MALMÖ, port in S. Sweden. The Jewish community, now the second largest in Sweden, was founded by Polish Jews in 1871, when it numbered 250. In 1900 the congregation appointed its first rabbi and in 1903 the first synagogue was built. During World War II Malmö was the port of entry for Jewish refugees rescued from Denmark. The community has grown rapidly and in 1968 numbered 1,700. Haquinus Stridzberg's *Kohen Gadol sive Pontifex-Maximus Ebraeorum* was printed in Malmö in 1689.

Bibliography: H. Valentin, *Judarna i Sverige* (1964); L. Herz, in: JJSO, 11 (Dec. 1969), 165–73. [Ed.]

MALTA, Mediterranean island. That Jews were present there in Roman times is attested by the discovery of a catacomb with the symbol of the **menorah*. There must have been a community under Arab rule (870–1090) and in 1240 there were 25 Jewish families there and eight in the neighboring island of Gozo. During the Middle Ages the two islands were part of the Kingdom of Sicily, and a great deal is known of their history from materials preserved in the Sicilian archives. The communities came to an end with the expulsion of the Jews from Sicily in 1492. From 1530 to 1798 the islands were ruled by the Knights of St. John, who in the course of their forays against the Muslims captured and brought back to Malta large numbers of Jewish prisoners. The Societies for Redeeming the *Captives (Ḥevrot Pidyon Shevuyim) in Venice and elsewhere were mainly engaged in raising funds for ransoming the Jewish prisoners in Malta, where the Venetian society kept a permanent Christian agent. Under the latter's auspices, the Jewish slaves were able to maintain a synagogue for worship, and there was also a cemetery. A regular community, mainly deriving from North Africa, began to develop during the last days of the rule of the Knights and under British rule (from 1800). In 1804 the *blood libel raised against the handful of Jews was firmly suppressed by the English poet S. T. Coleridge, then colonial secretary on the island. The community remained small, numbering 16 families in 1968. [C.R.]

Relations with Israel. Israel established friendly relations and cooperation with Malta even before the latter achieved independence in 1964. In the late 1950s the leader of the Maltese Labor Party, Dom Mintoff, tried to mediate between Israel and Egypt, albeit unsuccessfully. In 1966 an Israel embassy was established with a resident chargé d'affaires, while Israel's ambassador in Rome also serves as nonresident ambassador to Malta. Israel experts assisted in the development of dairy, poultry, and afforestation projects. Israel's exports to Malta exceeded $1,000,000 in 1970. [Ed.]

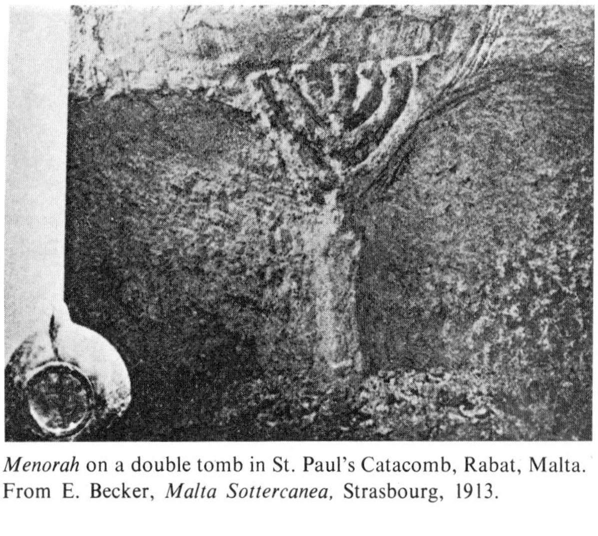

Menorah on a double tomb in St. Paul's Catacomb, Rabat, Malta. From E. Becker, *Malta Sottercanea*, Strasbourg, 1913.

Bibliography: C. Roth, *The Jews of Malta* (1931; =offprint from JHSET, 12 (1928–31), 187–251); S. Assaf, *Be-Oholei Ya'akov* (1943), 107–15; Roth, Mag Bibl, 113; idem, *Personalities and Events* (1961), 112–35.

MALTER, HENRY (1864–1925), rabbi and scholar of medieval Jewish philosophy. Malter was born in the village of Bonze, Galicia. His father was his teacher and provided him with the fundamentals of a rabbinic education. Hardly past childhood, Malter became interested in secular knowledge, having somehow obtained access to *Ha-Maggid*, a Hebrew periodical with a Haskalah viewpoint. At the age of 16 in search of broader knowledge he journeyed to Lyck and from there to Berlin. While earning his living by teaching Hebrew, he prepared himself for entering the university and at the same time continued his Jewish education at the Veitel-Heine-Ephraimsche Lehranstalt. There he attracted the attention and became the favorite pupil of Moritz *Steinschneider, who encouraged his interest in medieval Jewish bibliography, and whose book in that field, *Juedische Literatur* (1850), Malter translated into Hebrew as *Sifrut Yisrael* (1897). With his work on the influence of the 11th-century Muslim philosopher Al-Ghazzali on Jewish thought, *Die Abhandlung des Abu Hamid al-Gazzali* (1894), Malter earned a doctorate in philosophy from the University of Heidelberg. In 1898 he received a rabbinical diploma from the Lehranstalt fuer die Wissenschaft des Judentums. The newly founded library of the Berlin Jewish community then invited him to become its librarian. He held this post for a year. Malter went to the United States in 1900 at the invitation of the Hebrew Union College in Cincinnati to teach medieval Jewish philosophy. He also taught Bible and rabbinic law and literature, and at the same time served as rabbi at the Shearith Israel congregation in Cincinnati. However, he disagreed with the theological attitudes of American Reform Judaism and was, therefore, in conflict with Kaufmann *Kohler, then president of Hebrew Union College; consequently, he left the college in 1907. Thereafter, in New York he collaborated with J. D. Eisenstein on the Hebrew encyclopedia *Ozar Yisrael* contributing articles on Jewish literature, among others. With the opening of Dropsie College in 1909, Malter assumed the chair of talmudic literature which he occupied to the end of his life. He was a stimulating teacher in Talmud and particularly in medieval philosophy and ethics. Painstaking in his scholarship, Malter published a number of important essays in the *Jewish Quarterly Review* and elsewhere. His chief published work is *Saadia Gaon, His Life and Works* (1921). The study is based on a meticulous review of every fragment, including *genizah* material, by and about the head of the Sura academy in the tenth century. It is a model of a biography of a scholar by a scholar: it deals with *Saadiah's eventful life, analyzes his works, and in a bibliographical section shows his influence by citing the numerous references to him in the course of

Henry Malter, rabbi and scholar of medieval Jewish philosophy. Jerusalem, J.N.U.L., Schwadron Collection.

the centuries. Two other books, both published posthumously, deal with the talmudic treatise *Ta'anit: Treatise Ta'anit of the Babylonian Talmud* (1928), critically edited on the basis of manuscripts and old editions, and *Massekhet Ta'anit min Talmud Bavli* (1930), a critical edition of the text with notes and explanations on the basis of 24 manuscripts. With Alexander *Marx, Malter edited the *Gesammelte Schriften* of Moritz Steinschneider, of which only the first volume appeared (1925).

Bibliography: A. Marx, *Essays in Jewish Biography* (1947), 255–64; D. Druck, in: *Der Amerikaner*, 20 (April 28, 1922), 4; (May 5, 1922), 6; A. Marx, in: AJYB, 28 (1926), 261–72, also in: A. Marx, *Studies in Jewish History and Booklore* (1944), 409–17.

[S.G.]

MALTZ, ALBERT (1908–), U.S. playwright and novelist. Maltz, who was born in Brooklyn, wrote his first play in 1931 in collaboration with George Sklar. Entitled *Merry-Go-Round*, it was an exposé of corrupt Tammany politics in New York City. Maltz became associated with the left-wing Theater Union for which he wrote an antiwar drama, *Peace on Earth* (with George Sklar, 1933) and *Black Pit* (1935). From the late 1930s he began writing novels, notably *The Happiest Man on Earth* (1938); *The Underground Stream* (1940); *The Cross and the Arrow* (1944), which was made into a motion picture; and *The Journey of Simon McKeever* (1949). He also published essays and the scenarios for films including *This Gun for Hire* (1942), *Destination, Tokyo* (1943), and *Naked City* (1948). In 1947 Maltz was indicted during the McCarthy era, with nine other Hollywood writers, and spent nine months in prison. After his release in 1951 he settled in Mexico. A later novel was *A Long Day in a Short Life* (1957).

Bibliography: H. R. Warfel, *American Novelists of Today* (1951), 277; S. J. Kunitz (ed.), *Twentieth Century Authors*, first suppl. (1955).

[M.H.H.]

MALVANO, GIACOMO (1841–1922), Italian diplomat.. Born in Turin, he was secretary general of the foreign ministry from 1876 to 1885. Malvano was minister to Tokyo from 1887 to 1889 when he resumed the post of secretary general of the foreign office, which he held until 1907. Malvano was a senator from 1896 and later was appointed to the Council of State, eventually becoming its president. He was also president of the Italian Geographic Society for many years.

An opponent of Zionism, Malvano refused to assist Theodor Herzl on his visit to Rome (Jan. 26, 1904) on the ground that he was only "a modest civil servant." Herzl ironically refers to him, "He is a clerk in the wholesale firm of 'Italy, Inc.'" [G.R.]

MALZBERG, BENJAMIN (1893–), U.S. psychiatric statistician and epidemiologist. Malzberg was born in New York City and from 1923 to 1928 served as statistician to the Department of Welfare of New York State. After serving on the Committee on State Hospital Problems, he moved to the New York State Department of Mental Hygiene in 1940, becoming the director of its statistical bureau in 1944, its consultant in 1956. Malzberg performed numerous studies of a statistical and epidemiological nature. Among his early researches were "Mortality among Patients with Mental Disease" (1934); "Hereditary and Environmental Factors in Dementia Praecox and Manic-Depressive Psychoses" (with associates, 1938); "Social and Biological Aspects of Mental Disease" (1946). *Migration and Mental Disease* appeared in 1956, as did his important study *Mental Disease among Jews in New York State* (1960). *Mental Disease among Jews in Canada* appeared in 1963 and *Ethnic Variations in Mental Disease in New York State* in 1966. His studies also covered the mental health of the Negro and alcoholic psychoses. In his studies of mental illness among Jews, Malzberg demonstrated a higher incidence of psychotic depression among Jews than among white non-Jews (as measured by hospital admissions). His research confirmed the general knowledge that the incidence of alcoholism was very low among Jews.

[Lo.M.]

MAMLUKS (lit. slaves), a military class (see below) which ruled Egypt from 1250 to 1517. Under the Mamluk sultans in Egypt, Palestine, Syria, and adjacent regions in North Africa and Asia Minor, oriental Jewry suffered greatly at the hands of the government and Muslim zealots. In view of the length of the Mamluk rule this deterioration of the Jews' situation had far-reaching consequences. The animosity of the Muslims was directed essentially against the Christian subjects of the Mamluk state, particularly against the Copts, who at the beginning of this period represented a strong sector of the Egyptian population; but when fanaticism started, the Jews also suffered. Under the rule of the Baḥris, the first Mamluk dynasty (1250–1381), the antagonism between Muslims and non-Muslims developed into actual persecution. During that of the second dynasty, the Circassians (1381–1517), too, there was a long series of vexations. In this period the Jews of Egypt and Syria were very much weakened and humiliated and their numbers decreased considerably. The paucity of the Cairo *Genizah* documents from this period indicates the great change in Egyptian Jewry; whereas these archives of Cairo Jewry contain many documents from the 11th and 12th centuries, there are relatively few preserved from the Mamluk period. On the other hand, the numerous Arab chronicles of the 14th and 15th centuries contain much information on the Jews. From the accounts of the Arab authors it appears that three main factors brought about the deterioration in the situation of non-Muslims: the structure of the Mamluk regime, the hostility against the "infidels" resulting from the struggle with the Franks in Syria and Palestine, and social tension.

The Mamluks were former slaves bought by the *Ayyubid sultans to serve in their armies. When they had overthrown their masters, they constituted a military feudal aristocracy which replenished its ranks by the periodical purchase of new slaves from various northern countries, such as southern Russia and the Balkan peninsula. Many of the later rulers of Egypt had been born as Christians and all of them were foreigners speaking a Turkish *"koine"* among themselves. Since they cruelly oppressed the indigenous population, depleting the country of its riches, they were haunted by the fear of revolts. They therefore curried favor with the theologians, a most influential group of the native intelligentsia. Although most of the Mamluks did not observe many prescripts of Islam, they behaved as if they were devout Muslims. Their ambition was to be considered the champions of the holy war against the Christians. They founded many seminaries of Muslim theology and were always ready to comply with the wishes of the *ulamā* asking for measures against the Christians and Jews. Whereas the Ayyubids had acquiesced in coexistence with the crusaders in Syria and Palestine from the foundation of the regime, the Mamluk sultans embarked on a war of extermination against the Christian principalities. This war, combined with intense political and religious propaganda, aroused strong fanaticism. The Muslim masses regarded all Christians as allies or spies of the Franks and other enemies of Islam, especially after the crusaders in Syria had concluded an alliance with the Mongols who invaded the Fertile Crescent in 1258. The antagonism between Muslims and

Detail of wall of the Serai, the Gaza Government House, built in the 13th century, showing typical Mamluk ornamentation. Courtesy Israel Department of Antiquities, Jerusalem.

non-Muslims was intensified by the frustration of both the indigenous middle class, which was excluded from participation in the government, and of the merchants and wealthy bourgeoisie, who were plagued by extortion. The Muslim intelligentsia was much embittered by the fact that many posts in government offices were filled by Christians and Jews.

When Damascus was reconquered from the Tatars in 1260, there were riots against the Christians and Jews. Five years later the Christians in Cairo were accused of arson committed either in revenge for the destruction of a church in Nazareth or at the instigation of their coreligionists in Acre. Thereupon Sultan Baybars I assembled many Christians and Jews and ordered that they be burned alive, but released them on condition that they pay a heavy tribute in annual installments. Under Baybars' successors non-Muslim officials were dismissed several times. Arab chroniclers sometimes mention only measures taken against Christians, but they state explicitly that Jews suffered during the dismissal of the officials in 1290 and the riots under al-Malik al-Ashraf Khalīl (1290–93). In 1301 the hatred of non-Muslims burst into severe persecution; riots occurred in several towns in Egypt and many Christians and Jews were compelled to adopt Islam, including all the Jews of Bilbeis, in Lower Egypt, according to the late Jewish-Egyptian chronicler Joseph b. Isaac *Sambari. All churches and synagogues in Cairo were closed; in Alexandria, houses of non-Muslims which were higher than those of their Muslim neighbors were destroyed. These were unprecedented acts. Furthermore, the government decreed that henceforth Christians must wear blue turbans; Samaritans, red; and Jews, yellow. In 1354 there was another general persecution of the non-Muslims. There were riots, Jews and Christians were forcibly converted to Islam, and non-Muslim government officials were dismissed, even those who embraced Islam.

In the second half of the 14th century restrictive laws and various vexations followed. Non-Muslim officials were dismissed in Damascus in 1356 and in 1363. At that time Jews and Christians were forbidden to ride horses and mules. They were allowed to ride donkeys only, using packsaddles and mounted so that both feet were on one side of the animal. In public baths they had to distinguish themselves by wearing little bells around the neck, and women had to wear one black and one white shoe. In 1365 Muslim zealots in Damascus searched Jewish and Christian homes for wine, and poured the wine they found into the streets and rivers. Restrictive laws were again enforced; Jewish and Christian women were forbidden to frequent the public baths. Although the frequency of these ordinances proves that the discriminatory laws were not systematically kept it is evident that their periodic enactment humiliated Jews and Christians whose communities were sizably weakened and diminished by the end of the rule of the Baḥrī Mamluks in 1381. The image of the non-Muslim communities in the chronicles from the reign of the Circassian Mamluks (1381–1517) is quite different. With the end of the crusaders' principalities, the non-Muslims were no longer accused of conspiring with the enemies of the sultan; hence, general persecutions of non-Muslims in Egypt and Syria ceased. Nevertheless, the tyranny of the second Mamluk dynasty was even worse than its predecessor. The frustration of the population increased and the sultans were always inclined to enforce the restrictive laws on the *dhimmīs* or extort heavy contributions from them. Under Sultan al-Malik al-Mu'ayyad Shaikh (1412–19) the authorities harassed the Jews and Christians in Egypt for drinking wine. In 1417 non-Muslims were ordered to dress simply in order that they should not resemble the Muslim judges. Furthermore, they were forbidden to ride swift asses. Two years later the non-Muslim officials were again dismissed from government posts. The tyrannical al-Malik al-Ashraf

Barsbāy (1422–38) readily complied with the suggestions of the Muslim zealots. Immediately after his accession he dismissed non-Muslim officials, and in 1426 again demanded the distinctive signs, ordering Jews and Christians to reduce the size of their turbans and put iron rings around their necks when going to public baths. Periodically, he sent constables to search the non-Muslim quarters of Cairo for wine. In 1448 the Sultan Jaqmaq (1438–53) prohibited non-Muslim physicians from treating Muslims, and in 1450 reinforced the regulations regarding their dress. In 1463 Sultan Khushqadam solemnly reinforced all the restrictive laws imposed on non-Muslims, with the exception of those which forbade them to be physicians and money changers. The last Mamluk sultans did not introduce new restrictions, but periodically imposed heavy tribute. Arab historians report that Qa'itbāy did thus in 1488 and 1491 and that similar contributions were extorted from the Jews in 1500 and 1501.

The Jews' situation in the Mamluk state is vividly depicted in the letters of Obadiah of *Bertinoro and his anonymous pupil, an Italian Jew who settled in Jerusalem at the end of the 15th century. In the capitals of Egypt and Syria there were still large communities, but in the other towns they had dwindled to small groups. Everywhere they were subject to legal discrimination and had to pay special taxes, e.g., on drinking wine. Their letters also stressed the general lawlessness and anarchy from which the Jews suffered. The authors of these travelogues, however, were not aware of the great change that Oriental Jewry had undergone under the impact of Mamluk rule. The flourishing middle class, once the support of the Jewish communities, had been ruined by the Mamluks and most Jews had become poor. Social discrimination and the hostility of the upper classes caused many of the Jewish physicians and other well-situated Jews to adopt Islam. A relatively great number of biographies of these apostates appear in the writings of Arab historians of this period. On the other hand, the Mamluk sultans allowed the Jews to retain their judicial autonomy in cases of civil law, and until the end of their rule recognized the *nagid* as head of all the Jewish communities in Egypt, Palestine, and Syria. The *negidim*, who had deputies in Jerusalem and Damascus, represented the Jews, Karaites, and Samaritans to the government. Until the end of the reign of the Baḥrī Mamluks, the post was held by the descendants of Maimonides. The last was David II. In the 15th century the post was filled by Jewish court physicians. The Mamluk sultans apparently did not interfere with Jewish settlement in Egypt and Syria after the Spanish expulsion (1492).

Bibliography: Ashtor, Toledot; Baron, Social[2] 3 (1957), 172.

[E.A.]

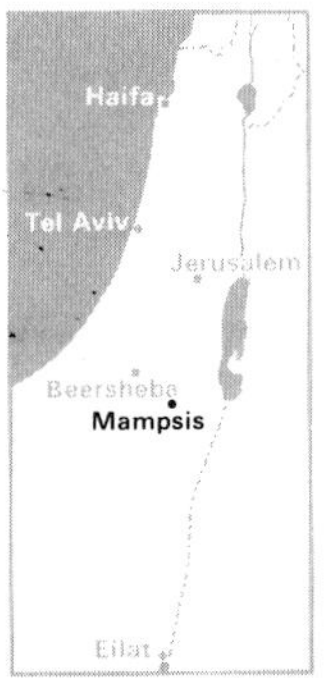

MAMPSIS, city in the Negev. According to Eusebius it was situated between Hebron and Elath, one day's march from Thamara (Onom. 8:8). The Madaba Map shows it between Beersheba and Thamara and calls it Maps. Ptolemy also refers to it as Maps. It appears in the episcopal lists of Palaestina tertia. Mampsis is identified with Kurnub where excavations were begun by A. Negev in 1966. The town, which is surrounded by a wall, consists of three hillocks. On the western side of the town are the remains of a palace including a guard room, audience hall, records room, and stairs leading to an upper story with balconies; nearby is a tower with office rooms. A complex of residential buildings extending over 1,900 sq. yds. (1,600 sq. m.) on the eastern hill included stables with mangers. Some of the rooms were decorated with frescoes; a hoard of 10,400 Roman tetradrachms was discovered there. Mampsis was apparently settled in about 50 C.E. and continued into Byzantine times; its ruins include two churches. A Nabatean and Roman military cemetery were found nearby. The remains of several dams were found in the vicinity.

Bibliography: C. L. Woolley and T. E. Lawrence, *The Wilderness of Zin* (1915), 121ff.; Kirk, in: PEFQS, 70 (1938), 218ff.; A. Reifenberg, *Milḥemet ha-Mizra ve-ha-Yeshimon* (1950), 62, 130; Applebaum, in: BIES, 30 (1956), 224ff.; Negev, in: IEJ, 16 (1966), 145ff.; 17 (1967), 48ff.; idem, in: *Zeitschrift fuer Kunstgeschichte und Archeologie*, 7 (1967), 67–86.

[M.A.-Y.]

MAMRAM (or **Mamran**; ממר"ם, ממר"מ, ממרנ"י, ממר"א and at times abbreviated to מ"מ), a form of promissory note distinguished by its brevity. In Hebrew sources it is mentioned for the first time during the 12th century in the *tosafot* of *Elhanan b. Isaac of Dampierre to the tractate *Avodah Zarah*. There is evidence of its use in Poland from the 14th century at least, but it was only during the 16th century that it became the distinctive promissory note used by Jewish merchants in their internal trade. There are various opinions on the etymological origin of this term, the most important being: a derivation from the Hebrew word המיר (*hemir*, "to change"); a contracted form of the Latin *in memoriam*; and a derivation from the word *membrana*, which in medieval Latin signified a scrap of parchment. The signature of the debtor appeared on one side of the document, while on the other, in the same place as the signature, the sum owed and the date of payment were recorded. According to the regulations of the community councils, the document had equal validity with the ordinary hand-written promissory note even though the lengthy traditional formula was absent. Since the name of the creditor was not mentioned in the *mamram*, it was payable to the person who presented it to the debtor. As a result, the *mamram* was purchased by one person from another by simple transfer without any written documentation. The brevity of the *mamram* and the possibility of its easy transfer gave it a great advantage over the ordinary bill, encouraging its popularity. It was most common in Poland, especially during the 16th century, and the trading of *mamramim* became a frequent occurrence.

Another kind of *mamram* frequently employed in Poland during the 16th century was the blank *mamram* (in Polish *membran goły*). Its principal feature was that neither the amount of the debt nor the date of payment were mentioned. The signature of the creditor appeared on one side and the other side was blank. It is evident that a document of this kind could only exist in a society where the honesty of the debtor was taken for granted. The blank *mamram* came to satisfy the demands of the commerce practiced by the Jews of Poland during that period and it was particularly suited for use at the large fairs then held in the country. The merchant did not bring large sums of cash to the fairs because of the many dangers attendant on his journey and many deals were concluded at the fairs on short notice. Thus the merchant was in need of credit during that time and the *mamram* document satisfied his requirements. Through its use merchants could borrow unlimited sums, which in turn permitted the orderly development of business. The *mamramim* thus fulfilled the functions later provided by banks. The blank *mamram* was also different in that it was signed not by the debtor but by the person providing the credit. When in need of funds, the debtor sold it and thus received the amount he required. Because the halakhic basis of the blank *mamram* was highly dubious some eminent rabbis objected to it and invalidated it and its use. Most authorities sanctioned it, however, because "it has already become the custom in these lands to collect by it according to the regulations of the countries." It was still in use among Polish Jews in the first half of the 19th century.

Bibliography: P. Bloch, in: *Festschrift . . . A. Berliner* (1903), 50ff.; A. Gulak, *Yesodei ha-Mishpat ha-Ivri,* 2 (1923), 142ff.; idem, *Oẓar ha-Shetarot* (1925), 214ff.; S. Dubnow, *Pinkas ha-Medinah* (1925), index; Halpern, Pinkas, index; idem, *Takkanot Medinat Mehrin* (1952), index; S. Lipschutz, *Ḥemdat Shelomo, Ḥoshen Mishpat* (1969); M. Breger, *Zur Handelsgeschichte der Juden in Polen im 17. Jahrhundert* (1932), 45ff.; J. Katz, *Tradition and Crisis* (1961), 70ff.

[Ed.]

MAMRE (Heb. מַמְרֵא), oak grove near *Hebron which was one of the favorite dwelling places of Abraham (Abram; Gen. 13:18); it is also the name of one of the clans of Hebron which was an ally of Abraham (14:13, 24). At Mamre, Abraham learned of the captivity of Lot and received the three angels (14:13; 18:1). It is described in Genesis 23:17 as having Machpelah "before" it; elsewhere, it is identified with Hebron (23:19; 35:27). In the time of Josephus, a tree some distance north of Hebron was

The site of Mamre (Rāmat al-Khalīl), with Herodian remains in foreground and ruins of the basilica of Constantine, upper left. Photo Werner Braun, Jerusalem.

assumed to be the "terebinth" of Abraham (Ant., 1:186; Wars, 4:533). In the Mishnah (Ma'as. 5:2), the site appears as Elath, one day's journey from Jerusalem, and in the Talmud (TJ, Av. Zar. 1:4, 38d) and the Midrash (Gen. R. 47:10) as Butnah (Butnan), the site of a famous trade fair where Hadrian sold the captives of the Bar Kokhba War into slavery. Later Christian sources refer to the site as a place of prayer; Constantine built a church there (which is shown on the Madaba Map). Jews, Christians, and pagans worshiped together there until the Arab conquest. The site is now identified with Rāmat al-Khalīl, 2 mi. (3.2 km.) north of Hebron. E. A. Mader, excavating there in 1926–28, cleared a Herodian enclosure wall, some blocks of which measure 14×4 ft. (4.3×1.2 m.). At its southwest corner was a well into which pilgrims threw gifts and money. In the eastern part of the enclosure, Constantine built a basilica measuring 60×50 ft. (19×16 m.), with a double narthex, a nave, and two aisles. Pottery from the ninth and eighth centuries B.C.E. indicates that the site was inhabited under the kings of Judah.

Bibliography: E. H. Mader, *Mamre,* 2 vols. (1957); D. Winton Thomas (ed.), *Archaeology and Old Testament Study* (1967), index.

[M.A.-Y.]

MAMZER (Heb. מַמְזֵר), usually translated as "bastard."

Definition. "If she cannot contract a legally valid marriage to this man, but can contract a legally valid marriage to others, her offspring [from the former] is a *mamzer.* Such is the case when a man has sexual relations with any of the *ervot* ["forbidden"; see *Incest] in the Torah" (Kid. 3:12; cf. Yev. 4:13). Thus, a *mamzer* is the issue of a couple whose sexual relationship is forbidden according to the Torah and punishable by **karet* or death. Because of this a marriage between them is void (Sh. Ar., EH 4:13), and thus, for example, the issue of a union between brother and sister or between a man and a woman validly married to another at the time is a *mamzer* (see *Adultery; Yev. 45b; Maim. Yad, Issurei Bi'ah 15:1; Tur and *Beit Yosef,* EH 4; Sh. Ar., EH 4:13). On the other hand, in Jewish law—unlike in other systems of law—the mere fact that a child is born (or conceived) out of lawful wedlock does not make him a *mamzer* and he is not an illegitimate child, i.e., one whose status or rights are impaired. The parents of the *mamzer* are indeed unmarried—either in fact or since they are so considered in law because of an absolute legal bar to a marriage between them—but unlike a man and a woman who, from the legal point of view, can marry each other but do not want to, the parents of the *mamzer,* owing to the said legal bar, cannot marry each other even if they want to. If one parent is non-Jewish this fact alone does not make the child a *mamzer* (see *Marriage; Yev. 45b; Maim. Yad, Issurei Bi'ah 15:3; Tur, EH 4; Sh. Ar., EH 4:19).

Consequences of the State of Mamzerut. These are twofold and relate to marriage and to personal status. (1) Marriage. The Bible lays down: "A *mamzer* shall not enter the congregation of the Lord" (Deut. 23.3), i.e., a marriage between a *mamzer* (male or female) and a legitimate Jew or Jewess is prohibited. If such a marriage is nevertheless contracted, it is legally valid but must be dissolved by divorce (see *Marriage, Prohibited). A marriage between two *mamzerim* is permitted (Yev. 45b; Kid. 69a, 74a; Maim. Yad., Issurei Bi'ah 15:33; Sh. Ar., EH 4:24) and so also is a marriage between a *mamzer* and a proselyte (Yev. 79b; Kid. 67a and *Rashi* thereto; 72b–73a; Maim. Yad, Issurei Bi'ah 15:7; Sh. Ar., EH 4:22). (2) Personal status. The offspring of a *mamzer* (whether male or female) and a legitimate Jew or Jewess are also *mamzerim,* since "*mamzerim* . . . are forbidden and forbidden for all time, whether they are males or females" (Yev. 8:3) and the rule is that in the case of a prohibited union the offspring follows the status of the "defective" parent (Kid., 3:12; see **Yuḥasin*). On the other hand, as the offspring of a union between a Jew and a gentile takes the status of the mother, a child born of a *mamzer* and a gentile mother will be gentile and not a *mamzer;* thus after proper conversion to Judaism, he will acquire the status of a legitimate proselyte and the fact that his father was a *mamzer* will be wholly irrelevant (Kid. 67a, *Rashi;* Maim. Yad, Issurei Bi'ah 15:3; Tur and *Beit Yosef,* EH 4; Sh. Ar., EH 4:20).

Except with regard to marriage, as stated above, the personal status of a *mamzer* does not prejudice him in any way. His rights of inheritance are equal to those of any other heir (Yev. 22b; Maim. Yad, Naḥalot, 1:7; Sh. Ar., ḤM 276:6). His birth releases his father's wife from the obligation of *levirate marriage and *ḥaliẓah.* The *mamzer* is eligible to hold any public office, the highest (i.e., that of a king), for he remains "thy brother" and "from among thy brethren shalt thou set a king over thee" (Deut. 17:15; Tos. to Yev. 45b). Furthermore, according to the Mishnah, "a *mamzer* who is a scholar [*talmid ḥakham*] takes precedence over a high priest who is an ignoramous [*am ha-areẓ*]" (Hor. 3:8).

Asufi ("a Foundling"). Sometimes a doubt may arise whether a child is legitimate or not and therefore he has the status of "doubtful" *mamzer.* One such case is that of a foundling, i.e., a child found abandoned in a public place when the identity of neither parent is known; in this case it is unknown whether the parents are legitimate or *mamzerim* (Kid. 4:12; Maim., Issurei Bi'ah, 15:13; Tur, EH 4; Sh. Ar., EH 4:31). If such a child is found in or near a place inhabited by both Jews and gentiles, so that it is impossible to know even if he is of wholly Jewish parentage or not, he is considered both a "doubtful" *mamzer* and a "doubtful" gentile, so that if he later marries a Jewess and then afterward she wants to marry another man, she will require a divorce because of this latter doubt (Ket. 15b; Maim. *ibid.* 15:25; Tur, EH 4; Sh. Ar., EH 4:33). If, however, such a child is found in or near an exclusively Jewish place, he is assumed to be of wholly Jewish parentage; but as the identity and hence the status of such parents (whether *mamzer* or legitimate) is unknown, he is considered a "doubtful" *mamzer* (Kid. 74a; Maim., Issurei Bi'ah 15:21 Sh. Ar., EH 4:31–36). Thus, he cannot marry either a legitimate Jewess (because he may be a *mamzer*) or a female *mamzer* (because he may in fact be legitimate). However, the suspicion of *mamzerut* only attaches to him if the circumstances in which he was found were such as to cast doubt on the status of legitimacy of his parents; for instance if it was clear that they did not care for his survival. If there is any indication at all that he was abandoned out of necessity, such as hunger or in time of war, or if there are some signs of minimal concern for his welfare and future, such as his being circumcised, clothed, or abandoned in a place (like a synagogue) where he is likely to be comparatively safe from danger or any other place where people are more likely to find and take care of him, then it is assumed that his parents are of unimpeachable status and so is he. Therefore no suspicion of *mamzerut* will be attached to him (Kid. 73b; Maim. Yad, Issurei Bi'ah 15:31; Tur, EH 4; Sh. Ar., EH 4:31).

Shetuki (lit. **"Undisclosed"**). The other case where the status of "doubtful" *mamzer* may arise is that of a child known to be born of an unmarried Jewish mother who either refuses to disclose the identity of the father or claims not to know it (Kid. 69a; Maim. Yad, Issurei Bi'ah 15:12). Since the father's status is unknown, the child is likely to be considered a "doubtful" *mamzer* (Kid. 74a; Maim. *ibid.; Arukh ha-Shulḥan,* EH 4:47). However, if the majority of the inhabitants of the district and of those who habitually visit there are Jews of unimpeachable status, it will be presumed that the father was also of such unimpeachable status and therefore no suspicion of *mamzerut* will be cast on the child (Tur, *Beit Yosef,* Baḥ EH 6 (at the end); Sh. Ar., EH 6:17–18; *Beit Shemu'el* 6, n. 31; but cf. Maim., Issurei Bi'ah 18:13–15; *Arukh ha-Shulḥan,* EH 4:34). The mother can always avert the suspicion of *mamzerut* being cast on her child by declaring that the father was a legitimate Jew or a gentile. In the latter case the child takes its status from the mother (i.e., he is a Jew; Kid. 74a; Maim. Yad, Issurei Bi'ah 15:12, 14; Sh. Ar., EH 4:26; *Arukh ha-Shulḥan,* EH 4:30, 31, 56).

Karaites. Halakhic problems concerning a "doubtful" *mamzer* have arisen in connection with the *Karaites because, while their form of *kiddushin* (*kiddushei-kesef* or *kiddushei bi'ah*) may be valid according to Jewish law (see *Marriage) their method of divorce does not accord with the *halakhah,* as their *get* (bill of divorce) is not in the form prescribed by the sages. Accordingly, a Karaite woman divorced by such a *get* is not properly divorced and remains a married woman *(eshet ish)* so that any child she bears to another man whom she marries on the strength of such a *get* is a *mamzer.* Since it is impossible to determine who, throughout the generations, remarried on the strength of such invalid divorce, Jewish law casts the suspicion of "doubtful" *mamzer* on all members of that community (*Beit Yosef,* EH 4—end; *Darkhei Moshe,* EH 4, n. 14; Rema, EH 4:37; *Turei Zahav,* EH 4, n. 24; *Ba'er Heitev,* EH 4, n. 49). Some *posekim,* however, did permit marriages between Karaites and Rabbanite Jews on varying halakhic grounds and such marriages were particularly prevalent in the 11th and 12th centuries. Especially noteworthy is the permission to contract such a marriage granted by David b. Solomon ibn Abi Zimra who based his decision on the grounds that the *kiddushin* of the Karaites are also invalid according to *halakhah,* as they are deemed to have taken place without witnesses, the witnesses of the *kiddushin* being disqualified according to *halakhah* (Resp. Radbaz, nos. 73 and 796). Thus, according to him, no stigma of *mamzerut* is to be attached to a child of a woman who married, was divorced, and then married another man, all in accordance with Karaite rites only, since—in Jewish law—she is regarded as never having been married at all. On the strength of this argument and for some additional reasons arising out of the specific circumstances of the case, in 1966 a rabbinical court in the State of Israel permitted the marriage of a non-Karaite Jewess to a Karaite man by whom she had become pregnant (see also *Oẓar ha-Posekim,* EH 4, n. 175).

Bibliography: ET, 1 (1951[3]), 202; 2 (1949), 71–74; *Ha-Ma'or,* 12 (1961), issue 9, p. 28 (English numbering of the same: 11 (1961), issue 7); S. M. Pasmaneck, in: HUCA, 37 (1966), 121–45; B. Schereschewsky, *Dinei Mishpaḥah* (1967[2]), 345–51; M. Elon, *Ḥakikah Datit* . . . (1968), 178–81. [B.Z.SCH.]

MAN, THE NATURE OF.

IN THE BIBLE

Names of Man. The idea of man is expressed in the Bible by a number of words that reflect various aspects of his nature. The following are the most important.

ʾADAM: collective, "men, human beings," also (in prose, with the article) "mankind," *Homo sapiens,* in distinction to other creatures (Gen. 6:7), or to God (Isa. 2:17). It is occasionally used of individuals (Neh. 2:10); etymologically it may be compared with Arabic *anam,* "creatures," "mankind." The plural is *bene ʾadam.*

ʾISH: "husband," "male," "individual" (Gen. 2:23–24; 13:16; 41:33; Hos. 2:18 [16]); very often used in collective sense (Josh. 9:6). In certain passages it has the meaning of "servant" or "soldier" (I Sam. 23:3, 12; cf. the expression *ʾish ha-ʾElohim,* "man of God"). The antithesis in Psalms 49:3[2] between *bene ʾadam* and *bene ʾish* apparently contrasts "men of low degree" with "men of high degree." Its etymology is uncertain. The plural *ʾanashim* is evidently from the same root as *ʾenosh.*

ʾENOSH: mostly a collective denoting the human race. Occasionally it is used of individuals (Isa. 56:2; Jer. 20:10). In antithesis to God it connotes frail, mortal man (Isa. 51:7, 12; Ps. 90:3; Job. 28:4). The word is probably related to the Arabic *anisa,* Ugaritic *ans* ("to be friendly, social"), Aramaic *enash,* and Arabic *ʾinsān* (pl. *ʾunās,* coll. *nās*). Other cognates show that it cannot be related to Arabic *anutha,* "to be weak."

GEVER: the adult male being in contrast to women and children (Ex. 10:11; Josh. 7:14). In poetry it often has a more general sense. The stem means "to be strong, mighty."

METIM: used only in plural, "males," "men," "people" (Gen. 34:30; Deut. 2:34; 4:27). In Isaiah 3:25 it may mean "warriors." The singular occurs in Ugaritic and other cognate languages and is possibly to be seen in names like Methushael and Methuselah.

According to this terminology, man is conceived as

both strong and weak, as a member of the human race and of the family unit, and as an individual.

Psychological Terms. Further insight into the nature of man is furnished by certain psychological terms that describe different aspects of the human personality. *Nefesh* can denote the essence of any living creature (Gen. 2:7); it may even be equated with the blood (Gen. 9:4; cf. Lev. 17:11). It signifies the "individual," "ego," "person" (Gen. 46:26; I Sam. 1:26; Job 16:4), and hence even "body" (Ex. 21:23). *Ru'aḥ* "spirit," is sometimes synonymous with *nefesh* (Gen. 6:17), but is also distinguished from the latter. It represents power and energy (Ex. 35:21; Isa. 31:3) that comes to man from without; it provides the impulse to higher life and finds expression in special skill (Ex. 28:3), might, or leadership (Judg. 3:10; Isa. 11:2). *Neshamah,* "breath," is not only the vitalizing element breathed into man by God (Gen. 2:7), but the divine spirit and lamp—the soul—within him (Prov. 20:27). In contrast to these spiritual aspects of man, *basar* signifies his physical nature, the living body (Gen. 2:23, 24), and, as such, it symbolizes human frailty (Isa. 40:6).

The Bible also regards certain organs as the seat of given psychological attributes. *Lev,* the "heart," is the center of thought (Ps. 45:2 [1]), conscience (I Sam. 24:6 [5]; Job 27:6), and emotion (love: Deut. 6:5; anger: Deut. 19:6; joy: Isa. 30:29; hatred: Lev. 19:17; courage: Jer. 48:41, and the like). By synecdoche, the heart represents the whole inner life of man (Gen. 6:5; Ps. 51:10; Ezek. 36:26; Prov. 4:23). *Kelayot,* the "kidneys" (in artificial "biblical" English "veins"), are likewise the source of emotion and conscience, and in conjunction with "heart" describe the fundamental character of man (Jer. 12:2; Ps. 7:10; 16:7; 26:2). *Me'ayim,* "bowels," are the seat of overpowering feelings (Isa. 16:11; 63:15; Lam. 1:20); modern versions sensibly substitute "heart" for "kidneys" or "bowels" in such contexts. *Kaved,* "liver," also means "being" (Lam. 2:11; cf. *Heart). *Raḥamim*—from *reḥem,* "womb"—means "compassion" (Deut. 13:18). *Yad,* "hand," is often used in a conative sense, indicating "power" (Deut. 2:7, 24; 32:36). Other shades of psychological significance are expressed by other parts of the body, e.g., face, eyes, ears, head, and so forth.

This extensive nomenclature points to the complexity of the human personality, but is not exhaustive. The complete picture of man's nature as envisaged by the Bible can only be seen in the full context of scriptural evidence.

Man's Origin. The key is to be found in the story of man's origin (Gen. 1:27; 2:7). He is not a descendant of the gods (as in certain pagan mythologies); the term child(ren) used with reference to man in relation to God (Deut. 14:1; Ps. 2:7) has in Scripture a metaphorical connotation. Nor is man the product (as some philosophical systems hold) of the blind forces of nature. He is the artifact of God, fashioned purposefully out of two diverse elements: his body is of the earth, but it is animated by the divine breath of life (Gen. 2:7). Yet man is not a dichotomy of body and soul (a view characteristic of Orphism and Platonism), and certainly not a trichotomy (I Thes. 5:23). His is a multifaceted unitary being—*nefesh ḥayyah,* "a living person" (Gen. 2:7). Of particular significance is the concept that all human beings, irrespective of ethnic and cultural differences, stem from two common ancestors, Adam and Eve. Humanity, despite its diversification, is essentially a single family, and men remain brothers even in the face of hate and murder (Gen. 4:9–10). To this inherent brotherhood and equality of all, even slaves (unlike the Greek view) were no exception (Job 31:13, 15). Furthermore, the world was divinely planned to be one of creaturely peace, harmony, and understanding; man, as well as other living beings, was not to destroy his fellow creatures even for food (Gen. 1:29–30; 2:19). The permission granted to Noah to eat flesh was a sad concession to a world that had lost its original idealism (Gen. 9:3). Monogamy is clearly viewed in the creation story as the proper state of marriage. Women play a pivotal role in numerous biblical stories, and there are women prophetesses, like Deborah and Huldah.

The Image of God. However, the Bible does not merely stress the creatureliness of man. It depicts him as the peak of creation. He climaxes the ascending course of the six days' work of the Beginning. He is formed by special resolve (Gen. 1:26) and in a unique manner (Gen. 2:7), and attracts to himself three of the six occurrences of the stem *bara'* ("to create") in the creation story. However, his crowning glory is contained in the statement that he was made in the divine "image" and "likeness" (for a suggested distinction between the two words see I. Epstein, in bibl., 224), which endows him with unique worth. Man alone among the creatures is capable of sustained thought, creativity, and awareness of God; the light of God is immanent in his spirit (Prov. 20:27). Hence he is given dominion (the "image" is the symbol of the Deity's presence) over the earth (Gen. 1:26, 28) and is privileged to commune with God and enjoy His fellowship (Gen. 2–3). In the language of later rabbinic literature, he became a "partner" of the Creator (Gen. R. ed. Ḥ. Albeck (1940), 73; cf. Shab. 10a). The dualism of man's status and significance within the unified framework of his psychophysical being is given unmatched expression by the Psalmist: "What is man that Thou art mindful of him . . . Yet Thou hast made him little less than the angels" (literally, "God-like beings"; 8:4–5).

Free Will. There is still another aspect of the divine image reflected in man, which plays a crucial role in the profound parable of the Garden of Eden. In a supreme act of self-limitation the Absolute God gave man freedom of moral choice. He could will to do right or wrong, to obey or disobey his Maker. It was heaven's greatest gift to man: he was not to be an automaton. However, the immediate consequences were calamitous. Man rebelled against the Creator; he introduced disharmony into the universal harmony. Sin was born and in turn begot suffering and death. History had begun. Israel was the first people to evince a sense of the historic.

While the Bible is unequivocal in its assertion of the reality of human responsibility for evil (Eccles. 7:29) and in condemning sin trenchantly as estrangement from and treason against God (this is the meaning of the story of Eden), it is no less emphatic in its affirmation of God's grace (Ps. 103:13–16) and readiness to forgive (Num. 14:20; Jer. 33:8). Sin is never final. It is punished, or rather punishes itself. However, retribution is part of the divine redemptive process. It helps man to seek atonement, which the divine love never fails to vouchsafe (Ezek. 33:11).

The road of redemption, however, is hard and long. Outside the Garden of Eden man's iniquity reaches new depths. Brotherhood as well as "sonship" are destroyed. Cain's example was widely imitated (Gen. 6:11). It almost seemed that the making of man was a divine error (Gen. 5–6), which only the Flood could expunge. At this point, however, a new providential principle manifests itself — the elective factor. The family of Noah is chosen from a doomed generation to be saved and to save the world. Later Abraham is elected to be a source of blessing to all mankind (Gen. 12:3). Israel, the seed of Abraham, were chosen to be "a kingdom of priests and holy nation" (Ex. 19:6). Though themselves far from perfect (Deut. 9:5), they were destined to become a light to the world (Isa. 60:3), illuminating the way of ethical and spiritual truth. To this end God made a covenant with Israel at Sinai (Deut. 5:2), which found detailed expression in the Torah. Religious and secular precepts are inextricably intermingled in the Law, for human life is a unity and must be dedicated to God's will in all its diversified aspects. God is served in the righteousness of human relationships—in love between man and man, which reflects God's image—as well as in divine worship. When the "image" is wronged, religious service becomes an abomination (Isa. 1:13–17). The path toward God is further delineated and interpreted by the Prophets, and even by figures (like Abraham, and Job, and some of Psalmists) who question God's moral government of the world. Revelation—the word of God understood in its broadest sense—is the great antidote to sin, leading man to repentance and regeneration. The relevance of this biblical teaching is not confined to Israel. In a deep sense, the Bible tells the story of Everyman in all generations. Even when Israel is the focal point of the Bible's concern, the universal concept of mankind is never ignored (Amos 9:7; Isa. 19:24–25). Israel's significance derives from its relationship to all humanity, whose significance, in turn, flows from man's relation to God. History is thus seen as the moral and spiritual drama of the human species.

The Afterlife. The beginning of that drama, with its hope and tragedy, was enacted in Eden. Inevitably the question arises: Where will the denouement take place? Has human life a divinely designed goal? Later Jewish theology, elaborated in apocryphal and rabbinic literature, answers these questions (solving at the same time the problem of theodicy) on the individual level, by postulating the belief in the afterlife. There the disembodied soul is judged, the wicked are condemned, and the righteous are rewarded with eternal bliss. This doctrine is unknown to Scripture. There is an unmistakable finality about the biblical conception of death (Ps. 146:4; Job 7:9; Isa. 38:18). The Bible is primarily concerned with the world; it seeks heaven upon earth in the form of the kingdom of God (Zech. 14:1), and continued life in descendants rather than in personal immortality (II Sam. 7:12). Nevertheless death does not mark the complete extinction of existence. The dead continue to live a shadowy, ghostlike existence in Sheol, a region of darkness and silence deep within the recesses of the earth. Yet the dead are not without consciousness (I Sam. 28:15ff.; Isa. 14:9ff.), nor beyond God's judgment (Ps. 139:8). Two holy men escaped death altogether: Enoch (Gen. 5:24) and Elijah (II Kings 2:11). In Job there is a yearning for continued life after death (14:13ff.; 19:26); in certain psalms the definite hope is expressed that death will not end the human fellowship with God (49:16; 73:24ff.). Whether resurrection is envisaged in Isa. 26:19ff. is a matter of exegesis, but it is certainly envisaged in Daniel 12:2. The preexistence of the soul is first taught in the Apocrypha (Wisd. 8:19ff.), but Jeremiah was "a thought of God" (B. Duhm) before ever he was formed in the womb (Jer. 1:5). Thus the Bible lacks a definite theology of the afterlife, and belief in resurrection is still vague and inchoate. Yet Scripture contains undoubted intimations of immortality, on which future epochs built their religious doctrines.

The End of Days. The true goal of history, however, is to be sought in "the end of days." It will be the age of regeneration, when the work of creation will be completed in accordance with God's original plan. Man and God, and man and man, will be reconciled. The treason man perpetrated in the Garden of Eden will be transmuted into universal voluntary obedience to God's will, and the crime of Cain will be atoned for in a state of international peace and brotherhood (Isa. 2:2–4; Micah 4:1–5). The immature knowledge man acquired from the forbidden fruit will give way to a higher wisdom. For inherently knowledge is good (Prov. 8); it is man's unwise use of it that vitiates it (Eccl. 1:18). A new earth and a new heaven will issue from the new heart and spirit of man (Isa. 65:17; Ezek. 36:26), and human communion with God will be restored (Joel 3:1–2). The Garden of Eden will, as it were, become worldwide, and the pristine glory of the reflected image of God in man will be renewed. The end of days is undated. It is an elusive horizon; yet its advent remains a prophetic certitude.

[I.A.]

IN RABBINIC THOUGHT

The Physical Nature of Man. The process of human gestation, and especially the preservation of the embryo, prompted the sages to the observation that these were evidence of both God's skill and solicitude in the fashioning of man (Ber. 10a; Nid. 31a; Lev. R. 14:3, 4; 15:2, 3; 34:3). The fact that every hair of man's head is fed through a separate root is cited as further evidence (BB 16a). From each of his parents, man receives five parts of his body and ten parts from God. From his father, he receives bones, veins, nails, brain, and white of the eye; from his mother, skin, flesh, blood, hair, and the pupil of the eye. To his formation, God contributes breath, soul, light of countenance, sight, hearing, speech, touch, sense, insight, and understanding. Hence, the rabbinic saying that there are three partners in man — his father and mother and God (Kid. 30b; Nid. 31a; TJ, Kil. 8:3, 31c; Eccl. R. 5:10, 2). A late Midrash (Mss. *Midrash ha-Ḥefeẓ*) describes the human body as possessing ten orifices, including the navel. The marvel is, the Midrash continues, that when the child is in the embryonic state, the navel is open and the other orifices are closed but when it issues from the womb, the navel is closed and other orifices are opened.

In the totality of his physical structure, man constitutes a microcosm (see *Microcosm and Macrocosm). An elaborate parallel, covering 30 items, is drawn between the various components of the human body and similar features in the physical world (ARN[1]:31). A hardly less complex parallel is found to exist between the organs of the human body and the structure and vessels of the Tabernacle (Mid. Tadshe, Beit ha-Midrash, Jellinek, vol. 3, 175f.; cf. the New Testament denomination of the human body as a tabernacle, II Cor. 5:1, 4; II Pet. 1:13, 14). A simpler summation of man's physical being is deciphered in the word *adam* ("man") as being an acronym (**notarikon*) for "dust" (*efer*), "blood" (*dam*) and "gall" (*marah;* Sot. 5a). They give a remarkably accurate enumeration of the 248 organs of the human body (Oho. 1:8). It may be fairly said that the rabbinic reflection on the complex mechanism of man's physical structure served as occasion for admiring reverence for the skill and wisdom with which God created him. Indeed, its unknown aspects suggested the argument that if man does not know his own body, he certainly cannot fathom God's acts (San. 39a). But for all its marvelous mechanism, it is destined, save for the soul, to return to the earth from which it originally came. Only one tiny bone remains indestructible and, in the time of resurrection, will serve as the nucleus out of which the body will be restored (Gen. R. 28:3; Eccl. R. 12:5; see *Luz of the Spine).

Nowhere in rabbinic literature is there any denigration of the human body so characteristic of contemporary Platonic, Stoic, and Gnostic thought. On the contrary, since even the body is conceived as having been created in the image of God, man is duty bound to honor it by maintaining it in a state of cleanliness. No less an authority than *Hillel termed such action a religious duty (Lev. R. 34:3).

Character. Since Genesis describes Adam as having been both created in God's image (1:27) and formed out of the dust of the earth (2:7), the sages declare that man possesses both heavenly and earthly qualities. In four respects, he is said to resemble the animals and the angels respectively. Like the angels, he possesses the power of speech, intelligence, upright posture, and glance of the eye. In his physical aspects, he resembles the animals (Gen. R. 12:8; 14:3). Indeed, God created man because he was not completely satisfied with either the angels or the animals. The former failed to satisfy him because they lacked the evil inclination. The animals, on the other hand, lacked the good inclination. God therefore created man, who possesses both a good and evil inclination and is confronted with the need to exercise free will. This is the origin of the ambivalent character of man. If he pursues evil, he is likened to an animal; if he chooses the good, he is likened to an angel (Gen. R. 14:3, 4). The contradictory nature of man is highlighted by the legend describing the sharp difference of opinion evoked by God's taking counsel with the angels as to whether or not man should be created. The angels that favored his creation contended that man would be affectionate and a doer of justice. Those who opposed his creation claimed that he would be quarrelsome and riddled with falsehood (Gen. R. 8:3–9; in the qualities of loving-kindness, righteousness, peace, and truth are hypostatized).

Man's moral ambivalence derives from the two inclinations within him: the good inclination *(yeẓer tov)* and the evil inclination *(yeẓer ra)* (see *Inclination, Good and Evil). The fact of human individuality exhibits God's power, for although all men are cast from the same mold since all are descendants of Adam, yet no two men are alike (Sanh. 4:5). Their physical differences are to be noted in their voice, taste, and appearance (ARN[1], 4).

In their attitude toward possessions, men fall into four distinct categories, ranging from the average to the wicked and the saint (Avot 5:10). It is assumed, as a legal principle, that all men become excited when their property is at stake (Shab. 117b, 153a). This concept is further reflected in the dictum that every artisan is hostile toward his fellow craftsmen (Gen. R. 19:6). It is assumed further, as a matter of legal principle, that in money matters no man is likely to regard himself as culpable (Ket. 105b). The rabbis look askance at him who has an excess of material things. They conclude that such a situation can only produce deplorable moral consequences (Tosef., Sot. 3:6; Ber. 32a; Sanh. 108a; Gen. R. 26:5; 28:6). Indeed, when a man is poor, he can be relied upon to have trust in God. Riches incline him to trust in his money and thus displace his piety (Tanḥ. Naso 28). For all the rabbinic recognition of the powerful influence of the economic motive on human conduct, a certain basic honesty is assumed as characteristic of all men. Hence, the assumption is made that a man makes no legal monetary claim unless there is some substance to it (Shevu. 40b), and that a man is not brazen as to deny outright the existence of his debt in the presence of his creditor (BM 3a). A man's basic character is recognizable by his drinking (how he behaves when under the influence of liquor), by his rectitude in financial transactions (Rashi's interpretation) and by his anger (to what extent he is able to control his temper). To this generalization, some add, also by his laughter (his good humor; Eruv. 65b).

Man and Woman. The difference in the origin of man and women described in Genesis served the sages as points d'appui for their observations on the contrast between the character and psychology of man and woman. The latter, having been fashioned from a more durable substance (man's rib-bone) than man (dust of the earth), can more readily withstand disagreeable circumstances and possesses greater inurement to pain (Tanḥ. Toledot 8). A woman, moreover, is blessed with greater native intelligence (instinct?; Nid. 45b). Whose intelligence matures sooner is a matter of opinion *(ibid.)*. A man is more hospitable towards guests and more generous than a woman (Sif. Num. Shlaḥ 100). An aggrieved man is more readily reconcilable than a woman (Nid. 31b). Peculiarly characteristic of woman is her proclivity to tears (BM 59a) and an inordinate curiosity (Toh. 7:9). At the time of her creation, God, anticipating woman's faults, sought to obviate them. He knew that she would be arrogant, wanton-eyed, an eavesdropper, a tattler, a meddler, and gadabout. Hence, he fashioned her from a chaste part of man's body that is free of these faults (Gen. R. 18:2; 45:5).

Destiny. The phenomena experienced in the theophany afforded the prophet Elijah (I Kings 19:11–12) are interpreted as symbolic of the four worlds through which man must pass. The wind symbolizes the evanescent quality of the life of this world. The earthquake represents the day of death, since on it man quakes and trembles. Fire is the symbol of man's judgment in Gehenna. The "still small voice" is the Last Judgment (Tanḥ. Pekudei 3). A more elaborate articulation of the worlds (i.e., stages) through which man passes in this life describes seven distinct phases. Each phase is marked by its own characteristics, few of which are flattering *(ibid.)*. All of life is clouded over by uncertainty, for a man goes on his way and knows not whether good or evil awaits him (Tan. Toledot 12). A trace of a tragic view of human destiny is to be discerned in a few rabbinic statements. Throughout his lifetime, man is caught in the impossible dilemma of either obeying his Creator *(yoẓer)* or his evil inclination *(yeẓer)*. Whichever he follows, he finds himself perpetually at odds with the other (Ber. 61a–b). Though man enters and leaves the world surrounded by love, both his entrance and exit are marked by sighing and weeping (Eccl. R. 5). The vanity of human ambition is expressed in the observation that man comes in to the world with his fists clenched, as if to say, "I will grasp the whole world"; he leaves with palms outstretched, as if to say, "See what I am carrying away" *(ibid.)*. Wherever man dies, there the earth will accept him, for the first man was created by God from dust gathered from the four corners of the earth (San. 38a–b; Tan. Pekude 3). Whether it were better for man to have been born or not to have been born is the subject of a prolonged controversy between the schools of Shammai and Hillel. The debate terminates with the decision that it would have been better for man never to have been born. But once having entered the world, "let him scrutinize his deeds" (Er. 13b). The pessimistic conclusion is unique and has no parallel in rabbinic literature. (Talmudic commentators have sought to temper it by interpretation. See Maharsha to Mak. 23b, and Urbach, in bibliography, pp. 224–6.)

Significance. Rabbinic thought considers all creation as having been called into being for the sake of man (Gen. R. 8:3–9); he is the only creature formed directly by the hand of God (Alphabet of R. Akiva 59); he was created last because he was to have dominion over all (Gen. R. 19:6). One man is worth the whole of creation (ARN[1] 31). R. Akiva is moved to exclaim: "Beloved is man who was created in the image (of God); still greater was the love in that it was made known to him that he was created in the image of God" (Avot 3:15). Man's likeness to God, a doctrine meant to emphasize the singular position of man in the world, is a common doctrine in rabbinic Judaism and occurs in a wide variety of contexts. (However, one meets the occasional notion that man was created in the image of the angels and not in that of God; (Gen. R. 14:3; 21:5). See Ginzberg, op. cit. in bibliography, vol. 5, p. 65, note 6 for a proposed explanation of this extraordinary view.) Man's superiority over the angels is to be found in his superior wisdom (Num. R. 19:3) and in his possession of free will

(Gen. R. 21:5). In poetic fashion, man is termed God's candle in the world (Tan. B. Gen. 28).

See also *Body and Soul; *Inclination, Good and Evil. [TH.F.]

Bibliography: I. Epstein, *The Faith of Judaism* (1954); Kaufmann Y., Toledot; U. Cassuto, *From Adam to Noah* (1961); N. W. Porteous, in: IDB, 3 (1962), s.v. (incl. bibl.); R. Gordis, *The Book of God and Man* (1965). IN RABBINIC THOUGHT: S. Schechter, *Some Aspects of Rabbinic Theology* (1923), ch. 15; W. Hirsch, *Rabbinic Psychology* (1947); G. F. Moore, *Judaism in the First Centuries of the Christian Era*, 3 vols. (1927–40), index, s.v. *Man;* Ginzberg, Legends, index, s.v. *Man;* E. Urbach, *Ḥazal* (1969), 190–226; H. Malter, in: JQR, 2 (1911/12), 453f.

MANĀKHA, town in Yemen in the mountains of Ḥarāz S.W. of Sanʿa, on the way from Sanʿa to Ḥudayda. Manākha was a prominent commercial center. It had an important Jewish quarter which served as a center for the Jewish population of nearby and faraway towns and villages, such as Madhmār, Jirwāh, Hawzān, and others. These Jews would get together on the weekly market day in Manākha, when the local Jews would also abandon their workshops and engage in trading. According to Eduard *Glaser's estimate, there were approximately 200 Jews in Manākha in the 1880s; others put their number at 1,000. In 1930 they numbered approximately 300. According to Joseph Halévy, there were some 500 Jews in Jirwāh. There was also a large number of Jews in Madhmār. At times the social and economic situation of the Jews of the region was better than in other parts of the country. They monopolized the coffee trade and some Jews of Manākha even had landholdings. Nevertheless, they were careful to maintain an external appearance of abject poverty, and their poor houses had the appearance of prisons. After the ascension of the imam Yaḥya (1904), the region, which was the stronghold of the Turkish authorities, underwent many upheavals. It is reported that in the years of famine and hardship (1906), approximately 1,700–2,000 Jews died in Manākha.

Bibliography: J. Saphir, *Even Sappir* (1886), 70; K. Rathjens and H. Wissmann, *Landeskundliche Ergebnisse* (1934), 67–73; E. Brauer, *Ethnologie . . .* (1934), index. [H.Z.H.]

MANARAH (Heb. מַנָרָה; derived from the Ar. **al-Manāra;** for a time the Hebrew name **Ramim,** "heights," was used), kibbutz near the Israel-Lebanese border on the Naphtali Ridge of Upper Galilee, affiliated with Ha-Kibbutz ha-Me'uḥad. Its founding in 1943 by pioneers from Germany and Israel-born youth was a bold enterprise. The settlers had to climb a 5 mi. (8 km.), steep footpath to reach the site—2,990 ft. (920 m.) above sea level—and withstand isolation in a place where the winter is snowy and stormy, and where no water sources are present in summer. In the Israel *War of Independence (1948), the settlers held out under enemy siege. In violation of the cease-fire arrangements the surrounding positions were occupied by irregular Arab forces commanded by Fawzī al-Qāwuqjī (October 1948). The area and all of Galilee were liberated by Israel's "Operation Ḥiram." In the first years after 1948 the water problem was solved when a pumping installation was built to bring water from the Einan Springs in the Ḥuleh Valley 2600 ft. (800 m.) below. A highway was paved and the kibbutz, in addition to its hill farming (mainly deciduous fruit and vineyards in the vicinity), received fields and carp ponds in the valley. Manarah also has a metal factory. The crusader castle ruins of Hūnīn (Chasteau Neuf) are located nearby. [E.O.]

MANASSEH (Heb. מְנַשֶּׁה), elder son of *Joseph and the name of one of the 12 tribes of Israel. Manasseh was born to Joseph in Egypt by *Asenath, daughter of Poti-Phera (Gen. 41:50–51). The name is said to be symbolic of Joseph's turn of fortune. Manasseh is distinguished by several traditional historical peculiarities. Whereas ten of the tribes (or 11 if Levi is included) are conceived as immediate sons of Jacob, Manasseh and *Ephraim are presented as the sons of Joseph and, thus, as the grandsons of Jacob. This feature of the tradition is in part a device to retain the number 12 as normative for the tribal roster. There are in fact two basic versions of the tribal roster: (1) the enumeration which counts Joseph as one tribe and includes Levi and (2) the enumeration which subdivides Joseph into Ephraim and Manasseh and omits Levi. It is commonly believed that the former is the older reckoning dating to the time when Joseph was still a single tribal entity and when Levi was as yet a secular tribe. The second is assumed to stem from a later period when Joseph broke into two segments and Levi became a priestly tribe and was dropped from the tribal roster. However, it may also be argued that the tribal league of 12 members did not become the normative until David made the old tribes into administrative subdistricts of his kingdom, in which case the version including Ephraim and Manasseh was older. Once the kingdom divided after Solomon's reign, the 12-fold tribal roster became a sacral tradition and Levi had to be included for religious reasons. To retain the number 12, Ephraim and Manasseh were coalesced under the heading Joseph. This bracketing of Ephraim and Manasseh as Joseph within the 12-tribe roster points, however, to an older affinity between the two tribes reflected in some texts (e.g., Gen. 41:50–52; 48:8–22; Deut. 33:13–17; Josh. 17:14–18). Ephraim and Manasseh were geographically contiguous, occupying the fertile mountains and small plains extending northward from Bethel to the plain of Jezreel in the region later to be known as Samaria. Manasseh lay to the north of Ephraim. The relationship between the two tribes is portrayed in the Bible as ethnic; they migrated into the central highlands as one people who later divided under the decentralizing pressure of settlement in rather different geographical-agricultural and cultural-political zones. It is, however, conjectured by some scholars that they were ethnically distinct and had entered the land separately, but were closely linked in a common religious conversion. The decision on this point depends largely on whether Ephraim and Manasseh are seen as Exodus tribes or are regarded as early converts to the religion brought to them by Levi or other tribes. The rivalry and struggle for priority between Manasseh and Ephraim is strongly attested in the traditions. In most tribal lists Ephraim is named first, which reflects its political predominance as epitomized in the leadership of Ephraimites (e.g., Joshua and Jeroboam I). By contrast, some lists name Manasseh first (Num. 26:28–37), which accords with the genealogical claim that Manasseh was the firstborn of Joseph (Gen. 41:50–52). This discrepancy between Ephraim's genealogical subordination and its historical dominance has been harmonized by inserting an etiology that accounts for the greater blessing which Jacob gave to Ephraim (Gen. 48:17–20). That Manasseh is sometimes represented as having priority probably points to its larger territory and population, to the prominence of the Manassite city of Shechem, and to the tribe's political leadership under Gideon.

Yet another traditional historical peculiarity of Manasseh is its stylization as a "half-tribe" in the central highlands west of Jordan and as a "half-tribe" in the highlands east of Jordan. It appears that colonists from the Manassite holdings in the Samarian highlands crossed the

Jordan eastward and settled on the slopes of the Gilead Mountains from the Jabbok River northward to the Sea of Galilee. Since the biblical account of the conquest tradition pictured all Israel as entering the Land of Canaan from the east as a unit, the presence of Israelites in Transjordan is explained by an initial occupation of Transjordan by two and a half tribes: Reuben, Gad, and the half-tribe of Manasseh (Num. 32). There are scholars, however, who believe that all these Transjordan settlements were the result of movements from the western highlands eastward across the Jordan. Historically, the Transjordan settlement was relatively light and always tenuous prior to the monarchy; even under the monarchy it was precarious except when a strong king secured the frontiers against the Arameans, Ammonites, and Moabites. The colonization of Transjordan by Manassites was matched by Ephraimite colonization in the same region (Judg. 12:4; II Sam. 18:6), and it is strongly suspected that Reuben and Gad were either offshoots of more established tribes in the western highlands or transplants of reduced or decimated tribes originally located in cis-Jordan. That Manasseh alone was credited with territory on both sides of the Jordan is probably an index of its greater success in colonization.

Another name for Manasseh was Machir (Judg. 5:14). Machir elsewhere is credited as a major clan within Manasseh, the latter's "firstborn" and "the father of Gilead" (Gen. 50:23; Josh. 17:1). If Machir was the original name of the tribe, Manasseh would have been introduced once colonization had extended the group holdings and the need was felt for a more inclusive term. The adoption of the term Manasseh would probably also have been a function of the desire to relate the tribe more closely to Ephraim, the two being regarded as "sons of Joseph."

Manasseh's territorial holdings as described in Joshua 17 and in Judges 1:27–28 appear in an account of the tribal allotments at the time of the Conquest, which some exegetes regard as an incomplete and mutilated sketch of the tribal administrative subdistricts of David's kingdom. The boundary of Manasseh with Ephraim to the south is given with some precision. The borders with Issachar and Asher to the north have been obscured as a result of redaction of the sources. Similar uncertainty exists in delimiting the Transjordan holdings of Manasseh in relation to Gad. It is doubtful whether before the time of David Manasseh settled the coastal plain on the west, the Carmel highlands on the northwest, the plain of Jezreel to the north, or the plain of Beth-Shean on the northeast. In Transjordan, Manassite colonization, it is supposed, hardly penetrated beyond the crest of the Gilead Mountain Range and perhaps some distance up the Jabbok Valley. The major settlements in west Manasseh, prior to the expansion under David, were Shechem, Dothan, Tirzah, Thebez, Arumah, Ophrah, Bezek, and Arubboth. In east Manasseh the major towns were Jabesh-Gilead and Abel-Meholah. The settlements of Succoth, Penuel, Zarethan, and Zaphon, located in or around the Jabbok Valley and its juncture with the Jordan, may also have been Manassite, although some of them are attributed to Gad. Among the clans of Manasseh (Josh. 17:2–3) are Canaanite cities, such as Shechem, some of which probably remained non-Israelite down to David's time, even though surrounded by Israelites. The approximate position of several of the clans in the west Jordan highlands can be plotted on the basis of their occurrence as place names in the Samaria Ostraca (Albiezer, [A]sriel, Helek, Hoglah, Noah, Shechem, Shemida). [N.K.G.]

In the Aggadah. Manasseh emerges in the *aggadah* as his father's right-hand man. He was sent by Joseph to spy on his brothers after they entered Egypt (Tanḥ. B., Gen. 202). He is identified as the interpreter between Joseph and his brothers (Gen. 42:23) when his father feigned ignorance of Hebrew (Gen. R. 91:8), and it was he who overcame Simeon despite his martial prowess and cast him into prison (Tanḥ, Va-Yiggash, 4). As the steward of his father's house Manasseh also prepared the repast for Joseph's brothers (Tar. Pseudo-Jon. Gen. 43:16), and was later sent to search the sacks for the silver cup (Tanḥ. B., Gen. 197). On the flag of the tribe of Manasseh was embroidered a wild ox, an allusion to Deuteronomy 33:17, which refers to Gideon (Judg. 6:11), a descendant of Manasseh (Num. R. 2:7).

For the relationship between Ephraim and Manasseh see *Ephraim in the *Aggadah.* [Ed.]

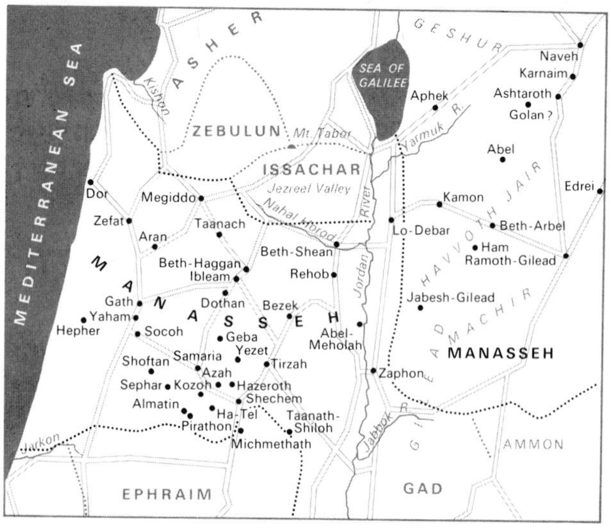

Territory of the tribe of Manasseh. After Y. Aharoni, *Lexicon Biblicum,* Dvir Co. Ltd., Tel Aviv, 1965.

Bibliography: EM, 5 (1968), 45–51 (incl. bibl.); M. Noth, in: PJB, 37 (1941), 50–101; idem, in: ZAW, 60 (1944), 11–57; J. Simons, in: PEQ, 79 (1947), 27–39; idem, in: *Orientalia Neerlandica* (1948), 190–215; M. Naor, *Ha-Mikra ve-ha-Areẓ,* 1 (1952), 145–6; 2 (1954), 63–68; E. Danelius, in: PEQ, 89 (1957), 55–67; 90 (1958), 32–43; E. Jenni, in: ZDPV, 74 (1958), 35–40; W. Phythian-Adams, in: PEQ, 61 (1929), 228–41; IDB, 3 (1962), 252–4; 4 (1962), 705; Aharoni, Land, index; Z. Kallai, *Naḥalot Shivtei Yisrael* (1967), 142–51, 248–54, 259, 375ff. In the Aggadah: Ginzberg, Legends, index.

MANASSEH (Heb. מְנַשֶּׁה; perhaps "one who causes [an earlier deceased, child] to be forgotten"), king of Judah (698–643 B.C.E.), son of *Hezekiah. Manasseh ascended the throne at the age of 12 and reigned for 55 years (II Kings 21:1). In those years Assyrian power reached its pinnacle; Manasseh's reign coincided with more than half of Sennacherib's (705–681 B.C.E.), all of Esarhaddon's (680–669), and most of Ashurbanipal's (668–627). During most of Manasseh's reign, Judah was a submissive dependent of Assyria. Manasseh is mentioned, together with 22 kings of Syria, Palestine, and Cyprus, in one of Esarhaddon's inscriptions relating that he imposed forced labor upon them, making them convey timber and stones for the construction of his palace in Nineveh (Pritchard, Texts, 291). Most of these kings, including Manasseh, are also mentioned in one of Ashurbanipal's inscriptions which recounts that their armies accompanied him to Egypt in his campaign against *Tirhakah (687; Pritchard, Texts, 294). Several scholars hold that part of Manasseh's army remained in Egypt as a garrison, and that they were the first inhabitants of the Jewish settlement in *Elephantine. Further evidence of Judah's subordination to Assyria is found in a fragment of an inscription from the period between Sargon and Esarhaddon, which lists the tribute of Judah after that of Ammon and Moab, the amount of the former being smaller than that of the latter. This probably relates to the period after *Sennacherib's campaign in Judah, when the country was impoverished.

The Book of Kings does not mention any political events during Manasseh's reign, but in Chronicles it is stated that, because he did what was displeasing to the Lord, the Lord caused the Assyrian officers to oppose him and put him in chains, transporting him to Babylon, where he submitted to God's will and was returned to Jerusalem and his throne (II Chron. 33:10–13). To the degree that there is any historical validity to the story, the imprisonment was probably brought about by an attempted revolt against Assyria, and not by foreign religious practices, which would be a sign of submission to Assyria. The tradition that he was transported to Babylon appears strange, unless the Assyrian king happened to be there due to a Babylonian revolt. It is likely that Manasseh was involved in the revolts which broke out against Assyria at the time of Shamash-shumukîn's revolt in Babylon against his brother Ashurbanipal (668–631). Further evidence of Manasseh's efforts to overthrow Assyrian domination may be seen in the fortification of Jerusalem and his appointing of officers over all the walled cities in Judah (II Chron. 33:14), although these events may refer to a later period. The account of Manasseh's return from imprisonment to the throne is given credence by the policy of Ashurbanipal, who, having exiled rebellious Egyptian princes to Assyria, came to favor Neco (671–663), the father of Psammetichus I, and returned him to Egypt as vassal ruler.

Manasseh abolished the religious reforms of his father Hezekiah and introduced alien rites into the Temple (II Kings 21:3). This was very likely a course forced upon him by the Assyrian overlords. Ashurbanipal imposed religious duties upon several Chaldean states in southern Mesopotamia after crushing their attempted revolt. (However, his actions in defeated territories need not be conclusive evidence concerning his policies in lands ruled by his vassals.) In any event, the abolition of Hezekiah's deeds was undoubtedly also a part of the internal struggle in Judah between those who had supported a policy of acceptance of Assyrian domination since the time of Ahaz and the devout circles around the prophets. It was a ruthless struggle, and Manasseh is described as having shed "very much innocent blood..." (II Kings 21:16). According to II Chronicles 33:12ff., Manasseh fully repented upon his return from Babylon, but this does not agree with II Kings 21:16, which relates that he died without repenting. It appears unlikely that the destruction of Jerusalem would have been so emphatically attributed to the sins of Manasseh had he completely repented as described in Chronicles. [J.Li.]

In the Aggadah. Manasseh's mother was the daughter of the prophet Isaiah, and married King Hezekiah after his miraculous recovery (Ber. 10a). Manasseh and his brother Rab-Shakeh soon showed their total dissimilarity from their parents. Once, when Hezekiah was carrying his two sons on his shoulders to the schoolhouse, he overheard their conversation. One said, "Our father's bald head might do well for frying fish." The other rejoined, "It would be good for offering sacrifices to idols." Enraged by these words, Hezekiah threw his sons to the ground. Rab-Shakeh was killed by the fall, but Manasseh escaped unhurt (Dik. Sof., Ber. 10a). His name is derived from נשה (*nashah;* "he forgot"), in that he forgot his God and indulged in idolatry, murder, and other abominable acts (Sanh. 102b). After his father's death, Manasseh began to worship idols. He destroyed the altar and set up an idol with four faces, copied from the four figures on the divine throne of Ezekiel, so that from whatever direction a man entered the Temple he saw a face of the idol (Sanh. 103b). Manasseh also made another idolatrous image so heavy that it required 1,000 men to carry it. New bearers were employed daily because the king had each group executed at the end of the day's work *(ibid.)*. He expunged the name of God from the Scriptures *(ibid.)* and delivered public lectures whose sole purpose was to ridicule the Torah (Sanh. 99b). He also committed incest by violating his sister (Sanh. 103b).

Manasseh sat in judgment on his own grandfather, Isaiah, and condemned him to death. The indictment against him was that his prophecies contradicted the teachings of Moses. Isaiah refused to defend himself, knowing that his efforts would be of no avail and preferring that his grandson act out of ignorance rather than from wickedness. He fled for safety and when he pronounced the Ineffable Name a cedar tree swallowed him up. Manasseh ordered that the tree be sawn in two, causing the prophet's death (Yev. 49b). Manasseh was carried off to Babylon in the 22nd year of his reign (SOR 24) and there placed in a heated oven. In his torture, he prayed in vain to the idols he had formerly worshiped, and at last besought the God of his fathers. The angels pleaded with the Almighty not to accept his penance. The plea was not accepted, God saying, "If I do not accept him I will be closing the door of repentance in the face of all repentant sinners." Immediately a wind arose and carried Manasseh back to Jerusalem (TJ, Sanh. 10:2, 28c).

Manasseh is included among those who have no share in the world to come. Despite his restoration to Jerusalem, the rabbis felt that he had forfeited eternal life because of his previous sins. R. Judah, however, held that he was also restored to his portion in paradise (Sanh. 10:2). Manasseh possessed a profound knowledge of the Torah and could interpret Leviticus in 55 different ways (Sanh. 103b). He justified his actions by pointing to the corrupt behavior of his times. R. Ashi once announced a lecture about him, saying, "Tomorrow, I shall speak about our colleague, Manasseh." That night, the king appeared to Ashi in a dream and asked him a ritual question which Ashi could not answer. Manasseh then revealed the solution to him. Amazed by the king's scholarship, R. Ashi asked why one so erudite had worshiped idols. Manasseh answered, "Had you lived at my time, you would have caught hold of the hem of my garment and sped after me" (Sanh. 102b). [Ed.]

Bibliography: Bright, Hist, 271–99; Nielsen, in: *Fourth World Congress of Jewish Studies,* 1 (1967), 103–6; EM, 5 (1968), 41–45 (incl. bibl.); Ginzberg, Legends, 4 (1947[2]), 277–81; 6 (1946), 370–6.

MANASSEH, PRAYER OF, brief penitential psalm incorporated among the books of the *Apocrypha. According to II Chronicles 33:11ff. Manasseh, king of Judah, repented his sins when he was taken to Babylonia in fetters (cf. also II Baruch 64:8). Shortly before the beginning of the Christian Era, an unknown author drew up a prayer appropriate for the occasion. Its style is comparatively simple and clear, concise and expressive, breathing throughout a spirit of deep and genuine religious piety. Its contents may be summarized as follows: O, God whose might and mercy are immeasurable (verses 3–7a), Thou hast promised forgiveness not for the righteous but for sinners (verses 7b–8). I have committed many iniquities and am now weighed down with sin. Therefore I confess my transgressions, and implore forgiveness (verses 11–13). Thou wilt save me in Thy mercy, and I will praise thee continually. For all the host of heaven sings thy praise, and thine is the glory for ever. Amen (verses 14–25). It is disputed whether the prayer was composed in Hebrew,

Aramaic, or Greek. The theology and literary style of the Prayer appear to be more in accord with the teachings of Palestinian than of Hellenistic Judaism. The two main ideas that permeate the prayer are the infinite mercy of God, and the efficacy of true repentance.

The position of this ancient prayer in biblical texts varies considerably. Its first appearance in literary history is in the *Didascalia Apostolorum*. In several Greek manuscripts (including codex B, 5th century C.E.) it is included among the 14 odes appended to the Psalter. In medieval manuscripts of the Vulgate it often follows II Chronicles. Several Syriac, Armenian, Ethiopic, and Old Slavonic manuscripts have the prayer, some at the close of the Psalter, some at the end of II Chronicles. Among printed Bibles its position varies. In editions of the Vulgate printed before the Council of Trent, the Prayer stands after II Chronicles; in official printings of the Vulgate after the Council, it is placed in an appendix after the New Testament. In Luther's German Bible it stands at the close of the Apocrypha. Among English versions it usually stands among the Apocrypha before I Maccabees, although in the Geneva Bible (1560), widely used by the Puritans, it is included among the canonical books, following II Chronicles. The Roman Catholic Douai Bible of 1609–10 places it in an appendix after II Maccabees.

Bibliography: Schuerer, Gesch, 3 (1909[4]), 458–60; Ryle, in: Charles, Apocrypha, 1 (1913), 612–24; R.H. Pfeiffer, *History of New Testament Times* (1949), 457–60; B.M. Metzger, *Introduction to the Apocrypha* (1957), 123–8. [B.M.M.]

MANASSEH (Menasseh) BEN ISRAEL (1604–1657), Amsterdam scholar. Manasseh, who was born a Marrano in Madeira, was baptized as Manoel Dias Soeiro. His father, Gaspar Rodrigues Nuñez, escaped from Lisbon after appearing as a penitent in an *auto-da-fé and settled in Amsterdam, where he took the name Joseph b. Israel and called his two sons Ephraim and Manasseh respectively. Manasseh made prodigious progress in his education. He became a member of the Ḥevrah for Talmud Torah at the age of 12, began to frequent the yeshivot when he was 14, made his first public oration in Portuguese when he was 15, and at 17 wrote his first book, *Safah Berurah*, a grammatical work (unpublished). He succeeded R. Isaac *Uzziel as preacher to the Neveh Shalom congregation in 622. His extraordinarily extensive knowledge in the theological rather than the talmudic sphere and his linguistic abilities made him a forerunner of the Jewish scholars of the 19th century who attempted to present Judaism in a sympathetic manner acceptable to the Christian world. He founded the earliest Hebrew printing press in Amsterdam (1626), where he continued to publish works in Hebrew and Spanish (or Portuguese) for the remainder of his life. *Penei Rabbah*, his index to the Midrashim, appeared in 1628. The first part of his *Conciliador* (1632, in Spanish; afterward in Latin),

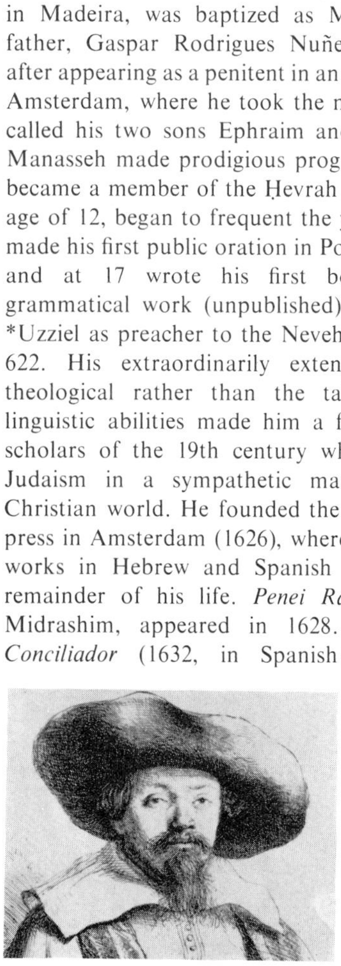

Figure 1. Etching of Manasseh Ben Israel by Rembrandt van Rijn. Jerusalem, Israel Museum. Photo David Harris, Jerusalem.

reconciling apparently discordant biblical passages, gained him a great reputation in Christian circles (the remaining three parts appeared in Spanish only, 1641–51). This was followed by a series of works also largely directed to non-Jews: *De Creatione* (1635, Latin only); *De Termino Vitae* (1634, Latin only); *De Resurrectione Mortuorum* (1636); and *De Fragilitate Humana* (1642). Beside other

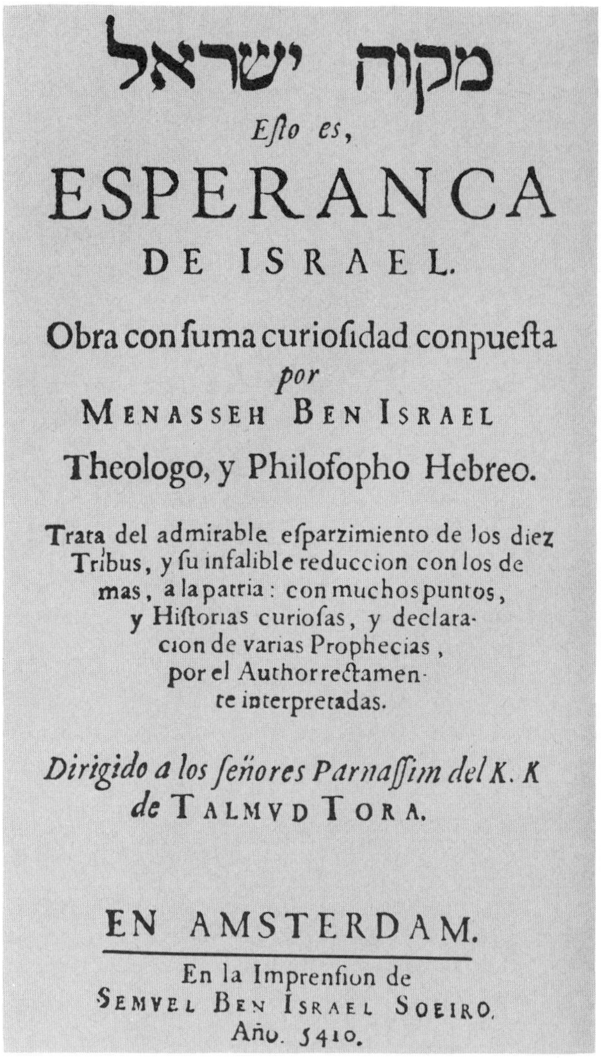

מקוה ישראל

Esto es,

ESPERANCA

DE ISRAEL.

Obra con ſuma curioſidad conpueſta

por

MENASSEH BEN ISRAEL

Theologo, y Philoſopho Hebreo.

Trata del admirable eſparzimiento de los diez Tribus, y ſu infalible reduccion con los de mas, a la patria: con muchos puntos, y Hiſtorias curioſas, y declaracion de varias Prophecias, por el Author rectamente interpretadas.

Dirigido a los ſeñores Parnaſſim del K. K de TALMVD TORA.

EN AMSTERDAM.

En la Imprenſion de SEMVEL BEN ISRAEL SOEIRO. Año. 5410.

Figure 2. Title page of *Esperança de Israel*, the Portuguese edition of *The Hope of Israel* by Manasseh Ben Israel. Amsterdam, Cecil Roth Collection.

minor works, he produced *Thesouro dos Dinim*, a code of Jewish law for returned Marranos (1645–47); *Piedra Gloriosa*, with engravings by Rembrandt (1655); and *Nishmat Ḥayyim* (1651) on the nature of the soul. For these works, as well as his synagogue sermons (at which gentile scholars and notables were often present), he was regarded in the world of scholarship as the leading representative of Hebrew learning. He had close personal relationships with luminaries such as *Grotius and *Rembrandt, who painted and engraved his portrait. Though continuing to serve the Amsterdam community in various capacities, he was never its official rabbi. In 1640, when he intervened in a quarrel between the synagogue authorities and his brother-in-law, Jonas Abrabanel, he was put under the ban. Despite his publishing activities, his income was never adequate, and in 1640 he planned to emigrate to *Brazil. When after the Puritan revolution the return of the Jews to England was proposed, Manasseh took a prominent share in the negotiations. In 1650 he dedicated the Latin edition of his work, *The Hope of Israel*, describing the reported discovery of the Lost *Ten Tribes in South America, to the English parliament in an effort to solicit their goodwill. At the same time, he entered into discussions with various Englishmen by correspondence and in person, on the possibility of permitting the return of the Jews; this, in his view, had messianic implications, because it would complete the dispersion of the Jews to *Keẓeh ha-Areẓ* ("the end of the earth"), the medieval Hebrew term for Angle-Terre (cf.

Deut. 28:64). Because of political circumstances and his own health, Manasseh did not avail himself of an opportunity to go to England in 1652, though his friend Manuel Martinez (David Dormido *Abrabanel) and his son Samuel Soeiro conducted some negotiations on his behalf. Eventually however, he went there in 1655, and submitted his petition to *Cromwell for the recall of the Jews. Although this was not formally granted, assent was given to a subsequent petition which merely asked for permission to establish a synagogue and acquire a cemetery. This arrangement eventually proved providential, since it placed no conditions on the return of the Jews. During his stay in England, Manasseh wrote *Vindiciae Judaeorum* (1656) to defend the Jews against the attacks which were then being made on them. He was bitterly disappointed at the apparent frustration of his hopes, although Cromwell showed his personal sympathy by granting him a pension of £100 a year. He returned to Holland in the autumn of 1657, but died at Middelburg shortly after his arrival.

Bibliography: C. Roth, *Life of Menasseh ben Israel* (1934); Roth, Mag Bibl, index; idem, in: JHSET, 11 (1924–27), 112–42; idem, in: V. D. Lipman (ed.), *Three Centuries of Anglo-Jewish History* (1961), 1–25; Lehmann, Nova Bibl, index; Kayserling, Bibl, 68–70; L. Wolf, *Menasseh ben Israel's Mission to Oliver Cromwell* (1901); M. Wilensky, *Shivat ha-Yehudim le-Angliyyah* (1944); A. Yaari, *Mi-Beit Defuso shel Menasheh ben Yisrael* (1947). [C.R.]

MANASSEH BEN (Porat) JOSEPH OF ILYA (1767–1831), one of the forerunners of the *Haskalah in Lithuania and Russia. He was born in Smorgon, Lithuania, and was renowned as a child for his remarkable memory and intellectual precocity. He received a talmudic education in the home of his father, who was a *dayyan*. In 1784 he married and went to live in the house of his father-in-law, a wealthy merchant in Ilya. Manasseh was among the disciples and intimates of *Elijah b. Solomon Zalman, the Gaon of Vilna, and became friendly with Joseph Mazal from Viasyn, who owned an excellent Hebrew library including scientific and research works. Gradually he reached theoretical and practical conclusions tending toward increasing rationalism and called for some change in *halakhah*. In his works his attitude to Talmud study is based on these conceptions. In several places, for example, he challenged the Talmud and Rashi's understanding of certain pronouncements of the Mishnah. He regarded natural sciences with respect and was critical of the Kabbalah. Demanding the abrogation of halakhic commands that were not an integral part of the basic, early law and that people could not carry out in actual life, he advocated the principle of alteration and leniency in *halakhah*, according to changing trends. He likewise called for a changed and orderly curriculum of traditional studies (see also *Judah Loew b. Bezalel): first the Bible, Mishnah, and *Gemara* and, for talented youth, secular studies as well.

Manasseh has been credited with the invention of several agricultural machines which the unsophisticated environment rejected. Raising the problem of the poor in Jewish society, he called for justice for them, as "the overwhelming majority of these people lack their basic needs, are hungry and thirsty, have no garment against the cold, and their spirit is faint within them." Social responsibility and service for society he regarded as a duty, even at the cost of personal advantage. He attacked the custom of *kest*, by which a newly married couple was supported for several years by the wife's parents, since he was in favor of productivization. Regarding trade as "robbery," he called for "proper leadership" to enable the Jewish masses to earn their livelihood through crafts. From time to time he suggested that the leading rabbis confer to deliberate on the problems of a "general improvement" of Jewish conditions and culture. Manasseh was persecuted. A rabbinical convention deliberated his excommunication and he was prevented from going to Berlin. He therefore completed his studies in the Polish and German languages at home and read antiquated scientific works in those languages, thus gaining a sketchy knowledge in this field. To make a living, he later worked as a private teacher in various places in Russia and Galicia. It was then that he became acquainted with Nachman *Krochmal and other Galician *maskilim*.

Manasseh was a prolific writer, but it was not easy for him to publish his writings, because none of them was issued with approbation of the rabbis. His *Pesher Davar* (Vilna, 1807) was burnt by many rabbis. When he attempted to publish his principal work, *Alfei Menasheh*, in Volhynia, the printer burned the manuscript and the copies that had already been printed as soon as he became aware of the content of the work; when it was printed in Vilna (1822), the author was required to omit a paragraph which alluded to reforms in *halakhah*. His *Binat Mikra* (Grodno, 1818), written in the form of unsystematic novellae, deals with the cantillation marks of the Bible as factors in syntax and meaning. In his pamphlet *Sama de-Ḥayyei* (Yid. trans. *Lebn-Mittel*), he sought to present his views to the people at large and to outline "proper and useful behavior for life in this world." Though he had intended to publish additional pamphlets, no more appeared, possibly because of the opposition of the rabbis and community leaders. After *Sama de-Ḥayyei*, Manasseh published anonymously the pamphlet *Shekel ha-Kodesh*, in which he apologized to those who considered him "a nonconformist in several matters," and suggested that his opponents "choose several men who would be willing to clarify their opinions with me."

Manasseh visited *ḥadarim* and encouraged young men to study mathematics and sciences. In 1827 the Jews of his native town elected him as their rabbi, but he resigned after a year, refusing to be involved in the cruelty of the *Cantonist mobilization. He died in a cholera epidemic. Most of his literary remains were destroyed in the fire which broke out in Ilya in 1884, but some extracts appeared in the second volume of *Alfei Menasheh* (1904), published by his grandson Isaac Spalter, head of a yeshivah in Smorgon. Circles of pupils and admirers cherished his memory, and using this tradition, M. *Plungian, one of the first Lithuanian *maskilim*, wrote his biography of Manasseh, *Ben-Porat* (Vilna, 1858). *Maskilim* of the 19th century (M. *Lilienblum, R. A. *Braudes, and others) used Manasseh's opinions against rabbis of the old school.

Bibliography: S. I. Stanislawski, in: *Ha-Shilo'ah*, 18 (1908), 274–7; S. Rosenfeld, in: *Ha-Tekufah*, 2 (1918), 250–88; Z. Rejzen, *Fun Mendelsohn Biz Mendele* (1923), 183–260; Zinberg, Sifrut, 6 (1960), 153–61; Klausner, Sifrut, 3 (1953), 25–32; B. Katz, *Rabbanut, Ḥasidut, Haskalah*, 2 (1958) 187–203; R. Mahler, *Divrei Yemei Yisrael ba-Dorot ha-Aḥaronim*, 4 (1956), 63–68. [Y.S.]

MANCHESTER, city in northern England. Its Jewish community, the second largest in Britain, dates from about 1780, the first synagogue being founded by two brothers, Lemon and Jacob Nathan, formerly of Liverpool. A cemetery was acquired in 1794 and the first local charity was the Manchester Jewish Philanthropic Society (1804) which provided winter relief for poor resident Jews. After a temporary schism in the congregation in 1840, a more serious split followed during the rabbinate of S. *Schiller-Szinessy and led to the establishment of a Reform synagogue in 1856. Two years later, the original community moved to its new synagogue ("the Great") on Cheetham Hill still in use in the 1970s. The early settlers and

The Great Synagogue of Manchester, built in 1857. Photo *Manchester Evening News and Chronicle.*

community leaders came mainly from Liverpool and included a tailor, a pencutter, and an optician. Nathan Meyer *Rothschild's first residence in England was in Manchester, from where he exported cotton goods from 1798 to 1805. The second half of the 19th century brought to the city substantial merchants from Central Europe, some political refugees from the 1848 liberal risings in Europe, Rumanian Jews fleeing from the 1869 persecutions, and in the 1870s young men escaping service in the Russian army. In 1871, small groups arrived from North Africa and the Levant, areas connected with the Manchester cotton industry, forming the nucleus of the flourishing 20th-century Sephardi congregations of south Manchester. The most significant influx, however, resulted from the great Russo-Polish immigration of 1881–1914. The Jews of Manchester spread northward, settling in the adjacent city of Salford and in the suburban districts of Prestwich and Whitefield. In the 20th century, the south Manchester Jews spread into the suburban areas of Cheshire.

Some of the earlier immigrants became waterproof-garment manufacturers, an industry developed by Jews which flourished until it was superseded by the technologically superior "rainproof," in the manufacture of which Jews were not prominent. The Russo-Polish immigrants followed the usual immigrant trades of tailoring and capmaking. There were also large numbers of jewelry travelers, hawkers, and street-traders. Communal institutions proliferated. The first Jewish school was founded in 1842, and by 1904, 2,300 pupils were being educated in Jewish schools. A Board of Guardians on the London pattern was founded in 1867. Many small *ḥevrot* were opened by immigrants. In the 20th century, Manchester had its own *bet din* and *sheḥitah* board and a Jewish hospital. The representative body, the Council of Manchester and Salford Jews, had 68 synagogues and organizations affiliated to it in 1969. The Jewish population of Greater Manchester was 31,500 in 1969.

As Manchester was the home of Chaim *Weizmann from 1904 to 1916, the city became the training ground of some of the outstanding British Zionists, personalities prominent also in British life: Lord Simon *Marks, Harry *Sacher, Leon *Simon, Israel and Rebecca *Sieff. In civic life, too, Jews played an increasingly important role. Nathan and Sarah *Laski were followed by a large number of Jewish lord mayors of both Manchester and Salford. Several Jews were Labor members of parliament for Manchester constituencies, especially after 1945, including Harold and Leslie *Lever and Frank Allaun. The novelist Louis *Golding lived in Manchester and set several of his novels in the city.

Bibliography: C. Roth, *Rise of Provincial Jewry* (1950), 83–84; JYB; V. D. Lipman, *Social History of the Jews in England, 1850–1950* (1954), index; L. P. Gartner, *The Jewish Immigrant in England, 1870–1894* (1960), index; Ch. Weizmann, *Trial and Error* (1949), index.

[V.D.L.]

MANCHURIA, N.E. region of China, adjacent to the Soviet Union. After the Russian Revolution of 1917 many refugees sought shelter in Manchuria, including some 5,000 Jews. Most of them gravitated to *Harbin, but small groups settled in Dairen, Mukden, and other cities. Those Jews who were not employed by the Chinese Eastern Railway worked as educators, physicians, or merchants. The Japanese occupied Manchuria (1931–45); as Axis partners during World War II they accepted the anti-Semitic policy of their Nazi ally and their treatment of the Jews was oppressive. After the Japanese defeat in 1945, civil war broke out in Manchuria between the Chinese Nationalists and the Communists. Those Russian Jews who did not succeed in escaping before the Communist takeover eventually returned to the Soviet Union.

See also *Mongolia.

Bibliography: H. Dicker, *Wanderers and Settlers in the Far East* (1962), 17–60. [R.L.]

MANCROFT, family of British politicians. ARTHUR MICHAEL SAMUEL, first BARON MANCROFT (1872–1942), English politician and philanthropist. Born into a wealthy family long-settled in the Mancroft district of Norwich, Arthur Samuel became head of one of the family manufacturing concerns but retired in 1912 to devote himself to public affairs. He contributed large sums and devoted service to various causes in Norwich, including the Castle Museum and Picture Gallery, and was lord mayor of Norwich from 1912 to 1913. During World War I he worked at the War Office and later at the Ministry of Supply where he dealt with arms contracts. Samuel was elected to Parliament as a Conservative from 1918, and became parliamentary secretary to the Board of Trade and minister for the Department of Overseas Trade. From 1927 to 1929 he was financial secretary to the Treasury. In 1932 he was made a baronet and in 1937 was raised to the peerage as Baron Mancroft. His writings include the biography *Piranesi* (1910); *The Herring: Its Effect on the History of Britain* (1918); *The Mancroft Essays* (all written under the name Arthur Michael Samuel); and numerous articles on economic and financial matters. While not active in communal affairs, Lord Mancroft occasionally defended Jewish interests in and out of Parliament.

Lord Mancroft was succeeded by his son, STORMONT MANCROFT, the second baron Mancroft (1914–). He was undersecretary to the Home Office from 1954 to 1957, when he became parliamentary secretary to the Ministry of Defense. He entered the cabinet as minister without portfolio, but resigned in the following year. In 1964 Stormont Mancroft was the central figure in a controversy which broke out when he was appointed chairman of the Board of the Norwich Union Insurance company, with which his family had long been associated. Although he had never shown any Jewish or Zionist interests, he was removed from the post as a concession to Arab pressure. [V.D.L.]

MANDATE FOR PALESTINE. The mandate system was established after World War I by the Treaty of Versailles for the administration of the former overseas possessions of Germany and parts of the Turkish Empire. Its purpose was to implement the principles of Article 22 of the Covenant of the League of Nations, which said in paragraph 4:

> Certain communities formerly belonging to the Turkish Empire have reached a stage of development where their existence as independent nations can be provisionally recognized, subject to the rendering of administrative advice and assistance by a Mandatory until such time as they are able to stand alone. The wishes of these communities must be a principal consideration in the selection of the Mandatory.

Class A of the mandates included former Turkish provinces constituted as Palestine, Iraq, and Syria. The first two were assigned to the administration of Great Britain and the third to France. The mandates for Iraq and Syria ended in 1932 and 1936, respectively, their main purpose having been to prepare the countries to be able "to stand alone." The mandate for Palestine differed from the other "A" mandates in that its primary purpose was the establishment of a national home for the Jewish people, as stated in its preamble, paragraph 3, "putting into effect the declaration originally made on November 2, 1917 [the *Balfour Declaration] by the Government of His Britannic Majesty, and adopted by the other Allied Powers . . ." Moreover, the reason for the establishment of a national home for the Jewish people in Palestine is related to the recognition of "the historical connection of the Jewish people with Palestine and to the grounds for reconstituting their national home in that country" (para. 3). Great importance was attached to the wording of this paragraph, as it made it clear that Palestine was not just a country in which a national home should be built, but was taken as the historic land of the Jews. Therefore the national home is to be reconstituted, and not just constituted, there (see *White Papers).

The second article of the mandate makes it the responsibility of the mandatory power, i.e., Great Britain, to place "the country under such political, administrative, and economic conditions as will secure the establishment of the Jewish national home, as laid down in the preamble." To this is added the aim of "the development of self-governing institutions," an intentionally vague phrase that implied the gradual preparation of Palestine for self-rule as a process parallel to the establishment of the Jewish national home (particularly when compared with the Mandate for Iraq (Mesopotamia)). The fulfillment of the main purpose of the Palestine mandate was to be assured by establishing "an appropriate Jewish Agency for the purpose of advising and cooperating with the Administration of Palestine," by facilitating Jewish immigration into Palestine, encouraging close settlement by Jews on the land (art. 6), and "facilitating the acquisition of Palestinian citizenship by Jews" (art. 7). The Zionist Organization was recognized as such an agency until the establishment of the *Jewish Agency in 1929 (art. 4).

The Hebrew language was recognized as one of the three official languages of the country (art. 22). The Mandate was also to safeguard the "civil and religious rights of all the inhabitants of Palestine, irrespective of race and religion" (introd. and art. 2) and to set up the judicial system so that it assured the rights of all and respected the "personal status of various peoples and communities" and that religious interests (in particular waqfs) be "fully guaranteed" (art. 9). Also many other articles dealt with religious autonomy for the various religions strongly emphasizing this as one of the important functions of the mandate (see arts. 13, 14, 15, 23). Each community was allowed to maintain its own schools in its own language (art. 15); and no modification of the mandate was possible without the consent of the League of Nations (art. 27). According to Article 25 of the mandate, "In the territories lying between the Jordan and the eastern boundary of Palestine as ultimately determined, the Mandatory shall be entitled, with the consent of the Council of the League of Nations, to postpone or withhold application of this mandate as he may consider inapplicable," and by virtue of this saving clause, Transjordan was severed from the territory destined to include the Jewish national home (see *White Papers).

The mandate for Palestine was given to Great Britain at *San Remo on April 25, 1920, and a civil administration (which superseded the British Military Administration), headed by Sir Herbert *Samuel, was effected on July 1, 1920. The mandate itself was ratified by the Council of the League of Nations on June 24, 1922. A special American-British Palestine Mandate Convention was ratified in March 1925, as the United States was not a member of the League of Nations. In this convention the United States agreed to the terms of the mandate and Great Britain agreed that no modification in these terms would be possible without the assent of the United States (art. 7); thus any modification in the mandate needed the assent of both the League of Nations and the United States. The mandate terminated with the establishment of the State of Israel on May 14, 1948.

See also *Israel: Historical Survey (1880–1970); *Palestine Inquiry Commissions; *Balfour Declaration.

Bibliography: League of Nations, *Mandate for Palestine* (1922); reproduced in W. Laqueur (ed.), *The Israel-Arab Reader* (1969), 34–61; U. S. Department of State, *Mandate for Palestine* (1927, 1931[2]); Ch. Weizmann, *Trial and Error* (1949), 347–64 and index; N. Bentwich, *The Mandates System* (1930); B. Joseph, *British Rule in Palestine* (1948).

[D.EF.]

MANDEL, ARNOLD (1913–), French author and journalist. Of Polish immigrant parentage, Mandel was born in Strasbourg. A libertarian radical until World War II, Mandel rediscovered his Jewish identity as a soldier in North Africa in 1940, and then in occupied France. He fled to Switzerland, where he was interned until 1944, after which he fought in the Maquis. From 1945, Mandel was one of the chief spokesmen for French Jewry. Under the influence of Samson Raphael *Hirsch and of ḥasidic mysticism, he returned to neo-Orthodoxy. His knowledge of Yiddish and of Jewish lore made him one of the few able interpreters of Yiddish literature in France. A prolific writer, Mandel defined the originality and distinctiveness of Jews—particularly French Jews—in the modern world. His works deal mainly with his search for identity in a gentile world, and with his intellectual and spiritual quest for a Judaism both modern and Orthodox. They include *L'Homme-Enfant* (1946); *Chair à Destin* (1948); *Les Temps incertains* (1950); *Les Vaisseaux brûlés* (1957); *Le petit livre de la sagesse populaire juive* (1963); *La Voie du Hassidisme* (1963); and *Les Cent Portes* (1968). Mandel contributed to most Franco-Jewish periodicals, particularly *La Terre retrouvée, Evidences,* and *L'Arche.*

[P.AU.]

MANDEL, GEORGES (Jeroboam Rothchild; 1885–1944), French statesman, born in Chatou, near Paris. Mandel became a close associate of Georges Clemenceau in 1903, after joining Clemenceau's staff at *L'Aurore,* a radical daily newspaper which campaigned for the rehabilitation of Alfred *Dreyfus. When Clemenceau became prime minister in 1906, he appointed Mandel head of his office *(chef de cabinet),* a position Mandel held until 1909, and again from 1917 to 1919 in Clemenceau's war cabinet. At the peak of World War I Mandel was put in charge of the trials dealing with treason and defeatism. In 1920 he was elected a deputy and after 1935 he was appointed minister a number of times. As cabinet minister he urged France's speedy rearmament to meet the threat of German National Socialism and in 1936 he opposed Germany's remilitarization of the Rhineland. As minister of the interior in Paul Reynaud's government (from May 1940 to the fall of France), Mandel ordered the arrest of numerous suspected Nazi sympathizers and also interned Jewish refugees from Germany and Austria. After the retreat of French troops, he opposed Pétain's and *Laval's policy of capitulation and collaboration. Pétain had Mandel arrested in Bordeaux, but upon his release he went to Morocco to organize the renewal of combat. Arrested a second time, Mandel was taken to prison in France and assassinated by the Vichy militia in 1944. Mandel did not participate in Jewish community life.

Memorial plaque for Georges Mandel at the entrance to the French Ministry of the Interior, Paris. Photo M. Ninio, Jerusalem.

Bibliography: G. Wormser, *Georges Mandel, l'homme politique* (1967); P. Coblentz, *Georges Mandel* (1946); J. M. Sherwood, *Georges Mandel and the Third Republic* (1971).

[L.L.]

MANDEL, MARVIN (1920–), U.S. politician. Mandel, born in Baltimore, Maryland, the son of East European immigrants, was raised in an Orthodox, Yiddish-speaking home. After graduation from the University of Maryland (1942) and service in the army during World War II, Mandel practiced law in Baltimore until his election to the lower house of the Maryland legislature in 1951. In 1963 he was chosen speaker of the Maryland House of Delegates, and also served as chairman of the Maryland State Democratic Committee. When Spiro T. Agnew, Maryland's Republican governor, was elected vice-president of the U.S. in 1968, Mandel was elected governor by legislature vote. As speaker he was credited with helping push through the legislature tax reform, a fair housing law, and the repeal of the state anti-miscegenation law. A former state commander of the Jewish War Veterans, Mandel was active in Jewish communal affairs. [B.P.]

MANDELBAUM, BERNARD, see supplementary entries.

MANDELBAUM, DAVID GOODMAN (1911–), U.S. anthropologist, born in Chicago. Mandelbaum joined the faculty of the University of Minnesota and from 1943 to 1946 was in the U.S. Army. In 1946 he moved to the University of California at Berkeley, becoming professor and serving as a director of educational resources in anthropological projects (1959–62). His major interests were the ethnology of Southeast and South Asia, anthropological theory, and applied anthropology. His works include: *The Plains Cree* (1940), *Soldier Groups and Negro Soldiers* (1952), and *Change and Continuity in Jewish Life* (1955). He edited *Culture, Language, and Personality* (1956), and *Resources for the Teaching of Anthropology* (1963).

[E.FI.]

MANDELBERG, AVIGDOR (Victor; 1870–1944), physician; delegate to the Second Russian Duma. Born in Berdichev, Mandelberg graduated from the faculty of medicine of the University of Kiev (1893) and settled in St. Petersburg, where he took a part in the organization of workers' circles and their intellectual activities. He was exiled for his activities to Irkutsk, eastern Siberia, in 1899 for four years, and while there, he joined the Social Democratic Labor Party, playing an active role in its organization in Siberia. Upon his release he attended his party's second congress as a delegate of the Siberian alliance and joined the Menshevik faction. He then returned to Siberia, took part in the revolutionary activities of 1905, and was elected to the Second Duma (1907), avoiding any collaboration with the three other Jewish delegates, who had joined the Kadet faction (the Russian Liberals). After the dismissal of the Second Duma and the arrest of the Social Democrats, he escaped abroad. He lived in Italy and returned to Russia with the outbreak of the revolution of 1917. When the Bolsheviks came to power, Mandelberg left for Siberia, emigrating to Palestine in 1920. He was chief physician of Kuppat Ḥolim of the *Histadrut and one of the founders of the League against Tuberculosis. In 1941 he helped found the League for Friendship with the Soviet Union (V League) and was a member of its central committee. Among his works should be mentioned: *Iz perezhitogo* ("Experiences," 1910) and *Me-Ḥayyai* (1942).

Bibliography: Ha-Ligah li-Ydidut Yisrael–S.S.S.R., *Dr. Avigdor Mandelberg, Dappim le-Zikhro* (1946). [Y.S.]

MANDELKERN, SOLOMON (1846–1902), Russian lexicographer, Hebrew poet, and translator. Mandelkern was born in Mlynow and in his youth was among the Ḥasidim of Menahem Mendel of Kotzk. However, he soon

Solomon Mandelkern, Russian lexicographer and Hebrew poet. Jerusalem, J.N.U.L., Schwadron Collection.

came under the influence of Haskalah. At the age of 19 he divorced his very pious wife and went to study at the newly founded rabbinical seminaries of Vilna and Zhitomir. He also studied Semitic languages at the University of St. Petersburg. From 1873 to 1880 Mandelkern served as assistant to the government-appointed rabbi at Odessa, being one of the first to preach in Russian. During this period he studied law at the university and compiled a history of Russia, *Divrei Yemei Rusyah* (3 vols., 1875), on behalf of the "*Society for the Propagation of Culture among Russian Jews." Because of his personal animosity toward its editor Alexander *Zederbaum Mandelkern submitted a false report of a *blood libel in Bessarabia for publication in the periodical *Ha-Meliẓ*. When it was discovered, the periodical was forced to suspend publication, and Mandelkern, to leave Russia. He studied at Jena and afterward settled in Leipzig, where he devoted himself to research. An early supporter of Ḥibbat Zion and Herzl's Zionism, he attended the first Zionist Congress in Basle in 1897. Mandelkern's great contribution to Jewish scholarship is his monumental Bible concordance *Heikhal ha-Kodesh* (1896, 1959^{8}; abridged edition, *Tavnit Heikhal*, 1897), the fruit of 20 years of scholarly labor. This concordance was a great improvement on its predecessors and was the first to follow the Jewish arrangement of the Hebrew Bible. In later editions of the work by F. Margolin and M. Goshen-Gottstein (1967^{7}) and H. M. Brecher and A. Avrunin (1955, with an English introduction by A. M. Freedman and Hebrew bibliographical essay on concordances by A. R. Malachi) many of its imperfections were corrected. Mandelkern had also begun to work on a Talmud and Midrash concordance, which, however, remained fragmentary and has not been published. Mandelkern's output as a writer, poet, and translator of poetry was equally considerable. They include an early ode to Czar Alexander II, *Teshu'at Melekh Rav* (1866), on his escape from an attempted assassination; a love poem *Bat Sheva* (1866), which earned him praise from Adam ha-Kohen (1896^{2}); aphorisms, *Ḥiẓẓim Shenunim* (1864); and an anthology *Shirei Sefat Ever* (3 vols., 1882–1901), which contained apart from his own poetry translations of great poets from various languages. He also translated Byron's *Hebrew Melodies* into Hebrew as *Shirei Yeshurun* (1890); Mapu's *Ahavat Ẓiyyon* into German, *Thamar* (1885; 1897^{2}, without mentioning the author), and *Ashmat Shomeron* as *Suende Samarias* (1890); and into Russian *Bogdan Chmielnicki* (1878) and Lessing's Fables (1885). Mandelkern expended great mental and physical efforts producing his works and soliciting buyers for his concordance, even traveling to the U. S. in 1899, and late in his life suffered mental illness. He also became increasingly interested in the theory and practice of spiritualism.

Bibliography: Klausner, Sifrut, 5 (1956^{2}), 243ff., incl. bibl.; S. Verba, in: *Hadoar*, 32 (1953), 524–5; G. Bader, *ibid.*, 829; R. Malachi, *ibid.*, 35 (1956), 93ff., 115; Y. H. Zagorodski, in: *Sefer ha-Shanah*, 4 (1903), 291–300. [Ed.]

MANDELSHTAM, LEONID ISAAKOVICH (1879–1944), Soviet physicist. Mandelshtam was born in Odessa and entered the New Russian (Novorossiyskiy) University in Odessa in 1897. He was expelled one year later for taking part in student protests and completed his education at the University of Strasbourg. He returned to Russia in 1914 and in 1918 was appointed professor at the Odessa Technical Institute. In 1925 he became professor of physics at Moscow University. Mandelshtam's main scientific works were in the fields of optics, theory of oscillations, and radiophysics. In his work *Ob opticheski odnorodnykh i mutnykh sredakh* ("On optically isotropic and cloudy media," 1907) he disproved J. W. Rayleigh's theory about molecular dispersion of light and showed that the medium must be anisotropic to be able to disperse light. He made several important contributions to the nonlinear theory of oscillations, and together with N. D. Papaleksi invented a new method of creating electrical oscillations. In radiophysics Mandelshtam solved several problems of propagation of radio waves over the surface of the earth. He also proposed the idea of exact distance measurements with the help of radio waves and together with Papaleski built radiointerferometric distance measuring devices. He also wrote papers about statistical and quantum physics and relativity theory, the philosopical basis of which has been criticized lately by the scientific community. From 1931 to 1936 Mandelshtam served as coeditor with Abram Fyodorovitch *Joffe of *Khimicheskiy Zhurnal*, the journal of the Russian Physico-Chemical Society, Leningrad.

Mandelshtam was awarded the Stalin Prize in 1942 for his work on nonlinear oscillations and propagation of radio waves. In 1945 the Academy of Sciences established two prizes in his name for the best work in physics and radio-physics.

Bibliography: I. V. Kuznetsov (ed.), *Lyudi russkoy nauki*, 1 (1948), 260–71; A. A. Semyonov, in: *Voprosy filosofii*, 3 (1953), 199–206; N. D. Papaleski, in: *Uspekhi fizicheskikh nauk*, 27 no. 2 (1945). [G.E.T.]

MANDELSHTAM, OSIP EMILYEVICH (1891–c. 1938), Soviet-Russian poet. Born into an assimilated Warsaw family, Mandelshtam spent most of his life in Leningrad and became thoroughly identified with the Russian intelligentsia. In 1934 Mandelshtam was arrested, allegedly for writing an epigram satirizing Stalin, was released, then rearrested and exiled to the Far East, where he died in a prison camp. According to some sources, he was insane at the time of his death and was killed by fellow prisoners for stealing their bread.

Mandelshtam is generally acknowledged as one of the most accomplished, refined, and erudite poets in all Russian literature. A vocal opponent of the symbolist movement in Russian poetry, he was a co-founder of acmeism, a literary movement born on the eve of World War I which denounced the symbolists' predilections for mysticism,

Osip Mandelshtam, Soviet-Russian poet. From N. Mandelshtam, *Hope Against Hope*, New York, 1970.

eroticism, and religiosity, proposing instead a return to classical simplicity, clarity, and an emphasis on craftsmanship. His works include the collections *Kamen* ("Stone," 1913) and *Tristia* (1922). His verse is often nourished by historical and literary motifs, particularly from ancient Rome and Greece. His lyric poetry is notable for its highly original imagery, its exquisite craftsmanship, and its rich use of the Russian language. The Revolution of 1917 left almost no imprint on his verse, which remained singularly apolitical and aloof from the ideological preoccupations so characteristic of Russian poetry of the period.

Both Mandelshtam's verse and his poetry demonstrate a painfully neurotic self-hating awareness of his Jewish antecedents. This is particularly true of his collection of essays *Shum vremeni* (1925), which were translated as "The Noise of Time" in C. Brown's *Prose of Osip Mandelstam* (1965). On several occasions he mocks what he describes as the correct but lifeless and artificial-sounding Russian speech of various Russian Jews, including his own father (it is worth noting that he presents his own failure to learn the Hebrew script as probably due to a psychological bloc). Mandelshtam is allergic to "Jewish smells" and to the sounds of the Jewish "jargon" (Yiddish). He detests and fears "the black and yellow stripes" of the *tallit*. Yet he never attempted to conceal his Jewish origin, but continued to brood and write about it. In 1970 his widow Nadezhda published a biography *Hope Against Hope*.

Bibliography: C. Brown, in: O. Mandelshtam, *Sobraniye sochineniy*, 1 (1964), I–XXVI (Eng.); G. P. Struve, *ibid.*, XXVII–LXXX; E. M. Rais, *ibid.*, LXXXI–CII; B. A. Filipov, *ibid.*, 2 (1966), I–XVIII; Y. Gilboa, in: *Maariv* (Dec. 8, 1967), 14–15. [M.F.]

MANDELSTAMM, BENJAMIN (1805–1886), Hebrew author. Born in Zagare, the older brother of Leon *Mandelstamm, he received both a traditional and a secular education. In the 1840s, he moved to Vilna and became one of the extremists in Haskalah circles. In a memorandum which he presented to Max *Lilienthal when the latter visited Vilna in 1842 during his survey of the condition of Russian Jewry, Mandelstamm accused Russian Jewry of six faults which were responsible for their backwardness: (1) Russian Jews do not speak the Russian language, but rather some confused tongue; (2) they dress quaintly; (3) they do not participate sufficiently in the arts; (4) nor in the crafts; (5) they have no factories; and (6) they are neither farmers nor herdsmen. The only solution recognized by Mandelstamm was harsh governmental intervention "forbidding the printing of the Talmud, completely removing from circulation books on the Kabbalah and Ḥasidism, dissolving the *ḥeder* thus removing the teachers (*melammedim*) who devour the children, and educating the children of Israel in Russian." When the enlightened community of Vilna established its own synagogue (*Tohorat ha-Kodesh*), Mandelstamm criticized it sharply for not daring to reform its liturgy and religious customs. In 1877 his writings and memoranda were published in Vienna under the title *Ḥazon Binyamin ben Yosef mi-Ma'aleh ha-Shekedim* (*Ḥazon la-Mo'ed*) with an introduction by Pereẓ *Smolenskin, a collection of great importance for the history of the Russian Haskalah during the 1840s. Mandelstamm also published a collection of aphorisms entitled *Mishlei Binyamin* (in *Ha-Asif*, 1885 and 1886).

Bibliography: Kressel, Leksikon, 2 (1967), 403–4; Zinberg, Sifrut, 6 (1960), 209–12, 214–6. [Y.S.]

MANDELSTAMM, LEON (**Aryeh Loeb**; 1819–1889), writer and adherent of the *Haskalah in Russia. Born in Zagare (Lithuania), Mandelstamm had a thorough religious and general education. In 1840 he became the first Jew to enroll at a Russian university (Moscow) and in 1844 graduated in oriental languages from the University of St. Petersburg. His research concerned the history of political regimes in ancient Israel. During his student years, he produced a book of poetry in Russian (1840). In 1846, after further studies at German universities, Mandelstamm was appointed in charge of Jewish affairs in the Ministry of Education in succession to M. *Lilienthal. He was mainly concerned with establishing a network of government schools for Jews, and supervising the Jewish *ḥeder* and *talmud torah* schools. For this purpose he traveled extensively throughout the *Pale of Settlement and prepared textbooks; these were published by means of funds raised through the *candle tax, and even private Jewish teachers were required to buy them. The books, which contained texts accompanied by German translations, included selections from the Mishnah, an anthology of Maimonides' writings, the Bible along with the *Biur* of Moses *Mendelssohn and his pupils, and the *Kevod Melekh* of R. Jehiel *Heller, which stressed the Jew's religious duty to respect secular kings and rulers. Mandelstamm was dismissed in 1857 as a result of attacks by his opponents among the *maskilim* and wealthier Jews of St. Petersburg who accused him of wasting funds and engaging in activities for his own profit. During his period in office, Mandelstamm corresponded with and met Haskalah leaders and prominent Hebrew writers, often arranging for them to be given posts. After losing his job, he lived for many years in Germany where he engaged in trade and in contracting. He wrote for both the Jewish and general press, and published, in German, several collections of studies in Bible and Talmud. The translation of the Pentateuch into Russian which Mandelstamm had produced in Germany was forbidden in Russia because of the general prohibition on scriptural works which were not approved by the Church. In 1872, however, permission was given to import and reprint his work there, provided that the translation was accompanied by the original Hebrew version. Toward the end of his life Mandelstamm returned to St. Petersburg where he died forgotten and in poverty.

Bibliography: *Ha-Meliẓ*, no. 198 (Sep. 5, 1889), M. P. (Kantor), *ibid.*; no. 199 (Sep. 6, 1889), *ibid.*, no. 201 (Sep. 8, 1889); S. Ginzburg, *Amolike Peterburg* (1944), 74–87; M. Margulis, *Voprosy yevreyskoi zhizni* (1889), 71–147; Ginsburg, in: *Perezhitoye*, 1 (1908), 1–50; L. S. Dawidowicz, *The Golden Tradition* (1967), 154–60. [Y.S.]

MANDELSTAMM, MAX EMMANUEL (1839–1912), ophthalmologist and leading member of the Zionist and Territorialist movements in Russia. Mandelstamm was born in Zagare, Lithuania. His father Ezekiel Mandelstamm, the brother of Leon *Mandelstamm and Benjamin *Mandelstamm, was an educated merchant who wrote a biblical lexicon entitled *The Book of Names* (1862). Mandelstamm was among the first Russian Jews to study in a Russian high school, but he received his main education at the German University of Dorpat (Estonia). After he completed his medical studies at Kharkov University, he continued his studies in ophthalmology in Berlin. Upon his return to Russia he opened a clinic in Kiev and became well known as an expert ophthalmologist throughout southern Russia. Mandelstamm also served as a lecturer in ophthalmology at Kiev University, but he left the university when his candidacy as an associate professor was not approved.

The pogroms in southern Russia at the beginning of the 1880s moved Mandelstamm into the field of Jewish public activities. He was the head of the Committee to Support Victims of Pogroms. At the conference of representatives of Jewish communities in St. Petersburg in 1881, he was the only one to support emigration from Russia as a radical solution to the problems the Jews faced there. From that time, emigration from Russia became the basis for his outlook on public affairs. In 1883 he participated along with L. *Pinsker, M. L. *Lilienblum, and H. *Shapira in a meeting in Odessa at which the foundations of the *Ḥibbat Zion movement in Russia were laid. His wide-ranged organizational work then began and came to an end only after sharp opposition from the authorities.

Mandelstamm joined the Zionist Organization at the First Zionist Congress and from then on was one of *Herzl's most devoted associates and one of the most faithful political Zionists among the Russians. Herzl depicted him in *Altneuland* as the first president of the Jewish state—"an ophthalmologist from Russia, Dr. Eichenstam." He was elected to the Zionist Actions Committee and at the Second Zionist Congress was appointed deputy of the Kiev district. At the Sixth Zionist Congress, Mandelstamm was among the enthusiastic supporters of the *Uganda Scheme and fought for its acceptance even at the *Kharkov Conference. He organized the supporters of the plan to meet the challenge of the Russian Zionists. After the Seventh Zionist Congress he joined I. *Zangwill and participated in the founding conference of the *Jewish Territorial Organization (J.T.A.). The pogroms that accompanied the first Russian Revolution (1905–06) strengthened his conviction that it was imperative to organize the flight of the Jews from Russia through Territorialism. He headed the emigration office established by the Territorialists in Kiev that concerned itself basically with organizing the emigration of Jews destined for *Galveston, Texas (under the Galveston Plan) with the aim of creating a Jewish Territorialist center in the southern United States.

Max Emmanuel Mandelstamm (right), ophthalmologist, with Theodor Herzl. Courtesy Central Zionist Archives, Jerusalem.

Bibliography: D. A. Friedman, in: *Ha-Refu'ah*, 18, no. 4 (1940); Y. Slutsky, in: *He-Avar*, 4 (1956), 56–76; 5 (1957), 44–68; Th. Herzl, *Complete Diaries* (1960), index; I. Klausner, *Be-Hitorer Am* (1962), index; idem, *Mi-Kattowitz ad Basel* (1965), index. [Y.S.]

MANDRAKE (Heb. דּוּדָאִים, apparently connected with דוֹד "beloved"; in the Talmud יַבְרוּחַ), a herb. The *Mandragora officinarum* grows in all regions of Israel. Its thick perennial root penetrates the earth deeply, at times bifurcating. It has no stalk and its large leaves straddle the surface of the

Mandrake *(Mandragora officinarum)*, plant with fruit. Courtesy J. Feliks, Jerusalem. Photo Yosaif Cohain.

ground forming a kind of hollow from whose center violet flowers grow. The yellow fruits, resembling the tomato, ripen in March and April and their intoxicating odor spreads far. The mandrake is mentioned in a description of Israel's spring: "The mandrakes give forth fragrance" (Song 7:14). Many legends circulated about mandrakes. Josephus knew of a plant having medicinal properties, identified by some with mandrake, to uproot which it was necessary to tie a dog to the roots. The animal pulling them out immediately met a vicarious death for its master (Wars, 7:183ff.). An allusion to such a legend is found in the Talmud which forbids the recital of biblical verses while uprooting the mandrake (TJ, Shab. 6:2, 8b). In his *Guide of the Perplexed* (3:29), Maimonides mentions the superstitions of the "deluded" about mandrakes. Similar legends circulated among various peoples almost to the present day. Some connect the legend about the remarkable powers of mandrakes with the biblical story of Reuben, who found mandrakes in the field during the wheat harvest and handed them to his mother Leah (Gen. 30:14–17). Since, however, it was the mother who subsequently conceived and not Rachel who received them, the biblical story may be intended to emphasize that mandrakes do not possess these reputed powers, and that conception and childbirth are a divine gift.

Bibliography: Loew, Flora, 3 (1924), 363–8; R. Patai, *Adam va-Adamah*, 1 (1942), 219; *Ha-Refu'ah*, 22 (1942), 7; 1–4; H. N. and A. L. Moldenke, *Plants of the Bible* (1952), 137–9, no. 132; J. Feliks, *Olam ha-Ẓome'aḥ ha-Mikra'i* (1968²), 192. [J.F.]

MANÉ-KATZ (originally **Emanuel Katz;** 1894–1962), French painter. Mané-Katz was born in Kremenchug, Ukraine. In 1913 he went to study in Paris. He returned to Russia during World War I, working and exhibiting in Petrograd. After the October Revolution of 1917 he returned to Kremenchug, where he taught art. As the city was the scene of continued fighting during the Civil War, there was little chance for him to work and in 1921 he migrated to Paris. He painted assiduously, and a decade

"Rabbi with Torah" by Mané-Katz, 1960. Oil on canvas, 46½×36¼ in. (118×92 cm.). Geneva, Oscar Ghez Collection.

later won a Gold Medal at the Paris World's Fair for his painting "The Wailing Wall." In 1939, Mané-Katz was mobilized and on the fall of France was imprisoned briefly by the Germans. He managed to get to the United States, but returned to Paris after the war. Mané-Katz was an eminent Jewish representative of the School of *Paris. His output was prodigious. He painted so fervently and with so little concern for detail that he seems to be carried away by his own exuberance. His color is sometimes blatant, but rarely coarse. His smaller works, particularly those of the 1920s, show an intensity of expression and a baroque ecstasy. The subject matter of his early works is exclusively Jewish—ḥasidic rabbis, talmudic students, fiddlers and beggars of the Pale of Settlement with meager bony faces and deep-set eyes, the same haggard figures placed against an almost barren background. He later painted the sights of Paris, orchestras, bullfights, the scenery of the Riviera, portraits, and numerous flower pieces, usually with a childlike delight in raw colors. He made several sculptures. He died in Israel and left his collection, including many fine specimens of Jewish ritual art, to the city of Haifa.

Bibliography: M. Ragon, *Mané-Katz* (Fr. and Eng., 1961); A. Werner, *Mané-Katz* (Eng., 1960); J. Aimot, *Mané-Katz* (Fr., 1933). [A.W.]

MANESSIER DE VESOUL (Menssier de Vezou; d. 1375), *"procureur-général"* and *"commissaire"* of the Jews of Langue-d'Oyl (central and northern France) during the reign of *Charles V (1364–80). He was a member of the family of Héliot de *Vesoul, a banker of that town during the early 14th century, and in 1349 he himself was expelled from Vesoul. It was Manessier who, in 1359, negotiated with Charles, duke of Normandy (subsequently King Charles V) for the return of the Jews to France and then acted as the financial intermediary between the Jews of northern France and the monarchy—to his own personal profit as well. In 1374 he secured a further ten-year extension of Jewish right of residence in France. When the Jews were once more obliged to wear a distinctive *badge, he and all his family were exempted. It is not certain whether it was this Manessier or a namesake who was involved in a lawsuit in 1365. After his death (between June 28 and October 1375), his children, his eldest son in particular, succeeded to his functions and privileges (which included complete exemption from the payment of taxes). When his son Joseph was converted to Christianity in 1382 he recovered the family properties, which had previously been seized. Nothing is known of the family after this.

Bibliography: L. Lazard, in: *Annuaire des Archives Israélites de France*, 7 (1890/91), 52–56; R. Anchel, *Juifs de France* (1946), 115f. [B.BL.]

°**MANETHO** (third century B.C.E.), Greco-Egyptian historian. Manetho, native of Sebennytos, Egypt, served as priest in Heliopolis. Thoroughly versed in Egyptian lore, he was also associated with the religious policy of the Ptolemaic dynasty, in particular with the introduction of the cult of Serapis. Manetho was the first Egyptian to give an account of the history of his country in Greek. A number of fragments from this work are preserved in *Contra Apionem* of *Josephus, who apparently did not draw from Manetho's work at first hand, but from extracts in Hellenistic Jewish historians. The fragments fall into two categories, the first of which describes the origin of the rule of the *Hyksos in Egypt (Jos., Apion, 1:73ff.). Manetho (in accordance with later Egyptian accounts) writes that the Hyksos were a nation of alien conquerors who set fire to Egyptian towns, razed the temples of the gods, and treated the natives with cruelty. After their expulsion from Egypt, the Hyksos crossed the desert on their way to Syria, and in "the country called Judea" built a town, which they named Jerusalem. Although Manetho does not mention the Jews by name, he is clearly referring to them. Josephus himself distinguishes between the first group of fragments of Manetho's writings and the second (*ibid.*, 1:228ff.), "where he had recourse to fables and current reports." In this second group of fragments it is stated that the Egyptian king Amenophis wished to be granted a vision of the gods and on the advice of his namesake, Amenophis son of Paapis, decided to purge the country of lepers and other polluted persons. He collected 80,000 people and sent them to work in the quarries east of the Nile. Afterward, acceding to their request, he assigned them Avaris, the ancient capital of the Hyksos, for settlement. Here they appointed as their leader one Osarsiph, a former priest of Heliopolis. Osarsiph decreed that his people should neither worship the gods nor abstain from the flesh of animals reverenced by the Egyptians, and cultivate close connections only with members of their own confederacy. Similarly, he sent representatives to the inhabitants of Jerusalem, who had been expelled from Egypt. Osarsiph's people defeated the Egyptians in a concerted effort, their behavior to the inhabitants being far worse than that of the Hyksos in their day. Here Manetho identifies Osarsiph with Moses.

Some historians completely deny the authenticity of Manetho's entire Osarsiph story, while some object only to his identification of Moses with Osarsiph. However, there are no convincing reasons for doubting the intended identification. The Osarsiph story throughout has much in common with such Egyptian tales as the "Prophecy of the Lamb" or the "Potter's Oracle," which could easily be fused with anti-Jewish elements. The biblical account of the Exodus challenged the Egyptians to provide a suitable answer, and anti-Jewish feelings were common in Egypt even before its conquest by the Greeks. It is therefore unnecessary to postdate Manetho's account to the later Ptolemaic period. The descriptions of the historian *Hecataeus show how easily the story of the Exodus was assimilated into the tale of the expulsion of the strangers because of calamities visited on the Egyptians. Nor was Manetho necessarily the first to combine the story of the lepers with Moses and the Jews. A synthesis, similar though not completely identical, is encountered in subsequent writers. Nevertheless, Manetho may undoubtedly be considered a central figure in the emergence of the anti-Jewish polemical writings of Alexandrian-Greek literature.

Bibliography: V. Tcherikover, *Hellenistic Civilization and the Jews* (1959), 361–4; Schuerer, Gesch, 3 (1909[4]), 529–31; A. von Gutschmid, *Kleine Schriften,* 4 (1893), 419ff.; E. Meyer, *Aegyptische Chronologie* (1904), 71ff.; Meyer Gesch, 2 pt. 1 (1928), 420–6; F. Staehelin, *Antisemitismus des Altertums* (1905), 9ff.; W. Helck, *Untersuchungen zu Manetho und den aegyptischen Koenigslisten* (1956), 38ff.

[M.St.]

°**MANETTI, GIANNOZZO** (1396–1459), Hebraist and humanist. Manetti acquired a wide knowledge of Hebrew language and literature and was even taught to speak Hebrew by a Jewish teacher (later baptized) who lived with him. Manetti took lessons also from a Florentine Jew named Immanuel (probably the loan-banker Manuelo of San Miniato), giving him instruction in philosophy in exchange. Many of the Hebrew manuscripts in the Vatican library were originally in Manetti's possession. He made a Latin translation of the Psalms, which he defended against its critics in a five-volume work. In 1447 Sigismondo Malatesta of Rimini organized a religious *disputation at his court between Manetti and Jewish scholars.

Bibliography: U. Cassuto, *Ebrei a Firenze nell' età del Rinascimento* (1918), 275–7; C. Roth, *Jews in the Renaissance* (1959), 103, 139–40, index; Vespasiano da Bisticci, *Vite di uomini illustri,* ed. by L. Frati, 2 (1893), 33–200 (abbr. Eng. tr. by W. G. and E. Waters, *Vespasiano Memoirs* (1926), 372–95); W. Zorn, *Gianozzo Manetti, seine Stellung in der Renaissance* (Endingen, 1939).

[U.C./Ed.]

MANGER, ITZIK (1901–1969), Yiddish poet, dramatist, and novelist. Manger, who was born in Czernowitz, learned Yiddish folklore and poetry from his father. His first poem was published in 1921 in the Rumanian Yiddish journal *Kultur* and his first book of poems was *Shtern Oyfn Dakh* ("Stars on the Roof," 1929). In this volume, he combined the simplicity of folksongs and of the Yiddish bards with sophisticated stanzaic structures and technical skill. The poems express delight in the entire universe, and find beauty and value even in suffering and sorrow.

Itzik Manger, Yiddish poet. Drawing by Alva, 1941. Courtesy Lewis Sowden, Jerusalem.

Four years later he published more mature poems in *Lamtern in Vint* ("Lantern in the Wind," 1933). In his *Khumesh Lider* ("Pentateuch Songs," 1935), patriarchal figures are portrayed as contemporary Jews, with the thoughts, feelings, and failings of Jews living in the villages of Eastern Europe. For example, when Abraham welcomes the three angels, he is Reb Avrohom the pious Jew, smoking a pipe and wearing a silk skullcap; and when he talks to Sarah, colloquial Yiddish epigrams naturally spice his conversation. Manger's *Megile-Lider* ("Scroll Songs," 1936) recreated the tradition of the Purim play in the form of dramatic lyrics. To the original story of the Book of Esther, he added new incidents and characters, such as the rivalry between the tailor's apprentice Fastrigosse and King Ahasuerus for the love of Queen Esther. These ironic and sentimental lyrics were enthusiastically received when staged as a musical in Israel in 1967 and the next year in English in the United States (music by Dov Seltzer).

Manger also adapted A. *Goldfaden's plays for a post-Goldfaden generation; most successfully *Di Kishufmakherin* ("The Witch") and *Drey Hotzmakhs* (1936, 1937). He paid tribute to Goldfaden, Eliakum Zunser, Berl Broder, and other predecessors in his volume *Noente Geshtalten* (1938, 1961). His most piquant tale is the imaginative novel, *Dos Bukh fun Gan-Eydn* (1939; English tr. by L. Wolf, *The Book of Paradise,* 1965). He depicts Shemuel-Abba, formerly an angel and now a newborn babe who relates his prenatal adventures in Paradise. The story is a double-edged satire on the Eden that people imagine and on the crass realities of shtetl life and foibles.

Soon after the appearance of this work, Manger had to flee the Nazis. He escaped to London where he lived until 1951, when he moved first to New York, and, in 1967, to Israel. Manger's poems were translated into Hebrew, the principal European languages (in English in S. Betsky, *Onions and Cucumbers and Plums* (1958) and in J. Leftwich's *The Golden Peacock* (1961)), and were included in the UNESCO anthology of world poetry in 1961. His short story *The Adventures of Hirschel Summerwind* is in I. Howe and E. Greenberg, *Treasury of Yiddish Stories* (1965), 438–46.

Bibliography: 1961 edition of *Noente Geshtalten,* incl. bibl. by E. H. Jeshurin; LNYL, 5 (1963), 435–43; M. Ravitch, *Mayn Leksikon* (1945), 125–7; N. Meisel, *Forgeher un Mitzeitler* (1946), 394–407; S. Bickel, *Shrayber fun Mayn Dor* (1958), 133–44; J. Glatstein, *In Tokh Genumen* (1956), 306–14; S. Liptzin, *Maturing of Yiddish Literature* (1970), 232–8; Y. Mark, in: JBA, 28 (1970/71).

[S.L.]

MANI (**Mana II**; fourth century C.E.), Palestinian *amora.* His teachers were firstly his father *Jonah, R. Yose (TJ, Ter. 8:9, 46a; Sanh. 3:6, 21a), and then R. Judah III (TJ, Pes. 6:1, 33a; Beẓah 1:1, 60a); he also referred to Hezekiah as his teacher (TJ, Ber. 3:5, 6d, et al.). He visited Caesarea where he attended lectures by R. Isaac b. Eliashib (Ta'an. 23b) and other scholars of that town (e.g., Oshaya b. Shemi, Zerikah, etc). In his early years he lived in Tiberias, but later R. Ḥanina (or Hananiah), the head of the academy in Sepphoris, retired in his favor (TJ, Pes. 6:1, 33a) and he remained there until his death (Eccl. R. 11:3). He held halakhic discussions with Zeira II (Mak. 22a). Z. Frankel dates his death in 399 C.E. (the view of I. Halevy that it was before 355 is untenable). It is not known whether he outlived R. Judah III (the statement in Weiss, Dor, vol. 3, p. 102 is due to a mistranslation of a passage in TJ, Ber. 3:1, 6a: "When R. Judah's sister died, Mani did not attend her funeral"). He appears to have been strict and uncompromising in his halakhic rulings, and he expressed his strong doubts as to the correctness of the permission granted by his father and R. Yose for bread to be baked on the Sabbath for the army of Ursicinus (c. 353 C.E.; TJ, Sanh. 3:5, 21b), despite that fact in a case of extreme emergency he permitted the bakers of Sepphoris to sell their bread in the market on the Sabbath for the army of Proclus (*ibid.;* see Lieberman, in: JQR, 36 (1946), 352–3). He also refused to agree that agricultural activity take place during the sabbatical year in a place called Yabluna on the grounds that it was not in Ereẓ Israel proper. On one occasion he strongly disapproved of his teacher, Judah, making appointments for money (TJ, Bik. 3:3, 65d). Most of his teachings are in *halakhah,* but the few in *aggadah* are of great interest. He explained Saul's reluctance to exterminate the Amalekites, including their children and cattle, on the grounds that they were innocent according to the Torah (Yoma 22b). He also taught that reciting the *Shema* at its proper time was greater than studying the Torah (Ber. 10b). Mani was apparently not altogether easy to get on with. Not only was he not on good terms with the patriarch and his household, who distressed him so much that he had to pray for relief, but in his domestic life he was also unhappy (Ta'an. 23b).

In addition to R. Mani, there was an earlier *amora* called Mana and it is not always certain which is meant. In Ecclesiastes Rabbah 5:4–5 both are found.

Bibliography: Weiss, Dor, 3 (1904[4]), 102–3; Halevy, Dorot, 2 (1923), 373–84; Hyman, Toledot, s.v.; Epstein, Mishnah, 399–404; Ḥ. Albeck, *Mavo la-Talmudim* (1969), 398. [H.FR.]

MANI, family in Iraq and Ereẓ Israel. According to family tradition the family is of Davidic origin and its name is an acrostic of *Mi-Geza Neẓer Yishai.*

ELIJAH BEN SULEIMAN (1818–1899), one of the best-known Iraqi rabbis, was born in Baghdad, where he studied at the Beit Zilka rabbinical academy and was one of the outstanding pupils of R. Abdallah *Somekh. In 1856 he settled in Ereẓ Israel, first in Jerusalem, but two years later he moved to Hebron. He played a prominent role in the development of the Jewish community there. In 1865 he was appointed chief rabbi of Hebron and retained this post until his death. By nature an unassuming and generous man, he was outspoken and adamant in matters of religious observance. He made several journeys on behalf of the Hebron community: to India in 1873; Egypt, 1872 and 1878; and Baghdad 1880. In 1879–80 a fierce argument broke out between R. Elijah and two prominent members of the community, Mercado Romano and R. Raḥamim Joseph Franco, which split the community into two factions. In the end R. Elijah's views prevailed. R. Elijah wrote several books dealing with traditional and mystical Jewish studies. Of these, the following were published: *Zikhronot Eliyahu,* a collection of religious precepts, arranged in alphabetical order, of which two parts appeared

Suleiman Menahem Mani, chief rabbi of Hebron. From O. Avisar (ed.), *Sefer Ḥevron,* Jerusalem, 1970.

(Jerusalem, 1936, 1938); and *Karnot Ẓaddik* (Baghdad, 1867). Many of his responsa were published in the Jerusalem *Me'assef* and in the writings of contemporary rabbinic scholars. [A.B.-Y.]

SULEIMAN MENAHEM (1850–1924), Elijah's eldest son, was appointed *rosh av bet din* in Hebron when his father died. After the death of Ḥayyim Hezekiah *Medini, he was elected chief rabbi of Hebron. ISRAEL (1887–1966), the son of SHALOM EZEKIEL, Elijah's second son, studied law in Paris. During the British Mandate he was appointed magistrate (1927) and district judge in Jaffa (1932). In 1936 he became the first Jewish judge in the newly established Tel Aviv district court. ISAAC MALCHIEL (1860–1933), Elijah's fourth son, became a district judge in Hebron. He was an enthusiastic supporter of *Herzl. In 1901 he moved to Jerusalem to practice law. From 1926 to 1929 he was district judge in Jaffa. His sons-in-law were Daniel *Auster and Giulio *Racah. ELIJAH MOSES (1907–), great-grandson of Elijah, during the Mandatory regime served as a lecturer in the Jerusalem law school. In 1948 he was appointed judge in the district court of Jerusalem, and from 1962 he served as a justice of the Supreme Court of Israel. His brother ABRAHAM (1922–) was professor of physics at the Hebrew University of Jerusalem. MAZAL (Mathilda) *MOSSERI was the daughter of Isaac Malchiel. [ED.]

Bibliography: M. Mani, *Rabbi Eliyahu Mani* (1936); A. Ben-Yacov, in: *Ḥemdat Yisrael... le-Zekher Rabbi Ḥ. Ḥ. Medini* (1946), 89–97; O. Avisar (ed.), *Sefer Ḥevron* (1970), 100–7, 132–4, 153–4.

MANICHAEISM, a system of religious beliefs and doctrines named after Mani or Manes (c. 215–275), who lived and taught in Persia. In his youth he seems to have associated with Jewish-Christian (Elchasaite) sectarians. Manes was put to death for his heretical doctrines, but his teachings spread from the Middle East to Rome and to North Africa where they had numerous adherents in the fourth century. Manichaean documents have also been found in Chinese Turkestan. A curious mixture of diverse gnostic, Persian-Zoroastrian, and other dualistic doctrines (see *Dualism), Manichaeism preached a severe asceticism, including vegetarianism, and survived in small and often clandestine sects into the Middle Ages.

Several heretical movements in medieval Christianity are thought to have been influenced, directly or indirectly by Manichaean sects. Manichaean doctrines seem to have been very influential also during the first centuries of Islam, as witnessed by the anti-dualistic polemics of orthodox apologists and theologians. Dualistic attacks on traditional teachings appear in the ninth and tenth centuries and had to be countered by a polemic reminiscent in some ways of the early rabbinic polemic against gnostic dualism *(shetei rashuyyot).* Saadiah argues against dualism both in his *Book of Beliefs and Opinions* and in his polemical tract against Ḥiwi al-Balkhi. The dualism, however, which he attacked was not just of the Zoroastrian type but seems to have been indebted to contemporary Manichaeism.

Bibliography: G. Widengren, *Mani and Manichaeism* (1965); J. Darmesteter, in: REJ, 28 (1889), 1–15; H. Puech, *Le Manichéisme* (1949). [R.J.Z.W.]

MANI-LEIB (pseudonym of **Mani-Leib Brahinsky;** 1883–1953), Yiddish poet. Mani-Leib arrived in the U.S. in 1905 after having participated in the Russian revolutionary movement. He immediately began to publish original poems in the New York Yiddish daily *Forward,* in leading Yiddish periodicals, and, above all, in the anthologies of the American Yiddish literary movement Di Yunge, whose impressionistic, anti-traditional, art-for-art's-sake poetic principles he helped to establish and followed faithfully. His most prolific year was 1918 when 11 of his books and booklets appeared. His ballads and tales for children were sung and recited in Yiddish schools. In 1925 he was coeditor, with Zishe *Landau and Reuben *Iceland, of

"Night of the Vigil." Initial-word panel and decorated border of a *piyyut* for Passover Eve, from the *Siddur of the Rabbi of Rizin.* South-East Germany, c. 1460. Jerusalem, Israel Museum, ms. 180/53, fol. 296v ($7\frac{3}{8} \times 5\frac{3}{4}$ ins/18.5 × 14.5 cm.).

Insel, one of the principal anthologies of Di Yunge. Mani-Leib was a neoromantic who discovered beauty everywhere. His reputation continued to grow after his death, when several volumes were publised: *Lider un Baladn* ("Songs and Ballads," 2 vols. 1955); *Sonetn* ("Sonnets," 1961); the former volume was reprinted in 1963 with parallel Hebrew translations by Shimshon Meltzer, and an introduction by Itzik *Manger, who was in many respects a kindred spirit. Many of Mani-Leib's lyrics have been set to

Mani-Leib, Yiddish poet. Courtesy YIVO, New York.

music. The second volume of his *Lider un Baladn* contains an extensive bibliography of works by and about him.

Bibliography: Rejzen, Leksikon, 2 (1927), 306–10; LNYL, 5 (1963), 450–7; J. Glatstein, *In Tokh Genumen* (1956), 113–21; S. D. Singer, *Dikhter un Prozaiker* (1959), 5–54; S. Bickel, *Shrayber fun Mayn Dor* 2 (1965), 43–49; A. Tabachnik, *Dikhter un Dikhtung* (1965), 140–69. [S.L.]

°**MANIN, DANIELE** (1804–1857), Italian patriot. Manin's father belonged to the Jewish Medina family who had been converted to Christianity. In 1848 he became president of the revived Venetian Republic and was ultimately appoint-

Daniele Manin, Italian patriot. Jerusalem, J.N.U.L., Schwadron Collection.

ed "dictator." The revolutionary government which he headed distinguished itself by its moderation and financial profits. His cabinet included two Jews: Leon *Pincherle as minister of agriculture and Isaac Pesaro Maurogonato as minister of commerce. After leading fruitlessly the heroic resistance of the city in the long siege by the Austrians, he went into exile in Paris, where he died.

Bibliography: G. M. Trevelyan, *Manin and the Venetian Revolution* (1923); C. Roth, *Venice* (1930), 364–6; Milano, Italia, 363; A. Ottolenghi, in: RMI, 5 (1930/31), 25–35. [G.R.]

MANISCHEWITZ, HIRSCH (1891–1943), U.S. Orthodox rabbi, business executive, and philanthropist. Manischewitz, who was born in Cincinatti, Ohio, was educated in Palestine at several yeshivot during 1901–14. While there he helped organize charitable organizations, and, upon his return to Cincinnati in 1914, he continued his philanthropic activities, serving as president of the Orthodox Jewish Orphan's Home. With his brothers he helped maintain the Rabbi Ber Manischewitz Yeshivah of Jerusalem from 1914 until 1943. Moving to New York in 1931, Manischewitz served from that time until his death as an officer of the family B. Manischewitz Baking Co. and helped to build it up into one of the largest manufacturers of Jewish food

Hirsch Manischewitz, U.S. rabbi, business executive, and philanthropist. Courtesy Elaine Sorki, Haifa. Photo Stern, Herstatt, New York.

products in the United States. He was the U.S. representative of over 30 Palestinian and European institutions and organizations of Jewish higher learning. He also served as vice-president of the Mizrachi Organization of America, and executive board member of Yeshiva College and of the Orthodox Jewish Congregations of America and Canada. [ED.]

MANISSA, identical with the ancient Magnesia, today the chief town of the Turkish province bearing the same name, N.E. of *Izmir. A Jewish community probably existed in Manissa from the first century C.E., but there is no extant information on it. During the Byzantine period, there was a congregation in the town and a synagogue, Eẓ ha-Ḥayyim.

After 1492 groups of Jews expelled from Spain arrived in Manissa; they founded two congregations and two synagogues, Lorca and Toledo. Later, as a result of a dispute which broke out in the town, a third congregation, Shalom, was established. At the end of the 15th century, there were more than 100 Jewish families in the town. With the rising importance of Izmir, and as a result of a plague which broke out in the town in 1617, many families left for Izmir. During this period the local rabbi was R. Aaron *Lapapa. At the beginning of the 19th century, the synagogues were renovated and a plot of land was consecrated for a new cemetery. In 1837, 200 Jews died of the plague. In 1838 the Jewish community numbered about 1,200. There were blood libels against the Jews in the town in 1883 and 1893. In 1891 the first school for boys was founded, and in 1896 this was followed by a school for girls. Both were administered by the Alliance Israélite Universelle. At the beginning of the 20th century the Jewish community numbered about 2,000, out of a total population of some 40,000. During this period two additional synagogues were built. After the conquest of the region by the Greeks in 1919, the Jews continued to support the Turks. They did not fly the Greek flag on their institutions and did not attend the Congress (August 1922) which demanded autonomy for Izmir and its surroundings. When the Greeks retreated in 1922, a great fire broke out in the town, as a result of which a number of Jewish institutions, including the yeshivah, were destroyed. In the late 1930s the community numbered only 30 families. The principal occupations of the Jews were commerce—the export of agricultural products (fruit, tobacco, and raisins) and the import of manufactured goods—and crafts—tailoring, shoemaking, money changing; there were also some farm owners. A few Jews served as physicians in the government hospitals, as judges, and as translators in the foreign consulates of the town. In the mid-20th century many families emigrated to the U.S., South Africa, Egypt, and Israel. By 1970 no Jews were living in Manissa.

Bibliography: Rosanes, Togarmah, 1 (1930^2), 172–3; 5 (1937–38), 57–58; A. Galanté, *Histoire des Juifs d'Anatolie*, 2 (1939), 70–100.

[A.H.]

MANITOBA, province of Canada, in mid-continent, bordered on the south by the United States. The Jewish population of Manitoba is virtually identical with that of metropolitan *Winnipeg; in 1936 90.8% and in 1961 96% of the province's Jewish population lived in Winnipeg. The other centers with organized Jewish communities in 1961 were Portage La Prairie, 111 Jews; Brandon, 101; and Flin Flon, 60.

Among the first Jewish settlers in Manitoba were Jews of Alsatian origin. The mass who settled later and formed the bulk of the community were from Russia and Eastern Europe, a large number coming from the Ukraine and the Volhynia area and others from Belorussia. In 1881 the Manitoba census showed 33 Jewish families in the province—21 families in Winnipeg and 12 in other parts of the province. Manitoba's first congregation was organized in Winnipeg in 1882. By 1891 a total of 791 Jews lived in the province; there were 1,514 in 1901, 10,636 in 1911, and 16,669 in 1921. For almost 40 years, from 1931 to 1970, the Jewish population of Manitoba remained fairly stable at 18,000–20,000, largely as a result of emigration from Manitoba to other Canadian provinces, the United States, Israel, and elsewhere.

Manitoba Jewry has from the outset been as conscious of its ethnicity—emphasizing the Yiddish language and East European folkways and culture—as of its religion. In this respect the community, while perhaps not unique, has built an image of its own, aided by the ethnic variety of Manitoba society.

Jews in Political Life. A. A. Heaps, English-born Labor leader who figured in the Winnipeg strike of 1919, served in the federal parliament for Winnipeg North from 1926 to 1940, first as Labor and later as Co-operative Commonwealth Federation (CCF) member. David Orlikow, a former school trustee who served in the provincial legislature from 1958 to 1962, was elected in 1962 to the federal parliament for the CCF party and in subsequent polling for its successor, the New Democratic Party (NDP).

The first Jewish cabinet member of the provincial legislative was Maitland *Steinkopf, who served as provincial secretary and minister of public utilities in the Progressive Conservative government in 1962–66. He was succeeded in the cabinet by Sydney Spivak, who was minister of trade and commerce. In 1969 five Jewish members were elected to the Manitoba legislature, more than have been elected in one session in any other Canadian provincial legislature. Four were members of the governing party, the NDP, and the fifth, Sydney Spivak, sat in the Opposition ranks. Three of the NDP members attained cabinet rank, something unprecedented in Canadian parliamentary history. These cabinet members were Saul Cherniack, Q.C., deputy premier and minister of finance, a former president of the Jewish Welfare Fund of Winnipeg and of the western region of the Canadian Jewish Congress; Saul Miller, minister of education and youth affairs, a former CJC staff member; and Sydney Green, minister of health and social services. The fourth NDP member elected in 1969 was Cy Gonick, a university professor regarded as spokesman for the radical wing of the party.

Manitoba's first Jewish provincial legislator was S. Hart Green, grandson of Solomon *Hart of New Brunswick; Green served as a Liberal in the legislature in 1910–14 for a constituency with a non-Jewish majority. The second Jew to serve in the legislature was Captain William Tobias, a Conservative who served in 1927–32. Marcus Hyman, a Labor representative, served in 1932–39. Morris Gray (Gurarie), a Russian-born travel agent and an active member of the Labor Zionist movement, served as CCF/NDP member of the legislative assembly for Winnipeg from 1941 to his death in 1966.

J. Freedman was mayor in Flin Flon in 1970, a town of 10,200 with a Jewish population of 60. In 1968 he was elected to his sixth two-year term since 1952. The Pas, a town in northern Manitoba with no organized Jewish community (pop. 5,031), in 1970 had a Jewish mayor, Harry Trager.

Bibliography: A. A. Chiel, *Jews in Manitoba; a Social History* (1961), incl. bibl.; idem, *Jewish Experiences in Early Manitoba* (1955); S. Rosenberg, *Jewish Community in Canada* (1970), 75–90.

[B.G.K.]

MANKOWITZ, WOLF (1924–), English novelist and playwright. Mankowitz was born and raised in London's East End. He studied English at Cambridge, then, like his father, became an antique dealer, revealing his expertise in *Wedgwood* (1953), *The Portland Vase* (1952), and *A Concise Encyclopedia of English Pottery and Porcelain* (1957) with R. G. Haggar. He turned increasingly to literature and wrote a number of books inspired by his childhood recollections of the East End. These include *A Kid for Two Farthings* (1953), the title of which was suggested by the Passover allegorical ditty **Ḥad Gadya; Make Me An Offer* (1952); *The Boychick* (1954); and *The Mendelman Fire* (1957). In his early writing, Mankowitz's Jewishness was somewhat muted, revealing itself merely in a preference for Jewish characters. His typical mingling of humor and pathos comes out strongly in the play, *The Bespoke Overcoat* (1955), a Jewish reworking of a Russian tale by Gogol. Like several of his other stories, this was made into a motion picture. Mankowitz was primarily a humorist with a talent for elaborating anecdotes, but he gradually developed a more astringent tone in his writing, e.g., *Expresso Bongo* (1960), a satire on the world of "pop" music, and in his satirical novel about film-makers, *Cockatrice* (1963). He later devoted himself to screen-writing and to publicity work in support of the Ḥasidic sect of Lubavich.

Bibliography: S. J. Goldsmith, *Twenty 20th Century Jews* (1962), 69–75; JC (March 22, 1968).

[Ed.]

MANN, ABRAHAM AARON OF POSNAN (mid-17th century), Hebrew writer. Mann, who was a *ḥazzan* in Poznan, wrote a short work, *Urim ve-Tummim* (Amsterdam, 1653), dealing with such matters as the proper way to fulfill the ethical commandments, repentance, and the way to achieve the state of **devekut* and the love of God. Instructions are also given regarding correct social behavior, in accordance with Jewish ethics, based directly on talmudic and midrashic ideas. The work is divided into short paragraphs (each beginning with a different letter of the alphabet), arranged in a *notarikon* system forming the author's name several times. The work likewise includes a short ethical poem, also arranged in a *notarikon* system, and, at the end, several brief sermons.

Bibliography: Steinschneider, Cat Bod, 4274; Benjacob, Oẓar, 30, no. 596.

[Y.D.]

MANN, FREDERIC RAND (1903–), U.S. public figure. Mann, who was born in Gomel, Russia, was taken to the U.S. at the age of two. A successful businessman, he had a varied public career. He was appointed a member of the U.S. Mint Assay Commission in 1943, served as director of commerce and city representative of Philadelphia, and as Pennsylvania state government commissioner of the Delaware River Port Authority. President Johnson appointed Mann the first U.S. ambassador to Barbados (1967) and U.S. special representative to the Caribbean islands of Antigua, Dominica, Grenada, St. Lucia, and St. Kitts-Nevis (1968). Active in Jewish affairs, Mann was vice-president of the American Committee for the Weizmann Institute of Science, a founder of the Israel Philharmonic Orchestra, which is housed in the Mann Auditorium in Tel Aviv bearing his name, and treasurer of Dropsie College in Philadelphia. [ED.]

MANN, JACOB (1888–1940), scholar of the *Genizah* period and of the Jews under the Fatimids, and particularly of the *Genizah* fragments. The son of a *shoḥet* from Przemysl, Galicia, where he received a traditional Orthodox

Jacob Mann, authority on the Cairo *Genizah*. From *American Jewish Yearbook, 1941–42.* Philadelphia, Pa.

education, Mann went to London in 1908 where he pursued his secular studies. At the same time he pursued rabbinic studies at Jews' College and qualified for the ministry in 1914. Soon after, he began publishing learned papers, including his excellent series, "The Responsa of the Babylonian Geonim as a Source of Jewish History" (in JQR, 7 (1916/17); 11 (1920/21)). The field in which he was later to distinguish himself as a great scholar was *Genizah* research. Mann for the first time undertook to collect and explain all the documents from the period preceding the Crusades to the fall of the Fatimids. His book, *The Jews in Egypt and in Palestine under the Fatimid Caliphs* (2 vols., 1920–22; printed with introd. by S. D. Goitein, 1970), was a masterpiece *sui generis.* By establishing the dates of a great number of the largely undated *Genizah* documents, Mann provided the chronological framework for the history of the Jews in the Near East. He revealed the great role played by the Jerusalem gaonate in the period before the Crusades and shed new light on the various forces within the Jewish communities then living in the lands ruled by the Fatimids. Although Mann neglected the Arabic documents, abstained avowedly from drawing general conclusions, and was mainly interested in the communal history of the Jews, his work is of lasting value as a great collection of hitherto unknown sources, which he ably deciphered and annotated. After the first volume of the above-mentioned book appeared, Mann went to the United States, first as lecturer at the Hebrew College in Baltimore and a year later as professor at the Hebrew Union College in Cincinnati. There he taught Jewish history and Talmud and continued his research. His second major work, *Texts and Studies in Jewish History and Literature* (2 vols., 1931–35, repr. 1970), contains various documents concerning European Jewry and Geonica and texts elucidating the history of the Karaites in the Near East and in Eastern Europe. In the last years of his life Mann embarked on the study of one of the most difficult branches of Hebrew literature, the Midrashim. In his work, *The Bible as read and preached in the Old Synagogue; a study in the cycles of the reading from Torah and Prophets, as well as from Psalms and in the structure of the Midrashic homilies,* he tried to establish the dependence of the Midrashim from the chapters of the Torah and from the *haftarot* which were read on the Sabbath on cycles of three and one-half years respectively. The first volume of the book was published in 1940. Material left by Mann for the second volume was prepared for publication by Isaiah Sonne; after the latter's death the work was continued by Victor Reichert; it appeared in 1966.

Bibliography: R. Mahler, in: *Yivo Bleter,* 16 (1940), 170–81, incl. bibl.; 17 (1941), 92. [E.A.]

MANN, MENDEL (1916–), Yiddish novelist and painter. Born in Poland, he grew up in villages near Plonsk, and his stories depict with great affection the quietness of rural life and the kindly disposition of villagers. He also studied painting in Warsaw and had several successful exhibitions. After fleeing the Nazis, he fought with the Red Army and upon his discharge in 1945, settled in Lodz where he published his first volume of poems, *Di Shtilkeyt Mont* ("Silence Calls," 1945). A year later, after the pogrom of Kielce, he left Poland and found refuge in the U.S. zone of Germany. There he published his second volume of poems, *Yerushe* ("Heritage," 1947). In 1948 he emigrated to Israel and settled as a farmer in a village on the outskirts of Tel Aviv. He published four volumes of short stories, but his international reputation was based on his war trilogy: *Bay di Toyrn fun Moskve* (1956; *At the Gates of Moscow,* 1963), *Bay der Vaysl* ("At the Vistula," 1958), and *Dos Faln fun Berlin* ("The Fall of Berlin," 1960), an epic which focused on the Jewish lieutenant Misha and a young Jewish woman doctor, both persecuted by a Soviet commissar because of their Jewish origin and character. Mann's protest against force and brutality was also expressed in his book *Nakht iber Glushina* ("Night Over Glushina," 1957). In Tel Aviv, Mann was coeditor of the Yiddish literary monthly *Di *Goldene Keyt.* After a decade in Israel, he was overcome by restlessness and a longing for Paris, the center of art, and went there to settle. His trilogy was translated into eight languages including English and French and widely praised. In Paris he wrote his novel, *Al Naharoys Poyln* ("By the Rivers of Poland," 1962), which dealt with Jewish life in Poland between the two world wars. Then his main interest shifted to painting again and in 1967 an exhibition in Paris won the acclaim of art critics.

Bibliography: LNYL, 5 (1963), 431–4; M. Ravitch, *Mayn Leksikon,* 3 (1958), 250ff.; A. Lis, *Heym un Doyer* (1960), 122–6; J. Glatstein, *Mit Mayne Fartogbikher* (1963), 427–32; S. Bickel, *Shrayber fun Mayn Dor,* 2 (1965), 408–19. [J.SCH.]

°**MANN, THOMAS** (1875–1955), German novelist and the leader of Germany's anti-Nazi intellectuals. Mann married Katja Pringsheim, daughter of Alfred Pringsheim (1850–1941), professor of mathematics at Munich University, who was Jewish. It was the Berlin Jewish publisher, Samuel *Fischer, who launched him on his literary career. He introduced positive Jewish characters in three of his masterpieces—*Koenigliche Hoheit* (1909), *Der Zauberberg* (1924; *The Magic Mountain,* 1927), and *Doktor Faustus* (1947; Eng., 1949)—but before the rise of Hitler avoided involvement in Jewish matters. When Jacob *Wassermann, in 1921, voiced his despair at the prevalence of anti-Semitism in Germany, Mann answered his fellow-novelist that Germany was the country least suited for the growth of this evil. When Hitler came to power, Mann, unlike his brother Heinrich (1871–1950) and his children, at first remained silent about the Nazi regime, hoping that it would prove to be only a brief aberration of the German people. Nevertheless, he went into voluntary exile. In 1936 he broke his silence on the persecution of German Jews. While disclaiming the appellation "philo-Semite," Mann expressed his repugnance for German anti-Semitism as the product of a racial myth designed for the rabble, and urged Jews not to despair: having survived many storms in the past, they would outlive this new oppression too. The Nazis promptly deprived him of German citizenship. During the early Nazi years he was at work on his prose epic *Joseph und seine Brueder* (4 vols., 1933–42, *Joseph and his Brothers*, 1934–45), the most profound treatment of this biblical theme in literature. At the beginning of World War II he broadcast regularly to Germany from the B.B.C. until, in 1941, he went to the United States. He lived there until 1952, when he moved to Switzerland.

In 1942, when news of the extermination of the Jews reached him, Mann broadcast the information, hoping it would reach German listeners. In 1943 he called attention to the "maniacal resolution" of the Nazis to exterminate the Jews totally. He begged the United States not to cling bureaucratically to its immigration laws while millions of Jews were being massacred, but to prove by a modification of those laws that the war was indeed being waged for humanity and human dignity.

His eldest child, ERIKA MANN (1905–1969), trained as an actress, directed *Die Pfeffermuehle*, an anti-Nazi cabaret. She went into exile after 1933 and was in the U.S. from 1936, became a war correspondent, and eventually settled in Switzerland. Her works include *Zehn Millionen Kinder. Die Erziehung deutscher Jugend im 3. Reich* (1938) and *Das letzte Jahr* (1956), a biography of her father. She was an outspoken critic of post-World War II German democracy. Her brother, KLAUS MANN (1906–1949), an anti-Nazi writer and journalist, also resumed his career in the U.S. He wrote various novels and an autobiography, *The Turning Point* (1944; German ed., 1952). He and his sister also published *Escape to Life* (1939), about the talented victims of Hitlerism. Klaus Mann committed suicide in Cannes. His public views on the Jewish question from the years 1936–48 were published in 1966 (*Sieben Manifeste zur juedischen Frage*, ed. by W. A. Berendsohn).

Bibliography: A. Eloesser, *Thomas Mann, sein Leben und sein Werk* (1925); K. Hamburger, *Thomas Manns Roman "Joseph und seine Brueder"* (1945). [S.L.]

MANNA (Heb. מָן), referred to as "bread from heaven" (Ex. 16:4; cf. Ps. 105:40). Manna is described in Exodus as coming down in the wilderness of Sinai within the area of the Israelites' encampment every morning except on Sabbaths in the form of "a fine, scale-like thing, fine as the hoarfrost on the ground." The Israelites collected "an *omer* a head," which they ate within 24 hours, for if left until the next morning it bred worms and rotted. When the sun shone on the ground the manna melted. The double portion collected on the sixth day, however, did not rot and sufficed also for the Sabbath when no manna fell. In form "it was like coriander seed, but white; and the taste of it was like wafers made with honey." For 40 consecutive years the Israelites ate the manna, "until they came to the land of Canaan" (Ex. 16:26–36).

Some, drawing an analogy between the manna and the quails, which also miraculously descended to the children of Israel, contend that, like the latter, the manna was a phenomenon of nature which sometimes occurs in the wilderness of Sinai. Something similar is stated by Josephus (Ant. 3:26ff.): "And to this very day all that region is watered by a rain like to that which then the Deity sent down for men's sustenance." As early as from the time of St. Anthony (c. 250–355 C.E.), Christian pilgrims tell of a tradition, current among the monks of the monastery of St. Catherine in Sinai, that the biblical manna comes from the secretion of insects on the branches of tamarisk trees, which to this day grow in the wadis of the southern Sinai mountains. Bodenheimer has suggested a similar explanation of the origin of the manna. Two genera of coccidae parasitize on tamarisk trees of the species *Tamarix mannifera*. On those growing in the Arabah Valley, in the lowlands of the southern Negev, and in Sinai, there are large numbers of the coccus *Najacoccus serpentinus minon*, which is covered with a pocket in the form of an elongated tube in which it lays its eggs. Another coccus, the *Tradutina mannipara*, lays its eggs in a cone-like pocket. These two coccidae extract the sap, rich in carbohydrates, of the branches of the tamarisk, the excess carbohydrates which their bodies cannot absorb being secreted in the form of drops of transparent liquid that congeal into white globules, composed chemically of glucose, fructose, and a very small quantity of pectin. The globules melt in the heat of the sun. A large proportion of these globules of "manna" is eaten by ants, which collect them in their nests. In years of plentiful rain, the Sinai Bedouin, who also call the globules *man*, gather as much as 600 kilograms (about 1,300 lbs.) of them, which they use as a substitute for honey.

Figure 1. *Tamarix mannifera* tree growing near St. Catherine's Monastery in the Sinai Peninsula. Some scholars believe this was the source of manna. Photo Richard Cleave, Jerusalem.

Although there is some resemblance between this "manna" and that described in the Pentateuch, and despite the importance of the early tradition supporting that identification, it is very doubtful whether this is the manna of the Bible, lacking, as it does several features of the biblical food. There is the additional fact that the nutritional value of the "manna" produced by the cocci of the tamarisk is very slight, since it contains no proteins at all, whereas the Pentateuch speaks of the manna as "bread" and as a basic food. And finally, the quantity of this "manna" is not enough to feed a tribe or even a family, let alone a nation wandering in the wilderness. Some identify the biblical manna with the *Lecanora esculenta*, a species of lichen, large quantities of which are sometimes borne by winds to the central Asian steppes and to the heights of the Atlas Mountains. This species, however, has thus far not been found in the Arabian Peninsula or in the neighborhood of Israel. [J.F.]

In the Aggadah. Manna was one of the ten objects created in the twilight on the eve of the Sabbath of Creation (Avot 5:6). It was ground by the angels in heaven (Tanḥ. B., Ex. 67), where manna is constantly being prepared for the future use of the pious (Ḥag. 12b). Manna deserved its name, "bread of the angels" (lit. "bread of the mighty" לֶחֶם אַבִּירִים, Ps. 78:25) because those who ate it became equal to the angels in strength. Furthermore, like angels, they had no need of relieving themselves since the manna was entirely dissolved in their bodies (Tanḥ. B., Ex. 67), and it was not until they sinned by complaining about the taste of the manna that they once again had to relieve themselves like ordinary mortals (Yoma 75b). Each day sufficient manna to sustain the Jewish people for 2,000 years fell (Tanḥ. B., Ex. 66), and this spared the Israelites the need of carrying it during their wanderings, and thus also of enjoying it while it was still hot. Receiving a new supply every day constantly made them turn their hearts to God for their daily bread (Yoma 76a).

Before the manna fell, a north wind swept the surface of the desert, which the rain then washed clean; dew next descended and was congealed into a solid substance by the wind so that it would serve as a table for the manna which next fell from heaven; it was then covered by another layer of dew which protected it from vermin and insects (Mekh., Va-Yassa, 4). The manna fell directly in front of the homes of the righteous, but the average person had to go out and gather it, and the wicked had to go far from the camp to attain their share (Yoma 75a). At the fourth hour of the day when the manna melted, it formed a river from which the righteous will drink in the hereafter. The heathens also attempted to drink out of these streams, but the manna that tasted so delicious to the Israelites had a bitter taste in their mouths. They could enjoy it only indirectly, by catching and eating animals that drank of the melted manna; even in this form it was so delicious that the heathens cried, "Happy is the people that is thus favored" (Tanḥ. B., Ex. 67). There was no need to cook or bake the manna. It contained the flavor of every conceivable dish.

Figure 2. Aaron distributing portions of manna. Detail from the 14th-century *Sarajevo Haggadah* (fol. 29) from Spain. Sarajevo National Museum.

One had only to desire a specific food, and the manna assumed its taste (Yoma 75a). To the child it tasted like milk, to the adolescent like bread, to the old like honey, and to the sick like barley steeped in oil and honey (*ibid.*). The manna exhaled a fragrant odor, and served the women as perfume and cosmetics. Together with manna, precious stones and pearls also fell down from heaven to the Israelites (Yoma 75a).

The amount of manna gathered by each family was found to correspond to the number of its members. This rendered the manna useful in solving many difficult problems. For instance, when two people came before Moses, one accusing the other of having stolen his slave and the other claiming to have bought the slave, Moses deferred his decision to the following morning, when the quantity of manna in their respective houses revealed to whom the slave truly belonged (Yoma 75a). When, many centuries later, the prophet Jeremiah exhorted his contemporaries to study the Torah, they responded by saying, "How shall we maintain ourselves?" The prophet then brought forth the vessel with manna which had been placed in the Temple, and exclaimed: "O generation, see ye the word of the Lord; see what it was that served your fathers as food when they applied themselves to the study of the Torah. You, too, will be supported by God in the same way if you will devote yourself to the study of the Torah" (Mekh., Va-Yassa, 6). When the destruction of the Temple was imminent, the vessel with manna was concealed along with the Ark and the sacred oil. In the messianic period, the prophet Elijah will restore all those hidden objects (*ibid.*).

[Ed.]

Bibliography: F. S. Bodenheimer, *Ha-Ḥai be-Arẓot ha-Mikra*, 2 (1956), 297–302; F. S. Bodenheimer and O. Theodor, *Ergebnisse der Sinai-Expedition 1927* (1929); Kaiser, in: ZDPV, 53 (1930), 63–75; Ginzberg, Legends, index; B. J. Malina, *Palestinian Manna Tradition* (1968).

MANNE, MORDECAI ẒEVI (1859–1886), Hebrew lyric poet and artist. Born near Vilna, he was sent at the age of 13 to study at yeshivot in Minsk. After his talent for painting was discovered he went to Vilna and enrolled at its school of art. He taught himself Russian and general studies, and wrote his first poems, lyrical studies of nature. In 1880 he was accepted as a student at the Academy of Arts in St. Petersburg (Leningrad). On the recommendation of A. *Zederbaum, Manne's studies were subsidized by A. Kaufman, a wealthy communal leader, and he served as his Hebrew secretary. He contributed poems and articles to *Ha-Meliẓ* and *Ha-Ẓefirah* under the pen name Ha-Meẓayyer ("the painter"; also Heb. acronym of—Mordecai Ẓevi yelid Radoshkewitz). In 1884 he went to Warsaw and contributed to Nahum *Sokolow's *Ha-Asif* and S. P. *Rabinowitz' *Keneset Yisrael*, designing the covers of both anthologies. A victim of tuberculosis, his health deteriorated after 1884. At the end of his life he wrote a popular poem, *Masat Nafshi*, wherein he expressed his longing for Palestine. Only a part of his poems and articles were published during his lifetime; his collected works appeared after his death, edited by his friend, A. L. Schoenhaus (1897).

Manne's poetry displays an individual lyricism, and he is at his best in descriptions of nature, in which his talents as writer and painter fuse. His poems are clearly influenced by the classical Russian and German poetry which he translated extensively. In his critical articles he wrote that "the poem and the poetic phrase have no purpose outside themselves, they are in themselves a purpose." Manne dreamed of "artists who loved their people and their religion," and who would devote themselves to depicting the beauty, the sacred values, and the history of Israel. A list of his works translated into English appears in Goell, Bibliography, p. 34.

Bibliography: *Kol Kitvei Manne* (1897), preface by Schoenhaus; J. Klausner, *Yoẓerim u-Vonim*, 1 (1944), 258–72; H. Toren, in: *Moznayim*, 22 (1946), 18–26, 97, 101, 156–63, incl. bibl.; Waxman, Literature, 4 (1960²), 207–10. [Y.S.]

MANNES, LEOPOLD (1899–1964), U.S. pianist and co-inventor with Leopold *Godowsky of the Kodachrome color process. He was born in New York, the son of David Mannes, the violinist and conductor of the New York Symphony Orchestra. He studied musical composition in Rome and was an accomplished pianist. He worked with Godowsky and together they found a successful method of producing color film. They experimented in the Eastman Kodak Laboratories in Rochester, New York. In 1939 Mannes left Rochester and joined his father as codirector of the Mannes School of Music. In 1953 he reorganized it as Mannes College of Music of which he was president. [Ed.]

MANNHEIM, city in Baden, W. Germany. Jews first settled in Mannheim (which was founded in 1606) around 1652, and the first rabbi, Naphtali Herz, served from 1657 to 1671. The community was granted a highly favorable charter in 1660. A cemetery was acquired a year later (in use till 1839), and a synagogue and *mikveh* were built in 1664. In 1663 there were 15 Jewish families in the town, two of them Portuguese, founders of a Portuguese community that later maintained its own schoolteacher and enjoyed particular privileges. In 1674 the *ḥevra kaddisha (Kippe)* was established. By 1680 there were 78 Jewish families in Mannheim; in 1689 they aided the burghers in the defense of the city against the French; on its destruction they took refuge in the communities of *Heidelberg and *Frankfort. Eighty-four families had returned to the city by 1691 when a new charter was issued. Modeled on the first one, it included the Portuguese, fixed the number of tolerated families at 86 (increased to 150 in 1698), established an interest rate of 5%, and abolished the yellow *badge. The charter of 1717 (also including the Portuguese) raised the number of tolerated families to 200 and permitted an interest rate of 10%. The favorable position of the Jews there is expressed in a contemporary reference to Mannheim as "New Jerusalem." There were many local followers of *Shabbetai Ẓevi in the community, vigorously opposed by its rabbi, Samuel Helmann (1726–51). In 1708 the synagogue and *ḥeder (klaus)*, donated by Lemle Moses Rheinganum, was consecrated and later endowed with 100,000 gulden (it remained in use until 1940). Soon after it was considerably enlarged. An unsuccessful attempt was made when the Jewish charter was renewed in 1765 to establish a separate Jewish quarter. Political emancipation came in 1807, followed by full civil rights in 1862. The main synagogue was consecrated in 1855. A public elementary school was in existence between 1821 and 1870. The number of families increased from 225 in 1761 to 247 in 1771, and the number of Jews in Mannheim rose from 940 in 1801, to 4,249 in 1885, 6,402 in 1913, and 6,400 (2.3% of the total population) in 1933. The community issued a monthly bulletin (1922–38) and maintained a *Lehrhaus* (school for adults) between 1922 and 1938, as well as numerous charitable, cultural, and social organizations. Jews were active in the social, cultural, and political life of the city.

Drawing of the main synagogue of Mannheim, consecrated in 1855, and destroyed in 1938 by the Nazis. Courtesy Mannheim Municipality.

The interior of the synagogue was demolished on April 1, 1933. By 1938 only 3,000 Jews remained. On Nov. 10, 1938, the main synagogue was burned and the community was forced to transfer the remains of 3,586 bodies interned in the old cemetery to the public one. On Oct. 22, 1940, 2,000 Jews were deported to the concentration camp of *Gurs and the remainder to Auschwitz a year later. After World War II, Jews returned to Mannheim; they numbered 68 in 1945 and 386 in January 1970. A new synagogue was opened in 1957.

Bibliography: F. Hundsnurscher and G. Taddey, *Die juedischen Gemeinden in Baden* (1968), 186–96; I. Unna, in: JJLG, 17 (1926), 133–46; idem, in ZGJD, 1 (1929), 322–8; 3 (1931), 277–8; B. Rosenthal, *Heimatgeschichte der badischen Juden* (1927), 110, 129, 330f.; idem, in: ZGJD, 5 (1934), 192–9; 7 (1937), 98–102; idem, in: *C. V. Kalender* (1930), 13–18; H. Eppstein-Strauss, in: *Juedische Wohlfahrtspflege und Sozialpolitik*, 1 (1930), 465–72. [L.Lew./Ed.]

MANNHEIM, HERMANN (1889–), lawyer and criminologist, pioneer of the teaching of criminology in Britain. Born in Russia of German parents, Mannheim was educated in Germany. He combined his work as a judge in the Berlin criminal and appeals court with that of a professor of criminal law at Berlin University. When in 1933 his career in Germany came to an end he had already achieved a position of both judicial and academic eminence. In 1934 Mannheim settled in England where he continued his studies in the sociological and psychological problems connected with crime and punishment and introduced the systematic teaching of criminology into British universities. His courses at the London School of Economics, where the post of reader in criminology was created for him in 1946, were attended by social scientists, lawyers, psychologists, and psychiatrists from all over the world. In those years Mannheim already wrote some of his influential books, among them: *The Dilemma of Penal Reform* (1939), *War and Crime* (1941), and *Criminal Justice and Social Reconstruction* (1946, 2nd ed. 1949, 3rd ed. 1967). He took a leading part in the establishment and the development of almost every important scientific and public activity aiming at the study of crime, the understanding of the offender, and the peno-correctional treatment of delinquents and criminals. For several years he served as president of the scientific committee of the International Criminological Society. He was co-founder and coeditor of the *British Journal of Criminology* (1950–66) and of the International Library of Criminology. The London Institute for the Study and Treatment of Delinquency, and the Howard League for Penal Reform were among the causes to which he dedicated his life. In 1955 he published (together with L. T. Wilkins) his: *Prediction Methods in Relation to Borstal*

Training, the first examination in Britain of the efficacy of penal methods. The Home Office adopted its findings in the administration of the Borstal and prison services. His textbook, *Comparative Criminology* (2 vols., 1965), is the definitive statement on the study of crime in the United States, Britain, and Continental Europe, dealing with the causes of crime, the sociological, psychological, and physical factors involved, and also critically analyzing the various methods used in criminological research. He edited *Pioneers in Criminology*, which has become one of the basic readings for the student of criminology in the Anglo-Saxon world.

Bibliography: T. Grygier et al. (eds.), *Essays in Honour of Hermann Mannheim* (1965), includes a full bibliography. [Z.H.]

MANNHEIM, KARL (1893–1947), sociologist. Born in Budapest, Mannheim was a student of Max Weber in Heidelberg. He was professor of sociology in Frankfort in 1930, emigrating in 1933 to London, where he taught at the London School of Economics until his death.

Combining influences coming from Marx, Dilthey, and Max Weber, Mannheim became—together with the philosopher Max Scholer—the initiator of the sociology of knowledge. This branch of sociology is based on the conviction that cognition is not a purely intellectual act but formed by vital relations which are non-theoretical in character and largely defined by the position of the actor in the social structure. Cognition is based on volition and volition, in turn, on the antecedents and concrete circumstances of a person's life. Mannheim denied that this view was leading to sociological relativism or to a disparagement of the spirit; rather, in his opinion, the mind was to be set free by the recognition of the nonrational roots of a consciousness.

After his emigration, Mannheim's interest turned largely toward the problem which was posed by the rise of Nazism, namely, how democracy in a period of mass movements could be prevented from sliding into totalitarian dictatorship. Mannheim's thesis was that *laissez-faire* liberalism, through loosening all societal bonds, would carry with it the danger of totalitarianism and that a fighting democracy would have to "plan for freedom"; the intention ought to be to guarantee the values of personality by means of social regulation. He even went so far as to suggest the cooperation of sociology and theology to that end. Mannheim's early work, *Ideologie und Utopie* (1929; Eng. trans., 1936), opposes "utopian" thinking, carried by the discontented and emphasizing change, to "ideological" thinking which is essentially conservative in nature. Still earlier appeared *Die Strukturanalyse der Erkenntnistheorie* ("The Structural Analysis of Knowledge"; 1922), "Das Problem einer Soziologie des Wissens" (in: *Archiv fuer Sozialwissenschaft und Sozialpolitik*, 53 (1925), 577–652). and "Das Konservative Denken" (in: *Archiv fuer Sozialwissenschaft und Sozialpolitik*, 57 (1927), 68–142; 470–95). The major works of Mannheim's second period are *Man and Society in an Age of Reconstruction* (1940) and *Diagnosis of our Time* (1943). Three posthumous publications were: *Freedom, Power and Democratic Planning* (1950), *Essays on Sociology and Social Psychology* (1953), and *Systematic Sociology* (1958).

Bibliography: J. J. P. Maquet, *Sociology of Knowledge . . . a Critical Analysis of the Systems of Karl Mannheim and Pitirim A. Sorokin* (1951); D. Kettler, *Marxismus und Kultur: Mannheim und Lukacs in den ungarischen Revolutionen [1918/19]* (1967); E. Manheim, in: *The American Journal of Sociology*, 52 (1947), 471–4 (includes list of his publications); A. Salomon, in: *Social Research*, (1947), 350–64. [W.J.C.]

MANNHEIMER, ISAAC NOAH (1793–1865), Vienna preacher and creator of a moderate, compromise Reform ritual. Born in Copenhagen, he was the son of a Hungarian *ḥazzan*. He received his general education at the local secular school and studied Hebrew literature and Talmud

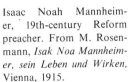

Isaac Noah Mannheimer, 19th-century Reform preacher. From M. Rosenmann, *Isak Noa Mannheimer, sein Leben und Wirken*, Vienna, 1915.

with R. Gedaliah Moses, the liberal pedagogue of Copenhagen. While attending the university of Copenhagen he continued with his talmudic studies. When in 1816 the Danish government issued regulations for Jewish religious instruction, he was appointed head teacher of religion (*Hauptkatechet*) and entrusted with the task of examining his students and preparing them for confirmation. The first confirmation took place with considerable fervor on May 9, 1817, with the accompaniment of organ music and in the presence of high state and university officials. He held services every Wednesday evening for adherents of *Reform Judaism that were characterized by the total elimination of the Hebrew language and the use of music by Christian composers. Mannheimer preached in the Danish language, much to the dismay of the traditional majority of the community who lodged an official protest with the government. In 1821 he went to Berlin to conduct services in the Reform synagogue, then to Vienna, and back to Copenhagen. He finally left Copenhagen to preach in 1823 in Hamburg and then went to Leipzig. At the suggestion of Lazar *Biedermann, he was asked in 1824 to officiate at the new Seitenstetten Synagogue in Vienna. Since Jews in Vienna were not permitted to constitute a community at that time, he was officially known as headmaster of the religious school. Mannheimer became one of the leading preachers of the 19th century, attracting all segments of the Jewish population; he adhered to an inspirational rather than didactic concept of preaching. His sermons, in which the *aggadah* was translated into modern terms, remained classical in form and content, yet they were the least rule bound and formalistic of contemporary sermons. Moreover, he was not reluctant to acknowledge his debt to Christian masters of the art of preaching. In his mature years in Vienna he rejected radical Reform and adopted a middle course in his service, eliminating some traditions without destroying their essence. He insisted on Hebrew as the language of worship, retained the prayers of Zion and Jerusalem, did not incorporate organ music into the service, and vigorously defended circumcision as a ritual of fundamental importance. In creating a form of worship known as "worship according to Mannheimer" (or "the Viennese rite") he prevented a split in the community, and became a pioneer in this type of service in the communities of Austria, Hungary, and Bohemia. His service was also imitated in some German communities.

Despite his moderate Reform tendencies, Mannheimer was strongly attacked by the *Orthodox community. He helped to foster reforms in religious education, retaining Hebrew as an important element and introduced birth, marriage, and death registers into the community. He also helped to found a number of charitable and cultural organizations and fought for the rights of the Jews in general society; with great persistence he sought to gain legal recognition of the Viennese community. Together with 24 Austrian rabbis he achieved the abolishment of the *oath *more judaico*, although his own modified form was not fully accepted. In 1842 he successfully defeated the proposal of Professor Rosas to limit the number of Jewish medical students.

During the revolution in 1848 Mannheimer delivered an eloquent eulogy on two of its Jewish victims who were buried together with Christian victims in a Christian cemetery (March 17). On March 31, 1848 he published a "Declaration on the Jewish Problem" and submitted an effective draft law to the political commission. In the same year the city of Brody elected him to the Reichstag, where, in cooperation with A. *Fischhof and the rabbi D. B. *Meisels, he succeeded in obtaining the removal of the "Jews' tax." Nevertheless, he warned the Jewish community against pleading on its own behalf. Jewish emancipation, he said, might be discussed, but only after it had been broached by the non-Jews. In the Reichstag he made a striking plea for abolishing the death penalty. The Vienna community, whose subservient attitude to the government he criticized, tried to restrict his liberal activity, in part out of concern that his outspokenness might embroil them with the increasingly reactionary forces in the government. They even sought to censor his utterances in the Reichstag. Reluctantly Mannheimer eventually withdrew from political life.

Mannheimer's most important literary work is the exemplary German translation of the prayer book and the festival prayers (Vienna, 1840, later in a number of editions). Of his sermons there have been published *Prädikender holdne ved det mosaiske Troessamfunds Andagts övelser i Modersmaalet i Sommerhalbaaret 1819* (Copenhagen, 1819), and *Gottesdienstliche Vortraege ueber die Wochenabschnitte des Jahres* (vol. 1, on Genesis and Exodus, 1834); *Gottesdienstliche Vortraege gehalten im Monat Tishri 5594* (1834). A posthumous edition of additional sermons was published by B. Hammerschlag (1876). Some of his sermons on Genesis and Exodus were translated in Hebrew by E. Kuttner and published under the title *Mei No'aḥ* (1865). Of importance, too, are his *Gutachten fuer das Gebetbuch des Hamburger Tempels* (1841), and *Gutachten gegen die Reformpartei in Frankfurt a. M. in Angelegenheit der Beschneidungsfrage* (1843).

Bibliography: G. Wolf, *Isak Noa Mannheimer* (1863); idem, *Geschichte der Kultusgemeinde in Wien* (1861), 43–54; M. Rosenmann, *Isak Noa Mannheimer...* (1915²); idem, in: AZDJ, 86 (1922), 30f.; M. Bisstritz (ed.), *Mannheimer-Album* (1864); MGWJ, 61 (1917), correspondence with L. Zunz; L. A. Frankel, *Zur Geschichte der Juden in Wien* (1853), 66f.; L. Geiger, in: AZDJ, 59 (1895), 271–3; M. Grunwald, *Vienna* (1936), index; A. Altmann, *Studies in 19th Century Jewish Intellectual History* (1964), index; S. Baron, in: PAAJR, 20 (1951), 1–17; G. Weil, in: JJS, 8 (1957), 91–101.

[B.Su./Ed.]

MANNHEIMER, THEODOR (1833–1900), Swedish banker. Mannheimer is regarded, with A. O. Wallenberg, a non-Jew, as the founder of modern Swedish banking. Born in Copenhagen, he settled in Goteborg, Sweden in 1855 and began his business career in the grain trade. Subsequently, he turned to banking, and by 1864 became managing director of the newly founded Skandinaviska Kreditaktiebolaget (Scandinavian Joint Stock Credit Company, now known as the Skandinaviska Banken), which was the first of its kind in Sweden. Under Mannheimer's leadership the Skandinaviska Banken soon became Sweden's most important financial institution, chiefly concerned with placing securities for industries and communications. Mannheimer was also deeply involved in railway and mining enterprises. From 1870 to 1876 and from 1881 to 1894 he was a member of the Goteborg municipal council.

Bibliography: *Svenska män och kvinnor*, 6 (1949). [H.V./Ed.]

MANOAH OF NARBONNE (end of 13th and first half of 14th century), Provençal scholar. No biographical details are known of him. Even the name of his father is uncertain (see Hurvitz in bibl.). Some (Geiger, according to Isaac b. Sheshet, resp. no. 85, and Samuel b. Meshullam Gerondi, *Ohel Mo'ed* pt. 1, Jerusalem 1886 ed., 88b) are of the opinion that his father's name was Simeon; others (Zunz, Gross, and the New York-Schulsinger publishers of Maimonides Yad) without giving reasons state that it was Jacob. A third view is that there were two scholars named Manoah—one, the subject of this article, whose patronymic is unknown, and a second, the son of Simeon, mentioned in the above responsa, who was the author of *Hilkhot Terefot*. Manoah's teachers were Meir b. Simeon ha-Me'ili and Reuben b. Ḥayyim. Internal evidence suggests that he was active in Narbonne (ch. 12 of *Hilkhot Tefillah:* "the custom of this town, Narbonne" quoted in the *Shem ha-Gedolim* of Azulai).

Of his works in the sphere of rabbinical literature, that on Maimonides' *Mishneh Torah* on the laws of leavened and unleavened bread, *shofar*, the Day of Atonement, *sukkah*, and *lulav* has been published (Constantinople, 1718; with the commentary of Simeon Sidon, 1879). An additional portion on the laws of the reading of the *Shema*, prayer, and the priestly and other blessings is extant in manuscript (Moscow-Guenzburg no. 123). This may be the manuscript seen by Ḥ. J. D. Azulai (*Shem ha-Gedolim*, 1 (1852), 126 no. 46). An excerpt from this section was published by Hurvitz in *Talpioth*, 9 (1965). This work is much quoted by Joseph Caro in his *Beit Yosef* and *Kesef Mishneh*.

Bibliography: A. Geiger, *Kevuẓat Ma'amarim*, ed. by S. A. Poznański (1910), 254; S. M. Chones, *Toledot ha-Posekim* (1910), 348; Hurvitz, in: *Talpioth*, 9 (1965), 136–76, 490–3.

[S.Z.H.]

MANOSQUE, town in the department of Basses-Alpes, S. E. France. Jews are mentioned in Manosque from 1240. In 1261 the community was already sufficiently numerous to maintain two butcher's stores. Before the *Black Death in 1348, there were about 30 Jewish families in Manosque. The Jews owned at least one synagogue and cemetery. They lived in their own street, the Carriera Judaica, on the site of the present Rue Bon-Repos. When an epidemic broke out in 1364, the services of a Jewish physician were still called for. However, from 1370 on there were frequent anti-Jewish disturbances, the most violent in 1455 and 1495. In 1498 the town obtained the expulsion of the Jews.

Bibliography: Gross, Gal Jud, 361f.; E. Baratier, *Démographie provençale...* (1961), 70; C. Arnaud, *Histoire d'une famille provençale* (1888), 450f.; D. Arnaud, *Etudes historiques sur... Manosque*, 1 (1847), 51ff.

[B.Bl.]

MANS, LE (Heb. מנש), capital of the department of Sarthe, W. France. A Jew, Vaslinus, is mentioned as a moneylender there between 1104 and 1115. In 1138, the Jews of Le Mans were the victims of a local persecution. They lived in the quarter formed by Rues Marchande, Saint-Jacques, Falotiers or de Merdereau, Barillerie, Ponts-Neufs and de la Juiverie, and owned a synagogue and a cemetery (in the parish of Sainte-Croix), which was also used by other Jews in the vicinity. They probably also had their own market and a hospital. Another local persecution may have occurred in about 1200, since several Jewish converts are found in Le Mans in 1207, and around 1216, Berengaria, the widow of Richard the Lion-Hearted, Lady of Le Mans, disposed of the so-called "school of the *Juiverie*," i.e., the synagogue. There is again mention of a Jewish quarter during the second half of the 13th century, the Jews of Le Mans then being under the jurisdiction of the bishop. Reference to Jewish scholars of Le Mans is found in rabbinical literature from the end of the ninth century, the most celebrated being *Avun the Great (tenth century) and *Elijah b. Menahem ha-Zaken (11th century). The Jews were expelled from Le Mans in 1289 at the same time as those of Maine and Anjou. During World War II many of the Jews in Le Mans were deported. A new community was formed after the war, many of its members coming from North Africa. It numbered 400 in 1969. A stained-glass window dating from the 12th century which depicts the allegorical Synagogue can be seen in the Cathedral of Le Mans.

Bibliography: B. Blumenkranz, in: *Mélanges... R. Crozet*, 2 (1966), 1154; Z. Szajkowski, *Analytical Franco-Jewish Gazetteer* (1966), 256; Gross, Gal Jud, 392–3. [B.Bl.]

MANSFELD, ALFRED (1912–), architect. Born in Russia, he went to Paris in 1933 and in 1935 to Ereẓ Israel and worked from 1936 as an independent architect, mainly in Haifa. He designed and built several housing schemes in Haifa (including Ramat Hadar), and also various public buildings, including the Institute for Jewish Studies of the Hebrew University in Jerusalem (Mount Scopus) and the Hydraulic Institute of the Technion (with M. Weinraub). In 1963, his design for the international airport at Lydda was awarded first prize. He designed and built (in partnership with Dora Gad, interior decorator), the Israel Museum in Jerusalem (1959–65). From 1949, he lectured at the Faculty of Architecture of the Technion, and from 1954 to 1956 he was dean of the faculty.

Civic and commercial center at Kiryat Eliezer, Haifa, designed by Alfred Mansfeld.

Bibliography: R. Pedio, *Profilo dell'architetto Alfred Mansfeld* (It., 1965), with Eng. preface. [A.E.]

°**MANṢŪR** (**Al**; full name: **al-Manṣūr Ibn Abī ʿĀmir**; in Christian sources, **Almanzor**; d. 1002), chamberlain (Ar. *ḥājib*) of Caliph Hishām II (976–1013) of Spain. Al-Manṣūr in effect ruled *Umayyad Spain as virtual dictator and in 996 assumed royal titles. His reign marked the climax of the Umayyad political, economic, cultural, and military supremacy in Spain. A religious fanatic, al-Manṣūr embarked on a lengthy and successful campaign against the Christians in northern Spain (against Catalonia in 985), in which he ruthlessly destroyed Christian holy places. He, however, did not harm the Christian and Jewish communities in his domain. The responsa of R. Ḥanokh of Cordoba attest to the conversions of Jews to Islam under al-Manṣūr, who intensified and increased Muslim preaching and other religious activities. Spain was extremely prosperous during his reign and Jewish immigration therefore increased. The Jews came mainly from North Africa (present Morocco and Algeria), together with many Berbers, whom al-Manṣūr employed in his military campaigns. The military security and economic stability contributed to an efflorescence of Jewish culture, *halakhah*, poetry, etc. (see *Spain). The 12th-century historian Abraham *ibn Daud recalls "King" al-Manṣūr's appointment of Jacob *ibn Jau, a wealthy and opportunistic silk merchant, to the position of *nasi* in charge of all Jewish communities in his domain. Al-Manṣūr empowered Ibn Jau to collect taxes from whomever he desired. He had Ibn Jau imprisoned one year later for not collecting enough money from the Jews. Al-Manṣūr's son ʿAbd al-Malik al-Muẓaffir succeeded him, thus founding the Amirid dynasty.

Bibliography: E. Levi-Provençal, *Histoire de l'Espagne Musulmane*, 2 (1950), 196–272; Ashtor, Korot, 1 (1966²), 244–8; Abraham ibn Daud, *Sefer ha-Qabbalah—the Book of Tradition*, ed. and tr. by G. D. Cohen (1967), 69. [Ed.]

MANSURA (**El Manṣura; al-Manṣūra; Al-Mansurah**), town of Lower Egypt, on the right bank of the eastern arm of the Nile. Founded during the 13th century, Mansura has become an important center for the cotton commerce in modern times. The Jewish population grew under Turkish rule and by the 17th century there was an organized community led by the rabbis Elijah Shushi (Shoshi) and Shabbetai ha-Kohen. During the middle of the 19th century, Jacob *Saphir found 40 families in the town, most of whom had come from Cairo and Damietta. During the second half of the 19th century, when blood libels were brought against the Jews in various Egyptian towns, the Jews of Mansura were also accused. In 1877 during Passover, the Jews were accused of having slaughtered a Muslim child in order to use his blood for the baking of *mazzot*. At the end of the 19th century, the number of Jews was about 500 and it continued to increase at the beginning of the 20th century. A well-organized community was set up in 1918 and educational and charitable institutions were established. A Zionist association was also founded in the town. After World War I there was a decrease in the population. In 1927 there were still 563 Jews there, but a few years later there were only 150 to 200 Jews left, and by 1971 the community no longer existed.

Bibliography: J. Saphir, *Even Sappir* (1866), 8a; J. M. Landau, *Jews in Nineteenth-Century Egypt* (1969), 38–40. [E.A./J.M.L.]

MANSURAH, SAADIAH BEN JUDAH (19th century), Yemenite scholar living in Sanʾa. He was author of *Sefer ha-Maḥashavah*, which appeared under the title *Sefer ha-Galut ve-ha-Ge'ullah* (1955), which consists of seven sections written in rhymed prose. Like the *Sefer ha-Musar* of R. Zechariah al-Ḍāhri, it describes the hardships endured by the community of Sanʾa in his time. The principal hero is Eitan ha-Ezraḥi (i.e., Abraham the Patriarch) and the narrator Ḥazmak (i.e., Saadiah, after the "*Atbash" method of interchanging Hebrew letters) is the poet himself. The narrator tells the founder of the nation of the misfortunes of Yemenite Jewry, and the latter in turn relates the servitude of Israel in the Egyptian exile. He deals with the exiles into which Israel was sent, with the return to Zion and the redemption of the people. The last section consists of eulogies of the rabbis of Yemen and the author himself. Mansurah also wrote poems and prayers, the subject of which is exile and redemption, as well as an introduction to Yemenite poetry. In the field of *halakhah*, he wrote *Sha'ar ha-Moda'it* on the laws of *sheḥitah* and *terefot*.

Bibliography: S. Mansurah, *Sefer ha-Galut ve-ha-Ge'ullah* (1955), introd. [Y.R.]

MANSURAH, SHALOM BEN JUDAH (d. c. 1885), Yemenite scholar. A member of one of the distinguished families of San'a, Mansurah was the brother of the poet Saadiah Mansurah. In addition to his knowledge of the Torah, he also engaged in popular and natural medicine and was renowned as a practical kabbalist. In 1854 he was appointed leader of the Jews of San'a. Three of his works on Torah and *halakhah* (in manuscript) are known. In addition to his own writings, he corrected many works of others. His notes in the margins of books, both published and in manuscript (especially those of R. Yiḥya Ṣalaḥ), are numerous.

Bibliography: A. Koraḥ, *Sa'arat Teiman* (1954), 45. [Y.R.]

MANTINO, JACOB BEN SAMUEL (d. 1549), physician and translator. Mantino was apparently of Spanish origin but he spent most of his life in Italy. After graduating in medicine at Padua in 1521, he developed a flourishing practice in Bologna, Verona, and Venice, especially among the upper classes. At the same time he became known for his translations from Hebrew into Latin of philosophical works, mainly those of Averroës and Avicenna. In the stormy debate on the annulment of the marriage between Henry VIII of England and Catherine of Aragon he opposed Henry's supporters, thus earning the gratitude of Pope Clement VII, and at his request Mantino was appointed lecturer in medicine in Bologna in 1529. In 1533 the pope invited him to Rome where, unlike his protector, Mantino took a strong stand against the messianic claims of Solomon *Molcho. In 1534 Pope Paul III appointed him his personal physician and in 1539–41 professor of practical medicine at the Sapienza in Rome. In 1544 he returned to Venice. Five years later he left for Damascus as personal physician of the Venetian ambassador. He died soon after his arrival there.

Bibliography: Kaufmann, in: REJ, 27 (1893), 30–60, 207–38; Milano, Italia, 242, 625, 631; idem, *Ghetto di Roma* (1964), 60, 68f.; C. Roth, *Jews in the Renaissance* (1959), index; Ravà, in: *Vessillo Israelitico*, 51 (1903), 310–3; Muenster, in: RMI, 20 (1954), 310–21. [A.Mil.]

MANTUA, city and province in N. Italy, an important Jewish center in late medieval and modern times.

History. The first record of a Jewish settlement in Mantua dates from 1145, when Abraham *ibn Ezra lived there for a while. A small Jewish community existed during the heyday of the city-republic. Sometime after the Gonzaga had become lords of Mantua, Jewish bankers were invited to start operations in the capital and province. Subsequently the Jewish population increased, reaching 3,000 by 1600. The merchant and artisan population soon outnumbered the bankers. Some 50 Jewish settlements of varying size flourished in the province, the major ones being *Bozzolo, *Sabbioneta, Luzzara, Guastalla, Viadana, Revere, Sermide, and Ostiano. The Jews were protected by a series of privileges granted them by popes, emperors, and the Gonzaga rulers. A Christian loan bank (**monte di pietà*)

Figure 1. Ark of the Law in the Scuola Norsa, the synagogue of Mantua. Courtesy J. Shaw, London.

was established in Mantua in 1486 to compete with Jewish banking, but initially at least had little success. Anti-Jewish riots took place at Mantua in the 15th century, fostered by the Church and aided and abetted by the business competitors of the Jews. There was also an isolated case of *blood libel in 1478. At the end of the 15th century the regulation imposing the Jewish *badge was introduced in Mantua. Rioting in 1495, after Duke Francesco Gonzaga's indecisive encounter with the French forces at Fornovo, resulted in the confiscation of the house of the leading Jewish banker in the city, Daniel *Norsa, and the erection of the Church of the Madonna della Vittoria on the site. David *Reuveni visited Mantua in 1530, but failed to obtain the support of either the ruler or the Jews. Two years later Solomon *Molcho was burned at the stake there.

The Counter-Reformation began to affect the Jews of Mantua adversely in the last quarter of the 16th century. Restrictive measures and anti-Jewish propaganda culminated in riots and murder. The worst outrage occurred in 1602, when seven Jews were hanged on a charge of blasphemy at the instigation of a Franciscan rabble-rouser. Some ten years later the Jews of Mantua were confined to a ghetto. The worst disaster in their history befell Mantuan Jewry in 1629–30, when they were despoiled of their possessions during the sack of the city by the German troops and then banished. A moving account of the disaster and of the return of the survivors is the contemporary *Ha-Galut ve-ha-Pedut* ("Exile and Deliverance") by Abraham *Massarani (Venice, 1634). The events of 1630 decimated the Jewish community which never quite recovered its former importance. In 1708 the duchy of

Mantua came under Austrian rule. In the last quarter of the 18th century Mantua became the chief center in the struggle for Jewish civil rights in Austrian Lombardy. On the Jewish side were ranged R. Jacob *Saraval of Mantua and Benedetto *Frizzi of Ostiano who had to contend with the lawyer G. B. Benedetti of Ferrara and G. B. G. d'Arco, a political economist. When in 1797 the French revolutionary army captured Mantua the ghetto was abolished, its gates were torn down, and the ghetto square was renamed Piazza della Concordia. After its recapture by the Austrians in 1799, however, several Jewish "revolutionaries" were banished from Mantua, among them Issachar Ḥayyim Carpi of Revere, who described the events in his *Toledot Yishak* (1892). The French again ruled Mantua from 1801 to 1814 and R. Abraham Vita *Cologna of Mantua was among the foremost personalities in the Napoleonic *Sanhedrin. During the last period of Austrian rule in Mantua (1814–66) there occurred yet another blood libel (1824), and in 1842 anti-Jewish riots took place.

The Jews of Mantua, like their coreligionists elsewhere in Italy, took an active part in the Italian Risorgimento. Among them were Giuseppe *Finzi of Rivarolo, one of the "martyrs of Belfiore," and the writer Tullo *Massarani. When Mantua was incorporated in the Kingdom of Italy (1866) the last restrictions affecting the Jews were removed. At that time the Jewish population reached 2,795, its highest figure since 1603. Subsequently migration and assimilation reduced the community. In 1931 the community numbered only 669 Jews. The anti-Jewish measures of the Fascist regime (see *Italy) seriously affected the Jews of Mantua, coming to a climax under the German domination in 1943–45. A concentration camp was set up in Mantua. Many Mantuan Jews were deported to the death camps, and over 50 perished. Only some of the survivors returned to Mantua after the war. In 1969 approximately 150 Jews lived in Mantua and maintained one of the former synagogues with irregular services.

Cultural Life. During its heyday in the 16th and 17th centuries the community of Mantua made important contributions to the development of Jewish communal institutions in Italy. The assembly of all taxpayers elected a "large" council, which in turn elected a "small" or executive council of seven to ten members. Alongside these, several smaller executive committees functioned. The chief officers were two *massari* (ממונים). Communal regulations, especially those pertaining to taxation, were published in Hebrew at regular intervals, as were also sumptuary laws for the restriction of ostentation in clothing and festivities. The synagogues of Mantua included the Great Synagogue of the Italian rite, and several smaller synagogues of the Ashkenazi and Italian rites. The community maintained a public school system and welfare institutions, including medical services for the poor. The rabbinical court had extensive powers until the grant of Jewish emancipation. Its procedure was laid down in the *Shuda de-Dayyanei* ("Judges' Verdict") of 1677–78.

Mantua was an important Jewish cultural center during the Renaissance in Italy. Prominent scholars in the 15th century included *Judah Messer Leon, rabbi, physician, and philosopher; R. Joseph *Colon, the greatest rabbinical authority in Italy; Mordecai *Finzi, mathematician, astronomer, doctor, and banker; and Baruch de Peschiera, scholar and merchant. Abraham *Conat, a physician and talmudist, founded at Mantua about 1475 one of the first Hebrew printing presses; the first dated work issued was the *Tur Oraḥ Ḥayyim* (1476). His wife Estellina assisted him as a printer. Other Hebrew printers active at Mantua included: Samuel Latif (1513–15), Joseph b. Jacob Shalit and Meir Sofer, both of Padua, Jacob ha-Kohen of Gazzuolo (1556–76), Samuel Norsa and his sons Isaac and Solomon (16th century); the Perugia and d'Italia families (17th and 18th centuries). The Hebrew press in Mantua was the second largest in Italy after Venice. Sixteenth-century scholars included Azariah de' *Rossi, author of *Me'or Einayim;* the versatile Abraham Yagel *Gallico; R. Azriel *Diena of Sabbioneta; the preacher Judah *Moscato; several members of the *Norsa (Norzi) family including Jedidiah Solomon Norsa, author of *Minḥat Shai;* the brothers Moses, David, and Judah *Provençal, rabbis and scholars; Abraham Colorni, engineer and inventor; members of the *Finzi, *Cases, *Fano, *Rieti, and Sullam families; the *Portaleone family, physicians for three centuries; and Judah Leone b. Isaac *Sommo, playwright, poet, and author of the famous "Dialogues on the Theater." Mantua was the most important center of Jewish participation in the Renaissance theater. The community provided its own theater company, which put on comedies and other plays for court performances throughout the 16th and early 17th centuries. The Jews of Mantua were also active in music and the dance. The greatest Jewish composer in Mantua and the first composer of modern Jewish music was Salamone de' *Rossi, whose sister "Madama Europa" acted on the Mantuan stage. Other Jewish musicians, dancers, and actors at Mantua included Abramo dall' *Arpa and his nephew Abramino; Isaac *Massarani; Angelo de' Rossi; and Simone Basilea. In the 17th and 18th centuries there lived at Mantua the *Basilea family of rabbis and scholars, including Solomon Aviad Sar-Shalom *Basilea; Judah Briel, rabbi and polemicist; Moses *Zacuto, mystic and poet; Samson Cohen Modon, rabbi and poet; Jacob Saraval, rabbi, polemicist, traveler, and preacher; the brothers Jacob and Immanuel *Frances, poets; the Cases family, rabbis, physicians, and scholars; and Samuel *Romanelli, poet and playwright. Outstanding modern Jewish personalities include Marco *Mortara,

Figure 2. The Great Synagogue, Mantua, demolished in the 1920s. Courtesy Italian Synagogue, Jerusalem.

rabbi and bibliophile; Tullo Massarani, writer; and Vittore *Colorni, jurist and historian.

Bibliography: S. Simonsohn, *Toledot ha-Yehudim be-Dukkasut Mantovah,* 2 vols. (1962–64); Milano, Bibliotheca, index, s.v. *Mantova;* Milano, Italia, index, s.v. *Mantova;* M. Mortara, *Indice Alfabetico dei Rabbini . . .* (1886), passim; Roth, Italy, index; idem, *Jews in the Renaissance* (1959), index; D. W. Amram, *Makers of Hebrew Books in Italy* (1909), 30ff., 323ff.; M. Steinschneider and D. Cassel, *Juedische Typographie* (1938), 14, 23, 26ff.; H. D. Friedberg, *Toledot ha-Defus ha-Ivri be-Italyah* (1956[2]), 15ff. [SH.SI.]

°**MANUEL I** (1469–1521), king of Portugal 1495–1521. He was termed Manuel the Great because of the achievements of his reign: Vasco da Gama's discovery of the sea passage to India via the Cape of Good Hope (1498) and the acquisition of Brazil (1500). For the Jewish citizens, however, Manuel's reign brought an end to their life in Portugal. Initially Manuel was well disposed to Jews. He retained the esteemed Abraham b. Samuel *Zacuto as his astronomer, and removed the Jewish disabilities imposed by his predecessor John II. But in 1496 the king entered a politically motivated marriage with Princess Isabella of Spain, daughter of *Ferdinand and Isabella, who made their consent conditional to Manuel's ridding Portugal of the Jews. On Dec. 4, 1496, an edict was passed ordering every Jew to leave Portugal before November 1497, on penalty of death. Manuel assured the Jews of every assistance in travel and free departure with their belongings. As the mass emigration got under way, Manuel realized that the loss of his Jewish citizenry would have dire economic results for Portugal. To stem the departures, he ordered all Jews desiring to emigrate to come to Lisbon, supposedly for embarkation. When some 20,000 had convened in Lisbon, Manuel herded them together for forced conversion. On May 30, 1497, he decreed that the Conversos would be free from the Church's discipline for 20 years. When the king learned soon after that the Conversos were emigrating in large numbers, he quickly withdrew their liberty to dispose of property and emigrate. When some 4,000 of the *New Christians were massacred by a Lisbon mob in 1506, Manuel responded by executing the Dominican friars who had incited the riot, and restored all previous rights and immunities to the New Christians, only to reverse his decision in the year of his death.

Bibliography: Graetz, Hist, 4 (1894, repr. 1949), 372–81, 485–8; Roth, Marranos, 55–66, 86, 196; M. Kayserling, *Geschichte der Juden in Portugal* (1867), 120–56, 334; J. Mendes dos Remedios, *Os Judeus em Portugal* (1895), 275–342; S. Usque, *Consolation for the Tribulations of Israel,* tr. by M. A. Cohen (1965), 5–7, 202–5. [ED.]

°**MANUEL I COMNENUS,** Byzantine emperor (1143–1180). He added humiliating procedures to the standard *oath *more judaico* requiring that the Jew spit on his circumcision. But he also continued to permit the Jews to use the older and less offensive formula of the oath. Manuel confirmed Jewish access to ordinary courts, giving them recourse to the protection of imperial law, thus abolishing the practice of having Jews summarily tried by a minor local official. Manuel had a Jewish physician who may have influenced him to moderate his position toward the Jews. The economic and cultural life of Byzantine Jewry during Manuel's reign is described by Benjamin of Tudela.

Bibliography: M. N. Adler (ed.), *Itinerary of Benjamin of Tudela* (1907), 10–14; J. Starr, *Jews in the Byzantine Empire 641–1204* (1939), 221–3, and index; Baron, Social[2], 4 (1962), 194f.; Patlagean, in: REJ, 124 (1965), 138–51. [AN.SH.]

MANUSCRIPTS, HEBREW, term which includes religious and secular books, as well as letters and documents written on papyrus, parchment, hides, and paper in Hebrew characters, sometimes using them for the writing of languages other than Hebrew, e.g., Aramaic, Yiddish, Ladino, etc. Hebrew manuscripts have been preserved in archives and public and private libraries. It has been estimated that there are about 60,000 manuscripts (codices) and about 200,000 fragments, most of which have come from the Cairo *Genizah* (and a certain number from the Judean Desert).

500 B.C.E.–500 C.E. Documents and letters, some with accurate dates, have been preserved from the period of 500 B.C.E. to 500 C.E. The most important of them are a collection of *papyri from Yeb (*Elephantine) and Assuan in Egypt (494–407 B.C.E.); papyri from Edfu, also in Egypt, are thought to belong to the third century B.C.E., as are parts of the Book of Jeremiah and fragments of II Samuel among the *Dead Sea Scrolls. The other scrolls from the Judean Desert are regarded as dating from the second century B.C.E. to the Bar-Kokhba War (132–135), including some written or dictated by him (see bibl. nos. 1–5).

500–1500. No material is available which can be proven with any certainty as belonging to the first centuries of this period. The oldest manuscripts of the period date from the end of the ninth century. Information has been published on a biblical manuscript in Leningrad dated to 846. On the other hand, some of the fragments found in the Cairo *Genizah* belong, without doubt, to the beginning of this period and possibly even to the end of the previous one. The development of Hebrew paleography should make it possible to determine with greater accuracy the dates of these most valuable fragments.

BIBLE AND BIBLE EXEGESIS. The oldest dated biblical manuscripts are: Prophets as vocalized by Moses b. Asher, which was found in the Karaite synagogue of Cairo and written in Tiberias in 895; Latter Prophets, with Babylonian punctuation, in the Saltykov-Shchedrin Library in Leningrad (No. 3), was copied in 916; and a Pentateuch which was copied by Solomon b. Buya'a (who also prepared, according to a note at its end, the so-called *Keter Aram Ẓova,* later vocalized by Aaron b. Asher) in 929 and vocalized by his brother Ephraim b. Buya'a (it appears that both were active in Tiberias). This particular *Keter Aram*

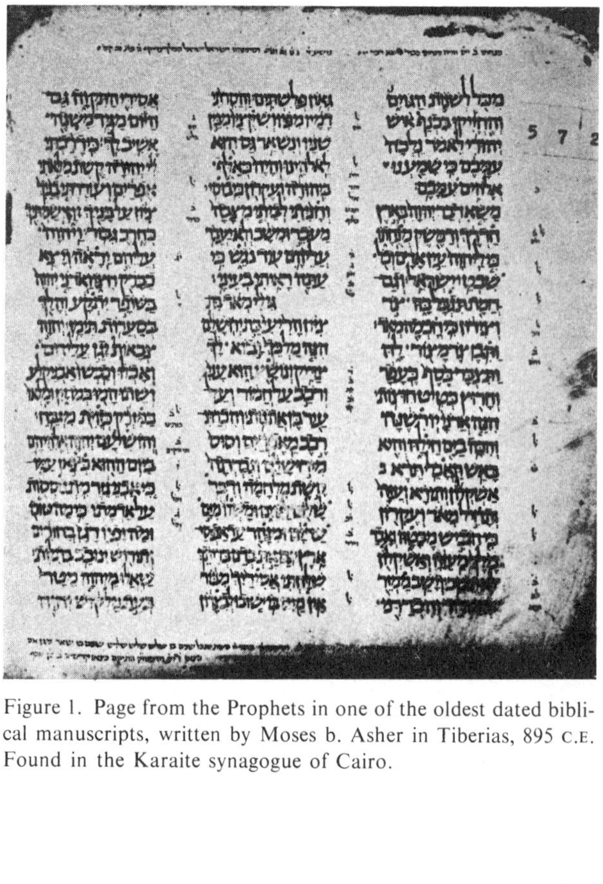

Figure 1. Page from the Prophets in one of the oldest dated biblical manuscripts, written by Moses b. Asher in Tiberias, 895 C.E. Found in the Karaite synagogue of Cairo.

Figure 2. Page from *Keter Aram Ẓova,* copied by Solomon b. Buya'a in Aleppo, and vocalized by Aaron ben Asher, tenth century, Jerusalem, Ben-Zvi Institute.

Figure 3. Page from the complete manuscript of the Babylonian Talmud, copied by Solomon b. Samson in 1342, probably in France. Munich, Bayerische Staatsbibliothek, Cod. Heb. 95, fol. 248r.

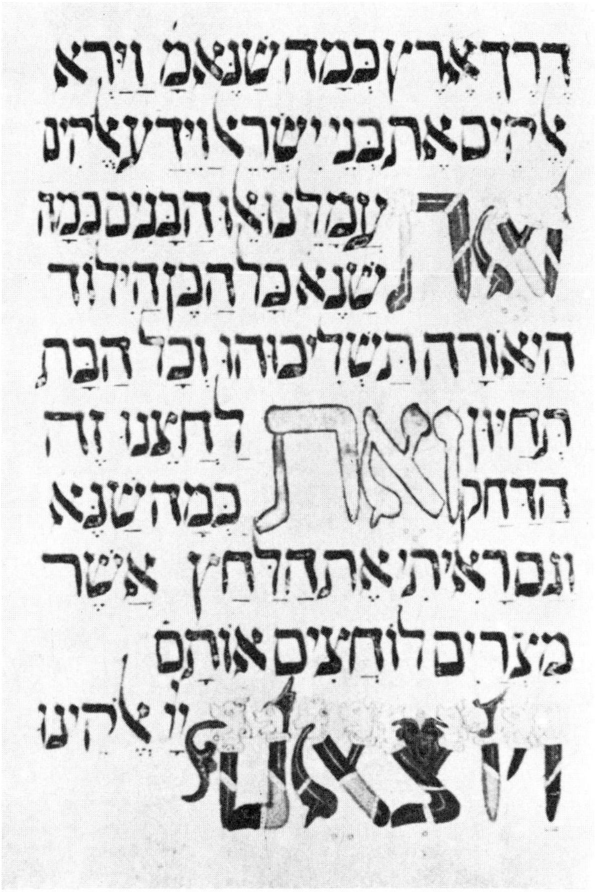

Figure 4. Page from the *Golden Haggadah,* Spain, c. 1320. London, British Museum, Add. Ms. 27210.

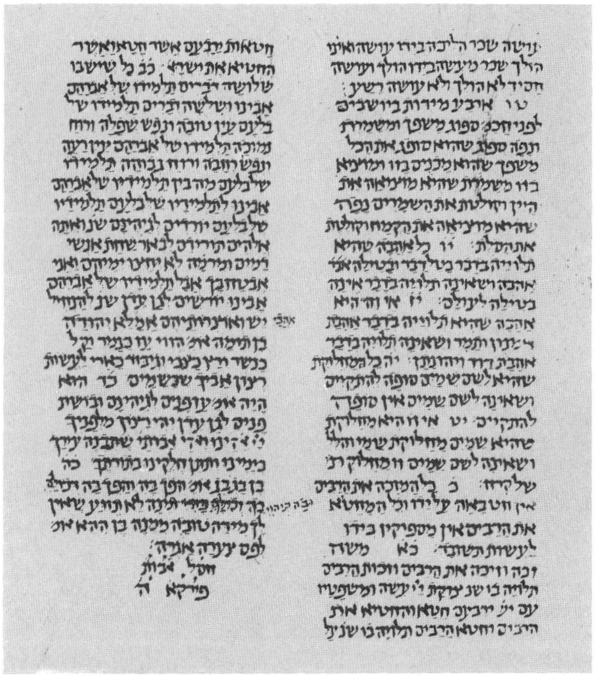

Figure 5. Page from an early Mishnah manuscript, 12th–14th centuries. Budapest, Library of the Hungarian Academy of Sciences, Kaufmann Collection, Ms. 50.

Figure 6. Opening of Genesis from a Pentateuch and Haftarot with the greater and lesser masorah, San'a, Yemen, 1496. From Cambridge, Westminster College.

Zova (*keter,* "crown" being an appellation for a Bible codex; *Aram Zova,* "Aleppo") is at the Ben-Zvi Institute, Jerusalem (see bibl. nos. 5–7). There are biblical manuscripts in the Saltykov-Shchedrin Library and others, which, according to their *colophons, were written during the tenth century, but doubts have been raised as to the reliability of these colophons. Finally, there is the Bible manuscript (Leningrad B 19A) which was written in 1009 in Egypt. The text is complete and the date appears to be authentic.

MISHNAH, TOSEFTA, TALMUD, AND HALAKHIC MIDRASHIM. The oldest dated manuscripts of the Mishnah are: Paris Manuscripts 328/9, the complete text with Maimonides' commentary and written and vocalized by Joab b. Jehiel, the "Physician of Beth-El," from the province of Cesena (Italy), between 1399 and 1401. Individual orders *(sedarim),* written and vocalized (in part) from 1168 *(Zera'im, Nezikin, Kodashim),* are in Oxford (nos. 393, 404), and *Mo'ed* of the same set is in the Sassoon Library (no. 72). Not dated but definitely early works are: Kaufmann Number 50 (facsimile edited by G. Baer, 1929) and Parma Number 138. The oldest Tosefta manuscripts are Erfurt Number 159, which was thought to have been written in 1150, and Vienna Number 46. The oldest dated halakhic Midrashim are: Sifra of 1073 (Vatican Library, no. 31) and Sifra of 1291 (Oxford, no. 151), which also includes the *Mekhilta.* The only manuscript of the Jerusalem Talmud, which was written in 1299 by *Jehiel b. Jekuthiel b. Benjamin, the Physician, is at Leyden. There is also only one complete extant manuscript of the Babylonian Talmud (Munich, Bayerische Staatsbibliothek, Cod. Heb. 95). It was written "on the twelfth of the month of Kislev, in the year 103 of the sixth millennium" (1342) by Solomon b. Samson, probably in France (facsimile edited by H. Strack, 1912). At the end of this manuscript several minor tractates are added. Individual tractates from 1176 and after have been preserved in the Library of Florence, as well as a manuscript from 1184 in the Hamburg Library and in the Jewish Theological Seminary Library (Av. Zar., 1290).

AGGADIC MIDRASHIM. Among the extant manuscripts of aggadic Midrashim are *Genesis Rabbah* and *Leviticus Rabbah* from 1291 (*Bibliothèque Nationale* of Paris, no. 149). There is a manuscript from the same year of the *Pesikta de-Rav Kahana* in the Bodleian. The Parma Library possesses a manuscript from 1270 (no. 1240) which contains *Song of Songs Rabbah, Lamentations Rabbah, Tanḥuma, Pesikta Rabbati, Midrash Proverbs,* and others.

MISCELLANEA. Thousands of medieval manuscripts in the fields of philosophy and Kabbalah are extant; these are as numerous as those in medicine, astronomy, astrology, geography, and other natural sciences. A considerable number of these manuscripts are translations from Greek, Arabic, and other languages spoken and written in the countries of the Diaspora. Polemics, poetry, philology (grammar, dictionaries, *masorah*), history, sectarian literature, *halakhah* (responsa, novellae, codes, ritual compendiums), ethics, and homiletics are well represented, as is liturgy (*siddurim* and *maḥzorim*). Due to their constant use many tens of thousands of them were stored away in *genizot* after being worn and damaged. Occasionally autographs were also preserved, i.e., either manuscripts from the hand of the author, such as Maimonides' Mishnah commentary and miscellaneous writings (ed. S. D. Sassoon, 1966), or confirmations of the correctness of the copy as the one added by Maimonides to a copy of his code: "Corrected from my [original] copy, I, Moses, son of Maimon of blessed memory" (Oxford Ms. 577).

1500–1970. Manuscripts of this last period are also extant; some of them were published, some not. A considerable number of the manuscripts of this period were written in countries where there were no Hebrew presses (e.g., the Yemen). They were either contemporary works or those of earlier periods, but some were copied from printed works which had reached them from Western countries and are therefore of no original value. Manuscripts written by the authors themselves are of special importance because of

Figure 7. Carpet page from the *Second Leningrad Bible,* Egypt, Fostat 1008/10, containing masoretic text and masorah in micrographic letters. Leningrad, Saltykov-Shchedrin Library, Ms. B. 19a., fol. 489 v.

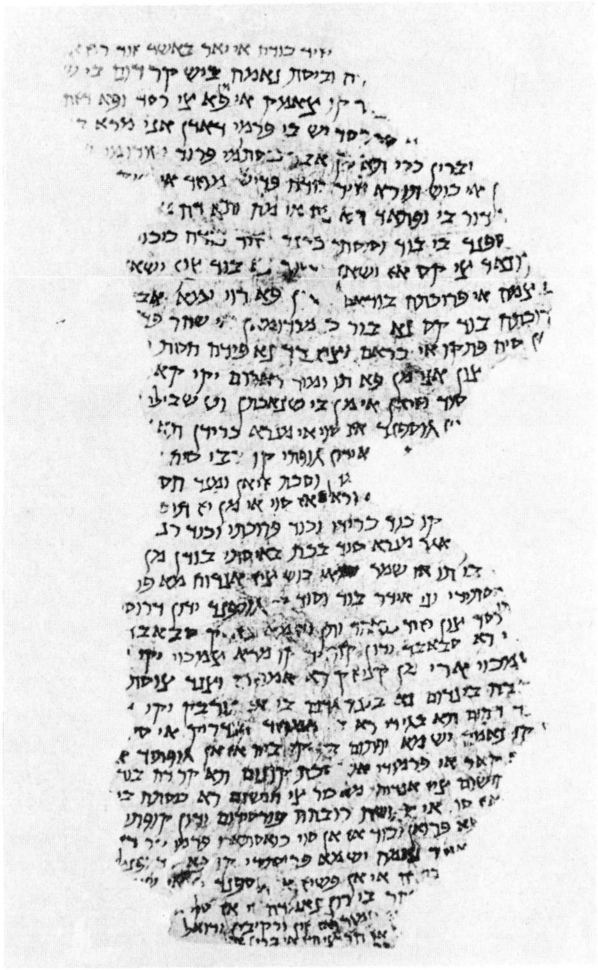

Figure 8. Mercantile document in Persian written in Hebrew characters, c. 800 C.E. London, British Museum, Ms. Or. 8212, No. 166.

their corrections. They make it possible to reconstruct the original text and compare it with other copies, either handwritten or printed editions. Early authorities, who wrote in the early years after the appearance of printing, made use of manuscripts of classic books and commentaries. In later centuries this practice naturally waned.

Owners and Other Lists. At the beginning and the end of manuscripts it was customary to note the name of the owner, with a formula such as "a man should always sign his name in his book lest a man from the street come and say it is mine." Owners, who usually were scholars, often added notes of their own to the text. At times, the names of several generations of a single family appear in these lists, and well-known names in Jewish literature and history are found among the owners, e.g., a manuscript of Maimonides' *Guide* (1472, Parma 660) belonged successively to David, Abraham, and Moses Provençal (father, son, and grandson).

Modern manuscript catalogs generally register these notes and lists in detail. The same pages were also used to commemorate family and general events, and documents which are sometimes of great historical value were also copied on them, although they may have no connection with the contents of the manuscript. Among this material are lists of books describing whole or parts of private collections. Such lists shed light on the cultural standards of various periods and environments. The prices of the manuscripts which are mentioned in them are of particular interest (see *Book trade).

For further information see *Alphabet, *Books, *Colophon, *Censorship, **Genizah*, *Illuminated Manuscripts.

Collection of the Material. The Institute for the Photography of Hebrew Manuscripts was founded in 1950 by the Israel Government (Ministry of Education and Culture) in order to enable a comparative processing and registration of all possible material. In 1962 the institute was placed under the authority of the Hebrew University and became affiliated with the National and University Library. During its 20 years of activity the Institute has photographed—mainly in the form of microfilms—approximately half of the collections of manuscripts and fragments scattered throughout the libraries of the world. The most important works which had not been previously published in the form of facsimiles were enlarged by the Institute, as were all the fragments which reached it. Some of the material has been listed in the publications of the Institute (bibl. nos. 24–27). The Jewish Theological Seminary of America houses the Louis Ginzberg Microfilm Collection, which aims at the microfilming of important Hebrew manuscripts from all over the world. The list below cites all libraries containing over 100 Hebrew or Samaritan manuscripts. The numbers of the manuscripts and fragments are given in parenthesis, and the names of the authors of the catalogs and the year of their publication are given after the colon. The numbers of the manuscripts given here are not always identical with those which are classified in the catalogs, as additions were acquired after their publication.

Austria. VIENNA: *Nationalbibliothek* (216; 308 fragments): A. Z. Schwarz (1925); *Bibliothek der Isr. Kultusgemeinde* (215): A. Z. Schwarz-Oesterreich (1932; 40 Mss. transferred to the Jewish Historical Institute, Warsaw).

Denmark. COPENHAGEN: *The Royal Library* (244): N. Allony-E. Kupfer (1964).

England. CAMBRIDGE: *Trinity College Library* (160): H. Loewe (1926); *University Library* (1,000; 100,000 fragments): S. Schiller-Szinessy (1876); *Westminster College Library* (3,000 fragments). LEEDS: *University Library* (371): C. Roth (Alexander Marx Jubilee Volume; 1950). LETCHWORTH: *D. S. Sassoon Collection* (1,220): D. S. Sassoon (1932). LONDON: *Bet Din and Bet Ha-Midrash* (161): A. Neubauer (1886); *British Museum* (includes the first part of the Gaster Collection, 2,467; 10,000 fragments): G. Margoliouth (1899–1935); *Jews College Library* (Montefiore Collection: 580); H. Hirschfeld, in: JQR (1902–03). MANCHESTER: *John Rylands Library* (second part of the Gaster Collection: 750; 10,000 fragments): E. Robertson (only the Samaritan Mss.; 1938–62). OXFORD: *Bodleian Library* (2,650; 10,000 fragments): A. Neubauer-A. E. Cowley (1886–1906).

France. PARIS: *Bibliothèque de l'Alliance Universelle* (338; 4,000 fragments): M. Schwab, in: REJ (1904, 1912); B. Chapira, in: REJ (1904); *Bibliothèque Nationale* (1459); H. Zotenberg (1886); *Ecole Rabbinique de France* (172): M. Abraham, in: REJ (1924–25). STRASBOURG: *Bibliothèque Nationale et Universitaire* (176; 292 fragments): S. Landauer (1881).

Germany. BERLIN: *Preussische Staatsbibliothek* (510): M. Steinschneider (1878–97); N. Allony-D. S. Loewinger (1957). FRANKFORT: *Stadt- und Universitätsbibliothek* (400; 10,000 fragments): R. N. N. Rabbinowitz (1888); N. Allony-D. S. Loewinger (1957; including the Merzbacher Collection; 10,000 *Genizah* fragments lost during World War II). HAMBURG: *Stadtbibliothek* 476); M. Steinschneider (1878; including the Levy Collection). MUNICH: *Bayerische Staatsbibliothek* (476): M. Steinschneider (1895); E. Roth (1966).

Hungary. BUDAPEST: *Hungarian Academy of Sciences* (Kaufmann Collection: 595; 600 fragments): M. Weisz (1906); D. S. Loewinger-A. Scheiber (1947); *Library of the Jewish Theological Seminary* (315; 400 fragments): D. S. Loewinger (1940).

Italy. FLORENCE: *Biblioteca Mediceo Laurenziana* (187): A. M. Biscioni (1757). LEGHORN: *Talmud Torah* (134): C. Bernheimer (1915). A part transferred to the Jewish National and University Library in Jerusalem. MANTUA: *Comunità Israelitica* (167): M. Mortara (1878). MILAN: *Biblioteca Ambrosiana* (183): C. Bernheimer (1933). N. Allony-E. Kupfer (*Aresheth;* 1960). PARMA: *Biblioteca Palatina* (1,552): G. B. De-Rossi (1803); P. Perreau (1880). ROME: *Biblioteca Casanatense* (230): G. Sacerdote (1897). *Biblioteca Apostolica Vaticana* (see Vatican, below). TURIN: *Biblioteca Nazionale* (247): B. Peyron (1880). (A great part destroyed by fire in 1904.)

Israel. JERUSALEM: *National and University Library* (6,000): G. Scholem (1930); B. Joel (1934). N. Ben-Menahem (120); *Hechal Shlomo* (150): J. L. Bialer (1966–69); *Mosad ha-Rav Kook* (1,000): N. Ben-Menahem in: *Aresheth,* 1 (1959), 396–413; *Ben-Zvi*

Institute (1,100); *Schocken Library* (400). RAMAT GAN: *Bar Ilan University Library* (Margulies Collection: 750). TEL AVIV: *Bialik House* (200).

Netherlands. AMSTERDAM; *Portugeesch Israelitisch Seminarium Etz Haim—Livraria D. Montezinos* (160): N. Allony-E. Kupfer (1964); *Universiteitsbibliotheek* (Rosenthaliana; 305); M. Roest (1875); N. Allony-E. Kupfer (1964). LEIDEN: *Bibliotheek der Universiteit* (118): M. Steinschneider (1858).

Poland. WARSAW: *Jewish Historical Institute* (1,500): E. Kupfer-S. Strelcyn (Przegląd Orientalisticzny; 1954–55). WROCLAW (formerly Breslau): *Jewish Theological Seminary of Breslau* (405): D. S. Loewinger-B. Weinryb, 1965 (partly transferred to the Jewish Historical Institute in Warsaw).

Switzerland. ZURICH: *Zentralbibliothek* (238): L. C. Wohlberg (1932); N. Allony-E. Kupfer (1964).

U.S.A. CINCINNATI: *Hebrew Union College Library* (1,500). LOS ANGELES: *University Library* (Rosenberg Collection from Ancona; the third part of the Gaster Collection, etc., 400). NEW HAVEN: *Yale University Library* (300): L. Nemoy (Journal of Jewish Bibliography; 1938–39). NEW YORK: *Columbia University* (1,000); *Jewish Theological Seminary of America* (10,000; 25,000 fragments): E. N. Adler (1921); *JTS Registers* (1902ff.); *Jewish Institute of Religion—Hebrew Union College* (200); *Jewish Teachers Seminary Library* (120); *R. H. Lehmann Collection* (400); *The New York University, Jewish Culture Foundation Library* (114); *Yeshiva University* (1,000); *YIVO Institute for Jewish Research Library* (1,200). PHILADELPHIA: *Dropsie College for Hebrew and Cognate Learning* (256; 500 fragments): B. Halpern (1924). SAN FRANCISCO: *California State Library* (Sutro Collection, 167): W. M. Brinner (1966).

U.S.S.R. LENINGRAD: *M. S. Saltykov-Shchedrin State Library* (1,962; 15,000 fragments; including the Firkovich Collections): A. Harkavy-H. L. Strack (1875); A. I. Katsch (1957/58; 1970). *Asiatic Museum* (2,347). MOSCOW: *Lenin State Library* (Ginzburg Collection, 2,000).

Vatican. VATICAN: *Biblioteca Apostolica Vaticana* (801): U. Cassuto (1956); N. Allony-D. S. Loewinger (1968).

Bibliography: C. Burchard, *Bibliographie zu den Handschriften vom Toten Meer* (1959, 1965); E. Sachau, *Aramaeischer Papyrus und Ostraka* (1911); N. Avigad, in: *Scripta Hierosolymitana*, 4 (1958), 56–87; idem, *Ha-Pale'ografyah shel Megillot Yam ha-Melah*... (1963), 107–34; G. R. Driver, *Aramaic Documents of the Fifth Century* (1954); I. Ben-Zvi et al., *Meḥkarim be-Keter Aram Ẓova* (1960); I. Yevin, *Keter Aram Ẓova*... (1969); L. Zunz, in: ZHB, 18 (1915), 58–64, 101–19; A. Freimann, *ibid.*, 11 (1907), 86–96; 14 (1910), 105–12; idem, in: *Alexander Marx Jubilee Volume* (1950), 231–342 (Eng. sect.); S. Poznański, in: ZHB, 19 (1916), 79–122; C. Bernheimer, *Paleografia Ebraica* (1924); S. A. Birnbaum, *Hebrew Scripts* (1954–57; 1 vol. of plates; Part 1 not publ.); C. Sirat and M.Beit-Arié, *Manuscripts médiévaux en caractères hébraiques*... (1969); *Reshimat Kitvei-Yad*... (1960), includes *"Kitvei-Yad... Faksimiliyyot"*: 54–69; S. Shaked, *A Tentative Bibliography of Geniza Documents* (1964); S. Loewinger and A. Scheiber, (eds.) in: *Geniza Publications in Memory of D. Kaufmann* (1949), xiii–xv; A. Scheiber, *Héber kodexmaradványok*... (1969); *Die hebraeischen Uebersetzungen des Mittelalters und die Juden als Dolmetscher* (1893); Shunami, Bibl. (for the literature on and from M. Steinschneider); M. Steinschneider, *Vorlesungen ueber die Kunde hebraeischer Handschriften* (1897; Hebrew edition by A. M. Habermann, in: *Aresheth*, 4 (1966), 53–165; separate ed., 1965); A. Freimann, *Union Catalog of Hebrew Manuscripts and their Location*, 2 (1964); N. Allony and D. S. Loewinger, *List of Photographed Manuscripts, Austria-Germany* (1957); N. Allony and A. Kupfer, *List... Belgium, Denmark, Holland, Spain, and Switzerland* (1964); N. Allony and D. S. Loewinger, *List... Vatican Library* (1968); D. S. Loewinger and E. Kupfer, *List... Parma Library* (in preparation); D. S. Loewinger, *Sekirah al Pe'ullot ha-Makhon*... (1965); idem, in: *Haaretz* (Sept. 21, 1969); M. Beit-Arié, in: KS, 43 (1967/68), 411–28; 45 (1969/70), 435–46.

[D.S.LOE./E.K.]

MA'ON (biblical **Maon**, Heb. מָעוֹן). (1) City in Judah, the dwelling place of Nabal (I Sam. 25:2, 3); there was also a desert of the same name (I Sam. 23:25). Maon belonged to the seventh district of Judah (Josh.15:55). In talmudic sources it is called Maon of Judah to distinguish it from Bet Maon near Tiberias (Mekh. Yitro 1). The place is identified with Tell Maʿīn, about 4 mi. (7 km.) S.E. of Yaṭṭa. (2) The Maonites, a tribe, oppressed Israel along with the Zidonians and the Amalekites (Judg. 10:12). This tribe may be identical with the Meunim whose tents were destroyed by the Simeonites (I Chron. 4:41) and were later defeated by Uzziah, king of Judah (II Chron. 26:7). The area in which this tribe was located is in dispute. (3) Site southwest of Gaza, called Menois in Roman times. It was the westernmost point of the Palestinian limes(Codex Theodosius 7:4, 30; *Notitia Dignitatum in partibus Orientis* 34:19, 2). The place is shown on the Madaba Map. Eusebius mistakenly identified it with the Madmannah of Joshua 15:31 (Onom. 130:7). It is now identified with Ḥorvat Ma'on (Khirbat al-Maʿin) near Nirim, southeast of Gaza. A kibbutz called Ma'on was established near the site in 1949. Remains of mosaic pavements and other debris show that the area contained an extensive settlement from the fourth century C.E. onward. The most interesting building is a synagogue which was excavated in 1958. It is oriented toward the northeast and consists of a hall, 14.8 × 11.8m., with two rows of four columns forming the nave and two aisles. In the vicinity was a ritual bath *(mikveh)*. The stone-paved aisles and narthex form a sort of ambulatory around the mosaic-paved nave. The design of the mosaic shows a vine

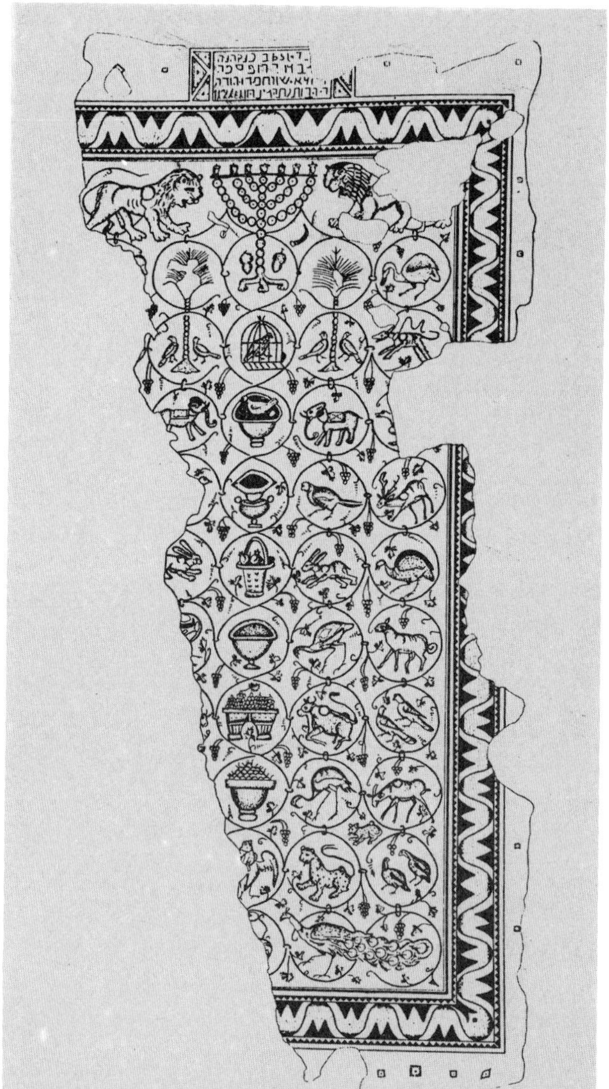

Drawing of the floor mosaic of the synagogue at Ma'on, near Nirim, southeast of Gaza, sixth century C.E. From *Bulletin of the Louis M. Rabinowitz Fund*, No. 3, Jerusalem, December 1960.

trellis issuing from an amphora flanked by peacocks; the trellis forms medallions within which pairs of various animals are represented. The section of the pavement nearest to the apse has symbolic designs: two palm trees with doves at their bases and above them a *menorah* with two *etrogim*, a *shofar*, and a *lulav*, flanked by two lions. The Aramaic inscription mentions the congregation as a whole and three individual donors of a gold dinar each. The pavement, which dates to the early sixth century, has an interesting parallel in a church pavement found at nearby Shellal.

Bibliography: (1) Beyer, in: ZDPV, 54 (1931), 228; Noth, in: PJB, 30 (1934), 35. (2) EM, s.v. (includes bibliography). (3) Alt, in: PJB, 26 (1930), 33; Abel, Geog, 2 (1938), 180; Avi-Yonah, Geog, index; idem, *Madaba Mosaic Map* (1954), 74; Levi et al., in: BRF, 3 (1960), 1–40. [M.A.-Y.]

MA'OR KATAN (Lucerna, Lutzerner, Luzerner), family of physicians in Vienna and Prague in the 17th century, who intermarried with the *Fraenkel-Teomim family. The family is well known mainly because of their internal correspondence from 1619, preserved in the Viennese imperial archives. The first of the family, MOSES BEN LOEB (d. 1605), was elected in 1570 and 1573 as physician of the Frankfort community. He presented a certificate by the *bet din* of Mantua that he belonged to the Freistaedtl family there. His son, JUDAH LEIB (Leva, Leo Lucerna Hebraeus Aulicus; d. 1635), was physician and at the same time rabbi in Vienna. He built himself a synagogue in his house, and left unpublished books. His grandson, Menahem Mendel *Auerbach, describes him in his *Atteret Zekenim* (1702), para. 572. Another son, AARON, was employed by the Prague Jewish community in 1619 as physician, attending Christians as well. Through his mother and his wife he was related to Yom Tov Lipmann *Heller, who in his *Ma'adanei Melekh* on *Ḥullin* 66b acknowledges information supplied by Aaron. Besides attaining the degree of doctor of medicine he was also a doctor of physics and philosophy from the university at Padua, and was the only Jewish physician fully recognized by the Vienna medical faculty.

Bibliography: B. Wachstein, *Die Inschriften des alten Judenfriedhofes in Wien*, 1 (1912), index; A. Landau-B. Wachstein, *Juedische Privatbriefe aus dem Jahr 1619* (1911), index; G. Kisch, in: JGGJČ, 6 (1934), 15; I. Kracauer, *Geschichte der Juden in Frankfurt a. M. (1150–1824)*, 2 (1927), 260; M. Grunwald, *Vienna* (1936), index. [M.LA.]

MA'OZ ḤAYYIM (Heb. מָעוֹז חַיִּים), kibbutz in central Israel, in the Beth-Shean Valley near the Jordan River, affiliated to Ha-Kibbutz ha-Me'uḥad. It was founded in 1937 during the 1936–39 Arab riots, as the first *tower and stockade village east of Beth-Shean, by four groups, three of whom set out a few months later to establish further kibbutz outposts: *Kefar Ruppin, *Mesillot, and *Neveh Eitan. Most of the founders of Ma'oz Ḥayyim were Israel-born. In the Israel *War of Independence (1948), the kibbutz held an advanced defense position; it again suffered repeated shelling in the period after the *Six-Day War (1967). The kibbutz economy is based on cotton, fruit orchards, carp ponds, and dairy cattle, and an agricultural machinery factory. Nearby, the Ma'oz Bridge (known in Arabic as Jisr e-Shaikh Husain جسر الشيخ حسين) spans the Jordan, over what is assumedly the ford used by the Midianites in their flight from Gideon's army; by Pompey in 63 B.C.E.; by the Arab-Muslim army in 635 C.E.; and by Saladin in 1187 when he invaded the country. The name, "Ḥayyim's Stronghold," commemorates Ḥayyim *Sturman, a Ha-Shomer veteran killed by Arabs on a land-purchasing mission in the Beth-Shean Valley. [E.O.]

MA'OZ ẒUR (Heb. (יְשׁוּעָתִי) מָעוֹז צוּר; "O Fortress, Rock (of My Salvation)," see: Isa. 17:10), initial words and title of a hymn sung, in the Ashkenazi ritual, in the synagogue and at home after the kindling of the *Ḥanukkah lights. The song originated in Germany probably in the 13th century (Zunz. Lit Poesie, 580); the author is an otherwise unknown poet by the name of Mordecai as shown by the acrostic of the first five stanzas. Some scholars indentify him with Mordecai b. Isaac, the author of the Sabbath table hymn *Mah Yafit*. The original *Ma'oz Ẓur* consists of six stanzas, the first expressing Israel's messianic hopes for the reestablishment of the ancient Temple worship. The following three stanzas praise God for the deliverance of Israel from the Egyptian bondage, from the Babylonian exile, and from *Haman's plot. The fifth stanza summarizes the miracle of Ḥanukkah, and the last one is a plea for the speedy redemption of Israel. The reference in it to *Admon*—as a synonym for Edom—has been understood to refer to the German Emperor Frederic Barbarossa (1121–90 C.E.). This last verse is now omitted and does not figure in most *siddur* editions, though its acrostic חֲזַק (*ḥazak*, "strong"), seems to show that it is part of the original composition. Another six verses have been added to *Ma'oz Ẓur* in the course of time by various authors, the first, so it is claimed, by Moses *Isserles. The theme of these additions, too, is a plaint against persecution by Edom and Ishmael (Christians and Arabs), and a prayer for divine vengeance and redemption. An English version of this hymn, called *Rock of Ages*, was written by M. *Jastrow and G. *Gottheil. It differs slightly from the original Hebrew text, with its strong plea for vengeance. Some editions of British prayer books (J. H. Hertz, 1963, p. 950) even tampered with the Hebrew text itself. In Conservative and Reform synagogues the English version is sung in addition to or instead of *Ma'oz Ẓur*. [ED.]

Musical Rendition. The most commonly sung melody of *Ma'oz Ẓur* is of West European Ashkenazi origin and may be dated from around the early 15th century. E. *Birnbaum and A. Z. *Idelsohn, on the basis of the similarity of isolated motives, related it to a group of early Protestant chorales and a German soldiers' song. There is a much closer correspondence in the entire melodic line to the church melody *Patrem omnipotentem* which appears in several Bohemian-Silesian manuscripts, the earliest of which is dated 1474. The earliest notation attesting to the use of the melody for *Ma'oz Ẓur* so far located is found in the manuscript of Judah Elias of Hanover (1744) as a "melodic reminder" in settings of *Hodu* for Ḥanukkah. The first printed version appears in Isaac *Nathan's *Hebrew Melodies* (1815) set to Byron's "On Jordan's Banks." None of the standard sources of the 19th and early 20th centuries has the repetition of the last sentence of the stanza, which is a recent and inept "improvement." In Ashkenazi usage, from the beginning of the month of Kislev onward and during the week of Ḥanukkah, various prayers are also sung to the *Ma'oz Ẓur* melody or feature its motives. Other melodies also exist, but their distribution is limited. The melody of the Tedesco (German-Italian) Jews was first notated by the gentile composer Benedetto Marcello in his *Estro poetico-armonico* (Venice, 1724, 1803[2]). It is still sung in Italy, and sometimes also in Israel and the United States. However, the standard West European Ashkenazi melody

X XII X
INTONAZIONE DEGLI EBREI TEDESCHI SOPRA
מעוז צור ישועתי וגו
מעוז צור ישועתי לך נאה לשבח תכון בית
תפלתי ושם תודה נזבח לעת תכין מטבח
מצר המנבח אז אגמור בשיר מזמור חנוכת המזבח
Presto
Violoncello.

EXAMPLE 1. Melody for *Ma'oz Ẓur* of German Jews in Italy, from Benedetto Marcello, *Estro poetico-armonico,* Vol 3, Venice, 1803², p. 12. The notation, from right to left, is followed by the beginning of Marcello's own composition, based on the melody, for voice, violoncello, and basso continuo. Jerusalem, J.N.U.L.

שמחת הנפש

EXAMPLE 2. German melody for *Ma'oz Ẓur,* from Elhanan Kirchhan (Kirchhain), *Simḥat ha-Nefesh,* part 2, Fuerth, 1726/27, fol. 6b. Superscribed in Judeo-German *Sing das Gesang mit Andacht/die Hanukkah Teg acht.* At the end of the first line, the flat sign before the *g* should be placed before the *a.* Jerusalem, J.N.U.L.

EXAMPLE 3

Ma—oz ẓur ye—shu—a—ti le-kha na—eh le-shab-be—ah
tik—kon bet te—fil—la—ti ve-sham to—dah ne-zab-be—ah le—
—et ta-khin maṭ-be—ah miẓ—ẓar ham—nab—be—ah
az eg—mor be—shir miz-mor ha-nuk—kat ham—miz—be—ah

EXAMPLE 3. The conventional Ashkenazi melody for Maoz Ẓur.

has become the dominant and representative one, in spite of objections to its "non-Jewish" character.

Sources: STANDARD MELODY: Idelsohn, Melodien, 6 (1932), pt.1 no. 53; pt. 2 no. 43, both "*Hodu* for Ḥanukkah" from cantors' manuals of the end of the 18th century; Idelsohn, Melodien, 8 (1933), no. 311. Judah Elias of Hanover, Ms. dated 1744, two *Hodu* for Ḥanukkah published by A. Nadel: one, no foliation indicated, in *Der Orden Bne Briss* (Sept.–Oct. 1935), 95; another *Hodu* no. 215, in *Musica Hebraica,* 1–2 (1938), 28, 69. The Ms. is lost; John Braham and Isaac Nathan, *A Selection of Hebrew Melodies . . . by Lord Byron* (London, 1815), 31–36 ("On Jordan's Banks"); Ms. formerly in the possession of the Lieben family of Prague, dated 1820 or 1826, lost, 2 copies made in 1920, one in Jewish Museum, Prague (no no. given), one in JNUL, Jacob Michael Collection of Jewish Music, Ms. no. JMA 4705. fol. 16a. Published by H. Avenary in *Taẓlil,* 7 (1967), 127; A. Baer, *Baal T'fillah* (1883²), no. 188; E. Birnbaum, *Chanuca Melodie "Maos Zur" fuer Pianoforte bearbeitet* (1889), textless; M. Wodak, *Hamnazeach* (1898), no. 94. GERMAN-ITALIAN: Benedetto Marcello, *Estro poetico-armonico* (Venice, 1724–26, 1803²), tom. III, xii–xiv, setting for 1 voice and 2 instruments, prefaced on p. xii by notation of the synagogal tune. Published in Idelsohn, Melodien, 6 (1932), appendix, no. 2 (p. 231), and elsewhere. GERMAN: Elhanan Kirchhan (Kirchhain), *Simḥat ha-Nefesh* (Fuerth, 1726/27), fol. 6b, textless, but with superscription in Judeo-German "Sing the song with devotion on the eight Ḥanukkah days" and fits the meter and rhythm of *Ma'oz Ẓur.* Published a) Facsimile ed., 1926, b) Idelsohn, Melodien, 6 (1932), appendix, no. 7 (p. 233). SILESIAN-POLISH: (based on *Eli Ẓiyyon*). Idelsohn, Melodien, 9 (1932), no. 413, after E. Kirschner, in *Mitteilungen zur juedischen Volkskunde,* 16 (1905), 113. MORAVIA: Ms. Lieben (1820 or 1826; see above) fol. 16b. HASIDIC: attributed to R. Mordecai "The *ḥazzan* of Saslaw" pupil of the Ba'al Shem Tov, fl. c. 1770, in M.S. Geshuri *Ha-Niggun ve-ha-Rikkud ba-Ḥasidut,* 1 (1956), 270. ḤASIDIC-GUR: L. Levi (see bibl.), music supplement p. 12. ITALY-GORIZIA: L. Levi (see bibl.), loc. cit.

[B.B.]

Bibliography: Landshuth, Ammudei, 202; Abrahams, Companion, ccv–vi; Davidson, Oẓar, 3 (1930), 159 no. 1955; J. T. Levinski, *Sefer ha-Mo'adim,* 5 (1954), 180f.; A. Carlebach, in: *Shanah be-Shanah 5730* (1969), 270–4; Hertz, Prayer, 275; *Union Prayer Book,* 1 (1924), 354; *Sabbath and Festival Prayer Book* (1946), 365. MUSICAL RENDITION: L. Levi, in: *Sefer ha-Mo'adim,* 5 (1954), 182–5; D. Kaufmann, in: *He-Assif,* 2 (1885), 298; Zunz, Lit Poesie, 422, 429; H. Avenary, in: *Taẓlil,* 7 (1967), 125–8; Idelsohn, Melodien, 9 (1932), xii; idem, in: HUCA, 11 (1936), 569–91; E. Werner, in: MGWJ, 81 (1937), 393–416.

MAPAI (initials of Heb. **Mifleget Po'alei Ereẓ Israel**), also called Israel—formerly Palestine—Labor Party. The party was founded in 1930 by the union of *Aḥdut ha-Avodah and *Ha-Po'el ha-Ẓa'ir as "a Zionist-Socialist party faithful to the ideal of national redemption and the ideal of socialism in the homeland." Among its founders were Berl *Katznelson, David *Ben-Gurion, Izhak *Ben-Zvi, and Yosef *Sprinzak. Though it had only 5,000 members in 1930, Mapai immediately became the dominant party in the Jewish community and the labor movement. It obtained 27 out of 71 places in the Asefat ha-Nivḥarim (Elected Assembly of the Yishuv) in 1931, and 165 out of 201 at the 1933 *Histadrut convention. At the 18th Zionist Congress in 1933, the labor delegation was the strongest, numbering 138 out of 318, and four Mapai members—David Ben-Gurion (chairman 1935–1948), Eliezer *Kaplan, Moshe Shertok (*Sharett), and Berl *Locker—were elected to the Jewish Agency Executive of ten. Mapai also controlled the Ḥever Ha-Kevuẓot and Ha-Kibbutz ha-Me'uḥad collective movements and the *Moshav movement.

Mapai's approach to socialism was pragmatic rather than Marxist; its aim was not so much the conquest of power by labor, as a gradual advance, in Ben-Gurion's phrase, *mi-ma'amad le-am* ("from class to nation"). It regarded labor as the central force in the nation, responsible for the achievement of national aims, and called for the unification of all the labor parties. It had to contend with the right-wing *General Zionists and the *Revisionists on the one hand, and with the left-wing *Ha-Shomer ha-Ẓa'ir on the other, while cooperating with the religious Zionists and, later, the moderate General Zionists. It was the leading member of the World Union (Iḥud Olami) of *Po'alei Zion and belonged to the Second (Socialist) International.

A leftist group in Mapai, Si'ah Bet ("Faction B"), criticized the reformist tendencies of the majority, who—it also complained—monopolized key positions. The struggle came to a head at the Kefar Vitkin Convention in 1942, which prohibited factions within the party. As a result, Si'ah Bet broke away in 1944, supported by over half of Ha-Kibbutz ha-Me'uḥad, and formed Ha-Tenu'ah le-Aḥdut ha-Avodah (see *Aḥdut ha-Avodah (2)). Despite the split, Mapai retained its absolute majority in the Histadrut, though reduced from 69.3% in 1942 to 53.8% in 1944. It remained the strongest party in the Asefat ha-Nivḥarim (63 delegates out of 171 in 1944), and retained a dominant position in the Jewish Agency Executive.

The party was divided over the Peel Commission's partition proposals in 1937, but decided, against the opposition of Katznelson and others, to accept the principle of partition. Later, it adopted the demand for the establishment of Palestine as a Jewish Commonwealth after the war, approved by the *Biltmore Conference in 1942. It called for participation by Jewish military units in the war against the Nazis, combined with opposition to the White Paper restrictions (1939) on Jewish immigration and land settlement, on the basis of Ben-Gurion's slogan: "We will fight the war as if there were no White Paper, but we will fight the White Paper as if there were no war." It advocated self-defense through the *Haganah under the authority of the Jewish national institutions (Jewish Agency and Va'ad Le'ummi), and the use of physical resistance and even armed force to combat British measures against clandestine immigration, while opposing terrorist reprisals against individual Arabs and all-out rebellion against the Mandatory government.

During the preparations for the establishment of the independent Jewish state, Mapai was allotted ten seats out of 37 in the National Council and four out of 13 in the National Administration, which became the Provisional State Council (legislature) and the Provisional Government respectively when the State of Israel was proclaimed. It won 46 out of 120 seats at the elections to the First Knesset in 1949, 45 in 1951, 40 in 1955, 48 in 1959, and 42 in 1961, and was supported by two to five members of associated Arab lists. It was the dominant force in all Israel cabinets, holding, among others, the portfolios of prime minister, defense, foreign affairs, finance, education, agriculture, and police. In the Jewish Agency, it held the chairmanship of the Executive and headed the Departments of Finance (for most of the post-1948 period), Land Settlement, and Immigrant Absorption. In the Histadrut, it maintained its absolute majority until 1965 and its representatives held leading positions in all its organs. Mapai nominees headed most of the local authorities and held the mayoralties of Jerusalem (1955–1965), Tel Aviv (from 1959), and Haifa (from 1951).

Mapai was badly shaken by the *Lavon Affair, which broke out in September 1960, and its aftermath, in which Ben-Gurion was opposed by a considerable section of the party (see also *Israel, State of, Parties and Politics, and *Ben-Gurion). After removing Lavon from the position of Histadrut secretary-general on Feb. 4, 1961 by 159 votes to 96, Mapai took no further official part in the affair and rallied behind Ben-Gurion at the 1961 elections; but it was still divided over his demand—which he continued to press after his resignation from the premiership in favor of Levi *Eshkol in 1963—for a judicial inquiry into the actions of the cabinet committee which had exonerated Lavon. The dispute was exacerbated by the struggle for the succession to party leadership between a group of younger men, headed by Moshe *Dayan and Shimon *Peres, who were supported by Ben-Gurion, and the veterans led by Eshkol and Golda *Meir. Mapai's tenth convention in 1965 supported Eshkol's rejection of the demand for an inquiry and approved his proposal for an Alignment with Aḥdut ha-Avodah by majorities of about 60%. Ben-Gurion and his followers thereupon established the independent *Rafi list and were expelled from the party. The Alignment gained 50.88% of the votes in the Histadrut elections in September 1965 (Mapai, 33.85% and Aḥdut ha-Avodah, 17.03%), and 45 seats in the Knesset elections in November (36 and 9 respectively).

The Six-Day War and Dayan's co-option to the cabinet as minister of defense paved the way for the healing of the breach. After lengthy negotiations, Mapai, Aḥdut ha-Avodah, and Rafi merged to form the *Israel Labor Party, with 55 parliamentary seats.

Bibliography: L. Fein, *Politics and Political Parties in Israel* (1967). [M.L.]

MAPAM (initials of Heb. **Mifleget ha-Po'alim ha-Me'uḥedet;** "United Workers' Party"), a pioneering, left-wing, labor-Zionist Israel party, founded in 1948, when the *Ha-Shomer ha-Ẓa'ir Workers' Party merged with *Aḥdut ha-Avodah-Po'alei Zion. Party unity was threatened from the first by an extreme left-wing group led by Moshe *Sneh, which demanded unswerving support for the Soviet Union's policies, going so far as to condone the *Slánský Trial in Prague (1952), at which the Zionist Movement was accused of espionage and subversion in the Communist countries and a prominent member of Mapam, Mordekhai Oren, was sentenced to 15 years' imprisonment. In 1953, after a rift which shook the party violently, the group was expelled. Aḥdut ha-Avodah members attempted to transform Mapam into a federation, and most of them left in 1954 to reconstitute their own party when a motion was carried accepting Arabs as members.

Mapam's policies are based on both Zionist and socialist principles. It aims at the concentration of the majority of the Jewish people in its homeland, with pioneering activities as the main motive force of the process. It supports not only the building of a new Israel society and economy, but also the class struggle and links with international socialism. Its declared aims are the achievement of socialism in Israel through the democratic hegemony of the labor movement, by the establishment of labor, public, and state enterprises; labor settlement led by the kibbutz; state ownership of the land; participation of private capital, together with labor and the state economy, in intensive development; efforts to avoid profiteering and parasitism; planned economy to ensure full employment and high productivity, as well as to reduce the gap between the classes by raising the standard of living of the underprivileged. Mapam strives for the separation of state and religion, freedom of conscience and worship for all faiths, and complete equality for the Arab minority.

Mapam regards the effort to achieve peace with the Arab peoples as a fundamental principle of Israel policy and believes that Israel's integration into the Middle East can only be achieved by peaceful means. However, so long as the Arabs do not respond to offers of peace negotiations without prior conditions, Israel must maintain her defensive preparedness. According to a peace plan published by Mapam after the 1967 Six-Day War, Israel must hold the occupied territories until a peace settlement is reached with the Arab governments. Mapam envisaged a peace settlement as based primarily on an agreement of close cooperation with Jordan.

Mapam regards the *Histadrut as the mainstay of Israel society. In the elections to its tenth convention (1965), Mapam received 14.51 per cent of the votes. Mapam was a member of the coalition governments during the third, fourth, and sixth Knesset (1955–61 and from 1966), its

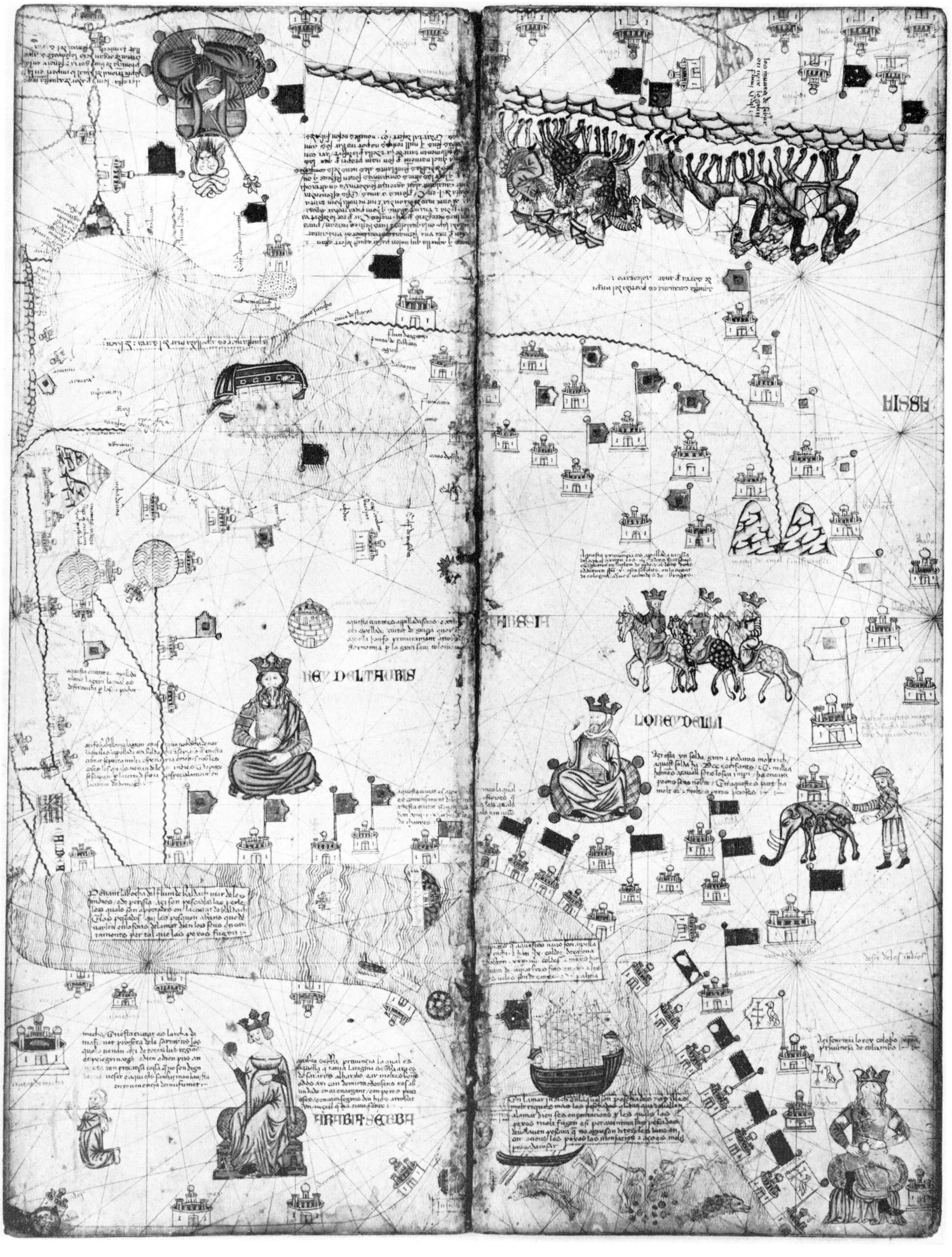

Plate from the "Catalan Atlas," a set of portolano maps drawn by Abraham Cresques and his son Judah (Jaime), in 1375–77 for Don Juan, heir to the French throne. The atlas was later presented to Charles VI of France. This double leaf shows the geography of the East, with the Volga and its delta and the Caspian sea at upper left drawn upside down. At upper right is a caravan, also drawn upside down, on its way to China. In the center of the map is the star of Bethlehem, with the three kings approaching from the right. The globe to the left of the star represents the Persian city of Shiraz. At bottom left is the Persian Gulf, with Mecca below it, depicted as a walled city with three minarets. The enthroned female figure is the Queen of Sheba. Paris, Bibliothèque Nationale, Ms. Espagnol 30, fol. 3v–4.

representatives holding the portfolios of housing and health. Nineteen of its candidates were elected to the first Knesset; 15 to the second, nine (after the split with Aḥdut ha-Avodah) to the third, fourth, and fifth Knesset, and eight to the sixth. In January 1969 it joined the Israel Labor Party in an alignment based on joint action in national and municipal affairs, close cooperation in the Histadrut, and organizational independence for the partners.

Mapam publishes a daily newspaper, *Al ha-Mishmar* ("On Guard"), as well as an Arabic weekly, *Al Marsad*.

Bibliography: M. Ya'ari, *From Vision to Reality* (1963); idem, *What Faces our Generation* (1958); Mapam, *United Workers' Party of Israel* (1965); American Ha-Shomer ha-Ẓa'ir, *Israel Horizons* (1953–); P. Merḥav, *Toledot Tenu'at ha-Po'alim be-Ereẓ Yisrael* (1967); M. Ya'ari, *Kibbutz ha-Galuyyot be-Aspaklaryah shel Yameinu* (1954); idem, *Be-Siman Aḥdut ve-Aẓma'ut* (1968); Mapam, *Ve'idat ha-Iḥud* (1948).

[N.P.]

MAP MAKERS. The first reference to a map is found in Ezekiel 4:1. The prophet is bidden to outline on an unburned brick, a plan of a city under siege, such as are found on Babylonian monuments. Nearer to real map making is a rudimentary map of the borders of Ereẓ Israel which Maimonides attached to one of his responsa (ed. Freimann, no. 346, 311).

The earliest examples of real maps known to have been designed by Jews belong to the so-called portolano maps, which are charts of the coastlines of the oceans, mostly of the Mediterranean, designed for the use of navigators. Portolanos are first mentioned in connection with reports on the second Crusade of Louis IX, king of France, in Tunisia in 1270. They were drawn with surprising precision and distances are also remarkably accurate. These maps, whose origin is still somewhat of a mystery, may preserve an ancient Greek and Byzantine tradition of sea charts, with Jews serving, as in other branches of science, as intermediaries between antiquity and the Middle Ages. Jews on the Spanish island of Majorca, as well as from Alexandria and Safed, have signed their names as makers of portolanos.

The 14th and 15th Centuries. Abraham *Cresques, cartographer and maker of portolanos, worked at Palma in Majorca, then part of the kingdom of Aragon. As the "master of maps and compasses" to the king of Aragon, he is said to have produced in 1376–77, together with his son, the six large leaves of the "Catalan Atlas," which were presented by his sovereign to Charles VI of France. His son Judah, also a geographer and cartographer, was forcibly baptized in 1391 and christened Jaime (or Jacome) Ribes de Majorca; he became director of the nautical observatory at Sagres. Another Jewish cartographer of Majorca—who is conjectured to have belonged to Abraham Crescas' family—was Ḥayyim ibn Rich. He, too, was converted at the time of the persecutions in 1391, adopting the name Juan de Vallsecha. He was probably the father of the Gabriel de Vallsecha who made another famous *mappa mundi* in 1439—now one of the treasures of the Institute of Catalan Studies in Barcelona; it belonged to Amerigo Vespucci—in which the meridian of the Azores is used for the first time in the history of cartography. Another Majorcan cartographer of Jewish birth was Mecia de Viladestes, a map of whose (dated 1413) is preserved in the Bibliothèque Nationale in Paris.

Other Jewish Map Makers. Judah Abenzara (or ibn Zara) is known as the maker of three portolano maps (Alexandria, 1497, in the Vatican College Library, Cincinnati; and the third with his signature followed by the words "Safed in Galilee, October 1505"). Gerard de Jode (de Judeis; 1509–1591), a maker of maps and publisher in Antwerp, was apparently of Jewish origin. A not very successful competitor of Abraham Ortelius, he published single maps and atlases. His work was based on sound geographical knowledge and was executed with elegance and technical perfection. His son Cornelius de Judeis (1558–1600) was his partner and successor. Abraham b. Jacob was an engraver at the end of the 18th century in Amsterdam. He engraved the map of Palestine in the Passover *Haggadah* which was printed by Moses Wesel in Amsterdam in 1696. It was the first map with Hebrew lettering. Aaron b. Ḥayyim of Grodno's map of Palestine appeared in his *Moreh Derekh* (Grodno, 1839^2), which was printed by Meir Isaac Bajarski. Ḥayyim Solomon Pinia of Safed made a pictorial map of the Holy Land, which was edited by Joshua Alter b. Moses b. Phinehas Feinkind of Turek and lithographed by S. Litmanowitz in Turek (near Kalisz, Poland) in 1875; the text is in Hebrew. Another edition with a supplementary German text is lithographed on fabric.

See also *Maps of Ereẓ Israel, *Jerusalem, Cartography.

Bibliography: E. G. Ravenstein, in: EB, 17 (1911^{11}), 633–53; G. Hoelscher, *Drei Erdkarten*... (1949); H. M. Z. Meyer, in: M. Avi-Yonah et al., *Jerusalem: the Saga of the Holy City* (1954), 59–76 (incl. bibl.); C. Roth, *Jewish Contribution to Civilization* (1956^3), 59–61; G. Grosjean and R. Kinauer, *Kartenkunst und Kartentechnik* (1970), 29ff.

[H.M.Z.M.]

MAPS OF EREẒ ISRAEL. Graphic descriptions of Ereẓ Israel relating to its topography and history and based on factual data, are not only extremely valuable sources for the reconstruction of the physiographic and anthropogenic conditions prevailing there at the time they were drawn, but are also nearly always far more important as documents which give evidence on contemporary developments of cartography in general. In this respect the cartographic representation of Ereẓ Israel differs fundamentally from that of any other country. The main reason for that was its unique status as its special significance for believers in the three monotheistic religions which had such a decisive influence upon the culture and history of the Occident. Consequently Ereẓ Israel became a main—at times almost a sole—object of cartography for several countries. There are innumerable maps depicting the "Holy Land," and they date back to the very dawn of cartography. Another important aspect is that there is no major break in the cartographic representation of Ereẓ Israel over more than a millennium and a half; thus the subsequent depictions of the country reflect the general developments of cartography and at times are even the principal reason for it. This resulted from the fact that the "Holy Land" was treated as a very special, even unique, geographical-historical and even cosmological object, involving specific problems as to adequate cartographic expression and therefore necessitating techniques and means that were not applied at all, or applied only partially and usually much later in maps dealing with other countries.

Ereẓ Israel in Ancient Cartography. Only four map-like documents dating back to classical times are known at present. Of these only one has been preserved in the original (Madaba Map mosaic), while the three others exist in medieval copies only.

MADABA MOSAIC. This mosaic, partly destroyed when a church floor in Madaba was unearthed, is a typical pictorial map whose subject is the biblical countries, i.e., besides the land of Israel—to which it is mainly devoted—it depicts parts of Lower Egypt, Sinai, and southern Syria. For further details see *Madaba Map. It became one of the most important and reliable sources for the reconstruction in particular of the anthropogenic landscape of Ereẓ Israel in the Byzantine period.

THE PTOLEMAEUS MAPS. In the maps which are ascribed to

Claudius Ptolemaeus, a second-century Alexandrian cartographer, and which are drawn presumably to illustrate his treatise *Γεωγραφικὴ ὑφήγησισς* (preserved only in medieval copies), Ereẓ Israel is represented in the map entitled "The fourth part of Asia." Its scale is very small; nevertheless, it is of great value since it contains much information pertinent to Ereẓ Israel in the period of the Antonine dynasty. From the cartographic point of view its greatest importance lies in the fact that (as will be detailed below) it changed thoroughly all the fundamental long-held clichés concerning the representation of the Holy Land, and introduced northern orientation and an exact scale by the use of the longitude and latitude grid.

THE PEUTINGER TABLE (TABULA PEUTINGERIANA). The Peutinger Table seems to have been one of the very common road maps in use in the Roman Empire. The original table seems to have been drawn in the third century, and the extant copy probably dates from the 13th century. It is exceedingly long in proportion to its width (682 ×33 cm.), and its main subject, to which all other details are subordinated, is a communications network of the contemporary Roman Empire, specifically emphasizing its stations and the distances between them. Originally drawn in one piece, it was apparently cut into a series of sections of equal size later on. Ereẓ Israel is depicted on it in the lower portions of the sections IX and X. It is assumed that the copy does not differ appreciably from the original; the most pronounced variances are, significantly, several "Christian" additions localizing, illustrating, and explaining sights and events of Christian-biblical interest and thus mainly found in the portion depicting Ereẓ Israel and the adjacent regions. It has been assumed, therefore, that this preserved map was copied in order to serve as a guide to pilgrims traveling to Ereẓ Israel and Rome. The map is not drawn to any scale, and the location of the provinces represented on it is dictated merely by the space provided by the elongated shape of the map which led to extreme distortions in their outlines and situation.

THE "SAINT JEROME MAPS." There are two maps known as the Saint Jerome Maps, both of these copies drawn in the third century. They are included in a manuscript in St. Jerome's *De hebraicis quaestionibus et interpretationibus nominum Veteris et Novi Testamenti,* and their contents provide evidence that the originals were produced at the time of the Church Fathers, but not necessarily by Jerome himself. Both are rather crude black-ink sketches very generalized in style and content, and were thus important as precursors of a great number of maps drawn by monks in the medieval period. One of the drawings depicts the Roman Empire according to its division into provinces, emphasizing the places of special interest to Christians. As a portion of this map is missing, only the northern part of Ereẓ Israel appears on it: the Mt. Hermon area and the sources of the Jordan (designated here as "Jor" and "Dan"—a toponymic deduction from the name of the river that prevailed throughout the Middle Ages). The second sketch contains both the whole of Ereẓ Israel and the adjacent countries, Egypt, Syria, and Mesopotamia. Some of the most characteristic features of almost all the "scholastic" medieval maps are also present here: Ereẓ Israel occupies the central part of the drawing and is represented out of all proportion to the surrounding countries, which appear as small unimportant appendages. Similarly, only places and topographical features of biblical interest appear on this map sketch.

In the Middle Ages. Although in general, cartography in the Middle Ages was of a low standard, cartography of Ereẓ Israel reached a peak in this period, both in quantity and quality. For several centuries, Ereẓ Israel was the sole, or at least the most important and prominent, subject of map making. Two kinds of maps existed in the Middle Ages:

a. World maps *(mappae mundi),* almost all of which were of an abstract nature, and were largely the work of monks. Their purpose was to explain and illustrate contemporary ecclesiastical views of cosmography and geography; which, rather than being based on a knowledge of reality, were based on the Scriptures, as interpreted by the Church Fathers and the scholastics, as well as by the writings of ancient polyhistors such as Pliny, Pomponius Hella, and Solinus. Not only was the content of these world maps decisively influenced by the Bible; even their shape (a circle or rectangle) was a result of dogmatic interpretations of certain biblical passages. The world maps are "oriented," i.e., their top denoted the East, the presumed site of Paradise (which is shown on many of these maps as a geographical actuality). In all the maps, Ereẓ Israel occupies a prominent place, in many instances as much as a sixth of the entire space (as for example in the famous "Anglo-Saxon" map). In some of the maps, which are so abstract in conception and drawing as to represent mere cartograms, Ereẓ Israel takes up so much space that the other countries tend to appear as insignificant background only. The description of Ereẓ Israel on these maps consists entirely of biblical topography, with an addition of explanations and traditional identifications of places. Furthermore, from the beginning of the Crusades up to the 16th century, Jerusalem, believed to be the "navel of the world," was placed at the very center of all world maps. This of course, dictated the whole framework, structure, and composition of the map, fulfilling the role played in present maps by the reference location of the poles and the equator. The proportionally great detail of the historio-geographical and physiogeographic facts in which traditional particulars of Ereẓ Israel were depicted or verbally denoted on the maps (such as Mt. Gilboa, Mt. Tabor, various springs, caves, trees, holy places, etc.), however, made it necessary to invent new forms for expressing such details, and this seems to have had a lasting effect upon the development of symbols and signs used in maps in the following centuries. Among medieval maps there were many sketchlike maps of Jerusalem, that were generalized and geometrical and served as guides to pilgrims and Crusaders.

b. The portolano maps, which appeared in the late Middle Ages, were used mostly for purposes of navigation and were probably derived from charts developed as early as the Byzantine period. Many Jewish cartographers were involved in the production of this kind of map, in particular those of the Catalan school, centered in Majorca. The most renowned representatives of this school were Abraham and Judah (Jaime) Cresques; the latter drew the Catalan Atlas, the most beautiful and advanced project of the portolano cartography. Although on these maps Ereẓ Israel no longer occupies a disproportionate amount of space, it continues to exhibit many specific aspects, both as to content and cartographic execution. Since these maps were sea charts aimed at serving navigation, they concentrated primarily on the delineation of coastlines and the location of ports, and show hardly any details of the interior, except perhaps for a flag (banner?) signifying the political control of the country. An exception is made in the case of Ereẓ Israel, for which the relevant portion of the map shows great inland detail, such as the Jordan and its lakes, holy places, and important churches and monasteries. The Red Sea is shown in red or crimson (whereas other bodies of water are shown in blue or light green); a white strip marks the site where the Israelites are presumed to have crossed the Red Sea. It has become increasingly certain that the portolano maps served as the basis of the few regional maps made in the Middle Ages (at least the few that have been preserved). All of these maps (with one exception, which also contains Britain; see the Matthew Paris map, below) have Ereẓ Israel as their subject. Considering the period in which they were made, these are exceptional maps: a) They are the outcome of either direct observation or factual and critically adapted information. b) Their contents are of a topical nature, describing Ereẓ Israel during and after the time of the Crusader Kingdom of Jerusalem, though they also contain many details based on biblical tradition—so important for every Christian pilgrim in the Middle Ages but not corresponding to the reality of the country and in contrast to the factual content of the map. c) They generally serve a practical purpose, i.e., as guides for armies or pilgrims. d) Some of the maps and techniques exhibit specific features that denote marked progress in cartography and were used in the maps of other countries only much later.

The outstanding medieval maps of Ereẓ Israel that have been preserved are the following: 1. A large map (2,080 sq. cm.), preserved at Florence, that is extraordinary not only with regard to its delineation of the coast, which corresponds closely to reality as is the rule with portolano maps, but also as to its wealth of detail. The details, however, are of a much lower standard; for example, the markings of locations—which is a major subject of all medieval maps—are out of proportion to the areal extension of the map. The map is oriented to the East, in contrast to the portolanos, thus reflecting the prevailing influence of the *mappae mundi* and their affinities. 2. A sketch map of Ereẓ Israel at Oxford, whose portolano origin is evidenced by its orientation to the North. It contains a great number of topical details, including some based on observation, such as a

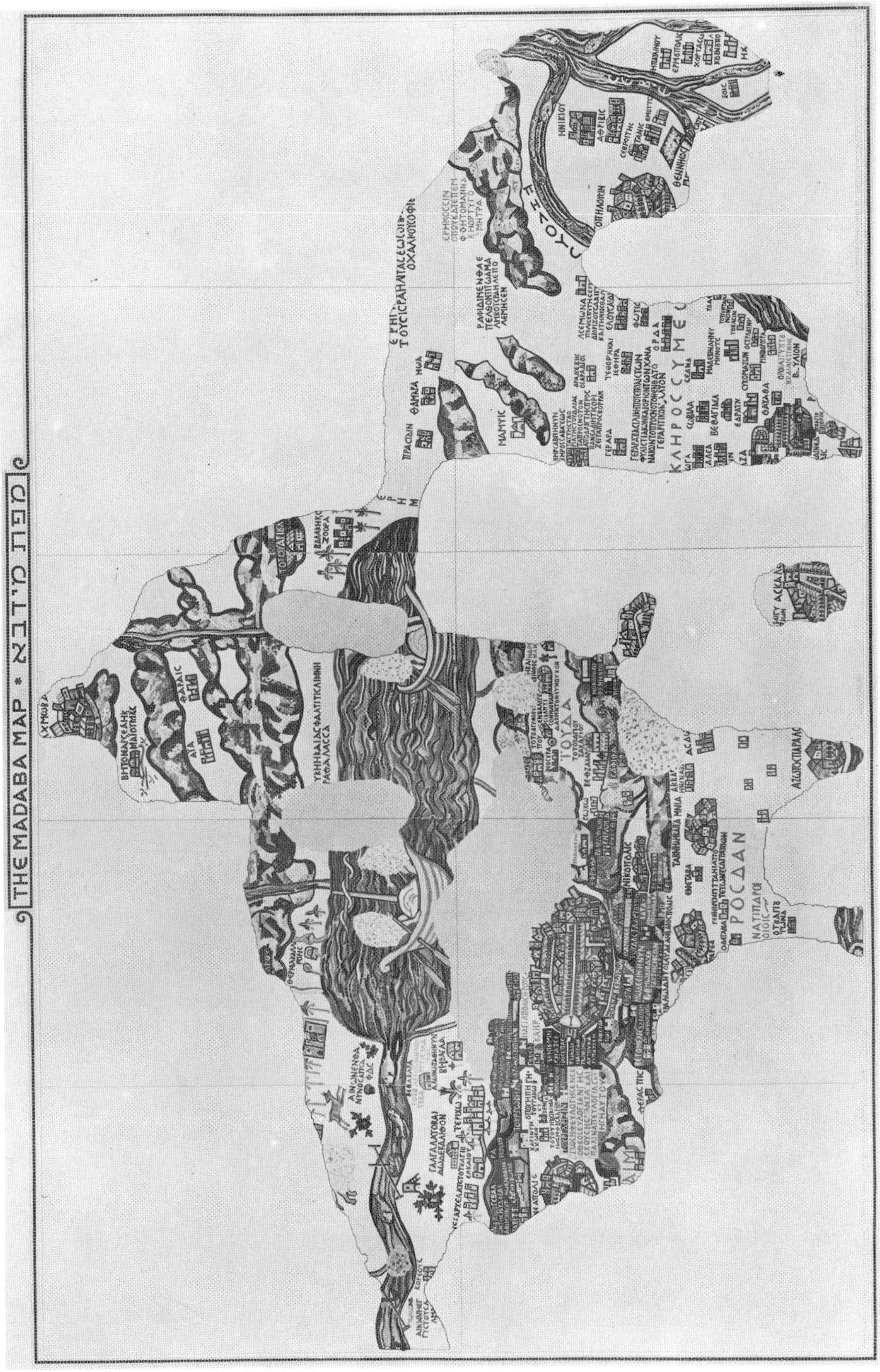

Figure 1. The mosaic map of Ereẓ Israel forming the floor of a sixth-century church at Madaba, Jordan. From *Atlas of Israel,* Survey of Israel, Jerusalem, 1970. Based on Palmer and Guthe's reproduction, 1906.

unique description of the road leading from the coast to Jerusalem. 3. Another map kept at Florence, outstanding in the quality of its illustrations and colors, but inferior in content to the two maps mentioned above. Because of its highly heraldic and ornamental designs and its wonderful coloring, it represents one of the most pronounced examples of the artistry employed in the late Middle Ages. 4. A map drawn by Matthew Paris of England (1250 C.E.), outstanding for its unique description of the road system and its allusions to caravan traffic between Ereẓ Israel and Syria. Some places, especially Acre, the most important Crusader fortress, are depicted in great detail in a separate small vignette. Paris was also the author of an illustrated road guide (England to the Holy Land) which is unique in cartography. The map has the form of a long strip and signifies with miniature designs the stops along the route between the two countries; the stops were usually churches or monasteries that pilgrims customarily visited, and even the roads leading from one stop to the next are indicated by two parallel lines. 5. Medieval cartographic presentation of the Holy Land

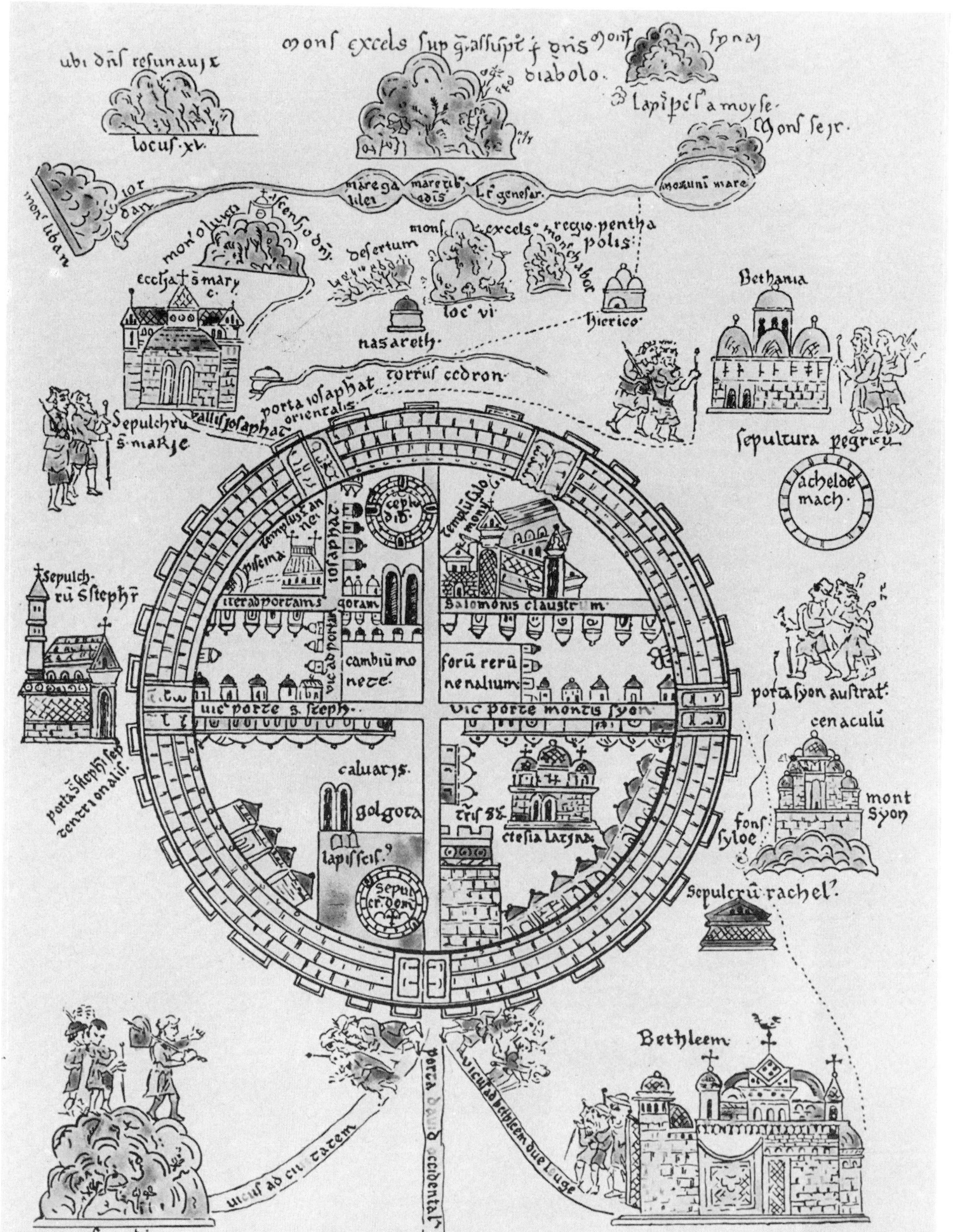

Figure 2. Pictorial map of Jerusalem and Ereẓ Israel from a 12th-century Latin manuscript. East is at the top. Brussels, Bibliothèque Royale de Belgique, No. 9823–24, p. 157.

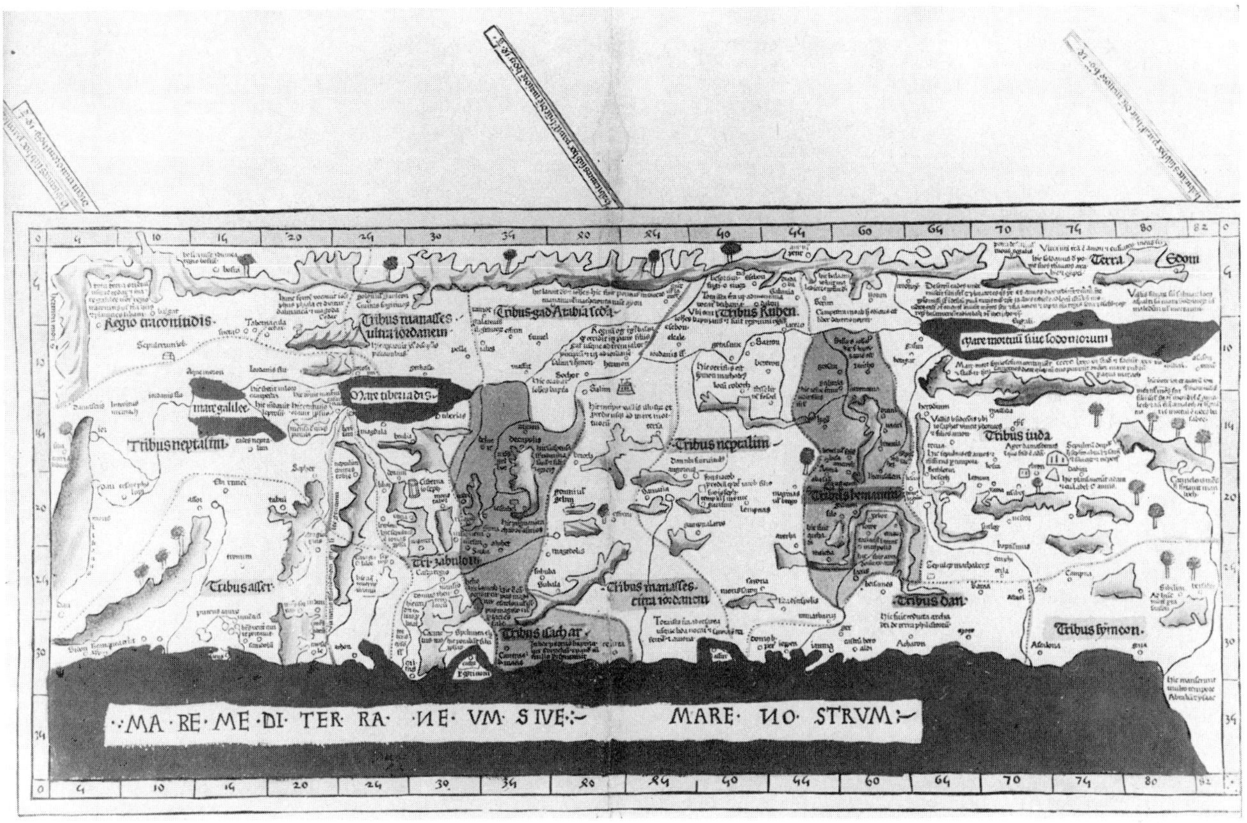

Figure 3. Map of Ereẓ Israel of non-Ptolemaic design, executed by Pietro Vesconte for *Liber Secretorum Fidelium Crucis* by Marino Sanuto, early in the 14th century. From Donnus Nicholas (ed.), *Claudii Ptolemei viri Alexandrini Cosmographie . . .*, Ulm, 1482. Jerusalem, J.N.U.L.

reached its climax in a series of maps and sketches attached to a memoir by the Venetian Marino Sanuto, appealing for a renewal of crusading *(liber secretorum fidelium crucis)*. The map appendage consists of a map of Ereẓ Israel, a rather stereotyped *mappa mundi*, a map of the Near Eastern countries, and a detailed, extremely accurate sketch of Acre, and a far more conventional one of Jerusalem. It is now established that at least the maps of Israel and of the Near East were drawn by Pietro Vesconte, a noted portolano cartographer. The map of Ereẓ Israel is an astounding piece of work, anticipating various future cartographical developments by several centuries. It is not only relatively exact in scale—a characteristic common to most portolanos as far as the coasts are concerned—but also exhibits a grid of longitudinal and latitudinal lines equally spaced throughout at the distance of 1 "leuca" (approx. 2,500 meters). The location of the towns and villages, at least those existing at the time, is rather exact, as are the sites of most topographic features represented in the map. Another extraordinary feature is the wealth of information (besides the usual indication of biblical sites, the areas assumedly occupied by the tribes of Israel, and pertinent remarks and explanations derived from the Bible) on the contemporary situation, based, as were the above-mentioned features of the map, on the author's personal observation and/or intensive study of the memoir. Because of its relative accuracy and abundance of detail, the map served as a pattern for other maps during the Renaissance period; however, its grid was generally replaced by the Ptolemaic latitude and longitude grid. 6. A map drawn by William Wey in the 15th century. It is a typical medieval depiction of Ereẓ Israel, in which all the elements of medieval presentation of this country are incorporated and superbly executed, in particular the pictorial embellishments and the coloring (illumination).

Ereẓ Israel in Arab Cartography of the Middle Ages. In general, medieval Arab maps were more exact, more detailed, and more comprehensive than European maps, but in technique they were far more uniform and stereotyped, employing outlines and symbols of a strictly geometric nature. In Arab maps, Ereẓ Israel did not occupy the most prominent place. The best and most comprehensive Arab map of Ereẓ Israel was made by Idrissi, whose cartographic works represent a mixture of Moslem and Western European style and content.

In Modern Times. The cartographical representation of Ereẓ Israel underwent some fundamental changes in modern times: 1. As a result of constantly growing geographical knowledge (gained from the works and maps of Ptolemaeus) and the extensive discoveries of whole continents, accompanied by the development of the sciences, in particular those dealing with the earth—its astronomical position, movements, and surface nature, Jerusalem could no longer be regarded as the "navel of the world" and ceased to be used as the center of world maps. 2. The mathematical and astronomical fixing of locations—by means of lines of longitude and latitude—based upon the method used by Ptolemaeus and arrived at by exact measurements, made it possible to establish the proper outlines of the countries and their relative size. Each map was now based on a distance scale and it was no longer possible to exaggerate the size of Ereẓ Israel in comparison with the other countries of the world. 3. However, whereas the maps of other countries usually contained only details of a contemporary nature, maps of Ereẓ Israel retained their historical character. The main purpose of these maps was to describe the topographical and geographical background of the events described in the Bible and the Gospels, and they ignored the actual landscape of the country, and in particular, the anthropogenic features (villages, roads, etc.). For this reason, a contemporary map of Ereẓ Israel *(tabula moderna)* was usually attached to the Ptolemaeus maps, made to a much larger scale, orientated to the East, and containing many traditional topographical designations. Most of these maps were based on that of Sanuto. Nevertheless, for a variety of reasons, maps of Ereẓ Israel retained their special importance in the early modern period: 1) For various historical and religious reasons (the Reformation, Bible translations), the invention of printing made maps of Ereẓ Israel the most popular and most widely distributed maps; they were also the first to be produced in print. 2) The competition resulting from the wide demand for maps of Ereẓ Israel that provided the location of sites mentioned in the Bible, caused these maps to become generally the most splendid and beautiful ones produced in this period; this applies particularly to the signs and symbols used on the maps, the decoration of the margins, and the cartouche, i.e., the part of the map separated by an ornamental enclosure containing the title of the map, its author, the scales, sources, and so on. The historical content, that seemed to illustrate the background of the Bible and Gospels with the little contemporary geographical detailing that was available during the Renaissance period, made it possible to experiment with the maps and even led to innovations as regards scales, symbols, shading, coloring (illumination), etc. Thus the first indication of magnetic variation was made on a map of Ereẓ Israel.

Ereẓ Israel in the Era of Atlases. The magnificent atlases produced during and after the Renaissance, in Western and Central Europe, usually contained at least two maps of Ereẓ Israel, which were the works of different cartographers and were scarcely compatible with each other. One of the maps forms an integral part of each atlas and is usually based on Ptolemaeus; it is oriented to the North, contains some slight changes in the delineation of the coast and some additional relief features and hydrographic details, and a wealth of place-names mentioned in the Scriptures, in the works of Josephus and so on. Thus, in essence, the map depicts Ereẓ Israel as it is shown in "The fourth part of Asia" by Ptolemaeus. There are numerous instances, however, in which the Ereẓ Israel map in the atlas is oriented to the East and is much closer in content and nature to the Sanuto map, with the important addition of the use of the astronomic longitude and latitude grid derived from Ptolemaeus. The second map of Ereẓ Israel (and sometimes even a third, produced by yet another cartographer) is found among the numerous addenda *(additamentum)* that were attached to the atlases in this period. Important Ereẓ Israel maps in this period were produced by Ortelius, Mercator, Tilemanus Sigenensis, Laicstein, Blaeu, Janszon, Homann, Sanson, Seutter, de Lille, Bonne, and d'Anville. The maps made by the last three cartographers mentioned (who represent the French school) were superior to others in the precision of their content and may be regarded as the most advanced maps prior to those of the 19th century. There were also maps of Ereẓ Israel that were attached to the numerous cosmographies published in this period (of which that by Sebastian *Muenster was the most widely distributed). Even more important, as a source for the maps appearing in the atlases, were the various works on Ereẓ Israel, which contained maps made to a large scale. Among these, mention should be made of the works of Jacob Ziegler, Adrian Adrichomius (1590), and last and most important, Hadrianus Relandus' *Palaestina ex monumentis veteribus illustrata,* which contains a number of detailed and relatively precise maps, especially one showing the relief and the consequent physiographic division of the country in the coastal plain, the mountains, the Valley of the Jordan and the Transjordan plateaus. Only a single map of Israel, made in 1483 by Bernard Breitenbach, is based entirely on the author's personal observation and describes the country as he saw it. Combining both the medieval and modern cartographic style, the map enjoyed great popularity.

In the 18th and 19th Centuries. The first mapping of Ereẓ Israel based partly on topographical survey was made in connection with Napoleon's campaign in Egypt and Ereẓ Israel. The main result of this was a series of 47 maps of Egypt, Sinai, and Ereẓ Israel, named the Jacotin maps after their author (1810). Six of the maps depict parts of Ereẓ Israel, especially those parts through which the army passed on its invasion of the country. The scale is 1:100,000, and the maps show precise details of the areas where measurements were taken by means of the trigonometric methods that had developed in Europe by this time (based on the theodolite and the principle of triangulation). Thus, even the representation of relief on these maps was relatively exact and adequate. Relative differences in height and the diverse gradients of the slopes are shown by hachuring (i.e., expressing the gradient of the slope by discontinuous, proportionally dimensioned lines extending down from the summit to the base of the slope; the steeper the slope the

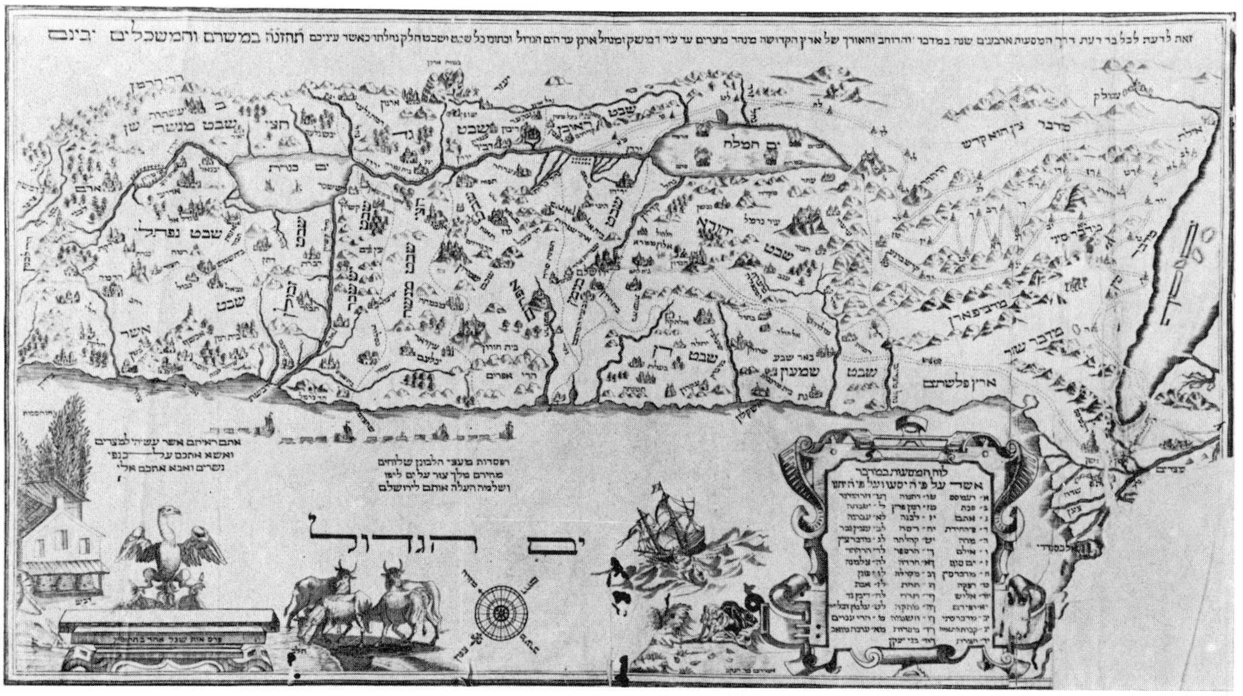

Figure 4. The first map printed in Hebrew. Made by Abraham ben Jacob, it appears in the *Amsterdam Haggadah,* 1695. Jerusalem, J.N.U.L.

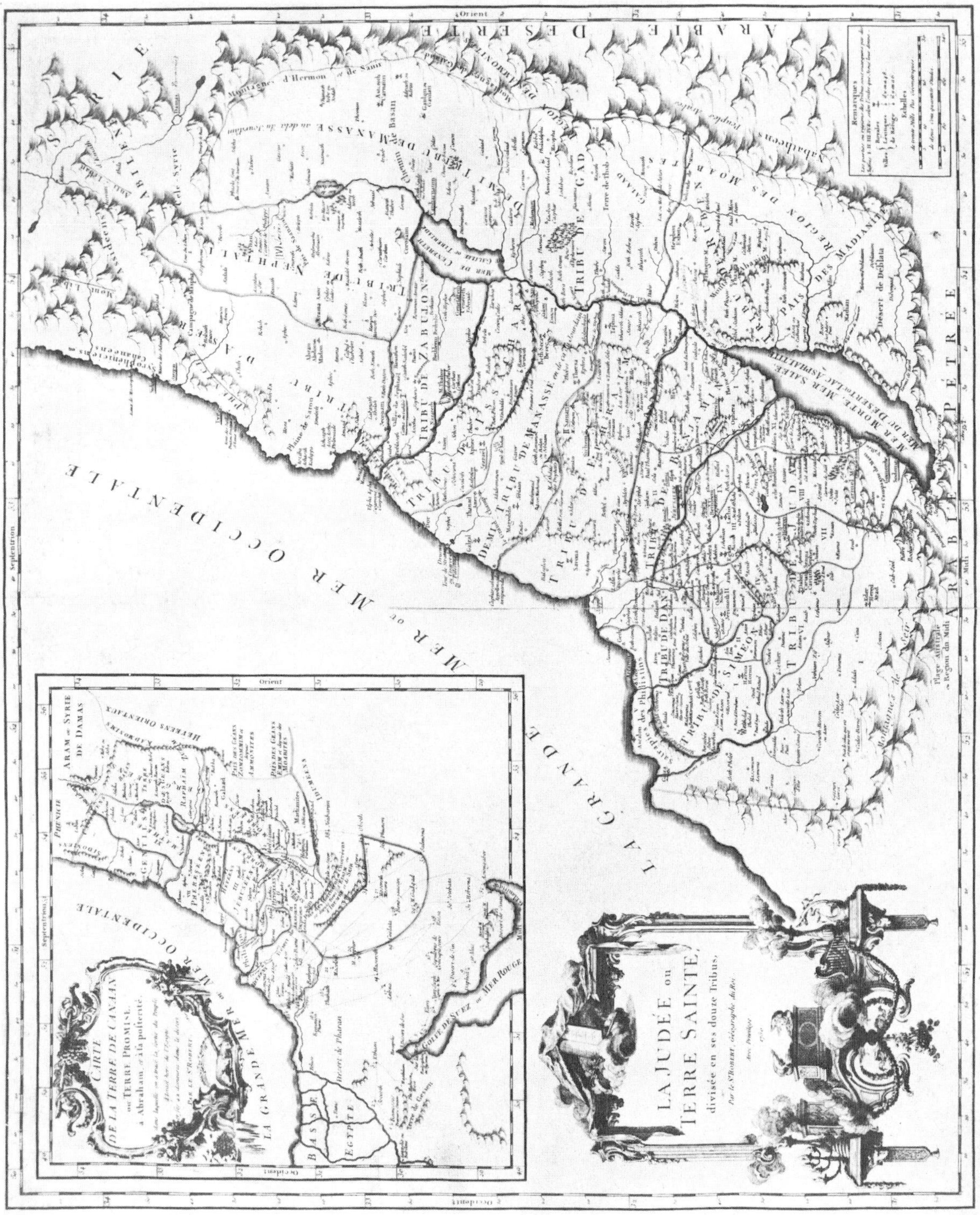

Figure 5. Map of Ereẓ Israel, drawn by Sr. Robert, geographer to the king of France, 1750. The large map shows the land divided among the 12 tribes, while the insert shows the 42 stopping-places of the Israelites on their way from Egypt. Jerusalem, Moshe and Alice Shalvi Collection.

shorter but thicker the hachure line and vice versa), and in general, the rest of the details shown on the maps, i.e., symbols and so on, are of a high standard. Some of the place-names are given in Arabic script, in addition to Latinized transcription. For a period of about 50 years these were the maps used in the exploration of the country.

Toward the end of the 18th century and in the first half of the 19th century, Ereẓ Israel became the subject of numerous exploratory voyages and expeditions, as though it was still "unknown territory." Although the emphasis was on the archaeological and historical aspects of the country, much attention was also paid to its natural conditions including its physiography. In particular, interest was centered on the Jordan Valley and the Dead Sea, because they formed the lowest depression on earth. The works produced by such itinerant scholars and explorers as Seetzen, Burckhardt, Buckingham, and Robinson generally included sketch maps of some areas and sites, and an overall map of the country. Outstanding among these maps is the one attached to Robinson's work, drawn by Kiepert, the well-known German cartographer. An American naval expedition, led by Lynch, executed a map survey of the Jordan River and the Dead Sea. All these works were summarized in *Erdkunde von Asien* ("Geography of Asia") the famous work by Ritter, which also contains a comprehensive list of all known maps of Ereẓ Israel, from ancient times up to the 19th century. A companion to Ritter's work, the atlas by Zimmermann, contains detailed maps of Ereẓ Israel, to the scale of 1:333,333. All the maps listed above were used as an important source for the study of the landscape of Ereẓ Israel in the first half of the 18th century. The final work of this period of individual research and mapping was the map of Van de Velde (scale 1:315,000), one of the most beautiful maps of Ereẓ Israel of this time.

In the second half of the 19th century, the existing maps were felt to be insufficient to meet the requirements of the growing interest in the country, especially for archaeological purposes. The Palestine Exploration Fund (PEF) was established in Britain to carry out a systematic survey of Ereẓ Israel "from Dan to Beer Sheba." The work of the fund was preceded by a survey of the coastline and the adjoining hinterland, ordered by the British Admiralty (1858–1862). They established not only the exact outline of the coastline but also a fixed number of points that were of great help in the survey that followed. An early project undertaken by the Fund was a survey of the Sinai Peninsula, aimed at establishing the route of the Exodus and the location of Mt. Sinai. The maps of Jebel Katerina (the presumed location of Mount Sinai) and Jebel Serbal, whose relief is expressed by form lines, are among the finest maps of the entire area. The first undertaking of the Fund in Ereẓ Israel proper was a survey of Jerusalem and its surroundings (1864), carried out with a precision hitherto not applied in the Near East. In the resulting maps the relief was presented by the hachuring method. In 1871 an expedition of the Fund, led by Conder and later on by Kitchener, embarked upon the main mapping project. The survey encompassed the entire country, from the Qasimiye River up to south of the Dead Sea, and resulted in a set of 26 sheets, made to the scale of 1:63,360 (inch to mile), as on the British topographical maps, and based on a precise triangulation (two base-lines), leveling (Acre-Sea of Galilee, Jaffa-Dead Sea), and altimetric measurements. The relief is represented by means of shading and tinting. In many instances the height is also given in figures; rivers and springs are shown in blue; the various kinds of vegetational cover are indicated by accordant symbols, as are also anthropogenic features. The maps are particularly accurate in the location of the many existing ruins of ancient places of settlement; much effort was also devoted to establishing the names of places and their proper transliteration. The Fund published its *Memoirs*, and they serve to this day as an important geographical and historical source.

"The Survey of Western Palestine" was followed by efforts to carry out a similar survey of Transjordan, which, however, failed for a variety of reasons. Only the Deutscher Palaestina Verein eventually carried out a survey of Gilead, executed to the same scale as the maps of PEF. The maps of the PEF and, to some extent, the German maps too, served as a basis for Ereẓ Israel maps that were produced up to the conquest of Palestine by the British. Among later maps based on those of the PEF, the most important was the Bartholemew map, in which the relief is expressed by contour lines and the subsequent altitude zones are also indicated by varying coloring. In World War I the existing maps were adapted to military requirements, with the help of aerial photography. The maps employed by the British army were made to a scale of 1:40,000, those of the German army to 1:50,000. Shortly before World War I a survey of the Sinai Peninsula was carried out by Newcombe, to a scale of 1:125,000; this included the Negev and the relief was represented by contour and form lines. Shortly after its establishment, the Mandatory government embarked upon a new survey of the country, using up-to-date methods. Two series of maps were printed, one a topo-cadastral set, made to a scale of 1:20,000, and the other a topographical set made to a scale of 1:100,000. This survey was also restricted to the area of Ereẓ Israel extending from the northern political boundary to somewhat south of Beersheba, and consisted of 16 sheets. In these maps the relief was presented by contour lines with a verticle interval of 25 meters. Agricultural areas appear in green and the hydrographic network in blue. The mapping was executed with comprehensive triangulation and fieldwork. Other maps produced by the Mandatory government were maps of the major cities and villages (scale 1:10,000) and a geographical map of the country (1:250,000). During the Mandatory period, efforts were also made to produce a Hebrew map of the country (Press, Brawer, Lief). These were necessarily adaptions of 19th-century maps and those issued by the government Survey Department but they made important contributions to the proper identification of localities, and the use of historical place-names and Hebrew transliteration. With the establishment of the state, "Survey of Israel" became one of its basic governmental institutions in view of the country's ever-expanding exigencies, in particular those connected with economic-demographic planning. These were met by extensive triangulation, leveling which also resulted in a dense altimetric network, new additions (Hebrew) of totally revised and updated map series 1:20,000 and 1:100,000, largely improved not only by the above-mentioned measurements but also by the thorough use of photogrammetric techniques. The 100,000 series is continuously supplemented by a far more comprehensive one at a scale of 1:50,000. The Israel atlas (Heb. 1956–64) and its English edition (1970)—the latest additions to the series of "National Atlases"—summarize both the history and the development of the cartographic representation of the country and its present state in all the fields given to cartographic expression.

Bibliography: L. Bagrow, *History of Cartography* (rev. and enlarged by R. A. Skelton, 1964; orig. Ger., 1951), index s.v. *Palestine;* R. Roehricht, *Bibliotheca Geographica Palestinae* (enlarged and ed. by D. Amiran, Jerusalem, 1963², Ger.); H. M. Z. Meyer, *The Holy Land in Ancient Maps* (Jerusalem, 1965³); Z. Vilnay, *The Holy Land in Old Prints and Maps* (1965²); *Old Maps of the Land of Israel.* Exhibition. Maritime Museum, Haifa. Catalog by H. M. Z. Meyer (1963); M. Avi-Yonah, *The Madaba Mosaic Map* (1954); K. Miller, *Weltkarte des Castorius, genannt die Peutinger'sche Tafel* (1888); B. von Breydenbach, *Die Reise ins Heilige Land . . . 1485* (with the repr. of Reuwich's woodcut map, 1961); Z. Vilnay, *The Hebrew Maps of the Holy Land* (Jerusalem, 1968²); *The World Encompassed. An Exhibition of the History of Maps.* Catalog. Baltimore, Md. (1952); R. A. Skelton, *Decorative Printed Maps of the 15th to 18th Centuries* (1952); C. R. Beazley, *The Dawn of Modern Geography*, 3 vols. (1897–1906, repr. 1949); J. E. Bailey, *Palestine Geography in the Seventeenth Century*, 4 (1872); I. Schattner, *The Maps of Palestine and their History* (Jerusalem, 1951); Y. Karmon, in: IEJ, 10 (1960), 155–73; C. R. Conder, *Tent Work in Palestine* (1878); *Atlas of Israel* (Amsterdam, 1970). [Is.Sc.]

MAPU, ABRAHAM (1808–1867), creator of the modern Hebrew novel. One of the principal exponents of the Haskalah movement in Eastern Europe, he is best known for his first and most successful novel *Ahavat Ẓiyyon* ("The Love of Zion," Vilna, 1853), which represents a turning point in the development of modern Hebrew literature. The son of an indigent and scholarly teacher, Mapu was born in Slobodka, a poverty-stricken suburb of Kovno, where he early acquired a reputation as a brilliant student, and, having mastered much of the talmudic learning of the day, he was considered fit for independent study at the age of 12. Following his marriage at 17, Mapu continued his studies in the home of his wealthy father-in-law in Kovno. After a brief flirtation with Ḥasidism, he resumed an interest in Kabbalah and mysticism, previously fostered by his father. This occasioned a period of close contact with Elijah

*Ragoler. The chance finding of a copy of the Psalms with a Latin translation in Ragoler's home aroused his interest and he taught himself Latin, virtually an unknown study among pious Jews in Eastern Europe. Eventually he

Abraham Mapu, creator of the Hebrew novel. Jerusalem, J.N.U.L., Schwadron Collection.

acquired a fair proficiency in French, German, and Russian, in spite of the prevailing hostility in Orthodox circles to the learning of languages. These studies plus an interest in such equally neglected subjects as Bible, Hebrew grammar, and modern literature, laid the foundations of his subsequent achievements.

Throughout his life Mapu struggled to maintain his family. He became a teacher of young children and was invited in 1832 to tutor the children of a wealthy merchant in the nearby town of Georgenberg. While separated from his family for two or three years, he was drawn to the Haskalah movement, and on his return to Kovno, he began to disseminate its doctrines among the local youth. In 1837 Mapu moved his family to Rossyieny, where he taught for about seven years. In spite of his economic hardship, Mapu found the cultural atmosphere of Rossyieny attractive. There his friendship with Senior *Sachs engendered a profound interest in the history of ancient Israel. In an attempt to improve his finances Mapu returned to Kovno in 1844. His wife died in 1846, and the following year he moved to Vilna to tutor the son of the wealthy but unlettered Judah Opatov. Despite Vilna's reputation as a great center of Haskalah Mapu found the city no more congenial than the house of his harsh employer. On learning of Mapu's appointment to teach at a government school in Kovno in 1848, Opatov assaulted him physically. Mapu, deeply humiliated, fled the house. He avenged the insult by modeling the character of the boorish upstart, Ga'al, in his novel *Ayit Ẓavu'a* ("The Hypocrite") on his former employer. From the Hebrew writers of Vilna, however, Mapu acquired the taste for Romanticism which permeates his novels.

As the new post proved permanent, Mapu settled in Kovno and remarried in 1851. For about ten years domestic happiness and improved financial circumstances coincided with his most fruitful literary period. His growing reputation was enhanced in 1857 by the personal congratulations of the Russian minister of public institutions, Norov, a single honor which induced Mapu to include a poem in Norov's honor in the introduction to his lost novel *Ḥozei Ḥezyonot* ("The Visionaries"). But from 1860 his health began to fail beneath the burdens of overwork and persecution by the pious opponents of Haskalah who managed to influence the censors to delay or even forbid his publications. His meager resources were further undermined by his second wife's long illness, from which she died in 1863. His later years were relieved only by a short visit to St. Petersburg in 1861, where his first acquaintance with opera appealed to his romantic imagination. The loneliness of his last years was aggravated by a disease of his fingers, which made every line he wrote an agony.

Although Mapu was 45 when *Ahavat Ẓiyyon* was published he seems to have labored on the novel, despite its modest length, for more than 20 years. While the plot may well have been originally modeled on the allegorical dramas of M. Ḥ. *Luzzatto, the influence of Senior Sachs directed Mapu's attention toward the Bible, so that the first Hebrew novel also became the world's first novel in a biblical setting. *Ahavat Ẓiyyon* won immediate acclaim, and its continued popularity is attested by at least 16 editions, as well as translations into many languages including English, French, German, Russian, Arabic, Judeo-Arabic, Judeo-Persian, Ladino, and Yiddish. The more liberal spirit prevailing in Russia during the early reign of Alexander II prompted Mapu to choose a contemporary setting for his second novel *Ayit Ẓavu'a*. Of the five parts comprising this long and rambling novel, the first was published in Vilna in 1858, the second in 1861, and the third in 1864. A second edition containing all five parts appeared posthumously in Warsaw in 1869. About ten editions show its popularity. Mapu had been simultaneously composing a third novel, *Ḥozei Ḥezyonot*, depicting the period of the pseudo-Messiah, *Shabbetai Ẓevi. Reputed to have been in ten complete parts, the work was sent to the censor in 1858, together with the first two parts of *Ayit Ẓavu'a*. Whereas the publication of the latter was subject only to irritating delays, the campaign of the fanatical opponents of Haskalah persuaded the censor to forbid publication of *Ḥozei Ḥezyonot* altogether. The manuscript disappeared, and only a seven-chapter fragment remains. Mapu never completely recovered from this loss. To avoid the persecution of his opponents, he reverted to a biblical background for his fourth and last novel, *Ashmat Shomron* ("The Guilt of Samaria," Vilna, first part, 1865; second part, 1866). Again, this achieved some ten editions.

Apart from his novels, Mapu published several books designed to improve the clumsy educational methods of his day. Two of his textbooks, *Ḥanokh la-Na'ar* and *Der Hausfranzose*, appeared in Vilna in 1859. The former outlines the author's method for teaching elementary Hebrew, while the latter comprises a primary textbook for the study of French. Written in German but with Hebrew characters, it constitutes an interesting example of the attempts made by the exponents of Haskalah to broaden the cultural interests of the Jewish community. A third textbook, *Amon Pedagog* (Koenigsberg, 1867), again deals with the teaching of Hebrew. But even within the framework of a textbook, his creative talent emerges in the form of a story, later published separately by J. Klausner under the title *Beit-Ḥanan* (Jerusalem, 1920), which is unfolded section by section to illustrate the rules to be explained. *Amon Pedagog* served as a standard textbook until the end of the century, and went through five editions.

Mapu's creativity contains both strongly imitative and highly original features. The influence of the Bible is naturally most conspicuous in the setting, style, and language of the two historical novels, *Ahavat Ẓiyyon* and *Ashmat Shomron*, which depict life in ancient Israel in the days of Isaiah. In less measure it also extends to *Ayit Ẓavu'a* which portrays contemporary Jewish life mainly in his native Lithuania. Aspects of his novels were derived from other sources, principally Hebrew and French writers. His limited inventiveness is demonstrated by his frequent borrowing of dramatic devices and by the many repetitions and similarities which occur in his stories.

Of the Hebrew writers who influenced Mapu, M. Ḥ. Luzzatto's example may be discerned in the plots, dramatic devices and symbolic names, as well as in the didactic and ethical ideas, and the interest in nature. From N. H. *Wessely, whom he held in almost equal esteem, Mapu derived less specific but no less important elements, such as the linguistic narrative possibilities inherent in the Bible. Moreover, the social and educational reforms advocated in Wessely's series of open letters, *Divrei Shalom ve-Emet* found an enthusiastic echo in Mapu's novels, especially *Ayit Ẓavu'a*. Among Hebrew prose writers, the Galician exponents of Haskalah, J. *Perl and I. *Erter exerted considerable influence on Mapu. From their satires on the shortcomings of society, he learned how to use melodrama and far-fetched incidents. The letters and dreams which Perl and Erter frequently introduce as convenient media for their satirical purposes are a characteristic feature of Mapu's novels. Many of his characters embody their demands for radical changes in outlook and occupation in Jewish society.

Mapu's novels also owe a considerable debt to the French romantic novelists, the elder Dumas and Eugène Suë. Like Dumas, Mapu turned his attention to the national past, infusing an historical situation with heroism and romantic love, and introducing historical personages side by side with his own creations. From Dumas, Mapu learned the art of creating atmosphere and of clothing his plots in a romantic historical mantle while the influence of Eugène Suë is particularly noticeable in Mapu's novel of contemporary life. But whereas the violence and intrigue encountered in Suë's *Mystères de Paris* are perfectly in keeping with its background of the Paris underworld, the attempt in *Ayit Ẓavu'a* to superimpose such elements on a back-cloth of Jewish society in Eastern Europe, which was characterized by sobriety, timidity, and a rigid control of the passionate emotions, is primarily responsible for the incongruity of the setting and the plot.

The original and creative element in Mapu's writings does not lie in the external forms of his novels. The structure, dramatic techniques, and characterizations, stereotypes personifying vice and virtue, all lean heavily on previous writers, and all display grave weaknesses and limitations. For Mapu's own generation, however, the plots, particularly of the historical novels, were the most attractive and fascinating aspect of his work, both because this literary medium was unknown in Hebrew literature, and because the adventure and excitement provided so striking a contrast to the colorless lives of most of his readers. The vivid descriptions of heroism and action, the free expression of emotion, and above all the colorful scenes of a people living unrestricted in its own land, inflamed the imagination of a life-starved generation. His success in arousing imagination and emotion, and his ability to transfuse a somewhat dry and intellectual literature with the feelings of heroism and romantic love constitute the most striking elements of his achievement. By fostering pride in the national past and focusing attention on the land of Israel, Mapu provided an emotional stimulus for generations of young readers. Indeed, the contribution of his novels to the rise of the Jewish national movement from which Zionism later emerged must be regarded as an important factor in modern Jewish history.

Mapu's use of language was equally remarkable. The restricted vocabulary of biblical Hebrew and its limited dialogue seriously curtail its suitability for the modern novel. The narrative power of the biblical story stems, moreover, from its tantalizing brevity and its ruthless pruning of extraneous detail. The Bible story relates a series of events in sequence of time, with little analysis or speculation. It presents a skeleton narrative, leaving the reader to supply the flesh and blood. But the novel demands techniques of a different kind. It is expansive and has to supply those very elements and details which the Bible is so careful to omit. Yet Mapu adopted a medium for expansion whose main strength lies in strict omission, knowingly risking the constant comparison of his own creation with the lofty grandeur of the original. Mapu attempted to solve the problem of language by using his material to the full. The entire Bible became a source for his invention. His style constitutes a fusion of elements of the prose and the poetry of the Bible. Appropriating and refashioning at will, he molded the material to suit his purpose, while retaining much of its original spirit. In spite of the frequent introduction of entire phrases and complete images, he avoided the danger of producing a jumbled patchwork of biblical snippets. So smoothly do they merge with the texture of his own style that the result is neither an imitation nor a parody of the Hebrew Bible. This sensitivity to language is one of the most attractive features of his novels. But Mapu was well aware that he had stretched his material to the limit. In *Ayit Ẓavu'a* he deliberately introduced post-biblical elements, and himself protested that biblical Hebrew was not an adequate vehicle of expression for the modern novel. His writing may be regarded as the consummation of the neo-biblical style advocated by the exponents of Haskalah. No major Hebrew novelist attempted to emulate his achievements.

Although aesthetically the least satisfying, it was *Ayit Ẓavu'a* with its emphasis on social and educational reform which exerted most influence on subsequent Hebrew writers. The realistic elements of Mapu's social novel may be traced in the words of many writers, including P. *Smolenskin, J. L. *Gordon, R. A. *Braudes, M. D. *Brandstaedter, and S. J. Abramowitsch (*Mendele Mokher Seforim), all of whom furthered the positivist and social aspects of his work. Indeed, the realistic novel depicting the problems of contemporary society has continued to occupy a dominant position in Hebrew literature.

For the Hebrew reader, Mapu's first novel, *Ahavat Ẓiyyon*, was uniquely influential. It opened the prospect of a free and independent life to a people hopelessly fettered by political, social, and economic restrictions. Its significance lies in the fresh possibilities of art and life which it revealed, and in the new awareness it promoted. As the first Hebrew novel, it represents the first expression of a people's longing for a fuller and better life. The English translations of **Ahavat Ẓiyyon* were published under various titles: *Amnon, Prince and Peasant*, tr. by F. Jaffe (1887); *In the Days of Isaiah*, tr. by A. M. Schapiro (1902); the same translation was published later under the title *The Shepherd Prince* (1922 and 1930); *The Sorrows of Noma*, tr. by J. Marymont (1919). His letters were published by B. Dinur under the title *Mikhtevei Avraham Mapu* (1971).

Bibliography: D. Patterson, *Abraham Mapu* (Eng., 1964); Waxman, Literature, 3 (1960[2]), 267–78; Klausner, Sifrut, 3 (1950[3]), 269–360 (incl. bibl.).

[D.P.]

MAQAM, a term in music which designates a particular system of musical composition prevalent in the Near East. The system includes a complex of rules covering the scale, the characteristic motives, the placement of these motives within the scale, and their sequence—initial, medial, or final—in the melodic structure. There are also associations with certain tempos, rhythms, poetic genres, and moods or occasions. A *maqām* does not exist in itself as a set of written rules or as a concrete melodic prototype: it is realized only through improvisation-in-performance, which is the way composition is carried out in the Near Eastern musical cultures. About 12 to 15 such *maqāmāt* are known throughout the Near East, some of them with subsidiary forms which bring the total number up to between 20 and 25, and there is some regional variation as to nomenclature or content. The *maqām* system of musical composition is basically similar to the East European Ashkenazi **Shtayger*, the Persian *Dastgah* and the Indian raga systems. A similar principle probably underlies the modes of ancient Greek music. It has been proposed, with weighty arguments, that the puzzling designations found in the headings of many *Psalms ("upon the *sheminit*," "upon *yonat-elem-reḥokim*," etc.) may also not be names of instruments, or of scales, or of prototype melodies, but of *maqām*-like melodic schemes; and such are probably also the superscriptions and subscripts of the song texts found in Assyrian and Babylonain cuneiform documents.

The Near Eastern Jewish communities use the local *maqāmāt* for the creation and classification of many of their liturgical and para-liturgical melodies. Even the cantillation of the masoretic accents is submitted to a "maqamic correlation," and is obviously affected by it in its melodic content. In the singing of the **bakkashot* and such, i.e., in everything which is outside the liturgy proper, melodic assimilation may of course be complete. The following selection of "maqamic correlations" is based mainly on the research of A. Z. *Idelsohn; *maqām Sīgah* can be correlated with the Pentateuch, Ruth, Ecclesiastes, Esther, and the **Amidah* for the High Holy days; *maqām Bayyāt* with the prophetic books and Lamentations; *maqām ʿAjam* (Persian name: *Naurūz*, "The New Year's Day"), associated with exaltation, magnificence, and actual or symbolical wedding functions and ceremonies, with Simḥat Torah, Shavuot, the seventh day of Passover, and *Shabbat Shirah; maqām Nawa* with Sabbath Eve (cf. **Lekhah Dodi*) and Sabbath morning; and *maqām Ṣabā* with circumcisions, and prayers on Sabbaths on which the weekly portion of the Bible mentions circumcision.

In Syria, the **Musaf* prayer for each Sabbath and festival has its own appropriate governing *maqām*. The *bakkashot* are often organized according to a progression of different *maqāmāt*, with the recitation of a Psalm between the single or grouped *bakkashot* serving as a melodic vehicle for modulation from one *maqām* to the other. Such modulations are also made in the festive recitation of the Ten Commandments, the *ḥazzan* displaying his virtuosity by skillfully passing through the maximum number of *maqāmāt*.

All the above are unwritten conventions. The written indication of the *maqām* is found in all manuscript and printed collections of *piyyutim* produced in the Near East since the time of Israel *Najara, who was apparently the first to compose and organize his *piyyutim* according to this system. In his *Zemirot Yisrael* the poems are divided by *maqāmāt*, in the following order: *Ḥusseini, Rast, Dūgah, Sīgah, Nawa, Busilik* (a Turkish *maqām*), *Ḥusseini, Naurūz-ʿAjam, Uzāl*, and *Iraq*. The practice has continued to this day, and even recent songs have been fitted into the system, so that in the collection *Shirei Yisrael be-Ereẓ ha-Kedem* of the Adrianople community (Constantinople, 1922) the anthem **Ha-Tikvah* can be found in *maqām Nihawand*.

Bibliography: Idelsohn, Melodien, 4 (1923), 53–112; A. Z. Idelsohn, in: *Sammelbaende der Internationalen Musikgesellschaft*, 15 (1913–14), 1–63; idem, in: MGWJ, 57 (1913), 314ff.; J. Chailley, in: *Acta Musicologia*, 28 (1956), 137–63; H. Farmer, in: *New Oxford History of Music*, 1 (1957), 447–50.

MAQĀMA (pl. *maqāmāt*), a narrative in rhymed prose, interlaced with short metrical poems. The *maqāma* originated in about the tenth century C.E. with the Arab poet, Ibn al-Fātiḥ Aḥmad ibn Ḥusaynī (Al-Hamdhānī). Derived from the Arabic word *maqām* ("place"; cf. Hebrew *makom*), *maqāma* refers to the place where people gathered to listen to rhetoric. In Hebrew the accepted name for this genre is *maḥberet* (pl. *maḥbarot*). The classical *maqāma* was created when a talented and quick-witted fellow, skillful at mockery and jest, appeared at the "place" flaunting his erudition, particularly in language and literature, and delighted listeners (and ultimately readers) with humorous remarks and stories. At the "place" he frequently encountered an acquaintance of similar abilities. The two, pretending not to know each other, engaged in an amusing conversation which culminated in the mutual recognition of their friendship. Shortly after they were introduced as spoken expressions, *maqāmāt* were put into writing. In the course of time other humorous stories and pieces in rhymed prose began to be called *maqāmāt* even though they did not contain the typical gay talk of the classical *maqāma*. The author of the first known Hebrew *maqāma* is Solomon *ibn Zakbel who lived in Muslim Spain during the first half of the 12th century. Later authors of Hebrew works in this genre are Joseph *ibn Zabara, who wrote *Sefer ha-Sha'ashu'im* and Judah ibn Shabbetai, who wrote *Minḥat Yehudah Sone ha-Nashim*. However, the greatest writer of the Hebrew *maqāma* is Judah *al-Ḥarizi, whose *Taḥkemoni* contains 50 *maqāmāt*. Al-Ḥarizi said that he composed the book to prove that it was possible to use Arabic literary forms in Hebrew. Under the title *Maḥbarot Itti'el* he translated into Hebrew the *maqāmāt* of Al-Ḥariri (1054–1121), the greatest Arabic exponent of this genre. Al-Ḥarizi greatly influenced such later Hebrew poets as Abraham ibn Ḥasdai, Jacob b. Eleazar, and Immanuel of Rome. Particularly worthy of mention is Isaac ibn *Sahula whose *Meshal ha-Kadmoni* (compiled in 1281), based on Jewish themes, was written in conscious contrast to the Arabic *maqāma*. The Hebrew style of the *maqāma*, especially of those written in later periods, has occasionally appealed to contemporary authors, the best example being Bialik's *Alluf Bazlut ve-Alluf Shum* ("Lord Onion and Lord Garlic").

Bibliography: C. Brockelmann, in: EI, 3 (1936), 174–7; H. A. R. Gibb, *Arabic Literature* (1963), 100–2, 123–5; I. Perez (ed.), *Maḥbarot Itti'el* (1951), 13–17; I. Goldziher, *Kiẓẓur Toledot ha-Sifrut ha-Aravit* (1952), 81f.; A. M. Habermann, *Toledot ha-Piyyut ve-ha-Shirah* (1970), 194–6, 201–7; N. Gubrin in: *Me'assef le-Divrei Sifrut, Bikkoret ve-Hagut*, 8–9 (1968), 394–417.

[A.M.H.]

MAQUEDA, small town in Castile, central Spain, on the territory of the Order of *Calatrava. Because of the resemblance to the biblical name of Makkedah (Josh. 10:10, 28, etc.), some Jewish commentators (cf. Isaac *Abrabanel's commentary to Kings) asserted that the Spanish city had been founded by Jews from Makkedah who had been exiled by Nebuchadnezzar. Conversely, Moses *Arragel tried to demonstrate to the head of the Order of Calatrava that Makkedah in Ereẓ Israel had been founded by the king of Maqueda in Spain. The beginning of Jewish settlement in Maqueda probably coincided with the transfer of the region to the ownership of the Order of Calatrava in 1177.

In 1238, Ferdinand III ordered the community to make the Church an annual payment of 30 denarii symbolizing the amount of money received by Judas Iscariot. In 1290 the community paid an annual tax of 11,162 maravedis. During the reign of Ferdinand IV (1295–1312), the tax was reduced from 8,000 to 5,000 maravedis to dissuade the Jews from leaving Maqueda. Alfonso XI confirmed this reduction in 1316, but the amount of tax for services collected from the Jews there remained unchanged. The Jews earned their livelihood from the same occupations as the other inhabitants of the region, including agriculture.

During the persecutions of 1391 its two synagogues were sacked. In 1415, the antipope *Benedict XIII answered an appeal sent by the apostate rabbi of the community, who had been maintained from the vineyards and fields which it owned and was left without means of subsistence. Benedict authorized him to take possession of the synagogue appurtenances and property.

By the beginning of the 15th century, the community had been reestablished, and in 1430 Moses Arragel completed there the translation of the Bible into Spanish commissioned by Don Luis de Guzman, head of the Order of Calatrava. The role played in 1464–65 by R. Maymaran, rabbi of Maqueda, in persuading Conversos to return to Judaism, emerges from the trial of Ḥayyim Fichel by the Inquisition held at *Huesca in 1489. The community still paid 50,000 maravedis in taxes in 1491. The status of the community may be gauged from the fact that a meeting of representatives of the communities of Castile was convened there in the fall of 1484, when important decisions concerning the practice of usury by the Jews in the kingdom were passed. After the decree of expulsion of 1492 was issued, Ferdinand ordered that inquiries should be made among the Jews of Maqueda to discover whether they were ready to adopt Christianity. The king ordered that watch should be kept over the synagogue until its future was decided and that a register should be made of Jewish property, of the debts owed to Jews, and those they owed to others. In the folklore of the Sephardim, stories were preserved about simple-minded Jews of Maqueda of the same type as those recounted about the Jews of *Chelm.

Bibliography: Baer, Urkunden, index; Beinart, in: *Tarbiz*, 26 (1956/57), 78; idem, in: *Estudios*, 3 (1962), 7–10; F. Cantera, *Sinagogas españolas* (1955), 243–4; Suárez Fernández, Documentos, index; C. O. Nordström, *Duke of Alba's Castillian Bible* (1967), 12, 16, 20, 32, 234.

[H.B.]

MAR (Aram. מָר; lit. "lord"), a term of respect and endearment used in addressing an important person. Daniel addressed the king as *mari* ("my lord"; Dan. 4:16). The rabbis related that King *Jehoshaphat rose from his throne upon seeing a scholar, embraced him, and exclaimed, "My master, my master; my teacher, my teacher" (Ket. 103b; Mak. 24a). In Babylonia *mar* was used as a deferential and respectful form of address. A son reporting his father's teachings was urged to say, "thus said my father, my master" (Kid. 31b). When *Rav acted as interpreter for Shila, the latter asked him to cease, proclaiming Rav his "master" upon perceiving his greatness (Yoma 20b). Abbaye referred to his uncle and teacher, Rabbah b. Nahamani, simply as *Mar*, without adding any name (Pes. 101a). Tavyomi's colleagues always called him *Mar* and he is therefore always referred to in the Talmud as "*Mar bar Rav Ashi" (Kid. 31b). *Mar* finally became a title preceding the name, and it became customary in Babylonia to call scholars *mar* and not *rav*. This was particularly so in the case of the two famous contemporaries of Rav, Mar *Samuel and Mar *Ukba, as well as Mar *Zutra. When a passage already quoted in the Talmud is quoted again for the purpose of further elucidation, it is introduced with the words "*Mar* said," which in the context merely means "It has been stated above" (e.g., Ber. 2a).

In modern Hebrew *Mar* is used as a term of address like the English "Mister."

Bibliography: Hyman, Toledot, 897ff.; J. Schechter, *Oẓar ha-Talmud* (1963), 244.

[Ed.]

MAR BAR RAV ASHI (d.c. 468), Babylonian *amora*. Mar was the son of *Ashi, the compiler of the Babylonian Talmud. His real name was Tavyomi, and so he signed himself (BB 12b), Mar being a title of honor. He is extensively quoted in the Babylonian Talmud. He possessed great authority, and according to a tradition of Rashi (to Ḥul. 76b) the *halakhah* follows him except in two cases. He studied under his father, who headed the famous academy of Mata Meḥasya, near Sura. On the death of Ashi, Mar stayed on under his successor Maremar (Ber. 45b). His companions were Ravina (the younger, Ber. 36a), Judah b. Maremar, and *Aḥa of Difti (Ber. 45b). In 455 he became head of the academy after competing for the post with *Aḥa. The *aggadah* describes his appointment as an example of prophecy having been given to fools. Mar was standing in the manor of Maḥoza when he heard a lunatic exclaim: "The man to be elected head of the academy of Mata Meḥasya signs himself Tavyomi." He quickly went to Mata Meḥasya and arrived in time to sway the voting in his favor (BB 12b). It was due to Mar that the editing of the Talmud begun by his father was completed in the following generation. The *aggadah* also relates that Mar had great knowledge of the ways of demons and great power over them (Ḥul. 105b). Sherira Gaon in his letter reports that in the time of Mar, King Yezdegerd III, who was hostile to the Jews, was swallowed by a dragon while he was in his bed (ed. by B. M. Lewin (1921), 95). Mar had a brother Sama and a sister, and a dispute between them over the bequest of their father was arbitrated by Ravina (Ket. 69a). He was a wealthy man (Git. 7a). He was succeeded by Rabbah Tosfa'a.

Bibliography: Bacher, Trad, index; Hyman, Toledot, 897–9; Ḥ. Albeck, *Mavo la-Talmudim* (1969), 445f.

[D.J.B.]

MAR BAR RAVINA (fourth century), Babylonian *amora*, famous for his saintly character. In his youth, he was carefully tended by his mother, who provided him with clean garments every day, so that he could study in comfort (Er. 65a). Although well-to-do, he lived austerely, fasting by day except on Pentecost, Purim, and the eve of the Day of Atonement (Pes. 68b). At his wedding, a note of seriousness was struck by Rav Hamnuna Zuta who, when asked to sing for the guests, chanted to them, "Alas for us that we are to die" (Ber. 31a). An even sadder note was injected at his son's wedding when Mar, seeing that the company was in a merry mood, deliberately broke a precious cup to dampen their spirit (Ber. 30b–31a). This is probably the origin of the custom of breaking a cup at a Jewish wedding ceremony. It seems likely that his austere piety was also influenced by the ever-present memory of the destruction of the Temple, and his negative attitude to gentiles was a logical corollary of his mourning for the glory that had departed from Zion. Thus, he held that even gentiles who observed the seven Noachide laws did not thereby earn any heavenly reward (Av. Zar. 2b–3a). He also had an extremely low opinion of Balaam—the arch-prophet of the gentile world—whom he charged with bestiality (Sanh. 105a) and singled out as the only major sinner against whom biblical passages could be expounded so as to discredit him (Sanh. 106b). Mar bar Ravina had a reputation as a pious, God-fearing man (Ber. 39b; Shab. 61a), who regarded the profanation of God's name as the most heinous sin (Kid. 40a). He was also credited with miraculous escapes from grave perils (Ber. 54a). Characteristic of his piety was his prayer which is still recited at the conclusion of the Eighteen Benedictions: "O my God, keep my tongue from evil and my lips from speaking guile. And to them that curse me may my soul be silent; yea, let my soul be as the dust to all. Open my heart in thy law, and let my soul pursue thy commandments . . ." (Ber. 17a).

Bibliography: Hyman, Toledot, 900f.; Ḥ. Albeck, *Mavo la-Talmudim* (1969), 368.

[M.A.]

Maror zeh ("this bitter herb") from a "Brother" to the *Rylands Spanish Haggadah*. In the center panel, a large artichoke is held by two men. The man in the lower panel is pointing at his wife while reciting *"maror zeh"*, a jocular custom in many European Jewish communities during the Middle Ages. Spain, 14th century. London, British Museum, Or. ms. 1404, fol. 18 ($10\frac{7}{8} \times 9\frac{1}{4}$ ins/27.5 × 23.5 cm.).

MARBURG, city in Hesse, W. Germany. A document dated May 13, 1317—the first to mention Jews in Marburg—indicates that they then had an organized community and a synagogue, and lived in a special quarter. The community was annihilated during the *Black Death persecutions (1348/49), but Jews were living in the town once more by 1364. In the middle of the 15th century they were apparently expelled from Marburg; the synagogue was demolished in 1452 and the cemetery passed into non-Jewish hands. The Jewish population eventually returned, only to be driven out again by a decree of 1523. However, in 1532 Duke Philip abolished the decree and permitted the Jews to reside there for a six-year period. In subsequent years the number of Marburg Jews remained low: six families in 1744 and eight in 1776. Jews from outside the town were permitted to remain there only during the annual fairs. The number of Jews increased during the course of the 19th century, reaching 512 (2.5% of the total population) in 1905. From 1823 Marburg was the seat of the district community organization and later of the district rabbinate. The community maintained a synagogue (built in 1897), a school, a convalescent home, and a number of other institutions. Hermann *Cohen, professor at the local university, founded the Marburg school of Neo-Kantianism. In 1933 there were about 325 Jews in Marburg. On Nov. 10, 1938, the synagogue was burned down. By May 17, 1939, only 143 Jews remained; ten survived the war, while the rest left or were deported in 1941–42. About 300 Jews lived in Marburg between 1945 and 1948, but by 1959 only 50 remained.

The Marburg synagogue, built in 1897 and burnt by the Nazis on *Kristallnacht,* 1938. Courtesy Foto Marburg.

Bibliography: L. Munk, *Zur Erinnerung an die Einweihung der neuen Synagoge in Marburg* (1897); FJW (1932–33), 191–4; Germ Jud, 2 (1968), 522–3; M. Hirschhorn, in: *Juedische Wohlfahrtspflege und Sozialpolitik,* 3 (1932), 342ff.; 6 (1937), 29ff.

[Ed.]

MARCEAU, MARCEL (1923–), French mime. Marceau was born in Strasbourg, the son of a butcher who was executed by the Nazis during World War II. Marceau worked for the French underground, helping Jewish children to cross the border into Switzerland. In 1944, he entered Charles Dullin's School of Dramatic Art and two years later joined the company of Jean-Louis Barrault. In 1947 he created his character "Bip," a flour-faced clown always in conflict with the physical world. Thereafter Marceau toured either as a solo artist or with a small company, his silent eloquence winning audiences in many parts of the world. Most of Marceau's programs consisted

Marcel Marceau, French mime. Courtesy Baruch Gillon, Tel Aviv. Photo Darrell Armstrong.

of small sketches featuring "Bip," but in 1951 he created an extended drama, *The Overcoat,* based on the novel by Gogol. He also made a number of films. Marceau described mime as "the art of expressing feelings by attitudes and not a means of expressing words through gestures."

Bibliography: Y. Karsh, *Portraits of Greatness* (1959), 124.

[S.J.C.]

MARCK, SIEGFRIED (1889–1957), German philosopher. Marck, who was born in Breslau, became a professor there in 1924. After the Nazis came to power, he taught at Dijon, France, and from 1940 in Chicago. Marck's thought derives from the Marburg neo-Kantians. He compared the fundamental concepts of Kant, Hegel, and Marx in his *Kant und Hegel* (1917), and *Hegelianismus und Marxismus* (1922). He applied *Cassirer's and *Kelsen's concepts in his *Substanz- und Funktionsbegriff in der Rechtsphilosophie* (1925). His main work, *Die Dialektik in der Philosophie der Gegenwart* (2 vols., 1929–31), develops his own "critical dialectic." Marck also wrote *Der Neuhumanismus als politische Philosophie* (1938), and *Grosse Menschen unserer Zeit* (1954).

Bibliography: *National Cyclopaedia of American Biography,* 43 (1961), 257–8.

[R.H.P.]

MARCKWALD, WILLY (1864–1950), German organic chemist. Marckwald was born in Jakobskirch, Silesia, and was professor at Berlin University from 1899. He was also director of the chemistry department of the university's physico-chemical institute. In 1910 he was appointed a privy councillor, and was president of the German Chemical Society from 1928 to 1931. When the Nazis rose to power, he escaped to Brazil. Marckwald's scientific papers dealt with the physical properties of organic compounds, stereochemistry, and radioactivity. He was the first to isolate the element polonium in pitchblende, which helped toward the discovery of radium. He observed changes caused by light in the color of certain compounds, and called this phenomenon "phototropy."

Marckwald wrote *Ueber die Beziehungen zwischen dem Siedepunkte und der Zusammensetzung chemischer Verbindungen* (1888), *Die Benzoltheorie* (1898), and *Radium in Biologie und Heilkunde* (1911–12). [S.A.M.]

MARCOUSSIS (originally **Marcous**), **LOUIS** (1883–1941), French painter. Marcoussis was born in Warsaw. As a student at the Academy of Fine Arts in Cracow he was one of the avant-garde Young Poland group which was strongly inclined to French culture. In 1903 he moved to Paris to study. When his father was no longer able to support him, he lived by contributing frivolous drawings to *La Vie Parisienne* and *L'Assiette au Beurre.* Marcoussis visited the United States in 1934 and his engravings were shown in

"Still Life," oil by Louis Marcoussis, 1925. New York, formerly Helena Rubinstein Collection. Photo courtesy Parker-Bernet-Sotheby, New York.

New York and Chicago. When the Germans occupied Paris in 1940 Marcoussis and his wife happened to be staying in a village in central France where he was able to live in safety until his death the following year. Marcoussis is listed generally among the cubists. Yet in his early still lifes, the element of fantasy is stronger than the purely analytical one. He was an excellent print-maker, who made illustrations for books by Gérard de Nerval, Guillaume Apollinaire, and Tristan Tzara. In his portraits, he abandoned cubism for a tight classical style.

Bibliography: J. Lafranchis (ed.), *Marcoussis* (Fr., 1961). [A.W.]

MARCULESTI, Jewish agricultural colony in Bessarabia. It was founded in 1839 on an area of 549 hectares leased by 239 settlers from Podolia from a private owner. In 1888 the land was acquired by the settlers, but because of the *May Laws of 1882 it was registered under the name of a Christian property owner. According to the census of 1897 there were 1,336 Jewish inhabitants. However, the survey conducted by the *Jewish Colonization Association in 1899 records 292 families (1,534 individuals), of whom 123 were landowners (with an average of 4.5 hectares to a family). Under the agrarian reform in Rumania in 1922, 105 Jews in Marculesti received plots of land. In 1901 a school was opened which was directed by the writer Shelomo *Hillels. Of the 541 members registered in the local loan fund in 1925, 195 were farmers. In 1930 the Jewish population numbered 2,319 (87.4% of the total). *Tarbut elementary and high schools functioned there during the 1930s. The colony was destroyed when the Germans and Rumanians invaded Bessarabia in July 1941, after its incorporation within the Soviet Union. On the 8th of that month, about 1,000 Jews living there were murdered. In September–November 1941 a transit camp was established in Marculesti for Bessarabian Jews who were deported to *Transnistria. Ada *Maimon and Rabbi Y. L. *Maimon (Fishman), who served as the rabbi of the colony from 1900 to 1905, were born in Marculesti. [EL.F.]

MARCUS, AARON (1843–1916), scholar, writer on Kabbalah and Ḥasidism. Marcus was born and educated in Hamburg, studied at the yeshivah of Boskovice (Moravia) but also acquired a wider philosophical education. In 1861 he left for Cracow where he joined the Ḥasidim. Between 1862 and 1866 he made several long visits to the ḥasidic rabbi of Radomsk, Solomon Rabinowicz. He later maintained close relations with many ḥasidic leaders in Poland and Galicia. A major part of his literary work (mainly in German but with a small amount in Hebrew) was devoted to the defense of Ḥasidism and an explanation of ḥasidic doctrines and Kabbalah. His work testifies to great erudition, but has proved unacceptable by the current standards of modern critical scholarship. In his work he defended traditional Judaism against modern Bible criticism and scientific materialism. At the same time, he tried to find confirmation for new insights in philosophy and science in Jewish religious literature, particularly in the writings of Ḥayyim b. Moses *Attar, M. Ḥ. *Luzzatto, and of Ḥabad Ḥasidism. Marcus was one of the few Orthodox Jews in Germany who totally adopted Ḥasidism in theory and practice. He published: *Hartmanns inductive Philosophie des Unbewussten im Chassidismus* (2 pts., 1889–90); *Der Chassidismus* (under the pseudonym Verus, 1901, 1927[3]); *Barsilai, Sprache als Schrift der Psyche* (1905); an edition of Jacob of Marvège's responsa *She'elot u-Teshuvot min-ha-Shamayim* with a commentary *Keset ha-Sofer,* 1895, 1957[2]); *Keset ha-Sofer* (Bible annotations, largely in Ms., 1912); and *Juedische Chronologie* (vol. 1, posthumously, 1935). From 1898 to 1899 Marcus edited *Krakauer Juedische Zeitung,* a paper he published as a vehicle for his ideas. He became an enthusiastic supporter of Theodor Herzl and his *Judenstaat* (see his *Theodor Herzls Judenstaat . . .,* 1897; second ed. 1919 with a eulogy of Marcus, thus becoming one of the pioneers of religious Zionism, though later he turned toward the anti-Zionist Agudat Israel.

Aaron Marcus, German scholar. Jerusalem, J.N.U.L., Schwadron Collection.

Bibliography: Moeller, in: *Jeschurun* (ed. Wohlgemuth), 4 (1917), 154–60; T. Herzl, *Diaries*, ed. by R. Patai, 1 (1960), 347; H. Schwab, *Chachme Ashkenaz* (Eng., 1964), 94 (incl. bibl.); M. Marcus, *A. Marcus, die Lebensgeschichte eines Chossid* (1966); G. Scholem, in: *Beḥinot*, 7 (1954), 3–8. [EJ]

MARCUS, DAVID DANIEL (1902–1948), U.S. soldier, commander of the Jerusalem front in the Israel *War of Independence. Marcus was born on New York's Lower East Side. In 1920 he entered the West Point Military Academy, graduating in 1924. He also studied law, and, when he left the army in 1927, was employed in the U.S. Attorney General's Office. In 1934 Mayor Fiorello La Guardia invited him to join the New York City Department of Correction, and in 1940 he was sworn in as a commissioner of correction. After the outbreak of World War II in Europe he rejoined the army with the rank of lieutenant colonel as divisional judge advocate and divisional headquarters' commander. In 1943 he was called to the Civil Affairs Division of the War Department and attended the meetings of the "Big Five." On D-Day he volunteered to participate in the airborne assault, parachuting into Normandy despite his lack of previous training. In 1945 he was on the staff of General Lucius D. Clay's military government in Germany. Recalled to Washington, he was appointed head of the War Crimes Branch. In 1947 he retired from the army with the rank of colonel and returned to legal practice, after being awarded a number of major U.S. and British decorations.

At the request of the *Jewish Agency and the *Haganah, he went to Palestine at the end of January 1948, serving as David *Ben-Gurion's military adviser under the *nom de guerre* of Mickey Stone. He immediately perceived the special spirit and conditions of the new Israel army which was emerging from the underground. After a brief visit to the United States, he returned to Israel in May 1948 and on May 28, 1948, was appointed commander of the Jerusalem front. Marcus was the first officer to receive the new rank of *alluf* (brigadier general). Before dawn on June 11, he went outside the perimeter fence of his headquarters in Abu Ghosh and was accidentally killed by a sentry. His body was transferred with military honors to the United States and buried at West Point. A village in Judea, Mishmar David, is named after him.

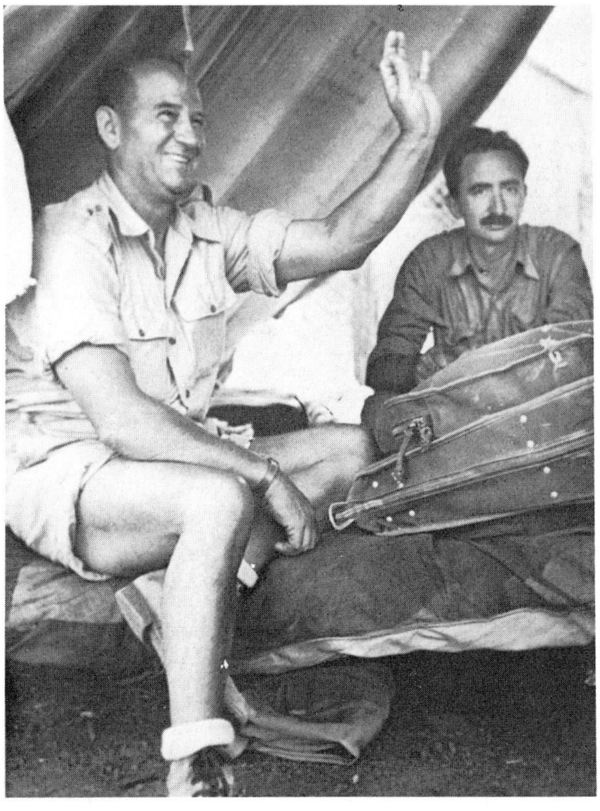

David Marcus, in a tent on the "Burma Road" to Jerusalem, 1948. Courtesy Government Press Office, Tel Aviv.

Bibliography: N. Lorch, *The Edge of the Sword* (1961), index; I. Berkman, *Cast a Giant Shadow* (1962; movie, 1965). [J.WA.]

MARCUS, ERNST (1856–1928), German jurist and philosopher. Marcus studied law and was a judge. As a philosopher, he was a Kantian who opposed the new interpretations offered by H. *Cohen and L. *Nelson. For Marcus the "thing-in-itself" remained central, deducible from reason. He developed a theory of the *a priori* "organism" which the "I" constructs. He wrote many works on Kant including *Kants Revolutionsprinzip* (1902); *Das Erkenntnisproblem* (1905); *Die Beweisfuehrung in der Kritik der reinen Vernunft* (1914); and *Kants Weltgebaeude* (1917). He also wrote *Theorie einer natuerlichen Magie* (1924). Using Kant's theory, Marcus criticized Einstein in his *Kritik des Aufbaus der speziellen Relativitaetstheorie* (1926) and in *Die Zeit- und Raumlehre Kants* (1927).

Bibliography: S. Friedlaender, *Der Philosoph Ernst Marcus als Nachfolger Kants* (1930); idem, *Kant gegen Einstein* (1932). [R.H.P.]

MARCUS, JACOB RADER (1896–), U.S. rabbi and historian. Born in Connellsville, Pennsylvania, he graduated from the University of Cincinnati and then from Hebrew Union College, whose faculty he joined in 1920 after his World War I military service. Receiving his Ph.D. in history from the University of Berlin in 1925, he returned to Hebrew Union College and, between 1928 and 1947, published several important studies of Central European Jewry. He began to emphasize American Jewish history during the 1940s and established it as an academic discipline. He founded the American Jewish Archives at Hebrew Union College in 1947, initiated its semiannual journal in 1948, established the American Jewish Periodical Center in 1956, and published pioneering books on early American Jewish life. His three-volume magnum opus, *The Colonial American Jew*, appeared in 1970. Active also in nonacademic life, he helped found Cincinnati's Jewish Community Council in the early 1930s, went abroad in 1936 to study Soviet Jewry, and served as president of the Central Conference of American Rabbis (1949–50) and of the American Jewish Historical Society (1956–59). For more data on Marcus and a listing of his publications 1916–58, see S. Chyet and H. C. Zafren, in: *Essays in American Jewish History* (1958), 1–22 (biography), 493–512 (bibliographical list). [S.F.C.]

Jacob Rader Marcus, U.S. rabbi and historian. Courtesy American Jewish Archives, Cincinnati, O.

MARCUS, JOSEPH (1897–), Hebrew scholar. Born in Derevno, Russia (Vilna province), Marcus was taken to the United States in 1910. He was ordained by the Jewish

Theological Seminary in 1924. After briefly holding several rabbinical positions, he assisted Israel *Davidson in the preparation of the latter's *Ozar* ("Thesaurus of Medieval Hebrew Poetry"); later he assisted *Bialik and *Rawnitzki in preparing their editions of the poems of Ibn *Gabirol and Moses *ibn Ezra, copying for them poems from the Seminary's *genizah* collection. In the course of this work (1929), Marcus discovered a leaf from a hitherto unknown Hebrew manuscript of *Ben Sira (Ecclesiasticus). After holding positions in various Jewish libraries, followed by a brief return to the rabbinate, Marcus became librarian and instructor in medieval Hebrew literature at the Hebrew Teachers College of Boston in 1946. In 1963 he settled in Israel, where he became librarian at the Mosad ha-Rav Kook in Jerusalem.

Marcus' works include: *A Fifth Manuscript of Ben Sira* (1931); *Ginzei Shirah u-Fiyyut* ("Liturgical and Secular Poetry of the Foremost Medieval Poets," 1933); *Studies in the Chronicle of Ahimaaz* (1934); *Iggerot Bialik* (1935); *Yozerot le-Arba Parashiyyot* (1965); and studies on the poetry of Isaac ibn *Ghayyat. [R.P.S.]

MARCUS, RALPH (1900–1956), U.S. scholar of Hellenistic Judaism. Born in San Francisco the son of the talmudic scholar Moses Marcus, Marcus was educated at Columbia, where he wrote his doctoral dissertation on *Law in the Apocrypha* (1927), and at Harvard where he studied with Harry A. Wolfson (1925–27). He taught at the Jewish Institute of Religion, at Columbia (1927–43), and at the University of Chicago (1947–56).

Marcus is best known for editing, translating, and annotating four volumes of Josephus and two of Philo in the Loeb Classical Library series. His notes show an unusual wealth of lexical and historical knowledge, and his translations are accurate and lucid. His invaluable appendixes on select points in Josephus are careful, critical monographs. His bibliographies in these volumes and in separate works (PAAJR, 16 (1946/47), 97–181; *Jewish Studies in Memory of G. A. Kohut* (1935), 463–91) show his mastery of the literature and his critical acumen. He successfully undertook the extraordinarily difficult task of translating Philo's *Quaestiones et Solutiones* from the Armenian and restored the Greek in numerous places.

Marcus' lexicon to Josephus, continuing the work of Thackeray, reached the letter *epsilon*. His 62 articles excel in etymologies, grammatical and lexical points, and in

Ralph Marcus, scholar of Hellenistic Judaism. Courtesy Alice Marcus, Chicago, Ill.

utilizing his vast knowledge of the various languages of the classical and Jewish worlds. Marcus intended to write a history of the Jews during the Second Temple period, and many of his most fertile ideas for future work in the field are found in his "The Future of Intertestamental Studies" (in: H. R. Willoughby's *The Study of the Bible* (1947), 190–208). Marcus also wrote semi-popular articles on Hellenistic Judaism for L. Finkelstein's *The Jews* and L. W. Schwarz's *Great Ages and Ideas of the Jewish People*, as well as for the *Encyclopaedia Britannica*. In the controversy between H. A. Wolfson and E. R. Goodenough on Philo, Marcus strongly supported Wolfson's contention that Philo closely parallels Pharisaic Judaism (*Review of Religion*, 13 (1949), 368–81). Toward the end of his life Marcus became much involved in the controversies surrounding the Dead Sea Scrolls. He connected the Qumran Covenanters with the Essenes and discerned in them a strong gnosticizing flavor.

Bibliography: G. E. von Grunebaum, in: JNES, 16 (1957), 143–4; BRE, 3 (1958), 44–46, a list of his works. [L.H.FE.]

MARCUS, SIEGFRIED (1831–1898), German inventor, born in Malchin. Marcus joined the Berlin engineering firm of Siemens und Halske in 1848 and worked on the establishment of telegraphic communication between Berlin and Magdeburg. In 1852 he settled in Vienna, where from 1860 he had his own laboratory. In 1864 he patented a petrol-driven automobile. A car he built in 1875 was preserved in the Vienna Industrial Museum. His patents included an electric lamp (1877), telegraphic relays, a microphone, a loudspeaker, electric fuses for submarine mines, and other devices which were developed by others in later years.

Siegfried Marcus, German inventor.

Bibliography: *Zeitschrift der Oesterreicher Ingenieure und Architekten* (1928), 262; Skowronnek, in: *Umschau*, 35 (1931), 743f.; Postal, in: *American Hebrew*, 129 (1931), 405, 416. [S.A.M.]

°**MARCUS AURELIUS ANTONINUS** (121–180 C.E.), Roman emperor, 161–180 C.E., adopted son and successor of Antoninus Pius; the ideal philosopher-king as envisaged by political thought of the period. Ironically enough, the years of his reign were spent in war defending the borders of the Roman Empire. In 164–5 C.E., Aurelius' general Avidius Cassius captured Seleucia and the Parthian capital Ctesiphon, bringing the Mesopotamian Jews temporarily under Roman rule. When Cassius later proclaimed himself emperor in Syria, the Jews are supposed to have supported him, as a result of which Aurelius "crushed them by means of his preses and legates" (Marcellinus, 23:3). Aurelius held a highly unfavorable opinion of the Jews of Palestine. After passing through the country on his way to Egypt, where he was harassed by their importunities and turbulence, he exclaimed "I find these people [the Jews] to be worse than the Marcomanni, the Quadi, and the Sarmatae!" (*ibid.*, 22:5). There may be an allusion to Marcus Aurelius in the *Sybilline Oracles (5:51). Possibly some characteristics of this philosopher-emperor find expression in the portrayal of the *Antoninus found in the Talmud.

Bibliography: H. D. Sedgwick, *Marcus Aurelius* (1922), 216–7, 226–7; S. Krauss, *Antoninus und Rabbi* (1910). [U.R.]

MARCUSE, HERBERT (1898–), philosopher and social theorist. Born in Berlin, he studied in Berlin and Freiburg, where he was influenced by Heidegger. In World War I he served in the German army and, as a delegate from his unit, participated in the abortive German "revolution" of 1918–19. In his works elements of Schillerian aesthetics, existentialist ontology, and utopian political thought are combined with a modified Marxist outlook and a modified

Herbert Marcuse, philosopher and social theorist. Photo Dominic Capezza, New York.

Hegelian (dialectical) method to produce what Marcuse calls "Critical Theory": a critical, "negating" analysis of prevailing social, political, and cultural institutions and theories.

A member of the Frankfort Institut fuer Sozialforschung, Marcuse left Germany in 1933, moving with the Institute to Geneva, then (1934) to New York. His first important work, "Neue Quellen zur Grundlegung des historischen Materialismus" (in *Die Gesellschaft*, vol. 9, 1932), an interpretation of the then newly discovered "Economic and Philosophical Manuscripts" of Karl Marx, established him as a pioneer in the exploration of "Marxist Humanism." He contributed to the Institute's *Studien ueber Autoritaet und Familie* (1936), and wrote a number of critical essays for its journal, notably "Der Kampf gegen den Liberalismus in der totalitaeren Staatsauffassung" (in *Zeitschrift fuer Sozialforschung*, vol. 3, 1934), in which Fascist-Nazi ideology is shown to be the ideology of capitalism in its monopolistic phase, and thus not so much antagonistic to, as an outgrowth of, liberalism—the ideology of capitalism in its (earlier) competitive phase.

After serving in the O.S.S. and the State Department (1941–50),. Marcuse was a fellow, successively, of the Russian research centers at Columbia and at Harvard. His first full-fledged academic appointment was in 1954, as professor of politics and philosophy at Brandeis University. He left there in 1965 to become professor of philosophy at the University of California, San Diego.

In *Reason and Revolution; Hegel and the Rise of Social Theory* (1941, 1954^2) he contrasted the negative (critical) social theory stemming from Hegel with the positive (positivistic) social theory founded by Comte. Marcuse next undertook a number of critical studies: of Freud's pessimistic theory that civilized society is necessarily repressive (*Eros and Civilization*, 1955); of Russia's Stalinized Marxism (*Soviet Marxism*, 1958); and of the repressive nature of a successful capitalist society (*One-Dimensional Man*, 1964.) Such a society, Marcuse argues, can satisfy material wants and employ industrial skills while it suppresses genuinely human needs and faculties and reduces man to a single, conformist dimension in order to maintain the established order and to secure the production of a surplus for the benefit of the ruling elements.

In later years Marcuse became something of a hero and an authority to many members of the *New Left. His essay on "Repressive Tolerance" (in H. Marcuse et al., *Critique of Pure Tolerance*, 1965), in which he argues that only progressive (i.e., radical) values and movements ought to be tolerated, while toleration should be denied to repressive (i.e., rightist) values and movements, was influential among young radicals.

Marcuse's critique of a capitalist system which satisfies—and tolerates—only those needs which it itself generates (precisely because it can satisfy them to its profit) while it perpetuates domination and exploitation is resumed in *An Essay on Liberation* (1969).

Bibliography: G. Kateb, in: *Community* (Jan. 1970), 48–63; A. Macintyre, *Herbert Marcuse: an Exposition and a Polemic* (1971).

[H.Lu.]

MARCUSE, LUDWIG (1894–1971), German essayist. Born in Berlin, Marcuse began his career as a drama critic and as the biographer of Buechner (1922) and Strindberg (1924). During his last years in Germany, he also published perceptive biographies of *Boerne (1929) and *Heine (1932). The implicit parallels between Heine's age and his own are prominent in the latter. In 1939, Marcuse escaped to the U.S. In 1945 he became professor of German literature and philosophy at the University of Southern California. He was increasingly drawn to the history of ideas: significant works in this field are his *Pessimismus, ein Stadium der Reife* (1953) and *Amerikanisches Philosophieren* (1959). These are stylized, luminous histories of ideas, written for the literate layman. In his autobiographical *Mein zwanzigstes Jahrhundert* (1960) he records a vast array of intellectual experiences, and presents a kaleidoscope of personalities in Germany, France, the U.S., and Israel.

[H.v.H.]

MARCUSE, MOSES (late 18th century), physician and Yiddish writer who grew up in Germany. In his book *Sefer Refu'ot* ("Book of Medicines," 1790) he claims to have studied medicine at the University of Koenigsberg, but his name does not appear in the University's matriculation lists. In 1774 he went to Poland and practiced medicine in several communities. The declared aim of *Sefer Refu'ot* was to transmit elementary knowledge of hygiene in Yiddish to those to whom no doctor was available. The book appears to have gone into a second edition, but only three copies have survived, and it has become a bibliographical rarity. Large extracts from it were published by Noah Prylucki (*Zamlbikher*, 2 (1917), 1–55). Marcuse goes beyond purely medical information; as an early pioneer of enlightenment among Eastern European Jews, he calls for a change of occupations among Jews and for a different type of education. The book is important for Jewish cultural history since it records customs, living habits, and economic conditions among the Jewish masses, familiar to him as a practicing physician.

Bibliography: Rejzen, Leksikon, 2 (1927), 345–7; LNYL, 5 (1963), 519ff.; Z. Rejzen, *Fun Mendelssohn biz Mendele* (1923), 83–104; Zinberg, Sifrut, 5 (1959), 98–108.

[Ed.]

MARCZALI, HENRIK (1856–1940), Hungarian historian. Marczali was born in Marcali, where his father, Mihály Morgenstern, was rabbi. At the University of Budapest he gained distinction as a lecturer and historical scholar, but because he refused to renounce Judaism, he was denied a full professorship until 1895. Marczali was the first Jew to obtain a chair at Budapest University. He was elected to the Hungarian Academy of Sciences in 1893, but was dismissed from his post in 1924. A historian of the positivist school and a pioneer of source criticism in Hungary, Marczali wrote many works, notably the three-volume *Magyarország története II, József korában* (1885–88; *Hungary in the Eighteenth Century*, 1910); *A magyar történet kútfőinek kézikönyve* ("Handbook of the Sources of Hungarian History," 1901); and *Az 1790/1-diki országgyülés* ("The Sessions of the Diet During the Years 1790–91," 1907). Internationally recognized as one of Hungary's outstanding historians, Marczali also edited volumes 2–4 of the *Monumenta Hungariae Judaica* (1937–38).

Bibliography: G. Szekfű and Z. Tóth, in: IMIT, 65 (1943), 125–37; *Magyar Irodalmi Lexikon*, 2 (1965), 186, includes bibliography; E. Lederer, in: *Századok*, 96 (1962), 440–69.

[AL.SCH.]

MARDIN, town in Turkish Kurdistan. A Jewish community existed in Mardin from the Middle Ages to the 20th century. In 1291 Abinadab b. Saadiah Halevi of Mardin copied Maimonides' *Moreh Nevukhim (Guide of the Perplexed)* in Arabic. During the middle of the 14th century, a Jew of Mardin named Najīb al-Dawla Abraham b. Yeshu'ah held a government position (Neubauer, Cat, nos. 180, 1249). At the beginning of the 19th century the number of Jews was small, but an ancient synagogue and holy places, such as the so-called Cave of the Prophet Elijah, were preserved. In 1827 the traveler *David D'Beth Hillel found in the town "about six locally born, poor Jewish families with a small synagogue." *Benjamin II relates that in 1848 there were 50 Jewish families, most of whom worked on the land. They spoke Hebrew and their leader was the *nasi* Mu'allim Moses. The number of families remained unchanged during the second half of the century, but the community was dispersed during the 20th century.

Bibliography: A. Ben-Jacob, *Kehillot Yehudei Kurdistan* (1961), 139.

[A.B.-Y.]

MARDUK (Heb. מְרֹדָךְ, Jer. 50:2), patron deity of the city of Babylon. Although known as a minor god as early as the third millennium, Marduk became an important local deity at the time of the advent of the First Babylonian Dynasty as can be seen mainly from the literary introduction of the *Hammurapi Stele and other documents. However, he was elevated to the rank of the chief deity and national god of Babylon only during the Middle Babylonian period and especially during the reign of Nebuchadnezzar I (c. 1100 B.C.E.; post-Kassite period) and not, as is commonly assumed, during the reign of Hammurapi (1848–1806 B.C.E.). This can be ascertained from the diffusion during the Old and Middle Babylonian periods of the name Marduk as a component of personal names or as a titular deity in legal and other procedures. Apart from its appearance in Jeremiah 50:2, the name Marduk is found in the Bible in personal names such as *Evil-Merodach and *Merodach-Baladan. In Jeremiah 50:2, the name of Marduk is paralleled by the word *bel* (Heb. בֵּל), a transliteration of the Akkadian attribute of Marduk, *belum*, "lord" (Sumerian *EN*), which he inherited in the second millennium from Enlil, the "former" most powerful god of the Mesopotamian pantheon. (According to the Old Babylonian conception expressed in the introduction to the Hammurapi Code, he received at this time only the *illilūtu*, the governorship of the people, which had formerly rested on Enlil.) The origin of Marduk's name is unknown but there are some suggested etymologies, the most accepted being from Sumerian *(A) MAR. UTU (K)*, "the young bull [or calf] of Samaš [Utu] the Sungod." This explanation was well known in the Babylonian tradition. (For "the 50 names of Marduk" see below.) Another etymology, put forward by Th. Jacobsen, is "the son of the storm" (or "maker of storm"?), *Marud(d)uk*, which brings the form of his name closer to the Aramaic-Hebrew transliteration.

Marduk's rise to the status of national god was slow but exceptionally comprehensive. It is very possible that, apart from being an historical process, his elevation was deeply influenced by his connection—not entirely proven—with Enki (Ea), the benevolent god of wisdom, incantations, and the sweet waters of the deep (Sum. *ABZU*, Akk. *apsû*), from Eridu, the most ancient holy city of Sumer.

This connection with Enki was maintained in the theology and practice of the cult of Marduk, e.g., in his identification with Asalluhi, the son of Enki, active in healing or exorcistic incantations, and in the naming of his temple in Babylon *Esagila* ("the house of the [high] raised head") after that of Enki in Eridu. Thus Marduk emerges as a national and popular god of the "second [younger] generation," who exercises influence in every walk of life as the healer and saviour of the Babylonians. In this capacity he appears in incantations, prayers, hymns, philosophical poems (e.g., *Ludlul bêl nêmeqi*, "I praise the God of wisdom," a variant of which was known also in Ugarit, see *Job), and epics such as the *Erra Epic*, where the "disappearance" of Marduk because of displeasure wreaks havoc in the world and brings about the temporary rule of Erra, the god of destruction.

Marduk is the hero of *Enūma eliš* ("When above . . ."), the Babylonian creation myth. In this myth the Son of the Storm is appointed by the gods to lead the fight against Tiāmat (Heb תְּהוֹם, "Ocean") who has planned to destroy them. In the struggle between these two personified natural elements, Marduk gains the upper hand. At the end of the didactic-cultic epic the assembly of gods praises Marduk with 50 name-exegeses and builds the *Esagila* in his honor.

Enūma eliš was read aloud in front of Marduk's statue during the *akītu* (New Year), Babylonia's most important festival. In these ceremonies the statues of Marduk and his son Nabû (Heb. נְבוֹ) were carried from Marduk's temple in Babylon to the house of the *akītu* festival outside the city walls. The elaborate ritual of this festival, known chiefly from a late (Seleucid) edition, greatly influenced many theories about supposed parallel developments in the Israelite cult (see *Psalms, *Kingship).

The cult and theology of Marduk began its expansion during the renewed expansion of Babylonian culture beyond Babylon in the Middle Babylonian-Assyrian period. Marduk was accepted into the Assyrian royal pantheon after Aššur and other important gods. The Babylonian elaboration of the theology of Marduk which expressed itself also in speculative identification and the absorption of the functions of other gods into that of Marduk (this was not exclusive to Marduk), as well as the identification of Marduk with the Babylonian national entity, had momentous consequences in that in the course of time Marduk became identified as a symbol of Babylonian resistance to Assyria. On the other hand, the conception of Marduk decisively influenced the cult of Aššur who was also elevated to a parallel or even higher position. Thus, for example, in the Assyrian version of *Enūma eliš*, Aššur takes the place of Marduk. The tension between the two nations resulted in a most decisive dislike of Marduk in the middle of the first millennium. After the "experiments" of *Tiglath-Pileser III and *Sargon, who were kings of Babylon in every respect, came *Sennacherib who during most of his reign was uniformly anti-Babylonian and "anti-Marduk," and who expressed this by destroying Babylon and *Esagila*. The emblems and statues of Marduk went into "captivity" many times. The return of the statue of Marduk, which was always connected with Babylonian resurrection, was interpreted as a theological change of destiny and as a punishment inflicted by Marduk on Babylon's enemies, as in the case of Sennacherib. Thus, this antagonism became a major issue in the entire destiny of the Ancient Near East in the middle of the first millennium. A very striking example of this antagonism is found in an Assyrian satirical, quasi-theological composition (correctly reinterpreted by W. von Soden) which, far from being an "apotheosis" of the "dead and resurrected Marduk" (as was suggested earlier), is a "mock trial" of Marduk ending probably with his "execution," as a god who—from the point of view of the Assyrians and other peoples—caused much enmity and treachery (see below). This trial is a "logical" continuation of that of the god Kingu and of his execution in *Enūma eliš*, where Marduk was the judge.

In the time of the final Assyrian period (Esarhaddon, Ashurbanipal) and the Neo-Babylonian Dynasty, from Nabopolossar on, and again in the Early Persian period (Cyrus), Marduk was the chief god of Babylon. Because they opposed the oppressive measures of Nabonidus, the last Neo-Babylonian king, the priests of Marduk were those who made possible the peaceful occupation of Babylon by Cyrus (539; see also *Babylon; *Mesopotamia).

Marduk in the West and in the Bible. Marduk is first mentioned in the West (Syria-Palestine) in Akkadian documents from Ugarit (Middle Babylonian period around 1350; see: *Ugaritica*, 5 (1968), 792) where, as mentioned, one version of the philosophical treatise *Ludlul bêl nêmeqi* was known. Also there is an incantation letter against *nambul* ("The Wrong"; "The Bad") directing him to appear before Marduk. The first appearance of Marduk in Palestine occurs in the same period and takes the form of the personal name of Šulum-Marduk in the *Tell el-Amarna letters (EA). According to EA 256:20, as interpreted by Albright (in BASOR, 89 (1943), 12ff.), the royal house at ʿAštartu (the contemporary king being A-ia-ab (=Job)) was called "The House of Šulum-Marduk." Marduk was known also among the Hittites, and Middle Babylonian cylinder seals dedicated to him have been found at Thebes, Greece. In the first millennium Marduk's name appears in Assyrian and Aramean treaties from Sefire that were concluded with King Matiʾilu of Arpad. In the Bible, apart from Marduk (see above), Bel (his appellative attribute) together with his son Nabû (see above) is mentioned in Isaiah 46:1 and Jeremiah 51:44. In both these prophecies divine judgment (not the judgment of a "rival" as in the case of Aššur) is pronounced against a symbolic polytheistic entity within the framework of a particular stage in history. The historical placement of these verses is difficult. Nevertheless, the announcement of biblical-prophetic judgment is consistent with the attitude of the other antagonists to Marduk and Babylon, described above.

Bibliography: S. A. Pallis, *The Babylonian Akitu Festival* (1926); W. F. Albright, in: BASOR, 89 (1943), 12; E. Dhorme, *Les Religions de Babylonie et d'Assyrie* (1949), 139–50; F. M. Th. Boehl, *Opera Minora* (1953), 282–312; W. von Soden, in: ZA, 51 (1955), 130–66; 53 (1957), 229–34; Pritchard, Texts, 60–72, 331–4; H. Schmoekel, in: *Revue d'assyrologie et d'archéologie orientale*, 53 (1959), 183ff.; H. Tadmor, in: *Eretz-Israel*, 5 (1959), 150–63; W. G. Lambert, in: W. S. McCullough (ed.), *The Seed of Wisdom* (1964), 3–13; B. Meissner, *Die Keilschrift*, ed. by K. Oberhuber (1967), 153–4; Th. Jacobsen, in: JAOS, 88 (1968), 104–8; P. Artzi, in: EM, 5 (1968), 442–5. [P.A./RA.K.]

MAREK, PESACH (**Piotr**; 1862–1920), historian of Russian Jews and Yiddish folklorist. After completing his law studies at the University of Moscow, Marek was among the founders of the Benei Zion society of the Moscow Zionists in 1884. Among his studies published in the journal **Voskhod* were articles on Jewish printing in Russia (1888), on the history of Moscow's Jews (1893, 1895, 1896), and on the Jewish Community Council of Belorussia (1903). His most important contribution was *Di Yidishe Folkslider in Rusland* ("Yiddish Folk Songs in Russia," 1901), which he compiled with Saul *Ginsburg. This volume laid the foundation for later studies in the field. Marek's sketches for a history of Jewish education in Russia, published in 1909, embraced the period from 1844 to 1873 and dealt with both traditional and secular systems of education. Marek also wrote for Russian-Jewish historical periodicals and was a contributor to the Russian Jewish encyclopedia.

Bibliography: Rejzen, Leksikon, 2 (1927), 338–42; LNYL, 5 (1963), 504–5. [Y.S.]

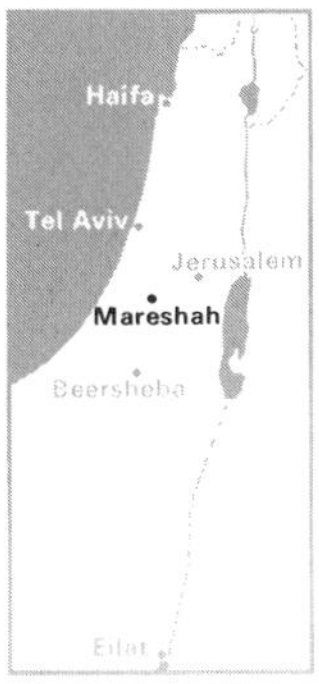

MARESHAH (or **Marissa**; Heb. מָרֵשָׁה), city in Judah connected with the families of Shelah and Caleb (I Chron. 2:42; 4:21). It was in the fourth district of the territory of the tribe of Judah (Josh. 15:44). Mareshah was one of the cities fortified by Rehoboam (II Chron. 11:8–9). It was the home town of the prophet Eliezer the son of Dodavahu (II Chron. 20:37) and possibly also of the prophet Micah (Micah 1:1; Jer. 26:18). In Persian or Hellenistic times, a Sidonian colony settled there and it served as an administrative center (Zeno Pap. 59006, 59015, 59537). Its population, however, was mostly Edomite, and as such, Mareshah served as a base for the Seleucid armies at war with Judah

Painting from one of the Hellenistic tombs found near Mareshah, third century B.C.E. Courtesy Hebrew University, Department of Archaeology, Jerusalem.

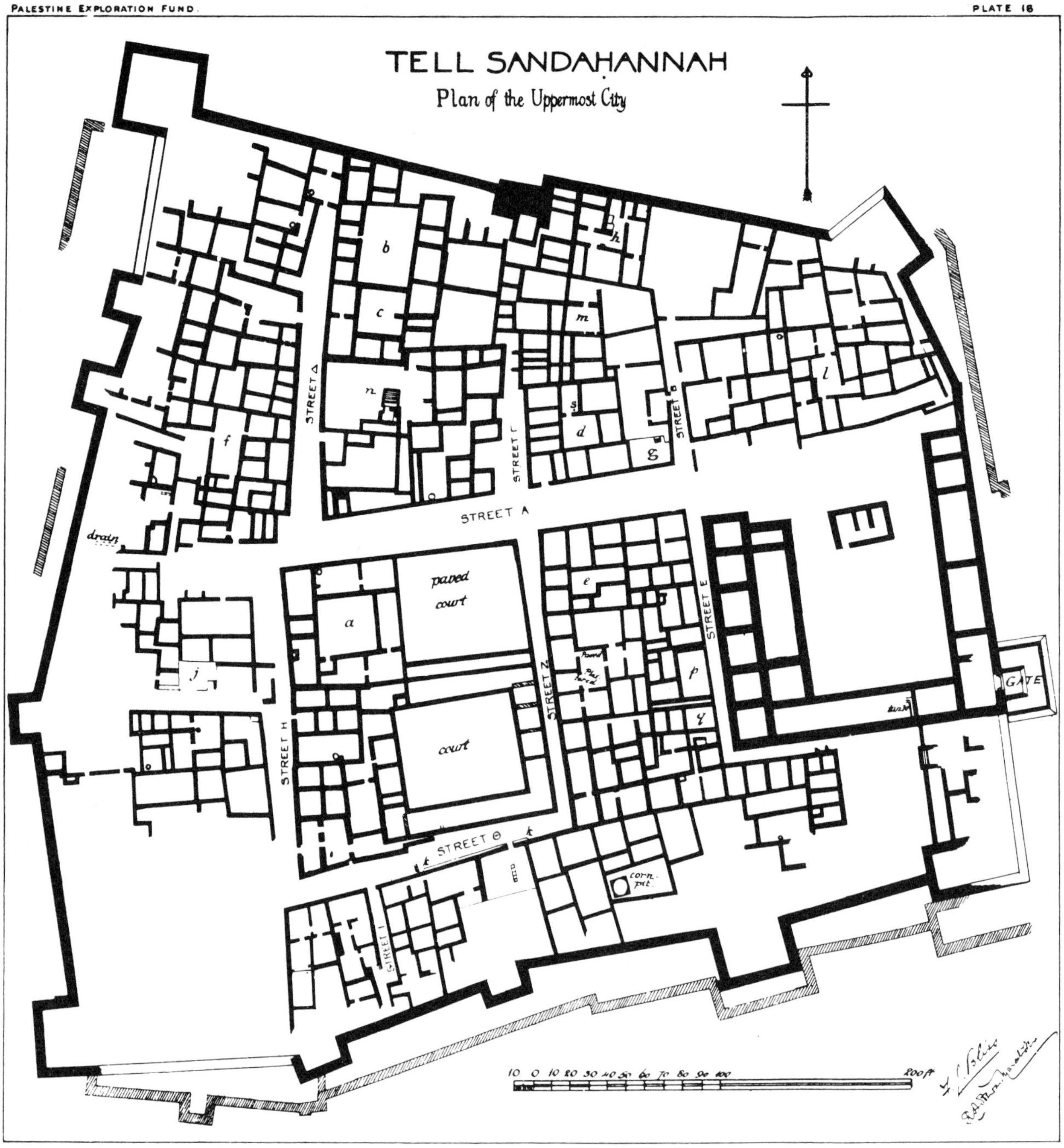

Plan of the Hellenistic city of Mareshah, dating from the second century B.C.E. From F. J. Bliss and R. A. S. Macalister, *Excavations in Palestine*, London, 1902.

Maccabee, who ravaged its territory (I Macc. 5:66; II Macc. 12:35). John Hyrcanus conquered it with the rest of Idumea and it remained in Hasmonean possession until Pompey. In 40 B.C.E., shortly after its "liberation" by Pompey, the Parthians completely destroyed it (Jos., Ant., 12:353; 14:75, 364; Wars, 1:269). After the destruction of the city, *Bet Guvrin became the center of the region. Robinson identified it with Tell Ṣandaḥanna, south of Bet Guvrin. Bliss and Macalister, excavating there in 1900, uncovered the Hellenistic stratum, which contained a city wall nearly square in plan (measurements, at its widest points: 520 ft. (156 m.) wide from east to west; 500 ft. (150 m.) wide from north to south). Inside, the town was laid out in the so-called Hippodamic plan, with streets intersecting at right angles. This plan was slightly distorted at a later stage of the town's existence. In the eastern part of the town were a marketplace and a temple. Ptolemaic inscriptions, pottery, and execration texts on limestone tablets were the main finds. In 1902, Hellenistic tombs with paintings and inscriptions were found near Mareshah. The principal tomb is decorated with representations of real and mythological animals; the inscriptions are of one Apollophanes, head of the Sidonians at Mareshah, and his family. The tomb was used from the second to the first century B.C.E. and the inscriptions indicate a gradual assimilation of the Sidonians into the Idumean and Jewish populations there. Other tombs of similar character were found in 1925 and 1962.

Bibliography: F. J. Bliss and R. A. S. Macalister, *Excavations in Palestine* (1902), 52ff; 204ff.; J. P. Peters and H. Thiersch, *Painted Tombs in the Necropolis of Marissa* (1905); Abel, in: RB, 34 (1925), 267–75; E. Oren, *Archaeology*, 18 (1965), 218–24. [M.A.-Y.]

MARGALIOT (Margulies), MORDECAI (1909–1968), scholar of midrashic and geonic literature. Margaliot was born in Warsaw and emigrated to Palestine as a child; he studied at the Mizrachi Teachers' Seminary in Jerusalem and he was one of the first graduates of the Hebrew University. He taught rabbinical literature at the Hebrew

University 1950–57, and from 1958 midrashic and geonic literature at the Jewish Theological Seminary in New York.

In 1938 he published a scholarly edition of *Ha-Ḥillukim she-Bein Anshei Mizraḥ u-Venei Ereẓ Yisrael* ("Differences in Religious Customs Between Babylonian and Palestinian Jewries"), a small compilation, which in his view was written in Palestine about the year 700 C.E. This was followed in 1942 by an edition of *Halakhot Keẓuvot* ascribed to *Yehudai Gaon, which, according to Margaliot, was composed in southern Italy in the middle of the ninth century.

He also edited *Midrash ha-Gadol* on Genesis (1947) and Exodus (1956); *Hilkhot ha-Nagid* (1962), on Samuel ha-Nagid as halakhist, and *Sefer ha-*Razim* (1966), a treatise on magic from the talmudic period, which he reconstructed from fragments found in various libraries. This work provided new, important insights into Jewish magic and mysticism. His major work was a critical edition of *Midrash Va-Yikra Rabbah,* 5 vols. (1953–60), which is considered to be a model of critical editing of a midrashic text. Margaliot also contributed to scholarly publications and was the editor of two popular biographical dictionaries, one on the sages of the Talmud and the *geonim, Enziklopedyah le-Ḥakhmei ha-Talmud ve-ha-Ge'onim,* 2 vols. (1946), and the other of later rabbinical scholars, *Enẓiklopedyah le-Toledot Gedolei Yisrael,* 4 vols. (1946–50).

Margaliot's wife Rachel wrote *Eḥad Hayah Yeshayahu* (1954, 1956[2]), a defense of the unity of the Book of Isaiah.

Bibliography: Tidhar, 4 (1950), 1720–21; 17 (1968), 5247; Kressel, Leksikon, 2 (1967), 419–20. [T.P.]

MARGALIOT, REUBEN (1889–1971), rabbinic scholar and author. Born in Lemberg (Lvov), Margaliot qualified as a rabbi, but remained in business, eventually as a bookseller. Having been active in the Mizrachi movement in Lvov, he settled in Israel in 1935, becoming librarian of the Rambam Library in Tel Aviv. He devoted several studies to ḥasidic lore such as *Or ha-Me'ir* and *Marganita de-R. Meir* (1926, 1964); and *Hillula de-Ẓaddikaya* (1929, 1961). At a later stage he turned to Kabbalah, producing a monumental annotated edition of the Zohar (1964[4]), of the *Tikkunei Zohar* (1948), of M. Ḥ. Luzzatto's *Zohar Ḥadash* (1953), and of the early kabbalistic work *Sefer ha-Bahir* (1951). He also wrote *Sha'arei Zohar* (1956), a comparative study of the Zohar's system. Margaliot also wrote on the *Emden-*Eybeschuetz controversy and received a reply from G. Scholem (1941).

Earlier he had also published sermons and homiletical material and annotations to Ḥayyim b. Moses *Attar's pentateuchal commentary *Ner la-Ma'or* (1932, 1959). He wrote biographies of S. Edels (1912); of Ḥayyim b. Moses Attar (1925); of Maimonides' son Abraham (1930), whose *Milḥamot Adonai* he published in 1953; as well as *Le-Toledot Anshei Shem bi-Lvov* (1950), on the scholars of his native city. On Talmud and *halakhah* Margaliot wrote among others *Margaliyyot ha-Yam* (novellae on tractate *Sanhedrin,* 1958) and *Nefesh Ḥayyah* on the Shulḥan Arukh *Oraḥ Ḥayyim* (1954[2]). Of special interest is a study of the halakhic aspects of a political resettlement of Ereẓ Israel (*Kavvei Or,* 1921) written under the impact of the Balfour Declaration. Among halakhic studies in a more modern vein and idiom are his *Yesod ha-Mishnah va-Arikhatah* ("Foundations of the Mishnah and its Redaction," 1956[4]); and *Meḥkarim be-Darkhei ha-Talmud* ("Studies in Talmudic Methodology," 1967). Also of importance are his editions of medieval texts, particularly his annotated *Sefer Ḥasidim,* attributed to Judah b. Samuel (12th century), first published in 1924 and republished many times since. Margaliot also prepared an edition of the responsa of the tosafist *Jacob of Marvège (*She'elot u-Teshuvot min ha-Shamayim,* 1957[3]); of the disputations of Naḥmanides with Pablo Christiani in Barcelona in 1263 (with a biography of Naḥmanides, 1929); and of Jehiel of Paris of 1240 (1928, 1944). He received the Israel Prize in 1957 for his research on Kabbalah and Ḥasidism.

Bibliography: Kressel, Leksikon, 2 (1967), 421–3. [ED.]

MARGARITA (Margalita), ANTON (b. c. 1490), apostate and anti-Jewish writer. Although the son of a rabbi, Samuel son of Jacob *Margolioth of Regensburg, while he was still a Jew he denounced the Regensburg community to the authorities. He converted to Catholicism in 1522, and later became a Protestant. He was a lecturer in Hebrew at Augsburg, Meissen Zell, Leipzig, and from 1537 until his death, at Vienna University. In his first anti-Jewish book, *Der Gantz Juedisch Glaub . . .* (first published in Augsburg, 1530), Margarita modeled himself on similar writings by the apostates Johannes *Pfefferkorn and Victor von *Carben. In an attempt to ridicule the religious precepts of the Jews, their customs, and their habits, he accused them of lacking charity, of reviling Christianity (in the **Aleinu* prayer), and finally of treason. The large number of Jewish prayers in his own translation included in the book reveal his ignorance of Jewish writings (as noted by Johann *Wagenseil in his Latin translation of tractate *Sotah* (Altdorf, 1674), 1105) and his scanty knowledge of Hebrew. The book formed the basis of a religious disputation between *Joseph (Joselmann) b. Gershom of Rosheim and Margarita held at the Diet of Augsburg of 1530 at the instance of Emperor *Charles V. When Joseph of Rosheim succeeded in proving that the apostate's allegations were unfounded, Margarita was imprisoned and later banished from Augsburg. However, his book was reprinted many times (Frankfort, 1544, 1561, 1689; Leipzig, 1705, 1713) and was widely read. It particularly influenced Martin *Luther, who quoted it

Der gantz Jüdisch glaub
mit sampt ainer gründtlichen vnd war-
hafften anzaygunge/ Aller Satzungen / Ceremonien/
Gebetten/ Haymliche vnd offentliche Gebreüch / deren sich dye
Juden halten / durch das gantz Jar / Mit schönen vnd ge-
gründten Argumenten wyder jren Glauben. Durch
Anthonium Margaritham Hebrayschen Leser
der Löblichen Statt Augspurg / beschri-
ben vnd an tag gegeben.
M. D. XXX.

Title page of *Der Gantz Juedisch Glaub,* the first anti-Jewish book by Anton Margarita, Augsburg, 1530. Courtesy J. Michman, Jerusalem.

many times in his *Von den Juden und ihren Luegen*. Margarita was also the author of *Dar Muschiach Schon Khomen* (1534).

Bibliography: Wolf, Bibliotheca, 1 (1715), 202–4; 3 (1727), 129–30; 4 (1733), 789; G. Wolf, *Studien zur Jubelfeier der Wiener Universitaet* (1865), 28–29; L. Geiger, in: ZGJD, 2 (1888), 324–5; H. Breslau, *ibid.*, 5 (1892), 310–2; A. Fuerst, *Christen und Juden* (1892), 191; J. Mieses, *Die aelteste gedruckte deutsche Uebersetzung des juedischen Gebetbuches . . . und ihr Autor Anton Margalita* (1916); Graetz, Hist, 4 (1949), 551; Baron, Social[2], 13, 223ff.; Josef Ish Rosheim, *Sefer ha-Minḥah* (1920), introd., 25ff. [B.Su./Ed.]

MARGET, ARTHUR W. (1899–1962), U.S. economist. Born in Chelsea, Mass. After serving with the U.S. army during World War I he taught at Harvard and at the University of Minnesota. In World War II he again joined the armed forces and rose to the rank of lieutenant colonel. After the war he was chief of the finance and economic division of the United States element of the Allied Commission for Austria, and during 1947–48 was chief of the United States finance division in Paris. In 1950 he joined the Board of Governors of the Federal Reserve System in Washington, and became the director of its international finance division. In 1961 he resigned and went to Guatemala as regional adviser to the State Department's Agency for International Development. His major publication is *The Theory of Prices*, 2 vols. (1938–42). [J.O.R.]

MARGHITA (Hung. **Margitta,** also **Margita;** referred to by the Jews as מארגארעטען (**Margaretten**)), town in Transylvania, W. Rumania. Until the end of World War I and between 1940 and 1945 it formed part of Hungary. Jews began to settle there during the 18th century. A geographical-historical description of Hungary which was published in 1799 mentions Jewish inhabitants among the Hungarians and Rumanians. The first Jewish settlers appear to have come from the neighboring village Petra. A community headed by a rabbi has probably existed by the close of the 18th century. The synagogue was erected in 1862. In 1885 the community also became a center for the Jews of the surrounding region. The Jewish population numbered 944 (18% of the total population) in 1900 and 1,623 (26.7%) in 1930.

From its inception the community was an Orthodox one. The influence of Ḥasidism was felt, particularly between the two world wars. The rabbis of the community included R. Joshua Aaron Ẓevi Weinberger, author of the *Mahariaẓ* responsa (first half of the 19th century); his descendants succeeded him in the rabbinical office until the liquidation of the community. For a short period, from 1850, R. Hillel *Lichtenstein was rabbi of the town. The students of the community's yeshivah included some who came from far away, and their numbers occasionally rose to 350. The last rabbi, who perished in the Holocaust, was R. Mordecai Azriel Weinberger; he was also the last head of the yeshivah. A Jewish press functioned in Marghita between the two world wars.

At the time of the Holocaust, in the summer of 1944, the local Jews were taken to the district capital of *Oradea-Mare and deported from there to Auschwitz. After the war some Jews returned to the town, numbering about 500 in 1947. Their numbers gradually decreased through emigration to Israel and other countries, so that they were finally reduced to 10 families in 1970 (out of a total population of 12,000). [Y.M.]

MARGOLIES, ISAAC BEN ELIJAH (1842–1887), Polish rabbi and author. Born in Kalvarija, S.W. Lithuania, the son of a rabbi, Margolies devoted himself in his early youth solely to talmudic studies. After his marriage in 1862 to the daughter of a prominent member of the community of Merech in Vilna province, he took up residence there and began to take a keen interest in the Haskalah. This interest aroused the hostility of anti-Haskalah zealots, which, together with reverses in his father-in-law's business, compelled him to seek employment elsewhere. After spending some 15 years as a teacher, particularly in the house of Ezekiel Jaffe in Kovno, Margolies was appointed rabbi of Druskinnikai in Grodno province. There too he was persecuted by the opponents of the Haskalah, and two years later he accepted the invitation of the congregation of Anshei Kalvarija in New York, where he became renowned as a public lecturer and teacher. Margolies is the author of two works, *Ma'oz ha-Talmud* (1869) and *Ma'oz ha-Yam* (1871), in which he uses his outstanding talmudic knowledge to defend the Talmud against its critics. He is also the author of *Sippurei Yeshurun* (1877), an anthology of aggadic and talmudic literature written in a pleasant and easily readable Hebrew. Margolies contributed to the Hebrew periodicals *Ha-Maggid*, *Ha-Shaḥar*, *Ha-Meliẓ*, and *Ha-Ẓefrah*.

Bibliography: *Ha-Asif*, 4 (1887), 72–74 (first pagination); *American Hebrew*, 32 no. 1 (Aug. 12, 1887), 8. [An.L.L.]

MARGOLIES, MOSES SEBULUN (1851–1936), U.S. Orthodox rabbi. Rabbi Margolies, who was born in Kroza, Russia, was educated at the yeshivot of Kroza and Bialystok. After serving as rabbi of Sloboda (1877–89), he went to the U.S. to assume the post of chief rabbi of Boston's Orthodox community. Margolies became rabbi of the prosperous and influential Congregation Kehilath

Moses Sebulun Margolies, rabbi and president of Rabbi Isaac Elchanan Yeshiva. From *American Jewish Historical Quarterly*, Vol. 54, New York, 1964.

Jeshurun, New York, in 1906 and held that post until his death. He introduced the system which supervised the distribution of kosher meat in New York City and served as president of the Union of Orthodox Rabbis of the United States and Canada. Margolies founded both the New York *kehillah* and the Central Relief Committee (later absorbed by the American Jewish Joint Distribution Committee). An early Zionist, Margolies was a member of the Mizrachi Organization of America. Margolies, who was president of the Rabbi Isaac Elchanan Yeshiva for several years, foresaw the need for Jewish institutions providing both a religious and secular education. The Ramaz School in New York is named after him.

Bibliography: *New York Times*, (Aug. 26, 1936). [Ed.]

MARGOLIN, ARNOLD (1877–1956), Ukrainian lawyer. Born in Kiev, the son of a rich sugar manufacturer, Margolin was well known for his role in pogrom trials, and especially in the *Beilis case. He was disbarred for his stand against the czarist court authorities but his rights were

Arnold Margolin, Ukrainian lawyer. Jerusalem, J.N.U.L., Schwadron Collection.

restored after the revolution. After M. *Mandelstamm's death in 1912, Margolin became, together with Dr. I. Jochelman, the leader of the Territorialist Organization in Russia (see *Territorialism). In 1918 he was appointed associate justice of the highest Ukrainian court, and later deputy minister of foreign affairs in the Ukrainian government. Although he resigned in March 1919 after the *Proskurov pogrom, he nevertheless defended the*Petlyura government, considering that the pogroms were perpetrated only by the Black Hundreds (see *Union of Russian People) and other agitators. In 1919 he became the diplomatic representative of the Ukrainian government in England, and in 1922 he left London for the United States, where he was a journalist and lecturer. He was admitted to the bar association of Massachusetts in 1929 and to that of Washington, D. C., in 1936. Margolin wrote several books, among them *Ukraina i politika antanty* ("Ukraine and the Policy of Entente," 1922), *The Jews of Eastern Europe* (1926), and *From a Political Diary* (1946).

Bibliography: E. Tcherikower, *Di Ukrainer Pogromen in Yor 1919* (1965), 186–9; J. Frumkin (ed.), *Russian Jewry* (1966), 164, 199. [Ed.]

MARGOLIN, ELIEZER (1874–1944), one of the commanders of the *Jewish Legion during World War I. Born in Belgorod, Russia, Margolin settled in Ereẓ Israel with his family in 1892 and lived in Reḥovot. He was outstanding in agricultural labor and in affairs of self-defense. With the death of his parents and the difficult economic situation in the country, he went to Australia in 1900 and worked in agriculture and trade there. During World War I he joined the Australian army. He was noted for his heroism on the Gallipoli front (1915–16) and became acquainted with Vladimir *Jabotinsky and the volunteers of the Zion Mule Corps from Ereẓ Israel. He was transferred to the French front under the command of General *Monash and achieved the rank of lieutenant colonel. Jabotinsky met with him in London and offered him the command of the Second Battalion of the Jewish Regiment, which consisted mostly of Jewish volunteers that had arrived from the U.S. and Canada, the 49th Royal Fusiliers (among its members were Izhak *Ben-Zvi and David *Ben-Gurion). Margolin accepted the offer and, with the agreement of the military authorities, arrived in Palestine in the summer of 1918 as commander of the battalion. He also cultivated friendly relations with the Ereẓ Israel volunteers of the third battalion of the Jewish Legion, disregarding the norms of military hierarchy. His battalion broke through the Turkish front on the Jordan River and captured the Transjordanian town of Salt, of which he was made military governor.

In December 1919, when the Legion was officially given its Jewish name, First Judeans, with the seven-branched *menorah* as its symbol, Margolin became its commander. Margolin constantly struggled against the hostile attitude toward the Legion of the British military command and military authorities in Palestine. But his sense of order could not be gainsaid; he never revealed his deep relationship to the *yishuv* and the first nucleus of its self-defense network to the outside world. With the riots that broke out in Palestine in the spring of 1920, the armed legionnaires were dispersed, with Margolin's knowledge, throughout the Arab villages, an act that prevented further bloodshed. Margolin argued with his superior officers for his right to command the Legion in this manner, an attitude that was not usually accepted in military circles.

Eliezer Margolin, commander of the World War I Jewish Legion. Jerusalem, J.N.U.L., Schwadron Collection.

With the gradual dismantling of the Legion, the British Military High Command decided to establish the Palestine Defense Force, composed of a Jewish and an Arab unit. Margolin was destined to be the commander of the Jewish unit (March 1921). Riots again broke out in Jerusalem and Tel Aviv-Jaffa (spring of 1921), and on May 1 Joseph *Brenner and his friends were killed. Jewish legionnaires, including discharged ones, took arms out from the military camp in Sarafand without Margolin's knowledge and used them to stop the riots. Margolin arrived in Tel Aviv on May 2, mobilized both in-service and discharged soldiers, and provided them with arms from the military stores. This act served as a pretext to abandon the plan of the Palestine Defense Force and finally disband the Legion. Margolin resigned from the army, rather than face a court martial, returned to Australia, and went into business. Throughout his life he longed to return to Ereẓ Israel. In 1950 his remains were transferred to Israel and reinterred in Reḥovot. A childhood friend from Reḥovot, the Hebrew author Moshe *Smilansky, described Eliezer Margolin in one of his stories, named after the Arab and Bedouin nickname for him, "Ḥawaja Nazar."

Bibliography: Tidhar, 5 (1952), 2324–25; M. Smilansky, *Mishpaḥat ha-Adamah*, 3 (1951), 167–76; B. Dinur (ed.), *Sefer Toledot ha-Haganah*, 1–2 (1954–63), index; Ever Hadani, *Am be-Milḥamto* (1953[3]), 178–81; E. Gilner, *War and Hope; a History of the Jewish Legion* (1969), index.

[G.K.]

MARGOLIN, MOSES (1862–?), Zionist writer. After completing his studies at the University of St. Petersburg Margolin was appointed secretary of the editorial board of the Russian *Entsiklopedicheskiy Slovar* ("Encyclopedic Dictionary") of Brockhaus-Efron and of several other Russian encyclopedias. He was active in Jewish public life, in the *Society for the Promotion of Culture among the Jews of Russia, the *Jewish Colonization Association, and other organizations. In 1904 he was one of the editors of the Russian-language Zionist newspaper, *Yevreyskaya Zhizn*. In his studies in Jewish history Margolin attempted to demonstrate the legitimacy of the historic development of the Jewish people. He deals with this in *Osnovye techeniya v istorii yevreyskago naroda* ("Basic Trends in the History of the Jewish People," 1900,

1917[2]) and in *Yevreyskaya zemlya* ("A Jewish Land," 1918). Under the Soviet regime Margolin belonged to the small group of Jewish intellectuals who attempted to continue their research work in Jewish history; he contributed until 1930 to the publications which these circles published. No information about his subsequent fate is known. [Y.S.]

MARGOLIOT, MOSES BEN SIMEON (d. 1781), Lithuanian rabbi and commentator on the Jerusalem Talmud. Margoliot was born in Kedziniai, near Kovno, Lithuania. His pupils included *Elijah of Vilna, then a boy of seven. Margoliot served as rabbi in several communities in the Samogitia region of Lithuania.

His main claim to fame rests on his important commentary on the Jerusalem Talmud, to all intents and purposes the first of its kind. His commentary is divided into two parts: *Penei Moshe*, an explanation of the text; and *Mareh ha-Panim* which gives the parallel passages in the Babylonian Talmud, and attempts to explain the differences between the two with regard to both text and content. Only part of his commentary, to the order *Nashim* (Amsterdam, 1754), and to the order *Nezikin* and the tractate *Niddah* (Leghorn, 1770), was printed with the text in his lifetime. His commentaries to the remaining tractates were published after his death (to *Berakhot*, Leghorn, 1785?) and the full commentary was not published until 80 years after his death, together with the text of the Talmud (Zhitomir, 1860–67). It has become the standard commentary on the Jerusalem Talmud and has been printed in almost every edition, affording ample evidence of Margoliot's vast erudition in Talmud and rabbinic literature as a whole. He paid careful attention to problems of the text, and had at his disposal many early manuscripts. He was the first to realize the vital importance of the Tosefta for an understanding of the Jerusalem Talmud, and he had an ancient manuscript of it which was superior to the printed text of his day both in completeness and accuracy. Margoliot also endeavored to acquire the knowledge of the natural sciences requisite for a proper understanding of the Jerusalem Talmud. In 1779, when he was nearly 70 years of age, his name is found among the students enrolled in the botanical department of the University of Frankfort on the Oder. His interest in botany was undoubtedly due to his desire better to understand the agricultural laws in Ereẓ Israel found in the order of *Zera'im* in the Jerusalem Talmud, but to which there is no **Gemara* in the Babylonian.

Margoliot's commentary is one of the two standard commentaries on the Jerusalem Talmud, of much greater importance than that of David *Fraenkel, and has become indispensable to the student. From his introduction to the commentary, it is clear that he wandered from country to country. For several years he served as a rabbi in Amsterdam, during which time his commentary to the order *Nashim* was printed. He was in London for some time before 1754, and was in Leghorn when his commentary to the order *Nezikin* was published there. The statement by Joshua Heschel *Lewin in his book *Aliyyot Eliyahu*, 28 that Margoliot traveled to Vilna after the publication of his commentary to *Nashim*, and there met R. Elijah of Vilna, must be regarded with reservation, because the latter never saw his commentary. In his commentary, Margoliot mentions two of his works: *Be'er Mayim Ḥayyim*, a commentary to the tractates *Shabbat* and *Eruvin*, and *Penei ha-Menorah*, on the Pentateuch. He died in Brody, Galicia.

Bibliography: Gelber, in: JJLG, 13 (1920), 132; Lewin, *ibid.*, 15 (1923), 92–94; L. Ginzberg (Ginzburg), *Perushim ve-Ḥiddushim ba-Yerushalmi*, 1 (1941), 55–58 (Eng. introd.). [A.D.]

MARGOLIOTH (Margoliouth, Margulies, Margolies, and various other spellings), family that traditionally traces its descent from *Rashi. The name derives from *margalit* (מרגלית), Hebrew for "pearl." The earliest identifiable member of the family was Jacob of Regensburg (see Jacob *Margolioth). Jacob's son Samuel may be identical with SAMUEL MARGOLIOTH, nominated elder of Great Poland and Masovian Jewry in 1527 by Sigismund I. Samuel's son was Anton *Margarita, the apostate anti-Jewish writer. Another son, MOSES (1540?–1616), was rabbi at Cracow and head of the yeshivah there. NAPHTALI MARGOLIOTH (b. 1562) embraced Christianity in 1603, as Julius Conrad Otto. He became professor of Hebrew at Altdorf and later returned to Judaism. Samuel's grandson MENDEL (d. 1652), rabbi at *Przemysl, had eight sons, all distinguished talmudists. The most outstanding member of this line, which was widely dispersed throughout Eastern Europe, was EPHRAIM ZALMAN *MARGOLIOTH. There was a MOSES MARGULIES among the first inhabitants of the Vienna ghetto, founded in 1620. His son, MORDECAI (Marx Schlesinger), was leader of the Vienna community at the time of the 1670 expulsion. Some members of the family settled permanently in Eisenstadt. Those who later returned to Vienna called themselves Margulies-Jaffe and registered themselves as "Schlesinger."

Bibliography: J. Mieses, *Die aelteste gedruckte deutsche Uebersetzung des juedischen Gebetbuches aus dem Jahre 1530 . . .* (1916); B. Wachstein, *Die Grabschriften des alten Judenfriedhofs in Eisenstadt* (1922); L. Loewenstein, *Geschichte der Juden in der Kurpfalz* (1895), 93. [ED.]

MARGOLIOTH, EPHRAIM ZALMAN BEN MENAHEM MANNES (1760–1828), rabbi and author. Ephraim studied under his uncle, Alexander Margolioth, rabbi of Satanov, Isaac of Ostrow, author of *Berit Kehunnat Olam*, and Ezekiel *Landau. In his youth he was rabbi of Ohanov, but later left the rabbinate, according to some reports declining an offer of the rabbinate of Frankfort. Ephraim settled in Brody and went into business, in which he was highly successful. He owned commercial establishments in Vienna and it was said of him: "From the time of the minister Saul *Wahl there has not been Torah and wealth such as belong to Margolioth." He spent most his time in study, leaving the conduct of his business to his partner Simeon Dishze. He also studied esoteric works with a group of kabbalists at Brody, and had a sound knowledge of history. Margolioth wrote many books and exchanged responsa with the greatest rabbis of his time, with some of whom he maintained close relations. He was involved in the controversy caused by Joshua Heshel *Ẓoref's book *Ha-Ẓoref* and established the fact that it had strong leanings toward Shabbateanism. He also contended with the communal leaders of Brody over the leniency extended to the wealthy *parnasim* under the prevailing system of communal taxation and demanded their full participation in community expenditure.

Margolioth gave his approbation to a great number of books, including many by ḥasidic rabbis. His own works, which appeared in many editions, and many of his halakhic decisions have been accepted.

His works include: *Beit Efrayim*, part 1 entitled *Peri Tevu'ah*, with commentary *Rosh Efrayim* (Lemberg, 1809); part 2 Shulḥan Arukh, *Yoreh De'ah* (*ibid.*, 1810); responsa *Beit Efrayim* (*ibid.*, 1818); and another collection of responsa *Beit Efrayim* (Brody, 1866); *Shem Efrayim*, on Rashi's commentary to the Pentateuch and *haftarot* (Ostrow, 1826); *Zera Efrayim* on the *Pesikta Rabbati* (Lemberg, 1853); *Yad Efrayim*, on Shulḥan Arukh, *Oraḥ Ḥayyim* (in Dubno ed. of Shulḥan Arukh, *Oraḥ Ḥayyim*, 1820). He also wrote *Ma'alot ha-Yuḥasin*, a genealogical book on the families

Landau, Margolioth, etc. (Lemberg, 1900). R. Ẓevi Hirsch *Chajes of Zolkiew was among his pupils.

Bibliography: J. A. Kamelhar, *Dor De'ah*, 2 (1928), 145–9; Rubinstein, in: *Hadorom*, 4 (1958), 3–13; Rabinowitz, in: *Zion*, 6 (1941), 80–84; *Arim ve-Immahot be-Yisrael*, 6 (1955), 65–66. [Y.AL.]

MARGOLIOTH, JACOB (d. between 1499 and 1512), rabbi of Regensburg (Ratisbon), originally from *Worms. In 1497 he corresponded with Johannes *Reuchlin on kabbalistic literature. Margolioth was considered a halakhic authority by his contemporaries and praised by them. His son SAMUEL, father of the apostate Anton *Margarita, succeeded him as rabbi of Regensburg until the expulsion in 1519; he subsequently moved to Posen (Poznan), where he served as *av bet din* of Great Poland until after 1537. Another of Jacob's sons, ISAAC EIZIK (d. 1525), was a member of the *bet din* of R. Jacob *Pollak of Prague. Jacob's *Seder Gittin ve-Ḥaliẓah* has been preserved in two copies, one made by his son Isaac (Bodl. Ms. 2010/3) and the other by his son SHALOM SHAKHNA under the title *Yam she-Asah Shelomo* (Bodl. Ms. 803). Part of his work was printed at the end of *Tur Even ha-Ezer* (Berlin, 1702). A privilege of Frederick III dated 1487 mentions a second JACOB MARGOLIOTH (d. before 1492), of Nuremberg. A halakhic declaration by him is noted in the responsa of R. Judah *Minz (no. 13), on the legality of a declaration of refusal *(me'un)* to marry. R. Elijah *Capsali named Jacob Margolioth as one of the supporters of R. Moses *Capsali in his bitter controversy (1475–80) with R. Joseph *Colon (*Likkutim Shonim*, 1869, p. 16), but it is unclear to which of the two he was referring.

Bibliography: M. Wiener, in: MGWJ, 12 (1868), 345–51; S. Wiener, *Pesak ha-Ḥerem shel ha-Rav Ya'akov Pollak* (1897), 67–68; Graetz-Rabinowitz, 6 (1898), 436–7; A. Freimann, in: *Festschrift... M. Philippson* (1916), 89–90; J. Mieses, *Die aelteste gedruckte deutsche Uebersetzung des juedischen Gebetbuches aus dem Jahre 1530* (1916), 12–26; A. Marx, *Studies in Jewish History and Booklore* (1944), 123, no. 66; R. Straus, *Urkunden und Aktenstuecke zur Geschichte der Juden in Regensburg* (1960), no. 672 [A.D.]

MARGOLIOTH, JUDAH LOEB (1747–1811), rabbi and preacher, one of the precursors of the Haskalah in Eastern Europe. Margolioth, who was born in Zborov, Galicia, served as rabbi in various East European communities and from 1805 in Frankfort on the Oder. He was familiar with medieval and contemporary Hebrew scientific literature as well as with contemporary Haskalah literature. In his books of sermons, he emphasized social justice and criticized the rich. He opposed Ḥasidism but also objected to the study of philosophy which he regarded as undermining faith. Thus he criticized *Mendelssohn for advocating freedom of ideas in Judaism in his book, *Jerusalem*, but advocated the study of Hebrew grammar, the sciences, and mathematics. He wrote *Or Olam al Ḥokhmat ha-Teva* ("Light of the World—On Science," Frankfort on the Oder, 1777). The main point of the book is the classification of the "wisdoms" into science, mathematics, physics, and metaphysics; and the art of leading men: politics, economics, and ethics. The book was well received and was enthusiastically praised by Russian and Polish rabbis. His other works include interpretations of the Torah, responsa, sermons, and linguistic studies. Margolioth's books give expression to the mood of Eastern European Jews in the early days of the Haskalah, and demonstrate the initial willingness among certain Orthodox elements to accept social reforms and even secular studies, but their disillusionment when they witnessed the radical results of Enlightenment.

Bibliography: Zinberg, Sifrut, 3 (1957), 290–1, 314–7; 5 (1959), 137–40; Kressel, Leksikon, 2 (1967), 419; Klausner, Sifrut, 1 (1952), 85–86; B. Dinur, *Be-Mifneh ha-Dorot* (1955), 264–5; R. Mahler, *History of the Jewish People in Modern Times*, 4 pt. 1 (1956), 40–44. [Y.S.]

MARGOLIOUTH, DAVID SAMUEL (1858–1940), classical scholar and orientalist. Born in London the eldest son of the convert missionary Ezekiel Margoliouth, Margoliouth was educated at New College, Oxford, where he later was a fellow (1881–89). In 1889 he was appointed professor of Arabic at Oxford University, holding the position until his retirement in 1937. In 1899 he was ordained and in 1913 he became moderator in oriental languages at London University, where he also delivered the Hibbert lectures. Margoliouth was honored by many learned societies; in 1915 he was elected as a member of the British Academy, and from 1934 to 1937 he was president of the Royal Asiatic Society. Margoliouth was an outstanding scholar in the fields of Islamic history and literature and was an important editor of medieval Arabic texts. Among his extensive writings the following are of particular Jewish interest: *A Commentary on the Book of Daniel by Jephet ibn Ali...* (edited and translated, 1889); *The Place of Ecclesiasticus in Semitic Literature* (1890); *The Origin of the "Hebrew Original" of Ecclesiasticus* (1899); and *Relations Between Arabs and Israelites Prior to the Rise of Islam* (Schweich lectures 1921, published 1924). He also edited Whiston's English translation of Josephus (1906).

Bibliography: S. Murray, in: DNB (1931–40), 597–9. [ED.]

MARGOLIOUTH, MEIR OF OSTRAHA (Ostrog; d. 1790), ḥasidic rabbi in Poland; a disciple of *Israel b. Eliezer the Ba'al Shem Tov. He was descended from a celebrated rabbinical family. From a very early age he and his elder brother became devoted and loved disciples of the Ba'al Shem Tov. R. Meir, who gained a reputation as one of the greatest scholars of his age, served as rabbi in Jaslo and later in Horodenka (Gorodenka); in 1755 he was appointed rabbi in the Lvov region and in 1777 was appointed *rabbi Ostraha*, a title officially confirmed by the King of Poland, Stanislas II Augustus, which established his authority over all the rabbis of the district. He wrote works on *halakhah* and Kabbalah, and also long didactic poems. His great prestige helped to promote Ḥasidism, which at that time gave it important support. He had five sons, all of whom became noted rabbis and scholars. His works are *Meir Netivim* (Polonnoye, 1791–92); *Sod Yakhin u-Vo'az* (Ostrog, 1794); *Derekh ha-Tov ve-ha-Yashar* (Polonnoye, 1795); and *Kotnot Or* (Berdichev, 1816).

Bibliography: M. Biber, *Mazkeret li-Gedolei Ostraha* (1907), 198–209, 270–3; S. Buber, *Anshei Shem* (1895), 137–49, 202. [A.ST.]

MARGOLIOUTH (Margalita), MOSES (1818–1881), English priest. Margoliouth, who was Jewish by birth, was born in Suwalki, Poland. In his youth he studied in yeshivot, and in 1837 he left Poland for Liverpool, where under the influence of Jewish converts to Christianity he himself became a Christian in 1838. After his studies at Trinity College, Dublin (1840–44), he served as curate in Liverpool (1844). From 1877 until his death he served as vicar in Little Linford in Buckinghamshire. Among his works are: *The Fundamental Principles of Modern Judaism Investigated* (1843 with Margoliouth's autobiography); *The History of the Jews of Great Britain* (1857); and *A Pilgrimage to the Land of My Fathers* (1858), a travelogue of Palestine.

His nephew, GEORGE MARGOLIOUTH (1853–1952), like his uncle Moses Margoliouth, converted to Christianity and became an ordained priest of the Church (1881). Margoliouth excelled in biblical and oriental studies and was in charge of the Hebrew, Syriac, and Ethiopic manuscripts of the British Museum from 1891 to 1914. His works included *The Liturgy of the Nile* (Palestine Syriac Text, Translation and Vocabulary; 1896); *The Palestine Syriac Version of the Holy Scriptures* (London, 1897); and the *Catalogue of the Hebrew and Samaritan Manuscripts in the British Museum* (3 vols.; 1909–15), which has served scholars as an important bibliographical guide to this most important collection. [A.T.]

MARGOLIS, MAX LEOPOLD (1886–1932), U.S. biblical and Semitic scholar. Born in Russia, Margolis received a thorough training in Bible and Talmud as well as in modern sciences and languages in his native country and in Berlin. In 1889 he went to the United States. His first field of specialization was the text-criticism of the Talmud to which his dissertation was devoted. His earliest work reveals meticulous attention to detail, thorough mastery of the subject, rigorous application of the inductive method, and brilliance and solidity in the conclusions. At the end of his fellowship year at Columbia University, Margolis was called to the Hebrew Union College in Cincinnati as assistant professor of Hebrew and biblical exegesis. During his incumbency he published his *Elementary Textbook of Hebrew Accidence* (1893), a succinct and original contribution to Hebrew grammar and phonetics, as well as several works dealing with Reform Jewish theology. In 1897 he went to the University of California at Berkeley to teach Semitic languages and in 1905 returned to the Hebrew Union College as professor of biblical exegesis. He resigned from the Hebrew Union College in 1910, after he and other faculty members differed with the College president regarding educational philosophy and Zionism—Margolis was a strong Zionist. He went to Europe to complete his work on his pioneering and still classic *Manual of the Aramaic Language of the Babylonian Talmud,* which appeared both in English and in German (1910). The Jewish Publication Society chose Margolis to be secretary of the Board of Editors and editor-in-chief of their new translation of the Bible into English. To this major task he devoted himself until 1917. After the translation appeared, his mimeographed *Notes on the New Translation of the Holy Scriptures* (1921), which served as the basis of the work, appeared in a tome of 646 pages for private circulation. When Dropsie College was opened in Philadelphia, Margolis became professor of biblical philology, a position he occupied from 1909 until his death. Two brief popular works *The Story of Bible Translations* (1917) and *The Hebrew Scriptures in the Making* (1922) were never expanded into full-length scholarly treatments because his energies were increasingly absorbed by his vision of a truly critical edition of the Septuagint. Choosing the Book of Joshua, he collated all the existing Greek manuscripts and by dint of minute and brilliant analysis established the principal recensions of the Septuagint, which he called Palestinian, Egyptian, Syrian, Constantinopolitan, and Mixed. On the basis of these he then recreated what he regarded as the original septuagintal text. While some scholars have differed with his underlying theory as to the nature of the Greek translation, *The Book of Joshua in Greek* (1931) is considered a work of brilliant scholarship. In the area of septuagintal studies, he also published scores of technical papers. In the field of biblical exegesis he published a brief but valuable English commentary on Micah, *Holy Scriptures with Commentary: Micah* (1908), and Hebrew commentaries on Zephaniah and Malachi in the Kahana Bible Commentary Series (1930). The book by which he is perhaps most widely known is a one-volume *History of the Jewish People* (1927, 1962[2]) written in collaboration with Alexander Marx. Within the confines of a single volume the multitude of details of nearly 40 centuries of Jewish history were compressed with conciseness, clarity, and completeness. Moreover, the entire work is informed by a broad philosophic grasp of the subject, a rare balance and objectivity of treatment, and a warm love for the Jewish people and its heritage.

Max Leopold Margolis, U.S. biblical and Semitic scholar. From *American Jewish Yearbook, 1933–34,* Philadelphia, Pa.

Bibliography: R. Gordis (ed.), *Max Leopold Margolis: Scholar and Teacher* (1952), includes an annotated bibliography of Margolis' writings. [R.Go.]

MARGOLIS-KALVARYSKI, HAIM (1868–1947), pioneer and administrator of Jewish settlement in Ereẓ Israel. Born in the province of Suwalki (then Russian Poland) where his parents were landowners, Margolis-Kalvaryski was active from his youth in the *Ḥibbat Zion movement. After studying agriculture in Montpellier, France, he went in 1895 to Ereẓ Israel and became the secretary of *Benei Moshe in Jaffa. He taught at the *Mikveh Israel Agricultural School and later worked at *Mishmar ha-Yarden on behalf of Baron Edmond de *Rothschild's administration. In 1900 he became administrator of the settlements that the *Jewish Colonization Association (ICA) founded in Lower Galilee. Margolis-Kalvaryski established a training farm for the settlers at Sejera and brought over Russian peasant families who had converted to Judaism. Between 1901 and 1905, Margolis-Kalvaryski founded the settlements Sejera (*Ilaniyah), *Yavne'el, *Kefar Tavor, Beit Gan, and *Menaḥemiyyah. In 1906 he was appointed manager of the settlements in Upper Galilee.

In 1913 he and Nahum *Sokolow met Arab leaders in Damascus to try to reach an understanding between them and the Zionist Movement. During World War I he defended the settlers imprisoned and persecuted by the Turks, and helped establish collective settlements including *Ayyelet ha-Shaḥar, *Tel Ḥai, *Maḥanaim, and *Kefar Giladi. In 1920 Margolis-Kalvaryski negotiated with the short-lived Arab government in Damascus and attempted to save the settlements in Upper Galilee from attacks through negotiations with local Arab leaders. He became manager of the ICA (see *Jewish Colonization Association) setttlements in northern Palestine, a member of the Palestine Government Advisory Council, and a member of the Va'ad Le'ummi (until 1929). Between 1923 and 1927 he was head of the Arab Bureau of the Zionist Executive and between 1929 and 1931 headed the joint bureau for Arab affairs of the *Jewish Agency Executive and the Va'ad Le'ummi.

Margolis-Kalvaryski saw Ereẓ Israel as a common homeland for Jews and Arabs belonging to a Middle East federation. He was a founder of *Berit Shalom and similar groups which sought to reach agreement with the Arabs. In his later years he opposed official Zionist policy, which, in his opinion, was not sufficiently active in this direction. He wrote on Arab-Jewish relations in *She'ifoteinu,* 2, 3 (1931–33) and in *Be'ayot ha-Zeman* (1948). The moshav Margaliyyot in Upper Galilee is named after him.

Bibliography: *Be'ayot ha-Zeman,* no. 27 (1947); A. Ever-Hadani, *Ha-Hityashevut ba-Galil ha-Taḥton* (1955), 18–162; M. Smilansky, *Mishpaḥat ha-Adamah,* 3 (1954), 176–84. [Y.S.]

MARGOSHES, SAMUEL (1887–1968), Yiddish journalist, editor, and Zionist leader. Born in Galicia, he early joined the Zionist movement, and emigrated to the United States in 1905. From the Jewish Theological Seminary he received his rabbinical degree in 1910 and later a doctorate in Hebrew literature. From Columbia University he received his doctorate in philosophy. After engaging in various communal, educational, and relief activities before, during, and after World War I, he began his long association with the New York Yiddish daily, *The Day*, in 1922. He served as editor (1926–42), English columnist, and commentator on Jewish events.

Margoshes espoused the causes both of Zionism and of Diaspora Jewry. For him the survival and growth of the Jewish people everywhere were of prime importance. The strengthening of the State of Israel, while a necessary means to achieve this objective, was for him not an end in itself. Hence, he emphasized the need for Yiddish as well as Hebrew, and the building of an American center of Judaism as well as the Israel center, both interdependent and influencing each other's development, economically, politically, and spiritually. As vice-president of the Zionist Organization of America, he participated in World Zionist congresses and served on the Zionist General Council for many years.

Bibliography: Rejzen, Leksikon, 2 (1927), 326–8; LNYL, 5 (1963), 487–90; S. Kahan, *Meksikaner Viderklangen* (1951), 176–9.
[S.L.]

MARGULES, MAX (1856–1920), Austrian meteorologist. Born in Brody, Margules lectured in Vienna on mathematics and physics from 1880 to 1882. His refusal to convert to Christianity blocked his academic advancement and he left the university to become secretary of the Central Institute of Meteorology in Vienna. He held this post for 24 years. In 1906, still refusing to convert and disappointed with his lack of academic success under the Austro-Hungarian academic system, he retired on early pension. He left the field of meteorological research, set up a chemical laboratory in his home, and concentrated on independent research. The post-World War I inflation rendered his small pension insufficient to live on, and he died from malnutrition.

Max Margules, Austrian meteorologist. Jerusalem, J.N.U.L., Schwadron Collection.

Margules' first group of writings dealt with the changes of barometric pressure and their diurnal double fluctuations due to inner oscillations and waves in the free atmosphere of the earth. The second group of writings dealt with the effect of hot and cold air masses on climate. In the 1890s, he organized a network of closely spaced stations in a 60-kilometer circumference around Vienna, fitted with thermo-barographs. He showed the progress of the cold and hot waves of pressure and storms, and was able to arrive at an understanding of the phenomenon. In 1901 he showed that the kinetic energy in storms would have to be much greater in order to be produced by the pressure gradient. His conclusion later replaced the accepted theory on the generation of winds. Margules published his most important work on the energy of storms in 1903 (in *Jahrbuch der Zentralanstalt fuer Metereologie und Geodynamik*). Here he replaced "the energy of the storm" with the "potential energy of distribution of masses on the vertical plane" known as the Margules equation. This introduced a three-dimensional distribution of energy in place of the previously accepted two-dimensional distribution. He stressed that the study of air masses in their space expansion led to an understanding of their movements, and proved the impossibility of understanding the problem according to methods of surface barometers only.

Bibliography: J. C. Poggendorff, *Biographisch-literarisches Handwoerterbuch*, 3 (1898); 4 (1904); 5 (1926); Wininger, Biog, s.v. *Margulies, Max*, includes bibliography.
[D.Ash.]

MARGULIES, EMIL (1877–1943), lawyer and Zionist leader. Born in Sosnowiec, Poland, Margulies became an ardent Zionist as a young man and, after his settlement in Bohemia, had a great share in the development of Zionism there and in the west Austrian district. At the Tenth Zionist Congress (1911), he submitted a new statute for the Zionist Movement. Throughout his life he was a "political" Zionist, and in 1923 he was co-founder of the Radical Zionist Fraction (Democratic Zionists), fighting against the enlargement of the *Jewish Agency by non-Zionists. Parallel to his Zionist activities, Margulies was one of the principal founders of the Czechoslovak "Jewish Party," of which he became president for a time. He also actively participated in the work on international minority problems and was a Jewish representative to the Congress of National Minorities. Margulies attained world renown through his action in the *Bernheim Petition. In 1939 he settled in Palestine, where, together with some colleagues, he opened an office for legal advice.

Bibliography: M. Faerber, *Dr. Emil Margulies* (Ger., 1949); Tidhar, 4 (1950), 1680–81.
[O.K.R.]

MARGULIES, SAMUEL HIRSCH (1858–1922), Galicia-born rabbi and scholar. Margulies laid the foundations of his talmudic-rabbinical knowledge at home and studied at the Breslau Jewish Theological Seminary and at the universities of Breslau and Leipzig. He served as rabbi at Hamburg (1885–87), as district rabbi of Hesse-Nassau (Weilburg, 1887–90), and then as chief rabbi of Florence. When in 1899 the *Collegio Rabbinico Italiano was transferred to Florence, Margulies became its head, and thus trained several generations of Italian Jewish spiritual leaders. Altogether he did much to revive Jewish life and consciousness in Italy and to foster contacts between Italian and other European Jewries. He founded *Rivista Israelitica*, the learned journal of his seminary (1904–15), and was one of the initiators of the weekly *Settimane Israelitica* (later named *Israel*). Margulies also established several charitable institutions in Florence.

Samuel Hirsch Margulies, chief rabbi of Florence. Jerusalem, J.N.U.L., Schwadron Collection.

His scholarly works include an edition of Saadiah's Arabic translation of the Psalms from a Munich manuscript with German translation and commentary (1884, chs. 1–20; the work was completed later by other scholars); *Dichter und Patriot* (life and work of D. Levi, 1896); *Schwertlied Ezechiels* (also in Hebrew, in *Scripta Universitatis... Hierosolymitanarum*..., 1 (1923)); articles in his own and other periodicals; and volumes of sermons, among them *Discorsi Sacri* (1891, repr. 1956). An autobiographical note appeared in his *Discorsi e Scritti vari* (1923).

Bibliography: D. Disegni, in: L. Jung (ed.), *Guardians of Our Heritage* (1958), 447ff.; J. M. Pacifici, in: L. Jung (ed.), *Men of the Spirit* (1964), 645ff.

[U.C./Ed.]

MARḤAB AL-YAHŪDĪ IBN AL-ḤĀRITH (d. 629), warrior of Arabia, renowned for his courage. His family is said to have been of Ḥimyarite origin and several other members gained fame as warriors. They were mentioned by many Muslim historians, and were noted for their outstanding courage. Marḥab's two brothers, al-Ḥārith and Yāsir, distinguished themselves in the Khaybar war against Muhammad. Zaynab, a woman famous in Islam, who attempted to poison Muhammad to avenge the death of her husband, father and uncle in that war, was also a member of the family. Arab sources refer to him as Marḥab al-Yahūdī (Marḥab the Jew), omitting mention of his father's name. The references to the woman Zaynab are somewhat confused. One source states that al-Ḥārith was "Zaynab's father and Marḥab's brother" (al-Maqrīzī, 1:314). The same source, however, refers to Zaynab as "Zaynab the Jewess, al-Ḥārith's daughter, and Marḥab's sister." Marḥab and his brother, Yāsir, both composed poetry in the *rajaz* meter. Arab historians and biographers of Muhammad state that Marḥab died in a duel during one of the battles at Khaybar. The story, as preserved by the ninth-century historians al-Wāqidī and Ibn Hishām, states that during the siege by Muslim forces of one of the Khaybar fortresses, Marḥab threw a heavy millstone over the walls of the fort, killing Maḥmūd ibn Maslama. His cousin Ali ibn Abu Ṭālib promptly challenged Marḥab's brother to a duel and killed him. Marḥab, singing an *urjūza* (poem in *rajaz* meter), then came to avenge his brother's blood and met Maḥmūd ibn Maslama's brother, Muhammad ibn Maslama. In the duel Marḥab's sword stuck in his adversary's shield and Mūhammad then struck Marḥab a mortal blow. Marḥab's second brother, Yāsir, was also killed in a duel, while Zaynab's husband fell in battle. The distraught Zaynab, having lost her husband and her brothers, attempted to poison Muhammad in revenge, but he was saved by his foresight. There are opposing traditions as to whether Muhammad had Zaynab killed, or released her after her conversion to Islam.

Bibliography: A. P. Coussin de Perceval, *Essai sur l'histoire des Arabes*..., 3 (Paris, 1847), 195–8; Graetz, Hist, 3 (1894), 82–84; Ibn Hishām, Abd el-Malik, *Kitāb Sīrat Rasūl Allah, Das Leben Muhammeds*, ed. by F. Wuestenfeld (1859), 670–1; Ibn Saad, *Kitāb al-Ṭabaqūt al-Kabīr... Biographien Muhammed's*..., ed. by J. Horovitz, 2 pt. 1 (1909), 80–81; al-Wāqidī, *The Kitāb al-Maghāzī*, ed. Marsden Jones, 2 (London, 1966), 645, 653–4; al-Maqrīzī, Ahmad ibn Ali, *Imtāʿ al-Asmāʿ*, ed. Mahmud M. Shākir, 1 (Cairo, 1941), 187, 311–16, 321–2; al-Diyārbakrī, Hussein ibn Muhammad, *Taʾrīkh al-Khamīs*..., (Cairo, 1283 H. (1866 C.E.)), II, 50–3; al-Ḥalabī Ali ibn Burhān al-Dīn, *Insān al-ʿUyūn*, 3 (1320 AH, 1902 C.E.), 43–46; H. Z. Hirschberg, *Yisrael ba-Arav* (1946), 55, 148, 251.

[Sh.M.]

MARḤESHVAN (Heb. מַרְחֶשְׁוָן), the post-Exilic name of the eighth month of the Jewish year, frequently shortened to Ḥeshvan (Heb. חֶשְׁוָן). Its pre-Exilic name is Bul (I Kings 6:38). The name occurs in the *Antiquities* of Josephus, **Megillat Ta'anit*, and later branches of rabbinic literature, but nowhere in the Bible. It is believed to be etymologically connected with *Arahsammu*, the Assyrian for "eighth month." The zodiacal sign of this month is *Scorpio*. Like *Kislev, it consists of 29 or 30 days in either common or leap years (see *Calendar). The 1st of Marḥeshvan never falls on Sunday, Tuesday, or Friday. In the 20th century, Marḥeshvan, in its earliest occurrence, extends from October 6th to November 4th (3rd), and, in its latest, from November 4th to December 3rd (2nd). Historic days in Marḥeshvan comprise: (1) 6th of Marḥeshvan, the marking of the blinding of King Zedekiah at the command of Nebuchadnezzar (II Kings 25:7), once observed as a fast (Meg. Ta'an. 13); (2) 7th of Marḥeshvan, the commencement in Ereẓ Israel of the Prayer for *Rain, inserted in the ninth benediction of the **Amidah* prayer (Ta'an. 1:3); (3) 17th of Marḥeshvan, the commencement of the Flood (Gen. 7:11), and of a series of fasts by pious individuals in their intercession for rain in years of drought (Ta'an. 1:4); (4, 5, 6) 23rd, 25th, and 27th of Marḥeshvan, formerly commemorative of the respective victories of the Hasmoneans and Pharisees over the Greeks, Samaritans, and Sadducees (Meg. Ta'an. 8).

[E.J.W.]

MARI, one of the principal centers of Mesopotamia during the third and early second millennia B.C.E. The archaeological and epigraphical discoveries there are of prime significance for the history of Mesopotamia and Upper Syria, and for Bible research, especially as to Hebrew origins and the formative stages of Israelite history. Mari (sometimes *Ma'eri* in the cuneiform sources) was located at Tell Ḥarīrī, at present some 1.5 mi. (2.5 km.) west of the Euphrates, near Abu Kemal, around 15 mi. (25 km.) north of the modern Syrian-Iraqi border. It was in an optimal position for contacts with the West and its location on the river artery, yet immediately adjacent to the desert, was decisive in the shaping of its fortune and character.

Figure 1. Statue of Lamgi-Mari, king of Mari, found at the temple of Ishtar and ascribed to the first half of the third millennium B.C.E. From A. Parrot, *Mari, Editions Ides et Calendes*, No. 7, Paris, 1953.

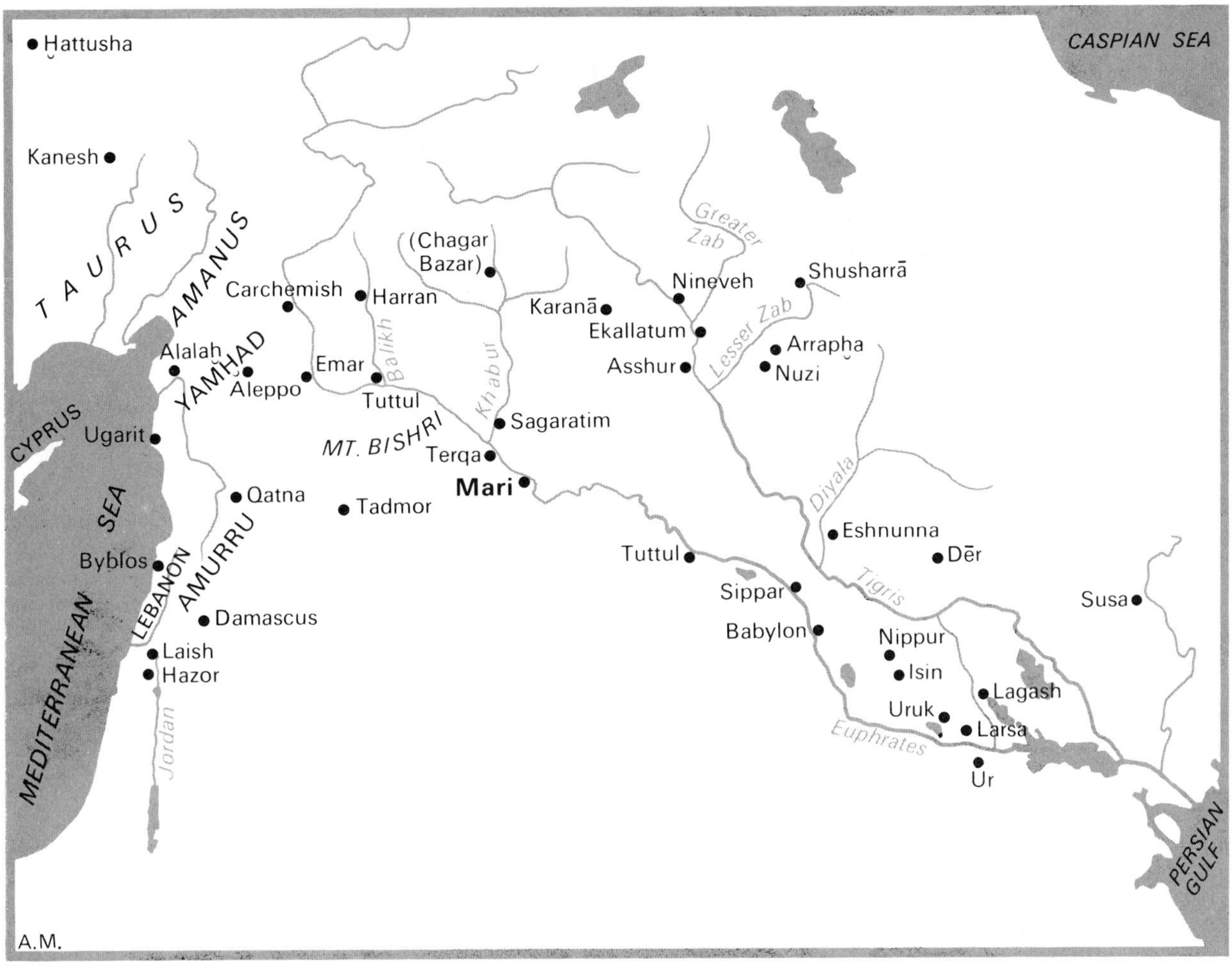

The Near East in the Mari Age.

A. Excavations and Discoveries. The French excavations at Mari, instituted in 1933 under the direction of A. Parrot, have continued (with a break during and after World War II) into their 20th season in 1971.

The archaeological evidence indicates that Mari was founded at the end of the fourth millennium B.C.E. (Jemdat Nasr period), reaching a cultural-artistic peak during the first half of the third millennium B.C.E. Dating to this period (known as "Early Dynastic II-III," or "pre-Sargonic") are a ziggurat and several sanctuaries: the temples of Dagan (where the earliest list of the Mari pantheon was discovered), Shamash, Ninḫursag, and Ishtar, and the pair of temples of Ishtarat and Ninni-Zaza. In the latter three, there came to light many inscribed statues of local kings (such as Lamgi-Mari, Iku-Shamagan, and Iblul-Il), lesser royalty, and courtiers. Although Sumerian culture was predominant, the character of the cultic installations, the appearance of bearded figures in art, and especially the occurrence of particular divine and private names are all clearly indicative of a basic Semitic element from earliest times, with Semitic rule there centuries before the rise of Akkad.

Since 1964, the excavations have revealed two superimposed palaces from pre-Sargonic times, most impressive in themselves, including a royal chapel with an earthen altar (cf. Ex. 20:24), the sacred tradition of which was preserved even in the Old Babylonian palace built there some 700 years later (see below). Within the palace complex, a jar came to light containing a "treasure" including a lapis lazuli bead with a votive inscription mentioning Mesannepada, founder of the First Dynasty at Ur. This indicates a close contact between Mari and Ur at an early date, as do other finds from Mari, such as shell inlays essentially identical with those of the "Ur Standard" (war panel). The pre-Sargonic palace was destroyed either by Eannatum of Lagash (mid-25th century B.C.E.) or, rather, by Lugal-zaggesi of Uruk (mid-24th century B.C.E.).

After Sargon's conquest, in the second half of the 24th century B.C.E., Mari became a vassal city within the empire of Akkad; among the epigraphic evidence from this period are the names of two daughters of Naram-Sin, king of Akkad. In the final two centuries of the third millennium B.C.E., Mari was a sort of loose dependency of Third-Dynasty Ur, flourishing anew under (local) governors who bore the title *šakkanakku* (eight of whom are known by name). Indeed, a ruler of Mari is known to have given his daughter in marriage to a son of Ur-Nammu, king of Ur.

The preeminence of Mari throughout the third millennium B.C.E. is well reflected in epigraphic sources: in the Sumerian King List it appears as the seat of the tenth postdiluvian dynasty; in the inscriptions of Eannatum mention is made of the penetration and repulse of forces from Mari as far south as Lagash; and it also appears in the inscriptions of Sargon and Naram-Sin of Akkad. At the close of the third millennium B.C.E., Ishbi-Irra, "a man of Mari," founded the Isin Dynasty and facilitated the collapse of the empire of Third-Dynasty Ur. After an obscure period of two centuries (from which several economic texts and 32 inscribed liver models are known), Mari reached its final period of glory in the 18th century under West Semitic rule. This latter was quashed by Hammurapi, king of Babylon, and Mari never regained its former position.

In the 13th century, Tukulti-Ninurta I conquered the

meager settlement there and stationed a garrison in the city for a short time. The uppermost layer on the site dates to the Seleucid-Roman period.

In the second half of the second millennium B.C.E., Mari was still sufficiently important to be mentioned in the *Nuzi documents (horses and chariots were sent there), in recently found texts at *Ugarit ("Ishtar of Mari" in an alphabetic text, and in an epithet of another deity in a Hurrian text), and in the Egyptian geographical lists of Thutmosis III and probably also of Ramses III. The land of Mari appears in the neo-Assyrian geographical treatise describing Sargon's Akkadian empire (on the basis of which W. F. Albright identified Mari with Tell Ḥarīrī, long before the start of excavations there). Finally, Mari is mentioned in a Greek itinerary, in the (Aramaic) form *Merrhan*.

THE OLD BABYLONIAN PALACE AND ROYAL ARCHIVES. The main discoveries at Mari are from the period of its domination by the West Semitic dynasties, in the last quarter of the 19th century and the first half of the 18th century B.C.E. (according to the middle chronology; or 64 years later according to the low chronology). Several temples of this period were built over corresponding sanctuaries of pre-Sargonic times—the temples of Ishtar, Ninḫursag, and Shamash; a second temple of Dagan, also known as the "lions' temple" (from bronze lions found flanking its entrance), was founded by the late third millennium B.C.E. This latter deity, the biblical *Dagon, held a prime position in the West Semitic pantheon, and at Mari bore the titles "King of the Land" and "Lord of all the Great Gods."

The outstanding architectural discovery from this period, however, is the royal palace—a structure of unparalleled magnificence and widespread fame in its time. This residence, enlarged successively by each of the West Semitic rulers at Mari, reached its zenith under Zimri-Lim, with an area of about eight acres and including over 300 chambers, corridors, and courts. Besides the private quarters for the royal family and entourage, there are administrative offices, a scribal school, quarters for visiting dignitaries, a royal chapel, a throne room, and a reception chamber. Service areas included guard quarters, workshops, and storerooms. A special elegance was provided in several halls and courts by multicolored frescoes depicting chiefly ritual and mythological scenes, including an investiture of a king (Zimri-Lim?) in the presence of several deities. This ceremony occurs in an idealized garden, its trees guarded by "cherubim" and symbolically watered by four streams flowing from a single source—all reminiscent of the biblical Paradise story. Many of the figures in these murals are depicted as typical West Semites.

The discovery of greatest impact on historical and biblical research comprises the more than 20,000 cuneiform tablets from the several archives in the palace, written in the Babylonian language (see below). So far, some 3,000 documents have been published by the Assyriologists G. Dossin (dean of the Mari epigraphers), M. Birot, J. Bottéro, Mme. M. L. Burke, A. Finet, J. R. Kupper, and the late G. Boyer and Ch.-F. Jean, mostly in the series *Archives royales de Mari* (henceforth, ARM, 1–13 (1946–67)). Though only a small portion of the total, these texts have shed much light on the administrative, economic, cultural, and political facets mainly of Upper Mesopotamia and Upper Syria in the 18th century B.C.E.—regions previously known only vaguely.

The archives were found to be distinguished according to subject. The political-diplomatic archives (ARM, 1–6 and 13) include correspondence between the king of Mari and his agents, both at the palace and abroad, as well as with foreign potentates. The 1,000 such letters published so far (as against the 350 at *Tell el-Amarna!) provide the earliest insight into the complexities of suzerain-vassal relationships, diplomatic protocol, and the fluctuating alliances and plots rampant in the Ancient Near East. A noteworthy class of letters is the unusually extensive women's correspondence (thus far, only cuneiform copies of 179 documents

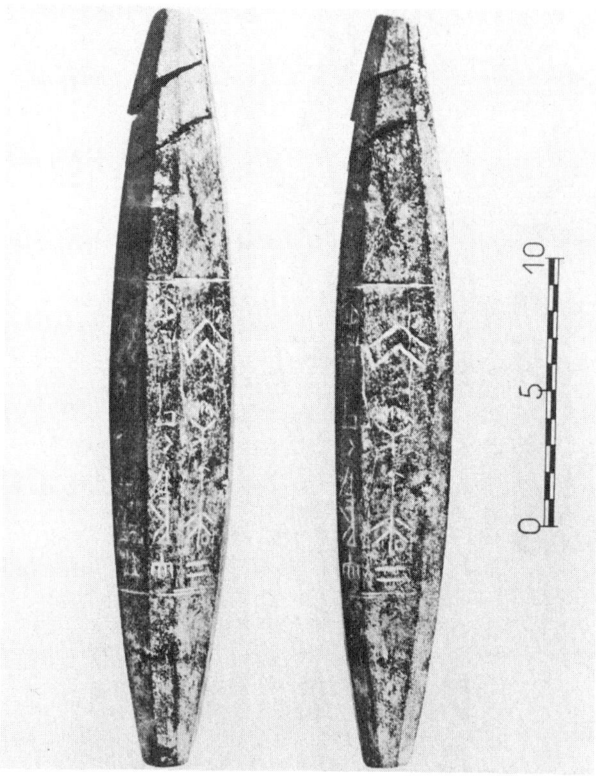

Figure 2. Two views of a lapis lazuli bead with the votive inscription mentioning Mesannepada, king of Ur, from the first half of the third millennium B.C.E. From A. Parrot, *Mission Archéologique de Mari, IV: Le "trésor" d'Ur*, Paris, 1968.

Figure 3. Bronze lion from the temple of Dagan, beginning of the second millennium B.C.E. From A. Parrot, *Mari . . .*, Paris, 1953.

have been published, in ARM, 10), revealing the prominent role of women in activities of the realm. The outstanding case is that of Shibtu, Zimri-Lim's queen (chief wife), who enjoyed the king's utter confidence, representing his interests during his absence from the city and exercising considerable influence in her own right.

The majority of documents (ARM, 7, 9, 11, and 12) are economic or administrative in nature, dealing with the maintenance of the palace, official trade abroad, lists of goods, and rosters of persons in royal employ (such as a list of nearly 1,000 captives [?] from the Harran-Nahor region engaged in the manufacture of clothing for the palace). Of a unique category are the some 1,300 tablets containing lists of daily provisions for the palace, often summarized by month. Though dealing only with "vegetarian" foodstuffs and beverages, they shed light on Solomon's "provisions for one day" and possibly also his monthly quantities (cf. I Kings 4:22–23, 27 [5:2–3, 7]; cf. also Neh. 5:17–18). The royal table at Mari, known to have entertained hundreds of guests on occasion, was served by spacious kitchens—in one of which were found numerous molds for preparing fancy cakes some bearing animal and goddess motifs (cf. Jer. 44:19).

Dozens of legal tablets were also found, mostly contracts concerning transactions and loans of silver or grain (ARM, 8), revealing that the palace served as a sort of exchange. Of exceptional interest is an adoption contract which ensured the "primogeniture" of the "eldest" (i.e., first adopted) son, stipulating that he receive a double portion of the inheritance; this is in full accord with biblical law (cf. Deut. 21:15–17).

The very few literary and religious compositions found at Mari include a lengthy Ishtar ritual in Babylonian, as well as six texts in Hurrian. That Hurrian was used occasionally in diplomatic correspondence is known from the only other tablet at Mari in that language, a letter written to Zimri-Lim.

B. Mari under West Semitic Rule. The origins of the West Semitic, or "Amorite," dynasties are shrouded in darkness, though there are clues pointing to North Syria for the local line at Mari. Thus, the theophoric name element *-Lim* (perhaps derived from the word for "folk," "people"; cf. Ugaritic *l'im* and Heb. *le'om*) is found at both Aleppo, in the dynastic name Yarim-Lim, and Mari, in the royal names Yagid-Lim, Yaḫdun-Lim, and Zimri-Lim. It is also present in the name of Yashi-Lim, ruler of Tuttul (probably the one at the mouth of the Balikh River), and Ibbit-Lim, ruler of Ebla (probably Tell Mardikh), both several generations earlier than the above. Furthermore, the title "king of Mari, Tuttul, and the land of Ḫana" was borne by both Yaḫdun-Lim (Disc Inscription) and Zimri-Lim (cf. a fragmentary inscription from Terqa, between Tuttul and Mari). And, indeed, the site of ancestor worship for both the local and the "Assyrian" dynasties at Mari lay at Terqa, around 44 mi. (70 km.) to the northwest, at the mouth of the Khabur River. Hence, the immediate origin of the West Semitic rulers at Mari would appear to be in the Terqa region.

The Reign of Yaḫdun-Lim. The historical figure of Yagid-Lim, founder of the local dynasty at Mari, is vague, and none of his records have been found. Nor have many tablets from the reign of his son, Yaḫdun-Lim, been published, though in 1965 an archive of some 300 of his economic texts came to light. It is known, however, that Yaḫdun-Lim was able to stabilize his kingdom, establishing his dominance over the entire Middle Euphrates region, as is evident from the dozen known year-formulas and especially the two extant royal inscriptions from his reign.

The shorter inscription (the "Disc Inscription") relates that Yaḫdun-Lim fortified Mari and Terqa, founded a fortress on the desert fringe (naming it after himself—Dur-Yaḫdun-Lim), and laid out an extensive irrigation system (boasting that "I did away with the water bucket in my land"). The other text, the Foundation Inscription of the Shamash temple, is a splendid literary composition relating his campaign to the Mediterranean coast and the "Cedar and Boxwood Mountain," where he obtained several types of choice wood, "and made known his might." However, this was probably only a passing episode and not a lasting conquest. Thirty-five economic texts published in 1970 are dated by two year-formulas for one Sumu-Yamam, an obscure character who ruled at Mari either before or after Yaḫdun-Lim. Also elusive is his kinship—whether to the local dynasty or otherwise—for the few other references to

Figure 4. The royal palace at Mari (north at bottom). From A. Parrot, *Mari* . . ., Paris, 1953.

him, such as in a "letter to a god" (ARM, 1, 3), are inconclusive. This same letter also reveals the assassination of Yaḫdun-Lim (or Sumu-Yamam) in a court conspiracy, much to the benefit of Shamshi-Adad, scion of a rival West Semitic dynasty, who established himself in Assyria, swiftly gaining control over large portions of Mesopotamia.

The Assyrian Interregnum. Yahdun-Lim's removal facilitated a take-over by Shamshi-Adad, who installed his son, Yasmaḫ-Adad, as viceroy at Mari. Under his father's tutelage, Yasmaḫ-Adad reorganized the local administration, cultivated ties with neighboring lands, and secured his flank against marauding nomads. Though his brother Ishme-Dagan, upon succeeding to the throne of Assyria, promised to maintain the protective policy of their father, Yasmaḫ-Adad was left adrift only three or four years later, when he was defeated by Eshnunna, a West Semitic kingdom beyond the Tigris. Altogether, Assyrian control of Mari lasted some 20 years.

The Kingdom of Zimri-Lim. Thus, the stage was set for the advent of Zimri-Lim, the son of Yaḫdun-Lim, who in the interim had lived in exile under the wing of Yarim-Lim, king of Yamḫad (capital, Aleppo). Yarim-Lim, who had become Zimri-Lim's father-in-law, was most instrumental in restoring him to the throne of Mari. Thirty-two year-formulas are known for Zimri-Lim's reign—though many of them may have been alternate designations for the same year, for (chronologically) he cannot have ruled for so long a period. Zimri-Lim's reign, during the tumultous interval between Assyria's decline and the rise of the empire

Figure 5. Multicolored wall-painting of a sacrifice, from the palace at Mari. From A. Parrot, *Mission Archéologique de Mari, II: Le palais —peintures murales,* Paris, 1958.

of Hammurapi, marks Mari at its apogee. It is this period which is best represented by the archives found at Mari which provide a thorough insight into the organization of the kingdom. Interestingly, several of Zimri-Lim's letters have been found in the royal archives at Tell el-Rimah (between the Upper Khabur and the Tigris), probably to be identified with the city of Karana, mentioned in the Mari correspondence. Mari had become a principal political force in Mesopotamia, alongside Babylon, Larsa, Eshnunna, Qatna, and Yamḫad (as is known from a contemporary political report). Relying heavily on his diplomatic cunning, Zimri-Lim developed an elaborate intelligence system—within his sphere of influence and beyond it. Frequent alliances, as with Yamḫad and Babylon, were designed to meet the danger of the moment—e.g., now against Eshnunna, then against Elam. His military endeavors were directed mainly against the hostile tribal federation of the Yaminites (the previously subdued Ḫanean tribes were already in his service; for both, see below). This political situation crystallized hand in hand with the development of economic ties branching out as far as the island of Dilmun (in the Persian Gulf), Elam (in the east), Arrapḫa and Shusharra (in southern Kurdistan), Cappadocia (in the north), Phoenicia and Palestine (in the west), and even Kaptara (Crete, in the Mediterranean). Indeed, tolls from caravan and riverine trade were one of Zimri-Lim's principal sources of income. This golden age at Mari came to an abrupt end, however, when Hammurapi turned on his former ally and conquered the city in his 32nd year, during the consolidation of his empire (in 1759 B.C.E.—middle chronology; or 1695 B.C.E.—low chronology). Two years later he ordered the razing of the city to the ground.

MARI AND THE WEST. Mari was bound closely with the lands to the west—Syria, and even northern Palestine—in economy, politics, culture, religion, and ethnic background. Already noted were the ties between the local dynasty at Mari and that of the kingdom of Yamḫad; Zimri-Lim's queen, Shibtu, was from Aleppo and he appears to have held land there, which was either a patrimony or received as a dowry. Similarly, the rival Assyrian dynasty at Mari secured political ties in the west through the marriage of Yasmaḫ-Adad to a princess from Qatna, Yamḫad's southern adversary. Another form of contact with the west is the already-mentioned campaign by Yaḫdun-Lim and the later expedition by Shamshi-Adad to the Levant. Zimri-Lim is also known to have visited various places in the west: Yamḫad, where he had presented a statue to "Adad the great god of Aleppo," and Ugarit, where he was accompanied by a select bodyguard (*ṣabum beḫru;* see below).

The region farther southwest is only sparingly mentioned in the Mari archives, but references are found to Byblos on the Phoenician coast and the land of Amurru in southern Syria (the Apum of the Mari texts is most probably only that in the Khabur region, and not the one around Damascus, known from the contemporary Egyptian Execration Texts and various later sources). In northern Palestine, Hazor is noted several times in the Mari archives as the destination of diplomatic and economic emissaries. In one instance, emissaries passing through Mari are on their way to Yamḫad, Qatna, and Hazor, and a fourth place whose name is broken (the traces in ARM, 6, 23:23 may perhaps be restored to read "Megiddo," rather than "Egypt" as is sometimes proposed, which surprisingly does not appear in the Mari archives). In an economic document published recently, Aleppo, Qatna, and Ugarit are listed, alongside Hazor ("Ibni-Adad, king of Hazor") and Laish ("Waritaldu at Laish," the later Dan north of Hazor), as destinations of large consignments of tin, a commodity of major importance among the exports to the west (it being alloyed with copper to produce bronze). On the other side of the ledger, Mari imported from the west horses and fine woods (from the Qatna region), various precious vessels of Syrian and "Cretan"

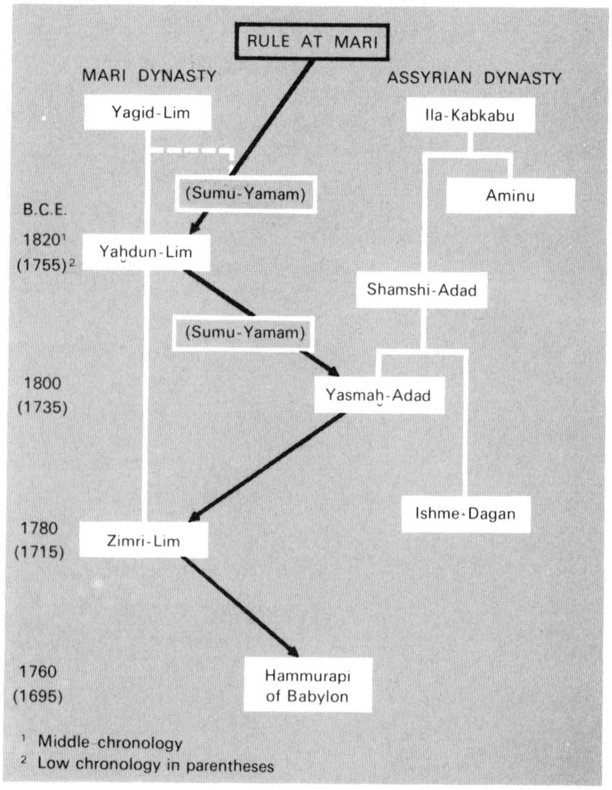

style, Cypriot copper, fabrics, and garments (especially from Aleppo and Byblos), and large quantities of foodstuffs, such as honey, wine, and olive oil.

C. Mari and the Bible. The Mari documents have a manifold bearing upon early Israelite history: chronological, if the so-called patriarchal age is placed in the first third of the second millennium B.C.E. (Middle Bronze Age II) (keeping in mind that even the oldest portions of the Bible are of much later date); geographical, for the patriarchal homeland (Aram-Naharaim) lay within Mari's horizons; ethnic-linguistic, the Hebrews being of the same West Semitic (or Amorite) stock as that strongly manifest at Mari; and sociological, for the descriptions of tribalism comprise the most extensive insight into the nomadic and settled phases of the Israelite tribes.

1. PATRIARCHAL HOMELAND. The cities of Harran and Nahor (cuneiform *Naḫūr*), in the Upper Balikh Valley—which figure in the Bible as ancestral habitats of the Patriarchs—are well documented as important dependencies controlled by governors from Mari (one of whom, Itur-asdu at Nahor, is the subject of ARM, 14). Both cities were foci of tribal foment: at the temple of Sin in Harran, a treaty between the "kings" of Zalmaqum and the Yaminites was sworn against Mari; while at Nahor reinforcements had often to be called in to quell local uprisings inflamed by the *Ḫabiru. Alongside the West Semitic peoples in this region was a considerable Hurrian element (note the typically Hurrian name of King Adalshenni, who at one time gained control over Nahor), which may well have left an imprint upon the initial ethnic and cultural composition of the Hebrews. The picture revealed in the Mari archives, of far-reaching tribal migrations (such as those of Yaminite groups) and caravan conditions between the Euphrates region and Syria-Northern Palestine, is a realistic backdrop for the biblical narratives of the patriarchal wanderings between Aram-Naharaim and Canaan.

2. ETHNO-LINGUISTIC AFFINITIES—THE WEST SEMITIC IDIOM. Evidence for the West Semitic (or *Amorite) origin of the majority of the people figuring in the Mari documents is revealed in the onomasticon and specific linguistic features of the Mari dialect. Many of the hundreds of proper names known from the Mari texts are paralleled in the Bible, especially in the patriarchal narratives and the Exodus-Conquest cycle, but at Mari often with (other) theophoric components; e.g., Jacob and Ishmael—i.e., *Ḫaqba-Ḫammu/-aḫim/* etc. and *Yasmaḫ-El/-Adad/-Baʿal/* etc. Parallels even for the divine names YHWH and Shaddai, and the epithet *Ẓur* (the "Rock") are possible (e.g., *Yawi-ila/-Adad/* etc., and the *Šadu/i-* and *Ṣura/i-* names). The names of the Israelite tribes of *Levi and *Benjamin also seem to have their parallels. Thus, the tribal designation at Mari, *DUMU.MEŠ-yamin(a)*, "Yaminites," bears the same connotation as Benjamin—"son(s) of the South" (though it is preferable not to render the logogram for "sons" as West Semitic *ba/inū*, which would yield *Ba/inū-yamina*, a form conveniently homophonic with the Hebrew *Binyamin*). The West Semitic imprint on the standard Babylonian language in use at Mari is evident to a certain extent in phonology, morphology, syntax, and, especially, vocabulary. The lack of terms in this standard Babylonian for certain specific features in the society and way of life of the population of the Mari region necessitated the freqent adoption of West Semitic expressions in the shape of either Babylonian words employed in new, West Semitic connotations or out-and-out loanwords from the West Semitic—words well represented in biblical Hebrew (often in exalted language, as also at Mari). Besides the linguistic yield, a comparative study of the West Semitic loanwords at Mari and their Hebrew cognates may broadly illuminate the nature of the societies involved. Thus, a list of such lexical items would include:

Geographical terms—*ḫamqum* = Hebrew *ʿemeq*, "valley"; *k/qaṣum* = Hebrew *qaẓeh*, "(desert) frontier"; *ḫen* (as a place-name) = Hebrew *ʿayin*, "spring"; points of the compass—*aqdamātum* = Hebrew *qedem*, "east"; *aḫarātum* = Hebrew *aḥar, aḥor*, "west"; north and south were preserved in the tribal names *DUMU.MEŠ-simʾal*= Hebrew *semol*, and *DUMU.MEŠ-yamina*= Hebrew *yamin;* fauna—*ḫa(ya)rum*= Hebrew *ʿayir*, "donkey foal"; *hazzum*= Hebrew *ʿez*, "goat"; *ḫiglum*= Hebrew *ʿegel*, "calf" (referring to a zoomorphic vessel at Mari); flora—*suḫrum*= Hebrew *seʿorah*, "barley"; *ḫimrum*= Hebrew *ḥemer*, "a fermented drink"; military terms—*be(ḫ)rum*= Hebrew *baḥur*, "(select) trooper"; *bazaḫātum*, "military outpost"(cf. Heb. root *bẓʿ*); *sag/qbum*, "guard" (later Heb. *zaqif?*); note perhaps *madārum*= later Hebrew *mador(?)*, "dwelling place"; *mas/škabum*= Hebrew *mishkav*, "a lodging"; probably *sablum*= Hebrew *sevel*, "corvée"; and *yagâtum* = Hebrew *yagon*, "sorrow."

A series of West Semitic terms is also found for tribal organization and institutions (see below, Nos. 3 and 4), which were quite foreign to contemporary Mesopotamia and therefore found no adequate means of expression in the pure Babylonian lexicon; cf., e.g., the set of terms for various tribal units: *gāyum* = Hebrew *goy; ḫibrum* = Hebrew *ḥever;* and perhaps *ummatum* = Hebrew *ʾummah*. West Semitic verbs unknown in standard Babylonian but with cognates in biblical Hebrew include the following: *ḫakûm*, "to wait"; *ḫalûm*, "to be ill"; *ḫarāšum*, "to be silent"; *naḫālum*, "to inherit, apportion"; *naqāmum*, "to avenge" (only in personal names); *qatālum*, "to kill"; *šapāṭum*, "to judge, govern" (and see below).

3. PATRIARCHAL TRIBAL SOCIETY. The Mari archives provide the most abundant and fruitful source material concerning West Semitic tribes of any Ancient Near Eastern source—shedding invaluable light on Israelite tribal society, its structure and organization, as well as its institutions. The wide range of the tribes mentioned at Mari—from fully nomadic to fully sedentary—and their confrontation with the indigenous population, bear directly upon an understanding of the gradual process of the Israelite settlement in Canaan and their ensuing relationship with its inhabitants. The most revealing material at Mari concerns the broad tribal federations of the Ḫaneans and Yaminites. The former were concentrated principally along the Middle Euphrates and comprised an appreciable segment of the general population (and of the army) of Mari. Indeed, the Middle Euphrates region became known as the "land of Ḫana," and "Ḫana" was applied also to a type of soldier and a kind of wool. The name, which was

Figure 6. A school for scribes in the palace. From A. Parrot, *Mari . . .*, Paris, 1953.

Figure 7. Multicolored wall painting showing the investiture of a king, from the palace at Mari. From A. Parrot, *Mission Archéologique de Mari II: Le palais—peintures murales*, Paris, 1958.

basically gentilic, also came to denote in general the generic concept of a (semi-) nomad; it seems to be in this sense that Zimri-Lim was called "king of the Ḫaneans," in parallel to "king of the Akkadians"—which together reflect the two main population strata, seminomadic and indigenous sedentary (see below). The Yaminites were in general less settled and posed the greater threat in this period, both to the rest of the population and to the authorities. In their subtribes (Ubrabu, Amnanu, Yaḫruru, Yariḫu, and the affiliated Rabbeans), they were dispersed over a wide arc from the city of Sippar (and even as far south as Uruk) and the eastern banks of the Tigris around to the Khabur and the Balikh valleys up to the Euphrates bend, where their main concentration lay. In the west, they had crossed the Euphrates toward Mount Bisir (Jabal Bishri) and encroached upon the land of Amurru in southern Syria. Little mention is made in the Mari archives of the *DUMU. MEŠ-sim'al*, the "sons of the north," who roamed the "upper country" in the Harran region, or of the Sutu, the fully nomadic tribe which appears more often in subsequent history. This latter ranged in the Syrian steppe and the Bishri mountains, raiding the adjacent oasis of *Tadmor (spelled *Tadmer* at Mari) on at least one occasion. The Mari archives are surprisingly silent on the "Amorites" as a definite tribal entity (though one reference is made to a *gāyu Amurum* as a sub-clan of the Ḫaneans); in general, the designation (both spelled phonetically and in the logogram *MAR.TU*) is restricted to the land of Amurru, far to the west, or to the military titles "great-of-Amurru" and "scribe-of-Amurru" (the latter only at Mari).

Patterns of Settlement. The tribal society depicted in the Mari archives is essentially dimorphic, i.e., it encompasses both nomadic and urban modes, with their inherent distinctions and interactions, social as well as economic. Tribal groups would sometimes undergo a gradual process of sedentation, splitting into partly settled and partly nomadic factions (cf. ARM 8, 11), or leading a life of transhumance—in the steppe or desert in the grazing season and in urban bases during the "off" months.

Depending on the stage of sedentation, the Ḫaneans and Yaminites dwelt in towns and hamlets (both designated at Mari as *ālāni*, literally, "cities"; the term *kaprum*, "village," is rare in this context) and engaged in urban-agricultural pursuits (as well as herding), or in temporary encampments *(nawūm)* and engaged in purely pastoral pursuits. At Mari, the standard Babylonian word *nawūm*, "desert, uncultivated field," or even "a savage," took on the West Semitic connotation of a pastoral abode, precisely the connotation of the Hebrew *naweh* (primarily in poetic usage in the Bible). An illustration of this dual mode of life, is found in the distinctions *Ḫana ša nawīm*, loosely, "steppe Ḫaneans," and *ḫibrum ša nawīm*, the nomadic faction of a partly settled clan (in this case, of Yaminites).

Another type of settlement originating among nomadic and seminomadic populations was the *ḫaṣārum* (pl. *ḫaṣirātum*), which, rather than an enclosure for sheep or cattle (as usually assumed), denotes a dwelling place, as does the cognate Hebrew term *ḥaẓerim*, referring to settlements of the Ishmaelites, the Avvites, and the "sons of Kedar" (Gen. 25:16; Deut. 2:23; and Isa. 42:11 (cf. Jer. 49:33), respectively).

Tribal Leadership. The Mari archives indicate that tribal leadership was in the hands of family heads (cf. the biblical *bet-'av*, "family," the basic unit of the patriarchal tribal organization), called *abū bītim*, "father of the household" (pl. at Mari *abūt bītim*, a West Semitic form, equivalent to Heb. *'avot*). The actual tribal rulers were elevated from among these family heads, leading to the use of the term *abū bītim* for certain officials, and occasionally *abū* served as a synonym for "tribal chiefs," e.g., *abū Ḫana* and *abū Idamaraṣ*. As in pre-monarchical Israel, the council of the "elders" *(šībūti)* appears in the Mari documents as a central institution, deciding on matters of war and peace, functioning in treaty making, and representing the tribe before the authorities.

A capital role in the tribal organization, unknown outside the Mari texts, is that of *sugāgum/suqāqum* (meaning unknown), whose function is somewhat vague.

Figure 8. Cake mold representing a goddess, from the kitchen of the palace at Mari. From A. Parrot, *Mission Archéologique de Mari II: Le palais—documents et monuments*, Paris, 1959.

He may have been a sort of mukhtar, chief of a tribal unit or village appointed (or at least approved) by the Mari authorities from among the local leadership; this office *(sugāgūtum)* was sometimes purchased with money or sheep.

At the head of the tribal hierarchy stood the "kings" (Akk. *šarru,* p. *šarrāni*), who usually appear in the Mari texts as wartime leaders—again suggesting a special West Semitic connotation (in this case, military), much like the Hebrew *sar*. Thus, Yaḫdun-Lim's royal inscriptions record that he defeated "seven kings, fathers *(abū)* of Ḫana" and, on another occasion, "three Yaminite kings." This plurality of "kings" must be understood as referring to subtribal rulers that collectively comprised the tribal leadership; such a structure is also found among the Midianites (Num. 31:8; Judg. 8:12), the early Arameans (I Sam. 14:47), and perhaps the Edomites (Gen. 36:31 ff.).

4. Tribal Traditions—Functional and Religious. The convergence of the West Semitic tribes at Mari with urban Mesopotamia involved a dual process of friction and strife alongside symbiosis and mutual adaptation; this interaction between a tribal heritage and an established civilization was characteristic also of the settlement of Israelite tribes in Canaan. In Mari, this was especially evident at the court, where despite the process of assimilation of Sumero-Akkadian civilization, much of tribal tradition was still preserved. The advice of the palace prefect to Zimri-Lim on a point of protocol may thus be interpreted: "[If] you are the king of the Ḫaneans, you are, moreover, a 'king of the Akkadians.' [My lord] should not ride horses [i.e., in tribal fashion]. May my lord drive in a wagon and mules [i.e., in a "civilized" manner], and may he [thus] honor his royalty" (ARM, 6, 76:20–25). This same distinction is found, too, at the early Israelite court, though there the mule was ridden (II Sam. 13:29; 18:9; I Kings 1:33) and the horse yoked to the chariot (I Sam. 8:11; II Sam. 15:1; I Kings 1:5).

Tribal heritage from the nomadic phase did persist in spite of the curbs of sedentation and acquiescence to royal administration of Mari. Tribal customs and institutions, legal, military, and political procedures, and ritual or religious practices all find expression in the Mari texts. These traditions, largely unknown outside Mari, serve to illuminate early Israelite practices. Here are some of the major points.

Making a Covenant. In the largely illiterate society of the tribe, treaties were concluded not by means of documents but solely by symbolic acts—in the cases recorded in the Mari texts, by the ritual of "killing an ass-foal" (note the purely West Semitic expression applied here—*ḫa(ya)rum qatālum*). (Another symbolic expression in this context is *napištam lapātum,* "to touch the throat.") In one case, a possible ploy was made to introduce other animals into the ritual: in a report on a peace treaty made between the Ḫaneans and the land of Idamaraṣ, a Mari official in the Harran region tells his king that "they brought to me a whelp and a goat, but I obeyed my lord and did not give (permission for the use of) a whelp and a goat. I caused 'the foal, the young of a she-ass' (cf. Gen. 49:11; Zech. 9:9) to be slaughtered" (ARM, 2, 37:6–12). The Bible mentions a parallel ceremony, involving the cutting in two of young animals (cf. the covenant between God and Abraham—Gen. 15:9–10; and one with the leaders of Judah during the Babylonian siege of Jerusalem—Jer. 34:18–19). In all these ceremonies, the common denominator is the ritual sacrifice of young and tender animals.

Census. The Mari authorities used to take periodic censuses of the tribes, both nomadic and settled. This activity was denoted by the terms *ubbubum* (D-stem of

Figure 9. Foundation inscription of King Yaḫdun-Lim on a brick found in the Shamash temple at Mari. From G. Dossin, *Syria* 32, 1955.

ebēbum), "to cleanse," and its derivative *tēbibtum* (literally, "cleansing," "purification"), and is most likely West Semitic in origin. The purpose of the census seems to have been military conscription, taxation, and land distribution, although at least originally it was accompanied by a ritual of purification, similar to that associated with the census of the Israelites in the wilderness (which involved a tax, the payment of which was regarded as a ritual expiation, Heb. *kippurim;* cf. Ex. 30:11–16). Some scholars, however, view the *tēbibtum* as a purely administrative procedure to clear persons or property of legal or financial claims (as would be indicated by the fact that it is carried out by secular, not religious, officials).

Patrimony. The Mari legal documents employ, inter alia, the West Semitic term *naḫālum,* "to inherit or apportion," in referring to land transfers effected within a quasi-familial inheritance framework and not in the normal sales procedures. This type of transaction was inherently a part of the patriarchal tribal system, in which land ownership was not on an individual basis but was a patrimony (*niḫlatum* at Mari = Heb. *naḥalah*). The patrimony could not, theoretically, be transferred other than by inheritance, and, therefore, various means were contrived to circumvent this rule. The Israelites upheld a similar custom, where the patrimony was considered an inalienable possession, "the Israelites must remain bound each to the ancestral portion of his tribe" (Num. 36:7; cf. Lev. 25:13, 25–28; I Kings 21:1ff.; Ezek. 46:16–18).

The "Judge." The Mari documents employ several derivatives of the West Semitic root *špṭ* (verb: *šapāṭum;* participle: *šāpiṭum;* abstract nouns: *šipṭum* and *šapiṭūtum*), which may serve to elucidate the biblical cognates *shafoṭ, shofeṭ,* and *mishpaṭ,* usually translated as "judge" (verb and noun) and "norm or law," respectively. However, neither in the Mari documents nor in the Bible is the primary connotation of these terms judicial (for which the Akkadian employs *dayānu*); rather, they connote the much broader concept of governorship and rule. Thus, the *šāpiṭum* and his counterpart in the Book of Judges, the *shofeṭ,* were actually prominent tribesmen who had acquired an authority far exceeding that of a mere "justice" (and cf. the later Punic *suffetes*). The expression *šipṭam nadānum/šakānum,* met with in the Mari documents, corresponds to the bibical *sim mishpaṭ*, "lay down a ruling" (by a duly authorized person) employed in connection with the authoritative acts of a Moses, a Joshua, and a David (cf. Ex. 15:25; Josh. 24:25; I Sam. 30:25).

The Ban. A peculiar expression at Mari, *asakkam akālum* (lit. "to eat the *asakku*"), refers to the infringement of a taboo or the profaning of something revered, and may be a loan translation of some West Semitic concept paralleling that of the biblical ban *(*ḥerem)*. The *asakku* of a particular deity, and/or king, is frequently invoked in penalty clauses of contracts, in oaths, and in royal decrees as the sacrosanct and inviolable element. The closest parallel between Mari and the biblical practice is in the impositon of the ban on spoils of war (cf., e.g., the Achan incident, Josh. 7). However, whereas the biblical ban functioned on a purely religious plane (whatever was banned was exclusively God's), the taboo at Mari was applicable also on a human level, and its infringement there, though theoretically still considered a capital offense, was expiated by payment of a simple fine.

God of the Father. Among the central religious concepts of the Hebrew Patriarchs is the "God of the/my/your/his father," i.e., a personal, innominate deity, revered by subsequent offspring (cf. Gen. 28:13; 31:5, 29, 42, 53; 32:10; 49:25; Ex. 3:6, 15; 15:2, etc.). A direct parallel occurs in one Mari text, where the king of Qatna swears "by the name of the god of my father" (ARM, 5, 20:16; and cf. Gen. 31:53), and in another, recently published, where Hammurapi (undoubtedly Yarim-Lim's successor as king of Aleppo) is appealed to "by the name of (the god) Adad, Lord of A[leppo] and the god of [your] father" (ARM, 10, 156:10–11). It is significant for the biblical comparison that both instances are in the west, as are all other references to such a deity outside Mari—in the slightly older Assyrian tablets from Cappadocia, the later texts from Ugarit (in Akkadian, Ugaritic, and Hurrian), and, again at Qatna, in temple inventories and in an Amarna letter sent from there.

Prophetic Revelation. The earliest definite references to intuitive divination are found in some 25 Mari texts, revealing a religious phenomenon independent of, but alongside, current external mantic techniques. The diviner-prophets of Mari largely acted as the unsolicited and spontaneous mouthpieces of deities by means of ecstatic trances, dreams, and the like. Apart from male and female laymen imbued with such esoteric abilities, there were cult diviners, usually attached to sanctuaries (e.g., the Dagan temple at Terqa, or the temple of the goddess Annunitum at Mari)—professionals designated by such Akkadian terms as *muḫḫûm* (fem. *muḫḫūtum*), "frenzied one" and *āpilum* (fem. *āpiltum*), "respondent." These appellatives may well be loan translations of West Semitic nomenclature, such as the biblical terms *navi'*, "prophet," and *meshugga'*, "frenzied one, possessed," as well as certain applications of the root *'nh*, "to respond."

The eminence of biblical prophecy lies in its socio-ethical pathos, its religious ideology, and its popular level—all of which are missing in the Mari material, where the ruling interests alone are promoted, satisfying local and immediate material demands. Despite this obvious shortcoming, the very manifestation at Mari of intuitive divination—revealing a consciousness of prophetic mission among West Semitic tribes in a period predating Israelite prophecy by centuries—places the history and investigation of Near Eastern prophecy in general, and both earlier and later biblical prophecy in particular, in an entirely new perspective (see also *Prophets and Prophecy).

Bibliography: General Surveys: A. Parrot (ed.), *Studia Mariana* (1950), includes bibliography; idem, *Mari* (1953); Ch.-F. Jean, *Six campagnes de fouilles à Mari 1933–1939* (1952); A. Malamat, in: EM, 4 (1962), 559–79; G. E. Mendenhall, in: *Biblical Archaeologist Reader*, 2 (1964), 3–20; J. R. Kupper (ed.), *La civilisation de Mari (XVe recontre assyriologique internationale* = RAI, 15, 1967); A. Petitjean and J. Coppens, in: *Bibliotheca Ephemeridum Theologicarum Lovaniensum*, 24 (1969), 3–13 (incl. bibl.). On A: Archaeological Reports: A. Parrot, *Mission Archéologique de Mari:* vol. 1, *Le temple d'Ishtar* (1956); vol. 2, pt. 1, *Le palais—architecture* (1958); vol. 2, pt. 2, *Le palais—peintures murales* (1958); vol. 2, pt. 3, *Le palais—documents et monuments* (1959); vol. 3, *Les temples d'Ishtarat et de Ninni-Zaza* (1967); vol. 4, *Le trésor d'Ur* (1968); idem, in: *Syria*, 46 (1969), 191–208 (17th campaign); 47 (1970), 225–43 (18th campaign). Others: W. F. Albright, in JAOS, 45 (1925), 225–6; 46 (1926), 220–30; M. Rutten, in: *Revue d'assyriologie et d'archéologie orientale*, 35 (1938), 36–52; I. J. Gelb, *ibid.*, 50 (1956), 1–10; M. Civil, *ibid.*, 56 (1962), 213; G. Dossin, *ibid.*, 61 (1967), 97–104; D. O. Edzard, in RAI, 15 (1967), 51–71; P. Carlmeyer, *ibid.*, 161–9; J. R. Kupper, in: JCS, 21 (1967), 123–5; A. Moortgat, in: *Baghdader Mitteilungen*, 3 (1964), 68–74; 4 (1968), 221–31; M. C. Astour, in: JAOS, 88 (1968), 738; idem, in: *Ugarit Forschungen*, 2 (1970), 2; E. Sollberger, in: *Revue d'assyriologie et d'archéologie orientale*, 63 (1969), 169–70; A. Caquot, in: *Syria*, 46 (1969), 246–7. Old Babylonian Archives: *Archives royales de Mari:* vol. 1, G. Dossin, *Correspondance de Šamši-Addu* (1950); vol. 2, Ch.-F. Jean, *Lettres diverses* (1950); vol. 3, J. R. Kupper, *Correspondance de Kibri-Dagan* (1950); vol. 4, G. Dossin, *Correspondance de Šamsi-Addu* (1951); vol. 5, G. Dossin, *Correspondance de Iasmaḫ-Addu* (1952); vol. 6, J. R. Kupper, *Correspondance de Baḫdi-Lim* (1954); vol. 7, J. Bottéro, *Textes économiques et administratifs* (1957); vol. 8, G. Boyer, *Textes juridiques* (1958); vol. 9, M. Birot, *Textes administratifs de la salle 5 du palais* (1960); vol. 10, G. Dossin, *La correspondance féminine* (1967; cuneiform only); vol. 11, M. Lurton Burke, *Textes administratifs de la salle 111 du palais* (1963); vol. 12, M. Birot, *Textes administratifs de la salle 5 du palais* (1964); vol. 13, G. Dossin, et al., *Textes divers* (1964); vol. 15, J. Bottéro and A. Finet, *Répertoire analytique des tomes 1 à V* (1954); G. Dossin, in: *Syria*, 19 (1938), 105–26; 20 (1939), 97–113; idem, in: *Revue d'assyriologie et d'archéologie orientale*, 35 (1938), 1–13; W. von Soden, in: *Die Welt des Orients*, 1 (1947–52), 187–204; F. Thureau-Dangin, in: *Revue d'assyriologie et d'archéologie orientale*, 36 (1939), 1–28; G. Goossens, *ibid.*, 46 (1952), 137–54; E. Laroche, *ibid.*, 51 (1957), 104–6; I. Mendelsohn, in: BASOR, 156 (1959), 38–40; A. L. Oppenheim, *Letters from Mesopotamia* (1967), 96–110; A. Malamat, in: *Qadmoniot*, 1 (1968), 80–87; P. Artzi and A. Malamat, in: *Orientalia*, 40 (1971), 75–89. On B: G. Dossin, in: *Syria*, 32 (1955), 1–28; idem, in: *Revue d'assyriologie et d'archéologie orientale*, 64 (1970), 17ff., 97ff.; W. F. Leemans, *ibid.*, 49 (1955), 201–4; idem, *Foreign Trade in the Old Babylonian Period* (1960), 176–81; B. Landsberger, in: JCS, 8 (1954), 35–36; J. M. Munn-Rankin, in: *Iraq*, 18 (1956), 68–110; J. R. Kupper, *Les nomades en Mésopotamie au temps des rois de Mari* (1957); H. Lewy, in: *Die Welt des Orients*, 2 (1959), 438–53; idem, in: RAI, 15 (1967), 14–28; I. J. Gelb, in: JCS, 15 (1961), 27–47; A. Goetze, in: JSS, 4 (1959), 142–7; D. O. Edzard, in: *Fischer Weltgeschichte*, 2 (1965), 165–91; K. A. Kitchen, *Ancient Orient and the Old Testament* (1966), index; W. Roellig, in: RAI, 15 (1967), 97–102; J. J. Finkelstein, in: JCS, 20 (1966), 95–118; A. Malamat, in JAOS, 88 (1968), 87–97; W. F. Albright, *Yahwe and the Gods of Canaan* (1968), index, s.v. *Mari;* J. M. Sasson, *The Military Establishments at Mari* (1969). On the West: F. M. Tocci, *La Siria nell'età di Mari* (1960); G. Dossin, in: *Bulletin de l'Académie royale de Belgique (classe des lettres)*, 38 (1952), 224–39; 40 (1954), 417–25; J. R. Kupper, in: CAH², vol. 2, ch. 1 (1963); A. Malamat, in: *Eretz-Israel*, 5 (1958), 67–73; idem, in: JBL, 79 (1960), 12–19; idem, in: *Studies in Honor of B. Landsberger* (1965), 365–73; idem, in: J. A. Sanders (ed.), *Essays in Honor of N. Glueck* (1970), 164–77; idem, in: IEJ, 21 (1971); B. Mazar, in: IEJ, 18 (1968), 65–97. On C 1–3: G. Dossin, in: *Mélanges Dussaud*, 2 (1939), 981–96; idem, in: *Revue d'assyriologie et d'archéologie orientale*, 52 (1958), 60–62; 62 (1968), 75–76; M. Noth, in: *A. Alt Festschrift* (1953), 127–52; idem, *Urspruenge des alten Israel im Lichte neuer Quellen* (1961); A. Finet, *L'accadien des lettres de Mari* (1956); idem, in: *Syria*, 41 (1964), 117–42; idem, in: *Revue d'assyriologie et d'archéologie orientale*, 60 (1966), 17–28; W. L. Moran, in: *Orientalia*, 26 (1957), 339–45; D.

O. Edzard, in: ZA, 19 (1959), 168–73; H. Klengel, in: *Orientalia*, 29 (1960), 357–75; idem, in: *Archiv Orientální*, 30 (1962), 585–96; idem, in: *Das Verhaeltnis von Bodenbauern und Viehzuechtern in historischer Sicht* (1968), 75–81; P. Fronzaroli, in: *Archivio Glottologico Italiano*, 45 (1960), 37–60, 127–49; J. C. L. Gibson, in: *Glasgow University Oriental Society Transactions*, 18 (1959–60), 15–29; idem, in: JSS, 7 (1962), 44–62; P. Artzi, in: *Oz le-David (Ben-Gurion)* (1964), 71–85; H. B. Huffmon, *Amorite Personal Names in the Mari Texts* (1965); G. Buccellati, *The Amorites of the Ur III Period* (1966); A. Malamat, in: JAOS, 82 (1962), 143–50; idem, in: RAI, 15 (1967), 129–38; W. von Soden, in: *Die Welt des Orients*, 3 (1966), 177–87; Lambert, Klima, Cazelles, Rowton, in: RAI, 15 (1967); M. Weippert, *Die Landnahme der Israel. Staemme* (1967), 102–23; J. Klima, in: *Das Verhaeltnis von Bodenbauern . . .* (1968), 83–89; L. R. Bailey, in: JBL, 87 (1968), 434–8. On C 4: G. Dossin, *Studies in Old Testament Prophecy (Th. H. Robinson Volume)* (1950), 103–10; W. von Soden, in: *Die Welt des Orients*, 1 (1947–52), 397–403; M. Noth, in: BJRL, 32 (1950), 194–206; idem, in: *Annuaire de l'Institut de Philologie et d'Histoire Orientales et Slaves*, 13 (1955), 433–44; idem, in: JSS, 1 (1956), 322–33; G. Wallis, in: ZAW, 64 (1952), 57–61; G. E. Mendenhall, in: BASOR, 133 (1954), 26–30; M. Held, *ibid.*, 200 (1970), 32–40; E. A. Speiser, *ibid.*, 149 (1958), 17–25; idem, in: JBL, 79 (1960), 157–63; A. Malamat, in: *Eretz-Israel*, 4 (1956), 74–84; 5 (1958), 67–73; idem, in VTS, 15 (1966), 207–27; idem, in: *Biblical Essays, Proceedings of the 9th Meeting, Die Ou Testamentiese Werkgemeenskap in Suid-Afrika* (1966), 40–49; W. Richter, in: ZAW, 77 (1965), 40–72; R. de Vaux, in: *Ugaritica*, 6 (1969), 501–17; C. Westermann, *Forschung am Alten Testament* (1964), 171–88; F. Ellermeier, *Prophetie in Mari und Israel* (1968); H. B. Huffmon, in: BA, 31 (1968), 102–24; J. G. Heintz, in: VTS, 17 (1969), 112–38; W. L. Moran, in: *Biblica*, 50 (1969), 15–55; idem, in: Pritchard, Texts^{3}, 623–31; J. F. Ross, in: HTR, 63 (1970), 1–28.

[A. Ma.]

MARIAMNE (Mariamme). Mariamne I (60?–29 B.C.E.) was the daughter of *Alexander the son of Aristobulus, the granddaughter of John Hyrcanus, and the second wife of *Herod. Herod's aim in contracting this marriage was to establish his standing with the royal house. Herod was only betrothed to her, but not yet married, when in 40 B.C.E. he was forced to flee to Idumea from Antigonus, who was supported by the Parthians, and he had placed Mariamne together with the other women of the royal household in the fortress of Masada for safety. When Herod's sovereignty over Judea was ratified by the Roman senate on the recommendation of Mark Antony, he went in 37 B.C.E. to Samaria to marry Mariamne while his army was still besieging Jerusalem. Herod's love for Mariamne was unbounded, but it was met by hatred of him on her part, because Herod had put to death practically all the members of her family. Aware of Herod's feelings for her, she was bold enough to speak harshly to him, which others feared to do. In addition to this, however, her anger was directed against the rise of the new dynasty which had replaced her own—the *Hasmonean—and this caused her to act disdainfully toward the members of the royal Idumean family, particularly to Herod's mother and his sister Salome. As a result these two harbored a grudge against her and were malevolently provocative toward her, fabricating such libels about her as that she had sent her portrait to Antony in Egypt.

When Herod went to visit Antony he entrusted his wife to Joseph, the husband of Salome, ordering him to put Mariamne to death should Antony sentence him to death. Joseph informed Mariamne of this with the intention of showing her how great was the love Herod bore her. When Herod returned from his journey he discovered from Mariamne that Joseph had revealed this secret order to her. According to one account in Josephus, it was then that in his rage Herod ordered both Joseph and Mariamne to be put to death. A parallel account, however, is given by Josephus in the section dealing with Herod's journey to Octavius at Rhodes after the battle near Actium. The first story belongs to the period before 31 B.C.E., while the second is later. It seems that both stories were true, but that the execution of Mariamne took place in 29 B.C.E., and that on the previous occasion Herod did not go so far as to murder his wife. Mariamne bore Herod three sons and two daughters. One of the sons died in his youth. The other two, Alexander and Aristobulus, were executed on the order of their father in 7 B.C.E.

Mariamne II (d. circa 20 B.C.E.), the daughter of Simeon b. Boethus the high priest, was the third wife of Herod. She belonged to a priestly family from Alexandria. Her son, also named Herod, was designated to succeed to the throne after Antipater. It was because of this that although Mariamne II knew of Antipater's intentions to kill his father, she held her peace. As a result, when the plot of Antipater was discovered, Herod erased from his will the name of his son Herod II as his heir and sent Mariamne away.

Bibliography: Jos., Wars; Jos., Ant.; A. Schalit, *Koenig Herodes* (1969), index; Klausner, Bayit Sheni, 3 (1950^{2}), 261, 268; 4 (1950^{2}), 14–18, 153f. (Mariamne I); 4 (1950^{2}), 42, 153 (Mariamne II); A. H. M. Jones, *Herods of Judea* (1938), index.

[Al.L.]

MARIANOS (sixth century), artist who—together with his son Ḥanina—designed the pictorial mosaic floor of the Bet Alfa (Ḥefẓi-Bah) synagogue near Beth-Shean. Their names also appear in an ornamental mosaic floor adjoining a synagogue at Beth-Shean. They are known only through these two mosaics. The inscription in Greek at Bet Alfa reads: "May the craftsmen who carried out this work, Marianos and his son Ḥanina, be held in remembrance." Below this inscription, a partially destroyed Aramaic legend dates the mosaic to the reign of the Byzantine emperor Justin (I), viz., 518–527 C.E. It is clear, that as local Galilean artists, they worked in the standard Greco-Oriental manner of the time, combining Eastern frontality, patterning, and lack of modeling and perspective, with Western costumes, composition, and mosaic technique. The similarity of their work to mosaics in other sixth-century synagogues of the Palestinian littoral indicates that they followed standard patterns. The style of their work appears to reflect rug designs. In the Bet Alfa mosaic the motifs of the border

Greek inscription in the floor mosaic of the Bet Alpha synagogue commemorating Marianos and his son, Ḥanina, who executed the mosaic. From E. L. Sukenik, *The Ancient Synagogue of Beit Alpha*, Jerusalem, 1932.

designs and of two of the three panels, that of the zodiac and of the holy symbols, are paralleled elsewhere (e.g., the sixth-century synagogue of Tiberias). The third panel located just inside the entrance to the prayer room depicts the sacrifice of Isaac, combining an artistic and symbolic complexity that belies the direct, seemingly naive manner in which the mosaic is worked. (See *Bet Alfa.)

Bibliography: B. Goldman, *Sacred Portal* (1966); E. L. Sukenik, *Ancient Synagogue of Beth Alpha* (1932); N. Tsori, in: *Israel Exploration Journal*, 13 (1963), 148–9. [B.Go.]

°**MARIA THERESA** (1717–1780), empress of Austria from 1740. She continued the hostile policy of *Charles VI, her father, against the Jews. Her passionate hatred, nurtured from childhood, culminated in the expulsion of *Prague Jewry (1744), which she revoked in 1748 after international intervention on behalf of the Jews. She declared in 1777 that she knew "no worse plague for the state than this nation, because of its deceitfulness, its usury," and noted that the Jews "bring the state more harm than good." She granted audiences to Jews from behind a partition. In spite of this, she profited from the services of such individuals as Diego d'*Aguilar, Israel von *Hoenigsberg, and Wolf *Wertheimer. Pursuing a mercantilist policy on the advice of Joseph von *Sonnenfels she granted special privileges to Jews, allowing them to establish factories with the condition that gentile labor be employed. She forbade the baptism of Jewish children against the will of their parents, and in 1754 issued the *General Polizey Ordnung* ("statute") for Moravian Jewry based on the long-standing *Shai Takkanot*. In 1742 she confirmed the judicial autonomy of Lombardian Jewry (reconfirmed in 1752 and 1764), and in 1744 refrained from carrying out her intention of expelling the Jews from *Naples. In 1753 she permitted the reestablishment of a prayer room at *Usov (Maehrisch-Aussee) and in 1762 reconfirmed the privileges of Mantuan bankers. The unified toleration tax introduced in 1749 in Hungary was called *"malke-geld"* ("queen money"); it was fear for the loss of the revenue from this tax that induced the empress to prohibit the spread of blood libels in 1764. Despite her concern for ensuring the revenues of the kingdom, her hatred of the Jews found frequent expression. In 1746 she ordered the expulsion of Jews from Buda (Ofen; see *Budapest) and *Timisoara, and in 1774 she expelled the Jewish community from *Hodonin (Goeding), her private domain. In 1752 she had a census taken of the Jews living in Vienna, checked personally on them every three months lest their number multiply illegally, and in 1764 issued a new statute for Lower Austria. Under her rule, as a result of the annexation of Galicia (1772) and Bukovina (1775), the Hapsburg monarchy became the country with the largest population of Jews.

Medal in honor of the revocation of Maria Theresa's edict expelling the Jews of Prague, struck by the Dutch Jews in 1745. New York, Jewish Museum, Daniel M. Friedenberg Collection.

Bibliography: M. Grunwald, *Vienna* (1936), 139–44; R. Pick, *Empress Maria Theresa* (1966), index s.v. *Jews;* H. Tietze, *Juden Wiens* (1935), 98–110; B. Mevorakh, in: *Zion*, 28 (1963), 125–64 (bibliography about Prague expulsion: 125–7 in remarks 1–5); idem, in: *Meḥkarim . . . le-Zekher Ẓevi Avneri* (1970), 188–232; H. Gold, *Juden und Judengemeinden Maehrens* (1929), 220, 338; S. Simonsohn, *Toledot ha-Yehudim be-Dukkasut Mantovah* (1963), index; R. Kestenberg-Gladstein, *Neuere . . . Boehmens*, 1 (1969), index; C. Schieber, in: *Zeitschrift fuer die Geschichte der Juden*, 1 (1964), 55–58, 153–7; A. Newman, in: JHSET, 22 (1970), 30–37. [M.La.]

MARI BEN ISSUR (first half of the fourth century), Babylonian *amora*. Mari's father was a non-Jew who became converted to Judaism after his son was conceived and was henceforth known as Issur the Proselyte (BB 149a). According to Rashi (Ber. 16a, BM 73b) his mother was Rachel, the daughter of Samuel (Mar or Samuel Yarḥina'-ah) who had been taken captive (Ket. 23a); Mari is therefore identical with the Mari b. Rachel and the "Mari, the son of Samuel's daughter" who are often mentioned in the Babylonian Talmud, and he was called after his mother because of his non-Jewish paternity. This view is upheld by Samuel b. Meir (Rashbam to BB 149a) but is contested by the *tosafot* (ad loc.) since according to the Talmud the daughters of Samuel were ransomed from captivity in Ereẓ Israel and married Simeon b. Abba, one after the other, all dying shortly after the marriage (Ket. 23a; TJ, Ket. 2:6, 26c). Moreover there is a chronological difficulty in identifying the daughter of Samuel, who died in 256, with the mother of Mari, who died in the second half of the fourth century. Issur, after his conversion to Judaism, became friendly with R. Safra (BM 31b) and particularly with Rava and under their influence Mari attended the *bet midrash* and devoted himself to study. Issur left Mari 12,000 *zuz* which he deposited with Rava (BB 149a). Mari had two sons: Mar Zutra and Adda Saba, contemporaries of Ashi (Kid. 65b).

Bibliography: Hyman, Toledot, 903–5; Ḥ. Albeck, *Mavo la-Talmudim* (1969), 369. [D.J.B.]

MARIBOR (Ger. **Marburg**), city in Styria, now in Slovenia, N. Yugoslavia; until 1918 in Austria. The first important Jewish settlement in Maribor dates from the end of the 12th century. Jews were merchants and artisans, and also owned mills, fields, and vineyards as security for loans. During the late Middle Ages they had a part in the banking business between Central and Southern Europe, and their commercial ties extended to Italy, Hungary, and Bohemia. They traded mainly in wood, cheese, wine, and cloth. After Styria became part of Austria, the expulsion decrees were applied to the Jewish inhabitants there; Jews were expelled from Maribor in 1496 and the synagogue was converted into a church. Exiles from Maribor are known to have settled in Italy and in the town of Split, where they took the name Morpurgo ("of Marburg"). Individual Jews again settled in Maribor after *emancipation in Austria (1867). Others found refuge in Graz, Trieste and Sopron (Oedenburg). After Styria became part of Yugoslavia in 1918, the few Maribor Jews became affiliated with the community of Varaždin.

Bibliography: Milica Detoni, in *Jevrejski Almanah* (1956/57), 72–74; Germ Jud, 2 (1968), index s.v. *Marburg (Drau)*. [Ed.]

°**MARIE-BENOÎT** (pseudonym for **Pierre Peteul,** also known in Italy as **Padre Benedetti;** 1895–), Catholic priest who rescued many Jews during World War II. Born in the French village of Bourg d'Iré (Maine-et-Loire), Marie-Benoît entered the Capuchin Order. He served five years in the French Army during World War I, after which he continued his studies at the Capuchin College in Rome, receiving recognition as a scholar of Hebrew and Judaism.

When Nazi Germany invaded France (1940), Marie-Benoît moved to Marseilles, where he built up an efficient organization for smuggling Jewish and other refugees into Spain and Switzerland. In July 1943 he opened negotiations with the Pope for a rescue plan to transfer 30,000 Jews from southern France to North Africa. In this project Marie-Benoît was aided by Angelo *Donati. When Italy surrendered to the Allies (Sept. 8, 1943), Marie-Benoît was forced to give up his rescue plan and left France to avoid arrest by the Gestapo. He then transferred his activities to Italy, where he became director of the DELASEM (Delegazione Assistenza Emigrati Ebrei), the committee for assistance to Jewish emigrants, which had gone underground. The committee mainly provided hundreds of false documents to rescue Jews. In December 1966 Marie-Benoît was awarded a medal in recognition of his rescue work by the *Yad Vashem Commission of the Righteous Gentiles.

Bibliography: J. Horty, in: *Commentary*, 2 (1946), 507–13; P. Friedman, *Their Brothers' Keepers* (1957), 55–59.

[Av.Le.]

MARIENBAD (Czech. **Mariánské Lázně**), town in W. Bohemia, Czechoslovakia. The first Jew settled in Marienbad in 1820; prior to this time Jews only went to Marienbad during the health cure season. The Jewish community grew, as did the town, during the 19th century, drawing its settlers mainly from the Drmouly (Duerrmaul; see *Chodová Planá) and *Lázně Kynžvart (Koenigswart) communities. Many foreigners also settled there. Instrumental in the development of Marienbad was the professor and balneologist Samuel *Basch, whose statue was removed by the Nazis, and reerected in 1970. On the initiative of Prague notables a Jewish hospice with a prayer room was built in 1861, with the help of gifts from Jewish visitors. Another balneologist, Heinrich Enoch *Kisch, also lived in Marienbad, contributing greatly to its development. He was the head of the Jewish hospice and a street was named for him. In 1875 a congregation was constituted and in 1884 a synagogue was dedicated. Marienbad was very popular among Russian Jewry at the end of the 19th century. According to the municipal election statute (in force until 1918), no Jew could be elected to the municipal council. The community numbered 405 in 1930 (3.3% of the total population). In 1937 the great assembly (*Keneset ha-Gedolah*) of *Agudat Israel was held in Marienbad. At the time of the Sudeten crisis (1938) most of the community left the town, those who remained were arrested by the Nazis. The synagogue was burned down and its site is now a park. In 1945 a community was refounded, mostly by army veterans from *Subcarpathian Ruthenia. It numbered 196 in 1949. For a period of time there was a yeshivah for survivors of the Nazi persecutions in the town. In 1970 Marienbad was a center of Jewish life in Czechoslovakia as its Jewish old-age home (with a prayer room and a *kasher* restaurant) had about 100 residents from all over the country.

Synagogue of Marienbad, dedicated in 1884 and burned by the Germans after their occupation of the Sudetenland in 1938. Courtesy H. Gold, Tel Aviv.

Bibliography: J. Steiner, in: H. Gold (ed.), *Juden und Judengemeinden Boehmens*... (1934), 396–7; J. C. Pick, in: *Jews of Czechoslovakia*, 1 (1968), 378; R. Iltis (ed.), *Die aussaeen unter Traenen*... (1959), 23; *Věstnik židovských náboženských obce v Praze*, 16 no. 6 (1954), 47; Yad Vashem BJCE.

[M.La.]

MARIJAMPOLE (Rus. **Mariampol**), city in S. Lithuanian S.S.R. In 1856 there were 2,853 Jews in Marijampole; in 1897 there were 3,268 (c. 49% of the total population); and on the eve of World War I, 5,000. Many of them were admitted to Russian boys' and girls' secondary schools. In addition to the traditional *ḥadarim*, a "reformed *ḥeder*," where Hebrew was the language of instruction, was established. During World War I the Jews were expelled and a number were imprisoned for allegedly collaborating with the enemy. In 1923 there were 2,545 Jews (21% of the total). The majority of them earned their livelihood from trading in agricultural produce and small industry. There were also some landowners and smallholders. The Jews of Marijampole engaged in extensive nationalist political and cultural activities. They established welfare and cultural institutions of a high standard, including the first Hebrew secondary school in Lithuania (1919). There was also a farm which provided training for *ḥalutzim* in the vicinity of the city. When the Germans occupied the city in 1941, the Jews were concentrated in a local ghetto together with other Jews from the surrounding area. Over 7,000 of them were massacred at the beginning of September 1941.

Bibliography: *Lite*, 1 (1951), 1563–67, 1839–42.

[D.Le.]

MARINI, SHABBETHAI ḤAYYIM (**Vita;** c. 1690–1748), rabbi, poet, and physician. Born in Padua, Marini studied there under Isaac Ḥayyim Cohen de *Cantarini, whom he succeeded in the rabbinate of the town. Marini was renowned for his sermons which fascinated not only members of the Jewish community but many educated Christians as well. He was also held in high esteem as a physician.

Marini's main work is a Hebrew translation of the first three books of Ovid's *Metamorphoses*, based on the Italian paraphrase by Giovanni Andrea dell' Anguillara. Originally Marini planned a joint translation with Isaiah *Bassano. Marini, however, completed the translation alone, and it is not certain whether Bassano's 100 octaves are included in Marini's 850. The translation, entitled "*Shirei ha-Ḥalifot le-Oved*," was to have been published in Mantua, but

Marini died when only one sheet had been printed. The original manuscript of the translation is in the municipal library in Mantua (Ms. 77 Comunità Israelitica). Others are: Parma, de Rossi, Ms. 1110 Budapest, Kaufmann Ms. 547; British Museum, Ms. Add, 26916, Vienna, Ms. 91. A longer excerpt of the translation was published in S. D. Luzzatto's letters.

Marini also wrote numerous poems for special occasions, including an elegy on the death of his teacher Cantarini and a wedding poem which could be read either as Italian or as Hebrew. The Mantua and the Vienna manuscripts of the Ovid translation contain 34 of Marini's poems (mostly sonnets), and a fragment of his poetic paraphrase of *Pirkei *Avot.* Isaiah Romanin wrote an elegy on Marini's death (Oxford, Bodleian Library, Ms. Mich. 439, fol. 376).

Bibliography: G. B. De' Rossi, *Dizionario Storico degli Autori Ebrei,* 2 (Parma, 1802), s.v. 39f.; Fuerst, in: *Literaturblatt des Orients,* 1 (1840), 124; Ghirondi-Neppi, 342–4; S. D. Luzzatto, *Iggerot Shadal,* 3 (1882), 394f., 404, 416, 419; Steinschneider, in: *Vessillo Israelitico,* 27 (1879), 3ff.; 28 (1880), 149; Schirmann, Italyah, 389–94. [J.H.Sch.]

MARINOFF, JACOB (1869–1964), Yiddish poet and editor. Born in Russia where he was a blacksmith, he later worked in a tailor shop in London (1891–93) and then emigrated to the U.S. and lived in Denver, where he sought to regain his impaired health. From 1895 he contributed poems to Yiddish periodicals. In 1909 he cofounded *Der Groyser Kundas,* a journal for humor, wit, and satire, which he edited for almost two decades. Among the contributors to the weekly, which had a large circulation and influenced Jewish public opinion, were *Shalom Aleichem, *Yehoash, A. *Reisen, M.L. *Halpern, A. *Lutzky, and M. *Nadir. Marinoff was the author of three volumes of verse, of which the most significant was *Shpil un Kamf* (1938), and coeditor of the collection *Humor un Satire* (1912).

Bibliography: Rejzen, Leksikon, 3 (1927), 333–7; LNYL, 5 (1963), 500–2; N. B. Minkoff, *Pionern fun Yidisher Poezie in Amerike,* 3 (1956), 169–218. [S.L.]

MARITAIN, °JACQUES (1882–) and **RAÏSSA** (1883–1960), French writers who took a positive stand on the Jewish issue during the Nazi era. Raïssa Oumansoff, a Russian Jew, was taken to Paris as a child, and there in 1904 she married Jacques Maritain, a Protestant by birth and a former disciple of Henri *Bergson, who became one of the foremost protagonists of neo-Thomism. Having lost touch with their respective religions, the Maritains became Catholics in 1905. These experiences were sensitively narrated by Raïssa Maritain in *Les grandes amitiés* (1941; *We Have Been Friends Together,* 1942). The conversion, which pained and scandalized their families, paradoxically induced the young couple to meditate on the Jewish destiny. Raïssa's poems, essays, and diary reveal a very pure, mystical approach, the source of which she described: "My maternal grandfather was a Ḥasid, and my father's father was a great ascetic sage. This is my inheritance." Through Raïssa, Jacques Maritain learned that "inspiration and spiritual sources of life come from the people chosen by God." When the times demanded that he speak up for the Jews, the philosopher became the man of action. From the moment the Nazi persecutions began, Maritain spoke out and he continued to champion the Jews while an exile in the U.S. during World War II, as French ambassador to the Vatican after 1945, and following the establishment of the State of Israel. Jacques Maritain's many articles and statements on the subject (1926–61) were collected by the author in a single volume, *Le Mystère d'Israël* (1965).

Bibliography: J. Maritain (ed.), *Journal de Raïssa* (1963); D. A. and I. J. Gallagher, *The Achievement of Jacques and Raïssa Maritain: a Bibliography, 1906–61* (1962). [M.-C.G.]

MARITIME LAW. The Talmud discusses many laws concerning shipping, and sea and river journeys—such as the sale of ships, instances of shipwreck salvage and rescue, rules of passage at sea, lading and charter agreements, and also various details of the laws of the Sabbath and ritual purity applicable to ships. Such laws do not, however, serve to create a distinct branch of maritime law proper, since they are interwoven into the wider principles of the laws of *contract and *damages (contrary to the view expressed by J. Dauvillier, in: *Revue Internationale des Droits de l'Antiquité,* 6 (1959), 33–63). Although in this field special shipping customs, if any, are followed, this is no more than an application of the general principle of contract law relating to local or trade customs (Rashba, Resp., vol. 2, no. 268).

With regard to the sale of ships, as with other sales, reference is made to accessories which are customarily sold with the ship and others which are considered as being independent and must therefore be purchased separately (BB 5:1). It is also stated that it was the practice of shipowners to receive not only the hire for the ship but also payment for its loss if shipwrecked (BM 70a). On arrangements for sea traffic it is stated: "Where two boats sailing on a river meet; if both attempt to pass simultaneously, they will sink; whereas if one makes way for the other, both can pass [without mishap]. Likewise if two camels met each other while on the ascent of Beth-Horon [which is a narrow pass; see Josh. 10:10 and 11] . . . if one is laden and the other unladen, the latter should give way to the former; if one is nearer [to its destination] than the other, the former should give way to the latter. If both are equally near or far, make a compromise between them, and the one [to go through] must compensate the other" (Tosef. BK 2:10; Sanh. 32b). If a person hires a ship for carriage of cargo and it sinks in mid-journey, he must pay for half the journey; if, however, he hires a specific ship for shipping a specific cargo, he loses the hire if he has already paid for it but is not obliged to pay if he has not already done so (BM 79b and Tos.). In a case where a man hired boatmen to deliver goods, stipulating that they guarantee against any accident (see **Ones*) occurring on the way, and the river dried up during the journey, it was held that the boatmen had not guaranteed against this possibility since such an accident was not foreseeable (Git. 73a).

Various *halakhot* were decided with regard to shipwrecks. Thus when a boat is in danger of sinking and part of the cargo is thrown overboard to lighten the vessel, the resulting loss is not apportioned equally amongst the cargo owners, nor is it calculated according to the value of the goods of each owner, but the loss is apportioned according to the weight of the cargo of each owner—provided that this does not conflict with local maritime customs (BK 116b). In one instance a donkey being transported threatened to sink the boat and was thrown overboard, whereupon it was decided that no compensation was payable to its owner, since the deed was justified on the grounds of self-defense, the donkey being considered as pursuing with intent to kill (BK 117b). An interesting *halakhah* concerning maritime insurance is related: "The sailors can stipulate that whoever loses a ship shall get another one, but if the boat was lost due to his own negligence or if he sailed to a place to which boats would not normally sail, he would not be provided with another boat." The same rule applies also to carriers on land (Tosef. BM 11:26; BK 116b).

In the post-talmudic period many responsa dealt with trade customs (see e.g., Rashba, Resp., vol. 2, no. 268), some of them marine customs. Solomon b. Abraham *Adret (RaSHBa), who lived in Barcelona where the well-known collection of marine customs *Consulat de Mar* was compiled, records the custom of depositing goods with a merchant traveling by sea for the latter to trade therein at the risk of the depositor—leaving the sailor exempt from liability for accident (his resp. vol. 2, no. 325; vol. 1, no. 930 and cf. no. 924). Also mentioned is the custom of paying the full wages, even if the journey for which the employee was hired was not completed due to accident overtaking the employer (Rashba, Resp., vol. 6, no. 224).

In the State of Israel maritime law is based on Israel legislation, conforming with the law of the maritime nations in those matters and also with Ottoman-French laws and English law.

Bibliography: Krauss, Tal Arch, 2 (1911), 338–49; Herzog, Instit, 2 (1939), 252–4, 268–70. [SH.A.]

MARITIME (Atlantic) PROVINCES, the four easternmost provinces of Canada—New Brunswick, Nova Scotia, Prince Edward Island, and (since 1949) Newfoundland. About 10% of Canada's population lives in these relatively undeveloped coastal provinces. Jewish centers in the provinces reached their peak population in 1921; since then some have declined, others have remained stable. Prince Edward Island, which in 1961 had only 22 Jews in a population of about 105,000, has no organized Jewish communities.

New Brunswick. In 1961 New Brunswick's population was 515,697, with a Jewish population of 1,218. The Jewish population has been stable at about 1,200 since 1921. In 1871 there were 48 Jews in the province; the community grew to 55 in 1881, 73 in 1889, and by 1901 included 376. Fredericton, the provincial capital, has a community of about 230 Jews (1970); its synagogue is Sgoolai Israel.

The first settler in New Brunswick was Solomon *Hart, an Alsatian, who went to Saint John in 1858. He was shortly followed by a brother-in-law, Amsterdam-born Nathan Green. Their combined families constituted a Jewish settlement of 15. Twenty years later two brothers, Abraham and Israel Isaacs, arrived from London. Like Nathan Green, they too were cigar makers. In 1880, when the city had 46 Jews, a burial ground was consecrated. In 1896, when there were 30 Jewish families, a congregation—Ahavath Achim—was organized. The synagogue was built in 1898 and consecrated in January 1899. Since its merger with another congregation it has been known as Shaarai Zedek. The Saint John Jewish community numbered about 848 in 1921, and about 500 in 1970. Both Saint John and Halifax are port towns and at an early stage developed local immigrant aid services, long before the establishment of a national society; Saint John established these services in 1896.

Jews settled in Moncton in the 1880s. Growth was slow—by 1891 there were only 10 Jews in the city. A rabbi was engaged in 1909, but a synagogue—Tiferes Israel—was not completed until 1924. Moncton's Jewish population, the bulk stemming from Probyan, Lithuania, is estimated (1970) at 300. Michael M. Baig has served as its mayor.

Newfoundland. Newfoundland, with 253 Jews in a population of 457,853 (1961), had two organized Jewish communities: St. John's, 130 Jews; and Cornerbrook, 40. Jack Marshall of Cornerbrook, elected to the federal parliament in 1968, became Canada's first Jewish member for the Conservative party since 1870.

Nova Scotia. In 1961 the total Nova Scotia population was 737,007 and the Jewish population was 2,230. *Halifax had 1,160 Jews; Sydney, 415 (stable at about 400 since 1921), and 2 synagogues; Glace Bay, 251 (441 in 1921, up to 320 in 1970), with one synagogue; and New Waterford, 58 Jews. Truro and Amherst each had 21.

Jews in Public Life. Despite their geographic isolation from larger Jewish centers, Jews in the Maritime Provinces have been closely linked with Canadian and world Jewry. As early as 1903 the then tiny community of Glace Bay was represented at the third national conference of Canadian Zionists in Montreal, as were Sydney, Saint John, and Yarmouth four years later in Ottawa. The Federated Zionist Organization of Canada and the Canadian Jewish Congress share a Maritime Provinces headquarters office in Halifax.

Prominent Jews in public life have included Percy Gaum of Sydney, who served as Progressive Conservative member of the Nova Scotia legislature for Cape Breton, 1956–70, and was appointed minister of public welfare in 1968 and, in 1969, minister of mines; he was responsible for the Human Rights Act. Harry Smofsky was mayor of Bridgetown, N.S.; Leonard Kitz, mayor of Halifax; Bernard Flam served as alderman in Chatham, N.B., and Hubert Lynch as councilor and deputy mayor of Yarmouth, N.S. Joseph Zatzman served as councilor in Dartmouth, N.S. Two Jews have served as judges in the Atlantic Provinces, both in Nova Scotia; Nathan Green was appointed magistrate in Halifax in 1959, and Justin Dubinsky, a Glace Bay lawyer, was named to the Supreme Court of Nova Scotia in 1967.

Bibliography: B. G. Sack, *History of the Jews in Canada* (1965); S. Rosenberg, *The Jewish Community in Canada*, 1 (1970). [B.G.K.]

MARK, BERNARD (Berl; 1908–1966), scholar and historian. Born in Lomza, Mark studied law at Warsaw University. Prior to World War II, he published articles in Polish and Yiddish on literary history and edited left-wing periodicals. Between 1932 and 1939, he published a two-volume work in Yiddish entitled *Geshikhte fun di Sotsiale Bavegungen in Poyln* ("The History of Social Movements in Poland," 1938–39). During World War II, he lived in the Soviet Union, where he was active on the Jewish *Anti-Fascist Committee, and in the Związek Patriotów Polskich ("Polish Patriots' Union"). In Moscow he published his first work on Jewish anti-Nazi uprisings in Poland. Upon returning to Poland (1946), he published a series of essays and collections of documents on Holocaust subjects. In 1949, Mark was appointed director of the *Jewish Historical Institute in Warsaw, and editor of its *Bulletin* and *Bleter far Geshikhte.* In 1954 he was appointed an associate professor. Mark visited Israel in 1957 and lectured at the Second World Congress of Jewish Studies. He strengthened the ties between the Jewish Historical Institute and research institutions in Israel, e.g., *Yad Vashem and the Central Archives for the History of the Jewish People (Jerusalem). His main works are: *The Extermination and the Resistance of the Polish Jews During the Period 1939–1944* (1955); *Dokumenten un Materialen vegn Oyfshtand in Varshever Geto* (1953); *Der Oyfshtand in Varshever Geto* (1963), translated into Polish, German, and Dutch; *Di Yidishe Tragedye in der Poylisher Literatur* (1950); *Di Umgekumene Shrayber fun di Getos un Lagern un Zeyere Verk* (1954); *Der Oyfshtand in Byalistoker Geto* (1953[2]); and *Di Geshikhte fun Yidn in Poyln* (1957). [N.ECK.]

MARK, YUDEL (1897–), Yiddish educator, philologist, and author. Born in Palanga, Lithuania, Mark became active in Jewish politics while studying at Petrograd University (1915–18). In Libava (Liepaja), Latvia, he organized the local branch of the Yidishe *Folkspartei, later becoming the secretary-general of the Jewish National Council in Lithuania (1923), and secretary and vice-president of the Folkspartei in the same country. From 1930 to 1934 he was the editor of the daily *Folksblat.* Mark was the

Yudel Mark, Yiddish educator and philologist.

founder (1920) and principal of the Yiddish Real-Gimnazye of Vilkomir (Ukmerge), the first of its kind in Lithuania, and between 1927 and 1930, taught Yiddish at various schools and seminaries. After settling in the U.S. in 1936, Mark continued his activity in the field of Yiddish education. He settled in Israel (Jerusalem) in 1970.

Mark's first literary publication appeared in the Kovno (Kaunas) daily *Nayes* (1921), and he subsequently contributed extensively to a wide range of Yiddish political, literary, and educational publications, such as *Eynheytlekhe Folkshul* (1922). In addition he edited various Yiddish periodicals. His books include a Yiddish school grammar, *Shul-Gramatik* (1922), various textbooks on Yiddish language teaching, Yiddish literature, Jewish history (*Der Yidishe Poyps,* c. 1947; *Dovid ha-Reuveni un Shloyme Molkho,* 1941), biography, as well as children's books in Yiddish. Among his translations into Yiddish are works of Thomas Mann and Erich Maria Remarque. He also edited various books, notably the *Groyser Verterbukh fun der Yidisher Shprakh* (2 vols., 1961) jointly with Judah A. *Joffe; further volumes were in preparation (1971).

Among Mark's attainments as a linguist are his numerous studies on Yiddish grammar and style, on the Hebrew-Aramaic component in the Yiddish language, and his stylistic analyses of the Yiddish authors. He was also the editor of the *YIVO's *Yidishe Shprakh* (1941–68).

Bibliography: Rejzen, Leksikon, 2 (1927), 342–4; LNYL, 5 (1963), 510–4.

[MOR.SCH.]

MARKAH (Heb. מרקה; fl. second half of fourth century C.E.), well known and venerated Samaritan poet who wrote in Aramaic. The great esteem in which he is held by Samaritan tradition is shown by his epithet "Founder of Wisdom" in the Samaritan chronicle *Tolidah* or "Fountain of Wisdom" (Yanbūʿ al-Ḥikma) in that of *Abu al-Fath and by the legend that the name Markah (מרקה) was bestowed upon him because it has the same numerical value as the name Moses (משה), which no other human being is allowed to bear. Actually, Markah is an Aramaized form of the Latin name Marcus. According to the Samaritan chronicles, he was the son of the liturgical poet Amram Darah whose byname, Tūta, is explained as a development of the Latin name Titus.

Like his father, Markah wrote liturgical poems, part of which belong to the earliest portions of the Samaritan common prayer book, the *Defter* (see *Samaritan Language and Literature). His style is more elaborate than that of his father, and none of his poems is composed in the style of "Verses of Durran" (see *Amram Darah). The verses of his poems are arranged in an alphabetic acrostic and the number of lines in each verse is nearly always equal. Once his name is contained in the acrostic of the first four verses of a poem. Through his terse and polished style, he succeeds in conveying the fiery religious feelings of his soul. That is why many of his expressions became fixed figures of speech used by later Samaritan poets.

The work that established Markah's fame and gained him the epithet "Founder of Wisdom" is his great midrashic composition *Meimar* or *Tevat Markah,* a compendium of exegetical and theological teachings. It is divided into six books, the main subjects of which are: the wonders revealed to Israel from Moses' call to Israel's victory at the Red Sea; a commentary on Exodus 15; a commentary on Deuteronomy 27:9–26; the commission of Joshua and instructions to various classes of the people, whereby priests are witnesses to Israel and to themselves; a commentary on Deuteronomy 32; Moses' death; speculations about the 22 letters of the alphabet. There are many thoughts and figures of speech shared by this work with Markah's poems. All extant manuscripts, the earliest dating from the 14th century, contain recognizable later additions.

Bibliography: Z. Ben-Ḥayyim, *Ivrit va-Aramit Nosaḥ Shomron,* 3 pt. 2 (1967), 15–16, 133–262; J. A. Montgomery, *The Samaritans* (1907), 294–5; A. E. Cowley, *Samaritan Liturgy,* 2 (1909), xx–xxi and index; J. Macdonald, *Memar Merqah,* 2 vols. (1963), incl. bibl.; J. Bowman, *Transcript of the Original Text of the Samaritan Chronicle Tolidah* (1955), 16b; Abū'l-Fath ibn Abi'l-Ḥassan al-Sāmirī, *Annales Samaritani . . .*, ed. E. Vilmar (1865).

[AY.L.]

MARKEL, LESTER (1894–), U.S. journalist who was responsible for changing the nature of the Sunday newspaper. Born in New York City and trained at Columbia University's School of Journalism, Markel was from 1923 to 1964 Sunday editor of the *New York Times.* It was he who conceived the idea of separate Sunday sections, which would bring the reader the news in greater depth than was possible in daily papers. He was personally responsible for the *Times Magazine,* the "Book Review," and the "Arts and Leisure" section. In 1935 he instituted the "News of the Week in Review," a report in perspective of the week's events, which won Markel and the *New York Times* a Pulitzer Prize. Markel wrote and lectured widely. In 1951, he founded the International Press Institute to foster the free flow of information and freedom of the press in general. In 1964, he became associate editor of the *New York Times* and head of its department of public affairs. He also started a television series in which he and others discussed the news in depth.

[S.KA.]

MARKET DAYS AND FAIRS. The nomadic nature of early medieval trade and the wide ranging contacts of Jewish merchants throughout the period made Jewish traders early and eager participants in market days and fairs, in spite of the religious and social problems attendant on such participation, especially in Christian countries. As merchants were prominent in European Jewish leadership and *autonomy, fairs were suitable meeting places for deliberating Jewish affairs. Around 825 Archbishop *Agobard complained that the day on which the *Lyons weekly market was held had been changed from Saturday to suit Jewish traders. In the following three centuries there are many references in both Hebrew and Christian sources to Jews attending fairs, particularly in cities of the Rhineland such as Cologne and *Treves. *Gershom b. Judah mentions a fair at a sea or river port during which the assembled merchants from various communities enacted an ordinance. *Champagne and *Provence, believed to be where the fairs began, had many Jewish communities, whose members in all probability participated in them. Jewish attendance at markets and fairs decreased after the era of the *Crusades when moneylending and pawnbroking became the major source of Jewish livelihood in northwestern and central Europe. In other areas, where the trade in goods formed an important Jewish occupation, their attendance continued.

The 16th century, in Eastern and subsequently in central Europe, witnessed the creation of economic and social patterns adapted to the attendance of large numbers of Jews of various fairs and markets. In *Poland-Lithuania it was expressly forbidden to fix the dates of fairs and markets on the Sabbath or Jewish holidays. The Jews' commercial rights at fairs and markets were the only ones not challenged by competing Christian merchants. When persecutions in 1539–40 resulted in Lithuanian Jews ceasing to travel to fairs, the nobility appealed to the king to suppress the persecutions at once. One of the most important fairs was the "Gromnice" (February 2), when many Jewish merchants and heads of communities convened at *Lublin; much trade was done and debts and taxes were gathered. Others fairs took place in *Brody, *Gniezno, *Gdansk (Danzig), *Torun, *Lvov, and *Cracow, and there were innumerable lesser ones as well. As the fairs bore the names of their patron Christian saints, these became common usage and were inscribed on official and business documents. The distinctive creation of Polish Jewry, the *Councils of the Lands, was an outgrowth of a *bet din* which officiated at the Lublin fairs. Meetings of the councils took place there regularly, twice a year, during the 16-day spring and summer fairs; sometimes they were held during the *Jaroslaw fairs in the fall. The Lithuanian Council also convened during fairs, and common sessions took place at *Leczyna. One of the tasks of the Councils was regulating the nomination of a **parnas* and **dayyan* for the duration of the fair. As both positions carried wide powers, they had to be judiciously distributed among the contending lands. In Poland-Lithuania the social aspects of the fair were as significant as the economic and communal leadership ones. N. N. *Hannover described a mid-17th-century fair: "the head of the yeshivah journeyed with all his pupils to the fair on market day . . . and at each fair there were hundreds of heads of yeshivot, thousands of pupils, and tens of thousands of youths and Jewish merchants . . . And whoever had an eligible son or daughter went to the fair and arranged a match, for everyone could find one to his liking. And at every fair hundreds of matches were made, and sometimes thousands; and the children of Israel, men and women, wore kingly vestments at the fair" (*Yeven Meẓulah*, 1966, 86f.). Meir b. Gedaliah (Maharam) of *Lublin (1558–1616) described another aspect of Jewish life at the fairs: "It is a regular custom that at every fair a place is determined as a synagogue for daily prayer, and every Sabbath scholars and yeshivah students and leaders of the land and people congregate there and read the Torah" (Responsa, 84).

Figure 1. "In the Market of Lemberg" (Lvov), drawing by J. Pennell in *The Jews at Home*, London, 1892.

Jews had been expelled from Breslau in 1455, but they were never absent from the fairs. In 1537 the municipal council opposed an attempt by Ferdinand I to levy a special poll tax on Jewish visitors to the fairs. A century later, at the request of the textile guilds and the imperial authorities and despite the opposition of the local merchants, Jews were permitted to be in the town a few days before and after the fairs. In 1697 the authorities divided the Jews into five categories whose duration of stay depended on the scope of their economic transactions.

Jews attended the fairs as a corporation of merchants based on their communities or countries of origin. These corporations were also responsible for nominating their officials: a *parnas ha-yarid*, in charge of keeping order and representing the fair corporations; a *dayyan ha-yarid*, who held regular judicial authority and was empowered by the chief rabbi of the land (first mentioned in 1698); supervisor of ritual law; and *shames (shammash)*, the distinctive Breslau functionary, who was permitted to remain between the fairs and guarantee the continuity of business transactions. First mentioned in 1673, he was elected by his *Judenschaft*, authorized by the Councils of the Lands, recognized by the Breslau municipal council, sworn in, and allowed to wear a sword. In 1696 there were ten *shamosim* at the fair, one each for the four Polish lands and one for Bohemia, *Moravia, *Glogau, *Posen, *Leczno, and Zuelz. The number of Jewish visitors at a fair in 1685 was 332, and they practically monopolized Polish trade, particularly in textiles, silks, spices, tobacco, and above all in furs.

Jewish attendance at fairs within the Austrian Empire was encouraged by Emperor *Maximilian I, who in 1494 permitted Jews to attend markets in the imperial cities from which they had been expelled on payment of three florins *Mautgeld* ("body tax"; see **Leibzoll*). This right, confirmed by his successors in return for extraordinary taxation, became the legal cornerstone of Jewish economic activity. *Joseph II eventually abolished the *Leibzoll* and declared all markets open to Jews (1782/83). In practice, however, many restrictions remained in force until 1848. At *Brno, for example, the Jews were allowed to enter through only one gate *(Judentor)* at fixed hours, were restricted to one market, and forced to lodge in one inn, the *Neue Welt* in the Krona suburb. They struggled for many years for the right to erect stalls. Complaints by Christian merchants against underselling and inferior wares were continuously raised, and peddlers (called *pinkerljuden*) were particularly harassed at the Brno fairs. The Council of Moravia regulated the supervision of dietary laws at the fairs, distributed stalls before the fairs commenced, and prohibited the Jews from being at the fair on the day before it opened. There was a tendency to establish Jewish communities near locations of major and minor markets and fairs.

There were a great many fairs in central Europe. Many

Figure 2. Engraving of the Cracow goose market, by Walery Eljasz. From M. Balaban, *Historja Żydow w Krakowie,* 1936.

Jewish calendars recorded dates of fairs, which Jews attended as peddlers who both bought and sold wares, as merchants buying goods wholesale for retailing, and sometimes as popular performers like jugglers. Registers of the special scales for weighing feathers at the *Linz markets of 1594 and 1603 show that there were 131 Jewish traders in feathers and only 12 Christian dealers. Other important commodities were leather, skins, old clothes, and new clothes and textiles imported from Bohemia. In 1714 Bohemian *"Federjuden"* had to have special permission to attend because of the plague. About 300 Jews dealing in similar articles attended the *Krems fairs annually; in 1701 the Moravian Jews boycotted it because a Jew had been arrested as a thief.

The records of Zurzach fairs in Switzerland mention the *Judengeleit (Leibzoll),* a tax of between 7 and 19 batzen according to age and wealth which was a considerable source of income. The number of Jews attending grew from about 150 in the mid-18th century to about 200 at its close; most foreign Jews were from Gailingen, *Hohenems, and communities in *Baden, *Alsace, and Swabia, which were composed primarily of peddlers and merchants. More than three quarters of the households of the nearby communities of Endingen and *Lengnau attended these fairs. Although Jews were not tolerated throughout most of Switzerland they were allowed and encouraged to attend the fairs, particularly the *livestock merchants. In France in 1741, the controller-general of finances wrote a circular letter to all provincial governors asking them about the commercial activities of the Jews. Unanimously they replied that Jews should not be excluded from the fairs and markets because they helped keep down prices. The monopolistic guilds were forcing up prices, while the outside merchants, who came for the duration of the fair, forced them down. An endemic source of strife and litigation between Jews and local merchants and the authorities was the constant attempt to sell outside the market, or not on market days, or on the way to or back from markets, or to remain in the area after the fair was over. In Italy Jews were to be found at the major fairs and often participated in the festive processions which inaugurated them. The community of *Mantua bought and erected stalls at the fairgrounds for its members; there was an unsuccessful attempt to prohibit their use in 1740. A Jewish community had the right to tax Jewish merchants attending the fairs for the use of communal amenities. In 1720 the Jewish communities of the duchy of Parma tried, without success, to tax Jewish merchants attending the Parma city fairs (where there was no community). A long dispute (1748–51) between the community of *Verona, which had attempted to exact a business tax from foreign visitors at the fairs, and the communities of Mantua, *Ferrara, and *Modena ended with rabbinical authorities in Italy and Germany deciding against Verona's action.

European rulers were aware of the economic benefits resulting from Jewish participation in fairs. Joachim II, elector of *Brandenburg, expelled the Jews in 1510 but subsequently allowed them to attend fairs. After the 1573 expulsion from Brandenburg, Posen Jews regularly received permission to attend the *Frankfort on the Oder fairs. Elector Frederick William (1640–88) encouraged Polish Jews to attend fairs in his realm long before he admitted 50 Jewish families from Austria to settle and trade freely throughout his lands (1671). Though Jews were rigorously excluded from *Saxony, the internationally important *Leipzig fairs needed Jews to participate in large numbers. Between 1675 and 1764, 82,000 Jews attended the biannual *Leipzig markets; their number fluctuated according to political and economic factors, but grew steadily from about 400 a year in the mid-17th century to twice that amount by the end of the century and continued to grow; they generally constituted about one-fifth of the total attendance. Their number increased from an average of 1,073 in the 1780s to 3,370 in the 1800s and 6,444 in the 1830s, when they formed around one-quarter of the participants. Between 1675 and 1764 the majority of Jewish participants came from Central Europe, though the number of East European Jews was increasing slowly, eventually amounting to one-third of the total Jewish attendance in the early 19th century. The attendance lists of the fairs offer a true mirror of 18th-century Jewish society. Members of the leading families attended (see *Bacharach, *Fraenkel, *Gomperz, *Ephraim, *Itzig families, and Samuel *Oppenheimer, David *Oppenheim, and Samson *Wertheimer). *Glueckel of Hameln recorded her husband's transactions at fairs with Jost *Liebmann, the Court Jew. The leading *Court Jews of the day, Alexander David, Behrend *Lehmann, and Leffmann *Behrends, were also present. Jewish visitors to Leipzig congregated in the Bruehl, which became in effect a Jewish quarter for the duration of the fairs. The *Landrabbiner* of *Anhalt had rabbinical jurisdiction there and those who died at the fair were buried in Dessau. At Leipzig Jews bought wares worth about half a million thalers annually between 1773 and 1775, primarily textiles. Officially they sold wares worth one-fifth of that amount, but the sales figure was not the true one, for the "scales tax" *(Wagegold)* was 1% of all sales; it was not until 1813 that it was reduced to 0.5%, the same as the Christian tax. In addition the city exacted a high entrance fee. *"Volljuden,"* who did not enjoy special privileges and protection and were the majority, paid six thalers each and three for a wife or servant. Jewelers paid eight thalers and cooks *(Judenkoch)* ten thalers and 12 groschen.

Figure 3. Petticoat Lane, a 19th-century engraving of the market in the heart of London's Jewish quarter.

Marriage scene from opening of *Tur Even ha-Ezer*. Mantua (?), 15th century. Vercelli, Seminario Vescovile, fol. 13v ($13\frac{3}{8} \times 9\frac{7}{8}$ ins/33.7×24.9 cm.).

In the *Pale of Settlement and Austrian Galicia the market square and the regular market days became the center of the *shtetl* and the heart of its economy. To a large extent the economic and social life in these townships was regulated by buying from peasants and selling to them on the fixed market day in the appointed place; taverns were therefore erected around the market square. Jewish emigrants carried over this type of market (with some changes) into large cities in Western Europe; an example is the Petticoat Lane Market in London.

Bibliography: R. Mahler, *Toledot ha-Yehudim be-Polin* (1946), index, s.v. *Yarid;* M. Breger, *Zur Handelsgeschichte der Juden in Polen im 17. Jahrhundert* (1932), 15ff.; B. D. Weinryb, *Neueste Wirtschaftsgeschichte der Juden in Russland und Polen* (1934), index, s.v. *Messe;* S. Dubnow, *Pinkas ha-Medinah* (1925), index, s.v. *Yarid;* Halpern, Pinkas, s.v. *Yarid;* D. Evron, *Pinkas ha-Kesherim shel Kehillat Pozna* (1967), index, s.v. *Yarid;* S. Simonsohn, *Toledot ha-Yehudim be-Dukkasut Mantovah* (1964), index, s.v. *Yarid;* I. Halpern, *Takkanot Medinat Mehrin* (1952), index, s.v. *Yarid;* H. Gold (ed.), *Die Juden und Judengemeinden Maehrens* (1929), 144ff.; F. Guggenheim-Gruenberg, *Die Juden auf der Zurzacher Messe im 18. Jahrhundert* (1957); A. Hertzberg, *The French Enlightenment and the Jews* (1968), index, s.v. *Fairs;* Z. Szajkowski, *Franco-Judaica* (1962), index, s.v. *Markets;* A. F. Pribram, *Urkunden und Akten zur Geschichte der Juden in Wien* (1918), index, s.v. *Markt, Jahrmarkt;* L. Moses, *Die Juden in Niederoesterreich* (1935), 91–94; idem, in: A. Engel (ed.), *Gedenkbuch . . . Kuratoriums* (1936), 90–101; V. Kurrein, *Die Juden in Linz* (1927), 26–38; idem, in: JGGJČ, 4 (1932), 481–4; A. Weldler-Steinberg and F. Guggenheim-Gruenberg, *Geschichte der Juden in der Schweiz* (1966), 21–86; B. B. Brilling, *Geschichte der Juden in Breslau von 1454 bis 1702* (1960); R. Markgraf, *Zur Geschichte der Juden auf den Messen in Leipzig* (1894); M. Freudenthal, *Leipziger Messgaeste* (1928); W. Harmelin, in: YLBL, 9 (1964), 239–66. [H.W.]

MARKISH, PEREZ (1895–1952), Soviet Yiddish poet, novelist, and playwright. Born in Volhynia, Markish received a traditional Jewish education and prepared for entrance to a university. He served in World War I and was discharged after being wounded. Markish was the youngest member of the Kiev lyric triumvirate, made up of David *Hofstein and Leib *Kvitko, who expressed the modern trends in Yiddish poetry and acclaimed the new Soviet revolution.

In 1921, Markish left Russia, lived in Poland and France, and visited England and Palestine. From 1921 to 1926 he wrote impressive poems about the anti-Jewish pogroms in the Ukraine, expressing Jewish sorrow and hope. One of the founders of the Warsaw *Literarishe Bleter,* he also coedited the expressionist *Khaliastre Almanakh* (1922), in Warsaw together with I. J. *Singer, and in Paris, with Oizer *Varshavsky, with illustrations by Marc *Chagall.

In 1926 he returned to the Soviet Union where among his best-known published works were the epic poem *"Brider"* (1929), the novels *Dor Oys, Dor Ayn* (1929), *Farklepte Tsiferblatn* (1929), and *Dem Balgufs Toyt* (1935). Markish wrote about industrialization, collectivization, and other aspects of life in the Soviet Union, and also an "Ode to Stalin" (1940), in harmony with the party demands regarding literature. In 1939 he was awarded the Order of Lenin. In his many works during World War II, he expressed hatred of the enemy, great Soviet patriotism, and sorrow at the extermination of the Jews. His 20,000-line epic poem *"Milkhome"* abounds in praise of Stalin, but neither this nor his previous ode to Stalin saved him from arrest in 1948. He was accused, together with other Jewish writers, of Jewish nationalism and executed on August 12, 1952.

Markish showed great vigor in his poetry. He was a master stylist and gave full expression to deep feelings and emotions,

Perez Markish, second from right. With him are (right to left) Mendel Elkin, Daniel Leibl, and Uri Ẓevi Greenberg. Jerusalem, J.N.U.L., Schwadron Collection.

though at times overladen with pathos. Rehabilitated after Stalin's death, his poems were again published in 1957, not in the original Yiddish, but in a rendering into Russian by 42 different translators who thus joined in paying tribute to him. In 1959, his uncompleted poem *"Yerushe"* and in 1964, his prose epic *Dor Oys, Dor Ayn,* were published abroad in Yiddish. His novel of Polish Jewish heroism during World War II, *Trit fun Doyres* (1966), was published posthumously in Soviet Russia; ironically, the novel is replete with praise for the regime and political system.

Bibliography: Rejzen, Leksikon, 2 (1927), 348–53; LNYL, 5 (1963), 523–8; S. Niger, *Yidishe Shrayber in Sovet Rusland* (1958), 229–61; J. Glatstein, *In Tokh Genumen* (1947), 31–39; Baal-Machshoves, *Geklibene Verk* (1953), 302–6; S. Bickel, *Shrayber fun Mayn Dor* (1958), 287–304; *A Shpigl Oyf a Shteyn* (1964), 373–512, 751–6; C. Madison, *Yiddish Literature* (1968), 404–9; M. Vortman, *Peretz Markish* (1937); Shunami, Bibl, no. 3934. [E.SCH.]

MARKON, ISAAC DOV BER (1875–1949), Russian scholar and librarian. Markon was born in Rybinsk on the Volga and studied at the St. Petersburg University under D. *Chwolson and at the *Hildesheimer Rabbinical Seminary and University of Berlin. He was librarian at the Imperial Public Library in St. Petersburg (1901–17), instructor at the Higher Courses of Oriental Studies (1908–11), instructor and later professor of Jewish studies at the university in St. Petersburg (1917–20), and professor at the Belorussian University at Minsk (1922–24). He also served for a time on the scholars' advisory committee for the Czarist Ministry of Education. For four years he was an editor of the Russian Jewish encyclopedia *Yevreyskaya Entsiklopediya* and planned the publication of a new encyclopedia, *Oẓar ha-Yahadut,* of which a prospectus appeared in 1914. He founded and edited the quarterly *Ha-Kedem* (with A. Sarzowski) which appeared from 1907 to 1909 in Hebrew and German. Markon left Russia for Berlin in 1926 where he joined the editorial staff of the *Encyclopaedia Judaica* and the *Eshkol Enẓiklopedyah Yisre'elit,* in charge of the departments of *Karaism and bibliography. For a time he also lectured at the Rabbinical Seminary. In 1928 Markon was appointed librarian of the Hamburg Jewish community. As he was a Jewish Soviet citizen, he was expelled from Germany in 1938. He went first to Holland and in 1940 escaped to England, where he joined the Montefiore College at Ramsgate.

Markon's first step in Jewish scholarship was his prize-winning comparison of Christian canonical with talmudic and Karaite marriage law (Russ., 1901). In the same field are his *Mekorot le-Korot Dinei Nashim* (about

Isaac Dov Ber Markon, scholar. Jerusalem, J.N.U.L., Schwadron Collection.

laws relating to women) 1, pt. 1 (1908) and various editions of Karaite works. Markon also published a study of the Slavonic glosses in the *Or Zaru'a* by Isaac b. Moses of Vienna (1906). With D. Guenzburg he edited the *Festschrift . . . A. Harkavy* (1908). Autobiographical reminiscences by Markon appeared in *Meẓudah* (2 (1944), 187ff.; 3 (1945), 341ff.; 4–6 (1948), 474ff.) as well as in some of his letters in G. Kressel (ed.) *Genazim* (1 (1961), 244ff.).

Bibliography: Kressel, Leksikon, 2 (1967), 429. [Ed.]

MARKOVA, ALICIA (Dame Lilian Alicia Marks; 1910–), ballerina. Born in London, she joined Diaghilev's company at the age of 14. After Diaghilev's death in 1929, she appeared at the Camargo Society in London, at Marie *Rambert's Ballet Club, and at Sadler's Wells. She and Anton Dolin were the first stars of the Vic-Wells Ballet in 1933 and two years later they formed the Markova-Dolin Company, Light, precise, and commanding great technique, she won recognition as a classical dancer, and played

Alicia Markova in "The Dying Swan." Courtesy D. Marks, London. Photo Jack Blake, London.

a major role in the growth of modern ballet in England. She was with the Ballet Russe de Monte Carlo (1938–41); Ballet Theatre, U.S. (1941–46); was co-founder of the Festival Ballet (1952), and made guest appearances with the Royal Danish Ballet, the Royal Ballet, and at the Metropolitan Opera.

She was created a Dame of the British Empire (1963) and became director of the Metropolitan Opera Ballet, New York (1963); Markova became professor of ballet at the University of Cincinnati (1970). She told much of her own story in *Giselle and I* (1960).

Bibliography: A. Chujoy and P. W. Manchester, *Dance Encyclopedia* (1967), 603–5; C. W. Beaumont, *Complete Book of Ballets* (1937), index; A. Haskell, *Ballet* (1938), 199. [Ed.]

MARKS, HAYMAN (1772–1825), early U.S. merchant and Mason. Marks, whose place of birth is unknown, was among the early Jewish settlers of Richmond, Va. Mention of him is found in several documents involving litigation. A well-known citizen of Richmond, he was one of the signers of a petition to the Virginia legislature asking for the incorporation of a bank there. Marks later moved to Philadelphia, where he became active in Congregation Mikveh Israel, ultimately becoming its president (1815–18). Marks was known to be a member of the Masonic fraternities of both Richmond and Philadelphia. His wife was Grace Judah, of the New York *Judah family. [Ed.]

MARKS, MARCUS M. (1858–1934), U.S. clothing manufacturer, civic official, and philanthropist. Marks was born in Schenectady, N. Y., and joined his father's clothing manufacturing firm, M. Marks and Son, which he later headed (1890–1913). From 1913 to 1917 Marks served as Manhattan borough president under the reforming mayor John P. Mitchel, establishing open public markets, welfare work, and joint trial boards for civil service employees. He was active in a variety of public causes. He was president of the National Daylight Association in 1917. As president of the National Association of Clothiers, he promoted the idea of cooperation among merchants, particularly in labor relations. As a member of Theodore Roosevelt's Nobel Prize Committee on Industrial Peace, Marks mediated many labor disputes. He was a founder and leader of several peace groups, of the Educational Alliance, of the Hospital Saturday and Sunday Association, and of the Tuberculosis Preventorium for children. An advocate of university exchange study between the U.S. and Europe, he served as chairman of the selection committee of the Institute of International Education. [Ed.]

MARKS, SAMUEL (1845–1920), South African industrialist and financier. Marks, who was born in Neustadt-Sugrind, Lithuania, emigrated to the Cape in 1868. With the Lewis brothers, he founded the firm of Lewis and Marks, which eventually controlled large industrial and mining undertakings in the Transvaal. The partners began as traveling traders ("tochers"). When diamonds were discovered they moved to Kimberley, where they opened the first general store in a prefabricated wooden building brought from the Cape by wagon. Lewis and Marks established themselves in the Transvaal in the 1880s, first on the Barberton gold workings and later on the Rand and in Pretoria. Marks, who was popularly known as Sammy, was noted for his salty humor and his fondness for biblical quotations. He understood the Boer outlook, particularly that of his friend President Kruger. He assisted the

Transvaal government financially, obtained industrial concessions, and acquired land on the Vaal River on which he founded the town of Vereeniging. He developed rich coal deposits in the area, established fruit farms, and planted

Samuel Marks, South African pioneer and financier. Courtesy Fieldhill Publishing Co., Johannesburg.

extensive forests. He also started the manufacture of bricks, glass, and leather goods and pioneered the steel industry. In 1897 Marks accompanied a deputation to Kruger asking, with indifferent results, for the repeal of laws which placed disabilities upon Jews in common with other non-Protestants and *uitlanders* ("foreigners"). In the conflict between the Boers and the British he commanded the respect of leaders on both sides and was a mediator in the negotiations which ended the South African War in 1902. He served as a senator in the first Union Parliament in 1910. Marks donated £10,000 for the statue of President Kruger which now stands in the center of Pretoria. In 1896 he helped endow the first chair in Hebrew studies at the South African College, later the University of Cape Town, and in 1905 founded a Hebrew school in Pretoria.

Bibliography: L. Herrman, *History of the Jews in South Africa* (1935); P. H. Emden, *Randlords* (1935), index; G. Saron and L. Hotz (eds.), *Jews in South Africa* (1955).

[Ed.]

MARKS, SIMON, LORD (1888–1964), industrialist and philanthropist. Born in Manchester, Simon Marks was the son of Michael Marks, who emigrated in 1882 from Russia to the U.K. where he began as a peddler. In 1884 he opened a market stall in Leeds and later a number of Penny Bazaars in the Midlands. They grew into the great multiple-store chain of Marks & Spencer Ltd. Simon Marks was elected chairman of the board in 1917 and from then on, until he died at his office desk, steered the firm to phenomenal commercial and financial success. His close business associate was Israel Moses (later Lord) *Sieff; they had

Simon Marks (extreme right) at a conference in Washington, D.C., c. 1937. With him are (right to left) Sir Herbert Samuel, Stephen Wise, and Lord Bearsted. Courtesy Yad Vashem Archives, Jerusalem. Photo Underwood and Underwood, Washington, D.C.

married each other's sisters. The high quality of their goods and business probity set a tradition in British retail merchandising. Indeed it was said that they were largely responsible for a quiet revolution in British life by raising living standards through making high quality goods available at popular prices.

From their mid-20s Marks and Sieff were loyal and devoted supporters of Chaim *Weizmann in his Zionist activities originally in Manchester and later in London, and were joined by other members of their families. In 1919 Marks went as secretary of the Zionist delegation to the Versailles Peace Conference. Later he became chairman of the Keren Hayesod Committee, vice-president of the Zionist Federation and in 1950 was elected a member of the Zionist Executive. He was president of the Joint Palestine Appeal at his death. Marks participated with Weizmann and the Zionist leadership in political negotiations with successive British governments and in other Zionist efforts until the State of Israel was established. He and Lord Sieff were leading contributors to the Daniel Sieff Research Institute (1934) and later in the Weizmann Institute of Science (1949) both at Reḥovot, Israel. Their personal and family trust benefactions to public causes in Britain and Israel totaled tens of millions of pounds over six decades.

Marks rendered distinguished public service in the period between and during both world wars. He helped to found the Air Defense Cadet Corps in Britain in 1938 and headed wartime production coordination in the London and southeast England area. He was also an adviser to the Ministry of Petroleum Warfare and one of the first directors of British Overseas Airways. In 1944 he received a knighthood and 1961 was created a baron.

Bibliography: G. Rees, *St. Michael, A History of Marks and Spencer* (1969); I. Sieff, *The Memoirs of Israel Sieff* (1970).

[J.L.M.]

MARKSON, AARON DAVID (1882–1932), Hebrew author and educator. Born in Lithuania, Markson went to the United States in 1904, and taught Hebrew in New York and other cities. He contributed essays and stories to Hebrew periodicals, edited a miscellany *Mi-Keren Zavit* (1921), and translated Mark Twain's *The Prince and the Pauper* (1923). His writings were posthumously collected in *Kitvei A. D. Markson* (1938), which also contains autobiographical material, a brief memoir by his daughter, and evaluations of his work by several authors.

Bibliography: Waxman, Literature, 4 (1960^2), 1080; Kressel, Leksikon, 2 (1967), 430.

[Ei.S.]

MARKUS, LUDWIG (1798–1843), historian. Born in Dessau, Germany, he studied medicine, but abandoned it to take up philosophy and astronomy. In 1825 he moved to Paris, and from 1830 until 1838 he taught German at the Royal College at Dijon.

An active member of the Society for Jewish Culture and Science in Berlin, one of his lifelong passions was the study of the Falashas of Abyssinia. This earned him Heinrich *Heine's sobriquet, "King of Abyssinia." He wrote *Histoire des Wandales* (1836) in which he traced the rise and collapse of the Vandal empire in Africa, and in 1842, published *Géographie ancienne des états Barbaresques*. Suffering from recurrent fits of depression, Markus died penniless in a Paris insane asylum. Baroness de Rothschild paid for the funeral, and Heine wrote an obituary.

Bibliography: Elbogen, in: MGWJ, 81 (1937), 177–85; H. Heine, *Saemtliche Werke*, 14 (1964), 43–58.

[G.S.]

MARLI, SAMUEL (Raphael) BEN MAẒLI'AḤ (d. 1617), Italian rabbi and author. One of the outstanding scholars of Italy, Samuel, like his father, served in a variety of offices in the Mantua community and was in charge until his death of collecting funds for Ereẓ Israel. In 1587 he was appointed rabbi of the community and was apparently also the head of a yeshivah. According to S. D. Luzzatto his name means "of Arles." During the time Marli was rabbi, the Jews of Mantua were confined to a ghetto prepared for them at their own cost, and Marli was one of the members of the committee which dealt with matters affecting the ghetto. His signature is found on many of the community's documents and regulations. He was highly praised by the scholars of his time, and although he published no works, a few of his responsa and letters have been published in the works of his contemporaries and preserved in manuscript. Some of his *piyyutim* were published in the *Ayyelet ha-Shaḥar* and in the *Siddur mi-Berakhah* of Italian rite (Mantua, 1653), as well as later in Schirman's *Mivḥar ha-Shirah ha-Ivrit be-Italyah.* Marli prepared and may have published a special essay which is still in manuscript, "to demonstrate to the nations and princes that a Jew is not permitted to curse or to act wrongly toward any man." He is also mentioned among those who supplied Azariah dei Rossi with material for his *Me'or Einayim,* and was among the rabbis who forbade the use of the *mikveh* of Rovigo (Moses Porto in: *Palgei Mayim,* p. 55). Hananiah Eliakim Rieti composed a eulogy on his death.

Bibliography: Ghirondi-Neppi, 337; S. Simonsohn, *Toledot ha-Yehudim be-Dukkasut Mantovah,* 1 (1964), 649.

[Y.AL.]

°**MARLOWE, CHRISTOPHER** (1564–1593), English playwright. *The Jew of Malta* (c. 1590) portrays the monstrous Jew, Barabas; T. S. Eliot described the play as a savage farce. Indeed it has elements of melodrama and exaggeration which suggest that Marlowe was not completely serious in his portrayal of the Jew. Barabas is a rich merchant whose wealth is expropriated and whose house is turned into a nunnery by order of the governor of Malta. In revenge, Barabas indulges in an orgy of slaughter, poisoning his daughter Abigail, her lover, and many others. Malta being besieged by the Turks, Barabas enters upon a career of political intrigue, first betraying the island to the enemy and then plotting the destruction of the Turkish commander. But Barabas is himself betrayed and perishes in a boiling cauldron. The story represents a mingling of traditional anti-Semitism (in the Middle Ages the Jews were often charged with poisoning the wells) with the late 16th-century taste for the "political thriller." Barabas, a disciple of Machiavelli, practices political stratagems with a view to gaining power in the state. From this point of view his Jewishness is no more than incidental, the main interest being focused on his "Italian" villainy. Barabas' conspiracy with the Turks may have been suggested by the career of Joseph *Nasi. *The Jew of Malta* was almost certainly in Shakespeare's mind when he wrote *The Merchant of Venice* some years later. Like Shakespeare's Jew, Barabas has a beautiful daughter who becomes a Christian, and a comic servant, Ithamore, who directs the audience's laughter against the Jew. This latter feature may be a relic of the medieval religious drama in which the Devil was frequently accompanied by a comic figure, the Vice. In spite of his negative portrayal of the Jew, Marlowe undoubtedly projected into the portrait some of his own restlessness, as well as his notorious dislike of the Establishment.

Bibliography: J. L. Cardozo, *Contemporary Jew in the Elizabethan Drama* (1925); M. J. Landa, *Jew in Drama* (1926), index; H. Michelson, *Jew in Early English Literature* (1926), 70ff.; T. S. Eliot, *Selected Essays* (1932), 118–25; H. Sinsheimer, *Shylock* (1947), 51–54; H. Levin, *Overreacher: a Study of Christopher Marlowe* (1954), index; H. Fisch, *Dual Image* (1959), 25–29.

[H.F.]

MARMOR, KALMAN (1879–1956), Yiddish writer and literary scholar. Born in Mishagola, near Vilna, he left Russia in 1899 for Switzerland, where he studied at the universities of Freiburg and Berne. He was a founder of the World Union of Po'alei Zion, active in its American sector, and editor of its weekly, *Der Yidisher Kemfer.* In 1906, Marmor came to the U.S. and joined the Po'alei Zion; later, in 1914, he joined the American Socialist Party and in 1919 the American Labor Alliance, which became the Workers Party and later the Communist Party. Marmor began his literary career in 1901 in *Der Yidisher Arbeter,* published by the Bund, and contributed to Yiddish periodicals in Europe and the U.S. In 1922, he joined the New York Yiddish Communist daily *Morning Freiheit* and remained a contributor until his death.

From 1933 to 1936, Marmor lived in Kiev, working in the Institute for Jewish Studies of the Ukrainian Academy of Sciences. While at the Institute, he prepared editions of the works of Aaron *Liebermann, Joseph *Bovshover, and David *Edelstadt. His monograph about Liebermann, as well as the collection of Liebermann's works which he annotated and translated into Yiddish, were lost when the Institute was liquidated by the Soviet government in 1936. He rescued only Liebermann's letters, which were later published in New York. The first two volumes of his edition of the works of David Edelstadt, written from an extreme party point of view, were published in Moscow in 1935. The manuscript of the third volume found its way to the YIVO Institute in New York. After the liquidation of the Kiev Institute and the arrest of its personnel, Marmor, as an American, was allowed to return to the U.S.

Marmor was a productive writer, an able researcher and collector of historical material, but he lacked the talent for critical evaluation. His publications include: *Der Onhoyb fun der Yidisher Literatur in Amerike* (1944); *Joseph Bovshover* (1952); *Dovid Edelshtat* (1950); *Jacob Gordin* (1953); and an autobiography, *Mayn Lebns-Geshikhte* (1959). Marmor also edited the complete works of Morris Vinchevsky, in ten volumes.

Bibliography: Rejzen, Leksikon, 2 (1927), 491–500; LNYL, 6 (1965), 113–9; A. Pomerantz, *Di Sovetishe Harugey Malkhus* (1962), 360–85.

[E.SCH.]

MARMOREK, ALEXANDER (1865–1923), bacteriologist and Zionist leader. He was born in Mielnice, Galicia, and studied in Vienna and at the Pasteur Institute in Paris, where he became assistant and subsequently *chef de travaux.* Early in his studies, he discovered an antidote (antistreptococcus) against puerperal fever. In 1903 he addressed the Paris Académie de Médecine and claimed the discovery of the toxin of the tubercle-bacillus and of the antituberculosis vaccine. This discovery was hotly debated

Alexander Marmorek, bacteriologist and Zionist leader. Jerusalem, J.N.U.L., Schwadron Collection.

in expert circles and was finally accepted as an invariably successful cure if prescribed up to a certain stage of the disease. With this discovery, Marmorek also initiated the serum study that led to the modern treatment of typhus and diabetes. Marmorek was also an ardent Zionist. In Vienna he belonged to *Kadimah, the first students' society to join *Herzl after the publication of *Der Judenstaat.* With his brothers Oscar and Isidor, he belonged to the circle of Herzl's closest friends and was repeatedly consulted on political steps contemplated by the Zionist leader. He was elected member of the Zionist General Council at the first 11 Zionist congresses (1897–1913). After Herzl's death Marmorek remained an adherent of Herzl's political Zionism and, next to Max *Nordau, became the foremost spokesman of the opposition, when "practical" Zionists assumed the movement's leadership in 1911. After World War I he strongly opposed *Weizmann's policies and refused to participate at the 12th Zionist Congress (1921). In his articles and speeches he emphasized that the Palestine Mandate was not the fulfillment of Herzl's idea of a Jewish state. Marmorek was chairman of the French Zionist Federation and one of the co-founders of *L'Echo Sioniste,* the Zionist monthly published in Paris. He founded the Jewish Popular University in Paris, chiefly for the benefit of foreign Jews who settled there. As a foreign national he was unable to remain in Paris during World War I and served as a doctor with the Allied armies in Eastern Europe.

His brother OSCAR (1863–1909) was an architect and Zionist leader. Born in Skala, Galicia, he studied in Vienna and Paris. He built a great number of important buildings in Vienna and Austria and also some synagogues, in which he attempted a style based on his studies of old Jewish architecture. He attained fame through his pavilion "Venice in Vienna" at the world exhibition of 1900 in Vienna.

Oscar Marmorek joined Herzl after the publication of *Der Judenstaat* and was elected to the Zionist Executive at the first six Zionist congresses. He was a co-founder of *Die *Welt.* Herzl depicted him in *Altneuland* as Architect Steineck. He died by his own hand.

Bibliography: D. Jacobson, *A. Marmorek* (Fr., 1923); JC (July 20, 1923); *Die Welt* (April 16, 1909); L. Jaffe, *Sefer ha-Congress* (1950), 339–40; M. I. Bodenheimer, *Prelude to Israel* (1963), index; M. Schach, *Asher Ittam Hithalakhti* (1951), 123–42. [O.K.R.]

MARMORSTEIN, ARTHUR (1882–1946), rabbi, scholar, and teacher. Born in Miskolc, Hungary, Marmorstein was descended from a long line of Hungarian rabbis known not only for their talmudic learning but also for their familiarity with secular literature. He studied at the yeshivah of Pressburg and the rabbinic seminaries of Budapest and Berlin. After visiting libraries for some time in England, Italy, and France, transcribing manuscripts, Marmorstein served for six years as rabbi at Jamnitz (Jemnice), Czechoslovakia. From 1912 until his death he taught at Jews' College, London. Marmorstein's scholarship embraced many subjects. His initial training at the universities was in Semitics, with special emphasis on Assyriology. He was particularly fascinated by the aggadic sections of the Talmud and by liturgy. Though Marmorstein contributed to many areas of Jewish scholarship, he is noteworthy for his studies in rabbinic theology, the subject of his two important volumes *Doctrine of Merits in Old Rabbinic Literature* (1920) and *Old Rabbinic Doctrine of God* (2 pts., 1927); both were reprinted in one volume with an introduction by R. J. Zwi Werblowsky (1968). Other important essays on rabbinic theology by Marmorstein were collected and published under the title *Studies in Jewish Theology* (1950). Marmorstein's work is characterized by painstaking detail in the collection of sources, which are important for the study of rabbinic religion.

Bibliography: E. Marmorstein, in: *A. Marmorstein, Studies in Jewish Theology: Marmorstein Memorial Volume* (1950), xv–xlvi (incl. bibl.). [A.T.]

MAROR (Heb. מָרוֹר), the traditional "bitter herb" which the children of Israel were commanded to eat with unleavened bread and the paschal offering both in Egypt (Ex. 12:8) and "throughout their generations" (Num. 9:11). The plural, *merorim,* occurs in the Bible in the verse: "He hath filled me with *merorim,* he hath sated me with wormwood" (Lam. 3:15), referring to a bitter vegetable, parallel to wormwood (cf. Deut. 32:32). The rabbis included under *merorim* plants whose common features are: "bitterness, possessing sap, with a grayish appearance" (Pes. 39a), meaning wild or cultivated vegetables, with leaves of a silvery-grayish-green color, that have a milk-like sap and leaves with a bitter taste. This definition can apply to a number of plants, particularly some of those belonging to the family of Compositae. Thus the Tosefta and the Talmud *(ibid.)* enumerate a number of such vegetables with which the duty of eating *maror* on the night of the *seder* can be fulfilled. The Mishnah enumerates five: *ḥazeret* ("*lettuce"); *olshin* ("chicory," see *vegetables); *tamkah* (according to Maimonides "wild chicory" but impossible to identify with certainty); *ḥarḥavina,* a plant of the family of Umbelliferae, of which the most common is *Eryngium creticum;* and *maror.* Some of the Compositae are called *murār* or *marāra* in Arabic. In the Jerusalem Talmud *maror* is described as a "bitter vegetable with a silvery appearance, and possessing sap" (Pes. 2:5, 29c; the same description as the Babylonian Talmud gives for all the varieties of *merorim*). These characteristics agree most with the plant *Sonchus oleraceus,* called in Arabic *murār.* This is a weed, widespread in gardens, fallow fields, and on the roadsides throughout Israel. Its soft leaves are at times eaten as salad by the poor, some also eating the juicy root. The plant is filled with a milk-like sap, the underside of the leaves is a bluish-silvery

Maror in an illumination from the *Sarajevo Haggadah,* Spain, 14th century. The bunch of lettuce in the shape of an artichoke indicates that a graphic tradition of the artichoke as *maror* may have survived when the plant was no longer used. Sarajevo National Museum, fol. 27.

color, and the green plant has a bitter taste and is hardly edible. According to Pliny "this is a healthy food, recommended as a remedy for various ailments" (*Historia Naturalis* 22:88–90; 26:163). The Samaritans use only the leaves of the wild lettuce *Lactuca scariola* for *maror*.

See also *Seder.

Bibliography: Loew, Flora, 1 (1928), 415–20, 424–40; H.N. and A.L. Moldenke, *Plants of the Bible* (1952), 74f., nos. 62–67; J. Feliks, *Kilei Zera'im ve-Harkavah* (1967), 57–60; J. Feliks, *Olam ha-Ẓome'aḥ ha-Mikra'i* (1968²), 194–6. [J.F.]

°**MARR, WILHELM** (1818–1904), German anti-Semite. Marr started his political career in the 1848 social protest movement in his native Hamburg, later joining an anarchist atheistic group in Switzerland as an exile. His 1862 anti-Semitic pamphlet *Der Judenspiegel* ("Jews' Mirror") was followed by the influential "The Victory of Judaism over Germandom, Considered from a Non-Religious Point of View," reaching its 12th edition in 1879. The religious issue was replaced by racism, the words Jews and Judaism by "Semite" and "Semitism" which, with the prefix "anti," were to gain general currency. He epitomized the current slogans of Jewish economic and cultural domination. Having first brought racist ideas to a wide audience, Marr introduced in 1879 the word "anti-Semite" into the political vocabulary by founding the League of Anti-Semites (Antisemiten-Liga), which organized lectures and published a short-lived monthly. The "league" failed as an organization, but it was historically important for it was the first effort of creating a popular political movement based on anti-Semitism. His later anti-Semitic pamphlets were poorly received and he retired from political agitation. Marr exerted a decisive influence upon T. *Fritsch and other anti-Semites. There is no proof for the often repeated assertion that he was of Jewish origin.

Bibliography: P. W. Massing, *Rehearsal for Destruction* (1946), 6–10; A. Bein, in: *Between East and West. Essays Dedicated to . . . Bela Horovitz* (1958), 165, 173; P. G. J. Pulzer, *The Rise of Political Anti-Semitism in Germany and Austria* (1964), 47–52, 95, 113; M. Meyer, in: YLBI, 11 (1966), 142–5; *Treitschke's History of Germany in the 19th Century*, 7 (1919), 304f. [T.O.]

MARRAKESH, one of the former capitals of *Morocco, situated at the foot of the High Atlas Mountains in a palm forest. Marrakesh was founded in 1062 by Yūsuf ibn Tāshifīn (reigned 1061–1107), a ruler of the *Almoravides. A Jewish community was established there. However, Ibn Tāshifīn's son and successor, Ali (1106–43), forbade the Jews of Aghmat-Ailan, an important commercial center further to the east which was exclusively inhabited by wealthy Jews, to live in Marrakesh, under penalty of death. The Jewish community was reconstituted in 1232—after it had been devastated earlier by the Almohads in 1147; its members were later massacred in the course of a revolt. After the conquest of southern Morocco by Abu Yūsuf the Merinid in 1269, Jews once more settled in Marrakesh. The community was headed by R. Judah Djian (d. c. 1310) of Jaén (southern Spain).

In 1492 and 1496 a large number of Jewish refugees from Spain, and especially from Portugal, immigrated to Marrakesh, but the nucleus of the community still consisted of Atlas Jews. During the 16th century, however, many Marranos immigrated to Marrakesh, which then became an important center of reconversion to Judaism for the New Christians. The Spanish-Portuguese Jews thus gained control of the entire community, which their descendants thereafter continued to dominate. For a long time they lived in two quarters of their own and were completely separated from their autochthonous coreligionists, who were mainly to be found in the Mawasin quarter. In 1557 the sultan al-Ghālib Billah concentrated all the Jews in the mellah. They numbered more than 25,000. One year later an epidemic of cholera killed 7,500 people. After this catastrophe, the community enjoyed a great period of prosperity. It lent an extremely large sum of money to the ruler ʿAbd al-Malik and was largely responsible for his enthronement in Marrakesh in 1576. Under the rule of the Saʿdian sharifs (1523–1659) the Jews of Marrakesh and their agents along the coast monopolized the principal industries and the commerce of Morocco. All the sharifs chose their physicians, bankers, advisers, and ambassadors from the Jewish upper classes. At the close of the period of Saʿdian rule, a Jew governed Marrakesh. In 1675 Mulay Ismāʿīl the Alawid allowed his soldiers to plunder Marrakesh because its population had supported his rebel nephew, and the Jews were subjected to all manner of atrocities.

Having lost its role as the capital, Marrakesh nevertheless retained its economic importance. Its Jews, especially after 1745, lived in better conditions than anywhere else in Morocco. Muhammad ibn Abdallah (1757–1790) established the seat of his government there. The favorite of this sultan was Samuel Sunbal, who lived in Marrakesh and was a scholarly kabbalist; he promoted Torah studies there. The flourishing yeshivot of the town were headed by talmudic scholars such as R. Abraham *Corcos, *av bet din* from 1735 to 1780, and his student Abraham *Pinto, or by kabbalists such as R. Solomon Amar, R. Abraham Azulai, and R. Shalom Buzaglo. Many foreigners also came to study under these teachers, e.g., the kabbalist Ḥiyya Cohen de Lara (d. 1738) of Amsterdam who completed his studies in Marrakesh.

The community was cruelly persecuted when Mulay Yazīd seized the town in 1792. Traditionally, the Jewish community was governed by the same families, of which the Corcos family was one. In spite of the favors which the

Figure 1. Ḥanukkah lamp from Marrakesh, 19th century, brass with colored glass, width 8½ in. (22 cm.). Jerusalem, Israel Museum. Photo David Harris, Jerusalem.

Figure 2. Etching of Marrakesh, with "The Jewes Churches" on the extreme right (H), and "The gate of ye Jewes dwellings" on the extreme left (K). From *Africa* by John Ogilby, London, 1670. D. Corcos Collection, Jerusalem. Photo Anatol Lewkowicz, Jerusalem.

sharifs bestowed upon certain Marrakesh Jews, the community never regained the general prosperity which it had enjoyed during the period of the Saʿdian sharifs. In addition to 200 or 300 wealthy families, some of whom even lived in opulence, there were 2,000 families who barely earned their livelihood and a further 2,000 who were poverty-stricken. This situation persisted until modern times. Until 1920 the mellah of Marrakesh was the largest in Morocco and was the center of considerable activity. During the 19th century the Jewish population increased by the arrival of groups from Jewish communities from the Atlas region, where they had lived in insecurity. [D.Co.]

Contemporary Period. The 1951 census indicated 16,392 Jews in Marrakesh. There were 10,007 Jews in Marrakesh according to the 1960 census. After the Six-Day War, and the various attacks on Jews throughout Morocco, there was a mass exodus from the town. Prior to this there had been (since 1899) Alliance schools in Marrakesh, attended by 3,026 pupils in 1953, and an Oẓar ha-Torah school, with 350 pupils in 1961. There were also Lubavicher, ORT, and other educational institutions, bringing the total number of pupils to 4,392 in 1961. In 1970 the community of Marrakesh consisted of a few hundred people who had long since left the mellah and whose material situation was particularly favorable. [H.J.C.]

Bibliography: J. Benech, *Essai d'explication d'un Mellah—Marrakech* (1949); D. Corcos, in: JQR, 54 (1963/64), 287; 55 (1964/65), 53–54; idem, in: *Sefunot*, 10 (1966), 90–93; Hirschberg, Afrikah, index; Miège, Maroc, index; Chouraqui, *Between East and West* (1968), index.

MARRANO, term of opprobium used to denigrate the New Christians of Spain and Portugal. Various origins for the term have been suggested. These include the Hebrew *marit ayin* ("the appearance of the eye"), referring to the fact that the Marranos were ostensibly Christian but actually Judaizers; *moḥoram attah* ("you are excommunicated"); the Aramaic-Hebrew *Mar Anus* ("Mr. forced convert"); the Hebrew *mumar* ("apostate") with the Spanish ending *ano;* the Arabic *mura'in* ("hypocrite"); and the second word of the ecclesiastical imprecation *anathema maranatha*. However, all such derivations are unlikely. The most probable, as clearly shown by Farinelli's study, is from the Spanish word meaning swine, a word already in use in the early Middle Ages, though Y. Malkiel argues plausibly for a derivation from the late Arabic *barrān, barrānī*, meaning an outsider or stranger, and a coalescence of this word with the term marrano "pig, pork" derived from Latin *verres* "wild boar." The term probably did not originally refer to the Judaizers' reluctance to eat pork, as some scholars hold. From its earliest use, it was intended to impart the sense of loathing conveyed by the word in other languages. Although romanticized and regarded by later Jewry as a badge of honor, the term was not as widely used, especially in official circles, as is often believed. In Latin America as a rule it is not found in official documents and there is little evidence of its unofficial use in most places.

See also **Anusim; *Chuetas;* *New Christians; *Conversos.

Bibliography: Roth, Marranos, 27f.; A. Farinelli, *Marrano: storia di un vituperio* (1925), 36; Y. Malkiel, in: JOAS, 68 (1948), 175–84. [Ma.C.]

MARRANO DIASPORA. *New Christians began to leave *Spain in the wake of the mass conversions of 1391 and *Portugal after the forced conversions in 1497. The tide of emigration ebbed and flowed, but was always stimulated by the advent of new disasters, such as the introduction of the *Inquisition into Spain in 1481 and Portugal in 1536, and the recrudescence of intensive persecution of the Marranos, as in Portugal after 1630. To stem this continuing exodus, as early as the last decade of the 15th century the authorities in both countries issued decrees prohibiting the emigration of New Christians, and these were frequently renewed. Even the so-called irrevocable permission to emigrate which the New Christians purchased from Philip III in 1601, during the union of Spain and Portugal, was short-lived, being rescinded in 1610. However, these decrees were frequently evaded: Marranos regularly left the Peninsula clandestinely, or secured permission to take business trips abroad from which they never returned. There are even cases of their leaving for the ostensible purpose of making a pilgrimage to Rome. Once the authorities became aware of such stratagems they tried to intercept Marranos as they moved through Europe to places where they could practice Judaism openly, and men like Jean de la Foix in Lombardy acquired notoriety for his inhuman treatment of those who fell into his hands. There were even instances where the highest authorities in the Peninsula closed their eyes to New Christian emigration, particularly when it involved their settling in *Latin America, where their skills and enterprise were desperately needed. Furtively and openly, in trickles and in torrents, thousands of New Christians left the Iberian Peninsula during the nearly three and a half centuries of the Inquisition's power.

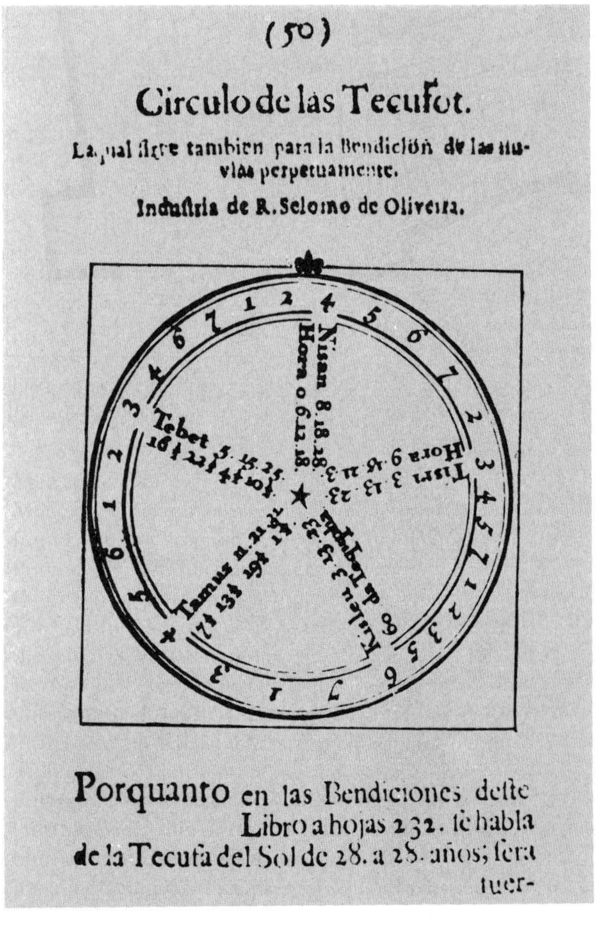
(50)

Circulo de las Tecuſot.

La qual ſirve tambien para la Bendición de las lluvias perpetuamente.

Induſtria de R. Selomo de Oliveira.

Porquanto en las Bendiciones deſte Libro a hojas 232. ſe habla de la Tecuſa del Sol de 28. a 28. años; ſera tuer-

Figure 1. Calendar page from the *Orden De Bendiciones,* a prayer book for Marranos who had returned to Judaism. Amsterdam, 1687. Cecil Roth Collection.

Not all the New Christians leaving the Peninsula were secret Jews. Many were devout Catholics and had no intention of changing their faith; others were religiously ambivalent or even apathetic. Some of these may have shared the general insecurity of all New Christians in the Peninsula; some may have feared implication in inquisitional proceedings because of the activities of their relatives or friends; some may have wished to hide their Jewish origins in foreign lands; and others may simply have been attracted by new challenges and opportunities. It was people like these who evoked apologies for Judaism such as Samuel *Usque's classic *Consolaçam às tribulaçoens de Israel* (1553; *Consolation for the Tribulations of Israel,* 1965), intended to persuade them to return to their ancestral religion. At the same time, considerable numbers of the New Christians were Marranos, or secret Jews, and were passionately dedicated to Judaism. This was particularly true of the Portuguese New Christians. By the 16th century the term "Portuguese" was already synonymous with the word "Jew" in much of Europe, Asia, and Latin America. During the Inquisition's extended sway over the Peninsula, the emigrating Marranos could plan to travel to four different kinds of countries: Muslim lands, Protestant territories as they came into being, Catholic countries outside the jurisdiction of Spain and Portugal, and Catholic countries within the peninsular orbit.

Muslim Countries. These were the most natural places of refuge for Marranos seeking to live openly as Jews, for they were the archenemies of the Christians and Spain and Portugal were particularly hated. *Morocco had already become a haven of refuge for both Jews and Conversos at the end of the 14th century, but many more Jews and Marranos were attracted to the *Ottoman Empire at the end of the 15th century and during the 16th. Sultan *Bayazid II (Bajazet II; 1481–1512) mocked King Ferdinand for impoverishing Spain and enriching the Ottoman Empire through his expulsion of the Jews. In the 16th century numerous cities in the Ottoman Empire had Jewish settlements, among them *Cairo, *Jerusalem, *Safed, *Damascus, *Constantinople with some 50,000 Jews, and *Salonika where the population of the Marranos exceeded that of the other Jews and the non-Jews as well.

Protestant Countries. Next to the Muslim countries the Protestant lands offered the best prospects, for here too the Catholics were detested, and the Inquisition was a hated institution because it was no more tolerant of Protestant heretics than Judaizers. In places like *England and *Hamburg and other German cities, Marranos began their existence as titular Catholics and secret Jews before the Reformation. They continued in this double life long after those areas had broken with Rome, for the Protestant authorities were not eager to grant official acknowledgment to the presence of Jews in their midst. In Hamburg, destined to become one of the wealthiest and most productive Marrano centers, the settlement of Jews was not officially authorized until 1612 and Jewish public worship not until 1650. In England, where Jews had been expelled in 1290, the Marranos who settled originally in *London and *Bristol were never officially acknowledged as Jews. Spokesmen for the Marranos, both Christians and Jews, including *Manasseh Ben Israel, failed in their efforts to secure the formal recognition of Jewish resettlement. Rather than being officially granted, the resettlement was "connived at": the question was simply ignored and Marranos were allowed to live undisturbed as Jews. Actually this connivance, or de facto resettlement through official silence, proved salutary for the Jews, since the failure to grant official permission for

Figure 2. Meeting of Marranos in Oporto, Portugal, 1932. Capt. Barros Basto, organizer of the community, is seen at the left corner of the podium. Photo Edvardo Correia, Oporto.

their presence made it impossible to impose particular disabilities on them. From the middle of the 17th century at least, the Marranos were treated like all other nonconformist citizens. In 1664 the crown granted Jews an official charter of protection, thus further facilitating the development of the Marrano community. The ex-Marranos and their descendants continued to be the dominant element in British Jewry until the 19th century.

In *Amsterdam the Marranos did not arrive until around 1590, some 11 years after the Union of Utrecht (1579) and the birth of the United Provinces of the Netherlands as a Protestant state. Here too they had to wait until 1615 before Jewish settlement was officially authorized, but the Marranos in Amsterdam differed from those in other Protestant countries in that they openly practiced Judaism almost from the moment of their arrival. Thanks to the Marranos, Amsterdam became one of the greatest Jewish centers in the world in the 17th century; it had some of the finest academies and produced some of the greatest Jewish thinkers. Amsterdam was also a haven for oppressed Jews from other places, including France in 1615 and Eastern Europe after the *Chmielnicki massacres (from 1648). Erstwhile Marranos from Holland were among the first settlers in Surinam and Curaçao, where a substantial Sephardi community came into being after 1650. Other former Marranos were also found in Barbados and in other parts of the West Indies, including Martinique and the Leeward Islands.

Other Catholic Countries. The Catholic lands outside the control of Spain and Portugal did not offer so secure a haven as the Ottoman Empire or the Protestant countries, but they had the advantage of being outside the orbit of the peninsular Inquisitions. At the same time these areas were not without their inherent dangers, in the form of envy or rooted prejudice on the part of the local population, pressures from the Spanish and Portuguese Inquisitions upon the local authorities, and even the possibility of persecution galvanized by local initiative, and, in the case of the Papal States, an indigenous Inquisition. As a result, the existence of many of these Marrano communities, even if unclouded and prosperous for a time, was seldom free from molestations.

In the Papal States the Marranos' presence was noticeable in places like *Rome and even more so the seaport of *Ancona, where they thrived under benevolent popes like Clement VII (1523–34), Paul III (1534–49), and Julius III (1550–55). They even received a guarantee that if accused of apostasy they would be subject only to papal authority. But Paul IV (1555–59), the voice of the Counter-Reformation, dealt them an irreparable blow when he withdrew all protection previously given the Marranos and initiated a fierce persecution against them. As a result of the anti-Marrano campaign, 25 Judaizers were burned alive in the spring of 1556; 26 others were condemned to the galleys, and 30 more who had been arrested were liberated only after they had paid a substantial bribe. Thanks to the intervention of the Marrano patroness, Gracia Mendes *Nasi, the sultan at Constantinople secured the release of all Marranos who were his subjects. Plans were laid to boycott Ancona and transfer all the Marranos' former business to neighboring *Pesaro, in the friendlier territory of the duke of Urbino, but the project failed, and the duke even expelled the Marranos from his territory. A document of 1550 indicates that there were some Marranos among the Spanish and Portuguese merchants in Florence who traded on a large scale with Spain and her colonies. In *Ferrara, under the house of Este, the Marranos formed a large and thriving community by the middle of the 16th century, one of the most notable in their entire Diaspora. The dukes protected them until 1581, when Duke Alfonso II, bowing to ecclesiastical pressure, allowed many of them to be arrested. Three were eventually sent to Rome to be burned at the stake in February 1583. Marranos settled in *Venice in the 15th and early 16th centuries but were subjected to decrees of expulsion in 1497 and again in 1550. Thereafter the city policy began to change. Venice not only welcomed Marranos but kept the Inquisition at bay. Theologians like Paolo Sarpi even claimed that the Judaizers were outside the jurisdiction of the Inquisition because they had been baptized by force. Equally fortunate was the situation in the grand duchy of *Tuscany. In an attempt to woo the Marranos to Pisa and *Leghorn, Ferdinand II issued a charter in 1593 granting them protection against harassment in matters of faith. As it was in decline at the time, Pisa did not attract many Marranos, but Leghorn did: the community there thrived and by the end of the 18th century its population approached 5,000. Emmanuel Philbert granted a special privilege to induce Jews to settle in the duchy of Savoy, intending mainly to settle Marranos from Spain and Portugal in Nice in order to develop the city into a central trading port with the East. The privilege enraged Philip II of Spain, who considered the whole plan as seriously damaging Spain's interests in the Mediterranean as well as an incitement to Marranos to return to Judaism. The joint pressure of Spain and the Holy See led to the rescinding of the privilege and on Nov. 22, 1573 the duke ordered a group of Marranos who had returned to Judaism to leave his territory within six months. This decree was probably not put into effect until 1581 when Charles Emmanuel I ordered the expulsion of all Portuguese Jews from the duchy.

In *France the Marranos had to maintain some semblance of Catholicism for more than two centuries, but they were seldom molested in their secret practice of Judaism. Though they were called "New Christians" or "Portuguese merchants," their Jewishness was an open secret. In the large settlements they lived in their own quarters, had their own burial grounds, developed their own schools and communal institutions, and even trained their own rabbis after first importing them from abroad. In the course of time they gradually reduced their Catholic practices and eventually abandoned Church marriage and even baptism. In 1730 they were officially recognized as Jews. Their more formal communities were situated at *Bordeaux and *Bayonne and there were numerous lesser settlements in such places as *Toulouse, *Lyons, Montpellier, La *Rochelle, *Nantes, and *Rouen. Bayonne was the center of a cluster of communities, including *Biarritz, *Bidache, *Peyrehorade, and *Saint-Jean-de-Luz. In this last town the Marranos had the misfortune of being expelled in 1619, and then, after a partial return, seeing the town captured by the Spaniards in 1636.

Other Territories. But in the far-flung Spanish and Portuguese possessions, in the Aragonese territories of *Sicily, *Sardinia and *Naples, in *Hapsburg territories like Flanders, or the colonial territories in the Far East or in the Americas, the situation of the Marranos was always precarious. There they lived continually under the shadow of the Inquisition; even where a tribunal of the Holy Office was not in operation, there were episcopal Inquisitions and occasional inquisitional "visitors" sent from the home countries to galvanize the search for heretics. Sicily and Sardinia, with Inquisitions introduced in 1487 and 1493 respectively, were practically free of Judaizers by the middle of the 16th century. There was opposition to introducing the Spanish Inquisition into Naples, but the papal Inquisition took over and managed to destroy most of the Marrano community by the middle of the 17th century. The situation of the Marranos was no less precarious in *Antwerp, where they began to arrive early in the 16th century, frequently to begin a trek across Europe to the Ottoman Empire. In 1526 New Christians' stay in the city was restricted to a 30-day period and though settlement was fully authorized 11 years later, Judaizing was strictly prohibited. With the decline of Antwerp, the center of Marrano life in the Low Countries shifted to Amsterdam.

In their colonies the Portuguese set up an Inquisition at *Goa and the Spaniards established one in the *Philippines. Episcopal Inquisitions were always present in Latin America: *Brazil never had a formal tribunal, but tribunals were established in the Spanish colonies at Lima (*Peru, 1570), Mexico City (1571), and Cartagena (1610). Latin America in particular attracted considerable numbers of New Christians. The advantage of these territories was that they offered the New Christians a familiar culture and the possiblity of direct even if infrequent contact with the mother countries. For New Christians wishing to live fully as Catholics, the distances from the Peninsula and the sparseness of the population of most of the territories aided in the obliteration of the record of their Jewish origins. On the other hand, these factors also facilitated the Marranos' practice of Judaism.

Activities of the Marranos. Religious considerations were important in determining the direction of the flight of many of the Marranos, but they were not the only ones. Of great and sometimes decisive importance were the economic and social opportunities available in the various lands open to them at the time of their escape. These opportunities often made it more desirable for Marranos to continue living as secret Jews in Catholic lands (even those under Spanish and Portuguese domination) than to seek a refuge where they could practice Judaism openly. Conversely, in each of the territories where the Marranos—or for that matter all New Christians—appeared, they were allowed to enter and remain because they served definite economic, social, and political ends. In almost every one of their new homes they quickly rose to prominence in international and domestic trade, and banking and finance. They helped to establish great national banks and were prominent on the stock exchanges. They played an important role in large trading companies, such as the *Dutch East Indies and *West Indies Companies, and even in the rival company established at Portugal to help oust the Dutch from Brazil.. As well as insurance companies, they established manufacturing plants for soap, drugs, and other items, and made signal contributions in minting, handicrafts, armaments, and shipbuilding. In the area of international trade they assumed virtual dominance and controlled, frequently to the point of monopoly, the traffic in such commodities as coral, sugar, tobacco, and precious stones. The Marranos' common background and culture, their presence in the leading commercial centers, and often their ties of kinship, enabled them to establish an efficient and closely knit international trading organization. Great banking and trading families, like that founded by Francisco Mendes at Lisbon, had branches throughout Europe. The Marranos' international connections served to stimulate communications between nations and their separate competitive development. In this way the activities of the New Christians fostered the stability of their countries of settlement and facilitated their transition from a medieval to a modern economy. The Marranos also attained prominence in the professional life of the lands of their dispersion. From their midst came great diplomats like João Miguez, the duke of Naxos (Joseph *Nasi), and his mother-in-law, Gracia Mendes Nasi (Beatriz de Luna), who also distinguished herself as a great philanthropist and patron of the Jewish arts, as well as the equally colorful Diego *Texeira de Sampaio (Abraham Senior Texeira). The Marranos produced scientists like Immanuel Bocarro Frances, distinguished physicians like *Amatus Lusitanus (Juan Rodrigo), Elijah Montalto (Felipo Rodrigues), and Antonio Ribeiro Sanchez, and a host of other distinguished names in secular literature, theater, and music.

Reciprocally, many of the states and nations in their Diaspora gave the Marranos an opportunity to develop their own institutions and culture, The printing press became a foremost instrument in the development of this culture. Ferrara's press, which published the famous translation of the Bible into Spanish and Samuel Usque's *Consolaçam as tribulaçoens de Israel* in Portuguese in addition to liturgical and other works, was the center of Marrano culture in the middle of the 16th century. By the end of the 16th century, Venice had the leading press and in the next century it was situated in Amsterdam. Other cities, too, like Leghorn, Hamburg, and London, had important presses, and printing in numerous smaller places helped to spread further Jewish culture. Especially noteworthy is the extensive literature published by these presses. Including prayerbooks and sermons, books of precepts and customs, translations into Spanish and Portuguese of classics in Jewish philosophy and thought, apologetical works and polemics, and also novels, poetry, and plays, it was particularly directed toward the Marranos who had left the Iberian peninsula and sought to find themselves in Judaism, although still assailed by doubts.

Marrano writers of note are far too numerous to mention them all. Among the more important ones were such men as the apologists Immanuel *Aboab, Saul Levi *Morteira, Lorenzo *Escudero (Abraham Ger or Abraham Israel Peregrino), Isaac *Cardozo, Isaac *Orobio de Castro, and David *Nieto; poets like David *Abenatar Melo, Daniel *Lopez Laguna, Solomon Usque, João (Moses) *Pinto Delgado, and Daniel Levi (Miguel) de *Barrios; playwrights like Antonio Enriquez *Gomez and Antonio Jose da *Silva; and versatile writers like the prolific Joseph *Penso de la Vega, writer of plays, short stories, and one of the earliest and most comprehensive treatises on the stock exchange. Many Marranos also attained fame outside the Jewish fold. The aristocracy of many societies in Europe and the Americas was enriched by these people and their descendants. Frequently, like Benjamin *Disraeli, they attained the highest diplomatic, military, and administrative positions. Like their Jewish counterparts, they also made a name for themselves in the business and cultural world.

An authentic Marrano community was discovered by Samuel *Schwartz in Portugal in 1917; and from time to time there emerge individuals or even groups whose faith is not Jewish who have retained some of the practices and customs of the Marranos, at times even without awareness of their Jewish ancestry.

Bibliography: Roth, Marranos, 195–375; Roth, Italy; M. A. Cohen (translator), in: S. Usque, *Consolation for the Tribulations of Israel* (1965), 3ff.; idem, in: *The Jewish Experience in Latin America* (1971); idem, in: AJHSQ, 55 (1966), 277–318, 451–520; H. Kellenbenz, *Sephardim an der unteren Elbe* (1958); H. C. Lea, *The Inquisition in the Spanish Dependencies* (1908), esp. bibl.; H. J. Zimmels, *Die Marranen in der rabbinischen Literatur* (1932); Rosanes, Togarmah, 4–6 (1934–45 = *Korot ha-Yehudim be-Arzot ha-Kedem*); S. Ullmann, *Histoire des Juifs en Belgique*, 2 vols. (1932–34); J. S. da Silva Rosa, *Geschiedenis der portugeesche Joden te Amsterdam* (1925); S. Assaf, in: *Zion*, 5 (1932); I. S. Revah, in: REJ, 118 (1959/60), 30–77; see also works by J. T. Medina in bibliography to *Inquisition.

[Ma.C.]

MARRIAGE. This article is arranged according to the following outline.

THE CONCEPT

In Jewish teaching, marriage is the ideal human state and is considered a basic social institution established by God at the time of creation.

In The Bible. The purposes of marriage in the Bible are companionship and procreation: "It is not good that the man should be alone; I will make him a help meet for him . . . Therefore shall a man leave his father and his mother, and shall cleave unto his wife, and they shall be one flesh" (Gen. 2:18, 24); and "Be fruitful, and multiply, and replenish the earth . . ." (Gen. 1:28). The biblical conception of marriage is essentially monogamous (Gen. 2:24), and although in biblical times polygamy was common among the upper classes (Judg. 8:30; II Sam. 5:13; I Kings 11:1–8), the many references to marriage in the *Wisdom

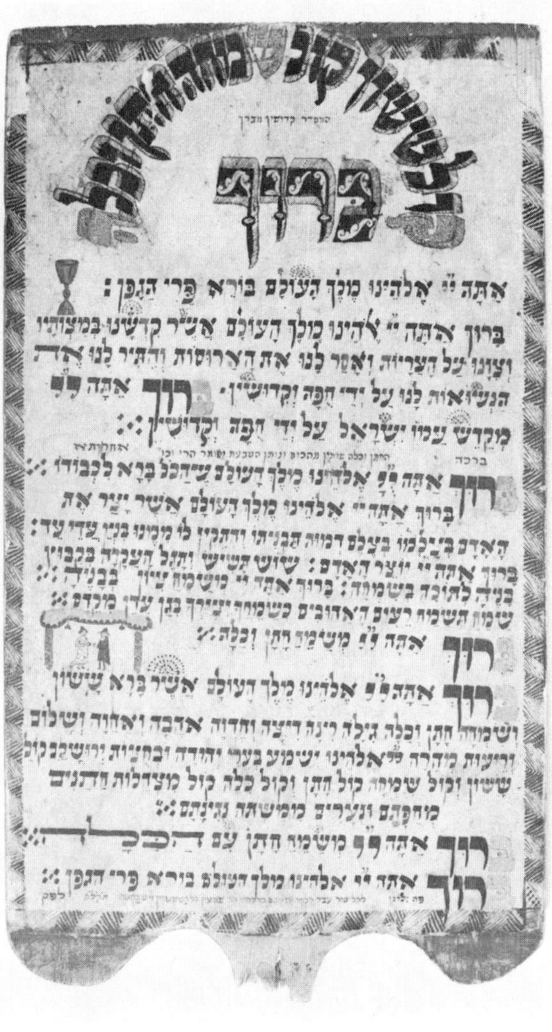

Figure 1. Blessings recited in the marriage ceremony, executed by Simon Glatstein, Bratislava area, 1771. The paper is mounted on a wooden frame, the handle of which has been broken. Jerusalem, Israel Museum, Feuchtwanger Collection, donated by Baruch and Ruth Rappaport. Photo R. Milon, Jerusalem.

Figure 2. A Frankfort bridal procession, with musicians preceding the bride, who walks under a canopy. Engraving by Peter Fehr from Schudt, *Juedische Merkwuerdigkeiten*, Frankfort on the Main, 1717.

literature seem to take it for granted that a man had only one wife (Ps. 128; Prov. 12:4; 18:22; 19:14; 31:10–31 Ecclus. 25:1; 26). The prophets using marriage as a metaphor for God's attachment to Israel (Isa. 61:10; 62:5; Ezek. 16; Hos. 2:21–22; also Song of Songs, if interpreted metaphorically) clearly have monogamous marriage in mind, since God did not enter into such a special relationship with any other people.

Marriages were usually arranged by parents (Gen. 21:21; 24; 28:2), but the bride's consent was asked on occasion (Gen. 24:5, 58), and romantic unions were not uncommon (Gen. 29:20; Judg. 14; I Sam. 18:20; II Sam. 11:2–4; I Kings 2:17; II Chron. 11:21). It was usual to marry within the clan (Gen. 24:4; 28:2; 29:19), and in a leviratic situation (*levirate marriage) this was obligatory (Gen. 38:9; Deut. 25:5; Ruth 3:12–13). Certain marriages, involving close relatives (Lev. 18; 20; Deut. 23:1–8; 27:20–23), priests, widows, and divorced women (Lev. 21:7; Deut. 24:4), are forbidden. While marriages outside the clan occurred, they were strongly opposed both as a measure against idolatry (Ex. 34:15–16; Deut. 7:3–4; 28:4), and to preserve Jewish distinctiveness (Ezra 9:12; 10:17; Neh. 10:31; 13:23–28). Fruitfulness in marriage is a great blessing and childlessness a tragedy and disgrace (Gen. 8:17; 9:1, 7; 13:16; 17–18; 22:17; 30:1–23; Ps. 127:3–5; 128). Marriage is the means to true companionship: "Whoso findeth a wife findeth a great good" (Prov. 18:22; cf. 12:4; 14:1; 19:14; 31:10–31); "live joyfully with thy wife whom thou lovest" (Eccles. 9:9). But where marital harmony no longer prevails (particularly in the case of the wife's *adultery), the marriage can be dissolved by *divorce (Deut. 24:1–4), though Malachi (2:14–16) warns that God deplores the resort to divorce.

In Sectarian Teaching. The Essenes in general rejected worldly pleasures, including marriage, and practiced continence (Jos., Wars, 2:120). The Covenanters of Qumran did not appear to have been strictly celibate as once was thought. It is clear that some members married and had children (*Zadokite Document*, 20:7–8; 13:20; *Damascus Document*, 4:7). The *Order of the Community* ruled that a young man should not have intercourse before 20 years of age (1:4–11). Archaeologists have found the remains of a few women and children at Qumran but it is not clear to what extent this indicates marriage. The New Testament has a negative attitude to the sexual impulse and regards celibacy as a higher ideal than marriage (Matt. 19:10; I Cor. 7). Marriage is a concession to human weakness (I Cor. 7), but once entered into, it is a sacrament dissolved only by death (Matt. 19:16; Mark 10:9); though some hold that Jesus allowed divorce in cases of adultery (Matt. 5:31–32; 19:9; Mark 10:12; Luke 16:18).

In Rabbinic Literature. In contrast, rabbinic teaching sees celibacy as unnatural. It is not he who marries who sins; the sinner is the unmarried man who "spends all his days in sinful thoughts" (Kid. 29b). Marriage is not only for companionship and procreation; it also fulfills one as a person: "He who has no wife is not a proper man" (Yev. 63a); he lives "without joy, blessing, goodness . . .Torah, protection . . .and peace" (Yev. 62b); he may not officiate as high priest on the Day of Atonement (Yoma 1:1), and probably not as **sheli'aḥ ẓibbur* on the High Holy Days (Isserles to Sh. Ar., OḤ 581:1, based on Yoma 1:1 and Yev. 37b). Sexual desire is not evil or shameful. When regulated and controlled in marriage, it serves beneficial ends: "Were it not for the *yeẓer ha-ra* ("evil inclination" here sexual urge), no man would build a house, marry a wife, or beget children" (Gen. R. 9:7). He who, by denying his legitimate instincts, fails to produce children "is as if he shed blood, diminished the Image of God, and made the *Shekhinah* depart from Israel" (Sh. Ar., EH 1:1, based on Yev. 63b–64a), and he will have to account for his actions in the world to come (Shab. 31a). Marriage is so important that a man may sell a Torah scroll in order to marry (Meg. 27a) and a woman will tolerate an unhappy marriage rather than remain alone (Yev. 113a, Kid 7a). One should never approach marriage lightly. To make a successful match is as hard as the parting of the Red Sea (Sot. 2a, et al.), and it requires the infinite wisdom of God himself (Gen. R. 68:3). Hence, although in one view a person's marriage is predestined (Sot. 2a), the individual must choose wisely: "Hasten to buy land; deliberate before taking a wife" (Yev. 63a). Marriage should not be for money (Kid. 70a), but a man should seek a wife who is mild-tempered, tactful, modest, and industrious (Sot. 3b), and who meets other criteria: respectability of family (Ta'an. 4:8; BB 109b), similarity of social background (Kid. 49a) and of age (Yev. 44a; Sanh. 76a–b), beauty (Ber. 57b; Yoma 74b), and a scholarly father (Pes. 49b). A man should not betroth a woman until he has seen her (Kid. 41a). Early marriage is preferred: "18 for marriage" (Avot 5:21). If one is not married by 20, God curses him (Kid. 29b–30a). Only a person intensively occupied in Torah study, e.g., *Ben Azzai, may postpone marriage (Yev. 63b; cf. Ket. 63a; Sot. 4b); though in Babylon it was suggested that one should first marry and then study (Kid. 29b). A practical order of procedure, derived from Deuteronomy (20:5–7) states; "First build a house, then plant a vineyard, and after that marry" (Sot. 44a). As far as a girl is concerned, if her father does not find her a husband while she is young (from the age of 12), she may become unchaste and he will have transgressed the commandment in Leviticus 19:29: "Profane not thy daughter to make her a harlot" (Sanh. 76a).

Polygamy, while theoretically still possible, was discouraged, and was almost unknown among talmudic rabbis. Marriage was not a sacrament in the Christian sense, since its dissolution through divorce, though regrettable, was possible. It is **kiddushin*, a sacred relationship (analogous to **hekdesh*), whereby the wife is consecrated to her husband and forbidden to all others during the duration of the marriage (Kid. 2a–b). At the same time, it is not a mere legal contract devoid of spiritual content. Thus, while the husband acquires rights over his wife's *ishut* ("wifehood"), though not over her person, and he undertakes duties toward her: e.g., supplying her with food and clothing, and adhering to the conjugal rights (Ex. 21:10), both parties must seek to raise their marriage to the highest level by means of mutual consideration and respect. The husband must deny himself in order to provide for his wife and children (Ḥul. 84b). He must not cause his wife to weep (BM 59a). If he loves her as himself and honors her more

Figure 3. Engraving of an Ashkenazi marriage in Amsterdam, with the bridal couple standing beneath a *tallit*. From Bernard Picart, *Cérémonies et coutumes réligieuses de tous les peuples du monde*, Amsterdam, 1723.

Figure 4. "Marriage Ceremony of Portuguese Jews," a drawing by Bernard Picart, 1721, showing the groom about to break the glass by throwing it into a dish. Amsterdam, Stedelijk Museum.

Figure 5. Engraving of an 18th-century German wedding in the open, under a portable canopy. On the buttress of the synagogue is a *Traustein*, the "marriage stone" against which the bridegroom broke the traditional glass. From J. Bodenschatz, *Kirchliche Verfassung der heutigen Juden*, Frankfort and Leipzig, 1748.

than himself, he will merit the blessing in Job (5:24) "And thou shalt know that thy tent is in peace" (Yev. 62b). If husband and wife are worthy, God will dwell with them; otherwise, there will be a consuming fire between them (Sot. 17a; PdRE 12). The rabbis, like the prophets, use marriage to symbolize other perfect relationships: e.g., God and Israel, Israel and the Torah, and Israel and the Sabbath.

In Medieval and Modern Times. The positive attitude of the rabbis to marriage was maintained in post-talmudic literature and Jewish practice. Asceticism and celibacy continued to be rare. Polygamy was finally prohibited among Ashkenazi Jews by a ban attributed to R. *Gershom b. Judah (see *Bigamy; *Monogamy). Early marriage became general practice. Divorce, though relatively easy to obtain, was not common, partly due to the social pressures of the closed Jewish society since the family was firmly established as the basis of Jewish life (see I. Abrahams, *Jewish Life in the Middle Ages* (1932^{2}), 99ff.). With the cultural changes which followed the emancipation, the Jewish marriage rate tended to be lower than the non-Jewish one, divorce and mixed marriage increased, early marriage was uncommon, and the urban Jewish birth rate fell (see A. Ruppin, *The Jews in the Modern World* (1934), 277f., 316ff.; J. Freid (ed.), *Jews and Divorce* (1968)). These trends intensified after World War II as environmental attitudes were increasingly being reflected among Western Jewry. Marital stability has been relatively less and traditional moral codes have been questioned. To counteract these tendencies, Jewish communities are promoting marriage education and guidance, largely through rabbis and social welfare agencies.

See also *Bigamy, *Celibacy, *Divorce, *Family, *Husband and Wife, *Mixed Marriage, *Monogamy, Prohibited *Marriages.

[R.AP.]

MARRIAGE CEREMONY

In the Bible. There is hardly any data about the marriage ceremony in the Bible. The act of marriage is called simply "taking" ("when a man taketh a wife," Deut. 24:1; "and there went a man of the house of Levi, and he took a daughter of Levi," Ex. 2:1). However, from the story of Jacob and Leah it is obvious that some sort of celebration took place: "And Laban gathered all the people of the place and made a feast" (Gen. 29:22) and later, when Jacob complained that he had been cheated and demanded Rachel, the daughter for whom he had worked, he was told: "Wait until the bridal week of this one is over and we will give you that one too" (Gen. 29:27). No details are recorded as to the nature of the feast or the bridal week. The same is true in the case of Samson (Judg. 14:12) except that there it is said that the groom posed a riddle to his companions and gave them the seven days of the feast to solve it. It appears that processions for both the bride and groom were a central part of the celebrations and were accompanied by music (Ps. 78:63; I Macc. 9:39) and there is ample reference to special marriage attire and adornment. From Deuteronomy 22:15 it seems that the exhibition of evidence of the bride's virginity (the blood-stained sheet) was part of the ceremony. It is reasonable to presume that even in the earliest times the act of marriage must have been accompanied by some ceremony; the biblical authors, however, give no direct description of it and usually refer to it only in passing or as a figure in their imagery.

In the Talmud. In the talmudic period—and presumably for a considerable time before then—the marriage ceremony was in two parts. The first, called *kiddushin* or *erusin* (betrothal; but see below, Legal Aspects, for the difference between this concept and what is commonly called betrothal), was effected by the bridegroom handing over in the presence of two witnesses any object of value (more than a *perutah*) to the bride and reciting the marriage formula, "Behold, you are consecrated unto me with this ring according to the law of Moses and Israel." On this occasion two benedictions were recited, one over wine and the other for the actual act. The second reads: "Blessed art Thou, O Lord our God, King of the universe, who has hallowed us by Thy commandments, and hast given us command concerning forbidden marriages; who hast disallowed unto us those that are betrothed (to us—variant in some rites), but hast sanctioned unto us such as are wedded to us by the rite of the nuptial canopy and the sacred covenant of wedlock. Blessed art Thou, O Lord, who hallowest Thy people Israel by the rite of the nuptial canopy and the sacred covenant of wedlock" (Hertz, Prayer, 1011). This benediction is already recorded in the Talmud (Ket. 7b), and since cohabitation of the bride and groom was forbidden until the second ceremony, the *nissu'in* (see below, and Legal Aspects), which in the case of a virgin usually took place a year later, it appears that the benediction was in fact a warning to the betrothed couple not to cohabit until that ceremony.

The second part of the ceremony took place at a later date and was called *nissu'in* (marriage proper). It was also called *ḥuppah* (see below) after either the groom's house to which the bride was led or the canopy, symbolic of that house, under which the ceremony took place. Originally *nissu'in* was effected by the bride entering the groom's house and cohabiting with him. On the occasion of the *nissu'in* a series of benedictions was recited (see below). After this stage the couple were completely married and liable to all the responsibilities and privileges of that state (see also below, Legal Aspects).

There is ample evidence in the Talmud that the wedding ceremony was accompanied by great rejoicing and sometimes even hilarity. The question of how one should dance before the bride was discussed and even occasioned a difference of opinion between the schools of Hillel and Shammai (Ket. 16b–17a). Although Rashi interprets the phrase "*keizad merakdim*" used there as meaning "what does one say" in order to fit the continuation of the text, the phrase must be understood in its literal sense "how does one dance." Judah b. Ilai is recorded as having danced before the bride with a myrtle branch and Samuel b. Rav Isaac was rebuked by his colleagues for having performed what seems to have been a juggling dance. The Talmud, however, justified his behavior entirely. Rav Aḥa went so far as to dance with the bride on his shoulders, something which astonished the other rabbis (Ket. 17a). Indeed the custom of shattering a glass at the marriage ceremony (see below) stems, according to the medieval commentators, from Mar berei de-Ravina and Rav Ashi who deliberately smashed expensive glassware at their sons' weddings in order to reduce the unseemly hilarity of the rabbis who were present (Ber. 31a). Until the destruction of the Temple both the bride and groom wore distinctive headresses, sometimes of gold (Sot. 9:14, 49a; Git. 7a; for details see *Crowns, Decorative Headdresses, and Wreaths). For the marriage of a virgin (as opposed to a widow or divorcee) special rites took place. She went out in a *hinnumah* (variously interpreted as a bridal veil or a special bridal litter used in the marriage procession); dried corn was distributed to the children (Ket. 2:1); games were played before the bride; a goblet of tithe wine was passed before her; according to some, a sealed (opened for a widow or divorcee) barrel of wine was used instead (Ket. 16b). The performance of all these ceremonies was sufficient evidence that the bride had been a virgin and was thus entitled to the larger *ketubbah* (see *Virgin). The bridal procession took precedence over a funeral procession and King Agrippa was praised by the rabbis for giving right of way to a bridal procession although his, being the royal procession, had precedence. At Tur Malka the disturbances which destroyed the town were started, according to talmudic legend, when Roman legionnaires took the hen and rooster which led a marriage procession as a fertility symbol (Git. 57a). Participation at the marriage ceremony and celebrations was considered a *mitzvah* and he who entertained the bride and groom was compared to one who had sacrificed a thanksgiving offering (Ber. 6b). The groom was required to devote at least three days to the preparation of the wedding feast and even if a parent of the bride or groom died on the set day of the marriage its consummation took place and the funeral was held afterward (Ket. 3a). The wedding of a virgin originally took place on a Wednesday (Ket. 1:1). This is explained in the Babylonian Talmud by the fact that the court sat on Thursdays and thus if the groom claimed that the bride had not been a virgin he could immediately complain to the court. However, it does appear that superstition was involved and that Wednesday was considered an auspicious day (cf. TJ, Ket. 1:1). A widow was married on Thursday so that her husband should devote at least three days to her without going back to his work. However, even in talmudic times the requirement that weddings be held on specific days fell into disuse for which a variety of reasons is given. It seems that in talmudic times the exhibition of the stained bridal sheet was discouraged. Originally the *shushbinim* ("friends," i.e., groomsmen) were appointed to ensure that no trickery was employed by either side (Tosef., Ket. 1:4 and Ket. 12a). For a virgin seven festive days were celebrated which, for the bride and groom, had something

Figure 6. An 18th-century wedding in Venice, attributed to Pietro Longhi (1707–1785). Oil on canvas, 35½×25 in. (90×64 cm.). Photo Pietro Fiorentini, Venice.

Figure 7. Paintings of a bride and groom from Persia with inscription in Judeo-Persian indicating that the bride is applying a blue cosmetic to her eyes and the groom is playing a *tar,* late 18th century. Oil on canvas, each 31×24 in. (78×60 cm.). Jerusalem, private collection. Photo David Harris, Jerusalem.

of the status of a religious holiday. The marriage benedictions were recited at meals (for details see below) and neither bride nor groom was allowed to mourn.

Post-Talmudic Period. The most imporant development in the marriage ceremony was the joining of the two parts, *erusin* and *nissu'in,* into one ceremony performed at one time. This took place during the Middle Ages and was presumably because of the uncertain and perilous conditions in which the Jews lived. It was also exceedingly inconvenient to have an interval between the two ceremonies since on the one hand the parties were prohibited from cohabiting while on the other all the stringencies of the married status applied to them. Thus from the beginning of the 12th century it became customary to perform both ceremonies together, a practice which has been universally followed except for a few oriental communities (see Freimann, bibl., 29ff.). Other developments are the addition of various prayers to the ceremony, the inclusion of a sermon by the officiating rabbi and, in some present-day communities, the invocation of a blessing on the bridal couple.

The ceremony may be performed anywhere. In many communities—particularly Sephardi and Oriental—it is performed inside the synagogue although there are halakhic opinions against it. In some places it is performed in the hall where the subsequent festivities are held and some circles (ultra-Orthodox Jews and Ḥasidim and generally among Ashkenazim in Israel) it is invariably performed in the open. This latter custom is perhaps due to the fact that ideally the ceremony takes place after nightfall and the stars above are associated with God's assurance to Abraham that He would "make your descendants as numerous as the stars of heaven" (Gen. 22:17; see Isserles to Sh. Ar., EH 61:1). In the western hemisphere Sunday is a popular day for weddings because of the convenience to the guests, while Tuesday is favored in Orthodox circles because of the repetition of the sentence "And God saw that this was good" in the biblical account of the creation on that day (Gen. 1:10, 12). However, any day of the week is valid except Sabbath; festivals, the *three weeks between the 17th Tammuz and the Ninth of Av, and the *sefirah* period between Passover and Shavuot (there are exceptional days in the last-mentioned period, notably Lag ba-Omer: see *Omer). According to the general Sephardi custom marriages are not performed on Lag ba-Omer but are performed from the following day onward. Usually a person in mourning for a parent does not marry until the year of mourning is out although in certain circumstances it is permitted to marry earlier (Sh. Ar., YD 392). There are no specific requirements for the way in which the bride and bridegroom dress. It is customary for the bride to wear white and for her to have a headdress and a veil. The bridegroom in some Orthodox circles wears a **kitel* either as an evocation of death or since his wedding day is compared to the Day of Atonement when the *kitel* is worn. In some communities the bridegroom wears a *tallit,* as does, in some, the officiating rabbi. In many oriental communities brides wear elaborate costumes richly embroidered and ornamented which were loaned from bride to bride; the Yemenite bridal costume is an outstanding example (see also *Dress).

The ceremony is presently performed as follows. Before being led to the *ḥuppah* (wedding canopy; see below) the bridegroom, in the presence of witnesses, undertakes, by an act of *kinyan* (see *Acquisition) the obligations of the *ketubbah.* This is done by the groom taking a piece of cloth, handkerchief, or some other object from the officiating rabbi, lifting it and returning it. The witnesses then sign the document and in many communities (including the State of Israel) the groom also signs. The groom is then escorted to the place where the bride is waiting (many modern synagogues have a special bride's room) and lets down her veil over her face, at which time the rabbi or cantor pronounces the blessing invoked on Rebekah "O sister! May you grow into thousands of myriads" (Gen. 24:60). This ceremony is known in Yiddish as *"bedeken di kale"* (lit. "covering the bride") and is not practiced by Sephardi Jews. The groom is then led to the *ḥuppah* by his and the bride's father (or two other male relatives or friends if he or the bride has been orphaned) and stands facing Ereẓ Israel, in Israel itself facing Jerusalem, and in Jerusalem facing the Temple site. The bride is then led to the *ḥuppah* by her mother and the groom's mother, usually to the accompaniment of a blessing of welcome chanted by the rabbi or cantor, the text of which is: "He Who is supremely mighty; He Who is supremely praised; He Who is supremely great; May He bless this bridegroom and bride." It is customary among Ashkenazim for the bride to be led in seven circuits around the groom which is presumably to be associated with the magic circle to ward off evil spirits. The bride then stands at the right hand of the groom, and, where customary, the rabbi delivers the sermon; the ceremony proper then begins. The rabbi recites the blessing over a goblet of wine and the marriage blessing (see text above) after which the father of the bridegroom gives the goblet to the bridegroom and he drinks, and then the mother of the bride gives the bride the goblet, from which she drinks. In many communities the officiant gives the goblet to the bride and groom. The groom then places the ring (see below) on the forefinger of the bride's right hand and recites the marriage formula (see above). In some communities the glass is crushed by the groom at this stage. The *ketubbah* is then read out loud by the rabbi or some other man whom the bridal couple wish to honor. In many communities it is read in the original Aramaic and followed by a précis in the vernacular; in Israel a Hebrew précis is often substituted. The purpose of the reading of the *ketubbah* is to divide between the two parts of the ceremony. The celebrant (rabbi, cantor, or some other person) then recites the seven marriage benedictions (see below) over a goblet of wine. In many places it is customary to have different men recite the different benedictions. The father of the bride then gives the groom to drink from the goblet and the mother of the groom does likewise to the bride. In most rites the groom crushes a glass under his right foot and where customary the rabbi invokes the *priestly blessing. The couple are then escorted to a room where they remain alone for some time, usually breaking their fast together (see below, Legal Aspects, for reasons). The breaking of the glass by the groom is explained by some authorities as a token of the seriousness desirable in even the most happy moments (see above, In the Talmud); however, the act has become understood over the ages as a sign of mourning for the destruction of Jerusalem. In some communities the bridegroom threw the glass against a special wall instead of treading on it. It has been suggested that originally the glass was broken to frighten away evil spirits. In some rites the memorial prayer, *El Maleh Raḥamim*, is recited for departed parents if either member of the couple is an orphan.

THE MARRIAGE BENEDICTIONS. These benedictions, commonly known as the *Sheva Berakhot* (Heb."seven benedictions"—when recited with the benediction over wine) are recorded in the Talmud (Ket. 7b–8a) where they are called *Birkat Ḥatanim* ("the bridegroom's benediction"). When recited under the *ḥuppah* the benediction for wine precedes the other six which are:

1) "Blessed art Thou . . . who hast created all things to Thy glory.

2) . . . Creator of man.

Figure 8. Jewish wedding in Morocco ("Noce juive au Maroc") by Eugène Delacroix, 1839. Oil on canvas, 40 x 56 in. (100 x 142 cm.). Paris, The Louvre.

Figure 9. Niello key casket, probably given to a bride, Ferrara(?), Italy, c. 1470. The front is decorated with illustrations of the three commandments incumbent on a woman: setting aside a portion of the dough, ritual immersion, and blessing the Sabbath lights. On the lid are listed items of household linen with dials to indicate quantity. Height, 2½ in. (6.6 cm.), length, 5 in. (13 cm.), width, 2½ in. (6 cm.), depth, 1½ in. (4 cm.). Jerusalem, Israel Museum. Photo R. M. Kneller, Jerusalem.

3) ... who hast made man in Thine image, after Thy likeness, and hast prepared unto him, out of his very self, a perpetual fabric. Blessed art Thou, O Lord, Creator of man.

4) May she who was barren (Zion) be exceedingly glad and exult, when her children are gathered within her in joy. Blessed art Thou, O Lord, who makest Zion joyful through her children.

5) O make these loved companions greatly to rejoice, even as of old Thou didst gladden Thy creature in the garden of Eden. Blessed art Thou, O Lord, who makest bridegroom and bride to rejoice.

6) Blessed art Thou ... who hast created joy and gladness, bridegroom and bride, mirth and exultation, pleasure and delight, love, brotherhood, peace, and fellowship. Soon O Lord, our God, may there be heard in the cities of Judah, and in the streets of Jerusalem, the voice of joy and gladness, the voice of the bridegroom and the voice of the bride, the jubilant voice of bridegrooms from their canopies, and of youths from their feasts of song. Blessed art Thou, O Lord, who makest the bridegroom to rejoice with the bride" (Hertz, Prayer 1013).

This series of benedictions raises some problems from the point of view of their formulation since normally only the first should begin with the formula "Blessed art thou ...." Rashi (to Ket. 7b–8a) gives the following explanation. The first benediction is not for the bridal couple but in honor of the assembled congregation; the second is a benediction in honor of the creation of Adam and the next three are for the couple being married, while the last is an invocation for all Israel including the couple. The series begins with the blessing over wine because of its festive nature. The blessings are recited at the marriage ceremony and at every meal during the next seven days at which there is "a new face," i.e., somebody who was not present at any previous recitation for that couple. This rule applies to all the seven days except the Sabbath, which is itself considered to be a "new face." At the meals the series is recited immediately following the grace after meals, which itself is introduced by a special invocation. The series then ends with the benediction over the wine and both the bride and groom and the person who led the grace drink from the wine. A *minyan* (ten males) is required for the recitation of the marriage benedictions both at the *ḥuppah* and after the grace; if no *minyan* is present the last of the marriage benedictions may be recited as long as there are three males (Sh. Ar., EH 62 and see also: *Grace after Meals). In talmudic times special formulas were added to the grace after meals for some considerable period before the actual wedding and after it. The present-day custom is limited to the recital of the benedictions for the seven day period immediately following the wedding, except in the case of a marriage between a widower and widow when it is recited on the first day only.

Ḥuppah (Heb. חֻפָּה). The term originally referred to the bridal canopy or the bridal chamber (Gen. R. 4:4) and sometimes to the wedding itself (Avot 5:21). In ancient times the *ḥuppah* was the tent or room of the groom into which, at the end of the betrothal period, the bride was brought in festive procession for the marital union (cf. Ps. 19:6; Yad, Ishut 10:1). In talmudic times it was customary for the father of the bridegroom to erect the *ḥuppah* (Gen. R. 28:6; Ber. 25b; Sanh. 108a). In *Bethar (near Jerusalem) the custom was to make the staves or beams of the *ḥuppah* from a cedar and pine tree which were planted for this purpose at the birth of male and female children respectively (Git. 57a). The *ḥuppah* was sometimes made of precious scarlet and gold cloth (Sot. 49b; TJ, Sot. 9:16, 246). The Talmud tells that God made ten *ḥuppot* for Adam and Eve and that He will build such *ḥuppot* for the pious in the world to come (BB 75a). In the early Middle Ages, the *ḥuppah* was not usually used at weddings; this is obvious from the phrasing of Isserles (Sh. Ar.) who regarded it as a novelty (Isserles to Sh. Ar., YD, 391; *ibid.*, EH 55:1). In France the groom covered the bride's head with his *tallit* as a symbol of his sheltering her. This custom was based upon the words of Ruth to Boaz: "Spread . . . thy cloak over thy handmaid; for thou art a near kinsman" (Ruth 3:9). This ceremony was also called *ḥuppah* and was the custom among the Jews of North Africa. Since in talmudic times the *ḥuppah* was the place of marital union and therefore required privacy, medieval responsa dealt with the question whether the act of entering the *ḥuppah* was sufficient to constitute marriage or whether it was only to be regarded as a symbol which would still require the couple to retire in privacy (cf. Tos. to Suk. 25b and see below, Legal Aspects). In the late Middle Ages the *ḥuppah*, consisting of a cloth spread on four staves, was placed inside the synagogue (Isserles to Sh. Ar., YD 391:3), but later it was moved to the courtyard of the synagogue, either because it was deemed improper to have the *ḥuppah*, as a symbol of the marriage tent, erected inside the synagogue or because of the need to accommodate the wedding party (and see above). In modern Israel, for the weddings of soldiers on active duty, the *ḥuppah* often consists of a **tallit* which is supported by four rifles held by friends of the bride and groom.

THE RING. Although the act of marriage can be effected in different ways (see below, Legal Aspects) it has become the universal Jewish practice to use a ring, except in a very few oriental communities where a coin is used. The ring, which must belong to the bridegroom, should be free of any precious stones but can be of any material (usually it is of gold or some other precious metal) as long as its value is more than a *perutah*, the smallest denomination of currency in Talmud times. In the ceremony the groom gives the ring to the bride as an act of acquistion and the bride, by accepting it, becomes his wife. Generally the groom places the ring on the forefinger of the bride's right hand; there are, however, many varied customs as to which finger the ring is placed on. In some Reform and Conservative congregations in the U.S. the "double ring" ceremony is practiced in which the bride also gives a ring to the groom and recites a marriage formula. Since, according to the *halakhah*, it is the groom who is acquiring the bride, this innovation raises serious halakhic doubts which, according to some authorities, even affect the validity of the marriage. [R.P.]

VARIOUS CUSTOMS. The marriage ceremony marks a crucial period in man's life cycle and it is only natural that it became surrounded by a multitude of different customs which generally had one of two purposes: to protect the couple from malignant spirits and to invoke God's blessing of fertility on the marriage. Many of the customs were adopted by the Jews from their non-Jewish environment and thus some are of almost a universal character. Many customs, however, are merely manifestations of the good-will and joy felt at the happy occasion. Among Ashkenazi Jews the most widely practiced customs, besides breaking the glass which has been interpreted as a defense against evil spirits (but see above) are that the women leading the bride to the *ḥuppah* carry lighted candles as do other members of the marriage party and that the bride makes seven circuits around the groom under the canopy. It is customary for the bride and groom to refrain from seeing each other for a time preceding the wedding. The actual duration of this period varies in the different communities from about one week to one day, i.e., that of the wedding itself until the ceremony. The bridegroom has precedence over all others to be called to the Torah reading on the Sabbath before the wedding (a ceremony known as *oyfrufn* in Yiddish) and in some Ashkenazi communities the bride, if she is an orphan,

Figure 10. *Traustein* from the outer wall of the synagogue in Bingen, Germany, inscribed with the initial letters of the phrase "the voice of mirth . . ." from Jeremiah 7:34. Red sandstone, 20×30 in. (51×76 cm.). Jerusalem, Israel Museum. Photo R. M. Kneller, Jerusalem.

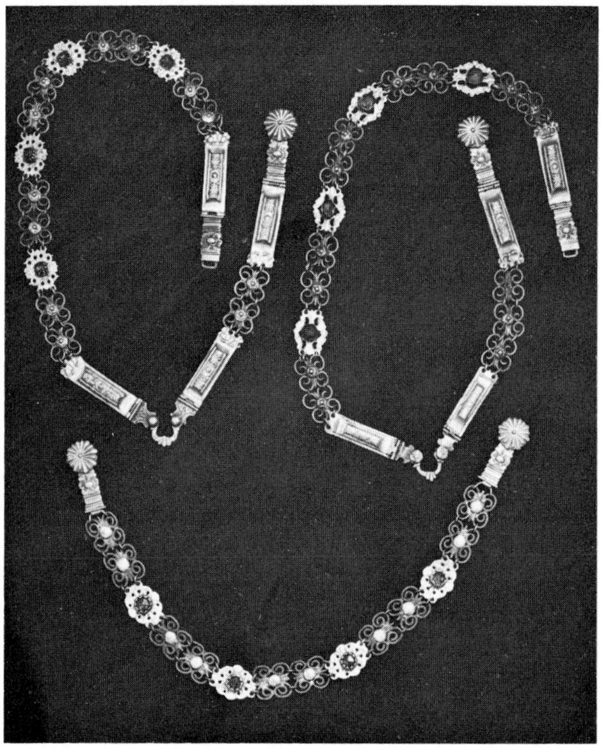

Figure 11. Pair of marriage belts with chain to link the bride's to the groom's. Gilded bronze with carneols, Germany, 17th century. Belts of this type were the most distinctive wedding gift in Germany during this period. Jerusalem, Sir Isaac and Lady Wolfson Museum in Hechal Shlomo. Photo David Harris, Jerusalem.

visits the cemetery some time before the wedding. The bride and groom usually fast on the day of the wedding itself until after the ceremony unless it takes place on a day when fasting is forbidden, such as a new moon. A peculiar custom, common in Eastern Europe as well as in oriental communities, was for the bride and groom to attempt to tread on the other's foot at the end of the ceremony, the one who succeeded thus being assured of dominance in their life together. In many places among both Ashkenazim and Sephardim it was and is customary to throw rice, wheat, nuts, and candies at the groom on various occasions during the marriage cycle; at the wedding itself, and particularly when the groom was called to the Torah reading on the Sabbath prior to the wedding. The bride's entry into her future home was marked by many ceremonies. In Libya and Djerba the groom would drop an earthenware pitcher of water from the roof and the bride would enter the house by walking through the water and broken pottery. In Jerusalem the Sephardim used to break a specially baked cake, called *ruskah*, above the heads of the bride and groom, while in Baghdad a loaf was cut above the head of the groom. In Afghanistan a fowl was slaughtered to mark the occasion. In Djerba the bride broke open eggs on the doorposts of the house and in Daghestan and Gruzia (Russian Georgia) the doorposts were smeared with butter and honey. In Salonika the groom would stand at the head of the stairs when the bride first entered the house and scatter sweetmeats, rice, and coins at her feet as she came in. In Georgia the groom would set a white fowl free from the roof of the house on that occasion and drop rice, wheat, and raisins on the bride's head. In Libya the groom broke the glass at the wedding ceremony when it was almost full of wine which would spill on the floor as a sign of plenty; whereas the groom in Georgia would put the wedding ring into the glass of wine after he had drunk from it, give it the bride to drink, extract the ring, and formally present it to her with the declaration. In Kurdistan the bride would hold a male infant as the assembled guests called out "May your first be a boy too." In Morocco fish was always served at the wedding meal and the subsequent festivities as a fertility symbol and in Salonika the groom would buy live fish and put them in water in a brass bowl; on the eighth day after the wedding the bride jumped three times over this bowl to the blessings of the guests "May you be as fertile as the fish." In Persia the groom would plant three sticks in the courtyard of his house and uproot them on the sixth day after the wedding and throw them behind him to ward off evil spirits. In most oriental communities the *ḥinnah* is celebrated the night before the wedding. In this ceremony the women of both families and female friends (men are entirely excluded) gather at the home of the bride and there her hands are painted with red henna. This ceremony is to ward off the evil eye and is sometimes accompanied by a ceremonial compounding of the dye by the bride's mother and feeding the bride seven times during the evening. Among the mountain Jews of Libya nearly all weddings take place two days before Sukkot. On the second day of the festival all the grooms participate in foot races symbolic of "And he is as a bridegroom coming out of his chamber, and rejoiceth as a strong man to run his course" (Ps. 19:6). Afterward celebrations are held at their homes. In all communities the groom is honored on the Sabbath after his wedding at the synagogue, where he is given precedence to be called to the reading of the Torah. In some communities special *piyyutim* are recited on this occasion and in many the groom is seated in a place of honor with a ceremonial canopy spread above him (Kurdistan). In Libya a second Torah scroll is taken out and an additional section (Gen. 24:1–4) is read. This is also the custom in Tunisia where the section is translated into Arabic. In Tunisia the groom is

Figure 12. Moroccan bridal costume, 1920s. Courtesy D. Corcos, Jerusalem.

Figure 13. Wedding party at the Western Wall in Jerusalem immediately after the Six-Day War. Courtesy Government Press Office, Jerusalem.

invited to the bride's home on the Sabbath preceding the wedding and has to find a roast chicken which has been especially hidden. On the fifth day after the wedding a competition between bride and groom is arranged in which they each have to dissect a large cooked fish for serving. The groom is always at a disadvantage in that he is given a blunt knife. In some communities (Afghanistan and, in a modified form, Yemen) it was sometimes customary to arrange a private wedding ceremony the night before the announced day. On the morrow the announced ceremony would also be held. This was in order to outwit evil spirits or malicious persons who had cast spells on the couple. At the ceremony it was also common for a relative of the couple to hold a pair of scissors and cut paper or cloth for its duration. In Kurdistan the officiating rabbi would publicly warn the assembled guests not to cast spells. The custom of examining the bride's linen after the first night for spots of blood as a proof of her virginity was very widespread and is still practiced in some oriental communities. The mother of the bride would preserve the sheet or underclothing to uphold the family honor if later required. [R.Ka./R.P.]

LEGAL ASPECTS

In Jewish law, marriage consists of two separate acts, called *kiddushin* and *nissu'in* respectively. The *kiddushin* (also called *erusin*) is an act performed by a man and a woman which leads to a change in their personal status, i.e., from bachelorhood to a personal status which remains unchanged until the death of either party or their *divorce from one another. However, the *kiddushin* alone does not bring about all the legal consequences of this change of status, as all those will follow only from a further act between the parties, namely the *nissu'in*. The common usage of the term *erusin*, which refers merely to *shiddukhin*, i.e., engagement (see *Betrothal), is therefore not identical with its legal meaning.

Modes of Effecting Kiddushin. There are three ways of effecting a *kiddushin*, namely by way of *kesef* ("money"), *shetar* ("deed"), or *bi'ah* ("cohabitation").

Kesef. The bridegroom, in the presence of two competent witnesses, transfers (see *Acquisition) to his bride money or its equivalent—today normally an unadorned ring—to the value of at least one *perutah*, for the purposes of *kiddushin*. It is customary for the bridegroom—after the officiating rabbi has recited the *Birkat ha-Erusin*—to place the ring on the bride's right-hand forefinger while addressing her with the words: *Harei at mekuddeshet li be tabba'at zo ke-dat Moshe ve-Yisrael* ("Behold, you are consecrated unto me by this ring, according to the law of Moses and of Israel"; Kid. 2a, 5b; *Rema* Sh. Ar., EH 27:1); i.e., by transferring the ring to the bride the groom signifies his intent to reserve her exclusively to himself and by accepting it she signifies her consent. Hence it is necessary that the ring belong to the bridegroom and not to the bride, since a person cannot alienate something that is not his own, nor can a person acquire something that already belongs to him (Kid. 5b; 6b; 47a; Sh. Ar., EH 27:1, 7; 31:2).

Shetar. In the presence of two competent witnesses, the bridegroom hands over to the bride a deed in which is written, besides the names of the parties and the other particulars required for the purposes of a *kiddushin* by *shetar*, the words, "Behold you are consecrated unto me with this deed according to the law of Moses and of Israel" and the bride accepts the deed with the intention of thereby becoming consecrated to the bridegroom (Kid. 9a; Sh. Ar., EH 32:1, 4). Delivery of the deed is therefore not merely evidence that the *kiddushin* has taken place before, but is the means whereby the tie is created, and in this respect it differs from the **ketubbah* deed which the bridegroom has to give to the bride after completion of the *kiddushin* (see also *Civil Marriage).

Bi'ah. If a man in the presence of two competent witnesses, addresses to a woman the words, "Behold you are consecrated to me with this cohabitation according to the law of Moses and of Israel," and in their presence he takes her into a private place for the purpose of *kiddushin*, she will, upon their cohabitation, be reserved to him (Kid. 9b; Sh. Ar., EH 33:1). Although valid this mode of *kiddushin* was regarded by the scholars as tantamount to prostitution, and they decreed that any person employing it was punishable by *flogging (Kid. 12b; Yad, Ishut 3:21; Sh. Ar., EH 26:4; 33:1). On the other hand, this mode of *kiddushin* has served as the basis for the halakhic presumption that a man does not cohabit with a woman for the sake of prostitution (Git. 81b; *Rema* EH 33:1), and for the various rules founded on that presumption (see *Husband and Wife; *Divorce).

In practice, in present times, only *kiddushei kesef* is

Figure 14. Yemenite bride in Israel smearing henna on her father's finger. Photo Werner Braun, Jerusalem.

Figure 15. Yemenite bride and groom in traditional dress, Israel, 1969. Photo Werner Braun, Jerusalem.

observed since the other two modes of *kiddushin* have long become obsolete. The version "Behold you are reserved . . . according to the law of Moses and of Israel" (which does not appear in the TB and is only found in the Tosefta (Ket. 4:9) and in the TJ, where the version is "according to the law of Moses and of the Jews" (*Yehudai;* Ket. 4:8), means that the bridegroom reserves the bride unto himself "according to the law of Moses"—i.e., the law of the Torah—"and of Israel"—i.e., in accordance with the rules of the halakhic scholars as applied in Israel, so that the *kiddushin* shall be valid or void in accordance with the regulations laid down by the scholars (Yev. 90b; Ket. 3a; Git. 33a; *Rashi* and Tos. ad loc.; see also *Rashbam* and Tos. to BB 48b). The version thus formulated provided the basis for the *halakhah* which empowered and authorized the scholars, in certain circumstances, to invalidate a *kiddushin* retroactively in such a manner that even if it was not defective in principle it was deemed to be void *ab initio.* The question whether this power to make regulations for the annulment of the *kiddushin* is conferred also on the rabbis of the times after the redaction of the Talmud has remained in dispute. One opinion is that a *kiddushin* which is valid according to talmudic law, even though it is celebrated contrary to a *takkanah* which expressly prohibits the celebration of a *kiddushin* in any manner except as therein provided (e.g., in the presence of a rabbi and a quorum of ten), will not be declared void *ab initio* and the woman will not be free to marry another man unless she first obtains a divorce (out of precautionary stringency; Resp. Ribash no. 399; see also Resp. Rashba, vol. 1, nos. 1185 and 1206 where no absolute decision is arrived at; Resp. Ḥatam Sofer, EH 1:108; ET, 2 (1949), 137–40; see also *Agunah, *Takkanot).

The Nissu'in. The act of *nissu'in* requires that the bride, after completion of the *kiddushin,* be brought to the bridegroom under the *ḥuppah* before two competent witnesses, for purposes of the marriage proper, i.e., the *nissu'in* "according to the law of Moses and of Israel." There are different opinions concerning the import of the term *ḥuppah.* One view is that the bride must be brought to the home of the groom for the *nissu'in* (Ran to Ket. 2a, *Beit Shemu'el* 55, no. 4), an interpretation forming the basis of the present custom of bringing the bride to a place symbolizing the domain *(reshut)* of the bridegroom, i.e., to the place where a canopy is spread across four poles and where the bridegroom is already waiting. According to another opinion *ḥuppah* embraces a private meeting (יחוד) between bridegroom and bride, at a place set aside for the purpose, as an indication of their marriage proper (Ket. 54b, 56a; Rosh 5:6; Yad, Ishut 10:1, 2; Isserles EH 55:1, 61:1; Sh. Ar., EH 55:2). In order to dispel doubt, custom requires that, in addition to *ḥuppah,* the couple also have the said private meeting.

Legal Consequences. As already indicated, the legal consequences of the act of *kiddushin* differ from those of the act of *nissu'in.* The *kiddushin* creates a legal-personal tie between the parties which can only be dissolved upon divorce or the death of either party, and the *arusah* ("affianced bride") is regarded as a married woman *(eshet ish)* for all purposes under the *de-oraita* law, which thus renders invalid a *kiddushin* between herself and any other man (Kid. 5; Yad, Ishut 1:3; Sh. Ar., EH 26:3). The *arus* too is prohibited, as is a married man proper, from taking an additional wife, and although in his case the prohibition stems not from the *de-oraita* law but from the *ḥerem de-Rabbenu Gershom* (see *Bigamy), the prohibition for the *arus* is as stringent as it is for a married man proper (*Rema* EH 1:10; *Oẓar ha-Posekim* EH 1, n. 65; other scholars differ, see *Taz* EH 1, n. 15). *Kiddushin* alone, however, does not serve to call into being the mutual rights and duties existing between husband and wife (see *Husband and Wife), and, in particular, cohabitation between them is prohibited (*Rashi,* Ket. 7b; Sh. Ar., EH 55:1, 6). This prohibition is also contained in the Consecration Blessing in the words, "and has prohibited us the *arus* but has permitted us those who are married to us by *ḥuppah* and *kiddushin*" (see Ket. 7b and Sh. Ar., EH 34:1). The *arus* is also not liable for the maintenance of his bride except after the lapse of 12 months from the time of the *kiddushin,* or any lesser period of time agreed upon between them, and then only if he has failed to marry her notwithstanding her demand and readiness to be married to him (Ket. 2; 57a, Sh. Ar., EH 55:4; 56:1, 3 and commentaries). The *arusah* also has no *ketubbah,* unless the bridegroom executed such a deed in her favor at the *kiddushin* stage (Ket. 54b; Sh. Ar., EH 55:6). The absolute change in their personal status, with all the rights and duties it entails is created by the *nissu'in.*

Manner of Celebrating Kiddushin and Nissu'in. In order to avoid irregularities which might possibly bring about complications, custom decrees that the *kiddushin* be solemnized by a rabbi who supervises that everything is done according to law. It is also the generally accepted custom that there shall be present a least a *minyan* (ten men). Custom further decrees that the bridegroom shall always recite the above-mentioned formulation in the precise words, "Behold, you are consecrated . . . etc.,"; although post-factum the *kiddushin* will not be invalidated if any like version with a similar content is used, any change

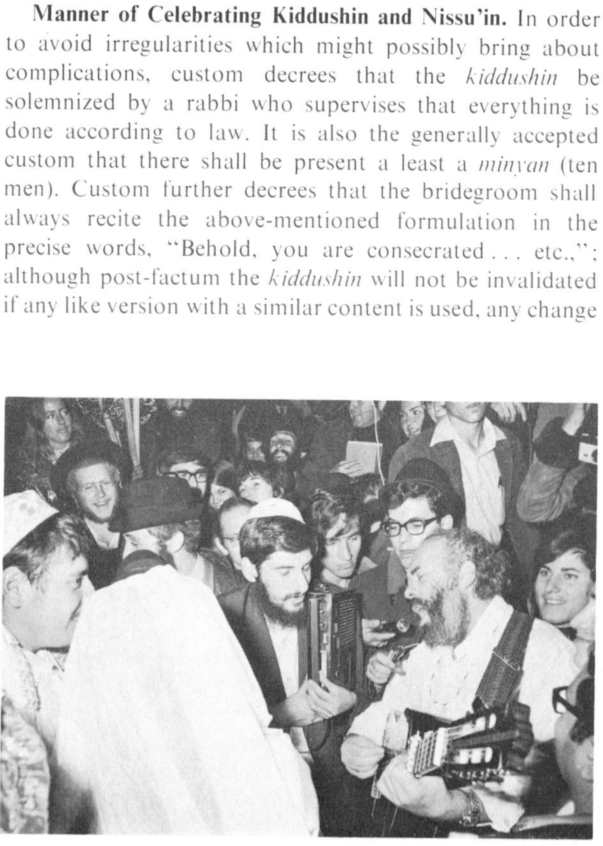

Figure 16. Wedding of an American couple on Mt. Zion, Jerusalem, 1970, with Shelomo Carlebach playing the guitar. Photo G. Drachsler, Jerusalem.

Figure 17. Wedding of Cochin Jews in Israel, 1954. Photo Werner Braun, Jerusalem.

in the recognized version should be avoided at the outset (Yad, Ishut 10:6; Resp. Rosh 37:1; Sh. Ar., EH 55:3 and *Rema* EH 61). The presence of two competent witnesses at both stages of the marriage ceremony is mandatory; as they do not merely serve as eyewitnesses but their presence is an essential part of the legal act, their absence will invalidate both the *kiddushin* and the *nissu'in*. Hence if a man and a woman acknowledge that there were not two witnesses present at their marriage, their acknowledgement *(hoda'ah)* that they are married will not serve as a basis for determining that this is the case (Kid. 65a; Yad, Ishut 4:6; Sh. Ar., EH 42:2). Conversely, if two competent witnesses testify to the celebration of a marriage between a particular couple, they will be regarded as duly married notwithstanding their own denial of the fact (Warhaftig 132, 139). For a full description see above. Theoretically, *kiddushin* being an act of legal effect, it may also be performed between the parties through an agent; i.e., the bridgroom may appoint an agent to enter, on his behalf, into a *kiddushin* with a particular woman and the woman may do likewise for the purpose of accepting *kiddushin*. However, it is a *mitzvah* for each personally to take and be taken in marriage (Yad, Ishut 3:19; Sh. Ar., EH 35, 36). Similarly, in principle, the couple may celebrate a conditional *kiddushin* in such a manner that, provided all the rules applicable to conditions are observed (Sh. Ar., EH 38:2) and the condition itself fulfilled, the *kiddushin* will be valid from the start, or from the time of fulfillment of the condition, in accordance with the stipulation of the parties, but will be invalid if the condition is not fulfilled (Sh. Ar., EH 38). However, on account of the possible complications arising therefrom, and the stringency of the laws concerning a married woman, no conditions are permitted in *kiddushin* or *nissu'in*.

Legal Capacity of the Parties. Since marriage is an act of legal effect, it can be celebrated only by parties who have legal capacity. Hence if one of the parties to a marriage is a minor, acting independently, it will be invalid. In Jewish law a male is a minor *(katan)* until the age of 13 years; from the age of 13 years and one day he is a major (called *gadol*) and only then may he contract a valid marriage (Kid. 50b; Yad, Ishut 2:10; 4:7; Sh. Ar., EH 43:1). A female is a minor *(ketannah)* until the age of 12 years; from the age of 12 years and one day until the age of $12\frac{1}{2}$ years she is called a *na'arah* (Yad, Ishut 2:1). Although as a *na'arah* she is considered a major (*gedolah;* Yad, Ishut 2:6), her marriage (when she is acting independently) will only be valid if she is orphaned of her father, but if he is alive, since a *na'arah* remains under her father's tutelage *(reshut)*, her marriage, when she is acting independently will be valid only after the tutelage ceases to exist, namely when she becomes a *bogeret*, i.e., when she reaches the age of $12\frac{1}{2}$ years and one day (Kid. 43b, 44b; Yad, Ishut 2:2, 3:11–13, 4:8 and Gerushin, 11:6; Sh. Ar., EH 37:11, 155:20, 21; see also *Legal Capacity). As regards the validity of a marriage entered into by a minor represented by his parents, see *Child Marriage.

For the same reason, i.e., lack of legal capacity, a marriage to which an idiot *(shoteh)* is party will be invalid when it is clear that such a party is a complete idiot (Yev. 69b; 96b; Sh. Ar., EH 44:2; 67:7). However, if such person be of sound, although weak, mind his marriage will be valid (Tur and *Beit Yosef*, EH 44; the statement attributed to Isserles, in Sh. Ar., EH 44:2 is apparently a printing error, see *Beit Shemu'el*, ad loc., n. 4; *Ḥelkat Meḥokek*, ad loc. n. 2). In case of doubt as to the soundness of a person's mind, as when he has lucid intervals, his *kiddushin* will, out of apprehension, be regarded as a doubtful *kiddushin* and the parties will not be permitted to marry anyone else except after their divorce (out of precautionary restriction גט מחומרא (Sh. Ar., loc. cit.). A *deaf-mute (*ḥeresh*, Yad, Ishut 2:26) is precluded, by Pentateuchal law, from entering into a *kiddushin* since his/her legal capacity is the same as that of the minor or the idiot. However, the scholars regulated that a *kiddushin* entered into by a deaf-mute shall be valid (Yev. 112b; Yad, Ishut 4:9; Sh. Ar., EH 44:1), but they did so without creating any obligations between parties to such a marriage. Hence if one of the parties is a deaf-mute, none of the legal obligations flowing from marriage will devolve on them—neither the obligation of *ketubbah* (i.e., in places where no *ketubbah* deed is written), nor of a *ketubbah* condition, nor of maintenance (Sh. Ar., EH 67:8–10), except possibly where a deaf-mute expressly undertakes these pecuniary obligations in the *ketubbah* deed (PDR 8:65, 69–71; 74–77). The *ḥerem de-Rabbenu Gershom* does not apply to a husband who was a deaf-mute at the time of his marriage, nor does a deaf-mute's express undertaking not to take an additional wife or not to divorce his wife against her free will have any binding force, since he is incapable of undertaking obligations—at any rate as regards matters of a non-pecuniary nature (PDR loc. cit.).

In the State of Israel. Matters of marriage in the State of Israel are governed by Jewish law, in accordance with the provisions of sections 1 and 2 of the Rabbinical Courts Jurisdiction (Marriage and Divorce) Law, 5713/1953. As regards the customs relating to the celebration of *kiddushin* and *nissu'in*, *takkanot* were issued at an Israeli rabbinical

Figure 18. Triple wedding at kibbutz Yad Mordekhai, 1962. Courtesy Government Press Office, Tel Aviv.

conference in 1950, imposing a strict ban on anyone solemnizing *kiddushin* and *nissu'in* contrary to the accepted customs.

By virtue of the Marriage Age Law 1950 (as amended in 1960) a woman may not be married before the age of 17 years. This law further renders it a punishable offense for any person to marry a woman under the age of 17 years (it is no offense for the bride), or to solemnize or assist in any capacity in the celebration of the marriage of such a woman, or for a father or guardian to give her away in marriage, unless prior permission of the competent district court has been obtained—the latter being empowered to give this on the grounds specified in the law (see *Child Marriage). No minimal age is specified for the bridegroom. This offense, although punishable, has no effect on the personal status of the parties; i.e., if the marriage is valid according to Jewish law, the fact that the offense has been committed will in no way affect the validity of the marriage, whether the question arises in relation to a matter of Jewish or of civil law, in the rabbinical or in the civil courts. However, in the event of a marriage with a woman below the said minimum age, the law provides that application may be made to the rabbinical court—by the persons and in the circumstances specified in the law—in order to oblige the husband to grant his wife a divorce. It must be emphasized that this provision does not create grounds for action for divorce under Jewish law, so that in fact it is a dead letter, for in matters of divorce the rabbinical courts apply Jewish law only. [B.-Z. Sch.]

Bibliography: General: de Vaux, Anc. Isr, 24–38; P. Elman (ed.), *Jewish Marriage* (1967); L. M. Epstein, *Sex Laws and Customs in Judaism* (1948); D. R. Mace, *Hebrew Marriage; A Sociological Study* (1953); R. Patai, *Sex and Family in the Bible and the Middle East* (1959); P. and H. Goodman, *The Jewish Marriage Anthology* (1965; incl. bibl.). The Ceremony: I. Abrahams, *Jewish Life in the Middle Ages* (1932), 179–228; I. Jakobovits, *Order of the Jewish Marriage Service* (1959); J. L. Lauterbach, in: HUCA, 2 (1925), 351–80; E. Brauer, *Yehudei Kurdistan; Meḥkar Antologi* (1948); *Yahadut Luv* (1960), 393–5; J. Yehoshu'a, *Yaldut bi-Yrushalayim ha-Yeshanah; Ha-Bayit ve-ha-Reḥov bi-Yrushalayim ha-Yeshanah* (1966), 59–78; M. Many, *Ḥevron ve-Gibboreiha* (1963), 88–100; M. Attias, in: *Saloniki, Ir va-Em be-Yisrael* (1967), 185–7; J. Saphir, *Even Sappir*, 1 (1866), 81a f.; 2 (1874), 74a–86a; D. S. Sassoon, *Massa Bavel* (1955), 200–3; H. Mizrahi, *Yehudei Paras* (1959); Z. Kasdai, *Mi-Malkhut Ararat* (1912), 59–62; Ben-Jacob (ed.), *Yalkut Minhagim mi-Minhagei Shivtei Yisrael* (1967); Y. Ratzaby, *Bo'i Teiman* (1967), 328–30; M. Zadoc, *Yehudei Teiman* (1967), 208–12; J. Kafih, *Halikhot Teiman* (1961), 110–56. Legal Aspects: M. Mielziner, *The Jewish Law of Marriage and Divorce* ... (1901); J. Neubauer, *Beitraege zur Geschichte des biblisch-talmudischen Eheschliessungsrechts* (1920); Gulak, Yesodei, 3 (1922), 19–22; Gulak, Oẓar, 17–58; idem, in: *Tarbiz*, 5 (1933/34), 384f.; L. M. Epstein, *Marriage Laws in the Bible and the Talmud* (1942); E. Neufeld, *Ancient Hebrew Marriage Laws* ... (1944); A. Freimann, *Seder Kiddushin ve-Nissu'in Aḥarei Ḥatimat ha-Talmud ve-ad Yameinu* (1945); ET, 1 (1951[3]), 257–61; 2 (1949), 137–40, 182–6; 4 (1952), 420–7, 631–51; 5 (1953), 138–52, 168–79; 6 (1954), 710–2; 7 (1956), 43–46; 12 (1967), 154–8; M. Vogelmann, in: *Sinai*, 43 (1958), 49–55; N. Sachs, in: *No'am*, 1 (1958), 52–68; O. Joseph, in: *Sinai*, 48 (1960/61), 186–93; H. Albeck, *ibid.*, 145–51; M. Silberg, *Ha-Ma'amad ha-Ishi be-Yisrael* (1965[4]); K. Kahana, *The Theory of Marriage in Jewish Law* (1966); E. Berkowitz, *Tenai ba-Nissu'in u-va-Get* (1966); Z. W. Falk, *Jewish Matrimonial Law in the Middle Ages* (1966); B. Schereschewsky, *Dinei Mishpaḥah* (1967[2]), 32–51; Elon, Mafte'aḥ, 246–51; idem, *Ḥakikah Datit* ... (1968), 31–37, 164, 183f.

MARRIAGE, PROHIBITED. A marriage is prohibited whenever there is a legal impediment to a *kiddushin* (see *Marriage) between the particular parties. In some cases the prohibition has the effect of rendering the marriage, if it is celebrated nevertheless, null and void *ab initio;* in other cases it does not invalidate the marriage, but provides a ground for having it terminated by divorce.

Prohibited and Void. This category includes: (1) Marriages which are גִּלּוּי עֲרָיוֹת (*gillui arayot*) according to pentateuchal law, i.e., punishable by **karet* or death, namely: (a) marriages between parties related to one another within the prohibited degrees of kinship: i.e., the marriage between a man and his mother, daughter, sister, and certain other relatives (Lev. 18:6ff.; Kid. 67b and codes); the marriage between a man and the sister of his wife is also void during the latter's lifetime (i.e., even after divorce), as is marriage with his brother's widow (except in the case of the levirate widow) or divorced wife: such marriages are punishable by *karet* (Yad, Issurei Bi'ah, 2:1, 9; Sh. Ar., EH 15:22, 26; 44:6; see also *Levirate Marriage); and (b) marriage between a man and a married woman, such *adultery being punishable by death (see also *Bigamy); (2) A marriage with a non-Jewish partner (Sh. Ar., EH 44:8; see also *Mixed Marriage); (3) Other cases enumerated in Shulḥan Arukh, *Even ha-Ezer* 15.

Prohibited but Valid. In this category are included marriages which, although prohibited, do not constitute *gillui arayot* according to pentateuchal law and therefore are valid and not terminable unless by the death of either party or by divorce (Sh. Ar., EH 15:1; 18; 44:7). Since these marriages are nevertheless prohibited and remain tainted with the prohibition during their subsistence, their dissolution by divorce is generally compelled, whether or not either or both of the parties consented to, or had prior knowledge of, the true situation. Marriage prohibitions of this kind derive either from the pentateuchal law imposed and punishable as a plain prohibition only (Yad, Ishut 1:7) or from the rules laid down by the scribes, i.e., marriage prohibited, as "incest of a secondary [minor] degree," not by the Torah but only by rabbinical enactment (*ibid.*, 1:6; Sh. Ar., loc. cit.). The following are examples of such prohibitions:

(1) A married woman who has sexual relations with anyone but her husband becomes prohibited to the latter as well, and also to her lover even after her divorce from her husband (Sotah 27b; Sh. Ar., EH 11:1; 178:17). If she has had sexual relations of her own free will, she is prohibited to her husband forever, i.e., he must never remarry her after divorce from him even if in the meantime she has not married anyone else (Sh. Ar., EH 13). If she has been raped (see *Rape), she is prohibited to her husband only if he is a priest, but if he is an ordinary Israelite, she is permitted to him. He need not divorce her and, if he has done so, he may remarry her provided she has not married someone else in the meantime (Sh. Ar., EH 6:10, 11). Similarly, the adulteress is also prohibited for all time from marrying her lover, i.e., even after divorce from her husband or his death (Yev. 24b and Rashi ad loc.; Sh. Ar., EH 11:1). This is because her lover has destroyed her family life, inasmuch as, owing to the adultery, he has rendered her prohibited to her husband. By the same token, and because the wife of an ordinary Israelite does not become prohibited to her husband when someone else has sexual relations with her against her own free will, some scholars are of the opinion that although beforehand she is prohibited to such a lover in order to penalize him, if they have nevertheless married each other, he will not be compelled to divorce her (Sh. Ar., EH 11; *Ba'er Heitev* n. 5 and *Beit Shemu'el* n. 2; but cf. *Rema*, EH 159:3, and *Ba'er Heitev* n. 6; *Oẓar ha-Posekim*, EH 11:1, n. 44).

(2) A divorcee who has remarried and her second marriage has also been terminated (by divorce or death) is therefore prohibited to her former husband, in terms of an express prohibition in pentateuchal law (Deut. 24:4).

(3) A priest is prohibited by an express prohibition in the pentateuchal law from marrying a divorcee, a *zonah*, or a

*ḥalalah (see *Yeḥasin; Lev. 21:7; Sh. Ar., EH 6:1). This prohibition is still in force (*Rema*, EH 3:6; PDR 5, 219, 221) despite the lack of certainty that all those known as priests are in fact the descendants of Aaron, for all of them are merely presumed to be priests (Yad, Issurei Bi'ah, 20:1). A divorced woman remains prohibited to a priest even if after her divorce she has remarried and become a widow (*Ḥokhmat Shelomo*, EH 6:1; Sh. Ar., EH 66:11, Isserles, *Ḥelkat Meḥokek*, 66, n. 41). A priest is forbidden to remarry even his own former wife (Resp. Ribash no. 348; see also *Divorce). For the purposes of the above prohibition, the term *zonah* is not to be interpreted in its ordinary sense—i.e., a woman who has sexual relations other than within matrimony (Yev. 61b). Here it refers to a woman who is not a Jewess by birth, such as a proselyte, and also to a woman who has cohabited with a man to whom she must not be married by virtue of a general prohibition (i.e., not one relating to the priesthood as such) e.g., if she has cohabited with a non-Jew or a **mamzer* (Yev. 61a and Rashi; Sh. Ar., EH 6:8).

(4) A Jewish man or woman must not marry a *mamzer (et)*. For details see **Mamzer*.

(5) A married man is prohibited, according to the decree of Rabbenu *Gershom, to marry another woman while his marriage still subsists. If contracted, the second marriage is valid but the parties will be compelled to a divorce (see *Bigamy).

(6) Marriage with a divorcee or widow is prohibited before the lapse of 90 days from the date of her acquiring her new status, in order to avoid doubt concerning the descent of her offspring; similarly, for the good of her child, it is forbidden to marry a pregnant woman or nursing mother until the child has reached the age of 24 months (Sh. Ar., EH 13:1, 11–14; for further instances of prohibited, but valid marriages see Sh. Ar., EH 15).

Legal Consequences of Prohibited Marriages. Family Law Aspects. So far as the parties themselves are concerned, no legal consequences at all attach to a marriage which is forbidden as עֶרְוָה (incestuous) according to pentateuchal law, and there is therefore no need for them to be divorced (Sh. Ar., EH 15:1, and Ha-Gra thereto, n. 3; Sh. Ar., EH 44:6); their children will be *mamzerim*. Only a marriage of a married woman to another man, although invalid, requires that the woman obtain a divorce not only from her husband but also from the paramour (see *Divorce; *Bigamy; **Agunah*).

In the case of prohibited but valid marriages either party is entitled to demand a divorce, whether or not either or both parties were aware of the impediment at the time of the marriage or at any time thereafter. In case of the other party's refusal, divorce may be compelled, except in the case of a marriage contracted within 90 days of dissolution of the wife's previous marriage (*Rema*, EH 13:10). The need for divorce is also relaxed with reference to marriage with a pregnant woman or nursing mother (PDR 4:60). On the status of children born of such marriages, see **Yuḥasin*.

Civil Law Aspects. Since the law requires that a prohibited marriage be dissolved, there is no place for the imposition of reciprocal marital rights and duties which are designed to sustain the marriage. In principle this is the position whenever the husband has married his wife without knowing that she is prohibited to him (לֹא הִכִּיר בָּהּ, *lo hikkir bah*). However, if he has done so knowingly, there will be no justification for his release from a husband's marital duties, and these he must fulfill, with the exception of those likely to impede dissolution of the marriage. This distinction between the husband's knowledge or lack of it is drawn mainly in regard to the most important cases of prohibited but valid marriages, i.e., cases of plain prohibition (אִסּוּרֵי לָאו, *issurei lav*); (for the prohibitions concerning other cases of prohibited marriage, see Sh. Ar., EH 116:2ff.). Since a man who marries without knowing that his wife is prohibited to him is released from all the marital duties of a husband, the wife will not be entitled to receive her "main" or minimal **ketubbah* and therefore also not to fulfillment of the *ketubbah* conditions since "the *ketubbah* conditions are as the *ketubbah* itself" (Ket. 54b and Rashi ad loc. s.v. *tena'ei ketubbah;* see also *Husband and Wife). Similarly, the wife will not be entitled to *maintenance, either during the husband's lifetime or as his *widow (Yad, Ishut 24:2; Sh. Ar., EH 116:1). In the same way, the wife too will be released from all her matrimonial duties, since these are imposed on her by law only in return for her husband's actual fulfillment of his duties toward her (see **Ketubbah;* *Husband and Wife; *Dowry). The husband will, however, remain liable for her *ketubbah* "increment" (*tosefet ketubbah*), as this is not an obligation imposed on him by law but one that he has voluntarily undertaken to fulfill for as long as she is willing to remain his wife, and this the law has forbidden her to do, independently of her own will in the matter (Yad, Ishut 24:3; *Taz*, EH 116, n. 3).

In cases where the husband knowingly contracts a prohibited marriage, the scholars regulated that in principle he should not be released from any of the matrimonial duties imposed upon the husband by law. Hence, in these circumstances he, or his estate, will be liable to his wife or widow for her *ketubbah* (including the *tosefet*) as well as its conditions as in every regular marriage. However, since everything should be done in order to bring about the dissolution of such prohibited marriages, the scholars further ruled that the husband was exempt from maintaining his wife during his own lifetime, in order to discourage her from remaining his wife (Sh. Ar., loc. cit, and *Taz* n. 1). He will consequently not be entitled to her handiwork, since he is entitled to this only in return for actually maintaining her. Divergent opinions are expressed in the codes concerning the husband's usufruct of his wife's property. According to some of the *posekim* the husband does not have this right, since it is in return for the obligation to ransom his wife from captivity, a duty which does not hold in the case of a prohibited marriage (see *Dowry) as marital life with her is forbidden to him; therefore the husband must return the equivalent of any benefit he may have derived from this source (see, e.g., Yad, Ishut 24:4 and *Maggid Mishneh* ad loc.). Other *posekim* are of the opinion that only when the wife is taken captive must the husband make available for purposes of her ransom, the equivalent of the fruits of her property that he has enjoyed, but otherwise he will be exempt from compensating her in this regard (see, e.g., *Ḥelkat Meḥokek* n. 4 and *Beit Shemu'el* n. 2 to EH 116). Since the marital rights afforded by law to the wife in respect of her husband are conditional on the existence of corresponding legal duties of her husband toward her and, in the same way, the wife's duties to her husband do not exist independently but are in return for her enjoyment of her rights against him (Yad, Ishut 12:1–4)—a position which depends on his knowledge or ignorance of the prohibited nature of the marriage—her knowledge or ignorance in this respect is of no legal significance.

In the State of Israel. Apart from rules of private international law, the problem of prohibited marriages is governed by Jewish law (see sects. 1, 2 of the Rabbinical Court Jurisdiction (Marriage and Divorce) Law, 5713/1953.

Bibliography: ET, 1 (1951[3]), 206–9; 2 (1949), 20f., 65, 84f.; 6 (1954), 343–54; 12 (1967), 49–67; Elon, Mafte'aḥ, 5–7; B. Schereschewsky, *Dinei Mishpaḥah* (1967[2]), 51f., 56–62, 203–6.
See also bibliography to *Marriage.

[B.-Z. Sch.]

MARSALA, town in Sicily. Though Jews probably lived in Marsala in Roman times, the first mention of them is made in a royal decree of 1374, in which approval was given for the enlargement of the synagogue. Toward the end of the 14th century the community protested against the abuses inflicted on them by the citizens, who forced them to attend church functions, and stoned them when they returned to their own quarter. Royal decrees of 1402 and 1405 exempted the Jews from the authority of the bishop, restored the ritual bath which had been confiscated, and restricted the taxes paid by the Jews to one-tenth of those imposed on the whole town. Every year, on October 16, councillors *(proti)* were elected to administer the community affairs. On the expulsion of the Jews from Sicily in 1492, about 2,600 Jews were forced to leave the town. The synagogue was converted into a church.

Bibliography: G. di Giovanni, *L'ebraismo della Sicilia* (1748), 329–36; B. and G. Lagumina, *Codice Diplomatico dei Giudei di Sicilia* (1884–1909); Milano, Italia, index; Roth, Italy, index; Lionti, in: *Archivio Storico Siciliano*, 8 (1883), 149–55; Zunz, Gesch, 484–534.

[J.S.S.]

MARSCHAK, JACOB (1898–), U.S. economist. Born in Kiev, Marschak taught at the University of Heidelberg from 1930 to 1933. From 1933 to 1939 he lectured at All Souls College, Oxford, and was the director of its Institute of Statistics. In 1940 he became professor of the graduate faculty of the New School for Social Research in New York City, which he left in 1942 to teach at the University of Chicago, directing at the same time the Cowles Commission for Economic Research (1943–48). He was a professor of economics at Yale from 1955 to 1960, in which year he was appointed to the same post at the University of California at Los Angeles. His major interests were microeconomics, econometrics, and business administration. His publications include *Kapitalbildung* (with Walther *Lederer, 1936), *Economic Aspects of Atomic Power* (coeditor, 1950), *Studies in Econometric Methods* (with W.C. Hood and others, 1953); and *Income, Employment, and the Price Level* (1965).

[J.O.R.]

MARSEILLES, capital of the department of Bouches-du-Rhône; second largest town in France. The earliest presence of Jews in Marseilles can be traced to at least the sixth century. In 574 there was a sufficient number to provide asylum for the Jews who fled from *Clermont-Ferrand to escape the coercive measures of Bishop *Avitus, who sought to convert them. In 591 Bishop Theodore of Marseilles also attempted to compel the Jews of the town to accept baptism, but Pope *Gregory I intervened in their favor. Although scant information is available on the Jews of Marseilles during the early Middle Ages, the importance of their settlement there is confirmed by the names of sites alluding to them. At the close of the tenth century there is mention of a *valle Judaica* in a quarter of fields and vineyards and at the end of the 11th century a vineyard named *rua Judaica*. During the 12th century, the Jews formed two communities: one in the upper part of the town, which was under the jurisdiction of the bishop; the other in the lower town, which belonged to the viscount. However, both communities were placed under the authority of the bishop. (It was this right which Frederick I Barbarossa ratified for Bishop Peter in 1164.) These two groups are mentioned by *Benjamin of Tudela, who also indicates that the yeshivot and the scholars were established in the upper town. As would be expected, the merchants settled in the lower part in the vicinity of the port, from where they traded with Palestine, Egypt, North Africa, Spain, and Italy, dealing mainly in wood, spices, textiles, metals, pharmaceutics, various products for dyeing, and slaves. Commercial partnerships with Christians were very common. Moneylending was rare; the Jews were more often borrowers than lenders, although at the close of the 12th century, they did advance loans to the Monastery of Saint Victor and to the squire of Trets. Although in 1257 the statutes of Marseilles granted Jews the status of citizens, they were nevertheless subject to some important restrictions; they were prohibited to work in public on Christian festivals, or to take an oath in a lawsuit against Christians, and no more than four Jews were allowed to embark on a ship bound for Egypt. No later than the middle of the 14th century, all the Jews of the town had united into a single community, led by three officers who administered the schools, the three synagogues, the almshouse, and the *mikveh*.

During the 14th century, the right of the Jew to be equal to other citizens of Marseilles was extended to his having the right to be different as well. Thus, although it was forbidden for all other citizens to sell flour in any place but on the bridge, a municipal ordinance of 1359 authorized Jews to sell or buy flour for unleavened bread *(mazzot)* in the Jewish quarter. Similarly, in 1363 it was stipulated that whereas all other inhabitants were to sweep the street before their houses on Saturday, Jews were permitted to do so on Friday. Finally, in 1387 Jews were exempted on evenings of Jewish festivals from the general obligation to walk about with a lamp after curfew.

Although they lived in a harbor on the crossroads of extensive international commerce, the Jewish population remained relatively stable; new arrivals in the town constituted hardly more than 10% of the population. (A higher percentage occurred once, approximately 30%, in 1351, after an influx caused by the *Black Death persecutions.) Although Jews participated little in the maritime trade, limiting their transactions practically to Spain, they were well represented in the town's internal commerce, many of them acting as brokers. The Jewish surname Sabonarius has led to the belief that it was the Jews who introduced the soap industry to Marseilles. They had a virtual monopoly over coral craftsmanship, although those engaged in this occupation made very little money. Poorly off, too, were the Jews who earned their livelihood as laborers, porters, stonecutters, and tailors. Since they dealt only in small sums, even Jewish moneylenders were not notably wealthy. Jews did, however, distinguish themselves in the medical field, the number of Jewish physicians in the town often exceeding that of their Christian colleagues. During the 15th century, Jewish economic life suffered a setback and the population engaged only in retail trade, mainly in the sale of wheat and textiles. Jews also suffered more than the rest of the population when the town was plundered by the Aragonese in 1423, most of them being reduced to a state of poverty, and their economic recovery was achieved with great difficulty.

Late in 1484 and early in 1485, shortly after the incorporation of *Provence into France (1481), the Jewish quarter of Marseilles was attacked. Plunder, destruction, and murder ensued, and the Jews of Marseilles began to flee. In 1486, however, the municipal council restrained their emigration and drew up an inventory of their belongings. Severe upheavals in the composition of the community are reflected in the lists of the heads of families after that time, and at least one half of the community's members were relatively new arrivals. Jews from Spain began to arrive in large numbers, particularly after 1491. As a result of the expulsion of Spanish Jewry in 1492 many shipowners of Marseilles amassed fortunes. The Spanish Jews hired vessels at exorbitant prices for transportation to

Italy or Constantinople, and many of these ships called at the port of Marseilles, the unfortunate exiles often attempting to remain in the city without the authorization of the municipal council. A general expulsion order for Provence was issued in 1500 and enforced in 1501. For about 20 years, conversions increased considerably as great numbers of Jews chose this alternative to evade expulsion.

Benjamin of Tudela refers to Marseilles as a "town of learned men and scholars." Among those he mentions is R. *Isaac b. Abba Mari of Marseilles, commentator and author of prayers. Several members of the Ibn *Tibbon family also lived in Marseilles, or were born there. (Records of a rabbinical lawsuit in this family about 1250 mention family relationships and marriages between the Jews of Marseilles and those of *Naples, *Aix-en-Provence, and *Montpellier.) *Nissim b. Moses of Marseilles was the author of a commentary—which some regard as "almost rationalist"—on the Pentateuch, entitled *Sefer ha-Nissim* or *Ma'aseh Nissim*. Samuel b. Judah ha-Marsili (also known as Miles Bonjudas) was born in Marseilles in 1294. He translated several philosophical and scientific works from Arabic into Hebrew. Judah b. David (also known as Bonjudas Bendavi or Maestre Bonjua), a talmudist and physician of the late 14th/early 15th century, emigrated to Italy, as did the talmudist and commentator Jacob b. David *Provencal (second half of the 15th century).

A second community was established in Marseilles for a brief period during the second half of the 17th century. As a result of an edict issued by Louis XIV in 1669 which granted tax exemption for the port of Marseilles, two Jews of Leghorn, Joseph Vais Villareal and Abraham *Athias, settled there in 1670 with their families. Their commercial success rapidly attracted other Jews. The local authorities soon protested against the presence of Jews and particularly objected to two places of Jewish worship. They obtained an expulsion order which was applied in 1682. Despite successive renewals of the expulsion order, a new community was founded in 1760. About 1768, it owned a small synagogue and in 1783, a cemetery. Although its membership had not grown to any considerable extent, a split occurred at the end of 1790, and both the municipality and the civil court were called upon to intervene to settle the differences. Thus reunited, the community established a new synagogue and a cemetery in 1804. The community was then composed of about 300 members, of whom over one third were needy. The Jewish population increased rapidly, to 450 in 1808, 1,000 in 1821, and 2,500 in 1865. At this time several new institutions were set up, including schools for both boys and girls, an almshouse, and the synagogue in the Rue de Breteuil which was still in use in 1970.

Holocaust Period and After. During World War II, between 1940 and 1942, Marseilles was in the "free zone." Along with *Lyons, it was the city in the southern zone where the greatest number of Jews and Jewish organizations and institutions found sanctuary. After the Allied landing in North Africa and the German occupation of France, there was a vicious hunt for Jews in Marseilles, accompanied by increased arrests and deportation. As a result the resistance movement also increased its activities. The synagogue on Rue de Breteuil was pillaged, the facade destroyed, the prayer books and the Torah scrolls burned. When the Germans left the city, about 5,000–10,000 Jews who were then in Marseilles—Jews from Provence and Alsace, immigrants from Eastern Europe, Sephardi Jews from the East Mediterranean, and Jews from North Africa—rebuilt the community and the synagogue. Near Marseilles the former military camp of Grand Arenas became a transit camp for Jewish survivors migrating to Palestine. From 1956, the Jewish population in Marseilles grew rapidly. The city attracted Jewish immigrants from North Africa, and in 1962 it became their main port of entry into France. In 1969, there were an estimated 65,000 Jews in Marseilles, making it the third largest Jewish community in Western Europe. Although the community's buildings and institutions expanded they could not keep pace with the population growth. In 1969 Marseilles and the immediate vicinity had a dozen synagogues with services to accomodate each religious tradition. It also had three community centers, a Jewish primary school, an *Ort vocational school, and a network of activities and organizations including youth movements. A consulate general of Israel was located in Marseilles.

Bibliography: Gross, Gal Jud, 366ff.; B. Blumenkranz, *Juifs et chrétiens*... (1960), index; R. Aubenas, *Recueil de lettres des officialités de Marseille*..., 2 (1938), 37, 40–42, 54–55; A. Crémieux, in: REJ, 46 (1903), 1–47, 246–68; 47 (1903), 62–86, 243–61; 55 (1908), 119–45; 56 (1908), 99–123; I. Loeb, *ibid.*, 16 (1888), 73–83; R. Busquet, *ibid.*, 83 (1927), 163–83; J. Weyl, *ibid.*, 17 (1888), 96–110; Z. Szajkowski, *ibid.*, 121 (1962), 367–82; idem, *Analytical Franco-Jewish Gazetteer* (1966), index; M. Zarb, *Privilèges de... Marseille* (1961), 90, 142; *Histoire du commerce de Marseille*, 1 (1949), 290–3; 2 (1951), 89–96; 3 (1951), 24–31; 4 (1954), 537–9; D. Hauck, *Das Kaufmannsbuch des Johan Blasi* (1965), index; A. Latil, in: *Répertoire des travaux de la societé de statistique de Marseille*, 30 (1867), 122–53. [B.Bl.]

MARSHAK, SAMUEL YAKOVLEVICH (1887–1964), Zionist and Russian poet. Marshak was born in Voronezh. Though his father received a solid religious education, Marshak himself seems to have experienced traditional Judaism only when he lived, as a child, with his observant grandparents in Vitebsk. There, for half a year, he studied Hebrew with a teacher by the name of Khalameyzer, whom he lovingly remembered and described in his childhood reminiscences *V nachale zhizni* ("At Life's Beginning," 1960). But it seems that he mastered Hebrew, as well as ancient and modern Jewish literature, sufficiently well to be able to translate it into Russian. Marshak received his formal education in Russian high schools in St. Petersburg and also in the Crimean town Yalta, where he lived in Maxim *Gorki's house.

According to his second autobiographical note *"O sebe"* ("About Myself"), published posthumously as an introduc-

Samuel Yakovlevich Marshak, Russian poet. From B. M. Sarnov, *Samuil Marshak*, Moscow, 1968.

tion to the eight-volume collection of his writings, he "began being published in almanacs in 1907." But actually his first verse had already appeared in Russian-language Jewish journals (*Yevreyskaya Zhizn, Molodaya Iudeya*) in 1904–07, all of them enthusiastically Zionist, such as poems on the death of *Herzl (*"20 Tammuz"* and *"Na grobe"*), poems based on biblical themes (from Ezekiel and Song of Songs), on midrashic legends, about the Spanish inquisition, and programmatic Zionist poetry (especially for youth), etc. Later he published his poetry, including translations from *Bialik, in the Zionist *Razsvet*, in which, after a visit in 1911 to Ereẓ Israel, he also published his observations and impressions of the various Jewish communities in the country. In his poem "Palestina," published in 1916 in *Yevreyskaya Zhizn,* he contrasted the Jewish plight in Russia during World War I to the elation he experienced in Ereẓ Israel. His poem *"Ierusalim,"* which depicts his journey to the Holy City, was included in the Russian-language anthology of Jewish poetry *Safrut* (1918). The *Evrejskaya Anthaloga* ("Hebrew Anthology"), which appeared in Moscow in 1918, edited by L. *Jaffe and V. *Khodasevich, published Marshak's translations from Bialik, Z. *Shneur and D. Shimonovich (*Shimoni).

As a high school student, during his stay in Gorki's house in Yalta, he was active until the summer of 1906 in organizing Zionist youth circles of Molodaya Iudeya ("Young Judea"). Under the influence of the clandestine *Po'alei Zion delegate, Isaac Shimshelevich (later Izhak *Ben-Zvi, the second president of Israel), Marshak became an activist of the illegal Po'alei Zion movement, and his address at Gorki's house even served as a liaison between the center of the movement in Poltava and its delegate in the Crimea. According to Ben-Zvi's letters, seized by the Czarist police, Marshak was active in organizing the Po'alei Zion branch in Yalta and the distribution of *Yevreyskaya Rabochaya Khronika* ("Jewish Workers' Chronicle"). During his stay in London (1912–13) Marshak was still in touch with Po'alei Zion, and Ber *Borochov mentions him in one of his letters to a London friend. Thus, from his high school days in Yalta until after the Russian Revolution, when he participated in the editing of the Russian-language anthologies of Jewish literature in Moscow, Marshak was a dedicated Zionist. This chapter in his life has been completely omitted from Marshak's biographies and autobiographical notes published in the Soviet Union.

[M.Mi.]

Most historians of Russian writing would probably accept Marshak's designation by his friend Maxim Gorki as the founder of Soviet children's literature. His first children's book was *Detki v kletke* ("Children in a Cage," 1923). There is hardly a Russian child or young adult who does not know some of Marshak's verse by heart. His nursery rhymes, songs, and verse form part of the Soviet kindergarten and school curriculum, and his plays have long been among the mainstays of the Soviet children's theater. There are few ideological elements in his verse, in which he usually exhorts children to be truthful, to obey their parents, to study diligently, and to be kind to animals. Four volumes of his writings, including his first autobiographical note, appeared in 1957–60. Marshak was also famous as a translator of the great European poets, including Shakespeare, Blake, Byron, and Heine.

Marshak's sister, YELENA YAKOVLEVNA ILINA (pen name of Liya Yakovlevna Preis, 1901–1964), was a well-known children's writer in her own right, and his brother, M. ILIN (pen name of Ilya Yakovlevich Marshak, 1895–1953), was probably the best-known Soviet writer of popular science, particularly for children. [M.F.]

Bibliography: B. E. Galanov, *S. Ya. Marshak . . .* (Rus., 1956); B. M. Sarnov, *Samuil Marshak . . .* (Rus., 1968); M. Minc, in: *Beḥinot,* 1 (1970).

MARSHALL, DAVID SAUL (1908–), Singapore labor politician. Marshall was born of a Sephardi family of Iraqi origin. He went to London to study, and after being admitted to the English bar returned to Singapore to practice law. He entered politics as a member of the Legislative Assembly and became president of the Workers' Party. When the island was granted partial independence in 1955, Marshall led the United Labor Front party to victory in the elections and became chief minister and minister for commerce, serving in these positions until 1956. In 1963 he was elected to Singapore's Legislative Assembly. Marshall was president of the Singapore Jewish Welfare Board from 1946 to 1953. [M.R.]

David Saul Marshall, Singapore labor politician, at the United Nations. Courtesy Singapore Jewish Welfare Board. Photo Max Machol, New York.

MARSHALL, LOUIS (1856–1929), lawyer and communal leader. Born in Syracuse, New York, the son of German-Jewish immigrants, Marshall graduated from Syracuse High School and served a two-year apprenticeship in a local law office. In 1876 he left for New York City where he completed the two-year Columbia Law School course in one year. Returning to Syracuse, Marshall joined a prominent law firm and in 1894 became a partner in the leading New York firm of Guggenheimer, Untermyer, and Marshall.

Marshall specialized in constitutional and corporate law. Many of the numerous cases that he argued before the U.S. Supreme Court were of major constitutional significance. His legal eminence was recognized by appointment or election to three constitutional conventions in New York State (1890, 1894, and 1915). Although he never sought public office, he was at one time seriously considered for appointment to the Supreme Court. A leading supporter of the Republican Party, Marshall participated in local and national politics, led in the establishment of the New York State College of Forestry, and served on numerous non-sectarian committees and boards.

In New York City, Marshall joined the German-Jewish elite and quickly became the chief spokesman for this group in matters affecting the Jewish community at home and abroad. His national leadership became evident in 1911 during the successful campaign against the United States-Russian Commercial Treaty of 1832, which was being used by the Czarist regime to discriminate against American Jews. Marshall's eloquence, legal knowledge, and skillful management, joined with intense public pressure, resulted in congressional action leading to abrogation of the treaty.

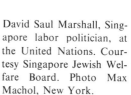

Louis Marshall, U.S. lawyer and president of the American Jewish Committee. Etching by Hermann Struck. Jerusalem, Israel Museum. Photo David Harris, Jerusalem.

In 1912 Marshall became president of the American Jewish Committee and held this post until 1929. During World War I, he participated in a bitter internal power struggle within the Jewish community over the establishment of an American Jewish Congress in preparation for peace negotiations. Playing a key role as mediator, Marshall joined the Jewish delegation to the Paris Peace Conference in 1919, where he supported the granting of national minority rights to the Jews of the new East European states.

Marshall vigorously attempted, without success, to block the American publication of the anti-Semitic *Protocols of the *Elders of Zion,* imported from Europe in the immediate postwar years. American Jewry was shocked when the *Dearborn Independent,* a publication owned by Henry Ford, embarked in 1920 on a crusade to popularize and elaborate the distortions and misrepresentations emanating from the *Protocols.* Unable to dissuade Ford directly, Marshall utilized quiet pressure and influential intermediaries in an attempt to abate this anti-Semitic campaign. Finally, in 1927, after lawsuits brought by individuals maligned by the *Independent,* Ford agreed to cease his attacks and to sign a formal apology to the Jews prepared by Marshall.

Marshall participated in the legal defense of Leo *Frank, who was convicted and subsequently lynched in Georgia for a murder he allegedly committed in 1913. He played a significant part in the campaign to delay the imposition of progressively harsher immigration-restriction legislation. His intervention in 1922 helped reverse Harvard University's announced intention to impose a quota system on Jewish students. He quietly opposed the powerful Ku Klux Klan and vigorously condemned the perpetrators of the Massena ritual murder libel in 1929.

Marshall was a dedicated Jew. He served as president of Temple Emanu-El in New York, the most important Reform Jewish congregation in the United States. At the same time, he served as chairman of the board of directors of the *Jewish Theological Seminary. During World War I, he was president of the American Jewish Relief Committee and helped organize and guide the *American Jewish Joint Distribution Committee. Although not a political Zionist, Marshall acknowledged the need for Palestine as a center of Jewish settlement, especially after the United States severely limited immigration in the early 1920s. He cooperated with Chaim *Weizmann in attempting to arrange a *modus vivendi* which would allow wealthy and influential non-Zionists to share in the support of Palestine without actually becoming Zionists. Weizmann's and Marshall's efforts, opposed by Stephen Wise and other American Zionists, finally came to fruition after many years of discussion. In August 1929, shortly before Marshall's fatal illness, a pact was ratified in Zurich for the establishment of a *Jewish Agency, which would include both Zionists and non-Zionists in the management of Jewish colonization in Palestine under the terms of the British mandate. Marshall's death was a blow to the full implementation of the venture, but his work helped create a tradition of American non-Zionist support that was of great value in the crucial decade after World War II.

Believing in the indivisibility of civil rights, Marshall was a consistent champion of other minorities. Active in the National Association for the Advancement of Colored People, he fought major legal battles on behalf of Negroes. In 1920, alarmed at hysterical anti-Bolshevism, Marshall defended five socialist assemblymen, who were refused their seats in the New York State Legislature.

Marshall's period of leadership coincided with the great era of mass Jewish immigration to the United States and the integration of the immigrants into an urbanized, industrialized society. Representing the native Jewish establishment, he nevertheless displayed a remarkable sensitivity to the needs and desires of the Jewish immigrants, encouraging, guiding, criticizing, but not patronizing. Aided by American democratic traditions and the political power of Jewish voters, Marshall generally used the traditional methods of intercession and quiet diplomacy to achieve his ends. While not uniformly successful, his dignity, sincerity, devotion, and strength combined to produce what a contemporary called "the foremost leader of American Judaism . . . the American Jew par excellence."

His son, GEORGE MARSHALL (1904–), conservationist, served as an economist with the National Recovery Administration from 1934 to 1937. Marshall devoted his efforts to the cause of conservation. He was managing editor of *The Living Wilderness* from 1957 to 1961 and was a director of the Sierra Club and the California Conservation Council.

Another son, JAMES MARSHALL (1896–), lawyer and educator, studied law at Columbia University and was associated with his father's firm, Guggenheimer, Untermyer, and Marshall from 1920 to 1930. After independent practice from 1930 to 1934, he became a member of the firm of Marshall, Bratter, Greene, Allison and Tucker. In addition to numerous other civic responsibilities, Marshall was a member of the New York City Board of Education from 1938 to 1952 and served as its president from 1938 to 1942. Active in Jewish communal life, he held important posts in the American Jewish Committee, Joint Distribution Committee, Jewish Publication Society, and American Friends of the Hebrew University.

A third son, ROBERT MARSHALL (1901–1939), served as director of the forestry division of the U.S. Office of Indian Affairs from 1933 to 1937. He became chief of the division of recreation and soil conservation of the U.S. Forest Service and held the position until his death.

Bibliography: C. Reznikoff (ed.), *Louis Marshall: Champion of Liberty*, 2 vols. (1957); M. Rosenstock, *Louis Marshall, Defender of Jewish Rights* (1965); American Jewish Committee, in: AJYB, 10–31 (1908–29); Adler, in: AJYB, 32 (1931), 21–55; Dawidowicz, in: JSOS, 25 (1963), 102–32. [Mo.Ro.]

°**MARSUS, C. VIBIUS,** successor to Petronius as Roman governor of Syria (42 C.E.). Marsus appears to have regarded the Judean king Agrippa I with more than the average Roman suspicion toward Jewish leaders, and went as far as to inform the emperor *Claudius of these suspicions. When Agrippa began to fortify the walls of the northern side of Jerusalem, the act was immediately reported by Marsus to the emperor. Claudius ordered the immediate cessation of the fortification, suspecting that a revolution was on foot. Marsus again intervened in Judean affairs when he disbanded the meeting of vassal kings convened by Agrippa at Tiberias. From that time, according to Josephus, Agrippa was at odds with Marsus. Marsus was succeeded in Syria by Cassius Longinus in 45 C.E.

Bibliography: Jos., Ant., 19: 316, 326–7, 240–2, 363; 20:1; Pauly-Wissowa, 2nd series, vol. 16 (1958), 1973–75 (under the name C. Vibius Marsus). [I.G.]

MARTHA, daughter of *Boethus, mentioned in the Talmud as one of the wealthiest women in Jerusalem in the period preceding the destruction of the Temple (70 C.E.). She is apparently to be identified with Miriam, daughter of Boethus (Lam. R., 1:47), whose family rose to a position of prominence in Herod's time. After the death of her first husband she married *Joshua b. Gamla. According to the Talmud she paid three measures of golden coins in order to have Joshua appointed high priest (Yoma 18a), a position he held for two years (63–65). Her wealth was proverbial and her priestly sons too were numbered among the wealthy citizens of Jerusalem. During the war, however, when hunger prevailed in Jerusalem, she died as a vagrant seeking a morsel of food (Git. 56a). The rabbis saw in her tragic death a fulfillment of the mosaic prophesy of woe (Deut. 28:56).

Bibliography: Schuerer, Gesch, 2 (1907[4]), 273; Graetz, Hist, 2 (1949), 249, 306; Klausner, Bayit Sheni, 5 (1951[2]), 22–23, 291.

[L.Ro.]

°**MARTI, KARL** (1855–1925), German Bible scholar. Marti taught at Basle university (1881–91), and was professor of theology (from 1895) and of Semitic philology (from 1901) in Berne until his death. Marti wrote critical studies on Jeremiah (1889) and Zechariah (1892), and a concise grammar on biblical Aramaic (1896; 1911[2]). He edited the second edition of A. Kayser's *Theologie des Alten Testaments* (1894; 1907[5]), bearing the title *Geschichte der israelitischen Religion,* a critical evaluation of biblical religion based on the *Wellhausen-Graf reconstruction of Israel's history. In the *Kurzer Hand-Commentar zum Alten Testament,* of which he was a coeditor, he wrote the volumes on Isaiah (1900), Daniel (1901), the Minor Prophets (1904), and the introductory volume, *Die Religion des Alten Testaments unter den Religionen des vorderen Orients* (1906; *The Religion of the Old Testament,* 1907). In the series *Die Heilige Schrift des Alten Testaments* he annotated Deuteronomy (1909), Daniel, and the books of Joel, Obadiah, Zechariah, Haggai, and Malachi of the Minor Prophets (1910). Among his numerous articles on biblical studies and Judaica there is a strongly biased one on the nature of the Christian mission to the Jews ("Zur Judenmission," in: *Kirchenblatt fuer die reformierte Schweiz,* 1886).

Bibliography: For a bibliography of K. Marti's writings until 1923, see: W. Baumgartner, in: BZAW, 41 (1925), 323–31.

[Z.G.]

°**MARTIAL (M. Valerius Martialis;** c. 40–104 C.E.), Roman epigrammatist. Martial ridiculed the Jewish rite of circumcision (*Epigrammaton,* 7:55) and speaks mockingly of women who fast on the Sabbath (*ibid.,* 4:4). In common with other classical writers (e.g., Augustus, Strabo, Pompeius Trogus, Persius, and Petronius), Martial confuses the Sabbath with a fast day, probably the Day of Atonement. He referred to licentious Jews who shared vices with their fellow Romans (*ibid.,* 7:30). Martial scolded a circumcised rival poet from Solymae (Jerusalem) for plagiarizing his verses, while criticizing them (*ibid.,* 11:94). In common with other Roman satirists (e.g., *Juvenal), he depicts unfavorably Jewish life in Rome, expressing indignation at the constant growth of that community which he considered strange.

Bibliography: Reinach, Textes, 287–9; M. Radin, *The Jews among the Greeks and Romans* (1915), 302, 325–6, 329–30.

[S.Ra.]

°**MARTIN,** name of five popes, two of whom were significant in Jewish history.

Martin IV, pope 1281–85. Although he employed a southern French Jewish physician, Martin IV was generally repressive in his actions concerning the Jews. He directed the inquisitors to proceed against lapsed Jewish converts (March 1, 1281), and issued an instruction to the archbishops and bishops of France not to hamper the work of the Inquisition, even suspending the right of sanctuary in the case of Jewish converts suspected of falling away from the faith. A series of articles specifying reforms for Portugal (1284) is partly concerned with the position of the Jews.

Martin V, pope 1417–31. On the whole Martin V was well-disposed toward the Jews. In the first two years of his reign he confirmed the Jews of Germany, Savoy, and Rome in their former privileges, and received favorably a delegation of Italian Jews and another from Spain. In 1419 (and again in 1422 and 1429) he issued a bull protecting the Jews in their synagogues. He resisted the imposition of the *badge, but ordered the Jews to abstain from work on Sundays and feast days. His aim seems to have been to encourage the fullest possible intercourse between Jews and Christians, excepting from his protection only those Jews who conspired to overthrow the Christian faith. His personal relations with Jews appear to have been good: he employed Elijah b. Shabbetai Be'er as his physician, and gave the Jewish physicians in the Papal States every encouragement in the practice of their profession. Martin may have been the pope who discussed theology with Aaron b. Gerson Abulrabi of Catania. To some extent he seems to have striven to moderate the worst excesses of the Inquisition. In 1418, after receiving a complaint that the Jews of Avignon practiced sorcery, infected simple Christians with Jewish superstitions, and demanded interest at a rate of 10%, he instructed the local inquisitor to proceed against them, but he soon attempted to restrain the inquisitor's zeal. The same situation was repeated in his dealings with John of *Capistrano, against whose excesses many of his edicts of protection were probably directed. Thus in 1422 he issued an edict forbidding forcible baptism, since "a man who is known to have undertaken Christian baptism unwillingly rather than of his own accord cannot be supposed to possess true Christian faith," but barely a year later he was induced to withdraw it. In May 1427 John of Capistrano persuaded the queen of Naples (Joanna II) to cancel the privileges of the Jews in her kingdom, but Martin's intervention resulted in the repeal of this edict in the following August.

Bibliography: E. A. Synan, *Popes and Jews in the Middle Ages* (1965), 121; 135–6; REJ, 3 (1881), 218 (on Bull of 1281); Roth, Italy, 157ff.; S. Grayzel, *The Church and the Jews in the XIIIth Century* (1966), 274.

[N.de-L.]

MARTIN, DAVID (1918–), Australian poet and novelist. Born in Hungary, Martin was educated in Germany, but left in 1935 with the rise of Nazi power, spending a year on a kibbutz in Ereẓ Israel. He fought in the Spanish Civil War, and lived in London from 1938, working for various newspapers and the European Service of the B.B.C. He moved to Australia in 1949, and was briefly editor of the *Sydney Jewish News.* His works include verse collections such as *Battlefields and Girls* (1942); *From Life* (1953); and *The Gift* (1966); and the novels, *Tiger Bay* (1946); *The Stones of Bombay* (1950); *The Young Wife* (1962); and *The King Between* (1966). Martin contributed stories, criticism, and occasional verse to Jewish publications in England, the U.S.A., and Australia. One of his best-known poems, "I am a Jew," was published in his *Collected Poems, 1938–1958* (1958). His other major Jewish works are a play, *The Shepherd and the Hunter* (1946), dealing with the Palestine problem in the 1940s, and the autobiographical novel, *Where A Man Belongs* (1968), which deals with aspects of contemporary Jewish life.

Bibliography: J. Hetherington, *Forty-two Faces* (1962), 127–32, incl. bibl.

[G.F.C.]

°**MARTINEZ, FERRANT,** archdeacon of Écija, one of the leading anti-Jewish agitators in Castile during the last quarter of the 14th century. Preaching in public in *Seville, Martínez demanded that the 23 synagogues in the town should be destroyed and the Jews confined to their own quarter. As vicar-general of the archbishop of Seville, he secured the right of jurisdiction over the Jews of the town and its environs and demanded their expulsion from Écija and other rural districts. In 1378 the Jewish community of Seville appealed to King Henry II of Castile, but his letter to the archdeacon commanding him to desist was ignored. The Jews turned to his successor John I in 1382 but John's edict of 1383 also did not deter Martínez. In 1388 the Jewish community of Seville finally resolved to summon the archdeacon before the supreme court of the crown. In his defense, Martínez claimed that his actions were beneficial to Church and crown and that he had acted with the consent of his superior, the archbishop. Due to the intervention of Queen Leonora in favor of the archdeacon, little resulted from the trial. Even the archbishop of Seville's prompt removal of Martínez from office was fruitless, for after the deaths of King John and the archbishop in 1390 the archdeacon was reinstated to his former position. Immediately after his reinstatement, he ordered that all synagogues within his jurisdiction be destroyed. The intervention of King Henry III, who demanded that Martínez rebuild the synagogues and resign from office, went unheeded. As a result of his continued activities, riots broke out throughout Castile in 1391 and spread rapidly to Aragon. In the ensuing destruction and massacres, many Jews were forced to accept baptism. In 1395 Martínez was imprisoned on the order of the king, but he was soon released; after his death the people revered him as a saint.

Bibliography: Baer, Urkunden, 1 (1929), 699ff.; 2 (1936), 210ff., 231ff., 244ff.; Baer, Spain, 2 (1966), index s.v. *Ferrant Martinez*.

[ED.]

°**MARTÍNEZ DE OVIEDO, GONZALO** (d. 1340), major-domo *(dispensero de la casa del rey)* of King Alfonso XI of Castile. He instigated the proposal to expel the Jews from the kingdom of Castile. When in the royal service, Martínez enjoyed the protection of the Jewish courtier Joseph de *Écija. According to Solomon *ibn Verga in *Shevet Yehudah*, he was jealous of his Jewish master and petitioned the king to sell him Joseph and nine other Jews, including the physician Samuel *ibn Waqar. The king granted his request and the two courtiers R. Joseph and R. Samuel died under torture in prison. Martínez' influence increased until he was appointed head of the Order of Alcántara. When Abu al-Malik, son of the sultan of Morocco, declared war on Castile in 1339, Martínez advised Alfonso to expel all the Jews from the kingdom and confiscate their property. In spite of the objections of some of the court ministers, the king accepted his suggestion and the Jews of several towns were arrested and their property seized. Martínez led the troops who defeated the Moroccan army, but after his victory he lost favor with the king, probably as a result of the intervention of Alfonso's mistress Doña Leonor de Guzmán; he was arrested, charged as a traitor, and executed by royal command. Ibn Verga relates that all the tyrant's property was sold to Jews and his ring handed over to the courtier Moses, probably Moses *Abzardiel.

Bibliography: Baer, Spain, 1 (1961), 354ff.; S. ibn Verga, *Shevet Yehudah*, ed. by A. Shochat (1947), 53ff.

[ED.]

°**MARTINI, RAYMOND** (1220–1285), Spanish Dominican friar and polemicist. Born in Subirat, Catalonia, Raymond lived for a long time in a monastery in Barcelona, temporarily also in Tunis where he engaged in missionary activity among Jews and Arabs. He studied Hebrew and other oriental languages at the college of Murcia, founded to train selected friars in the conduct of religious disputations with Jews and Muslims for the purpose of converting them to Christianity. Raymond was able to read rabbinical writings with ease. He took an active part in the disputation with Naḥmanides at *Barcelona in 1263 where Pablo *Christiani was the Christian spokesman (see *Barcelona, Disputation of). In 1264 he was appointed a member of the first censorship commission to examine Jewish books for passages allegedly offensive to Christianity. After the disputation of Barcelona, Raymond Martini became one of the chief executors of the anti-Jewish policy of the church.

Raymond's main work is his *Pugio Fidei* ("The Dagger of Faith"; c. 1280), divided into three parts of which the second and third are devoted to anti-Jewish polemics. The last part contains extracts from the Talmud, the Midrash, and later rabbinical writings (Rashi, etc.). The book is clearly an attempt to regain the ground lost after the Christian failure in the disputation of Barcelona. Raymond's polemics are innovative in that he derives his "proofs" of the truth of Christianity or falsehood of the Jewish faith not solely from the Old Testament but mainly from the Talmud and other rabbinical literature. Thus, according to Raymond, Jesus is also announced as Messiah in the *aggadah*, and the talmudic passage, according to which "the commandments will be abolished in the Hereafter" (Nid. 61b) after the advent of the Messiah, heralds the abrogation of the Jewish laws after the advent of Jesus. Furthermore, Raymond claims that the emendations to the Bible undertaken by Ezra's collaborators and cited in the Talmud as *tikkun soferim* have distorted the original text. But his own interpretation of the aggadic text was not always correct, and by arbitrary grouping of sentences out of their original context he often gave them a christological meaning.

Pugio Fidei became the most important and widely circulated medieval anti-Jewish polemic, and supplied polemical source material to disputant friars, Christian scholars, and Jewish apostates (see *Nicholas of Lyre, *Abner of Burgos, *Pablo de Santa Maria, *Arnold of Villanova, Joshua *Lorki (in his *Hebraeomastix*, especially for the disputation of *Tortosa)). The manuscript, which was lost for a long time, was brought to light by Justus Scaliger and published by Joseph de Voisin under the title *Pugio Fidei . . . adversus Mauros et Judaeos* (Paris, 1651). A second edition was published by I. B. Carpzov (Leipzig, 1678), who added an anti-Jewish preface "*Introductio in Theologiam Judaicam*" and a biography of the author. Another anti-Jewish book written by Raymond Martini, *Capistrum Judaeorum*, was less important and never printed.

Solomon b. Abraham *Adret took part in a disputation with Raymond or with one of his disciples. Adret wrote a small apologetic work refuting Raymond's main fictitious proofs from the *aggadah* for the validity of Christianity, without mentioning the author's name or work. These refutations, as well as a detailed defense of *tikkun soferim* against charges of forgeries of the biblical text, are also included in Adret's aggadic commentary *Ḥiddushei Aggadot* (see: Rashba, Resp., 4 (1958), nos. 31 and 187, and J. Perles, 30–56, Heb. sect.).

Bibliography: Baer, Spain, index; idem, in: *Sefer Zikkaron le-Asher Gulak* . . . (1942), 29ff.; A. L. Williams, *Adversus Judaeos* (1935), 248ff.; J. Rosenthal, in: *Perspectives in Jewish Learning*, 3 (1967), 48ff.; Graetz, Gesch, 7 (1894), 124f., 150ff.; J. Quetif, *Scriptores Ordinis Praedicatorum* . . ., 1 (Paris, 1719), 396–8; Wolf, Bibliotheca, 1 (1715), 1016ff.; 3 (1727), 989ff.; 4 (1733), 572ff., 968; J. Perles, *R. Salomo b. Abraham b. Adereth* (Ger. 1863), 54ff., 77f.; S. M. Schiller-Szinessy, in: *Journal of Philology*, 16 (1887), 131–52; L. Levy, in: ZHB, 6 (1902), 30f.; P. Browe, *Judenmission im Mittelalter und die Paepste* (1942), 77, 103f., 108, 120, 122, 272; S. Lieberman, *Sheki'in* (Heb. with Eng. summary, 1939), index; idem, in: HJ, 5 (1943), 91; Zunz-Albeck, Derashot, 144–5; H. Merḥavyah, *Ha-Talmud bi-Re'i ha-Nazerut* (1970), index.

[B.SU./ED.]

MARTON, ERNÖ JECHEZKEL (1896–1960), editor and leader of Transylvanian and Hungarian Jewry. Born in Dicsőszentmárton (now Târnăveni, Rumania), Marton was the son of the city's rabbi. Toward the end of World War I, he participated in Hungarian public life and in 1918 he was appointed general secretary to the district governor. But he quickly left this position, moved to Kolozsvár, and took part in the "Zionist revolution" that was then taking place among the Jews of Transylvania. He joined the group that established the Hungarian-language Zionist newspaper *Uj Kelet* ("The New East") and was soon appointed editor in chief (1919). From then until his death he was editor of the paper (in Cluj and later in Tel Aviv). Marton was elected to major posts in the Zionist Movement in Transylvania.

Ernö Jechezkel Marton, Hungarian Jewish leader and newspaper editor. Courtesy J. Marton, Jerusalem.

Marton was one of the founders and leaders of the Jewish Party in Rumania and succeeded in convincing Rumanian politicians to view the Jews of Transylvania as a national minority. In 1919 he was elected to the city council of Cluj on behalf of the Jewish Party and was appointed vice-mayor. In 1932 he was chosen on the same list as a member of the Rumanian parliament, where he defended the rights of the Jews.

During World War II, with the reannexation of Cluj to Hungary (1940), the publication of *Uj Kelet* was discontinued. Marton moved to Budapest and joined the executive of the Hungarian Zionist Movement. In 1944, when the Nazis occupied Hungary, he moved to Bucharest and organized rescue activities on behalf of Hungarian Jewry. He renewed his ties with Rumanian politicians and designed a program for the large-scale rescue of Hungarian Jews. With the liberation of Hungary, Marton headed a convoy to Budapest to organize welfare programs for the survivors of the ghetto. In 1946 Marton settled in Palestine. Two years later, together with David Dezsö Schoen, he renewed publication of *Uj Kelet* in Tel Aviv. He also founded the World Federation of Hungarian Jews and was its first chairman. In addition to numerous articles that appeared for decades in his newspaper, he also published books of ideological problems of Zionism. His most important work is *A magyar zsidóság családfája* ("Family Tree of Hungarian Jewry," 1941), in which he developed new theories on the history of the Jews in Hungary. The book also appeared in English translation in *Hungarian Jewish Studies* (1966), 1–59.

Bibliography: B. Vágó, in: *Hungarian Jewish Studies* (1966), 177–222. [Y.M.]

MARTOV, JULIUS (Iulii Osipovich Tsederbaum; 1873–1923), Russian revolutionary, leader of Menshevism. Born in Constantinople, where his father represented the Russian Steamship Co. and a St. Petersburg newspaper, Martov was the favorite grandson of Alexander *Zederbaum, the Hebrew writer and founder of *Ha-Meliz*, but his father, Osip, was a conscious assimilationist. Active in revolutionary student circles in St. Petersburg, he was arrested and exiled to Vilna, where he worked from 1893 to 1895 in the Jewish social democratic organization (which in 1897 became the *Bund). In a programmatic address (later published as *A Turning Point in the History of the Jewish Labor Movement*), Martov urged the creation of a "separate Jewish workers' organization to lead the Jewish proletariat in the struggle for its economic, civil, and political emancipation"; it would use Yiddish as its language of agitation and champion "equality of rights for Jews."

Returning to St. Petersburg in October 1895, he joined *Lenin as co-founder of the "Union of Struggle for the Emancipation of the Working Class," was arrested in 1896 and was exiled to Siberia. After his term of exile, Martov, together with Lenin and Alexander Potresov, founded the Marxist journal *Iskra* and joined its editorial board abroad (1901–05). He participated in *Iskra's* crusade against revisionism and "economism" and, reversing his earlier stand on the Jewish question, vigorously opposed the national "separatism" of the Bund, urging Jewish socialists to "assist the organization of the vast majority of the [Russian] proletariat" rather than waste their revolutionary talents on their "own little corner" in the *Pale of Settlement.

Martov broke with Lenin at the Second Congress of the Russian Social Democratic Party (1903), opposing his bid for personal domination of the party. He led Menshevik opposition to Lenin's scheme of a narrow party of professional revolutionaries, advocating a broad, inclusive workers' party adapted to Russian semi-illegal conditions.

During the 1905 Revolution Martov returned to Russia, worked in the St. Petersburg Soviet and edited social-democratic newspapers. In 1906–12 he lived abroad, mainly in Paris, where he edited the Menshevik *Golos sotsialdemokrata*. He supported cooperation with the Bolsheviks and sought to combine legal with underground activities.

During World War I Martov was a central figure of the pacifist Zimmerwald movement. He thwarted Lenin's attempt to turn the movement into a Bolshevik-dominated tool for civil war and the destruction of the Second International. Upon his return to Petersburg on May 9, 1917, Martov led the faction of Menshevik-Internationalists, who opposed the "defensist" policies of the Menshevik majority and advocated the establishment of a popular front government.

After the Bolshevik seizure of power in October 1917, Martov, together with Raphael *Abramowitz, urged the creation of a socialist coalition goverment in a vain attempt to prevent the Bolsheviks from establishing a minority dictatorship. He became the leader of a vociferous, semi-loyal opposition that tried to function in the Soviet system by making the Bolsheviks respect their own Soviet constitution. Martov denounced the Bolshevik terror, whether directed against "bourgeois" newspapers, liberal parties, the Czar's family, church dignitaries, or Socialist Revolutionaries, and thus became the revolution's "true voice of conscience." But he supported the Soviet regime against counterrevolution and foreign intervention. When the Menshevik Party was finally outlawed, Martov was allowed to leave Russia (1920). He settled in Berlin to lead the Mensheviks in exile and assist the underground Menshevik remnant in Russia. He edited the *Sotsialistichskii Vestnik* and was a leader of the short-lived "Vienna International," which tried to thwart the Comintern's bid to take over the western, independent left-wing parties.

Brave, honest, and gentle, and a beloved figure of Russian and European socialism—even the Bolsheviks mourned him as their "most sincere and honest oppo-

Marriage

Plate 1. Wedding rings, 17th and 18th centuries. They are embellished with a house or a roof symbolizing the establishment of a new home, and the majority are inscribed *mazzal tov.* Left to right, top: silver gilt, Italy, 18th century; silver filigree, N. Africa, 18th century. Bottom: silver gilt, Austria, 17th–18th century; gold filigree and cloisonée enamel, Italy, 18th century; wrought and repoussé gold, Italy, 17th century. Jerusalem, Israel Museum. Photo David Harris, Jerusalem.

Plate 2. "Jewish Wedding" by Moritz Oppenheimer, 1861. In this painting of a German marriage ceremony, a *tallit* serves as the *ḥuppah.* The bridal couple have their belts symbolically tied together. The tablet with a *Magen David* on the wall of the synagogue is a marriage stone *(traustein),* at which the bridegroom will hurl a glass of wine to intoxicate and injure the Devil. On the steps stands a *badḥan* in his jester's costume. Oil on canvas, $14\frac{1}{2} \times 10\frac{3}{4}$ in. (37×27.5 cm.). Jerusalem, Israel Museum. Photo David Harris, Jerusalem.

Plate 3. Double-beakered marriage cup for use by the bride and bridegroom, S. Germany, 18th century. Silver, partly gilt, with engravings including doves, symbolizing love, and two quotations from the marriage service. Height 6 in. (15.2 cm.). Jerusalem, Michael Kaufman Collection. Photo David Harris, Jerusalem.

4

5

6

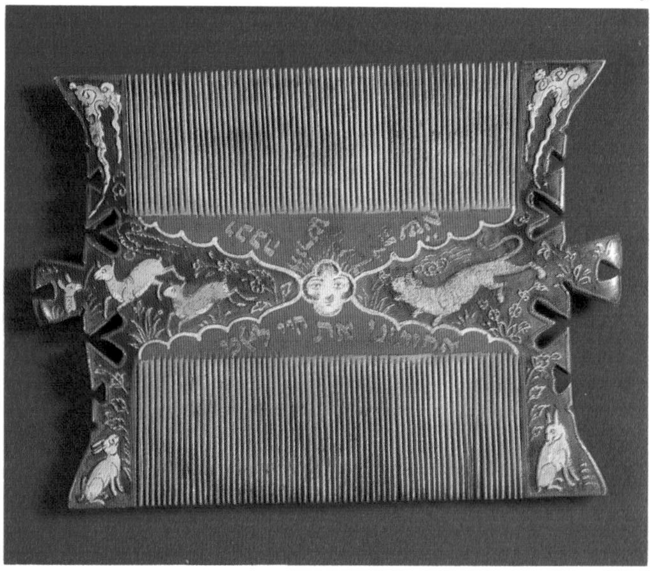

PLATE 4. China platter depicting a marriage ceremony, England, 1769. It forms part of a hand-painted coffee service in salt glaze Staffordshire ware, designed as a wedding gift. New York, Jewish Museum. Photo Eric Politzer, New York.

PLATE 5. Painting of a bride by Isidor Kaufmann (1853–1921). The traditional East European wedding garments include a *brusttuch*. New York, Oscar Gruss Collection. Photo Eric Politzer, New York.

PLATE 6. Comb for a bride, Persia, 19th century. The ornamentation includes a woman's face, birds and flowers. The inscriptions include blessings (Gen. 24:60) and invocations against the evil eye. Painted wood, 5×3½ in. (12.5×9 cm.). Jerusalem, Sir Isaac and Lady Wolfson Museum in Hechal Shlomo. Photo David Harris, Jerusalem.

nent"—Martov personified the dilemma of revolutionary socialists with humanitarian and democratic commitments when facing the amoral authoritarianism of Lenin and the Soviet regime.

Martov believed that the advent to socialism would also solve the problem of the Jewish people. He was deeply shaken by the pogroms of 1905–06 and by the *Beilis trial, remained personally involved in the struggle against anti-Semitism, and wrote a little book *Russkii narod i evrei* ("The Russian People and the Jews," 1908).

His works, fragmentary and scattered, include: *Istoriia rossiiskoi sotsial-demokratii* ("History of the Russian Social-Democracy" 1918; in German translation published as *Geschichte der russischen Sozialdemokratie*, Berlin, 1926), *Obshchestvennye i umstvennye techeniia v Rossii 1870–1905* ("Social and Intellectual Trends in Russia 1870–1905, 1924); *Razvitie krupnoi promyshlennosti i rabochee dvizhenie v Rossii* ("The Development of Heavy Industry and the Workers' Movement in Russia," 1923). He was chief editor of the monumental Menshevik study *Obshchestvennoe dvizhenie v Rossii v nachale XX veka* ("The Social Movement in Russia at the Beginning of the 20th century," 4 vols., 1909–1914), which is his major scholarly achievement. His moving autobiographical *Zapiski sotsialdemokrata* ("Notes of a Social Democrat," 1923) is his literary masterpiece.

Bibliography: I. Getzler, *Martov, A Political Biography of a Russian Social Democrat* (1967); A. M. Bourguina, *Russian Social Democracy: the Menshevik Movement, A Bibliography* (1968); *Sotsialisticheskii vestnik* (April 10, 1923); *Martov i ego blizkie*, (1959); A. V. Lunacharsky, *Revolutionary Profiles* (1967); O. Blum, *Russische Koepfe* (1923); Z. Shazar, *Or Ishim* (1963).

[I.GE.]

MARWICK, LAWRENCE (1909–), librarian and oriental scholar. Born in Poland, Marwick emigrated in 1929 to the United States. During World War II he served in the U.S. intelligence corps. From 1948 he was head of the Hebraic section of the U.S. Library of Congress and after the war he was the assistant director of the Board of Jewish Education in St. Louis. In 1954–56 he lectured in Arabic and Islamic studies at Dropsie College and from 1961 in modern Hebrew literature and Arabic at New York University. Marwick was a member of the American Academy of Jewish Research, and the board of governors of Dropsie College. He wrote *A Handbook of Diplomatic Hebrew* (1957), and edited Solomon b. Jeroham's *Arabic Commentary on the Book of Psalms, Chapters 42–72* (1956).

[ED.]

MARX, ADOLF BERNHARD (1795–1866), German musicologist. Born in Halle, he was originally a lawyer, but in 1830 became professor of music at Berlin University, a post that had been intended for but declined by the 21-year-

Adolf Bernhard Marx, German musicologist. Jerusalem, J.N.U.L., Schwadron Collection.

old Felix Mendelssohn. In 1850 he helped to found the school still known as the Stern Conservatory and taught there till 1856. He wrote operas, lieder, a piano sonata, a symphony, and an oratorio *Moses* (1843), but achieved no importance as a composer. His theoretical and critical works, however, retain their value, the most important being a four-volume work on composition, *Die Lehre von der musikalischen Komposition* (1837–47); *Ludwig van Beethoven, Leben und Schaffen* (1859); *Gluck und die Oper* (2 vols., 1863); and a work on the interpretation of Beethoven's piano works (1863). Marx's memoirs, *Erinnerungen aus meinem Leben*, were published in two volumes in 1865, and a collection of his articles appeared in three parts, from 1912 to 1922.

Bibliography: K. E. Eicke, *Der Streit zwischen Adolph Bernhard Marx und Gottfried Wilhelm Fink um die Kompositionslehre* (1966); Baker, Biog Dict; s.v.; Grove, Dict; MGG; Riemann-Gurlitt.

[A.EI./ED.]

MARX, ALEXANDER (1878–1953), historian, bibliographer, and librarian. Born in Elberfeld, Germany, Marx grew up in Koenigsberg (East Prussia). His studies were

Alexander Marx, historian and bibliographer. Courtesy American Jewish Historical Society, Waltham, Mass.

interrupted by a year in a Prussian artillery regiment where he excelled in horsemanship. Later he studied at the University of Berlin and at the *Rabbiner Seminar (Berlin), marrying Hannah the daughter of D. Z. *Hoffmann, rector of the Rabbiner Seminar in 1905. In Berlin, he was influenced by Moritz Steinschneider. In 1903 Marx accepted Solomon Schechter's invitation to teach history at the Jewish Theological Seminary of America and be its librarian.

His mastery of the materials of history and of languages became proverbial. He published articles in many languages and was at home in classical and Semitic languages. Marx contributed monographs and articles to journals on a wide variety of subjects, published two volumes of collected essays (*Studies in Jewish History and Booklore* (1944); *Essays in Jewish Biography* (1947)), and with Max L. *Margolis wrote *A History of the Jewish people* (1927). This pioneering work, stressing economic and social life, organization and legal status, offers the general reader a soundly researched, authoritative, and objective Jewish history in one volume. Marx amassed a private collection of 10,000 books. The J.T.S. library on his arrival in 1903 contained 5,000 volumes and 3 manuscripts. At his death it possessed 165,000 books and over 9,000 Hebrew, Samaritan, Aramaic, and Yiddish manuscripts, comprising the largest Judaica collection in the world. Marx's ability to determine a manuscript's age merely by looking at it was legendary. His annual reports of the library's growth, containing a detailed description of materials acquired, were eagerly awaited by bookmen and scholars.

In 1926 Marx was elected to the Medieval Academy of America; he served as president of the American Academy for Jewish Research (1931–33), president of the Alexander Kohut Memorial Foundation, vice-president of the American Jewish Historical Society, and member of the publications committee of the Jewish Publication Society of America.

His sister, Esther, married S. Y. *Agnon. [M.EP.]

His brother MOSES (1885–) was also a bibliographer and librarian. Best known for his contributions to the field of

Hebrew incunabula and 16th-century Hebrew printing, he was a founder of the Soncino Gesellschaft and a Berlin publisher. He issued, inter alia, bibliophile editions of early works by his brother-in-law S. Y. Agnon, and co-edited with Aron Freimann in the 1920s the *Thesaurus Typographiae Hebraicae Saeculi XV*. In 1926 he went to the United States and joined the staff of the Hebrew Union College Library in Cincinnati. Retiring as head cataloger in 1963, he served briefly as curator of rare books and then settled in Israel. Much of Marx's research in early Jewish printing remained unpublished. [S.F.C.]

Bibliography: *Alexander Marx Jubilee Volume*, 2 vols. (Eng. and Heb., 1950), 481–501, incl. bibl.; A. S. Halkin, in: AJYB, 56 (1955), 580–8; *Festschrift fuer A. Freimann* (1935), 91–96; *Gershon Soncino's Wanderyears in Italy* (1936), index; *Sefer ha-Yovel li-Khevod A. Marx* (1943), 1–10 (introd.).

MARX, KARL HEINRICH (1818–1883), German social philosopher and the chief theorist of modern socialism. His system, named Marxism, became in the 20th century a new creed for hundreds of millions of socialists, often hardening into a dogma, particularly in the communist movement and in the Soviet Bloc, the People's Republic of China, and other communist countries. Born in the Rhineland town of Trier (then West Prussia), Marx was the son of Jewish parents, Heinrich and Henrietta Marx. Heinrich Marx became a successful lawyer and when an edict prohibited Jews from being advocates, he converted to Protestantism in 1817. In 1824, when Karl was six years old, his father converted his eight children. Karl Marx was educated at the high school in Trier and studied history and philosophy at the universities of Bonn and Berlin. He was strongly influenced by Hegel's philosophy and joined a radical group known as the Young Hegelians. In 1841 he received his degree of doctor of philosophy at the University of Jena where he presented his dissertation on the "*Differenz der demokritischen und epikureischen Naturphilosophie.*" When his connection with the Young Hegelians prevented him from obtaining a teaching position at the University of Bonn, he turned to journalism. He became the editor of the liberal Cologne daily *Rheinische Zeitung* in 1842. In the following year he married Jenny von Westphalen, daughter of a high Prussian official. Soon afterward, the *Rheinische Zeitung* was suppressed and the young couple went to Paris where Marx expected to edit the *Deutsch-Franzoesische Jahrbuecher*. In fact only one issue was brought out (1844).

The young Marx's ideas attracted the attention of older radicals and socialists. Moses *Hess, one of the editors of the *Rheinische Zeitung*, wrote in a letter to the German-Jewish writer Berthold *Auerbach: "Dr. Marx, as my idol is called, is still a very young man; he will give medieval religion and politics their last blow. He combines the deepest earnestness with the most cutting wit. Imagine Rousseau, Voltaire, Holbach, Lessing, Heine, and Hegel united in one person. I say united, not lumped together—and you have Dr. Marx." While evolving from his philosophy as a Young Hegelian to his own concept of man as creating himself by labor, he transmitted in his writings a passionate yearning for a new, free society in which socialist man will transcend the imposed "alienation" from state-controlled society and from his labor and its fruits. An article contributed to the *Deutsch-Franzoesische Jahrbuecher* by Friedrich Engels led to a lifelong friendship between Marx and Engels. Engels, a fellow Rhinelander of socialist and Hegelian leanings, was the son of a wealthy industrialist with factories in Germany and England and was able to support Marx financially for the rest of his life. Marx, who maintained personal friendly contact with Heinrich *Heine, was one of the editors of *Vorwaerts*, a German newspaper published in Paris, which contained sharp attacks against the Prussian government. Its ambassador in Paris protested and Marx was expelled from France.

He went to Brussels where he wrote "*Misère de la philosophie, Response a la philosophie de la misère de M. Proudhon*" (1847), an attack on the Utopian social order advocated by Proudhon. Marx argued that the capitalistic society leads to the strengthening of the proletariat, a class which of necessity must become revolutionary and must overthrow the contemporary social organization based on exploitation. Socialist theorists should not waste their time in describing how society should be ideally built, but rather analyze what is going on in the present world.

In 1845, while in Brussels, Marx renounced his Prussian citizenship, and thus became "stateless." (Sixteen years later he vainly tried to regain it with the help of Ferdinand *Lassalle. He also applied for British citizenship, but the Home Office rejected his application (1874) on the grounds that "this man was not loyal to his king.") Marx cooperated with the "League of the Just" which became "The League of the Communists" (Bund der Kommunisten) which had its headquarters in London. He attended its second congress in London at the end of 1847 and together with Engels presented a new program for the League called *The Communist Manifesto*. It was published in February 1848 under the title *Manifest der Kommunistischen Partei* and rapidly became the best known work of modern socialism. It began with the words "A specter is haunting Europe—the specter of Communism," and postulated that "The history of all hitherto existing society is the history of class struggles. Freeman and slave, patrician and plebeian, lord and serf, guild-master and journeyman, in a word, oppressor and oppressed, stood in constant opposition to one another, carried on uninterrupted, now hidden, now open fight, a fight that each time ended, either in a revolutionary reconstitution of society at large, or in the common ruin of the contending classes." It ended with the words "The proletarians have nothing to lose but their chains. They have a world to win. Working men of all countries, unite!" A month after the publication of the Manifesto, Marx was expelled from Belgium and went to Paris. He left for Cologne soon afterward, following the outbreak of revolution in Germany, and became editor of the Cologne daily *Neue Rheinische Zeitung*. When the revolution failed and political reaction set in, he was expelled first from Cologne and then from Paris. He settled in London soon afterward where, in spite of the financial assistance that he received from Engels, he led the hard life of a political exile until his death.

From 1852 to 1861 Marx partly supported himself by being the London correspondent of the *New York Tribune*, commenting on current world affairs. He also drafted a resolution of English workers congratulating Abraham Lincoln on his election as president of the United States. For years he was an almost daily visitor to the British Museum Library, where he studied the great economists, many governmental "Blue Books" on industrial and labor relations, gathering material for his magnum opus "*Das Kapital, Kritik der politischen Oekonomie*" the first volume of which appeared in Hamburg in 1867. (Volumes 2 and 3 were completed and edited by Engels in 1885 and 1893 respectively.) Marx's other writings include *Die Klassenkaempfe in Frankreich 1848–1850* (1850; Eng. translation *The Civil War in France*, 1852); *Der achtzehnte Brumaire des Louis Bonaparte* (1852), and *Zur Kritik der politischen Oekonomie* (1859; Eng. trans. *Critique of Political Economy*, 1904).

Marx was not only a theoretician, he also took active part in the labor and socialist movement, and especially in

The grave of Karl Marx in Highgate Cemetery, London. Photo M. Ninio, Jerusalem.

the International Workingmen's Association (The First International), being a leading member of its General Council. But he lacked the qualities of a popular leader and his followers constituted a small minority of the association.

Marx's System. Marx had an exceptionally powerful mind and a rare capacity for research; his knowledge was encyclopedic. His influence on the modern world has been compared to that of the great religions, or Newton and Darwin. His work is the more difficult to understand as *Das Kapital* remained unfinished, and certain aspects of his doctrine only slightly sketched. His (and Engels') system—Marxism—is also known under the names of "economic" or "materialistic determinism," "dialectical materialism," or "scientific" (as opposed to "utopian") socialism. From Hegel he took the dialectical method, but ultimately applied it in a sense opposite to Hegel's idealist philosophy.

In what Marx calls "the social production" men enter into relations that are indispensable and independent of their will. These "relations of production" correspond to a definite stage of development of the material powers of production. The totality of these "relations of production" constitutes the real basis on which rises a legal and political "superstructure," and to which correspond definite forms of social consciousness. The consciousness of men does not determine their existence, but on the contrary, is determined itself by their social existence. At a certain stage of their development, the "material forces of production" come in conflict with the existing "relations of production" or—what is but a legal expression of the same thing—with "the property relations" within which they had been at work before. From forms of development of the forces of production these relations turn into their fetters. Then comes the period of social revolution. With the change of the economic basis the entire immense superstructure is more or less rapidly transformed. The bourgeois relations of production are the last antagonistic form of the social process of production, the productive forces in the womb of bourgeois society creating the material conditions for the ultimate socialist solution of that antagonism.

Marx's theory of value, which he considered as the very basis of his whole economic theory, is Ricardian in origin. The value of a commodity, according to Marx, is determined by the amount of labor socially necessary for its production. Of indispensable importance in the system is Marx's concept of "surplus value." The activity of the capitalist employer is represented by the formula $M-C-M^1$. With money (M), he buys the commodities (C) needed for production, and then sells the finished product for money (M^1). It is evident that M^1 is larger than M, else the whole process would involve no more than gratuitous trouble to the capitalist. Thus the labor power produces more than its value. This surplus value is the evidence and measure of the exploitation of the laborer by his employer.

Marx and the Jews. Marx's father Heinrich, whose original name was Hirschel ha-Levi, was the son of a rabbi and the descendant of talmudic scholars for many generations. Hirschel's brother was chief rabbi of Trier. Heinrich Marx married Henrietta Pressburg, who originated in Hungary and whose father became a rabbi in Nijmegen, Holland. Heinrich received a secular education, obtained a law degree, detached himself from his family and eventually also from his religion. Marx's mother spoke German with a heavy Dutch accent and never learned to write a grammatical letter in German. Intellectually she had little in common with her husband and son.

Karl Marx's attitude to Jews and Judaism evolved into what was later described as "self-hatred." At the age of 15 he was solemnly confirmed and became deeply attached to Christianity and German culture. Great influence on him was exercised by his future father-in-law, Baron Johann Ludwig von Westphalen, who was a neighbor of his family. But later his relations with other members of his wife's aristocratic family became strained. For them he was a Jew, an atheist, a nonconformist, a man lacking in good manners.

Marx's first essay in the *Deutsch-Franzoesische Jahrbuecher* was entitled *Zur Judenfrage* ("About the Jewish Question"), in which he criticized Bruno Bauer's book on the topic. Bauer had insisted that the Jewish question was essentially a religious one, insoluble unless the Jews gave up their faith and joined the society of the state as atheists or non-Jews. Although Marx favored political emancipation of the Jews, he used violent anti-Jewish language to present his view. Judaism for him was synonymous with the hated bourgeois capitalism. "The chimerical nationality of the Jew is the nationality of the merchant, of the moneyed man generally . . ." "What is the secular basis of Judaism? Practical need, self-interest. What is the worldly cult of the Jew? Huckstering. What is his worldly god? Money . . . Out of its entrails bourgeois society continually creates Jews . . . Emancipation from huckstering and from money, and consequently from practical, real Judaism, would be the self-emancipation of our era." Marx's essay is a striking evidence of his complete ignorance of Jewish history and culture, an ignorance surprising in light of his otherwise encyclopedic knowledge. Marx expressed his antagonism to Jews on a number of occasions: in his "Thesis on Feuerbach," in his articles for the *New York Tribune*, and in *Das Kapital*. In his private correspondence there are many derogatory references to Jews, who were for him the symbol of financial power and capitalist mentality, and also to Ferdinand Lassalle to whom he referred in his letters to Engels in typical anti-Semitic clichés. The only sympathetic account of Jews to emerge from Marx's pen is that which described their life and tribulations in the city of Jerusalem (New York Tribune, April, 15, 1854).

For six years Marx lived in London at 28 Dean Street, the house of a Jewish lace dealer. While on holiday he met the Jewish historian Heinrich *Graetz in Carlsbad and sent him his book on "The History of the Commune" as a present. Two years prior to his death the wave of anti-Jewish pogroms occurred in Russia (1881) and the influx of Jewish immigrants into London began. But there is no evidence of Marx's reaction to these events. His beloved daughter Eleanor, however, who acted as his secretary, considered herself Jewish, took interest in her ancestors, and had a warm appreciation for the Jewish workers in the East End of London. (She committed suicide in 1898 after an unhappy marriage to Edward Aveling.)

Marx's Jewish origin became a catalyst of anti-Jewish emotions. Already his rival in the First International, the Russian anarchist Michael *Bakunin did not refrain from anti-Jewish outbursts while attacking Marx. Later it served right-wing propagandists, particularly the fascist and Nazi regimes of the 1930s and 1940s, as a means to spice their anti-socialism with outright violent anti-Semitism. They used the term "Marxism" as denoting a sinister, worldwide "Jewish" plot against their national interests. In the Soviet Union, where Marxism-Leninism became the obligatory ideology, Marx's Jewish origin was generally mentioned in research works and encyclopedias until the 1940s, but from the later 1940s, when *Stalin's policy became anti-Jewish, it has been studiously concealed.

Collected Editions. The Marx-Engels (later the Marx-Engels-Lenin, and still later Marx-Engels-Lenin-Stalin) Institute in Moscow started in 1927 the publication of an academic edition of the collected works of Marx and Engels. In 1935 the publication was interrupted. There appeared: *Marx-Engels, Historisch-kritische Gesamtausgabe; Werke, Schriften, Briefe* first part: *Saemtliche Werke und Schriften mit Ausnahme des "Kapital"* (7 vols., 1927–35); third part: *Der Briefwechsel zwischen Marx und Engels* (4 vols., 1929–31). The volumes published thus far include the writings of Marx and Engels up to 1848 and all the known correspondence between Marx and Engels, 1844–83. The early volumes were edited under the direction of D. Ryazanov. An earlier collection is Franz Mehring's edition, *Aus dem literarischen Nachlass von Karl Marx, Friedrich Engels und Ferdinand Lassalle* (4 vols., 1902). D. Ryazanov edited the *Gesammelte Schriften von Karl Marx und Friedrich Engels 1852 bis 1862* (2nd ed., 1920). For a bibliography of Marx's works, see Ernst Drahn, *Marx-Bibliographie* (2nd ed., 1923). Reliable and good selective bibliographies on Marx, Engels, and cognate subjects are found in Donald Drew Egbert and Stow Persons (eds.), *Socialism and American Life* (vol. 2, 1952, pp. 34ff., and passim).

Bibliography: F. Mehring, *Karl Marx: the Story of his Life* (1936, repr. 1951), incl. bibl.; K. Korsch, *Karl Marx* (Eng., 1963), incl. bibl.; L. Schwarzschild, *The Red Prussian: the Life and Legend of Karl Marx* (1948); I. Berlin, *Karl Marx: his Life and Environment* (1963³), incl. bibl.; C. Tsuzuki, *The Life of Eleanor Marx* (1967); J. Lachs, *Marxist Philosophy: a Bibliographical Guide* (1967); R. Payne, *Marx: a Biography* (1968), incl. bibl.; M. Rubel, in: IESS, 10 (1968), 34–40, incl. bibl. On Marx and the Jewish Question: E. Silberner, *Ha-Sozyalizm ha-Ma'aravi u-She'elat ha-Yehudim*, pt. 2 (1955), 133–64, 448–51, includes detailed bibliography; idem, in: HJ, 9 no. 1 (1949), 3–52. [S.Lev./Ed.]

MARX BROTHERS, U.S. theatrical comedy team. Zany and irreverent, their wild and impromptu humor appealed to lowbrows and intellectuals alike. Originally, there were five Marx Brothers. All were part of a vaudeville act called "Six Musical Mascots" (their mother, Minnie, a sister of the vaudeville actor Al *Shean, was the sixth). The brothers, all born in New York, were Chico (Leonard, 1891–1961), Harpo (Adolph, later Arthur, 1893–1964), Gummo (Milton, 1894–), Groucho (Julius, 1895–), and Zeppo (Herbert, 1901–). When their mother left the act, they became "The Nightingales" and played in vaudeville as singers and comedians until they reached the Palace Theater in New York in 1918. They made their Broadway debut in 1924 in a revue called *I'll Say She Is*. By that time, the brothers had developed a distinct comic style. Chico donned a pointed hat over a deadpan face and affected an Italian accent. He was also an accomplished piano player, and he frequently broke the comedy with a turn at the keyboard. Harpo, with a battered hat over a frizzled wig of blond curls, never spoke during the act. He used two means to communicate—a bulb horn on stage and a romantic harp. He played the harp at concerts as well as in films. Groucho, wearing a swallowtail coat, chewing a long cigar and wearing a large black moustache, was master of the insult. After the brothers' film career had ended, Groucho confirmed his reputation as a wit as the master of ceremonies on a T.V. weekly quiz show. Zeppo, the straight man of the team in the movies, left the act in the early 1930s, and became a successful theatrical agent. Gummo, who was in the act only briefly, also became a successful agent. Their succession of stage and film comedies—such as *The Cocoanuts* (1929); *Animal Crackers* (1930); *Horsefeathers* (1932); *Duck Soup* (1933); *A Night at the Opera* (1935); and *A Night in Casablanca* (1946)—were considered cinema classics which continued to attract audiences on their many replays. Harpo's autobiography, *Harpo Speaks*, appeared in 1961. Groucho wrote *Groucho and Me* (1959), an autobiography, and *Memoirs of a Mangy Lover* (1963). His prolific and unconventional correspondence was published as *The Groucho Letters* in 1967.

Groucho (left), Chico, and Harpo, three of the Marx Brothers. Courtesy Personality Posters (U.K.), London.

Bibliography: A. Eyles, *The Marx Brothers* (1966); K. S. Crichton, *The Marx Brothers* (1951); O. Levant, *A Smattering of Ignorance* (1940, 1959²), on Harpo Marx. [S.Ka.]

MARYLAND, state on the E. coast of the U.S., one of the 13 original states. Religious intolerance and a one-crop tobacco economy caused Jews, with rare exceptions, to avoid the colony during the first century and half after its establishment in 1634. The first definitely identified Jew, Jacob Lumbrozo, was arrested in 1658 under the Act Concerning Religion (Toleration Act) of 1649, which imposed the death penalty for denial of Christianity. Lumbrozo was saved by an amnesty proclaimed while he was awaiting trial. Following the American Revolution, religious toleration and economic expansion attracted Jews to Maryland, and by 1825 there were about 150 Jews in the state. Despite continuous efforts to attain civic equality, it was only in 1826 that the "Jew Bill" passed whereby Jews were enabled to hold public office without submitting to a Christian oath. The credit for this achievement is chiefly

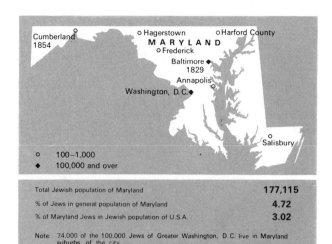

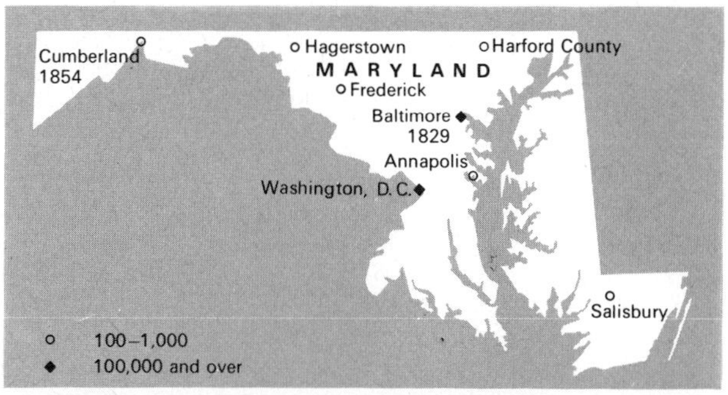

Total Jewish population of Maryland	177,115
% of Jews in general population of Maryland	4.72
% of Maryland Jews in Jewish population of U.S.A.	3.02

Note: 74,000 of the 100,000 Jews of Greater Washington, D.C. live in Maryland suburbs of the city

due to Solomon *Etting, Jacob I. *Cohen, Jr., and the non-Jewish legislator Thomas Kennedy. Between 1830 and 1870 over 10,000 Jews, primarily from Germany, settled in the state. East European Jews began to trickle into Maryland during the 1860s, and in great numbers from the 1880s. The Jewish population exceeded 40,000 in 1897, with about 50,000 in 1908. It was over 65,000 in 1924, when immigration quotas were introduced. The period of the Nazi persecutions and that of post-World War II brought an additional 5,000 Jewish immigrants. *Baltimore, the largest city in Maryland (population 914,000), is also its largest Jewish center (estimated population 106,000). After World War II, with the growth of the Jewish population in the Washington area, over 50,000 Jews settled in Montgomery and Prince Georges counties, which are suburbs of Washington that are part of Maryland. Outside these Washington suburbs and Baltimore there were only about 2,300 Jews in the rest of the state (1970), and only one other community, Annapolis, had a Jewish population of 1,000. In 1970 the estimated Jewish population of Maryland was 160,000 out of a total of 3,874,642. Marvin *Mandel was elected governor in 1968.

Bibliography: J. H. Hollander, in: AJHSP, 1 (1892), 25–40; 2 (1894), 33–44; E. M. Altefeld, *Jew's Struggle for Religious and Civil Rights in Maryland* (1924); A. Vossen Goodman, *American Overture* (1947), 133–49. [I.M.F.]

MARZOUK, MOSHE (1926–1955), Cairo-born Karaite Jew of Tunisian origin who was tried by a military court in Cairo on charges of spying for Israel and was executed on Jan. 31, 1955. In 1954 three Jews were arrested in Egypt and accused of setting fire to the USIS Library in Alexandria. Their arrest led to the discovery of a spy ring in Egypt and the imprisonment of ten other Jews, among whom were Marzouk and Samuel Azaar. Two of the prisoners managed to escape and the others were brought to trial on Dec. 10, 1954. According to the indictment, the accused had gathered information for Israel, carried out acts of sabotage, and spread false reports in Egypt designed to create public unrest. During the course of the trial, Max Bennet—described as the leader of the ring—committed suicide, after which Marzouk became the chief suspect. It was alleged that he had organized the Cairo group, had been trained in Israel, and had arranged wireless transmissions to Israel.

During his student days at the Cairo Medical School, Marzouk had become convinced that the future of all Egyptian Jews lay in their migration to Ereẓ Israel. He dedicated his life to the realization of his Zionist ideals and, while working as a doctor at the Jewish Hospital, organized the self-defense of the Cairo Jewish Quarter, helped to send young Jews to Israel, and, although he himself could have left, stayed at his post and worked for Israel.

SAMUEL AZAAR (1929–1955), a native of Alexandria of Turkish parentage, had been active in Zionist youth movements at an early age. A youth of great promise, he was awarded a scholarship that enabled him to study electronic engineering. Like Marzouk, he chose to stay in Egypt and carry out his mission. During the trial he was described as the head of the Alexandria group and was accused of operating an underground workshop to manufacture sabotage devices.

The trial of the ten defendants came to an end on Jan. 27, 1955. Two were acquitted, six were sentenced to prison terms ranging from five years to life, and Marzouk and Azaar were sentenced to death. In Israel, "Kedoshei Kahir" (the Martyrs of Cairo) as they came to be known were honored and commemorated in various ways.

Bibliography: H. M. Sachar, *From the Ends of the Earth: The Peoples of Israel* (1964), 328–66. [M.SHA.]

MASADA (Heb. מְצָדָה, *Meẓadah*), Herod's royal citadel and the last outpost of the Zealots during the Jewish War against Rome (66–70/73). Masada is situated on the top of an isolated rock on the edge of the Judean Desert and the Dead Sea Valley, approximately 15½ mi. (25 km.) south of En-Gedi. On the east the rock drops sharply approximately 1,300 ft. (400 m.) to the shore of the Dead Sea; its western side is approximately 330 ft. (100 m.) high above sea level. The rock is rhomboid shaped, very narrow in the north and broad in the center and measures approximately 1,950 ft. (600 m.) from north to south and approximately 1,000 ft. (300 m.) from east to west in the center. Its natural approaches are steep and arduous and include the "snake path" mentioned by Josephus on the east; the "white rock" (the Leuce of Josephus) on the west; and approaches on the cliff's northern and southern sides. The name Masada appears only in Greek transcription; it may be an Aramaic form meaning the *meẓad* ("stronghold").

History. The only significant source of information about Masada are the writings of Josephus (Ant., 14, 15; Wars, 1, 2, 4, 7) who relates that it was first fortified by the high priest Jonathan and named Masada by him (Wars, 7:285). Scholars disagree as to the identity of this Jonathan—whether he was referring to the brother of Judah Maccabee (mid-second century B.C.E.) or Alexander Yannai (103–76 B.C.E.) who was also called Jonathan. In another passage Josephus attributes Masada's construction to "ancient kings" (Wars, 4:399). In 40 B.C.E. Herod fled from Jerusalem to Masada with his family to escape from Mattathias Antigonus, who had been made king by the Parthians. He left his family, his brother Joseph and 800 men there to defend it against a siege by Antigonus (Ant., 14:361–2; Wars, 1:264, 267). According to Josephus the defenders almost died of thirst during the siege but were saved when a sudden rainstorm filled the creeks and pits on the summit of the rock. Herod, returning from a trip to Rome, raised the siege and carried his family off to safety (Ant., 14:390–1; 396, 400; Wars, 1:286–7, 292–4). Subsequently "Herod furnished this fortress as a refuge for himself, suspecting a twofold danger: peril on the one hand from the Jewish people, lest they should depose him and restore their former dynasty to power; the greater and more serious from Cleopatra, queen of Egypt" (Wars, 7:300). Herod's transformation of the rock of Masada into a mighty fort apparently took place between 37 and 31 B.C.E. when most of its buildings and fortifications were erected. Although there is no information on Masada immediately after Herod's death, it can be assumed that a Roman garrison was probably stationed there from 6 to 66 C.E.

Figure 1. Masada from the south, with the Dead Sea and oasis of En-Gedi in the background. The arrow points to the Roman siege ramp. Courtesy National Parks Authority, Tel Aviv.

when, at the outbreak of the Jewish War Menahem, son of Judah the Galilean, attacked Masada at the head of a band of Zealots and captured it "by stratagem" (Wars, 2:408, 433). After Menahem was murdered in Jerusalem by Jewish rivals, *Eleazar, son of Jair, son of Judah (i.e., Menahem's nephew) escaped to Masada where he became its "tyrant" until its fall in 73 C.E. During this period Masada served as a place of refuge for all who were in danger of capture; Simeon bar Giora also stayed there for a time. In 72 C.E. the Roman governor Flavius Silva marched against Masada—the last remaining Zealot stronghold—at the head of the Tenth Legion, its auxiliary troops, and thousands of Jewish prisoners of war. After a prolonged siege a breach was made in the wall of Masada, whereupon Eleazar persuaded his followers to kill themselves rather than fall into the hands of the Romans. Josephus describes the dramatic last hours of Masada, Eleazar's speech to the Jewish defenders, the mass suicide of 960 men, women, and children and the burning of the buildings and stores of food. He quotes the story told by two women who together with five children survived by hiding in a cave. After Masada's conquest, Silva left a garrison there. Masada is also briefly mentioned by Pliny (*Natural History* 5:17, 73).

History of Exploration. Masada was correctly identified for the first time in 1838 by the Americans E. Robinson and E. Smith who viewed the rock which the Arabs called al-Sabba through a telescope from En-Gedi. The site was first visited in 1842 by the American missionary S. W. Wolcott and the English painter Tipping and next by members of an American naval expedition in 1848. Ten years later, F. de Saulcy drew the first plan of Masada. C. Warren in 1867 heading the "Survey of Western Palestine" climbed Masada from the east along the "snake path" and in 1875, C. R. Conder, on behalf of the survey, drew plans which were the most accurate up to that time. The first detailed study of the Roman camps was made by A. V. Domaszewski and R. E. Bruennow in 1909. Others followed in the beginning of the 20th century, foremost among them, the German A. Schulten, who surveyed Masada for a month in 1932. The major impetus for the extensive excavations of the site was provided by enthusiastic Israel scholars and amateurs, especially S. Guttman who correctly traced the serpentine twistings of the "snake path" and, with A. Alon studied Herod's water system (1953). He also excavated and restored one of the Roman camps. Large-scale Israel surveys were conducted for ten days in 1955 (headed by M. Avi-Yonah, N. Avigad et al.) and again in 1956 (headed by Y. Aharoni and S. Guttman) which established the general outline of the buildings and prepared new plans of the rock. Masada was mainly excavated in two seasons of 11 months (1963–65) by Y. Yadin, a large staff of archaeologists, and thousands of volunteers from all parts of the world. Almost the entire built-up area of the rock was uncovered as well as one of the Roman camps, and restoration of the buildings was carried out at the site simultaneously.

Early Settlements. Remains of a Chalcolithic settlement (4th millenium B.C.E.) including plants, cloth, mats, and

Figure 2. Northern area of Masada showing: 1. storage complex, with reconstructed storerooms at left; 2. upper terrace of the Northern Palace with living quarters and porch; 3. middle terrace with circular pavilion; 4. lower terrace. Courtesy Y. Yadin, Jerusalem.

Figure 3. Volunteer cleaning a floor mosaic in the Western Palace. Courtesy National Parks Authority, Tel Aviv.

potsherds were found in a small cave on the lower part of the southern cliff. Some sherds, but no evidence of building, were found on the summit from the Iron Age II (tenth–seventh centuries B.C.E.). As to the buildings attributed by Josephus to "Jonathan the high priest," only a few of the cisterns may possibly be pre-Herodian, but the discovery of tens of coins from the reign of Alexander Yannai indicates that Josephus' reference was most likely to Yannai and not to Jonathan the Hasmonean.

Herodian Period. One of Herod's first undertakings at Masada was undoubtedly the water system he constructed to ensure an adequate supply of water. It consisted of a drainage system to carry rainwater from the two wadis west of Masada to a group of cisterns in the northwestern slope of the rock. The water was deflected by dams and flowed along open plastered channels to 12 cisterns which were cut in two parallel rows. Each cistern had a capacity of up to 140,000 cu. ft. (4,000 cu. m.) and together could hold about 1,400,000 cu. ft. (40,000 cu. m.) The cisterns are mostly square in shape and have two openings, one leading from the aqueduct, and a second higher one, connected with an inner staircase for drawing out water. Other cisterns dug into the summit of Masada were filled with water brought by hand from the cisterns on the slope. Herod enclosed the entire summit of Masada, except for the northern tip, with a casemate wall (a double wall with the inner space divided into rooms). Its circumference measures about 1,400 m. (1,530 yd.) which corresponds exactly with the 7 *stadia* of Josephus' description. About 70 rooms, 30 towers, and four gates were found in the wall. The gates were elaborately built and consisted of a square room with two entrances, benches along the walls, stone slab pavements, and frescoes. They include the "snake path" gate in the northeast; the western gate in the middle of the western wall; the southern ("cistern") gate which led to a group of cisterns; and the northern ("water") gate near the bathhouse which served mainly for bringing water from the upper row of cisterns and was probably also the gate for the northern part of Masada.

NORTHERN PALACE. Herod constructed the most important buildings in the northern part of Masada—the highest point of the rock. Josephus gives a detailed account of a royal palace situated beneath the walls of the fortress on the western side facing north. Up to the 1950s this was believed to be a large building on the western side of the site but Israel explorers, including members of youth movements, discovered that the palace described was actually located on the north where it was daringly constructed on the very edge of the precipice. This palace, or more correctly, royal villa commanded a magnificent view of the

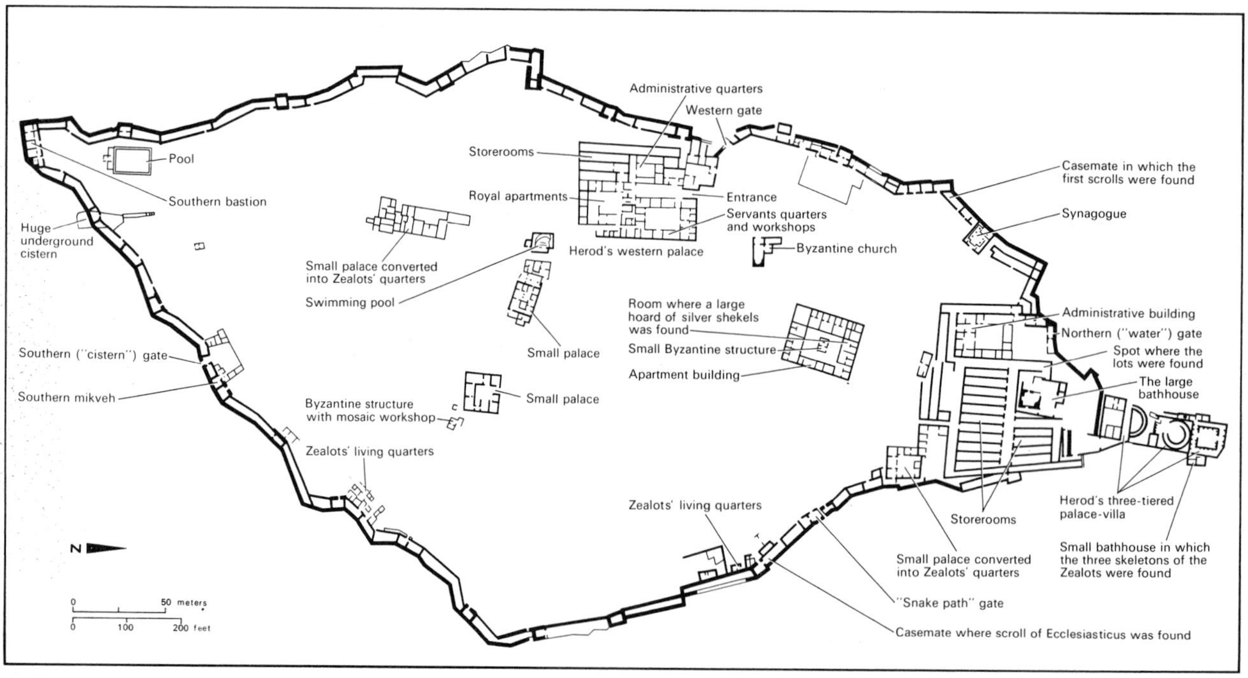

Plan of the fortress of Masada. After *Encyclopaedia of Archeological Excavations in the Holy Land.* Jerusalem, 1970.

surroundings as far as En-Gedi, and was built in three tiers, the upper containing the living quarters whereas the lower ones were designed for pleasure. The upper terrace is an extension of the narrow tip of the summit and contains a large semicircular balcony bounded by a double wall. A four-room building south of it with two rooms on each side of a court was apparently Herod's private abode. Its black and white mosaic floor in geometric designs is one of the earliest mosaics found in Israel. The walls and ceilings were decorated with frescoes. To the south a great white plastered wall separated the palace from the rest of Masada and left only a narrow passageway at its eastern end for a staircase. Columns had probably stood on the facade of the building and round the semicircular balcony. The middle terrace, approximately 65 ft. (20 m.) beneath the upper one, contained two concentric circular walls which served as a platform for a columned building. A staircase on the west led to the upper level and on the east stood a large room with traces of frescoes; between them was a roofed colonnade. This terrace was apparently designed for relaxation and a leisurely enjoyment of the view. The bottom terrace, approximately 50 ft. (15 m.) below the middle one, tapers to a narrow point; great supporting walls were built to form a raised square platform which was surrounded by low walls forming porticoes. Both the inner and exterior walls contained columns composed of sandstone drums plastered and fluted to resemble large monolithic columns. Frescoes on the lower part of the walls were painted to imitate stone and marble paneling. In the eastern corner of the terrace was a small bathhouse built in Roman style.

WESTERN PALACE. In addition to the palace-villa, Herod constructed a main official palace on the western side of Masada in the largest building found on the site, covering an area of nearly 37,500 sq. ft. (4,000 sq. m.). Containing scores of rooms and installations this palace was a self-sufficient unit and consisted of four wings: (1) Royal apartments in the southeast built around a large central court with a large reception hall leading into the throne room. In the hall was a magnificent richly colored mosaic pavement with circles and border ornaments of plant and geometric designs. This wing also contained service rooms

Figure 4. The synagogue (1), with a smail room at left probably used for ritual objects, and the adjacent casement wall (2). Courtesy Y. Yadin, Jerusalem.

as well as bathrooms with tubs, a cold water pool, and other installations, all paved with mosaics. (2) Servants quarters and workshops in the northeast around a central court and including a potter's workshop. (3) Storerooms in the southwest. (4) Administrative quarters in the northwest. Three small richly decorated palaces nearby probably housed members of Herod's family. Near one of them was a large swimming pool with broad plastered steps leading to the water. Two large rectangular buildings, apparently an administrative center and residence of high officials, were found in the north. A circular building with some 80 small niches set in rows in the inner walls on the southern part of the summit may have served as a columbarium for the gentile garrison troops.

BATHHOUSE. South of the Northern Palace was a large bathhouse with four rooms and a court built in traditional Roman style. The largest room, the *caldarium* (hot room), had a *hypocaust* (heating room) beneath it and its floor stood on about 200 tiny columns, mostly made of brick. The walls of the rooms were faced with perforated clay pipes through which an adjacent furnace drove hot air into the room. Its general plan resembles Roman bathhouses at Pompei and Herculaneum and especially in Herodian palaces at Jericho, Herodium, etc. The other rooms, the *frigidarium* (cold room), *tepidarium* (tepid room), and *apodyterium* (entrance room) were lavishly decorated with frescoes and mosaic floors which were later replaced by triangular tiles.

STOREHOUSES. The public storerooms, situated east and south of the bathhouse, consisted of long narrow rooms built of large stone slabs in two main blocks: a small one containing four rooms in the north and a larger one in the south with 11 rooms. Oil, wine, flour, etc. were each kept in a separate room in special storage jars. Food, weapons, and other costly goods were also stored in small storerooms attached to public buildings. During the Herodian period at Masada, the buildings were constructed in two main phases over a long period of time. Many amphoras for holding wine were dated (the year of the consul C. Sentius Saturninus, i.e., 19 B.C.E.), and inscribed that they had been sent to Herod, king of Judea. From the period of the Roman garrison stationed at Masada between the time of Herod and the Jewish War hundreds of coins were found from the reigns of Archelaus, Agrippa, and the procurators.

Period of the Zealots (66–73). The many finds from this brief seven-year period throw much light on the character of the Zealots, their way of life at Masada, and the end of the Jewish War. The sumptuous palaces and small number of dwelling rooms in the Herodian buildings could not be easily adapted for dwellings for the Zealots and were therefore used as command posts, public buildings, etc. Their decorative architectural parts were dismantled for building materials and furniture: floors, roofs, columns, tables, etc. The Northern Palace, which was covered with a thick layer of ashes, apparently served as an administrative center and defense post. On the bottom level near the bathhouse were parts of skeletons of a man, woman, and child. The woman's scalp and braids and leather sandals were preserved intact and nearby were hundreds of silverplated armor scales, arrows, and fragments of a *tallit*. The skeletons undoubtedly represent the remains of an important commander of Masada and his family. The

Figure 5. *Mikveh* built by the Zealots in the southern casemate wall, c. 66–73 C.E. 1. water conduit; 2, 3, 4. pools; 5. opening in the inner wall leading to the *mikveh*. At right, 6, 7, 8. three of the camps built by the Romans at the foot of the mountain, 73 C.E. Courtesy Y. Yadin.

Western Palace was also found covered with a thick conflagration layer. The rooms and courts of the small palaces were partitioned to serve as dwellings for large numbers of Zealot families. Alabaster and gold vessels and two hoards of shekels found under floors indicate that important leaders were housed in them. Some of the storerooms were found completely destroyed by fire while others had been left intact, apparently, as stated by Josephus, to prove to the Romans that they had not been driven to death by hunger. Most of the Zealots were housed in the casemate wall and in shacks of mud and small stones adjoining the wall and other buildings. Cooking stoves and niches for the cupboards were built into the wall. In rooms which had not been burnt remains of their daily life were strewn on the floors: clothing, leather, baskets, glass, stone and bronze objects, etc. Piles of charcoal with remnants of personal belongings indicate that they had collected all their possessions at the end and had set fire to them. Hundreds of coins and several scroll fragments were found in the rooms. The towers served mainly as public rooms or workshops, such as bakeries or tanneries.

MIKVA'OT (ritual baths). Two *mikva'ot* were found, one at the north and the other at the south, built exactly according to halakhic law which prescribed that part of the water of a *mikveh* must be supplied by rainwater flowing directly into it. The southern *mikveh* was built in a casemate and consists of three plastered pools. The largest one was for storing rainwater collected from the roof through a conduit and was connected by a narrow hole with a smaller pool (for immersion). Through the hole some of the rain-water could be mixed with other water brought by hand. A third small pool served for actual washing. An entrance hall and dressing room were added outside the wall. An elongated hall with a bench extending along three sides of the wall in one of the small palaces may have been a *bet midrash*.

SYNAGOGUE. A rectangular building from the time of the Zealots was found in the wall. Oriented toward Jerusalem, it contained four tiers of plastered benches along the walls and two rows of columns in the center. Lamps and an ostracon inscribed *ma'aser kohen* ("priest's tithe") were found here as well as parts of two biblical scrolls, Ezekiel and Deuteronomy, hidden in pits dug into the floor. In a corner was a room for ritual objects. This building, which was undoubtedly a synagogue, is the earliest known and the only one preserved from the time of the Second Temple (a similar synagogue was found later—in Herodium). It had originally been built by Herod on a different plan and may also have served as a synagogue in his time.

ZEALOT REMAINS. Twenty-five skeletons of men, women, and children were found thrown in a heap in a small cave on the southern cliff. Most of the skulls were of the type found in the Bar Kokhba caves in Naḥal Ḥever and it can be assumed that they are remains of Zealots. They were buried at Masada with full military honors in 1969.

COINS. Numerous coins struck during the Jewish War (66–70) were found both in large hoards (of 350, 200, and 100 coins) and in small numbers. Mostly ordinary bronze coins, they also include 37 silver shekels and 35 half-shekels representing all the years of the war and including the rare Year Five. This was the first discovery of shekels in a dated archaeological stratum.

OSTRACA. More than 700 ostraca were found mostly written in Hebrew or Aramaic. Since they can be dated exactly between 66 and 73 C.E. they are of great paleographic value and they also shed much light on the organization of life at Masada and the national and religious character of the defenders who scrupulously observed the ritual laws. About half of them were found near the storerooms. These bore single or several letters in Hebrew and may have been connected with the Zealot's rationing system during the siege. Others indicate tithes and names on others may be those of priests or levites. Eleven small ostraca each inscribed with a single name and all written by the same person may be the lots described by Josephus which the last ten survivors at Masada drew to choose who would kill the other nine and then himself. The names appear to be nicknames; one inscribed "ben Jair" may stand for Eleazar son of Jair, the commander of the Zealots.

Figure 6. Plaits and sandals of a young woman *in situ*. Courtesy Y. Yadin, Jerusalem.

SCROLLS. Parts of 14 biblical, apocryphal, and sectarian scrolls found at Masada are the first scrolls discovered outside of caves in a dated archaeological stratum. The biblical scrolls are mostly identical with the Masoretic Text but some show slight variations. These include parts of the books of Psalms, Genesis, Leviticus, Deuteronomy, and Ezekiel. Apocryphal scrolls include part of the original Hebrew text of the Wisdom of Ben Sira 39–44, dated to the first century B.C.E. and several lines of the Book of Jubilees. A fragment of a sectarian scroll of the Songs of Sabbath Service is identical with a scroll found at Qumran. It is important for dating the Dead Sea Scrolls and because it indicates that members of the Dead Sea Sect (apparently Essenes) took part in the Jewish War.

Roman Siege. Flavius Silva's effort to conquer Masada is still clearly visible. He surrounded the fortress with a siege wall (circumvallation) fortified by towers to prevent the 960 defenders from escaping. Round the base of Masada he set up eight camps including a large one in the east (Camp B) and in the northwest (F). The latter served as his headquarters and near it on the western slope he built an assault ramp of beaten earth and large stones on which was erected a siege tower from which the wall was attacked with a battering ram, catapults, and flaming torches. After the fall of Masada a Roman garrison was stationed there for at least 40 years, from 73 to 111, to which the latest coin find dates. Remains of the garrison troops were found in Camp F and also on Masada itself.

Byzantine Period. A group of monks settled at Masada in the fifth and sixth centuries, after a series of earthquakes

Figure 7. Some of the iron arrows, two with their original wooden shafts, found near the skeleton of a Zealot fighter. Courtesy Y. Yadin, Jerusalem.

Figure 8. Stone vessels found in Zealot dwelling chamber within the casemate wall. Courtesy Y. Yadin, Jerusalem.

had caused considerable damage to many of the buildings. They erected a small church with mosaic pavements of which little remains aside from a beautiful colored floor in a side room with 16 round medallions containing representations of fruits, flowers, plants, etc. West of the church was a refectory and kitchen. These last occupants of Masada dwelt in small stone cells scattered over the summit and in caves.

Since the completion of Masada's reconstruction, it has become one of Israel's major tourist sites. In 1971 a cable car was inaugurated on the eastern (Dead Sea) side. For Israel youth it is a unique symbol of courage and, on its summit, the recruits of the Israel Armored Corps swear their oath of allegiance: "Masada shall not fall again."

Bibliography: Y. Yadin, *Masada, Herod's Fortress and the Zealot's Last Stand* (1966), incl. bibl.; Livneh, in: *Ha-Teva ve-ha-Areẓ*, 10 (1954), 507ff., Alon and Avi-Yeftaḥ in: *Mi-Bifnim*, 16 (1953), 468–76; Kadman, in: IEJ, 7 (1957), 61–65; Y. Aharoni, *Meẓadah* (1957); M. Livneh and Z. Meshel, *Meẓadah* (1966).

[Y.YA.]

°**MASARYK, JAN GARRIGUE** (1886–1948), Czechoslovak diplomat and statesman, son of president Thomas G. *Masaryk. From 1925 to 1938 Masaryk was his country's envoy in London, but resigned after the Munich Pact (Sept. 30, 1938), which compelled Czechoslovakia to give up the Sudetenland. In 1940 he was appointed foreign minister of the Czechoslovak exile government in London and retained the post after Czechoslovakia's liberation in 1945 and after the Communist takeover on Feb. 25, 1948. On March 10, 1948, his corpse was found beneath the window of the Czernin Palace in Prague, in which the Foreign Ministry was situated. It is still controversial whether he was murdered for political reasons or committed suicide. During his stay in London he formed ties of friendship with Chaim *Weizmann and became an ardent supporter of Zionism. He fought against anti-Semitism during and after the Nazi period. In one of his speeches, Masaryk stated: "Every anti-Semite is a potential murderer whose place is in prison." Due to his intervention, Czechoslovakia allowed the Jewish refugees of the *Beriḥah to cross its territory and actively supported the proposal to establish a Jewish state. He believed that "to establish a Jewish state is one of the greatest political ideas of our time."

Bibliography: V. Fischl (Avigdor Dagan), *Hovory s Janem Masarykem* (1952); Ch. Weizmann, *Trial and Error* (1949), index.

[CH.Y.]

°**MASARYK, THOMAS GARRIGUE** (1850–1937), Czech philosopher and statesman, first president of *Czechoslovakia from its foundation (1918) until his retirement (1935). Born into a poor family in Hodonin (southern Moravia), as a child he was imbued with the popular Catholic anti-Semitism of his surroundings and was brought up to believe in the *blood libel. Impressions gained from Jewish schoolmates and a peddler made him change his opinions, a stage which he expressed in a sketch, *Náš pan Fixl* ("Our Mr. Fuechsel"). He studied at Vienna University where Theodor *Gompertz was one of his teachers. In 1882 he was appointed professor of philosophy at the newly founded Prague Czech University. He founded his "Realistic Party" and was elected to the Austrian parliament in 1907, and again in 1911. In his *Scientific and Philosophical Crisis of Contemporary Marxism* (1898) he asserted that, contrary to Marx's definition, Jews are a homogeneous nation, although they have given up their language. Masaryk conceived Zionism mainly in the moral sense. Impressed by the views of *Aḥad Ha-Am, he published in 1905 an essay on him. Believing that it was impossible to be a Christian and an anti-Semite, Masaryk considered that it was his duty to eradicate anti-Semitism from his people. In 1899 he took a leading stand in the *Hilsner blood libel case, "not to defend Hilsner, but to defend the Christians against superstition," publishing two pamphlets on the affair (see bibliography of Hilsner). He was attacked by the anti-Semitic mob and his university lectures were suspended because of student demonstrations against him. Similarly, in 1913 he came to the defense of Menahem Mendel *Beilis. He was enthusiastically received by U.S. Jewry upon his visit there in 1907. As a political émigré during World

Thomas Masaryk in Jerusalem with Joseph Ḥayyim Sonnenfeld, center, rabbi of Jerusalem's ultra-Orthodox community, 1927. Courtesy J. Buxbaum, Jerusalem.

War I, he established connections with Jewish and Zionist leaders such as Louis Brandeis, Julian Mack, Louis Marshall, Stephen Wise, and the Bohemian-born congressman Adolf Joachim Sabath as well as with Naḥum Sokolow and later Weizmann. When elected president of Czechoslovakia (1918) he declared that Jews would enjoy equal rights with other citizens and expressed sympathy with Zionism. He also supported the claims for recognition of the right of a Czechoslovak citizen to declare his nationality as Jewish.

By his personal example Masaryk did much to combat anti-Semitism in Czechoslovakia. In 1927 he visited Palestine, taking a special interest in the new settlements, their social problems and aspirations, and the newly established Hebrew University. In 1930 a Masaryk forest was planted near Sarid, and in 1938 *Kefar Masaryk, a settlement founded by pioneers from Czechoslovakia, was named after him. Tel Aviv conferred honorary citizenship on him in 1935.

Bibliography: E. Rychnovsky et al., *Masaryk and the Jews* (1941); K. Čapek, *President Masaryk Tells His Story* (1934); T. G. Masaryk, *Making of a State* (1927); O. Donath, *Masaryk und das Judentum* (1920). [CH.Y.]

MĀSHĀ'ALLAH (Heb. **Manasseh**) **B. ATHAŇ** (754–813), astronomer. Mashā'allah was probably born in Egypt, which is possibly the reason why he was also called al-Miṣrī, the Egyptian, but part of his life was spent at the court of the caliphs al-Manṣūr and al-Ma'mūn in Damascus. His name appears in many different versions, such as Macha Allah al Mesri, Mashallah, Messahalla, Messahalac, Messalahach, Masalla, Mescallath, Macelama, Macelarama—mainly due to distortions in Latin manuscripts.

Mashā'allah was one of the earliest independent and original scientific thinkers and scholars. His main efforts led to the transfer of astronomical knowledge from the East to the West by means of later translation; he also adapted Arabic data for the Cordoba astronomical tables. Unfortunately, none of his writings appears to have survived in the original texts and the main source is Latin translations, some of which give rise to confusion, since they list the same works under different titles. Mashā'allah may also have written an interesting astrological treatise in Hebrew *She'elot*, which was translated about 1146–48 by Abraham *ibn Ezra. In 1493 and again 1519 there appeared in Venice a smaller treatise on lunas and solar eclipses, *Epistola de rebus eclipsium et de conjunctionibus planetarum in revolutionibus annorum mundi* ... translated by Johannes Hispalensis from a Hebrew text. Some of the available manuscripts list 12 short chapters, all beginning with the words "Mashā'allah says ..." His treatise on the astrolabe was translated into Latin and English (R. T. Gunther, *Chavuv and Messahalla on the Astrolabe* (1929). A crater on the moon is named after him.

See also *Astrolabe, *Astronomy, and *Astrology.

Bibliography: Steinschneider, Arab Lit, 15–23; Steinschneider, Uebersetzungen, nos. 378–9; G. Sarton, *Introduction to the History of Science*, 1 (1927), 531; Brockelmann, Arab Lit, supplement, 1 (1937), 391; F. J. Carmoly, *Arabic Astronomical and Astrological Sciences in Latin Translation* (1956), 23–38. [A.BE.]

MASHĀʿIRĪ, AL-, family in Iraq. The al-Mashāʿirī family members in Babylonia during the 13th century included some distinguished personalities who occupied important positions in the state. They are mentioned by *Eleazar b. Jacob in his poems (see *Divan R. Eleazar b. Jacob ha-Bavli*, Jerusalem, 1935). They included: ISAAC MUHADHDHIB AL DAWLA IBN AL-MASHĀʿIRI and his sons, ELEAZAR, ELIEZER, and OBADIAH (poem 8); and ELEAZAR AMĪN ABU (OR IBN) MANṢŪR IBN AL-MASHĀʿIRĪ and his sons, EZEKIEL, YESHU'AH, and ISAAC (poem 185). The nature of their public positions is unknown. In the Arabic chronicle of Ibn al Fūṭī, a Jewish state official named MAHADHDIB AL-DAWLA NAṢR IBN MASHĀʿIRĪ is mentioned. In 1284 during the rule of the Mongol governor Arghūn (1284–91), he was appointed adviser in affairs of the state to the government dīwān. In 1289 when *Saʿd al-Dawla ibn al-Ṣāfi became vizier of the Mongolian Empire, he, in turn, appointed Muhadhdhib al-Dawla Naṣr as commissioner of Babylonia. Muhadhdhib occupied this position until his assassination in 1291. Some scholars believe that he is the same person as the above-mentioned Isaac Mahadhdhib al-Dawla.

Bibliography: Mann, Texts, 1 (1931), 268, 300, 304; Fischel, Islam, 95, 104, 115; idem, in: *Tarbiz*, 8 (1936/37), 234–5; A. Ben Jacob, *Yehudei Bavel* (1965), 38–39, 63–64; idem, in: *Zion*, 15 (1949/50), 59–61. [A.D.]

MASHGI'AḤ (Heb. מַשְׁגִּיחַ; "overseer" or "inspector"), designation of the person entrusted by the rabbinate with the supervision of *kasher* butcher shops, food factories, hotels, and restaurants. He is to ensure that the food products sold or prepared in those places comply with the requirements of the traditional *dietary laws. The *mashgi'aḥ* must be an observant Jew and know all the particulars of the dietary laws. He is, however, not competent to decide on his own whether a product is *kasher* or not. In some places the *mashgi'aḥ* is also called *shomer* (i.e., "watchman"). [ED.]

MASHIV HA-RU'AḤ (Heb. מַשִּׁיב הָרוּחַ; "He causes the wind to blow"), a phrase in the *Amidah* prayer, inserted after the first verse of the second blessing. It has two variants. The one for the winter season, "Thou causest the wind to blow and the rain to fall" is said from the last day of *Sukkot (after the Prayer for *Rain) until the last day of *Passover (until the Prayer for *Dew), and "who causest the dew to descend" is recited during the summer months in Ereẓ Israel, but only in the Sephardi ritual elsewhere. The praise of God as the dispenser of rain is referred to in the Mishnah (Ber. 5:2; Ta'an. 1:2) which ordains that it should be mentioned together with resurrection of the dead, as the sustenance of the living and the resurrection of the dead are both manifestations of the *gevurot* ("powers") of God. Another prayer for rain is recited in the ninth blessing of the *Amidah*.

Bibliography: Elbogen, Gottesdienst, 44ff., 518ff.; JE, 5 (1903), 643–5. [ED.]

"Mashiv ha-ru'aḥ" plaque, hung in the synagogue during the season in which the prayer was recited. Hamburg, 18th century, carved walnut. 10×15 in. (26×38 cm.). Hamburg, Altonaer Museum.

MASIE, AARON MEIR (1858–1930), physician. Born near Mogilev, Belorussia, Masie studied at the yeshivah in Mir and moved to Berlin in 1878, where he joined the Union of

Aaron Meir Masie, developer of Hebrew medical terminology. Courtesy Jerusalem Municipal Archives. Photo Ben Dov, Jerusalem.

Hebrew Socialists, founded by Aaron *Liebermann. In 1879 he was sentenced to a term in prison together with his comrades. Set free, he went to Zurich where he attended the Institute of Technology and came under the influence of Russian socialists, leading to his activity in the student revolutionary movement. Deeply affected by the 1881 pogroms, Masie actively supported the idea of a Jewish state. He joined the Jewish nationalist movement, and decided to study medicine so that he might have a profession which would be useful in Ereẓ Israel. Graduating in 1887, he went to Paris where he specialized in ophthalmology, and in 1888 he settled in Rishon le-Zion. There he was appointed medical officer for the Rothschild settlements in Ereẓ Israel.

From 1900, he lived in Jerusalem where he was active in medicine and in various cultural spheres. He was mainly interested in the revival of Hebrew, and saw his life task in the development of a Hebrew terminology in medicine and in the natural sciences. A member of the Va'ad ha-Lashon, he advised Eliezer *Ben-Yehuda in medical terminology. He published a monograph, *Maḥalat ha-Shivtah* ("Meningitis," 1910), and articles in *Ha-Ẓefirah, Ha-Or, Ha-Refu'ah* (vol. 2, 1923), and *Leshonenu* (vols. 1 and 2, 1928–30). Masie's dictionary of medical terms, *Sefer ha-Munaḥim li-Refu'ah u-le-Madda'ei ha-Teva*, was completed by S. *Tchernichowsky and published posthumously in 1934.

Bibliography: Slouschz, in: *Kovez ha-Ḥevrah ha-Ivrit la-Ḥakirat Ereẓ Yisrael ve-Attikoteha*, 3 (1935), 5–24 (incl. bibl.); *Sefer ha-Yovel... Petaḥ Tikvah* (1929), 433–43; M. Smilansky, *Mishpaḥat ha-Adamah*, 3 (1951²), 106–17; J. Saphir, *Ḥalutzei ha-Teḥiyyah* (1930), 50–55; Munker, in: KS, 12 (1935/36), 19–28, no. 70. [J.Kl./Ed.]

MASKIL (**Maschil**; Heb. מַשְׂכִּיל). (1) A term used in the superscription of 13 psalms (Ps. 32, 42, 44–45, 52–55, 74, 78, 88, 89, 142), and possibly also in 47:8. The Babylonian Talmud (Pe'ah 117a) explains such psalms as written by the psalmist with divine inspiration and then publicly proclaimed by another person called a *turgeman*, who added his own commentary. Both medieval and modern commentators have related the term to the root *skl* ("have understanding," e.g., Isa. 44:18; Ps. 2:10) and explain that a *maskil* is a didactic psalm. However the content of some of the psalms which have this superscription is not didactic in nature. Therefore, *maskil* is more likely a musical term signifying the proper accompaniment or melody for the recitation of the psalm (so David Kimḥi; see II Chron. 30:21–22—*maskilim*). See also *Psalms.
(2) An adherent of the *Haskalah movement.

Bibliography: C. A. and E. G. Briggs, *The Book of Psalms*, 1 (ICC, 1927), 9–11; J. Hempel, in: IDB, 3 (1962), 295; M. Dahood, *Psalms*, 1 (1966), 194; E. J. Kissane, *The Book of Psalms* (1964), 24. [Ge.B.]

MASKILEISON (Maskil le-Eitan), ABRAHAM BEN JUDAH LEIB (1788–1848), Russian rabbi and author. Born in Radoshkovich, Belorussia, Maskileison studied under his father, who was *av bet din* of Khotimsk in the district of Mogilev. Abraham served as *av bet din* in Novogrudok. Toward the end of his life he moved to Minsk, where he died. He lived in poverty all his life. He was the author of *Maskil le-Eitan* (Vilna, 1818), novellae to the tractates of orders *Mo'ed* and *Kodashim*. His reputation as a result of this work was such that the title of his book (from Ps. 88:1) became his own designation and family name. *Be'er Avraham* (1844), his novellae to tractate *Berakhot* and the order *Mo'ed*, was published by his son Aaron. In the introduction Abraham lists the seven aims of the work among which were to give explanations of those passages of Talmud in which the tosafists found difficulties, an exposition of those passages of Rashi where the tosafists disagree with him, and a profound examination of those laws of Maimonides for which the commentators were unable to find sources.

Some of his works were published posthumously: *Naḥal Eitan* (1855), published by his son Naphtali, contains novellae on the first two parts of Maimonides' *Mishneh Torah*, as well as novellae by Maskileison's brother Moses Nisan, compiled when he was 16. *Miẓpeh Eitan*, novellae and glosses to tractates of the Talmud, was published in the Zhitomir edition of the Talmud (1858–64). It was subsequently republished in the Vilna Talmud with additional material to the author's manuscript entitled *Tosefet Merubbah*. *Yad Avraham* (Vilna, 1880) is on the Shulḥan Arukh, *Yoreh De'ah*. His glosses and novellae on Maimonides' *Mishneh Torah* were assembled from various manuscripts and collected in the *Yad ha-Ḥazakah* (1900) under the title *Yad Eitan*. Comments and novellae on the *Ein Ya'akov* were assembled in *Ahavat Eitan* (1883–84). His notes on the *Sifrei* were published in S. Luria's edition (1866).

His sons included Aaron, Moses Nisan, and Naphtali. Moses Nisan was *av bet din* of the community of Shumiachi and author of the *Ḥikrei Halakhot* (1875), consisting of 32 halakhic studies, *pilpulim*, and *novellae*. Particularly well known was Naphtali (1829–1897), a book dealer and an accomplished scribe and poet, to both talmudists and *maskilim*. His main work is his critical edition, with additions, of the *Seder ha-Dorot* (1877–82) of Jehiel *Heilprin. Aaron's son was Abraham Isaac Maskileison (1840–1905), born in Smolevichi, where in 1874 he was appointed rabbi, an office he held for 15 years. He then served in Haslovich. He was a member of Ḥovevei Zion. In 1904 he was appointed rabbi of Stoypitz where he remained until his death. He left works in manuscript which were lost. Reuven *Katz, the chief rabbi of Petaḥ Tikvah, was his son-in-law.

Bibliography: N. Maskileison, in: A. Maskileison, *Naḥal Eitan* (1855), 4–8 (introd.); Fuenn, Keneset, 41; B. Z. Eisenstadt, *Rabbanei Minsk ve-Ḥakhameha* (1899), 27, 43, 67f.; Z. Harkavy, *Le-Ḥeker Mishpaḥot* (1953²), 5–15; R. Katz, in: A. Maskileison, *Maskil le-Eitan* (1966²), introd.; *Yahadut Lita*, 3 (1967), 71; Kressel, Leksikon, 2 (1967), 431f. [Y.Ho.]

MAṢLI'AḤ ṢĀLIḤ (d. 1785), Babylonian liturgical poet. He and his son Nissim (d. after 1816) wrote poems and *piyyutim* on various subjects. Some of these were published in regular and festival prayer books according to the rite of the Jews of Baghdad and its surroundings. Others were published by A. Ben-Jacob in *Shirah u-Fiyyut shel Yehudei Bavel ba-Dorot ha-Aḥaronim* (1970) which includes poems written in the Spanish meter in honor of events and personalities (rabbinical emissaries, etc.). Ṣāliḥ held the rabbinical seat of Baghdad from 1773 to 1785, and enquiries were addressed to him from Syria, Persia, Kurdistan, and other places on halakhic problems and community organization. Torah novellae of the father and the son are to be found in the works of their contemporaries.

Bibliography: A. Ben-Jacob, *Yehudei Bavel* (1965), 121–4. [A.B.-Y.]

MASLIANSKY, ZVI HIRSCH (1856–1943), popular Yiddish orator, the most eloquent and influential *maggid* on the American scene at his time. Masliansky was born in

Zvi Hirsch Masliansky, Yiddish orator and Zionist. Jerusalem, J.N.U.L., Schwadron Collection.

Slutsk, Belorussia. He taught at the Polish *talmudei torah* and at the yeshivah of Pinsk (1882–90), where one of his students was Chaim Weizmann. Stirred by the pogroms of 1881, he became a proponent of the idea of a return to Zion. He was active in Ḥibbat Zion, and fellow-Zionists M. M. Ussishkin, M. L. Lilienblum, Aḥad Ha-Am, and L. Pinsker encouraged him in his activity as a wandering preacher of Zionism. His fame as an impassioned orator spread rapidly throughout Russia. Compelled to leave the country in 1894, he undertook a lecture tour of Central and Western Europe and in 1895 emigrated to New York. During the three decades that followed, he helped popularize Zionism, wielding a great influence upon Yiddish-speaking immigrants, especially through his Friday evening sermons at the Educational Alliance on East Broadway. He combined the qualities of a *maggid* and those of a modern speaker. He was able to hold the attention of a popular audience and scholars as well. His imposing figure further strengthened the impression he made. He was also active in U.S. Zionist organizations.

Masliansky founded and coedited the daily *Die Yidishe Velt* (1902–05). His Yiddish sermons were published as *Maslianskys Droshes fir Shabosim un Yomim Toyvim* (2 vols., 1908; Eng. tr. *Sermons by Reverend Zevi Hirsh Masliansky*, 1926). He also published a memoir, *Fertsik Yor Lebn un Kemfn* ("Forty Years of Life and Struggle," 1924), and a collection of Hebrew articles, *Kitvei Masliansky* (1929).

Bibliography: L. Lipsky, *Gallery of Zionist Portraits* (1956); Rejzen, Leksikon, 2 (1927), 321–4; LNYL, 5 (1965), 467–70; EẒD, 3 (1965), 293–8; M. Danzis, *Eigen Licht* (1954), 223–8; M. Zablotski and J. Massel, *Ha-Yiẓhari: Toledot Zevi Hirsh Masliansky* (1895). [S.L.]

MASLOW, ABRAHAM H. (1908–1970), U.S. psychologist. Maslow was professor and chairman of the psychology department at Brandeis University from 1951. He was president of the American Psychological Association. Maslow was best known as a personality theorist, interested in motivational structure. In his work, he conceptualized within a phenomenological frame of reference that emphasizes the inherent goodness of man. He postulated a hierarchical theory of human motivation, wherein needs arrange themselves in a hierarchy from basic biological needs to those of self-esteem and self-actualization. Maslow's books include: *Principles of Abnormal Psychology* (1951) with B. Mittelmann; *Motivation and Personality* (1954); *New Knowledge in Human Values* (1959); and *Toward a Psychology of Being* (1962). [Ma. S.]

MASNUT, SAMUEL BEN NISSIM (13th century), talmudist and leader of Aleppo Jewry. Scarcely any biographical details are known of him, even the place from which his family originated being uncertain since some manuscripts mention Toledo and others Sicily. Judah *al-Ḥarizi, who visited Aleppo about 1218, waxed eloquent in praise of "Samuel b. Rabbenu Nissim of Aleppo." He wrote a special composition in his honor called *Iggeret Leshon ha-Zahav* (published by Z. H. Edelmann in *Divrei Ḥefeẓ,* 1853). Because of the similarity of the names and the places, scholars are inclined to regard the two as identical, in spite of an explicit statement by Samuel in one of his commentaries (Dan. 7:25) to the effect that it was written in 1276, which would make him about 90 years old at the time. Masnut's renown rests on his extensive midrashic commentary, *Ma'yan Gannim,* which apparently embraced most, if not all, of the Bible. The following parts have been published: Genesis (1962), which the editor entitled *Midrash Bereshit Zuta;* Job (1889); and Daniel and Ezra (1968). His commentary on Chronicles is extant in manuscript, and is remarkably similar verbally to the commentary of David *Kimḥi. Fragments of his commentary on Numbers have also been preserved. Masnut's work is totally unlike other midrashic commentaries, even those of *David ha-Nagid and Jacob b. Hananel *Sikili—who were near him in place and time and bear some resemblance to him—in that he rarely uses his own words in the presentation of his commentary. It is, in effect, a verbal amalgam of different and independent midrashic sources woven together into a unique exegetical fabric. His familiarity with halakhic and aggadic sources (for which he rarely gives references) is quite exceptional. His books contain important halakhic material for research on the history of *halakhah,* the texts of the Talmuds and the Midrashim, and particularly the various Aramaic **targumim,* of which he made frequent use. A *piyyut* by Masnut for the morning service of the Day of Atonement has been preserved in the liturgy of Algeria and Tunisia.

Bibliography: Samuel b. Nissim Masnut, *Ma'yan Gannim . . . al Sefer Iyyov* (1889), introd. by S. Buber (ed.); idem, *Midrash Bereshit Zuta* (1962), introd. by M. Kohen (ed.), and 331–8; idem, *Ma'yan Gannim . . . al Sefer Daniel ve-Sefer Ezra* (1968), introd. by S. Land and S. Schwarz, and 164–71; A. Kasher, in: *De'ot,* 23 (1963), 59–62. [I.T.-S.]

MASORAH. See Supplementary Entries.

MASORETIC ACCENTS (Musical Rendition).

HISTORICAL DEVELOPMENT.

In Jewish tradition, the formal reading of certain of the books of the Bible in worship and in study is carried out with a musical intonation linked closely with the masoretic accents of the text and governed by fixed rules and practices (see *Masorah; in supplementary articles). Public reading from the Bible is attested much earlier than the establishment of the written systems of accentuation. In the Bible itself, such readings are mentioned only in connection with special occasions (cf. Deut. 31:12; II Kings 22:1–3; Neh. 8:8, 10:30). The practice was not a prominent part of the Temple liturgy but became so in the *synagogue. Talmudic sources attest the detail with which the practice was regulated, citing the choice and order of the scriptural passages for Sabbaths and weekdays (Monday and Thursday) and the feasts, the qualifications of the reader, the translation of each verse into the vernacular, the *somekh* ("supporter") who aided the reader, or the replacements of the lay reader by a specialist (sometimes the **ḥazzan*). As to the musical element, the sources merely say that the Bible was to be read and studied only by melodic recitation (cf. Meg. 32a; Song R. 4:11). It is doubtful whether the terms *pissuk/piskei te'amim* (the division by the *te'amim*)

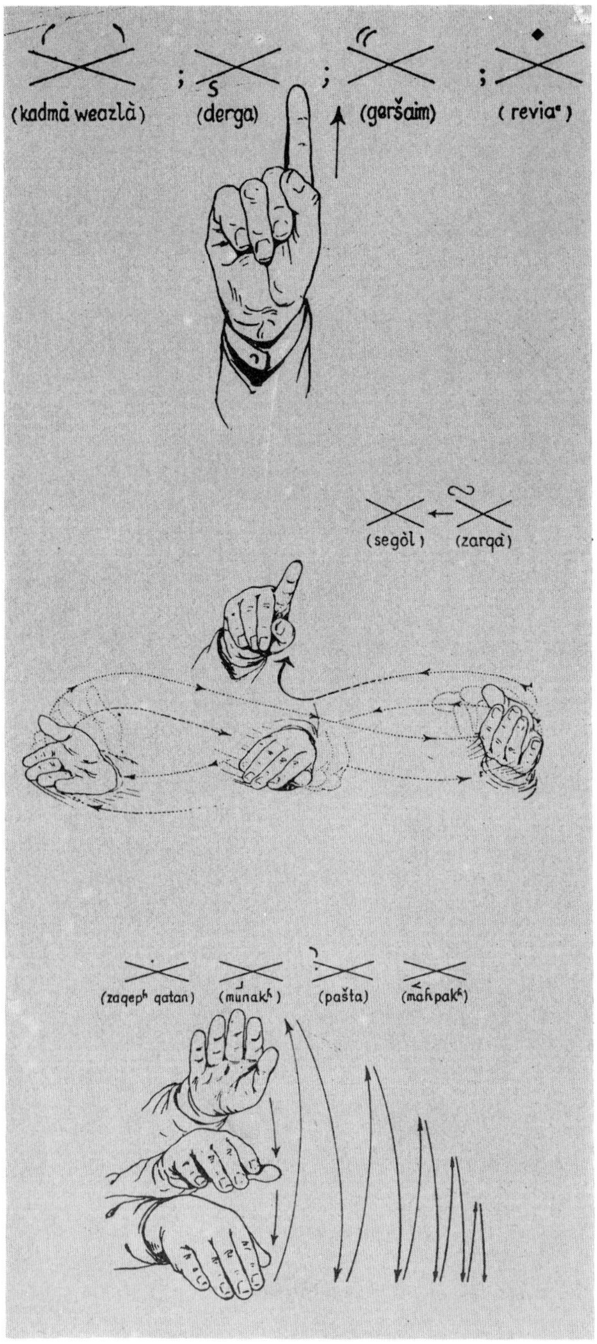

Figure 1. Hand movements indicating the accents and their melody, used as memory aids and prompting signs for the reader. Shown here are the movements still practiced in Rome. Several other communities preserve relics of a similar practice, although the movements are not identical. From I. Adler, "Histoire de la musique réligieuse juive," in J. Porte (ed.), *Encyclopédie des musiques sacrées,* vol. 1, 1968, 472–3.

refer to the melodic element, although they are connected with the aide-memoire movement of the reader's or *somekh's* hand (Meg. 3a; Ned. 37a; Ḥag. 6a; see Figure 1). The talmudic usage of the term *te'amim* is still not sufficiently clear; however, considering the strict regulation of every other element of the scriptural reading, it is inconceivable that the melodic rendition could have been left to the ad hoc invention or choice of the reader.

A comparison with the practices of "scriptural" reading in other religious traditions—such as Vedic recitation in India or Buddhist recitation in Japan and other countries—reveals that none is spoken or sung but they are "cantillated"; that this cantillation is based upon strict conventions handed down by oral tradition (which were described explicitly only in the respective Middle Ages of each culture); and, most important, that a basic similarity of constructive principles (not of melodic content) can still be recognized in all such practices throughout the Asian continent, including all Jewish traditions throughout the Diaspora. The melodic structure in all these traditions is of the kind defined by Curt *Sachs as "logogenic," where the musical element is generated by the words, bonded to the verbal and syntactical structure, and subordinated to the communication of the text, with no attempt at musical autonomy.

This "pan-Asiatic" style must already have been present in cantillated Bible reading in the synagogue preceding the period in which the system of written accents began to be developed. The Tiberian system of accent signs and vowel signs and their functions was based on existing practices not only of the pronunciation and grammatical basis and syntactical structure of the text, but also of its musical rendition. The earliest surviving treatise of this system, *Ben-Asher's *Dikdukei he-Te'amim,* mentions the *ne'imah* (melody) in the characterization of several of the accents. Neither this nor the preceding "Palestinian" and "Babylonian" systems seem to show the intention of establishing a complete correspondence between each accent sign and a specific and different melodic motive, which implies that no such correspondence existed in practice at that time, and that there was no intention on the part of the masoretes to create it artificially.

Comparative studies of the living traditions of the present and the evidence gleaned from the medieval and later masoretic treatises reveal that only in the Ashkenazi Diaspora was the system developed and augmented with the aim of having each accent sign expressed by a distinct melodic formation. The farthest point along this path is reached by the Ashkenazi cantillation of the Torah. Even there, however, one finds different accent signs expressed by identical melodic formations (e.g., *segol, zakef,* and *tippeḥa* in the "Polish-Lithuanian" tradition), or identical accent signs expressed by different melodic formations (e.g., the *darga* preceeding a *tevir* as against the *darga* preceding a *munaḥ-revi'a,* in the Western Ashkenazi tradition). Other traditions are still more limited in their repertoire of distinct melodic motives and content themselves with the expression of the divisive accents, or even of the major divisive accents only. This style is probably not the result of any erosion or loss of knowledge, but may well be the surviving evidence of the earliest stages of the system, perhaps even of the

Figure 2. The earliest known notation of Pentateuch cantillation. Western Ashkenazi, perhaps notated by Johann Boeschenstein. In J. Reuchlin, *De accentibus et orthographia linguae hebraicae,* Hagenau, 1518, fol. [83b]–[87a]. First opening, fol. [83b]–[84a]. The motives are given in the tenor part, while the *discantus, altus,* and *bassus* parts are mere harmonizations in contemporary art-music style, added arbitrarily to enhance the presentation. Jerusalem, J.N.U.L.

EXAMPLE 1. Beginning of A. Z. Idelsohn's comparative table of Pentateuch cantillation motives. From A. Z. Idelsohn, *Melodien,* vol. 2, 1922, 44 and 45, also reproduced in his *Music,* 44–45.

EXAMPLE 2. "Table of Accents" for the Pentateuch, as read in the *ḥeder* in Tunis, with different intonation from the one used regularly in the synagogue. Such a cantillated sequence of the accent names is used for *ḥeder* instruction in many communities, often being called, from its initial motive, *lu'aḥ zarka* (*zarka* table). Transcribed by A. Herzog from a version recorded by him in Jerusalem in 1962. From A. Herzog, *The Intonation of the Pentateuch in the Ḥeder of Tunis,* 1963, 9, ex. 3b.

Proto-Tiberian or Palestinian or Babylonian ones. In all traditions, the rendition of the accents of the prophetic books, the *haftarah,* and the Hagiographa is also partial and selective as is their rendition in the special style used for study in the **ḥeder.*

Practice. The musical rendition of the text in conformity with the accent signs is based on the convention (as described above) of each sign or group of signs representing a certain melodic motive. The graphic symbol does not stand for an absolutely predetermined sequence of tones. As in all music cultivated by oral tradition, the motives exist as "ideals" to be realized in performance, within certain margins of flexibility. Preservation of the "ideals," i.e., the style, is assured by several factors: the support of the well-defined and strict doctrine of the grammatical and syntactical functions of the accents; the deliberate teaching, by which the tradition is handed on from generation to generation; and the constant public practice of the system in the synagogue, where not only the layman's rendition (when "called up to read") but even that of the specialized reader, *ba'al kore*—not always, and in some communities never, identical with the *ḥazzan*—is always subject to the critical ear of the more learned members of the community. The margin of flexibility, on the other hand, makes it possible to link, or rather blend, the motives as they are recalled and enunciated successively by the reader so as to create a melodic organism. The style itself remains constant, but each reader may interpret it with a certain individuality and will never repeat his previous performance precisely when he reads the same passage upon another occasion.

Theoretically, the accent signs are divided into only two categories: the accents of the "twenty-one books" (טעמי כ"א) and those of the Psalms, Proverbs, and Job (טעמי אמ"ת). In practice, the musical renditions show a much greater diversity of styles. These are determined by (1) the text, i.e., the specific book, chapter, verse, or contents; (2) the liturgical circumstances; (3) the medium of performance; (4) regional stylistic traditions; (5) the above-mentioned margin for individual interpretation.

STYLE DETERMINED BY TEXT. Separate melodic conventions exist for the Pentateuch (Torah), the prophetic books (*haftarah*), and for several of the Hagiographa (cf. The Five *Scrolls, Musical Rendition). These may not be interchanged, and explicit prohibitions are found in several rabbinic sources (e.g., *Sefer Ḥasidim,* par. 302). Nevertheless there is a kind of infiltration of motives from one book to the other, as evinced by the appearance of motives from the cantillation of the Torah in that of the *haftarah.* Some motives may also be common to more than one book, such as certain motives in the cantillation of the Book of Esther and Lamentations in the Ashkenazi tradition. In principle, however, each book has its distinct and characteristic "melody," i.e., melodic style.

Most regional traditions have special "festive" styles for the reading of certain chapters or paragraphs—the *Song of the Sea, the *Decalogue, and often also for the Blessing of Moses (Deut. 32) and the *Priestly Blessing (Num 6:24–26), and also a "low" intonation for the "rebuking" text of Deut. 28:15–68. The Ashkenazi tradition is particularly rich in special intonations. A kind of "roster formula" is used for some verses in the story of the wanderings in the desert (Num. 10 and 33). Another intonation emphasizes the importance of certain single verses in the Torah (see A. Baer, *Baal T'fillah* (1883[3]), 39–40, nos. 117, 118, 121). Another one is used for the dramatic turning points in the Book of Esther (1:22; 2:4, 15, 17; 3:15; 4:1, 14; 5:7, 13:6, 10). Chapters and verses referring to calamities, such as several verses in the Book of Esther, are read in the style of the Book of Lamentations.

EXAMPLE 3. "Table of Accents" for the Pentateuch, according to the Eastern Ashkenazi ("Poland-Lithuania") tradition. From S. Kisselgoff, A. Zhitomirsky, and P. Lwow (eds.), *Lider-Zamlbuch far der yidisher shul un familye,* 1914[3], 133.

Verses or parts thereof which denote supplication and the request for pardon are intoned in the style in which the Torah is read on the High Holy Days (see below). In the reading of the Book of Esther in the Ashkenazi tradition there is even one "quotation" from the prayer mode of the High Holy Days (Esth. 6:1) and another from that of the *selihot (ibid. 6:3).

Style Determined by Liturgical Circumstances. During the three pilgrimage festivals the reading is more festive, with more ornamentations and prolongations. The atmosphere of the Ninth of *Av influences the reading of the *haftarah* on the preceding Sabbath, the reading of the Torah on the Ninth of Av itself, which should be in a "low" voice and is sometimes rendered "almost without the accents," and its *haftarah* (which is often read with a verse-by-verse translation into the vernacular—Arabic or Ladino). The Ashkenazim of Holland read the Torah on the Ninth of Av in a style related to the *haftarah* style of the Polish-Lithuanian region. On the High Holy Days and *Hoshana Rabba, the Ashkenazi tradition has a special style for the reading of the Torah ("in a low melody, as if plaintive," as mentioned in the *maḥzor* ed. Sabionetta, 1557). On the Sabbath nearest to the wedding day, among some Near Eastern communities, the section "And Abraham was old" (Gen. 24) is read in front of the bridegroom in a special festive style. Other modifications applied on Hoshana Rabba and Shavuot are described below.

Style Determined by the Medium of Performance. When part of the regular prayer service, the reading of the Torah, *haftarah,* or Scrolls is always carried out by a single reader. On certain other occasions, however, the reading may become communal. On the night of Hoshana Rabba and Shavuot, when there are assemblies for "studying" the Torah, chapters or sections are cantillated in alternation by several members of the group. The style is an abbreviated version of the regular Torah style, or that of the study of the Torah in the *ḥeder.* Cantillation by the entire congregation according to the accents is found in the Sephardi communities for the **Shema Yisrael* (i.e., Deut. 5:7 and 11:19) during prayer and for the "Thirteen Divine Attributes" (i.e., Ex. 34:6–7) during the *seliḥot.* In the *ḥeder,* the study of the Torah is traditionally carried out through constant, loud repetition by all the children together. This was done in many communities in a special intonation, related to the accents but more simple in structure than the one practiced by the adults in the synagogue. There are also other kinds of "*ḥeder* tunes" based upon the sequence of accented (long) and unaccented (short) syllables in the text, similar to those found in the group recitation of passages from the Mishnah and other prose texts in many Near Eastern communities (cf. *Talmud, Musical Rendition). It can be assumed that the "*ḥeder* tunes" have remained unchanged for very long periods, since under these circumstances there is no inducement, or indeed any possibility, for personal expression and initiative and the melodic element is wholly subjugated to the pedagogical task.

Regional Stylistic Traditions. A. Z. *Idelsohn's assumption (see bibliography, and frequently repeated in later writings) that the living traditions of masoretic cantillation developed out of one common—i.e., pre-Exilic—base does not seem to be confirmed by a more thorough examination. This is one of the central problems in research of Jewish music (cf. *Music, Introduction), and, by its very nature, this research is particularly prone to conscious or unconscious wishes to justify a foregone conclusion that there is, indeed must be, a common base. In the present state of research, it may tentatively be proposed that while the principle of cantillation as such is a common heritage (see introduction, above), the diverse regional and functional styles observable today stem from an albeit small number of distinct source styles. It can be assumed that several "melodies" for the reading of the Bible were current and equally legitimate at the time in which the forms of synagogal worship began to be stabilized. Later, by processes which we are unable to reconstruct, some of these "melodies" and melodic elements were accepted as normative by one or several communities, were attached to specific books, and were sanctified by custom. It must always be remembered that the accent signs themselves are not, and never were, a sound script with the same possibilities and limitations of the music notation which

Example 4. Analytical presentation of three formations of the "*tevir* complex" in the combination of *tevir, etnaḥta,* and *sof pasuk,* in the reading of the Pentateuch, Eastern Ashkenazi tradition. From J. L. Ne'eman, *Ẓelilei ha-Mikra,* vol. 1, 1955, 110.

EXAMPLE 5. Exodus 12:21–22 as rendered in the "Babylonian" (Iraq), "Syrian," and Amsterdam Sephardi communities. From A. Z. Idelsohn, *Melodien*, vol. 2, 1922, preface, 33, 34, 37.

developed in Western Europe. They are only reference aids to the evocation of "motivic ideas" which, in themselves, are an orally transmitted patrimony. Some late medieval and renaissance writers mention the "style of the Sephardim," but with hardly any concrete definitions which would enable its character to be understood (Simeon b. Ẓemaḥ *Duran, *Magen Avot;* the Karaite Elijah *Bashyazi (1420–90) in his *Sefer ha-Mitzvot* (ed. 1870), fol. 71 and 81; Elijah *Levita in his *Tuv Ta'am*).

The living traditions of the present may be classified according to five major regional styles: (1) Yemenite, (2) Ashkenazi, (3) Middle Eastern and North African, (4) Jerusalem Sephardi, (5) northern Mediterranean local diverse styles.

(1) The Yemenite Style. This is particularly rich in distinct sub-styles for the biblical books and for particular chapters and in various divisions among single and group performers. One of the "*ḥeder* tunes," built upon the pentatonic scale, is related to the Ashkenazi Torah style.

(2) The Ashkenazi Style. This is the earliest to be documented in musical notation, in Johannes *Reuchlin's *De accentibus...* (1518) and soon afterward by several other scholars. The melodic elements have been preserved most tenaciously among the Western Ashkenazi communities, including southern Germany. The Eastern Ashkenazi Torah style (known as "Polish-Lithuanian") is somewhat different from the Western one. The *haftarah* style is particularly developed in Eastern Europe, and is nowadays common to both the Eastern and Western Ashkenazi communities.

(3) The Middle Eastern and North African Style. This is the style designated by Idelsohn as "oriental." Its distribution, with many sub-styles, ranges from Cochin to Algeria, through Persia, Bukhara, Iraq, Syria, Kurdistan, the Caucasus, and North Africa. There is a close connection between this and the styles of the European Sephardi communities in Italy, France, Holland, England, and America. It can also be traced in some Balkan communities (those of the "Romaniote" rite). Its influence is also noticeable in the intonation of the Song of Songs of the "Polish-Lithuanian" tradition. The earliest notation of this style was published in 1699 in the Hebrew Bible edited by Daniel Jablonski, to whom it was given by David de Pinna, a *parnas* in the Portuguese community of Amsterdam.

(4) The Jerusalem Sephardi Style. This is the style designated by Idelsohn as "oriental Sephardic." It is found around the eastern shores of the Mediterranean, from Turkey and the Balkan communities to North Africa, and centered in Ereẓ Israel. Due to the prestige of its association with Jerusalem and Ereẓ Israel, it overlaid and frequently even ousted many local traditions throughout the Mediterranean countries. The Torah style in this tradition cannot represent the pre-expulsion Spanish tradition, since it is found neither in North Africa nor among the European Sephardim, but is based upon the Maqam *Sigah*. It seems to be a relatively recent development, but this phenomenon needs further study before a conclusion can be confirmed.

(5) The Northern Mediterranean Styles. Several communities in this area, such as Rome and *Carpentras (in Provence), have distinct local styles of their own. The Carpentras tradition survives only in notation (M. and J. S. Cremieu, *Zemirot Yisrael*, c. 1887), since the community itself no longer exists.

In Israel, the "ingathering of the exiles" has caused a major deterioration in many of the local and regional traditions brought into the country, since the immigrants often could not keep up their homogenous associations centered around the synagogue. The breakdown of the traditional education system (there is no organized *ḥeder* of any community except the East Ashkenazi) has also broken the chain of tradition. The regional styles tend to disappear, yielding

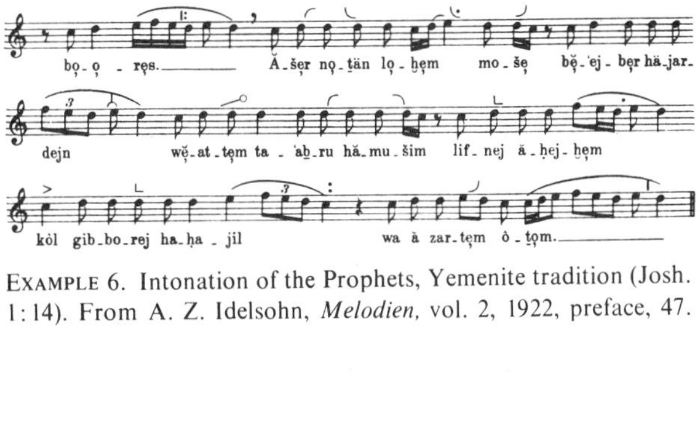

EXAMPLE 6. Intonation of the Prophets, Yemenite tradition (Josh. 1:14). From A. Z. Idelsohn, *Melodien*, vol. 2, 1922, preface, 47.

EXAMPLE 7. Intonation of the Prophets, two Western Ashkenazi traditions (Isa. 43:10; *ibid.*, 56:7). From A. Baer, *Baal Tfillah*, 1883[3], 37–39.

to two dominant and dominating styles: the East Ashkenazi is gradually adopted in most Ashkenazi synagogues and the "Jerusalem Sephardi" prevails, especially for the reading of the Torah, in the synagogues of all the Near Eastern and North African communities. In the latter, the virtuoso status and ambitions of the *ḥazzan* or *ba'al kore* and the influence of the maqam-based Arabic art music at present come near to completely eroding the traditional base of masoretic cantillation proper.

See also *Music; the Five *Scrolls, Musical Rendition; *Psalms, Musical Rendition; and articles on the musical traditions of the various major communities.

Bibliography: MUSICAL RENDITION: Sendrey, Music, nos. 1931–2155; S. Rosowsky, *Cantillation of the Bible—the Five Books of Moses* (1957); Idelsohn, Music, 35–71; Idelsohn, Melodien, 2 (1922), 33–53 and examples in vols. 1, 3, 4, 5, and 8; C. Sachs, *Rise of Music in the Ancient World* (1943), 78–89 and passim; J. L. Ne'eman, *Ẓelilei ha-Mikra* (1955); idem, *Kera be-Ta'am* (1967); M. Perlmann, *Dappim le-Limmud Ta'amei ha-Mikra*, 3 vols. (1958–61); A. Herzog, *Intonation of the Pentateuch in the Ḥeder of Tunis* (1963); H. Avenary, *Studies in the Hebrew, Syrian and Greek Liturgical Recitative* (1963); idem (H. Loewenstein), in: *Zeitschrift fuer Musikwissenschaft*, 12 (1930), 513–26; idem, in: *Bat Kol*, 2 (1961), 56–58; L. Levi, in: *Italyah*, ed. by M. A. Shulvass, 1 (1945); E. Gerson-Kiwi, in: DBI, suppl. 5 (1957), 1449–62; idem, in: *Die Musikforschung*, 13 (1960); idem, in: *Journal of the International Folk Music Council*, 13 (1961), 64–67; S. Levin, in: JBL, 87 (1968), 59–70.
[AV.HE.]

MASSACHUSETTS, New England state of the U.S. Massachusetts had a population of 6,000,000 in 1969, of whom 275,000 were Jews. In 1917 the state's Jewish population was 190,000; by 1937 it had risen to 263,000, dropping to 223,000 in 1959, and then rising over the following decade. Nearly 80% of the Jews in the state in 1969 lived within an hour's ride of *Boston. A 1969 study by the Combined Jewish Philanthropies of Greater Boston reported 176,000 Jews in its areas of service and 32,000 more lived in adjacent towns of metropolitan Boston. Three-fourths of Greater Boston Jewry resided in the suburbs to the north, west, and south. Boston itself, including Dorchester, Mattapan, Brighton, and Roxbury, had only 40,000 Jews. Only 14,000 remained in Dorchester-Mattapan, compared to 50,000 in the mid-1950s. The Chelsea-Malden-Revere section, 40% Jewish in the 1940s, in 1969 had only 28,000 Jews, and the number was declining steadily.

The shift from the older neighborhoods in and around Boston to the suburbs created substantial new Jewish communities in Newton-Wellesley (35,000); Brookline (29,500); Cambridge-Belmont-Lexington-Concord-Waltham-Woburn (16,000); Natick-Framingham (6,000); the Massachusetts Bay north shore towns of *Lynn, Swampscott, Nahant, Salem, and Saugus (20,000); and the southern suburbs (23,000). Thousands of young Jewish scientists, engineers, and manufacturing entrepreneurs work in the industrial complex that lines Route 128 west of Boston, and they have given a new élan to the Jewish communities that have sprung up in the expanded Boston suburbs.

Beyond metropolitan Boston there were 35 cities and towns with 100 or more Jewish residents in 1970. The largest Jewish populations were to be found in *Springfield (12,000), *Worcester (10,000), *Fall River (5,000), New

Bedford (3,600), Lawrence (2,100), Lowell (2,000), Pittsfield (2,000), Haverhill (2,300), and Holyoke (1,300). At the end of the 1960s there were about 200 synagogues in 85 communities, most of them erected in the 1960s either as the first houses of worship in newly settled areas or as replacements for older sanctuaries in communities where Jewish residence antedated the massive move out of Boston. There are synagogues in Plymouth and Salem, as well as on Cape Cod (in Hyannis) and Martha's Vineyard, two popular seashore resorts. The newest congregation in New Bedford, Tifereth Israel Synagogue (Conservative), was founded in the 1920s. This congregation and Ahavath Israel (Orthodox) were still serving the community in 1970. Pittsfield has three synagogues: Ahavath Sholem, Knesses Israel (Conservative), and Temple Anshe Amunim (Reform), founded 1867. Lawrence has four congregations: Sons of Israel (1894), Congregation Anshi Sfard (1899), which first worshiped in various halls (briefly in City Hall), dedicated its first synagogue in 1905 and in 1955 merged with Tifereth Israel Congregation (founded 1941), Anshai Sholom, and Temple Emanuel (Reform). Holyoke has two synagogues: Sons of Zion (Conservative), formed in 1901, and Rodphey Sholom (Orthodox). Rodphey Sholom originated in 1899 when the local lodge of the Order of Brith Abraham assumed religious as well as fraternal functions and organized a synagogue which became Rodphey Sholom.

Early History. Aaron *Lopez, a ship owner, was the first Jew naturalized in Massachusetts (at Taunton, 1752). In 1777 he founded the first Jewish community in Massachusetts, at Leicester near Worcester. The families of Lopez and of Jacob Rodriguez *Rivera, numbering 61 people, stayed in Leicester until after the Revolution.

Massachusetts' first permanent Jewish community was established in the late 1830s in Boston, where Central European settlers established the state's first Jewish congregation, Ohabei Shalom, in the 1840s. For about 100 years the Boston Jewish community exercised a powerful influence on the growth of new settlements throughout the state.

The first Jews to take up permanent residence outside Boston were German and East European peddlers who replaced the itinerant Yankee traders in the 1840s and 1850s. Typical of these was Abraham *Kohn, later a figure in the Republican Party in Illinois. In 1842 and 1843, Kohn carried a pack through central and northern Massachusetts, praying alone in the fields, sometimes with his brother and partner, Judah, or with other Jewish peddlers he met on the way. Peddlers like Kohn settled down and became storekeepers; they were followed by tailors, watchmakers,

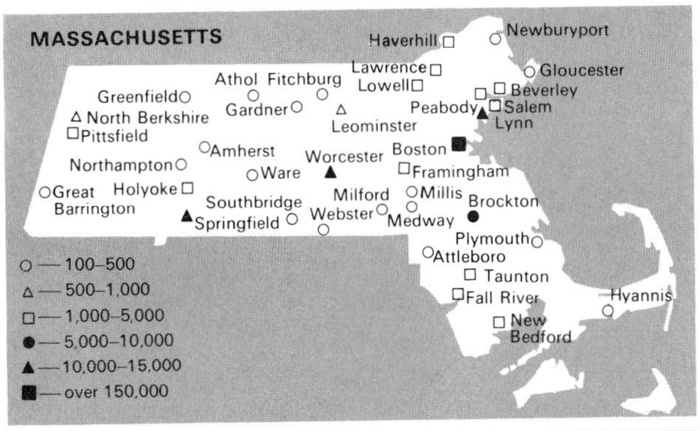

Total Jewish population of Massachusetts	259,635
% of Jews in general population of Massachusetts	4.75
% of Massachusetts Jews in Jewish population of U.S.A.	4.42

Jewish communities in Massachusetts. Population figures for 1968.

Figure 1. Temple Emanuel of Worcester, Massachusetts.

cigarmakers, shoemakers, and dealers in dairy products, leather goods, provisions, lumber, and kerosene.

These merchants established themselves in the factory and mill towns, including Pittsfield (1850), where most were of German origin; Worcester (1860); Holyoke (1873; first congregation, Agudas Achim, founded 1895); Springfield (1881); Fall River (1881); Lawrence (late 1880s); Lynn (1893); and Haverhill (1897). Some Sephardi Jews lived in New Bedford, which has a Jewish cemetery said to date from the post-Revolutionary era, as late as the 1850s, when the first German Jews arrived. One of these was Leopold *Morse, who served in Congress from a Boston district in 1877–85 and again in 1887–89. A burial society, Bnay Israel, was formed in New Bedford in 1857. The first Jewish burial took place the same year. East European Jews arrived in New Bedford about 1877, the earliest of them being Isaac Goodman and Simon Siniansky. The first *minyan* was formed in 1879; services were held in Siniansky's house. The first congregation, Ahabath Achim, was founded in 1893 and purchased a cottage house as its first synagogue. A new synagogue was dedicated in 1899. In 1898 Congregation Chesed Shel Emes was incorporated; it occupied a new synagogue building in 1903. Springfield also had a colony of Sephardi Jews in the 1830s, but the first Russian arrivals found no trace of them. German and Polish Jews arrived in Worcester in the late 1860s.

Contemporary Life. Massachusetts is the home of two major national Jewish institutions: the nonsectarian *Brandeis University, in Waltham, and the *American Jewish Historical Society, whose headquarters is on the Brandeis campus. The *Menorah Society, the first Jewish intercollegiate movement, was organized at Harvard University in 1906.

Jewish charitable institutions are coordinated by the Combined Jewish Philanthropies of Greater Boston and by counterpart organizations in 12 other cities, including Jewish welfare federations in New Bedford, Pittsfield, Lawrence, and Holyoke. Outside Boston, B'nai B'rith maintains Hillel foundations for Jewish college students at Brandeis University; Clark University (Worcester); Nichols College (Dudley); Amherst College and the University of Massachusetts (Amherst); Harvard, Radcliffe, and the Massachusetts Institute of Technology (Cambridge); Tufts University and Jackson College (Medford); Lowell Technical Institute; and Smith College (Northampton). Jewish community centers (JCCs) and YM-YWHAs are affiliated

Figure 2. Nineteenth-century wood engraving of the first synagogue in Boston, Massachusetts. Cincinnati, Ohio, American Jewish Archives.

with the Greater Boston Associated JCCs, and similar institutions are maintained in Fitchburg-Leominster, Haverhill, Lawrence, Lynn, New Bedford (JCC founded as YMHA 1911), Springfield, Worcester, Holyoke (JCC founded as YMHA in 1918), and Pittsfield. Lawrence is also seved by the Jewish Family Service. Four Jewish weeklies are published in the state: the *Jewish Advocate*, in Boston; the *Jewish Times*, in Brookline; the *Jewish Civic Leader*, in Worcester; and the *Jewish Weekly News*, in Springfield.

George Feingold, who was the Republican nominee for governor when he died in 1958, was the first Jew to win statewide elective office, serving three terms as attorney general (1952–58). Springfield, Worcester, Holyoke, and Pittsfield (Daniel Englander, elected 1902) have had Jewish mayors. In 1961 Jacob J. Spiegel was named to the State Supreme Court, the first Jew to serve in that office; he was still serving on the court in 1970. Abraham *Ratshesky was ambassador to Czechoslovaskia under President Hoover (1930–32). David K. *Niles was one of President Franklin D. Roosevelt's key White House aides and later served President Truman in a similar capacity (1942–51). Maxwell H. *Rabb served as secretary to the Cabinet under President Eisenhower (1953–58).

Bibliography: L. M. Friedman, *Pilgrims in a New Land* (1915); idem, *Jewish Pioneers and Patriots* (1942); J. R. Marcus, *Early American Jewry*, 2 vols. (1951–53); B. Postal and L. Koppman, *Jewish Tourist's Guide to the U.S.* (1954), 219–41. [B.P.]

MASSADAH (Heb. מַסָּדָה), kibbutz in northern Israel, in the Jordan-Yarmuk valley, affiliated with Iḥud ha-Kevuẓot ve-ha-Kibbutzim. Massadah was founded in 1937, during the Arab riots, as a tower and *stockade settlement by pioneers from Poland. In the Israel *War of Independence the village had to be evacuated before the onslaught of the Syrian army (May 1948) and was completely razed, but the site was taken back 24 hours later by Israel forces and the

Figure 1. Hoisting the iron walls of the watchtower at kibbutz Massadah on its first day of settlement, March 22, 1937. Courtesy Keren Hayesod, United Israel Appeal, Jerusalem.

Figure 2. Kibbutz Massadah, a tower and stockade settlement in the Jordan Valley, 1939. Courtesy J.N.F., Jerusalem.

kibbutz was rebuilt. After the *Six-Day War (1967), the village came frequently under shelling. Its farming is based on fruit, crops, and carp ponds. In 1968 the population of the kibbutz was 285. [E.O.]

MASSARANI, TULLO (1826–1905), Italian author and statesman. Born in Mantua, Massarani studied law and painting, at the same time taking part in the conspiratorial struggle for the unification of Italy. As a result of the failure of the 1848 revolution and his collaboration with Mazzini's followers, he had to take shelter in Switzerland and later lived the life of a refugee in Germany and France. On the proclamation of the Kingdom of Italy in 1860 he returned to Milan. He was elected to parliament for three legislative periods (1860–67), and in 1876 was appointed senator. He also held municipal offices.

An extremely prolific writer, Massarani introduced the works of Heinrich *Heine to Italian readers. He left a great number of critical essays, historical, political, and autobiographical writings, translations and verse, which were collected after his death in 24 volumes (1906–11). Massarani's criticism does not delve beneath the surface, but reveals a broad and up-to-date culture in which scholarship is blended with a journalistic approach. Among his most important works are *L'idea italiana attraverso i tempi* (1869), *Eugenio Camerini, i suoi studi e i suoi tempi* (1877), and *Carlo Tenca e il pensiero civile del suo tempo* (1886). During his latter years he devoted himself to an original and erudite study of laughter (1900–02). Massarani's essays earned him a high reputation among European art critics, and in 1878 he was elected chairman of the international jury of art at the Paris Exhibition.

Bibliography: G. Natali, *Il pensiero e l'arte di Tullo Massarani* (1910); B. Croce, *La letteratura della nuova Italia* (1950^{3}). [G.R.]

MASSARANO, JACCHINO or **ISACCHINO** (16th century), Italian choreographer. In 1583 he was commissioned to provide the dances for Bernardo Pino's *Gli Ingiusti Sdegni* which was performed by the Jewish Theater in Mantua in honor of the marriage of the duke's heir, Vincenzo Gonzaga, who was an intimate friend. The following year, when Vincenzo visited Ferrara, he was sent to supervise a similar performance there. In 1591, the poet Manfredi corresponded with Massarano and also commissioned him to supervise dances for him. When Giovanni Guarini's *Pastor Fido*, the most famous play of its day, was staged at the ducal palace in Mantua, in 1598, Massarano was commissioned to supervise the "Blindfolded Dance" for the ballet. He was also appointed choreographer for one of the Jewish theater's biggest performances, *Accessi de Amor fatta* by Niccolo Grassi in 1605, when 64 members of the company took part, and in the following year he choreographed the Tasso's *Delli Intreghi de Amor*. Massarano was also a composer, teacher, and singer. He was father of Abraham Massarano, historian and author of *Ha-Galut ve-ha-Pedut* (Venice, 1634).

Bibliography: C. Roth, *Jews in the Renaissance* (1959), 284–5 and index; S. Simonsohn, *Toledot ha-Yehudim be-Dukkasut Mantovah*, 2 (1964), index and bibl.; A. D. Ancona, *Origini del Teatro in Italia* (1891^{2}), index; E. Faccioli, *Mantova, la storia, le lettere, le arti* (1962). [Ed.]

MASSEKHET (pl. **Massekhtot;** Heb. מַסֶּכֶת, pl. מַסֶּכְתּוֹת; lit. "a web," idiomatically a tractate; cf. Lat. *textus*), a main subdivision of each of the six orders, or *sedarim*, of the Mishnah. Each mishnaic order is divided into a number of *massekhtot;* each *massekhet* is divided into chapters, and each chapter into Mishnayot or paragraphs in the Babylonian Talmud and into *halakhot* in the Jerusalem Talmud. The total number of tractates of the entire Mishnah, which was originally 60, was subsequently, by a further minor subdivision, increased to 63. *Massekhet* also designates the corresponding *Gemara* tractates. Beginning with the *editio princeps* (1520–23, Venice), in all standard editions of the Babylonian Talmud each *massekhet* has a fixed number of folio pages. The most voluminous tractate, numbering 176 folios, is *Bava Batra;* the smallest is *Horayot* numbering 14. In the Jerusalem Talmud the original pagination of the tractates has been preserved only in the Venice edition of 1522–23, and in its later reprints. As there is no *Gemara* on all mishnaic tractates, the number of *massekhtot* in the Babylonian Talmud is only 37 and in the Jerusalem Talmud 39. Occasionally the term *massekhet* is also applied to rabbinical books outside the Talmud.

See also *Talmud; *Mishnah; and *Minor Tractates.

Bibliography: Epstein, Mishnah, 981–3. [J.K.M.]

MASSELL, SAM JR. (1927–), U.S. lawyer and politician. Massell, who was born in Atlanta, Georgia, served as a flying instructor in the U.S. Army Air Force during World War II. In 1961 he made his first attempt to win public office and was elected to the office of vice-mayor as a Democrat. He held the position until 1969 when he was elected Atlanta's youngest and first Jewish mayor with a victory margin provided by a white liberal and poor black coalition. In the course of the campaign Massell charged that members of the "power structure," meaning the corporations and civic groups who had long ruled Atlanta, were anti-Semitic. Active in Jewish affairs, Massell was a member of the American Jewish Committee, Jewish War Veterans, and the B'nai B'rith. [Ed.]

MASSERMAN, JULES HOMAN (1905–), U.S. psychiatrist and psychoanalyst. Born in Chudnov, Poland, Masserman was taken to the United States in 1908. He first taught at the University of Chicago and in 1952 was appointed professor of neurology and psychiatry at Northwestern University's medical school. Masserman's thought and experience in psychiatry and psychotherapy are set forth in his textbook *The Principles of Dynamic Psychiatry* (1946, 1961) and in *The Practice of Dynamic Psychiatry* (1955). These works represent a theoretical and clinical attempt to correlate various physiological and psychological concepts of behavior into a comprehensive system (biodynamics), and to base a therapy upon this. He conducted many animal experiments to check, clarify, and extend psychological premises about human beings. He also added "un-defenses," such as the general delusion of invulnerability and immortality by which man denies danger and death, to the Freudian concepts of defenses against anxiety. Masserman's later works include *Transcultural Problems of Youth* (1969), and he directed many instructional motion pictures, such as *The Dynamics of Experimental Neurosis* (1944). He edited the annuals *Science and Psychoanalysis* and *Current Psychiatric Therapies*, and was associate editor of *Psychosomatics*. He was also president of the American Academy for Psychoanalysis and of other learned associations. In 1969 he became president of the International Association of Social Psychiatry. [Lo.M.]

MASSU'OT YIẒḤAK (Heb. מַשּׂוּאוֹת יִצְחָק), moshav shittufi in the Coastal Plain, 8 mi. (13 km.) N.E. of Ashkelon, affiliated to the Ha-Po'el ha-Mizrachi Moshav movement. Massu'ot Yiẓḥak was originally founded in 1945 by pioneers from Hungary and Czechoslovakia as a kibbutz in the Hebron Hills, the second village in the Eẓyon Bloc, under the name Massu'ot ("Beacons"). The name Yiẓḥak was added in honor of Chief Rabbi I. H. *Herzog in a ceremony attended by him. Along with the other three settlements of the Eẓyon Bloc, Massu'ot Yiẓḥak fell in the Arab Legion's onslaught (May 13, 1948), and was completely destroyed, its surviving defenders being taken to Jordan as prisoners of war. After their release and return to Israel, they established their village on the present site (1949), several years later deciding to go over to the moshav shittufi settlement form. In 1969 the village was based on intensive agriculture and had a metal factory. Its population in 1968 was 403. [E.O.]

Prayers at Massu'ot Yiẓḥak on the day of its foundation, October 7, 1945. Courtesy J.N.F., Jerusalem. Photo Rosenblit.

MASTBAUM, JOEL (1884–1957), Yiddish novelist. Born in Poland, he lived in Warsaw from 1905 to 1933, working as a house painter until he could support himself with his writing. In 1933 he emigrated to Palestine and wrote many stories about his experiences there. Overtaken by World War II while visiting Poland, he managed to return to Tel Aviv and described in articles and in a Hebrew volume his 60 days under the Nazis. Mastbaum was a romantic impressionist, emphasizing moods rather than scenes. His most important works of fiction were: *Marita's Glik* ("Marita's Fortunes," Yiddish, 1923; Hebrew, 1941), about three Jewish generations in Poland; *Fun Roytn Lebn* ("Red Life," 2 vols., 1921–23), about the revolutionary youth of 1905; *Salamandra* (1926), on Jewish workers in a glass foundry; *Nokhemkes Vanderungen* ("The Wanderings of Nokhemke," 1925), an adventurous romance beginning in a Polish town and ending in Buenos Aires. A projected trilogy of Palestine between 1933 and 1948 was left uncompleted; only the first volume, *Der Koyakh fun der Erd* ("Power of the Earth," 1951), was published.

Caricature of Joel Mastbaum, by Ross. Courtesy Genazim, Tel Aviv.

Bibliography: Rejzen, Leksikon, 2 (1927), 316–21; LNYL, 5 (1963), 464–7; S. Niger, *Dray Doyres* (1920), 263–73; M. Ravitch, *Mayn Leksikon*, 1 (1945), 128–30; 3 (1958), 254ff.; S. Bickel, *Shrayber fun Mayn Dor* (1964), 348–52. [M.Rav.]

MASTEMA (Heb. מַשְׂטֵמָה), the name of the devil in the Book of *Jubilees. He is there identical with Satan and on one occasion the author speaks also (1:20) about spirits of Belial. Like other works originating in the broader movement within which the Dead Sea Sect came into existence, the Book of Jubilees is characterized by a dualistic trend, and in it the devil Mastema plays a great role, being the opponent of the forces of righteousness. He is the chief of evil spirits. After the flood a tenth part of his spirits received permission from God to execute the power of his will on the sons of men and the other nine parts were imprisoned in the place of condemnation. Not God, but Mastema caused Abraham's testing by proposing that God should require Abraham to sacrifice Isaac in order to test his love and obedience. He, and not God, sought to slay Moses on his return to Egypt at the lodging place (Ex. 4:24) and he also helped the Egyptian sorcerers against Moses and slew all the firstborn in the land of Egypt.

The name is found in Hosea 9:7, 8 as a common noun meaning "enmity." It was not translated in the Greek version of the Book of Jubilees but transcribed in Greek characters, and thus it came into the Latin and Ethiopian versions of the book. But the normal meaning of the name is seen in the term "the prince of the Mastemah" *(sar ha-Mastemah)* in the same book, meaning also "the prince of enmity." The same title occurs in its Hebrew original in the introduction of the medieval Hebrew Book of Asaph the Physician in the same context as Mastema in Jubilees chapter 10, an additional indication that this introduction depends on a Hebrew Book of Noah written by an ancient Jewish author from the same circles as those in which the Book of Jubilees originated. Mastema, i.e., the Satan, is also mentioned in the (Greek) Acts of Philip chapter 13 (*Acta Apostalorum Apocrypha*, 2 (1903), 7). The common noun *mastema* occurs in the Dead Sea Scrolls in connection with Belial, another name of the Satan frequent in the Dead Sea Scrolls and similar literature, where he is also named "the angel of Mastema." Thus the term is typical of the whole dualistic trend in ancient Jewish literature.

Bibliography: R. H. Charles (ed.), *The Book of Jubilees* (1902), 80 n. 8; S. Muntner, *Mavo le-Sefer Asaf ha-Rofe* (1957), 149; M. Baillet, J. T. Milik, and R. de Vaux, *Les petites grottes de Qumrân* (1962), 135; J. Licht (ed.), *Megillat ha-Serakhim* (1965), 93; J. M. Allegro, *Qumran Cave*, 4 (1968), 70. [D.Fl.]

MASTER, ARTHUR M. (1895–), U.S. cardiologist. Master, who was born in New York, worked at Mt. Sinai Hospital in that city. In 1942 he was appointed cardiac consultant at the National Naval Medical Center in Bethesda, Md., and in 1947 became clinical professor of medicine at Columbia University. In his book *The Electrocardiogram and X-ray Configuration of the Heart* (1939) he showed how variations in the size and shape of the heart and its chambers and their relative positions may affect the electrocardiogram. He showed that acute coronary insufficiency was a complete entity which may be prevented and even cured. He designed the well-known diagnostic "two-step test" named after him; this tolerance test of myocardial reserve measures the response of the heart rate and blood pressure to a standardized amount of exercise.

Bibliography: S. R. Kagan, *Jewish Medicine* (1952), 342f. [S.M.]

MASTIC, the shrub *Pistacia lentiscus*, known as "medicinal mastic." It exudes a gum which in the Midrash is called *mastikhe*. It has been identified by some with the *lot* (AV "myrrh," JPS "laudanum") mentioned among "the choice products of the land" which Jacob sent to Egypt with his sons (Gen. 43:11; Gen. R. *ibid.;* but see *laudanum). The Tosefta (Shab. 12:8) states that *mastikhe* may not be chewed on the Sabbath since it is a medicine. Dioscorides states that "Its gum serves for medicine and tooth powder. It is smeared on the skin of the face to make it shine. When chewed it sweetens the breath and contracts the gums. The best mastic comes from the island of Chios" (*De materia medica* 1:89). To the present day a special variety of the shrub whose gum is sold as medicinal mastic is grown on the island of Chios. It is widely distributed throughout Israel, particularly in the wadis of the Judean hills, but the medicinal properties of its sap have not yet been tested. It would appear that it is to be identified with *bakha* (pl. *bekha'im*) of the Bible (II Sam. 5:23; I Chron. 14:14–15; AV "mulberry"; RV "balsam"), the name being connected with the "weeping" *(bokhim)*, i.e., the excretion of the sap. The valley through which the pilgrims walked to the Temple was called *emek ha-bakha* (Ps. 84:7) because of the shrubs of that name growing there. The phrase was however regarded as meaning "the vale of tears" and it thus became a synonym for the exile.

Bibliography: H. N. and A. L. Moldenke, *Plants of the Bible* (1952), 177f., no. 161; J. Feliks, *Olam ha-Ẓome'aḥ ha-Mikra'i* (1968^2), 102. [J.F.]

MAT, MOSES (c. 1551–c. 1606), Galician rabbi. Mat was born in Przemysl where his father Abraham died a martyr's death. An intimate disciple of Solomon Luria, he taught in Belz. Subsequently he lived in Vladimir-Volynski, where his father-in-law resided and where Mat wrote his *Matteh Moshe*, a compendium of Jewish ritual law. The book was completed in 1584 and printed in Cracow about six years later, when Mat was already rabbi and head of the yeshivah of Przemysl. Later he lived in Lyuboml. He spent the last years of his life in Opatow. In 1590 Mat was one of the leading rabbis of Poland who signed an ordinance strictly forbidding the "buying" of rabbinical positions. Mat also wrote: *Taryag Mitzvot* (Cracow, 1581), a versification of the 613 commandments, which he composed at the age of 22; a commentary on the Pentateuch and on the Five Scrolls with a supercommentary on the commentary of *Rashi on these books, both of which were published after his death by his son ABRAHAM under the title *Ho'il Moshe* (Prague, 1611); and *Minhagei Maharshal* (printed in the 1870 Przemysl edition of Jacob Ẓemaḥ's *Nagid u-Meẓavveh*) which describes the customs and conduct of his teacher, Luria. Some of Mat's responsa are quoted or mentioned by his contemporaries Benjamin *Slonik and Joel *Sirkes. In his *Ho'il Moshe* he mentions novellae which he wrote on the treatise of *Yevamot*, but which have not been published.

Bibliography: J. Kohen-Zedek, *Shem u-She'erit* (1895), 30–43; Halpern, Pinkas, 15, 62; Raphael, in: *Sefer Yovel... S. Federbush* (1960), 316–29; also separately: *Hanhagat Maharshal* (1961); idem, in: *Sinai*, 63 (1968), 96.

[T.P.]

MATA MEḤASYA, town situated in S. Babylonia, on the Euphrates River near *Sura where the river divides into two. In geonic responsa Sura is often identified with Mata Meḥasya; thus Sherira Gaon in his famous letter at the end of the tenth century (ed. by B. M. Lewin (1921), p. 79, Spanish version) wrote that: "after Rav came to Babylon in 219 he left Nehardea moving to a place where there was no Torah, viz., Sura, which is Mata Meḥasya" (the French version reads: "Sura which is called Mata Meḥasya"). The same identification is found in the work of Benjamin of Tudela in the 12th century. However, it would seem that the two places are not identical. They were two separate settlements near each other; and elsewhere in his letter (p. 84) Sherira Gaon explicitly distinguishes between the two places, stating that the school of Huna, the pupil and successor of Rav in the academy of Sura, was situated "near Mata Meḥasya." The Talmud also clearly distinguishes between the two places (Beẓah 29a). Mata Meḥasya is not mentioned in the Talmud before the time of *Ashi, who headed the Sura academy in the years 367–427. He extended the academy and transferred it to Mata Meḥasya (pp. 90–92). Of its inhabitants Ashi said: "The people of Mata Meḥasya are 'stouthearted' (cf. Isa. 46:12), for they see the glory of the Torah twice a year [in the **kallah* months of Adar and Elul], and never has one of them been converted" (Ber. 17b). R. Mesharsheya praised the scholars of Mata Meḥasya, saying: "Rather sit on the rubbish heap of Mata Meḥasya than in the palaces of Pumbedita" (Hor. 12a).

[M.BE.]

MATHEMATICS. There are no passages of any significant mathematical interest in the Bible, where mathematical knowledge seems to have been of an elementary, rule of thumb nature. In the Talmud mathematical reasoning appears quite often in the discussion of halakhic problems, even if it is never treated as a subject in its own right.

Talmudic Period. The mathematical knowledge of the rabbis was derived from Mesopotamian scientific traditions from the Romans (cf. Eruv. 76b, referring to the sages of the Roman province of Caesarea) and from the Greeks. However, it lacks the sophistication of Greek mathematics and tends to be mostly practical approximations for the purpose of solving halakhic problems. Thus, for example, π (the ratio of the circumference of a circle to its diameter) was taken by the rabbis to have the value of three (Eruv. 1:5), whereas in the third century B.C.E. Archimedes had already given a more exact value. A value of $3\frac{1}{7}$ is found in the *Mishnat ha-Middot* (dating according to S. Gandz from the second century C.E. but more probably later than the ninth century C.E.). The justification for the value of three given by the Talmud is not a mathematical derivation but a reference to a verse in I Kings 7:23, where the "Sea of Solomon" is said to have been ten cubits in diameter with a circumference of 30 cubits, the ratio thus being three. Many other calculations of the rabbis were based on the assumption that $\pi = 3$, and are therefore to that extent approximations (cf. Oho. 12:6; Suk. 8a; Eruv. 76b). Equally approximate is the rabbinic value for the diagonal of a cubit square $1\frac{2}{5}$ cubits (Suk. 8a).

The rabbis were also in possession of certain measuring instruments and techniques. Thus Rabban Gamaliel is said to have had a tube resembling a telescope or astrolabe by means of which he could estimate the Sabbath distance of 2,000 cubits as well as heights and depths (Eruv. 41b, 43b). The calculations presumably involved similar triangles (cf. Rashi, ad loc.). The rabbis had rule of thumb methods for measuring heights relative to the lengths of the shadows of the object and the observer (*ibid.*), and also had a knowledge of solid geometry (Eruv. 14b). For their astronomical calculations the rabbis must have had a grasp of basic trigonometrical theory, though nowhere in their discussions of the calendar or the New Moon is this made explicit. The construction of a calendar was a secret matter and the prerogative of the Palestinian authorities; hence the reticence over details in the talmudic passages on this subject (cf. Ber. 63a).

Rabbinic mathematics never progressed beyond an elementary stage, partly due to a lack of interest in abstract mathematical reasoning on the part of the talmudic rabbis. An added drawback was the lack of a decimal system including an adequate notation and a symbol for zero. The rabbinic system was alphabetical, the letters being taken to represent consecutive numbers, i.e., *alef* = one, *bet* = two, etc., higher numbers being formed by a combination of letters. One possible interpretation of a statement as referring to the decimal system in use in Persia (Bek. 60a) may indicate that the rabbis were aware of the decimal system. The use of the alphabetical system was reinforced because of its connection with **gematria*, which in turn had religious associations. The *gematria* method of summing the value of the letters of a word or group of words and equating them with words having a similar numerical value was often used in halakhic discussion. For instance, the duration of pregnancy was accepted as 271 days because the Hebrew word for pregnancy has a numerical value of 271 (Nid. 38b).

Middle Ages. Because of the association of mathematics with speculative knowledge in Greek philosophy, the spread of Greek learning among Arab and Jewish scholars also meant the spread of Greek mathematical theory. Added to this was a knowledge of Indian mathematics, possibly brought to the Arab world by Radhanite Jewish merchants.

The earliest known Jewish scholar who contributed to medieval mathematical knowledge was the Egyptian astronomer Masha Allah (c. 754–813), known in Latin as Messahalla. About the same period Sahl Rabban al Ṭabari was active in the field of geometry. Two centuries later a Jewish convert to Christianity, Moses Sephardi (baptized as Petrus Alfonsi), who became physician to Henry I, was instrumental in introducing Arabic mathematical-astronomical knowledge to England. One of the most outstanding figures of this period was the 12th-century Spanish scholar *Abraham b. Ḥiyya. He is known for his encyclopedic work, *Yesodei ha-Tevunah u-Migdal ha-Emunah*, written in Hebrew and dealing with mathematics, astronomy, optics, and music. Another of Abraham b. Ḥiyya's work that deals with geometry is entitled *Ḥibbur ha-Meshiḥah ve-ha-Tishboret*. It was written to help Jews in southern France measure their fields, and was translated into Latin in the 12th century by his colleague Plato of Tivoli as *Liber embadorum*. This introduced Arabic trigonometry and mensuration to the West, and had considerable influence on the development of European mathematics. It gave the close approximation of 1.4143 ($1\frac{2}{5} + \frac{1}{10}$) for $\sqrt{2}$ and 3.141593 for π, and was the first Hebrew work to show that the area of a circle is πr^2.

Abraham *Ibn Ezra, poet and biblical commentator, was the author of a number of mathematical works, including *Sefer ha-Eḥad* and *Sefer ha-Mispar*. He introduced the decimal system of enumeration into Hebrew mathematics, using the Hebrew letters of the numbers one to nine plus the zero symbol. The theory of permutations and combinations which he employs in astrology (number of possible conjunctions of the "seven planets") and in grammar (number of possible Hebrew roots) is worth noting. He also throws some light on the passage of the decimal place value system from its Indian origins into Arabic mathematics.

*Maimonides, though making no direct contribution to mathematical theory, was clearly aware of advances in mathematical astronomy, which he applied in his *Hilkhot Kiddush ha-Ḥodesh* (laws for fixing the date of the New Moon and determining the lunar calendar). Euclid's *Elements* was translated into Hebrew by Moses b. Samuel ibn *Tibbon in the 13th century, and extracts from Euclid were included in the encyclopedic *Midrash ha-Ḥokhmah* of Ibn Tibbon's contemporary Judah b. Samuel Cohen. The classical Hebrew work on mathematical astronomy was written in the early 14th century by Isaac b. Joseph *Israeli, under the title *Yesod Olam*. This work also contained introductions on geometry and trigonometry. *Levi b. Gershom was the leading Jewish mathematician of the 14th century. He wrote extensively on various branches of mathematics and astronomy, and his *De sinibus chordis et arcuibus* emphasized the importance of the sine function in the application of trigonometry to astronomy. Particularly interesting is the theory of permutations and combinations enclosed in his *Ma'aseh Ḥoshev*. Another mathematician of repute in this period was Kalonymus b. Meir (1286–1328), also known as Maestro Calo, who translated a large number of mathematical works into Hebrew.

In the 15th century both Mordecai *Comtino and his pupil Elijah *Mizraḥi wrote on arithmetical and algebraic topics. The latter also included a discussion of geometry in his *Melekhet ha-Mispar*. A century later David *Gans, the historian and colleague of Tycho Brahe and Kepler, contributed to the development of algebraic theory in his works *Ma'or ha-Katan, Migdal David*, and *Perozedor*. His contemporary, Joseph Solomon *Delmedigo, wrote about plane and spherical trigonometry and symbolic algebra in his *Sefer Elim*. *Elijah b. Solomon Zalman of Vilna (18th century), the most outstanding talmudist of his age, wrote a work containing treatises on trigonometry, geometry, and to a lesser extent algebra. The work was published after his death under the title *Eliah Wilna und sein elementargeometrisches Compendium* (1903).

Modern Period. With the opening of European universities to Jewish students and the spread of enlightenment in general, the situation changed greatly. Already in the 19th century there were a number of outstanding Jewish mathematicians including Karl Gustav *Jacobi, James Joseph *Sylvester, Leopold *Kronecker, and many more who have played key roles in the 20th century (see following list).

See also *Physics; *Numbers, Typical and Important.

Bibliography: S. Gandz, *Studies in Hebrew Mathematics and Astronomy* (1970); W. M. Feldman, *Rabbinical Mathematics and Astronomy* (1931); M. Steinschneider, *Mathematik bei den Juden* (1893–1901, repr. 1964); B. Zuckermann, *Das Mathematische im Talmud* (1878); L. Finkelstein (ed.), *The Jews*, 2 (1960³), 1376ff.; A. Mieli, *La Science Arabe et son rôle dans l'évolution scientifique mondiale* (1938); O. Neugebauer, *Exact Sciences in Antiquity* (1952); J. Ginsburg, *Ketavim Nivḥarim* (1960), preface; G. Sarfatti, *Munaḥei ha-Matematikah ba-Sifrut ha-Ivrit ha-Madda'it bi-Ymei ha-Beinayim* (1968), bibl.: 231–41. [B.S./ED.]

ALPHABETICAL LIST OF MODERN MATHEMATICIANS INCLUDING CAPSULE ARTICLES

The individuals whose names are marked with an asterisk in the list below form the subject of articles in their appropriate alphabetical position in the Encyclopedia.

AMIRA, BINYAMIN (1896–1968), Israel mathematician. Born in Mogilev-Podolsk, Russia, Amira was taken to Palestine in 1900. He founded the Institute of Mathematics at the Hebrew University, Jerusalem. He also founded the *Journal d'analyse mathématique*, which appeared in 17 volumes from 1955 to 1966.

ASCOLI, GUIDO (1887–1957), Italian mathematician, see *Ascoli family.

***BESICOVITCH, ABRAM SAMOILOVITCH** (1891–), English mathematician.

***BONDI, HERMANN** (1919–), English mathematician.

***CANTOR, MORITZ BENEDICT** (1829–1920), German mathematician.

COHEN, PAUL JOSEPH (1934–), U.S. mathematician; professor of mathematics at Stanford University from 1963. His main interests were set theory, harmonic analysis, and partial differential equations. He wrote *Set Theory and the Continuum Hypothesis* (1966).

***COURANT, RICHARD** (1888–), French mathematician.

DVORETSKY, ARYEH (1916–), Israel mathematician. Born in Chorol, Russia, Dvoretsky went to Palestine in 1922 and studied at the Hebrew University, Jerusalem, where he became professor of mathematics in 1951. As dean of the faculty of science (1955–56) and as vice-president (1959–61) he adopted a policy of fostering basic research designed to keep pace with advances in contemporary mathematics. He was also chief scientist to the Israel Defense Forces. His special fields of study were mathematical statistics, the theory of probability, and functional analysis.

EISENSTEIN, FERDINAND GOTTHOLD (1823–1852), German mathematician. Eisenstein was brought up in poverty and succeeded in studying at a university despite considerable family opposition. In 1847 he became a lecturer at Berlin University. He made important contributions to algebra and to elliptic functions and their applications to number theory.

***ENSHEIM, MOSES** (1750–1839), mathematician and Hebrew versifier.

***FEJÉR, LEOPOLD** (1880–1959), Hungarian mathematician.

***FEKETE, MICHAEL** (1886–1957), Israel mathematician.

FRAENKEL, ABRAHAM ADOLF (1891–1965), Israel mathematician. Born in Munich, Fraenkel received a thorough education in talmudic and Jewish studies in addition to mathematics. He held chairs of mathematics at Marburg (from 1922) and Kiel (1928). From 1929 to 1931 he was visiting professor at the Hebrew University, Jerusalem, and accepted a permanent chair there in 1933. Fraenkel made important contributions to set theory. His publications are listed in *Essays on the Foundations of Mathematics Dedicated to A. A. Fraenkel on his Seventieth Birthday*, ed. by Y. Bar Hillel (1966).

***FUBINI, GUIDO** (1879–1943), Italian mathematician.

GELFAND, IZRAIL MOISEVICH (1913–), Soviet mathematician. Gelfand was appointed professor of mathematics (1943) at the Academy of Sciences Institute of Mathematics, Moscow, and was awarded the Stalin prize in 1951. He made important contributions to group theory, ring theory, differential equations, trigonometric series, and generalized functions. He was one of the discoverers of the general theory of normed algebras, which provides an application of the theory of Banach spaces, and general theory of linear representation of locally compact groups.

GELFOND, ALEKSANDR OSIPOVICH (1906–), Soviet mathematician. Gelfond was appointed professor of mathematics at Moscow University in 1931. He made important contributions to number theory, complex analysis, and theory of transcendental numbers. Of his works, the following were translated into English: *The Solution of Equations in Integers* (1961) and *Transcendental and Algebraic Numbers* (1960).

***GINSBURG, JEKUTHIEL** (1889–1957), U.S. mathematician and Hebrew writer.

***HADAMARD, JACQUES SOLOMON** (1865–1963), French mathematician.

***HAUSDORFF, FELIX** (1868–1942), German mathematician.

HENSEL, KURT (1861–1941), German mathematician. Professor of mathematics at Marburg from 1901, Hensel wrote on number theory and algebra. He edited *Crelle's Journal fuer Mathematik* (1901–36), and wrote the authoritative article "Arithmetische Theorie der algebraischen Funktionen" for *Encyklopaedie der mathematischen Wissenschaften* (1921).

***HURWITZ, ADOLF** (1859–1919), German mathematician.

***JACOBI, KARL GUSTAV JAKOB** (1804–1851), German scientist and mathematician.

***KĀRMĀN, THEODORE VON** (1881–1963), U.S. aerodynamicist.

***KRONECKER, LEOPOLD** (1823–1891), German mathematician.

***LANDAU, EDMUND** (1877–1938), German mathematician.

LEFSCHETZ, SOLOMON (1884–1972), U.S. mathematician. Born in Moscow, Lefschetz received his doctorate in 1911 at Clarke University. During the years 1907 to 1910 he was employed by the Westinghouse Electric Manufacturing Company at Pittsburgh. He began his academic career in 1911 as an instructor at the University of Nebraska and after a number of appointments became research professor at Princeton University after 1933. He made important and significant contributions to algebraic geometry, topology, and differential equations. Among his published works are: *Algebraic Topology* (1942); *Algebraic Geometry* (1953); *Differential Equations* (1957), and *Stability Theory of Liapunov*.

***LEVI-CIVITA, TULLIO** (1873–1941), Italian mathematician.

***LEVITSKY, JACOB** (1904–1956), Israel mathematician.

***LEVY, LUCIEN** (1853–1912) and **PAUL** (1886–), French mathematicians.

***LIPSCHITZ, RUDOLF OTTO SIGISMUND** (1832–1903), German mathematician.

***MINKOWSKI, HERMANN** (1864–1909), German mathematician.

***MORDELL, LOUIS JOEL** (1888–), English mathematician.

***NEUMANN, JOHANN LUDWIG VON** (1903–1957), Hungarian and U.S. mathematician.

***NOETHER, EMMY** (1882–1935), and **MAX** (1844–1921), German mathematicians.

***PEKERIS, CHAIM LEIB** (1908–), Israel mathematician.

***ROSENHEAD, LOUIS** (1906–), English mathematician.

***ROTH, KLAUS FRIEDRICH** (1925–), English mathematician. His specialty is the theory of numbers. He was professor at the University of London from 1961 to 1966, when he took the post of professor of pure mathematics at the Imperial College of Science and Technology in London. Translating from the Russian of Ivan M. Vinogradov, Roth co-edited (with A. Davenport) *Method of Trigonometrical Sums in the Theory of Numbers* (1954). He published *Rational Approximations to Irrational Numbers* (1962), a pamphlet which spans the field of Diophantine Approximations, from the guarded attitudes of the Pythagoreans toward the concept of irrationality, to the current methods in the substitution of irrational numbers by rational ones.

***SCHUR, ISAIAH** (1875–1941), Russian-born mathematician who worked in Germany and Palestine.

SCHWARTZ, LAURENT (1915–), French mathematician. During World War II Schwartz was a refugee at Clermont-Ferrand. After holding chairs at Nancy and Paris he was appointed professor of mathematics at the Ecole Polytechnique in Paris in 1959. He made contributions to the theory of distributions, potential theory, and partial differential equations. He was also interested in human rights; he was a member of several committees, including the Bertrand Russell International Tribunal Against American War Crimes in Vietnam.

***SCHWARZ, KARL HERMAN AMANDUS** (1843–1921), German mathematician.

SEGRE, BENIAMINO (1903–), Italian mathematician. Segre was professor of mathematics at Bologna University until he was dismissed in 1938 under the Fascist anti-Jewish laws. He was then invited to England by the Society for the Protection of Science and Learning and spent the years until 1946 at the universities of London, Cambridge, and Manchester. He returned to his chair at Bologna in 1946 and moved to Rome in 1950. He was elected president of the Accademia Nazionale dei Lincei in 1968. Segre made important contributions to geometry. His books include *Non-singular Cubic Surfaces* (1942) and *Arithmetical Questions on Algebraic Varieties* (1951).

***SEGRE, CORRADO** (1863–1924), Italian mathematician.

SERRE, JEAN-PIERRE (1926–), French mathematician. Born in Bages, Serre was appointed professor of mathematics at the Collège de France in 1956. He made important contributions to the topology of homotopy groups, algebraic geometry, local fields, and number theory.

STEINHAUS, HUGO DYONIZY (1887–), Polish mathematician. Steinhaus was one of the founders of the so-called 'Lvov school' in mathematics; with S. Banach he founded its organ, *Studia Mathematica*, which he continued to edit. From 1920 to 1941 he was professor at the University of Lvov, and in 1945 became professor at Wroclaw. In 1961–62 he taught at the University of Sussex, England. Apart from serious mathematical works such as *Theorie der Orthogonalreihen* ("Theory of Orthogonal Rows," with S. Kaczmarz, 1935), *Sur la localisation d'objets au moyen des rayons* (1938), and *Sur les fonctions indépendantes* (1948), Steinhaus popularized his subject in books such as *Kalejdoskop matematyczny* (1938; *Mathematical Snapshots*, 1960[2]), and *Orzel czy rzeszka* ("Heads or Tails," 1961), and also wrote on the subject of establishing paternity, as in *Dochodzenie ojcowstwa i alimentów* (1958; *Remarks . . . on the Establishment of Paternity and Maintenance Rights*, 1958).

***SYLVESTER, JAMES JOSEPH** (1814–1897), English mathematician.

TOEPLITZ, OTTO (1881–1940), German mathematician. Toeplitz was professor of mathematics at Kiel (1920) and Bonn (1928–35) until his dismissal by the Nazis. He immigrated to Palestine in 1939 and held an adminsitrative post at the Hebrew University. He contributed to many branches of research in pure mathematics; his main interest was in matrix algebra. He wrote *Von Zahlen und Figuren* (1930), and published articles on Plato's mathematical ideas in *Quellen und Studien zur Geschichte der Mathematik, Astronomie und Physik*, a periodical which he helped found.

***VOLTERRA, VITO** (1860–1940), Italian mathematician.

***WEIL, ANDRÉ** (1906–), U.S. mathematician.

***WIENER, NORBERT** (1894–1964), U.S. mathematician.

MATKAH (IBN), JUDAH BEN SOLOMON HA-KOHEN (first half 13th century), Spanish philosophical writer. Judah was born in Toledo and was a disciple of Meir *Abulafia. In 1245, he wrote, in Arabic, an encyclopedic work on logic, physics, metaphysics, psychology, geometry, astronomy, and other topics, based on the writings of Aristotle, Euclid, Ptolemy, and a work on astronomy by al-Biṭrūjī. This work also includes philosophical commentaries on Genesis and several chapters of Psalms and Proverbs. Judah translated his own work into Hebrew under the title *Midrash Ḥokhmah*, of which there are several manuscripts extant (Bodleian Library, Mich. 551; Poc. 343; Hunt 57; Opp. Add. 4°, 10; Mich. 400; and Parma, De Rossi, 421). In Christian tradition this work is known by the name *Inquisitio sapientiae*. Judah also composed a special summary of al-Biṭrūjī's theories of astronomy, as well as a work on astrology, entitled *Mishpetei ha-Kokhavim* (Bodleian Library, Mich. 71). Judah maintained a correspondence with the emperor Frederick II, and apparently also traveled to Italy to see the emperor or to take part in a program of translations sponsored by him.

Bibliography: Graetz, Hist, 3 (1949²), 565–6; G. Sarton, *Introduction to the History of Science*, index s.v. *Judah b. Solomon ha-Kohen;* Neubauer, Cat, 470–1, 682, 691; Steinschneider, Uebersetzungen, index s.v. *Jehuda b. Salomo Kohen;* idem, in: *Ozar Neḥmad*, 2 (1857), 234. [Ed.]

MATSAS, NESTORAS (1932–), Greek author, painter, and motion picture director. Born in Athens, Matsas was in hiding during the Nazi occupation of Greece. During this time he was baptized into the Greek Orthodox Church, but his Jewish background and tragic memories of the war were to find expression in several of his books. When he was only 16 some of his stories appeared in the periodical *Nea Estia*. In 1950 he published three plays: *Animenei* ("Unmarried"), *Fleghomeni batos* ("Burning Bush"), and *Yiom Kipur* ("Yom Kippur"). *Animenei*, written in collaboration with K. Asinakopoulos, was a considerable stage success. His first novel was *Klisti ourani* ("Closed Heavens," 1955), a story of life in the slums of Athens. He also published several volumes of short stories. Two of Matsas' most significant works are on Jewish themes. *I meghali irini* ("The Great Peace," 1957), a collection of three short novels, dealing with an Athens Jewish family, is dedicated to the author's father "who sleeps in the barren earth of Auschwitz." Another novel, *O Messias* ("The Messiah," 1959), describes the tragic fate of a Greek Jew who survives imprisonment in Dachau but who, on his return to Greece, entertains the delusion that he is the Messiah. Other books by Matsas include two children's novels, the prizewinning *Khoris aghapi* ("Without Love," 1960) and *To koritsi me t'asteria* ("The Girl with the Stars," 1968); *To paramithi tou Theofilou* ("The Fairy Tale of Theophilos," 1963), a fictional biography of a Greek painter that was awarded the National Prize for Literature; *Plevsate vorios Sporadhon Skyiathos* ("Travel North to the Sporades, Scyathos," 1964), verse written in the style of the Psalms and containing "Letters from Joseph to the sleeping Rebecca"; and *O mikros stratiotis* ("The Little Soldier," 1967), an anti-war novel. Matsas wrote the scripts for many documentary films and directed feature films. [R.D.]

MATTATHIAS, priest from the village of Modi'in, and first leader of the uprising of the *Hasmoneans against *Antiochus IV Epiphanes (167 B.C.E.). A number of discrepancies appear regarding the genealogy of Mattathias, and it is not certain that he was a native of Modi'in. According to I Maccabees 2:1 Mattathias was "the son of Johanan, son of Simeon, a priest of the family of Joarib (יְהוֹיָרִיב; cf. I Chron. 24:7) who "moved away from Jerusalem and settled in Modi'in." Josephus twice alludes to Mattathias' background. In Antiquities 12:265 he is described as "living in Modi'in in Judea . . . the son of Johanan, the son of Simeon, the son of Asamonaius, a priest of the family of Joarib, and a native of Jerusalem." In Wars 1:36 Mattathias is called simply "son of Asamonaius, a priest of a village called Modi'in." It appears that the name "Asamonaius" or "Hasmonean" is a family title, although later rabbinic tradition regards "Hasmonai" as a particular person e.g. " . . .'neither did I abhor them' [Lev. 26:44]—in the days of the Greeks, when I raised up for them Simeon the Righteous and Hasmonai and his sons, and Mattathias the high priest" (Meg. 11a; some variants however omit "Hasmonai and his sons"). The anachronistic description of Mattathias as high priest is also found in tractate *Soferim* (20:6, ed. M. Higger (1937), 346), and was inserted into the special prayer recited on Ḥanukkah.

Although a number of minor differences exist, the general descriptions of Mattathias' activities, transmitted by Josephus and in I Maccabees are fairly similar. A

"Mattathias," a late 19th-century sculpture by Boris Schatz. formerly Sofia, King Boris of Bulgaria Royal Collection. Courtesy Bezalel Schatz, Jerusalem.

company of Greek officers arrived at Modi'in with the intention of forcibly implementing the king's ordinances regarding sacrifices to idols. As Mattathias was held in high esteem by the villagers, he was ordered to begin the sacrificial offerings. When Mattathias refused, another Jew proceeded to fulfill the officer's command. Mattathias then attacked and killed both that Jew and the Greek officer at hand (named Appeles in Jos., Ant.; Bacchides in Jos., Wars), and together with his sons and a number of similarly minded fellow countrymen sought refuge in the desert and mountains of Judea. One such group of fugitives was attacked on the Sabbath. Refusing to defend themselves on the day of rest, the group, numbering about 1,000, was almost totally annihilated. This led Mattathias to decree that defensive military action is permissible on the Sabbath (cf. M. D. Herr, in: *Tarbiz*, 30 (1961), 243–4). Both I Maccabees and Josephus further attribute to Mattathias the circumcision of all those uncircumcised children brought up under the influence of enforced Hellenization. Mattathias led the rebellion for only one year, and before his death appointed two of his five sons to continue as leaders of the revolt: *Judah Maccabee was declared military commander, and *Simeon the Hasmonean counselor. Of Mattathias' other three sons, *Johanan b. Mattathias and *Eleazar b. Mattathias both met violent deaths during the early years of the uprising while *Jonathan, who succeeded Judah, was killed by treachery in 161 B.C.E.

See also *Maccabees.

Bibliography: A. Buechler, in: REJ, 34 (1897), 69–76; B. Niese,

Kritik der beiden Makkabaeerbuecher (1900), 44–47; E. Bickerman, *From Ezra to the Last of the Maccabees* (1962), 96ff.; Schuerer, Hist, 29–30; Klausner, Bayit Sheni, 3 (1950²), 13–19; W. R. Farmer, *Maccabees, Zealots and Josephus* (1956), index. [I.G.]

MATTATHIAS (15th century), Spanish or Provencal Hebrew poet, sometimes identified with Mattathias ha-Yiẓhari. The **maqāma, Aḥituv ve-Ẓalmon,* attributed to Mattathias and written before 1453 was inspired by the religious *disputations held in Spain. Its action is simple. The pagan queen of a legendary island sends three messengers, Zalmon, Eker, and Ahitub, to inquire into the religions of the world. Seven years later, the messengers return and engage in a stormy discussion. Zalmon, who was in Hebron and became converted to Islam, accepts the arguments of Ahitub, himself converted to Judaism in Spain, and becomes a Jew. Eker, converted to Christianity in Constantinople, argues in favor of that religion; however, since the queen and her court, persuaded by Aḥitub, have also adopted Judaism, Eker hangs himself in anger, bringing the story to an end. Another *maqāma, Begidat ha-Zeman,* likewise written before 1453, also bears the name of a poet known as Mattathias; it is assumed that both were written by the same author. The *maqāmat* resemble each other in style and vocabulary. The second is written in the first person and the personal element is important. The author repents the sins of his youth, describing his experiences so that his tale might serve as a warning.

Bibliography: Schirmann, Sefarad, 2 (1956), 648–62; Assaf, in: *Ba-Mishor,* 7 no. 286 (1946), 8; Zunz, Gesch, 129; Renan, Ecrivains, 432–3; Gross, Gal Jud, 256–7; Davidson, Oẓar, 4 (1933), 451. [Yo.D.]

MATTATHIAS BEN SIMEON, son of *Simeon the Hasmonean. During the winter of 135 B.C.E., Mattathias, together with his mother and brother Judah, was seized at a banquet given in Simeon's honor by his son-in-law *Ptolemy, who was governor of Jericho. Simeon was killed, probably at the instigation of the Syrian monarch Antiochus VII Sidetes, but a third son of the high priest, John *Hyrcanus, managed to escape. Ptolemy withdrew to the nearby fortress of Dok, where the two brothers and their mother were tortured in full view of the grief-stricken Hyrcanus, who was unable to take the stronghold. When the sabbatical year came around, it was impossible to maintain an army for any great length of time, and Hyrcanus was forced to withdraw. Ptolemy thereupon killed the woman and her two sons and fled to Philadelphia (but according to Maccabees they were slain together with their father; I Macc. 16:15ff.; Jos., Wars, 1:54ff.; Jos., Ant., 13:228ff.).

Bibliography: Schuerer, Hist, 66; Graetz, Hist, 1 (1891), 530. [I.G.]

MATTATHIAS HA-YIẒHARI (14th–15th century), Spanish scholar. He was a descendant of a Narbonne family which emigrated to Aragon after the expulsion from France in 1306. Mattathias, who had a profound knowledge of philosophy, was apparently a pupil of Ḥasdai *Crescas. A commentary on Psalm 119 is attributed to him (Venice, 1546, partly translated into Latin by Philippe d'Aquin, Paris, 1629). Mattathias also wrote a number of other works, including a commentary on *Avot* (extant in Ms.) and homiletical explanations to the Pentateuch, known only by later references. It is possible, however, that at least some of them were written by an earlier Mattathias ha-Yiẓhari, perhaps his grandfather. He played a prominent but not over-courageous part in the Disputation of *Tortosa (1413–14), where he was one of the representatives of the Saragossa community.

Bibliography: Baer, Spain, index; Renan, Ecrivains, 432f.; S. Buber, *Midrash Tehillim* (1891), introd.; A. Pacios López, *Disputa de Tortosa* (1957), index. [Ed.]

MATTERSDORF (official name since 1924, **Mattersburg;** Hung. **Nagymarton**), town in *Burgenland, Austria; one of the "Seven Communities," and after 1813 one of the "Five Communities." The town was traditionally divided into two districts, Izraelita-Nagymarton and Keresztény ["Christian"]-Nagymarton. The Jewish neighborhood comprised a separate administrative unit (see **Politische Gemeinden*) until 1902. Jews are traditionally believed to have settled there in about 800 or 1222. A tablet on the synagogue wall dates its building to 1354. At any rate, Jews were already living there before the Turkish conquest in 1526, when Mattersdorf absorbed numerous refugees from *Sopron. In 1569 there were 67 Jews living in 11 houses. After 1622 the community came under the protection of the Esterházy family. In 1694 the Esterházys granted the "Seven Communities" letters of protection, subsequently renewed four times and newly formulated in 1800. Some of the Jews were expelled by Leopold I in 1671, but were allowed to return in 1675. The community was looted several times by the Turks. In 1744, 352 Jews inhabited 30 houses; in 1770, 179 Jewish families were registered; in 1785, 767 persons lived in 43 houses; permission was granted to build 12 more houses in 1818. They paid fees to the towns of Sopron and *Wiener Neustadt for the right to trade within their boundaries. In 1848 there were 1,500 Jews in the town (one-third of the total population). From the beginning of the 20th century their numbers declined due to emigration to larger towns; in 1902 they had fallen to 752 and at the time of the *Anschluss* (1938) to 511.

The centuries-long autonomy gave rise to a powerful communal regime, which regulated not only religious but also economic and social life. Among the prominent rabbis who served the community were Gershon b. Abraham *Chajes, Jeremiah *Mattersdorf, Issachar Baer b. Samson *Bloch, Moses *Sofer, and Simon *Sofer. The Mattersdorf yeshivah attracted students from all over Europe. In 1938 the Nazis destroyed the synagogue and other communal institutions and damaged the Jewish quarter. Part of the community emigrated and the remainder were deported to the death camps. The remains of the Jewish quarter were demolished during development projects, and by 1970 only an old cemetery was left to commemorate this ancient community. About 7,000 documents from the community's archives have been preserved in the central state archives in Eisenstadt. A Kiryat Mattersdorf was founded in Jerusalem in 1963 and some of its inhabitants originated from there.

Synagogue of Mattersdorf, Austria, destroyed by the Nazis in 1938. Courtesy Dr. Shiver, Netanyah.

Bibliography: MHJ, 1–12 (1903–69), indexes; F. P. Hodik, in: M. Gold (ed.), *Gedenkbuch der untergegangenen Judengemeinden des Burgenlandes* (1970); 91–115; J. J. Greenwald, *Mazzevet Kodesh* (1952); M. Pollák, in: IMIT (1900), 164–6. [Y.M.]

MATTERSDORF, JEREMIAH BEN ISAAC (d. 1805), Hungarian rabbi and author. Born in Oswiecim, Galicia, Mattersdorf originally had the family name of Rosenbaum, but took the name Mattersdorf after serving as rabbi of the community of that name in Burgenland. He was appointed rabbi of Mattersdorf (now Mattersburg) around 1770 and stayed there until about 1801, when he went to Abaujszanto, remaining until his death. Mattersdorf was renowned for his extensive knowledge of *halakhah.* His spiritual authority extended beyond the borders of Hungary. In 1791 he gave his approbation to the edition of the Talmud published by Joseph Hraschanszky, who called him one of the most distinguished rabbis of the generation. In Mattersdorf he headed a yeshivah which had among its students Aaron *Chorin, the pioneer of religious reform in Hungary. Among Mattersdorf's works is a commentary to Ḥayyim Shabbetai's *Moda'a ve-Ones* (Lemberg, 1798) under the title *Moda'ah Rabbah,* published along with his son Joab Mattersdorf's commentary *Moda'ah Zuta.* He gave approbations to a number of works, and is mentioned in the responsa of Moses *Sofer. L. Loew states that he wrote the comments on the *Sha'arei Shibbolet* of Isaac b. Reuben, but this work has been attributed to other authors.

Bibliography: L. Loew, *Gesammelte Schriften,* 2 (1890), 257; M. Pollák, in: IMIT, (1900), 164–6; J. J. Greenwald, *Ha-Yehudim be-Hungaryah* (1913), 53f.; P. Z. Schwartz, *Shem ha-Gedolim me-Erez Hagar,* 1 (1913), 51b no. 243. [Y.M.]

MATTHIAS BEN THEOPHILUS, the name of two high priests at the close of the Second Temple period.

MATTHIAS BEN THEOPHILUS I (early first century C.E.) was for all practical purposes the first high priest originating from Ereẓ Israel to be appointed by Herod after *Aristobulus III. He succeeded *Simeon b. Boethus, the king's father-in-law, and preceded Joezer b. Boethus (see *Boethusians). Josephus notes that Matthias was a Jerusalemite (Ant., 17:78). He also relates that on one occasion Matthias was prevented from officiating on the Day of Atonement through being ritually unclean, and *Joseph b. Elem had to officiate in his place (*ibid.,* 165). This incident is also recorded in the Talmud (Yoma 12b; TJ, *ibid.,* 1:1, 38d). Herod, although on his deathbed, replaced Matthias as he held him partially responsible for the disorders in the Temple caused by the two patriots, Judas b. Sepphoraeus and Matthias b. Margalus. It would appear that Matthias was connected in some way with the house of *Anan and presumably it was no coincidence that one of Anan's sons was named Matthias (Jos., Ant., 19:316, 342) and another *Theophilus (*ibid.,* 18:123; 19:297). It is possible that the elder Anan married the daughter of Matthias.

MATTHIAS BEN THEOPHILUS II (late first century C.E.) was appointed high priest by Agrippa II in succession to *Joshua b. Gamala (*ibid.,* 20:223). It seems probable that he was the son of Theophilus b. Anan. His period of office witnessed the outbreak of the Jewish War (66 C.E.).

Bibliography: MATTHIAS BEN THEOPHILUS I: Derenbourg, Hist, 160; Schuerer, Gesch, 2 (1907[4]), 270 no. 5; Klausner, Bayit Sheni, 4 (1950[2]), 163, 165; A. Schalit, *Koenig Herodes* (1969), 635, 638. MATTHIAS BEN THEOPHILUS II: Graetz, Hist, 2 (1893), 249ff., 752ff.; Schuerer, Gesch, 2 (1907[4]), 273, no. 27; Klausner, Bayit Sheni, 5 (1951[2]), 24, 235. [M.ST.]

MATTIAH (Mattityahu) BEN ḤERESH (second century C.E.), *tanna.* Born in Ereẓ Israel, Mattiah was among a group of scholars who fled Ereẓ Israel after the fall of *Betar. However, when they reached Puteoli (an Italian port, now Pozzuoli), love of Ereẓ Israel overcame them, and they returned (Sif. Deut. 80). It must have been later that Mattiah finally moved to Rome, where he established a great yeshivah (Sanh. 32b). When *Simeon b. Yoḥai visited Rome to protest to the emperor against the Palestinian governor's emergency decrees, Mattiah consulted him on points of *halakhah* and *aggadah* (Me'il. 17a; Yoma 53b).

His most famous halakhic decision is that all the Sabbath prohibitions may be overruled in order to save human life (Yoma 8b.) He is quoted in both the Babylonian and Jerusalem Talmuds (e.g., Yev. 61b; TJ, Sanh. 10:1, 27c), although relatively few of his halakhic decisions reached Ereẓ Israel. It may have been his isolation from his Palestinian colleagues which prompted his most famous maxim, "Be a tail to lions, and not a head to foxes" (Avot 4:15; in TJ, Sanh. 4:10, 22b, the phrase is contrasted with the Roman proverb, "Be a head to foxes, rather than a tail to lions").

Mattiah's piety was legendary. The *Tanḥuma* relates that on one occasion, he deliberately blinded himself rather than be seduced by Satan (who appeared to him in the guise of a beautiful woman). He only accepted healing at the hands of the angel Raphael, after a divine promise that he would not be tempted again (Yal., Gen. 161).

Bibliography: Hyman, Toledot, 913–5, s.v.; Bacher, Tann, 1 (1903[2]), 380–4. [ED.]

MATTNAH (second half of third century C.E.), Babylonian *amora.* He studied under *Samuel (Mar Samuel) and was considered one of his outstanding pupils (Er. 6b; Mak. 3b). He quotes numerous halakhic decisions in his name (Ket. 43b; Nid. 27a; et al.) He also studied under *Rav (Shab. 24a). He was a younger colleague of *Judah b. Ezekiel (Kid. 70b), and when, after the death of Rav and Samuel, R. Judah taught at Pumbedita, Mattnah taught at the neighboring town of Popuna (Ḥul. 139b). He is one of the authors of the tradition that the fourth blessing of the Grace after Meals ("He who is good, and bestows good") was instituted by the rabbis after permission was granted to bury the slain of *Bethar, whose bodies had miraculously not decomposed (Ber. 48b). Mattnah had three sons, Aḥadboi, Tobi, and Ḥiyya (Nid. 60b; BB 151a), all of whom were scholars. Among the sages of the next generation who were his pupils and who quote decisions in his name was R. Zeira (Ber. 36a). Another *amora* called Mattnai lived in the fourth century. He was a pupil of Ḥisda (Kid. 32a), and a colleague of Abbaye (Ket. 35b).

Bibliography: Hyman, Toledot, 915–7. [ED.]

MATTUCK, ISRAEL ISIDOR (1883–1954), rabbi, leader of Liberal Judaism in England. Born in Lithuania, Mattuck was taken as a child to the U.S. where he trained for the Reform rabbinate. After serving at Far Rockaway, N.Y., and at Lincoln, Nebraska, he was invited by C. G. *Montefiore to London in 1911 to become the spiritual leader of the small but growing Liberal Jewish synagogue and eventually of a widespread Liberal movement in the British Isles. He was a co-founder and for many years chairman of the *World Union of Progressive Judaism. Among his published works are: *What are the Jews?* (1939); *Essentials of Liberal Judaism* (1947); *Jewish Ethics* (1953); and *Thought of the Prophets* (1953). Mattuck also edited *Aspects of Progressive Jewish Thought* (1954), a *Festschrift* in honor of Leo Baeck's 80th birthday.

Bibliography: JC (Jan. 1, April 9, 1954). [ED.]

"This *mazzah,*" a full-page miniature from the *Barcelona Haggadah.* The round wafer in the middle of the panel is decorated with four identical shields of the Barcelona coat of arms and four blank shields. The *mazzah* represents the roundel of the world, with the four winds blowing trumpets in the corners. The five musicians in the lower arcade allude to the harmony of the universe. On top of the panel, between the initial words, is a man holding two decorated *mazzah* wafers. Barcelona, 14th century. London, British Museum, Add. ms. 14761, fol. 61 ($10\frac{7}{8} \times 7\frac{1}{4}$ ins/27.5 × 18.2 cm.).

MA'TUK, SULAYMAN BEN DAVID (18th century), *paytan* and astronomer who lived in Baghdad. Ma'tuk was a descendant of R. Ma'tuk, the *nasi* of the Jewish community of ʾAna. The latter fled to Baghdad with his family in the first quarter of the 17th century, under the threats of the tyrannical governor who had persecuted the community. Of Sulayman's *piyyutim*, 16 are known, and about half of them were included in books published in Baghdad and India; they are still familiar to Iraqi Jews. During the lifetime of his grandson R. Judah b. Jacob, the family name was changed to Yehuda. The family's descendants include two modern scholars, the brothers R. Isaac Yahuda and Prof. Abraham Shalom *Yahuda.

Bibliography: A. Ben-Jacob, *Yehudei Bavel* (1965), 95. [A.B.-Y.]

MATZ, ISRAEL (1869–1950), U.S. manufacturer, philanthropist, and patron of Hebrew literature and scholarship. Matz, who was born in Kalvarija, Russian Poland, emigrated to America in 1890. He became an accountant, later entering the drug business. In 1906 he founded the Ex-Lax Company and served as its president. Long an admirer of Hebrew authors, Matz aided Eliezer *Ben-Ye-

Israel Matz, U.S. patron of Hebrew literature. Jerusalem, J.N.U.L., Schwadron Collection.

huda in the publication of his Hebrew-language thesaurus. From 1922 to 1925 he was publisher of the Hebrew monthly *Ha-Toren*, edited by Reuben *Brainin. Matz was also a founding patron and honorary chairman of the Hebrew monthly *Bitzaron*. He established the Israel Matz Foundation in 1925 for the support of Hebrew authors. A pioneer Zionist, in 1928 he founded a company in Palestine called Gan Ḥayyim for the development of an orange plantation. Matz also contributed to various schools of higher learning.

Bibliography: Orlans, in: *Hadoar*, 30 (1950), 396–7. [Ja.Ka.]

MAURITIUS, island in the Indian Ocean about 500 mi. E. of Madagascar, where Jewish refugees from Central Europe—passengers of the *Atlantic*—were put into detention during World War II after being forcibly deported from Palestine by the British as "illegal" immigrants (see **Patria*). On their arrival in Mauritius (Dec. 26, 1940), they numbered 1,580 persons: 1,320 landed in Haifa on Aug. 26, 1945, after the ban on their return was rescinded; 128 died while in Mauritius; 212 men joined the Allied forces, 56 of whom entered the *Jewish Brigade. About 60 children were born after the original strict regulation on separation of the sexes in the camp was abolished. The detainees consisted of a Maccabi-He-Ḥalutz transport from Czechoslovakia, remnants of the Jewish community of Danzig, and a transport launched from Vienna. They were interned in the town of Beau Bassin, the men in a former prison, the women in adjacent huts of corrugated iron. They were not brutally treated, but were afflicted by tropical diseases, such as malaria, and by a lack of suitable clothing; food was often inadequate. Considerable moral and material assistance was given by Jewish organizations, particularly the South African Jewish Board

Detainees from Mauritius preparing to disembark at Haifa, August 26, 1945. Courtesy Central Zionist Archives, Jerusalem.

of Deputies, the Zionist Federation, and the Jewish Agency. The detainees conducted manifold communal and cultural activities; they struggled for release and retransfer to Palestine through the Zionist Association of Mauritius, to which about 70% of the detainees belonged. Their struggle was supported by official Jewish institutions which regarded the "Exile in Mauritius" as a political challenge and an infliction of needless suffering upon refugees from the Holocaust through the implementation of the anti-Jewish Palestine White Paper of May 1939. The ultimate liberation of the detainees was hailed as a moral and political success for the Zionist movement. [A.Z.]

Relations with Israel. In 1960, while Mauritius was still a British colony, Israel, represented by a consul general, extended it technical aid particularly through scholarships for young Mauritians to study medicine in Jerusalem and technical assistance on the spot. Mauritius became independent in 1968 and joined the United Nations. An Israel delegation attended the celebration, and full diplomatic relations were established between the two countries, Israel's ambassador in Tananarive (Malagasy) serving as nonresident ambassador to Mauritius. Offers for new scholarships in Israel, as well as Israel assistance by experts in agriculture and other fields, were accepted by Mauritius. Mauritian professionals trained in Israel founded a Mauritius-Israel Friendship Society. Strong Indian influence in Mauritius, as well as Muslims of Pakistani origin who constitute 17% of its population, make themselves felt in Mauritius' attitude and policy toward Israel. These have also been influenced by American-Soviet naval competition in the Indian Ocean. The general attitude to Israel, however, is basically friendly, with the elder generation still remembering with sympathy the Jewish refugees from Europe exiled there in 1940, and the mutual relations between the countries remained fruitful. [Z.Lo.]

Bibliography: Zwergbaum, in: *Yad Vashem Studies*, 4 (1960); 191–257; idem, in *Gesher*, 66 (March 1971), 92–104; D. Trevor, *Under the White Paper* (1948), index; M. Basok (ed.), *Sefer ha-Ma'pilim* (1947), passim; Yad Vashem, *Ha-Sho'ah ve-ha-Gevurah be-Aspaklaryah shel ha-Ittonut ha-Ivrit—Bibliografyah*, 2 (1966), 12871–970.

MAUROIS, ANDRÉ (originally **Emile Herzog**; 1885–1967), French biographer, novelist, and essayist. Born in Elbeuf, Maurois was descended from Alsatian industrialists who moved to Normandy after the Franco-Prussian War. Raised in a staunchly patriotic home, he experienced anti-Semitism as a student at the time of the *Dreyfus Affair and was influenced by the philosopher Alain (Emile Chartier). He spent ten years in his father's factory and his experiences there were later used in his fiction. A French liaison officer and interpreter with a Scots division during World War I, he published a light-hearted book about his

British army comrades, *Les Silences du Colonel Bramble* (1918; Eng. tr., 1919) using his pseudonym, André Maurois, for the first time. He followed it with *Les discours du docteur O'Grady* (1922). Maurois earned a reputation as

André Maurois, French writer. Jerusalem, J.N.U.L., Schwadron Collection. Photo Henri Manuel.

an acute interpreter of the English scene and as an outstanding biographer. During the 1920s and 1930s he published *Ariel, ou la vie de Shelley* (1923; Eng. tr., *Ariel*, 1924); *La vie de Disraeli* (1927; Eng. tr., 1927); *La vie de Lord Byron* (1930; Eng. tr., 1930), and historical works such as *Edouard VII et son temps* (1933; Eng. tr. 1933) and *Histoire de l'Angleterre* (1937; Eng. tr., 1937). In writing his biographies, Maurois combined documentation, erudition, and imagination, to unfold the psychological development of his subjects. His books in this genre include studies of Voltaire (1935), Chateaubriand (1938; Eng. tr., 1938), George Sand (1952; Eng. tr. 1953), and Hugo (*Olympio*, 1954). Two outstanding biographies were *A la recherche de Marcel Proust* (1949; *Proust, a biography*, 1950) and *Promethée, ou la vie de Balzac* (1965). Maurois also wrote short stories and several semiautobiographical novels, notably *Bernard Quesnay* (1926; Eng. tr., 1927); *Climats* (1928; *Whatever Gods May Be*, 1929; and *Le cercle de famille* (1932; *The Family Circle*, 1932). In the first of these he told the story of his refugee Alsatian family.

After the armistice of 1940, Maurois supported the Vichy regime, but then violently opposed Hitler and fled to the U.S., where he taught at Princeton until the end of the war. He claimed that the Jews of the Diaspora had to choose segregation, assimilation, or some difficult intermediate path. Himself a convinced assimilationist, he nevertheless remained interested in problems of Jewish identity, to which he referred in the first part of his *Mémoires* (1942; *I Remember, I Remember*, 1942). In later years he confessed to "a deep sadness" within himself and praised the intellectual enrichment which the Jews had brought to French literature. Maurois' other works include: *Aspects de la biographie* (1928; Eng. tr., 1929); *Magiciens et logiciens* (1935; *Prophets and Poets*, 1935); *Histoire des Etats-Unis* (2 vols., 1943–44; Eng. tr., 1948); and *Histoire de la France* (1947; Eng. tr., 1949); and the autobiographical works *Portrait d'un ami qui s'appelle moi* (1959) and *Mémoires 1885–1967* (1970). His collected works appeared in 16 volumes (1950–55). He was elected to the French Academy in 1938.

Bibliography: G. Lemaître, *André Maurois* (Eng., 1939); Chaigne, in: A. Maurois, *Poésie et action* (1949); J. Suffel, *André Maurois* (Fr., 1963). [S.D.B.]

°**MAURRAS, CHARLES** (1868–1952), French nationalist writer and anti-Semitic politician. In association with *Daudet, Maurras founded *L'*Action française*—both the newspaper and the movement by that name. His call for a return to the traditional values of *"la vieille France"* and his extreme political attitudes are reflected in all his books, especially *Quand les Français ne s'aimaient pas* (1916), *Mes idées politiques* (1937), and *La contre-révolution spontanée* (1943). Maurras' love of monarchy, hierarchy, and the rural virtues was paralleled by his hatred of the republic, democratic institutions, and the *"métèques"* (a word he coined himself), i.e., recently naturalized foreigners, and above all the Jews. He believed that the Jews—together with their allies the Freemasons, the Protestants, and the *métèques*—sought to control the entire political life of France. The *Dreyfus Affair (which obsessed him for the rest of his life) was for him the supreme example of Jewish dominance. Nevertheless, his passion for the French nation did not prevent Maurras from welcoming Hitler as a savior from democracy and the Jews, and he hailed the German invasion of France in 1940 as the "divine surprise." When the Jews in occupied France were forced in May 1942 to wear the Jewish badge, Maurras regarded it as a suitable opportunity to rid France, too, of the "Jewish scourge." For his subsequent collaboration with the Germans, Maurras was condemned in January 1945 to life imprisonment.

Bibliography: R. F. Byrnes, *Antisemitism in Modern France*, 1 (1950), index; E. Nolte, *Three Faces of Fascism* (1966), passim; E. R. Tannenbaum, *The Action Française* (1962), index. [Ed.]

MAUSS, MARCEL (1872–1950), French ethnologist, sociologist, historian of religion, and polyhistorian. Born at Epinal, Mauss was a nephew of Emile *Durkheim, who guided his education and greatly influenced him. His early interests were mainly philosophy and the history of religion. He taught the latter subject throughout his life, but enriched the entire domain of social science and contributed to the growth of the French school of anthropology. Mauss was professor of the history of religions of noncivilized peoples at the Ecole des Hautes Etudes in Paris and also taught at the Collège de France. In 1925 he helped to found the ethnological institute of Paris University, of which he became joint director. He worked with his uncle in both practical and theoretical studies, carrying forward some of Durkheim's basic ideas such as the total social fact, collective representations, and the correspondence of morphological social structure with moral, legal, and symbolic facts. He was one of the team of young scholars assembled by Durkheim for his journal *L'Année sociologique* (1898–1913), and directed its section on religion. He revived the journal after World War I. Of Mauss's works on anthropology, the best known outside France is *Essai sur le Don* (1926; *The Gift*, 1954), an elaborate study of the relation between exchange patterns and social structure. Mauss was active in French political life participating in the support of *Dreyfus, and in the socialist and cooperative movements. He never recovered from the mental breakdown caused by the brutalities of the German occupation, though he published two more works before his death.

Bibliography: C. Lévi-Strauss, in: G. Gurvitch and W. E. Moore (eds.), *Twentieth Century Sociology* (1945), 503–37; idem, in: M. Mauss, *Sociologie et anthropologie* (1950), introd.; R. Needham, in: E. Durkheim and M. Mauss, *Primitive Classification* (1963), introd.; S. Lukes, in: IESS, 10 (1968), 78–82; J. Gugler, in: *Homme*, 64 (1964), 105–12 (bibliography). [E.Fi.]

MAUTHAUSEN, Nazi concentration camp in Austria 12½ mi. (20 km.) S.E. of Linz, established in April 1938 shortly after the annexation of Austria to Nazi Germany. The *S.S. employed its prisoners in the local granite quarry called "Wienergraben," that was incorporated into the camp. Initially, Mauthausen served as a concentration camp for Austrian anti-Nazis. Its commander from February 1939 to May 1945 was Franz Ziereis about whom it was stated that "he gave his son fifty Jews for target practice as a birthday

Mauthausen and its satellite camps. Based on H. Maršalek and J. Kohl, *Wegweiser durch das ehemalige Konzentrationslager Mauthausen* (1960).

present" (see Presser p. 54). Starting as a satellite of *Dachau, Mauthausen became an independent camp in the spring of 1939, and expanded continually, with several satellites of its own throughout Austria (Gusen, Ebensee, and others) by the end of the war. After the outbreak of World War II it became a camp for anti-Nazis from all over occupied Europe and in 1940 was graded in category III, the harshest category of concentration camps (Dachau was in category I). Mauthausen received the so-called "protective custody" prisoners whose "return was not desired" (RU = *Rueckkehr unerwuenscht;* see *Camps, Concentration and Extermination). Himmler specially ordered the death of a prisoner in Mauthausen to be communicated to his family only after incineration. The camp had the highest death rate of all the concentration camps with regard to "protective custody" prisoners. Of over 10,000 Spanish Republicans who were interned there early in 1941, handed over by the Vichy regime, only 1,500 were still alive after one year.

Work conditions were intolerable; the prisoners had to carry heavy stones up the 186 steps of the "Wienergraben." In November 1941 Russian prisoners of war began arriving, destined for immediate liquidation by death through overwork and starvation. The camp authorities used a special measuring installation to shoot their victims in the nape of the neck. Prisoners were also killed by phenol injections or gassed at the euthanasia installation at Hartheim until a gas chamber was constructed at Mauthausen. From the beginning of 1942 prominent citizens from occupied territories arrested under the "night and fog decree" were brought there. Recaptured prisoners of war were executed under the "bullet decree" *(Kugel-Erlass).* When prisoners of other camps were caught for clandestine activities, those not immediately executed were sent to Mauthausen for punishment. Following *Heydrich's death, hundreds of Czech prisoners were killed.

In May 1941 about 400 Jewish "hostages" from *Amsterdam arrived via *Buchenwald; they were all killed within three days in the forced-labor quarry which also served as a place of execution. There were another two shipments of Jews from Holland to Mauthausen (end of 1941 and 1942) who were killed after a short time in the camp. Up to 1944 Jews never stayed alive for more than three days. When the camps in the East were evacuated, thousands of prisoners from *Auschwitz, including Jews, were brought to Mauthausen. Hungarian Jews arrived in 1944, and after the evacuation of Hungary, thousands of Hungarian Jews who had slaved at the so-called "Southeast Rampart" were brought. The name of Mauthausen was particularly feared by Holland's Jews, and the Germans took advantage of this fear to suppress resistance to their measures against the Jews. The Jews in Mauthausen were singled out for especially cruel treatment compared to that given non-Jews (see *Anklageschrift in der Strafsache gegen Fritz Woehrn et al.* (1968), 98–102, 228–35). Shortly before the capitulation it was planned to exterminate all Mauthausen prisoners in a subterranean aircraft-construction hangar in Gusen, but the plan was not carried out. Mauthausen was liberated by U.S. troops in May 1945. In the main camp the prisoners had rebelled. Ziereis hid in the camp but was shot by a U.S. patrol several days later when he tried to escape. Of the 335,000 prisoners estimated to have passed through Mauthausen and its satellites, 122,767 were murdered.

The execution chamber of Mauthausen concentration camp. From B. Baum, *Die letzten Tage von Mauthausen,* Berlin, 1965.

Bibliography: G. Reitlinger, *Final Solution* (1968²), index; IMT, *Trial of the Major War Criminals,* 23 (1949), index; J. Presser, *Destruction of the Dutch Jews* (1969), index; P. Tillard, *Mauthausen* (Fr., 1945); H. Maršálek, *Mauthausen mahnt* (1951); H. Maršálek and J. Kohl, *Wegweiser durch das ehemalige Konzentrationslager Mauthausen* (1960²); M. Riquet, *L'Europe à Mauthausen, tragédie de la déportation 1940–1945* (1954). [Y.Re.]

MAUTHNER, FRITZ (1849–1923), German author and philosopher. Mauthner, who was born in Horice, Bohemia, came of an assimilated family and remained estranged from Judaism. His *Erinnerungen* (1918) provides a fascinating account of his early upbringing. After law studies at Prague, he settled in Berlin, where he became editor of the *Magazin fuer Literatur* and wrote reviews for the *Berliner Tageblatt.* A naturalistic writer and a socialist, he was a co-founder of the *Freie Buehne,* but later turned to writing historical fiction and philosophical works. Mauthner first attracted attention with *Nach beruehmten Mustern* (1878), witty parodies of 22 of his contemporaries, including Berthold *Auerbach, Gustav Freytag, Paul *Heyse, and Richard Wagner. This was followed by many novels, novellas,

Fritz Mauthner, German philosopher and satirist. Jerusalem, J.N.U.L., Schwadron Collection.

satirical sketches, and fairy tales. The subject of his novel *Der neue Ahasver. Roman aus Jung-Berlin* (1881) was anti-Semitism. Mauthner's *Beitraege zu einer Kritik der Sprache* (3 vols., 1901–2) dealt with the psychology and science of language, and with the role of grammar and logic. In his *Woerterbuch der Philosophie, neue Beitraege zu einer Kritik der Sprache* (2 vols., 1910) he subjected more than 200 philosophical concepts to critical examination. A militant agnostic, Mauthner was denied academic appointments because of his anti-religious stand and political views. *Der Atheismus und seine Geschichte im Abendlande* (4 vols. 1920–23) claimed that all dogmas—religious or scientific—were mere human inventions and that their origin, efflorescence, and decline had their basis in history. Mauthner then sought to show how the West had begun to shake off the once dominant concept of God. His work was thus intended to trace the disintegration of this concept, an "anthropomorphic illusion" that had held peoples spellbound for several millennia. From 1911 until his death he lived in Meersburg, near Lake Constance, where he edited the *Bibliothek der Philosophen*.

Bibliography: G. Landauer, *Skepsis und Mystik* (1923[2]); T. Kappstein, *Fritz Mauthner, der Mann und sein Werk* (1926), incl. list of his works; W. Eisen, *Fritz Mauthners Kritik der Sprache* (1929); G. Weiler, in: YLBI, 8 (1963), 136–48. [S.L.]

MAWZA', a salty and barren stretch of land between *Mocha and *Aden, notorious for its harsh, hot climate. The expulsion of the Jews of Yemen to Mawza' was the worst calamity that befell them in recent centuries. They were exiled in 1678, when the Imam, Aḥmad ben Ḥasan, sought to reestablish the old ordinance forbidding more than one religion in the Arabian Peninsula; he gave the Jews the choice of converting to Islam or leaving the country. Three years earlier the Imam had ordered the destruction of all synagogues in Yemen and had prohibited public prayer by Jews. The order applied to all parts of the country and the Jews made their way to Mawza'. Among the exiles was R. Shalem *Shabazi, Yemenite Jewry's greatest poet, who described his people's plight in his poems. The houses that the Jews had left behind were destroyed or sold cheaply, and all their valuables were either lost or stolen. Many died en route, and those who reached Mawza' suffered from disease and starvation; as many as two-thirds of the exiles did not survive. The expulsion of the Jews deprived Yemen of all its artisans, and the Muslim population came to realize that they could not do without them. The district governors petitioned the central authorities in San'a to bring the Jews back, and a year after their expulsion the Imam permitted their return. The "Exile of Mawza'" caused far-reaching changes in the demography of Yemenite Jews. Many communities were not restored. New communities were set up and small communities which could not reestablish themselves on their own joined the neighboring villages.

Bibliography: Ratzabi, in: *Sefunot*, 5 (1961), 339–95. [Y.R.]

°**MAXIMILIAN I** (1459–1519), king of Germany from 1486 and Holy Roman emperor from 1493. His Jewish policy, like that of his father, *Frederick III, was erratic and motivated by financial considerations. In 1496 he expelled the Jews from *Carinthia and *Styria, after the estates there had undertaken to reimburse him for the loss of Jewish taxes, but he permitted them to settle in *Burgenland. He forbade Jews to live in *Vienna, with the exception of his agent Hirschel of Zistersdorf, with whom he "had to have patience" because he was so much in his debt. In 1509 he gave power to Johannes *Pfefferkorn to confiscate Jewish books and to destroy those which were offensive to Christianity. Reversing this decree in 1510, he ordered expert opinions to be asked from the universities as well as from Johannes *Reuchlin, Victor von *Carben, and Jacob van *Hoogstraaten. After banning Reuchlin's *Augenspiegel* in 1512, a year later he ordered both sides to keep silent. He issued a decree forbidding rabbis to apply the **ḥerem* (ban) against those appealing to gentile courts. Under his rule, *Joseph (Joselmann) b. Gershom of Rosheim became the *shtadlan* of German Jewry, and in Moravia the first **Landrabbiner* was appointed.

MAXIMILIAN II (1527–1576), from 1564 ruler of the Hapsburg dominions and Holy Roman emperor, successor to *Ferdinand I. His policy toward the Jews was generally lenient, though he suspected them of supporting the Turks. In 1567 he reaffirmed the charters of Bohemian Jewry, promising to maintain their rights to practice trades they had previously engaged in, and issued decrees against usury. Foreign Jews were forbidden to trade in his dominions without explicit license. Against the will of the local ruler, in 1570 he permitted the Jews free passage through the duchy of *Brunswick (Braunschweig), and asked the *Worms municipality not to harass its Jews because their rights were long standing. While permitting seven families to settle in Vienna in 1571, a year later he decided to concentrate them in one building in the center of the city for easier surveillance, then expelled them in the same year. Maximilian was the first to grant a Jewish craftsman, a diamond cutter from *Breslau (Wroclaw), a permit to pursue his craft. The baptized Jew, Paul Rizius (Ricci, d. 1542), was his court physician.

Bibliography: MAXIMILIAN I: J. E. Scherer, *Die Rechtsverhaeltnisse der Juden in den deutsch-oesterreichischen Laendern* (1901), 447–9; M. Brod, *Johannes Reuchlin und sein Kampf* (1965), index; Baron, Social[2], 13 (1969), 182–91, passim; S. Stern, *Josel of Rosheim* (1965), index; M. Grunwald, *Vienna* (1936), index. MAXIMILIAN II: A. F. Pribram, *Urkunden und Akten zur Geschichte der Juden in Wien* (1918), index; Baron, Social[2], 14 (1969), 148–52; Bondy-Dworský, 462–550; M. Wiener, in: MGWJ, 10 (1861), 241–53; G. Wolf, *ibid.*, 361–3, 456–60. [M.LA.]

MAXIMON (Maximowski), SHALOM DOV BER (1881–1933), essayist and educator. Maximon, who was born in Skvira, left Russia at the age of 21 and traveled to Galicia,

Switzerland, France, and England. In London he met Aḥad Ha-Am who exerted a permanent influence on his writings. He was also befriended by Brenner who published his first article in *Ha-Me'orer.* In New York, he was employed by the Bureau of Jewish Education and edited a paper for children, *The Jewish Child.* He was also one of the founders and editors of the monthly *Ha-Toren* in 1913, and edited the pedagogical journal *Shevil ha-Ḥinnukh* for two years (1927–29). He was a member of the faculty of Hebrew Union College School for Teachers in New York and in 1930 was appointed registrar of Hebrew Union College in Cincinnati. Maximon contributed articles to Hebrew periodicals in Europe and Palestine. Most of his articles were collected in his book *Gevilim* ("Rolls of Parchment," 1925).

Bibliography: *Sefer Maximon* (New York, 1935); A. Epstein, *Soferim* (1934), 215–21; Kressel, Leksikon, 2 (1967), 414f.; S. I. Feigin, *Anshei Shem* (1950), 206–11. [EI.S.]

°**MAXIMUS, MAGNUS CLEMENS (Maximus the Usurper;** d. 388 C.E.), Roman emperor 383–388. A native of Spain, Maximus was proclaimed emperor by the army in Britain in 383. To secure his position Maximus invaded Gaul and occupied it, defeating the western emperor Gratian. In a treaty negotiated with the eastern emperor Theodosius, Maximus received recognition of his conquests in return for an assurance that he would honor the sovereignty of Valentinian II (Gratian's brother) in Italy, Western Illyricum, and Africa. He violated his promise and he invaded Italy in 388. Theodosius together with the Franks, Goths, Alanis, and Huns took up arms against him, and within two months Maximus was deserted by his troops and forced to take refuge in Aquileia. He subsequently capitulated and was executed in August 388.

The relationship between Maximus and the Jews is difficult to establish because of the paucity of sources available. The only substantial document of relevance is a letter sent by St. Ambrose to the emperor Theodosius in December of 388. In it, St. Ambrose admonishes Theodosius for his punishment of those involved in the burning of a synagogue in the East. He argues that the imperial punishment imposed upon those involved in the crime should be rescinded, and that the local bishop who instigated the affair should not be held financially responsible for the renovation of the synagogue. St. Ambrose reminds Theodosius of the many offenses committed against Christians by the "scheming Jews," and goes on to suggest that penalties for civic offenses should be viewed differently when there are religious considerations. He further asks the question: "Shall a place be provided out of the spoils of the Church for the disbelief of the Jews?"

To illustrate his point Ambrose utilized the recent example of Maximus. According to Ambrose, Maximus condemned the burning of a synagogue in Rome on the basis that it was a breach of public order. Ambrose records the hostile reaction of the Roman people to this course of action, their charges that Maximus had converted to Judaism, and their grim prophecies of Maximus' downfall. Ambrose clearly hoped that Theodosius would profit from the mistake of his former adversary, and adopt a more lenient attitude toward those involved in Jewish persecutions.

Bibliography: [St.] Ambrosius, in: PL 16 (1845), Epistola 40: 23, p. 1109f.; Paulus Orosius, *Historiae adversum paganos,* 7:34, 9 and passim; Sulpicius Severus, *Dialogus tertius,* 11:2; Zosimus, *Historiae novae,* liber 4; Pauly-Wissowa, 28 (1930), 2546–55 (no. 33). [J.M.O.]

MA'YAN BARUKH (Heb. מַעְיַן בָּרוּךְ), kibbutz on the Israel-Lebanese border near the Tannur waterfall, affiliated with Iḥud ha-Kevuẓot ve-ha-Kibbutzim. It was founded in 1947 by South African and Rhodesian World War II veterans, joined by Israel-born youth and immigrants from the United States, Great Britain, and other countries. Its founding at the time was regarded as an act of defiance against the British administration which imposed martial law on Tel Aviv and the Jewish sectors of Jerusalem. In the Israel *War of Independence (1948), the kibbutz resisted strong Syrian contingents who attempted to penetrate into the Ḥuleh Valley, and in the years preceding the *Six-Day War (1967) Ma'yan Barukh was repeatedly shelled by the nearby Syrian positions. Its economy is based on fruit orchards, irrigated field and garden crops, and dairy cattle. The kibbutz maintains a local museum. Its name, "Baruch's Spring," commemorates Baruch (Bernard) Gordon, a South African Zionist. [E.O.]

MA'YAN ẒEVI (Heb. מַעְיַן צְבִי), kibbutz in central Israel, on Mt. Carmel near Zikhron Ya'akov, affiliated with Iḥud ha-Kevuẓot ve-ha-Kibbutzim. It was founded in 1938, initially as tower and *stockade settlement, by pioneers of Maccabi ha-Ẓa'ir youth from Germany, Austria, and Czechoslovakia. In 1969 Ma'yan Ẓevi had 540 inhabitants. Its economy is based on farming and carp ponds below on the Carmel Coast plain, as well as dairy cattle and poultry. The kibbutz runs a factory for plastic goods and a mechanical workshop. The name, "Spring of Ẓevi," commemorates Ẓevi Henri Frank, a director of the *Jewish Colonization Association (ICA) in Palestine. [E.O.]

MAYBAUM, IGNAZ (1897–), Reform rabbi and theologian. Born in Vienna, Maybaum served as rabbi at Bingen (Rhineland), Frankfort on the Oder, and Berlin. In 1939 he emigrated to England. From 1947 to 1963 he was minister of the Edgeware Reform Synagogue (London) and lecturer on theology and homiletics at the Leo Baeck College (established 1956). In addition to publications in his German period (*Parteibefreites Judentum,* 1935; *Neue Jugend und alter Glaube,* 1936) he wrote books in English including *Synagogue and Society* (1944); *Jewish Mission* (1951); *Sacrifice of Isaac* (Leo Baeck College Publication, no 1, 1959); *Jewish Existence* (1960); *The Faith of the Jewish Diaspora* (1962); and *The Face of God after Auschwitz* (1965). In his writings Maybaum considers the theological and religious problems presented by the Holocaust and the dual existence of the Jewish people in the Diaspora and its ancient homeland. He was a nephew of Sigmund *Maybaum.

Bibliography: JC (Feb. 24, 1967), 13. [ED.]

MAYBAUM, SIGMUND (1844–1919), rabbi and lecturer on homiletics. Born in Miskolc, Hungary, Maybaum studied at the yeshivot of Eisenstadt (under I. *Hildesheimer) and Pressburg (Bratislava) and at the university and rabbinical seminary of Breslau. He officiated as rabbi in Dolni-Kubin, Hungary (1870–73), and Zatec, Bohemia (1873–81). In 1881 he was called to Berlin, where from 1888 he also lectured on homiletics at the *Hochschule fuer die Wissenschaft des Judentums. In 1903 he was appointed professor. Active in the association of rabbis in Germany, in 1897 Maybaum was among those rabbis who protested against the idea of convening the Zionist Congress in Germany. His works include: *Die Anthropo-*

Sigmund Maybaum, German rabbi and professor of homiletics. Jerusalem, J.N.U.L., Schwadron Collection.

morphien und Anthropopathien bei Onkelos und den spaeteren Targumim (1870); *Die Entwicklung des alt-israelitischen Priestertums* (1880); *Die Entwicklung des israelitischen Prophetentums* (1883); and *Juedische Homiletik* (1890). His important article on the life of Leopold *Zunz appeared in 1894 (in the 12th report of the Hochschule). Maybaum was an excellent preacher and his sermons were published in several volumes. A jubilee volume was published on the occasion of his 70th birthday.

Bibliography: M. Cahn, *Religioese Stroemungen...* (1912), passim. [N.N.G.]

MAYER, DANIEL (1909–), French socialist politician, Born in Paris, Mayer was a journalist by profession, and wrote for the socialist newspaper *Le Populaire.* After the fall of France during World War II, he reorganized the Socialist Party, clandestinely editing the *Populaire,* and after the Liberation became its general secretary. Mayer was a member of the Chamber of Deputies from 1946 to 1958 and from 1946 to 1949 held a number of ministerial offices —labor, public health, and veteran's affairs. He was also president of the parliamentary committee on foreign affairs. He left parliament in 1958 to devote himself to the League for Human Rights of which he was president. Mayer was an active figure in Jewish affairs as president of *ORT. After the *Six-Day War, when French policy toward Israel took a hostile turn, Mayer emerged as a vigorous defender of the

Daniel Mayer, French socialist politician. Courtesy Moshe Catane, Jerusalem.

Israel cause both as a speaker and writer. His publications include *Etapes yougoslaves: producteur citoyen, homme* (1962); *Pour une histoire de la gauche* (1966); *Les Socialistes dans la Résistance* (1968). [S.C.]

MAYER, GUSTAV (1871–1948), German historian. Born in Brandenburg, he became professor of history, democracy, and socialism at the University of Berlin in 1920. He wrote extensively on socialism and the history of the German labor movement. Gustav's unbiased writings contributed to the appreciation of the historical significance of A. Lasalle, *Marx, and his friend Friedrich Engels about whom Mayer wrote an important biography. Among his books were: *Johann Baptist von Schweitzer und die Sozialdemokratie* (1909); *Die Anfaenge des politischen Radikalismus im vormaerzlichen Preussen* (1912); *Der deutsche Marxismus und der Krieg* (1916); *Aus der Welt des Sozialismus* (1927); *Bismarck und Lasalle, ihr Briefwechsel und ihre Gespraeche* (1928); *Friedrich Engels, eine Biographie* (2 vols., 1933; Eng., 1936). When the Nazis came to power Mayer emigrated to Holland where in 1949 his *Erinnerungen* were published. [Ed.]

MAYER, LEO ARY (1895–1959), orientalist. Born in Stanislav (Austrian Poland), he settled in Palestine in 1921 and was successively inspector of antiquities and librarian and keeper of records for the Department of Antiquities. In

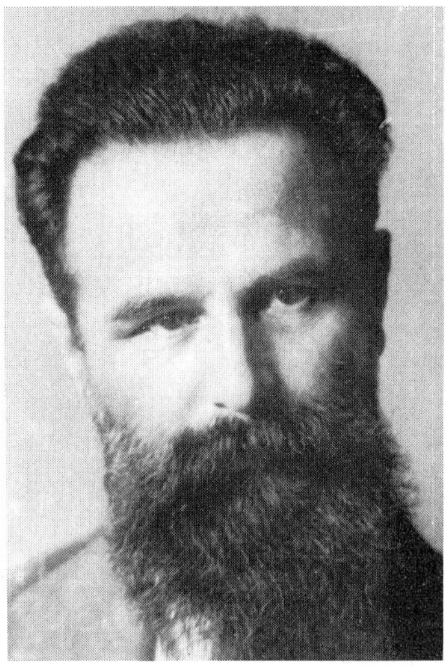

Leo Ary Mayer, Israel orientalist. Courtesy Hebrew University, Jerusalem.

1925 he was appointed lecturer in the Institute of Oriental Studies of the Hebrew University. From 1932 to 1958 he was professor of Near Eastern art and archaeology there. He held numerous positions: head of the Institute of Oriental Studies; dean of the faculty of humanities; rector of the Hebrew University (1943–45); president of the Israel Exploration Society (1940–59); and president of the Israel Oriental Society. With E. L. Sukenik, he excavated the Third Wall of Jerusalem and with A. Reifenberg the Eshtemoa synagogue. Mayer specialized in Islamic art, costume, epigraphy, and numismatics. His published works include *Saracenic Heraldry* (1933), *Mamluk Costume* (1952), bibliographies of Jewish art and numismatics, and a comprehensive work on Muslim artists, *Islamic Architects and their Works* (1956). A museum of Islamic art and culture in Jerusalem was named after him. [M.A.-Y.]

MAYER, LEOPOLD (1827–1903), U.S. community leader and businessman. Mayer, who was born in Abendheim, Germany, emigrated to the United States in 1850. Settling in Chicago, he engaged in private tutoring of Hebrew and German and became known as "Lehrer Mayer." Mayer exerted great influence on the development of the new Jewish community in Chicago, particularly in religious education and in the movement toward Reform Judaism. In 1851 he conducted the first bar mitzvah service at Kehillath Anshe Maarab (K.A.M. Congregation) and also was a founder of the Hebrew Benevolent Society. In the former, Mayer advocated reforms in worship, including the adoption of the "living language German" in the ritual and preaching, but was unsuccessful in this effort. In 1859 he joined eight others, including Bernard *Felsenthal, to form the Jewish Reform Society (Juedischer Reformverein), which in 1861 founded Sinai Congregation, the first Reform congregation in the city. Mayer actively espoused the

Union cause in the Civil War, and, with several other Jews, raised $10,000 to outfit a Jewish company of 100 recruits who formed the Concordio Guard. Later he and his brother entered the banking business.

Bibliography: M. A. Gutstein, *Priceless Heritage* (1953).

[M.A.G.]

MAYER, LEVY (1858–1922), U.S. attorney. Mayer was born in Richmond, Virginia, and was brought up in Chicago. He graduated from Yale Law School, and in 1876 became assistant librarian of the Chicago Law Institute, a position he held for six years. During this period he edited and revised the works of Judge David Rorer on interstate law, published as *American Interstate Law* (1879). Mayer became associated with the law firm Kraus, Mayer, and Stein, which he ultimately headed when it became Mayer, Meyer, Austrian and Platt. His major interest was corporation law, and he became one of the leading corporation lawyers in the country. He was a founder of many U.S. and international corporations and was identified with some celebrated law cases. Mayer served as a member of the State Council of Defense of Illinois during World War I. He was a member of the American Economic Association and the American Academy of Political Science. He was associated with the Zion Temple in Chicago, and was secretary of the Zion Literary Society. [M.A.G.]

MAYER, LOUIS BURT (1885–1957), U.S. motion picture executive. Born in Russia, he was taken to Canada at the age of two. In 1907 Mayer bought a burlesque theater in Haverhill, Mass., began showing films there, and soon owned all the theaters in the city. Moving to Hollywood in 1918, he formed the Louis B. Mayer Pictures Corporation, which merged to form Metro-Goldwyn-Mayer in 1924, with Mayer as vice-president in charge of production. His bold use of talent and his gift for understanding public taste made MGM enormously successful. He made *The Merry Widow* in 1925, and he turned the early Goldwyn production of *Ben Hur* (1927) into one of the greatest of silent pictures. A string of money-making successes included *The Good Earth* (1932), the *Andy Hardy* series, and *Treasure Island* (1950).

Mayer was a great exponent of the star system. In addition to "finding" Greta Garbo and Greer Garson, he helped to establish such stars as Norma Shearer, Lon Chaney, Joan Crawford, and Clark Gable. The powerful "L.B.," as he was called, liked films with children and presented such child stars as Jackie Cooper, Mickey Rooney, Peter Lawford, Judy Garland, and Elizabeth Taylor. He also knew how to find managerial talent. At MGM, where he remained a power until 1951, he had a

Louis B. Mayer, U.S. motion picture executive. Photo Karsh, Ottawa.

series of brilliant production men, from Irving Thalberg to Dore Schary. For seven years he was the highest paid executive in the United States. From 1931 to 1936, he was president of the Association of Motion Picture Producers.

Bibliography: B. Crowther, *Hollywood Rajah* (1960); *Current Biography Yearbook 1958* (1958); *New York Times* (Oct. 30, 1957), 29; (Nov. 1, 1957), 27; G. Jessel, *Elegy In Manhattan* (1961), 103–6.

[H.C.]

MAYER, RENÉ (1895–1972), French politician who was prime minister of France in 1953. Born in Paris, Mayer became a lawyer and fought in the French Army in World War I. In 1919 he was made an auditor in the Conseil d'Etat

René Mayer, French politician. Courtesy Moshe Catane, Jerusalem.

and was later given a senior post as Maître des Requêtes. He lectured at the Ecole Libre des Sciences Politiques from 1922 to 1932. He was vice-president and secretary-general of the Chemins de fer du Nord and from 1933 to 1940 was administrator of Air France, but in September 1940 was compelled by the Vichy government to give up these positions and shortly afterward he joined the Resistance. Mayer became a member of the French Committee for National Liberation in 1943 and in the following year was made minister of transport in the provisional government. He was elected to the National Assembly as a Radical Socialist in 1946 and was made minister of finance in the Pleven cabinet (1947–48). From 1949 to 1951 he was minister of justice in successive governments and after serving as minister of finance for a second term (1951–52), he became prime minister in January 1953. As prime minister, Mayer based his policy on friendship with Great Britain and a strong European defense community. His government fell the following May and Mayer was later active in the movement for European integration, becoming chairman of the Coal and Steel Authority (1955–58). Mayer played an active part in Jewish affairs and was a member of the Central Consistoire of French Jews. He was a member of the Executive of the *Alliance Israélite Universelle and after 1946, its vice-president. [S.C.]

MAYER, SALLY (1875–1953), Italian Jewish leader and philanthropist. Born in Alsheim, Germany, Mayer settled in Italy in 1891 and gave a great impetus to the paper industry of the Vita family, which, thanks to his activity, became one of the country's most important economic concerns. He was also active in Jewish and Zionist affairs. After World War II, he became president of the Milan Jewish community, the second largest in Italy, to which he devoted himself with great energy. He rebuilt the synagogue of Milan, destroyed in an air raid, and reopened the Jewish school there. All other Jewish and Zionist organizations in Milan and Italy, however, also benefited from his generosity and dynamism. Mayer was also a patron of non-Jewish welfare institutions in Milan and in Abbiate Guazzone, where his paper mills were located.

His son, ASTORRE MAYER (1906–), born in Milan, graduated as an engineer and carried on and expanded his father's enterprises in both the industrial and Jewish fields. For some years he was president of the Italian Zionist Federation and led the Jewish community in Milan. He also was honorary consul general of Israel there. He was president of the Standing Conference on European Jewish Community Service and other Jewish welfare and cultural institutions. Mayer also promoted important industries

Sally Mayer, Italian communal leader. Courtesy I. Haimovic, Tel Aviv.

in Israel, the foremost being the Ḥaderah Paper Mills, of which he was a founder.

Bibliography: G. Romano, in: *Scritti in memoria di Sally Mayer* (1956). [G.R.]

MAYIM AḤARONIM (Heb. מַיִם אַחֲרוֹנִים; lit. "latter waters"), term for the ritual washing of the hands after a meal, and before the recitation of the Grace After Meals. The twofold injunction "Sanctify yourselves and be ye holy" (Lev. 20:7) was interpreted as commanding ritual ablution both before the meal and before the recitation of the Grace After Meals (Ber. 53b). The *amoraim* even contended that *mayim aḥaronim* was more important than washing before the meal (Yoma 83b; Ḥul. 106a). According to the Talmud, the duty was particularly insisted upon in order to prevent the danger of touching one's eyes with the salt which was used as a condiment during the meal (Ḥul. 105b). Because the variety of salt referred to by *Judah b. Ḥiyya in the Talmud was a particularly potent one (*melaḥ sedomit,* "salt of Sodom"), containing an admixture of the acrid potash of the Dead Sea, *tosafot (ibid.)* maintained that the duty did not apply in France, where this particular salt is not to be found. This view is contested, however, by the Shulḥan Arukh (OḤ 181:10). No blessing is said before the performance of *mayim aḥaronim* (Sh. Ar., OḤ 181:7). [Ed.]

MAY LAWS, a series of "temporary laws" applying to Jews confirmed by Czar Alexander III in May 1882 and repealed in March 1917 by the revolutionary provisional government. The pogroms which broke out in southern Russia in 1881 brought the Jewish problem into prominence. Reports by higher government officials placed the blame on the Jews and pointed to the failure of the relatively liberal policy of Alexander II. On the basis of these reports, the minister of the interior Ignatiev wrote to Czar Alexander III:

> The principal, indeed exclusive cause of this [anti-Jewish] movement is the economic situation; over the last 20 years the Jews have gradually gained control of commerce and industry; they have also acquired, mainly by purchase or lease, much land, and by their unity they have generally made every possible effort to exploit the general population, especially the impoverished classes. They have thus fomented a wave of protest, which has taken the unfortunate form of violence. Now that the government has firmly suppressed the riots and lawlessness in order to protect the Jews, justice demands that it immediately impose severe regulations which will alter the unfair relations between the general inhabitants and the Jews and protect the former from the harmful activity of the latter.

Accordingly, on Aug. 22 (Sept. 3), 1881, the czar ordered the formation of special committees in the districts inhabited by Jews. Composed of representatives of the various classes and communities and presided over by the governor of the province, the committees were to determine "which kinds of Jewish economic activity had a harmful effect on the lives of the general inhabitants." This directive predetermined the attitude adopted by the committees. During their deliberations of September-October 1881 accusations against the Jews were made by the representatives of the peasants and townspeople, while the Jewish representatives endeavored to defend themselves. Their conclusions were passed on to a special committee formed to draft legislation. While the latter was in session during the winter of 1882, an anti-Jewish campaign was fomented by the press (with the support even of the Russian revolutionary movement Narodnaya Volya) and there were renewed outbreaks of violence in towns such as Warsaw and Balta. With the consent of the government, Jewish leaders assembled twice in St. Petersburg (September 1881 and April 1882) to discuss the government proposals, the most far-reaching of which suggested a planned mass emigration of Russian Jewry or the settlement of many Jews on the plains of Central Asia. Against these extreme measures some intercessionary moves were made behind the scenes, and outraged liberal public opinion in Western Europe also had some influence.

As a result, the "temporary regulations" of May 3 (15), 1882 stated: (1) Jews are forbidden to settle outside the towns and townlets; (2) deeds of sale and lease of real estate in the name of Jews outside the towns and townlets are canceled; and (3) Jews are prohibited from trading on Sundays and Christian holidays. The "temporary laws" satisfied the demands of the Russian rural merchant class which sought to be rid of its Jewish rivals in the villages of the Ukraine and Belorussia. In effect they were a contraction of the *Pale of Settlement, since Jews were confined to towns and townlets only. These laws were binding in the 15 "Russian" provinces of the Pale of Settlement (but not in the provinces of the "Kingdom of Poland"). Until 1904 they also applied to those Jews who had been granted the right of residence throughout the empire (with the exception of university graduates). The police were charged with the implementation of these laws, which became a source of constant police extortion and harassment of Jews still living in the villages. Over the years, the May Laws were interpreted with increasing severity. Thus in 1887 the Jews living in villages prior to 1882 were forbidden to move from one village to another.

Examining the legislation concerning the Jews between 1883 and 1888, the Pahlen Commission condemned the "temporary laws" and advocated that they be abolished, but its recommendations were rejected by the government. At the beginning of the 20th century, criticism of the "temporary laws" was voiced by the generally anti-Jewish Russian ministers of the interior Sipyaghin and *Plehve. It was decided on May 10, 1903 to authorize Jewish residence in 101 villages, which in the meantime had developed and in practice became townlets. On the outbreak of World War I, there were 300 villages of this kind. Echoes of the May Laws are found in the Jewish literature of Russia (cf. Shalom Aleichem, *Tevye der Milkhiger;* Ḥ. N. Bialik, *Ha-Ḥazozerah she-Nitbayyeshah;* S. Ben-Zion, *Ḥayyim shel Parnasah, etc.*).

Bibliography: Gessen, in: *Pravo* (1908) no. 30, 1632; Dubnow, Hist Russ, 2 (1916), 309–12; Elbogen, Century, 210–20; Dinur, in: *He-Avar,* 10 (1963), 5–60. [Y.S.]

MAYMERAN (Maimoran, Mimran), family of rabbis and diplomats in Morocco and Algeria, originally from Marrakesh. R. Meir Maymeran (early 17th century) of Ereẓ

Israel sent a letter recommending Isaac Cansino to collect funds in Oran (Algeria) for his *hekdesh* ("poor house"). Maymeran was the head of a largely Shabbatean Marrakesh community in the second half of the 17th century. The two best known members of the Maymeran family were JOSEPH (d. 1683) and his son ABRAHAM (d. 1723), who served as financial advisers to the ruler Moulay Ismail (1672–1721) in Meknès. Joseph was instrumental in formulating and negotiating the commercial treaties between Morocco and The Netherlands in 1682. According to the priest Busnot, Joseph played a major role in bringing Ismail to power, but Ismail caused Joseph's fall by an "accident." Abraham succeeded his father as the king's favorite, continuing the negotiations with the Dutch and obtaining commercial privileges from the British and French as well. Abraham was involved in ransoming captives in 1688, and like his father was the head of Moroccan Jewry, on whose behalf he attempted to lighten the king's heavy taxation. His rival in the community was Moses *Benatar. Abraham's nephew SAMUEL negotiated with the English and the Dutch, and a relative, Moise, dealt with the French.

Bibliography: J. M. Toledano, *Ner ha-Ma'arav* (1911), 121f.; Hirschberg, Afrikah, 2 (1965), 105, 267–76; idem, in: H. J. Zimmels et al. (eds.), *Essays Presented to Chief Rabbi Israel Brodie*... (1967), 161–2; P. de Cenival, in: *Hesperis*, 5 (1925), 176f.; I. D. Abbou, *Musulmans andalous et judéo-espagnols* (1953), 309–12; SIHM, index.

[ED.]

MAYZEL, NACHMAN (1887–1966), Yiddish editor, literary critic, and historian. Born in Kiev, Mayzel stemmed from a family of rabbis and rich Kiev merchants and was related to the Yiddish novelists David *Bergelson and *Der Nister, whose fame he helped to spread. He made his debut with essays in Hebrew (1905) and in Yiddish (1909), and after the Revolution of 1917, founded the publishing house, Kiev Farlag, which issued more than 100 books. He also edited periodicals and anthologies of the Kiev Culture League. Settling in Warsaw in 1921, he helped to found its Culture League and continued his activity as editor and literary critic. He later described this dynamic period in his volume *Geven Amol a Lebn* (1951). He founded and coedited the weekly *Literarishe Bleter*, which exerted a significant influence upon Yiddish literary activity in Poland between the two world wars. He participated in the Jewish World Congress of Culture (1937) in Paris, which launched YKUF, the international Yiddish Culture League. Emigrating to New York in 1937, he furthered the growth of YKUF's American section and edited its monthly organ *Yidishe Kultur* from 1939 to 1964, and then settled in Israel at kibbutz Alonim. Mayzel was a prolific

Nachman Mayzel, Yiddish writer. Courtesy Kibbutz Alonim.

writer, composing more than 40 books and hundreds of major articles. *Noente un Vayte* (2 vols., 1924–26) contained his most valuable early articles. His studies on I. L. *Peretz and on *Mendele Mokher Seforim contributed important new knowledge. His book *Dos Yidishe Shafn un der Yidisher Shrayber in Sovetnfarband* (1959) surveyed, in 20 essays, Russian Yiddish literature from 1917 until the tragic autumn of 1948 when Yiddish cultural institutions were liquidated and their leaders silenced. In his last years in Israel he completed studies on Chaim *Zhitlowsky (1965) and on the influence of national literatures upon each other, with special emphasis on the influence of foreign literatures upon Yiddish writers (1966).

Bibliography: Rejzen, Leksikon, 2 (1927), 380–4; *Yidishe Kultur*, 28 no. 5 (1966), 1–8; 28 no. 6 (1966), 31–57; LNYL, 5 (1963), 578–87.

[S.L.]

MAZAR (Maisler), BENJAMIN (1906–), Israel archaeologist and historian. Born in Ciechanowiec in Poland, he studied at the universities of Berlin and Giessen. In 1929 he settled in Palestine, becoming the secretary of the Jewish Palestine Exploration Society (1929–43). Mazar joined the

Benjamin Mazar, Israel archaeologist and historian, and president of the Hebrew University of Jerusalem, 1953–61. Courtesy Hebrew University.

staff of the Hebrew University in 1943 and in 1951 he was appointed professor of the history of the Jewish people in the biblical period and the archaeology of Palestine. He was appointed rector of the university in 1952 and president in 1953, holding both positions until 1961. In 1959 he became president of the Israel Exploration Society. He was also chairman of the Archaeological Board of Israel and a member of the Israel Academy of Sciences and Humanities. In 1968 he received the Israel Prize for Jewish Studies. Mazar directed archaeological excavations at *Ramat Raḥel (1931), *Bet She'arim (1936–40), Tell Qasile (1949 ff.), and *En-Gedi (1957–66). He conducted the historic excavation along the outside of the southern and western sections of the Temple enclosure in Jerusalem and the Tyropoeon Valley (1967ff.). Besides over 300 articles, including excavation reports, Mazar has published *Untersuchungen zur alten Geschichte und Ethnographie Syriens und Palästinas* (1930); *Toledot ha-Meḥkar ha-Arkheologi be-Ereẓ Yisrael* ("History of Palestine Exploration," 1935); *Toledot Ereẓ Yisrael* ("History of Palestine" part I, 1937); *Israel in Biblical Times*—a Historical Atlas (1941); and the first volume of *Beth Shearim* (1944, 1957[2]). He headed the editorial board of the biblical encyclopedia *Enẓiklopedyah Mikra'it* (1950–).

Bibliography: H. Beinart, in: *Eretz Israel*, 5 (1958), 1–8.

[M.A.-Y.]

MAZE, IDA (1893–1962), Canadian Yiddish lyricist. Born in Kapulie near Minsk (the birthplace of her distant relative, *Mendele Mokher Seforim), she was taken to Montreal at the age of 14. Following the death of one of her children in 1928, she began to write Yiddish lyrics which were published under the title *A Mame* ("A Mother," 1931) and were followed by the larger collection *Naye Lider* ("New Songs," 1941) and by songs for children. Her lyrics were influenced by the impressionistic poets of England and America and by the American Yiddish literary group Di *Yunge.

Bibliography: LNYL, 5 (1963), 402ff.; M. Bordo-Rivkin, *Lider un Iberblikn* (1958), 70–74. [M.Rav.]

MAZEH, JACOB (1859–1924), Zionist leader and Hebrew writer. Born in Mogilev, Belorussia, he was orphaned in childhood and given a traditional education in his grandfather's home. Later he read and was influenced by the Haskalah, in particular by the works of E. *Zweifel. At the age of 16, he entered a Russian secondary school in *Kerch, Crimea, and in 1886 completed his studies at the law faculty of the Moscow University. After the pogroms of 1882, he joined the *Ḥibbat Zion movement and was one of the founders of the *Benei Zion society (1884). In his article *Elleh Hem ha-Ashamot* in *Ha-Meliẓ* (1888) Mazeh rebuked his generation for negligence in the education of their children, charging exorbitant rates of interest, forging currency, evading public welfare activities, despising work, and "lack of positive love of our fathers." He represented the Benei Zion at the founding conference of the Committee for the Support of Farmers and Craftsmen in Palestine (Odessa, 1890), and organized a group of wealthy men for settlement in Ereẓ Israel. Traveling there as their emissary, he even opened negotiations for the purchase of the *Mahanaim land in Galilee for the project, which was brought to a halt as a result of the Moscow expulsion (1891).

Jacob Mazeh, Zionist leader and Hebrew writer. Jerusalem, J.N.U.L. Photo Archives.

In 1893, after S. Z. *Minor was removed from his position as *kazyonny ravvin* ("government-appointed rabbi") of the Moscow community, Mazeh was appointed as his successor. Being both a *maskil* and a man steeped in Jewish tradition and nationalism, he was an exception to the usual type of *kazyonny ravvin.* He became the spiritual leader of his congregation and its representative before the local authorities, who were noted for their hatred of the Jews. A brilliant orator, Mazeh was well-known for his numerous activities in Jewish public life, which included the promotion of Hebrew culture and the foundation of the Ḥovevei Sefat Ever Society. His appearance as the defense expert on Jewish law at the *Beilis trial in Kiev (1912), when he refuted the evidence of the prosecution "experts," made him famous among Jews everywhere. After the 1917 Revolution, he was a deputy at the all-Russian Constituent Assembly representing the Jewish National List and was also among the founders and devoted workers of the *Tarbut organization. He supported the *Habimah theater during its early years. With the establishment of the Soviet regime, Mazeh interceded with the authorities in order to assure the rights of Hebrew language and culture. In 1920 he participated in the last Zionist Council of Russia. He refused to sign the declaration of the representatives of the various religions in which they denied that religion was persecuted in the U.S.S.R. In his last years, deprived of his functions under the Communist regime, Mazeh wrote his memoirs, which are marked by dignity and humor. He was unable to complete them as he became blind in 1922. The chapters which were brought out of Russia and published in Ereẓ Israel (*Zikhronot,* 4 vols., 1936) are a valuable source for the history of Russian Jewry and Hebrew literature. Mazeh wrote under the pseudonyms Saadiah, Jacob ha-Kohen, Aharoni, and Kochav.

Bibliography: Z. Rabiner, *Sefer ha-Rav Mazeh* (1958). [Y.S.]

MAZER, U.S. family of business executives. Abraham Mazer (1876–1953) was born in Goshcha, Ukraine. He went to the United States at the age of 17 and started a paper business in Hartford, Connecticut, later managing it from New York City. In 1952 the company, the Hudson Pulp and Paper Corporation, had a sales volume of $36 million and plants in four states and held half a million acres of woodland in Florida and Maine. Mazer played a leading role in the United Jewish Appeal, the Federation of Jewish Philanthropies, and the Jewish National Fund. He supported Yeshiva University in New York, and the Hebrew University of Jerusalem, and founded the Abraham Mazer Free Loan Bank of Israel. His three sons, Jacob (1898–1968), Joseph M. (1899–), and William (1905–), took over the corporation's executive posts. They were active in Jewish charity work, taking a special interest in undertakings benefiting Israel. The family sponsored the American-Israeli Paper Mills in Ḥaderah, Israel. [Ed.]

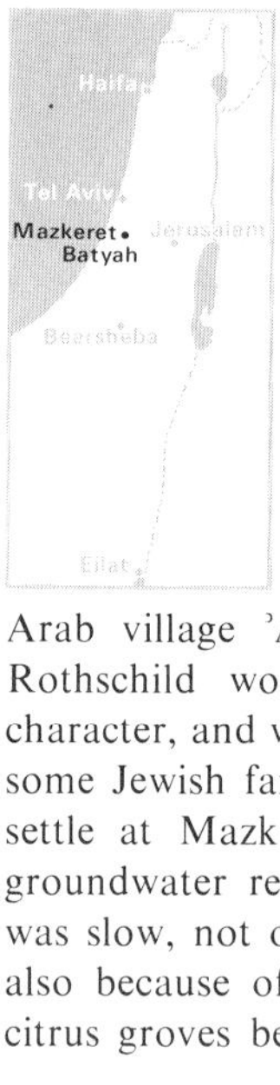

MAZKERET BATYAH (Heb. מַזְכֶּרֶת בַּתְיָה; "Memory of Batyah"), moshavah with municipal council status, in the Coastal Plain of Israel southeast of Reḥovot. It was the first village founded upon Baron Edmond de Rothschild's initiative (1883), and was known up until the early 1900s mostly by the name of Ekron (see *Kiryat Ekron). The name Ekron was given in the desire to identify the moshavah with the biblical site *Ekron from which the neighboring Arab village ʾAqir (أقير) also took its name. Baron Rothschild worked to give the village a truly rural character, and was aided by the *Ḥovevei Zion in bringing some Jewish families who had been farmers in Russia to settle at Mazkeret Batyah. Until the 1940s, when rich groundwater reserves were tapped, the village's progress was slow, not only because little water was available but also because of bad communications. After the change, citrus groves became prominent. New immigrants settled

Mazkeret Batyah (Ekron), southeast of Reḥovot, c. 1920. Courtesy Central Zionist Archives, Jerusalem.

there and more arrived in the first years after 1948. A further phase of expansion began in the mid-1960s and by 1969 the village had 845 inhabitants. Its name commemorates Baron Edmond de Rothschild's mother. [E.O.]

MAẒLI'AḤ (Heb. מַצְלִיחַ), moshav in central Israel, near Ramleh, affiliated with Tenu'at ha-Moshavim. Founded in 1950 by *Karaites from Egypt, it was named after Felel al Maẓliaḥ, a Karaite leader who lived in Jerusalem, and it is one of the principal Karaite centers in Israel. In 1969 Maẓli'aḥ had 690 inhabitants. Citrus groves, other fruit orchards, irrigated field and garden crops, and dairy cattle constitute its principal farm branches. [E.O.]

MAẒLI'AḤ BEN SOLOMON HA-KOHEN (d. 1139), the first of the Egyptian *geonim.* His father, R. *Solomon b. Elijah ha-Kohen, left Tyre and settled in Ḥadrak (near Damascus), where he founded the Yeshivah Ereẓ ha-Zevi. Upon his father's death, R. Maẓli'aḥ, who had no doubt studied at the yeshivah when it was still in Tyre, headed this institution. For some unknown reason R. Maẓli'aḥ left Syria and arrived in Fostat in 1127. The yeshivah which he founded within the synagogue of the Jerusalemites occasionally rivaled that of Damascus because its leaders felt that it also possessed the right to refer to itself as yeshivat Ereẓ ha-Ẓevi (i.e., of Ereẓ Israel). R. Maẓli'aḥ assumed the title of *rosh yeshivat Ge'on Ya'akov* ("*rosh yeshivah* of the Glory of Jacob"). It appears that his spiritual influence was important and that it extended to the whole of Yemen. Many letters and documents issued by his *bet din* are extant. Upon his death, he was succeeded by R. *Moses b. Nethanel ha-Levi, who was his deputy and *av bet din* in the yeshivah.

Bibliography: Mann, Egypt, index s.v. *Maṣiaḥ Gaon;* Mann, Texts, 1 (1931), 255f.; idem, in: HUCA, 3 (1926), 293; S. D. Goitein, *A Mediterranean Society* (1967), 260, 380, 485 n. 15; idem, in: *Sinai,* 33 (1953), 227ff.; S. Assaf, *Be-Oholei Ya'akov* (1943), 91.
[A.D.]

MAẒRANUT (Heb. מַצְרָנוּת; **Abutter**), the right of preemption available to the owner of land over the abutting land of his neighbor, when the latter is sold. The rule is not a provision of strict law but is derived from a rabbinical enactment to compel any prospective purchaser to yield to the abutting neighbor, in terms of the Pentateuchal injunction to "do that which is right and good in the eyes of the Lord" (Deut. 6:18; see also BM 108a and Rashi *ibid.*). For the other prospective purchaser does not sustain a great loss, since he will find land elsewhere, and should not burden the abutting neighbor with property in two separate localities. The right of the *maẓran* ("abutting neighbor") is a proprietary right *(in rem)* in the neighboring land itself (*Nimmukei Yosef* BM *ibid.*), similar to the right of a creditor in the case of lien or mortgage and other *jura in re aliena.* In applying this enactment, the scholars did not impose on the purchaser a duty to resell the land to the abutter, but rather endowed the abutter with the right to receive the land on the conclusion of the (putative) sale—without any additional act of acquisition being required—the purchaser thus becoming the agent of the abutter in regard to all the conditions of the sale to which the former agreed. Accordingly the purchaser is subject to all the laws governing an agent and holds the land in question on behalf of the abutter, the latter only acquiring actual title to it if and when he pays the price paid by the purchaser and fulfills the remaining terms agreed by the purchaser. As the abutter's right originates from the purchaser's obligation to "do what is right and good," if the latter is a non-Jew—to whom the obligation is not applicable—the corresponding right will also not accrue to the abutter (Rashi to BM 108b). The abutter also forfeits his preemptive right if he had indicated, by speech or conduct, that he does not wish to avail himself thereof (Sh. Ar., ḤM 175:32).

The abutter's right or preemption, being an application of the equitable principle to "do what is right and good," is a flexible right (Resp. Rashba vol. 1, no. 915) and does not prevail where it is not supported by the factors of "right and good." Thus the law of *maẓranut* does not apply if the exercise of the preemptive right would cause loss to the seller or purchaser or any loss to the public in general, or if the abutter were to derive no benefit therefrom. Consequently, the law of *maẓranut* is not applicable to a gift (BM 108b) as the recipient cannot get another gift in its stead and he would therefore suffer a loss (Ran, Kid. 59a). For the same reason the right of preemption is precluded when the purchaser is a woman since "it is not fitting for her to search in many places." Nor does the right exist in the following cases: when the purchaser is a co-owner of the land together with the seller, or if he is the mortgagee, for a sale of the land to such parties invokes the factors of "right and good" in their own cause; when the coins offered by the purchaser are of greater weight or more marketable than those offered by the abutter, for here the seller would lose; when all the seller's assets are sold to a single purchaser, lest the sale as a whole is prejudiced; when the landowner sells a distant field in order to purchase one that is nearer, or when the land is sold to defray funeral expenses or taxes or to provide maintenance for a widow, or when an orphan's land is sold, for in such cases the seller would suffer if he waited for the abutter. Furthermore, an abutter who wishes to cultivate the land must yield to a purchaser who wishes to build a house there, as public interest prefers habitation. Similarly, the preemptive right is excluded whenever its exercise would cause a loss in any other manner to the seller or purchaser, provided only that the judge is satisfied that there is no evasion of the abutter's right *(ibid.).*

The law of *maẓranut* is mentioned neither in the Mishnah nor in the Palestinian Talmud, but only in the Babylonian Talmud by the *amoraim* of Babylonia. It may be assured that in Ereẓ Israel conditions were not such as to justify the application of the preemptive right on the equitable ground of doing "right and good." The scriptural injunction teaches that the standards of proper conduct between man and his fellow is determined in accordance with the prevailing circumstances of the time and place and the scholars applying it created different rules accordingly (*Maggid Mishneh* to Maim. Yad, Shekhenim concl.). In post-talmudic times the right of preemption was customarily applied (in France, Germany, Spain, and in the Orient) and, in many places, also in relation to buildings even though it is doubtful whether the law was so extended in the talmudic period (*Piskei ha-Rosh* BM 9:34). In modern times the law of *maẓranut* has been less and less frequently applied although the rabbinical courts of the State of Israel have given several decisions in which various problems have been determined in accordance with these laws.

In the State of Israel the law of *maẓranut* was abolished by the Israel Land Law, 1969.

Bibliography: M. Bloch, *Das mosaisch-talmudische Besitzrecht* (1897), 59f.; ET, 4 (1952), 168–95; M. Silberg, *Kakh Darko shel Talmud* (1961), 105–110.
[Sh.A.]

MAZUR, ELIYAHU (1889–), communal worker and businessman in Poland and Israel, son of Ẓevi Meir Mazur, rabbi in Zagorow and later in Warsaw. His public activity encompassed political, economic, and social fields. He was a member of both the world executive of *Agudat Israel and of its executive board in Poland. He served as president of the Jewish community council *(kehillah)* of Warsaw from 1931 to 1937, when Maurici *Meisel was appointed commissar by the government. He also acted as director of the administrative council of the Ḥakhmei Lublin yeshivah. Mazur was the largest importer of rice in Poland, and he established rice-processing factories in the port of Gdynia. He was a member of the board of the Polish chamber of commerce. In 1940 he escaped from Poland and immigrated to Ereẓ Israel, where he continued to pursue his public and economic activities. In 1948 he was elected to the first *Knesset as a delegate of Agudat Israel.   [Y.Ar.]

MAẒẒAH (Heb. מַצָּה), unleavened bread. Like its antithesis, *ḥameẓ* ("fermented dough," or "leavened bread"), *maẓẓah* in Jewish observance is connected with the injunction that it was to be offered up with sacrifices on the altar (Lev. 2:4, 5, etc.) and that it is the only bread which is permitted for use during *Passover. The reason for the latter institution is that the children of Israel "baked the *maẓẓot* of the dough which they had brought forth out of Egypt, for it was not leavened; because they were thrust out of Egypt and could not tarry" (Ex. 12:39), i.e., the speed with which *maẓẓot* could be prepared identifies it with the bread made in the Bible when there was no time to prepare ordinary bread (cf. Gen. 18:6; 19:3). *Maẓẓah* is the antithesis of *ḥameẓ* in another respect. Only grains capable of fermentation are valid for the manufacture of *maẓẓah*. Such grains are therefore limited to the five species—wheat, barley, spelt, rye, and oats (see *Ḥameẓ). In practice, however, only wheat is used, except by the Karaites (see below). The manifold precautions which must be taken at the various stages of the *maẓẓah*'s production are designed to prevent any fermentation of the flour.

The Flour. The flour suitable for the baking of *maẓẓah* can be divided into three categories of decreasing stringency: (1) "guarded flour" which is closely supervised from the time the wheat is harvested; (2) "Passover flour," the supervision of which to prevent fermentation begins with the milling of the wheat; and (3) ordinary flour. The first is used for the preparation of *maẓẓah shemurah* (see below),

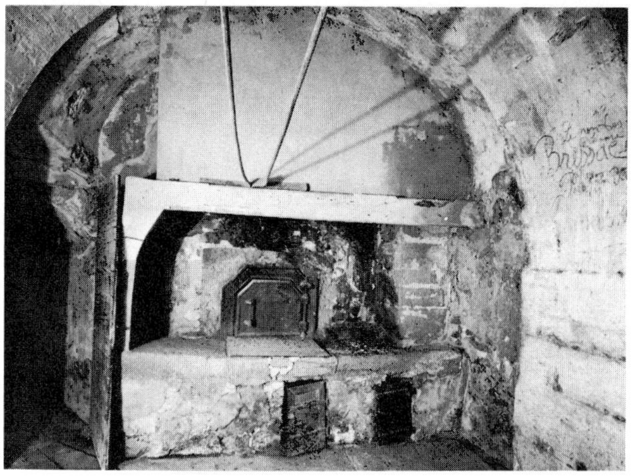

Figure 2. *Maẓẓah* bakery built in Carpentras, southeastern France, 1625. Photo F. Meyer, Carpentras.

the third is permitted only in times and conditions of emergency, and the second is used to make ordinary *maẓẓah*.

The Preparation. It is laid down that under normal conditions of climate and temperature flour mixed with water begins to ferment in the time it takes to walk a (Roman) mile (Pes. 46a), which is estimated variously from 18 to 24 minutes. The shortest time is adopted today. Should the temperature of the water be above normal, however, the process is accelerated, but it can be retarded by the continual manipulation of the dough. Perforation of the dough to enable the escape of air bubbles is also an efficacious retardant. In order to reduce the water to normal temperature, only "water which has rested" (Pes. 42a, i.e., water which has been left in a vessel overnight) is used, and the mixture of flour and water is constantly manipulated until it is ready for baking as thin perforated wafers. Care is taken that the whole process from kneading to final baking does not exceed the 18 minutes. No ingredients but flour and water are permitted for valid *maẓẓot*. Although it is accepted that salt is not a fermenting agent, its use in *maẓẓot* is forbidden as a precaution against fermentation (Sh. Ar., OḤ 455:5). The introduction of machine-made *maẓẓot* in the middle of the 19th century sparked a violent

Figure 1. The preparation and baking of *maẓẓot*, in a woodcut from Holland, 17th century. From J. Leusden, *Philologus Hebraeo-Mixtus*, Utrecht, 1663. Jerusalem, J.N.U.L.

Figure 3. *Maẓẓah* piercers from either southern Germany or Alsace, 19th century. Basle, Jewish Museum. Photo D. Widmer, Basle.

4 

5 

6 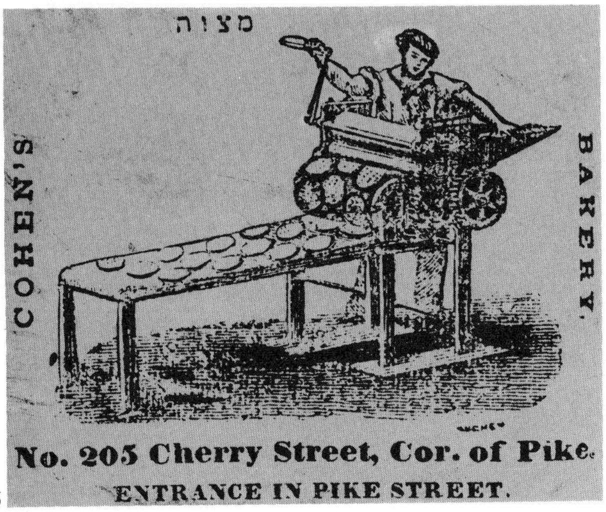

Figure 4. Board for the preparation of *mazzah*, colonial period, Newport, Rhode Island, Touro Synagogue Collection. Photo John Hopf, Newport, R.I.

Figure 5. The beginning of the passage, *Mazzah zu* ("This unleavened bread"), set in a *mazzah*-shaped panel in a *Haggadah* from Spain, 14th century. Sarajevo, National Museum, *Sarajevo Haggadah*, fol. 26.

Figure 6. An early *mazzah* machine in a New York bakery, 1855. From H. Grinstein, *The Rise of the Jewish Community in New York*, Philadelphia, 1945.

and extended halakhic controversy, whose faint echoes are still heard to the present day (Freehof, p. 188, see bibliography). The controversy centered on whether the machine process caused fermentation, i.e., did the milling by heavy machinery cause the wheat to exude a moisture which brought about fermentation and, especially, did the pieces of dough which adhered to the machinery have the same effect?

The Duty of Eating Mazzah. Whereas the prohibition against eating *hamez* or having it in one's possession applies to the whole of Passover, the positive duty of eating *mazzah* applies only to the first night (in the Diaspora the first two nights). In Temple times this duty was based on the verse "with *mazzah* and bitter herbs shall they eat it," i.e., the Paschal lamb (the verse actually pertains to the Second Passover in Iyyar for those unable to observe it in Nisan (Num. 9:11), but it was applied to the normal Passover) and in general based on the verse "In the evening ye shall eat *mazzot*" (Ex. 12:18). For this reason there is the widespread custom of eating only *"mazzah shemurah"* on the night of the *seder*, although some, as a special act of piety, eat it throughout the festival. For the same reason, on the *seder* night two blessings are made over the *mazzot*, (*"Mozi, Mazzah"* in the *mnemonic of the Order of the *seder*) the one over "bread," the other on the positive commandment to eat *mazzah*. According to the letter of the law one must abstain from eating *mazzah* on the eve of Passover from the time that the eating of *hamez* is forbidden, i.e., from 10 a.m. on the 14th of Nisan, but the custom has been adopted of abstaining from eating *mazzah* for the month before Passover so that its novelty can be enjoyed. *Mazzah* is referred to as *lehem oni*, "the bread of affliction" (Deut. 16:3). On this basis the Karaites make *mazzah* only from barley, which was used to make the poor man's bread. The same phrase is used in the talmudic discussion of whether *mazzah* made from flour mixed with wine, oil, honey, or eggs instead of water may be used on Passover. Although if there is no admixture of water it is not regarded as fermenting, *mazzah* made from any such ingredient is forbidden on the first night since it constitutes *mazzah ashirah*, the *"mazzah* of opulence," in contrast to the "bread of affliction" (Pes. 36a). Generally, *"mazzah ashirah"* was permitted only for the sick or the aged (OH 462).

Bibliography: S. Zevin, *Ha-Mo'adim ba-Halakhah* (1959[7]), 241–5; S. B. Freehof, *The Responsa Literature* (1955), 182–9; P. Goodman, *Passover Anthology* (1961), 176–9, 432–7. [L.I.R.]

MAZZUVAH (Heb. מַצּוּבָה), kibbutz near the Israel-Lebanese border S.W. of Hanitah, affiliated with Ihud ha-Kevuzot ve-ha-Kibbutzim. Founded in 1940 by *Youth Aliyah graduates originating from Germany and Austria Mazzuvah joined Hanitah and *Eilon as a third border outpost in western Galilee. In its initial years, the kibbutz was confronted with the task of heavy reclamation work on its hilly soil, a lack of water and high incidence of malaria, and with sea winds damaging fruit orchards. By 1948 most of these difficulties had been overcome. In 1969, Mazzuvah's economy was based predominantly on hill farming (fruit orchards) and a weaving plant. The name dates back to talmudic times (Tosef., Shev. 4:9; TJ, Dam. 2:1, 22d); and is preserved in the Arabic name for the site, Khirbat Maʿṣūb. Remants were found of antique buildings, including a Greek tomb with a Greek and Phoenician inscription dating from 222–221 B.C.E. testifying that an Astarte sanctuary had been erected at the spot. [E.O.]

ME-AM LO'EZ, an 18th-century ethico-homiletical Bible commentary in *Ladino, the outstanding work of Judeo-Spanish literature. The commentary, conceived on an encyclopedic scale, was begun by Jacob *Culi, who felt that, after the chaos left by the *Shabbetai Ẓevi heresy, there was a need for the reabsorption of the masses into Orthodox Judaism. Because of their ignorance of the Hebrew language they had no access to traditional literature, and gradually turned away from religious observance. As is clear from his preface to the first volume, on Genesis, this is what Culi had in mind when, in about 1730, he undertook the writing of this work. His aim was to popularize Jewish lore by means of extracts from the Mishnah, Talmud, Midrash, Zohar, and the biblical commentaries—in fact all the branches of rabbinical literature—translated into the Ladino vernacular. Culi originally intended to call his work *Beit Ya'akov,* but quoting from Psalms 114:1, "When Israel went forth out of Egypt, the house of Jacob from a people of strange language," he finally called it by the original Hebrew of that phrase, *Me-Am Lo'ez.* Written in an unpretentious, popular style and in an attractive form, *Me-Am Lo'ez* was to put the elements of Jewish life at the disposal of people unable to use the sources. It deals with all aspects of Jewish life, and often with life in general, with history, ethics, philosophy, and biblical exegesis. It comments on the prescriptions of the Law and clarifies them with a profusion of detail. Culi's idea was to compile the first part of his commentary around the weekly portion of the Pentateuch, assembling, verse by verse, all the material that had any bearing on the section. This was linked together by anecdotes, legends, historical narrative and folklore. The easy, colloquial style of the work gives it a conversational quality. The first volume of *Me-Am Lo'ez* was published in Constantinople in 1730. No work designed to instruct the Jewish masses had ever proved so popular.

When Culi died in 1732 he was about to publish his commentary on the first part of Exodus. He left many unfinished manuscripts on the other books of the Bible, which later writers used as the basis for their continuation of his work. Isaac b. Moses Magriso completed the volumes on Exodus (2 vols., Constantinople 1733, 1746), Leviticus (1753) and Numbers (1764). Isaac Behar Argüeti wrote only a part of his commentary on Deuteronomy (1772). Both Magriso and Argüeti followed Culi so faithfully that the *Me-Am Lo'ez* on the Pentateuch may be considered a unified work. Using the same method, others sought to cover the rest of the Bible and complete the undertaking. Joseph di Trani of Constantinople wrote on Joshua (2 vols. 1850, 1870); Raphael Ḥiyya Pontremoli on Esther (1864); Raphael Isaac Meir ibn Venisti on Ruth (1882); Isaac Judah Abba on Isaiah (1892); Nissim Moses Abod on Ecclesiastes (1898); and finally Ḥayyim Isaac Sciaky worked on the Song of Songs (1899). There may have been other volumes, written in the spirit of Culi, that are no longer extant or that were destroyed before printing. One such work was Isaac Peraḥyah's commentary on Jeremiah, lost in the 1917 fire in Salonika. The commentaries on Genesis and Exodus were the most popular. There were at least six editions of Genesis between 1730 and 1897, and eight of Exodus between 1733 and 1884. The different places of printing show the popularity of the work among the Sephardim of Turkey and the Balkans, and there was even a partial Arabic translation in North Africa. Those who did not own the expensive complete set (sometimes given as a dowry) studied it in reading groups. For a long time the *Me-Am Lo'ez* was the only literature for thousands of Sephardi Jewish families, and its reading was often considered a religious duty. It was so well thumbed by generation after generation that very few sets remain in existence. The *Me-Am Lo'ez* played a role in Sephardi culture parallel to, but wider than, that of the Yiddish **Ẓe'enah u-Re'enah* in the Ashkenazi world, its main difference being that it was not intended primarily for women. As a vast synthesis of everything that had been written in Hebrew, the *Me-Am Lo'ez* was directed to all—men, women, and even children. A Hebrew translation was undertaken by A. Yerushalmi (*Yalkut Me-Am Lo'ez,* vol. 1, 1967), as well as an edition in Latin transliteration by the Ibn Tibbon Institute at Granada University, Spain (*Me'am Lo'ez. El gran comentario bíblico Sefardí,* vol. 1, 1964).

Bibliography: M. Molho, *Le Meam-Loez* (Fr., 1945); M. D. Gaon, *Maskiyyot Levav* (1933); A. Yaari, in: KS, 10 (1933), 271–4; idem, *Ha-Defus ha-Ivri be-Kushta* (1967), index of books; M. J. Bernardete, in: *Homenaje a Millás-Vallicrosa,* 1 (1954), 127, 146–51; C. Crews, in: *Proceedings of the Leeds Philosophical and Literary Society, Literary and Historical Section,* 9 (1960), 13–106; O. Camhy, in: *Le Judaïsme Sephardi,* 19 (1960), 829–34; M. J. Bernardete et al., *In Search of our Sephardic Roots* (1970).

[H.G.]

MEARS, OTTO (1841–1931), U.S. railroad builder. Mears was born in Russian Lithuania and was brought to California in 1854. He served in the Civil War. In 1865 he settled in Saguache County, Colorado, as a merchant, later becoming county treasurer and Indian commissioner. He was a road and railroad builder, constructing most of the principal roads in southwest Colorado, building a railroad in Ouray County in 1888, and participating in building and later

Stained glass portrait of Otto Mears, U.S. railroad builder, in the Colorado state capitol. Courtesy Mrs. S. H. Uchill, Denver, Colorado. Photo R. W. Lee.

serving as president of the Denver and Rio Grande Southern Railway. Mears was a presidential elector (1876), lieutenant governor (1883), and state capitol commissioner (1889). A monument honoring him is near Ouray.

Bibliography: DAB, incl. bibl.; J. H. Baker and L. R. Hafen (eds.), *History of Colorado*, 5 (1927), 412–3; L. R. Hafen, in: *Colorado Magazine*, 9 (1932), 71–74; S. Jocknick, *Early Days on the Western Slope of Colorado and Campfire Chats with Otto Mears* (1913); F. Hall, *History of the State of Colorado*, 4 (1895), 510; B. B. Postal, *Jewish Tourist's Guide to the U.S.* (1954), 77–78; W. F. Stone, *History of Colorado*, 4 (1919), 640–1.

[R.E.L.]

ME'ASSEF (Heb. מְאַסֵּף; lit. "collector"), first Hebrew organ of the *Haskalah. Founded in 1783 in Koenigsberg by pupils of Moses Mendelssohn, *Me'assef* was devoted to the education of youth, the increased use of the Hebrew language, and raising the general culture level of the people. Although the organ was planned as a monthly, it actually appeared as a quarterly whose numbers were collected into annual volumes. The first three volumes were published in Koenigsberg in 1784–86; the next three in Berlin, 1788–90; four issues of the seventh volume in Breslau, 1794–97; and three volumes of the renewed *Me'assef* in Berlin, Altona, and Dessau (1809–11) after which it ceased publication. The editors in Koenigsberg were Isaac *Euchel (who also participated during the first period in Berlin) and Mendel Bresselau; in Berlin and Breslau they were Aaron *Wolfsohn-Halle and Joel *Loewe (Brill). The renewed *Me'assef* was edited by the poet, Shalom *Cohen. Many of the articles published in the periodical were unsigned. Mendelssohn's occasional contributions, for instance, do not bear his name. However, Naphtali Herz *Wessely, who was advisor to the organ, was an exception to this practice and signed his many poems and articles. In addition to Haskalah writers, a number of moderate rabbis also contributed to the periodical. The radicalism of Wolfsohn-Halle not only led religious Jews to shun *Me'assef*, but also caused Wessely to cease writing for it. The organ's moderate Haskalah policy, which avoided breaking with tradition, was restored only when publication was renewed under Cohen. In the spirit of Haskalah, *Me'assef's* literary section published poems in praise of wisdom and nature, in denigration of obscurantism and idleness; festive poems, ethical parables, and hymns of praise to notable persons and kings. It also published linguistic articles, biblical exegesis, historical studies, biographies of famous Jews, reviews, news relevant to the Jewish world, translations of works from world literature, and supplements in German, which were occasionally printed in Hebrew letters. In its support of Hebrew, *Me'assef* sometimes criticized Eastern European Jews for their use of Yiddish. In its advocacy of pure language, the periodical sought to remain faithful to the language and metaphorical style of the Bible. Yet, despite this, it quoted rabbinical sayings and Aramaic expressions. Although its reportage of news and its educational articles were of immediate practical value, *Me'assef* was mainly literary in character and somewhat detached from the concerns of daily life. The periodical hoped, perhaps naively, to prepare Jews for emancipation. Nevertheless, there occasionally appeared writings of a Jewish nationalist nature, such as Judah Halevi's *Ẓiyyon ha-Lo Tishali* printed in the 1789 volume, and the yearnings for Zion expressed in a number of the poems published in the renewed *Me'assef*. *Me'assef* became the symbol of the Haskalah movement, and Haskalah writers were called the "generation of *Me'assefim*." *Maskilim* of this time long lamented its demise and for many years the *Bikkurei ha-Ittim* (1821–32) of Vienna reprinted "the best of *Ha-Me'assef*." Raphael Fuerstenthal's publication, which appeared in Breslau in 1829, was named Ha-Me'assef. Even beyond the borders of Germany, *Me'assef's* content and form were, for generations, the prototype for Haskalah organs.

Bibliography: S. Bernfeld, *Dor Tahpukhot* (1914); M. Eliav, *Ha-Ḥinnukh ha-Yehudi be-Germanyah* (1960); B. Z. Katz, *Rabbanut, Ḥasidut, Haskalah* (1956), 248–66; Graetz, Hist, 5 (1949), 291ff.; Klausner, Sifrut, 1 (1952); R. Mahler, *Divrei Yemei Yisrael, Dorot Aḥaronim*, 2 (1954), passim; P. Sendler, *Ha-Be'ur la-Torah shel Mendelssohn ve-Si'ato* (1941); Ḥ. Sheli, *Meḥkar ha-Mikra be-Sifrut ha-Haskalah* (1942); B. Wachstein, in: *YIVO Bleter*, 13 (1938); Kressel, Leksikon, 1 (1965), 87–89, 346, 378f., 645–8, 697f.; 2 (1967), 126–8, 391–401, 632f.; Waxman, Literature, index.

[Ts.Ts.]

MEAT (Heb. בָּשָׂר, *basar*), the flesh of animals permitted for consumption. (For its meaning as human flesh and symbolic connotation see *Flesh.) The Talmud points out (Sanh. 59b) that according to the biblical account the consumption of meat was forbidden from Adam until Noah (Gen. 1:29) and was specifically permitted first to Noah (*ibid.* 9:3). Apart from this, however, there is no suggestion of vegetarianism in the Bible. On the other hand, meat is never included among the staple diet of the children of Israel, which is confined to agricultural products, of which the constantly recurring expression in the Bible is "grain and wine and oil" (Deut. 11:14), or the seven agricultural products enumerated in Deuteronomy 8:8. (It has however been suggested that Deuteronomy 11:15 refers to the eating of meat.) In point of fact, meat was regarded in the Bible as a luxury for which the children of Israel would yearn "when the Lord enlarges your territory" (Deut. 12:20), and the lusting of the children of Israel after the "fleshpots of Egypt" (Ex. 16:3 and Num. 11:4) was regarded as highly reprehensible. From Deuteronomy 12:20–22, R. Ishmael (Ḥul. 16b–17a) deduces that during their sojourn in the wilderness the children of Israel were permitted to eat only meat from an animal which had actually been sacrificed and that it was only when they entered the land of Israel that "meat of desire," i.e., the meat of all permitted animals, could be eaten as desired without the animal being sacrificed. R. Akiva, however, interprets it to mean that in the wilderness any method of killing an animal, even stabbing (*neḥirah*) was permitted, but that after their entry into the land only the meat of animals which had been slaughtered by *sheḥitah* could be eaten. All agree, however, that the reference is only to "cattle" which could be offered as sacrifices, but that the meat of "beasts" (nondomesticated animals, the "gazelle and the hart") was freely permitted (cf. Deut. 12:22). That the flesh of birds was permitted is clear from Exodus 16:13 and Numbers 11:31–33. The only limitation on the consumption of meat to non-Jews ("the children of Noah") is the prohibition against meat cut from a living animal (based on Gen. 9:4; see *Noachide Laws). For Jews however only the flesh of "clean" animals was permitted, and that, only after *sheḥitah* and the removal of forbidden blood and fat. The seething of meat in milk was forbidden (Ex. 23:19 et al.) and interpreted to include eating meat and milk together or deriving any benefit from it. It has been suggested that this prohibition is because such practices were connected with heathen fertility rites (Maim. *Guide* 3:48; see *Dietary Laws). In the talmudic period, meat was regarded as the diet of the well-to-do, and as a feature of festive occasions rather than a staple diet. It was regarded as obligatory only on Sabbaths and festivals since "there is no joy without meat and wine" (Pes. 109a). The immensely wealthy Eleazar b. Azariah laid it down that only a person who possesses 100 *maneh* may eat meat daily; otherwise it should be eaten only on the Sabbath. In the amoraic period, however, it seems to have become more common. In Ereẓ Israel, R. Johanan said that owing to the prevailing physical weakness, "whoever has a penny in his pocket should run to the shopkeeper" (to buy meat daily), while the Babylonian Naḥman said that one should even buy it on credit (Ḥul. 84a). Its nutritive value was recognized. It was specially recommended for pregnant women as they would thus have robust children (Ket. 60b–61a). On the basis of homiletical exposition of Leviticus 11:46, R. Judah ha-Nasi suggested that only those engaged in the study of the Torah were permitted to indulge in meat (Pes. 49b). Poultry was more highly regarded as a delicacy than meat, and meat than fish (Num. R. 21:25). Of poultry the most delectable was the chicken, of meat, the ox (BM 86b). Among the things to be avoided by a convalescent, since they "bring on his sickness again in a severe form," are "beef, fat meat, roast meat, and poultry" (Ber. 57b). As the consumption of meat was associated with joy, abstention from it was a symbol of mourning. For the same reason meat is not eaten by a mourner on the day of burial or in the period of national mourning from the first until the Ninth of *Av (Sh. Ar., OḤ 551:9). After the destruction of the Temple there were those who sought to adopt asceticism, including abstention from meat, but it was strongly opposed (BB 60b).

See also Cruelty to *Animals.

Bibliography: Eisenstein, Dinim, 66f.; ET, 4 (1952), 675–741.

[L.I.R.]

MECKLENBURG, former duchy in E. Germany. Before the middle of the 14th century Jews were to be found in Wismar, Rostock, Parchim, Krakow, Guestrow, Schwerin, Friedland, and perhaps also in Borzenburg and Malchin. A Jewish community is first mentioned in 1279 at Rostock and there were communities from around the same time in Parchim and Guestrow. The other cities had only a few families. The Jews were allowed to engage only in moneylending. A Jew, Salathiel, bought a house and loaned money to the duke and to the city of Schwerin. Accusations of desecrating the *Host in Krakow am See (1325) and Guestrow (1330) and the *Black Death persecutions in Rostock, Parchim, and Wismar practically wiped out Mecklenburg Jewry. After another accusation of desecrating the Host, in Sternberg in 1492, 27 Jews were burned at the stake and all Jews were expelled from the duchy.

From 1679 Jewish merchants from Hamburg, often of Sephardi extraction, were granted letters of protection and commercial privileges, and some became Court Jews. One of them, Michael Hinrichsen (Portugies) of *Glueckstadt (d. 1710), court jeweler and tobacco agent, settled in Schwerin, where he rapidly gained ascendancy. He employed a rabbi so that he might study Talmud with him, and opened a synagogue in his home. He was the first Jew in Germany to be freed (in 1701) from payment of the *Leibzoll* ("body tax") for his lifetime. His descendants continued to hold leading positions in Mecklenburg economic and public life for five generations. The first *Landesrabbiner,* Jeremias Israel, appointed in 1763, was a member of his family. A growing number of communities were established by privileged Jews and their households despite a 1755 enactment making illegal all forms of landholdings. Tax records of 1760 show 141 taxpaying Jews residing legally in the duchy. In this period the history of Mecklenburg Jewry is linked with that of O. G. Tychsen (1734–1816), orientalist, professor, and unsuccessful missionary, who meticulously recorded the history of the local Jews as well as supporting their emancipation. A ducal order (May 30, 1772), that burials be postponed for three days in order to eliminate the possibility of "false" deaths, induced the Jews of Mecklenburg to apply to Moses *Mendelssohn, who advised them to erect burial halls, a decision which was contested by more Orthodox rabbis.

On Feb. 22, 1811, M. R. Hinrichsen and I. Mendel presented a petition for emancipation. Although the estates demanded basic reforms in Judaism, the liberal duke, Franz Friedrich I (d. 1839), nonetheless issued an emancipatory edict two years later (March 25, 1813), based on the Prussian model. Markets were not to be held on Jewish holidays and support was given to Jewish rights within the German Confederation. On Sept. 11, 1817, under pressure from the estates, the duke suspended emancipation. During the *Hep! Hep! disturbances (1819) troops had to be called in to Guestrow to suppress the riots. The estates continued to oppose the duke's liberal attitude toward individual Jews and rejected a law of 1830 granting the Jews occupational and economic liberties. In 1847 the estates at last supported emancipation, which endured briefly until 1850; the Jews were not fully emancipated until 1869.

In 1839 statutes were enacted granting autonomy to rabbinical organizations. A year later Samuel *Holdheim was elected *Landesrabbiner* and introduced far-reaching and controversial reforms. Holdheim was active in the struggle for emancipation and succeeded in having the degrading medieval formula of the Jewish *oath changed. He was followed by the even more radical David Einhorn (1847–51), whose denial of circumcision as a prerequisite of Judaism was attacked by Franz *Delitzsch, the Christian missionary and scholar. For the sake of peace, and on the order of the government, the rabbinate was subsequently filled by Orthodox rabbis.

Mecklenburg Jewry increased from 2,494 persons in 1810 to 3,318 (0.64% of the total population) in 1845. The small communities (11 with more than 100 persons in 1850) subsequently declined numerically, and due to the emigration of Jews to the big cities, the larger ones did not grow. The numbers decreased to 1,413 (0.22%) in 1910 and to 1,225 in 1932. Rostock, the largest city, which excluded Jews until 1867, was then the main community, with about 350 members, followed by Guestrow (120), Parchim (48), and Schwerin (200). The fate of Mecklenburg Jews during World War II was similar to that of the rest of German Jewry. In 1970, very few Jews resided in the state of Mecklenburg.

Bibliography: Germ Jud, 2 (1968), 528–9; L. Donath, *Geschichte der Juden in Mecklenburg* (1874); Neuman, in: *Juedische Familien Forschung,* no. 5 (1926), 98–101; Gruenfeldt, in: *Zeitschrift fuer Demographie und Statistik der Juden* 8 (1912), 1–7; Silberstein, in: *Festschrift zum 25 jaehrigen Bestehen der juedischen theologischen Seminars Fraenkelscher Stiftung,* 2 (1929), 303–66; idem, in: *Festschrift zum 70 Geburtstage Martin Philipson* (1916); Sterling, in: HJ, 12 (1950), 134; H. Kellenbenz, *Sephardim an der unteren Elbe* (1958), 436–46; H. Schnee, *Die Hoffinanz und der moderne Staat,* 2 (1954), 293–315; 5 (1965), 105ff., S. Stern, *The Court Jew* (1950), index.

[H.W.]

MEDALIE, GEORGE ZERDIN (1883–1946), U.S. lawyer and Jewish community leader. Medalie was born in New York's lower East Side to Russian immigrants. He served as assistant district attorney of New York County (1910–15). Subsequently founding his own law firm, Medalie also served in various advisory and public legal capacities. As U.S. attorney for the Southern District of New York from 1931 he vigorously prosecuted racketeers and smugglers. One of several assistants whom he later helped attain public careers in elective office, was Thomas E. Dewey. Medalie himself was the Republican nominee for the U.S. Senate in 1932. In 1945 Dewey, then governor of New York, appointed him to an interim term as associate justice of the Court of Appeals, the highest state court. Medalie was prominent in local legal associations, and was a leader of the New York Jewish Community. He was on the board of directors of both the Joint Distribution Committee and the UJA. As chairman of the American Jewish Committee's Overseas Committee, he devoted his efforts to securing equal rights for Jews in the countries to which they returned after World War II. From 1941 to 1945 he served as president of the Federation of Jewish Philanthropies. As president of the Jewish Board of Guardians in 1931 Medalie gave strong support to the development of psychiatric casework. He was chairman of the Mayor's Committee on Unemployment Relief during the Depression and served on many other government committees.

Bibliography: AJYB, 48 (1946–47), 93–100; J. Willen, in: AJYB, 42 (1946–47), 93–100 (portrait). [Ed.]

MEDALISTS. Pewter, seal, and gem engraving were traditional Jewish professions, often handed down from father to son through several generations. By the 18th century, this practice had developed into medal engraving and Jewish medalists were employed at several Protestant courts of northern Germany and Scandinavia. Members of the *Abraham-Abramson family were among the leading 18th-century medalists. The *Jacobson family rose to prominence at Copenhagen in the same period. Philipp *Aron, active from about 1750 to 1787, and his brother Abraham (1744–1824), did portrait medals for the courts of Mecklenburg and Stockholm, as did Meir Loeser and his son Nathan at the turn of the century. About the same time Abraham Jacobs and Abraham Heilbut spent their active careers working in their native Hamburg. An important 18th-century Russian medalist was Samuel *Judin, while the *Simon family flourished in Belgium and France. The three *Wiener brothers from Belgium are considered among the finest 19th-century medalists, as were Avenir and Abraham *Griliches in Russia. France was the home of several distinguished 19th-century Jewish medalists such as René Stern, court engraver to Napoleon III, and E.-A. Soldi. One of the few Jewish medals by the French sculptor Emmanuel Hannaux has an excellent portrait of Narcisse *Leven, president of the Alliance Israélite Universelle. S. F. *Beer engraved the commemorative for the Second Zionist Congress. Aaron Kohn (early 19th century, Germany) is noteworthy for his religious medals, such as his 1817 **Tashlikh* prayer and his 1837 circumcision medals. In the

Figure 2. Medal designed by a Belgian medalist, F. Weiner, for the inauguration of the new synagogue of Maastricht, Holland, 1841. Silver, diam. 1½ in. (4 cm.). Jerusalem, Israel Museum (Feuchtwanger Collection, donated by Baruch and Ruth Rappaport). Photo R. Milon, Jerusalem.

Figure 3. Medal by I. W. Loewenbach of the new synagogue, Munich, struck in 1826. Silver, diam. 1½ in. (4 cm.). New York, Jewish Museum, Daniel M. Friedenberg Collection.

Figure 1. Medal by Jacques Elion struck in honor of the opening of the Amsterdam Jewish Orphanage, April 30, 1865. Copper, diam. 2½ in. (6 cm.). New York, Jewish Museum, Daniel M. Friedenberg Collection.

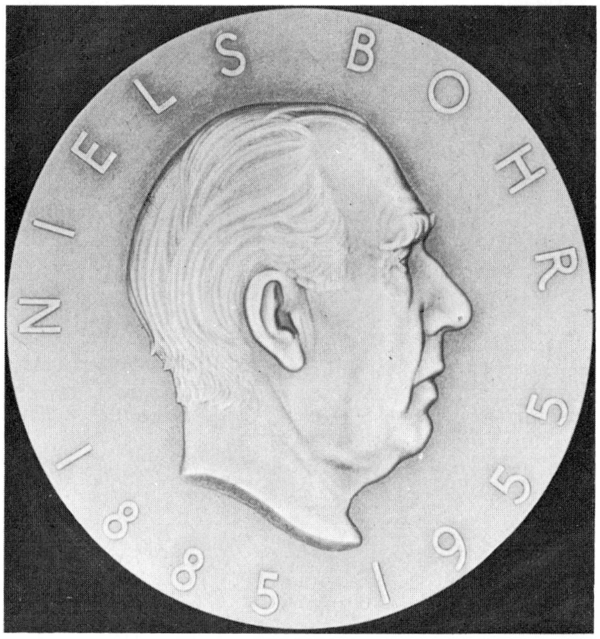

Figure 4. Medal by Harald Salomon in honor of Niels Bohr. Diam. $2\frac{1}{2}$ in. (6 cm.).

same period Asher Wappenstein (1780–1852) of Vienna engraved patriotic commemoratives. I. W. Loewenbach of Munich struck Bavarian nationalist medals from the 1820s through the 1860s. He also did the earliest German synagogue medal, issued in 1826 for the new synagogue at Munich. H. Oppenheim is well known for his medals dealing with his home city of Frankfort on the Main. On the other hand, Leo Horovitz, son of the Frankfort rabbi Marcus *Horovitz, concentrated mainly on Jewish subjects. Dutch Jewish medalists of this period were M. C. de Vries Jr., A. L. Snoeck, and Jacques *Elion, the last having been preceded by his father Samuel Cohen Elion. Two Americans, both born in the Austrian Empire, achieved distinction. One was Moritz *Furst; the other, Isidore Konti, a gifted sculptor as well, struck the 1905 commemoration of the 250th anniversary of Jewish settlement in the United States. Among 20th-century Jewish medalists are Victor D. *Brenner (U.S.), Benno *Elkan (Germany and England), and Harald Salomon (Denmark). Fulop O. Beck (b. 1873) is considered one of the best medalists of the 20th century; though baptized he executed medals for many important Jews. Ede Telcs (1872–1958), also a Christian convert, became the official medalist for Hungary during World War I. Other noted 20th-century Jewish medalists include the Germans Hugo Kaufmann and Arnold *Zadikow; the Austrians Emil Fuchs and Arthur Loewental; the Dutch Loecki Metz; the Hungarian István Csillag; the French Boris Bernstein, Simon Goldberg, and Esther Gorbato; Paul *Vincze, in England, as well as the Americans Abram Belskie, Michael Lantz, Albert W. Wein, and Adolph Block. The American sculptors Leonard Baskin and William *Zorach have done occasional medals. Boris *Schatz, Ivan Sors, F. J. Kormis, and A. Eisenberg are known for their medals of Jewish subject matter. Israel has a new group of medalists, including Miriam Karoli, Zvi Narkiss, Gabriel and Maxime Shammir, the team of Rothschild and Lippmann ("Rcli"), Alex Berlyne, Mordechai Gumpel, Jacob Zim, Josef Bass, and Moshe Zipper.

See *Medals.

Bibliography: L. Forrer, *Biographical Dictionary of Medalists* (1902–30); D. M. Friedenberg (ed.), *Great Jewish Portraits in Metal* (1963); idem, in: *The Numismatist* (July 1969); O. C. Gaedechens, *Die neuren Hamburgischen Muenzen und Medaillen* (1843); T. Hoffmann, *Jacob Abraham und Abraham Abramson—55 Jahr Medaillenkunst (1755–1810)* (1927); L. Kadman, *Israel's Money* (1963); M. Stern, *Aus dem Berliner Juedischen Museum* (1937).

[D.M.F.]

MEDALS. The significance of Jewish medals is both historical and artistic; they illustrate the history of the Jews in the widest sense of the word. Opinions widely differ on the classification of Jewish medals. Bruno Kisch (see bibliography) gives the following classification:

1. Symbolic representation, biblical personages and scenes, imitation shekels, and biblical medals. (This group should really not be included among Jewish medals, since in most cases they were made neither by, nor for Jews.)
2. Medals referring to political events in connection with Jews, such as the granting of religious freedom, Zionistica, etc.
3. Medals referring to Jewish communities, inaugurations and jubilees of synagogues, or institutions, schools, etc.
4. Medals of Jewish personalities, such as rabbis, physicians, philanthropists, etc.
5. Marriage and anniversary medals, tokens, amulets.

Though no medals exist from talmudic or biblical times, the Talmud (BK 97b) speaks of portrait coins bearing the likeness of biblical personages. Probably the oldest Jewish medal extant (1497 or 1503) is one associated with the name of Benjamin b. Elijah Be'er the physician, with a long and enigmatic Hebrew inscription with a text also in Greek and Latin, surrounding what may be intended to represent a Roman emperor. In the 16th century, during the Renaissance, portrait medals were made by or for rich Jewish families. The best known of these is that of Gracia *Nasi (1556), in all probability the younger of the two ladies known by that name. Dating roughly from the same period are the portrait medals of Elijah de Latas (or Lattes; 1552) and Abramo Emanuele Norsa (1557). Mention may be made also of the medals struck for Marranos in Antwerp, such as Luis Perez (1597) and Ursula Lopez, widow of Martin Perez (1580).

At the end of the 17th century, the so-called *"Korn Jude"* medals are found, a typical example of anti-Semitica. These medals, made of silver, copper, and tin, all show more or less the same picture: on the front a bearded man wearing a Jew's hat, a stick in his hand, and carrying a sack of grain on his back, on which sits the devil who rips the sack open. Around this picture is the inscription *"Du Korn Jude"* and under it a date with the word *Theurezeit.* On the reverse side is a corn measure and the verse (Prov. 11:26): *Wer Korn inhaelt, dem fluchen die Leuthe. Aber Seegen kommt ueber den, der es verkauft, Sprueche* ("He that withholdeth corn, the people shall curse him; but blessing shall be upon the head of him that selleth it," Proverbs). Other examples of anti-Semitic medals are the "Federjude" medals of the same period. The figure represented is a Jew in a feather hat, carrying a large sack on his back and a money bag in his hand. Similarly anti-Jewish feeling in Germany is expressed by the medals struck on the occasion of the execution of Jew "Suess" *Oppenheimer in 1738. The medals are in silver, lead, and bronze. In the 18th and 19th centuries baptism was for many Jews a way out of the difficult circumstances in which they lived, and this led to the striking of baptismal medals. Among such is a satiric medal in silver, circa 1700. On the front is a clergyman holding a Bible, who pours water on the head of a kneeling Jew carrying a millstone around his neck. On the reverse side is an anti-Semitic text, and on the rim *Wenn die Maus die Katze frisst, dan wird ein Jud ein wahrer Christ* ("When the mouse eats the cat, then a Jew becomes a true Christian"). Political accusations against the Jews were also known. When in 1686 the city of Ofen (the old German name for Buda, see *Budapest) was

Figure 1. Obverse of the Benjamin b. Elijah Be'er medal, the earliest known medal associated with a Jew, 1497/1503. Cast bronze, diam. approx. 7 in. (17.7 cm.). New York, Jewish Museum, Daniel M. Friedenberg Collection.

Figure 2. "Israel Liberata" coin celebrating the tenth anniversary of the State, 1958. The reverse is a facsimile of a "Judaea Capta" coin recording Vespasian's conquest in 70 C.E. Courtesy Israel Government Medals and Coins Corporation, Jerusalem.

Figure 3. Medal issued by the Ashkenazi community of Amsterdam in 1735 to celebrate the arrival of Eleazar b. Samuel Shmelka, chief rabbi of Brody, to take up his post as rabbi of the community. Pewter, diam. 2 in. (5 cm.). Jerusalem, Israel Museum (Feuchtwanger Collection, donated by Baruch and Ruth Rappaport). Photo R. Milon, Jerusalem.

Figure 4. A German *Korn Jude* medal, associating Jews with the rise in the price of grain during the famine of 1694. Pewter, diam. 1½ in. (3.8 cm.). New York, Jewish Museum, Daniel M. Friedenberg Collection.

Figure 5. Israel medal marking the 30th anniversary of the beginning of immigration blockade-running, 1964. Courtesy Israel Government Medals and Coins Corporation, Jerusalem.

Figure 6. Medal commemorating Franz Joseph I's proclamation allowing Jews in Galicia, Bukovina, and Cracow to purchase land, 1860. Pewter, diam. 3 in. (7.6 cm.). New York, Jewish Museum, Daniel Friedenberg Collection.

Selective List of Jewish Medals

1. Renaissance Medals:

1503 (or 1497)	Benjamin ben Elijah Be'er (medallion)
1552	Elijah de Latas (De Lattes) and his mother, Rica de Latas
1556	Gracia Nasi
1557	Abramo Emanuele Norsa (Norcia)

2. Jewish Emancipation Medals

1745	Repeal of Edict of Maria Theresa expelling Jews from Prague and Bohemia
1781	Edict of Toleration of Emperor Joseph II
1782	idem, issued by Dutch Jews after Emperor visited the Netherlands (four variants)
1790	Homage to Landgrave Ludwig X of Hesse and Darmstadt
1790	Homage to Landgravine Louise Caroline Henriette of Hesse and Darmstadt (two variants)
1796	Emancipation of Jews in Batavian Republic (i.e., Holland)
1805	Alexander I of Russia frees Jews from a special tax
1806	Sanhedrin of Napoleon
1808	Enfranchisement of the Jews of Westphalia (by Abraham Abramson)
1836	Homage to Gabriel Riesser (for role in German Jewish emancipation)
1840	Montefiore and Crémieux at Cairo on behalf of Jews held in accusation of ritual murder (The Damascus Affair)
1846	Jubilee of emancipation of Jews in The Netherlands
1848	Emancipation of Jews in the Kingdom of Sardinia (Dedication to Count Roberto d'Azeglio)
1848	Commemoration of the German Revolution (a plank listed on medal is "Emancipation of the Jews")
1854–55	Presentation by Italian Jews to Albert Cohen, 15th Sivan 5614, on his receiving assurances from Sultan Abdal-Mejid that the Jews in Palestine would receive equal rights with Christians
1860	Proclamation of Right for Jews in Galicia, Bukovina, and Cracow to buy real estate (for Franz Joseph I)
1864	Intercession in Morocco of Sir Moses and Lady Judith Montefiore
1881	100th Anniversary of Joseph II's Edict of Toleration

3. Commemorative Medals (Including a few anti-Semitic because of their importance)

1670	300th Anniversary of the alleged desecration of the Host at Brussels. This medal was reissued in 1820, on the 450th anniversary and then again in 1870, the last being philo-semitic
1686	Participation of the Jews in the defense of Ofen (Buda) against Austria (two variants)
1696	Satire on the followers of Shabbetai Ẓevi (Christian in origin)
1700	The Useless Baptism of Jews
1711	Fire in the Frankfort on the Main Ghetto (three variants by C. Wermuth; Separate one by Johann Linck)
1721	Fires in the Frankfort Ghetto
1738	Hanging of Jew Suess (five variants); also portrait
1791	Wilhelm (Jewish) School in Breslau, Jewish
1800	Inauguration of the Adat Jeshurun (Reform) Synagogue in Amsterdam
1810	Building of the Bordeaux Synagogue
1826	Dedication of the New Synagogue in Munich, by I.W. Loewenbach, Jewish medalist
1841	Hamburg Jewish Hospital (Solomon Heine on obverse as benefactor)
1841	Opening of the Jewish Home for Aged at the Hague; by J. Weiner, Jewish medalist
1841	Opening of the New Maastricht Synagogue
1841	25th Anniversary of the Jewish Loan Institute at Hamburg
1843	Laying of the Foundation Stone of the Hebrew National School at Birmingham
1843	First Jewish Girl's Confirmation at Warsaw; by Eichel, Jewish medalist
1848	Destruction of the Rothschild Chateau at Surenne

4. Important Early Tokens

1671 and 1714	Burial Pass Permits for the Amsterdam Ḥevra Kaddisha
1697–1812	English "Jew Brokers" Medals
c. 1780	Moses Benjamin Foa

1780–1793	Lord George Gordon as a Jew (nine variants)
1790	Daniel Mendoza (five variants)
1791	Mendoza and Ward
5. Important Portrait Medals Before 1850	
1735	Eleazar b. Samuel Shmelka, welcomed as rabbi by Ashkenazi community of Amsterdam (by Joel, Jewish medalist)
c. 1774	Moses Mendelssohn (by Jacob Abraham and son, Abraham Abramson)
1793	Daniel Itzig's 70th Birthday (by Abraham Abramson)
1794	Homage to Marcus Herz (by Jacob Abraham and Abraham Abramson)
1803	73rd Birthday of Lipmann Meyer (by Anton Friedrich Koenig)
c. 1816	Memorial to Gershom Mendes Seixas (by Moritz Furst)
1836	Memorial to Nathan Mayer Rothschild (pub. by Hyam Hyams)
1837	Memorial to Ludwig Boerne (by H. Oppenheim)
1837	Elias Henschel (Breslau): 50th Anniversary of graduation as doctor (by Lesser—possibly a Jew)
1839	Johann Stieglitz
1842	Memorial to Chief Rabbi Solomon Hirschel (pub. by Hyam Hyams)
1844	70th Birthday of Solomon Mayer Rothschild
1846	"Rachel," Elisa-Rachel Felix
1847	Giacomo Meyerbeer
1847	Jubilee of Ḥakham Isaac Bernays of Hamburg

captured from the Turks by Leopold I of Austria, the Jewish community was massacred. As a memento of the event a satiric medal was struck showing a Turk and Jew melting metal in a furnace, the Turk holding the tongs and the Jew the bellows, while ingots appear at the bottom. "Who mints money for peace now that the Turk and Jew are tired of war?" is the ironic inscription.

Two medals were struck on the occasion of the fire in the Judengasse at Frankfort on the Main in 1711, one in three variants. That with the variants by Christian Wermuth is one of the most vicious anti-Semitic pieces extant. In 1735 a medal was struck in Amsterdam—by Joel Levi—with a Hebrew text to mark the arrival there of *Eleazar of Brody, who had been invited to become rabbi of the Ashkenazi congregation. A portrait of Moses *Mendelssohn, one of the forerunners of the Emancipation in Germany, was made about 1774 jointly by the Jewish medalist Jacob Abraham (1723–1800) and his son, Abraham Abramson (1754–1811). The Emancipation of the Jews was the occasion of commemorations and frequently led to the striking of medals. (The most important medals in this group are listed in Section 2 of the appended list.) The Emancipation of the Jews caused a revival of Jewish communities especially in Western Europe, and an extensive development of Jewish intellectual life. In Germany and Austria, in particular, hundreds of medals were struck on the occasion of various events.

Large numbers of Jewish medalists and sculptors were engaged in the making of medals. Besides the German and Dutch medals there are also a number of French, Italian, and English medals, many American and a few Polish, Scandinavian, and Russian ones. [A.Po.]

In Israel. The first commemorative medals and coins were issued in Israel in 1958 on the tenth anniversary of the state, as part of the activities of the Anniversary Committee set up by the Prime Minister's Office. In 1961 a special Israel Government Coins and Medals Corporation was set up, whose charter provides for a board of directors on which a number of ministries are represented and which appoints a director general. State medals are struck for the following purpose: to commemorate events of national or international significance in the field of culture, science, history, and the various stages of Israel's development and achievement. In keeping with Jewish tradition, living personalities are not commemorated. Commemorative coins are issued by the Bank of Israel and are legal tender, while official state medals are the monopoly of the Coins and Medals Corporation. Apart from the purposes mentioned, these coins and medals have a great publicity value both among Diaspora Jews and in official circles of other states. They earn revenue and foreign currency for the Israel treasury; the income is earmarked for the restoration and preservation of historical sites in Israel.

The first medal issued in 1958 was the Liberation Medal showing the Roman "Judaea Capta" coin on the obverse and "Israel Liberata" on the reverse. This was followed by the Valor medal of 1959, with the symbol of the Israel Defense Forces on the obverse and the Trumpeldor Memorial on the reverse. A medal of the same year commemorated the jubilee year of the founding of Tel Aviv, while a Bar Kokhba medal was struck in 1960, after the Bar Kokhba letters were found in the Dead Sea Caves. More than 100 subjects had been commemorated by 1970, among them the Warsaw Ghetto Rising (1963), Masada (1964), the Rothschild family (on the opening of the new Knesset, 1966), the Sinai Campaign (1966), the Jewish Legion, the Balfour Declaration (1967), and El Al Airlines (1969). There is also a very popular bar mitzvah medal (1961).

Figure 7. Medal commemorating the 16th Chess Olympics, held in Israel in 1964. Courtesy Israel Government Medals and Coins Corporation, Jerusalem.

Commemorative coins are issued every year on the occasion of Israel Independence Day (1958–). A series of Ḥanukkah coins was struck (1958–63), as well as special gold coins to mark the Herzl centenary (1960), the Six-Day War of 1967, and the reunification of Jerusalem (1968). Half-shekels (1961, 1962) to be donated to charity on Purim, and Redemption of the Firstborn shekels (1969) for the *Pidyon ha-Ben* ceremony have been struck for religious use.

Each medal and coin is accompanied by an illustrated prospectus, in various languages, telling the story behind the medal, as well as numismatic technical details such as mintage figures, metal, weight, diameter, name of the artist, and the place of striking. In order to distinguish state medals from privately issued medals, official medals carry on their edge the emblem of the state and the words "State of Israel" in Hebrew and in English and are engraved with serial numbers. After minting the designated number of medals, the dies from which they were struck are destroyed in the presence of official witnesses. Official catalogs are issued periodically by the corporation and are also published in the *Israel Numismatic Bulletin*.

Bibliography: D. M. Friedenberg (ed.), *Great Jewish Portraits in Metal* (1963); idem, in: *The Numismatist* (July 1969), 891–918; C. Roth, *Jews in the Renaissance* (1959); L. A. Mayer, *Bibliography of Jewish Art* (1967), index; M. Stern, *Aus dem Berliner juedischen Museum* (1937); T. Hoffmann, *Jacob Abraham und Abraham Abramson—55 Jahre Medaillenkust (1755–1810)* (1927); A. Polak, *Joodse penningen in de Nederlanden* (1958); Kisch, in: HJ, 7 (1945), 135–66 (8 plates); Nahon, in: RMI, 28 (1962), 377–88 (4 plates); B. Kirschner, *Deutsche Spottmedaillen auf Juden*, ed. by A. Kindler (1968); S. Haffner, *History of Modern Israel's Money, 1917 to 1967* (1967), incl. bibl.; F. Bertram and R. Weber, *Israel's 20-year Catalog of Coins and Currency* . . . (1968). [Y.Av./I.Z.]

MEDEM, VLADIMIR (pseudonym **M. Vinitski;** 1879–1923), prominent *Bund leader in Russia and Poland. He was born in Libau (Liepaja), Courland, to an army medical officer, who was an extremely assimilationist liberal and had him baptized into the Orthodox Church. In his youth Medem regarded himself as a Russian, and the influence of his association with Jews at the secondary school of Minsk was only revealed later. He studied law in Kiev, became acquainted with the writings of Plekhanov and Lenin, and identified himself ideologically with Marxism. As a result of his role in a students' strike (1899) he was expelled from the university, and after a brief term of imprisonment returned to Minsk. His interest in the Jewish masses was now aroused and he felt himself attracted to them. This evolution, which led him to join the Bund, became for him the way back to Jewish identity. It was precisely this lengthy journey which later won him admiration within the Bundist

Vladimir Medem, Bund leader. Jerusalem, J.N.U.L., Schwadron Collection.

masses. He was a member of the Bund committee of Minsk and wrote for its organ, *Der Minsker Arbeter*.

After being imprisoned and suffering from a kidney disease, he succeeded in escaping to Berne, Switzerland. He was active in the Russian student circles there and at the end of 1901 was elected first secretary of the Bund organization abroad. He represented the Bund at the Second Convention (1903) of the Russian Social Democratic Party in London. After the convention he was appointed to the Committee Abroad of the Bund. During the years 1905–08, Medem was also active in Russia as one of the leading contributors and editors of the Bund newspapers *Posledniya Izvestiya* and *Nashe Slovo*. At the Seventh Convention (1906) of the Bund, he was elected to its central committee. He was deeply concerned with the national question, and it was he who formulated the so-called neutralist attitude toward the future fate of the Jewish nation which was adopted by the Bund as its official position ("neutralism"). It was only in 1910 that he began to retreat from this position and recognized the need for a positive attitude on the national future of the Jews. He was among the first to call for an active interest by the Bund in the Jewish community organization *(kehillah)*; he demanded actual action in the question of Yiddish schools, the right to rest on the Sabbath, and the right of employment for Jewish workers. He played an active role in the revival of the Bundist press during the years 1912–13 (*Lebnsfragen* Vienna, and *Di Tsayt*, St. Petersburg). In 1915, as a result of the Russian retreat during World War I, he was freed before completing a two-year term of imprisonment in Warsaw. During the German occupation he was the ideological leader of the Bund in Poland. He began to speak and write in Yiddish. His anti-Zionist writings became increasingly violent, but he renewed the demand for Jewish national-cultural autonomy. He was even in favor of collaboration with middle-class elements in the field of Yiddish culture. During the years 1919–20, when pro-Communist tendencies gained the upper hand within the Bund, Medem found himself isolated in his violently critical attitude toward Bolshevism and its methods. At the beginning of 1921 he emigrated to the U.S. where he contributed to the Jewish daily, **Forward*. His autobiography (*Fun Mayn Lebn*, 2 vols., 1923) is of both literary and historical value.

Bibliography: *Vladimir Medem—tsum Tsvantsikstn Yortsayt* (1943), incl. bibl.; LNYL, 6 (1965), 22–29; B. Dinur et al., *Kelal Yisrael* (1954), 538–41; J. Pinson, in: JSOS, 7 (1945), 233–64; L. Dawidowicz, *The Golden Tradition, 1772–1939* (1967). [M.M.]

MEDES AND MEDIA (מָדַי; in Akkadian inscriptions: *Madai*), a people of Indo-Iranian origin that inhabited the mountainous area of Iran and the northeastern and eastern region of Mesopotamia. In the biblical passage enumerating Noah's sons, Madai, the progenitor of the Medes, like those of other Indo-Iranian peoples, is included among the sons of *Japheth (Gen. 10:2). The Medes are first mentioned in the historical inscriptions of the Assyrian kings of the end of the ninth century B.C.E., Shalamaneser III and his son Shamshi-Adad V. The Assyrian kings in military campaigns against Media, which then stretched southeast of Lake Urmiah, inflicted heavy losses on its population. Although the Medes did not as yet have a central kingdom, they succeeded in repelling the Assyrian kings in sporadic encounters and by evasive tactics. In the eighth century B.C.E., *Tiglath-Pileser III, in his campaigns which extended from Ararat to the mountains south of the Caspian Sea, subdued the Medes. Annexing Media to Assyria, he deported 65,000 of its population, whom he replaced with inhabitants of other countries. However, in the days of *Sargon II, at the end of the eighth century B.C.E., Media, under the leadership of a Median called Dayaukku, revolted against Assyria. In Sargon's military operations conducted in 716–15 B.C.E. against the centers of revolt, Dayaukku was captured and exiled to Hamath in Syria, whereupon 22 Median rulers, submitting to the sovereignty of Assyria, presented a gift to the king. Dayaukku is undoubtedly identical with Deioces, who is mentioned by Herodotus (1:96–101) as having united the tribes of Media and as having been its first king, reigning for 53 years. However, according to contemporary Assyrian sources, he was merely the forceful local chieftain of a region lying between Assyria and Ararat. Apparently a later tradition attributed to him a royal title and the establishment of the Median Empire. Media became a united empire under the leadership of Kaštarita (according to the Persian pronunciation; in Assyrian: *Kastarītu*) who formed a military pact against the Assyrians in the region of the Zagros Mountains and rose to be king of Media (in the first half of the seventh century B.C.E.). The present tendency is to identify Kaštarita with Phraortes king of Media who, according to Herodotus (1:102), reigned 22 years, subdued the Persians, and was killed when advancing on Nineveh. Having consolidated their position at the end of the reign of Ashurbanipal king of Assyria (668–627 B.C.E.), the Medians, in the wars between Babylonia and Assyria in the days of the last Assyrian kings (626–616 B.C.E.), joined forces with the Babylonians, attacked Nineveh, and, after conquering it, assisted in the capture of Haran. The Medes (called in contemporary Babylonian documents *Ummān manda*, that is, barbarians) were then ruled by Cyaxares (in Babylonian: *Umakištar*), who, Herodotus reports (1:100–4), defeated the Scythians. After the overthrow of Assyria, Cyaxares extended his sway over the northern part of the Assyrian Empire, as well as over large sections of Iran, Armenia, and Asia Minor. When unable in 500 B.C.E. to conquer Lydia, Cyaxares, through the mediation of the kings of Babylonia and Cilicia, made a treaty with the Lydians. This consolidation of Media under Cyaxares, constituting as it did a danger to Babylonia, finds expression in utterances of the prophets of Israel who saw in the army of Media a relentless foe rising to destroy Babylonia (Isa. 13:4–6, 17–19, 21:1–10) and uniting with other northern peoples to bring about, at God's command, the overthrow of the kingdom of the Chaldeans (Jer. 51:11–14, 25–36). Astyages (Ass. *Ištumègu*) the son of Cyaxares and the last king of Media (584–550 B.C.E.) attempted to oust Babylonia from the region of Haran. However, after *Cyrus king of Persia had revolted against Astyages and defeated him, Media became part of the Persian Empire (550 B.C.E.). The revolts which broke out against Persian rule at the beginning of *Darius I's reign were unsuccessful, and Media was incorporated into two Persian satrapies (the 11th and the 18th). Nevertheless it occupied an honorable and special position in the Persian Empire, as is reflected in the biblical combination (in Esther and Daniel) of "Persia and Media" or "Media and Persia," e.g., "the seven princes of Persia and Media" (Esth. 1:14); "the kings of Media and Persia" (10:2); or "the laws of the Persians and the Medes" (1:19). The Bible apparently expresses a view, then prevalent, about the part played by the two empires in the historical events preceding the fall of Babylonia. According to this view, not only did the one empire supplement the work of the other but the Persian Empire was the natural heir of Media. Echoes of this view appear in Daniel's vision of the destruction of Babylonia by the Medes and Persians (Dan. 5:26–28; cf. 6:1, 29; 8:20) as well as in the prophecies in Isaiah and Jeremiah concerning the overthrow of Babylonia by Media (see above).

See also *Persia.

Bibliography: J. von Prašek, *Geschichte der Meder und Perser* (1906); Luckenbill, Records, index, s.v. *Madai, Matai, Medes, Media;* J. Levy, *Forschungen zur alten Geschichte Vorderasiens* (1925); C. J. Gad, *The Fall of Nineveh* (1926); idem, in: *Anatolian Studies*, 8 (1958), 72–78; Landsberger and Bauer, in: ZA, 3 (1927), 81–88; F. W. Koenig, in: *Der Alte Orient*, 33 (1934), 3–4; G. G. Cameron, *History of Early Iran* (1936); C. C. Torrey, in; JAOS, 66 (1946), 1–15; H. L. Ginsberg, *Studies in Daniel* (1948), 5–23; R. G. Kent, *Old Persian*... (1950); R. Ghirshman, *Iran* (1954), 72–126; D. J. Wiseman, *Chronicles of Chaldean Kings* (1956); idem, in: *Iraq*, 20 (1958), 11ff.; I. M. Dyakonov, *Istoria Midii* (1956), incl. bibl.; R. Labat, in: JA, 249 (1961), 1–12. [Sh.Ab.]

MEDICINE. From the beginning of their history until modern times Jews have exercised a tremendous influence on the development of medical science. They have always been solicitous in their care for the sick and held the medical profession in great esteem. In ancient times medicine and religion were closely connected. The priests were the custodians of public health. The dispute as to the propriety of human interference in sickness—regarded as divine retribution—ceased to trouble the Jews, because they came to regard the physician as the instrument through whom God could effect the cure. Jewish physicians therefore considered their vocation as spiritually endowed and not merely an ordinary profession. By the same token, great demands were made of them, and the ethical standards have always been very high.

The importance of medicine and physicians among the Jews is best seen in the long line of rabbi-physicians, that started during the talmudic period and continued until comparatively recently. Various factors were responsible for this combination of professions. Medicine was sanctioned by biblical and talmudic law and had an important bearing upon religious matters. Since teaching or studying the word of God for reward was not considered ethical, the practice of medicine was most often chosen as a means of livelihood. This trend was further strengthened by the fact that during the greater part of the Middle Ages the Jews were excluded from almost all other occupations, including public office, and medicine was left as one of the few dignified occupations by which they could earn their living.

Jews have contributed to medicine both by the creation of new medical concepts and by the transmission of medical knowledge. It was through the medieval Jewish physician-translators that the medical knowledge of the East and much of ancient Greek medical lore was preserved and transmitted to the West. A general survey of Jews in medicine may be divided into three broad periods: (a) biblical and talmudic times, which covers the period from antiquity until roughly the fourth to fifth centuries C.E.; (b) a middle period from approximately the sixth century C.E. to the beginning of the 19th century; and (c) the last two centuries, during which Jews throughout the world have excelled not only in the practice of medicine but in all fields of medical research and teaching. It is significant that over 20% of all winners of the Nobel Prize for medicine up to the end of the 1960s were Jewish.

The high standard of medical science in Israel must be mentioned. Not only have Israel physicians successfully met the challenge of medical problems in a developing country with a mixed population, but they have continued the ancient Jewish medical tradition by teaching and giving practical aid to those developing countries striving to attain the scientific levels of the 20th century.

IN THE BIBLE

The main source of information on ancient Hebrew medicine is the Bible, which refers to medicine as it pertains to religious or civil laws or when important characters are involved. No general ancient Hebrew medical documents are extant, although the Talmud reports that King *Hezekiah canceled the "Medical Book" (Ber. 10b; Pes.

56a) and that a scroll on pharmacology was lost. From earliest times, the Jewish faith sought to suppress *magic customs and practices in every field of life, including those concerned with the health of its members. The Hebrews were doubtlessly influenced in their medical concepts and practices by the surrounding nations, particularly by Egypt, where medical knowledge was highly developed. Prevailing superstitions and beliefs in magic medicine were far less accepted and practiced by the Jews, however, than by their neighbors. But like their contemporaries, the ancient Hebrews attributed health and disease to a divine source.

Healing was in the hands of God and the role of doctors was that of helpers or instruments of God. There are numerous references to physicians and men of healing throughout the Bible. It is always implied, however, that although man may administer treatment, it is God who heals: "I am the Lord that healeth thee" (Ex. 15:26). The title *rofe* ("healer") was therefore never adopted by ancient Jewish physicians; where it occurs it invariably refers to foreign doctors, who were usually assumed to be helpless because they were not aided by God. Pharmacists and midwives are also mentioned. Hebrew priests had no authority as physicians but rather held the position of health wardens of the community, charged with enforcing the laws pertaining to social hygiene.

The uniqueness of biblical medicine lies in its regulations for social hygiene, which are remarkable not only for their period but even by present-day standards. Hygiene and prophylaxis became religious dogmas intended for the welfare and preservation of the nation. Of the 613 commandments, 213 are of a medical nature. Prevention of epidemics, suppression of prostitution and venereal diseases, frequent washing, care of the skin, strict dietetic and sanitary regulations, rules for sexual life, isolation and quarantine, the observance of a day of rest—the Sabbath—these and other provisions inhibited the spread of many of the diseases prevalent in neighboring countries.

The Hebrews were aware of the fact that contagious diseases are spread by direct contact as well as by clothing, household utensils, etc. To prevent the spread of epidemics or infectious maladies they therefore compiled a series of sanitary regulations. These included precautionary or temporary isolation, quarantine, burning or scalding of infected garments and utensils, thorough scrubbing and smoking out of houses suspected of infection, and scrupulous inspection and purification of the diseased person after recovery (Lev. 13–14). Anyone coming into contact with a corpse or carrion, or suffering from purulent discharges from any part of his body, also required a thorough cleansing of himself and his belongings before being allowed back into the encampment (Num. 19: 7–16; Lev. 15:2–13). The garments, weapons, and utensils of soldiers returning to the camp after a battle had to be thoroughly cleansed and disinfected to prevent the spread of diseases possibly picked up during contact with the enemy (Num. 31:20, 22–24). The danger of infectious bowel diseases spreading through excrement was also recognized and the Bible instructs how to keep the camp clean (Deut. 23: 13–14).

Diseases and Remedies. Many diseases are mentioned in the Bible. Among them are: *shaḥefet*—phthisis (Lev. 26:16); *ʿafolim*—leishmaniasis (Deut. 28:27); *yerakon (yeraqon)*—ikterus (Deut. 28:22); *sheḥin pore'aḥ ʾavaʿbuʾot*—pemphigus (Ex. 9:9); *zav*—gonorrhea-leukorrhea (Lev. 15); *dever*—pest (Deut. 28:21); *shivron motnayim*—lumbago (Ezek. 21:11); *nofel ve-galui ʿenayim*—epilepsy (Num. 24:4); *rekav (reqav) ʿaẓamot*—osteomyelitis (Prov. 14:30). Although not specifically mentioned by name, eye diseases such as blepharitis ciliaris and gonorrheal ophthalmia undoubtedly existed, and senile cataract probably occurred frequently among the ancient Hebrews: "Now the eyes of Israel (Jacob) were dim for age so that he could not see" (Gen. 48:10). The dimness of sight rather than blindness is indicative of cataract. Various forms of skin disease are referred to in Deuteronomy: "The Lord will smite thee with the boil of Egypt, and with the emerods, and with the scab, and with the itch, whereof thou canst not be healed" (Deut. 28:27). The Hebrew word *ẓaraʿat,* which has been translated as leprosy, was probably a generic term for a number of skin ailments, many of which were considered curable (Lev. 13). However, leprosy in the modern sense was also known, and rigid quarantine, which did not exclude kings (II Chron. 26:21), was imposed on lepers. The term *maggefah* refers to plague, epidemics, and contagious diseases in general, very often of a venereal type. A bubonic plague described in I Samuel 5 mentions rodents, who are known to be carriers of the disease. Various types of wounds are mentioned: *makkah* is the generic term for wound; *makkah teriyyah* is a festering wound; *makkah ʾanushah,* a wound which will not heal, often fatal; *peẓaʿ*, a stab wound; *ḥabburah,* a boil or hematoma; and *mazor,* a septic boil.

With the one exception of the incurable serpent bite (Num. 21:9), biblical remedies and treatments are all of a rational character and do not involve incantations or magic rites, nor do they include the so-called "filth pharmacy." Biblical therapeutics consisted of washing; the use of oils, balsams, and bandages for wounds and bone fractures; bathing in therapeutic waters (II Kings 5:10), especially in the case of skin diseases; sun rays, medicated drinks, etc. Among medicaments mentioned by name are myrrh, sweet cinnamon, cassia, galbanum, niter, and the mandrake *(dudaʾim)* which was considered to possess aphrodisiac properties. The modern method of mouth-to-mouth artificial respiration was also known, as testified by the accounts of Elijah and Elisha (I Kings 17:22; II Kings 4:34–35). The only surgical operations mentioned are circumcision and castration, and these were not specifically Jewish practices. *Embalming, though unusual, was not forbidden.

Anatomical Knowledge. The Hebrew had more than a passing knowledge of anatomy. This is attested by the language used in instructions concerning methods of sacrifice and by passages of poetry where the names of organs and limbs are used metaphorically. The heart is mentioned frequently as the seat of emotion and intellect, and the functions now ascribed to the brain were then thought to emanate from the heart. No word for brain is mentioned, the word *mo'aḥ* in Job refers to marrowbone.

It is interesting to note that the Bible has a distinctive nomenclature for parts of the body and types of illnesses. Thus, for example, body defects or deformities are described solely by words constructed in the *piʿel* grammatical form: *ʾiṭṭer*—paralyzed, left-handed; *ʾillem*—dumb; *ʿivver*—blind; *pisse'aḥ*—lame; *gibben*—hunchback. Descriptions of mental or nervous diseases appear in the *piʿalon*-form: *dikkaʾon*—depression; *shiggaʿon*—madness; *iẓẓavon*—nervousness; *ʾivvaron*—mental blindness; *shikkaron*—drunkenness. Somatic illnesses appear in the *paʿelet (paʿalat)* form; *dalleket (dalleqet)*—inflammation; *shaḥefet*—tuberculosis; *yabbelet*—acne; *ʾaẓẓevet*—neuritis; *baheret*—leukoderma, vitiligo; *sappaḥat*—psoriasis; *ẓaraʿat*—lepra, skin diseases; *gabbaḥat*—loss of hair. Trauma of the body is formed according to the *paʿul* model: *shavur*—fractured; *ḥaruẓ*—split; *maʿukh*—crushed; *natuk (natuq)*—disjointed; *raẓuẓ*—smashed; *ẓaruʾa*—infected; *paẓuʿa*—wounded. Many anatomical terms have the ancient two-letter root, while most Hebrew words derive from three letters. Thus לֵב *lev*—heart; דָּם *dam*—blood; פֶּה *peh*—mouth; חֵךְ *ḥekh*—gums; שֵׁן *shen*—tooth; יָד *yad*—hand.

THE TALMUDIC ERA

The period surveyed in this section extends roughly from the second century B.C.E. to the sixth century C.E. The historical events of that period had a profound influence on the thought and way of life of the Jews and consequently on the development of Jewish medical art as well. As a result of the Babylonian Exile, of Greek rule followed by the Hasmonean Wars, the rise of Christianity and the Exile after the destruction of the Second Temple, the Jewish community became wide open to influences from neighboring countries and to foreign philosophies, which had their effect on every walk of life, including medicine.

Sources and Influences. The sources for this period are the Apocryphal books, Greco-Roman writings of Jews and non-Jews, the Mishnah, the Jerusalem and Babylonian Talmuds, the Midrashim, and, in part, the recently discovered Dead Sea Scrolls. None of these sources is a medical book as such. Except for a few cases, such as the praise of medicine and the physician by *Ben Sira, medical matters are dealt with mainly to illustrate points of ritual, or civil and criminal law. In the Talmud, a few medical matters are dealt with extensively in the tractates *Ḥullin, Nega'im* and *Bekhorot.* The influence of Persian and Babylonian magic medicine is clear from references to *amulets, the *evil eye, *demons, etc. The Greek influence on Jewish medical thought was considerable, but we find that the scholars were not blind adherents of the humoral pathology, but rather followers of anatomic pathology. This was doubtless based on their experiments and observations of sick animals before and after slaughter, as well as on their studies of human bodies and corpses. One of the interpretations given to the name of the sect known as *Essenes is אסיים, "healers." Their medicine mainly influenced Christian medicine and medical thought. They studied and collected herbs and roots for healing purposes, though their chief remedies were prayer, mystic formulas, and amulets. Abiding faith was all that was considered necessary for curing physical and mental diseases as well as chronic defects such as blindness, lameness, and deafness. The medicine mentioned in the New Testament is almost entirely of this type of miracle cure. By contrast, the attitude of Jewish scholars of the time, and later those of the Talmud, is generally a scientific one.

The talmudic attitude toward the sanctity of human life and the importance of health is expressed in numerous statements: "The saving of life *(pikku'aḥ nefesh)* takes precedence over Sabbath" (Yoma 85a). "Whoever is overzealous in fasting should be regarded as a sinner" (Ta'an. 11a). It was also decreed that when treating the sick or a woman in childbirth, even though no danger to life was involved, the sanctity of the Sabbath could be profaned.

Status of the Physician. The Talmud does not regard calling upon a physician for medical aid as a failure to rely upon God to restore health: "Whoever is in pain, let him go to the physician" (BK 46b). The profession of physician—as an instrument of God—was held in high esteem: "Honor the physician before need of him. Him also hath God apportioned . . . The skill of a physician shall lift up his head; and he shall stand before nobles . . ." (Ecclus. 38). The Talmud enumerated ten things that must be in a city where a scholar lives, and these include a physician and a surgeon. From this statement it may also be concluded that the number of practicing physicians was relatively great.

Specialists as known in Egypt did not exist. However, the Talmud names two types of physician, *rofe* and *rofe umman* ("skilled physician" and "surgeon"). Patients visited the physician in his home and not, as in Greece, in the marketplace. A special regulation was therefore enacted which required anyone renting premises to a physician to

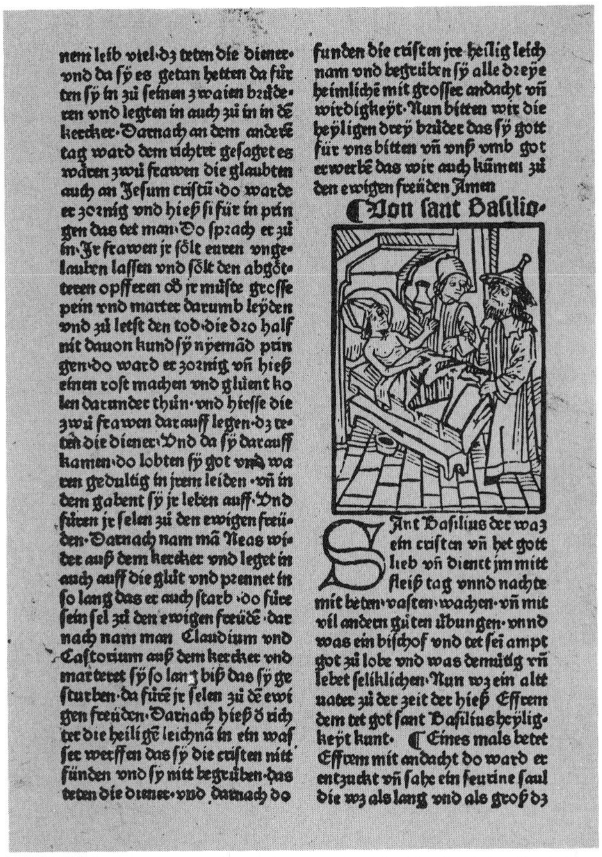

Figure 1. The sick St. Basil (c. 300) with his Jewish physician, Ephraim, who wears a medieval Jewish hat. From Hans Schobsser, *Plenarium,* Augsburg, 1487.

obtain the prior agreement of his neighbors, since the cries and noise of visiting patients might disturb them (BB 21a). *Hospitals were apparently nonexistent in this period, although certain temple halls, and later on, parts of the poorhouses and synagogues, were set aside for the sick. However, mention is made of operation rooms, which had to be walled with marble for cleanliness—*"battei shayish."* There were communal or district physicians, whose duties included assessing the character and extent of any physical disability sustained in cases of injury in order to determine damages (Sanh. 78a). They were also required to judge the degree of physical endurance of a person sentenced to corporal punishment (Mak. 22b). "The victim of an assault could refuse to be treated by a physician coming from a distance since he would not be sufficiently concerned with the welfare of his patient" (BK 85a).

A physician had to receive adequate fees, and free medical service was not approved because "A physician who takes nothing is worth nothing" (BK 85a). At the same time, Jewish physicians had special consideration for the poor and needy—a tradition which was maintained throughout the centuries. Abba Umana (fourth century C.E.) was reputed as a physician and a charitable man. In order not to discourage needy patients he would hang a box on the wall where anyone could put in, unnoticed, the fee he thought he could afford for medical treatment. Abba Umana refused to take fees from poor students and would return them their money so that they could use it for convalescence (Ta'an. 21b). If, in spite of every care, a licenced physician injured a patient or caused his death, he was not—as among many other peoples—held guilty (Sanh. 84b). Jewish physicians were apparently organized in some type of guild which had as its insignia the *ḥarut*—the branch of a palm or a balsam bush (Jews at that time regarding balsam as the best remedy for wounds; cf. Pliny, Hist. Nat., 12:54).

Jewish doctors had an excellent reputation and practiced throughout the then-known civilized world. A physician Theudas is mentioned in *Bekhorot* (4:4) as a famous doctor from Alexandria. Aulus Cornelius *Celsus, writing in the first century C.E., refers to salves compounded by skilled Jewish physicians. *Galen reports on the Jewish physician Rufus Samaritanus in Rome in the first–second centuries C.E. Similar references are made by Marcellus Empiricus, Aetius of Amida, and Paulus of Aegina. Pliny (Hist. Nat., 37.60.10) mentions a "Babylonian physician—Zechariah," undoubtedly a Jew, who dedicated his medical book to King Mithridates. The emperor Antoninus Pius (86–161 C.E.) requested R. Judah ha-Nasi to supply him with a physician for his house slaves from among his circle of students. The personal physician of St. Basil (c. 300 C.E.) was the Jew, Ephraim. The bishop Gelasius refers to his Jewish physician Telesinus as his "trusted friend." At the same time, numerous restrictions against Jewish doctors were already being promulgated by Christian bishops and emperors. These only serve to show how large the number of practicing Jewish physicians was at the time.

The study of medicine was included in the curriculum of talmudic schools and many Talmud scholars were themselves physicians. Among them were R. Ishmael, R. Ḥanina b. Dosa, R. Hananiah b. Ḥama, Joseph ha-Rofe of Gamla, Tobiah ha-Rofe of Modi'in, and Minjomi (Benjamin). The most distinguished of them was *Samuel b. Abba ha-Kohen, also called Mar Samuel Yarḥina'ah (165–257), to whom many remedies and much anatomical knowledge is attributed. He was also the personal physician of the Persian king, Sapur. In addition, the Talmud mentions *askan bi-devarim,* which might be described as a research scientist, who occupied himself more with the study of animal and human anatomy and physiology than with the actual practice of medicine.

Talmudic Anatomy. The preoccupation with regulations concerning ritually unclean meat, the physical qualifications for priesthood, rules concerning menstruous women, defilement, etc. accounts for the extraordinary anatomical knowledge of talmudic scholars. For full details see *Anatomy.

Talmudic Embryology. A great deal of material on this subject can be found in the Talmud and in the Midrashim, some of it of an imaginary or legendary character but most of it surprisingly accurate. Abba Saul describes the development of an embryo in its sixth week (Nid. 25b). Simlai describes the parts, posture, and nourishment of an embryo in the womb. Scholars accepted the opinion that the embryo is a living organism from the time of conception (Sanh. 91b). In contrast to Aristotle, who regarded the seed as a mosaic of individual creative factors corresponding to each of the parts of the human body and assumed that each limb is derived from the parallel limb of the father, the talmudic scholars regarded the seed as one single summary of all the creative forces of the organism and did not acknowledge the individual influence of one limb on the embryo. "The seed is mixed, otherwise blind would beget blind and one-limbed a one-limbed" (Ḥul. 69a). The Talmud also accepts the equal share of the male and female in forming the organism.

Pathology and Etiology. In examining the ritual fitness of animals and the cleanliness and purity of members of the community, talmudic scholars had numerous opportunities of observing and diagnosing diseases. They described various pathological conditions of the lungs and knew the existence of pulmonary infections (Ḥul. 47b). Disturbances of the circulatory system were recognized by the paleness or flush of the body (Yev. 64b). The diagnosis of certain skin diseases was determined according to the form, temperature, and secretion of the wound and the color of the hair round it. The observation of such a wound could last up to three weeks (Neg. 10). Scholars were able to recognize macula of the cornea, keratitis, and detached retina (Bekh. 38a). R. Ishmael describes diphtheria as an epidemic disease which causes painful death through strangulation. The pathology of hemophilia as a lack of viscosity in the blood preventing coagulation is described, and the circumcision of an infant in a hemophilic family was forbidden. It was also recognized that the female is the transmitter of this disease (Yev. 64a; Ḥul. 47b). A large number of lung, liver, kidney, and stomach diseases were described as being caused by worms (Ḥul. 48a; Shab. 109b; Git. 70a). Lack of fluids was thought to lead to digestive disturbances (Shab. 41a). It was recognized that fear accelerates the pulse and causes heartbeats (Sanh. 100b); that falling from a great height may cause fatal internal injury (Ḥul. 42a); that injury to the spinal cord causes paralysis (Ḥul. 51a); and that restraint of the gall causes jaundice. Fevers and colds were thought to be caused by negligence (BM 107b). According to R. Eleazar the gall (humor) and according to Mar Samuel the air (pneuma) could cause disease. It was generally accepted that blood is the chief cause of disease (BB 58b). Overeating, excessive drinking of intoxicants, and sexual excesses were also thought to cause disease. It was realized that animals and insects, in particular flies, are carriers and transmitters of infectious diseases (Ket. 77a), and that contaminated water may also cause illness (Av. Zar. 30a).

Remedies, Treatments, and Surgery. The medicines mentioned in the Talmud include powders, medicated drinks, juices, balsams, bandages, compresses, and incense. Meat and eggs were considered to be the most nourishing foods (Ber. 44b); fried food or food containing fat was regarded as difficult to digest (57b). The eating of vegetables throughout the year and the drinking of fresh water at every meal were recommended (*ibid.* 57b, 40a). Baths and mineral waters were regarded as general strengthening tonics and as therapeutics for certain skin diseases (Shab. 40a, 109a; Ket. 77b). Herbs were used for constipation and purges were recommended in serious cases, except for pregnant women (Pes. 42b). The use of opium as an analgetic and hypnotic drug was known, and warning was given against overdosing (TJ, Av. Zar. 2:2, 40d). Anything useful for healing purposes was permitted at any time, even on the Sabbath (Ḥul. 77b). Surgeons operated in special halls—*"battei shayish"* (see above). "Sleeping drugs"—*sammei de-shinta*—were used as anesthetics. From descriptions of operations we learn of trepannings, amputations, and removal of the spleen (cf. Sanh. 21b; Ḥul. 57a; Git. 56a). A cesarean was also performed, but it is not clear whether the operation was done on a living or on an already dead body. In general, the life of the mother had priority and therefore the killing of a foetus during a difficult birth was allowed (Tosef., Yev. 9:4). Wound edges were cut in order to ensure complete and clean healing (Ḥul. 54a). Surgeons wore special operation aprons (Kelim 26:5).

Hygiene and Prophylaxis. The main contribution of talmudic medicine lies not so much in the treatment of illness but rather, as in the Bible, in the prevention of disease and the care of community health. The hygienic measures advocated were of a practical as well as of a religious, ethical nature. A principle which recurs a number of times is that "bodily cleanliness leads to spiritual cleanliness" (Av. Zar. 20b; TJ, Shab. 1:3, 3b). Hygienic regulations applied among other things to town planning, climatic conditions, social community life, family life, and care of the body. Mention is made of a disinfectant composed of seven ingredients used for cleansing infected clothing (Zev. 95a). A town was required to have a physician and a bathhouse. Clothing had to be changed before eating. Mar Samuel declared that diseases may be carried by caravans from land to land (Ta'an. 21b). Members of a family with a sick person among them were to be avoided. The digging of wells in the neighborhood of cemeteries or refuse dumps was forbidden (Tosef., BB 1:10). It was forbidden to drink uncovered water for fear of snake venom (Av. Zar. 30a). Food had to be fresh and served in clean dishes. Kissing on the mouth was discouraged, and kissing only on the back of the hand was recommended in order to prevent contagion. During epidemics, the population was advised to avoid crowding in narrow alleyways because of the danger of contagion in the air. For body care, the Talmud recommends physical exercises, massage, sunlight, employment, and above all cleanliness. Mar Samuel states: "The washing of hands and feet in the morning is more effective than any remedy in the world" (Shab. 108b). Excesses of any kind were regarded as harmful. The Talmud also concerned itself with the health of future generations and forbade marriage to epileptics or the mentally retarded (Yev. 64b; 112b). Surprisingly enough, talmudic pathology had very little influence on medieval medicine, not even on such outstanding physicians as *Maimonides and Isaac *Israeli, who were certainly well versed in the Talmud. The medical authority of Galen was so preeminent that all other medical theories and practice were regarded as banalities or even heresy. Scholars warned against the unselective use of talmudic remedies because they are not equally effective in all countries and at all times. Nonetheless, the hygienic laws and regulations of the Talmud, as well as many of its anatomical and pathological findings, appear in the light of modern knowledge to have enduring validity.

THE MIDDLE PERIOD

The medieval period of Jewish history does not coincide exactly with the common historical definition of the Middle Ages in Western civilization, but may be said to extend from the second–third centuries C.E. until the 19th century when, in most Western countries, Jews were granted full emancipation.

The large variety of climates, environments, and customs to which the Jewish people were exposed during their migrations in exile naturally had a profound influence on the development of their medical thought and knowledge. Thus, for example, there is a description of *diabetes mellitus* in the writings of Maimonides. According to him, this was a disease quite common in the warm Mediterranean countries with which he was acquainted but practically unknown in Northern Europe. Talmudic scholars give a precise description of *ratan* ("filariasis") and its treatment—a malady unknown in Europe. Similarly, the prevalence of eye diseases in the Orient greatly encouraged the development of ophthalmology and, when Jewish eye doctors migrated to Europe, they quickly acquired an excellent reputation among their Christian colleagues.

However, the merit of Jewish doctors of that period lay not only in their individual achievements as physicians, but in their work as translators and transmitters of Greek medicine to the Arabs and later on of Arab medicine to Europe. Jewish scholars, and among them physicians, had command of the three most important scholastic languages of the time—Latin, Arabic, and Hebrew—and, in some cases, Greek. This enabled them to translate most of the Arab and Greek medical works into Hebrew and Latin or vice versa. Knowledge of Hebrew was considered extremely important in the study of medicine. The English scholar Roger *Bacon (c. 1220–c. 1292) declared that Christian physicians were ignorant in comparison with their Jewish colleagues because they lacked knowledge of the Hebrew and Arabic in which most of the medical works were written. Vesalius, the great 16th-century anatomist, made a point of learning Hebrew to facilitate his studies, and gives Hebrew terms together with their Greek equivalents in his work *Fabrica* (see also *Frigeis, Lazaro De). Mosellanus, in his rectorial address at the University of Leipzig in 1518, urged Christian medical students to learn Hebrew so that they might study the medical lore "hidden in the libraries of the Jews." The close religious and family ties linking the various Jewish communities also helped to spread medical knowledge and facilitate rapid communication. As merchants and travelers the Jews met the best minds of their period and became acquainted with drugs, plants, and remedies from many parts of the world.

Nevertheless, although Jewish physicians were frequently held in great esteem by their non-Jewish colleagues as well as by kings and bishops, they suffered from persecution and restrictions, especially in the Christian world. From the fourth century C.E. onward there were innumerable regulations, papal bulls, and royal ordinances forbidding Jewish physicians to practice among non-Jews, to hold official positions and, later on, to study at universities. The fact that, despite these threats and restrictions, Jewish physicians continued in their profession and even held high positions at the courts of the very authorities who preached against them, attests to the esteem with which they were regarded for their medical skill. In this respect the Muslims were much more tolerant: although persecutions of Jews erupted from time to time in Muslim territories, physicians were not singled out, and consulting them was not forbidden.

The large number of Jewish physicians during these centuries may also be explained by the fact that Jews still regarded the medical profession as a spiritual vocation compatible with the career of a rabbi. Many scholars took up the medical profession as an honorable way of earning a living. This was made comparatively easy because the curriculum of talmudic schools often included the philosophies and sciences of ancient and contemporary times. Very often, therefore, medieval Jewish physicians were simultaneously rabbis, scholars, scientists, translators, grammarians, or poets, and as men of wide general knowledge they frequently attained high official positions in the countries in which they lived.

The Byzantine Era. While Greek science and culture declined in the Byzantine Empire and the Jews living there suffered under oppression, Jewish, as well as Nestorian and Jacobite, physicians and scholars sought to save what they could of Hellenistic science. The Babylonian talmudic centers of Sura and Pumbedita flourished at this period. Although the teaching languages of the period were Hebrew, Syrio-Aramaic, and Persian, it was Greek medicine which was taught, strongly influenced by Hebrew, Babylonian, Persian, and Indian traditions. This becomes apparent from the medical work left by Asaph b. Berechiah, called *Asaph ha-Rofe or Asaph Judaeus, who lived about the sixth century C.E. somewhere in the Middle East. Together with Johanan b. Zavda, Judah ha-Yarḥoni and other Jewish scholars, he founded a medical school. His work, the oldest known medical book written in Hebrew, encompasses all the then-known wisdom of Greek, Babylonian, Egyptian, and Persian medicine, as well as something of Indian medicine. His medical technique is based on old Hebrew traditions. No Arab influence is apparent, which points to the fact that the book was composed before the seventh century. Most of the remedies mentioned were known in the Middle East generally. The book includes chapters on anatomy, embryology, physiology, hygiene, fever and pulse lore, urology, and a rich antidotarium. The oldest known Hebrew translation of the *Aphorisms* of Hippocrates, as well as chapters of Dioscorides and Galen, are also to be found in it. The book contains a "physician's oath," modeled on Hippocrates but far surpassing it in ethical content. The book of Asaph is not only significant to modern historians: it had considerable influence on medical history, particularly as far as Hebrew medical terms are concerned.

The Arab Period in the East. Following the Arab conquest of the Middle East and Spain, Jewish communities and centers of learning started to flourish at Faiyum in Egypt, Kairouan in Tunisia, and Cordova in Spain. Studies often included ethics, philosophy, sciences, and medicine. Students acquired experience in medicine by assisting practicing physicians. About a hundred years after the Arab conquest of the Middle East, the name of the Jewish physician Māsarjuwayh of Basra is mentioned as the first of a long list of men who translated a great number of Greek and Syrian works into Arabic. Unfortunately all his works have been lost, and he only appears as a frequent reference. Rabbān al-Ṭabarī (Sahl), a Jew converted to Islam who lived in Persia at the beginning of the ninth century, was a noted physician, mathematician, and astronomer. He was the first to translate *Ptolemy's *Almagest* into Arabic. His son Ali al-Tabarī Abu al-Ḥasan, also a convert, served as court physician to caliphs from 833 to 861, and was renowned as an ophthalmologist. His *Paradise of Wisdom* dealt with medicine, embryology, astronomy, and zoology and was one of the first original Arabic medical textbooks. He is best known as the teacher of the Arab physician Rhazes. One of the most outstanding medical personalities of the period was Isaac Judaeus (Isaac Israeli). He is believed to have been the first medical author in Arabic whose works were brought to Europe, and his books on fever, diet, uroscopy, and the ethical conduct of physicians were regarded as classics for several hundred years. His outstanding pupils were Abu al-Jazzār (a non-Jew) and *Dunash b. Tamim. It was said of him that he "lived a hundred years, was unmarried, shunned riches, and wrote important books more precious than silver or gold" (Saʿīd b. Ahmad, tenth-century Arab scholar). Israeli's books were first translated into Latin by the monk Constantinus Africanus (1020–87) and were all printed in Lyons in 1515.

Jewish physicians also flourished in Europe during this period. Among them was Zedekias (d. 880), the first registered Jewish doctor in Franco-Germany. He was personal physician to Louis the Pious and to his son Charles the Bald, and was known as the "wonderful physician" (Muenz).

The School of Salerno. From the ninth to the 12th century a medical study center existed in Salerno in southern Italy uninfluenced, either deliberately or by accident, by the Arab culture which penetrated into Southern Europe. The beginnings of the School of Salerno are associated with the name of the distinguished Jewish physician Shabbetai *Donnolo, of Oria, Calabria. His most famous medical work, *Sefer ha-Yakar,* lists 120 different remedies and their composition. Greek medicine is often referred to and Hebrew terms such as those used by Asaph ha-Rofe are frequently found in it. There is, however, no evidence that the author knew or accepted Arab medical wisdom, even though by that time many Arabic medical works had reached southern Italy by way of the Saracens of Sicily. It is interesting to note that *Sefer ha-Yakar* was also the first Hebrew prose written on European soil. References to other Jewish physicians practicing in Salerno and to Hebrew as a language of instruction are to be found in various records of the time. Benjamin of Tudela (12th century) refers to the physician Elijah whom he met when visiting Salerno. On the whole, however, the Jews who transmitted Arab philosophy and medical science had little influence on the School of Salerno, which endeavored to uphold the Greek medical tradition.

The Arab-Spanish Period. The Jews played an influential part in the cultural history of the period, starting with the Arab conquest of Spain in the eighth century and ending with their final expulsion from Granada in the 15th century. As statesmen, physicians, mathematicians, philosophers, and poets they attained high positions at the courts of both Moorish and Christian princes. At the Caliphate of Cordova (tenth century) was Ḥasdai *ibn Shaprut who, together with a monk, translated Dioscorides from Greek into Arabic. About a century later, Ephraim b. al-Zafran served as physician to the caliph of Egypt. Zafran was a renowned author and bibliophile and left a library of over 20,000 books. Another famous Jewish physician of the 11th century was Salāma ibn Ramḥamūn who lived in Cairo and whose works include a treatise on the causes of scant rainfall in Egypt and another discussing why Egyptian women grow stout early in life. *Judah Halevi (end of 11th century), the famous Spanish poet-physician, exerted great influence on his contemporaries and on later generations. Jonah ibn *Bikhlarish (11th century) of Andalusia, court physician to the sultan of Saragossa, was one of the first Jewish scholars to learn Latin. In about 1080 he compiled a dictionary of drugs in Syriac, Persian, Greek, Latin, and Spanish which is believed to be the earliest work of its kind. Sheshet b. Isaac *Benveniste, who served as court physician to the king of Barcelona, was the author of a famous gynecological treatise in Arabic. The most important Jewish physician-philosopher of the period was Maimonides. Born in Cordova, he fled with his family to North Africa and soon attained a worldwide reputation as a religious legislator, philosopher, and physician. In 1170 he became personal physician to the family of Sultan Saladin of Egypt and continued to serve them until his death. Maimonides wrote ten medical works, of which the most important ones were *Pirkei Moshe* ("Aphorisms of Moshe") and *Regimen Sanitatis.* Maimonides' whole concept of medicine is based on the conviction that a healthy body is the prerequisite for a healthy soul. This enables a man to develop his intellectual and moral capabilities and leads him toward the knowledge of God and thus to a more ethical life. He regards healing as the art of repairing both the defects of the body and the turmoil of the mind. A physician must therefore have not only the technical knowledge of his profession, but also the intuition and skill to understand the patient's personality and environment. Maimonides divides medicine into three main fields: preventive medicine—the care of the healthy; the curing of the sick; and the care and treatment of the convalescent, including the aged. Though leaning heavily on the medical teachings of the ancient Greeks, Maimonides warns against blind belief in so-called authorities and upholds the value of clear thought and experiments. His medical observations, diagnoses, and methods of healing mentioned in his works on asthma, poisons, his medical responsa, and commentaries on the *Aphorisms* of Hippocrates contain innovations in their day and many of them are still valid. Maimonides wrote his medical books in Arabic: most of them were soon translated into Hebrew and Latin.

Southern France. At the end of the 12th and the beginning of the 13th century, Jewish centers of learning were established in southern France—in Avignon, Lunel, Montpellier, Béziers, and Carcassonne. Conditions for Jews in these regions were generally somewhat better than those in Spain, although they did not escape restrictions,

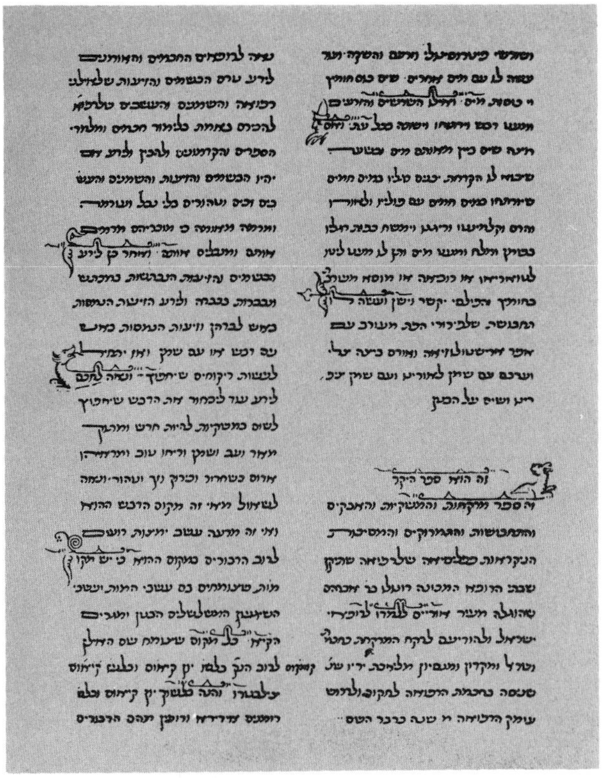

Figure 2. First page of Shabbetai Donnolo's book of remedies, *Sefer ha-Yakar,* included in a Hebrew medical manuscript, Italy, c. 1300. Jerusalem, J.N.U.L., Friedenwald Collection.

expulsion, and persecution. For a period of two to three hundred years, papal bulls and Synod decrees alternated in forbidding and then allowing Jewish physicians to practice their profession. The principal service rendered by Jewish scholars of southern France, many of whom had emigrated from Spain and Portugal, was the translation of Arabic works into Hebrew and Latin. Since some of the original Arabic works had been lost, it was only through their Hebrew translations that they were preserved. The important early 11th-century medical work, the Canon of *Avicenna, was translated into Latin and Hebrew a number of times. The work of translation was accompanied by great scholarly activity. The medical school of Montpellier owed its foundation largely to Jewish scholars, and various records mention "private" schools in which Hebrew law, science, and medicine were taught for a stipulated fee. During the 15th and 16th centuries, when certain universities were closed to Jews, Hebrew translations of Arabic and Greek medical works were made specifically for Jewish medical students.

The most notable of the long list of distinguished translators was the *Tibbon family (Judah b. Saul, Samuel, Moses), who during the 12th and 13th centuries translated most of the well-known scientific and philosophic works including those of Maimonides, from Arabic into Hebrew. Other eminent translators of the period were Jacob b. Makhir (Prophatius Judaeus) a member of the Tibbon family; Zerahiah ibn Shealtiel Ḥen; and Jacob ha-Katan, translator into Hebrew of Nicolai's antidotarium and of Averroes' treatise on diarrhea. Of special interest is Abraham Shem Tov of Tortosa, who practiced in Marseilles toward the end of the 13th century. His works, especially his translation of Abu al-Qāsim al-Zahrāwī's *al-Tatzrif,* are of particular importance because he introduced a new Hebrew terminology based mainly on terms used in the Talmud. In other works he deals with the necessity of studying basic sciences with apprenticeships in hospitals, and with the behavior required of the physician when visiting patients, especially poor ones. Another distinguished translator-physician was Moses Farrachi b. Salem (Ferragut) of the 13th century. He studied medicine at Salerno, and at the request of the king of Naples translated Rhazes' *Continens* and other Arabic medical works into Latin.

Jewish influence was so strong that in Montpellier, portraits of Jews were included in the marble plaques commemorating the early masters of the university. Apparently there was also a Jewish school of medicine in Lunel, which did not, however, attain the eminence of the University of Montpellier. A large part of the information on the early history of the latter and its relations with Jewish scholars is to be found in the history written by one of its graduates, Jean *Astruc (1684–1766), a man of Spanish-Jewish descent, later professor of medicine there and subsequently physician to Louis XV. The Saporta family, also of Marrano descent, has a prominent place in the history of Montpellier during the 16th century. Louis (I) Saporta came from Lerida, was appointed city physician in Marseilles in 1490 and from 1506 to 1529 served as professor at Montpellier University. His son Louis (II) studied medicine there, and his grandson Antoine became successively royal professor, dean, and chancellor of the university (1560). His great-grandson Jean became professor in 1577 and vice-chancellor in 1603. The family then emigrated to the French colonies of America and the name does not appear in the later history of Montpellier. The Sanchez family, already well-known in Portugal and Spain, also became prominent in medicine in southern France. The most distinguished member was Francisco *Sanchez (1562–1632), who was appointed professor of medicine and philosophy at Montpellier and later at Toulouse, and published many medical treatises. Jean Baptiste Silva (1682–1742), a native of Bordeaux who graduated in medicine from Montpellier, became physician to the grand duke of Bavaria, Prince Luis Henry of Conde, and Voltaire.

Benvenutus Grapheus, from Jerusalem, one of the most famous eye doctors of the Middle Ages, lived in the 12th century. He taught and practiced in Southern Europe and probably also in Salerno. His observations of and recommended cures for eye diseases prevailing in Southern Europe and other Mediterranean countries are of extraordinary accuracy and his works, which were translated into many European languages, were the most popular textbooks on ophthalmology of the period. There were also Jewish women physicians practicing at this time. Among them was Sarah La Migresse, who lived and practiced in Paris toward the end of the 13th century. In Marseilles a record has been found of an agreement signed in 1326 between Sara de Saint Gilles, widow of Abraham, and Salvet de Bourgneuf, whereby the former undertook to teach the latter "Artem medicine et physice," and to clothe and care for him for a period of seven months. In return, Salvet agreed to turn over to his teacher all his fees as physician during that period. Sarah of Wuerzburg received a licence from Archbishop Johann II in 1419 and developed a lucrative medical practice. Rebekah Zerlin of Frankfort (c. 1430) became famous as an oculist.

Christian Spain and Portugal. During the major part of the 13th and 14th centuries Jewish physicians in Catholic Spain enjoyed the protection and support of the reigning monarchs though toward the end of that period the Inquisition became more active. The list of prominent physicians of that period is a long one and only a few can be mentioned here. One of the most important was al-Fakhār (d. 1235), who received the title of *nasi* ("prince") at the court of Ferdinand III in Toledo. Another, Nathan b. Joel *Falaquera (second half of 13th century), wrote a medical book in Hebrew on the theory and practice of medicine, therapeutics, herbs and drugs, and hygiene. He used medical and botanical terms found in the Talmud. Abraham b. David Caslari of Narbonne and Béziers was the author of *Aleh Refu'ah* ("The Leaf of Healing," 1326), a treatise on fevers, divided into five books, to be used as a vademecum on these matters, and of a treatise on pestilential and other fevers, written in 1349 when the Black Death decimated the population of Provence, Catalonia, and Aragon. In 1360, Meir b. Isaac *Aldabi, a native of Toledo who went to Jerusalem in the middle of the 14th century, completed his comprehensive *Shevilei Emunah* a collection of philosophic, mystic, and talmudic teachings including chapters on human embryology, anatomy, physiology, pathology, and rules of health.

After the Expulsion. At the end of the 15th century the Jews were expelled from Spain and Portugal. Even before that many eminent physicians had emigrated to North Africa, Turkey, Greece, Italy, and Holland. Many were forced converts and some continued to practice in Spain and Portugal until the 18th century, despite their precarious position in those countries, where they were under constant threat of persecution. It is a historical fact that the Marranos and their descendants were leaders and pioneers in medicine in Europe and Asia for several centuries, from the Renaissance until modern times. Many of them distinguished themselves particularly in medical literature. The 16th century was a time of immense exploration, discovery, and progress. During this period—the beginning of the medical renaissance—many distinguished Jewish physicians, fleeing the Iberian Peninsula, won a worldwide reputation in other lands. Among them was *Amatus Lusitanus, who studied and practiced in Salamanca, Lisbon, Antwerp, Italy, and Greece and whose life was a saga of adventurous flights from one country to another. His principal works were *Centuria*, the description of 700 cases of disease and a translation of and commentary on Dioscorides. He is also famous for his unrelenting battle against superstition and medical quackery.

Some Distinguished Families. Abraham b. Samuel *Zacuto, called Diego Roderigo, was born in the Spanish city of Salamanca in 1452 and emigrated to Portugal and Tunis, where he became famous as a physician and astronomer. His great grandson, *Zacutus Lusitanus, born in Lisbon in 1575, became a physician in Salamanca and later fled to Amsterdam, where he became one of the foremost critics of his time. He wrote a history of medicine in 12 volumes, *De medicorum Principum*, and was also known for his code of ethics for physicians, *Introitus medici ad praxim*.

Dionysus Brudus (1470–1540), a physician at the Portuguese court who later lived in Antwerp, wrote important works on Galenism and on phlebotomy. His son Manuel Brudus practiced in Venice, England, and Flanders and published works on diet for febrile diseases which were widely read. Luiz Mercado (16th–17th century) of Valladolid wrote a medico-philosophical work *De Veritate* (1604), as well as numerous works on fevers, gynecology, pediatrics, hereditary diseases, and infectious maladies. Isaac *Cardozo, born in Portugal in 1610, became court physician to King Philip IV in Madrid. The 15th-century physician and poet Francesco Lopez de Villalobos was one of the first to describe lues (syphilis). In 1498 he also published a description of bubonic plague. Roderigo *Lopez was an internist and anatomist who fled the Inquisition in 1559 and became physician to Queen Elizabeth I of England. In 1594 he was accused of plotting to poison Elizabeth and sentenced to death.

The family of de *Castro produced many distinguished physicians. The most famous was Roderigo de Castro (c. 1550–1627), author of a gynecological work, *Universa Muliebrium Medicina*, and physician to the king of Denmark and various German dukes and princes. His son Benedict de Castro (b. 1597) started practicing in Hamburg and later became physician to the queen of Sweden. He was the author of *Apologia*, a medico-historical work which described the achievements of Jewish doctors and defended them against anti-Semitic charges. Orobio de Castro fled the Inquisition and settled in Amsterdam, where he became a famous physician and leader of the Jewish community. Jacob de Castro Sarmento (1692–1762), born in Portugal, settled in England and was admitted as a fellow of the Royal Society in 1730. His work *Agua de Inglaterra* reveals a profound knowledge of the therapeutic properties of quinine. The 18th-century Jacob Rodrigues *Pereira was a pioneer in the education of deaf-mutes. Born in Spain, of Marrano parents, he escaped the Inquisition, settled in Bordeaux, and embraced Judaism. At the age of 19 he started his campaign for improving the status of the deaf-mute, and continued in his chosen task for 46 years, showing great ability in teaching speech to the congenital deaf-mute. He invented a sign language for the deaf and dumb. The fate of Antonio Ribeira Sanchez illustrates how far-reaching was the influence of Jewish physicians at that period. A Portuguese Marrano, he fled from the Inquisition to Holland at the beginning of the 18th century and became the pupil of the famous Dutch physician, Boerhaven. In 1740 he went to Russia as personal physician to the czarinas Elizabeth and Catherine II. However, when his Jewish origin became known he was threatened with death and with great difficulty escaped to Paris, where he became an eminent physician and introduced soblimat into the therapy of syphilis.

A large number of Jewish physicians also settled in Turkey, where private citizens as well as sultans, viziers, and pashas valued their skill and medical knowledge and their high standard of ethics. In the 15th century Joseph *Hamon, a Granada physician, went at an advanced age to Constantinople, where he became court physician. For almost a century some member of the Hamon family held the position of court physician and exercised great public influence. Marrano physicians were also among the East India pioneers. Foremost among them was Garcia de *Orta, born in Portugal. In 1534 he went to India and there studied and collected oriental plants and drugs. His

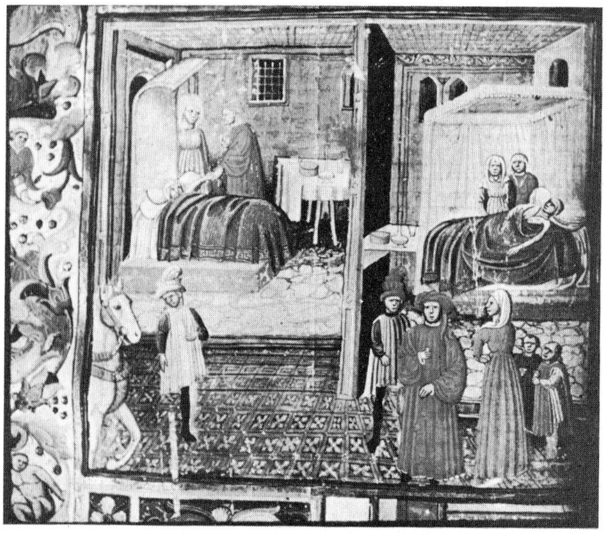

Figure 3. The treatment of the sick (detail) illustrated in a Hebrew illuminated manuscript from Book Four of the Canon of Avicenna, Ferrara, 15th century. Bologna, University Library, Ms. 2197, fol. 402r.

Figure 4. Luis Mercado (1525–1611), the Marrano physician to King Philip of Spain, Naples, and Sicily. From the frontispiece to Mercado's *El Libro de la Peste.* New York, Academy of Medicine.

Colloquios dos simples Drogas e cosas medicinas de India, which appeared in 1563 in the form of dialogues, is not only the first but also the most important contribution on this subject to European medicine of that time. Twelve years after his death his body was exhumed and burnt by the Inquisition as a suspected Jew. To this same group belongs Cristoval d'*Acosta (1515–80), a Marrano physician and botanist born in Mozambique, who lived and traveled in India and in the Middle East. He completed and enlarged the work of de Orta.

Italy. Numerous Italian Jewish physicians were also rabbis and leaders of their communities, especially in Rome, Ferrara, Mantua, and Genoa. The Italian universities, notably those of Padua and Perugia were among the few that allowed Jews to enter the medical faculties at a time when most other European universities were closed to them. The Jewish communities of Italy were also enriched by the influx of Jewish and Marrano scholars and physicians fleeing the persecution of the Inquisition in other countries. At various periods Jews acted as personal physicians to popes, cardinals, bishops and dukes. Thus Pope Nicholas IV (1287–92) had at his court the physician Isaac b. Mordecai, better known as Maestro Gajota. In 1392 Boniface IX made Angelo, son of Manuele the Jew, his physician and familiar. Immanuel b. Solomon, known as *Immanuel of Rome, was a practicing physician of note, who wrote on various physical and psychic ailments. *Hillel b. Samuel of Verona, who practiced in Ferrara, was a physician and translator of distinction. Another famous physician and translator was *Kalonymus b. Kalonymus, a native of Arles in southern France who later moved to Rome. He translated some of Galen's writings from Arabic into Hebrew and became famous for his accuracy and literary style. Special privileges and tax exemptions usually accompanied the appointment of court physicians. However, the periods of leniency to Jews were usually followed by periods of restriction and persecution. It has been suggested that the popularity of Jewish physicians in Italy in spite of the innumerable restrictions, the bitter attacks, and the calumnies was due to the superstitious belief of Christians in the "magic" arts of the Jews. They also admired Jewish doctors for their unselfish devotion to their calling, and it is not irrevelant that there was a scarcity of Christian physicians, especially during times of epidemic.

THE 15TH AND 16TH CENTURIES. A number of distinguished Italian Jews appeared in the field of medicine during the 15th and 16th centuries. Saladino Ferro d'Ascoli (15th–16th century) was acknowledged as the leading pharmacist of his time, and his work on pharmacology was the basic textbook for all pharmacists until the 18th century. Bonet de *Lattes (d. 1515), a native of Provence, became physician to Popes Alexander VI and Leo X. He also served as judge of the highest Italian court of appeal and rabbi to the Jewish community of Rome. Philotheus Eliajus *Montalto (d. 1616) fled to Italy from the Portuguese Inquisition. In 1606 he became physician to the Grand Duke Ferdinand of Florence and in 1611 personal physician to Queen Marie de Medici of France. By order of the queen he was buried in a Jewish cemetery in Amsterdam. His work *Archipathologia,* dealing with diseases of the nervous system and mental disturbances, was widely used in his time and often referred to by later medical writers. Roderigo de Fonseca in the 16th century earned his reputation by his clear diagnoses and descriptions of internal diseases, fevers, surgery, and pharmacology. Benjamin *Mussafia distinguished himself as physician, philologist, scholar, and rabbi. He served as personal physician to the Danish king Christian IV. One of the most outstanding personalities of the time was Rabbi Jacob *Ẓahalon, born in Rome and later physician in Ferrara. In his book *Oẓar ha-Ḥayyim* he described contemporary hygienic measures as well as the bubonic plague in Rome in 1656. He used numerous new Hebrew medical terms and redefined the moral obligations of the Jewish physician to his profession. Joseph Solomon *Delmedigo studied medicine in Padua and was a pupil of Galileo. After many years of study and travel he settled in Poland and became personal physician to Prince Radziwill. He is famous as a rabbi, physician, philosopher, and mathematician. During the 17th and 18th century the family of Conegliano became prominent as physicians and medical teachers in Venice. David de Pomis (1525–1593) of Spoleto became physician to Pope Pius IV. Apart from various medical treatises, he wrote the famous *De Medico Hebreo Enarratio Apologica,* a scholarly defense of the Jewish physician. The Jewish community in Italy, however, declined during the second half of the 17th and the 18th centuries. Only with the French Revolution and the conquest of Italy by Napoleon did the Jews of Italy come into their own again.

The Northern Countries. In the northern countries—Germany, Poland, Russia—there were Jewish physicians of note only from the middle of the 17th century onward, many of them refugees from the countries of the Inquisition. However, as early as the 11th century a medical book had been written in Hebrew by R. Saadiah of Worms. Gradually, the universities of the German states opened their doors to Jews. Around the middle of the 17th century the grand duke of Brandenburg permitted Jews to enter the University of Frankfort on the Oder. One of the first to study there was Tobias b. Moses *Cohn of Metz. However, he was unable to obtain his degree and therefore went to Padua to receive his MD. He practiced in Poland and later became physician to five successive sultans in Constantinople. His *Ma'aseh Tuviyyah* is almost an encyclopedia and includes medicine, sciences, philosophy, and part of a dictionary. From the beginning of the 18th century the number of practicing Jewish physicians in Germany, Czechoslovakia, England, and Poland increased. Jewish physicians of that period include Marcus Eliezer *Bloch, a

Figure 5. A physician examining his patient's urine. Miniature from a 15th-century Hebrew miscellany of medical and philosophical treatises, N. Italy (Padua?). Cambridge University Library, Dd. 10.68.

famous general practitioner in Berlin during the mid-18th century; Gumperz (Georg) Levison, who distinguished himself as a practitioner, medical author, and organizer in England and in Sweden during the second half of the 18th century; Elias *Henschel, a pioneer in modern obstetrics; and Marcus *Herz, an outstanding philosopher, teacher, and physician. [S.M.]

19TH AND 20TH CENTURIES

Nineteenth Century. When Joseph II of Austria proclaimed the Act of Tolerance in 1782 and when, shortly thereafter, the French Revolution brought in its wake emancipation to Jews throughout Western Europe, the gates of European medical schools were thrown open to Jewish students. The importance of the contribution made by Jewish doctors to subsequent medical progress is enormous. The quality and quantity of this contribution is reflected in rosters of Nobel laureates and winners of other awards, dictionaries of eponymic syndromes and diseases, and lists of medical authors and investigators. Spanning nearly two centuries and extending over many lands, Jewish participation in modern medicine defies rigid categorization within frameworks of countries and centuries. Frequent demographic changes have occurred as a result of global events which did not always coincide with the "turn" of a century. In fact, a future historian might choose the 1930s as the watershed decade, during which the mainstream of Jewish medical activity became diverted from Europe to America, coinciding with the rise of American medicine vis-à-vis that of Europe.

The geographic distribution of Jews practicing medicine in the 19th century reflected the incongruity between the size of Jewish communities and their number of medical practitioners and scientists. Because of restrictions practiced by Russian medical schools, the youth of the world's largest Jewish community went abroad to pursue their medical studies. Those who returned had to pass special examinations in order to obtain a license. Not until 1861 were they admitted to the army and civil service, and only in 1879 were they granted permission to live beyond the *Pale of Settlement. Even when Jewish physicians successfully overcame the main restrictions and hardships, they were rarely permitted to participate fully in university-centered medical activities.

On the other hand, Jewish doctors were extensively involved in the academic-scientific life of Central and Western Europe. In Austria and Germany, this involvement did not, however, come about suddenly. Although the gates of the universities were open for admission, the inner doors to academic recognition remained partially closed during the first half of the century. At best, a Jew could hope to become a *privatdocent* or a "titular" professor. And even after the struggle for academic recognition had been won, Jews were not welcome in "establishment"-controlled specialties, such as surgery. As a result they tended to cultivate fields that did not attract their non-Jewish colleagues.

An outstanding example of this trend is dermatology-venereology. When Ferdinand von Hebra took over the Kraetze Klinik in Vienna, he was able to recruit only Jewish assistants, some of whom—Moritz *Kaposi, Isador Neumann (1832–1906), and Heinrich Auspitz (1835–1886)—became world famous. In Germany, where dermatology was often referred to disdainfully as "Judenhaut," Paul *Unna, Oskar *Lassar, and Josef *Jadassohn established reputations as pathfinders in their specialty. In Switzerland Bruno Bloch (1878–1933) made Zurich an international teaching center. The predilection for neglected fields may also account for Jewish preeminence in biochemistry, immunology, *psychiatry, and in hematology, histology, and microscopic pathology—sciences which were collectively referred to at the time as "microscopy." The microscope attracted Jewish physicians, many of whom combined the study of microscopy with the practice and teaching of clinical medicine. Outstanding among these men were Ludwig

Figure 6. Prayer for health in time of plague, Mantua, 18th century. Cecil Roth Collection. Photo David Harris, Jerusalem.

*Traube, a great teacher and pioneer of experimental pathology, anatomy, and neurohistology; Robert *Remak, a pathfinder in embryology, neurohistology and electrotherapy; Moritz *Romberg, the founder of neuropathology; and the surgeon Benedict *Stilling, whose discovery of nerve nuclei was a turning point in basic neurology. These investigators laid the foundation of modern neurology, which numbered among its great names Leopold *Auerbach, Ludwig *Edinger, and Herman *Oppenheim—discoverers of many neurologic disorders now bearing their names.

Microscopy was also pursued by investigators who were exclusively devoted to basic science. To this category belong the histologist-anatomist Jacob *Henle, who anticipated the germ theory of infection; Gabriel *Valentin, who enriched every branch of basic science; the histologist-pathologist Julius *Cohnheim, who proved that pus cells are derived from the blood; the physiologists Hugo *Kronecker, Rudolf *Heidenhain, Nathan *Zuntz, and Hermann *Munk, who were trailblazers in this field; and Carl *Weigert, whose novel concepts and staining techniques advanced many sciences, particularly bacteriology. Jewish contributions to bacteriology date back to the botanist Ferdinand Cohn (1828–1898), who established the vegetable nature of bacteria (1853). These contributions increased during the latter part of the century when bacteriology and the allied science of immunology became integral parts of medicine. Jews became conspicuous in the discovery of bacteria and the development of immunologic methods for diagnosing and preventing bacterial infection. Prominent in this field were Fernand *Widal, who devised a test for typhoid fever and for its prevention; Mordecai Waldemar *Haffkine, who prepared vaccines against cholera and plague; August von *Wasserman who researched antitoxins and antisera; and Nobel laureate Paul *Ehrlich, the father of hematology, chemotherapy, and theoretical immunology.

At the same time, clinical medicine was also receiving Jewish contributions. Among the outstanding internists were Heinrich von *Bamberger, for his contributions to cardiology; Hermann *Senator, for his work on the kidney; and Ottomar Rosenbach (1851–1907) for his researches in functional disease and psychotherapy. Outstanding pediatricians were Edward Henoch (1820–1910) who described a bleeding disease named after him; Adolf *Baginsky who investigated nutrition and infectious diseases; and Max Kassowitz (1842–1913) who shed light on congenital syphilis and rickets. Jews were also prominent in otolaryngology, a specialty founded by Adam *Politzer, and in ophtalmology, with the contributions extending from 1810, when George Gerson (1788–1844) investigated astigmatism, to the close of the century, when Karl *Koller began to use local anesthesia in the treatment of eye diseases. Obstetrics and gynecology owe much to Samuel *Kristeller, Wilhelm Freund (1833–1917), and Leopold *Landau for new concepts, observations, and operative techniques. X-ray therapy was founded in 1897 by Leopold Freund (1868–1944). Even surgery, a specialty not too accessible to Jews, numbered many notables. Anton Wolfeer (1850–1917) performed the first gastroenterostomy in 1881, James Israel (1848–1926) pioneered urologic surgery, and Leopold Von Dittel (1815–1898) devised new surgical techniques and instruments. Jewish doctors also contributed to the history of medicine. Noted historians were August *Hirsch, Judah *Katzenelson, and Julius *Pagel.

It is apparent from some of the aforementioned names that Jewish contributions to medicine were not confined to German-speaking countries. In France, many Jewish doctors attained eminence. Julius Sichel (1802–1868) established the first eye clinic in Paris in 1830; Michel Levy (1809–1872) introduced new concepts in the field of public health; Georges Hayem (1841–1933) pioneered hematology; and Fernand Widal made a world impact with his work on the detection and prevention of typhoid fever. In Denmark the great anatomist Ludvig *Jacobson and the pioneer in occupational diseases, Adolph *Hannover were active during the first half of the century; and the epidemiologists Carl *Salomonsen and "the father of pediatrics in Denmark," Harold Hirschprung (1830–1916) during the second. Holland was the home of the physiologist Van Deen (1804–1869); Italy of the anatomist-physiologist-psychiatrist, Cesare *Lombroso; and Poland, of the anatomist Ludwig *Hirszfeld, the neurologist Samuel Goldflam (1852–1930) and the ophthalmologist Ludwig *Zamenhof, the creator of Esperanto. England knighted its greatest laryngologist Sir Felix *Semon. Even restrictive Russia honored the distinguished ophthalmologist. Max *Mandelstamm with the title "Privatdocent" and the physiologist, Elie de-*Cyon with a professorship (1872).

In America, where the Jewish community was small and medical science was not yet advanced, Jewish contributions to medicine were modest, and as often related to organization, administration, and of the foundation of hospitals as to scientific pursuits. The ophthalmic surgeon Isaac Hays (1796–1879) was editor of the influential *American Journal of Medical Sciences* (1827) and one of the founders of the American Medical Association. Jacob da Silva *Solis-Cohen, a pioneer in laryngology who performed the first laryngectomy for laryngeal cancer (1867) was the acknowledged "father" of organized instruction in his specialty. Another "father"—that of American pediatrics—Abraham Jacobi was the founder of the American Pediatric Society and in his later years (1910), the president of the American Medical Association. Jewish doctors were also active in establishing and staffing Jewish hospitals that provided training for Jewish interns and residents. In time these hospitals became important research centers affiliated with medical schools that absorbed many Jewish students.

Twentieth Century. Jewish participation in world medicine underwent little change during the early years of the 20th century, apart from an increasing trend toward practical application of accumulated basic knowledge. During this period, August von Wasserman introduced the first diagnostic test (1906) and Paul Ehrlich the first effective drug for syphilis (1910). Casimir *Funk revolutionized nutrition through its use of vitamin B (1911–14) in the treatment of beri-beri. Anticipating other substances with similar functions, he created the term "vitamin." Joseph *Goldberger introduced nicotinic acid (1914) for pellagra, and Alfred *Hess, vitamin C for scurvy. Markus *Hajek of Vienna devised new techniques in nasal and laryngeal surgery, and Gustav *Bucky invented the X-ray diaphragm that bears his name. While many Jewish doctors were making history, some were writing it. Outstanding among the historians were Max Neuberger (1868–1955) in Austria, Charles *Singer in England, Arturo Castiglioni (1874–1953) in Italy, and Harry *Friedenwald, Victor Robinson (1886–1947), and Saul Jarcho (1906–) in the U.S.

The early years of the 20th century also witnessed a continued immigration to the U.S. that changed the "ethnic" and cultural pattern of American Jewry and its medical representation. The first Jewish doctors in the U.S. were of Sephardi origin, and during the second part of the 19th century Jewish immigrants from Germany assumed leading roles in communal affairs and medicine. Russian Jews, who began emigrating after the pogroms of the 1880s, added a third element, which was destined to grow in numbers and influence. World War I, the Russian Revolution, and the *Balfour Declaration had demographic and political consequences that profoundly influenced Jewish participation in medicine. Many Russian Jews moved to large university centers, where they had previously been forbidden to reside. As a result of this movement and of the new policy of open university admissions which remained in force until unofficial quotas reappeared during the later years of Stalin's rule, the number of Jewish doctors greatly increased. Neither their number nor their achievements can be readily determined, however, because of the isolation of Russian Jewry from the Western world.

In the countries that broke away from the Russian and Austro-Hungarian empires, the Jewish population had at first been augmented by an influx of refugees from Russia. This increase, however, was later offset by emigration due to unfavorable economic and political conditions. The emigration increased sharply in the 1930s after the rise of the Nazi Party; the majority of those who escaped in time or survived the Holocaust emigrated to the United States and Israel. Physicians who found refuge in America arrived at a propitious time. The 1930s and the 1940s marked the beginning of the golden age of scientific medicine, ushered in by the discovery of antibiotics and cortisone and advances in molecular biology and medical technology. The hub of activity was the United States. Rid of vestiges of intolerance and receptive to new talent, the country's medical establishment and public welcomed the newcomers. Jewish hospitals, such as Mount Sinai in New York and Michael Reese and Mount Sinai in Chicago, as well as non-Jewish hospitals, research foundations, and universities absorbed many of them into the mainstream of medical progress.

Jewish physicians in the United States greatly outnumber those in other countries. In the State of New York there are about 7,500 practicing Jewish doctors as compared with 5,500 in Israel and 3,000 in France. More than 17,000 of the approximately 27,000 U.S. Jewish physicians in private practice reside in the thickly populated states of New York, California, Illinois, Pennsylvania, New Jersey, and Massachusetts. Approximately 4,700 doctors are general practitioners, 6,500 specialize in internal medicine and its branches, 3,000 in surgery, 2,900 in obstetrics and gynecology, 1,000 in ophthalmology, 800 in radiology, 650 in dermatology, and 600 in otolaryngology.

The distribution of U.S. Jewish doctors among the specialties is uneven. Whereas in occupational medicine they are represented by only 5%, they comprise 20% of internists and more than 30% of psychiatrists. On the whole, Jewish doctors constitute about 9% of the physician population in the United States—a number which exceeds threefold the percentage of Jews in the total population.

The Jewish contribution to American medicine—and for that matter to world medicine—cannot, however, be assessed entirely in terms of numbers of practicing physicians. Equally, if not more important, is the scope and the quality of Jewish participation in the advance of medical science as reflected in research and education.

Contributions to Medical Science. Chemotherapy, Immunology, and Hematology. Ehrlich's dream of a "magic bullet," which would destroy all bacteria as salvarsan does the spirochetes, was partially realized by the discovery of sulfonamides and antibiotics. Isolated in England by the Nobel Prize winner Sir Ernst Boris *Chain in 1940, penicillin was first produced in the United States. Streptomycin was isolated in 1944 and neomycin in 1948 by Selman *Waksman of Rutgers University. Important contributors to progress in antibiotics were Harry Eagle (1905–) and Maxwell Finland (1902–), who devised painstaking methods of evaluating antimicrobial agents so as to ensure their safe and effective use. Jewish investigators also helped harness immunology to practical use in controlling infectious diseases. Bela *Schick devised a diagnostic skin test for diphtheria, and Jonas *Salk and Albert *Sabin eliminated the threat of poliomyelitis through their vaccines.

Originally limited to the study of serology and resistance to infection, immunology soon expanded to include allergy, isoimmunity, autoimmunity, immunosuppression, and immunology of malignancy—all disciplines touching on matters of fundamental biologic importance and clinical relevance. Discoveries of blood groups by Nobel Prize winner Karl *Landsteiner, and his associates Philip *Levine, and Alexander Wiener (1907–) were conceptual breakthroughs as well as major practical achievements. Not only did these discoveries provide insight into the nature of isoimmunity and hemolytic disease of the newborn, but they also ensured the reasonable safety of transfusions, which was also the original concern of Ernest Witebsky (1901–1969). He subsequently devoted his energies to autoimmunity, and experiments provided proof of antibody formation by the host organism against its own tissues. Witebsky's associate, Felix Milgrom (1919–), elucidated the mechanisms of host tolerance and its breakdown. Another distinguished hematologist who later turned to immunology, William *Dameshek, became a pathfinder in immunosuppression. The first to treat acute leukemia with an antimetabolite, he steadily expanded his interest to organ transplantation and immunotherapy of malignant diseases. His associate, Robert Schwartz (1928–), made important observations on immunosuppressive therapy in relation to cancer. Robert Epstein (1928–) performed successful bone marrow transplantations. Michael Heidelberger (1888–), "the father of immunochemistry," measured quantitative relations of antigen-antibody reactions by biochemical methods. He also contributed to the study of allergies, pioneered in France by Alexander *Besredka of the Pasteur Institute. Also impressive are Jewish contributions to non-immunologic aspects of hematology. Maxwell *Wintrobe's researches on red-cell morphology, blood indices, iron metabolism, and nutritional aspects of blood diseases made him a central figure in American hematology. More recently, Ernest Jaffe (1925–) contributed to the understanding of hemoglobin synthesis, and Ernest Beutler (1928–) shed light on enzyme deficiencies in red blood cells.

Metabolism and Endocrinology. Progress in these fields received impetus from fundamental insights into metabolic processes, provided by such giants of biochemistry as Max *Meyerhof, and Sir Hans Adolph *Krebs. However, even before the biochemical breakthroughs, Jewish clinical investigators made important advances in metabolic diseases, particularly diabetes: in 1899, Oskar Minkowski (1855–1931) demonstrated the association of diabetes with the pancreas, and in 1920 Moses Barron (1883–) described observations on the pancreas that suggested to Banting his experimental approach in the discovery of insulin. More recently Rachmiel Levine (1910–) helped clarify the mechanism of insulin action and the metabolic derangements in diabetes. Isadore Snapper investigated correlations of bone and joint disease with metabolic and endocrine disturbances. Seymour Reichlin (1924–) has conducted important researches in endocrinology.

Heart, Lung, and Kidney Diseases. The fields of cardiovascular, pulmonary, and renal diseases have many Jewish contributors. Arthur *Master introduced the concept of coronary insufficiency and the "Master Step Test" for its detection; Louis Katz (1897–) elucidated principles of cardiovascular hemodynamics, metabolism, and electrophysiology—fields of research also enriched by Simon Dack (1908–), Richard Bing (1909–), Eugene Braunwald (1929–), and Eliot Corday (1913–). New approaches to the study of the pulmonary circulation have been introduced by Alfred P. Fishman (1918–). Arthur Maurice Fishberg (1898–) provided insights into correlations of pathologic changes with clinical manifestations of kidney disease. In 1934 Harry Goldblatt (1891–) demonstrated the mechanism of secondary hypertension caused by renal vascular disease. Kurt Lange (1906–) investigated immunologic, biochemical, and pathological facets of kidney disease in children.

GASTROENTEROLOGY. At the turn of the century, Max Einhorn (1862–1953) introduced important new concepts and diagnostic devices that advanced the growth of this specialty. Samuel Weiss (1885–) made contributions to investigate techniques and laboratory diagnosis. In 1931 Burrill *Crohn described the bowel disease which bears his name; and Heinrich Necheles (1897–), Joseph Kirsner (1909–), and Leon Schiff (1901–) have contributed to the understanding of the pathophysiology and therapy of a wide range of gastrointestinal and liver diseases.

NEUROLOGY. Neurology owes much to the Nobel laureate physiologist Joseph *Erlanger for his research on the functions of individual nerves. Deserving special mention among the numerous Jewish neurologists are Israel *Wechsler, for his standard *Textbook of Clinical Neurology* (1927), Bernard Alpers (1900–), for his investigations of neurosyphilis and cerebral arteriosclerosis, and Benjamin Boshes (1907–), for his studies on Parkinsonism. Leo Alexander (1905–) was noted for his researches on multiple sclerosis.

DERMATOLOGY. A field traditionally chosen by Jewish doctors, dermatology has continued to exert its appeal. Marion Sulzberger (1895–), a pupil of Bruno Bloch of Zurich, became the leading dermatologist-venereologist in the United States early in the century. Stephen Rothman (1894–1963) was a pathfinder in physiology of the skin and Herman Pinkus (1905–), in its histopathology.

PEDIATRICS. Initiated by Abraham Jacobi (1830–1919), American pediatrics has attracted many Jewish physicians. Isaac A. *Abt and Julius Hess (1876–) were trailblazers in child nutrition and care of the premature infant. Henry *Koplik added to the knowledge of infectious diseases in children, Louis *Diamond contributed to pediatric hematology, and Alexander Nadas (1913–) to pediatric cardiology. Henry Schwachman (1910–), researched cystic fibrosis.

SURGERY, OBSTETRICS, AND GYNECOLOGY. Jewish participation in these specialties is impressive. Isidor Ravdin (1894–) contributed to chemotherapy of cancer; Charles Elsberg (1871–1948) introduced new methods in the treatment of spinal-cord tumors. A pioneer in thoracic surgery, Max Thorek (b. 1871) founded the International College of Surgeons. Adrian *Kantrowitz contributed to methods and techniques of cardiac surgery and an innovator in the field of neurosurgery. Irving Cooper (1922–) pioneered in the introduction of an operative procedure for the treatment of Parkinson's disease.

In obstetrics, Joseph de Lee (1869–1942) occupies a special place. His authoritative text and contributions to the literature, to teaching, and to practice made him an undisputed leader in his specialty during the first half of the century. Isidor S. Rubin (1883–1958) made many important contributions to gynecology, and is best remembered for his fallopian tube patency test for sterility. Problems of sterility and fertility at the present time command the attention of many Jewish gynecologic endocrinologists.

RADIOLOGY. U.S. Jewish radiologists have enriched every branch of their specialty. Outstanding contributions have been made by Hymer Friedell (1911–) to radiation biology, by Harold G. Jacobson (1912–) to neuroradiology and Leo Rigler (1896–), who was president of the American Radiologic Society, to the radiology of the chest and abdomen.

PATHOLOGY. U.S. Jewish pathologists have helped advance their specialty. Among those who achieved eminence are Hans Popper (1905–) and Fenton Schaffner (1920–) in pathology of liver disease; David Spain (1913–) in cardiac pathology and Averile Liebow (1911–) in pulmonary pathology; Benjamin Castleman (1906–) in pathology of parathyroid glands; and Paul *Klemperer in that of connective tissue disorders.

PUBLIC HEALTH. Jews were active in public health and hygiene. Sigmund Goldwater (1873–1942) founded the first occupational disease clinic in New York in 1915. Milton J. Rosenau (1869–1946), his contemporary, promoted important measures for the prevention of epidemics in America and abroad. More recently, Jeremiah Stamler (1919–) has conducted important epidemiologic studies on environmental factors influencing coronary heart disease.

EDUCATION AND PUBLICATIONS. Jews have played a prominent part in these interrelated fields. Abraham *Flexner is still remembered for his "Flexner Report" (1906), which charted the subsequent course of medical education in the United States. After World War II a steadily increasing number of Jews have joined the teaching staffs of medical schools. Many have also contributed to teaching by authoring textbooks and editing medical journals. The best known medical editor, Morris *Fishbein, edited the *Journal of the American Medical Association* from 1924 until 1949, and played a leading role in shaping the policies of American medicine. Also active in the editorial field are Alexander Gutman (1902–), editor of the *American Journal of Medicine* and Alfred Soffer (1922–), editor of *Chest*.

Other Countries. Other countries also have provided opportunities for Jewish creativity. Canada shares with the United States such notables as Maxwell *Wintrobe, and has produced the noted pediatrician Alton Goldbloom (1890–1962) and the pioneer of myocardial vascularization, Arthur Vineberg. England honored Sir Ludwig *Guttemann, Lord *Cohen, Lord Rosenheim, and Sir Solly *Zukerman for their achievements as teachers, researchers, clinicians, and spokesmen for the profession. France was the home of Nobel Prize winners Andre *Lwoff and Francois *Jacob and of Jean Hamburger (1909–), its leading authority on immunology of renal transplantation. Switzerland was the home of the Nobel laureate Tadeus *Reichstein, who isolated cortisone, and Pierre Rentchnick (1923–), the country's foremost authority on public health and hygiene. Sweden sheltered the Nobel Prize winner Robert *Barany and, more recently, the Hungarian-born leader of Swedish cancer research, George Klein. Sweden is also the home of the endocrinologist Carl Luft, well-known for research on diabetes.

LATIN AMERICA. Because of geographic remoteness from the larger Jewish centers, Jewish contributions to medicine in Latin America have received less recognition abroad than they deserve. In Argentina, where Jewish immigration began in 1889, the figure of the pioneer physician Noah Yarchi is still remembered and revered. The doctors who followed in his footsteps helped sustain the health and morale of the colonists and the early settlers in the cities. With the establishment of the Ezra Hospital in Buenos Aires in 1921, a center was provided for medical activity; it grew in importance as the Jewish population increased. Prominent in every phase of professional and academic life of the country—Professor Quiroga was president of the Academy of Medicine of Buenos Aires and Ricardo Rodriguez, the dean of the Medical Faculty of La Plata—Jewish physicians publish the *Journal Archives de Medicina Argentina-Israel.* In Brazil, with a Jewish population of 140,000, and other Latin American countries with much smaller settlements, Jewish participation in medicine increased significantly after the arrival in the 1930s and 1940s of refugee doctors who brought the sophisticated approach of European medicine. Many Jewish physicians rose to eminence. Victor Soriano of Montevideo, Uruguay, was the editor of the *World Journal of Neurology.* Mexico had 120 Jewish doctors in 1970, many of whom attained professional distinction. Characteristic of the medical pioneers' sense of Jewish identity was their publication—early in the century, when their number was very small—of a medical journal, *Ars Medici.*

POLAND. Despite poor economic conditions, Jews in pre-Hitler Poland maintained 40 hospitals where many of the country's 3,500 Jewish doctors provided services. Poverty, backward technology, and a hostile academic environment prevented Jewish scientists from attaining the achievements reached by their colleagues in Western Europe. Still, their contributions were far from negligible. Edward Platau, the dean of Polish neurologists, researched meningitis and brain tumors; Adolf Beck investigated physiology of nerves; Samuel Goldflam studied reflexes, myasthenia gravis, and periodic paralysis; Zygmunt Bychowski investigated traumatic epilepsy and multiple sclerosis; Henry K. Higier explored the vegetative nervous system; Anastaszy Landau was prominent in metabolic research; Stanislaus Klein in hematology; Seweryn Sterling in social medicine; Gerszon Lewin in tuberculosis, and Aron Solowiesczyk, who was killed during the Warsaw ghetto revolt, in surgery. The scientific potential of Jewish doctors in Poland was not destined to develop. During the German occupation they devoted their energies to caring for people doomed to starvation, torture, and death. Many distinguished themselves by acts of dedication and heroism. Over 2,800 were killed. The tragic events in Poland were paralleled by similar developments in other German-occupied territories.

SOUTH AFRICA. South Africa has about 750 Jewish doctors, many of whom attained eminence. Among them may be mentioned Philip *Tobias, president of the Royal Society of South Africa, Maurice Shapiro an immuno-hematologist, the head of the country's transfusion services, S. Joel Cohen a gynecologist, M. M. Sussman a specialist in internal medicine, Valva Shrire in cardiology, and Jack Wolfowitz in surgery. Jack Penn, a plastic surgeon, played a great part in facial operations for Israel soldiers wounded in the War of Independence. A number of doctors emigrated to England, the United States, and Israel where they achieved distinction in various fields.

ISRAEL. Physicians have been prominent in the Zionist movement since its inception. The first Jewish physician in Palestine, Simon Fraenkel, was sent to Jerusalem in 1843 by Moses Montefiore. Menahem Stein was the first Jewish doctor in Jaffa (1882), Hillel *Yaffe the first in Haifa (1890), and Bathsheba Yunis (1880–1947) the first in Tel Aviv. Leib Pashkovsky was the first surgeon to settle in Palestine (1906). In 1912, the year the Medical Association was founded in Tel Aviv, there were 35 Jewish doctors in the country, the majority specially trained in ophthalmology, dermatology, and parasitology to face the country's prevalent diseases. Prominent among the early specialists were Aryeh *Feigenbaum, the ophthalmologist; Aryeh Dostrovsky, the dermatologist; Israel J. Kligler, the bacteriologist, the founder of the Pasteur Institute in Jerusalem (1913); Aryeh Boehm, who was responsible for many improvements in public health; and Moshe Sherman the otolaryngologist who became the founder and first president of the country's Medical Association. Although public health remained a major preoccupation, increased control of malaria, rabies, trachoma, and other infectious diseases allowed more time for other specialties. Chaim Sheba, surgeon-general of the Israel Army, helped raise the standard of his specialty and its teaching. Important contributions were made by Moshe *Rachmilewitz in hematology, Karl Braun in cardiology, Lipman *Halpern in neurology, and others in their respective fields.

The number of Jewish physicians in Israel increased sharply after the Balfour Declaration in 1917, and the pace of their immigration accelerated with each wave of persecution in Europe. As a result, the number of physicians per capita became the highest in the world, to be reduced only recently by the arrival of new immigrants. In 1970 the number of doctors in Israel was 5,500, of whom 2,600 were employed by the Kuppat Ḥolim. The Israel Medical Association, founded in 1929, has helped to raise the standards of the profession and improve service to the public during the difficult years of economic hardship and political and military tension. The Association's official organ, *Harefuah,* founded in 1913, has maintained a high scientific and journalistic standard. The Non-Resident Fellow Project of the Association has helped forge close links with Jewish doctors in the Diaspora.

Immigration of eminent scientists during the 1930s and 1940s, expansion of hospitals, founding of the *Hadassah-Hebrew University Medical School (1949), of the Weizmann Institute (1944), and of the Tel Aviv Medical School (1965), have advanced medical research and made it an integral part of Israel medicine.

Saul *Adler, a world authority of parasitology and tropical medicine, contributed to research on amebiasis, leishmaniasis, and relapsing fever. Bernhard and Hermann *Zondek continued their endocrinologic research, which had been interrupted by the European upheaval. A trailblazer in the treatment of female sterility Bruno Lunenfeld made the Tel Hashomer Hospital a world center of fertility research. Michael Sela, the immunologist, of the Weizmann Institute, devised new techniques for the study of antibody responses at the molecular level; David Erlick, Haifa, improved techniques of renal transplantation; Moshe Prywes, educator and editor of the *Israel Journal of Medical Sciences,* contributed to medical education, and Hanoch Midwidsky to the promotion of postgraduate studies. Andre de Vries (1911–) was head of the medical department of Beilinson hospital and wrote extensively in hematology.

Historians of medicine in Israel have included Sussman *Muntner, Joshua B. *Leibowitz, and David Margalit.

See also *Biology; *Chemistry; *Psychiatry; *Israel, State of, Science and Research, Health Services.

[S.VA.]

Bibliography: SOURCES: S. Muntner, in RHMH, 11 (1951), 23–38; 12 (1952), 21–23; idem, in: *Miscellanea Mediaevalia,* 4 (1966); idem, in: *Korot,* 1 no. 1–2 (1952); idem, in: *Sinai: Sefer Yovel* (1958), 321–37; Saladino di Ascoli, *Sefer ha-Rokeḥim* (1953); C. Roth, in: *Speculum,* 28 (1953); Steinschneider, Uebersetzungen. GENERAL: H. Friedenwald, *Jews and Medicine,* 2 vols. (1944); S. Muntner, *Le-Korot ha-Safah ha-Ivrit ki-Sefat ha-Limmud be-Ḥokhmat ha-Refu'ah* (1940); J. Seide, *Toledot ha-Refu'ah* (1954); R. Kagan, *Jewish Medicine* (1952). IN BIBLE AND TALMUD: C. J. Brim, *Medicine in the Bible* (1936); J. L. Katzenelson, *Ha-Talmud ve-Ḥokhmat ha-Refu'ah* (1928); S. Muntner, in: *Leshonenu,* 14 (1946); idem, *Sexology in the Bible and the Talmud* (1961); idem, in: *Refu'ah Veterinarit* (1944), 6–22; (1945), 5–22; M. Perlman, *Midrash ha-Refu'ah* (1926); J. Preuss, *Biblisch-Talmudische Medizin* (1911); W. Steinberg, in: *International Record of Medicine,* no. 12 (1960); nos. 2 and 4 (1961). MIDDLE PERIOD: E. A. W. Budge, *Syrian Anatomy, Pathology and Therapeutics* (1913); A.

Feigenbaum, in: *Acta Medica Orientalia*, 14 (1955), 26–29, 75–82; J. Leibowitz, in: *Dappim Refu'iyyim*, 11 no. 3 (1952); D. Margalit, *Ḥakhamei Yisrael ke-Rofe'im* (1962); S. Muntner, in: *Leshonenu*, 10 (1939/40), 135–49, 300–17; idem, *Alilot al Rofe'im Yehudiyyim be-Aspaklaryah shel Toledot ha Refu'ah* (1953); idem, *Mavo le-Sefer Asaf ha-Rofe* (1957); S. Donnolo, *Kitvei Refu'ah*, 2 vols. (1949); I. Judaeus, *Hebrew Physician* (1963). MODERN PERIOD: R. Landau, *Geschichte der juedischen Aerzte* (1895); H. Friedenwald, *Jewish Physicians and the Contributions of the Jews to the Science of Medicine* (1897); F. H. Garrison, *An Introduction to the History of Medicine* (1929[4]); S. R. Kagan, *Jewish Medicine* (1952); idem, *The Jewish Contribution to Medicine in America* (1934); idem, *American Jewish Physicians of Note* (1942); L. Falstein (ed.), *The Martyrdom of Jewish Physicians in Poland* (1963); L. Šik, *Juedische Aerzte in Jugoslawien* (1931); L. Gershenfeld, *The Jews in Science* (1934); C. Roth, *The Jewish Contribution to Civilization* (1956[3]); V. Robinson, *Pathfinders in Medicine* (1912); R. Taton (ed.), *A General History of Science*, 3 (1965), 494–548; 4 (1966), 502–62; M. Einhorn (ed.), *Harofé Haivri* (1928–65); I. Simon (ed.), *Revue d'Histoire de la Médicine Hebraïque* (1948–68); *Medical Leaves*, 5 vols. (1937–43); *Harefuah* (1920–70); A. Castiglioni, in: L. Finkelstein (ed.), *Jews, Their History, Culture, and Religion*, 2 (1960[3]), ch. 31, 1349–75.

ALPHABETICAL LIST OF ENTRIES INCLUDING CAPSULE ARTICLES

The individuals whose names are marked with an asterisk in the list below form the subject of articles in their appropriate alphabetical position in the Encyclopaedia.

***ABT, ISAAC ARTHUR** (1867–1955), U.S. pediatrician.

ADAM, LAJOS (**Louis**; 1879–1946), Hungarian physician. His appointment in 1927 as assistant professor at the University of Budapest aroused violent opposition in anti-Semitic circles, but in 1930 he was appointed full professor and director of the surgical clinic. In 1946 he became *Rector Magnificus*. His contribution to the technique of local anesthesia was of great importance. Among other books he wrote *A helí érzéstelenités kézikoenyve* ("The Handbook of Local Anesthesia").

***ADLER, SAUL** (1895–1966), Israel physician and parasitologist.

***ALBU, ISIDOR** (1837–1903), German physician and public health specialist.

***AMATUS LUSITANUS** (**João Rodrigues**; 1511–1568), physician and medical researcher.

***ASAPH HA-ROFE** (sixth-century), physician.

ASCOLI, ALBERTO ABRAM (1877–1957), Italian physician and educator (see *Ascoli).

ASCOLI, MAURIZIO (1876–1958), Italian pathologist (see *Ascoli).

ASCOLI (d'Ascoli), JACOB BEN ABRAHAM ROFE (15th century), Italian rabbi, physician, and liturgical poet (see *Ascoli).

ASCOLI, VITTORIO (1863–1931), Italian pathologist (see *Ascoli).

AXELROD, JULIUS (1912–), U.S. physiologist, pharmacologist, and Nobel Prize laureate. In 1949 he joined the staff of the National Institute of Mental Health, Bethesda, Maryland, and in 1954 was appointed chief of pharmacology. Axelrod specialized in the field of biochemical mechanism, drug and hormone actions, and glandular research. He identified the mechanisms that regulate the formation of noradrenalin in nerve cells, as well as the mechanisms in its inactivation. He shared the 1970 Nobel Prize for physiology and medicine with Bernard *Katz and Wolf von Euler.

***BAGINSKY, ADOLF ARON** (1843–1918), German pediatrician.

***BALLIN, SAMUEL JACOB** (1802–1866), Danish physician.

***BAMBERGER, HEINRICH VON** (1822–1888), Austrian physician.

***BARANY, ROBERT** (1876–1936), Austrian otologist.

***BARNETT, SIR LEWIS EDWARD** (1865–1946), New Zealand surgeon.

***BARUK, HENRI** (1897–), French neurologist.

***BENDER, MORRIS B.** (1905–), U.S. neurologist.

***BENVENUTUS GRAPHEUS HIEROSOLYMITANUS** (c. 12th century), oculist.

***BERENBLUM, ISAAC** (1903–), Israel pathologist.

***BERNARD, HAIM DAVID** (1782–1858), Polish professor of medicine.

***BERNHEIM, HIPPOLYTE** (1840–1919), French neurologist.

BERNSTEIN, NATHAN OSIPOVITCH (1836–1891), Russian physiologist and civic leader. The grandson of Solomon Eger, chief rabbi of the Posen provinces, Bernstein moved to Odessa in 1849 with his parents. He studied medicine at the University of Moscow. From 1871 he lectured without official appointment at the New-Russian University at Odessa (1865). He wrote a textbook on physiology, and succeeded Leo Pinsker as editor of the Russian-Jewish periodical *Zion*. Bernstein was president of the Medical Society of Odessa for 14 years, and became both a city councillor and an honorary Justice of the Peace. He was a director of the Odessa Talmud Torah.

***BESREDKA, ALEXANDER** (1870–1940), French immunologist.

***BLOCH, IWAN** (1872–1922), German physician and medical historian.

***BLOCH, MORDECAI ELIEZER** (1723–1799), German physician and zoologist.

BODIAN, DAVID (1910–), U.S. anatomist. Born in Chicago, Bodian investigated the nervous system, concentrating on the synaptic function and structure of invertebrate neurons (a portion of the pituitary gland). His study of the neurohypophysis (in the pituitary gland) was concerned with the cytological aspects of neurosecretion. Bodian also studied the pathology of poliomyelitis, dealing with the problems of interaction between the virus and host tissues. Bodian was elected to the U.S. National Academy of Sciences.

***BONDAVIN, JUDAH BEN DAVID** (**Bonjudas** or **Bonjusas**; 14th century), French physician and rabbi.

***BRANDES, LUDWIG ISRAEL** (1821–1894), Danish physician and philanthropist.

***BREUER, JOSEF** (1842–1925), Austrian physican, neurophysiologist and precursor of psychoanalysis.

***BRUDO, MANUEL** (c. 1500–c. 1585), Marrano physician and author.

***BUCKY, GUSTAV** (1880–1963), roentgenologist.

***BUERGER, LEO** (1879–1943), U.S. pathologist, urologist, and surgeon.

***CANNSTADT, KARL FRIEDRICH** (1807–1850), German physician. Cannstadt was born in Regensburg. His monograph on a cholera outbreak in Paris led to his being invited to establish a cholera hospital for the Belgian government. In 1844 he was appointed professor of internal medicine at Erlangen University. His *Handbuch der medizinischen Klinik* (1841) shows him to have been one of the first to substitute clinical observation for speculative natural philosophy. Another notable work was *Die Krankheiten des hoeheren Alters und ihre Heilung* (1839), and from 1841 he edited the *Jahresbericht ueber die Fortschritte der gesamten Medizin in allen Laendern*.

***CASTRO, BENDITO DE** (**Baruch Nahamias**; 1597–1684), physician and author.

***CASTRO, RODRIGO DE** (1550–1627), Marrano physician.

***CASTRO SARMENTO, JACOB** (**Henrique**) **DE** (1691–1762), Marrano physician.

CHERKASKY, MARTIN (1911–), U.S. medical administrator. Born in Philadelphia, where he trained to be a Hebrew teacher before becoming a physician, Cherkasky was appointed director of Montefiore Hospital, New York in 1951. In 1956, he was appointed clinical associate professor of environmental medicine and community health at the State University of New York, Downstate Medical Center, and in 1967 professor and chairman of the Department of Community Health at the Albert Einstein College of Medicine of Yeshiva University.

***COHEN, HARRY S.** (1885–1969), U.S. surgeon, medical inventor, and author.

***COHEN, HENRY, LORD** (1900–), English medical administrator and diagnostician.

COHEN, IRVIN J. (1908–), U.S. medical administrator. Born in New York, he began practicing as a pediatrician but later turned to hospital administration; he was director of the Veterans Administration Hospital in New York, Baltimore, and Washington, D.C., from 1946–62. He then became executive vice-president of the Maimonides Medical Center, Brooklyn, N.Y. In addition, he was appointed professor and chairman of the Health Care and Hospital Administration Program of the State University of New York in 1967.

***COHN, EDWIN JOSEPH** (1892–1953), U.S. biochemist.

***COHN, TOBIAS** (1652–1729), physician.

***COHNHEIM, JULIUS** (1839–1884), German pathologist.
***CONEGLIANO, ABRAHAM JOEL** (16th–17th century), Italian physician and mathematician.
***CONEGLIANO, ISRAEL** (c. 1650–c. 1717), Italian physician and politician.
***CONEGLIANO, SOLOMON** (1642–1719), Italian physician and lecturer.
***CROHN, BURRILL BERNARD** (1884–), U.S. gastroenterologist.
***CYON, ELIE DE** (1843–1912), Russian physiologist.
***DAMESHEK, WILLIAM** (1900–), U.S. hematologist.
***DAVIDOFF, LEO MAX** (1898–), U.S. neurosurgeon.
DAVIDSOHN, ISRAEL (1895–), U.S. pathologist. Born in Tarnopol, Austria, Davidsohn qualified in Europe before emigrating to the United States in 1923. He became pathologist and director of laboratories at Philadelphia's Mount Sinai Hospital (1926–30). He then moved to Mount Sinai Hospital, Chicago, where he was director of experimental pathology. He also taught at Rush Medical College (1934–41) and the University of Illinois College of Medicine (1941–47) and from 1947 to 1968 was professor and chairman of the pathology department at the University of Chicago Medical School. His main field of research was immunohematology.
***DE LEE, JOSEPH B.** (1869–1942), U.S. obstetrician and gynecologist.
***DE VRIES, ANDRE** (1911–), Israel physician and educator.
***DIAMOND, LOUIS L. KLEIN** (1902–), U.S. hematologist and pediatrician.
***DONNOLO, SHABBETAI** (913–c. 982), Italian physician.
DOSTROVSKY, ARYEH (1887–), Israel dermatologist. Born in Caro, Russia, Dostrovsky studied medicine at several European universities before settling in Palestine in 1919. From 1920 to 1956 he was head of the Department of Skin and General Diseases at the Hadassah Hospital, Jerusalem. He was the first dean of the Hebrew University-Hadassah Medical School (1948–53). Dostrovsky laid the foundation for the development dermatology in Israel, and was a specialist in the problem of leprosy in Ereẓ Israel. He was a member of the expert advisory panel of the World Health Organization on venereal diseases and treponematosis, and was coeditor of *International Dermatologica.*
***DRESSLER, WILLIAM** (1890–), U.S. cardiologist and electrocardiographer.
***EDINGER, LUDWIG** (1855–1918), German neurologist.
***EHRLICH, PAUL** (1854–1915), German chemist, physician and Nobel Prize laureate.
EINHORN, MAX (1862–1953), U.S. internist and gastroenterologist. Born in Grodno, Russia, he emigrated to the U.S. where he became professor of medicine at the New York Postgraduate Medical School of Columbia University from 1896 to 1940. He was visiting physician at New York's Lennox Hill Hospital and consulting physician to several other hospitals. His major work was on gastric, digestive, and intestinal disorders.
***EINHORN, MOSES** (1862–1953), U.S. internist and gastroenterologist.
***ERLANGER, JOSEPH** (1874–1965), U.S. physiologist and Nobel Prize laureate.
***FALAQUERA, NATHAN BEN JOEL** (13th century), Spanish physician.
***FEIGENBAUM, ARYEH** (1885–), Israel opthalmologist.
***FINKELSTEIN, HEINRICH** (1865–1942), German pediatrician.
***FISHBEIN, MORRIS** (1889–), U.S. medical editor.
FISHMAN, WILLIAM HAROLD (1914–), U.S. biochemist. Born in Winnipeg, Canada, he joined the Bowman-Gray School of Medicine, North Carolina, in 1941, the University of Chicago in 1945, and the Tufts-New England Center Hospital in 1948, where he became director of cancer research in 1957. He contributed many papers and co-edited the books *Physiopathology of Cancer* (1955, 1959) and *Chemistry of Drug Metabolism* (1961).
***FRIEDENWALD, HARRY** (1864–1950), U.S. physician and medical historian.
***FRIGEIS, LAZARO DE** (16th century), Italian anatomist.
***FRIZZI, BENEDETTO** (1756–1844), Italian physician and author.
***FROEHLICH, ALFRED** (1871–1953), U.S. pharmacologist, born in Vienna.
***FUNK, CASIMIR** (1884–1967), U.S. biochemist.
***GARLOK, JOHN H.** (1896–1965), U.S. surgeon.
GLICK, DAVID (1908–), U.S. biochemist. Born in Homestead, Pennsylvania, he became professor of physiological chemistry at the University of Minnesota in 1950. In 1961 he became professor of pathology and head of the division of histochemistry at Stanford University Medical School, California.
***GLUCKMAN, HENRY** (1893–), South African physician and politician.
***GOLDBERGER, JOSEPH** (1874–1929), U.S. public health specialist.
***GOLDSTEIN, KURT** (1876–1966), U.S. neurologist and psychiatrist.
***GOTTLIEB, BERNHARD** (1885–1950), dental scientist.
GROB, DAVID (1919–), U.S. physician. Born in New York City, Grob graduated in medicine from Johns Hopkins University, where from 1955 to 1958 he was associate professor of medicine. From 1958 he was director of medical services at Maimonides Medical Center in New York. He was at the same time professor of medicine at New York State University, and from 1952 its assistant dean. Grob has written extensively, including textbooks. His major interests are neuromuscular diseases and anticholinesterase chemical compounds.
***GROSSMAN, MORTON IRVIN** (1919–), U. S. gastroenterologist.
***GRUBY, DAVID** (1811–1898), Hungarian physician.
***GUTTMACHER, ALAN F.** (1898–), U.S. obstetrician.
***GUTTMAN, ALEXANDER B.** (1902–), U.S. physician.
***HAFFKINE, MORDECAI WALDEMAR** (1860–1930), bacteriologist, immunologist, philanthropist, and Bible scholar.
***HAJEK, MARKUS** (1861–1941), Austrian laryngologist.
***HALBERSTAEDTER, LUDWIG** (1876–1949), Israel radiologist.
***HALPERN, LIPMAN** (1902–1968), Israel neurologist.
***HANNOVER, ADOLPH** (1814–1894), Danish physician and histologist.
***HEIDENHAIN, RUDOLF** (1834–1897), German physiologist.
***HELPERN, MILTON** (1902–), U.S. pathologist.
***HENLE, JACOB** (1809–1885), German anatomist and pathologist.
***HIRSCH, AUGUST** (1817–1894), German historical and geographical pathologist.
***HIRSCH, RACHEL** (1870–1953), German physician.
***HIRSCHBERG, JULIUS** (1843–1925), German ophthalmologist.
***HIRSCHFELD, ISADOR** (1882–1965), U.S. dental surgeon.
***HIRSZFELD, LUDWIK** (1884–1954), Polish physician, immunologist, serologist, and microbiologist.
HOLLANDER, FRANKLIN (1899–1967), U.S. physiologist. Born and educated in New York City, Hollander became assistant professor of physiology at New York Medical College from 1927 to 1932. From 1936 until his death, he was chief of the Gastrointestinal Physiology Research Laboratory at New York's Mount Sinai Hospital and assistant clinical professor of physiology at Columbia University's College of Physicians and Surgeons. He was consultant to a number of hospitals and health institutes. He wrote extensively on gastrointestinal physiology and served on several editorial boards of medical journals.
***HUARTE DE SAN JUAN, JUAN** (1529–1589), physician and author.
***IBN YAḤYA, GEDALIAH BEN TAM** (16th century), physician.
ILLOWAY, HENRY (1848–1932), U.S. physician, son of Bernard *Illoway.
***ISAAC BEN TODROS** (14th century), French physician.
***JACOB, FRANCOIS** (1920–), French molecular biologist and Nobel Prize laureate.
***JACOB HA-KATAN** (13th century), medical translator.
***JACOBI, ABRAHAM** (1830–1919), U.S. pediatrician.
***JACOBSON, LUDVIG LEWIN** (1783–1843), Danish physician, anatomist, and naturalist.
***JADASSOHN, JOSEF** (1863–1936), German dermatologist.
JANOWITZ, HENRY D. (1915–), U.S. gastroenterologist. From 1956 to 1961, Janowitz was chief of the Gastrointestinal Clinic at New York's Mount Sinai Hospital, and in 1967 became professor of clinical medicine at its medical school. From 1960 to 1967 he was assistant clinical professor of medicine at Columbia University's College of Physicians and Surgeons. Janowitz was president of the New York and American Gastroenterological Associations.

***JEITTELES, JONAS** (1735–1806), physician from Prague.
***JOSEPH BEN AḤMAD IBN ḤASDAI** (12th century), Spanish medical scholar.
***KAGAN, SOLOMON R.** (1889–1955), U.S. medical historian.
***KANTROWITZ, ADRIAN** (1918–), U.S. surgeon.
***KAPOSI (Kohn), MORITZ** (1837–1902), Austrian dermatologist.
***KATZ, SIR BERNARD** (1911–), English physiologist and Nobel Prize laureate.
***KATZENELSON, JUDAH L.** (1847–1917), Russian medical historian.
***KISCH, BRUNO** (1891–1961), U.S. physiologist and biochemist.
***KLEMPERER, PAUL** (1887–1964), U.S. pathologist.
***KOLLER, KARL** (1857–1944), U.S. ophthalmologist.
***KOPLIK, HENRY** (1858–1927), U.S. pediatrician.
***KRISTELLER, SAMUEL** (1820–1900), German obstetrician and gynecologist.
***KRONECKER, HUGO** (1839–1914), Swiss physiologist.
***LAMPRONTI, RABBI ISAAC HEZEKIAH BEN SAMUEL** (1679–1756), Italian rabbi, physician, and philologist.
***LANDAU, LEOPOLD** (1848–1920), German gynecologist.
***LASSAR, OSKAR** (1849–1907), German dermatologist.
***LEVINE, PHILIP** (1900–), U.S. immunohematologist.
***LEVINSON, ABRAHAM** (1888–1958), U.S. pediatrician.
***LOEB, JACQUES** (1859–1924), U.S. physiological chemist.
***LOEB, LEO** (1869–1959), U.S. pathologist.
***LOEWI, OTTO** (1873–1961), biochemist and Nobel Prize laureate.
***LWOFF, ANDRE** (1901–), French biologist, physician, and Nobel Prize laureate.
***MACHT, DAVID I.** (1882–1961), U.S. pharmacologist.
***MAGNUS, RUDOLF** (1873–1927), German physician and pharmacologist.
***MAIMONIDES** (1135–1204), philosopher, halakhist, and physician.
***MASTER, ARTHUR M.** (1895–), U.S. cardiologist.
***MER, GIDEON** (1894–1961), Israel epidemiologist.
***MEYERHOFF, MAX** (1874–1945), ophthalmologist and medical historian.
***MICHAELSON, ISAAC CHESAR** (1903–), Israel ophthalmologist.
***MUNK, HERMANN** (1839–1912), German physiologist.
***NATHAN, MORDECAI** (15th century), French physician.
***OLITZKI, ARYEH LEO** (1898–), Israel bacteriologist.
***OPPENHEIM, HERMAN** (1858–1919), German neurologist.
***OPPENHEIMER, KARL** (1864–1926), German pediatrician.
***ORENSTEIN, ALEXANDER JEREMIAH** (1879–), South African physician.
***ORTA, GARCIA DA** (1500–1568), Marrano physician.
***PAGEL, JULIUS LEOPOLD** (1851–1912), German physician and medical historian.
PAGEL, WALTER (1898–), pathologist and historian of science (see *Pagel, Julius Leopold).
PENN, JACK (1919–), South African plastic surgeon. He served during World War II and commanded the Brenthurst Military Hospital for Plastic Surgery in Johannesburg. During the War of Independence he took a unit to Israel and did valuable work among the wounded; he was again in Israel after the campaigns of 1956 and 1967. Penn was a professor at the University of the Witwatersrand.
***PLAUT, HUGO CARL** (1858–1928), German bacteriologist.
***POLITZER, ADAM** (1835–1920), Austrian otologist.
***PREUSS, JULIUS** (1861–1913), German medical historian.
***RACHMILEWITZ, MOSHE** (1899–), Israel hematologist.
RAPPAPORT, HENRY (1913–), U.S. pathologist. Born in Austria, he trained in Europe and the U.S. In the late 1940s he was assistant professor of pathology at George Washington University School of Medicine and pathologist and chief of laboratories at Mount Alto Veterans Administration Hospital, Washington, D.C. He headed the reticulo-endothelial pathology and hematology section of the Armed Forces Institute of Pathology, Washington, D.C., from 1949 to 1954. Rappaport moved to the University of Chicago, where he became professor of pathology and director of surgical pathology. He was a member of the WHO committee for nomenclature and histopathologic classification of leukemias and lymphomas. He wrote *Tumors of the Hematopoietic System* (1966).
REMAK, ERNEST JULIUS (1849–1911), German neurologist (see *Remak).
REMAK, ROBERT (1815–1865), German neurologist (see *Remak).
***RIBEIRO, SANCHEZ** (1688–1782), Marrano physician.
***ROMBERG, MORITZ HEINRICH** (1795–1873), German neurologist.
***ROSALES, JACOB HEBRAEUS** (c. 1593–c. 1688), Portuguese physician, mathematician, astrologist, and poet.
***ROSENHEIM, MAX, BARON** (1908–1972), English physician and educator.
***SABIN, ALBERT B.** (1906–), physician.
***SACHS, BERNARD** (1858–1944), U.S. neurologist.
***SALOMONSEN, CARL JULIUS** (1849–1924), Danish physician and bacteriologist.
***SCHICK, BELA** (1877–1968), U.S. pediatrician.
***SCHOENHEIMER, RUDOLF** (1897–1941), German biochemist.
SELDIN, HARRY M. (1895–), U.S. oral surgeon. Born in Russia, Seldin was taken to the U.S. in 1905. From 1919 to 1924 he was an instructor in the dental department of New York University, and headed its department of general anesthesia from 1926–31. He was associate director of the dentistry division of the Department of Hospitals, New York City, from 1928 to 1930, and director from 1930 to 1934. In 1934 he was appointed consulting oral surgeon to the Harlem Hospital in New York and in 1942 to the Peekskill Hospital in Westchester County, New York. Seldin played a leading part in the establishment of the Hebrew University-Hadassah School of Dentistry in Jerusalem founded by the Alpha-Omega Fraternity. He was governor of the Hebrew University and of Tel Aviv University. In 1960 he founded the Harry M. Seldin Center of Oral-Maxillary Surgery at the Rambam Hospital in Haifa. Seldin was the author of a textbook on oral surgery, and his achievements in this field earned him academic honors and the highest awards of his profession in the United States and abroad.
***SEMON, SIR FELIX** (1848–1921), English physician.
***SENATOR, HERMANN** (1834–1911), German internist.
***SHEBA (Schieber or Schiber), CHAIM** (1908–1971), Israel physician and hospital administrator.
SHEDLOVSKY, THEODORE (1898–), U.S. physical chemist. Born in St. Petersburg, Russia, he went to the U.S. in 1908. From 1927 he worked at the Rockefeller Institute for Medical Research (now the Rockefeller University), and became professor there in 1957. He wrote mainly on the electrochemistry of solutions and of biological fluids and was the author of *Electrochemistry in Biology and Medicine* (1955). He became a member of the U.S. National Academy of Sciences.
***STARKENSTEIN, EMIL** (1884–), pharmacologist, born in Bohemia.
***STEINACH, EUGEN** (1861–1944), physiologist and biologist.
STEINBERG, MARTIN R. (1904–), U.S. medical administrator. Born in Russia and educated in the U.S., he was appointed assistant professor of otolaryngology at the graduate school of the University of Pennsylvania in 1935. In 1948 he became director of New York City's Mount Sinai Hospital and in 1964 he was also appointed professor and chairman of the department of administrative medicine of the Mount Sinai School of Medicine. He was president of the Greater New York Hospital Association and of the Hospital Association of New York State.
***STERN, LINA SOLOMOVNA** (1878–1950), Russian physiologist and biologist.
***STILLING, BENEDICT** (1810–1879), German surgeon.
***TELLER, ISSACHAR BAER** (17th century), physician and surgeon from Prague.
***TICHO, ABRAHAM** (1883–1960), Israel ophthalmologist.
***TRAUBE, LUDWIG** (1818–1876), German pathologist.
***UNNA, PAUL G.** (1850–1929), German dermatologist.
***VALENTIN, GABRIEL GUSTAV** (1810–1883), German embryologist, physiologist, and anatomist.
***VILLANOVA, ARNALDO DA** (1240–1311), Spanish scholar and physician.
***VORONOFF, SERGE** (1866–1951), Russian surgeon and physiologist.
***WAKSMAN, SELMAN ABRAHAM** (1888–), U.S. microbiologist and Nobel Prize laureate.

***WASSERMAN, AUGUST VON** (1866–1926), German bacteriologist and immunologist.
***WECHSLER, ISRAEL SPANIER** (1886–1962), U.S. neurologist.
***WEIGERT, CARL** (1845–1904), German pathologist.
***WERTHEIMER, CHAIM ERNEST** (1893–), biochemist.
***WIDAL, FERNAND G.** (1862–1929), French physician.
***WIENER, ALEXANDER S.** (1907–), U.S. immunohematologist.
***WINTROBE, MAXWELL MYER** (1901–), U.S. hematologist.
WOLF, ABNER (1902–), U.S. neuropathologist. Born and educated in New York City, Wolf was appointed professor of neuropathology at the College of Physicians and Surgeons from 1951 and at Columbia Presbyterian Medical Center from 1964. Wolf served as president of the American Association of Neuropathologists (1951–52) and the New York Neurological Society (1956–57). He was a member of numerous professional societies and published extensively. He was editor in chief of the *Journal of Neuropathology and Experimental Neurology* from 1963.
***YAHR, MELVIN D.** (1917–), U.S. neurologist.
***ZACUTUS LUSITANUS** (1575–1642), Marrano physician.
ZAMENHOF, STEPHEN (1911–), U.S. biochemist. Born in Warsaw, the nephew of Ludwig *Zamenhof; he went to the U.S. in 1939. He worked at Columbia until 1964, when he became professor of microbial genetics and biological chemistry at the School of Medicine of the University of California in Los Angeles. His scientific papers were concerned with nucleic acids, enzymes, growth hormones, immunology, and genetics. He wrote *The Chemistry of Heredity* (1959).
***ZIMMERMAN, HARRY M.** (1901–), U.S. neuropathologist.
ZONDEK, BERNHARD (1891–1966), endocrinologist and gynecologist (see *Zondek).
ZONDEK, HERMANN (1887–), endocrinologist (see *Zondek).
ZONDEK, MAX (1868–1933), German physician (see *Zondek).
ZONDEK, SAMUEL GEORG (1894–1970), physician (see *Zondek).
***ZUELZER, GEORGE** (1870–1949), German hormonologist.
***ZUNTZ, NATHAN** (1847–1920), German physiologist.

MEDINA (Ar. **Madīna;** ancient name, **Yathrib**), city in fertile valley of the *Hejaz in northern *Arabia. Along with *Tayma and *Khaybar, Medina was a leading Jewish community in ancient Arabia. Prior to the expulsion of most of Medina Jewry by *Muhammad (620s) the oasis was largely inhabited by Jews. According to legend, the Jewish community dates from Moses' war against the Amalekites, the Babylonian Exile (c. 586 B.C.E.), Antiochus IV's persecutions, and the defeat by Rome (70 C.E.). In any case, by the early centuries of the Christian era the population of Medina consisted mostly of Jewish tribes (according to some Arabs, up to 20 tribes), either of Judean-Palestinian, mixed Judeo-Arabic, or Arab proselyte origin. Remains of their life survive, including castles, courtyards, and wells, the first of which were dug by the *Naḍīr tribe who inhabited the best lands and cultivated date palms west of the city. The two other major tribes were the *Qurayẓa, who occupied an area in the southeastern part of the town, and the *Qaynuqāʿ, who were among the earliest settlers and resided in the central market. Other tribes included the Thaʿlaba (northeast of the city) and the Anī, a tribe of Arab proselytes who lived in the Qubā' area (south of Medina). There was a continuous Arab migration to the area and many Arab tribes assimilated into the Jewish milieu, accepting Judasim and acquiring skills such as writing, which up to that time was known only by Jews. The two major Arab tribes, the Aws and the Khazraj, settled in the area, coming from South Arabia in the middle of the fifth century. They came because the breaking of the Ma'rib dam had ruined their lands. Some of the Arabs lived among the Jews, others in areas far from Jewish settlement. They were subjects of the Jewish tribes. The Khazraj gained some independence from the Jews in later times after a bloody battle, which according to legends originated as a request of the Jewish king Faytun to exercise the *jus primae noctis* on Arab subjects. Henceforth domination of Medina gradually passed to Arabs; the Jewish tribes aligned themselves with the Aws or the Khazraj, who threatened to confiscate the Nadīr lands. Fighting between these two major tribes and their Jewish clients (Nadīr and Qurayẓa with Aws; the Qaynuqāʿ with the Khazraj) characterized the sixth century and is recalled in Arabic poetry, including that of the Jew *Samuel b. Adiya. The bloody battles ended with the victory of the Aws and peaceful settlement with the Khazraj. Shortly before Muhammad's arrival in Medina the Jewish population had reached between 8,000 and 10,000, forming a majority of the city's inhabitants. The presence of so large and vital a Jewish community (though Arabic in language, customs, and behavior) provided an atmosphere conducive to the acceptance of monotheism among Arabs. Hence, Muhammad's message found a receptive audience among many Arabs and a few Jews. Most Jews, however, scorned Muhammad, deriding his prophetic pretensions and adaptations of biblical material. Suspicious of the effect of such vehement opposition, Muhammad began to expel the Jewish tribes with whom he had formerly signed an agreement. The Qaynuqāʿ and the Naḍīr were expelled from Medina in 624 and in 626 respectively. The Qurayẓa men were annihilated in 627 and the women and children were sold into slavery. The Jewish tribes apparently did not assist one another or unite against the common enemy, each meeting its fate as an individual tribe. The small Jewish population which remained in Medina was powerless and could not cause Muhammad much trouble. The community eventually dwindled and died out.

Bibliography: Baron, Social², 3 (1957), 60–80; H. Z. Hirschberg, *Yisrael ba-Arav* (1946), index; H. Hirschfeld, in: REJ, 7 (1883), 167–93; 10 (1885), 10–31; S. D. Goitein, in: *Tarbiz*, 3 (1932), 410–22; A. Katsch, *Judaism and the Koran* (1954), index; W. M. Watt, *Muhammad at Medina* (1956), 192–220; M. ibn Isḥāq, *Life of Muhammad*, tr. by A. Guillaume (1955), index. [ED.]

MEDINA, SAMUEL BEN MOSES DE (known by the acronym **Maharashdam;** 1506–1589), rabbi, halakhic authority, and communal leader of Salonika. Medina was descended from a distinguished family of scholars which originated from Spain. He was one of the three outstanding **posekim* of Salonika of the 16th century; the others being Joseph ibn *Lev and Solomon b. Abraham ha-Kohen. Medina was dogged by misfortune throughout his life. Orphaned in his childhood, his sister and two of his sons-in-law died in his lifetime and the burden of the maintenance of his widowed daughters and their many children fell upon him. The death of his elder brother, a man of means who had educated him and supported him financially, added to these burdens. The death of his eldest son left a permanent mark on him and affected his health. He was obliged from time to time to undertake journeys, in all probability in order to improve his financial position. Until his position in Salonika was established, he devoted himself completely to study, finding in it consolation for his sorrows. Medina founded a yeshivah in Salonika in which he introduced the system of teaching of the great Spanish talmudic scholars from the time of Isaac *Campanton and his successors. It had many disciples, a number of whom became famous and he himself says that some of them were worthy of heading yeshivot themselves. They include Aaron Abayuv, Joseph ibn Ezra, Abraham di Boton, David Naḥmias, and Abraham ibn Aruz. The yeshivah was supported by Donna Gracia Mendes (*Nasi) and was highly praised by his contemporaries.

Medina was the accepted halakhic authority both in his own and succeeding generations for European Turkey and the Balkans. Queries were addressed to him from all parts of the Ottoman Empire and Italy and his published responsa number over 1,000. Jacob Alfandari *(Maggid me-Reshit)* compares him and Solomon ha-Kohen to "Maimonides and the Rosh (Jacob b. Asher) in their time." Ḥayyim *Shabbetai says of him "He was an expert judge and of encyclopedic knowledge and one must not deviate an iota from his decisions" (*Torat Ḥayyim* 3:70). Some even went so far as to take an oath by the names of these two rabbis to give authority to their decisions (Aaron Sasson, *Torat Emet* 80). Although many scholars such as Isaac Adarbi, *Moses of Trani, Jacob Samut, and even his own maternal grandson Samuel *Ḥayyun disagreed with him, his decision always prevailed. His decisions were incorporated in those of Eastern European scholars in later generations. For historians his responsa constitute a most important source for the period in all its aspects, and his decisions are often quoted in modern times by judges in Israel in support of their decisions.

Medina's personality and character emerge clearly from his many responsa. He imposed his authority on litigants by the power of his personality and succeeded in enforcing just compromises even when there was no basis for them in law. This firmness and self-confidence were revealed even in his youth (cf. J. Caro, Responsa *Avkat Rokhel,* 219). They find striking expression in his stern rebuke to the scholars of Safed, who included Caro, for presuming to intervene in the affairs of the community of Salonika (Resp. YD 80) and he did not refrain from sharp and vigorous language, especially in his polemics.

Medina was original in his method. He would give a decision in accordance with his own judgment when he found no precedent in the *halakhot* of his predecessors. Utterly fearless, he was alive to all problems which arose from the special circumstances of his time and place, and many of his responsa deal with the social and economic problems which exercised the minds of his contemporaries. Medina applied himself to the communal orgaization of the Spanish exiles, which he established on a solid juridical basis. In the controversies which reigned in Salonika and elsewhere as a result of the glaring gap between the rich and the poor, Medina maintained the right of the wealthy members of the community to regulate the direction of communal affairs. According to him it was not numbers but quality which counted and it was right that, as had been the custom in Spain, the leadership of the community should be in the hands of those who bear its financial burden, providing they were loyal to religious principles. With all his respect for local custom, he strove to make it accord with the *halakhah* as he saw it. Where that custom differed from that in force in Spain, he justified the latter on halakhic grounds and encouraged its gradual adoption, whether in the liturgical usage or in matters of *sheḥitah,* etc. Unlike his predecessors his consistency in this matter did not meet with great opposition. Medina's decisions with regard to **anusim* are important and are stamped with the same original approach as he showed in other matters for which there was no legal precedent. He regarded the community of Salonika and especially its educational institutions as being in a unique position, and as a result demanded a greater financial support for them than for the institutions in Ereẓ Israel.

Side by side with his intensive halakhic activity Medina filled certain communal offices. He was the rabbi of the most important and largest congregations of Iberian communities in Salonika among them those of "Gerush" (i.e., of the exiles) and Lisbon, and went to Constantinople on missions on behalf of Salonika. He was called on to decide in the serious disputes which arose in Salonika and other communities, and succeeded in preventing schisms. His authority is seen in the fact that his signature appears on the majority of the communal regulations *(haskamot)* which have come down. Unlike many of his contemporaries of Spanish provenance Medina did not engage in Kabbalah, nor did he enter deeply into philosophy and secular studies. He was the man of *halakhah* and the communal leader par excellence. Despite his often unsatisfactory financial position he refused to take advantage of the exemption from taxes granted to scholars. Toward the end of his life legends were woven about him.

Medina's responsa were published during his lifetime in two volumes (Salonika, 1585?–87) and an improved edition in three volumes (Salonika 1594–98). A considerable number also appear in the works of other scholars, while others are still in manuscript. Thirty of his sermons were published in *Ben Shemu'el* (Mantua, 1622) and his novellae on a number of tractates of the Talmud are still in manuscript.

Medina's son Moses was a man of means and a scholar. He was responsible for the founding of a Hebrew printing press in Salonika in 1594 and published his father's responsa. He succeeded his father as rabbi of the Portugal community in Salonika.

Moses had two sons, Judah and Shemaiah. The former, a *dayyan* in Salonika, was murdered by an assassin hired by a Jew because of a verdict given against him. This tragedy caused his brother, who was also a scholar and communal leader of Salonika, to move to Venice where he became one of its scholars. He published his grandfather's *Ben Shemu'el,* and some of his poems were published in *Ḥadashim la-Bekarim* (Mantua, 1622).

Bibliography: Conforte, Kore, index; Jacob Luzzatto, *Kehillat Ya'akov* (Salonika, 1584), preface; Azulai, 1 (1852), 176 no. 122; A. Danon, in: REJ, 40 (1900), 206–30; 41 (1900), 98–117, 250–65; I. S. Emmanuel, *Histoire des Israélites de Salonique* (1936), 167–75; idem, *Maẓẓevot Saloniki* (1967), index; Rosanes, Togarmah, 2 (1937–38²), 115–18; M. S. Goodblatt, *Jewish Life in Turkey in the XVIth Century, as Reflected in the Legal Writings of Samuel de Medina* (1952); M. Molho, in: *Sinai,* 41 (1957), 36–48; J. Katz, in: *Tarbiz,* 27 (1958), 204; I. R. Molho and A. Amarijlio, in: *Sefunot,* 2 (1958), 35–39; I. Kister, in: *Saloniki Ir va-Em be-Yisrael* (1967), 38–41.

[Jos.H.]

MEDINA, SIR SOLOMON DE (c. 1650–1730), army contractor and the first professing Jew in England to receive a knighthood. He was probably born in Italy but lived in Holland until William of Orange's invasion of England in 1688, which he helped to finance. An English example of the *court Jew, he was principal army contractor to the duke of Marlborough during the War of the Spanish Succession (1701–14), supplying money, provisions, and particularly intelligence. These transactions ultimately contributed to the duke's downfall. Medina was active in and contributed generously to the London Sephardi community but died abroad in poverty. He is wrongly identified with the Jew whose bankruptcy was blamed by *Voltaire for his financial difficulties.

Bibliography: Roth, England, 193, 287–8; Roth, Mag Bibl, index; A. M. Hyamson, *Sephardim of England* (1951), index.

[V.D.L.]

MEDINACELI, town in Castile, N. Spain, near Sigüenza. A Jewish community existed there as early as the 12th century. The *fuero* ("municipal charter") of Medinaceli gave the Jews a status equal to that of the Christians and Moors in legal matters. In the 13th century the community numbered 20 to 30 families. Jewish occupations included agriculture, viticulture, commerce, and crafts. In 1280 Abraham of Medinaceli made an agreement, valid for four years, with the bishop of Sigüenza to open and exploit salt mines (see *Salt Trade). The bishop was to supply Abraham with the necessary equipment, finance the project, and provide him with lodging. In 1290 the communities of

Medinaceli and Sigüenza together paid annual taxes and services amounting to 34,217 maravedis, which indicates considerable prosperity. The community continued to exist throughout the 15th century. It was taxed 91 castellanos in 1485 as a contribution to the war against Granada. The synagogue, which passed to the Church after the expulsion of the Jews from Spain in 1492, was restored by the government.

Bibliography: Baer, Spain, 1 (1961), 192, 200; Baer, Urkunden, index. [H.B.]

MEDINA DEL CAMPO, town in N. Castile, between *Olmedo and Rueda. The Jewish community was particularly prosperous during the 13th century: in 1290 its annual tax amounted to 44,000 maravedis. By the 14th century the community consisted of between 50 and 100 householders. In 1313 the regulations on Jewish affairs of the regional council of *Zamora were applied to Medina del Campo. They covered the employment of Christians in Jewish homes, the distinctive badge to be worn by the Jews, the prohibition on practicing medicine, interest rates, and the dismissal of Jews from public functions. Nothing is known of how the community fared during the persecutions of 1391, but afterward a *Converso community existed there. In 1459 Medina del Campo was the center of the activities of the monk *Alonso de Espina against Conversos suspected of practicing Judaism. During that year he found 30 Conversos who had undergone circumcision. Some of the Conversos prepared to depart for North Africa. One of them, the physician Magister Franciscus, circumcised himself and immigrated to Ereẓ Israel. Therefore, like *Huesca and Ciudad Real, in the 1450s and 1460s Medina del Campo was a center for the return to Judaism. After the edict of expulsion (1492), those who left the town presumably crossed the borders of the kingdoms of Navarre and Portugal. The last rabbi of the community was Isaac Uzziel, who probably settled in Salonika after the expulsion.

Bibliography: Baer, Spain, index; Baer, Urkunden, 2 (1936), index; B. Llorca, in: *Sefarad,* 2 (1942), 119; A. Marx, *Expulsion of the Jews from Spain* (1944), 85, 100; Suárez Fernández, Documentos, index. [H.B.]

MEDINA DE POMAR, town in Castile, N. Spain. The Jewish settlement here was one of the flourishing communities in 13th-century Castile. Like other Jews in the area, Jewish residents of Medina de Pomar owned vineyards and lands and engaged in commerce and crafts. Joseph Nasi and *Abraham Benveniste de Soria, both of Medina, supplied grain and money to the army stationed on the border in 1429–30. On March 12, 1475, two Jewish cloth merchants, Josi Leal and Moses Sasson, complained that the authorities had prohibited visiting Jews from trading and buying goods in Medina. Conversely in 1490 the Jews of Medina complained to the crown that the Bilbao municipal council had banned visiting Jews from staying there overnight and that they had therefore been unable to attend the fair at Medina del Campo. After the edict of expulsion of the Jews from Spain in 1492, the Jews of Medina de Pomar asked the crown for redress because the Christians had refused to pay their debts. Ferdinand and Isabella ordered the municipal authorities to deal with the matter expeditiously to enable the Jews to leave on time.

Bibliography: Baer, Urkunden, index; F. Cantera, *Sinagogas españolas* (1955), 244f.; Suárez Fernández, Documentos, index. [H.B.]

MEDINAH. In Hebrew writings emanating from the Muslim-influenced areas, *medinah* is used to mean city. In Ashkenazi culture, especially in the later Middle Ages and early modern times, *medinah* denotes a region embracing several or many communities organized as a territorial unit for the purpose of *autonomy and leadership.

See also *Councils of the Lands and **Landjudenschaft.*

Bibliography: J. Katz, *Tradition and Crisis* (1961), 122–34. [ED.]

MEDINI, ḤAYYIM HEZEKIAH BEN RAPHAEL ELIJAH (1832–1904), rabbi. Medini was born in Jerusalem. He studied under Isaac *Covo and Joseph Nissim *Burla. His father died in 1853, and in that same year he traveled to Constantinople where he stayed for 14 years. For a while he

Ḥayyim Hezekiah Medini, rabbi and halakhic scholar. Jerusalem, J.N.U.L., Schwadron Collection.

earned his living as a private tutor but lectured publicly without remuneration. He attracted many disciples, some of whom later became rabbis. From 1867 to 1899 he was rabbi of Karasubazar in the Crimean peninsula and succeeded in raising the previously low spiritual standard of the community. He instituted local *takkanot,* abrogated strange customs or amended and restored them to their proper origin, and founded schools and yeshivot. He opposed *Firkovich, showing that his claim that the people of Crimea were descended from the Karaites was without foundation. He was an ardent Zionist, and in his works there are many passages extolling the virtue of settling in Ereẓ Israel, the forthcoming redemption, and on the duty of settling in Israel and supporting its poor. He became seriously ill in 1878 and it seems that he was then given the additional name of Ḥayyim. In 1899 he returned to Jerusalem where he was received with great honor. His books won for him a reputation, and religious and halakhic problems were addressed to him from the whole Jewish world. In 1901 he heard that there was a proposal to appoint him **rishon le-Zion* (Sephardi chief rabbi), but unwilling to accept this office he moved to Hebron where he served as rabbi until his death. He founded a yeshivah there, meeting part of its maintenance from his private resources. His fame as a man of saintliness spread to the non-Jews who honored him and regarded him as a wonder worker.

Medini's fame rests principally on his *Sedei Ḥemed,* which he began in the Crimea, a halakhic encyclopedia of exceptional originality, 13 of the 18 volumes of which were published during his lifetime (Warsaw, 1891–1912). It is one of the most monumental halakhic works, and is still extensively used. It contains rules of talmudic and halakhic methodology, an alphabetical list of the various laws, and responsa. In addition, it contains bibliographical research and articles on the lives of Jewish scholars and of the history of Ereẓ Israel. At the beginning of volume 14 is his lengthy ethical will which reflects his lofty spiritual and moral stature. He wrote a supplement to it, entitled *Pakku'at ha-Sadeh* (in *Ha-Me'assef*, 5, Jerusalem (1900), supplement). Among his other works are: *Mikhtav le-Ḥizkiyyahu* (Smyrna, 1868), talmudic novellae and responsa on *Oraḥ Ḥayyim; Or Li* (*ibid.*, 1874), novellae and responsa—published anonymously in memory of his only son who died in 1868; *Ne'im Zemirot* (Warsaw, 1886), *piyyutim* which it was the custom to recite every morning. Several of his poems were published at the beginning of *Sedei Ḥemed*, volume 6. Many of his responsa and approbations are to be found in the works of contemporary rabbis.

Bibliography: Benayahu, in: *Ḥemdat Yisrael* (collection of essays in his memory), ed. by A. Elmaleh (1946), 183–212, 203 (bibl.); Burla, *ibid.*, 213–5; Avisar, *ibid.*, 216–28; A. Ben-Jacob, in: *Hed ha-Mizraḥ*, 3 (1944/45), no. 30; M. Benayahu, *ibid.*, L. Jung (ed.), *Men of the Spirit* (1964), 107–21.

[A.B.-Y.]

MEDITATION (Heb. *Hitbonenut*), a term which first appears in kabbalistic literature, from the middle of the 13th century, referring to protracted concentration of thought on supernal lights of the divine world and of the spiritual worlds in general. Many sources, however, in this connection use the terms *kavvanah, or *devekut ("cleaving") of thought to a particular subject, and of "contemplation of the mind." The kabbalists did not distinguish between the terms meditation and contemplation—a distinction prevalent in Christian mysticism. In the kabbalistic view, contemplation was both the concentrated delving to the depths of a particular subject in the attempt to comprehend it from all its aspects, and also the arresting of thought in order to remain on the subject. The arresting and delving in spiritual contemplation do not serve, therefore, to encourage the contemplating intellect to advance and pass on to higher levels, but first of all to gauge to the maximum its given situation; only after having tarried in it for a protracted period does the intellect move on to a higher step. This, then, is contemplation by the intellect, whose objects are neither images nor visions, but non-sensual matters such as words, names, or thoughts.

In the history of the Kabbalah a different contemplation preceded this one: the contemplative vision of the *Merkabah, for which the ancient Merkabah mystics of the tannaitic and amoraitic period strove, and which was described in the *Heikhalot Rabbati* of the *heikhalot* literature. Here the reference is to an actual vision of the world of the chariot which reveals itself before the eyes of the visionary. Therefore the term *histakkelut* is used here in the exact sense of the Latin term *contemplatio* or the Greek *theoria*. The contemplation of the Merkabah mystics, in the first period of Jewish mysticism, provided the key, in their opinion, to a correct understanding of the heavenly beings in the heavenly chariot. This contemplation could also be achieved by way of preparatory stages which would train those who "descend to the Merkabah" to grasp the vision and pass on from one thing to another without being endangered by the audacity of their assault on the higher world. Even at this stage, the vision of the Merkabah is bound up with immunization of the mystic's senses against absorption of external impressions and concentration through an inward vision.

In the Kabbalah, the conception of the ten *Sefirot*, which reveal the action of the Divine and comprise the world of emanation, was superimposed upon the Merkabah world. This contemplation of divine matters does not end, according to the Kabbalah, where the vision of Merkabah mystics ended, but is capable of ascending to greater heights, which are no longer the objects of images and vision. The concentration on the world of the *Sefirot* is not bound up with visions, but is solely a matter for the intellect prepared to ascend from level to level and to meditate on the qualities unique to each level. If meditation activates at first the faculty of imagination, it continues by activating the faculty of the intellect. The *Sefirot* themselves are conceived of as intellectual lights which can only be perceived by meditation. The Spanish kabbalists in the 13th century knew of two types of meditation: one which produces visions similar in kind if not in detail to the visions of the Merkabah mystics, and the second which leads to the communion of the meditating mind with its higher sources in the world of emanation itself. *Moses b. Shem Tov de Leon describes in one of his books how an intuition of the third *Sefirah* (*Binah*) flashes up in the mind through meditation. He compares this to the light which flashes up when the rays of the sun play on the surface of a bowl of water (MGWJ, 1927, 119).

The instructions on the methods to be employed in performing meditation form part of the hidden and secret teachings of the kabbalists which, apart from some general rules, were not made public. The kabbalists of Gerona mention it in connection with the description of the mystic *kavvanah* in prayer, which is described as a meditation concentrating upon each word of the prayer in order to open a way to the inner lights which illuminate every word. Prayer, according to this idea of meditation, is not just a recitation of words or even concentration on the contents of the words according to their simple meaning; it is the adherence of man's mind to the spiritual lights and the mind's advancement in these worlds. The worshiper uses the fixed words of the prayer as a banister during his meditation which he grasps on his road of ascension so that he should not be confused or distracted. Such meditation results in the joining of human thought to the divine thought or the divine will—an attachment which itself comes to an end, or is "negated." The hour of prayer is, more than any other time, suitable for meditation. *Azriel of Gerona said: "The thought expands and ascends to its origin, so that when it reaches it, it ends and cannot ascend any further . . . therefore the pious men of old raised their thought to its origin while pronouncing the precepts and words of prayer. As a result of this procedure and the state of adhesion which their thought attained, their words became blessed, multiplied, full of [divine] influx from the stage called the 'nothingness of thought,' just as the waters of a pool flow on every side when a man sets them free" (*Perush ha-Aggadot*, 1943, 39–40). In such meditation, which progresses from one stage to another, there was also a certain magic element, as can clearly be deduced from the detailed description in another piece by Azriel called *Sha'ar ha-Kavvanah la-Mekubbalim ha-Rishonim*. Meditation does not only ponder and penetrate its object; it has the power to bring about changes in its object and likely to cause transformations as it reaches the common root of opposing extremes. In most descriptions of the methods of meditation which were preserved from the golden era of Spanish Kabbalah, however, this magic element was concealed or completely glossed over in silence.

A detailed elaboration of the doctrine of meditation is to be found particularly in the teachings of Abraham *Abulafia. The whole of his *Ḥokhmat ha-Ẓeruf* was designed, he believed, to teach a lasting and safe approach to meditation. It consists principally of instruction concerning meditation on the Holy Names of God and, in a wider sense, meditation on the mysteries of the Hebrew alphabet.

This meditation, which is not dependent on prayer, was described in his more important manuals as a separate activity of the mind to which man devotes himself in seclusion at given hours and with regular guidance by an initiate teacher. Here again the point of departure is the mortification of the activity of the senses and the effacement of the natural images which cling to the soul. Meditation on the holy letters and names engenders pure rational forms in the soul, as a result of which man is able to comprehend the exalted truths. At certain stages of this meditation, there appear actual visions, such as are described in the work *Ḥayyei ha-Olam ha-Ba* for instance, but these are only intermediate stages on the road to pure contemplation of the mind. Abulafia negates from its very start the magical element which was originally attributed to such meditation.

The difference between the Christian and the kabbalistic doctrines of meditation resides in the fact that in Christian mysticism a pictorial and concrete subject, such as the suffering of Christ and all that pertains to it, is given to the meditator, while in Kabbalah, the subject given is abstract and cannot be visualized, such as the Tetragrammaton and its combinations.

Instruction in the methods of meditation were widespread in the works of early kabbalists and these methods continue to be found after the expulsion from Spain among several kabbalists who were influenced by Abulafia. An anonymous disciple of Abulafia has left (in *Sha'arei Ẓedek*, written in 1295) an impressive description of his experiences in the study of this meditation. The works *Berit Menuḥah* (14th century) and *Sullam ha-Aliyyah* by Judah *Albotini, one of the exiles from Spain who settled in Jerusalem, were also written in the same spirit.

The most detailed textbook on meditation into the mystery of the *Sefirot* is *Even ha-Shoham* by Joseph ibn Ṣayah of Damascus, written in Jerusalem in 1538 (Ms. National and University Library, Jerusalem; see G. Scholem, *Kitvei Yad be-Kabbalah* (1930), 90–91). The kabbalists of Safed paid much attention to meditation, as is evident from *Sefer Ḥaredim* (Venice, 1601) of Eleazar *Azikri, from chapter 30 in Moses *Cordovero's *Pardes Rimmonim* (Cracow, 1592) and the *Sha'arei Kedushah* of Ḥayyim *Vital, part 3, chapters 5–8, propounds his doctrine on the subject. Here the magic aspect attached to meditation is once more emphasized, even though the author explains it in a restricted sense. The last steps in the ascension of the meditating mind which seeks to bring down the influx of the supernal lights to earth require meditatory activities of a magic nature, which are known as *Yiḥudim* ("Unifications"). The practical importance of these doctrines, whose influence can be recognized throughout the whole of late kabbalistic literature, should not be underrated. The doctrines of adhesion and meditation in 18th-century Ḥasidism are also definitely based on the form given to them in Safed. This doctrine was not written down in its entirety in the writings of Isaac *Luria's disciples and its major part was preserved orally. In Jerusalem's kabbalistic yeshivah Bet El practical guidance on meditation was handed down orally for about 200 years and the initiates of this form of Kabbalah refused to make the details of their practice public knowledge.

Bibliography: G. Scholem, *Kitvei Yad be-Kabbalah* (1930), 24–30, 225–30; idem, *Reshit ha-Kabbalah* (1948), 142–6; idem, in: KS, 1 (1924), 127–39; 22 (1946), 161–71; idem, in: MGWJ, 78 (1934), 492–518; R. J. Z. Werblowsky, in: *History of Religions*, 1 (1961), 9–36.

[G.Sch.]

MEDZIBEZH (**Medzhibozh;** Pol. **Miedzyborz;** Yid. **Mezhibezh**), small town in Khmelnitsky oblast, Ukrainian S.S.R.; until 1793 in Poland and then under Russia, until 1917 in the province of Podolia. The Jewish community of Medzibezh is one of the oldest in the Ukraine—Jews are mentioned there in 1518—and until the *Chmielnicki persecutions of 1648 one of the largest in Podolia. During the first half of the 17th century, Joel *Sirkes officiated as rabbi. The community suffered severely at the hands of the Cossacks in 1651, 1664, and again at the beginning of the 18th century. In 1765 there were 2,039 Jews registered in the community of Medzibezh and the nearby villages. The founder of Ḥasidism, *Israel b. Eliezer Ba'al Shem Tov, made the town his seat from about 1740 until his death in 1760 and was buried there. The *zaddikim* *Baruch b. Jehiel, Israel's grandson, and R.*Abraham Joshua Heschel of Apta also lived and were buried there. From 1815 to 1827 a printing press published ḥasidic and kabbalistic works in Medzibezh. From 1,719 in 1847 the number of Jews grew to 6,040 (73.9% of the total population) in 1897, then fell to 4,614 (58.2%) in 1926. The community was destroyed after the German occupation in 1941.

Bibliography: Ḥ. D. Friedberg, *Toledot ha-Defus ha-Ivri be-Polanyah* (1950²), 150; M. Spektor, *Mayn Lebn*, 2 (1926), 74–101; M. Osherowitch, *Shtet un Shtetlekh in Ukraine*, 1 (1948), 47–59.

[Y.S.]

MEEROVITCH, MENACHÉ (1860–1949), member of *Bilu and one of the key figures in Jewish settlement in Ereẓ Israel. Born in Nikolayev, south Russia, Meerovitch graduated from a government institute as an agronomist. After the 1881 pogroms in south Russia, he participated in the establishment of the first *Ḥibbat Zion association in Warsaw and joined the Bilu society. At the end of 1882 he went to Constantinople and took part in the activities of Bilu's political bureau, which was trying to obtain Turkish consent to Jewish agricultural settlement in Ereẓ Israel. He then joined his comrades at *Rishon le-Zion and was active in the settlement's public life.

Meerovitch, who used the pen name Mi-Ziknei ha-Yishuv, wrote letters and articles on life in Ereẓ Israel that were published in the Russian Jewish press, the Yiddish- and German-language Zionist press, and Hebrew papers. He was one of the first to discuss practical agricultural problems and, in 1893/94, edited the first agricultural paper in the country, *Ha-Ikkar* ("The Farmer"). In his Russian book *Opisaniye Yevreyskikh Koloniy v Palestine* ("A Description of the Jewish Settlements in Palestine," 1900), he summarized the achievements of Ereẓ Israel agriculture in its first 25 years.

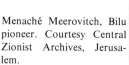

Menaché Meerovitch, Bilu pioneer. Courtesy Central Zionist Archives, Jerusalem.

Meerovitch was active in the work of the Ḥibbat Zion association in Jaffa and headed it from 1903 to 1904. He was among the founders of Aguddat ha-Koremim (Vintners Association) in 1903 and of the Judean Settlement Association in 1913. During

World War I he participated in the Jewish community's representative body to the Turkish authorities. From 1918 to 1920 Meerovitch was a member of the Va'ad Le'ummi. His articles and memoirs are of great importance to the historian of Jewish settlement in Ereẓ Israel. Some were collected in book form during his later years: *Ḥevlei Teḥiyyah* ("Pangs of Resurrection," 1930); *Me-ha-Shevil el ha-Derekh* ("From the Path to the Road," 1935, with an annotated list including index of his articles); *Minḥat Erev* ("Evening Rest," 1940); *Mi-Bilu ad va-Ya-'apilu* ("From Bilu to Immigration," 1947). The moshav Talmei Menasheh in the Coastal Plain is named after him.

Bibliography: M. Smilansky, *Mishpaḥat ha-Adamah*, 3 (1954), 141–50; Tidhar, 2 (1947), 823–5; D. Idelovitch (ed.), *Sefer Rishon le-Ẓiyyon* (1941), 89–92. [Y.S.]

MEGED, AHARON (1920–), Israel writer and editor. Born in Wloclavek, Poland, his family emigrated to Palestine in 1926. He joined kibbutz Sedot Yam, and worked at the port of Haifa. Meged left the kibbutz in 1950 and settled in Tel Aviv where he edited the journal *Ba-Sha'ar*. Together with a number of friends, he founded the bi-weekly literary magazine *Massa* which became the weekly literary supplement of the daily *La-Merḥav*. From 1960 to 1971 he served as Israel's cultural attaché in London.

In his prose, which often has strong autobiographical elements, Meged moved from the realism of his early works to surrealism and back to realism. His first short story collection, *Ru'aḥ Yamim* ("Sea Winds," 1950), was inspired by life in Sedot Yam. *Ḥedvah va-Ani* ("Ḥedvah and I," 1964), a realistic novel, tells of the misfortunes of a kibbutz member who had to leave the kibbutz, much against his will, at the inducement of his wife. The protagonist is the first example of Meged's anti-hero, so typical of his later writings. Lonely, tortured by thoughts of his shortcomings, fearing above all ridicule and abasement, the anti-hero is always the outsider in an otherwise congenial and united society. In *Mikreh ha-Kesil* (1960; *Fortunes of a Fool*, 1962), he is the only "good man" who fails to join the "society of the wicked." Meged's most ambitious work, the novel *Ha-Ḥai al-ha-Met* (1965; *The Living on the Dead*, 1970), describes in unflattering terms modern Israel society, and makes the accusation that the great expectations of the first

Aharon Meged, Israel writer and editor. Courtesy Genazim, Tel Aviv.

pioneers have not been fulfilled by their successors. Meged's stories and novels have been translated into several languages and his plays including *Genesis*, *Hannah Szenes*, and the comedy *I Like Mike* have been produced in Israel and abroad. (A list of his works translated into English appears in Goell, Bibliography.) His brother MATTI (Matityahu) MEGED (1923–), poet and literary critic, wrote a number of works that made their mark on the modern Hebrew literary scene. *Ha-Migdal ha-Lavan* (stories, 1949) and *Or ha-Soreg* (novel, 1953) are among his best-known fictional works; *Ha-Drama ha-Modernit* (1966), an edition of essays on drama, and *Dostoevski, Kafka, Beckett* are critical works. He lectured in Hebrew literature at the University of Haifa.

Bibliography: Kressel, Leksikon, 2 (1967), 313–4; R. Wallenrod, *The Literature of Modern Israel* (1956), 212; Waxman, Literature, 5 (1960[2]), 41–42; G. Avinor, in: *Moznayim*, 18 (1964), 258–63. [G.Av.]

MEGIDDO (Heb. מְגִדּוֹ), ancient Canaanite and Israelite city, identified with Tell al-Mutasallim on the southern side of the Jezreel Valley, approximately 22 mi. (35 km.) S.E. of

Figure 1. Tablets from the ivory hoard found in the palace of stratum VIIa (1350–1150 B.C.E.). Jerusalem, Rockefeller Museum, Israel Department of Antiquities.

Haifa. The site was excavated in 1903–05 by G. Schumacher and in 1925–39 by the Oriental Institute in Chicago, under the direction of C. S. Fisher, P. L. O. Guy, and G. Loud. Small additional soundings were made by Y. Yadin in 1960 and later years. The excavations revealed the existence of over 20 levels, beginning with the Chalcolithic period in the fourth millennium (Stratum XX). In the Early Bronze Age (Canaanite period), represented in Strata XIX–XVI, the first temples were built, as well as a round high-place and a wall, 26 ft. (8 m.) thick. Three temples of the megaron type, consisting of a porch with two columns, a hall with a roof supported by two columns and an altar near the southern wall, may also have been built in the Early Bronze Age, although originally attributed to Stratum XV. The Middle Bronze Age city is represented by Strata XV–X, with Strata XIV–XIII corresponding in time to the 12th dynasty of Egypt. The statue of an Egyptian official called Thuthotep, which was found in the excavations, indicates that an Egyptian governor probably resided there at that time. Like all the Canaanite cities, Megiddo fell to the Hyksos (Strata XII–X; 18th–16th centuries B.C.E.). The conquerors strengthened the wall and built a glacis and a gate with the

Figure 2. The gate area on the north side of the tell, showing buildings of various periods: 1. earliest gate, with part of its break wall, 19th century B.C.E.; 2. gate from Late Bronze period (16th–15th century B.C.E.); 3. street and basalt steps leading from Late Bronze gate; 4. eastern section of Solomonic gateway (tenth century B.C.E.); 5. part of Ahab's gate (9th century B.C.E.). Photo Richard Cleave, Jerusalem.

Figure 3. Tel Megiddo from the north, with the Jezreel Valley in the background. The major visible structures are: 1. gate area; 2. water installation pit; 3. south stables complex; 4. silo; 5. Schumacher's shaft; 6. round high place; 7. three temples of the megaron type; 8. north stables complex; 9. Israelite fortifications. Photo Werner Braun, Jerusalem.

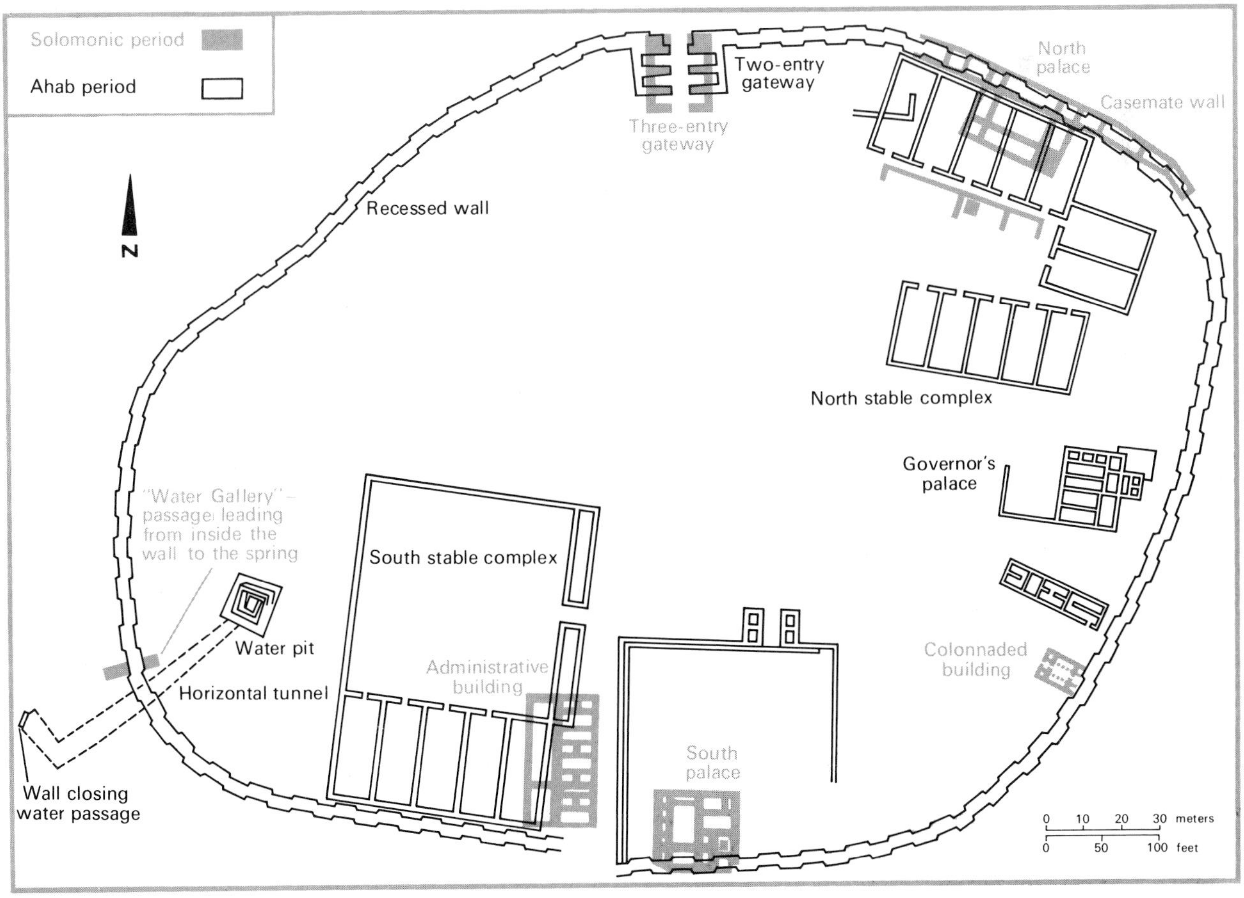

Plan of Megiddo in the time of Solomon and Ahab (tenth-ninth century B.C.E.). Based on *Encyclopedia of Archeological Excavations in the Holy Land,* Jerusalem, 1970.

entrance between two guardrooms in the style typical of the period. In a large palace near the gate were found jewels and ivories, which attest to the prosperity of the city at that time. In approximately 1469 B.C.E. (Stratum IX), Thutmosis III suddenly appeared before the walls of Megiddo, after passing through the Aruna Valley giving the city access to the coast. He overcame a coalition of Canaanites and Hittites and captured the city after a siege of seven months; the rich plunder he seized indicates the wealth of Megiddo. From then until Stratum VII the city remained under Egyptian sovereignty, with the presence of both a local king and an Egyptian commander and garrison. In the el-Amarna period, the king of Megiddo, Biridya (an Indo-Iranian name), was hard pressed by the Ḫabiru and Labaya of Shechem (EA, 242–5). This Late Bronze Age city, dating to the period of Egyptian rule, witnessed the erection of a fortified temple, similar to that discovered at Shechem; according to the latest researches, such temples originate in the last phase of the Middle Bronze Age. Under one of the rooms of the Stratum VII palace (el-Amarna period) was found a rich treasure of gold, ivory, and lapis lazuli. A cuneiform tablet dating to this level contains a fragment of the Gilgamesh epic. The palace was rebuilt in Stratum VIIA and in it were discovered inscriptions of Ramses III and Ramses VI and a hoard of 200 ivory tablets. This stratum marks the last wealthy and fortified Canaanite city, which was destroyed in the second half of the 12th century B.C.E. The next city, Stratum VI (late 12th–11th centuries B.C.E.), was poor and unfortified and of an unclear ethnic composition.

According to biblical tradition, Megiddo did not fall to Joshua, although its king was defeated (Josh. 12:21; cf. Josh. 17:11–13; Judg. 1:27–28). Most scholars date its capture only to the time of David. Solomon fortified the city (I Kings 9:15) and included it in his fifth district (I Kings 4:12). The Solomonic gate with three guardrooms is identical in plan with the gates at Hazor and Gezer (cf. I Kings 9:15). A large palace built of well-hewn ashlar masonry and adorned with proto-Aeolic capitals was probably the residency of Solomon's governor, Baana, son of Ahilud. The city was largely occupied by three units of five rectangular stables and one unit of two stables, with feeding troughs between pillars and a capacity of 492 horses. Yadin, however, attributes these stables only to the time of Ahab, who rallied 2,000 chariots against Shalmaneser III at the Battle of Karkar. A water installation, built sometime in the Israelite period consists of a pit 81 ft. (25 m.) deep, with stairs leading to a horizontal tunnel 224 ft. (70 m.) long and to a spring in the slope of the hill, which was thus connected with the city inside the walls. The Israelite city (Stratum IV) perished in 733/2 B.C.E. with the conquest of Tiglath Pileser III. The Assyrian king made Megiddo the capital of a province, which included Galilee and the Jezreel Valley. The Stratum III city was rebuilt on a uniform plan, with two large public buildings in the Assyrian style. Within the city was a silo, 23 ft. (7 m.) deep, with stairs curving around the inside and leading to the bottom. Stratum II (630–609 B.C.E.) probably dates to the time of Josiah of Judah, who fell in the battle against Pharaoh Necoh near Megiddo. To this event can be attributed the association of war with the Megiddo Valley in Zechariah 12:11 and with *Armageddon in Revelation 16:16. The last settlement at Megiddo was a small city of the Persian period. Both Napoleon (in 1799) and *Allenby (1918) defeated the Turks at Megiddo. The tell has been developed for visitors with a small museum demonstrating the history of Megiddo. On his visit to Israel in 1964 Pope Paul VI was received by President Shazar at Tell Megiddo.

A kibbutz was founded in 1949 by settlers of Polish origin near the ancient mound and is affiliated with Kibbutz Arẓi Ha-Shomer ha-Ẓa'ir.

Bibliography: P. L. O. Guy and M. Engberg, *Megiddo Tombs* (1938); H. May, *Material Remains of the Megiddo Cult* (1935); R. S. Lamon, *The Megiddo Water System* (1935); R. S. Lamon and M. Shipton, *Megiddo*, 1 (1939), 2 (1942); Y. Yadin, in: *Bi-Ymei Bayit Rishon*, ed. by A. Malamat (1961), 66ff.; Aharoni, Land, index; EM, s.v. (incl. bibl.).
[M.A.-Y.]

MEGILLAH (Heb. מְגִלָּה; "scroll"), designation of each of the five scrolls of the Bible (*Ruth, *Song of Songs, *Lamentations, *Ecclesiastes, *Esther). When the scroll is not specifically named, the term *Megillah* most commonly refers to the scroll of Esther which is read on *Purim.

See *Purim; *Scroll of Esther; *Scrolls, Five. [Ed.]

MEGILLAH ("Scroll"), tenth tractate in the order *Mo'ed*, in the Mishnah, Tosefta, and Babylonian and Jerusalem Talmuds. *Megillah*, in four chapters, deals with liturgical readings from the Bible, especially with the reading of the *Scroll of Esther on *Purim to which the word *megillah* particularly refers, and with related subjects. The regulations concerning the reading of the Scroll of Esther on Purim are largely dealt with in the first two chapters of the tractate. Chapter 1 is primarily concerned with determining on which day of Adar the *megillah* is to be read, there being a difference between walled cities on the one hand and open towns and villages on the other. Only the first half of this chapter (*mishnayot* 1–4) deals with the *megillah*, while the remainder (5–11) is a collection of various *halakhot*, which were included because they are all introduced by the same formula ("The only difference between A and B is . . . "). According to J. N. Epstein (Tanna'im, 257) this group belongs to the Mishnah of R. Akiva (Tosef. 1:7–21, gives a similar but longer group of such *halakhot*). Chapter 2 first discusses the appropriate way of reading the *megillah*, e.g., whether reciting by heart and reading in a language other than Hebrew are valid. It goes on to deal with the technicalities of writing a *megillah* to be used for public reading, e.g., whether it must be written on parchment, or whether paper may be used. Among other questions discussed is the qualification of the reader, and whether women or minors are fit to read it. There is also much extraneous matter in this chapter. Chapter 3 starts with a discussion on the sanctity of the synagogue and its appurtenances, but its main contents are the public readings from the Pentateuch and *haftarah*. Chapter 4 continues with the main subject but deals with other liturgical questions (e.g., public reading of the *Shema*, priestly blessings, etc.). The sequence of the chapters as set out above is the one found in current editions of the Mishnah, Jerusalem Talmud, and Tosefta, but in the Babylonian Talmud the order of the last two chapters is reversed. The reason is that since the first Mishnah of chapter 4 opens with the words "He who reads the *megillah*," it was thought appropriate that this chapter follow the first two, which deal mainly with the *megillah*.

Various strata can be detected in the Mishnah. In addition to the above-mentioned groups from the Mishnah of R. Akiva, R. Johanan attributes Mishnah 1:1 to Akiva (Meg. 2a). According to Epstein, Mishnah 2:6 belongs to Eleazar b. Simeon (cf. Men. 72a), Mishnah 3:1 is from the *mishnayot* of Menahem b. Yose, and Mishnah 3:6 from that of Judah b. Ilai; according to the *Gemara* (9b) the second part of 1:9 is Meir's, while its first part is of unknown origin. The order of the paragraphs in the Tosefta to *Megillah* usually corresponds to that in the Mishnah. It includes a vivid description of gatherings in Jerusalem for the performance of *mitzvot* (4 (3):15). There is a great deal of *aggadah* in the Babylonian Talmud. Deserving of particular

Illustration for the tractate *Megillah,* showing the unrolling and reading of the Scroll of Esther on Purim, from a title page of the Hebrew-Latin Mishnah illustrated by Mich. Richey, Amsterdam, 1700–04. Jerusalem, J.N.U.L.

mention are geographical notes (5b–6b), the observations on the origin of the Targums (3a) and of the Septuagint (8b–9b), the extensive aggadic Midrash to Esther, which is practically a complete Midrash to the Book of Esther (10a–17a) and the arrangement of the **Amidah* (17b–18a). Of linguistic interest is the reference to the confusion of the letter *alef* with *ayin* in certain places, and the problem of correct pronunciation of the letters *he* and *ḥet.* There is less aggadic material in the Jerusalem Talmud than in the Babylonian. Unlike the latter, the Jerusalem Talmud does not give any *aggadot* about the story of Purim. It does, however, deal with the problem of the inclusion of the Book of Esther in the canon (1:7; 70d), and also has lengthy discussions on the laws of writing Torah scrolls and on the divine names (1:11; 71b–72a). It also gives the list of dates included in **Megillat Ta'anit* (1:6; 70c).

Bibliogrpahy: Ḥ. Albeck, *Shishah Sidrei Mishnah, Seder Mo'ed* (1958), 349–53; Epstein, Tannaim, index. [A.Z.E.]

MEGILLAT SETARIM (Heb. מְגִלַּת סְתָרִים; lit. "concealed scroll"). On two occasions (Shab. 6b; BM 92a), *Rav mentions that he found a *Megillat Setarim* in the academy of R. Ḥiyya containing laws in the name of Isi b. Judah. The first is that there are 39 principal categories of work *(avot melakhah)* forbidden on the Sabbath, but culpability is incurred only on account of one (this is the actual statement quoted, although the Talmud finds it inconceivable and emends it to "there is one for which culpability is not incurred"). In the second he states that the law in Deuteronomy 23:25, "When thou comest into thy neighbor's vineyard, then thou mayest eat grapes until thou have enough at thine own pleasure," applies to anyone entering the vineyard, and not only to a laborer employed there, on which Rava commented, "Isi would make it impossible to live," since a man would soon have his vineyard stripped, and there also the statement is then qualified as a result.

Rashi (ad. loc.) explains that the scroll was concealed because it was forbidden in general to commit the Oral Law to writing but since these laws were not generally taught, they were written down to save them from oblivion. I. H. Weiss is of the opinion that they contained views which Judah ha-Nasi rejected, and they were kept concealed out of respect for him, but this view is most improbable. All the *beraitot* were excluded from the Mishnah, and they contained many views that he had rejected, yet there is no suggestion that they were suppressed. Kaplan maintains that these scrolls were kept concealed because their contents were unsuitable for publication, and in addition he suggests that "concealed" means that they were written in a cryptic manner, in order to conceal their meaning. However, there is nothing particularly cryptic in the language of the passages quoted. Nevertheless it certainly would have been dangerous to make these laws widely known, and that would also explain why these are the only laws mentioned.

Bibliography: I. H. Weiss, Dor, 2 (1904^{4}), 168–9; M. Kaplan, *Redaction of the Babylonian Talmud* (1933), 277–8. [H.Ft.]

MEGILLAT TA'ANIT (Heb. lit. "scroll of fasting" but see below), a list of 36 days on which there were significant victories and happy events in the history of the Jews during the Second Temple, as a result of which the rabbis forbade fasting on them, as well as, in some cases, the delivery of memorial addresses for the dead *(hespedim).* The title should therefore be taken as meaning "the scroll of (the days of prohibited) fasting." The work received its present form close to the time of the destruction of the Second Temple or at the latest during the Bar Kokhba era. It is written in Aramaic and with extreme brevity. According to a tannaitic source (Shab. 13b) it was compiled by "*Hananiah b. Hezekiah (b. Garon) and his company," but the appendix to the *megillah* gives the author as Eliezer, the son of this Hananiah, one of the leading rebels against the Romans (Jos., Wars, 2:409). S. Zeitlin regards it as a literary remnant of the rebel party. If this is accepted, the purpose of the list of victories was to strengthen the spirit of heroism and faith in the success of the revolt. The value of the *megillah* for historical research lies in the parallels it provides to the facts and dates mentioned in Josephus. In the period following the conclusion of the Talmud a scholium was appended to the *megillah,* written in mishnaic Hebrew and based upon the Hebrew original of I Maccabees, the talmudic literature, and various oral traditions unknown from any other source. The historical value of this appendix is limited. In the course of time copyists and editors added notes and explanations, taken in particular from the Babylonian Talmud, so that two versions evolved, a Sephardi and an Italian.

The dates included in the *megillah* from before the Hasmonean era are: the second Passover (14th Iyar) and Purim. Those from the Hasmonean era are: the 23rd of Iyyar when the defenders of the *Acra left Jerusalem, an event mentioned in I Maccabees 13:49–53; the 14th of Sivan, "the seizure of the citadel Zur," identified by Graetz with Beth-Zur conquered by Simeon the Hasmonean (see I Macc. 11:65–66; 14:33); the 15th and 16th of Sivan, in memory of the conquest of Beth-Shean and the valley (of Jezreel) by the sons of John Hyrcanus (see Jos., Ant. 13:280; Jos., Wars 1:66); the 23rd of Marḥeshvan when they removed the *soreg* from the Temple (according to the appendix it meant a place "which the gentiles built, on which they stationed harlots"); the 25th of Marḥeshvan, in memory of the capture of Samaria by John Hyrcanus and his sons (see Jos., Wars 1:64; Jos., Ant. 13:275–81); the 21st of Kislev, "the day of Mt. Gerizim," in memory of the destruction of the Samaritan temple by John Hyrcanus (see Jos., Ant. 13:255/6); the 25th of Kislev, Ḥanukkah, for which festival the appendix mentions several reasons, including that when the Hasmoneans were victorious and found all the temple vessels ritually unclean, "they brought seven iron spits, covered them with white metal, and commenced the lighting"; the 28th of Shevat, when King

Antiochus was driven out of Jerusalem (according to the appendix the reference is to Antiochus IV (Epiphanes), but it is probable that it actually refers to Antiochus VII (Sidetes) of the time of John Hyrcanus; see Jos., Ant. 13:245); and the 13th of Adar, the day of Nicanor, in memory of the defeat of this Syrian commander (see I Macc. 7 and II Macc. 15). The dates from the period of Roman rule over Judea include the third of Kislev, when the "emblems" (the images of the Emperor) were removed from the Temple court, apparently in the time of Pontius Pilate (see Jos., Wars 2: 169), and the 22nd of Shevat, when the edict of Gaius Caligula ordering the erection of a statue of him in the Temple was rescinded (see Jos., Wars, 2: 195–203). From the period of the Jewish war with Rome are the 25th of Sivan, when the tax collectors were removed from Judea and Jerusalem, apparently a reference to the suspension of the tax payment to the emperor in 66 C.E., a matter mentioned in the long speech of King Agrippa (Wars 2:345–401); and the 17th of Elul, when the Romans departed from Jerusalem, although it is not known to what incident this refers.

A number of dates appear to allude to victories of the Pharisees over the Sadducees, but the details are not clear, Apart from the two days, the 12th of Adar, "the day of Trajan," which some connect with the emperor Trajan, and the 28th of Adar, which the appendix attributes to the abrogation of Hadrian's edicts, the *megillah* contains no events after 67 C.E. These memorial days were observed until the third century, but later "*Megillat Ta'anit* was rescinded" (TJ, Ta'an. 2: 13, 66a; RH 18b). A 13th-century manuscript of the work is extant in the Palatine library in Parma (De Rossi collection no. 117). *Megillat Ta'anit* was first published in Mantua in 1513. A critical edition, with introduction and commentary was published by H. Lichtenstein (see bibl.).

Bibliography: Graetz, Gesch, 3 pt. 2 (1906⁵), 559–77; S. Zeitlin, *Megillat Ta'anit as a Source for Jewish Chronology and History in the Hellenistic and Roman Periods* (1922); H. Lichtenstein (Z. Avneri), in: HUCA, 8–9 (1931–32), 257–351; H. Mantel, in: *Sefer Zikkaron le-Y. Avineri* (1970); B. Z. Lurie, *Megillat Ta'anit* (Heb. ed., 1964). [N.N.G.]

MEGILLAT YUḤASIN (Heb. מְגִלַּת יֻחֲסִין; "genealogical scroll"), a work mentioned by *tannaim* and *amoraim* as having been found in Jerusalem and containing genealogical information on traditions of importance in *halakhah* and in *aggadah*. Simeon b. Azzai (the *tanna* living at the beginning of the second century C.E.) relates that he found a *Megillat Yuḥasin* "in Jerusalem in which was written: so and so is a **mamzer* from a married woman; the Mishnah [teaching] of Eliezer b. Jacob is little but well sifted; [King] Manasseh killed [the prophet] Isaiah" (Yev. 49b). Similarly Levi (the *amora* of the end of the third century) states that he found in *Megillat Yuḥasin* in Jerusalem details of the family origin of Hillel, Yose, Nehemiah, Ḥiyya, Yannai, and others (TJ, Ta'an. 4:2, 68a; Gen. R. 98:10; ed. Theodor–Albeck 1259). Josephus too (Apion 1:30ff.) testifies to the existence of genealogical documents in Israel, particularly of priestly families. According to him, the priests in Egypt and in Babylon notified the center in Jerusalem of details of their marriages and of the patriarchal families into which they married. The Talmud (Pes. 62b) also mentions a "*Sefer Yuḥasin,*" but it does not appear to have any connection with the aforementioned *Megillat Yuḥasin.* It is difficult to determine its exact nature from the data given in the Talmud, but it seems to have been a kind of Midrash or *baraita* to the Book of Chronicles. According to Rashi (Pes. 62b), the work contained "reasons for the Laws of the Torah," but from a statement of *Amram Gaon (*Oẓar ha-Ge'onim* to Pes. p. 80, no. 190) it seems that the work served as a commentary and supplement to the genealogical lists in the biblical books. The Talmud there states that Simlai requested Johanan to teach him *Sefer Yuḥasin* but the latter refused to accede to his request. It also states in the name of Rav that from the time the *Sefer Yuḥasin* was concealed the sages became weak and their vision was dimmed.

See also *Genealogy. [Y.D.G.]

MEḤILAH (Heb. מְחִילָה; "waiver"), the renunciation, repudiation, abandonment, or surrender of some claim, right, or privilege. *Meḥilah* may be the waiver of a present right or *lien or the waiver of the right to a future increment; in the latter case, it is usually referred to as *silluk* (TJ, Ket. 9: 1, 32d; Ket. 83a).

Range of Applicability. *Meḥilah* cancels any debt, lien, or *obligation regardless of origin. Thus, debts arising out of *loans, *sale, *leasing and *hiring, *labor, *partnership, and *surety; liens on *property put up as collateral; obligations originating in *contract or *tort—all are effectively cancelled by *meḥilah* on the part of the creditor. Nor is the effectiveness of *meḥilah* curtailed by the form of the obligation; it applies with equal vigor whether the obligation is an oral or written one, whether it is attested to by witnesses or not (Gulak, Yesodei, 2 (1922), 111–4, 162f.).

Silluk, i.e., the waiving of future accretions, however, is only of limited effectiveness. This is due to the general reluctance of Jewish law to grant effective control over things that have as yet not come into existence (*davar she-lo ba la-olam;* see *Contract). Thus, if, on the one hand, a person possesses a present right, claim, or lien, *silluk* cannot dissolve it; only *meḥilah* can do so. If, on the other hand, the future right, claim, or lien is so remote as to have no specific relationship to this particular person, his *silluk* is equally ineffective since it pertains to *davar she-lo ba la-olam.* However, if the future right, claim, or lien, although not in existence, has by the operation of circumstances at least achieved a likelihood of accruing to a specific person, then his *silluk* is effective. Thus, the ability of a man to waive the rights of usufruct in his wife's property depends upon the status of his relationship with her; if he has already married her *(nissu'in),* his claim on her usufruct is a present one; hence his waiver must be in the form of *meḥilah,* and his *silluk* is no longer effective. If he has not entered into the first stage of *marriage *(erusin),* the usufruct in her property has as yet not come into existence (it is a *davar she-lo ba la-olam*); hence it is sufficiently remote as to vitiate the effectiveness of either form of waiver, that of *meḥilah* and that of *silluk.* If, however, he has entered into the first stage of marriage *(erusin)* but has not yet consummated the marriage *(nissu'in),* the right of usufruct, although not yet in existence, has achieved sufficient likelihood of accruing to him as to have endowed him with the power, not of *meḥilah,* but of *silluk* (Ket. 83a–84a, and codes).

The effectiveness of *silluk* with regard to obligations (i.e., rabbinic origin; see **Mishpat Ivri*) that have as yet not come into existence is undisputed among the early authorities (**rishonim;* see *Authority, Rabbinical). Its effectiveness with regard to obligations which are *mi-de-oraita* (i.e., biblical origin; see **Mishpat Ivri*) that have as yet not come into existence presented these scholars with two major difficulties: (1) it is an established rule of law that conditions contrary to biblical law are void (BM 7: 11). (2) The Talmud rules that biblical rights of succession, which are *mi-de-oraita,* such as those of a son to inherit his father's estate (in contradistinction to the right of a husband to inherit his wife, which is *mi-de-rabbanan*), cannot be waived (cf. Ket. 83a). The first difficulty was overcome by the limitation of the rule to non-monetary conditions on the one hand, and by the limitation of the power of waiver to monetary obligations on the other. The second limitation was overcome by construing *mi-de-oraita* rights of inheritance as being unique in that they inhere in the heirs even before the death of the owner of the estate; hence *silluk*, as the waiver of future rights, is impossible (*Keẓot ha-Ḥoshen* 209 n. 11).

Waiver is limited to rights; it is ineffective as a mode of transfer of real property or of chattel (*Rema* ḤM 241:2).

Legal Analysis. It has been pointed out that in the realm of rights, where it is effective, waiver does not constitute a transfer; rather it is mere withdrawal. A creditor who waives his claim does not transfer his right to the debtor and thereby extinguish the claim; on the contrary, he withdraws his right or removes his lien from the debtor and his estate. The effectiveness of *meḥilah*, therefore, is independent of the wishes of the debtor. Thus, if a creditor waives the debt due to him and the debtor refuses to avail himself of the waiver, the waiver nevertheless takes effect. Had *meḥilah* been viewed as a kind of transfer, it would have failed to take effect inasmuch as the debtor, as transferee, had declined (cf. Herzog, Instit, 2 (1939), 229). The juridic basis of waiver is the insistence of the law that the obligatory nature of monetary obligations is always dependent upon the will of the party to whom the obligation is due; the suspension of this will, e.g., by waiver, automatically extinguishes the obligation (Rambam, nov., BB 126b).

Formal Requirements. *Meḥilah* requires no formal mode (*meḥilah einah ẓerikhah kinyan;* Yad, Mekhirah 5:11 and Ishut 17:19; Tosef to Sanh. 6a s.v. *ẓerikhah*). It is effective by parole alone. Some authorities, however, do require a formal *kinyan* to validate the waiver of a creditor who retains possession of the debtor's promissory note (cf. commentaries to Sh. Ar., ḤM 12:8; see also *Acquisition). There is no formal requirement that witnesses validate a waiver of indebtedness. The function of witnesses is evidentiary, preventing the creditor from subsequently denying his act of waiver or from alleging that the act was made in jest. For this purpose, the witnesses need not have been formally appointed; their mere presence suffices (Sh. Ar., ḤM 81:29).

Implied Waiver. Waiver may be express or implied. Thus, the mere declaration of the creditor that the debtor owes him nothing absolves the latter of all obligation; for although he knows that the creditor's statement is incorrect, it is nevertheless construed as an implied waiver (Sh. Ar., ḤM 75:11; Rema, ḤM 40:1; but cf. *Siftei Kohen*, ḤM 81, n. 72). Asher Gulak has pointed out the similarity between this waiver implied in the creditor's denial of the debtor's indebtedness with the *acceptilatio* in Roman law. This was an oral form of dissolving obligations by having the debtor ask the creditor, "What I have promised you, have you received it *(habesne acceptum)*?" and the creditor answering, "I have *(habeo)*." The effectiveness of the Roman *acceptilatio* was limited, however, to the dissolution of obligations created by verbal contracts *(verbis);* it was ineffective in dissolving obligations created by real *(re)* and written *(litteris)* contracts. This limitation does not exist in Jewish law where the creditor's declaration of receipt of payment dissolves all obligations, regardless of origin (cf. Gulak, Yesodei, 2 (1922), 112f.). Implied waiver serves as the operational rationale of a number of legal rules. Thus, the rule that monetary conditions contrary to law are valid is justified on the grounds that the parties entering into the agreement governed by said conditions have implicitly waived their (monetary) rights (Rashi Kid. 19b; see also Contract). Similarly, the rule that overreaching *(*ona'ah)* that involves less than one-sixth of the fair price need not be returned to the injured party is explained on the basis of an implied waiver on the part of the latter (Yad, Mekhirah 12:3; cf. Sma. ḤM 227 n. 2). Again, the lapse of the right of a widow who no longer lives on her husband's estate to collect her *ketubbah* after 25 years, in localities where written *ketubbot* are not used, is based upon implied waiver (Ket. 104a; Yad, Ishut 16:23; see also *Limitation of Actions).

Legal Rules Limiting its Effectiveness. Some of the legal rules governing waiver may be summarized as follows:

(1) The power of waiver applies to claims estimable in money *(manona ityaḥiv li-meḥilah);* it is thus inapplicable to modes of effectuating marriage and divorce (Kid. 7a; Git. 64a). (2) Waiver need not be made in the presence of the debtor, but the debt does not lapse until the waiver has come to his knowledge (*Arukh ha-Shulḥan*, ḤM 241:4; but cf. Herzog, Instit, 2 (1939), 231f.). (3) If co-debtors are named in one promissory note and the creditor waives the obligation of one of them, the other's obligation remains intact and is actionable (opinion of Sh. Ar., ḤM 77:6; disputed by *Rema, ad loc.). If the debtors are correal, however, i.e., where each is bound severally to discharge the entire liability, the creditor's waiver of the obligation to one of them cancels the liability of all *(ibid.)*. (4) A waiver of the lien on an obligation, retaining, however, the obligation itself, must be accomplished by a *kinyan* in order to be effective (*Derishah*, ḤM 111, n. 10). (5) A creditor may effectively waive part of the obligation, or he may postpone the date of payment by waiving the time stipulated in the **shetar* (Sh. Ar., ḤM 66:24, and *Siftei Kohen, ibid.*, n. 83). (6) A waiver, in order to be effective, must be related to an object that is definite or to a quantity that is fixed; obligations that are vague, limitless, or unknown are unaffected by *meḥilah* (Yad, Mekhirah 13:3; Sh. Ar., ḤM 232:7). (7) Waiver is ineffective if made through error (see *Mistake; Tos. to BM 66b, s.v. *hatam;* cf. Herzog, Instit, 2 (1939), 299); if made under duress (see **Ones*, Tos. to BB 48a, s.v. *amar*); if made in jest (Yad, Mekhirah 5:13 and Ishut 17:19); and if made by minors and, presumably, by deaf-mutes and mentally incompetents (BM 22b; see *Legal Capacity). (8) The effectiveness of *meḥilah* is disputed in cases where the creditor retains possession of the debtor's promissory note or his *pledge, some authorities requiring a formal *kinyan* to supplement the waiver by parole (Sh. Ar., ḤM 12:8; 241:2, and commentaries).

Bibliography: I. S. Zuri, *Mishpat ha-Talmud*, 5 (1921), 25; Gulak, Yesodei, 1 (1922), 159; 2 (1922), 111–4, 162f.; Herzog, Instit, 2 (1939), 115, 132ff., 229–33, 299f.; Elon, Mafte'aḥ, 123–9. [A.Kir.]

MEḤIẒAH (Heb. מְחִיצָה; "partition"), designation of the partition screen in synagogues between the space reserved for men and that, generally in the rear or upstairs, for women. The origin of the *meḥiẓah* derives from the talmudic description of the festivities *(Simḥat Beit ha-Sho'evah)* held on the second evening of the feast of Tabernacles in the court of women of the Temple (Suk. 5:2; Mid. 2:5). The Talmud states that men and women were allotted separate space (Suk. 51b–52a, Tosef., Suk. 4:1). Further sources for the separation of the sexes, as practiced in traditional synagogues, are to be found in midrashic literature like *Pirkei de-Rabbi Eliezer* 41, where it is stated in the name of R. Pinḥas that men and women stood separately when the Israelites assembled at Mount Sinai to receive the Ten Commandments (see also PdRE 23). Remains of galleries

Latticed *meḥiẓah* of the women's gallery of the Vittorio Veneto Synagogue, Italy, 1701. Jerusalem, Israel Museum.

discovered in ancient Palestine synagogues have been taken as belonging to the women's sections.

Most European synagogues of the Middle Ages had a separate women's gallery called *Weibershul* fenced off by an iron grille or a non-transparent curtain. In synagogues where there was no balcony, the *meḥiẓah* was made of latticework serving as a partition between the seats of the men in front and those of the women in the rear. References to the custom of *meḥiẓah* in the Middle Ages can be found in the responsa literature of that period such as *Mordecai b. Hillel's commentary to Shab. 3, note no. 311, where it is stated "We are permitted to erect on Sabbath the partition-curtain between men and women during the time of the sermon" (see also *Sefer ha-Maharil* of Jacob Moellin (ed. Cremona (1565), 38a, 50b, 59b). The abolition of the *meḥiẓah* by the Reform movement in Europe in the early part of the 19th century was strongly opposed by the leading rabbinic authorities in Hungary and Poland, such as Moses *Sofer, Moses *Schick, and Elijah *Guttmacher, who regarded this innovation as an illicit change and, consequently, ruled that any synagogue without *meḥiẓah* is unfit for prayer.

In most Conservative synagogues in the United States, the *meḥiẓah* has been abolished and men and women sit together, or, in some cases, one side of the synagogue is reserved for the men and the other for the women, without an actual partition. In Reform synagogues the segregation of men and women has been entirely abolished based on the fact that the Bible nowhere commands the separation of men and women during public worship or assemblies (see Deut. 31:12; Neh. 8:2–3). These modern trends met with vigorous opposition in the last decade on the part of Orthodox Jewry in the United States, which has come to regard the retention of the *meḥiẓah* as a cardinal principle and as a mark of the preservation of the Orthodox character of the synagogue. In several congregations the Orthodox minority turned to the courts for legal redress and were granted relief by court orders enjoining the synagogue board from changing the status quo, as in the case of congregation Beth Tefilas Moses of Mount Clemens, Michigan (Court Order of Sept. 21, 1959). Similar litigations were dealt with by the state courts in New Orleans, Louisiana and by the Superior Court of Pennsylvania (no. 178, October Term, 1954), all of which ruled in favor of the party demanding the retention of the *meḥiẓah*.

Bibliography: J. B. Agus, *Guideposts in Modern Judaism* (1954), 133ff.; idem, in: *Conservative Judaism*, 11 no. 1 (1956), 11ff.; Elbogen, Gottesdienst, 49; B. Litvin, *Sanctity of the Synagogue* (1959; Orthodox viewpoint); HALAKHIC RESPONSA: Moses Schreiber, *Ḥatam Sofer* (1855), to Sh. Ar. ḤM 190, OḤ 28; Moses Schick, *Maharam Schick* (1880) to Sh. Ar. OḤ 77; Hillel Lichtenstein, *Teshuvot Beit Hillel* (1908), no. 50; Ḥayyim Halberstam, *Divrei Ḥayyim* (1875), no. 18; Elijah Guttmacher, *Zikhron Shelomo* (1933), 70–72. [M.Y.]

MEHLSACK, ELIAKIM BEN JUDAH HA-MILZAHGI (c. 1780–1854), Polish talmudist. "Milzahgi" is a derivation of Mehlsack, the German name for Samila in Poland where Eliakim was born. He settled in Galicia and lived his last years in Lvov and Brody under the patronage of Isaac Berish *Blumenfeld of Brody, devoting his life to Jewish scholarship. In 1837 he published *Sefer Ravyah* (=**R**abbi **E**liakim **b.** **J**udah **h**a-Milzahgi), a criticism of the *Gottesdienstliche Vortraege* of *Zunz and the *Toledot* of Solomon Judah *Rapoport. Unlike Zunz, who conceded the correctness of some of Mehlsack's remarks, Rapoport took umbrage at them and replied scathingly in *Kerem Ḥemed* (6 (1841), 96–109). Although he wrote almost 70 books, only *Sefer Ravyah* was published. Mehlsack also published an attack against the forgeries of A. *Firkovich in the German-Jewish press. Most of his works were about Talmud and Kabbalah, but *Mirkevet Esh* ("Train of Fire") argues that one is permitted to travel by train on the Sabbath. The manuscript was sent to S. *Holdheim, the leading Reform rabbi, who reproduced parts of it in a German-Jewish periodical. According to Gershom Scholem, Mehlsack's unpublished study of the Zohar, *Zohorei Ravyah*, at the Hebrew National and University Library is the most significant book written on the Zohar during the 19th century. Extant also is his commentary on the Book of *Raziel (London, Jews College Ms. 347). His treatise on the principle of the Kabbalah and a commentary on the *Pesikta de-Rav Kahana* have not survived.

Bibliography: P. Lachower, in: *Keneset*, 6 (1941), 299–300; G. Kressel in: KS, 17 (1940), 87–94 (his bibliography); G. Scholem and I. Joel (eds.), *Kitvei Yad be-Kabbalah* (1930), 40 no. 13; Zunz-Albeck, Derashot, 20–21; S. D. Luzzatto, *Iggerot Shadal*, ed. by E. S. Graeber, pt. 4 (1882), 602–5. [Z.Av./G.K.]

MEHRING, WALTER (1896–), German poet and author. The son of a writer, Mehring was born and raised in Berlin, where he studied art history. A friend of Kurt *Tucholsky, he joined the Berlin branch of the Dada movement and published his early expressionistic poems in Herwarth *Walden's *Sturm*. During the years 1920–33 Mehring, who became a brilliantly witty spokesman of the moderate left, worked on the staff of the *Weltbuehne*. His satirical light verse followed the tradition developed by Wedekind, Ringelnatz, and Brecht, and his *chansons* dealt with the life of the vagabond, symbolizing the disillusionment of his age. Mehring's best-known collection of poems is *Die Gedichte, Lieder und Chansons des Walter Mehring* (1929), notable for its sarcastic criticism of contemporary society. His comedy, *Der Kaufmann von Berlin* (1929), outraged the Nazis. On their accession to power in 1933, they planned to arrest him but he escaped to France. During World War II Mehring escaped from an internment camp to the U.S., where he remained from 1941 until after World War II, when he settled in Ascona. His other works include *Das politische Cabaret* (1919); *Die Nacht des Tyrannen* (1937); *No Road Back* (1944), a work published in English and German; and *Berlin-Dada* (1959). Mehring also wrote *Die verlorene Bibliothek. Autobiographie einer Kultur* (1952). [R.K.]

MEI AMMI (Heb. מֵי עַמִּי), kibbutz in central Israel, in the Iron Hills of Samaria, affiliated with Ha-No'ar ha-Ẓiyyoni, founded in 1963 as a *Naḥal outpost on the pre-1967

Jordanian border. In August 1967 a civilian group took over the village, whose construction—including the reclamation of its hilly land—was aided by the Jewish community of Miami, Florida. Accordingly, the name chosen, meaning "Water of My People," is similar in sound to Miami. [E.O.]

MEIDNER, LUDWIG (1884–1966), German painter. Meidner was born in Bernstadt, in Silesia. At nineteen, he went to Breslau to study art. For a time he eked out a living in Berlin, sketching for fashion magazines, but in 1906–08 studied in Paris. In 1908 he returned to Berlin where in 1912, with Jakob *Steinhardt and Richard Janthur, Meidner founded the group *Die Pathetiker.*

Though an ardent pacifist, Meidner was drafted into the German army, and served throughout World War I. In January 1918 he was given furlough to attend his one-man show of prewar paintings in Berlin. One of its major features was the oil, "I and the City," in which he presented himself as a large, tortured, brooding figure, with exploding streets, factories, and tenements in the background. The show caused a great stir and Meidner suddenly became one of the foremost representatives of expressionism in Central Europe. After the war, Meidner was prominent in the *Novembergruppe,* an association of artists and intellectuals eager to bridge the gap between the public and the nation's creative minds.

Self-portrait etching of Ludwig Meidner, German expressionist artist, 1921. $9\frac{3}{4} \times 7$ in. (23.5×18 cm.). Jerusalem, B. M. Ansbacher Collection.

Meidner was deeply attached to Judaism, and for a time during the early Nazi period taught drawing at the Jewish secondary school "Yawne" in Cologne. In 1939 he escaped to England. During the air raids on London he served as night watchman in a morgue. Here, for a few pounds each, he painted portraits of deceased people from photographs. In 1952 he returned to Germany, and for a time lived in the Jewish Old Age Home in Frankfort. A portrait commission by the German president Theodor Heuss led to his rediscovery; this enabled him to have a studio for the last years of his life. On his eightieth birthday in 1964, he was awarded the Grosses Verdienstkruez of the Federal Republic of Germany. Meidner's most important works are those painted before World War I. Apart from his apocalyptic landscapes and his Jewish themes, his most significant creations are his disturbingly intense self-portraits and portraits of friends. His wife Elsa Meidner also made a reputation as a painter.

Bibliography: T. Grochowiak, *Ludwig Meidner* (1966). [A.W.]

MEIER, JULIUS (1874–1937), U.S. governor. Meier was born in Portland, Oregon. He became president and general manager of his family's mercantile firm, Meier and Frank Company in Portland. Meier developed the Columbia River highway system. During World War I, he was northwest regional director of the Council of National Defense. When his former law partner, the Progressive Republican candidate for governor in 1930, died during the campaign, Meier reluctantly agreed to run as an Independent against a regular Republican and a Democrat and won. During his term as governor (1931–35), he fostered conservation of the state's natural resources, formation of the state police system, and establishment of a nonpolitical judiciary, and he demanded rigid economies in state expenditures. While governor, he served as president of

Julius Meier, governor of Oregon. From M. Schappes, *The Jews in the United States,* New York, 1958.

Congregation Beth Israel in Portland (1933–35), which his father had helped to found.

Bibliography: H. M. Corning (ed.), *Dictionary of Oregon History* (1956), 165; R. Neuberger, in: *Opinion,* 4 no. 9 (1934), 10–12; J. J. Nodel, *The Ties Between* (1959), 128; E. Pillsbury, in: *American Hebrew,* 129 (1931), 509–22; B. Postal, *Jewish Tourist Guide to the U.S.* (1954), 520–3; UJE, s.v. [R.E.L.]

ME'ILAH (Heb. מְעִילָה; "sacrilege"), eighth tractate in the Mishnah, Tosefta, and Babylonian Talmud order *Kodashim. Me'ilah* contains six chapters and deals with the unlawful use and enjoyment of *hekdesh* (i.e., things consecrated to the Temple, especially sacrifices). The scriptural basis is Leviticus 5:15–16, which lays down that a person inadvertently committing a trespass "in holy things," shall bring a guilt offering, make restitution for the loss caused, and pay an additional fine. Chapters 1 and 2 discuss the various offerings and sacrificial portions to which the law of *me'ilah* applies, and define the moment from which an offering is considered *hekdesh* for the purpose of this law. Chapter 3 is concerned with exceptional instances of illicit enjoyment of *hekdesh,* which are not

Engraving for the tractate *Me'ilah,* showing the profane use of a sacrifice consecrated to the Temple, from a title page of the Hebrew-Latin Mishnah illustrated by Mich. Richey, Amsterdam, 1700–04. Jerusalem, J.N.U.L.

affected by the law of *me'ilah*. Chapters 4 and 5 include the problem of determining the minimal value of misappropriation to which the law applies, and especially whether illicit enjoyment that causes no loss to *hekdesh* constitutes *me'ilah*. Chapter 6 deals with trespass by proxy. The Tosefta is divided into three chapters. The Babylonian *Gemara* enlarges on the teaching of the Mishnah but, with the exception of the remarkable *Ben Temalyon story (17b), there are no aggadic digressions. *Me'ilah* was translated into English in the Soncino edition of the Talmud (1948). [A.Z.E.]

°**MEINERTZHAGEN, RICHARD HENRY** (1878–1967), British soldier, administrator, and supporter of Zionism. During World War I he served on the East African front and was on the staff of General *Allenby's army, which conquered Palestine. He was chief political officer in Palestine and Syria in the postwar military administration, and in a dispatch to the Foreign Office (1919), accused the military administration of hostility to the principles of the *Balfour Declaration, expressing the view that Arab opposition to Zionism would not last once it was known that the British government was determined to carry through its pledge of a national home to the Jewish people. He joined Herbert *Samuel's staff when the latter was appointed high commissioner of Palestine. Meinertzhagen was also attached to the British delegation to the Paris Peace Conference as an advisor (1919–1920), and from 1921 to 1924 he was military advisor to the Middle Eastern Department of the Colonial Office. He remained a firm friend of Zionism, and his *Middle East Diary 1917–1956*, published in 1959, is a valuable record as well as source for correcting the misinterpretations of history related to the Balfour Declaration and the subsequent period. He was also an enthusiastic ornithologist, and his book *Birds of Arabia* (1954) threw much light on the bird life of Palestine.

Bibliography: J. Lord, *Duty, Honour, Empire: The Life and Times of Colonel Richard Meinertzhagen* (1971). [M.R.]

°**MEINHOLD, JOHANNES FRIEDRICH** (1861–1937), German Bible scholar. Meinhold taught at Greifswald and Bonn. He wrote on the history of the Hagiographa (1889) and on the compilation of Daniel (1884, 1889), maintaining that the basic corpus of Daniel (2:4b–6:29) was composed around 300 B.C.E. and that Daniel 1:2–2:4a and 7–12 were added in the Hasmonean period. His views on the role of Israelite wisdom and prophecy, the documents contained within the Hexateuch, and the composition of Ruth reflect the strong influence of the classical Wellhausen school. It also characterizes his *Einfuehrung in das Alte Testament* (1919, 1932[3]). In addition to studies on Genesis 14 (1911), the Decalogue (1927), and the role of the biblical Sabbath (1905), he wrote a history of the Jewish people (1916). His *Jesus und das Alte Testament* (1896) clashed with accepted Christian positions, but his *Altes Testament und evangelisches Christentum* (1934), an apology for keeping the Hebrew heritage within the Christian tradition, argued that the national ethical religion of Israel was fulfilled in the primitive church's faith in resurrection. He was also coeditor with Hans Lietzmann of the Hebrew-Greek text of Amos for *Kleine Texte fuer theologische Vorlesungen und Uebungen*. [Z.G.]

MEININGEN, city in E. Germany. The medieval Jewish community suffered persecutions in 1243 because of a *blood libel, in 1298 during the *Rindfleisch disturbances, and during the *Black Death massacres in 1349 when it was destroyed. The synagogue was transformed into a chapel in 1384. Jews continued to live in nearby villages, which in 1803 were incorporated into the newly created duchy of Saxe-Meiningen. The duchy's Jewry law of 1811 laid down disabilities regarding residence, marriage permits, and economic pursuits. Only a few Jews were allowed to live in Meiningen itself; after the *Hep! Hep! riots (1819) only one family remained. By 1844, 29 persons lived there. At that time 1,500 Jews lived in the duchy; the seat of the rabbinate was in the nearby village of Walldorf, where 550 Jews lived (35% of the total population) in 1844, when the ducal authorities approved the Saxe-Meiningen synagogue regulations stressing religious reforms. The Saxe-Meiningen Jewry law of 1856 granted citizenship to Jews owning substantial business, and that of 1868 to all the duchy's Jews. By 1870, 470 Jews lived in Meiningen, 490 in 1898, 359 in 1913 (2.08% of the total), 293 in 1925 (1.6%), and 192 in June 1933. In 1871 the rabbinate was transferred to Meiningen, a cemetery acquired in 1874, a synagogue consecrated in 1883, and a *ḥevra kaddisha* founded in 1885. In 1856 Jewish and Christian financiers founded the Central-German Credit Bank in Meiningen. The banks of B. M. Strupp (formerly a merchandise firm) and D. Mannheimer (founded in 1871) were important in industrial financing far beyond the duchy's limits. Gustav Strupp (1851–1918) was chairman of both the Chamber of Commerce and the Jewish community, and a member of the Landtag (1903–18). From the 1870s Jews were admitted to the bar, and some were appointed judges. Anti-Semitism was strong in Meiningen: the anti-Semitic vote in 1898 and the Nazi vote in 1932 far exceeded the national average. The synagogue was burned in 1938 and by the end of that year only a few Jewish families remained, with 16 children attending the Jewish school. Records on deportations are missing. No Jews returned to Meiningen after 1945.

Bibliography: T. Oelsner, in: JSOS, 4 (1942), 256, n. 36, 358–74, 378 and n. 166; *Handbuch der juedischen Gemeindeverwaltung und Wohlfahrtspflege* (1913), 202; (1928), 167, 319; J. Jacobson, in: MGDJ, 6 (1962), 59–97; Germ Jud, 2 (1968), 530; S. Colodner, *Jewish Education under the Nazis* (1964), 62; P. H. Emden, *Money Powers of Europe in the 19th & 20th Centuries* (1937), 208. [T.O.]

MEIR (second century C.E.), *tanna*, one of the leaders of the post-Bar Kokhba generation. Essentially a halakhist, he played a decisive part in the development of the *Mishnah.

According to the *aggadah*, Meir was a descendant of proselytes. One tradition holds that his real name was Nehorai (or Mesha; the Aramaic form of Meir), but that he was called Meir ("the illuminator") because he "enlightened the eyes of the sages of the *halakhah*" (Er. 13b; see Dik. Sof.). His main teacher was *Akiva, but he also studied under *Ishmael and *Elisha b. Avuyah. One of the five ordained by *Judah b. Bava during the persecutions following the Bar Kokhba revolt, he was also ordained by Akiva. In the account of this ordination it is emphasized that he was given precedence over Simeon b. Gamaliel, which is indicative of his status and importance. The persecutions compelled him to flee from Ereẓ Israel. On his return after the savagery had abated, he was among the sages who assembled in the Valley of Rimmon to intercalate the year; afterward he was one of those who convened at Usha for the assembly that led to the renewal of the office of *nasi* and of the Sanhedrin, which had been abolished during the revolt and the subsequent oppression.

When Simeon b. Gamaliel was appointed *nasi*, R. Nathan was appointed *av bet din*, and Meir, *ḥakham*. There are differences of opinion about the nature of this office, but it appears that the leadership of the nation at that time consisted of three persons: the *nasi* and the *av bet din*, who presided over the Sanhedrin and his deputy the *ḥakham*. However, Meir's participation in the assemblies at the Valley of Rimmon and Usha, in which the *nasi* did not participate, seems to indicate that his influence and power were considerable. This did not suit Simeon b. Gamaliel, who took steps to strengthen the status of his office vis-à-vis the Sanhedrin. Nathan and Meir endeavored to dismiss Simeon but without success, but the *nasi* was equally unsuccessful in having them removed from the *bet ha-midrash* (Hor. 13b–14a). The tradition of the Jerusalem Talmud (MK 3:1, 81c) which asserts that "they wished to excommunicate Meir" also testifies to a conflict between Meir and his colleagues in the leadership, although the excommunication was not put into effect. The failure of the attempt may probably ascribed to the **takkanah* adopted at Usha "not to excommunicate an elder." Nevertheless, as a punishment for his opposition to the *nasi*, it was decreed that all subsequent statements made by Meir should be introduced anonymously, the author being quoted merely as *"aḥerim"* ("the others").

On one subject Meir was of one mind with Simeon b. Gamaliel: both stood for moderation toward the Roman government. It may be assumed that his doctrine of moderation was the result of the Bar Kokhba revolt and the suffering which it brought in its train. In general, it should be noted that despite the extreme attitude adopted by Meir in some spheres, he was also liberal in his approach. This liberal attitude is noticeable in all his contacts with the non-Jewish world (see *Oenomaus of Gadara), and in his sayings concerning foreign culture. Three hundred fox *fables are ascribed to Meir, of which three are given (Sanh. 38b). It should also be noted that Meir was the only *tanna* who kept up relations with Elisha b. Avuyah after the latter's apostasy.

Meir's contribution to the *halakhah* and the compilation of the Mishnah was considerable. "The Mishnah of Meir" was one of the main bases of the Mishnah whose final editing was undertaken by Judah ha-Nasi. The Talmud states "an anonymous *mishnah* represents the view of Meir following that of Akiva" (Sanh. 86a; cf. TJ, Yev. 4:11, 6b). This tradition means that, generally speaking, the early *halakhot* of the Mishnah were reported in the style and form taught by Meir, who had received them from his teacher Akiva. In point of fact the Mishnah contains anonymous statements of other *tannaim*, and sometimes Meir can be found disagreeing with an anonymous *mishnah*, because of the fact that Judah ha-Nasi also used the *mishnayot* of other tannaim. Nevertheless, the Mishnah of R. Meir laid the foundation of the Mishnah of Judah ha-Nasi. Meir frequently spoke in praise of living in Ereẓ Israel: "Whoever lives permanently in Israel and speaks the holy language . . . he is assured of a share in the world to come" (TJ, Shek. 3:4, 47c). Meir died in Asia (probably Ezion-Geber). Before his death he ordered his body to be taken to Ereẓ Israel, and requested that until then his bier be put on the shore in order that it may be lapped by the sea that washes the shores of Ereẓ Israel (TJ, Kil. 9:4, 32c).

Meir was the spiritual father of the *Kehilla Kaddisha de-vi-Yrushalayim*, which in its way of life calls to mind the *ḥavurot* of the Temple period (see **ḥaver*). The three fundamental tenets of the *Kehilla Kaddisha*, study, work, and prayer were highly extolled by him. The importance he attached to knowledge comes to the fore in his comment on the mishnaic provision (Hor. 3:8) that a **mamzer* who is a scholar takes precedence over a high priest who is an ignoramus. Meir goes further and says that even a gentile who occupies himself with the Torah is the equal of a high priest (BK 38a.; Av. Zar. 3a). Meir uses strong language to express his contempt for the ignoramus: "Whosoever marries his daughter to an **am ha-areẓ* is as though he bound her and laid her in front of a lion" (Pes. 49b). His extreme attitude in demanding study of Torah emerges clearly in the saying: "Whoever forgets one word of the Torah is accounted by Scripture as if he had forfeited his life" (Avot 3:8). He required that one should not be satisfied with acquiring knowledge of the Torah, but should also teach it to others (Sanh. 99a). Together with the study of Torah, Meir stresses the importance of labor: "A blessing rests only upon labor" (Tosef. Ber. 7:8); "A man should always teach his son a clean craft" (Kid. 4:14). He similarly stresses the importance of prayer: " 'And it came to pass as she prayed long' [I Sam. 1:12] this implies that whoever prays long is answered" (TJ, Ber. 4:17c; et al.). Punctiliousness in ritual purity was another major concern of Meir. In a discussion in connection with the ritual purity demanded of the *ḥavurot* of Temple times and the concept of *am ha-areẓ* as regards tithes and purity, Meir takes a more stringent view than his colleagues. According to him anyone not eating ordinary food in ritual purity belongs to the category of the *am ha-areẓ* while his colleagues apply the term only to someone who disregards the duty of giving tithes. Such stringency with regard to abstinence and ritual purity apparently was part of the principles of the *Kehilla Kaddisha*. As Meir not only preached these standards of purity but carried them out in practice, he was accorded the epithet of "holy," granted to only a few in the Talmud. His contemporary, Yose b. Ḥalafta, called him: "A great man, a holy man, a modest man" (TJ, Ber. 2:7, 5b), while Simeon b. Lakish called him "holy mouth" (Sanh. 23a).

Meir had a tragic family life. His wife *Beruryah was the daughter of the martyred *Hananiah b. Teradyon. After the Bar Kokhba War her sister was taken to a brothel from where Meir rescued her (Av. Zar. 18a). His two sons died simultaneously while he was busy in the college, and according to a legend quoted by Rashi (Av. Zar 18b), Beruryah herself was seduced by one of the scholars.

Bibliography: Hyman, Toledot, 865–78; I. Konovitz, *Rabbi Meir* (Heb., 1967); A. Blumenthal, *Rabbi Meir* (Ger., 1888); Bacher, Tann; Frankel, Mishnah, index; A. Buechler, *Der galilaeische Am ha'Areṣ des zweiten Jahrhunderts*, in: *XIII. Jahresbericht der Israelitisch-Theologische Lehranstalt in Wien* (1906), esp. 157–90; Alon, Toledot, 2 (1961[2]), index; M. Avi-Yonah, *Bi-Ymei Roma u-Bizantiyyon* (1952[2]), 1–21; Safrai, in: *Zion*, 22 (1957), 183–93.

[A.O.]

MEIR (Myerson), GOLDA (maiden name **Mabovitch;** 1898–), Israel prime minister and Labor leader. She was born in Kiev, Russia, where her father was a skilled carpenter. Because of the family's extreme poverty, they emigrated to the United States in 1906 and settled in Milwaukee, where Golda graduated from high school and enrolled in the Milwaukee Normal School for Teachers. Childhood memories of Russian pogroms, intensified by the anti-Jewish massacres during the civil war in Russia after 1917, led her to embrace Zionism and, being a socialist as well, she joined *Po'alei Zion in 1915. A gifted orator in Yiddish and

Figure 1. Golda Meir, fourth prime minister of Israel. Courtesy Government Press Office, Tel Aviv.

Figure 2. Golda Meir, as minister plenipotentiary to the U.S.S.R., presenting her credentials to Vaslov, the Deputy Chairman of the Supreme Soviet, 1948. Courtesy Foreign Ministry, Jerusalem.

English, the young girl quickly attracted attention; however, she rejected the role of a "Diaspora Zionist" and in 1921 settled in Palestine with her husband Morris Myerson, joining kibbutz *Merḥavyah. Although Golda Meir rapidly adjusted to the hard conditions, including malaria, then prevailing in the kibbutz, she soon became involved in political and social activities that took her from Merḥavyah. In 1928 she became the executive secretary of *Mo'eẓet ha-Po'alot and was sent as an emissary to the Pioneer Women's Organization in the United States from 1932 to 1934.

Upon her return to Palestine in 1934, she was invited to join the Executive Committee of the *Histadrut. Golda Meir rapidly rose in the hierarchy of the Palestine labor movement, and was appointed head of the Political Department of the Histadrut, a task which proved to be invaluable training for her subsequent role as leading statesman of Israel. In the 1940s, during the struggle with the Mandatory government, she was in the forefront of the conflict as an organizer of its various facets. When the British, determined to crush the *Haganah and Jewish resistance, arrested the leaders of the *yishuv* in June 1946, Golda Meir was chosen to be acting head of the Political Department of the Jewish Agency, instead of the arrested Moshe Shertok (*Sharett), thus becoming the principal Jewish representative in the difficult negotiations with the Mandatory power. After Sharett, upon his release from the camp in Latrun, left for the United States to take charge of the fight for the partition plan at the U.N., Golda Meir served as the head of the Political Department in Jerusalem until the establishment of the state in 1948.

During the Arab attacks between November 1947 and the proclamation of the State of Israel, Golda Meir engaged in two major endeavors. In January 1948, she visited the United States and proved extremely successful in presenting the case of the embattled *yishuv* and enlisting the aid of U.S. Jewry. On May 10, 1948, four days before the proclamation of the state, she made a dangerous and dramatic journey across the Jordan in order to meet secretly with King Abdullah, hoping to persuade him not to join the attack on the newborn Jewish state. After the establishment of Israel she was appointed minister to Moscow, a post she held until April, 1949. Her presence elicited an extraordinary congregation of Jewish masses at the Moscow Great Synagogue on the High Holidays—the first dramatic expression of long-suppressed Jewish identity in the Soviet Union.

After the elections to the First Knesset in 1949, to which she was elected on behalf of the *Mapai party, Golda Meir was appointed minister of labor. She initiated large-scale housing and road-building programs and vigorously supported the policy of unrestricted immigration despite the great economic difficulties faced by the young State of Israel. In 1956 she became foreign minister of Israel and held the post until 1965.

As one of the few women to hold so high an office, Golda Meir became a famous figure on the international scene and displayed an extraordinary capacity to convey, in public and in private talks with foreign statesmen and representatives, the moral aspect of Israel's vital interests. She was frequently active at the United Nations, especially in the period following the *Sinai Campaign; and her speeches from its rostrum became central events of the General Assemblies' debates. Among her main achievements in foreign relations was extension of Israel aid to the emergent African nations and the establishment of friendly relations with them. Upon her retirement from the Foreign Ministry, Golda Meir became secretary-general of Mapai, and after the *Six-Day War (1967) she was instrumental in bringing about the union of Mapai, *Rafi, and *Aḥdut ha-Avodah, becoming the secretary-general of the new unified *Israel Labor Party. After the death of Levi Eshkol on Feb. 26, 1969, Golda Meir became the fourth prime minister of Israel. In 1969 she paid an official visit to President Nixon in Washington and subsequently led her party to victory in the general elections. She again became prime minister retaining at first the broad coalition of "national unity" established on the eve of the Six-Day War. She dramatically voiced the identification and solidarity of Israel and its government with the Soviet Jews who courageously engaged in an open struggle for their right to settle in Israel. Her concept of Israel as a focal center of a united Jewish people the world over was a conspicuous element in her activities as prime minister.

In August 1970 she accepted the American peace initiative, based on a stoppage of the "war of attrition" with

Figure 3. Golda Meir with President Richard Nixon, at the White House, September 1969. Courtesy Government Press Office, Tel Aviv.

Egypt and an Israel pledge to withdraw to "secure and recognized boundaries" under a general peace settlement. In consequence *Gaḥal seceded from the government of national unity, and Golda Meir continued to lead the remaining coalition and the nation as a whole in the delicate relations with the U.S. government and other international factors. She won great popularity as an outstanding "team leader" of the coalition government and as an exponent of the national consensus on Israel's crucial interests while entering the new phase of indirect negotiations with Egypt. Her collected papers, *This is Our Strength*, edited by H.M. Christman with an introduction, appeared in 1962.

Bibliography: M. Syrkin, *Golda Meir: Woman with a Cause* (1963); idem, *Golda Meir: Israel's Leader* (1969); E. Agres, *Golda* (Heb., 1969), photo album and text; P. Mann, *Golda* (1971).

[M.Sy.]

MEIR, JACOB (1856–1939), Sephardi chief rabbi of Ereẓ Israel. Born in Jerusalem, the son of a well-to-do merchant, Caleb Mercado, Meir studied Talmud under Menahem

Jacob Meir, Sephardi chief rabbi of Ereẓ Israel. Courtesy Jerusalem Municipality Historical Archives. Photo Ben Dov, Jerusalem.

Bekhor Isaac and Kabbalah under Aaron Azriel. In 1882 he was sent to Bukhara, as the first emissary to visit that country. Meir, enthusiastically welcomed, was instrumental in encouraging the immigration of Bukhara Jews to Ereẓ Israel. In 1885, 1888, and 1900 he visited Tunisia and Algeria as an emissary. In 1888–99 he was a member of the *bet din* of R. Jacob Saul *Elyashar in Jerusalem. Meir was one of the promoters of the revival of spoken Hebrew in Palestine. Under Turkish rule, he often interceded with the authorities on behalf of the Jewish community; he also encouraged the construction of new Jewish quarters of Jerusalem. In 1899 he was appointed deputy head of the *bet din* of R. Raphael Isaac Israel. In 1906 he was a candidate for the chief rabbinate of Jerusalem, in succession to Elyashar, but his opponents, supported by the *ḥakham bashi* in Turkey, prevented his election. In 1908 he was elected chief rabbi of Salonika, where he remained until 1919. He was elected chief rabbi of Jerusalem in 1911, but the Jews of Salonika prevented him from assuming the office. When in 1921 the chief rabbinate was established in Palestine, Meir was elected (together with Rabbi A. I. Kook) as chief rabbi of Palestine with the title of *rishon le-Zion*. He was decorated by the sultan of Turkey and by the kings of Greece and England, and was awarded the French Legion of Honor. Meir even received decorations from Hussein, king of the Hejaz. Two manuscripts of his were lost in a fire in Salonika. To celebrate his 80th birthday, his friends published *Zikhron Me'ir* in his honor.

Bibliography: M. D. Gaon, *Yehudei ha-Mizraḥ be-Ereẓ Yisrael*, 2 (1938), 361–71; P. Grajewsky, *Zikkaron la-Ḥovevim ha-Rishonim*, no. 110 (1933).

[G.B.-Y]

MEIR BA'AL HA-NES, TOMB OF, a building on the shores of Lake Kinneret. According to R. Moses *Basola "people gathered there for prayer morning and night, stating that it was the tomb of one called R. Meir who took a vow that he would not lie down until the Messiah came, and was buried there in an upright position." At present it is a large building consisting of two *battei midrash* (one for Ashkenazim and one for Sephardim) covering the tomb. Some scholars connect the grave with the *tanna* *Meir, who established his school in Tiberias (TJ, Ḥag. 2:1) and has a miracle related about him (Av. Zar. 18 a/b). There are however different traditions about his place of burial, as he died in Asia and said "Place my bier (*'arsi*) on the sea shore" (TJ, Kil. 9:4, 32c). In the 13th century the tomb was connected with R. Meir Kaẓin, or Meir b. Jacob who immigrated to Ereẓ Israel with Jehiel of Paris (see Vilnay in bibl.). The name of Meir b. Isaac, author of **Akdamut* for Shavuot, has also been connected with him (*Oẓar Yisrael*). It is customary to arrange a great celebration at his grave on the 14th of Iyyar (Second Passover) which is comparable to the one in *Meron on Lag ba-Omer. The tomb was exceptionally well publicized in the Diaspora by the emissaries of Ereẓ Israel, as well as in their emissarial *iggerot* (letters). Beginning with the 18th century a Meir Ba'al ha-Nes box was found in almost every Jewish home, and housewives dropped small change into it just before kindling the Sabbath lights. Due to the miraculous deeds connected with the tomb, it was customary to contribute money, candles, or oil for lighting as a specific protection against all kinds of ailments and dangers; it was also done in the hope of finding something lost, of having children, or of driving away evil thoughts. It is clear, however, that the box also symbolized the longing for Ereẓ Israel (for the way in which the money was distributed, see Vilnay in bibl.). Craftsmen created art objects connected with Meir Ba'al ha-Nes. In spite of the opposition on the part of both rabbis and *maskilim* to the celebration and the boxes, the practice still continues.

Tomb of Meir Ba'al ha-Nes near Tiberias. Courtesy Keren Ha-yesod, United Israel Appeal, Jerusalem.

Bibliography: *Kerem Ḥemed,* 2 (1836), 16–39; *Yerushalayim,* ed. by A. M. Luncz, 1 (1880/81), 48f., 102–4; *Va-Titpallel Ḥannah,* 2 (1890); I. Ben-Zvi (ed.), *Masot Ereẓ Yisrael le-Rabbi Moshe Bassola* (1938), 75; Yaari, Sheluḥei, 927 (index); J. Braslavski, *Ha-Yadata et-ha-Areẓ* 1 (1955[6]), 88, 90, 286; Z. Vilnay, *Maẓẓevot Kodesh be-Ereẓ Yisrael* (1963[2]), 315–24; M. Ish-Shalom, *Kivrei Avot* (1948), 186–9; S. H. Kook, *Iyyunim u-Meḥkarim,* 2 (1963), 101–95. [M.H.]

MEIR BEN BARUCH HA-LEVI (d. 1404), German scholar; colleague of Abraham *Klausner. Meir came from Fulda. His chronology is obscure, but it is now generally held that his first rabbinic post was in Erfurt, where Hillel "Ha-Zaken" of Erfurt was his pupil, and that he subsequently became rabbi of Frankfort, moving to Nuremberg in 1383, and returning two years later to Frankfort. In 1391 he was imprisoned as a result of a false accusation and upon his release in 1392 became rabbi of Vienna, where he appears to have remained until his death. Meir is frequently mentioned in the works of the leading scholars of his own and the following generation, among them Jacob *Moellin, Judah *Minz, Israel *Isserlein, and Israel *Bruna, who cite his customs and rulings (under the name Maharam Segal or Maharam Sal) regarding them as authoritative. Meir's central role in Jewish life of the 14th century is reflected by the part he played in the celebrated dispute about 1393 between *Johanan Treves and Isaiah b. Abba Mari, the pupil of Johanan's father, Mattathias Treves. When Johanan was appointed to succeed his father as chief rabbi of France, Meir conferred upon Isaiah—who was apparently the greater scholar—the title *morenu,* which authorized him to assume the chief rabbinate in place of Johanan. This intervention of Meir, a German, in the affairs of the French community, aroused the opposition of many leading scholars, including *Isaac b. Sheshet, who nevertheless refers to Meir with extraordinary respect. This incident has led some scholars to believe that it was Meir who reinstated ordination in Germany, but the view is now regarded as very doubtful.

Bibliography: Breuer, in: *Zion,* 33 (1968), 15–25, 44f.; Graetz-Rabbinowitz, 6 (1898), 12f., 37–39; A. Hershman, *R. Isaac bar Sheshet Perfet and his Times* (1943), 203–13; J. Even Shmuel (Kaufman), *Yom Tov Lipman Muelhausen* (1927), 2f.; Schweinburg-Eibenschitz, in: *Neuzeit,* 34 (1894), 347ff.; M. Stern, *Die Israelitische Bevoelkerung der deutschen Staedte,* 3 (1894–96), 325f.; G. Wolf, *Geschichte der Juden in Wien* (1876), 14. [I.T.-S.]

MEIR BEN BARUCH OF ROTHENBURG (c. 1215–1293), teacher, scholar, tosafist, and supreme arbiter in ritual, legal, and community matters in Germany. He was born in Worms into a family of scholars, many members of which were important leaders in the communities of Germany. In his responsa he mentions two uncles and 12 other relatives bearing the title *Ha-Rav,* a title reserved, in this period, for talmudic scholars of high standing, mainly for heads of yeshivot. Meir often quotes their opinions and legal decisions in order to bolster his own views; hence they must have been well-known and highly esteemed scholars. Meir's father Baruch was an outstanding member of this scholarly family. He was credited with a wide knowledge of talmudic lore, was a member of the *bet din* of the community of Worms, and was often chosen to act as judge. He also bore the honorific title *Ha-Rav;* several halakhic decisions were recorded in his name; and his epitaph, preserved to this day, was written in highly laudatory terms. His teaching and guidance contributed greatly to the intellectual growth of his son. At the age of 12 Meir joined the well-known school of R. Isaac b. Moses, the author of the *Or Zaru'a,* in Wuerzburg, where he studied for about six years. While in that city Meir also studied under R. Samuel b. Menahem, in whose name, in later years, he quoted important decisions in law and ritual. Subsequently Meir moved to Mainz, where he studied under his relative R. Judah b. Moses ha-Kohen. Finally, he went to France and studied under the great tosafists *Samuel b. Solomon of Falaise, also known as Sir Morel of Falaise, and *Jehiel of Paris, known as Sir Vivo. Meir was in France in 1240 when these two teachers took part in the famous disputation with Nicolas *Donin over the Talmud. He was still there two years later, in 1242, when he witnessed the public burning of the Talmud, on which occasion he wrote his famous elegy *Sha'ali Serufah ba-Esh,* "Inquire, oh thou who art burned by fire, about the welfare of those who mourn for thee . . .," which is included to this day in the *Kinot* of the Ninth of *Av according to the Ashkenazi rite.

After this occurrence Meir returned to Germany and within a few years settled in Rothenburg, where he remained for more than 40 years, until 1286. Students flocked to his school from all the communities of Germany and its neighboring countries. Occasionally he would visit other towns for private or community business, but his home and his famous school remained in Rothenburg. His fame as a great talmudic authority spread rapidly even to other countries. In 1249, when a serious dispute arose between the communities of Bohemia and those of Moravia regarding the payment of taxes by these communities, the matter was referred to Meir for final settlement. Apparently at this early period he was already reputed to be the greatest scholar of his generation. For nearly half a century Meir acted as the supreme court of appeals for Germany and its surrounding countries. Rabbis, judges, and members of

Figure 1. Representation of Meir b. Baruch of Rothenburg in a detail from the *Rothschild Miscellany,* Italy, c. 1470. Jerusalem, Israel Museum, IM 180/51, fol. 79v. Photo David Harris, Jerusalem.

courts of arbitration sent him their questions regarding law and ritual. Individual complaints that the local courts decided contrary to talmudic law were also sent to him. He was the arbiter between communities and their members, between settlements and new settlers, and between various communities in their mutual relationships. They turned to him during their greatest crises. About a thousand of his responsa have survived, more than the combined number which have been preserved from all the other tosafists.

Meir sent his responsa to the communities of Germany, Austria, Bohemia, Italy, France, and even to Solomon b. Abraham Adret of Spain. In his lucid style and terse language he gave short, clear, and unequivocal answers to the inquirers. Sometimes he complains of the large number of responsa he is forced to write, apologizes for abbreviating the introductory greetings, is impatient with long and drawn-out questions, occasionally displays genuine anger when a case is repeatedly brought up before him because of persistent litigants, flares up in spirited temper when a litigant threatens to apply to the secular courts, and allows his passion to rise to a crescendo when confronted with serious crime. Sometimes he complained that those who addressed their queries to him overestimated his prerogatives as a talmudic scholar, and asked him to decide matters over which he had no jurisdiction. He was often unwilling to answer queries dealing with taxation, since the laws of taxation depended principally on local custom and procedures. He was very careful not to become involved in disputes and quarrels of the communities. Nevertheless, his opinion was often earnestly sought in matters involving community rights and taxes "in order to avoid the outbreak of a great quarrel."

The type of question sent to Meir speaks eloquently of the position he held in the esteem of his contemporaries. The great majority of Meir's responsa deal with business transactions, real estate, inheritance, marriage contracts, partnerships, agents, sureties, trustees, community government, community property, settling rights, and taxation. The preponderance of queries regarding civil cases and their abundance are eloquent proof of his importance as a communal leader of the first rank. Nevertheless, the opinion of many modern historians to the contrary notwithstanding, Meir held no official position as judge, as head, or as chief rabbi, of German Jewry as a whole. He was neither elected to such a position by the communities, nor was he appointed to it by the emperor. It is true that during the last two decades of his life he often took a somewhat authoritative stand in his relation to the communities. He once convoked a synod of the communities and scholars, and urged them to adopt an ordinance to the effect that a rebellious wife when divorced should forfeit her right to her *ketubbah*. On one occasion he wrote to the Jews of Wuerzburg that they should change their customary procedure in the sale of real estate, and the change was adopted in spite of the fact that some members of that community were reluctant to abandon their ancient practice. In a responsum Meir wrote: "On many occasions have individuals, whose wealth consisted of ready cash, desired to transfer the burden of taxation to real estate owners, but we did not permit them to do so." This seems to imply that in such cases Meir exercised the authority of a chief rabbi, although a thorough study of his responsa proves that he held no such official position.

Meir was highly honored and in many cases his word was law. He enjoyed this authority, however, on account of his scholarship; because many leaders of the German communities had been his students who owed him respect and even obedience; and because the Talmud was the "constitution" of community government, and Meir, the greatest scholar

Figure 2. Tombstone of Meir b. Baruch of Rothenburg at the old Jewish cemetery of Worms. Photo Shiver, Netanyah.

of the land, was its best and most authoritative interpreter. His authority was based on his knowledge of talmudic law and on his intellectual attainments, both of which enabled him to arrive at a correct decision in questions of law or ritual. Thus he once wrote to the leaders of the Rhine communities in high-spirited defiance: "You, the aforementioned community leaders, probably delude yourselves with the idea that since your permission is required before a person may divorce his wife, no scholar is permitted to render decisions in ritual law unless he receives your authorization. No, this is not true, for the Torah is free to anyone who is capable of arriving at a correct decision." (I. A. Agus (ed.), *Teshuvot Ba'alei ha-Tosafot* (1954), 143). In the community of Rothenburg, however, Meir probably did hold an official position as judge, cantor, and head of the yeshivah. His house in Rothenburg was probably provided for him by the community since it contained 21 rooms, including a *bet midrash* and rooms for his students. He did not depend on his salary for a livelihood, engaging in business. The major part of his time, however, was devoted to his studies, his students, and his correspondence with the leaders of the communities.

Meir's role in the final formulation and fixing of the law and the ritual of Ashkenazi Jewry can hardly be overestimated. His numerous responsa—collected, copied, and seriously studied for generations—greatly influenced the work of codifiers of the subsequent centuries and thus helped standardize legal procedure and civil law. He introduced certain modifications in the ritual of prayer and religious **minhag* in the synagogue and at home, and instituted many customs which later became standard practice throughout Germany and Eastern Europe. His impact on the life, the organization, and the behavior of subsequent generations was exercised mainly through the work of his students, who followed him everywhere—at home, in school, in the synagogue, and even in prison. They studied his behavior, customs, and ceremonies, and later recorded their observations in their halakhic works together with Meir's decisions on law and ritual. One student in particular, R. Samson b. Zadok, was a veritable Boswell. In his *Tashbeẓ,* he described in great detail Meir's customs and practices from the moment he rose in the morning until he went to bed at night, on weekdays, Sabbaths, and festivals. This book became popular in Germany, Austria, Bohemia, and Poland, and its details were eventually incorporated in the codes.

Meir's influence, therefore, was exerted along three main channels: (1) his students became the leaders of a number of communities in Germany, Austria, and Bohemia, and imprinted his views upon the life of the members of these communities and the surrounding territories; (2) he had a profound influence on his most eminent student, Asher b. Jehiel, and on the latter's son Jacob, the author of the *Arba'ah Turim,* and thus directly affected the final *halakhah* incorporated in the Shulḥan Arukh; (3) the *Mordekhai, Agudah, Haggahot Maimuniyyot, Sha'arei Dura,* and *Tashbeẓ,* classical works compiled by his students mainly on the basis of his decisions, responsa, and customs, were thoroughly studied by the scholars of succeeding generations and thus became the foundation for the work of R. Moses *Isserles, who incorporated the Ashkenazi usage in the Shulḥan Arukh. By far the greatest number of the views and decisions of Isserles incorporated in the above-named code stem directly or indirectly from the work and practices of Meir.

In the more than 80 of his responsa dealing with public law and community government, Meir gave the clearest and most incisive expression and explanation of the ideas of human freedom, government by consent, limitation of the power of the majority, and group responsibility—that formed part of Jewish law on the highest level of comprehension—of any other Jewish scholar before him or since. The principles of Jewish public law that man is absolutely free, that the legitimacy of government is derived solely from the free and uncoerced consent of the governed, and that the legislative power of the majority is limited to certain areas only and cannot encroach upon the private and inalienable rights of the individual were most forcefully and most clearly explained in his responsa. He thus greatly strengthened the democratic form of government of the communities—a form they derived traditionally from the forefathers of Franco-German Jewry—and it was eventually copied by the municipal governments and the guilds of the burgher class that arose in close contiguity with these Jewish communities. Thus in the 15th century, in the legislation intended for the benefit of the whole group the principle "majority rules" was applied, while particular legislative acts that encroached upon the rights and the immunities of the individual did not become law unless unanimous agreement by the membership of the group was achieved (Otto v. Gierke, *Das deutsche Genossenschaftsrecht,* vol. 2, pp. 230–2, and 478–9). This division of legislation into two categories and the requirement of unanimity in the second category, paralleled in practically every detail the form of community legislation, so clearly described by Rabbi Meir, could only have been the result of direct copying by the burghers and town communes of the community system of government that antedated their own by several centuries. Meir's peaceful life as a scholar and teacher was rudely interrupted by the turbulent political events that followed the termination of the interregnum and the election of Rudolph I of Hapsburg as emperor of Germany. In order to reestablish the right of the emperor to tax the Jews, which during the interregnum of 1254–1273 had been claimed by the local dukes, Rudolph I began to press the claim that the term *servi camerae* ("serfs of the treasury")—which in the 13th century began to gain ascendancy as the legal description of the political status of the Jews—really meant that the Jews were the slaves of the treasury of the empire, that their persons and their possessions were therefore the property of the treasury of the empire, and that the emperor therefore possessed the right to tax the Jews over and above the taxes they paid to the local rulers; and in 1286 he did impose such a tax on them. As a result thousands of Jews decided to leave Germany. Meir, especially outraged at this attempt to enslave the Jews, became the leader of the widespread exodus. In the spring of 1286, he "set out to go across the sea together with his family, his daughters, and his sons-in-law." However, while he was waiting for his followers in Lombardy, he was recognized by an apostate who informed against him, with the result that the ruler of that town, Count Meinhardt of Goerz, arrested Meir and delivered him to Rudolph I. The emperor put him in prison, first in Wasserburg and then in Ensisheim, until the day of his death. The Jews made great efforts to effect the release of their beloved teacher—at one time agreeing to pay 23,000 pounds of silver to the emperor, but stipulating that the money was a payment of ransom and not of taxes—but without success. Rudolph I was determined to use the great devotion of the Jews to their teacher to force them to admit the right of the emperor to tax them. However, since a payment of taxes would be an admission that they were slaves, the Jews found it impossible to agree. Meir, therefore, remained in prison, and even after his death in 1293, his body was not delivered to the Jews until 1307 when it was redeemed by Alexander b. Salomo Wimpfen for a large sum of money and buried in Worms.

Rabbi Meir wrote *tosafot* and novellae to 18 tractates of the Talmud—the *tosafot* to *Yoma,* in the printed text of the Talmud are from his pen; commentaries to the two orders of the Mishnah *Zera'im* and *Tohorot;* compendia of laws for special purposes, such as *Hilkhot Eruvin, Halakhot Pesukot, Hilkhot Berakhot, Hilkhot Semaḥot, Hilkhot Sheḥitah, Hilkhot Hatmanah;* a collection of customs connected with the marriage ceremony and with the wording of the *ketubbah;* and, most important, nearly 1,000 responsa found in the following collections which differ to a great extent in content: Cremona, 1557; Prague, 1608 (reprinted in Sudilkov, 1835, and in Budapest, 1895); Lemberg, 1860; and Berlin, 1891–92; aside from those incorporated in the works of his students. Some of his responsa were published from manuscripts by I. Z. Kahana (Jerusalem, 1943) and by I. A. Agus (see bibl.). Meir also composed liturgical poems (in addition to the above-mentioned "Inquire thou who art burnt by fire . . .") and a collection of masoretic explanations (in I. Z. Kahana's *Teshuvot, Pesakim u-Minhagim,* 1 (1957), 3–41).

Bibliography: I. A. Agus, *Rabbi Meir of Rothenburg,* 2 vols. (1947); S. Back, *Rabbi Meir b. Baruch aus Rothenburg* (1895); H. J. Zimmels, *Beitraege zur Geschichte der Juden in Deutschland im 13. Jahrhundert* (1926); J. Wellescz, in: REJ, 58 (1909), 226–40; 59 (1910), 42–58; 60 (1910), 53–72; 61 (1911), 44–59; Urbach, Tosafot, 405–46.

[I.A.A.]

MEIR BEN ELIJAH (early 19th century), author of the ethical and educational work, *Naḥalat Avot* ("The Inheritance of the Fathers," Vilna, 1835). Although written in the form of an *ethical will—the author seemingly directing his teachings toward his own sons—the book is intended for the ethical betterment of the general public. Meir's principal concern is demonstrating the way to achieve reverence toward God, but he also deals with man's struggle against his own evil inclination, the best methods by which to educate one's children, proper behavior at home and in the synagogue, and social and religious ethics. The book is prefaced by a *piyyut*, with the *notarikon* of the author's name, and two opening statements, one encouraging sinners to repent, and the other insisting on repeated study of ethical literature. Among his major sources are the *Zohar and *Sefer *Ḥasidim*, which he quotes frequently; the *Shenei Luḥot ha-Berit* by R. Isaiah ha-Levi Horowitz; and a more contemporary source—*Nefesh ha-Ḥayyim* by R. Ḥayyim of *Volozhin. In addition, Meir mentions *Ma'alot ha-Torah*, a work composed by his grandfather. Meir also wrote a commentary on the tractate *Avot*, *Derekh Avot*, printed in Vilna, 1836. [Ed.]

MEIR BEN ELIJAH OF NORWICH (13th century; also called **Meir of England**), liturgical poet and *ḥazzan*. Meir's family came from France, and his father was apparently a *dayyan*. Meir lived in Norwich and was among those exiled from England in 1290. His *piyyut "Oyevi bi-Me'erah Tikkov"* ("Thou wilt curse mine enemy with execration") was composed on this exile, as its heading states: "For the severity of the exile and the killings, the imprisonment, and the destruction of property." A great Torah scholar, Meir was the only known English *paytan*. His *piyyutim* contain some elements of the Ashkenazi *piyyut* and some of the Spanish. Strong phrases on the suffering of the nation find their expression through his poetry. His *piyyut* for Passover *Mitnasse ba-Marom al Keruvo* ("Uplifted on High upon His Cherub" called by him "Who is like Thee") is one of the longest acrostics in the Hebrew *piyyut*. Besides the alphabet, autobiographical information is also contained in the acrostic. Meir's secular poems, which he called *ḥaruzot* ("stanzas")—16 in all, with an additional poem explaining the form and the construction of the poems—are written in the meter of the Spanish-Hebrew poetry, but do not have its glitter and originality. Sent to one of his friends, the poems were arranged in an order unknown in the poetry of others, namely in four parts *("banim")* following the letters of his name Meir *(Benei M(-em) Benei A(-lef)*, etc., i.e., poems whose stanzas begin with the letters *mem, alef*, etc.). The first two letters of each stanza are also repeated at the end of the stanza.

Bibliography: V. D. Lipman, *The Jews of Medieval Norwich* (1967), with the poems edited by A. M. Habermann; Davidson, Oẓar (1933), 432; A. Berliner, in: *Magazin fuer die Wissenschaft des Judenthums*, 16 (1889), 52–55; Zunz, Lit Poesie, 328; Roth, England, 127; Urbach, Tosafot, 279; J. Schirmann, in: KS, 43 (1967/68), 450–1; A. Berliner, *Hebraeische Poesien des Meir ben Elia aus Norwich* (1887). [A.M.H.]

MEIR (Moses Meir) BEN EPHRAIM OF PADUA (d. 1583), scribe, printer, and teacher in Mantua. Meir was presumably born in Padua but lived in Mantua, where he served in various communal capacities. Meir's exceptional talent and his skill as a scribe were attested to by his disciple, Abraham *Portaleone. Meir noted down detailed descriptions of all 43 Torah scrolls written by him. Questions addressed to his close friend, Moses b. Abraham *Provencal, the rabbi of Mantua, indicate Meir's rabbinical scholarship, as does his treatise on the diacritical marks of the Torah, *Rimzei ha-Tagim*. In 1556 Meir founded a printing establishment at Mantua, in collaboration with Jacob b. Naphtali of Garolo (d. c. 1570), and his considerable contribution to the printing of Hebrew books included the first edition of the Zohar (1558–1560).

Bibliography: D. W. Amram, *The Makers of Hebrew Books in Italy* (1909), 323–33; *Kaufmann*, in: JQR, 11 (1899) 266–90; S. Simonsohn, *Toledot ha-Yehudim be-Dukkasut Mantovah*, 2 (1964), 531f. [Ed.]

MEIR BEN ḤIYYA ROFE (1610?–1690?), scholar and emissary of Hebron, Palestine. Born in Safed, the son of *Ḥiyya Rofe, Meir was orphaned in boyhood. He studied in Hebron, leaving about 1648 as an emissary to Italy, Holland, and Germany. On his return journey, he stayed for two years in Italy to publish *Ma'aseh Ḥiyya* (Venice, 1652), his father's talmudic novellae and responsa. In Amsterdam he had influenced the wealthy Abraham Pereira to found a yeshivah in Hebron to be called Ḥesed le-Avraham, of which Meir himself became a scholar. Meir was in Gaza in 1665 when *Nathan of Gaza began to prophecy on the messianism of *Shabbetai Ẓevi. In a subsequent letter to Amsterdam, to Abraham Pereira, he wrote that "Nathan of Gaza is a wise man fit for the divine presence to rest upon him," and urged Pereira to come to Gaza. Pereira reached Venice, but returned to Holland. Meir maintained his belief even after Shabbetai Ẓevi's conversion in 1666. In 1672 Meir left, again as an emissary of Hebron, for Turkey. He stayed for a time in Adrianople, where he was in contact with Shabbetai Ẓevi. On Shabbetai's exile to Albania in 1673, Meir returned to Gaza where he stayed with Nathan and even copied his writings for his own use. He then traveled again to Italy, and from 1675 to 1678 resided in the home of the Shabbatean Abraham *Rovigo. Throughout his stay in Italy Meir did much to encourage those who believed in Shabbetai Ẓevi and spread the writings of Nathan of Gaza. During the last ten years of his life he was recognized as the outstanding scholar of Hebron.

Bibliography: Yaari, Sheluḥei, 160–1, 464–6; Benayahu, in: *Sinai*, 35 (1954/55), 61–62; idem, in: *Yerushalayim, Meḥkerei Ereẓ Yisrael*, 5 (1955), 152–6, 176–80, 186; Scholem, Shabbetai Ẓevi, index: Tishby, in: *Sefunot*, 3–4 (1960), 71–130. [A.Ya.]

MEIR BEN ISAAC OF TRINQUETAILLE (12th century), Provençal scholar. Knowledge of Meir is largely derived from Menahem b. Solomon *Meiri's introduction to his commentary on *Avot*. Born in Carcassonne, the young Meir b. Isaac was brought by his father to Posquières to study under *Abraham b. David, and after many years Meir became his pupil-colleague. Meir's retort to his teacher, when the latter attempted to force his opinion upon him in a halakhic matter, has become well known: "Do not make light of my honor. For if you are unique among teachers, I am unique among pupils." From Posquières Meir apparently went to Trinquetaille, near Arles. In Meir's comprehensive work *(Sefer ha-Ezer)*, written in defense of the *halakhot* of Isaac *Alfasi against the *hassagot* of *Zerahiah b. Isaac ha-Levi (the author of *Ha-Ma'or*), the influence of Meir's great teacher who wrote a similar book is clearly recognizable. Although the book has not been preserved, it is quoted by the *rishonim*—among them *Manoah b. Jacob (who also mentions Meir's *Ḥibbur ha-Mukẓeh*, and *Estori ha-Parḥi, Meir's great-grandson. Menahem b. Solomon Meiri also claims family connection with him.

Meir's son, Nathan of Trinquetaille, was a well-known scholar and a disciple of the eminent tosafist, *Isaac b. Abraham. He later became the teacher of *Naḥmanides, Samuel b. Isaac ha-Sardi (see *Sardi), and Meir b. Simeon ha-Meili. Naḥmanides, Sardi, and Estori ha-Parḥi in particular, quote Nathan frequently. From their quotations it is clear that Nathan wrote a comprehensive work on civil law which was divided into *she'arim* ("gates") as well as a commentary on the Torah. Nathan's commentary on tractate *Shevu'ot* is always mentioned.

Bibliography: Gross, Gal Jud, 246f.; idem, in: MGWJ, 27 (1878), 378ff.; I. Twersky, *Rabad of Posquieres* (1962), 245f. [I.T.-S.]

MEIR BEN ISAAC SHELI'AḤ ẒIBBUR (also called **Nehorai;** d. before 1096), preacher and liturgical poet of Worms. Meir was considered authoritative in the sphere of liturgy and custom among the Franco-German communities. He appears also to have compiled a custumal for the whole year. Many of the great scholars of Germany and France in his own and in the following generations frequently mention him with esteem and cite his words: Rashi in his prayer book and in his commentary to Scripture, the *tosafists, *Simḥah of Vitry in the *Maḥzor Vitry,* *Abraham b. Azriel in his *Arugat ha-Bosem,* Jacob *Moellin, in his custumal, and others. Several legends were created about him. Meir compiled **piyyutim* and **selihot* in Hebrew and Aramaic, more than 50 of which are extant. A number of his *piyyutim* for the festivals were accepted by the Franco-German and Polish communities and were published innumerable times in *maḥzorim* and among *seliḥot.* The best known of his *piyyutim* is the Aramaic **Akdamut Millin,* which is customarily said to the present day in Ashkenazi communities during Shavuot after the reading of the first verse of the Torah reading (Ex. 19:1); a number of scholars, however, introduced the custom of saying it before the reading of the Torah. It was translated into Hebrew by Gabriel *Polack (*Literaturblatt des Orients* (2 (1850), 554–5) and *Ben Gorni* (1851, 52–55)), and by others as well. It has also been translated into other languages (into English by Joseph Marcus in *Maḥzor,* United Synagogue of America, 1927). *Menahem b. Ḥelbo wrote commentaries on Meir's *piyyutim.* Two of his sons—Jacob and Isaac—are known; the latter perished in the pogroms of 1096.

Bibliography: Zunz, Lit Poesie, 145–52, 248–50, 610; Zunz, Poesie, index; Landshuth, Ammudei, 162–7; Elbogen, Gottesdienst, 334–5; Germ Jud, 1 (1934), 446–7; E. E. Urbach (ed.), Abraham b. Azriel, *Arugat ha-Bosem,* 4 (1963), index; Davidson, Oẓar, 4 (1933), 432; D. Goldschmidt, in: KS, 34 (1958/59), 391–2; H. Schirmann, in *Divrei ha-Akademyah ha-Le'ummit ha-Yisre'elit le-Madda'im,* 3 (1969/70), 36–37, 55, 61–62. [A.D.]

MEIR BEN SAMUEL OF RAMERUPT (c. 1060–c. 1135), one of the first tosafists of northern France. Meir's teachers were the scholars of Lorraine, *Isaac ha-Levi of Worms, *Eliezer of Mainz, and *Rashi, whose daughter, Jochebed, he married. Of his sons, three, who were also his pupils, are especially known—*Samuel b. Meir (Rashbam), *Isaac b. Meir, and Jacob b. Meir *Tam. His son-in-law was Samuel of Vitry, father-in-law of the tosafist *Isaac b. Samuel ha-Zaken. For a certain period Meir apparently dwelt with his father-in-law in Troyes, but he moved to Ramerupt during Rashi's lifetime, founding a *bet ha-midrash* there. He is sometimes designated *ha-yashish* ("the venerable") or "the father of the rabbis." Meir wrote commentaries to the Talmud, similar to those of his father-in-law and of his son Samuel. One extant section of his commentaries was incorporated in the commentary of Rashi to the Talmud and some of his *tosafot* are included in the *tosafot* of the standard Talmud editions. Halakhic statements by him are quoted in the *Sefer ha-Yashar* of his son Jacob Tam, in the *Or Zaru'a,* in the *Sefer ha-Ittur,* and elsewhere. Biblical comments by him are quoted by his son Samuel in his commentary to the Pentateuch. These are permeated by a spirit of literal exegesis and it is probable that the son was influenced in this by the father. The present text of **Kol Nidrei* is the result of amendments introduced by him into the original formula. There are extant responsa written to him by Rashi, and also a responsum written by them jointly. Meir also composed a *seliḥah, Avo Lefanekha* ("I come before Thee").

Bibliography: Urbach, Tosafot, 38–42, and index. [Z.K.]

MEIR BEN SAMUEL OF SHCHERBRESHIN (Pol. **Szczebrzeszyn;** mid-17th century), *paytan* and chronicler who lived in a small town near Lublin, Poland. His known writings consist of *Shir Mizmor le-Yom ha-Shabbat* ("Psalm for the Sabbath," Venice, 1639) and a rhymed account in Hebrew of the *Chmielnicki persecutions of 1648–49, written during the summer of 1650, and which is to be read "at all times, but especially during the three weeks of mourning between the 17th of Tammuz and the Ninth of Av and on the 20th of Sivan," the latter being the fast day in commemoration of the persecutions. The work was published during the same summer in Cracow, under the title *Ẓok ha-Ittim* ("Sufferings of the Times"). In the spirit of the accounts of the sufferings during the First *Crusade (1096), the author describes the persecutions of his own day as related to him by fugitives and, in part, as he witnessed them himself in Zamosc and the surrounding region in the summer of 1649. *Ẓok ha-Ittim* is of greater historical importance than the other Jewish chronicles of these persecutions, which were mostly written and published some time after the events by refugees in distant places who could not, for various reasons, give all the details.

Bibliography: H. Y. Gurland, *Le-Korot ha-Gezerot al Yisrael,* 4 (1889–90), 7–61; Halpern, in: *Zion,* 25 (1960), 17–56. [I.HA.]

MEIR BEN SIMEON HA-ME'ILI (first half of 13th century), Provençal talmudist and communal leader. Meir's main center of activity was *Narbonne, and he cites many of its customs in his works. His principal teacher was his uncle, *Meshullam b. Moses, and Meir frequently cites him and his customs. He also studied under *Nathan b. Meir of Trinquetaille. There are references to his connections with Naḥmanides, another pupil of Nathan b. Meir. Among his other activities, Meir engaged in disputations with Christian eccelesiastics and was one of the chief speakers in a delegation of the Jewish leaders of Narbonne and Capestang who interceded with the cardinal of Narbonne concerning discriminating laws which it was proposed to issue against the Jews. He was spokesman of the community at the court of the emperor, and before ministers and church leaders. According to Gross and Scholem, his work *Milḥemet Mitzvah* (Ms. Parma, cat. De Rossi (1803) no. 155 only part of which was published; see below) was written between 1230 and 1240. The work itself, however, gives the date 1245, and it seems to contain matters of a still later date (see Gross in: MGWJ, 30 (1881), 296). The work contains an account of his disputation with the bishop of Narbonne, a defense of Judaism against the allegations of Christians, explanations of biblical verses dealing with the coming of the Messiah, and a commentary on the **Shema* and the 13 divine attributes. Meir also appears in this work as a vehement opponent of a certain circle of kabbalists, to whom he attributes heretical views. Questioning the authenticity of *Sefer ha-Bahir,* he sharply criticizes its contents, together with other kabbalistic works. These criticisms were included in an "epistle" sent to "our rabbis in every town." His work was also directed against the ideas of some kabbalists based on works which, according to Meir, were forgeries attributed to well-known scholars. At the end of this epistle he gives Meshullam's commendation to his activity.

Only latterly have his works begun to be published, under the title *Sefer ha-Me'orot:* novellae to (1) tractates *Berakhot* and *Pesaḥim* (1964); (2) to *Shabbat* (1964); (3) *Mo'ed Katan* and *Ḥullin* (1964); (4) *Eruvin* (1967); (5) *Yoma, Sukkah, Beẓah, Rosh Ha-Shanah, Ta'anit* and *Megillah,* and the minor tractates (1967). His commentary on the **hoshanot* was published in *Sefer ha-Mikhtam,* edited by A. Sofer (1959). The *Milḥemet Mitzvah* contains five sections (504 columns) and a fragment of it was published by G. Scholem (bibl.) and the end of section four with part of section five in *Sefer ha-Me'orot*, volume one. Also known are his novellae to the order *Kodashim* (mentioned by Bezalel Askenazi in *Kelalei ha-Talmud* no. 37; A. Marx, in: *Festschrift . . . D. Hoffmann* (1914) Heb. pt. 181); *Me'or Torah*, a commentary on the weekly portions of the Pentateuch; sermons (for Passover, the New Year, and Tabernacles in the manner of the sermons of Abraham b. David and Naḥmanides); and a pamphlet called *Meshiv Nefesh* defending Maimonides' *Hilkhot Yesodei ha-Torah* in his *Mishneh Torah* against his critics.

Bibliography: Renan, Rabbins, 558–62; Neubauer, in: *Israelitische Letterbode*, 3 (1877–78), 20f.; idem, in: REJ, 10 (1885), 98f.; idem, in: JQR, 4 (1892), 358; H. Gross, in: MGWJ, 30 (1881), 295–305, 444–52; 554–69; Gross, Gal Jud, 423–25; Meshullam b. Moses, *Sefer ha-Hashlamah le-Seder Nezikim*, ed. by J. Lubetzky, 1 (1885), introd. 5 n. 2, 14; idem, *Sefer ha-Hashlamah al Massekhet Berakhot*, ed. by M. Schochor (1892) introd. by H. Brody, 14; J. Lubetzky, *Bidkei Battim* (1896), introd. 9, 12, 14f., 22f.; G. Scholem in: *Sefer Bialik* (1934), 146–50; M. Y. Blau (ed.), *Sefer ha-Me'orot le-Rabbenu Meir b. R. Shimon . . . ve-Sefer ha-Hashlamah le . . . Meshullam b. R. Moshe . . . al Massekhtot Berakhot u-Fesaḥim* (1964), introd; Dinur, Golah, 1 pt. 1 (n.d.[2]) 136f., 180 n. 35, 2 pt. 1 (1965[2]), 290 n. 35, 291 no. 44, 2 pt. 3 (1968[2]), 168–70, 339 n. 119; S. Stein, in: JJS, 10 (1960), 45–63. [S.Z.H.]

MEIRI, MENAHEM BEN SOLOMON (1249–1316), Provençal scholar and commentator of the Talmud. Meiri was born in Perpignan where he spent his whole life. His family, regarded as one of the most distinguished in Provence, originated from Carcassonne and Narbonne. Few biographical details are known of Meiri. In his youth he was orphaned of his father, and his children were taken captive while he was still young (Introduction to *Kiryat Sefer*), but no details of this personal tragedy are known. Meiri's principal teacher was *Reuben b. Ḥayyim. His reference to *Jonah Gerondi as "my teacher" does not necessarily mean that he studied under him: it may merely mean that he studied his works. Among the contemporary scholars with whom he maintained close ties was Solomon b. Abraham *Adret; they exchanged many responsa and Adret's teachings assisted him in the writing of his monumental work. Meiri was one of the participants in Adret's polemic against Maimonides which ended in Adret's excommunicating any person who read philosophical works in his youth. In a letter to *Abba Mari b. Moses Joseph, who handled the entire affair and collected the relevant correspondence, Meiri disassociated himself from the attitude of Adret and his colleagues, upholding freedom of thought for the scholars of each country, and freedom from intervention by outside scholars. Extracts from Meiri's letter (republished by D. Kaufmann along with the reply by Joseph b. Simeon in the name of Abba Mari under the title *Ḥoshen Mishpat* in the *Jubelschrift . . . L. Zunz* (1884; Heb. sec. 142–74), reveal his great interest in philosophy and other secular sciences, and reflect his pride in the local scholars who had acquired proficiency in them.

Meiri occupies a central position in the sphere of the talmudic creativity of Provence, not only due to his extraordinary literary fecundity and the comprehensive scope of his works, but also because he summarizes the teachings of his predecessors during the previous three centuries. In effect he puts the seal upon the literary efforts in this area of Jewish culture. His literary activity covered halakhic rulings, talmudic exposition, biblical exegesis, customs, ethics, and philosophy. The vast majority of Meiri's works remained in manuscript until very recently, probably on account of their exceptional length, which made it practically impossible to copy them in full. A small number of his books were published in the second half of the 18th century and the majority of them—from the beginning of the 20th century up to the present day. A great contribution to this project was by A. *Sofer (Schreiber). An exception is his commentary to the Book of Proverbs which was first published in Portugal in 1492, and then included in the *Kehillot Moshe* edition of *Mikra'ot Gedolot* (Amsterdam, 1724).

Meiri's chief work is the gigantic *Beit ha-Beḥirah* on the Talmud, in which he was engaged from 1287 to 1300. In it he summarizes the subject matter of the Talmud, giving both the meaning and the *halakhah* derived from it. It follows the order of the Mishnah. The work covers the orders of *Mo'ed*, *Nashim*, and *Nizikin*, and the tractates, *Berakhot*, *Ḥallah*, *Ḥullin*, *Niddah*, *Tamid*, *Middot*, and *Mikva'ot*. *Beit ha-Beḥirah* has been republished almost in its entirety in recent years from a single complete manuscript (Parma). Of particular interest is the introduction to his commentary on *Avot*, in which he gives the chain of tradition of Torah study from its outset to his own time. It contains valuable material for the knowledge of the history of Torah study in Spain and Provence, and was copied out in full and completed (updated) to his own time by Isaac *Lattes in his *Sha'arei Ẓiyyon* (ed. by S. Buber, 1885). In addition to *Beit ha-Beḥirah*, Meiri wrote commentaries on the Talmud which were expository rather than halakhic in orientation. Although the manuscripts in this group of a number of tractates are still extant, none has been published, except for the commentary to *Avot* and the *Beit ha-Beḥirah* to the tractate, *Beẓah* (ed. by I. S. Lang and K. Schlesinger, 1956), which apparently belong to this group. Meiri follows an original method of exposition. He develops his theme from its origin and for this reason he assigns a separate section to the Mishnah and explains it before turning to the later development and discussions in the later literature. Each tractate and its individual chapters is preceded by a short preface outlining the subject in general terms. The discussion begins with a presentation of the fundamental principles involved and proceeds with an explanation of the opinions of each of the *amoraim*. The author in conclusion sums up and collates these opinions, giving the relevant *halakhah* as he sees it. An abundance of comments handed down by German, Provençal, and Spanish scholars with their different interpretations are incorporated, but each one is given separately to prevent confusion on the part of the reader. Meiri was one of the few rabbis of his time to make extensive use of the Jerusalem Talmud in order to clarify the parallel discussions in the Babylonian Talmud, and his works are therefore of added importance for research on the Jerusalem Talmud and its variant readings. Meiri's style contributes much to the lucidity of his presentation. His Hebrew is accurate, precise, and simple. In addition, he succeeded in finding the golden mean between the generally contradictory aims of expository comprehensiveness and halakhic definitiveness. These features endeared the *Beit ha-Beḥirah* to scholars and its volumes are now repeatedly republished in spite of their great length.

Meiri adopted the unusual practice of designating his predecessors by epithet rather than by name, e.g., "the greatest of authors" (Maimonides), "the greatest of *posekim*" (Alfasi), "the early scholars of Narbonne," "the former scholars of Catalonia," and "the great scholars of Provence." As a result it is difficult now to determine to whom he is referring, especially as he often employs the same epithet for many scholars who, in his opinion, belong to the same "genre." On the other hand, it is clear that Meiri utilized all the rabbinic literature available to him, so that his work may be considered the first effort to create a kind of *"Shitah Mekubbeẓet,"* a digest which gives a synoptic and comprehensive presentation of the whole expository and halakhic activity up to his own time, ignoring individual efforts and establishing it upon a collective or local basis. His admirable style makes it impossible to detect the verbatim quotations which no doubt he gives from the sources, since it became one harmonious whole. He employed this method only in *Beit ha-Beḥirah*.

Meiri wrote several other important works. His first, written in his youth, was *Ḥibbur ha-Teshuvah* devoted entirely to ethics and repentance. It clearly reveals the influence of the *Malmad ha-Talmidim* of Jacob *Anatoli, the first Provençal scholar to stimulate interest in the meaning of the precepts as distinct from their observance. It may be assumed that toward the end of his life Meiri revised the work, which in its present form, bears the character of a well constructed sermon book. Extracts from it were published in various places; it was published in its entirety for the first time in 1950.

Meiri's commentary to Proverbs, and even more, his commentary to Psalms (1936), reveal all his exegetical and stylistic characteristics as well as his love for explicitness. In them he draws upon the Midrashim and the accepted ethical and wisdom literature of the Middle Ages, such as **Ben ha-Melekh ve-ha-Nazir* and *Muserei ha-Filosofim*, and also makes frequent use of the works of the great grammarians, such as Abraham *ibn Ezra, Jonah *ibn Janaḥ, and the *Kimḥi family. Corrections to the text of the commentary to Psalms were published in *Kobez al Jad*, New Series, 4 (1946), 229–40. Another of his works, *Kiryat Sefer* (1863–81), contains the laws of writing the **Sefer Torah*, including lists of those words written *plene* and those written defectively, and of the "open" and "closed" sections of the Torah. *Kiryat Sefer*, composed in 1306, was considered for many years as one of the three basic works on the laws of writing a *Sefer Torah*—all the great *posekim* and masoretes making use of it. *Kiryat Sefer* was based upon Provencal and Spanish traditions as well as upon a copy of a *Sefer Torah* written by Meir *Abulafia for his own use. However, 150 years after Meiri's death, more and more of Abulafia's manuscripts of *Masoret Seyag la-Torah* were circulated, which did not correspond with the *Sefer Torah* Meiri had written and as a result the reliability of *Kiryat Sefer* began to be called into question. Meiri wrote *Magen Avot* (ed. by I. Last, 1909) to uphold the customs of Provence in general and Perpignan in particular, against those of Spain, particularly Gerona, held by *Naḥmanides and brought by his disciples to Provence after its annexation to Spain during the reign of John I (1213–1276). In its 24 chapters, each devoted to the discussion of a different custom, Meiri asserts the value and superiority of these local traditions as against the great authority of Naḥmanides.

In recent years many collections of extracts from Meiri's works, arranged according to subject, have been published, including a commentary to the Passover *Haggadah* (1965; ed. by M. M. Meshi-Zahav); *Sefer ha-Middot* (idem (ed.), 1966), a guide to proper conduct; and an anthology of his biblical expositions (1957), by J. I. Gad. Meiri stands out as the embodiment of the highest qualities which characterized Provençal Jewry: greatness in Torah combined with a leaning toward, and an appreciation of, philosophy, secular erudition, and the sciences in general; unswerving attachment to custom and tradition coupled with a high-minded tolerance of gentile society, and brilliant Torah creativity, brought to expression in fluent, even poetic Hebrew. Meiri was also the last Provençal scholar to embody this synthesis.

Bibliography: S. B. Sofer, *Or ha-Me'ir* (1942); M. N. Zobel, in: *Eder ha-Yakar ... Mukdashim le-S. A. Horodezky* (1947), 88–96; S. K. Mirsky, in: *Talpioth*, 4 (1949–50), 1–90; J. Katz, in: *Zion*, 18 (1953), 15–30; I. Preis-Horev, in: KS, 14 (1937–38), 16–20 no. 56; I. Ta-Shema, *ibid.*, 45 (1970); D. Hoffmann, *Der Schulchan Arukh und die Rabbinen ueber das Verhaeltniss der Juden zu Andersglaeubigen* (1894[2]), 4–7; J. Stein, in: MGWJ, 82 (1938), 46–56; J. Lévi, in: REJ, 38 (1899), 103–22; S. Deutschlaender, in: *Festschrift ... J. Rosenheim* (1931), Heb. pt., 82–86; S. K. Mirsky, in: A. Sofer and S. K. Mirsky (eds.), *Ḥibbur ha-Teshuvah le-R. Menaḥem b. Shelomo ha-Me'iri* (1950), 1–80. [I.T.-S.]

MEIR JEHIEL HA-LEVI (Holzstock, Holzstick) OF OSTROWIEC (1851–1928), ḥasidic rabbi and scholar. Meir Jehiel was born to a poor family of humble origin, but through his outstanding gifts became one of the foremost

Meir Jehiel ha-Levi of Ostrowiec, ḥasidic rabbi and scholar. Jerusalem, J.N.U.L., Schwadron Collection.

leaders of Orthodox Jewry. He was a pupil of Elimelech of Grodzisk and like him settled in Ostrowiec, where many thousands of Ḥasidim became his disciples. Meir Jehiel was acknowledged as one of the greatest scholars of his age, and for a time no important decision on *halakhah* or Jewish life was made without consulting him. His form of Ḥasidism was original; his sermons were based on complicated equations from **gematria* by which he interpreted many texts in *halakhah* and *aggadah*. He was of an ascetic turn of mind, and made a long series of fasts over forty years. As he did not permit his books to be printed in his lifetime, only a fraction of his sayings and writings has been preserved. His son Ezekiel (1887–1943), rabbi of Nasielsk, was his successor. Some of his sayings are found in: *Or Torah*, edited by his disciple Judah Joseph Leibush (1920) and in M. Nomberg's *Omer Man* (1912). [A.St.]

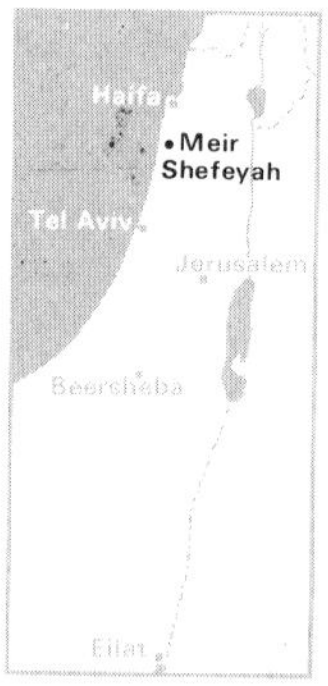

ME'IR SHEFEYAH (Heb. מֵאִיר שְׁפֵיָה), agricultural school and youth village in central Israel, on the southern slope of Mt. Carmel near *Zikhron Ya'akov, founded in 1892 by Baron Edmond de *Rothschild to provide farmsteads for the sons of Zikhron Ya'akov settlers. In 1904, after the Kishinev pogrom, Israel *Belkind established a home at Me'ir Shefeyah for orphans of the pogrom. In World War I, the Herzlia High School was transferred there from Tel Aviv when the Turkish authorities ordered the city's evacuation. In 1923 a youth village was set up, which was included in the 1930s in the network of *Youth Aliyah. The population, including pupils, reached about 450 in 1969. The name is composed of the Hebraized form of the former Arabic name of the place, and the name of Mayer Amschel *Rothschild. [E.O.]

MEIR SIMḤAH HA-KOHEN OF DVINSK (1843–1926), talmudic scholar. His brilliance was such that he is said to have annotated the halakhic work of a distinguished rabbi when only 13 years old. At the age of 17 he went to Eishishok where he studied under R. Moses Danishevsky. Meir Simḥah married the daughter of Ẓevi Paltiel, a wealthy man from Bialystok who supported him while he continued his studies under the local rabbi, Yom Tov Lipman Halpern, the author of *Oneg Yom Tov* (1880). With the publication of his work, *Or Same'aḥ* on Maimonides (1902–26), Meir Simḥah became widely renowned as an outstanding talmudic scholar and commentator. His novellae *Or Same'aḥ* to *Baba Kamma* and *Bava Meẓia* were published in Jerusalem (1948), and his novellae to most of the tractates of the orders *Nashim* and *Nezikin*, together with some responsa and occasional notes were printed in 1967 from a manuscript identified as his in the Jewish National and University Library. In these fundamental and classic works of rabbinic literature, he shed new light on the Talmud and codifiers, displaying vast erudition, great depth, and profound logic. On the advice of R. Jacob Ḥarif of Zagare and R. Joseph B. *Soloveichik of Brest-Litovsk, he was invited to become rabbi of Dvinsk, a position he occupied for 40 years. Meir Simḥah earned the high esteem of all communal circles, not only in Dvinsk, but far beyond its borders. In 1906 he declined the offer of a rabbinical position in Jerusalem, as a result of the entreaties of the community of Dvinsk who wrote to the leaders in Jerusalem that were he to leave, "not only would we, God forfend, be destroyed, but also the entire Diaspora. For he is the authority able to answer anyone who enquires concerning the word of the Lord. It is not for you, people of Jerusalem, to do such a thing." In 1911 he presided jointly with Isaac Jacob Rabinovitz, the rabbi of Ponevezh, over the Central Committee of Rabbis, the representative body of Russian Jewry in its relations with the government. During World War I most of the Dvinsk community fled, and only a few of the poorest inhabitants remained. Meir Simḥah stayed with them, declaring that as long as there were nine Jews in the city he would be the tenth.

In his work on the Pentateuch, *Meshekh Ḥokhmah* (1927), he drew freely on his vast knowledge of the two Talmuds and of the halakhic and aggadic Midrashim, giving new and profound interpretations. The book, which contains original reflections, attained wide popularity. *Zera Avraham* (1929) by Abraham Luftvir, consists of an exchange of correspondence between Luftvir and Menahem *Ẓemba, and also includes some fine specimens of Meir Simḥah's responsa to him.

Bibliography: *Yahadut Lita*, 3 (1967), 65f.; S. Y. Zevin, *Ishim ve-Shitot* (1966[3]), 155–87. [Mo.Ha.]

MEISEL, MAURICI, last president of the Warsaw Jewish community before the Holocaust (1937–39). In the elections held in 1936, after *Agudat Israel had been in power for six years, the *Bund increased its strength to become the largest party. As the three most prominent groups (the Zionists, the Orthodox, and the Bund) could not reach agreement on the establishment of an effective administration, the government dissolved the community council. Meisel was appointed community president, and a committee of independent personalities, including Adam *Czerniakow, Mark Lichtenbaum, Kaminer (Orthodox), and the lawyer Zondelewicz, was formed to assist him. Meisel himself was a leader of the merchants' association and an assimilationist in outlook. The attitude of the parties' delegates and the public toward the government appointment was negative. Meisel was essentially an administrator who sought to assure regular and vital services while obeying the instructions of the authorities; the latter supported him in the face of violent criticism from the public and the Jewish press. When the Nazis invaded Poland, he fled from Warsaw; the mayor appointed Adam Czerniakow in his place.

Bibliography: H. M. Rabinowicz, *Legacy of Polish Jewry* (1965), 123–4. [M.Lan.]

MEISEL (Meisl, Meysl, Miška, Akhbar, Maušel, Konír), MORDECAI (Marcus, Marx) BEN SAMUEL (1528–1601), Prague financier, philanthropist, and head of the Jewish community. He was considered by *Graetz the "first Jewish capitalist in Germany." Although the source of his fabulous wealth is not known, it enabled him to finance large transactions in support of *Rudolph II, to whom he was appointed counsellor, during the Turkish wars. His business was based on the special privilege granted him to loan money not only against pledges but also against promissory notes and real estate. (The illegality of such practices according to Bohemian law was one of the pretexts for confiscating Meisel's estate, which amounted to over half a million florins, after his death.) He also acted as purveyor of luxuries and art objects. Meisel is first mentioned in business relations with his father-in-law, Isaac Rofe (Lékař), in 1569. Another of his business associates was Veit (Ḥayyim) Vokatý. He used his wealth for philanthropic activities of all kinds; the epitaph on his tombstone records: "None of his contemporaries was truly his equal in deeds of charity." With the support of his first wife, Eve, he built the Meisel Synagogue in 1597, for which Rudolph II granted him tax immunity and the right to display in it the "flag of David." Rudolph further decreed that the synagogue might not be entered by officers of the law. It remained Meisel's property until his death, when it was taken over by the community. (From 1963 it housed the synagogue silver collection of the Jewish State Museum.)

Meisel purchased land for the expansion of the Jewish cemetery and the construction of a *bet tohorah* (where the dead were prepared for burial). He financed the building of

Tombstone of Mordecai Meisel in the Prague cemetery.

a hospital, a *bet midrash,* a *mikveh,* and a *klaus.* The tradition that he also built the Jewish town hall cannot be proved. He had the streets of the Jewish quarter paved and donated large sums to all other charities, especially for the ransoming of captives. He also sent money to Jerusalem and granted considerable loans to the Cracow and Poznan (Posen) communities (possibly because of their connections with *Judah Loew b. Bezalel).

About Meisel's second wife, Frumet (d. 1625), there is diverse information. On one hand, she is said to have supported him in his philanthropic activities, and on the other hand, she is reported to have refused Meisel's dying request to give to Judah Loew a large sum for his charities. That she was Meisel's wife is not mentioned on her gravestone. When Meisel died, childless, he willed his property to his two nephews, both named Samuel. Although the emperor was represented at Meisel's funeral, all Meisel's property was seized in the name of the emperor, his heirs tortured to make them disclose any "concealed" assets, and Meisel's will itself declared void. A lawsuit was initiated, to which the entire community became a party, claiming the right to part of the inheritance because it had been forced to pay interest on it. In the course of this lawsuit, the *ḥerem* was pronounced on the impoverished Meisel family and one of them was refused burial. Although the main part of the estate burned down in the conflagration of 1689, an agreement between the community and the family was not reached until 1699.

Bibliography: J. R. Marcus, *The Jew in the Medieval World* (1965), 323–6; O. Muneles (ed.), *The Prague Ghetto in the Renaissance Period* (1965), index; Bondy-Dworský, nos. 859, 967–9, 971–3; H. Volavková (ed.), *Guide to the Jewish Museum in Prague,* 2 pts. (1948–57), index; idem, *A Story of the Jewish Museum in Prague* (1968), 259–66; H. Schnee, *Die Hoffinanz und der moderne Staat,* 5 (1966), 219–22; B. Kisch, in: HJ, 3 (1941), 86–88; 4 (1942), 71–73; G. Wolf, in: ZGJD, 2 (1888), 172–81.

[M.La.]

MEISEL, MOSES BEN MORDECAI (c. 1758–c. 1838), Torah scholar and *maskil;* born in Vilna. In his youth Meisel was one of the disciples closest to the Vilna Gaon *Elijah b. Solomon Zalman. He was familiar with German literature and became deeply interested in the writings of Moses *Mendelssohn. However, he was also in secret contact with R. *Shneur Zalman of Lyady, the founder of the *Ḥabad movement, and when this became known, he fled to Germany, fearing persecution by the Vilna religious establishment. During the Napoleonic Wars he conferred with the representatives of the French government on several occasions. After acceding to R. Shneur Zalman's request to stop these talks with people close to Napoleon, he was suspected of collaborating with the Russian army and was compelled to flee. He went to Ereẓ Israel but returned to Lithuania after the French defeat. During the early 1820s he went once more to Ereẓ Israel and in his last years was closely associated with Sir Moses *Montefiore. He wrote *Shirat Moshe* (Shklov, 1788), on the 613 precepts. Meisel died in Hebron.

Bibliography: S. Fuenn, *Kiryah Ne'emanah* (1860), 246–7; M. Teitelbaum, *Ha-Rav mi-Ladi* (1910–13), 31, 156–8. [A.Cy.]

MEISEL, NOAH (1891–1956), Latvian politician, born in Nesvizh, Belorussia. From his student days Meisel was a member of the *Bund. In World War I he served in the Russian army as a medical officer. After Latvia became independent (1918) he was appointed municipal health officer in Daugavpils (Dvinsk) and also served as a member of the city council and the Jewish community council. Later, he was elected to the Latvian parliament, where he represented the Bund. After the Fascist takeover (1934) he was arrested together with other Socialist deputies and spent some time in prison. He visited the United States, but did not stay there, returning to Latvia. In 1940, when the Soviet forces overran Latvia, Meisel was arrested—as were other Socialist and democratic leaders—and deported to the far north of the U.S.S.R., where he eventually died.

Bibliography: *Yahadut Latvia* (1953), index; J. S. Hertz, *Doyres Bundistn,* 2 (1956), 236–40; LNYL, 5 (1963), 585–6. [Jo.Ga.]

MEISELS, DAVID DOV (1814–1876), Polish rabbi. Mesels was the son of Aryeh Judah Jacob who served as *av bet din* of Piotrkow and Kilatow. He was known in his youth as a prodigy *(illui).* He was appointed *av bet din* of Dobra at the age of 18 and later served in the same capacity at Nasielsk. From 1851 until his death he was rabbi of Lask. He was regarded as one of the outstanding talmudists of his generation and gained the deep respect of the ḥasidic rabbi of Gur, Isaac Meir, author of the *Ḥiddushei ha-Rim.* Meisels' important works, published by his sons, are *Ahavat David,* on the laws of invalid witnesses (1884); *Ḥiddushei ha-Radad,* novellae on tractate *Pesaḥim* (1891); *She'elot u-Teshuvot ha-Radad,* responsa on *Oraḥ Ḥayyim* and *Even ha-Ezer* (1903); and *Binyan David,* on the Book of Lamentations (1913). Of his sons, Jacob, author of the *Toledot Ya'akov,* succeeded his father as rabbi of Lask; Phinehas Elijah served as rabbi of Rakov and Ze'ev Wolf was a distinguished Ḥasid at Tarnow.

Bibliography: P. Zelig, *Ir Lask va-Ḥakhameha* (1926), 71–75.

[A.Cy.]

MEISELS, DOV BERUSH (1798–1870), rabbi and Polish patriot. Scion of one of the most ancient families of Cracow, he was a descendant of Moses *Isserles. He studied under his father Isaac, who was rabbi of Kamenets-Podolsk, Ukraine. After his marriage to the daughter of the wealthy Solomon Borenstein, he settled in Cracow, where he opened a bank in partnership with Horowitz, the bank bearing the names of both partners. In 1832, after a difficult struggle against R. Saul Landa, Meisels was elected rabbi of the town. R. Saul Landa and his followers did not recognize this election and they established their own *bet din.* The divergences of opinion between the two *battei din* were tremendous; what one of them permitted the other prohibited. Both rabbis vigorously fought the emergence of Haskalah in Cracow and they were violently attacked by the *maskilim* in the pages of their *Algemeyne Tsaytung.* During the period of his rabbinate in Cracow, and even before then, Meisels played a central role in the communal life of the Jews of Cracow. Being extremely wealthy, he distributed the whole of his rabbinical salary to charitable institutions thus gaining the esteem of the masses. Many of the inhabitants of Cracow, which was then under Austrian rule, joined the Polish Revolt which broke out in Warsaw in 1830 against Russian rule. Meisels supported the rebels and

Dov Berush Meisels, Cracow rabbi and Polish patriot. Jerusalem, J.N.U.L., Schwadron Collection.

he personally financed the purchase of arms and the expenses of the rebels. In general, Meisels was an enthusiastic Polish patriot and he proved it on several occasions.

During the revolution of 1844, Meisels again supported the rebels. At a central prayer service held in the synagogue, Meisels called upon the congregation to join the rebels and to support them, even taking part in mass demonstrations in the street. In 1846 he was elected to the Senate of the Cracow Republic (the Free City of Cracow) and in 1848 was a member of the Polish delegation to the Austrian emperor which appealed for the liberation of the political prisoners. In the elections to the Austrian parliament which were held on December 31, 1848, Meisels was elected as the first Jew, obtaining a large majority over the other Jewish candidates. During the same year, he was also elected as one of the 40 councillors of the municipality of Cracow. In 1851, Meisels lent his assistance to projects for Jewish agricultural settlement, but these did not materialize. In parliament, Meisels joined forces with the Radicals. His sharp reply of: *"Juden haben keine Rechte"*—"Jews have no Right(s)"—to the speaker of parliament who had asked him why he sat with the Leftists, has become renowned. In 1854 his great rival, R. Saul Landa, died and two years later, Meisels became chief rabbi of Warsaw. He was received with much enthusiasm by all circles, though his election followed upon a violent dispute. In Warsaw, he also fought together with the Poles, joining their demonstration and assisting the Polish patriots.

In November 1861, he was arrested for closing the synagogue of Warsaw in defiance of the czarist authorities and was compelled to leave the town after a lengthy imprisonment. London and Amsterdam offered him their rabbinical seats, but in 1862 he was authorized to return to Warsaw, which he preferred. He was again expelled and deported to Cracow, but he was pardoned and returned to Warsaw—but from then he engaged exclusively in study. When he died in Warsaw the whole population attended the funeral, as a manifestation of the desire for Polish independence; the Russians prohibited the publication of obituaries on him, in revenge for his political activities against them. Meisels published *Ḥiddushei Maharadam* (Warsaw, 1870), consisting of novellae on the *Sefer ha-Mitzvot* of Maimonides. His son, Israel, was *dayyan* in Cracow and rabbi in Shedletz (Polish: Siedlce) from 1858–1867. He then returned to Cracow, where he died in 1875. His second son, Solomon, lived in Vienna.

Bibliography: *Sefer Cracow* (1959), 62ff.; *Me'ir Einei ha-Golah*, 2 (1954²), 12f.; D. Flinker, *Arim ve-Immahot be-Yisrael*, 3 (1948), 108–12; A. Levinson, *Toledot Yehudei Varshah* (1953), 158–64; E. Kupfer, *Ber Meisels* (Yid.; 1952); M. Kamelhar, *Rabbi Dov Ber Meisels, Gadol ba-Torah, Medinai ve-Loḥem* (1970); J. Shatzky, *Geshikhte fun Yidn in Varshe*, 21 (1948), 226–39 and index; 3 (1953), index. [Y.Al.]

MEISELS, UZZIEL BEN ẒEVI HIRSCH (1743–1785 or 1786), ḥasidic rabbi in Poland. Meisels was a member of an old rabbinic family in Poland, and a descendant of Moses *Isserles whom he calls "my grandfather" in his works. He served as *av bet din* in Rychwal (Bogatynia), Ostrowiec, and Nowy Dwor. Attracted to Ḥasidism he became a disciple of *Dov Baer, the Maggid of Mezhirech, and with his brother Isaac became one of the propagators of Ḥasidism in Poland. A considerable portion of his teachings in the yeshivah has been lost. His works include: *Ez ha-Da'at Tov*, novellae on tractates *Ketubbot* (1863) and *Shabbat* (1866); *Menorah ha-Tehorah* (1883/84), on *Tur, Oraḥ Ḥayyim, Hilkhot Shabbat*; and *Tiferet Ẓevi* (1803), on tractate *Beẓah*. The rest were published posthumously by his grandchildren in *Tiferet Uzzi'el*. This work includes selections on the Bible and moralistic ḥasidic sermons, combined with kabbalistic themes, though even these reflect the style of the halakhist, and contains many sayings of the founders of Ḥasidism, Meisels was called עבד ה׳ ("Servant of the Lord") *eved* being the initial letters of Uzziel ben Dreizel (his mother's name). [P.Me.]

MEISL, JOSEPH (1883–1958), historian and archivist. Born in Brno, he became an official of the Berlin Jewish community in 1908, rising to general secretary, and was later librarian of the community's important library. After the Nazis seized power, Meisl settled in Jerusalem. There he founded (and to 1957 directed) the General *Archives for the History of the Jewish People. Before and after World War II he was able to transfer valuable archival material from Central and Eastern Europe to the archives.

Writing mainly in German, Meisl made considerable contributions to Jewish historiography. His works include: *Geschichte der Juden in Polen und Russland* (3 vols., 1921–25); *Haskalah, Geschichte der Aufklaerungsbewegung unter den Juden in Russland* (1919), a history of the Haskalah movement in Russia; and *Die Juden im Zartum Polen* (1916). He also wrote studies on well-known Jewish historians: H. *Graetz (1917), S. *Dubnow (1930), and his father-in-law S.P. *Rabinowitz (Heb., 1943). In 1939 he published his study of Sir Moses *Montefiore's (abortive) endeavors to raise the educational and economic standards of Jerusalem Jewry, while his important edition of the minutebooks of the Berlin Jewish Community, 1723–1854 *(Pinkas Kehillat Berlin)* was published posthumously in 1962 by Shaul Esh. Meisl was a coeditor of the *Festschrift zu S. Dubnows siebzigstem Geburtstag* (1930).

Bibliography: N.M. Gelber, in: *Ḥokhmat Yisrael be-Ma'arav Eiropah*, ed. by S. Federbush, 2 (1963), 170ff. [G.K.]

MEISSEN, former margravate in Saxony, city near Dresden, E. Germany. Jews are mentioned as resident in the margravate of Meissen in the first decade of the 11th century. An organized community in the city of Meissen dates only from the 12th century, when a synagogue and a cemetery were maintained. The Jews lived at first in a *Judendorf* outside the city walls near the "Jewish gate." In 1265 Duke Henry the Illustrious enacted a liberal decree securing the Jewish community undisturbed participation in the city's life for some 80 years. During this period they made their living as pawnbrokers and moneylenders. Their communal life flourished and they established the first Jewish school in Saxony. In 1330 Emperor Louis IV transferred the protection of the Jews in Meissen to Frederick the Grave of Thuringia. During the *Black Death persecutions of 1349 the community was destroyed. Although it was never reestablished within the city itself during medieval times, Jewish moneylenders and tradesmen remained as taxpayers within the margravate. A partial expulsion took place in 1411, but the decree was rescinded in 1415. In 1425 Frederick the Warlike granted them protection for a yearly fee; however, during the course of the Hussite Wars (see John *Huss) Frederick the Mild ordered the expulsion of all Jews from Meissen and Thuringia in 1430. They were not permitted entry into Saxony as a whole until the end of the 18th century. The modern community in the city of Meissen was founded in the 19th century but it never achieved the status of its medieval counterpart. The city had a population of 32 Jews in 1890 that remained stable until 1904, but by 1933 all of them had been absorbed by *Dresden.

Bibliography: Germ Jud, 1 (1963), 225–6; 2 (1968), 531–3, incl. bibl.; A. Leicht, *Die Judengemeinde in Meissen* (repr. 1890); A. Levy, *Geschichte der Juden in Sachsen* (1900), passim; S. Neufeld, *Die Juden im Thueringisch-Saechsischen Gebiet waehrend des Mittelalters*, 2 vols. (1917–27), passim; FJW, 323. [A.Sha.]

MEITNER, LISE (1878–1968), physicist and one of the small group responsible for the discovery of atomic fission. Born in Vienna, she moved to Berlin in 1917 and there joined the distinguished chemist Otto Hahn, with whom she worked in collaboration, researching into radioactive substances. Lise Meitner was one of the first women to become a professor at the University of Berlin (1926). From 1917 she was for over 20 years head of the physics department in the Kaiser Wilhelm Institute for chemistry in Berlin.

After the *Anschluss* in 1938, she left Germany and settled in Stockholm, working on the staff of the Nobel Institute. There she received a letter from Hahn describing his discovery with Fritz Strassmann that, when a uranium atom was disintegrated by a neutron, an atom of barium was thereby produced. While holidaying near Gothenburg in December 1938, she discussed this with her nephew, Otto *Frisch, who was working in Denmark with Niels *Bohr. The two physicists immediately realized the significance of Hahn's work, which meant that the uranium atom was split into roughly equal parts, accompanied by a tremendous release of energy. Frisch called this "fission," a term borrowed from biology. Lise Meitner visited the United States after 1945, but returned to Sweden and became a citizen in 1949. Both before and after World War II she received many honors. She eventually retired to Cambridge, England, where she died.

Bibliography: *New York Times* (Oct. 28, 1968); E. Yost, in: *Science Digest* (May 1962), 83–88. [M.Gol.]

MEITUS, ELIAHU (1892–), Hebrew poet, writer, and translator. Born in Kishinev, Meitus studied at the Sorbonne but during World War I returned to Russia. After the war he served as headmaster of a Hebrew gymnasium in Bessarabia, and later taught in the teachers' seminary in Jassy (Rumania). In 1935 he settled in Palestine, where he taught literature in secondary schools. His first poem appeared in *Ha-Shilo'aḥ* (1910), when he was studying in Odessa. He came to the attention of Bialik, then the literary editor of that periodical, and became a member of the "Odessa group" of Hebrew writers. Subsequently, Meitus published poems and articles in the Hebrew press in Russia, Rumania, and elsewhere. After he settled in Palestine, Meitus' writings appeared regularly in the newspapers, particularly in the daily *Al ha-Mishmar.* He translated extensively (from French, Rumanian, Russian, and Yiddish), mainly works of fiction, but also poetry and nonfiction. Four collections of his poetry have appeared: *Shirim* (1943), *Balladot mi-Nof ha-Yaldut* (1954), and *Bi-Keẓeh ha-Gesher ha-Sheni* (1967, sonnets). He also compiled an anthology of modern Hebrew poetry, *Shiratenu ha-Ḥadashah* (1938).

Bibliography: M. Avishai, *Bein Olamot* (1962), 153–6; A. Cohen, *Soferim Ivriyyim Benei Zemannenu* (1964), 204–6; Kressel, Leksikon, 2 (1967), 345–6. [G.K.]

MEKHILTA OF R. ISHMAEL (Aram. מְכִילְתָּא דְּרַבִּי יִשְׁמָעֵאל) halakhic Midrash on Exodus.

The *Mekhilta of R. Ishmael* is a tannaitic production comprising a collection of *beraitot.* The Aramaic word *mekhilta,* signifying "a measure," was used by the *amoraim* in the sense of a collection of halakhic material and especially of halakhic *beraitot* (cf. the evolution of the Greek word *κανών*). The appellation *"Mekhilta"* as the title of the work is first mentioned by the Babylonian *geonim* in the tenth century C.E. in the form of *Mekhilta ve-Elleh Shemot* and *Mekhilta de-Ereẓ Yisrael.* Somewhat later there occurs, for the first time in the writings of R. Nissim Gaon, the form *Mekhilta of R. Ishmael,* apparently after the principal beginning of the Midrash: "R. Ishmael says, Moses showed Israel the new moon" (*pisḥa* 1 [2]).

The *Mekhilta of R. Ishmael* is an exegetical Midrash which interprets Exodus, chapter by chapter and verse by verse, and often, too, all the words in a verse. It commences with Exodus 12:1, continues consecutively to Exodus 23:19, and then contains expositions on Exodus 31:12–17 and 35:1–3. Consisting of a compilation of various expositons, which were redacted excluding everything connected with the section dealing with the Tabernacle, by the editor of the Midrash, on the halakhic portion of Exodus, the *Mekhilta of R. Ishmael* also includes the narrative sections, incorporated in the principal part (Ex. 12:1–23:19). These narrative sections (Ex. 12:29–42, 51; 13:17–16:27; 16:35–19:25), whose verses constitute more than half of those expounded in the Midrash, account for the fact that the aggadic portion of the *Mekhilta of R. Ishmael,* which is mainly an halakhic Midrash, does not fall short of the halakhic one.

The work is divided into nine tractates: *Pisḥa* (Ex. 12:1–13:16); *Va-Yehi Be-Shallaḥ* (13:17–14:31); *Shiraṭa* (15:1–21); *Va-Yassa* (15:22–17:7); *Amalek* (17:8–18:27); *Ba-Ḥodesh* (19:1–20:26); *Nezikin* (21:1–22:23); *Kaspa* (22:24–23:19); and *Shabbeta* (31:12–17; 35:1–3). Each tractate is divided into sections (of which there are 82 in manuscripts of the work), and each section was originally subdivided (the subdivision is preserved in manuscripts) into *halakhot* ("paragraphs"). This division, which is according to subject matter, is very old and unconnected with the weekly portions of the reading of the Torah, under the influence of which it was, however, in the course of time corrupted. Thus two tractates were subdivided into two (*Amalek Be-Shallaḥ* and *Amalek Yitro; Shabbeta Ki Tissa* and *Shabbeta Va-Yakhel*), while two others, *Nezikin* and *Kaspa,* were combined as *Mishpatim.* As a consequence of this, the division into sections was also corrupted, while that into *halakhot* was completely discarded in the printed versions.

As in all halakhic Midrashim, neither the tractates nor the sections have proems (*Homiletics), but in one instance there is something in the nature of a proem (Amalek 1): "R. Joshua and R. Eleazar Ḥisma say, This verse is written here and interpreted by Job (8:11), for it is stated: 'Can the rush shoot up without mire? Can the reed-grass grow without water?' Is it, then, possible for the rush to grow without mire and without water . . . ? So, too, it is impossible for Israel to exist without the words of the Torah, and because they separated themselves from the words of Torah. the enemy came upon them. For the enemy comes only because of sin and transgression, and hence it is said: 'Then came Amalek.'" According to its entire form and its position, this exposition bears the character of a classic proem (familiar from the aggadic Midrashim of the *amoraim*) in that it opens with a verse taken from elsewhere, interprets it, and then connects it with the beginning of the section, on which the principal exposition centers.

Some sections conclude with an epilogue containing a message of consolation to Israel, a promise of their future redemption, or a reference to their mission.

The language of both the halakhic and aggadic homilies in the Midrash is a pure rabbinic Hebrew, with an admixture of Greek and Latin words.

Since the literature of the sages (the Talmuds as well as the aggadic Midrashim) contains *beraitot* in the name of R. Ishmael, or of a *tanna* of the school of R. Ishmael, which are quoted anonymously in *Mekhilta of R. Ishmael,* M.

Ish-Shalom (Friedmann), and following him many scholars, concluded that the work is indeed the product of Ishmael's school. In time, further proofs were adduced in support of this conclusion, which became an integral part of an entire theory about the division of the halakhic Midrashim into two distinct types, one of which emanated from the school of Ishmael, the other from that of Akiva. In any event the *Mekhilta of R. Ishmael* belongs to type A of the halakhic Midrashim. On the division into types and its significance, as also Ḥ. Albeck's arguments against the interpretation of the facts, see **Midreshei Halakhah*. Although constituting no proof that the *Mekhilta of R. Ishmael* belongs to the school of Ishmael, it is noteworthy that many *tannaim* from among his pupils and from his *bet midrash* are mentioned in it. Since this work, like the other halakhic Midrashim, was apparently unknown to the rabbis of the Talmuds, it was probably, compiled and redacted in Ereẓ Israel not earlier than the end of the fourth century C.E.

The *Mekhilta of R. Ishmael* was first printed at Constantinople in 1515, then at Venice in 1545, and since then several times. It has also appeared with various commentaries. In the 19th century some editions, with an introduction and comments, were issued by scholars (I. H. Weiss, 1865; M. Friedmann (Ish-Shalom), 1870). An excellent critical edition, based on manuscripts and on the first printed versions, and with comments, was started by H. S. Horowitz and completed after his death by I. A. Rabin (1931). Another critical edition, with English translation, was issued by J. Z. Lauterbach (Philadelphia, 1933–35).

Bibliography: Zunz-Albeck, Derashot, 27; M. Friedmann (ed.) *Mekhilta de-Rabbi Yishma'el* (1870), introd.; D. Hoffmann, *Zur Einleitung in die halachischen Midraschim* (1888); Ḥ. Albeck, *Untersuchungen ueber die halakischen Midraschim* (1927); idem, *Mavo la-Talmudim* (1969), 79–143; J. Z. Lauterbach, in: HUCA, 1 (1924), 427–66; Epstein, Tanna'im, 545–87. [M.D.H.]

MEKHILTA OF R. SIMEON BEN YOḤAI (Aram. מְכִילְתָּא דְרַבִּי שִׁמְעוֹן בֶּן יוֹחַאי), halakhic Midrash on Exodus consisting of a collection of *beraitot*, from the period of the *tannaim*. In the Middle Ages the Midrash was also known as *Sifrei de-Vei Rav, Mekhiltin de-R. Akiva*, and *Mekhilta de-Sanya*. The last title, as also the present, was based on its opening sentence. "R. Simeon b. Yoḥai says, Why did the Holy One blessed be He reveal Himself from the heavens on high and speak to Moses from the midst of the bush" (*seneh*, "bush" = *sanya* in Aramaic). (See also **Mekhilta of R. Ishmael*.) The *Mekhilta of R. Simeon b. Yoḥai* is an exegetical Midrash which expounds Exodus chapter by chapter and verse by verse. It begins with Exodus 3:1, but because of the state of its preservation (see below) it is impossible to tell whether it continued expounding each chapter and verse consecutively, and where exactly it ended. It also contains aggadic expositions on the narrative passages of Exodus. Originally the Midrash was subdivided into sections and the sections into paragraphs or *halakhot*. Because of its state, however, even the details of its division are not wholly clear. The language of the Midrash is a pure rabbinic Hebrew but of a somewhat later type, with an admixture of Greek and Latin words. The Midrash was regarded as belonging to the type of halakhic Midrashim that issued from the school of Akiva (see **Midreshei Halakhah*). Some scholars, however, ascribed it indeed to Simeon b. Yoḥai while others contended that Hezekiah or Rav was its author or compiler. All these conjectures are apparently without substance. The *Mekhilta of R. Simeon b. Yoḥai* belongs to type B of the halakhic Midrashim, and in that group is closest to **Sifrei* on Deuteronomy. It contains many comparatively late features, particularly in its language. Most of its aggadic passages are similar to those in the *Mekhilta of R. Ishmael*, from which they were apparently taken. On the basis of all these factors and, furthermore, since the Midrash was unknown in its present form to the rabbis of the Babylonian and Jerusalem Talmuds, the date of its redaction in Ereẓ Israel is to be assigned to not earlier than the commencement of the fifth century C.E. From the geonic period onward, the *Mekhilta of R. Simeon b. Yoḥai* was frequently quoted by medieval scholars and was still known in the 16th century, but was not printed. From the 17th century it was thought to have been lost. When in the 19th century a small extract from the beginning of the Midrash was discovered in a manuscript, M. Friedmann (Ish Shalom), who first identified it, began to collect the extracts from the *Mekhilta of R. Simeon b. Yoḥai* quoted in medieval literature. After him, I. Lewy showed that many *beraitot* of the Midrash are to be found in *Midrash ha-Gadol* (of David b. Amram *Adani). When further fragments, from the Cairo **Genizah*, were discovered and published, D. Hoffmann issued an edition, together with an introduction and notes, of the Midrash (1905), compiled from *Midrash ha-Gadol* on Exodus and containing also several small *Genizah* fragments. Since the author of *Midrash ha-Gadol* did not indicate his sources, however, and also freely adapted and changed, abbreviated and expanded, subdivided and combined them, Hoffmann's edition is far from being a true reflection of the *Mekhilta of R. Simeon b. Yoḥai*. In the course of time more *Genizah* fragments were discovered. J. N. Epstein began to prepare a critical edition, with an introduction and notes, of the Midrash, based on fragments chiefly from the *Genizah*, and containing extracts from *Midrash ha-Gadol*. The work was completed after Epstein's death by E. Z. Melamed (1955), but the manuscripts contain, it seems, only slightly more than half of the original Midrash.

Bibliography: M. Friedmann (ed.), *Mekhilta de-Rabbi Yishma'el* (1870), introd.; I. Lewy, *Ein Wort ueber die Mechilta des Rabbi Simon*, in: *Jahresbericht... Fraenckelscher Stiftung* (1889); D. Hoffmann, in: JJLG, 3 (1906), 191–215; L. Ginzberg, in: *Festschrift I. Lewy* (1911), 403–36; S. Horovitz, in: *Jahresbericht des Rabbinerseminars in Breslau* (1919); Ḥ. Albeck, *Untersuchungen ueber die halakischen Midraschim* (1927); idem, *Mavo la-Talmudim* 1 (1969), 82–83; J. N. Epstein and E. Z. Melamed (eds.), *Mekhilta de-Rabbi Shimon ben Yoḥai* (1955), introd.; Epstein, Tanna'im, 725–40. [M.D.H.]

MEKHLIS, LEV ZAKHAROVICH (1889–1953), Soviet army officer. Born in Odessa, Mekhlis was conscripted into the czarist army and during World War I served in an artillery regiment. He joined the Red Army during the civil war of 1918–21, becoming military commissar of a brigade in the Ukraine. For several years Mekhlis was an official of the Communist party central committee and after 1930 worked on the newspaper *Pravda*. He was head of the Red Army's political administration from 1937 to 1940 when he became U.S.S.R. people's commissar of state control. Following the outbreak of World War II, Mekhlis served in the Red Army on several fronts and was promoted to lieutenant-general. His many decorations included the award of four Lenin medals. After the war he served for a short period as U.S.S.R. minister of state control.

Bibliography: *Bolshaya Sovetskaya Entsiklopediya*, 27 (1954), 388; *Sovetskaya Istoricheskaya Entsiklopediya; Sovetsky entsiklopedichesky slovar.* [Mo.K.]

MEKIẒE NIRDAMIM (Heb. מְקִיצֵי נִרְדָּמִים; "rousers of those who slumber"), the first society for the publication of medieval Hebrew literature in every branch of intellectual activity, in scholarly editions. The aim of the society was both to propagate a knowledge of Jewish scholarship and to establish personal contact between scholars. The structure of the society—which still continues—provided for a board of directors, consisting of the best qualified scholars in their field, and annual subscriptions from members. The Mekiẓe Nirdamim was founded in 1862 by E. L. *Silbermann in Lyck, founder-editor of the first Hebrew weekly **Ha-Maggid*, with the cooperation of Chief Rabbi Nathan M. *Adler (London), M. *Sachs (Berlin), and S. D. *Luzzatto. There was a certain amount of opposition—for a variety of reasons—which included a lack of faith in the possibility of the renaissance of Jewish culture, an opposition to the publication of non-rabbinic texts, and an opposition in principle to the exclusive use of Hebrew, which was established as a rule by the society, and/or an opposition to its founders by such scholars as A. *Geiger and M. *Steinschneider. Support was found, however, among Polish and Russian scholars and even in rabbis such as Samuel and Mattityahu *Straschun, S. *Ganzfried, M. L. *Malbim, and by 1864 the number of subscribers, from a great many countries, stood at 1,200. In the same year the first four publications were issued, among them the first installment of S. D. Luzzatto's edition of Judah Halevi's *Diwan*. The adherence of Moses *Montefiore in 1865 brought with it the support of many who had been aloof. After a decade's activity, there was a pause until, in 1885, the society resumed its work in Berlin, guided by A. *Berliner, A. *Harkavy, and others. It was then that the series *Kobeẓ al Jad* was initiated (26 volumes by 1970), devoted to the publication of smaller manuscripts and documents. In 1934 the seat of the Mekiẓe Nirdamim was transferred to Jerusalem. By 1970, 110 works had been issued. S. Y. *Agnon served as president of the society (1954–70), and was succeeded by Gershom *Scholem.

Bibliography: *Ḥevrat Mekiẓe Nirdamim: 1864–1964* (1964), includes complete bibliography of books published by the society.

[I.T.-S.]

MEKLENBURG, JACOB ẒEVI (1785–1865), rabbi and biblical commentator. Meklenburg was born in Inowroclaw, Poznania. Unwilling to enter the rabbinate, he engaged

Jacob Ẓevi Meklenburg, biblical commentator. Jerusalem, J.N.U.L., Schwadron Collection.

in business, but in 1831, after his business had failed, he accepted an invitation from the community of Koenigsberg to serve as their rabbi, and he remained there until his death. An opponent of religious reforms, he fought against the reformist ideas advocated in his community by Joseph Lewin Saalschuetz.

Meklenburg's major work was a commentary on the Pentateuch, *Ha-Ketav ve-ha-Kabbalah*, in which he sought to demonstrate the conformity between the oral tradition and the written law. His commentary, which contains numerous original interpretations, was first published in Leipzig in 1839. It was reprinted twice during his lifetime, with his additions and included a German translation of the text of the Pentateuch based on Meklenburg's commentary, by Jonah Kossmann. A fourth printing was begun some time before Meklenburg's death, but was interrupted because of differences between the publisher and the printers. In 1880, Abraham Berliner published a new edition with additional material from manuscripts left by the author. Meklenburg was also the author of a commentary on the prayer book, *Iyyun Tefillah*, first published in 1857 with the *siddur* of R. Jacob *Lorbeerbaum of Lissa; it, too, was reprinted several times. A number of rabbinic works carry introductory notes or approbations by Meklenburg.

Bibliography: D. Druck, in: *Horeb*, 4 (1937), 171–9; N. Ben-Menahem, in: *Sinai*, 65 (1969), 327–32.

[T.P.]

MEKNÈS, town in Morocco. Jews settled in the region of Meknès before the advent of Islam. A Hebrew inscription has been found and the remains of a synagogue were uncovered in the excavations of Volubilis, which is near Meknès. A *kinah* of Abraham *ibn Ezra mentions Meknès among the communities which suffered at the hands of the *Almohads. A chronological note testifies that such persecutions occurred in 1140, and adds that in 1247, during the wars of the *Merinids, many Jews lost their lives or were forcibly converted to Islam, while in the earthquake of 1340 "several courtyards caved in, as well as the synagogue and the *bet ha-midrash* of R. Jacob." According to traditions preserved in writing, the "Mahrit" synagogue, still existing in Meknès, was first built in the 13th century, destroyed in the earthquake of 1630 and rebuilt in 1646 by the *Toledanos upon their arrival in Meknès. It is similarly stated that the "Tobi" synagogue was built in 1540. It would therefore seem that Jews already at that time lived in the present mellah area as well as in the Medina in which an "Aaron Street" is, according to tradition, named after the then leader of the community. The sharif Mulay Ismail (1672–1727), the real founder of the *Alawid dynasty, moved his capital to Meknès and granted the Jews additional land for construction of buildings. The *nagid* Abraham Maymerān and other wealthy Jews then built luxurious houses. Christian emissaries from Europe who stayed in them were astonished by their beauty. Near the mellah, Ismail built a beautiful quarter for his officials and servants.

From then until the 19th century the community of Meknès was one of the best developed and organized in Morocco. It was a city of *ḥakhamim* and authors, as well as merchants and men of action who frequently visited Tetuán, Salé, Rabat, and Fez on their affairs. The community was organized and its institutions functioned accordingly. The taxation on meat, wine, and other products constituted a source of income for the community, which with the addition of local donations, was able to supply the minimal requirements of the needy and those engaged in studies. The community maintained regular relations with Ereẓ Israel, whose emissaries returned home with considerable funds. The education of the children was entrusted to many teachers; at a more advanced age the youths were employed in the crafts or commerce, while the more talented pursued their studies in yeshivot.

As capital of the country and residence of the sharifs (rulers) Meknès was also the center of Jewish activities at the court. The leaders of the Meknès community acted as *negidim* (see **Nagid*) of Moroccan Jewry and agents of the sharifs. Among them were members of the *Maymerān family (Joseph and his son Abraham), as well as the Toledanos, the Ibn Attars, the Ben Māmāns, the Ben Quiquis, and others. The most prominent rabbinic scholars and *dayyanim* in Meknès during the 18th–20th centuries come from the Berdugo and Toledano families, many of whom wrote responsa. From 1790 and during the 19th century Meknès lost its importance as the capital and the Jewish community suffered pogroms frequently.

Entrance to the old mellah of Meknès, Morocco. Jerusalem, Israel Museum Photo Collection, Department of Ethnography. Photo Shulman, 1953.

There was an important change for the better in the situation of the Jews with the formal establishment of the French Protectorate in 1912. From then on the Jews enjoyed relative security and economic stability, as well as elementary human rights. There were also changes in the field of religious education with the arrival of R. Ze'ev Halperin, a Russian scholar who came from Britain in 1912. He introduced reforms in the system of study of the yeshivot and gathered the young men of the town, for whom he founded a *kolel avrekhim* (advanced yeshivah), the first of its kind in Meknès and probably the whole of Morocco. He founded an *Ez Ḥayyim* society for laymen which organized regular studies and whose members supported the young men of the Bet El yeshivah with their contributions. As a result of this activity the yeshivah produced a nucleus of *ḥakhamim* who later officiated as rabbis in Meknès and other communities. The fame of Meknès yeshivot spread far and they attracted students from many parts of the country. After World War II, a Ḥabad yeshivah was founded (in conjunction with *Oẓar ha-Torah).

The government allocated new areas near the mellah for the Jews to live in, and a new quarter, known as the "new mellah," was built. The construction was modern, being scattered and not surrounded by a wall. Many beautiful synagogues were also built, including the beautiful "Toledano" and Joseph Mrejen synagogues, as well as a large Jewish school, Em ha-Banim, in which all the children of the community studied (the needy were exempted from the payment of tuition fees). Its expenses and the salaries of the teachers were provided from community funds. In 1947 approximately 1,200 pupils attended this school. The Alliance Israélite Universelle built two large schools, one for boys and another for girls, which were attended by about 1,500 boys and girls in 1950. According to the 1947 census the Jewish community numbered 15,482 (about 3,000 others were not included in the census for various reasons). Most of the Jews of Meknès emigrated to Israel after the establishment of the state and both the old and the new mellahs are now inhabited for the most part by Muslims. [Ha.Be.]

Contemporary Period. The Jewish population of Meknès, which numbered 12,445 in the 1951 census report, dropped in 1960 to 10,894 (according to the census of that year), and in 1968, after the large-scale emigration of Moroccan Jewry, to about 2,000–3,000. During the 1950s the Jewish schools had 3,182 pupils, but the number dropped off in the 1960s. Most of the charitable and social welfare organizations, which included branches of WIZO and the World Jewish Congress, were closed. In 1970 the Meknès community, although reduced, was one of the more vital of the Moroccan provincial communities. A considerable Jewish petite bourgoisie lived there with communal life centering around the two main synagogues. Only a few dozen Jews remain in the old mellah, and most live in the modern Jewish neighborhood. [H.J.C.]

Bibliography: Hirschberg, Afrikah, index; idem, in: H. J. Zimmels et al. (eds.), *Essays Presented to... Israel Brodie...* (1967), 153–81; A. Chouraqui, *La condition juridique de l'Israélite marocain* (1950); idem, *Between East and West* (1968), index; B Meakin, *Land of the Moors* (1901), 277–87; R. Attal, in: *Tefuzot ha-Golah*, 1 (1964), 42ff.

MEKOROT (Heb. "Sources") **WATER COMPANY,** company established in 1937 as a joint undertaking of the *Histadrut, the *Jewish Agency, and the *Jewish National Fund, to develop a water supply project in the western part of the Valley of Jezreel. Its first managing director was Levi *Eshkol. After World War II, Mekorot extended its operations to a regional project in the Negev and a smaller project in central Israel. During the *War of Independence (1948) it constructed an emergency water supply system for Jerusalem and, after the war, embarked upon a major development program encompassing the entire country. In 1962 Mekorot officially became Israel's National Water Supply Agency.

In the early 1950s the projects executed were mainly connected with ground and spring water. In the mid-1950s further major regional projects were carried out. In the later 1950s and early 1960s the main emphasis was upon the National Water Carrier (Jordan Project), and subsequently systems utilizing flood runoff and reclaimed sewage were constructed. From the early 1960s the company also operated abroad, mainly in the construction of water supplies in developing countries.

The Israel government was a shareholder in the company from 1948 and held one-third of the shares in 1967. Another third was held by the Histadrut, and the rest equally by the Jewish Agency and the Jewish National Fund. In 1967 the share capital of Mekorot was IL228,000,000 ($76,000,000). Its 1966 water sales were 820,000,000 cu. m. (1,074,000,000 cu. yds.) and its income was IL78,000,000 ($26,000,000). The assets up to 1967 were IL818,000,000 ($273,000,000).

Open section of the National Water Carrier channel in western Galilee. Courtesy Government Press Office, Tel Aviv.

The company had approximately 1,730 permanent and 600 temporary employees. Mekorot owned a number of subsidiary companies including the Water Resources Development (International) Ltd. for its foreign operations, the paid-up share capital of which was IL3,900,000 ($1,300,000) in 1967.

Bibliography: *Mekorot Water Company Ltd. and its Role in Israel's Development* (1963); *Sheloshim Shanah li-Mekorot* (1967).

[A.Wi.]

MELAMED, EZRA ZION (1903–), Israel talmudic scholar and philologist. Born in Shiraz, Persia, Melamed was taken to Palestine by his father, R. R. *Melamed when he was two. He worked at the Ministry of Education (1952–56), and was appointed professor of Bible at the Hebrew University (1964) and of Talmud at Bar Ilan (1961) and at Tel Aviv (1964) universities. He was elected to the Hebrew Language Academy in 1956 and to the Higher Archaeological Council in 1963. Melamed's major works are in the fields of talmudic literature; *Midreshei Halakhah shel ha-Tanna'im be-Talmud Bavli* (1943), in which he collected *beraitot* in the Babylonian Talmud based on verses from the Pentateuch, and *Ha-Yaḥas she-Bein Midreshei Halakhah la-Mishnah ve-la-Tosefta* ("Relations Between Halakhic Midrashim and Mishnah and Tosefta," 1967). Melamed devoted much labor to editing the scientific legacy of his teacher Jacob Nahum *Epstein, including *Mekhilta de-Rabbi Shimon bar Yoḥai* (1955), *Mevo'ot le-Sifrut ha-Tanna'im* (1957), *Mevo'ot le-Sifrut ha-Amora'im* (1962), and *Dikduk Aramit Bavlit* (1960). He also edited B. de Vries' *Meḥkarim be-Sifrut ha-Talmud* (1968), and prepared textbooks and popular works, including *Pirkei Minhag ve-Halakhah* ("Chapters of Custom and Halakhah," 1955), and *Parashiyyot me-Aggadot ha-Tanna'im* ("Chapters of Tannaitic *Aggadot*," 1955). Among his other writings are *Tafsir Tehillim bi-Leshon Yehudei Paras* ("Psalms in Judeo-Persian," 1968) and *Millon Arami-Ivri le-Talmud Bavli le-Mathilim* ("Aramaic-Hebrew Dictionary of the Babylonian Talmud for Beginners," 1969), as well as articles in scientific journals. Of special significance is his edition of Eusebius' geographical work *Onomastikon*, which he translated from the original (1938). Because of his involvement with the Persian and other oriental communities (whom he served as honorary rabbi) and his familiarity with their traditions of custom and language, Melamed served as an important source on such community traditions. [M.Z.Ka.]

MELAMED, MEIR (second half of 15th century), financier in Spain during the period of the expulsion. A Hebrew author of the period calls him the "king's secretary," apparently because he held office in one of the royal accounting departments. In official documents he is referred to as "Rabbi" and not "Don," as were most of the other Jewish tax farmers, which indicates that he was a scholar. He lived mainly in Segovia. In 1487 he succeeded his aged father-in-law Abraham *Seneor as chief administrator of tax farming in the kingdom. On June 15, 1492, he and Abraham Seneor were baptized with great ceremony at Guadalupe, Ferdinand and Isabella acting as godparents. As a Christian he adopted the name Fernando Pérez Coronel. On June 23, 1492, he was appointed chief accountant *(contador mayor)*. He also became a permanent member of the royal council and was town councillor *(regidor)* in Segovia.

Bibliography: Baer, Spain, index, s.v. *Meir Melamed*· Baer, Urkunden, index; Suárez Fernández, Documentos, index. [Ed.]

MELAMED, RAḤAMIM REUVEN (1854–1938), Persian rabbi and preacher. Born in Shiraz, he moved to Jerusalem in 1906, established a yeshivah in his own home, and served as rabbi to the Persian Jews. He wrote many commentaries in both Hebrew and *Judeo-Persian to the Pentateuch, the Scrolls, *Avot*, and portions of the Zohar: among them *Kisse Raḥamim* (1911), *Yeshu'ah ve-Raḥamim* (1912), *Ẓedakah ve-Raḥamim* (1926), *Ḥayyei Raḥamim* (1929), *Zikhron Raḥamim* (1930), and *Seder Leil Pesaḥ* (in Hebrew and Persian, 1930), all published in Jerusalem. Some of his works were republished by his son, Ezra Zion *Melamed.

Bibliography: M. D. Gaon, *Yehudei ha-Mizraḥ be-Ereẓ Yisrael*, 2 (1937), 437–8. [W.J.F.]

MELAMED, SIMAN TOV (d. c. 1780), spiritual leader of the Jewish community in *Meshed. A poet, philosopher, and author of many treatises in Hebrew and *Judeo-Persian, he composed **azharot* (1896) in Judeo-Persian (portions of which were written in Persian, as well as Aramaic and Hebrew). A manuscript of his commentary to *Pirkei Avot* is in the possession of Hebrew Union College, Cincinnati, together with other of his writings. His major work is his philosophical-religious *Sefer Ḥayyat al-Rukh* (published 1898), which combines a commentary on Maimonides' teachings on the 13 articles of faith and a treatise on Israel's existence in the Diaspora and ultimate salvation. The work shows a strong influence of the Sufic ideas of *Baḥya ibn Paquda's *Ḥovot ha-Levavot* and other Jewish and Muslim medieval thinkers. In the tradition of Meshed's Jews, Siman Tov Melamed is also remembered as a staunch defender of Judaism in theological disputations which the Shiʿa clergy arranged between him, Muslims, and Jewish converts.

Bibliography: W. Bacher, in: ZHB, 14 (1910), 51ff.; A. Yaari, *Sifrei Yehudei Bukharah* (1942), nos. 33, 39, 161; E. Neumark, *Massa be-Ereẓ ha-Kedem*, ed. by A. Yaari (1947), 95; W. J. Fischel, in: L. Finkelstein (ed.), *The Jews*, 2 (1960^3), 1174, 1177; E. Spicehandler, in: SBB, 8 (1968), 114–36. [W.J.F.]

°MELANCHTHON (Schwarzerd), PHILIPP (1497–1560), German reformer and theologian. Born at Bretten in Baden, Melanchthon was a great-nephew of the Hebraist and Christian kabbalist Johann *Reuchlin, who taught him Hebrew and supervised his education at Pforzheim. In 1518, at the age of 21, Melanchthon was appointed professor of Greek at Wittenberg but within a year he had sided with Martin *Luther in the struggle with Rome, thus alienating Reuchlin, who later disinherited him. Melanchthon was Luther's principal assistant in translating the Old Testament into German (1523–34). Widely respected as a humanist and theologian, he favored study of the Kabbalah, but condemned its later accretions. One of his addresses on the importance of Hebrew, *De studio linguae Ebraeae*, appeared in 1549. Although Melanchthon was influenced by Luther's anti-Semitism, he avoided its cruder excesses and in 1539, at the Frankfort religious assembly, publicly denounced the blood libel that had resulted in the martyrdom of 38 Brandenburg Jews in 1510.

Bibliography: K. Hartfelder, *P. Melanchthon als Praeceptor Germaniae* (1889); G. Ellinger, *Philipp Melanchthon* (Ger., 1902); F. Hildebrandt, *Melanchthon: Alien or Ally?* (1946); C. L. Manschreck, *Melanchthon, the Quiet Reformer* (1958); H. Sick, *Melanchthon als Ausleger des Alten Testaments* (1959); G. Kisch, *Melanchthons Rechts- und Soziallehre* (1967); Baron, Social[2], 13, 229ff. [Ed.]

MELAVVEH MALKAH (Heb. מְלַוֵּה מַלְכָּה; "escorting the queen"), term used to describe the meal and festivities at the end of the Sabbath. This gesture of farewell to the "queen" (Sabbath) is designed as the counterpart of the festivities which greeted her arrival. The origin of the custom has been traced to the Talmud. R. Ḥanina asserted that the table should be (festively) laid at the termination of the Sabbath, although only a small amount of food would be eaten (Shab. 119b). The *melavveh malkah* was later seen by both *Jacob b. Asher and Joseph *Caro to be the fulfillment of R. Ḥidka's injunction to celebrate four meals on the Sabbath (Shab. 117b). It was in the context of this injunction that the *melavveh malkah* later assumed the image of a virtually voluntary extension of the Sabbath. Isaac *Luria, for example, believed that not until the *melavveh malkah* was over did the sinful dead return to hell from their Sabbath rest, and the kabbalists and Ḥasidim were so reluctant to relinquish the honored Sabbath guest, that they used the *melavveh malkah* as a means of prolonging the Sabbath day as long as possible. They used the occasion to chant special **zemirot* and to relate ḥasidic tales. The *melavveh malkah* is also known as *se'udat David* ("King David's banquet"). As such it serves as a reminder of the legend that King David, having been told by God that he would die on the Sabbath (Shab. 30a), used to celebrate his survival each new week with special joy *(Ta'amei Minhagim)*.

One of the favorite *melavveh malkah* hymns is *Eliyahu ha-Navi* ("Elijah the Prophet"), attributed by some authorities to *Meir of Rothenburg. It welcomes the prophet as the herald of the Messiah. According to legend, Elijah is expected to announce the salvation of Israel at the first opportunity after the termination of the Sabbath. Medieval *paytanim* devoted several other *zemirot* to the *melavveh malkah* festivities. Among the most notable are *Be-Moẓa'ei Yom Menuḥah* by Jacob Menea (14th century); *Addir Ayom ve-Nora, Ish Ḥasid* by Jesse b. Mordecai (13th century), and *Amar Adonai le-Ya'akov*.

Bibliography: Eisenstein, Dinim, 227; H. Schauss, *Guide to Jewish Holy Days* (1962), 27, 30, 35.

[H.Ra.]

MELBOURNE, capital of Victoria, Australia. General population (1970) 2,400,000; Jewish population 34,500. The 15 Port Phillip Association members who founded Melbourne in 1835 included two Jews. Melbourne is today the only Jewish community of any size in the State of Victoria. During the 19th century however a considerable number of Jews settled in other centers in the State, but, as will be seen from the accompanying tables, the country communities practically disappeared. Details will be found at the end of the article. The Melbourne Jewish community was established in 1841.

Early Metropolitan Settlement. Jews clustered around shops and businesses in the center of the city in Collins, Bourke, and Elizabeth streets and in 1847 opened the first synagogue (Melbourne Hebrew Congregation) in that area. The influx in the 1850s and 1860s led to settlement in working-class districts in the suburbs adjoining the city—Fitzroy, Carlton, Richmond, and East Melbourne. The East Melbourne Congregation was founded in 1857 with Moses Rintel as minister, most of the congregants being immigrants from Germany and Austria. At the turn of the century this congregation was led by the patriarchal figure, Rev. Jacob Lenzer.

There were continuous movements of Jews from their first areas of settlement to new areas. In the wake of such a group movement the St. Kilda Synagogue was opened in 1872. In the period before compulsory education the Melbourne Hebrew School was established as a day school in 1874 and continued till 1886, when it was closed because of financial difficulties. In 1888 the three congregations (Melbourne, East Melbourne, and St. Kilda) established the United Jewish Education Board, which conducted part-time Hebrew schools in various centers. As they moved from area to area the Jews ascended in the social and occupational ladder and by 1900 the most popular occupations were textile manufacturing, general dealing, and skilled trades such as tailoring, watchmaking, and cabinetmaking. Small draper shop-owners were beginning to acquire large retail stores. Carpenters were opening furniture factories. Less than 3% were in the professions. During the first decades of the 20th century there gradually developed a struggle for communal supremacy between the earlier immigrants who lived south of the Yarra River, and who were more prosperous and assimilated, and the more recent immigrants, mostly from Eastern Europe, who were concentrated north of the river, and who were Yiddish speaking, with an Orthodox background, Yiddish culture, and strong Zionist leanings.

Concurrently, a change took place in the centers of Jewish activity. Whereas until the first decades of the 20th century life centered around the synagogues, in the next decades a shift took place, non-synagogal bodies being organized and gradually taking a more prominent place in communal leadership. The synagogues in the first decades of the 20th century were the Melbourne Hebrew Congregation (first at Bourke St. in the city; after 1930 at Toorak Road) and the St. Kilda Synagogue south of the Yarra, and the East Melbourne Synagogue and the Carlton Synagogue (established 1927), north of the Yarra. Some smaller *minyanim* had also been formed, notably the Woolf Davis Chevra, run by the family of J. E. Stone, and the Talmud Torah Hascola at North Carlton. A number of societies mainly in the hands of the south of the Yarra element were already in existence—the Philanthropic Society, Aid Society, Welfare Society, Sick Visiting Society, the Chevra Kadisha (founded 1910), the United Shechita Board and the Beth Din. A number of bodies began to spring up north of the Yarra. In

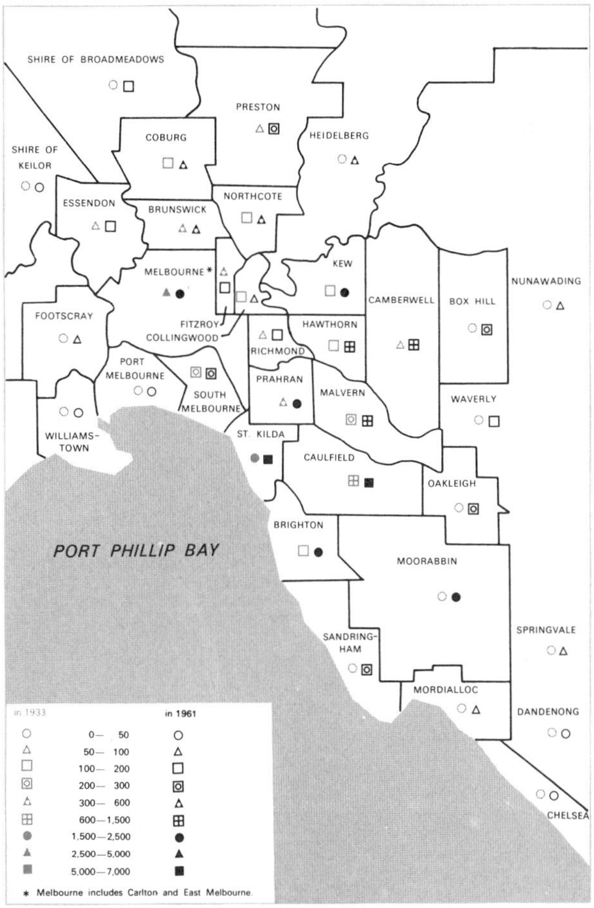

Jewish population of Melbourne and suburbs for 1933 and 1961. Based on *Journal of the Australian Jewish Historical Society*, 1968.

1912 new immigrants had helped to form a center of Yiddish culture, the "Jewish National Library-Kadimah" which apart from its book collection held regular cultural meetings including Yiddish lectures and plays.

The Judean League of Victoria was founded in 1921 as a roof-organization for non-synagogal activity, sports, literary, cultural, social, and Zionist activity. Its headquarters in its heyday at Monash House, Carlton, was a vibrant center of Jewish activity every night of the week for three decades. Its founder and leading spirit was Maurice *Ashkanasy. The struggle between the two elements ended in 1948 with a democratic representation unifying the whole community and putting an end to the era of Anglo-Jewish patrician control and of the congregational dictatorship in communal affairs. The place of Melbourne (later Victorian) Jewish Advisory Board (established in 1921), a strictly synagogal body, was taken by the Victorian Jewish Board of Deputies (in 1948) which gave a new direction to communal activities, and brought about the formulation of a community viewpoint on all matters affecting both local Jewry, such as public relations, immigration and a deepening of Jewish cultural values, and wider Jewish issues such as Zionism and anti-Semitism. There was also a move from voluntary philanthropy to organized professional social services. It operated through the following committees: education, social welfare, immigration, public relations, appeals

Table 1. Victorian Jewry—Places of Settlement 1861–1961 (slight differences in the tables below are due to non-inclusion of Jews in rural areas on a consistent basis)

Victoria	1861		1881		1901		1921		1933		1947		1954		1961	
Melbourne Metropolis																
Males—Number	1074		1876		2606		3533		4552		7322		11915		14747	
% of all males	57.8		78.3		85.4		89.5		92.9		95.1		97.6		98.3	
Females—Number	722		1467		2509		3394		4352		6896		11533		14737	
% of all females	69.0		75.9		87.9		91.0		94.5		95.6		97.7		98.7	
Persons—Number	1796		3343		5115		6927		8904		14218		23448		29484	
% of all persons	61.9		77.2		86.6		90.2		93.7		95.4		97.6		98.5	
Other Cities	m	f	m	f	m	f	m	f	m	f	m	f	m	f	m	f
Ararat	12	6	5	2	8	2	5	1	4	1	5	1	7	4	4	4
Ballarat	163	78	180	175	135	131	42	49	40	30	34	38	19	26	25	26
Bendigo	140	68	68	72	57	35	16	19	10	4	9	2	6	5	4	6
Castlemaine	23	10	9	8	3	2	2	2	3	1	—	—	1	5	1	1
Geelong	86	42	28	30	46	34	37	47	48	41	33	40	25	36	28	34
Maryborough	14	6	13	3	3	3	1	—	—	—	—	1	—	—	—	1
Mildura							2	1	2	1	7	10	4	3	3	2
Shepparton							—	—	5	9	7	7	14	12	14	9
Stawell			13	8	2	1	1	—	1	1	4	5	—	1	2	—
Wangaratta			6	2	—	—	5	1	4	5	5	3	3	2	1	—
Warrnobool	1	1	1	—	1	3	4	6	5	4	7	8	3	2	3	2
Others	51	11	43	84	22	19	72	62	26	25	27	20	93	78	76	67
Total	490	222	366	384	277	230	187	188	148	122	138	135	175	174	161	152
% of all m or f	26	21	15	20	9	8	5	5	3	3	2	2	1.4	1.5	1.1	1.0
Rural—Total	293	102	154	83	168	117	229	146	198	128	236	183	121	98	85	50
% of all m or f	16	10	6	4	6	4	6	4	4	3	3	3	1	1	0.6	0.3
Goldfields	608	259	355	310)												
Shepparton									44	39	53	57	28	29	15	9

Table 2. Jewish Population of Melbourne (census totals) 1871–1961

Total	1871	1891	1901	1921	1933	1947	1954	1961
Melbourne	1576	2426	2272	1959	2800	3003	2613	1677
Inner East	308	1370	985	869	571	369	552	311
Northern	13	100	86	508	764	1145	2577	2165
Western	5	79	96	136	132	195	249	260
Southern	116	356	348	382	249	264	308	268
South Eastern	319	1019	1186	2826	3991	8140	12986	17732
Outer South East	2	7	5	39	84	192	1385	2525
Eastern	8	160	130	210	308	865	2461	3692
Outer Eastern	—	11	6	15	12	58	242	622
Totals	2547	5528	5114	6944	8911	14231	23373	29252
Percentage								
Melbourne	61.9	43.9	44.4	28.2	31.4	21.1	11.2	5.7
Inner East	19.9	24.9	19.3	12.5	6.4	2.6	2.4	1.1
Northern	0.5	1.8	1.7	7.3	8.6	8.0	11.0	7.4
Western	0.2	1.4	1.9	2.0	1.5	1.4	1.1	0.9
Southern	4.6	6.4	6.8	5.5	2.8	1.9	1.3	0.9
South Eastern	12.5	18.4	23.2	40.7	44.8	57.2	55.6	60.6
Other South East	0.1	0.1	0.1	0.6	0.9	1.3	5.9	8.7
Eastern	0.3	2.9	2.5	3.0	3.5	6.1	10.5	12.6
Outer Eastern	0.0	0.2	0.1	0.2	0.1	0.4	1.0	2.1
	100.0	100.0	100.0	100.0	100.0	100.0	100.0	100.0

coordination, youth, organization and statistics, and congregational. The struggle was fought out on a number of points, including the question of the *kashrut* of frozen meat exported to Palestine, prepared under the supervision of the United Shechita Board and its chief *shoḥet* Rabbi I. J. Super (who served the community as *shoḥet, mohel,* and teacher for more than half a century), which was challenged by Rabbi J. L. Gurewicz, disciple of Chaim Ozer *Grodzinsky of Vilna and the respected leader of the Orthodox Carlton Synagogue in its heyday. The main issues however were the battle against anti-Zionist elements in the mid-40s, the struggle for the establishment of a Jewish day school, the continuing cleavage between the Orthodox and the Liberals, a stubborn but losing battle for the greater use of Yiddish, the attitude to anti-Semitism, and the problem of public relations.

Silencing the Anti-Zionists. Early efforts to spread Zionism were not successful. The Victorian Zionist League, founded in 1902, was short-lived. In 1913 the Victorian Zionist society, Hatechiah, was formed. In the 1920s following the Balfour Declaration and Britain's acceptance of the Palestine Mandate, there was some influential support from the well-established families and in 1921 the community, then numbering only 7,700, contributed £26,000 to the Palestine Restoration Fund. In 1923 the Palestine Welfare League was formed and in 1927 the Zionist Federation of Australia was launched. The movement was still not popularly known nor widely supported, though Sir John *Monash, as honorary president of the Federation, and Rabbi Israel Brodie, as president, added considerable prestige. However, as soon as there appeared to be an apparent clash of interests between Britain and the Zionists the Melbourne Jewish Advisory Board disassociated itself from the declarations and appeals of the Zionist movement. This first occurred in 1928 when the Zionist Federation appealed for free access to the Western Wall. During the 1930s there was steady Zionist growth with organizations such as the Ivriah and the Young Zionist League coming into being and the Jewish National Fund making its very modest beginnings. The State Zionist Council was created to coordinate all Zionist activity and to represent all Zionist bodies on the Board of Deputies. By 1944 the president of the Zionist Federation, Alec Masel, became president of the Victorian Jewish Advisory Board and from then on there has been a Zionist majority on the Board, which meant that the Zionist position was put in the name of the whole community. After World War II the Board demanded the urgent repeal of the 1939 White Paper, the finding of a solution by the Allies for the victims of Nazism, and that the Australian government bring the views of Australian Jewry before the British prime minister, Attlee. The Board of Deputies took a leading part in combating anti-Zionist propaganda of the groups led by Sir Isaac *Isaacs (see *Australia) and in 1946, despite the desire to avoid criticism of so eminent an Australian, it dissociated itself from his views, and supported the ideal of a Jewish state, but denounced terrorism. Victorian Jewry has remained strongly pro-Israel.

The Day School Movement. The greatest single act of the Victorian Jewish Board of Deputies was the establishment of Mount Scopus College—the first Jewish day school in Australia. In 1948 after previous abortive attempts, at the crucial stage the vote was carried by the Zionist, foreign-born elements in the Board over the opposition of the Australian-born members. Compulsory religious education at the college was later introduced. The college is a communal school administered by the Board of Deputies, and its establishment gave tremendous impetus to the whole future of Jewish education in Australia (see *Education). The next

Figure 1. Sir Benjamin Benjamin, mayor of Melbourne 1887–89. Caricature by Phil May. Sydney, N.S.W., Mitchell Library.

largest school was the Lubavich Yeshivah College, founded in 1955 by Rabbi Zalman Serebryanski, and later headed by Rabbi I. D. Groner. Its sister-school, Beth Rivkah Ladies' College, founded and directed until 1970 by (Mrs.) Susi Herz, was Australia's only Jewish girls' school, and likewise offered courses to university entrance standard in addition to a program of intensive Torah and Hebrew studies. In 1968 some 2,750 pupils (roughly 40% of the children of school age) were served by Melbourne's network of day schools.

Orthodox-Liberal Cleavage. After the establishment of the first Liberal Congregation in 1935 it was not possible to attain Orthodox-Liberal amity. The Board established two congregational committees to overcome this problem. While in the 1940s Orthodox rabbis would appear on the same platform with a Liberal rabbi, the strengthening of the Orthodox groups from the 1940s with the establishment of ultra-Orthodox congregations, such as Adass Israel, the Lubavicher Ḥasidim, and the modern Orthodox Mizrachi congregation, have prevented cooperation even on lay issues. The ultra-Orthodox who do not practice separatism exceed 10% of Melbourne Jewry. The Liberal movement unsuccessfully tried to obtain official representation at the Chaplaincy of the Defense Department and for civic and government functions.

Communal Public Relations. The chief source of disunity in the community from the 1950s revolved around the Jewish Council to Combat Fascism and Anti-Semitism. Formed in the 1940s by the Jewish War Effort Circle to adopt a more militant attitude on anti-Semitic manifesta-

Figure 2. The Toorak Synagogue. Courtesy *The Herald* and *Weekly Times,* Ltd., Melbourne.

tions (the previous official policy being to remain silent and inconspicuous) the Council functioned in the late 1940s as the public relations committee of the Victorian Jewish Board of Deputies. However, Communist affiliations and sympathies of some members of the Council were alleged to compromise the community's public relations. The Council views on world affairs were always close to the official Soviet line. They refused to act in regard to the persecution of Jews in Eastern Europe or to the treatment of Jewry behind the Iron Curtain. They claimed that the deportation of Jews from Hungary and Rumania (1950–51), the Prague Trials (1952), and the Doctors' Plot (1953), were all fictitious issues. As a result, the Board of Deputies set up its own public relations committee and the Council continued to function outside the Board. Subsequently it modified its views on many issues. This conflict often had its echoes in the daily press as well as in the federal parliament.

Religious Activities. As in Australia as a whole about 80% of the Jews belong to Orthodox congregations and about 20% to Liberal. Of the Orthodox congregations, the Adass Israel congregation of Hungarian migrants is educationally and communally self-contained. The Mizrachi group is active in educational and youth work; while both branches of the Lubavich center have pioneered full-time tertiary institutions: the Yeshivah Gedolah Rabbinical Academy (founded 1966) which serves communities as far afield as Sydney and New Zealand, and a teachers' seminary for girls (1971).

Prominent Personalities. One of the key personalities who had a lasting influence on the development of Melbourne Jewry was Rabbi Jacob *Danglow, whose ministry at St. Kilda Hebrew Congregation extended over 50 years. Another important figure was Rabbi Israel Brodie (later chief rabbi of the British Commonwealth), chief minister of the Melbourne Hebrew Congregation and *av bet din* from 1923 to 1937, where he wielded great influence, and his regular practice of visiting every community in Australia fostered a federal consciousness. During the years of the depression he rendered singular service to Jewish unemployed. Also outstanding was Prof. Newman H. Rosenthal, science master at Xavier (Catholic) College and principal of the United Jewish Education Board (1923–40). A pioneer of visual aids and films in education, he was professor of the department of audio-visual aids at Melbourne University (1946–66). He advocated the establishment of a Jewish day school as early as 1932 in view of the fact that 600 Jewish children lived within a radius of one mile from the center of Carlton. Other leading personalities were Rabbi Dr. H. Sanger, minister of Temple Beth Israel (Liberal synagogue) from its foundation in 1935 and prominent in interfaith activities; Samuel Wynn was a leading Zionist and organizer of many United Jewish Appeals; Leo Fink, head of the Overseas Relief Fund during World War II and later leader in welfare and immigration activities; rabbis L. M. Goldman (chaplain to A.I.F. in World War II), Dr. H. Freedman, H. Stransky, and Dr. I. Rapaport—all ministers of the Melbourne Hebrew Congregation between 1937 and 1971; Rabbi H. J. Gutnick, minister of Elwood Synagogue, and his brother S. Gutnick of the Caulfield Synagogue; Rabbi R. Lubofsky of the St. Kilda Hebrew Congregation; Abe Feiglin, principal of Mount Scopus College from its inception in 1949 to 1969; the Zionist leaders S. Wertheim, Dr. A. L. Patkin, Mrs. Ida Wynn, N. Jacobson, and J. Solvey, the communal leaders Joseph and David Feiglin, A. Bloch, W. M. Lippman, and I. J. Leibler; and Benzion Patkin, whose stubborn and long-standing advocacy of a Jewish day school eventually led to the establishment of Mount Scopus College.

The Contemporary Community. The Jewish population more than doubled between 1947 and 1971. The number of Jewish organizations grew from 90 in 1940 to more than 180 Jewish organizations in 1971, including 16 Orthodox synagogues, three Liberal synagogues, two homes for the aged, a sheltered workshop for old people, three group foster homes, four migrant hostels, seven day schools, 18 part-time schools, ten kindergartens, a Hillel Foundation, a Jewish book club, a library, an art gallery, one English-Yiddish newspaper, 16 Zionist groups, 21 welfare and social groups, three burial societies, ten educational bodies, 14 cultural groups, 17 youth clubs, 16 sporting bodies, one ex-servicemen's association, and 21 *landsmanschaften.* WIZO has 15 separate societies and 3,000 members.

Against the backdrop of the conflict between the poorer, foreign-born and the more affluent acculturated group the Melbourne Jewish community, despite its relatively small size, developed from the 1940s into an extremely virile and intensively Jewish community. The areas of first settlement north of the Yarra are no longer populated by Jews and the united cohesive community has expanded into many of the higher-class outer suburbs. The 1961 census of Melbourne Jewry shows that it is predominantly middle-class; 51.2% were employers (8% in the general population), 24% were self-employed (14%) and 18.4% (75%) were employees. In 1940–59 Jews constituted 5.05% of all university graduates, with a strong preference for medicine, law, and arts.

Despite minor and frequent anti-Semitic manifestations, relations with the non-Jewish community have always been ideal and the Jewish contribution to the State's life and development have often been given recognition by political leaders. The city of Melbourne's two most honored citizens were Jews: Sir John Monash and Sir Isaac Isaacs. Monash was honored at his death in 1931 by more than one million

Figure 3. The Adass Israel Synagogue in Melbourne, designed by E. Fooks. Photo Mark Strizig, Richmond.

Figure 4. The Lubavich Yeshivah College in Melbourne. Photo S. Cylich, Melbourne.

people who lined the route of the state funeral procession. Sir Isaac Isaacs was also given a state funeral.

Early Settlement in the Country Towns of Victoria. The 1841 census shows only one Jewish family residing in the country districts, probably Abraham Levy, a shopkeeper, at Geelong. By 1849 there were 33 families at Geelong and the first regular services were held at the home of Benjamin Goldsmid Levien. In 1851 a cemetery was acquired. The community reached its peak in 1861 (128 settlers) when its synagogue was dedicated. In 1868 Samuel Herman (1793–1879), *av bet din* of Victoria, was appointed by the chief rabbi of Great Britain as minister. Numbers declined so that by 1886 the community led by Morris Jacobs held services only on the High Holidays, though weekly Hebrew classes continued until 1948. Since 1968 no *minyan* has existed, even on the Day of Atonement. Geelong Jews serving as mayor included Julius Solomon, Solomon Jacobs, Morris Jacobs, Benjamin Rosenberg (Geelong West) and Zillah Crawcour (Newtown and Chilwell), the first woman to hold such office in Australia. The gold rush in 1851 attracted many migrants, including thousands of Jews from England and Europe. The Jewish storekeeper was a prominent and colorful figure in most of these gold-mine towns. Against overwhelming odds these pioneers tried to preserve their religious tradition but many married out of the faith, while others returned to Melbourne as soon as their financial position permitted.

In the 1850s half of Victorian Jewry resided in the provincial towns, but by 1861 this number declined to 38%. The most popular center was *Ballarat. Majorca, Talbot, and Amherst saw the coming and going of Jewish settlers. Julius Solomon, son of an early storekeeper, was mayor of Talbot in 1905 at the age of 25, the youngest person to have held such office in Victoria. Isidor Solomon was a founder of the borough council of Majorca. Services were held in Talbot, Amherst, and Maryborough at various times. The Hon. Nathaniel Levi was elected to the Victorian Legislative Assembly for Maryborough district in 1860. Matthew Mitchell became the mayor of Maryborough in 1858 and was later a member of the board of the Melbourne Hebrew Congregation. Alexander Lowenstein, a tobacconist, was four times elected mayor of Maryborough. In 1867 he presented Prince Alfred, duke of Edinburgh, with an illuminated address of welcome and in 1887 laid the foundation stone of the Maryborough Town Hall. Stawell was another center for Jewish families, one of its earliest residents being S. Isaacson, a draper, some of whose descendants played a prominent part in public life. M. G. Sloman J. P. was mayor of Prahran. Other early settlers in the country districts include Jacob Joseph J.P., president of Lowan Shire council in 1875; Sigismund Jacoby, a member of the Hamilton borough council in the 1870s and later mayor of St. Kilda; Louis Hurwitz, a solicitor, mayor of Hamilton in 1904; the Hon. Pharez Phillips, member for Wimmera district in the first Commonwealth parliament in 1901; Hyman O. Hart, mayor of Daylesford in 1873; and Reuben Tobias, five times mayor of Queenscliff. These pioneering Jewish families left a respected name in the country districts of Victoria. The only development in a country district in the 20th century was at Shepparton. In 1913 the brothers Moses and Baer Feiglin, and a group of East European and Palestine migrants, founded a culturally self-sufficient Jewish farming settlement there. The community maintained a synagogue, *mikveh,* and migrant hostel, and retained a *shoḥet*-cum-*melamed* who bicycled his way to outlying homesteads. The population reached 189 in 1946. In 1948, six Russian migrant families of Lubavicher Ḥasidim settled, and founded Australia's first full-time yeshivah, which later moved to Melbourne, as did the majority of the local orchardists. From 1950 the Australian Zionist Federation's *Hachsharah* Training Farm was situated at nearby Toolamba.

Bibliography: P. Y. Medding, *From Assimilation to Group Survival* (1958), incl. bibl.; L. M. Goldman, *Jews in Victoria in the 19th Century* (1954), incl. bibl.; I. Solomon, in: *Journal of the Australian Jewish Historical Society,* 2 (1946), 332–48; N. Spielvogel, *ibid.,* 2 (1946), 356–8; R. Apple, *ibid.,* 4 (1955), 61.

[I.P./Y.Ri.]

MELCHIOR, family prominent in Denmark since the mid-18th century. Originally from Hamburg, where the family had lived since the 18th century, Moses Melchior (1736–1817) arrived in Copenhagen in 1750. He became a successful dealer in leather and tobacco and in 1795 founded the import-export firm of Moses and son G. Melchior, which is still in existence. His son Gerson (1771–1845) took over the business on his father's death, and enlarged it by importing sugar, rum, and tea. He was one of the leaders of the Copenhagen Jewish community One of his sons, Nathan Gerson (1811–1872), was a prominent ophthalmologist. He lectured at Copenhagen University and in 1857 became a director of the Ophthalmological Institute in Copenhagen. Another son, Moritz Gerson (1816–1884), succeeded his father as head of the firm in 1845, establishing branches in the Danish West Indies and in Melbourne, Australia. Melchior was a member of the *landsting* (upper house of the Danish parliament) from 1866 to 1874 and was the first Jew to belong to the Danish Chamber of Commerce, becoming its president in 1873. Active also in the Jewish community, he served as a trustee and was made president in 1852. The writer Hans Christian Andersen was a friend and frequent guest in his house. His brother Moses (1825–1912) succeeded him in 1884, opening a New York office in 1898. He was well known for his philanthropy, contributing to many Jewish and general causes. Carl Henriques (1855–1931) took over the business after his brother's death and expanded it. He organized many athletic associations and sports clubs in Denmark and became their patron. Like his brother, he was the president of the Copenhagen community (1911–29). His son Harald Raphael (1896–) succeeded him in the firm, which deals in the import of coffee, tea, rice, cocoa, and vanilla.

Bibliography: *Moses og søn G. Melchior, Et dansk handelshus gennem 6 generationer* (1961), Eng. summary 53–56; *Dansk Biografisk Haandleksikon,* s.v.; *Dansk Biografisk Leksikon,* s.v.

[Ed.]

MELCHIOR, CARL (1871–1933), German banker. Melchior, who was born in Hamburg, studied law and later became a judge there. In 1900 he was appointed legal counsel to the bank M. M. Warburg and Co. and in 1917 became a partner in the bank. During World War I, he served as a captain with the German Army and was badly wounded. After his recuperation, he worked for the German government's Zentraleinkaufsgesellschaft (ZEG), which was charged with importing foodstuffs. During 1918–19 Melchior took part in the financial and economic negotiations following the armistice. He subsequently played a prominent part in the lengthy negotiations which eventually paved the way for Germany's reacceptance into the community of nations and displayed a mastery of financial and legal issues, diplomatic tact, and attention to detail. After Germany's admission to the League of Nations, Melchior became a member of the League's finance committee and in 1928–29 its chairman. He also served as a member of the board of the Bank for International Settlements in Basle until 1933. After Hitler's accession to power, he was active in the preparation for the formation of the *Reichsvertretung der Juden in Deutschland.

Bibliography: *Carl Melchior, Ein Buch des Gedenkens und der Freundschaft* (1967). [J.O.R.]

MELCHIOR, MARCUS (1897–1969), chief rabbi of Denmark. Born in Fredericia of an old Danish family, Melchior received his rabbinical diploma in 1921 from the Hildesheimer Seminary. He served as rabbi in Tarnowice, Poland (1921–23), in Beuthen, Germany (1925–34), and as rabbi of the Danish refugees in Sweden (1943–45). From 1947 he was the chief rabbi of Denmark. Melchior endeavored to promote understanding between all the religious trends in Judaism, while personally advocating the modern Orthodox one. He supported Zionism short of advocating *aliyah*. The main spokesman of Danish Jewry before the gentile community, Mechior was considered one of the prominent orators in Denmark. He supported the establishment of relations and furthering of understanding with West Germany. Among his books are: *Jødedommen i vor tid* (1966[2]), *En jødedommens historie* (1962); *Levet og oplevet* (1965; *A Rabbi Remembers*, 1968; also Ger. tr.); and *Tænkt og Talt* (1967). He translated into Danish (1961) Shalom Aleichem's *Tevye de Milkhiger*. He was succeeded in the chief rabbinate by his son Bent. [Ed.]

Marcus Melchior, chief rabbi of Denmark. Lithograph by Harald Isenstein, 1964. Jerusalem, Israel Museum. Photo David Harris, Jerusalem.

MELCHIZEDEK (Heb.: מַלְכִּי צֶדֶק; "legitimate/righteous king"; the English spelling follows LXX Μελχισεδεκ), king of Salem (or Jerusalem; cf. Ps. 76:3) according to Genesis 14:18–20. He welcomed *Abraham after he had defeated the four kings who had captured his nephew, Lot. Melchizedek brought out bread and wine and blessed Abraham. Finally, it is related that "he gave him a tithe of everything" although who gave the tithe to whom became a subject of considerable dispute (see below). The biblical account states that "he (Melchizedek) was priest of God

Abraham preparing to shear Melchizedek, from 16th-century Greek *Sacred History of the Old Testament*. According to legend, Abraham found Melchizedek living as a caveman, and convinced him to believe in one God. Sinai Peninsula, St. Catherine's Monastery, Ms. 1187, fol. 1, 52v.

Most High" (וְהוּא כֹהֵן לְאֵל עֶלְיוֹן). Melchizedek's priesthood was a source of numerous post-biblical speculations which were intensified by the difficult verse Psalms 110:4: "The Lord has sworn/and will not repent/Thou art priest for ever/after the manner of Melchizedek" (אַתָּה כֹהֵן לְעוֹלָם עַל־דִּבְרָתִי מַלְכִּי צֶדֶק). It is generally believed that the Melchizedek mentioned here and the one in Genesis are the same. Some interpreters, however, maintain that the Melchizedek of Psalms is not a person but a title, presumably because the name is written as two separate words (מַלְכִּי צֶדֶק).

The first documents mentioning Melchizedek in various contexts appear from around the beginning of the Christian era. The earliest is probably the fragmentary scroll discovered in cave 11 at Qumran and published by A. S. Van der Woude (in OTS, 14, 1965) and again with certain corrections by M. de Jonge and A. S. Van der Woude (in NTS, 12, 1966). Although this text "is a midrashic development which is independent of the classic Old Testament loci" (J. A. Fitzmyer, JBL, 86, 1967), it is clear that the eschatological and soteriological functions it attributes to Melchizedek draw on the perplexing figure of the biblical Melchizedek. In the Qumran text, Melchizedek is described as passing judgment, in the time of the tenth or last Jubilee, on Belial and those of his sort. The judgment takes place in heaven, and immediately there follows the "day of slaughter" prophecied by Isaiah. Here, Melchizedek is both judge and executor of his own decree, and in all likelihood he is to be identified with the Angel of Light, who figures in the dualistic doctrine of the Qumran sect (I. Gruenwald, in: *Mahanayim*, 124 (1970), 94). Melchizedek is also mentioned in another Qumran text, the Genesis Apocryphon (22:13–17), where the biblical story of the meeting between Abraham and Melchizedek is retold. Here it is Abraham who offers the tithe to Melchizedek: "And he [i.e., Abraham] gave him a tithe of all the goods of the king of Elam and his companions" (cf. Heb. 7:2 followed by the Christian translations of Genesis where, however, Melchizedek, not Abraham, is the subject of the verse). The question of who gave the tithe to whom was of considerable importance in rabbinical literature. In several places Melchizedek is stated to be a descendant of Noah, and is even identified with Shem the son of Noah. The same sources maintain that his priesthood was taken away from him and bestowed upon Abraham because he blessed Abraham first and only afterward blessed God (Gen. 14:19–20; cf. Ned. 32b; Lev. R. 25:6). Abraham's priesthood is also mentioned in connection with Psalms 110 (Gen. R., 55:6). In other rabbinical sources Melchizedek is mentioned among the four messianic figures allegorically implied by the "four smiths" of Zechariah 2:3. Melchizedek's messianic functions are also elaborated in two other literary documents. At the end of several manuscripts of the Slavonic Book of Enoch appears the story of the miraculous birth of Melchizedek as the son of Nir, Noah's brother. He is transported to heaven and becomes the head of a line of priests leading down to messianic days. There will presumably be another eschatological Melchizedek who will function as both priest and king. In symbolizing Mechizedek as Jesus in his three functions as messiah, king, and high priest (see below) the author's ingenuity combines all the motives singled out in the above-mentioned sources. A gnostic sect whose particular theological position is unknown called itself after Melchizedek. [I.GR.]

In Christian Tradition. The two brief and somewhat enigmatic references to Melchizedek in the Bible provided the New Testament with a subject for typological interpretation. In the Epistle to the Hebrews (7:1–7), Melchizedek (king of justice—Zedek; of peace—Salem) is described as unique, being both a priest and a king, and because he is "without father, without mother, without genealogy"; he is eternal, "having neither beginning of days nor end of life." In this respect Melchizedek resembles Jesus, the son of God, and thus is a type of the savior.

Abraham, and therefore Levi "in the loins of his father" (*ibid.* 9–10), paid the tithe in submission to Melchizedek. Since in Christian tradition Jesus is high priest "after the order of Melchizedek" and "not after the order of Aaron" (*ibid.* 7:11, 17–21), Jesus' priesthood is excellent, superior to that of Abraham's descent, and transcends all human, imperfect orders (Heb. 7:23–28; 8:1–6). To Christians the objection that Jesus, like Aaron, was "in the loins" of the patriarch, and consequently paid the tithe was met by the Church Fathers with the argument that Jesus, though descended from Abraham, had no human father. [IL.S.]

Bibliography: H. L. Strack and P. Billerbeck, *Kommentar zum Neuen Testament*, 4 (1928), 452–65; Rowley, in: *Festschrift Bertholet* (1950), 461ff.; A. Vaillant, *Le livre des secrets d'Hénoch* (1952); Yadin, in: *Scripta Hierosolymitana*, 4 (1958), 36–55; idem, in: IEJ, 15 (1965), 152–4; Panikkar, *Kairos*, 1 (1959), 5–17; J. Maier, *Vom Kultus zur Gnosis* (1964), 37ff.; Flusser, in: *Christian News from Israel* (1966), 23ff.; J. A. Fitzmyer, in: JBL, 86 (1967), 25–41; A. R. Johnson, *Sacral Kingship in Ancient Israel* (1967²), 35–53; S. Paul, in: JAOS, 88 (1968), 182. IN CHRISTIAN TRADITION: Friedlaender, in REJ, 5 (1882), 1–26, 188–98; 6 (1883), 187–99; Barody, in: RB, 35 (1926), 496–509; (1927), 25–45.

MELDOLA, Sephardi family of rabbis and scholars. The family originated in the 15th century in Meldola, northern Italy; the legend that they descended from Spanish exiles cannot be substantiated. The first of the family to attain prominence was JACOB MELDOLA, rabbi in Mantua in the 16th century. His son SAMUEL MELDOLA or MENDOLA was both a rabbinic scholar and physician to the Mantuan court. In the next generation members of the family settled in Leghorn, entering thus into the tradition of Sephardi life. For the next 200 years they provided rabbis, printers, and leaders to the Sephardi communities in Holland, Italy, France, and England.

Bibliography: E. Castelli, *I banchi feneratizi ebraici nel Mantovano*... (1959), index; Mortara, Indice, 38; Ghirondi-Neppi, 79, 311, 355–7. [C.R.]

MELDOLA, RAPHAEL (1754–1828), British rabbi; son of Moses Hezekiah Meldola (1725–1791), professor of oriental languages in Paris. Raphael was born in Leghorn, received rabbinical ordination there from Ḥ. J. D. *Azulai in 1796, became a *dayyan* in 1803, and in 1804/05 was appointed haham of the Sephardi community in London—an office vacant since the death of Moses Cohen d'*Azevedo in 1784. Energetic and capable, he helped to reform the educational institutions of his community in the face of missionary activities, introduced a choir into the synagogue and cooperated cordially with Solomon *Hirschell, the Ashkenazi chief rabbi. On the other hand, his belligerent nature was responsible for periodic friction with the members of his community. Notwithstanding his imperfect knowledge of English he corresponded extensively with Christian scholars. Before leaving Leghorn, he had published there *Ḥuppat Ḥatanim* (1797), a handbook on the laws of marital life. He also published sermons and memorial poems: part of his catechism *Derekh Emunah (The Way of Faith)* appeared with his English translation after his death (1848). His son DAVID (1797–1853), who succeeded him as presiding rabbi though not as haham of the Sephardi community in London, was one of the founders of the **Jewish Chronicle*, and ineffectively opposed the movement for religious reform among London Jewry in 1840. A grandson of Raphael's was the British scientist, Raphael *Meldola.

Bibliography: DNB, s.v.; Roth, Mag Bibl, index; M. Gaster, *History of the Ancient Synagogue*... Bevis Marks (1901), 159–64; A. M. Hyamson, *Sephardim of England* (1951), index; Barnett, in: JHSET, 21 (1968), 1–38 (bibl. of Meldola's publications 13–14). [V.D.L.]

Raphael Meldola, haham of the London Sephardi community. Engraving by Joshua Lopez from a painting by E. B. Barlin. London, Alfred Rubens Collection.

MELDOLA, RAPHAEL (1849–1915), British chemist and naturalist. Meldola was the grandson of Raphael *Meldola, the haham of the London Sephardi community. He worked at the Royal Mint (1868–71), with a firm of color manufacturers, and at the Royal College of Science. In 1875 he led a Royal Society expedition to the Nicobar Islands to

Raphael Meldola, British chemist and naturalist. Jerusalem, J.N.U.L., Schwadron Collection.

observe a total eclipse of the sun. He spent several years as a schoolteacher and in industry and in 1885 became professor of chemistry at Finsbury Technical College, a position he held for over 30 years. Meldola's early investigations were in the fields of natural history and entomology as well as astronomy, but his main interest was dyestuffs. "Meldola's Blue" was the first oxazine dye, and he also discovered the first alkali green. In 1904 he published *Chemical Synthesis of Vital Products.* Meldola played an important role in the British chemical profession and was president of the Chemical Society and of the Institute of Chemistry, as well as a fellow and vice-president of the Royal Society. After his death the Society of *Maccabeans, of which he had been president, instituted the Meldola Medal of the Royal Institute of Chemistry in his memory.

Bibliography: J. Marchant (ed.), *Raphael Meldola* (Eng. 1916); A. Findlay and W. H. Mills, *British Chemists* (1947), 96–125.

[S.A.M.]

°**MELITO OF SARDIS** (c. 120–185 C.E.), bishop of Sardis (Asia Minor) and Christian author. Together with other bishops of Asia Minor, Melito continued to celebrate Easter on the 14th of Nisan, the eve of Passover. He visited Palestine to learn about the canon of the Old Testament (from which he excerpted passages pertaining in some way to Jesus). Only brief quotations from Melito's works were known until the mid-20th century, when two papyrus copies of his homily on the Passion were published. As a result of this discovery, Latin, Coptic, Georgian, and two Syriac translations of this treatise could be identified. The bishop delivered the treatise as a sermon after the biblical account of the Exodus was read on Easter, precisely the time when the Jews observed the Passover feast. The coincidence of observances and Melito's animosity toward Judaism caused his sermon, which was written between 160 and 170 C.E., to become one of the most important documents of early Christian anti-Judaism. After a theological introduction, Melito gives a dramatic description of Egypt's sufferings at the time of the Exodus. Influenced by the Midrash on Exodus 10:21, the darkness that engulfed Egypt is described as tangible. However, the events surrounding the Exodus were only a prefiguration of the Passion of Christ, the true Passover lamb. The earlier model no longer had validity and usefulness, because the prefigurations of the Old Testament had become a reality in the New Testament. The second part of the sermon is the oldest and one of the strongest accusations of deicide made against the Jews in early Christian literature. Jews are, among other things, described as having themselves crucified Jesus; and the murder is clearly defined as deicide: "God has been murdered, the King of Israel has been slain by an Israelite hand" (§ 96). In view of the tragic events suffered by the Jews of this period—the destruction of the Temple and the defeat of Bar Kokhba—Melito could say that, in consequence of the deicide, "Israel lay dead," while Christianity, "the broad grace," was conquering the whole earth. The sermon, nevertheless, attests the antiquity of the Passover *Haggadah.* Paragraph 68 of the sermon contains a Greek version of part of the introduction to *Hallel* in the *Haggadah;* and paragraphs 84–85 and 88 derive from the famous Passover litany *"Dayyeinu."*

Bibliography: Eusebius Pamphili, *Ecclesiastical History,* 2 vols. (1926–32), index; T. Otto, *Corpus Apologetarum Christianorum,* 9 (1872), 374-478, 497–512; E. J. Goodspeed, *Aelteste Apologeten* (1914), 306–13; C. Bonner, *Homily on the Passion* (1914); M. Testuz (ed. and tr.), *Papyrus Bodmer XIII, Méliton de Sardes, Homélie sur la Pâque* (1960); O. Perler, *Méliton de Sardes sur la Pâque, sources Chrétiennes* (1966); J. Blank, *Meliton von Sardes vom Passa* (1963); E. Werner, in: HUCA, 37 (1966), 191–210.

[D.FL.]

MELITOPOL, city in Zaporozhe oblast, Ukrainian S.S.R. According to the 1897 census there were 6,563 Jews and 454 *Karaites in Melitopol (45.7% of the total population). On April 19, 1905, a mob attacked Jewish houses, but a Jewish *self-defense group managed to prevent a pogrom. In 1910 Melitopol had a *talmud torah* and two private schools for boys and two for girls. Joseph *Trumpeldor was active in the town and the first *ḥalutzim* he organized left from there for Palestine. By 1926 the Jewish population rose to 8,583 (33.6% of the total). When the town was occupied by the Germans during World War II the Jews were murdered. In 1970 the estimated Jewish population was about 800; there was no synagogue.

Bibliography: *Voskhod,* nos. 17, 18, 19 (1905); Dubnow, Hist Russ, 3 (1920), 115.

[ED.]

MELOKHIM BUKH, a poetic adaptation of biblical history and one of the great national epics in Old Yiddish literature. Neither the author nor the date of its composition is known with certainty. In all probability it is a work of the 15th century, though Fuks (see bibl.), in his critical edition, believes it to date from the 14th century. Yiddish national epics, which left a considerable mark on creative medieval Yiddish literature, flourished in the 15th century and were very popular among the Yiddish-speaking masses. This folk literature was modeled on the Germanic epics from which the metric romance and heroic epic were derived. Later, Jewish writers turned to biblical sources and national sagas and ultimately created a Jewish national epic. The highly skilled author of the *Melokhim Bukh,* basing his epic on the great period in Jewish history recorded in the Books of Kings, treated the subject with poetic freedom and imagination. Apart from the historical books, he employed traditional material, drawing extensively on the Talmud and Midrash, thus embellishing his historical narrative with numerous legends and tales from the ancient *aggadah.*

The author of the *Melokhim Bukh,* like the author of the **Shmuel Bukh,* was a poet of great creative power who took pride in the Jewish heritage and was fascinated by the glories of the ancient Jewish past. The grandeur of King Solomon's reign and the heroic deeds and gallant exploits of the later kings of Judah and Israel are described in a colorful, often idealized fashion.

The epic concludes with Nebuchadnezzar's destruction of the Temple and the ensuing Exile, which were considered just punishment for the Jewish people's sins and disloyalty to God. Like many traditional works of the period, this epic contains a didactic and moralizing tendency. For example, in the last stanza, the author again refers to the hatred and enmity among the Jews, which he believed caused the destruction of the Temple and the Exile. In the final strophe he laments the tragic fate of the Jewish dispersion and concludes with the traditional eschatological note:

We have suffered long, several hundred years,
Could we only leave off envy and enmities,
Our fate will better and this will doubtessly happen,
Sure, we will see with our eyes the coming of the Messiah, the son of David.

The *Melokhim Bukh* consists of 2,262 strophes of four lines, each composed in the metric form of the Nibelungen (Hildebrand) stanza. The poet shows great skill in handling verse, and although he borrowed the style, technique, terminology, and diction of the contemporary German epics, songs, and rhymed biblical paraphrases, his work remained, in essence, a Jewish creation in content and spirit. Well within the Jewish tradition, his narrative is permeated with the spirit of great piety, national pride, and religious pathos. High dramatic tension is successfully combined with vivid realism. The work's didacticism is relieved by its rich store of folklore and some genuine folk humor and wit. Often humanizing historical events and tales of adventure, the author created a refined and attractive epic narrative. The work represents a successful fusion of the cultural influences from the world at large and the traditional lore of the people.

The Author. The poet who created the *Melokhim Bukh* remains anonymous, but evidence indicates that he was a German Jew who emigrated to northern Italy, where many Ashkenazi communities flourished at the close of the Middle Ages, and where he composed his epic. The author was undoubtedly a man of Jewish learning, familiar not only with the Bible but also with rabbinic literature, the Talmud and Midrash, and such medieval commentators as Rashi, David Kimḥi, and R. Levi b. Gershom. At the same time he was well versed with the style and technique of the literature written in Middle High German, which he adapted to his purpose in a masterful way. The vast amount of traditional and historical material served the author in creating a large canvas packed with heroic deeds and tragic events. This outstanding and popular national epic is second in importance only to the *Shmuel Bukh.*

The original manuscript of the epic has not survived. The extant copy, made in Italy in the 16th century, is a shorter version of the printed edition. The copy is known as the codex Wilmersdorf and is in the Rosenthaliana Library in Amsterdam. The epic was first published in Augsburg in 1543, a year earlier than the *Shmuel Bukh* (Augsburg, 1544). However, the publishers considered both epics to be one entity, and they apparently were accepted as such by the readers. The title page of the *Shmuel Bukh* reads: "*The Shmuel [Bukh]* is the first part of the *Melokhim Bukh,* as they belong together." Apart from the *editio princeps* (Augsburg, 1543), two more editions are known: Cracow, 1582, and Prague, 1607.

Bibliography: F. Folk (ed.), *Das Schemuelbuch des Mosche Esrim Wearba* (1961); L. Fuks, *Das Altjiddische Epos Melok̲îm Bûk̲,* 2 vols. (1965); Ch. Shmeruk, in: *Di Goldene Keyt* (1967), no. 59, 208ff.; J. I. Meitlis, in: *The Zukunft* (New York), 74 (1967), 13–17; W. Staerk, in: MGWJ, 63 (1919), 20ff.; Steinschneider, Cat Bod, 184f.; idem and A. Leitzmann, *Die juedisch-deutschen Bibelueberstezungen* (1923); M. Erik, *Die Geshikhte fun der Yidisher Literatur-Geshikhte* (1928); A. A. Roback, *The Story of Yiddish Literature* (1940); I. Zinberg, *Di Geshikhte fun der Literatur bay Yidn,* 6 (1943), 117, 123–33, 294, 306, 378; N. B. Minkoff, in: *The Jewish People, Past and Present,* 3 (1952), 145ff.; Waxman, Literature, 2 (1960), 617ff. [Y.J.M.]

MELON, two plant species belonging to different botanical genera: the watermelon and the muskmelon.

(1) The watermelon (Heb. אֲבַטִּיחַ, *avati'aḥ*) is the *Citrullus vulgaris.* The Bible mentions it among the vegetables eaten by the Israelites in Egypt, for which they hankered in the wilderness (Num. 11:5). The Hebrew name may possibly be connected with the verb בטט *(btt)* meaning to swell or grow. Watermelons were a familiar plant in Egypt, and a papyrus from the 21st dynasty preserves a pictorial representation of one. The *avati'aḥ* is frequently mentioned in rabbinical literature. It was comparatively cheap (Ma'as. 2:6) and was usually eaten when ripe, though some ate it as a vegetable while it was still unripe (Ma'as. 1:5).

(2) The muskmelon, *Cucumis melo,* is called in the Mishnah *melafefon* (מְלָפְפוֹן), a name of Greek origin. It is not known if it was grown in biblical times and no Hebrew name exists for it. The Palestinian Targum identifies the biblical *avati'aḥ* with *melafefonya,* i.e., the muskmelon, but this does not appear likely, since in a number of places in the Tosefta and Talmud they are mentioned together (Tosef., Kil. 1:1). Some held that these two species do not constitute a mixed species *(*kilayim; ibid.)* for "a man takes a seed from the upper part of the *avati'aḥ* and plants it—and it becomes a *melafefon*" (TJ, Kil. 1:2, 27a), i.e., these species may be interchangeable. This view was taken over from Greek and Roman agricultural folklore which assumed that the characteristics of species were subject to change. An echo of this view is found in the Palestinian Targum in the philological explanation of the name *melafefon* given by R. Judah: "A man takes one seed from the upper part of an *avati'aḥ* and one seed from the upper part of an apple and puts them into the same hole, they grow together and become a hybrid species, that is why in Greek it is called *melafefon.*" The Greek μηλοπέπον and the Latin *melopepo* both mean "apple-watermelon" probably because the taste of the muskmelon is reminiscent of both the apple and the watermelon. According to Pliny the *melopepo* originated in Campania from a species of cucumber which looked like a quince (Natural History 19:67). There is certainly no substance for these views, which are based on the polymorphism of the family Cucurbitaceae. The plant *Cucumis melo* var. *Chate,* identified with the *kishut, kishu'im* (see *Cucumber), that belongs to the same botanical genus (and apparently even to the same species) as the muskmelon, is especially polymorphic. It could be that pollination between these two species gives rise to hybrids and is the reason for the *halakhah* that the *kishut* (*Chate* melon or cucumber) and the *melafefon* do not constitute *kilayim* (Kil. 1:2). Despite the ruling of the Academy for the Hebrew Language, modern Hebrew has adopted the name *melafefon* for cucumber.

Bibliography: Loew, Flora, 1 (1928), 528–54; B. Chizik, *Ẓimḥei ha-Delu'im be-Ereẓ Yisrael,* 1 (1937); H. N. and A. L. Moldenke, *Plants of the Bible* (1952), 315 (index), s.v.; J. Feliks, *Kilei Zera'im ve-Harkavah* (1967), 44–53; idem, *Olam ha-Ẓome'aḥ ha-Mikra'i* (1968²), 164f. [J.F.]

Harvesting muskmelon in the Arabah. Photo Werner Braun, Jerusalem.

MELTON, SAMUEL MENDEL (1900–), U.S. industrialist and philanthropist. Melton was born in Saros, Austro-Hungary. His family emigrated in 1904 to Toledo, Ohio. He established the Capitol Manufacturing and Supply Company in Columbus, as well as several pipe and nipple companies, which later merged with the Harsco Corporation (1968) and became a leader in the metals industry. Melton extended the Capitol Company to Israel in 1949 and deeded it to various Israel institutions in 1955. Active in numerous communal and national Jewish organizations, he was a member of the UJA "cabinet" and the board of the Jewish Theological Seminary, where he founded the Melton Research Center (1959) to develop Jewish educational materials. He established professorships in Judaica at the Ohio State University and the Hebrew University (1965), a vocational school in Bat Yam, Israel, and the Samuel Mendel Melton Foundation (1951).

[E.GR.]

MELTZER, ISSER ZALMAN (1870–1953), talmudic scholar and yeshivah head. Born in Lithuania, Meltzer studied in Volozhin under Ḥayyim Soloveichik and Naphtali Ẓevi Judah Berlin, and later under the Ḥafeẓ Ḥayyim in Radin. All of these exercised a profound influence upon him, Soleveichik by his talmudic methodology, Berlin by his love for Ereẓ Israel, and the Ḥafeẓ Ḥayyim by his humility and his ethical approach. In 1892 he married Beila Hinda, daughter of R. Faivel Frank of Ilukste. His wife possessed considerable scholarly abilities and throughout his life assisted him in transcribing his works and in arranging them for publication. In 1894 he was appointed by R. Nathan Ẓevi *Finkel one of the principals of the *Slobodka yeshivah and in 1897 the head of a yeshivah for advanced students in Slutsk, where Jacob David *Willowski was the rabbi. Hundreds of students flocked to the yeshivah, and when Willowski emigrated to Ereẓ Israel in 1903 Meltzer succeeded him as rabbi of Slutsk. After the Bolshevik Revolution in 1917 the yeshivah moved to Kletsk in Poland. Meltzer, however, refused to leave his community in Slutsk, despite his suffering at the hands of the Bolsheviks, including imprisonment for teaching Torah. In 1923 he left Russia for Kletsk and in the same year participated in the founding conference of the *Agudat Israel in Vienna, at which he was elected to the Mo'eẓet Gedolei ha-Torah. In 1925 he became head of the Eẓ Ḥayyim Yeshivah in Jerusalem. In Ereẓ Israel, he devoted himself almost entirely to the dissemination of Torah and the strengthening of yeshivot. As a fervent Zionist, he exercised a moderating influence in the councils of the Agudah. In 1935 his first work appeared, *Even ha-Ezel* on the *Mishneh Torah* of *Maimonides which is regarded as a fundamental work of its kind. Seven volumes appeared during his lifetime, the other posthumously. He also edited and wrote commentary to the novellae of Naḥmanides (1928/29).

Isser Zalman Meltzer, talmudic scholar and yeshivah head. Courtesy Agudat Israel World Organization, Jerusalem.

Bibliography: S. Zevin, *Ishim ve-Shitot* (1966[3]), 337–60; D. Katz, *Tenu'at ha-Musar,* 3 (1957), 37–42 and passim; *Yahadut Lita* (1960), index; A. Rothkoff, in: *Jewish Life* (March 1971), 51–57.

[MO.HA.]

MELTZER, SHIMSHON (1909–), Hebrew poet. Born in Tluste (eastern Galicia; present-day Tolstoye), Meltzer emigrated to Palestine in 1933, after having taught in Horodenka (Gorodenka), Galicia. For a time he taught secondary school in Tel Aviv, but from 1937 he engaged in editorial work; first in the daily **Davar,* and later in the Am Oved publishing house and in the children's magazine *Davar li-Yladim.* From 1959 he was on the editorial staff of the Zionist Library publications of the Jewish Agency.

His first poems were published in *Ba-Derekh,* the magazine of the teachers' seminary in Lvov where he studied. After his arrival in Ereẓ Israel his poetry appeared mainly in *Davar,* but also in various literary journals. He published a number of volumes of poems and ballads including: *Be-Shivah Meitarim* (1939); *Me'ir ha-Keleizemar Na'asah Komisar* (1940); *Asarah She'arim* (1943); *Alef* (1945, 1963[2]), memoirs of the *ḥeder; Sefer ha-Shirot ve-ha-Balladot* (1950); and *Or Zaru'a* (1966). Meltzer attempted to capture the folk flavor of Eastern European Jewry by using ḥasidic tales and motifs in his ballads. His collection of essays on literature is entitled *Devarim al Ofnam* ("Words and their Forms," 1962). Meltzer translated extensively from Polish-Jewish writers, especially from Yiddish writers, dramatists, and poets. For English translations of his works, see Goell, Bibliography, 1033–38.

Shimshon Meltzer, Hebrew poet.

Bibliography: D. Zakkai, *Keẓarot* (1956), 470–1; A. Cohen, *Soferim Ivriyyim Benei Zemannenu* (1964), 195–8; I. Cohen, *Sha'ar ha-Soferim* (1962), 355–8; J. Lichtenbaum, *Bi-Teḥumah shel Sifrut* (1963), 105–9; D. Sadan, *Bein Din le-Ḥeshbon* (1963), 105–11.

[G.K.]

MELUN, capital of the department of Seine-et-Marne, 26 mi. (42 km.) S. of Paris. The first explicit reference to Jews in Melun dates from the middle of the 12th century: in his will, Simon of Beaugency mentions a Jew of Melun among his creditors. From the beginning of the 13th century, there is evidence of a Rue des Juifs and an *"escole des Juis"* (the synagogue). There is no record of a medieval Jewish community after the expulsion of the Jews from the Kingdom of France in 1306. Scholars of Melun took part in the *synod convened by *Samuel b. Meir (Rashbam) and Jacob b. Meir *Tam. Meshullam b. Nathan of Melun, previously from Narbonne, lived in Melun from 1150. During the second half of the 12th century, Jedidiah of

Melun also lived in the town. Judah b. David of Melun was one of the four rabbis who confronted Nicholas *Donin at the famous *disputation organized by *Louis IX (St. Louis) in 1240. Preserved in the municipal library of Melun is a *maḥzor* of the 14th century for the New Year and Day of Atonement according to the French rite (Ms. No. 14): it had previously been in the possession of the Carmelite monastery of Melun and is possibly of local origin. On the eve of World War II there was a very small community in Melun. It increased in the postwar period, mainly as a result of the arrival of Jews from North Africa, and numbered over 500 in 1969.

Bibliography: S. Rouillard, *Histoire de Melun* (1628), 352f.; M. Schwab in: REJ, 13 (1886), 296–300; G. Leroy, *Histoire de la ville de Melun* (1887), 126, 167: Gross, Gal Jud, 351–5; J. Thillier and E. Jarr, *Cartulaire de Ste-Croix d'Orléans . . .* (1906), 13. [B.BL.]

MEM (מֵם; ם, מ), the 13th letter of the Hebrew alphabet; its numerical value is 40. In proto-Sinaitic and early proto-Canaanite inscriptions the *mem* was drawn as a pictograph representing water *(mayim)* ~ or ≀. In the later proto-Canaanite script the vertical zigzag prevailed, which turned into ≀ in the tenth century B.C.E. Phoenician script. Later, the *mem* consisted of a zigzag-shaped head and a downstroke. The Hebrew forms were: → (cursive) and (formal); hence the Samaritan . From the eighth and seventh centuries B.C.E., the Phoenician *mem* was written , which in the Aramaic became . In the late fifth century B.C.E. and later Aramaic cursive the downstrokes were bent leftward. Thus the medial and final variations evolved. These are prototypes of the Jewish medial מ and final ם *mem* forms. The Nabatean *mem* was drawn without lifting the pen , and this led to the Arabic م. The ancestor of the Latin M, the Archaic Greek developed from the early Phoenician *mem*.

See *Alphabet. [JO.NA.]

MEMEL (Lith. **Klaipėda**), a Baltic port in W. Lithuanian S.S.R. The town was founded in the 13th century; the earliest existing document in which Jews are mentioned is dated April 20, 1567, and refers to an edict expelling the Jews from the city. In 1664 the elector of Brandenburg permitted a Jewish merchant from the Netherlands, Moses Jacobson de Jong, to settle in Memel, and eventually Jews were allowed to visit the city for the annual trade fairs. Only after the emancipation of Jews in Prussia (1812) were they able to settle freely in Memel.

In the 19th century the community consisted of Eastern European and Prussian Jews. The former had settled in the port in connection with their trans-Baltic business and formed the majority of the Jewish population (in 1880 they accounted for 80% of the total number of Jews). In later years there was an increased influx of Jews from Germany. The number of Jews grew from 887 in 1867, to 1,214 in 1900, and to over 2,000 in 1910. Each group had its own synagogue and communal institutions, but the official community administration was run by German Jews. Israel *Lipkin (Salanter), founder of the Musar movement, lived and taught in Memel 1860–80, founding a *bet midrash* and societies for Torah Study, and publishing here the short-lived periodical *Ha-Tevunah* (1861). Isaac *Ruelf, one of the spiritual leaders of German Jewry, was rabbi of Memel from 1865 to 1898 and devoted much effort to alleviating the plight of Russian Jews. Ruelf was succeeded by Emanuel *Carlebach (until 1904), M. Stein (until 1915), L. Lazarus (until 1932), and S. Schlesinger (until 1939).

After World War I, the League of Nations adopted the Memel Convention (1924), whereby it became an autonomous region under Lithuanian rule. As the country's only port, it played an important role in the economic life of Lithuania, and there was a steady influx of Jews into the city in the interwar period. In March 1939 it had a Jewish population of approximately 9,000 (17% of the total). Most of the Jews were engaged in commerce but there were also a few industrialists. The Memel district also had a few Jewish-owned estates, some of which were made available for *hakhsharah.* On March 22, 1939, the Germans occupied Memel and incorporated it into the Reich. Most of the Jews managed to flee to *Lithuania, where they later shared the fate of their coreligionists. In 1970 the estimated Jewish population was less than 1,000. There was no synagogue, cemetery, or organized religious life.

Bibliography: I. Ruelf, *Zur Geschichte der Juden in Memel* (1900); Gringauz, in: *Lite,* 1 (1951), 1427–38; Shulman, in: *Yahadut Lita,* 3 (1967), 281–3; A. Carlebach, *Adass Jeshurun of Cologne* (1964), 25–28; L. Scheinhaus, in: *Memeler Dampfboot* Aug. 15, 1928). [JO.GA.]

MEMMI, ALBERT (1920–), French author and sociologist. Memmi, a native of Tunis, fought with the Free French during World War II. After completing his studies he returned to Tunis, where he became head of a psychological institute. In 1959, he joined the Centre National de la Recherche Scientifique in Paris, and became a teacher at the Ecole Pratique des Hautes Etudes where he was appointed a professor in 1966. He specialized in the social effects of colonization, finding a similarity between the situation of the Jew and that of colonized peoples. Though an advocate of independence for the countries of the Maghreb, he was well aware that one of its consequences would be the mass exodus of North African Jewry. Memmi's first two books were novels, both largely autobiographical. *La statue de sel* (1953; *Pillar of Salt,* 1955), is the story of a North African Jew's emergence from a narrow Jewish society through the discovery of French culture, and his eventual disillusionment with an idealized Western humanism. *Agar* (1955; *Strangers,* 1958) describes the isolation of a Tunisian Jew, rejected by both Frenchmen and Arabs. Memmi was still dealing with the same problem a decade later in essays such as *Portrait d'un Juif* (1962; *Portrait of a Jew,* 1963) and its sequel, *La libération du Juif* (1966; *The Liberation of the Jew,* 1966). He portrays the Jew as a "shadow figure," neither wholly assimilated nor anxious to lose his distinctiveness, concluding that "Israel is our only solution, our one trump card, our last historical opportunity." Memmi's sociological studies appeared in various journals and in *Le Français et le racisme* (1965). He published an *Anthologie des écrivains nord-africains* (1964) and a *Bibliographie de la littérature nord-africaine d'expression française 1945–1962* (1965). He also wrote essays on Jewish subjects for *L'Arche, Evidences,* and *Commentary.*

Albert Memmi, French novelist and sociologist.

Bibliography: Sartre, in: *Les Temps Modernes*, no. 137–8 (1957), 289–92; Camus, in: A. Memmi, *La statue de sel* (1953), preface; A. Khatibi, *Le Roman Maghrébin* (1968); Di-Nour, in: *Dispersion et Unité*, 8 (1967), 81–92.

[JA.K.]

MEMMINGEN, city in Bavaria, W. Germany. Jews were present in Memmingen by the second half of the 13th century, since the city statutes of 1270 contain references to Jewish moneylending activities. In 1344 the bishop of Augsburg excommunicated the city for nonpayment of its debts to a Jew; the burghers thereupon threatened to bury their dead in the Jewish cemetery. The Jews made their living in the city in 1373. By 1500, however, there were no *Judengasse*. The community was destroyed during the *Black Death persecutions of 1348, but Jews were again living in the city in 1373. By 1500, however, there were no longer Jews there. The privilege of *Judenfreiheit* ("freedom from Jews"), granted in 1541, was renewed in 1559. Many Jews who had formerly lived in Memmingen concentrated in Fellheim, a nearby village, and there maintained a settlement numbering 379 persons (63% of the population) in 1810 (during World War II it again served as a center for refugees). Jews from Fellheim often visited Memmingen for trading purposes during the 17th and 18th centuries. In 1862 the first Jew received citizenship in Memmingen. A community comprising 100 members was formed in 1875 and 20 years later it had grown to 231. A synagogue was dedicated in 1909. The community subsequently declined: from 194 in 1900, to 161 in 1933, and 104 on Jan. 1, 1939. The Jews, who were mainly textile manufacturers and livestock merchants, were severely hit by the Nazi boycott of Jewish business establishments, and considerable numbers emigrated despite the many obstacles they encountered. In 1938 the synagogue and Jewish homes were looted and destroyed and in the spring of 1942 the community was liquidated. In 1968 there were two Jews in Memmingen.

Bibliography: J. Miedel, *Die Juden in Memmingen* (1909); FJW (1932–33), 304; W. Rapp, *Geschichte des Dorfes Fellheim* (1960); D. Linn, *Das Schicksal der juedischen Bevoelkerung in Memmingen, 1933–1945* (1962); Germ Jud, 2 (1968), 534–6; PK.

[ED.]

MEMORBUCH, a community prayer book once common in Jewish communities throughout Central Europe. It consisted of three major parts: (1) a collection of prayers usually intoned by the reader while standing at the *almemar* (see *Bimah) such as the order of blowing the *shofar* and reading the Scroll of Esther, different forms of the *Mi She-Berakh* prayer, etc; (2) a necrology of distinguished persons, either of local or of general Jewish importance; (3) a martyrology of persons and places. The last has been subjected to minute research by scholars, particularly by S. *Salfeld. According to one view the *Memorbuch* received its name from being placed, for the convenience of the reader, on the *almemar*, while another holds that it is derived from the Latin *memoria*.

The custom of reading the names developed after the massacres of the *Rhine communities during the First Crusade; to this list were added the names of the martyrs of the *Rindfleisch massacres and other catastrophes. The list of martyrs who perished during the *Black Death persecutions (1348–49) was of such magnitude that mainly names of places were recorded. It became the custom to read off the list of thousands of names in ceremony on the Sabbath before Shavuot (when the massacres of the First Crusade took place); at a later date it was also read off on the Sabbath before the Ninth of Av although the author probably intended it to be read in part each Sabbath. Rabbi Jacob b. Moses Levi of Mainz (see *Moellin), the codifier of the Ashkenazi *minhag*, made the reading of the full list obligatory for Rhenish communities while non-Rhenish

Page from the martyrology of the *Memorbuch* kept by the community of Frankfort on the Main from 1629 to 1907. It records the names of individual communities which have suffered persecution and ends with a general prayer for the souls of the martyrs. Jerusalem, J.N.U.L.

ones were to read only the list of places. The *Memorbuch* of the Mainz community, begun by Isaac b. Samuel of Meiningen in 1296, was supplemented and became the complete and authoritative version for all other copies. (Salfeld considered the early version to be that of the Nuremberg community, a view not accepted by M. Weinberg, a later authority.) It was updated by mention of the catastrophes of 1492 in *Mecklenburg, and 1510 in *Brandenburg, and by the names of communities which perished in the *Chmielnicki massacres (1648). As no community could be complete without the *Memorbuch*, it was frequently copied in the 17th and 18th centuries.

The *Memorbuch* was expanded in the different localities to include names of esteemed local personages, lists of deceased, as well as prayers of purely local use and origin. It was therefore never printed and gradually fell into disuse in the mid-19th century, through the unification and standardization of services and ritual.

The earliest *Memorbuecher* (excluding that of Mainz) appeared in about 1600, but between 1650 and 1750 a large number were commenced (based on that of Mainz), for many communities were established in this period. The *Memorbuch* reflected the religious life of the community and accompanied it in its tribulations and migrations; refugees from Vienna (1670) continued using their *Memorbuch* in Fuerth; refugees from Fulda (1671) took theirs with them to Amsterdam and subsequently back to Fulda. Some communities had more than one *Memorbuch* (Fuerth Jewry had five complementary ones). *Memorbuecher* were particularly common among communities in rural areas; it is estimated that there were about 150 in Bavaria alone and a few hundred more in *Baden, *Wuerttemberg, *Hesse, *Alsace, and *Switzerland. The *Memorbuch* continues to serve the historian as an important source for the social and religious history of the Jews and is frequently cited.

Bibliography: M. Weinberg, *Die Memorbuecher der juedischen Gemeinden in Bayern* (1938); idem, in: JJLG, 16 (1924), 253–320; 18 (1926), 203–16; C. Duschinsky, *Gedenkbuecher "Memorbuecher" von Offenbach a. M. und anderen deutschen Gemeinden* (1924); A. Neubauer, in: REJ, 4 (1882), 1–30; Salfeld, Martyrol; W. H. Lowe, *The Memorbuch of Nuremberg* (1881); L. Loewenstein, in: ZGJD, 1 (1887), 195–8; 2 (1888), 86–99. [Ed.]

MEMORIAL LIGHT (Heb. נֵר נְשָׁמָה; "the light of the soul"), a light kindled on the anniversary of the death of a relative. It is lit on the eve of the anniversary, according to the Hebrew calendar, and should burn without interruption for 24 hours. A memorial candle is also kindled when a person dies (it is placed near his head until the burial) and during the seven-day mourning period, or according to some customs during the *sheloshim* ("30 days") after the death. In some communities, it is customary to kindle memorial lights on the eve of the *Day of Atonement.

It is generally believed that the custom of memorial lights, as well as that of **yahrzeit*, originated in Germany in the Middle Ages and spread from there to other Jewish centers. The medieval custom easily linked up with earlier notions of light as a symbol for the soul as found, e.g., in Proverbs 20:27 "The spirit of man is the lamp of the Lord" or in the story about R. *Judah ha-Nasi who asked on his deathbed that a light be kindled in his room after his death (Ket. 103a). In some synagogues memorial lights are lit on the anniversary of departed members of the congregation who have bequeathed money for that purpose. Near the lights (electrical bulbs are used nowadays), nameplates indicate the persons who are being commemorated.

See also **Yahrzeit*.

Bibliography: I. Abrahams, *Jewish Life in the Middle Ages* (1932²), 156 and n. 2; Eisenstein, Dinim, 274; H. Rabinowicz, *Guide to Life* (1964), 106. [Ed.]

MEMPHIS (a Greek name derived from the Egyptian *Mn-nfr*, "established and beautiful"), ancient city in Lower Egypt, approximately 12 mi. (c. 19 km.) south of Cairo, lying partly under the site of modern Mit Riheina. According to tradition, Memphis was founded by the legendary Egyptian king Menes in about 3000 B.C.E. The Egyptian name *Mn-nfr* originally designated the pyramid of King Pepi I (c. 2300 B.C.E.), and was eventually extended to the town that grew up around it. By the end of the second millennium the name was probably vocalized "Menufi," although a papyrus from the late 20th Dynasty (c. 1184–1087 B.C.E.), gives the variant reading *Mnf*, from which the Coptic *Menfi*, Arabic *Menf*, and Hebrew *Mof* were derived.

Until the founding of Alexandria, Memphis played a paramount role in Egypt. As the administrative capital, it had many palaces and temples, particularly that of Ptah, the city's chief god; the remains of these structures can still be seen on the site. Literary texts, lavish in their praise and descriptions of the city, indicate that it was a cosmopolitan metropolis with a large, resident foreign population which included Jews (cf. Jer. 44:1); this has been confirmed by archaeological excavation. The eventual destruction of Memphis is predicted in Isaiah 19:13; Jeremiah 2:16; 46:14, 19; and Ezekiel 30:13. The city was not in fact destroyed, although it was besieged and taken by the Persians.

Bibliography: W. F. Petrie, *Memphis*, 1 (1909); idem, *The Palace of Apries* (1909); idem, *Meydum and Memphis* (1910), 38–46; W. F. Petrie et al., *Tarkhan I and Memphis V* (1913); A. H. Gardiner, *Ancient Egyptian Onomastica*, 2 (1947), 122–6. [Al.R.S.]

MEMPHIS, city in Tennessee; population (1968 estimate) 563,000 and Jewish population (1965 estimate) of 9,200. Memphis was first settled in 1818 and the first known Jewish settler, David Hart, arrived in 1838. In the 1840s Jews began to settle in larger numbers, and they acquired land for a cemetery in 1848. In 1850 a Hebrew Benevolent Society was formed, and by 1853 the Jews were "regularly organized" for purposes of worship. In 1854, B'nai Israel Congregation (Children of Israel) with 36 members, was granted a charter by the state legislature. The congregation worshiped in rented halls until 1857, and in 1858 converted a bank building into a place of worship. Rev. Jacob J. Peres, a native of Holland, was the first spiritual leader. In 1860 the relationship between the congregation and Rev. Peres was severed and a new congregation, Beth El Emeth, was organized. From 1860 to 1870 R. Simon Tuska was rabbi of Congregation Children of Israel.

Though Memphis suffered little or no damage during the Civil War, Jews did enlist in the army of the Confederacy. From 1863 to 1866 Congregation Children of Israel sponsored a nonsectarian school—Hebrew Educational Institute. The school was to provide educational opportunities during the disruption caused by the war. Following the death of Rabbi Tuska in 1870, Rabbi Max Samfield was elected rabbi of the congregation in 1871 and served until 1915. In addition to serving the congregation, Samfield published *The Jewish Spectator* from 1885 until his death. This paper served the Jews of Memphis and the mid-South.

In 1884 the Orthodox Baron Hirsch Congregation was organized and in 1891 converted a church as a place of worship. The first rabbi was Benjamin Mayerowitz. Congregation Anshe Sphard was organized in 1898. Beth Sholom, a Conservative congregation, was established in 1950 and in 1967 dedicated its new synagogue. A B'nai B'rith Lodge was organized in 1856 and in 1927 the B'nai B'rith Home was established to serve the Jews of Memphis and the mid-South. It was completely rebuilt in the 1960s and dedicated in 1968 as the B'nai B'rith Home and Hospital. The Jewish Community Center was organized in 1949 and in 1968 dedicated a $2,000,000 edifice. Jews have been active in the economic, political, and civic life of the community. Rev. Peres and his two sons, Israel and Hardwig, served on the Memphis Board of Education. The Peres family was perhaps one of the most distinguished in the community. The Goldsmith family, leading merchants, were known as benefactors of the community for three generations. Abe Plough, a native of Tupelo, Mississippi, was generally regarded as the foremost citizen of the community by virtue of his philanthropy. Jews have served as presidents of the bar association and the medical society. [J.A.W.]

MENAHEM (Heb. מְנַחֵם; "comforter"; in Assyrian inscriptions **Me-ni-ḫi-im-me, Mi-in-ḫi-im-mu**), king of Israel, c. 746/6–737/6 B.C.E., son of Gadi (II Kings 15:17). Menahem seized the throne after assassinating *Shallum son of Jabesh (15:14). Shallum and Menahem may possibly have competed for the throne during the decline of the house of *Jehu. It is widely believed that both were among the officers from Gilead, a group which had been influential from the beginning of Jehu's reign (cf. II Kings 9:1ff.; 15:25). Both Jabesh (the name of the principal city of Gilead) and Gadi (the name of a tribe) are designations pointing to the fact that both Menahem and Shallum were of Transjordanian origin. The struggle between the two was conducted with great cruelty. II Kings 15:16 states: "At that time Menahem sacked Tiphsah and all who were in it and its territory." Tiphsah is Thapsacus which is on the River Euphrates, east of Aleppo. From this statement it appears that Menahem's campaign extended to the Euphrates. However, most scholars maintain that in light of the political-military situation of the Kingdom of Israel since the end of the reign of *Jeroboam II, it is not possible that Menahem ruled over such a large kingdom, and they therefore accept the Lucian version of the Septuagint, where Tappuah appears instead of Tiphsah (cf. Josh. 16:8; 17:8). In view of the biblical chronological data with regard to Menahem and *Pekah, several scholars concluded that Menahem ruled only in the mountain of Ephraim, while at the same time Pekah ruled in eastern Transjordan. It appears that Pekah first served as Menahem's military commander, but later rebelled with the help of Aram, and became an independent ruler in Gilead, although nominally he was still considered the military commander of Menahem and Pekahiah.

According to the biblical account, during Menahem's reign, Pul, the king of Assyria (i.e., Pulu, the name given to *Tiglath-Pileser III when he became king of Babylon in the latter part of his reign), extended his campaign into Israel; Menahem paid him 1,000 talents of silver in order to retain his throne (II Kings 15:19). The annals of Tiglath-Pileser III mention "Menahem of Samaria" (the city; this designation may be considered as attesting the limited area of his administration) among the kings who paid tribute to Assyria in 738 B.C.E., immediately after the defeat inflicted by the Assyrian king on *Uzziah, King of Judah. It is questionable whether the biblical account of Menahem's tax and the account of Menahem's tax in the Assyrian source refer to the same event. It is Y. Yadin's opinion that the *Samaria ostraca belong to the last years of Menahem's reign and bear some relation to the tribute paid to the king of Assyria, to which every "mighty man" of wealth was required to contribute 50 shekels (II Kings 15:20). Apparently the Assyrian recognition of Menahem as the vassal king of Israel strengthened his status and helped stabilize his regime. Menahem needed Assyrian support both against rebel bases within his domain and against neighboring states, including the state of Judah (cf. Hos. 5:8–11). It is possible to assume that most of the prophecies of Hosea 4–14 reflect the period of Menahem (H. Tadmor).

Bibliography: Bright, Hist, 252–4; Kittel, Gesch, 2 (1923), 351ff., 516; E. R. Thiele, *The Mysterious Numbers of the Hebrew Kings* (1951), 73ff.; Y. Yadin, in: *Scripta Hierosolymitana,* 8 (1961), 19–25; H. Tadmor, *ibid.,* 248–66; M. Haran, in: *Zion,* 31 (1966), 18–38; idem, in: *Fourth World Congress of Jewish Studies,* 1 (1967), 33–35 (Heb. pt.), 252 (Eng. summ.); H. L. Ginsberg, *ibid.,* 92–93 (Eng. pt.); EM, 5 (1968), 30–33 (includes bibliography).

[J.L./B.O.]

MENAHEM BEN AARON IBN ZERAḤ (c. 1310–1385), codifier. Menahem was born in Estella, Navarre, where his father had settled after leaving his native France, on the expulsion of the Jews in 1306. In 1328 riots broke out against the Jews of Navarre and the Estella community suffered severely. All of Menahem's family, including his parents and four brothers, were killed, and he himself was severely wounded, but his life was saved by a Christian friend of the family. When he recovered he went to Toledo and studied in the yeshivot there. Among his teachers were Joseph b. Shuʿayb and Judah the son of *Asher b. Jehiel (the Rosh). From Toledo he went to Alcalá and studied under Joseph b. al-ʿAysh, succeeding him on his death in 1361. In Alcalá also, there were troubles and suffering. Fratricidal war had broken out in Spain between the two aspirants to the throne, Henry of Trastamara and Pedro the Cruel, and many Jewish communities suffered as a result. Menahem escaped to safety through the help of the royal courtier Don Samuel *Abrabanel, and Menahem praises him in the introduction to his *Ẓeidah la-Derekh.*

In Toledo Menahem compiled his *Ẓeidah la-Derekh,* a code of laws dealing in the main with the laws concerning the daily way of life. The work has an added importance on account of the introduction, which contains valuable historical material, including important details of the method of study in the yeshivot of France and Germany, as well as contemporary incidents in the history of the Jews in Spain. The book was designed as an abridged code for the upper classes who, because of their preoccupation with material concerns, had no time to refer to the sources. He writes reprovingly of those Jews who, because of the demands of the times, began to disregard the observance of the precepts. Although he shows great erudition in his knowledge of the Talmud and codes and was acquainted with the teachings of the earlier Spanish, French, and German scholars, he relies mainly for his halakhic rulings on those of Asher b. Jehiel.

Menahem gives much information about the different customs of the Jews of Spain, France, and Germany, as well as of various communities (see pp. 71, 82, 88, 104, 110, 116 in the Warsaw edition of 1880). He had some knowledge of medicine, and in the code he includes the need to preserve one's bodily health (see pp. 28–33; et al.). He also knew astronomy and believed in astrology (pp. 98–120). Although he criticized philosophy, he appears to have engaged in its study to some extent (104–48). In these sciences, however, Menahem merely gleaned from the works of others. His work reflects contemporary conditions. He complains that many of the youth, particularly children of the wealthy, were careless in the observance of the precepts and scoffed at the words of the sages, and some were even licentious in matters of sex (pp. 68–81). The book is divided into five *ma'amarim* ("articles"), which are divided into *kelalim* ("principles"), which are subdivided into chapters. The first *ma'amar* discusses prayer and the blessings; the second, the *halakhot* of **issur ve-hetter;* the third, laws of marriage; the fourth, the festivals; and the fifth, fasting and mourning, the Messiah, and the resurrection. It was first published in Ferrara in the printing press of Abraham Usque in 1554. In addition to his major work, three small works by Menahem are extant in manuscript: an abridgment of Baḥya ibn Paquda's *Ḥovot ha-Levavot, Hilkhot Sheḥitah u-Vedikah,* and *Menaḥem Avelim;* it is possible however, that they are simply abridgments from his *Ẓeidah la-Derekh* (see A. Freimann, in: *Annuario di Studi Ebraici* (1934), 166ff.).

Bibliography: Weiss, Dor, 5 (1904[4]), 126–8, 210; A. Freimann, in: *Annuario di Studi Ebraici,* 1 (1935), 147–67; H. Tchernowitz, *Toledot ha-Posekim,* 2 (1947), 191–8; Urbach, Tosafot, 15, 210, 454, 465; Baer, Spain, 1 (1966), 373, 378, 419, 450f.

[S.E.]

MENAHEM BEN ḤELBO (11th century), one of the first commentators on the Bible in northern France. Little is known of his life. He was the uncle of Joseph *Kara, who transmitted Menahem's comments to *Rashi. Apparently he lived for some time in Provence, and it is his influence which accounts for the presence of Arabic words as well as some Provençal forms of French in Rashi. Menahem was also called "Kara," which shows that his principal occupation was biblical commentary. He also wrote comments on the *piyyutim.* Menahem collected his commentaries in book form which he called *pitronim* ("solutions"). They covered all the Prophets and the Hagiographa, but not the Pentateuch upon which, apparently, he did not attempt to comment. His books are no longer extant as they were apparently superseded by Rashi's commentaries. Fragments, however, were collected by S. A. Poznański from quotations, especially by Joseph Kara, and also from the works of commentators in Germany (published by Poznański in *Festschrift N. Sokolow* (1904), 389–439 with Menahem's commentary on the *piyyutim,* and also separately).

Menahem was the first commentator in France to interpret the Bible according to the simple meaning of the text, although he also gave homiletical interpretations. He often limited himself to explaining difficult words and phrases, relying extensively on the Targum (e.g., Isa. 1:8). He employed many French words and terms in his commentary and had little recourse to grammar. Zunz is of the opinion that Menahem did not commit his comments on the *piyyutim* to writing, but transmitted his explanations of *Kallir's *piyyutim* orally. There is now evidence that he also wrote commentaries to other *piyyutim*.

Bibliography: Abraham b. Azriel, *Sefer Arugat ha-Bosem*, ed. by E. E. Urbach, 4 (1963), 3–6. [Av.G.]

MENAHEM BEN JACOB (also known as **R. Menahem of Worms;** 1120?–1203), rabbi and liturgical poet in Worms. Menahem, whose tombstone bore the inscription *posek, darshan* ("preacher"), and *paytan*, was a member of the *bet din* of *Eleazar b. Judah, the author of *Roke'aḥ*, and Kalonymus b. Gershom. His relatives included Gershom *ha-Gozer and *Eliezer b. Joel ha-Levi. From the words of the latter, it appears that Menahem was influential in ruling circles. None of his teachings has been preserved, but 33 of his *piyyutim* are known. These include *yoẓerot, kinot*, and *seliḥot*, some of which were published in various places. Among them is the *kinah, Alelai Li Ki Va'u Rega Almon ve-Shakhol*, on the martyrs of Boppard of 1179 and of the islands of the sea (i.e., Britain) of 1190; the *piyyut Maẓor Batah ha-Ir* refers to the siege of Worms by Emperor Otto IV in 1201. Some of his *piyyutim* are signed "Ẓemaḥ," which in *gematria* is equal to "Menahem." In one manuscript he is mentioned as R. Menahem b. Jacob of Lutra (which is Bavarian Kaiserslautern in the Rhenish Palatinate); Zunz assumed that he was identical with Menahem b. Jacob, the *paytan* of Worms. If so, then Menahem was born in Lutra.

Bibliography: Davidson, Oẓar, 4 (1933), 434; Zunz, Lit Poesie, 294–8; Berliner, in: *Kobez al-Jad*, 3 (1887), 3–9 (2nd pagination); Schechter, in: JHSET, 1 (1893–94), 8–14; Germ Jud, 1 (1934), index; V. Aptowitzer, *Mavo le-Sefer Ravyah* (1938), 382–4; A. M. Habermann, *Sefer Gezerot Ashkenaz ve-Ẓarefat* (1946), 147–51, 239f., 260. [Ed.]

MENAHEM BEN JACOB IBN SARUQ (Saruk; tenth century), Spanish author and lexicographer. Born in Tortosa, he moved at an early age to Cordova, where Isaac, the father of *Ḥisdai ibn Shaprut, became his patron. After Isaac's death, Menahem went back to his native town for a short interlude, and then returned to Cordova, where he lived under the patronage of Ḥisdai and worked as his seretary. Besides eulogies on Ḥisdai's parents, Menahem composed Ḥisdai's famous letter to the king of the *Khazars. Ḥisdai encouraged him to compile his *Maḥberet*, a biblical dictionary in Hebrew. However, Menahem endured poverty because Ḥisdai was not a very generous patron. Later, when Menahem fell into disgrace, Ḥisdai even persecuted his former protégé and forced him to return to Tortosa. Here Menahem wrote a touching letter of complaint to Ḥisdai, a gem of epistolary style and an important historical document concerning its author's life.

Menahem's most important work, intrinsically and historically, is the *Maḥberet*, whose original name was probably *The Book of Solutions*. Because Menahem's dictionary was originally written in Hebrew, its style surpasses that of biblical dictionaries of greater quality translated into Hebrew from Arabic, such as Judah ibn *Tibbon's translation of *Ibn Janaḥ's *Book of Roots*. More importantly, because the dictionary was in Hebrew, it was also understood by Jews in Christian countries where it exerted great influence. For example, in France, the *Maḥberet* was used extensively by *Rashi. Menahem carefully refrained from linguistic comparisons between Hebrew and Arabic, presumably as Hebrew was considered a holy language. Menahem's theological concern is further reflected in his attempt to show that *ehyeh* which is referred to as a name for God in Exodus 3:14 is not derived from the verb *hayah* ("to be").

Often original in terminology, the dictionary attempts, without reference to its predecessors, a systematic summation of the lexicographical and grammatical knowledge of the time. Menahem shows awareness of ellipses and pleonasms occurring in the Bible, and brings into relief poetic parallelism, or constructions in which, as he put it, "one half instructs us in the meaning of the other." However, he did not have a systematic knowledge of grammar, and his approach tended to the empirical. Although Menahem carried out the investigation of the Hebrew roots systematically and built his dictionary accordingly, he thought that letters of the root that disappear in conjugation are not radical, and therefore established, on the synchronic level, biliteral and even uniliteral roots, e.g., *nâṭâh*, root ṭ; *hikkâh*, root k. Thus, the *Maḥberet* can only be regarded as a summary of past achievements and it was, according to some authorities, reserved to Menahem's pupils to initiate the new period of linguistic research. Shortly after the *Maḥberet* appeared, it was vehemently attacked by *Dunash b. Labrat who claimed that certain definitions were likely to lead the reader to erroneous interpretations of *halakhah* and belief. The expectation that the dictionary would therefore become a source of heresy explains the bitterness of the attack. Menahem himself did not reply to Dunash's criticisms, but three of Menahem's pupils took it upon themselves to defend their master. One of the pupils was Judah ibn Daud whom some scholars think is identical with Judah b. David *Ḥayyuj, the great initiator of the theory of the triliterality of Hebrew roots, while other scholars consider this identification doubtful. However, Isaac ibn *Gikatilla, another of the three, was the teacher of Ibn Janaḥ, the greatest medieval Jewish lexicographer and philologist. The controversy between the two camps continued; Yehudi b. Sheshet defended his master Dunash against the attacks of Menahem's pupils, and the famous tosafist Jacob b. Meir *Tam in his *Book of Decisions* (appended to the Filipowski ed. of the *Maḥberet*) tried to prove that Menahem's definitions were valid. However, a modern scholar, D. *Yellin, demonstrated that, from the scientific point of view, Dunash's criticisms were generally well founded (*Sefer Zikkaron le-A. Gulak ve-S. Klein* (1942), 105–14; *Leshonenu*, 11 (1941–43), 202–15).

Bibliography: W. Bacher, in: ZDMG, 49 (1895), 342–67; idem, in: J. Winter and A. Wuensche (eds.), *Die juedische Litteratur*, 2 (1894), 145–9; H. Hirschfeld, *Literary History of Hebrew Grammarians and Lexicographers* (1926), 24–31; Ashtor, Korot, 1 (1966²), 160–170, cf. also 310f. as to the identification of Judah ibn Daud with Judah Ḥayyuj; the *Maḥberet* was edited by Z. Filipowski (1854) from five manuscripts; for additions from a Berne Ms. see D. Kaufmann, ZDMG, 40 (1886), 367–409; the response of Menahem's pupils, *Liber Responsonuim*, was edited by S. G. Stern (1870; where introd. 23–37 Menahem's epistle to Ḥisdai first edited by S. D. Luzzatto, in: *Beit ha-Oẓar*, 1 (1847), 26a–33a is reprinted. It was re-edited by Schirmann, in: *Sefarad*, 1 (1955), 8–30). [Y.Bl.]

MENAHEM BEN MICHAEL BEN JOSEPH, medieval Karaite scholar. He was author of a Hebrew polemical epistle in verse addressed to "Akylas the Proselyte, in care of Saadiah the Rabbanite," dealing with the laws of slaughtering. S. P. *Pinsker, who first published the poem, assumed that it was directed against *Saadiah Gaon and that therefore the author must have lived in the first half of the tenth century. His vocabulary, however, is that of a Byzantine Karaite of a later date, presumably the 12th century, and he is very likely identical with Menahem b. Michael, the author of several hymns included in the Karaite liturgy.

Bibliography: S. Pinsker, *Likkutei Kadmoniyyot* (1860), index s.v. *Menaḥem Giẓani ha-Goleh;* S. Poznański, *Karaite Literary Opponents of Saadiah Gaon* (1908), 11–12. [L.N.]

MENAHEM BEN MOSES HA-BAVLI (d. 1571), rabbi and author in Ereẓ Israel. Despite his surname ("the Babylonian"), Menahem appears to have come from Italy; his ancestors probably lived in Babylon. Until 1525 Menahem served as *dayyan* in Trikkola, Greece. In 1527 he was living with his family in Safed, among whose scholars his name is included. There, with his brother Reuben, he engaged in business connected with the wool-dyeing industry. After 1546 he moved to Hebron, apparently being among the Safed rabbis who renewed the Jewish settlement in that city in the middle of the 16th century. Menahem achieved renown through his *Ta'amei ha-Mitzvot* (Lublin, 1571), in which he briefly sets forth the reasons for the precepts. In the introduction Menahem refers to a lengthy work he had written called *Ta'amei Mitzvot ha-Arukot*. One of his responsa on divorce was published among those of Joseph *Caro to *Even ha-Ezer* (Salonika, 1598, 80a, *Dinei Gittin ve-Gerushin*, no. 10).

Bibliography: Ben-Yaakov, in: *Ḥemdat Yisrael, Koveẓ le-Zikhro shel... Ḥ. Ḥ. Medini* (1946), 89–97; M. Benayahu, in: KS, 29 (1953/54), 173f.; 31 (1955/56), 399f.; Roth, *ibid.*, 399; Dimitrovsky, in: *Sefunot*, 7 (1963), 67. [Ed.]

MENAHEM BEN SOLOMON (first half of 12th century), author of the midrashic work *Sekhel Tov*. Menahem's country of origin is unknown. The foreign words in his book are Italian, but it is difficult to establish on this basis that he lived in Italy since he does not mention the *Arukh* of *Nathan b. Jehiel of Rome though it was written about 50 years earlier. Similarly, all that is known of Menahem is that two halakhic responsa were addressed to him apparently by Solomon b. Abraham, the nephew of Nathan of Rome (included in the *Shibbolei ha-Leket*, pt. 2, still in manuscript). Menahem's fame rests on his *Sekhel Tov*, an aggadic-halakhic midrashic anthology arranged according to the weekly scriptural readings. Only the first two parts of the book, to Genesis and Exodus, have been preserved and published by S. Buber (*Sekhel Tov*, 1900), who added a detailed introduction. However, many early scholars possessed complete manuscripts from which they frequently quote, particularly the author of the *Asufot* (in manuscript) who lived in Germany at the beginning of the 13th century. The *Sekhel Tov* was written, according to its author, in 1139, with the aim of explaining the verses in accordance with the Midrashim and Hebrew philology. Apart from the talmudic and midrashic sources, the only works he quotes are the *She'iltot* of *Aḥa of Shabḥa, the *Halakhot Gedolot*, *Hananel b. Ḥushi'el, Isaac *Alfasi, and the Midrash *Lekaḥ Tov* of *Tobiah b. Eliezer. Menahem's comprehensive knowledge of *halakhah* is evident from his work; in some places he actually assembles collections of *halakhot* on specific subjects, such as the laws of the Sabbath, **eruv*, Passover (in the weekly portion *Yitro*), etc. Still more marked is his great interest in linguistic topics and Hebrew grammar, which in fact constitute the underlying basis of the whole work. Indeed, Menahem devoted another work to this subject, *Even Boḥan;* only a minor part, of which fragments alone have been published, is extant in manuscript. This work was completed in 1143. It was divided into 50 *she'arim* ("gates"), constructed on a most complicated system. Only five of these "gates" remain, all of which deal with the study of the roots of Hebrew verbs, and they are of considerable importance for scriptural exegesis. The work mentions by name only the Targums of Onkelos and of Jonathan b. Uzziel, and also Eliezer ha-*Kallir, but it is based on the works of *Menahem ibn Saruq and *Dunash b. Labrat, although they are not mentioned by name. Menahem's knowledge of grammar did not exceed theirs; like them he too assumed the existance of verbal roots of two and even of one letter, and his table of the conjugations is far from perfect. Besides these authors, he also used Saadiah Gaon's translation of the Scriptures. Some regard the book as the first attempt at a treatise on the Hebrew language.

Bibliography: Bacher, in: *Jubelschrift... H. Graetz* (1887), 94–115; idem, in: *Oẓar ha-Sifrut*, 5 (1895), 257–63. [I.T.-S.]

MENAHEM THE ESSENE (first century B.C.E.), a contemporary of *Herod, to whom prophetic powers were attributed. Josephus relates how Menahem "had once observed Herod, then still a boy, going to his teacher, and greeted him as 'king of the Jews.'" The pious Essene added, however, that Herod would abandon justice and piety and thus bring upon himself the wrath of God. When Herod had reached the height of his power, he sent for Menahem and questioned him about the length of his reign. Menahem succeeded in satisfying the king, albeit with an ambiguous answer, and hence (according to Josephus) Herod continued to hold all Essenes in honor. L. Ginzberg suggests that Menahem is to be identified with the Menahem mentioned in the Mishnah (Ḥag. 2:2). This Menahem was, together with *Hillel, one of the heads of the Sanhedrin, who left his post (presumably to join the Essenes) and was succeeded by *Shammai. There is little evidence, however, to support his view. Talmudic discussions of the Mishnah tend to describe the mishnaic Menahem in terms far more fitting to *Menahem son of Judah the Galilean, a patriot leader during the uprising of 66–70 C.E.

Bibliography: Jos., Ant., 15:373–8; Klausner, Bayit Sheni, 3 (1950²), 115; 4 (1950²), 148; A. Schalit, *Koenig Herodes* (1969), 459; L. Ginzberg, *On Jewish Law and Lore* (1955), 101. [I.G.]

MENAḤEMIYYAH (Heb. מְנַחֲמִיָּה), moshav in northern Israel with municipal council status, southwest of Lake Kinneret, affiliated with Ha-Iḥud ha-Ḥakla'i. Menaḥemiyyah was founded as a moshavah by the Jewish Colonization Association (ICA) in 1902, as part of the *ICA enterprise to establish villages in Galilee based on grain production. Menaḥemiyyah's progress was slow, and it suffered from the frequent attacks by Bedouins in the vicinity. In the 1920s, a gypsum quarry was opened nearby to supply the Haifa "Nesher" cement works. Later, World War II veterans ("Ya'el") joined the first settlers. Following the Israel *War of Independence (1948), new immigrants, mainly from North Africa and Rumania, settled in Menaḥemiyyah. In 1969 the moshav had 585 inhabitants. Its name is based both on the previous Arabic name of the site—Milḥamiyya—and the first name of Herbert *Samuel's father. [E.O.]

MENAHEM MENDEL BEN ISAAC (second half of 16th century), tax collector, architect, and builder in Kazimierz, near *Cracow. Menahem Mendel was born in Brest-Litovsk, and from 1560 to 1568 was the king's tax farmer in the Zhmud (Zemaitkiemis) region of Lithuania. In 1572 he moved to Kazimierz, and by 1581 he had become one of the elders of the *kahal*. From the early 1570s, he constructed flour mills and city walls, and was noted as a designer and builder of bridges. During the Polish campaign against Russia (1579–82), King Stephen Báthory was accompanied by Menahem Mendel, who built bridges over the Dvina and military installations for the sieges of Polotsk, Velizh, and Pskov. In 1587, since he had supported the defeated Austrian archduke Maximilian, he was compelled to leave Poland. Upon his arrival in Vienna, he was given a modest allowance by the court. On July 4, 1589, he proposed that Emperor Rudolph II finance the building of a bridge over the Danube, between Vienna and Nussdorf, at an estimated outlay of 30,000 *Rheingulden*. Menahem Mendel was to levy tolls to repay the investment. After two years of deliberations the project was deferred indefinitely and Menahem Mendel returned to Kazimierz. In 1592 King Sigismund III Vasa of Poland deputed him to arrange a match between the king's aunt, Ann Jagellon, and an Austrian archduke. All trace of Menahem Mendel vanishes after this point.

Bibliography: M. Balaban, in: *Nowy Dziennik* (Nov. 15, 1919); idem, *Dzieje Żydów w Krakowie i na Kazimierzu*, 1 (1931), 139, 159, 162; M. Bersohn, *Dyplomataryusz dotyczący Żydów w dawnej Polsce* (1910), 108 no. 171; Schwarz, in: *Jahrbuch fuer Landeskunde von Niederoesterreich* (1913), suppl. 1. [A.Cy.]

MENAHEM MENDEL OF PEREMYSHLANY (b. 1728), ḥasidic leader. In his youth he joined the group of *Israel b. Eliezer, the Ba'al Shem Tov, and in the late 1750s is mentioned as a participant at a "third Sabbath meal" gathering (Israel *Loebel, *Sefer Vikku'aḥ* (Warsaw, 1798), 9b). In 1764, he went to Ereẓ Israel together with R. *Naḥman of Horodenko (Gorodenka) and settled in Tiberias. Before his emigration, he visited Cekinowka and Soroki, townlets on both banks of the Dniester, where he occupied himself in the "redemption of captives" *(pidyon shevuyyim)*. He is identical with R. Mendel of Cekinowka mentioned in *Shivḥei ha-Besht* (Kapust, 1815), 19. As for the reason for his emigration, one of his intimates has written: "He emigrated to the Holy Land because emissaries started traveling to him urging that he occupy himself with community affairs" (A. Rubinstein, in: *Tarbiz*, 35 (1965/66), 177), which probably signifies that they came to him as a *ẓaddik* and miracle-worker *(*Ba'al Shem)* and he refused to assume such a role.

R. Mendel represents the extreme enthusiast among the first generations of the ḥasidic movement. His teachings abound in radical expressions which aroused violent opposition, such as: "One should not be exceedingly meticulous in every act performed, because this is the intent of the evil inclination; even if, Heaven forbid, one has sinned—one should not be overtaken by melancholy" (*Darkhei Yesharim* (Zhitomir, 1805), 4b, 5a). Like other disciples of the Ba'al Shem Tov, he considered devotion to God the pivot of ḥasidic doctrine and conduct. In contrast to others, however, he thought that Torah study and the practice of devotion were not compatible; study was therefore to be restricted so as not to restrain the process of approximation to the Creator. "If we divert our thoughts from devotion to God, and study excessively, we will forget the fear of Heaven . . . study should therefore be reduced and one should always meditate on the greatness of the Creator." R. Mendel considered prayer the most suitable manner in which to achieve devotion, and that prayer must be restrained and not, as was the opinion of Ḥasidim of other schools, vociferous. In general, it was his view that devotional conduct should be based on contemplative concentration attainable by seclusion from society and cessation of all occupation. His principal teachings were published in his booklet *Darkhei Yesharim ve-hu Hanhagot Yesharot* (Zhitomir, 1805); in *Likkutei Yekarim* (Lvov, 1792); and in *Yosher Divrei Emet* (1905), of R. Meshullam Feivush of Zbarazh.

Bibliography: Dubnow, Ḥasidut, index; A. Rubinstein, in: *Tarbiz*, 35 (1965/66); J. Weiss, in: *Tiferet Yisrael—I. Brodie Jubilee Volume* (1967), 158–62. [A.Ru.]

MENAHEM MENDEL OF SHKLOV (d. 1827), rebuilder of the Ashkenazi community of Jerusalem at the beginning of the 19th century; he was born in Shklov. His father was R. Baruch Bendet, who was a *maggid*. Menahem Mendel was one of the outstanding pupils of R. *Elijah b. Solomon the Gaon of Vilna. He himself recounts: "I did not withdraw from his presence; I held onto him and did not leave him; I remained in his tent day and night; I went where he went, slept where he slept, and my hand never left his hand." After the death of his teacher in 1794 he worked with R. Elijah's sons on the arrangement and publication of his works. Through his initiative the following of Elijah's works were published in the course of nine years: R. Elijah's commentary on Proverbs; his annotation on *Seder Olam Rabbah* and *Seder Olam Zuta;* his interpretation of the Shulḥan Arukh, *Oraḥ Ḥayyim;* his commentary on *Avot,* and others.

In 1808 Menahem Mendel immigrated to Ereẓ Israel and settled in Safed where he established *battei midrash* for study and prayer and became the leader of the community of Ashkenazim-Perushim (followers of the Vilna Gaon), which then numbered around 150 persons. From Safed he maintained a correspondence with his friend R. *Israel of Shklov and entreated him to act on behalf of the economic consolidation of the community and even encouraged him to emigrate to Palestine. As a result of philosophical and traditional conflicts with the ḥasidic community of Safed Menachem Mendel drew close to the Sephardi rabbis and their *bet midrash*.

When a plague broke out in Safed in 1812 he fled with others to Jerusalem. He probably reached the decision at that time to remain there permanently, but he set up his home in the city only in 1816. At the same time he rented the courtyard of the yeshivah of R. Ḥayyim ibn *Attar as a place for Torah study and prayer. This action should be seen as the renewal of the Ashkenazi community of Jerusalem, after a lapse of about 100 years. In his letters abroad he requested that **ḥalukkah* funds be transferred to the new community. Here, too, however, he maintained friendly relations with the *rishon le-Zion* R. Solomon Moses Suzin who aided him in consolidating his community. Despite the numerous difficulties—resulting from the non-legalization of the residence of the Ashkenazim in the city—the Ashkenazim under Mendel's leadership continued to live in Jerusalem. After his death, his son Nathan Nata was appointed in his place. Mendel was a prolific author and wrote about ten books dealing mainly with the teachings of Kabbalah and mysticism.

Bibliography: Frumkin-Rivlin, 3 (1929), 138ff.; *Yerushalayim*, ed. by A. M. Luncz, 13 (1919), 223ff. [Ye.Ka.]

MENAHEM MENDEL OF VITEBSK (1730–1788), ḥasidic leader active in Belorussia, Lithuania, and Ereẓ Israel. He was a disciple of *Dov Baer the Maggid of Mezhirech, and headed a congregation in Minsk during the lifetime of his teacher; in *Zemir Ariẓim ve-Ḥarvot Ẓurim* (Warsaw, Bialystok, 1798), a pamphlet written by one of the **Mitnaggedim*, he is mentioned by the name of Mendel of Minsk. When the first wave of opposition to *Ḥasidism erupted (1772), he visited Vilna on two occasions—on the second occasion, accompanied by his disciple *Shneur Zalman of Lyady—and attempted to meet *Elijah b. Solomon the Gaon of Vilna in order to point out to him the merits of Ḥasidism, but the Gaon refused to receive him and "he closed the door upon us twice." Ḥasidic tradition also regards him as one of the leading spokesmen at the meeting which was convened in Rovno in the house of Dov Baer after the imposition of the *ḥerem* on the Ḥasidim in 1772. The persecutions of the *Mitnaggedim* made him leave Minsk, and in 1773 he settled in Gorodok, from where he spread Ḥasidism in the Vitebsk and Mogilev provinces (assisted by *Israel of Polotsk, *Abraham b. Alexander Katz of Kalisk, and Shneur Zalman of Lyady).

In 1777 Menahem Mendel went to Ereẓ Israel, accompanied by Abraham of Kalisk and Israel of Polotsk, at the head of a group of 300 persons, of whom only some were Ḥasidim. He became the leader of the ḥasidic *yishuv*, and sent emissaries to Russia in order to raise funds for its support. In Ereẓ Israel ḥasidic immigrants also encountered hostility among the Jewish community, as a result of the initiative of some *Mitnaggedim*, who addressed special letters on the subject to Ereẓ Israel. In the wake of the disputes which broke out, Menahem Mendel moved to Tiberias, where he erected a ḥasidic synagogue. He became related by marriage to one of the prominent Sephardim of Jerusalem. After his arrival in Ereẓ Israel Menahem Mendel remained the spiritual leader of the Ḥasidim of Belorussia, who maintained a correspondence with him. He continued to guide them in their conduct and interpreted the principles of Ḥasidism to them. Menahem Mendel did not consider himself to be a *ẓaddik* who could bless his Ḥasidim with the bounties of Heaven. He regarded his function of *ẓaddik* as being restricted to teaching and guidance in divine worship and not as that of a "practical" *ẓaddik*.

Teachings. In his teachings, Menahem Mendel remained faithful to those of the Maggid. Following him, he regarded the *ẓimẓum* (contraction) of divine emanation and its restriction as a condition for revelation, because that which is not limited cannot be conceived, just as thought is conceived by restriction and contraction into letters. The worlds were created by divine will as an act of mercy, by the contraction of the divine emanation, because of the deficiency of the recipients. "When one teaches a small child, he must be instructed in accordance with his young intelligence . . . in accordance with the ability of reception of his mind" (*Likkutei Amarim* (1911), 17a). Divinity is restricted in every place (the world is not His abode, but He is the abode of the world). It is the duty of man to adhere to the Divinity in the material creation and to redeem the Divine Presence from its exile in the material world This can be achieved by various methods: (1) By widening the conception of man as the wisest and most capable of understanding, "when he has attained wisdom and studies the Torah, he then creates new heavens and a new earth" (*ibid.*). (2) By *devekut* (devotion) to God. Man is a part of the Celestial Divinity. The root of his soul is to be found in the world of *Aẓilut* (emanation) and he is therefore able to commune with God without the obstruction of any interruption or barrier. Menahem Mendel emphasizes prayer with devotion and *kavvanah* (intention). "With his prayer, he is a groomsman who brings the Divine Presence before God" (*ibid.*, 31b). In order to attain the virtue of *devekut:* (a) "He must consecrate his person and his meditation to wisdom to the extent that he, so to say, has no further existence," i.e., spiritual self-denial. (b) By self-abnegation in the moral aspect and by the cultivation of other ethical values, such as humility, compassion, etc. With the consciousness of his own worthlessness, he is to regard himself as naught so that he become enwrapped with awe (as a result of which he will rise to speculative contemplation), which is the gateway to love. This degree of love will attach him to all men and his spiritual elevation will be followed by the uplifting of all of them in perfect contact and *devekut*. His occupation in secular affairs is to resemble the coming and goings of a man who immediately returns to his home (i.e., to his condition of *devekut*). (3) By the observation of the precepts it is within the power of man to knit together the whole of the world, to control it and exert his influence in the heavenly spheres; he should therefore accustom all his limbs to the precepts. When observing a precept, he must realize that the reward of the precept is the actual observance of the precept itself (the observance of the precept for its own sake). Similarly, he emphasizes that there must be fear of sin and not fear of punishment. The perfect fear is a sublime degree which surpasses *ẓimẓum;* it is the fear of God's majesty, a constant fear before which all the other fears are contracted and "happy is the man that feareth always" (Prov. 28:14). He stresses the importance of faith even beyond logic and rational reason.

On worship through corporeality, he argues that one must not follow "the heretics who say that a man must be at a lower degree so that he may ascend from there, a drop which must needs precede a rise; may there not be such a thought in Israel" (*Likkutei Amarim*, 25b–26a).

His main works were: *Peri ha-Areẓ* (Kopys, 1814); *Peri ha-Eẓ* (Zhitomir, 1874); *Eẓ Peri* (Lvov 1880); *Likkutei Amarim* (Lvov, 1911). His letters appeared in *Nefesh Menaḥem* (Lvov 1930).

Bibliography: A. S. Heilman, *Beit Rabbi*, 1 (1903), 11–22; A. Yaari, *Iggerot Ereẓ Yisrael* (1943), 308–24; W. Rabinowitsch, *Lithuanian Ḥasidism* (1970), index; R. Mahler, *Divrei Yemei Yisrael*, vol. 1, book 3 (1955), 246–8; Dubnow, Ḥasidut, index; Horodezky, Ḥasidut, vol. 2, 13–35; H. Liberman, in: KS, 36 (1960), 127–8; L. I. Newman, *The Hasidic Anthology* (1934), index; M. Buber, *Tales of the Hasidim*, 1 (1968[4]), 175–81; B. D. Kahana, *Ḥibbat ha-Areẓ* (1968); M. Wilensky, *Ḥasidim u-Mitnaggedim* (1970), index.

MENAHEM OF MERSEBURG (first half of the 14th century), one of the leading scholars of Saxony, Germany. Menahem as a pupil of Isaac b. Ḥayyim of Oppenheim (apparently to be identified with the son of *Ḥayyim b. Isaac Or Zaru'a, who was a pupil of *Meir b. Baruch of Rothenburg). Menahem was renowned in his time as a talmudic scholar, and was particularly well known for his *takkanot* which determined relations between the individual and the community in all matters affecting the communal life of the Jew—especially in the subjects of taxation, personal injuries, and fines. Especially important was the *takkanah* in which he abolished the right of *me'un* (see *child marriage; responsa Judah *Mintz (Venice, 1553) no. 13), which had been a cause of great tragedies in Jewish family life, particularly as a result of the widespread custom of child marriage. Some 150 years later his *takkanah* gave rise to violent controversy when some wanted to explain it as having been instituted only in cases where the child had been influenced to exercise it (see Jacob *Falk). Solomon *Luria writes in the *Yam shel Shelomo* to *Yevamot* (13: 17): "It has become customary during recent years not to permit *me'un*, this having originated with Menahem, author of *Me'il Ẓedek*, who carefully weighed up and enacted many restrictive and preventive measures and was a great expert and scholar, and his *takkanot* and restrictions spread throughout the whole of Germany." Here the name of Menahem's book is mentioned; only fragments of it have been preserved. Quotations from it are found in talmudic works of the 15th and 16th centuries, particularly in those of Jacob *Weil and Solomon *Luria, as well as in the glosses of Moses Ḥazzan to the *Minhagim le-Kol ha-Shanah* of *Isaac of Tyrnau, and in the *Shitah Mekubbeẓet* of Bezalel *Ashkenazi. Jacob *Weil describes Menahem of Merseburg as an eminent scholar in his generation living in Saxony. "He laid down many laws and decisions which he collected, and from them compiled an extensive work. That book is to be found in Saxony and the *minhag* of Saxony completely follows it. Many of these rulings have been extracted from his book and are in my possession ..." (Resp. Maharyu 133). These words were written in reply to questioners who were unaware of Menahem's identity and turned to Weil for information. In fact, at the end of the printed editions of the responsa of Jacob Weil there is a small collection, extracted from the *Me'il Ẓedek*, entitled *Nimmukei Menaḥem Merseburg*. It is entirely devoted to the judicial relations between individuals and communities. Among Menahem's pupils was Yom Tov Lipmann *Muelhausen, author of *Seder Tikkun ha-Get* which was based on his tradition (*Yam shel Shelomo*, Git. 2:5).

Bibliography: Joseph b. Moses, *Leket Yosher*, ed. by J. Freimann, 2 (1904), xiiv. [I.T.-S.]

MENAHEM SON OF JUDAH, patriot leader at the outset of the Roman War (66–70 C.E.). He was the son of *Judah of Galilee, leader of the insurgents against the census of *Quirinus in 6 C.E. and must therefore have been well on in years at the time of the outbreak of the war. His most successful exploit was the capture of *Masada in the early stages of the war and his subsequent distribution of the contents of the armory to his followers. Menahem now led his forces to Jerusalem where the insurgents were besieging the royal palace and forced the Romans to surrender. Convinced that he could act as the leader of the rebels, he proceded with a purge of the army, putting to death the former high priest *Ananias and his brother *Hezekiah. His assumption of power, however, was unacceptable to the Jerusalem insurgents (headed by *Eleazar son of Ananias) who, according to Josephus, were unwilling to fight for their freedom against the Romans only to become enslaved under a despot of lowly origin. When Menahem came to pray in the Temple Court, dressed in royal garb and accompanied by an armed guard, Eleazar and his men attacked him. Menahem was killed, and his followers forced to flee (Jos., Wars 2:443ff.). They regrouped themselves at Masada under *Eleazar son of Jair, a relative of Menahem, where they held out even after the fall of Jerusalem. The opposition of the Jerusalemites to Menahem and his followers was apparently due to a number of factors, among them the opposition of the Jerusalemites to revolutionary social changes and to the alleged messianic pretensions of Menahem. Geiger identifies Menahem with the Menahem mentioned in talmudic sources (TJ, Ḥag. 2:277d; Ḥag. 16b) and with the Menahem b. Hezekiah mentioned in the *aggadah* as the Messiah, born on the date of the destruction of the Temple (TJ, Ber. 2:4, 5a). Following the publication of the Dead Sea Scrolls, attempts have been made to identify the *Teacher of Righteousness mentioned there with Menahem the insurgent leader or his relative Eleazar son of Jair. These suggestions must be treated with reserve, pending further research.

Bibliography: Graetz, Hist, 2 (1949), 260–1; Klausner, Bayit Sheni, 4 (1950²), 149, 175; 5 (1951²), 145–8; M. Hengel, *Die Zeloten* (1961), 365ff.; M. Stern, in: *Ha-Ishiyyut ve-Dorah* (1964), 70–78; G. R. Driver, *The Judean Scrolls* (1965), 276f.; 366f.; C. Roth, *The Dead Sea Scrolls* (1965), index. [L.Ro.]

MENAHEM ẒIYYONI (late 14th-early 15th century), kabbalist and exegete who lived in Cologne, where he signed a document in 1382, probably as rabbi of the community. His father was R. Meir Ẓiyyoni. Nothing else definite is known about his life, his career, or his teachers. He is known only through his major work, *Ẓiyyoni*, a homiletical commentary on the Torah (first printed in Cremona in 1559 and again there in the following year after the first impression had been destroyed by fire), and by the treatise *Ẓefunei Ẓiyyoni* (partly preserved in Ms.), one of the major early kabbalistic books dealing in detail with the powers of evil and demonology. Menahem Ẓiyyoni was one of the few kabbalists in 14th-century Germany, and his work demonstrates that he was heir to two different esoteric traditions: the Spanish kabbalah, including the Zohar, the *Sefer ha-Bahir*, and the exegetical works of Naḥmanides; and the esoteric theology of the 12th–13th-century movement of the Ḥasidei Ashkenaz. He quotes frequently from Eleazar b. Judah of Worm's *Sodei Razayya*, referring to him as *"ish sodi"* ("my esoteric authority"). These two traditions are also reflected in his subject matter: the customary kabbalistic questions on the emanation of the *Sefirot* alongside the Ashkenazi-ḥasidic conception of the *Kavod* ("divine glory") and its relationship to the prophets. He composed a *kinah* for the Ninth of Av which was incorporated in the Ashkenazi liturgy.

Bibliography: Davidson, Oẓar, 4 (1933), 435; A. Kober, *Cologne* (1940), 358; Y. Dan, *Torat ha-Sod shel Ḥasidut Ashkenaz* (1968), 259f. [Y.D.]

MENAḤOT (Heb. מְנָחוֹת; "meal-offerings"), second tractate in the order *Kodashim*, in the Mishnah, Tosefta, and Babylonian Talmud (there is no Jerusalem Talmud to this tractate). *Menaḥot* has 13 chapters and deals, as its name indicates, with the various meal-offerings in the Temple. Chapters 1–3 discuss in great detail the defects in the sacrificial act, especially wrongful intent and omission, which render the offering unfit (*pasul* or *piggul*). Chapter 4 continues with the same subject, listing instances of omissions which do not invalidate the offering; the last part deals with the meal-offering of the high priest (Lev. 6:13–16). Chapters 5 and 6 are mainly concerned with the preparation of the meal-offering. Chapter 7 deals with the loaves of the thanksgiving-offering (Lev. 7:12), of the consecration-offering (Lev. 8:26), and of the Nazirite-offering (Num. 6:15). Chapter 8 gives the ingredients of the meal-offering (flour, oil, wine, etc.) and the manner in which they were processed and prepared. Chapter 9 gives valuable information on the liquid and dry measures used in the Temple. Chapter 10 deals with the offering of the *omer* ("sheaf of the waving"; Lev. 23; 15–22), and Chapter 11 with the meal-offering of the barley of the new harvest (Lev. 23:16) and the shewbread (Lev. 24:5–9). Chapter 12 is mainly on vows concerning meal-offerings and drink-offerings. Chapter 13 discusses the problem arising out of sacrificial vows which were inaccurately defined. It also mentions, incidentally, the temple of *Onias. The Mishnah ends with a homily on the fact that the Bible employs the phrase "a sweet savor unto the Lord" equally with regard to offerings of cattle (Lev. 1:9), fowl (Lev. 1:17), and meal (Lev. 2:2) in order to emphasize that "it matters not whether one offers much or little, provided one's heart is directed towards heaven." The Tosefta, also 13 chapters, ends with a homily on the causes of the destruction of the Temple, and, quoting Isaiah 2:2–3, visualizes the future Temple as a universal one.

The first three chapters of the tractate have language patterns similar to the first four chapters of *Zevaḥim*. The similarity between Mishnah 3:1 and *Zevaḥim* 3:3 is especially striking. Epstein (Tannaim, 156f.) points to various strata in the Mishnah: *mishnayot* 3:5–4:4 end are from the Mishnah of R. Simeon, while *mishnayot* 1:3–4 belong to Judah b. Ilai (cf. Zev. 1:2; 6:7). Mishnah 3:4, quoted in the name of Simeon, appears in the Tosefta in the name of his son Eleazar. Apparently Eleazar had recorded his father's sayings together with his own, and thus the editor of the Tosefta attributed it to Eleazar. The Tosefta

Engraving for the tractate *Menaḥot*, showing the preparation of the meal-offering, from a title page of the Hebrew-Latin Mishnah illustrated by Mich. Richey, Amsterdam, 1700–04. Jerusalem, J.N.U.L.

includes several groups of *beraitot*. Thus 1:2–4 contrasts the laws of *sheḥitah* ("slaughtering"), *kemiẓah* ("scooping out" with the hand) and *melikah* ("nipping" the neck of a bird). In the group 4:9–14 each of the passages starts with the word *kamaẓ* ("he scooped"), and the group 12:11–13:12 consists of laws concerning the dedication of offerings to the Temple. The Tosefta includes some aggadic material: Moses' blessing of the nation after the erection of the Tabernacle (7:8); God's evaluation of the sacrifices (7:9); an account of the golden tables, and candelabra, and of the shewbread of the Temple (11:6–18); and the corruption of the priests (13:18–21) and the sins that brought about the destruction of Shiloh and of the First and Second Temples: "Why was the First Temple destroyed? Because of the idolatry, incest, and shedding of blood that prevailed. But at the Second Temple we know that they toiled in the study of Torah and were heedful of the tithes: why then were they exiled? Because they loved money and hated one another. This teaches that hatred of man for his fellow is heinous before the Omnipresent and is regarded as being as grave as idolatry, incest, and murder" (13:22). The Babylonian *Gemara* has some interesting aggadic passages. There is a remarkable story to demonstrate the merits of wearing *ẓiẓit* as a safeguard against immorality (44a); a most interesting homily of R. Ezra (53a); and passages on the Jewish attitude toward Greek culture (64b, 99b) and on the origin of the Temple of Onias (109b). Several of the *aggadot* in *Menaḥot* emphasize the spiritual implications of sacrificing. A poignant *aggadah* by R. Isaac states that when the poor offer God a meal-offering, in spite of its negligible value, God honors the giver as though he had offered up his soul (104b). Regarding its *halakhot*, large portions of the text are taken up by extraneous material; e.g., 28a–44b deal mainly with the *menorah*, *mezuzah*, *teffillin*, and *ẓiẓit*. In the printed editions the sequence of the chapters in the Babylonian Talmud differs from that of the separate Mishnah edition; the 10th Mishnah chapter is 6th, and consequently the mishnaic 6th, 7th, 8th, and 9th chapters become the 7th, 8th, 9th, and 10th respectively. *Menaḥot* was translated into English and published by the Soncino Press, London (1948).

Bibliography: Ḥ. Albeck, *Shishah Sidrei Mishnah-Kodashim* (1959), 59–62; Epstein, Amora'im.

[A.Z.E.]

MENASCE, DE, Egyptian family which went to Egypt from Spain, by way of Ereẓ Israel and Morocco.

JACOB DAVID DE MENASCE (1802–1885) was president of the Cairo Jewish community and leader of the Austrian subjects in Egypt. He received the hereditary title of baron from the emperor Francis Joseph. In 1871 he settled in Alexandria, where he established the Menasce synagogue in 1873 and a large Jewish school (1881). His son BAKHOR DE MENASCE (1830–1884) was president of the Alexandria community and active in Jewish philanthropy. Three of his sons became well-known: JACQUES (1850–1916), head of the local community from 1890 to 1914, helped to found the Menasce hospital, financed jointly by his family and the community. FELIX (1865–1943) was president of the community from 1926 to 1933. In 1918 he founded the Zionist Pro-Palestine Society and aided pioneers traveling to Ereẓ Israel through Alexandria. ALFRED (1867–1927) was a member of the Alexandria municipal council for many years and honorary consul of Hungary. In 1925, after a teacher in a Christian school had repeated stories of the *blood libel before Jewish pupils, he reacted by becoming the principal benefactor in the establishment of a Jewish vocational school in the city. Felix's son GEORGES (b. 1900) was known in Egypt for his art collection and generosity, especially on behalf of Jewish causes. He settled in England. Another son, JEAN (b. 1910), who became a Jesuit priest in France, wrote a book on Ḥasidism (*Quand Israel aime Dieu*, 1931), following a visit to Poland.

Bibliography: J. M. Landau, *Ha-Yehudim be-Miẓrayim* (1967), index.

[H.J.C.]

MENDEL, wealthy family prominent in Hungary in the late 15th and early 16th centuries. It appears that the family went there from Germany and they seem to have been in Buda from 1470. On the suggestion of the royal treasurer, the apostate János Ernuszt, King Matthias Corvinus (1458–90) granted to members of the Mendel family the office of **Praefectus Judaeorum*. Probably the family was friendly with Ernuszt or may even had been related to him. First to hold the office was JUDAH (c. 1470). He was succeeded by his son JACOB (1493–1522), who was particularly respected. A record of his seal, inscribed with his initials, still exists. Next in office was ISRAEL (1523–26), who was followed by ISAAC (1527–39). With the expulsion of the Jews from Buda to Turkey (1526; see *Budapest) and the conquest of the town the family declined; the office of *Praefectus Judaeorum* also ceased to exist at that time. A prominent member of the family was MENDEL SCHWARTZ, one of the most important financiers of the Hungarian capital. He is mentioned for the last time in 1526. Members of the Mendel family were also to be found in other Hungarian towns, such as in Sopron, but those mentioned in Pressburg were almost certainly identical with the Buda branch, who also owned houses in Pressburg.

Bibliography: S. Kohn, *A zsidók története Magyarországon* (1884), 220–2; S. Büchler, *A zsidók története Budapesten* (1901), 48–51; Sz. Balog, *A magyarországi zsidók kamaraszolgasága* (1907), 68–69; B. Mandl, in: *Mult és Jövő*, 5 (1915), 304–5; *Magyar Zsido Lexikon* (1929), 586; P. Gruenwald, in: *N. M. Gelber Jubilee Volume* (1963).

[A.KU.]

MENDELE MOKHER SEFORIM (Abramowitsch, Shalom Jacob; 1835–1917), Hebrew and Yiddish writer. Mendele's life and work encompass several periods in the development of Jewish society in Russia: the Haskalah, *Ḥibbat Zion, and Zionism. He lived to the onset of the Russian Revolution as well. Mendele began his literary career as an essayist and writer of fiction during the Haskalah period in Russia and reached his artistic maturity during the period of national renaissance after 1881. He was instrumental in the founding of modern literary Yiddish and the new realism in Hebrew style, and left his mark on the two literatures thematically as well as stylistically.

Knowledge of Mendele's life, especially his childhood, which is depicted in minute detail, comes mainly from his autobiographical works, *Ba-Yamim ha-Hem* ("In Those Days"; first published in Hebrew in 1903, 1904, 1910, 1917) and *Reshimot le-Toledotai* ("My Life Story"; in *Sefer Zikkaron* (1889), 117–26), and his many letters.

Mendele was born in the small town of Kapuli in Belorussia. After the death of his father, Mendele, aged 13, left Kapuli and wandered through Lithuania, studying at various yeshivot. Traveling throughout Volhynia, Ukraine, and Podolia, he absorbed many impressions of Jewish life which he later recorded in his writings. He lived in Berdichev from 1858 to 1869, in Zhitomir from 1869 to 1881, and, except for a short stay in Geneva from 1905 to 1907, in Odessa from 1881 to 1917. During the first literary period, which began in the 1860s, Mendele wrote literary and social criticism (*Mishpat Shalom*, 1860; *Ein Mishpat*, 1867), works of popular science in Hebrew (*Toledot ha-Teva* (Natural History), vol. 1 1862; vol. 2 1867; vol. 3, 1873), and Hebrew and Yiddish fiction—in Hebrew: *Limmedu Heitev* ("Learn Well," 1862); *Ha-Avot ve-ha-Banim* ("Fathers and Sons," 1868); in Yiddish: *Dos Klayne Menshele* ("The Little Man"), *Dos Vinshfingeril* ("The Wishing Ring," 1865); *Fishke der Krumer* ("Fishke the Lame," 1869).

In his writings on social and literary problems Mendele showed lively interest in the education and public life of Jews in Russia. He was preoccupied by the question of the role of Hebrew literature in molding the Jewish community. Concerned as he was with problems of Jewish society, Mendele took an active part in public life in Berdichev: he founded a philanthropic association to help the poor and, in his Yiddish play, *De Takse* ("The Tax," 1869), denounced the infamous meat-tax which fell heaviest upon the poor. Adopting the objectives of Russian positivist literature of the 1860s, the young Mendele demanded that contemporary Hebrew literature be actively involved in current problems of the Jewish community. Hebrew literature, he contended, should influence and inspire Jewish life. Hence his endeavors to teach the sciences to the mass of Jews and to aid the people in obtaining secular education in the spirit of the Haskalah. His advocacy of the study of the sciences is expressed, among other places, in the first version of his Yiddish novel, *Dos Vinshfingeril*, and particularly in his compilation, *Toledot ha-Teva*, whose zoological terminology based on talmudic sources has influenced modern Hebrew usage. The literary quality of his description of nature in general and animal behavior in particular is indicative of the artistry of his later fiction. In the 1870s Mendele devoted himself to traditional Jewish literature; he compiled original translations-adaptations of *Zemirot Yisrael* (1875) and *Perek Shirah* (1875), and planned to translate the prayer book and the Book of Psalms into Yiddish, but this project remained unfinished and only small parts are extant. Concurrently, Mendele published the first version of his allegorical novel, *Di Kliatshe* ("The Nag," 1873) and his allegorical poem, *Yudel* (1875), which is based on the history of the Jewish people. He also produced "practical" literature, e.g., the calendar, *Der Nitslikher Kalendar* (1875–85), which includes information in Yiddish on natural sciences and Jewish history. Also in this category is his Yiddish translation from Russian of the regulations concerning compulsory service in the Russian army (1874).

Although Mendele continued writing and publishing in Hebrew throughout the 1870s, this decade was mainly devoted to writing in Yiddish. The return to Hebrew writing came in 1886 with the publication of his story, *Be-Seter Ra'am* ("The Secret Place of Thunder"), his first Hebrew belletristic work since 1866, when he had published the novel, *Ha-Avot ve-ha-Banim*. Mendele's Hebrew writing became his main concern in the 1890s, when in addition to continuing to publish his short stories in Hebrew he rewrote his Yiddish novels *Dos Vinshfingeril* and *Fishke der Krumer* in Hebrew, entitling them *Be-Emek ha-Bakha* ("In the Valley of Tears," 1904) and *Sefer ha-Kabbeẓanim* ("Book of Beggars," 1909) respectively. Between 1890 and 1911 he continued to write original works in Hebrew, to recast his Yiddish works into Hebrew, and to re-edit his Yiddish fiction. The result was the publication in 1909–11 of his complete Hebrew works in three volumes and in 1911–13 of his Yiddish works in 16 volumes. By this time Mendele had become the acknowledged classicist of both Hebrew and Yiddish literature and enjoyed critical recognition and wide popularity in Jewish society.

Social Views. Mendele's work and activity oscillate between two antithetical poles: satirical chastisement of the ghetto Jew on the one hand and apologetic love of the Jewish people on the other. Though one can distinguish periods in which his approach tended toward radical criticism and periods in which it tended toward sympathetic understanding, often both tendencies exist simultaneously in the same work, expressive of Mendele's deep sense of ambivalence.

An apologetic approach is discernible in articles written as early as 1865, which were collected and published as *Ein Mishpat* ("Critical Eye," 1866). In his discussion of Jewish education he defends the study of the Talmud and traditional Jewish literature, and indulges the people's belief in legends and imaginary literature, knowing it was a means of escaping the reality of exploitation and persecution. The element of Russian patriotism in the novel *Ha-Avot ve-ha-Banim* (1868) is offset by the critical tone of the first Yiddish version of his allegorical story, *Di Kliatshe* (1873), in which he boldly decries the economic and civil repression of Russian Jews and anti-Semitic agitation in the Russian press of the 1870s.

Figure 1. Mendele Mokher Seforim, Yiddish and Hebrew writer. Jerusalem, J.N.U.L., Schwadron Collection.

Mendele records the plight of Russian Jewry suffering

Figure 2. Mendele Mokher Seforim with his family, c. 1905. Jerusalem, J.N.U.L., Schwadron Collection.

tyranny and hate from without and the exploitation by the Jewish upper classes from within. Further, he expresses the ambiguities and contradictions within the Jewish spirit through his use of legend and his imaginative conception of character. In spite of the fact that Mendele continues the Haskalah tradition of derisively satirizing folk beliefs (e.g., in *Masot Binyamin ha-Shelishi*, "Travels of Benjamin the Third," 1897), he retains the use of legend as an artistic vehicle for allegories such as *Di Kliatshe—Susati*, or as an evocation of the intimate and authentic experiences of Jewish childhood as in *Be-Emek ha-Bakha*. Steeped as they are in allusions to the Talmud and Midrash, Mendele's writings, both serious and humorous, evidence his abiding attraction to legend.

As he passed from the Haskalah period to that of Ḥibbat Zion and then Zionism, Mendele's indecisiveness about the solutions to the problems of Jewish society is reflected in his works. In his Haskalah period the young Mendele rejects assimilation in principle and expresses respect and appreciation for the unique significance of the Hebrew language and of Jewish tradition, its festivals and customs (*Ha-Avot ve-ha-Banim*). During the Ḥibbat Zion period Mendele was among the authors who were alert to ideological changes and to spiritual agitation within Jewish society after the pogroms of the 1880s. In his Hebrew story, *"Bi-Yshivah shel Ma'lah u-vi-Yshivah shel Mattah"* ("The Heavenly and Earthly Academies," 1894–95), he describes the split in Jewish society between the assimilationists, the Orthodox, and Ḥovevei Zion adherents, and recounts their many arguments. Mendele Mokher Seforim himself, who appears as a character in the story, takes an indecisive stand. He articulates various arguments, in turn advocating Haskalah, traditionalism, and Ḥibbat Zion nationalism, but without finally choosing one of them. The story, in which the use of dialogue abounds, actually ends in an ideological draw. At the same time Mendele does not hesitate to criticize manifestations of provincialism and superficiality among Ḥibbat Zion officials who took their public responsibility lightly (*Bi-Ymei ha-Ra'ash*, 1894). He continued to praise the Haskalah and its achievements in his long discursive digressions in one of the later versions of the novel, *Be-Emek ha-Bakha* (1907–09).

Literary Achievement. In his autobiographical works Mendele's characters are drawn from Jewish life in towns and cities in Russia, Lithuania, and Belorussia, where he spent his childhood and youth. His principal stories portray characters from Volhynia and southern Russia, with the action taking place in Berdichev, Zhitomir, Odessa and other towns in the Jewish Pale of Settlement. However, these places are usually concealed by significant names which satirically describe the qualities of their inhabitants, such as "Kislon" (Heb.) or "Glupsk" (Yid.), literally meaning foolishness and ignorance; "Batlon" (Heb.) or "Tuneyadevka" (Yid.), implying naïveté and impracticability; and "Kabẓi'el" (Heb.) or "Kabẓansk" (Yid.), connoting beggary. Although Mendele was deeply immersed in Jewish lore he also was influenced by the traditions of European fiction. His story *Masot Binyamin ha-Shelishi* (Yid., 1879; Heb., 1896) was inspired by Cervantes' *Don Quixote*, and his *Dos Klayne Menshele* and *Fishke der Krumer—Sefer ha-Kabbeẓanim* reflect the Russian satirical tradition of Gogol and of Saltykov-Shchedrin and the techniques of the picaresque novel. Mendele was successful in several literary genres. He revealed a special affinity for the autobiographical story (*Ba-Yamim ha-Hem*, Yid., *Shelomo Reb Kayims*) and for the biographical novel (*Dos Vinshfingeril—Be-Emek ha-Bakha*), often using the technique of building his story around the personality of a narrator who appears in various situations. For example, in *"Bi-Yshivah shel Ma'lah u-vi-Yshivah shel Mattah,"* the character "Mendele Mokher Seforim" wanders from town to town as a publisher of written and oral personal confessions, last wills, and autobiographical treatises purported to have been received from their authors for translation, adaptation, and distribution so that these annals might serve people as a moral lesson. The technique of taking on the guise of a character who functions as narrator furnishes Mendele with many opportunities for ironic play and enables him to achieve artistic distance from his story. Assuming the position of observer, as it were, serves him particularly well in those stories.

Mendele complained at times that the Jewish milieu was boring, lacked the raw materials for literary plots and heroes capable of exceptional deeds. He did adopt the typical patterns of the sentimental adventure story in *Fishke der Krumer—Sefer ha-Kabbeẓanim*, a character novel in which surprising situations occur and extraordinary characters are depicted. On the other hand Mendele devotes a great deal of space to rambling ruminations about ideas and movements. These digressions contain sentimental harangues on the fate of the suffering individual, and the condition of Jewish society as a whole (particularly in *Di Kliatshe—Susati*). This type of digression encroaches upon the story proper, weakening its structure and its artistic effect. Even in his later and stylistically more elaborate works, he did not relinquish his desire to instruct and reform.

Style. Mendele's Hebrew style went through a number of stages. In the 1860s he was still under the influence of Abraham *Mapu's biblical-rhetorical style, a style particularly apparent in his stories. However, the essays of the same period clearly indicate a break with the pseudo-biblical rhetoric (*meliẓah*) of the Haskalah and an attempt to enrich Hebrew with talmudic and midrashic references. In the 1870s, in his Hebrew commentaries on his Yiddish translations of *"Perek Shirah"* and *"Zemirot shel Shabbat"* in *Zemirot Yisrael*, and in the appendices to *Toledot ha-Teva*, Mendele used a more rabbinic Hebrew style. He carried on the tradition of expanding the Hebrew language established by such early Haskalah writers as Mendel (Lefin) *Levin, Joseph *Perl, and Eliezer *Zweifel, whose style absorbed elements of mishnaic Hebrew, the language of medieval philosophical literature, and of ḥasidic literature which was influenced by spoken Yiddish. Mendele's search for Hebrew equivalents for Yiddish popular speech is seen in his first Hebrew story, *"Limmedu Heitev"* (1862), in which he attempts to translate popular proverbs literally and simply. The process of creating a Hebrew style composed of many elements reached its peak in the late 1880s, when Mendele "returned" to Hebrew literature. His style came to reflect the earnest simplicity of the prayer book and the wit of talmudic sayings employed in the everyday Yiddish speech of scholars.

Mendele wrote in both languages throughout his career, but he did so with unequal emphasis, writing predominantly in Hebrew in some genres, and predominantly in Yiddish in others. Writing in both languages produced interaction between his Hebrew and Yiddish style. In his use of Yiddish there are abundant references and allusions to the Talmud, prayer book, and *piyyutim*, and in his use of Hebrew there are popular idioms taken from Yiddish and expressed in a Hebrew equivalent. Although Mendele began writing in Yiddish for the practical purpose of reaching a larger reading public, he eventually came to regard his work in Yiddish to be of intrinsic artistic value in its own right. Mendele's original use of language, especially Hebrew, serves him as an effective instrument for satire and irony not only because it is apposite but often because it is unexpected; for example, phrases originally expressing the sacred are deliberately applied to the profane—i.e., the description of earthly, everyday phenomena. He defined the quality of his new Hebrew style thus: "Let us create a Hebrew style, a live creature, talking, clearly and precisely, the way people do in this time and place, and let its soul be Jewish." This style, a natural synthesis of content and form, has left its imprint on Hebrew fiction to this day.

Textual Development—The Versions. Mendele is an author who continually reworked his novels and stories—enlarging and polishing them. This characteristic is partially explained by the fact that his long literary career spanned several movements and ideologies. From an artistic point of view, it may also be attributed to Mendele's genius and his striving for artistic perfection. *Dos Vinshfingeril* and *Fishke der Krumer*, which developed from thin booklets into extensive and complex novels, are typical examples of works that Mendele expanded. The various versions of his works, and particularly the jubilee edition, evince both a rethinking and a rephrasing of his ideas. Thus he moderated his satiric-admonitory stance in the novel *Ha-Avot ve-ha-Banim* (1868) and minimized the propagandist-enlightenment element in *Dos Vinshfingeril* (1865). To *Di Kliatshe* (1873) Mendele later added allusions to the state of Russian Jews at the beginning of the 20th century. Subsequent versions of works also underwent changes in structure, e.g., the use of a more sophisticated framework in his last edition of *Fishke der Krumer—Sefer ha-Kabbeẓanim*, and the transition from the autobiographical point of view of *Dos Vinshfingeril* to that of the omniscient author in later Yiddish and Hebrew versions. In the process of bilingual recreation in later adaptations of his works, Mendele introduced important variations in content and style. Mendele did not merely translate his works from Yiddish into Hebrew but rather reshaped them. The comparative study of the several versions of his works in Yiddish and Hebrew, a study which is still incomplete, indicates a reciprocal influence of the works in both languages. In some cases, e.g., in *Di Kliatshe—Susati*, and *Dos Vinshfingeril—Be-Emek ha-Bakha*, it appears that a number of the chapters added later in the Hebrew versions served as the basis for the final versions of those works in Yiddish. The careful study of the versions of Mendele's work in Yiddish had already been carried out in the Soviet Union in the 1930s, but this study almost completely disregarded the interrelationship of the Yiddish and Hebrew versions. The academic edition of Mendele's collected works, in preparation at the Hebrew University in Jerusalem (begun 1965) will stress the organic relation of the several versions in both languages.

Criticism of Mendele's Work. Mendele's Yiddish and Hebrew writings attracted attention from the start, but critical interest in them grew especially in the 1880s, after he had published his major works. This interest increased in the 20th century as Mendele's works won admiration on the one hand and drew reserved and even negative reaction on the other. From the ideological point of view, critics were interested in his attitude to the Ḥibbat Zion movement and his stand on the social problems of the oppressed multitudes in Russia. Some regarded Mendele as the preacher, loyal to his people and calling for a radical change in Diaspora life. The documentary character of Mendele's description of life in the ghetto, intended to serve as a historical testimony to the Jewish way of life in the 19th century, was highly appreciated. Yet critics used Mendele's documentary method as an argument against his work. They thought his "realistic" portrayal of the harshness and cruelty of ghetto life to be a distortion and falsification of Jewish existence there. While originally praised for faithfully depicting 19th-century East European Jews and their circumstances, later, particularly in the last generation, Mendele's work was held to be educationally "dangerous," especially for the young reader who was a stranger to that Jewish existence. Opinions also differed concerning the artistic significance of Mendele's works; while critics admired his delightful descriptions of nature, and his epic achievement in recreating Jewish types of the *shtetl*, they felt that his power was restricted to the depiction of general types, only inadequately revealing the life of the individual Jew and his spiritual struggles. Critics also believed that the influence of Mendele's style on the Hebrew writers of Bialik's generation was detrimental to the discovery of their individual creative personalities. The unfavorable evaluation of Mendele in the last generation notwithstanding, literary research and critical interest in his work have not decreased. At present the approach of critics is balanced and direct, especially in the analysis of his Hebrew work. Mendele's critics now neither advocate nor condemn but rather discuss his works in the light of their inherent

Figure 3. Mendele Mokher Seforim on his 70th birthday in 1905, with Yehoshua Rawnitski (seated left), A. Levinsky (seated right), S. Ben-Zion (standing left), and Ḥayyim Naḥman Bialik (standing right). Courtesy Beit Bialik, Tel Aviv.

satiric-ironic nature, pointing out the writer's ambivalent alternation between satire and sentiment and his simultaneous attraction to and repulsion from Jewish life in the ghetto. Special interest has been shown in Mendele's style, its linguistic figures, e.g., simile and metaphor, and its relation to description and plot. Critics have also studied the interaction between his Yiddish and Hebrew writing, a relationship essential to a fuller understanding of his work. A fresh approach to his work might open up new horizons for the contemporary reader, helping him to rediscover Mendele's art.

Bibliography: Shunami, Bibl, no. 3144–55; Mendele Mokher Seforim, *Reshimat Ketavav ve-Iggerotav le-Hatkanat Mahaduratam ha-Akademit* (1965); Rejzen, Leksikon, 6 (1965), 48–72; A. Gurstein, in: *Tsaytshrift* (Minsk), 2–3 (1928); Klausner, Sifrut, 6 (1958), 315–457; N. Mayzel, *Dos Mendele-Bukh* (1959); I. Nusinov, *Fun Bukh tsu Bukh, Shriftn* (Kiev, 1928); Ch. Shmeruk, in: *Fourth World Congress of Jewish Studies, Papers*, 2 (1968), 25–30; idem, in: *Ha-Sifrut*, 2 (1968), 337–42; S. Werses, *ibid.*, 23f; idem, in: *Molad*, 20 (1962); idem, in: *Di Goldene Keyt* (1965–66), no. 51, 188–210; D. Miron, in: Mendele Mokher Seforim, *Limmedu Heitev* (1969), introd.; G. Shaked, *Bein Seḥok le-Dema* (1965); I. Rabinovich, *Major Trends in Modern Hebrew Fiction* (1968), index; A. A. Roback, *The Story of Yiddish Literature* (1940), 95–105; H. Ormian, in: *YIVO Annual*, 5 (1950), 292–312; S. Spiegel, *Hebrew Reborn* (1930), 243–66, 457f.; Waxman, Literature, 4 (1960), 124–49; S. Liptzin, *Flowering of Yiddish Literature* (1963), index. For English translations see, Goell, Bibliography, no. 2271–2308, 2831–32. [S.WE.]

MENDELSOHN, ERIC (1887–1953), architect. He was born in Allenstein, Germany and was a member of the revivalist movement in European architecture from the 1920s onward. His early works, especially his sketches made during World War I and the buildings designed in the early twenties (such as the observatory near Berlin, 1920), are of an expressionist character. His later buildings are noteworthy, against the background of the contemporary style, for the originality of their shapes and their monumental nature. He built a large number of business-houses and large office blocks in Berlin and in other towns in Germany, as well as factories and dwelling-houses. When Hitler seized power in 1933, Mendelsohn left Germany and worked in Britain and Palestine until the outbreak of World War II. Between 1934 and 1939, he built in Palestine the villa and library of Zalman Schocken in Jerusalem, the Anglo-Palestine Bank in Jerusalem, the Hadassah hospital on Mount Scopus, Chaim Weizmann's villa in Reḥovot, part of the Hebrew University's Faculty of Agriculture at Reḥovot, and the Haifa government hospital. When World War II broke out, he went to the United States, and from 1945 onward, built in various places. His works include the Maimonides Health Center in San Francisco, and many synagogues, in which he tried to acheive a monumental impression without adherence to any traditional style. These include synagogues in St. Paul, Minnesota; Washington, D.C.; Baltimore, Maryland; Dallas, Texas; Saint Louis, Missouri. He wrote the autobiographical *Letters of an Architect* (1967).

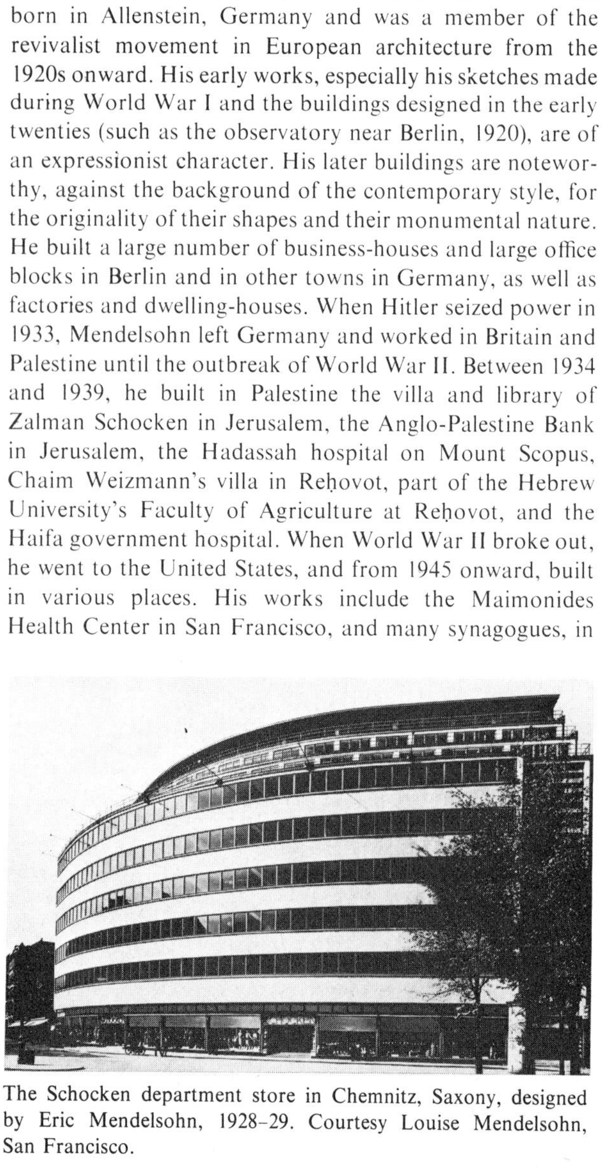

The Schocken department store in Chemnitz, Saxony, designed by Eric Mendelsohn, 1928–29. Courtesy Louise Mendelsohn, San Francisco.

Bibliography: A. Whittick, *Eric Mendelsohn* (Eng., 1956²); W. Eckardt, *Eric Mendelsohn* (Eng., 1960). [A.E.]

MENDELSOHN, FRANKFURT MOSES (Moses ben Mendel Frankfurt; 1782–1861), Hebrew scholar and writer. Born in Hamburg, he received a traditional education but, under the influence of N. H. *Wessely, became attracted to Haskalah. He engaged mainly in literary work, writing in both German and in Hebrew. His main work is *Penei Tevel* (published posthumously in Amsterdam in 1872), a collection of poetry and prose in the style of the *maqāmāt* of *Al-Ḥarizi. The book contains satire, polemics, epic poems on biblical themes, and a history of the Hebrew Haskalah movement at the turn of the 18th century. He was an uncle of S. R. *Hirsch.

Bibliography: E. Duckesz, *Ḥakhmei Ahav* (1908), 120–1; G. Kressel, *Ivrit ba-Ma'arav* (1941), 36–41; Ḥ. N. Shapira, *Toledot ha-Sifrut ha-Ivrit ha-Ḥadashah* (1967²), 503–10. [G.K.]

MENDELSOHN, SHELOMO (1896–1948), Yiddish critic. Born in Warsaw, he early showed his brilliance in talmudic studies. While enrolled at Warsaw University, he taught Jewish history and literature at Polish secondary schools. From 1917 he was coeditor of *Dos Folk* and a leader of the Folk Party. In 1928 he joined the Bund and eight years later was elected to the Jewish *kehillah*. He emigrated to the United States in 1941 and joined the editorial board of *Undzer Tsayt*. In 1947 the Bund sent him to Europe, where he organized Jewish educational, cultural, and communal organizations. His articles on literature were published in various Yiddish journals. His literary criticism includes works on Shlomo *Ettinger, H. D. *Nomberg, and J. J. *Trunk.

Bibliography: H. S. Kashdan, *Shloyme Mendelson* (1949). [I.H.B.]

MENDELSON, YOSEF (José; 1891–1969), Argentine Yiddish editor and writer. Born in Cherkassy, Ukraine, Mendelson began his Yiddish literary publication in 1912 with an article on Peretz *Smolenskin in the Russian-Zionist monthly, *Die Yidishe Hofenung*. In the same year, he emigrated to Argentina, where he taught Hebrew, later continuing in journalism. With Z. Brokhes he co-edited the fortnightly, *Der Kolonist*, in which he also published articles on Yiddish and Spanish writers. Having begun to write for *Di Yidishe Tsaytung* in 1917, he edited that publication from 1923 to 1929. Likewise, together with Y. Helfman he edited the Yiddish monthly *Argentina* (1921), aside from periodicals. Mendelson edited the anthologies *Oyf di Bregn fun La-Plata* (1919), *50 Yor Yidishe Kolonizatsye in Argentine* (1939), and *Rashi-Bukh* (1940). *Amol in a Halben Yoyvl*, a collection of his writings, was published in 1943. His translations into Yiddish include many Russian, Spanish, French, and English novels. Among his other works were plays and writings about artists, sculptors, etc. From 1943, he directed the Hebrew-Yiddish Teachers Seminary in Buenos Aires.

Bibliography: LNYL, 6 (1965), 39–41. [I.H.B.]

MENDELSSOHN, family of scholars, bankers and artists. The founder of the family was MOSES *MENDELSSOHN (1729–1786). His wife FROMET (1737–1812), was a great-granddaughter of the Viennese Court Jew, Samuel *Oppenheimer.

Moses' eldest son, JOSEPH (1770–1848), had a banking

business, at times in partnership with his brother Abraham (1776–1835). The bank helped transfer the French indemnity after Napoleon's defeat, and was later active mainly in German and foreign railway issues and state loans,

Joseph Mendelssohn (1770–1848), banker. Jerusalem, J.N.U.L., Schwadron Collection.

particularly Russian. Mendelssohn and Co. were bankers and correspondents for many foreign commercial banks, central banks, and governments, but did not launch any industrial ventures of their own. After World War I the bank opened an issuing house in Amsterdam. The Berlin house was absorbed by the Deutsche Bank in 1939. Joseph was the friend and patron of Alexander von *Humboldt, the naturalist, and for many years chairman of the corporation of Berlin merchants. He and his brother Abraham were co-sponsors of the enlightened circle of Jewish notables, Gesellschaft der Freunde. His nephew, Abraham's son, the composer Felix Mendelssohn Bartholdy (for the Bartholdy see Felix *Mendelssohn) urged him to go through with his old project of an edition of his father's collected works, on the suggestion of F. A. Brockhaus, the noted publisher; in this he was aided by his son, Georg Benjamin (1794–1874), professor of geography at Bonn University. Joseph himself contributed to this

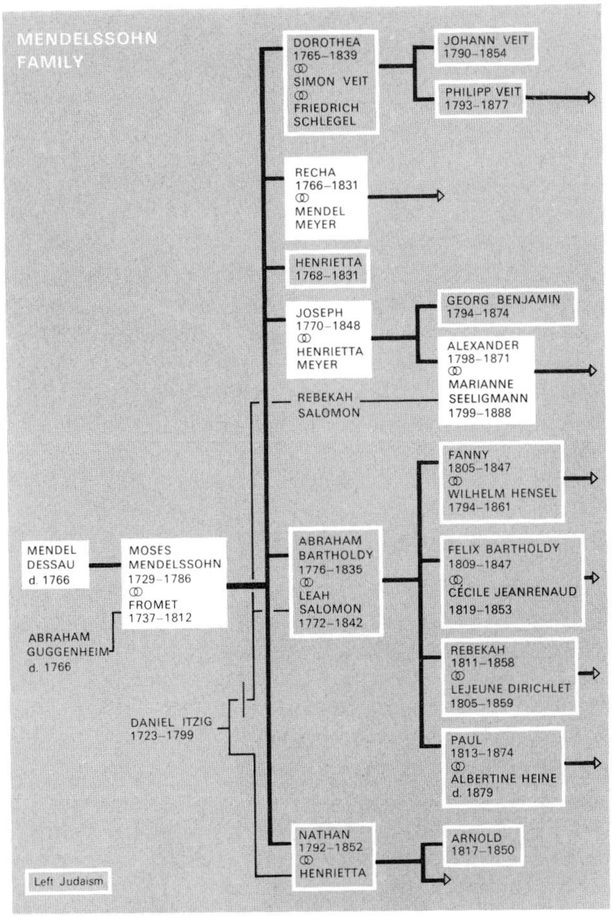

Based on S. Hensel, *The Mendelssohn family*, 1729–1874.

project, for which he wrote his father's biography. Of Joseph's sons, Georg Benjamin was baptized; Alexander (1798–1871), head of the bank, remained a Jew. Through social contacts with the *Hohenzollerns Joseph's grandson Franz (1829–1889) and Abraham's grandson Ernst (1846–1909) were elevated to the hereditary nobility.

In 1804, Abraham married Leah Salomon, granddaughter of Daniel *Itzig, and thereby became a naturalized Prussian citizen, ahead of the bulk of his coreligionists. He served for many years as municipal councillor without pay. A deist and rationalist by conviction he brought up his children as Protestants in order to improve their social opportunities. He and his wife embraced Christianity in 1822 "because it is the religious form acceptable to the majority of civilized human beings" (in a letter to his daughter Fanny). This decision to convert was influenced by the current *Hep! Hep! riots (1819).

Later Mendelssohn-Bartholdy descendants include Albrecht Mendelssohn-Bartholdy, editor of the *Europaeische Gespraeche* in Hamburg, who died in exile in England. Felix *Gilbert, a historian, at the Institute of Advanced Study, Princeton, New Jersey; the philosopher Leonhard *Nelson (1882–1927); Kurt Hensel, a West German diplomat posted to Tel Aviv in 1968. Carl Mendelssohn-Bartholdy (1838–1897), assisted by his uncle Paul (1813–1874), wrote the first biography of his father Felix. Felix's nephew Sebastian Hensel (1830–1898) was the first family chronicler.

Moses' eldest daughter, Dorothea (Brendel, 1765–1839), was married twice: to the banker Simon Veit (see *Veit family) and to Friedrich Schlegel, man of letters. Her sons, Johannes *Veit (1790–1854) and Philipp Veit (1793–1877), were painters of the Romantic "Nazarene" school. Henriette (Sorel; 1768–1831), Moses' youngest daughter, resembled her father in character. She never married, having his deformity. She served as governess and teacher in Vienna and Paris, where she was head of a boarding school. The intellectual luminaries of the age, Madame de Staël, Spontini, Benjamin Constant, and the Schlegels formed part of her salon. In 1812 she became tutor to the French general Sebastiani's daughter. In that year, following her mother's death, she was baptized into the Catholic Church, taking the name Marie (a few years earlier she had rebuked her sister Dorothea for doing the same). Moses' youngest son, Nathan, had a son, the physician Arnold Mendelssohn (1817–1850), a supporter and confidant of Ferdinand *Lassalle.

Bibliography: S. Hensel, *Mendelssohn Family*..., 2 vols. (1882; tr. of *Die Familie Mendelssohn*, 3 vols., 1879); E. Werner, *Mendelssohn; a New Image of the Composer*... (1963); idem, in: HUCA, 26 (1955), 543–65; M. A. Meyer, *Origins of the Modern Jew* (1967), index; J. Jacobson, in: YLBI, 5 (1960), 251–61; 7 (1962), 279–82; H. G. Reissner, *ibid.*, 4 (1959), 93–110; A. Altmann, in: BLBI, 11 (1968), 73–116; E. Achterberg and M. Mueller-Jabusch, *Lebensbilder deutscher Bankiers*... (1963); H. M. Z. Meyer, *Moses Mendelssohn Bibliographie* (1965); M. Peez, *Henriette Mendelssohn* (Ger., 1888). [H.G.R.]

MENDELSSOHN, FELIX (Jakob Ludwig Felix; 1809–1847), composer. Born in Hamburg, Felix was the grandson of Moses *Mendelssohn and the son of Abraham Mendelssohn, a successful banker first in Hamburg and later in Berlin, and Lea Mendelssohn, the granddaughter of Daniel *Itzig (see *Mendelssohn family). His parents had their children baptized and later converted to Christianity themselves. Felix grew up in an intellectual, cultivated atmosphere. The Sunday morning concerts at his parents' Berlin home were notable occasions attended by many celebrities, and most of Mendelssohn's early music was

Felix Mendelssohn playing for Goethe in Weimar. Jerusalem, J.N.U.L., Schwadron Collection.

written for these gatherings. Abraham Mendelssohn added the name Bartholdy (after a property that had belonged to his wife's brother) to the family name, stating that "A Christian Mendelssohn is an impossibility." He wished his son to go by the professional name of Felix M. Bartholdy, but he refused to comply and in 1829 conducted under the name Felix Mendelssohn. (His sister Rebecca often signed her letters Rebecca Mendelssohn Meden (the latter meaning "never" in Greek) Bartholdy.)

Mendelssohn advanced rapidly as a composer and pianist. His String Octet, completed in 1825, is a major work of chamber music. Two years later the first public performance of his overture to *A Midsummer Night's Dream* took place, and in 1829, Mendelssohn performed what some believe to be his greatest achievement: the revival of J. S. Bach's *St. Matthew Passion* (at the Singakademie in Berlin), which initiated the renewed popularity of Bach's works. That same year, he made the first of many journeys to England, where his popularity grew. This trip was the first episode in a three-year grand tour which included Scotland, Italy, Switzerland, and France. Some important works of this time, reflecting impressions of his travels, are the *Hebrides Overture* and the *Italian* and *Scotch* symphonies.

In 1833, Mendelssohn was appointed musical director of the Dusseldorf Music and Theater Society; he also supervised the city's church music and directed the subscription concerts of the Society's orchestra. Far more to his liking was his appointment as director of the Gewandhaus concerts in Leipzig in 1835. He continued to be identified with this city for the rest of his life. In 1835 he completed his oratorio *St. Paul* for the Lower Rhine Festival in Duesseldorf (May 1836). Then he traveled to Frankfort to direct the Caecilien-Verein.

In 1840 Mendelssohn was the most famous living composer in Central Europe. It was therefore inevitable that Frederick William IV, who wished to ensure Prussia's cultural and political supremacy, would summon him to court. In spite of the frustrations of bureaucracy, Mendelssohn did accomplish some good work there, notably the complete incidental music to *A Midsummer Night's Dream.* During this period he also continued writing his many *Songs Without Words,* the most popular piano pieces of their genre. In 1843 he returned to Leipzig and founded the conservatory which became the most renowned institution of its kind in Germany in the 19th century. Mendelssohn's last years saw many triumphs, the greatest of which was the première of *Elijah* in Birmingham (1846). But his strenuous existence as pianist, conductor, composer, and pedagogue had worn him out prematurely. His sister Fanny's sudden death in May 1847 was a shock to his already weakened system, and he died six months later in Leipzig.

FANNY CAECILE (Zipporah) MENDELSSOHN (1805–1847) was unusually close to her brother Felix, and her marriage to the painter Wilhelm Hensel in 1829 did not weaken this bond. Felix relied upon her musical taste and advice, and six of her songs which were published along with his (without identification) are stylistically indistinguishable from his work. Under her own name, she published four books of piano pieces, two books of solo songs, and one book of part-songs. After her death, a few more piano pieces, some songs, and a piano trio in D major were published.

Bibliography: G. Grove, *Beethoven, Schubert, Mendelssohn* (Eng., 1951); S. Hensel, *Mendelssohn Family 1729–1847,* 2 vols. (1882); J. Horton, *Chamber Music of Mendelssohn* (1946); F. Mendelssohn, *Letters,* ed. by G. Selden-Goth (1945); J. Petitpierre, *Romance of the Mendelssohns* (1948); P. Radcliffe, Mendelssohn (Eng., 1954, 1967[2]); E. Werner, *Mendelssohn: A New Image of the Composer and his Age* (1963); J. Werner, *Felix and Fanny Mendelssohn,* in: *Music and Letters,* 28 (Oct., 1947), 303–38; P. Young, *Introduction to the Music of Mendelssohn* (1949); Grove, Dict, s.v.; MGG, s.v.; Riemann-Gurlitt, s.v.; Baker, Biog Dict, s.v.

[DI.N.]

MENDELSSOHN, MOSES (**Moses ben Menahem,** acronym **RaMbeMaN,** or **Moses of Dessau;** 1729–1786), philosopher of the German Enlightenment in the pre-Kantian period and spiritual leader of German Jewry. Born in Dessau, Mendelssohn during his early childhood suffered from a disease which left him with a curvature of the spine

Figure 1. Portrait of Moses Mendelssohn by D. Rode. Jerusalem, J.N.U.L., Schwadron Collection.

and permanently affected his nervous system. The son of a Torah scribe, Mendelssohn received a traditional Jewish education under the influence of David *Fraenkel, who was then rabbi of Dessau. When the latter was appointed rabbi of Berlin in 1743, Mendelssohn followed him there in order to pursue his studies and to acquire a general education. He earned his livelihood with difficulty at the same time studying diligently and acquiring broad education. In addition to his fluent knowledge of German and Hebrew, he became familiar with Latin, Greek, English, French, and Italian. His teachers were young educated Jews, such as Israel M. Zamosz, who taught him mathematics, Abraham Kisch, and A. S. Gumpertz. During this period he met the writer and dramatist G. E. *Lessing (1754) and a deep and lifelong friendship developed between them. In 1750 he became a teacher in the house of Isaac Bernhard, owner of a silk factory; in 1754, he was entrusted with the bookkeeping of the factory and eventually he became a partner in the enterprise. During the whole of his lifetime he worked as a merchant, while carrying out his literary activities and widespread correspondence in his free time. Only in 1763 he was granted "right of residence" in Berlin by the king. In 1762, he married Fromet Guggenheim of Hamburg, and they had six children (see *Mendelssohn family). In 1754 Mendelssohn began to publish—at first with the assistance of Lessing—philosophical writings and later also literary reviews. In 1763, he was awarded the first prize of the Prussian Royal Academy of Sciences for his work *Abhandlung ueber die Evidenz in metaphysischen Wissenschaften*. However, when the academy elected him as member in 1771, his election was not ratified by King Frederick II. In 1769, he became embroiled in a dispute on the Jewish religion, and from then on, he confined most of his literary activity to the sphere of Judaism. He was also active on behalf of the Jews in practical affairs. He was as outstanding in his conversation as in his writing, and a circle of intellectuals gathered regularly at his home to discuss general and Jewish subjects. He was famous among both Jews and non-Jews for his wide knowledge, his sharp intellect and his moderate, patient, and modest character.

Philosophy. One of his first publications, *Briefe ueber die Empfindungen* (1755, "Letters on the Emotions"), laid the groundwork for a new understanding of the nature of beauty. Elaborating his views later in *Philosophische Schriften* (2 vols., 1761), Mendelssohn formulated a new psychological theory which defined and justified the autonomy of aesthetic judgments, stressing their independence from logical criteria or ethical purposes. His theory pa' ed the way for notions later expressed by Schiller, Goethe, and Kant in his *Critique of Pure Reason.* Some s'holars maintain that Lessing could not have developed the views in his *Laokoon* (1766) without Mendelssohn's influence.

Philosophy of Religion. As a philosopher of religion Mendelssohn did not create an original system; he continued mainly in the tradition of classical rationalism current in the 17th and 18th centuries. His philosophy incorporates the dominant themes of Enlightenment philosophy; its emphasis on reason as the sole medium by which man acquires knowledge fulfillment; its notion that man is endowed with eternally valid innate ideas of absolute goodness and truth; its belief that all men "are to be accounted by nature as equal" (Pufendorf); and its eudaemonistic orientation which sees the purpose of philosophy not in the discovery of truth but in the achievement of happiness by the individual and society through the perfection of man. The starting point of Mendelssohn's philosophy of religion is his theory of knowledge. With Locke, Shaftesbury, and, especially, Leibniz, he distinguishes between eternal truths *(vérités de raison)*, which are self-evident to reason, and historical or temporal truths *(vérités de fait)*, requiring the evidence of sense experience. Among the truths self-evident to reason are the belief in a wise and merciful God and the immortality of the human soul. These metaphysical truths, which are the essential elements of the religion of reason, are the themes of his two major religio-philosophical works, *Morgenstunden* (1785) and *Phaedon* (1767). In the former Mendelssohn seeks to demonstrate the rationality of the belief in the existence of God. He treats the subject as a principle of general metaphysics and man's universal religion of reason. *Morgenstunden* was prepared for the instruction of his oldest son Joseph, and Alexander and Wilhelm von *Humboldt, the former a close friend of Joseph. In it Mendelssohn expands views already outlined in *Abhandlung ueber die Evidenz in metaphysichen Wissenschaften* (1764).

Existence of God. Mendelssohn's favorite proof for God's existence is a modification of the ontological argument: Man finds the idea of a Supreme Being in his consciousness. Since this idea cannot have arisen out of man's limited and fragmented experiences—we have no direct knowledge of anything remotely resembling the idea of divine perfection—it is a priori and belongs to the category of concepts that precede all experience and enable us to comprehend the universe, including space, time, and causality. Although these concepts do not arise from experience, they are not subjective because they determine the character of universal experience. Further, there is a necessary connection between the concept of an absolutely perfect beng and his existence. a being which is absolutely real, or perfect, must have existence among its attributes; otherwise, it would be lacking the full complement of its unconditioned possibility.

Immortality of the Soul. The question of the immortality of the soul is examined in Mendelssohn's chief philosophical work, *Phaedon* (1767; Eng. tr. 1784), modeled on Plato's dialogue of the same name. As early as 1760 Mendelssohn had expressed the wish to translate and rewrite Plato's text in the light of modern psychology. He was encouraged in this project by his correspondence with Thomas Abbt (1738–1760), a professor at the University of Frankfort, about the destiny of man and the soul and its fate after death. Mendelssohn develops his thesis along Leibnizian lines: An infinite number of souls or monads constitutes the inner substance of the universe. Things that perish do not cease to exist; they are dissolved into their elements. The soul must be such an element or substance, rather than a compound, since it is the soul which imposes a unifying pattern on the diverse and changing elements of the body. Hence it is neither weakened by age nor destroyed by death. However, this line of argument demonstrates only that the soul is imperishable but not that it will retain its consciousness in a future state. That it will possess its consciousness is guaranteed by the goodness of God, who has implanted in man the idea that his soul is immortal. To assume that this notion is deceptive would be incompatible with God's goodness and justice. "If our souls were mortal, reason would be a dream. . . . We would be like animals destined only to seek food and to perish."

Freedom of the Will. Mendelssohn's belief in the existence of God and the immortality of the soul, though developed as doctrines of the universal religion of reason, are in harmony with the dominant views of Jewish tradition. He differs from Jewish tradition, however, in his conception of free will. Inasmuch as every act of will must have a cause or motive, human freedom, if defined as an uncaused act, is logically impossible. Man's will can be free

Figure 2. Etching of Moses Mendelssohn (left) with Gotthold Lessing (standing) and the Lutheran theologian, Johann Caspar Lavater. Jerusalem, J.N.U.L., Schwadron Collection.

only in the sense that it is determined or aroused by a recognition of the good. But if man is not truly free, the sinner cannot be responsible for his misdeeds; why then should he be punished? Mendelssohn answers that divine punishment or retribution is not an end in itself; it is the means of purging the sinner to prepare him for life in the world to come. Divine justice is superseded by divine goodness, which never excludes man permanently from the bliss of eternal life. Mendelssohn's general philosophical position was soon challenged by Kant and his successors, whose critical idealism negated the presuppositions of the Enlightenment philosophy.

Critic of German Literature. During the period in which his first philosophical writings appeared, Mendelssohn also began to publish critical articles in the periodical *Bibliothek der schoenen Wissenschaften und der freien Kuenste* (1757–60) of the bookseller and publisher Friedrich Nicolai (1733–1811), his closest friend after Lessing. While his first reviews were mainly concerned with philosophical works, he also took up literary criticism which was published in Nicolai's second periodical *Briefe die neueste Literatur betreffend*, behind which Mendelssohn was a moving spirit. At this time German literature which was still young was struggling for recognition and a position in the cultural life of Germany which was dominated by Latin and French. Nicolai, Lessing, J. G. Herder, and others accomplished a kind of cultural revolution by adopting German as the language in which to express their revolutionary ideas. Mendelssohn, the Jew, became a natural ally of these writers, who did not identify with the academic and intellectual establishment, which, in turn, looked upon them, "Nicolai's sect" with contempt and suspicion. Like them, Mendelssohn was not a member of the establishment; like them, he sought to renovate his spiritual world and was distinguished for his universal humanist aspirations; which, like them, he chose to express in German. Mendelssohn found himself so much at ease in this cultural milieu that he embarked upon an offensive war in support of the use of the German language, even venturing to criticize King Frederick II himself for the publication of a book of poems in French. "Will the Germans never be aware of their own value? Will they forever exchange their gold (i.e., their basic thinking) for their neighbors' tinsel?" (French literature). It is against this background that the personality of Mendelssohn and the cultural heritage which he handed down to future generations must be assessed. The aesthetic writings of Mendelssohn attest to the supreme value which he attributed to beauty and above all to poetry. Mendelssohn's philosophic style in German was recognized by all, including Lessing, Herder, and Kant, as one of the most excellent of his time, but his talent for poetic expression was limited, a fact which he admitted himself.

The Dispute with Lavater. Although it was against his nature and his intentions, Mendelssohn was compelled publicly to defend his personal Judaism and the right of the independent existence of the Jewish religion before the society of his time. "I wanted to refute the world's derogatory opinion of the Jew by righteous living, not by pamphleteering," he said. During this period various Protestant circles sought the means to rescue Christianity from the onslaught of rationalism or even to unite the religion of reason and enlightenment with the traditional Christian religion. In this struggle, the integration of the Jews into the general society through conversion was to serve as a proof for the supremacy of Christianity. In line with these aspirations, John Casper Lavater (1741–1801), a talented Swiss clergyman given to irrational tendencies, publicly challenged the now-famous Mendelssohn to defend the superiority of Judaism to Christianity. As a young man, he had met Mendelssohn in Berlin (1763) and had been deeply impressed by his tolerant attitude toward Christianity, his appreciation of its moral value, and his general philosophic approach. In the summer of 1769, he translated into German a section of *La Palingénésie philosophique* by the Calvinist Charles Bonnet (1720–1793), professor of philosophy and psychology in Geneva, which was an apology for Christianity against deistic views and was based on contemporary rationalistic convictions and opinions. Lavater dedicated this translation to Mendelssohn, calling upon him "to do what wisdom, love of truth, and honor require, and what Socrates would have done had he read the treatise and found it irrefutable" or in other words, as Mendelssohn explained in his reply, "to abandon the religion of my fathers and to embrace the faith advocated by Bonnet." The astounded Mendelssohn was compelled to answer the attack in public, which he did in a polite and restrained but definite style (*Schreiben an den Herrn Diaconus Lavater zu Zuerich*, 1770). From the very start, he based his counterargument on the personal question which had been asked of him, which he rejected as unbecoming from a personal, and unjustified from an objective point of view. His loyalty to Judaism, he claimed, was the consequence of a decision based on the studies, the inquiries, and the deliberations of his youth. He maintained that he refrained from entering into a polemic on religious questions for three reasons. First the Torah was given solely to the Jewish people who are therefore the only ones bound by it; all other men are only obliged to abide by the rules of natural religion—the religion of reason ("*Noachide Laws"). Also, Judaism is devoid of any missionary tendencies, discouraging those who seek to convert. This removes the need for a dispute on religious questions. Second, fundamental conceptions should not be subjected to debate, even if they are based on error, as long as they serve as the basis for the morality of society and do not infringe upon natural law. His third reason was a practical one: As a Jew in a country such as Prussia where the Jews enjoy only relative freedom, it is preferable to refrain from a dispute on the religion of the majority. "I am a member of an oppressed people," he said. Mendelssohn, thus, did not deal with the fundamental questions which Lavater had sought to pose; he did not publicly attack Christianity and did not justify his Judaism by means of fundamental proofs. He nevertheless gave vent to his thoughts on the subject in *Gegenbetrachtungen ueber Bonnets Palingénésie*, which was not published until the middle of the 19th century, and in letters, some of which were addressed to Bonnet himself. The polemic between Mendelssohn and Lavater persisted during the winter of 1769–70, but was brought to an end when Lavater, who also encountered the discontent of his Protestant colleagues, apologized. The above exchanges, however, gave rise to a general debate which continued until the beginning of 1771. A large number of booklets and pamphlets were published, the overwhelming majority of them attacking Mendelssohn. This controversy upset Mendelssohn to such an extent that for over seven years he suffered from a nervous disease which prevented him from pursuing his philosophic studies. For Mendelssohn, these years proved to be a kind of catharsis. He came to realize that his Judaism committed him beyond the boundaries of his personal loyalty that was expressed in the observance of precepts, and that it conditioned his life not only in its external circumstances but also erected a barrier between himself and his enlightened colleagues and demanded of him a fundamental appraisal of his position in the two worlds: in Judaism and in his universal philosophic outlook. As a result of the crisis, Mendelssohn returned with greater vigor to the original sources of Judaism, especially to the Bible. From then on he considered it his obligation to attend to the betterment of the status and the condition of the Jews and he felt himself compelled to devote a place in his philosophic system for his belief in the Jewish religion. Among the results of this spiritual struggle was his work *Jerusalem*, which secured Mendelssohn's place in the history of Jewish thought.

The Activities for the Improvement of the Civic Status of the Jews. Mendelssohn was sharply conscious of living in the Exile and being a man without a homeland. However, before the controversy with Lavater, he did not actively campaign for the improvement of the civic status of the Jews, but concentrated on maintaining the best possible relations with the authorities. From the 1770s, Mendelssohn became actively involved in the struggle for the protection and the civil rights of the Jews. He willingly replied to anyone who came to him for counsel or guidance, endeavoring to assist within the limits of his means any Jew who had been overtaken by misfortune or became embroiled with the authorities. He also came to the aid of Jewish communities involved in conflicts with the authorities, taking advantage of his recognized status in order to request help from various renowned personalities whom he had befriended. When new decrees against the Jews of Switzerland were anticipated, he even turned to Lavater (1775); when the community of Dresden was threatened by an expulsion order, he addressed a personal letter to one of the leading officials of Saxony, who ranked among his admirers (1777); the community of Koenigsberg appealed to Mendelssohn (1777) to refute the accusation that the prayers, particularly *Aleinu*, were anti-Christian. In the wake of Mendelssohn's explanations, the royal order requiring the presence of a government-appointed "supervisor" in the synagogue when prayers were recited was also abrogated. On two occasions, Mendelssohn collaborated directly with the Prussian government; upon the request of the chief rabbi of Berlin, Ẓevi Hirsch Levin, Mendelssohn provided the authorities with a German summary of the laws of matrimony connected with rights of possession, which were then transferred from the jurisdiction of the rabbinical tribunals to that of the civil courts (*Die Ritualgesetze der Juden*, 1778). Of even greater importance was the statement on the Jewish oath which Mendelssohn wrote in 1782 in collaboration with the judge E. F. Klein (1743–1810), one of the architects of the reformed Prussian legislation, which was under preparation. The proposed version of the oath was essentially based on the traditional version of the *Judeneid*, but Mendelssohn demanded that the use of Yiddish be replaced by German. However, Mendelssohn was not always in agreement with the rabbis. In 1772 he advised the Jews of Mecklenburg to consent to the demand of the authorities to arrange the burial of the dead after three days because this practice did not violate the law of the Torah and was even to be recommended on medical grounds. As he had anticipated, this opinion was rejected by the rabbis, and a sharp correspondence on this subject developed between himself and Jacob Emden. Of decisive importance were the contributions which Mendelssohn brought to the debate on the question of the civic status of the Jews in the modern state. Cerf Berr, the leader of Alsatian Jewry, requested that Mendelssohn write a memorandum on the question of the rights of the Jews to be submitted to the French Council of State. The objective was to ameliorate the situation of the Jews to refute the accusations of the Jew-baiter F. J. A. Hell. Believing that it was Gentiles—enlightened Christians who sought an improved society—who should raise this question, Mendelssohn turned to Ch. W. von *Dohm, whose *Ueber die buergerliche Verbesserung der Juden* became the classic work in the struggle for emancipation. It is not clear whether Mendelssohn was only the initiator of the work or whether he also collaborated in the writing of it; whatever the case, he was not completely satisfied with it in every aspect. He expressed his views in his introduction to the German translation of the defense writ of Manasseh Ben Israel, *Vindiciae Judaeorum* (1782). In this first public argument on the subject of the civic status of the Jews, Mendelssohn set out with the fundamental optimism of the Enlightenment, expecting that the natural evolution of society would bring with it the solution to the Jewish question, stating that "it is a fortunate coincidence that the betterment of the situation of the Jews is identical with the progress of mankind." In this introduction, Mendelssohn emphasized that the character of the Jews and the categories of their occupations had been imposed on them, thus defending them against Dohm's contention that they should improve themselves. It was, however, not only incumbent upon the Christians to cease their humiliation and persecution of the Jews. The Jews on their part were also required to abandon those attitudes which were opposed to the freedom of man and particularly the freedom of thought. On this point, he opposed Dohm who favored the right of imposing the *ḥerem* and even recommended a limited judicial autonomy for the community. He also rejected autonomous Jewish jurisdiction, calling for "government-appointed judges" to whom one would turn, without any relation to his religious attachment. The views of Mendelssohn and Dohm aroused criticism and controversies. Among the critics were J. D. Michaelis (1717–1791), a theologian and professor of Semitic languages, who in 1754, in his review of Lessing's play *The Jews*, had rejected the possibility that a Jew could exemplify a noble person. Mendelssohn had then clashed with him for the first time, in *Theatralische Bibliothek*, published anonymously in 1755. Michaelis argued in his review of the work of Dohm that because the Jews awaited the arrival of the Messiah and their return to Zion, they would never identify completely with their host country. Their precepts would also prevent them from fulfilling civic obligations, such as military service. Mendelssohn retorted by arguing that messianic hopes of the Jews belonged to the domain of the "Church" and the text of their prayers, but did not in any way influence their civic conduct. He strongly advocated the obligation "to defend the fatherland," arguing that in such cases people know how to adapt their opinions to their civic commitment. The publication of Dohm's work coincided with the publication of the *Toleranzedikt* of Joseph II. At first, Mendelssohn regarded the edict as a harbinger of an improvement of the situation, but he was rapidly sobered and soon feared the hidden intentions of the reforms whose purpose was to lead the Jews to conversion. At the end of his *Jerusalem*, he explicitly addressed himself to those who advocated an amalgamation of religions instead of tolerance. Here he expressed his view that he was not ready to deviate from the Mosaic law in order to gain civic rights. A true union of religions would only be forseen at the "end of days," when the knowledge of God would fill the universe.

Mendelssohn was much more consistent in his philosophical views than in his political ones. He admitted that he did not understand politics and that history did not interest him and that he did not understand it. He was nevertheless on the alert with regard to those political phenomena which directly affected his fundamental views. Thus, for example, he clearly understood the significance of the new rules which were set down in the United States on the subject of the relationship between church and state. Although Mendelssohn generally lacked, as did most of the members of the Enlightenment, a historical perspective, he nevertheless revealed a deep understanding in his reply to the "person of high rank," who in 1770—at the time of the disputation with Lavater—submitted to him a project for the establishment of a Jewish state in Palestine. The author appears to have been a Saxon landlord, Rochus Friedrich zu Lynar, who had formerly served as the Danish diplomat and administrator; his motives may have been religious ones, as were those of Lavater. Mendelssohn rejected his suggestion on the grounds that the Jewish people were no longer capable—after their lengthy servitude—of being moved by the spirit of freedom, or even of joining forces for the execution of such a great act. In addition the execution of this project required tremendous sums and the Jews were not wealthy. Further he assumed that the realization of the project could only take place through a generalized European war, otherwise it would certainly be held up by one of the powers. This pessimistic attitude, which failed to envisage any possible future for the Jewish people as a nation, was shared by many of the Jewish personalities of the Haskalah.

Mendelssohn's Jerusalem. Among the reactions to Mendelssohn's introduction was the pamphlet, published anonymously in 1782, entitled *Das Forschen nach Licht und Recht in einem Schreiben an Herrn Moses Mendelssohn auf Veranlassung seiner merkwuerdigen Vorrede zu Menasseh Ben Israel*. Its author was Josef von Sonnenfels, an apostate who had secured a position for himself among the intellectuals of Vienna. The pamphlet accused Mendelssohn of having undermined the authority of traditional Jewish religion by arguing for the abolition of the *ḥerem*: "Clearly, ecclesiastical law armed with coercive power has always been one of the cornerstones of the Jewish religion of your fathers. How then can you, my dear Mr. Mendelssohn, continue to adhere to the faith of your fathers yet shake the entire structure by removing its very foundation since you deny the ecclesiastical law, given by Moses, which derives its authority from divine revelation?" On this occasion, Mendelssohn felt that it was his duty to provide an answer and explain and justify his stand, which he did in his *Jerusalem: oder, Ueber religioese Macht und Judenthum* (1783). In this book he summarized and completed his thoughts, arguments, and notes of the previous 13 years.

During the course of his disputation with Mendelssohn, Lavater had already mentioned the problem of the former's attitude toward revelation and miracles upon which Christian dogma was based. He endeavored—through Bonnet—to prove to Mendelssohn their theoretic truth. In contrast, Sonnenfels, who did not believe in Christian dogma but accepted Christianity in the abstract attire of rationalist religion, was anxious to point out to Mendelssohn that since he had also ceased to believe in revelation it was incumbent upon him to abandon the traditional Jewish religion, which was no longer adapted to the present era, in order to embrace modern Christianity whose fundamentals were compatible with the religion of reason. This presentation of the problem exposed Mendelssohn to the following questions: if indeed he believed in revelation and the existence of miracles (a) why did he believe in the revelation at Sinai and not in the revelation of Jesus? (b) how can he reconcile belief in the revelation at Sinai with the universal religion of reason according to which every man can attain the truth through the power of his intellect and does not require its special revelation by God? (c) why does he reject religious coercion in Judaism if, in his opinion, the authority of the Torah is derived from God who revealed it to the Jews and compelled them to observe it? In contrast to his procedure at the time of the dispute with Lavater, Mendelssohn detached the problems from their personal context and dealt with them against the background of a general clarification of the roles of the Church and the state, and the relationship between them. He devoted the first chapter of *Jerusalem* to this question and the second chapter to the place of Judaism within this general framework.

State and Church. According to the common understanding of the Enlightenment, the state's task is to provide for the welfare of its citizens by regulating their life on the ground of a contract. The church's task, on the other hand, is to take care of man's soul. The secular society, i.e., the state—Mendelssohn explains—deals with deeds while religion's sphere comprises men's convictions and their relationship to God, whereas, therefore, the first addressing itself to man's will, may use coercion, the second may only speak to man's mind and attempt to convince. Thus, the domain of religious thought and practice must be independent of any power of coercion, whether of the state or of the church. Mendelssohn, however, actually builds his image of the ideal society and his demand for toleration on grounds different from those of the Christian philosophers. Locke, he points out, claims that "the state as a state has no right to take notice of the differences between religions, because religion inherently has no bearing or influence on temporal affairs." But Mendelssohn's is the Jewish conception of the oneness of the world: true welfare in this life is one and the same as eternal bliss hereafter. Both are attained by fulfilling one's obligations in this world "the vestibule to the innermost chamber" as he says quoting *Avot* (4:16). The aim of state and church is one, only the state attains it through deeds, the church through conviction.

JUDAISM. Following the approach of Enlightenment philosophy, he maintains that if the true doctrines of religion are based on reason, divine revelation is no longer needed as a source of truth, for revelation cannot disclose any ideas which cannot be discovered by man's reason. In taking this position, Mendelssohn divorces himself sharply from the views of earlier Jewish philosophers, especially Maimonides, for whom man's knowledge of truth is derived from both reason and revelation. For Maimonides too, the truth is essentially rational; it cannot contradict reason. Nevertheless, it requires the support of revelation in order to reach the masses of the common people who do not know philosophy and are unable to discover the truth by their own efforts. Mendelssohn rejects the notion that truth can be derived from two sources. It is superfluous and therefore illogical to assume that revelation can disclose a truth at which man can arrive by his own capacity to reason. Revelation cannot convince any man of the validity of something his reason cannot understand. Mendelssohn is aware that his rejection of revelation on philosophical grounds clashes with the classic self-image of Judaism which conceives itself as based on the Sinaitic covenant between God and Israel. If Judaism is revealed, it cannot be a religion for Mendelssohn, or if it is a religion it cannot have been revealed. He resolves this dilemma by defining Judaism not as a "revealed religion" but as "revealed law." The central religious tenets of Judaism—the existence and unity of God, divine providence, and the immortality of the soul—are not specific Jewish notions but doctrines of the general religion of reason, which require no proof or act of revelation to be intelligible. What distinguishes the Jew from the non-Jew is not his religion, which is the common property of all men of reason, but the unique laws, statutes and commandments that were disclosed at Sinai. That God spoke at Sinai is for Mendelssohn a *vérité de fait*, an established historical fact, because it was witnessed by the entire people of Israel with incontrovertible clarity. All people are destined to attain felicity, but Jews can attain it only by observing the Sinaitic laws. For him the God of reason and the God of Sinai are one and the same: the benevolent Creator and Sustainer of the world whom reason can affirm, and the King and Guardian of Israel who spoke at Sinai and ordained the laws that govern Jewish life. This "revealed legislation" has an additional function in that it prescribes rules of life that "guide the seeking mind to divine truths—partly eternal, partly historical—on which the religion of this [the Jewish] people was based." In emphasizing that the observance of the *mitzvot* constitutes Jewish particularity and is indispensable to Jewish existence, he adapts a theory previously formulated by the Christian theologian Faustus Socinus (1539–1604), who asserts that God can reveal to man laws but not metaphysical truths. Socinus, therefore, defines religion objectively as the giving of law and subjectively as its observance. For Mendelssohn, several conclusions follow logically from his definition of religion and revelation: (1) No miracle can validate the truth of any faith or doctrine that cannot be established by reason. Miracles can at most support or confirm rational truths, but they cannot establish them. (2) For the same reason Judaism does not possess dogmas. It addresses itself to man's will but does not attempt to control his thoughts. "Faith accepts no commands; it accepts only what comes to it by way of reasoned conviction." Judaism requires conformity in act but grants freedom in matters of doctrine. (3) If, as Mendelssohn firmly believed, a knowledge of truth is indispensable to the achievement of man's happiness, truth has to be accessible to all people without distinction of race or creed. No religion, not even his own Judaism, can be the sole instrument through which God discloses his truth. (4) Freedom of thought and doctrine requires equal respect for all religious ideas. "Let every man who does not disturb the public welfare, who obeys the law, acts righteously toward you and his fellow men be allowed to speak as he thinks, to pray to God after his own fashion or after that of his fathers, and to seek eternal salvation where he thinks he may find it."

Nevertheless Mendelssohn discusses the difference between the Jewish religion, which brings man closer to eternal truths through his daily conduct which is regulated by the Torah, and other ancient religions, which conceal the truth through idolatry. In ancient Judaism, in contrast to idolatry, there was a complete identification between religion and state. Thus a violation of the honour of God was a political crime and was chastised accordingly. This situation was brought to an end as a result of the destruction of the Temple. There is also no further validity in the punishments for those "political crimes," because they could only be applied as long as God was also the sovereign of the Jewish State. It was thus "Jerusalem"—that is, classic Judaism—which for Mendelssohn embodied the true religious might *("religioese Macht")*, united all contrasts, led to the eternal truths, and elevated the Jew toward felicity in this world and in the world to come.

There is no justification for the claim that there is no actual connection between the first and second parts of this world. The clarification of the relationship between church and state was required by Mendelssohn in order to justify the original unity between the universal God and the sovereign of the Jewish people, when in the ancient past, church and state were one. Furthermore, it was only on the basis of the limitation of the right of the state to interfere with the internal world of man that Mendelssohn could argue in favor of the right of the Jews to serve God after their own manner within the framework of the Christian states. The contradiction lay in the fact that the claim for the individual freedom of the religious man was voiced in the name of Judaism which, even in Mendelssohn's own view, was a coercive system. His supposedly historical explanation does not do away with the fundamental contradiction. Neither does his basic explanation remove the practical opposition between two compulsory constitutions: that of the state and that of Judaism. Critics of Mendelssohn's day were already aware of all these problems. It was to a lesser extent that they realized that Mendelssohn drew his view that the world was one and that there existed only one reality from the depths of Jewish thought, and that he was loyal to the conception of the unity of the world of the one God, even though he gave a rationalistic explanation to this.

Attitude to Christianity. Mendelssohn's views on Christianity were not expressed in concentrated form but are scattered throughout his notes, writings, and letters. He believed that Christianity is based on dogmas which are opposed to reason and natural religion, and he objects to its claim that only those who believe in Jesus and his miracles can perceive the truth and are worthy of eternal life. The Christian interpretations of the words of the Jewish prophets which supposedly herald the coming of Jesus are, in his opinion, completely unfounded. "The difference between the Old and the New Testament as I see it is therefore: the first harmonizes with my philosophical convictions or at least does not contradict them, the latter asks for a belief I am not able to provide." He regarded interpretations of the Christian intellectuals Bonnet and Sonnenfels as false and was vigorously opposed to any attempt to convert the Jews.

Activities in the Realm of Jewish Culture. One of the first literary activities of Mendelssohn was his anonymous collaboration with one of the first Jewish periodicals of Germany, the *Kohelet Musar* (its two issues appear to have been published during the middle 1750s), published in immaculate biblical Hebrew. Mendelssohn manifested zeal for Hebrew as for German, because, in his opinion, pure language was the basis of all culture, while he looked upon Yiddish with distaste, regarding it as a jargon, which fosters "immorality of the common man." *Kohelet Musar,* one of the first buddings of the *Haskalah, was later developed, with the participation of Mendelssohn, by *Ha-Me'assef.* Among Mendelssohn's publications in Hebrew was *Millot ha-Higgayon* (1761), an explanation on the logic of Maimonides, giving men the opportunity to deal with a rational subject independent of the discussion about religion. In 1770 he published a commentary on Ecclesiastes. As early as 1770, in a letter to Michaelis, he had mentioned the publication of a translation of Psalms into German (it was not published until 1783), which was to act as a counterbalance to the translations and commentaries written in the spirit of Christianity. The principal work among his biblical translations was, however, the translation of the Pentateuch with the *Biur* (*Be'ur;* 1780–83; see *Bible: Translations, German). The German text was written, in accordance with the custom which prevailed among German Jews, in Hebrew characters, and the commentary, *Biur,* in Hebrew. The *Biur* was essentially based on traditional exegesis, although Mendelssohn introduced a number of modern conceptions and emphasized aesthetic aspects. The translation aroused the anger of such traditional rabbis as Raphael Kohen of Altona and Ezekiel *Landau of Prague, and after the publication of a sample of the translation entitled *Alim li-Terufah* (1778), there were threats of a ban against the reading of it. Three printings of the translation were published during the lifetime of Mendelssohn, but an attempt to publish it in Latin characters was unsuccessful. Mendelssohn's claim in his introduction that he had at first undertaken the transation for his children and that it was only upon the entreaties of Solomon *Dubno, their teacher, who wrote the commentary to the Book of Genesis, that he decided to publish it, contradicts the testimony in a letter to Hennings, which states that it was by this method that he sought to propagate culture among his coreligionists. Mendelssohn was unaffected by the opposition of the rabbis. When Dubno regretted his collaboration in the enterprise, Mendelssohn was assisted by Naphtali Herz Wessely, Naphtali Herz Homberg and Aron Jaroslaw in the writing of the commentary. Mendelssohn's translation of the Song of Songs with commentary was published posthumously (1788). Although Mendelssohn maintained friendly relations with the members of the "philanthropist" movement of school reform, who also founded a school "Philanthropin" in Dessau and invited Jews to participate, he was not directly involved in educational activities, and it appears that he was skeptical as to the utility of a progressive general education as long as the Jews were still "held in political servitude." He nevertheless supported the Juedische Freischule founded by his disciple David *Friedlaender, and also contributed to the *Lesebuch fuer juedische Kinder,* in which he published a translation of Maimonides' 13 Articles of Faith. Apart from the storm which broke out over the translation of the Pentateuch, Mendelssohn maintained particularly good relations with the community of Berlin. In 1763 the community exempted him from the payment of taxes for life and in 1771—after the disputation with Lavater and the proposal of the Academy to elect him as member—he was appointed *parnas.*

Mendelssohn, Lessing, and Spinoza. Mendelssohn's friendship with Lessing became one of the cornerstones of his life. It was Lessing who secured Mendelssohn a place in the circle of intellectuals, and Mendelssohn affirms that he was accustomed to think of Lessing as a reader and a critic when he wrote his philosophical works. As is well known, the protagonist of Lessing's *Nathan the Wise* is regarded as a portrayal of Mendelssohn. While Mendelssohn and Lessing generally agreed on philosophical questions concerning religion and the problem of tolerance, Mendelssohn opposed certain views that Lessing advanced in his last work, *Die Erziehung des Menschengeschlechts,* and argued against them in his *Jerusalem.* In his last work, Lessing affirmed that the spirit of man was dependent on evolution. Reason was, therefore, no longer the primary comprehensive and static factor, which was given to every man in every period in the same measure, as was the opinion of the Enlightenment, but was revealed to man and took form in a gradual process. This invalidated Mendelssohn's conception of a single historic revelation. On this occasion Mendelssohn, however, still refrained from engaging in a fundamental argument with Lessing. He was unable to do so when the question of Lessing's attitude toward Spinoza was raised. While Mendelssohn recognized the importance of Spinoza, he objected to his radical conclusions with regard to religion in general and Judaism in particular. He thus developed a "refined Spinozism" which he professed first in his *Philosophische Gespraeche* (1755) and which he again propounded in his last work *Morgenstunden.* According to Mendelssohn, the world is to be regarded as detached from God, in addition to its immanent existence within God—according to the pantheistic outlook of Spinoza. This enables Mendelssohn to uphold the concept of the creation of the world by God and divine providence which metes out reward and punishment—which Mendelssohn regarded to be the basis of moral conduct. Mendelssohn was compelled to dissociate himself from Spinoza's attitude toward Judaism as expressed in the latter's *Tractatus Theologico-Politicus.* Both Mendelssohn and Spinoza defined the powers of the state and religion in order to assure freedom of religion. However, whereas Spinoza essentially sought to liberate religion from the coercive measures employed by the state, Mendelssohn also called for the avoidance of coercive measures within the domain of religion itself. Mendelssohn also challenged Spinoza's appraisal of the revelation at Sinai. Both shared the opinion that revelation of a religious truth was an impossibility, but Spinoza characterized Judaism as being based on the revelation of a political constitution which created a theocracy and which had lost its practical validity with the destruction of the Temple, while Mendelssohn maintained that it had retained its validity and that the ancient Jewish state was a unique phenomenon that cannot be characterized by such general conceptions. It was because Mendelssohn was very close to Spinoza in his point of departure and his approach that he was compelled to keep his distance and dissociate himself from that which was condemned as his "atheism." At the time of the publication of his *Morgenstunden,* Mendelssohn was personally attacked on religious questions for the third time in his life—on this occasion for his divided attitude to Spinoza. F. H. Jacobi, in his *Lehre des Spinoza in Briefen an den Herrn Moses Mendelssohn,* claimed Lessing had admitted to him during the last years of his life that he had been a Spinozist. This attack struck at the very foundation on which Mendelssohn had established himself: he was publicly confronted with the conflict on the doctrine of Spinoza, while it was said that Lessing, the philosophical mentor, had deserted their common struggle and Lessing, the friend, had deceived him. Mendelssohn attempted to refute all three arguments in his work *An die Freunde Lessings* (1786), and thus extricate himself from the ruinous conclusions of the claim of Jacobi. The tremendous strain and emotion sapped Mendelssohn's strength and a few days after he had given his manuscript in for publication he died, apparently of a heart attack.

Appreciation and Influence. The death of Mendelssohn was greatly mourned by both Jews and gentiles. His first biography was published in Hebrew less than three years after his death by his disciple and companion, Isaac

*Euchel (1788). Mendelssohn became a legend even during his own lifetime, and he was regarded as the embodiment of the humanist ideal. He was a charismatic personality whose influence withstood the changes of the time, even though his philosophical position did not withstand the undermining of its foundation by Kant—a fact which Mendelssohn recognized toward the end of his life. Moreover, he, the great defender of Judaism, actually undermined it because he subjected it to the test of the searching rationalism of the Enlightenment, although he sought to prove that it could withstand this test. The strength of the rationalism upon which he had based himself was, however, incapable of spanning the gulf between traditional Judaism, from which he had emerged, and the world of rationalistic thought, in which he had grown; between his inferior civic status as a Jew and his emancipated status in the circle of intellectuals; between his Jewish pride and his violent criticism of the social and cultural character the Jews of his time; between his loyalty to *halakhah* and the cultural treasury of Judaism, on the one hand, and his despair over the prospect that the Jewish people would not find its place in a gradually changing world, on the other. His life became a testimony of the basic conflict of the emancipation—the conflict between assimilation and the safeguarding of the singularity of Jewish life, between equality of civic and individual right and the minority status, the conflict of the modern Jew in the Diaspora, who seeks integration while at the same time desiring to preserve his Jewish identity. Mendelssohn's personal solution was made possible because of his personal qualities and the specific spiritual climate of the German intellectual society at the outset of his career. When this climate underwent a change towards the end of his life, and as the struggle between rationalism and romanticism gained in impetus, his arguments appeared to be devoid of any real foundation. Those non-Jews who challenged his system were either those who had developed an emotional culture of Christian romanticism, or rationalists such as Kant. Both exploited Mendelssohn's argument that Judaism was a revealed legislation in order to abuse it as a "ceremonial law," a fossil of an ancient era which had become obsolete—a claim which Kant bequeathed to German philosophy. Indeed, Jewish thinkers of the 19th century were also compelled to dissociate themselves from Mendelssohn's views and to seek a new spiritual basis for Judaism. The hidden ambivalence of Mendelssohn's position was matched by the open ambivalence of his non-Jewish admirers in their attitude toward him. This was the case with not only Kant himself but also J. G. Hamann (1730–1788), who wrote a whole book against *Jerusalem*, Herder, Lavater, and even Jacobi. On the other hand, among the Jews in the course of time, the basic conflict of Mendelssohn's position erupted into an open conflict when various and contradictory trends of Judaism all claimed to find support in his image and in his words. It was also Mendelssohn who set the example for the deep identification of German Jewry with the German culture and language and the aversion to Yiddish and the culture of Eastern European Jewry. It was, however, the latter which developed modern thinking through the Haskalah. Even during his own time, Mendelssohn was not the only one among the Jews of Germany to contribute to the Enlightenment, but his personality and his life seem to have embraced all the factors of the transition period of the emancipation, and has become the symbol of that era.

There are two editions of Mendelssohn's collected works: *Gesammelte Schriften* (7 vols., 1843–45) by G. B. Mendelssohn, and *Gesammelte Schriften* (7 vols., uncompleted, 1929–38), by I. Elbogen, E. Mittwoch, and F. Bamberger. In addition, A. Altmann edited Moses Mendelssohn's *Fruehschriften zur Metaphysik* (1969). The following works have been translated into English: by M. Samuels; *Memoirs of Moses Mendelssohn* (1825), *Jerusalem, Treatise on Ecclesiastical Authority and Judaism* (1838), and *Jerusalem and other Jewish Writings* (by A. Jospe, 1969).

Bibliography: H. M. Z. Meyer, *Moses Mendelssohn Bibliographie* (1965); Shunami, Bibl., no. 5. 3953–57; A. Altmann, in: BLBI, (1968), 73–115; Badt-Strauss: *Moses Mendelssohn, der Mensch und das Werk* (1929); I. A. Euchel: *Toledot Rabbenu ha-Ḥakham Moshe Ben Menaḥem* (1788); M. Kayserling, *Moses Mendelssohn, sein Leben und seine Werke* (1888[2]); H. Walter, *Moses Mendelssohn, Critic and Philosopher* (1930); M. A. Meyer, *The Origins of the Modern Jew* (1967), 11–56; Guttmann, Philosophies, 291–303; idem, in: *Bericht der Hochschule fuer die Wissenschaft des Judentums*, 48(1931), 31–67; N. Rotenstreich, *Jewish Philosophy in Modern Times* (1968), 6–29; idem, in: YLBI, 11 (1966), 28–41; B. Berwin, *Moses Mendelssohn im Urteil seiner Zeitgenossen* (1919); F. Bamberger, in: MGWJ, 72 (1929), 81–92; idem, in: K. Wilhelm (ed.), *Wissenschaft des Judentums im deutschen Sprachbereich* (1967), 521–36; *Gedenkbuch fuer Moses Mendelssohn* (1929); ZGJD, 1 (1929); S. Rawidowicz, in: *Sefer Bialik* (1934), 99–140; P. Sendler: *Ha-Be'ur la-Torah shel Moshe Mendelssohn* (1951); E. Cassirer, *The Philosophy of the Enlightment* (1955); I. Eisenstein-Barzilay, in: JQR, 52 (1961), 69–93, 175–86; J. Katz, in: Zion, 29 (1964), 112–32; B. Mevorah, *ibid.*, 30 (1965), 158–70; A. Altmann, *ibid.*, 32 (1968), 47–58. [A.Jo./L.Y.]

MENDES (Mendez), family in England of Marrano origin. FERNANDO MENDES (d. 1724), a Marrano physician, arrived in London in 1669 and practiced there, later becoming court physician (the story that he arrived as physician to Catherine of Braganza, wife of Charles II, is due to a confusion with Antonio Mendes, who attended her on her return to Portugal in 1692 (see JHSET, 16 (1952), 226–7)). His wife was a professing Jew, but his reluctance to declare himself a Jew caused anger and distress among his

Fernando Mendes, Marrano physician, painted by his daughter, Catherine da Costa, 1721. London, Jews' College, Montefiore Library. Courtesy Spanish and Portuguese Jews' Congregation, London.

wealthy relatives. His daughter CATHERINE (Rachel), who married her cousin Anthony (Moses) da Costa, was the first known Anglo-Jewish portrait painter. Fernando's grandson, MOSES MENDES (d. 1758), amassed a fortune as a stockjobber. Baptized and married to a gentile, he acquired a reputation as a successful dramatist and wit. His musical entertainment *The Chaplet* (London 1749, 1753, 1756) was the earliest published contribution of a Jew to English belles lettres, while his farce *The Double Disappointment* was presented at Covent Garden theater in 1760. His sons took their mother's name, Head, and the family passed out of Anglo-Jewish history, though achieving some prominence in English life; Moses' grandson, SIR FRANCIS BOND HEAD (1793–1875), for example, became lieutenant governor of Upper Canada. A kinsman of Moses, SOLOMON MENDES (d. 1762), was a patron and associate of writers.

Bibliography: L. Wolf, in: JHSET, 5 (1902–05), 5–33; A. Rubens, *ibid.*, 14 (1935–39), 95–97; A. M. Hyamson, *Sephardim of England* (1951), index; J. Picciotto, *Sketches of Anglo-Jewish History* (1956²), index; Roth, England, index; Roth, Mag Bibl., 137, 409ff.; idem, *Anglo-Jewish Letters (1158–1917)* (1938), 99–114, 121–6, 133–40, 144–7; *Gentleman's Magazine* (Jan., 1812), 21–24.

[V.D.L.]

MENDES (Mendiz), family of rabbis and merchants in Morocco and Algeria of Spanish-Portuguese origin. JOSEPH MENDES (mid-16th century) was rabbi of the community of Spanish exiles (Heb., *megorashim*) in Fez and a signatory of its *takkanot*. GIDEON (late 17–early 18th century), a merchant of Amsterdam, served as consul of the Netherlands in Salé from 1703 and was active in promoting commerce and negotiating treaties with Morocco. His son JOSHUA was a merchant in Salé and in Amsterdam. A contemporary R. ISAAC was a rabbi and an international merchant in Agadir and spent time in London trading with European countries. His son JACOB remained in Agadir and one of his daughters married the rabbi and thinker Khalifa b. *Malca.

Bibliography: Hirschberg, Afrikah, 2 (1965), 268–72; J. Ben-Naim, *Malkhei Rabbanan* (1931), 107; SIHM, index. [ED.]

MENDES, U.S. Sephardi family of rabbis. FREDERIC DE SOLA MENDES (1850–1927) was born in Montego Bay, Jamaica, where his father, ABRAHAM PEREIRA MENDES (1825–1893), was at that time rabbi. Frederic became preacher at the New Synagogue, London, in 1873 but in the same year was appointed to Congregation Shaarey Tefillah, New York. He served there for 47 years, as assistant to S. M. *Isaacs (to 1877) and then as rabbi (to 1920). Mendes led his congregation within the orbit of Reform and became a member of the Central Conference of American Rabbis. He was one of the founders of the *American Hebrew* (1879) and served as a member of the original editorial board of the Jewish Publication Society's English translation of the Bible. For a period he was an editor of the *Jewish Encyclopedia.* Frederic's brother HENRY PEREIRA MENDES (1852–1937) was born in Birmingham, England. In his early youth he was educated at Northwick College, a boarding school founded by his father in London which offered a combination of religious and secular education. Henry studied at University College, London, and took the medical degree at the University of the City of New York. Henry served as rabbi to the new Sephardi congregation of Manchester from 1874 to 1877 and then emigrated to New York to take up his post as *ḥazzan* and rabbi at Shearith Israel congregation, serving there until 1923. Championing an enlightened modern Orthodoxy, Mendes used his privileged position as rabbi at Shearith Israel to work closely with all sectarian and social elements in Jewish life. In facing the problems affecting Jewry, he followed his belief in *kelal Yisrael* ("the totality of Israel"). He was one of the founders and leaders of the Union of Orthodox

Henry Pereira Mendes (1852–1937), U.S. Orthodox leader and Zionist. Courtesy American Jewish Archives, Cincinnati, Ohio.

Congregations of America, the Jewish Theological Seminary, the New York Board of Jewish Ministers, and—at the personal request of Theodor Herzl—the Federation of American Zionists. He was a prolific writer on Jewish and general themes for the *American Hebrew,* which he and his brother helped establish, and wrote scores of books and pamphlets. Some of his better-known books are *Looking Ahead* (1899), *Bar Mitzvah* (1938), *Esther and Harbonah* (1917), *Jewish Religion Ethically Presented* (1905), *Jewish History Ethically Presented* (1898), *Mekor Ḥayyim: Mourners Handbook* (1915), and *Derekh Ḥayyim: Way of life* (1934).

Bibliography: D. de S. Pool, *H. Pereira Mendes . . .* (1938); E. Markovitz, *Henry Pereira Mendes* (Eng., 1962), incl. bibl.; idem, in: AJHSQ, 55 (1965/66), 364–84. [S.D.T./E.MA.]

MENDÈS, CATULLE (1841–1909), French poet. Mendès was born in Bordeaux. His father was a banker of Sephardi origin and his mother a Catholic. At the age of 18 he went to Paris,

Grave of Catulle Mendes, French poet, at Montparnasse Cemetery, Paris. Photo M. Ninio, Jerusalem.

where in 1861 he founded *La Revue fantaisiste*—the first of several journals issued by the French Parnassian poets. It stressed their anti-utilitarianism and their devotion to art. He also contributed to the serialized anthology *Le Parnasse contemporain* (1866–76), which he later described in *La Légende du Parnasse contemporain* (1884). A versatile, "decadent" poet, Mendès had a prolific output—some 150 volumes over four decades. They include verse collections—*Poésies* (3 vols., 1892), *Poésies nouvelles* (1893), and *Choix de poésies* (1925); neo-Romantic plays such as *La Femme de Tabarin* (1887), *Médée* (1898), and *La Reine Fiammette* (1899); and several novels, notably *Monstres parisiens* (1882), *Les Folies amoureuses* (1877), and *Zohar* (1886). Mendès also wrote short stories; a study of Richard *Wagner, of whose music he was the French champion; and, in collaboration with the lyric poet Ephraïm *Mikhaël, the dramatic poem *Briséis* (1899). The *Rapport sur le mouvement poétique français 1867–1900* (1902) reveals considerable critical insight. Mendès, who married the daughter of the poet Théophile Gautier (1811–1872), was killed in a railroad accident.

Bibliography: A. Bertrand, *Catulle Mendès, biographie critique* (1908); A. Schaffer, *Parnassus in France* (1929), 46–71; M. Souriau *Histoire du Parnasse* (1929); J. F. Herlihy, *Catulle Mendès, critique dramatique et musical* (1936).

[S.D.B.]

MENDES, DIOGO (b. before 1492–d. c. 1542), Marrano merchant, born in Spain, and descended from the *Benveniste family. With his brother Francisco (d. 1536), he established a business in spices and precious stones. He settled in *Antwerp, and on his brother's death was joined there by the latter's widow, later Gracia *Nasi. Mendes became a magnate in the spice trade and made large-scale loans to the governments of the Low Countries, Portugal, and England. Taking advantage of a network of factors and agents throughout Europe, he organized an "underground railway" to facilitate the flight of Marranos from Portugal, via the Low Countries (and sometimes England) to Italy and Turkey. In 1535, he and his sister-in-law, Gracia Nasi, headed the group of *New Christians who sought the help of the papal nuncio to stop the activity of the *Inquisition in Portugal. Arrested in 1532 on a charge of Judaizing, Mendes managed to exculpate himself, but after his death in Antwerp, the same charge led to the sequestration of his property.

Bibliography: L. Wolf, *Essays in Jewish History* (1934), 75–81; J. Vroman, *L'Affaire Diego Mendez* (1937); C. Roth, *House of Nasi: Doña Gracia* (1947); J. A. Goris, *Les Colonies marchandes méridionales à Anvers* (1925); P. Grunebaum-Ballin, *Joseph Naci, duc de Naxos* (1968).

[C.R.]

MENDÈS-FRANCE, PIERRE (1907–), French statesman. Born and educated in Paris, his university thesis *Le Redressement Financier Francais en 1926 et 1927* (1928) attracted considerable attention and his later study, *L'Oeuvre financière du gouvernement Poincaré* (1928) was used as propaganda by the left-wing parties and made Mendès-France one of the leading financial experts of the Radical party.

At the age of 16 Mendès-France joined the Radical Socialist Party and in 1932 was elected to the National Assembly, being its youngest member. In the same year he outlined an economic program for the party which was accepted at its conference at Toulouse. He supported the Popular Front government of 1936–38 and in 1938 was an undersecretary to the treasury. An advocate of resistance to the Nazis even before World War II, Mendès-France organized an opposition to the Vichy government after the fall of France and was imprisoned by the Pétain government. He escaped to England in 1941 and joined the Free Fench under General De Gaulle who later made him finance commissioner of Algeria. From 1944 to

Pierre Mendès-France, French statesman. Courtesy French Embassy Press and Information Division, New York.

1945 he was minister of economic affairs and in 1946 he was appointed French governor of the Bank for Reconstruction and Development. In the same year he returned to parliament and in 1954, after a series of cabinet crises, became prime minister with a huge majority of 419 out of 617 deputies.

As premier, Mendès-France offered France a "new deal," promising to end the Indochina war, tackle the problems of European defense, and enact wide-reaching economic reforms. His prestige rose considerably when he ended the war and introduced the plan for a Western European Defense Community with a British military commitment for the defense of Europe. In February 1955 he was defeated over his North Africa policy to grant independence to Morocco and Tunisia and resigned. From January to May 1956 Mendès-France was minister without portfolio but resigned following disagreement with the prime minister, Guy Mollet, on the Algerian policy. He remained an important figure in French politics and frequently opposed De Gaulle's policies. In 1968, he formed a new party, the Parti Socialiste Unifié, which he headed. Mendès-France was a consistent supporter of Zionism and outspoken in his championship of the cause of Israel. He was an ascetic in his private life and once aroused controversy when he urged Frenchmen to abandon their wine drinking for milk, his favorite beverage. He wrote extensively on politics and finance. His books are widely read and some have been translated into other languages. They include: *La Banque Internationale* (1930); *Liberté, Liberté Chérie* (1943; *The Pursuit of Freedom*, 1956); *Gouverner c'est choisir* (3 vols., 1953–58); and *La République moderne* (1962; *A Modern French Republic*, 1963).

[M.R.]

MENDLOWITZ, SHRAGA FEIVEL (1886–1948), U.S. educator and Orthodox Jewish leader. Mendlowitz was born in Vilag, Austria-Hungary, and studied under R. Samuel Rosenberg of Hunsdorf and R. Simḥah Bunim Schreiber of Pressburg. He went to the United States in 1913, and for seven years was teacher-principal in the *talmud torah* of Scranton, Pennsylvania. In 1921 he became principal of Yeshiva Torah Vadaath in the Williamsburg section of Brooklyn. Under his guidance the new school developed into a leading American yeshivah and as a result Williamsburg became a center of Orthodoxy. Mendlowitz, who was close to his pupils, inspired them with a feeling of total dedication to Orthodoxy. He later organized a high school for secular studies under the auspices of the yeshivah, the second such school in the United States. In 1941, he set up a school in Spring Valley, New York, which was later to serve as a *kolel* for the graduates of Yeshiva

Torah Vadaath. He was instrumental in founding *Torah Umesorah, a national society for Hebrew day schools, in 1944.

Bibliography: A. Gross and J. Kaminetsky, in: L. Jung (ed.), *Men of the Spirit* (1964), 553–72. [ED.]

MENDOZA, province in Argentina and capital city of the province.

The Province. Population 825,535 in 1960; Jewish population numbered two in 1895, 2,439 in 1947, and 2,767 (above the age of five, or about 3,000 altogether) in 1960 according to the census, an imprecise accounting because some Jews refused to delare their religion. Jews had settled in the province as agriculturists and plantation owners by the end of the 1880s. In 1904–05 Jews from Yekaterinoslav attempted to settle in Palmira, but after a short time found they could not meet the difficult terms of their settlement contract and were compelled to leave. A similar attempt to settle there in 1913 likewise failed. In 1943 there were Jews in 24 out of the 123 towns and villages in the province. In 1964 only San Martín, San Rafael, and the capital city of the province, Mendoza, had organized Jewish communities affiliated with the Va'ad ha-Kehillot (see *Argentina). The province is well known for its grapevines and since 1952 there has been industrial production of strictly kosher wine.

The City. Population about 100,000 in 1960; Jewish population in 1966 approximately 1,100 families. In 1909 there were some 600 Jews in the city—approximately 500 from Eastern Europe and the remainder from France and Sephardi countries. The first community organization, Sociedad Israelita de Beneficencia, was established in 1910, and continues to function. Its membership in 1968 was 577 families. The Sociedad, which comprises the Ashkenazim of Mendoza, owns a large community building, a synagogue, and a cemetery, and plays an important role in the operation of all Jewish institutions in the city. The Sephardi community established in 1918 the Sociedad Israelita de Socorros Mutuos. In 1943 it comprised about 60 families and has come to maintain its own synagogue and cemetery. The Sephardi and Ashkenazi organizations, however, cooperate in running the school, the Macabí Social Club, and the country club (purchased in 1954).

Various welfare institutions were established in the city but they became superfluous and no longer exist. The financial institution Asociación Israelita de Crédito Mutual has become the Jewish bank Crédito de Cuyo with branches in other provinces. The bank and the Ashkenazi community cooperated in financing the erection of the beautiful Max Nordau Jewish School, which in 1968 had an enrollment of 277 students (75 in kindergarten, 168 in elementary school, and 34 in high school). Local committees of the Jewish National Fund and of the United Jewish Appeal are active in Mendoza as well as the local committee of *DAIA, the umbrella organization of Argentinian Jewry. The Progressives, a pro-Communist group whose number in 1966 was estimated at 80 families, maintain their own committee and a school named after I. L. Peretz. The majority of Jews in Mendoza are engaged in business and some own vineyards and fruit plantations. Jewish participation in the liberal professions and in the local university has been increasing. [D.B.R.N.]

Building of the Sephardi community in Mendoza, Argentina. Photo D. B. Rubenstein Novick.

MENDOZA, DANIEL (1764–1836), English boxing champion. Born in Aldgate, London, Mendoza learned at a young age to defend himself with his fists. In 1780 he won his first professional fight. A natural middleweight, Mendoza became the father of scientific boxing by devising defensive moves that enabled him to fight against much heavier opponents. His ring success brought him to the attention of the Prince of Wales and he became the first boxer to receive royal patronage. Mendoza's ascendancy to boxing heights, and his acceptance by royalty, helped ease the position of the Jew in the English community. He proudly billed himself as "Mendoza the Jew." He opened his own boxing academy and became a teacher. He went on tour and gave boxing exhibitions in England, Wales, Scotland, and Ireland. Mendoza lost the title to John Jackson on a ninth-round knockout on April 15, 1795. He wrote *The Art of Boxing* (London, 1789) and *The Memoirs of the Life of Daniel Mendoza* (London, 1816). In 1954 Mendoza was one of the inaugural group chosen for the Boxing Hall of Fame in the United States.

The great fight between Daniel Mendoza and Richard Humphries at Odiham, Hampshire, Jan. 9, 1788. The accompanying account reveals that Mendoza (right), despite his extraordinary skill, was eventually forced by his opponent's superior strength and weight to give up the contest. London, Alfred Rubens Collection.

Bibliography: H. D. Miles, *Pugilistica*, 1 (1880); H. U. Ribalow, *Fighter from Whitechapel* (1962). [J.H.S.]

MENE, MENE, TEKEL, U-FARSIN, enigmatic inscription referred to in *Daniel 5:25, which appeared on a wall, written by a detached hand. The narrative in Daniel 5:1ff. relates that King *Belshazzar of Babylonia made a feast for 1,000 of his lords, wives, and concubines. During the feast, wine was drunk from the vessels which had been taken out of the Temple in Jerusalem, and the guests at the feast praised (or perhaps sang to—the Aramaic *shabbaḥ le-* can mean either) the gods of gold and silver, bronze, iron, wood, and stone. Suddenly, the fingers of a man's hand appeared and were seen writing something on the wall of the king's palace. The king became alarmed and summoned all his wise men, but they were unable to read or interpret the writing. The queen then suggested that Daniel, a sage whom Nebuchadnezzar used to consult and found matchless, be brought before the king. Daniel was summoned to Belshazzar. After rebuking the king for his arrogance toward the Lord, for drinking wine from the holy Temple's vessels, and for worshiping man-made gods, Daniel read and interpreted the writing as follows: *mene, mene, tekel (teqel)*, and *parsin*. *Mene:* God has numbered *(menah)* the days of your kingdom and will bring it to an end; *tekel:* you have been weighed *(teqilta)* in the balance and found wanting; *parsin:* your kingdom has been divided *(prisat)* and given over to the Medes and Persians *(Paras)*.

The narrative presents four basic problems. The first question concerns the actual designation of the words *mene, mene, tekel*, and *parsin*. C. Clermont-Ganneau was the first to suggest that the words refer to weights of monetary units. Thus, *mene* (Aramaic *mene;* Heb. *maneh*) is a mina; *tekel* (Aram. *teqel;* Heb. *shekel*) is the shekel; and *u-farsin* (of which the *u* is simply the copulative) is two half-minas. The word **פרש** has been found on half-mina weights in bilingual Aramaic-Akkadian inscriptions and also occurs in the Talmud (Aramaic *peras*) in the sense of a half-mina. Most scholars have accepted Clermont-Ganneau's explanation of the words and at most add that the first *mene*, unlike the second (5:15), is the Aramaic passive participle (equivalent to the Heb. *manui*, "counted") and is to be read as, "it was counted: *mene, tekel* and *parsin*."

The second question to be asked is why the characters of the inscription baffled the Chaldeans, who should have been able to read easily a few simple Aramaic words. The narrative clearly indicates that the wise men could not decipher the writing, as the king promised a great reward for the man who read the writing (5:7). Daniel solved the riddle by first reading the script; only afterward did he explain it (5:25ff.). Talmudic sages suggest that the letters of the inscription were written in reverse order or in accordance with the *Atbash* (see **Gematria*) sequence (Sanh. 22a). A. Alt proposes that only the initials and not the whole words were written, and he bases his view on the premise that it can be corroborated from archaeological evidence that names of weights were often designated by initials only; Aramaic contracts from the fifth century B.C.E. attest to this practice. Alt, therefore, assumes that what was written were the initials *M. M. T. P. P.* (ממתפ״פ). H. L. Ginsberg points out that in the Aramaic contracts the word *tekel* is generally written *shkl* and abbreviated as *sh*, and it is possible that even after the more modern spelling *tkl* was adopted, the abbreviation *sh* was retained. Therefore the legend on the wall may have been not *M. M. T. P. P.* but *M. M. Sh. P. P.*, which made it harder for the king's regular sages to recognize it as a series of abbreviations. Daniel, however, realized that the letter *shin* was the initial of the obsolete spelling *shkl*, for *tekel*, and so he read for the two *mem's*—*mene mene*, for the *shin*—*tekel*, and for the two *pe's*—*parsin*.

A third problem is the variance between the written version on the wall (5:25): *mene, mene, tekel*, and *parsin* and the words in Daniel's version: *mene, mene, tekel* and *peras* (5:26ff.). Most ancient versions (Vulg., Theod., and

Rembrandt's "Belshazzar's Feast," containing the words *"mene, mene, tekel, u-farsin,"* 1634. London, National Gallery.

Jos., Ant., 10:239ff.) give the written version (verse 25) also as *mene, tekel, peras*. Since, however, Daniel interprets the last expression as meaning both *perisat* and *paras*, the Masoretic Text's version of verse 25 can be upheld, and the reading in verses 26 and 28 could be the result of haplography. The doubling of the word *mene* at the beginning, Ginsberg believes, was suggested by the doubling of *nafelah*, "fallen," in Isaiah 21:9, "Fallen, fallen is Babylon."

The fourth and last problem is concerned with what the words actually refer to. These words were probably used not only to indicate monetary values but also to express estimates of character. Thus, these words presumably referred to a situation of degeneration. God has weighed the kings of Babylon and has found them to be steadily decreasing in weight. P. Haupt and J. D. Prince hold that the phrase refers to Nebuchadnezzar *(mene)*, Belshazzar *(tekel)*, the Medes (*peres*, a half-*mene*, i.e., half the greatness of Nebuchadnezzar) and the Persians (*peres*, a half-*mene*, i.e.; half the greatness of Nebuchadnezzar). E. G. Kraeling believes that the phrase was applied to the occupants of the neo-Babylonian throne after Nebuchadnezzar: Awêl-Marduk (Evil-Merodach), Labâshi-Marduk, Nabonidus, and Belshazzar.

Bibliography: C. Clermont-Ganneau, in: JA, 8 (1886), 36ff.; idem, *Recueil d'archéologie orientale*, 1 (1888), 136–59; J. D. Prince, *Mene Mene Tekel Upharsin* (1893); A. Kamphausen, *Daniel* (Ger., 1896), 28; H. Bauer, *Vierter deutscher Muenzforschertag zu Halle, Festgabe den Teilnehmern gewidmet* (1925), 27–30; J. A. Montgomery, *Daniel* (ICC, 1927), 262ff.; E. G. Kraeling, in: JBL, 63 (1944), 11–18; O. Eissfeldt, in: ZAW, 63 (1951), 105; A. Alt, in: VT, 4 (1954), 303–5; H. L. Ginsberg, in: EM, 5 (1968), 10–13.

[D.Bo./M.Ze.]

MENELAUS (d. c. 162 B.C.E.), high priest in the time of Antiochus Epiphanes. Menelaus was the brother of Simeon and Lysimachus, both mentioned in II Maccabees. According to II Maccabees 3:4, Simeon and Menelaus belonged to the tribe of Benjamin, and Simeon did not therefore belong to a priestly family. This raises a difficulty and attempts have been made to amend the text, or to suggest that he belonged to a priestly family named Benjamin or Miamin (cf. I Chron. 4:24). It seems preferable to accept the reading found in some Latin manuscripts which reads "Bilgah" instead of Benjamin. Bilgah was the name of one of the priestly divisions (I Chron. 24:14) and probably Menelaus and his brothers belonged to it. The statement of Josephus (Ant., 12:238–9) that Menelaus was a brother of *Jason and a son of *Onias III, is certainly erroneous. Menelaus was one of the leaders of the Hellenists and one of the extremists among them. When sent by the high priest Jason to Antiochus Epiphanes, he intrigued against his principal, bribed Antiochus and received from him appointment as high priest (II Macc. 4:23–24). At the beginning of his tenure of office he plundered the Temple of its gold vessels (*ibid.*, 4:32). He also instigated the murder of Onias III (*ibid.*, 4:34). His appointment and policy aroused the opposition of the people and caused uprisings and disturbances. Jason attempted to seize the high priesthood back from him, but Menelaus succeeded in retaining power, chiefly with the assistance of the Syrians. He remained loyal to Antiochus and sent him large amounts of money. As leader of the Hellenists he must be considered responsible to a great extent for the persecution of Antiochus (see Bickermann in bibl.; cf. II Macc. 13:4). It seems, however, that later, when it became clear that this policy brought no advantage to the Hellenists, he was partly responsible for the more conciliatory policy of Antiochus Epiphanes (164 B.C.E.; II Macc. 11:29). Later he lost favor in the court of the Seleucids and on the advice of Lysias was put to death (apparently in 162 B.C.E.).

Bibliography: F. M. Abel, in: *Miscellanea Giovanni Mercati*, 1 (1946), 52–58; Rowley, in: *Studia Orientalia Ioanni Pedersen... Dicata* (Eng. 1953), 303–15; V. Tcherikover, *Hellenistic Civilization and the Jews* (1959), 70–74, 216–20, and index; E. Bickermann, *From Ezra to the Last of the Maccabees* (1962), 106f. See also *Antiochus.

[U.R.]

MENES, ABRAM (1897–1969), historian. Born in Grodno, Poland, Menes became engrossed in the problems of socialism early in his youth; at the age of 20 he founded an illegal *Bund branch in Grodno, which engaged in educational work and the distribution of illegal socialist literature. After World War I he devoted himself to public affairs, becoming the vice-chairman of the Grodno Jewish community. After moving to Berlin in 1920, where he studied Jewish history and Bible, Menes, together with Nahum *Shtif and E. *Tcherikower, laid the foundations of

Abram Menes, Yiddish writer and historian. Courtesy YIVO, New York.

*YIVO (the Institute of Jewish Research). In 1933 he moved to Paris, and became one of the leading contributors to the *Yiddish Encyclopedia*, writing on a wide range of historical subjects. He continued his work on the editorial board of the encyclopedia even after settling in the U.S. (1940), where he also joined the staff of the Yiddish daily, *Forward*.

Menes' main area of interest in Jewish history was its economic and social aspects. Articles on these subjects, covering the talmudic period as well as late 19th-century Russian Jewry, appeared in YIVO's historical publications. Together with Raphael *Abramowitz, Menes wrote *Leyenbukh tsu der Geshikhte fun Yisroel* ("A Layman's History of Israel," 1923). Another favorite topic of his was the history of the Jewish Workers Movement and of socialism: *Der Onhoyb fun der Yidisher Arbeter-Bavegung un ir Shoyresh in Yidishen Folks Lebn*, published in the *Zukunft* (40 (1935), 539–44), is an investigation into the problems of socialism, in general, and in particular among the Jews. His essays on significant events in Jewish history, in both the preexilic and postexilic periods, were published in *Oyfn Sheydveg*, an independent publication of Jewish culture, art and literature, and cultural philosophy, edited by E. Tcherikover and I. Efroikin. These essays mark a turning point in Menes' approach to Jewish history: "The time has come to amend Heine's youthful error and to replace 'le credit' with 'la religion'—the belief in man with the belief in God." Mention should also be made of his contribution, "Jewish History," to the volume "Jews" in the *Yiddish Encyclopedia*, in which he wrote on the biblical and talmudic periods. His articles in the *Forward* dealt to a large extent with Jewish holidays. His writings on the problems of methodology in Jewish history are of significance to scholars in the field.

Menes' writings on Jewish ethics, sociology, and philosophy continued to be based on the principle that "there can be no faith in man without a feeling of sanctity."

Jacob Glatstein described Menes as a historian "who has introduced a new evaluation of Jewish history."

Bibliography: LNYL, 6 (1965) 72–78. [I.H.B.]

°**MENGELE, JOSEF** (1911–), doctor of the Auschwitz extermination camp. Born in Guenzburg, Germany, he studied medicine and philosophy. (He was deprived of both these academic degrees in 1961 and 1964, respectively.) Declared medically unfit to serve at the front in World War II, he was, at his own request, appointed doctor of the Auschwitz camp where, from 1943 to 1945, he initiated a series of cruel, "medical" experiments, which caused the death of many Jewish inmates. He "investigated," from a genetic aspect, the phenomenon of twins and of dwarfs. He participated in the selection of tens of thousands of prisoners in the Birkenau camp (see *Auschwitz), destined to die in the gas chambers. The figure of Mengele decreeing life or death by a flick of his finger has become one of the symbols of the Holocaust; he was called by the camp inmates "the Auschwitz monster." Up to 1951 Mengele lived under his own name in various places in Bavaria, Germany. The search for him started only in 1953, after he escaped from Germany. It is known that in 1954 he was granted Argentinian citizenship. In Argentina he represented the Karl Mengele and Sons factory for agricultural machinery, a firm managed by his brother in Guenzburg. Mengele was traced by organizations of former Nazi victims, both Jewish and non-Jewish. His extradition was demanded by the government of West Germany, but Mengele escaped from Argentina. His disappearance was also, apparently, connected with the apprehension of *Eichmann. Various conflicting news items subsequently appeared in the world press concerning the whereabouts of Mengele. Mengele's name was often mentioned by witnesses at the Eichmann trial in Jerusalem and at numerous trials in West Germany, in particular at the *Auschwitz trials held in Frankfort on the Main in 1963–65. He figures in Rolf Hochhut's play *The Deputy* (1963).

Bibliography: M. Nyiszli, *Auschwitz: a Doctor's Eyewitness Account* (1960); O. Kraus and E. Kulka, *Death Factory* (1966). [E.Br.]

MENKEN, U.S. family. SOLOMON MENKEN (1787–1853), who was born in Westphalia, Prussia, arrived in the U.S. from Holland in 1820 and soon established a wholesale drygoods business in Cincinnati, where he was one of the first Jewish settlers. His eldest son, JULES MENKEN (1836–1890), was a lieutenant in the Cincinnati Home Guards during the Civil War. NATHAN DAVIS MENKEN (1837–1878), his second son, was a merchant and soldier. During the Civil War, he held the rank of cavalry captain and was cited for bravery. He later joined his younger brother's Memphis business. He died assisting victims of yellow fever during an 1878 epidemic. JACOB STANWOOD MENKEN (1838–c.1900), Solomon's third son, was born in Cincinnati. A merchant and philanthropist, he founded the large Menken and Co. department store in Memphis in 1863, and was active in organizing the Children's Christmas Club and the first Southern kindergarten for Negroes. S. STANWOOD MENKEN (1870–1954), Nathan's son and great-great-grandson of Haym *Solomon, was born in Memphis, Tenn. A lawyer and publicist, he was educated at Cornell and Columbia Law School and admitted to the New York bar in 1894. Active in New York City politics, he organized the Hall of Records Association in 1896, the Democratic League (1908), and the National Security League of America (1915). [Ed.]

MENKEN (née **Theodore**), **ADAH ISAACS** (1835–1868), U.S. actress, known mainly for her flamboyant way of life. The first of her four husbands was a musician, Alexander Isaac Menken, whose name she kept after he divorced her. Her stage career began in 1856 in New Orleans. Probably not a great actress, she had an arresting stage personality, and displayed her dark, slim beauty with a boldness that created a sensation wherever she appeared. The first American actress to wear flesh-colored tights, she made her most spectacular appearance in the play *Mazeppa* (adapted from Byron's poem) in which she rode up a steep ramp strapped to a fiery horse. She mixed in the circle of American literary bohemians that included Walt Whitman, Bret Harte, and Mark Twain. In London in 1864 her *Mazeppa* angered the press, but she won the literati with her poems. Dickens, Charles Reade, and Rossetti were her friends. Swinburne described her as the world's delight and claimed she was his mistress. She enjoyed triumph in Paris in 1866; won over Gautier and George Sand; and became the mistress of the elder Dumas. Though she invented fanciful accounts of her origin, which was obscure, she took a militant pride in her Jewishness. In 1857 she led a protest against the exclusion of Jews from the House of Commons. She never performed on the Day of Atonement and kept a Hebrew Bible under her pillow. Her two books of poems, *Memoirs* (1856) and *Infelicia* (1868), teem with biblical allusions. She died in Paris, and Baron Lionel de *Rothschild erected a memorial on her grave in Montparnasse.

Bibliography: A. Lesser, *Enchanting Rebel* (1947); B. Falk, *Naked Lady* (1934); P. Lewis, *Queen of the Plaza* (1964). [Ed.]

MENKES, ZYGMUNT (1896–), U.S. painter. Menkes was born in Lvov, Galicia. He grew up in a religious atmosphere and worked as a house painter until he was able to enter the Cracow Academy of Fine Arts. After a short time in Berlin, he went in 1923 to Paris. In 1936 he settled in New York. Menkes' pictures, cheerful still lifes, introspective portraits, and vivid landscapes have a decidedly French accent. He resisted the trend toward abstract art and never veered from recognizable subject matter. Primarily a

"The Flute Player" by Zygmunt Menkes. Photo J. J. Breit, New York.

colorist, his work showed an increasing tendency toward flatness and two-dimensionality. Menkes frequently used Jewish themes in his earlier work. One of his best-known canvasses is "The Torah" (1927), in which a group of East European Jews are shown lifting up a partly unrolled Torah scroll. [A.W.]

MENORAH (Heb. מְנוֹרָה; "candelabrum"), the name given to the seven-branched candelabrum which, according to the Bible, was a prominent feature of the *Tabernacle erected by the people of Israel in the wilderness, as well as in the Jerusalem Temple. In archaeological finds in Ereẓ Israel and Syria dating from the Middle Bronze Period onward, lamps have been uncovered in the form of a deep bowl, with seven spouts on its rim for inserting wicks. At the high place *(bamah)* discovered at Nahariyyah, several bowls, similar to those of the Middle Bronze Period, have been found. Some lamp bowls have a clay, stone, or metal stand, thereby transforming them into *menorot*. At Taanach such a *menorah* has been unearthed, consisting of a small bowl with seven spouts, set on a stand whose circumference, narrowing in the middle to form a grip, broadens out at the bottom into a base for placing it on the ground.

The Tabernacle. Among the vessels of the Tabernacle mentioned in the Priestly Code, reference is made to a *menorah* of gold, whose form is given in two parallel passages (Ex. 25:31–40; 37:17–24). A pattern of this *menorah* was, it is related, shown by God to Moses at Mount Sinai (Ex. 25:40), as He also showed him the pattern of the Tabernacle and all its furniture (Ex. 25:9). Six branches, three on each side, curved upward from the *menorah's* central shaft, which stood on a base (Ex. 25:31; Num. 8:4) whose precise shape cannot be determined. The shaft and each of the branches were ornamented respectively with four and three carvings of cups made like almond-blossoms, each subdivided into a knop and a flower. Under every two branches that were of one piece a knop was carved on the central shaft, making a total of three knops "for the six branches going out of the *menorah*" (Ex. 25:35). These three knops were probably an integral part of the cups on the central shaft and not, as some (A. R. S. Kennedy, S. R. Driver, and others) hold, in addition to its four cups. The fourth cup was at the top of the central shaft, above the places where the branches joined it. The uppermost cups of the branches were similarly at their top, with all of them—as well as that of the central shaft—ending at the same height. The flowers on these uppermost cups served as receptacles for the seven lamps.

The entire *menorah* was carved from one ingot of gold, "beaten work" (Ex. 25:31), and its vessels, also of gold and including the lamps, were carved separately (Ex. 25:37–38). The *menorah* was placed in front of the veil *(parokhet)* "on the side of the Tabernacle toward the south . . . over against the table" (Ex. 26:35; 40:24). When the lamps burnt they gave "light over against it" (Ex. 25:37) "in front of the *menorah*" (Num. 8:2–3), that is, the spouts of the lamps and the wicks faced northward, so that their shadow was cast on to the wall. The measurements of the *menorah* are not given in the Bible but the Talmud stated that its height was 18 handbreadths, which are three short cubits (Men. 28b; Rashi to Ex. 25:35). The use to which the Tabernacle *menorah* was put is described in the Priestly Code. The lamps *(nerot)* are said to have burned from evening to morning (Lev. 24:3), were lit at dusk and trimmed in the morning by the high priest (Ex. 30:7–8), and hence are called *ner tamid* (a perpetual lamp; Ex. 27:20; Lev. 24:2), that is, they were lit according to a fixed routine and for the nighttime only. This is specifically mentioned in connection

Figure 1. Panel on the Arch of Titus showing the carrying of the *menorah*, with a double octagon base, as part of the spoils in the triumphal procession following the subjugation of Judea in 70 C.E. Courtesy Government Press Office, Tel Aviv.

Seven-branched *menorah* being lit by Aaron, who stands on a high pedestal. A full-page miniature at the end of a Pentateuch. The *menorah* has knops, flowers, bowls and lamps in its branches (Ex. 25:31–40). Two biblical scenes are depicted beneath the branches of the *menorah:* on the right, Solomon's Judgment; on the left, The Sacrifice of Isaac. Pentateuch, megillot, haftarot and Job; written in Poligny by Joseph, the Scribe of Pontarlier in 1300. Paris, Bibliothèque Nationale, ms. Heb. 36, fol. 283v ($20\frac{1}{4} \times 14$ ins/51.4×35.5 cm.).

Figure 2. Coin with depiction of a *menorah* on a triangular base. Inscribed with the name of Mattathias Antigonus (40–37 B.C.E.), it is believed to date from the last year of his reign. Diam. $\frac{5}{8}$ in. (1.6 cm.). Jerusalem, Israel Museum, Israel Department of Antiquities Collection. Photo David Harris, Jerusalem.

Figure 3. Stone *menorah* from the third-century synagogue of Hammath near Tiberias. The branches are decorated with alternating pomegranates and blossoms and above are grooves for terra-cotta lamps. Jerusalem, Israel Museum. Photo David Harris, Jerusalem.

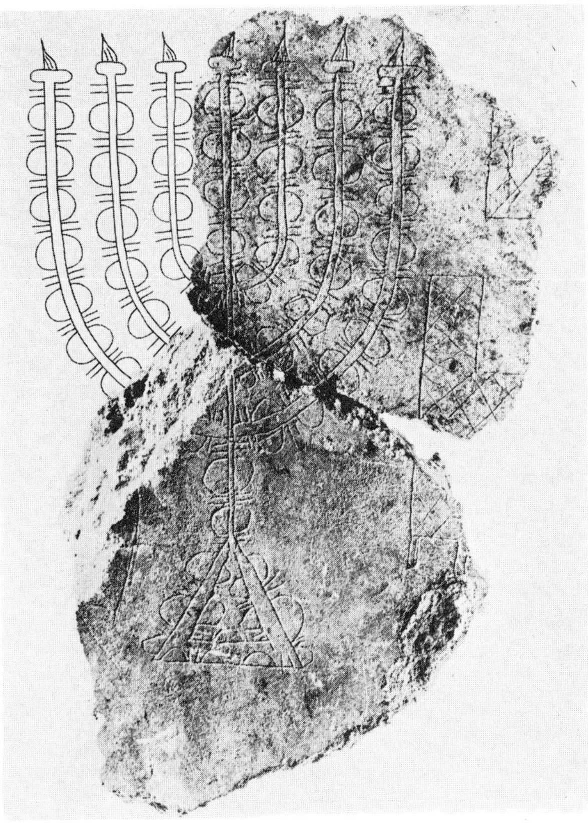

Figure 4. Plaster fragments of the earliest known representation of the Temple *menorah*, from the reign of Herod (37 B.C.E.–4 C.E.), found in excavations of the Old City of Jerusalem, 1969. Height 8 in. (20 cm.). Courtesy N. Avigad, Hebrew University, Jerusalem. Photo Zev Radovan, Jerusalem.

with the lamp in the sanctuary at Shiloh (I Sam. 3:3). However, in the Second Temple (see below) three of the lamps burnt throughout the day, the rest being lit in the evening (Jos., Ant., 3:199).

The First Temple. In the Temple built by Solomon there were ten *menorot* of gold, five along the northern and five along the southern wall of the *Heikhal* (the hall; I Kings 7:49; II Chron. 4:7). These were ornamented with carvings of flowers and furnished with appliances of gold for tending the lamps (I Kings 7:49–50), the number of which on each *menorah* is not stated. Some scholars hold that the passage listing the golden vessels made by Solomon for the house of the Lord (I Kings 7:48–50) is a later addition; but this view should be rejected. All the vessels of gold in Solomon's Temple, including the ten *menorot*, were cut in pieces at the end of Jehoiachin's reign by the Chaldeans who entered the *Heikhal* during their siege of Jerusalem (II Kings 24:13). Hence neither vessels of the *Heikhal* nor *menorot* are mentioned in the description of the Temple in Ezekiel's vision (Ezek. 41:1–4), for this description is apparently based largely on the actual appearance of the Temple in Jerusalem after the exile of Jehoiachin.

The *menorot* in Solomon's Temple may have had branches, and these may have numbered seven on each *menorah*. For the *Heikhal*, which Solomon built and which measured 40 by 20 cubits (I Kings 6:2, 17), was too large for only ten lamps to give it adequate illumination. Hence it is probable that each of the ten *menorot* had not one but several lamps, arranged on a central shaft and on branches, and that they numbered seven. Further support for the similarity between the *menorot* of Solomon and the one in the Tabernacle is to be found in the fact that the former, too, were ornamented with carvings of flowers (7:49), resembling the latter which had "cups made like almond-blossoms" and flowers. Moreover, the *menorot* in Solomon's Temple were made of pure gold (*ibid.*, loc. cit. *zahav sagur*, apparently the equivalent expression for *zahav tahor* used in the Priestly Code; see Ex. 25:31, 39; et al.; see *Metals). The vessels of the *menorah* in the Tabernacle consisted of lamps, tongs, snuff-dishes, and oil vessels (Ex. 25:37–39; Num. 4:9); the first three are among those mentioned in connection with the *menorot* in Solomon's Temple (I Kings 7:49–50).

In addition to the vessels in the *Heikhal*, there were others in Solomon's Temple treasuries whose collection was started already in the days of David (II Sam. 8:10–11), and which were left as objects consecrated to God but not used in worship. The passage in the Book of Chronicles enumerating the gifts prepared for the Temple by David before his death refers to the *menorot* of gold and silver in the Temple treasuries (I Chron. 28:15; and cf. 28:12). When the First Temple was destroyed the Chaldeans removed from it all these vessels, among which *menorot* are again included (Jer. 52:19), but they were not those of the *Heikhal*. No actual specimen of the *menorah* in the Tabernacle nor of one with a different number of branches has up to the present been uncovered in archaeological finds. Only reproductions of the *menorah* of the Second Temple are extant (see below).

Although according to the critical views the Priestly Code's account of the subject is legendary tradition, the artistic and architectonic elements of its description are undoubtedly based on an actual art style and derived from reality. Many scholars of the Wellhausen school held that the Tabernacle *menorah* was a literary projection of the one in the Second Temple. Their theory proceeds from that school's basic view that the Priestly Code was compiled at the beginning of Second Temple times, and hence its need to explain the entire Tabernacle as an imaginary reflection of the Second Temple. If, however, it is maintained that the Priestly Code was committed to writing earlier and is the production of the Jerusalem pre-Exilic priesthood, it must necessarily be held that the *menorah* described in it reflects a historic situation preceding the Second Temple. That the *menorot* in Solomon's Temple provided the pattern for the *menorah* in the Tabernacle is, indeed, not impossible.

The Second Temple. According to rabbinic legend, when the Temple was about to be destroyed the *menorah* was hidden away and it was later brought back by the exiles (see L. Ginzberg, *Legends of the Jews*, 4 (1913), 321; 6 (1928), 410–1). In reality, however, the *menorah* of the Tabernacle, as a hallowed emblem mentioned in the Pentateuch, had an influence on the interior of the Second Temple, in which from the outset one *menorah* as in the Tabernacle, and not ten, as in the Temple of Solomon, was placed. The *menorah* in the Temple of necessity had to conform to that in the Pentateuch, which became its archetype. The force that the *menorah* of the Tabernacle had in Second Temple times as a hallowed and binding emblem can be seen from the claim, incorporated by the Chronicler in Abijah's speech, that the people of Judah, keeping the commandments of the Lord, every night lit the lamps of the *menorah* of gold (II Chron. 13:11). Elsewhere, however, the Chronicler repeats the evidence of the Book of Kings by stating specifically that in the First Temple there were ten *menorot* and not one (see above). This contradiction between the enduring and binding validity of the *menorah* mentioned in the Pentateuch and the ten *menorot* in Solomon's Temple was met by the Sages with the above-mentioned statement that the *menorah* made by Moses was used during the entire existence of the First Temple, where all the *menorot* were placed on the south side, five on its right side and five on its left, and that of Moses in the middle (Men. 98b).

The golden *menorah* which stood in the Second Temple in the early stage of its history (it is referred to by Ben Sira—26:17) was removed in 169 B.C.E. by Antiochus Epiphanes IV (I Macc. 1:21). Judah Maccabee made new Temple vessels, including the *menorah*, after the cleansing of the Temple (I Macc. 4:49–50; II Macc. 10:3). According to the Talmud the first one was made of iron overlaid with tin (or with wood): "When they grew richer they made it of silver; when they grew still richer, they made it of gold" (RH 24b, Av. Zar. 43b); according to Josephus (Ant., 12:238), however, it was made of gold from the outset. It was seen by Pompey and his men when they entered the Temple (*ibid.*, 14:7) and remained in Herod's Temple until its destruction (Jos. Wars, 5:216–7). After the destruction of the Temple it was borne by the Romans in Titus' triumphal procession (*ibid.*, 7:148–9) and depicted with the other vessels on the wall of the triumphal arch called after him (see below). Elsewhere, however (*ibid.*, 6:387–8), Josephus relates that during the siege of Jerusalem by Titus one of the priests went out and handed over to him two lamps of gold similar to the lamp in the Temple. On the erroneous assumption that the reference is to the *menorah*, some maintain that there were in the Second Temple several copies of the *menorah* of the *Heikhal*, one of which was carried in the triumphal procession (see below). In the Second Temple three of the lamps of the *menorah* burnt throughout the day, the rest being lit in the evening (Jos., Ant., 3:199). The Talmud states that the priest who entered used to clean and trim the lamps except its two eastern ones which he found burning, and that its western lamp burnt continuously, and from it the priest relit the *menorah* at dusk (Tam. 3, 9; 6, 1; Sifra, Emor, 13, 7; Sif. Num. 59; Yoma 33a; et al.). If the western lamp was extinguished it was interpreted as boding ill for the future (Yoma 39b). Josephus (Apion, 1:22) similarly reports in the name of Hecataeus that on the Temple *menorah* there was a light

Figure 5. *Menorah* with a tripod base in relief on a stone capital from the fifth-century synagogue at Caesarea. Courtesy Israel Department of Antiquities, Jerusalem.

Figure 6. *Menorah* from the mosaic floor of the third–fourth-century synagogue at Jericho. Courtesy Israel Department of Antiquities, Jerusalem.

Figure 7. *Menorah* in a third-century fresco from the catacomb at the Villa Torlonia, Rome. From Beyer and Lietzmann, *Die juedische Katakombe der Villa Torlonia in Rom*, Berlin and Leipzig, 1930.

Figure 8. *Menorah* on the side of a fourth-century sarcophagus from the Vigna Randanini, Rome. Courtesy Soprintendenze alle Antichita, Rome.

Figure 9. *Menorah* represented in relief on a marble slab from the third-century synagogue at Priene in Asia Minor. Berlin, Staatliche Museen, Fruehchristlich-byzantinische Sammlung.

→

Figure 10. Ceramic lamp from Ereẓ Israel, third/fourth century, decorated with a *menorah*. Jerusalem, Israel Museum, Reifenberg Collection. Photo R. M. Kneller, Jerusalem.

Figure 11. *Menorah* depicted on a bronze amulet from Syria, fourth/fifth century. Jerusalem, Israel Museum, Reifenberg Collection. Photo David Harris, Jerusalem.

Figure 12. Ring with a representation of the *menorah*, from Ereẓ Israel, third/fourth century. Tel Aviv, I. Einhorn Collection. Photo David Harris, Jerusalem.

Figure 13. *Menorah* formed from the words of Psalm 67 on a silver amulet from Persia, 19th century. Haifa, Ethnological Museum and Folklore Archives. Photo Oskar Tauber, Haifa.

(φῶς) which was never extinguished by night or by day. According to some, the western lamp mentioned by the sages refers to the second of the two easterly lamps, according to others, to the middle lamp, designated as "western" because its spout faced westward, that is, toward the inner sanctum, the Holy of Holies (see Rashi to Shab. 22b, and to Men. 98b; Maim. Yad, Beit ha-Beḥirah, 3, 8). According to the latter interpretation the tradition of the sages accords with Josephus' statement (Ant., 3:199) that three lamps burnt throughout the day, that is, the two eastern and the western lamps. [M.Ha.]

Menorah on the Arch of Titus. The most important testimony for the form of the Temple *menorah* is the candelabrum on the Arch of Titus in Rome, which ought to be considered in conjunction with Josephus' description. Only three sides of each octagon of the arch are visible. They show reliefs within a threefold frame: in the middle shield of the upper cone two eagles face each other and hold a garland in their beaks; the other shields have different types of sea-monsters. The upper part of the *menorah* is, by and large, in accordance with biblical tradition and archaeological evidence. The hanging leaf-ornament of the middle shaft shows the oriental (Persian) origin (cf. the pillars of Persepolis). The problem of the Arch of Titus *menorah* is, however, its pedestal, which consists of two octagonal casings, a smaller above the larger, giving a cone-shaped form. Though its proportions are rather large, it does not necessarily cast doubt on the fidelity of the sculptor, since this was a peculiarity of Roman—and later Christian—artists. What does make this representation of the pedestal suspect is that according to all Jewish sources (cf. Men. 28b) and archaeological finds the Menorah stood on three legs, usually lion's paws. These paws are particularly distinct in the Nirim Mosaic (see below). The Bible speaks of the *yerekh* of the candelabrum (Ex. 25:31), which Rashi explains as a plate with three legs (see S. Shefer (ed.), *Enẓiklopedyah le-Inyenei ha-Mishkan* . . ., 1 (1965), 126ff.), and so it appears in the wall painting of *Dura-Europos and perhaps on the coin of Mattathias Antigonus, the only ancient coin depicting a *menorah*. The few extant specimens of this coin are, however, badly preserved, one only showing, besides the plate, a rudimentary foot.

This divergence between the Arch of Titus and the sources has given rise to a lively controversy beginning with Relandus' *De Spoliis* . . . (1716) which maintained, on the basis of the biblical prohibition of depicting animals, that the pedestal of the *menorah* on the Arch of Titus could not be an authentic reproduction. In point of fact, as E. Cohn-Wiener pointed out, there is a difference in style between the lower and upper parts of the *menorah*. The upper part, dating from the time of the later Hasmonean kings (see above), shows characteristics of late Hellenistic style, whereas the pedestal is typical of a later Roman style. Important too, is the evidence of Josephus, who must have seen the *menorah* often, both in Jerusalem and in Rome, and who has proved reliable in matters such as these, e.g., the Masada excavations. Whether his description supports or contradicts the authenticity of the Arch of Titus *menorah* depends on the interpretation of the relevant words used by him. According to W. Eltester (in bibl. cf. Michel-Bauernfeind's edition of Josephus, Wars, 2, 2, 1969), the words ὁ μὲν γὰρ μὲσος ἦν κίων ἐκ τῆς βὰσεως πεπεγὼς should be translated "the central shaft arose firmly from the pedestal," seeming to confirm the Arch of Titus representation which indeed gives this impression of weight and firmness. Another interpretation would be that the central shaft "stretched" out of its pedestal, that it was of one piece with it. This would not only be in accordance with the biblical injunction of Numbers 8:4 (cf. Ex. 25:31, 36; 37:17, 22), but also with Josephus' statement preceding the above quotation that the *menorah* was different from those in general use. These were put together from separate parts (cf. Pliny, Nat. Hist. 34, 6, 11).

Various suggestions have been made to solve the difficulty. Chief Rabbi Isaac Herzog, after summing up all other proposals, suggested that the original pedestal had been broken in the transport from Jerusalem to Rome and was replaced by the work of a Roman artist. Another hypothesis is that of W. Wirgin (IEJ 11, 1961, no. 3) who suggests that in order to carry the *menorah* in the triumphal procession without mishap, a Roman artist built a box-shaped covering from relief plates—well known from Roman censers—around the base to give it greater stability. A third suggestion is that the *menorah* on the Arch of Titus had as its model another *menorah*, perhaps one given as a gift to Rome by Herod. In fact Josephus (Wars, 6:388) relates that after the capture of Jerusalem, a priest handed to Titus "two lampstands similar to those deposited in the Temple." The Talmud (Ḥag. 26b, 27a) also mentions duplicates and triplicates of all Temple vessels in case the original ones were defiled. The Jerusalem Talmud (Ḥag. 3:8; 79d) and the Tosefta (Ḥag. 3:35) report the cleansing of the *menorah* on the Sabbath which provoked the derision of the Sadducees. This would not have been done had there been a duplicate but in any case it does not solve the problem of the Arch of Titus, since the duplicate would have been an exact replica of the original.

Reproductions of the Temple Menorah. Though the *menorah* of the Arch of Titus was widely known—the medieval pilgrims' guide *Mirabilis Urbis Romae* mentions the *arcus septem lucernarum*—it was not copied in late antiquity or the Middle Ages. While church candelabra and manuscript illustrations have animal feet, only one example of the Arch of Titus type is known: the Gothic candelabrum in Sta. Maria i Vulturella near Rome (see bibl. P. Bloch).

Several sketches of the *menorah* have been preserved from the time of the Second Temple in Jason's Tomb, Jerusalem (see Rahmani, in: *Atiqot*, 1964, Plate XII no. 1 and 2), and in the two pieces of plaster excavated in the Jewish Quarter of the Old City of Jerusalem in 1969, an artisan's sketch; three feet or triangle-basis are visible, but with knobs on them, a feature not corroborated by any other ancient literary or archaeological source (reproduced in *Jerusalem Post*, Weekend Magazine, 5/XII/1969; see Avigad, in Qadmoniot, 3, 1970, 28–29).

The Later History of the Menorah. Vespasian deposited the *menorah* together with the other booty in the special Peace Temple which he erected after the Jewish War (Jos.

Figure 14. *Menorah* in the center of a painted wooden *"shiviti"* plaque, Persia (?), 18th/19th century. New York, Jewish Museum.

Figure 15. The *menorah* on the emblem of the State of Israel, patterned after that on the Arch of Titus. Courtesy Government Press Office, Tel Aviv.

Wars 7:148–50; ARN[1] 41, 133). The subsequent fate of the candelabrum is uncertain. Procopius of Caesarea, the sixth-century Byzantine historian, in his introduction to the history of the Gothic War, reports that the "treasures of the Jews" were carried in Belisarius' triumphal procession in Constantinople (Byzantium) after his victory over the Vandals, who had taken them to Carthage after their sack of Rome in 455. Procopius goes on to relate that a Jew had warned a high official at Justinian's court not to keep the sacred vessels in Byzantium, as they had manifestly brought ill luck to Rome and Carthage, whereupon the Emperor had sent them hurriedly to Jerusalem, where they were deposited in one of the churches. As the result of the Persian and Arab invasions of the seventh century, their fate once more became unknown. This story has little credibility; no other source, such as the reports of the pilgrims, can be adduced in its support, nor is the *menorah* mentioned explicitly in this story.

On the other hand, medieval sources speak of the presence of the candelabrum in Constantinople. The seventh-century apocalypse *Milḥemet Melekh ha-Mashi'aḥ* ("War of the King Messiah") mentions Temple vessels deposited in the palace library of Emperor Julian. The learned emperor Constantine Porphyrogenitus (905–59) reports that a Heptalychnos, i.e., a seven-branched candelabrum, was lit for solemn processions. The imperial palace is said to have included a "Dome of the Seven-branch Candelabrum" It is not clear whether all these reports refer to the original *menorah* or a later copy. If the one or the other was really in Constantinople during the Middle Ages, it must have shared the fate of other ancient masterpieces when the town was sacked in 1204 in the course of the Fourth Crusade. It may appear odd that no reference to it is found in later medieval chronicles.

See also *Temple Vessels; *Symbolism. For Ḥanukkah candelabra, see *Ḥanukkah lamps. [He.S.]

In Kabbalah. From the early days of Kabbalah, the *menorah* appears as a symbol of the structure of the *Sefirot*. As far as is known, it was *Asher b. David, in his *Perush Shem ha-Meforash* (published in *Ha-Segullah* (1932) pamphlet 2ff.), who first explained the *menorah* in kabbalistic symbolic terms as reflecting the world of the *Sefirot*. He was followed by *Baḥya b. Asher and especially by Menaḥem *Recanati and others. There is little difference between the interpretations of Recanati and Asher b. David. The basic idea is that the *menorah*, despite the fact the it is composed of branches, bowls, etc., is not a combination of parts but is one solid whole made from "one bar." Similarly, the world of the *Sefirot*, despite its multiplicity, is a unity. The seven branches symbolize the seven lower *Sefirot*. Asher b. David and, following him, Recanati, placed special emphasis on the middle branch, which is equal to the *Sefirah Tiferet* ("glory"), which is called the "middle line." This *Sefirah* is directed toward the "attraction of the body" of man, in contrast to the other lower *Sefirot* which are directed toward the arms and legs. The middle branch, which stands on the *menorah* itself, toward which all the other branches face, therefore naturally stands for the "middle line." This *Sefirah* is imbued with abundance flowing from above which is transferred from it to the others. The oil which is put in the branches and is the force for the light of the *menorah* signifies the dynamic stream influenced by the **Ein-Sof*. This stream is the inner soul of all the *Sefirot* which operate within every *Sefirah*. For the same reason—these kabbalists maintain—the Torah calls the seven lower *Sefirot* "lights" and days of the week according to Genesis. The oil as a symbol of the streaming of abundance from above is a commonplace idea in kabbalistic literature. There were kabbalists who explained that the oil and the light indicate the three higher *Sefirot*.

According to the view of several kabbalists that Divine Providence is exercised through the *Sefirot*, Recanati interprets the saying of Zechariah (4:10): "These seven are the eyes of God," to mean that God governs by means of the seven *Sefirot* symbolized by the seven branches of the *menorah*.

The *Zohar itself gives no details of the symbolic significance of the parts of the *menorah*. In the *Tikkunei Zohar* the symbolism differs from that of the kabbalists mentioned above. In one place the *menorah* symbolizes an angelic power outside that of the *Sefirot*. The wick stands for the last *Sefirah*, *Malkhut*, equated with the *Shekhinah;* the oil is the *Sefirah Yesod* ("foundation"); and the light is the *Sefirah Tiferet* (*Tikkunei Zohar*, Introd., 146, ed. R. Margulies).

In a 14th-century kabbalistic manuscript Psalm 67 is interpreted as signifying the *menorah* and the counting of the *omer* (Vatican Ms. no. 214). A reproduction of the text of the psalm in the form of a *menorah* has since become widespread among oriental Jews and appears both in prayer books and in the form of amulets on walls in homes and, especially, synagogues. [E.G.]

THE MENORAH IN ART

After the destruction of the Temple the *menorah* became "the most important Jewish pictorial motif, and from an implement it became an emblem." Out of 1,207 reproductions in the third volume of Goodenough's standard work, *Jewish Symbolism in the Greco-Roman World* (see bibliography), no less than 182 are representations of the *menorah*. This number has considerably increased through later findings. Here only a short review of the various kinds of archaeological remnants together with the most important examples can be given (the numbers refer to Goodenough).

Synagogues. Actual Menorah. Upper part of brass *menorah* from En-Gedi (Barag-Porat, in *Qadmoniot* 3, 1970, 97–100, back-cover; see below).

Stone Fragments and Capitals. Stone screen from Ashkelon (575, 576), from El Ḥamma (629), stones from Eshtemoa and Naveh (615, 618); Capitals in Capernaum (478), Beit Jibrin (542), and Caesarea (997, 998); on a column in Gaza mosque Djami-el-Kebir (584); and on stones in Pergamon (877), Priene (878), and Ostia.

Mosaic Floors. In Beth Alpha (639); Hammath-Tiberias (in both these and many others are two *menorot* right and left of the Ark); and Maon (Nirim, see above; the Nirim *menorah* is reproduced on the Israel 50 lira banknote).

Paintings. The only preserved example is in Dura-Europos, and it is a conical base with three feet near Ark (602). It appears twice in narrative paintings: Aaron in the Temple (Goodenough vol. 11, color-plate X), and Moses giving water to the tribes (color-plate XII).

On Tombs. Sculptures. In Bet She'arim, a *menorah* on the head of a warrior (56).

On Doors of Tombs. Ibelin: YMHEY 17 (1953), nos. 3 and 4; Kefar Yassif (44); Kefar Tamra, near Shefar Am (Haifa Municipal Museum), which shows the *menorah* on the top of a date tree.

Fresco and Sarcophagus in the Torlonia Catacomb, Rome (817, 818). In the catacombs the *menorah* is often the only indication of Jewishness.

Sarcophagi in Vigna Randanini Catacomb, Rome (789). (Now in the Museo di Terme.) The *menorah* is in a medallion, borne by two winged Victorias; on gentile sarcophagi such medallions show the head of the buried person or a Medusa. Here the *menorah* is the distinctive emblem of Judaism on an artifact common to other religions as well.

LEAD SARCOPHAGI IN THE ISRAEL MUSEUM, JERUSALEM. The same type as made for pagans, Christians, and Jews. On the Jewish sarcophagi (from Bet She'arim) *menorot*—in contradistinction to the ornaments—are pressed on the three sarcophagi (see bibl. Katz reproductions nos. 104, 120).

TOMBSTONES. Frequently in catacombs (e.g. Randanini and Monteverde in Rome: 33 example in Goodenough).

OSSUARIES (rare): *menorah* (220, not certain): Ḥanukkah lamp (198).

Varia. GLASS-BOTTLES: 391, 411, 424, 428, 961.

GOLD-GLASSES. From catacombs (963–974), with peculiar techniques: between two layers of glass is the golden design (mostly ritual objects, Ark, lions).

LAMPS. Bronze. K. Katz, *From the Beginning*, pl. 109, p. 126: Reifenberg Collection, now on loan to Israel Museum; ceramic lamps: with various numbers of holders for oil lamps, but very frequently with a *menorah* design (more than 40 reproductions in Goodenough).

AMULETS, SEALS, RINGS, CORNELIANS. On these small artifacts too, the *menorah* is the most frequent symbol indicating the Jewishness of the owner (1012–1027). A good example is a glass amulet (third–sixth centuries) showing a *menorah* among other ritualia (Hechal Shlomo Museum).

The Middle Ages. Representations of the *menorah* are found frequently in medieval manuscripts, Jewish and Christian, of both Spanish and Franco-German origin, depicted alongside other Temple vessels. Earlier even, and of particular importance in this context, is the one in the *Codex Amiatinus* (Italy, c. 500, see bibl. H. Strauss and P. Bloch), which no doubt still reflects an older, classical-oriental tradition (cf. Strauss, in *Ereẓ Yisrael*, 6, 1960, 126/7; Roth, *Warburg-Courtauld 16*, 1953, 37–38). B. Narkiss, *Hebrew Illuminated Manuscripts* (1969), reproduces (and describes in detail) five medieval manuscripts with *menorah* representations: Plate 1: Bible (Leningrad), probably from Egypt (Introduction, 23); Plate 6: Cervera Bible (Portugal, *ibid.*, and note 53); Plate 16: Farḥi Bible (Spain-Provence, Introduction, 23); Plate 23: British Museum (11639, Franco-German, *ibid.*, 28, note 95); and Plate 24: Pentateuch (French, *ibid.*, 26; note 96). In the British Museum plate, Aaron is twice depicted lighting the *menorah* (*ibid.*, 114a and 122b), the differences in style suggesting two artists. The frequency of this representation may be connected with the fact that it is based on Numbers 8:2–3 and with its ample treatment by the Midrash. All five examples reflect faithfully and impressively their local background: the first three, the influence of the iconoclastic Islamic art, including the playful one of the *Reconquista* in no. 2: the burning lights turned toward the center and the variant of the oil flowing in the same direction; while the last two show the influence of the late Gothic French environment with their wealth of figures and drolleries. Numerous seven-branched candelabra may also be found in medieval French, German, and Italian churches.

A hitherto unpublished *menorah* with its appurtenances (Ex. 25, 38) painted in gold and color, is contained in a Spanish 14th-century Bible-manuscript on parchment, which was shown in an exhibition of the Jewish National and University Library (Jerusalem April-May 1970, Catalogue No. 6). This *menorah* has three feet with rather rare knobs (as in the recently excavated piece of plaster from the Old City of Jerusalem, see above), and snuffdishes like goblets with coats of arms: the tongs hang from the outer branches of the candelabrum and are shown in perspective before and behind the branches. It is apparently the work of an artist of the late Middle Ages, already accustomed to perspective. It frequently appears as an emblem also on book plates showing *Ḥanukkah lamps, printers' marks, and community seals.

Modern Times. In modern times the *menorah* has continued to be used as a religious symbol, particularly in synagogue art: wall-paintings, stained glass windows, mosaics, and—in spite of the talmudic prohibition (see below)—as a seven-branched metal candelabrum. In imitation of the ancient mosaics, some synagogues place a *menorah* to the right and the left of the Ark. The *menorah* representations in modern American synagogues reveal the problem of expressing ancient symbols in terms of modern art. In many cases little is left of the original tree-and-branches motive, but in some this has been preserved, in spite of modern simplicity. Independently of the synagogue, Benno *Elkan created several tree-shaped bronze *menorot*, of which one stands in Westminster Abbey, London, and another in the vicinity of the Knesset building in Jerusalem. Marc *Chagall incorporated a lighted *menorah* and olive leaves (Deut. 33:24) in his Tribe of Asher window (Hadassah Synagogue, Jerusalem). The Warsaw Ghetto memorial (1963) embodies two outsize *menorot* flanked by lions. The U.S. Jewish artist Ben *Shahn, who is responsible for the mosaic in the Ohev Shalom synagogue in Nashville, Tenn. (Kampf, *ibid.*, 134–6), has produced as its sketch a *menorah* (with *shofar*) in tempera (Ben Shahn, 1966, no. 116) and another one as the colored frontispiece of a Passover *Haggadah* illustrated by him (1965). Jankel *Adler has a *menorah*—together with several ritualia—in his "Jewish Still-Life" painted in the 1930s. In literature Stefan *Zweig devoted his short story *Der begrabene Leuchter* ("The Buried Candelabrum; 1937) to the saga of the *menorah*. The Arch of Titus *menorah* was adopted as the official symbol of the State of Israel, expressing the idea of Judaea Resurrecta, 2,000 years after the last Hasmonean prince had used the same symbol on his coins.

According to the Talmud it was forbidden to make an exact copy of the seven-branched candelabrum (RH 24b; Av. Zar. 43b; Men. 28b), and this prohibition is largely observed to the present day. On the other hand, the discovery of the upper part of a small bronze *menorah* during the excavations of a synagogue of the Byzantine period at En-Gedi (see above) shows that this prohibition was not always observed. It is possible that the bar of brass connecting the seven branches on their upper end which is also found in mosaic, stone-and-oil-lamp-representations of the same time (Bet Alfa, Ashkelon, oil lamp from Syria: Goodenough 3, p. 941) may have invalidated the above prohibition. J. Gutmann suggests that since the prohibition is found in a *baraita* in the Babylonian Talmud only, it was not accepted in Palestine. Gregorovius reports (*History of the City of Rome* ... 2, 2, 3) that in the time of King Theodoric (c. 500) the Jews of Rome used to assemble in their synagogue on Sabbaths and festivals to the light of a gilded seven-branched candelabrum. The Ḥanukkah lamp, having eight branches, did not violate the talmudic law. [HE.S.]

Bibliography: A. R. S. Kennedy, in: *Hastings Dictionary of the Bible*, 4 (1914), 663–4; K. Galling, in: ZDPV, 46 (1923), 23–29; Galling, Reallexikon, 348–9; Gressman, Bilder, 134. fig. 467; E. Cohn-Wiener, *Die juedische Kunst* (1929), 73–75; M. Kon, in: PEQ, 82 (1950), 25–30; G. Widengren, *The King and the Tree of Life in Ancient Near Eastern Religion* (1951), 64–67; S. R. Driver, *Exodus* (1953, Cambridge), 275–8; Goodenough, 4 (1954), 71–77; Y. Herzog, in: *Sinai*, 36 (1955); M. Dothan, in: IEJ, 6 (1956), 19; Ḥ. Albeck, *Seder Kodashim* (1957), 427, 429; W. Eltester, *New Testament Studies*, 3 (1957), 102–4; Y. Levi, *Olamot Nifgashim* (1960), 255–8; E. Peterson, *Judentum und Gnosis* (1959), 31ff.; W. Wirgin, in: IEJ, 11 (1961), 151–3; M. Haran, in: *Scripta Hierosolymitana*, 8 (1961), 277–8; idem, in: IEJ, 13 (1963), 54–55, 57; A. Negev, in *Eretz-Israel*, 8 (1967), 193–210; L. Yarden, *Tree of Light* (1971). IN KABBALAH: I. Weinstock, *Be-Ma'gelei ha-Nigleh ve-ha-Nistar* (1970), index; G. Scholem, *Ursprung und Anfaenge der Kabbala* (1962), 348; idem, in: *Judaica*, 19 (1963), 97–98; *Lu'aḥ ha-Areẓ 5708* (1947–48). IN ART: K. Katz et al. (eds.), *From the Beginning* (1968); P. Bloch, in: *Wallraf-Richartz Jahrbuch*, 23 (1961), 55–190; idem, in: *Monumenta Judaica* (1963), 21–25 and plates 76–88, 97, 100, 102; C. Roth, in: PEQ, 87 (1955), 151–64; H. Strauss, in: *Warburg and Courtauld Institute Journal*..., 12 (1959), 6–16; idem, in: *Muenster am Hellweg*, 15 (1962), no. 4, 60–63; S. S. Kayser and G. Schoenberger (eds.), *Jewish Ceremonial Art* (1959^2), 14–15, 120ff.; D. Sperber, in: JJS, 16 (1966), 135–59; J, Gutmann, in: ZNTW, 60 (1969), 289–91; M. Simon, *Recherches d'histoire judéo-chrétienne* (1962); A. Kampf, *Contemporary Synagogue Art* (1966), index; Roth, Art, index; J. Zwarts, *De zevenarmige Kandelaar* (1935); Schuerer, Gesch 1 (1901), 636–7; 2 (1898), 342–4; 3 (1898), 717.

MENORAH, a German-language, monthly illustrated journal for science, art, and literature. It was founded in

Vienna in 1923 by Paul Diamant "to serve as a bridge between the different sections of the Jewish people." A year later the journal passed into the hands of Norbert Hoffmann, who edited it together with his wife until it ceased publication in 1932. Some contributions appeared in Hebrew and in English. *Menorah* consistently maintained a high level of scholarship and of literary and artistic quality. Though politically independent, *Menorah* tended to support the Zionist *Revisionist movement and published articles by its leader, Vladimir *Jabotinsky.

Bibliography: S. Federbush (ed.), *Ḥokhmat Yisrael be-Ma'arav Eiropah*, 2 (1963), 403–6. [Ed.]

MENORAH ASSOCIATION AND MENORAH JOURNAL, U.S. Jewish campus organization and periodical. Both grew out of the Harvard Menorah Society, a Jewish campus group formed in 1906 by Henry *Hurwitz, at the time an undergraduate at the university. Influenced by the "new humanism" then being propounded in Cambridge by such figures as William James and George Santayana, the society sought to pursue the study of humanistic values in Judaism and to develop a positive intellectual relationship to Jewish tradition and belief. Similar groups soon formed on other American campuses, and in 1913 an intercollegiate Menorah Association was established which eventually numbered some 80 chapters. The association became largely defunct in the 1930s, but as the first attempt to establish an intercollegiate Jewish body of its kind it helped pave the way for such later organizations as the *B'nai B'rith Hillel societies.

The *Menorah Journal*, first published in 1915, was similarly dedicated to the promotion of a "Jewish humanism." Appearing bimonthly from 1915 through 1927, monthly from 1928 to 1930, and irregularly thereafter until 1962 for a total of 157 issues in all, it featured articles and fiction by leading Jewish scholars, intellectuals, and writers, and reproductions of contemporary Jewish art. It served for several decades as a center for lively controversy in American Jewish life. The *Journal* lost much of its prominence in the years after World War II, but like the Menorah Association, it was in many ways the prototype of the successors that displaced it.

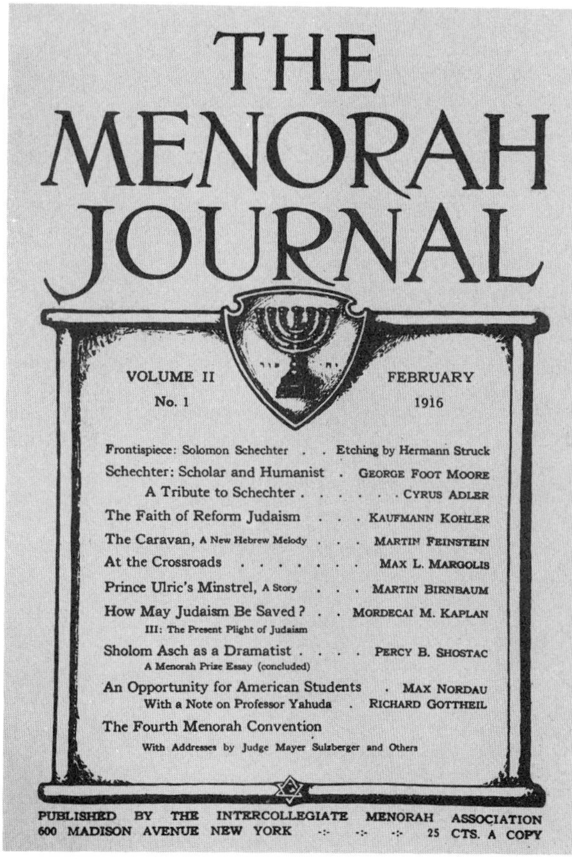
THE MENORAH JOURNAL

VOLUME II No. 1 FEBRUARY 1916

Frontispiece: Solomon Schechter . . Etching by Hermann Struck
Schechter: Scholar and Humanist . George Foot Moore
A Tribute to Schechter . . . . . . Cyrus Adler
The Faith of Reform Judaism . . . Kaufmann Kohler
The Caravan, A New Hebrew Melody . . . Martin Feinstein
At the Crossroads . . . . Max L. Margolis
Prince Ulric's Minstrel, A Story . . . Martin Birnbaum
How May Judaism Be Saved? . . Mordecai M. Kaplan
III: The Present Plight of Judaism
Sholom Asch as a Dramatist . . . . Percy B. Shostac
A Menorah Prize Essay (concluded)
An Opportunity for American Students . Max Nordau
With a Note on Professor Yahuda . Richard Gottheil
The Fourth Menorah Convention
With Addresses by Judge Mayer Sulzberger and Others

PUBLISHED BY THE INTERCOLLEGIATE MENORAH ASSOCIATION
600 MADISON AVENUE NEW YORK 25 CTS. A COPY

Cover of *The Menorah Journal*, Vol. II, No. 1, New York, February, 1916. Jerusalem, J.N.U.L.

Bibliography: L. W. Schwartz (ed.), *The Menorah Treasury* (1964); H. M. Kallen, in: *Menorah Journal*, 49 (1962), 9–16; R. Alter, in: *Commentary*, 39 no. 5 (1965), 51–55. [H.H.]

MENTAL ILLNESS. Man has been subject to mental illness from the earliest known times. The Bible makes frequent reference to it among Jews, and describes recognizable types of mental disturbances. The reference in Leviticus 20:27: "A man also or a woman that divineth by a ghost or a familiar spirit . . ." apparently included the mentally ill and, almost definitely, people subject to hysterical conditions. In Saul's personality, a brooding homicidal paranoia was overlaid by suicidal depression. Some of the prophets seem to have experienced states of ecstasy, and there are indications of neuroses among them.

The legal tenets of the Talmud regarding mental illness indicate the existence of conditions ranging from grave types of psychoses to those which develop out of physical states. The writings of the noted Jewish physicians of the medieval period, which were generally based on their practice among Jewish patients, reveal that mental illnesses were frequently encountered. They included melancholia, mania, and other serious psychotic states, states of anxiety, and psychosomatic conditions. The "wonder" cures of the 18th-century folk healers *(ba'alei shem)* provide evidence of the hysterical nature of the emotional disturbances they treated. In dealing with possession by a dybbuk, which was of the same nature, they were carrying on the practice of the Kabbalists in Safed, in Ereẓ Israel.

Toward the end of the 19th century mental disturbances were clearly classified into two major categories. The first is psychosis, where there is profound disturbance of perception (e.g., hallucination), thought (e.g., delusion), and mood (e.g., depression), and accompanying vagaries of behavior, but the patient does not understand that he is disturbed. The second category is neurosis (and deviations of personality), where the disturbance is less profound and the individual retains his perception of reality and knows that he is disturbed, but suffers from worry and guilt, or anxiety, or medically unexplained physical symptoms. Psychotic, neurotic, and "normal" personalities shade imperceptibly into each other and have more in common than appears from these categories. Thus agreement about diagnosis is not constant. Theories of the causes of mental illness fall into three main groups: physical (including genetic); psychological (which has to do with the control of instinct and the personal development of the child within the family); and social (which has to do with the effect of general social influence or stresses and deprivations). Modern theory seeks an explanation for many cases in a varying combination of all three factors.

In the study of mental illness, the analysis of large numbers by statistical methods (epidemiology), and comparison between groups, may provide clues to understanding its nature and causation and the mental health situation and needs of a particular group. The most important epidemiological method is the comparison of the incidence (frequency) of new cases. Incidence is measured as a rate: the number of new cases occurring per year in a given number of the population. In this article, incidence and all other rates are noted per 100,000 of the population concerned. A rough but fairly reliable incidence may be determined by calculating the rate of new cases hospitalized per year. More reliable information is obtained by noting all the cases which appear at both mental hospitals and clinics. Prevalence of illness refers to all the cases—old and new—that exist at any given moment, either in an institution or at home. Prevalence is obtained by a total survey of the community.

Knowledge about mental illness among Jews at the

present time is confined mainly to those in the United States and Israel, since by and large it is only in these countries that specific reference to Jews is made in hospital statistics. In Israel, statistics of mental illness are provided by the Mental Health Services of the Ministry of Health. The statistics available on the rates of mental disturbances among Jews and other significant observations about them are presented here under three headings: psychoses; neuroses; and other indicators of mental ill health.

Psychoses. Depression (manic-depressive, affective psychosis—including involutional melancholia in the aging). This is a relatively significant mental illness among Jews. The U.S. statistics of the 1920s for manic-depressive and involutional illnesses from hospitals in New York City, Illinois, and Massachussets, showed Jews to have had slightly lower first-admission rates than non-Jews (including Negroes). However, the painstaking work of Benjamin *Malzberg reveals that in 1949–51, Jews in New York State had a notably higher rate of first admission to private and public hospitals than white non-Jews (27 *v.* 15). These rates are crude, i.e., per 100,000 of the total population of all ages. The crude rate for Jews in Israel in 1958 was about the same (24) as for New York Jews. However, Jews in Israel born in Central and Eastern Europe had in 1958 twice the rates (50,46) as for New York Jews of the same origin and descent. As usual, the rate is about twice as high in women as in men. On the other hand, in Israel in 1958, Asian-African born showed only half the rate of European-born Jews and Israel-born Jews even less. The Oriental-born rates were somewhat lower than that for New York Jews and probably only of a slightly higher order than for white non-Jews in New York. Israel-born Jews seem to have had the lowest rates of all these groups, despite the higher proportion among them of those of European rather than Oriental descent.

The Israel rates of first admission for psychotic depressive conditions in 1966 seem to bear out all these conclusions and show that:

1) European-born Jews in Israel have a notably higher rate (45) than their non-Jewish European counterparts (Sweden: 21).

2) Asian-African-born Jews in Israel have a markedly lower hospital rate (23) than those born in Europe, lower than the known rate for Jews in New York, and resembling that for European non-Jews.

3) Israel-born Jews of both European and Afro-Asian descent show an even lower rate (16) than the Afro-Asian-born and, *a fortiori*, a lower rate than European-born immigrants. Israel-born Jews have a lower rate than those known for Jews and even non-Jews in New York State. Israel-born Jews in 1966 had a clearly lower crude rate than Swedes (1964) and New Zealanders (1967), the ratio being 6:21:27. The rate for Israel-born over the age of 15 was only 17. The age-specific rate for the population over 15 is a finer measure than the crude rate, since mental illness usually manifests itself after that age. To these conclusions must be added Malzberg's proof of the higher incidence of depressive psychosis in New York State among Jews of European birth and descent than among non-Jews.

The hypothetical reasons for the higher incidence of depressive psychoses in Jews of European birth in Israel and those of European birth and descent in the U.S. may well include the family and social tensions accompanying their profound, achievement-oriented ethical system. This has been incorporated in their personality as a sense of individual conscience and responsibility, the control of aggression, and sobriety. This psychosocial system does not allow of easy solutions and the camouflage of problems by the use of alcohol and other reality-denying behaviors. Furthermore, it is known that closed Orthodox societies in the West tend to produce more depression. The very high incidence of depression among European-born Jews in Israel is undoubtedly the result of persecution and concentration-camp experiences, underlaid by tendency to depression and exacerbated by migrational upheavals.

The hypothesis that there is an hereditary element in the Jewish tendency to depression is probably not tenable in the light of the moderate rate among Asian-African-born Jews. The apparent generational change manifested as a lower incidence of this psychosis in Israel-born Jews also argues against genetic causes. The speculation that the higher incidence is the result of the known readiness of Jews to seek psychiatric help cannot hold much water. The high rates for European-born Jews as compared to Asian-African-born Jews in Israel, where all psychotics have an almost equal chance of hospitalization, rule out that factor. It is certain, therefore, that European Jews have a higher rate of psychotic deression than non-Jews. Research in Israel has proved that Jewish women, like all women, have a depression rate about 100 per cent higher than men. In 1966, the rate for Israel-born women (27), because of the particularly low rate for Israel-born men (7), was four times as high as for men.

Schizophrenia. This form of insanity is characterized by profound disturbances such as hallucinations, delusions, and social withdrawal. In this universally found psychosis, the crude rates of first hospitalizations were approximately the same for Israel Jews in 1958 (39) as those given by Malzberg for New York Jews in 1949–51 (36). However, closer examination reveals marked differences in the Israel Jewish population. In 1958, Asian-African-born immigrants of 15-plus showed a considerably higher incidence of first admissions for schizophrenia (57–80) than Central-European-born (44) and East-European-born (34), Israel-born (81) had the highest incidence. Among the Asian-African-born, Yemenite immigrants had the lowest rate and Turkish the highest.

The high rate of schizophrenia in the Israel born is difficult to explain and may have something to do with the inter-generational adjustment between them and their foreign-born parents, and with the pressures of mass immigration. However, in 1966 the Israel-born rate in the population over the age of 15, while it had declined, was still the highest (67). In that year the incidence in the Asian-African-born had fallen to 51, indicating that their former high rates were due to transient stresses of immigration and sociocultural change. In 1966 the Asian-African rates were only slightly higher than the European-American, and definitely lower than the Israel-born ones. The total European-American-born crude rate in Israel in 1966 stood at 45, which is about the same as the European-born rate for 1958, but appreciably higher than the earlier-known rate for New York Jews. In every case the schizophrenic rate in Israel Jews still appears to be higher than earlier rates for non-Jews. The general urban crude rate in the U. S. in 1929–31 was 27. In New York in 1949–51 it was 32 for non-Jews. In New Zealand in 1963–67 the general crude rate was 21, while the figures for Jews in Israel in 1958 and 1966 were 39 and 37, and higher if "psychotic episodes" are included. In Israel, among the Asian-African-born the male rate predominates, among the European-American-born the female rate is in excess of the male.

Paranoia. This generally rather firm diagnostic category has often been said to be more common in Jews than in non-Jews. Malzberg's work in New York did not bear this out. However, in Israel in 1958, higher first admission rates were diagnosed among European-born Jews (10) and among the Asian-African-born (8–20). The latter was probably a reaction to migration and change, and not always true paranoia. The Israel-born had the same rate in 1958 as Jews and white non-Jews in New York (0.7). In New Zealand in 1967 the rate was 1.0. More recent information indicates no abatement, but rather an increase, in the rates of paranoia diagnosed and treated among the foreign-born Israelis. It was especially marked in women of European-American origin (21 for the 15-plus age group).

It should be noted that among Jews in Israel in 1966 the incidence of all psychoses of a functional, or non-organic nature (schizophrenic, effective, psychotic episode, paranoiac) was approximately the same for the Israel and Asian-African-born (107 and 100 respectively for the 15 plus) and for European-American-born (121). As elsewhere, foreign-born immigrants in Israel in the 15-plus group have higher total rates of first admission to hospital than the native-born, but the differences are not very significant (1966: Israel 188, Asian-Africa 218, European-American 226).

Malzberg showed that Jews have about the same total rate of first admissions as white non-Jews. The Israel rate was later discovered to be about 12 per cent higher than both. In the Midtown Manhattan study, *Mental Health in the Metropolis* (1962), Leo Srole and Thomas Langner found that Jews showed a far higher prevalence of all treated disorders than Protestants and Catholics, but for cases normally treated in hospital approximately the same rate as Protestants and less than Catholics. Jews generally had the lowest rate for serious impairment of mental health. Because Jews were found less frequently in the lower socioeconomic strata, their seriously impaired rates were lower. This leads to the conclusion that the rate of the more severe conditions for which treatment was sought in the U.S. was not greater among Jews than among non-Jews. In Israel, European-American-born Jews had a definitely higher rate for all psychoses (including organic conditions) than Jews of other origins.

Neuroses and Allied Conditions. The available hospital statistics in New York City (Bellevue Hospital, 1938) and in New York State (Malzberg's study, 1949–51) indicate a higher rate of neuroses in Jews than in non-Jews. A higher rate of neuroses for Jews was reported among military selectees in Boston in 1941–42. The rate for first admissions to Illinois State mental hospitals, however, was lower for Jews.

Leo Srole notes that in the early 1950s the prevalence rate of treated neuroses for Jews was twice that of Catholics and Protestants. In the Manhattan study, Jews also yielded considerably higher patient rates for disorders usually treated in an ambulatory facility. While in the community survey they showed the lowest seriously impaired rate, their mental health was generally not as satisfactory as that of Catholics and Protestants, from which it is to be concluded that neurosis rates in New York are higher among Jews than among non-Jews.

In Israel in 1958 Jews had a hospital first admission rate which was definitely higher for neuroses than Jews in New York (1949–51:21 *v.* 12). Furthermore, the Asian-African-born had generally twice the rate (15 plus) of the European- and Israel-born. The highest rate (65) was among those born in Iran, who had particular adjustment problems and also showed an apparently greater tendency to paranoid reactions. In 1966 the general Israel rate for neuroses was even higher than in 1958 (30), but the two groups of immigrants had approximately the same rate (±40). This is accounted for by the steep rise in the first admission rate for neurosis among European immigrants and some subsidence in the rate among Oriental immigrants.

Concentration-camp survivors, while generally known to have made a good social adjustment in Israel, were in a large proportion of cases deeply affected by the trauma they had suffered. Their emotional reactions often included anxiety, depression, and difficulty in reestablishing relations. Kibbutz-born Israelis appear to have the usual emotional disturbances, and in average proportions. They do not, however, manifest homosexuality or delinquency.

For personality (character, behavior disorders), Malzberg's study of hospitalization showed a crude rate slightly less for Jews in New York (1.5) than for white non-Jews. Israel Jews in 1958 showed a very much higher hospital incidence rate. The Asian-African-born in Israel showed remarkably high rates in the population over the age of 15 (36–48), as did the Israel-born (50), when compared to the European-born (15–25). This accords with their rates for schizophrenia, and like these they decreased in 1966 (Asian-African-born 25, Israel-born 23). This indicates that these reactions were the product of immigration and social upset and that they were reduced after social adaptation. In 1958 and 1966 the rates for personality disorders among the European-American-born were the lowest in Israel (9).

Other Indicators of Mental Ill Health. ALCOHOLISM. Jews are traditionally known for their sobriety. In the 1920s their rate for arrests for drunkenness in Warsaw was 30 *v.* 1,920 for Christians. In 1925 the rate of admission to public and private mental hospitals in New York City was 0.1 for Jews and 5.9 for non-Jews. A similar picture held in Massachussets and Illinois State hospitals. In the Boston examination of military selectees, Jews had the lowest incidence of alcoholic psychosis of all ethnic groups. Malzberg found only two cases during a three-year period (1950–52) in Canada, where the Jewish population was 240,000. He also states that he found an intemperate employment of alcohol in 2.2 per cent of Jewish first admissions in New York as against 18 per cent of non-Jewish first admissions. In the New Haven psychiatric census of 1950, no alcoholic Jews were found among the patients at any treatment site.

In a census in Israel in 1964 analysing cases found in mental hospitals, only 21 (0.3 per cent) presented alcoholic problems. In 1966, however, a total of 152 alcoholic cases were admitted to hospital (2 per cent of all cases admitted). This was the total crude rate of 6.6 (for men 12.5), which resembles the earlier rates for non-Jews in the U.S. (urban total rate 7, males 12). However, this rate constituted about one in ten of which only four were Israel-born; 26 were from Europe-America (rate 3) and 44 from Asia-Africa (rate 7). It is evident, therefore that alcoholism in Israel is a problem relating almost entirely to male immigrants, especially those from Asia and Africa. However, social changes in the country and the growing consumption of alcohol may conceivably increase its incidence, in spite of the intense social cohesion in Israel.

It is possible that a part of the real incidence of neurosis and depression in many non-Jewish populations is masked by or expressed through alcoholic overindulgence. In Jews it may well be that emotional difficulty is expressed through neurosis and depression rather than through the escape into and physical self-destruction of alcoholism (see *Drunkenness).

DRUG ADDICTION. Drug addiction is relatively speaking not new or uncommon among Jews in Israel. In 1966 and 1967 91 Jews with a primary diagnosis of addiction were admitted to hospital for treatment. Thirty-two of these cases were admitted for the first time (23 males, 9 females). They were composed equally of immigrants from Europe-America and Afro-Asia, with only five or six Israel-born. In 1970 there were probably rather more than 400 hard-core addicts in Israel. Drug addiction is known to be associated in the underworld with criminality and with pimping and prostitution, but a few of the cases were related to medical treatment. The New Haven study of 1950 revealed no drug addicts among Jews. A comparison of half-year figures for 1966 with 1970 shows a rise of first admissions related to drugs (from 20 to 39) with an especial increase of the number of younger Israel-born Jews. In 1970, despite the absence of statistical study, the abuse of drugs was known to have spread to groups of Jewish youth in the U.S. A few who visited Israel after the Six-Day War required treatment. Some of the older immigrants to Israel from North Africa and the Middle East had been in the habit of smoking marijuana, but it became much less evident among them in Israel and was not used by their children except among delinquents and small marginal groups. Following the Six-Day War, with the occupation of the West Bank and the flood of volunteers and students from North America, the use of marijuana increased in marginal groups. The occasional and apparently temporary use of a small amount of marijuana even appeared among groups of pupils at secondary schools.

Suicide. Emile *Durkheim demonstrated at the end of the last century that Jews had a lower suicide rate than Protestants and Catholics. It was estimated that in 1925 the suicide rate for Jews in New York was ten as compared to a similar general average yearly rate for the period 1950–59 in the U.S., a rate of three in Ireland, and one of 23 in Denmark. In Israel in 1952–58 the general rate was ten (and 15 for the population above 15 years of age in 1949–59). While the suicide rate in Israel represents a mid-point between extremes in other nations, it has special characteristics. The female rate relative to the male rate is unusually high. In European countries males usually have a suicide rate three or four times that of females. In Israel in the years 1949–59, female rates were never less than half that of males and in two of those years equaled that of males. This has been explained as a result of the social equality and shared burdens of the sexes in Israel. A slackening of religious Orthodoxy may be a factor, but high female ratios are not found in other egalitarian societies. It is more probably a result of the high incidence of depression, especially among older Western women in Israel. Since 1949 at least 70 percent of female suicides have occurred in women over the age of 31, which is also the age associated with the onset of depression.

The high ratio of suicides in women as compared to men among Jews in Europe can be seen from a report by Arthur *Ruppin in 1940. Of the suicides of Jews in Warsaw between 1927 and 1932, 49.4 percent were women. Ruppin ascribes this to the difficult psychological situation of Jewish girls who, in the secular environment of the Polish capital, had lost touch with their Orthodox parents. Another striking fact is the very low suicide rate in Israel among the Asian-African- and Israel-born. However, attemped suicide is becoming more frequent among young women from Oriental homes in Israel. This is probably related to the psychological conflict described by Ruppin, who ascribes rising rates of suicide among Jews generally to growing secularity. Where Durkheim quotes a rate of 18 for Jews in Prussia in 1890, Ruppin gives a rate of 50 for 1926. Since 1956 the suicide rate in Israel has gradually declined. In 1964 it was 12 for the population above the age of 15, while the rate for the general population was 7.6. This decrease may also be related to the general readaptation which followed the absorption of the mass immigration of the early 1950s.

Criminality and Delinquency. While no statistics exist, criminality was known to be rare among Jewish communities in the Diaspora and has generally been so in Ereẓ Israel as well. However, delinquency has been found, especially among the less privileged Oriental, near-slum groups in Israel's cities. Striking evidence of the stress which followed the mass immigration is seen in the high rates of crimes of violence (murder, attempted murder, and manslaughter) and causing death by negligence from 1949 until about 1956–57. The rate for murder dropped from 45 in 1949 to one in 1962. The total rate of these crimes of violence decreased from 20 in 1950 to five in 1960. This again indicates adaptation after the tensions caused by mass immigration.

The percentage of juvenile delinquency rose from 0.7 in 1949 to 1.0 in 1957. The proportion was higher for Oriental groups. In 1957 children of all groups of immigrants constituted 69 per cent of the delinquents. Delinquency and criminality are not encountered among kibbutz-born children. The incidence of juvenile delinquency among Oriental groups indicates problems which at times arise out of cultural and social changes in their families. On the other hand, the palpable increase in delinquency among children from a "good" socioeconomic background highlights the difficulties being encountered by some developed city families in the modern, technologically advanced society of Israel.

Bibliography: L. Miller, in: N. Petrilowitsch (ed.), *Contributions to Comparative Psychiatry* (1967), 96–137; idem, in: A. Jarus et al. (eds.), *The Child and the Family in Israel* (1970); B. Malzberg, *Mental Health of Jews in New York State. 1949–1957* (1963); L. Srole and Th. Langner, in: *Mental Health in the Metropolis*, 1 (1962), 300–24; M. Mandel, J. Gampel, and L. Miller, *Admission to Mental Hospital in Israel—1966* (1971); L. Eitinger *Concentration Camp Survivors in Norway and Israel* (1964). [Lo.M.]

MENUHIN, YEHUDI (1916–), violinist. Menuhin was born in New York, the son of parents who were both educated at the Herzlia Gymnasium in Tel Aviv and had left Palestine to settle in the U.S. He himself spoke Hebrew in his early years. Yehudi started to learn the violin at the age of five, and appeared as soloist with the San Francisco Orchestra when he was eight. He was taken to Europe in 1927, and continued his studies with Georges Enesco and with Adolf Busch. In 1928, he captivated Paris, London, and New York. By 1933 he had played in 63 different cities and retired for two years to California. He had played the Bach, Beethoven, and Brahms violin concertos under Bruno *Walter in Berlin, performed 75-year old Elgar's violin concerto under the composer's baton in London and Paris, and played under Fritz Busch and Toscanini in New York. When he reappeared on the stage his reputation was so great, that he was instantly booked for years ahead.

Yehudi Menuhin, violinist. Courtesy B. Gillon, Tel Aviv. Photo David Farrell, London.

World War II intervened, and Menuhin spent the years 1939–45 playing for U.S. and Allied Forces and giving benefit concerts for wartime causes. In 1944 he was the first allied soloist to play in liberated Paris and in 1945 he was invited to play in Moscow. He became an active member of UNESCO's international Musical Council of which he served as president. In 1957 Menuhin initiated his own music festival at Gstaad in Switzerland, and in 1959 another at Bath in England, which he directed until 1968. His great contribution to the development of Britain's musical life in the postwar decades included the establishment of a school for musically gifted children. Among the many composers who wrote specially for him were Ernst *Bloch, Béla Bartók, Paul *Ben-Haim, and Sir William Walton. He paid the first of several visits to Israel in 1950. In 1970 he was awarded the Jawaharlal Nehru Prize for International Understanding. Yehudi Menuhin's sisters, HEPHZIBAH (1920–) and YALTA (1921–) both gifted pianists, appeared with him in chamber music recitals and in concert tours. Two other pianists—his son JEREMY and his son-in-law FOU TS'ONG—enabled the Menuhin family to make some extremely interesting combined concert appearances and recordings.

Bibliography: N. Wymer, *Yehudi Menuhin* (1961); R. Magidoff, *Yehudi Menuhin: the Story of the Man and the Musician* (1956); H. O. Spingel, *Yehudi Menuhin* (Ger., 1964); Baker, Biog Dict.; Grove, Dict; Riemann-Gurlitt.

[U.T.]

ME'OT ḤITTIM (Heb. מְעוֹת חִטִּים; "wheat money"), collection made before *Passover to ensure a supply of flour for unleavened bread (*maẓẓot*) for the poor. Residence in a town for 12 months obliged one to contribute to or entitled one to receive communal funds known as *Kimḥa de-Fisḥa* ("flour for Passover"; TJ, BB 1:6, 12d). In medieval Europe it was customary for the communal rabbi and seven notables to draw up a list of those eligible to donate and to receive the tax, at the beginning of the month of Nisan. The custom was codified by *Isserles (OḤ 429:1). In modern times, the term has been broadened to include all the holiday needs of the poor at Passover (e.g., wine, fish, meat).

See also *Charity; *Passover.

Bibliography: E. Ki-Tov, *Sefer ha-Toda'ah*, 1 pt. 2 (1960), 22f.; Eisenstein, Dinim, 342.

[ED.]

MEPHIBOSHETH (Heb. מְפִיבֹשֶׁת), a son of Jonathan and a grandson of Saul; called Merib-Baal (מְרִיב־בַּעַל) or Meribaal (מְרִיבַעַל) in the genealogy of the house of Saul (I Chron. 8:34; 9:40) where the name is parallel to Eshbaal (see *Ish-Bosheth). The original form in I Chronicles is obviously, *boshet*, "shame" having deliberately been substituted for *ba'al*, "lord," which later generations objected to because it was the name of the pagan god Baal. Mephibosheth, the sole heir of the house of Saul (cf. II Sam. 9:1ff.), became lame at the age of five as the result of a fall from the hands of his nurse when she hurriedly picked him up in order to flee after receiving the news of the death of Saul and Jonathan (II Sam. 4:4). David treated Mephibosheth compassionately, refusing to deliver him over to the Gibeonites to be hanged with the other descendants of Saul (21:7), inviting him to eat at the royal table, and restoring him to the fields of Saul (9:1ff.). These kindnesses toward Mephibosheth can be explained as the fulfillment of David's oath to Jonathan (I Sam. 20:15, 42; II Sam. 21:7) and perhaps even of his oath to Saul (I Sam. 24:22). The story telling of David's generosity, however, makes no mention of the oaths, perhaps thereby implying that David's magnanimity was motivated not only by his oath but also by a plan to keep the descendants of the preceding dynasty under observation and to impress upon his own monarchy the stamp of continuity and legitimacy. Reasons of state become particularly evident in David's attempts to draw closer to the Benjamites and those who had been allied with Saul (II Sam. 3:19; 9:4–5; 17:27; 19:17, 18, 21; I Chron. 12:1–9). During Absalom's revolt Mephibosheth did not take any action and apparently remained loyal to David (II Sam. 19:25–32). *Ziba failed in his attempt to impute to Mephibosheth the ambition of receiving the monarchy from the people (II Sam. 16:1–4; 19:25–30).

[SH.AB.]

In the Aggadah. Mephibosheth was an outstanding scholar. David called him "My teacher," and consulted him on all matters (Ber. 4a), and in the Talmud his name, used metaphorically to denote a noted scholar (Erub. 53b; "out of my mouth, humiliation"), indicated that he humiliated even David by his learning (*ibid.*). Nevertheless, David saved his life (cf. II Sam. 21:7) by praying that Mephibosheth should not be made to pass before the Ark and thus risk being condemned to death as were the rest of Saul's sons (Yev. 79a). Because David gave ear to Ziba's slander against Mephibosheth, the Temple was destroyed TJ, Yev. 4a). The later division of the kingdom was a punishment for David's decision that Mephibosheth and Ziba were to divide the land (II Sam. 19:29; Shab. 56b).

[ED.]

Bibliography: H. P. Smith, *The Books of Samuel* (ICC, 1912), 310–3, 374–6; W. Caspari, *Die Samuelbuecher* (1926), 579–80; Noth, Personennamen, 119, 143; M. Z. Segal, *Sifrei Shemuel* (1956), 255, 293, 332, 352–3; J. Lewy, in: HUCA, 32 (1961), 36–37; H. W. Hertzberg, *Samuel* (Ger., 1960²), 298–301. IN THE AGGADAH: Ginzberg, Legends, 4 (1954), 76; I. Ḥasida, *Ishei ha-Tanakh* (1964), 265.

MER, GIDEON (1894–1961), Israel expert on malaria and epidemiologist. Mer was born in Ponevez (Panevezys), Lithuania, and gave up the study of medicine in 1913 to emigrate to Palestine. On the outbreak of World War I he was expelled by the Turkish authorities as an enemy alien and went to Egypt, where he responded to *Trumpeldor's call for volunteers to found a Jewish brigade. He was one of the first to join the Mule Corps and served with distinction at Gallipoli. After the war, Mer obtained work in the anti-malaria service under Professor *Kligler, who persuaded him to return to Europe to complete his medical studies. In 1928, at the invitation of the Hebrew University of Jerusalem, he rejoined Kligler on the staff of the malaria research station at Rosh Pinnah, and in 1935 was appointed professor.

In World War II, Mer served as an expert on malaria first with the Australian army in the Middle East and then the British with the British forces in Iraq, Persia, and Burma. In Burma he carried out the first large-scale experiments on the use of D.D.T. After the war he returned to Rosh Pinnah and in 1948 served as brigade medical officer in the Palmah. With the founding of the State of Israel Mer was appointed head of the department of preventive medicine of the Israel army, but returned to his research station at Rosh Pinnah in 1951. Mer's work in the field of malaria control earned international recognition. His greatest contribution to the study of the bionomics of anopheles was his method of age grouping of the female anopheles by the size of the ampulla of the ovary.

Bibliography: L. Dror et al. (eds.), *Gideon G. Mer . . .* (Heb. 1962; = *Beri'ut ha-Ẓibbur*, 5 (1962), 149–219).

[ED.]

MERAB (Heb. מֵרַב; probably from the root *rbb*), the eldest daughter of King *Saul (I Sam. 14:49). Saul promised Merab as a wife for *David, upon the condition that David fight Saul's wars against the Philistines (18:17–18). Saul did not fulfill his part of the bargain (18:19). Instead he gave Merab to *Adriel the Meholathite, and *Michal, her younger sister, became the wife of David. The conditional promise of marriage is similar to I Samuel 17:25, where Saul promises his daughter to the person who defeats Goliath. II Samuel 21:8 mentions the five sons of Michal and Adriel. The text should, however, read Merab instead of Michal on the basis of the Lucianic version of the Septuagint, the Peshita, and two masoretic texts.

Bibliography: de Vaux, Anc Isr, 32. [Ed.]

MERANO, town in the province of Bolzano, N.E. Italy, near the Austrian border. Only around the middle of the 19th century did a few Jewish families, mainly from Central Europe, settle in Merano, the area having been under *ḥerem* since 1475 (see *Trent). In 1905, a community was constituted in Merano, encompassing the communities of Trent and Bolzano. In 1918 Merano passed from Austrian to Italian rule. In 1931, 780 Jews lived there, many of whom were foreign citizens. During World War II the Jews in Merano had to face the hostility of the German-speaking population, as well as the Nazi occupation: 25 Italian Jews from Merano are known to have died in the extermination camps; many more were executed or disappeared. There were 64 Jews in Merano in 1945, and about 30 in 1970. [S.D.P.]

The synagogue in Merano, Italy. Courtesy Italian Synagogue Collection, Jerusalem.

°**MERCIER, JEAN (Joannes Mercerus;** d. 1570), French Hebraist. Born in Uzès, near Nîmes, Mercier was a pupil of François Vatable, whom he succeeded as professor of Hebrew at the Collège Royal, Paris, in 1546. Unlike his master, Mercier was a prolific writer, publishing works on Hebrew and Semitic grammar, Latin translations and editions of the Targums, Bible commentaries, and other books of Jewish interest. Owing to his sympathy with the Reformers during the French religious wars, Mercier was obliged to take refuge in Venice in 1567 and, after returning to France, he died of the plague. One of his best-known works was the *Libellus de abbreviaturis Hebraeorum, tam Talmudicorum quam Masoritarum et aliorum rabbinorum* (Paris, 1561), later exploited by Guy *Le Fèvre de la Boderie, which reveals Mercier's interest in the Kabbalah and cites scholars such as *Reuchlin and *Galatinus. However, from remarks in his commentary on Genesis (Geneva, 1598), published after his death by Théodore de Bèze, his enthusiasm for later kabbalistic literature clearly waned. Mercier translated almost the whole of Targum Jonathan b. Uzziel on the Prophets; and he wrote annotations to Santes *Pagnini's *Thesaurus* (*Oẓar Leshon ha-Kodesh;* Lyons, 1575, etc.). His other works include: *Besorat Mattei* (1955), a Hebrew version of the gospel of Matthew; *Luḥei Dikduka Kasda'ah o Arama'ah: Tabulae in grammaticen linguae Chaldaeae* (Paris, 1560); *Aseret ha-Devarim: Decalogus*, with the commentary of Abraham ibn Ezra, in Hebrew and Latin (Lyons, 1566–68); and the posthumous *De notis Hebraeorum liber* (1582), revised by another French Hebraist, Jean Cinqarbres (Quinquarboreus; d. 1587). Among those who studied under Mercier was the Huguenot leader and author Philippe de Mornay (Du Plessis-Mornay, 1549–1623).

Bibliography: F. Secret, *Les Kabbalistes Chrétiens de la Renaissance* (1964), 208–9; Steinschneider, Cat. Bod., 1748.
[G.E.S.]

MERCURY (Mercurius; in talmudic literature מֶרְקוּלִיס, Merkulis), Roman god of merchants and wayfarers, identical with the Greek god Hermes. The rabbis of the Talmud discussed Mercury more than any other pagan deity and apparently considered him almost synonymous with idolatry. Thus, where one *baraita* states, "He who sees Mercurius should recite 'Blessed (be God) who has patience with those who transgress His will'" (Ber. 57b), the parallel source reads simply, "He who sees idolatry ..." (Tosef., *ibid.*, 7[6]:2). Similarly, the Midrash interpreted the general prohibition against erecting statues or pagan monuments (Lev. 26:1) as referring to statues of Mercury on the roads (Sifra, Be-Har, 9:5). The rabbis were also aware of certain modes of worship connected with Mercury, and thus the Mishnah proclaims: "He that throws a stone at a Mercurius is to be stoned, because this is how it is worshiped" (Sanh. 7:6). The trilithon, or three stones erected as part of the Mercurius, was also known, and therefore "R. Ishmael says: Three stones beside a Mercurius, one beside the other, are forbidden, but two are permitted" (Av. Zar. 4:1). So well known, in fact, was Mercurius worship in Palestine that it is mentioned even in popular proverbs: "As one who throws a stone at Mercurius is guilty of idolatry, so one who teaches a wicked pupil is guilty of idolatry" (Tosef. Av. Zar. 6[7]:18). Rabbis were constantly confronted with Mercury, and according to one talmudic account, a Mercurius was erected in the field of R. Simeon, son of Judah the Patriarch, but he succeeded in having it dismantled by the local authorities (TJ, Av. Zar., 4:1, 43d).

Bibliography: S. Lieberman, in: JIR, 36 (1945/46), 366–8; 37 (1946/47), 42–54. [I.G.]

MERCY (Heb. רַחֲמִים), a feeling of compassion tempered with love, which engenders forgiveness and forebearance in man and which stimulates him to deeds of charity and kindness. This quality, inherent in man's attitude toward his loved ones, is an essential characteristic of God who "pitieth like a father" (Ps. 103:13; Isa. 49:15; Ex. 20:6; 34:6; Micah 7:8), and of the descendants of Abraham, renowned for their compassion. As God is known as *Raḥamanah* ("the Merciful"), so are the people of Israel distinguished as "merciful sons of merciful fathers" (Yev. 79a). In accordance with the tradition of the *imitation of God—"as He is merciful so be you merciful" (Shab. 133b)—mercy transcends familial bounds to encompass the entire range of human relationships (Ecclus. 18:13; Gen. R. 33:1). Just as God is bound by His covenant of mercy with His people (Deut. 13:17; 30:3; II Kings 13:23), so is the Jew bound by specific commandments to act mercifully toward the oppressed, the alien, the orphan, the widow, indeed, every living creature (Deut. 22:6; 25:4; Prov. 19:17; Git. 61a; Moses Cordovero, *Tomer Devorah*, ch. 3). The exercise of mercy is the fulfillment of a covenantal obligation, and, in turn, enhances moral sensibility (Suk. 49b; BB 9b). The stress placed upon maintaining charitable institutions in Jewish communal life is an outgrowth of this view of mercy. Man's recognition of God as "the Merciful One" finds its verbal expression in his prayers (Num. 19:19; Ps. 106:1), wherein he implores God to deal compassionately even with the undeserving man (Ex. 34:7; Sot. 14a; Ber. 7a). Because of the imperfection of every mortal, even such righteous men as Abraham are dependent on God's mercy. Recognizing human frailty, God forgives transgressors, especially those who themselves are forgiving (Ecclus. 28:2; Shab. 151b; BM 85a; Ex. R. 12:1). The firm belief that "it is because of the Lord's mercies that we are not consumed, because His compassions fail not" (Lam. 3:22) has sustained the Jewish people through many periods of travail (Hos. 12:7). God's mercifulness does not negate the principle of divine justice, but rather complements it and reinforces its efficacy (see *God, Justice and Mercy of). In analyzing the 13 attributes by which God manifests Himself, the rabbis point to the positive interaction of mercy and justice in God's relation to the world (RH 17a, b; Lev. R. 29:3). This combination of justice and mercy in God is denoted in the two names of God, *Elohim* and YHWH, the first of which designates justice, the second, mercy. God resolves the tension between strict judgment and mercy in favor of the latter (Ps. 89:3; Prov. 20:28). Philo expresses this in his statement: "God's pity is older than his justice" (Deus, 16). Judaism can thus demand of its judges the seemingly contradictory qualities of impartiality and compassion (Ex. 23:3; Ket. 9:2; Sanh. 6b). The principle of mercy assumes an overriding significance in the administration of Jewish law, where rules of equity qualify strict legalism: "... execute the judgment and show mercy and compassion every man to his brother" (Zech. 7:9).

Bibliography: G. F. Moore, *Judaism*, 2 (1946), 154 and 169; C. G. Montefiore and H. Loewe, *A Rabbinic Anthology*, index; Orḥot *Ẓaddikim* (Prague, 1581); I. Heinemann, *Ta'amei ha-Mitzvot be-Sifrut Yisrael*, 2 (1956), index s.v. *ḥemlah*. [Z.Sz.]

MEREMAR (d. 432), Babylonian *amora* of the end of the fourth and beginning of the fifth centuries. According to the *Sefer Kabbalah* of Abraham *ibn Daud, Meremar succeeded Ashi as head of the academy of Sura (427–32). He was a pupil of the elder Ravina (Yev. 75b) and transmitted to the younger Ravina in the name of the latter's father the teachings of Joseph (Ned. 60b) and of Papi (Ned. 90a). He transmitted a statement once in the name of R. Dimi (Git. 19b), but he could hardly have known him personally, since Dimi lived in the first half of the fourth century. Among his colleagues were Mar Zutra (Suk. 45a) and Ashi (Ber. 30a). His pupil the younger Ravina, who visited him later in Sura (Pes. 117b), is mentioned frequently (Shab. 81b; Git. 19b; BM 72b, 104a; et al.), and Aḥa of Difti (Ber. 45b; Ḥul. 47a) is also apparently a pupil of Meremar. He was succeeded as head of the academy by Idi b. Avin. Meremar had a son Judah who was a colleague of Mar b. Rav Ashi and the above-mentioned Aḥa (Ber. 45b).

Bibliography: Hyman, Toledot, 908–10; Ḥ. Albeck, *Mavo la-Talmudim* (1969), 438f. [D.J.B.]

MERGENTHEIM (Bad Mergentheim), city in Wuerttemberg, W. Germany. Jews settled in Mergentheim in the first half of the 13th century; 16 Jews were murdered during the *Rindfleisch massacres of 1298. Jews are mentioned again in 1312; they suffered during persecutions in 1336 and again during those of the *Black Death in 1349 when a number of Jews were martyred. They reappeared in the city, however, in 1355, and during the next century prospered, in large part through moneylending. The Jewish population remained small throughout the 14th and 15th centuries. In 1516 there was only one Jew in the city, but by the end of the century the population rose again. In 1590 a cemetery plot was put to use in Unterbalbach for the Jews of that town as well as those of surrounding communities, including Mergentheim. This cemetery was enlarged in 1702 and remained in continuous use throughout the modern period. During the early 17th century only **Schutzjuden* were permitted in the city; all other Jews were restricted to an eight-day stay. Throughout the century every attempt was made by the municipal authorities to restrict Jewish economic activities. Nonetheless, the Jewish families managed to build a synagogue in 1658; this was enlarged in 1762. By 1700 there were 40 Jewish residents, among them the *Court Jews Calman Model and Hirsch Manasses. At this time Jewish commercial interests included trade in horses, livestock, corn, and wine. By the end of the century these had expanded into wholesale trade and banking. In 1728 Mergentheim became the seat of the **Landrabbiner*, an office filled with distinction between 1742 and 1763 by Naphtali Hirsch Katzenellenbogen (see *Katzenellenbogen Family). In 1799 there were 90 Jews; 110 in 1830; 176 in 1869; 250 in 1886; and 276 in 1900.

On Nov. 9/10, 1938, Jewish stores and homes were demolished; the rabbi, M. Kahn, was physically assaulted and the interior of the synagogue destroyed. By 1939 there were only 87 Jews left in the city. In 1941 and 1942, 41 Jews were deported to concentration camps. The community's Torah scrolls and sacred objects were saved from destruction and turned over to an American army chaplain after the war. In 1946 the synagogue was renovated but shortly thereafter was closed again and subsequently demolished. All that remained of the Mergentheim Jewish community in 1970 was the cemetery in Unterbalbach.

Bibliography: Germ Jud, 2 (1968), 538–9, incl. bibl.; P. Sauer, *Die juedischen Gemeinden in Wuerttemberg und Hohenzollern* (1966), 37–43, incl. bibl.; FJW, 338. [A.Sha.]

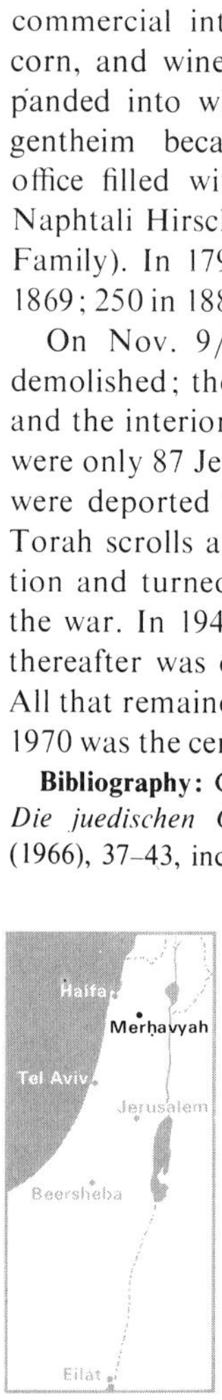

MERḤAVYAH (Heb. מֶרְחַבְיָה; "God's Wide Space"), (1) kibbutz in the Jezreel (Ḥarod) Valley, Israel, E. of Afulah and at the foot of Givat ha-Moreh, affiliated with Kibbutz Arẓi Ha-Shomer Ha-Ẓa'ir. In 1909, the first holding in the Jezreel Valley was acquired at Merḥavyah by Jews through the efforts of Yehoshua *Hankin on behalf of the Palestine Land Development Company. Initially, a group of *Ha-Shomer established a farm there (1911). They persevered in spite of the malaria and the attempts of the Turkish authorities and their Arab neighbors to make them leave the place. Merḥavyah soon became a workers' cooperative according to Franz *Oppenheimer's ideas. During World War I, German pilots set up a temporary camp there. The cooperative dispersed after the war and another group founded a settlement, joined by veterans of the *Jewish Legion, which, however, did not succeed. In 1929 a group of Ha-Shomer ha-Ẓa'ir pioneers from Poland established its kibbutz on the site. It became the movement's organizational center, including the Kibbutz Arẓi secretariat, archives, printing press, and the Sifriat Poalim publishing house. In 1969, the kibbutz, with 550 inhabitants, based its economy on intensive farming, and also had a factory for plastic pipes and a metal workshop. (2) moshav founded on part of the Merḥavyah lands in 1922 by a group of Third Aliyah pioneers from Eastern Europe. Merḥavyah, affiliated with Tenu'at ha-Moshavim in 1969, engaged in intensive agriculture with field and garden crops, dairy cattle and poultry as prominent branches. Its population in 1968 was 42. [E.O.]

Stamp issued by the Israel Post Office in honor of the jubilee of Merḥavyah, designed by M. and G. Shamir. Jerusalem, B. M. Ansbacher Stamp Collection.

MÉRIDA, city in W. Spain, capital of the ancient Lusitania. Located at an important road junction, it had one of the oldest communities in Spain. A folk legend relates that the Jewish settlement there dated from the arrival of captives brought by Titus after the destruction of the Second Temple; the exiles were "the nobles of Jerusalem . . . among them there was a maker of curtains [for synagogue arks] by the name of Baruch who was also skilled in silk-work. These people remained in Mérida where they raised families . . ." (Ibn Daud, *Sefer ha-Qabbalah*, ed. by G. Cohen (1967), 79). There was a Jewish settlement in Mérida in the late Roman and Visigothic periods. A Jewish tombstone inscription in Latin, probably dating from not later than the fourth century, embodies Latin translations of Hebrew formulas commonly found on Jewish tombstones of the period. After the Arab conquest, there was an important Jewish community in Mérida. Its prominent families included those of Ibn Avitur and Ibn al-Balia.

During Christian rule the Jewish quarter was situated near the Church of Santa Catalina, formerly the synagogue. From 1283 the tax paid by the community was 4,000 maravedis. The Jews in Mérida suffered during the 1391 persecutions, and a *Converso group existed there during the 15th century. However the amount of tax paid by the community in 1439 (2,250 maravedis) shows that it was relatively flourishing. Because of its proximity to the Portuguese border, the exiles from Mérida went to Portugal when the Jews were expelled from Spain in 1492.

Bibliography: Ashtor, Korot, 1 (1966²), 230–2; Baer, Urkunden, 2 (1936), index; J. M. Millás, in: *Sefarad*, 5 (1945), 301ff. (cf. plate between 300–1); C. Roth, *ibid.*, 8 (1948), 391–6; J. Ma. Navascués, *ibid.*, 19 (1959), 78–91; Cantera-Millás, Inscripciones, 410ff.; H. Beinart, in: *Estudios*, 3 (1962), 9f., 14, 27–30; Suárez Fernández, Documentos, 69, 81, 257–7; A. Marcos Pon, in: *Rivista di Archeologia Cristiana*, 32 (1956), 249–52 (It.) [H.B.]

MERINIDS (Banu-Marīn), Berber dynasty ruling over *Morocco and part of *Algeria from the mid-13th to the mid-15th centuries. Their center was *Fez, which they rebuilt. The first Merinids had Jewish courtiers, from the Ruqaṣa (or Waqāṣa) family, who had a great influence on the rulers. This aroused the jealousy of the Muslims, who incited the court against the Jews. According to the Arab historians these events occurred in the years 1286–1310. Under Merinid rule the Jewish population increased considerably as a result of the arrival of refugees from Spain, particularly in Fez. In the 15th century there was a great deal of anti-Jewish agitation as a result of the increased fanaticism and propaganda on the part of the sharifs in the wake of Spanish attacks on Morocco. In some places Jews were prohibited to reside near Muslim holy places. As the sharifs (descendants of Muhammad) and the *Wattasid families gained power the situation of the Jews worsened. It temporarily improved when the king ʿAbd al-Ḥaqq (d. 1465) appointed the Jewish physician Hārūn as vizier, thus offending the Muslims. Hārūn is described by the Egyptian merchant ʿAbd al-Bāsiṭ as being intelligent and giving sound advice. Muslim fanatics murdered Hārūn and the king and attacked the Jewish population of Fez in 1465, thus bringing an end to Merinid rule. The events are described by ʿAbd al-Bāsiṭ and in Jewish histories written in the 19th century, which were based upon oral traditions and are referred to in an anonymous poem composed about 15 years after the event. During the Merinid period important Jewish communities existed in Fez and Taza. The Algerian rabbis corresponded with Simeon b. Ẓemaḥ *Duran and his son Solomon Duran in the mid-15th century. Jews were also involved in the negotiations to free the infante Ferdinand of Portugal, who was held captive in Fez in 1438–39.

Bibliography: Hirschberg, Afrikah, 1 (1965), 281–2, 288–94. [Ed.]

MERKABAH MYSTICISM or **MA'ASEH MERKAVAH** (Heb. מַעֲשֵׂה מֶרְכָּבָה), the name given to the first chapter of Ezekiel in Mishnah *Ḥagigah*, 2:1. The term was used by the rabbis to designate the complex of speculations, homilies, and visions connected with the Throne of Glory and the chariot (*merkavah*) which bears it and all that is embodied in this divine world. The term, which does not appear in Ezekiel, is derived from I Chronicles 28:18 and is first found with the meaning of Merkabah mysticism at the end of Ben Sira 49:8: "Ezekiel saw a vision, and described the different orders of the chariot." The Hebrew expression *zanei merkavah* should possibly be interpreted as the different sights of the vision of the chariot in Ezekiel, chapters 1, 8, and 10 (according to S. Spiegel, in: HTR, 24 (1931), 289), or as the different parts of the chariot, which later came to be called "the chambers of the chariot" (*ḥadrei merkavah*). It has been suggested (by Israel Lévi in his commentary on Ben Sira, *L'Ecclesiastique*, 1 (1898), and 2 (1901)) that the text be corrected to *razei merkavah* ("secrets of the chariot"). The divine chariot also engrossed the Qumran sect; one fragment speaks of the angels praising "the pattern of the Throne of the chariot" (Strugnell, in: VT, 7 supplement (1960), 336). In Pharisaic and tannaitic circles Merkabah mysticism became an esoteric tradition (see *Kabbalah) of which different fragments were scattered in the Talmud and the Midrash, interpreting *Ḥagigah* 2:1. This was a study surrounded by a special holiness and a special danger. A *baraita* in *Ḥagigah* 13a, which is ascribed to the first century C.E., relates the story of "A child who was reading at his teacher's home the Book of Ezekiel and he apprehended what *Ḥashmal* was [see Ezek. 1:27, JPS "electrum"], whereupon a fire went forth from *Ḥashmal* and consumed him." Therefore the rabbis sought to conceal the Book of Ezekiel.

Many traditions relate to the involvement of *Johanan b. Zakkai, and later of *Akiva in this study. In the main, details about the conduct of the rabbis in the study of Merkabah are found in the Jerusalem Talmud *Ḥagigah 2* and the Babylonian Talmud, *Shabbat* 80b. According to the manuscript of the latter source the prohibition on lecturing to a group was not always observed and the tradition adds that a transgressor, a Galilean who came to Babylonia, was punished for this and died. In the Babylonian Talmud, *Sukkah* 28a, Merkabah mysticism was put forward as a major subject *(davar gadol)* in contrast to the relatively minor subject of rabbinic casuistry. Traditions of this type are found, for example, in *Berakhot* 7a, *Ḥullin* 91b, *Megillah* 24b, and at the beginning of *Genesis Rabbah*, *Tanḥuma*, *Midrash Tehillim*, *Midrash Rabbah* to Leviticus, Song of Songs, and Ecclesiastes. Several traditions are preserved in *Seder Eliyahu Rabbah* and in small tractates, such as *Avot de-Rabbi Nathan* and *Massekhet Derekh Ereẓ*. In contrast with the scattered fragments of these traditions in exoteric sources, books, and treatises collecting and developing *Ma'aseh Merkavah* according to the trends prevailing in different mystic circles were written at the latest from the fourth century on. Many of the treatises include early material but numerous additions reflect later stages. *Re'iyyot Yeḥezkiel*, the major part of which was found in the Cairo *Genizah* (published in S. A. Wertheimer, *Battei Midrashot*, 2 (1953²), 127–34), depicts historical personalities and the context is that of a fourth-century Midrash. Scraps of a second- or third-century Midrash on the *Ma'aseh Merkavah* were found in pages of the *Genizah* fragments. These sources do not yet show any sign of the pseudepigraphy prevailing in most surviving sources; in these the majority is formalized, and most of the statements are attributed to Akiva or to Ishmael. Several of the texts are written in Aramaic, but most are in Hebrew, in the language of the rabbis. A great deal of material of this type has been published (mostly from manuscripts) in collections of minor Midrashim such as A. Jellinek's *Beit ha-Midrash* (1853–78), S. A. Wertheimer's *Battei Midrashot*, E. Gruenhut's *Sefer ha-Likkutim* (1898–1904), and H. M. Horowitz' *Beit Eked ha-Aggadot* (1881–84). *Sefer Merkavah Shelemah* (1921) includes important material from the manuscript collection of Solomon Musajoff. Some of the texts included in these anthologies are identical, and many are corrupt.

The most important are: (1) *Heikhalot Zutrati* ("Lesser *Heikhalot*") or *Heikhalot R. Akiva*, of which only fragments have been published, mostly without being recognized as belonging to the text. The bulk of it is in a very difficult Aramaic, and part of it is included in *Merkavah Shelemah* as *"Tefillat Keter Nora."* (2) *Heikhalot Rabbati* ("Greater *Heikhalot*," in *Battei Midrashot*, 1 (1950²), 135–63), i.e., the *Heikhalot* of Rabbi Ishmael, in Hebrew. In medieval sources and ancient manuscripts the two books are at times called *Hilkhot Heikhalot*. The division of *Heikhalot Rabbati* into *halakhot* ("laws") is still preserved in several manuscripts, most of which are divided into 30 chapters. Chapters 27–30 include a special tract, found in several manuscripts under the title *Sar Torah*, which was composed much later than the bulk of the work. In the Middle Ages the book was widely known as *Pirkei Heikhalot*. The edition published by Wertheimer includes later additions, some of them Shabbatean (see G. Scholem, in *Zion*, 7 (1942), 184f.). Jellinek's version (in *Beit ha-Midrash*, 3, 1938²) is free of additions but suffers from many corruptions. (3) *Merkavah Rabbah*, part of which is found in *Merkavah Shelemah*, mostly attributed to Ishmael, and partly to Akiva. Perhaps this work contained the most ancient formulation of *Shi'ur Komah* ("the measurement of the body of God"), which later was copied in manuscripts as a separate work that developed into *Sefer ha-Komah*, popular in the Middle Ages (see G. Scholem, *Jewish Gnosticism* ... (1965), 36–42). (4) A version of *Heikhalot* which has no name and was referred to in the Middle Ages as *Ma'aseh Merkavah* (G. Scholem, *ibid.*, 103–17). Here statements of Ishmael and Akiva alternate. (5) Another elaborate treatise on the pattern of *Heikhalot Rabbati*, but with differing and partly unknown new details; fragments have been published from the Cairo *Genizah* by I. Greenwald, *Tarbiz*, 38 (1969), 354–72 (additions *ibid.*, 39 (1970), 216–7; (6) *Hekhalot*, published by Jellinek (in *Beit ha-Midrash* (vol. 1, 1938²), and later as *III Enoch or the Hebrew Book of Enoch* (ed. and trans. by H. Odeberg, 1928). Unfortunately Odeberg chose a later and very corrupt text as a basis for his book, which he intended as a critical edition. The speaker is R. Ishmael and the work is largely made up of revelations about Enoch, who became the angel Metatron, and the host of heavenly angels. This book represents a very different trend from those in *Heikhalot Rabbati* and *Heikhalot Zutrati*. (7) The tractate of *Heikhalot* or *Ma'aseh Merkavah* in *Battei Midrashot* (1 (1950²), 51–62) is a relatively late elaboration, in seven chapters, of the descriptions of the throne and the chariot. In the last three works a literary adaptation was deliberately made in order to eradicate the magical elements, common in the other sources listed above. Apparently they were intended more to be read for edification rather than for practical use by those who delved into the Merkabah. (8) The Tosefta to the Targum of the first chapter of Ezekiel (*Battei Midrashot*, 2 (1953²), 135–40) also belongs to this literature.

A mixture of material on the chariot and creation is found in several additional sources, mainly in *Baraita de-Ma'aseh Bereshit* and in *Otiyyot de-Rabbi Akiva*, both of which appear in several versions. The *Seder Rabbah de-Bereshit* was published in *Battei Midrashot* (1 (1950²), 3–48), and in another version by N. Séd, with a French translation (in REJ, 3–4 (1964), 23–123, 259–305). Here the doctrine of the Merkabah is connected with cosmology and with the doctrine of the seven heavens and the depths. This link is also noticeable in *Otiyyot de-Rabbi Akiva*, but only the longer version contains the traditions on creation and the Merkavah mysticism. Both extant versions, with an important supplement entitled *Midrash Alfa-Betot*, were published in *Battei Midrashot* (2 (1953²), 333–465). M. Margaliot discovered additional and lengthy sections of *Midrash Alfa-Betot* in several unpublished manuscripts. Again, these works were arranged more for the purposes of speculation and reading than for practical use by the mystics. The doctrine of the seven heavens and their angelic hosts, as was developed in Merkabah mysticism and in cosmology, has also definite magical contexts, which are elaborated in the complete version of *Sefer ha-*Razim* (ed. by M. Margalioth, 1967), whose date is still a matter of controversy.

In the second century Jewish converts to Christianity apparently conveyed different aspects of Merkabah mysticism to Christian Gnostics. In the Gnostic literature there were many corruptions of such elements, yet the Jewish character of this material is still evident, especially among the Ophites, in the school of Valentinus, and in several of the Gnostic and Coptic texts discovered within the last 50 years. In the Middle Ages the term *Ma'aseh Merkabah* was used by both philosophers and kabbalists to designate the contents of their teachings but with completely different meanings—metaphysics for the former and mysticism for the latter.

See also *Throne of God.

Bibliography: Scholem, Mysticism, 40–70; idem, *Jewish Gnosticism, Merkabah Mysticism and Talmudic Tradition* (1965); P.

Bloch, in: MGWJ, 37 (1893); idem, in: *Festschrift J. Guttmann* (1915), 113–24; Néher, in: RHR, 140 (1951), 59–82; J. Neusner, *Life of Rabban Yohanan ben Zakkai* (1962), 97–105; M. Smith, in: A. Altmann (ed.), *Biblical and Other Studies* (1963), 142–60; B. Bokser, in: PAAJR, 31 (1965), 1–32; J. Maier, *Vom Kultus zur Gnosis* (1964), 112–48; E. E. Urbach, in: *Studies in Mysticism and Religion presented to G. G. Scholem* (1968), 1–28 (Heb. section).
[G.Sch.]

MERNEPTAH (Egyptian, **Mr-n-Ptḥ;** "the beloved of Ptah"), king of Egypt (reigned c. 1224–1214 B.C.E.). Most scholars believed that Merneptah was the pharaoh of the *Exodus until the discovery of the "Israel" stela at Thebes in 1896. This stela, dated to the fifth year of Merneptah's reign, states in the second line that "Israel is laid waste, his seed is not." Since in this part of the stela "Israel" is the only name containing the Egyptian determinitive sign of a people and not of a land, many scholars have presumed that at this time Israel was a nomadic people located somewhere in or near Palestine. However, others think that this may be merely due to a scribal error. Although the major historical texts of Merneptah deal with the repulsion of a Libyan invasion of the Egyptian Delta in the fifth year of his reign, the concluding lines of the "Israel" stela and his use of the epithet "reducer of Gezer" in a Nubian inscription may attest to the crushing of a revolt in Palestine early in his reign. A few other miscellaneous texts of the period (notably *Papyrus Anastasi* I) show that the Egyptians had a thorough geographic, topographic, and toponymic knowledge of Palestine and Syria, particularly along the main arteries of traffic.

Bibliography: Pritchard, Texts, 376–8, 475–9; A. H. Gardiner, *Egypt of the Pharaohs* (1961), 271ff.; R. O. Faulkner, in: CAH^2, 2 (1966), ch. 23. [Al.R.S.]

MERODACH (Heb. מְרֹדַךְ), a Babylonian god (Jer. 50:2), whose name also enters into the composition of the personal names *Merodach-Baladan (= Berodach-Baladan; II Kings 20:12; Isa. 39:1), *Evil-Merodach (II Kings 25:27; Jer. 52:31), and *Mordecai.

See *Marduk. [Ed.]

MERODACH-BALADAN (Heb. מְרֹדַךְ בַּלְאֲדָן; Akk. ^{d}Marduk-ap-la-iddin; "Marduk has given a son"), Babylonian king (722–710 B.C.E.). Assyrian inscriptions place the origin of Merodach-Baladan in the land of Bît-Iakin, a Chaldean kingdom near the coast of the Persian Gulf ("Sealands"). This is more probable than Merodach-Baladan's claim that he was the son and legal heir of the Babylonian king Erība-Marduk. In 731 B.C.E., Ukin-zer of Bît Amukkani, a Chaldean, wrested the kingship of Babylonia from the pro-Assyrian king Nabu-nadin-zer. Merodach-Baladan, who also had designs on the kingship, supported the Assyrian king Tiglath-Pileser III, against Ukin-zer. He was thus able to strengthen his position among the Chaldean tribes, increase his influence in Babylonia, and forge an alliance with Elam, without interference from Tiglath-Pileser III or Shalmaneser V, both of whom exercised sovereignty over Babylonia (729–722 B.C.E.).

With the death of Shalmaneser V, Merodach-Baladan seized the Babylonian throne (722/721 B.C.E.). This marked the beginning of violent struggles between Merodach-Baladan and the Assyrians. By 720, Sargon II was preparing for war against Merodach-Baladan, who had the support of the Elamites. Conflicting reports have been preserved of this battle, which took place in the plain of Dêr, east of the Tigris. Merodach-Baladan ruled Babylonia until 710, when, through neglect and economic exploitation, he incurred the enmity of the native Babylonian population in the large urban centers which had been loyal to him, although he enjoyed the support of the Chaldean and Babylonian tribes which were largely concentrated in the southern part of the country.

Therefore, it is not surprising that when Sargon II waged war against Merodach-Baladan in 710, he was warmly received by the urban population. Sargon defeated Merodach-Baladan's armies and conquered his fortresses, causing Merodach-Baladan to flee south to Bît-Iakin, where he waited for an opportunity to regain the throne. Seeing in the widespread disturbances that arose after the death of Sargon (705) the opportunity to resume his rule over Babylonia, Merodach-Baladan, in 703, with the support of the Elamites and much of the Babylonian population, reestablished his rule there. He found an ally in *Hezekiah, who was at that time planning a revolt against Assyria, exploiting the latter's political goals for his own benefit. Hezekiah could help Merodach-Baladan by distracting the attention of the Assyrians to the west. This appears to be the background of the biblical narrative concerning the good-will delegation sent by Merodach-Baladan to Hezekiah of Judah in 701 B.C.E. after Sennacherib's campaign there (II Kings 20:12–19; Isa. 39:1–8; II Chron. 32:31). However, it is doubtful that political conditions in Palestine after the Assyrian campaign were favorable for Merodach-Baladan and Hezekiah to form an alliance.

In 703 B.C.E. Sennacherib conducted a campaign against Merodach-Baladan, defeating the Elamite and Babylonian armies surrounding Kish. Merodach-Baladan fled to the "Sealands," and from there continued to rule over Bît-Iakin and the southernmost part of Babylonia. After Sennacherib returned from his campaign in the west in 701, he waged war against Merodach-Baladan (700). The Chaldeans were no match for the Assyrians, and Merodach-Baladan fled further along the Persian Gulf to the region bordering on Elam, dying there in 694. [B.O.]

In the Aggadah. Merodach-Baladan is praised for honoring his father. He added his father's name Baladan to his own when acting as regent during the incapacity of his father, and signed documents in the name of both his father and himself (Sanh. 96a). When told that the sun had reversed its course on the day that Hezekiah miraculously recovered from his illness, he acknowledged the superiority of God, though previously he had been a sun worshiper. He thereupon addressed a letter to Hezekiah the original introduction of which was "Peace to Hezekiah, Peace to the God of Hezekiah, and Peace to Jerusalem." Realizing, however, that he had been disrespectful in not placing God first, he took steps and recalled his messengers in order to change the wording. As a reward he was told: "You took three steps for the honor of My name . . . I will therefore raise up from thee three kings [Nebuchadnezzar, Evil-Merodach, and Belshazzar], who shall rule from one end of the world to the other" (Est. R. 3:1). [Ed.]

Bibliography: H. W. F. Saggs, *The Greatness that was Babylon* (1962), 109–20; J. A. Brinkman, in: *Studies Presented to A. Leo Oppenheim* (1964), 6–53; idem, in: JNES, 24 (1965), 161–6; P. Artzi, in: EM, 5 (1968), 445–9; Ginzberg, Legends, 4 (1913), 275, 300; 6 (1928), 368, 430; I. Y. Ḥasida, *Ishei ha-Tanakh* (1964), 269.

MERON or **MEROM** (Heb. מֵרוֹם). (1) A city appearing in the lists of Canaanite cities conquered by Thutmosis III (no. 12 or 85) and by Ramses II, and later in the list of Tiglath-Pileser III's conquests in 733/2 B.C.E. The "waters of Merom" (Josh. 11:5, 7), near which Joshua defeated Jabin, king of Hazor, and his allies, have been associated for a long time with (2) below. However, some scholars prefer a location slightly more to the north of Tell el-Khureibeh, about 7 mi. (12 km.) northwest of Hazor. Its

identification with Lake Ḥuleh, proposed by earlier scholars, is unfounded. (2) Josephus lists a Meroth, presumably Meron, in Upper Galilee among the villages fortified by him in 66 (Life, 188; Wars, 2:573). Elsewhere, he mentions his locality as marking the western limit of Upper Galilee (Wars, 3:40), but this possibly refers to (1) above, if western is emended to northern. It appears in the form Meiron in talmudic sources (Tosef., Dem. 4:13). The names of several talmudic sages are associated with the place, the most famous one being R. *Simeon b. Yoḥai and his son *Eliezer, who, according to tradition, were buried there. To this day, a popular festival is held at Meron on Lag ba-Omer, and it is mentioned as early as 1522 by R. Moses Basola (see *Hillula de-Rabbi Shimon Bar Yoḥai; *Lag ba-Omer). It was also the seat of the priestly family of Jehoarib, the first in the list of such families; apparently it was settled after the Bar-Kokhba war. The name Meron appears in this connection in various poems of Kalir and other liturgical authors. The present-day village of Meron stands near the remains of an ancient synagogue of the early (Galilean) type, with the facade, a main gate flanked by two side doors, oriented south toward Jerusalem. The western wall was cut into the rock against which the synagogue stands. It is the longest of the Galilean synagogues (24 m.) but in all other respects, the plan is the usual one of a hall with no fixed place for the ark, and two lengthwise rows of columns joined at the back by a transverse row. [M.A.-Y.]

Remains of the facade of the Meron synagogue, second/third century, with the left entrance reconstructed. Courtesy Government Press Office, Tel Aviv.

(3) Moshav in northern Israel, in central Upper Galilee, at the foot of Mt. Meron, affiliated with the Ha-Po'el ha-Mizrachi Moshavim Association. Founded in 1949, near the yeshivah and remnants of the ancient Meron synagogue, by immigrants from Hungary and Czechoslovakia, it specializes in hill farming, with deciduous fruit orchards, vineyards, and poultry as major branches. [E.O.]

Bibliography: J. Aharoni, *Hitnaḥalut Shivtei Yisrael ba-Galil ha-Elyon* (1957), 95ff.; H. Kohl and C. Watzinger, *Antike Synagogen in Galilaea* (1916), 80ff.; Avi-Yonah, Geog, 142; EM, s.v. (incl. bibl.).

MERON (originally **Maierzuk**), **HANNA** (1923–), Israel actress and star of the *Cameri Theater in Tel Aviv. Born in Berlin, she appeared on the German stage and in Fritz Lang's movie "M" as a child before going to Palestine in 1933. She trained at the Habimah Studio, served in a British Army entertainment unit during World War II, and in 1945 joined the newly founded Cameri Theater. She was subsequently responsible for some of the company's

Hanna Meron in the title role of the Cameri Theater's production of *Hedda Gabler,* 1966. Photo J. Agor, Bat Yam.

greatest successes. Her realistic portrayal of the title role in *Pick-Up Girl* shocked some and delighted others. Possessing incisive style and vitality, she was particularly successful in modern, sophisticated comedy. She also distinguished herself in a wide range of parts that included Micka in Moshe Shamir's *He Walked in the Fields,* Eliza in *Pygmalion,* Rosalind in *As You Like It.* Elizabeth in Schiller's *Mary Stuart,* and the title role in Ibsen's *Hedda Gabler.* She was active in the management of the Cameri Theater and helped to shape its policy. In 1968, she played the lead in the musical *Hello Dolly.* In 1970, she lost a leg as a result of an Arab attack in Munich airport on Israel passengers. However, on her recovery she resumed her performances on the Israel stage.

Bibliography: M. Kohansky, *The Hebrew Theater* (1969), index.
[M.K.]

MEROZ (Heb. מֵרוֹז), an unidentified locality, which is cursed in the Song of Deborah (Judg. 5:23) because the inhabitants refused to help the prophetess and Barak in their war against Siserah. Suggested identifications for Meroz are Mazar on Mt. Gilboa or al-Ruz near al-Lajjūn.

Bibliography: J. J. Garstang, *Joshua-Judges* (1931), 396; Abel, Geog, 2 (1938), 385; A. Alt, in: ZAW, 58 (1941), 244ff. [M.A.-Y.]

MERRICK, LEONARD (1864–1939), English novelist, and short-story writer. Born of a London family named Miller, Merrick at first tried to make a career on the stage. His first novel, *Violet Moses* (1891), crude in technique, especially in its portrayal of Jewish types, was not included in his collected works. He won attention in 1898 with *The Actor-Manager,* followed by *The Quaint Companions* (1903), the story of a Negro tenor and his white wife; he also wrote *Conrad in Quest of his Youth* (1903), and *The Position of Peggy Harper* (1911). Merrick's best achievement was his three volumes of short stories, *The Man Who Understood Women* (1908), *A Chair on the Boulevard* (1921), and *While Paris Laughed* (1918), where he excelled in the delineation of French Bohemian types as seen through English eyes. Merrick developed a humorous and satiric style, but his stories were later criticized as too contrived. He never won popularity, but was highly regarded by his fellow writers, a number of whom, including Wells, Hewlett, Barrie and Pinero, wrote prefaces to the collected edition of his works, issued in 1918. [L.S.]

MERSEBURG, city in E. Germany. The Jewish community of Merseburg was one of the oldest in Germany. As early as 973 Emperor Otto II granted Bishop Gisiler authority over "the Jews, the merchants, and the mint in the city." King Henry II renewed this privilege in 1004. In 1234 three Jews lent 80 silver marks to the burgrave of Merseburg. In 1269 the convent of Pegau sold properties to repay debts to Merseburg Jews. In this period R. Ezekiel of Merseburg addressed a number of halakhic queries to *Meir b. Baruch of Rothenburg. Another scholar of the period was R. Samuel of Merseburg. The cemetery of the community dated at least from 1362. The assertion that there was a persecution in 1349–50 rests on a confusion between similar names of localities. In a Hebrew source *Menahem of Merseburg, author of *Nimmukim*, was a leading German rabbi in the second half of the 14th century. In 1434 the Jews of the Merseburg bishopric paid 100 gilders coronation tax to King Sigismund II, in 1438 a 3% income tax to King Albert II, and in 1440 a coronation tax again. At an unknown time thereafter the Jews left the city which underwent economic decline and internal tension. In 1556 the Saxon historian Ernst Brotuff wrote, "Formerly many Jews lived in Merseburg who had their own synagogue with a courtyard in the small street west of the Cathedral chapter." In 1565 Merseburg came under the rule of Saxon, where no Jews were tolerated, and in 1815 under Prussia, which lifted the restrictions in the new territories only in 1847. By 1849, 34 Jews lived in Merseburg; there were 23 in 1871, 16 in 1880, 20 in 1903, 29 in 1905, 20 in 1913 (five families), and 40 in 1925. They were affiliated with the Jewish community in Weissenfels. Records for the years 1933–45 are missing. No Jews settled in Merseburg after 1945.

Bibliography: Salfeld, Martyrol, 78, n. 4; FWJ (1928–9), 293; *Deutsche Reichstagsakten*, publ. by Hist. Kommiss. Bayer, Ak. d. Wissenschaften (1867–1961), 11, 305–7; 13, 465; 14, 671; G. Kisch, *Forschungen zur Rechts-und Sozialgeschichte der Juden*... (1955), 54; Baron, Social[2], 4 (1957), 65–66; T. Oelsner, in: YIVOA, 2 (1958–9), 193; idem, in YLBI 7 (1962), 189; S. Neumann, *Zur Statistik der Juden in Preussen* (1884), 47; H. L. Mursek, *Merseburg* (1963), passim; Germ Jud, 1 (1963), 226–28; 2 (1968), 539–40. [T.O.]

MERSIN (Icel), provincial capital and harbor on the Mediterranean coast in Cilicia (now in Turkey). In ancient times there was a Jewish community in the town. In 107 B.C.E., some of its Jewish inhabitants were transferred to the Bosphorus region by Mithridates IV, king of Pontus. No information is available on the existence of a Jewish community during the Middle Ages. From the 19th century, however, there were a number of Jews in the town who had come from various Turkish towns (especially Salonika) and were engaged in commerce. In 1909, there was a *blood libel, in which one of the heads of the local Gatenyo family was accused of using Greek blood for the baking of *mazzot*. The accusation was withdrawn after the intervention of the Greek patriarch of Istanbul. During the late 1930s, the community consisted of about 35 families. With the establishment of the State of Israel most Jews left Mersin to settle there.

Bibliography: A. Galante, *Histoire des Juifs d'Anatolie*, 2 (1939), 303f. [A.H.]

MERTON, family of British and German industrialists and philanthropists. ABRAHAM LYONS MOSES (1775–1854), whose sons later dropped the name Moses and called themselves Merton, shared in the founding of the Jews' Orphan Asylum and with Henry Solomon endowed a number of almshouses in 1838. RALPH MERTON (1815–1883), his son, settled in Frankfort and joined the metal firm of his father-in-law, Philip Abraham Cohen, after whose death, Merton expanded the company and renamed it Metallgesellschaft. It became one of the most important metal and metalurgical concerns in Germany. He maintained close business relations with his brother, HENRY R. MERTON (1848–1929), who headed Henry R. Merton and Co. of London, which held a dominant place in England parallel to that of Metallgeschellschaft in Germany. Both firms had strong associations with the American Metal Company in New York. Because of its connections with the German firm, the British Merton company was liquidated during World War I and reorganized as two separate firms under the names of H. Gardener and Co. Ltd. and the British Metal Corporation. Both H. Gardener and Co. and the British Metal Corporation were later incorporated into a new company, the Amalgamated Metal Corporation Ltd. Ralph Merton's son, WILLIAM (WILHELM) MERTON (1848–1916), who was born in Frankfort, became the head of the Metallgesellschaft in Frankfort. A generous philanthropist, he founded the Academy for Social and Commercial Sciences which later formed the basis of the University of Frankfort in Frankfort and supported the institution for many years. Under Hitler, the Merton family lost control of the Metallgesellschaft and took refuge in England.

Bibliography: P. H. Emden, *Jews of Britain* (1943), index; P. Stein, *Wilhelm Merton* (1917); C. Fuerstenberg, *Lebensgeschichte eines deutschen Bankiers* (1931). [M.M.B.]

MERTON, ROBERT KING (1910–), U.S. sociologist. Born in Philadelphia, Merton, a student of George R. Simpson, Pitirim Sorokin, and Talcott Parsons, taught at Harvard and Tulane universities and from 1941 at Columbia University. He was president of the American Sociological Association and a member of the Board of the Center for Advanced Study in the Behavioral Sciences at Stanford University.

Merton, whose thinking was influenced by Marx, Durkheim, Simmel, and Weber, is one of the leading American theorists in the social sciences. Essentially, he interpreted the task of sociology as the understanding of the ways in which social structures shape and channel the values, attitudes, and actions of persons. Among the numerous concepts first formulated or felicitously reformulated by Merton are "theories in the middle range" (as against sweeping theories in the grand style), "manifest and latent functions," "self-fulfilling prophecy," the latter elaborating a theorem of W. I. Thomas, and others. His most significant contributions can be located in four areas. First, he provided an objective analysis of various kinds of deviant behavior which has been widely used in research on delinquency, criminality, and social movements. Second, he made significant contributions to the sociology of science, especially about the impact of religion on science, about multiple discoveries in science, rivalry among scientists, and unintended consequences of scientific discoveries. Third, he was interested in the study of bureaucracy, partly refining Durkheim's concept of "anomie," partly complementing Max Weber's structural approach with an analysis of the psychological consequences of bureaucratic organization. Fourth, he advanced the study of adult socialization focusing especially on the activation of attitudes by key personalities and on the concept of the reference group. Generally, he has emphasized the interdependence of theory and research; the collection of essays which he published under the title *Social Theory and Social Structure* (1957[2]) is one of the most influential books in American sociology.

Other significant publications of Merton are *Science, Technology, and Society in Seventeenth Century England* (1938); "The Sociology of Knowledge," in Gurvitch and Moore, *Twentieth Century Sociology* (1945); *Mass Persua-*

sion (1946); *Continuities in Social Research* (1950); he was one of the editors of *Reader in Bureaucracy* (1952); *Focused Interview* (with M. Fiske and P. Kendall, 1952²); *Contemporary Social Problems* (with R. Nisbet, 1966²); *On Theoretic Sociology* (1967); and numerous papers, chiefly dealing with topics of the sociology of knowledge. [W.J.C.]

MERV (Modern **Baīram Alī**), ancient city in Turkmen S.S.R. According to a tradition reported by the 12th-century Muslim historian al-Bayhaqī, Ezra the scribe is said to have traveled from Palestine to Merv, building a synagogue which was still in existence in the 11th century. In connection with tax reforms carried out in the time of the caliph Omar II (717–720), a certain Akiva the Jew, of Merv, is mentioned as being responsible for the collection of taxes from the Jews there. That a Jewish community continued in existence is attested by a disputation held in Merv in 1336 between Christian monks and one of the leaders of the community, and by a *Judeo-Persian dictionary composed there in 1473. Nineteenth-century European travelers (J. *Wolff, E. N. *Adler, etc.) refer to the numbers and occupations of the Jews in Merv. After the forced conversion of the Jewish community in *Meshed (1839), many **jadīd al-Islām* converts found refuge in Merv. No recent information is available.

Bibliography: W. J. Fischel, in: *Zion*, 1 (1935), 49–74; idem, in: HJ, 7 (1945), 29–50. [W.J.F.]

MERZBACHER, family of numismatists. ABRAHAM MERZBACHER (1812–1885), rabbi, banker, numismatist, and bibliophile, was born in Baiersdorf (near Erlangen), Bavaria. After a short career as rabbi of Ansbach, in 1840 he entered the banking firm of J. N. Oberndoerffer at Munich, which was also the leading German coin dealer, and later the house of Rollin et Feuardent in Paris—Rollin was a foremost European expert in numismatics. He exposed the "Becker Counterfeits," a famous case of counterfeiting of ancient coins. He became an expert on Polish medals, and also took a special interest in Jewish coins and medals, building up a valuable collection. In 1873 he retired from business and turned to collecting rare Jewish manuscripts and prints to assist R. N. N. *Rabbinovicz in his monumental *Dikdukei Soferim* (*Variae Lectiones in Mischnam et in Talmud Babylonicum*, 1876ff.), also financing its publication. His library grew to over 4,000 volumes, including 156 manuscripts and 43 incunabula, and eventually became part of the city library of Frankfort (see *Libraries). Merzbacher was also active in the Jewish community, becoming a member of the central committee of the Alliance Israélite Universelle. He also used to practice—gratis—as a *mohel*. Merzbacher's son EUGEN (1845–1903) also became a numismatist. Born in Munich, he took the *shekel as subject for his thesis (*De Siclis* . . . 1873). Merzbacher had a vast knowledge of classical and modern coins, but his main interest was in Jewish numismatics.

Bibliography: *Mitteilungen der Bayerischen Numismatischen Gesellschaft* (1885), fasc. 4., on Abraham; *ibid.* (1903), on Eugen; J. Perles, *Trauerrede . . . A. Merzbacher* (1885); R. N. N. Rabbinovicz, *Ohel Avraham* (1888), catalog of A. Merzbacher's library; L. A. Mayer, *Bibliography of Jewish Numismatics* (1966), nos. 457–60. [A.KI./ED.]

MERZBACHER, GOTTFRIED (1843–1926), German explorer. Born in Baiersdorf, Bavaria, Merzbacher founded a successful fur business in Munich. He retired at 45 to concentrate on the scientific research of mountain areas. He explored in Africa, North America, the Caucasus, and from 1892 climbed mountains in Arabia, Persia, and India. He published the reports of these expeditions in scientific journals. From 1902 to 1908 he climbed the Central Tien Shan range of Asia and his findings were published by the Bavarian Academy of Sciences. His book *Aus den Hochregionen des Kaukasus* (1901) became a classic. [ED.]

MERZBACHER, LEO (1810–1856), first U.S. Reform rabbi. Merzbacher, who was born in Fuerth, Bavaria, studied rabbinics under R. Moses Sofer. He went to the United States in 1841 and took up a teaching position with Congregation Rodeph Shalom in New York. In 1843 Congregation Anshe Chesed, New York, appointed him preacher and teacher at a monthly salary of six dollars. A sermon critical of the practice of married women covering their hair led to nonrenewal of his appointment, whereupon his partisans in the congregation united with the recently formed Cultus Verein to establish Congregation Emanuel with Merzbacher as its rabbi (1845). The reforms made by the new congregation were minimal in character. Confirmation was introduced in 1848 and Merzbacher compiled a shortened prayer book in 1855. He was one of the founders of the Independent Order of True Sisters. Sickness limited Merzbacher's activities, and he seems to have had little impact either on his own congregation or on the New York Jewish community. [S.D.T.]

MESENE, the land of southern Mesopotamia extending from about 24 mi. (40 km.) below Kut al-Amāra to the Persian Gulf. This area was also called Characene, a term giving political identification derived from Charax Spasinu, name of the fortified capital city of the district. During the late Middle Ages the name was replaced by that of the new capital and port of the district, Basra. The economy of Charax depended on her role as the main port and relay point for east-west trade on the upper Persian Gulf. During the first and second centuries C.E. overland trade developed via Mesene with the Nabatean city of *Petra and with the Syrian desert emporium of Palmyra (Tadmor), and through these centers with the rich Roman west.

A Jewish community existed in Mesene from at least the late Parthian period. During the reign of Artabanus V (209–27 C.E.) a Jewish merchant of Meṣhān converted Izates, prince of Adiabene, to Judaism (see *Charax Spasinu). At this time a second Jewish merchant of Meṣhān similarly converted a number of women of that city (Jos., Ant. 20:2, 4).

In talmudic sources of the third century C.E. the Jews of Babylonia refer to Mesenean Jews as imprudent (Kid. 49b), unfit and of tainted descent (Kid. 71b), since "whosoever did not know his family and his tribe made his way there" (Yev. 17a). Marriage between Babylonian Jews and the Jews of the northern Mesenean city of *Apamea was forbidden (Kid. 71b). The city of Meṣhān (Charax) is described as being lower than hell, and Harpania, a second city of Mesene (perhaps a variant spelling of Apamea), as being lower still than Meṣhān (Yev. 17a). This hostility shown by Babylonian Jews may have been caused, in part, by the adoption of elements of Mandeanism by the Jews of Mesene. It has also been noted that the practice of allowing the Jewish dead of Harpania to lie while the shroud was woven (Sanh. 48b) would indicate an adaptation by the Jews of that city of the Zoroastrian practice of exposing a corpse before burial (see Obermeyer, 197). A possible preference by Mesenean Jews for the Jerusalem Talmud may have further contributed to their being disliked by the Jews of Babylonia.

Bibliography: Neubauer, Géogr, 325, 329, 382; E. Peterson, in: ZNW, 27 (1928), 55–98; J. Obermeyer, *Die Landschaft Babylonien* . . . (1929), index; S. Nodelman, in: *Berytus*, 13 (1960); J. Hansman, in: *Iranica Antiqua*, 8 (1967). [ED.]

MESHA (Heb. מֵישַׁע), king of Moab in the ninth century B.C.E. (see *Moab). The name is formed from the root *yšʿ*, "to deliver, save." In II Kings 3:4 it is stated that Mesha was a sheep breeder. He was subjugated by *Ahab and paid him tribute. After Ahab's death, the king of Moab, most likely Mesha, revolted and ceased paying tribute (II Kings 3:4–5; cf. II Kings 1:1). *Jehoram son of Ahab conducted a military campaign against Moab to subjugate it (II Kings 3:6ff.).

Most of the information on Mesha is contained in the stele which he erected at Dibon (see *Mesha Stele). The first three lines of the inscription mention that Mesha's father Chemoshyat, whose name is known from a stele found in Kerak (Kir of Moab; W. L. Reed and F. V. Winnett, in: BASOR, 172 (1963), 6), ruled over Moab for 30 years, and that Mesha succeeded him. Mesha resided at Dibon, situated north of Arnon, and called himself "King of Moab, the Dibonite." The stele then relates how *Omri, king of Israel, took possession of the land of Medeba in the northern part of the plain, and subjugated Moab "his days and a part of the days of his son, forty years." The phrase "his son" obviously refers to Ahab. However, all the days of Omri and Ahab together are considerably fewer than 40 years. Moreover, the Bible relates that the king of Moab revolted after Ahab's death, rather than during his lifetime. Among the many attempts to explain the discrepancy between what is recorded in the Bible and in the Mesha Inscription, the most acceptable theory is that the number 40 is not to be taken literally, but is the conventional length of a generation (cf. Num. 32:13; Ps. 95:10). Mesha apparently revolted twice, once during the reign of Omri's son Ahab, as is related in the stele, and once after Ahab's death, as is stated in the Bible. If this theory is correct, the following sequence of events can be proposed: Moab revolted against Israel following the division of Solomon's kingdom, or at the latest in the days of Baasha. The Moabites even reached north of the Arnon and captured the plateau, including the land of Medeba. The king's residence was established at Dibon, at the latest in the days of Mesha's father. Omri waged war against Moab, recapturing Medeba and several cities in the plateau. For various reasons, the Israelite king preferred to leave Dibon in Moabite hands and was content to receive yearly tribute as a token of subjugation. In Ahab's time, Mesha revolted against Israel. It is not clear if Ahab fought against Mesha, since the stele contains the expression "king of Israel" (lines 10–11, 18), which may refer to either Omri or Ahab. It is more likely that the reference is to Omri (cf. line 7), since Ahab was occupied with wars against the Arameans (but see *Ben-Hadad). Mesha first concentrated upon preparing fortifications for a confrontation with Israel. He secured communications between Dibon and Moab proper by building roads across the Arnon (line 26). He fortified Aroer, strengthened the acropolis (*qarḥoh*) of Dibon, and prepared the city for withstanding a siege by digging ditches and building a cistern (*ʾswḥ*; vocalization uncertain) inside the city. Upon the death of Ahab, Mesha exploited Israel's defeat at Ramoth-Gilead and the weakness of *Ahaziah son of Ahab; he erupted northward, capturing all the cities of the plain. He reached Nebo, which he destroyed, killing its population of 7,000 people, "because I consecrated it to Ashtar-Chemosh." Jehoram, king of Israel, combined forces with *Jehoshaphat, king of Judah, and the king of Edom and invaded Moab from the south, through Edom (II Kings 3:20), reaching the city of Kir-Hareseth in the heart of Moab. The battle in the city of Horonaim in southern Moab and its capture by Mesha, which is related at the end of the inscription, should be connected with this campaign. The biblical account agrees, stating that Jehoram's campaign ended in failure and that he was forced to withdraw without conquering Moab. The Bible attributes the failure to a ritual act performed by the king of Moab: "Then he took his eldest son that should have reigned in his stead and offered him for a burnt offering upon the wall. And there came great wrath upon Israel; and they departed from him, and returned to their own land" (II Kings 3:27).

Bibliography: Y. Liver, in: PEQ, 99 (1967), 14–31. [B.O.]

MESHA STELE, an inscribed basalt stele, measuring about 40 inches (one meter) high and about 28 inches (70 centimeters) wide, erected by *Mesha, king of Moab, at Dibon (today, Dhībân), probably in the third quarter of the ninth century, B.C.E. The shape of the stele, with a flat base and rounded top, is characteristic of those erected by kings of that period. Unlike many other memorial inscriptions, the Mesha stele has no relief on the upper part. It was found at Dibon in 1868 by F. A. Klein, a Prussian missionary. Prior to its acquisition by the Louvre, it was smashed by Bedouins, who, observing the great interest it aroused among Europeans, assumed that it contained a treasure or ghost. The inscription was deciphered with the aid of a squeeze made by Clermont-Ganneau of all but the last few lines. The language of the inscription is Moabite, which is closely related to Hebrew, though it diverges from it in several grammatical features. The alphabetic Canaanite-Hebrew script is well shaped and clear; the words are separated from each other by dots, and the sentences by vertical lines. Mesha dedicated the stele to his deity Chemosh out of gratitude for the latter's deliverance of the

Cast of the Mesha stele. Jerusalem, Rockefeller Museum, Israel Department of Antiquities. Photo Zev Radovan, Jerusalem.

Moabites from Israelite rule, and for his help in the conquest of the plain. The stele (lines 4–9) relates, "As for Omri, king of Israel, he humbled Moab many years [lit. days], for Chemosh was angry with his land. And his son followed him and he also said 'I will humble Moab.' In my time he spoke [thus], but I have triumphed over him and over his house, while Israel hath perished forever" (cf. II Kings 1:1; 3:4–5). However, by describing the events in the first person, Mesha's real intention was probably to perpetuate his own victories over Israel.

Bibliography: A. H. Van Zyl, *The Moabites* (1960), 247ff., incl. bibl.; W. F. Albright, in: JQR, 35 (1944/45), 247–70; EM, 4 (1962), 925–9, incl. bibl.; Pritchard, Texts, 320–1; H. Donner and W. Roellig, *Kanaanaeische und aramaeische Inschriften*, 1 (1962), 33; 2 (1964), 168–79.

[B.O.]

MESHECH (Heb. מֶשֶׁךְ), a nation from Asia Minor, identified today with Muški of Assyrian souces (beginning about the 12th century B.C.E.) and with Μόσχοι of classical sources. In the table of nations (Gen. 10:2; I Chron. 1:5) Meshech appears after Javan and Tubal as one of the sons of Japheth. Meshech, again with Javan and Tubal, is mentioned in Ezekiel 17:13 as slave traders and merchants of copperware. This description appears to be historically accurate. The mention of Meshech together with Tubal and *Gog (Ezek. 38:2–3; 39:1), derives from the legend about Gog which gained currency in the time of Ezekiel.

Bibliography: E. A. Speiser, *Genesis* (1964), 66; R. D. Barnett, in: CAH², vol. 2, ch. 30 (1966), incl. bibl.; EM, 5 (1968), 531–2, incl. bibl.

[Ed.]

MESHED (Ar. **Mashhad**), capital of Khurasan, N.E. Iran. In 1740 Nādir Shāh moved 40 Jewish families from the city of *Kazvin to Meshed, a holy city of Shi'ite Islam. The small community began to flourish under his protection, attracting an increasing number of Jews from other Persian communities, and was the home of the outstanding scholar, poet, and philosopher Siman Tov *Melamed (see *Judeo-Persian). With the assassination of Nādir Shāh in 1747, the Jews of Meshed were exposed to persecution, and after the ascent of the Qājar dynasty toward the end of the 18th century their situation became precarious. Meshed did not escape the wave of annihilation which swept the Jewish communities of Tabriz, Maragheh (Rizaiyeh), Urmia, and Lar between 1834 and 1848. In March 1839 (Nisan 12, 5599), on the day of mourning for Hussein, grandson of Muhammad, a fanatical mob, incited by a false rumor,

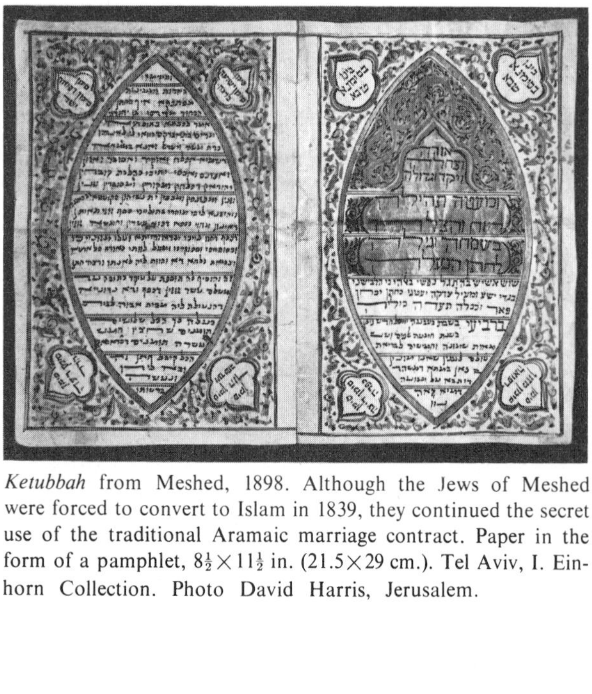

Ketubbah from Meshed, 1898. Although the Jews of Meshed were forced to convert to Islam in 1839, they continued the secret use of the traditional Aramaic marriage contract. Paper in the form of a pamphlet, 8½×11½ in. (21.5×29 cm.). Tel Aviv, I. Einhorn Collection. Photo David Harris, Jerusalem.

poured into the Jewish quarter, burned the synagogue, and destroyed the scrolls of the Law. They would have murdered the entire Jewish community had the Muslim leaders not promised that all the Jews of Meshed would be converted to Islam. With this forced conversion, the Jewish community in Meshed officially ceased to exist and the Jews became **Jadīd al-Islām* (sing.) or New Muslims.

Once the disorders had died down, Meshed Jews continued secretly to practice Jewish observances in almost every detail. Officially however, they were Muslim and some of their leaders were urged by Muslim religious leaders to make the pilgrimage to Mecca and Medina in order to demonstrate their allegiance to Islam. The forced conversion led to a continuous wave of migration to other parts of the Jewish Diaspora, east and west. *Jādidim* (Hebraized form of the Ar. *Jadīd*) fled to Herat and other cities in Afghanistan, to Turkestan, Samarkand, and Bukhara, establishing new settlements or augmenting existing ones, and also reached Bombay, London, and Jerusalem. The latter became the home of the largest and most important colony of *Jadidim*, with two synagogues of their own. During the British Mandate and increasingly after the creation of the State of Israel, Meshed Jews settled in Jerusalem.

[W.J.F.]

Contemporary Period. Most of the converted Jews of Meshed went to Israel by 1955, and there is no exact figure of the number who remained, though it is estimated at about 2,000. The 1956 census in Iran showed 400 Jews, as the forced converts were counted as Muslims, who had a synagogue and practiced their religion openly, but their school was closed in around 1954. The descendants of the forced converts, however, have continued to pray in secret as Jews, while openly practicing Muslim religious ceremonies and appearing to be Muslims until they could leave for Israel. About 2,000 of the descendants of the forced converts have been living in Teheran, where they have maintained several separate synagogues. The converted Jews of Meshed engaged mainly in trade, and among them were a number of wealthy families. They were noted for their willingness to help each other and their brethren outside the city. Despite the fact that their ancestors had zealously observed the Jewish faith in secret for the past 130 years, the younger generation has tended to abandon Judaism, and there have been cases of mixed marriages. Those who resettled in Israel have become an integral part of the Jewish population of the country and one of them, Mordekhai Zar (b. 1914) a former *Jadīd* of Meshed (who lived a double religious life in his youth), was a labor member of the Knesset from 1961 and deputy speaker from 1969.

[H.J.C.]

Bibliography: Fischel, in: *Zion*, 1 (1935), 49–74; idem, in: *Commentary*, 7 (1949), 28–33; I. Ben-Zvi, *Meḥkarim u-Mekorot* (1966), 319–34.

MESHULLAM BEN JACOB OF LUNEL (12th century), Provençal scholar. A master of *halakhah*, Meshullam also occupied himself with secular studies. He was a wealthy man and philanthropist, and together with his sons provided for the support and maintenance of the disciples and scholars who flocked to his *bet ha-midrash*. Benjamin of Tudela describes him and his five sons as being "great and wealthy scholars, Joseph, Isaac, Jacob, Aaron, and Asher the ascetic, who had no concern with worldly matters, but devoted himself to study day and night, fasting and refraining from eating meat, and an outstanding talmudist, together with their brother-in-law Moses" (*The Itinerary of Benjamin of Tudela*, ed. by E. N. Adler (1907), 3). Around them there gathered an outstanding group of talmudic scholars and seekers after knowledge, who became known as "the company of Lunel." In consequence *Lunel became famous as an important center of study. Many of them and their disciples were among the great scholars of that generation, including Samuel b. Moses, "the lion of the group," who apparently was head of the *bet din*, *Abraham b. Isaac of Narbonne, author of *Ha-Eshkol*, his son-in-law *Abraham b. David of Posquières, and *Samuel b. David. This center even attracted scholars from Spain. As Judah ibn *Tibbon notes, Meshullam was distinguished in fields of study other than Talmud. This was in contrast to Jewish scholars before him in Christian countries, who occupied themselves essentially with the Talmud, either because they regarded it as their sole avocation or because of lack of books on general sciences (which were then written in Arabic). Meshullam sponsored the translation of books on grammar, theology, rhetoric, ethics, and parables (cf. introduction to the *Ḥovot ha-Levavot* of *Baḥya b. Joseph ibn Paquda, translated by Ibn Tibbon on the instruction of Meshullam). Meshullam himself also composed halakhic works, as well as books on "parables of wisdom and ethics" that are no longer extant. He is known to have written a book called *Issur Mashehu*, on minute quantities of forbidden foods, mentioned by Solomon b. Abraham *Adret in his novellae to *Ḥullin* (93b Jerusalem, 1 (1963), ed. 227). From a fragment of the *Issur Mashehu* of Abraham b. David of Posquières published by S. Assaf (*Sifran shel Rishonim* (1935), 185–98) "which I wrote before my teacher Meshullam" it is clear that Abraham b. David wrote it in answer to a work of the same title by Meshullam so as to discuss critically the latter's views. It was recently discovered and published by Y. Kafaḥ in the responsa of the Rabad which he edited (1964, 241ff. no. 207). According to Solomon ibn Verga (in *Shevet Yehudah*) Meshullam died in 1170, but the date is not certain.

Bibliography: Meshullam b. Moses of Béziers, *Sefer ha-Hashlamah le-Seder Nezikin*, ed. by J. Lubetzki, 1 (1885), introd., VI; Abraham b. Isaac of Narbonne, *Sefer ha-Eshkol*, ed. by S. Albeck, 1 (1935), introd., 10; Benedikt, in: *Tarbiz*, 22 (1950/51), 100f.; S. Assaf, *Sifran shel Rishonim* (1935), 185f.; I. Twersky, *Rabad of Posquières* (1962), index. [S.Z.H.]

MESHULLAM BEN KALONYMUS (10th–11th century), rabbi and *paytan*. Born into a rabbinical family from *Lucca, his grandfather was R. Moses the Elder who was taught by Abu Aaron the secrets of the Kabbalah. Meshullam's father (see *Kalonymus family) was a well-known talmudic scholar and *paytan*. His teacher was *Solomon b. Judah ha-Bavli. Meshullam himself was a famous talmudist and liturgical poet, often called "the Great." His works include a commentary on *Ethics of the Fathers*, of which only one extract is extant; responsa, dealing with explanations of talmudic passages and with matrimonial, legal, and ritual matters and including a responsum against the Karaites; and liturgical poems, of which the best known are a composition for the morning service of the Day of Atonement and "*Ammiẓ Ko'aḥ*," the version of the **Avodah* adopted in the Ashkenazi rite. His responsa, apart from their intrinsic value, are important sources of information for the social and economic history of the Jewish communities of pre-Crusade Europe. He is the first author in Europe to mention the commercial law of Ma'arufya. His answers are usually brief and concise, and devoid of argumentation. His decisions are based mainly on the Babylonian Talmud but also refer to the writings of the *geonim*. Both *Gershom Me'or ha-Golah and *Rashi held Meshullam in high regard. The center of Meshullam's activity is uncertain. Responsa by *Sherira and *Ḥai Gaon point to Italy as does the title "of Rome"

Part of the tombstone of Meshullam ben Kalonymus, Mainz, 1020. Mainz, Mittelrheinisches Landesmuseum.

sometimes given him. Later he settled in Mainz where his tombstone was discovered. His works helped to establish Rhineland scholarship and stimulated the development in France and Germany of a powerful poetical tradition.

Bibliography: Rapoport, in: *Bikkurei ha-Ittim*, 10 (1829), 40–41, 111; 11 (1830), 100; Carmoly, in: *Israelitische Annalen*, 1 (1839), 222; Schirmann, Italyah, 27–36; Roth, Dark Ages, index; Zunz, Vortraege, 378; Zunz, Lit Poesie, 107; Wiener, in: MGWJ, 3 (1854), 236–7; Gross, *ibid.*, 27 (1878), 249–50; Davidson, Oẓar, 4 (1933), 451 (index); *Ginzei Schechter*, 2 (1929), 194–235, 279–87. [Yo.D.]

MESHULLAM BEN MOSES (c.1175–c.1250), scholar of Béziers and one of the most prominent scholars of Provence in the 13th century. Meshullam, born in Lunel into one of the distinguished families of Provençal Jewry, went to Béziers with his father, Moses b. Judah, one of the leaders of the community and friend of *Abraham b. David of Posquières and *Zerahiah ha-Levi Gerondi. Meshullam's maternal grandfather was *Meshullam b. Jacob of Lunel. His sister's son was *Meir b. Simeon ha-Me'ili of Narbonne, author of *Ha-Me'orot*. Among Meshullam's grandsons were the renowned 14th-century talmudists and scholars of the *Lattes family. Meshullam typifies the remarkable Provençal blending of Torah and general culture. He is known to have taken a definite stand against the new trend favoring the study of Kabbalah, then making inroads among the Jews of Provence, and supported his sister's son, Meir, in his opposition to the *Sefer ha-*Bahir*. Meshullam was highly regarded in France and Spain, and even *Naḥmanides, when he complained to Meshullam of the baseless aspersions emanating from Béziers against the family of Jonah *Gerondi, couched his remarks in highly respectful terms (*Kitvei ha-Ramban*, ed. by C. B. Chavel (1963), 360–4). There is a reference to correspondence between them in Naḥmanides' novellae to the tractate *Eruvin* (still in manuscripts). *Jedaiah ha-Penini, who studied in Meshullam's yeshivah at the age of 15, has left an account of his master's eminence and wisdom, along with a very detailed and impressive description of the program of study in the yeshivah which closed with Meshullam's death.

Meshullam is chiefly renowned for his *Sefer ha-Hashlamah,* designed to complete the *halakhot* of Isaac *Alfasi, explaining its difficult passages, adding *halakhot* that do not appear in it, updating it with the Provençal tradition of scholarship, and dealing with criticisms of the work, including those of *Zerahiah ha-Levi Gerondi in his *Ha-Ma'or*—all this in order to give it uncontested authority. Indeed, Menahem *Me'iri, who wrote more than 50 years later, refers to Alfasi in the same breath as the *Sefer ha-Hashlamah,* thus showing it to be the standard version of Alfasi in his locality (see introduction to Meiri's commentary on *Avot* ed. by B.Z. Prag, 1964). Meshullam based his work chiefly upon the teachings of the earlier scholars of Provence, and shows especially high regard for Abraham b. David of Posquières, though he does not hesitate to disagree with him upon occasion.

Publication of *Sefer ha-Hashlamah* was begun during the last century and the greater part of it, comprising the orders *Mo'ed* and *Nezikin,* and the tractate *Ḥullin,* has already appeared. Those chiefly responsible for its publication were: Judah *Lubetzky—*Nezikin* (Paris, 1885–87; Warsaw, 1907), with an extensive commentary, *Torat ha-Hashlamah;* Moses Herschler in the series *Ginzei Rishonim* (1962–), and Abraham Ḥaputa, who also added an extensive commentary, *Reshit ha-Hashlamah* (1961–). The *Sefer ha-Hashlamah Yevamot* was published in the Vilna (Romm) edition of the Talmud under the title *Tosafot Ḥad mi-Kamai.* Some of Meshullam's *hassagot* on Maimonides to *Shabbat, Eruvin,* and *Shevu'ot* in (J. Lubetzky, *Bidkei Battim,* 1896), show he was apparently unaware of Abraham b. David's *hassagot* on Maimonides.

Bibliography: Meshullam b. Moses of Béziers, *Sefer ha-Hashlamah le-Seder Nezikin,* ed. by J. Lubetsky, 1 (1885), introd.; idem, *Bidkei Battim* (1896); Neubauer, in REJ, 20 (1890), 244–8; I. Twersky, *Rabad of Posquières* (1965), 252f.

[I.T.-S.]

MESHULLAM BEN NATHAN OF MELUN (12th century), talmudist in northern France. Meshullam was born in Narbonne, where he eventually became a member of the *bet din* of *Abraham b. Isaac of Narbonne. From there he went to head the community of Melun. Meshullam became involved in a long and bitter dispute with Jacob *Tam, who accused him of abrogating ancient customs and replacing them with new ones; of introducing many lenient rulings; of exaggerated emendment of the text of the Talmud; of slighting *Rashi and French scholars in general; and of unwarranted independence in *halakhah.* Tam cited, among other instances, permitting a gentile to touch wine-vinegar, permitting ritual immersion for women in the daytime because of the danger from attacks by gentiles at night (an accusation denied by Meshullam), and abrogating the blessing over the Sabbath candles. Tam's complaint to the community of Melun resulted in a lengthy correspondence between the two men, which has in part been preserved (*Sefer ha-Yashar le-Rabbenu Tam,* Responsa vol. ed. by F. Rosenthal (1898), nos. 43–50). Meshullam defended himself vigorously against all the accusations of Tam, accusing him (though in much milder language) of essentially the same things and refusing to accept the slightest external interference in matters of Torah. The fact that Meshullam could base himself on existing halakhic traditions which differed in origin from those held by Tam, and his mastery of the Talmud, stood him in good stead in his dispute with Tam, the greatest scholar of his generation. Meshullam is frequently mentioned in the printed *tosafot.* Meshullam's son, Nathan, and his descendants after him (with the family name of Official) were renowned as the family of the *Mekanne'im* ("Zealots") because of its many noted polemists, who, for several generations, engaged in disputes with high church dignitaries.

Bibliography: Kahn, in: REJ, 1 (1880), 222–46; 3 (1881), 1–38; Urbach, *ibid.,* 100 (1935), 49–77; Urbach, Tosafot, 62–71 and index; Z. Malter, in: *Mi-Mizraḥ u-mi-Ma'arav,* 4 (1899), 9–16; J. Rosenthal, in: *Aresheth,* 2 (1960), 142–3.

[I.T.-S.]

MESHULLAM PHOEBUS BEN ISRAEL SAMUEL (1547–1617), Polish rabbi. Meshullam's exact birthplace is unknown. Before becoming *av bet din* in Cracow, he held a similar position in Brest-Litovsk. It appears that in 1590, while in Brest-Litovsk, he introduced regulations to prevent work being done on the Sabbath. These regulations afford an insight into the economic situation of the Jews of Poland and Lithuania in the 16th and 17th centuries. They were first published in an abbreviated form in *Kevod Ḥakhamim* (Venice, 1700) by Judah Leib Poḥovitz, and then more fully by I. Sonne (see bibliography). Although the year of Meshullam's arrival in Cracow is not certain, his presence there is recorded in 1609, when he gave a ruling as to which *haftarah* should be recited when the New Moon of Av falls on a Sabbath. While in Cracow, he participated in the meetings of the *Council of Four Lands, and it is possible that even the aforementioned regulations gained the approval of the council. A recognized and respected halakhic authority, Meshullam gave numerous rulings on synagogue customs. The most famous of his disciples was Joel *Sirkes. Meshullam had a wide knowledge of languages other than Hebrew, and was well versed in medical matters, as is evident in his responsa on these subjects. Nothing is known of his family and children except that he had two sons: SAMUEL, who became *av bet din* in Przemysl, and JOSEPH (d. 1648), who was *av bet din* in Cracow. Meshullam died in Cracow.

Few of his works remain but his responsa are found in contemporary works, including those of *Meir b. Gedaliah of Lublin, in *Turei Zahav* by *David b. Samuel ha-Levi, and in *Bayit Ḥadash* by Joel Sirkes. Meshullam's work, *Sefer Shemot Gittin,* on the names used in bills of divorce, is mentioned by Abraham *Rapaport in his *Eitan ha-Ezraḥi.* Meshullam also edited responsa by Moses b. Isaac *Mintz from manuscripts in his possession.

Bibliography: J. M. Zunz, *Ir ha-Ẓedek* (1874), 49–52; Sonne, in: *Horeb,* 2 (1935), 237–46; Halpern, Pinkas, 22, 63, 456, 483–8; Ben-Sasson, in: *Zion,* 21 (1956), 183–206; Feldman, *ibid.,* 34 (1969), 90–97; Lewin, in: *Sinai,* 65 (1969), 109.

[ED.]

MESHULLAM ZALMAN HA-KOHEN (late 18th and early 19th century), preacher and moralist in Fuerth, Bavaria. His first work, *Bigdei Kehunnah* ("Priestly Garments," Fuerth, 1807), contains responsa on various laws in the Shulḥan Arukh and *novellae on the talmudic tractates *Gittin* and *Bava Meẓia. Naḥalat Avot* ("Heritage of our Fathers," Fuerth, 1811), his second work, was written when the author was 70 years old. Utilizing the form of the *ethical will, the book was intended to educate both the author's children and pupils. After an introduction in rhymed prose, the work comprises sermons on ethical subjects—both personal and social—the commandments, and devotion to God. [ED.]

MESHWI (or **Misḥawayh,** a form of Moses) **AL-ʿUKBARĪ** (second half of the ninth century), Jewish sectarian of Ukbara, near Baghdad. Later *Karaites refer to him as Meshwi Ba'albaki, since his followers emigrated from Babylonia to Syria in the tenth century. No details are known of the life of Meshwi, founder of a sectarian movement whose members are known as Misḥawayhites. No writings of his are known, and his opinions and teachings have been preserved only in the writings of his opponents. His teachings differed in many ways from Rabbinic and Karaite Judaism. This is particularly evident in his calendar computations. According to Meshwi the first day of Passover must always fall on a Thursday, Shavuot on a Sunday, and the Day of Atonement on a Saturday. As he claimed that the day spanned from dawn to dawn, his followers observed the Sabbath from the dawn of Saturday to the dawn of Sunday. He also claimed that no sacrifices were offered at the Tabernacle on Saturdays, interpreting Numbers 28:10 to mean that the burnt-offering must be sacrificed on Friday for Saturday. Many deviations from tradition were ascribed to him by his opponents: in his commentary on Leviticus Saadiah Gaon refers to Meshwi's permitting the fat of animals which were not sacrificed at the altar to be eaten. The 11th-century Karaite scholar, Tobias b. Moses, attacked him as a heretic for declaring many pentateuchal laws void. Meshwi may have been influenced by his contemporary, the heretic Hiwi al-Balkhī. Remnants of the Mishawayhites survived until the 12th century; *Benjamin of Tudela, who met them in Cyprus, relates their heretical manner of observing the Sabbath, and Abraham *ibn Ezra, in his commentary on Exodus 16:24 and in his epistle on the Sabbath, refers to their interpretation of Genesis 1:5 and their observance of the Sabbath. It is striking that the interpretation of *Samuel ben Meir (Rashbam) of Gen. 1:5 corresponds to that of Meshwi.

Bibliography: Ankori, *Karaites in Byzantium* (1959), 372–417 and index; S. A. Poznański, in: REJ, 34 (1897), 161–91; L. Nemoy, in: HUCA, 7 (1930), 330, 389–90; Y. Rosenthal, in: *YIVO-Bleter*, 21 (1943), 79.

[J.M.R.]

MESILLAT ZION (Heb. מְסִלַּת צִיּוֹן; "Roadway to Zion"), moshav affiliated with Tenu'at ha-Moshavim in the foothills of Judea on the highway leading to Jerusalem, near the entrance to the Sha'ar ha-Gai gorge (the moshav's initial name was Sha'ar ha-Gai). Mesillat Zion was founded in 1950 initially as a "work village" whose inhabitants were employed in land reclamation and in planting the nearby Martyrs' Forest and other woodlands. Its inhabitants originate from Cochin, India. The moshav's economy is based on vineyards, deciduous fruit orchards, poultry, and flowers.

[E.O.]

MESILLOT (Heb. מְסִלּוֹת; "Roadways"), kibbutz in central Israel, at the foot of Mt. Gilboa, affiliated with Kibbutz Arẓi Ha-Shomer ha-Ẓa'ir. It was founded in 1938 as a tower and stockade village by pioneers from Bulgaria who had participated in establishing *Ma'oz Ḥayyim and worked there. The kibbutz' economy is based on intensive field crops, fruit orchards, dairy cattle, carp ponds, and poultry, and on a factory for steel cables. [E.O.]

MESKIN, AHARON (1898–), Israel actor, a founding member of *Habimah. Meskin was a Russian government official, when in 1917, he heard of the establishment of the Habimah studio in Moscow and applied for admission. He played his first major role in 1924 as *The Golem* in H. Leivick's play of that name and from that time ranked as a leading member of the company. He subsequently played many leading roles, both in Israel and on tour abroad, among his most effective being Othello and Shylock. A tall man with a rough-hewn face and a striking deep voice, Meskin endowed his roles with dignity and humanity. In 1960 he was awarded the Israel Prize. He was the first chairman of the Israel section of the International Theater Institute.

Bibliography: D. Lazar, *Rashim be-Yisrael*, 2 (1955), 297–301.

[M.K.]

MESOPOTAMIA, see Supplementary Entries.

MESQUITA, family name of prominent American and European Sephardim of Marrano descent. The merchant Luis de Mesquita (or Amesquita), of Segovia, Castile, took up residence in Mexico and was reconciled at an *auto-da-fé there in 1646. Benjamin Bueno de Mesquita, who went to Jamaica from Portugal in the 1660s, petitioned the English authorities for the right to trade with the crown, which foreign merchants could not ordinarily do. Permission was granted in 1664, but soon thereafter he and two sons were banished from Jamaica on an extraneous charge. He then went to New York where he died in 1683 (the earliest date on any tombstone in New York's Jewish cemeteries). Joseph Bueno de Mesquita, one of these sons, became prominent in New York and around 1700 had important financial dealings with Lord Bellamont, the colonial governor. On behalf of Congregation Shearith Israel he purchased a burial ground, the Chattam Square cemetery, from William Merett. Joseph's will gives the name of the other brother, Abraham Bueno de Mesquita who was then living at Nevis in the British West Indies. The name Mesquita appears also in Europe. Moses Gomez de Mesquita (1688–1751) was haham of London's Spanish-Portuguese Jews from 1744.

See also *Bueno family.

Bibliography: A. M. Hyamson, *Sephardim of England* (1951), index s.v. *Bueno de Mesquita and Gomez de Mesquita;* J.

Moses Gomez de Mesquita, haham of the London Sephardi community. Engraving by J. Faber after a portrait by S. Da Silva. Cecil Roth Collection.

Picciotto, *Sketches of Anglo-Jewish History* (1956), 465; M. Gaster, *History of the Ancient Synagogue...* (1901), passim; I. S. Emmanuel, *Precious Stones of the Jews of Curaçao* (1957), index; J. R. Rosenbloom, *Biographical Dictionary of Early American Jews* (1960), 112. [ED.]

MESSEL, German family. AARON MESSEL (1784–1848) founded the banking house of A. Messel & Co. in Darmstadt which his son SIMON BENJAMIN MESSEL (1817–1859) continued. Simon's son L. E. W. L. MESSEL (1847–1915) apparently left Judaism. He settled in England, and his granddaughter ANNE was mother of Anthony Armstrong-Jones, Earl of Snowden, who in 1960 married Princess Margaret, sister of Queen Elizabeth II of England. RUDOLPH MESSEL (1848–1920) also settled in England where he was a successful chemist and engineer. ALFRED MESSEL (1853–1909) distinguished himself as an architect in Germany. He renounced Judaism in the 1890s. OLIVER MESSEL (1904–), a grandson of L. E. W. L. Messel, achieved distinction in England as a theatrical producer, stage designer, and painter. [S.D.T.]

MESSERER, ASAF MIKHAILOVICH (1903–), dancer and teacher of the Bolshoi Ballet, Moscow. Messerer, who was born in Vilna, graduated from the Bolshoi School in 1921 and was soon dancing important roles, including Siegfried in *Swan Lake*. He had a brilliant technique, performing feats of virtuosity seldom accomplished by men. He revolted against traditional mime, which he replaced with expressive acting, and was equally brilliant in *danseur-noble* parts, and in demi-character roles. His first choreographic work, in collaboration with Igor Moiseyev, was a new production of *La fille mal gardée* (1930). He restaged the last act of *Swan Lake* in 1936, and his later works include *Sulla* (1952) and *Ballet School* (1962). Messerer retired from dancing in 1954, but remained with the Bolshoi company as a teacher and principal choreographer. SULAMITH MESSERER (1908–), Asaf's sister, was also a dancer and teacher for the Bolshoi Ballet. She entered the company from the Bolshoi School in 1926. Her first important role was that of Lise in *La fille mal gardée* (1929). Other outstanding roles were those of Swanilda in *Coppélia* and Kitri in *Don Quixote*. She was an athletic dancer more suited to demi-character than classical roles. She became a teacher in the Bolshoi School in 1938, and continued as a principal instructor after retiring from dancing in 1950. Asaf Mikhailovich and Sulamith Messerer received the title of People's Artist of the U.S.S.R. The ballerina Maya *Plisetskaya was their niece.

Bibliography: M. Abrahamski (ed.), *Bol'shoy Teatr SSSR* (Russ., 1958), 398–403. [M.B.S.]

MESSIAH, an anglicization of the Latin *Messias*, which is borrowed from the Greek Μεσσιας, an adaptation of the Aramaic *meshiḥa* (מְשִׁיחָא), a translation of the Hebrew *(ha-melekh) ha-mashi'aḥ* (הַמָּשִׁיחַ [הַמֶּלֶךְ]), "the Anointed [King]"; a charismatically endowed descendant of David who the Jews of the Roman period believed would be raised up by God to break the yoke of the heathen and to reign over a restored kingdom of Israel to which all the Jews of the Exile would return. This is a strictly postbiblical concept. Even *Haggai and *Zechariah, who expected the Davidic kingdom to be renewed with a specific individual, *Zerubbabel, at its head, thought of him only as a feature of the new age, not as the author or even agent of its establishment. One can, therefore, only speak of the biblical prehistory of messianism. It may be summarized as follows: *Stage I.* At the height of David's power there appears the doctrine that the Lord had chosen David and his descendants to reign over Israel to the end of time (II Sam. 7; 23:1–3, 5) and had also given him dominion over alien peoples (II Sam. 22:44–51 = Ps. 18:44–51; Ps. 2). To quote II Samuel 22:50–51 (= Psalm 18:50–51; all the arguments against dating this composition later than the age of David seem forced): (50) For this I sing Your praise, O Lord among the nations/and hymn Your name://(51) "He who grants wondrous victories to his king/and deals graciously with his anointed *(mashi'aḥ)*, with David, and with his offspring, evermore."//David is here, as Saul was before him (I Sam. 24:6; 26:9; II Sam. 1:14, 16), and as he expects descendants of his to be after him, the Lord's anointed in the sense that he was anointed as a sign of consecration to the Lord (see *Kingship, *Oil), not, of course, in the sense of "the Messiah" described at the beginning of this article. Because anointing is an act of consecration, Deutero-*Isaiah speaks of Cyrus as the Lord's "anointed" in the purely derived sense of a non-Israelite-king chosen by the Lord for a great destiny and a great mission (Isa. 45:1). Thus "Stage I" of the prehistory of messianism is the doctrine that David's present position of power will endure throughout his lifetime and be inherited by an endless chain of succeeding links in his dynasty. Stage II began with the collapse of David's empire after the death of Solomon. There arose the doctrine, or hope, that the House of David would again reign over Israel as well as Judah and again exercise dominion over neighboring nations. This hope was expressed (a) probably by reinterpretation of compositions like Psalm 18 in a prophetic sense and (b) in so many words in prophecies like Amos 9:11–12; Isaiah 11:10; Hosea 3:5 (the phrase—a Judahite interpolation—"and (the Israelites will seek) their king David"); Ezekiel 37:15ff., especially verses 24ff. (and see *Isaiah A, Panel 3, Field A, on Isa. 9:1–6 [2–7]). *Stage III.* Isaiah's shifting of the emphasis from the perpetuity of the dynasty to the qualities of the future king: the foundation of his throne will be justice, he will be distinguished by his zeal for justice, and, finally, he will be charismatically endowed for sensing the rights and wrongs of a case and for executing justice. (See not only the passage in *Isaiah just cited on Isa. 9:1–6 [2–7], but also Isaiah B I, 4 on Isa. 16:4–5 and, in particular, *Isaiah A, Panel 3, Field B on Isa. 11:1ff., where the origins of this idea are discussed). The "*Immanuel prophecy" in Isaiah is completely irrelevant, so far as one can see and the echoes of ancient Canaanite-Ugaritic mythology that have been "discovered" there are as dubious as those in the figure of the *Ancient of Days in Daniel 7. Without "stage III" in its biblical prehistory, the development of the postbiblical idea of "the Messiah" would not have been possible. [H.L.G.]

Second Temple Period. The title "Messiah" (משיח) as a designation of the eschatological personality does not exist in the Old Testament; it occurs only from the time of the Second Temple after the Old Testament period. However for ancient Judaism the idea of eschatological salvation was more important than the concept of Messiah. Hence there are books from the Second Temple period where the Messiah does not occur, even if they refer to eschatological salvation. Such a book, for instance, is the Book of *Tobit, in which the salvation of Jerusalem, the return of the Diaspora, and the conversion of nations to the God of Israel is described but a personal Messiah is lacking. The same also applies to the Book (Wisdom) of *Ben Sira and probably the Book of Daniel. In the latter, the messianic figure of the *son of man is explained as a symbol for the holy ones (or saints) of the Most High (chap. 7). In the Assumption of *Moses (chap. 10) the eschatological figure

Figure 1. The Messiah, on a white donkey, being led into Jerusalem by the prophet Elijah. From a *Haggadah,* Munich, 15th century. Munich, Staatsbibliothek, Cod. hebr. 200.

is the angel of God but a human agent of the salvation is not mentioned. It seems also that in the more ancient form of the *Amidah* a personal messiah was not mentioned, but only the hope of the return from the Diaspora and the building of the eschatological Jerusalem and the Temple. Even in such ancient Jewish prayers where the concept of Messiah occurs the word *mashi'aḥ* is lacking.

In the time of the Second Temple there was a greater variety of messianic figures than later. The Old Testament Book of Zechariah already makes mention of two messianic figures, the high priest and the messianic king. This idea did not disappear from the rabbinic literature where the priest of righteousness *(kohen zedek)* is sometimes mentioned together with the Davidic king Messiah. These two figures, the priest and the king, are important for the eschatology of the *Dead Sea Sect, the eschatological high priest being more important than the scion of David. The third figure occurring in the *Dead Sea Scrolls with the two messiahs is the prophet of the Last Days. Thus in the Dead Sea Scrolls there are three messianic figures which correspond to the three main functions of the ideal Jewish state, in which kingdom, priesthood, and prophecy shall exist (see I Macc. 14:41). The three eschatological figures of the Dead Sea Scrolls are therefore based upon a broader ideological concept. These three figures are reflected later in the theological concept of of the ancient Jewish sect of the Ebionites (see *Jewish Christian sects) according to which Jesus united in himself the function of king, priest, and prophet. The importance of the Davidic Messiah in Judaism who weakened or caused the disappearance of the other messianic figures was the outcome especially of the Old Testament heritage because the eschatological king is hinted at in the Hebrew Bible.

The oldest description of the eschatological king is in the third book of the Sibylline Oracles (c. 140 B.C.E.) and in the Vision of *Seventy Shepherds in the Book of Enoch which was written approximately a decade earlier. However the prevalence of the Davidic Messiah in the apocryphal literature became common from the time when the Maccabean Aristobulus I accepted the title of a king. This was seen as a usurpation of the rights of the family of David; hence as a reaction, the Davidic Messiah received his central importance as can be seen from the Psalms of Solomon written approximately in 63 B.C.E. (especially in the 17th Psalm). The other component of the political messianic hope in Judaism was caused by the Roman occupation, and so in later books the Davidic Messiah is the only figure which occurs. He thus appears in IV Ezra and in the Syrian Apocalypse of Baruch. A further proof of the expectation of the Davidic Messiah can be found in the New Testament where Jesus is identified with the Davidic Messiah. Even the name "Christians" and the word "Christos" are Greek translations of the word "Messiah" (Christos = the anointed one). This hope was not only an abstract one: from the first century C.E. there were *messianic movements centered on messianic pretenders. Such a list of messianic pretenders occurs in Acts 5:36–37. One of the names there is Judas the Galilean, who was the founder of the *Zealots. Thus this movement was centered on a family with messianic pretensions. Josephus (Wars 2:444–448) states that Judas' son, Menahem, was murdered in the Temple, being "arrayed in royal robes." Apparently after Judas' death his partisans transferred the status of pretender to the kingship to his son.

The most important historical messianic figure was surely *Bar Kokhba, though he himself did not sign as king and names himself only *nasi.* He was already seen by others as the messiah, and it is important that on his coins his name also occurs with that of a priest Eleazar. Both Josephus and the Talmud also mention other messianic pretenders from the first and beginning of the second centuries C.E. The first messianic interpretation of a biblical verse occurs in the Greek translation of the Pentateuch (Num. 24:17) where the word "scepter" is translated in the Greek by "man" (see also the Greek translation of Num. 24:7). The Greek translation of the Pentateuch dates back to the third century B.C.E. Possibly the designation of the Messiah as "man" is a proof that the special concept of son of man already existed in the early third century B.C.E. Philo, who did not like to refer explicitly to the eschatological hopes of Israel, mentions the hope of the coming of the Messiah in connection with this Greek interpretation of the biblical verse. The above shows that messianic concepts were manifold in the time of the Second Temple, and there were even numerous aspects to the function of the Messiah. All depended upon the spiritual and theological approach of the various Jewish trends, but the Messiah or messiahs were always human beings, even if sometimes supernatural qualities were connected with them. The political aspect, if it prevailed, did not always eliminate the supernatural. However, the Messiah was always an agent of God and never a savior in the Christian meaning. The Davidic origin of the kingly Messiah was supposed; but, as it seems, the messianic pretender had to prove his authenticity by his deeds—in the period of the Second Temple Davidic descendants were not traceable. [D.FL.]

Messiah in Rabbinic Thought. In rabbinic thought, the Messiah is the king who will redeem and rule Israel at the climax of human history and the instrument by which the kingdom of God will be established. While the Bible stresses the nature of the age called the "end of days," the

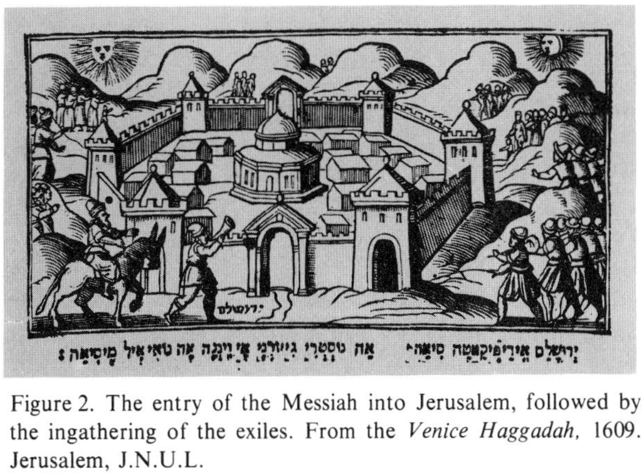

Figure 2. The entry of the Messiah into Jerusalem, followed by the ingathering of the exiles. From the *Venice Haggadah,* 1609. Jerusalem, J.N.U.L.

rabbis focus as well on the person of their regent, who gives the messianic age *(yemot ha-mashi'aḥ)* its very name. "Messiah" *(Mashi'aḥ)* means "annointed" and in the Bible can refer either to a king or a priest. The *aggadah* restricts the term to the eschatological king, who is also called *malka meshiḥa* ("king messiah") in the Targums, *ben David* ("son of David"), and *mashi'aḥ ben David* ("Messiah, son of David"). The Messiah was expected to attain for Israel the idyllic blessings of the prophets; he was to defeat the enemies of Israel, restore the people to the Land, reconcile them with God, and introduce a period of spiritual and physical bliss. He was to be prophet, warrior, judge, king, and teacher of Torah.

A secondary messianic figure is the Messiah son of (i.e., of the tribe of) Joseph (or Ephraim), whose coming precedes that of the Messiah, son of David, and who will die in combat with the enemies of God and Israel. Though some (e.g., Torrey, Segal) claim that this figure is described in pre-Christian apocalyptic and apocryphal works, most scholars note that the first unambiguous mentions of this doctrine occur in tannaitic passages of uncertain date (Suk. 52a) and in the Targums (Pseudo–Jon., Ex. 40:11; Pesh., Song 4:5). The genetic function of the doctrine is similarly unclear: Messiah ben Joseph has been seen as the symbolic embodiment of the reunification with the ten tribes of Israel, as the Samaritan Messiah, and as a figure whose martial character and death testify to the impact of the abortive revolt under *Bar Kokhba upon the Jewish imagination.

There are a number of developmental accounts of the messianic idea. Klausner argues that the nationalist-naturalist base of the idea was "spiritualized" after the political and military debacle of the Bar Kokhba revolt; Mowinckel claims virtually the same results due to the acceptance of apocalyptic and spiritualizing elements. It is true, on the whole, that the later Midrash is more extravagant and inventive than the earlier sources in the elaboration of many messianic motifs; the relative sobriety of the earlier sources contrasts markedly with the portrait drawn in the apocalyptic literature. The earliest sources speak little of messianic origins. Subsequently there is the belief that he was born at Beth-Lehem (cf. Micah 5:1) or Jerusalem on the day of the Temple's destruction. He is then hidden—either in Rome or (in the later Midrash) in heaven, where he pines over the agony of people and his own impotence—to come forth at the time of the Redemption. Some have him present at the creation of the world; for some the "name" (i.e., concept) of the Messiah existed before creation; in yet others (assumed late), the Messiah himself exists before the world (PR 36:161).

The prophetic books do not all assume a personal messiah, nor do they identify him. The rabbis agree he is of Davidic lineage (based on Hos. 3:5 and Jer. 30:9), nor is this idea necessarily post-Bar Kokhba. Some expected a resurrected David, and others a messiah named David. Hezekiah, king of Judah, was a potential messiah: Johanan b. Zakkai announced the "coming" of Hezekiah in what some take to be a messianically oriented deathbed declaration. The name Menahem b. Hezekiah, which may refer to an anti-Roman patriot rebel or may simply be symbolic of "comfort," is also found. Various *amoraim* derive the name of the Messiah from the names of their masters; there is also a puzzling identification of the Messiah and *Judah ha-Nasi (Sanh. 98b). The messianic "name" is sometimes meant descriptively, as when Yose ha-Gelili said that the Messiah's name is *Shalom* ("peace"). The early sources do not mention a "suffering Messiah." In the Targum to Isaiah 53:3–6 suffering is the historical lot of the people, who are reconciled to God by the prayers of Messiah; the toils of Messiah are those of constructive achievement. Third-century sources speak of a suffering Messiah, or a leprous Messiah; still later, his suffering atones for Israel (Sanh. 98b; PR 37:162b). The vicarious atonement of all righteous for the wicked is a general aggadic theme, however.

The Messiah is generally assumed to be man, though writ large. As such, he can come either riding a donkey, in subdued fashion (cf. Zech. 9:9), or triumphantly riding the clouds (Dan. 7:13). That the Messiah is fully human is dramatically shown by Akiva's knowledgement of the rebel leader, Bar Kokhba, as the Messiah. (Yet Akiva also declared that the Messiah would occupy a throne alongside God!) One talmudic source does apparently attribute immortality to Messiah (Suk. 52a), and the Midrash (mostly later) singles him out among the immortals of Paradise. The Messiah does not displace either God or Torah in rabbinic thought. Thus, Hillel (fourth century) can deny the coming of Messiah (for which he is rebuked), though he doubtless expected Israel's redemption. So too, the Midrash can delare that the ultimate author of redemption is not Messiah but God, and His kingship is stressed in the liturgy as well (Mid. Ps. to 31:1; 36:1; 107:1).   [G.J.B.]

The Doctrine of the Messiah in the Middle Ages. Jewish ideology in the Middle Ages did not receive from the ancient period a coherent, unified concept of the Messiah, messianic times, and the signs of the messianic age. Apocalyptic literature of the Second Temple period (see above) differed greatly from the biblical concept of the Messiah and his times, and talmudic literature and the various Midrashim included many contrasting views about this problem. In the Middle Ages messianic ideas were a product of medieval thought and experience, based on some ancient sources, but developed within medieval Hebrew literature and thought. During the last decades of Byzantine rule in Palestine, in the last years of the sixth century and the beginning of the seventh century, the political upheavals in the Middle East—especially the continuous wars between the Byzantines and the Persians—gave rise to a body of messianic literature, which was destined to play a major role in shaping the image of the messianic age in the eyes of medieval Jewry. The most important work which was written at that time was the Book of *Zerubbabel. In this pseudepigraphical work Zerubbabel, the last ruler of Judea from the House of David, tells his visions concerning the happenings at the end of days and the time of the Messiah. According to this work, the appearance of the Messiah will be preceded by the appearance of a satanic king of Rome, who will be the son of Satan and a stone sculpture of a woman; his name will be *Armilus (=Romulus, the first

Figure 3. Woodcut of the Messiah's entry into Jerusalem by Sigmund Forst. From *The Jewish Observer,* New York, September 1965.

king of Rome who will also be the last). Armilus will conquer the whole world, vanquish all the traditional enemies of Rome, especially Persia, and will unify the whole world under his religion. He will be a spiritual Satan as well as an emperor. According to the descriptions, the writer seems to see in him a new incarnation, or a new appearance, of Jesus. The whole world will believe in him and see him as god and emperor, except the Jews. The war of the Jews against this monster will be conducted, at first, by the Messiah son of Joseph, assisted by a woman named Hephzibah. The Messiah son of Joseph will gather all the Jews to Palestine and Jerusalem, but Armilus will overcome him and kill him; Jerusalem will be saved by Hephzibah. Then Hephzibah's son, the Messiah son of David, will arise, overcome Armilus, and the messianic age will begin.

It is possible that this story, which is rich in detailed descriptions of the persons and the wars, and contains detailed dates for all the occurrences included in it, was written under the influence of the great victories achieved by the Byzantine emperor, Heraclius, against the Persians; for a Jew living in Palestine at that time it seemed that the emperor was about to conquer the whole world and reunite the empire with the Christian religion. The author believed that the Messiah was not going to overcome an enfeebled, divided Roman-Christian empire, but that his victory should be against an empire which would be physically and spiritually as strong as possible. Only after such unity is achieved by a Christian "messiah" can the Jewish Messiah appear and overcome the enemy.

A vast literature developed around the Book of Zerubbabel—apocalyptic literature describing the end of the Diaspora, the wars of the Messiah, and the final victory. It is difficult to date the various works in this literature; some of them may even be earlier than the Book of Zerubbabel. One of the most important works in this apocalyptic literature is the *"Otot Mashi'aḥ"* ("The Signs of the Messianic Age"), in which ten occurrences are described as foreshadowing the imminent appearance of the Messiah. This literature had an enormous impact upon medieval Jewry.

One of the main characteristics of this apocalyptic literature is the complete absence from it of any doctrinal religious or ideological elements. In these works the future is described as an inevitable end of the world as known and the beginning of a new one. In none of these works is there any explanation as to why anything is going to happen, or what a Jew should do in order to help in the great task of bringing about the redemption. The apocalyptic future is given as a story, not as a theological doctrine. This fact became very meaningful in the Middle Ages, when Judaism was divided between conflicting ideologies and theologies; there was nothing in this apocalyptic description which could make it unacceptable to any Jewish ideology. A philosopher, an Ashkenazi Ḥasid, a kabbalist, or a rabbinic traditionalist, could accept the apocalyptic future as described in the Book of Zerubbabel and related works. Thus the appeal of this body of literature became universal to all Jews, in all countries, in both medieval and early modern times. Another characteristic which helped these ideas to be accepted and believed by all Jews is that this literature contained many elements taken from biblical and talmudic sayings about the messianic age. There was no conflict between the texts from ancient times and the apocalyptic literature of the early Middle Ages; what was fragmentary and incomplete in the ancient texts was developed in the latter into a complete, coherent picture, in which it was as easy to believe as if it sprang directly from the traditional sources.

This does not mean that other, non-apocalyptical concepts of the messianic age did not exist in the Middle Ages among Jewish thinkers. Thus, for instance, whereas Eleazar *Kallir, in describing the messianic age, used images similar to those in the apocalyptic literature, his predecessor and probable teacher, the *paytan* *Yannai, used more quiet, non-apocalyptical images in referring to the redemption. Most of the philosophers did not accept the apocalyptic picture, even though *Saadiah Gaon, the first systematic Jewish philosopher, included in his *Book of Beliefs and Opinions* a paraphrase of the Book of Zerubbabel when describing the messianic age. *Maimonides and his followers regarded the coming of the Messiah as a political deliverance of the Jews from the rule of the gentiles, without any upheaval in the order of the world and without any apocalyptic elements. Maimonides also opposed messianic speculation, and rejected rumors from Yemen and other places that a Messiah had come (see *Messianic Movements). However, other philosophers held different opinions. Abraham bar Ḥiyya, a rationalist philosopher with neoplatonic tendencies, wrote a major work, *Megillat ha-Megalleh,* attempting to establish, by astrological calculations, the date of the coming of the Messiah.

Messianic speculation and attempts to find such dates were a constant feature of Jewish culture in the Middle Ages and early modern times. Dozens of dates were proposed as the dates of the beginning of the redemption, which was divided into many stages; sometimes different dates for different stages were also given. Sometimes the dates set for redemption coincided with great upheavals in the world and terrible persecutions of the Jews—like the beginning of the persecutions by the crusaders (1096), the years of the Black Death in Europe, the Expulsion from Spain (1492), or the persecutions in Poland and the Ukraine (1648). But, even though one date after the other was refuted, the explanation was that the Jews were not sufficiently righteous to accept the Messiah, and a new date was set. The generations preceding and following the Expulsion from Spain were especially rich in such speculations, but in fact every age engaged in such speculations, with very little differences in method and ideological concepts.

Among the theological movements in the Middle Ages the ideas of apocalyptical eschatology clashed with the ideas of personal eschatology, the personal reward that a devout person will received upon his death in the next world. Evidently, when emphasis was put upon personal redemption in the Garden of Eden the descriptions of national deliverance upon the coming of the Messiah tended to be somewhat blunted. This may have been one of the reasons why Maimonides and his school de-emphasized the apocalyptic nature of the redemption. However, among the masses of the people, belief in the apocalyptic redemption did not diminish.

A good example for this conflict can be found in the movement of the *Ḥasidei Ashkenaz in the late 12th and early 13th centuries. In their popular works the teachers of Ashkenazi Ḥasidism, Judah he-Ḥasid and *Eleazar b. Judah of Worms, explained the dangers of engaging in messianic speculation and in the belief in false messiahs. Several passages in the *Sefer Ḥasidim* are dedicated to this question. However, from other souces, esoteric works, and contemporary documents, a different picture is obtained. It was believed that Judah he-Ḥasid knew when the Messiah was to come, but he died before he could reveal it to his disciples. Judah himself explained in one of his esoteric works that there are a few righteous people in every generation who know this date, but they have to keep it a secret; there is no doubt that he included himself among them. A passage describing the appearance of the Messiah was deleted from the *Sefer Ḥasidim*, but is found in manuscripts. There is a document from the Cairo *Genizah* from which it can be learned that when a person appeared claiming to be the Messiah, the community appealed to Eleazar of Worms for advice, and he seemed to believe in the veracity of the miracles worked by that person. Even though Ashkenazi Ḥasidism put the main emphasis on personal redemption, belief in messianic speculation and the imminent appearance of the Messiah was still very strong even among their leaders.

From the 13th century on, especially after the publication of the *Zohar*, messianic speculation and messianic belief was centered in kabbalistic literature, and culminated in the great kabbalistic-messianic movement, Shabbateanism. See also *Kabbalah; *Shabbetai Ẓevi and Shabbateanism; and *Messianic Movements. [Y.D.]

In Modern Jewish Thought. Classical Reform in the last century reinterpreted the doctrine of the Messiah in two ways. First, it substituted the belief in a messianic age for the belief in a personal Messiah. Secondly, the messianic hope was severed from its traditional associations with a return of the exiles to Zion, these associations being viewed as too particularistic. The destruction of the Temple and the exile of the Jewish people were seen not as calamities but as affording greater opportunities for the fulfillment of Judaism's "mission" to all mankind. The whole world would become perfected and, through the example of Judaism, monotheism would be the religion of all men. Progress in the Western world, in terms of greater liberalism, Jewish emancipation, social reforms, and better educational facilities, was hailed as the dawn of the messianic age of which the prophets had dreamed. References to a return to Zion were erased from the prayer book. The principles regarding the Messiah in the Reform "Pittsburgh Platform" (1885) read: "We recognize in the modern era of universal culture of heart and intellect the approaching of the realization of Israel's great messianic hope for the establishment of the kingdom of truth, justice, and peace among all men. We consider ourselves no longer a nation, but a religious community, and therefore expect neither a return to Palestine, nor a sacrificial worship under the sons of Aaron, nor the restoration of any of the laws concerning the Jewish state."

The Reform vision of messianism as a perfect world just around the corner and of the Jews as the brave carriers of a universalistic message ready to be heeded by all was rendered hollow by the rise of Zionism with its stress on the Jews as a nation and its emphasis on a physical return to Palestine, culminating in the emergence of the State of Israel; the threat of anti-Semitism and the Holocaust in which six million Jews were murdered; and the disillusionment that set in after the two world wars. Even as early as 1937 the "Pittsburgh Platform" was considerably modified by a conference of Reform rabbis in Columbus, Ohio. A statement by the conference dealing with the messianic question reads: "In all lands where our people live, they assume and seek to share loyally the full duties and responsibilities of citizenship and to create seats of Jewish knowledge and religion. In the rehabilitation of Palestine, the land hallowed by memories and hopes, we behold the promise of renewed life for many of our brethren. We affirm the obligation of all Jewry to aid in its upbuilding as a Jewish homeland by endeavoring to make it not only a haven or refuge for the oppressed but also a center of Jewish culture and spiritual life. Throughout the ages it has been Israel's mission to witness to the Divine in the face of every paganism and materialism. We regard it as our historic task to co-operate with all men in the establishment of the kingdom of God, of universal brotherhood, justice, truth and peace on earth. This is our messianic goal."

There is a tendency among some modern Jewish thinkers to invoke once again the traditional idea of messianism as a direct, divine intervention, in which a "new heart" will be created for men, rather than as automatic human progress towards an ideal state. Even a determined non-supernaturalist like Mordecai Kaplan can write (*Questions Jews Ask* (1956), 183): "We can no longer believe that any person or semi-divine being, is divinely destined to rule as the Messiah and usher in the millennium. Nevertheless, the idea of the Messiah can still figure symbolically to express the valid belief in the coming of a higher type of man than this world has yet known." Will Herberg (*Judaism and Modern Man* (1951), 227–35) is typical of the new school of thought. History cannot redeem itself. It proceeds and ends in catastrophe from which it must be redeemed by God. Even the most perfect world state could do no more than enforce peace throughout the world, but the hatred and conflicts among men would remain. The "peace" in the messianic age dreamed of by the prophets is, on the other hand, an inner harmony that needs no external sanctions. To attempt to reduce the prophetic vision of perfection to the level of perfectionist utopianism is to throw confusion into both practical politics and the ultimate insights of religion. It is not surprising, therefore, to find voices raised, also outside the Orthodox camp, in favor of retaining the doctrine of the personal Messiah sent by God.

Orthodoxy retains unimpaired the traditional doctrine. The Messiah is a scion of the House of David. He will reign in Jerusalem, will rebuild the Temple, and will reinstitute the sacrificial system. Many Orthodox rabbis were at first opposed to Zionism in that it seemed to substitute a purely human redemption for the redeemer sent by God. But with the establishment of the State of Israel the widely held Orthodox view was to see the events in Israel as *atḥalta de-geulla*, "the beginning of the redemption," i.e., the foundations laid by humans, under God's guidance, ready to receive the building to be erected by God's direct act. Among Orthodox rabbis there is no lack of speculation on the meaning of contemporary events in the light of the messianic hope. Thus M. Kasher (*No'am*, 13 (1970), end) has tried to read: "Then the moon shall be confounded, and the sun ashamed; for the Lord of hosts will reign in Mount Zion, and in Jerusalem, and before His elders shall be glory" (Isa. 24:23) as a prophetic vision in which the moon landings coincide with the establishment of the State of Israel. In the writings of A. I. Kook the argument is advanced that the Jewish people had become too "spiritual," too remote from the world. To pave the way for the Messiah the concrete realities of a modern state based on Jewish principles of justice and compassion are essential. Kook accepted the theory of evolution even in the moral sphere in that it is evidence of the movement of the whole of creation toward its ultimate fulfillment, as in the messianic hope (*Orot ha-Kodesh* (1938) V, 19–22). [L.J.]

Bibliography: General: J. Klausner, *The Messianic Idea in Israel* (1955); A. H. Silver, *A History of Messianic Speculations in Israel* (1927); S. Mowinckel, *He That Cometh* (1956); Kaufmann Y., Toledot, 3 (1960), 626–56; G. von Rad, *Old Testament Theology*, 1 (1962), 306–24; 2 (1965), 165–79; H. L. Ginsberg, in: *Conservative Judaism*, 22 no. 1 (1967), 2–11. Second Temple Period: D. Flusser, in: IEJ, 9 (1959), 99–109; M. Hengel, *Die Zeloten* (1961); J. Liver, *Toledot Beit David* (1959); E. Sjöberg, *Der Menschensohn im aethiopischen Henochbuch* (1946); P. Volz, *Die Eschatologie der juedischen Gemeinde im neutestamentlichen Zeitalter* (1934); M. Zobel, *Gottesgesalbter; der Messias und die* *messianische Zeit in Talmud und Midrasch* (1938); F. Hahn, *Christologische Hoheitstitel* (1964); In the Aggadah: Ginzberg, Legends, 7 (1938), 306–9 (index); J. Even-Shemuel, *Midreshei Ge'ullah* (1954[2]); G. F. Moore, *Judaism*, 2 (1927), 323–76; W. D. Davies, *Torah in the Messsianic Age* (1952), 50–85; Baron, Social[2], (1952), 351f.; 5 (1957), 138ff.; Kaufman, in: *Molad*, 16 (1958), 197–203; E. E. Urbach, *Ḥazal, Pirkei Emunot ve-De'ot* (1969), 639 (index): J. Liver, *Toledot Beit David* (1959). Doctrine of the Messiah in the Middle Ages: J. Even-Shemuel, *Midreshei Ge'ullah* (1954[2]); A. Z. Aešcoly, *Ha-Tenu'ot ha Meshiḥiyyiot be-Yisrael* (1956); B. Z. Dinur, *Yisrael ba-Golah*, 2/3 (1968). 358–453; J. Dan, *Torat ha-Sod shel Ḥasidei Ashkenaz* (1968), 241ff.; idem, in: *Ha-Ummah*, 30 (1970), 237–55; G. Scholem, *The Messianic Idea in Judaism* (1971); In Modern Jewish Thought: J. H. Greenstone, *The Messiah Idea in Jewish History* (1943); S. S. Schwarzschild, in: *Judaism*, 5 (1956, 123–35; L. Jacobs, *Principles of the Jewish Faith* (1964). 368–97.

MESSIANIC MOVEMENTS.

Basic Elements. The pattern on which Jewish messianic movements were based crystallized in the late Second Temple period, and furnished Jews in following generations with certain basic elements. These, when confronted by certain typical challenges, culminated in messianic movements of varying scope. The term "messianic movement" in Jewish history applies to a movement centered around or expressing the yearning for a king or leader of the house of David and for a new ideal political existence for the Jewish people that would serve as a reassertion of independence and cause their return to Ereẓ Israel, as well as acting as a model and focus for a united and better mankind. Experiencing the miracle of Jewish redemption, mankind would attain an ideal world where true faith and real harmony would prevail. Jewish prayers for redemption, while seeking the advent of the king and the kingdom, also ask "may they all blend into one brotherhood to do Thy will with a perfect heart," and express the hope that with this change of heart, "Thou shalt reign over all whom Thou hast made, Thou alone" (in evening service *(Arvit)* for Rosh Ha-Shanah). This formulates the abiding hope of the Jew while in the **galut*. The basis of the movements is intense longing for the messianic era. Up to the 18th century it was both an article of faith and an emotional necessity among Jews to hope constantly for the immediate advent of the Messiah. Yet this persistent element did not of itself necessarily lead to the emergence of such movements. Jewish messianic history includes periods and religious trends in which people experienced intense and wholehearted hopes for the Messiah while being lukewarm toward active messianic movements. Thus the *Karaites throughout the Middle Ages had a deep-seated feeling of being in exile; Karaite settlers in Jerusalem in the tenth century called themselves *Avelei Zion ("Mourners for Zion"), organizing their life and patterning their thought on the basis of this attachment to Zion. Yet only one Karaite messianic movement is known for certain. The Rabbanite *Ḥasidei Ashkenaz longed for the Messiah, yet only rarely is any active striving for a Messiah mentioned in their relatively extensive writings. Indeed, some of the expressions they use appear to satirize computations of the date of the coming of the Messiah (J. Wistinetzki (ed.), *Sefer Ḥasidim* (1924), 461, no. 1706). They even warned their readers: "If you see that a man has prophesied the advent of the Messiah, know that he is engaged either in sorcery or in dealings with devils; or that he uses the power of the Divine Name . . . One has to say to such a man: 'Do not talk in this manner' . . ., eventually he will be the laughingstock of the whole world . . . . they teach him calculations and secrets to bring shame on him and on those who believe him" (*ibid.*, 76–77, no. 212).

This attitude displayed by mystics and ascetics in opposing activist messianism finds even sharper expression in the views of the 13th-century mystic, Naḥmanides. In his disputations with the representatives of Christianity, Naḥmanides told the Spanish king at *Barcelona in 1263:

> Our Law and Truth and Justice are not dependent upon a Messiah. Indeed, you yourself are more important to me than a Messiah. You are a king and he is a king. You are a gentile sovereign and he is a king of Israel. The Messiah is but a king of flesh and blood like yourself. When I serve my Creator under your jurisdiction, in exile, torment, and subjection, exposed constantly to universal contempt, I merit great reward; for I offer of my own flesh a sacrifice to God, and my reward in afterlife will be so much the greater.

(*Kitvei Rabbenu Moshe ben Naḥman*, ed. by H. D. Chavel, 1 (1963), 310).

The basic consideration put forward here is that the greatness of the individual suffering under alien rule can be as rewarding as redemption. In a work addressed to Jews Naḥmanides wrote:

> Even if we thought that it is the will and purpose of God to afflict us with political enslavement on this earth [forever], this would in no way weaken our adherence to the precepts of the Torah, for the sole rewards which we anticipate are those of the world to come—the beatitude of the soul which, having escaped hell's torments, enjoys the bliss of paradise.

He continues that he believes in the Messiah and redemption because it is true and because it gives him comfort to face the adversities suffered by the Jewish people; but this is not a necessary or sustaining element of his Jewish faith (*Sefer ha-Ge'ullah*, pt. 2; *ibid.*, 279–80).

The extreme wing of modern *Orthodoxy in Judaism and most of the adherents of *Neo-Orthodoxy—in particular *Agudat Israel in the period before the Holocaust and, later, *Neturei Karta—continued, under changed and secularized conditions, old attitudes of messianism which were halfhearted toward a messianic movement. Messianic-prompted efforts have been made toward an ingathering of the Jews without an express connection with either Ereẓ Israel or political independence (see Anan b. David, *Sefer ha-Mitzvot*, ed. by A. Harkavy (1903), 6–7). Jacob *Frank in the 18th century had a savage desire for armed Jewish power and a Jewish settlement on the land—but all this was to be achieved on the soil of Poland. Thus, the modern movement of *territorialists can claim some ancient though rare precedents in traditional Jewish messianic trends.

Within this ideological framework and set of attitudes, the emergence of an active messianic movement required a challenge that would break through the tranquility of the regular messianic hope to turn it into fervent and directed effort, and create a revolutionary constellation. There were elements in Jewish historical consciousness encouraging such active responses to various and widely differing challenges. One element basic to Jewish messianism is anticipation of the "birth pangs of the Messiah" *(ḥevlei Mashi'aḥ)*—the time of troubles and turbulence that precedes his coming. Hence, periods in which terrible massacres of Jews occurred (e.g. during the *Crusades or the *Chmielnicki massacres) have also been periods of fervent messianic expectations and movements. Jewish historical conception—and for that matter Christian also—interpreted Daniel's apocalyptic vision of the four evil beasts (7:2ff.) as denoting four successive evil empires. The fourth will be succeeded by the everlasting dominion of "one like unto a son of man." He will be given "dominion and glory and a kingdom that all the peoples, nations, and languages should serve Him." This conception enabled Jews to view great historical and political transformations—the fall and rise of empires and kingdoms, or revolutions and counterrevolutions—as the death throes of the fourth and last beast-kingdom and the harbingers of the messianic eternal kingdom.

The person to lead the messianic movement—the Messiah himself—was viewed from two different angles. Jews—in particular since the parting of the ways with Christianity—saw the Messiah as a man and not God; in the first place, as a national king. But here the agreement ends. Some, like *Maimonides in the 12th century, stressed that the Messiah will himself die even though his life will be a long one. He will first be tested as the successful warrior-king of Israel and proved its lawful ruler by devotion to Torah. Mankind will follow this new exemplary Jewish state. Nature will not change its laws, though society will become perfect (Yad, Melakhim (1962), 417). Along with this rationalistic conception of the Messiah, there is also a miraculous one, in which the person of the Messiah sometimes attains semi-divine heights. The 17th-century pseudo-Messiah, *Shabbetai Ẓevi, concluded a letter:

> I will have to give full reward to all those who believe truly, men, women, and children—from the Lord of Peace and from me, Israel your Father, the bridegroom coming out from under the marriage canopy, the husband of the dear and virtuous Torah, this beautiful and virtuous matron, the man set on high, the Messiah of God, the lion of the upper regions and the deer of the high regions, Shabbetai Ẓevi (his letter to Venice, in: J. Sasportas, *Ẓiẓat Novel Ẓevi*, ed. by I. Tishby (1954), 129).

The rationalistic attitude sometimes reached the extreme of conceiving a Messiah-like political leader. The 14th-century rationalist, Joseph b. Abba Mari ibn *Kaspi, theorizes about:

> the imminent actual possibility of our coming out from this *galut*, becoming free to rule ourselves, without a Lord. Thus, while being confined as slaves in egypt, God took us out from there with a high hand. Now why should not this be even easier for Him in these days? Is there no longer any material available with which this Creator may create a man like Moses, or even of smaller stature, who shall come before the kings and they will give in to him, as Pharaoh gave in the end, though in the beginning Pharaoh hardened his heart to him (*Tam ha-Kesef*, ed. by Last (1913), 44ff., sermon 8).

The miraculous conception of the Messiah evolved a complex of superhuman traits, anticipated actions, and achievements; the Messiah is to take the crown from the head of the alien sovereign by his virtue of appearance alone and redeem and avenge the Jews by miraculous means.

According to the rationalistic image of the Messiah, he should be "a very eminent prophet, more illustrious than all the prophets after Moses" (Maim., *Iggeret Teiman*, ed. A. S. Halkin (1952), 87). In Maimonides' view prophecy necessitated the highest intellectuality. These criteria were not accepted by most of the messianic movements, whose leadership was largely charismatic. It is related of a pseudo-Messiah who appeared around the end of the seventh century, *Abu ʿIsā (Isaac b. Jacob al-Iṣfahanī), that, "the most wonderful thing about him in the opinion of his followers is the fact that although he was, as they say, an illiterate tailor and could neither read nor write, he produced books and pamphlets without having been instructed by anyone" (Jacob al-Kirkisānī's account of the Jewish sects, ed. by L. Nemoy, in: HUCA, 7 (1930), 328). Not many of the messianic claimants had such humble intellectual beginnings, but practically none of them was regarded by his contemporaries as preeminent among scholars of his day, though some were known as considerable scholars. The most widespread of the messianic movements, that of Shabbetai Ẓevi, had for its leader a man of less than 40 years old, while its great prophet, *Nathan of Gaza, was 21 when he announced the Messiah and died at the age of 36. It is hardly surprising that men of rationalistic bent rarely saw the embodiment of their ideal in the actual messianic claimants who arose, whereas those inclined to follow a Messiah seldom found a man to rouse them in the Maimonidean ideal. This generally created a situation in which the supporters and opponents of the movement were driven into two opposing camps.

The messianic movements envisioned the coming of the Messiah as an historic breakthrough, a new lease of divine grace, and, according to some theories, as a basic change in the cosmos and divine relationships. Hence a phenomenon accompanying many messianic movements was some proposed change in the way of life of Jews. This ranged from the extreme innovations introduced by the New Testament of early Christianity, through minor variations in the law introduced by early medieval messianic movements, up to the orgiastic tendencies and activities of the Shabbatean movement and even more of the Frankists.

The Movements. Early Manifestations. Some consider the events surrounding *Zerubbabel of the house of David and his mysterious disappearance (c. 519/518 B.C.E.) as the first messianic movement. The charismatic leadership of the first *Hasmoneans and the devotion they inspired is by rights part of the messianic movement cycle, but for the open question of the claims of this house as opposed to the claims of the house of David. The political and moral ferment created with the rise of *Herod and his house, and even more so with the advent of undisguised Roman rule in Judea, led to the emergence of many messianic leaders and influenced new concepts concerning their aims and leadership. *Jesus of Nazareth was one of many Jews who in this turbulent period claimed to be bringing redemption to the people and who were eventually crucified for announcing their message. *Judah the Galilean told Jews about ten years before the birth of Jesus that it was shameful for them to be "consenting to pay tribute to the Romans and tolerating mortal masters after having God for their Lord" (Jos., Wars, 2:118). Judah and his comrade, "the Pharisee Saddok," were regarded by the hostile *Josephus as the founders of the Zealots. They had "a passion for liberty that is almost unconquerable since they are convinced that God alone is their leader and master" (Jos., Ant., 18:23). With these men there began a heroic and tragic line of short-lived kings, martyred leaders, and brave fighters for freedom. Combating both the Romans and the Herodians, they developed the concept of inaugurating the reign of the "Kingdom of Heaven" for God's elected people here and now. There were many such leaders; it is almost certain that not all of them are mentioned in the extant sources. It is difficult to be certain about their ideas and types of leadership, for the accounts of their activities are subject to distortion either by uncritical admirers or by tendentious enemies. In the case of some of them, not only Jesus, miraculous elements enter the conduct of their leadership. Of *Theudas it is related that he influenced "the majority of the masses to take up their possessions and to follow him to the Jordan River." He stated that he was a prophet and that at his command the river would be parted and would provide them an easy passage (Jos., Ant., 20:97ff.; see also Acts 5:35–39). For this, he and many of his followers paid with their lives, about 45 C.E. Also mentioned is a Jew from Egypt, "who had gained for himself the reputation of a prophet"; followed by "about thirty thousand" Jews, he went to "the Mount of Olives. From there he proposed to force an entrance into Jerusalem" and to free it from the Romans. Many of his followers were killed in battle (Jos., Wars, 2:261ff.). How he was regarded by the Romans appears clearly from the fact that the Christian apostle *Paul was mistaken for him (Acts 21:37–38). It is almost certain that *Menahem b. Judah was considered a Messiah by the Zealots, as possibly was Simeon *Bar Giora.

The unflinching heroism displayed by the warriors in the great revolt against the Romans (66–70/73 C.E.) is comprehensible only in the context of a messianic movement. Some consider that the reason why the Jews did not despair when their messianic leaders had fallen in battle was because of their belief in the Messiah in the person of the son of Joseph (see *Messiah), who is destined to fight and die before the coming of the Messiah in the person of the son of David. Even Josephus—who tried to conceal the messianic motives of the great revolt—once had to reveal that "what more than all else incited them to the war was an ambiguous oracle, likewise found in the sacred Scriptures, to the effect that at that time one from their country would become ruler of the world" (Wars, 6:312; cf. Tacitus, *Historiae,* 5:13, and Suetonius, *Lives of the Caesars,* Vespasian, 4). The *Qumran scrolls also point to messianic hopes and suffering as activating factors in the life and thoughts of this sect, though lacking the Davidic element.

As the great revolt, the precedent of many types of messianic leadership and activity, lay crushed, many new concepts of messianic challenge and response entered the Jewish mind and imagination as the legacy of this period. One trend of Jewish messianism which left the national fold was destined "to conquer the conquerers"—by the gradual Christianization of the masses throughout the Roman Empire. Through Christianity, Jewish messianism became an institution and an article of faith of many nations. Within the Jewish fold, the memory of glorious resistance, of the fight for freedom, of martyred messiahs, prophets, and miracle workers remained to nourish future messianic movements.

Jewish messianic revolt against the Roman Empire did not cease with the severe defeat of 70 C.E. The Jewish revolt against Emperor *Trajan in 115–17, which spread like wildfire through Egypt, Cyrenaica, and Libya, had a messianic king-figure at its head. Simeon *Bar Kokhba was at first only one of several messianic figures, though he became the dominating one in the uprising of 132–35 C.E. It is related that the great *tanna,* *Akiva, "when he saw [him] would say: 'This is the king Messiah' " (TJ, Ta'an. 4:8, 68d). It was only after the death of this semi-legendary figure that the messianic movements began to aim at redeeming the Jews and carrying them back to renewed greatness. Symptomatic of this change is the story about the Jew who appeared in 448, approximately, in Crete and, "said that he is Moses and promised the many Jews on this island to bring them through the sea without ships to Judea." He fixed a certain date for this miracle, and ordered them to jump into the sea; several of them drowned (Socrates Scholasticus, *Historia Ecclesiae,* 12:33).

Early Middle Ages. The challenge of the appearance of the victorious Arabs and the Muslim caliphate on the world scene gave rise to a new upsurge of Jewish messianic movements. They again assumed a warlike temper, while utilizing social tensions within the Jewish community and some of the military tactics used among Muslims to attain their aims. About 645 there is mention of a Jew who "asserted that the Messiah had come. He gathered around him weavers, carpet makers, and launderers, some 400 men. They burned down three [Christian] sanctuaries and killed the chief of that locality." The leader of these craftsmen was crucified, after his followers and their families had been massacred (Nestorian Chronicle, as quoted in: Baron, Social[2], 5 (1957), 184). Similar movements relying on miracles are recorded in Muslim Spain and its vicinity in the eighth to ninth centuries.

Much more significant was the movement led by the above-mentioned Abu ʿĪsā. His teachings include many significant halakhic variations. According to the Karaite sources, he followed the Rabbanite rite and laws in many matters for tactical reasons so that the Rabbanites did not persecute his followers. Abu ʿĪsā acknowledged the prophecy of Jesus and Muhammad, regarding them as prophets for their own followers only. This practical motivation and tendency to temporize was belied by the direction his movements took: Abu ʿĪsā led a battle and fell in the fighting, though some of his followers later believed "that he was not killed, but entered a hole in a mountain and was never heard of [again]" (Kirkisānī, ed. by L. Nemoy, in: HUCA, 7 (1930), 328, 382–3). Those who followed him in the Islamic lands in the eighth to ninth centuries, like *Yudghan and Mushka, resembled him in inaugurating changes in aspects of religion and in their warlike spirit.

The Later Middle Ages. With the *Crusades, certain new features in messianism appeared. In the Balkans a general movement of repentance was induced by crusader violence. At *Salonika, in 1096, Jews and Christians reported "that Elijah . . . had revealed himself openly, and not in a dream, to certain men of standing." People saw "many signs and miracles." There was widespread excited anticipation. It was reported that, under the impression that the redemption was at hand, "the Jews were idly neglecting their work." They sent letters to Constantinople to appraise them of the good news. Other communities sent to inquire about it. There was also a rumor "that all the Byzantine congregations were together in Salonika, and would leave from there" for Ereẓ Israel (J. Starr, *The Jews in the Byzantine Empire 641–1204* (1939), 203–6 no. 153). This was apparently a messianic movement without a Messiah. Jews were united by general feelings of excitation, rumors, and indeterminate tidings.

Maimonides heard that a miracle-working Messiah had appeared—at Lyons in France or Leon in Spain—about 1060. He also heard a tradition that in approximately 1100 a man had been influenced by a dream to proclaim himself Messiah. The man, Ibn Aryeh, was flogged and excommunicated by the community leaders, and with this the affair ended. In the first half of the 12th century messianic ferment was strong in Jewish communities everywhere. About 1121, *Obadiah, the Norman proselyte, met a Karaite *kohen*, Solomon, who prophesied that within two-and-a half months all the Jews would be gathered together in Jerusalem, "for I am the man whom Israel is waiting for." The proselyte was amazed that a man of Aaronide descent should claim messiahship: "It is 19 years since I entered the Covenant and I never heard that Israel is looking for redemption at the hands of a son of the tribe of Levi—only at the hands of the prophet Elijah and the King Messiah of the seed of King David" (J. Mann, in: *Ha-Tekufah,* 24 (1928), 336–7). This encounter in the Near East reveals how deep-rooted, even in the case of a proselyte, was the concept that the Messiah should be of Davidic descent, whereas in sectarian circles the ancient sectarian concept of an Aaronide Messiah (as shown in the *Dead Sea Scrolls) still persisted.

More or less about the same time, in 1120/21, there was messianic excitation in Baghdad centered around a young prophetess (see S. D. Goitein, in: JQR, 43 (1952/53), 57–76). In 1127 approximately the same occurred in Fez, Morocco, where the man, Moses Al-Dar'i, a great scholar—and admired by Maimonides even after he proclaimed his messiahship—announced the coming of the Messiah.

> He told them that the Messiah was about to appear on the first night of Passover. He advised them to sell all their

property and to become indebted as much as possible to the Muslims, to buy from them a thing worth a dinar for ten dinars, and thus to fulfill the words of the Torah [Ex. 12:36], for after Passover they would never see them. As Passover came and went and nothing happened, these people perished for they had sold all their property and their debts overwhelmed them (*Iggeret Teiman*, 103).

Nevertheless, Maimonides expressed satisfaction that this Moses managed to escape to Ereẓ Israel:

there he died, may his memory be blessed. As has been told to me by those who have seen him when he left, he prophesied all that happened later on to the Maghreb Jews, the main outlines as well as the details (*ibid.*, 103).

The story is not only remarkable in demonstrating the influence wielded by the Messiah on large groups of Jews, and their obedience to his instructions, but also instructive since this movement occurred soon after the visit to Fez of Muhammad ibn Tumar, the founder of the *Almohads, and the public discussions he held there with the leaders of the Muslim establishment. Maimonides' attitude to Moses, his blessing him after his death, and his statement that his prophecies were true, reveal that even such a consistent rationalist could be inconsistent with regard to messianic movements.

The first half of the 12th century also saw the remarkable messianic movement led by David *Alroy. Though the dates and personalities are very confused in the sources mentioning this event, they all indicate that it occurred in the first half of the 12th century, and in the remote eastern districts of the Muslim Empire. Most traditions indicate his great and widespread influence and an extensive campaign of written and oral propaganda. All of them agree about the military character of the movement. The apostate to Islam, *Samuel al-Maghribi, relates that Alroy attempted to take the fortress of Amadiyah, in the mountains of Azerbaijan, by the stratagem of having masses of his believers enter the fortress with hidden weapons (tactics resembling those used by the earlier Muslim founder of the Assassins, Hasan ibn al-Sabbah, with regard to the fortress of Alamut). The apostate adds that:

When the report about him reached Baghdad two Jewish tricksters, cunning elders, decided to forge letters by Menahem to the Jews of Baghdad bringing them the good tidings which they had been expecting since of yore; that he would appoint for them a certain night in which all of them would fly to Jerusalem. The Jews of Baghdad, their claim to sagacity and pride in craftiness notwithstanding, were all led to believe it. Their women brought their moneys and jewels in order that it all might be distributed on their behalf, as charity to those whom the two elders considered deserving. In this manner the Jews spent the bulk of their wealth. They donned green garments and on the night gathered on the roofs expecting, he asserted, to fly to Jerusalem on the wings of angels. Women began to weep over their nursing infants; what if the mothers should fly before their children or the children before their mothers? The children might suffer because of the delay in feeding (*Ifḥām al-Yahūd: Silencing the Jews*, ed. and trans. by M. Perlmann (1964), 73).

Despite its obvious intention to ridicule, this tale cannot be dismissed out of hand, for this readiness among Jews to believe in miracles is also found in Maimonides' story about the movement in North Africa.

About 1172 a Messiah appeared in the Yemen. Maimonides' hostile reaction to him shows that he had a clear and proclaimed revolutionary social aim, incomprehensible to Maimonides:

He told them that each man shall distribute all his money and give to the poor. All those who obey him are fools and he is a sinner; for he acts against the Torah. For according to our Torah a man should give as charity only part of his money and not all of it . . . No doubt his heart and mind that have misled him to say that he is a Messiah have also brought him to tell the people to leave all their property and give it to the poor. Thus they will become poor and the poor rich, and according to his law they [the former poor] will have to return to them [the now impoverished rich] their money. In this fashion money will go back and forth between rich and poor unceasingly (*Iggeret Teiman*, 89).

Maimonides advised the communities to proclaim him a madman or put him to death (*ibid.*, 93, 95). Later on, in a letter to the scholar of Marseilles, Maimonides related further details about the movement and its end. By this time he knew that the man in the Yemen was only:

saying that he is a messenger to smooth the path for the King Messiah. He told them that the Messiah [is] in the Yemen. Many people gathered [around him] Jews and Arabs and he was wandering in the mountains . . . He gave them new prayers . . . After a year he was caught and all who were with him fled." Asked by his Arab captor for proof of the divine source of his message, the Yemen Messiah "answered him: 'Cut off my head and I will come back to life immediately,'" and so he was killed. Maimonides heard that there were still many foolish people in the Yemen who believed that he would arise and lead them yet (A. Marx, in: HUCA, 3 (1926), 356).

In the 1240s a new source of messianic excitation accompanied the rumors and hopes centering around the news of the Mongol advance into European countries. Meshullam da Pierra in a poem was certain that:

in our days the kingdom shall be renewed for the lost nation and the scattered communities. Tribute will be brought to the son of David, and gifts to my counts and dukes. My Temple will be rebuilt . . . There are tribes that have been exiled and now they have left the land of the living. Proof that God has sent them is that many rulers have come to harm . . . Babylonia, Aleppo, and Damascus were taken [by the Mongols in 1260] . . . My Savior has broken through the mountainous wall.

To about the same time should be ascribed the information that "women in the land of Canaan [i.e., Bohemia] were reciting the entire Book of Isaiah by heart and ignorant people knew by heart all the prophecies of consolation" (J. Wistinetzki (ed.), *Sefer Ḥasidim* (1924), 77 no. 212).

Spain and the Marranos. At the end of the 13th century the kabbalist Abraham b. Samuel *Abulafia saw himself as the Messiah or the harbinger of the Messiah and tried to spread the word through apocalyptic writings. Solomon b. Abraham *Adret had to oppose the "prophet of Avila" who prophesied the coming of the Messiah in 1295 and had a large following in Avila. There is some information that there was an upsurge of messianic excitation around 1350 (see *Shemariah of Negroponte). The catastrophe of the persecutions of 1391 in Christian Spain led to widespread messianic ferment. In the vicinity of Burgos there appeared a prophet who foretold the imminent coming of the Messiah. At the Disputation of *Tortosa the Christian protagonist claimed that "in our day R. Ḥasdai *Crescas has announced a report and preached to congregations in the synagogues that the Messiah had been born in Cisneros, in the kingdom of Castile." Crescas entertained, it would seem, even more earthly hopes. He imagined the realities of the Second Temple period "as if the king of Egypt, who now reigns over the land of Israel, were to grant permission to Jews living elsewhere in his empire to go and rebuild the sanctuary, on the condition that they submit to his rule" (in his *Or Adonai*). In a letter of that time from which all proper names have been carefully deleted, it is related that a certain teacher taught that the calamities of the period should be seen as the birth pangs of the Messiah; there was a proliferation of confused messianic tidings:

This one writes about the Lord's Messiah, that he shall

surely come by Passover time, and that one says: 'Behold, he stands already at our walls . . .' Another declares that if the Feast of Tabernacles should arrive and there is yet no Messiah, then surely it is God's will to have us die and to harden our hearts from his fear. But before he has done talking, yet another comes and says: 'It is rumored that a prophet has arisen in Israel who has seen a vision of the Almighty . . . The Lord revealed himself in a dream at night and assured him of great amelioration: misery and grief shall flee the years wherein we have seen evil shall be no more; lo, this presages good, this proclaims salvation (Baer, Spain, 2 (1966), 158–62).

As the position of the Jews in Christian Spain steadily deteriorated, messianic hopes were kept alive. The fall of Constantinople in 1453 awakened great messianic hopes and speculations both in the communities of Spain and among Ashkenazi Jewry. Among the forced converts (**anusim*) men and women prophesied the coming of the Messiah. Letters from the Constantinople community related tales about the birth of the Messiah, the place of his activity, and mode of living. A mother and daughter told their Converso friends: "The gentiles do not see us [do not understand us], for they are blind and know not that the Lord our God hath decreed that for a time we should be subject to them, but that we shall now surpass them [have the upper hand], for God hath promised us that after we go to those lands [overseas], we shall ride on horses and pass them by" (*ibid.*, 292–5). Even on the eve of the expulsion of the Jews from Spain, both Jews and *anusim* actively harbored these hopes. About 1481 a Converso told a Jew, when at his request the latter read the messianic prophecies to him: "Have no fear! Until the appearance of the Messiah, whom all of us wait for, you must disperse in the mountains. And I—I swear it by my life—when I hear that you are banished to separate quarters or endure some other hardship, I rejoice; for as soon as the measure of your torments and oppression is full, the Messiah, whom we all await, will speedily appear. Happy the man who will see him!" One Marrano was certain that the Messiah would possess the philosopher's stone and be able to turn iron into silver. He also hoped that "in 1489 there will be only one religion" in the world. Even after the expulsion many Marranos expressed these hopes and were punished for them by the Inquisition (*ibid.*, 350ff.).

Ferment in the 16th to 18th Centuries. In the 16th century there were numerous expressions of messianic expectation. In 1500–02 Asher *Lemlein (Lammlin) preached repentance and the imminent coming of the Messiah. He had great influence. The grandfather of the chronicler David *Gans "broke up the oven that he had for baking *mazzot*, being sure that next year he would be baking *mazzot* in the Holy Land" (*Ẓemaḥ David*). From the end of the 15th century tales originating in and letters from Jerusalem show messianic hopes centering around the *Ten Lost Tribes of Israel. Joseph *Ḥayyun commenting on the verse "In his days Judah shall be redeemed and Israel will live secure" (Jer. 23:6) wrote:

He [Jeremiah] said that Judah shall be redeemed and not that Israel shall be redeemed, for Israel need no redemption for they are not in *Galut*. I mean the Ten Tribes, for they are a great people and they have kings—according to what has been told about them—but Judah needs redemption, whereas [the people of] Israel will then live secure in Ereẓ Israel, for now they are not living so secure as they are abroad. What is more, they fight continuously with the gentiles around them (his commentary to Jeremiah, British Museum, Add. Ms. v 27, 560, fol. 106).

The great Mishnah commentator Obadiah of *Bertinoro wrote in 1489 from Jerusalem to his brother in Italy:

Jews have told us that it is well known, as related by reliable Muslim merchants, that far away, a journey of 50 days through the desert, there lies the famous *Sambatyon River; it surrounds the whole country where the Children of Israel live like a thread. It throws up stones and sand, resting only on the Sabbath. The reason why no Jew goes to this country is because they avoid desecrating the Sabbath. According to their tradition all of them—the descendants of Moses—are saintly and pure like angels; there are no sinners among them. On the outer side of the Sambatyon River there are Children of Israel as numerous as the sands of the seashore, kings and lords, but they are not as saintly and pure as those living on the inner side of the river (A. Yaari, *Iggerot Ereẓ Yisrael* (1943), 140).

Obadiah believed in the existence of a Jewish realm beyond and around the miraculous river which was not only independent and strong but also consisted of two circles of life—an inner, more holy one, and an open, less holy one. Messianic expectations in this period centered actively around these images and fantasies as shown, for example, in the writings of *Abraham b. Eliezer ha-Levi from Jerusalem.

With the advent of David *Reuveni and Solomon *Molcho many Jews were convinced that they were seeing and hearing a prince of those tribes and one of his devoted companions. About the same time many Jews pinned their hopes on Martin *Luther as a man who had come to pave the way for the Messiah through gradually educating the Christians away from their idolatrous customs and beliefs. In Safed, messianic hopes were strong in the circles around Isaac b. Solomon Ashkenazi *Luria and Ḥayyim b. Joseph *Vital. The latter once dreamed:

I stood on the peak of the great mountain to the west of Safed . . . over Meron village; I heard a voice announcing and saying, 'The Messiah is coming and the Messiah stands before me.' He blew the horn and thousands and tens of thousands from Israel were gathering to him. He said to us, 'Come with me and you shall see the avenging of the destruction of the Temple.' We went there; he fought there and defeated all the Christians there. He entered the Temple and slew also those who were in it. He commanded all the Jews and told them, 'Brethren, cleanse yourselves and our Temple of the defilement of the blood of the corpses of these uncircumcised ones and of the defilement of the idolatry that was in it.' We cleansed the Temple and reconstructed it as it was, the daily burnt offering was brought by the arch-priest who looked exactly like my neighbor Rabbi Israel (his *Sefer ha-Ḥezyonot* (1954), pt. 2, no. 2, p. 41).

This blend of the Safed reality and messianic visions of war and glory expresses the intensity of messianic hopes in kabbalistic circles that found expression in Shabbetai Ẓevi in the 17th century. Most communities became involved with Shabbetai Ẓevi and the messianic movement he led in the 1660s. In it many aspects of the messianic movements reached their highest expression, to be faced by crisis: his followers fervently believed that the Messiah would achieve a miraculous victory and were cruelly disappointed when Shabbetai Ẓevi collapsed before the terror of punishment; the masses of his followers repented, but repentance proved of no avail. The movement stimulated Jews to feelings of liberation, but they remained subjugated; orgiastic aspects developed which discredited the movement. The movement led by Jacob Frank in the 18th century introduced the elements of nihilism, licentiousness, and severance of the connection between messianism and Ereẓ Israel.

Scholars are divided as to whether in its origins Ḥasidism bore traits of a messianic movement or whether it was on the contrary a kind of sublimation of messianism.

The Modern Period. In modern times the *Haskalah (Enlightenment) and *Reform wings of Judaism increasingly tended to regard their activity in spreading pure and rational monotheism as a kind of collective movement of messianic "mission." In his letters Leopold *Zunz referred many times to the European revolution of 1848 as "the Messiah." Even many Jews who left the faith tended to invest secular liberation movements with a messianic glow. Martin *Buber expressed the opinion that the widespread Jewish activity in modern revolutionary movements stemmed both from the involvement of the Jew with the state and his criticism of it through his messianic legacy (see *disputations).

Zionism and the creation of the State of Israel are to a large extent secularized phenomena of the messianic movements. The ideology of the Zionist religious parties, *Mizrachi and *Ha-Po'el ha-Mizrachi, tends to regard them—in particular the achievements of the State of Israel—as an *athalta di-ge'ulla* ("anticipation and beginning of redemption"), thus retaining the traditional concepts held by messianic movements in conjunction with the new secularized aspects of the State and its achievements.

Jewish messianism, though appearing in many shapes and permutations, has been and continues to be an activist element in world culture. For Jews it has retained, through the leaders and movements to which it has given rise, the life-force of charisma, and the binding spell of Jewish statehood and kingship to be realized immediately through God's will, through the passion and devotion of His people. Some have spoken of "the price" that Jews and Judaism have had to pay for disappointment and disenchantment after every failure of the messianic movements. Against this are to be set the benefits that these visionary movements gave to a suppressed people—in inspiring them to activity, revitalization, and a sense of sacrifice.

Bibliography: J. Klausner, *The Messianic Idea in Israel* (1955); A. H. Silver, *A History of Messianic Speculation in Israel* (1959^2); A. Z. Aescoly, *Ha-Tenu'ot ha-Meshihiyyot be-Yisrael* (1956); Y. Baer, *Yisrael ba-Ammim* (1955); M. Hengel, *Die Zeloten* (1961); Baron, $Social^2$, index; S. Yeivin, *Milhemet Bar Kokhva* (1946); Scholem, Shabbetai Ẓevi; J. Liver, in: HTR, 52 (1959), 149–85; H. H. Ben-Sasson (ed.), *Toledot Am Yisrael*, 3 (1969), s.v. *Meshihim;* idem, *The Reformation in Contemporary Jewish Eyes* (1970).

[H.H.B.-S.]

MESSINA, seaport in Sicily. About 1171 *Benjamin of Tudela found 200 (families of?) Jews in Messina. Between 1279 and 1282 the community received the famous kabbalist Abraham *Abulafia, who gave instruction there to two disciples, Abraham and Nathan. In 1347 some Jews of Messina were accused of the ritual murder (see *Blood Libel) of a Christian boy and consequently sentenced to death, an event which was commemorated by a marble inscription in the cathedral. At that time, the Jews lived in a separate quarter called the Paraporto or Giudecca. Although the various communities in Sicily were under the jurisdiction of the **dienchelele*, at one stage the Jews of Messina were exempt from it. Their community was administered by councillors *(proti)*, who, with the assent of the elders, had the authority to excommunicate offenders against Jewish law. When he was *dienchelele*, Moses *Bonavoglia (Ḥefeẓ) of Messina intervened with Alfonso V in 1428 on behalf of the Sicilian Jews and succeeded in having the order concerning conversionist sermons revoked: in 1440 he constructed an assembly hall for the synagogue. In 1487–88 Obadiah of *Bertinoro was in Messina for some months. He gives a vivacious account of the conditions of the community in a letter to his father in Città di Castello. A manuscript of *Naḥmanides' commentary on the Pentateuch, revised and corrected by the scholars of Messina, formed the basis of the 1490 Naples edition. There were 180 Jewish families in the city in 1453. When the Jews were expelled from Sicily in 1492, some 2,400 of them left Messina. In 1728 permission was given for the return of Jews to Messina and the reestablishment of a synagogue, but the experiment was unsuccessful.

Bibliography: Elbogen, in: RI, 1 (1904), 108–11; G. De Giovanni, *L'ebraismo della Sicilia* ... (Palermo, 1748), index; B. and G. Lagumina, *Codice diplomatico dei giudei di Sicilia*, 3 vols. (1884–1909), passim; E. N. Adler, *Jewish Travellers* (1930), 214; Roth, Italy, index; idem, *Gleanings* (1967), 291–7; Milano, Bibliotheca, index; Milano, Italia, index.

[J.S.S.]

MESTEL, JACOB (1884–1958), Yiddish poet, actor, and theater director. Born in Eastern Galicia, his first lyrics appeared in the Lemberg *Togblat* and were collected in the booklet *Ferkholemte Shoen* ("Dream Hours," 1909). He gained his first professional theatrical experience in Vienna (1910–14), and after serving as an officer during World War I, he directed the Freie Juedische Folksbuehne (1918–20). Emigrating to the United States in 1920, in 1923 he joined Maurice *Schwartz's Yiddish Art Theater, and then directed his own group Artef, where he experimented with bold theatrical innovations. From 1926 he and Jacob *Ben-Ami produced Yiddish plays in New York and on tours which included South America. Author of *Literatur un Teater* (1962), he co-edited the leftist monthly *Yidishe Kultur* and the first three volumes of Zalman Zylbercweig's *Leksikon fun Yidishn Teater.* From 1950 to 1958 he was editor of the YCUF publishing house.

Jacob Mestel in the film of Sholem Asch's *Uncle Moses*, produced by Maurice Schwartz, 1932. Courtesy YIVO, New York.

Bibliography: Rejzen, Leksikon, 2 (1929), 458–61; LNYL, 6 (1965), 78–81; Z. Zylbercweig, *Leksikon fun Yidishn Teater*, 2 (1934), 1369–74; M. Neugroeschel, in: *Fun Noenten Over* (1955), 298–305; D. S. Lifson, *Yiddish Theater in America* (1965), 116–25, 436–51.

[S.L.]

METALS AND MINING. In the Bible. Six metals are mentioned in the Bible and in many passages they are listed in the same order: gold, silver, copper, iron, tin, and lead. Antimony is also mentioned. The metals are referred to in various contexts, including methods of mining, metallurgical processes of extracting the metal, and preparing finished products. The strategic and economic importance of metals and of metal craftsmen is stressed. The prophets employ figures of speech based on the properties of metals and the stages of their treatment. These metals have been uncovered in excavations in Ereẓ Israel in the form of vessels and slag. At Tell Jemmeh, Tell Kasila, Timnah, and other sites, furnaces for smelting iron and copper have been found dating from different periods. The only explicit biblical reference to a foundry is to that of King Solomon "in the plain of Jordan ... in the clay ground" where Temple vessels were produced (I Kings 7:46). Utensils for smelting are mentioned mainly as metaphors—"But you the Lord took and brought out of Egypt, that iron blast furnace" (Deut. 4:20). Isaiah speaks of refining silver in a furnace (Isa. 48:10); while Proverbs (27:21) describes the refining of gold and silver in a furnace. Ezekiel compares Israel with the process of refining metals: "The house of Israel has become dross unto Me; all of them, silver and bronze and tin and iron and lead in the furnace, have become dross" (Ezek. 22:18). The prophet was apparently well acquainted with the technical process of refining and smelting silver, and describes how silver is extracted from its ores by means of bellows, leaving slag behind. The working of metals was executed by special smiths and craftsmen, the first of whom was "... Tubal-Cain, who forged all implements of copper and iron" (Gen. 4:22). The Bible speaks of the high qualifications necessary for the specialized metalwork of the Tabernacle: "I have endowed him with a divine spirit of skill, ability, and knowledge... to make designs for work, in gold, silver, and copper" (Ex. 31:3–5). Solomon was forced to bring the craftsman Hiram from Tyre to work in copper (I Kings 7:13–14). The Bible describes the Philistine monopoly of metalsmiths and their strategic importance: "Now there was no smith to be found throughout all the land of Israel; for the Philistines said, 'Lest the Hebrews make themselves swords or spears'" (I Sam. 13:19). The great importance attributed by Nebuchadnezzar to craftsmen and smiths is evident in his deporting them from Jerusalem together with Jehoiachin's army to prevent a possible revolt (II Kings 24:15–16). The methods of working metal after its extraction varied according to the type of metal and the use to which it was put: casting, hammering, gilding, preparing metal, wires, etc.

GOLD (Heb. *zahav*). Gold is one of the rare metals found as an element in nature. It is extracted from the earth by a process of collecting and washing. Specialized goldsmiths employed two methods in working gold. The first consisted of beating it with a hammer into very thin sheets which was possible because of the gold's softness. The sheets were used for, among other things, gilding, and also for making gold wire: "They hammered out sheets of gold and cut threads..." (Ex. 39:3). The second method consisted of melting the gold and then casting it (Ex. 25:12). In the process of melting, the gold was also refined; refined gold, which was necessary for certain purposes (I Chron. 28:18), is apparently identical with "pure gold" (Ex. 25:17).

In various biblical passages words are mentioned that are explained as synonyms of gold: *segor* (Job 28:15); *paz* (Ps. 21:4; Lam. 4:2); *ketem* (Prov. 25:12); *ḥaruẓ* (Ps. 68:14; Prov. 3:14); and *baẓer* (Job 22:24; sometimes understood as "gold ore" or "ingots"). In addition, there are adjectives describing gold, some of which may designate types of gold. The various kinds of gold mentioned in the Bible are summarized in the Talmud (Yoma 44b–45a): "There are seven kinds of gold: gold; good gold (Gen. 2:12); gold of Ophir (I Kings 10:11); fine gold (*ibid.* 10:18); beaten gold (*ibid.* 10:17); pure gold (*ibid.* 6:20); gold of Parvaim (II Chron. 3:6)." In the talmudic discussion concerning the different types of gold, Ophir gold is said to be derived from the place name *Ophir, whereas the other adjectives are said to designate metallic or commercial qualities of gold: *zahav mufaz,* "fine gold," because it resembles *paz* ("a shining jewel"); *zahav shaḥuṭ,* "beaten gold," because it is spun like thread (Heb. *ḥuṭ*); *zahav sagur,* "pure (lit. "locked") gold," indicates such fine quality that when its sale begins all the other shops lock up; *zahav parvaim,* "gold of Parvaim," is said to look like the blood of a bullock (Heb. *par*), but it may also designate a place-name.

The Bible mentions various places from which gold was brought into Ereẓ Israel. Scholars do not agree as to the identification of most of these places but in all probability they include the countries in which gold mines were located in the biblical period: Egypt, Sudan, Saudi Arabia, and India. Among the places cited is the "land of *Havilah" (Gen. 2:11–12), which scholars locate either in southeast Sudan, northwest Ethiopia, or in the southern Sinai Peninsula. The location of Sheba (I Kings 10:6–10) is also disputed (see *Sabea); some scholars place it in Ethiopia and others consider it the name of one of the regions or tribes in southern Arabia. Ophir, which was reached by ships from Ezion-Geber (I Kings 9:26–28; 10–11; 22:49), is identified by *Josephus with India, but, like Havilah and Sheba, it has also been located in Saudi Arabia. Uphaz has not been identified (Jer. 10:9). Parvaim (II Chron. 3:6) is either a place in Arabia or an adjective describing gold as in the talmudic explanation mentioned above.

As early as the patriarchal period, gold was used for manufacturing jewelry and fine vessels (Gen. 24:22) whose value was measured by the amount of gold they contained. Gold was a symbol of wealth and position and served as capital but not as a means of payment. Silver served as currency, but gold bullion as payment is mentioned only once in the Bible: "So David paid Ornan 600 shekels of gold by weight for the site" (I Chron. 21:25; but cf. Num. 22:18; 24:13; II Sam. 21:4; I Kings 15:19; Ezra 8:25f.). The Mishnah explains that "Gold acquires silver, but silver does not acquire gold" (BM 4:1), i.e., gold is valuable as property while silver is a means of payment. At the time of the Exodus from Egypt, the Israelite women borrowed from their neighbors "objects of silver, and gold, and clothing" (Ex. 12:35). Aaron broke off golden earrings to make the golden calf (*ibid.* 32:3). The fullest descriptions of the use of gold are found in the accounts of the building of the Tabernacle in the desert and of Solomon's Temple. In the Tabernacle, gold leaf and gold casts were used, for which the gold was contributed by the Israelites: "And these are the gifts that you shall accept from them: gold, silver, and copper" (Ex. 25:3). The finest craftsmen executed the work (*ibid.* 31:4). Solomon obtained gold for the Temple and his palace from the booty taken in King David's wars (II Sam. 8:7; 12:30) and from trade with Ophir on Hiram's ships (I Kings 9:28). Gold vessels of all kinds denoted wealth and nobility and were also important in ritual. At the same time, the principal idols were made of gold and silver and the prophets inveighed against the worship of these graven images (Isa. 30:22). The wealth and prestige of silver and gold in the form of property and of idols was used as a symbol by the prophets: "Neither their silver nor their gold shall be able to deliver them ..." (Zeph. 1:18). Wealth and gifts of splendor were associated with gold: the Queen of Sheba brought Solomon "... very much gold" (I Kings 10:2); "and the whole earth sought the presence of Solomon to hear his wisdom ... every one of them brought articles of ... gold" (*ibid.* 10:24–25). The shields of Solomon's guard were made of gold (*ibid.* 14:26), and when Ahasuerus made a great banquet for the nobility of his court, he served them from "golden goblets" (Esth. 1:7).

SILVER (Heb. *kesef*). The main minerals in which silver appears in nature are natural silver and silver sulfides. Silver is commonly found in association with gold and copper, and sometimes with lead. Silver was known to man in earliest antiquity; articles of silver have been found in Ereẓ Israel from as early as the Middle Bronze Age. Silver mines in ancient times were located in Spain, Egypt, and Anatolia. According to the Bible, silver, like other metals, was brought by Solomon from *Tarshish (II Chron. 9:21) and Arabia (9:14). Silver was extracted from its ore by smelting, with the use of bellows, and the slag containing lead was separated from the silver (Jer. 6:29–30). Job was acquainted with the technical process of extracting silver: "Surely there is a mine for silver, and a place for gold which they refine" (Job 28:1). Ezekiel also describes the method of extracting silver and mentions slag containing bronze, iron, lead, and tin (Ezek. 22:20–22).

Because of the high value of silver, it was used as a means of payment from earliest times, in preference to gold which was extremely soft. Payment in silver took the form of bullion ("400 shekels of silver," Gen. 23:15) or was weighed on scales. The biblical verse "Here, I have with me the fourth part of a shekel of silver" (I Sam. 9:8) clearly indicates the use of coins. The Temple tax was also paid in silver coins ("a half-shekel," Ex. 30:13). In the Bible the shekel designates a unit of weight (Heb. *mishkal*), from which the term *shekel is apparently derived. Weighing the silver was replaced by standard units of weight, which became *coins; later the coins were counted, as, for example, "I herewith give your brother 1,000 pieces of silver" (Gen. 20:16).

Silver was also used for making vessels for the Tabernacle and the Temple. It was a symbol of wealth and position as in the description of the palace of Ahasuerus ". . . silver rings and marble pillars, and also couches of gold and silver . . ." (Esth. 1:6). When "all the kings of the earth" came to hear Solomon they brought him gifts of gold and silver (II Chron. 9:23–24). The most outstanding description of a king's wealth is the chariot bought in Egypt by Solomon for 600 shekels of silver (I Kings 10:29). Job describes kings and counselors "who filled their houses with silver" (Job. 3:15). Among biblical figures of speech and similes based on silver is: "Your silver is become dross" (Isa. 1:22), i.e., the very valuable metal is transformed into something worthless like the slag formed during its reduction. The smelting and refining of silver is used as a symbol of the Israelites: "For Thou, O God, hast tested us; Thou hast tried us as silver is tried" (Ps. 66:10). Trade in silver becomes a symbol of trade in general; although it is an honest trade, it is transcended by the acquisition of wisdom "For the gain from it is better than gain of silver" (Prov. 3:14).

COPPER (Heb. *neḥoshet*). The copper referred to in the Bible is not pure copper but an alloy of copper and tin. This alloy—bronze—was the most useful and important metal from the beginning of the third millennium B.C.E. to the 13th century B.C.E. when it began to be replaced by iron. Copper mines in the Ancient Near East were located in Cyprus (from which the name copper is apparently derived), Sinai, and Egypt. It was the main metal extracted in Ereẓ Israel in antiquity and is the only one mined there today. Copper is usually extracted from sulfide minerals, and partly from silicates, and carbonates; very small amounts of native copper are also found.

The Arabah contains copper mines in three main centers: (1) Faynān (biblical Punon, Num. 33:42), around 25–30 mi. (40–50 km.) south of the Dead Sea in the eastern Arabah; (2) the area of Wadi Abu Khushayba, around 8 mi. (13 km.) southwest of Petra; (3) and in the Timna-Amram region which also extends southwest of Elath. The copper deposits appear in the form of concentrates in the white Nubian sandstone with a base of *Evronah* complex formation of the Lower Cretaceous period. The concentrates are connected with the layer of fossilized trees in the sandstone and are composed mainly of sulfides, carbonates, silicates, and copper oxides. They have a high copper content which reaches as much as 30–40%. N. Glueck, the first to describe these deposits in detail, attributes the beginning of copper mining and smelting activities to the Kenites, Kenizzites, and Kadmonites (Gen. 115:19), who inhabited the area and were related to Tubal-Cain (i.e., the Kenite), the first metalsmith (*ibid.* 4:22). In Glueck's opinion they were nomadic tribes who wandered in the Arabah and were metallurgical specialists. He also associates the Edomites with the metal industry and its trade through the Arabah and the Red Sea. The area was conquered by David, and Solomon continued to work the mines and develop international trade, mainly by way of Ezion-Geber; his metallurgical industry was located in the plain of the Jordan "in the clay ground between Succoth and Zarethan" (I Kings 7:46). Glueck suggests that copper was even exported from the Arabah by Solomon, and also that the protracted wars between Judah and Edom during the period of the Kingdom of Judah were over control of the copper mines in the Arabah.

Excavations carried out between 1959 and 1969 by the Arabah Expedition headed by B. Rothenberg concluded that the copper mines in the Timna area are not to be attributed to the time of Solomon. Rothenberg distinguished three periods at the site: the Chalcolithic period (fourth millennium B.C.E.), the Early Iron Age, and the Byzantine period (third–fourth centuries C.E.). Rothenberg suggests that Egyptian kings in the 14th–12th centuries B.C.E., and not the kings of Israel and Judah, sent mining expeditions to the Arabah, and that the copper mines and the smelting installations were operated by the Egyptians together with the Midianites, Kenites, and Amalekites. Among the finds in an Egyptian temple discovered in Timna was a copper snake which dates it to the time of the Exodus. According to the excavator, the Kenites and the Midianites employed highly developed methods of copper production that ceased with the Israelite Conquest; only commercial activities, and not production, were undertaken in the period of the Monarchy by way of Ezion-Geber and the Red Sea to Ophir and Sheba. Rothenberg also emphasizes that a metallurgical center was located in the Succoth-Zarethan area where imported raw copper was made into finished products (I Kings 7:46). The copper was extracted from its ore by smelting in an oven and then cast. Heat was produced by charcoal from acacia trees which grow in the Arabah.

Much copper was used in manufacturing vessels for the Temple and especially for the Tabernacle: clasps, sockets, rings, posts of the enclosure, lavers, etc. (Ex. 26–36). The biblical description of copper weapons indicates a highly developed military culture, e.g., the description of Goliath: "He had a helmet of bronze on his head, and he was armed with a coat of mail, and the weight of the coat was 5,000 shekels of bronze" (I Sam. 17:5–7). Copper was fashioned into a symbol for the Israelites in the desert in the form of a serpent of copper made by Moses (Num. 21:9; see *Copper Serpent); it was preserved by the Israelites up to the time of Hezekiah who destroyed it, calling it *Nehushtan (II Kings 18:4). The destruction of the Temple is emphasized by the removal of the copper; after the Temple was burnt, the Babylonians destroyed all the objects in it and carried away a great many copper objects to Babylonia and "the bronze of all these vessels was beyond weight" (II Kings 25:13, 16). In its use in vessels for the Tabernacle and Temple and for weapons, copper symbolized strength and rigidity—"The skies above your head shall be copper" (Deut. 28:23). It also denoted drought—"I will make your skies like iron and your earth like copper" (Lev. 26:19). The word for chains (*neḥushtayim*) is also derived from copper. Not only the heaven and earth but also the Israelites are compared with rigid copper: "your forehead copper" (Isa. 48:4).

IRON (Heb. *barzel*). Job was acquainted with the technical process of extracting iron from iron ore: "iron is taken out of the earth" (Job. 28:2). Isaiah described the smith's technique of working iron with the help of charcoal to produce steel suitable for making vessels (Isa. 54:16). The Bible speaks of Tubal-Cain as the first metalsmith (Gen. 4:22; see above discussion of copper). Some scholars identify the family of Japheth, to whom Tubal-Cain was related, with peoples who inhabited the coast of the Black

Sea. Iron was first exploited by the Hittites in Asia Minor and it was brought to Syria and Ereẓ Israel by Phoenician merchants. Another source of iron was Tarshish, and "massive iron" was brought from Vedan and Javan (Ezek. 27:12–13, 19).

The Early Iron Age in Ereẓ Israel corresponds roughly with the period of the Philistines (from c. 1200 B.C.E.). The iron in the hands of the Philistines may have been connected with their maritime trade and with imports by merchants from the north. Iron mines were apparently located in the mountains of iron in the hill region of Edom (Josephus mentions an "Iron Mountain" near Gerasha) and also in southern Lebanon, but these were probably of little importance. Iron was used primarily for weapons, and ironsmiths were thus of prime importance in the military organization. The Philistines succeeded in securing control of all the smiths—apparently ironsmiths: "Now there was no smith to be found throughout the land of Israel" (I Sam. 13:19). Whoever needed the services of ironsmiths for sharpening everyday tools, such as agricultural implements, was forced to go to the Philistines. Iron implements (a plow and a spade) have been found at Tell Jamma and also furnaces for smelting iron; the earliest finds come from Tell al-ʿAjūl where a dagger with an iron blade and copper handle were also discovered. As early as the biblical period, iron was employed extensively in everyday life: war, agriculture, building, religion, trade, and household utensils. Iron weapons included chariots (Josh. 17:16); horns (I Kings 22:11); swords and spears (I Sam. 13:19; II Sam. 23:7); "iron objects" (Num. 35:16); and fetters (Ps. 105:18); while iron agricultural tools included sledges (Amos 1:3) and yokes (Jer. 28:14). In building, iron was used in door bars (Isa. 45:3), nails for doors of gates (I Chron. 22:3), and hammers and axes (I Kings 6:7); in religion, it was used for statues of gods (Dan. 5:4); and in trade, for weights (I Sam. 17:7). Household utensils made of iron included: bedsteads (Deut. 3:11) and pens (Job 19:24).

Iron often appears in figures of speech in the Bible, but it mainly symbolizes the material from which instruments of war were made. Its use was prohibited in building an altar (Ex. 20:25): "an altar of unhewn stones, upon which no man has lifted an iron tool" (Josh. 8:31). The Mishnah elaborates: "for iron was created to shorten man's days, while the altar was created to lengthen man's days; what shortens may not rightly be lifted up against what lengthens" (Mid. 3:4). Solomon carried the ban against using stones hewn with iron in building the altar even further when he built the Temple, "so that neither hammer nor axe nor any tool of iron was heard in the Temple," while it was being built (I Kings 6:7). In the Talmud a discussion is held on whether the prohibition against the use of iron tools applied only to the Temple site or to the quarry as well (Sot. 48b), for Solomon built three rows of hewn stone in the inner court (I Kings 6:36). In the description of David's battle with Goliath, spiritual values are contrasted with iron weapons symbolizing war, as Goliath appears with a sword, spear, and javelin, opposite David's faith in God (I Sam. 17:45, 47). Iron also denotes strength: "iron yoke" (Deut. 28:48), "your neck is an iron sinew" (Isa. 48:4), and has a special meaning in Psalms 107:10.

TIN (Heb. *bedil*). Tin was known to, and utilized by, the ancient Egyptians. There was an extensive international trade in tin that was alloyed with copper to make bronze—the copper of the Bible. Tin was mentioned by Ezekiel as one of the products imported by the Phoenicians from Tarshish (27:12). It appears in the Bible together with the other metals, gold, silver, copper, iron, and lead, for example, in connection with the laws of their purification after being captured as booty (Num. 31:22). Tin is mentioned by Ezekiel as one of the components of the slag obtained by reducing silver from its ore (22:18–22) and by Isaiah: "smelt away your dross as with lye, and remove all your tin" (1:25). No specific tin vessels are mentioned in the Bible.

LEAD (Heb. *ʿoferet*). The ancient sources of lead were Asia Minor and Syria, and it was included among the metals brought by the Phoenicians from Tarshish (Ezek. 27:12). Lead galena is found today at the foot of Mount Hermon; however, nothing is known of its extraction in antiquity. Because of its high specific gravity, it served as weights for fishermen's nets—"they sank like lead in the majestic waters" (Ex. 15:10), from which the simile "to sink in water like lead" is derived. The plumb line may also have been made of lead (Amos 7:7). Lead served also as a cover of utensils because of its high specific gravity (Zech. 5:7–8). The verse, "... that with an iron pen and lead they were graven in the rock for ever!" (Job. 19:24), seems to indicate that as early as biblical times, lead was used for writing; because of the softness of lead, writing implements were made of stone filled with lead. Lead is mentioned several times in the Bible together with the other metals (e.g. Num. 31:22). Lead, or lead minerals, may have been used for cosmetics and dyes.

ANTIMONY (Heb. *pukh*). No objects made of antimony are known, but it appears in copper alloys. Unlike the other metals, the Bible does not mention antimony as a metal but only its use as a mineral—as eye shadow. Kohl for painting the eyes (II Kings 9:30; cf. Ezek. 23:40) is translated in the Vulgate as stibium. [U.S.W.]

In Rabbinic Literature. Rabbinic literature—the Talmuds in particular—contains a wealth of information on metals and metallurgy (though not on their primary production by mining), on the use of the various metals in manufacture, on metal artifacts, and so on. The growth of terminology as well as the use of terms borrowed from Greek, Latin, and even Persian is an indication on the progress from biblical times in the refining process and in the use of metals, though the basic metals remained more or less the same. As distinct from the Bible, rabbinic literature has generic terms for metals, generally *mattekhet* from the biblical root (*ntk*, "to smelt"), and in the Middle Ages also *metilin* or *metil* from the Greek *μέταλλον* or Latin *metallum*. Metals mentioned in rabbinic literature are gold, silver, copper (brass and bronze), iron, tin, lead, and antimony or stibium. A number of terms exist for metal sheets, bars, or lumps: *eshet* or *ashashit niska* ("cast metal"), particularly a bar of silver or gold; *ḥarakhah* ("lumps of metal [iron ore]"), before smelting; *milela* for gold ore as broken in the mine; *peitalon* (Gr. *πέταλον*; "metal or gold leaf"), for which there is also a Hebrew word *(tas)*; and also the more general term *golem* (pl. *gelamim*), meaning any raw, unfinished material. There is also a whole range of terms for old and broken metal which could be used again, the most general of which is *gerutei* (pl. *geruta'ot*) or *gerumei* (in Gr. *γρύτη*), "junk iron" still used in modern Hebrew for junk, rubbish, but other derivations have been suggested (see S. Krauss in JE 8, 515 and Kohut, *Arukh ha-Shalem* s.v.). *Asimon* (Gr. *ἄσημος*) is uncoined bullion or coins on which the stamping has worn off.

The social standing of metalworkers was high, but they maintained fine distinctions between them, with the gold- and silversmith *(zehavim, kassafim)* ranking higher than the ordinary smith *(nappaḥ)*; cf. the description of the separate seats occupied by different craftsmen in the great synagogue of Alexandria in Sukkah 51b. The metalworker is called *nappaḥ* as he has to blow *(nafaḥ)* the fire with the *mappu'aḥ* ("bellows") in order to soften the metal. The gold- and silversmith is also called *meẓaref*, though this is occasionally applied to the coppersmith as well. For fuel, the smith used *peḥam* (charcoal), which he had to make himself, and the *peḥami* is therefore both the charcoal burner and the blacksmith (cf. the story of R. Gamaliel's visit to the home of R. Joshua b. Hananiah, who was a needle maker; Ber. 28a). For the smelting of gold, straw was used as fuel. When taken from the fire with *ẓevat* ("tongs," cf. Avot 5, 6), the metal was beaten with the *pattish* ("hammer") or *kurnas* (Gr. κέαρνον) on the *saddan* ("anvil") made by the *sadna'ah*. The term "beat with the hammer" became typical for every kind of manufacture. Rabbinic literature contains many further details on the various activities of the blacksmith and other instruments which he uses (see Krauss, Tal Arch, 2 (1911), 299ff.) There is an equally great variety of implements and vessels, which were made from the various metals. Metals were used in every kind of manufacturing process, in agriculture, for domestic and personal needs, for weapons and armaments, for coins, and Temple use. Gold and silver were the main raw material of women's ornaments (*ibid.*, 307ff.).

GOLD. Both Talmuds and some Midrashim have slightly differing lists of seven varieties of gold, most of which occur already in the Bible (TJ, Yoma 4:4, 41d; Yoma 44b; Num. R. 12:4; Song R. 3:10, no. 3; for the talmudic discussion on the various names for gold see above, in the biblical section). Various information is given on the smelting of the gold used for the making of the **menorah* by Moses (TJ, Shekalim 6:4, 50b), Solomon, and in the Second Temple (Song R. 3:10, no. 3). According to the Midrash, gold had, in any event, been created for its use in the Temple (Ex. R. 35:1). It does not deteriorate (Me'il. 5:1 19a). In Solomon's time, weights were made of gold (PdRK 169a). The gold (and silver), which the Israelites carried away from Egypt, is a frequent subject of *aggadah* (see Ber. 32a). So are the golden tables of the rich (Shab. 119a; Ta'an. 25a; Tam. 32a). The members of the Sanhedrin of Alexandria sat on golden chairs in the famous basilica (Suk. *ibid.*, and parallels). Famous, too, is the golden tiara (*Yerushalayim shel zahav*) which R. Akiva gave to his wife (Shab. 59a). His colleague R. Ishmael had a bride fitted with a golden tooth to make her more attractive (Ned. 66b; cf. Shab. 6, 5). Rich men in Jerusalem would tie their *lulavim* with threads of gold (Suk. 3, 8) and offer their firstfruits in baskets of silver or of gold (Bik. 3, 8).

SILVER (Heb. *kesef*). The term *argentariyya* and similar forms (Gr. ἀργεντάριος, Lat. *argentarium*) is used in TJ, *Peah* 8:9, 21b and the Midrash (PdRK 106b) for table silver (and gold) and *martekha* for silver slag (Git. 69b).

COPPER, BRASS, BRONZE (Heb. *neḥoshet*). The word *beronza* ("bronze") is found in medieval rabbinic literature (Heilprin, *Seder Dorot*, 1 (1905), 104). The Greek word χαλκός which like *neḥoshet* means copper as well as the alloys brass and bronze, though later the latter only, is used in the Babylonian Talmud (BK 100b) for copper caldron (so also in Gr.; see Jastrow, Dict. s.v.); in the Jerusalem Talmud (BB 4:6, 14c) for the copper (caldron) room in a bathhouse; the Targum often used the form *karkoma* (χαλκωμα), Greek for anything made of copper, etc. (see S. Krauss, *Griechische und lateinische Lehnwoerter* (1898), 299). The term *peliza* (a kind of bronze, see JE, 8, 516) is used in *Bava Kama* (113b, Ms., see Rabbinowicz, Dik Sof, BK 140). According to the Midrash (Lev. R. 7:5; Tanḥ., Terumah 11), the copper covering on the altar of the Tabernacle would miraculously not melt in spite of the perpetual fire. Bronze tablets were used to inscribe international treaties, such as the one between Judah Maccabee and Rome (I Macc. 8:22; Jos., Ant. 12:416) and his brother Simeon and Sparta (I Macc. 14:18). Mishnah *Parah* (12:5) mentions a "hyssop of brass." Nathan b. Jehiel's *Arukh* quotes from the lost *Midrash Yelammedenu* the term *konekhi* (Gr. κόγχη), a copper shell or bowl (for oil). Corinthian bronze (*kelinteya*), famous for its quality and shine, was used for the Nicanor gates of the Herodian Temple (Eliezer b. Jacob, Yoma 38a; Tosef. *ibid;* 2:4).

IRON (Heb. *barzel, parzel, parzela*). As to the sources of iron ore, the Palestinian Targum translates the place-names Kadesh and Wilderness of Zin (Sinai) as "Mountain of Iron" (Num. 33:36; 34:4). The Mishnah (Suk. 3:1) and Josephus (War 4:454) mention an Iron Mountain near Gerasa in Transjordan (Avi-Yonah, Geog. 162). Indian iron was used for making weapons (Av. Zar. 16a), and Indian swords were the very best available (Tanḥ., Va-Etḥannan, 6). *Parzelayyah* is used as a generic term for iron tools (Lev. R. 24:3; TJ, Nid. 2:6, 50b, as a simile for a sharp mind). He who bathes in hot water without showering himself afterward with cold water is like iron that has been treated in the fire without being put into cold water afterward (Shab. 41a). According to R. Eliezer, it is permitted on the Sabbath to cut wood on which to burn coal to forge a knife for a circumcision which is to occur on that day (*ibid.* 19:1, 130a). The Talmud speaks of *even sho'evet*, a magnetic stone which attracts iron (Sot. 47a).

TIN. The terms used for this metal are either *ba'aẓ* or *avaẓ, kassitera, kassiteron*, and *gassiteron* (Gr. κασσίτερος). Both *ba'aẓ* and *kassitera* are used in the same passages (Men. 28b and elsewhere), which implies that they were two different metals or kinds of the same metal. The Temple *menorah* was not to be made of them, but when the Hasmoneans cleansed the Temple and needed a new *menorah* (the golden one having been carried off by Antiochus IV) they made it of seven spears plated with tin (*ibid.*) It was forbidden to make weights out of metal—tin and lead being mentioned specially—because metal wears away (BB 89b and Tos. ad loc.; Tosef. *ibid.*, 5:9). The traveler Pethahiah of Regensburg (12th century) reports that in Babylonia people were summoned to synagogue by a tin instrument. In the later Middle Ages up to modern times tin was used extensively for objects of *ritual art such as Ḥanukkah *menorot, seder, Kiddush*, and *Havdalah* plates, etc.

LEAD. Lead is called *avar* in rabbinic literature, also *karkemisha* in the Palestine Targum (Num 31:22; Job 19:24). *Ḥullin* 8a (cf. Neg. 9:1) mentions "lead from its source" as a naturally hot substance causing injury. The water reservoirs below the Temple Mount were said to be lined with lead (Letter of Aristeas 90). Lead was also used as a writing material (Shab. 104b, see Rashi). A wick of hot lead was used to carry out the death sentence by burning (Sanh. 52a), and water pipes were made of lead (Mik. 6:8). The term *alsefidag* (of Persian origin) is used in geonic literature for white lead (Kohut, Arukh, 4 (1926), 82).

ANTIMONY OR STIBIUM. Antimony or stibium, called *koḥal*, was used in the form of a powder for painting the eyelids (verb *kaḥal*). From the word *koḥal* the modern Hebrew word for blue (*kaḥol*) is derived. Both the noun and the verb are used in many talmudic passages (e.g., Shab. 8:3; 10:6, 80a; Ket. 17a). A species of hyssop is called *ezov koḥalit* (Neg. 14:6 and elsewhere), probably after a district (Kid. 66a) in Transjordan (see Jastrow, Dict. s.v.), which may, in turn, have derived its name from the metal; cf. the "hyssop of brass" in *Parah* 12:5, mentioned above.

ḤASHMAL. The mysterious *ḥashmal* (Ezek. 1:4; 8:2) is interpreted in Ḥagigah (13a–b) as fire-spouting dragons. Translators called it amber or galena (lead-ore), while in modern Hebrew it has become the word for electricity (cf. S. Munk (ed.), *Guide des égarés*, 2 (1961), 229 n. 4).

VALUE OF METALS. The relative value attached to metals

can be seen from the pages concerning the Temple *menorah* (Men. 28b), where they are listed either in descending order—gold, silver, tin, lead—or ascending order—iron, tin, silver, gold. The relative value of metals depended on the currency situation, the coins made of less valuable metal being considered currency in relation to those of the more valuable one, which is then considered commodity but not currency (see BM 4:1; Mishnah lists gold, silver, and copper in descending order, whereas the same Mishnah in the Jerusalem Talmud (BM 4:1, 9c) puts silver before gold).

SYMBOLISM OF METALS. The symbolism of metals representing the Four Kingdoms in Daniel 2 and 3 is expanded in *Exodus Rabbah* (35:5), "Gold is Babylon; silver is Media; copper is Greece; iron is Edom (Rome); etc." A symbolic meaning is found by *Midrash Tadshe* 11 in the fact that of the two altars in the Tabernacle and Temple one was overlaid with gold (the soul) the other with copper (the body). On account of the Golden Calf, gold became a symbol of sin, and therefore a *shofar* mouthpiece was not to be overlaid with gold (RH 27a; cf. Maharil, *Hilkhot Rosh Ha-Shanah*), nor did the high priest officiate on the Day of Atonement in the Holy of Holies in his golden vestments but in white linen ones (*ibid.* 26a). At the same time, the gold plate on the incense altar of the Tabernacle and Temple was to atone for the sin of the Golden Calf (Yal., Ex. 368). Iron is also a metaphor for strength of character, and a scholar who is not as hard as iron is no scholar (Ta'an. 4a; cf. Men. 95b concerning Rav Sheshet). Similarly the Evil Inclination may be as hard as iron, but the Torah, which is likened to an (iron) hammer (Jer. 23:29), will smash it (Suk. 52b; see Tos. ad loc.). Some students may find their studies as hard as iron (Ta'an. 8a), but two scholars studying together sharpen each other's mind as one piece of iron sharpens the other (*ibid.* 7a). As wine cannot be preserved in golden or silver vessels but only in the humblest of vessels (earthen ones), so the words of the Torah will not be preserved in one who is in his own eyes like a gold or silver vessel but only in one, who is like the lowliest of vessels (Sif. Deut. 48).

[ED.]

Jews as Metalworkers and Miners. A study of the part played by Jews in the mining and metal industries proves that there has been too great a tendency to minimize their participation in the promotion and development of these branches. It is true that the objective restrictions which kept the Jews off the land and prevented their ownership of it, especially in medieval society, contributed in no small measure to limiting their opportunities of exploiting natural resources in general and various metals in particular. Yet despite all this the Jews succeeded, at different times and in various countries, in penetrating several branches connected with the mining of metals, their contribution to the advance of the industry being at times of great significance.

PRE-MODERN PERIOD. Very little information on the exploitation of the earth's resources has come down to us from the mishnaic and talmudic periods. Until the end of the fourth century there were copper mines at Punon, at the south of the Dead Sea, and *Jerome (340?–420) testifies that mining was discontinued there during his lifetime. The literature of these periods frequently mentions coal and copper refiners; it may be assumed that the "refiner" mentioned in the Mishnah (Ket. 7:10) is merely a copper smelter. As mentioned, the separation of Jews from the land in the Middle Ages had implications for the mining industry. In those times mining was frequently connected with agricultural labor, and thus in Germany, for instance, there were farmers who were engaged in extracting iron ore in their free time. It is therefore evident that since the Jews were cut off from agriculture their opportunities for extracting metals were limited. Added to this, in Christian Europe minerals were considered crown property, so that private ownership of mines was impossible. Yet in spite of all these restrictions Jews were to be found in various branches of the mining industry, as lessees and managers, traders in metals, and even miners. As for precious metals, there can be no doubt that their employment as minters of coins, especially in absolutist Europe at the time when *Court Jews flourished, brought them into direct contact with gold and silver mining (see *Mintmasters and Moneyers). A similar state of affairs prevailed with regard to the extraction of precious stones (see *Diamond Industry and Trade), since the Jews were prominent in the international trade in luxury goods and in purveying them to royal courts, at least from the days of the Carolingian kingdom up to the time of the absolutist states in modern Europe. In such countries as Spain and Poland, where Jews played an outstanding part as colonizers, they were prominent as lessees of salt mines (see *Salt Production).

There were also Jews in different countries throughout the Middle Ages who were engaged in extracting both heavy and light metals of various kinds. In England, for instance, Jews had worked in tin mining in Cornwall in 1198. Joachim *Gaunse appeared in 1581 and suggested to the English government new methods for processing copper. When it became known that he was a Jew from Prague he was arrested by the authorities and his fate is unknown. In Sicily, there was a long tradition of Jewish activity in the mines from the times of the emperor Tiberius, who sent 4,000 Jewish youths as slaves to the mines. Jews were commonly engaged there not only in the manufacture of metalware but also in mining silver and iron. In spite of the opposition of the local authorities, a royal decree of 1327 ordered Sicilian officials to support Jewish mine prospectors and miners. At the beginning of the 15th century two Jews of *Alghero received special authorization to exploit the resources of the region, on condition that half the output be handed over to the crown. Attempts by Jews to extract metals in Germany are also known: in 1625 Duke Frederick Ulrich of Brunswick asked the theologians of the University of Helmstedt if he might be allowed to hand over the lead trade to two Jews and authorize them to move freely through his state for that purpose. After the members of the faculty had agreed, these Jews mined lead from the Harz Mountains.

MODERN PERIOD. In modern times the part played by Jews in the mining and metal industries of Germany reached considerable dimensions. After Aron Hirsch (1783–1842) had established a firm for buying and selling copper in 1805 Halberstadt became the cradle of the modern German nonferrous metal trade. In 1820 he became a partner in founding copper enterprises in Werne and Ilsenburg. When his son Joseph (1809–71) joined the business its name was changed to Aron Hirsch and Son. In 1863 they acquired the copper works of Heegermuehle, near Eberswalde. A branch was established in New York in 1894 and the firm began to take an interest in the metal enterprises of France, Belgium, and England and the mines of Australia, America, and Eastern Asia. At the close of the 19th century Aaron Siegmund Hirsch initiated the establishment of the zinc enterprises of *Vladivostok. The firm of Hirsch Kupfer- und Messingwerke A.G. was founded in 1906; World War I and the economic crisis of 1929–32 caused it to be liquidated in 1932. Dr. Emil Hirsch (1870–1938) then founded a new enterprise in Berlin, the Erze und Metalle Hirsch A.G., with a branch in Amsterdam, but the firm was liquidated when the Nazis came to power. Philipp Abraham Cohen, a descendant of the Hanover banking family, transferred the family business to

Frankfort in 1821. In Hanover they had been connected with the mining enterprises in the Harz Mountains. Philipp Abraham Cohen's son-in-law established the metal-trading firm of Henry R. Merton and Co. in London. In the meantime the Frankfort firm extended its scope and traded in American copper and tin from the Dutch Indies. This enterprise was also involved in the nickel and aluminum trades, and until 1873, when the Deutsche Gold und Silber-Scheideanstalt was established, in the silver trade too. In 1881 the branches in England and Frankfort established the Metallgesellschaft, Frankfort on the Main, which became the leading German firm in the metal trade. Among other enterprises, they established the Usine de Désargentation (de-silverizing plant) in Hoboken, near Antwerp. In 1896, together with the firms of Hirsch and Beer, and Sondheimer and Co., they undertook zinc and lead mining. The Metallurgische Gesellschaft (Lurgi) was established in 1897; together with the Metallgesellschaft, it founded the Berg und Metallbank A.G. in 1906. Once the firm had successfully overcome the post-World War I crisis, branches were established in Amsterdam, Basle, Brussels, Copenhagen, Madrid, Milan, Prague, Stockholm, and Vienna. It was liquidated as a Jewish firm when Hitler came to power.

The Jews of Russia, too, had considerable achievements to their credit in the mining of certain metals and in associated industries. In 1807 there were 253 Jewish copper and tin workers in Minsk, Kiev, and Yekaterinoslav, that is, 6.8% of the Jewish craftsmen in these towns. ICA (*Jewish Colonization Association) statistics of 1897 reveal that there were then 15,669 Jewish smiths and 11,801 Jewish craftsmen in the various branches of the metal industry. The Jews were also well represented in the development of the industry: in Moscow four metal factories were established by Jews between 1869 and 1878, and a further two factories in the Moscow area between 1878 and 1880. Of the 96 large iron and tin plants in Odessa in 1910, 88 belonged to Jews. The laws of 1882 and 1887 excluded the Jews from the mines, but in spite of this they played a considerable role in the gold mines. Descendants of exiles and Jewish settlers in Siberia were among the pioneers of gold mining there. The director of the largest gold-mining enterprise in Russia in 1913, Lena Goldfields Co., was Baron Alfred Guenzburg; Jews were represented in the Gold Mining Co., and also in the platinum mines: of the five directors of the A.G. Platinum enterprise in 1912, two were Jews.

In the U.S. there were several prominent Jewish firms engaged in copper extraction. In 1813 Harmon *Hendricks established in Belleville, New Jersey, the Soho Copper Rolling Mills, later known as the Belleville Copper Mills. His descendants were prominent in the metal trade. In 1891 Meyer *Guggenheim (1828–1905), formerly a peddler and dry-goods merchant, acquired copper mines and then established an enterprise in Aguas Calientes, Mexico. Together with his sons he founded the mining company of M. Guggenheim's Sons. In 1901 they merged with the American Smelting and Refining Co. and the Guggenheim sons directed the enterprise. The firm initiated the acquisition and development of a copper mine in Alaska, developed copper mines in Mexico, and even extended its activities to Australia, Canada, and Africa.

Coal, which had been practically unknown in medieval Europe, was introduced into various branches of industry in England at the beginning of the 17th century because of the rise in the price of firewood. The Industrial Revolution increased the importance of coal, which came into use in the other countries of Europe during the 18th and the beginning of the 19th centuries. In Eastern and Central Europe the Jews were pioneers in developing coal mines. In Poland, prospecting by Solomon Isaac of *Bytom led to the establishment of two large coal mining enterprises in 1790: the Krol mine near Chorzow and the Królowa Ludwika mine near Zabrze, which were worked for about 50 years. Between 1874 and 1879 many Jews studied at the mining school of Tarnowskie Gory; they were later employed as miners and engineers in Upper Silesia. Jews participated in the wholesale coal and iron trade until World War II. The large coal concern of *Katowice was a development of the important coal firm of Emmanuel Friedlander and Co. Their activity in the coal mines led them to develop an interest in mining other metals and brought them into various branches of the metal industry. In 1805 there were three copper foundries in Podolia employing 42 Jewish workers; in Warsaw a Jewish iron factory, which employed 200 Jewish workers, was established in 1848. Until 1938, when the cartel organizations introduced their policy of ousting all factories not connected with international concerns, the iron foundry of Cracow belonged to Jews. In the wholesale iron trade, the old-established Warsaw firms of Priwess, and Freilach and Carmel were prominent; both prospered between the two world wars. According to the census of 1931, 1,462 Jews were employed in the mines (including 853 miners); 33,318 Jews were employed in metal foundries and in the metal and machinery industries (9,185 manual workers), and 4,209 Jews in the minerals industry (1,440 manual workers). The great majority of the Jews employed in the metal branch (73.9%) were craftsmen.

The Jews of Germany, too, were active in the coal industry in that country; many of them entered it via the coal trade or real estate business. Fritz Friedlaender-Fuld (1858–1917), an apostate, extracted coal in the Rybnik region. Eduard Arnhold (1849–1925), who had been director of the Caesar Wollheim coal firm, supervised a considerable part of the mining industry of Upper Silesia. Paul Silberberg succeeded his father as director of a lignite mine (Fortuna) in 1903.

In various parts of Czechoslovakia the Jews were the first to extract coal. The first person to exploit the coal mines of Ostrava-Karvina (Moravia), in 1840, was David Gutmann of Lipnik nad Becvu (see Wilhelm von *Gutmann). After obtaining the support of the Rothschild family, who owned iron works in Vitkovice, they established joint iron and mining enterprises there. At the beginning of the 20th century some of the coal mines of Kladno were owned by Jews, among them Leopold Sachs. The *Petschek family was active in the development of the lignite coal mines, particularly in northern Bohemia. Their competitor and former employer was Jakob *Weinmann. [J.KA.]

In South Africa Jews were among the pioneers in the exploitation of South Africa's mineral resources. They were early in the field when industrial development started during the second half of the 19th century, and they remained prominent in the opening up of the country's coal, diamond, gold, and base metal mines. Jews like Barney *Barnato, the *Joel brothers, Lionel *Phillips, the *Beit brothers, and the *Albu brothers were among the prospectors, explorers, diggers, and financiers who flocked to the diamond fields at Kimberley in the 1870s. Sammy *Marks began coal mining on a large scale in the Transvaal and laid the foundations of the steelworks at Vereeniging. When the industrial focus moved to Johannesburg with the discovery of gold there in 1886, the Kimberley Jews played a foremost role in the creation of the great mining groups which developed the Witwatersrand. Here Sir Ernest *Oppenheimer created the powerful Anglo-American Corporation, headed the De Beers group, and stabilized the diamond market through the Diamond Corporation. Oppenheimer also pioneered the copper industry in Northern Rhodesia (now Zambia) and after World War II led the development of the new goldfields in the Orange Free State and in the Eastern Transvaal. During this period A. S. Hersov and S. G. Menell created the Anglo-Vaal mining and industrial group. Jewish financiers also promoted the exploitation of platinum, manganese, and asbestos deposits. [Ed.]

As for the oil industry (see *Petroleum), which was first developed in the second half of the 19th century, not only did the Jews participate in it (especially in Central and Eastern Europe) but Jewish industrialists were among the first to engage in the commercial exploitation of petroleum products.

From the above it is clear that the notion that Jews succeeded in forming part of the metal industry in the Diaspora only in secondary branches, close to the consumer, ignores the specific part they played in developing the primary branches. Even if this part was not quantitatively significant, there is no doubt that it was qualitatively important. It would appear that in those times and countries in which Jews were able to enter these branches of industry they engaged in them with great success.

Jewish Craftsmen in the Metal Trades. Many successive generations of Jews were engaged in various crafts connected with the metal industries. This continuity of occupation could be preserved chiefly in Muslim countries, where the Jews were enabled to conduct a more varied economic life than in Christian Europe. This was also true of such countries as Spain and Sicily which, although conquered by the Christians, still preserved modes of life from the days of Muslim domination. Jews were especially noted for arms manufacture. Jewish armorers are mentioned in the Mishnah (Av. Zar. 1:6), and Josephus describes the preparation of arms during the Jewish War (see, e.g., Jos., Wars, 3:22). *Dio Cassius, the historian of the second to third centuries C.E., relates that before the *Bar Kokhba War Jewish smiths deliberately manufactured defective weapons so that they would be rejected by the Romans and could later be used by Bar Kokhba's soldiers. From this account it can also be deduced that the Romans conscripted Jewish craftsmen to manufacture their arms. When *Muhammad gained control of *Medina, in southern Arabia, many of the weapons he obtained for his army were manufactured by local Jewish artisans. The "coats of mail of David" (probably named after a Jewish smith) were then famous in Arabia. The Jews of Portugal, too, excelled in this craft; their expulsion in 1496 brought a considerable number of them to Turkey, where they made a significant contribution to strengthening the military might of the Ottoman Empire.

The agent of the king of France in Constantinople during the first half of the 16th century tells of the numerous Marranos who revealed to the Turks the secrets of manufacturing cannons, guns, warships, and war machines. Obadiah of *Bertinoro found many Jewish copper- and ironsmiths in *Palermo in 1487. When an expulsion decree was issued against the Jews of Sicily, in the wake of the expulsion from Spain, the local authorities complained that tremendous loss would result "because almost all the craftsmen" in Sicily were Jews; their expulsion would deprive the Christians of "workers who manufacture metal utensils, arms, and ironware." A similar complaint was heard in Portugal as a result of the expulsion order of 1496.

Many Jewish craftsmen and artisans were engaged in the metal industry in Christian Spain. In 1365 three Jewish smithies are mentioned in Toledo, and there were also Jewish workshops in Avila, Valladolid, Valdeolivas near Cuenca, and Talavera de la Reina; a Jewish tinsmith, Solomon (Çuleman) b. Abraham Toledano of Avila, is mentioned in a document of 1375; at the close of the 14th century Jewish smiths were called upon to repair the copper fountain of Burgos. Before 1391 many Jewish smiths, engravers, and goldsmiths lived in Barcelona. From a Saragossa register of 1401 we learn that there were many Jewish engravers and artisans in copper and iron. The local engraver's synagogue was used for the meetings of the community administration.

Jewish metalworkers continued to pursue their crafts along traditional medieval lines in various Muslim lands, where manual occupations were often despised and therefore pursued by religious minorities, particularly Jews. The report of the French consul on the condition of the Jews in Morocco at the close of the 18th century speaks of Jewish armorers there. The traveler *Benjamin II relates that Jews were employed in the iron industry in Libya in the middle of the 19th century. There are also reports on Jewish smiths who manufactured horseshoes there at the beginning of the 20th century. R. Ḥayyim *Habshush, who guided the researchers Joseph *Halevy and Eduard *Glaser in their search for ancient manuscripts in Yemen during the second half of the 19th century, was a coppersmith. Visiting that country in the late 1850s R. Jacob *Saphir found many Jewish smiths. Yom Tov Ẓemaḥ reports that in 1910 the three remaining Jewish smiths of San'a were compelled to move to the provincial towns because of unemployment.

See also *Goldsmiths, *Petroleum, and *Salt. [J.Ka.]

Bibliography: In the Bible: M. Narkiss, *Metal Crafts in Ancient Palestine* ... (1937), 113–25; N. Glueck, *Copper and Iron Mines in Ancient Edom* (1937), 51–60; idem, *The Other Side of the Jordan* (1954), 150–89; Albright, Arch; R. W. Forbes, *Studies in Ancient Technology*, 7 (1966); B. Rothenberg, in: PEQ, 94 (1962), 5–71; idem and A. Lupu, in: *Archaeologia Austriaca*, 47 (1970), 91–130; S. Abramsky, in: EM, 5 (1968), 644–61 (incl. bibl.). In the Talmud: Krauss, Tal Arch, 2 (1911), 219–315; 3 (1912), 371; idem, in: JE, s.v.; M. D. Gross, *Oẓar ha-Aggadah*, 1 (1954), 223–5 (gold and silver). Jews as Metalworkers and Miners: Baer, Urkunden, index; I. Abrahams, *Jewish Life in the Middle Ages* (1917, repr. 1960), 221, 226ff.; G. Caro, *Sozial und Wirtschaftsgeschichte der Juden im Mittelalter und in der Neuzeit*, 2 (1920), index s.v. *Metall;* Baron, Social², 273; L. Hermann, *A History of the Jews in South Africa* (1935), 226–40; L. Berger, in: I. Halpern (ed.), *Beit Yisrael be-Polin*, 1 (1948), 211–3; A. Marcus, in: YIVOA, 7 (1952), 176–81; M. Hendel, *Melakhah u-Va'alei Melakhah be-Am Yisrael* (1955); M. Wischnitzer, *A History of Jewish Crafts and Guilds* (1965), index s.v. *blacksmiths, coppersmiths*, etc.; I. M. Dijur, in: J. G. Frumkin et al. (eds.), *Russian Jewry* (1966), 140ff.; G. Saron and L. Hotz (eds.), *The Jews in South Africa* (1955), passim; *The Jews of Czechoslovakia*, 1 (1968), 371–7; S. M. Auerbach, in: YLBI, 10 (1965), 188–203; J. Jaros, in: BZIH, no. 35 (1960), 87–99.

METAPHYSICS, the philosophic discipline that deals with ontology and cosmology. The Jews through the end of the medieval period did little original work in metaphysics, drawing mainly on other, primarily secular, authorities. The major systems employed were *Platonism, *Kalam, *Neoplatonism, and *Aristotelianism, which appear in Jewish works largely in mixed form, containing elements borrowed from one another as well as from other philosophies, such as *Stoicism. Moreover, the Kalam only constitutes a metaphysics in the broadest sense. While there was no one period in which any one of these metaphysical systems was exclusively subscribed to by the Jews, the periods of dominance for each were: Platonism, the first centuries before and after the Common Era; Kalam, the tenth century; Neoplatonism, the 11th and 12th centuries; and Aristotelianism, the 12th century through the end of medieval times. The foremost representatives respectively among the Jews employing these systems were: *Philo, *Saadiah, Solomon *ibn Gabirol, and

*Maimonides. The Jewish philosophers were primarily interested in meeting the challenges that various metaphysics presented to their Judaism and their understanding of revelation. Metaphysics, pursued scientifically through reason, produced ostensibly different conclusions about God, the universe, and salvation from those conveyed by the literal meaning of Scriptures. The religious thinker who valued human reason and did not wish to repudiate what was considered its profoundest activity met the challenge by reconciling and synthesizing metaphysics with Scripture. This was usually accomplished by partially limiting the validity of metaphysics, and partially by interpreting the literal meaning of Scriptures. Philo, in his great works of metaphysical and scriptural synthesis, formulated the basic methods for reconciling reason and revelation, which were employed throughout medieval philosophy not only by the Jews, but by the Muslims and Christians as well. It may be noted that not all Jews acquainted with metaphysics found its claims to truth convincing. Thinkers such as *Judah Halevi and Ḥasdai *Crescas met the challenge of metaphysics, not by reconciliation, but with trenchant critiques of its conclusions. As the validity of metaphysical knowledge in post-Cartesian thought came increasingly under attack from within philosophy itself, which concentrated primarily on the problems of epistemology, there existed little need for Jewish thinkers to meet speculative claims in the grand medieval style. However, in modern thought new challenges arose from rationalism and idealism, the scientific and empirical philosophies, and from existentialism which required the continued involvement of Jewish thinkers in philosophic thought.

Bibliography: Guttmann, Philosophies; Husik, Philosophy; H.A. Wolfson, *Philo, Foundations of Religious Philosophy* ..., 2 vols. (1947).
[A.J.R.]

METATRON (Matatron), angel accorded a special position in esoteric doctrine from the tannaitic period on. The angelology of *apocalyptic literature mentions a group of angels who behold the face of their king and are called "Princes of the Countenance" (Ethiopic *Book of Enoch*, ch. 40, et al.). Once Metatron's personality takes a more definitive form in the literature, he is referred to simply as "the Prince of the Countenance."

In the Babylonian Talmud Metatron is mentioned in three places only (Ḥag. 15a; Sanh. 38b; and Av. Zar. 3b). The first two references are important because of their connection with the polemics conducted against heretics. In *Ḥagigah* it is said that the *tanna* *Elisha b. Avuyah saw Metatron seated and said, "perhaps there are two powers," as though indicating Metatron himself as a second deity. The Talmud explains that Metatron was given permission to be seated only because he was the heavenly scribe recording the good deeds of Israel. Apart from this, the Talmud states, it was proved to Elisha that Metatron could not be a second deity by the fact that Metatron received 60 blows with fiery rods to demonstrate that Metatron was not a god, but an angel, and could be punished. This imagery recurs frequently in different contexts in Gnostic literature and is associated with various figures of the heavenly realm. It is however thought that the appearance of Metatron to Elisha b. Avuyah led him to a belief in *dualism.

The story in tractate *Sanhedrin* also confers on Metatron a supernatural status. He is the angel of the Lord mentioned in Exodus 23:21 of whom it is said "... and hearken unto his voice; be not rebellious against him ... for My name is in him." When one of the heretics asked R. *Idi why it is written in Exodus 24:1 "And unto Moses He said 'Come up unto the Lord'," instead of "Come up unto Me," the *amora* answered that the verse refers to Metatron "whose name is like that of his Master." When the heretic argued that, if that were so, Metatron should be worshiped as a deity, R. Idi explained that the verse "be not rebellious against (תמר) him" should be understood to mean "do not exchange (תמירני) Me for him." R. Idi added that Metatron was not to be accepted in this sense even in his capacity as the heavenly messenger. Underlying these disputations is the fear that speculations about Metatron might lead to dangerous ground. The Karaite *Kirkisānī read in his text of the Talmud an even more extreme version: "This is Metatron, who is the lesser YHWH." It is quite probable that this version was purposely rejected in the manuscripts.

The epithet "lesser YHWH" is undoubtedly puzzling, and it is hardly surprising that the Karaites found ample grounds for attacking the Rabbanites over its frequent appearance in the literature they had inherited. The Karaites viewed it as a sign of heresy and deviation from monotheism. The use of such an epithet was almost certainly current before the figure of Metatron crystallized. The explanations given in the latter phases of the *Heikhalot* literature (Hebrew *Book of Enoch*, ch. 12) are far from satisfactory, and it is obvious that they are an attempt to clarify an earlier tradition, then no longer properly understood. This tradition was connected with the angel Jahoel, mentioned in the *Apocalypse of Abraham* (dating from the beginning of the second century), where it is stated (ch. 10) that the Divine Name (Tetragrammaton) of the deity is to be found in him. All the attributes relating to Jahoel here were afterward transferred to Metatron. Of Jahoel it is indeed appropriate to say, without contrived explanations, that his name is like that of his Master: the name Jahoel contains the letters of the Divine Name, and this therefore signifies that Jahoel possesses a power exceeding that of all other similar beings. Apparently, the designation "the lesser YHWH" (יהוה הקטן) or "the lesser Lord" (אדני הקטן) was first applied to Jahoel. Even before Jahoel was identified with Metatron, designations such as "the greater Jaho" or "the lesser Jaho" passed into Gnostic use and are mentioned in various contexts in Gnostic, Coptic, and also in Mandean literature, none of which mentions Metatron. The name *Yorba* (יורבא) in Mandean in fact means "the greater Jaho" but he has there been given an inferior status as is characteristic of this literature in its treatment of Jewish traditional concepts.

Two different traditions have been combined in the figure of Metatron. One relates to a heavenly angel who was created with the creation of the world, or even before, and makes him responsible for performing the most exalted tasks in the heavenly kingdom. This tradition continued to apply after Jahoel was identified with Metatron. According to this tradition, the new figure took over many of the specific duties of the angel *Michael, an idea retained in certain sections of the *Heikhalot* literature up to and including the Kabbalah. The primordial Metatron is referred to as Metatron Rabba.

A different tradition associates Metatron with Enoch, who "walked with God" (Gen. 5:22) and who ascended to heaven and was changed from a human being into an angel—in addition he also became the great scribe who recorded men's deeds. This role was also already delegated to Enoch in the Book of Jubilees (4:23). His transmutation and ascent to heaven were discussed by the circles who followed this tradition and elaborated it. The association with Enoch can be seen particularly in the *Book of Heikhalot*, sometimes also called the *Book of Enoch*, of R. *Ishmael Kohen ha-Gadol, or the Hebrew *Book of Enoch* (H. Odeberg's edition (see bibl.) includes an English translation and a detailed introduction). The author links the two traditions and attempts to reconcile them. But it is clear that chapters 9–13 allude to the primordial Metatron, as Odeberg points out.

The absence of the second tradition in the Talmud or the most important Midrashim is evidently connected with the reluctance of the talmudists to regard Enoch in a favorable light in general, and in particular the story of his ascent to heaven, a reluctance still given prominence in the Midrash *Genesis Rabbah*. The Palestinian Targum (Gen. 5:24) and other Midrashim have retained allusions to Metatron in this tradition. Instead of his role of heavenly scribe, he sometimes appears as the heavenly advocate defending Israel in the celestial court. This transposition of his functions is very characteristic (Lam. R. 24; Tanḥ. *Va-Etḥannen;* Num. R. 12, 15). A number of sayings of the sages, in particular in *Sifrei, Parashah Ha'azinu*, 338, and Gen. R. 5:2, were explained by medieval commentators as referring to Metatron on the grounds of a corrupt reading of Metraton instead of *metator* ("guide").

In certain places in Merkabah literature, Metatron completely disappears and is mentioned only in the addenda that do not form part of the original exposition, such as in *Heikhalot Rabbati*. The descriptions of the heavenly hierarchy in *Massekhet Heikhalot* and *Sefer ha-*Razim* also make no mention of Metatron. On the other hand, Metatron is a conspicuous figure in the *Book of the Visions of Ezekiel* (fourth century) although he is mentioned without any reference to the Enoch tradition. This source mentions a number of the other secret names of Metatron, lists of which later appear in special commentaries or were added to the Hebrew *Book of Enoch* (ch. 48). Explanations of these names in accordance with ḥasidic tradition are given in the *Sefer Beit Din* of Abraham Ḥamoy (1858), 196ff., and in another version in the *Sefer ha-Ḥeshek* (1865). According to the traditions of certain Merkabah mystics, Metatron takes the place of Michael as the high priest who serves in the heavenly Temple, as emphasized particularly in the second part of **Shi'ur Komah* (*Sefer Merkavah Shelemah* (1921), 39ff.).

One can, thus, detect different aspects of Metatron's functions. In one place he is described as serving before the heavenly throne and ministering to its needs, while in another he appears as the servitor (*na'ar*, "youth") in his own special tabernacle or in the heavenly Temple. In the tannaitic period, the duty of the "prince of the world" formerly held by Michael was transferred to him (Yev. 16b). This conception of Metatron's role as the prince of the world since its creation contradicts the concept of Metatron as Enoch who was taken up to heaven only after the creation of the world.

It is already observed in *Shi'ur Komah* that the name Metatron has two forms, "written with six letters and with seven letters," i.e., מטטרון and מיטטרון. The original reason for this distinction is not known. In the early manuscripts the name is almost always written with the letter *yod*. The kabbalists regarded the different forms as signifying two prototypes for Metatron. They again distinguished between the various components that had been combined in the Hebrew *Book of Enoch* in their possession. They identified the seven-lettered Metatron with the Supreme emanation from the *Shekhinah*, dwelling since then in the heavenly world, while the six-lettered Metatron was Enoch, who ascended later to heaven and possesses only some of the splendor and power of the primordial Metatron. This distinction already underlies the explanation given by R. *Asher b. David to *Berakhot* (see G. Scholem, *Reshit ha-Kabbalah* (1948), 74–77; and idem, *Les Origines de la Kabbale* (1966), 225–31).

The origin of the name Metatron is obscure, and it is doubtful whether an etymological explanation can be given. It is possible that the name was intended to be a secret and has no real meaning, perhaps stemming from subconscious meditations, or as a result of glossolalia. To support the latter supposition are a number of similar examples of names with the suffix—on: *Sandalfon (סנדלפון), Adiriron (אדירירון), etc., while the doubling of the letter *t* (טט) is characteristic of names found in the Merkabah literature, e.g., in an addition to *Heikhalot Rabbati*, 26:8. Among numerous etymological derivations given (see Odeberg, 125–42) three should be mentioned: from *matara* (מטרא), keeper of the watch; from *metator* (מיטטור), a guide or messenger (mentioned in *Sefer he-Arukh* and the writings of many kabbalists); from the combination of the two Greek words *meta* and *thronos*, such as *metathronios* (μεταθρόνιος), in the sense of "one who serves behind the throne." However, the duty to serve the heavenly throne was associated with Metatron only at a later stage and does not agree with the earlier traditions. It is highly doubtful whether the "angel of the Countenance" entering "to exalt and arrange the throne in a befitting manner" mentioned in *Heikhalot Rabbati* (ch. 12) can in fact be Metatron, who is not mentioned at all in this context. The Greek word *thronos* does not appear in talmudic literature. The origin of the word, therefore, remains unknown.

In contrast to the lengthy description of Metatron found in the Hebrew *Book of Enoch*, in later literature the material relating to him is scattered, while there is hardly a duty in the heavenly realm and within the dominion of one angel among the other angels that is not associated with Metatron. This applies particularly to kabbalistic literature (Odeberg, 111–25). Extensive material from the Zohar and kabbalistic literature has been collected by R. Margalioth in his work *Malakhei Elyon* (1945, 73–108). In books dealing with practical Kabbalah there are no incantations of Metatron, although his name is frequently mentioned in other incantations.

Bibliography: H. Odebeg, *III Enoch or the Hebrew Book of Enoch* (1928); Scholem, Mysticism, 67–70; idem, *Jewish Gnosticism* (1965), 43–55; idem, *Les Origines de la Kabbale* (1966), 132–5, 225–31, 263.

[G.Sch.]

METCHNIKOFF, ELIE (1845–1916), Russian biologist, born at Ivanovka, near Kharkov. Mechnikoff's father was an officer of the Imperial Guard, his mother was Jewish (her family name was Neakovich). After graduating from the

Elie Metchnikoff, Russian biologist. Jerusalem, J.N.U.L., Schwadron Collection.

University of Kharkov he went to Germany for further training in biology. A succession of important discoveries in embryology earned Metchnikoff a reputation for originality and acuteness of observation, and in 1870 he was appointed professor extraordinarius at the University of Odessa.

The political upheavals and persecution of the Jews that followed the assassination of Czar Alexander II led Metchnikoff to leave Odessa in 1882. He went to Messina, a place especially favorable for the study of marine organisms. Here, during the course of studies on jellyfish and sponges, he began to turn his attention to the remarkable behavior of certain amoeba-like cells that ingest and destroy foreign particles in the body. Metchnikoff developed the theory that these cells, which he named "phagocytes," served to engulf and digest bacterial invaders of the organism. He set forth this thesis in an essay "The Struggle of the Organism Against Microbes" (1884).

In 1888 Pasteur invited him to Paris and gave him a laboratory at the Ecole Normale. When the Pasteur Institute was established, Metchnikoff became its subdirector. To this laboratory Metchnikoff attracted large numbers of investigators, whose researches established the validity of the phagocytosis theory.

Metchnikoff later became interested in the problems of biological aging. In *Etudes sur la nature humaine* (1903; *The Nature of Man,* 1904) he advanced the idea that senile changes result from toxins produced by bacteria in the intestine. To prevent these "unhealthy fermentations," Metchnikoff advocated the inclusion of sour milk in the diet. In 1908 Metchnikoff shared the Nobel Prize for Medicine with Ehrlich for his work on immunity.

Bibliography: O. Metchnikoff, *Life of Elie Metchnikoff, 1845–1916* (1921), incl. bibl.; H. Zeiss, *Elias Metschnikow, Leben und Werk* (1932), incl. bibl.; A. Besredka, *Histoire d'une idée* (1921); T. Levitan, *Laureates, Jewish Winners of the Nobel Prize* (1960), 111–5. [M.L.G.]

METHUSELAH (Heb. מְתוּשֶׁלַח), patriarch of mankind, son of *Enoch, father of *Lamech, and grandfather of *Noah (Gen. 5:21–25). The name has been variously explained as meaning "man of the weapon" or "man [worshiper] of [the deity] Salah." Methuselah in the genealogy of Seth (Gen. 5:2–21, P) is the counterpart of Methusael in that of Cain (4:18, J). The parallel is even more exact in the Septuagint which transcribes "Methuselah" in both instances. Methuselah according to the Bible lived 969 years, longer than any of the pre-Abrahamic fathers of the human race. Babylonian tradition attributes exaggerated longevity—tens of thousands of years—to its heroes. U. Cassuto believes that the Bible wishes to negate the fantastic figures which attribute to kings a longevity that is unnatural to human beings and that makes them godlike. Not even Methuselah attained the age of 1,000 years, a single day of the Almighty (Ps. 90:4). If the biblical story be compared with the prevailing Babylonian tradition, the many years of Methuselah seem a modest, even a short life-span. The Bible diminished the exaggerated ages attributed to people in the Ancient Near East, but still preserved the tradition of assigning extraordinary longevity to great men.

Bibliography: K. Budde, *Die biblische Urgeschichte* (1883), 93–103; A. Ehrenzweig, in: ZAW, 38 (1919/20), 84; E. G. Kraeling, *ibid.*, 40 (1922), 154–5; M. Tsevat, in: VT, 4 (1954), 41–49, 322; U. Cassuto, *A Commentary of the Book of Exodus 1* (1961), 287. [Ed.]

METMAN-COHEN, YEHUDAH LEIB (1869–1939), educator in Ereẓ Israel. Born in Ostiya, a village in the Ukraine, Metman-Cohen was ordained as a rabbi. He joined *Benei Moshe, and in 1904 settled in Ereẓ Israel, where he became headmaster of the school in *Rishon le-Zion. In 1906, he founded the first Hebrew high school in Jaffa, the Herzlia Gymnasium with 17 pupils and four teachers, and directed it until 1912; he was its headmaster again during World War I. Metman-Cohen was one of the

Yehudah Leib Metman-Cohen (1), with his wife Fania (2), and the first graduating class of the Herzlia Gymnasium in Jaffa, which included Dov Hos (3), Moshe Shertok (Sharett) (4), and Eliyahu Golomb (5). Jerusalem, J.N.U.L. Photo Collection.

founders of Tel Aviv (1909) and one of the initiators of Ir Gannim (1913), which eventually became *Ramat Gan. His publications included textbooks on the teaching of technical subjects in Hebrew and works on Hebrew language.

His wife, Fania (1874–), was one of the first teachers at the Hebrew high school in Jaffa and was active in the Women's Federation for Equal Rights. [A.A.]

°METTERNICH, PRINCE KLEMENS WENZEL VON (1773–1859), Austrian statesman. A supporter of Jewish rights in the German Confederation and abroad—although in Austria itself he did little for the Jews—at the Congress of Vienna he consistently supported the liberal policy of Karl August von *Hardenberg and Wilhelm *Humboldt (see Congress of *Vienna). He repeatedly warned the senate of *Frankfort on the Main not to infringe upon the rights of its Jewish community and sent letters of protest to *Hamburg, *Luebeck, and *Bremen when they deprived their Jewish citizens of their civil rights. During the 1819 Hep! Hep! riots he cautioned the Frankfort authorities against letting matters get out of control. Metternich ordered his diplomatic agents to reveal France's complicity in the 1840 *Damascus blood libel affair. A frequenter of the sophisticated Jewish salons of Vienna, he associated, for business and pleasure, with the patrician Jewish banking families to such a degree that the *Rothschilds were suspected of aiding his escape from revolutionary *Vienna in 1848. His right-hand man, Friedrich von Gentz, was also sympathetic to Jewish causes.

Bibliography: M. J. Kohler, *Jewish Rights at the Vienna Congress* (1918), index; S. Baron, *Die Judenfrage auf dem Wiener Kongress* (1920), index; N. M. Gelber, *Aktenstuecke zur Judenfrage am Wiener Kongress* (1920); idem, in: JJLG, 18 (1926), 217–64; I. Kracauer, *Geschichte der Juden in Frankfurt a. M.*, 2 (1927), 498–521; M. Gruenwald, *Vienna* (1936), index. [Ed.]

METULLAH (**Metulah**; Heb. מְטוּלָּה, מְטֻלָּה), northernmost Israel village (moshavah). It stands on the Israel-Lebanese border, on the hill chain connecting the *Naphtali Ridge with the *Hermon Massif and separating the *Ḥuleh Valley from the Iyyon Valley in Lebanon. Metullah was founded in 1896, on Baron Edmond de *Rothschild's initiative, by young settlers specially chosen for their ability to defend the isolated site. Metullah progressed slowly until the 1950s, when water and electricity were supplied to the village, and new immigrants settled there. The village's economy is based on deciduous fruit orchards, vineyards, field crops, and cattle, but it also seves as a summer resort. The name Metullah is derived from the Arabic. The population at the end of 1969 numbered 350. [E.O.]

METZ (Heb. מיץ), capital of the Moselle department, N. E. France. Even if Simon, bishop of Metz in 350, was really of Jewish origin (as a later source affirms) this does not prove that Jews were present in the town during that period. However, their presence is confirmed from 888 at the latest; a *Church council held in Metz at that date forbade Christians to take meals in the company of Jews. There is a reference earlier than the 11th century to a Jew called David perhaps renting a vineyard. It was in Metz that the series of anti-Jewish persecutions accompanying the First Crusade began, claiming 22 victims in the town in 1096. Among the scholars of the Early Middle Ages, foremost was *Gershom b. Judah ("Light of the Exile"); although he lived mainly in Mainz he was born in Metz, as was his disciple Eliezer b.

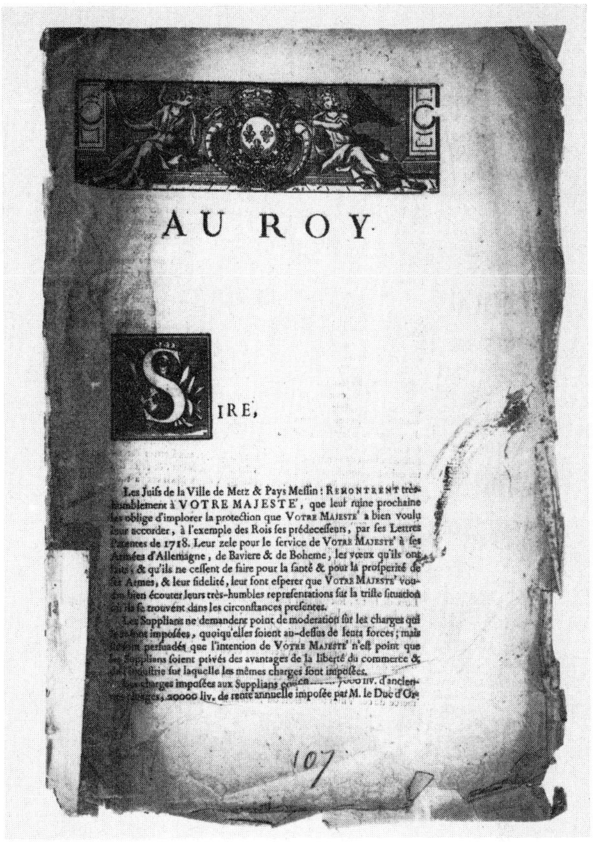
AU ROY.

SIRE,

Les Juifs de la Ville de Metz & Pays Messin: Remontrent très-humblement à VOTRE MAJESTE', que leur ruine prochaine les oblige d'implorer la protection que Votre Majeste' a bien voulu leur accorder, à l'exemple des Rois ses prédecesseurs, par ses Lettres Patentes de 1718. Leur zele pour le service de Votre Majeste' à ses Armées d'Allemagne, de Baviere & de Boheme, les vœux qu'ils ont faits, & qu'ils ne cessent de faire pour la santé & pour la prosperité de ses Armes, & leur fidelité, leur font esperer que Votre Majeste' voudra bien écouter leurs très-humbles representations sur la triste situation où ils se trouvent dans les circonstances présentes.

Les Supplians ne demandent point de moderation sur les charges qui leur sont imposées, quoiqu'elles soient au-dessus de leurs forces; mais ils sont persuadés que l'intention de Votre Majeste' n'est point que les Supplians soient privés des avantages de la liberté du commerce & de l'industrie sur laquelle les mêmes charges sont imposées.

Les charges imposées aux Supplians consi...... 7000 liv. d'anciennes charges, 20000 liv. de rente annuelle imposée par M. le Duc d'Or

107

Figure 1. First page of a petition by Metz Jews to Louis XV in 1745, requesting permission to engage freely in commerce and industry. Jerusalem, C.A.H.J.P.

Samuel. There was also the tosafist David of Metz. The medieval Jewish community occupied a whole quarter, the *Vicus Judaeorum*, whose memory is perpetuated in the street named "Jurue." In 1237 every Jew who passed through Metz was compelled to pay 30 deniers to the town, but was not permitted to live there. In the 15th century successive bishops, whose residence had been transferred to Vic, tolerated the Jews under their jurisdiction and granted them privileges (1442). In Metz itself, however, the Jews were permitted to stay only three days.

After the French occupation (1552), the first three Jewish families were admitted to reside there as pawnbrokers (1565/67); they were followed by others, and in 1595, 120 persons established a community which Henry IV and his successors took under their protection. Through the arrival of Jews from the Rhine areas, their number increased to 480 families in 1718 and almost 3,000 persons in 1748. Assigned to the Rhimport quarter, they governed themselves by elected trustees and levied numerous taxes, which grew more burdensome after the introduction of the Brancas tax (1715), originally gifts given by the community mainly to the duke of Brancas. The debts of the community became enormous: 500,000 livres at the time of the Revolution. With the consent of the king, the chief rabbi—often renowned for his erudition like Jonah Teomin-Fraenkel of Prague (1660–69), Gabriel b. Judah Loew *Eskeles of Cracow (1694–1703), and Jonathan Eybeschuetz (1742–50)—was chosen from abroad. He judged lawsuits between Jews but from the 18th century the parliament sought to assume this right, and to this end ordered a compendium of Jewish customs to be deposited in its record office (1743).

From the beginning of the 17th century the community owned a cemetery, a synagogue, and an almshouse. In 1689 free and compulsory elementary schooling was introduced, and in 1764 a Hebrew press. The Jews were, however,

Figure 2. The great synagogue of Metz, built in 1850. Photo Lorraine, Metz.

hampered in their economic activities by legal disabilities. An oligarchy, at whom sumptuary laws were aimed, achieved great wealth. The poverty of the masses, however, increased. Hostility toward the Jews reached its peak at the time of the execution of Raphael *Lévy (1670) for alleged ritual murder, but before the Revolution the jurists Pierre Louis Lacretelle (1751–1824) and Pierre Louis *Roederer of Metz, future members of the National Assembly, called for their emancipation. The latter organized the famous concourse of the academy of Metz on this subject (1785). In 1792 Lafayette, commanding the army at Metz, assured the religious freedom of the Jews, which was later suspended during the Reign of Terror (1794). The *consistory created in Metz in 1808, which included Moselle and Ardennes, served 6,517 Jews. The yeshivah (Ecole Centrale Rabbinique), which was promoted to the status of Rabbinical Seminary of France in 1829, was transferred to Paris in 1859; the synagogue was rebuilt in 1850 and the almshouse in 1867. Debts arising out of taxes not abolished by the Revolution devolved on the descendants of the former community. After the German annexation (1871) about 600 Jews moved to France, although immigrants soon arrived from other parts of Germany. After 1918, when the region reverted to France, there was a massive influx of immigrants from Eastern Europe and the Saar region. The Jewish population of the city numbered about 2,000 in 1866; 1,407 in 1875; 1,900 in 1910; and 4,150 in 1931. [G.C.]

Hebrew Printing. In 1764 Moses May set up a Hebrew printing press in Metz, and issued in association with the royal printer Joseph Antoine a Yiddish translation of Daniel Defoe's *Robinson Crusoe* (1764) and the first edition of Bezalel *Ashkenazi's *Asefat Zekenim* (*Shitah Mekubbeẓet,* to tractate *Beẓah,* 1765). These were followed by a great number of rabbinic and liturgical works, some by the outstanding rabbis of Metz, such as Aryeh Leib b. Asher's novellae *Turei Even* (1781). May's venture in publishing a small-scale edition of various talmudic tractates from 1768 onward brought about his financial ruin. His son-in-law and successor Godechau-Spire printed some "enlightened" literature in Hebrew, such as a volume of riddles by Moses Ensheim (1787). May and his successors were active until 1793. Other Hebrew printers in Metz were Ephraim Hadamar and Seligmann Wiedersheim and successors, who continued until 1870, when the German annexation of Alsace-Lorraine led to the closure of this press.

Holocaust Period and After. Under German occupation in World War II, Metz, like the rest of Moselle and Alsace, was made *judenrein* following the flight of the population and particularly brutal expulsions after the entry of the Germans. About 1,500 Jews died after being deported, among them rabbis Bloch and Kahlenberg. The two synagogues and the workhouse were plundered and defiled. The great synagogue was used as a military warehouse. After the liberation the reorganized Jewish community was more united than before the war. In 1970 Metz had about 3,500 Jews (including some 40 families recently arrived from North Africa) and a well-organized communal body. It was the seat of the consistory of Moselle, which comprised 24 communities with a total of about 5,500 Jews; the largest communities were Thionville with 450; Sarreguemines with 270; Sarrebourg with 180; and Forbach with 300. In Metz itself, in addition to the great synagogue (Ashkenazi rite) with a seating capacity of 700, there are four smaller places of worship, including one Polish and one Sephardi. The community also ran a *talmud torah* center with 180 pupils from six to 13, a kindergarten with a kosher canteen, a workhouse, a *mikveh,* and a *ḥevra kaddisha.* [ED.]

Bibliography: Gross, Gal Jud, 346ff.; R. Anchel, *Juifs de France* (1946), 153–212; N. Netter, *Vingt siècles d'histoire* ... (1938); J. Schneider, *La ville de Metz* ... (1950), 288f.; R. Clement, *Condition des juifs de Metz* ... (1903); A. Cahen, in: REJ, 7 (1883), 103–15; 204–26; 8 (1884), 255–74; 12 (1886), 283–97; 13 (1886), 105–26; Germ Jud, 2 pt. 2 (1968), 228ff.; H. Contamine, *Metz et la Moselle* ..., 1 (1932), 44–46; 2 (1932), 352–9; A. Hertzberg, *French Enlightenment and the Jews* (1968), index.

METZGER, ARNOLD (1892–), German scholar and author. Metzger was born in Landau in the Palatinate and began his career at the Hochshule fuer die Wissenschaft des Judentums in Berlin, where he taught from 1934 to 1937. In the face of rising Nazism he escaped to England, and then spent time in the United States where he became associated with Simmons College, Boston. After the war he returned to Germany, accepting a professorship in philosophy at the University of Munich. Much of his writing treats those areas of philosophy that touch on psychology; his contributions center on the phenomenology of recollection, perception, and the longing for death. His early books include *Phaenomenologie und Metaphysik* (1933); better known are his works on free will and determinism *Freiheit und Tod* (1955), on transcendentalism *Daemonie und Transzendenz* (1964), and on the ramifications of technology for the human personality *Automation und Autonomie* (1964). His later interests include existentialism, social philosophy, and the American pragmatic school in juxtaposition to the German metaphysical schools. In this connection he wrote "William James and the Crisis of Philosophy" (*In Commemoration of William James,* 1942). [ED.]

MEUNITES (Heb. מְעוּנִים), an Arab tribe which lived on the border of the kingdom of Judah. Along with "the Philistines ... and the Arabians that dwelt in Gur-Baal" (II Chron. 26:7), the Meunites paid a tax to *Uzziah king of Judah. At about the time of Hezekiah, the Meunites were attacked by the tribe of Simeon, which reached "to the entrance of Gedor, even unto the east side of the valley" (I Chron. 4:39–41). An inscription of the Assyrian king Tiglath-Pileser III indicates that at about this time (eighth century B.C.E.) the Meunites lived near the Egyptian border, which extended to the "Brook of Egypt" (Wadi el-Arish). There is no basis for J. A. Montgomery's identification of the Meunites of Chronicles with the Mineans, one of the south Arabian kingdoms whose economic activities and settlements reached as far as the oases in northern Arabia, or for A. Musil's location of them in the region of Ma'an in southern Transjordan. These theories are based upon references to the M(ε)ιναῖοι in the Septuagint and in works of the classical historiographers of the third century B.C.E. and later; the conditions reflected in these sources are later and do not conform to those of the eighth century B.C.E. [I.EPH.]

MEVASSERET ZION (Heb. מְבַשֶּׂרֶת צִיּוֹן; "Herald of Zion"), Israel urban settlement with municipal council status, 5 mi. (8 km.) W. of Jerusalem. On a 2,600 ft. (799 m.) high hilltop the Romans erected a fortress, Castellum, to secure the road to Jerusalem. The Crusaders renewed it, calling it Castellum Belveer. This strategic spot became a small Arab village which preserved the ancient name (al-Qastal). During the Israel *War of Independence (1948), it changed hands in heavy battles, but finally (April 9) fell into Jewish hands. In 1951 the settlement Ma'oz Zion ("Stronghold of Zion") was established at the foot of Qastal Hill to house immigrants from Iraqi Kurdistan who worked in the nearby *Solel Boneh stone quarry, reactivated after the War of Independence. They developed fruit gardens and auxiliary farms. In 1956 a laborers' garden suburb, Mevasseret Yerushalayim, was established east of Ma'oz Zion, on a ridge close to the armistice lines of the time and north of *Moẓa. Its inhabitants found employment partly in the fruit orchards, in the Arazim Valley stretching south and east of Mevasseret Yerushalayim, and partly in Jerusalem. In 1963 Ma'oz Zion and Mevasseret Yerushalayim merged into one municipal unit, Mevasseret Zion which in 1969 had 4,160 inhabitants. [E.O.]

MEVORAKH BEN SAADIAH (11th century), *nagid* and leader of the Jewish community in Egypt. Mevorakh was a descendant of a family of scholars and physicians, and was himself a distinguished scholar; therefore, he is referred to in letters as *Sanhedra Rabba* ("member of the Sanhedrin"). His fame as a physician was such as to gain him an appointment at the Egyptian royal court. He succeeded his brother Judah as *nagid* in about 1080. At that time *David b. Daniel b. Azariah arrived in Egypt to wrest the leadership from the heads of the Egyptian community. He instigated others to bring false accusations against Mevorakh and forced the latter's banishment from the Egyptian capital to Fayyum and later to Alexandria. After some time Mevorakh succeeded in proving his innocence, and was reinstated as court physician and *nagid*. His triumph over David b. Daniel was complete by 1094. He wielded much influence with al-Malik al-Afḍal the Fatimid regent, and remained in his position until the beginning of the 12th century.

Bibliography: Mann, Egypt, 1 (1920), 169, 188ff.; 2 (1922), 249ff.
[E.A.]

MEVORAKH HA-BAVLI (11th century), *paytan* and poet. Although his family was Babylonian, Mevorakh lived in Ereẓ Israel or its surroundings. In the Cairo *Genizah*, parts of his *divan* were found, including both religious and secular poems, some of which have been published by various scholars. He was one of the first poets in the oriental countries supported by philanthropic contributions, and, in his poems, explicitly appeals for support, adding praise for those who furnish it. In one of his poems, he mentions the philanthropist Abraham b. Samuel, from whom he requested a "night shroud" (i.e., a sheet), and, in another, one of his friends, R. *Abiathar b. Elijah ha-Kohen, the author of *Megillat Evyatar*. An acrostic bearing the name of the recipient, Yasa (?) ha-Kohen, appears in still another poem.

Bibliography: S. Abramson, in: *Tarbiz*, 15 (1944), 216; M. Zulay, in: *Haaretz* (Oct. 3, 1948); A. M. Habermann, in: *Maḥanayim*, 36 (1958), 112f.; J. Schirmann, *Shirim Ḥadashim min ha-Genizah* (1965), 79–86.
[ED.]

MEXICO, a federal republic in southern North America; area 760,373 sq. mi. (1,970,000 sq. km.); population 48,000,000 (1970), Jewish population approximately 45,000 (1970).

Colonial Period. A number of Marranos who were known as New Christians (i.e., nominal Catholics of Jewish birth or extraction) went to Mexico with Cortés, who conquered the country in 1521. In 1523, when Mexico was closed to all but those who could show Catholic ancestry for four generations and thus qualify for a certificate of **limpieza de sangre,* some Spanish and Portuguese Marranos managed to procure these certificates through corruption. The immigration of others, who came from other European countries posing as "old" Christians, continued to some extent throughout the colonial period. Veracruz and Campeche were the ports of entry for settlers coming from Europe, and Acapulco for those coming from Brazil, Chile, and Peru. Although the first auto-da-fé at which Marranos were burned at the stake was held in Mexico City as early as 1528 (when the conquistador Hernando Alonso was among the victims), comparatively few Crypto-Jews were seized prior to the formal establishment of an independent tribunal of the Holy Office of the Inquisition in Mexico City in 1571. Soon thereafter the instances of Marrano persecution increased both in frequency and intensity. It has been said that by 1550 there were more Spanish Crypto-Jews than Spanish Catholics in Mexico City.

In spite of accounts to the contrary, Luis de *Carvajal, the governor of the territory now part of northeastern Mexico, was not a Jew but a devout Catholic of Christian origin. His sister married a Marrano, and one of her children was designated the heir and successor to the governor. This nephew of Carvajal's who adopted his name and is known as Luis de *Carvajal el Mozo ("the younger") was disinherited, however, when the governor discovered his inclination toward Judaism. Luis el Mozo, his mother, and three sisters were burned at the stake on Dec. 8, 1596, together with five other Crypto-Jews. From 1596 to 1659 there was hardly a public auto-da-fé at which at least one Crypto-Jew was not penanced. The years 1642 to 1649 were the worst period of Inquisitional persecution. The great auto-da-fé of April 11, 1649, included 109 victims of whom all except 13 were executed; these were "reconciled" with the Church and, although they were to be sent back to Spain, many of them never left Mexico.

In spite of these persecutions, Marranos continued to settle and prosper in Mexico. The development of trade and commerce there was largely due to their enterprise. Although the Inquisition's pursuit of them is attributed to fear of a rumored Portuguese attempt to capture Mexico with the help of the Portuguese (mostly Marranos) already there, it may also have been due to economic jealousy of Marrano merchants and the venality of the three Inquisitors of that era, who confiscated entire fortunes. The Marranos engaged in every aspect of colonial life and ran the gamut of occupations.

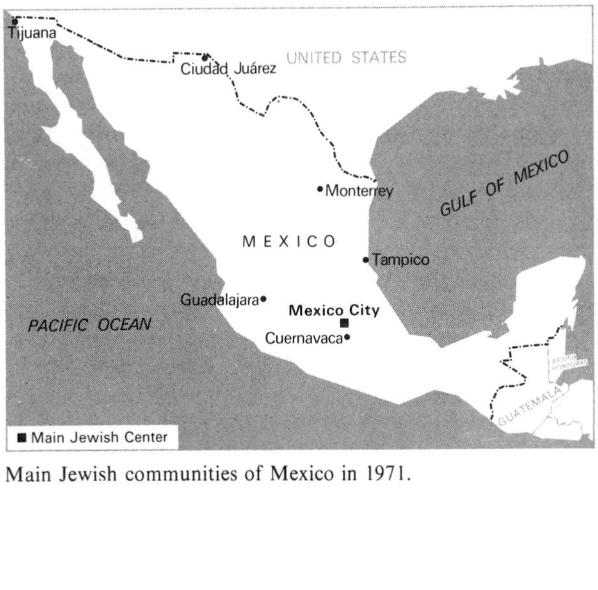

Main Jewish communities of Mexico in 1971.

Many held official positions for the crown and even in the Church itself. The Italian Ricardo Ossado, said to be a Jew who had escaped from Mexico, wrote a compendium of Maya herbs, medicines, and diseases known as *El Libro del Judio* (c. 1647), which served as a reference work for almost 300 years. Although Marranos lived in every part of New Spain, their principal centers were in Mexico City, Veracruz, and Guadalajara. According to the records of the Mexican Inquisition, communal prayers were held regularly in private homes.

The form of religious observance among the Mexican Marranos was similar to that of their secret coreligionists in Spain, Portugal, and in other parts of the Diaspora. It was characterized by exaggerated attention to fasts and acts of penitence and the inevitable neglect of some fundamental rites and observances of traditional Judaism. There are some indications, however, that Mexican Crypto-Judaism was closer to the norms of traditional Judaism than were the practices of Marranos in Catholic Europe. Many Jews immigrated to Mexico under the impression that in the relaxed conditions of the New World they could afford to be somewhat less circumspect. Even circumcision seems to have been a common practice, and dietary laws were approximately observed. The Crypto-Jews of Mexico were in communication with European and Near Eastern Jewish communities. Occasionally funds were raised for Ereẓ Israel, the collection being called *farda*. There is evidence that people with a greater degree of knowledge went from community to community to instruct the local inhabitants in Jewish tradition. The Inquisitional records sometimes refer to these teachers in exaggerated terms, giving the impression that they were rabbis and talmudic scholars in the true sense.

From the middle of the 17th century, Inquisitional activity against Mexican Marranos showed a marked decrease. In the auto-da-fé of 1659 only four Marranos figured among the 32 victims, and in succeeding years the proportion was even lower. In 1712, a solitary Judaizer was reconciled, and as late as 1788 a clerk in Holy Orders, Raphael Gil Rodriguez, was sentenced to relaxation for the same offense, though he professed repentance at the last moment and escaped capital punishment. Marrano immigration into Mexico in the 18th century decreased considerably as a result of changing conditions and increasing tolerance in other countries. For several years the Mexican Inquisition was directed to desist from searching for Jews, and during the last decades of the colonial era those apprehended were usually prominent personalities suspected of liberal opinions. Throughout the colonial period approximately 1,500 persons were convicted of being Judaizers, observing the Laws of Moses, or following Jewish practices. The number actually burned at the stake was less than 100, but almost an equal number died in the Inquisition cells and more than 192 plus another 32 sentenced to serve in *obrajes* and jails and 46 women to serve as charwomen in hospitals for up till five years were consigned to the galleys. punished by confiscation of property, jail sentences, wearing of the *sambenito*, etc. The descendants of the Marranos of the colonial period assimilated in the 19th century. Some Mexicans today claim Jewish ancestry.

1821–1900. The abolition of the Inquisition during the first third of the 19th century did not remove the stigma of *judío*, because the Church continued to charge the Jews with deicide and Holy Week remained the occasion to burn effigies of Judas. The original cry "Death to Judas" often became "Death to the Jews," a custom which still exists in small Mexican villages. At the beginning of Mexican Independence in 1821, the number of Jews greatly diminished and the remainder were small merchants and traders whose primary foreign contact was with Jews in the West Indies and Caracas. Mexico secured its first international loan in 1821 from the Jewish banking firm Goldschmidt of London. From 1825 to 1835 there was some Jewish immigration from Germany but there is no record of any communal life until 1862. Maximilian, emperor of Mexico from 1864 to 1867, had brought with him many Belgian, French, Austrian, and Alsatian Jews. In 1862 over 100 Jews met to discuss the construction of a synagogue in the capital, but nothing developed and services continued to be held in private homes. Maximilian's personal physician was Samuel Basch, an avowed Jew. The overthrow of Maximilian by Benito Juárez did not harm the Jews since Juárez was a devout believer in freedom of religion.

The Jewish population grew slowly, and by 1885 the first organized congregation had come into existence. Assimilation and intermarriage were prevalent. Jews were not known as Jews but as Mexicans, Frenchmen, or Germans. Jews were the subject of novels and were mentioned in histories of Mexico. *La hija del judio*, a novel, ran first as a serial in a newspaper in Mérida and became a popular book. During the late 19th century there was immigration of East European Jews from Russia and Galicia. The European Jewish press sometimes connected this immigration with Jewish colonization projects, and in 1891, when the Baron de Hirsch Fund was established in New York and the Jewish Colonization Association (ICA) in London, various plans were proposed for large-scale agricultural settlement of Jews in Mexico. These, however, did not materialize. In 1899, when the first Jewish immigrants from Syria arrived in Mexico, Francisco Rivas Puigcervez began the publication of a literary weekly, *El sábado secreto*, later *La luz del sábado*, dedicated to Sephardi history and language.

1901–1950. Unrest in the Ottoman Empire caused many Sephardi and Levantine Jews to emigrate to Mexico where their Ladino language and physical appearance facilitated their absorption into the general population. In 1901 the Arabic-speaking Jews maintained religious services in a private home, and in 1905 and 1908 Oriental, Sephardi, and Ashkenazi religious services were held in hotels. The Jews from Aleppo established their first association in 1909; and the first Jewish communal organization in Mexico, Alianza Monte Sinai, was established by Ashkenazi and Sephardi Jews in 1912. By the 1960s, however, the Alianza was composed exclusively of Damascene Jews. The Alianza sponsored financial aid to individuals, religious services, the building of a *mikveh*, and it also brought to Mexico ritual slaughterers, Hebrew teachers, and a *mohel*. Through personal contact with the leader of the Mexican revolution, President Francisco Madero (1910–13), the first Jewish cemetery was acquired.

The Mexican revolution, together with the riots and insecurity which came in its wake between 1913 and 1917, brought about a noticeable decrease in the Jewish population; but the extreme liberal constitution enacted in 1917, which gave Mexico the image of being a wholly secular state, strengthened the legal basis for Jewish existence in the country. After World War I, Jewish immigration from Eastern Europe began again and at an increased rate. But during the first years most of the immigrants used Mexico only as a stopping place on their way to the United States. As of 1924, however, most immigrants were barred from continuing on to the U.S. by that country's restrictive immigration legislation and were compelled to remain in Mexico under difficult conditions. The new immigrants settled in every part of the country, and prospered as peddlers and proprietors of small stalls in public markets.

They introduced into Mexico the system of buying on credit which helped to raise the standard of living for the Mexican peon and servant class by allowing them to buy shoes, socks, stockings, ties, thread, and other commodities on the installment plan.

B'nai B'rith contributed thousands of dollars to Mexico's Jews between 1924 and 1930. The Young Men's Hebrew Association (formed in Mexico in 1918) helped the immigrants by conducting classes in Spanish and in various vocations, and by providing them with an opportunity for social life. In 1929–30, because of the economic depression and the agitation of German and French storekeepers against stall operators in the Lagunilla market, a virulent anti-Semitic drive was started under the aegis of the National League Against Chinese and Jewish Penetration. This movement had the temporary support of two members of the Chamber of Deputies, the Mexican Chamber of Commerce, and the two leading papers, *Excelsior* and *El Nacional*. Leaders of the *American Jewish Committee complained to the United States Department of State which then made unofficial entreaties on behalf of the Jews to the Mexican government, and the movement abated. The anti-Semitism forced the Jewish peddlers and stall operators to leave the public market and to open private stores, which ultimately raised their economic status. Banco Mercantil, a Jewish bank founded in 1929, has provided Jews with ready financing for the purchase of machinery, especially in every branch of the clothing and soft-goods industry. Investment and expansion in this industry has created employment and diminished the necessity for importing these items. In 1931, the Cámara de Comercio Israelita was established as a coordinating institution.

The increased immigration of Ashkenazim brought about the establishment of their communal organization, Niddeḥei Israel, which began operation in 1922 as a *ḥevra kaddisha*. It assumed communal functions and was officially converted into a *kehillah* on Jan. 1, 1957. The arrival of Ashkenazim also brought about the establishment, in 1923, of the Zionist Federation, which united the various Zionist groups within the Mexican Jewish community. Because of the prevalent use of Yiddish in the Ashkenazi organizations, as well as the Sephardim's lack of interest in the internal Zionist controversies, a separate Sephardi Zionist organization, Benei Kedem, was founded in 1925. During the 1920s and 1930s, organizations of the *Bund and the Jewish Communists existed in addition to the Zionist Movement. In the 1920s the Sephardim and Ashkenazim established separate welfare and women's groups, as well as their respective social and cultural organizations, La Fraternidad and Idischer Kultur Tsenter. The Colegio Israelita, established in 1924, became the foundation for the extensive Jewish educational network which exists today.

The number of obstacles to Jewish immigration increased during the 1930s and culminated in the 1937 Constitution which established the principle of immigration by quota. Within this framework, Poland and Rumania, for example, countries where Jewish emigration was high, were restricted to 100 entry visas a year. Thus only a limited number of Jews persecuted in Europe succeeded in entering Mexico. During the Holocaust years 1943–44, Mexico agreed to take in several hundred refugees, but only for the duration of the war. Supported by the Mexican Fascists, Las Camisas Doradas, and the German embassy, anti-Semitism increasing during the early years of World War II. Only with Mexico's entry into the war against the Axis powers in May 1942, was anti-Semitism subdued. The Jewish community began the organized fight against anti-Semitism with the establishment in 1932 of the Federación de Sociedades Judías, which functioned on a limited scale for several years. In 1938 the Comité Central Israelita de México was founded as an umbrella organization for all Jewish institutions and became the only representative body recognized by both the Jewish community and the government.

The economic prosperity that Mexico enjoyed during the war and during the 1950s also raised the economic status of the Jewish community and increased the number of economic areas in which Jews participated. A 1950 survey conducted among the Ashkenazim found 52 professions and branches of economic activity represented. At this time the Jewish population of Mexico was estimated at 27,000, of which 60% of the economically active population engaged in various branches of commerce, 15% in industry, and 8% in the liberal professions. The remaining Jews were laborers and clerks. There has been an increasing tendency toward Jewish participation in the liberal professions, mostly medicine, engineering, and the natural sciences. The economic boom has enabled a considerable part of the Jewish population to become affluent in a country where there is still widespread poverty. Accompanying the economic gains were the expansion of existing Jewish institutions, and the establishment of new bodies, especially the Centro Deportivo Israelita in 1949.

Contemporary Position. According to the 1960 National Census 110,750 citizens registered as *Israelitas*, but this number includes various Protestant sects which consider themselves *Israelitas*, together with some smaller Indian groups which aroused great interest by claiming Jewish descent. The recognized Jewish community which adheres to Jewish ways of life was estimated in 1967 at 31,000 persons, of whom approximately 17,000 were Ashkenazim (central organization Niddeḥei Israel); about 5,500 were Sephardim (communal organization Unión Sefaradí de México); about 5,000 were Damascene and Aleppo Jews (communal organization Alianza Monte Sión and Zedaca Umarpé); about 1,500 were German Jews (principal organization Ha-Tikvah Menorah); and about 2,000 were Hungarian and American Jews (organized around *Emunah and Beth Israel Community Center). A larger figure of 40,000 Mexican Jews, however, takes into account an estimated 25% of "marginal" Jews who do not belong to the organized community. The vast majority of Mexican Jewry is concentrated in the capital, Mexico City, but small communities exist in Monterrey and Guadalajara; and individual Jews live in Tijuana, Veracruz, Puebla, and Cuernavaca. The Comité Central, which comprises seven communal organizations—and for some years included the Jewish Communists—is affiliated with the *World Jewish Congress, and maintains strong ties with the American Jewish Committee, and with B'nai B'rith (whose first lodge was established in 1934 and which was one of the founders of the Comité Central). An even more comprehensive organization, the Centro Deportivo Israelita (C. D. I.), has about 20,000 members from every group in the community, and constitutes the largest organization within Mexican Jewry. The C. D. I. offers its members extensive social and cultural activities, as well as a wide variety of facilities for sports, entertainment, and relaxation. It also has played an important role in bringing together the diverse groups of the younger generation, which are not divided by the linguistic differences separating their parents.

With a view toward developing Jewish education, an extensive network of schools encompassing all Jewish communal organizations was set up. In 1967 this network comprised ten educational institutions with 4,749 students, of which six were connected with the Va'ad ha-Ḥinnukh of the Ashkenazi community. Four schools—Colegio Israelita, Tarbut, Yavneh, and I. L. Peretz—had an enrollment of

Figure 1. Congregants of the Mexican sect of Casa de Dios (House of God), who regard themselves as Jews.

2,913 students and represented different approaches to Hebrew, Yiddish, and religion. Other members of the Va'ad ha-Ḥinnukh are a yeshivah with 156 Ashkenazi and Sephardi pupils; a teachers' seminar with 71 students, scores of whose graduates teach in the Jewish schools; Monte Sinai with 752 students, established by Damascene Jews; Colegio Sefaradi with 638 students, established by Sephardim; and Zedaca Umarpé with 70 students and a yeshivah, Keter Torah, with 149 students, established by the Jews from Aleppo. All of the institutions are day schools, and some of them include all grades from kindergarten through university preparatory class. It is estimated that the educational system comprises about 65% of all Jewish school-age children. Communal organizations and the parents bear the considerable financial costs of the system, while the State of Israel contributed 30 of the 160 teachers.

The central role played by the Ashkenazi community also includes sponsoring cultural activities. Since 1962 it has held an annual music month in which singers and cantors from outside Mexico participate with the Zamir choir maintained by the *kehillah.* Other cultural activities are carried on by the various congregations, women's organizations, and Zionist parties. In 1967 Mexico City had 14 synagogues and 11 officiating rabbis. Two of the synagogues—Beth-El and Beth Israel, founded in 1963 and 1953 respectively—are Conservative; the rest are Orthodox, with the exception of those synagogues maintained by the Aleppo Jews which are ultra-Orthodox. In the towns of Monterrey and Guadalajara there are joint Ashkenazi and Sephardi congregations which operate schools and perform religious and cultural services. The Jews of the capital city communicate with the Jews in cities of the interior through the Jewish press which therefore plays an important role in the education and daily life of the Jewish community. Among the better known periodicals are: *Der Weg,* a bi-weekly Yiddish and Spanish paper; *Di Shtime* (1939–), a Yiddish bi-weekly; *Prensa Israelita* (1948–), a Spanish weekly; *Horizonte* (1964–), *Tribuna Israelita* (1946–), and *Revista Israelita de México,* Spanish monthlies; *Forois* and *Fraynd,* Yiddish monthlies; *Voz Sefardi,* a Spanish review; and *Meksikaner Lebn; Dos Vort* (1947–); *Oyfn Shvel;* and *Freeland.* Another cultural enterprise was the publication of a 10-volume Jewish encyclopedia *Enciclopedia Judaica Castellana* published in Mexico in 1948–51. The lessening of anti-Semitism during World War II did not lead to its disappearance. Sporadic outbursts occurred in 1954 and during the 1960s, the latter influenced by the Arab struggle against Israel and Zionism. Mexico's freedom of speech and press have not only enabled anti-Semites to make the country a center for the publication of Nazi and anti-Semitic propaganda, but have also foiled many efforts by the Comité Central to suppress such publications. From 1965 anti-Semitic propaganda was accompanied by occasional acts of violence against Jewish communal property.

"JUDAIZING" MESTIZOS. During the late 1930s, the Jews of Mexico City heard reports that there were *Israelitas* in Venta Prieta, a small village 65 miles from the capital. The *Israelitas* of Venta Prieta are mestizos, or Mexicans of mixed Indian and European ancestry, and in 1964 consisted principally of two families and numbered about 50 people. When first meeting Jews from Mexico City, the *Israelitas* made the impossible claim that they were descendants of the Carvajal family which came to Mexico in 1580. Later they varied the account of their ancestry, but historical research has disclosed inconsistencies in each new version. The original leader of the sect was Baltazar Laureano Ramirez, one of the founders of a branch of the Iglesia de Dios (Church of God). This Church is a Protestant sabbatarian sect which believes in the Mosaic laws as well as the Immaculate Conception, the Trinity, and Christ. The disciples of this sect term themselves *Israelitas* since they claim descent from the 12 sons of Jacob-Israel. Due to a rift between Baltazar Laureano and his brother, Laureano, a minister of the Church, Baltazar "converted" his disciples in Mexico City and Venta Prieta from Protestantism to Judaism. The Venta Prieta flock has long disavowed him and his successor. The present congregation has a small one-room synagogue in which it practices Jewish rites to the best of its ability.

Another group of mestizos in Cocula, state of Guerrero, contend that the two great-grandfathers or founders of their group were "brown-skinned Jews" who came to Cocula from Yucatan in 1850. They acknowledge that the two men married non-Jewish women and that intermarriage with the local people has been the general practice among them. The group, which numbers about 30, live in a primitive area; their religious practices are minimal and biblical.

Another sect, Beth-El or Casa de Dios (House of God), and numbering several thousand, came into being about 1949. They believe in the Old and New Testaments and consider Jesus and the Apostles as prophets in the Hebraic tradition. They register as *Israelitas* in the Mexican decennial census which shows three religious categories: Catholic, Protestant, and *Israelita.* They admit that they adopted Judaism after trying other faiths and denominations. Prior to this century, none of the above-mentioned groups had any religious objects or other tangible evidence of Jewish identity. None of the groups is recognized as Jewish by the rabbinate of Mexico or the State of Israel.

[S.B.L./HA.LE.]

Relations with Israel. Together with most of the members of the UN, Mexico voted for the establishment of the

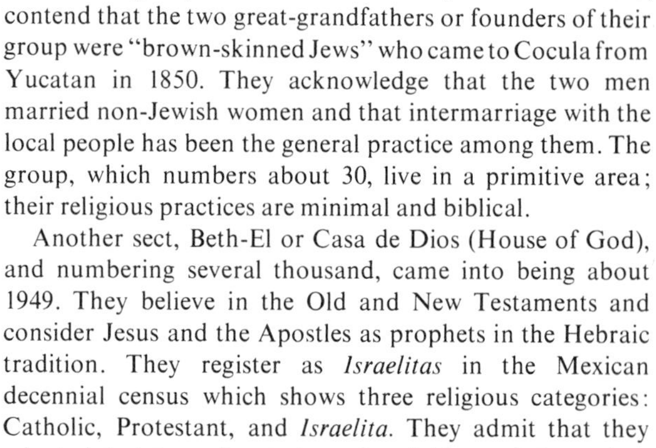

Figure 2. Mexican exhibits at the Israel Museum, part of the cultural exchange between the two countries. Courtesy Israel Museum, Jerusalem.

United Nations Special Committee on Palestine (UNSCOP) on May 15, 1947. On the other hand, it abstained in the vote on the plan to partition Palestine on Nov. 29, 1947. Mexico recognized Israel on April 4, 1949, and on May 11 of the same year voted in favor of accepting Israel into the UN. In July 1952 the two states agreed to establish diplomatic relations and exchange legations. The Israel legation in Mexico was established on Nov. 5, 1953, and the Mexican legation in Israel was established in August 1956. The legations were raised to the status of embassies in June 1959. The Mexican embassy is located in Tel Aviv, as Mexico voted for international administration over Jerusalem on Dec. 9, 1949.

In line with Mexico's traditional policy toward problems in various areas of the world, her government has adopted a neutral stance toward the Middle East conflict, which is expressed by Mexico's consistent abstentions in the UN votes on Middle Eastern issues. Nonetheless, public support and sympathy of certain groups toward Israel are in evidence in Mexico, especially in professional and cultural circles. After the Six-Day War (1967), Mexico was among the major forces behind the Latin American resolution raised in the General Assembly to counter the Yugoslav resolution, which demanded Israel's unconditional withdrawal from territories captured during the hostilities.

In July 1969 a cultural pact was signed between the two countries. In the framework of cultural exchanges, a permanent exhibit of 250 valuable cultural articles contributed by the Mexican government and various Mexican personalities is on view in the Israel Museum in Jerusalem. In turn, a permanent exhibit of Israel cultural articles is on show in the Mexican Cultural Museum. A building on the campus of the University of Tel Aviv has been named in honor of Mexico, and the Institute for Mexican-Israel Cultural Relations is especially active in Mexico.

A trade agreement was signed between the two states on July 25, 1952. In 1968 Israel exports to Mexico reached the sum of $882,000 and in 1969 it was $1,128,000; the major exports were textiles, chemicals, diamonds, and electrical and electronic equipment. In 1968 Israel imported $360,000 worth of goods from Mexico, and in 1969 the sum rose to $409,000; the major import product was graphite. Although the Jews of Mexico identify with the State of Israel, the number who have settled in Israel has been limited to a few hundred, including some students. [N.Y.]

Bibliography: S. B. Liebman, *Guide to Jewish References in the Mexican Colonial Era 1521–1821* (1964); idem, *The Enlightened: The Writings of Luis de Carvajal el Mozo* (1967); idem, *The Jews in New Spain: Faith, Flame and the Inquisition* (1970); H. C. Lea, *The Inquisition in the Spanish Dependencies* (1908), 191–298; Roth, Marranos, index; S. B. Liebman, in: *Hispanic American Historical Review*, 43 (1963), 94–108; idem, in: AJA, 19 (1967), 144–74, incl. bibl.; idem, in: *Reconstructionist*, 27 no. 13 (1961), 18–22; idem, in: *Jewish Spectator*, 27 no. 2 (1962), 22–23; Wiznitzer, in: AJHSQ, 51 (1961/62), 168–214, 222–68; Ricard, in: *Revue d'Histoire Moderne*, 14 (1939), 516–24; Toro, in: *Los Judiós en la Nueva España* (1932); B. Lewin, *Màrtires y Conquistadores judios en la America Hispana* (1954); idem, *La Inquisición en Hispanoamérica* (1967²), incl. bibl.; EJC, 7 (1950), 426–75. CONTEMPORARY PERIOD: I. T. Lerner, *Mexican Jewry in the Land of the Aztecs: A Guide* (1967²); R. Patai, in: *Menorah Journal*, 38 no. 1 (1950), 54–67; S. Kahn, *Yidish Meksikanish* (1945); J. Shatzky, *Yidishe Yishuvim in Latayn-Amerike* (1952), 143–58; E. Gutman, in: *Hoy*, no. 139 (Oct. 1938), 38–43; J. Beller, *Jews in Latin America* (1969), 17–34; A. Tartakower, *Shivtei Yisrael*, 3 (1969), 109–20.

MEYER, ANNIE NATHAN (1867–1951), U.S. educator and writer. Annie Nathan was born in New York to a family of colonial stock (see *Nathan). She undertook college studies at home for two years in order to pass the examinations of Columbia University's Collegiate Course for Women, because women were not permitted to attend lectures. She completed her studies when she was 20 years old and the following year married ALFRED MEYER, a prominent New York physician, who devoted most of his long career to fighting tuberculosis.

After her marriage she became active in founding a college for women within a university, there being no women's college of scholastic standing at that time. She advocated her cause on the speaker's platform and in the press, obtained financial contributions, and negotiated with the trustees of Columbia University. Ultimately, her efforts resulted in the opening of Barnard College in 1899, of which she was a lifelong trustee.

Although Annie Meyer considered herself a feminist, she opposed the women's suffrage movement. Decrying unintelligent use of the vote, she called for the inclusion of an educational clause in the suffrage bill. She also opposed women in business and wrote two plays dealing with that theme, *The Dominant Sex* (1911) and *The Advertising of Kate* (produced on Broadway in 1921). Another play, *Black Souls* (produced and published in 1932), deals with race relations. She was the author of many other works, including plays, novels, social studies, magazine articles, and art reviews. Her autobiography *It's Been Fun* was published in 1951.

Annie Meyer was an active lecturer and publicist. To Jewish students she spoke about the "challenge of prejudice" and pride in Judaism. Her efforts on behalf of the Negroes was similar in nature; she spoke of the difficulties of the emancipated Negro in a society that rejects him and of his struggle to achieve dignity and recognition.

Bibliography: D. Askowith, *Three Outstanding Women* (1941).

[ED.]

°**MEYER, EDUARD** (1855–1930), German Bible critic and historian. Born in Hamburg, Meyer was professor of ancient history at the universities of Breslau (from 1885), Halle (from 1889), and Berlin (1902–22). While he supported *Wellhausen's critical views on Pentateuchal composition, in his *Die Entstehung des Judenthums* (1896, 1965²) he opposed Welhausen's position concerning the authority of the documents mentioned in Ezra and the list of names referred to in Nehemiah, suggesting that a late date for Ezra does not allow for the development of Judaism as is known from the sources. In writing his classic *Geschichte des Altertums* (5 vols., 1884–1902; 1925–58²) he examined all available documentary evidence but failed to appreciate the contributions of archaeologists in regard to early Phoenician and Israelite history. He wrote, among other things, on the culture and history of the Sumerians (*Sumerier und Semiten in Babylonien*, 1906) and the Hittites (*Reich und Kultur der Chetiter*, 1914). He was one of the first to interpret the papyrus finds from Elephantine, and his *Die aeltere Chronologie Babyloniens, Assyriens, und Aegyptiens* (1925) reached very sound conclusions which are still widely refered to by students of the chronology of the ancient world. His *Ursprung und Anfaenge des Christentums* (3 vols., 1921–23) dealt with the history of Judaism and early Christianity, and it reflected the bias of classical biblical criticism, which respected prophetic Judaism, but saw talmudic Judaism as a fossil of rabbinic casuistry. [Z.G.]

MEYER, EUGENE (1875–1959), U.S. banker, government official, and newspaper editor and publisher. Born in California, he formed the banking firm of Eugene Meyer, Jr., and Co. in 1901. For 16 years he played a leading role in developing oil, copper, and automotive industries. During World War I he entered government service as an adviser on nonferrous metals to the War Industries Board. In 1918 he was named managing director of the War Finance Corporation, and under President Hoover he served as governor of the Federal Reserve Board and organized the Reconstruction Finance Corporation (1932). He was also the first chairman of the Reconstruction Finance Corporation. In 1933, he bought the then moribund *Washington Post* at a public auction, pumped new life into it, absorbed the Washington *Times-Herald,* and raised the *Washington Post* daily circulation to 400,000. After World War II, Meyer accepted an appointment by President Truman to become first president of the International Bank for Reconstruction and Development, and continued to serve on various commissions under President Eisenhower. The Washington Post Company, owner also of *Newsweek* magazine and a number of radio stations, was later headed by Meyer's daughter, Katherine Graham.

Bibliography: *Current Biography,* 20 (Oct. 1959), 30. [I.R.]

MEYER, JONAS DANIEL (1780–1834), Dutch jurist and public figure. Meyer was a grandson of Benjamin *Cohen, a prominent Dutch Jew and friend of William V of Orange. A child prodigy, Meyer was awarded the Ll.D. at the age of 16 for a thesis on the American revolutionary Thomas Payne, whom he attacked for the latter's disapproval of religious ceremonies, particularly those of the Jews. Meyer was the first Jew in Holland to be admitted as a lawyer, but although the period in which he lived saw the official granting of civil rights to Jews, anti-Jewish prejudices continued. In 1808, on becoming king of Holland, Louis Napoleon appointed Meyer director of the *Royal Gazette,* a member of the Institute of Sciences, and a court magistrate in Amsterdam. Meyer retained this position under King William I of Orange until he resigned in 1817. In 1815 the king appointed him secretary of a government committee for the drafting of a new Dutch constitution, but anti-Semitic prejudice prevented him from being appointed to higher positions and he returned to private practice. He appeared in 1817 on behalf of Louis Napoleon in a lawsuit against William I.

In 1827 Meyer returned to public life as secretary of a royal commission to prepare a new Dutch history. He was given the Order of the Netherlands Lion—the first Jew to receive this award. In 1808 Meyer was largely instrumental in reuniting the old Ashkenazi congregation of Amsterdam and the dissident liberal congregation of Adath Yeshurun. In 1809 he became chairman of the Dutch consistory of Jewish communities and in 1815 the first chairman of the Hoofdcomissie tot de Zaken der Israëliten. He was also chairman of a commission for drafting a program for Jewish schools in Amsterdam and together with Carel *Asser, Meyer drew up a

Jonas Daniel Meyer, Dutch jurist. Detail of oil portrait by Louis Moritz. Amsterdam, Rijksmuseum.

report disclosing the appalling social and educational situation of the Jews of Amsterdam. In 1873, a square separating the Sephardi and the main Ashkenazi synagogues in the center of the Jewish quarter of Amsterdam was named after him. Meyer's legal works include *Principes sur les questions transitoires* (Amsterdam, 1813) on legal problems which arose from the introduction of the Code Napoléon in Holland, and *Esprit, origine et progrès des institutions judicaires des principaux pays de l'Europe* (6 vols., 1819–23), a history of legal institutions in England, France, Holland, and Germany. He was a member of the French Academy, the Royal Academy in London, of the academies of Brussels and Torino, and of the Netherlands Society for Literature.

Bibliography: N. de Beneditty, *Leven en Werken van J. D. Meyer* (1925). [H.Bo.]

MEYER, LEON (1868–1957), French politician. Born in Le Havre, Meyer was a cousin of the Jewish anti-Dreyfusard journalist, Arthur Meyer. Having established a position for himself as a coffee merchant, he was elected to the city council in 1912 and as mayor of Le Havre in 1919. In 1921 Meyer became a radical-socialist member of the Chamber of Deputies and served as undersecretary of state in two administrations, first in 1925 and again in 1929. In 1932 he became minister of mercantile marine, in which post he made a substantial contribution to France's shipbuilding industry and to the development of the port of Le Havre. An outspoken critic of the Popular Front coalition of 1936, in which the radical socialists participated, Meyer fell out of favor with his own party. He devoted himself entirely to local politics until the fall of France in 1940, after which he took no further part in public affairs. [S.C.]

MEYER, MARTIN ABRAHAM (1879–1923), U.S. Reform rabbi and scholar. Meyer, who was born in San Francisco, California, was ordained by the Hebrew Union College in 1901. Meyer served as rabbi of Congregation Beth Emeth, Albany, New York (1902–06); Temple Israel, Brooklyn, New York (1906–10); and Temple Emanu-el, San Francisco (1910–23). From 1911 to 1923 he was lecturer in Semitics at the University of California. During World War I, Meyer became a supporter of both Zionism and the movement for an American Jewish Congress. In 1918–19 he served with the Red Cross in France. Meyer, who was associated with several social service organizations in San Francisco, served as president of the Big Brothers movement and the California Conference on Social Work, and as a member of the California Commission of Charities and Corrections (1911–20). He helped to organize small Jewish communities in the area, was director of the Jewish Education Society of San Francisco and of the Pacific Coast branch of the Jewish Chatauqua Society, and was a board member of several national Jewish organizations. Meyer's publications include: several articles on the condition of the Jews in Palestine; *History of the City of Gaza from the Earliest Times to the Present Day* (1907); and the two-volume *Methods of Teaching Post-Biblical History and Literature* (1915).

Bibliography: AJYB, 27 (1925/26), 246–59. [S.D.T.]

MEYER, PAULUS (alias **Pawly** originally **Kremenetzki, Eliezer Baruch Ashkenazi;** 1862–?), renegade who published testimony claiming that he had witnessed a ritual murder. Meyer, a native of Ostrow (Poland), acted during the 1880s as a Protestant missionary among the Jews in Germany. He came into conflict with the *Judenmission* there and published pamphlets against it, attacking H. L. *Strack and others. In 1892 missionary periodicals identified him as an impostor and swindler and he was expelled by the police from Prussia and Saxony. Meyer went to Vienna in 1893 and contacted Joseph *Deckert. On August *Rohling's recommendation, Deckert suggested to Meyer that he write a "scientific" book on the *blood libel. On May 11, 1893 the *Vaterland* published a letter by Meyer in which he claimed to have been present at a ritual murder in his native town in 1875, naming several participants. Joseph Samuel *Bloch took up the case. With the assistance of Nahum *Sokolow and Ḥayyim Selig *Slonimski, he discovered the persons accused by Meyer and, in some cases, their heirs. Joseph Kopp, who had represented Bloch in the Rohling controversy, persuaded them to sue for defamation of character. Throughout the trial Meyer denied having written or signed the letter or been responsible for its contents, although he admitted that the handwriting was that of his fiancée. The jury found him, Deckert, and the *Vaterland* guilty and they received a nominal sentence. The outcome, however, was symbolically important in the context of the anti-Semitic agitation of the 1890s.

Bibliography: J. S. Bloch, *My Reminiscences* (1923), 385–570; H. L. Strack, *Das Blut im Glauben und Aberglauben der Menschheit* (1900), index. [M.La.]

MEYER, RICHARD MORITZ (1860–1914), German literary historian. Born and educated in Berlin, Meyer became professor of literature at Berlin University in 1903. His books enjoyed a remarkable popularity extending far beyond his immediate scholarly circle. His prizewinning biography of Goethe was published in 1895. He wrote a monograph on Nietzsche (1913). Meyer's outstanding achievement was his *Die deutsche Literatur des 19. Jahrhunderts* (1900; enlarged edition ed. by Hugo *Bieber, 1923). [R.K.]

MEYER, VICTOR (1848–1897), German organic chemist. Meyer, the son of a Berlin textile printer, obtained his doctorate at Heidelberg *magna cum laude* before he was 19. He worked with Bunsen at Heidelberg and Baeyer in Berlin, and in 1872, despite his youth, was appointed professor of general chemistry at the Zurich Polytechnic. He was professor at Goettingen University from 1885 to 1889 and at Heidelberg from 1889 until his death. Meyer invented the term "stereochemistry" and made basic contributions in the field of organic compounds. As well as being one of the foremost organic chemists of his generation and an outstanding lecturer and speaker, he was an accomplished musician, but he was dogged by ill-health and committed suicide. Meyer's biography was written by his brother, Richard Emil Meyer (1846–1926), who was also an organic chemist of distinction. He held professorships at the Technische Hochschule of Braunschweig and at Heidelberg and was editor of the *Jahrbuch der Chemie* from 1891 to 1918. [S.A.M.]

MEYERBEER, GIACOMO (Jacob Liebmann-Beer; 1791–1864), German composer, remembered mainly for his spectacular operas. Meyerbeer was born in Berlin, where his father Jacob Herz Beer was a prominent banker; his brothers were Wilhelm *Beer and Michael *Beer. His musical gifts appeared early, and his grandfather Liebman Meyer Wulf was so impressed with the boy's genius that he made him his sole heir on condition that he added "Meyer" to his name. After studying with the composer Clementi, he went to live and work with the Abbé Vogler in Darmstadt. There he composed his first opera, *Jephthas Geluebde*, which was performed at Munich in 1813 with moderate success. His next dramatic work, *Die beiden Kalifen*, was a failure when produced in Vienna in 1814. Discouraged, Meyerbeer went to Italy. Between 1818 and 1824 he composed a series of successful Italian operas, among the most popular being *Romilda e Costanza*, *Semiramide riconosciuta*, *Emma di Resburgo*, and *Il crociato in Egitto*. His change of name from Jacob to Giacomo symbolized his "conversion" to the new Italian style.

In 1826, Meyerbeer was invited to the first performance of *Il crociato* in Paris. Its favorable reception led to his later career as a composer of French grand opera. His first in a

Portrait of Giacomo Meyerbeer, opera composer. Jerusalem, J.N.U.L., Schwadron Collection.

series of brilliant successes in this genre, *Robert le Diable*, was produced in 1831, and within a year it was being presented in many European cities. Meyerbeer, aided by his librettist Eugène Scribe, gave the public what it wanted: a sensational story, novel stage effects, showy singing, and colorful orchestration. This formula was repeated many times, most notably in *Les Huguenots* (1836), *Le Prophète* (1843), and *L'Africaine* (*Vasco da Gama*; 1838–64), first produced in French and English a year after the composer's death. While vigorously promoting his own career, Meyerbeer was always ready to help other composers. For example, he warmly recommended Wagner's *Rienzi* for production in Dresden, and during his period as royal director of opera in Berlin (1842–47) he introduced the *Flying Dutchman* to the repertoire there. Wagner however violently attacked the music and personality of his one-time friend. Meyerbeer remained faithful to Judaism. Meyerbeer's popularity continued for some years after his death—in 1895 *Le Prophète* attained its 150th performance in London—but his reputation declined in the 20th century.

Bibliography: M. Cooper, *Fanfare for Ernest Newman* (1959), 38–57; W. L. Crosten, *French Grand Opera: an Art and a Business* (1948), passim; H. Becker, *Der Fall Heine-Meyerbeer* (1958); B. Van Dieren, *Down Among the Dead Men* (1935), 142–74; *Giacomo Meyerbeer, 1791–1864, exposition...* (Fr. and Heb., Jerusalem, Jewish National Library, 1964); Istel, in: *Musical Quarterly*, 12 (1926), 72–109; J. Kapp, *Meyerbeer* (1920); A. Hervey, *Giacomo Meyerbeer* (1913); MGG, s.v.; G. Meyerbeer, *Briefwechsel und Tagebuecher*, ed. by H. Becker, 2 vols. (1960–70).

[D.N.]

MEYERHOF, MAX (1874–1945), ophthalmologist and medical historian. He was born in Hildesheim, Germany. In 1903 he went to Egypt and served as chief of the Khedivial Ophthalmic Clinic. He returned to Germany in 1914 to serve as a medical officer in the German army and after the war settled in Hanover as a practicing oculist. He returned to Cairo in 1923 and stayed there until his death. During his lifetime, Meyerhof published over 300 books, monographs, and treatises on ophthalmology and medical history. He made special studies of the various eye diseases endemic in Egypt and North Africa, especially of trachoma and its complications, of glaucoma, lepra of the eye, etc. His book, *Ueber die ansteckenden Augenleiden Aegyptens* appeared in 1909. He also wrote on the history of ophthalmology and pharmacology among Spanish Muslims and Jews and did research on medieval Arab medicine from unpublished documents in Cairo and other libraries. He edited and translated the Arabic text of the famous medieval ophthalmologist Ḥunain ibn Isḥāq, *The Book of the Ten Treatises on the Eye* (1928), and was one of the first to study

Maimonides as a physician; he translated and published for the first time Maimonides' glossary of drugs *L'Explication des noms de drogues* (1940). In recognition of his many services as an oculist and medical historian, Meyerhof received many honors and decorations from medical societies all over the world. Meyerhof also contributed to the organization of medical care for the poor in Egypt.

Bibliography: S. R. Kagan, *Jewish Medicine* (1952), 527f.; I. Fischer (ed.), *Biographisches Lexikon der hervorragenden Aerzte*, 2 (1933), s.v.; *Works of Max Meyerhof* (1944), compiled by U. ben Ḥorin. [S.M.]

MEYERHOF, OTTO (1884–1951), German biochemist and Nobel Prize winner. Meyerhof, who was born in Hanover, was first concerned with psychology (he wrote a book *Contributions to a Psychological Theory of Mental*

Otto Meyerhof, German biochemist and Nobel Prize winner. Jerusalem, J.N.U.L., Schwadron Collection.

Diseases) and philosophy (he edited a journal *Abhandlungen der Friesschen Schule*, mainly for neo-Kantian philosophers), and worked in Krehl's clinic and at the Marine Zoological Laboratory in Naples. In 1913 he joined the University of Kiel, where he became professor of physiological chemistry (1918–24). In 1923 Meyerhof was awarded the Nobel Prize in physiology and medicine (shared with A. V. Hill) "for his discovery of the fixed relationship between the consumption of oxygen and the metabolism of lactic acid in the muscle." An associated phenomenon is known as the Pasteur-Meyerhof effect. In 1924 Meyerhof became head of a division in the Kaiser Wilhelm Institute of Biology in Berlin-Dahlem, and in 1929 head of the department of physiology in the Institute for Medical Research in Heidelberg. He elucidated the roll played by ATP (adenosine triphosphate) in energy transfer in biological systems and introduced the term "energy coupling." He was forced to leave Germany in 1938, and became director of research at the Institut de Biologie Physicochimique in Paris. When the Germans conquered France, he escaped, first to southern France, and then to America. He then became research professor of physiological chemistry at the University of Pennsylvania's medical school.

Bibliography: Nachmansohn, in: *Science*, 115 (1952), 365–8; idem, in: *Biochimica et Biophysica Acta*, 4 (1950), 1–3; T. N. Levitan, *Laureates: Jewish Winners of the Nobel Prize* (1960), 124–7. [S.A.M.]

MEYERHOFF, HANS (1914–1965), U.S. philosopher. He was born in Brunswick, Germany, and went to the U.S. in 1934. From 1943 to 1948 he worked for the U.S. government. From 1949 on he taught philosophy at the University of California at Los Angeles. He wrote *Time in Literature* (1955), an analysis of scientific and literary renderings of time. He edited *The Philosophy of History in Our Time* (1959), and translated works by Max Scheler and Paul Friedlander. His publications include articles on philosophy, literature, psychology, and politics. He died in an automobile accident. A free speech plaza at the Los Angeles campus of the University of California is named after him. [M.M.M.]

MEYERHOFF, JOSEPH (1899–), U.S. businessman, communal worker, and philanthropist. Meyerhoff was born in a small town near Poltava, Russia, and was taken to the United States in 1906, settling with his family in Baltimore, Maryland. From 1921 he headed his own building and real estate firm, which developed new communities, especially in the Baltimore area, and shopping centers in many cities. Meyerhoff was associated with the United Jewish Appeal, of which he served as general chairman, 1961–64 and a member of the executive committee thereafter, and with the PEC Israel Economic Corporation, of which he was president, 1957–63 and later as chairman of the board and the executive committee. He also was chairman of the Israel Education Fund of the UJA, 1965–67. He served on the board of directors of many national and international Jewish organizations and institutions, including the Hebrew University in Jerusalem, 1961–67. A philanthropic leader in his local Baltimore Jewish community, his local interests included the Sinai Hospital of Baltimore, of which he served as vice-president and chairman of the board, 1943–59, and Associated Jewish Charities and Welfare Fund Campaign of Baltimore, of which he was general chairman, 1951–52. Meyerhoff served the state of Maryland as chairman of the State Planning Commission, 1956–63, as member of the State Board of Public Welfare, 1953–57, and in other capacities. [Ed.]

MEYERS, EDUARD MAURITS (1880–1954), Dutch jurist, who as professor of law at the University of Leiden from 1910 to 1950 influenced several generations of Dutch lawyers. Born in Den Helder, Meyers was admitted to the bar in 1903. He practiced law in Amsterdam until 1910, when he was made professor of civil and private international law at Leiden. After 1928 he was substitute counselor in the High Court of Justice at The Hague. Meyers' numerous books were largely devoted to the history of civil law. His work, *The Labor Contract* (1908), became a standard treatise on the subject and was followed by *Legal Decisions Regarding the Law on Labor Contracts* (1909). His textbook on succession, *Le droit ligurien de succession en Europe occidentale* (1928), and his *L'Histoire des principes fondamentaux du droit international privé à partir du Moyen Age* (1934) brought him further distinction. Following the Nazi invasion of Holland, Meyers was dismissed from his post and was sent to *Theresienstadt concentration camp for the duration of the war. His arrest led to a public demonstration by students at Leiden. They were addressed by the dean, Professor R. P. Cleveringa, who described Meyers as a great lawyer, a "faithful, honest child of his people," and a "noble and true son of our nation." Cleveringa was himself imprisoned for this speech. After World War II, Meyers was commissioned to draft a new civil code for Holland , but died before its completion. [H.Bo.]

MEYERSON, EMILE (1859–1933), French chemist, historian, and philosopher of science; son of Malvina Meyerson, Polish novelist. Born in Lublin, Poland, Meyerson studied in Germany, mainly in Heidelberg with the noted chemist R. W. Bunsen. He later emigrated to Paris where he worked as an industrial chemist, editor, and administrator of the Jewish colonization association (ICA). Although never appointed to a university post, Meyerson came to be recognized as an unusually erudite scholar of the interrelationships among the natural sciences, the history of philosophy, and cultural developments, particularly since the rise of modern science in the 16th century. His knowledge embraced the most recent work on Einstein's theory of relativity and the early quantum theory of Max Planck and Niels Bohr. Meyerson wished to understand the nature of explanation both in the natural sciences and elsewhere. He believed that the philosopher of science has to have a thorough knowledge of the history of science, and of how scientists themselves conceived of their own work. His own philosophy, though abstract, was based on vast scholarly research which led him to conclude that rational understanding consisted in the discovery of those factors of permanence underlying processes of change, and the search for those identities found within the evident flux of experience or the incompletely rationalized world of most scientific work. Reality nevertheless seemed to Meyerson to be only partially open to rational understanding. Its sensual

Emile Meyerson, French philosopher of science, Jerusalem, J.N.U.L., Schwadron Collection.

factors, for instance, which are so important for epistemological theory, remain unexplained. A complete understanding of nature thus seems to elude the grasp of a reasoned science. Meyerson's works include: *Identité et Réalité* (1908; *Identity and Reality*, 1930); *De l'explication dans les Sciences* (2 vols., 1921); and various essays.

Bibliography: T. R. Kely, *Explanation and Reality in the Philosophy of Emile Meyerson* (1937), incl. bibl.; G. Boas, *A Critical Analysis of the Philosophy of Emile Meyerson* (1930); L. de Broglie et al., in: *Bulletin de la Société francaise de Philosophie*, 55 no. 2 (1961), 55–105, issue devoted to Meyerson and Milhaud.

[R.S.C.]

MEYERSTEIN, EDWARD HARRY WILLIAM (1889–1952), English poet and novelist. The son of a well-known philanthropist, Meyerstein was educated at Harrow and Oxford. He worked for some years in the manuscripts department of the British Museum. Though a noted scholar, especially in Greek and Roman literature, Meyerstein was mainly drawn to poetry. He published a number of volumes of verse elaborate in diction and reminiscent of the fashions of the 1890s. They included *The Door* (1911); *New Odes* (1936); *Briancourt* (1937); *Sonnets* (1939); *The Visionary* (1941); *In Time of War* (1942); *Three Sonatas* (1948); and *The Delphic Character* (1951). *The Unseen Beloved* was published posthumously in 1953. Meyerstein also wrote several novels, outstanding among which was the trilogy *Terence Duke* (1935), a study in viciousness. Few of his works retained their popularity, but his careful and detailed life of Thomas Chatterton (1930) is one of the best extant studies of that romantic poet. A melancholy and eccentric bachelor, Meyerstein is unsympathetically portrayed in the character of Brunstein in Arnold Lunn's novel, *The Harrovians* (1913). His own account of his youth appears in *Of My Early Life* (1958).

Bibliography: Wain, in: *Encounter*, 19 (Aug. 1962), 27–42.

[P.D.H.]

MEYERSTEIN, EDWARD WILLIAM (1863–1942), British philanthropist. Meyerstein was a highly successful member of the London Stock Exchange, who was renowned as "the great benefactor of hospitals." He had a very special interest in the Middlesex Hospital in London, which received his gift of £350,000 to make possible its expansion. Other institutions which were beneficiaries of his generosity were the Queen Victoria College Hospital, Tonbridge, the Kent County Ophthalmic Hospital at Maidstone, the Westminster, St. Mary's, and Princess Elizabeth of York hospitals in London. From 1937 to 1938 and from 1941 to 1942 he served as the high sheriff of Kent. He was knighted in 1938 for his benefactions to health services. His son, Edward Harry William *Meyerstein, was a writer of prose and poetry.

Bibliography: JC (Feb. 6, 1942), 18.

[Ed.]

MEYUḤAS, ABRAHAM BEN SAMUEL (d. 1767), rabbi and kabbalist in Jerusalem, his birthplace. Abraham studied under Israel Meir Mizraḥi in the Yeshivah Bet Ya'akov founded by Jacob Israel Pereira, and married the daughter of Tobias *Cohn. His life was one of suffering and affliction. He was orphaned as a child and lost his sight at the age of 30. Abraham was the author of: *Sedeh ha-Areẓ*, homilies on the Torah, in three parts (pts. 1 and 2, Salonika, 1784, 1798; pt. 3, Leghorn, 1788); *Diglo Ahavah*, a commentary on the *Derekh Eẓ ha-Ḥayyim* of Isaac *Luria: it was arranged by Meir *Poppers and included the latter's own work, *Or Zaru'a; Ha-Ma'or ha-Katan*, on the *Eẓ Ḥayyim* by Ḥayyim *Vital; and *Si'aḥ ha-Sadeh*, on the *Kavvanot* ("Meditations") of Isaac Luria, together with homilies and notes. Raphael *Meyuḥas was his brother. One of Abraham's sons, Benjamin Moses (d. 1804), was responsible for publishing part 1 of *Sedeh ha-Areẓ*, and another, Joseph Jacob, an emissary of the Hebron community, published the other two parts while engaged on his missions.

Bibliography: Michael, Or, 121, no. 253; Frumkin-Rivlin, 2 (1928), 118; 3 (1929), 86, 90–91; Yaari, Sheluḥei, 556–7, 598; idem, *Meḥkerei Sefer* (1958), 138–9.

[A.D.]

MEYUḤAS, MOSES JOSEPH MORDECAI BEN RAPHAEL MEYUHAS (1738–1805), chief rabbi of Jerusalem. Moses studied in the *bet midrash* Bet Ya'akov. When only 15 years of age he answered questions on *halakhah*. After 1778 he was one of the members of the *bet midrash* Keneset Israel founded by Ḥayyim ibn *Attar. After the death of his father-in-law Yom Tov *Algazi, Moses succeeded him as Sephardi chief rabbi *(rishon le-Zion)* in 1802. He was on friendly terms with Ḥ. J. D. *Azulai. The titles of all his works include the word *mayim* from the initials of his name (he even signed his responsa "Mayim Meyuḥas"). They are: *Sha'ar ha-Mayim* (Salonika, 1768), novellae on the laws of *terefot* in *Yoreh De'ah*, on tractate *Ḥullin* and responsa; *Berekhot Mayim* (*ibid.*, 1789), novellae to the Shulḥan Arukh; *Mayim Sha'al* (*ibid.*, 1799), responsa, including the work, *Mayim Rishonim*, novellae written in his youth, to the *Mishneh Torah* of Maimonides. Many of his novellae and responsa, among them *Penei ha-Mayim* and *Ein ha-Mayim*, remain unpublished.

Bibliography: Frumkin-Rivlin, 3 (1929), 183–6; M. D. Gaon, *Yehudei ha-Mizraḥ be-Ereẓ Yisrael*, 2 (1938), 401f.; M. Benayahu, *Rabbi Ḥayyim Yosef David Azulai* (Heb., 1959), 350f.

[A.D.]

MEYUḤAS, RAPHAEL MEYUḤAS BEN SAMUEL (?1695–1771), chief rabbi *(rishon le-Zion)* of Jerusalem. Meyuḥas was born in Jerusalem and studied in the yeshivah Bet Ya'akov, which he subsequently headed. In 1723 when the troubles of the Jewish community of Jerusalem were aggravated because of the harsh rule of its governor, Yussuf

Pasha, Raphael was sent by Abraham *Yiẓḥaki, the *rishon le-Zion*, to Constantinople to plead for the governor's removal. Meyuḥas served as *av bet din* in Jerusalem, his colleagues including Isaac Zerahiah *Azulai and, much later, his son Ḥ. J. D. *Azulai. In 1756 on the death of Israel Jacob *Algazi, he was appointed *rishon le-Zion*. In one of his rulings Raphael endeavored to bring about a rapprochement between the Karaites and the Rabbanites, permitting the Karaites to send their children to the *talmud torah*. Tradition has it, however, that Raphael later recanted his ruling. He was the author of: *Minḥat Bikkurim* (Salonika, 1752) on the Talmud; *Peri ha-Adamah* in 4 parts (*ibid.*, 1752–57 (64?)), novellae on Maimonides' *Mishneh Torah* with responsa—appended to the fourth part are homilies called *Penei ha-Adamah; Mizbaḥ Adamah* (*ibid.*, 1777) on the Shulḥan Arukh. Raphael was the brother of Abraham b. Samuel *Meyuḥas and the father of Moses Joseph Mordecai *Meyuḥas.

Bibliography: Frumkin-Rivlin, 3 (1929), 85–90; S. Assaf, *Be-Oholei Ya'akov* (1943), 203; Yaari, Sheluḥei, index, s.v. *Meyuḥas Meyuḥas;* M. Benayahu, *Rabbi Ḥayyim Yosef David Azulai* (Heb., 1959), index; idem (ed.), *Sefer ha-Ḥida* (1959), 28–31. [A.D.]

MEYUḤAS, YOSEF BARAN (ben Raḥamim Nathan; 1868–1942), leader of the Sephardi community in Ereẓ Israel, writer, and educator. Born in Jerusalem, from 1884 Meyuḥas taught in various schools, including the Evelina de Rothschild School, and was headmaster of the Ezra Teachers Seminary and the municipal school for boys. In 1888 he was one of the founders of the lodge of "Jerusalem" *B'nai B'rith—the first in Ereẓ Israel—and a founder of the Sha'arei Ẓedek quarter of Jerusalem. Meyuḥas was also a leader of the Ḥibbat ha-Areẓ Society, which founded *Moẓa, near Jerusalem. One of the first Ereẓ Israel Sephardim to take an Ashkenazi wife, he married Margalit, the daughter of Y. M. *Pines. His was among the first families to follow Eliezer *Ben-Yehuda's example of speaking Hebrew. Meyuḥas was among the founders of the Ginzei Yosef u-Midrash Abrabanel Library, which formed the nucleus of the *Jewish National and University Library. From 1920 to 1931 he was president of the city council of Jews in Jerusalem. From his youth, he contributed to the Hebrew and Ladino press on matters of culture, education, and literature and became a specialist on Sephardi folklore, oriental communities, the Arabs of Palestine, and the history of the Jews of the Orient and of the *yishuv*. He published a number of works and some have remained in manuscript. [A.A.]

MEZAḤ (Segal), JOSHUA HA-LEVI (1834–1917), Hebrew and Yiddish author. Born in Lithuania in the Kovno region, near Zagare, Mezaḥ (whose pen name derives from the initials of "Mi-Zager Ḥadash"), lived in many different Jewish settlements in Russia and Rumania, and for the last 25 years of his life in Vilna. From 1861 he wrote for most of the Hebrew and Yiddish newspapers existing at the time. His first book was *Ha-Emunah ve-ha-Haskalah* ("Faith and the Enlightenment," 1874). A collection of articles containing descriptions of the social shortcomings of various Jewish communities was published as *Mikhtavim mi-Sar shel YaM* ("Letters from Yehoshu'a Mezaḥ," 5 vols., 1884–88). *Tefaḥ Megulleh* (1886), for the greater part written by Judah Leib *Gordon, was an attack upon Alexander *Zederbaum, the editor of *Ha-Meliẓ*. In *Bamat Yiẓḥak* (1890), Mezaḥ wrote about the Yiddish theater, and *Ha-Eshel* (2 pts., 1893–94) contains selections from his tales, poems, and essays. He also wrote two plays, *Tummat Ivriyyah* (1904), and *Alilat Shav* (1908). He edited *Gan ha-Perahim* (1891), and, together with Reuben Asher *Braudes, the short-lived biweekly *Ha-Yahadut* (1885). After the 1890s Mezaḥ wrote almost nothing in Hebrew; but he published many popular short stories and popular booklets in Yiddish which were circulated in hundreds of thousands of copies, sometimes anonymously and often without receiving remuneration. Mezaḥ spent the end of his life in poverty. A bibliography of his works in Yiddish was compiled by A. J. Goldschmidt in Ẓ. Shabad (ed.), *Vilner Zamlbukh*, 1 (1917), 192–201.

Bibliography: Rejzen, Leksikon, 2 (1927), 366–74: Kressel, Leksikon, 2 (1967), 335–6. [Y.A.K.]

MEZEI, MÓR (1836–1925), Hungarian lawyer and politician. Graduating from law school in 1864, Mezei was admitted to the bar by special royal permission, since Jews were excluded from the legal profession until 1867. While still a student he joined the movement for Jewish emancipation. From 1861 he was secretary of the Izraelita Magyar Egylet ("Union of Hungarian Israelites"), and later editor of the union's official journal, *Magyar Izraelita*. In 1868–69 he was secretary of the General Congress of Hungarian Jews. It was largely through his efforts that the Jewish religion was officially recognized in Hungary (1895). From 1905 through 1925 he was president of the National Bureau of Hungarian Israelites, and was also active in general public affairs. He was a member of parliament (1893–1901), as a representative of the Liberal Party. His brother ERNŐ (1851–1932), a journalist and politician, also studied law at Budapest University. From 1874 to 1910 he was the political leader-writer of *Egyetértés* (Concord"), the mouthpiece of the opposition Independence Party. In 1881 Mezei was elected member of parliament for Miskolc, but his parliamentary career was cut short when he submitted embarrassing questions in parliament in connection with the *Tiszaeszlar blood libel. Previously, Mezei had written several pamphlets against the policy of the Liberal Party leader Kálmán *Tisza, who pursued a conciliatory policy toward the Hapsburg regime, *Tisza Kálmán a miniszterelnök* ("K. Tisza the Premier," 1875), *Tisza Kálmán 1877-ben* ("Tisza in 1877," 1877). His other works include a book describing his travels in Italy, *Bolyongások az olasz ég alatt* ("Roaming under Italian Skies"). At the beginning of the 20th century, Mezei, who was opposed to Zionism, corresponded with Theodor *Herzl. In a letter that later became famous, Herzl warned him of the fate in store for the assimilationist Jewry of Hungary.

Bibliography: Zs. Groszmann, in: IMIT, 58 (1936), 197–208; J. Rákosi, in: *Zsidó Evkönyv*, 2 (1928–29), 111–2. [J.Z.]

MEZEY, FERENC (1860–1927), Hungarian lawyer and communal worker. Mezey studied law at the university of Budapest and took an interest in Jewish affairs from his student days. In the *Tiszaeszlar blood-libel case, he assisted the counsel for the defense, K. Eötvös. During the 1890s Mezey was one of the founders of the movement seeking institutional equality for the Jewish religion (granted in 1895). From 1902 he was the secretary of the national bureau of the Hungarian Jews, and its president in the last year of his life. Between 1889 and 1916 he was also secretary of the *ḥevra kaddisha* of Pest (see *Budapest), and was instrumental in establishing social welfare institutions. Mezey was also president of the administrative council of the rabbinical seminary. He founded the Jewish Museum of Budapest (1916), and was editor of the periodical **Magyar Zsidó Szemle*. An extreme assimilationist and anti-Zionist, Mezey sought to foster religious life organized within the religious institutions in order to repair the breach between the two factions of Hungarian Jewry, and helped to promote the influence of *Neologism.

Bibliography: L. Blau, in: *Magyar Zsidó Szemle*, 45 (1928), 97–100; idem, in: IMIT, 44 (1929), 11–25; Ö. Kálmán, *M. F. élete és működése* (1929). [J.Z.]

MEZHIRECH (Pol. **Miedzyrzec;** Ukrainian **Mezhirichi**), village in Rovno oblast, Ukrainian S.S.R. In Jewish sources Mezhirech is called *Mezrits Gadol* to distinguish it from Miedzyrzec Podlaski in the province of Lublin and Miedzyrzec in the province of Poznan. An organized Jewish community existed there from the 18th century. Among the celebrated Jewish personalities who lived there were the kabbalist R. *Jacob Koppel b. Moses Lipschuetz and R. *Dov Baer of Mezhirech; as a result of the latter's presence the town became a center of the ḥasidic movement. In 1847 the Jewish community numbered 1,808 persons. At the close of the 19th century the Jews of Mezhirech established and developed a factory producing brushes, which became known throughout Russia. During 1910–12 the annual turnover of this firm amounted to over 50,000 rubles. There were 2,107 Jews (67% of the total population) living in the town in 1897 and 1,743 (73%) in 1921. The town was occupied by the Soviet army in 1939, and, in July 1941, by the Germans, who murdered, robbed, and conscripted the Jews into forced labor, with the assistance of the local Ukrainians. About 1,500 Jews of Mezhirech were massacred in October 1941. Most of the remainder were slaughtered in August of the following year; only 150 succeeded in escaping, some to Soviet Russia and about 50 others to the forests, where they joined the partisans.

Bibliography: Halpern, Pinkas, index; B. Wasiutyński, *Ludność żydowska w Polsce w wiekach XIX i XX* (1930), 85; I. Schiper, *Dzieje handlu żydowskiego na źiemiach polskich* (1937), index; H. Tenenbaum, *Bilans handlowy Królestwa Polskiego* (1916), 161; B. Brutzkus, in: *Sozialwissenschaft und Sozialpolitik*, 61 (1929), 275. [EH]

MEZŐFI, VILMOS (1870–1947), Hungarian politician and journalist, leader of the socialist agrarian movement. Born in Debrecen, Mezőfi was a watchmaker's apprentice who became a journalist and columnist in liberal newspapers. He joined the Social Democratic Party and edited their daily newspaper, *Népszava*. He also edited the workers' literary magazine, *Népolvasótár*.

Mezőfi played a leading role in the Social Democrats' attempt to organize agricultural workers. He was elected to the Hungarian parliament in 1905 where he advocated universal suffrage and pressed for immediate land reform. He left the party in 1910 when he found that it was not applying itself to this question. After World War I Mezőfi joined the newly formed small landowners' party and edited its journal *Szabad Szó* ("Free Word"). He continued to be active in Hungarian politics after the counterrevolution of 1920. In 1938 legislation was introduced to deprive Jews of their civic rights. Mezőfi vigorously fought the proposals and helped to organize the defense of the Jewish community. He was elected president of the 14th synagogue district of Pest in 1941.

Among Mezőfi's many writings are *A szociáldemokrácia evangéliuma* ("Gospel of Social Democracy") and *A munkabérek Magyarországon az 1896–1898 években* ("Wages in Hungary During the Years 1896–1898," 1899). In 1937 he published a pamphlet, *Irás a zsidókról* ("Script on the Jews"), directed to the agricultural population to combat the anti-Semitic Nazi propaganda which was being distributed among them.

Bibliography: *Magyar Irodalmi Lexikon*, 2 (1965), 226; *Magyar Életrajzi Lexikon*, 2 (1969), s.v. [B.Y.]

MEZUZAH (Heb. מְזוּזָה), parchment scroll affixed to the doorpost of rooms in the Jewish home. The original meaning of the word *mezuzah* is "doorpost" (cf. Ex. 12:7). Its etymology is obscure; it has been suggested that it is derived from the Assyrian *manzazu*, but this is by no means certain. The Bible twice enjoins (Deut. 6:9 and 11:20) "and ye shall write them (the words of God) upon the *mezuzot* of thy house and in thy gates"; by transference, the word was

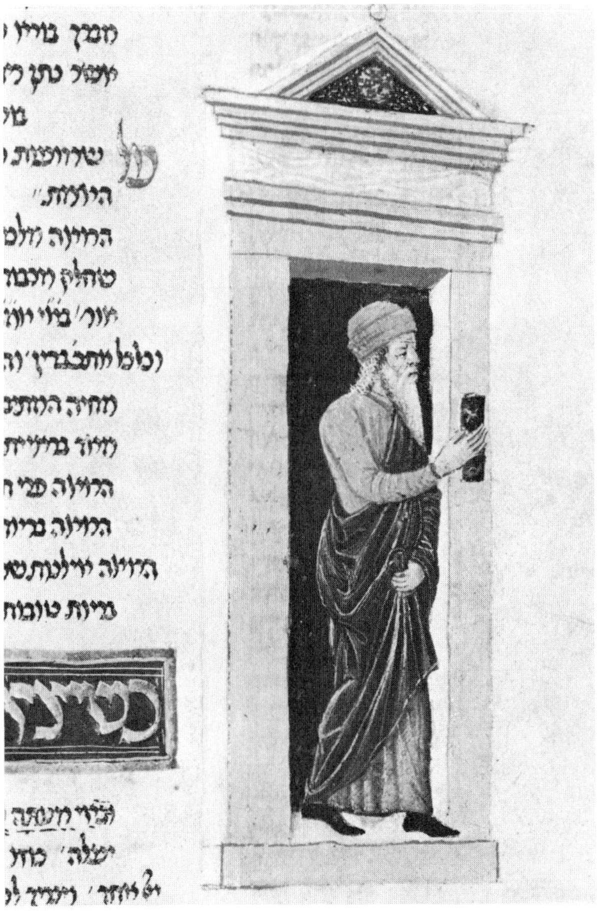

Figure 1. Man touching the *mezuzah* as he leaves a house. Detail from illustration in the *Rothschild Miscellany*, north Italy, Ferrara(?), c. 1470. Jerusalem, Israel Museum, Ms. 180/51, fol. 126v. Photo David Harris, Jerusalem.

Figure 2. Wooden *mezuzah* in the shape of a fish, Eastern Europe, 19th century(?). New York, Jewish Museum.

4

5

Figure 3. Silver *mezuzah*, Russia, 19th century, decorated with an Ark with hinged doors, and engraved foliage. Formerly Feinberg Collection, Detroit, Mich. Photo Manning Bros., Highland Park, Mich.

Figure 4. Embroidered velvet cover for a front-door *mezuzah* given by a bride to her husband, Morocco, 19th century. The silver-thread embroidery includes the bride's name, Simḥah Ḥamou. Cecil Roth Collection. Photo David Harris, Jerusalem.

Figure 5. A modern silver *mezuzah* designed by the 20th-century U.S. artist, Ilya Schor. Photo J. J. Breit, New York.

made to apply not to the doorpost, but to the passages which were affixed to the doorpost in accordance with this injunction. The *mezuzah* consists of a piece of parchment, made from the skin of a clean animal, upon which the two passages in which the above-mentioned verses occur (Deut. 6:4–9 and 11:13–21) are written in square (Assyrian) characters, traditionally in 22 lines. The parchment is rolled up and inserted in a case with a small aperture. On the back of the parchment the word שַׁדַּי ("Almighty," but also the initial letters of שׁוֹמֵר דְּלָתוֹת יִשְׂרָאֵל "Guardian of the doors of Israel" (Kol Bo 90, 101:4)), is written, and the parchment is so inserted that the word is visible through the aperture. It is affixed to the right hand doorpost of the room, or house, or gate, where it is obligatory (see below), in the top third of the doorpost and slanting inward. A blessing "Who hast commanded us to fix the *mezuzah*" is recited when affixing it. The earliest evidence for the fulfillment of the commandments of the *mezuzah* dates from the Second Temple period. A *mezuzah* parchment (6.5 cm. × 16 cm.) has been found at Qumran (Cave 8) in which are written some sentences from Deuteronomy (10:12–11:21) but not from the *Shema* (*Discoveries in the Judean Desert of Jordan* (1962), 158–61). The Samaritans make their *mezuzot* out of large stones and attach them to the lintel of the main door of their houses or place them near the doorway. They carve on them the Ten Commandments or the "ten categories by which the world was created." Sometimes they use abbreviations and initial letters of the ten or single verses in praise of God. *Mezuzah* stones of this sort are found in Israel dating from the early Arab and perhaps even Byzantine era. The Karaites do not make the *mezuzah* obligatory. Nevertheless, the *mezuzot* that they do attach are made of a tablet of blank plate in the form of the two tablets of the law but without writing on them and they fix them to the doorways of their public buildings and sometimes to their dwelling places.

In the Middle Ages the custom obtained of making kabbalistic additions, usually the names of angels, as well as symbols (such as the **magen david*) to the text. The custom was vigorously opposed by Maimonides. He declared that those who did so "will have no share in the world to come." With their "foolish hearts" "they turn a commandment" whose purpose is to emphasize the love of God "into an amulet" (Yad, Tefillin 5:4). Despite this, there is one clear reference in the Talmud to the efficacy of the *mezuzah* as an amulet, though from the context it need not be regarded as doctrine. In return for a material gift sent by *Ardavan to *Rav, the latter sent him a *mezuzah*, and in answer to his surprised query replied that it would "guard him" (TJ, Pe'ah 1:1, 15d; Gen. R. 35:3). To a similar context belongs the story of the explanation of the *mezuzah* given by *Onkelos the proselyte to the Roman soldiers who came to arrest him: "In the case of the Holy One, blessed be He, His servants dwell within, while He keeps guard on them from without" (Av. Zar. 11a).

Maimonides' decision prevailed, and the *mezuzah* today contains only the two biblical passages. However, at the bottom of the obverse side there is written the formula כולו במוכסלכולו, a cryptogram formed by substituting the next letter of the alphabet for the original, it thus being the equivalent of יהוה אלהינו יהוה ("the Lord, God, the Lord"). This is already mentioned by *Asher b. Jehiel in the 13th century in his commentary to the *Hilkhot Mezuzah* of Alfasi (Romm-Vilna ed. p. 6b).

The *mezuzah* must be affixed to the entrance of every home and to the door of every living room of a house, thus excluding storerooms, stables, lavatories, and bathrooms, and must be inspected periodically (twice in seven years) to ensure that the writing is still readable. The custom has become widespread and almost universal at the present day to affix the *mezuzah* to the entrance to public buildings (including all government offices in Israel) and synagogues. There is no authority for this, unless the building or room is also used for residential purposes (Levi ibn Ḥabib, Resp. no. 101), and the Midrash (Deut. R. 7:2) actually asks the rhetorical question, "Is then a *mezuzah* affixed to synagogues?" As the scriptural verse states, it is also to be affixed to "thy gates." It is thus obligatory for the entrances to apartment houses. On the gates of the suburb Yemin Moshe in Jerusalem, which stand since their erection in 1860, the *mezuzot* are still to be seen. After the Six-Day War *mezuzot* were affixed to the gates of the Old City of Jerusalem. In the responsa *Sha'ali Ẓiyyon* of D. Eliezrov (1962, pt. 2, nos. 9–10), who served as rabbi to the Jewish political prisoners at Latrun during the British Mandate, there are two responsa from him and Rabbi Ouziel, Sephardi chief rabbi of Israel, as to whether *mezuzot* were obligatory for the rooms and cells of the camp.

In the Diaspora the *mezuzot* must be affixed after the householder has resided in the home for 30 days; in Israel, immediately on occupation. If the house is sold or let to a Jew the previous occupier must leave the *mezuzah*. It is customary, among the pious, on entering or leaving to kiss the *mezuzah* or touch it and kiss the fingers (Maharil, based on the passage from Av. Zar. 11a quoted above).

The Talmud enumerates the *mezuzah* as one of the seven precepts with which God surrounded Israel because of His love for them. Of the same seven (the *ẓiẓit* being regarded as four) R. *Eliezer b. Jacob stated, "Whosoever has the **tefillin* on his head, the *tefillin* on his arm, the *ẓiẓit* on his garment and the *mezuzah* on his doorpost is fortified against sinning" (Men. 43b). The *mezuzah* is one of the most widely observed ceremonial commandments of Judaism. In modern times the practice developed of wearing a *mezuzah* around the neck as a charm. Some of the cases in which the *mezuzah* is enclosed are choice examples of Jewish art, and the artistic *mezuzah* case has been developed to a considerable extent in modern Israel.

See also *Amulet; *Ceremonial Objects.

Bibliography: Eisenstein, Dinim, 214f.; F. Landsberger, in: HUCA, 31 (1960), 149–66; J. Trachtenberg, *Jewish Magic and Superstition* (1939), 146ff.; V. Aptowitzer, in: REJ, 60 (1910), 38–52.

[L.I.R.]

MIAMI, metropolitan area located in Dade County on the southern tip of Florida, including Miami, Miami Beach, and 24 incorporated municipalities, as well as unincorporated territory. The permanent Jewish population is difficult to ascertain because of seasonal residents. The official figure is 100,000, but is probably closer to 200,000. As one of the largest Jewish communities in the United States, which attracts thousands of visitors, Miami has become a national center for Jewish organizational activity.

Early History. Efforts by individuals to develop the area made little progress until the extension of the railroad into the area in 1896. Among the residents of the city and its environs were 25 Jews. Some had drifted into Miami from Key West, which had imposed a discriminatory tax on itinerant peddlers and had suffered a decline in its cigar industry. The first Jewish resident of Miami was Samuel Singer, who came from Palm Beach in 1895. Isidor Cohen arrived in 1896. He, like most of the other Jewish pioneers, sold dry goods in a small store along the river. A Jewish congregation was organized for the High Holidays in 1896. By the turn of the century only three Jewish pioneers were left, of whom Isidor Cohen was the most noteworthy by virtue of his participation in both general and Jewish community activities until his death in 1951.

In 1912, when the number of settlers had reached 75, Cohen was instrumental in founding B'nai Zion, a regular congregation. It was reorganized and renamed Beth David in 1917 and is now referred to as "the pioneer synagogue." Five years later it established the city's first permanent Hebrew school. Initially the congregation included Orthodox, Conservative, and Reform elements, and both Conservative and Orthodox services were conducted. However, the Reform group broke away in 1922 and organized Temple Israel. It built what is still considered one of the most beautiful synagogue structures in the area. Beth Abraham, a small Orthodox congregation, also began to hold services about 1925, and Beth Jacob, another Orthodox synagogue, the first Jewish congregation on Miami Beach, received its charter in 1927. These four synagogues served Greater Miami until the next great increase in population, just before and after World War II. A Zionist Society was formed after World War I, a United Jewish Aid Association was founded in 1920, a B'nai B'rith lodge in 1922, a chapter of the National Council of Jewish Women in 1921, followed in 1926 by Hadassah and the Workmen's Circle. The tremendous influx of new settlers attracted by the Miami land boom of the 1920s swelled the general population from 69,000 to 110,000, while the number of Jews rose from 2,000 in 1925 to 3,500 in 1930. Although the conditions of the time brought marginal dealers in real estate to Miami, many others, particularly lawyers and builders, arrived determined to become a permanent part of the burgeoning community. Among those pioneers were Stanley C. Myers, Baron de Hirsch Meyer, and the Simonhoff brothers. The growing number of winter visitors and settlers from New York, Philadelphia, and Chicago encouraged the establishment of local branches of national Jewish organizations.

The United Jewish Aid Association, which assisted indigent invalids who had come to Miami for their health, changed its name in 1927 to the Jewish Welfare Bureau of Miami, later to the Jewish Social Service Bureau, and finally to the Jewish Family Service. The increase in local poor as a result of the 1926 collapse of the Miami real estate boom, plus the problems of helping sick and needy visitors during the difficult 1930s, resulted in the Greater Miami Federation of Jewish Welfare Funds, which was organized in 1938. The first president was Stanley C. Myers. By 1940 the Jewish population of Greater Miami was 7,500, with the greatest increase in Miami Beach, where a new congregation was established. The Miami Beach Jewish Center, later known as Temple Emanu-El, obtained the services of Irving Lehrman as its rabbi. In 1970 it numbered over 1,200 member families.

World War II to 1970. Congregation Beth Sholom began during World War II as a soldier's congregation in Miami Beach, and had a membership in 1968 of over 1,000 families. It is a Liberal congregation, led (in 1970) by Rabbi Leon Kronish. Although the greatest concentration of Jewish population in Greater Miami was (1970) in Miami Beach, where about 80% of the population was estimated to be Jewish, the trend of younger families during the 1950s and 1960s was to move to North Miami Beach and Southwest Miami, each of which numbered about 30,000 Jewish residents. There were also centers of Jewish population in the city of Miami and the surrounding communities. The growth and mobility of the Jewish community was reflected in the increase in the number of houses of worship in the new areas of settlement. There were seven synagogues in North Miami Beach, of which Beth Torah with 665 families was the largest. The Reform Synagogue Beth Am in the southwest area of Miami boasted the largest religious school, with 1,200 students, in Greater Miami, and Beth David with a membership of over 750 families established an auxiliary school building in the suburbs. There were 46 officially recognized congregations, in addition to small unofficial groups and seasonally active synagogues. Jewish community life centered around the synagogue rather than in organizations.

The Bureau of Jewish Education of Greater Miami was established in 1944, as a coordinating agency for autonomous congregational and independent schools. It was supported almost entirely by the local federation, and the number of affiliated and assisted schools rose from four in 1944, to 10 in 1950, and to 42 in 1967, while the school population rose from 1,140 to 11,703. An Orthodox day school, the Hebrew Academy, in Miami Beach, was founded in 1947 and had 506 students in 1968. A day school under Conservative auspices, the Solomon Schechter School of Temple Emanu-El, was organized in 1961. The YMHA, first organized in 1913 and reactivated in 1933, was soon joined by a YWHA and a branch of the YMHA on the Beach. In 1951 the branches of this association were amalgamated. The YMHA also purchased new quarters, which expanded its program of social group work and leisure time activities. In 1970 the membership was over 6,000. Miami's first extra-synagogal Jewish women's organization was the National Council of Jewish Women, which sent assistance to European refugees stranded in Cuba, organized the first Jewish Sunday School at Beth David, participated in the organization of the Jewish Welfare Bureau, and helped furnish the synagogue. The Council assisted in the resettlement of European refugees in cooperation, first, with the Jewish Welfare Bureau and, later, with the local immigration authorities. During the 1960s it was concerned with refugees from Cuba, of whom 2,500–3,000 were Jewish.

Zionist Activity. Local Zionist activity, which reached its low point in 1938–39, was renewed with the formation of the Miami Beach Zionist District in 1941. It had 1,200 members by 1945 and became a major center of national Zionist activities. The Miami branch of the Jewish National Fund, which had long been the recipient of local funds, was organized in 1941. The Miami branch of the American Zionist Emergency Council, formed in 1945, sponsored community-wide meetings to further the Zionist cause. In 1968 Hadassah had a membership of 8,500, and there were seven Mizrachi groups and nine Pioneer Women chapters. The interest of the Jews of Miami in Israel was also indicated by the 17,000 contributors to the Combined Jewish Appeal in 1967, their purchase of $6,300,000 worth of Israel bonds in 1967, and the investments in Israel hotels and oil fields by local businessmen.

Economic Life. Tourism, the city's largest industry, was also the most important activity among Jews. The second largest economic activity among Jews involved building and real estate and the savings and loan associations which serve them. Third were the services and retail trade, which were about 40% Jewish owned. There were also a large number of Jewish professionals, including dentists, lawyers, social workers, accountants, and doctors, and a growing number were involved in such small manufacturing as the needle trades, furniture production, and paper industry.

Miami Beach, the focus of tourism, began as a restricted resort, but by 1970 was estimated to be 80–85% Jewish. Most of the hotels on the Beach were owned and managed by Jews, although an increasing number were controlled by outside syndicates. The entry of considerable Jewish capital into the hotel industry came in the 1930s and continued through the 1940s and 1950s. During the 1960s building concentrated on high-rise rental building and condominiums, rather than hotels.

Political Life. A great increase in the political activity of Jews has resulted from their overwhelming increase in population on a percentage basis in Miami Beach and their growth in absolute numbers in other parts of Greater Miami. Since 1930, when Baron de Hirsch Meyer was elected to the City Council of Miami Beach, there has been a series of Jewish mayors and Jewish councilmen, although most municipal appointees were not Jewish. Jews were also becoming involved in municipal politics of other towns and in state politics as well. Abe Aronowitz was mayor of the city of Miami in 1953. He received extensive support from the general as well as Jewish community.

Local and National Institutions. The local population boom after World War II resulted in the founding of institutions to fill new needs. Mt. Sinai Hospital, established in 1945, moved to its $10,000,000 plant in 1960. In 1959 Cedars of Lebanon Hospital was founded by a group of 75 Jewish physicians. The Jewish Home for the Aged was organized in 1944 with a bequest from a Jacksonville gentile. Its original capacity of 38 beds was soon inadequate, and therefore it was necessary to relocate the home on a larger tract of land and to almost double the number of beds. Many additional facilities for the aged have been built, as a survey has indicated a median age of 61 years for Miami Beach's population. Miami has become the most popular retirement home for Jews in America. Branches of many national Jewish organizations have been formed in Miami since the late 1930s. The Jewish War Veterans established a chapter in Miami in 1937. The American Jewish Congress, which was organized in 1939, had in 1970 a large and active women's membership of over 1,000 and a men's group, which was established in 1958. In 1941, spurred on by the growing climate of anti-Semitism, the Sholem Lodge of B'nai Brith helped organize the Florida Regional Office of the Anti-Defamation League, which opened an office in Miami. In 1952 the American Jewish Committee also opened a Miami branch, which succeeded in attracting many younger second generation Miamians from influential families. The Yiddish element of Jewish life in Miami still predominates in South Beach, largely among older members of the community, and there is also a Yiddish school and a radio program in Yiddish. There has never been a Yiddish newspaper in the community. The English language newspaper *Jewish Unity* was published from 1926–1935, when it was purchased by the *Jewish Floridian*, an Anglo-Jewish weekly founded in 1927 by J. Louis Shochet. In 1969 the *Jewish Floridian* was owned and edited by Fred *Shochet, son of the founder, and had a circulation of 18,000.

The Greater Miami Jewish community has developed as a result of migration from urban centers in the Northeast and Midwest, and this has resulted in the formation of *landsmannschaften* organized by former residents of Chicago, Detroit, St. Louis, Newark and other cities. Miami is known as the "campaign capital of American Jewry," and this role has given the maturing local community added responsibilities and signficance.

Bibliography: I. Lehrman and J. Rappaport, *Jewish Community of Miami Beach* (1956); Simonhoff, *Under Strange Skies* (1953), 274–331. [Gl.R.]

MICA (Heb. מִיכָא; "who is like [El]"), son of *Mephi-Bosheth, son of Jonathan, son of Saul (II Sam. 9:12). In the genealogical list of the tribe of Benjamin (I Chron. 8:34, 35; 9:40, 41) he is called Micah (Heb. מִיכָה). Thanks to *Jonathan, his grandfather, and Mephi-Bosheth, his father, Mica no doubt benefited from David's generosity (II Sam. 9:12; cf. 19:24–29).

For his descendants, see *Benjamin. [Ed.]

MICAH (Heb. מִיכָה), the sixth book in the collection known as the Twelve Minor Prophets within the subdivision "Later Prophets" of the second division of the Hebrew Bible (the Prophets). In the Septuagint translation, where the order varies, Micah usually comes immediately after Hosea and Amos.

The Content of the Book. The title (1:1) specifies the name, country, and date (in the days of Jotham, Ahaz, and Hezekiah, kings of Judah) of Micah's prophecy "concerning Jerusalem and Samaria." This is followed by a diatribe against Israel and Samaria (1:2–7). Critics have suggested that verse 1:5b, dealing with the "cult places" *(bamot)* of Judah—which are hardly a concern of Micah—is a gloss inspired by 3:12. In the succeeding lamentation (1:8–16), over the birthplace of the prophet and the neighboring towns, misfortune strikes at the gates of Jerusalem (12) but does not pass beyond them. The prophetic "I" makes its first appearance in verse 15. In verse 16, as the form of the

Hebrew verb shows, a female person is addressed; no doubt the daughter of Zion of verse 13, or, following the reading of some manuscripts of the Septuagint, "Fair Israel." In fact the "kings of Israel" did suffer a reverse at Achzib, as verse 14 indicates.

In 2:1 the threat is no longer directed against cities but against men who, having dispossessed others and defrauded them of their holdings, shall themselves be dispossessed. This section of chapter 2 may be dealing with social injustices (8–12) or, like Hosea 5:9–11, with a territorial dispute between tribes. Actually it is a clan (*mishpaḥah,* 2:3), which has angered the Lord and it is a stranger who reaps the benefit of the vengeful spoliation, without right of repurchase. The key phrase is in verse 7: the Lord does not abandon Israel. The sense of the passage becomes clearer if the prophet is assumed to be warning the ministers of Judah, who wish to expand at the expense of Israel. From this the conclusion can be drawn that the Lord, the sole King, steps into the breach and gathers His people together despite Judah's policy. In a new soliloquy (3:1) the prophet personally attacks the "leaders" and "magistrates" of Israel (without any mention of kings) who ignore the law and devour each other in quarrels through which the people suffer. Consequently, the Lord no longer answers and the prophets are confused. Curiously enough, the same mode of address is repeated in verse 9, where it is clearly the authorities of Jerusalem that are accused. Chapter 3 culminates with a prediction of the destruction of Jerusalem, corresponding to that of Samaria in 1:6. Jeremiah 26:18 makes it clear that this text had great repercussions, reaching the ear of Hezekiah and precipitating his reforms.

The allusion to Jerusalem and Zion is followed by the insertion of the famous passage, which appears also in Isaiah (2:2–4), concerning the universal reign of peace, with the Lord issuing instructions on Mount Zion. After the profession of faith in 4:5 ("We walk in the name of the Lord, our God"), a new oracle announces the reign of the Lord, who assembles the crippled. The daughter of Zion regains her former sovereignty and is victorious as far as Babylonia. The text here appears to reflect the intense diplomatic activity following the death of *Sargon that put *Merodach-Baladan on the throne of Babylonia for several months and caused him to dispatch a mission to *Hezekiah (II Kings 20) approximately 15 years before the latter's death (I Kings 20:6), which is dated at 687 B.C.E.

J. T. Willis has demonstrated the unity of the section (4:14–5:5) on Beth-Lehem-Ephrathah. Though the latter is too small to be a fighting unit, from there the leader (*moshel,* the term "king" is avoided) of Israel will arise. The allusion to a Davidide is clear, inasmuch as his wellsprings, or origins, can be traced from ancient times. The schism between Israel and Judah is compared to the abandonment of the Israelites by this Davidide until the day when she who is destined to give birth does so, be she either the *almah* of Isaiah 7:14 or the daughter of Zion in 4:10. The leader presides over the ingathering but here this is presented as a return of Judah to Israel (cf. Deut. 33:7). This shepherd is capable of organizing a coalition against Assyria of seven shepherds and eight *nesikhim* ("princes") and of assuring peace. This passage is therefore linked with the preceding one, as B. Renaud has pointed out. It likewise connects with the following verses: 6–8, where the remnant of Israel is seen as present in the midst of the nations as a sign of the Lord's blessing or curse.

In contrast, chapter 5:9–14 returns to the theme of the extermination of idols (as in 1:7 against Samaria; cf. Isa. 2:6–22) with an allusion to the cities of the country (as in 1:10–15). This passage is linked with chapter 6 (verse 1 "hear ye"; cf. 5:14). Here the presentation follows the *riv* ("forensic pleading") pattern. The Lord recalls his acts of salvation, citing the plot of Balaam. The people respond by asking what type of sacrifice is proper; must they make an offering of the firstborn? The famous verse 8 replies that it has already been revealed to man what is required of him: justice, mercy, and humility before the Lord. Chapter 6:9–16 is a new soliloquy to an unnamed town, and probably to a tribe. The resemblance to Amos 8:4–5 and the allusion in verse 16 to Omri and the house of Ahab make it probable that the passage alluded (at least originally) to Samaria. The tribe may be Ephraim, since in the oracles of Hosea and Isaiah the kingdom of the North dismembered by *Tiglath-Pileser III is called Ephraim (Isa. 9:7 (8)).

The prophetic "I" again appears in 7:1 in a lamentation on civil discord (cf. 3:3; Isa. 10:17ff.). This "I" reappears from verse 7 onward where the prophet speaks in the name of Israel, which reproaches its "enemy" for having rejoiced at its downfall. It is probable that (as in 2:8) the enemy is in this case Judah, since the question raised by the "enemy": "Where is your God?" is the reproach of the Judeans against the Israelites who did not recognize the choice of the sanctuary at Zion. Verse 10b is reminiscent of 3:12 on the ruin of Jerusalem. Chapter 7:14–20 is a prayer imploring the Lord to become the shepherd of His people once again (the geographical terms are of the North, Carmel, Bashan, and Gilead, alienated in 733 B.C.E.) as He promised to Jacob and Abraham. This rare reference probably aimed at encompassing both Judah and Israel in the same gathering.

Composition. The book is composed of independent but more or less connected sections. Ordinarily, these sections are redivided into three: chapters 1–3 speak of condemnation, 4–5 of consolation, and 6–7 of a mixture of condemnation and consolation. The visions of consolation are generally attributed to the years following the Exile and are assumed to have been added to the original oracles of Micah at the time when the book was put together (Renaud). There are two objections to this simplistic view: (1) It disregards the importance of the kingdom of the North and its downfall in 722 in the religious thought of Israel. This strain in Micah was given great emphasis by F. C. Burkitt, O. Eissfeldt, and J. T. Willis; (2) It neglects the influence of the cultural traditions in the sanctuaries (including Jerusalem) on the prophetic oracles. E. Hammershaimb and B. Reicke have stressed this fact. In the ancient Orient, as at the beginning of the monarchy, prophecy announced good tidings rather than misfortune.

The Prophet and His Time. R. Weil emphasized the importance of historical events known from II Kings 20–22 for an understanding of Micah. His birthplace, Moresheth-Gath, near Lachish, is known as far back as the El-Amarna period (tablet 335:7). This region had suffered since the days of the Syro-Ephraimite war against Judah, which commenced under *Jotham (II Kings 15:37; cf. Micah 1:1 and probably 1:13) and continued up to the time of the Assyrian campaign against Gath and Ashdod in 733, 720 (the Assyrian speaks of *nsk* as in Micah 5:4), and 712 (cf. Isa. 20). Meanwhile Samaria had fallen. Hezekiah, who had probably been associated in the kingship from 729/7, became in any case the sole king after 716/5. He shared the views of Micah (Jer. 26:18), who attacked the leaders of Jerusalem (but never the king), and his political activities disturbed Sargon. Perhaps it was at this time that the mission of Merodach-Baladan took place and the oracles on the deliverance of the daughter of Zion were delivered, but this mission probably dates from 703, the time of the general revolt against Sennacherib which was to end in 701 with a new occupation of Lachish and the region. The book, which closes on a melancholy tone and contains a pronouncement against Jerusalem directed at the "high places of Judah," reflects the prophet's disappointment in the monarch, but still keeps a note of hope. The rabbis held that Micah's prophecies were redacted and canonized by the Men of the Great Assembly (BB 15a; see Great *Synagogue).

The Theological Problem. Micah recognized only one king of Israel, YHWH. He recalls the exigencies of His justice toward Jerusalem and Samaria alike. However, he regards it as the will of YHWH that all Israel rally united around the dynasty which issued from Beth-Lehem. This dynasty has some connection with Ephraim, and is a guarantee of the nation's hope. Unlike Isaiah, Micah is a man from the country and he lacks Isaiah's love of the Holy City. If he cites David it is not as the founder of the sanctuary of the Ark at Zion but as a man who likewise came from the country, from Beth-Lehem. David was born there in the clan of Ephrathah and was recognized by the Israelites of the North as being their flesh and blood (II Sam. 5:1). Micah resembles Amos, another countryman.

This difference between Micah and Isaiah does not preclude many analogies in the theology of the two prophets: the fidelity of the Lord endures despite his "wrath" (Micah 7:9; Isa. 9:11, 16); He remains the light of the faithful (Micah 7:8; Isa. 10:17); He is King of Israel (Micah 4:7; Isa. 6:1); and He has chosen the Davidide dynasty for the salvation of the people (Micah 5:1; Isa. 7:1–9; 9:6). Finally, the theology of Micah shares points in common with that of Hosea and *Deuteronomy when he speaks of *ḥesed* ("mercy"; 7:18, 20), "the love of *ḥesed*" (6:8), and when he places mercy and humble submission to God above sacrifices (6:8; cf. Hos. 6:6). This prophet who, unlike the others, reveals himself as "full of strength, the spirit of YHWH, and justice and valor" takes on his shoulders the burden that the descendants of David should have assumed (Isa. 11:2–3). [He.C.]

In the Aggadah. According to one opinion, Micah was a contemporary of Isaiah (SOR 20; and Pes. 87b); according to another, he was one of the post-Exilic prophets (PdRK 16, 128b). The verse: "He hath shewed thee, O man, what is good; and what doth the Lord require of thee, but to do justly, and to love mercy, and to walk humbly with thy God?" (Micah 6:8) is a quintessence of the 613 commandments of the Bible (Mak. 24a). [Ed.]

Bibliography: F. C. Burkitt, in: JBL, 45 (1926), 159–61; K. Elliger, in: ZDPV, 57 (1934), 81–152; R. Weil, in: RHR (1940), 146–61; H. L. Ginsberg, in: *Eretz Israel*, 3 (1954), 84; idem, in: JAOS, 88 (1968), 47–49; Pritchard, Texts, 286–7; H. Tadmor, in: *Journal of Cuneiform Studies*, 12 (1958), 80–83; O. Eissfeldt, in: ZDMG, 112 (1962), 259–68; idem, *Einleitung in das Alte Testament* (1964[3], rev. ed.); B. Renaud, *Structure et attaches littéraires de Michée IV–V* (1964); E. Hammershaimb, *Some Aspects of Old Testament Prophecy* (1966); B. Reicke, in: HTR, 60 (1967), 349–67; C. Cazelles, in: *Fourth World Congress of Jewish Studies*, 1 (1967), 87–89; J. T. Willis, in: VT, 18 (1968), 529–41; Kaufmann Y., Religion, 395–8. In the Aggadah: Ginzberg, Legends, index; I. Ḥasida, *Ishei ha-Tanakh* (1964), 260.

MICAIAH (Micah; Heb. מִיכָה, מִיכָיְהוּ), an Ephraimite in whose house was a shrine. Micaiah lived in the hill country of Ephraim though the exact location of his dwelling is not known. According to the Talmud (Sanh. 103b), his house was in Gareb, 3 mi. (5 km.) from Shiloh, which is perhaps Khirbet Arabah, about 2½ mi. (4 km.) west of Shiloh. The Bible relates that Micaiah took 1,100 pieces of silver from his mother but returned them because of her curse (Judg. 17–18). The mother consecrated the money to God: she gave 200 pieces of silver to a silversmith to make a graven image and a molten image and the rest she apparently consecrated to the shrine of God in her house. In the shrine were placed the graven and molten images, and an *ephod and teraphim. It is difficult to ascertain their significance: the images were apparently cultic symbols while the ephod and teraphim were used for asking counsel of God (Judg. 17:3–5; 18:3–7, 14–15, 18–21). At first one of Micaiah's sons served as a priest but later a young levite who had come to the hill country of Ephraim from Beth-Lehem in Judah was hired as a "father and priest." The men of the tribe of Dan, passing through Ephraim on their way to capture Laish, forced the young levite to accompany them and take the graven image. Henceforth the image stood in the sanctuary of the city of Dan and the young levite, whose name was Jonathan the son of Gershom, son of Moses (or son of Manasseh), served there as a priest; and his sons continued to serve "until the day of the captivity of the land" (18:30). This ancient story, which is connected with the description of the capture of Laish in the north, may possibly reflect cultic customs during the period of the Judges when affluent men set up their own houses of God and used the cultic objects to inquire of God. Along with local attendants (or in their place) they installed levites who worked for wages and whose merit as inquirers of God was greatly valued as "father and priest." The purpose of the story of Micaiah is to explain how the sanctuary was established in Dan and how a body of priests—perhaps descendants of Moses—came to be based there after having had their beginning in a private house of God in the hill country of Ephraim. The Bible stresses the greater importance of priestly service "unto a tribe and a family in Israel" as against serving "the house of one man" (18:19) and draws a parallel between the end of the sanctuary at Dan and that at Shiloh, perhaps as a result of some unknown historical event. From Judges 18:30–31 it can be concluded that the worship of Micaiah's graven image at Dan did not continue after the destruction of Shiloh.

Bibliography: Ha-Ḥevrah le-Ḥeker ha-Mikra be-Yisrael, *Iyyunim be-Sefer Shofetim* (1957), 184–208, 547–84; Y. Kaufmann, *Sefer Shofetim* (1964), 8–9, 56–57, 267–77; Noth, Personennamen, 107, 144; G. F. Moore, *Judges* (ICC, 1949), 365–402. [Sh.Ab.]

MICAIAH (Heb. מִיכָיְהוּ; in II Chron. 18:14, Micah, Heb. מִיכָה), son of Imlah, prophet who foretold the death of *Ahab (I Kings 22:7–28). Before embarking on the campaign of Ramoth-Gilead, Ahab and his ally *Jehosaphat king of Judah consulted prophets who unanimously prophesied: "Go up; for the Lord will give it into the hand of the king" (22:6; cf. 22:12). When Micaiah was called, he at first expressed the view of the other prophets, but only in an ironic mockery, and when the king adjured him to speak "nothing but the truth in the name of the Lord," he described two visions he had had: one, of the Israelites scattered over the hills like sheep without a shepherd, which the Lord explained to mean, "these have no master, let every one of them return to his house in peace"; and one, of a meeting of the heavenly council at which it was decided that Ahab should be lured to his death in battle at Ramoth-Gilead by a spirit of falsehood in the mouths of his prophets. Micaiah, who firmly repeated the prediction that the king would not return home alive, was then imprisoned for the duration of the campaign.

It appears that Micaiah was known as a prophet even before this, and the king of Israel says of him "I detest him, for he does not prophesy good concerning me, but evil" (22:8). It thus appears that Micaiah was not one of the court prophets, who as a rule acquiesced and encouraged the king. However, he did not bear animosity toward the king and tried, in his prophecy, to prevent his death and the defeat of Israel. His personality was distinguished by prophetic independence and a firm, uncompromising stand not only against the king and his ministers but against all the 400 prophets gathered in the king's court, who in his opinion were not merely false prophets, but became messengers of falsehood through a divine temptation. He was not a rebuking prophet and was not eager to prophesy as were the messenger-prophets. Nor is there any proof that he was one of the prophets who advised the people, like Elisha. His prophecy was similar to that of the classical prophets in his obdurate and unusual stand and his readiness to suffer and be tortured for the sake of truth.

From a political point of view, too, Micaiah differed from the other prophets who in their extreme nationalism were violently anti-Aramean and urged the king to fight against Aram without compromise (I Kings 20:22).

See also *Ahab; *Prophecy. [SH.AB.]

In the Aggadah. In the Aggadah, Micaiah is identified with the anonymous prophet who "came near unto Ahab" and foretold the destruction of the Aramean army (I Kings 20:13; SOR 20, p. 52). Later, when he predicted the death of Ahab in battle, the false prophet Zedekiah b. Chenaanah challenged his prophecy, claiming that Elijah had previously prophesied that the dogs would lick Ahab's blood in the field of Naboth, and he would not therefore be slain on a battlefield three days' journey from there. However, both prophecies were fulfilled. Ahab fell in Ramoth-Gilead, but his blood was licked by the dogs in Samaria, when they washed the slain king's chariot there (I Kings 22:28; Jos., Ant. 8:15, 4). [ED.]

Bibliography: J. A. Montgomery, *The Book of Kings* (ICC, 1951), 335–41; B. Oppenheimer, in: *Sefer Urbach* (1955), 89–93. IN THE AGGADAH: Ginzberg, Legends, index; for further bibliography see *Prophecy.

°MICHAEL II, Byzantine emperor (820–829) to whom strong Judaizing leanings were ascribed, partly because of his iconoclasm. A tenth-century chronicler states that Michael relieved Jews of financial burdens and that he "loved Jews above all mortals" since he was himself half Jewish and had been brought up by Jews. It is possible that Michael may have come under Jewish influence as a native of Amorium in Phrygia, a province noted for Judeo-Christian syncretism, including sects which kept the whole of Jewish law except circumcision and had close contact with Jews. However, the main impetus for imputing pro-Jewish sentiments to Michael came from the desire of the succeeding dynasty, the Macedonian, to discredit the founder of the Amorian dynasty.

Bibliography: J. Starr, *Jews in the Byzantine Empire 641–1204* (1939), index; idem, in: HTR, 29 (1936), 93–106; G. Caro, in: MGWJ, 53 (1909), 576–80; F. Doelger, *Regesten der Kaiserurkunden des Ostroemischen Reiches von 565–1453*. 1 (1924), no. 414; Baron Social², 3 (1957), 178. [AN.SH.]

°MICHAEL VIII PALAEOLOGUS, Byzantine emperor (1259–1282). In 1261 Michael recaptured Constantinople from the Latins, who had held it from 1204, and restored an independent if greatly reduced empire. Unlike his predecessors in Nicaea, he had no reason to suspect his Jewish subjects of having contact with Jews in hostile territory and was anxious to gain their support. Therefore as recorded by Jacob ben Elijah, the only contemporary Hebrew source, he called together the leaders of the Jewish communities and promised them religious tolerance, as well as thus ending a series of nearly 40 years of persecutions (see *Epirus). Michael also persuaded his son and co-emperor Andronicus II Palaeologus (1282–1328) to continue and expand this policy, so that the Jews of Constantinople—as distinct from Jewish merchants of hostile Venice living in Constantinople—were allowed to live and build synagogues wherever they wished—to the displeasure of Patriarch Athanasius I.

Bibliography: J. Starr, *Romania* (1949), 20–23; J. Mann, in: REJ, 82 (1926), 372–3; P. Charanis, in: *Speculum*, 22 (1947), 75–76. [AN.SH.]

MICHAEL, HEIMANN JOSEPH ḤAYYIM (1792–1846), German merchant and bibliophile. Michael was born in Hamburg and lived there all his life. He assembled one of the finest collections of Hebrew manuscripts and books, a library containing 5,471 printed books and 862 manuscripts of which 60 were autographs and 110 were written between 1240 and 1450. He maintained a lively correspondence, partly in German in Hebrew letters and partly in an attractive Hebrew, with L. *Zunz (in the years 1832–46), S. J. *Rapoport, and S. D. *Luzzatto. This correspondence is a treasury of bibliographical information.

Heimann Joseph Ḥayyim Michael, Hebrew bibliophile. Jerusalem, J.N.U.L., Schwadron Collection.

A detailed catalog of Michael's collection, *Oẓerot Ḥayyim*, with notes by Moritz Steinschneider and an introduction by L. Zunz, appeared in 1848. After Michael's death his friend M. Isler appealed to all friends of Jewish scholarship, wealthy German Jewry in particular, to preserve the priceless collection in Jewish hands and to save it from being sold abroad. The appeal was in vain, and Michael's library was dispersed, the books going to the British Museum in London and the manuscripts to the Bodleian at Oxford (see *Libraries) for a little over £1,000.

Michael's encyclopedic work, *Or ha-Ḥayyim* (1891; repr. Jerusalem, 1965, with additional notes by N. Ben-Menahem), based on his very rich collection, contains the biographies and bibliographies of medieval Jewish scholars.

Bibliography: A. Berliner, in: JJLG, 4 (1906), 269–74; A. Marx, *Studies in Jewish History and Booklore* (1944), 221–4 and passim; H. Michael, *Orha-Ḥayyim* (1965²), introd. [N.B.-M.]

MICHAEL, JAKOB (1894–), U.S. financier and philanthropist. Born in Frankfort, he began his business career in 1910 with his father-in-law's metal-trading firm, Beer Sondheimer. Demobilized from the German army in 1917, he became active in trade and industry, but in 1933 left Germany for Holland, and in 1939 moved to the United States where he continued his activities in various industrial enterprises. He was prominent in many Jewish philanthropic, educational, and scientific institutions. He financed a high school and a children's home in Pardes Hannah, Israel; an institute of bio-medical research at the Einstein College of Medicine, New York; the institute of nuclear science at the Weizmann Institute in Israel, and a college of Hebraic studies at Yeshiva University, New York. Much of his attention was devoted to religious institutions, and his special interests included the collecting of Jewish ceremonial objects and Jewish music. He donated a collection of 25,000 items of Jewish music to the Hebrew University and many valuable books and ceremonial objects to the Israel

Museum (including a complete synagogue taken from Vittorio Veneto in Italy). [J.O.R.]

MICHAEL (Michaes, Michall), MOSES (Moshe bar Jehiel; 1675–1740), ship owner and international trader, born in Harzfeld, Germany. Michael immigrated to New York, and from 1717 shipped large quantities of foodstuffs, sometimes lumber and candles, to Curaçao, and supplied its garrison with flour and other foodstuffs. Michael usually traveled with his cargo on board his schooner *Abigail.* From 1721 to 1722 he was in partnership with Michael Asser of Boston; from 1731 to 1732, with his son Michael Michaels (d.1736). In 1729 he paid for the privilege of placing the first cornerstone of New York's Mill Street Synagogue. He died in Curaçao.

Bibliography: H. A. Alexander, *Notes on the Alexander Family of South Carolina and Georgia* (1954), 98–105; I. S. Emmanuel, *Precious Stones of the Jews of Curaçao* (1957), 260–5. [I.S.E.]

MICHAEL AND GABRIEL, two *angels named in Daniel 10:13, 21; 12:1 and Daniel 8:16; 9:21 respectively.

The Attributions of Proper Names to Angels. Michael and Gabriel are usually cited as the earliest instance of the practice of attributing proper names to angels; and it is just the contrast between the anonymity of the seraphim in Isaiah 6:2, 6 on the one hand and the explicit naming of Gabriel in Daniel 9:21 and of Michael in Daniel 10:21 on the other that is cited by R. Simeon b. Lakish as proof that the names of the angels were something that the returning exiles brought with them from Babylonia (TJ, RH 1:2, 56d). But these are not strictly the oldest examples. According to the critical view, the Book of *Daniel is of later authorship than those of *Zechariah and *Job; yet "the Satan [Accuser]," Zechariah 3:1–2; Job 1:6–12; 2:2–7 is a virtual proper name, and it is retained as the name of the angel in question throughout Jewish literature; but these passages too are post-Exilic. A special early instance is Beth-El (Jer. 48:13), a real proper name shortened from (Ha) El-Beth-El, Genesis 31:13; 35:7, "The Numen of Beth-El," who was the special tutelary genius of Jacob and of the nation Israel (see the Book of *Hosea B-b; H. L. Ginsberg, in: JBL, 80 (1961), 339–47). Already the E document of the Pentateuch has made an angel of this being (Gen. 31:11), and Deutero-Hosea, who in Hosea 12:3–5, 13 palpably draws on the E story of Jacob embedded in Genesis 25 and 27–35 (and modifies it for his own purposes), refers to the being alternately as *ʾelohim,* "a divine being" (Hos. 12:4) and *malʾakh,* "an angel" (Hos. 12:5).

Michael (*Mikhaʾel,* מִיכָאֵל, "Who is like God?"—in ten passages the name of as many men: Num. 13:13; I Chron. 5:13, 14; 6:25; 7:3; 8:16; 12:21; 27:18; II Chron. 21:2; Ezra 8:8). Daniel 10:2–11 states that Daniel practiced asceticism for three full weeks in his endeavor to move Heaven to reveal to him what he wanted to know. At the end of that period a frightening figure appeared to him. He fell on his face in terror, but the being helped him to his feet and told him that he had been sent to deliver a message to him. In 10:12–21 he then explains that Daniel's petition had been received favorably on the very first day, but the speaker was unable to leave his post for 21 days because he was holding in check "the prince [*sar,* שַׂר] of the kingdom of Persia"; at the end of that period, however, he was relieved in this task by "Michael, one of the chief princes *[sarim],*" whom he left there "with the kings of Persia." He himself will only stay with Daniel long enough to inform him "what will befall your people at the end of the days" (verse 14), for he will have to "return to fight with the prince of Persia and when he retires—there comes the prince of Greece ... and there is none who shares my efforts against all these but your (pl., i.e., the Jews') prince, Michael." At the climax of history, it is "Michael, the great prince who stands guard over your fellow countrymen," who will arise and save them (12:1). It will be seen that *sar*—properly "dignitary," "official," or "minister," but here better "prince" in view of the designation of God in 8:25 as "the *sar* of *sarim*"—means "angel," that every nation is conceived of as having an angelic representative, and that the author conceives of these representatives as engaging in clashes with each other which prefigure clashes between the respective nations. Obviously, the germ of this idea is Deuteronomy 32:8, which reads, according to the text of the Septuagint and a fragment from Qumran: "When the Most High gave nations their countries,/ When he set the divisions of man,// He established peoples' homelands/to the number of the divine beings."// For "the divine beings" (*bene ʾel,* lit. "children of God"), the Masoretic Text reads "the Israelites" (*bene Yisraʾel,* lit. "the children of Israel"). The latter, however, is a conflation of the Septuagint-Qumran reading בני אל and a variant שרי אל which is presupposed by the above Daniel passages (H. L. Ginsberg, in: *Eretz-Israel,* 9 (1969), 45, n. 4). On the other hand the writer in Daniel diverges from his source in one important respect. The next verse in Deuteronomy 32, namely verse 9, specifically makes an exception of Israel: the latter is not apportioned to any *ben ʾel* or *sar ʾel* ("But YHWH's people is his own portion,/ Jacob is his own allotment.") All the passages cited above from Daniel 10–12 are from the pen of Apoc III (see *Daniel, Book of, B).

Gabriel (*Gavriʾel,* גַּבְרִיאֵל). This angel is the creation of Apoc IV, the author of Daniel 9 and of sundry interpolations in chapters 7, 8, 11, and 12 (see *Daniel B). In chapter 9 itself, Gabriel appears to the apocalyptist (9:21) in the first year of Darius the Mede (9:1, see *Daniel B) in answer to his prayer for enlightenment on the subject of the 70 years of Jeremiah (Jer. 25:11–12; 29:10). Gabriel explains that those 70 years are in reality 70 weeks of years *(septennia),* and proceeds to sketch the course that history will take during those 70 hebdomads. This is closely analogous to the role that is played in Apoc III (chs. 10–12) by an angel who is not named but merely described, who appears to Daniel in the third year of Cyrus in response to three weeks of mourning, and tells him in astonishing detail what is destined to take place from that date until the horrors of Antiochus IV. Apoc IV wished to imply that his Gabriel was

Silver amulet, including the names of Gabriel and Michael (sixth line from bottom), as among the angels invoked to ward off evil. Persia, 18th century. Haifa, Ethnological Museum and Folklore Archives. Photo Oskar Tauber, Haifa.

identical with this informant of Apoc III, and this he did in a subtle way. Apoc III's informant explains to him in 10:12–13 that Daniel's petition for enlightenment was favorably received at the very beginning of his quasi-fast, and the delay was only due to the informant's being tied down with keeping the prince of Persia at bay (see above). Then in 10:20–21 he goes on to say that he has barely enough time at his disposal to impart to Daniel "that which is written in the book of truth [or, that which is written in the book, truly]" because he must presently go back to the combat with the prince of Persia, and after that with the prince of Greece, "and there is none who shares my efforts against these but your [i.e., the Jews'] prince Michael," after which Apoc IV interpolates (11:1) "and ever since the first year of Darius the Mede [the date of 9:1, on which Gabriel appeared to the seer] I have been standing by him to strengthen and support him." The implication is clearly this: "The same cause that prevented me from coming to you during the past three weeks also explains why I have not appeared to you for such a long time since my last visit." In other words, the unnamed linen-clad one of chapters 10–12 is identical with the Gabriel of chapter 9. Apoc IV has also taken steps to identify with the latter the originally unnamed being of Apoc II (ch. 8). Daniel 8:15 reads. "And when I, Daniel, beheld the vision *[ḥazon]* I asked [prayed] for an explanation, and lo, there was standing before me one having the appearance of a man *[gaver]*." Inspired by this last word, Apoc IV interpolated here, "(16) And I heard somebody's voice between [the banks of?] Ulai. He called out, 'Gabriel *[Gavri᾽el]*! Explain the statement *[mar᾽eh]* to him.' " *Mar᾽eh* must mean "statement," and the reference must be to the statement about the evenings and mornings in verse 14, in view of verse 26; and verses 13–14 and 26a—also, by the way, verse 27b—are, just like verse 16, interpolations of Apoc IV in the text of Apoc II (the original text of ch. 8), so that they may be described as II-d. In 9:21b, then, when Apoc IV tells how he was visited by "the man [here the Hebrew has *ha-᾽ish*, but the Aramaic original doubtless had *gavra* here as well as *gevar* in 8:15] Gabriel who had appeared to me before in the vision," he is referring back to chapter 8 as interpolated by himself. [H.L.G.]

In the Aggadah. Michael and Gabriel, along with Uriel and Raphael, are the four angels who surround the throne of the Almighty (Num. R. 2:10; cf. Enoch 9:1). Michael, as the constant defender of the Jewish people (PR, 46), is considered greater than Gabriel (Ber. 4b). The *aggadah* consistently identifies Michael and Gabriel with the anonymous divine messengers or angels mentioned in the Bible. Thus, they were two of the three angels who visited Abraham after his circumcision (Gen. R. 48:9), Michael's task being to announce the future birth of Isaac while Gabriel's was to destroy Sodom (Gen. R. 50:2). It is Michael who called to Abraham at the **Akedah*, telling him not to offer up Isaac (*Midrash Va-Yosha* in A. Jellinek, *Beit ha-Midrash*, 1:38). It was either Michael or Gabriel who wrestled with Jacob (Gen. R. 78:1) and appeared to Moses at Horeb (Ex. R. 2:5). It was Michael who rescued Abraham from the fiery furnace (Gen. R. 44:13) and also informed him of the capture of Lot (PdRE, 27). He also accompanied the servant of Abraham in his mission to find a wife for Isaac (Gen. R. 59:10). Michael and Gabriel were called upon to record that the birthright was sold to Jacob by Esau (Gen. R. 63:14). They were both among the angels who accompanied God when He came down on Mount Sinai (Deut. R. 2:34). Although they were considered the kings of the angels, they were afraid of Moses (Eccles. R. 9:11, 2), and they refused to take his soul, so that God himself had to do so. Michael and Gabriel then stood at either side of Moses' bier (Deut. R. 11:10). On the day that Solomon married the daughter of Pharaoh-Neco, Michael came down from heaven and stuck a reed in the sea, round which matter settled, and upon this Rome, the future destroyer of Israel, was built (Song R. 1:6, 4). Michael smote Sennacherib and his army, and Gabriel delivered Hananiah, Mishael, and Azariah (Ex. R. 18:5) from the fiery furnace. Michael acted as the defender of the Jews against every charge which Haman brought against them (Esth. R. 7:12). It was Michael who pushed Haman against Esther to make it appear as if Haman intended to violate her (Esth. R. 10:9). Both Michael and Gabriel will be among those who will accompany the Messiah, and they will then contend with the wicked *(Otiyyot de-Rabbi Akiva Shin)*. Michael is made up entirely of snow and Gabriel of fire, and though they stand near one another they do not injure one another, thus indicating the power of God to "make peace in His high places" (Job 25:2; Deut. R. 5:12). Michael also occupies an important place in the interpretation of biblical stories in later Midrashim, e.g., *Exodus Rabbah*, *Midrash Avkir*, and *Midrash Konen*. [A.Ro.]

In the Kabbalah. The motifs of Michael and Gabriel as found in the *aggadah* are in general repeated in the Kabbalah, but Michael is given an added importance.

In the *Heikhalot* and Merkabah literature of the late talmudic period and the period of the *geonim*, Michael plays a central role in the realm of the Chariot. He is the guardian of the south side, the figure of the lion in the Chariot, and so on (the descriptions vary in the different versions of this literature). In any case he is one of the four archangels, despite the interchange of names in the list. G. Scholem has deduced, from a statement in *Perek Re'iyyot Yeḥezkel* (Wertheimer, *Battei Midrashot*, 2 (1955), 132–3) and from other sources, that at first Michael and *Metatron were identical—the guardian of the interior and the highest figure in the domain of the angels in the Merkabah literature and in the Kabbalah which succeeded it—and that some of the descriptions of Michael in talmudic and midrashic literature were later transferred to the figure of Metatron. He is outstanding as guardian and protector of Israel in Merkabah literature and in the European mystical literature of the Ḥasidei Ashkenaz and early kabbalistic circles. A central role in bringing about the redemption was attributed to him in midrashic and Merkabah literature. Such descriptions of the role of Michael relied mainly on sayings in the Book of Zerubbabel and other apocalyptic works dating from the end of the ancient era and the beginning of the Middle Ages, in which Michael was assigned the role of revealer and bringer of tidings. (As there is in the various versions an interchange between Michael and Metatron, it does indeed seem that the two figures are basically identical.)

In kabbalistic literature Michael is allotted the role of grace in the Merkabah, angel of the right, representing the *Sefirah Ḥesed* ("grace"). In several places in the *Zohar Michael symbolizes the *Sefirah Ḥesed* itself (Zohar 1:98b–99a, *Sitrei Torah;* 2:147, et al.). All the symbols of grace (the right side, silver, water, etc.) are to be found in the descriptions of the angel Michael. He is frequently described as a high priest, and the Zohar and later kabbalists (e.g., Moses Cordovero) portray him as bringing the souls of the righteous before the Almighty, an act which led to their inclusion in the world of emanation *(aẓilut)*. [Y.D.]

Bibliography: H. L. Ginsberg, *Studies in Daniel* (1948). IN THE AGGADAH AND IN KABBALAH: J. Kaufman (Ibn Shemuel), *Midreshei Ge'ullah* (1954), 73ff.; R. Margulies, *Malakhei Elyon* (1945), 87–89, 108–35; I. Tishby, *Mishnat ha-Zohar*, 1 (1949), 463–9; Ginzberg, Legends, 7 (1967^3), 311–2 and index; G. Scholem, *Jewish Gnosticism* . . . (1960), 43–45.

°**MICHAELIS, JOHANN DAVID** (1717–1791), German Bible scholar. Born in Halle, Michaelis was the son of the theologian and orientalist Ch. B. Michaelis. In 1746 he was appointed professor of oriental languages in Goettingen. While he was at first a pietist of the Halle school, after a stay in England (1741–42) he advocated, somewhat inconsistently, a moderately rationalistic orthodoxy. His *Einleitung in die goettlichen Schriften des Neuen Bundes* (1750; 1787–88[4]) was the first textbook on the historical-critical approach to the New Testament. His early works included a Hebrew grammar textbook (Halle, 1745) and a compendium of Jewish marriage laws *Ehegesetze Moses* (Goettingen, 1755). In his *Gruendliche Erklaerung des mosaischen Rechts* (Frankfort, 6 vols., 1770–75) he interpreted the laws of the Pentateuch as the work of the statesmanlike wisdom of Moses whose aim was the separation of Israel from the heathens. He popularized the conclusions of biblical scholarship in a translation of the Bible with notes (13 vols., 1769–83). He also wrote an introduction to the Old Testament, *Einleitung in die Schriften des Alten Bundes* (1787). In 1761 he suggested to the king of Denmark that a scientific expedition be sent to Arabia. Through his extremely diverse academic and literary activities he enjoyed a worldwide reputation; however, in his later years, as a result of weaknesses of character and of scholarship, he became progressively isolated.

Bibliography: J. M. Hassencamp, *Leben des Herrn J. D. Michaelis, von ihm selbst beschrieben* (1793); R. Smend, *Johann David Michaelis* (Ger. 1898); R. Kittel, in: *Realencyklopaedie fuer protestantische Theologie und Kirche,* 13 (1903), 54ff.; E. Kutsch, in: RGG[3], 4 (1960), 934–5 (incl. bibl.).

[R. SM.]

MICHAELIS, LEONOR (1875–1949), German biochemist. Born in Berlin, he worked with Paul *Ehrlich at the City Hospital where he directed the bacteriology department from 1906 to 1922. In 1908 he was appointed professor of medicine at the University of Berlin, and from 1920, professor of physical chemistry. From 1922 to 1926 he was professor of biochemistry in Nagoya, Japan. In 1926 he went to the Johns Hopkins University in the U.S. and then to the Rockefeller Institute for Medical Research in New York. He contributed many scientific papers on topics concerned with casein, blood pH in biological systems, the behavior of dyestuffs in biological media, and respiration. His books included *Hydrogen Ion Concentration* (1926), *Praktikum der physikalischen Chemie inbesondere der Kolloidchemie fuer Mediziner und Biologen* (1930[4]; *Practical, Physical and Colloid Chemistry for Students of Medicine and Biology,* 1925), and *Oxydations-Reduktion Potential* (1929; *Oxidation Reduction Potentials,* 1930).

[S.A.M.]

MICHAELIS, SIR MAX (1860–1932), South African mining magnate and philanthropist. Born in Eisfeld, Germany, Michaelis worked in a Frankfort banking house before emigrating to South Africa in 1876. He settled in Kimberley where he formed a diamond-buying company which was later taken over by De Beers. Michaelis is best known for his interest in and benefactions to art and education. He established scholarships in South Africa and England, including the Jewish War Memorial Scholarship at Oxford. He donated funds to the University of Cape Town for a school of fine arts which was named after him. In 1912 he bought the Hugh Lane collection of Dutch masters, which he presented to the South African nation as the nucleus of the Michaelis Art Gallery in Cape Town. Michaelis contributed to the Johannesburg Art Gallery, City Library and to hospitals. He was knighted in 1924.

Bibliography: P. H. Emden, *Randlords* (1935), index.

[L.HO.]

MICHAELSON, EZEKIEL ẒEVI BEN ABRAHAM ḤAYYIM (1863–1942), Polish rabbi, biographer, and bibliographer. He was a child prodigy, and in one of his works he cites responsa which he claims to have written at the age of 12. Orphaned in his early youth, he was forced to move from one place to another. In 1884 he was invited to become rabbi of the important community of Zamosc, but he refused. In the same year, he was elected rabbi of Karsinbrod. There he was harassed by enemies and was even arraigned in court as a result of a false accusation. In 1893 he became rabbi of Plonsk and from then on was known as "the rabbi of Plonsk." At the outbreak of World War I he was on a visit to Carlsbad and was unable to return home. In 1922 he was elected a member of the rabbinical council of Warsaw, and engaged in many communal activities. When the German forces entered Warsaw he was working in the community archives and in 1942 he was taken to *Treblinka where he died.

Bust of Sir Max Michaelis by Moses Kottler, 1923. Cape Town, the Michaelis Collection.

An exceptionally prolific writer whose knowledge of family lineages was unequaled, Michaelson published many books in such diverse fields as *halakhah, aggadah,* history, biography, and bibliography.

His best-known works are: *Degan Shamayim* on tractates *Berakhot* and *Rosh Ha-Shanah* (appended to Israel Jonah Landau, *Ein ha-Bedolah* 1901); responsa *Beit Yeḥezkel,* 1924); *Pinnot ha-Bayit,* novellae (1925); *Siddur Beit ha-Oẓar* (1931 (1929)); responsa *Tirosh ve-Yiẓhar* (1936). His most famous biographies are those of R. Israel Jonah of Kempen, R. Meshullam Zalman Ashkenazi, R. Joseph *Te'omim, R. Shabbetai *Bass, R. *Phinehas of Korets, the Margolioth family, R. Solomon *Ganzfried, R. Ẓevi Hirsh Ẓemah, and R. Jacob Aryeh of Radzymin, all appended to his editions of their works. During the Holocaust, three large chests containing his manuscripts were lost. They included *Imrei Yeḥezkel* on the Pentateuch and *Me'at Ẓevi* on the other books of the Bible.

Bibliography: N. Shemen, *Di Biografie fun a Varshever Rov ha-Rov Ẓevi Yeḥezkel Michaelson* (1948); *Elleh Ezkerah,* 2 (1957), 195–202.

[I.AL.]

MICHAELSON, ISAAC CHESAR (1903–), Israel ophthalmologist. Born in Scotland, he taught at Glasgow University and served with the Royal Army Medical Corps in World War II. During Israel's War of Independence in 1948, he was specialist adviser to the Israel Government and from 1953 served as professor of ophthalmology at the Hebrew University-Hadassah Medical School in Jerusalem. He set up eye clinics in Liberia, Malawi, Tanzania, and Rwanda and trained local doctors and medical assistants to run them. The Ophthalmology Research Laboratories administered by Michaelson and his colleagues from Hadassah Hospital in Jerusalem serve an estimated patient-population of 20 million in Africa.

A specialist on the diseases of the inner eye, Michaelson is the author of *Circulation of the Inner Eye in Man and Animals* (1952) and, with Ballantyne, of *Textbook of Diseases of the Eye* (1970²). Michaelson was awarded the 1960 Israel Prize for medicine. [L.HA.]

MICHAL (Heb. מִיכַל), the youngest daughter of King *Saul (Sam. 14:49), who loved *David and was given to him in marriage after he had killed 200 Philistines (in the Septuagint—100). Michal's father had insisted on this as the condition for the marriage contract—"a hundred Philistines' foreskins," instead of a dowry (18:27–29), hoping of course that David would lose his life in the attempt to collect them. Michal, who loved David, was given to him instead of *Merab the elder, who had been promised to him but had been given to *Adriel the Meholathite (17:15; 18:17–20).

Michal demonstrated her loyalty to David in deceiving her father's messengers, who had been sent to murder David in his own home (19:17ff.). By the time Saul's messengers discovered the deceit, David had had time to escape. Later Saul gave Michal to *Paltiel son of Laish from Gallim (25:44). When David reigned in Hebron, he asked Ish-Bosheth, the son of Saul, to bring Michal back apparently under pressure from Abner, who was about to defect to David. He did in fact take her from her husband and restore her to David (II Sam. 3:12–16). No doubt the demand was politically motivated, at least in part. David was trying to induce Israel (the northern tribes) to follow the example of Judah and accept him as its king (II Sam. 2:5–7), and his marriage to a daughter of Saul who might become the mother of his successor would be an added inducement to the men of Israel to act upon his suggestion.

Page from the *Pierpont Morgan Picture Bible*, France, 13th century. Upper register, Saul promises Michal to David if he slays 100 Philistines. Lower register, David kills 200 Philistines. New York, Pierpont Morgan Library, Ms. 638, fol. 29v.

When David leaped and danced in front of the Ark as it was brought to Jerusalem, Michal jeered that he had exposed himself "as one of the vain fellows shamelessly uncovers himself." David answered her in anger, referring to his being chosen as king, "above thy father, and above all his house" (6:16, 20–23). Michal remained childless (6:23). The masoretic text of II Samuel 21:8 mentions five children of Michal by *Adriel of Meholah, but the latter was in fact the husband of Merab (see above). Some versions (LXX, the Syriac; cf. Sanh. 19b) have Merab here instead of Michal. [SH. AB.]

In the Aggadah. Michal's love for David is compared to that of Jonathan; whereas the latter saved David from Saul outside the palace, Michal did so inside the palace (Mid. Ps. 59:1). She is identical with Eglah (mentioned in II Sam. 3:5 as David's wife), and was so called because like a heifer (*eglah*) she refused to accept the yoke of her father (Mid. Ps. 59:4). This love was returned. Although David married Merab after Michal's death he continued to refer to "My wife, Michal" (II Sam. 3:14; Sanh. 19b). Michal's marriage to Palti (I Sam. 25:44) was illegal, since she was already bethrothed to David (Sanh. *ibid.*), and she had no marital relations with him (*ibid.*). She is stated to have worn *tefillin* (Er. 96a).

When rebuking David (II Sam. 6:20), Michal made a forceful comparison between the modesty which Saul displayed when covering his feet (I Sam. 24:4), and David's behavior (Num. R. 4:20); it was on account of this criticism that she was punished with childlessness (Sanh. 21a). [ED.]

Bibliography: Bright, Hist, 172, 176–7, 186; de Vaux, Anc Isr, index, s.v. *Mikal;* Morgenstern, in: ZAW, 49 (1931), 54–55; Stoebe, in: ZAWB, 77 (1958), 224–43; EM, s.v. incl. bibl.

MICHALI, BINYAMIN YIZHAK (1910–), Hebrew writer, literary critic, and editor. Born in Bessarabia, Michali lived in Bucharest from 1933 to 1939, where he was active in Zionist circles. He went to Ereẓ Israel in 1939 and joined the staff of the archives of the *Histadrut. He was a leading member of the Israel Writers' Association for many years and one of the chief editors of its journal, *Moznayim.* His first articles in Yiddish as well as Hebrew appeared in the Labor Zionist press. He published several books on modern Hebrew writers dealing in particular with the younger schools (*Olamam shel Benei ha-Areẓ,* 1951, and *Peri ha-Areẓ,* 1966, and *Ḥayyim Hazaz, Iyyunim bi-Yẓirato,* 1968) and edited several anthologies and journals of contemporary Hebrew literature.

Bibliography: I. Cohen, *Sha'ar ha-Te'amim* (1962), 197–9; Kressel, Leksikon, 2 (1967), 348. [G.K.]

MICHALOVCE (Hung. **Nagymihály**), town in N.E. Slovakia, Czechoslovakia. Jews lived in the nearby village of Pozdisovice (Hung. Pasdios) until 1867, when the community of Michalovce was founded. It developed rapidly, mainly because the town was on the railroad line. The synagogue was one of the most imposing buildings in the town. The community was a stronghold of Orthodoxy in Hungary, and in 1865 the convention of rabbis which decided on secession of the Orthodox congregations was held there. The Michalovce community itself did not split and remained Orthodox. In 1926 a ḥasidic synagogue, seating 300, was consecrated. Between the world wars Michalovce was the most important community of the region. Nearly all the wholesale merchants, physicians, and lawyers in the town were Jews. The Zionist and Hebrew revival movements were especially active, mainly due to the support of R. Simeon Ehrenfeld (1905–32). There were three yeshivot. The community numbered 2,809 in 1921 and 3,386 in 1930 (c. 30% of the total population). In spring

1939 the era of persecutions and arrests began. There were 3,955 Jews in Michalovce in 1941. From May 1942 onward approximately 2,000 of them were deported to the Nazi death camps; around 15% of them survived. The community was reestablished immediately after the war; between 1945 and 1948 it numbered approximately 800, some 500 of whom originated from other localities. The large *bet midrash* had been destroyed, but the synagogue was restored. The number of Jews declined to 400 in 1957 and to between 200 and 250 in 1967. The municipality paid the salary of one communal functionary. A *shoḥet* came once a week from *Kosice. In 1970, although the community was still active, the building of the ḥasidic synagogue was used as an automobile repair shop, while the former *maẓẓah* bakery housed the municipal printing press. The Hungarian writer Erzsi *Szenes was born in Michalovce.

Bibliography: M. Ben-Zeev (ed.), *Sefer Michalovce ve-ha-Sevivah* (1969), Heb., Eng., and Hung.; R. Iltis (ed.), *Die aussaeen unter Traenen...* (1959), 165–7; M. Lányi and H. Propperné Békefi, *A szlovenszói zsidó hitközségek története* (1933), 246ff. [M.La.]

MICHEL, JUD (d. 1549), also known as "the rich Michel," financier and soldier of fortune. According to legend Michel was an illegitimate son of one of the dukes of Regenstein, who were his benefactors at the beginning of his career but later became his bitter enemies. His loans to rulers of *Hesse, the Palatinate, and lesser principalities are first recorded in the early 1530s. Michel, who had no official title (see *Court Jew), stood in the relationship of vassal to Philip the Magnanimous of Hesse, for whom he had to muster five horsemen, as well as to the elector of the Palatinate and the margrave of Ansbach. When the duke of Regenstein repudiated a promissory note, Michel first warned and challenged him and then instigated acts of arson against his property. Called before the imperial court, he fled to Silesia where he organized effective support from nobility and *Ferdinand I, to whom he had once loaned 2,000 gold gulden. Michel subsequently entered the service of Joachim II, elector of *Brandenburg, with whom he conducted intricate economic transactions against the dukes of Regenstein, vassals of the elector. He owned two houses in *Berlin and one in *Frankfort on the Oder, although the latter town objected to his presence there. In 1544 his wife, Merle, was accused of attempting to poison the wells and in 1546 he was accused of illegal slaughtering; in both cases Joachim intervened on his protégé's behalf. He was kidnapped while on a mission in 1549; his abductors were arrested and brought to Saxony and Michel was released on Joachim's command. Shortly after Michel died in dubious circumstances as the result of a fall down stairs. Michel made a singular impression on his contemporaries, including Martin *Luther, who reported having heard of a rich Jew who traveled throughout Germany, drawn by 12 horses. In dress and manners he conducted himself like a rich nobleman, surrounded by Jewish servants, and thus attended the Diets of the empire.

Bibliography: H. Schnee, *Die Hoffinanz und der moderne Staat*, 1 (1955), 23–38; 5 (1965), 194, no. 80. [Ed.]

MICHEL-LÉVY, AUGUSTE (1844–1911), French petrologist and mining engineer. Michel-Lévy, who was born in Paris, was appointed director of the French geological survey and national inspector of mines in 1874. He was also a professor at the Collège de France. The most distinguished petrologist of his time, he was the first scientist to use the polarizing microscope to examine magmatic rocks and minerals. He extended this work by laboratory experiments in melting and crystallization, and with his collaborator F. Fouqué, was the pioneer of experimental petrology. He formulated fundamental queries which continue to pose major problems in the discussion of magmatic process as, for example, the role of volatiles (1875) and the mode of emplacement of granitic magmas through the assimilation of country rocks and bed-by-bed injection. The Fouqué-Lévy system became the standard one in the French teaching of petrography. Together with Fouqué, Michel-Lévy wrote *Minéralogie micrographique* (1879), *Synthèse des minéraux et des roches* (1882) and *Structure et classification des roches éruptives* (1889). He was a member of the French Academy.

This distinction was also conferred on his son, Albert-Victor (1877–1955), also a petrographer. He was born in Autun. Albert-Victor's main research was on the composition of the Vosges mountain range. He succeeded in producing artificial metamorphism in rocks by using pressure at high temperatures. [Ed.]

MICHELSON, ALBERT ABRAHAM (1852–1931), U.S. physicist; the first American to be awarded a Nobel Prize for science. He was born in Strelno, Prussia, and was taken by his family to the United States at the age of two. Michelson graduated from the naval academy at Annapolis in 1873. However, after spending two years at sea he resigned to become an instructor in physics at the naval academy (1875–79). He spent a year in Washington and then two years studying in Germany. He returned to the U.S. in 1883 to become professor at the Case School of Applied Science in Cleveland until 1889. From 1889 to 1892 he was at Clark University and finally he was professor at the University of Chicago (1892–1929). He was awarded the Nobel Prize in physics in 1907. Michelson was a remarkable experimentalist able to secure astonishing accuracies with the simplest apparatus. His lifelong interest was the velocity of light, and this was the subject of his first experiment even in his mid-20s when he was an instructor at the U.S. naval

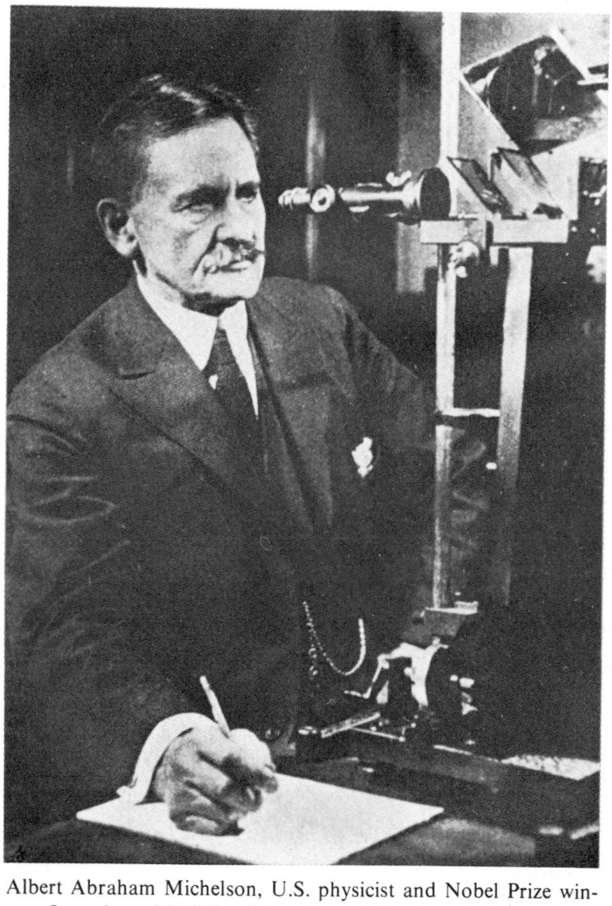

Albert Abraham Michelson, U.S. physicist and Nobel Prize winner. Jerusalem, J.N.U.L., Schwadron Collection.

academy at Annapolis. At that time physicists believed in the existence of an ether that filled all space, was at absolute rest, and through which light traveled in waves. There was then no way of measuring the motion of any body relative to the ether and leading scientists doubted whether this could be done. If it could be measured, two beams of light should show interference fringes denoting the difference. By measuring the width of the fringes it should be possible to show the earth's exact velocity when compared with the ether. Not only would the earth's absolute motion be determined, but also that of all bodies in the planetary system whose motions relative to the earth were known. For his experiment Michelson developed the interferometer, an instrument now used to measure wavelengths of light and other wavelengths of the radiation spectrum. He carried out his first experiments in Berlin in 1881 in Helmholtz' laboratory. In 1887, together with Edward Williams Morley, he performed one of the most important experiments in the history of science, which provided a new starting point for the great theoretical developments in 20th-century physics. The conclusion of the experiment indicated that light travels with the same velocity in any direction under any circumstances, and the implication was that the ether did not exist. This became one of the basic concepts which led *Einstein in 1905 to his special theory of relativity. The proving of this revolutionary theory of the absolute speed of light under any conditions has become the underlying principle of modern physics, astronomy, and cosmology and is considered to be, perhaps, the one absolute natural law in the universe. As a great experimentalist, Michelson established in 1892/93 the meter in terms of the wavelength of cadmium. He also determined the diameter of Jupiter's satellites and was the first person to measure the dimension of a star, Alpha Orion. Michelson wrote *Velocity of Light* (1902), *Light Waves and Their Uses* (1903), and *Studies in Optics* (1927).

Bibliography: B. Jaffe, *Michelson and the Speed of Light* (1961), incl. bibl. [M.Gol.]

MICHELSON, CHARLES (1869–1948), U.S. editor, journalist, and political publicist. Michelson, who was born in Virginia City, Nevada, ran away from home at the age of 13. He worked as a sheepherder, miner, and teamster, before going to work for the Virginia City *Chronicle* as a reporter. He subsequently worked for San Francisco newspapers, before going to Cuba as a correspondent for Hearst's New York *Journal* in 1896. Soon after his arrival Michelson was imprisoned briefly in Morro Castle, but was released in time to cover the Spanish-American War. After the war, Michelson worked for several other newspapers. From 1917 to 1929 he was chief of the Washington bureau of the New York *World*. In 1929 the Democratic National Committee hired Michelson as the first full-time publicity director, the first ever employed by a political party. Within two years of his appointment, Michelson was the ghostwriter of hundreds of press releases attacking the Hoover administration. After Roosevelt's election, Michelson also did publicity work for the Treasury Department, the Civilian Conservation Corps, and as public relations director of the National Recovery Administration (NRA). His weekly column, "Dispelling the Fog," was distributed free to newspapers throughout the country. The Republican Party considered Michelson a key factor in the electoral successes of the Democratic Party. Michelson retired in 1942, returning briefly as associate director of publicity in 1944. He wrote his memoirs, *The Ghost Talks* (1944). [Ed.]

MICHELSTAEDTER, CARLO (1887–1910), Italian philosopher and poet. Michelstaedter was born into a well-known family, his mother being a relation of Samuel David Luzzatto and his father a descendant of Isaac Samuel Reggio. He was greatly influenced by the writings of Schopenhauer, Nietzsche, and Ibsen and based his philosophy on the assumption that all human endeavor, spiritual or physical, is merely an illusion. Michelstaedter's fundamental pessimism is expressed in his *Dialogo della Salute* (1912) and, in a more poetic fashion, in his *Poesie* (1912). He spent the last years of his short life in his native Gorizia preparing a thesis on "The Concept of Persuasion and Rhetoric in the Writings of Plato and Aristotle." After completing the second volume of this work (*La persuasione e la retorica,* 1913) Michelstaedter committed suicide. In this last book he anticipated the main doctrines of European existentialism. Michelstaedter's philosophical outlook led him to the extreme step of taking his own life out of inner conviction. His works, all posthumously published, were widely circulated and greatly influenced Italian philosophy and literature after World War II. A critical edition of Michelstaedter's complete works, including the first collection of his letters, was published in 1959.

Bibliography: C. Pellizzi, *Gli spiriti della vigilia* (1924), 13–73; G. Chiavacci, in: *Giornale critico dela filosofia italiana,* 5 (1924), nos. 1–2; T. Moretti-Costanzi, in: L. Pelloux (ed.), *Esistenzialismo, saggi e studi* (1943); E. Garin, in: *Cronache di filosofia italiana* (1955), 36–41; A. Piromalli, in: *Saggi critici di storia letteraria* (1967), 165–81; G. Chiavacci et al., in: *La fiera letteraria* (July 13, 1952); L. Soperchi, in: *Rivista di Psicologia,* 28 (1932), 26ff., 280ff., incl. bibl. [G.R.]

MICHIGAN, one of the N. central states of the U.S.; state with a population (1968) of 8,374,000, including 97,995 Jews, of whom 84,500 are in Metropolitan *Detroit.

Ezekiel Solomon (d. c. 1808), the state's first Jew, went to Fort Michilimackinac (Mackinac) in 1761, when Michigan was part of British Canada. He was captured by the Indians during the 1763 massacre of Mackinac but was ransomed. An extensive fur trader, he was a founder of Michigan's first Board of Trade and a partner of the Mackinac Company, a combine of some 30 traders. Although married to a Christian, he was an important member and frequently an officer of Montreal's Congregation Shearith Israel. A state historical marker, dedicated to Solomon, was placed in 1964 at the restored Fort Michilimackinac by the Jewish Historical Society of Michigan. Gershon Levy, Benjamin Lyon, and Levy Solomons, partners of Ezekiel, also traded at Mackinac. Two of them were captured during the 1763 Indian uprising but gained their freedom. Jacob Franks—nephew of the American patriot David Salisbury *Franks—and his nephew, John Lawe, served with the British forces in Mackinac during the War of 1812.

The Mackinac bridge, the world's second largest suspension bridge, was designed by David B. Steinman. Lawrence A. Rubin was executive secretary of the Mackinac Bridge Authority. Ann Arbor was the first community, where a colony of Jews settled in the 1840s, during the German-Jewish immigration. The first to arrive were the Weil brothers (Solomon, Moses, Leopold, Marcus, and Jacob) and their parents. The first services were held in 1845 and the first private cemetery acquired about 1848. Originally located in what is now downtown Ann Arbor, the cemetery was condemned by the city and the remains of the interred transferred to the Jewish section in Forest Hill Cemetery. By 1873 the last of the Weil brothers moved to Chicago. The present Jewish community, numbering 2,000, dates back to the arrival of Osias Zwerdling in 1903. The B'nai B'rith Hillel Foundation at the University of Michigan (Dr. Herman Jacobs, director) shares its quarters with the Beth Israel Congregation (Conservative). Temple Beth Emeth, Reform, was organized in 1966. The Jewish

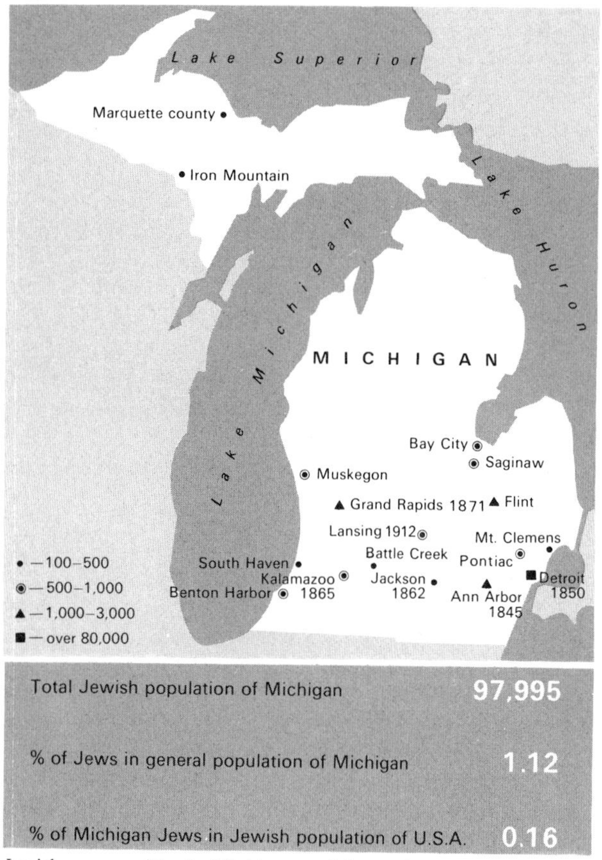

Jewish communities in Michigan and dates of establishment. Population figures for 1968.

Cultural School was formed in 1965 and the Jewish Community Council in 1966. The university has about 4,000 Jewish students, with numerous Jewish professors on its faculty, some of national note.

Jacob Hirsch and Jacob Levy went to Jackson (200 Jews) in 1842. The Hebrew Benevolent Association was formed in 1858 and a cemetery purchased. Temple Beth Israel, Reform, began in 1862. Maurice Heuman served as mayor of Jackson. Mannes Israel arrived in Kalamazoo (800 Jews) in 1844. His son, Edward, was the astronomer of General A. W. Greeley's Arctic Expedition of 1881. Congregation B'nai Israel, Reform, started in 1865 and Congregation of Moses, Conservative, in 1886. Samuel Folz served as mayor of Kalamazoo. Charles, Henry, and Emanuel Lederer were in Lansing (900 Jews), Michigan's capital, in 1849. Mount Hope Cemetery was acquired in 1898. Congregation Shaarey Zedek, Reform, was founded in 1912 and the Jewish Welfare Federation in 1939. The B'nai B'rith Hillel Foundation at Michigan State University (Rabbi Abraham Zemach, director) is in East Lansing. About 1,800 Jewish students are enrolled at the university, in addition to Jewish professors.

Julius Houseman went to Grand Rapids (1,300 Jews) in 1852. He was mayor of Grand Rapids and a member of Congress, the first and only Michigan Jew to have been elected to the U.S. Congress. His son-in-law, David Amberg, served in the Civil War, and his grandson, Julius Amberg, was an assistant secretary of war in World War II. In 1857 a Hebrew Benevolent and Burial Society was organized and a cemetery purchased. Temple Emanuel, Reform, was incorporated in 1871 and Congregation Ahavas Israel, Conservative, a merger of two Orthodox congregations, was formed in 1938. The Jewish Community Fund began in 1940. Bay City has a population of 700 Jews. Congregation Anshe Chesed was organized in 1872 and Congregation Shaarey Zedek in 1880. The Jewish community is now served by Temple Israel, Conservative, which is successor to Temple Abraham, organized in 1914. The Northwestern Michigan Jewish Welfare Federation was formed in 1940. Benton Harbor's Jewish community dates back to 1882. Its 880 Jews are served by Temple Beth El, Reform, Congregation B'nai Sholom, .Conservative, and the Arthur Sidney Mendel Educational Center. Saginaw with 560 Jews supports Congregation B'nai Israel, Conservative (founded in 1890), and Temple Beth El, Reform (organized in 1903). The Jewish Welfare Federation opened in 1949.

Flint, having 3,000 Jews, claims Harry Weingarden and his wife as the first Jewish settlers (1905). Congregation Beth Israel, Conservative, is an outgrowth of the Jewish Community Center started in 1910. Temple Beth El, Reform, was organized in 1927. The Jewish Community Council began in 1936. Muskegon, with 525 Jews, is served by Congregation B'nai Israel, Reform, which was organized in 1901. Mount Clemens (420 Jews) has an Orthodox congregation, Beth Tefilath Moses, which was founded in 1912. South Haven, with 315 Jews, organized its First Hebrew Congregation, Orthodox, in 1920. Pontiac's (700 Jews) Jewish Community Center was incorporated in 1923 and was the forerunner of Temple Beth Jacob, Reform, which was organized in 1932. Congregation B'nai Israel, Conservative, was founded in 1934. Battle Creek (245 Jews) supports the Jewish Center, Orthodox (organized in 1935), and Temple Beth El, Reform. Small Jewish communities also exist in Alpena, Hancock, Iron Mountain, Ishpeming, Mt. Pleasant, Midland, Monroe, Petoskey, Port Huron, and Traverse City.

Bibliography: D. E. Heineman in: AJHSP, 13 (1905), 47–70; United States, Work Projects Administration, The Michigan Historical Records Survey Project, *Inventory of the Church and Synagogue Archives of Michigan: Jewish Bodies* (1940), mimeographed; I. I. Katz, *The Beth El Story, with a History of the Jews in Michigan before 1850* (1955).

[ED.]

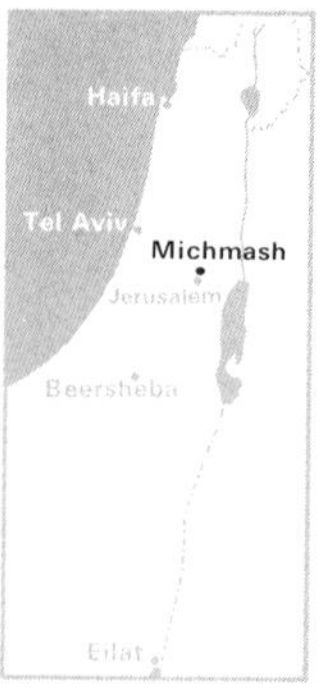

MICHMASH or **MICHMAS** (Heb. מִכְמָשׂ, מִכְמָס, מִכְמַשׁ), city of the tribe of Judah, originally belonging to the tribe of Benjamin, situated between Jerusalem and Beth-El in a strong strategic position north of the deep Wadi al-Suwaynīṭ. Saul gathered part of his army there (I Sam. 13:2) and the main part of the Philistine forces later encamped in the city prior to the battle of Michmash, fleeing by way of Aijalon after their defeat (I Sam. 13–14). It is mentioned in Isaiah's description of the advance of the Assyrian army, where it is placed between Aiath and Geba (Isa. 10:28), and in the lists of those returning from the Babylonian Exile (Ezra 2:27; Neh. 7:31). Jonathan the Hasmonean resided there for a time before assuming the high priesthood (I Macc. 9:73). In the Mishnah, the wheat of the place is highly praised (Men. 8:1). Eusebius calls it a very big village, 9 mi. (c. 14 km.) from Jerusalem and in its territory (Onom. 132:3–4). Michmash is identified with Mukhmās, approximately 6 mi. (c. 10 km.) northeast of Jerusalem.

Bibliography: Abel, Geog, 2 (1938), 386; Aharoni, Land, index; EM, 4 (1962), 961–2.

[M.A.-Y.]

°**MICKIEWICZ, ADAM** (1798–1855), Polish poet. Born in Lithuania, Mickiewicz became involved in student nationalist politics at Vilna University and in 1826 was expelled from the country and ordered to live in Russia. In 1829 he was given permission to go abroad, and started the journeying from one European city to another that was to last for the rest of his life. It was during the period 1823–32 that he wrote his great drama *Dziady* (3 vols. (Paris, 1832); partial trans. *Forefathers' Eve*, 1928), in which he drew a picture of the future savior of Poland which has been interpreted as referring to himself. According to the vision of one of the characters, this savior would be "a son of an alien mother; his blood, the blood of ancient heroes; and his name—forty-and-four." Mickiewicz's mother, descended from a converted Frankist family, was an "alien"; and his own name, Adam (אדם), omitting the unvoiced "A" (א), has the numerical value of 44. Such kabbalistic notions were gleaned from the writings of the French mystic, Louis-Claude de Saint-Martin. Although Mickiewicz at first occasionally referred slightingly to the Jews, even in his biblically-influenced *Księgi narodu polskiego i pielgrzymstwa polskiego* "Books of the Polish Nation and the Polish Pilgrimage," Paris, 1832), he soon revised his attitude. In this he was influenced by the mystical philosopher Andrzej Towiański, who considered the Jews, together with the French and Poles, to be a "chosen nation" and whose Messianic nationalism drew inspiration from Mesmer, Swedenborg, and the Kabbalah. Thus the idealized Jew, Jankiel, in Mickiewicz's masterpiece, the great epic *Pan Tadeusz* (1834) is an ardent Polish patriot. In the lectures he gave as professor of Slavonic languages and literatures at the Collège de France in Paris (1840–44), Mickiewicz was at pains to praise the Jews and defend them against their detractors. In a sermon delivered in a Paris synagogue on the Fast of the Ninth of Av, 1845, he expressed his sympathy for Jewish suffering and yearning for Ereẓ Israel. Although he dreamed for years of the conversion of the Jews to Christianity, he was greatly disappointed at the assimilationist tendencies of French Jews. In one of the statutes of the Polish legion which he organized in Italy in 1848 to fight against Russia Mickiewicz wrote: "To Israel, our elder brother: honor, fraternity, and help in striving towards his eternal and temporal goal. Equal rights in all things." When the Crimean War broke out in 1853, Mickiewicz went to Constantinople to help raise a Polish regiment to fight against the Russians. He hoped to include Jewish units, and was prepared to assure them the right to observe the Sabbath and all other religious obligations. His chief assistant, a French medical officer named Armand Lévy, was a Jewish nationalist, and it is possible that the two men believed that the creation of Jewish units would be a first step towards the revival of the Jewish nation in its own land. Mickiewicz died suddenly before his mission in Constantinople was completed.

Bibliography: A. G. Duker, in: M. Kridl (ed.), *Adam Mickiewicz, Poet of Poland* (1951), 108–25; S. Scheps, *Adam Mickiewicz: ses affinités juives* (1964); R. Brandstaetter, *Legjon żydoswki Adama Mickiewicza* (1932 = *Miesięcnik żydowski*, 2 (1932), 20–45, 112–32, 225–48); W. Feldman, *Stosunek Adama Mickiewicza do Żydów* (1890); P. Kon, in: *Źródłamocy*, 1 (1924), bibl. of Heb. and Yid. trans.; R. A. Braudes (Broydes), *Adam Mickiewicz* (Heb., 1890); F. Kupfer and S. Strelcyn, *Mickiewicz w przekładach hebrajskich* (1955). [Y.A.K.]

MICROCOSM (from Gr. *mikros kosmos;* "small world"), term in the Western philosophical tradition referring to man as an epitome of the universe (the macrocosm) in his parts and structure. The Arabic (*ʿālam ṣaghīr*), Hebrew (*olam katan*), and Latin (*mundis minor*) terms are literal equivalents of the Greek. The term is said to be first attested in Aristotle (*Physics*, 8:2, 252b, 26–27), though the motif is older; indeed, the notion that some aspect of reality (the city, sanctuary, man) reflects the cosmos is both ancient and widespread. Though the broad diffusion of the microcosm motif in late antiquity (in Gnostic, Hermetic, neoplatonic, neopythagorean, Orphic, and stoic writings) complicates the study of original sources, its occurrence in medieval Arabic and Hebrew texts is mainly the result of neoplatonic influence. The analogy was frequently invoked to argue for the existence of a world soul or mind which directs and orders the physical universe as the soul does the body. The idea that man exemplifies all being was also used to buttress the theme of man's superiority, dignity, or freedom: as *nodus et vinculum mundi*, he epitomizes the entire scale of being (spiritual and material) and determines his own place, unlike angels and beasts whose nature is fixed. The elaboration of the neoplatonic hypostases was, in effect, a projection of human psychology to the supersensible world. Furthermore, the neoplatonic notion that the human mind is potentially a *κόσμος νοητός* ("intelligible world") implies that by knowing the intelligibles man becomes identical with all being. Microcosmic speculation tended to combine with astrology (correspondence between heavenly bodies and parts of the human body), medicine (universal and human nature, parallel between the four elements and the four humors), and magical practice (universal sympathy). Philo frequently compares man as microcosm *βραχὺς κόσμο* to the universe (Conger, in bibl., 16–18; H. A. Wolfson, *Philo*, 1, (1948), 424, n.), stressing the parallel between the human and cosmic minds (*logoi;* e.g., Op. 69–71). He is said to have drawn his theory of the microcosm from Greek and rabbinic sources (A. Altmann in bibl., 20). Among the latter is found a long list of gross analogies between parts of the world and parts of man in *Avot de-Rabbi Nathan* (ARN^2 31, 92). (For other rabbinic sources, see Altmann, 21, n.) In medieval Jewish philosophy the motif is frequently cited, being part of the common stock of popular philosophy found in such works as the Epistles of the *Brethren of Sincerity. It is mentioned, for example, by *Saadiah Gaon in his commentary on the *Sefer Yeẓirah* (ed. by M. Lambert (1891), 67ff., 91), where he compares God to life and intelligence and sets forth a series of analogues between the universe, the sanctuary, and man (followed by Abraham ibn Ezra in his commentary on Ex. 25:40; see Altmann, in bibl., 25–26); by *Baḥya ibn Paquda (*Ḥovot ha-Levavot*, 2:4), and by *Judah Halevi in his *Kuzari* (4:3), where he quotes "the philosophers" who compared the world to a *macranthropos* ("large man") and man to a microcosm, implying that God is the spirit, soul, mind, and life of the world. (For other citations of the microcosm motif by medieval Jewish philosophers, see Conger, in bibl., 37ff., and Altmann, in bibl., 27–28.)

The microcosm theme was productive in *Israeli, Ibn *Gabirol, and Joseph ibn *Ẓaddik. Israeli links it to his definition of philosophy as self-knowledge: "This being so, it is clear that man, if he knows himself in both his spirituality and corporeality, comprises knowledge of all, and knows both the spiritual and the corporeal substance, and also knows the first substance which is created from the power of the Creator without mediator . . . " (A. Altmann and S. M. Stern (eds.), *Isaac Israeli* (1959), 27; see comments, *ibid.*, 28–30, 203–8, and Altmann, in bibl., 22–23). The same combination of philosophy as self-knowledge and the consequent knowledge of all is found in Ibn Ẓaddik's *Sefer ha-Olam ha-Katan* (Introd.). Ibn Ẓaddik adds that this knowledge leads to knowledge of the Creator. (See also *Sefer ha-Olam ha-Katan*, pt. 2, Introd., where Job 19:26 is cited as a proof verse—"And from my flesh I shall behold God"; cf. Altmann-Stern, 208; Altmann, in bibl., 23, 25; and Vajda, in bibl., 97 and n. 3, who cites the similar combination of the microcosm and *γνῶθι σεαυτόν* ("know yourself") themes by Abraham ibn Ezra.) In a more primitive vein, reminiscent of *Avot de-Rabbi Nathan* and the microcosm passage in the Iranian *Greater Bundahišhn* (trans. by B. T. Anklesaria (1956), 245), Ibn Ẓaddik (pt. 2, ch. 1), referring to "the ancients," compares the members of the human organism to the heavenly bodies (head to the outer sphere, nostrils to Venus, mouth to Mars, tongue to Mercury, vertebrae to the signs of the zodiac, eyes to the sun and moon, ears to Saturn and Jupiter), while the arteries are compared to the seas and rivers, the bones to the mountains, the hair to the plants, and the four humors to the four elements (see Altmann, in bibl., 24; and Vajda, in bibl., 113, who brands this a *"néoplationisme vulgarisé"*). Nothing so gross appears in Ibn Gabirol's *Mekor Ḥayyim*. Though the term for microcosm *(ʿālam ṣaghir=mundis minor)* appears but once (3:2, 10; see S. Pines, in *Tarbiz*, 27 (1958), 220), Ibn Gabirol makes ample use of the motif. Following the general principle that the inferior is an exemplar of the superior, man as microcosm is said to exemplify the macrocosm. The correspondence is utilized to demonstrate, for example, that the most simple substance is not in contact with the substance that bears the nine categories (3:2, 10, see also 3:58). The action of the particular will is invoked in order to explain that of the universal will (5:37).

Maimonides had little use for the popular philosophy of the Brethren of Sincerity and says he never read Ibn Ẓaddik's *Sefer ha-Olam ha-Katan* (in his letter to Ibn Tibbon; A. Marx (ed.), in: JQR, 25 (1934–35), 378–9), but in a central chapter of the *Guide* (1:72) he sets forth an elaborate analogy (with qualifications) between the whole of being and man, the parallel par excellence, being that between God vis-à-vis the universe and the rational intellect vis-à-vis man. It is on the basis of this parallel that man is called a microcosm. In his structure man exemplifies the unity within diversity and the hierarchical ordering of the universe (an idea which appears frequently in the writings of al-Fārābī). With this analogy in the *Guide* microcosmic speculation in Jewish philosophy reaches its peak, from which it ebbs with the decline of Jewish neoplatonism occasioned by the rise of Jewish Aristotelianism in the post-Maimonidean era. A notable exception is Judah *Abrabanel (Leone Ebreo), the Renaissance neoplatonist, who set forth analogies between the heavens and parts of the body (astrological microcosm; cf. Ibn Ẓaddik) in the second dialogue of his *Dialoghi d'amore* ed. Carmella (1929), 84f.; trans. by F. Friedberg-Seeley and J. H. Barnes (1937), 93ff.).

Bibliography: A. Altmann, *Studies in Religious Philosophy and Mysticism* (1969); G. Vajda, in: *Archives d'histoire doctrinale et littéraire du moyen âge*, 24 (1949), 93–181; D. Levy, in: *The Encyclopedia of Philosophy*, 5 (1967), 121–5 (with good bibl.); G. P. Conger, *Theories of Macrocosms and Microcosms in the History of Philosophy* (1922); M. Doctor, *Die Philosophie des Josef (Ibn) Ẓaddik* (1895); H. Schipperges, in: P. Wilpert (ed.), *Antike und Orient im Mittelalter* (1962), 129–53 (with extensive bibliography); R. Allers, in: *Tradition*, 2 (1944), 319–407; A. Goetze, in: *Zeitschrift fuer Indologie und Iranistik*, 2 (1923), 60–98. [J.Kr.]

°**MICZYŃSKI, SEBASTIAN** (late 16th–early 17th century), anti-Jewish agitator and professor of philosophy at Cracow University. In 1618 Miczyński published a venomous anti-Semitic lampoon entitled *Zwierciadło korony polskiej* ("The Mirror of the Polish Crown"). It is a catalog of demagogic denunciations accusing the Jews of all the misfortunes that had befallen the kingdom of Poland and its people. Through reports of *blood libels and accusations that they had desecrated icons and profaned Catholic festivals, the Jews are presented as the implacable enemies of Christians. Miczyński also presents the Jews as traitors and spies in the pay of Turkey, and lays special emphasis on the wealth of the Jewish merchants and craftsmen who compete with their Christian neighbors, driving the guilds and towns to ruin. The pamphlet seriously disturbed the Jews of *Cracow. When riots broke out in the town, the *parnasim* of the community appealed to King Sigismund III Vasa. The king promptly prohibited the circulation of the pamphlet, but in spite of his order it was reprinted in a second and enlarged edition during the same year; it was published for a third time in 1648. Miczyński's work is an important link in the chain of Polish anti-Semitic literature.

Bibliography: K. Bartoszewicz, *Antysemityzm w literaturze polskiej 15–17 wieków* (1914); M. Bałaban, *Historja Żydów w Krakowie i na Kazimierzu*, 1 (1931), 171–7. [A.Cy.]

MIDDLESEX COUNTY, NEW JERSEY, on the eastern coast of New Jersey, southwest of New York City, U.S.; estimated total population in 1870 was 570,000; Jewish population figures were unavailable. The majority of Jewish settlers in Middlesex County were traders and peddlers. Most of the information about Jewish immigrants comes from court and land records. Aaron and Jacob Lozada owned a grocery and hardware store in Bound Brook, on the border between Middlesex County and Somerset County, as early as 1718, and helped form a synagogue ten years later. The next mention of a synagogue, Congregation Anshe Emeth of New Brunswick, is found in an 1861 land record. A court record from 1722 lists Daniel Nunez as town clerk and tax collector of Piscataway Township and justice of the peace for Middlesex County. Perth Amboy was an important Jewish center for Jewish merchants from the time that it was named capital of East Jersey in 1685. The first Jewish religious sevice was held here in 1890 in the home of a local Jewish resident. A *mikveh* was constructed shortly thereafter and Rosh Ha-Shanah and Day of Atonement services were held at the Perth Amboy Savings Bank. When the size of the Jewish community increased, a building was purchased in about 1900 under the name of the Hebrew Mutual Aid Society. This subsequently became Congregation Shaarey Tefiloh which was dedicated on October 29, 1903. In 1904 a burial ground was purchased and a free Hebrew school was organized. The founders of the second congregation came from Perth Amboy, Metuchen, and South Amboy. It was incorporated on August 2, 1895. The first meeting places were in homes. In 1897 a synagogue was built and called Temple Beth Mordecai after a deceased son of Henry Wolff, one of the founders. In April 1927 the temple was dedicated. The Perth Amboy YMHA was formed in 1908 and was the first YMHA built in the state to have its own building rather than a rented one.

Middlesex County's prominent political figures included: David T. Wilentz of Perth Amboy, the first Jewish New Jersey attorney general (1934–44), prosecutor in the Lindbergh kidnapping trial, and New Jersey national Democratic committeeman (1964–70); his son Robert Wilentz, also of Perth Amboy, state assemblyman from 1966 to 1970; Arthur J. Sills of Metuchen, state attorney general from 1962 to 1970; Donald Wernik, mayor of Metuchen in 1970; and Norman Tanzman of Woodbridge, who was elected state senator in 1962. In 1970 the Jews of Middlesex County were mainly engaged in the professions and as business executives. [B.D.S.]

MIDDOT (Heb. מִדּוֹת; "measures"), tenth tractate of the order *Kodashim* (in some codices and early editions it is ninth; in current Talmud editions the 11th and last). It is found in the Mishnah only. This tractate gives, in five chapters, exact details and measurements of the building of the Temple and of its component parts, intended perhaps to serve as a guide for the rebuilding of the Temple. The description is of the Temple of Herod. It is not based on a plan drawn up in Temple times, but depends on the

Engraving for the tractate *Middot*, with a scale representation of the Temple, from a title page of the Hebrew-Latin Mishnah illustrated by Mich. Richey. Amsterdam, 1700–04. Jerusalem, J.N.U.L.

memory of sages who saw the Temple and who after its destruction gave an oral description of it to their disciples. The main reporter seems to have been *Eliezer b. Jacob I, who figures prominently in this tractate. He is thought to have seen the Temple while it was still standing, but he may also have learned much about its inner arrangements from his uncle who actually served in it (1:2). That the descriptions are based on memory is evident from the controversies on factual points (1:9; 2:6; 3:4, 6; et al.); moreover, Eliezer b. Jacob is repeatedly reported to have "forgotten" certain details (2:5; 5:4). In fact this tractate was considered the original *mishnah* ("teaching") of Eliezer b. Jacob; the final redaction of Judah ha-Nasi contains, of course, the variant traditions of the other authorities as well (see Yoma 16a–17a; TJ, Yoma 2:3, 39d).

See also *Temple.

Bibliography: Ḥ. Albeck, *Shishah Sidrei Mishnah*, 5 (1959), 313–5. [A.Z.E.]

MIDIAN, MIDIANITES (Heb. מִדְיָן , מְדָנִים Gen. 37:28, מְדְיָנִים), name of a people or a group of (semi-) nomadic peoples in the Bible (LXX, Madian, or Madiam; 1QIs[a] 60:6, מדים). The Midianites are among the sons of Abraham and Keturah who were sent to "the land of the East" (Gen. 25:1–6). "Midianite traders" are mentioned in the episode about the sale of Joseph (Gen. 37:28). *Jethro, Moses' father-in-law, was a Midianite priest living in the land of Midian (Ex. 2:15–3:1); he met Moses in the wilderness of Sinai (Ex. 18:1–5), and the members of his family accompanied the Israelites in their wanderings in the desert (Num. 10:29–32). The elders of Midian displayed hostility toward the Israelites on the plains of Moab (22:7) and the Israelites fought the Midianites, killing many of them (31:1–20).

This episode was connected with the attempt to entice the Israelites to worship Baal-Peor, in which the daughters of Midian participated (25:6–18). In the period of the Judges, the Midianites exerted harsh pressure on Israel (Judg. 6:1–7), and Gideon defeated them far from the borders of Ereẓ Israel, in Karkor (8:10), which was probably in Wadi Sirḥān in Transjordan, on the border of the desert. After this war, the Midianites ceased to be a political or military factor.

The range of the Midianites' wanderings was very broad: from the neighborhood of Moab (Gen. 36:35; Num. 22:4,7; 25:1, 5, 15) and the kingdom of Sihon the Amorite (Josh. 13:21) in the border region of Transjordan, along the border of the Arabian desert (cf. Judg. 8:21, 24) west of Edom (I Kings 11:18), to the Sinai Desert and the trade route between Ereẓ Israel and Egypt (Gen. 37:28). In Greek-Roman and Arabic sources Midian is mentioned in Arabia, as well as on the shore of the Red Sea, and, according to Josephus (Ant. 2:257), this is the biblical Midian (cf. Eusebius, Onom. 124:6). This Midian is identified, according to the tradition of the Arabic geographers, with modern Maghāyir Shuʿayb (=the caves near Akaba). It appears that the Midianites' settlement in Arabia occurred in a later time, when their living area was reduced, but it is possible that the settlement in North Arabia during the Hellenistic-Roman period was a continuation of the biblical settlement. Among the sons of Keturah are mentioned tribes which inhabited North Arabia—Ephah and Dedan (Gen. 25:3–4)—and it is also possible that from there the Midianites spread to the north, the east, and the west. In the Bible the Midianites are also designated by the inclusive typological title "Ishmaelites" (Judg. 8:24). Some scholars discern a connection between the Midianites and the Kushu tribes mentioned in the Egyptian Execration Texts from the 18th century B.C.E., who wandered in the southern deserts of Ereẓ Israel (cf. Cushan, Hab. 3:7). This may be hinted at in the story of the "Cushite woman" whom Moses married (Num. 12:1).

The name Midian is attributed to groups of tribes or peoples (cf. Gen. 25:4), as is attested by the nature of the monarchy in Midian. The Bible mentions "the five kings of Midian" during the war in the wilderness (Num. 31:8) and Zebah and Zalmunna in the war of Gideon (Judg. 8:1ff.). The Midianite kings are called "chieftains" *(nesiʾim)* and "princes" (*nesikhim;* Josh., 13:21; Ps. 83:12), very fitting titles for a tribal organization united in groups; Zur, a prince of Midian, is explicitly called "the tribal head of an ancestral house in Midian" (Num. 25:15). Their typically (semi- and eventually complete) nomadic character made them close to other similar tribes—Amalekites and Kedemites. The Midianites in Transjordan followed the cult of the Moabite Baal-Peor, while those who inhabited the Negev and the Sinai became close to the Kenites or even identified with them (cf. Num. 10:29; Judg. 1:16; 4:11) and the Hebrews. The Midianites were known as shepherds (Ex. 2:17) and traders (Gen. 37:28, 36). From time to time, they, together with neighboring tribes, broke into the permanent settlements around them. The Bible describes them as robbers (Judg. 6:5). During the Monarchy the Midianites lived within the confines of their place of origin, North Arabia, and they were known as middlemen in the frankincense *(levonah)* and gold export from Sheba in South Arabia (cf. Isa. 60:6). During the Hellenistic period the Nabateans mined much gold in the land of Midian and exported it via the port of Macna (Strabo, *Geographica,* 17:784). There has been no systematic scientific research of Midian in North Arabia.

See also *Arabia, *Nabateans, *Tema. [Sh.Ab.]

In the Aggadah. Midian and Moab had always been enemies but, fearing that Israel would subdue them, they composed their differences and entered into an alliance (Sanh. 105a). They succeeded in inducing the Israelites to commit fornication with the daughters of Midian only by first making them drunk. For this reason, Phinehas forbade the drinking of gentile wine (PdRE, 47). The hatred of the Midianites for Israel was solely on account of the observance of the Torah by Israel (Num. R. 22:2). The Midianites are sometimes identified with the Moabites, who lost their claim to special consideration as descendants of Lot (Deut. 2:9), the nephew of Abraham, because they tried to induce Israel to sin (*Yelammedenu* in Yal. 1, 875). The command to Moses to make war upon the Midianites before his death was because, having no reason for their hatred against Israel, they nevertheless joined the Moabites and outdid them in their enmity. Moses did not lead the war in person because he had found refuge in

Midian when he was a fugitive from Egypt. He delegated the command to Phinehas as he had been the first to take action against them by slaying the Midianite princess, Cozbi (Num. R. 22:4). [Ed.]

Bibliography: R. F. Burton, *The Gold Mines of Midian* (1897); idem, *The Land of Midian* (1898); E. Glaser, *Skizze der Geschichte und Geographie Arabiens,* 2 (1890), 261ff.; E. Meyer, *Die Israeliten und ihre Nachbarstaemme* (1906), 326ff. 381–2; H. Grimme, in: OLZ, 13 (1910), 54–59; H. Gressmann, *Mose und seine Zeit* (1913), 416ff.; A. Musil, *The Northern Hegâz* (1926), 109ff., 267ff., 278–98, 321ff.; W. J. Phythian-Adams, in: PEFQS (1930), 193ff.; L. E. Binns, in: JTS, 31 (1930), 337–59; A. Reuveni, *Shem, Ham, ve-Yafet* (1932), 16–18, 68–69; Albright, Stone, 195–6; idem, in: BASOR, 83 (1941), 36, n. 8; M. Noth, in: ZAW, 60 (1944), 23ff.; B. Mazar, in: Eretz-Israel, 3 (1954), 20; S. Abramsky, *ibid.,* 118–9; Y. Kutscher, *Ha-Lashon ve-ha-Reka ha-Leshoni shel Megillat Yeshayahu* (1959), 82; G. W. van Beer, in: BA, 23 (1960), 3, 70–95; A. Grohman, *Arabien* (1963), 21, 38–92. In the Aggadah: Ginzberg, Legends, 7 (1938), 313; A. Rosmarin, *Moses im Lichte der Aggadah* (1932), index.

MIDRASH (Heb. מִדְרָשׁ), the designation of a particular genre of rabbinic literature constituting an anthology and compilation of homilies, consisting of both biblical exegesis (see *Hermeneutics) and sermons delivered in public (see *Homiletics) as well as *aggadot* or *halakhot* (see **Midreshei Halakhah*) and forming a running aggadic commentary on specific books of the Bible. The name Midrash derives from the root *drsh* (דרש) which in the Bible means mainly "to search," "to seek," "to examine," and "to investigate" (cf. Lev. 10:16; Deut. 13:15; Isa. 55:6; et al.). This meaning is also found in rabbinic Hebrew (cf. BM 2:7: "until thou examine *[tidrosh]* thy brother if he be a cheat or not"). The

Title page of *Midrash Ḥamesh Megillot,* the second part of *Midrash Rabbah,* printed by Daniel Bomberg, Venice, 1545. Jerusalem, J.N.U.L.

noun *"Midrash"* occurs only twice in the Bible (II Chron. 13:22 and 24:27); it is translated in the Septuagint by βίβλος, γραφή i.e., "book" or "writing," and it seems probable that it means "an account," "the result of inquiry (examination, study, or search) of the events of the times," i.e., what is today called "history" (the word history is also derived from the Greek root ἱστορέω which has a similar meaning). In Jewish literature of the Second Temple period the word Midrash was first employed in the sense of education and learning generally (Ecclus. 51:23), "Turn unto me, ye unlearned, and lodge in my house of Midrash," which the author's grandson translated into Greek by 'Ἐν τῷ οἴκῳ τῆς παιδείας, "house of instruction or of study"; compare the similar development of the Latin *studium* which originated in the verb *studeo* which means "to become enthusiastic," "to make an effort," "to be diligent," etc. and only in a secondary sense, in the post-Augustan era, in the sense of learning (with diligence and the noun *studium* passed through the same stages of meaning; cf. Ger. *studium;* Fr. *étude,* etc).

Darosh both in its nominal and verbal forms is sometimes found in the literature of the *Dead Sea sect as the designation for a certain method, a special technique of learning things—in *halakhah* and in *aggadah*—through rigorous study and painstaking, searching inquiry into the verses of the Bible. This method of Midrash was both ideologically and halakhically one of the fundamentals of the life of the sect: "and that his deeds appear in accordance with the Midrash of the Torah as followed by the holy upright men" (Damascus Covenant 8:29–30; cf. the Manual of Discipline 8:25–26: "If his way is perfect in company, in Midrash, and in counsel"; cf. also *ibid.* 6:24 and 6:6). The nature of this Midrash is testified to by the explicit words: "When these become a community in Israel with such characteristics they separate themselves from the company of the wicked men to go thither to the wilderness to make clear there the way of the Lord, as is written [Isa. 40:3], 'and in the wilderness clear ye the way . . . make plain in the desert a highway for our God,' that being the Midrash of the Torah [which] he commanded through Moses, to do in accordance with all that is revealed in every era and as the prophets revealed through his holy spirit" (Manual of Discipline 8:12–16); i.e., the Midrash of the Torah is the lesson derived from the verse (4:21–5 5:11). A different method of interpretation is the **pesher,* although the Midrash could also contain *pesharim* (see 4Q 174 Florilegium, 1–2, I 14–19, in: J. M. Allegro, *Discoveries in the Judean Desert,* V: Qumran Cave 4, I (1968), p. 53f.). This technique of biblical exegesis which is largely similar to that customary among the Greek grammarians, the students of the classical texts of Homer, and among the Roman rhetoricians, the exponents of Roman law, is found among the Jews for the first time in the Dead Sea sect (see particularly Book of *Jubilees). Only in a later era was that method adopted (see **Derashah*) by the sages also (see *Shemaiah, *Avtalyon, *Hillel), although it is not quite clear how they arrived at it, whether by way of the Dead Sea sect—on the principle of the need to utilize the weapon of their opponents to smite against them—or directly from the Hellenistic world; it is possible that both elements played their part.

Midrashic Literature. Suggestions to the effect that the *Liber Antiquitatum Biblicarum* (pseudo-Philo) is a Midrash are without foundation. It is very possible that along with the *pesharim* the Dead Sea sect also produced complete works belonging to the class of Midrash, but from the works of the sect published up to 1971, no conclusions can be drawn. In fact, complete works belonging to the genre called Midrash are known only from rabbinic literature (on the question of committing *aggadot* to writing, see **Aggadah*). It is very possible that the earliest Midrash to come down is the Passover **Haggadah*, the earliest and chief element of which is a Midrash to Deuteronomy 26:5–8 (cf. Sif. Deut. 301). A great part of the midrashic *aggadah* of the tannaitic period is included side by side with the midrashic *halakhah* in the halakhic Midrashim. On the other hand there are no substantial midrashic *aggadot* from the tannaitic era, even though such works as the **Seder Olam Rabbah* and the **Baraita de-Melekhet ha-Mishkan* have a midrashic nature, nor is there extant any Midrash that can be regarded as an independent work which, it can be stated with certainty, was compiled in Babylon. The existing Babylonian Midrashim, even as more or less complete works, are embedded in the Babylonian Talmud (cf. the Midrash on the Book of Esther in Meg. 10b–17a, and on Lamentations in Sanh. 104a–b), and both in quantity and quality (form, style, and technique) these Midrashim are clearly much inferior to those compiled in Ereẓ Israel; in addition, more than half of the material in them originated in Ereẓ Israel.

From the point of view of the period of their arrangement and collection the aggadic Midrashim can be divided into three groups: early, middle, and late. The determination of the time of the editing and arranging of the various Midrashim is by no means a simple matter. It is nearly impossible to determine with even approximate certainty the period when a Midrash or aggadic work was compiled (see **Pirkei de-R. Eliezer*). However, it is possible to arrive at a relative date, that is, to determine the relation of a particular Midrash to others (see the table below). To do this one cannot rely on the historical allusions alone or merely on the names of the sages mentioned in the Midrash, nor can one rely on the first mentions of the Midrash and its first citations, since all the Midrashim contain much material from different and extended eras. The lack of historical allusions after a definite period do not suffice to testify to its compilation immediately after that period, just as the lack of mention of a Midrash and of its citation until a certain period does not prove that it was edited at the date nearest to the beginning of that period. In neither case can one rely on the *argumentum a silentio*. A more reliable method for determining priority and lateness among Midrashim is the relationship between the various Midrashim—the use one makes of another—as well as their relationship to other sources. Thus, for instance, where Midrash A and Midrash B contain parallels, it is possible to determine whether A drew on B, or B on A, or whether both drew on a third common source, extant or not. After one arrives by use of this method, though with great caution, at a determination of precedence, it becomes clear that other additional indications exist (literary forms, language, style, etc.).

The Early Midrashim (the Classical Amoraic Midrashim). This period, from which it seems only seven Midrashim have come down, is the golden age of the aggadic Midrashim. The most developed and perfect literary forms and constructions are already found in the oldest aggadic Midrash, **Genesis Rabbah*, proving that many generations of development preceded the literary crystallization. Since in general such perfect and developed literary constructions and forms are found neither in the halakhic Midrashim nor in their aggadic section (although here and there mere beginnings can be found), it is probable that the main development of the literary forms came in the amoraic era. Toward the close of this period the assembling, collecting, and editing was begun.

Among its most perfect forms, one should mention the classical proem at the beginning of a complete Midrash or of a chapter, which served fundamentally as the introduction to a homily delivered in public. The classical proem is a prelude to a homily on a certain verse by citing a verse from another source (in most cases from another book, or even from a different section of the Bible, usually the Hagiographa) and connecting it with the chief verse of the homily, the proem concluding with the verse with which the homily itself begins. Thus, for example, the proem to Lamentations 1:1 begins with a verse from the Pentateuch, while the proems to the Pentateuch Midrashim open with a verse usually from the Hagiographa. The proem, scarcely found in the tannaitic literature, was greatly developed and perfected in the time of the *amoraim*, in order to attract, stimulate, and rouse the curiosity of the audience and to emphasize the unity of the biblical books. When gathering and assembling the material the compilers and editors of the Midrashim followed the method of the actual preachers of the homilies and placed the proems at the beginning of the Midrashim and of the various sections. They did not always have proems readily available and in consequence created artificial proems themselves (combining different sayings and a number of homilies together). Sometimes they greatly enlarged the proems so that a simple proem became compound, i.e., it included a number of homilies independent in themselves. Classical proems in their pure form are almost wholly confined to the early Midrashim: *Genesis Rabbah; Leviticus Rabbah; Lamentations Rabbah; Esther Rabbah I; *Pesikta de-Rav Kahana; Song of Songs Rabbah;* and *Ruth Rabbah*. These Midrashim all consist of a collection of homilies, sayings, and *aggadot* of the *amoraim* (and also of the *tannaim*) in Galilean Aramaic and rabbinical Hebrew, but they also include many Greek words.

It seems that all these Midrashim, which are not mentioned in the Babylonian Talmud, were edited in Ereẓ Israel in the fifth and sixth centuries C.E. Two types can be distinguished: exegetical and homiletical. The exegetical Midrash (*Genesis Rabbah, Lamentations Rabbah*, et al.) is a Midrash to one of the books of the Bible, containing comments on the whole book—on each chapter, on every verse, and at times even on every word in the verse. The homiletical Midrash is either a Midrash to a book of the Pentateuch in which only the first verse (or verses) of the weekly portion is expounded (in accordance with the early *triennial cycle that was current in Ereẓ Israel, e.g., **Leviticus Rabbah*), or a Midrash that is based only on the biblical and prophetic reading of special Sabbaths and festivals, in which, also, only the first verses are expounded (eg., *Pirkei de-Rav Kahana*). In both cases, in contrast to the exegetical Midrashim, the homiletical Midrashim contain almost no short homilies or dicta on variegated topics, but each chapter (or section) constitutes a collection of homilies and sayings on one topic that seem to combine into one long homily on the specific topic.

The Difference Between the Early Midrashim and Later Midrashim. In the Midrashim of the middle period a decline is already discernible in the developed literary constructions and forms, especially in the proem, which is not the classical proem but merely an inferior and artificial imitation. After the Muslim conquest there is a gradual strengthening in the influence of the pseudepigraphic and the apocalyptic literature of the Second Temple era (see *Apocrypha and Pseudepigrapha), which had been disregarded by the talmudic rabbis (particularly because of the controversy with Christianity; see *Church Fathers). This influence is apparent both in content and form. In content, there is an increase not only in homilies which refer to angels and demons, the garden of Eden and hell, but even complete topics from apocalyptic literature. In form, there is an

Table of the *Midreshei Aggadah* according to types and periods.

Aggadic Works	Midrashim	Date C.E.	The Era
	Genesis Rabbah	400–500	Classical Amoraic Midrashim of the Early Period (400–640)
	Leviticus Rabbah		
	Lamentations Rabbah		
	Esther Rabbah I		
Apocalyptic and Eschatological Midrashim	*Pesikta de-Rav Kahana*	500–640	
	Songs Rabbah		
	Ruth Rabbah		
Megillat Antiochus	Targum Sheni	640–900	The Middle Period (640–1000)
Midrash Petirat Moshe ("Death of Moses")	Midrash Esfah		
Tanna de-Vei Eliyahu ("Seder Eliyahu")	Midrash Proverbs		
Pirkei de-R. Eliezer	Midrash Samuel		
Midrash Agur (called "Mishnat R. Eliezer")	Ecclesiastes Rabbah		
Midrash Yonah	Midrash Ḥaserot vi-Yterot		
Midrash Petirat Aharon	*Deuteronomy Rabbah*		
Divrei ha-Yamim shel Moshe	*Tanḥuma*		
Otiyyot de-R. Akiva	*Tanḥuma (Buber)*		
Midrash Sheloshah ve-Arba'ah	*Numbers Rabbah II*		
Midrash Eser Galuyyot	*Pesikta Rabbati*	Tanḥuma Midrash (Yelammedenu) (775–900)	
Midrash va-Yissa'u	*Exodus Rabbah II*		
	Va-Yeḥi Rabbah		
	The manuscripts of the Tanḥuma Yelammedenu Midrashim		
Throne and Hippodromes of Solomon	Midrash Tehillim I	900–1000	
Midreshei Ḥanukkah	Exodus Rabbah I		
Midreshei Yehudith	*Aggadat Bereshit*		
Midrash Hallel	Aggadat Shir ha-Shirim (Zuta)		
Midrash Tadshe	Ruth Zuta		
	Ecclesiastes Zuta		
	Lamentations Zuta		
Midrash Aseret ha-Dibberot	Midrash Shir ha-Shirim	1000–1100	The Late Period (1000–1200)
Midrash Konen	Abba Guryon		
Midrash Avkir	Esther Rabbah II		
Alphabet of Ben Sira	Midrash Tehillim II		
Midrash va-Yosha			
Sefer ha-Yashar			
Pesikta Ḥadta	Panim Aḥerim le-Esther (version 1)	1100–1200	
Midrash Temurah	▼ Lekaḥ Tov (c. 1110)		
	Midrash Aggadah, Genesis Rabbati, Numbers Rabbah I } all based on the work of Moshe ha-Darshan		
	▼ Yalkut Shimoni	1200–1300	The Period of Yalkutim (anthologies) 1200–1550
	▼ Midrash ha-Gadol	1300–1400	
	▼ Yalkut Makhiri		
	▼ Ein Ya'akov	1400–1550	
	▼ Haggadot ha-Talmud		

Notes: Names in italics are homiletical Midrashim; those marked by ▼ are anthologies; the rest are exegetical.

increase in the type of aggadic work which does not belong to the genre of Midrash at all. This type is not a compilation but a unified work impressed with the seal of the author, who is a narrator but chooses to attribute his words to the ancients and to ascribe to them statements which they never made (see **Tanna de-Vei Eliyahu*). The increase of pseudepigraphic matter can also be seen in authentic Midrashim. In contrast to the early Midrashim there was also an increase of Midrashim and aggadic works in which the *aggadah* is connected with *halakhah* in a variety of forms, some of which are merely transferred from Second Temple literature (e.g., *Pirkei de-R. Eliezer*) and some are the result of internal development by the sages (e.g., *Tanḥuma Yelammedenu*). In addition there is also a difference in language. The Galilean Aramaic of the early Midrashim progressively disappears, as does rabbinical Hebrew. Instead there is progressive use of artificial Hebrew, apparently pure and polished and becoming freer from the influences of Aramaic or the admixture of Greek words.

The Middle Period. To the period from the Muslim conquest (c. 640 C.E.) to the end of the tenth century belong many variegated midrashic and aggadic works. In addition to the exegetical and homiletical types of Midrash, the above-mentioned composition by a single person belongs to this period. The most important group of Midrashim of this period—all of which are homiletical—are those of the **Tanḥuma Midrash (Yelammedenu)* group in which the old and the new are used indiscriminately. Of the exegetical Midrashim, particular mention may be made of *Ecclesiastes Rabbah, Midrash Samuel, Midrash Proverbs* (greatly influenced by the apocalyptic and *Heikhalot* literatures), *Midrash Tehillim I, Exodus Rabbah I,* and the series of smaller *Midrashim *(Midreshei Zuta)* to four of the five *scrolls. In all these too, marks of the old and the new, both in content and in form, appear together. Among the aggadic works the most important are: *Seder Eliyahu Rabbah* and *Seder Eliyahu Zuta; Pirkei de-R. Eliezer* (compiled apparently close to 750); *Midrash Agur,* also called *Mishnat R. Eliezer;* and a further series of smaller compositions. In most of them external influences from the Muslim *(Pirkei de-R. Eliezer)* or Byzantine (*The Throne and Hippodrome of Solomon,* etc.) eras can be seen.

The Late Period. To the period of the 11th and 12th centuries belong the very latest Midrashim. Of these special mention should be made of *Midrash Abba Guryon, Esther Rabbah II, Midrash Tehillim II,* and the series from the school of *Moses ha-Darshan that already border on the anthologies with regard to their period of composition as well as to content. In these Midrashim there is hardly a trace of even an imitation of the classical proem, the Hebrew is completely medieval, and the pseudepigraphic influence both in content and form is still more pronounced. Among the aggadic works of this period particular mention must be made of the *Sefer ha-Yashar* (see *Midrashim, Smaller in supplementary entries, vol. 16) where the Muslim influence is most recognizable.

The Yalkutim (Anthologies). From the beginning of the 12th century, scholars in various countries assembled anthologies from various Midrashim and aggadic works. To these belong such works as the **Midrash Lekaḥ Tov* (or the *Pesikta Zutarta*) to the Pentateuch and the five *scrolls (of Tobiah b. Eliezer); the **Yalkut Shimoni* to the whole of the Bible (assembled in Germany at the beginning of the 13th century); **Midrash ha-Gadol* to the Pentateuch and scrolls; and the **Yalkut Makhiri* to various biblical books. Anthologies of the *aggadot* in the Babylonian and Jerusalem Talmuds were also collected, especially close to the beginning of the age of printing. Most of the anthologies quote their sources with the original wording and indicate them (an exception being the *Midrash ha-Gadol*).

Bibliography: Zunz-Albeck, Derashot; H. L. Strack, *Introduction to the Talmud and Midrash* (1945), pt. 2; A. G. Wright, *The Literary Genre Midrash* (1967); J. Bowker, *The Targums and Rabbinic Literature, and introduction to Jewish interpretations of Scripture* (1969); G. Vermes, *Scripture and Tradition in Judaism* (1961); Ginzberg, Legends; S. M. Lehrman, *The World of the Midrash* (1961). [M.D.H.]

MIDRASH ASERET HA-DIBBEROT (Heb. מִדְרַשׁ עֲשֶׂרֶת הַדִּבְּרוֹת; "Midrash of the Ten Commandments"), a collection of stories, occasionally connected by short homiletic passages, from the geonic period. Various scholars have ascribed different dates to it, ranging from the seventh century to the 11th. The collection cannot be dated later than the 11th century because in that century both Rabbi *Nissim of Kairouan and later the anonymous collector of the legends published by M. Gaster as *Sefer ha-Ma'asiyyot, The Ancient Collections of Agadoth. The Sefer ha-Ma'asiyyot and Two Facsimiles* (1894) made use of stories included in it. The work was apparently composed at the beginning of the geonic period, but later stories were added and have created confusion regarding both the number of stories included and the structure of the book as it appears in the several printed versions and the 20 extant manuscripts.

The collection was called a "Midrash" although its contents do not justify the name. It is basically a narrative work, one of the first medieval Hebrew works in the field of fiction. Its treatment of the midrashic material can be described as revolutionary: whereas traditional Midrashim place primary importance on homiletic material with only occasional use of stories, this work is primarily composed of stories, with the homiletic passages relegated to secondary importance. This stress on the fictional element is one of the characteristics of the new attitude toward the story introduced in medieval times (see *Fiction).

The work, which is based on the Ten Commandments, is correspondingly divided into ten parts. However, there is not always a close connection between the midrashic story and the commandment on which it is supposed to be based. This explains the material occasionally introduced into a story to create the impression of such a connection. In some versions the work is called *Midrash shel Shavu'ot* or *Haggadah le-Shavu'ot,* leading one to believe that it was used on Shavuot, the festival on which the receiving of the Ten Commandments is celebrated. However, there is no proof that any Jewish community ever used this work during Shavuot. Noy (see bibl.) concludes plausibly that the arbitrary connection between the *Midrash Aseret ha-Dibberot* and the commandments and Shavuot is merely an attempt to give a religious veneer to a collection of essentially secular stories which had no other purpose than to entertain.

Some of the stories in the collection are originally found in the Talmud and represent a medieval retelling of the talmudic *aggadah.* Others are derived from more ancient sources, like the Apocrypha and Pseudepigrapha: the story of Judith is told in a different version (without mentioning her name), and the story of the woman and her seven sons from the Book of Maccabees is also retold. However, most of the stories are folktales, either Jewish in origin or Jewish versions of international folktales found in a variety of versions in many languages (Noy lists among them the international types Aarne-Thompson 976, 670, 899, 2040, and others). Some of these stories are still current today among oral storytellers.

The number of stories composing the collection differs from version to version, some containing no more than 17 and others nearly 30. One manuscript (Parma 473) has 44 stories. As there are some which appear in only one version, the total number of stories connected with this work is over 50. A large number of stories (12) are concerned with the commandment "Thou shalt not commit adultery"; an erotic element is also found in stories related to other commandments. Women, frequently courageous and devout, are the heroines of many of the stories. From the religious point of view, the stories seem to imply an extreme devotion to the observance of the commandments, far beyond that required by the *halakhah.* The collection can also be described, therefore, as one of the earliest ethical works written in the Middle Ages.

Bibliography: D. Noy, in: *Fourth World Congress of Jewish Studies, Papers,* 2 (1968), 353–5 (Heb.); A. Jellinek, *Beit ha-Midrash,* 1 (1938), 62–92; M. M. Kasher (ed.), *Torah Shelemah,* 16 (1954), 189–99; J. L. Maimon (Fishman), *Haggadah shel Shavu'ot* (1924); M. Gaster, *The Exempla of the Rabbis* (1924), 142–8.

[Y.D.]

MIDRASH HA-GADOL (Heb. מִדְרַשׁ הַגָּדוֹל), a 13th-century rabbinic work on the Pentateuch, emanating from Yemen and consisting mainly of excerpts of older rabbinic texts of the talmudic period. The Midrash is anonymous, but it is now certain that it was written by a native of Aden, David b. Amram *Adani. Adani writes in clear, limpid Hebrew prose, introducing each weekly portion with a proem in rhymed verse. His work is of importance not only because of the author's original contributions to the literature of *halakhah* and *aggadah,* but also because of the multitude of extracts which he incorporates from ancient tannaitic Midrashim either unknown, or only partially known, from other sources. Thus, for instance, the *Midrash ha-Gadol* has enabled scholars to reconstruct large portions of the lost **Mekhilta of R. Simeon b. Yoḥai,* the **Sifrei Zuta,* and the *Mekhilta of R. Ishmael* on Deuteronomy. In addition, the *Midrash ha-Gadol* is valuable for the accuracy of its quotations from known sources, such as the Talmud and the Midrashim. Its readings have made it possible to correct the texts of older works which have survived in garbled form. The *Midrash ha-Gadol* is also notable for its contribution to the study of the code of *Maimonides, as it preserves many sources available to Maimonides but otherwise unknown. Not only does Adani frequently quote the code on which the Yemenites largely, if not exclusively, base their religious rulings, but his work enables students to reconstruct the older authorities on whom Maimonides had based his rulings. As a result, many difficulties which had puzzled students of Maimonides over the generations have been solved. The *Midrash ha-Gadol* first came to the notice of European scholars in the 19th century. The text was brought to Europe in manuscript in 1878 and sold to the Royal Library in Berlin by M. W. Shapira, whose name is associated with the alleged forgery known as the *Shapira fragments. Since then, other manuscripts have been acquired by the major libraries in the western world. Solomon Schechter in his edition of the *Avot de-Rabbi Nathan* (1887) was the first to make extensive use of this Midrash and he edited the first part (on Genesis) in 1902. Different parts of the Midrash have been edited by other scholars: Exodus by D. W. Hoffmann (1913–21), Leviticus by Nahum E. Rabinowitz (1932), and Numbers by Solomon Fisch (partial edition, 1940; reissued in complete form with Hebrew commentary and introduction, 2 vols., 1957–63). Genesis and Exodus were re-edited by M. Margulies (*Margalioth; 1947, 1956), and Numbers by Z. M. Rabinowitz (1967). There exist two Yemenite commentaries on the Midrash, one entitled *Segullat Yisrael* ("The Treasure of Israel"), dated 5440 (i.e., 1680) by R. Israel b. Solomon ha-Kohen, containing only a few interpretations and these of only slight value, and the other (anon.), the *Sefer ha-Margalit* ("Book of the Pearl"), containing explanations in Hebrew and Arabic of difficult words. The *Midrash ha-Gadol* is still a standard work of rabbinic homily for the Yemenite community and circulates widely in manuscript.

Bibliography: J. Riqueti, *Ḥokhmat ha-Mishkan* (Mantua, 1676), 5, 6, 13; S. A. Poznański, in: HHY, 3 (1886), 1–22; S. Schechter, *Avot de-Rabbi Nathan* (1887), introd.; D. Z. Hoffman (ed.), *Mekhilta de-Rabbi Shimon ben Yoḥai* (1905); idem, *Midrash Tanna'im,* 2 vols. (1908–09); S. Liebermann, *Midreshei Teiman* (1940); S. Fisch, *Midrash ha-Gadol* (1940), 1–136; M. Kasher, *Ha-Rambam ve-ha-Mekhilta de-Rashbi* (1943), introd.; M. Margulies, *Midrash ha-Gadol, Shemot* (1956), 5–15; Y. L. Nahum, *Mi-Ẓefunot Yehudei Teiman* (1962), 181–205; Y. Ratzaby, in: *Tarbiz,* 34 (1965), 263–71; Z. M. Rabinowitz, *Midrash ha-Gadol, Ba-Midbar* (1967), 5–16.

[S.F.]

MIDRASHIM, SMALLER. See Supplementary Entries.

MIDRASH LEKAḤ TOV (מִדְרַשׁ לֶקַח טוֹב), a late 11th-century Midrash on the Pentateuch and Five Scrolls by Tobias b. Eliezer. The author called it *Lekaḥ Tov* ("good doctrine") on the basis of its opening verse (Prov. 4:2): "For I give you good doctrine" which he chose with allusion to his name (for the same reason he begins his interpretations of the weekly portions of Scripture and of the Scrolls with a verse containing the word *tov,* "good"). The book was called *Pesikta* by later scholars, and also, in error, *Pesikta Zutarta.* Tobias lived in the Balkans (Buber), and his Midrash contains allusions to contemporary historical events and specific reference to the martyrs of the First Crusade of 1096 (in the portion *Emor* and in his commentary on the verse "Therefore do the maidens love thee": Song 1:3). Zunz defined the Midrash as a composition which is "half exegesis and half *aggadah,*" but even in the "half *aggadah*" the exegetical commentary aspect is conspicuous. Tobias took the ideas he needed from the Babylonian Talmud, the halakhic Midrashim, and the early aggadic Midrashim (including some no longer extant), as well as from the early mystical literature and used them as the basis of his Midrash. He did not however quote them literally nor as a rule did he mention their authors. He translated Aramaic passages as well as Greek and Latin terms into Hebrew; abridged the language of the early authors; and even combined their sayings and refashioned them. He tended to quote scriptural verses from memory, which explains the many variations from the standard text.

The work also contains hundreds of explanations by Tobias himself, some in the style of the midrashic literature and some giving the literal meaning. He expounds the **keri* and the **ketiv,* the **masorah,* **gematriot,* and **notarikon* and also gives many mnemotechnical devices in the manner of the rabbis. His literal explanations are based on the rules of grammar, vocalization, accentuation, etc. It is noteworthy that he explains anthropomorphic verses and statements as parables and frequently repeats: "The Torah speaks in the language of men." This tendency is without doubt an aspect of his violent struggle with the Karaites which finds expression in the Midrash in many places. His practical aim is also conspicuous when he deals with certain *halakhot* whose performance was apparently neglected in his time. Tobias' Midrash was frequently quoted soon after it was written, but until the end of the last century only the *Lekaḥ Tov* to Leviticus, Numbers, and Deuteronomy had been published (first edition, Venice, 1746). It was published in full, Genesis and Exodus by S. Buber (1884), Leviticus, Numbers, and Deuteronomy by Meir Katzenellenbogen of Padua (1884) from the Venice edition with corrections; The Song of Songs was published by A. W. Greenup (1909); Ruth by I. Bamberger (1887), Lamentations by J. Nacht (1895), and again by Greenup (1908); Ecclesiastes by G. Finberg (1904); Esther by Buber in the *Sifrei de-Aggadata al Megillat Esther* (1886).

Bibliography: S. Buber, *Midrash Lekah Tov* (1884), introd.; Zunz-Albeck, Derashot, 145f., 441–3; L. Ginzberg, *Ginzei Schechter*, 1 (1928), 253–97. [Y.El.]

MIDRASH PROVERBS or **AGGADAT PROVERBS** (Heb. מִדְרָשׁ מִשְׁלֵי ; cf. Arukh. s.v. *nakad* 3), Midrash on the Book of Proverbs, also frequently but wrongly referred to as Midrash *Shoher Tov*. The Midrash is distinguished by an exegetical style demonstrated both in the choice of its contents and the manner in which they are quoted. The compiler selected passages which largely explained the texts of Proverbs according to the literal meaning, and very frequently reworded them. As a result several of the characteristics of the early Midrash disappear and the exegetical method prevails. There are few proems, introductory words are rare, the few statements depend upon abstruse allusions, and the discussions in general are brief. A departure from the method of the early Midrashim is further conspicuous in two respects: in the formulation of disputes, and in the ascription of dicta to early scholars. The sources of the Midrash are the Mishnah, Tosefta, Mekhilta, and Sifrei. A phenomenon worthy of mention is the compiler's use of *Heikhalot* literature (to which Zunz drew attention; see *Merkabah Mysticism). The editor also made use of amoraic Midrashim, *Genesis Rabbah, Leviticus Rabbah, Pesikta de-Rav Kahana, Songs Rabbah,* and *Ecclesiastes Rabbah,* and he also knew the two versions of *Avot de-Rabbi Nathan.* He had no acquaintance with the Jerusalem Talmud, although there are numerous quotations from the Babylonian Talmud. From this, Buber concluded that it was compiled in Babylon, and not in Italy as claimed by Zunz, and conjectured from this and the quotations from it in geonic works of the eighth century, that it was edited after the final editing of the Babylonian Talmud. Although the quotations in the geonic writings are doubtful (Albeck) it is nevertheless certain that it cannot be as late as the end of the geonic period, despite the contrary view of Zunz.

The Midrash in its present state is incomplete. Parts of sections and whole sections are missing. The last third is particularly fragmentary, though the discussion of the last chapter (31) is given in detail. More Midrashim to this chapter are extant, namely *Midrash Eshet Hayil* (in S. A. Wertheimer, *Battei Midrashot*, 2 (1953²), 146–50); *Midrash Eshet Hayil* in the *Midrash ha-Gadol* to Genesis (ed. by M. Margulies (1947), 368–74); and L. Ginsberg published a fragment from a new edition of *Midrash Proverbs* (*Ginzei Schechter*, 1 (1928), 163–8). These apparently reflect different editions of the Midrash. Another version of the *Midrash Eshet Hayil,* which was collated in 1512 by Moses b. Joseph Albiladah of Yemen, is based upon ancient sources, and shows affinities in some details with the Ginsberg version (published in J. L. Nahum, *Mi-Zefunot Yehudei Teiman* (1962), 209–22). The most important printed editions of the Midrash are Constantinople 1517, Venice, 1547, and Prague, 1613. Subsequently the printers relied chiefly upon the Prague edition, which relied upon the Venice edition (whose reading is doubtful, as Buber has shown), and added to it the glosses, *Ot Emet*, of Meir b. Samuel Benveniste. In 1893 S. Buber published a new edition of great value based upon three manuscripts, as well as the Constantinople edition. Additional manuscripts of the Midrash are now available.

Bibliography: Zunz-Albeck, Derashot, 133, 412f.; S. Buber (ed.), *Midrash Mishlei* (1893), introd. [Y.El.]

MIDRASH SAMUEL (Heb. מִדְרָשׁ שְׁמוּאֵל, *Midrash Shemu'el*), the only Midrash to a book of the early prophets. It contains 32 chapters—24 on I Samuel and eight on II Samuel—which appear to be the contents original to the time of composition. The Midrash, a compilation chiefly from early works, contains tannaitic material from the Mishnah, Tosefta, *Mekhilta*, and *Sifrei*, as well as amoraic material from the early aggadic Midrashim: *Genesis Rabbah, Leviticus Rabbah, Lamentations Rabbah,* and the *Pesikta de-Rav Kahana.* The author also included material from later Midrashim: *Song of Songs Rabbah, Ecclesiastes Rabbah, Ruth Rabbah, Esther Rabbah, Pesikta Rabbati,* and the *Tanhuma* Midrashim (the question of whether he made use of the *Midrash Tehillim* is still unresolved). The Midrash also contains original material, however, both early, dating from the *tannaim* and the first *amoraim,* and late. The state of the Midrash seems to indicate that it is based upon an earlier Midrash on Samuel, with additions by the editor, mostly from existing material but also some of his original interpretation. Among indications of the editing are the interlacing of exegetical and homiletical matter, which is uncommon in early Midrashim. The Midrash however is, in the main, homiletical. Other evidence of later editing is to be seen in the artificial character of most of its 14 proems, as well as the incorporation of homilies which are irrelevant to the scriptural verse or the subject matter under discussion—apparently resulting from routine copying of the sources (Albeck).

Nothing is known of the author. Zunz's assumption that the work is to be dated no earlier than the 11th century appears probable. There is overwhelming evidence, however, that it was edited in Palestine. Its sources, as has been stated, are Palestinian, as are all the *amoraim* mentioned in it. It contains no passages from the Babylonian Talmud. The language contains elements from the Palestinian Midrashim and it contains many Greek words such as are found in the Palestinian Midrashim. Both the conditions reflected by the Midrash and the problems dealt with point clearly to a Palestinian background. Rashi was the first to mention and quote the Midrash, and it is frequently mentioned by later authorities (Buber, introd., p. 28). It is referred to by many names: *Midrash Samuel, Aggadat Samuel, Midrash Et La'asot* (from its opening words, Ps. 119:126). It is also sometimes erroneously referred to as *Shoher Tov,* the name of *Midrash Tehillim,* together with which it was published (Venice, 1546). The book was first published in Constantinople in 1517, the Venice edition being the second. It was published a third time in Prague in 1613 with the commentary of Isaac b. Samson Katz, son-in-law of *Judah Loew b. Bezalel of Prague, and has been frequently reprinted since. The best edition is that of S. Buber (Cracow, 1893) based on the printed editions of the Parma manuscript. For a commentary to *Avot* of the same name see Samuel ben Isaac *Uceda.

Bibliography: Zunz-Albeck, Derashot, 133, 413–4; S. Buber, *Midrash Shemu'el* (1893), 7–40. [Y.El.]

MIDRASH TANNAIM (Heb. מִדְרָשׁ תַּנָּאִים ; *Mekhilta* on Deuteronomy), a tannaitic work which is a collection of *beraitot,* comprising fragments of a halakhic Midrash on Deuteronomy. D. Hoffmann conjectured that in ancient times there was an halakhic Midrash, also on Deuteronomy, of the school of R. Ishmael, similar to *Mekhilta of R. Ishmael.* Indeed, in the Cairo **Genizah* several fragments of such a Midrash were found, which were published by S. Schechter (in *JQR,* 16 (1904), 446–52, 695–9). Later Hoffmann issued an edition of *Midrash Tannaim* on Deuteronomy, with an introduction and notes (1908–09), compiled from *Midrash ha-Gadol* on Deuteronomy, with the addition of the above-mentioned *genizah* fragments. Since, however, the author of *Midrash ha-Gadol* did not indicate his sources, and even adapted, abbreviated, and expanded, subdivided, and combined them, Hoffmann's edition has to be treated with great caution. Still later, yet another *genizah* fragment was discovered which was likewise published by Schechter (in *Festschrift I. Lewy* (1911) Heb. pt. 187–92). The fragments, totaling six folios, constitute only an extremely small part of the lost Midrash, which was subdivided into sections, and the sections into *halakhot*. More cannot be said of its structure, nor is the date of its redaction or even its original name known. It is, however, clear that it belonged to a type A of the halakhic Midrashim (see **Midreshei Halakhah*).

Bibliography: D. Hoffmann (ed.), *Midrash Tanna'im* (1908–09), introd.; Ḥ. Albeck, *Untersuchungen ueber die halakischen Midraschim* (1927), 156f.; J. N. Epstein, in: *Abhandlungen . . . H. P. Chajes* (1933), 60–71 (Heb. pt.); Epstein, Tanna'im, 631–3; Ḥ. Albeck, *Mavo la-Talmudim* (1969), 84. [M.D.H.]

MIDRASH TEHILLIM (Midrash Psalms; Heb. מִדְרַשׁ תְּהִלִּים), an aggadic Midrash on the Psalms, called also *Aggadat Tehillim*, and *Shoḥer Tov* because of its opening verse, Proverbs 11:27. The Midrash embraces most of the Psalms. Despite the fact that most manuscripts and printed editions, as well as the copy that was before the author of the *Yalkut Shimoni*, lack homilies for Psalms 96, 97, and 98, they are included in the glosses of Abraham Provençal and in some manuscripts (see Jellinek and Buber). In several manuscripts and printed editions there is no Midrash to Psalm 15 but the Midrash to it is added to that of Psalm 14. The only psalms to which there is definitely no Midrash are 123 and 131. Zunz rightly conjectured that the Midrash on Psalms 119–50 differs from that to the preceding Psalms. From the differences of language and subject matter, the definite omission of the names of the authors, and the expository character of this section, he came to the conclusion that it was of later date than the earlier portion.

Zunz's claim was verified through the researches of Buber. In six manuscripts and in the edition printed in Constantinople (1512), the Midrash concludes with Psalm 118. Only two manuscripts and those before Provençal contain a short fragment of a homily on Psalm 119. Buber also showed that the homilies of Psalms 122–137 were copied from the *Yalkut*, and since the latter contains no homilies to Psalms 123 and 131, these are also wanting in the Midrash. Zunz concluded from an examination of the sources, the methods employed, linguistic usages, and details of its contents (see especially Mid. Ps. 63:2; 6:2) that the first part is also late and that it was edited in Italy in the last centuries of the geonic period. From his examination of the manuscripts, Buber claimed that the original work had been added to by later copyists, and that its "youthfulness" is the result of these interpolations. According to him, Zunz erred in his identification of historical allusions in the work and was misled by errors in the names of persons and places (see his notes to Mid. Ps. 9:8). In his opinion the language of the original portions of the Midrash, its style, the manner of its homilies, and the *amoraim* mentioned in it, as well as the sources upon which it draws, are evidence of its antiquity and its Palestinian origin.

Buber, however, was mistaken, as has been shown by Ḥ. Albeck, who proved that the author of this Midrash also drew upon late Ereẓ Israel Midrashim. Albeck also bases his argument for late dating on an examination of the form of the proems and points to the signs of deterioration in them: the connection with the verses being interpreted is faulty, the terminology is inconsistent, the proems are mainly anonymous, and their formulation is at times defective. Albeck claims, furthermore, on the basis of the many differences between the manuscripts, the many additions in several of them, the errors in their arrangement, and the significant differences in the repetition of the same homily, that the present *Midrash Tehillim* consists of groups of Midrashim to the Psalms. This too is the reason, in his view, for the lack of uniformity in the methods of interpreting the Psalms: some are interpreted at length, every single verse being discussed, while in others homilies are found for only a few verses. It may be concluded, therefore, that the period of composition of the Midrash extended over some centuries. Obviously it is not identical with the *Midrash Tehillim* which Simeon b. Judah ha-Nasi taught Ḥiyya (Kid. 33a; and see also Av. Zar. 19a), even though it apparently contains material from as early as this period (third century). Its concluding section is definitely from the 13th century, and not as Mann suggested, that parts of it derive from an early "short" Midrash to Psalms.

Despite the lack of uniformity in this Midrash, its fragmentary nature on the one hand and the many additions to it on the other, it has retained many fine qualities and is one of the most beautiful in aggadic literature: it has exalted language and colorful themes, cites many stories and parables, and makes extensive and tasteful use of the hermeneutics of aggadic interpretation. L. Rabinowitz, adapting the main theory of Mann in his "The Bible as Read and Preached in the Old Synagogue," claims that one could assume a triennial reading of the Psalms paralleling that of the Torah, and from this it is possible to understand the contents of its homilies. This claim, however, is still far from being proved.

The Midrash has been frequently published: Constantinople, 1512, Venice 1546, Prague 1613, etc. Of great value are the Warsaw editions of 1873 and 1875, with the commentary of Aaron Moses Padua; the 1891 Vilna edition of Buber, for which he utilized eight manuscripts and the glosses of Abraham Provençal; and the English edition of Braude (1959). Important fragments of the *Midrash Tehillim* were published by: A. Jellinek, *Beit ha-Midrash*, 5 (1873), 70–86 (glosses by A. Provençal); J. Mann, in: HUCA, 14 (1939), 303–32; and M. Arzt, in: *Alexander Marx Jubilee Volume* (1950), Hebrew section, 49–73.

Bibliography: S. Buber (ed.), *Midrash Tehillim* (1891), introd.; Zunz-Albeck, Derashot, 131f., 407–12; L. Rabinowitz, in: JQR, 26 (1935–36), 349–68; W. G. Braude (trans.), *The Midrash on Psalms*, 1 (1959), introd. [Y.El.]

MIDRASH VA-YISSA'U (Heb. מִדְרַשׁ וַיִּסָּעוּ), a medieval Midrash in Hebrew about the legendary wars of Jacob and his sons. The name derives from the first word of Genesis 35:5, with which the Midrash opens. The original name of the work is probably "The Book of Wars of the Sons of Jacob," a name which is preserved in Naḥmanides' commentary on the Book of Genesis (to Gen. 34:13), the earliest reference to the existence of the legend. The small book contains three chapters: The first describes a war of Jacob and his sons against the army of Ninevites, who came to Palestine to subdue the whole world. Characteristic of this chapter are exaggerations which are lacking in the two other chapters, a style possibly influenced by the Book of Josippon. This chapter does not appear in some manuscripts, although two of them consist of it only, which indicates that it was possibly a later addition to the Midrash. The second chapter describes the wars of the sons of Jacob against the Amorite kings seven years after Jacob and his family withdrew from Shechem (Gen. 35:5) because of the defilement of Dinah and the events which followed. The story of the victory over the Amorite kings is opposed to that of the biblical narrative, where Jacob fears that he will be outnumbered and destroyed. However, the story of the victory is hinted at in Genesis 48:22, a verse which is quoted to this effect in the Midrash. The third chapter describes the war between Jacob and his sons and Esau and his sons, in which Esau is killed by Jacob and Esau's descendants become tributary to Jacob's family.

The medieval Hebrew book (with the exception of the first chapter) is a free translation from Greek (or Latin) of an old Jewish (Hebrew or Aramaic) text from the time of the Second Temple, a text which was also used by the authors of the Book of Jubilees and the Testaments of the Patriarchs: the wars against the Amorites are narrated in the Testament of Judah, chapters 3–7, and in an abbreviated form in Jubilees 34:1–9; and a parallel narrative to the war against Esau and his sons is preserved in Jubilees 37 and 38:1–14, and in an abbreviated form, in the Testament of Judah, chapter 9. The medieval *Midrash Va-Yissa'u* is of great importance for a reconstruction of the original ancient Jewish text. The ancient text, which was used by the Book of Jubilees and the extant Testament of Judah, and is the basis of chapters 2–3 of *Midrash Va-Yissa'u,* could have been a separate work. It seems more probable, however, that the common source of all three works, in their description of the war of Jacob and his sons against the Amorite kings and against Esau, was an older and more expanded form of the Testament of Judah than its extant form in the Testament of the Patriarchs, a situation similar to that of the Testament of *Levi and the Testament of *Naphtali. Some scholars see in the description of the wars against the Amorites and Esau a tendentious projection into the biblical past of the wars of John Hyrcanus against the Samaritans and Edomites, the descendants of Esau, and a historical justification of these wars. *Midrash Va-Yissa'u* was used, expanded, and rewritten in the medieval *Sefer ha-Yashar* (Book of Jashar). A critical edition was published with an introduction by J. Z. Lauterbach in *Abhandlungen zur Erinnerung an H. P. Chajes* (1933, Heb. pt. 205–22).

Bibliography: S. Klein, in: ZDPV, 57 (1934), 7–27; A. Jellinek, *Beit ha-Midrash,* 3 (1938[2]), ix–xiv, 1–5; R. H. Charles (ed.), *The Greek Versions of the Testaments of the Twelve Patriarchs* (1908), li, 235–8; idem (ed.), *The Testaments of the Twelve Patriarchs* (1908), lxv, 69–79; idem (ed.), *The Book of Jubilees* (1902), 200–4, 214–21; Ginzberg, Legends, 5 (1925), 315f., 321f.; Y. M. Grintz, *Perakim be-Toledot Bayit Sheni* (1969), 105f., n. 2. [D.FL.]

MIDRESHEI HALAKHAH (Heb. מִדְרְשֵׁי הֲלָכָה; "Midrashim of the *halakhah*"), the appellation given to a group of tannaitic expositions on four books of the Pentateuch. Like many of the *Midreshei Aggadah* (see *Midrash) they consist of expositions of the biblical books chapter by chapter, verse by verse and even sometimes the individual words in the verse. The *Midreshei Halakhah* deal primarily with the *halakhah* to be derived from the Bible, even though they also contain *aggadah.* In fact, in those books in which the narrative element exceeds the legislative, there is sometimes more *aggadah* than *halakhah.* Since there is no legislation in the Book of Genesis, the *Midreshei Halakhah* are only on Exodus, Leviticus, Numbers, and Deuteronomy. All the *Midreshei Halakhah* are collections of **beraitot,* a part of the tannaitic literature, and their language, like the Mishnah and the Tosefta, is the Hebrew of the type employed by the sages.

At the beginning of modern research into the *Midreshei Halakhah,* about the middle of the 19th century, only four such works were known, one on each of the above-mentioned four books of the Pentateuch: the **Mekhilta of R. Ishmael* on Exodus, **Sifra* on Leviticus, **Sifrei Numbers,* and **Sifrei Deuteronomy.* At that time M. Friedmann (Ish-Shalom) called attention to an affinity between the *Mekhilta of R. Ishmael* and other works which had issued from R. Ishmael's *bet midrash.* Subsequently D. *Hoffmann pointed out four differences between two distinct types of *Midreshei Halakhah* (see table).

Division of Midreshei Halakhah according to Types.

	Type A ("*de-vei* R. Ishmael")	Type B ("*de-vei* R. Akiva")
Exodus	†*Mekhilta* (of *R. Ishmael)*	*Mekhilta* of *R. Simeon ben Yoḥai*
Leviticus	(fragments?)	†*Sifra*
Numbers	†*Sifrei* on Numbers	*Sifrei Zuta*
Deuteronomy	*Mekhilta* on Deuteronomy = *Midrash Tannaim*	†*Sifrei Deuteronomy*

The Midrashim that were known in the middle of the 19th century are marked with a †.

These four differences may be enumerated as follows: (1) Whereas the two Midrashim *Mekhilta of R. Ishmael* and *Sifrei Numbers* (type A) contain very many statements by *tannaim* known as the pupils of R. *Ishmael b. Elisha (such as R. Oshaiah and R. Jonathan), the names of these *tannaim* occur infrequently in the two Midrashim *Sifra* and *Sifrei* on Deuteronomy (type B), where the names of sages, known to be the pupils of R. *Akiva, are in the majority. (2) In the type A Midrashim there are many anonymous *beraitot* which are quoted elsewhere, mainly in the two Talmuds, in the name of a *tanna de-vei* ("of the school of") R. Ishmael. However, this is not the case with the type B Midrashim. (3) In the type A Midrashim extensive use was made of the hermeneutical rules and principles (see *Hermeneutics) characteristic of Ishmael and his *bet midrash,* whereas those characteristic of R. Akiva and his *bet midrash* are more frequently used in the type B Midrashim. (4) In the type A Midrashim the entire terminology is wholly different from that in the type B Midrashim (for example: *maggid [ha-katuv]* in contrast to *melammed;* and many others).

Accordingly, Hoffmann concluded that the *Midreshei Halakhah* are to be divided into two types, the one, type A, which came from R. Ishmael's *bet midrash,* the other, type B, which emanated from that of R. Akiva. Later when manuscript fragments, the remnants of other *Midreshei Halakhah* which had been lost, began to be discovered, Hoffmann on the basis of these differences was able to determine precisely to which family or type these fragments belonged and even to attempt to reconstruct them from later compilations of the Middle Ages. It also soon became evident that there had formerly existed two complete sets of tannaitic *Midreshei Halakhah* on all four books of the Pentateuch which contain *halakhah* (Exodus, Leviticus, Numbers, and Deuteronomy). As the entire set of the type B Midrashim was discovered *(Mekhilta of R. Simeon ben Yoḥai, *Sifrei Zuta),* it became possible to trace and identify remnants of the *Midreshei Halakhah* on Leviticus and Deuteronomy belonging to type A (see **Midrash Tannaim,* **Sifra*). The division laid down by Hoffmann became one of the cornerstones of the research into the literature of the sages, and his interpretation also (that is, the identification of type A as *de-Vei* R. Ishmael and type B as *de-Vei* R. Akiva) has been acepted since his time until the present time by almost all scholars.

Ḥ. Albeck, however, while accepting the actual division, disputed Hoffmann's interpretation. Of the four distinctive features which according to Hoffmann distinguish the two types, the first three—the frequency with which the names of the various sages are mentioned, the identification of the anonymous *beraitot,* and the use of hermeneutical rules and principles—are not absolute but only relative. Thus, for example, the *Mekhilta of R. Ishmael* also contains statements in the name of sages who were pupils of Akiva, although to a lesser extent than in the name of those who were pupils of Ishmael; conversely, the *Mekhilta of R. Simeon ben Yoḥai* also includes hermeneutical methods and principles characteristic of R. Ishmael's *bet midrash*, but to a lesser degree than those characteristic of R. Akiva's school. Only the fourth distinctive feature that distinguishes the two types—the different terminology—is absolute, for here it is not a question of a relatively greater or lesser frequency but an absolute difference (save for individual exceptions).

Albeck therefore came to the conclusion that since the entire identification of type A with *de-Vei* R. Ishmael and of type B with *de-Vei* R. Akiva is based only on criteria 1–3 (criterion 4 [terminology] has no relevance to the difference between R. Ishmael and his *bet midrash* and R. Akiva and his *bet midrash*), and since these criteria are themselves only relative, Hoffmann's identification has not been decisively proved. At most it may be said that the type A Midrashim contain a greater amount of material from R. Ishmael's *bet midrash*, and the type B Midrashim a greater amount from R. Akiva's *bet midrash*, but no more. Furthermore, the Midrashim of both types have much material in common. Thus the clear division into two distinct types is based only on different terminology, the work of redactors, compilers, and systematizers of the Midrashim, who flourished in the days of the *amoraim* (see later). According to Albeck, therefore, types A and B represent merely two different redactions produced in two different *battei midrash* having no connection with either R. Ishmael or R. Akiva. Albeck also, on the basis of the criterion of terminology, divides type B into two sub-types—the one, *Sifra* and *Sifrei Zuta*, the other, the *Mekhilta of R. Simeon ben Yoḥai* and *Sifrei Deuteronomy*—both of which, he holds, are of a later date. Albeck also investigated the relation of the extant *Midreshei Halakhah* to the Talmuds and found, as is the case also with the Tosefta, that the present *Midreshei Halakhah* were unknown to both the Jerusalem and the Babylonian Talmuds. Albeck therefore concluded that the arrangement and redaction of the *Midreshei Halakhah* are comparatively late, dating from the latter half of the fourth, the beginning of the fifth centuries C.E.

Bibliography: Epstein, Tannaim, 501 (partial bibl.), and ff.; Ḥ. Albeck, *Untersuchungen ueber die halakischen Midraschim* (1927); idem, *Mavo la-Talmudim* (1969), 79–113; D. Hoffmann, *Zur Einleitung in die halachischen Midraschim* (1886–88). [M.D.H.]

MIDSTREAM, U.S. Jewish monthly. *Midstream* was founded as a quarterly in 1955 by the Theodor Herzl Foundation with the object of creating a serious Zionist periodical that would have an intellectual impact upon American Jewish life. Under the editorship of Shlomo *Katz, the magazine has published articles and fiction of merit on various aspects of U.S. Jewry and Israel. In 1965 it became a monthly. Its circulation in 1970 was estimated at 9,000.

Bibliography: S. Katz (ed.), *The Midstream Reader* (1960).

[ED.]

MIEDZYRZEC PODLASKI (Pol. **Międzyrzec Podlaski**; called **Mezhirech** or **Mezrich** by the Jews), town in Lublin province, E. Poland. An organized Jewish community existed in the town from the middle of the 17th century. Between 1689 and 1692, the *parnasim* of the community of Miedzyrzec Podlaski waged a stubborn struggle against the leaders of the community of *Tykocin (Tiktin) for the hegemony over the Jewish communities in the vicinity of *Mielec. A magnificent synagogue, which was still standing in 1970, was erected in Miedzyrzec Podlaski at the beginning of the 18th century. The owners of the town during the 18th century, the Czartoryski family (see Adam *Czartoryski), encouraged Jews to settle in order to develop the town. At the fair held twice a year in the town, local Jewish merchants, as well as those from other towns, played an important role. In 1714 the community of Miedzyrzec Podlaski and the Jews of the surrounding villages which were under its jurisdiction paid 1,000 zlotys as poll tax. In 1759 a compromise was reached between the communities of Miedzyrzec Podlaski and *Lukow: the Jews living in the surrounding villages and townlets would pray in Miedzyrzec on the High Holidays and would also bury their dead there; they would pay their taxes one year to one community and the next year to the other. In the 19th century, during the period of Russian rule, there were no residence restrictions in Miedzyrzec Podlaski. Around the middle of the 19th century, the influence of Ḥasidism spread among the Jews there. At the time of the political agitation in Poland (1861), a Hebrew manifesto on the contemporary problems was circulated among the Jews of the town. In 1863 a number of the local Jewish craftsmen assisted the Polish rebels supplying them with equipment and food. During the second half of the 19th century, a Jewish working class emerged which found employment in the sawmills, the tanneries, the production of ready-made clothing, and hauling. The organized Jewish proletariat and youth participated in the 1905 revolution. At the end of 1918, a Jewish self-defense group was active in the town. Between the two world wars, branches of all the Jewish parties were established, as well as Jewish educational institutions (*Tarbut, CYSHO, Beth Jacob). During the 1920s a weekly, *Podlashier Lebn*, was published. [A.CY.]

Holocaust Period. Before the outbreak of World War II, there were about 12,000 Jews in the town and they constituted 75% of the total population. During the first year of Nazi occupation, about 4,000 Jews from other places were forced to settle there. In December 1939, 2,300 Jews from Nasielsk, Pultusk, Rupiń, and Serock were deported to Miedzyrzec Podlaski. In April 1940 over 1,000 Jews from Slovakia were deported there, followed by 600 Jews from Cracow, Mlama, and Mielec. In June 1940 about 2,300 men were deported to six forced labor camps organized in the vicinity of the town. Almost all of them perished. On Aug. 25–26, 1942, the first deportation to the *Treblinka death camp took place. Other deportations followed on Oct. 6–9, 1942, and Oct. 27 of that year. Over 11,000 Jews perished in these deportations, but hundreds succeeded in fleeing into the surrounding forests. Some of them organized small guerrilla units that operated in the vicinity.

In October 1942 the Germans issued a decree about the establishment of a ghetto in Miedzyrzec Podlaski. Jews who fled into the forests were encouraged to return and promised that no more deportations would take place. The Germans managed to concentrate over 4,000 Jews in the ghetto. In December 1942 about 500 of them were deported to the Trawniki concentration camp, where all of them perished. On May 2, 1943, the ghetto was liquidated and all its inmates were deported to the Treblinka death camp and exterminated there. Only about 200 Jews were left in a forced labor camp, but they too were executed on July 18, 1943, when the town was declared *judenrein*. After the liberation of the town in July 1944, 129 Jewish survivors settled there, but after a short time they left because of the inimical attitude of the local Polish population. Organizations of former residents of Miedzyrzec Podlaski are active in Israel, the United States, and Argentina. [S.KR.]

Bibliography: Halpern, Pinkas, index; Cracow, Archiwum PAN, 3795 (= C.A.H.J.P., HM 6739); B. Wasiutyński, *Ludność żydowska w Polsce w wiekach xix i xx* (1930), 35; A. Eisenbach et al. (1963), index. HOLOCAUST: J. Horn (ed.), *Mezrich Zamlung: Isum* (comps.), *Żydzi a powstanie styczniowe, materiały i dokumenty 10 Yortsayt* (1952).

MIELEC, town in Rzeszow province, S.E. Poland. The Jewish community of Mielec was first organized in the middle of the 17th century. The *Council of Four Lands decided in 1757 that the Mielec community should pay an annual tax of 1,200 zlotys to the *Opatow *kahal*. In 1765 there were 585 Jewish poll tax payers in Mielec and 326 in the surrounding villages; among the former were 12 tailors, three hatters, three bakers, two goldsmiths, five butchers, three *shoḥatim*, four musicians *(klezmer)*, and three jesters *(badḥanim)*. In the 19th century Mielec came under the influence of the Ḥasidim of *Chortkov and *Ropczyce and descendents of the *ẓaddik* of Ropczyce were rabbis there. The few wealthy Jews exported timber, dealt in grain, livestock, feathers, and building materials, and ran sawmills, but the majority engaged in petty trade, tailoring, shoemaking, smithery, and building. There were also some Jewish farmers in the nearby villages. An elementary school was established by the *Baron de Hirsch fund in 1900, as well as a Beth Jacob school for girls. In 1907 the Zionist association, Benei Yehudah, was founded. During the elections of 1907 and 1913 there were anti-Jewish riots in the town. In 1917 a "Borochov circle" was organized, as well as a Jewish library and sports clubs. The Jewish population of the town remained relatively static, increasing from 2,766 (56% of the total population) in 1880 to 2,819 (57%) in 1900 and 3,280 (53%) in 1910, then falling to 2,807 (50%) in 1920. Zionist parties, *He-Ḥalutz and *Agudat Israel, were active in Mielec between the two world wars.

[A.Cy.]

Holocaust Period. By September 1939 the population had reached 4,000. On Sept. 13, 1939, the eve of Rosh Ha-Shanah, the Germans set a synagogue aflame and pushed 20 persons into the burning building. Those who tried to escape were shot. German soldiers sent some Jews into the slaughterhouse and set it aflame. Then the soldiers entered the *mikveh* and murdered the Jews present. On Sept. 15, 1939 (second day of Rosh Ha-Shanah), a second synagogue was set aflame. Jews suffered from administrative and economic restrictions, from the local Germans living at Czermin, and from forced labor at the camp near the Berdechow airport.

Early in January 1942 the General Government decided on the deportation of the Mielec Jews. Orders were given to deport 2,000 persons, and on March 7–9, 1942, the order was executed in greater dimensions. The sick and old were shot on the spot; others were transferred to the Berdechow airport, where a *Selektion* was made. A group of youths was sent to the labor camp at Pustkow; the remaining population was sent to Parczew, Wlodawa, Hrubieszow, Miedzyrzec, Susiec, and other towns in the Lublin district. The Jewish population there eased the suffering of the Mielec refugees by providing lodgings and public kitchens. Some months later, the Mielec refugees and these Jewish communities were exterminated.

Mielec was among the first cities that the General Government made *judenrein*. Near the workshops of the Heinkel airplane company, Mielec had a labor camp under the direct auspices of the S.S. At first the camp employed 250 forced laborers, 80 of whom were from Mielec and others from Wielopole Skrzynskie. The population at the camp increased with the deportation of Mielec Jews in the winter of 1942. By the summer the population reached 1,000, including Jews from Tarnobrzeg and Huta Komarowska. The mortality rate at the camp reached more than 15 per day, excluding the sick who were shot. The camp was liquidated on Aug. 24, 1944. Some of the prisoners were transferred to Wieliczka and the rest to the camp at Flossenburg. Some 200 persons of the Mielec community survived. [Ar.W.]

Bibliography: Halpern, Pinkas, index; R. Mahler, *Yidn in Amolikn Poyln in Likht fun Tsifern* (1958), index; B. Wasiutyński, *Ludność żydowska w Polsce w wiekach xix i xx* (1930), 111, 146, 150, 156; M. Balaban, *Historja żydów Krakowie i na Kazimierzu*, 1 (1931), 351, 540; Y. Keitelman, in: *Fun Noentn Over* (1955), 401–51.

MIELZINER, MOSES (1828–1903), Reform rabbi and scholar. Born in Czerniejewo (Szubin, province of Posen), Mielziner came from a long line of rabbis. After Jewish and general studies in Germany, he was ordained by such diametrically opposed men as his teacher J. Oettinger and S. *Holdheim. He served as preacher and teacher in Waren (Mecklenburg), but had to leave because of opposition by the Orthodox *Landesrabbiner*. After a short time in Randers, Denmark, he was head of the Jewish school in Copenhagen from 1857 to 1865. He then emigrated to the United States, where he became rabbi of the Anshei Ḥesed congregation in New York. When his synagogue merged with another one in 1873, Mielziner opened a private boys' school and also taught at the Temple Emanu-El preparatory school for rabbinical students out of which the *Hebrew Union College at Cincinnati eventually developed. There he became professor of Talmud and rabbinical literature (1879), and at the death of I. M. *Wise in 1900, acting president. He took an active part in the work of the *Central Conference of American Rabbis, the *Jewish Publication Society of America, and the *Jewish Encyclopedia*.

Mielziner's published works include his Ph.D. thesis, first published in German (*Die Verhaeltnisse der Sklaven bei den Hebraeern*, 1859) and later in English (*Introduction of Slavery among the Ancient Hebrews*, 1894, repr. 1931), which was much quoted by the abolitionist movement in the United States 1861–62. His best work is *Introduction to the Talmud* (1894, 1968[4]), which remains a most widely used reference book. He also wrote *Jewish Law of Marriage and Divorce and its Relation to the Law of the State* (1901[2]) and shorter studies on Jewish law. Mielziner also published sermons and wrote some Hebrew poetry.

Bibliography: E. McKenna Friend Mielziner, *Moses Mielziner, a Biography* (1931); contains bibliography; W. Rosenau, *A Tribute to Moses Mielziner* (1929).

[Ed.]

MIESES, FABIUS (1824–1898), Hebrew writer and scholar. Born in Brody (Galicia), Mieses moved to Cracow in 1840. Subsequently he lived in Brody (1846–54), Breslau (1854–67), and Leipzig (from 1867). Mieses wrote extensively in the Hebrew journals of his day, publishing poems as well as articles on Judaism, philosophy, and topical subjects. His major work, the first of its kind in Hebrew, is *Korot ha-Filosofyah ha-Ḥadashah* ("History of Modern Philosophy," 1887), of which only the first volume appeared in print. He also wrote in German, contributing regularly to *Orient*.

Bibliography: I. A. Guenzig, *Elleh Toledot ha-Rav Fabius Mieses* (1890), first published in *Oẓar ha-Sifrut*, 3 (1890); Kressel, Leksikon, 2 (1967), 345.

[G.K.]

MIESES, MATTHIAS (1885–1945), Yiddish philologist. Born in Galicia, he was a prolific writer in Hebrew, Polish, and German. His main interest, however, was Yiddish, about which he wrote much, although little in the language itself. His Hebrew articles in defense of Yiddish against its detractors involved him in a controversy with Nahum *Sokolow. At the *Czernowitz Yiddish Conference of 1908, he created a sensation with his well-reasoned, scholarly espousal of Yiddish. I. L. *Peretz asked for the widest possible distribution of Mieses' speech. In his German study on the origin of Yiddish, *Die Entstehungsursache der juedischen Dialekte* (1915), a pioneer work in Yiddish philology, Mieses fought for the emancipation of the so-called Jewish "jargon" and its recognition as a language on a par with other European national languages. Another work on Yiddish was *Die jiddische Sprache* (1924). Mieses spent his last years in Cracow and was sent to Auschwitz with all remaining Jews as the Russian troops approached that city. He died on the way at the Glewitz station.

Bibliography: Z. Rejzen, Leksikon, 2 (1927), 375–9; LNYL, 6 (1965), 566–9; M. Ravitch, *Mayn Leksikon*, 2 (1947), 42–44; Kressel, Leksikon, 2 (1967), 344. [S.L.]

MIESIS, JUDAH LEIB (1798–1831), leading member of the Galician Haskalah movement in the early 19th century. Born in Lvov, to a wealthy, prominent family, Miesis

Judah Leib Miesis, supporter of the Galician Haskalah, Jerusalem, J.N.U.L., Schwadron Collection.

received a broad general education as well as a traditional Jewish one. His home was a meeting place for young *maskilim*, whom he encouraged and helped, and to whom he made available his large library. His first literary effort was the publication of a new edition of David *Caro's *Tekhunat ha-Rabbanim* (1822). Miesis' main work is *Kinat ha-Emet* ("The Zeal for Truth," 1823, 2nd ed. Lemberg, 1879), written in the form of a dialogue between Maimonides and Solomon Ḥelma (author of a commentary on Maimonides, *Mirkevet ha-Mishneh*). In the body of the work, as well as in an appendix containing quotations from Jewish scholars down through the ages, Miesis attacks the obscurantist beliefs in spirits, demons, mystical powers, and all the superstitious views fostered by the Orthodox rabbis. His highly rationalistic approach and his outspoken criticism of traditional beliefs were so extreme that even a number of *maskilim*, including his colleague and friend S. J. Rapoport, felt that he had gone too far and dissociated themselves from his views. Miesis also published a number of articles in the Hebrew journals (*Ha-Ẓefirah, Bikkurei ha-Ittim, Kerem Ḥemed*). He died of cholera in 1831.

Bibliography: Waxman, Literature, 3 (1960²), 165; R. Mahler, *Ha-Ḥasidut ve-ha-Haskalah* (1961), s.v.; Zinberg, Sifrut, 6 (1960), 29–35; Klausner, Sifrut, 2 (1960³), 267–82; Kressel, Leksikon, 2 (1967), 343f. [G.K.]

MIGDAL (Heb. מִגְדָּל; "Tower"), moshavah in the Ginnosar Valley, N. W. of Lake Kinneret, established in 1910 by Jews from Moscow who hired laborers to work their land. In 1921 it became a camp for Third *Aliyah pioneers working on the construction of the Tiberias-Rosh Pinnah road. These laborers founded *Gedud ha-Avodah, the "Labor Battalion," at Migdal. From 1924 Jews from England and America acquired parcels of land at Migdal and some of them went to settle. Lord *Melchett's farm was among those established at the time. After 1948 the moshavah was enlarged as new immigrants settled. Banana, date palm, and other fruit orchards, out-of-season vegetable gardens, and dairy cattle constitute Migdal's principal farming branches. It also has resorts. Its population numbered 535 in 1970. The historical name of the site is *Magdala. [E.O.]

MIGDAL HA-EMEK (Heb. מִגְדַּל הָעֵמֶק; "Tower of the Valley"), town with municipal council status in Lower Galilee, 4 mi. (7 km.) S.W. of Nazareth, founded in 1952 with the aim of absorbing inhabitants of transitory immigrant camps in the vicinity. Real progress started at the end of the 1950s, when industrial enterprises opened there. The population increased from 1,650 in 1955 to 8,200 in 1968 when 67% of the inhabitants were from Morocco and other North African countries, 19% from Rumania, and 7.5% from Iraq, while 1% were veteran Israelis and the rest from different countries. Approximately half of the town's gainfully employed worked in local factories, the largest of which were leather and cosmetic plants and produce mainly for export. In 1969 it was said to have the highest "export-dollar" income per capita in the country. Its educational network comprised 2,700 pupils in 1968, and maintained two comprehensive high schools. The town overlooks a beautiful landscape, with a wide view over the Jezreel Valley in the south, and is surrounded by extensive woodlands, among them the *Balfour Forest. [E.O.]

MIGDOL (Heb. מִגְדֹּל), (1) Canaanite city, mentioned in the list of cities conquered by Thutmosis III (no. 71) with Socoh (Ra's al-Shuwayka) and Yaham (Khirbat Yamma). It is identified with Khirbat Majdal southeast of *Ḥaderah. Sherds of the Late Bronze Age were found on the site. (2) Egyptian border fortress near Baal-Zephon (Ex. 14:2; Num. 33:7), inhabited by Jews in Jeremiah's time (Jer. 44:1; Ezek. 29:10). It is the Greek Magdolos and the Migdol of Baalsephon in the demotic Cairo papyrus (31.169). It is present-day Tell al-Khayrī near Pelusium. [M.A.-Y.]

MIGRATION. See Supplementary Entries.

MIHAILENI (Rum. **Mihăileni**), town in Moldavia, N.E. Rumania. When the town was founded in 1792 only Jews from the other side of the border were permitted to settle in the locality. The prayer house of the Jews and their ritual bathhouse were exempted from taxes, and during the first year Jewish merchants did not have to pay taxes. In 1834 the town became the property of the prince of Moldavia, Michael Sturdza. Eager to develop the town, he granted Jewish craftsmen special privileges, exempting them from taxes for five years. He also encouraged merchants to settle there by granting loans. From a population of 516 in 1820 the number of Jews reached 2,472 (67.6% of the total population), in 1859. In 1903 there were 248 Jewish and 58 Christian merchants in the town. The majority of the Jews were engaged in commerce, especially the fur trade. Jewish carriers plied their trade throughout the whole area; they had their own prayer house. An organized community dates from 1897. A Jewish primary school was founded in 1899. After World War I, with the Rumanian annexation of Bessarabia and Bukovina, Mihaileni lost its position as a frontier town. In 1930 only 1,490 Jews (32%) remained in the town. In the same year, the Jewish Party obtained the majority of votes in the local council elections. The peasants preferred it to the other parties, asserting that the Jews were more capable administrators. The election, however, was canceled by the authorities. On the eve of World War II there were nine prayer houses, a ritual bath, a primary school, and a cemetery in Mihaileni. The Hebrew author of the Haskalah period Marcus *Strelisker lived and died in Mihaileni. The Yiddish poet Jacob *Groper (1890–1966) was born there.

In World War II the Jews of Mihaileni were deported to *Transnistria. Few returned to Mihaileni after the war; the majority emigrated. The Jewish population numbered 680 in 1947, 400 in 1950, and about ten families in 1969.

Bibliography: PK Romaniya 180–1; E. Schwarzfeld, *Impopularea, reîmpopularea şi întemeierea tîrgurilor şi tîrguşoarelorîm Noldova* (1914), 26–33, 43, 82–83, 101–3; M. Schwarzfeld, in: *Analele Societăţii istorice Juliu Barasch*, 2 (1888), 28–29, 117; *Fraternitatea*, 4 (1882), 345. [Th.L.]

MI'ILYA (Ar. معليا), Christian-Arab village in northern Israel, in western Upper Galilee, west of *Ma'alot. Mi'ilya constitutes an important center in Israel for the Greek-Catholic faith, to which almost all its 1,390 inhabitants (1969) belong. Tobacco, deciduous fruit, vineyards, and olive groves, on land reclaimed from rocky slopes, are the base of the village's economy. According to archaeological evidence, Mi'ilya has been inhabited since the second millennium B.C.E. Although few remains from the earlier periods have been preserved, the crusader fortress built by German knights in the 13th century C.E. (Chasteau du Roi or Castrum Regis) has remained almost intact and still forms the village's nucleus. Another crusader fortress, Montfort (Burg Starkenberg), lies nearby in the Chezib River gorge. [E.O.]

MIKHALEVICH, BEINISH (pseudonym of **Joseph Izbitski**; 1876–1928), leader of the *Bund in Russia and Poland. Mikhalevich was born at Brest-Litovsk into a working-class family and at the age of 18 he joined a socialist circle. On the establishment of the Bund, he was active in Bialystok and Warsaw, set up its local organs there, and also wrote in its central newspaper *Arbeter Shtime*. After a period of arrest by the czarist police, he took part in the establishment of the Garber Bund and edited its organ *Der Kemfer*. In the following years—between repeated arrests, exile, and flight—he was an organizer, speaker, publicist, and propagandist of the Bund. In the internal struggles he belonged to the "soft" group which supported the Bund's return to the Russian Social Democratic party (1906), and during the period of reaction, after the short-lived constitutional aftermath of the revolution, he belonged to the "anti-liquidators," who demanded to continue illegal activities. Mikhalevich was the first to discuss the problem of the relationship between the Bund and the Jewish *kehillah* (the organized Jewish community) (1907). In 1912 he became a member of the central committee of the Bund and edited its weekly *Tsayt* in St. Petersburg. During World War I he was active in welfare and educational institutions in Vilna until his imprisonment by the German occupation forces for a leaflet he wrote against forced labor.

The leftward turn of the Bund in independent Poland decreased Mikhalevich's political standing and he devoted himself mainly to writing and to social and cultural work. He wrote in the Bund organ *Folkstsaytung*, and gave a historical-biographical description of the Jewish workers' movement in three volumes: *Zikhroynes fun a Yidishn Sotsialist* (1921–23). He took part in the founding of the Central Yiddish School Organization (CYSHO) and until his death served as its chairman, visiting the U.S. in 1923–24 as its emissary and promoting the establishment of the Society for Helping Children's Institutions Overseas. He was also a member of the Jewish community council in Warsaw (1925–28). One of the outstanding polemicists against Zionism, Mikhalevich was popular even among his opponents because of his honesty and attachment to Jewish values.

Bibliography: LNYL, 5 (1963), 608–12; I. Cohen, *War's Tribulations and Aftermath* (1943), 361; idem, in: *Beinush Mikhalevich Gedenk Bukh* (1951), incl. bibl.; A. Litvak, *Mah she-Hayah* (1945), 237–45; A. S. Stein, *Ḥaver Artur* (1953), index; J. S. Hertz et al. (eds.), *Geshikhte fun Bund*, 3 vols. (1960–66), indexes. [M.M.]

MIKHMORET (Heb. מִכְמֹרֶת; "Fishing Net"), moshav village, and vocational school in central Israel, near *Kefar Vitkin, founded in 1945 by World War II veterans, some of whom had learned fishing in Holland. The moshav is affiliated with Tenu'at ha-Moshavim. Its economy is based on citrus groves, dairy cattle, and carp ponds. The village Mikhmoret Bet has developed the neighboring beach, one of the finest in the country, as a seaside resort. The fishery and seafaring school Mevo'ot Yam ("Approaches to the Sea") constitutes a central maritime training institute. In 1970 the three sections of Mikhmoret had a population of 720. [E.O.]

MIKHOELS, SOLOMON (stage and public name of **Solomon Vovsi**; 1890–1948), Yiddish actor; head of the Moscow State Jewish Theater; chairman of the Jewish *Anti-Fascist Committee. Born in Dvinsk, Mikhoels studied law at St. Petersburg. In 1918 he joined Alexander *Granovsky's Jewish drama studio, the next year following Granovsky to Moscow, where the group became the State Jewish Theater. He was Granovsky's chief actor, and succeeded him to the directorship in 1928. Mikhoels, whose distinction lay in his command of both tragic and tragicomic roles, first attracted attention in 1921 in a performance of *Shalom Aleichem's *Agents*. He was soon playing such famous Yiddish roles as Shimele Soroker in

Solomon Mikhoels as King Lear in the Jewish State Theater production in Moscow, 1935. Jerusalem, C.A.H.J.P.

Two Hundred Thousand, Hotsmakh in Goldfaden's *The Witch*, Benjamin in *The Travels of Benjamin the Third* by *Mendele Mokher Seforim, and Shalom Aleichem's Tevye. One of his most notable performances was King Lear in the production by Sergei Radlov in 1935. From August 1941, Mikhoels, as chairman of the Jewish Anti-Fascist Committee, launched fervent appeals to "our Jewish brethren" in the West to help the Soviet war effort against Nazi Germany. In 1943 he and the poet Itzik *Fefer traveled on behalf of the Anti-Fascist Committee to the U.S., Canada, Mexico, and England, where they were enthusiastically received by the Jewish public. At the end of World War II, when survivors of the Holocaust and Jews returning from evacuation in Soviet Asia tried to resettle in their old homes, Mikhoels gradually became their spokesman and protector, interceding for them with the Soviet authorities. He apparently was also connected with the "Crimean project" which aimed at the settlement of homeless Jews in the Crimea. On Jan. 13, 1948, while on an official mission in Minsk on behalf of the State Committee for Theater Prizes, Mikhoels was brutally killed, ostensibly by hooligans or in a car accident, but in reality (as later admitted in the Soviet press) by order of the Soviet secret police. (Svetlana Alliluyeva, Stalin's daughter, testified (in her book *Only One Year*) that her father was personally involved in covering up Mikhoels' assassination and presenting it as an accident.) On January 16 Mikhoels was eulogized at his state funeral in Moscow in which many thousands of Jews participated. Mikhoels' assassination was the first step in the process of liquidation of all Jewish cultural institutions and of most outstanding Yiddish writers, artists, and actors which took place during the last years of Stalin's rule. Five years after his death, Mikhoels' name was mentioned in the press in connection with the *Doctors' Plot as "the well-known Jewish bourgeois nationalist" who served as contact man between U.S. intelligence and the "criminal doctors," one of whom was Professor Vovsi, a relative of Mikhoels. During the de-Stalinization in the mid-1950s Mikhoels was de facto rehabilitated. In Tel Aviv a square was named in his honor in 1962, on the tenth anniversary of the execution of the Jewish writers in the U.S.S.R.

Bibliography: B.Z. Goldberg, *The Jewish Problem in the Soviet Union* (1961), index; K. L. Rudnitskiy (ed.), *Mikhoels'* (Rus., 1965); Sutskever, in: *Di Goldene Keyt*, no. 43 (1962); I. Ionasovich, *Mit Yidishe Shrayber in Rusland* (1959), passim. [B.E./J.LE.]

MIKULOV (Ger. **Nikolsburg**), town in S. Moravia, Czechoslovakia. The Mikulov community was the largest and most important in Moravia, and was the seat of the *Landesrabbiner* ("chief rabbi") from apparently as early as 1574 until 1851. A Jew from Mikulov, a moneylender, is mentioned in a document of 1369, but there is no mention of Jews in the oldest known city record of 1414. An inscription in the synagogue (burned down in 1719) was dated 1450. The community was probably founded by expellees from Austria (1420), reinforced in 1454 by those from *Brno (Bruenn) and *Znojmo (Znaim). The charter granted the Jews in 1591 guaranteed a self-elected communal administration (the revised charter of 1612 (renewed in 1708) removed the Jews from the jurisdiction of the town to that of the lord). In 1593 the Jews were permitted to trade in textiles. On the conquest of the town by the Swedes (1642), the Jews raised a quarter of the town's contribution. Refugees from the *Chmielnicki massacres came to Mikulov in 1648. In 1653 the **ḥevra kaddisha* was founded. In 1657 there were 145 families in the town. Their number was augmented in 1670 by expellees from Vienna, who at first kept apart from the local community, maintaining their own institutions and endeavoring to return to Vienna. A hospital for infectious diseases was built in 1680. Jews who were captured on the conquest of *Belgrade were ransomed in 1688 and settled in Mikulov. Almost the entire Jewish quarter, including the old synagogue and all records, was destroyed in a fire in 1719. The concomitant plunder led to a conflict between the central authorities and the local lord over military intervention. Under the leadership of Samson *Wertheimer, communities throughout Europe offered assistance to the Jews of Mikulov. The municipality bought up building sites to avoid the enlargement of the Jewish quarter, whose boundaries were fixed by an imperial commission in 1720.

The prosperity of the community depended on its connection with the cultivation of wines and the wine trade and on the town's position on the main road between Brno and Vienna. Many of the Jews were carters. The Jewish wine merchants leased vineyards, vats, and cellars or bought up the grape crops, paying in advance of the harvest. Jews also distilled spirits and produced the special Moravian plum jam *(povidl)*. In the 17th century, the Jews undertook to supply the whole town with candles, and in the 18th century the purveyors of gold and silver to the imperial mint lived in Mikulov. The community *takkanot* from the 18th century are preserved in the National Library in Jerusalem. The Jewish tailors, shoemakers, and butchers were organized into guilds, with their own synagogues. However, most members of the community earned their livelihood in peddling, mainly in the villages of Austria.

Mikulov, the center of all activities of Moravian Jewry, was especially prominent when Samson Raphael *Hirsch held office as chief rabbi (1846–51). A German-language school, connected with a textile workshop, was opened in 1839. Joel Deutsch founded the Jewish institute for the deaf and dumb in 1844 (transferred to Vienna in 1852). Mikulov became a political community (*Politische Gemeinde) after 1848. After the economic importance of the community had declined when the Vienna–Brno railroad line bypassed Mikulov, many of its members left (after 1848), moving mainly to Brno and Vienna, where a "Verein der Nikolsburger" ("association of Nikolsburgers") grew up. The rapid decline in the community was reflected in the number of synagogues: 12 until 1868, five until the beginning of the 20th century, and then only two. The number of permitted families allotted under the *Familiants Laws was 620. From 3,020 persons in 1793, the community increased to 3,237 in 1830 and 3,680 in 1857, then fell sharply to 1,500 in 1869; 1,213 in 1880; 1,061 in 1890; 900 in 1900; 778 in 1913; 573 in 1921; and 437 in 1930 (5.6% of the total population).

Town of Mikulov depicted on a silver *seder* plate with the Jews shown leaving the town gate as part of the Exodus, first half of 19th century. Prague, State Jewish Museum.

The yeshivah of Mikulov was renowned, and many well-known rabbis held office in the town; nearly all of them were simultaneously chief rabbis of Moravia (see *Moravia). The scholar Abraham *Trebitsch lived in Mikulov and Aloys and Joseph von Sonnenfels were natives of the town.

In 1936 a Moravian Jewish museum was founded in Mikulov; it was transferred to Brno at the time of the Sudeten crisis, and from there to the Central Jewish Museum in Prague. The community dispersed at this time; many of its members were deported to the Nazi extermination camps from Brno in 1941 and 1942. It was not reestablished after World War II. The synagogue was demolished as a public hazard in 1950.

Bibliography: B. M. Trapp and V. R. Koenig, in: H. Gold (ed.), *Juden und Judengemeinden Maehrens* (1929), 417–50; A. Willmann and H. Flesch, *ibid.*, 45–52; I. Herrisch, *ibid.*, 193–7 (on Lednice); Y. Z. Kahane, in: *Arim ve-Immahot be-Yisrael*, 4 (1950), 210–310 (bibl. 310–3); E. N. C. Roth, *Takkanot Nikolsburg* (1961); A. Engel (ed.), *Gedenkbuch . . . Kuratoriums . . .* (Ger., Czech, and Heb., 1936); D. Feuchtwang, in: *Kaufmann Gedenkbuch* (1900), 369–84; ide, in: *Juedisches Archiv*, 1 (1928), nos. 3–4, 1–3; L. Loew, *Gesammelte Schriften*, 2 (1890), 165–218; B. Brilling, in: *Zeitschrift fuer die Geschichte der Juden in der Tschechoslowakei . . .*, 2 (1931/32), 243–7; L. Moses, *ibid.*, 5 (1938), 85–108; A. Z. Schwarz, in: *Studies . . . in Memory of A. S. Freidus* (1929), 170–81; A. Scheiber, in: *Yeda-Am*, 5 (1958/59), 71–73; M. Freudenthal, in: MGWJ, 46 (1902), 268–70; W. Mueller, *Urkundliche Beitraege* (1903), passim; Baron, Community, 3 (1942), index; S. Simonsohn, *Ha-Yehudim be-Dukkasut Mantovah*, 2 (1965), index, s.v. *Nikolsburg;* M. H. Friedlaender, *Kore ha-Dorot* (Ger., 1876); G. Deutsch, in: *Die Deborah*, 2 (1902), 354–62; Y. Heilperin, *Takkanot Kehillot Mehrin* (1952), index; A. Freimann, in: ZHB, 20 (1917), 36f.; M. Steinschneider, in: HB, 5 (1862), 128. [M.LA.]

MIKVA'OT (מִקְוָאוֹת; "Ritual Baths"), the sixth tractate in the order of the *Tohorot* in the Mishnah and the Tosefta. The tractate consists of ten chapters and deals wholly with the details of the **mikveh*. Chapter 1 classifies *mikva'ot* according to the grade of their purity and purifying effect, from ponds or ditches containing less than 40 *se'ah* (c. 750 liters; see *Weights and Measures) and therefore invalid, to those of the highest grade, consisting of *mayim ḥayyim* ("pure spring water"). Chapter 2 discusses cases of "doubtful impurity" (e.g., if a person is not sure whether he has immersed properly or whether the *mikveh* was ritually fit), and then deals with the problem of *mayim she'uvim* ("drawn water"). Chapters 3 and 4 continue with various aspects of *mayim she'uvim*, e.g., how a *mikveh* invalidated by *mayim she'uvim* can be made ritually fit, or how to direct rainwater from a roof into a *mikveh* without letting the water pass through a "vessel" in order to prevent the water's becoming *mayim she'uvim*. Chapter 5 deals mainly with the fitness of springs, rivers, and seas as *mikva'ot*. Chapter 6 is concerned with the question of a body of water linked with a *mikveh*, or two *mikva'ot* connected so that the water of the one "touches" the water of the other *(hashakah)*, which is of great significance in the construction of the modern *mikveh*. Chapter 7 discusses the minimal requirement of 40 *se'ah*, especially whether snow, ice, etc. may complete that measure. Chapter 8 first deals with the halakhic difference between *mikva'ot* of the Holy Land and those of other countries; it then discusses problems touching on seminal issue and menstruation. Chapter 9 discusses the problem of *ḥaẓiẓah* ("interposition"). Chapter 10 deals with vessels or any other artifact requiring purification in a *mikveh*.

All the Tosefta manuscripts of *Mikva'ot* contain seven chapters, but the printed one contains eight chapters. The Tosefta quotes traditions about queries raised by the inhabitants of Asia (Ezion-Geber, on the shore of the Red Sea) with the scholars of Jabneh during the three pilgrim festivals (4:6); about R. Gamaliel and Onkelos the Proselyte bathing in the sea at Ashkelon (6:3); and about discussions which took place among 32 scholars in Lydda (7(8):11). Although there is no Babylonian or Jerusalem Talmud on *Mikva'ot*, several of its Mishnayot are explained in the Babylonian Talmud; for example, Mishnah 4:1 is explained in *Shabbat* 16b, Mishnah 7:2 in *Yevamot* 82b and *Zevaḥim* 22a, Mishnah 7:4 in *Shabbat* 144b, Mishnah 8:4 in *Ḥullin* 24b, Mishnah 9:1 in *Shabbat* 57a, and Mishnah 9:5 and 6 in *Shabbat* 114a. This tractate was translated into English by H. Danby (1933) and The Soncino Press (1948).

Engraving for the tractate *Mikva'ot*, showing immersion in a natural pool, from a title page of the Hebrew-Latin Mishnah illustrated by Mich. Richey. Amsterdam, 1700–04, Jerusalem, J.N.U.L.

Bibliography: Ḥ. Albeck, *Shishah Sidrei Mishnah, Seder Tohorot* (1959), 337–9. [A.Z.E.]

MIKVEH (Heb. מִקְוֶה; "a collection [of water]"), a pool or bath of clear water, immersion in which renders ritually clean a person who has become ritually unclean through contact with the dead (Num. 19) or any other defiling object, or through an unclean flux from the body (Lev. 15) and especially a menstruant (see *Ablution; Purity and Impurity, Ritual). It is similarly used for vessels (Num. 31:22–23). At the present day the chief use of the *mikveh* is for the menstruant (see **Niddah*), since the laws of ritual impurity no longer apply after the destruction of the Temple. Nevertheless, since according to the *halakhah* the contracting of marital relations while the wife is in the state of *niddah* is a particularly severe offense, punishable by **karet*, and according to one opinion in the Talmud (not, however, accepted as *halakhah*), that a child born of such a union is a **mamzer*, the rabbis insisted on the meticulous adherence to the laws of immersion in a *mikveh* before his mother could resume marital relations. They are also obligatory for the immersion of proselytes, as part of the ceremony of *conversion. In addition immersion in the *mikveh* is still practiced by various groups as an aid to spirituality, particularly on the eve of the Sabbath and festivals, especially the Day of Atonement (see *Ablution) and the custom still obtains, in accordance with Numbers 31:22–23 to immerse new vessels and utensils purchased from non-Jews.

It is emphasized that the purpose of immersion is not physical, but spiritual, cleanliness. Maimonides concludes his codification of the laws of the *mikveh* with the following statement:

Figure 1. Photograph and schematic plan of the southern *mikveh* at Masada, built strictly according to ritual requirements. 1. plastered conduit. 2. pool for collecting rainwater. 3. the actual *mikveh*, connected to 2. by a pipe. 4. pool for washing hands and feet before entering the *mikveh*. Courtesy Y. Yadin, Jerusalem.

> It is plain that the laws about immersion as a means of freeing oneself from uncleanness are decrees laid down by Scripture and not matters about which human understanding is capable of forming a judgment; for behold, they are included among the divine statutes. Now 'uncleanness' is not mud or filth which water can remove, but is a matter of scriptural decree and dependent on the intention of the heart. Therefore the Sages have said, 'If a man immerses himself, but without special intention, it is as though he has not immersed himself at all.'
>
> Nevertheless we may find some indication [for the moral basis] of this: Just as one who sets his heart on becoming clean becomes clean as soon as he has immersed himself, although nothing new has befallen his body, so, too, one who sets his heart on cleansing himself from the uncleannesses that beset men's souls—namely, wrongful thoughts and false convictions—becomes clean as soon as he consents in his heart to shun those counsels and brings his soul into the waters of pure reason. Behold, Scriptures say, 'And I will sprinkle clean water upon you and ye shall be clean; from all your uncleannesses and from all your idols will I cleanse you [Ezek. 36:25]' (Yad, Mikva'ot 11:12).

Although Maimonides in this passage states that lack of intention invalidates the act under all circumstances, a view which is found in the Tosefta (Ḥag. 3:2), the *halakhah,* as in fact codified by him (Yad, *ibid.* 1:8), is that the need for intention applies only for the purpose of eating holy things, such as *ma'aser* and **terumah.* For a menstruant, and before eating ordinary food, though intention is desirable in the first instance, its lack does not invalidate the immersion. The importance of intention in the laws of ritual impurity is further illustrated by the fact that the rabbis permitted fig cakes which had been hidden in water—an action that would normally make the food susceptible to uncleanness—because they had been put there in order to hide them and not in order to wet them (Makhsh. 1:6). This stress on intention passed from Judaism into Islam. "Purity is the half of faith" is a saying attributed to Muhammad himself and in general the laws of uncleanness in Islam bear a striking resemblance to those of Judaism (*Encyclopedia of Islam,* s.v. *Tahara*).

According to biblical law any collection of water, drawn or otherwise, is suitable for a *mikveh* as long as it contains enough for a person to immerse himself (Yad, *ibid.* 4:1). The rabbis, however, enacted that only water which has not been drawn, i.e., has not been in a vessel or receptacle, may be used; and they further established that the minimum quantity for immersion is that which is contained in a square cubit to the height of three cubits. A *mikveh* containing less than this amount (which they estimated to be a volume of 40 *se'ah,* being between 250–1,000 liters according to various calculations) becomes invalid should three *log* of drawn water fall into it or be added. However, if the *mikveh* contains more than this amount it can never become invalid no matter how much drawn water is added. These laws are the basis for the various ways of constructing the *mikveh* (see below). To them a whole talmudic tractate, **Mikva'ot,* is devoted, and Maimonides assigns them a whole treatise of the same name. The laws can be conveniently divided into two parts, the construction of the *mikveh* itself, and the water which renders it valid or invalid.

The *mikveh* is valid, however built, providing that it has not been prefabricated and brought and installed on the site, since in that case it constitutes a "vessel" which renders the water in it "drawn water" (*"mayim she'uvim";* Mik. 4:1). It may be hewn out of the rock or built in or put on the ground, and any material is suitable. It must be watertight, since leakage invalidates it. It must contain a minimum of 40 *se'ah* of valid water, and, although it was originally laid down that its height must be 47 in. (120 cm.)

Figure 2. Women immersing food utensils in a *mikveh* in an illustration from a 14th-century *Haggadah* from Spain. London, British Museum, Or. Ms. 2737, 90a.

to enable a person standing in it to be completely immersed (Sifra 6:3), even though he has to bend his knees (Sifra 6:3) it was later laid down that providing there is the necessary minimum quantity of water, immersion is valid while lying down.

The Water. All natural spring water, providing it is clean and has not been discolored by any admixtures is valid for a *mikveh.* With regard to rainwater, which is ideal for a *mikveh,* and melted snow and ice (even if manufactured from "drawn" water) which are also valid, care must be taken to ensure that the water flows freely and is not rendered invalid by the flow into it being stopped, thus turning it into "drawn water." In addition the water must not reach the *mikveh* through vessels made of metal or other materials which are susceptible to ritual uncleanness. This is avoided by attaching the pipes and other accessories to the ground, by virtue of which they cease to have the status of "vessels." Similarly the *mikveh* is emptied from above by hand, by vacuum, or by electric or automatic pumps. The emptying through a hole in the bottom is forbidden since the plug may be regarded as a "vessel" as well as giving rise to the possibility of a leakage.

There is, however, one regulation with regard to the *mikveh* which considerably eases the problems of assuring a supply of valid water. Once it possesses the minimum quantity of 40 *se'ah* of valid water even though "someone draws water in a jug and throws it into the *mikveh* all day long, all the water is valid." In addition "if there is an upper *mikveh* containing 40 *se'ah* of valid water, and someone puts drawn water in the upper *mikveh,* thus increasing its volume, and 40 *se'ah* of it flows into the lower pool, that lower pool is a valid *mikveh*" (Yad, Mikva'ot 4:6). It is thus possible to exploit limitless quantities of valid water.

Various Forms of Mikveh. The above regulations determine the various kinds of *mikveh* which are in use. In

Figure 4. A medieval *mikveh* uncovered during excavations in Cologne, Germany, 1956–57. From Z. Asaria, *Die Juden in Koeln,* Cologne, 1959.

rare cases where there is a plentiful supply of valid water, spring or rain- (or sea-) water which can constantly replenish the *mikveh,* the only desiderata which have to be complied with are to ensure that the water does not become invalidated by the construction of the *mikveh,* rendering it a "vessel" or by going through metal pipes which are not sunk in the ground, as detailed above.

Since, however, *mikva'ot* are usually constructed in urban and other settlements where such supplies are not freely available, the technological and halakhic solution of the valid *mikveh* depends essentially upon constructing a *mikveh* with valid water and replenishing it with invalid water, taking advantage of the fact that the addition of this water to an originally valid one does not invalidate it.

The following are among the systems used:

1. The basic *mikveh* consists of the minimum valid

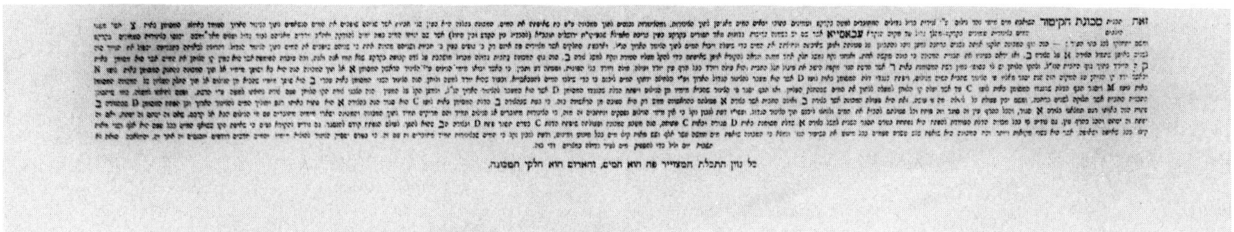

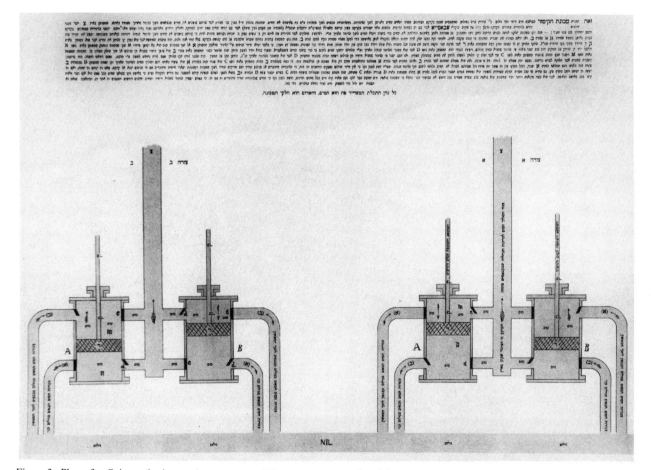

Figure 3. Plan of a Cairo *mikveh* pumping system enabling water to enter from the Nile in a continuous flow. From Raphael Aaron b. Simeon, *U-mi-Ẓur Devash,* Jerusalem, 1912.

Figure 5. Cross section drawing of the medieval *mikveh* of Friedburg, Germany, dug more than 60 ft. (18 m.) below ground. Courtesy J. Schoenberger, Jerusalem.

amount of 40 *se'ah* of rainwater. To this rainwater, ordinary water may subsequently be added through a trough which is absorbent, dug in the ground, or one made of lean concrete at least three handbreadths (c. 30 cm.) long, and one wide. Through this device the added water is regarded as coming from the ground and not through a "vessel." The resultant mixture of both types of water passes into the *mikveh* through a hole in the dividing wall. Since the added water is regarded as "seeding" the original valid water, it is called the *ozar zeri'ah* ("store for seeding").

2. In a second system the added drawn water is not previously mixed with the rainwater, as in the previous case, but flows directly onto the basic rainwater *mikveh* through an aperture in the wall of the *mikveh*, the diameter of which must be "the size of the spout of a water bottle" (c. 2 in.; 5–6 cm., Mik. 6:7). This method is called *ozar hasnakah* ("the store produced by contact"). Both the above methods, though they answer the halakhic needs, have their disadvantages in operation and in maintenance, particularly through the exhaustion of the rainwater and the stagnation of the standing water. The other systems are aimed at overcoming these drawbacks.

3. The *"dut,"* a cistern or tank built into the ground to store rainwater. When changing the water in the *mikveh*, it is filled each time with at least 21 *se'ah* of rainwater from the cistern and water is then added from the "store for seeding" by conduction. The water in the *mikveh* is brought into contact with the "contact store" by the method mentioned above. Though indeed this method overcomes the many shortcomings and halakhic problems, it nevertheless requires an extensive area for the cistern, and large areas of roof and pipes for filling with considerable amounts of rainwater in the winter.

4. Both a "store for seeding" and a "contact store" are built on each side of the *mikveh*. Each store has an aperture connecting its water with that of the *mikveh*.

5. A single "store" consisting of both "seeding" and "contacting."

6. A "store" upon a "store." A "contact store" is built on two stories joined by an aperture with the diameter of "the spout of a bottle." The water of the *mikveh* is validated by means of the hole in the party wall between the *mikveh* and the upper "store."

7. A "contact store" under the floor of the *mikveh*, connected by means of a hole the size of "the spout of a water bottle."

The *mikva'ot* of Jerusalem as well as the oldest *mikva'ot* in other towns of Ereẓ Israel are built in general by the method of the "contact store" as well as by the "store of seeding." In the new settlements and elsewhere the *mikva'ot* are built in the main only by the method of the "store of seeding" (a system approved by Rabbi A. I. Karelitz, the "Ḥazon Ish"). Latterly *mikva'ot* have been built by the method of two "stores."

In recent years vast improvements have been made in the hygienic and other aspects of the *mikveh*. An early enactment, attributed to Ezra, that a woman must wash her hair before immersing herself (BK 82a) may be provided for by the now universal custom of having baths as an adjunct to *mikva'ot*, the use of which is an essential preliminary to entering the *mikveh*, and especially in the United States they are provided with hairdressing salons and even beauty parlors.

Figure 6. *Mikveh* in the basement of the 18th-century synagogue of Carpentras, France. Photo F. Meyer, Carpentras.

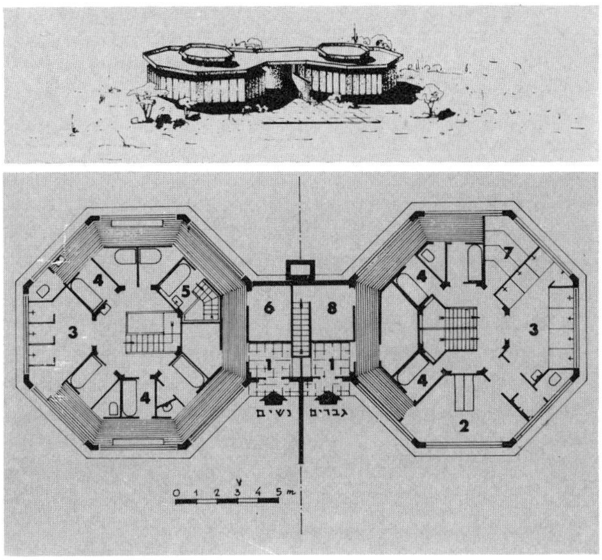

Figure 7. Plan (above) and architect's drawing of a *mikveh* for Ashdod, Israel. Men's facilities are on the right, women's on the left. 1. entry, 2. dining room, 3. showers, 4. baths, 5. private *mikveh,* 6. powder room, 7. steam room, 8. storage area and passage to boiler room. Courtesy J. Schoenberger, Jerusalem.

As will have been seen the regulations for constructing the *mikveh* are complicated and its construction requires a considerable knowledge of technology combined with strict adherence to the *halakhah,* and it should be built only after consultation with, and under the supervision of, accepted rabbinic authorities. Nevertheless in order to increase the use of this essential requirement of traditional Judaism, a book has been published which consists almost entirely of instructions for making a valid "Do it yourself" *mikveh* (see D. Miller in bibl.).

History. Data is lacking for a historical account of *mikveh,* particularly with regard to its construction and development in ancient times. There is scant information about the *mikveh* for priests—the Sea of Solomon in the first Temple. The few references in the Bible (I Kings 7:23f.; II Chron. 4:2f.) are insufficient to cast light on the enigma of this huge *mikveh* containing, according to the rabbis, the volume of 150 *mikva'ot* (ER. 14a), on its construction and functions. There is more information about the period of the Second Temple, when, in its closing years, even the common people were particular about the laws of cleanness, as is seen by the fact that (Jos., Ant. 18:38) when Herod founded Tiberias he was obliged to supply its inhabitants with many benefits to induce them to stay in the locality, since it was built on ancient tombs and the people avoided "uncleanness breaking through."

Certain districts of Jerusalem were planned *ab initio* in conformity with the requirements of the laws of cleanness and of the *mikva'ot,* practiced in the city. The unclean walked in the "current," i.e., in the middle of the road or the bridge, and the clean on the sidewalks (Shek. 8:1). The obligation of purification in a *mikveh* before entering the area of the Temple was recognized even by foreign kings who ruled in Jerusalem (Jos., Ant. 12:145). The crowds of festival pilgrims were in need of many valid *mikva'ot* before entering Jerusalem. According to the *halakhah* all the *mikva'ot* of Ereẓ Israel were clean, even in the towns with mixed populations (Mik. 8:1). The *bet din* would appoint special supervisors to examine the construction, the validity, the measurements, and the cleanliness of the *mikva'ot* (Tosef., Shek. 1:2) which also served the crowds of pilgrims who streamed to Jerusalem for the festivals. The paucity of the rainfall of Ereẓ Israel on the one hand, and the punctiliousness of Torah in matters of uncleanness with

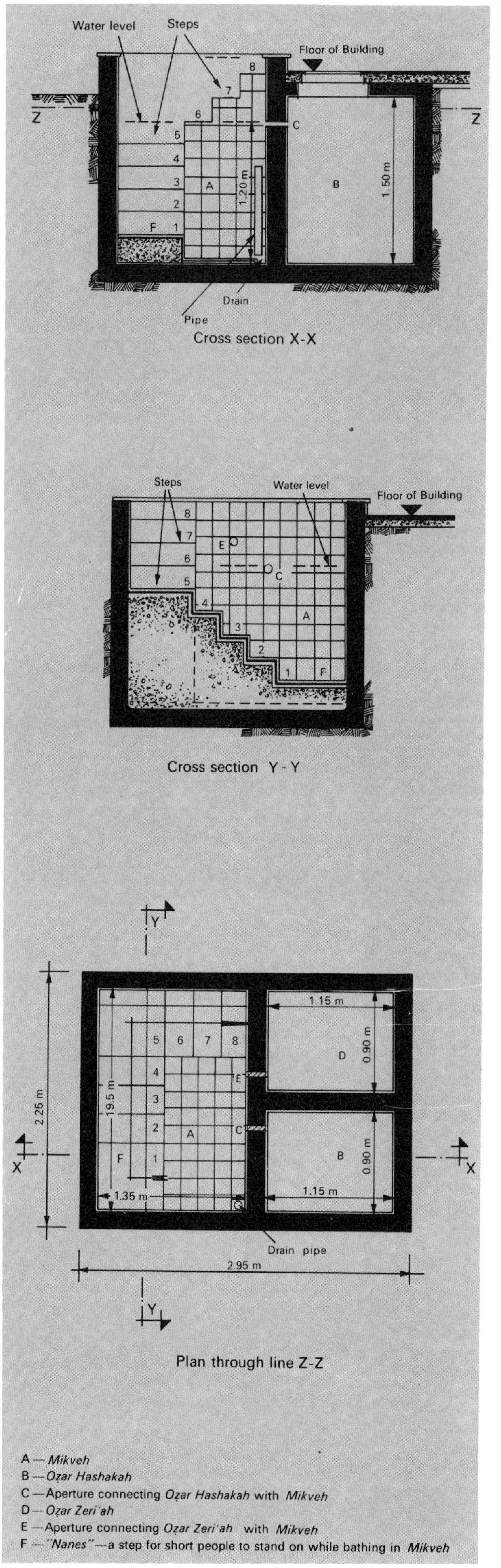

Figure 8. *Mikveh* designed according to halakhic principles. Courtesy J. Schoenberger, Jerusalem.

the precepts of washing and bathing on the other, required the overseeing of economy in rainwaters. They utilized water in caves (Zav., end and Bertinoro thereto), springs, and rivers in building *mikva'ot* (Mik. 1:4; et al.). In Jerusalem there was the pool of Siloam popularly called to this day "the *mikveh* of the high priest Ishmael." There is also mention of the "trough of Jehu" whose location is unknown (Yev. 15a). The multitude of *mikva'ot* gave rise to new halakhic problems, which were sometimes brought before the supreme legislative body to the Chamber of Hewn Stone (Eduy. 7:4). There were many *mikva'ot* on the Temple Mount, one in the chamber of lepers situated in the northwest corner of the court of women (Mid. 2:5). In the view of the rabbis it served not only for the cleansing of lepers, but for anyone entering the court (Yoma 30b). Even during the fratricidal war on the Temple Mount the laws of ritual immersion were strictly adhered to (Jos., Wars, 4:205). The Temple itself contained pools in various places for the priests to bathe (Commentary to Tam. 26b), even in the vaults beneath the court (Tam. 1:1). The high priest had special *mikva'ot* in the Temple, two of which are mentioned in the Mishnah; one above the water gate in the south of the court (Mid. 1:4), and one on the roof of the Parva chamber (Mid. 5:3), apparently to the north of the court (Moses Ḥefeẓ, *Ḥanukkat ha-Bayit* (Venice, 1696) no. 27) for immersion in the holy place on the Day of Atonement. There was an additional place for immersion on the Mount of Olives (Par. 3:7), which was connected with the burning of the *red heifer. A special ramp led to it from the Temple Mount, which was built as an arched way over another arched way to avoid uncleanness from a grave in the depths below. The requirements of the *halakhah* for the purification of the high priest in a *mikveh* were much more stringent than those for ordinary priests and the people. In the period being dealt with of the return to Zion and the Second Temple, important changes occurred in the country in physical habits of hygiene—washing in a bath for pleasure—and this also affected problems of bathing in a *mikveh*. The many sources in both Talmuds testify to these customs from abroad which had no small influence on the *halakhah*.

Archaeological remains of the Second Temple period—such as the *mikva'ot* in Masada, in Maon (Nirim), and in *Herodium—prove that the *mikveh* of today has indeed remained faithful to its prototype of the time of the Mishnah and the Talmud. From Israel the *halakhot* of the *mikveh* and its construction spread to Europe, first and foremost to Italy. Eleazar b. Yose taught a *halakhah* on the topic of cleanness in Rome and his colleagues agreed with it (Tosef., Nid. 7:1). The close connection between Italy and Germany through the medium of the scholars of Alsace and the communities of Spires, Worms, and Mainz brought the spread of the *halakhot* of Ereẓ Israel and their *mikva'ot* were built according to the traditional format. In the Middle Ages the *mikveh* constituted civically an integral part of the Jewish center and synagogue, not merely in Byzantine Israel (Huldah, Maon-Nirim, etc.) but also in Italy, Germany, Bohemia, Lithuania, Poland, and other places. The most ancient remnants of *mikva'ot* in Germany have been uncovered in Cologne from 1170, Spires 1200, Friedberg 1260, Offburg 1351, in Andernach, too, in the 14th century. The most typical is in Worms—a subterranean building with 19 steps descending to the entrance hall and then another 11 steps to the *mikveh* itself. A similar *mikveh* exists in Cairo and in the vault of the Tiferet Israel synagogue in Jerusalem. In Europe the architectural lines were influenced by the environment and by the builders who were generally not Jews (who had no entry to the trade guilds). The architectural and other details of their construction are remarkable by their precision—the outer and inner ornamentation, the capitals of the pillars, beautiful inscriptions, etc; a mixture of oriental and European elements created architectural solutions for the special problems of building the *mikveh*. In place of Roman modes, the Gothic and Baroque left their mark on the outer and inner style.

In many instances the *mikva'ot* of the Middle Ages served as bathhouses because of the order forbidding Jews to wash in the rivers together with Christians.

The views of the halakhic authorities in all generations differed with reference to many details of the *mikveh*. From this stemmed the great difference in the ways of building and in the systems of installation. Modern technology demands solutions of many problems, such as the permissibility of the use of reinforced concrete, porous concrete for the trough of validation, floor tiles to prevent leaking of the water. In every generation the authorities of each generation have delved deeply into the sources of the *halakhah* and its reasons, and from them have come to clear decisions for the planner and builder, leaving extensive scope for his imagination and his ability to coordinate *halakhah* with technology.

Bibliography: N. Telushkin, *Tohorat Mayim* (1964[3]); D. Muenzberg, *Mivneh Mikva'ot ve-Hekhsheram* (1963); Krauss, Tal Arch, 1 (1910), 209ff.; ET, 11 (1965), 189–222; *The Secret of the Jew* (1930, 1938[2]); E. Roth (ed.), *Die alte Synagoge zu Worms* (1961), 46–51, 65, illus. nos. 25–27; H. Kroner, *Zur Geschichte der juedischen Ritualbaeder in Wuerttemberg* (1914); R. Lanciani, *The Ruins and Excavations of Ancient Rome* (1897); I. Abrahams, *Jewish Life in the Middle Ages* (1932); R. Krautheimer, *Mittelalterliche Synagogen* (1927); D. Kotlar, in: *Miscellanea di Studi in memoria di Dario Disegni* (1969); C. M. Bassols, in: *Sefarad*, 28 (1968); J. Millás-Vallicrosa, *ibid.*, 25 (1965).

[D.Ko.]

MIKVEH ISRAEL (Heb. מִקְוֵה יִשְׂרָאֵל), Israel agricultural school, E. of Tel Aviv-Jaffa. Established in 1870, it is the oldest Jewish rural community in Ereẓ Israel. The school was founded by the *Alliance Israélite Universelle on the initiative of Charles *Netter, who visited the country for the

Figure 1. Entrance to the Mikveh Israel agricultural school. Courtesy Government Press Office, Tel Aviv.

Figure 2. Model of the original Mikveh Israel school on show at the centenary exhibition, June 1970. Courtesy Government Press Office, Tel Aviv.

first time in 1868. He then visualized such a school as the beginning of a future network of Jewish villages. In 1870 Netter obtained a lease of 650 acres (2,600 dunams) of land from the Turkish government, personally receiving the firman from the sultan in Constantinople. In the summer of 1870 he opened the school, which he directed until 1873, gaining support from the *Anglo-Jewish Association and from individuals and interesting Baron Edmond de *Rothschild in the enterprise. In 1882 the first *Bilu pioneers found work and were trained at Mikveh Israel immediately upon their arrival in the country and a few months later ten of them set out to found *Rishon le-Zion. During his visit to Ereẓ Israel in 1898, Theodor *Herzl greeted Kaiser William II at the entrance of Mikveh Israel. From 1914 to 1955 Eliyahu *Krause directed the school. Numerous species of fruit and forest trees were tried out there in the early years, and under Krause, Mikveh Israel became a pioneering ground for the introduction and improvement of new farm branches. Hebrew became the language of instruction soon after Krause had taken over. In the Israel *War of Independence (1948), the school was attacked several times. Since the 1930s Mikveh Israel has become an important education center for *Youth Aliyah. In 1968 it had 940 inhabitants (pupils, teachers, instructors, and other personnel). It consists of a state school and a state-religious school. Mikveh Israel has been instrumental in developing novel techniques in citrus and other farm branches, introducing avocado cultivation and the acclimatization of many livestock strains. The school has a cultural center; a library, named after Krause; a botanical garden; and a collection of 130 citrus species. The Mikveh Israel wine cellars produce select wines and liqueurs. The name is taken from Jeremiah 14:8 and 17:13 and means "Israel's Hope."

[E.O.]

MILAN, city in Lombardy, N. Italy. The presence of Jews in Milan in the Roman period is attested by three Jewish inscriptions, two of which refer to the "father of the community." In 388, *Ambrose, bishop of Milan, expressed regret for failing to lead his congregation in burning down the synagogue which instead had been destroyed "by act of God." It was soon rebuilt, but about 507 was sacked by the Christian mob, whose action was condemned by the Ostrogothic ruler Theodoric. The community presumably continued in existence, though there is little evidence in succeeding centuries except for vague references to Jewish merchants and farmers in the tenth century. With the spread of Jewish communities through northern Italy in the 13th century that of Milan was also revived, but in 1320 the *podestà* issued a decree expelling the Jews, in 1387 Duke Gian Galeazzo Visconti granted privileges to the Jews in the whole of *Lombardy; these were confirmed by Francesco Sforza and his successors. When in 1452 Pope Nicholas V approved the Jewish right of residence in the duchy, he specifically authorized the construction of a synagogue in Milan. Pope Pius II demanded a levy of one-fifth on the possessions of the Jews to subsidize a Crusade (1459), but was opposed by Duke Francesco Sforza. In 1489, under Ludovico il Moro, the Jews were expelled from the entire Duchy. They were soon readmitted, except to Milan itself where a Jew could only stay for three days. Similar conditions continued under the last Sforza dukes and after 1535, when the Duchy of Milan came under Spanish rule. In 1541 Emperor Charles V confirmed that Jews were allowed to live in various towns of the territory, but not in Milan. Thus, when the Jews were finally expelled in 1597, there were none in Milan itself. In 1714, when Lombardy came under Austrian rule, Jews began to return to Milan, and by the middle of the 19th century they numbered approximately 500; a synagogue was built in 1840. In 1848 some were active in the rising against Austrian rule. In 1859 Milan became a part of the new Italian kingdom and the Jews received full rights.

Because of the great commercial and industrial development around Milan which now followed, the city became a center of attraction for new immigrants. In 1900, 2,000 Jews resided there and in 1931, 6,490. [A.Mil.]

Holocaust Period. After Hitler assumed power many refugees arrived from Central and Eastern European countries; this flow continued illegally during the first years of war. About 800 Jews were deported from Milan during the war. Many were captured and killed by the Germans in the towns and villages where they had taken refuge. During the autumn of 1943, the Germans carried out an anti-Jewish raid, in the course of which the community synagogue was destroyed.

Contemporary Period. At the end of the war, 4,484 Jews were living in Milan and were joined temporarily by many refugees from camps in Lombardy. A number of Jewish immigrants came to Italy after 1949 from Egypt and, to a lesser degree, from other Arab countries; 4% came from Israel. The Jewish population of Milan in 1965 numbered 8,488 persons out of total of 1,670,000 inhabitants, with the Sephardi and Oriental element predominating. After the *Six-Day War (1967), some 3,000 Jews, who fled persecution in Egypt, and above all in Libya, sought temporary refuge in Italy. Assimilation was widespread, especially among the Italian element, with the proportion of mixed marriages fluctuating around 50%. The general socioeconomic status of the community was middle class or upper-middle class, with the characteristic concentration in the wholesale and export-import business.

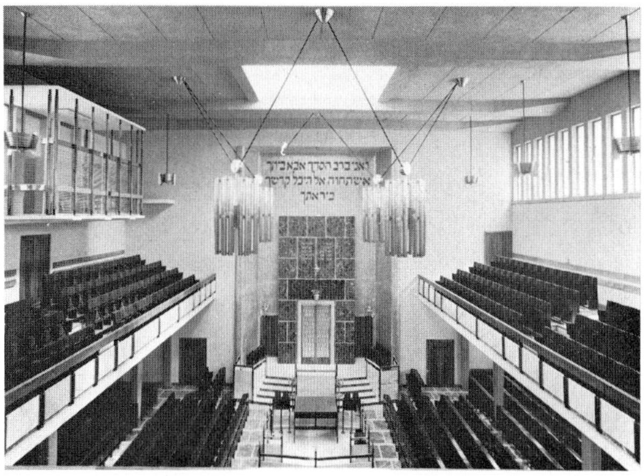

The new synagogue of Milan, built 1953. Courtesy Luisella Mortara-Ottolenghi, Milan.

The community of Milan has a Hebrew school with about 1,000 students. Beside the central synagogue, which follows the Italian rite, there are seven other synagogues and houses of prayer of Italian, Oriental, Persian, and Ashkenazi rites, as well as a rest home for elderly people. In 1967 there were 8,700 Jews in Milan, making the community the second in importance in Italy. The following Jewish journals appear irregularly: *La Rassegna Mensile d'Israel, Il Bollettino della Comunità di Milano, Hed ha-Ḥinnukh ha-Yehudi,* and *Quaderni del Bollettino.* [S.D.P.]

Bibliography: Milano, Bibliotheca, index; Kaufmann, in: REJ, 20 (1890), 34–72; Ferorelli, in: *Vessillo Israelitico,* 63 (1925), 227–38, 337–9; A. Sarano, *Sette anni di vita e di opere della communità israelitica di Milano (1945–52)* (1952). See also bibliography to *Lombardy.

MILANO, ATTILIO (1907–1969), historian of Italian Judaism. Milano was born in Rome, where he studied law and economics. He emigrated to Israel in 1939 with the inception of the racist laws in Italy, settling in Ramat ha-Sharon, where he worked as a manufacturer. Milano's historical studies deal mostly with the economic and social conditions of various Italian Jewish groups, particularly stressing the study of the causes and consequences of usury and relations with the Roman Catholic Church. His *Bibliotheca Historica Italo-Judaica* (1954, 1964, and RMI, 1966) is an indispensable bibliographical tool for the study of Italian Jewry; it includes articles published in various periodicals by Milano himself. Among his important works are *Storia degli Ebrei Italiani nel Levante* (1949), *Storia degli Ebrei in Italia* (1963), and *Il Ghetto di Roma* (1964). He was editor of the department for Italian Jewish history of the *Encyclopaedia Judaica.*

Bibliography: E. S. Artom, in: RMI, 29 (1963), 227–30; G. Romano, *ibid.,* 35 (1969), 369–73; idem, in: *Quaderni della labronica,* n. 3 (1969), 5–12; idem, et al., in *Scritti in memoria di Attilio Milano,* RMI, 36 (1970), 13–47. [A.M.R.]

MILBAUER, JOSEPH (1898–1968), poet. Born in Warsaw, Milbauer was raised in Brussels where, in 1914, he met *Shalom Aleichem, some of whose works he later translated. He went to Paris in 1921. Milbauer's early verse collections were well received. During the 1930s he was for a time editor of the *Univers Israelite,* but his outspoken Zionist opinions brought him into conflict with the paper's directors, and he resigned. Milbauer fought in both world wars and was a prisoner of war but after some harrowing experiences arrived in Ereẓ Israel as an illegal immigrant in 1944. He headed the French desk at the *Keren Ha-Yesod, and was a co-founder of a French literary circle which developed into the Association des Amitiés Israël-France. Milbauer published several more volumes of poetry, often inspired by the landscape of Israel. His other works include: translations of S. Y. *Agnon, Ḥ. N. *Bialik, and S. *Tchernichowsky and the anthology *Poètes yiddisch d'aujourd'hui* (1936).

Bibliography: C. Vigée, in: *L'Arche,* 134 (1968), 63–64. [P.T.]

MILETUS, city in Asia Minor captured by Alexander the Great in 334 B.C.E. According to a document cited by Josephus (Ant. 14:244–6), the inhabitants of Miletus during the Roman period attacked the Jews, "forbidding them to observe their Sabbaths, perform their native rites or manage their produce [tithes] in accordance with their custom." The Roman proconsul, Publius Servilius Galba, the author of the aforementioned document, was informed at Tralles of the inhabitants' actions by Prytanis, the son of Hermas and a citizen of Miletus. The proconsul subsequently ruled in favor of restoring the rights of the Jewish population. An inscription from the Roman theater refers to "the place of the Jews who are also called God-fearing." A ruined building dating from the late Roman-Byzantine period has been surmised by some to have been a synagogue.

Bibliography: Schuerer, Gesch, 3 (1909[4]), 16, 110, 125, 174; Juster, Juifs, 1 (1914), 252 n. 3; Frey, Corpus, 2 (1952), 14–15; E. L. Sukenik, *Ancient Synagogues in Palestine and Greece* (1934), 40–42; Mayer, Art, nos. 816–7. [I.G.]

MILEYKOWSKY, NATHAN (Netanyahu; 1879–1935), Zionist preacher. Born near Kovno, Lithuania, Mileykowsky was educated in the Volozhin yeshivah and ordained in the rabbinate. While in Volozhin he displayed talent as a preacher and speaker and spent two years with the preacher J. L. *Yevzerow. At the age of 20, he was sent by Y. *Tschlenow on a propaganda tour of Siberia, and from that time he became a preacher and speaker on behalf of Zionism. In 1908 he settled in Poland, taught in the Hebrew high school of M. Krinski, in Warsaw, and participated in its management. He continued his propaganda tours in the cities and towns of Poland. During World War I he was a preacher in the Ohel Ya'akov synagogue in Lodz. In 1920 Mileykowsky settled in Palestine, where he served as the principal of a school in Safed. From 1924 to 1929 he was sent to England, Carpatho-Russia (then part of Czechoslovakia), and the United States on a mission for the Jewish National Fund and the Keren Hayesod. Toward the end of his life, he settled in Herzliyyah and was active in the Farmers' Association. During the *Arlosoroff murder trial (1933–34), he set up a committee for the defense of the accused. Some of his speeches are included in his anthologies *Ha-Nevi'im ve-ha-Am* ("The Prophets and the People," 1913) and *Folk un Land* (1928).

Bibliography: Tidhar, 1 (1947), 186–7; EẒD, 3 (1965) 417–9; LNYL, 5 (1963), 621. [Y.S.]

MILHAUD, DARIUS (1892–), French composer. Milhaud was born in Aix-en-Provence and was descended from an old Jewish family that claimed to have been among the first settlers in southern France after the fall of Jerusalem. He entered the Paris Conservatory at the age of 17, was soon attracted by the theater, and between 1910 and 1916 he composed *La Brebis egarée, Agamemnon,* and *Le pauvre matelot.* He became acquainted with the composer Eric Satie and the writers Paul Claudel and Jean Cocteau and, when Claudel was appointed French minister to Brazil, he asked Milhaud to become his secretary. Milhaud spent almost two years (1917–18) at Rio de Janeiro, and his musical impressions of Brazil echo in many of his compositions. After his return to Paris, he joined a circle of progressive artists, the musicians of which formed an inner circle later known as "Les Six." A versatile and prolific composer, Milhaud wrote music for concert, stage, and screen, and for voice and orchestra. South American rhythms, U.S. jazz, Jewish synagogal traditions (especially those of his native region, the *Comtat Venaissin), 12-tone music, and trends and styles of great divergence merge in his works. Yet the mixture is always unmistakably his own.

Milhaud's most important contributions to 20th-century music are to be found in some of his operas: *Les Choëphores* (1915), *Esther de Carpentras* (1925, with text by Armand *Lunel); *Christophe Colomb* (1928); *Bolivar* (1943); and the biblical opera *David* which Milhaud composed with Lunel for the Jerusalem Festival of 1954. Milhaud wrote concertos for almost every orchestral instrument, ballets, short and full-scale symphonies, chamber music, songs, piano music, and cantatas. Among the best known of his compositions on Jewish themes are his

Service Sacré (1947), and two song cycles with piano accompaniment: *Poèmes juifs* (1916) and *Chants populaires hébraïques* (1925). He also wrote musical settings of Psalms for solo voices and chorus; the ballet *La Création du Monde* (1923); a piano suite, *Le Candélabre à sept branches* (1951); and music for various festival prayers.

Darius Milhaud, French composer.

When France collapsed in 1940 Milhaud emigrated to the U.S. and became a professor at Mills College, Oakland, California. After 1947 he divided his time between the U.S. and Paris, where he became a professor of composition at the Conservatory. The story of his life and musical beliefs was told in *Notes sans musique* (1949; *Notes Without Music*, 1953), which also appeared in Hebrew, and in *Entretiens avec Claude Rostand* (1952). During his later years Milhaud suffered from rheumatoid arthritis which confined him to a wheelchair for long periods of time.

Bibliography: P. Collaer, *Darius Milhaud* (Fr., 1947); H. H. Stuckenschmidt, *Schoepfer der neuen Musik* (1958), 204–16; P. Claudel, *Correspondence Paul Claudel and Darius Milhaud 1912–1953* (1961); Grove, Dict.; Riemann-Gurlitt; MGG.

[P.E.G.]

MILICH, ADOLPHE (1884–1964), French painter, born in Tyszowce, Poland; a member of the school of Paris. He originally worked as a sign painter, finally settling in Paris in 1920. During the German occupation he lived in Switzerland. Milich worked in oils and watercolors, and painted landscapes, still lifes, large compositions of women bathing, and portraits. He particularly loved the Mediterranean landscape of Provence and of the area around Lugano. His painting owes much to his long study of the old masters. Among modern painters, the strongest influence is that of Cézanne. Milich cultivated his own idiom regardless of fashion. His work is well thought out and serene, and is characterized by its joyful color harmonies.

Bibliography: G. Huisman, *Milich* (Fr., 1949); Roth, Art, 665.

[ED.]

Watercolor landscape by Adolphe Milich. Jerusalem, J. Leron Collection. Photo Erde, Tel Aviv.

MILITARY SERVICE. Jews served in the national armies of most countries in which they settled. However, in many states they were denied the right to bear arms before the 20th century since they were considered to be second-class citizens not fitted to fight for their country. A major consideration motivating the Jewish desire to fight in the armed forces of the countries of their adoption was that they hoped that the acceptance of this obligation would entitle them to civic rights. For this very reason states which denied Jews civil rights frequently restricted their service in their armies. In the 20th century however, Jews participated fully in modern warfare as the following table of participation of Jews in the two world wars shows.

WORLD WAR I	
U.S.	250,000
Great Britain	50,000
British Commonwealth	8,000
Czarist Russia	450,000
Austria-Hungary	275,000
Italy	8,000
France	35,000
Germany	90,000
Bulgaria	6,000
TOTAL	1,172,000

WORLD WAR II	
U.S.	550,000
Great Britain	62,000
Canada	16,000
South Africa	10,000
Australia and New Zealand	3,000
Palestinian Units in British army	35,000
Belgium	7,000
Holland	7,000
U.S.S.R.	500,000
Greece	13,000
France	46,000
Poland	140,000
Czechoslovakia	8,000
TOTAL	1,397,000

The above figures were published by the United Nations and do not include Jewish partisans who fought against Nazi Germany. Jews served in all the services and a few became army commanders, for example the Italian general Giorgio *Liuzzi. More recently, the military achievements of the Israel army during the War of Independence (1948–49), the Sinai Campaign of 1956, and the *Six-Day War (1967) focused attention on the quality of the Jewish soldier.

United States of America. Jews first did military service early in the colonial period in the form of militia duty. Asser *Levy insisted on his right to be allowed to stand guard duty against attack by Indians, and other early members of the community of New Amsterdam demanded the right of helping to defend the settlement and, when necessary, sprang to arms in a common effort to repel hostile assaults, earning full admission as citizens of the colony (1657). Later, in the 1750s, Jews served in the conquest of Canada in which Aaron *Hart led a battalion against the French in Canada, and Judah Hays commanded a 16-ton privateer, the *Duke of Cumberland*. During the American War of Independence (1775–83), a considerable number of Jews volunteered for the colonialist armies and several acquired considerable distinction, among them Isaac *Franks, David Salisbury *Franks, Lewis *Bush, and Solomon Bush. In this war some U.S. companies included a considerable number of Jewish soldiers, such as that commanded by Major Benjamin Nones (d. 1826), a French Jew who served under the command of Lafayette and George Washington. During the second war between the United States and Great Britain from 1812 to 1814 there were a small number of Jews in the U.S. army most of whom were volunteers or members of militia companies. Joseph Bloomfield (d. 1823) held the rank of brigadier general and Aaron Levy (d. 1829) became a lieutenant colonel. Two naval officers achieved fame in this war. Captain John Ordraonaux (1778–1841) seized nine British prize vessels and later captured a British frigate and Uriah Phillips *Levy volunteered for the U.S. navy in 1812 and rose to become commodore nearly half a century later. Levy's ship was captured by the British after sinking 21 merchant vessels and he spent the last 16 months of the war in a British prison. His subsequent career in the face of anti-Semitic opposition opened the way for future generations of U.S. Jewish sailors among whom Claude C. *Bloch rose to become admiral of the U.S. fleet over a century later. In the following decades many Jews held senior posts in the U.S. forces; in the Nones family there were four naval officers who rose to the rank of captain. During the Mexican War (1746–48) the Jews of Baltimore formed a volunteer corps and Jonas Phillips Levy, brother of Uriah Phillips Levy, was promoted to naval captain. In the American Civil War (1861–65) Jews flocked to the colors of both Union and Confederacy armies. About 6,000 Jews fought on the Union side and a smaller number in the Confederate forces, though the exact figures are in dispute. The Confederate forces contained many prominent Jews, including Judah Phillip *Benjamin, the secretary of war, David de Leon (1813–1872), the first surgeon general, and 23 staff officers. The naval captain, Levi Myers Harby, distinguished himself in the defense of Galveston and commanded a fleet of gunboats on the Sabine River. On the Union side seven Jews were awarded the Congressional Medal of Honor: Leopold Karpeles, Benjamin Levy, Abraham Cohn, David Obranski, Henry Heller, Abraham Grunwalt, and Isaac Gans. Several Jews rose to the rank of general during the war including Frederick Knefler (1833–1901), a Hungarian by birth, who volunteered for the Union army on the outbreak of war as a private and was the first Jewish brevet major general; Edward S. Salomon (1836–1913), who was made governor of Washington Territory in recognition of his military feats at the battles of Frederickston, Mainfordsville, and Gettysburg; and Leopold C. Newman (1815–1863), who was killed in action. Max Einstein and Phillip J. Joachimson (1817–1890), who organized the 59th New York volunteer regiment, were made brigadier generals in the Union army. Jews played no conspicuous part in the Spanish-American War of 1898. Nevertheless, it is noteworthy that hostilities broke out following the sinking of the U.S.S. *Maine*, commanded until shortly before then by the Jewish officer Adolph Marix, and over 100 of nearly 5,000 Jews who fought in the U.S. army were killed. A few Jews were active in various Latin American armies including Jacob Baiz who was a brigadier general in the army of Honduras and Sam Dreben known as the "fighting Jew" who fought in Nicaragua in 1910, and was subsequently a colonel in the armies of Honduras and Mexico. In World War I a quarter of a million Jews fought in the armies of the United States, representing 5% of the total Jewish population of the United States, whereas only 3% of the total U.S. population served in World War I. Over 15,000 Jews were killed or wounded in the 18-month campaign. Nearly half of the 77th Division, the National Army unit from New York, consisted of Jews and there were approximately 10,000 Jewish officers, including three generals, Milton J. Foreman (1863–1935), Charles Laucheimer (1859–1920) and Abel Davis (1878–1937). Three Jews also rose to high rank in the navy during World War I: Rear Admiral Joseph Strauss (1861–1948) who commanded the battleship *Nevada* and was later responsible for placing a barrage of mines across the English Channel, Commander

Figure 1. Adolph Marix, first Jewish rear admiral in the U.S. Navy. From J. G. Friedman and L. A. Falk, *Jewish War Veterans of America*, 1954.

Walter F. Jacobs, who commanded a flotilla of minesweepers, and Captain Joseph K. *Taussig who was responsible for the safe escort of convoys against submarine attacks. Six Jews won the Congressional Medal of Honor: William Sawelson, Benjamin Kaufman (1894–), Sydney G. Gumpertz (1879–1953), Charles W. Hoffman, Samuel Sampler, and Philip C. Katz. In addition over 200 Jews were awarded the Distinguished Service Cross. The Jewish contribution to the U.S. fighting force in World War II was no less impressive. Over half a million U.S. Jews fought in the Allied armies, many of whom crossed the Canadian border early in the war to volunteer for the Canadian army before the United States entered the fighting. More than 50,000 Jewish servicemen were killed or wounded and two Jewish soldiers were awarded the Congressional Medal of Honor, one of whom was Lieutenant Raymond Lussman who single-handedly killed 17 German soldiers and captured another 32. An outstanding army officer who fell in battle was Major General Maurice Rose (1899–1945) who commanded the U.S. third armoured division in the final offensive against Germany in 1945 and who was killed at Paderborn only a few weeks before the end of the war. In addition Lewis *Strauss was promoted to rear admiral during World War II. In 1953 Hyman *Rickover, a naval captain in World War II, was promoted to rear admiral and retired in 1958 with the rank of vice admiral. Jews also played an important part in the United States armies in Korea and in Vietnam; 150,000 Jews saw service in the Korean War and nearly 30,000 Jews fought in Vietnam, where Ben Sternberg (1914–) served as major general. [Ed.]

Great Britain. Until the repeal of the 1673 Test Act in 1828, professing Jews were debarred by religious tests from serving as officers in the regular armed forces of the crown. English Jews were, however, like their counterparts, the Continental Court Jews, prominent as army contractors for pay and supplies in the 18th century: the most famous were Sir Solomon de *Medina, the associate of Marlborough, and Abraham Prado (the diary and letter-book of the latter's subordinate, David Mendes da Costa, have survived). Aaron *Hart was commissary officer at the taking of Montreal and settled in Canada. Professing Jews could serve in the ranks and a number served especially in the navy, among them Barnett Abraham Simmons (later minister in the Penzance synagogue) and Isaac Vallentine, founder of the *Jewish Chronicle*. When invasion threatened, volunteers were enlisted and many professing Jews served, particularly in the London Volunteers. Jews could hold

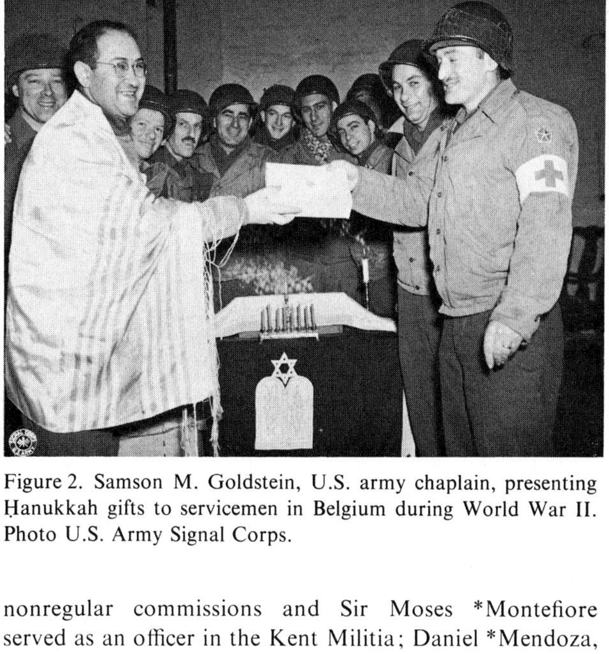

Figure 2. Samson M. Goldstein, U.S. army chaplain, presenting Ḥanukkah gifts to servicemen in Belgium during World War II. Photo U.S. Army Signal Corps.

nonregular commissions and Sir Moses *Montefiore served as an officer in the Kent Militia; Daniel *Mendoza, the boxer, was a sergeant in the Fifeshire, then Aberdeenshire, Fencibles. There were a number of officers of Jewish origin before 1828—Wellington said 15 served under him at Waterloo in 1815—but they were presumably converts or at least not professing Jews: the most famous were the descendants of Meyer Low Schomberg, physician to the Great Synagogue; among his sons were Captain Sir Alexander Schomberg R.N. (Royal Navy), founder of a naval and military dynasty still flourishing, and Lieutenant Colonel Henry Schomberg, probably the first Anglo-Jewish army officer.

After the repeal of the Test and Corporation Acts, some professing Jews entered the army and became regular officers, particularly in the Indian army (e.g., Captain Lionel Gomez da Costa, who died of wounds at Lucknow in 1857, and Ensign Edmund Helbert Ellis, who died in 1851 at the age of 22), in which Indian native Jews had previously served. The most distinguished soldier in the community was Col. Albert E. W. *Goldsmid. An increasing number of professing Jews served in the ranks, including veterans of the Crimean War. Judaism was not, however, recognized in the British army as a separate denomination until 1886, partly owing to the efforts of Trooper Woolf Cohen of the 5th Lancers. In the South African War (1899–1902), between 3,000 and 4,000 Jews served, with 127 killed in action; many of those serving were South African "colonials" and "outlanders," notably Colonel Sir David *Harris who commanded the Kimberley Town Guard during the siege. During World War I the number of Jews in the British army rose to 50,000. Several Anglo-Jewish families provided large numbers of Jewish soldiers. The *Rothschild family contributed five officers, the *Sassoon family 14 officers, and five sons of Arthur *Sebag-Montefiore held commissions, while 41 descendants of Sir Isidore *Spielmann were said to have served as officers. Five Jewish soldiers won the Victoria Cross: Captain Robert Gee, Lieutenant Frank Alexander De Pass, Sergeant Issy Smith (Shmulevitsch), and Privates J. White and Leonard Keysor; 50 Jewish soldiers received the Distinguished Service Order. In addition the Jews formed their own unit, the Zion Mule Corps, which fought at Gallipoli and in the Dardanelles in 1915. Later, three Jewish units, the 38th, 39th, and 40th battalions of the Royal Fusiliers participated in the conquest of Palestine in 1918 under General Allenby (see *Jewish Legion). The regiments were disbanded after World War I. In World War II over 60,000 Jews fought in the British army. Jewish soldiers included volunteers from Central and Eastern Europe who were not British subjects and Palestinian volunteers who enlisted after the German advance across North Africa threatened the *yishuv* in Palestine. Two Jewish soldiers won the Victoria Cross in World War II: Captain David Hirsch, and naval lieutenant T. Gould. Several others rose to high military rank including Major General William Beddington (1893–), Brigadier Sir Edward Beddington (1884–1966), who was deputy director of military intelligence at the War Office, Brigadier Barnard Goldstone (1896–), Brigadier Fredrick Morris (1888–1941), Brigadier Bernard Schlesinger (1896–1945), and Brigadier Frederick *Kisch, who was killed in action. In addition, Irish-born Abraham Briscoe (1892–) was the first Jew to reach the rank of air-commodore in the Royal Air Force. Jewish soldiers also fought in the British army in Korea and in Egypt where Brigadier Edmund Meyers (1906–) was chief engineer to the British forces at the Suez Canal. Major General James A. *D'Avigdor-Goldsmid became colonel of the 4/7th Dragoon Guards and director-general of the Territorial army.

British Commonwealth. No discrimination existed against Jews serving in the armed forces of Canada, Australia, and South Africa and a number of Jewish officers rose to high rank. In World War I Lieutenant General Sir John *Monash commanded the Australian army corps in France from June 1918 and was responsible for the breach of the German lines on August 8 which led to the collapse of German resistance. He was considered the outstanding army commander of World War I and in 1930 was promoted to full general. Major General Sir Charles Rosenthal also achieved prominence in the Australian army during World War I, commanding the ANZAC artillery and later the second Australian army division under Monash's supreme command. Another Australian, Private Leonard Keysor, was awarded the Victoria Cross during the Gallipoli campaign of 1915. In World War II 16,000 Jews fought in the Canadian army in Europe and North Africa, and one of them, Colonel Phinias Rothschild (1914–), was later promoted to major general and quartermaster-general of the Canadian army. 10,000 Jews fought in the South African army in which Major General Alexander Ohrenstein was director-general of the medical services.

[V.D.L.]

Czarist Russia. Before 1827 Jews were exempted from military service on payment of a money tax. In that year, however, on the accession of Nicholas I, Jews were conscripted into the Russian army for periods of up to 25 years. Ten Jews for every thousand males were conscripted,

Figure 3. English caricature of the Jew as a fighter during the Napoleonic Wars. London, 1803. Cecil Roth Collection. Photo David Harris, Jerusalem.

Figure 4. Members of the Zion Mule Corps, a British army unit which fought at Gallipoli and in the Dardanelles in 1915. Courtesy Haganah Historical Archives, Tel Aviv.

recruitment being of boys aged between 12 and 25 while those under 18 were placed in special schools (see *Cantonists). Jewish soldiers were subjected to persistent pressure to convert, young Jewish children were seized and pressed into military service for 25-year periods, and Jews were excluded from the ranks of officers. Not unnaturally Jews sought every opportunity to evade military service in Russia under these conditions. These conscription laws did not apply to Jews in Polish terriotries annexed by Russia at the end of the Napoleonic wars. Thousands of Jews fought in the czarist army in the Crimean War (1854–56) and about 500 were killed. In 1864 a monument was erected to the Jewish soldiers who fell in the siege of Sebastopol and one Jewish soldier, Chaim Zaitchikoff, was congratulated by Prince Gortchakoff for his valor. Following the accession of Alexander II the condition of the Jews improved slightly and they were given the right to be promoted to sergeant while demobilized Jewish soldiers were allowed to live outside the *Pale of Settlement. The seizure of Jewish children for military service was abolished and the maximum period of service was reduced to 15 years. In 1874 a law was enacted introducing universal military service obliging all Russian citizens to report for military service at the age of 21. The effect of the new law was to grant Jews equality with the rest of the population but half a century of enforced service in the Russian army had already conditioned them to avoid enlistment wherever possible. Nevertheless, many thousands of Jews fought in the Russo-Turkish War of 1877. They were not allowed to become officers though as an exception to the rule Captain Zvi Hertz *Zam was permitted to enter the officers' school in 1874 after eight years of service; however, he was promoted to captain only after more than 40 years of service in the Russian army. Another exception was Joseph *Trumpeldor, who refused to be discharged from service after he lost his right arm in action. The acute shortage of doctors in the Czarist army also led to Jews being admitted as surgeon officers. On the outbreak of World War I nearly 400,000 Jews were drafted into the Russian army and the number increased to nearly half a million by 1917. Several thousands won awards for bravery on the battlefield.

Austro-Hungary. The Austro-Hungarian Empire generally adopted an enlightened policy toward its Jews. In 1782 Joseph II granted civic rights to the Jews and six years later Jews were declared fit for military service, though the right was at first restricted to serving in the supply corps in the province of Galicia where most Jews lived. Later Jews were allowed to serve in all branches of the Hapsburg army. During the Revolutionary and Napoleonic wars (1792–1813) many Jews served in the Austro-Hungarian army. Some were allowed to become officers. In 1818 Jews were officially accepted as officers even in the conservative cavalry regiments. Nevertheless, several professing Jews rose to the rank of general in the Hapsburg army, among them Field Marshal-Lieutenant Joseph *Singer who was chief of staff of the Third Army, and Major General Alexander von *Eis and Field Marshal-Lieutenant Eduard von *Schweitzer, both of whom commanded major Austrian army units. The comparatively generous treatment of Jews in the Austro-Hungarian army led many Jews to take up a military career, especially as certain other professions were closed to them. In 1855 there were 157 Jewish officers in the Hapsburg army and by 1893 this number had risen to 2,179 or 8% of all the officers in the Hapsburg army. A number of Jews also became prominent in the navy, including Tobias von Oesterreicher, who was the first Austrian Jew to be promoted to rear admiral, and two battleship commanders (sea captains), Friedrich Pick (1839–1908) and Moritz von Funk (1831–1905). Nearly 300,000 Jews fought in the Austro-Hungarian army during World War I. Among 2,500 officers were three field marshal-lieutenants, Eduard von Schweitzer, Adolph Kornhaber (1856–1925), and *Hazai Samu, and five major generals, Simon *Vogel, Johann Mestitz, Leopold Austerlitz, Emil von *Sommer, and Márton Zöld. Nearly 30,000 Jewish soldiers were killed during the four years of war, including 600 Austrian Jewish officers. After the collapse of the Hapsburg Empire Jews played an increasingly smaller part in the armed forces of both Austria and Hungary, and following the advent of Fascist and pro-Nazi regimes in the 1930s they ceased to serve in the armed forces altogether. One outstanding figure of the post-World War I period was General Vilmos Böhm (1880–1947) who was commander in chief of the Hungarian army during the four-month Soviet dictatorship of Béla *Kun in 1919.

U.S.S.R. Following the Revolution of February 1917, Jews were granted equal rights and for the first time were allowed to become army officers. Many were transferred to officers' schools and on graduating received the rank of sub-officer *(praporshchik)*. When the Bolsheviks seized power in November 1917, many Jewish soldiers fought in the Red Army organized by Leon *Trotsky, aided by Skliansky and Jacob Sverdlov. Four divisional commanders were Jews and a few units consisted solely of Jews such as the brigade commanded by Joseph Furman. After the civil war J. B. Goldberg became commander of a reserve army. Among Jews who obtained senior army commands were Grigori Stern, Jan Gamarnik, and Feldman. Most of them were executed during Stalin's purges, a notable exception being Stern, who was sent to the Far East (1935), where he routed the Japanese army which had invaded Soviet territory. He later commanded the Soviet

Figure 5. Captain of the air fleet Michael Plotkin, a Hero of the Soviet Union.

Far Eastern Forces with the rank of full general and drove the Japanese from Mongolian territory. Stern's army was assisted by air force units under Yaacov *Smushkevich, appointed commander in chief of the Soviet air force in 1940.

World War II. Following the outbreak of World War II,

Figure 6. "Jewish recruits complaining about having to learn exercises." A caricature of Jews in the Prussian army, c. 1780. Nuremberg, Germanisches Museum.

the Soviet Union annexed the Baltic states and territories in eastern Poland and Belorussia thus incorporating a large number of Jews within its borders. After the German invasion of Russia, Polish and Belorussian soldiers in the Soviet army were considered of suspect loyalty and were transferred to labor battalions. In December 1941, however, the order was revoked and Jews from the Baltic states were permitted to serve in all units of the Soviet army. Subsequently four Lithuanian Jews were made Heroes of the Soviet Union. The Soviet Jewish historian Jacob Kantor estimated that almost half a million Jews fought in the Soviet army in World War II of whom at least 140 were awarded the title Hero of the Soviet Union (the official Soviet figure is 107). Jews constituted a disproportionately large number of senior officers, largely because the percentage of Jews having a university education was higher than that of other nationalities. More than 100 Jews held the rank of general, as the following partial table shows:

No. of Jewish Generals	Corps
13	Engineering and Mechanical
13	Artillery
10	Tank
10	Medical
6	Infantry
5	Air Force Engineering
4	Air Force
4	Quartermaster Service
2	Veterinary Service
2	Navy
2	Cavalry
1	Communications

Jewish generals were particularly prominent as field commanders, notably General Jacob *Kreiser. Other Jewish commanders at the battle of Stalingrad included Lt. gen. I. S. Beskin and Major gen. (later Lt. gen.) Matvey Weinrub. Jewish generals also held key commands during the final assault on Berlin. Lieutenant General Hirsh Plaskov was artillery commander of the Second Guards Army, Lieutenant General Semion Krivoshein commanded one of the first corps to break into Berlin in the spring of 1945, and Lieutenant General Weinrub was artillery commander of the Eighth Guards Army. Special mention should also be made of the Jewish Cossack commander, Major General Lev Dovator, who was killed during the first Soviet offensive in December 1941, Lieutenant General David Dragunski, who was twice made a Hero of the Soviet Union, and Major Caesar Konikov, whose courageous defense of the fishing village of Stanichka for seven months led to the village being renamed Kunikovo after his death. In addition Colonel General Leonti Kotlyar was commander of the engineering corps and six Jews held the rank of major general in the medical services (where there were a large number of Jewish doctors and nurses): Vovsy, Levitt, David Entin, Reingold, Gurvich, and Slavin. A number of Jews were given the award Hero of the Soviet Union in the Soviet air force, among them Michael Plotkin, who flew in the first Soviet bombing raid on Berlin in August 1941, Henryk Hofman, and four women: Polina Gelman, Zina Hofman, Lila Litvak, and Rachel Zlotina, who belonged to a women's air regiment. Two Jewish Soviet submarine commanders became Heroes of the Soviet Union—Israel Fisanovich and Isaac Kabar—as did Abraham Sverdlov who commanded a flotilla of torpedo boats. Jews were also prominent among the partisans, constituting more than 20,000 men in separate units in the Polish-Russian border areas. The Soviet official history of the war mentions the names of several Jewish partisan heroes, among them N. S. Kagan, one of seven Moscow Komsomol members hanged by the Germans while on a mission behind enemy lines, L. E. Bernstein, commander of the Pozharski unit which joined the Slovak rising against the Germans, and Vladimir Epstein, who escaped from Auschwitz to form a partisan unit in Poland. (See also *Partisans.)

After World War II. Although famous Jewish generals such as Dragunski and Kreiser retained their popularity after World War II, Soviet policy toward the Jewish soldier changed for the worse, in accordance with general Soviet policy toward the Jews. It is believed that nearly all the Jewish generals of World War II were retired by 1953 as

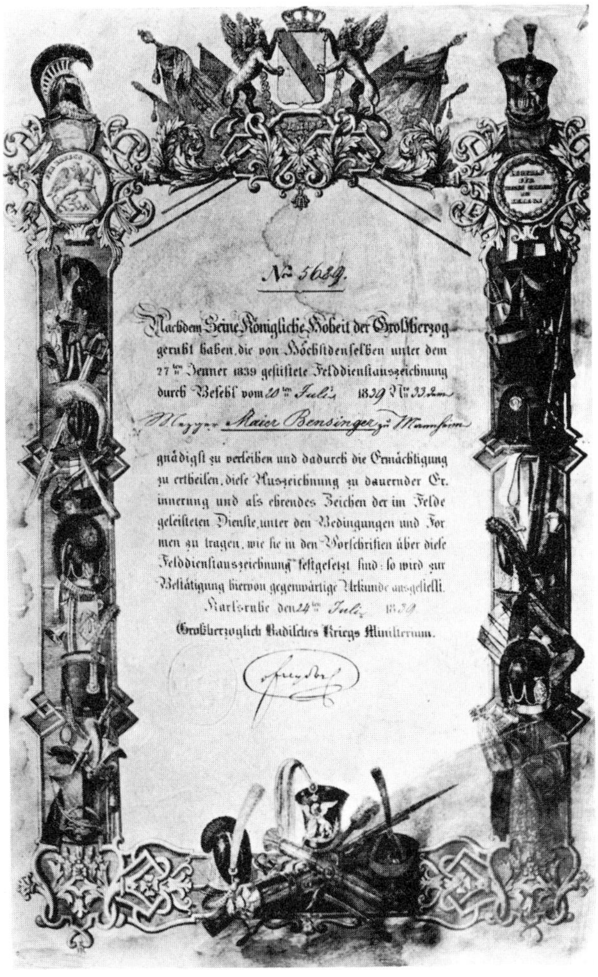
№ 5689.

Nachdem Seine Königliche Hoheit der Großherzog geruht haben, die von Höchstdenselben unter dem 27ten Jenner 1839 gestiftete Felddienstauszeichnung durch Befehl vom 20ten Juli 1839

Maier Bensinger zu Mannheim

gnädigst zu verleihen und dadurch die Ermächtigung zu ertheilen, diese Auszeichnung zu dauernder Erinnerung und als ehrendes Zeichen der im Felde geleisteten Dienste, unter den Bedingungen und Formen zu tragen, wie sie in den Vorschriften über diese Felddienstauszeichnung festgesetzt sind: so wird zur Bestätigung hiervon gegenwärtige Urkunde ausgestellt.

Karlsruhe den 24ten Juli 1839

Großherzoglich Badisches Kriegs Ministerium.

Figure 7. Certificate permitting Maier Bensinger, a butcher of Mannheim, to wear his service decoration. Karlsruhe, 1839. Jerusalem, C.A.H.J.P.

were nearly 300 Jewish colonels and lieutenant colonels. By 1970 the number of Jewish senior officers on active service in the Soviet army had declined drastically. [ED.]

Italy. Before the beginning of the 19th century Jews were forbidden to bear arms in any of the Italian states or to be a member of any military organization. The French Revolution, however, led to the demand for equal rights in Italy as elsewhere and the Jews were among the beneficiaries of progressive legislation. Following the conquest of north Italy by Napoleon, Italian Jews even established their own units and fought with the emperor all over Europe. However, during the reactionary period in north Italy following the final defeat of Napoleon in 1815, Jews were debarred from military service. After the decree of March 1848 granting Jews full equality in Piedmont, 235 Jews volunteered for the Piedmontese army in the war against Austria. Enrico *Guastalla was among the Italian soldiers who captured Rome in 1849, and among the Piedmontese troops fighting on the allied side in the Crimean War (1854–56) was Colonel Cesare Rovighi who later became aide-de-camp to King Victor Emanuel I. In the war against Austria, 1859–60, 260 Jews volunteered for the Piedmontese armies and several were awarded medals. There were 11 Jews among the 1,000 led by Garibaldi who captured southern Italy and Sicily from the Bourbons and Enrico Guastalla later became one of Garibaldi's chief lieutenants. In 1870, 236 Jews were among the victorious Italian army which conquered Rome. Jewish soldiers were subject to no restrictions in the army of united Italy and the percentage of Jewish officers was disproportionately large. Many Jews held the rank of general in the Italian army. They included Lieutenant General Achille Coen (1851–1925), Lieutenant General Emanuele *Pugliese, Lieutenant General Roberto *Segre, Lieutenant General Angelo *Arbib (Arbid), Lieutenant General Angelo Modena, and others. Other Jewish soldiers rose to high military rank, among them Lieutenant General Giuseppe *Ottolenghi who was minister of war from 1902 to 1904. In all, several thousand Jewish officers and men fought in the Italian army in World War I.

Other Jewish officers included four major generals: Carlo Archivolti (1873–1944), Armando *Bachi, Adolfo Olivetti (1878–1944), and Giacomo Almagia (1876–1947), and 12 brigadier generals. Five Jews became admirals in the Italian navy. Augusto Capon, Franco Nunes (1868–1943), and Guido Segre (1871–1942) were full admirals, and Vice Admiral Paolo Marani (1884–1950) and Rear Admiral Aldo Ascoli (1882–1956) commanded ships in the invasion of Abyssinia in 1935. In November 1938 a new law was promulgated prohibiting Jews from serving in the armed forces and all the Jewish generals and admirals were forced to retire. During World War II no Jews fought in the army of Benito Mussolini, and some joined the partisan underground movement. Nevertheless two Jews were specially recalled to service because of particular skills: these were Rear Admiral Pontremoli and Major General Umberto Pugliese (1880–). The latter was given the task of raising Italian naval vessels sunk by the British at Taranto. After World War II Giorgio *Liuzzi who was one of the senior officers retired in 1938 was recalled to active service and was chief of staff of the Italian army from 1956 to 1958 with the rank of lieutenant general. [ED.]

Germany. In the early Middle Ages Jews were accorded the right to bear arms. Later on, however, with the deterioration in their social and political standing after the upheavals of the *Crusades, this right was gradually withdrawn until by the middle of the 13th century Jews, numbered with women, children, and clerics, as being forbidden to bear arms. Exceptions to this rule were rare during the following centuries (see Jud *Michel), though Jews were very prominent as military *contractors (purveyors of livestock, fodder, food, uniforms, etc.) in the 17th and 18th centuries.

The first German Jews conscripted in modern times were from the left bank of the Rhine occupied by revolutionary and Napoleonic France. German states under French influence followed suit (*Westphalia). In 1812 Prussia decreed that Jews were liable to military service and when the War of Liberation broke out a year later many hundreds volunteered, 82 of them receiving decorations. Nevertheless, *Frederick William II repudiated his promise that war veterans could receive positions, irrespective of religion, and even wounded veterans suffered discrimination. The sole Jewish officer in the army during his reign was Major Meno Burg (1787–1853), who owed his position to the influence of the king's brother, the commander of the artillery. It was commonly accepted that Jews were inferior soldiers and that their service was mainly of educational and assimilatory value.

In 1845 the first Jewish officers were commissioned into the Prussian reserve forces, the *Landwehr*. Until about 1885, Jewish officers, primarily university graduates, were commissioned by co-option; but after this date virtually none became officers, despite their exemplary service in the Austro-Prussian (1866) and Franco-Prussian (1870–71) wars, because of growing anti-Semitism. An exception was Walther von *Mossner, the sole senior Jewish officer in the Prussian army, and he owed his position to personal connections with the king and converted to Christianity during his career. Most German states followed Prussia's discriminatory policy (particularly Hanover) while others were more liberal, Bavaria permitting Jewish officers to rise to the upper ranks in the standing army. During the 1848 Revolution Jews enlisted in the National Guard, where they were reluctantly accepted. That year the first Jewish doctor was commissioned in Prussia, and subsequently, due to the lack of physicians, the medical corps harbored Jewish officers in large numbers without permitting them to become senior officers.

Many thousands of Jews fought in the German army in World War I. About 2,000 Jewish officers were commissioned and 12,000 Jews were killed in battle. Nevertheless, during and after the war there was an ugly upsurge of accusations that Jews had either not enlisted or shirked front-line service. To combat this propaganda the Reichsbund juedischer Frontsoldaten, an association of Jewish war veterans, was founded. In 1917 the War Ministry ordered a thorough survey conducted to find the number and proportion of Jews serving in front-line units. The results and the dubious manner in which they had been obtained became the subject of a bitter public controversy. In fact, the percentage of Jews was almost equal to that of Christians; that it was not higher is explained by the diminishing birthrate among German Jewry (between 1880 and 1930) which resulted in a lower proportion of those of military age relative to the non-Jewish population. After World War I the small professional army of the Weimar Republic contained few Jews, who were all removed in 1933. [H.W.]

France. During the Middle Ages Jews were generally excluded from military service except in times of emergency. Their position remained unchanged until 1789 when, following the outbreak of the French Revolution, all Frenchmen, including Jews, were made liable for military service. Many Jews served in Napoleon's armies, among them Brigadier General Marc-Jean-Jerome Wolffe (1776–1848) who commanded the first cavalry brigade of the Grande Armée and Captain Alexandre Marcquefoy who

Figure 8. "The Return of the Volunteer," a painting by Moritz Oppenheim (1800–1882) showing a Jewish soldier being welcomed home. New York, Oscar Gruss Collection. Photo Frank Darmstaedter, New York.

was awarded the Legion of Honor by Napoleon himself; 800 Jews were estimated to be serving under Napoleon in 1808, among them a number of Italians and Poles. Berek (Berko) *Joselewicz, the Polish patriot, commanded a regiment in Napoleon's Polish Legion. The outstanding Jewish soldier in Napoleon's army was Henri *Rottenbourg who was made major general in 1814. Nevertheless, conditions of the Jewish soldiers were made difficult by the refusal of many commanding officers to allow Jews into their ranks and the restrictions on the rights of promotion.

During the early part of the 19th century an increasing number of Jews fought in the French army and a few achieved considerable prominence, among them Colonel Martin Cerfbeer, Captain Abraham Lévy, Captain M. Vormess, and Captain Benoît Lévy who were all awarded the Legion of Honor. No exact details are available as to the number of Jews who fought in the Crimean War (1854–56) but several won awards for gallantry, among them Leopold *See and Colonel Abraham Lévy. In the Italian war of 1859 See and Lévy were again decorated as was Major Adolph Abraham, and in the Franco-Prussian War (1870–71), Colonel Jules Moch and Captain Halphen broke through the Prussian lines after the French army had been surrounded at Metz. In that war Major Franchetti was posthumously decorated having fallen during the siege of Paris. During the Third Republic (1870–1940) Jews entered the French army in unprecedented numbers and 23 rose to the rank of general. Although subject to no official restrictions, Jews were frequently the target of anti-Semitic attacks, the most notable occasion being the *Dreyfus case. The outstanding Jewish officers of the period before World War I were major generals Leopold See, Aimé *Lambert, Alvarez Lévy, and Naquet-Laroque (1843–1921), and brigadier generals Edgar Wolffe (c. 1840–1901), Gabriel Gustave Brisac (1817–c. 1890), Adolphe Hinstin (c. 1820–c. 1890), Bernard Abraham (1824–c. 1900), and Adolphe Aron (c. 1840–c. 1910). On the outbreak of World War I several hundred Jews volunteered for the French army, among them captains Charles Lehmann and René Frank, both of whom had fought in the Franco-Prussian War 44 years earlier. About 50,000 French Jews, over 20% of the total Jewish population, fought in the French army between 1914 and 1918, and an additional 4,000 Jewish refugees from Eastern Europe volunteered. Twelve French Jews held the rank of general, among them Lieutenant General *Valabrègue, major generals Naquet-Laroque and Justin Dennery (1847–1928), who were recalled from retirement, major generals Camille Baruch Levi (1860–1933) and Jules Heymann (1850–1928) and brigadier generals René Alexandre (1864–1931), Lucien Lévi (1859–1932), Paul Emile Grumbach (1861–1931), Gédéon Geismar (1863–1931), and André Weiller (1865–c. 1940). Of 39 French Jewish airmen who fought in World War I, all but four were killed in battle and the total number of French Jews killed in action exceeded 8,000. Several Jews rose to the rank of general after World War I, among them Major General Pierre Boris, Major General Raymond Laroque and Brigadier General Albert Baumann (1869–1945).

Before the French collapse in June 1940 General Boris was made general inspector of the French artillery. Major General Charles Huntzinger and Major General Pierre Brisac were all permitted by the Vichy régime to retain their rank despite the racial laws against Jews. Similarly the Vichy régime gave Samuel Meyer the award of the Legion of Honor for bravery while André Gutman received the award of the Croix de Guerre for bravery in action. The French army included one regiment almost entirely made up of Polish Jews. Following the French defeat in June 1940 many French and East European Jews joined the Free French under Charles de Gaulle in London, among them Ingénieur-Général Louis *Kahn who was director of naval construction. Jews were also prominent in the French resistance, among them Roger Carcassonne who led the resistance movement in North Africa. In 1944, following the liberation of France, General Boris was one of several Jewish officers reinstated in the French army, and in 1945 General *Dassault commanded the French artillery. After World War II a small number of Jews served in the French army in Indo-China.

Poland. Jewish settlement had begun in Poland by the 12th century and Jews were conscripted principally to reinforce the local militia and help build fortifications. They were not expected to take any important part in the Polish army until the Tatar attacks on eastern Poland at the end of the 16th century. Jews were recruited into defense units and some were taken prisoner, a fact recorded in the orders of the Russian czar Michael (1613–1645). A Jewish unit was formed under the command of one Mozko and in some cities the general mobilization of Jews was ordered. Jews were also prominent in the wars against Sweden (1655–60). During the 18th century, Catholic pressure was brought to bear against Jews fighting in the Polish army and the number of Jews serving fell from over 2,000 to a few hundred. During the uprising in the year following the second partition of Poland of 1793, numbers of Jews joined the revolutionary army along with other Poles and many Jews fought in the Polish force which drove the Russians out of Warsaw. Later in 1794, a Jewish cavalry legion was formed under the command of Berek Joselewicz, initially numbering 500 men and later nearly 2,000. The Jewish legion distinguished itself in the defense of Warsaw but was completely wiped out in the Russian massacre in the suburb of Praga after the collapse of the rebellion. At the turn of the 19th century a number of Jews joined Napoleon's army and fought for France in Italy and Eastern Europe. Joselewicz himself commanded a regiment of Polish cavalry, and another Polish Jew, Caspar Junghof, was awarded the Legion of Honor. Similarly Jews volunteered for the army of the Grand Duchy of Warsaw established by Napoleon in 1807. Among them was Josef *Berkowicz, the son of Joselewicz, who fought with other Poles in the French army which invaded Russia in 1812.

After the defeat of Napoleon in 1814, Jews in the area of Poland under czarist rule played an active part in the Polish uprisings of 1830, 1848, and 1863. During World War I, Polish Jews fought in units of both the armies of the Allies and the central powers. A number of Polish Jews in the Russian Austro-Hungarian and French armies were decorated. After the war thousands of Jews fought in the Polish army against Russia, among them Colonel Goldman, Colonel Karaffa-Kreutenkraft, and Colonel Floyar-Reichman. Nevertheless, Polish anti-Semitism per-

Figure 9. "*Yahrzeit* at the Front," a painting made during the Franco-Prussian War, by Moritz Oppenheim, 1870. New York, Oscar Gruss Collection. Photo Frank Darmstaedter, New York.

Figure 10. Austrian Jewish soldiers praying at the Western Wall in Jerusalem during World War I. Courtesy Central Zionist Archives, Jerusalem.

meated the army and all the other organs of state, and although there were never less than 20,000 Jews in the Polish army between the wars, very few Jewish soldiers held high military rank. An outstanding exception was Bernhard *Mond who was promoted to colonel in 1924 and on the outbreak of World War II commanded the Fifth Infantry Division with the rank of major general. The condition of the Jewish soldier improved during the nine-year rule of Joseph Pilsudski (1926–35) but deteriorated after his death. Nevertheless, 400,000 Jews were recruited into the Polish army on the outbreak of World War II and many thousands were killed in battle during the four weeks of fighting. A large number of Jewish soldiers were taken prisoner by the Russians and interned in the Soviet Union. In 1942 an agreement between the U.S.S.R. and the Polish government in exile resulted in the formation of a Polish army in Russia under General Anders. Although Jews were generally excluded from this army, usually on the pretext that they were unsuitable for military service, 4,000 fought in General Anders' army in Western Europe while over 5,000 Jews fought in a second Polish army in Russia, a large number of them holding officer's rank. In addition many more Jews fought in Polish units serving in the armies of other Allied states.

Despite the fact that the Jewish population of Poland was decimated by the Holocaust, a large number of Jews joined the Polish army and after World War II many held senior ranks. Following the *Six-Day War in 1967, however, nearly all of them were removed from their posts.

Rumania. Rumania became an independent kingdom in 1881. Restrictions were subsequently placed upon the right of Jews to serve in the armed forces despite the fact that nearly 1,000 Rumanian Jews had fought against the Turks in the Balkan War of 1877. An outstanding Jewish soldier in the Rumanian army was Colonel Maurice Brociner (1855–1942) who was decorated for gallantry in 1877 and in 1882 was made secretary to Charles I, king of Rumania. In 1896 a law was enacted prohibiting Jews from volunteering for the Rumanian army but in 1913, following the involvement of Rumania in the Balkan Wars, the law was rescinded. During World War I, 20,000 Jews fought in the Rumanian army, including several hundred officers. Thirty-seven Jewish officers and 845 men were known to have died. After World War I a large number of Jews served in the Rumanian army, and some rose to the rank of officer. During World War II, however, Nazi pressure led the Rumanian government to remove all the Jews from the Rumanian army. Few Jews served in the army of Communist Rumania after 1945.

Bulgaria. Following Bulgarian independence in 1878 Jews were given equal rights with the rest of the population. Bulgarian Jews fought in the Turkish army when Bulgaria was under Turkish rule, and after independence they joined the Bulgarian army in their thousands. Many Jewish soldiers distinguished themselves during the Serbo-Bulgarian war of 1885 and were described by Prince Alexander of Bulgaria as "true descendants of the ancient Maccabeans." Despite growing anti-Semitism no restrictions were placed on Jews entering the army or even the officers' training schools. Five thousand Jews fought in the Bulgarian army in the Balkan Wars (1912–13) and several hundreds of them were killed. In World War I a number of Jews reached senior army ranks, among them three Jewish colonels Graziani, Tajar, and Mushanov. Over 700 Jews were killed in the war, among them 28 officers. Between the wars, Jewish soldiers continued to enjoy equal rights in the Bulgarian army until 1940 when Bulgaria allied herself with Nazi Germany. All Jews were removed from the Bulgarian army and organized into labor units to perform manual work. Many of them were later sent to concentration camps but some succeeded in joining the partisans headed by the Fatherland Front. After the war most of Bulgaria's surviving Jews emigrated to Israel and hardly any joined the army of Communist Bulgaria.

Greece. Greek Jews were subject to continual persecution for many years after Greek independence in 1821. Very few Jews joined the army until the outbreak of the Greco-Turkish War of 1897 in which 200 Jews fought in the Greek army. Abraham Matalon rose to the rank of colonel during World War I and was one of several Jewish soldiers to have been decorated. The total number of Greek Jews fighting in World War I was estimated at 500. Many Jews fought in the Greek army against Italy in 1940 and by 1942 when the Germans invaded Greece over 13,000 Jews had been recruited, many of them from Salonika and Macedonia where there were large concentrations of Jews. Five hundred and thirteen Jews were known to have been killed in action, among them Colonel Mordechai Parisi, who was killed after holding off an entire Italian brigade for nine days. A monument was erected in his memory in his native town of Chalcis and 25 Greek towns have streets named after him. Following the German conquest of Greece, many Jews were deported to concentration camps. Among the Greek Jews deported to Auschwitz was Colonel Baruch who set fire to part of the gas chambers and was later killed by the Nazis. A few Greek Jews joined the partisan movement in the mountains of northern Greece and some fought in the Allied armies in North Africa.

Switzerland. Before 1850 Jews were exempted from military service upon payment of a tax. In 1866 Jews were granted equal rights including the obligation of military service but even before the law of 1866 certain cantons permitted Jews to bear arms, the first of them being Aargau where the civil authorities acceded to a request of Marcus Dreyfus, head of the Jewish community. In 1855 Moritz Meyer from Aargau was made an officer and several other Jews became officers during the latter part of the 19th century. Several hundred Jews were recruited into the Swiss army for border defense during the two world wars and two Jewish soldiers rose to the rank of colonel: A. Nordman and his son Jean Nordman.

Holland. Jews were allowed to bear arms in Holland from the 17th century when the country became an independent state under the House of Orange. In 1808, during Napoleonic rule, Jews were granted equal rights and were therefore obliged to do military service along with the rest of the population. The number of Jews serving in the Dutch army grew steadily during the 19th century and a few Jewish soldiers were singled out for merit, one of them, Michael Kohen (b. 1877), being decorated for outstanding bravery in the fighting in Surinam. Thousands of Jews fought against the Nazi invasion of Holland in May 1940 and a small number of them succeeded in escaping to Britain to continue fighting from there. After World War II, hardly any Jews served in the Dutch armed forces.

Other Countries. A small number of Jewish soldiers rose to fame in India, the Middle East, and North Africa, some of them serving as soldiers of fortune. Some of the Jewish soldiers of fortune achieved fame in the Turkish army in which several thousand Jews fought during the Balkan wars of the 19th century. Fischel-Freind (1885–1928), a Polish Jew, became a colonel in the Turkish army and was later governor of Syria with the title Magyar Mahmud Pasha. An English Jew, Stephen Lakeman (1812–1897), was briefly a Turkish general with the title Mazar Pasha. In addition David Effendi Molcho, a Jew from Salonika, was made head of the Turkish navy's medical services with the rank of vice admiral. Another Jewish soldier of fortune was Rubino *Ventura who held military commands both in Persia and in India during the 19th century. A small number of Indian Jews reached high military rank in the British army, among them Subadar major Haskelji Israel Kolatkar who was killed during the Burmese campaign of 1887 and Subadar major Shalom Moses Penkar of the 15th Bombay Infantry unit. Indian Jews fought in the two world wars and after Indian independence, some became senior officers, and one of them, Colonel Joseph Ephraim Jhirad, was killed in the 1965 war against Pakistan. North African Jews were prominent in World War II both in the French and British regular armies and in the French underground. Thus Maurice Guedj (1913–1945), a Tunisian lawyer, joined the Free French air force and won numerous decorations. He was killed in action in January 1945. Leaders of the underground included José *Abulker, Pierre Smadja, and Raoul and Edgar Bensoussan. Jews were not prominent in the Algerian war against the French after 1955 or in the armies of the Arab North African states after independence.

Women in Military Service. There is no record of Jewish women serving in the army of any modern state until 1813 when Louise Grafemus (Esther Manuel; 1785–1852), in search of her husband in the Russian army, joined the Prussian infantry disguised as a man. She was twice wounded and rose to become a sergeant major before her sex was discovered. Louise Grafemus was awarded the Iron Cross and returned to her home in Hanau with great honor. During the 19th century women played an increasing part in the conduct of wars in auxiliary capacities such as nurses. Thus nurse Woolf was decorated by King George V for her services in the British army in World War I and several Jewish women became nursing officers in the Allied forces in World War II. During World War II women went into active service for the first time as auxiliary troops; in Russia they served with men in the front lines during the initial invasion by Germany and afterward. A number of Soviet Jewish women became famous through their bravery in action, among them Lyudmila Kravetz who was made a Hero of the Soviet Union when as a medical sergeant she took command of her unit when all the officers were killed and advanced against the enemy. Riva Steinberg (d. 1944), who was killed trying to rescue a Russian soldier from a burning aircraft, was posthumously decorated, and Mary Ykhnovich, a senior battalion commander, Sarah Meisel, Klara Gross, and Lea Kantorovich, a nurse, were all cited for bravery under fire. Another Russian Jewess, Gitta Schenker, a telephone operator, took command of an infantry battalion during the battle of Stalingrad. However, the most famous Jewish heroine of World War II was Hannah *Szenes who was parachuted into Yugoslavia to organize Jewish resistance and was captured and killed.

See also *Israel, Defense Forces.

Conclusion. In most states Jews were not called upon to do military service until well into the 19th century since the obligation to take up arms was considered a privilege to which Jews were not entitled. Even where they did fight they were usually restricted in their right to hold officer's rank (as in Prussia and Russia) or were excluded from certain branches of the army such as the general staff in Austria-Hungary. In the 20th century most restrictions on Jews as soldiers were removed but only in France, Italy, and Austria-Hungary was the number of Jewish senior officers relatively high. Vilmos Böhm and Giorgio Liuzzi were the only Jews to become commanders in chief of an army, the former when he held this post in the short-lived regime of Bela Kun in Hungary, the latter in Italy. Three other Jews reached the rank of full general: John *Monash, Grigori Stern, and Jacob *Kreyzer; and three Jews the rank of full admiral: Ben Moreel (1892–), Augusto *Capon, and Roberto Segre (1872–1942). One Jew, Jacob *Smushkevich, was commander of an air force.

See also *Israel, Defense Forces; *Partisans. [ED.]

Jewish Chaplaincy. In most countries of Europe where Jews have volunteered or been enlisted into the armed forces, provision has been made for the appointment of chaplains to look after the religious needs of servicemen and women in times of war and peace. One can generally say that from the middle of the 19th century, following the political emancipation of the Jews, Judaism became a recognized denomination having more or less the same privileges and obligations as those of other denominations. Commissioned chaplains were given relative military rank, senior chaplains having the relative rank of colonel, lieutenant colonel, or major. This was the case in Austria, France, Prussia, Britain, Belgium, Italy, Holland, and Poland. In Britain in 1889 Judaism was recognized as a denomination for the purpose of chaplaincy in the forces. The first Jewish chaplain was Rabbi Francis L. Cohen who was appointed in 1892. In European countries, such as Italy and Belgium, chaplains were first commissioned during World War I when the number of Jews serving in the various national armies increased considerably. In World War I Jewish chaplains, with the approval, and sometimes at the request of the superior commanding officer, rendered service to the Jews in occupied territories. Thus German Jewish chaplains acted as intermediaries between the German army authorities and Jewish civilians in Poland and in northern France. They also provided religious

Figure 11. Turkish army recruits from Jewish high schools and *battei midrash* in Palestine, 1915. Courtesy Jerusalem Municipality Historical Archives. Photo Ben Dov, Jerusalem.

appurtenances and Passover requirements (such as *mazzot* and *haggadot*). British chaplains performed similar services for Jewish civilians in northern France and Belgium. They were supported by chaplains attached to the forces of Australia, New Zealand, Canada, and South Africa, and chaplains also served with the Jewish units serving in Palestine and Egypt. A number of chaplains in both the Allied and central armies were decorated for bravery. An outstanding example of bravery was that of Rabbi A. Bloch of the French army who was killed by a shell in 1914 after seeking a crucifix for a severely wounded Frenchman when there was no priest available. During World War II there was a further increase in the number of chaplains in the Allied forces. On the other hand the Dutch government in exile, for the first time, appointed a Jewish chaplain, Chief Rabbi S. Rodrigues Pereira, to look after the religious requirements of Dutch Jews serving with the Allies. In the Polish army Rabbi J. Mieses was senior chaplain to be succeeded by Rabbi B. Steinberg who was killed during the Katyn massacre in 1943. Jewish chaplains served with the Polish army in Russia, the Middle East, and Europe. The last senior chaplain in the Polish army was Rabbi David Kahana who served from 1945 to 1952. Jewish chaplains were also attached to the Jewish infantry group made up of Palestinians and Jews from other British army units who served in the western desert, in Italy, and with the army of the Rhine. As in World War I, a number of Jewish chaplains were decorated for gallantry in the Allied armies, among them Grand Rabbi Jacob Kaplan of the French army who was awarded the Croix de Guerre. The duties of chaplains during the two world wars were extensive and involved a considerable amount of travel. They were required to organize religious services whenever possible, particularly during the festivals and High Holy Days, to distribute service prayer books and religious literature, visit the sick and wounded in hospitals and casualty clearing stations, and bury the dead. They were also required to assist observant soldiers in following the religious requirements of their faith without detriment to their army duties and to deal with the many welfare and social problems affecting the domestic life of the soldier. At the end of World War II chaplains were additionally required to help bury Jews who had died in concentration camps and to help those who survived as far as possible. As in the case of chaplains of other denominations, Jewish chaplains were requested to use their influence in maintaining the morale and fighting spirit of the troops. They were encouraged to participate in educational and recreational programs designed to improve the mind and outlook of the serviceman. In the Royal Air Force a scheme of moral leadership courses was devised to guide and train officers and men who had shown a talent for leadership to apply their potential in the groups to which they were attached.

[I.B.]

IN THE UNITED STATES. The Jewish military chaplaincy in the United States began in 1862 during the U.S. Civil War. Before then army chaplains had to be ordained Christian clergymen, selected by the officers of the regiments to which they were assigned. By an Act of Congress of 1862, a regularly ordained minister of any religious denomination could be commissioned as a chaplain. Three rabbis were commissioned as chaplains in the Union forces: Rabbi Jacob Frankel of Philadelphia, who served the six Philadelphia military hospitals; Rabbi Bernhard Gotthelf, of Louisville, Kentucky, who served 18 army hospitals in Kentucky and Indiana; and Rabbi Ferdinand L. Sarner of Brith Kodesh Congregation, Rochester, New York, who was elected chaplain of the 54th New York Volunteer Regiment and was wounded at Gettysburg.

No Jewish chaplains served in the Spanish-American War (1898), although Rabbi Emil G. *Hirsch and Rabbi J. Leonard Levy of Philadelphia were commissioned. Rabbi Joseph *Krauskopf of Philadelphia spent the summer of 1898 at military camps in the United States and in Cuba as a field commissioner for the National Relief Commission, and conducted religious services for Jewish personnel. A number of other rabbis also conducted services at camps adjacent to the communities in which their congregations were located.

In 1917 the *National Jewish Welfare Board (J.W.B.) was organized to serve the religious and morale needs of Jewish soldiers and sailors in the U.S. armed forces during World War I. One of the duties assigned to the J.W.B. by the government was the recruiting and endorsing of Jewish military chaplains. In October 1917 Congress authorized the appointment of chaplains-at-large of "faiths not now represented in the body of Chaplains of the Army." As a result, 149 of the 400 English-speaking rabbis in the United States volunteered, and 34 received the ecclesiastical endorsement of the J.W.B.'s Chaplains Committee. Of these, 26 received commissions. The first Jewish chaplain commissioned was Rabbi Elkan C. Voorsanger of St. Louis, who earned two decorations for gallantry under fire, and became senior chaplain of the 77th Division.

After World War I, some chaplains maintained reserve commissions, and a number of younger rabbis enlisted in the reserves between 1918 and 1940. As World War II approached, the chaplaincy underwent a major reorganization. Cyrus *Adler was succeeded by Rabbi David de Sola *Pool as chairman of the J. W. B. Chaplaincy Committee, and the committee was renamed Committee on Army and Navy Religious Activities (CANRA) of the J.W.B. Rabbi Phillip S. *Bernstein was named executive director. By the time the United States entered World War II, 24 Jewish chaplains were on active duty. By the end of the war 311 rabbis had been commissioned and served in the armed forces; seven died in service, among them Alexander Goode who was one of four chaplains who lost their lives on the military transport, S.S. *Dorchester*. CANRA provided the chaplains with vast supplies of religious literature, equipment, and kosher foods in a supply line that reached around the world. Two tasks of special importance performed by Jewish chaplains were their work as leaders in the first penetration of areas cut off from Jewish contacts during the Nazi occupation, and their aid to concentration camp survivors. After World War II the chaplaincy became a career for some, and a way for the promotion of senior Jewish chaplains to key administrative chaplaincy posts. Many of those who did not choose a career in the chaplaincy retained their reserve commission. Only 18 Jewish chaplains remained on active duty at the outbreak of war in Korea in 1950. Twelve Jewish chaplains were decorated in that war.

After World War II CANRA was renamed to emphasize its function within the J.W.B. organization, which finances it, first as the Division of Religious Activities and, after the outbreak of the Korean war, as the Commission on Jewish Chaplaincy of the J.W.B. Reform, Conservative, and Orthodox rabbis rotated as commission chairmen for three-year terms. The commission instituted a draft to supply 100 Jewish chaplains; it drew from all rabbis and newly ordained students eligible for military service who had not already served in the forces, and required a two-year tour of duty. From 1950 to 1968 the draft brought 485 rabbis into the chaplaincy, about a third of all the rabbis ordained by the major Jewish seminaries of the United States during the period. The commission also used civilian rabbis who had their own congregations to provide

Figure 12. Rabbi Alexander Goode (far right) and the three other army chaplains lost with the U.S.S. *Dorchester* in 1943, on a memorial stamp issued in 1948. Jerusalem, B. M. Ansbacher Collection.

chaplaincy services at military bases, academies, and hospitals and nonmilitary federal installations where no full-time Jewish chaplain was assigned. About 800 rabbis were involved in this program up to 1970. In 1969, reacting to anti-Vietnam sentiment among rabbinical students, the commission substituted a voluntary system for the drafting of newly ordained rabbis. When the Vietnam war led to a new military buildup, four Jewish chaplains were assigned to duty in that country. From 1966 to 1970, 11 chaplains were decorated. In 1970 Jewish chaplains were serving 611 domestic installations and hospitals, as well as in more than 40 foreign countries.

Publications and Child Education. In the 1950s and 1960s religious-lay cooperation and interdenominational harmony were strikingly evident in the work of the Jewish Chaplaincy Commission's responsa and publication committees. The former formulated mutually acceptable answers to questions of religious practices under military conditions. The latter published prayer books, *Haggadot*, hymnals, and a library of pamphlets on the Sabbath, holy days, festivals, Jewish ethics, and Jewish history, all widely distributed and serving as excellent expositions of Judaism to non-Jews in the military. In 1954 the commission published the first standardized religious school curriculum for the children of servicemen, rewritten in 1965 as "Unified Jewish Religious Education Curriculum." It is particularly important because of the growing number of service children who live far from civilian synagogues and Jewish schools. Religious education for service children has become a prime task of the Jewish chaplains, who prepare many youngsters for bar and bat mitzvah as part of an organized program of elementary Jewish training. [B.P.]

Bibliography: M. Kaplan, *Ha-Loḥem ha-Yehudi bi-Ẓeva'ot ha-Olam* (1967), incl. bibl.; J. Ben Hirsch, *Jewish General Officers* (1967), incl. bibl.; G. Loewenthal, *Bewaehrung im Untergang* (1966), J. Lazarus, *Juifs au combat* (1947); F. Servi, *Israeliti italiani nella guerra 1915–18* (1921); J. G. Fredman and L. A. Falk, *Jews in American Wars* (1963); A. L. Lebeson, *Pilgrim People* (1950); S. Wolf, *The American Jew as Patriot, Soldier, and Citizen* (1895); P. S. Foner, *Jews in American History 1654–1865* (1945), 16–27, 36–42, 63–78, incl. bibl.; P. Wiernik, *History of the Jews in America* (1931), 87–97, 229–41, 417–20; W. Ziff, in: D. Runes (ed.), *Hebrew Impact on Western Civilization* (1951), 240–312; Z. Szajkowski, in: PAAJR, 26 (1957), 139–60, incl. bibl.; Comite zur Abwehr antisemitischer Angriffe in Berlin, *Juden als Soldaten* (1896); M. Fruehling, *Biographisches Handbuch* (1911); Wiener Library, *German Jewry* (1958), 201–4; H. Fischer, *Judentum, Staat und Heer in Preussen* (1968); R. Ainsztein, in: L. Kochan (ed.), *Jews in Soviet Russia* (1970), 269–87. Jewish Chaplaincy Outside the U.S.: I. Brodie, in: AJYB, 48 (1946/47), 58ff.; *Ha-Gedudim ha-Ivriyyim be-Milḥemet ha-Olam ha-Rishonah* (1968); A. Tabian, *Australian Jewish Historical Society Transactions*, 6 (1965), 344; *South African Jewry in World War II* (1950); *Illustrierte Neue Welt* (June 1970), 26; *L'Aumônerie militaire belge* (1966), 88; Redier et Honesque, *L'Aumônerie militaire française* (1960). In the U.S.: L. Barish (ed.), *Rabbis in Uniform* (1962); O. I. Janowsky et al., *Change and Challenge: A History of Fifty Years of JWB* (1966), 80–83; *JWB Circle*, 1 (1946–), index.

Distinguished Jewish Servicemen. The individuals whose names are marked with an asterisk in the list below form the subjects of articles in their appropriate alphabetical position in the Encyclopaedia.

AGUILAR, SIR CHARLES LAWRENCE D' (1821–1912), English general (see *Aguilar, Diego D').

AGUILAR, SIR GEORGE CHARLES D' (1784–1855), English lieutenant general (see *Aguilar, Diego D').

***ARBIB (Arbid), ANGELO** (1865–1922), Italian lieutenant general.

***ARBIB, EDOARDO** (1840–1906), Italian soldier.

***ARBIB, EMILIO** (d. 1933), Italian general.

***ASCOLI, ETTORE** (1873–1943), Italian lieutenant general.

ASHANSKI (Oshyanski), ABEL-AARON ITSKOVICH (1825–1899), Russian soldier, and the only Jew ever to reach the rank of regimental sergeant in the Czarist army. Ashanski was called up for service in an army labor battalion in 1846, but because of his good service and impressive physique he was transferred in 1863 to the czarina's own cavalry regiment. In 1874 he was promoted regimental sergeant and served in this rank until 1896. Ashanski was given a state funeral, and was buried in the old Jewish cemetery of St. Petersburg.

***BACHI, ARMANDO** (1883–1943), Italian lieutenant general.

***BAR-LEV, HAIM** (1924–), Israel chief of staff.

BEDDINGTON, CLAUDE (1868–1940), English cavalry officer (see *Beddington).

BEDDINGTON, SIR EDWARD HENRY LIONEL (1884–1966), English brigadier (see *Beddington).

BEDDINGTON, WILLIAM RICHARD (1893–), English major general (see *Beddington).

***BENJAMIN, ERNEST FRANK** (1900–1969), English colonel, World War II commander of the Jewish Brigade.

***BERNHEIM, LOUIS** (1861–1931), Belgian lieutenant general.

***BLOCH, CLAUDE** (1878–1967), U.S. admiral.

CAPON, AUGUSTO (1872–1944), Italian admiral. Capon commanded a corvette during the Italo-Turkish War (1911–12) and was a frigate commander during World War I. He later became chief of naval intelligence and in 1931 was promoted to admiral. The Italian racial laws of 1938 forced him to resign his commission and in 1944 he was seized by the Nazis. He subsequently perished in Auschwitz.

***COHEN, MORRIS ABRAHAM** (1887–1970), general in the Chinese army.

***CORNBLAT, ISIDORE CYRIL** (1914–), Canadian air vice-marshal.

***DASSAULT, DARIUS PAUL** (1882–), French general.

***D'AVIGDOR-GOLDSMID, JAMES ARTHUR** (1912–), English general.

DAVIS, ABEL (1878–1937), U.S. army officer. Born in Lithuania, Davis was taken to Chicago as a child and served in the Illinois National Guard during the Spanish-American War of 1898. He fought in France in World War I and won awards for gallantry in the battles before Amiens, St. Hilaire, and in the Argonne. He was later made a brigadier general in the Illinois National Guard. Davis was active in Jewish affairs as director of the Associated Jewish Charities and in 1921 was chairman of the *American Jewish Relief Committee conference.

***DAYAN, MOSHE** (1915–), Israel chief of staff and minister of defense.

DISKIN, CHAIM (c. 1923–), Russian military physician of World War II and Hero of the Soviet Union. When his unit was annihilated, he continued firing and singlehanded put several German tanks out of action. He was then only 18 years old. No longer fit for active service, Diskin was allowed to study medicine and returned to serve as an army physician attaining the rank of major general. He later became a professor at the Army Medical Academy.

***DORI, YAAKOV** (1899–), Israel chief of staff.

DRAGUNSKI, DAVID ABRAMOVICH (1910–), Soviet army officer. Born near Bryansk, Dragunski commanded a tank brigade on the Ukrainian front in World War II and was twice awarded the title Hero of the Soviet Union. He was subsequently promoted to lieutenant general. Dragunski was one of a number of Soviet Jews who in 1970 publicly declared their allegiance to the U.S.S.R. and their hostility to Israel and Zionism.

DREBEN, SAM (1878–1925), U.S. soldier of fortune. Born in Russia, Dreben emigrated to the United States in 1898 and volunteered for the army. He fought in China during the Boxer Rebellion of 1900 and later in Nicaragua, where he became known as the "fighting Jew." In 1916 he volunteered as a colonel in the Mexican army and in 1918 fought in France, where he won the Distinguished Service Cross. Dreben donated a large sum of money to the *American Jewish Joint Distribution Committee and helped fight the Ku Klux Klan in Texas in the 1920s.

***EIS, ALEXANDER VON** (1832–1921), Austro-Hungarian major general.

***ELLSBERG, EDWARD** (1891–), U.S. rear admiral.

FELDMAN, HERMAN (1889–), U.S. army officer. Born in New York, Feldman joined the army as a private in the field artillery. During World War I he was sent to France and was commissioned in the field artillery. During World War II Feldman again served in the quartermaster corps being eventually promoted to major general. From 1949 until his retirement in 1951 he was quartermaster of the U.S. army.

FOA, RAIMONDO (1877–1940), Italian army officer. Born in Casale Monferrato, he was commissioned in 1899 and fought in the Italo-Turkish War (1911–12). He was an artillery commander in World War I and in 1919 worked in the technical service of the artillery. Foa became director of the Terni Ordnance Arms factory in 1927. He was promoted to the rank of lieutenant general in 1937.

FOMIN, YEFIM MOISEYEVICH (d. 1941), Soviet soldier. In 1941 Fomin was a captain and commissar of a regiment during the Brest-Litovsk campaign. When the Germans broke through the Russian lines, Fomin conducted the defense of the Brest-Litovsk fortress for weeks after the rest of the front had retreated. Severely wounded, he was captured with the fall of the fortress and because he was a Jew, he was executed. He was posthumously made a Hero of the Soviet Union and a factory and a street in Brest-Litovsk were named after him.

***FRANKEL, SAMUEL BENJAMIN** (1905–), U.S. rear admiral.

GAMARNIK, YAN BORISOVICH (1894–1938), Soviet army political officer. Gamarnik was head of the political administration of the Soviet army from 1917 until the purge of 1937. Sometime Ukrainian, Belorussian, and ultimately U.S.S.R. Central Committee member, he also served as deputy people's commissar for defense and chief editor of the Red Army journal *Krasnaya Zvezda*. He committed suicide in 1938. His wife and the wife of Ḥayyim Nahman Bialik were sisters.

GOLDBERG, J. B. (1884–1946), Soviet army commander. In 1919, Lenin personally entrusted him with the command of the reserves and with the task of setting up a corps of reserves for the whole of the Red Army fighting on the Eastern front. Within two years Goldberg created a force of half a million men In 1922 he was appointed deputy head of the air force.

GOLDSMID, ALBERT EDWARD WILLIAMSON (1846–1904), English colonel (see *Goldsmid).

GOLDSMID, SIR FREDERICK JOHN (1818–1908), English major general (see *Goldsmid).

***GUASTALLA, ENRICO** (1828–1903), Italian lieutenant colonel.

HARBY, LEVI MYERS (1793–1870), U.S. naval officer. Born in Georgetown, South Carolina, Harby joined the navy as a boy and was captured by the British during the war of 1812. He was cashiered from the navy in 1836 for siding with the secessionist Texans but was later reinstated. Promoted to captain, he fought in the Mexican War (1846) and the Bolivian War of Independence. Harby fought on the Confederate side in the American Civil War and distinguished himself in the defense of Galveston.

***HAZAI, SAMU** (1851–1942), Hungarian general.

JOSEPHTAL, LOUIS MAURICE (1869–1929), U.S. naval officer. Born in New Rochelle, N.Y., Josephtal joined the New York naval militia in 1891 and during the Spanish-American War (1898) was an assistant paymaster. During World War I he was a captain (paymaster) at the naval militia headquarters. In 1923 he was appointed rear admiral in the supply corps and was later commander of the New York naval militia. An observant Jew, Josephtal was active in Jewish affairs and was a director of Mount Sinai Hospital for many years.

KATUNIN, ILYA BORISOVICH (1908–1944), Soviet airman and Hero of the Soviet Union. Katunin commanded a squadron of fighter planes during an attack on enemy ships and his plane was hit and caught fire. Instead of bailing out, Katunin directed his plane at one of the boats and crashed into it; the boat and its crew sank, Katunin dying with them.

***KLEIN, JULIUS** (1901–), U.S. major general.

KNEFLER, FREDERICK (1833–1901), U.S. army officer. Born in Hungary, Knefler emigrated to the United States in 1859 and volunteered for the Unionist army in 1861 on the outbreak of the Civil War. He rose from the rank of private to captain in the 11th Indiana regiment within a year and from captain to colonel within another year. Later he fought under General W. T. Sherman and was promoted to brevet brigadier general in 1865 shortly before the end of the war.

KRAVETS, LYUDMILA (c. 1920–), Soviet heroine of World War II. In the final Russian assault on Berlin in 1945, she was the medical sergeant of her unit. When all the officers were killed, she took command of the unit and captured an enemy position. For her bravery she was made a Hero of the Soviet Union.

***KREISER, JACOB GRIGORYEVICH** (1905–1969), Russian army commander in World War II.

KRULEWITCH, MELVIN LEVIN (1895–), U.S. soldier. Born in New York City, he was a sergeant in the U.S. army in France during World War I. After practicing law for several years he returned to the army. During World War II Krulewitch was decorated for meritorious service at Iwo Jima. He was a military observer in Israel in 1948 and in Korea in 1950, and retired in 1956 with the rank of major general.

***LAMBERT, AIMÉ** (1825–1896), French lieutenant general.

***LASKOV, ḤAYYIM** (1919–), Israel chief of staff.

LAWTON, SAMUEL T. (1894–), U.S. army officer. Born in Peoria, Illinois, Lawton was admitted to the bar in 1905 but enlisted in the Illinois national guard in 1909. He fought on the Mexican border and in France during World War I as a captain. He later served in Germany and Luxembourg, and returned to the United States to command a field artillery brigade. He was major general commanding the 33rd division from March 1941 to April 1942, and remained on active service until his retirement in 1948.

LÉVY, ABRAHAM EUGÈNE (1826–1917), French army officer. Lévy joined the French army in 1845 and was distinguished for his bravery during the Crimean War of 1854–56. He was promoted to brigadier general in 1880, one of the first Jews so appointed. Lévy refused to convert to Christianity to further his career.

***LEVY, URIAH PHILLIPS** (1792–1862), U.S. naval commodore.

LICHTMACHER, LAZAR (1880–?), Russian soldier, the only Jew to be decorated in the czarist army during the Russo-Japanese War. On June 24, 1905, wounded and alone, he repulsed a Japanese attack. He was awarded all the classes of the St. George Cross.

***LIPTON, MAURICE** (1916–), Canadian air-commodore.

***LIUZZI, GUIDO** (1866–?), Italian lieutenant general.

***LIUZZI, GIORGIO** (1896–), Italian chief of staff.

MAKLEFF, MORDECHAI (1920–), Israel chief of staff (see *Makleff).

MARIX, ADOLPH (1848–1919), U.S. naval officer. Born in Germany he was taken to the United States by his father, Henry Marix, who was an official translator to the U.S. Treasury. Adolph Marix was appointed to the U.S. Naval Academy at Annapolis and in 1872 joined the judge advocate-general's department. He commanded a number of ships between 1894 and 1898 including the *U.S.S. Maine* until shortly before its mysterious sinking in the Bay of Havana. Marix was appointed judge advocate in the court of enquiry into the sinking, and his findings led to the U.S. declaration of war on Spain. Subsequently, he was president of the navy board which experimented in the use of submarines and in 1908 was promoted to rear admiral, the first Jew to attain that rank.

***MEKHLIS, LEV ZAKHAROVICH** (1889–1953), Soviet general and political commissar.

MOCH, JULES (1829–1881), French colonel, one of the first Jews to reach this rank in the French army. He fought with distinction in the Crimean War in 1854–55, and in the conquest of Rome in 1859, as well as in the Franco-Prussian War of 1870–71. He was the first Jew to be an instructor and examiner at the Military Academy of Saint-Cyr. Moch, proud of his Jewishness, was one of the founders of the Club Militaire which after his death became the moving spirit behind the incitement against Captain *Dreyfus.

MODENA, ANGELO (1867–?), Italian army officer. Born in Reggio Emilia, Modena graduated from the military academy and joined the general staff. He lectured at the military academy from 1907 to 1911 and fought in the Tripolitan War of 1911. During World War I, Modena commanded the 208th infantry regiment. He successfully held the Zugna-Torta heights following the Italian retreat in 1917, and was promoted to major general with command of the 32nd infantry division. In 1927 he became corps commander.

MOLCHO, DAVID EFFENDI ISAAC PASHA (1839–1909), vice admiral of the Ottoman navy. Born in Salonika, Molcho was descended from an established family of Salonika rabbis. Molcho entered the College of Military Medicine and upon graduation joined the Turkish armed forces as a surgeon. He was promoted to lieutenant colonel in 1877 and was later appointed inspector general of the health services. He was made a vice admiral in 1902.

***MONASH, SIR JOHN** (1865–1931), Australian general, commander of the Australian forces in World War I.

***MOND, BERNHARD STANISLAW** (1877–1944), Polish major general.

***MORDECAI, ALFRED** (1804–1887), U.S. major.

MOREEL, BEN (1892–), U.S. admiral. Born in Salt Lake City, Moreel worked as an engineer and in 1917 joined the U.S. navy engineer corps. In 1937 he was made chief of the bureau of yards. During World War II Moreel organized the naval construction battalions known as Seabees and became a vice admiral in 1944. He retired as a full admiral in 1958, the first engineering officer to reach this rank.

OESTERREICHER, TOBIAS VON (1831–1893), Austro-Hungarian rear-admiral. After serving in wars in Hungary, Italy, France, and Prussia, in which he commanded vessels and was decorated, he became a naval captain at the age of 38 and commanded a battleship. He was raised to the nobility and in 1881 he became a rear admiral. Until 1883 he occupied a key position in the Ministry of War and on his retirement received the personal thanks of Emperor Francis Joseph I for his services. On his death, he was given a state funeral.

***OTTOLENGHI, GIUSEPPE** (1838–1905), Italian general and minister of war.

PHILLIPSON, IRVING JOSEPH (1882–), U.S. army corps commander. Graduated from West Point in 1904, he saw action in the Philippines in 1906–07 and in the Meuse-Argonne battles of World War I. In World War II he was chief of staff of the Second Corps area and in 1941 was promoted to major general. In 1942 he was sent to Washington to plan and administer the aid to be given to the wives and dependents of soldiers' families. Phillipson introduced many needed reforms in this field.

POPPER, SIEGFRIED (1848–1933), Austro-Hungarian rear admiral and naval engineer. From 1871 to 1904 he served as an engineer on battleships and was then appointed head of naval construction with the rank of rear admiral. Popper developed new methods of naval warfare and almost all the Austrian battleships of his time, as well as torpedo boats and fast destroyers, were constructed under his direction. After his retirement he served in the Technische Hochschule in Vienna but was dismissed through Nazi pressure in 1933.

***PUGLIESE, EMANUELE** (1874–), Italian lieutenant general.

***RABIN, YIẒHAK** (1922–), Israel chief of staff.

RABINOVICH, ZALMAN KHAIMOVICH (d. 1944), Soviet army officer. Rabinovich commanded a parachutist unit which was dropped behind the German lines in the Russian assault on Minsk. He was killed in battle and a monument to him was erected at the entrance to the town bearing the inscription: "Here lies the commander of parachute company 69, lieutenant colonel Zalman Khaimovich Rabinovich, liberator of the town."

***RICKOVER, HYMAN GEORGE** (1900–), U.S. vice admiral.

***ROSE, MAURICE** (1898–1945), U.S. major general.

ROTHSCHILD, ROBERT PHINIAS (1914–), major general in the Canadian army. He held various staff and regimental commissions during World War II and was Canadian military attaché to Greece (1947–50). In 1962 he was promoted to acting major general and quartermaster-general of the Canadian army.

***SADEH, YIẒHAK** (1890–1952), creator of the Palmaḥ.

SCHOMBERG, SIR ALEXANDER (c. 1716–1804), English admiral (see *Schomberg).

SCHOMBERG, SIR ALEXANDER WILMOT (1774–1850), English admiral (see *Schomberg).

SCHOMBERG, HENRY (c. 1715–1755), English lieutenant colonel (see *Schomberg).

SCHOMBERG, ISAAC (1753–1813), English commissioner and deputy comptroller of the navy (see *Schomberg).

***SCHWEITZER, EDUARD VON** (1844–1920), Austro-Hungarian field marshal lieutenant.

***SEE, LEOPOLD** (1822–1904), French general.

***SEGRE, ROBERTO** (1872–1936), Italian lieutenant general.

***SELIGMAN, HERBERT SPENCER** (1872–1951), English brigadier general.

***SHMUSHKEVITCH, YAACOV** (1902–1941), Soviet air force commander.

***SINGER, JOSEPH** (1797–1871), Austro-Hungarian field marshal lieutenant.

***SOMMER, EMIL VON** (1868–1946), Austro-Hungarian major general.

STERN, GRIGORY (d. 1940), Soviet army officer. Stern was chief adviser to the Republican army in Spain from 1936 to 1937 when he was sent to the Far East as chief of staff of the Soviet Far Eastern forces. He defeated the Japanese at the battle of Lake Khasan and was promoted to colonel general and given command of the Soviet forces. In the following year he defeated the Japanese at the battle of Khalkhin-Gol and drove them out of Soviet Mongolia. Stern died during the Finnish campaign.

TAUSSIG, EDWARD DAVID (1847–1921), U.S. rear admiral (see *Taussig).

TAUSSIG, JOSEPH KNEPLER (1877–1947), U.S. rear admiral (see *Taussig).

***VALABREGUE, MARDOCHEE GEORGES** (1852–1930), French general.

***VENTURA, RUBINO** (1792–1858), Italian soldier, commander of the army of Lahore.

VOGEL, SIMON (1850–1917), Hungarian soldier. Born in Karczag, Vogel joined the Austro-Hungarian army as a private but was selected for the officers' school and fought in the Bosnian campaign. Teaching at the Kassa cadet academy, Vogel was introduced to Emperor Francis Joseph I, and was promoted to colonel with command of a regiment. He was made governor of Sarajevo in 1903 and represented the Austrian army at the marriage of King Alphonso XIII of Spain in 1906. In 1909 he became a major general and retired soon afterward.

WEINRUB, MATVEY, Soviet lieutenant general, Hero of the Soviet Union. In World War II, at the battle of Stalingrad he commanded the armour of the 62nd army and his small tank force twice succeeded in preventing the Germans reaching the Volga. Weinrub was promoted to major general with command of the armoured division of the 8th guards army which recaptured the Donets coalfield and Odessa and advanced to Berlin.

***WEIZMAN, EZER** (1924–), Israel air force commander.

XIMENES, SIR DAVID (1776–1848), English army officer. Born in London, into a distinguished Jewish family, Ximenes joined the British army and served in North America. He returned to Britain in 1805 and commanded the 62nd Regiment in Ireland. He later fought in Italy, Spain, and Portugal. Ximenes was knighted in 1832 and retired with the rank of lieutenant general in 1847.

***YADIN, YIGAEL** (1917–), Israel chief of staff.

YAKIR, YONAH (d. 1937), Soviet general. Born in Kishinev, Yakir commanded the 45th division of the Red Army during the Civil War and was later promoted to general with command of the Kiev district. He was one of the founders of the Red Army armoured corps and in 1937 was made military commander of the Ukraine and a member of the Supreme Military Council. Shortly afterward Yakir was arrested on charges of spying and executed. He was posthumously rehabilitated in 1945 and a postage stamp was issued in 1954 in his memory.

***ZAM, ZVI HERZ** (1835–1915), captain, only Jewish officer in the Russian army in the 19th century.

ZÖLD, MÁRTON (b. 1865), Austro-Hungarian general. Born in Hungary, Zöld passed out of the military academy in Budapest and was seconded to the infantry. In 1914 he commanded a battalion against Serbia and Montenegro, and was awarded a Hungarian knighthood for valor on the Russian front. In the same year he commanded a regiment on the Italian front. After the establishment of an independent Hungarian state, Zöld was made a full general. He was active in Jewish affairs.

ẒUR, ẒEVI (1923–), Israel chief of staff.

MILK. The milk most commonly mentioned in the Bible is that of sheep and goats (Prov. 27:27; Deut. 32:14), but cows' milk was also known and was consumed at least in the form of curds (Isa. 7:21–22). Milk is considered among the finest of foods (Deut. 32:14; Isa. 55:1) and is used as a term of abundance (Joel 4:18; Isa. 60:16), as the standard of whiteness (Lam. 4:7) and, with honey, of sweetness (Song 4:11). A "land flowing with milk and honey" refers to the abundant fertility of Canaan (e.g., Ex. 3:8, 17; Num. 13:27; Deut. 6:3; Jer. 11:5) and of Egypt (Num. 16:13). The prohibition against boiling a kid in its mother's milk (Ex. 23:19; 34:26; Deut. 14:21) most probably refers to a Canaanite sacrificial custom. Some scholars believe that this practice is referred to in Ugaritic text 52, line 14, but the textual restoration is uncertain. Boiling in milk—called "its mother's milk"—is a common way of preparing a kid or a lamb among modern Arabs, but it has no ritual significance for them. [T.S.F.]

In Halakhah. The milk of clean animals such as cows, sheep, and goats, etc., although it comes "from the living" (*min ha-ḥai,* Bek. 6b), is permitted for consumption, but not the milk of unclean animals or of those suffering from visible disease which causes the animal to be ritually unfit for consumption *(terefah)*, or that of an animal which after ritual slaughtering is found to have suffered from such a disease. In the latter case, all milk which the animal produced during the three days before it was slaughtered is forbidden to be used (Sh. Ar., YD 81:2). Milk bought from a non-Jew is forbidden for consumption out of fear that he may have mixed it, either through carelessness or in order to improve it, with milk of unclean animals. If a Jew was present at the milking, the milk may be used (*ibid.*, 115:1). There are, however, opinions that nowadays, even if the Jews did not supervise the milking, the milk is permitted since the law of the land forbids adulterating the milk. By many authorities butter made by gentiles is permitted for consumption on the grounds that butter cannot be produced from the milk of unclean animals (Av. Zar. 35b, Maim. Yad, Ma'akhalot Asurot, 3:12, 15, 16).

See also *Dietary Laws. [Ed.]

Bibliography: C.H. Gordon, *Ugaritic Text-Book* (1966), 174; Eisenstein, Dinim, 68; ET, 5 (1953), 84–91; S. Lieberman, *Ha-Yerushalmi ki-Feshuto* (1934), 39–42.

MILKWEED, plant of the Euphorbiaceae family. Many genera comprising scores of species are found in Israel. Attempts have been made to identify them with plants mentioned in the Bible, but such attempts are without foundation. One plant mentioned in the Mishnah belongs to the Asclepiadaceae family: the *Calotropis procera,* the mishnaic *Petilat ha-Midbar* ("desert wick," Shab. 2:1). It is a shrub growing in the salt Jordan valley and the Arabah. It has large leaves and its fruit is like a big lemon, but instead of juice it contains many seeds enveloped in shining silky fibers. These are used for making cushions, and wicks too can be prepared from them, but since the oil does not rise well in the fiber its use for the Sabbath lamp is forbidden (Shab. *ibid.*). The popular name of the fruit is "Sodom apple," which has no connection with "the vine of Sodom" (Deut. 32:32). Milkweed is mentioned by Josephus (Wars 4:484) who points out that this fruit of Sodom appears edible but on being opened turns to dust. The reference is to the seeds, which have hairy adhesions by which they are broadcast.

Bibliography: Loew, Flora, 1 (1928), 282f.; J. Feliks, *Olam ha-Ẓome'aḥ ha-Mikra'i* (1968[3]), 82. [J.F.]

MILL, JOSEPH SOLOMON (John; 1870–1952), pioneer of the *Bund. Born in Panevezys, Lithuania, Mill was left on his own when his family emigrated to the United States. From an early age he established close relations with Polish families, acquainting himself with the complex nationality problems of the region. He joined revolutionary circles under the influence of Z. *Kopelson. From 1890 he was a most active member of the Jewish Social Democratic organization in Vilna, except for intervals of imprisonment (1892), military service, and studies at the University of Zurich. He established ties with the leaders of the Polish Social Democrats, Rosa *Luxemburg, and L. *Jogiches, who led the Social Democratic "circles" in Vilna at the end of the 1880s. In 1895 Mill went to Warsaw as the head of a group interested in laying a foundation for a Jewish workers' society that later became a branch of the Bund there. He fought the Polish Socialist Party and its group of Jewish members and succeeded in uniting Lithuanian and local workers into one Jewish association. After the arrest of Bund members in 1898, Mill fled the country, and together with Kopelson initiated the establishment of the Bund "committee abroad." He was the editor of its organ *Der Yidisher Arbeter* (nos. 6–11), and initiated the setting up of the Bund archives. At the third congress of the Bund (1899) Mill was the first to demand that the claim to national autonomy be included in its program. For many years he headed the organizational affairs of the Bund and its "committee abroad" until he emigrated to Chicago in 1915. In the United States he worked at his profession of dental technician, and was active in the *Jewish Socialist Verband and the Socialist Party, holding the position of Jewish secretary and translator. He wrote for Jewish socialist periodicals and published important memoirs entitled *Pionern un Boyer* (2 vols., 1943–46).

Bibliography: LNYL, 5 (1963), 624–6, incl. bibl.; J. S. Hertz et al. (eds.), *Geshikhte fun Bund,* 3 vols. (1960–66), indexes; M. Mishkinsky, in: *Asufot,* 14 (1970), 81–131. [M.M.]

°**MILLÁS VALLICROSA, JOSÉ MARIÁ** (1897–1970), Spanish scholar and historian. Millás Vallicrosa was born in Santa Coloma de Farnés, Spain. From 1925 onward he was professor of Hebrew studies at the University of Barcelona, having also taught at the University of Madrid. Millás Vallicrosa did research into the history of Spanish Jewry, medieval Hebrew poetry, the Bible, and the history of the sciences. He also translated medieval works from Hebrew and Arabic into Spanish. One of his important studies on Spanish Jewry is *Documents hebraics de jueus catalans* (1927), in which he compiled and explained Hebrew documents of the Catalonian Jews in the 11th–12th centuries. Another work of his is *Assaig d'història de les idees físiques i matemàtiques a la Catalunya medieval* (1931), on the history of the development of science in Catalonia. In the field of the history of science, Millás Vallicrosa's studies on Abraham ibn Ezra and *Abraham bar Ḥiyya are notable, while in the research into Hebrew poetry and literature a special place is occupied by his work *La poesía sagrada hebraico-española* (1940). He suggested that antecedents of poetic forms in medieval Hebrew poetry in Spain can be traced to biblical poetry (in *Sefarad,* 1 (1941), 45–87). In this field he also published the studies *Yehuda ha-Leví, como poeta y apologista* (1947), and *Šĕlomō ibn Gabirol, como poeta y filósofo* (1945). Millás Vallicrosa published scores of articles in scholarly journals, including *Al-Andalus, Sefarad, Revue Internationale de l'Histoire des Sciences,* and *Osiris: Archeion.* Many of his pupils earned scholarly reputations among them his own sons. His wife, Francisca Vendrell, also a scholar, studied the history of medieval Spanish Jewry. A two-volume *Homenaje . . .* containing scholarly articles by Jewish and non-Jewish scholars was published in honor of Millás Vallicrosa in

1954–56. A list of his works was published under the title *Títulos y Trabajos de Profesor D. José M. Millás Vallicrosa* (1950). [H.B.]

MILLER, ARTHUR (1915–), U.S. playwright. Born in New York City, Miller worked in a Michigan automobile factory to finance his studies, became a newspaper editor, and first began writing in the late 1930s. He acquired an international reputation after World War II, following the publication of two plays and of *Focus* (1945), a novel about anti-Semitism. The play *All My Sons* (1947) revealed his ability to portray characters involved in emotional conflicts, but his reputation was really established with *Death of a Salesman* (1949), which won the Pulitzer Prize for drama. The play, later made into a motion picture, owed its success to the delineation of Willy Loman, the unsuccessful traveling salesman, and was regarded as an indictment of the false sense of values of American life.

In 1950, engaged by the problem of freedom of speech, Miller wrote an adaptation of Henrik Ibsen's *An Enemy of the People*, and in 1953, in his own play *The Crucible*, he turned to the Salem witch trials of 1692, and spoke for freedom of conscience during the period of Senator McCarthy's anti-communist campaign. This play was screened as the *Witches of Salem*. *A View from the Bridge* (1957) again won a Pulitzer Prize. It showed Miller still striving for significant realistic drama and imaginative dramatic form. The film script, *The Misfits* (1961), written after his marriage to the screen star Marilyn Monroe, and acted in by her and Clark Gable, was an unusually sensitive, though commercially unsuccessful, study of loneliness and divorce. Miller returned to the theater with an autobiographical drama, *After the Fall* (1964), based largely on his life with Marilyn Monroe, whom he had divorced in 1962, and relating his own conflicts in love and friendship to the state of the world. *Incident at Vichy* (1966) dealt with the arrest of a number of Frenchmen, including some Jews, during the Nazi occupation. *The Price* (1968), depicting a dramatic conflict between two brothers, had as a central character an old Jew who acted as a wise commentator. Miller stated his intention as a dramatist as being to "bring to the stage the thickness, awareness, and complexity of the novel." He endeavored to give postwar American drama depth of purpose and content, and a sense of tragic conflict in terms of contemporary American life. Widely regarded in the 1950s as America's leading dramatist, his reputation faded somewhat in the 1960s as realistic drama itself passed out of critical fashion. For the collected edition of his plays published in 1958, he wrote a 50-page introduction which clarified his purpose and explained his methods of work. Translated into many languages, the plays were internationally popular. Miller was elected president of the International P.E.N. Club in 1965, in which position he strove vigorously to organize protests against literary censorship and repression all over the world.

Arthur Miller, U.S. playwright, with his wife, Marilyn Monroe. Courtesy Jewish Theatrical Guild, New York.

Bibliography: D. Welland, *Arthur Miller* (1961); B. Nelson, *Arthur Miller* (1970); L. Moss, *Arthur Miller* (1967); S. Huftel, *Arthur Miller, The Burning Glass* (1965); R. Hogen, *Arthur Miller* (University of Minnesota Pamphlets on American Writers, no. 40, 1964); J. Gassner, *Theater at the Crossroads* (1960), 194–5, 197–204; *Contemporary Authors*, first rev. (1967), incl. bibl.

[J.Mer.]

MILLER, EMANUEL (1893–1970), English psychiatrist. Born in London, Miller studied medicine at Cambridge University and the London Hospital and lectured in psychology at Cambridge for a brief period after 1924. He became a psychiatric specialist in 1940 and in 1946 was made a Fellow of the Royal College of Physicians. One of the foremost psychiatrists in Britain, Miller was founder and honorary director of the East London Child Guidance Clinic and chairman and honorary president of the Association of Child Psychiatry. He showed a keen interest in the development of medicine in Israel and in 1953 was elected president of the British Friends of Magen David Adom. His publications include *Modern Psychotherapy* (1930) and *Neurosis in War* (1940). His wife, Betty Miller (née Spiro; 1910–1965), born in Cork, Ireland, was the author of various novels including *Farewell Leicester Square* (1940), *A Room in Regent's Park* (1942), *On the Side of the Angels* (1945), and *The Death of the Nightingale* (1949). She also wrote a biographical study, *Robert Browning: A Portrait* (1952) and was elected a Fellow of the Royal Society of Literature. Their son Jonathan Miller (1934–) qualified as a doctor but established his reputation as an actor in the revue *Beyond the Fringe*, a satire on various aspects of British life from Shakespeare to the Royal Family, which played in London and New York. Later he directed many successful theatrical and television productions, frequently winning acclaim for his originality. [Ed.]

MILLER, IRVING (1903–), U.S. rabbi and Zionist leader. Rabbi Miller, who was born in Kovno, Lithuania, was taken to the U.S. in 1912. Ordained a rabbi at Yeshivath Rabbi Isaac Elhanan in 1926, he served congregations in Youngstown, Ohio (1926–1928), Chelsea, Mass. (1928–30) and Far Rockaway, N.Y. (1930–46), before becoming rabbi of Congregation Sons of Israel, Woodmere, N.Y. (1946–63). Extremely active in Jewish affairs, Miller's posts included: secretary-general of the World Jewish Congress (1942–45); president of the American Jewish Congress (1949–52); president of the Zionist Organization of America (1952–54); president of the American Zionist Council (1954–63); chairman of the Conference of Presidents of Major American Jewish Organizations (1961–63); and member of both the national cabinet of the United Jewish Appeal and the Actions Committee of the World Zionist Organization. [Ed.]

MILLER, ISRAEL (1918–), U.S. rabbi and educator. Miller was born in Baltimore, Maryland, and was ordained at Yeshiva University (1941). During World War II Rabbi Miller was a chaplain in the Army Air Corps. He served as rabbi of the Kingsbridge Heights Jewish Center, Bronx, for 25 years prior to becoming assistant to the president of Yeshiva University for student affairs. Rabbi Miller, an Orthodox rabbi who participated in the whole spectrum of Jewish communal affairs, was chairman of the American Zionist Council. He was chairman of the American Jewish Conference on Soviet Jewry and the Commission on Jewish Chaplaincy of the National Jewish Welfare Board, and was president of the Rabbinical Council of America. [L.BE.]

MILLER, LOUIS (1917–), Israel psychiatrist. Born in Somerset West, South Africa, he went to Israel in 1948 and established psychiatric and psychological services in the Israel army and air force. In 1949 Miller became director of psychiatry in Israel's Ministry of Health, where he planned and initiated its regional hospital and community services. In 1954 he entered the field of public health and developed a family health and community organization program for the Jerusalem region. In 1959 he returned to his post of director of Mental Health Services, and in 1970 became chief national psychiatrist. In 1966–67, as visiting professor at Northwestern University, he planned and initiated a community mental health program in Chicago for the State of Illinois. His contributions to mental health theory, research, and practice were concerned particularly with the effects of socio-cultural and community influences on mental health and ill health and its treatment. He integrated this approach with the biological and psychological interpretations of personality. His publications include studies concerning the incidence of psychiatric conditions in various cultures in Israel, immigration and mental health, child rearing on the kibbutz and among Tripolitanian Jews, aging, urbanization and social change. He was chairman of the National Committee for the Study of Drug Abuse. [ED.]

MILLER, LOUIS E. (pseudonym of **Louis E. Bandes;** 1866–1927), Yiddish editor and labor leader. Miller was born in Vilna and became involved in socialist and revolutionary activities in his boyhood. He fled from Russia at 14 and participated in émigré revolutionary circles in Berlin, Switzerland, Paris, and, after 1886, in New York. In the U.S. Miller worked in a shirt factory, and helped found the first shirtmakers union among Jewish workers. Miller was also deeply involved in the political life of socialist and other labor organizations. In his early years he remained close to organizations which used Russian as their language, but in 1889 he represented the Yiddish-language-oriented United Hebrew Trades at the Second International in Paris.

Miller was most influential as editor and writer in Yiddish. In 1890, with Philip *Krantz, Morris *Hillquit, and Abraham *Cahan, he founded the Yiddish-socialist *Die Arbeiter Zeitung* (1890). In 1897 he joined Cahan in launching the daily *Forward* (1897). In 1905 he broke with Cahan, the editor in chief of this daily, and founded his own paper *Die Wahrheit* (1905) which stressed Jewish national aspirations no less than socialism. When World War I broke out, he espoused the cause of the Allies, while most of his daily's 100,000 readers favored Germany as against czarist Russia. The paper continued to lose circulation, and he preferred to resign rather than to keep silent. He attempted several journalistic ventures after 1917, but never regained his earlier influence with the Yiddish reading masses.

Bibliography: Rejzen, Leksikon, 2 (1927), 409–14; LNYL, 5 (1963), 628–31. [A.T.]

MILLER, SHAYE (1895–1958), Yiddish novelist. Born in a Ukrainian village near Novograd-Volinsk, he emigrated to the United States at the age of 17 and settled in Los Angeles ten years later. He began to publish Yiddish short stories at the age of 22, translated Maeterlinck, Tagore, and Wedekind, and published ten volumes of impressionistic stories. His novel *Dor Hafloge* ("The Lost Generation," 1948) dealt with the decay, in the new American environment, of an Eastern European Jewish family which symbolized the pre-World War I generation of transition. The stories of *Nekhtn* ("Yesterday," 1956) deal largely with Los Angeles Jews: Miller gives a panoramic view of the charlatans, the noble characters, and the ordinary men and women who were caught up in California's boom-psychosis of the 1920s and ended their lives tragically during the Great Depression of the early 1930s. He stressed the nostalgia for old-fashioned Jewishness which assailed the Jews who had wrested themselves loose from early Jewish roots and who found their materially successful life empty of meaning in later years. Miller is a master of dialogue, accurately reproducing the speech, intonations, and gestures of his marginal, semi-assimilated Jews. His posthumously published essays *Skeptishe Makhshoves* ("Sceptical Thoughts," 1959) deal with basic questions of American-Jewish cultural survival and cast light upon his own personality and approach to literary craftsmanship.

Bibliography: Rejzen, Leksikon, 2 (1927), 417ff.; LNYL, 5 (1963), 631–4; J. Glatstein, *In Tokh Genumen* (1960), 328–33; S. Bickel, *Shrayber fun Mayn Dor* (1958), 327–34. [S.L.]

MILLET, name for the religious communal organization of non-Muslims in the Ottoman Empire. The Koran uses *milla* for religion or rite, e.g., religion of the Jews and Christians (2:114), and the religion of Abraham (2:124; 3:89). It is assumed that a Jewish communal organization was already in existence for some time in the areas occupied by the Ottoman Turks in the 14th and early 15th centuries. Even before the capture of Constantinople in 1453 the Ottoman conquerors of the Balkans had granted the Christian population religious, juridical, and administrative autonomy. Muhammad II the Conqueror (1451–81) organized all non-Muslim communities and recognized their religious leaders as heads of the respective millets. Each head had jurisdiction over and responsibility for the members of his millet, and even in matters of taxation, the apportionment of the whole amount was left to him. R. Moses *Capsali was the first to be appointed (1461?) head of the Jews in Constantinople (see also **ḥakham bashi*). The powers of the second head, R. Elijah b. Abraham Mizraḥi (1485?–1526), were in fact restricted to religious matters of the Jews in Constantinople. Mizraḥi clearly had nothing to do with the collection of taxes and the representation of the Jews with the various authorities. That the collection of taxes was not the concern of the official representatives of the millet is confirmed by many sources. In fact, the opposite is true: the various tax collectors, toll farmers, cashiers, and bankers of the pashas, in so far as they were non-Muslims, were the natural spokesmen of their communities by virtue of their functions and influence at court. In his time *Kakhya Shealtiel was the official spokesman who represented the Jews of the city—especially in the matter of tax collection—before the authorities. Mizraḥi's judgment in the case of Kakhya Shealtiel repeatedly mentions the representatives of the congregations in Constantinople. The representative's title of *memunneh* (lit. "appointee") is one of the titles designating the persons elected by the congregation to manage its affairs; other titles are *parnas, barur, kazin,* and the ancient collective designation, *tovei ha-ir.* The powers, number, manner of election, and period of tenure of these functionaries varied greatly. Their main task was the collection of communal taxes (especially the *gabella*), which were used to maintain the children of the needy at school and to finance charitable purposes. The mode of imposition and amount of the taxes were also different; as a rule, the consent of the whole congregation or at least of the taxpayers was required. The congregations of expellees and immigrants from Europe usually retained the practices they had followed in their countries of origin. The veteran residents likewise maintained their ancestral tradition according to which public affairs were looked after by the elders, who were the heads of prominent and influential families.

In connection with the reforms in the Ottoman Empire in the 19th century, the structure of the millet organization underwent many changes. The regulations of the Greek community (*Rum milleti*) were finally drafted and approved in 1862 and those of the Armenian community (*Ermeni milleti*) in 1863. The submission of proposals for the reorganization of the Jewish community (*Yahudi milleti*), as required by the *Khaṭṭi hümayun* (imperial decree) of 1856, was delayed due to internal dissension. The "Organizational Regulations of the Rabbinate" (*ḥakham Khane niẓam namesi*) was approved finally in 1865 (see *community and *ḥakham bashi*). The tenor of the regulations reveals a desire to limit the powers of the *ḥakham bashi*, and they remained in force so long as the Ottoman Empire existed; only under the republic did they lapse de facto—without being officially replaced.

Bibliography: R. Gibb and H. Bowen, *Islamic society and the West*, 1 pt. 2 (1957), index and 219–26; G. Young, *Corps de Droit Ottoman*, 2 (1905), 148–55; A. Galanté, *Documents Officiels turcs concernant les Juifs de Turquie* (1931), 10–27; H. Z. Hirschberg, in: A. J. Arberry (ed.), *Religion in the Middle East*, 1 (1969), 185f., 200–2; B. Lewis, *Emergence of Modern Turkey* (1961), 329–30. [H.Z.H.]

MILLET, the *Panicum miliaceum*, a summer plant of the Gramineae family, whose small seeds are utilized as fodder or are sometimes ground to produce a poor quality flour. It is regarded by some as identical with *doḥan*, one of the ingredients of the flour mixture that Ezekiel was commanded to eat for 390 days (Ezek. 4:9). The probability is, however, that *doḥan* is *sorghum. *Doḥan* is mentioned a number of times in rabbinic literature together with *orez* ("rice"), *peragim*, and *shumshemin* ("sesame"; Shev. 2:7), as summer plants from which occasionally bread is made (Ḥal. 1:4). *Peragim* cannot therefore be poppy as is stated in the *Arukh* of Nathan b. Jehiel (and as the word is used in modern Hebrew), since the poppy is a winter plant and is used only as a spice. From Syrian Aramaic it would seem that *peragim* is to be identified with millet, an identification compatible with the talmudic sources.

Bibliography: Loew, Flora, 1 (1928), 738–40; H.N. and A.L. Moldenke, *Plants of the Bible* (1952), index; J. Feliks, *Olam ha-Ẓome'aḥ ha-Mikra'i* (1968^{2}), 154f. [J.F.]

MILLIN, PHILIP (1888–1952), South African Supreme Court judge. Millin began his career as a journalist in Johannesburg and Cape Town, studying law at the same time. On graduation in 1913 he began to practice in Johannesburg. He became a King's Counsel in 1927, and was chairman of the Bar Council for several years. He was appointed to the Supreme Court in 1937. As chairman of the Company Law Amendment Inquiry Commission he drafted the "Millin Report," which led to important changes in company law. He was also the coauthor of *Mercantile Law of South Africa* (1917 and several other editions), a standard work. For some years Millin was vice-president of the South African Friends of the Hebrew University. His wife was the novelist, Sarah Gertrude *Millin.

Bibliography: S. G. Millin, *The Measure of My Days* (1955). [L.S.]

MILLIN, SARAH GERTRUDE (born **Liebson;** 1889–1968), South African novelist. Born in Lithuania, she grew up near Kimberley and married Philip *Millin. After publishing several novels, she made her name with *God's Step-Children* (1924), a story of the colored people of Cape Province. None of her subsequent novels had the same popular impact, though at least one of them, *Mary Glenn* (1925), a rural tragedy, showed great power of projecting atmosphere and passion. Turning to biography, she published a life of Cecil Rhodes (1933), and *General Smuts* (2 vols., 1936). A prolific writer on South African and world affairs, Sarah

Sarah Gertrude Millin, South African novelist. Courtesy Fieldhill Publishing Co., Johannesburg.

Gertrude Millin produced among other works short stories of South Africa and during World War II she wrote her war diaries in six volumes (published 1944–48), in which she devoted much attention to Palestine. Returning to fiction, she broadened her scope in *King of the Bastards* (1949) and *The Burning Man* (1952). She wrote two volumes of autobiography, *The Night is Long* (1941) and *The Measure of My Days* (1955).

Sarah Gertrude Millin's style was terse and her objectivity in fiction carried to the point where it often seemed that she disliked the people she wrote about. In her later years she often expressed conservative and controversial views on South Africa's race relations and color policies (apartheid). In 1966 she edited and contributed to a volume of essays, *White Africans are Also People*, in defense of Rhodesia and South Africa. Sarah Gertrude Millin, although interested in Jewish affairs, took no part in Jewish life. She occasionally introduced Jews in her stories, as in *The Coming of the Lord* (1928). [L.S.]

MILLO (Pasovsky), JOSEF (1916–), Israel theatrical producer. Born in Prague, Millo was taken to Israel in 1921 but received his theatrical training in Prague and Vienna. On

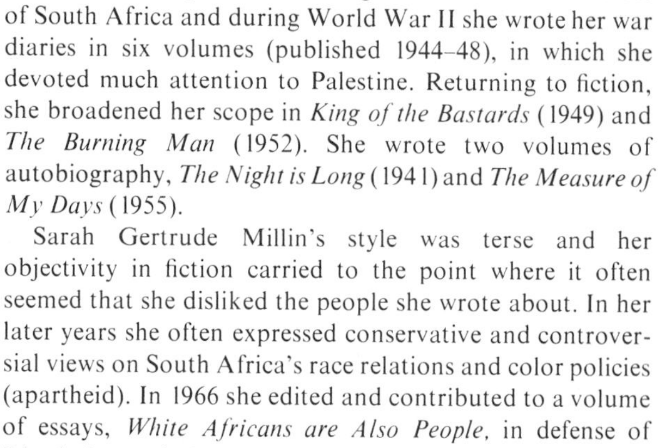

Josef Millo, Israel theatrical producer and director. Courtesy Government Press Office, Tel Aviv.

returning to Israel he worked with a marionette troupe (1937–41), acted for two years with the satirical theater "Ha-Matate," and in 1942 founded the Cameri Theater, which he directed until 1959. In 1961 he founded and became director of the Haifa Municipal Theater. Millo inaugurated a naturalistic school of Israel drama and strongly influenced the younger generation of actors and writers. He directed about 100 plays, including works by Bertolt Brecht and Shakespeare, himself playing many leading roles. He was considered to have shown new trends in modern Hebrew drama with N. Shaham's *They Will Return Tomorrow* and M. Shamir's *He Walked Through the Fields.* He was also responsible for the film version of the latter (1967). Millo translated into Hebrew Goldoni's *The Servant of Two Masters* and Čapek's *The World We Live In.* He directed plays at drama festivals in Paris (1956), Venice (1965), and other European cities.

Bibliography: Ohad, in: *Teatron* (Heb., June–Aug. 1963), 23–26.

[Ed]

MILLSTONE (Heb. רֵחַיִם), an instrument used for grinding grain. The word has a dual ending, indicating an instrument composed of two parts: an upper millstone (Heb. *rekhev,* Deut. 24:6) and a lower millstone (talmudic Heb. *shekhev*), which, however, was called *reḥayim* as well *(ibid.).* Other terms for both millstones are *pelaḥ* (Judg. 9:53, in combination with *rekhev* for upper millstone; Job 41:16, in combination with *taḥtit,* lower millstone), and *taḥanah* (Eccles. 12:34). The mill was worked by slaves (Ex. 11:5; Judg. 16:21—Samson; Isa. 47:2; Lam. 5:13). The manna too was ground by millstones (Num. 11:8). Abimelech was killed with an upper millstone by the woman of Thebez (Judg. 9:53). Grain would be spread out between the upper and lower millstones, and the friction and pressure of one stone upon the other would break the kernels and grind them into flour. The desired friction was achieved by passing the upper stone back and forth over the lower one, as is illustrated in early Egyptian pictures. Millstones of this type have been found in abundance in excavations in Ereẓ Israel, for example at Gezer, Megiddo, and Hazor. This type of millstone was in use until the end of the Israelite period.

Upper millstone, basalt, found at Capernaum, Roman period (37 B.C.E.–324 C.E.). Haifa, Dagon Museum. Photo P. Dorn.

Only at the end of the Persian period did another type of millstone come into use, in which the desired friction was achieved by means of the circular motion of the upper stone—which turned on an axle—upon the stationary lower stone. Millstones were essential household items, and it was forbidden to remove them from their owner's possession, for example, as a pledge for a loan (Deut. 24:6). In talmudic times a distinction was made between "hand mills" or "human mills," usually worked by the housewife and standing in a special room or place, and a mill operated by a donkey, which was both larger and of a more complicated construction. Water mills are mentioned but were rare.

Bibliography: J. A. Wilson and T. G. Allen, *Megiddo,* 1 (1939), pl. 114, no. 11; C. C. McCown, *Tell En-Naẓbeh,* 1 (1947), pl. 91, nos. 1, 2, 4; R. Amiran, in: *Eretz Israel,* 4 (1956), 46–49; Y. Yadin et. al., *Hazor,* 3–4 (1961), pl. 233, nos. 20, 21; Krauss, Tal Arch 1 (1910), 95–97.

[Z.Y.]

MILNER, MOSES MICHAEL (Mikhail Arnoldovich; 1886–1953), composer, born in Rokitno, Ukraine. As a child he sang in the choirs of several famous *ḥazzanim,* including J. S. *Morogovski (Zeidel Rovner), and then studied at the Kiev and St. Petersburg conservatories. From 1912 to 1919 he was conductor of the choir of the Great Synagogue in St. Petersburg, and then worked as singing teacher and choral conductor in various posts. From 1924 to 1931 he was musical director and conductor of the Yiddish Theater in Moscow and Kharkov, musical director of the Jewish Voice Ensemble in Leningrad (1931–41), and coach of the choir of the Leningrad Bolshoi Theater from 1941 until his death.

Milner's renown began with the publication of his songs in 1914 by the *Society for Jewish Folk Music which he had helped to found. His works indicated new possibilities for the harmonization of traditional melodic material in the dramatic style of Moussorgsky. Until the mid-1930s he wrote many works on Jewish themes, mainly for the stage. The opera, *Die Himlen Brenen,* based on S. *An-Ski's *Dibbuk* and adapted by M. Rivesman, performed in 1923, was later denounced as reactionary and its performance was forbidden. Among his other works are: *Der Najer Veg* (1933); *Josephus Flavius* (1935), based on L. *Feuchtwanger's novel; stage music for the Habimah performances of H. Leivik's *Golem* and R. *Beer-Hoffmann's *Jaakobs Traum;* and a ballet, *Ashmedai.* In addition, he also wrote settings of Jewish folk songs and liturgical texts. After the repression of Jewish art, Milner turned to more general subjects and wrote a symphony (1937); a symphonic poem, *The Partisans* (1944); and a piano concerto.

Bibliography: I. Heskes and A. Wolfson (eds.), *Historic Contribution of Russian Jewry to Jewish Music* (1967), 74–79 (=*Jewish Music Festival,* 23rd, New York, 1966); Sendrey, Music, index; L. Saminsky, *Music of the Ghetto and the Bible* (1934), index; I. Rabinovitch, *Of Jewish Music* (1952), index; B. C. Steinpress (ed.), *Entsiklopedicheskiy muzykalny slovar* (1959); G. Bernandt, *Slovar Oper* (1962).

[H.B.-D.]

MILOSZ, OSCAR (originally **Oscar Venceslas De Lubicz-Milosz,** 1877–1939), French poet, mystical writer, and diplomat. Milosz, who was born in Chereya, Belorussia to a Lithuanian nobleman and the baptized daughter of a Warsaw Hebrew teacher, was raised as a Catholic. He nevertheless retained a warm regard for his Jewish heritage and developed a keen interest in the Kabbalah. At the age of 12 he was taken to Paris, where he later studied Hebrew and Assyrian at the Ecole des Langues Orientales. He was Lithuania's minister resident in Paris (1919–26) but, despite his eventual assumption of French citizenship, remained attached to his ancestral land, which inspired his *Contes et fabliaux de la vieille Lithuanie* (1930) and *Contes lithuan-*

iennes de ma Mère L'Oye (1933). In his poetry Milosz progressed from erotic mysticism to spiritual and metaphysical speculation. Among his early works were *L'Amoureuse initiation* (1910), a novel in the form of a poetic monologue, and two plays, *Miguel Mañara* (1912; Eng. tr. in *Poet Lore*, 1919), and *Méphiboseth* (1914), the second of which dealt with David and Bathsheba. His mystical experiences inspired two metaphysical works, *Ars magna* (1924) and *Le Poème des Arcanes* (1927). These mingle Catholic theology with mystical and kabbalistic doctrine, stressing the belief that man possesses the ability to perceive reality as it is seen by God and that this faculty, at present hidden, will one day be recovered. In his *Arcanes*, Milosz glorified the Jewish people as the servant of humanity who "preserved the sacred treasure of the original Revelation in all its purity through a thousand vicissitudes for the sole purpose of the world's future regeneration." *Les origines ibériques du peuple juif* (1932), a product of Milosz' last, kabbalistic, and eschatological period, attempted to prove, by comparing Andalusian and biblical place-names and Basque and Hebrew etymology, that the Hebrews emigrated to Canaan from southern Spain.

Bibliography: A. Richter, *Milosz* (Fr., 1965); J. Buge, *Milosz en quête du divin* (1963); A. Godoy, *Milosz, le Poète de l'Amour* (1961); G. I. Židonis, *O. V. de L. Milosz* (Fr., 1951); J. Rousselot, *O. V. de L. Milosz* (Fr., 1949). [Ed.]

MILSTEIN, NATHAN (1904–), U.S. violinist. Born in Odessa, Russia, he was a child prodigy and studied with L. *Auer and E. Ysaye, making his debut in 1914. He toured Russia after the revolution with Vladimir *Horowitz and Gregor *Piatigorsky but left for Paris in 1925 where he soon became famous as a soloist. He went to the United States in 1929, and first appeared there with the Philadelphia Symphony Orchestra under Stokowski. He made his home in the United States but toured widely and gained a reputation as one of the great virtuosos of his time. He wrote arrangements and cadenzas for the violin.

Bibliography: B. Gavoty, *Nathan Milstein* (Fr., 1956, Eng. tr., 1956); *The International Who is Who in Music* (1951). [U.T.]

°**MILTON, JOHN** (1608–1674), English Puritan poet, whose works contain an unusual concentration of biblical and Judaic sentiments. Milton may have learned Hebrew while he was at Cambridge from the Semitic scholar, Joseph Mede (1586–1638). His knowledge of Hebrew and Aramaic was sufficient to enable him in later years to read the Hebrew Bible and probably also the classical Hebrew commentators. On the other hand, it seems certain that he had no first hand knowledge of Talmud or Kabbalah, although he read the works of Maimonides and other post-biblical texts in the Latin translations of Johannes *Buxtorf. The result of these studies is apparent in two tracts, *Doctrine and Discipline of Divorce* (1643), and *Tetrachordon* (1645), obviously prompted by his own unhappy marriage. In pleading for more liberal divorce laws, Milton tends to view the Hebrew legislation on the subject in Deuteronomy as the normative code for Christians. He was attacked as a flagrant heretic by many fellow Presbyterians, including William Prynne (1600–1669), who was later to oppose the reentry of the Jews into England. In 1659 he became Cromwell's Latin secretary, and continued to maintain his covenant faith in the God who had chosen England as the messiah-nation and himself as the prophet-poet of Reformation. The end of the Commonwealth in 1660 found him a blind, abandoned, and aging revolutionary.

Milton's great epic poem, *Paradise Lost* (1667), which seeks to "justify the ways of God to men," frames the biblical account of the Creation and the fall of Man in the Christian tradition, relating the battles in fall of the angels; however, its fundamental emphasis is on human freedom and responsibility. This indicates Milton's relative proximity to Hebraic norms and his remoteness from the deterministic views of the more orthodox Puritans. *Paradise Lost* also reflects in part Milton's early acquaintance with Sylvester's English translation (1605) of *Du Barta's epic *On the Creation*. In *Samson Agonistes* (1671), he clearly identifies himself with his hero, the Hebrew judge, "Eyeless in Gaza at the mill with slaves," whom God had nevertheless chosen for special tasks and revelations. Biblical and Judaic elements are also prominent in the sonnets *On His Blindness* (1651?–5) and *On the Late Massacre in Piedmont* (1655), and in the pamphlet *Areopagitica* (1644).

Milton's most heretical work, the *De Doctrina Christiana* (written c. 1658–60, but published in 1825), which rejects the orthodox view of the Trinity, indicates his virulent Puritan objection to the Jewish priesthood and ritual code. His theological and philosophical position was marked by considerable internal conflict as he sought to resolve the tensions set up between the Hellenic, Hebraic, and Christian elements of his cultural inheritance. Milton's biblical verse had a considerable influence on the romantic poets Blake, Wordsworth, and Coleridge.

Bibliography: D. Saurat, *Milton, Man and Thinker* (1924); H. F. Fletcher, *Milton's Semitic Studies*... (1926); W. B. Selbie, in: E. R. Bevan and C. Singer (eds.), *Legacy of Israel* (1927), 407–31; M. Kelley, *This Great Argument*... (1941); D. Daiches, *Milton* (1957); Wolfe, in: *Journal of English and Germanic Philology*, 60 (1961), 834–46; H. Fisch, *Jerusalem and Albion*... (1964); idem, in: R. D. Emma and J. T. Shawcross (eds.), *Language and Style in Milton* (1967); H. F. Fletcher, *Milton's Rabbinical Readings* (1967). [H.F.]

MILWAUKEE, city situated in S.E. Wisconsin on the shore of Lake Michigan with an estimated Jewish population of 23,900 (1968). Jewish settlement dates back to 1844 when the Shoyer brothers, Moses Weil, Isaac Neustadtl, and Solomon Adler arrived. Most of the immigrants who followed came from Germany, Bohemia, Hungary, Austria, and some from France and England. The Jewish population grew from 70 families in 1850 to 200 in 1856, and to 2,074 persons in 1875. Czarist persecutions beginning in 1882 generated a flow of immigrants to Milwaukee, so that by 1895 Russian Jews represented 39% of the Jewish population of 7,000. An estimated 22,000 Jews resided in the city in 1925. The rise of Nazism in Germany brought approximately 900 Jewish refugees to Milwaukee from 1938 to 1950.

Pioneer Jews earned their livelihood as country peddlers, clothiers, and grocers. By the 1860s they were well represented in clothing manufacturing, grain, meatpacking, and were notable in Great Lakes transportation. In 1895 practically all clothing factories and shops were Jewish-owned, and remained so into the 1920s. Wholesale dry goods, knitting goods, and yarn mills owed their development to Jewish initiative. They led also in flour milling, soap and tobacco manufacturing, and department store enterprises. East European immigrants used petty trade as a stepladder to retail and wholesale fields. In the 1920s Jews became clerical employees, and began to enter the arts and professions. By the early 1960s the small storekeeper faded in importance, while the peddler and junk dealer practically vanished as their sons attained prominence in the professions and business world. Harry E. Soref, inventor-founder, and Samuel Stahl and P. E. Yolles created Master Lock Company in 1921, the world's largest padlock manufacturer; Elmer L. Winter and Aaron Scheinfeld established Manpower, Inc. in 1948, with branches in Europe; Max

H. Karl founded Mortgage Guarantee Insurance Company in 1956, the largest private mortgage guarantee insurer; and Max Kohl built in 1927 the most extensive independently-owned food-department store chain in Wisconsin.

Figure 1. Harry M. Benjamin, acting mayor of Milwaukee 1875–76. Courtesy State Historical Society of Wisconsin, Madison.

The 1920s saw a rapid exodus of Jews from the immigrant district, northward and westward. By 1945 the center of population had shifted to northwest, while new areas of settlement had grown in the far northeast along Lake Michigan. These trends continued into the sixties. Jews actively participated in local and state political and civic affairs. The first Jew elected to the state legislature was Bernard S. Weil in 1851. Henry M. Benjamin, one of eight Jewish aldermen and councilors before 1900, served as acting mayor of Milwaukee from 1875 to 1876; three Jews sat on the Common Council after 1920. The judiciary included Charles L. Aarons (1926–50); Max Raskin, Socialist city attorney from 1932 to 1936, and Circuit Court Judge from 1965; Circuit Court Judge Maurice M. Spracker (1968); and former Wisconsin Supreme Court Justice Myron L. Gordon, Federal judge of the Wisconsin Eastern District from 1967.

Several Jews attained national and international prominence: Marcus *Otterbourg, U.S. consul at Mexico City (1861–67) and U.S. minister to Mexico, 1867; Victor L. *Berger, principal founder of the Social Democratic Party and first Socialist elected to the House of Representatives (1911–13; 1919–29); Golda *Meir (Myerson) who became prime minister of Israel; Joseph A. *Padway, general counsel, American Federation of Labor; and Wilbur J. *Cohen, undersecretary of Health, Education and Welfare. While Jews moved freely and held office in German and non-sectarian societies—sons of Hermann, Turnverein, Masons, etc.—they developed Jewish fraternal groups, such as B'nai B'rith, Kesher Shel Barzel, etc. Later, the Abraham Lincoln House provided social and recreational facilities. The new Jewish Community Center, built on the Lakefront in 1954, became the hub for recreational, social, and cultural activities, including the Yiddish "Perhift Players" performances. Milwaukee's only Anglo-Jewish weekly is *The Wisconsin Jewish Chronicle*, established in 1921 by Nathan J. Gould and Irving R. Rhodes, the latter being sole proprietor after Gould's death in 1941.

Congregation B'ne Jeshurun was organized in 1856 through a consolidation of congregations Emanu-El (1850) and Ahabath Emuno (1854), joined by Anshe Emeth (1855) in 1859. The congregation's first rabbi was Isidor Kalisch (1857–60). Disagreement between traditionalists and advocates of complete reform caused 35 members to withdraw and establish, in 1869, the "Reform Congregation Emanu-El." Its initial rabbis were Edward B. M. Browne (1870) and Moritz Spitz (1872–78). In 1927 Emanu-El and B'ne Jeshurun amalgamated under the name Congregation Emanu-El B'ne Jeshurun, with Samuel Hirshberg and Joseph L. Baron as co-rabbis. East European immigrants established synagogues shortly after they arrived: Beth Israel (now Conservative), whose roots date from 1886; B'ne Israel, 1887; Anshe Sfard, 1889; Agudas Achim, 1904; and Anshe Lubavich, 1906. Rabbi Solomon I. Scheinfeld (1860–1943), while serving Beth Israel (1892–93; 1902–43), was the recognized head of the city's Orthodox congregations during his tenure. Milwaukee's first Conservative congregation, Beth El Ner Tamid, was originally founded in 1921, with Dr. Louis J. Swichkow its rabbi from 1937. Jacob Twerski, a ḥasidic rabbi, guided Congregation Beth Yehudah from 1929 when it was organized. More recently established synagogues are Reform congregations Shalom (1951) and Sinai (1955), and Conservative Menorah (1957) and Anshe Emeth (1958). Eight cemeteries served the Jewish community.

A Bureau of Jewish Education, reorganized with a full-time director in 1944, serves as the operating, coordinating, and subsidizing agency for Jewish education in the city. The founding of the Federated Jewish Charities in 1902, of which the Hebrew Relief Association (1867) was a principal beneficiary, opened a new era as emphasis gradually shifted from general relief to individualized social services, reflected in the agency's most recent change in name to Jewish Family and Children's Service (1948). Incorporating leading local and national Jewish institutions and major overseas drives, the Milwaukee Jewish Welfare Fund was organized in 1938. Milwaukee's Jewish philanthropic and welfare institutions include Mount Sinai Hospital (1903), Milwaukee Home for Aged Jews (1904), and the Jewish Convalescent Hospital. The Milwaukee Jewish Council, a joint defense agency, was organized in 1938. Almost all national organizations are represented in Milwaukee by their local branches.

Bibliography: L. J. Swichkow and L. P. Gartner, *The History of the Jews of Milwaukee* (1963); *The Jewish Community Blue Book of Milwaukee and Wisconsin* (1924, 1925[2]); L. J. Swichkow, in: A. J. Karp, ed. *The Jewish Experience in America*, 3 (1969), 152–76.

[L.J.Sw.]

Figure 2. The Mount Sinai Medical Center, Milwaukee, Wis.

Come ye and let us go up to the mountain of the Lord
of His ways and we will walk in His paths for out of Z
Jerusa